A Reference Guide for English Studies

A Reference Guide
for English Studies

MICHAEL J. MARCUSE

UNIVERSITY OF CALIFORNIA PRESS

Berkeley   Los Angeles   Oxford

University of California Press

Berkeley and Los Angeles, California

University of California Press

Oxford, England

Copyright © 1990 by The Regents of the University of California

Library of Congress Cataloging-in-Publication Data

> Marcuse, Michael J. (1944–)
>   A reference guide for English studies.
>   Includes indexes.
>   1. English literature—Library resources.
>   2. Bibliography—Bibliography—English literature.
>   3. Reference books—English literature—Bibliography.
>   4. American literature—Library resources.
>   5. Bibliography—Bibliography—American literature.
>   6. Reference books—American literature—Bibliography.
>   7. Performing arts—Library resources.
>   8. Bibliography—Bibliography—Performing arts.
>   9. Reference books—Performing arts—Bibliography.
>
>   I. Title.
>   PR56.M37 1990   016.82'09   86–14675
>   ISBN 0–520–05161–0 (alk. paper)

Printed in the United States of America
1 2 3 4 5 6 7 8 9

For Gisela, for Deborah, and for Anne

CONTENTS

PREFACE

The purpose of *A Reference Guide for English Studies* is to introduce and describe unfamiliar reference sources that one may consult when dealing with any reference question arising from current teaching or research in any branch of English studies. For these purposes, English studies are defined as all those subjects and lines of critical and scholarly inquiry presently pursued by members of university departments of English language and literature. Put more boldly, this work aims to provide more help to more people than any single reference guide we in English studies have hitherto possessed.

HISTORY OF THE PROJECT

The work's title echoes that of Donald F. Bond's *Reference Guide to English Studies*, 2d ed. (1971) (see entry A–11), itself a more current version of the earliest work of this kind, Tom Peete Cross's *List of Books and Articles, Chiefly Bibliographical, Designed to Serve as an Introduction to the Bibliography and Methods of English Literary History*, first published in 1919 and revised every few years through mid-century. Indeed, the present volume began as a supplement to sheer-list student reference guides such as Bond's; the *Selective Bibliography for the Study of English and American Literature* by Richard D. Altick and Andrew Wright, 6th ed. (1979) (A–10); and *A Concise Bibliography for Students of English* by Arthur G. Kennedy and Donald B. Sands, 5th ed., rev. William E. Colburn (1972) (A–12). My original aim was to supplement these lists with descriptions sufficient to alert students to the characteristics and thus the potential uses of key reference works. Armed with such descriptions, beginning researchers would, I thought, spend less time consulting numbers of works that might possibly be of use and more time using appropriate tools to solve problems. I further anticipated that instead of relying on the reference librarian, students would use the guidance of my descriptions to become more self-sufficient in the research library.

A few years after I began composing and distributing mimeographed "summary characterizations," as I called those supplementary descriptions, two books were published that had similar intentions. First in 1976 came Margaret Patterson's *Literary Research Guide* (see A–14), and then in 1977 came the United States publication of Robert C. Schweik and Dieter Riesner's *Reference Sources in English and American Literature: An Annotated Bibliography* (A–16), which had been issued in Germany the previous year.

When I compared my "summary characterizations" with the annotations in these two books, I found that though our intentions were similar, I had a different view of the kind and amount of information that students might require in a reference guide for English studies. And when my students worked with first the one and then the other published guide, they discovered also that the brevity and descriptive character of their annotations—designed to help readers know about a work—were less helpful than my fuller and more dynamic, user-oriented summaries in making decisions about which tools to consult and in what order.

What we discovered was the difference between a guide designed for the use of a hypothetical beginner—deliberately and consistently introductory in its perspective on the discipline—and a guide available to the beginner but intended for a wider, more experienced audience and more than introductory use.

USE OF THIS GUIDE

The present work is of this more ambitious kind. It assumes serious use by students who are beginners only in their unfamiliarity with the material and who seek more than a passing acquaintance with the tools of their discipline. For it has become my view that the best way to educate the apprentice is to treat him or her as a junior colleague. To reduce or simplify goals in order to accommodate the limited means of the apprentice is to shackle him or her finally with triviality, since apprentices do not become masters by using dull tools or toying with their work. It is better in my opinion to support inexperience with patience and encouragement, good tools, and valuable work than to falsify expectations or trivialize the work for the sake of some easy sense of achievement.

A case in point was my decision to include foreign-language materials in this guide wherever I found them to be without English-language equivalents or to be otherwise worthy of note. To exclude all or most non-English-language reference materials on the grounds that English-speaking students lack foreign languages is to misrepresent the fact that scholars do indeed miss valuable resources under such circumstances. I did not want simultaneously to regret linguistic provinciality and to construct a reference work that made competence in foreign languages seem unnecessary for serious scholarship.

This example holds by analogy with my reasoning throughout this guide, where sophisticated works used by the advanced scholar are cited along with more accessible, elementary tools.

This work is not intended to be of particular use to the specialist in his or her own field. But it should prove informative whenever questions arise about adjacent or ancillary fields. The book therefore retains something of its original character as an information source for the uninitiated, but it also acknowledges that even the most experienced scholar may be an apprentice outside what seem to be increasingly narrow fields of primary specialization. In addition, the publication explosion of scholarly reference works during the last decades makes it possible that even in the familiar territory of a specialization the scholar will find here some unfamiliar works that supplement or complement tools already well-known and used. Or the scholar may notice here unrecognized features or unexplored uses for works already consulted regularly. In short, this work has been prepared on the assumption that one reference guide might properly serve both the student and the scholar—terms that I have long thought nearly synonymous.

Because of its broad scope the contents of this volume are difficult to characterize in themselves, for it is less their nature and more the scholarly functions they might serve that have led to their inclusion. Thus, where there are no available alternatives, works that are poorly organized, inaccurate, or significantly out of date are included (with appropriate cautions). Where, on the contrary, numerous works are available, the effort has been one of selectivity: appearing here will be the most current, the most accurate, the best organized, and the most useful of the lot. There is, in other words, a marked inequality among items included in this guide: in common is only my judgment of their utility as resources for a particular class of scholarly reference questions. Few works are cited that are concerned with one author or one work. The exceptions include Chaucer (see entries N–45, N–47), Shakespeare (see O–40 through O–59), and Milton (see O–28). Further exceptions include the two guides to major–author reference works (see M–60 and S–50). Finally there are occasional biographical or critical works that, though cen-

tered on one author or one work, range so widely in treatment as to constitute essential, or at least frequently recommended, reading for students of a particular period or genre (as, for example, Tolkien on *Beowulf*, Brower on Pope, or Ellmann on Joyce). Access to such works is easiest through the author–as–subject entries in the Index of Subjects.

This guide only occasionally cites article-length materials, on the grounds that most articles of surpassing value become anthologized or develop into books—and many such collections and books are cited in lists of frequently recommended works. There are, however, occasional exceptions to this limitation, dictated by my judgment that in a particular case an article is in fact of such importance or stands so utterly alone in its field as to make citation necessary.

OTHER USES OF THIS GUIDE

The primary use of this guide, then, is to locate appropriate tools to consult for a particular reference question. But it does have other uses. Because of its scope it provides a survey map of reference resources in contemporary English studies. Thus it will offer an initial reference bibliography for any field or subfield of English studies, including both basic and advanced reference tools, and both scholarly journals and frequently recommended scholarly books. Again, the specialist would not look here for that bibliography, having long since become aware of the tools of his or her trade. But the apprentice preparing for an examination in, say, English romanticism and the visitor from another specialization suddenly assigned to design and teach a course in children's literature, or a survey of commonwealth literature, or a general education course in the art of biography will turn with profit to the relevant sections of this guide.

Because of my intention to help the English–studies researcher become self-sufficient in the library, this guide also provides librarians with a fairly comprehensive introduction to and overview of a contemporary English studies reference collection. In comparison with general reference guides such as Sheehy (A–20), Walford (A–21), Malclès (A–22), or Totok (A–23), this guide is more specialized. It includes a wider range of tools and describes them from a more specific point of view—that of the research scholar. Thus it would be an appropriate resource for more specialized reference librarians, those concerned exclusively with English studies, or languages and literatures, or even humanities reference.

CAUTIONS ABOUT INTENTIONS

Given such broad purposes and extensive uses, it may be well to indicate forcefully what this volume is *not* intended to do. First, it does not claim bibliographical authority. While pains have been taken to make entries bibliographically accurate, my central concern and principal occupation have been to make them informative.

Readers needing precise citations will therefore wish to verify bibliographical information for all entries by consulting standard authorities such as the *National Union Catalog* (see B–10 and B–11).

A second use to which this guide should not be put is as a closed bibliography aiming at anything like completeness. As a guide, it is, in fact, extremely selective, even in the reference works it cites. The rationale for an item's inclusion is its utility as a current reference source and not simply the fact of its existence. And though I may have overlooked works that should be admitted under that principle, missing items, particularly if published before 1985, may have been considered and silently excluded on the grounds that something more useful was available. While I might have appended a list of the hundreds of works thus considered but excluded, I decided that such a list would serve too narrow a purpose for the space it would take and the offense it might cause. Suffice it to say, then, that many more inclusive bibliographies of reference tools are available in such standard works as Howard-Hill (M–1, O–45), the *New Cambridge Bibliography of English Literature* (M–11, N–11, O–11, P–11, Q–11, and R–11), Nilon (S–1), and the *Literary History of the United States* (S–10), to mention only four leading works of wide-ranging scope and much broader principles of inclusion (though they differ significantly one from another in this regard).

The third and most serious misunderstanding of this volume would be to see it as somehow presenting or representing a consensus or corporate evaluation of the reference system for English studies. For good or ill, this massive volume remains the work of a single individual. It has, then, a degree of coherence and evenness of treatment that no guide composed by a committee could hope to have. At the same time this single perspective is an obvious limitation, for no individual, however indefatigable, can hope to provide either the depth or the range attainable in a large collaborative project. It may be that a subsequent edition of this guide—one informed and corrected by the help of its users and critics in all specialities—will be able to carry a more general authority than is currently possible. Indeed, such a broadly based, authoritative guide to reference sources for English studies remains a *desideratum*. But the present volume must be regarded as a single individual's view of what, in the interim, will be most helpful.

ENTRY TYPES

There are three types of entries in this guide. First and most frequent are entries concerned with a single work of scholarly reference. Basic bibliographical information is provided along with a description of the reference work's history, purpose, principles of inclusion, arrangement, and special features. In addition, supplementary and complementary works are cited, along with cross-references to otherwise related tools.

For further guidance about the character and use of a particular reference work (and, given the caveats suggested above, to compare my annotations with additional or alternative sources of opinion) users are referred to section E.VI, Reviews, and to the Index of Subjects entries under "Reviews" and "Bibliographic essays."

The character of my annotations is deliberately dynamic, as they are intended to provide prospective *users* of a reference work with information concerning it. The prospective user will find my annotations sufficiently extensive to form what will turn out to be accurate expectations about a work's utility. Some white space has also been left for users of this guide to add further annotation of their own.

A second type of entry lists scholarly journals in particular fields. The most recent title of the journal is given (along with some previous titles); the current place of publication and publisher are cited (along with some former places and publishers); the beginning date and frequency (or range of frequencies) of publication are given; whether the journal includes reviews or a current bibliography is indicated; and whether and where it is cumulatively indexed is stated. The user should not (to repeat) rely on these entries only. For full, bibliographically authoritative publishing histories of each cited journal, see the *Union List of Serials* (D–90) and *New Serial Titles* (D–91), along with other serials authorities described in section D. See section D, also, for entries on general periodical indexes and guides to indexing and abstracting services that might cover a particular journal.

In these journal lists, my effort has been to strike a balance between including every possible journal in a field and including only the most important. There are nearly fifty such lists interspersed through the various sections and subsections of this volume; a master list appears on page xxxvii.

The third type of entry is the guide list of frequently recommended works in a particular field. The purpose of these lists is to present handy working bibliographies. Authors, titles, and places and dates of publication are indicated, along with Library of Congress call numbers. While every specialist will know of items that might readily be added or deleted from each list, few will find that an included item has no serious claim to a potential user's attention or that an item generally thought indispensable is missing. I urge users to regard these lists with all the suspicion proper to bibliographies assembled by a nonspecialist. In working with this type of entry especially the user should remember the caveats mentioned above and that this book presents the judgments of a single individual. There are about 150 such lists interspersed throughout the various sections and subsections of this guide; a master list appears on pages xxxix-xlii.

One subclass of entries in this category consists of the guides to major English and American authors (at M–60 and S–50 respectively). As is true of every other evaluative decision made in completing this guide, the designation of "major" status reflects my own judgment of where to draw the line. These lists could be enlarged easily and almost as easily contracted. In this case, as in so many others, a degree of arbitrariness is simply unavoidable and might as well not be disguised. In view of the ongoing, radical expansion of the canon, these sections will undoubtedly seem among the most conservative elements in this work, a work in which I have constantly tried to steer a moderate course between the tradition of English studies and the immediate scene in all of its tumultuous vitality.

ARRANGEMENT

Every reference work expresses its author's conception of the field it covers, and this work is no exception. But to interpret my expression correctly, some metadiscourse may prove helpful. I think it within neither my province nor my prerogative to predict the no-doubt related outcomes of the current critical wars in literary theory and the current contentions for control of the institutions of English studies. Nor have I wished to define the ultimate relationship which will emerge between English studies as practiced during the last twenty years and the tradition of studies which have gone before. I have, however, accepted the dual obligations to represent available reference tools, many of which emerge from traditions of study no longer current, and to represent possible reference queries which will emanate not only from the immediate present, but from the foreseeable future of English studies, whatever their various contemporary forms will take. I thus envision a large and relatively stable terrain, with relaxed but determinate, well-traveled borders to neighboring fields, which has recently been disturbed by natural disasters, zoning changes, and the arrival of various new inhabitants, variously related, whose presence is of uncertain duration and significance.

The arrangement of this guide is accordingly complex. I have chosen a table of contents which allows a set of twenty-four unequal sections (not called or considered co-equal chapters) on whole large topics of interest (Section B—Libraries, Section F— History and Ancillae to Historical Studies, Section Z—The Profession of English); broad general classes of reference works (Section A—General Reference Guides, Section C—National Bibliography, Section D—Serial Publications); large general categories of literary study (Section I—Language, Linguistics, and Philology; Section K—Literary Materials and Contexts; Section U— Theatre and Drama; Section W—Prose and Prose Fiction);

traditional periods of English literary study (Section N—Medieval, Section O—Renaissance, Section Q—Nineteenth Century); and the always anomalous field of American Literature—Section S.

I have placed new fields of study within sections where they seemed to find a plausible location (e.g. Folklore, Symbology, and Intellectual History in Section K—Literary Materials and Contexts; Children's Literature and Women's Studies in Section J—Literature; Commonwealth Literature in Section M—English Literature; Chicano Literature in Section S—American Literature; and Structuralism and Deconstruction within Section X—Literary Criticism and Literary Theory). *And I have relied throughout on my intention that the user would begin an inquiry with the Index of Subjects rather than the Table of Contents*, knowing that the index format would allow me most readily to point out where tools on particular topics or texts were located, since an inquirer's topic or text might include works found in half-a-dozen or more locations within this volume. Such reliance, I thought, freed me from having to design a table of contents by either ignoring or having to settle the very issues that make English studies today so exciting and so intractable. My arrangement is thus an act of evasion which is also, I believe, an act of appropriate modesty. Mediating between the evasions of the table of contents and the multiple access points of the index are the numerous cross-references, designed to guide a user to such related materials as I imagined would most likely interest him or her.

Main entries, lists of journals, and lists of frequently recommended works are arranged, then, in twenty-four major sections from A to Z (excluding J and V). Within sections, entries are further disposed into subsections. In general, the sequence of entries moves from more general to more specific works and from more distant subjects and types of tools to those more immediately and narrowly related to English studies. The lists of scholarly journals and of frequently recommended works generally come near the end of the sections or subsections to which they pertain.

Sections A through E concern the most general sorts of bibliographical and reference tools: bibliographies of bibliographies; general reference guides; encyclopedias; library guides; national bibliographies; periodical bibliographies, indexes, and finding lists; tools useful in locating and using dissertations, microforms, reprints, reviews, composite books, dictionaries of anonyms and pseudonyms, and both films and spoken recordings from literary works. Sections F, G, and H treat history and ancillae to historical study; biography and ancillae to biographical study; and manuscripts and archives, along with aids for their study. Section I, on language, linguistics, and philology, is followed by section K on literary materials and contexts, including reference works in the fields of folklore, mythology, Bible study, proverbs, quotations, symbology, and *stoff und motiv-geschichte*. The guides to historical contexts which conclude section K list in one place standard works in social and cultural history; works on costume and courtesy; works on the history of taste and related problems; works on intellectual history and the history of ideas; and finally studies in the history of learning, including education, scholarship, and librarianship. These lists alone make it imperative that users not expect to find all works pertinent to a certain broad subject area—Eighteenth–century studies, for example—enumerated in one place. Many are in section P, on the Restoration and Eighteenth Century, to be sure, but others are here in section K, and there are pertinent works in a dozen other sections, all of which are identified in the Index of Subjects.

Section L begins the specifically literary focus of this guide and treats general and comparative literature; general literary dictionaries; classical studies; and modern languages and literatures (except for the English language and its literatures); along with the newest fields of general literature: children's literature, and women and literature. Section M treats English literature, with separate sections on Scottish, Welsh, and Irish studies, along with Commonwealth literature and world literature written in English. Sections N through R cover the traditional periods of English literary history: medieval, Renaissance, Restoration and eighteenth century, nineteenth century, and twentieth century.

Section S treats American literature, with sections on local and regional literature and on ethnic American languages and literatures. The genres follow in sections T through W, treating poetry and versification; drama, theater, and film; and prose fiction and nonfictional prose respectively. Section X concerns reference works in the fields of literary theory, rhetoric, and composition; Y includes the fields of analytic and enumerative bibliography, textual criticism, the history of the book, book collecting, and libraries and librarianship. Section Z, finally, treats works concerning the profession of English, including historical studies, directories of scholars, expositions of purposes and methods of scholarship, and guides to research, to research methods and techniques, to computer–assisted research, to grants and fellowships, to publication, to the job market, to pedagogy, and to alternative careers. It thus brings the arrangement back full circle to the broadest and most general contexts for the work of English studies.

Within these twenty-four major sections, arrangement generally moves from guides and reviews of research to standard closed and serial bibliographies, to other reference works, such as encyclopedias, companions, dictionaries, and standard reference histories. Subsections of sections concerned with one period of literary history treat works on the poetry, drama, prose fiction, and nonfictional prose of the period. Subsections within the three genre sections include the major subgenres. Subsections in section L treat the major literatures of the world; those in section M treat each of the major Commonwealth English literatures; those in section S treat each of the major regional and ethnic American literatures. The Overview of the Organization of this Guide (pp. xxxi-xxxvi) will aid the user in grasping this organization more completely.

In arrangement of sections and sub-sections, I sought to steer a middle course between an overly simple and an overly elaborate organization. A very simple organization would have been entirely inadequate; a fully systematic arrangement would have left users entangled by complexity. Thus there are numerous divisions and subdivisions, but I have not sought to make them all follow a single system of categories; they are convenient rather than logical divisions and are meant to be overstepped or ignored as necessary in an individual researcher's use of the work.

Still there should be no illusions about the value of this arrangement. It is a relatively flexible and thus fairly realistic way of organizing a vast, various, and everexpanding volume of materials. I do not mean for the Short-Form Listing of all main entries (pp. xliii-lxxii) to be the only or even the best (though it will probably be the most frequently used) means of access to the contents of this volume. And I suspect that the experienced user will not treat it as such.

Given the Guide's functional emphasis and the multiplicity of uses to which almost any reference tool can be put, experienced users will learn to turn first to the detailed Index of Subjects. There in a single alphabet will be found the most convenient means of locating all the tools likely to be worth considering for a particular reference question. Index entries include not only the subject matter of reference works but also terms referring to their type ("indexes and indexing—newspaper," "student bibliographical guides"); their arrangement ("arrangement—chronological"); and the character of their entries ("short-title catalogs," "bibliography, descriptive").

In addition to the Index of Subjects, users will find an Index of Authors, Compilers, Contributors, and Editors; and an Index of Titles. There are also cross–references at the beginnings of most sections and subsections and cross-references within entries. These constitute yet another means of reorganizing this guide. My practice in cross-referencing has been to cite a work under any heading where it makes a fundamental contribution, either because it is itself a major tool (but classed in another section where it is also of the first importance) or because the paucity of available works is such as to make it an essential resource, though it is a work of more general utility. Cross-references between period and genre listings are examples of the first type; repeated cross-references to the *MLA International Bibliography* (L–50), the MHRA's *Annual Bibliography of English Language and Literature* (M–21), the *Year's Work in English Studies* (M–22), and *American Literary Scholarship*: *An Annual* (S–13) are examples of the second sort of cross-reference.

The full entry for each reference work appears, however, only once in the volume, in the place where it seemed to me most appropriately cited. These judgments are not always obvious in their logic, however, and I have had to rely on a number of rules according to which I have placed certain items.

If a work is confined to one literary period (or a part of a period), its main entry is placed within the section concerning that period. Thus, the *Old English Newsletter* is in section N, on medieval literature, subsection on Anglo-Saxon (N–22); the journal *Contemporary Literature* is in the list of scholarly journals in section R, on the twentieth century (R–18); and the standard work of F. O. Matthiessen on the American Renaissance is in the list of frequently recommended works on American literature (S–19).

If a work is confined to one genre, the work is in the section concerned with that genre. Thus Ian Watt's *The Rise of the Novel* is among frequently recommended works on the novel in section W, on prose and prose fiction (W–9), rather than in eighteenth–century studies, though no serious student of the eighteenth century will want to miss reading it, even if its scope is ultimately broader than a treatment of the eighteenth-century novel. In contrast, Ronald Paulson's *Satire and the Novel in Eighteenth Century England* is cited among the frequently recommended works for eighteenth-century studies (P–19), for though it treats the novel, its treatment is confined to novels of the eighteenth century. But Paulson's *Fictions of Satire*, which treats some eighteenth-century novels, is in section W, among frequently recommended works on satire (W–159), for its focus is broadly generic.

If a work treats one genre in one period, as in the above example, the entry is in the genre subsection of that period's section. A frequent exception is when such a work helps to constitute what might be regarded as a multivolume series, in which case it will be cited in the genre section. *The London Stage 1660–1800, 1800–1900,* and *1890-* will be found in section U, on drama and theater (U–77, U–78, U–79), rather than in sections P, Q, and R. Similarly, Chambers's *Elizabethan Stage*, though it is as essential a work of reference for the student of Renaissance drama as the stage calendars are for students of eighteenth-, nineteenth-, and twentieth–century theater, will nevertheless be found in section U beside his work on the medieval stage and the works of Bentley on the seventeenth-century stage and Harbage on Cavalier drama (U–73, U–74, U–75, U–76). Another important exception is when the work

is among several that together constitute the history of the genre. Thus Hallet Smith's *Elizabethan Poetry* is at T–49; Robert D. Hume's *Development of English Drama in the Late Seventeenth Century* is at U–80; and Kathleen Tillotson's *Novels of the Eighteen-Forties* is at W–49.

American literature is treated in a separate section, though works relevant to its study are found in virtually every section of this volume. When a work treats American or indeed another of the world literatures written in English along with British literature, it will most likely be found in section M, along with other works concerned exclusively with English (that is, British) literature. But the user with a question concerning some particular aspect of American literature or American studies would best consult the Index of Subjects, where references are made from a multiplicity of subject terms, rather than the table of contents, where each item if cited at all can be cited, alas, only once, no matter its complexity or variety.

OTHER FEATURES

Standard abbreviations and short titles for journals and major reference works are given in brackets after the full title. Also provided, when possible, are Library of Congress call numbers. Note, however, that LC numbers are uniform only in their first elements, the letters and numbers that identify the subject area of the work. Subsequent elements (and particularly those identifying authors and editions) may vary slightly in other libraries that nevertheless use the LC system. The numbers cited here are those actually used at the Library of Congress, where most of the work of preparing this Guide took place. Most users will find the deviation from this number at their research library relatively slight and will, therefore, have use for this feature.

Here and there some not-yet-published works are cited, but only when they are likely to be worth consulting as soon as they are published—that is, when they fill a gap in existing resources.

Features that some reference guides have included but that I have excluded are citation of Dewey decimal numbers (on the grounds of their infrequent use in research libraries); reference to the rapidly changing facts of microform versions or reprints (see the pertinent reference tools in section E.IV, on microforms, and E.V, on reprints); and reference to the even more rapidly changing facts of publication: prices, paperback editions, and in-print status (see tools in section C such as *Books in Print*, C–39).

SOME PECULIARITIES

One oddity that users will probably regret, but which I found expedient for indexing and other purposes, is my decision to delete initial definite and indefinite articles in English-language titles except in the titles of works of literature. Another peculiarity is my decision to exclude lists of frequently recommended works from the indexing process, save that the general subjects of those lists are included in the subject index.

There are also peculiarities arising from the once ground-breaking but now antiquated main-frame word processing and document design programs through which this book has been typeset. These include unusual hyphenation practices, particularly in foreign language words, and sufficient formatting difficulty to make it necessary sometimes to accept titles in one column whose description is in another. While an effort has been made to over-ride these automatic inelegancies, it has not been possible always to catch or to cure them.

One consequence of the unusual manner in which this book has been typeset is that it has taken several years to complete the process. While an effort has been made to add important new titles, they have sometimes for convenience sake been appended as ancillary titles to an earlier entry when they should under more flexible circumstances have changed places and become main entries themselves.

I am aware, also, of the unfortunate peculiarity that this volume fails consistently to practice nonsexist usage, particularly in my more than occasional employment of masculine pronouns and references in their "generic" sense. I have myself only recently been able to acknowledge the offensiveness of this practice and I apologize for it. I am also aware of, but was unable to act on the need to change "Afro-American" references to the preferred designation of "African-American."

FURTHER CONCERNS

Although I have worked alone on this guide, I have not been without the benefit of colleagues and friends who have given advice freely on most sections and whose help is acknowledged below. But the University of California Press and I recognize the opportunity that only publishing creates to secure the advice of hundreds of colleagues about errors of exclusion and inclusion, errors of fact, of emphasis, and of judgment. We will be grateful for the receipt of all such advice and hope to incorporate it in a revised edition. Needless to say, all such errors remain my sole responsibility.

It is difficult ever to let a book of this sort be published. As has been true for each of the last twelve years of work on *A Reference Guide for English Studies*, yet another year's tinkering will certainly improve it. But there is no end to such effort, and every year of tinkering brings on another year's worth of revised, supplemented, and new reference works that must be evaluated for inclusion. As it is, the entries in this volume are current only through 1985 or so, though I have made considerable effort to cite later items as they came to my attention. Because the entire text is stored on computer, it has been possible continuously to revise and update it until the point at which camera-ready copy was generated, roughly six months before actual publication. Still, if this book succeeds in being the guide I have intended to write, a later edition will certainly improve on this one.

I cannot conclude this Preface without referring users to the Acknowledgments. Though this has been a single and quite lonely project, my work has been supported at every turn by colleagues and friends. Without their interest, encouragement, and help, I would never have been able to bring it even to this provisional conclusion.

College Park, Maryland   Michael J. Marcuse
December 1989

ACKNOWLEDGEMENTS

Work on this Reference Guide began in the mid–1970's while I was associated with The Catholic University of America. I am grateful to my former colleagues and students in the English Department there for the opportunity to start this project. Among my students, I want particularly to thank David Arbogast, Walt Besecker, Verlyn Flieger, Karen Garlick, Anne McCallum, Bill Roen, Kathy Shapleigh, Will Wadsworth, and Josephine Williams.

Of those instrumental in the project's continuation, none were more continuously supportive than my colleagues Jon Wakelyn at Catholic University and Calhoun Winton at the University of Maryland. Jack Miles, former editor of the University of California Press and now the Book Review editor of *The Los Angeles Times*, provided all the editorial encouragement one could hope for. Little did I know when Jack sent me a copy of Dr. Johnson's prayer written on April 3, 1753, on beginning the second volume of his *Dictionary*, that I would refer to it so regularly over such a long time. Nor did I realize with what sympathy I would learn to read the Preface to that great work.

I want also to thank the numerous reviewers of this work at one stage or another in its development. Some of them I know by name and others remain anonymous to me; their careful comments have rescued the users of this guide from many an error. Among those I can name are Jackson Bryer, Theresa Coletti, Sherod Cooper, George Dillon, Robert Levine, Bill Peterson, Sam Schoenbaum, and Joseph Wittreich of The University of Maryland; Janet Gilligan of USIA; Richard K. Gardner, Robert L. Kinsman, and Thomas Wortham of the University of California at Los Angeles; and James Woodress of the University of California at Davis.

I appreciate also the many librarians who reviewed entries on their institutions, helping me to provide relatively accurate and current information. I must especially, if without name, acknowledge many Library of Congress staff members who answered hundreds of queries over the years. It is difficult to imagine working on this project elsewhere; the librarians and research facilities at the LC were invaluable at every turn. I am particularly grateful to the staff of the Stack and Reader Division and to Katherine Ann Gardner, Reference Collection Specialist and head of the reference collection in the Main Reading Room. I also want to acknowledge help received from Blue Gudekunst and the late Dorothy King of the Humanities Division of Mullen Library at Catholic University, and from Helen Baer, Susan Cardinale, Betty Day, and Martha Seabrook of McKeldin Library at The University of Maryland.

At Maryland I also received the welcome support of the English Department who collegially subsidized a semester without teaching or administrative duties during which I was able to complete a thorough revision of the main body of this work. My work was also supported at Maryland by the Graduate Research Board whose Book Subsidy Award helped to defray part of the cost of computerizing the text.

Without an abundance of secretarial help at Maryland both before and after computerizing, this project could not have been completed. For typing and retyping, proofreading, and constant good cheer, I thank Adrienne Brice, Ann Newton, Susan Nippes, and Mattie Patterson, all formerly with the English Department. For their rapid, high quality, and thoughtfully cooperative hard work, I thank Deb Mateik and Carol Warrington of the Maryland Computer Science Center. I am particularly grateful for their ability to cope with the many frustrations that arose while working with an antiquated main-frame document processing system in the face of newer and more tractable hardware and software which this project, alas, pre-dated.

Thanks also to Mitch Cahan for twice proofreading the entire manuscript as it was being transferred to computer, and to Molly Brennan for engineering that bit of good fortune at just the right time. I want also to thank my current research assistant, Robert Champ, for his help in putting the finishing touches on this work and in giving it a thorough proofreading. Finally, I want to record my gratitude to Aletha Hendrickson, my student, graduate assistant, colleague, and friend, for years of editorial assistance: this book would not have been finished without her help.

It is fitting to have read final proof of the pages of this guide in the Shirley Strum Kenny Library in the English Department at Maryland, for without the opportunity Shirley gave me in 1978, neither this book nor any other aspect of my academic work over the last twelve years would have been possible. And I was multiply blessed in having that opportunity enriched and extended by John Howard, Annabel Patterson, Richard Cross, and Deirdre David, to all of whom I give heartfelt thanks for many kindnesses over many years.

A separate paragraph must be given to acknowledge the extraordinary efforts of University of California Press copyeditor, Nicholas Goodhue, who took on an arduous task and has made this book better in almost every line.

I acknowledge also my colleagues, counselors, family, and friends for their encouragement, support, patience, and forbearance as I babbled on endlessly about this project and its repeatedly delayed conclusion. I thank Mendel Abrams, Steve Cohen, Linda Coleman, Frank Del Pino, Kevin Dungey, Jeanne Fahnestock, Betty Fern, Anne Franzak, Bob Gamble, Roger Hayhurst, Margaret Garrett, Gene Hammond, Jack Hofer, Joseph Horobetz, Ray Hylton, Susan Kleimann, Walter Knorr, Steve Lautermilch, Rick Lovely, David Marcuse, Deborah Marcuse, Estelle Marcuse, Gisela Marcuse, Peggy Pearl, Tom Phillips, Ingo Seeler, Karl-August Seeler, and Bruce Wine.

Death has claimed some of the most important people in my life. I remember the help and encouragement of Harry Marcuse, Hannah Pearl, Magdalena Seeler, and Beatrice Wilson.

It is with gratitude which surpasses the power of acknowledgment that I dedicate this work to Gisela, to Deborah, and to Anne.

M.J.M.

ABBREVIATIONS, ACRONYMS, AND SIGLA

AA	*American Archivist* H–8	*AfrS*	*African Studies* L–138
A and EB	*Analytical and Enumerative Bibliography* Y–38	*AfrSR*	*African Studies Review* L–138
		Afr-T	*Africa-Tervuren* L–138
AAS	*Asian and African Studies* L–148	AFS	*Abstracts of Folklore Studies* K–12
ABA	*American Biographical Archive* G–39	AGR	*American German Review* L–108
ABAA	Antiquarian Booksellers Association of America Y–77	AHA	American Historical Association F–1
		AHA Guide	*AHA Guide to Historical Literature* F–1
ABC	*American Book Prices Current* Y–72	AHC	*Arts and Humanities Citation Index* D–19
ABC	Association for Business Communication Z–25	AH	*American Humanities Index* D–18
ABCMA	*Annotated Bibliography of Canada's Major Authors* M–135	AHL	*America, History and Life* F–54
		AHR	*American Historical Review* F–10
ABELL	*Annual Bibliography of English Language and Literature* M–21	Ahumor	*American Humor* S–18
		AI	*American Image* X–38
ABHB	*Annual Bibliography of the History of the Printed Book and Libraries* Y–7	AICRJ	*American Indian Culture and Research Journal* S–18
ABMI	*Author Biographies Master Index* L–31	AIQ	*American Indian Quarterly* S–18
ABPR	*American Book Publishing Record* C–27	AJAS	*Australian Journal of American Studies* S–18
Abrams	see L–13		
ACLA	American Comparative Literature Association Z–25	AJFS	*Australian Journal of French Studies* L–78
ACLALSB	*ACLALSB Bulletin* M–108	AJP	*American Journal of Philology* L–48
ADB	*Australian Dictionary of Biography* M–129	AL	*American Literature* S–18
		ALA	American Library Association
ADD	*American Doctoral Dissertations* E–6	ALH	*American Literary History* S–18
ADE	Association of Departments of English Z–25	ALing	*Analecta Linguistica* I–15
		Allibone	see M–50
ADFL	Association of Departments of Foreign Languages Z–10	ALM	*American Literary Manuscripts* H–51
		ALMA	*Archivum Latinitatis Medii Aevi* N–18
AEB	*Analytical and Enumerative Bibliography* Y–14, Y–38	ALR	*American Literary Realism* S–18
		ALS	*American Literary Scholarship* S–14
AES	*AES Abstracts of English Studies* M–23	ALS	*Australian Literary Studies* M–127, M–128
AETA	American Educational Theatre Association U–8		
		ALT	*African Literature Today* L–138, M–118
Africa	*Africa: Rivista trimestrale di studie documentzione dell'Istituto italo-africano* L–138	Altick and Wright	see A–10
		American Catalogue	see C–28
AfricaL	*Africa: Journal of the International African Institute (London)* L–138	AmerS	*American Studies* S–18
		AmLS	*American Literary Scholarship* S–18
AfricaM	*Africa (Madrid)* L–138	AmSt	*Amerikastudien* S–18
AfrLJ	*Africana Library Journal* L–138	AN&Q	*American Notes and Queries* S–18, Z–58
AfrLS	*African Language Studies* L–138	AnBol	*Analecta Bollandiana* N–18

BUCOP	*British Union Catalogue of Periodicals* D–95	*CHEL*	*Cambridge History of English Literature* M–32
BUL-L	*Bibliographie unselbständiger Literatur— Linguistik* I–9	*ChildL*	*Children's Literature: An International Journal* L–179
BUR	*Bucknell Review* X–38	*ChinL*	*Chinese Literature* L–148
Burke	see G–18, G–19, G–20	*ChinaQ*	*China Quarterly* L–148
BUSL	*Bibliography of United States Literature* S–11	*CHR*	*Canadian Historical Review* F–10
		CHUM	*Computers and the Humanities* Z–75
C	Cambridge University Library B–50	*CIJE*	*Current Index to Journals in Education* Z–125
ca.	circa	*CJ*	*Classical Journal* L–48
CA	*Contemporary Authors* R–23	*CJIS*	*Canadian Journal of Irish Studies* M–93
CAA	*Contemporary American Authors* S–28	*CJL*	*Canadian Journal of Linguistics* I–15
CALL	*Current Awareness Library Literature* Y–93	*CL*	*Comparative Literature* L–9
CALM	*Calendars of American Literary Manuscripts* H–53	CLA	Children's Literature Association Z–25
		CLA	College Language Association M–25, S–18, Z–25
Camb	U.L. Cambridge University Library B–50	*CLAJ*	*CLA Journal* M–25, S–18
CanL	*Canadian Literature* M–143, M–148	Clio	see F–10, X–38
C&L	*Christianity and Literature* X–38	*CLS*	*Comparative Literature Studies* L–9
CANR	*Contemporary Authors: New Revision* R–23	CLU	University of California, Los Angeles (UCLA) Libraries B–39
CaOTU	University of Toronto Libraries B–39	CLU-C	William Andrews Clark Memorial Library, UCLA B–39
CAP	*Contemporary Authors: Permanent Series* R–23	*CMH*	*Cambridge Modern History* F–14
CAR	*Contemporary Authors: First Revision* R–23	*CN*	*Cultura neolatína* L–63
Case	see O–21	CNRS	Centre national de recherche scientifique I–10
CB	*Current Biography* G–55	Cokayne	see G–21, G–22
CBEL	*Cambridge Bibliography of English Literature* M–10, N–10, O–10, P–10, Q–10	COM	Computer Output Microfiche, Computer Output Microform B–13
CBI	*Cumulative Book Index* C–30	*ComM*	*Communication Monographs* X–165
CBRI	*Children's Book Review Index* L–179	*CompD*	*Comparative Drama* U–18
CCBEL	*Concise Cambridge Bibliography of English Literature 600–1950* M–10	*ComQ*	*Communication Quarterly* X–165
		Conch	*The Conch: A Sociological Journal of African Cultures and Literatures* L–138
CCC	*College Composition and Communication* X–165	*ConL*	*Contemporary Literature* R–18
CCCC	Conference on College Composition and Communication Z–25	*ConP*	*Contemporary Poetry* T–8
		Cooper	see C–25
CCHEL	*Concise Cambridge History of English Literature* M–33	*CP*	*Classical Philology* L–48
		CP	*Concerning Poetry* T–8
CCL	*Current Contents Linguistic* I–9	*CPM*	*Catalogue of Printed Music in the British Library to 1980* B–41
CCL	*Canadian Children's Literature* L–179		
CCM	*Cahiers de civilisation médiévale* N–18	*CQ*	*Classical Quarterly* L–48
CCP	*Catalogue collectif des périodiques* D–98	*CR*	*Classical Review* L–48
CCrit	*Comparative Criticism: A Yearbook* L–9	Crane and Kaye	see D–50
CDAB	*Concise Dictionary of American Biography* G–35	*CrevB*	*Conch Review of Books: A Literary Supplement on Africa* L–138
CD	*Comprehensive Dissertation Index* E–5	CRIS/History	see F–8
CE	*College English* X–165, Z–25	*Crit*	*Critique: Studies in Modern Fiction* R–18, W–8
CEAA	Center for Editions of American Authors S–50, Y–36	*CRL*	*College and Research Libraries* H–8
CEF	*Catalogue de l'édition française* C–57	*CRLN*	*Comparative Romance Linguistics Newsletter* L–63
CEd	*Communication Education* X–165		
CES	*Commonwealth: Essays and Studies* M–108	Crum	see T–10
		CS	Stanford University Libraries B–39
CHAL	*Cambridge History of American Literature* S–34	CSE	Center for Scholarly Editions Y–36
		CSHVB	*Computer Studies in the Humanities and Verbal Behavior* Z–75
ChauR	*Chaucer Review* N–18	CSmH	Henry E. Huntington Library and Art Gallery B–20
CHBE	*Cambridge History of the British Empire* F–20	*CTR*	*Canadian Theatre Review* U–18

CtY	Yale University Library B–21, H–27	
CU	University of California, Berkeley, Libraries B–39	
CUBI	see C–72	
D	Trinity College, Dublin B–56	
DAB	*Dictionary of American Biography* G–35	
DAE	*Dictionary of American English on Historical Principles* I–45	
DAEM	*Deutsches Archiv für Erforschung des Mittelalters* N–18	
DAH	*Dictionary of American History* F–57	
DAI	*Dissertation Abstracts International* E–7	
Davies	see F–32	
DCB	*Dictionary of Canadian Biography* G–35	
Debrett	see G–23	
DeRicci	see H–28	
DFo	Folger Shakespeare Library B–22	
DHLR	*D.H. Lawrence Review* M–60	
Dietrich	see D–13	
DLB	*Dictionary of Literary Biography* [Everyman's] M–51	
DLB	*Dictionary of Literary Biography* [Gale] M–58	
DLC	Library of Congress B–23	
DM	*Dublin Magazine* M–93	
DNB	*Dictionary of National Biography* G–10	
DOE	*Dictionary of Old English* I–36	
DQR	*Dutch Quarterly Review of Anglo-American Letters* M–25	
DramS	*Drama Survey* U–18	
DreiN	*Dreiser Newsletter* S–50	
DSA	*Dickens Studies Annual: Essays on Victorian Fiction* M–60, Q–18	
Dt	Trinity College, Dublin B–56	
DT	Trinity College, Dublin B–56	
duCangesee	I–69	
Duff	see C–4	
Dutcher	see F–2	
DVLG	*Deutsche Vierteljahresschrift für Literaturwissenschaft und Geistesgeschichte* L–57	
DWL	*Dictionary of World Literature* L–11	
E&S	*Essays and Studies* M–25	
EA	*Études anglaises* M–25	
EA	*Encyclopedia of Associations* Z–28	
EAL	*Early American Literature* S–18	
EC	*Études celtiques* M–93	
ECCB	*Eighteenth Century: A Current Bibliography* P–5	
ECF	*Eighteenth-Century Fiction* P–18	
EcHR	*Economic History Review* F–10	
ECLife	*Eighteenth Century Life* P–18	
ECr	*L'ésprit créateur* L–78	
ECS	*Eighteenth-Century STudies* P–18	
ECT&I	*Eighteenth Century: Theory and Interpretation* P–18	
ed.	edition	
EE	*English Education* Z–138	

EEMSF	*Early English Manuscripts in Facsimile* N–29	
EETS	Early English Text Society	
EF	*Études françaises* L–78	
EFT	*English Fiction in Transition* R–2	
EG	*Études germaniques: Revue trimestrielle* L–108	
EGL	*Essay and General Literature Index* E–81	
EHR	*English Historical Review* F–10	
E	*Études irlandaises* M–93	
EIC	*Essays in Criticism* X–13	
EIE	*English Institute* X–13	
EJ	*English Journal* X–165, Z–138	
ELH	*English Literary History* M–25, Q–25	
ELN	*English Language Notes* M–25	
ELR	*English Literary Renaissance* O–8, O–18	
ELT	*English Literature in Transition* R–2, R–18	
ELT	*English Language Teaching Journal* Z–138	
EngC	*The English Catalogue* C–13	
enl.	enlarged	
EnlE	*Enlightenment Essays* P–18	
ERIC	Educational Resources Information Center Z–125	
ES	*English Studies* M–25	
ESA	*English studies in Africa* M–118	
ESP	*English for Specific Purposes* I–15, X–165	
Espasa	see A–47	
ESQ	*ESQ: A Journal of the American Renaissance* S–18, S–50	
ESTC	*Eighteenth-Century Short Title Catalogue* C–12	
ETC	*Review of General Semantics* I–15	
ETJ	*Educational Theater Journal* U–18	
Evans	see C–22	
Expl.	*Explicator* T–8, T–31	
FC	*Film Comment* U–129	
FC	*Film Criticism* U–129	
FDP	*Four Decades of Poetry, 1890–1930* T–8	
FEN	*Freshman English News* X–165	
FF	*Folklore Forum* K–23	
FFC	*Folklore Fellows, FF Communications* K–23	
FG	*International Film Guide* U–129	
FHA	*Fitzgerald/Hemingway Annual* S–50	
FID	Fédération international de documentation	
Filby	see G–14	
FL	*Foundations of Language* I–15	
FM	*Le français moderne: Revue de linguistique française* L–78	
FMLS	*Forum for Modern Language Studies* L–57	
FoLi	*Folia Linguistica* I–15	
Follett	see I–52	
Folklore	see K–23	
Fortescue	see A–32	
Foster	see G–28	
Fowler	see I–34	

Foxon	see P–20	
FQ	*Film Quarterly* U–129	
FR	*French Review* L–78	
FS	*Feminist Studies* L–189	
FS	*French Studies: A Quarterly Review* L–78	
FU	University of Florida Libraries B–39	
G&R	*Greece and Rome* L–48	
GAZ	*Gesamtverzeichnis ausländischer Zeitschriften* D–98	
GAZS	*Gesamtverzeichnis ausländischer Zeitschriften und Serien* D–98	
GDZS	*Gesamtverzeichnis der deutschen Zeitschriften und Serien* D–98	
GEFR	*George Eliot Fellowship Review* M–60	
Genre	see L–9, X–13	
Georgi	see C–60	
Germanistik	see L–108	
GL	*General Linguistics* I–15	
GL	*Glotta: Zeitschrift für griechische und lateinische Sprache* L–48	
GL&L	*German Life and Letters: A Quarterly Review* L–108	
Glossa	see I–15	
Gn	*Gnomon: Kritische Zeitschrift für die gesamte klassische Altertumswissenschaft* L–48	
Goff	see C–4	
GQ	*German Quarterly* L–108	
GR	*Germanic Review* L–108	
Granger's Index	see T–20	
Grässe	see C–51	
Graves	see F–25	
Greg	see O–31	
GRM	*Germanisch-Romanische Monatsschrift* L–57	
Grose	see F–35	
GSLI	*Giornale storico della letteratura italiana* L–88	
GV	*Gesamtverzeichnis* C–67	
GW	*Gesamtkatalog der Wiegendrücke* C–4	
GZS	*Gesamtverzeichnis der Zeitschriften und Serien* D–98	
HAHR	*Hispanic American Historical Review* F–10	
Halkett and Laing	see E–92	
Hanham	see F–43	
Harvey	see M–40	
HDB	*Hasting's Dictionary of the Bible* K–41	
Heinsius	see C–61	
Hermes	see L–48	
Hinrichs	see C–63	
HIS	*Humanities in the South* Z–158	
Hispania	see L–95	
HJ	*Historical Journal* F–10	
HJAS	*Harvard Journal of Asiatic Studies* L–148	
HLAS	*Handbook of Latin American Studies* L–99	
HLB	*Harvard Library Bulletin* B–26	
HLB	*Huntington Library Bulletin* B–20	
HLQ	*Huntington Library Quarterly* B–20, Z–58	

HMC	Historical Manuscripts Commission H–60, H–61	
HMSO	Her Majesty's Stationery Office	
Hoefer	see G–9	
Holman	see L–12	
Howard-Hill	see M–1, O–45, Y–1	
HQ	*Hopkins Quarterly* M–60	
HR	*Hispanic Review* L–95	
HRHRC	Harry Ransom Humanities Research Center B–35	
HSCP	*Harvard Studies in Classical Philology* L–48	
HudR	*Hudson Review* Z–158	
Hyamson	see G–2	
IBBB	*Internationale Bibliographie des Buch- und Bibliothekswesens* Y–8	
IBF	*Internationale Bibliographie der Festschriften* E–85	
IBHS	*International Bibliography of Historical Sciences* F–4	
IBN	*Index Bio-bibliographicus Notorum Hominum* G–5	
IBR	*Internationale Bibliographie der Reprints* E–62	
IBR	*Internationale Bibliographie der Rezensionen* E–75	
IBRH	*Index to Book Reviews in the Humanities* E–73	
IBT	*International Bibliography of Theatre* U–15	
IBZ	*Internationale Bibliographie der Zeitschriftenliteratur* D–13	
ICN	Newberry Library B–25	
ICU	University of Chicago Libraries B–39	
IDB	*Interpreter's Dictionary of the Bible* K–40	
IEN	Northwestern University Libraries B–39	
IF	*Indogermanische Forschungen* L–108	
IFR	*International Fiction Review* W–8	
IHS	*Irish Historical Studies* M–93	
IJAL	*International Journal of American Linguistics* I–15	
IJBF	*Internationale Jahres-Bibliographie der Festschriften* E–85	
IJOH	*International Journal of Oral History* F–10	
IJPs	*International Journal of Psycholinguistics* I–15	
IJSL	*International Journal of the Sociology of Language* I–15	
IJSLP	*International Journal of Slavic Linguistics and Poetics* L–128	
IJSym	*International Journal of Symbology* K–79	
IMB	*International Medieval Bibliography* F–23	
IMEP	*Index of Middle English Prose* N–38	
IMEV	*Index of Middle English Verse* N–36, N–37	
IMU	*Italia medioevale e umanistica* L–88	
IncL	*Incorporated Linguist* I–15, I–106	
IndL	*Indian Literature* L–148, M–158	
IndLing	*India Linguistics* M–158	
InU	University of Indiana Libraries B–39	

IRAL	*International Review of Applied Linguistics* I–15
IRLI	*Italnianistica: rivista di letteratura italiana* L–88
IS	*Italian Studies* L–88
ISA	*Irregular Series and Annuals* D–101
ISBN	International Standard Book Number
ISSHP	*Index to Social Science and Humanities Proceedings* E–88
Italica	see L–88
IU	University of Illinois Libraries B–39
IUR	*Irish University Review* M–93
JAAC	*Journal of Aesthetics and Art Criticism* X–13, X–32, X–38
JAC	*Journal of Advanced Composition* X–165
JAC	*Journal of American Culture* S–18
JAF	*Journal of American Folklore* K–23
JAH	*Journal of American History* F–10
Jahresverzeichnis	see E–18
JAmS	*Journal of American Studies* S–18
JAOS	*Journal of the American Oriental Society* L–148
JapQ	*Japan Quarterly* L–148
JArabL	*Journal of Arabic Literature* L–148
JAsiat	*Journal asiatique* L–148
JASt	*Journal of Asian Studies* L–148
JBRS	*Journal of the Burma Research Society* L–148
JBS	*Journal of British Studies* F–10
JC	*Journal of Communication* X–165
JCF	*Journal of Canadian Fiction* M–148, W–8
JCL	*Journal of Commonwealth Literature* L–138, M–101, M–108
JCP	*Journal of Canadian Poetry* M–148
JEGP	*Journal of English and Germanic Philology* L–108, L–118
JEH	*Journal of Economic History* F–10
JEngL	*Journal of English Linguistics* I–15
JES	*Journal of Ethnic Studies* S–18
JFI	*Journal of the Folklore Institute* K–23
JGE	*Journal of General Education* Z–138
JH	*Journal of the History of Ideas* F–10, X–38
JHS	*Journal of Hellenic Studies* L–48
JIL	*Journal of Irish Literature* M–93
JJQ	*James Joyce Quarterly* M–60, M–93
JJS	*Journal of Japanese Studies* L–148
JKS	*Journal of Korean Studies* L–148
JL	*Journal of Linguistics* I–15
JLS	*Journal of Literary Semantics* I–15
JMH	*Journal of Modern History* F–10
JML	*Journal of Modern Literature* R–17, R–18
JMRS	*Journal of Medieval and Renaissance Studies* N–18
JNL	*Johnsonian Newsletter* M–60, P–9, P–18, Z–58
JNT	*Journal of Narrative Technique* W–8
Jones	see I–35
JPC	*Journal of Popular Culture* K–23
JPS	*Journal of the Polynesian Society* M–168
JPsyR	*Journal of Psycholinguistic Research* I–15
JRAS	*Journal of the Royal Asiatic Society of Great Britain and Ireland* L–148
JRS	*Journal of Roman Studies* L–48
JSoAL	*Journal of South Asian Literature* L–148, M–158
JSSE	*Journal of the Short Story in English* W–8
JTWC	*Journal of Technical Writing and Communication* X–165
JUFVA	*Journal of the University Film and Video Association* U–129
JWCI	*Journal of the Warburg and Courtauld Institutes* X–38
JWSL	*Journal of Women's Studies in Literature* L–188
Kayser	see C–62
Kelly	see C–26
Kenyon & Knott	see I–53
Klapp	see L–73
KSGT	*Kleine Schriften der Gesellschaft fur Theatergeschichte* U–18
KSJ	*Keats-Shelley Journal* M–60, Q–18, Q–26
KSMB	*Keats-Shelley Memorial Bulletin. Rome.* M–60, Q–18
L	British Library B–40
L&H	*Literature and History* X–38
L&	*Literature and Ideology* X–38
L&P	*Literature and Psychology* X–38, X–61
L&S	*Language and Speech* I–15
L&U	*Lion and the Unicorn: A Critical Journal of Children's Literature* L–179
LA	*Language Arts* Z–138
LALR	*Latin American Literary Review* L–95
Lang&S	*Language and Style: An International Journal* I–15
Langer	see F–11
Language	see I–15
Latham	see I–69
LATR	*Latin-American Theater Review* U–18
LC	Library of Congress A–33, B–12, B–13, H–23
LCR	*Literary Criticism Register* M–24
LCSH	*Library of Congress Subject Headings* A–33
LE&W	*Literature East and West* L–148
Lewis & Short	see I–65
LFQ	*Literature/Film Quarterly* U–129
LHUS	*Literary History of the United States* S–10, S–30
LHY	*Literary Half-Yearly* M–158
LI	*Lettere italiane* L–88
Liddell & Scott	see I–60
LIMC	*Lexicon Iconographicum Mythologiae Classicae* K–29
Ling & P	*Linguistics and Philosophy* I–15
LingA	*Linguistic Analysis* I–15
LingI	*Linguistic Inquiry* I–15
Lingua	see I–15
Linguistics	see I–15
LJ	*Library Journal* Y–98

LL	*Language Learning* I–15	
LLBA	*Language and Language Behavior Abstracts* I–7	
LLINQUA	*Language and Literature Index Quarterly* L–7	
LNHT	Tulane University Libraries B–39	
LNL	*Linguistics in Literature* X–165	
Lodge	see G–24	
LondC	*The London Catalogue* C–11	
LOP	*Language of Poetry* T–8	
Lorenz	see C–55	
Lowndes	see C–3	
LQ	*Library Quarterly* Y–38	
LR	*Les Lettres romanes* L–63	
LR	*Literary Research: A Journal of Scholarly Method and Technique* Y–14	
LRB	*London Review of Books* Z–153	
LSA	Linguistic Society of America Z–25	
LSoc	*Language in Society* I–15	
MA	*Le moyen âge* N–18	
MAE	*Medium Aevum* N–18	
MAL	*Modern Austrian Literature* L–108	
Malclès	see A–22	
M&H	*Medievalia et Humanistica* N–18	
Manuscripta	see H–8	
MARC	Machine readable cataloging Z–78	
MARC	Machine Readable Cataloging see Z–78	
Mathews	see I–46	
MB	Boston Public Library B–39, H–27	
McGuire	see L–40	
McNamee	see E–20	
MD	*Modern Drama* R–18, R–44	
MDAC	*Mystery and Detection Annual* W–8	
MdHi	Maryland Historical Society Library H–27	
MED	*Middle English Dictionary* I–38	
MeWC	Colby College Library B–39	
MFS	*Modern Fiction Studies* R–18, R–59, W–8	
MH	Harvard University Libraries B–26, H–27	
MHRA	Modern Humanities Research Association L–52, M–21, Z–25, Z–94	
Michaud	see G–9	
MIO	*Mitteilungen des Instituts für Orientforschung* L–148	
MissQ	*Mississippi Quarterly* S–18	
MiU	University of Michigan Libraries B–39, H–27	
MiU-C	Clements Library, University of Michigan B–39, H–27	
MLA	Modern Language Association L–50, Z–25, Z–94	
MLAIB	*MLA International Bibliography* L–50	
MLJ	*Modern Language Journal* L–57	
MLN	*MLN: Modern Language Notes* L–57, Z–58	
MLQ	*Modern Language Quarterly* L–57	
MLR	*Modern Language Review* L–57	
MLS	*Modern Language Studies* L–57	
MMLA	Midwest Modern Language Association Z–25	
MN	*Monumenta Nipponica: Studies in Japanese Culture* L–148	
MnU	University of Minnesota Libraries B–39	
Monatshefte	see L–108	
Mosaic	see L–9	
MoSW	Washington University Libraries see H–27	
Motif-Index	see K–2	
MP	*Modern Philology* L–57	
MPS	*Modern Poetry Studies* T–8	
MS	manuscript	
MS	*Mediaeval Studies* N–18	
MSEX	*Melville Society Extracts* S–50	
MSS	manuscripts	
MSS	*Manuscripts* H–8	
MTJ	*Mark Twain Journal* S–50	
MTLA	*Micropublisher's Trade List Annual* E–52	
MuK	*Maske and Kothurn* U–18	
Muret-Sanders	see I–85	
Muséon	see L–148	
MWA	American Antiquarian Society Library B–27, H–27	
MWH	Massachusetts Historical Society Library H–27	
NAIP	North American Imprints Programsee C–12	
Names	see I–15	
N&Q	*Notes and Queries* Z–58	
NCBEL	*New Cambridge Bibliography of English Literature* M–11, N–11, O–11, P–11, Q–11, R–11	
NcD	Duke University Libraries B–39	
NCF	*Nineteenth Century Fiction* Q–18, W–8	
NCMH	*New Cambridge Modern History* F–14	
NConL	*Notes on Contemporary Literature* R–18	
NCSTC	*Nineteenth Century Short Title Catalogue* C–14	
NCTE	National Council of Teachers of English Z–25, Z–129	
NCTR	*Nineteenth Century Theatre Research* Q–18, Q–62, U–18	
NcU	University of North Carolina B–39	
NDB	*Neue deutsche Biographie* G–61	
NED	*New English Dictionary on Historical Principles* I–33	
NEMLA	Northeast Modern Language Association Z–25	
Neohelicon	see L–9	
Neophil.	*Neophilologus* L–57	
NEQ	*New England Quarterly* S–18, S–101	
NHJ	*Nathaniel Hawthorne Journal* S–50	
NHPRC	National Historical Publications and Records Commission H–21	
NIC	Cornell University Libraries B–39	
Nicholson	see I–51	
Nilon	see S–1	
NIM	*Newspapers in Microform* E–56	
NjP	Princeton University Libraries B–39, H–27	
NLH	*New Literary History* X–13	
NLI	National Library of Ireland B–57	

REL	*Revue des études latines* L–48		*RTE*	*Research in the Teaching of English* X–165, Z–129, Z–138
RELO	*Revue de l'Organization internationale pour l'etude des langues anciennes par ordinateur* Z–75		*RusL*	*Russian Literature* L–128
			RusLing	*Russian Linguistics* L–128
Ren&R	*Renaissance and Reformation/Renaissance et Réforme* O–18		*RusR*	*Russian Review* L–128
RenD	*Renaissance Drama* O–18		*S&S*	*Science and Society* X–38
RenQ	*Renaissance Quarterly* O–6, O–18		*S&S*	*Sight and Sound* U–129
RER	*Review of Educational Research* Z–138		*SA*	*Studi Americani* S–18
RES	*Review of English Studies* M–25		*SAB*	*Shakespeare Association Bulletin* O–58
rev.	revised		*SAB*	*South Atlantic Bulletin* L–57
RF	*Romanische Forschungen* L–63		Sabin	see C–21
RFE	*Revista de filología española* L–95		Sader	see D–29
RFI	*Regionalism and the Female Imagination* L–189		*SAF*	*Studies in American Fiction* S–18, W–8
RFR	*Resources for Feminist Research* L–187		*SAIL*	*Studies in American Indian Literature* S–18
RG	*Reader's Guide to Periodical Literature* D–15		SAMLA	South Atlantic Modern Language Association Z–25
RHL	*Révue d'histoire littéraire de la France* L–74, L–78		*SAQ*	*South Atlantic Quarterly* Z–158
RHM	*Revista Hispánia moderna* L–95		*SB*	*Studies in Bibliography* Y–38
Rht	*Revue d'histoire du theatre* U–18		*SBHC*	*Studies in Browning and His Circle* M–60
RIB	*Revista interamericana de bibliografía* L–95		*SBL*	*Studies in Black Literature* M–118, S–18
RIE	*Resources in Education* Z–126		*SBTC*	*Shakespearean Bibliography and Textual Criticism* O–45
RILA	*Répertoire internationale de la littérature de l'art* X–45		SCA	Speech Communication Association Z–25
RILM	*Répertoire internationale de littérature musicale* X–40		*Scan*	*Scandinavica* L–108
RJ	*Romanistisches Jahrbuch* L–63		*ScanR*	*Scandinavian Review* L–108
RL	*Revista de literatura* L–95		*SCL*	*Studies in Canadian Literature* M–148
RL	*Revue de littérature comparée* L–9		SCMLA	South Central Modern Language Association Z–25
RLI	*Rassegna della letteratura italiana* L–88		*SCN*	*Seventeenth Century News* O–9, O–18, P–18
RLIN	Research Libraries Information Network Z–78		*SCraN*	*Stephen Crane Newsletter* S–50
RLiR	*Revue de linguistique romane* L–63		*ScS*	*Scottish Studies* M–78
RLJ	*Russian Language Journal* L–128		*SCT*	*Schriften der Gesellschaft fur Theatergeschicte* U–18
RLMC	*Rivista di litterature moderne e comparate* L–9		*SECC*	*Studies in Eighteenth Century Culture* P–18
RLT	*Russian Literature Tri-quarterly* L–128		*SEEJ*	*Slavic and East European Journal* L–128
RLV	*Revue des langues vivantes* L–57		*SEER*	*Slavonic and East European Review* L–128
RMS	*Renaissance and Modern Studies* O–18		*SEL*	*Studies in English Literature* M–25, O–7, O–18, O–32, P–4, P–18, Q–5
RNL	*Review of National Literatures* L–9		*Semiotica*	see I–15
Romania	see L–63		*SFBRI*	*Science Fiction Book Review Index* W–108
RomN	*Romance Notes* L–63			
Roorbach	see C–24		*SFNL*	*Shakespeare on Film Newsletter* O–58
RORD	*Research Opportunities in Renaissance Drama* O–18, O–33, U–18		*SFQ*	*Southern Folklore Quarterly* K–23
RP	*Romanische Bibliographie* L–60		*SFr*	*Studi francesi* L–78
RPA	*Recently Published Articles [in History]* F–6		*SFS*	*Science Fiction Studies* W–8
			SH	*Studia Hibernica* M–93
RPB	Brown University Libraries B–33		*ShakS*	*Shakespeare Studies* O–58
RPh	*Romance Philology* L–63		Shaw	see C–23
RPP	*Romanticism Past and Present* Q–18		*ShawR*	*Shaw Review* M–60
RQ	*Reference Quarterly* Y–38		Sheehy	see A–20
RR	*Rhetoric Review* X–165		Shipley	see L–11
RR	*Romanic Review* L–63		*ShJ*	*Shakespeare-Jahrbuch* O–58
RRQ	*Reading Research Quarterly* Z–138		*ShJE*	*Shakespeare Jahrbuch (East)* O–58
RSQ	*Rhetoric Society Quarterly* X–106, X–165		*ShJW*	*Shakespeare Jahrbuch (West)* O–58
RSTC	Revised *Short Title Catalogue* C–5		*ShN*	*Shakespeare Newsletter* O–53, O–58
RSVP	Research Society for Victorian Periodicals Q–18, Q–48, Z–25		Shoemaker	see C–25

SHR	*Scottish Historical Review* F–10		*TCBS*	*Transactions of the Cambridge Bibliographical Society* Y–38
ShS	*Shakespeare Survey* O–58		*TCL*	*Twentieth Century Literature* R–16, R–18
ShStud	*Shakespeare Studies (Tokyo)* O–58		*TDR*	*The Drama Review* R–18, U–18
SIGLASH	*Newsletter of the Special Interest Group on Language Analysis and Studies in the Humanities* Z–75		Term Catalogues	see C–8
			TESOL	Teachers of English to Speakers of Other Languages Z–25
Signs	see L–189		*TETYC*	*Teaching English in the Two-Year College* X–165
SIP	*Subject Index to Periodicals* see D–17			
SIR	*Studies in Romanticism* Q–18		*Text*	see I–15
SLang	*Studies in Language* I–15		*TheatreS*	*Theatre Studies* U–18
SlavR	*Slavic Review* L–128		Thieme and Becker	see A–70
SLJ	*School Library Journal* L–179		*THJCS*	*T'sing-hua Journal of Chinese Studies* L–148
SLJ	*Southern Literary Journal* S–18			
Slocum	see G–1		*ThR*	*Theatre Research International* U–18
SM	*Speech Monographs* I–15, X–165		Thrall, Hibbard & Holman	see L–12
SMC	*Studies in Medieval Culture* N–18			
SMed	*Studi medievali* N–18		*ThS*	*Theatre Survey* U–18
SN	*Studia Neophilologica* L–57		*THY*	*Thomas Hardy Yearbook* M–60
SNNTS	*Studies in the Novel* W–5, W–8		Tilley	see K–56
SOED	*Shorter Oxford English Dictionary on Historical Principles* I–33		*TLS*	*Times Literary Supplement* Z–151
			TN	*Theatre Notebook* U–18
SoR	*Southern Review* S–18		Totok-Weitzel	see A–23
SoSt	*Southern Studies* S–18		*TPA*	*T'oung Pao: Revue internationale de sinologie* L–148
SovL	*Soviet Literature* L–128			
SP	*Studies in Philology* L–57		*TPS*	*Transactions of the Philological Society* I–15
SQ	*Shakespeare Quarterly* O–50, O–58			
SR	*Sewanee Review* Z–158		*TQ*	*Theatre Quarterly* U–18
SR	Stationers' Register C–6		*TQ*	*Thoreau Quarterly* S–50
SRen	*Studies in the Renaissance* O–18		*TRev*	*Translation Review* I–106
SRO	*Shakespearean Research and Opportunities* O–58		*TRHS*	*Transactions of the Royal Historical Society* F–10
SS	*Scandinavian Studies* L–108		*TS*	*Today's Speech* X–165
SSF	*Studies in Short Fiction* W–8, W–52		*TSB*	*Thoreau Society Bulletin* S–50
SSI	*Short Story Index* W–55		*TSLL*	*Texas Studies in Literature and Language* L–57
SSL	*Studies in Scottish Literature* M–78			
SSSL	Society for the Study of Southern Literature Z–25		*TSWL*	*Tulsa Studies in Women's Literature* L–189
StAH	*Studies in American Humor* S–18		*TWI*	*Writing Instructor* X–165
Stationers' Register	see C–6		*TWT*	*Technical Writing Teacher* X–165
STC	*Short Title Catalogue* C–5		TxU	University of Texas Libraries B–35
StC	*Studia Celtica* M–93		Type-Index	see K–1
STC	*Short Title Catalogue* C–5			
STCL	*Studies in Twentieth Century Literature* R–18		UDC	Universal decimal classification A–21
			Ulrichs	see D–100
STTH	*Science Technology & the Humanities* Z–158		*ULS*	*Union List of Serials* D–91
Style	see I–15, X–165		USC	*United States Catalog* see C–30
SVEC	*Studies on Voltaire and the Eighteenth Century* P–18		*UTQ*	*University of Toronto Quarterly* L–57, Z–158
SWAL	*Southwestern American Literature* S–18		Valázquez	see I–75
Symposium	see L–57		Venn	see G–27
			Verbatim	see I–15
TA	*Theatre Annual* U–18		Vicaire	see C–53
Tanselle	see C–20		*VIJ*	*Victorians Institute Journal* Q–18
TAPA	*Transactions of the American Philological Association* L–48		ViU	University of Virginia Libraries B–39
			VLang	*Visible Language* I–15
TArts	*Theatre Arts Monthly* U–18		*VN*	*Victorian Newsletter* Q–18
TASJ	*Transactions of the Asiatic Society of Japan* L–148		vol.	volume
			VP	*Victorian Poetry* Q–18, Q–39
Taylor and Whiting	see K–58		*VPR*	*Victorian Periodicals Review* Q–18, Q–48

VQR	*Virginia Quarterly Review* Z–158	
VR	*Vox Romanica* L–63	
VS	*Victorian Studies* Q–18	
VWQ	*Virginia Woolf Quarterly* M–60	

W&L	*Women and Literature* L–189
WAL	*Western American Literature* S–18, S–117
Walford	see A–21
Watt	see A–30
WB	*Weimarer Beiträge* L–108
WC	*Wordsworth Circle* M–60, Q–18
WCWN	*William Carlos Williams Review* S–50
Webster's 2nd	see I–47
Webster's 3rd	see I–48
Wellesley Index	see D–12
Wells	see N–30
Wentworth	see I–54
Wentworth & Flexner	see I–55
WF	*Western Folklore* K–23
WHi	Wisconsin Historical Society Library H–27
WHIMSY	*World Humor and Irony Membership Serial Yearbook* W–157
Whitaker	see C–15
Whiting and Whiting	see K–55
WI	*Writing Instructor* X–165
Wing	see C–7
Wing *STC*	see C–7
WJSC	*Western Journal of Speech Communication* X–165
WL	*Women and Language* I–15
WLSP	*World List of Scientific Periodicals* D–96
WLT	*World Literature Today* L–148
WLWE	*World Literature Written in English* M–108
WPA	*Writing Program Administration* X–165
WP	*Words and Phrases Index* I–30
Wright	see I–41
WS	*Women's Studies: An Interdisciplinary Journal* L–189
WSJour	*Wallace Stevens Journal* S–50
WSL	*Die Welt der Slaven: Halbjahresschrift für Slavistik* L–128
WWR	*Walt Whitman Review* S–50

YCC	*Yearbook of Comparative Criticism* L–9
YCGL	*Yearbook of Comparative and General Literature* L–9
YER	*Yeats-Eliot Review* M–60
YES	*Yearbook of English Studies* M–25
YR	*Yale Review* Z–158
YWES	*Year's Work in English Studies* M–22
YWMLS	*Year's Work in Modern Language Studies* L–52
YWOES	*Year's Work in Old English Studies* N–22
ZAA	*Zeitschrift für Anglistik und Amerikanistik* M–25
ZCP	*Zeitschrift für celtische Philologie* M–93
ZDA	*Zeitschrift für deutsches Altertum* L–108
ZDMG	*Zeitschrift der Deutschen morgenländischen Gesellschaft* L–148
ZDP	*Zeitschrift für deutsche Philologie* L–108
ZFSL	*Zeitschrift für französische Sprache und Literatur* L–78
ZfV	*Zeitschrift für Volkskunde* K–23
ZGL	*Zeitschrift für germanistische Linguistik* L–108
ZRP	*Zeitschrift für romanische Philologie* L–60, L–63
ZS	*Zeitschrift für Slavistik* L–128
ZSP	*Zeitschrift für slavische Philologie* L–128

For further help with abbreviations, acronyms, and sigla, see the following reference works:

Leistner, Otto. *ITA: Internationale Titelabkürzungen von Zeitschriften, Zeitungen, wichtigen Handbüchern, Wörterbüchern, Gesetzen, u. s. w.* 3rd ed. 2 vols. Osnabrück: Biblio Verlag, 1981.   Z6945.A2 L4

Wellington, Jean Susorney. *Dictionary of Bibliographic Abbreviations Found in the Scholarship of Classical Studies and Related Disciplines.* Westport, Conn.: Greenwood, 1983.   PA99.W44

Alkire, Leland G. *Periodical Title Abbreviations.* 4th ed. 2 vols. Detroit: Gale, 1983.   Z6945.A2 W34

AN OVERVIEW OF THE ORGANIZATION OF THIS GUIDE

AN OVERVIEW OF ENTRIES LISTING JOURNALS [J]

AN OVERVIEW OF ENTRIES LISTING FREQUENTLY RECOMMENDED WORKS AND SIMILAR GUIDES [R]

A SHORT-FORM LISTING OF
ALL MAIN ENTRIES

Section E   MISCELLANY: Dissertations—General and National Lists; Dissertations—Subject Lists (National Literatures); Dissertations—Subject Lists in Fields of English and American Literature; Microforms; Reprints; Reviews; Indexes to Composite Volumes; Anonyma and Pseudonyma; Guides to Spoken Recordings; Guides to Films from Literary Works

Section F HISTORY AND ANCILLAE TO HISTORICAL STUDY: General and World History; British (and Irish) History—General; Medieval History; British (and Irish) History—Medieval; British (and Irish) History—Renaissance through Eighteenth Century; British History—Nineteenth Century and Twentieth Century; American (and Canadian) History; Chronological Ancillae—General; Chronological Ancillae—Literary; Topographical Ancillae— General; Topographical Ancillae— British and Irish; Literary Topography—British and Irish; Topographical Ancillae—American and Canadian; Literary Topography—American

Section G BIOGRAPHY AND BIOGRAPHICAL REFERENCES: Indexes, Bibliographies, and General Works; British Biography; American Biography; Contemporary Biography; South American and Continental Biography; Ancillae to Biographical Study

Section I LANGUAGE, LINGUISTICS, AND PHILOLOGY: Bibliographies—Language and Linguistics; Bibliographies—Dictionaries; Dictionaries—English; Dictionaries—American; Dictionaries—Scottish; Dictionaries—Foreign–Language; Translation—Bibliographies and Guides; Translation of Medieval Texts; Translation of World Literatures, Ancient and Modern

M–136 Watters and Bell, *On Canadian Literature, 1806–1960*

M–137 Moyles, *English–Canadian Literature to 1900: A Guide to Information Sources*

M–140 Stevens, *Modern English–Canadian Poetry: A Guide to Information Sources*

M–141 Fee, *Canadian Fiction: An Annotated Bibliography*

M–142 Hoy, *Modern English–Canadian Prose: A Guide to Information Sources*

M–143 "Canadian Literature: A Checklist," in *Canadian Literature*

M–144 "Canadian Literature: An Annotated Bibliography," in *Journal of Canadian Fiction*

M–145 *Oxford Companion to Canadian History and Literature*

M–146 *Oxford Companion to Canada Literature*

M–147 Sylvestre et al., *Canadian Writers/Écrivains canadiens*

M–148 [J] Scholarly Journals in Canadian Literature in English

M–149 [R] Some Frequently Recommended Works on Canadian Literature in English

XIII. India

M–150 Singh et al., *Indian Literature in English, 1827–1979: A Guide to Information Sources*

M–151 Alphonso-Karkala and Karkala, *Bibliography of Indo–English Literature*

M–152 Jain, *Indian Literature in English: An Annotated Bibliography*

M–153 *Bibliography of Indian English*

M–154 *BEPI: A Bibliography of English Publications in India*

M–158 [J] Scholarly Journals in Anglo–Indian Literature

M–159 [R] Some Frequently Recommended Works on Anglo–Indian and Indo–English Literature

XIV. New Zealand and the South Pacific

M–160 Thomson, *New Zealand Literature to 1977: A Guide to Information Sources*

M–168 [J] Scholarly Journals in New Zealand Literature and the Other English Literatures of the South Pacific (Excluding Australia)

M–169 [R] Some Frequently Recommended Works on New Zealand Literature and the Other English Literatures of the South Pacific (Excluding Australia)

XV. West Indies

M–172 Allis, *West Indian Literature: An Index to Criticism, 1930–1975*

M–173 Carnegie, *Critics on West Indian Literature: A Selected Bibliography*

M–174 Hughes, *Companion to West Indian Literature*

M–175 Herdeck, *Caribbean Writers: A Biobibliographical-Critical Encyclopedia*

M–176 Dance, *Fifty Caribbean Writers: A Biobibliographical Critical Sourcebook*

M–178 [J] Scholarly Journals in West Indian Literature in English

M–179 [R] Some Frequently Recommended Works on West Indian Literature in English

Section N MEDIEVAL LITERATURE: General; Anglo-Saxon; Middle English; Drama and Theater; Epic and Romance; Prose, Prose Fiction, Criticism, and Rhetoric; Medieval Latin

I. General

N–1 Rouse, *Serial Bibliographies for Medieval Studies*

N–2 Crosby et al., *Medieval Studies: A Bibliographical Guide*

N–3 Powell, *Medieval Studies: An Introduction*

N–4 *Lexikon des Mittelalters*

N–5 Fisher, *Medieval Literature of Western Europe: A Review of Research, Mainly 1930–1960*

N–6 *Progress of Medieval and Renaissance Studies in the United States and Canada*

N–7 "Bibliography of Editions and Translations [of Medieval Texts] in Progress," in *Speculum*

N–10 *Cambridge Bibliography of English Literature*, vol. 1, 600–1660, pp. 1–316

N–11 *New Cambridge Bibliography of English Literature*, vol. 1, 600–1660, cols. 1–806

N–12 Renwick and Orton, *Beginnings of English Literature to Skelton, 1509*

N–15 Greenfield, "Old English and Middle–English Bibliographical Guides," in Zesmer, *Guide to English Literature from Beowulf through Chaucer and Medieval Drama*

N–16 Matthews, *Old and Middle English Literature* [A Goldentree Bibliography]

N–17 Beale, *Old and Middle English Poetry to 1500: A Guide to Information Sources*

N–18 [J] Scholarly Journals in Medieval Studies

N–19 [R] Some Frequently Recommended Works in Medieval Studies

II. Anglo-Saxon

N–20 Greenfield and Robinson: *Bibliography of Publications on Old English Literature*

N–21 Robinson, *Old English Literature: A Select Bibliography*

N–22 "Old English Bibliography" and "The Year's Work in Old English Studies," in *Old English Newsletter*

N–24 "Bibliography for [year]," in *Anglo–Saxon England*

N–25 "Old English Research in Progress," in *Neuphilologische Mitteilungen*

N–27 Quinn and Quinn, *Manual of Old English Prose*

N–29 [R] Some Frequently Recommended Works in Anglo-Saxon Studies

III. Middle English

N–30 Wells, *Manual of Writings in Middle English, 1050–1400*

N–31 Tucker and Benham, *Bibliography of Fifteenth Century Literature*

N–32 Severs and Hartung, *Manual of Writings in Middle English, 1050–1500*

N–33 Simms, *Ritual and Rhetoric: Intellectual and Ceremonial Backgrounds to Middle English Literature*

N–35 Brown, *Register of Middle English Religious and Didactic Verse*

N–36 Brown and Robbins, *Index of Middle English Verse*

N–37 Robbins and Cutler, *Supplement to the Index of Middle English Verse*

N–38 Edwards et al., *Index of Middle English Prose*

Section T POETRY AND VERSIFICATION: Bibliographies, Bibliographical Guides, and Biobibliographies; Verse and Song Indexes; Anthologies and Collections—Bibliographies and Indexes; Indexes of Explication and Checklists of Criticism; Histories of English or American Poetry; The Language of Poetry; Prosody and Versification; Special Subjects—Bibliographies and Indexes

Section W PROSE FICTION AND NONFICTIONAL PROSE: Bibliographies—Prose Fiction; Checklists of Prose Fiction; Handbooks, Guides, and Indexes; Checklists of Criticism; Histories of the Novel; Short Fiction; The Picaresque; Gothic Fiction; Historical Fiction; Detective Fiction; Fantasy, Utopian Fiction, and Science Fiction; Nonfictional Prose; The Sermon, the Character, and the Essay; Travel Literature; Life-Writing; Humor and Satire

Section X THEORY, RHETORIC, AND COMPOSITION: Literary Criticism and Literary before ca. 1950 Theory; Literary Criticism and Literary Theory after ca. 1950; Literature and the Other Arts and Sciences; Rhetoric, Communications, and Discourse Theory; Style and Stylistics; Composition and the Teaching of Writing

I. Literary Criticism and Literary Theory Before Ca. 1950

Section Y BIBLIOGRAPHY: General Bibliographies and Guides; Analytical and Descriptive Bibliography and Textual Criticism—Basic Works of Reference; The History of Printing and the Book Trade; Rare and Used Book Trade—Catalogs and Sale Records; Book Collecting; Libraries and Librarianship

GENERAL WORKS

I. GENERAL BIBLIOGRAPHY OF BIBLIOGRAPHIES

Note that most bibliographies begin with a bibliography of bibliographies on that subject, theme, genre, author, or work; when available, these more specific tools are preferable to more general works. ABELL (M–21), for example, carries an annual bibliography of bibliographies on English Language and Literature. For general bibliographies of individuals, see also Arnim, *Internationale Personalbibliographie* (G–4) and the *IBN* (G–5). For bibliographies of major authors of English and American literature, see also the author guides (M–60 and S–50).

A–1 Besterman, Theodore. *World Bibliography of Bibliographies and of Bibliographical Catalogues, Calendars, Abstracts, Digests, Indexes, and the Like.* 4th ed., rev. and enl. 5 vols. Lausanne: Societas Bibliographica, 1965–1966.
Z1002.B5685

A closed, universal bibliography of primary and secondary bibliographies in all subjects and languages (except oriental). It is limited to "true bibliographies," separately published and arranged according to some permanent principle. The more than 117,000 short-title entries, briefly annotated with such information as number of items, are organized by subjects through the continuously paginated volumes, including subheadings (often not those that easily come to mind—see lists in the introduction), and under each heading chronologically by publication date. Special features include an index in volume 5 of subjects and authors (editors, translators, compilers) and of locations and libraries, with anonymous and serial bibliographies listed by title. There is considerable cross-referencing. The fourth edition brings the closing date for inclusion to 1963 and replaces previous editions.

The whole work has been supplemented by Alice F. Toomey, *World Bibliography of Bibliographies, 1964–1974*, 2 vols. (Totowa, N.J.: Rowman and Littlefield, 1977) [Z1002.T67]. Because of the narrowly defined principle of inclusion, however, this work should be supplemented by *Bibliographic Index* (A–2), Howard-Hill, *Index to British Bibliography* (M–1), and Nilon, *Bibliography of Bibliographies in American Literature* (S–1). Among the single volumes of subject-area bibliography extracted from the main work is *Literature, English and American: A Bibliography of Bibliographies* (Totowa, N.J.: Rowman and Littlefield, 1971) [Z2011.A1 B47].

A–2 *Bibliographic Index: A Cumulative Bibliography of Bibliographies.* Vol. 1–. New York: H. W. Wilson, 1938–.
Z1002.B595

An open, serial, universal subject index to bibliographies (selective, with emphasis on Germanic- and Romance-language items) presently indexing some 2,600 periodicals in addition to monographs. The work includes separately published bibliographies as well as those published in books and periodical articles, provided that they consist of at least fifty items. Bibliographies in theses and dissertations are excluded.

Bibliographic Index is currently published in April and August with a bound cumulation in December. An annual cumulation has been published since 1969 (vol. 9); retrospective volumes 1 through 8 cumulate periods of up to seven years, as follows: vol. 1 (1937–1942); vol. 2 (1943–1946); vol. 3 (1947–1950); vol. 4 (1951–1955); vol. 5 (1956–1959); vol. 6 (1960–1962); vol. 7 (1963–1965); and vol. 8 (1966–1968). The volumes are organized alphabetically by broad subject headings and subdivisions, and within each subject heading alphabetically by author or (before 1955) title. Under author-as-subject headings are listed bibliographies first of primary and then of secondary materials. There is considerable cross-referencing but no further indexing. Entries do note whether or not a bibliography is annotated. Readers are referred to *Bibliographische Berichte* (A–3) for supplementation in East European languages. Entries since November 1984 can be searched by computer through WILSONLINE (Z–78). The *Index* complements Besterman (A–1) and most other closed bibliographies of bibliographies because of its less restricted definition of items, and it supplements all closed bibliographies of bibliographies for current items.

A–3 *Bibliographische Berichte / Bibliographical Bulletin [BB].* Vol. 1–. Frankfurt: Klostermann, 1959–. Z1002.B5

This serial bibliography of bibliographies, published quarterly to 1962, semiannually to 1969, and annually to date, aims to present a current subject index to all recent primary and secondary bibliographies of all countries and subject areas. Limited to true bibliographies, the *Berichte* excludes those appended to books or articles that serve another purpose beyond enumerative bibliography. It now lists over 3,000 items each year; coverage is stronger for German works. Though generally more restrictive than *Bibliographic Index* (A–2), *Berichte* does include many more listings in oriental-, Slavic-, and Eastern-European-language materials. It therefore complements *Bibliographic Index* (A–2) in those areas while generally supplementing Besterman (A–1) and other closed bibliographies of bibliographies.   There may be inaccuracies in the listings, as many titles are taken from national bibliographies (see section C) and the majority are not seen by the compilers. There is occasional annotation.   An annual subject and author-as-subject index appears, but no index of compilers. There are quinquennial cumulative subject and author-as-subject indexes for volumes 1–5, 1959–1963 (1966), and volumes 6–10, 1964–1968 (1970).

A–4   **Collison, Robert L.   *Bibliographies, Subject and National: A Guide to Their Contents, Arrangement and Use.*** 3d ed., rev. and enl.   New York: Hafner; London: Lockwood, 1968.   Z1002.C7

This highly selective, informal, annotated guide to about 500 bibliographies is divided into two parts.   The first, Subject Bibliography, is further divided into ten headings covering authorship, book production, publishing, and bookselling; librarianship and encyclopedias; philosophy, psychology, and psychoanalysis; theology and religion; the social sciences; science; technology and industry; art, entertainment, and sport; languages and literatures; and geography, history, and biography.   The second part is devoted to universal bibliographies, bibliographies of bibliographies, national bibliographies, and bibliographies of serial publications.   Within each section is a discursive informal essay.   References to particular tools are presented in a quasi-facsimile reproduction of title pages; annotation is part of the essay.   The principles of selection are sometimes unclear, and commentary is often superficial and always rather personal.   An index of names and subjects is included and is especially valuable because the bibliographies included are not arranged in alphabetical order under topics and the location of particular tools would otherwise be difficult.

A–5   **Petzholdt, Julius.   *Bibliotheca Bibliographica: Kritisches Verzeichnis der das Gesammtgebiet der Bibliographie betreffenden Litteratur des In- und Auslandes, in systematischer Ordnung.*** Leipzig: Engelmann, 1866.   Z1002.P51

The first closed general bibliography of bibliographies, this one-volume work is a critical catalog of the whole field of bibliography, including both German and foreign works to 1861. The work is divided into three parts.   The first, introductory part deals with works on bibliography in general and with bibliographical systems.   The second, general part covers bibliographies citing universal or multilanguage entries over a universal or at least very wide range of subjects.   Included are bibliographies compiled by various authors along with special sections on anonymous and pseudonymous bibliography, the bibliography of incunabula, and prohibited books.   Also in part 2 is a considerable section on bibliographies produced by single authors on individuals and on lists of portraits.   The third and largest part covers bibliographies confined to one nation and/or one subject.   Included are national bibliographies for all European countries as well as America and the Orient. Subject bibliographies are divided into eight sections and include bibliographies in literary history and miscellaneous fields; philosophy and theology; mathematics, natural science, and medicine; pedagogy and folklore; political science, law, and military science; philology and belles-lettres; technology and the fine arts; and history (with maps).

After each entry there is a commentary in German which is usually explanatory and sometimes evaluative.   A title and subject index of some sixty-five double-column pages concludes the work.   Petzholdt is largely superseded by Besterman (A–1) and more modern bibliographies.   Nevertheless, the extended annotation and the date of compilation make this a valuable work for those seeking information on pre-nineteenth-century works of bibliography and reference. Archer Taylor's *History of Bibliographies of Bibliographies*

(New Brunswick, N.J.: Scarecrow, 1955) [Z1002.T32] provides a list of additional older titles for the student of earlier periods seeking contemporary reference books.

A–6   **Courtney, William P.   *Register of [British] National Bibliography, with a Selection of the Chief Bibliographical Books and Articles Printed in Other Countries.*** 3 vols. London: A. Constable, 1905–1912.   Z1002.C86

The original two volumes of this bibliography of bibliographies and reference works are arranged alphabetically by the *subjects* of the works cited.   This work is therefore, though dated, an easy-to-use guide, especially valuable for its references to pre-twentieth-century works in private collections and those printed for limited circulation.   The *Register* is closed and retrospective, although closing dates are not specified.   Some works in progress at the time of publication are listed; there is an appendix listing material obtained too late to list in the main body of the bibliography; and volume 3, published as a supplement in strict conformity to the structure of volumes 1 and 2, adds about 10,000 further entries to those found in the original volumes.   Materials covered include not only bibliographies in book form but also lists in periodicals, general reference works, calendars of manuscripts, and other sorts of compilations which, while not strictly bibliographies, contribute to the bibliographic control of an author or subject. The *Register* is restricted to English and American authors writing on English literature and major foreign literature, and foreign authors writing on English literature.   Courtney's principal guide in foreign bibliography is Henri Stein's *Manuel de bibliographie général* (Paris: A. Picard et fils, 1897) [Z1002.S81].   Omissions include sale catalogs, bibliographies of manuscripts, maps and charts, and catalogs of the free libraries that had sprung up in England during the last two decades of the nineteenth century.   Though not exhaustive, the register is useful both because of the alphabetical arrangement of entry subjects and because of the general index of seventy triple-column pages by subject and author-compiler. There is considerable cross-referencing both in the body and in the index.

A–7   ***Bulletin of Bibliography [and Magazine Notes] [BB].*** Vol. 1–.   Westwood, Mass.: F. W. Faxon, 1897–1981; Westport, Conn.: Meckler, 1982–.   Z1007.B94

The *Bulletin* publishes enumerative bibliographies, checklists, studies of reference works, and a record of new, changed, and discontinued periodicals.   Many of the bibliographies and checklists are on authors, genres, and other literary topics.   Publication has been irregular at times but is now quarterly with an annual author-subject index.   The *Bulletin* is also indexed annually in *Bibliographic Index* (A–2).   A *Cumulative Index (1897–1975)*, published in 1977, is divided into two main sections.   The first, an Index to Bibliographies and Articles, is an alphabetical author-subject index.   The second, an Index to Book Reviews, is an alphabetical author-title index to all books reviewed.   Another *Cumulative Index (1976–1980)* was published in 1982.

A–8   **Gray, Richard A.   *Serial Bibliographies in the Humanities and Social Sciences.*** Ann Arbor, Mich.: Pierian Press, 1969.   Z1002.G814

This selective bibliography seeks to identify and designate the salient characteristics of serial bibliographies most likely to be used by humanists and social scientists.   The bibliography, which has a Latin-alphabet language bias, includes ongoing and defunct publications, concealed and separately published bibliographies.   As a rule, Gray excludes the following categories: national bibliographies, library accessions lists, book-review sections of periodicals, monographic bibliographies in series, bibliography bulletins, bibliographies of periodical titles, bibliographies of government publications, and bibliographies that are primarily or exclusively listings of audiovisual materials. Occasionally, though, he does include such items from that list.

The bibliography is arranged by the Dewey decimal classification system in an attempt to show the relationship of specialized bibliographies to those more extensive in scope. In addition, the 1,409 entries are numbered sequentially. Each serial bibliography is fully described under its principal classification. Secondary entries are abbreviated and followed by cross-references to the primary entry. English translations are included for most of the foreign titles. Each entry includes dates of coverage as well as dates of publication. Following most main entries are descriptive codes that indicate the primary characteristics of the bibliography. A complete explanation of the codes appears on the inside covers of the volume. Characteristics specified include: 1—language of the editorial apparatus, 2—comprehensive or selective coverage, 3—countries and regions covered, 4—languages covered, 5—frequency of publication and/or cumulation, 6—types of publications included, with specification of dissertations, book reviews, research in progress, and use of abstracts, 7—bibliographic arrangement, 8—indexing practices, 9—type of annotation. Four indexes complete the volume. They include a title index; an author-publisher-sponsor index; a subject and keyword-in-context index; and a selected-characteristics index that sorts entries by types of publications included and type of annotation provided.

Another directory of serial bibliographies is the *Verzeichnis laufend erscheinender Bibliographien* prepared by the Deutsche Forschungsgemeinschaft (Wiesbaden: Franz Steiner, 1963) [Z1002.D4], with a total of 727 entries organized by subject field and concluding with indexes of subjects and titles.

A–9 **Wortman, William A.** *Guide to Serial Bibliographies for Modern Literatures.* New York: Modern Language Association, 1982.   Z6519.W67 1982

This extremely valuable guide identifies, describes, classifies, cross-references, and indexes some 700 serial bibliographies pertinent to the study of the modern literatures. It is disposed into six chapters, an introduction followed by chapters enumerating comprehensive bibliographies and general indexes; serial bibliographies treating English, American, and Commonwealth literature; serial bibliographies treating the non-English modern literatures; serial bibliographies on a total of sixty-one subjects related to the study of modern literature; and serial bibliographies for a total of 127 individual authors. Subjects include American studies, black studies, Celtic studies, and Scottish studies; drama, fiction, film, and poetry; linguistics, language, and language teaching; Arthurian studies, children's literature, classical literature, comparative literature and translation, critical and literary theory, and women's studies; as well as such fields as bibliography: enumerative, bibliography: analytical, book reviews, computers, dissertations and theses, economics and business, education, folklore, libraries, music, names, periodicals, science and technology, theology, and religion.

Chapters begin with helpful headnotes interrelating the major bibliographies cited for that domain. Serially numbered entries within chapters are arranged in descending order of comprehensiveness and accessibility. Current titles, places and names of publishers, beginning dates, and frequency of publication are given. Annotations are brief, describe the contents, structure, and special features of the bibliography, identify former or later works to which it is related, and offer occasional evaluative comments. An elaborate system of cross-references reminds users of the particular section(s) of major or more comprehensive bibliographies that pertain to the more specific field and that should therefore be consulted. There are occasional small errors in bibliographical details.

II. STUDENT REFERENCE GUIDES

There are many student reference guides cited in connection with the subject, national literature, or genre for which they provide guidance. See, among others, student guides for the following fields: history (F–3), American history (F–52), geography (F–90), art (A–71), music (A–75), philosophy (A–60), the social sciences (A–66), folklore (K–9), mythology (K–25), the Bible (K–35), French literature (L–70), Italian literature (L–80), Spanish literature (L–90), Spanish-American literature (L–96), German literature (L–110), Russian literature (L–122), children's literature (L–170), Medieval Latin literature (N–70), Shakespeare (O–40 and O–44), Romantic poetry (Q–23), Romantic prose (Q–24), Victorian poetry (Q–40), Victorian fiction (Q–43 and Q–44), Victorian prose (Q–42), Victorian periodicals (Q–47), American literature (S–4, S–5, and S–8), English poetry (T–1), English drama (U–12 and U–50), film (U–85), the English novel (W–1), the horror novel (W–70), detective fiction (W–90), and science fiction (W–100).

A–10 **Altick, Richard D., and Andrew Wright.** *Selective Bibliography for the Study of English and American Literature.* 6th ed. New York: Macmillan, 1979.
Z2011.A1A47 1979

The sixth edition of this most selective of all sheer-list reference guides follows the tradition established by the first edition of 1960 in citing items published in English which the compilers consider to be utterly indispensable reference tools for the graduate student of English and American literature. There is a clear emphasis on titles in literary history and in the historical contexts of literature. Entries are systematically arranged into some thirty-four unnumbered sections that proceed in an order thought to be helpful to the beginning scholar. The first four sections include references on The Scope, Aims, and Methods of Literary Scholarship; Bibliographical Handbooks; The Techniques of Research; and Scholarly Style. The fifth section enumerates standard Literary Encyclopedias and Handbooks. The sixth and seventh sections cite histories of English and American literature respectively and are each divided into subsections on General Histories, Period Histories, and Special Topics (linguistics, stylistics, folklore, histories of criticism, poetry, drama, and fiction). The eighth section is given to European, English, and American Cultural and Intellectual History. The ninth presents Guides to Libraries, while the tenth, eleventh, and twelfth sections list closed and serial bibliographies of English and American literature. The remaining sections cover more general classes of tools: General Reference Guides, Bibliographies of Bibliographies, Universal Bibliographies, Author Bibliographies, Subject Catalogues, Indexes to Composite Books, Guides to Anonymous and Pseudonymous literature, Encyclopedias, Dictionaries, Scholarly Periodicals (arranged by fields), General indexes of Periodicals and Newspapers, Aids for Tracing Particular Copies of Books, Analytical Bibliography, Book-Trade History, National Bibliographies, Microforms, Guides to Dissertations, Paleographical Handbooks, Guides to Manuscripts, Guides to Public Records, and a considerable number of references in History, Social History, and Biography.

The introductory essay on the use of scholarly tools, the short glossary of bibliographical terms, the list of "Some Books Every Student of Literature Should Read," and the author-title-subject index increase the value of this brief guide. It should be added that this work forms the bibliographical companion volume to Altick's *Art of Literary Research* (Z–40) and *Scholar-Adventurers* (see Z–41).

A–11 **Bond, Donald F.** *Reference Guide to English Studies.* 2d ed. Chicago: University of Chicago Press, 1971.

Z1002.B72 1971

This guide contains items published in Western languages before about 1970 judged by the compiler to be indispensable reference tools for the graduate student in English. The 1,549 serially numbered entries, giving minimal bibliographical information for each item, are occasionally annotated as to contents, arrangement, currency, supplementation, or value. The entries are disposed into thirty-two classes, some of which are further divided. The classification into a total of ninety headings and subheadings is by type of reference tool in the sections devoted to general humanistic research (1—Bibliography: General Works, 2—Bibliographies of Bibliographies, 3—General Bibliographies and Subject Indexes, 4—Encyclopedias, 5—Dictionaries of Quotations and Proverbs, 6—Literary and other Handbooks, 7—Library Catalogs, 8—Guides to Special Collections, 9—Bibliographies of Newspapers and Periodicals, 10—Scholarly Journals, 11—Learned Societies, 12—Dissertations, 13—Descriptive Bibliography, 14—Methods of Research and Preparation of Manuscript); by literary subject area in the sections given to literary reference works (15—Literature: General and Comparative, 16—Classical Antiquity, 17—The Middle Ages, 18—Incunabula, 19—English Literature, 20—Literatures of Ireland, Scotland, Wales, and the Commonwealth, 21—American Literature, 22—Romance Languages [and literatures], 23—German and Austrian Languages [and literatures], 24—Scandinavian, Russian, and Other [national] Literatures, 25—Bibliographies by genre and type); and by ancillary discipline in the section of references in subject areas other than English (26—Linguistics and Philology, 27—History, 28—Biography, 29—Genealogy and Heraldry, 30—Anonymous and Pseudonymous Literature, 31—Ancillary Subjects including auction records, education, fine arts, folklore, myth and custom, music, paleography, philosophy and psychology, prohibited books, religion, science, social sciences, and 32—Bibliographies: Miscellaneous Subjects including chapbooks, children's books, costume, courtesy books, dance, furniture, privately printed books, sport, travel, unfinished books). An index by author or compiler and a brief subject index further classify the entries. This is the most recent volume in a series of similar guides published since 1919 by the University of Chicago Press, all of which share the same general purpose and structure.

A–12 **Kennedy, Arthur G., and Donald B. Sands.** *Concise Bibliography for Students of English.* 5th ed. Revised by William E. Colburn. Stanford: Stanford University Press, 1972.

Z2011.K35 1972

This handbook, the most recent edition of a work that first appeared in 1940, is the most extensive of the sheer-list bibliographical guides for English studies. The 3,162 entries in this edition are disposed into three parts, on the literature itself, the book as a physical object and related topics, and the profession of English. These three parts are further disposed into twenty-one chapters, and they in turn are divided into a total of 125 serially numbered classes of materials, within which each entry is also serially numbered. The twelve chapters of Part I cover general works on literature in English, British literature, literature of the United States and Canada, poetry, drama, and theater, prose, the medieval period, the Renaissance, the Restoration and eighteenth century, the nineteenth century, the modern period, and literary criticism. The six chapters of Part II cover the fields of analytical and descriptive bibliography and textual criticism, manuscripts, publishing and the book trade, libraries, special topics (antiquarian books, microforms and reprints, computers, film and records, author-audience relationship, and censorship), and periodical bibliography. Part III has three chapters on the

purposes and methods of literary scholarship; on tools for the student, teacher, and scholar; and on works in allied fields (translation and world literature, children's literature, folklore, linguistics, and miscellaneous periodicals). Among the additional features adding to the principal value of this guide (which is the sheer quantity of standard works of history and criticism cited) are the provision of Dewey decimal class numbers and Library of Congress call numbers to each entry; a separate index of periodicals; an index of authors, editors, collaborators, revisers, translators, and assistants; and a rather general subject index. While an explicit effort has been made to avoid the citation of foreign-language titles, the perspective on English studies is quite broad, so that this is the best guide to use in the area of Commonwealth literature and world literature in English. A further attractive feature is the listing of classes of standard works of history and criticism in chronological order.

A–13 **Bateson, F. W., and Harrison T. Meserole.** *Guide to English and American Literature.* 3d ed. New York: Longman, 1976.   Z2011.B32 1976

The successor edition to Bateson's *Guide to English Literature*, first published in 1965, this handbook consists of twelve chapters that present, in essay or essaylike form, a bibliographical guide both to the primary works of English and American literature and to the standard bibliographies, histories, and critical works about English and American literature. The first chapter covers general works on English literature; the "interchapters"—2, 4, 6, and 8—provide a concise, idiosyncratic, but useful history of English literature, dealing with medieval (excluding Anglo-Saxon), Renaissance, Augustan, and Romantic literature respectively. The main chapters—3, 5, 7, and 9—provide reading lists for each of the periods, with the first part of each chapter discussing general works and the latter part presenting a series of bibliographical essays on the principal writers of the period. Chapter 10 is concerned with surveying modern literary criticism, while chapter 11 is entitled "Literary Scholarship: An Introduction to Research in English Literature." Chapter 12, by Meserole, deals with American literature. Among the especially valuable features of this guide are the author bibliographies giving dates, standard editions, standard critical works, and standard biographical and bibliographical studies. These appear in chronological order by the date of the author's birth. But if that date is not known, the index of subjects and authors-as-subjects which concludes the volume will help.

A–14 **Harner, James L.** *Literary Research Guide: A Guide to Reference Sources for the Study of Literatures in English and Related Topics.* New York: Modern Language Association, 1989.   Z2011.H34

This volume is the successor to Margaret C. Patterson's *Literary Research Guide*, 2d ed., 2d rev. printing (New York: Modern Language Association, 1984) [Z6511.P37 1984], first published by Gale Research in 1976. Designed for use in graduate student bibliography and methods courses, this work presents more than 2,200 numbered entries provided with lucid descriptive and evaluative annotations, including citations of selected reviews. Entries are disposed into twenty-one topical sections, as follows: A. Research Methods; B. Guides to Reference Books; C. Literary Handbooks, Dictionaries, and Encyclopedias; D. Bibliographies of Bibliographies; E. Libraries and Library Catalogs; F. Guides to Manuscripts and Archives; G. Serial Bibliographies, Indexes, and Abstracts; H. Guides to Dissertations and Theses; I. Data Bases; J. Biographical Sources; K. Periodicals; L. Genres; M. English Literature; N. Irish Literature; O. Scottish Literature; P. Welsh Literature; Q. American Literature; R. Other Literatures in English; S. Foreign-Language Literatures; T. Comparative Literatures; U. Literature-Related Topics and Sources.

Within national literature and period sections, Harner attempts to subdivide entries into sub-sections by type of reference work as follows: Research Methods; Guides to Reference Works; Histories and Surveys; Literary Handbooks, Dictionaries, and Encyclopedias; Annals; Bibliographies of Bibliographies; Guides to Primary Works (Guides to Collections, Manuscripts, Printed Works); Guides to Scholarship and Criticism (Surveys of Research, Serial Bibliographies, Other Bibliographies, Abstracts, Dissertations and Theses, Review Indexes, Related Topics); Language (Guides to Primary Works, Guides to Scholarship, Dictionaries, Thesauruses, Concordances, Studies of Language); Biographical Dictionaries; Microform Collections; Periodicals (Research Methods; Histories and Surveys; Guides to Primary Works; Guides to Scholarship; Scholarly Journals); Background Reading; Genres (Fiction—Research Methods, Guides to Reference Works, Histories and Surveys, etc.—Drama, Poetry, Prose). But the best guide to the organization of each section is the table of contents for that section which precedes its entries.

Among particularly valuable features are the inclusion of total pagination in main entry citations, reference to both Library of Congress and Dewey Decimal classifications, and the numerous references to selected reviews. Abundant cross references at the ends of sections and sub-sections, along with indexes of names, titles, and subjects facilitate access to the entries in this volume.

Although Harner's work is meant to replace Patterson, and is superior to it in scope and particularly in the quality of its annotations, there are a few features which still recommend Patterson's second edition, specifically its enumerations of titles in various series, including "British Writers and Their Work," "Critical Heritage Series," "Critical Idiom Series," "Essential Articles Series," "Gale Information Guide Library," "G. K. Hall Reference Guides," and the various Twayne series, and its helpful front matter. Harner is, however, to be congratulated for a revision so fundamental and so thorough as to render his work an independent achievement.

A–15 **Kehler, Dorothea. *Problems in Literary Research: A Guide to Selected Reference Works.*** 2d ed., rev. and enl. Metuchen, N.J.: Scarecrow Press, 1981.   Z6511.K4

Both a reference guide and a textbook, this work, first published in 1975, is a highly selective but very detailed guide to about 150 essential tools. The numbered entries are divided into a main body, giving elaborate annotation to about fifty works, and a list of nearly 100 supplementary works, each given a modest descriptive annotation. The annotations to works in the main body include a general description, a detailed summary of the contents of the tool, a precise account of its arrangement, a series of review questions to help fix salient characteristics in the student's mind, a series of sample research problems to use with the tool, and a very helpful series of additional notes pointing up further related tools and other useful matters. An author-title index concludes the volume.

A third edition was published in 1987, but could not be reviewed in time for full citation.

A–16 **Schweik, Robert C., and Dieter Riesner. *Reference Sources in English and American Literature: An Annotated Bibliography.*** New York: W. W. Norton, 1977.
Z2011.S415

The American edition of a work first published in Berlin under the title *English and American Literature: A Guide to Reference Materials.* The 1,207 serially numbered annotated entries in this excellent guide are divided into twenty-four sections: English Literature; American Literature; Literary Forms: Bibliographies, Indexes, and Handbooks; General and Comparative Literature; Literary Theory and Criticism; Inter-

disciplinary Literary Materials; The Literary Text: Printing, Textual History, Analytical and Descriptive Bibliography, and Editing; Guides to Scholarship and General Literary Reference Materials; Guides to General Reference Materials; General Bibliographies of Bibliography; National Bibliography; Microforms and Reprints: Guides and Bibliographies; Media: Guides, Bibliographies, and Indexes; Dissertations: Bibliographies, Indexes, and Abstracts; Serial Directories, Indexes, and Union Lists; Review Indexes; Indexes to Books, Collections of Essays, and Other Composite Works; Rare and Used Book Trade: Guides, Catalogues, Directories and Glossaries; Sources of Biographical Information; Sources of Information on Religion, Myth, Folklore, and Popular Custom; History; Dictionaries; Encyclopedias and Fact Books Supplementary to Encyclopedias; and Catalogs of and Guides to Libraries, Archives, and Other Repositories.

A detailed table of contents, cross-references, and indexes of subjects and authors, but not titles, make for relatively easy use of the work. Among the features of special value are a useful preface that discusses the principles of inclusion and arrangement followed, an introduction on "Using Reference Sources" that is one of the best available, and a handy glossary of terms used in enumerative bibliography. The greatest value of this guide, however, is the *absence* of an English-language bias that limits the value of most other student guides, and the inclusion of short but generally reliable descriptive annotations that most other student guides omit. Other guides produced for German students include Klaus Lubbers, *Einführung in das Studium der Amerikanistik* (Tübingen: Niemeyer, 1970) [PE2808.L8] and Gerhard Müller–Schwefe, *Einführung in das Studium der englischen Philologie,* 2d ed. (Tübingen: Niemeyer, 1968) [PE71.M8], both of which are done in the form of extended bibliographical essays. The most current volume of this kind is Paul S. Ulrich's *Wie finde ich anglistische Literatur* (Berlin: Berlin Verlag, 1980) [Z2015.A1 U57].

A–17 **Poulton, Helen J. *Historian's Handbook: A Descriptive Guide to Reference Works.*** Norman: University of Oklahoma Press, 1972.   Z6201.P65

This American student's guide is divided into eleven chapters presenting discursive bibliographical essays on selected reference materials judged indispensable to the working historian. Chapter titles are: The Library and Its Catalog; National Library Catalogs and National Trade Bibliographies; Guides, Manuals, and Bibliographies of History; Encyclopedias and Dictionaries; Almanacs, Yearbooks, Statistical Handbooks, and Current Surveys; Serials and Newspapers; Geographic Aids; Biographical Materials; Primary Sources (Manuscripts, Archives, Oral History, Diaries, Quotations and Speeches) and Dissertations; Legal Sources; and Government Publications. Where feasible, these essays are further divided by country or other appropriate subtopics.

The essays present titles of reference works, and footnotes give more complete bibliographical information for each work cited. As is characteristic of bibliographic essays, the annotation provided for any particular work is likely to be fairly brief, but reference works are consistently placed in systematic relationship to one another through the structure and organization of the essays themselves. The *Handbook* concludes with an index of titles and a general index of names and subjects.

A–18 **Hansel, Johannes. *Bücherkunde für Germanisten: Studienausgabe.*** 7th ed. Revised by Lydia Tschakert. Berlin: Schmidt, 1978.   Z2235.A2 H3

This is the latest revision of the standard student guide for Germanic studies which was first published (in a format that included more dated works and extensive information on manuscript holdings and the like) in 1959 with the subtitle *Wie sammelt man das Schrifttum nach dem neuesten Forschungs-stand?* In addition to the 1,192 entries citing works judged current, standard, and indispensable to the student of German language and literature, this guide includes brief but helpful introductory essays designed to teach the student to prepare systematically a bibliography of primary and secondary materials on any topic in Germanic studies. A five-step process is identified, and the reference works are grouped into five chapters according to the step in which they would be used. The first step is to check the closed bibliographies found in standard works. The second step uses closed current subject bibliographies. The third uses references in current issues of serial subject bibliographies. The fourth step (and chapter) refers to citations in current serial general bibliographies. The last step refers to current issues of relevant periodicals. Each chapter is further divided into relevant subtopics. The first has sections on general linguistics, general poetics, German language and linguistics, German literary history, and general reference tools (encyclopedias, biographical dictionaries, and reference works in ancillary fields including classics, folklore, theology, philosophy, art history, music history, history, sociology, and law). The second and third chapters are similarly disposed. The fourth is divided into sections on national bibliographies, dissertations, and bibliographies of periodicals. The last chapter is divided into sections listing periodicals in the fields of language and literature and listing general periodicals. An author-title index and a short subject-index complete the work.

For older works, more information on manuscript holdings, catalogs, and the like, the original edition of 1959 must be consulted. This work is complemented by Hansel's *Personalbibliographie zur deutschen Literaturgeschichte: Studienausgabe*, 2d ed., rev. and enl. by Carl Paschek (Berlin: Schmidt, 1974) [Z1002.H24], which lists for some 300 authors standard bibliographical aids, including surveys of research, lists of repositories with manuscript holdings, and organizations and journals devoted to their study. A briefer but even more systematic student guide is Paul Raabe's *Einführung in die Bücherkunde zur deutschen Literaturwissenschaft*, 8th ed. (Stuttgart: Metzler, 1975) [Z2231.R24], which includes a series of foldout tables listing the key bibliographical aids to searching primary and secondary literature for any period of German literary history. See also the reference guides cited in section L, below.

A-19 **Palfrey, Thomas R., Joseph C. Fucilla, and William C. Holbrook, comps. *Bibliographical Guide to the Romance Languages and Literatures.*** 8th ed. Evanston, Ill.: Chandler's, 1971.   Z7031.P15

This guide, first published in 1939 and revised continuously since then, lists 1,824 items occasionally annotated briefly and disposed into a general section and four additional parts covering the French; Italian; Portuguese and Brazilian; and Spanish, Catalan, and Spanish-American Languages and Literatures. The first part, General Romance Bibliography, is further disposed into sections on Methods of Research, Bibliographical Methods and Techniques, Thesis Preparation and Style Books, Universal Bibliographies, Bibliographies of Bibliographies, Special Bibliographies, Catalogues and Book Lists, Dissertations, General Romance Linguistics, Paleography and Chronology, Comparative Literature, General Romance Periodicals, Encyclopedias and Biographical Dictionaries, and Pedagogy. The subsequent parts covering national literatures are each divided into a general section (under which are subdivisions for bibliographies, linguistics, literature, periodicals, and history) and, in the case of the French, Italian, and Spanish parts, further divided into sections for each historical period, under each of which are the same subdivisions as are found in the general section. In the absence of any indexes, users are advised to study the fairly detailed table of contents before searching a particular reference.

Other reference guides to the Romance languages and literatures include Rupprecht Rohr, *Einführung in das Studium der Romanistik*, 2d ed., rev. (Berlin: Schmidt, 1968) [PC53.R6], and those cited in section L, below.

III. GENERAL REFERENCE GUIDES

A-20 **Sheehy, Eugene P. *Guide to Reference Books.*** 10th ed. Chicago: American Library Association, 1986. Z1035.1.S43

This is a revised, expanded, and updated version of the ninth edition which, in turn, continued a work that originally began in 1902, though with radical alteration of arrangement beginning with Constance M. Winchell's 8th edition. Through its long history the *Guide to Reference Books* has been designed to list works basic to both general and specific research in all fields. The current edition serves as an annotated reference guide to approximately 12,000 reference tools. The work is arranged by coded subject areas and divisions. The major areas and divisions are as follows: A—General Reference Works (AA—Bibliography, AB—Librarianship and Library Resources, AC—Encyclopedias, AD—Language Dictionaries, AE—Periodicals, AF—Newspapers, AG—Government Publications, AH—Dissertations, AJ—Biography, AK—Genealogy); B—The Humanities (BA—Philosophy, BB—Religion, BC—Linguistics and Philology, BD—Literature: General, English, Germanic, Romance, Slavic and East European, Classical, African, and Oriental, BE—Fine Arts, BF—Applied Arts, BG—Theater and Performing Arts, BH—Music, BJ—Sports, Recreation, and Travel); C—Social Sciences (CA—General Works, CB—Education, CC—Sociology, CD—Psychology and Psychiatry, CE—Anthropology and Ethnology, CF—Mythology, Folklore and Popular Culture, CG—Statistics and Demography, CH—Economics, CJ—Political Science, CK—Law, CL—Geography); D—History and Area Studies (DA—General History, DB—The Americas, DC—Europe, DD—Africa, DE—Asia, DF—Australia and New Zealand, DG—Oceania, DH—Arctic and Antarctic); and E—Science, Technology, and Medicine (EA—General Works, EB—Astronomy, EC—Biological Sciences, ED—Chemistry, EE—Earth Sciences, EF—Mathematics, EG—Physics, EH—Agricultural Sciences, EJ—Engineering, and EK—Medical and Health Sciences).

Entries are preceded by helpful introductory notes on the class of tools about to be presented or on reference problems associated with a particular subject matter. The items listed, each of which is serially numbered within the alphabetical series of subject divisions as given above, include bibliographies, guides, manuals, indexes, abstract journals, encyclopedias, dictionaries, handbooks, annuals, directories, histories, biographical works, atlases, and serial publications, each selected as a basic reference tool in the particular subject under which it is ordered. Annotations usually cover scope, arrangement, and critical limitations of the work. Most entries also include the Library of Congress call number. The guide has extensive headings, running titles, and an elaborate index (by author, subject, and most but not all title entries) almost 260 triple-column pages in length. Moderate cross-referencing also facilitates access. The closing date for entries is 1984–1985; the tenth edition supersedes all previous editions.

This work is complemented by Walford (A-21) and the other General Reference Guides and is supplemented by *ARBA, American Reference Books Annual* (A-25). Vastly more simplified introductions to reference works include such titles as Robert B. Downs, *How to Do Library Research* (Urbana: University of Illinois Press, 1966) [Z1035.D63].

A–21 Walford, A. J. *Guide to Reference Material.* 4th ed. 3 vols. London: The Library Association, 1980–1986.

Z1035.1.W33

Emphasizing the bibliography of recent reference books, Walford is international in scope but focuses on items published in Britain. The annotated main entries, with information on the scope, arrangement, and critical limitations of the nearly fourteen thousand items included, are disposed into three volumes, all organized according to the Universal decimal [subject] classification (UDC). The first volume, Science and Technology, 5/6, includes the subject areas of Mathematics and Natural Sciences (5—General, 51—Mathematics, 52—Astronomy, 53—Physics, 54—Chemistry, 55—Geology, 56—Paleontology, 57—Anthropological and Biological Sciences, 574—General Biology, 58—Botany, 59—Zoology) and the Applied Sciences (6—General, 61—Medicine, 62—Engineering, 63—Agriculture, 64—Domestic Science, 65—Management, Communication, 66—Chemical Industry, 67—Industries and Crafts Based on Processable Materials, 68—Specialized Trades, and 69—Building). The second volume, published in 1982, includes Philosophy, Psychology, and Religion (1—Philosophy and Psychology, 159.9—Psychology, 2—Religion, 22/28—Christianity, 29—Non-Christian Religions) and the Social and Historical Sciences (3—General Social Sciences, 31—Statistics, 32—Political Science, 33—Economics, 34—Law, 35—Public Administration, 36—Social Relief and Welfare and Insurance, 37—Education, 38—Commerce, 39—Customs and Traditions, 9—General Geography, Biography, and History, 91—Geography, Exploration, and Travel, 912—Atlases and Maps, 914–919—Guide Books, 92—Biography, 929—Genealogy and Heraldry, 93—History, 931—Ancient History, and 94—Medieval and Modern History). The final volume covers Generalia (0—Generalities, 02—Librarianship, 03—Encyclopedias, Dictionaries, and Reference Books, 05—Periodicals, and 087.7—Government Publications); Languages (4—General, 420—English, 430—German, 440—Romance, 482—Russian, 49—Oriental, African, and Other Languages); the Arts (7—General, 72—Architecture, 75—Painting, 77—Photography, 78—Music, 79—Entertainment and Sport) and Literature (8—General, 820—English, 830—German, 840—Romance, 87—Classical, 882—Russian, 89—Oriental, African, and Other Literatures).

Volumes 1 and 2 each contain a combined author-title-subject index (subjects are in capitals). Volume 3 contains a *cumulated* subject index of over twenty triple-column pages and an author-title index to the entries of the third volume only. Because of certain vagaries of the Universal decimal [subject] classification itself, use of the indexes is advisable, especially for readers unfamiliar with the UDC. Because of differing annotations and a British bias this work is complementary to Sheehy (A–20), and the two can be used profitably together.

A–22 Malclès, Louise Noelle, et al. *Les sources du travail bibliographique.* 3 vols. in 4. Geneva: Droz, 1950–1958.

Z1002.M4

This work is a now somewhat out-of-date closed bibliography, international in scope but with a French emphasis, of general and specialized bibliographies and reference works. The author has been chief librarian of the Sorbonne and the University of Paris and is a leading figure in bibliographical education. The work contains extensive annotations and detailed explanatory material. Citations are generally presented in chronological order, although fundamental works are often placed first within a subject area. Volume 1 begins with an overview of the discipline of bibliography and then contains entries for general bibliographies and reference works. It is divided into sections on bibliographies of bibliographies; universal bibliographies; books of the fifteenth and sixteenth centuries; printed library catalogs; collective catalogs; national bibliographies; encyclopedias; biographical dictionaries; periodical bibliographies and guides; periodical publications of learned societies; indexes of periodicals and collected volumes; bibliographies of Slavic and Balkan countries; and encyclopedias of the book and dictionaries of editorial, bookselling, and librarianship terminology.

The second part (in two volumes) contains specialized bibliographies in the human sciences. The first chapter of volume 1 contains an introduction to specialized bibliography. The remaining twelve chapters cover bibliography in the fields of prehistory, anthropology, ethnography, and sociology; general linguistics and linguistic geography; universal history and ancillary sciences; Greco-Latin antiquity and medieval Greek and medieval Latin cultures; medieval, modern, and contemporary history; European and American history and the bibliography of Africa, Asia, and Oceania; Romance languages and literatures (French, Provençal, Catalan, Italian, Spanish, Portuguese, Rumanian); Celtic languages and literatures; Germanic languages and literatures (German, English, American, Dutch, and Scandinavian); non-Indo-European languages of Europe; Finno-Ugric and Basque; world and European literary history and comparative literature; and religion. The second volume of part 2 continues with six further chapters on geography; art, archaeology, and musicology; law, political science, economics, and social science; philosophy; the language, literature, and history of the Slavic and Balkan countries; and the Near, Middle, and Far East.

The last volume treats of special bibliography in the natural sciences. The first two chapters concern the history of science and general reference works. The remaining eleven chapters cover the fields of mathematics; astronomy and astrophysics; physics, crystallography, and mineralogy; physical geography; chemistry; geology; general biology; zoology; botany and plant physiology; medicine; and pharmaceutics.

Each volume has a general table of contents. Extensive headings and subheadings as well as running titles make the location of particular fields or subfields fairly easy. Each volume also has a combined index (in capital letters) of authors, compilers, and editors and (in lowercase) of titles and subjects. Malclès's one-volume text for students of bibliography, *Manuel de bibliographie,* 3d ed. (Paris: Presses universitaires de France, 1976) [Z1002.M281976], is an introductory guide to the materials more extensively treated in the multivolume work.

A–23 Totok, Wilhelm, Karl-Heinz Weimann, and Rolf Weitzel. *Handbuch der bibliographischen Nachschlagewerke.* 5th ed., rev. and enl. Frankfurt: Klostermann, 1977.

Z1002.T68

This work, first published in 1953, is a handbook designed for the use of students of bibliography and reference works. It may be regarded as a German analogue to Sheehy (A–20), Walford (A–21), or Malclès (A–22), though it is more compact than any of the others. Entries are very sparsely annotated and disposed into a two-part structure of general and specialized bibliographies and reference works. The first part is divided into sections on bibliographies of bibliographies; international general bibliographies; library catalogs; national bibliographies; periodical bibliographies; lists of theses and dissertations; bibliographies of government and other official publications; incunabula; miscellaneous bibliographies (on books in print, reprints, translations, collected works, anonymous and pseudonymous literature, prohibited books); guides to learned societies, organizations, and research institutions; general encyclopedias; and biographical dictionaries.

The second part is divided into sections on library and information science; philosophy; theology; education and psychology; linguistics and literature (general linguistics, general literature, classical philology, Germanic languages and literatures, Romance languages and literatures, Slavic languages and literatures, oriental languages and cultures, South and East Asian languages and cultures, and African languages and cultures); the arts (the pictorial arts, archaeology, music, theater, film, and dance); history; law; economic and social sciences; geography; the natural sciences; medicine; agriculture; and technological sciences (e.g., architecture, engineering, physics, electronics, computer science, nutrition, etc.).

A reasonably detailed table of contents, marginal notations, headings, running titles, and an index of authors, titles, and subjects (in italics) make access to entries fairly easy. A valuable extra feature is the brief table of bibliographical terminology which follows the helpful introduction. A sixth edition was published in 1984.

For an earlier German bibliographic guide see Georg Schneider, *Handbuch der Bibliographie*, 4th ed., rev. and enl. (Leipzig: Hiersemann, 1930) [Z1001.S35]. Though out of date, this work remains valuable for the commentary and annotations it includes. The introductory theoretical and historical treatment of bibliography found in the first three editions was translated into English by Ralph Robert Shaw under the title *Theory and History of Bibliography* (New York: Columbia University Press, 1934) [Z1001.S36].

A–25 **American Reference Books Annual. [ARBA]** Vol. 1–. Littleton, Colo.: Libraries Unlimited, 1970–.   Z1035.1.A55

This yearly comprehensive review of all reference books recently published in the United States has since its beginning reviewed over 17,000 items. Each volume aims to cover all newly published closed ready-reference titles including bibliographies, guides, indexes, dictionaries, encyclopedias, directories, atlases, gazetteers, and concordances. Reference works that are annually updated, including some general encyclopedias, yearbooks, almanacs, and indexing and abstracting services, are reviewed initially and then at intervals of from three to five years to note changes in scope, editorial policy, and the like. Selected foreign reference titles that have an exclusive American distributor are often reviewed, though coverage is restricted to English-language publications. Selected government publications are also reviewed, as are reprints. Detailed tables of contents precede each volume's entries. In the most recent volume, reviews are disposed into the following fields: General (Bibliography, Periodicals, Publishing and Bookselling, Encyclopedias, Directories, Handbooks and Yearbooks, Abbreviations, Almanacs, Alternative Information Sources, Government Publications, Style Manuals and Biography); Library Science; Social Sciences and Area Studies; History; Ethnic Studies; Genealogy; Political Science; Law; Geography and Travel; Education; Recreation and Sports; Sociology; Women's Studies; Anthropology and Ethnology; Statistics and Demography; Economics and Business; Fine Arts; Applied Arts; Music; Theater; Films; Religion; Philosophy; Folklore and Popular Customs; Linguistics; Communication; Literature (General, American, British, Australian, Canadian, Classical Greek and Roman, Danish, French, German, Irish, Russian, and Spanish); General Science and Technology; Mathematics; Astronomy; Chemistry; Physics; Natural History and Biology; Botany; Zoology; Environmental Science and Energy Resources; Earth Sciences; Psychology; Medical Science; Agricultural Sciences; Engineering and Technology; Military Science.

Reviews are signed, and a list of contributors at the beginning of each volume identifies the professional affiliation of the reviewers. Many entries include reference to additional reviews of the item published elsewhere. A combined author-title-subject index (subjects in boldface) concludes each volume. Two five-year cumulative author-title-subject indexes have been published to date, covering 1970–1974 and 1975–1979.

Additional sources for reviews of new reference books include *Reference Services Review*, vol. 1–. (Ann Arbor, Mich.: Pierian, 1973) [Z1035.1.R43], which in each issue

provides a partly annotated bibliography of new reference books in all fields and indexes reviews of new reference books. A quarterly update under the title *Reference Sources* has been published by Pierian Press since 1977 [Z1035 .1.R45]. The indexes supplement the separately published *Reference Book Review Index, 1970–1972*, ed. Shirley Smith (Ann Arbor, Mich.: Pierian, 1975) [Z1035.1.S578], and *Reference Book Review Index, 1973–1975*, ed. M. and S. Balachandran (Ann Arbor, Mich.: Pierian, 1979) [Z1035.1. B34]. Balachandran also edited a *Subject Guide to Reference Books, 1970–1975* (Ann Arbor, Mich.: Pierian, 1980) [Z1035.1 .B343].

A third source is the triannual *Reference Book Review*, vol. 1–. (Dallas [place varies]: C. Northouse, 1976–) [Z1035.1.R44], which annually lists up to 150 reference books with descriptive and evaluative reviews.

Literary reference books are discussed at length in annual review essays in *YWES* (M–22), *YWMLS* (L–52), and *ALS* (S–14). In addition, see the regular reviews in *Literary Research* (Y–14).

IV. GENERAL SUBJECT INDEXES OF BOOKS

See section D for subject indexes of periodicals and section E for subject indexes to dissertations and composite volumes. Many library catalogs (section B) have subject arrangements, as do a number of national bibliographies (section C).

A–30 **Watt, Robert. *Bibliotheca Britannica; or, A General Index to British and Foreign Literature.*** 4 vols. Edinburgh: Constable, 1824.   Z2001.W34

This valuable four-volume "universal" bibliography contains the works of some 40,000 authors in its first two volumes and a key-word-in-title subject index (of about 150,000 items) to those works in the last two volumes. It is an indispensable tool for students of the eighteenth century and earlier, though less useful for medieval studies. The author volumes are alphabetical and generally give a short biography followed by a chronological list of works. Anonymous and pseudonymous authors' works are listed in the subject volumes. Under each subject heading, titles are arranged chronologically and are cross-referenced (by page number and letter location on the page) to the author volumes, where more complete information is given. The work is comprehensive in its coverage of editions and translations of the classics in England, "universal" for English works, and quite selective for foreign works. It is the first recourse for students of general subjects (e.g., topics in the history of ideas) in earlier periods and is especially helpful in locating treatments of such subjects in obscure works of contemporary or earlier date. Though it is sometimes inaccurate (watch the dates, especially) and the subject entries depend on titles of the works listed being both accurate and informative (which is not always the case), Watt is the most satisfactory tool of its kind ever produced. (The original manuscript slips are preserved in sixty-nine volumes in the Free Public Library at Paisley.) Special features include attention to early printing, with works listed under printers' names in addition to author and subject listings. Collected serial publications, such as transactions of societies, are analyzed under author and subject headings. English translations of foreign works are included and are another special feature. A handy source for verifying Watt's entries is the Averley compilation, *Eighteenth Century British Books: A Subject Catalogue* (P–13).

For further information about Watt and the history of his work see George Watson Cole, "Do You Know Your Lowndes?" *PBSA* 33 (1939): 5–9, and see Francesco Cordasco, *A Bibliography of Robert Watt, M.D., Author of the Bibliotheca Britannica* (New York: William F. Kelleher, 1950; reprint, Detroit: Gale, 1968) [Z6676.W31968]. For additional information about other early subject indexes see Archer Taylor, *General Subject Indexes since 1548* (Philadelphia: University of Pennsylvania Press, 1966) [Z695.T28]. It is organized by century and provides access to important early reference works in Latin and in the European languages. Descriptions are designed to alert scholars to the potential research uses of these tools.

A–31 **Peddie, Robert Alexander.** *Subject Index of Books Published up to and Including 1880.* 4 vols. London: Grafton, 1933–1948.   Z1035.P37

Peddie's index is an extensive subject index to pre–1880 titles using a very precise and narrow subject classification. The first series contains some 50,000 titles; it is supplemented by the second series; both are supplemented by the third; and all are further supplemented by the new series of 1948. Each supplement adds 50,000 titles, and the second and third series include all subject headings from the previous volumes, indicating by typographical signs (asterisks—1st, daggers—2d) whether the previous volumes show any titles under that subject heading. Under headings, entries are arranged in chronological order of publication, giving author, title, and date of publication. The subject headings are chosen so that further subdivisions are not needed: thus, for example, "musical instruments" is used but without reference to individual instruments, "trees" is not used, though "forestry" is; the names of particular instruments and kinds of trees are also used as headings. A regrettable feature is the paucity of cross-references between related subjects. Those present are relegated to the end of the first volume. An effort has been made to stress unusual titles and unusual subjects, on the grounds that access to these is most difficult. Most titles are of books, though pamphlets, dissertations, and reprints from periodicals are included when they are main sources of information on the subject in question. Each volume except the third has a small supplement in the back. The *British Museum Subject Index* (A–32) takes up with titles published after 1880.

A–32 *Subject Index of the Modern Works Added to the Library of the British Museum in the Years 1881–1900.* Edited by George K. Fortescue. 3 vols. London: William Clowes and Sons, 1902–1903. Quinquennial supplementary volumes (titles vary) for 1901–1970 have been published, 1906–1982.   Z1035.B86

This index to books published or reissued after 1880 uses rather general subject divisions. These are further subdivided as necessary and are provided with abundant cross-references to related subjects. Personal names are not used as subjects, since they are covered by cross-references in the General Catalogue (B–40). Entries give authors, places, and dates of publication. They are not always arranged alphabetically or chronologically under the alphabetically arranged subject headings or subheadings, so that one must read the full enumeration under the heading or subheading. No system such as that found in Peddie's index to books published before 1800 (A–31) indicates in later volumes of this index the subject headings also found in earlier ones. Hence, the pertinent volumes in each supplement and in the original series must be checked carefully. Though use of this subject index is more difficult and time-consuming than use of the indexes of Peddie and the Library of Congress (A–33), it is the only index of its scope available for books (provided that they were acquired by the British Museum) published after 1880 and not cata-

loged by the Library of Congress or participating libraries after 1950; it is thus the most extensive available subject index for books published between 1880 and about 1945. For more recent volumes the Library of Congress Catalog is much to be preferred, not only because it is more current but also because subject headings are narrower and the arrangement is more conducive to rapid use. But the headings used in the British Museum index are those likely to suggest themselves to the untutored user, while the Library of Congress system of headings must be studied before it can be readily used. This index may be complemented by the subject indexes of individual libraries, particularly that of the London Library (A–36).

A final set of volumes for 1971–1975 were published in 1986. Subject catalogs of acquisitions from 1976 onwards are published in microfiche. A printed text, *British Library General Subject Catalogue 1975–1985* (New York: K.G. Saur, Inc.) [Z921.L553] contains approximately seventy-five volumes, treating titles published since 1971 and cataloged since 1975. Entries are arranged alphabetically according to the subject headings of PRECIS (Preserved Context Index System), used also in the *British National Bibliography* (C–16).

A–33 *Library of Congress Catalog—Books: Subjects; A Cumulative List of Works Represented by Library of Congress Printed Cards.* 1950–1974. Publisher varies. New title: *Subject Catalog.* 1975–1982.   Z881.A1 C325

This has been the best current international subject index to books. Containing works cataloged by the Library of Congress, it appeared in quarterly issues, in an annual cumulation, and in quinquennial cumulations. The subject headings were rather specific, though not minutely so. For a summary, see the ninth edition of *Library of Congress Subject Headings [LCSH],* 2 vols. (Washington D.C., 1980) and its supplements, which were published quarterly and cumulated annually (1979, 1980, 1981, and 1982) [Z695.U4749 1980]. All materials cataloged by the Library of Congress since 1950 are included. Entries present bibliographical information, LC call number, Dewey decimal classification number, and LC card number. Quinquennial cumulations were published by private publishers for the years 1950–1954 (20 vols.), 1955–1959 (22 vols.), 1960–1964 (25 vols.), 1965–1969 (42 vols.), and 1970–1974 (100 vols.). Annual cumulations have been published by the library for the years 1975 (18 vols.), 1976 (17 vols.), 1977 (15 vols.), 1978 (19 vols.), 1979 (21 vols.), 1981 (15 vols.), and 1982 (17 vols.). No annual cumulation was published for 1980. However, an 11-volume fourth quarterly issue was published, containing additional material not found in standard quarterly issues.

The *Subject Catalog* ceased publication with the 1982 annual cumulation. It has been carried on in the *National Union Catalog* publications through the cumulating subject index to the four *NUC* publications (see B–13).

A–34 **Peabody Institute, Baltimore.** *Catalogue of the Library.* 13 vols. Baltimore, 1883–1905.   Z881.B2

This catalog of one of the most extensive nineteenth-century American libraries includes over 80,000 entries in its first part, which is arranged by author, title, and subject headings. Not only books but also periodicals, bound pamphlets, publications of learned societies, and various collections are analyzed. Detailed headings for subjects are followed by a listing first of books and then of periodical articles. Under author entries are included dates, works, and critical and biographical secondary works. A second part of the catalog, including the whole alphabet, supplements the first. Many cross-references add to the utility of this valuable subject index, which is limited only by the holdings of the institute at the turn of the century. In terms of range this subject index supplements Peddie (A–31) and subject indexes to periodicals (see section D).

A–35 **Catalogue of the Library of the Boston Athenaeum, 1807–1871.** Compiled by C. A. Cutter. 5 vols. Boston: The Athenaeum, 1874–1882. Z881.B74

Arranged alphabetically by author, by subject, and, where appropriate, by title, this catalog represents the holdings of the Boston Athenaeum, one of the major American libraries of the nineteenth century, from 1807 to 1871. There is a short preface citing entry methods and abbreviations, which is followed by a list of corrections. The entries on the 3,402 continuously numbered pages include the author's surname, the title of the work, and the place and date of publication of the work. Where a multivolume work is cited, its contents are listed. Since this collection is widely humanistic in scope and the catalog includes some analysis of composite volumes, this item may be considered another supplement to Peddie (A–31) for humanities subjects.

A–36 **Subject Index of the London Library…with Appendix and Synopsis of Headings.** Compiled by C. T. Hagberg Wright et al. 4 vols. London: Williams and Norgate, 1909–1955. Z921.L6

This is the index to the author catalog (B–45) of the London Library, arranged by subject headings in alphabetical order. Volumes 2–4 are additions to the original index, adding works acquired during the years 1909–1922, 1923–1938, and 1938–1953 respectively. The preface and following notes explain the indexing procedures followed. Each subject heading is followed by a list of general works on the subject, then by subheadings and lists of particular works, all alphabetical by author. General cross-references are at the end of each heading, particular cross-references at the end of individual subheadings. Where entries under a heading are numerous, an index has been placed at the top showing the subheadings into which it is divided. There is a list in volume 1 of the academic and learned societies whose publications are held by the library, along with information on the treatment accorded them (i.e., detailed subject analysis of the volumes, citation under general subjects only, or a combination of both). In addition, volume 1 contains an appendix listing subjects for books acquired too late to be entered in the body of the text. There is also a synopsis of headings by broad subject categories which clearly demonstrates the arrangement. Since the index is meant to be used in conjunction with the author catalog, there are several types of omissions: titles are shortened (full titles in the author catalog); initials of authors are omitted when the surname is uncommon and does not interfere with easy cross-reference to the author catalog; all bibliographical details are omitted; since they appear in the main author catalog, no personal-names-as-subjects occur, but a subheading "biography" appears under many subjects (e.g., a biographical study of Garrick would be under "Acting," subheading "Biography"); texts of works by Latin and Greek authors are omitted; and for English, French, and German literature there are no texts later than the fifteenth century or lists of dramatists, poets, or writers among the subjects. Since the four volumes are meant to be used in conjunction, volumes 2–4 do not repeat cross-references to cognate headings, though new ones are added. Throughout the volumes the headings of volume 1 are maintained, which results in some minor peculiarities: the USSR is cited "Russia," World War I is the "European War," and so on. (Consultation of the synopsis of headings in volume 1 should alleviate any difficulties this arrangement might occasion.)

A–39 **Subject Guide to Books in Print.** New York: R. R. Bowker, 1957–. Z1215.P973

A companion to *Books in Print* (C–30), this annual guide lists current data on in-print books published and distributed in the United States. Intended originally as a subject index to *Publishers Trade List Annual* (C–29), the work now has other sources, though it still derives entries primarily from *PTLA*. Since Library of Congress subject classifications are used, works not assigned LC subject headings are not indexed (i.e., single pieces of fiction, poetry, or drama, and Bibles), with the exception of collections and criticism of literary works. Each alphabetically arranged main entry includes author, editor, translator, title, edition, number of volumes, publisher, ISBN number, and price. Abbreviation keys for terminology and publishers are included; the latter key contains addresses for ordering material directly from publishing houses. There is also a *Subject Guide to Forthcoming Books* (New York: Bowker, 1967–) [Z1215.P974], which uses a narrower range of subject areas to provide a preliminary subject index to *Forthcoming Books* (see C–27).

V.   GENERAL ENCYCLOPEDIAS

A–40 **Encyclopaedia Britannica: A Dictionary of Arts, Sciences, Literature, and General Information.** 11th ed. 29 vols. Cambridge: Cambridge University Press, 1910–1911. AE5.E363

This is the last humanistically oriented edition of the British national encyclopedia, whose first edition in three volumes appeared in 1768–1771. Though somewhat more popular than the ninth edition in twenty-five volumes of 1875–1889, the eleventh still retains the character of a collection of scholarly monographs. Because it is more recent, the eleventh edition also contains more current information, though it obviously cannot be used when really up-to-date information is required. There are some shorter articles on specific topics, but the majority of articles are long, authoritative in their time, with bibliographies appended, and covering some 40,000 fairly broad, general topics. The user wanting information on a narrow topic is advised to consult first the index in volume 29. There are excellent orienting articles of greater extent than can be found in literary handbooks and most current literary encyclopedias on literary genres, forms, themes, and the like. When information is sought about the state of knowledge on a particular subject at some point in the past, use of the *Encyclopaedia Britannica* as a historical source is warranted. Additional information about other encyclopedias of historical interest may be found in Robert L. Collison, *Encyclopaedias: Their History throughout the Ages*, 2d ed. (New York: Hafner Publishing Co., 1966) [AE1.C61966]. See also S. Padraig Walsh, *Anglo-American General Encyclopedias, 1703–1967: An Historical Bibliography* (New York: Bowker, 1968) [Z5849.E5 W3].

The latest, fifteenth edition of the *Encyclopaedia Britannica*, now the most distinguished American national encyclopedia, was published in thirty volumes in 1974. The first ten volumes, the "Micropaedia," contain brief, ready-reference articles. There is a single-volume "Propaedia," which presents an outline of all knowledge and is designed to give a topical overview of the main encyclopedia, the nineteen-volume "Macropaedia," which contains some 4,200 long, signed articles with selective, briefly annotated bibliographies appended. In addition, there is a separate index volume to the full set. Cross-references between entries in the "Micropaedia" and the "Macropaedia" are abundant; their relationship is such that the user is advised always to begin with the "Micropaedia," or with the index volume. The "Propaedia" is designed for the beginner seeking an overview of a particular area of human knowledge and can provide a helpful orientation to the amateur inquirer. The fifteenth edition, also known as "Britannica 3," has been subjected to fairly severe criticism. The dependent user or prospective buyer is advised to consult the discussions in the *Booklist* 71 (1 June 1975): 1021–1028, and *Commentary* 61 (February 1976): 63–67, among others. Updating of "Britannica 3" is provided both by a policy of continuous revision and through the annual *Britannica Book of the Year.*

A–41 ***Chambers's Encyclopaedia.*** New rev. ed. 15 vols. Oxford: Pergamon Press, 1967. Reprinted with corrections, 1973.

AE5.C443

This is a completely new edition of the popular British encyclopedia first published 1850–1868. Unlike the *Encyclopaedia Britannica* (A–40), this work contains primarily short articles on very specific, even minute topics. Most are signed with initials and have been contributed by British scholars. When bibliographies are appended, they include both standard works and recent ones. The last "Index and Atlas" volume contains maps by John Bartholomew and Sons, including a series of historical maps. There is an index to the maps, a list of contributors and the principal articles contributed, a classified list of main articles, and a general subject index to the entire work. Users are advised to consult the general subject index first.

A–42 ***Encyclopaedia Universalis.*** 20 vols. Paris: Encyclopaedia Universalis France, 1968–1975.

AE25.E3

Sixteen volumes of this most recent major new French-language encyclopedia present signed articles preceded by brief summaries, with bibliographies and cross-references appended. Universal in scope, the well-illustrated articles, designed for the use of serious students, present detailed, thorough, often highly technical discussions. Biographical articles are found for major figures only. Volume 17, the Organum, intended to provide an overview of human knowledge, is disposed into four parts: the first, a series of signed essays on man and his knowledge; the second, a series of signed articles with bibliographies on topics and problems of immediate, contemporary concern; the third, a series of tables on epistemological relations illustrating the opening essays on human knowledge; and last, a series of predictive statistical tables on world affairs, 1960–2000, with supplementary discussion. The final three volumes comprise a Thesaurus-Index designed to serve as a detailed analytical index to the main body of the encyclopedia. The index includes cross-references to the main work, with or without a brief article; cross-references to other entries in the Thesaurus; and brief articles on very specific topics as well as brief biographical sketches without reference to the main work. The last volume of the Thesaurus-Index also contains a series of tables of world mythologies; calendars of dynasties and historical periods; tables of world peoples and ethnic groups; charts of alphabets with transcriptions and transliterations; and a series of miscellaneous tables of units, symbols, and Nobel Prize winners.

A–43 ***La Grande Encyclopédie: Inventaire raisonné des sciences, des lettres et des arts, par une société de savants et des gens de lettres.*** 31 vols. Paris: Lamirault, 1886–1902.

AE25.G7

This work, the major French-language encyclopedia of the nineteenth century, contains authoritative signed articles with brief bibliographies appended. Its values are parallel to those of the ninth, tenth, and eleventh editions of the *Encyclopaedia Britannica* (A–40), having special importance in the areas of medieval and Renaissance studies and for continental Europe-

an history, literature, and culture. It contains many valuable entries on Continental persons and places not treated as thoroughly or as carefully in other encyclopedic sources. There are some cross-references. It should be noted that the work was radically curtailed from letter T (vol. 30) to the end.

A–44 ***Grand Larousse encyclopédique en dix volumes.*** Paris: Libraire Larousse, 1960–1964. Supplements 1 and 2, 1969, 1975.

AE25.G64

This heavily illustrated modern French dictionary-encyclopedia contains mostly brief, unsigned articles written by some 700 specialists on very specific topics. Authors of principal articles are identified in a list at the end of each volume. Also at the end of each volume are collected the brief bibliographies (containing French-language titles only) to which readers are referred at the end of the more substantial articles. Supplementary volumes with the same structure appeared in 1969 (with articles prepared between 1958 and 1968) and in 1975 (covering materials prepared between 1968 and 1975). Asterisks indicate that articles on the same topics will be found in the original series or in the prior supplement. This work essentially supersedes the *Nouveau Larousse illustré,* 8 vols. (Paris: Larousse, 1898–1907) [AE25.L34], and the *Larousse du XXᵉ siècle,* 6 vols. (Paris: Larousse, 1956) [AE25.L365].

A–45 ***Brockhaus Enzyklopädie in zwanzig Bänden.*** 17th ed., rev. and enl. 24 vols. Wiesbaden: F. A. Brockhaus, 1966–1976.

AE27.G672

This contemporary seventeenth edition of the Brockhaus encyclopedia originally published in 1796–1810 is the standard current German-language dictionary-encyclopedia. Volumes 1 through 20 contain some 225,000 unsigned, generally brief articles, often illustrated and often with short bibliographies appended. Volume 21 contains a world atlas with some 255 topographical, travel, and thematic maps and an extended index to the atlas. Volumes 22 and 23 constitute a first supplement (1975–1976) and refer to the original articles by volume number whenever presenting additions or corrections. Other similar German dictionary-encyclopedias include *Der Grosse Herder: Nachschlagewerk für Wissen und Leben,* 5th ed., rev. and enl., 12 vols. (Freiburg im Breisgau: Herder, 1952–1962) [AE27.H5], which is written from a Roman Catholic point of view, and *Meyers enzyklopädisches Lexikon,* 32 vols., 9th ed., rev. (Mannheim: Bibliographisches Institut, 1971–) [AE27.M6], which includes some 100 "Sonderbeiträge" by famous scholars on especially current topics of interest.

A–46 ***Enciclopedia italiana de scienze, lettere ed arti.*** 41 vols. Rome: Istituto Giovanni Treccani della Enciclopedia italiana, 1938–1961.

AE35.E5

This is the standard Italian scholarly encyclopedia, prized for the lavish quantity and high quality of its illustrations, its authoritative signed articles with extensive bibliographies, and its special emphasis on all aspects of the humanities. Each of the thirty-five volumes of the main encyclopedia includes a list of contributors with professional affiliations and scholarly specializations. The thirty-sixth volume, which appeared in 1939, includes an analytical index and separate indexes to the color illustrations and to the maps included. The indexes cover the entire work and the first supplemental volume, which appeared in 1938. The first and all later supplements follow the format of the main work and refer to it all substantive additions and corrections to original entries. The first supplement also includes a list of errata for the entire work. The second supplement, published in 1948–1949 in two volumes, covers the period 1938–1948; it has its own indexes, list of contributors, and list of addenda and corrigenda. The third supplement, also in two volumes, was published in 1961. It covers the period 1949–1960 and has its own index and list of contributors.

A shorter Italian dictionary-encyclopedia, the *Dizionario enciclopedico italiano*, was published in twelve volumes (Rome: Istituto della Enciclopedia italiana, 1955–1961) [AE35.D516] and is currently being supplemented (fascicles 1–3 appeared in 1969–1970).

A–47 *Enciclopedia universal ilustrada europeo-americana.* 70 vols. plus supplements. Barcelona: Espasa, 1907?–.

AE61.E6

This monumental Spanish dictionary-encyclopedia contains illustrated brief articles as well as major articles with extended bibliographies and elaborate cross-references. A list of contributors appears in the seventieth and final volume of the original work. The original has been supplemented by a ten-volume "appendix" published 1930–1933, and some seventeen additional supplements issued biennially, the most recent of which covers the period 1969–1970 and was published in 1975. The supplemental volumes are not organized as dictionary-encyclopedias but are ordered instead by broad subject fields from aeronautics to tourism. Each volume has a detailed analytical index.

A–49 *New Columbia Encyclopedia.* Edited by William H. Harris and Judith S. Levey. 4th ed. New York: Columbia University Press, 1975.

AG5.C725 1975

This large single volume, published in previous editions under the title *Columbia Encyclopedia* (1st ed. 1935), is generally regarded as the best one-volume encyclopedia. Its 3,052 triple-column pages contain some 50,000 alphabetically arranged, relatively short articles, some with bibliographies appended, on the humanities, social sciences, biological and physical sciences, and geography. It is simultaneously an atlas (with long articles on the geography, history, and economics of individual countries); a gazetteer; a biographical dictionary (with more than 5,000 biographical articles); a companion to art, literature, and music; a dictionary of history and current events (with long articles on cultural movements and major historical events); a dictionary of science, technology, and mathematics; and a dictionary of the social sciences. There are some illustrations, including drawings, maps, and charts. As an example of its pattern of coverage, two columns are devoted to labor unions, four to Islam, five to the Reformation, and eight and a half to Shakespeare (including two large charts of his plays).

An abbreviated version of less than 1,000 pages, *Concise Columbia Encyclopedia*, was edited by Judith S. Levey and Agnes Greenhall (New York: Columbia University Press, 1983) [AG5.C7371983]. It contains some 15,000 entries and many of the tables, charts, maps, and other features of the greater work.

VI. SPECIAL ENCYCLOPEDIAS IN ANCILLARY FIELDS

A–50 *Encyclopaedia of Religion and Ethics.* Edited by James Hastings. 12 vols. and index. New York: Charles Scribner's Sons, 1908–1927.

BL31.E4

The *Encyclopaedia*, though dated, remains an extremely valuable "universal" reference work that aims to examine the whole range of theology and philosophy and relevant portions of anthropology, biology, economics, folklore, mythology, psychology, and sociology. It contains signed articles with full bibliographies on all religions and on every religious belief or custom; on ethical systems and movements; on philosophical ideas and moral practices; and on persons and places famous in the history of religion and morals. To avoid overlapping and yet treat each topic fully, subjects are described comprehensively in general articles, and particular topics are then treated more fully in separate discussions. The index volume lists all articles pertaining to general subjects such as "Church History"; particular subjects are also indexed, as are titles of books. There are also indexes of foreign words (by language) and Scripture passages as well as a list of contributors and their articles.

A more recent general encyclopedia of religion with long signed articles and full bibliographies is *Die Religion in Geschichte und Gegenwart: Handwörterbuch für Theologie und Religionswissenschaft*, 3d ed., rev. and enl., 6 vols. plus index (Tübingen: Mohr, 1957–1965) [BL31.R42]. Among the available one-volume dictionaries and encyclopedias of religion may be cited *Dictionary of Religion and Ethics*, ed. Shailer Mathews and Gerald Birney Smith (New York: Macmillan, 1921) [BL31.M3], with brief signed articles and a classified bibliography at the end of the volume, and *Encyclopedia of Religion*, ed. Vergilius T. A. Ferm (New York: Philosophical Library, 1945) [BL31.F4], with brief signed articles that are often followed by short bibliographies. For brief definitions of terms only, consult Donald T. Kauffman, *Dictionary of Religious Terms* (Westwood, N.J.: Revell, 1967) [BL31.K34], or Edgar Royston Pike, *Encyclopedia of Religion and Religions* (New York: Meridian Books, 1958) [BL31.P5 1958]. See also entries concerning Religion and Literature in Section X (X–30 ff.).

A–51 *Encyclopaedia Judaica.* Cecil Roth, editor in chief. 16 vols. New York: Macmillan, 1971–1972.   DS102.8.E496

The most recent, comprehensive Jewish encyclopedia, this work includes the fields of Judaism, Jewish philosophy, the Bible, the Talmud, and Jewish law; Hebrew and Semitic languages; Jewish history, the Second Temple period, the Holocaust, contemporary Jewry; the history, geography, and contemporary culture of the land of Israel; Judaism in America and Canada; Zionism; Jewish literature—medieval, modern Hebrew, and Rabbinical; modern Jewish scholarship; and the participation of Jews in world culture (including divisions of art, literature, medicine, music, the sciences, and other disciplines). The work incorporates articles from the German *Encyclopaedia Judaica*, 10 vols. (Berlin: Eschkol, 1928–1934) [DS102.8.E5], and the Hebrew *Encyclopaedia Hebraica* [AE30.E5] and is a product of efforts to continue and complete both of those works. Some 25,000 signed, authoritative articles, with bibliographies appended, are often illustrated and well cross-referenced. They range in length from capsule biographies to monographs of over 100,000 words. The last volume has a supplement and is to be further supplemented by yearbooks. The first volume contains an elaborate analytical index to the entire work; a detailed introduction; lists of editors and contributors to the encyclopedia; lists of general, rabbinical, and bibliographical abbreviations; rules of transliteration; and supplementary lists including a hundred-year Jewish calendar, 1920–2020, charts of the Hasidic dynasties, lists of Israeli place-names, Hebrew newspapers and periodicals, and a guide to the pottery of Judaic antiquity.

Two earlier English-language Jewish encyclopedias are of historical interest. They are *Jewish Encyclopedia*, new ed., 12 vols. (New York: Funk and Wagnalls, 1925) [DS102.8 .J65], and the *Universal Jewish Encyclopedia*, 10 vols. (New York: Universal Jewish Encyclopedia, 1939–1943) [DS102.8 .U5]. The best one-volume references are *Everyman's Judaica: An Encyclopedic Dictionary*, ed. Geoffrey Wigoder (London: Dent, 1975) [DS102.8.E68], planned as a mini-encyclopedia complementary to the *Encyclopaedia Judaica*, and the *New Standard Jewish Encyclopedia*, 5th ed., rev. Geoffrey Wigoder (Garden City, N.Y.: Doubleday, 1977) [DS102.8.S73].

A-52 ***New Catholic Encyclopedia.*** Prepared by an editorial staff at the Catholic University of America. William J. McDonald, editor in chief. 17 vols. New York: McGraw-Hill, 1967–1979.   BX841.N44

"An international work of reference on the teachings, history, organization, and activities of the Catholic church and on all institutions, religions, philosophies, and scientific and cultural developments affecting the Catholic church from its beginning to the present. This work is not a revision of the *Catholic Encyclopedia*, 16 vols. (New York: Catholic Encyclopedia Press, 1907–1914; supplement 1, 1922; supplement 2, 1951) [BX841.C24], which remains of historical value, but is a completely new work. There are about 17,000 separate articles, each signed by one of the 4,800 contributors (both Catholic and non-Catholic). Nearly all include bibliographies. Though international in scope, there is an emphasis on the Catholic church in the United States and in English-speaking countries. No biographies of living persons are included. Volume 15 gives details about each author and lists all his contributions. Additional features include considerable numbers of maps, charts, and illustrations; an elaborate system of cross-references; and, in volume 15, an extensive analytical index of some 350,000 entries. Volume 16 presents a supplement, 1967–1974.

A useful, one-volume dictionary that includes but is not limited to theological matters and that gives brief definitions of terms, names, and phrases is *Catholic Dictionary*, ed. Donald Attwater, 3d ed. (New York: Macmillan, 1958) [BX841-.C35].

A-53 ***Encyclopedia of Islam.*** New Edition. Edited by H. A. R. Gibb, J. H. Kramers, et al. Leiden: E. J. Brill, 1954–.   DS37.E523

This new edition, which is being published in English and French parallel editions in double fascicles of 128 pages each, will eventually replace the original four-volume *Encyclopedia of Islam: A Dictionary of the Geography, Ethnography and Biography of the Muhammadan Peoples*, ed. Martin Theodor Houtsma (Leiden: Brill; London: Luzak, 1913–1934; *Supplement*, 1938) [DS37.E5]. Each bound volume begins with a list of authors of articles, identifying those articles that are reprinted or revised from articles in the original edition or in the related one-volume *Shorter Encyclopaedia of Islam*, ed. H. A. R. Gibb and J. H. Kramers (Leiden: Brill, 1953) [DS37-.E52]. The new edition covers the same broad range of subjects as the earlier one, with long, signed, authoritative articles on topics associated with the Islamic religion, including beliefs, laws, and institutions; on the biography, history, customs, and manners of the Islamic peoples; and on the geography, industries, sciences, and political life of the Islamic community. The new edition has a special emphasis on economic and social topics and on Islamic art. Elaborate bibliographies are generally appended to articles, and there are abundant cross-references from English and French terms to the transliterated Arabic words that are the main entries. A general index and an atlas of the Islamic world are planned.

A-60 ***Encyclopedia of Philosophy.*** Paul Edwards, editor in chief. 8 vols. New York: Macmillan, 1967.   B41.E5

This encyclopedia, which sets out to cover both the whole of the discipline of philosophy—Eastern and Western, ancient, medieval, and modern—and many of the connections between philosophy and other disciplines, contains nearly 1,500 signed articles (some of them virtually monographs) useful to both the specialist and the intelligent layman. Some 900 of the articles are on individual philosophers. Appended to each article is an extended bibliography, sometimes classified and sometimes elaborately annotated. A list of the 500 specialist contributors with brief *vitae* and the titles of articles contributed is found at the beginning of volume 1. An elaborate analytical index occupies some 150 four-column pages in volume 8. For single definitions of terms, consult Alan Robert Lacey, *Dictionary of Philosophy* (Boston: Routledge and Kegan Paul, 1976) [B41.L32], which provides short articles, often with brief bibliographies added. Additional references may be found in the excellent volume, *Guide to Philosophical Bibliography and Research*, by Richard T. DeGeorge (New York: Appleton-Century-Crofts, 1971) [Z7125.D44]. Another useful guide is Herbert Guerry, *Bibliography of Philosophical Bibliographies* (Westport, Conn.: Greenwood, 1977) [Z7125.A1 G83]. See also entries concerning Philosophy and Literature in Section X (X–30 ff.).

A-61 ***Dictionary of the History of Ideas:*** **Studies of Selected Pivotal Ideas.** Philip P. Wiener, editor in chief. 4 vols. plus index. New York: Charles Scribner's Sons, 1973–1974.   CB5.D52

A selection of pivotal topics in intellectual history intended to exhibit central ideas through cross-disciplinary, historical, and analytical essays. An analytical table of contents in volume 1 divides the articles into the seven domains covered by the work: 1—ideas about the external order of nature; 2—ideas about human nature; 3—ideas in literature and the arts, aesthetic theory, and literary criticism; 4—ideas about, or attitudes toward, history, historiography, and historical criticism; 5—the history of economic, legal, and political ideas and institutions, ideologies, and movements; 6—the history of religious and philosophical ideas; and 7—the history of formal mathematical, logical, linguistic, and methodological ideas. Articles are signed and have bibliographies appended. Cross-references and an extensive analytical index volume make access to the contents quite easy. There is also an alphabetical list of articles and a list of contributors giving academic affiliations and the articles contributed.

See additional material on the history of ideas in Section F and in most other sections dealing with literature in general or in specific periods.

A-65 ***Encyclopaedia of the Social Sciences.*** Edwin R. A. Seligman, editor in chief, and Alvin Johnson, associate editor. 15 vols. New York: Macmillan, 1930–1935.   H41.E6

This now somewhat outdated interdisciplinary work aimed to trace connections between all of the social sciences. It includes signed expert articles of up to 20,000 words in length on all important topics in the sciences of politics, economics, law, anthropology, sociology, penology, and social work. Relevant portions of history, selected topics from the "semi-social sciences" of ethics, education, philosophy, and psychology, and selected topics from biology, geography, medicine, philology, and art are also covered. About one-fifth of the entire work consists of some 4,000 biographies of deceased persons whose work was significant to social science.

The articles are arranged in a continuous alphabetical order throughout the fifteen volumes with abundant cross-references. Most conclude with a list of further references to consult. Each volume contains a list of contributors and a table of contents naming each article and its author. The first volume contains a two-part introduction of nearly 350 pages on "The Development of Social Thought and Institutions" (a history from Greek antiquity to the 1920s) and on "The Social Sciences as Disciplines" (describing the history and character of social science throughout the world by nation or geographical region).

The work concludes with a three-part index, the first classifying each subject and biographical article under broad disciplinary and topical headings, the second analyzing the contents of the articles themselves, and the third providing an alphabetical list of contributors and their articles. This work is extended but not replaced by the more recent *International Encyclopedia of the Social Sciences* (A–66).

A–66 **International Encyclopedia of the Social Sciences.** Edited by David L. Sills. 18 vols. New York: Macmillan, 1968–1979.   H40.A2 I5

Designed to complement, not supplement, the *Encyclopedia of the Social Sciences* (A–65), this work consists of entirely new, specially commissioned, signed articles devoted to the concepts, theories, and methods of anthropology, economics, geography, history, law, political science, psychiatry, psychology, sociology, and statistics. There are also articles presenting modern social thought about the arts, the major religions, and many professions. Further articles discuss major societies of the world, area studies, regional sciences, and behavioral science. Also included are some 600 fairly long biographies of persons born after 1890 whose research and writings have had an impact upon the social sciences. A volume 18, *Biographical Supplement*, was published (Sills, N.Y.: Free Press, 1979), adding 215 further biographies.

Editorial aims include summarizing existing knowledge, aiding the standardization of terminology and research procedures, and counteracting the effects of specialization by combining in single entries materials from several different fields. Articles tend to be on broad topics with subarticles on aspects of the overall topic. They tend to use historical and descriptive material that is international in scope for illustrative purposes only, and to emphasize analytical and comparative aspects of each topic. Each is followed by a selected bibliography containing documentation of the article and suggestions for further reading. The articles are arranged in a continuous alphabetical order through volumes 1–16, with elaborate cross-references. Volume 17, the index, provides an alphabetical directory of contributors, a classification of topical and biographical articles designed to give users an overview of coverage in the different disciplines and subject areas, and a detailed analytical index of article contents. For brief, signed articles describing and defining about 1,000 basic concepts in the fields of sociology, political science, economics, social anthropology, and social psychology, consult *Dictionary of the Social Sciences*, ed. Julius Gould and William L. Kolb (New York: Free Press, 1964) [H41.G6], and for brief definitions of terms see *Dictionary of the Social Sciences*, ed. Hugo F. Reading (London: Routledge and Kegan Paul, 1976) [H41 .R42]. Another source of reference information is Gillian A. Burrington, *How to Find Out about the Social Sciences* (Oxford: Pergamon, 1975) [H62.5.G7 B87 1975]. The standard general reference guide is *Sources of Information in the Social Sciences*, ed. Carl M. White et al., 2d ed. (Chicago: ALA, 1973) [Z7161.W491973].

See also additional references on Literature and the Social Sciences in Section X (X–30 ff.).

A–70 **Allgemeines Lexikon der bildenden Künstler von der Antike bis zur Gegenwart.** Edited by Ulrich Thieme and Felix Becker (later Hans Vollmer). 37 vols. Leipzig: Engelmann, 1907–1950.   N40.T42

A biographical dictionary of some 150,000 artists and craftsmen of all places and times, up to the beginning of the twentieth century. Excluded are minor oriental artists, artists of local interest only, and modern "illustrators" and other commercial artists. Articles of varying lengths are signed, give lists of works for major artists, and provide sources of information. A list of contributors precedes volume 1. Volume 37 contains articles on anonymous masters whether known by place of work, by major composition, by some other rubric, by year, or by initials.

For artists of the twentieth century see the continuation, *Allgemeines Lexikon der bildenden Künstler des XX. Jahrhun-*

derts, ed. Hans Vollmer, 6 vols. (Leipzig: Seeman, 1953–1962) [N40.V6], the last two volumes of which contain a supplement to the entire forty-three-volume work.

A–71 **Encyclopedia of World Art.** Massimo Pallottino, editor in chief. 15 vols. New York: McGraw-Hill, 1959–1968.

N31.E4833

The simultaneously published English version of the *Enciclopedia universale dell'arte*, this work aims to provide a major historical synthesis covering the representational arts of all periods and countries. Architecture, sculpture, painting, and the decorative arts and crafts are included, without limits as to the time, place, or cultural environment of their creation. There are historical articles by cultural cycle, epoch, school, and artist; geographical articles presenting inventories of monuments; articles on artistic types and iconographies; on materials and techniques; on matters relating to the conservation, restoration, preservation, and evaluation of art; on art criticism and art historiography; and on broad questions of general aesthetics. Articles are long, signed, and authoritative, with extensive bibliographies appended. Lists of contributors with affiliations precede, and plates illustrating articles occupy roughly the last half of each volume. A complete list of contributors and their articles is found in volume 15, the index volume, which presents a detailed analytical index including names of persons and places, titles of works of art, and a wide range of subjects including styles, periods, materials, techniques, and concepts.

Among the shorter works available may be mentioned the five-volume *McGraw-Hill Dictionary of Art*, ed. Bernard S. Myers (New York: McGraw-Hill, 1969) [N33.M23], which uses illustrations and other materials from the fifteen-volume *Encyclopedia*, and the five-volume *Praeger Encyclopedia of Art* (New York: Praeger, 1971) [N33.P68]. Both have many signed articles and are extensively illustrated. The best one-volume reference source is the *Oxford Companion to Art*, ed. Harold Osborne (Oxford: Clarendon Press, 1970) [N33.O9]. See also the *Oxford Companion to Twentieth-Century Art*, ed. Harold Osborne (London: Oxford University Press, 1982) [N6490.O94], and the *Oxford Companion to the Decorative Arts* (London: Oxford University Press, 1975) [NK30.O93], now available in paperback (1985).

The standard special reference guides are by Mary Chamberlin, *Guide to Art Reference Books* (Chicago: ALA, 1959) [Z5931.C45] continued by Etta Arntzen and Robert Rainwater, *Guide to the Literature of Art History* (Chicago: ALA, 1978) [Z5931.A67], and Donald L. Ehresmann, *Fine Arts: A Bibliographic Guide to Basic Reference Works, Histories, and Handbooks*, 2d ed. (Littleton, Colo.: Libraries Unlimited, 1979) [Z5931.E47 1979]. See also additional references on Art and Literature in Section X (X–30 ff.).

A–75 **New Grove Dictionary of Music and Musicians.** Edited by Stanley Sadie. 20 vols. London: Macmillan, 1980.

ML100.N4B

This new and almost entirely rewritten encyclopedic work is the standard English reference book in all fields of music. It replaces the nine-volume fifth edition of *Grove's Dictionary of Music and Musicians*, ed. Eric Blom (1955) [ML100.G885] and its supplements, and becomes the current representative of the original work published in 1879 under the editorship of Sir George Grove. The work is universal in scope and intends to cover every topic that bears on music in any way. In contrast with its predecessor work, it includes popular music and musicians in significant numbers and has a much more extensive coverage of non-Western and folk music than was previously the case.

More than half of the articles are biographical in character, treating composers, performers, scholars, critics, theorists, musical organization administrators, persons eminent in the other arts (librettists, authors, dancers, and so on), music patrons, printers, publishers, and instrument producers. Music theory, terminology, history, genres, forms, instruments, places, and institutions are all included, as are massive articles on topics from aesthetics to electronic music, ethnomusicology, and popular music. Theoretical topics in the study of melody, harmony, and rhythm are included, as are articles providing bibliographies and reference materials. There are national bibliographies, and bibliographies of media and of genres. In addition, there are extensive articles on sources for the study of music history.

Some 2,500 contributors have produced signed articles with extensive bibliographies. There are classified bibliographies for each composer. In volume 20 there are two appendixes, the first providing an index of terms used in articles on non-Western music, folk music, and kindred topics, and the second giving an alphabetical list of contributors with the last known address of living contributors.

A valuable series of single-volume paperback excerpts, the *New Grove Composer Biography Series*, has been published in New York by W. W. Norton (1983) [LC numbers vary]. To date, the following have appeared in separate volumes: The Bach Family, Beethoven, Handel, Haydn, Masters of Italian Opera [Bellini, Donizetti, Puccini, Rossini, and Verdi], Mozart, Schubert, and The Second Viennese School [Berg, Schoenberg, and Webern]. Another excerpt is the *New Grove Dictionary of Musical Instruments*, 3 vols. (London: Macmillan, 1984) [ML102.I5 N48 1984].

Among shorter reference works may be cited Percy A. Scholes, ed., *New Oxford Companion to Music*, by J. O. Ward. 2 vols. (New York: Oxford University Press, 1983) [ML100.N5 1983] which contains about 1,500 biographical sketches in addition to articles on places, periods, works, instruments, forms, sound, scales, notation, music theory, and non-Western music. Scholes also prepared a *List of Books about Music in the English Language . . .: An Appendix to the Oxford Companion* (1979) [ML100.S37 1979]. See, in addition, *Baker's Biographical Dictionary of Musicians*, 7th ed., rev. Nicolas Slonimsky (New York: Schirmer, 1984) [ML105.B16 1984], which excludes nonbiographical materials, and Willi Apel, ed., *Harvard Dictionary of Music*, 2d ed., rev. and enl. (Cambridge: Harvard University Press, 1969) [ML100.A64 1969], which contains more than 5,700 entries but excludes biographical articles whether of composers, performers, publishers, organizations, or orchestras.

For historical study see Gerald Abraham, the *Concise Oxford History of Music* (Oxford: Clarendon Press, 1979) [ML160.A27], separate from the *New Oxford History of Music*, 10 vols. (London: Oxford University Press, 1954–) [ML160.N44], to which Abraham contributed the fifth volume, *Age of Humanism, 1540–1630*. In the field of music there is an excellent special reference guide by Vincent H. Duckles, *Music Reference and Research Materials: An Annotated Bibliography*, 3d ed. (New York: Free Press, 1974) [ML113.D83 1974]. See also Harold Diamond, *Music Criticism: An Annotated Guide to the Literature* (Metuchen, N.J.: Scarecrow, 1979) [ML113.D5].

See also additional references on Music and Literature in Section X (X–20 ff.).

LIBRARIES

See also section H, Manuscripts and Archives, and Section Y.VI on Scholarship concerning Libraries and Librarianship.

I. LIBRARY DIRECTORIES

B–1 *International Library Directory*. Edited by A. P. Wales. 3d ed. London: The A. P. Wales Organisation, 1969–1970.
Z721.I6

This directory lists the libraries of most countries in alphabetical order under the subdivisions of cities and towns except in the case of Canada, Argentina, Brazil, Colombia, France, the Philippines, the United States, Australia, and India, for which the division is by state or province and then by city or town. Abbreviations, explained in a list that precedes the directory proper, record for each library its type, its subject strengths, the languages of its holdings, the number of volumes, the number of periodicals held, and the name of the chief librarian. Information was gathered by questionnaire and thus is as accurate as the respondents individually made possible. Since there are only forty subject divisions, that category is of very limited use and does not permit identification of distinctive subject strengths of the kind that students of English and American language and literature may be interested in. It does, however, give a general idea of the character of each library listed.

The directory provides information on libraries in 150 nations, and it is thorough: there are 214 separate entries for libraries in Washington, D.C., for instance. Supplemented by other, more detailed sources of information such as Lewanski (B–2), Roberts (B–3), the *ASLIB Directory* (B–4), Young et al. (B–6), or Ash (B–7), this directory can be used as a first step in determining which libraries in a particular locality might be worth looking into for a particular research problem.

Similar coverage is also available in the *World Guide to Libraries*, 7th ed. (New York: K. G. Saur, 1985) [Z721.I63 W927 W4 1985], an updated English-language edition of the *Internationales Bibliotheks-Handbuch* (Munich: Verlag Dokumentation, 1970) [Z721.I63], a directory of more than 35,000 special and general libraries in 165 countries. The guide covers national, federal, regional, university and college libraries, and school and public libraries with 30,000 volumes or more. It also covers special, government, and business libraries with more than 3,000 volumes. It is arranged by continent, country, and library type. Entries typically include the library name and an English translation, the address, founding date, main departments, special collections, holdings statistics, and reference to data network and/or interlibrary loan participation. An index of library names concludes the volume.

For somewhat greater and more current detail on American libraries see the biennial *American Library Directory: A Classified List of Libraries in the United States and Canada*, 37th ed., 2 vols. (New York: Bowker, 1984) [Z731.A53]. The directory lists public, academic, and special libraries in the United States and Canada. Arrangement is geographic by state, region, or province, then city, and then by institutional name. Entries provide information obtained from libraries themselves or public sources. Included are addresses, telephone numbers, key personnel, history of the library, budget figures, holdings statistics, names of special collections, automation data, and information networks to which the library belongs. A variety of appendixes provide supplementary information about such matters as library networks.

B–2 **Lewanski, Richard C.** *Subject Collections in European Libraries: A Directory and Bibliographical Guide.* 2d ed. New York: R. R. Bowker, 1978. Z789.L4

This Directory provides a guide to special collections in over 6,000 European libraries (including those of Great Britain, Iceland, Cyprus, Malta, and Greenland, but excluding those of the Asiatic parts of the Soviet Union and Turkey) which is meant to complement the guide to North American libraries by Ash (see B–7). It is arranged by Dewey decimal subject classification, and the libraries with special strengths in that subject are listed alphabetically by country and then by locality. Entries are determined by the unique character and size of a library's collection in a particular subject and depend on the prior report of the collection as a special one. Each entry includes the name of the library, its exact address, the date of its foundation, the number of volumes in the special collection (or, occasionally, in the total collection), and a review of rules and restrictions imposed by the library administration, including opening hours. The extent, quality, and currency of information given is variable, since it was culled from a wide variety of sources, including some in need of revision and some of inferior quality. In addition, different libraries naturally have different views of what constitutes a special collection and describe their collections in different ways; such variation is even more pronounced between different countries. An alphabetically arranged subject index refers the user to the appropriate Dewey decimal number section of the volume. Each edition of the directory replaces previous editions.

Lewanski is also the author of the *European Library Directory: A Geographical and Bibliographical Guide* (Florence: Leo S. Olschki, 1968) [Z789.L39], which serves as a companion volume to his subject guide, giving descriptions of libraries and citing available catalogs and finding aids.

B–3 **Roberts, Stephen, Alan Cooper, and Leslie Gilder, comps.** *Research Libraries and Collections in the United Kingdom: A Selective Inventory and Guide.* Hamden, Conn.: Linnet Books, 1978.   Z791.A1 R6 1978

Brief, current descriptions of some 247 research libraries in England, Scotland, Wales, and Northern Ireland. The work is disposed into four sections, covering national libraries (or libraries of national scope), special libraries, and public libraries; university libraries; polytechnic libraries in England and Wales; and Scottish Central Institutions. Entries include the official name of the library and its parent institution or organization; the library's postal address, telephone number, and telex and telegraphic addresses; and the name of the librarian. The date of foundation and brief historical details follow, along with a brief description of present aims and principal facilities. General and special subject coverage, brief statistical details about holdings, and an enumeration of special collections of strength are followed by information about the classification system used, the catalogs maintained, and matters related to public access to holdings. Entries conclude with an enumeration of current publications about the library and a bibliography of further descriptions available in the literature.

The volume begins with a helpful bibliography of other printed guides to libraries in the United Kingdom, disposed into sections of general guides, guides covering specific subjects or forms of material, and guides to collections in area and regional studies. It concludes with indexes of subjects, names, and places, followed by a number list of the 247 libraries treated.

B–4 *ASLIB* **[Association of Special Libraries and Information Bureaux] *Directory.*** Vol. 1, *Information Sources in Science, Technology, and Commerce.* 4th ed. London: ASLIB, 1978. Vol. 2, *Information Sources in Medicine, the Social Sciences, and the Humanities.* 3d ed. London: ASLIB, 1970. Both volumes edited by Brian J. Wilson.   Z791.A1 A82

These volumes, which present 2,787 and 2,414 serially numbered entries respectively, together nearly double the coverage of the 1957 second edition of this standard directory of special libraries in Britain. Library entries are presented under the name of their locality, in strict alphabetical order by the official postal name of the town. Entries give addresses and telephone numbers, a characterization of the library, a definition of its scope, and a list of primary and (sometimes) secondary subjects collected. Statistics are given on the size of the collection, and a list of publications about the library concludes the entry. Each volume has two indexes, the first of names (identifying all organizations, institutions, societies, companies, libraries, and special collections cited) and the second of subjects. The subject index uses fairly broad terms and must therefore be supplemented by other sources giving a more detailed picture of a potentially useful library's actual holdings. It should be noted that the same library may be entered in both volumes, if its collections are in subjects that belong in each. The sources of information for this and most other directories are questionnaires completed by the libraries themselves, and the accuracy of entries depends on the precision of the responses.

For British library holdings on the United States see also Peter Snow, *United States: A Guide to Library Holdings in the United Kingdom* (H–50).

B–5 **Downs, Robert B.** *British and Irish Library Resources; A Bibliographical Guide.* 2d ed. London: Mansell, 1981.   Z1002.D63 1981

A bibliographical guide, the first edition of which appeared in 1973, containing some 5,000 serially numbered entries intended to record all published library catalogs, general and special; all checklists of special collections; calendars of manuscripts and archives; exhibition catalogs; articles describing library collections; guides to individual libraries and their holdings; directories of libraries, both general and in specialized fields; all union lists of periodicals, newspapers, and other serials; and all other descriptive, analytical, or critical records that might guide the scholar in assessing the resources for advanced study and research in libraries of England, Scotland, Wales, and Ireland. Designed to include all types of libraries, all subjects, and all categories of library materials, the work is arranged in the order of the Dewey decimal classification. Entries are often annotated. A comprehensive index of authors, compilers, authors-as-subjects, institutions, and subjects completes the volume. Downs is the author also of *American Library Resources* (B–8) and of *Australian and New Zealand Library Resources* (London: Mansell, 1979).

Since it is limited to published records, this guide should be supplemented by reports of holdings in such surveys as Lewanski (B–2), Roberts et al. (B–3), and the *ASLIB Directory* (B–4). But students are well advised to study all published materials about a library's holdings *before* traveling to it. The more that is known before arrival, the more efficient and productive a study visit can be.

B–6 **Darnay, Brigitte T.** *Directory of Special Libraries and Information Centers.* 10th ed. 3 vols. Detroit: Gale Research Co., 1987.   Z731.Y68

A guide, first published in 1963, to North Americn special libraries, research libraries, information centers, archives, and data centers maintained by government agencies, business, industry, newspapers, educational institutions, nonprofit organizations, and societies in the fields of science, technology, medicine, law, art, religion, history, social sciences, and humanistic studies. More than 18,000 special libraries and information centers are listed alphabetically in the base volume, *Special Libraries and Information Centers in the United States and Canada*, under the official name of the parent institution. Each serially numbered entry is based on survey information supplied by the libraries and lists the name of the sponsoring organization, the address of the library, the date of foundation, the important subjects represented in the collections, special or unique holdings, the number of holdings, services available to outside inquirers, names of staff members, and several other kinds of information enumerated in the introduction to the volume. The volume concludes with a subject index in which each listing is organized alphabetically by state or province, and then numerically by the library or center that holds materials on the subject. Volume 2, *Geographic and Personnel Indexes*, is arranged alphabetically by state (or province) and locality in the first case, and alphabetically in the second. Volume 3, *New Special Libraries*, consists of periodical supplements to Volume 1, with cumulative indexes.

Also available is *Subject Directory of Special Libraries and Information Centers*, 5 vols. (Detroit: Gale, 1977) [Z675.A2 Y68], in which the contents of an earlier edition of the directory have been rearranged into five subject-oriented volumes as follows: 1—Business and Law Libraries, including Military and Transportation Libraries; 2—Education and Information Science Libraries, including Audiovisual, Picture, Publishing, Rare Book, and Recreational Libraries; 3—Health Sciences Libraries, including all aspects of basic and applied medical sciences; 4—Social Sciences and Humanities Libraries, including Area/Ethnic, Art, Geography/Map, History, Music, Religion/Theology, Theater, and Urban/Regional Planning Libraries; and 5—Science and Technology Libraries, including Agriculture, Environment/Conservation, and Food Sciences Libraries. Each of the volumes also has an alternate-name index that refers readers to the main entry under which the library or center of that name appears. Note that libraries in the United States and Canada are always treated separately in this massive work, except in the subject index.

B–7 **Ash, Lee, et al.** *Subject Collections: A Guide to Special Book Collections and Subject Emphases as Reported by University, College, Public, and Special Libraries and Museums in the United States and Canada.* 6th ed., rev. and enl. 2 vols. New York: R. R. Bowker, 1985.

Z731.A85 1985

This directory, first published in 1958, provides a guide to special collections gathered from questionnaires sent out by the compiler. Subjects are arranged alphabetically; beneath each one are listed libraries reporting special strengths, alphabetically by state or province, then by city, then by the name of the library. Entries include addresses, notes, hours of operation, and restrictions for use imposed by library administrators. Notes vary depending on the type of information received from the library, as does the extent and quality of the entire directory, which depends on those responses for its data base. There are approximately 4,000 subjects included, plus innumerable citations of author, place, and name collections. It is estimated that the number of entries exceeds 90,000.

B–8 **Downs, Robert B. *American Library Resources: A Bibliographical Guide.*** Chicago: American Library Association, 1951. ***Supplement, 1950–1961.*** Chicago, 1962. ***Second Supplement, 1961–1970.*** Chicago, 1972. ***Third Supplement, 1971–1980.*** Chicago, 1981. ***Cumulative Index, 1870–1970***, edited by Clara Keller. Chicago, 1981.

Z1002.D6

With supplements, a bibliography of nearly 12,000 printed catalogs, union lists of books and serials, descriptions of special collections, surveys of holdings, calendars of manuscripts and archival materials, and similar items whether published separately as books or pamphlets or in periodicals or collected volumes. Annotated entries are serially numbered and arranged in Dewey decimal subject classes. Detailed indexes of authors, compilers, editors, libraries, organizations, and subjects conclude each volume. Since it lists, with rare exceptions, only published items, this guide does not always give an accurate picture of actual holdings, particularly in smaller or poorer libraries that may nevertheless have collections of interest to scholars. It should be used in conjunction with Young (B–6) and Ash (B–7). Although limited to bibliographies and indexes, the more recent date of Paul Wasserman and Esther Herman's *Library Bibliographies and Indexes: A Subject Guide to Resource Material Available from Libraries, Information Centers, Library Schools and Library Associations in the United States and Canada* (Detroit: Gale, 1975) [Z1002.W28] makes it a useful supplement to Downs.

B–9 **Esdaile, Arundel. *National Libraries of the World: Their History, Administration and Public Services.*** 2d ed. Revised by R. J. Hill. London: The Library Association, 1957.   Z721.E74 1957

First published in 1934, this volume introduces the national libraries in thirty-two countries. Included are articles on the national libraries in Great Britain (the British Museum—now the British Library—in London, the National Library of Scotland in Edinburgh, the National Library of Wales in Aberystwyth); France (La Bibliothèque nationale in Paris); Austria (Die Österreichische Nationalbibliothek in Vienna); Germany (Die Deutsche Staatsbibliothek in Berlin); Switzerland (La Bibliothèque nationale suisse / Die Schweizerische Landesbibliothek in Bern); Ireland (the National Library of Ireland in Dublin); Belgium (La Bibliothèque royale de Belgique in Brussels); The Netherlands (De Koniklijke Bibliotheek in The Hague); Luxemburg (La Bibliothèque nationale);

Italy (La Biblioteca nazionale-centrale in Florence, La Biblioteca nazionale centrale Vittorio Emanuele II in Rome, La Biblioteca nazionale Braidense in Milan, La Biblioteca nazionale Vittorio Emmanuele III in Naples, La Biblioteca nazionale in Palermo, La Biblioteca nazionale in Turin, and La Biblioteca nazionale marciana in Venice); Greece (the National Library in Athens); Spain (La Biblioteca nacional in Madrid); Portugal (A Biblioteca national in Lisbon); Denmark (Det Koneglige Bibliotek in Copenhagen); Norway (Universitetsbiblioteket in Oslo); Sweden (Kunigliga Biblioteket in Stockholm); Finland (the Library of the University of Helsinki in Helsinki); the Soviet Union (the Lenin State Library in Moscow and the Saltykov-Shchedrin Library in Leningrad); Bulgaria (the "Vassil Kolarov" State Library in Sofia); Poland (the National Library in Warsaw); the United States (the Library of Congress in Washington, D.C.); Canada (the National Library in Ottawa); Mexico (La Biblioteca nacional in Mexico City); Argentina (La Biblioteca nacional in Buenos Aires); Brazil (La Biblioteca nacional in Rio de Janeiro); Chile (La Biblioteca nacional in Santiago); Peru (La Biblioteca nacional in Lima); South Africa (the South African Public Library / Die Suid-Afrikaanse Openbare Biblioteek in Cape Town and the State Library / Die Staatsbiblioteek in Pretoria); Israel (the Jewish National and University Library in Jerusalem); Australia (the National Library of the Commonwealth in Canberra); and Japan (the National Diet Library in Tokyo).

The chapters generally include an account of the library's foundation and history, its constitution, administration, and divisions, and its buildings. The collections are described and the catalogs enumerated and described. The library's place in the respective national system is discussed, its finances and staffing are summarized, and a bibliography is appended.

Other works more or less parallel in purpose to Esdaile's introduction are Margaret Burton's *Famous Libraries of the World* (London: Grafton and Co., 1937) [Z721.B97], which includes chapters on many important but not national libraries such as the Bodleian in Oxford, the Vatican Library, the New York Public Library, and the Huntington Library in San Marino, California, among many others; and Colin Steele's *Major Libraries of the World: A Selective Guide* (New York: Bowker, 1976) [Z721.S82 1976]. In addition, there are fairly current, long articles on major libraries included among entries of the *Encyclopedia of Library and Information Science* (see Y–90).

II.   UNION CATALOGS

Other union catalogs cited in this volume include the *Library of Congress Catalog—Books: Subjects* (A–33); the *Union List of Libraries* (D–91), the *British Union Catalogue of Periodicals* (D–95); and the *National Union Catalog of Manuscript Collections* (H–22), as well as the national library databases OCLC and RLIN (see Z–78).

B–10 **Wehefritz, Valentin, ed. *International Loan Services and Union Catalogues.*** 2d, completely rev. ed. Frankfurt am Main: Klostermann, 1980.   Z695.83.I58 1980

A completely revised edition of the *Guide to Union Catalogues and International Loan Centers*, ed. L. Brummel and E. Egger (The Hague, 1961) [Z695.83.B68], this work (under the sponsorship of the International Federation of Library Associations) presents for each of the eighty countries considered an enumeration of the main national bibliographies both current and retrospective; all printed union catalogs; unprinted union catalogs with the year of their foundation, the number of titles cataloged, and the categories of material included; the international loan centers; the principal libraries with legal deposit functions, including the date when depositing began and whether the requirement is geographically or otherwise limited; and the principal special collections. Entries for each country were contributed by local authorities and vary considerably from one contribution to another. A series of introductory sections concern the technicalities of arranging for international loans of books. A register gives an alphabetical list of the countries covered and the pages to consult (in the text proper; countries are listed in alphabetical order according to their French names).

B–12 *National Union Catalog of Pre–1956 Imprints: A Cumulative Author List. [NUC]* 685 vols. *Supplement.* vols. 686–755. London: Mansell, 1968–1981.

Z881.A1 U518 / Z663.7.L5155

A cumulative author list of books printed before 1956, representing all Library of Congress printed cards plus the holdings reported to the National Union Catalog [*NUC*] by (about 1,000 other) participating libraries. Entries are either LC cards or the card submitted by a participating library and thus contain variable quantities of bibliographical information. Since the editing of the cards does not involve a bibliographical examination of the books themselves, two kinds of errors do occur regularly in the *NUC*. First, books that are bibliographically identical may appear as different because of differences in their reported descriptions; second, books that are bibliographically different may be treated as identical because the reported descriptions do not adequately differentiate between them. Entries for books in all languages using the Latin, Greek, and Gaelic alphabets are included. Each entry provides at the bottom a series of abbreviations indicating the libraries reporting the title among their holdings (a key to the major library abbreviations appears on the inside covers of each volume). There is some cross-referencing among the entries, which are arranged alphabetically by author or main entry, under each author alphabetically by title. The section on the Bible, volumes 53–56 of the complete work, was not published in order but appeared along with the last volumes of the original series in 1980. Extensive holdings of an author (e.g. Milton, John) are preceded by a table of contents that specifies how the entries are disposed.

The *Supplement* volumes include both new materials and Registers of Additional Locations for entries in the original volumes. They should regularly be consulted when searching the *NUC*.

The *NUC* replaces all earlier listings of pre–1956 printed matter held by the Library of Congress and/or in union catalog lists. The exceptions are volume 24 of the earlier *Library of Congress Author Catalog, 1948-1952* [Z881.U49 AZ] and volumes 27–28 of the *National Union Catalog 1953-1957* (see B–13), which list motion pictures, filmstrips, and phonorecords, and are not absorbed into the new catalog.

To celebrate the conclusion of the fourteen-year NUC: Pre–1956 publication project, a program sponsored by the Library of Congress Center for the Book was held on 27–28 January 1981. Proceedings were published with the title *In Celebration: The National Union Catalog, Pre–1956 Imprints*, ed. John Y. Cole. (Washington, D.C.: Library of Congress, 1981) [Z881.A1 U523]. See also the account of the project by David A. Smith, *"The National Union Catalog, Pre–1956 Imprints," Book Collector* 31 (1982): 445–62.

B–13 *National Union Catalog. A Cumulative Author List [of post–1955 imprints]. [NUC]* Washington, D.C.: Library of Congress, 1956–.   Z881.A1 U372 / Z663.7.L512

Through 1982 this serial catalog was published by the Library of Congress in a subscription pattern that included nine monthly issues (January, February, April, May, July, August,

October, November and December), three quarterly issues (March, June, and September), and an annual cumulation. The *National Union Catalog* (*NUC*) includes reproductions of printed cards for titles currently cataloged by the Library of Congress and entries for monographic titles as reported held by about 1,100 other North American libraries. Books, pamphlets, maps, and atlases are included in a single alphabet. To date, the following official cumulations have been published: 1953–1957 (28 vols.), 1958–1962 (54 vols.), 1963–1967 (72 vols.), 1956–1967 (125 vols.), 1968–1972 (128 vols.), and 1973–1977 (150 vols.). These multiyear publications are available from private publishers. Annual cumulations available from the library exist for 1978 (16 vols.), 1979 (16 vols.), 1980 (18 vols.), 1981 (15 vols.), and 1982 (21 vols.).

In January 1983 the *NUC* became a monthly publication produced in register/index, Computer Output Microform (COM) microfiche format only. In addition to the monthly issues of *NUC: Books* there is a new monthly national bibliography, *NUC: U.S. Books*, which lists only books published in the United States and cataloged by the Library of Congress and participating libraries. Also included in the *NUC* family of microfiche publications are the quarterly catalogs, *NUC: Cartographic Materials* and *NUC: Audiovisual Materials*. All issues contain a cumulating series of indexes for names, titles, subjects, and series. A fifth index, by geographic classification codes, is included for *NUC: Cartographic Materials*. Index fiche are cumulative; register fiche are additive. The entire *NUC* family of publications contains materials published in all languages, though all nonroman foreign-language materials have been romanized for this system. The new microfiche family of *NUC* publications replaces the book-form publications, *National Union Catalog: Subject Catalog* (A–33), *Chinese Cooperative Catalog*, and *Monographic Series* (D–107).

The supplementary *National Union Catalog: Register of Additional Locations* [*RAL*] identifies by LC card number and NUC number those additional libraries that have reported holding titles previously reported to the NUC. The following *RAL* cumulations have been published in book-form as part of the *NUC* multiyear cumulations listed above: 1963–1967 *NUC* cumulation, vols. 60–67; 1968–1972 *NUC* cumulation, vols. 105–119. A cumulative microfiche edition is available which includes all entries added to the automated data-base from 1968 to the present. This cumulation now contains over 33 million locations for more than 4.5 million entries. It is updated each quarter.

Motion pictures and filmstrips have been cataloged by the Library of Congress since 1948. A special volume (24) of the otherwise superseded 1948–1952 Library of Congress author catalogs contained cards on films; and the Library of Congress subject catalog (A–33) included films in its analysis, 1950–1954. From 1953 to 1972, separate annual volume and multiannual cumulations titled *Library of Congress Catalog: Motion Pictures and Filmstrips* [Z881.U49 A25] were published and appended to the *NUC* cumulations. Since 1972 there have been quarterly, annual, and quinquennial catalogs of *Films and Other Materials for Projection*, organized by titles and subjects. To date, the following cumulations have been published: in the 1953–1957 *NUC* cumulation, vol. 28; in the 1958–1962 *NUC* cumulation, vol. 53 (Titles) and vol. 54 (Subject Index); in the 1963–1967 *NUC* cumulation, two appended volumes; in the 1968–1972 *NUC* cumulation, four appended volumes; in the 1973–1977 *NUC* cumulation, seven appended volumes. From 1978 through 1982 there have been annual volumes, with the title changed in 1979 to *Audiovisual Materials*. From 1983 on, this catalog has been produced in COM microfiche in cumulating quarterly issues (see U–116).

Music and phonorecords have been cataloged since 1943 (music) and 1953 (records). From 1944 through 1953, music was included in the analysis of the subject catalog (A–33). Since 1953, semiannual, annual, and quinquennial cumulations of the *Library of Congress Catalog: Music and Phono-records* have been published [Z881.A1 C328]. In 1972 the name was changed to *Music, Books on Music, and Sound Recordings*. To date the following cumulations have been published: in the 1953–1957 *NUC* cumulation, vol. 27; in the 1958–1962 *NUC* cumulation, vols. 51–52; in the 1963–1967 *NUC* cumulation, three appended volumes; in the 1968–1972 *NUC* cumulation, five appended volumes; and in the 1973–1977 *NUC* cumulation, eight appended volumes. A seven-volume cumulation was prepared for 1978–1980, and annual volumes are available for 1981 (one vol.) and 1982 (two vols.). This catalog will eventually be automated also, but for the time being it will continue in printed form.

B–15 **Collison, Robert.** *Published Library Catalogues: An Introduction to Their Contents and Use.* London: Mansell, 1973.   Z695.87.C6

A two-part guide to the published library catalogs of the English-speaking world. The first part consists of a series of discursive essays on published library catalogs in various subject fields (general catalogs, auction sales catalogs, the book industries, philosophy and religion, the social sciences, science and technology, the arts and architecture, literature, history and biography, music, and geography). The essays refer by title and code to the entries in part 2, an enumeration of published library catalogs in alphabetical order by the name of the library and, within the series of each library's catalogs, in the numerical order of the code. Entries give complete short-form bibliographical information for each catalog listed. A short bibliography of related reference tools and a subject-author index conclude the volume.

A relatively new source is Bonnie R. Nelson, *Guide to Published Library Catalogs* (Metuchen, N.J.: Scarecrow, 1982) [Z710.N44] which contains a total of 429 numbered entries disposed into thirty-three subject divisions. The entries provide lengthy descriptive annotations. The volume concludes with a subject index and an index of libraries.

III. MAJOR LIBRARY CATALOGS AND GUIDES: NORTH AMERICAN LIBRARIES

Scholars intending to use a research library should always follow the policy of first studying about the library and its holdings in all available printed sources and then writing in advance with a precise description of the purpose of a visit.

B–20 **The Henry E. Huntington Library and Art Gallery. San Marino, California [CSmH].**

Founded in 1919 by Henry Edwards Huntington (1850–1927), a director of some forty corporations including thirteen railway companies, the Huntington Library is famous for containing one of the largest collections of incunabula in America (ca. 5,300 items) and one of the finest collections of English and American history and literature in the country. Special treasures include the Ellesmere manuscript of *Canterbury Tales* and some 230 other Middle English manuscript texts, more than 50 percent of all titles in the STC (C–4), the world's largest collection of Shakespearean quartos, the Larpent Collection of English plays 1737–1824 (to which a chronologically arranged *Catalogue* compiled by Dougald Macmillan was published in 1939) [Z2014.D7 H525], and more than 90 percent of all extant original manuscripts of Restoration plays. Substantial files of early newspapers are another important collection (D–50).

The best introduction to the library is *Founding of the Henry E. Huntington Library and Art Gallery: Four Essays* (San Marino: Huntington Library, 1969) [Z733.S25]. Also useful is John E. Pomret's *Henry E. Huntington Library and Art Gallery from Its Beginnings to 1969* (San Marino: Huntington Library, 1969) [Z733.S25 P6], which includes a bibliographical note (pp. 236–238), a subject index, and an enormous amount of information about the library's history, its benefactors, its holdings, its research institute, visiting scholars and their work, staff members and their work, and the library's magnificent setting. Brief descriptions of the library's research facilities and collections are also available in *HLB* 1 (1931): 33–104; *HLQ* 3 (1939): 131–45; *ShS* 6 (1953): 53–63; and in an article by Robert O. Dougan in the *Encyclopedia of Library and Information Science*, vol. 10 (New York: Dekker, 1973), pp. 390–398 [Z1006.E56]. An illustrated introduction to the entire institution is Elizabeth Pomeroy and Robert Schlosser, *Huntington: Library, Art Gallery, Botanical Gardens* (London: The Times Mirror, 1983) [N6750].

Current publications include *Huntington Library Quarterly*, 1937– (preceded by *Huntington Library Bulletin*, 1931–1937) [Z733.S24]. No complete current catalog of the Huntington's collection has been published, though there is a catalog of the original collection compiled by George Watson Cole (New York: Bowker, 1919; rev. 1920) [Z733.S24 C6]. A five-volume guide to the library's 2.5-million-piece manuscript collection is now available. The volumes include a *Guide to American Historical Manuscripts in the Huntington Library* (H–52), a *Guide to British Historical Manuscripts in the Huntington Library* (H–44), a *Guide to Literary Manuscripts in the Huntington Library* (H–24) and a *Guide to Medieval and Renaissance Manuscripts in the Huntington Library* (H–29). These guides replace all earlier works of this kind. Further details about published catalogs of special collections may be found using Downs (B–8) and other general tools.

Admission to the library is by written application. It should be noted that the Huntington has a fairly extensive program of fellowships to assist visiting scholars who wish to use the collection. For further information consult the guides to fellowships and grants (Z–80 ff.).

B–21 **The Yale University Libraries.** New Haven, Connecticut [CtY].

The Yale library, founded in 1701, is now the second largest university library in the world and the third largest library in the United States. More than 9,000,000 books are housed in forty-one distinct library units, the most important of which are the Sterling Memorial Library, which has housed the main Yale collection since its opening in 1931, and the Beinecke Rare Book and Manuscript Library, which since opening in 1963 has been the largest building in the world devoted exclusively to the preservation of rare books and manuscripts.

Among the outstanding Yale collections are the Yale Collection of American Literature, the Coe Collection of Western Americana, the German Baroque Literature Collection, the Osborne Collection of Manuscripts, and a very large (3,100 titles) collection of incunabula. Holdings in English literature and history, when combined with the extraordinary resources of the new Yale Center for British Art, make Yale the most important center for British studies outside England. The collections for seventeenth- and eighteenth-century English literature are particularly outstanding, as are the special collections of Arnold, Boswell, Byron, Carlyle, Coleridge, Conrad, Defoe, Dickens, Dryden, George Eliot and G. H. Lewes, Fielding, Goldsmith, Hardy, Johnson, Joyce, Kipling, Meredith, Milton, St. Thomas More, Ruskin, Shakespeare, Shaw, Sheridan, Stevenson, Thackeray, Walpole, and Wordsworth. Among the special collections of American authors are Cooper, Edwards, Franklin, Irving, Lewis, O'Neill, Pound, Stein, Wharton, Whitman, Wilder, William Carlos Williams, and Wright.

The most recent general guide is Merrily E. Taylor's *Yale University Library 1701-1978: Its History, Collections, and Present Organization* (New Haven: The Library, 1978) [Z733.Y182 T39] with detailed accounts of the many special collections, area collections, and individual collections that enhance the library's holdings. An extensive bibliography is appended (pp. 179–185). A charming illustrated guide is that by Wilmarth S. Lewis, *Yale Collections* (New Haven: Yale University Press, 1946) [I.D6342.A2 L4]. There is also an excellent and well-illustrated volume, *Beinecke Rare Book and Manuscript Library: A Guide to Its Collections* (New Haven, 1974) [Z733.Y18], which provides a series of chapters describing in detail its various collections. An updated version is in preparation and should appear in 1990. Current publications include the quarterly *Yale University Library Gazette*, published since 1926 [Z733.Y179].

B–22 **The Folger Shakespeare Library.** Washington, D.C. [DFo].

Opened in 1932, on a site and in a building bequeathed along with his extraordinary collection of Shakespeareana by Henry Clay Folger (1857–1930) and his wife, the Folger Shakespeare Library is under the administration of the Trustees of Amherst College. The library today boasts the finest collection of Shakespeare folios and quartos in the world; a superb collection of English books of the period 1475–1700, second only to the British Library in STC holdings; over 1,000 editions of Shakespeare's plays in English and foreign languages from the eighteenth, nineteenth, and twentieth centuries; an extensive collection of theatrical records with special emphasis on the history of Shakespeare performance; extensive manuscript holdings, including the Macro Manuscript of English morality plays (see H–25); letters and diaries of numerous actors and actresses; vast holdings of continental books, 1500–1750; and many other treasures. Betty Ann Kane's *Widening Circle: The Story of the Folger Shakespeare Library and Its Collections* (Washington, D.C.: Folger Library, 1976) [Z733.F6632 K34] with its many illustrations provides a useful guide to the library, its history, its collections, its academic programs and special activities, as well as a selected bibliography (p. 69). An older but still valuable history is Joseph Quincy Adams, *Folger Shakespeare Memorial Library* (Washington, D.C.: For the Trustees of Amherst College, 1942) [Z733.W3 F6]. Among briefer treatments may be cited those in *ShakS* 1 (1948): 57–78; *LQ* 19 (1949): 178–185; and articles both on Folger and on the library by Philip A. Knachel in the *Encyclopedia of Library and Information Science*, vol. 8 (New York: Dekker, 1972), pp. 578—582, 582–591 [Z1006.E57].

Printed catalogs of the Folger collections include the twenty-eight-volume *Catalog of Printed Books of the Folger Shakespeare Library* (Boston: G. K. Hall, 1970) with a *First Supplement* in three volumes (Boston: G. K. Hall, 1976) and a *Second Supplement* in two volumes (1981); the three-volume *Catalog of Manuscripts* (Boston: G. K. Hall, 1971) and the *Catalog of the Shakespeare Collection* (Boston: G. K. Hall, 1972) [Z8811.F65]. Since 1972, *Shakespeare Quarterly* (1950–) [PR2885.S63] has been an official publication of the Folger; it includes information on various aspects of the library's current state.

It should be noted that the Folger Institute of Renaissance and Eighteenth Century Studies sponsors a variety of graduate and postgraduate seminars and symposia and that there is an active program of fellowships to support visiting scholars for brief and extended programs of research in the library's collections.

B–23 **The Library of Congress.** Washington, D.C. [DLC].

Established in 1800 as a reference library for the Congress, the Library of Congress serves today as the national library of the United States. The Library of Congress is probably the world's largest library, with a collection that grows at the rate of over 25,000 new items every week. Some 26 million books and pamphlets; 36 million manuscripts (including the papers of twenty-three presidents); the world's largest collection of maps and atlases, numbering 3.91 million items; 6 million items in the music collection; 10 million prints and photographs; 900,000 sound recordings; 125,000 titles of motion pictures; and 7 million microforms constitute the current holdings. The collections are housed in three buildings on Capitol Hill, the Thomas Jefferson, John Adams, and James Madison Memorial Buildings. The newest of these, the Madison Building, was fully occupied in 1983. By virtue of the library's Copyright Office, two copies of every work seeking copyright registration have been deposited since 1870 or so. Though not all deposited items are retained by the library, about half are transferred to its permanent collections.

In addition to providing assistance to Congress (primarily through the Congressional Research Service), the LC serves as the bibliographical center for North America, maintaining the Dewey decimal classification system, the Library of Congress classification system, the centralized cataloging program (in book, card, and machine-readable tape form), the *National Union Catalog*, and the national interlibrary loan system.

Among the major catalogs published by the Library of Congress are the *National Union Catalogs* (B–12, B–13) and the *Subject Catalog* (A–33). Other important catalogs include those for serials (D–91, D–92), newspapers (E–56), microforms (E–50, E–52), and manuscripts (H–23). There are also dozens of catalogs of various special collections, including *Library of Thomas Jefferson* (1952–1959) [Z663.4.C4], *Lessing J. Rosenwald Collection* (1977), *Literary Recordings: A Checklist of the Archive of Recorded Poetry and Literature in the Library of Congress*, enl. ed. (E–106); the *Hans P. Kraus Collection of Hispanic American Manuscripts* (1974) [Z663.34.K7]; and the 1960 *Guide to the Study of the United States of America* (F–52). An excellent guide to this abundance was published in 1980 by Annette Melville, *Special Collections in the Library of Congress: A Selective Guide* (Washington, D.C.: Library of Congress, 1980) [Z733.U58 U54 1980], which describes 269 special collections, summarizing their history, content, scope, subject strengths, and organization. It concludes with an extensive subject and name index.

The most useful general guide is that by Charles R. Goodrum, *Library of Congress* (New York: Crown, 1974) [Z733.W6 G66], which includes an extensive bibliography. A briefer *Guide to the Library of Congress* by Goodrum and Helen W. Dalrymple (Washington, D.C.: Library of Congress, 1982) [Z733.L735 L48 1982] is well illustrated and organized to present both a history of the library and a systematic account of its reading rooms, procedures for their use, their collections, catalog uses and finding aids, and special services available through them. The recent volume by John Y. Cole, *For Congress and the Nation: A Chronological History of the Library of Congress* (Washington, D.C.: Library of Congress, 1979) [Z733.06.C565], is well illustrated and includes a brief bibliographical essay, pp. 177–179. There is also a substantial treatment of the Library of Congress by Mary C. Lethbridge and James W. McClung in the *Encyclopedia of Library and Information Science*, vol. 15 (New York: Dekker, 1975), pp. 19–93 [Z1006.E57], and a publication entitled *Librarians of Congress, 1802–1974* (Washington, D.C.: Library of Congress, 1977). The most elaborate work of all is Charles R. Goodrum's magnificent volume, *Treasures of the Library of Congress* (New York: Abrams, 1980) [Z733.U58 G66], with lavish illustrations and a text at once fascinating and filled with current and accurate information.

B–25   **The Newberry Library.** Chicago, Illinois [ICN].

Established in 1887 through provisions in the will of Walter Loomis Newberry (1804–1868), a wealthy Chicago banker, railroad financier, and civic leader, the Newberry Library is one of the foremost humanistic research libraries in the United States, with outstanding collections in the fields of bibliography and printing history, Italian Renaissance culture, music, American studies, and genealogy. The collections are very good in English literature and history, the history of cartography, and calligraphy. Among its holdings are more than 1.4 million volumes, 5 million manuscripts, and over 60,000 separate maps. Special collections include a great Melville collection; the papers of Sherwood Anderson and Malcolm Cowley; a large collection of Katherine Mansfield papers; the Edward E. Ayer Collection of Americana and American Indians (*Dictionary Catalogue*, 16 vols., Boston, 1961; *Supplement*, 3 vols., 1970); the John M. Wing Collection of Printing History (*Dictionary Catalogue*, 6 vols., Boston, 1962; *Supplement*, 3 vols., 1970); the William B. Greenlee Portuguese Collection (*Catalogue*, 2 vols., 1971); the Everett D. Graff Collection of Western Americana (*Catalogue*, Chicago, 1968); the Louis H. Silver Collection of Books and Manuscripts; and the Genealogy Collection (*Index*, 4 vols., Boston, 1960).

Guides to the library include the *Handbook of the Newberry Library* by George B. Utley, rev. ed. (Chicago: Newberry Library, 1938) [Z733.C525 H], which gives detailed information about the history, collections, and research facilities of the library, as well as references to many published checklists of various portions of the library's holdings (including courtesy books, French political pamphlets, Arthurian-legend materials, religions, fifteenth-century books, STC period holdings, and American Revolutionary pamphlets. More current than the Utley handbook is the illustrated guide by Lawrence W. Towner, *Uncommon Collection of Uncommon Collections: The Newberry Library*, 2d ed. (Chicago: Newberry Library, 1976) [Z733.C5255], and, also by Towner, a brief article in the *Encyclopedia of Library and Information Science*, vol. 19 (New York: Dekker, 1976), pp. 450–456 [Z1006.E57]. The history of the library may be traced, however, in issues of the irregularly published *Newberry Library Bulletin* (1944–) and *Newberry Newsletter* (1973–) [Z881.C5245]. That history may also be gathered from the recent volume, *Humanities' Mirror: Reading at the Newberry, 1887–1987*, edited by Rolf Achilles (Chicago: Newberry Library, 1987) [Z881 .C525 H8 1987a].

It should be noted that the library maintains a fairly extensive fellowship program to aid visiting scholars. Four research centers also provide fellowships in their respective fields: the Hermon Dunlap Smith Center for the History of Cartography; the D'Arcy McNickle Center for the History of the American Indian; the Family and Community History Center; and the Center for Renaissance Studies. More information about all of the fellowship programs may be found in the usual directories (see Z–80 ff.). The reading rooms are open to qualified users upon presentation of valid current identification.

B–26   **Harvard University Libraries.** Cambridge, Massachusetts [MH].

Harvard, the oldest library in the United States and the largest university library in the world, was founded in 1638, two years after the foundation of Harvard College. It is the second largest library in the United States, with collections numbering 10,700,000 volumes and pamphlets as of 1984. Many different libraries are a part of the university complex. The most important for literary studies are the Widener, which opened in 1915 and currently has a collection of more than 600,000 volumes on language and literature, and the Houghton, which opened in 1942 and contains Harvard's 430,000 rare books and manuscript collections numbering several million pieces.

The Widener, Harvard's main research library (with the rare book and manuscript collection next door in the Houghton), has very strong collections in the humanities generally; among the fields best represented are the classics; Slavic and Eastern European literature, history, and geography; French, German, Italian, Spanish, and Latin American history and literature; and British and American history and literature. There are major collections of Bibles and medieval texts; extensive holdings of incunabula (more than 3,700 items); a large collection of *STC* books (the *STC* revision is being done at Harvard–see C–5); strong collections in the theater, particularly in stage history and in Elizabethan and Jacobean drama; and a large printing and graphic arts collection.

British authors represented through strong collections include Bacon, Beerbohm, the Brontës, the Brownings, Burns, Byron, Carlyle, Lewis Carroll, Chaucer, Coleridge, Wilkie Collins, Dickens, Donne, Dryden, Etherege, Galsworthy, Gay, Goldsmith, Herbert, Housman, Johnson, Joyce, Keats (an incomparable collection), Kipling, Lamb, Masefield, Milton, St. Thomas More, Pepys, Pope, Ruskin, Shakespeare, Shaw, Shelley, Southey, Stevenson, Swinburne, Tennyson, Thackeray, Dylan Thomas, Wordsworth, and Yeats. Among the American authors there are substantial collections of Aiken, the Alcotts, Bryant, e. e. cummings, Dickinson, T. S. Eliot, Emerson, Faulkner, Hawthorne, Holmes, Howells, James, Longfellow, Amy Lowell, J. R. Lowell, Melville, Poe, Pound, E. A. Robinson, Steinbeck, Thoreau, Twain, Whitman, Whittier, and Thomas Wolfe. Continental authors for whom major collections will be found include Ariosto, Camoens, Cervantes, Dante, Goethe, Heine, Hofmannsthal, Machiavelli, Molière, Montaigne, Pascal, Petrarch, Rilke, Ronsard, Rousseau, Schiller, Strindberg, and Tasso.

A still useful guide, the first edition of which appeared in 1903, is Alfred Claghorn Potter's *Library of Harvard University: Descriptive and Historical Notes*, 4th ed. (Cambridge: Harvard University, 1934) [Z733.H34 P66 1934]. There is a brief pamphlet entitled *Houghton Library* (Cambridge: Harvard University Press, 1942) [Z733.H341 H7], with photographs illustrating the new facilities; it was prepared to accompany the exhibition celebrating the library's opening. More attractive and more recent is *Houghton Library 1942–1967: A Selection of Books and Manuscripts in Harvard Collections*, with an introduction by W. H. Bond (Cambridge: Harvard University Press, 1967) [Z881.H347], which commemorates the twenty-fifth anniversary of the Houghton by presenting facsimile illustrations of some 370 pieces from the collection. A fairly recent, brief history of the library is one by René Kuhn Bryant, *Harvard University Library, 1638-1968* (Cambridge: Harvard University Press, 1969) [Z733.H3373]. There is also a very substantial article by Edwin E. Williams in the *Encyclopedia of Library and Information Science*, vol. 10 (New York: Dekker, 1976), pp. 317–373 [Z1006.E57], with a sixty-three-item bibliography appended.

Computer-based shelflists of the Widener Library have been produced in various subject areas. Shelflists 35–38 cover the subject of English literature and were published in four volumes in 1971; volumes 26 and 27 are on American literature and were published in 1970. These shelflists present Harvard's holdings by call number (subject classification), chronologically by date of publication, and in an alphabetically arranged dictionary catalog by author and title. In 1981 the University Library began issuing its microfiche *Distributable Union Catalog*, an author-title-subject listing of computerized cataloging produced by Harvard libraries since July 1977. Monthly supplements are integrated into the main file twice yearly. The best source for current accounts of the library's history and collections is the *Harvard Library Bulletin*, 1947–1960, 1967–, for which there are cumulative indexes to volumes 1 through 10 and 11 through 14 [Z881.H3403].

B–27 The American Antiquarian Society Library. Worcester, Massachusetts [MWA].

Founded in 1812 as the first national historical society in the United States, the American Antiquarian Society has had the aim of preserving American history and culture and forwarding scholarship in these areas. The society's present library (the third in its history), built in 1910, houses the largest single collection of printed source material related to the history, literature, and culture of the United States through 1876. Its current holdings number more than 750,000 volumes, including 75,000 pre–1820 imprints, 3,000,000 issues of newspapers, and 20,000 volumes of early American periodicals, among them some 50,000 issues of amateur journals. These holdings make the American Antiquarian Society Library a major resource for American bibliography, and many of the major retrospective bibliographical projects have centered on its collections (see entries C–20, C–21, C–23, C–25, D–70, D–71). In addition to the above, there are valuable collections of official documents from the Revolution and the Civil War and virtually complete collections of American almanacs and yearbooks (about 18,000) as well as directories. The largest and choicest collection of American poetry, drama, fiction, essays, oratory, letters, wit and humor, children's books, and cookbooks to 1820 will be found at the American Antiquarian Society, along with major collections of American ballads, caricatures and cartoons, early genealogies, laws and legal publications, sheet music, psalmbooks and hymnals, schoolbooks, and songbooks, as well as extraordinary collections of regional, state, county, and local histories.

The library's catalog has been published in twenty folio volumes with the title *Dictionary Catalog of American Books Pertaining to the Seventeenth through Nineteenth Centuries* (Westport, Conn.: Greenwood, 1971) [Z1215.A264]. Also published in four volumes is the *Catalog of the Manuscript Collections of the American Antiquarian Society* (Boston: G. K. Hall, 1979) [Z1361.C6 A43]. In addition, there is a somewhat out-of-date *Guide to the Resources of the American Antiquarian Society* (Worcester, Mass.: American Antiquarian Society, 1937) [Z733.W898 G], which may be supplemented by Clarence S. Brigham's more recent *Fifty Years of Collecting Americana for the Library of the American Antiquarian Society 1909-1958* (Worcester, Mass.: Privately printed, 1958) [Z733.W898]. There is also a handsomely printed illustrated exhibition catalog with the title *Society's Chief Joys: An Introduction to the Collections of the American Antiquarian Society* with a foreword by Walter Muir Whitehall (Worcester, Mass.: American Antiquarian Society, 1969) [Z1212.A26].

B–30 The Research Libraries, The New York Public Library. New York City [NN].

Founded in 1895, the New York Public Library is the largest of American public libraries and the third largest library in the United States. It was created through the merger of the Astor Library (founded in 1848), the Lenox Library (founded in 1870), and the Tilden Foundation endowments. Housed in the main library at Forty-second Street and Fifth Avenue and three other locations in Manhattan are the Research Libraries, with over 6,000,000 volumes, some 25,000 linear feet of manuscripts, 358,000 maps, and 357,000 reels of film and microfilm. The eighty-three branch libraries have about 9,000,000 books, pictures, and audiovisual materials and 85,000 talking books for the blind.

The library's collections are known for their range and depth in almost any field. Literature is one of the special strengths of the General Research Division, with about 25 percent of the entire holdings devoted to this subject. Special literary collections include the J. E. Spingarn Collection of Criticism and Literary History; the Duychinck Collection of American Literature; the Arents Collections on the History of Tobacco and of Books Published in Parts; the Carl H. Pforzheimer Collection of Shelley and His Circle; the Spencer Collection of Illustrated Books in Fine Bindings; and, most important by far, the Berg Collection of English and American Literature, which has some 70,000 pieces, including first and important editions, original manuscripts, and autograph letters, particularly of the nineteenth and twentieth centuries. A *Dictionary Catalog of the Henry W. and Albert A. Berg Collection* was published in five volumes in 1969 (Boston: G. K. Hall) [Z2011.N55]. There is also a brief treatment of the Berg Collection in *PBSA* 48 (1954): 303–314.

Among major collections of English authors are those for Arnold Bennett, the Brontës, the Burney family, Bunyan, Lewis Carroll, Coleridge, Conrad, Defoe, Dickens, Donne, George Eliot, Galsworthy, Hardy, Kipling, Lawrence, Meredith, Milton, Shakespeare, Shaw, Thackeray, Woolf, and Wordsworth. The exceptional collections of American authors are those for Bryant, Cooper, T. S. Eliot, Emerson, Franklin, Hawthorne, Irving, Longfellow, J. R. Lowell, Melville, Mencken, Poe, Robinson, Thoreau, Twain, Noah Webster, Whittier, and Whitman.

Unlike the earlier *Guide to the Reference Collections of the New York Public Library* by Karl Brown et al. (New York: The Library, 1941) [Z733.N6 R4], which provides a still valuable though out-of-date overview, the more recent *Guide to the Research Collections of the New York Public Library* by Sam P. Williams (Chicago: ALA, 1975) [Z733.N6 W54] describes the collections subject by subject in great and useful detail and is current to about 1969. More recent yet is the brief article by John Mackenzie Cory in the *Encyclopedia of Library and Information Science*, vol. 19 (New York: Dekker, 1976), pp. 377–388 [Z1006.E57]. There is also a *History of the New York Public Library* by Harry Miller Lydenberg (New York: New York Public Library, 1923) [Z733.N585], which will be replaced, in time, with the new history by Phyllis Dain. Her first volume, *New York Public Library: A History of Its Founding and Early Years* (New York: New York Public Library, 1972) [Z733.N59], takes the story to 1913; a second, which will bring it to the present, is now in preparation. Not to be overlooked by the potential user is a charmingly written and illustrated volume by William K. Zinsser, *Search and Research: The Collections and Uses of the New York Public Library at Fifth Avenue and Forty-second Street* (New York: The Library, 1961) [Z733 .N63 Z5].

In addition to the published catalog of the Berg Collection, there are also printed catalogs for other important collections of the library. Among them is the massive *Catalog of the Theatre and Drama Collection* (U–30). Other dictionary catalogs include one in 9 volumes for the *Schomburg Collection of Negro Literature and History* (Boston: G. K. Hall, 1962) [Z1361.N39 N55 1962] with a First Supplement in 2 volumes (Boston: G. K. Hall, 1967), and a Second Supplement in 4 volumes (Boston: G. K. Hall, 1972); one for American History in 28 volumes (Boston: G. K. Hall, 1961), with a 9-volume supplement (Boston: G. K. Hall, 1964); one for the Dance Collection in 10 volumes (Boston: G. K. Hall, 1974) [Z7514.D2 N462 1974]; and one for the Local History and Genealogy collection in 18 volumes (Boston: G. K. Hall, 1974). Also published have been dictionary catalogs of the Manuscript Division in 2 volumes (Boston: G. K. Hall, 1967) and of the Rare Book Division in 21 volumes (Boston: G. K. Hall, 1971).

The *Dictionary Catalog of the Research Libraries of the New York Public Library, 1911-1971*, was published in 1983 by G. K. Hall [Z881.N59 1979]. This 800-volume work gathers together the 9,000,000 author, title, and subject entries in the Research Libraries' main card catalog to 1971. This basic catalog was supplemented by the *Dictionary Catalog of the Research Libraries, 1971-1981* [Z881.N59]. From mid–

1981 to the present, access to holdings is available through the RLG/RLIN data base and from a printed *Interim List* of holdings. The library's journal, *Bulletin of the New York Public Library* [Z881.N6B], was published 1897–1977; its successor is the *Bulletin of Research in the Humanities*, 1978–, edited jointly by the library and the State University of New York, Stony Brook. There are cumulative indexes for volumes 1–40, 41–50, and 51–66 of the *BNYPL*.

B–31 **The Pierpont Morgan Library.** New York City [NNPM].

Opened to public use in 1924, the Pierpont Morgan Library was originally the private collection of Pierpont Morgan (1837–1913) and J. P. Morgan, Jr. (1867–1943). The library building, completed in 1906, is on Thirty-sixth Street in Manhattan beside Pierpont Morgan's house, which was torn down to build an annex after the Library became a public institution in 1924. The Pierpont Morgan Library has the most extensive and finest series of medieval and ancient written records on the American continent. Its incunabula collection is generally thought the best, though not the largest, in the United States. Also exceptional is the collection of important printed books illustrating the history of printing (see the exhibition catalog, *Art of the Printed Book*, with 125 plates of illustrations, published in New York, 1973, which gives some idea of the range and richness of these holdings) and bindings from the fifth century to the present. The Library's treasures— including a magnificent collection of master drawings—give it a unique character; they are complemented by fine research holdings, including important collections relating to the Italian Renaissance, the Reformation in Germany, Tudor and Stuart England, and the American Revolution. An extraordinary number of authors' manuscripts, letters, and journals are held by the Library: among the English and American authors best represented are Jane Austen, Blake, the Brontës, the Brownings, Burns, Byron, Carlyle, Coleridge, Dickens, Galsworthy, Gilbert and Sullivan, Hawthorne, Keats, Meredith, Milton, Pope, Ruskin, Scott, Sir Phillip Sidney, Sterne, Stevenson, Swift, Thackeray, Thoreau, and Twain. The collections of music manuscripts and early children's books and manuscripts are also unsurpassed in America.

Four volumes in the series *Major Acquisitions of the Pierpont Morgan Library, 1924-1974* were published in 1974; they present facsimile illustrations in addition to their texts and are entitled *Medieval and Renaissance Manuscripts* [ND2920.P53 1974], *Early Printed Books* [Z240.P62 1974], *Autograph Letters and Manuscripts* [Z6621.P6512], and *Drawings* [NC25.N4 P536 1974] respectively. A second, revised edition of Frederick B. Adams's illustrated guidebook, originally published in 1964, is now out of print: *Introduction to the Pierpont Morgan Library* (New York: Pierpont Morgan Library, 1974) [Z733.N733 A53]. See also the briefer, recent article by Adams in the *Encyclopedia of Library and Information Science*, vol. 22 (New York: Dekker, 1977), pp. 250–262 [Z1006.E57].

B–33 **Brown University and the John Carter Brown Libraries.** Providence, Rhode Island [RPB].

The John Carter Brown Library in its present character began about 1846 as a private collection; it was given to Brown University in 1904. An almost complete listing of its holdings printed before 1701 is to be found in the third edition of the chronologically arranged *Bibliotheca Americana: A Catalogue of the John Carter Brown Library in Brown University*, 5 vols. (Providence: Brown University Press, 1919–1931) [Z1203.B89] and in the *Short-Title List of Additions: Books Printed 1471–1700* (Providence: Brown University Press, 1973) [Z881.P9665 1973]. A partial listing of the eighteenth-century holdings is to be found in volumes 3 and 4 of the second edition of the *Catalogue* (Providence, 1871 and

1875). One of its editors, Lawrence C. Wroth, has also written the *First Century of the John Carter Brown Library: A History with a Guide to the Collections* (Providence, 1946) [Z733.P963 W7]. Other publications useful in explaining the purpose and scope of the library are *John Carter Brown Conference, A Report of the Meeting . . . on the Early History of the Americas* (Providence: Brown University, 1961), and *Opportunities for Research in the John Carter Brown Library* (Providence: Brown University, 1968) [Z733 .P9626]. These make clear the library's concern with all aspects of the history of the impact of the Americas on Europe during the colonial period (1493 to ca. 1830), of which discovery, exploration, and settlement are merely the point of departure. A six–volume guide to *European Americana*-books about America published overseas between 1493 and 1750—is in production. Volumes 1 (1493–1600) and 2 (1601–1650) have already been published (New York: Readex Books, 1980–1982) [Z1203.E87].

In addition to the bibliography and descriptive guide to the collections contained in the 1968 *Opportunities for Research* volume, an illustrated catalog, *Collection's Progress: Two Retrospective Exhibitions* (Providence: Associates of the John Carter Brown Library, 1968) [Z1207.B872], gives a vivid impression of the range of the library's holdings. There is also a brief article on the library by Thomas R. Adams in the *Encyclopedia of Library and Information Science*, vol. 3 (New York: Dekker, 1970), pp. 378–382 [Z1006.E57], and the *Annual Reports* from 1901 through 1966 have been reprinted with an index (Providence: Brown University Press, 1972).

Of the other Brown University libraries, the most prominent are the John D. Rockefeller, Jr. Library, which houses the general collection, the Sciences Library, and the John Hay Library, which houses special collections, rare books, and manuscripts. Among the special collections may be mentioned important holdings for Blake, Dante, Poe, Thoreau, Whitman, and Zola, as well as a collection of materials on the legend of the Wandering Jew and one on the occult. The most important from a literary point of view is the Harris Collection of American Poetry and Plays, the largest collection in its field, with some 300,000 volumes, 30,000 broadsides, 500,000 pieces of sheet music, and 15,500 manuscripts. A *Dictionary Catalog* in thirteen volumes was published by G. K. Hall in Boston in 1972 [Z1231.P7 B72]; a two-volume *Supplement* appeared in 1977. Another important area of collecting interest is the history of science. The most notable single collection in this field is the Albert E. Lownes Collection, comprising twelve thousand volumes spanning the period from the fifteenth century to the Manhattan Project. In addition, detailed reports of acquisitions for the Harris Collection and other Brown University holdings are available through *Books at Brown* [Z733.P958 B6], which has been published irregularly since 1938. There is a history and description of the Brown University library system by David A. Jonah in the *Encyclopedia of Library and Information Science*, vol. 3 (New York: Dekker, 1970), pp. 382–408 [Z1006.E57].

B–35 **The University of Texas Libraries.** Austin, Texas [TxU].

Founded with the university in 1883, the library experienced extraordinary growth during the late 1950s, 1960s, and 1970s. It currently boasts a collection of more than five million books along with extensive manuscript and microform holdings. The rare materials are housed within the Harry Ransom Humanities Research Center (administered separately from the General Libraries), established in 1957, which has important research collections in American and French literature, photography, theater arts, the history of science, modern English literature, and bibliography. But the crown jewel of the Center's collections is the Carl H. Pforzheimer Library, consisting of 2,100 titles and approximately 250 manuscript groups of letters and documents covering the period from

1475 to 1700. Bacon, Donne, Milton, Shakespeare, and Spenser are among the major authors represented in this famed collection. There are also extensive files of early newspapers and periodicals (see D–50). In addition, the Benson Latin American Collection and the Barker Texas History Center, both administered by the General Libraries, are outstanding research collections.

Among the English and American authors particularly well represented in the Harry Ransom Humanities Research Center [HRHRC] collections are James Agee, Maxwell Anderson, Auden, Beckett, the Brownings, Byron, Conrad, Hart Crane, e. e. cummings, Defoe, Dickens, Dryden, T. S. Eliot, Faulkner, E. M. Forster, Galsworthy, Robert Graves, Graham Greene, Hardy, Lillian Hellman, Hemingway, Joyce, D. H. Lawrence, T. E. Lawrence, Sinclair Lewis, Edgar Lee Masters, Mansfield, Maugham, Arthur Miller, Henry Miller, Marianne Moore, O'Neill, Poe, Pope, Pound, Shaw, Sitwell, Swift, Dylan Thomas, H. G. Wells, Tennessee Williams, William Carlos Williams, and Yeats. Modern French authors include Céline, Cocteau, Genet, Gide, Giraudoux, and Sartre. In general, Texas shares with the Berg Collection in New York the distinction of being the major repository of twentieth-century English and American authors' manuscripts, and it has the finest modern French manuscript collections anywhere outside of France.

Glimpses of the extraordinary buying program at Texas can be caught in the *Library Chronicle* of the University of Texas, 1944— [Z881.T383]. Additional publications of the Humanities Research Center throw light on particular sections of the collection. Among these are the illustrated presentations of *Creative Century: Selections from the Twentieth Century Collections at the University of Texas* (Austin: University of Texas Press, 1964) [Z42.T37]; *One Hundred Modern Books From England, France and America: 1880–1950*, by Mary Hirth (Austin: University of Texas Press, 1971) [Z6519.H57]; and *Baudelaire to Beckett: A Century of French Art and Literature* (Austin: University of Texas Press, 1975) [Z732.T25 T46]. See also the brief article by John Lehmann, *TLS*, 10 July 1969, 758.

B–39 Other Major United States and Canadian Libraries of Importance for Students of English and American Language and Literature.

CU   **University of California, Berkeley, Bancroft Library**: American literature; Hispanic literature; Dickens, Durrell, Twain

CLU   **University of California, Los Angeles:** Sadleir collection of nineteenth-century fiction; children's literature

CLU-C   **UCLA, William Andrews Clark Memorial Library:** sixteenth-, seventeenth-, and earlier-eighteenth-century literature; Oscar Wilde and the 1890s

CS   **Stanford University:** Maugham

CaOTU   **University of Toronto:** Spanish and Portugese literature

FU   **University of Florida:** Latin American literature

ICU   **University of Chicago, Regenstein Library:** Renaissance studies; European drama; Slavic literature; American historical manuscripts

IEN   **Northwestern University:** Joyce

IU   **University of Illinois:** classics; philology and rhetoric; English prose fiction; Milton, Sandburg, Twain

InU   **University of Indiana, Lilly Library:** American poetry; Housman, Milton, Poe, Sterne, Wordsworth

LNHT   **Tulane University:** Latin American literature

MB   **Boston Public Library:** New England materials; Defoe

MeWC   **Colby College:** American literature

MiU   **University of Michigan, Hatcher Library:** theatre; Carlyle, Trollope

MiU-C   **University of Michigan, William L. Clements Library of Americana**

MnU   **University of Minnesota, Wilson Library:** American studies; children's literature; popular culture

NIC   **Cornell University:** Dante, Joyce, Shaw, Wordsworth

NNC   **Columbia University, Butler Library:** Swift; graphic arts and publishing history; American literature

NNU   **New York University:** fiction; the Fales collection; early American periodicals; Frost

NcD   **Duke University, Perkins Library:** American literature; the Old South; Wesleyana; Byron, Emerson, Whitman; French literature; Italian literature

NcU   **University of North Carolina:** fiction; Spanish and Portuguese literature; Shaw

NjP   **Princeton University:** the Victorian novel; twentieth-century literature; Cowper, Dickinson, Hemingway, Kipling, O'Neill, Wilde

OO   **Oberlin College:** Spanish and Portuguese drama

OU   **Ohio State University:** American fiction; Hart Crane, Hawthorne, Thurber; Romance periodicals

PPL   **The Library Company of Philadelphia:** seventeenth- and eighteenth-century American and European books; nineteenth-century Americana

PU   **University of Pennsylvania, Van Pelt Library:** eighteenth-century fiction, drama; Aristotle; English Bible; Byron, Dreiser, Swift, Whitman; witchcraft

ViU   **University of Virginia, Barrett Library:** American fiction; Gothic novels; Cather, Faulkner, Frost, Hawthorne, Hemingway, Poe, Tennyson, Thoreau, Twain, Whitman

IV. MAJOR LIBRARY CATALOGS AND GUIDES: BRITISH AND IRISH

Scholars intending to use a research library should always follow the policy of first studying about the library and its holdings in all available printed sources and then writing in advance with a precise description of the purpose of a visit.

B–40 The British Library [formerly, the Library of the British Museum].

Established in 1973, the British Library incorporates the library departments of the British Museum with their nucleus of books and manuscripts brought together when the museum was founded in 1753, along with all subsequent additions. Holdings now total some 10,000,000 books, over 700,000 maps and plans, some 1,250,000 items of printed music, over 500,000 newspapers, and more than 120,000 volumes of manuscripts. Also part of the new national library of Britain are the Science Reference Library, the Lending Division (formed from the previous National Lending Library and the National Central Library), and the Bibliographic Services Division, publisher of the British National Bibliography (see C–21). The India Office Library and Records became part of the British Library in 1982. The British Institute of Recorded Sound (renamed the National Sound Archive) became part of the library in 1983. Since 1757, when the old Royal Library was given to the British Museum, rights to deposit copies of every book, periodical, and newspaper published in Britain were transferred to the British Museum. As a result, the library has built up the most complete collection of British publications in the world.

The Reference Division of the British Library was formed from the library departments of the British Museum, of which the two leading departments for students of English and American language and literature are the Department of

Printed Books and the Department of Manuscripts.

The Department of Printed Books includes the Official Publications Library (formerly the State Paper Room), the Map Library, the Music Library, the Newspaper Library (at Colindale), and a number of other sections. Among the special collections that make this the finest library in the world for the study of English history and literature are the Thomason Collection of Civil War and Commonwealth Materials (*Catalogue*, 2 vols., London, 1908); the Garrick Collection of plays; the Burney Collection of seventeenth- and eighteenth-century newspapers (which is available on microfilm; see E–57); the King's Library, George III's collection, rich in English literature; and the Wise Collection of English literature. The library's buying policy, which has stressed the acquisition of materials in all the humanistic fields, has contributed to the collection's comprehensiveness. Thus holdings in incunabula and early printed books of both England and the continent are extensive. Indeed, the series of *Short-Title Catalogues* to early printed books of various countries held by the British Library constitute essential portions of the national bibliographic record of those countries. There is a now somewhat out-of-date guide to the catalogs of printed books by F. C. Francis, *Journal of Documentation* 4 (1948): 14–40 [Z1007.J9]. Among the most important are the *General Catalogue* with its *Supplements* and new edition now in progress (B–41), and the *Subject Indexes* (A–32). The series of national catalogs noted earlier includes the *Short-Title Catalogue of Books Printed in France and of French Books Printed in Other Countries from 1470 to 1600* (1924) [Z2162.B86]; *Short-Title Catalogue of French Books, 1601–1700, in the Library of the British Museum* (1973) [Z2162.B87 1973]; the *Short-Title Catalogue of Books Printed in the German-speaking Countries and German Books Printed in Other Countries from 1455 to 1600* (1962) [Z2222.B73]; the *Short-Title Catalogue of Books Printed in Italy and of Italian Books Printed in Other Countries from 1465 to 1600* (1958) [Z2342.B7]; the *Short-Title Catalogue of Books Printed in the Netherlands and Belgium and of Dutch and Flemish Books Printed in Other Countries from 1470 to 1600* (1965) [Z2402.B7]; and the volume of *Short-Title Catalogues of Spanish, Spanish-American and Portuguese Books Printed before 1601* (1966) [Z2682.B87], which reprints the three catalogs earlier published separately.

Of special importance to students of British and American Literature is the *Eighteenth Century Short-Title Catalogue* project (see C–13), the basis for which is the machine-readable and microfiche catalog of the British Library's eighteenth-century holdings. Another data base in process of creation is the ISTC (Incunable Short-Title Catalogue), a census of all known fifteenth-century printed books.

The Department of Manuscripts includes the famous Cotton Collection of Manuscript Books, dispersed at the Reformation, which along with the 7,660 volumes of the Harleian manuscripts and the 4,100 manuscripts of the Sloane Collection, constitutes the foundation of the department's holdings. Other special collections include the Royal, Lansdowne, Hargrave, Burney, King's, Arundel, Stowe, Ashley, and Yates Thompson Manuscripts. Additional manuscripts (over 60,000 volumes to date) and the Egerton manuscripts (over 4,000 volumes to date) are the two collections that are still being enlarged by new acquisitions. In addition, the department houses the Lord Chamberlain's collection of plays submitted for licensing, 1824–1968 (for earlier plays in this series see B–20), and copies of playscripts for new plays produced in Britain since 1968. Also collected by the department are charters, rolls, seals, papyri, and ostraca (potsherds with writing). Among the treasures especially interesting to students of English and American literature are the largest collection of Anglo-Saxon and Middle English manuscripts in existence, including the only manuscript of Beowulf. There is a brief but extremely handy guide to the manuscript collections and their many published and unpublished catalogs by M. A. E.

Nickson, *British Library: Guide to the Catalogues and Indexes of the Department of Manuscripts* (London: The Department, 1978) [Z6621.B837 B74]. A more detailed survey is T. C. Skeat's *Catalogues of the Manuscript Collections*, rev. ed. (London: British Museum, 1962) [Z6621.B844], first published in 1951 (see H–10 and H–11).

The standard history and survey of the collections remains that of Arundel Esdaile, *British Museum Library: A Short History and Survey* (London: Allen and Unwin, 1946) [Z792.B863 E8]. Briefer treatments include articles in *TLS*, 17 June 1955, p. 338, and 24 June 1955, p. 356; the chapter by Sir Frank Francis in Irwin and Staveley (B–44), pp. 13–30; a more recent article by Sir Frank Francis in the *Encyclopedia of Library and Information Science*, vol. 3 (New York: Dekker, 1972), 288–300 [Z1006.E57]; and articles by K. W. Humphreys, *Journal of Librarianship* 4 (January 1972), 1–13, and D. T. Richnell, *Journal of Librarianship* 5 (October 1973), 246–258 [Z671.J66]. Current publications include the semiannual *British Library Journal*, 1975– [Z921.B854 B73], which replaces the *British Museum Quarterly*, 1926– (indexes vols. 1–5 in vol. 6; vols. 6–10 in vol. 10) [AM101.B832] as a source of information about current acquisitions and similar news. The British Library has published every year since its formation an *Annual Report* (sixth, for 1978/79, issued 1979) [Z792.B593a].

B–41 **British Library General Catalogue of Printed Books to 1975 [BLC].** 360 volumes. London: Bingley; New York: Saur, 1979–1984.   Z921.L633 B74 1979

This listing of the printed books held by the British Library, which supersedes the 263 volume *General Catalogue of Printed Books* (London: Mansell, 1965–1968) [Z921.B8703] and its three supplements, is arranged alphabetically by author, by publishing body (if corporate organization), or by a proper name or adjective (if present in the title) in the case of anonymous works. Entries from the slip catalog in the main reading room of the British Library contain author (pseudonyms are often identified as such and accompanied by the author's real name), title, number of pages, edition, some publication information, format, indication of special features such as annotation, and location shelf-mark. Under author headings, books are listed alphabetically by title, and multiple editions appear in the order of their publication. Collected and selected works appear at the beginning or end. For further details consult the *Rules for Compiling Catalogues in the Department of Printed Books in the British Museum*, 2d ed. (London, 1936).

A special feature of the catalog is the inclusion under the names of persons (in the case of large headings, in an appendix) of works pertaining to that author with cross-references to their main entries. Included are subdivisions for complete works, collections of works, letters and other categories of works, individual works and books about them, selections, doubtful works, and works about the author.

Official publications and other works about or related to a country or locality are listed chronologically under the name of the country (there are eight volumes for "England"). There are also chronologically arranged titles cited under the names of sacred books and related works (there are four volumes for "Bible" and two for "Liturgies"). Further, there are abundant cross-references from personal names, and a few articles in serial publications are analyzed.

Supplemental volumes have been published for acquisitions *1976–1982* in fifty volumes (London: Saur, 1983), and for *1982–1985* in twenty-six volumes (London: Saur, 1986).

For the period since 1975 (including publications dated from 1971 but acquired after 1975) the library publishes annual microfiche catalog cumulations. These publications may also be searched through BLAISE-LINE's DPB database (see Z–78). Although compiled according to modern international standards, these catalogs continue to follow the practice of the pre–1975 general catalog of giving entries under persons-as-subjects.

Additional British Library catalogs include the *Catalogue of Printed Music in the British Library to 1980 [CPM]*, 62 vols. (London: Saur, 1980–1987); the forthcoming cumulative *British Catalogue of Music 1957–1985*, 10–12 vols. planned; and the *British Library Catalogue of Printed Maps, Charts and Plans*, 15 vols. (London: Saur, 1967), with a *Ten Year Supplement* (1977).

The companion set of publications to the *General Catalogue* and the special catalogs of music and maps is the *Subject Index*, which lists under alphabetical subject headings all publications (except belles-lettres) acquired by the library with publication dates after 1880 (see A–32). See also the subject arrangement of the eighteenth-century works in the catalog prepared by Averley et al. (P–13).

B–44   **Irwin, Raymond, and Ronald Stavely, eds.** *Libraries of London.* 2d rev. ed. London: The Library Association, 1961.   Z791.L852

Based on a series of seventeen lectures delivered in 1948, the first edition of this work (1949) sought to supplement the standard work, R. A. Rye's *Student's Guide to the Libraries of London, with an Account of the Most Important Archives and Other Aids to Study*, the third and last edition of which was published by the University of London Press in 1928 [Z791.L85 1928]. That work is now so out of date that the second edition of Irwin and Stavely is designed more nearly to replace it. The original seventeen chapters have been expanded to twenty-three, and the authors of lectures were invited to expand their presentations, which they have done. The authors of the individual chapters were chosen because of their personal affiliation with the library or library group being described. Individual chapters cover the history, collections, catalogs, services, and administration of the libraries they discuss. The chapters are as follows: I. The British Museum; II. The Library of the British Museum (Natural History) and Some Other Libraries of Natural History; III. The Science Library; IV. The Library of the Victoria and Albert Museum; V. The Patent Office Library; VI. The National Central Library; VII. The Parliamentary Libraries; VIII. Government Department Libraries; IX. The London Borough Libraries; X. The Guildhall Library; XI. The Libraries of the London County Council; XII. The University of London Library; XIII. The Library of University College, London; XIV. The Library of Political and Economic Science [in the London School of Economics]; XV. Other Libraries of the University of London; XVI. The London Library; XVII. Learned Society Libraries; XVIII. Technical and Professional Libraries; XIX. Industrial Libraries; XX. Ecclesiastical and Theological Libraries; XXI. Law Libraries; XXII. Medical Libraries; and XXIII. Music Libraries. An index of names and subjects concludes the volume.

Among the features of Rye's *Guide* are several that the more recent work does not duplicate. These include the detailed introductory history of libraries in London, the more elaborate histories of individual libraries discussed, treatment of commercial and subscription libraries (other than the London Library), treatment of libraries associated with the national newspapers, the enumeration of special libraries by special subject, and the detailed index and directory of more than 100 double-column pages that conclude the volume. For these features, students must still turn to Rye's 1928 *Guide*.

B–45   **The London Library.**

Founded in 1841 through the efforts of Thomas Carlyle and his friends, the London Library is a private subscription and circulating library from which members may borrow volumes for home use. It has been the aim of successive committees to build a permanent collection of standard and authoritative works in many languages. With a stock of approximately one million volumes, the library is strong in the fields of philosophy, philology, history, literature (both English and foreign, including fiction), topography, archaeology, biography, theology, bibliography, and art. There is a little general science and natural history, but no attempt has been made to acquire specialist works in the fields of medicine, law, the natural sciences, or technology. Extensive holdings of the publications of learned societies are a distinctive feature of the collection, as are many runs of periodicals, both current and defunct. The most recent *Catalogue of the London Library*, compiled by C. T. Hagberg Wright and C. J. Purnell in two volumes, was published in 1913–1914 [Z921.L6]. It has been supplemented by additional volumes covering acquisitions 1913–1920 (1920), 1920–1928 (1928), and 1928–1950 (1953). Subsequent accessions are cataloged on cards. A most valuable complement to the author catalog of the library is the *Subject Index*, issued in 1909, with supplements in 1923, 1938, and 1955 (A–36).

For more information about the London Library see *Carlyle and the London Library*, ed. Frederic Harrison (London: Chapman and Hall, 1907) [Z792.L6H]; Simon Nowell-Smith, "Carlyle and the London Library," in *English Libraries, 1800–1850* (London: H. K. Lewis for University College, London University, 1958), 59–78 [Z791.L8515]; the chapter by C. J. Purnell in Irwin and Stavely (B–44), 231–241; Nowell-Smith's "London Library Occasions," *TLS*, 18 February 1972, 187–188; and the special issue of *Adam International* edited by Miron Grindea (*Adam 1977*, nos. 387–400) [PN601.A3]. This issue has been separately published with the title *London Library* (Ipswich: Boydell Press, 1978) [Z792.L6 L65 1978]. The article in it by C. T. Hagberg Wright, "The Soul's Dispensary" (reprinted from the March 1922 issue of *Nineteenth Century and After*), is particularly recommended. A history of the London Library is in preparation by John Wells and publication is expected in 1991, the library's 150th anniversary year.

B–47   **The John Rylands University Library of Manchester.** Manchester, England.

Established in 1972 by the merger of the Library of the University of Manchester and the John Rylands Library, the library is today a unique amalgam of world-famous private collections and university scholarship. Its holdings number over 3.5 million books, some 20,000 manuscripts, and hundreds of thousands of archival items.

Dating from 1851, the library of the university was and is very much the product of local wealth and philanthropy. It was especially rich in early printed books in various subjects but particularly in the Renaissance, Humanism, and Italian Literature. The John Rylands Library was founded in 1899 by the widow of John Rylands (1801–1888) as a memorial to her industrialist husband. Originally intended as a working collection for students of theology, its purchase of such internationally famous private collections as the Spencer Library of early printed books and the Crawford Collection of rare manuscripts made it a center for the humanities. The original home of the Rylands Library, a most distinguished building architecturally, is now the Special Collections division for the whole library.

The holdings are impressive in many fields. There are about 4,500 incunabula, extraordinary runs of early printed books, including many unique English items, the two largest collections of Aldines in existence, a Bible collection of world renown, some sixty-three Caxtons, and innumerable other rarities. There is great strength in the fields of English history, the literature of the Italian and French Renaissance, the Reformation, the French Revolution, and numerous others. Among authors there are notably strong collections of Carlyle, Chaucer, Dante, Dickens, Gaskell, Johnson, Malory, Milton, the pre-Raphaelites, Ruskin, Swift, and Wesley. A useful pamphlet, *English Studies: A Guide to Research Resources* (Manchester: The Library, 1989) describes holdings in greater detail. Similar pamphlets are available for *French Studies* (1986) and *German Studies* (1987). The Library also houses such great archives and libraries as those of the *Manchester Guardian* and the Methodist Conference.

A catalog of STC holdings, compiled by E. Gordon Duff, was published in 1895 [Z921.M18]; a complete *Catalogue of the Printed Books and Manuscripts* of the John Rylands Library in three volumes followed in 1899 [Z921.M18]. A variety of catalogs and indexes have been published since then, but no complete current printed catalog exists. The *Bulletin of the John Rylands University Library of Manchester [BJRL]* [Z921.M18 B], published since 1903 and now appearing three times a year, includes handlists, catalogs and surveys of the principal collections of manuscripts and printed books.

Until a full history of the library can be prepared, the history and description of the Rylands collections by Henry Guppy, *John Rylands Library, Manchester: 1899-1935* (Manchester: Manchester University Press, 1935) [Z792.M21 1935], and the pamphlet by Edward Robertson, *John Rylands Library, Manchester: A Brief Descriptive Account* (Manchester: The Library, 1954) [Z792.M214], will have to be consulted. There is also an account by F. W. Ratcliffe, in the *Encyclopedia of Library and Information Science*, vol. 17 (New York: Dekker, 1976), 107–113 [Z1006.E57], an illustrated guidebook by F. Taylor and W. G. Simpson, *John Rylands University Library of Manchester* (Manchester: The Library, 1982) [Z792.J58], and the *John Rylands Research Institute Prospectus* (Manchester: The Library, 1987).

B–48 The Bodleian Library. Oxford.

Founded in 1602 by Sir Thomas Bodley, an Oxford scholar who had a brilliant career as a diplomat and Member of Parliament, the Bodleian Library, in England second in size only to the British Library, is the library of Oxford University. One of the earliest of all surviving European libraries, the Bodleian was refounded on the site of an earlier Oxford library, the history of which reaches back to the fourteenth century. The Bodleian is renowned for its vast holdings of medieval manuscripts and works relating to medieval studies and for an extraordinary collection of classical and other ancient manuscripts. Major collections of Dante, Petrarch, Boccaccio, and Erasmus, along with the Malone Collection of Elizabethan and Jacobean plays and literature and the Douce Collection of illuminated manuscripts and sixteenth- and seventeenth-century books, make the Bodleian also a center for Renaissance studies. Further special collections include one of the world's most extensive collections of English poetical manuscripts; extraordinarily large holdings of ephemeral publications (ballads, almanacs, tickets, playbills, etc.) and especially the John Johnson Collection of Printed Ephemera, a vast amount of material in the form of prospectuses, advertisements, type specimens, and similar items, for the history of printing and the book trade; the Harding Collection of libretti, plays, ballad operas, jest books, and sheet music; the Gough Collection of British Topography and Saxon and Northern literature; the Rawlinson, Tanner, and Wood collections of English literature; and an unusually full collection of early pamphlets and newspapers (see D–50). The Bodleian

secured deposit privileges under an agreement with the Stationers' Company in 1610 and further secured those privileges under provisions of the various copyright acts. It is not surprising, therefore, that although full advantage was not taken of those privileges until the nineteenth century, pre-eighteenth-century English holdings in the Bodleian's 5.2-million-volume collection are often stronger than those of the British Library, for the Bodleian's foundation predates the establishment of the British Museum by more than a century. Indeed, the Bodleian may be regarded as the predecessor to the British Library and as England's national library up to the mid-eighteenth century and in some respects up to the mid–nineteenth century.

The Bodleian occupies a number of buildings, but the centerpiece of the current establishment is still Duke Humphrey's Library, which has been in existence since the fifteenth century and is used as the manuscript Reading Room.

A survey of the Western manuscripts is provided by the seven-volume *Summary Catalogue of Western Manuscripts in the Bodleian Library at Oxford* (H–12). Several valuable additional catalogs for manuscripts remain unpublished; no catalogs of printed books have been published since the mid-nineteenth century. See the bibliography of E. H. Cordeaux and D. H. Merry, *Bibliography of Printed Works Relating to the University of Oxford* (Oxford: Clarendon Press, 1968) [Z5055.G7093], 492 ff., where the successive editions of the early printed catalogs are enumerated. The Clarendon Press has recently published in facsimile *First Printed Catalogue of the Bodleian Library 1605* [Z921.O94 B63 1987].

More detailed views of the collections may be obtained from Craster's standard *History of the Bodleian Library, 1845-1945* (Oxford, 1952) [Z792.O94 C82] and W. D. Macray's *Annals of the Bodleian Library*, 2d ed. (Oxford, 1890) [Z792.O94.M3]. A brief but authoritative overview may be found in *TLS*, 24 September 1954, 616. For its earlier history, I. G. Philip's *Bodleian Library in the Seventeenth and Eighteenth Centuries* (Oxford: Clarendon Press, 1983) [Z792.O94 P47 1983] is regarded as indispensable. See also the study by Alex Noel-Tod, *Bodleian Library in the Eighteenth Century* (Aberystwyth: College of Librarianship in Wales, 1980) [Z792.O94 N64 1980]. There are also brief accounts, primarily historical, of the library and its founder, also by I. G. Philip, in the *Encyclopedia of Library and Information Science*, vol. 2 (New York: Dekker, 1969), pp. 647–652, 653–655 [Z1006.E57]. Current publications include the irregular *Bodleian Library Record*, 1938–, which was preceded by the *Bodleian Quarterly Record*, 1914–1938 [Z792.O94.B6].

B–49 Morgan, Paul. *Oxford Libraries outside the Bodleian: A Guide.* 2d ed. Oxford: Bodleian Library, 1980.

               Z791.O98.M67

This guide, first published in 1974, was compiled to complement A. N. L. Munby's *Cambridge College Libraries* (B–51). The work is divided into two main sections. The first, occupying nearly three-fourths of the volume, presents entries for Oxford's thirty-five college and hall libraries, seventeen of which are older than the Bodleian. The second adds descriptions of twenty-four faculty, departmental, institute, and other libraries. Entries begin with statistics: total stock, number of current periodicals, number of incunabula, and number of STC titles. A short history of the library is followed by descriptive accounts of manuscript, archival, and printed book holdings. Entries end with a survey of catalogs (both published and unpublished) of the individual libraries' collections.

There are two appendixes. The first lists and briefly describes more than 100 special libraries in Oxford which are not given separate treatment in the main work. The second contains a "Select index of manuscript collections in Oxford libraries not listed in [H. O.] Coxe" [*Catalogus Codicum*

Manuscriptorum. Qui in Collegiis Aulisque Oxoniensibus Hodie Adservantur (Oxford: Oxford University Press, 1852)] [Z6621.O98]."

B–50 **The Cambridge University Library.**

The Cambridge University Library collection existed as early as the mid-fourteenth century, though it was formally established in the second decade of the fifteenth. The office of University Librarian was created in 1577, and the University Library was among the nine granted copyright deposit privileges in the Copyright Act of 1709. Its privileges go back to the Licensing Act of 1662. Originally located in the Old Schools, the library was moved to its current premises in 1934. With a collection of some 3,300,000 volumes, the library is among the most important and comprehensive in England. The collections include some 50,000 manuscripts, 800,000 maps, and more than 350,000 items of printed music. There are important special collections in history, logic, auction catalogs (including most of A. W. L. Munby's collection, see Y–65), Irish books, ballads and chapbooks, and, among individuals, Charles Darwin, Erasmus, Sterne, and Swift. Manuscript holdings are extensive. A *Catalogue of the Western Manuscripts* in five volumes plus index was published (Cambridge: Cambridge University Press, 1856–1867) [Z6621.C17]; a *Summary Guide to Accessions of Western Manuscripts (Other Than Medieval) Since 1867* (see H–13) by A. E. B. Owen was published (University Library, 1966) [Z6621.C173]. The library is strong in incunabula (a *Catalogue* published by Cambridge University Press of the 4,582 items was compiled by J. C. T. Oates in 1954) [Z240.C167] and in STC books (ca. 12,000), a catalog of which, *Early English Printed Books in the University Library, Cambridge*, was compiled in four volumes (Cambridge: Cambridge University Press, 1900–1907) by Charles Edward Sayle [Z2002.C17]. The library of Peterborough Cathedral, particularly strong in STC books, is deposited at the University Library. C. E. Sayle also wrote the *Annals of Cambridge University Library, 1278–1900* (Cambridge: University Library, 1916) [Z792.C185]. The current guide is by J. C. T. Oates, *Cambridge University Library: A Historical Sketch* (Cambridge: University Library, 1975) [Z792.C18 O27]; it is a virtual reprint of his article in the *Encyclopedia of Library and Information Science*, vol. 4 (New York: Dekker, 1970), 50–70 [Z1006.L57]. There is also a brief account in *TLS*, 26 March 1954, 207.

B–51 **Munby, A. N. L. *Cambridge College Libraries: Aids for Research Students.*** 2d ed., rev. and enl. Cambridge: W. Heffer and Sons, 1962.   Z792.M86

The aim of this now somewhat out-of-date guide is to survey the holdings of twenty-three college and hall libraries (six of which are older than the University Library), as well as the Fitzwilliam Museum and the Cambridge University Archives. The descriptions are preceded by a subject index to selected special collections. Descriptions begin with the date of foundation, name of the librarian, and hours of opening. The buildings are described, and a succinct account is given of manuscript holdings, printed books, and college archives. Printed and other catalogs are referred to in the course of the descriptions. The introduction surveys the work of predecessors in describing the Cambridge college libraries.

B–53 **The National Library of Wales / Llyfrgell Genedlaethol Cymru.** Aberystwyth [NLW].

A product of the continuous effort to preserve and maintain the Welsh national heritage, the National Library of Wales was granted a Royal Charter in 1907 and opened in temporary quarters in 1909; it has since acquired imposing permanent buildings. As one of the six libraries in the United Kingdom and Ireland currently entitled to legal deposit privileges, the NLW contains more than 2,000,000 printed works, some 30,000 volumes of manuscripts, 3,500,000 deeds and other documents, and very large collections of prints, drawings, and maps. A general reference library that includes a vast collection of English literature, the NLW specializes in the preservation of all materials related to Wales and the other Celtic nations. Among the library's strengths are the world's largest collections of books, periodicals, and manuscripts in Welsh and of books and manuscripts relating to the Welsh people, their history, language, and literature, as well as to the cultures of other Celtic peoples and countries. There are also special collections of Arthuriana, medieval French romances, ethnology and folklore, English dictionaries and grammars, incunabula, and private presses (including the Gregynog Press). Welsh literary manuscripts are an especially important part of the library's resources and include the "Black Book of Carmarthen," the "Book of Taliesin," and the "White Book of Rhydderch," which contains the earliest known complete text of the Mabinogion. Other treasures include the Hengwrt manuscript of Chaucer's *Canterbury Tales* and other important medieval manuscripts in English, French, and Latin. In its collections of graphic material the library specializes in Welsh topography.

There is a beautifully printed and lavishly illustrated volume by W. Ll. Davies, *National Library of Wales: A Survey of Its History, Its Contents, and Its Activities* (Aberystwyth: NlW, 1937) [Z792.A193 D], prepared to mark the twenty-fifth anniversary of the library. Issue 2 of volume 5 of the *National Library at Wales Journal* was devoted to a description of the work and collections of the library's three main departments. A more recent, informative pamphlet in Welsh and English is *National Library of Wales: A Brief Summary of Its History and Its Activities* (Aberystwyth, 1973) [Z792.W18]. There is also a brief but authoritative account in *TLS*, 10 July 1953, 452. Current publications include the semiannual *National Library of Wales Journal*, 1939– [Z921.A18 A3], and its supplementary annual *Handlist of Manuscripts*, 1941– . The annual *Bibliotheca Celtica: A Register of Publications Relative to Wales and the Celtic Peoples and Languages*, is also published by the library (1910–) [Z2071.B56]. It classifies books, articles, and pamphlets on all aspects of current and historical Celtic life and concludes with an index of authors and subjects. The *Subject Index to Welsh Periodicals* (1931–) [AI19.W4 L5], formerly published by the Welsh branch of the Library Association, is now also produced by the library.

B–54 **The National Library of Scotland.** Edinburgh [NLS].

The National Library of Scotland was established in 1925, incorporating all but the legal collections of the Library of the Faculty of Advocates, itself founded in the early 1680s and granted the privilege of copyright deposit by Act of Parliament from 1710. The current building was opened in 1956, and an extension was opened in 1989. The library's primary responsibilities are to collect books printed in the British Isles through its privilege of legal deposit and to enlarge, preserve, and make available its collections of books printed in Scotland or of Scottish interest or association; to acquire, catalog, and preserve manuscripts of all kinds and of all periods relating mainly to Scotland and the Scots; and to provide an extensive and representative selection of foreign books. The collection comprises over 5,000,000 printed books, over 1,000,000 maps, over 50,000 volumes of manuscripts, and a substantial collection of music scores. Special collections include chapbooks; children's books; plays of the sixteenth to eighteenth centuries; incunabula; early printed books; Spanish, Portuguese, and Latin American literature; Scandinavian history and literature; Lutheran pamphlets; and important collections relating to Berlioz, Burns, Carlyle, Handel, Scott, and Robert Louis Stevenson, among others.

A very helpful, brief *Guide to the National Library of Scotland* prepared by J. R. Seaton was published by the library in 1976 [no LC number], but it is no longer in print. Additional guides to the library include those in Esdaile (B–9) and Roberts (B–4); two authoritative articles in *TLS*, 28 August 1953, 555 and 6 July 1956, 416; and a recent article in the *Encyclopedia of Library and Information Science*, vol. 27 (New York: Dekker, 1979), 98–109 [Z1006.L57]. Catalogs of manuscript accessions are published from time to time and include *Catalogue of Manuscripts Acquired since 1925*, 4 vols. (Edinburgh: NLS, 1938–1980) [Z6621.E192]; *Summary Catalogue of the Advocates' Manuscripts* (Edinburgh: NLS, 1970) [Z6621.S3615]; *Notable Accessions of the Advocates' Library* (Edinburgh: NLS, 1965) [Z921.S28 1965a]; *Notable Accessions since 1925* (Edinburgh: NLS, 1965) [Z921 .S28 1965b]; *Accessions of Manuscripts, 1959–1964* (Edinburgh: NLS, 1964) [Z6621.S36]; and *Accessions of Manuscripts 1965–1970* [Z6621.S37]. The library publishes *Bibliography of Scotland* (Edinburgh: HMSO, 1978–) [Z2069.B52], a series of annual volumes covering current publications in Scotland or relating to Scotland, including articles from a wide range of periodicals. Recent publications include *Current Periodicals* (1982–); the *Scottish Gaelic Union Catalogue: A List of Books Printed in Scottish Gaelic from 1567 to 1973* (1984) [Z2039.G3 F47 1984]; the *Directory of Scottish Newspapers* (1984); the *Map Room* (1984); and *Scottish Family Histories* (1986) [Z5313.S4 F39 1986]. Also published are bibliographical catalogs based on the library's collection of printed books and catalogs of the many exhibits held to illustrate the range of the collections, among which are *English Literature* (1962) [Z2029.S35]; *Shakespeare* (1964); *Scottish Manuscripts* (1967) [Z2069 .S351]; *Celtica* (1967) [Z921.S27]; *Hugh Macdiarmid* (1967) [Z927.S27 no. 7]; *William Blake* (1969); *Scandinavia* (1970) [Z921.S27 no. 1]; *Sir Walter Scott* (1971) [PR5339 S5 1971]; *David Hume 1711 to 1776* (1976); *Scottish Architects at Home and Abroad* (1978) [NA975 .S36 1978]; *Treasures of the National Library of Scotland* (1979) [Z921.S27 no. 16]; *Northern and Western Isles in the Viking World* (1958); *Thomas Carlyle 1795 to 1881* (1981); *Eye of the Mind: The Scot and His Books* (1983) [Z921.S27 no. 24]; *Scots in India* (1986), *Scots in Russia* (1987), and *Scots in Australia* (1988). The library's *Annual Report* has been published since 1956.

B–56 Trinity College Library, Dublin.

Founded almost immediately after the 1591 foundation of the university, the library of Trinity College received the privilege of British and Irish copyright deposit with the Copyright Act of 1801, a privilege that has not been altered with political change. The library now has about 3,000,000 volumes. The old library was occupied in 1732; four further buildings including the Berkeley Library (1967) date from this century. The library's greatest treasure is the Book of Kells, generally regarded as one of the most beautiful and elaborate illuminated manuscripts in the world. There are a number of other important illuminated manuscript copies of the Gospels from various Irish monasteries. In addition, there are important collections of Irish authors, especially Berkeley, Swift, Synge, Wilde, and Yeats; a large collection of Bibles; and an unusually fine collection of early Continental printing. A nine-volume catalog of printed books was published 1864–1887; a catalog of manuscripts was published in 1900; and a catalog of Latin manuscripts will be published in 1990. A convenient guide is Peter Fox's *Trinity College Library, Dublin* (Dublin: Eason, 1982) [Z792.5.T7], and more extensive coverage of the collections is given in *Treasures of the Library, Trinity College Dublin*, edited by Peter Fox (Dublin: Royal Irish Academy, 1986) [Z792.5.T75 T75 1986]. The Friends of the Library publish the annual journal *Long Room*.

B–57 The National Library of Ireland, Dublin [NLI].

Founded in 1877 on the purchase by the state of parts of the library of the Royal Dublin Society (founded in 1731), the library moved into its present building in 1890. Though general, the collection is especially rich in works published in Ireland or related to the Irish people and their history, language, and literature. Altogether the library holds more than 500,000 books and more than 10,000 volumes of manuscripts, including over 1,200 volumes of Irish-language manuscripts, as well as some 100,000 other documents. It also holds over 6,000 reels of microfilm containing, among other things, a comprehensive collection of copies of Irish manuscripts in archives and libraries throughout the world.

Since 1927 the National Library has been a legal deposit library for all items published in the Republic of Ireland. Among special strengths are full sets of many Irish newspapers and periodicals. An author-subject-place index edited by R. J. Hayes to the contents of over 150 periodicals was published in nine volumes (Boston: G. K. Hall, 1970) with the title *Sources for the History of Irish Civilisation: Articles in Irish Periodicals* [Z2034.H35]. There are strong collections of Joyce, Shaw, Swift, and Yeats, as well as a large collection of Irish topographical prints, historical prints, photography, and maps.

The library has published the *Bibliography of Irish Philology and of Printed Irish Literature* (1913; supplemental volume, 1942) [Z2037.D81] and the eleven-volume union catalog, edited by Richard J. Hayes, *Manuscript Sources for the History of Irish Civilization* (Boston: G. K. Hall, 1965) [Z2041.D85], with a three-volume *Supplement* (1979). Descriptions of the library are in Esdaile (B–9) and by Patrick Henchy in the *Encyclopedia of Library and Information Science*, vol. 13 (New York: Dekker, 1975), pp. 82–88 [Z1006.L57].

B–59 Other British Libraries of Importance to Students of English and American Language and Literature.

Birmingham. **Public Libraries (Birmingham Reference Library)**: drama, children's books, Byron, Cervantes, Johnson, Milton, Shakespeare (*Catalogue* [O–49])

Cambridge. **Christ's College**: Milton

Cambridge. **Fitzwilliam Museum Library**: literary manuscripts, art history

Cambridge. **Magdalene College**: Pepys Library

Cambridge. **Pembroke College**: Gray, Spenser

Cambridge. **St. John's College**: Butler

Cambridge. **Trinity College**: English literature and literary manuscripts

Edinburgh. **University Library**: drama, Scottish literature, Shakespeare, literary manuscripts

Glasgow. **Public Libraries (the Mitchell Library)**: Celtic literature, Scottish literature, Robert Louis Stevenson

Glasgow. **University Library**: Hunterian books and manuscripts

Leeds. **University (Brotherton Library)**: sixteenth- to eighteenth-century English literature; maps, atlases, and travel literature; Anglo-French studies; the Brontës

London (see also listings in B–45)

London. **Guildhall Library**: county history, records of the City of London, works of More and Erasmus

London. **Institute of Historical Research**: history, bibliography, and reference collections

London. **University, King's College**: philology

London. **University (Sterling Library)**: theater, early education, Bacon, Shakespeare

London. **Victoria and Albert Museum**: Dickens, Swift

London. **Warburg Institute Library**: classical tradition, art history

Manchester. **Public Libraries**: the Brontës, Carlyle, Coleridge, DeQuincey, Emerson, Hazlitt, Hunt

Oxford. **Ashmolean Museum**: classical philology

Oxford. **Balliol College**: Browning, Dante

Oxford. **Christ Church College**: STC and Wing holdings

Oxford. **Merton College**: medieval history and literature

Oxford. **Pembroke College**: Aristotle, Johnson

Oxford. **The Taylor Institution Library**: philology, modern European languages and literatures, Voltaire

V. MAJOR LIBRARY CATALOGS AND GUIDES: CONTINENTAL LIBRARIES

Scholars intending to use a research library should always follow the policy of first studying about the library and its holdings in all available printed sources and then writing in advance with a precise description of the purpose of a visit.

B–60 **Welsch, Erwin K.** *Libraries and Archives in France: A Handbook.* 2d, rev. ed. New York: Council for European Studies, 1979.   Z797.A1 W44 1979

By far the best tool for any American scholar planning to undertake research in French libraries, this handbook first appeared in 1973. It is divided into two sections, one covering Paris and one the rest of France. A very useful discussion of the Bibliothèque nationale begins the main body of the text. It is followed by treatments of other Parisian libraries arranged by their subjects of specialization. Under literature, for example, are found discussions of the Bibliothèque de l'arsenal and the Bibliothèque Sainte-Geneviève. There are also sections on the libraries of the University of Paris and the Centre Georges Pompidou. Treatment of archives in the Paris region includes sections on the Archives nationales and other major collections. The second part combines the discussion of archives and libraries in each of the eighty-nine departments of France and is arranged in an alphabetical list of the departments. Information covered includes subject specializations, hours, holdings generally described, access rules and procedures, advice on the expeditious use of the collections, description of available catalogs, photocopying facilities, miscellaneous notes, and publications available about the library or archive and its holdings.

Bibliographies of works on French libraries, works on French archives, and works on departmental archives and libraries conclude the volume, along with appendixes on classification at the Archives nationales, classification at the departmental archives, and on locating manuscripts in French libraries. An annotated list of addresses useful to visiting American scholars is appended. Copies of this indispensable handbook may be ordered from the Council for European Studies, 1429 International Affairs Building, Columbia University, New York, NY 10027.

Other aids for potential users of French libraries are the brief article "Selected Parisian Libraries and How to Use Them" by Theodore and Josephine Greider, *PMLA* 88 (1973): 550–556, and the more extensive article on libraries in France by Paule Salvan in the *Encyclopedia of Library and Information Science*, vol. 9 (New York: Dekker, 1973), 37–66 [Z1006.E57].

B–61 *Catalogue générale des livres imprimés de la Bibliothèque nationale:* **Auteurs [1897–1959].** 231 vols. Paris: Bibliothèque nationale, 1897– 1981.   Z927.P2

This catalog of the holdings of the Bibliothèque nationale [BN] has various closing dates, depending on the date when each individual volume was issued. Holdings acquired and cataloged by that date are included; those processed later are not. But a corrected working copy of the Inventaire Général of the BN is available on microfiche, *Supplément sur fiches* (Paris: Chadwyck-Healey France, 1986). No volumes of the *Catalog* have closing dates later than 1959, however, for all works received and cataloged after 1959 are treated in the new *Catalogue générale des livres imprimés: Auteurs–collectivités–auteurs–anonymes* (Paris, 1965–) [Z927.P1957], which is published in quinquennial sets. A cumulation in twenty-three volumes of the *Nouveau catalog générale, 1960-1969* was published 1972–1975 [Z927.P222 1972]; one covering 1970–1979 is in preparation. The original *Catalogue générale* excludes title entries for anonymous works, periodicals, publications of learned societies, or government and corporate authors. Though limited to true single-author entries, the catalog does have distinctive bibliographical value in the fullness of information given and in the unusual feature of a title index for the works of a voluminous author which indicates the various volumes or editions in which a particular work may be found. The new catalog, as its title makes clear, includes entries both for the works of collective authors and for anonymous works.

Two guides published by the Bibliothèque nationale will help in locating other catalogs of holdings: Lydia Mériogot, *Les catalogs du département des imprimés* (Paris, 1970) [Z798.P216], and Lydia Mérigot and Pierre Gasnault, *Les catalogs du département des manuscrits: Manuscrits occidentaux* (1974) [Z6621.P1994]. See also Eugène-Gabriel Ledos, *Histoire des catalogs des livres imprimés de la Bibliothèque nationale* (Paris: Éditions des Bibliothèques nationales, 1936) [Z798.P22 L4]. The best short guide to the Bibliothèque nationale is that in Welsch (B–60), 12–19 and passim. There is also an article by Etienne Dennery in the *Encyclopedia of Library and Information Science*, vol. 2 (New York: Dekker, 1969), 435–448 [Z1006.E57]. The *Bulletin de la Bibliothèque nationale* has been published since 1976 [Z927.P22 B84]. The Reader's Office at the BN distributes a guide (available in English) for the use of both the published catalogs and the library's card indexes.

B–65 **Welsch, Erwin K.** *Libraries and Archives in Germany.* Pittsburgh: Council for European Studies, 1975.
Z675.R45 W45

This handbook, indispensable for any American scholar considering research in German libraries, is the second in a series sponsored by the Council for European Studies. It is divided into two main sections, on libraries and archives respectively. The first part, on libraries, has several chapters on introductory material concerning types of libraries, manuscript collections, finding research collections, and regional catalogs and union lists. There follow descriptions of the libraries in the Federal Republic of Germany. The major national libraries are treated first, including descriptions of the Deutsche Bibliothek in Frankfurt, the Staatsbibliothek preussischer Kulturbesitz in West Berlin, and the Bayerische Staatsbibliothek in Munich. Then follow the nonnational libraries by *Land* and locality. Descriptions of libraries in the German Democratic Republic are similarly divided: first the Deutsche Bücherei in Leipzig and the Deutsche Staatsbibliothek in East Berlin; then university, regional, and special libraries. Each description insofar as possible includes areas of collecting interest, mention of special collections, the size of holdings, and any special features; the hours; restrictions on use; availability of copying machines and other equipment; general notes; and a list of publications about the library and its holdings. Archives are similarly described in the second part of the volume, from the Bundesarchiv of the Federal Republic to special and local collections, and in less full detail for the central and special archives in the German Democratic Republic. Bibliographies of related books and articles conclude each of the two parts; a helpful discussion of travel in Germany for the use of visiting scholars is appended. The handbook is available from the Council for European Studies, 1429 International Affairs Building, Columbia University, New York, NY 10027.

There is an excellent guide to the West German library system by Gisela von Busse and Horst Ernestius, *Libraries in the Federal Republic of Germany*, 2d ed. (Wiesbaden: Harrassowitz, 1983) [Z801.A1 B82 1983], a revised and enlarged translated edition of *Das Bibliothekswesen der Bundesrepublik Deutschland: Eine Einführung*, 2d ed. (Wiesbaden: Harrassowitz, 1983) [Z801.A1 B8 1983]. There is also a series of articles by various authors on the German library system in the *Encyclopedia of Library and Information Science*, vol. 9 (New York: Dekker, 1973), 395–545, a table of contents to which is on page 395 [Z1006.E57]. Further, there is an excellent guide to special collections by Walter Gebhardt, *Spezialbestände in deutschen Bibliotheken* (Berlin: de Gruyter, 1977) [Z801.A1 G4].

B–70 **Lewanski, Rudolf J.** *Guide to Italian Libraries and Archives*. Edited by Richard C. Lewanski. New York: Council for European Studies, 1979.   Z809.A1 L48

This is the third in a series of guides to European libraries

and archives sponsored by the Council for European Studies and is the best single aid for the American scholar contemplating research in Italy. Archives and libraries are treated together. Introductory materials include an outline of Italian libraries and archives and a discussion of laws and regulations governing them. Descriptions of major archives and libraries follow, arranged by city. Subject collections are treated next, by subject. Sections on minor archives, on library-related services, and on Italian archives outside Italy conclude the main part of the handbook. Bibliographies of related books and articles, of United States literature on Italian libraries, of Italian catalogs and union catalogs, an English-Italian list of geographical names, and a bibliography of dictionaries of Italian archival and library terminology conclude the work. Entries on individual libraries and archives include address, major dates in the institution's history, statistics on holdings, a statement of scope and subject emphases, a list of special collections and unique items, information on catalogs available, hours, information about photocopying and microfilming facilities, restrictions on the use of the collections, and a list of books and articles on the library or archive and its holdings. Copies of this indispensable handbook may be ordered from the Council for European Studies, 1429 International Affairs Building, Columbia University, New York, NY 10027.

There is also an article on libraries in Italy by Savina A. Roxas in the *Encyclopedia of Library and Information Science*, vol. 13 (New York: Dekker, 1975), 122–139 [Z1006.E57].

RETROSPECTIVE AND CURRENT NATIONAL BIBLIOGRAPHY

I. GENERAL BIBLIOGRAPHIES AND GUIDES

For additional guides to national bibliography see also Collison, *Bibliographies: Subject and National* (A–4), Wehefritz (B–10), and the relevant sections of the general reference guides by Sheehy (A–20), Walford (A–21), Malclès (A–22), and Totok (A–23).

C–1 **Conover, Helen F.** *Current National Bibliographies.* Washington, D.C.: Library of Congress, 1955. Z1002.U583

A somewhat out-of-date guide to current national bibliographical control throughout the world. After a brief introduction citing related works on national bibliography, the work is disposed into the major areas of the world and by area into countries. The entries for each country (numbered serially throughout) list current national bibliographies and related works. Generally, they are subdivided into sections on general national bibliography, current periodical indexes, the bibliography of government publications, and the bibliography of newspapers and periodicals. Each listed work is described in a discussion of the various tools and their interrelationships which follows the enumeration in each section.

More schematic but more current are Gerhard Pomassl's *Comparative Survey of Existing National Bibliographies* (Paris: UNESCO, 1975) and his *Synoptic Tables concerning the Current National Bibliographies* (Leipzig: Deutsche Bucherei, 1975) [Z1002.S89]. Most recent is Richard H. A. Cheffins, *Survey of the Contents of Existing National Bibliographies* (Paris: UNESCO, 1977) [Z100.C46]. Pomassl's conception of national bibliography is as broad as Conover's; Cheffins considers only current national bibliographies properly so called, giving information on their arrangement, indexes, up-to-dateness, and contents. Additional useful information on national bibliographies may be found in Wehefritz's *International Loan Services and Union Catalogs* (B–10). Leroy Harold Linder's *Rise of Current Complete National Bibliography* (New York: Scarecrow, 1959) [Z1001.3 .L5] is a serviceable history of national bibliography; the series of bibliographical appendixes are especially valuable.

II. BRITISH AND IRISH NATIONAL BIBLIOGRAPHY

Both the *Cumulative Book Index* (C–30) and the *Guide to Reprints* (E–60) include works published in Great Britain. See also the *Biblioteca Celtica* (see B–53), the *Scottish National Bibliography* (see B–54) and the *Irish Publishing Record* (see B–57). For works on the history of the book trade in Britain and Ireland see also section Y.III. A vastly more complete enumeration of the resources available for the study of British national bibliography will be found in the second section of Howard-Hill, *Bibliography of British Literary Bibliographies* (M–1).

C–3 **Lowndes, William T.** *Bibliographer's Manual of English Literature, Containing an Account of Rare, Curious, and Useful Books, Published in or Relating to Great Britain and Ireland, from the Invention of Printing, with Bibliographical and Critical Notices, and the Prices at Which They Have Been Sold in the Present Century.* 4 vols. London: William Pickering, 1834. New ed. Revised, corrected and enlarged by H. G. Bohn. 10 parts in 6 vols. 1857–1864. Frequently reprinted from stereotyped plates throughout the nineteenth century by Bell and Daldy and George Bell and Sons. Z2001.L82

A closed retrospective bibliography, this work shares with Watt's *Bibliotheca Britannica* (A–30) the distinction of being the English monument to nineteenth century enumerative bibliography. Since it is most frequently available in a six-volume edition, the arrangement in six volumes will be described. Entries in volumes 1–5 are alphabetical by author, with title and keyword-in-title entries and cross-references. Volume 6, the appendix, lists publications of literary and scientific societies, printing clubs, private presses, and serials. The entries for the more than 50,000 distinct works treated contain author, title, and publication information as well as a bibliographical summary of editions and reprints, specification of the best to use, notes on distinctive features of the work (paper, binding, illustrations, dedications, number printed, identification of pseudonymous and, occasionally, anonymous authors), collations of the rarer works, locations of copies, recent prices of those with value in the antiquarian book trade (with sale catalog numbers), and comments about the work taken from the writings of critics and reviewers. Works in all fields except theology are included, provided that they were published in, or relate to, Great Britain or Ireland and were printed in whole or in part by 1834; theological works were to be treated in a later bibliography that Lowndes never completed.

Later reprintings by Bohn include further additions to and corrections (and corruptions) of the original. Information in any set of Lowndes must always be checked against additional authorities. Nevertheless, the work remains a mine of potentially valuable information. There is an instructive essay by George Watson Cole, "Do You Know Your Lowndes?" *PBSA* 33 (1939): 1–22, which also discusses Watt's *Bibliotheca Britannica*.

C–4 **Duff, E. Gordon.** *Fifteenth Century English Books: A Bibliography of Books and Documents Printed in England and of Books for the English Market Printed Abroad.* Oxford: For the Bibliographical Society, 1917.   Z240.D852

An author checklist with short titles, a descriptive bibliography, and a finding list (with examined copies marked) of incunabula printed in England or for the English market. The bibliographical descriptions (collations plus contents) of the 431 sequentially numbered items are followed by a list of facsimiles and then fifty-three full-page facsimiles illustrating the work of the most important printers. The volume concludes with an incomplete typographical index identifying by locality and printer the various type fonts used with the dates of their use for each of the incunabula listed.

Duff may be supplemented in various ways; full details are available in the relevant sections of David S. Berkowitz's *Bibliotheca Bibliographica Incunabula: A Manual of Bibliographical Guides to Inventories of Printing, of Holdings, and of Reference Aids; With an Appendix of Useful Information on Place-Names and Dating; Collected and Classified for the Use of Researchers in Incunabulistics* (Waltham, Mass.: Printed privately, 1967) [Z240.A1 B4]. See also Walter Heilbronner, *Printing and the Book in Fifteenth Century England: A Bibliographical Survey* (Charlottesville: University Press of Virginia for the Bibliographical Society, 1967) [Z151.2.H4]. Note the special catalogs of fifteenth- and sixteenth-century books held by the British Library (see B–40) and by others of the major British and Irish research libraries. American students will want to consult Frederick R. Goff's *Incunabula in American Libraries: A Third Census of Fifteenth-Century Books Recorded in North American Collections* (New York: Bibliographical Society of America, 1964) [Z240.G58], with its *Supplement* (New York: Bibliographical Society of America, 1973) [Z240.G6], to locate copies.

The definitive bibliography of incunabula, the *Gesamtkatalog der Wiegendrucke*, seven volumes of which were published in the period 1925–1940 (Leipzig: Hiersemann) [Z240.G39], has been resumed with the reprinting of the original volumes (Stuttgart: Hiersemann, 1968) and the delivery of fascicles for volume 8 and parts of volume 9 (Stuttgart: Hiersemann, 1972–) [Z240.A1 G47]. The most comprehensive catalog of incunabula is the on-line database, *ISTC* (Incunable Short Title Catalogue) which aims to include reference to every copy of every extant edition. The database can be searched through BLAISE-LINE (see Z–78), using author, title elements, place of publication, printer, or date.

C–5 **Pollard, A. W., and G. R. Redgrave, et al.** *Short Title Catalogue of Books Printed in England, Scotland, and Ireland and of English Books Printed Abroad 1475–1640* [*STC*]. London: Bibliographical Society, 1926. 2d ed., rev. and enl. [*RSTC, NSTC*] Begun by W. A. Jackson and F. S. Ferguson. Completed by Katherine F. Panzer. Vol. 1, A-H. London: Oxford University Press for the Bibliographical Society, 1986. Vol. 2, I-Z. London: Oxford University Press for the Bibliographical Society, 1976. Vol. 3, the *Index of Printers and Booksellers*, plus addenda and corrigenda, is in progress.   Z2002.P77

A closed retrospective national bibliography that attempts to list all editions and all issues of all books and other printed materials that fit the specifications of the title, provided that

copies were extant in one of the 133 British and 15 American libraries consulted. The 26,143 items, sequentially numbered, are arranged alphabetically by author (primarily) or main entry. They contain drastically abbreviated titles, with words abridged or eliminated except for the opening words, and without indication of omission. Anonymous works are filed under the first major word of the title. An effort has been made to preserve original spelling and to include as much publication information as possible, whether found cited in the book or deduced from bibliographical or other evidence. Stationers' Register (C–6) listings are noted, as are locations in the 148 libraries consulted, save that only one library in a community is cited and that the holding of more than one copy by a single library is not noted. Cross-references occur and may refer either to the entry number or to the heading or to both. The original *STC* has hundreds of "ghosts" and is thought to have listed only 90 percent of the extant works and only 80 percent of the extant editions and issues that fall within its limits. Until the revision is finished, one must for completeness consult a variety of supplements including those of the Huntington Library (see M–1, Howard-Hill, item 531), the Newberry Library (see Howard-Hill, item 533), and others enumerated in Howard-Hill. An *Index of Printers, Publishers and Booksellers* giving date(s) and entry number(s) where each name or initial appears was compiled by Paul G. Morrison (Charlottesville: Bibliographical Society of the University of Virginia, 1950; reprint with add. and corr., 1961) [Z200.P77 Index B]. See also the index to writers of prefatory matter and dedicatees in Franklin B. Williams, Jr., *Index of Dedications and Commendatory Verses in English Books before 1641* (London: Bibliographical Society, 1962).

Finding lists for Britain (David Ramage et al., a *Finding List of English Books to 1640 in Libraries in the British Isles* [Durham: Council of Durham Colleges, 1958]) [Z2002.P772 R3] and the United States (William Warner Bishop, a *Checklist of American Copies of "Short Title Catalogue" Books* 2d ed. [Ann Arbor: University of Michigan Press, 1950]) [Z2002.P772 B5] include also the enumeration of additions to the *STC* noted prior to the finding lists' respective dates of publication.

The revision has vastly expanded the number of locations recorded and roughly doubled the quantity of material presented. Titles are more fully transcribed, and there are extensive notes and commentaries on various items and groups of items. Original numeration is retained with the use of decimal points and sequential numbering for additions and corrections. For details of the revision see "*STC*: The Scholar's Vademecum," *Book Collector* 33 (1984): 273–304. Until the index volume is completed, the indexes to the original *STC* must be used. There is, however, an index by title prepared by A. F. Allison and V. F. Goldsmith, *Titles of English Books (and of Foreign Books Printed in England)*, vol. 1, 1475–1640 (Hamden, Conn.: Archon, 1976) [Z2001.A44 vol. 1]. This index excludes anonymous works and was based on an unauthorized use of an unrevised draft of volume 1 and proof of volume 2. It should be used with caution.

Microfilm copies of *STC* works are being made available through the project, *Early English Books 1475–1640* (Ann Arbor, Mich.: University Microfilms, 1938–) [Z2002.U574]. A series of annual indexes to completed reels is being published under the project title (see E–50).

C–6 **The Registers of the Company of Stationers of London [SR].**

The Company of Stationers, chartered in 1557 by Queen Mary, was granted a virtual monopoly on printing in England and a kind of copyright control through the right to register all proposed printing by its members except for publications printed by royal permission, to seize all works printed in violation of this right, and to imprison anyone printing without leave. The history of the company has been admirably told by Cyprian Blagden, *Stationers' Company: A History, 1403–1959* (London: Allen and Unwin, 1960) [Z329.S79 B5].

Among other activities of the Stationers' Company was the keeping of extensive records of transactions, including entries of books for copyright (as it were), enrollments of apprentices, books of fines, cash account books, lists of members and officers, minutes of official actions, and court records. These are of inestimable value in the study of publishing in England, and some though by no means all of them have been transcribed and made available in printed editions. Note, however, that ownership of a title or copyright is what is recorded: works were published which are not included here, and titles included may not have been published or may have a different title from the one recorded. For complete details on all the records see the "Note on the Records and on Secondary Sources," in Blagden, *Stationers' Company*, 300–303, and Robin Myers, "The Records of the Worshipful Company of Stationers and Newspaper Makers (1554–1912)," *Archives* 16 (1983): 28–38, reprinted in *Publishing History* 13 (1983): 89–104.

There is, to begin with, a *Transcript of the Registers . . . 1554–1640* [with a gap from 1571 to 1576], Edward Arber (London: Privately printed, 1875–1877) [Z2002.S79] in four volumes; volume 5, an index volume, was published in Birmingham, 1894. Arber transcribes, with some deletions and with extensive additions of supplementary materials, a considerable portion of the surviving records for this period. The index volume lists the printers and publishers of London between 1553 and 1640 and a chronology of London printing by printer through 1602–1603. An index of book-trade persons and places cited anywhere in the entire *Transcript* concludes the volume. Because of its idiosyncrasies this work should be used with Walter W. Greg's *Companion to Arber: Being a Calendar of Documents in Edward Arber's Transcript . . . with Text and Calendar of Supplementary Documents* (Oxford: Clarendon Press, 1967) [Z151.3.G68], which enumerates and summarizes in chronological order all documents interpolated by Arber in his transcript and transcribes additional relevant documents. The *Companion* has an extensive subject index.

H. R. Plomer transcribed and G. E. B. Eyre edited the three-volume *Transcript of the Registers . . . from 1640–1708* (London: Privately printed, 1913–1914) [Z2002.S791]. It continues the Arber transcription to 1708/9 but lacks the supplementary materials and is without an index. To these transcriptions may be added the *Records of the Court of the Stationers' Company, 1576 to 1602, from Register B*, ed. Walter W. Greg and Eleanore Boswell (London: Bibliographical Society, 1930) [Z329.S79], and the *Records of the Court of the Stationers' Company, 1602–1640*, ed. W. A. Jackson (London: London Bibliographical Society, 1957), both of which supplement Arber by including the court records he was not permitted to publish.

William P. Williams has an important discussion of the main desideratum in the use of these valuable records, "Indexing the Stationers' Register," *LRN* 2 (1977): 3–19. A new microfilm series, *Records of the Stationers' Company 1554–1920*, under the editorial direction of Robin Myers, is now being prepared by Chadwyck-Healey, Ltd. in Cambridge. It will include 115 reels of microfilm and a printed guide.

C–7 **Wing, Donald.** *Short-Title Catalogue of Books Printed in England, Scotland, Ireland, Wales, and British America and of English Books Printed in Other Countries, 1641–1700.* 3 vols. New York: For the Index Society, 1945–1951 [i.e., 1952]. Z2002.W5
2d ed., rev. and enl. 3 vols. New York: Modern Language Association, 1972–1988. Z2002.W52

The Wing volumes are intended to continue the closed retrospective national bibliography of Pollard and Redgrave to 1700 and were compiled on principles similar to those used for the earlier *STC* (see C–4). One significant difference involved a shift from continuous numbering to numeration through the letter of the alphabet under which the author or title entry is found, followed by a serial number marking the entry's place under that letter. Wing numbers in each volume thus run from A–1 to E–2926, E–2927 to 0–1000, and P–1 to Z–28. Another difference is the use of the first word of the title, rather than the first major word of the title, as the head word for all entries of anonymous works. In addition to bibliographical information, locations are given in up to five American and five British libraries for relatively common books, using a system of abbreviations devised by Wing and unique to him.

Supplements to the work include an *Index of Printers, Publishers and Booksellers in Donald Wing's Short-Title Catalogue* (Charlottesville: For the Bibliographical Society of the University of Virginia, 1955) [Z2002.W5 Index], compiled by Paul G. Morrison, and a series of addenda recording additional holdings at the Huntington Library and at the William Andrews Clark and other UCLA libraries; the library of Christ Church College, Oxford; English translations from the French; books printed in Scotland; holdings in the British Museum; books in the Library Company of Philadelphia; and Wing's own *Gallery of Ghosts*; *Books Published between 1641–1700 Not Found in the Short-Title Catalogue* (New York: MLA, 1967) [Z2002.W48]. There is also an index by title, *Titles of English Books (and of Foreign Books Printed in England)*, vol. 2, 1641–1700 (Hamden, Conn.: Archon, 1977) [Z2002.W520], prepared by A. F. Allison and V. F. Goldsmith, which must be used with caution because of its omission of all anonymous works as well as many entries in the first volume of the second edition. More useful is the index to the microfilm collection cited below.

All additions and corrections are being absorbed into the second edition, volume 1, of which (*A to England: Privy Council*) was published in 1972. Volume 2 (*England Anatomized to Oyes, Oyes, Oyes*) appeared in 1982, and volume 3 (P to Z) in 1988. To avoid disturbing the original numeration so far as possible, the new edition uses Wing numbers with supplemental lowercase letters to designate additions. An appendix in volume 2 lists all changes in entry numbers from the first to the second edition of volume 1 (A-E), thus helping somewhat with the confusion caused by the partial renumbering of entries. Though it incorporates all recorded additions and corrections to the first edition, the second is not a thoroughgoing *revision* of the earlier edition. It is not surprising, therefore, that further "Additions and Corrections to the Second Edition of Donald Wing's Short-Title Catalogue" have been published as a regular feature of *Studies in Bibliography* from volume 29 (1976) on. The new edition, under the editorship of Timothy Crist, is being done at Yale University, where complete records (including all the locations on file for each entry) are maintained. See the reviews of volume 1 in *PBSA* 72 (1978): 435–454 and of volume 2 in *AEB* 7 (1983): 243–50 and in *PBSA* 80 (1986): 255–62.

Microfilm copies of Wing works are being made available through the project *Early English Books 1641–1700 Selected from Donald Wing's Short Title Catalogue* (Ann Arbor, Mich.: University Microfilms, 1955–) [Z2002.E23]. Works filmed are being cataloged in MARC format and are searchable through OCLC (see Z–78). A series of annual and multiannual indexes to completed reels are being published under the project title (see E–50). These have been cumulated in *Accessing Early English Books, 1641–1700: A Cumulative Index to Units 1–32 of the Microfilm Collection*. 4 vols. (Ann Arbor, Mich.: University Microfilms International, 1981–1982) [Z2002.V586 1981] which gives author, title, subject, and reel-position Wing-number indexes to the first 25,000 titles in the collection. The indexes must be used with the first edition of volume 1.

C–8 **Arber, Edward, ed.** *Term Catalogues, 1668–1709 A.D., with a Number for Easter Term, 1711 A.D.: A Contemporary Bibliography of English Literature in the Reigns of Charles II, James II, William and Mary, and Anne. Edited from the Very Rare Quarterly Lists of New Books and Reprints of Divinity, History, Science, Law, Medicine, Music, Trade, Finance, Poetry, Plays, etc.; with Maps, Engravings, Playing Cards, etc. Issued by the Booksellers, etc. of London.* 3 vols. London: Privately printed, 1903–1906.   Z2002.A31

The Term Catalogues, England's earliest attempt at complete current national bibliography and a landmark in the history of current national bibliography, were issued by the book trade for each of the quarterly law terms, in November for Michaelmas Term, in February for Hilary Term, in May for Easter Term, and in June for Trinity Term. The catalogs, first compiled by booksellers Robert Clavell and John Starkey, were classified by broad subject groups (see the title for examples). Excluded were official publications, almost all Quaker and Roman Catholic books, and newspapers. Imperfect at first, the issues of the quarterly lists became increasingly satisfactory. Entries generally, but not always, include title, author, format, publisher or printer (often omitted), and price.

Arber's edition reproduces 161 of the 162 actually published quarterly lists as follows: volume 1, those from 1668 to 1682; volume 2, 1683–1696; and volume 3, 1697–1709 along with the list for Easter Term 1711. Approximately 20,000 items are cited. There are two rather short indexes in each volume, one of titles and the other of persons, places, and subjects.

In addition to the quarterly lists, the bookseller Clavell produced four cumulations, the first titled *Catalogue of All the Books Printed in England since the Dreadful Fire of London, in 1666, to the End of Michaelmas Term, 1672* [Z2002.C55]. It was published in 1673, with a supplement in 1674, followed by a second edition in 1675 extending coverage to Trinity Term 1674, a third in 1680 covering publications through Trinity Term 1680, and a fourth and last in 1696, which included publications to Michaelmas Term 1695. These have been reprinted in four volumes under the editorship of D. F. Foxon within the series titled *English Bibliographical Sources, Series 2: Catalogues of Books in Circulation* (Farnborough: Gregg, 1965) [Z2002.A2], which also includes the early lists of Andrew Maunsell (1595) and William London (1657, 1658, 1660). For many though not all uses, these lists have been incorporated in and superseded by the *Pollard-and-Redgrave* and *Wing STCs.*

C–9 **Growoll, Adolf.** *Three Centuries of English Booktrade Bibliography: An Essay on the Beginnings of Booktrade Bibliography since the Introduction of Printing and in England since 1595, with a List of the Catalogues . . . Published for the English Booktrade from 1595–1902 by Wilberforce Eames.* New York: For the Dibden Club, 1903.
          Z2001.A1 G8

Fully and correctly titled, this remains an authoritative historical account of the development of English national bibliography. Because of their detail, the entries in Wilberforce Eames's bibliography of book-trade catalogs are still of value. A recent study is LeRoy Harold Linder's *Rise of Current Complete National Bibliography* (New York: Scarecrow, 1959), chapters 2 and 3 [Z1001.3.L5].

C–10 **Foxon, D. F., ed.** *English Bibliographical Sources, Series 1: [Eighteenth-Century] Periodical Lists of New Publications.* London: Gregg Press, 1964–1966.   Z2002.A55

Until the *Eighteenth Century Short Title Catalogue* is completed (see C–12), researchers must use a miscellany of lists and catalogs to identify books published in England between 1700 and about 1775. The major sources to consult are *Bibliotheca Britannica* (A–30), Lowndes (C–3), Arber (C–8), and the *London Catalogue* (C–11). In addition, students may refer to many current periodical listings published in the eighteenth century. The most reliable and useful of such periodical lists have been reprinted under the editorship of D. F. Foxon, who has contributed valuable brief introductions to each volume. The series includes:

1. Monthly Catalogue [May] 1714–1717. Edited by Bernard Lintot. 3 vols., Reprint (3 vols. in 1 with a modern index) [Z2005.M64].
2. Monthly Catalogue [March] 1723–[February] 1730, with a biennial index for 1723 and 1724, and annual indexes 1725–1730. Edited by John Wilford. 4 vols. Reprint (4 vols. in 2) [Z2002.M65].
3. Register of Books, 1728–[March] 1732, extracted from the *Monthly Chronicle* (with annual indexes for 1728–1731) [Z2002.R4].
4. *Bibliotheca Annua.* London: 1699–1703/4. Classified lists with indexes to authors and titles for the 3d and 4th vols. 4 vols. Reprint (4 vols. in 2) [Z2002.B52].
5. *Annual Catalogue 1736–1737.* Edited by John Worral. 2 vols. Reprint (2 vols. in 1) [Z2002.A55].
6. Lists of Books from the *Gentleman's Magazine*, 1731–1751, collected with annual indexes and the [subject] index to the first twenty years compiled by Edward Kimber (1753). 4 vols. [Z2002.K5 1967].
7. Monthly Catalogues from *London Magazine*, 1732–1766, with the annual indexes and the [keyword-in-title] index for 1732–1758 compiled by Edward Kimber (1760) [Z2002.M64].
8. The [Monthly] Lists of Books from *British Magazine*, 1746–1750, collected with annual [subject] indexes. 4 vols. [Z2001.B73].

C–11 *London Catalogue of Books in All Languages, Arts and Sciences, That have been Printed in Great Britain, since the Year MDCC [LondC]. Properly Classed under the Several Branches of Literature and Alphabetically disposed under each Head. With Their Sizes and Prices. Carefully compiled and Corrected, with Innumerable Additions.* London: [For W. Harris], 1773.   Z2001.E5

The first important issue of a series of catalogs, variously titled, which summarize British books printed (primarily in London) since the beginning of the eighteenth century. Because of their division by broad subject classes and the omission of imprint dates, publishers, and sometimes even authors, these catalogs are of limited utility. But until an eighteenth-century STC is available, they can be used in conjunction with Watt (A–30), Lowndes (C–3), Arber (C–8), and the periodical lists (C–10) to gather a partial record of publications. New editions or important supplements of the *London Catalogue* were published in 1779, 1780, 1785, 1786, 1788, 1791, 1799, 1800, 1803, 1805, 1807, 1811, 1812, 1814, 1816, 1822, 1827, 1829, 1831, 1835, 1837, 1839, 1844, 1846, 1849, 1851, and 1855. Subject indexes to the series were published in 1848, covering 1814–1846, and in 1853, covering 1816–1851. The series was absorbed into the *English Catalogue* (C–13) in 1864. More complete details about the years covered in each of the editions and supplements may be gathered from Howard-Hill (M–1) and other usual sources.

Among features of particular interest to literary students are the classes of Poetry, Poetical Translations, and Dramatic Works; Novels and Romances; Miscellanies [including literary criticism]; History, Biography, Topography, Antiquities, Voyages and Travels; Latin, Greek, French, and Italian Books and Prose Translations from the Classics; and a section on School Books. Starting with the 1799 issue, these classes are all collapsed into one alphabetical list except for school-books, which are separately listed until the issue of 1827.

C–12 *Eighteenth Century Short Title Catalogue [ESTC].*

Discussion of an eighteenth-century *STC* has been more or less continuous since the achievements of Pollard and Redgrave (C–5) and Wing (C–7). In June 1976 a conference was held in London to determine the feasibility of an *ESTC*, which had been unsuccessfully attempted several times before. With over 300,000 items the British Library (which had been host to the conference) has the largest collection of eighteenth-century English imprints in the world. In 1977 the British Library began recataloging its eighteenth-century holdings and converting these records to machine-readable cataloging form (MARC), thus providing the essential first step in making an *ESTC*. An initial report on progress in this effort was published by R. C. Alston, the editor of the *ESTC*, and M. J. Jannetta under the title *Bibliography, Machine-Readable Cataloguing, and the ESTC* (London: British Library, 1978) [Z699.4.E17 A47]. It contains a summary history of the project, a discussion of working methods, a set of revised cataloging rules being used at both the British Library and at the many other contributing libraries, and a sample production, a catalog of British Library holdings of the works of Alexander Pope printed between 1711 and 1800.

To the recorded British Library holdings are being added records of eighteenth-century holdings at dozens of other libraries in Britain along with records of the North American Imprints Program (NAIP) at the Library of the American Antiquarian Society in Worcester, Mass. To these are being added records of imprints held by dozens of other libraries in North America which are being assembled by the North American office at Louisiana State University in Baton Rouge (*ESTC/NA*) under the direction of Henry L. Snyder. All contributing libraries are working with the cataloging rules first published in the Alston and Jannetta report and subsequently as the *Eighteenth-Century Short-Title Catalogue: The Cataloguing Rules*, rev. ed. (London: British Library, 1984) [no LC number].

In addition to this volume the British Library also published a volume of proceedings from a conference held at the University of London in July 1982 with the purpose of demonstrating the uses of an on-line *ESTC*. The volume's title is *Searching the Eighteenth Century*, ed. M. J. Crump and M. Harris (1983) [no LC number]. A further illustration of the uses of the *ESTC* is R. C. Alston, et al., *Check-list of Eighteenth-Century Books Containing Lists of Subcribers* (New Castle: Avero, 1983) [Z1016.A47 1983].

The *ESTC* group at the British Library has also been publishing an irregular newsletter, *Factotum*, since 1978 [Z124.F344]. A cumulative *Index to Factotum Numbers 1–20* was compiled by Charles Wheelton Hind and published in 1985. Along with the issues of this newsletter have been included a number of *Occasional Papers*. *Occasional Paper 1, Searching ESTC Online: A Brief Guide*, by R. C. Alston (1982), discusses the use in Britain and Europe of the British Library computer network BLAISE-LINE, on which the ESTC file has been available since 1982 (see Z–78). *Occasional Paper 2, Searching ESTC Online through RLIN. A Brief Guide*, by R. C. Alston and J. C. Singleton (1982), discusses parallel use in North America of the Research Libraries Information Network [RLIN] maintained by the Stanford-based Research Libraries Group, on which the *ESTC* file has been available also since 1982 (see Z–78). A revision was published by David Hunter, *Searching ESTC on RLIN* as *Occasional Paper 5* (1987). *Occasional Paper 3, The English Provincial Printer 1700–1800*, was published to coincide with an autumn 1983 ESTC/British Library exhibit. And, finally, *Occasional Paper 4, First Phase: An Introduction to the Catalogue of the British Library Collections for ESTC*, by R. J. Alston, was published in December 1983. It coincides

with the computer output microform (microfiche) publication of the British Library's *ESTC* holdings and thus signals the conclusion of the first phase of the *ESTC* project.

In contrast with the Pollard-and-Redgrave and Wing STCs, the *ESTC* contains records of each item comparable in fullness to the entries in the British Museum *General Catalogue* (B–41) and the *National Union Catalog* (B–12, B–13). Included are records for all books, pamphlets, and single sheets printed in any language in England, America, and the British colonies and possessions throughout the world, along with all items printed in English anywhere in the world between 1701 and 1800. Intentionally excluded from record are books destroyed during World War II, printed forms intended to be completed in manuscript, wholly engraved single-sheet items, and ephemera such as playbills, concert and theater programs, and playing cards.

Catalog entries begin with a personal name, corporate name, or pseudonymous heading. Within the listing for one author, entries have the following arrangement: collected works; selected works or collections of works in a single genre; individual titles separately published in alphabetical order; selected, abridged, and abstracted individual works. Corporate headings include official publications of Parliament, the *Bible*, appeal cases (cited under the name of the defendant and/or appellant), trials (cited under the name of the defendant), churches (cited under the name of the religious body), almanacs (cited under the name of the original compiler and under the title), prospectuses (cited with the work proposed by use of a uniform title), and advertisements (cited under the name of the vendor or promoter and under the title). Pseudonymous publications are entered under the author's real name if known, under the pseudonym if not, and also under the title. Title-page wording is transcribed exactly. Imprint statements give the place of publication, the significant elements of the rest of the publishing statement, and the date as given (with corrections in square brackets). Collation and format are given, with generally sufficient information to distinguish editions and issues of works. Notes explain as necessary authorship, language, nature of the work (verse, a catalog), subject, additional pertinent bibliographical features, bibliographical status, contents, references to bibliographical sources, and locations in Britain, North America, and the rest of the world.

Indexes include a chronological index with entries arranged by author and title within a given year; a place-of-publication index for all works printed elsewhere than London; and a genre index listing by date, author, and title all entries for almanacs, directories, single-sheet songs and ballads, prospectuses, and advertisements.

In addition to the microfiche edition of British Library ESTC holdings, the entire continuously expanding *ESTC* data base has been available since 1982 for on-line searching through BLAISE-LINE in Britain and Europe and through RLIN in North America. (see Z–78). Complete RLIN search instructions are found in Jonathan Lavigne, *Eighteenth Century Short Title Catalog*, 2d ed. (Stanford, Calif.: The Research Libraries Group, 1986). During the second, enrichment phase of the project, this will be the only way of using the "complete" *ESTC*. Eventually, however, a computer output microform version of the "enriched" *ESTC* will be published. It is expected to contain over 600,000 items, and if it were published in book form, it would occupy some fifty to sixty volumes.

Among other developments has been an agreement for the microform publication of selected titles from the *ESTC* by Research Publications of Woodbridge, Conn., in a program under the editorship of R. C. Alston. Some 200,000 volumes are expected to be included in the filming, which began in 1982 and will take until nearly the end of the century to complete.

C–13 ***English Catalogue of Books [EngC] . . . Comprising the Contents of the "London" and the "British" Catalogues, and the Principal Works Published in the United States of America and Continental Europe . . . Giving in One Alphabet, under Author and Title, the Size, Price, Month of Publication, and Publisher of Books Issued in the United Kingdom . . . 1801–.*** London: Sampson Low [and various other publishers], 1864–.   Z2001.E52

A closed, retrospective (to 1864) and then current national bibliography, with various titles. The first volume, compiled by Sampson Low, brought together listings in the various available catalogs for the period 1835–1862; this was followed by five other volumes in the nineteenth century covering 1863–1871 (1873), 1872–1880 (1882), 1881–1889 (1891), 1890–1897 (1898), and 1898–1900 (1901) respectively. A retrospective list for 1801–1836, edited by Robert Alexander Peddie and Quintin Waddington, was published in 1914 [Z2005.P97]. Since the beginning of this century there have been a series of cumulations covering three- to five-year periods.

Coverage has varied over the years. The first two volumes included important American and Continental publications; European publications were dropped after 1871, American publications after 1900. Beginning with the seventeenth cumulated volume covering 1952–1955, maps are listed separately at the end. Beginning with the cumulation for 1960–1962 a paperback section is found at the front of the volume. Separate subject catalogs indexing titles and topics were published for the periods 1837–1857 (1859), 1856–1876 (1876), 1874–1880 (1884), and 1881–1889 (1893). The 1801–1836 volume and those for the twentieth century incorporate the subjects, authors, and titles in one alphabet. Current volumes are based on the monthly cumulations of the weekly lists of publications included in the *Publishers' Circular and Booksellers' Record of British and Foreign Literature*, 1837–1958, first retitled *British Books*, 1959–1966, and then retitled *Publisher: The Journal of the Publishing Industry*, 1967–1970 [Z2005.P97]. The last cumulation issued was the one for 1963–1965; the last annual volume, that for 1968, and the last quarterly issue of the *Publisher* appeared in 1970. The *English Catalogue* is now defunct and has been replaced by the *British National Bibliography* (C–16).

C–14 ***Nineteenth Century Short Title Catalogue [NCSTC].*** Newcastle upon Tyne: Avero Publications, 1984–.
                                   Z2001.N55

The *Nineteenth Century Short Title Catalogue*, to cover publications 1801–1918, is to be prepared under the auspices of the Project for Historical Bibliography at the University of Newcastle upon Tyne in three phases: 1801–1815, 1816–1870, and 1871–1918. To be included are all works published in the United Kingdom, its colonies, the United States of America, all books in English published anywhere, and all translations from English.

Each publication phase will begin with a printed union catalog of all relevant works held by the Bodleian Library; the British Library; Cambridge University Library; the Library of Trinity College, Dublin; the National Library of Scotland; and the University Library of Newcastle upon Tyne. Phase 2 will add books at the Library of Congress and Harvard University Library. Primary entries are by author, with indexes appended of subjects and places of publication. In addition, an alphabetical list of titles will be prepared on microfiche.

The first such union catalog, Series I, treating books published 1801–1815, was published in five volumes (1984–1985). Volumes 1–4 list works by author, with subject and place of publication indexes. Entries give a serial reference number, an author, a short title including the first five words and all proper nouns, up to three subject classification numbers (which approximate to the first three figures of

the Universal Dewey Decimal Classification), an edition statement, and location symbols. Volume 5 contains general sections for Directories, England, Ephemerides, Ireland, London, Periodical Publications, and Scotland. In addition, a microfiche title index is included with volume 5.

Series II, treating books published 1816–1870 began publication in 1986, and is to appear at the rate of five volumes per year until all 50 volumes are in print. Subject and place of publication indexes are included in every fifth volume.

C–15 ***Whitaker's Cumulative Booklist: The Complete List of All Books Published in the United Kingdom during the Period, Giving Details as to Author, Title, Sub-Title, Size, Number of Pages, Price, Date, Classification, Standard Book Number, and Publisher of Every Book, in One Alphabetical Arrangement under Author, Title and Subject, Where This Forms Part of the Title.*** London: J. Whitaker and Sons, 1926–.   Z2005.W57

A closed, current national book-trade bibliography of new books, new editions, and new issues, which appears in quarterly cumulations, with annual and triennial or quinquennial cumulations [Z2005.W58]. Entries are based on the weekly author and short-title lists published in the *Bookseller* (1858–) [Z2005.B72] and on the classified cumulated list appearing each month in *Current Literature* (1908–1970) [Z2005.M67] now named *Whitaker's Books of the Month and Books to Come* [in the next two months] (1971–), [Z2005.W56]. Until 1976, entries in the cumulative booklist were classified according to broad subject area alphabetically by author, with full information provided as specified in the subtitle. A second list following the classification listed authors and titles. From 1976 on, there is a single listing that includes titles, authors, and some subjects. Also published by Whitaker was the *Reference Catalogue of Current Literature*, now titled *British Books in Print* (C–17).

C–16 ***British National Bibliography [BNB].*** London: Council of the British National Bibliography (now the Bibliographic Services Division of the British Library). 1950–.   Z2001.B75

This work, the current complete national bibliography for Britain and Ireland (except for Irish government publications), is based on the new books received by the Copyright Receipt Office of the British Library. Included are monographs, new editions, new serial titles, government publications, standards, and works published abroad; excluded are music, maps, patents, and audiovisual materials. Weekly issues present entries classified according to the eighteenth edition of the Dewey decimal classification; full bibliographic data are given. In addition, there are weekly and monthly indexes of authors, titles, and series, and a separate monthly detailed subject index. The issues and indexes are cumulated for January-April, May-August, then annually. To date, there are multiyear cumulations for 1951–1954, 1955–1959, 1960–1964, 1965–1967, 1968–1970, and 1971–1973. Separate volumes present the multiyear cumulated author and title indexes and the cumulated subject indexes [Z2001.B752]. Entries can be searched through BLAISE-LINE (see Z–78).

The other components that contribute to current national bibliography in the United Kingdom are the *British Union Catalogue of Periodicals—New Serial Titles* (D–95): H. M. Stationery Office's bibliography, *Government Publications* (1922–) [Z2009.G82]; the *British Catalogue of Music* (1957–) [ML120.G7 B7]; the *British National Film Catalogue* (see U–118); and the *Index to Theses Accepted for Higher Degrees in the Universities of Great Britain and Northern Ireland* (E–11).

C-17 *British Books in Print [BBIP]*. London: J. Whitaker and Sons, 1962–.   Z2001.R33

This index, the successor to [Whitaker's] *Reference Catalogue of Current Literature: A National Inclusive Book-Reference Index of Books in Print and on Sale in the United Kingdom*, 1874–1961, provides an author-title-subject index to entries in *Whitaker's Cumulative Booklist* (C-15). Entries include author, title, editor, translator, reviser, year of publication or latest edition, size, number of pages, presence of illustrations, binding (when not cloth), price, publisher's name, and ISBN. It is now an annual publication and appears in November. The *Reference Catalogue* originally was a collection of uniformly sized publishers' catalogs, bound together with a separate index. In 1936 the use of sales catalogs was discontinued, and a more complete bibliographical description was included in the index volume. Publication was biennial from 1936 to 1940, after which time it was suspended until 1951. Paperback publications are also indexed separately in *Paperbacks in Print* [Z1033.P3 P28].

III. UNITED STATES NATIONAL BIBLIOGRAPHY

Additional sources for United States national bibliography include the *National Union Catalog* (B-13), *New Serial Titles* (E-92), the *National Register of Microform Masters* (E-53), and *Guide to Reprints* (E-60). For works on the history of the United States book trade see also Section Y.III.

C-20 Tanselle, G. Thomas. *Guide to the Study of United States Imprints*. 2 vols. Cambridge: Belknap Press of Harvard University Press, 1971.   Z1215.A2 T35

The purpose of this monumental guide is to facilitate research by providing systematic references to all work relevant to the study of United States imprints; to provide a manual that can help in the identification, cataloging, or recording of a particular imprint; and to give sufficient information about each standard work included so as to aid in the deciphering of brief reference to such works. Entries are serially numbered with decimal numeration showing related and subordinated works; supplementary works are indented below their originals. The entries are disposed into nine sections. The first three, Basic Imprint Lists, are A—Regional Lists (arranged from larger to smaller regions of coverage, then chronologically); B—Genre Lists (ninety-two types are listed alphabetically; further arrangement is from larger to smaller regions of coverage, then chronologically); C—Author Lists (both groups and individuals, including major and minor figures). The next three sections, Related Lists, include D—Copyright Records (arranged from larger to smaller regions of coverage, then chronologically); E—Catalogues (including auction, dealers', exhibition, and both institutional and private library catalogs); and F—Book Trade Directories (national, then by state, and within states by locality, then chronologically). The last three sections, which along with the detailed index occupy volume 2, are concerned with Supplementary Studies. Section G contains Studies of Individual Printers and Publishers; section H contains General Studies of American Printing and Publishing; and section I contains Checklists of Secondary Material (that is, plain or annotated guides to materials found in one of the previous sections). In addition to the detailed index of authors, titles, and subjects, volume 2 also contains an appendix, "A Basic Collection of Two Hundred and Fifty Titles on United States Printing and Publishing." This, along with the extended introduction in volume 1, constitutes a valuable introduction to American bibliography. In addition, the student of English and American literature will find much of value in the genre and author list sections. Among the ninety-two genres (an outline of which will be found on p. viii of volume 1) are autobiographies, Bibles, biographies, children's books, diaries, drama, fiction, jest books, letter writers, murder literature, Negro Americana, outlaw literature, poetry, science fiction, sermons, translations, and travel literature, to mention only a few. Among the authors are not only American writers but also any writers for whom checklists or studies of their publication in America have been made. Though not completely parallel, Tanselle's extraordinary achievement in these volumes can be compared only to that of Howard-Hill (M-1); their works are similarly indispensable.

C-21 Sabin, Joseph. *Bibliotheca Americana: A Dictionary of Books Relating to America, from Its Discovery to the Present Time*. 29 vols. New York: J. Sabin (later the Bibliographical Society of America), 1861–1936.   Z1201.S2

A retrospective bibliography of 106,413 numbered entries originally intended to include everything printed about the political, governmental, military, economic, social, and religious history of the Western Hemisphere from its discovery until the date of publication, wherever published and in whatever language. The more recent the volume, the less inclusive it is, for Sabin's successors gradually narrowed the scope of the project. The introduction to volume 29 will clarify the changes introduced. Sabin himself died in 1881, by which time only the first twelve volumes had been published; Wilberforce Eames directed the work through volume 20 (1928), and R. W. G. Vail carried on to completion in 1936 the last series of volumes, 21–29, which are the most restricted.

The volumes are difficult to use. Works are generally listed under author, making subject searching nearly impossible. Anonymous entries are listed by title, but under a locality, society (or other corporate author), or a general subject heading. Entries contain standard short-form bibliographical information but also make symbolic reference to libraries where the item may be found. The whole work has been rendered much more accessible by the *Author-Title Index to Joseph Sabin's Dictionary of Books Relating to America* compiled by John Edgar Molnar in three volumes. (Metuchen, N.J.: Scarecrow, 1974) [Z1201.S222], which has approximately 520,000 entries. Molnar frequently identifies anonymous and pseudonymous entries and has a considerable number of cross-references. He uses short titles, however, and thus the user must refer to Sabin for complete information.

Laurence S. Thompson is now editing the *New Sabin: Books Described by Joseph Sabin and His Successors, Now Described Again on the Basis of Examination of Originals, and Fully Indexed by Title, Subject, Joint Authors, and Institutions and Agencies* (Troy, N.Y.: Whitston, 1974–) [Z1201.T45 E18]. To date, nine volumes and an index volume have been published (1983). Each volume of the *New Sabin* describes and indexes a series of works in, or eligible for citation in, the original Sabin, which are in print in microform. The entries are serially numbered throughout volumes 1–5, and the index volume cumulatively indexes all 13,513 items; volumes 6–9 continue the serial numeration through item 23,828. Each volume covers one or several microform series of Americana; those in volume 4, for example, are the entries in Wright's bibliography of American fiction (S-85) which are available in microfiche editions from the Lost Cause Press in Louisville, Kentucky. Though reviewers are agreed that the *New Sabin* does not in any way replace the original, there is consensus that the volumes published to date provide a useful supplement.

C–22 **Evans, Charles.** *American Bibliography: A Chronological Dictionary of All Books, Pamphlets and Periodical Publications Printed in the United States of America from the Genesis of Printing in 1639 down to and Including the Year 1820 [i.e., 1800], with Bibliographical and Biographical Notes.* 12 vols. Chicago: Privately printed, 1903–1934. Vol. 13, 1799–1800. Edited by Clifford K. Shipton. Worcester, Mass.: American Antiquarian Society, 1955. Vol. 14, Index. Compiled by Roger P. Bristol. Worcester, Mass.: American Antiquarian Society, 1959.   Z1215.E923

This closed retrospective national bibliography describes 39,162 items, including some that are not extant, with author or institutional author, full title of the book, place of publication, printer, date, number of pages, format, and sometimes notes on the location of copies and on auction prices. Arrangement of entries is chronological under the year of publication from 1638 to 1800, Evans having died before reaching his intended terminus of 1820 (but see C–23). Further arrangement of entries is alphabetical by author or title, with entries numbered serially throughout. The user must be cautioned that Evans sometimes placed items he had heard of but not seen under the wrong year and that an early item may be listed out of chronological sequence in a later volume because it was not located until after its proper volume had already been printed. Also items for which there are no extant copies *are* included. Alphabetical lists of authors, subjects, and printers and publishers are found at the end of each volume. But because the original subject indexes were so incomplete and were not cumulated, Bristol's new index volume 14 was produced. In addition to clarifying many obscure entries, the volume provides some cross-referencing and a full author-title index. A supplementary cumulative *Index of Printers, Publishers, and Booksellers* was published by Roger P. Bristol in 1961 (Charlottesville: Bibliographical Society of the University of Virginia) [Z1215.E9233]. *Supplement to Charles Evans' American Bibliography*, also edited by Roger P. Bristol (Charlottesville: University Press of Virginia for the Bibliographical Society, 1970) [Z1215.E92334], lists 11,282 imprints overlooked in the original work. It is arranged like the original but uses a "B" before each numbered entry to distinguish it from the Evans number. In it Bristol incorporates the various checklists of additions to Evans compiled by the Huntington Library, the Library of Congress, the New York Public Library, and so on (see Tanselle, C–20, for a complete enumeration, A 1.15 ff.). There is an *Index to the Supplement*, by Roger P. Bristol (Charlottesville: University Press of Virginia, 1970) [Z1215.E92334], which, together with the 1959 *Index* to the original, makes it possible to identify the more than 50,000 items printed in the United States through 1800. A revision of the entire work, the *National Index of American Imprints through 1800: The Short Title Evans*, was compiled by Clifford K. Shipton and James E. Mooney (Barre, Mass.: American Antiquarian Society, 1970) [Z1215.S495], in two volumes. It is serving as the bibliographical control for a project to place the entire contents of Evans on microform (see E–50).

It should be noted that the Wing *STC* (C–7), the *Eighteenth Century Short Title Catalogue* now in progress (C–12), and the *Nineteenth Century Short Title Catalogue* now in progress (C–14) incorporate titles published in America in the seventeenth, eighteenth and nineteenth centuries.

C–23 **Shaw, Ralph R., Richard H. Shoemaker, et al., comps.** *American Bibliography: A Preliminary Checklist for [1801 to 1819].* 22 vols. New York: Scarecrow Press, 1958–1966.   Z1215.S48

This is a closed retrospective national bibliography for the years 1801–1819, inclusive. The first nineteen volumes each contain entries for items published in one year arranged alphabetically by author. Their 51,960 serially numbered entries

provide a minimum of bibliographical information, along with the locations of titles using the NUC symbols. The quality of the entries is uneven because of the variety of secondary sources from which they were entirely drawn. Prefaces in volumes 1 and 6 explain the limitations and methodology of the work. Newspapers and periodicals are entered only once, while almanacs and similar annuals are listed for each year in which they appeared. Author-title indexes are located in each annual volume. Volume 20 contains an addendum of 1,768 items missed in the first nineteen, a list of sources used for all twenty volumes, and a list of *NUC* library symbols. There is a cumulative index of titles in volume 21 and a list of corrections and an author index in volume 22. The work was designed and executed to fill the gap between Evans's *American Bibliography* for 1638–1800 (C–22) and Roorbach's *Bibliotheca Americana* for 1820–1861 (C–24). There are some supplementary publications, for which see Tanselle (C–20), items A1.5 ff. The microfilming of all titles in Shaw and Shoemaker is under way (see E–50).

C–24 **Roorbach, Orville A.** *Bibliotheca Americana: Catalogue of American Publications, Including Reprints and Original Works, from 1820 to 1852, Inclusive.* New ed. New York: O. A. Roorbach, 1852. Supplement, October 1852 to May 1855 (1855). Addenda, May 1855 to March 1858 (1858). Vol. 4, March 1858 to January 1861 (1861).
Z1215.A3

A partly retrospective, partly current national bibliography, the 1861 edition of Roorbach contains over 24,000 titles of nineteenth-century American imprints to 1860. It updates the 1849 original edition and its 1850 supplement. Most entries in the new edition present authors, titles, number of volumes, size, binding, price, publisher, and date of publication. Biographical works are entered under the names of their subjects. There is also a list of periodicals published in the United States. The work is preceded by a list of publishers and their addresses. The three supplements report new publications as well as titles that have changed either publishers or price. For the period 1820–1833, Roorbach has been replaced by the *American Imprints* project of Shoemaker et al. (C–25).

C–25 **Shoemaker, Richard H.** *Checklist of American Imprints for 1820 [through 1829].* 10 vols. New York: Scarecrow Press, 1964–1971. *Title Index.* Compiled by M. Frances Cooper. Metuchen, N.J.: Scarecrow Press, 1972. *Author Index, Corrections and Sources.* Compiled by M. Frances Cooper. Metuchen, N.J.: Scarecrow Press, 1973. Z1215.S5

A continuation of Shaw and Shoemaker (C–23), containing 41,633 serially numbered entries disposed over ten annual volumes. In content and arrangement it is comparable to the Shaw and Shoemaker series except for the exclusion of periodicals. Shoemaker's *Checklist* is, in turn, being continued for the 1830s. To date, the following volumes have been published: for 1830, by Gayle Cooper (Metuchen, N.J.: Scarecrow, 1972) [Z1215.C66], with items 1–5,609; for 1831, by Scott Bruntjen and Carol Rinder Knecht Bruntjen (Metuchen, N.J.: Scarecrow, 1975) [Z1215.C44], with items 5,610–10,775; for 1832, by the Bruntjens (Metuchen, N.J.: Scarecrow, 1977), with items 10,776–17,207; for 1833, also by the Bruntjens (Metuchen, N.J.: Scarecrow, 1979), with items 17,208–22,795; and for 1834 (Metuchen, N.J.: Scarecrow, 1982), with items 22,796–29,893. It is expected that further volumes will appear biennially. This work, like the previous series by Shaw and Shoemaker, is based on the fifteen million slips of the "American Imprints Inventory" sponsored by the WPA during the Depression. As they are published, these volumes replace the parallel portions of Roorbach (C–24).

C–26 Kelly, James. *American Catalogue of Books (Original and Reprints) Published in the United States from January 1861 to January 1866 [vol. 2, 1866–1870 inclusive] with Date of Publication, Size, Price, and Publisher's Name.* 2 vols. New York: J. Wiley and Son, 1866–1871. Reprint (2 vols. in 1). Metuchen, N.J.: Scarecrow Press, 1967.　Z1215.A4

The successor to Roorbach (C–24), this work provides United States national bibliography for 1861–1870. The first volume carries a supplement on the Civil War; both volumes have an appendix containing "Names of Learned Societies and Other Literary Associations, with a List of Their Publications, 1861–66 [1866–70]." Kelly is supplemented by several trade publications enumerated in Tanselle (C–20), A 1.66 ff.

C–27 *Publishers' Weekly: The Book Industry Journal.* New York: F. Leypoldt [later, Office of Publishers' Weekly; then R. R. Bowker], 1872–.　Z1219.P98

This journal contains a weekly listing of books, pamphlets, maps, and atlases just published or announced for publication by the American book trade. Since 1974 the *Weekly Record* has been separately bound. The quantity and quality of information included has varied over the years. Since 1960 the weekly lists have been gathered in a monthly Dewey decimal classification of the cumulated entries under the title *American Book Publishing Record[ABPR]* [Z1219.A515]. Annual indexes were published 1962–1964. In 1966 appeared the first of the ongoing series *BPR Annual Cumulative*, gathering entries for the year 1965 [Z1201.A52]. And in 1968 the first in the ongoing quinquennial series, *BPR Cumulative 1960/64*, was published [Z1201.A52]. The monthly, annual, and quinquennial series exclude government publications and most serials, as well as dissertations and the publications of some small presses and the smaller university presses. Because of their author and title indexes and subject classification, however, they remain of value as the standard current Dewey decimal classification of American publishing. In 1978 Bowker published the *American Book Publishing Record Cumulative, 1950–1977: An American National Bibliography* in fifteen volumes [Z1215.B67 1978], which includes more than 920,000 author and title entries. In 1980 appeared *American Book Publishing Record Cumulative, 1876–1949: An American National Bibliography* in fifteen volumes [Z12.A55]. Both fifteen-volume sets are arranged with the first ten volumes in Dewey decimal classification order, volume 11 treating fiction and juvenile fiction, volume 12 non-Dewey-decimal-classified titles, and volumes 13 through 15 presenting indexes of authors, titles, and subjects respectively.

Students interested in works announced for publication will also want to consult the author and title listings in *Forthcoming Books* (1966–) [Z1219] and entries in *Subject Guide to Forthcoming Books* (1967–), both of which are published bimonthly.

C–28 *American Catalogue of Books . . . Books in Print and For Sale (Including Reprints and Importations) [1876–1910].* 8 vols. in 13. New York: Publishers' Weekly, 1880–1911. Reprint. New York: Peter Smith, 1941.　Z1215.A52

The two base volumes of this current national bibliography, which extends the record of United States publications from Kelly's *American Catalogue of Books* (C–26), present an author-title and a subject index to books in print as of 1 July 1876. Subsequent pairs of volumes cover authors-titles and subjects for the periods 1876–1884, 1884–1890, 1890–1895, and 1895–1900. From 1900 on, single volumes combining author-title and subject indexes in one alphabet cover publications for the periods 1900–1905, 1905–1907, and 1908–1910. Entries are based on information reported by publishers in the *Annual American Catalogue*, 22 vols. (1887–1911)

[Z1215.A6] and give date, size, and price in addition to author, title, and publisher.

C–29 *Publishers' Trade List Annual [PTLA].* New York: Office of the *Publishers' Weekly* (later R. R. Bowker Co.), 1873–.　Z1215.P97

This annual collects and indexes the current sales catalogs of the American book trade. A supplement enumerates the offerings of small and special publishers with lists of only a few pages' length. Coverage and arrangement have varied over the years. Currently the multivolume work provides an index to publishers in the main body and supplement. Also provided is a subject index to the publishers, citing them under the subject headings they chose to describe their offerings. These indexes are followed by the supplement mentioned above and then by the uniformly sized catalogs of each publishing house.

The *PTLA* is indexed in *Books in Print [BIP]* (New York: Bowker, 1948–) [Z1215.P972] by authors and titles; in *Subject Guide to Books in Print* (New York: Bowker, 1957–) [Z1215.P973]—see A–39; and in *Paperbound Books in Print* (New York: Bowker, 1955–) [Z1033.P3 P32] by authors, titles, and subjects. The base volumes of these indexes are published annually in November; supplements with additions, deletions, and corrections appear in May and in September.

C–30 *Cumulative Book Index [CBI]: A World List of Books in the English Language.* New York: H. W. Wilson, 1898–.　Z1219.M78

This is a current, international author-title- subject dictionary catalog of English-language books published. It appears monthly (except August) with semiannual (July and December), annual, and multiannual cumulations. Excluded are government publications, pamphlets, maps, music, and most ephemera. The author entries contain name, complete titles, series, edition, pagination, price, date, and publisher. Changes in the data of previously listed books are recorded as well. The *CBI* is particularly prized as a tool for bibliographic verification because of its high degree of accuracy. Entries after January 1982 are searchable through WILSONLINE (see Z–78).

The *Cumulative Book Index* serves as a current standard "national" bibliography. Its multiannual cumulations began in 1928 as permanent supplements to the four editions of Wilson's earlier *United States Catalog: Books in Print* [1898, 1903, 1912, 1928], published in Minneapolis and later New York [Z1215.U6]. The *U.S. Catalog* also contained author, title, and subject lists of books in print. Cumulations have been published for 1928–1932, 1933–1937, 1938–1942, 1943–1948, 1949–1952, 1953–1956 and biennially from 1957–1958 until 1967–1968. Thereafter only annual cumulations are available.

For current coverage of international English-language titles, see also *International Books in Print: English-Language Titles Published Outside the United States and the United Kingdom* [IBIP], published by K. G. Saur, Inc. The volumes for 1986 are published in two parts. *Part One: Author-Title List* in two volumes enumerates over 156,000 titles of in print books, pamphlets, and microforms. Entries include author or editor, date of publication, pagination, binding, price, ISBN, and publisher. *Part Two: Subject Guide* in two volumes arranges the title list in a total of 116 subject areas.

IV.   FRENCH NATIONAL BIBLIOGRAPHY

C–50   **Brunet, Jacques-Charles.** *Manuel du librairie et de l'amateur de livres.* 5th ed. 6 vols. Paris: Didot, 1860–1865. Supplement by P. Deschamps and G. Brunet. 2 vols. Paris: Didot, 1878–1880.   Z1011.B9 M5

Originally published in 1810, this is a selective, universal bibliography of some 47,500 rare, valuable, and unique books chosen by Brunet from those published in "the ancient and modern Romance languages" (i.e., Latin and French) from the beginning of printing through roughly 1825. Entries are alphabetical by author through volumes 1 to 5 and provide a range of information comparable to that given by Lowndes (C–3), including copious bibliographical notes for rare books, abundant illustrations, records of auction prices, current values, and the like. Supplementary volumes 7 and 8 supply about 10,000 additional entries for titles of the years 1860–1875 or earlier which were either unknown to Brunet or previously rejected by him. Volume 6 contains a "Table méthodique en forme du catalog raisonné," a classified subject index to the manual, with detailed instructions on its use; volume 8 provides a similar index to the *Supplement*. The indexes are broken into the general categories of Theology, Jurisprudence, Science and Arts, Belles-Lettres, and History (including literary history and bibliography). Books not rare or precious but relevant to a subject area are added here, though they are excluded from the first part of the work. See Donald B. McKeon's *Classification System of Jacques-Charles Brunet* (Baton Rouge: Louisiana State University Press, 1976) [Z696.A4 B78213 1976] for a commentary on and translation of Brunet's important introduction to the "Table méthodique."

Additional features in volume 1 include an alphabetical list of printers, publishers, and booksellers and a list of book catalogs used in the compilation of the *Manuel*. Separate sections listing encyclopedias, dictionaries, and periodical publications appear in volume 6. A supplementary *Dictionnaire de géographie ancienne et moderne, à l'usage du librairie et de l'amateur de livres* by P. Deschamps, published in 1870, is treated as volume 9 of the *Manuel*. The geographical dictionary lists countries, provinces, and towns of Europe by their ancient and Renaissance names and has a French-Latin dictionary of place-names for bibliophiles. There is also a bibliography of works concerned with the history of printing in Europe through the end of the eighteenth century. Brunet should be used in conjunction with Grässe (C–51) and Lowndes (C–3).

C–51   **Grässe, Johann Georg Theodor.** *Trésor de livres rares et précieux; ou, Nouveau dictionnaire bibliographique.* 6 vols. Dresden, 1859–1869. *Supplement* in 1 vol. Reprint. Paris, 1900; Berlin, 1922. *Second supplement.* Edited by G. G. Gorlich. Milan, 1950.   Z1011.G74

Based on the work of Brunet (C–50), which it is meant to supplement and complement, Grässe's work is also a selective, universal bibliography of rare, valuable, and unique books and includes many works valuable to scholarship without being of much economic value. Though he covers the same ground as Brunet, Grässe is less restrictive about the rarity of items included and places much more emphasis on German works; the two are best used together. Grässe has altogether more than 100,000 entries; the same type of bibliographical description for entries is found as in Brunet and Lowndes (C–3). Each volume includes a set of addenda and corrigenda; the supplements contain both new items and works cited in the original, with corrections.

C–52   **Quérard, Joseph M.** *La France littéraire; ou, Dictionnaire bibliographique des savants, historiens et gens de lettres de la France, ainsi que des littérateurs étrangers qui ont écrit en français, plus particuliérement pendant des XVIIIᵉ et XIXᵉ siècles. Ouvrage dans lequel on a inseré, afin de former une bibliographie nationale complete, l'indication 1) des réimpressions des ouvrages français de tous les âges; 2) des diverses traductions en notre langage de tous les auteurs étrangers, anciens et modernes; 3) celle des réimpressions, faites en France des ouvrages originaux de ces mêmes auteurs étrangers, pendant cette époque.* 12 vols. Paris: Didot, 1827–1864. Reprint. Paris: Maisonneuve et Larose, 1964.   Z2161.Q4

Both a dictionary of French authors and a "national" bibliography, Quérard includes all French works published anywhere from 1700 until the mid-nineteenth century; all reprints of French books from any period; translations into French from any ancient or modern language; and all foreign works reprinted in France. The work is arranged as an author list. Each author is given a short biography, followed by an alphabetical list of his works with their principal editions. Anonymous works, collections, and periodicals are found alphabetically by title in volumes 7 and 8. The first volume also includes a list of the secondary sources from which Quérard has drawn his information. The last two volumes have addenda and corrigenda to the first ten, with a list of anonymous and pseudonymous authors.

The work is supplemented by Quérard's later production, *La littérature française contemporaine XIX siècle: Dictionnaire bibliographique . . . accompagné de biographiques littéraires et de notes historiques et littéraires,* 6 vols. (Paris: Daguin, 1842–1857) [Z2161.Q41], which covers additional French authors of the first half of the nineteenth century in a format similar to that of *La France littéraire*. Both of Quérard's works are supplemented by Vicaire (C–53).

For pre-eighteenth-century French national bibliography, scholars must consult a combination of tools. Brunet (C–50) and Grässe (C–51) are helpful, as are Georgi (C–60) and Gustave Brunet's *La France littéraire au 15ᵉ siècle; ou, Catalogue raisonné des ouvrages en tout genre imprimés en langue française jusqu'à l'an 1500* (Paris: A. Franck, 1865) [Z240.B89], along with the appropriate *British Museum Short Title National Catalogue* (see B–40) and general bibliographies of incunabula. Avenir Tchemerzine's descriptive *Bibliographie d'éditions originales et rares d'auteurs français des XVᵉ, XVIᵉ, XVIIᵉ et XVIIIᵉ siècle,* 10 vols. (Paris: Pieé, 1927–1934) [Z2174.F5 T2], can also be of use. For the sixteenth century there is a new multivolume descriptive bibliography now in course of publication, Louis Desgraves's *Répertoire bibliographique des livres imprimés en France au seizième siècle* (Baden-Baden: Koerner, 1968–) [Z2162 .D47]. And for the seventeenth century one may consult the *Short Title Catalogue of French Books, 1601–1700, in the Library of the British Museum* (Folkestone: Dawsons, 1973) [Z2162.B87 1973], along with the new multivolume descriptive bibliography by Louis Desgraves, *Répertoire bibliographique des livres imprimés en France au XVIIᵉ siècle* (Baden-Baden: Koerner, 1978–) [Z2162.D47].

C–53   **Vicaire, Georges.** *Manuel de l'amateur de livres du XIXᵉ siècle, 1801–1893.* Éditions originales.—Ouvrages et périodiques illustrés—Romantiques.—Réimpressions critiques de textes anciens ou classiques.—Bibliothèques et collections diverses.—Publications des sociétés de bibliophiles de Paris et des départements.—Curiosités bibliographiques, etc., etc. 8 vols. Paris: A. Rouguette, 1894–1920.
                                                              Z2161.V62

A national bibliography, modeled on Brunet (C–50), which is rather selective but covers original editions, reprints, periodical publications, and collections published in France during the nineteenth century. Entries give full titles and bibliographical notes, auction prices, and information similar to that found in Brunet. Vicaire should be used in conjunction with Quérard (C–52).

C–54 *Bibliographie de la France; ou, Journal général de l'imprimerie et de la librairie [BibFr].* Vol. 1. Paris: Cercle de la librairie, Syndicat des industries du livre, 1811–.

Z2165.B58

The first part of this weekly publication, the standard national bibliography of France, is a record of publications received as copyright deposit in the Bibliothèque nationale. To it are attached a second and third part, both compiled by the French book trade, by whose central organization the whole work was published until 1972. Since then, it has been published jointly by the Cercle de la librairie and the Bibliothèque nationale.

Part 1, "Bibliographie officielle," is arranged by broad subject fields according to the Universal decimal classification. Entries include full bibliographical information and are serially numbered. The author-title index is keyed to the numeration. Part 1 is cumulated quarterly and annually. It is also regularly supplemented by various lists of special classes of publications: Suppl. A—a monthly, Universal decimal classification of new periodicals, with title index, which is cumulated annually; Suppl. B—an annual (since 1946) list of engravings, stamps, and photographs arranged by formal groups with an author index; Suppl. C—an irregularly issued list (since 1946) of music scores; Suppl. D—published from 1947 until 1970 and now discontinued, a list of theses, classified by disciplines and by universities; Suppl. E—an irregularly issued list (since 1948) of atlases, maps, and plans, arranged alphabetically by place; Suppl. F—issued irregularly since 1950, a list of official publications, arranged by offices, with an annual cumulative index of authors, catchwords, corporate bodies, and periodical titles; and Suppl. G—an annual list (since 1958) of sales catalogs.

Part 2, "Chronique," is a compilation of trade news, with occasional special features that may be of bibliographical interest. Part 3, "Annonces," contains book-trade advertisements with indexes of new publications. It is issued weekly and cumulated monthly, quarterly (April and October), semiannually (July), and yearly (December). The weekly issue, *Les livres de la semaine*, is arranged by subject classes, then alphabetically by author and title. *Les livres du mois* is also arranged by subject classes. In contrast, *Les livres du trimestre* and *Les livres du semestre* (now discontinued) were arranged as author and title indexes. *Les livres de l'année* [Z2161.L695] cumulates all of these lists, adding further items to them, in three separate indexes by author, title, and subject classes. The first part, the subject classification, contains main entries. This is followed by an index of titles, an index of authors, one of illustrators, and one of publishers, booksellers, and printers. Current prices are given, thus making this also a current books-in-print. In 1971 the title of the work was changed to *Les livres de l'année—Biblio* [Z2161.L6952] following the merger of the cumulations of part 3 of the *Bibliographie de la France* with the separate trade publication *Biblio: Catalogue des ouvrages parus en langue française dans le monde entier* (C–56). Now the work is arranged as a dictionary catalog of authors, first main word in title, and subjects. Entries include author, title, number of edition, editor, collation, series title, notes, ISBN, and price. There are abundant cross-references. The annual volumes are finally gathered in multiannual cumulations that serve as continuing supplements to *La librairie française: Catalog général des ouvrages en vente* (see C–55). To date there is a two-volume cumulation for 1933–1945 and one in three volumes for 1946–1955.

C–55 **Lorenz, Otto, [et al.].** *Catalogue général de la librairie française [1840–1925].* 34 vols. Paris: Lorenz [publisher varies], 1867–1945. Z2165.C35

This closed, retrospective national bibliography was designed to follow the work of Quérard (C–52). The first eleven volumes were compiled and published by Lorenz, by whose name the work is generally known. Volumes 12 through 28, part 2 (1886–1918) were compiled by D. Jordell; volume 28, part 3 through volume 32 by Henri Stein; and volumes 33 and 34 by the Service bibliographique Hachette. Coverage includes books and pamphlets, some theses and annuals, but excludes periodicals. Each volume is arranged in a single alphabet of authors, titles, and subjects, with many cross-references. Author and title entries list full title, publisher, date, edition, and pagination and sometimes have brief notes. Subject entries give author, title, publisher, and date. There are brief biographical notes on authors.

C–56 *Biblio: Catalog des ouvrages parus en langue française dans le monde entier [covering 1933–1970].* 39 vols. Paris: Service bibliographique [de la librairie] Hachette, 1935–1971. Z2165.B565

This is the annual cumulation of Hachette's *Biblio: Bibliographie, littérature,* 1–(October 1933–), which appeared in ten monthly or bimonthly (June-July, August-September) issues. Using the *Bibliographie de la France* (C–54) as a base, this current "national" bibliography adds notices of all French-language books published anywhere in the world, which makes it the French analogue to Wilson's *Cumulative Book Index* (C–30). Entries are arranged in a dictionary catalog of authors, titles, and keyword of subjects, with many cross-references. The main entry, by author, gives full title, publisher, date, size, price, pagination, and subject area. The annual volumes supply further additions to the cumulated monthly issues. In 1971 *Biblio* merged with *Les livres de l'année* to form *Les livres de l'année—Biblio* (see C–54).

C–57 *Catalogue de l'édition française [CEF]: Une liste exhaustive des ouvrages disponible publiés, en français, de par le monde.* Paris: VPC Livres, 1970–. Z2165.C3

The French equivalent of *Books in Print*, this annual presents author, title, and subject indexes to French books published anywhere which are currently available for purchase. The fifth edition of 1976 occupied six volumes. Entries present author, title, publisher, editor, pagination, year of publication, dimensions, name of the collection, and price. The subject index is arranged alphabetically under Universal decimal classification subject categories.

In 1972 a second French Books in Print, the *Répertoire des livres de langue française disponibles* (Paris: France-Expansion, 1972–) [Z2161.R43], began publication under the sponsorship of the Cercle de la librairie. The two series merged in 1977 and are currently published with the title *Les livres disponibles* [year]: *La liste exhaustive des ouvrages disponibles publiés en langue française dans le monde* (Paris: Cercle de la librairie, 1977–) [Z2161.L8]. The issue for 1978 is in three volumes and follows the structure of the CEF as described above.

V.   GERMAN NATIONAL BIBLIOGRAPHY

C–60   **Georgi, Gottlieb.** *Allgemeines europäisches Bücher-Lexicon . . . Vor dem Anfange des XVI seculi bis 1739* [i.e., **1757**]. 5 parts in 2 vols. Leipzig: Georgi, 1742–1753. Three supplements. Leipzig, 1750–1758. Reprint. Graz, 1966–1967.   Z1012.G35

The first four parts of this pioneering attempt at a "universal" European bibliography present works published in Latin and German before 1739; part 5 presents French works to 1739. The supplements cover Latin and German works of 1739–1747, 1747–1754, and 1753–1757. Entries are by author in alphabetical order. Six columns of material are given on each page: date, first name of author, last name, short title and description of the work, place of publication, and price. Though incomplete, this work is important for German national bibliography before 1700. It may be supplemented by Brunet (C–50) and, particularly, Grässe (C–51), as well as by the appropriate British Museum short-title national catalog (see B–40) and standard bibliographies of incunabula. Now in publication is the *Verzeichnis der im deutschen Sprachbereich erschienenen Drucke des XVI. Jahrhunderts: VD16* (Stuttgart: Hiersemann, 1983–) [Z1014.V47].

C–61   **Heinsius, Wilhelm.** *Allgemeines Bücher-Lexikon, oder, Vollständiges alphabetisches Verzeichniss aller von 1700 bis zu Ende [1892] erschienenen Bücher, welche in Deutschland und in den durch Sprache und Literatur damit verwandten Ländern gedruckt worden sind.* 19 vols. in 31. Leipzig: F. A. Brockhaus [publisher varies], 1812–1894.   Z2221.H47

This retrospective national bibliography by the bookseller Heinsius was initially based on the catalogs of the Frankfurt book fairs. Books, pamphlets, and periodicals are listed alphabetically by author or catchword title in multivolume cumulations. The base volumes 1–4 cover publications from 1700 through 1810. Subsequent volumes are often, though not always, quinquennial in coverage. Entries give author, title, pages, place of publication, publisher, date and price. For the period 1700–1827 there are appendixes listing novels and plays alphabetically by title; after 1868 there is an appendix listing maps and plans. Entries in Heinsius are included in the *Gesamtverzeichnis 1700–1910* (C–67).

C–62   **Kayser, Christian Gottlieb.** *Vollständiges Bücher-Lexikon, enthaltend alle von 1750 bis zu Ende des Jahres [1910] in Deutschland und in den angrenzenden Ländern gedruckten Bücher.* 36 vols. Leipzig: Tauchnitz [publisher varies], 1834–1911.   Z2221.K23

This retrospective and current national bibliography by the bookseller Kayser is basically an author list of books, pamphlets, and periodicals, comparable in structure to, and both complementing and supplementing, Heinsius (C–61). Entries give author, title, place of publication, publisher, date, number of volumes, pages, series name, and price. Some Austrian and Swiss publications are included. The first six volumes cover the period 1750–1832; thereafter volumes cover several years each. There are appendixes listing novels and dramas in the first series but not in later volumes. An appendix listing maps and plans appears from 1887 on. There are two subject indexes to entries in Kayser. The first, *Sachregister zu Kayser'schen Bücher-Lexikon* (Leipzig: Schumann, 1838) [Z2221.K23], covers the six volumes treating publications of 1750–1832. The second, *Sach und Schlagwortregister* (Leipzig: Tauchnitz, 1896–1912) [Z2221 .K23], indexes in five volumes entries for the period 1891–1910 (i.e., volumes 27–36), one index volume for ev-

ery two volumes of the main work. A further subject index by Karl Georg and Leopold Ost, *Schlagwort-Katalog: Verzeichnis der im deutschen Buchhandel erschienenen Bücher und Landkarten in sachlicher Anordnung*, 7 vols. in 12 (Hannover and then Leipzig: [publisher varies], 1889–1913) [Z2221.G34], includes titles in Heinsius (C–61), Kayser, and Hinrichs (C–63) under subject and form headings. Entries in Kayser are included in the *Gesamtverzeichnis 1700–1910* (C–67).

C–63   **Hinrichs, J. C., et al.** *Katalog.* [title varies]. 13 vols. Leipzig: J. C. Hinrichs, 1857–1913.   Z2221.H658

A variety of different catalogs, supplementing and complementing those of Heinsius (C–61) and Kayser (C–62), appeared at various intervals, published by the Hinrichs bookselling firm. Of these, the *Fünfjahres-Katalog der im deutschen Buchhandel erschienenen Bücher, Zeitschriften, Landkarten*, etc. is the most useful series of cumulations, covering titles and subjects, 1851–1912. The quinquennial catalogs supplement the Hinrichs series, *Halbjahresverzeichnis der Neuerscheinungen des deutschen Buchhandels* (Leipzig: Hinrichs, 1798–1852), and cumulate the semiannual catalogs issued after 1852 (see C–64). A three-volume *Repertorium über die nach den halbjährlichen Verzeichnissen 1871–1875* [i.e., 1885] *erschienenen Bücher, Landkarten*, etc. . . . *mit einem Sachregister* (Leipzig: Hinrichs, 1877–1878) serves as a subject index for publications of the period 1871–1885. Gustav Thelert published additions and corrections to all three booksellers' catalog series in his *Supplement zu Heinsius', Hinrichs' und Kaysers Bücher-Lexikon: Verzeichnis einer Anzahl Schriften, welche seit der Mitte des neunzehnten Jahrhunderts in Deutschland erschienen, in den genannten Katalogen aber garnicht oder fehlerhaft aufgeführt sind; mit bibliographischen Bemerkungen* (Grossenhain: Baumert, 1893) [Z2221.T38], which should be consulted when using any of the three series. Entries in Hinrichs are included in the *Gesamtverzeichnis 1700–1910* (C–67).

C–64   *Deutsche Nationalbibliographie [since 1960:] und Bibliographie des im Ausland erschienenen deutschsprachigen Schrifttums.* Leipzig: Deutsche Bücherei und Börsenverein der deutschen Buchhändler, 1931–.   Z2221.H67

This work is the successor to *Wöchentliches Verzeichnis der erschienenen und der vorbereiteten Neuigkeiten des deutschen Buchhandels* (Leipzig: Hinrichs, 1843–1930) [Z2225 .W84], compiled first by the publishing house of Hinrichs, then, from 1916, by the Society of Bookdealers, and from 1921 by the Deutsche Bücherei. Since 1960 its scope has been comparable for German-language publications to that of the *CBI* for English publications. Title and format have varied over the years. From 1931 on, two series have been published: *Reihe A*, a weekly list of "Neuerscheinungen des Buchhandels," including books, pamphlets, maps and atlases, new and ceased periodicals, and (in an appendix) sound recordings available from the book trade; and *Reihe B*, a semimonthly list of "Neuerscheinungen ausserhalb des Buchhandels," including theses (in every other issue until 1968), papers, institutional and governmental pamphlets and other documents, and ephemera, all published outside the book trade. Since 1969 a third series, *Reihe C*, provides a monthly list of "Dissertationen und Habilitationsschriften." The entries in all three series are arranged by broad subject areas and then alphabetically by author. Area 7 is the subject category for language and literature. An author-title-keyword index is published with every issue of each series, and the indexes of series A and B are cumulated quarterly. The entries of *Reihe A* and the most important ones from *Reihe B* (except dissertations, see E–18) are cumulated annually into the *Jahresverzeichnis der deutschen Schrifttums* [after coverage of 1967 publications: *Jahresverzeichnis der*

Verlagsschriften und einer Auswahl der ausserhalb des Buchhandels erschienenen Veröffentlichungen der DDR, der BRD, und Westberlins sowie der deutschsprachigen Werke anderer Länder], the first volume of which covered publications of 1945 (Leipzig: Verlag des Börsenvereins der deutschen Buchhändler, 1946–) [Z2221.J26]. This annual cumulation succeeds the pre–1945 semiannual cumulations with the title *Halbjahresverzeichnis der Neuerscheinungen des deutschen Buchhandels* (Leipzig: Hinrichs, 1798–1944) [Z2221.H66], published until 1916 by Hinrichs (C–63), then by the Börsenverein, and since 1931 by the Deutsche Bücherei. Two parts of this annual (or semiannual) cumulation are published: an author and keyword-in-title list and one by subject and keyword (in separate volumes since 1961).

In addition to the annual (or semiannual) cumulations, multiannual cumulations are available. These begin with the volumes of *Hinrichs' Katalog* (C–63) which cover the years 1875–1913. That series is followed by the *Deutsches Bücherverzeichnis: Eine Zusammenstellung der im deutschen Buchhandel erschienenen Bücher, Zeitschriften und Landkarten*, prepared by the Börsenverein, and covering in twenty-two volumes publications from 1911 through 1940 (Leipzig: Börsenverein, 1916–1943) [Z2221.K25]. Two volumes of *Ergänzung* (Leipzig: Deutsche Bücherei, 1949) [Z2221.H6712] supplement the *Deutsches Bücherverzeichnis* by listing publications that for political reasons were originally excluded from the official bibliographies. Multiannual cumulations were resumed in 1952 with volumes 22–28 listing some 310,000 titles published between 1941 and 1950, including those in the two volumes of *Ergänzung* under the title *Deutsches Bücherverzeichnis: Verzeichnis der in Deutschland, in Österreich, in der Schweiz und in übrigen Ausland erschienenen deutschsprachigen Verlagsschriften nebst den wichtigeren ausserhalb des Buchhandels erschienenen Veröffentlichungen und des innerhalb Deutschlands verlegten fremdsprachigen Schrifttums* (Leipzig: VEB Verlag für Buch- und Bibliothekswesen, 1952–) [Z2221.K25]. Subsequent volumes are quinquennial cumulations; all multiannual cumulations retain the two-part structure of author-title and subject-keyword lists and include books, periodicals, and maps. Entries from all of these cumulations are included in the *Gesamtverzeichnis 1911–1965* (C–68).

Also published by the Deutsche Bücherei in Leipzig is the *Bibliographie fremdsprachiger Germanica*, originally titled *Bibliographie fremdsprachiger Werke über Deutschland und deutsche Persönlichkeiten* (1963–) [Z2225.S586], a quarterly listing cumulated annually; the *Bibliographie der Übersetzungen deutschsprachiger Werke* (1954–) [Z2234.T7 B5], arranged by languages and published quarterly with an annual cumulation; and *Das gesprochene Wort. Jahresverzeichnis der literarischen Schallplatten* (1960–) [Z2221.D481], arranged by subject groups with an author and keyword index. A monthly classified *Bibliographie der Bibliographien* (1966–) [Z2221.A1 B5], the monthly *Deutsche Musikbibliographie* (1829–) [ML113.H82], the *Jahresverzeichnis der Musikalien und Musikschriften* (1943–) [ML113.H715], and the *Bibliographie der Kunstblätter* (1967–) [Z5961.G4 B52] complete the present-day contribution of the Deutsche Bücherei to current complete German national bibliography. Since 1945 many of these bibliographical works have had counterparts published under the auspices of the Deutsche Bibliothek in Frankfurt (see C–65).

ed monthly and quarterly (with entries added quarterly for titles in the Austrian and Swiss national bibliographies). *Reihe B*, published since 1965, is a monthly (since 1966, a semimonthly) list of "Erscheinungen ausserhalb des Verlagsbuchhandels" recording such publications as government reports, research reports, industrial publications and other nonbook trade materials but excluding theses and dissertations and all Austrian and Swiss publications. To it are appended indexes of authors and subjects which are cumulated annually. *Reihe C*, published since 1965, is a quarterly list of maps, alphabetically arranged by title, with indexes of authors, subjects, publishers, and publishing organizations, which are cumulated annually. Dissertations have been included since 1972 in a separate *Reihe H, Deutsche Bibliographie: Hochschulschriften-Verzeichnis*, a monthly list with author, title, and subject indexes that are cumulated annually. Since 1974 a quarterly *Schallplatten-Verzeichnis* cumulated annually has also been published.

The weekly and monthly lists are cumulated, more or less, into the *Deutsche Bibliographie: Halbjahres-Verzeichnis* (Frankfurt am Main: Buchhändler-Vereinigung, 1951–) [Z2221.F73]. Cumulation of the weekly lists was complete through 1964; since then, all of *Reihe A*, selections from *Reihe B*, and Austrian and Swiss publications received by the Deutsche Bibliothek have been included. Author-title and keyword-subject indexes are provided in separate volumes. Entries from these cumulations are included in the *Gesamtverzeichnis 1911–1965* (C–68).

The semiannual cumulations are further cumulated in a quinquennial series with the title *Deutsche Bibliographie: Fünfjahres-Verzeichnis: Bücher und Karten: Bibliographie aller in Deutschland erschienenen Veröffentlichungen und der in Österreich und der Schweiz im Buchhandel erschienenen deutschsprachigen Publikationen sowie der deutschsprachigen Veröffentlichungen anderer Länder* (Frankfurt am Main: Buchhändler-Vereinigung, 1953–) [Z2221.D47]. Cumulated are all materials published in Germany since 1945 and all German-language materials published by the book trade outside of Germany since that date, with the exclusion of theses and dissertations, music and books on music, and periodicals. Separate volumes provide author-title and subject-keyword indexes. An irregularly published multiannual *Deutsche Bibliographie: Zeitschriften-Verzeichnis* (Frankfurt am Main: Buchhändler-Vereinigung, 1954–) [Z6956.G3 F67] cumulates periodical publications from 1945 on. And a biennial *Deutsche Bibliographie: Verzeichnis amtlicher Drucksachen* (Frankfurt am Main: Buchhändler-Vereinigung, 1963–) [Z2229.D48] cumulates official publications from 1957/58 on.

C–66 *Verzeichnis lieferbarer Bücher / German Books in Print.* Frankfurt am Main: Verlag der Buchhändler-Vereinigung, 1971–.   Z2221.V47

This multivolume dictionary catalog of German books published in Germany, Austria, and Switzerland which are in print has author, title and keyword entries. There are abundant cross-references. A separate ISBN register is published, and a midyear supplementary volume is issued. A special feature is the enumeration under series names of all titles in that series.

C–65 *Deutsche Bibliographie: Wöchentliches Verzeichnis Amtsblatt der Deutschen Bibliothek [since 1969:].* Frankfurt am Main: Buchhändler-Vereinigung, 1947–.   Z2221.F74

Titled until 1952 *Bibliographie der Deutschen Bibliothek*, this work presents a weekly list of all books, periodicals (new and ceased), and maps published in German or Germany, as received by the Deutsche Bibliothek. There have been several changes in structure and frequency. Currently, the work appears in three sections. *Reihe A* is a weekly list of "Erscheinungen des Verlagsbuchhandels," disposed into twenty-six subject areas with entries arranged alphabetically by author or title and an author-title-keyword index that is cumulat-

C–67 Geils, Peter, and Willi Gorzny, eds. *Gesamtverzeichnis des deutschsprachigen Schrifttums (GV): 1700–1910.* 160 vols. planned. Munich: K. G. Saur Verlag, 1979–1987.   Z2221.G469

The purpose of this work is to cumulate in one alphabet through photolithographic methods the unchanged entries of some 183 sources of German national bibliography for the period 1700–1910. Sources include national bibliographies like Heinsius (C–61), Kayser (C–62), and Hinrichs (C–63), as well as Austrian and Swiss publications and subject bibliographies of various kinds. The introductory pages of the first volume include enumerations of the source volumes used both alphabetically by title and classified into forty-four categories of bibliographical type and subject area. Though entries are taken over from these sources without change and thus vary widely in their extent, accuracy, and principles of composition, the *Gesamtverzeichnis* (if used with care) provides convenient access to an extraordinarily diverse and extensive range of bibliographical tools. Users must study the introductory pages of volume 1, however, to learn precise rules for use. Among likely sources of confusion for the uninstructed user are the treatment of umlauts as if they were the unumlauted letters and the treatment of works by authors of the same name as if they were all by one author. A special microfiche edition of the *GV* is also available.

C–68 **Oberschelp, Reinhard, ed.** *Gesamtverzeichnis des deutschsprachigen Schrifttums (GV): 1911–1965.* 150 vols. Munich: [Saur] Verlag Dokumentation, 1976–1981.
Z2221.G47

The purpose of this work is to cumulate in one alphabet through photolithographic methods the unchanged entries of the standard German national bibliographies, including the *Deutsches Bücherverzeichnis* (C–64), the *Deutsche Bibliographie* (C–65), the *Deutsche Nationalbibliographie* (C–64), the Swiss and Austrian national bibliographies, the *Jahresverzeichnis* (E–18), and seven other sources of current national bibliography, 1911–1965. Though entries are taken over from their sources without change and thus vary in terms of the cataloguing principles according to which they are prepared, the volumes of the *Gesamtverzeichnis* provide a convenient means of checking through a multiplicity of sources all at once. Some 2,500,000 separate entries are to be included in the complete work. The introductory pages of the first volume provide an enumeration of the source works used in the compilation, an account of the technical process used to duplicate and interfile them, and an account of the various cataloging principles exhibited in the source materials and their implications for the correct use of the work. A special microfiche edition is also available. For a similar cumulation of German national bibliography, 1700–1910, see the *Gesamtverzeichnis des deutschsprachigen Schrifttums (GV): 1700–1910* (C–67).

VI. ITALIAN NATIONAL BIBLIOGRAPHY

C–71 **Pagliani, Atillio.** *Catalogo generale della libreria italiana dall'anno 1847 a tutto il 1899.* 6 vols. Milan: Associazione tipografico-libraria italiana, 1901–1922. 4 supplements in 11 vols. Milan, 1912–1958.
Z2341.A85

This standard retrospective bibliography of Italian-language publications (based on major library catalogs, catalogs of book dealers, and some 200 Italian bibliographies) originally covered the years 1847–1899. It is organized as both an author catalog (giving author, title, place, publisher, date, pagination, size, and original price) and a subject index. In the original series, three volumes are an author catalog and three provide a subject index. The first and second supplements have a combined subject index in four volumes covering 1900–1920. There is no subject index for the third and fourth supplements, which give author catalogs for 1921–1930 and 1931–1940 respectively. Maps and privately printed publications are included, as are dissertations. Periodicals are excluded.

For records of earlier publications see the appropriate national *Short-Title Catalogue* of British Museum holdings (see

B–40); the *Short-Title Catalogue of Books Printed in Italy and of Books in Italian Printed Abroad, 1501–1600, Held in Selected North American Libraries,* 3 vols. (Boston: G. K. Hall, 1970) [Z2342.S56]; and the retrospective bibliography now being published by Suzanne Michel and Paul-Henri Michel, *Répertoire des ouvrages imprimés en langue italienne au XVIIe siècle,* vol. 1– (Florence: Olschki, 1970–) [Z2342.M52].

C–72 *Catalogo cumulative 1886–1957 del Bollettino delle pubblicazioni italiane ricevute per diritto di stampa dalla Biblioteca nazionale centrale di Firenze [CUBI].* 41 vols. Nendeln, Liechtenstein: Kraus Reprint, 1968–1969.
Z2345.F65

A computer-generated cumulation of the nearly 640,000 entries from the *Bollettino delle pubblicazioni italiane ricevute per diritto di stampa* (Florence: Biblioteca nazionale centrale, 1866–1957) [Z2345.F63], a monthly classified list of Italian publications deposited for copyright, seventy-two volumes of which were published with annual indexes before it was discontinued, or rather continued by the *Bibliografia nazionale italiana* (C–73). The *Bollettino* included books, maps, official publications, academic publications, publications of learned societies, and music and music literature. Excluded were periodicals after the first number, and dissertations. *CUBI* is a dictionary author-title listing, volumes 40–41 of which provide a supplementary index of secondary authors (collaborators, commentators, and translators) cued both to the main entries in *CUBI* and to the original entries in the *Bollettino*. Complications resulting from the machine filing of entries make it necessary to read the prefatory materials in volume 1 before attempting an exhaustive search.

C–73 *Bibliografia nazionale italiana [BNIt]: Nuova serie del Bollettino delle pubblicazioni italiane ricevute per diritto di stampa.* Florence: Biblioteca nazionale centrale di Firenze, 1958–.
Z2345.F63

The current national bibliography of Italian publications, this is essentially a continuation of the *Bollettino delle pubblicazioni italiane* (C–72), based (as it was) on copyright deposit in the national library. It is issued monthly in a Dewey-decimal-classified order, with an author-title index. Included are books, new serial titles, selected official publications, theses published in book form, maps, music, recordings, and other audiovisual materials. The indexes cumulate into annual volumes. Annually, the titles of the monthly bibliography are cumulated into the *Catalogo alfabetico annuale* [1958–] (Florence: Biblioteca nazionale centrale, 1961–) [Z2341.B52]. Originally published separately but since 1963 in one dictionary catalog, are listed authors and titles from the monthly issues. An alphabetical index of secondary authors and publishers and a keyword index are also included. A supplement published in 1971 provides additional entries for the period 1958–1969.

C–74 *Catalogo dei libri italiani in commercio:* [Autori, soggetti, titoli]. Milan: Associazione italiana editori, 1970–.
Z2341.A83a

An Italian books-in-print, this work presents separate volumes listing authors, titles, and subjects for works from Italian publishers. Entries include date, format, pagination, price, and publisher. In the first years of its publication this catalog appeared in a single volume of author and title listings.

SERIAL PUBLICATIONS

I. BIBLIOGRAPHICAL GUIDES AND INDEXES TO INDEXES

D–1 **Vesenyi, Paul E.** *Introduction to Periodical Bibliography.* Ann Arbor, Mich.: Pierian Press, 1974. Z6941.V47

This guide is divided into two parts. The first is a historical and analytical introduction to periodical bibliography with eight chapters concerning definitions (chaps. 1 and 2), history (chaps. 3–6), depositories (chap. 7), and standardization (chap. 8). The second part is a selective annotated alphabetical list of periodical bibliographies, including indexes, abstracting services, union lists, directories, and miscellaneous items. About 85 percent of the entries are concerned with tools useful for periodicals in the humanities and social sciences. Vesenyi refers users interested in science periodicals to the guides published by the National Federation of Science Abstracting and Indexing Services (see D–4) and the International Federation of Documentation (FID), since he includes only the predominant periodical bibliographies in the sciences.

Entries in part 2 give the type of aid an item provides, its publisher, its date of origin or publication, its frequency, the indexes it provides, and a description of principles of inclusion and arrangement of entries. The work concludes with an author-title-subject index to part 1 and a subject classification of the bibliographies cited in part 2. In spite of various inaccuracies this work is of value to users of periodical bibliographies, indexes, union lists, and related tools.

D–2 **Kujoth, Jean Spealman.** *Subject Guide to Periodical Indexes and Review Indexes.* Metuchen, N.J.: Scarecrow Press, 1969. Z6293.K84

This index to about 2,000 indexes is divided into three sections. The first enumerates indexes by rather broad academic subject classes (e.g., "Humanities," "Language," "Literature"), under which pertinent indexes are listed alphabetically. The second section enumerates the titles of indexes in alphabetical order with brief descriptions of each—how published, how arranged, and (through codes) the contents of the index. Indicated for each index are the following kinds of information: whether it includes periodical articles, material other than periodical articles, general or popular materials, reviews (with specifications of the types of works reviewed), abstracts, annotations, or digests of indexed items, or quoted excerpts. The final part presents tables that summarize contents characteristics of all the indexes so that one can see at a glance which ones have a particular type of entry (e.g., theater reviews). Though no evaluations are given and descriptive annotations are brief, this is a handy guide to periodical and review indexes which is more extensive than the more current and detailed but less inclusive subject guide of Harzfeld (D–3).

D–3 **Harzfeld, Lois A.** *Periodical Indexes in the Social Sciences and Humanities: A Subject Guide.* Metuchen, N.J.: Scarecrow Press, 1978. AI3.H37

This work, inspired by and to some extent a revision of Kujoth's *Subject Guide* (D–2), enumerates current serial publications that analyze the contents of periodicals in the social sciences and humanities. Each entry gives detailed annotation on the scope, arrangement, and special features of the work. Entries are arranged in forty-eight alphabetically ordered subject categories and within each category alphabetically by title. The humanities fields covered include African Studies, Archaeology, Architecture, Art, Asian Studies, Classical Studies, Education, Ethnic Studies, Film, Folklore, History, History of Science, Humanities, Jewish Studies, Journalism, Language/Linguistics, Latin American Studies, Literature, Children's Literature, Literature—Fiction/Poetry/Plays, Medieval Studies, Music, Near Eastern Studies, Philosophy, Popular Culture, Religion, Slavic and East European Studies, Speech, Theater Arts, Women's Studies. There are also chapters on General—U.S. and General—Foreign indexes and chapters on Indexes to Book Reviews and to Reviews of Musical Recordings and Other Media. An index of titles, authors and compilers, and publishing or sponsoring institutions concludes the volume.

Paul Vesenyi's *European Periodical Literature in the Social Sciences and the Humanities* (Metuchen, N.J.: Scarecrow, 1969) [Z6955.Z9 V45] supplements the English-language focus of Harzfeld.

D–4 **Ireland, Norma Olin.** *Index to Indexes: A Subject Bibliography of Published Indexes.* Boston: F. W. Faxon, 1942. Z6293.I7

A selection of some 1,000 separate indexes arranged under 280 different subjects, this volume includes special indexes, indexes to sets of books (e.g., encyclopedias), periodical indexes, cumulative indexes to individual periodicals, and government document indexes. Cited, too, are indexes of individual books that are uniquely valuable aids to research in a particular subject. In general, only indexes published in the United States are included. Entries are arranged by subject headings that should be inventively checked. An author-title index concludes the work.

Though largely superseded by other reference works, this small volume is still of use since none of the more current aids is quite like it in conception or scope. See also the same author's *Local Indexes in American Libraries: A Union List of Unpublished Indexes* (Boston: Faxon, 1947) [Z6293.A5], which is also arranged by subject.

D–5 Chicorel, Marietta, ed. *Chicorel Index to Abstracting and Indexing Services: Periodicals in Humanities and the Social Sciences.* 2d ed. Chicorel Index series, vols. 11 and 11A. New York: Chicorel Library Publishing Corp., 1978.

Z6293.C54 1978

The aim of this work, first published in 1974, is to identify all the indexing and abstracting services in which any given humanities or social-science periodical is analyzed. The second edition, a distinct improvement over the very inaccurate first edition, includes some 50,000 periodicals, serials, services, and yearbooks in the humanities and social sciences. Entries are arranged as an alphabetical list of periodicals according to the first significant word of the title; generic words such as "journal" or "bulletin" have been inverted, so that the *Journal of English and Germanic Philology* appears under "English." Under each journal are enumerated all the abstracting and indexing services that cover that periodical. If even one periodical in a given subject is known, use of this index will enable the researcher to locate the indexes that treat it, and, through them, the other periodicals publishing material in this field. The second volume concludes with a directory of indexing and abstracting services and a list of the generic terms that are inverted in title citations.

Other guides to abstracting services include the two-volume work published by the Fédération internationale de documentation (FID), *Abstracting Services* (The Hague: FID, 1969) [Z695.93.I58 1969], an alphabetical listing with indexes by subject and country. Volume 1 with about 1,300 entries covers science and technology, while volume 2 presents about 200 entries in the social sciences and humanities. In addition, *Ulrich's Directory* (D–100) makes reference to leading indexing and abstracting services covering a given current periodical in the entry for that periodical.

D–6 Haskell, Daniel C. *Checklist of Cumulative Indexes to Individual Periodicals in the New York Public Library.* New York: New York Public Library, 1942.   Z6293.N45

By virtue of the extent of this library's periodical holdings, this somewhat out-of-date checklist remains a valuable tool. The compiler's intention was to include every index covering three or more volumes of any periodical file held by the New York Public Library. Periodicals are listed alphabetically by their most recent title. If there is more than one cumulative index available, the most inclusive is listed first, with minor indexes given in smaller print below. Notes detail the previous history of the periodical and describe the coverage of the available indexes. The work concludes with a few pages of addenda. Haskell is particularly valuable for pre-twentieth-century periodicals not indexed in more general works such as Poole (D–10) or the *Wellesley Index* (D–12). For additional aid in locating indexes to individual periodicals see also the more recent *Guide to Special Issues and Indexes of Periodicals* by Charlotte M. Devers, 2d ed. (New York: Special Libraries Association, 1976) [Z6951.S755 1976].

D–7 Marconi, Joseph V. *Indexed Periodicals: A Guide to 170 Years of Coverage in 33 Indexing Services.* Ann Arbor, Mich.: Pierian Press, 1976.   Z6941.M27

An alphabetically arranged list of some 11,000 periodical titles. Marconi identifies for each title the leading and widely available American, British, and Canadian periodical indexes

treating it, along with the years of coverage, from 1802 until mid-1973. Entries begin with the title of the indexed periodical, its dates of publication, and other information about its publishing history. This is followed by a chronological list of the relevant indexes, the numbers of the volumes that covered the periodical, and the dates of coverage.

This work is updated by installments in *Serials Review* (see D–99). Compared to the *Chicorel Index* (D–5), Marconi is less comprehensive but provides more information. For locating major indexes treating a particular nineteenth- or early-twentieth-century periodical, this is the superior work.

II. GENERAL INDEXES: PERIODICALS

Note that any bibliography that analyzes the contents of periodicals treating a particular subject or containing materials of a certain form is an index to that set of periodicals. Thus the *MLA International Bibliography* (L–50) is a general index to journals concerned with the subjects of the modern languages and literatures; the *Play Index* (U–48) is a general index to periodicals containing plays.

D–10 Poole, William Frederick. *Poole's Index to Periodical Literature [1802–1881].* Rev. ed. 2 vols. Boston: Houghton Mifflin, 1882. *First [-Fifth] Supplement* [1882–1906]. Boston: Houghton Mifflin, 1888–1908. Reprint. New York and Gloucester, Mass.: Peter Smith, 1958.   AI3.P7

A subject and keyword index to approximately 590,000 articles in some 480 English and American periodicals of the nineteenth century, this extraordinary work treats of writers as subjects when their work is being reviewed but *does not otherwise index by author.* The preliminaries to volume 1 include a list of the fifty-one cooperating libraries; a list of periodical "abbreviations, titles, and imprints" giving the title, years published, and number of volumes for each periodical indexed; and a "chronological conspectus of the serials indexed," which lists by year all the indexed serials in publication and the last volume number published that year. Entries in the index proper are arranged alphabetically by subject and make reference to the article title (sometimes altered), the author (in parentheses, sometimes misidentified), the periodical (by its "best-known" title), the volume (but ignoring all renumberings and without the year), and the page on which the article begins. The five supplements conform to the base volume both in preliminaries and in the main body. They cover publications of the years 1882–1887, 1887–1892, 1892–1896, 1897–1902, and 1902–1906 respectively. Taken together, the volumes present more than 590,000 references to periodical articles.

Fiction and poetry are generally indexed under titles. Reviews are entered under the name of the reviewed author. There are numberless inaccuracies and a few bothersome eccentricities. Corrections of some errors were published in the *Bulletin of Bibliography*, vols. 1–4 (1897–1900), and three important supplementary aids have been made available. The first, by Marion V. Bell and Jean C. Bacon, is titled *Poole's Index, Date and Volume Key* (Chicago: Association of College and Reference Libraries, 1957) [Z674.A75 no. 19]. In addition to a history of Poole's index and other valuable preliminaries, it presents a single alphabetical list of all the periodicals indexed in Poole with the volume numbers and the date of each volume. Bell and Bacon thus replaces the chronological conspectus as a source for verifying index coverage and identifying the years of publication for cited volume numbers.

The second supplemental aid, Vinton Dearing's *Transfer Vectors for Poole's Index to Periodical Literature, no. 1, Titles, Volumes and Dates* (Cleveland, 1963; Los Angeles,

1967) [AI3.P75], presents a bibliography of periodical titles with their name changes, an enumeration of the actual issue dates for each volume, and (in parentheses) the actual volume number if different from that given by Poole (i.e., Poole's volume 63, say, may actually be New Series, volume 12, etc.). The second volume of Dearing's *Transfer Vectors* was to be a key to Poole's sometimes inconsistent subject headings (i.e., the same subject is often treated under several different headings) but remains a desideratum.

The third available supplementary aid is C. Edward Wall's *Cumulative Author Index for Poole's Index to Periodical Literature, 1802–1906* (Ann Arbor, Mich.: Pierian, 1971) [AI3.W3 1971], which displays in one alphabetical sequence the more than 300,000 references to personal names which appear within parentheses in the original and supplementary volumes. It should be noted, however, that this work indexes Poole and not the nineteenth-century periodicals that Poole indexes. The "authors" remain unverified and in the form given in Poole's index.

All subsequent general periodical indexes are in some sense supplements to Poole. They include the thirteen volumes of the *Annual Index of Periodicals* (1890), which title changed to *Index to the Periodical Literature of the World* (1891–1893) and to *Index to the Periodicals of 1894–1902*, an annual international index published by Review of Reviews in London 1891–1903 of monthly and quarterly magazines (many not in Poole) [AI3.R5]; Alfred Cotgreave's *Contents-Subject Index to General and Periodical Literature* (London: Elliot Stock, 1900) [AI3.C7] with about 100,000 entries, indexing monographs, chapters in monographs, and anthologies, and supplementing Poole's index to peiodicals, particularly for the late nineteenth century; the *Nineteenth Century Readers' Guide to Periodical Literature 1890–1899* (D–11); and the *Wellesley Index* (D–12), in which the introduction to the first volume offers a valuable discussion of the strengths and limitations of Poole's monumental work.

D–11 **Cushing, Helen, and Adah U. Morris.** *Nineteenth Century Readers' Guide to Periodical Literature, 1890–1899, with Supplementary Indexing, 1900–1922.* 2 vols. New York: H. W. Wilson, 1944. AI3.R496

These are the first volumes in what was to have been an extensive retrospective index to nineteenth-century periodicals supplementing Poole (D–10). No more volumes were published, but those that were remain a valuable addition to available indexing. In contrast to Poole, these volumes use a standard list of subject headings, cross-references, and author/illustrator entries and thus serve as an author/illustrator and subject index to fifty-one general or literary periodicals. The work is also an author index to book reviews and a title index to short stories, novels, plays, and poems. Anonymous authors are generally identified. Of the fifty-one periodicals analyzed, only thirteen are English journals; the rest are American. There is a list of periodicals included which makes clear which fourteen among them were given supplementary indexing beyond 1899, and until when.

D–12 **Houghton, Walter E.** *Wellesley Index to Victorian Periodicals 1824–1900: Tables of Contents and Identification of Contributors with Bibliographies of Their Articles and Stories.* 4 vols. Toronto: University of Toronto Press, 1966–1988. AI3.W45

This is the most complete index available for some forty-eight principal nineteenth-century monthly and quarterly magazines. The first volume, published in 1966, presents the tables of contents and an author index for eight periodicals; volume 2, published in 1972, adds twelve more; volume 3, published in 1979, adds fifteen more; and volume 4, published in 1988, adds thirteen more. Because a very large percentage of the articles were published anonymously or pseudonymously, particularly before 1865, the most celebrated feature of the *Wellesley Index* is its identification of the authorship of most articles. The contributions of some 13,000 different writers have been identified.

Each of the volumes is divided into three parts. The first, Part A, is a listing, alphabetical by magazine, of the contents of each issue. These listings, which make possible an overview of the changing subject matter of nineteenth-century public opinion, are preceded in each case by a short history of the magazine being analyzed and a set of bibliographical notes. As the contents are enumerated, each article of a particular magazine is assigned a serial number. The exact title of the article is given, along with its pagination and its author. Entries also provide evidence for the attribution if the article was originally anonymous or pseudonymous; a list of names of translators or collaborators, if required; reference to other articles directly related to the entry; and a specification of its subject matter if the article's title is not sufficiently precise. It should be noted that verse is not included in the analysis of volume 1 and with very few exceptions is excluded from subsequent volumes as well. Reviews are included; entries specify the title of the book being reviewed and, for major works, supply the name of the reviewed author.

Part B presents an index of contributing authors, giving for each contributor a brief biographical note (including dates, profession, and reference to standard biographical treatments), then a list of all contributed articles in alphabetical order according to the name of the periodical and then in chronological order by the article entry numbers as given in Part A.

Part C presents an index of initials and pseudonyms found in the indexed periodicals, both those identified and those that remain unidentified. An appendix of additions and corrections to Parts A and B is found in each volume. In addition, volume 2 has an appendix of corrections and additions, however minute, to volume 1; volume 3 has an appendix of additions and corrections to volume 2 with additional changes to volume 1; and volume 4 completes the pattern. Other relations between volumes include abundant cross-references from the later to the earlier volumes. There are several important variations among the volumes, and the user is urged to consult the several introductions for detailed clarification of procedure.

For the magazines treated, the *Wellesley Index* is a radically more complete author index than Poole (D–10) or the *Nineteenth Century Readers' Guide* (D–11). The current volumes are not, however, a subject index, though they form the basis of one that is planned.

D–13 *Internationale Bibliographie der Zeitschriftenliteratur [IBZ] aus allen Gebieten des Wissens / International Bibliography of Periodical Literature Covering All Fields of Knowledge / Bibliographie internationale de littérature périodique dans tous les domaines de la connaissance.* Vol. 1–. Osnabrück: Dietrich, 1965–. AI9.I5

This international subject index to some 8,300 periodicals and annuals appears in semiannual issues of about thirty fascicles which form a number of annual volumes. More than 300,000 articles in German, French, English, and other periodicals are indexed each year. Entries are under relatively broad German subject headings, with cross-references from English and French headings. They give titles, authors, periodical code number (the key is at the beginning of each volume), and volume and page numbers. From 1967/68 on, the key to periodicals consulted is in one volume, the subject index is in a series of six or so volumes, and the author index, expanded to include full entries that can be used independently of the subject volumes, is in another six or so volumes.

This is the current form of an index that began in 1897, the *Internationale Bibliographie der Zeitschriftenliteratur mit*

Einschluss von Sammelwerken und Zeitungen, founded by Felix Dietrich (Leipzig [and later Osnabrück], 1897–1964), by whose name it is known. The work was published in three series, covering German and foreign periodicals and book reviews respectively. *Abteilung A*, titled *Bibliographie der deutschen Zeitschriftenliteratur mit Einschluss von Sammelwerken* [AI9.B5], was published in a total of 128 semiannual volumes, 1897–1944 and 1947–1964. Coverage varies from some 300 German periodicals indexed in the earliest volumes to well over 4,000 in the latest. Entries by German-language subject headings refer to titles and authors of articles and to journals or composite volumes by numerical code. There are author indexes to each half-yearly volume, which refer to subject headings under which articles by a given author may be found. The series is enlarged by twenty retrospective *Ergänzungsbände* that analyze German periodical volumes of the period from 1895 back to 1861.

Abteilung B, the complementary index to non-German periodical literature, *Bibliographie der fremdsprachigen Zeitschriftenliteratur / Répertoire bibliographique internationale des revues / International Index to Periodicals*, was published in twenty-two volumes, 1911–1921/25, and then in volumes 1–51 of a "Neue Folge," 1925–1943/44 and 1949/50–1964 [AI9.B7]. This series is of special value for French and other European periodicals; its coverage varies to nearly 4,500 indexed periodicals in recent volumes. Semiannual volumes have main entries arranged under German subject headings; the "Neue Folge" includes an author index in each semiannual volume.

The third series, *Abteilung C*, is titled *Bibliographie der Rezensionen und Referate*. Volumes 1–77, 1900–1943, present an author index to works reviewed, including at first only German reviews (1900–1910, 1916–1924) and later (1911–1915, 1925–1944) both German and foreign-language reviews in separate volumes [AI9.B6]. In 1971 the series was resumed as the *Internationale Bibliographie der Rezensionen wissenschaftlicher Literatur*, ed. Otto Zeller; it is being published in semiannual volumes that analyze some 1,000 periodicals and present three indexes, to subjects, to authors of books reviewed, and to reviewers. Retrospective volumes for the period 1945–1969 are planned (see E–75).

Users of both the combined *IBZ* and the earlier separate series A and B will find the *Index Generalis: Register der Schlagwörter, 1896-1974*, 2 vols. (Osnabrück: Dietrich, 1975) [AI9.I53], a helpful aid, since it presents an alphabetical list of all German-language subject headings found during the period 1896–1974, with indications of the volumes in which entries under the subject heading are given. It thus serves as an index of sorts to the entire massive work.

D–14 **Cumulated Magazine Subject Index, 1907–1949: A Cumulation of the F. W. Faxon Company's Annual Magazine Subject Index.** 2 vols. Boston: G. K. Hall, 1964.   AI3.C76

These volumes bring together a photographic reproduction of entries from the forty-three volumes of the Faxon index, subtitled *Subject Index to a Selected List of American and English Periodicals and Society Publications* [1907–1949], which was published in Boston from 1908 through 1952. The first volume's title was *Magazine Subject-Index to Seventy-Nine American and English Periodicals* (2 vols.). By the following year, 120 periodicals were included; the number of indexed works varies over the years but always consists of periodicals *not* treated in other major indexes such as the *Reader's Guide* (D–15) or the *Social Sciences and Humanities Index* (D–16). In contrast with those indexes, however, this one is *only* a subject index and does not include title or author entries except for works of fiction by noted authors, which are indexed under the author's name. Poetry, short articles, and most fiction are omitted. Drama is treated in Faxon's *Dramatic Index* (U–55), which was also published as Part II of the *Annual Magazine Subject Index*. Though this index is general in scope, it tends to emphasize periodicals related to the field of history, especially local history. There are a total of 253,000 entries, and, in all, some 356 different American, Canadian, and English magazines were analyzed.

D–15 **Readers' Guide to Periodical Literature (Unabridged): An Author-Subject Index to Selected General Interest Periodicals of Reference Value in Libraries [RG]** [1900–]. New York: H. W. Wilson, 1905–.   AI3.R45

This widely used general index is published semimonthly from September through January and March through June and monthly in February, July, and August. A bound cumulation appears each year. There are also multiannual cumulative volumes covering periods of from two to five years from 1900 through 1965. Indexed periodicals vary over the years; approximately 160 periodicals are now included in a dictionary catalog of authors, subjects, and, when necessary, titles. Cumulative volumes 2 and 3 (1905–1909, 1910–1914) include the analysis of composite volumes and thus serve as an unofficial supplement to the *A.L.A. Index* (E–80). Since 1953 some scientific periodicals have been analyzed. Entries give author, title, periodical, exact date, and inclusive pagination.

Reviews of fiction and drama are found under the subject author's name with cross-references to the title of the work. Reviews of motion pictures, musical comedies, and operas are treated under general headings (see the introductory pages). If included in the *Book Review Digest* (E–75), reviews are omitted in *Readers' Guide*.

Since 1936, Wilson has also published an *Abridged Readers' Guide to Periodical Literature* in monthly and annual (before 1965, biennial) cumulations. For the periods 1959–1970 [AI3.C84] and 1973–1978 [AI3.C86] users may find the unofficial *Cumulative Index to Periodical Literature* helpful. Published by the National Library Service Corporation in Princeton, these cumulations in seven and five volumes, respectively, bring together author and subject headings for the cumulated period and present individual citations under them in reverse chronological order. A further *Cumulative Index* for the period 1970–1973 is scheduled for publication. As in the *Readers' Guide*, drama and fiction references are found under authors' names; motion picture, theater, and opera reviews are found under generic headings. Materials indexed from January 1983 on, may be searched on WILSONLINE (see Z–78).

For indexes to additional contemporary popular magazines, the *Readers' Guide* may be supplemented by other current indexes. These include the quarterly *Alternative Press Index: An Index to Alternative and Radical Publications* (Baltimore, Md.: Alternative Press Centre, 1969–1970, 1974–) [AI3.A27]; the semiannual *Popular Periodical Index* (Camden, N.J.: Popular Periodical Index, 1973–) [AI3.P76]; the triannual *Access: The Supplementary Index to Periodicals* (Evanston, Ill.: John Gordon Burke, 1975–) [AI3.A23]; and the semiannual *New Periodicals Index* (Boulder, Colo.: Mediaworks, 1977–) [no LC number]. Since 1976 there have also been available the microform and hard-copy versions of *Magazine Index* (Belmont, Calif.: Information Access Corp.) [no LC number], providing indexing to some 370 popular magazines by author, title, and subject.

For Canadian publications the *Canadian Periodical Index / Index de périodiques canadiens* (1948–) [AI3.C242], with varying frequency and title, now published monthly, quarterly, and with an annual cumulation, provides a single-alphabet subject-author analysis of more than 100 Canadian periodicals.

D–16 Humanities Index. Vol. 1–. New York: H. W. Wilson, 1974–.   AI3.H85

This is the current form of an index that began in 1916 as the *Readers' Guide to Periodical Literature Supplement* [AI3.R49]. Its original purpose was to index scholarly journals in all fields that were not treated in the *Readers' Guide to Periodical Literature* (D–15). The original volume indexed publications for 1907–1915; subsequent publication was quarterly with an annual cumulation and a four-year cumulation. Beginning with volume 3, the multiannual cumulation for 1920–1923, the title was changed to *International Index to Periodicals*. The subtitle of the *International Index* has varied; beginning with volume 53 (1965), the main title was changed to *Social Sciences and Humanities Index*. The *Social Sciences and Humanities Index* split in 1974 to form two separate series, the *Social Sciences Index* [AI3.S62] and the *Humanities Index*.

Throughout its history this index series has followed the original pattern of quarterly, annual, and, until 1964, multiannual permanent cumulations. Indexing is by author and subject; current volumes include a separate book-review section with entry under the reviewed author. Coverage has varied; current volumes of the *Humanities Index* analyze some 300 periodicals in the fields of archaeology and classical studies, area studies, folklore, history, language and literature, literary and political criticism, performing arts, philosophy, religion and theology, and related subjects. Each issue of the *Index* is preceded by a list of periodicals covered. Materials indexed from February 1984 on may be searched on WILSONLINE (see Z–78). Coverage may be supplemented by the *British Humanities Index* (D–17), the *American Humanities Index* (D–18), and the *Arts and Humanities Citation Index* (D–19).

Note that the *Social Sciences Index* also includes much of interest to students of literature including such topics as autobiography, literature and society, politics and literature, and psychological aspects of literature.

D–17 British Humanities Index [BHI]. Vol. 1– [1962–]. London: The Library Association, 1963–.   AI3.B7

This index continues the series that originally began in 1915 with the title [until 1919: *Athenaeum*] *Subject Index to Periodicals*. Scope and arrangement have varied. Early volumes presented an author-subject index to various classes of subject matter, excluding fiction and essays. From 1923 through 1925 no index was published; from 1926 on, it was an alphabetical subject list to articles on specific subjects found in some 500 British and American (and some European) periodicals. Though many listings duplicate entries in Dietrich (D–13), the *Readers' Guide* (D–15), and the *International Index* (D–16), many British periodicals are included which are not analyzed elsewhere. European periodicals were dropped during World War II, and American periodicals were excluded after 1946; from 1947 on, the more than 300 titles analyzed have been entirely British. After the 1961 volume, the *Subject Index to Periodicals* split to form the *British Education Index* [Z5813.B7], the *British Technology Index* [Z7913.B7], and the *British Humanities Index*. The latter analyzes more than 350 British periodicals in the humanities and social sciences. Articles and reviews are indexed in helpful detail, with extensive cross-referencing. Publication is quarterly, with an annual cumulation. Entries are arranged alphabetically by subjects, with a separate author index occupying the second half of each annual volume.

D–18 American Humanities Index for [1975–] [AHI]. Troy, N.Y.: Whitston Publishing Co., 1976–.   AI3.A278

The first annual publication of this new author-subject index to American journals contained some 20,000 entries analyzing almost 100 scholarly, critical, and creative journals, most of which were not being indexed elsewhere. Published quarterly and annually, the work covers journals in the performing arts, language and linguistics, philosophy, black studies, and classical studies. Poems and stories are included, and reviews of fifty words or more are indexed under the names of both author and reviewer. More than 250 journals are currently analyzed, including a number of author newsletters.

D–19 Arts and Humanities Citation Index [AHCI] [1976–]. Philadelphia: Institute for Scientific Information, 1977–.   AI3.A63

This new computer-produced index, modeled on the earlier *Science Citation Index* (1961–) [Z7401.S365] and *Social Science Citation Index* (1973–) [Z7461.S65], presents a group of four different but interrelated indexes, named the "Source Index," the "Citation Index," the "Permuterm Subject Index," and the "Corporate Index" respectively. *AHCI* covers about 1,300 journals in the fields of art; architecture; classics; dance; film, TV, and radio; folklore; history; linguistics and philology; literature; music; philosophy; theater; and theology and religious studies. Articles, reviews, notes, and correspondence are indexed. In addition, some festschriften and other composite volumes are analyzed. The "Source Index" is an author index that provides a complete bibliographical description of each article. To facilitate comprehension, title-enrichment terms are introduced to clarify the subject and character of the indexed article. Titles are translated into English, with the language of the original work indicated; titles of works reviewed and of works as subjects remain untranslated, however. The author's institutional affiliation is provided, if known. The last part of the entry for an individual source is a list of all the works cited in the article, with author and short title. These data form the basis for the "Citation Index," which indexes all authors cited, giving short titles of their works and identifying the source article from which the citation is taken. Note, however, that the index does not discriminate a passing reference from a detailed discussion. Endnotes and footnotes are sources for citations, thus making the accuracy of the index dependent on the accuracy of the original notes. The "Permuterm Subject Index" is an alphabetical index of paired keywords in titles and subtitles (including enrichment terms), through all possible permutations of two terms. Finally, the "Corporate Index" presents an alphabetical list of all organizational affiliations of authors as given in the source article, with authors listed alphabetically under their home institutions.

Published in softbound issues covering January to April, and May to August, the indexes are also gathered into several hardbound annual cumulative volumes. Materials indexed from 1980 on are searchable online through BRS (see Z–78). By using these new indexes, researchers are able in one step to locate articles using the same or related keywords in their titles (Permuterm Index), to find articles citing a particular author or work (Citation Index), to scan through the citations of an article without looking it up (Source Index), and to locate groups of articles published by researchers with the same institutional affiliation (Corporate Index). Annual cumulations provide a complete introduction to the use of this index; the introduction should be consulted in undertaking a search for the first time. For a more elaborate discussion of this new form of indexing see Eugene Garfield, *Citation Indexing—Its Theory and Application in Science, Technology, and Humanities* (New York: Wiley, 1979) [Z697.S5 G37].

AHCI is supplemented by *Current Contents: Arts and Humanities* (Philadelphia: Institute for Scientific Information,

1978–) [no LC number], a weekly publication reproducing the tables of contents for all the periodicals, festschriften, and other composite volumes analyzed by the *AHCI*. A "Current Book Contents" section, displaying tables of contents from new books, a subject index to keywords in titles, and an Author Index and Address Directory are also included.

Another service provided by the Institute for Scientific Information (ISI) is the *Index to Social Science and Humanities Proceedings* (see E–88). Some items from this index, from *Current Contents*, and from *AHCI* may be ordered through *Genuine Article*, formerly OATS (Original Article Text Service), a document delivery service providing tear sheets or photocopies of articles.

III. GENERAL INDEXES: NEWSPAPERS

See also the *IBZ* (D–13), which includes newspapers.

D–20 **Lathrop Report on Newspaper Indexes: An Illustrated Guide to Published and Unpublished Newspaper Indexes in the United States and Canada**. Compiled by Norman M. and Mary Lou Lathrop. Wooster, Ohio: Lathrop Enterprises, 1979.   AI3.L38

Originally published as an annually updated, looseleaf work, this hardbound volume appeared only in this 1979–1980 edition. Both the looseleaf format and the hardbound work provide detailed descriptions with illustrations of all known published and unpublished newspaper indexes in the United States and Canada. A cross-index allows access to indexes by state, by newspaper title, by format, by indexing organization, and by subject. A chronology allows one to locate the oldest indexes, those with the longest coverage, and those covering special periods.

Another, similar, but less informative source is Anita Cheek Milner, *Newspaper Indexes: A Location and Subject Guide for Researchers*. 3 vols. (Metuchen, N.J.: Scarecrow, 1977–1982) [Z6951.M635], which is arranged by state, county, and city. Entries identify and locate commerically produced indexes as well as indexes prepared by libraries, societies, and individuals. There is some indication of dates, special topics, and the location of the index. Herbert O. Brayer's "Preliminary Guide to Indexed Newspapers in the United States, 1850–1900," *Mississippi Valley Historical Review*, vol. 33 (1946) [Z6293.B7], may also be of use within its relatively limited period of coverage.

No comparable special resources exist for British or Irish newspaper indexes.

D–21 **Palmer's Index to the [London] Times Newspaper [1790–1941]**. 456 [numbering varies] volumes. Corsham, Wilts.: Palmer, 1868–1943.   AI21.T5

An uncumulated quarterly index to the *Times* which uses broad topical headings (such as Accidents, Bankruptcies, Births, Civil Actions, Companies, Criminal Trials, Deaths, Executions, France, Law, Parliamentary Proceedings, Ship News, Theatres) and subheadings of personal names and more specific subtopics. The index was published in two series, current from September 1869, and retrospective from 1868 back to 1790. A retrospective volume for 1785–1790 is in preparation. From 1906 on, the *Official Index* (D–22) should be used in preference to Palmer's.

D–22 **Official Index to the [London] Times [1906–]**. London: The Times, 1907–.   AI21.T6

The title of this monthly and annual (1906–1913), semiannual (1914), quarterly (1914–1956), bimonthly (1957–1971), quarterly (1972–1976), and now (1977–) monthly index has varied. It is much more detailed than the unofficial Palmer's Index (D–21) and should be used in preference to it. Proper names, including authors of reviewed works, appear as subjects. Topics are treated under fairly specific subject headings. Some subjects are treated in elaborate systems of up to six levels of subheadings. Since 1973 this work has been indexing the *Sunday Times*, the *Times Education Supplement*, the *Times Higher Education Supplement*, the *Times Literary Supplement* (Z–151), and the daily *Times* itself.

Available for biographical inquiry is the new index to *Obituaries from the Times* (Westport, Conn.: Meckler, 1975–) [CT120.O16]. Currently volumes are available for 1951–1960 [CT120.O16], 1961–1970 [CT120.O165] and 1971–1975 [CT120.O17]; retrospective volumes will carry the index back to 1785, while current volumes will carry it forward in five-year periods.

D–23 **The New York Times Index [1913–]**. New York: The New York Times, 1913–.   AI21.N45

An index to the Late City edition of the *New York Times*, this work classifies the contents of the newspaper by subject, person, and organization name. Exact reference is made to articles by the date, page, and column of the newspaper. Plentiful cross-references to names and related topics aid the searcher; brief synopses of articles often answer questions without requiring reference to the paper itself. The index has been published with varying frequency: from 1913 through 1929, quarterly with no cumulations; in 1930, monthly with quarterly and an annual cumulation; from 1931 through 1947, monthly with an annual cumulation; from 1948 through 1977, semimonthly with an annual cumulation; since 1978, semimonthly with quarterly and an annual cumulation.

A *Prior Series* was published 1966 through 1974 in fifteen volumes [AI21.N452]. It indexes the *New York Times* for the period from 1851, when it started publication, through 1912, after which the current series began. In format and style it is similar to more current indexes, though abstracts of news are not as detailed nor as informative as are those of more recent volumes. Subject headings are also less extensively subdivided. For biographical inquiries see the *Personal Name Index for the New York Times Index, 1851-1974*, prepared by Byron A. Falk and Valerie R. Falk in twenty-two volumes (Succasunna, N.J.: Roxbury Data Interface, 1976–1983) [Z5301.F28 1976]. Five-year supplements are planned. Also available are a separate five-volume *New York Times Book Review Index* (see Z–150), and the *New York Times Obituary Index 1858-1969* (New York, 1970) [CT213.N47] with a total of more than 353,000 names in a single alphabet.

Among other major American newspaper indexes may be mentioned the *New York Daily Tribune Index* in thirty-one volumes, covering the period 1875–1906 [AI21.N5]; the current index to the *Wall Street Journal* (1958–) [HG1.W258]; the current subject index to the *Christian Science Monitor* (1960–) [AI21.C46]; and the series of unofficial current indexes to major United States newspapers prepared by the Indexing Center of the Bell and Howell Company (1972–), which includes indexes to the *Chicago Tribune* [AI21.C45 C47], the *Los Angeles Times* [AI21.L65 N49], the *New Orleans Times–Picayune* [AI21.T66], the *Washington Post* [AI21.W33 W36], and the *Christian Science Monitor* [AI21.C462 B44]. The NEWSEARCH database, which is cumulated each month into the NATIONAL NEWSPAPER INDEX database (1979–), indexes the *Christian Science Monitor*, the *New York Times*, the *Wall Street Journal*, the *Los Angeles Times*, and the *Washington Post*.

IV. GENERAL INDEXES: LITTLE MAGAZINES

D–27 **Index to Little Magazines** [1948–]. Denver, Colo.: Swallow [later Troy, N.Y.: Whitston Publishing Co.], 1949–1970.
AI3.I54

This generally biennial index to over fifty American little magazines excludes any title indexed in *Readers' Guide* (D–15) or other major periodical indexes. Entries are presented in a combined author-subject alphabet. Coverage varies from volume to volume, particularly with regard to the inclusion of reviews. This index can be supplemented by Marion Sader's *Comprehensive Index* (D–29), which includes the reviews found in the 100 English-language little magazines that she analyzes.

For subsequent indexes see *Access to Little Magazines* [1974–] (Evanston, Ill.: John Gordon Burke, 1977–) [AI3.A24], an annual author-title-subject index to some seventy American little magazines. The following retrospective volumes take coverage back to 1900: Stephen H. Goode, comp., *Index to Little Magazines 1943-1947* (Denver, Colo.: Swallow, 1965); *Index to Little Magazines 1940-1942* (Troy, N.Y.: Whitston, 1967); *Index to American Little Magazines, 1920-1939* (Troy, N.Y.: Whitston, 1969); and *Index to American Little Magazines, 1900-1919, to Which Is Added a Selected List of British and Continental Titles from the Years 1900-1950, Together with Addenda and Corrigenda to Previous Indexes* [in this series], 4 vols. (Troy, N.Y.: Whitston, 1974). One might also consult with benefit the "Annotated Bibliography of Selected Little Magazines" by Peter Martin which appears on pp. 666–750 of *Little Magazine in America: A Modern Documentary History*, eds. Elliott Anderson and Mary Kinzie (Yonkers, N.Y.: Pushcart Press, 1978) [PN4878.3.L5].

For British and Commonwealth little magazines see Bloomfield (D–28) and other titles listed there.

D–28 **Bloomfield, B. C. Author Index to Selected British "Little Magazines" 1930–1939.** London: Mansell, 1976.
AI3.B56

An author index to some seventy-three little magazines (listed on p. xi of the introduction) which includes about 11,000 entries. Each entry gives the author's name, the title (or a general title—review, poem, play), the periodical, volume and part number, date of publication, page reference, and a symbol that indicates the general type of contribution (bibliography, critical article, drama, theater review, illustration, music, creative prose, book review, verse). The introduction enumerates a group of magazines that were excluded. There is no subject index. Books reviewed are identified wherever possible. There are some cross-references.

British little magazines are also indexed in the *Comprehensive Index to English–Language Little Magazines* (D–29) and by author and subject in the biannual *Index to Commonwealth Little Magazines* [1964–], ed. Stephen H. Goode (Troy, N.Y.: Whitston, 1966–) [AI3.I48], the first volume of which covered thirty-three magazines for the years 1964–1965. Retrospective indexing to 1900 is planned.

D–29 **Sader, Marion, ed. Comprehensive Index to English-Language Little Magazines 1890–1970.** Series One. 8 vols. Millwood, N.Y.: Kraus-Thomson, 1976.
Z6944.L5 S23

This monumental work indexes by personal name the contents of some 100 little magazines over their entire run or through 1970–1971. A list of indexed magazines with their short titles appears on pp. xvii-xxix. Entries are arranged alphabetically by contributor or subject, with work by an individual preceding works about him. Entries provide, as appropriate, names of authors; title; names of editors, adapters, translators, compilers, illustrators, photographers, directors, or composers; a characterization of the type of item involved; the title of the magazine, issue number, date of issue, and pages of the article. The categories used to characterize items are enumerated on pp. xv-xvi of the introduction and include articles, poems, dramas, illustrations, photographs, lists, works of fiction, letters, essays, and reviews. It should be noted that anonymous works are entered under their subject, with unsigned contributions excluded unless a subject name could be assigned to the contribution. Untitled poems are entered by first lines. Reviewed books are entered under the author of the book, its subject(s), and the author of the review, unless signed with initials only. Unsigned reviews are entered by the author of the book. Initials for authors of substantial articles are used in the index only if no other way of entering the item could be found. With the noted exceptions, however, this is essentially a personal-name index.

It is important to remember that a broad definition of "little magazines" such as Sader's includes many primarily academic journals such as the *Drama Review*, *Modern Fiction Studies*, and *Twentieth Century Literature: A Scholarly and Critical Journal*.

V. PERIODICAL BIBLIOGRAPHY

See also Retrospective Bibliography, Historical Studies, and Finding Lists, section VII below.

D–35 **British Library. Catalogue of Printed Books to 1975 [BLC].** Volumes 252–254, Periodical Publications. London: Bingley; New York, Saur, 1979–1984.
Z921.B87

These three volumes of the *BLC* (B–41) present a geographical listing of periodical holdings acquired before 1975 alphabetically by place of publication.

In general, periodicals listed here are published monthly or less frequently; those published more often than once a month tend to be included in the *Catalogue of the Newspaper Library* (D–42). But in a complete search of British Library periodical holdings, both catalogs should be checked. In addition, special collections of early periodicals have their own catalogs. In particular, see the *Catalogue of the Thomason Collection of Civil War Publications* and the *Catalogue of the Burney Collection of Seventeenth and Eighteenth Century Newspapers*. An important supplement to all British Library catalogs of periodicals will be the listing now in preparation of pre–1920 periodicals held by the Bodleian.

VI. NEWSPAPER BIBLIOGRAPHY

See also Retrospective Bibliography, Historical Studies, and Finding Lists, section VII below.

D–40 **Price, Warren C. Literature of Journalism: An Annotated Bibliography [to 1957].** Minneapolis: University of Minnesota Press, 1959.
Z6940.P7

This standard bibliography of English-language works contains 3,147 serially numbered entries divided into thirteen sections according to their subjects. Annotations are both descriptive and evaluative. The sections cover entries on the history of journalism (primarily of the United States and Britain); biographical works; narratives of working journalists;

appraisals of related social, ethical, and legal issues; techniques of journalism; works on the education of journalists; studies and bibliographies of magazines; the periodical publications of the press; the management of the press; works concerned with matters of public opinion, propaganda, and public relations; works on radio and television; works on the foreign press; and, finally, bibliographies and directories of general works, works on special fields, and checklists of newspapers, magazines, almanacs, and directories. The volume concludes with author, subject, and anonymous-title indexes.

A supplement by Warren C. Price and Calder M. Prickett, *Journalism Bibliography, 1958-68* was published in Minneapolis in 1970 [Z6940.P69]. It contains 2,172 annotated entries arranged alphabetically by author but not otherwise classified. There is a single combined index of names (except of authors), subject headings, and titles.

D–42 **The British Library.** *Catalogue of the Newspaper Library Colindale.* 8 vols. London: British Museum Publications, 1975.   Z6945.B855 1975a

This catalog of what was formerly the British Museum Newspaper Library is a record of some half a million volumes and packets of daily and weekly newspapers and periodicals. Included are London newspapers from 1801 on; Scottish, Irish, and English provincial newspapers from 1700 on; and large collections of Commonwealth and foreign newspapers. New titles and amendments to titles are included for United Kingdom newspapers up to the end of 1970, and for Commonwealth and foreign newspapers up to the end of 1971. The work is disposed into two sections: the first four volumes provide a geographical catalog of the collection, while the last four provide an alphabetical title catalog. Volume 1 covers London newspapers and those of the London suburbs; volume 2 covers newspapers of England and Wales, Scotland, and Ireland; volumes 3 and 4 list foreign newspapers alphabetically by country and then by locality. The alphabetical title catalog arranges works of the same title alphabetically according to their place of publication and then chronologically within each place.

This work replaces the previous catalog of British Museum newspapers, issued as a *Supplement* to the *Catalogue of Printed Books: Newspapers Published in Great Britain and Ireland, 1801-1900* (London, 1905) [Z921.B86 1881 suppl. N]. For other periodical holdings of the British Library see the section of the *General Catalogue* devoted to *Periodical Publications* (D–35).

D–43 **[Muddiman, J. G., comp.]** *The Times.* London. *Tercentenary Handlist of English and Welsh Newspapers, Magazines, and Reviews [1620–1920].* London: The Times, 1920.
Z6956.E5 T5

This bibliography, based on the collections of the British Museum (including the Thomason and Burney special collections), is divided into two sections, for newspapers, magazines, and reviews published in London and its suburbs, and for those published in the provincial cities and towns of England and Wales. The listings are chronological by the first known date of publication, from the corantos of 1620 and 1621 to the newspapers, magazines, and reviews begun in 1919. At the end of each section is an index of titles. The volume begins with an introduction that provides a history of periodical publication in England and Wales. The introduction also indicates the work's incompleteness, particularly for eighteenth century periodicals. Annuals, yearbooks, publications of academies and scholarly societies, and several other classes of periodicals are excluded. Furthermore, experience has shown that the entire work must be used with caution and that entries must be verified elsewhere (primarily through the use of the *ULS*, D–91, and the *BUCOP*, D–95). A series of

additions and corrections by Roland Austin was published in *Notes and Queries*, ser. 12, vols. 8 (1921) and 10 (1922). To 1832, this work has been largely replaced by the bibliographies of Crane and Kaye (D–50) and Ward (D–53); and the *Waterloo Directory of Victorian Periodicals* (D–56), based partly on this *Handlist*, is the most current enumeration of periodicals 1824–1900; nevertheless the *Tercentenary Handlist* remains of value for the early twentieth century.

D–45 **Mott, Frank Luther.** *American Journalism: A History, 1690–1960.* 3d ed. New York: Macmillan, 1962.
PN4855.M63 1962

Each section of chapters in this standard work concludes with several pages of bibliographical notes. Short bibliographical essays on the history of American journalism during the periods 1690–1765, 1765–1783, 1783–1801, 1801–1833, 1833–1860, 1860–1872, 1872–1892, 1892–1914, 1914–1940, 1940–1950, and 1950–1960 provide orientation to the major scholarship. Complete bibliographical coverage will be found in Price (D–40). See also Mott's standard history of American magazines (D–76).

VII. RETROSPECTIVE BIBLIOGRAPHY, HISTORICAL STUDIES, AND FINDING LISTS

See also the extensive primary and secondary retrospective bibliographies of the periodical press in the *CBEL* (M–10) and the *NCBEL* (M–11). For periodicals specializing in individual authors, see Patterson, *Author Newsletters and Journals: An International Annotated Bibliography of Serial Publications* (L–33).

D–50 **Crane, Ronald S., and F. B. Kaye.** *Census of British Newspapers and Periodicals 1620–1800.* Chapel Hill: University of North Carolina Press, 1927.   Z6956.B5 C8

Originally published in *Studies in Philology* 24 (1927): 1–205, this work is a bibliography and United States finding list of pre-nineteenth-century British periodicals (including newspapers) which aimed at completeness but is now considerably out of date, particularly as a finding list. The 2,182 serially numbered entries cover virtually all recognized types of periodicals, including newspapers, magazines, reviews, essay sheets, and annuals. Scottish, Irish, and Welsh publications are listed. Entries are alphabetical by the earliest known title and include references to subsequent titles; initial and final dates of publication; names of editors, publishers, or printers; and frequency; followed by information about the files held by individual American repositories. Two indexes, one chronological and the other geographical, make possible searches for works published during a certain time or at a certain place outside London even when titles are not known. Because the bibliography was divided into two parts, reporting on those 970 periodicals for which files were available in the sixty-two American libraries surveyed and the 1,445 periodicals for which files were unavailable, both parts must be checked in bibliographical work. Consultation of the *ULS* (D–91) will confirm and update location data; the *BUCOP* (D–95) will provide supplementary locations in British repositories.

A number of supplements to Crane and Kaye have been published by various libraries. These include Anthony J. Gabler's "Check-List of English Newspapers and Periodicals before 1801 in the Huntington Library," *HLB* 2 (1931): 1–66; R. T. Milford and D. M. Sutherland, *Catalogue of English*

Newspapers and Periodicals in the Bodleian Library, 1622–1800 (Oxford, 1936), originally published in the *Oxford Bibliographical Society Proceedings and Papers* 4 (1934/35): 163–346 [Z1008.O98]; Powell Stewart's *British Newspapers and Periodicals 1632-1800* [in the University of Texas Library] (Austin, Tex., 1950) [Z6956.E5 S85]; and appendix C, the "Register of English Provincial Newspapers, 1701–1760," in R. M. Wiles, *Freshest Advices: Early Provincial Newspapers in England* (Columbus: Ohio State University Press, 1965) [PN5115.W5]. For periodicals published 1789 and later, see the work of William S. Ward (D–53). For secondary studies on the early English periodical see the bibliographies of Weed and Bond (D–52) and White (D–55).

D–51 **Nelson, Carolyn, and Matthew Seccombe.** *British Newspapers and Periodicals, 1641–1700. A Short-Title Catalogue of Serials Printed in England, Scotland, Ireland, and British America.* New York: Modern Language Association, 1988. Z6956.G6 N44 1987

This volume provides a comprehensive issue-by-issue union list of all known British serials of the Wing period. Serials are listed alphabetically by their first title, with cross-references to later titles. Entries are sequentially numbered (using an integer for the serial, and decimal numbers for individual issues). The first entry for a serial gives a uniform title with inclusive dates, followed by a headnote giving the format, average length, frequency of publication, editor or author if known, and bibliographical references. Subsequent entries are by issue, giving title, number, inclusive dates, place, imprint, year, and a list of libraries holding that issue.

Six indexes conclude the volume along with two large appendixes. The indexes cover period, editor/author, publisher/printer, place of publication, language, and subject. The first appendix summarizes serials publishes from January 1701 until the accession of Queen Anne in March 1702, and is also indexed. The second appendix discusses and as possible both enumerates and describes variant issues and reprints of the more widely circulated serials.

D–52 **Weed, Katherine Kirtley, and Richmond P. Bond.** *Studies of British Newspapers and Periodicals from Their Beginning to 1800: A Bibliography.* *Studies in Philology*, extra series, no. 2. Chapel Hill: University of North Carolina Press, 1946. P25.S82 no. 2

A bibliography of some 2,100 books and articles published before 1940. Entries are divided into sections covering bibliographies and bibliographical studies; the beginnings of the newspaper; general studies; studies of individual newspapers and periodicals; studies of individual editors, authors, and publishers; studies of the periodical press in particular towns or countries; studies of the contemporary periodical press in Europe and America. There is an author index. Additions and corrections were printed in *MP* 45 (1947): 65–66.

To supplement Weed and Bond, one may consult the bibliography of White (D–55) and the secondary bibliography of periodical publications in volumes 1 and 2 of the *New Cambridge Bibliography of English Literature* (M–11). A useful review of research is James E. Tierney, "The Study of the Eighteenth-Century British Periodical," *PBSA* 69 (1975): 165–86.

D–53 **Ward, Williams S.** *Index and Finding List of Serials Published in the British Isles, 1789–1832.* Lexington: University of Kentucky Press, 1953. Z6956.E5 W27

This list includes about 500 newspapers and periodicals published in the United Kingdom and Ireland during the romantic period for which files are located in British, American, or Canadian libraries. The list is geared for use with the *ULS*

(D–91) and the *Union Catalogue of the Periodical Publications in the University Libraries of the British Isles* (D–97). It may also be used with the newer *BUCOP* (D–95). Entries are in alphabetical order by earliest title and include the place of publication, volumes or serial numbers, the initial and final dates and frequency of publication, and indications of libraries holding files of each title, with information about the extent of the files.

When holding libraries are listed in the *ULS* or the *UCP*, they are not re-listed in Ward; instead a cross-reference to these volumes is given. For the period 1789–1800, Ward replaces the earlier Crane and Kaye *Census* (D–50). Ward published a "supplement" in the *BNYPL*, vol. 77 (1974). It may also be supplemented by the relevant sections of the *NCBEL*, vols. 2 and 3 (M–11). Other related publications by Ward include his bibliography of *Literary Reviews in British Periodicals, 1789-1820, With a Supplementary List of General (Non-Review) Articles on Literary Subjects*, 2 vols. (New York: Garland, 1972) [Z2013.W36], which lists more than 15,000 reviews of verse, novels, drama, and the like, with appendixes citing special articles on authors (including Shakespeare, Milton, Pope, and Johnson) and other literary topics. These include general articles on the contemporary literary scene, lists of articles on the various genres, and articles on operas and musical dramas. Subsequent volumes cover *Literary Reviews in British Periodicals, 1821-1826: A Bibliography with a Supplementary List of General (Non-Review) Articles on Literary Subjects* (New York: Garland, 1977) [Z2013.W36 1977], and *Literary Reviews in British Periodicals, 1789-1797: A Bibliography* (New York: Garland, 1979) [Z2013.W36 1979]. See also Ward's bibliography of secondary sources on periodicals of this period (D–54), and the bibliography by White (D–55).

D–54 **Ward, William S.** *British Periodicals and Newspapers, 1789–1832: A Bibliography of Secondary Sources.* Lexington: University of Kentucky Press, 1972. Z6956.G36 W37

Meant to be used in conjunction with Ward's *Index and Finding List* (D–53), this bibliography of 2,991 books and articles is arranged by topics and includes sections on the contents, editors, publishers, and readership of each of the periodicals indexed. Entries are sometimes annotated. There are separate indexes of authors, subjects, and library catalogs/union lists.

This work may be supplemented by the relevant sections of the *NCBEL*, volumes 2 and 3 (M–11).

D–55 **White, Robert B.** *English Literary Journal to 1900: A Guide to Information Sources.* Detroit: Gale Research Co., 1977. Z6956.G6 W47

This guide to secondary materials written in English since 1890 about British literary periodicals of the seventeenth, eighteenth and nineteenth centuries is divided into five chapters, concerned respectively with bibliographies and bibliographical aids, general studies, studies of individual periodicals, studies of authors and other persons important in the history of literary journals, and studies of literary journals in particular places. The 2,301 serially numbered entries are annotated. Within the various subsections, entries are alphabetical by author or other main entry. Indexes of authors, periodicals, persons, and places conclude the volume. It should be noted that the chapter treating authors and other persons provides a handy bibliography of the journalistic careers of such major English authors as Addison, Boswell, Dickens, Fielding, Johnson, and Swift.

Coverage is uneven, but better for eighteenth century works. See also Madden and Dixon (D–57) for nineteenth century periodicals and Stanton (D–58) for literary periodicals of the twentieth century.

D–56   ***Waterloo Directory of Victorian Periodicals, 1824–1900.***
Phase I.   Compiled by Michael Wolff, John S. North, and
Dorothy Deering.   Waterloo, Ontario: Wilfrid Laurier University Press, 1976.   Z6954.W38

This directory, sponsored in part by the Research Society for
Victorian Periodicals (RSVP), which also publishes the *Victorian Periodicals Newsletter* (Q–52), aims to present a comprehensive alphabetical list of the titles of all periodicals in
any subject area that were published in England, Ireland,
Scotland, and Wales at any time between 1824 and 1900.   A
computer-generated, serially numbered list of nearly 30,000
titles, this work is based on the collation of references in other
printed sources, specifically, Joel Wiener's *Descriptive Finding List of Unstamped British Periodicals 1830-1836* (London: Bibliographical Society, 1970) [Z6956.G6 W54]; the
British Museum General Catalogue of Printed Books: Periodical Publications (D–35); the *British Museum Catalogue of
Newspapers, 1801-1900* (see D–42); the *British Union Catalogue of Periodicals* (D–95); *Newspapers on Microfilm*
(E–56); Mitchell's *Newspaper Press Directory*; the *Union List
of Serials* (D–91); and the *Times Tercentenary Handlist of
English and Welsh Newspapers* (D–43).   Entries are listed
under the earliest known title, with cross-references from other titles.   In some cases the publishing body (rather than a title
beginning *Proceedings* or *Journal*) is used as the main entry;
there, too, cross-references are provided so that a scholar may
trace a periodical according to any of its titles.   Where
sources differ in their information, all conflicting opinion has
been recorded in the order of general reliability of the sources
(which is the order in which they are listed above).

If information was available in the sources consulted, entries
give the full title and subtitle; the numbering of series, volumes, and issues; the publication dates; the name of the editor
and his dates; the place and dates of publication; the publisher
and his dates; the printer and his dates; the price and dates of
effectiveness; size; frequency; presence of illustration; circulation figures and dates; the issuing body and its dates with
cross-reference from all its subsequent names; the presence of
indexes; notes; mergers with dates; and subsidiary and alternate titles.   Preliminary materials should be studied carefully
before using the volume.

This *Directory* can be used to verify publication information,
to distinguish between publications of the same title, to follow
the publishing history of a journal, to determine the range of
publications and thus the interests of a particular issuing body,
to aid in the location of particular issues, to survey the field of
Victorian periodical literature, and to refine bibliographical
control of Victorian periodicals.   Phase II will provide a comprehensive directory based on actual inspection of volumes,
with the addition of more extensive and complete descriptions
of each title than was possible in Phase I.   A Subject Guide to
Phase I is in preparation and will give a rough subject classification of titles for use until the Phase II directory is completed.

The first production of the shelf-checking Phase II of this
project is *Waterloo Directory of Irish Newspapers and Periodicals, 1800-1900* (Waterloo, Ontario: North Waterloo Academic Press, 1986).   This 1,000 page volume presents an alphabetical listing of newspapers and periodicals in all fields,
with daily to annual frequency.   Serially numbered entries for
more than 4,500 titles give subtitles, title changes, publications dates, series, editors, printers, proprietors, issuing bodies, size, price, circulation figures, frequency indexing information, subject, departments, illustrations, indexing, mergers, reference sources and studies, and locations of copies.
There are cross-references from all later titles and issuing bodies.   Indexes by subject, place, and personal name conclude
the volume.

D–57   **Madden, Lionel, and Diana Dixon.**   *Nineteenth-Century
Periodical Press in Britain: A Bibliography of Modern
Studies, 1901–1971.*   New York: Garland, 1976.

Z6956.G6 M3 1975

Originally published as a supplement to vol. 8, no. 3 (September 1975) of the *Victorian Periodicals Newsletter* (Q–52),
this annotated bibliography of 2,632 items is disposed into
four sections.   Section A includes bibliographies, finding
lists, and reports on bibliographical projects; section B covers
general histories of periodicals and newspapers; section C
treats individual periodicals and newspapers; and section D
presents studies and memoirs of individual proprietors, editors, journalists, and contributors.   Within sections, entries
follow a generally chronological arrangement.   The volume
concludes with an author index.   The work has many small
errors and should be used with caution.   For literary periodicals it may be supplemented by White (D–55) and, more fully, by Vann and VanArsdel, *Victorian Periodicals: A Guide to
Research* (Q–47).   In addition, it may be supplemented by the
relevant sections of the *NCBEL*, vol. 3 (M–11).   For current
references see the annual "Checklist of Scholarship and Criticism" in the *Victorian Periodicals Newsletter* (Q–48).

D–58   **Stanton,   Michael   N.**   *English   Literary   Journals,
1900–1950: A Guide to Information Sources.*   Detroit: Gale
Research Co., 1982.   Z2005.S73 1982

This brief volume is in two parts, the first presenting an annotated bibliography of specifically literary journals published
in England (not Scotland, Wales, or Ireland) during any part
of the period 1900–1950.   The second part, which occupies
about one-fifth of the volume, is a classified secondary bibliography of related material.   The entry for each journal covered in part 1 includes the following information: title, life
span, pertinent publication history, frequency of issue, names
and tenures of the editors, and a discussion of the journal's
aims and nature as well as its contents and notable contributors.   Part 2 is divided into four sections listing general reference works; background readings; works on autobiography,
biography, and letters; and works of critical and historical
commentary on individual literary journals.   The volume
ends with an index of authors and titles and an index of journals.

D–60   **Sullivan, Alvin.**   *British Literary Magazines.*   4 vols.
Westport, Conn.: Greenwood, 1983–86.   PN5124.L6 B74

This four-volume work is designed to provide detailed descriptions of the major literary magazines published in Britain
from the seventeeth century to the present, along with representative minor magazines.   The coverage of the individual
volumes is as follows: vol. 1, The Augustan Age and the Age
of   Johnson,   1698–1788;   vol. 2,   The   Romantic   Age,
1789–1836; vol. 3, The Victorian and Edwardian Ages,
1837–1913; and vol. 4, The Modern Age, 1914–1984.   Each
volume contains lengthy profiles written by specialist contributors on each of the included magazines.

The signed profiles, which vary in quality, offer discursive
accounts of the history, aims, notable associated persons, significant features, and social and cultural impact of the magazine.   After the commentary is a two-part reference section.
The first presents a bibliography of information sources listing
bibliographical authorities that treat the magazine, indexes,
reprint editions, and both American and British locations of
full or partial files.   The second part offers a publication history of the magazine, noting title changes, volume and issue
data, frequency of publication, publishers, and editors.   Volumes conclude with appendixes listing the magazine titles
covered in each of the volumes of the series, presenting a
chronology of social and literary events during the period of

the volume's coverage, and presenting special appendixes appropriate to the volume in question. Thus, volume 1 contains an appendix enumerating successors, imitators, and contemporaries of the *Tatler* and an appendix enumerating predominantly political journals with literary contents. Each volume concludes with an index of names, titles, and subjects and a list of contributors.

D–70 **Brigham, Clarence S.** *History and Bibliography of American Newspapers, 1690–1820.* 2 vols. Worcester, Mass.: American Antiquarian Society, 1947. Reprinted with additions and corrections. Hamden, Conn.: Archon Books, 1962.   Z6951.B86

This bibliography and finding list is of newspapers, not magazines, though, as Brigham notes, the distinction is somewhat arbitrary. Entries are by state, city within state, and then by most recent title of the newspaper. Annotations generally include the establishment date, name of establisher, and frequency; a history of the publication, with changes in proprietorship; and changes in the title. Locations are listed in order of importance, with the earliest files listed first and full details of the completeness of files provided. About 2,210 different newspapers are listed in the two volumes. Indexes of titles and printers are included in volume 2, along with lists of the libraries and private owners whose files are recorded. As with the original work (published serially 1913–1927), so the additions and corrections to these cumulated volumes were first published in the *Proceedings of the American Antiquarian Society* 71 (1961): 15–62; they have been appended in all printings of the two-volume set after the first. Gregory's *Union List* (D–71) supplements Brigham for newspapers beginning after 1820.

Brigham is complemented by Edward Connery Lathem, *Chronological Tables of American Newspapers, 1690–1820: Being a Tabular Guide to Holdings of Newspapers Published in America through the Year 1820* (Worcester, Mass.: American Antiquarian Society, 1972) [Z6951.L3], which arranges the newspapers by date, and then by state and locality, so that for any chronological period it is possible immediately to see what newspapers have been preserved for a particular locality or region.

D–71 **Gregory, Winifred, ed.** *American Newspapers 1821–1936: A Union List of Files Available in the United States and Canada.* New York: H. W. Wilson, 1937.   Z6945.A53

Presents, by state, and city within state, a list of more than 35,000 newspapers published in America between 1821 and 1936 with indication of locations where files are preserved in the United States and Canada. The files of nearly 5,700 depositories are cited, including county courthouses, newspaper offices, and private collections, as well as libraries. Excluded are titles found in the *Union List of Serials* (D–91), foreign newspapers, and the news organs of clubs and associations. The most recent title is used for individual newspaper entries, which are alphabetized under their last city of publication by their first important word (excluding the name of the city). Facts of publication are provided, including initial and final dates, frequency, places of publication, and changes in name. Entries conclude with a list of locations with indication of the extent of the file held at each. If the title of a newspaper is known but not its city of publication, consult Avis G. Clarke, *Alphabetical Index to the Titles in "American Newspapers 1821–1936: A Union List"* (Oxford, Mass.; 1958); "A Bibliography of Union Lists of Newspapers," compiled by Karl Brown and Daniel Haskell, is appended. This union list takes up where the list of Brigham (D–70) ends. For additional newspaper union lists see Tanselle (C–20), 1:135–137, and the general reference guides.

D–72 **Kribbs, Jayne K.** *Annotated Bibliography of American Literary Periodicals, 1741–1850.* Boston: G. K. Hall, 1977.   Z1219.K75

This work presents some 940 serially numbered periodicals published in the United States between 1741 and 1850 which, in the compiler's judgment, are of distinct literary interest. Of the works included, about 840 are annotated. Entries are listed alphabetically by the original title of the periodical. Annotation includes place of publication, dates of first and last issues, periodicity, editor, publisher, two locations of files, and a guide to the literary content of the periodical. The guide to literary content classifies but does not cite locations. Classes are Poetry (giving original poetry and selected poetry signed by the author), Prose (under the categories Biography, Travel, Essay, Familiar Essay, Criticism, Letters, and Book Reviews), Fiction (under the categories Essay Serials [with titles], Sketches, and Tales [with titles]), and Miscellaneous (under the categories Anecdotes, Extracts, Literary Notices, and News). Notes add further information of interest.

The work concludes with a valuable series of indexes. A chronological index listing dates of beginning, titles, places of publication, and closing dates is followed by a geographical index arranged alphabetically by state, then locality, and then title. An index of editors and publishers keyed to item numbers is followed by an index of names of literary figures and those of literary interest. An index of the titles of tales, novels, and drama cited, keyed to item numbers, concludes this volume.

D–73 *Literary Writings in America: A Bibliography.* 8 vols. Millwood, N.Y.: Kraus Thomson Organization, 1977.   Z1225.L58

These volumes present an unedited photographic reprinting of a 250,000-card catalog at the Van Pelt Library of the University of Pennsylvania which contains the results of an elaborate project to index creative American literature written between 1850 and 1940. The project, begun at the University of Pennsylvania in 1938 and terminated in 1942, was organized by the Work Projects Administration. The cards produced during the project are here arranged alphabetically by author and author-as-subject. They result from the analysis of some 2,000 volumes of magazines, some 500 volumes of literary history and biography, and more than 100 bibliographies. *Literary Writings* is thus both an index to periodicals and an index to composite books. The cards give authors and their dates, title of item, periodical, volume, date, and pagination. They also offer a characterization of the item by genre (article, biography, criticism, essay, fiction, letter, narrative, novel, sermon, short story, textbook, travel sketch, verse). Reviews are listed under both the reviewer and the author of the book reviewed.

While these volumes provide only the raw material for an important bibliography, they still serve a useful function in their unedited form if used with appropriate caution. A list of abbreviations for the periodicals indexed (which may not be complete) precedes the entries of volume 1.

D–74 **Chielens, Edward E.** *Literary Journal in America to 1900: A Guide to Information Sources.* Detroit: Gale Research Co., 1975.   Z6951.C57

An annotated bibliography of secondary material on pre-twentieth-century American literary periodicals, this work is disposed into eight chapters. The first two present an introduction and a bibliography of general studies. Chapters 3–6 treat general and individual literary journals associated with each of the "literary" regions of the United States: New England, the Mid-Atlantic, the South, and the West. Chapter 7 cites bibliographies and checklists of periodicals, and chapter

8 presents a bibliography of background studies. The appendixes A and B present a bibliography of works treating literary materials in nonliterary periodicals and one of material concerning Poe and the American literary periodical. Entries are unnumbered but generally annotated. An index of names and titles concludes the volume. It is supplemented by a second volume covering 1900–1950 (D–75).

Chielens has also edited the new volume, *American Literary Magazines: The Eighteenth and Nineteenth Centuries* (Westpost, Conn.: Greenwood, 1986) [Z1231.P45 A43 1986]. See also the new volume, *Magazines of the American South* by Sam G. Riley (Westport, Conn.: Greenwood, 1986) [PN4893.R54 1986] which profiles about ninety magazines from 1764 to the present. Essays are alphabetically arranged and include purpose, audience, editorial policies, bibliographies, and publication history. Riley has also compiled an *Index to Southern Periodicals* (Westport, Conn.: Greenwood, 1986) [Z6952.S6 R54 1986] which lists nearly 7,000 southern non-newspaper periodicals that began publication between 1764 and 1984. The main part of the volume provides a chronological listing, giving title, place(s) of publication, dates of publication, title changes or other alterations in publishing arrangements, and a list of some libraries that hold files of the periodical. An alphabetical list of titles, and a chronological listing by state are provided in appendixes.

D–75 **Chielens, Edward E. *Literary Journal in America, 1900–1950: A Guide to Information Sources.*** Detroit: Gale Research Co., 1977.   Z6951.C572

An annotated bibliography of secondary material on some 100 twentieth-century American literary periodicals, this work forms a supplement to Chielens's earlier work on the literary journal in America to 1900 (D–74), to which it is similar in format and intention. It is disposed into nine chapters. The introduction and a bibliography of general studies and views occupy the first two. Chapter 3 presents studies of general literary periodicals with large circulation, followed by studies of individual periodicals. Chapter 4 has the same arrangement for studies of little magazines of poetry, fiction, and art. Regional literary periodicals are treated in chapter 5, under general studies and then under both general and individual sections for each of the regions. Chapter 6 treats politically radical literary periodicals, while chapter 7 covers academic quarterlies of scholarship and criticism. Chapter 8 cites bibliographies and checklists of periodicals in the various categories treated. Chapter 9 lists background studies, and an appendix lists both general studies and studies of individual nonliterary periodicals that occasionally carry literary material. A combined author-editor- title index concludes the volume.

It should be noted that this work does not serve as an authoritative bibliography of literary periodicals; the annotations are not always reliable.

D–76 **Mott, Frank Luther. *History of American Magazines [1741–1930].*** 5 vols. New York: Modern Language Association of American [and later Cambridge: Harvard University Press], 1930–1968.   PN4877.M63 1938

These five volumes provide the standard history of American magazines, covering 1741–1850, 1850–1865, 1865–1885, 1885–1905, and 1905–1930 respectively. In general, the volumes are disposed in such a way that individual chapters treat types of magazines. There are thus a number of more-or-less self-contained chapters concerned with literary magazines during different periods of American history. Supplements to each volume give sketches of certain important magazines published during the periods 1741–1794, 1794–1825, 1825–1850, 1850–1865, 1865–1885, 1885–1905, and 1905-1930. For the last, posthumous volume, the sketches consti-

tute the only available material. Appendixes to volumes 1–3 present chronological lists of magazines founded 1751–1849, 1850–1864, and 1865–1884, respectively, with charts showing the chronological relations among the runs of the various magazines. Volumes 1–4 are indexed by names, titles, and subjects; there is also an elaborate cumulative index to all five volumes in volume 5.

D–80 **Hoffman, Frederick J., Charles Allen, and Carolyn F. Ulrich. *Little Magazine: A History and Bibliography.*** Princeton, N.J.: Princeton University Press, 1946. Reprinted with additions and some corrections, 1947.   PN4836.H6

The standard work on the subject of little magazines, this volume contains a 230-page discursive history and a 174-page annotated chronological checklist of little magazines published 1891–1945. There is also a detailed index to titles, title changes, and names of editors and contributors.

Among the more recent studies of the little magazine may be mentioned that by Ian Hamilton, the *Little Magazine*: *A Study of Six Editors* (London: Weidenfeld and Nicolson, 1976) [PN4878.3.H3] and that edited by Elliott Anderson and Mary Kinzie, the *Little Magazine in America*: *A Modern Documentary History* (Yonkers, N.Y.: Pushcart Press, 1978) [PN4878.3.L5], which was designed as a companion to Hoffman and consists of a collection of essay-memoirs by prominent and representative persons associated with little magazines. It concludes with "An Annotated Bibliography of [84] Selected Little Magazines" by Peter Martin, pp. 666–750, which is focused on little magazines with important runs after 1950 and thus supplements the bibliographical portion of Hoffman.

VIII. UNION LISTS OF SERIALS

D–90 **Freitag, Ruth S. *Union Lists of Serials: A Bibliography.*** Washington, D.C.: Library of Congress, 1964.
                                                    Z6945.U5 U53

This bibliography of 1,218 serially numbered union lists of serials aims at geographical and chronological comprehensiveness. Included are both union lists properly so called and other bibliographies of serials which give locations in more than one library of materials described. Both separately published lists and those included in journals or as parts of books are covered. Entries are arranged geographically by region or country (in some cases by state or city) and then alphabetically by author. Entries are annotated to describe the arrangement of the union list, the number and location of contributing libraries (using the *NUC* symbols for North American institutions), the number of serials included, and the presence of indexes. The bibliography concludes with three indexes of names, subjects, and places. The introduction describes the history of union lists of serials and enumerates bibliographies relevant to their study which were used in the compilation.

D–91 ***Union List of Serials in Libraries of the United States and Canada [ULS].*** Edited by Edna Brown Titus. 3d ed. 5 vols. New York: H. W. Wilson, 1965.   Z6945.U45 1965

A comprehensive list, first published in 1927, of serials holdings in 956 cooperating North American libraries. More than 156,000 different serials that began publication before the end of 1949 are enumerated. Excluded are government publications; administrative reports; almanacs; American newspapers; English and foreign newspapers published after 1820; alumni and intercollegiate publications; law reports and digests; publications of local, religious, labor, and fraternal organizations; and similar kinds of ephemeral serials. Entries are alphabetical by the *most recent* title (with slight modifications that can be learned from the introductory matter to vol. 1). Title changes, names of publishers, places and dates of publication, and number of volumes are indicated. There are cross-references from earlier or alternative titles. The list uses the *NUC* symbols to identify libraries, provides in the list of symbols information as to individual library loan and/or duplication policies, and indicates under each serial all the libraries reporting holdings of that title. Symbols show whether the reporting library's file is complete or, if incomplete, which items are held. The front matter to volume 1 includes explained sample entries that must be consulted before using this work.

For serials that began publication in 1950 or later, the record of North American library holdings is found in *New Serial Titles* (D–92). It should be noted that local and regional union lists tend to be more current and accurate than this work; their existence and scope can be learned from the Freitag bibliography (D–90).

D–92 **New Serial Titles: A Union List of Serials Commencing Publication after December 31, 1949 [NST].** Washington, D.C.: Library of Congress, 1953–. Z6945.U5 S42

This continuing supplement to the *Union List of Serials* (D–91) is published in eight monthly (since 1969), four quarterly, an annual, and five- or ten-year cumulations. The same information (based on holdings in some 800 participating libraries) is provided for all new, altered, or ceased titles as is found in the *Union List*. Cumulations to date include those for 1950–1960 in two volumes (1961), 1961–1964 in three volumes (1965), 1966–1969 in two volumes (1971), 1971–1975 in three volumes (1976–1977), 1976–1980 in two volumes (1980), and 1981–1985 in six volumes (1986) [Z6945.N4 1981–85]. Since 1981, *NST* has also been published in a Computer Output Microform (COM) format that is issued monthly and continuously cumulated. A twenty-year revised and supplemented *1950-1970 Cumulative* in four volumes was published in 1973 jointly by the Library of Congress and the Bowker Company. It includes additional locations and International Standard Serial Numbers. In addition, Bowker has published *New Serial Titles: 1950-1970, Subject Guide*, 2 vols. (New York, 1975) [Z6945.N42]. It is arranged alphabetically by title under country of publication within some 225 subject headings in Dewey decimal order. Library holdings are not indicated.

Since 1955 the Library of Congress has also published monthly issues of *New Serial Titles—Classed Subject Arrangement* [Z6945.U5 N38], ordered by Dewey decimal classification, with LC and some other library holdings indicated. These issues are not cumulated.

D–93 **Union List of Little Magazines [in the Libraries of Six Midwestern Universities].** Chicago: Midwest Inter-Library Center, 1956. Z6944.L5 I53

This volume presents the holdings of 1,037 little magazines in libraries of Indiana University, Northwestern University, Ohio State University, the State University of Iowa, the University of Chicago, and the University of Illinois. Entries are in alphabetical order by original title, with a history of all title changes. The list includes some titles for which there are no known holdings in any of the participating libraries.

D–95 **British Union Catalogue of Periodicals: A Record of the Periodicals of the World, from the Seventeenth Century to the Present Day, in British Libraries [BUCOP].** Edited by James D. Stewart et al. 4 vols. London: Butterworth's Scientific Publications, 1955–1958. *Supplement to 1960.* London: Butterworths, 1962. Z6945.B87

These four volumes list alphabetically by first main word of title some 140,000 periodicals held in about 440 libraries in Britain. Works issued by an organization, however, are listed under the organization's name, unless it is specified in the title. Many periodicals not listed in the North American *Union List of Serials* (D–91) are included. The classes of included material are magazines, journals, reviews; all *Acts, Proceedings,* and *Transactions* of academies, universities, societies, and institutions; the periodical reports of organizations which regularly contain research results; yearbooks and other annuals; and miscellaneous irregular series issued by universities, societies, and other corporate bodies. Titles or issuing organizations are listed under their earliest known name, with cross-references from later names, followed by a chronological listing of all known changes. An introduction in volume 1 explains conventions followed in the listings, which include sponsoring bodies, dates of publication, and locations of files with details about their extent. All locations of files are *not* given, however, except in the case of rare periodicals for which all reported holdings are included. Since it depends on some complete and some partial reports of holdings, this work is uneven in coverage and should be supplemented by the *Union List of Serials* when compiling a serials bibliography. *BUCOP* generally replaces the 1937 *Union Catalogue of the Periodical Publications in the University Libraries of the British Isles* (D–97), except for the latter's usefulness in discovering additional locations.

The 1962 *Supplement* [Z6945.B874] adds holdings for periodicals that began publication after the original series was issued and before 1960, as well as some entries for earlier periodicals missed in the original list. It also presents expanded and amended entries for some items included in the original volumes. This work, as supplemented, is continued by *New Periodical Titles* (D–96).

D–96 **British Union Catalogue of Periodicals, Incorporating World List of Scientific Periodicals: New Periodical Titles [NPT].** London: Butterworth's Scientific Publications, 1964–1981. Z6945.B874

Since 1964 the additions to the supplemented *British Union Catalogue of Periodicals* (D–95) and the fourth edition of the *World List of Scientific Periodicals Published in the Years 1900-1960* [WLSP], 3 vols. (Washington, D.C.: Butterworths, 1963–1965) [Z7403.W923], have been published jointly in quarterly issues and cumulated annually in two series. One combines all titles from the quarterly issues; the other includes scientific, technical, and medical titles only. There are also multiannual cumulations for each series covering 1960–1968 (London, 1970), and 1969–1973 (London, 1976). These works supplement the *BUCOP* and *WLSP* by providing entries for periodicals that began in or after 1960, changed titles, began a new series, or ceased publication. Entries are alphabetical by title or sponsoring organization as in the original *BUCOP* volumes and include sponsor, place of publication, dates of first (and/or last) issues, frequency, a history of previous or subsequent titles, and file locations in some, though not all, British libraries.

Since 1981, the British Library has published the quarterly, *Serials in the British Library* [Z6945.B874], a union list of serials acquired since 1976 by the library and sixteen other major libraries in the United Kingdom and in Ireland. The quarterly issues are cumulated annually and published in microfiche.

D–98 Other Major Union Lists of Periodicals.

In addition to the *ULS* and the *BUCOP*, there are several other major national union lists of periodicals. The Département des périodiques of the Bibliothèque nationale publishes the *Catalogue collectif des périodiques du début du XVIIᵉ siècle à 1939 [CCP], conservés dans les bibliothèques de Paris et dans les bibliothèques universitaires des départements* (1967–) [Z6945.P236], which covers holdings in some seventy-three French libraries alphabetically by title.

The Staatsbibliothek der Stiftung preussischer Kulturbestiz in Marburg published the *Gesamtverzeichnis ausländischer Zeitschriften und Serien [GAZS]: Hauptband, 1939–1958*, 5 vols. (Wiesbaden: Harrassowitz, 1963–1968), with *Nachträge* (Marburg: Staatsbibliothek der Stiftung preussischer Kulturbesitz, 1966–) [Z6945.S792] that add publications up to 1970 held in West German and West Berlin libraries. In progress is a *Gesamtverzeichnis der deutschen Zeitschriften und Serien [GDZS]*, which will cover German periodicals and serials from the seventeeth century to 1970. Also in progress is a continuation from 1971 of both these series under the title *Gesamtverzeichnis der Zeitschriften und Serien [GZS]*.

A work similar to the West German *GAZS* is published by the Anskunftsbüro der Deutschen Bibliotheken in the Deutsche Staatsbibliothek in East Berlin under the title *Gesamtverzeichnis ausländischer Zeitschriften 1939-1959 [GAZ]* (1964–). It supplements the earlier series, *Gesamtverzeichnis der ausländischen Zeitschriften 1914-1924* (Berlin: Preussische Staatsbibliothek, 1927–1929) [Z6945.P9 1929].

D–99 *Serials Review.* Vol. 1–. Ann Arbor, Mich.: Pierian Press, 1975–. PN4832.S47

This quarterly review of new periodicals includes (since 1984) a *Serials Review Index* that indexes by title reviews of serials in some eighty periodicals commonly held by academic, special, and public libraries. Indexed are such major reviewing journals as *AHR, AN&Q, CE, EHR, JAH, MLJ, MLR, MP, NYRB, NYTBR, N&Q, PBSA, RQ, Speculum,* and *TLS*. Other features include updating accounts of various periodical publications; long signed reviews of serial reference works; lists of recently published cumulative indexes to serials (updating Marconi, D–7); and accounts of important reference tools for serials librarianship. Each issue contains an index, and a cumulation was compiled by Linda Gabel, "*Serials Review*: Cumulative Index of Titles Reviewed in Volumes 1 through 5, 1975–1979," 6.1 (1980): 18 pp. between 38–39.

IX. DIRECTORIES OF CURRENT PERIODICALS

In addition to the following general directories, see the *MLA Directory of Periodicals: A Guide to Journals and Series in Langauges and Literatures* (Z–100).

D–100 *Ulrich's International Periodicals Directory: A Classified Guide to Current Periodicals, Foreign and Domestic.* 26th ed. 2 vols. New York: R. R. Bowker, 1987.
Z6941.U5 1983/84

This is the present edition of the most comprehensive directory of current periodicals in existence, the first edition of which appeared in 1932. The twenty-sixth edition gives information on more than 69,000 periodicals published throughout the world, including all periodicals currently in print

which are issued more frequently than once a year and which are usually published at regular intervals over an indefinite period. Annuals and irregularly published serials are covered in the companion volume, *Irregular Serials and Annuals* (D–101).

The main body of the directory is a subject listing of all the periodicals. Some 557 subject classes are used, within which periodicals are listed alphabetically by title. Full entries occur under only one subject class, with cross-references from other subjects a periodical may cover. Information gathered by direct mail inquiry is uneven. If provided, information given in individual entries includes parallel-language titles, translated titles, subtitle, and variant title information. This information is followed by notation of the languages used in the text, the year of first issue, the frequency of publication, the subscription price, notes on availability of back issues, the corporate author (sponsoring body), the publisher's name and address, and the name of the current editor. Special features (book reviews, bibliographies, abstracts, charts, illustration, etc.) are noted, and information about cumulated indexes is given, as is information about availability in microform. Indexing and abstracting organs are cited. Former titles are given at the end of each entry, along with a brief annotation clarifying the subject-matter specializations of the serial. Also associated with each entry are the Dewey decimal classification of the serial, a code indicating country of publication, the ISSN for both the current and former titles, and (if different from the main entry title) the key title used in assigning the ISSN.

Preliminaries of the volume include a user's guide, lists of abbreviations (including a list of the abbreviated titles of indexing and abstracting services cited), a set of notes on new and revised subject headings, a list of subject fields, and a cross-index of subjects. A new subject feature in the eighteenth edition is the creation of a heading "Abstracting, Bibliographies, Statistics" associated with each major subject. Formerly all such serials were listed together under the generic subjects "Abstracting and Indexing," "Bibliographies," and "Statistics" rather than associated with particular subject matters. The volume concludes with a list of serials that ceased publication, an index to the publications of international organizations, and an alphabetical title index with all variant, parallel-language, and former titles included.

Both *Ulrich's Directory* and its companion volume, *Irregular Serials and Annuals*, are supplemented by the quarterly *Bowker International Serials Database Update* (1985–), formerly *Ulrich's Quarterly* (New York, 1977–1984) [no - LC number], formerly the annual *Bowker Serials Bibliography Supplement*, 1972–1977) [Z6941. U522], which enumerates new titles, changes in titles, and cessations. Each new biennial edition of the two companion directories incorporates and thus replaces the previous editions and any intervening supplements. The Bowker International Serials Database can be searched through both DIALOG and BRS (see Z–78).

D–101 *Irregular Serials and Annuals: An International Directory, 1987–88*. 13th ed. New York: R. R. Bowker, 1986.
Z6941.I78

This is the current edition of the standard directory of annual and irregularly published serials which first was issued in 1967. Designed to complement *Ulrich's Directory* (D–100), this work follows the structure and format of the earlier guide. Some 34,500 current serial publications are covered in the fifth edition, including such classes of publications as proceedings, transactions, reports, yearbooks, handbooks, annual reviews, and monographic series that are in the "twilight" area between books and serials. Included are titles of any serial publications issued annually or less frequently than once a year, or issued irregularly; serial works published at least twice under the same title; and monographs that are announced as the first volume of a series.

Entries are arranged under 461 of the same subject headings as are found in *Ulrich's Directory*, with the same classes of information included (subject to availability from the publisher). There is a title index. Like its companion volume, *Irregular Serials and Annuals* is also supplemented by the *Bowker International Serials Database Update* (1985–) and its predecessors (see D–100) which should be consulted for changes occurring between biennial editions of the main directory. The Bowker International Serials Database can be searched through both DIALOG and BRS (see Z–78).

D–103 *Ayers Directory of Publications.* Philadelphia: Ayer, 1880–.
Z6951.A97

This directory and gazetteer of the American serial press has been published annually since 1880. It absorbed Rowell's *American Newspaper Directory*, 40 vols. (1869–1908) in 1910 and so can claim coverage since 1869. Currently the directory covers serial publication in the United States, Puerto Rico, the Virgin Islands, Canada, the Bahamas, Bermuda, and the Republics of Panama and the Philippines. Publications that have four or more issues annually are eligible for inclusion. There are fifteen separate classified lists in the 1979 *Directory*, most of which are organized by locality. Among these listings are ones for Foreign-language Publications, Jewish Publications, Black Publications, Magazines of General Circulation, Daily Newspapers, Daily Periodicals, Weekly, Semi-, and Tri-weekly Publications, and an alphabetical list of publishers. The main listing of daily, weekly, monthly, and quarterly newspapers is arranged by locality, with considerable gazetteer information provided. *Ayers Directory* serves, in fact, as the best alternative in the absence of a standard gazetteer of the United States. Entries include reference to the periodical title, editor, address, subscription rate, circulation figures, and frequency of publication. A series of maps show localities of publication. Since 1987, this directory is titled the *Gale Directory of Publications* and published by Gale Research, Inc., with a mid-year *Supplement* adding new newspapers, magazines, and other periodicals.

Similar information, less elaborately classified, is available in *Willing's Press Guide* (London: Willing, 1874–) [Z6956.E5 W5] for the serial press of the United Kingdom and the Commonwealth and, in a separate listing, for the principal serial press of Europe (as well as the United States).

D–104 *Standard Periodical Directory*. 9th ed. New York: Oxbridge, 1985.
Z6951.S78

This directory, which began publications in 1964, presents an alphabetical subject arrangement, within which more than 65,000 periodicals are enumerated. The name and address of the publisher, the editorial content and scope of the periodical, its year of foundation, frequency, cost, and total circulation are given. Indexes of titles and subjects conclude the volume.

X. CATALOGS OF BOOKS IN SERIES

D–105 **Baer, Eleanora A. *Titles in Series: A Handbook for Librarians and Students.*** 3d ed. 4 vols. Metuchen, N.J.: Scarecrow Press, 1978.   AI3.B3 1978

An index to 69,657 titles of books published before January 1975 in a series. The first two volumes list the series names in alphabetical order and within each series enumerate the author, title, and date of publication for each published volume number in the series. Each title is assigned an alphanumeric number from A1 through Z143. These numbers are used as means of reference from the author-title index that occupies volumes 3 and 4. Also in volume 4 are an alphabetical list of all series titles keyed to the page numbers in volumes 1 and 2 where the series is enumerated, and a directory of publishers with addresses. For more recent titles in series see the *Library of Congress Catalog*, *Monographic Series* (D–107).

D–107 **Library of Congress. *Monographic Series.*** Washington, D.C., 1974–1982.   Z663.7.L53

This catalog, published in three quarterly issues and an annual cumulation, was composed of all Library of Congress printed cards newly issued or revised which represent monographs that are part of a series. The cards are arranged in alphabetical order by the name of the series or by the name of the corporate body responsible for the series (in which case there is a cross-reference from the series title). Within each series, individual monographs are listed in numerical order, or in alphabetical order by author or title if the series is without numeration. From 1983 on, data available in this publication have been incorporated in the *National Union Catalog: Books* and the new *National Union Catalog: U.S. Books* (B–13).

In addition to this catalog, students interested in series publications will find the new serial publication *Books in Series: Original, Reprinted, In-Print, and Out-of-Print Books, Popular, Scholarly, and Professional Series*, 3d ed. (New York: Bowker, 1980) [Z1033.S5 B724] helpful. It lists more than 100,000 titles in more than 10,000 series alphabetically by series name but also provides separate author and title volumes citing all the monographs listed. See also *Titles in Series* (D–105), and for reprints of monographic series see the *Catalog of Reprints in Series* (E–63).

MISCELLANY

I. DISSERTATIONS—GENERAL AND NATIONAL LISTS

E–1 **Reynolds, Michael M.** *Guide to Theses and Dissertations: An International Annotated Bibliography of Bibliographies.* Rev. and enl. ed. Phoenix, Ariz.: Oryx Press, 1985.

Z5053.A1 R49 1985

Originally published in 1975, this work is an invaluable retrospective international listing of both separately published and embedded closed and serial bibliographies of theses and dissertations produced through 1983–1984. The volume is arranged by subject, with subject and institutional subdivisions. The 2,948 entries are serially numbered in alphanumeric order. Annotations indicate whether the bibliography is of theses or dissertations, whether completed or in progress, the number of items contained, the years within which the theses or dissertations were completed, the institution(s) or place(s) where they were undertaken, the subject coverage of the bibliography, the arrangement, and the indexes found. Annotations are not always sufficiently descriptive of the scope of an item to be relied on exclusively.

The nineteen subject divisions are: A—Universal; B—National bibliographies; C—Area Studies (subdivided); D—Special/Racial Groups (As Subjects and As Authors); E—Applied Sciences; F—Communications and Mass Media (including General, Film, Journalism, and Radio and Television); G—Education; H—Fine Arts (including Arts, Dance, Music, Photography, and Theater subdivisions); J—History; K—Home Economics; L—Languages and Literature (subdivided into sections on General, African Languages and Literature; Anglo-American Languages and Literature; Arabic Literature; Austronesian Linguistics; Chinese Linguistics; Children's Literature; Classical Studies; Comparative Literature; Folklore; Germanic Languages and Literature; Hebrew Literature; Indian Languages and Literature; Japanese Language and Literature, Languages and Linguistics; Philippine Literature; Romance Languages and Literature; Science Fiction; Slavic and East European Languages and Literature; Speech; Individual Authors); M—Law; N—Library and Information Services; P—Medical Sciences; Q—Philosophy; R—Psychology; S—Sciences; T—Social Sciences; and U—Theology and Religion.

The work is concluded by three indexes: of granting institutions for all citations limited to the theses of a single institution, of compilers' names and of journal titles, and a subject index designed to supplement the subject arrangement of the entire volume.

E–5 *Comprehensive Dissertation Index, 1861–1972 [CDI].* 37 vols. Ann Arbor, Mich.: University Microfilms, 1973. Supplements 1973–1977 cumulated in 19 vols. Ann Arbor, Mich., 1980. Annual supplements for 1978–. Z5053.X47

The original volumes and supplements of the *CDI* listed virtually all the dissertations for academic doctoral degrees (not professional or honorary) granted since 1861 by United States educational institutions, along with some dissertations of foreign universities. More than 417,000 dissertations are listed in the original volumes. The CDI is a computer-generated index based on keywords taken from dissertation titles. Many sources were used to compile the data including Library of Congress listings (E–6), *American Doctoral Dissertations* (E–6), and *Dissertation Abstracts International* and its predecessors (E–7). All institutions known to have had doctoral programs prior to 1932 were asked to complete questionnaires on dissertations accepted through 1935. A bibliography of sources consulted is included. Annual supplements indexing American doctoral dissertations accepted during the preceding year are issued. Those for the years 1973–1977 have been cumulated in nineteen volumes; further quinquennial cumulations are planned. In the original volumes entries are grouped by broad disciplinary categories (e.g., vol. 28, History; vols. 29–30, Language and Literature). Within each volume, headings direct the user to general subjects. Cross-references begin each section. The keywords-out-of-context appear in alphabetical order within each general subject, and under each are listed all dissertations having that word in their title. Order under each keyword is chronological, then alphabetical by university, then alphabetical by author. Each entry gives the title with the keyword in boldface in its context, the author, the degree, the date, university, number of pages, and the source of the listing. Entries for dissertations available from University Microfilms refer to the abstract in *DAI* (E–7) and also give a University Microfilm order number. Entries are also keyed to lists in *American Doctoral Dissertations* (E–6) and other bibliographies of dissertations. The author index occupies the last five volumes of the original *CDI*, the last three volumes of the quinquennial supplement cumulation, and the last part of the annual supplementary volumes. The CDI must be used in conjunction with other guides for non-American dissertations, and for dissertations granted by institutions that no longer exist or that no longer grant doctorates.

E–6 *American Doctoral Dissertations [1963/64–] [ADD].* Ann Arbor, Mich.: University Microfilms, 1965/66–.

Z5055.U49 A62

This is the annual classified listing of most dissertations accepted by American and Canadian universities. Entries are arranged by granting institution within broad subject headings ("Language and Literature") and subheadings ("Classical" or "Modern"). A table presents information on the current publication, preservation, and lending policies of each university. There is an author index.

The current series was preceded by the *Index to American Doctoral Dissertations* [1955/56–1962/63], 8 vols. (Ann Arbor, Mich., 1957–1964). The volumes of this series were published as extra numbers of *Dissertation Abstracts* (E–7). The indexes for 1955/56–1956/57 are in *DA*, vol. 16, no. 13 (1956), and vol. 17, no. 13 (1957); 1957/58 is treated in *DA*, vol. 18, no. 7 (1957/58); indexes to 1959/60–1962/63 appear as the 13th number of *DA*, vols. 20–23 (1959/60–1962/63). The format of this prior series is the same as that of current volumes and includes an author index.

The *Index to . . . Dissertations* was preceded by *Doctoral Dissertations Accepted by American Universities*, [1933/34–1954/55], 22 numbers in 18 vols. (New York: Association of Research Libraries, 1934–1956) [Z5055.U49 D6]. Compiled by the Association of Research Libraries, the annual numbers of this series have a format comparable to those of the more recent series. Both published and unpublished dissertations are cited, with bibliographic data given for published works. A "Publication and Presentation" section clarifies individual university arrangements for publication, preservation, and loan of presented theses. There is an author index at the end and an alphabetical subject index in the front matter of each annual number.

For American dissertations prior to 1933 the most comprehensive listing is the Library of Congress's *List of American Doctoral Dissertations Printed* [in 1912–1938], 27 vols. (Washington, D.C., 1913–1940) [Z5055.U49 U5], which records only printed dissertations received annually by the Library of Congress in four parts: an alphabetical author list (with a supplementary list of unrecorded dissertations published in previous years), a general subject list following the Library of Congress classification system, a detailed subject index, and a list of authors arranged alphabetically by granting institutions.

E–7 *Dissertation Abstracts International [DAI].* Series A and B, vol. 30– Ann Arbor, Mich.: University Microfilms, July 1969–.

Z5053.D57

Originally titled *Microfilm Abstracts* (vols. 1–11, 1938–1951), then titled *Dissertation Abstracts* (vols. 12–29, 1951–1969). Beginning with vol. 27 (1966), divided into two series: A—Humanities and Social Sciences, and B—Sciences. Volumes 1–29 (1938–1969) are cumulated in a *Retrospective Index*, 9 vols. in 11 (1970), volume 8 of which covers dissertations in the fields of communication, information, business, literature, and fine arts, and volume 9 of which is an author index to the whole retrospective cumulation. Beginning with volume 37 (1976), a third series, C—Foreign Dissertations, has now been published.

The base volumes give abstracts of dissertations from American, Canadian, and (since 1969) European universities associated with University Microfilms which are available for purchase in microfilm or xerographic reproductions. Issues include all dissertations filmed during the period they cover, irrespective of the date when the thesis may originally have been submitted for a degree. Abstracts are arranged by broad subject categories (e.g., language and literature) and within categories by university. Entries give author and title, the abstract, name of thesis adviser, and a unique identification number. Various indexes to authors and subjects are available for various periods; full details may be found in Reynolds (E–1). The *Retrospective Index* to volumes 1–29 is an alphabetical permuted keyword-in-title index covering some 150,000 dissertations. Entries give reference to the granting institution and to the volume and page number of the original *Abstracts* listing.

Currently, *DAI* is published monthly both in series A and B and in series C. Each issue has a keyword-in-title and author index; there is a cumulated annual keyword-in-title and author index to each series. In addition to searching the file oneself, one can take advantage of the University Microfilm computerized information retrieval program called *Datrix II*, which uses selected keywords to identify all dissertations in the system having titles that contain them. Information about the use of this service may be obtained directly from the company. Also available is a semiannual (quarterly since 1976) index, *Masters Abstracts: A Catalog of Selected Masters Theses on Microfilm*, vol. 1– (Ann Arbor, Mich.: University Microfilms International, 1962–) [Z5055.U49 M3], similar in format to *DAI*, listing masters' theses recommended for publication in microform by the faculty of one or another of some ninety granting institutions. The author and subject indexes are cumulated annually and quinquennially.

Another source of current M.A. thesis citations is *Master's Theses in the Arts and Social Sciences* [1976–] (Cedar Falls, Iowa: Research Publications, 1977–) [Z5055.U5 M465], an annual classified list of United States and Canadian theses with indexes of authors and institutions.

Because Harvard University did not participate in the University Microfilms disseratation publishing program until 1982, earlier Harvard dissertations are only available through interlibrary loan, except for those reprinted by Garland Publishing in the series, *Harvard Dissertations in American and English Literature* and *Harvard Dissertations in Comparative Literature*.

E–10 *Retrospective Index to Theses of Great Britain and Ireland, 1716–1950.* Edited by R. R. Bilboul and F. L. Kent. Vol. 1: *Social Sciences and Humanities.* Santa Barbara, Calif.: ABC-Clio, 1975.

No LC number

This volume brings together the titles of some 13,000 theses from all universities, indexed by subject (pp. 1–234) and by author (pp. 235–393). Further volumes will add some 40,000 additional titles in the fields of applied sciences and technology, life sciences, physical sciences, and chemical sciences.

The availability of pre–1950 theses is discussed in the brief work of P. D. Record, *Survey of Thesis Literature in British Libraries* (London: Library Association, 1950) [Z5035.G69 R4], which treats British theses identifying by university the deposit and availability policies in force and, in a second part, foreign theses available in British libraries. See also the updating of the second part of Record by R. S. Johnson, *Foreign Theses in British Libraries* (Cardiff: The Library, University College, 1971) [Z5053.J64].

For theses accepted in or after 1950 see the annual *Index to Theses Accepted for Higher Degrees in the Universities of Great Britain and Ireland* (E–11).

E–11 *Index to Theses Accepted for Higher Degrees in the Universities of Great Britain and Ireland* [since 1968:] *and the Council for National Academic Awards.* Vol. 1– [1950/51–]. London: ASLIB, 1953–. Z5055.G69 A84

This semiannual publication (annual through vol. 24, 1974) classifies, on the basis of their titles, British and Irish masters' and doctoral theses under broad general subject headings (e.g., Language and Literature) elaborately subdivided into chronological, historical, and other appropriate groupings. There is extensive cross-referencing. The serially numbered entries are listed within their proper subdivision alphabetically by the name of the granting university and then by author. Entries give authors, titles, degrees, and dates.

Each volume concludes with a keyword-in-title subject index, an author index, and a "Table of Availability" that provides information on access and lending policies of the various granting institutions. Note that classification depends on the title assigned a thesis, that information is secured by reports from the accepting universities, and that certain works are excluded (those associated with postgraduate diplomas from the University of London and those submitted in conjunction with a written examination).

For theses before 1950 see the *Retrospective Index to Theses of Great Britain and Ireland, 1716–1950* (E–10).

E–13 *Répertoire des thèses de doctorat soutenues devant les universités de langue française [1969/70–].* Vol. 1–. Quebec: Université Laval; later Montreal: Association des universités partiellement ou entièrement de langue française [AUPELF], 1970–. No LC number

Originally semiannual, after 1973 a bimonthly publication listing annually some 7,000 to 8,000 serially numbered theses that were presented to French-speaking universities in twenty countries. There are five parts: 1) a geographic index, 2) a subject index, 3) an index of thesis advisers, 4) an author index, and 5) a list by the number assigned each dissertation giving author, title, university, degree and date, and the name of the thesis adviser.

E–14 *Répertoire des thèses de doctorat européennes: Année [1969–].* Louvain: DeWallens, 1970–. Z5055.E85 R45

This annual computer-generated alphabetical author index published by the Bibliothèque général of the Université de Liège is a guide to Western European doctoral dissertations. Excluded, however, are the dissertations of Spain, Portugal, Italy, and East Germany. Entries give author's names, dissertation titles, dates, paginations, and university names. The entries, which number about 12,000 annually, are now disposed into three subject areas: sciences humaines, medicine, and science. The first few volumes had a slightly different arrangement. The annual volumes conclude with four indexes of keywords in titles by languages, one of French keywords, one of German, one of English, and one of keywords in other languages.

E–15 *Catalogue des thèses et écrits académiques [after 1959: Catalogue des thèses de doctorat] soutenues devant les universités françaises.* Fasc. 1–75 [1884/85–1958]. Paris: [Publisher varies], 1885–1959. 75 parts in 15 vols. *Catalogue des thèses de doctorat … Nouvelle série [1959–].* Paris: Cercle de la librarie, 1960–. Z5055.F8 C357

The official annual list of French dissertations, prepared from 1930 on by the Bibliothèque nationale. Arranged alphabetically by universities, 1884–1913, and by faculties (law, medicine, letters), universities, and authors since 1914. Entries generally give author, full title, place, date, size, and pagination of the thesis. An index of authors has been included since 1957 in the last fascicles of the original series and in the annual volumes of the new series. This new series is also known as *Supplément D* (C–54) of the *Bibliographie de la France.* Entries are serially numbered, and both the author and the keyword-in-title indexes are keyed to the entry numbers. An index by university is also keyed to the entry numbers.

In 1982 this work split into three separate annual publications, listing theses in the sciences; in medicine and the medical arts and sciences; and in law, economics, and the humani-

ties. This last has the title *Inventaire des thèses de doctorat soutenues devant les universités françaises; Droit, sciences economiques, sciences et gestion, lettres, sciences humaines, theologies* [1981–] (Paris: Université de Paris I, Bibliothèque de la Sorbonne, Direction des bibliothèques, des musées et de l'information scientifique et technique, 1982–) [Z5055.F69 I59].

E–17 **Mundt, Hermann.** *Bio-bibliographisches Verzeichnis von Universitäts- und Hochschuldrucken (Dissertationen) vom Ausgang des 16. bis Ende des 19. Jahrhunderts.* 13 fascicles in 2 vols. (incomplete). Leipzig: Carlsohn, 1936–1942. Completed by vol. 3, compiled by K. Wickert. Munich: Verlag Dokumentation, 1977. Z5033.M89

This catalog, the first two volumes of which (A-Ritter) were left incomplete until recently, attempts to include records of printed German dissertations along with items from Sweden, Norway, and Holland which were defended through the end of the nineteenth century and which include some biographical information about the persons involved. Entries are generally arranged alphabetically by the respondent (i.e., the "author" of the dissertation); if more than one respondent was involved in the examination, entry is then by the name of the *praeses* (i.e., the presiding officer at the doctoral examination). The third volume generally retains the structure of the original two but sets the closing date for entries at 1800. The first two volumes present a total of 28,989 serially numbered entries; the additional volume (with its earlier closing date) adds nearly 9,000 works to bring the total number to 37,834.

E–18 *Jahresverzeichnis der deutschen Hochschulschriften [1885–]* [current title: *Jahresverzeichnis der Hochschulschriften der Deutsche Demokratischen Republik, der Bundesrepublik Deutschland, und West Berlins].* Berlin and Leipzig: Börsenverein der deutschen Buchhändler, 1887–1936; Leipzig: VEB Verlag für Buch- und Bibliothekswesen, 1937–. Z5055.G39 B35

This is the standard annual listing of German dissertations and has been edited since 1937 by the Deutsche Bücherei, Leipzig. Arranged first by place, then university, then faculty (for theses in literature see the Philosophische Fakultät), serially numbered dissertations are then listed alphabetically by author. Entries include title, date, publication information, size, and whether reprinted in a journal or elsewhere. The scope of covered institutions has varied. Technische Hochschulen are included from 1913; all other Hochschulen from 1924. Author and keyword only author indexes are available.

Dissertations are also included in the *Deutsche Nationalbibliographie* (C–64), quarterly in "Reihe B: Neuerscheinungen ausserhalb des Buchhandels," from 1931 through 1967 and since 1968 in the monthly "Reihe C: Dissertationen und Habilitationsschriften." The "Reihe B" listings include only East German dissertations after 1946; there are quarterly and annual author and subject indexes. The "Reihe C" listings are disposed into twenty-four subject classes and cover all separately published German-language dissertations and academic lectures; monthly issues contain both author and subject indexes. Since 1972, dissertations have also been listed by the *Deutsche Bibliographie*, Frankfurt (E–19).

E–19 *Deutsche Bibliographie: Hochschulschriften-Verzeichnis [1971–],* Frankfurt am Main: Buchhändler-Vereinigung, 1972–. Z5055.G3 D486

This monthly listing, known also as "Reihe H" of the Frankfurt German National Bibliography (see C–65), lists only West German dissertations under broad subject fields. Entries give institution, faculty, date, publication, and availability information. Author, title, and keyword indexes in each issue are cumulated annually.

For complete bibliographic control this list should be used in conjunction with the Leipzig list cited in E–18.

II. DISSERTATIONS—SUBJECT LISTS (NATIONAL LITERATURES)

Dissertations are treated in many general reference tools. Besterman (A–1) lists bibliographies of theses under the heading "Academic Writings"; *Bibliographic Index* (A–2) cites such bibliographies under the heading "Dissertations." Gray, *Serial Bibliographies* (A–8), identifies those that cite dissertations. Among the bibliographies in English and American Literature which do cite theses, see the *MLA International Bibliography* (L–50), New's *Bibliography of Commonwealth Literature* (M–100), and *Western American Literature* (S–117), among many others.

E–20 **McNamee, Lawrence F.** *Dissertations in English and American Literature: Theses Accepted by American, British, and German Universities 1865–1964.* New York: R. R. Bowker, 1968. *Supplement 1* [Dissertations Accepted], 1964–1968. New York, 1969, *Supplement 2* [Dissertations Accepted], 1969–1973. New York, 1974.   Z5053.M32

This computer-generated work is based on the records of universities that fall within the scope indicated by its title. Arrangement of entries is by subject classes, so that a user can readily tell what work has been done on a topic. Numeric codes were devised for home universities and for subject classes. The subject code divides first into thirty-five chapters, each with up to 100 subdivisions. Where feasible, the first fourteen of these subdivisions are parallel, facilitating tracing across divisions: thus code 0411 is humor in the Middle English period, 0711 is humor in seventeenth-century English literature, 5011 is humor in the American colonial period, and 11 is generally the "humor" subdivision. The main body of the volume is in the numerical order of subject and subject subdivision codes; within each subdivision, dissertations are listed in chronological order. An appended cross-index of historical authors-as-subjects relates them to the authors of dissertations; an alphabetical listing of dissertation authors is keyed back to the subject code entries. The two supplements add nearly 12,000 dissertations to the 14,521 listed in the original volume; they also add theses accepted by British Commonwealth universities to the original scope. It is advisable to check the list of subject codes used and to study entries under all related subject codes when using this tool. Because of the imperfection of all subject classifications, this work can profitably be supplemented by the keyword-in-title *Comprehensive Dissertation Index* (E–5) and, where possible, by other subject-area bibliographies of dissertations such as Altick and Matthews (E–33) and Woodress (E–35).

E–21 **Mummendy, Richard.** *Die Sprache und Literatur des Angelsachsen im Spiegel der deutschen Universitätsschriften, 1885–1950: Eine Bibliographie/Language and Literature of the Anglo-Saxon Nations as Presented in German Doctoral Dissertations, 1885–1950: A Bibliography.* Bonn: H. Bouvier; Charlottesville: Bibliographical Society of the University of Virginia, 1954.   Z2011.M8

A seriously incomplete list of 2,989 dissertations submitted to German universities in the period 1885–1950, including the University of Strasbourg to 1918, and Austrian universities

from 1938 through 1945. Entries are disposed into three main divisions: (1) linguistics, subdivided by subject field; (2) literary science including poetics, literary criticism, and literary history; (3) theatrical science including the theory and history of the drama, subdivided by historical period. Entries include details of publication (form and place) not found in other lists.

The volume concludes with an author and a subject index. It is supplemented by McNamee (E–20) and by more recent bibliographies of dissertations in particular fields of English and American literature. In recent years, listings of German dissertations in the fields of English and American Literature have been published irregularly in the form of articles in or supplements to *Anglia: Zeitschrift für englische Philologie* (see Reynolds, L–24, L–25) and *English and American Studies in Germany* (E–22).

E–22 **Habicht, Werner, ed.** *English and American Studies in German: Summaries of Theses and Monographs: A Supplement to Anglia [1967–].* Tübingen: Niemeyer, 1969–.
PE3.A6 suppl.

An annual volume of serially numbered extended summaries in English of printed and typescript doctoral dissertations, *Habilitationsschriften*, and monographs. Summaries are by the author of the thesis. Entries identify the author, the German title, the translated title, whether the work is a dissertation, the location where it was written, the sponsoring professor, and publication information. Entries are in three divisions, I. Language, II. English Literature (including world literature in English and Comparative Studies), III. American Literature (including Canadian literature); after 1972 a fourth division was added, IV. General / Teaching of English. There are two indexes, one of thesis and monograph authors and the other of subjects and authors-as-subjects. Originally a guide to academic writings, this annual now cites more monographs than theses and thus supplements for German scholarship other serial bibliographies of English and American literature such as *MLA* (L–50) or *MHRA* (M–21).

E–23 **Gabel, Gernot U., and Gisela R. Gabel.** *Dissertations in English and American Literature: Theses Accepted by Austrian, French, and Swiss Universities, 1875–1970.* Hamburg: Gernot Gabel Verlag, 1977.   Z2011.G25

Designed to supplement Mummendey (E–21) and McNamee (E–20), this volume records 2,169 serially numbered dissertations in the subject areas of English and American literature accepted for degrees by Austrian (1,051), French (723), and Swiss (395) universities. Entries are grouped by period with chapters on literary history and criticism, Old and Middle English literature, sixteenth-century, seventeenth-century, eighteenth-century, nineteenth-century, and twentieth-century English literature, and two concluding chapters on American literature to 1900 and American literature of the twentieth century. Within each period, arrangement is alphabetical by literary author and text, then chronological, and finally (if necessary) alphabetical by the name of the thesis writer. In addition to the author and title of the dissertation, only the name of the university and date of acceptance are cited. The bibliography concludes with an author-subject (including author-as-subject) index.

E–24 **Naamen, Antoine.** *Guide bibliographique des thèses littéraires canadiennes de 1921 à 1976.* Sherbrooke: Editions Naamen, 1978.   Z6511.N26

This volume, which supersedes the earlier *Guide bibliographique des thèses littéraires canadiennes de 1921 à 1969* (Sherbrooke: Naamen, 1970) and its supplement, *Répertoire des thèses littéraires canadiennes, janvier 1969-septembre*

1971 (1972) [Z6511.B75], presents a classified list of 5,613 serially numbered theses by Canadian authors on literary subjects. The first part enumerates theses on topics of general and comparative literature. It is disposed into seven sections on culture, folklore, and the history of ideas; literary genres; literary history; world literature in French; comparative studies; translations; and philology and linguistics (i.e., sciences du langage). Entries are in chronological order beneath subject headings. The second part presents theses on individual authors classified alphabetically by author, and under each author, in chronological order by date of thesis submission. Entries in both parts give the name of the author, the thesis title, the degree, university, and year, pagination, name of the thesis director, and reference to publication information when applicable. The work concludes with five indexes, of thesis authors, of directors, of authors studied, of subjects (French, English, and foreign languages), and of literary works.

E–25 **Howard, Patsy C.** *Theses in English Literature, 1894–1970.* Ann Arbor, Mich.: Pierian Press, 1973.
Z2011.H63

This bibliography of 9,000 unpublished baccalaureate and masters' theses is based on information collected from files in colleges and universities of the American East, South, and Southwest. Though international in scope, most entries are for theses accepted by American, Canadian, or British institutions. The serially numbered entries are classified alphabetically by subject author, and under each class alphabetically by thesis author. Entries present author, title, degree, institution, date, and sometimes pagination. A list of institutions from which theses are cited and a table of contents precede the main body. The volume concludes with a general subject index including authors-as-subjects, and a separate index of thesis authors. A companion volume covers theses in American literature (E–26). For aid in finding masters' theses not in Howard, see Dorothy M. Black, *Guide to Lists of Master's Theses* (Chicago: ALA, 1965) [Z5055.U49 B55].

E–26 **Howard, Patsy C.** *Theses in American Literature, 1896–1971.* Ann Arbor, Mich.: Pierian Press, 1973.
Z1225.H67

This bibliography of 7,000 serially numbered unpublished baccalaureate and masters' theses is identical in scope and arrangement with its companion volume covering English literature (E–25).

III. DISSERTATIONS—SUBJECT LISTS IN FIELDS OF ENGLISH AND AMERICAN LITERATURE

E–30 **Pulsanio, Phillip.** *Annotated Bibliography of North American Doctoral Dissertations on Old English Language and Literature.* East Lansing, Mich.: Colleagues Press, 1988.

This work aims to be a comprehensive listing and treats nearly one thousand dissertations. They are enumerated under three main headings, General Works, Poetry, and Prose. Within each category entries are arranged chronologically, and give the following information: author's name, dissertation title, university, year, pagination, and the director's name (where known). Entries also include the *Dissertation Abstracts International* number (E–7), bibliographical information on the work if published in a dissertation series, a list of additional works discussed, and information on ordering a co-

py. Dissertations which appeared as books are enumerated in a separate bibliography. Cross-references and indexes of subject and author increase the ease of reference.

E–33 **Altick, Richard D., and William R. Matthews.** *Guide to Doctoral Dissertations in Victorian Literature, 1886–1958.* Urbana: University of Illinois Press, 1960. Z2013.A4

Lists 2,105 dissertations in ten chapters with abundant cross-references. The classification is into theses on General Topics (including movements and minor types), Themes and Intellectual Influences, Fiction, Drama, Poetry, Literary Criticism, Periodicals, Foreign Relations (with further subdivisions), and Individual Authors. Entries list author, title, institution, and year. The serially numbered entries are drawn from dissertations submitted in the United States (through 1958), the United Kingdom (through 1956), Germany (through 1956), Austria (through 1958), Switzerland (through 1958), and France (through 1958), dealing wholly or in part with British literature of the period 1837–1900. Authors who were "established" by 1900 are included; those who are associated with the romantic period, though they lived on beyond 1837, are not. The volume concludes with an index to authors of dissertations.

For dissertations completed after the closing dates see the bibliography in *Victorian Studies* (Q–38).

E–35 **Woodress, James.** *Dissertations in American Literature, 1891–1966.* 3d ed. Durham, N.C.: Duke University Press, 1968. Z1225.W8 1968

This edition of a work that first appeared in 1957 (2d ed., 1962) cites 4,700 completed dissertations from all countries alphabetically by subject. First, individual authors as subjects are listed, then thirty-three general subjects (some of which are further subdivided) including Drama, Fiction, Humor and Satire, Poetry, Criticism, Periodicals and Journals; the American Revolution, Civil War, Foreign Relations, Regionalism; Indians, the Negro; Folklore, Religion, and Fine Arts. Entries are serially numbered and give author, title, institution, and date. The table of contents and author index are keyed to entry numbers. There are many cross-references. This work is continued, though imperfectly, by the lists of completed dissertations in each issue of *American Literature* (S–12), which also has lists of dissertations in progress. But these lists are not by any means complete.

E–36 **"American Studies Dissertations in Progress [for 1956–]."** *American Quarterly*, vol. 8– (1956–). AP2.A3985

From vol. 27 (1975) on, titled "American Studies Research in Progress," this annual classified listing cites M.A. theses, Ph.D. dissertations, monographs, and other research projects in progress on all aspects of American studies. Entries are arranged alphabetically by author, and give titles, institutions, names of directors, the estimated date of completion, and the name of the publisher if the work is under contract. Entries are grouped into broad categories that vary from year to year and include such rubrics as Literature, Social Sciences, History and Biography, Regions, Plastic and Visual Arts, and Popular-Culture Studies. Within each such category entries are divided under the subcategories "New Listings" (i.e., work now in progress not previously listed or changed), "Completed," and "Withdrawn" (i.e., project abandoned).

E–38 **Emerson, O. B., and Marion L. Michael.** *Southern Literary Culture: A Bibliography of Masters' and Doctors' Theses.* Rev. and enl. ed. University: University of Alabama Press, 1979.   Z1251.S7 C3 1979

The updated version of a work originally published in 1955, this volume, prepared under the auspices of the Society for the Study of Southern Literature, presents approximately 8,000 titles on authors and topics associated with the literature of the Old and New South. It is disposed into three parts, the first of which lists theses on individual writers alphabetically by the name of each literary figure and then by thesis author. Part 2 is concerned with theses on the cultural, historical, and social backgrounds of Southern literature and is subdivided into sections on folklore, education, and theater history, among other topics. The last part includes theses on broader subjects such as Southern literature, bibliographies and checklists, comparative studies, and several others.

E–40 **Litto, Frederic M.** *American Dissertations on the Drama and the Theatre.* Kent, Ohio: Kent State University Press, 1969.   Z5781.L56

This computer-generated index to American doctoral theses on the theater to 1965 contains some 4,565 theses. Its goal is to cite any study offering primary or secondary information about the theatrical performing arts including drama, the legitimate stage, opera, film, radio and television, dance, and popular entertainments. Citations are drawn from a variety of sources, some of which are enumerated in the prefatory materials.

The volume is disposed into three sections. The first is a bibliography in the alphanumeric order of a reference code derived from the first four letters of the thesis author's last name, the author's initials, the last two digits of the year of the thesis, and the first letters of the first three significant words of the title. The entries present the name of the author, the title of the thesis, the academic department of the author, the degree granted, the university, and the date. Following the bibliography is an alphabetical author index keyed to the reference code for each author's thesis. The second main section is a Keyword-in-Context (KWIC) Index to every significant word in every dissertation title except such words as *drama* and *theater*, which appear too frequently to be of use in locating relevant theses. The last section is a subject index arranged by country, within country chronologically, and within chronological periods, by subjects such as individual authors, audience, and the like. Both the second and the third sections are also keyed to the reference code. Announced plans to publish quinquennial supplements have not been fulfilled.

IV. MICROFORMS

For a general bibliography of nonbook material see Hans Wellisch, ed., *Nonbook Materials: A Bibliography of Recent Publications* (College Park: College of Library and Information Services, University of Maryland, 1975) [Z688.N6 W44].

E–50 **Dodson, Suzanne Cates, ed.** *Microform Research Collections: A Guide.* 2d ed. Westport, Conn.: Meckler, 1984.
                                                    Z1033.M5 D64 1984

A selective guide, first published in 1978, to nearly 400 major research collections available in microform. Collections are listed in alphabetical order by "main" title, with cross-references in the index from alternative titles. Entries include publishing dates, publisher, format, price, citation of reviews

of the collection, discussion of collection arrangement and bases of bibliographical control, an enumeration of related bibliographies and indexes (both print and nonprint), and a descriptive account of the scope and content of the microform collection. Comments include quotations from publishers' brochures and from reviews of the collection under discussion. The volume concludes with an elaborate and comprehensive index to authors, editors, and titles of microform collections and cited reference sources; an index to subjects; and cross-references to alternate titles.

Among the major research collections available in microform and described in Dodson are the following series of particular interest to students of English and American language and literature (bibliographical controls are given in parentheses):

1. *American Autobiographies* (Kaplan; see G–41).
2. *American Culture Series, 1493–1875.* Selected by the American Studies Association. Compiled and edited by David R. Weiner, *Bibliography of American Culture* (Ann Arbor, Mich.: University Microfilms International, 1979) [Z1215.A583].
3. *American Fiction 1774–1900* (Wright; see S–85). *Cumulative Author Index to the Microfilm Collection* [Z1231.F4 R4].
4. *American Fiction 1901–1910* (Wright; see S–85).
5. *American Periodicals*, Series I (eighteenth century), II (1800–1850), III (1850–1900). See Jean Hoornstra and Trudy Heath, *American Periodicals, 1741–1900: An Index to the Microfilm Collection* (Ann Arbor, Mich.: University Microfilms International, 1979) [Z6951.H65].
6. *American Poetry* (Harris collection; see B–33).
7. *British and Continental Rhetoric and Elocution* (see X–102).
8. *British Manuscripts* (British Manuscripts Project; see H–19).
9. *British Periodicals in the Creative Arts* (Periodicals, 1770–1900). Index [Z5937.B75].
10. *British Records Relating to America in Microform* (Crick and Allman, see H–50).
11. *Early American Imprints: First Series, 1639–1800* (Evans, see C–22).
12. *Early American Imprints: Second Series, 1801–1819* (Shaw-Shoemaker, see C–23).
13. *Early American Newspapers 1704–1820* (Brigham, see D–70).
14. *Early British Fiction: Pre–1750* (Beasley, see P–40; and McBurney, see P–44).
15. *Early British Periodicals* (170 periodicals; University Microfilms). Fader, *British Periodicals of the Eighteenth and Nineteenth Centuries* [PN5124.P4 F3].
16. *Early English Books: Series 1: 1475–1640* (Pollard and Redgrave, see C–5). Guide: *English Books 1475–1640: A Partial List by STC Numbers* [Z2002.E2].
17. *Early English Books: Series 2: 1641–1700* (Wing, see C–7). *English Books 1641–1700: A Partial List by Wing Numbers* [Z2002.U583].
18. *Early English Courtesy Books 1571–1773* (Newberry Collection, see B–25).
19. *Early English Newspapers: 1622–1820* [the Burney Collection]. Guide: Susan M. Cox and Janice L. Budeit, *Early English Newspapers: Bibliography and Guide to the Microfilm Collection* (Woodbridge, Conn.: Research Publications, 1983).
20. *English and American Plays of the Nineteenth Century.* (Nicoll, vols. 4–6, see U–71). Index to the American Plays: Donald L. Hixon and Don A. Hennessee, *Nine-*

teenth Century Drama: A Finding Guide (Metuchen, N.J.: Scarecrow, 1977) [PS632.H57].

21. *English Cartoons and Satirical Prints, 1320–1832, in the British Museum.*

22. *English Linguistics 1500–1800* (Alston, see I–12).

23. *English Literary Periodicals* (233 journals of the eighteenth and nineteenth centuries).

24. *Nineteenth and Twentieth Century English and American Drama* (see U–38).

25. *Publications of English Local Record Societies, 1844-1957* (Mullins, see H–76).

26. *Selected Americana from Sabin's Dictionary* (see C–21).

27. *Three Centuries of Drama*, including the Larpent MSS at the Huntington Library among the 5,350 plays reproduced. Covered are British plays, 1500–1800 and American plays, 1714–1830 (Bergquist, see U–37).

28. *Victorian Fiction and other Nineteenth Century Fiction* (Sadleir, see Q–76).

Recently available is an *Index to Microform Collections* by Ann Niles (Westport, Conn.: Meckler, 1984) [Z1033.M5 I53 1984], which provides a list of the contents of some thirty collections and then indexes by author and title. Subsequent volumes will presumably index additional collections.

Among other microform series of interest to students of English and American literature may be mentioned the following:

1. *American Biographical Archive* (K. G. Saur), a cumulated collection of major and minor biographical reference works from the beginnings of American history to the early 20th century (G–39).

2. *Archivo Biografico de España, Portugal e Iberoamerica / The Spanish, Portuguese and Latin American Biographical Archive* (K. G. Saur), a cumulated collection of more than 300 original biographical reference works (G–68).

3. *Bibliography of German-Language Publications, 1700–1910* (K. G. Saur), a microform edition of the Gesamtverzeichnis des deutschsprachigen Schrifttums 1700–1900 (C–66).

4. *Bibliography of German-Language Publications, 1911–1965* (K. G. Saur), a microform edition of the Gesamtverzeichnis des deutschsprachigen Schrifttums, 1911–1965 (C–67).

5. *Bibliotheca Shakespeariana* (Microforms International), some 3,000 works in thirty subject units, including Shakespeare's Editors since Rowe, Theatres and Staging, Adaptations and Acting Versions, Shakespeare Bibliographies and Periodicals, and many others. Each unit has a subject guide prepared by its editor, who is in each instance a distinguished specialist in the field.

6. *British Biographical Archive* (K. G. Saur), a cumulated collection of original biographical reference works, containing nearly 450,000 entries pertaining to 250,000 individuals. Included are persons from England, Scotland, Wales, Ireland, and all British colonies to the date of independence or home rule, as well as persons generally associated with Britain (G–12).

7. *Charles Dickens Research Collection* (Chadwyck-Healey and Yushodo), including over 700 items from the J. F. Dexter Collection in the British Library and other major collections.

8. *Eighteenth Century* (Research Publications), including some 200,000 items from the *Eighteenth Century Short Title Catalogue* (C–13).

9. *Eighteenth Century English Provincial Newspapers* (Research Publications).

10. *German Biographical Archive: A Cumulation of the Most Important 18th- and 19th Century Biographical Reference Works / Deutsches Biographisches Archiv* (K. G. Saur), a cumulation of 262 reference works published between 1700 and 1910, containing some 400,000 entries (G–62).

11. *Nineteenth Century: Sources in English for the Study of the Period 1801–1900* (Chadwyck-Healey, in association with the British Library and Avero Publications), a massive project including Specialist Collections in Literature, Visual Arts and Architecture, Linguistics, Publishing, the Booktrade and the Diffusion of Knowledge, and a General Collection of Works in Politics, Economics, Geography, Agriculture, History, Law, Philosophy, Psychology, Religion, the Useful Arts, Education, Recreation, Science, Medicine, and Household Management. The first parts of the Literature Specialist Collection treat Women Writers and Children's Literature.

12. *Ninteenth-Century Children's Periodicals* (Greenwood Press), includes eleven periodicals published in the United States from 1836 to 1921.

13. *Renaissance Rhetoric: Key Texts, A. D. 1479–1602* (Microforms International), includes works by fifty-two authors from the Bodleian Library, selected by James J. Murphy, and published with a printed guide.

14. *Science Fiction Periodicals, 1926–1978* (Greenwood Press), includes twenty-one titles selected by Thomas D. Clareson.

E–51 **Union List of Microfilms.** Rev., enl., and cumulated ed. Ann Arbor, Mich.: Edwards, 1951. [Supplement] Cumulation 1949–1959. 2 vols. Ann Arbor, Mich.: Edwards, 1961.   Z1033.M5 P5

This national union catalog of microfilm holdings came out in two series. The first is a one-volume cumulation of some 25,000 films representing all holdings to 1949 of some 197 reporting institutions. Entries give the Library of Congress subject classification, bibliographical information, the *NUC* abbreviation of the library holding the microfilm, the type of film, and the *NUC* abbreviation of the location of the originals from which the film was made. A series of supplements for 1949–1952 and 1952–1955 have been replaced by the cumulation for 1949–1959 in two volumes. Cited are some 52,000 entries representing accessions reported by 215 libraries. Entries in both series are alphabetical by author or title in the case of serial or anonymous publications. Newspapers are included in the first series but excluded from the second since they were separately indexed in *Newspapers in Microform* (E–56). Dissertations are also omitted. For more recent microforms see the *National Register of Microform Masters* (E–52).

E–52 **Microforms in Print.** Incorporating International Microforms in Print. Westport, Conn.: Meckler, 1977–.
                                                   Z1033.M5 G8

This annual, cumulative bibliography combines the earlier *Guide to Microforms in Print* (Washington, D.C., 1961-1976) with the former *International Microforms in Print: A Guide to Microforms of Non-United States Micropublishers* (Weston, Conn.: Microform Review, 1974–1976) [Z1033.M5 V4 1974]. It lists books, journals, and other materials currently available in microform for purchase from United States and foreign micropublishers. Excluded are theses and dissertations. Each entry identifies the publisher, price, and type of microform; they are arranged in a single alphabet of authors, editors, or titles of books or journals. Newspapers are listed under their place of publication.

A separate *Subject Guide to Microforms in Print* (Washington, D.C.: Microcard Editions, 1962/63–) [Z1033.M5 G946

A] is published biennially and classifies the available microforms into some 135 subjects derived from the Library of Congress subject classification schedule, an index to which precedes the main body of the *Guide*.

Microforms in Print: Supplement (Westport, Conn.: Meckler, 1979–) [Z1033.M5 G835] is an author-title and subject listing of microforms published between the annual listings in *Microforms in Print*. Another bibliography of the trade is the *Micropublisher's Trade List Annual [MTLA]* (Weston, Conn.: Microform Review, 1975–) [Z1033.M5 M53], which provides an annual microfiche cumulation of the catalogs of all microform publishers, with an index of publishers.

E–53 **Library of Congress.** *National Register of Microform Masters [NRMM].* 1965–.   Z1033.M5 N3 or Z663.A43

An originally irregular but now annual supplement to the *Union List of Microfilms* (E–51), this register reports locations of master copies of all types of microform (including microfilm and microfiche) which are retained, for the sole purpose of making other microform copies available, by the more than 200 reporting repositories. Included are master microforms of books, pamphlets, serials, and foreign doctoral dissertations; excluded are technical reports, typescript translations, archival manuscript collections, and U.S. doctoral and masters' theses. The entries were arranged until 1970 by LC card number; since then, they have been given alphabetically by author or, in the case of serial or anonymous items, by title. Information includes years covered in the case of periodicals, type of microreproduction, and location. A six-volume cumulation for 1965–1975 with some 350,000 entries was published in 1975, replacing the annual volumes for that period.

The conversion of the *NRMM* to automated technique is now in progress. Machine-readable records are being produced in cooperative recataloging programs at major research libraries around the United States. Proposed is one final cumulation of the *NRMM* from 1976 through the date when the register will be produced in computer output microform.

E–56 *Newspapers in Microform [NIM].* 7th ed. 2 vols. Washington, D.C.: Library of Congress, 1973.   Z6951.U469

These volumes, subtitled respectively *United States 1948–1972* and *Foreign Countries 1948–1972*, replace the 1967 sixth edition [Z6945.U515 1973]. The United States volume lists 34,289 newspaper titles from more than 4,500 localities held in microform by some 843 libraries and commercial firms. Entries are by state, then by city of publication, and indicate dates of publication, changes of title, and changes in publishing arrangements. Notes show the type of microform held and the inclusive dates of its coverage. A title index concludes the volume.

The list of microformed foreign newspapers is also arranged geographically, listing 8,620 titles from 1,935 localities first by country and then by city of publication. Holdings are as reported by some 550 libraries and commercial firms. This volume also concludes with a title index. Both volumes have abundant cross-references.

Supplementing both 1973 volumes are annual volumes with the title *Newspapers in Microform* [1973–] [Z6945.N754]. The annuals for 1973–1977 have been cumulated in one volume (1979). The annual volumes and their cumulation are arranged according to the same principles as the original series. Discussion is under way to convert the catalog and its supplements to computer output microfiche.

See also the *Guide to Microforms in Print* (E–52) and *International Microforms in Print* (E–52) for newspaper titles available in microform. These works may also be supplemented by *Serials on Microfilm* [1973/1974] (Ann Arbor,

Mich.: University Microfilms, 1973) [Z6946.S47], which presents both title and subject lists of periodicals, newspapers, and other serials available from Xerox University Microfilms.

E–57 *Microform Review.* Vol. 1–. Westport, Conn.: Meckler, 1972–.   Z265.M565

This quarterly publication presents, in addition to articles of general interest, bibliographic aids including extensive reviews and evaluations of microform series both current and retrospective. Most issues carry a list of "Recent Articles on Micro Publishing." The author and title index in each issue cumulate up to the last issue of the volume. A *Cumulative Ten Volume Index 1972–81* is available (Meckler, 1983).

Another helpful bibliographical aid in this field is the volume by Felix Reichmann et al., *Bibliographic Control of Microforms* (Westport, Conn.: Meckler, 1972) [Z1033 .M5 R43], with its 200-page annotated "Microform Bibliography," disposed into sections covering microform catalogs and lists, collections, and series, manuscript and archival collections and reference books, followed by an author-title-subject index.

V. REPRINTS

E–60 *Guide to Reprints.* Kent, Conn.: Guide to Reprints [publisher has varied], 1967–.   Z1000.5.G8

An annual index by author or title (in the case of journals or sets of books) to works that were out of print and have been reprinted in full size, without recomposition of their text. Entries include original date of publication, date of reprint, publisher, and price; volume numbers and years of reprinted issues are given in periodical entries. For other guides to reprints in print see Ostwald (E–61) and the *International Bibliography of Reprints* (E–62).

This guide is updated by the quarterly *Announced Reprints* (Kent, Conn.: Guide to Reprints, 1969–) [Z265.A55], which includes forthcoming items announced by both U.S. and foreign reprint publishers. Each issue cumulates the previous numbers of the year.

A further source of information about reprints is the *Reprint Bulletin: Book Reviews* (Dobbs Ferry, N.Y.: Oceana Publications, 1955–) [Z671.R34], a quarterly with reviews of reprints on all subjects by North American publishers primarily. Entries are arranged by Dewey decimal classification numbers; each issue's author index cumulates entries up to the last issue of the volume.

E–61 **Ostwald, Renate.** *Nachdruck-Verzeichnis von Einzelwerken, Serien, und Zeitschriften aus allen Wissensgebieten (Reprints).* 2 vols. Wiesbaden: Nobis, 1965–1969.   Z1011.078

An international reprints-in-print listing (in alphabetical order by the main entry) of monographs, series, and periodicals. Entries show original place and date of publication; place, publisher, and date of the reprinted work; and indicate the item's place in a reprint series, along with the name of the series in which it was published. Volume 1 covers the period from about 1945 through 1965; volume 2 lists reprints available through the fall of 1967 and adds the works of important reprint series omitted from the first volume. An appendix in volume 2 lists the names of all the analyzed reprint series that were added. There is also a list of all reprint publishers treated in either volume. More current information about reprints in print may be found in the *International Bibliography of Reprints* (E–62).

E–62 ***Internationale Bibliographie der Reprints/International Bibliography of Reprints [IBR].*** Edited by Christa Gnirss. Munich: Verlag Dokumentation; New York: R. R. Bowker, 1976.   Z1033.R4 I572

This comprehensive bibliography of available reprints of books, serials, annuals, and periodical series published up to the end of 1973 is to be in two main sections, the first treating books and series and the second, not yet published, treating annuals and periodicals. The first section, containing some 52,000 reprinted titles, is divided into three parts, each in its own volume. Part 1 presents important preliminaries followed by an alphabetical list of authors, subjects, and titles of reprints, A-K. Part 2 concludes this list, while part 3 presents an index to titles and an index to reprint series, identifying the series numbers, along with authors and titles of each volume being published. For reprints published after 1973 this bibliography may be supplemented by reference to the *Bulletin of Reprints* (E–63).

E–63 ***Bulletin of Reprints.*** Vol. 11–. Munich: Verlag Dokumentation, 1974–.   Z1033.R4 B5

Volumes 1 through 10 of this work carry the title *Bibliographia Anastatica*: *A Bimonthly Bibliography of Photomechanical Reprints [BA]* (Amsterdam, 1964–1973). With volume 11 and the title change, publication became quarterly rather than bimonthly. Though there are cumulated indexes to volumes 1–5 (1964–1968) and 6–10 (1969–1973), these are superseded by the cumulated entries of the *International Bibliography of Reprints* (E–62), which should be consulted for pre–1974 publications and which the *Bulletin* may be said to update. Each issue presents an alphabetical listing by authors (and titles in the case of anonymous or periodical publications) of newly available reprints as well as selected older reprints missed in the *International Bibliography* and previous issues of the *Bulletin*. To be cited, a publication must be a photomechanical reprint involving no recomposition and not produced for sale by the original publisher, unless the original appeared before 1950. Entries give author; title; place and date of original publication; place, date, and publisher of the reprint; and price.

E–64 ***Catalogue of Reprints in Series.*** 1940–. Metuchen, N.J.: Scarecrow Press, 1940–.   Z1033.S5 C3

This irregularly published, more or less annual, catalog has been issued by a number of different publishers. Its goal at each edition (20th ed., 1965; suppl., 1967; 21st ed., 1972) has been to list (in part I), by author and title, all works reprinted as part of a series, giving the reprint series in which the work has appeared, with date and price. Also listed (in part 2) are the reprint series that are analyzed, with their publishers.

Other guides to reprinted serials include Sam P. Williams, *Reprints in Print—Serials*, 1969, 2d ed. (Dobbs Ferry, N.Y.: Oceana Publications, 1970) [Z1033.S5 W55], which includes about 10,000 entries representing reprints of scholarly serials and monographs in series in print at the end of 1969; and *Périodiques et publications en série concernant les sciences sociales et humaines. Liste de reproductions disponibles dans le commerce* [*microformes et réimpressions*] / *Periodicals and Serials concerning the Social Sciences and Humanities*: *Current List of Available Reproductions* (*Microforms and Reprints*), comp. Odette Paoletti and Odile Daniel (Paris: Maison des sciences de l'homme, Service bibliothèque-documentation, 1966–) [Z6941.P3], with biennial supplements.

E–68 ***Books on Demand.*** 3 vols. Ann Arbor, Mich.: University Microfilms, 1977.   Z1033.M5 U53

These three volumes present respectively an Author, Subject, and Title Guide to a distinctive "on demand" reprinting program through which xerographic hard copies of microfilmed, out-of-print titles are made available for purchase. Special emphasis is on out-of-print American scholarly and professional works in the social sciences and humanities.

Entries in the author and title volumes are alphabetical; the *Subject Guide* is disposed into some forty broad categories with a topical index identifying the subject under which a particular topic has been located.

Through special arrangements with some 300 publishers, titles are to be added to this program as they go out of print; supplements are planned to keep these three index volumes current.

VI. REVIEWS

Note that many general and special indexes of periodicals cite reviews. These include such references as *American Reference Books Annual* (A–25), *Canadian Periodical Index* (D–15), the *Index to Periodical Articles By and About Blacks* (S–122), the *Popular Periodical Index* (D–15), *America: History and Life* (F–54), *Reviews in American History* (F–10), the *Art Index* (A–71), the *Music Index* (A–75), and *Women Studies Abstracts* (L–186). Also note many bibliographies which cite reviews including, for example, closed bibliographies such as Howard-Hill (M–1) and serial bibliographies such as the *MLAIB* (L–50) and *ABELL* (M–21). See also the enumeration, Aids for Locating Contemporary Reviews (Z–66).

E–70 **Walford, A. J., ed.** ***Reviews and Reviewing: A Guide.*** Phoenix, Ariz.: Oryx Press, 1986.

This volume contains a combination of general essays in Part 1 on "The Art of Reviewing" by A. J. Walford and "The Administrative Role of the Book-Review Editor" by J. D. Hendry, and in Part 2, articles on Specialized Reviewing. The latter articles are bibliographical essays that describe major publications which review books, giving circulation figures, types of reviews published, types of books covered, average length of reviews, and other matters. The fields covered in these bibliographical essays are Reference Books (by Walford); Religion and Philosophy (by Michael J. Walsh); Social Sciences (by Joan M. Harvey); Life and Earth Sciences (by Anthony P. Harvey); Medicine (by Walford); Technology (by D. J. Grogan); Fine Arts (by Margaret Girvan); Music (by Walford); Literature and Language (by Walford); History, Archaeology and Geography (by Walford); Children's Books (by Grace Hallworth); and Audiovisual Materials (by Helen P. Harrison).

The volume concludes with two appendixes and an index. The first, a Select List of Indexes to Reviews is divided into three sections: Indexes Wholly Devoted to Reviews; Indexes That Include a Book Review Section, Entries, or References; and Retrospective Indexes to Reviews. The second appendix contains a Select and Annotated Bibliography.

E–72 **Gray, Richard A.** ***Guide to Book Review Citations: A Bibliography of Sources.*** Columbus: Ohio State University Press, 1969.   Z1035.A1 G7

A guide to 512 serially numbered bibliographies, indexes, and other reference works that cite book reviews from more than one periodical. The goal is to provide direction to reviews of any given book regardless of its date, subject, or the language of its text. Entries listing sources for such citations are arranged under broad general headings such as "Modern Languages, Philology, and Literature" with subheadings. Careful annotations specify the scope and arrangement of works listed. There is a brief glossary of foreign words and abbreviations followed by indexes of subjects, personal names, titles, chronology, and country of origin. One hopes that this uniquely valuable reference tool will be brought up to date in due course.

Additional guidance to indexes of reviews will be found in Kujoth (D–2) and Harzfeld (D–3). See also Jennifer Gallup, *Reference Guide to Book Reviews* (Vancouver: University of British Columbia Library, 1968) [Z883.B72 no. 24].

E–73 **Index to Book Reviews in the Humanities [IBRH].** Vol. 1–. Detroit (and later Williamston), Mich.: Phillip Thomson, 1960–.   Z1035.A1 I63

This formerly quarterly (to 1963) and now annual current index covers reviews published in more than 600 general and scholarly, primarily English-language, periodicals. Originally the *Index* cited only reviews of "humanities" books; since 1971 it has been covering all reviews in the "humanities" journals it analyzes. The first three volumes cite only reviews in English; starting with volume 4 (1964), reviews in any language have been included. Since 1970 some foreign journals have been added to the list of periodicals covered. "Humanities" fields include art and architecture; biography, personal narrative, and memoirs; drama and dance; folklore; history; language; literature; music; philosophy; travel and adventure. Excluded are archaeology, religion, and theology. After volume 2 (1971) history was excluded because it is covered in the *Index to Book Reviews in the Social Sciences / Book Review Index to Social Science Periodicals* [Z7161.A15 B65], which also covers journals in the fields of anthropology, biography, economics, education, geography, political science, sociology, and related subjects.

Entries are arranged alphabetically by the author of the book reviewed. The periodicals covered are enumerated in the front matter of each volume. Among those of importance to students of English and American Language and Literature are *Anglia*, *Archiv*, *Criticism*, *PQ*, *VP*, and *VS*. For relatively current (within six to eight months of publication) reviews of scholarly works in literary fields, this is the index of first resort; the most current reviews must be located by using the *Book Review Index* (E–74) and *Current Book Review Citations* (E–77) or by consulting the reviewing organs themselves. It is always wise to check several volumes after the publication date of the work one is interested in; an asterisk before an entry title means that earlier issues record other reviews of that title.

E–74 **Book Review Index.** Detroit, Mich.: Gale Research Co.; vols. 1–4, 1965–1968; vol. 8–, 1972–; retrospective vols. 5–7 for 1969–1971 published 1974–1975.   Z1035. A1 B6

A monthly index until 1969, this work is now published bimonthly; it has always cumulated quarterly and annually. It is thus the most current general index to current reviews of current books in more than 375 general, humanities, and social-science periodicals primarily published in North America. Publication was suspended from 1969 through 1971, but retrospective volumes were published to cover that period. A number of periodicals important to students of English and American literature are analyzed, including *AL*, *CL*, *Criticism*, *JAAC*, *JEGP*, *JHI*, *MLJ*, *MLR*, *MP*, *NYRB*, *NY Times Bk Rev*, *PBSA*, *PQ*, *QJS*, *RES*, *Speculum*, and *TLS*. The full list is in the front matter of each volume. Entries are alphabetical by the author of the book being reviewed, citing the title and the reviewer. An index of titles was added from volume 12 (1976) on. This work should be used in conjunction

with an *Index to Book Reviews in the Humanities* (E–73), which, though less current, contains references to reviews in many more scholarly periodicals.

E–75 **Internationale Bibliographie der Rezensionen wissenschaftlicher Literatur.** Edited by Otto Zeller. Vol. 1–. Osnabrück: Dietrich, 1971–.   Z5051.I64

A semiannual (now bimonthly) index to reviews of monographs and books in series which is intended to revive and extend the scope of Abteilung C of the *Internationale Bibliographie der Zeitschriftenliteratur* (see D–13), titled *Bibliographie der Rezensionen und Referate* [1900–1943], 77 vols. (Leipzig: Dietrich, 1901–1944) [AI9.B6]. Unlike the earlier work, which at first (1901–1910) covered German language reviews only and then both German and foreign language reviews in alternate issues, the new work, which indexes some 1,000 journals, includes all reviews in one treatment. And, also unlike the earlier work, which was arranged only by author of the book reviewed, the new work is arranged in four parts: *Periodica*—an index of periodicals analyzed; *Index Rerum*—an index of book reviews by subjects; *Index Auctorum*—an index of authors of reviewed books; and *Index Recensorum*—a particularly distinctive index of book reviewers. Retrospective volumes are being prepared to cover the period 1944–1970.

Because only the *Book Review Digest* (E–76) was available during the period of the older work, that work remains a uniquely valuable reference to the many reviews in English and American periodicals not treated in the *Digest*.

E–76 **Book Review Digest.** Vol. 1–. New York: H. W. Wilson, 1905–.   Z1219.C96

A monthly (except February and July) index cumulated semiannually and annually with excerpts to current English-language reviews of *selected* current works of fiction and nonfiction appearing in a list of about ninety English-language popular and general periodicals. Periodicals covered are listed in the front matter of each issue. Among those covered periodicals that are likely to have reviews of interest to students of English and American language and literature are *AL*, *JAAC*, *MLJ*, *NYRB*, *NY Times Book Review*, and *TLS*. Reviews are cited alphabetically by the author of the book reviewed, and entries give title and publication information along with an indication of the tenor of the review and salient excerpts arranged alphabetically by the name of the periodical in which they appeared. Generally no more than three (for fiction) or four reviews are excerpted, though all reviews appearing in the periodicals analyzed are cited for the sake of completeness. It is important to note, however, that before a reviewed work is selected for inclusion (i.e., before reviews of it are excerpted or cited), it must meet certain criteria. Generally these require that it be reviewed in two (fiction) or four of the covered periodicals within eighteen months of its United States publication date. The *Digest* concludes with a subject-title index, which is cumulated annually and quinquennially. A cumulative author-title index for 1905–1974 was published in four volumes (New York, 1976); also published was an unofficial author-title index, the *Cumulative Book Review Index 1905–1974* (Princeton, N.J.: National Library Service, 1975) [Z1035.A1 N3], which includes citation of all reviews in the *Book Review Digest*, the *Library Journal*, *Choice*, and the *Saturday Review*.

E–77 **Current Book Review Citations.** 1–. New York: H. W. Wilson, 1976–.   Z1035.A1 C86

A monthly index (except August) citing reviews published in over 1,200 North American and British journals. The list of analyzed journals includes *Booklist*, *Choice*, the *Library*

Journal, the *School Library Journal*, and citations to book reviews found in the various Wilson periodical indexes, including those in the *Humanities Index* (D–16), the *Social Science Index* (D–16), and the *Reader's Guide to Periodical Literature* (D–15). Monthly lists are cumulated annually under the title *Current Book Review Citations (Annual)* [Z1035 .A1 C87].

E–78 **Combined Retrospective Index to Book Reviews in Humanities Journals, 1802–1974.** Executive ed., Evan Ira Farber; Senior ed., Stanley Schindler. 10 vols. Woodbridge, Conn.: Research Publications, 1982–1984.

Z6265.C65 1982

This work provides access to reviews in some 150 journals. Entries are listed alphabetically by reviewed author, give titles, and then list reviews by reviewing journal.

A similar publication treats reviews in history, political science, and sociology journals, the *Combined Retrospective Index to Book Reviews in Scholarly Journals, 1886–1974*, Executive ed., Evan Ira Farber, 15 vols. (Arlington, Va., 1979–1982) [Z1035.A1 C64], which treats reviews in a total of 459 journals.

VII.   INDEXES TO COMPOSITE VOLUMES

Many other works analyze and index composite books. Among them see, for example, Cotgreave (D–10); the *IBZ* (D–13); and, for literary matters, the beginning "Festschriften" section of the *MLA International Bibliography* (L–50), where composite volumes analyzed in the bibliography are listed and assigned a code number by which their contents are identified. Indexes of the contents of genre anthologies such as those cited in sections T, U, and W are further examples.

E–80 *A.L.A. Index: An Index to General Literature, Biographical, Historical, and Literary Essays and Sketches, Reports*, etc. 2d ed. Boston: Houghton Mifflin, 1901. Supplement 1900–1910. Chicago: American Library Association, 1914.   AI3.A3

An index (first published in 1893) to English-language composite volumes that treat more than one subject. Arranged alphabetically by catchword subject, including authors' names as subject headings. Collections of essays, books of travel and general history, and reports and publications of associations and learned societies are among the types of volumes analyzed; both the original volume and the supplement include lists of all the composite books they treat. Altogether there are some 80,000 citations in the two volumes. This work is complemented and supplemented by the *Essay and General Literature Index* (E–81). Its use is facilitated by C. Edward Wall's *ALA Index to General Literature: Cumulative Author Index* (Ann Arbor, Mich.: Pierian, 1972) [AI3.W28].

E–81 *Essay and General Literature Index, 1900–1933: An Index to about 40,000 Essays and Articles in 2,144 Volumes of Collections of Essays and Miscellaneous Works [EGLI].* New York: H. W. Wilson, 1934. Supplements, 1934–.

AI3.E752

A detailed, single-alphabet author, subject, and occasionally title index to English-language collections of essays and other composite works, including annuals, with emphasis on titles in literature and the humanities. The supplemental volumes index collections published during the years 1934–1940,

1941–1947, and 1948–1954, respectively. Since 1955 the index has appeared in semiannual issues, annual volumes, and permanent volumes covering five years. To date, more than 250,000 essays, articles, and chapters have been listed. The ten permanent volumes covering 1900–1984 together index nearly 15,000 collected works, which are listed by author or editor and title in the volume *Essay and General Literature Index: Works Indexed* (New York: Wilson, 1972). Each volume of the actual index also lists the composite works that it analyzes. Thus the *Index* can be used both to find out the contents of, say, Van Nostrand's *Literary Criticism in America* (what essays are in it?) and also to find out the collections in which a particular essay has appeared. Main entries include the author, title of the essay, article, or chapter, and a reference to the collection in which the item may be found. There are extensive cross-references. Headings include both subjects and authors (both as authors and as subjects). The work can also be used to establish the authorship of essays of which only the title is known and to locate biographical treatments and literary criticisms subsumed in composite volumes. Note, however, that works of collected biography have been analyzed, since 1946, in *Biography Index* (G–4). Works indexed since 1985 may also be searched on WILSONLINE (see Z–78).

E–85 **The New York Public Library.   *Guide to Festschriften.* Vol. 1, *Retrospective Festschriften Collection of the New York Public Library, Materials Catalogued through 1971*. Vol. 2: *Dictionary Catalog of Festschriften in the New York Public Library (1972–1976) and the Library of Congress (1968–1976).*** Boston: G. K. Hall, 1977.

Z1033.F4 N48 1977

Volume 1 reprints the card catalog of the New York Public Library's massive festschriften collection, including not only volumes of essays in honor of scholars by colleagues, students, and friends but also volumes of collected essays celebrating occasions in the history of learned societies, institutions, and corporations. Entries are arranged alphabetically by the main entry, which is generally either the title of the volume or the name of the corporate body being celebrated. Cards are often quite detailed in the information they provide, giving in many cases the contents of the festschrift.

Volume 2 is a computer-generated interfiled dictionary catalog by main entry, subject, and secondary entries, of the New York Public Library festschriften acquisitions 1972–1976 merged with the record of those works included in the Library of Congress MARC data base. In contrast with the entries of volume 1, those in volume 2 do not require users to know the exact titles of the festschriften.

A seriously incomplete but nevertheless valuable index of festschriften published about 1850–1974, arranged as an alphabetical list of the names of honored persons and institutions, is Otto Leistner's *Internationale* [after 1988: *Jahres-*] *Bibliographie der Festschriften mit Sachregister/International* [after 1980: Annual] *Bibliography of Festschriften with Subject-Index [IBF/IJBF]* (Osnabrück: Biblio Verlag, 1976) [Z1033.F4 L43]. Entries do not analyze the contents of the volumes but do give titles, editors, publisher, date, and pagination. The subject index is rather general. The publisher's plans include retrospective volumes treating festschriften from the beginnings until 1979 and current annual volumes from 1980 on.

Among specialized bibliographies of festschriften in language and literature, see the following works:

Fucilla, Joseph G. *Universal Author Repertoire of Italian Essay Literature*. New York: S. F. Vianni, 1941.

Z6511.F8

Golden, Herbert H., and Seymour O. Simches. *Modern French Literature and Language: A Bibliography of*

Homage Studies. Cambridge: Harvard University Press, 1953.   Z2175.F375 G6

———. *Modern Iberian Language and Literature: A Bibliography of Homage Studies.* Cambridge: Harvard University Press, 1958.   Z7031.G6

———. *Modern Italian Language and Literature: A Bibliography of Homage Studies.* Cambridge: Harvard University Press, 1959.   Z2355.A2 G6

Griffin, Lloyd W., Jack A. Clarke, and Alexander Y. Kroff. *Modern French Literature and Languages: A Bibliography of Homage Studies.* Madison: University of Wisconsin Press, 1976.   Z2175.F45 G74 1976

Metzger, Bruce M. *Index of Articles on the New Testament and the Early Church Published in Festschriften.* Philadelphia: Society of Biblical Literature, 1951.
Z7772.L1 M4

Rounds, Dorothy. *Articles on Antiquity in Festschriften: An Index.* Cambridge: Harvard University Press, 1962.
Z6202.R6

Williams, Harry F. *Index of Medieval Studies Published in Festschriften, 1865–1946, with Special Reference to Romanic Material.* Berkeley and Los Angeles: University of California Press, 1951.   Z6203.W5

An extremely useful guide, "Festschriften Bibliographies and Indexes," *Bulletin of Bibliography* 42 (1985): 193–202, enumerates sixty-three bibliographies and indexes of festschriften.

E–88 **Index to Social Sciences and Humanities Proceedings [ISSHP],** Vol. 1–. Philadelphia: Institute for Scientific Information, 1979–.   Z7163.I5

This work, designed to complement the *Index to Scientific and Technical Proceedings* (1978–), provides a total of six different indexes to individual papers in published proceedings of conferences. The main entry gives a proceedings number; identifies the title, location, date, and sponsors of the conference; and then gives the title of the book or journal in which the proceedings were published along with pertinent publication information. The titles of individual papers follow, along with the names of all authors and the address of the first author of each paper. These entries are indexed in six ways: by general subject category (including such fields as literature, philology, linguistics, theater, and communication); by a permuted-term subject index in which every term in the titles of conferences, proceedings, and individual papers is paired with every other term; by conference sponsor; by author or editor; by meeting location; and by corporate bodies associated with the conference or its proceedings.

VIII. ANONYMA AND PSEUDONYMA

Anonymns and pseudonyms are also identified in the *National Union Catalog* (B–12, B–13), the British Museum *General Catalogue of Printed Books* (B–41), the *Wellesley Index* (D–12), the *Nineteenth Century Reader's Guide* (D–11), and many of the works of national bibliography, including Lowndes (C–3).

E–90 **Taylor, Archer, and Frederick J. Mosher. *Bibliographical History of Anonyma and Pseudonyma.*** Chicago: University of Chicago Press, 1951.   Z1041.T3

An extensively documented history of works with problematic authorship. Chapters treat homonyms, latinized names, pseudepigrapha, anonyma and pseudonyma, confus-

ing titles, and works with fictitious facts of publication. This history is followed by an annotated, classified bibliography of some 350 entries, with cross-references to the historical chapters in which items are more elaborately discussed. A separate, classified guide to dictionaries and other lists of anonyma and pseudonyma, by language or geographical area and by subject, aids users in finding works to assist in particular searches. The volume concludes with an index to the historical chapters.

The earlier work of Adah V. Morris, "Anonyms and Pseudonyms: An Annotated [classified] List," *LQ* 3 (October 1933): 354–372, reprinted separately by the University of Chicago Press, 1934 [Z1041.A1 M8], is not entirely superseded by the Taylor and Mosher volume.

E–92 **Halkett, Samuel, and John Laing. *Dictionary of Anonymous and Pseudonymous English Literature.*** New and enl. ed. Edited by James Kennedy et al. 9 vols. Edinburgh: Oliver and Boyd, 1926–1962.   Z1065.H17 1926

This dictionary of some 72,000 entries lists works by anonymous and pseudonymous authors alphabetically, by the first word of the title that is not an article. It first appeared in 1882 and is still regarded as the best source for identifying authors of anonymous and pseudonymous English literature. Entries include the format and pagination of the work, the place and date of publication, and the pseudonymous and real names of the author. Sources of attributions are often given. The first six volumes contain an alphabetical listing by titles; pages 273–449 of volume 6 contain the *first supplement* to the whole. Volume 7 provides an alphabetical index by author and an alphabetical list of pseudonyms, initials, etc.; pages 585–588 contain a *second supplement*. The first seven volumes cover works published before 1900. Volume 8 is an alphabetical listing by title of works published between 1900 and 1949 inclusive, with identification of anonyms and pseudonyms and indexes. Volume 9 consists of addenda to all eight previous volumes. Thus, for pre–1900 works volumes 1–6, the first supplement (in 6), the second supplement (in 7), and the addenda (in 9) must be consulted; post–1900 works will be found in volumes 8 and 9. For works published after 1950 the *British National Bibliography* (C–16) and the *National Union Catalog* (B–12, B–13) are the standard authorities. It should be noted that Halkett and Laing is derivative and that the authority of attributions resides in its sources, the four-page list of authorities in volume 1, and the specific citations in some other entries.

A new, completely revised and much enlarged edition of the entire work in six volumes plus index under the direction of John Horden of the School of English, Leeds University, is in progress. Volume 1, *Dictionary of Anonymous and Pseudonymous Publications in the English Language: 1475–1640* (London: Longman, 1980) [Z1065.D5], contains identification of authorship for some 4,000 works, including English translations from other languages. Entries are fully documented. Subsequent volumes will treat publications from 1641 on.

The standard guide to anonyms and pseudonyms for French literature is Joseph M. Quérard, *Les supercheries littéraires dévoilées*, 2d ed., ed. by Gustave Brunet and Pierre Jannet, including the *Dictionnaire des ouvrages anonymes par Antoine-Alexandre Barbier*, 3d ed., and a *table général des noms réels*, 7 vols. (Paris: Didot, 1869–1879) [Z1067.Q45]. For German literature the standard works are Michael Holzmann and Hanns Bohatta, *Deutsches Anonymen-Lexikon*, 7 vols. (Weimar: Gesellschaft der Bibliophilen, 1902–1928) [Z1068.H76], and, by the same authors, *Deutsches Pseudonymen-Lexikon* (Vienna: Akademischer Verlag, 1906) [Z1068.H77].

E–95 **Sharp, Harold S.** *Handbook of Pseudonyms and Personal Nicknames.* 2 vols. Metuchen, N.J.: Scarecrow Press, 1972. First Supplement. 2 vols. 1975.   Z1041.S43

Approximately 15,000 alphabetically arranged main entries give real names (in all capital letters) with birth and death dates, nationality, occupation, and a list of pseudonyms and nicknames used. The 25,000 pseudonyms and nicknames are interfiled in the alphabet of real names, with cross-references to the real names of persons who used them. The first supplement adds about 15,000 real names and another 25,000 pseudonyms and nicknames. Because this work is not limited by time or place, it is more comprehensive than other guides; the single alphabetical arrangement is also very convenient to use. A second supplement is expected.

For modern authors see also Frank Atkinson, ed., *Dictionary of Literary Pseudonyms: A Selection of Popular Modern Writers in English*, 2d ed. (Hamden, Conn.: Linnet, 1972) [Z1041.A84], which should, however, be used with caution.

IX.   GUIDES TO SPOKEN RECORDINGS

E–100 **Roach, Helen.** *Spoken Records.* 3d ed. Metuchen, N.J.: Scarecrow Press, 1970.   Z2011.R6 1970

This volume, the first edition of which appeared in 1963, presents in five chapters a series of discursive essays with enumerative discographies appended to each, listing all recordings selected for discussion. The chapter titles are An Introduction to Spoken Recording; Documentaries, Lectures, Interviews, and Speeches; Authors' Recordings; Readings by Other Than Authors; and Plays. The volume concludes with a "Selected Discography of Shakespeare's Plays"; two appendixes, one on the history of sound recording and the other listing recording companies with addresses; and an index of authors and titles.

E–102 **Some Current Guides to Spoken Recordings.**

The monthly *Schwann Record and Tape Guide* (Boston: Schwann, 1973–) [ML156.2.S385], successor title to the *Schwann Record Catalog* (Boston: Schwann, 1949–), has semiannual supplements (*Schwann–2*) [ML156.2.S3852] that list recordings of poetry, drama, prose, and speeches available for purchase in the United States and Canada. A British equivalent is Charles Fox, *Gramophone: Spoken and Miscellaneous Catalogue* (Kenton, Middlesex: General Gramophone Publications, 1965) [ML156.2.F65], which provides indexes to authors, titles, and performers on spoken recordings available in the United Kingdom.

E–103 **Words on Tape. *International Guide to the Spoken Word.*** Westport, Conn.: Meckler, 1984–.   No LC number

This annual guide to spoken-word cassettes lists some 7,000 available titles from about 100 publishers. Main entries are by title, listing author, reader, number of cassettes, playing time, price, and other costs. Author and subject indexes conclude each annual.

E–105 **Chicorel, Marietta.** *Chicorel Index to the Spoken Arts on Discs, Tapes, and Cassettes.* 2 vols. New York: Chicorel, 1973.   ML156.2.C52

This work, which constitutes volumes 7 and 7A of the *Chicorel Index*, enumerates more than 1,200 recorded plays, short stories, poems, essays, novels, and speeches. Each volume is a single alphabetical index of authors, titles, performers, and directors.

Also produced by Chicorel is the *Chicorel Index to Poetry in Collections in Print* [which are] *on Discs and Tapes* (New York: Chicorel, 1972) [PR1175.8.C4], which constitutes volume 4 of the *Chicorel Index*. It is an alphabetical list of titles, poets, first lines, readers, and directors. Main entries are by title and give full publishing information.

E–106 **Library of Congress.** *Literary Recordings: A Checklist of the Archive of Recorded Poetry and Literature in the Library of Congress.* New ed. Compiled by Jennifer Whittington. Washington, D.C.: Government Printing Office, 1981.   Z663.Z93 L5

A checklist current to May 1975 of more than 1,200 recordings in the library's Recorded Sound Section, arranged by the name of the recording artist. This edition supersedes those of 1961 and 1966. Serially numbered entries describe the contents of each recording; they are arranged alphabetically and then chronologically. The index includes the names of authors reading their own works; authors whose works are read by another person; editors, translators, and compilers of works; other names associated with a recording, such as readers, interviewers, announcers; and names of persons responsible for the mechanical production of the recording, including producers and directors.

X.   GUIDES TO FILMS FROM LITERARY WORKS

Further help in locating filmed versions of literary texts may be found in the film reference guides and encyclopedias (U–85 ff.), as well as in the bibliographical guides concerned with literature and film (U–98).

E–110 **Enser, A. G. S.** *Filmed Books and Plays: A List of Books and Plays from Which Films Have Been Made, 1928–1974.* London: Deutsch; New York: Academic Press, 1975.   Z5784.M9 E55 1975

This most recent version of a work first published in 1950 is limited to English-language film titles. It is in three parts. The Film Title Index lists about 3,500 films alphabetically by the British version of their titles, with the author and title (if different) of the novel, play, poem, or short story on which the film was based, and the name of its publisher. Also listed are the film's British producer and the date of its release in Britain. The second part, an Author Index, is arranged alphabetically by the name of the source author. A Change of Original Title Index, the third part, gives the published title of a source work, followed by the titles of films that depend on it although they have different titles.

E–111 **Dimmitt, Richard B.** *Title Guide to the Talkies.* 2 vols. New York: Scarecrow Press, 1965.   PN1998.D55

The guide lists 16,068 serially numbered, feature-length English-language sound films released from October 1927 through December 1963 alphabetically by their titles, with company and date. Provided are the author's name, publisher, date, or collection in which the original work was included, along with the name of the novel, play, poem, short story, or screenplay on which the film was based. For film titles that differ from their source names, there are cross-references from the original titles to the film titles. There is an author index in volume 2.

This work is continued by Andrew A. Aros, *Title Guide to the Talkies: 1964 through 1974* (Metuchen, N.J.: Scarecrow, 1977) [PN1998.A6695], which includes the information in Dimmitt's volumes plus some additional items. Foreign films released in the United States are included, and the 3,429 serially numbered entries give the distributor, the year of a film's general release, its story source, and its director. Authors and screenwriters are included in the index; directors are not.

E–112 **Thiery, Herman [Johan Daisne, pseud.].** *Dictionnaire fil-mographique de la littérature mondiale / Filmographic Dictionary of World Literature.* 2 vols. Ghent: E. Story-Scientia; Atlantic Highlands, N.J.: Humanities Press, 1971–1975. Supplement (A-Z), 1978.   PN1997.85.T5

This extraordinary work is designed to illustrate "how the whole of literature forms the basis of the seventh art." Both the original two volumes and the supplemental volume are disposed into three parts. The main body is arranged alphabetically by the source author's name, followed by the title of the film, the original title of the source (if different), the country and year of production of the film, the name of the director, and a cast list. Any remakes of the film are also noted. Following the main body is a large section of illustrative materials, mostly studio stills, also arranged alphabetically by the author's name. Finally there is an alphabetical index of titles, both of books and of films, using the title as cited in the work (i.e., in French, unless the original title is in English, German, or Flemish). Throughout, special attention is given to the work of minor authors. The *Supplement* is current to 1976/77 and also includes citations missed in the original edition [PN1997.85.T52].

E–115 **Leonard, William T.** *Theatre: Stage to Screen to Television.* Metuchen, N.J.: Scarecrow Press, 1981.

PN2189.L44

These volumes present alphabetically by title works that have been produced first for stage, then screen, and then television. Entries give source authors and dates, a synopsis, comment and critique, and biographical sketch of the author. Stage openings are described, including the cast, as are major revivals. Screen productions are described with the name of the producer, the cast, and other details. Finally, television productions of the work are identified, with programs and dates of airing.

At the end of the volume is an index to composers, lyricists, and librettists followed by an author-playwright index. The latter identifies the individual fiction author and the dramatizations, films, and television productions that emerged from his or her work.

A new work by Larry Langman, *Writers on the American Screen: A Guide to Film Adaptations of American and Foreign Literary Works* (New York: Garland, 1986) [Z5784.M9 L28 1986] may also prove valuable.

HISTORY AND ANCILLAE TO HISTORICAL STUDY

For frequently recommended background reading in English and American social and cultural history, the history of taste, intellectual history, and the history of education, see also K–90, K–92, K–95, and K–98. For works on historical fiction see section W.IX. For works on historiography and historical prose see also W–120 ff. For works on the interrelations between history and literature see also X–84. And for works on historical method in literary studies see section Z.IV and Z.V.

I.   GENERAL AND WORLD HISTORY

F–1   *American Historical Association's Guide to Historical Literature.* Edited by George Frederick Howe et al. New York: Macmillan, 1961.   Z6201.A55

This is the standard annotated bibliography of historical, biographical, political, geographic, and ethnographical literature relating to all periods and countries. More than 20,000 entries are disposed into some thirty-five main sections, each under the supervision of a specialist editor. The first division is general; subsequent divisions are by countries or geographical areas and roughly by periods. The main sections are as follows: A—History and Related Studies; B—General Reference Resources; C—World History and Universal Treatments; D—History of Religions; E—Regions, Peoples, and Cultures: General and Prehistoric; F—The Ancient Orient; G—Early History of Asiatic Peoples; H—Ancient Greece and the Hellenistic World; I—Rome: Republic and Empire; J—General: Eurasia and Northern Africa (ca. 476–1453); K—Medieval Europe; L—The Byzantine Empire; M—The Muslim World; N—Asia: General; O—China; P—Japan; Q—Southeast Asia; R—South Asia; S—The Middle East since 1450; T—Europe (General), 1450–1914; U—The Expansion of Europe; V—Western and Central Europe (VA—The United Kingdom and the Republic of Ireland, VB—Scandinavia and the Baltic States, VC—France and the Low Countries, VD—Spain and Portugal, VE—Italy, VF— Germany, Austria, and Switzerland); W—Eastern Europe; X—Russia and the Soviet Union (Including the Russian Empire in Asia); Y—The Americas: General; Z—Latin America; AA—British and Dutch America; AB—United States of America; AC—Africa; AD—Australia and New Zealand (with Antarctica); AE—Oceania; AF—Recent History; AG—The World Wars; AH—International Relations: Political; AI—International Re-

lations: Non-Political. An index of authors and of broad subject headings is included. Anonymous works are not indexed. By virtue of its scope this guide is highly selective, but every effort has been made to identify standard sources of information regarding the subjects covered. Emphasis is on English-language materials. Annotations are less full than those of the predecessor guide (F–2), and the index is not sufficiently detailed. Nevertheless, this is the most satisfactory and current general guide available.

Though rather out of date, Edith M. Coulter and Melanie Gerstenfeld's *Historical Bibliographies: A Systematic and Annotated Guide* (Berkeley: University of California Press, 1935) [Z6201.A1 C8 1935] may still be used with profit as a particularly well annotated descriptive and critical bibliography of bibliographies. Another is Günther Franz, *Bücherkunde zur Weltgeschichte vom Untergang des römischen Weltreiches bis zur Gegenwart* (Munich: Oldenbourg, 1956) [Z6201.F68]. Standard general bibliographies of bibliographies, such as Besterman (A–1) and *Bibliographic Index* (A–2), and general reference guides, such as Sheehy (A–20) and Walford (A–21), will also supplement both the coverage and the annotation of the *AHA Guide*.

F–2   **Allison, William Henry, et al.** *Guide to Historical Literature.* New York: Macmillan, 1931.   Z6201.G94

This volume, which is divided into twenty-six sections, with serially numbered entries in each, was compiled under the auspices of the American Historical Association and its special committee on bibliography under the chairmanship of George M. Dutcher. The sections, each edited by a distinguished scholar in the field, are as follows: A—History and Auxiliary Sciences; B—General History; C—Near East in Ancient Times; D—Ancient Greece and the Hellenistic World; E—Rome: The Republic and the Empire; F—History of Christianity; G—History of Mohammedanism and Moslem Peoples; H—Medieval Times, 500–1450; I—Modern Europe 1450–1870; K—Exploration and Colonial Expansion; L—Great Britain and Ireland; M—France; N—Spain and Portugal; O—Italy; P—Germany, Austria, and Switzerland; Q—Netherlands and Belgium; R—Scandinavian Countries; S—Russia, Poland, Czechoslovakia, and the Borderlands; T—Southeastern Europe and Southwestern Asia: The Balkans and the Near East since the Rise of the Ottoman Turks; U—Asia, Including India, China, and Japan; V—Oceania; W—Africa; X—United States; Y—Hispanic America; Z—British North America.

Each chapter has a table of contents displaying the structure of the chapter and the serially numbered entries in each section and subsection. The first index presents the general scheme of classification used in each chapter: the headings are Bibliography, Library and Museum Collections; Encyclopedias and Works of Reference; Geography and Atlases; Ethnography; Sourcebooks, Collections of Sources, Archive Publications; Shorter General Histories; Longer General Histories; Histories of Special Periods, Regions, or Topics; Diplomatic, Military, and Naval History; International Law; Constitutional and Legal History, Political Theory; Economic and Social History; Cultural History (General; Religious; Education, Thought, and Philosophy; Literature; Art, Music); Biography; Government Publications; Academic, University, and Society Publications; Periodicals.

The text is more nearly that of a discursive essay, beginning with an introduction and then proceeding to discuss short groups of entries as they are cited. The second index is to authors, periodicals, and academy publications cited. The work is, of course, out of date and has to some extent been replaced by the *AHA Guide* (F–1). It remains of value, however, as a record of the state of historical scholarship in 1930.

F–3 **Hepworth, Philip.** *How to Find Out in History: A Guide to Sources of Information for All.* New York and London: Pergamon Press, 1966.   D16.2.H4 1966

An extended bibliographical essay with information on reference works in history and biography. Chapters cover general works, general history, Europe including Britain and the Commonwealth, individual countries by continent, ancillary fields, and historical sources. There are illustrative sample pages from the most important tools. A brief index concludes the volume.

Aside from Poulton's *Historian's Handbook* (A–17) and Hepworth, general reference guides will provide names of further student guides in history. One of the best and most recent is Alan Edwin Day, *History: A Reference Handbook* (London: Bingley, 1977) [Z2016.D38 1977]; there is also a slim but very well annotated pamphlet by John Fines, *History Student's Guide to the Library* (London: Phillimore, 1973) [Z6201.F55]. The most extensive series of brief guides is published by the Historical Association, London, under the title *Helps for the Student of History.* Among the eighty-five works in this series are handy aids such as S. B. Chrimes and I. A. Roots, *English Constitutional History: A Select Bibliography* (no. 58, 1958) [Z6458.G7 C45]; Alum Grier Davies, *Modern European History, 1494-1788* (no. 58, 1967) [Z2000.D3]; William Parker Morrell, *British Overseas Expansion and the History of the Commonwealth* (no. 63, 1970) [Z2021.C7 M6 1970]; Theodore Carwell Barker, *Business History* (no. 59, 1971) [HG5353.B33 1971]; Owen Chadwick, *History of the Church* (no. 55, 1973) [Z7777 .C485 1973]; E. M. Johnston, *Irish History* (no. 73, 1972) [Z2041.J64 1972]; Helen Miller, *Early Modern British History, 1485-1760* (no. 79, 1970) [Z2016.M5]; and I. R. Christie, *British History since 1760* (no. 81, 1970) [Z2016 .C53].

F–4 *International Bibliography of Historical Sciences [IBHS] [1926–1939, 1974–].* Washington, D.C. [later Paris etc.]: International Committee of Historical Sciences, 1930–.
                                             Z6205.I61

This annual bibliography has been compiled through the work of the national historical committees of thirty-seven countries. Cited books and articles are of more than local interest, but history is interpreted broadly to include the political, constitutional, religious, cultural, economic, and social life of mankind. In principle, coverage is universal and cited works are in the language of their publication; the bibliography itself uses alternately English, French, German, Italian, and Spanish as the editorial language. Serially numbered entries (varying in number from nearly 5,000 in the first volume to nearly 8,500 in the most recent) are classified. Reviews of

books are cited under the entry for the book; otherwise there is no annotation. Before the main body of the work is a section titled "General Historical Bibliographies," which enumerates the major international or national bibliographies dealing with one or more of the historical disciplines or presenting the historical work of one country.

The current classification system (which has varied somewhat over the years) is as follows: A—Auxiliary Sciences; B—Manuals, General Works (Collected Works); C—Prehistory (and Proto-history); D—The Ancient East; E—Greek History; F—Roman History (Including Ancient Italy and the Roman Empire); G—Early History of the Church to Gregory the Great; H—Byzantine History (since Justinian); J—History of the Middle Ages; K—Modern History: General Works; L—Modern Religious History; M—History of Modern Culture; N—Modern Economic and Social History; O—Modern Legal and Constitutional History; P—History of International Relations; R—Asia; S—Africa (to Its Colonization); T—America (to Its Colonization); U—Oceania (to Its Colonization). Within each class, entries are alphabetical by author and cite the title of the work, place of publication, publisher, date, and pagination. Place and publisher (in the case of an article) are the journal title and the issue number and volume. Each volume concludes with an index of names (authors and personal names) and a geographical index of places, both keyed to entry numbers.

The last annual volume, published in 1976, covered works of 1973. Since then, publication has been biennial, as follows: double volumes 43 and 44 treating publications 1974–1975 (1979), 45 and 46 for 1976–1977 (1980), and 47 and 48 for 1978–1979 (1982). The gap created by not publishing the *International Bibliography* during the Second World War is filled, in part, by the British National Committee's *Bibliography of Historical Writings Published in Great Britain and the Empire, 1940-1945* (F–9).

F–5 *Historical Abstracts: Bibliography of the World's Historical Literature.* Edited by Eric H. Boehm. Vol. 1– (March 1955–). Santa Barbara, Calif.: ABC-Clio, 1955–. D299.H5

This quarterly bibliography originally covered only the period 1775–1945; since the publication of volume 17 (Spring 1971) it has been divided into two parts: A—Modern History Abstracts, 1775–1914, and B—Twentieth Century Abstracts, 1914-[present]. From vol. 19 (Spring 1973), coverage of Part A was extended back to 1450. Material concerned with only the United States and Canada is excluded because of its treatment in *America: History and Life* (F–54). All other aspects of history, except strictly local history, are covered, regardless of where in the world an article was published, whether the journal is standard or not, and the language of publication. Currently some 2,000 periodicals published in eighty-five countries are analyzed and some 9,000 to 15,000 serially numbered entries appear in the Spring, Summer, and Fall issues. The issues are divided into three parts. Part 1 treats general articles (on bibliography, methodology, historiography, the philosophy of history, archives, libraries and institutions, meetings, and pedagogy). Part 2 treats articles on topics (international relations, wars and military history, World Wars I and II, political history, social and cultural history, economic history, religion and churches, sciences and technology). Part B cites articles treating particular areas or countries. Citations give author, title, translation (if the original is not in English), name of journal, year, volume, issues, and pages. This is followed by a signed informational abstract. Reference is made to the presence of documentation, graphs, notes, etc. in the original article. Each of the issues contains a combined author-person-place-subject index. It should be noted that book reviews are not indexed.

The fourth issue of each year cumulates the indexes of the first three quarters. Since volume 16 (1970) the subject portion of the index has been designed to include keywords and phrases from article titles and abstracts, along with standard terms from a list of subject headings and free language terms as needed. Each article is cited under each subject, including biographic, geographic, or chronological descriptors, as appropriate. This new index is called the Subject Profile Index, or SPIndex. With each term are given the author, abstract number, and the other indexing terms associated with the title.

Five-year cumulated indexes of *Historical Abstracts* have been published. That for volumes 1–5 (1955–1959) appeared in 1963; one for volumes 6–10 (1960–1964) in 1965; and one for volumes 11–15 (1965–1969) in 1970. Indexes for volumes 16–20 of part A (1970–1974) and volumes 17–20 of part B (1971–1974) were published in 1979. Each five-year index contains a subject index with topical, geographical, and biographical entries, an author index, a list of periodicals abstracted, and an index to the sections of bibliographical news which were published as a supplement to *Historical Abstracts*. In addition, the complete data base is available for computer-aided searches through the Lockheed/DIALOG system.

F–6　***Recently Published Articles.*** Vol. 1–. Washington, D.C.: American Historical Association, 1976–.　　Z6205.A49a

Formerly a section, with variable title, of each issue of the *American Historical Review*, 1895–1975, this is now a triannual publication, appearing in February, June, and October of each year. About 15,000 references per year are taken from some 2,000–2,500 journals published throughout the world. Historical and literary journals as well as journals in sociology, political science, education, philosophy, economics, and current affairs are analyzed. Entries are disposed into the following twenty sections: General and Unclassified; Ancient; Medieval; Modern Europe—General; British Commonwealth and Ireland; France; Spain and Portugal; Low Countries; Northern Europe; Germany, Austria, and Switzerland; Italy; Eastern Europe; Soviet Union; Near East; Africa; East Asia; Southeast Asia; South Asia; Latin America; and the United States. Each section is compiled under the supervision of an individual section editor and is subdivided into a general section and appropriate special divisions. There are no indexes.

F–7　**Historical Association, London.** ***Annual Bulletin of Historical Literature.*** Vol. 1–. (1911–). London: Historical Association, 1912–.　　Z6205.H65

A highly selective survey, in the form of a series of bibliographical essays, of the year's work in history. Books and articles are treated, with emphasis on Britain and English-language materials. The *Bulletin* is divided into periods from ancient history to the twentieth century: relatively more space is devoted to the year's work in modern history. Each survey is written by a recognized authority; stress is placed on works that present new evidence or fresh interpretations of existing evidence. An index of names, but none of titles, is provided.

These bibliographical essays may be supplemented by the extensive signed reviews, classified lists of current publications, and annual indexes of the *American Historical Review* (1895–) and the *English Historical Review* (1886–) [DA20.E58]. See also *History: Reviews of New Books* (Washington, D.C.: Heldref, 1972–) [Z6205.H69], which presents in ten issues per year reviews of books on European, Asian, general, and American history. Author indexes in each issue are not cumulated annually; there is, however, a cumulative index to volumes 1–8.

F–8　***C.R.I.S.: The Combined Retrospective Index Set to Journals in History, 1838–1974 [CRIS/History].*** Annadel N. Wile, executive editor. 11 vols. Washington, D.C.: Carrollton Press, 1977–1978.　　Z6208.C18 D1

This new index analyzes the contents of 243 English-language periodicals in the field of history. Nine volumes contain a subject/keyword index; four volumes treat articles on world history, and five treat articles on American history. Each subject/keyword index uses 342 standard subject headings, chronological divisions as keywords, and keywords from titles. Volumes begin with a list of the standard subject headings. Titles with no significant keywords are cited first. Titles cited under chronological divisions as keywords appear next. Finally, titles with keywords are cited alphabetically by keyword. Entries give a reference title, the author, the year, volume, journal name, and the page on which the article begins. The nine subject and keyword volumes are followed by a two-volume author index that lists all articles alphabetically by author.

F–9　**Frewer, Louis Benson.** ***Bibliography of Historical Writings Published in Great Britain and the Empire, 1940–1945.*** Oxford: Basil Blackwell, 1947.　　Z6201.F7

Published for the British National Committee of the International Committee of Historical Sciences to fill in part the gap created by the cessation over the war years of the *International Bibliography of Historical Sciences* (F–4). Included are 5,315 serially numbered items classified in the same fashion as the entries in the *IBHS*. Books, articles, and reviews are included. Entries are not annotated. An index of persons and one of places conclude the volume.

Subsequent volumes published by the Institute of Historical Research have continued that of Frewer under the title *Bibliography of Historical Works Issued in the United Kingdom*. None are annotated, and all treat only books and pamphlets, excluding articles and reviews. The first, compiled by Joan C. Lancaster, treats works published 1946–1956 (London, 1957) [Z2016.L3]. There are 7,400 titles and an author index. The next three volumes were all compiled by William Kellaway. The first covers 3,801 serially numbered publications 1957–1960 (London, 1962) [Z6201.K4]; it, too, excludes articles and reviews. The index of authors and secondary authors includes also some series names, as well as the names of groups of people, persons, places, and institutions that are subjects of cited works. The second of Kellaway's compilations covers 1961–1965 (London, 1967) [Z6201.K41] and enumerates 4,800 titles with an index like the one in the first of his volumes. The third volume treats 1966–1970 (London, 1972) [Z6201.K42] and cites 5,315 serially numbered books and pamphlets. The index is like those of the two preceding volumes. The most recent volume is compiled by Rosemary Taylor and covers 5,281 serially numbered publications, 1971–1975 (London, 1977) [Z6201.T38 D20]. Its index is like those of its immediate predecessors. Another such compilation, treating publications of 1971–1975, may appear. Until its appearance, and for publications of 1976 and after, see the *Annual Bulletin of Historical Literature* (F–7).

F–10　**Scholarly Journals in History.**

AHR　　*American Historical Review.* Vol. 1–. Washington, D.C.: American Historical Association, 1895–. 5/yr (i.e., five issues per year). Reviews. *Guide to the AHR, 1895-1945* published in 1945. Indexes to vols. 1–10 (1895–1905), 11–20 (1905–1915), 21–30 (1915–1925), 31–40 (1925–1935), and 41–60 (1935–1955). See *Recently Published Articles* (F–6).　　E171.A57

BIHR   *Bulletin of the Institute of Historical Research.* Vol. 1–. London: Longmans, Green, 1923–. 2/yr. Reviews. Bibliographical notices including reports on archives and manuscript collections, summaries of unpublished historical theses, and addenda and corrigenda to the *DNB*, *OED*, and other standard reference works. Indexes to vols. 1–50 (1923–1977).
D1.L65

CHR   *Canadian Historical Review.* Vol. 1–. Toronto: University of Toronto Press, 1920–. 4/yr. Reviews. Indexes to vols. 1–10 (1920–1929), 11–20 (1930–1939).   No LC number

Clio   *Clio: An Interdisciplinary Journal of Literature, History, and the Philosophy of History.* Vol. 1–. Fort Wayne: Indiana University–Purdue University, 1971–. 3/yr [from 1980 4/yr]. Reviews. Bibliography (see X–87). Biennial cumulative indexes.
No LC number

Current History. Vol. 1–. Philadelphia: Current History, Inc., 1941–. 10/yr.   D410.C82

EcHR   *Economic History Review.* Vol. 1–. Utrecht: Aoosthoek, 1927–. Frequency varies. Reviews. Annual Bibliography of British Economic and Social History. Index to vols. 1–18 (1927–1948) and to 2d ser., vols. 1–23 (1948–1970).   HC10.E4

EHR   *English Historical Review.* Vol. 1–. London: Longman, 1886–. 4/yr. Reviews. July issues since 1924 (vol. 39) carry a list of selected current periodical articles, classified by geographical area, with brief content notes. Indexes to vols. 1–20 (1886–1905), 21–30 (1906–1915), 31–40 (1916–1925), 41–50 (1926–1935), 51–70 (1936–1955).
DA20.E58

HAHR   *Hispanic American Historical Review.* Vol. 1–. Durham, N.C.: Duke University Press, 1918–. 4/yr. Reviews. Bibliographical Section.
F1401.H66

HJ   *Historical Journal.* Vol. 1–. Cambridge: Cambridge University Press, 1923–. 4/yr. Reviews. Index for 1923–1974.   D1.H33

Historische Zeitschrift. Vol. 1–. Munich: Oldenbourg, 1859–. 6/yr. Reviews. Annual indexes. Periodic bibliographical surveys.   D1.H6

History: The Quarterly Journal of the Historical Association. Vol. 1–. London: F. Hodgson [publisher varies], 1912–. 3/yr. Reviews. Bibliographical notices. Annual index.   D1.H815

History and Theory: Studies in the Philosophy of History. Vol. 1–. Middletown, Conn.: Wesleyan University Press, 1960–. 3/yr. Reviews. Indexes to vols. 1–5 (1960–1966) in vol. 5 and to vols. 6–10 (1967–1971) in vol. 10.   D1.H8173

IJOH   *International Journal of Oral History.* Vol. 1–. Westport, Conn.: Meckler, 1980–. 3/yr. Reviews. Bibliography.   D16.I4 I57

Journal of Asian Studies. Former title: *Far Eastern Quarterly.* Vol. 1–. Ann Arbor, Mich.: Association for Asian Studies, 1941–. 4/yr. Reviews. Bibliography (see L–144).   DS501.F274

JAH   *Journal of American History.* Former title: *Mississippi Valley Historical Review* (1914–1964). Vol. 1–. Bloomington, Ind.: Organization of American Historians, 1914–. 4/yr. Reviews. Bibliography. 50-year index, 1914–1964, published 1973.   E171.J87

JBS   *Journal of British Studies.* Vol. 1–. Hartford, Conn.: Trinity College, 1961–. Reviews. DA20.J6

Journal of Ecclesiastical History. Vol. 1–. Cambridge: Cambridge University Press, 1950–. 4/yr. Reviews. Bibliography. Annual index. BR140.J6

JEH   *Journal of Economic History.* Vol. 1–. Atlanta, Ga.: Economic History Association, 1941–. 4/yr.
HC10.J64

Journal of Interdisciplinary History. Vol. 1–. Cambridge: MIT Press, 1970–. 4/yr. Reviews. Bibliography. Index to vols. 1–5 (1970–1975).
D1.J59

JMH   *Journal of Modern History.* Vol. 1–. Chicago: University of Chicago Press, 1929–. 4/yr. Reviews. Bibliography.   D1.J6

Journal of Psychohistory. Vol. 1–. New York: Association for Psychohistory, 1973–. 4/yr. Reviews.   D16.16.J68

Journal of Social History. Vol. 1–. Pittsburgh: Carnegie-Mellon University Press. 1967–. 4/yr. Reviews, Index to vols. 1–12 (1967–1978). HN1.J6

Journal of Southern History. Vol. 1–. Baton Rouge, La.: Southern Historical Association, 1935–. 4/yr. Reviews. Index to vols. 21–30 (1955–1964).   F206.J68

JHI   *Journal of the History of Ideas: An International Quarterly Devoted to Intellectual History.* Vol. 1–. Philadelphia: Temple University, 1940–. 4/yr. Reviews. Index to vols. 1–25 (1940–1964), 26–30 (1965–1969), 31–35 (1971–1974), 36–40 (1975-1979).   D1.J75

Local Historian: The Quarterly Journal of the Standing Conference for Local History. Vol. 1–. London: National Council of Social Service, 1952–. 4/yr. Reviews. Bibliography. Annual Index.
DA20.A44

Middle East Journal. Vol. 1–. Washington, D.C.: Middle East Institute, 1947–. 4/yr. Index to vols. 1–20 (1947–1966).   DS1.M5

NEQ   *New England Quarterly* (see S–101).

PP   *Past and Present: A Journal of Historical Studies.* Vol. 1–. Oxford: Oxford University Press, 1952–. 4/yr. Reviews. Index to nos. 1–53 (1952–1971).
D1.P37

RPA   *Recently Published Articles* (see F–6).

Reviews in American History. Vol. 1–. Baltimore: Johns Hopkins University Press, 1973–. 4/yr. Reviews. Review Articles. Bibliographic Essays.
Z1236.R47

Reviews in European History. Vol. 1–. Westport, Conn.: Redgrave, 1974–. 4/yr. Reviews. Review Articles. Bibliographic Essays.   D1.R219

SHR   *Scottish Historical Review.* Vol. 1–. Aberdeen: Aberdeen University Press for the Company of Scottish History, 1903–. 2/yr. Reviews. Index to vols. 1–12 (1903–1916), published 1918; to vols. 13–25 (1916–1928) published 1933.   DA750.S21

Slavic Reviews. Former title: *American Slavic and East European Review* (1945–1961). Vol. 1–. Columbus, Ohio: American Association for the Advancement of Slavic Studies, 1941–. 4/yr. Reviews.   D377.A1 A5

Social History: An International Journal. Vol. 1–. London: Methuen, 1976–. 3/yr. Reviews.
HN1.S56

TRHS *Transactions of the Royal Historical Society.* Vol. 1–. London: The Society, 1869–. 1/yr.

DA20.R914

William and Mary Quarterly: A Magazine of Early American History. Vols. 1–27; 2d ser. vols. 1–23; 3d ser., vol. 1–. Williamsburg, Va.: Institute of Early American History and Culture, 1892–1919; 1921–1943; 1944–. 4/yr. Reviews. Bibliography. Index to 3d ser., vols. 1–15 (1944–1958) and 16–30 (1959–1973).

F221.W71

For additional references to historical periodicals see Pierre Caron and Marc Jaryc, eds., *World List of Historical Periodicals and Bibliographies* (New York: Oxford University Press, 1939) [Z6201.A1 C3], which enumerates the 3,100 periodicals used for the *International Bibliography of Historical Science* (F–4); and the more recent work of Erich Boehm, Barbara H. Pope, and Marie S. Ensign, *Historical Periodicals Directory: An Annotated World List*, 5 vols. (Santa Barbara, Calif.: ABC-Clio, 1981–1983) [Z6205 .H654], which cites about 8,200 periodicals, annuals, and irregular serials, including all historical periods, countries, and fields (political, social, cultural, economic, religious, and intellectual history) and all the ancillary disciplines. Both current works and those that ceased publication after 1960 are covered, with bibliographical information and a short description of contents. It is arranged geographically by place of publication: vol. 1, USA and Canada; vol. 2, Europe: West, North, Central, and South; vol. 3, Europe: East and Southeast; USSR; vol. 4, Africa; Middle East; Asia and Pacific Area; Latin America and West Indies; and vol. 5, Addenda; International Organizations; Subject and Title Indexes to vols. 1–4. Notes on contents treat the periodical's subject matter, period, and area concentrations and note whether it contains book reviews, documents, bibliographies, or professional news. A briefer, less current aid is John Lavan Kirby, *Guide to Historical Periodicals in the English Language* (London: Historical Association, 1970) [Z6205.K55]. Briefer still is Dale R. Steiner, *Historical Journals: A Handbook for Writers and Reviewers* (Santa Barbara, Calif.: ABC-Clio, 1981) [Z6205.S73], which discusses current editorial and publishing policies for more than 350 North American history journals, with directory entries arranged alphabetically by journal title, followed by a subject index of journal titles. For the often valuable journals of state and local historical societies see Milton Crouch, *Directory of State and Local History Periodicals* (Chicago: ALA, 1977) [Z1250.C76]. And for somewhat parallel British work see Mullins's *Guide* (H–76).

F–11 **Langer, William L.** *Encyclopedia of World History, Ancient, Medieval and Modern, Chronologically Arranged.* 5th ed., rev. and enl. Boston: Houghton Mifflin, 1972.

D21.L27

This work is based conceptually on Karl Plötz's 1863 work *Auszug aus der [alten, mittleren, neueren, und neuesten] Geschichte*, 27th ed. (Würzburg: Plötz, 1967) [D21.P7 1967]. An English version of Plötz was published by William H. Tillinghast with the original title *Epitome of Ancient, Medieval, and Modern History* (Boston: Houghton Mifflin, 1883) [D21.P72]; the most recent edition of this English version, *Manual of Universal History*, appeared in 1933. The first edition of Langer appeared in 1940. Like Plötz, Langer treats in handbook fashion social, economic, and cultural history, in addition to political, military, and diplomatic history. The method used by both is a telescoped narrative that provides a quick but accurate survey of developments. The chronological sections are as follows: I—The Prehistoric Period, II—Ancient History, III—The Middle Ages, IV— Early Modern History, V—Modern History, VI—The First World War and the Interwar Years, VII—The Second World War

and the Aftermath to 1970, and VIII—Recent History. Appendixes present lists of Roman Emperors, Byzantine Emperors, Caliphs, Popes, Kings of England, Kings of France, Presidents of the United States, Member Nations of the United Nations, and lists of European and New World Universities. A detailed index of persons, places, and subjects concludes the work.

A new illustrated edition of Langer in two volumes was published by Harry N. Abrams, Inc. (New York, 1975) [D21 .L276]; the fifth edition text is accompanied by more than 2,000 photographs, maps, charts, and drawings.

F–12 **Cambridge Ancient History.** 12 vols. plus 5 vols. of plates. Cambridge: Cambridge University Press, 1923-1939. D57.C25 Rev. ed., vols. 3–11, 1951–1954. 3d ed., vols. 1–3, 1970–1977. A new edition of plates to vols. 1, 2, and 3, and 7 part 1; 1977–1984. D57.C252

This standard comprehensive work presents a history of the West from early Egyptian and Babylonian times to A.D. 324. Each volume is self-contained and consists of chapters written by specialists. Each volume concludes with an extensive bibliography and an analytical index. The five volumes of plates are keyed to the relevant portions of the text. There is no general index.

Among the shorter works on classical history see the *Larousse Encyclopedia of Ancient and Medieval History* (London: P. Hamlyn, 1963) [D59.H553 1963a] and Herman Bengtson, *Introduction to Ancient History* (Berkeley, Los Angeles, London: University of California Press, 1970) [Z6202.B413] as well as the *Chronology of the Ancient World* by Mellersch (F–74). Standard works in classical studies include Pauly's *Real-Encyclopädie der klassischen Altertumswissenschaft* and its abbreviated version (L–41); *Oxford Classical Dictionary* (L–42); Arey's *New Century Classical Handbook* (L–45); the serial bibliography *L'année philologique* (L–47); and the *Year's Work in Classical Studies* (L–47).

F–13 **Cambridge Medieval History.** Edited by H. M. Gwatkin et al. 8 vols. with portfolios of illustrations and maps for each vol. Cambridge: Cambridge University Press, 1911–1936. 2d ed. Edited by Joseph Robson Tanner et al. 1966–.

D117.C3

This standard comprehensive work covers the history of the Middle Ages, from the Christian Roman Empire to the Italian Renaissance. Each volume is self-contained, with a detailed bibliography and analytical index. Individual chapters are completed by specialists. There is no comprehensive index. An epitome by Charles William Previte-Orton, *Shorter Cambridge Medieval History*, 2 vols. (Cambridge: Cambridge University Press, 1952) [D117.P75], presents a concise version that incorporates more recent research. The revised edition, now in progress, also incorporates recent research. In contrast with the original work, however, the second edition is without bibliographies.

For brief treatments see also Harry Ezekiel Wedek, *Concise Dictionary of Medieval History* (London: P. Owen, 1964) [D114.W4 1964]. The interdisciplinary *International Medieval Bibliography* (F–23) provides more current references, as do many of the bibliographies and reference works cited in section N.

F–14   *New Cambridge Modern History [NCMH].* 14 vols.   Cambridge: Cambridge University Press, 1957–1970.   Vol. 13 is the general index, and vol. 14 is an atlas.   D208.N4

This new work is meant to supersede the original *Cambridge Modern History [CMH]*, ed. A. W. Ward et al., 13 vols. (Cambridge: Cambridge University Press, 1902–1926) [D208.C17].   It covers the period from the Renaissance to 1945, treating not only political history but also modern economic, social, and cultural history and presenting a comprehensive and authoritative account.   The original *CMH* has a less up-to-date but more extended treatment of seventeenth- and eighteenth-century European and American history; the new work is stronger for nineteenth-century and non-European history.   Individual volumes in the *NCMH* are self-contained with notes and analytical indexes but, unlike the original volumes, without full bibliographies.   Individual chapters are contributed by authorities who were also consulted by John Roach when he compiled *Bibliography of Modern History* (Cambridge: Cambridge University Press, 1968) [Z6204.R62], which serves as the bibliographical portion of the *New History*.   Its 6,040 serially numbered, often annotated entries, current through 1960, are arranged chronologically and topically to conform to the chapters of the *NCMH*.   English-language titles are emphasized.   There are three sections to the Roach bibliography, treating 1493–1648 (and keyed to *NCMH* vols. 1–4), 1648–1793 (*NCMH* vols. 5–8), and 1793–1945 (*NCMH* vols. 9–12).   An index of personal names and subjects, but not of authors, concludes the bibliography.

Shorter works include Richard B. Morris and Graham W. Irwin, eds., *Harper Encyclopedia of the Modern World: A Concise Reference History from 1760 to the Present* (New York: Harper, 1970) [D205.H35 1970].   This handbook is disposed into two parts, a "Basic Chronology" covering political, military, and diplomatic history by state, region, and area, and a "Topical Chronology" treating economic, social, and constitutional history as well as the history of science, of thought, and of culture.   There is a detailed analytical index.   An earlier work of the same sort is Alan W. Palmer, *Dictionary of Modern History, 1789-1945* (London: Cresset Press, 1962) [D299.P32], which emphasizes British affairs and political and historical figures.

II.   BRITISH (AND IRISH) HISTORY— GENERAL

F–15   *Writings on British History, 1901–1933.   A Bibliography of Books and Articles on the History of Great Britain from about 400 A.D. to 1914, Published during the Years 1901–1933 Inclusive, with an Appendix Containing a Selected List of Publications in These Years on British History since 1914.* Compiled by H. H. Bellot. 5 vols. in 7.   London: Jonathan Cape, 1968–1970.   Z2016.W74

Published under the sponsorship of the Royal Historical Society, these volumes present an exhaustive, unannotated, retrospective list (which does, however, cite the major reviews of books) divided into volumes as follows: vol. 1, Auxiliary Sciences and General Works; vol. 2, Middle Ages, 450–1485; vol. 3, Tudor and Stuart, 1485–1714; vol. 4, Eighteenth Century, 1714–1815 (in two parts); vol. 5, 1815–1914 (in two parts).   Volume 5, part 2 also includes the appendix.   An effort is made to avoid duplication between entries in this retrospective list and those found in widely available standard bibliographies such as the *BBH* series, which should also be consulted.   Emphasis is on English-language materials.

The retrospective volumes for publications 1901–1933 were preceded by a current bibliography with the same title which

was developed by Alexander Taylor Milne and which covers, in eight volumes, works published 1934–1945.   These volumes were published during the period 1937–1960; they are followed by volumes compiled under the auspices of the Institute of Historical Research by Donald J. Munro, *Writings . . . 1946-1948* (1973), *1949-1951* (1975); by J. M. Sims, *Writings . . . 1952-1954* (1975); by Sims and Jacobs, *Writings . . . 1955-1957* (1977); by H. H. Creaton, *Writings . . . 1958-1959* (1977); by Philpin Creaton, *Writings . . . 1960-1961* (1977); *Writings . . .1962–1964* (1979) by Heather J. Creaton, who has also prepared *Writings . . . 1967–1968* (1982), *Writings . . . 1967–1970* (1984), *Writings . . . 1971–1972* (1985), and *Writings . . . 1973–1974* (1986).   With the completion of this series through Writings of 1974 (except for 1965–1966), it has now linked up with the new *Annual Bibliography of British and Irish History* (F–16).

Though there is some variation among individual volumes, the arrangement of all is a classified one, with general materials appearing in part I.   These include sections on Auxiliary Sciences (Chronology, Dictionaries and Glossaries, Paleography and Diplomatic, Heraldry, Coinage and Numismatics, Costume, Arms and Armour, Iconography, Historical Geography); Bibliographies and Indexes; Archives and Collections; Historiography, Study and Teaching; British History in General (Comprehensive, Medieval, Modern, Political, Constitutional and Legal History, Economic and Social History, Ecclesiastical History, Educational History, Military and Naval History, Maritime History and Exploration, Foreign Relations, History of Arts and Crafts); English Local History and Topography; Wales; Scotland; Ireland; Genealogy and Family History; Collected Biography.   Part II has sections on the various periods of British history: Pre-Conquest, Early Medieval; Later Medieval; Tudor; Stuart; Eighteenth Century; 1815–1914.   There are subsections identical with those in part I, plus special subheadings appropriate to individual periods.   Serially numbered entries are alphabetically arranged within their subsections.   Book reviews are cited after the entry for the book reviewed both in the retrospective volumes for *Writings . . . 1901-1933* and in the series of volumes compiled by Milne, treating *Writings . . . 1934-1945*.   Indexes are of places, names, and subjects, keyed to entry numbers.

A massive individual bibliography of bibliographies is the work by David Berkowitz, *Bibliotheca Bibliographica Britannica; or, Bibliographies in British History: A Manual of Bibliography of Bibliographies, and of Bibliographies, Catalogues, Registers, Inventories, Lists, Calendars, Guides, Reference Aids, Directories, Indices, etc., Collected and Classified for the Use of Researchers in British History*, 2 books in 7 vols. (Waltham, Mass.: Privately printed, 1963–1969) [Z2016.B45].   Unannotated entries in book 1 treat general studies and guides to repositories and research materials.   Book 2 provides unannotated entries on British general, cultural, local, imperial, and Commonwealth history.

F–16   Royal Historical Society.   *Annual Bibliography of British and Irish History [for 1975–].* Edited by G. R. Elton.   Hassocks, Sussex: Harvester Press; Atlantic Highlands, N.J.: Humanities Press, 1976–.   Z2016.A55

Issued more promptly than the *Annual Bulletin* (F–7) is, each volume of this new annual current bibliography lists about 3,000 references to books, essays in composite volumes, and articles from some 500 journals.   Entries are listed according to the following classification: Auxiliary (including Bibliography and Archives, Aids, and Historiography); General; Roman Britain; England 450–1066; England 1066–1500; England and Wales 1500–1714; Britain 1714–1815; Britain 1815–1914; Britain since 1914; medieval Wales; Scotland before the Union; Ireland to ca. 1640; Ireland since ca. 1640.   The major sections are then further subdivided, generally into the following areas: General; Politics; Constitution, Administration, and Law; Foreign Affairs; Economic Affairs; Religion; Social Structure and Population; and Intellectual and Cultural Affairs. Author and subject indexes conclude each volume.

F–17 Steinberg, Sigfrid Henry, Ivor H. Evans, et al. *Steinberg's Dictionary of British History.* 2d ed. London: Edward Arnold, 1970. DA34.S7 1970

First published in 1963, this dictionary handbook is the work of a dozen contributors. Signed articles treat topics in the political, constitutional, administrative, legal, ecclesiastical, and economic history of England and of countries that are, or were, part of England and her overseas possessions or the British Empire or the Commonwealth for as long as their British connection lasted. The internal history of Scotland and Ireland is less fully treated than is that of Wales; such treatment as is found is from the point of view of relations with England. The histories of literature, music, the arts and architecture, philosophy, and science are generally excluded, as are purely biographical entries, for which users are referred to the *DNB* and related works (G–10). There are extensive cross-references. Bibliographies of definitive monographs are given; users are otherwise referred to the *Annual Bibliography of British and Irish History* (F–16), the *Writings on British History* (F–15), and the *Annual Bulletin of Historical Literature* (F–7).

A similar work, though by a single hand, is the compact *Dictionary of British History*, ed. J. P. Kenyon (New York: Stein and Day, 1983) [DA34.D52 1983], which covers in some 3,000 articles events and persons significant in British history. A chronology is appended which treats British, American, and Continental events.

F–18 *Oxford History of England.* G. N. Clark, general editor. 15 vols. Oxford: Clarendon Press, 1934–1971.
LC numbers vary.

Generally, each large volume of this standard reference history is written by an authority on the period and contains a preface, detailed table of contents, main body with specific running-titles on each page, a valuable and extensive annotated bibliography, and a detailed index of names and subjects. When only historical facts are wanted, *Steinberg's Dictionary of British History* (F–17) is more convenient to use. This work may be supplemented by *New History of England* (F–19).

1. R. G. Collingwood and J. N. L. Myres. *Roman Britain and the English Settlements.* 2d ed. 1937.
DA145.C583 1937
2. A. Peter Salway. *Roman Britain.* 1981. DA145.S26
3. F. M. Stenton. *Anglo-Saxon England, c. 550–1087.* 3d ed. 1971. DA152.S74 1971
4. A. L. Poole. *From Domesday Book to Magna Carta, 1087–1216.* 2d ed. 1955. DA175.P6 1955
5. Sir Maurice Powicke. *Thirteenth Century, 1216–1307.* 2d ed. 1962. DA225.P65 1962
6. May McKisack. *Fourteenth Century, 1307–99.* 1959.
DA230.M25
7. Ernest F. Jacob. *Fifteenth Century, 1399–1485.* 1961.
DA245.J3
8. J. D. Mackie. *Earlier Tudors, 1485–1558.* 1952.
DA325.M3
9. J. B. Black. *Reign of Elizabeth, 1558–1603.* 2d ed. 1959. DA355.B65 1959
10. Godfrey Davies. *Early Stuarts, 1603–60.* 2d ed. 1959.
DA390.D3 1959
11. G. N. Clark. *Later Stuarts, 1660–1714.* 2d ed. 1956.
DA435.C55 1961
12. Basil Williams. *Whig Supremacy, 1714–1760.* 2d ed., Revised by C. H. Stuart. 1962. Controversial.
DA498.W5 1962

13. J. Steven Watson. *Reign of George III, 1760–1815.* 1960. DA505.W38
14. Sir Llewellyn Woodward. *Age of Reform, 1815–70.* 2d ed. 1962. DA530.W6 1962
15. R. C. K. Ensor. *England, 1870–1914.* 1936.
DA560.E6 1936a
16. A. J. P. Taylor. *English History, 1914–1945.* 1965.
DA566.T38

Another convenient and frequently cited multivolume historical survey is the *Pelican History of England*, 9 vols. (Harmondsworth: Penguin, 1950–) [DA30.P4], in which the following individual volumes appear:

1. Ian Richmond. *Roman Britain.* 1964.
2. Dorothy Whitelock. *Beginnings of English Society* (from the Anglo-Saxon Invasion). 1952.
3. Doris Mary Stenton. *English Society in the Early Middle Ages (1066–1307).* 1965.
4. A. R. Myers. *England in the Late Middle Ages.* 1952.
5. Stanley T. Bindoff. *Tudor England.* 1950.
6. Maurice P. Ashley. *England in the Seventeenth Century.* 1975.
7. John Harold Plumb. *England in the Eighteenth Century.* 1950, 1968.
8. David Thomson. *England in the Nineteenth Century (1815–1914).* 1965.
9. *England in the Twentieth Century, 1914–1963.* 1965, 1981.

The most frequently recommended shorter history is by G. M. Trevelyan, *History of England*, 3d ed. (London: Longmans, Green, 1945) [DA32.T749 1945].

F–19 *New History of England [1460–1960].* A. G. Dickens and Norman Gash, general editors. Cambridge: Harvard University Press, 1977–. LC numbers vary

Each volume of this ongoing ten-volume work, designed for both the general and the student reader, is scheduled to cover approximately fifty years of English history. To each is appended a bibliography or bibliographical essay intended primarily to survey recent materials and to identify sources for specialized studies. To date, the following volumes have been published:

J. R. Lander. *Government and Community— England, 1450–1509.* 1980. DA250.L29
G. R. Elton. *Reform and Reformation—England, 1509–1558.* 1977. DA332.E497
J. R. Jones. *Country and Court—England, 1658–1714.* 1978. DA435.J66
W. A. Speck. *Stability and Strife—England, 1714–1760.* 1977. DA498.S68
Ian R. Christie. *Wars and Revolutions—Britain. 1760–1815.* 1982. DA505.C48 1982
Norman Gash. *Aristocracy and People—Britain, 1815–1865.* 1979. DA535.G37
Max Beloff. *Wars and Warfare—Britain, 1914–1945.* 1984.
DA566.7.B446 1984

F–20 *Cambridge History of the British Empire [CHBE].* J. Holland Rose, general editor. 8 vols. Cambridge: Cambridge University Press, 1929–1954. 2d ed. 1963–. DA16.C252

These volumes provide a comprehensive and authoritative history of Britain's imperial history and the history of the imperial and Commonwealth nations. Coverage of the individual volumes is as follows: vol. 1, The Old Empire from the Beginnings to 1783; vol. 2, The Growth of the New Empire,

1783–1870; vol. 3, The Empire Commonwealth, 1870–1919; vol. 4, British India, 1497–1858; vol. 5, The Indian Empire, 1858–1918; vol. 6, Canada and Newfoundland; vol. 7, Australia (part 1) and New Zealand (part 2); vol. 8, South Africa, Rhodesia, and the High Commission Territories (2d ed., 1963). Each volume is self-contained, with chapters by specialists, a classified bibliography, and an elaborate analytical index.

III. MEDIEVAL HISTORY

See also section N.

F–21 **Paetow, Louis J. *Guide to the Study of Medieval History.*** Rev. ed. Prepared under the Auspices of the Mediaeval Academy of America. Edited by Dana C. Munroe and Gray C. Boyce. New York: F. C. Crofts, 1931.   Z6203.P25

The first edition of this comprehensive scholarly and critical guide appeared in 1917. It is divided into three main parts, treating General Works, the General History of the Middle Ages (500–1500), and Medieval Culture (599–1300), respectively. Part 1 lists more than 1,200 serially numbered works, including reference books, some ancillary works, general modern historical works, and large collections of original source materials. Emphasis here and throughout is on English, French, and German works. Works restricted to English history are not included, and though both eastern and northern Europe are treated, primary concern is with western European history. Parts 2 and 3 are arranged topically: each topic is outlined, recommendations for reading are provided, and bibliographical references are made to entries in part 1 and to more specialized works. Material is listed in the order of its importance. There is an extensive index of authors, editors, translators, and subjects and titles of large collections. In 1980, Kraus issued a reprint of Paetow, revised and corrected with errata by Gray C. Boyce (pp. xxi-li) and an addendum by Lynn Thorndike (pp. liii-cxii).

For work since 1930 see Gray Cowan Boyce, comp. and ed., *Literature of Medieval History 1930–1975: A Supplement to Louis John Paetow's A Guide to the Study of Medieval History*, 5 vols. (Millwood, N.Y.: Kraus International Publications, 1981) [Z6203.P25 1980 suppl.]. Sponsored by the Medieval Academy of America, this supplement has been in preparation since the second edition of Paetow was published. It follows the original in format, with a virtually identical table of contents. Two important deviations are that Boyce extends the coverage of part 3, medieval culture, to 1500 and that he omits the topical outlines that preceded the listings of recommended readings and bibliographies in Paetow. The first volume contains a complete list of journal abbreviations, followed by a detailed "List of Subject Headings" that gives an overview of all chapter titles and subheadings used in the entire work. Individual entries are arranged in alphabetical order under the subheadings. They include occasional descriptive and evaluative annotation and reference to important reviews. The bibliography proper occupies the first four volumes; volume 5 provides an index of author and subject names. For materials published since 1975, the *International Medieval Bibliography* (F–23) and other serial bibliographies will provide current references.

F–22 **van Caenegen, R. C., with the collaboration of F. L. Ganshof. *Guide to Sources of Medieval History.*** New York: North-Holland Publishing Co., 1978.   Z6203.C25

This discursive guide is a revised and expanded edition of earlier versions which appeared in Dutch (*Encyclopedie van de Geschiedenis der Middeleeuwen* [Ghent, 1962]) and German (*Kurze Quellenkunde des west-europäishen Mittelalters*

[Göttingen, 1964]). It is in five main sections: (1) Typology of the Sources of Medieval History; (2) Libraries and Archives; (3) Great Collections and Repertories of Sources; (4) Reference Works for the Study of Medieval Texts; and (5) Bibliographical Introduction to the Auxiliary Sciences of History. Each of these sections contains a number of informative chapters enumerating and describing a full range of sources. Chapters on new historical applications such as metrology and computers are included. A detailed table of contents facilitates access, as does an index of names and anonymous titles.

F–23 ***International Medieval Bibliography [IMB] [1965–].*** Leeds, England: School of History, University of Leeds; and Minneapolis: Department of History, University of Minnesota, 1968–.   Z6203.I63

A quarterly and then semiannual bibliography of medieval history and civilization published under the auspices of the Medieval Academy of America, this work lists articles, notes, and review articles located in some 1,000 journals and 50–100 festschriften and other composite volumes. Analyzed journals and composite volumes are listed at the beginning of each issue. Some 4,400 serially numbered entries in current issues are disposed into rough subject categories, as follows: General; Administration; Archaeology; Architecture; Art-General, Painting, Sculpture; Bibliography; Crusades; Daily Life; Demography; Ecclesiastical History; Economic-General, Trade; Epigraphy; Folklore; Genealogy; Geography; Hagiography; Hebrew and Jewish Studies; Heraldry; Historiography; Intellectual History; Language; Law (including Canon Law); Literature—General, Prose, Verse; Liturgy; Local History; Manuscripts; Military History; Music; Numismatics; Onomastics; Palaeography and Diplomatic; Philosophy; Political History; Religious Orders; Science; Sources; Theology. Subdivisions are by geographical area and include: General; Baltic; British Isles; Byzantine Empire; eastern Europe; France; Germany; Iberia; Italy; Low Countries; Russia; Scandinavia; and South-Eastern Europe.

Entries give author, title, and standard bibliographical information; the date(s) characterizing the chronological range of the cited article; and the presence in the cited work of maps, bibliography, medieval texts, or illustrations. An author and a selective general subject index conclude each issue.

The *IMB* is the most comprehensive of the available serial bibliographies treating medieval history. Its competitors were the *International Guide to Medieval Studies: A Quarterly Index to Periodical Literature*, 12 vols. (Darien, Conn.: American Bibliographic Service, 1962–1977) [Z6203.I6], and the *Quarterly Checklist of Medievalia: An International Index of Current Books, Monographs, Brochures, and Separates*, 20 vols. (Darien, Conn.: American Bibliographic Service, 1958–1978) [Z6203.Q34], both produced by the American Bibliographic Service. The former, covering periodicals, festschriften, and published proceedings, has a somewhat more elaborate subject index; the latter has only an index of contemporary authors, editors, and translators. Also available are the *Bibliographie internationale de l'humanisme et de la Renaissance* (O–3) and the lists of current books and articles in *Speculum* (N–7).

F–24 ***"Bibliographie" in Cahiers de civilisation médiévale: Xᵉ-XIIᵉ siècles.*** Vol. 1–. Poitiers: Centre d'études supérieures de civilisation médiévale, 1958–.   CB3.C3

In each quarterly issue through 1970 and then in the fourth issue of the year appears a bibliography of books, articles, dissertations, and reviews on studies of the tenth through twelfth centuries. The more than 5,000 entries (which are serially numbered over the year) are listed under French subject headings that include names of authors and key terms of titles, with abundant cross-references. During the period when the bibliography was produced in quarterly issues, the fourth issue contained a supplement to the bibliographies of the first three quarters. The bibliography closes with an index of authors cited. It is particularly valuable for citations of French and European scholarship and should be consulted to supplement the coverage of such materials in British and American bibliographies.

IV. BRITISH (AND IRISH) HISTORY—MEDIEVAL

See also section N.

F–25 Graves, Edgar B. *Bibliography of English History to 1485 [BBH-Graves].* Oxford: Clarendon Press, 1975.
Z2017.B5

Based on the long-standard work of Charles Gross, *Sources and Literature of English History from the Earliest Times to about 1485,* 2d ed., rev. and enl. (London: Longman's, 1915) [Z2016.G87 1915], this authoritative volume was issued under the sponsorship of the Royal Historical Society, the American Historical Association, and the Medieval Academy of America. It is disposed into twenty-three chapters, in two major divisions. The first division is chronological and consists of fifteen chapters. The first three, concerned with General Works and Auxiliary Sciences, cover Bibliographical Guides, Journals of More than Local Scope, and Auxiliaries to Historical Study (Philology, Chronology, Palaeography, and Diplomatic, Seals and Heraldry, Biography and Genealogy; Geography and Place-Names, Numismatics, Archaeology, and Art). The next four chapters treat Archives and Libraries, Printed Collections of Sources, Comprehensive Modern Narratives, and Local History. Chapters 8–10 treat Prehistoric and Celtic Times, the Roman Occupation, and Celtic Britain after the Roman Occupation. Chapters 11–12 treat the Anglo-Saxon Period. Chapters 13–15, collectively titled From Normans to Tudors, cover Chronicles and Royal Biographies, Law Tracts, and Public Administrative Records. The remaining chapters, 16–23, constitute the second major division of the book and are topically defined, covering Political History, Military and Naval History, Land Tenure and Estates, Agrarian Society, Urban Society, the Church, Modern Studies of the Medieval English Church, and Intellectual History, respectively. An appendix enumerates the individual volumes of important series of concern to the historian of medieval England.

In all there are 7,225 serially numbered, descriptively and evaluatively annotated entries, more than double the number (3,234) found in the revised edition of Gross. It should be noted that entries concern *English* history only; students interested in the medieval history of Wales or Ireland are advised to consult a number of alternative bibliographies cited in the preface. There is an elaborate index of names, places, and subjects. The work is supplemented by *Writings on British History* (F–15) and the *Annual Bibliography of British and Irish History* (F–16).

F–26 Bonser, Wilfrid. *Anglo-Saxon and Celtic Bibliography (450–1087).* 2 vols. Berkeley and Los Angeles: University of California Press; Oxford: Basil Blackwell, 1957.
Z2017.B6

A standard work, containing more than 11,975 books and articles published through 1953. There is a list of the 422 periodicals and composite volumes analyzed. Entries are disposed in an extremely detailed, classified format. Main sections treat (1) General Topics and Historical Source Material,

(2) Political History, (3) Local History, (4) Constitutional History and Law, (5) Social and Economic History, (6) Ecclesiastical History and Religion, (7) Geography and Place-Names, (8) General Culture, (9) Archaeology, (10) Numismatics and Seals, (11) Epigraphy, and (12) Art. A detailed breakdown of the contents is presented in the preliminary pages of volume 1. Volume 2 contains two indexes, of authors, and of subjects, personal names, and place-names.

Bonser has also published *Romano-British Bibliography (55 B.C.-A.D. 449),* 2 vols. (Oxford: Basil Blackwell, 1964) [Z2017.B62], similarly authoritative, listing more than 9,300 items. Volume 2 is an index.

F–27 Altschul, Michael. *Anglo-Norman England, 1066–1154.* Cambridge: Cambridge University Press, 1969.   Z2017.A43

This is chronologically the earliest in coverage of a series of bibliographical handbooks for the advanced scholar sponsored by the Conference on British Studies and prepared by American historians. The work lists 1,800 serially numbered titles of books and articles that appeared before August 1968. Some entries are briefly and evaluatively annotated. Entries are disposed into fourteen standard divisions used in all volumes of this series: Bibliographies; Catalogues, Guides, and Handbooks; General Surveys; Constitutional and Administrative History; Political History; Social History; Economic History; Agricultural History; Science and Technology; Military and Naval History; Religious History; History of the Fine Arts; Intellectual History; and Historiography. Where appropriate, these chapters are further subdivided into standard sections treating Printed Sources, Surveys, Monographs, Biographies, and Articles, respectively. An index of authors, editors, and translators concludes each volume. Further volumes in this extremely well received series are cited at F–28, F–29, F–31, F–36, F–42, and F–45. More are planned.

F–28 Wilkinson, Bertie. *High Middle Ages in England, 1154–1377.* Cambridge: Cambridge University Press, 1978.
Z2017.W54

Another volume in the series of bibliographical handbooks for the advanced scholar sponsored by the Conference on British Studies. There are 2,259 serially numbered entries, which are current to 1976 and are disposed into the fourteen standard chapters and subdivisions, and indexed (see F–27).

F–29 Guth, Delloyd J. *Late Medieval England, 1377–1485.* Cambridge: Cambridge University Press, 1976.   Z2017.G87

Another volume in the series of bibliographical handbooks for the advanced scholar sponsored by the Conference on British Studies, this work presents a briefly annotated list of 2,500 entries, current to December 1974, disposed into the usual chapters and subdivisions, and indexed (see F–27).

V.   BRITISH (AND IRISH) HISTORY— RENAISSANCE THROUGH EIGHTEENTH CENTURY

See also section O and section P.

F–30 **Read, Conyers.** *Bibliography of British History: Tudor Period, 1485–1603 [BBH-Read].* 2d ed. Oxford: Clarendon Press, 1959.

This volume, the first edition of which appeared in 1933, was prepared under the direction of the American Historical Association and the Royal Historical Society. It is designed to follow the earlier volume in this series of definitive bibliographies of British history by Graves (F–25). The work is disposed into fourteen chapters, treating General Works; Political History; Constitutional History; The History of Political Theory; The History of Law; Ecclesiastical History; Economic History; Discovery, Exploration, and Colonization; Military and Naval History; Cultural and Social History (Education, Music, Science, and Fine Arts); Local History; Scotland (with subtopics parallel to the series of chapters on England); Ireland (with parallel subtopics); and Wales. The 6,543 serially numbered, descriptively and evaluatively annotated entries are current to 1956. The volume concludes with an index of authors and subjects (including persons).

F–31 **Levine, Mortimer.** *Tudor England, 1485–1603.* Cambridge: Cambridge University Press, 1968.   Z2017.5.L4

Another volume in the series of bibliographical handbooks for advanced scholars sponsored by the Conference on British Studies, this work has 2,360 entries, current to 1 September 1966, divided into the standard fourteen chapters and subdivisions, and indexed (see F–27).

F–32 **Davies, Godfrey.** *Bibliography of British History: Stuart Period, 1603–1714 [BBH-Davies].* 2d ed. Revised by Mary F. Keeler. Oxford: Clarendon Press, 1970.

Z2018.D25 1970

The original edition of this volume was published in 1928. Both it and its successor are part of the series of authoritative, descriptively and evaluatively annotated bibliographies issued under the direction of the American Historical Association and the Royal Historical Society, of which the works by Graves (F–25) and Read (F–30) are the chronologically preceding volumes. This volume contains 4,350 serially numbered entries, which are current to 1961/62, disposed in an arrangement of fifteen chapters. The chapters treat General Reference Works, Political History, Constitutional History, Legal History, Ecclesiastical History, Military History, Naval History, Economic History, Social History, Cultural History (Fine Arts, Music, Science, and Education), Local History, Colonial History, Wales (with subheadings as for England), Scotland (with subheadings), and Ireland (with subheadings). Within sections arrangement is alphabetical, in contrast with the chronological arrangement of entries in the first edition. There are some cross-references and a detailed index.

J. S. Morrill's critical bibliography, *Seventeenth-Century Britain, 1603-1714* (Hamden, Conn.: Archon, 1980) [Z2018 .M63], treats material of the period 1958–1979. There are sections on General Works, Government, Political History, Political and Constitutional Thought, Military and Naval Thought, Ecclesiastical History, Economic History, Social History, Local Studies, Cultural History, and Scotland, Ireland, and Wales. An appendix cites significant articles published 1958–1979.

F–35 **Grose, Clyde Leclare.** *Selected Bibliography of British History, 1660–1760.* Chicago: University of Chicago Press, 1939.   Z2016.C86

This volume presents some 3,801 serially numbered entries, plus more than 4,000 subordinate references. Treated are bibliographies, reference works, source materials, contemporary works, and later works concerning the history of Britain 1660–1760. Entries, which are descriptively and evaluatively annotated, are disposed in the first part into fifteen sections, as follows: Introductory Section, General Works on the Period, Constitutional History, Diplomatic History, Military History, Naval History, Economic History, Social History, Religious History, Cultural History, Local History, Wales, Scotland, Ireland and Colonial History. Following these sections, which treat of the entire period, are three further parts, treating the periods 1660–1688, 1689–1714, and 1715–1760, respectively. These have subsections covering the same topics as are found in the chapters of the first part, along with subheadings for selected events and biographical subjects special to each of the periods. In addition to many cross-references, there is a detailed index of authors, titles, names of persons, and subjects. Though somewhat out of date, this volume continues to be of value because it connects what the standard bibliographical guides of Davies (F–32) and Pargellis (F–38) separate, the Restoration and both the early and the mid-eighteenth century.

F–36 **Sachse, William L.** *Restoration England, 1660–1689.* Cambridge: Cambridge University Press, 1971.   Z2018.S3

Another volume in the series of bibliographical handbooks for the advanced scholar sponsored by the Conference on British Studies, this work has 2,350 serially numbered entries, current to January 1969, disposed into the usual chapters and subdivisions, and indexed (see F–27).

F–37 **Morgan, William Thomas, and Chloe Sizer Morgan.** *Bibliography of British History (1700–1715), with Special Reference to the Reign of Queen Anne.* 5 vols. Bloomington: Indiana University Press, 1934.   Z2018.M6

Originally issued as volumes 18–19 and 23–26, numbers 94–95 and 114–124, of *Indiana University Studies*, this often reprinted comprehensive bibliography of the reign of Queen Anne presents in twenty-five chapters Bibliographical Aids; Lists of Pamphlets and Memoirs Published before 1700 and in each of the years 1700 through 1716; Source Materials; Correspondence; Periodicals; Plays and Other Dramatic Works; Secondary Works; and Unpublished Manuscripts. Entries are serially numbered in alphanumeric order. Volumes 1–3 include chapters 1–24; volume 4 covers the last chapter on Unpublished Manuscripts, with its own index; volume 5 contains supplements to volumes 1–3 and a detailed index of authors, titles, and subjects.

Addenda by Pat Rogers were published in *PBSA* 69 (1975): 226–37 and *PBSA* 73 (1979): 93–107.

F–38 **Pargellis, Stanley, and Dudley Julius Medley.** *Bibliography of British History: The Eighteenth Century, 1714–1789 [BBH-Pargellis and Medley].* Oxford: Clarendon Press, 1951.   Z2018.P37 1951

This now quite dated work, issued under the direction of the American Historical Association and the Royal Historical Society, is part of a series of definitive annotated bibliographies of British history, of which the volumes by Graves (F–25), Read (F–30), and Davies (F–32) are the chronologically preceding works. The 4,558 serially numbered entries are elaborately classified into the following main sections: General Reference Works, Political History, Constitutional History,

Legal History, Ecclesiastical History, Economic History, Military History, Naval History, Social History, Cultural History, Local History, Scotland, Ireland, Wales, The American Colonies, India, and a final chapter on the Historical Manuscripts Commission Reports (see also H–61). Annotations of entries often refer to additional works. A detailed index concludes the volume.

More current bibliographical aid may be found in the relevant volume of the *New History of England* by Speck (F–19), in the *Annual Bibliography of British and Irish History* (F–16), and in the interdisciplinary bibliography on *Eighteenth Century* sponsored by the American Society for Eighteenth-Century Studies (P–4).

VI. BRITISH HISTORY—NINETEENTH CENTURY AND TWENTIETH CENTURY

See also section Q and section R.

F–40 **Brown, Lucy M., and Ian R. Christie. *Bibliography of British History, 1789–1851 [BBH-Brown & Christie].*** Oxford: Clarendon Press, 1977. Z2019.B76

Like the preceding volumes by Graves (F–25), Read (F–30), Davies (F–32), and Pargellis (F–38) in this series of authoritative bibliographies of British history, this one was issued under the direction of the American Historical Association and the Royal Historical Society. It has 4,782 serially numbered, descriptively and evaluatively annotated entries disposed into a total of fifteen major sections. These treat General Reference Works, Political History, Constitutional History, Legal History, Ecclesiastical History, Military History, Naval History, Economic History, Social History, Cultural History, Local History, Wales, Scotland, Ireland, and the British Empire. An extensive index of authors, titles, personal names, and subjects concludes the massive volume.

F–42 **Altholz, Josef L. *Victorian England, 1837–1901.*** Cambridge: Cambridge University Press, 1970. Z2019.A56

Another volume in the series of bibliographical handbooks for the advanced scholar sponsored by the Conference on British Studies, this work has 2,500 serially numbered entries, current to 1 January 1968, following the structure and arrangement of other volumes in the series (see F–27), though with less annotation than most.

F–43 **Hanham, H. J. *Bibliography of British History, 1851–1914 [BBH-Hanham].*** Oxford: Clarendon Press, 1976. Z2019.H35

This volume, issued under the direction of the American Historical Association and the Historical Society, is disposed into thirteen chapters, as follows: General; Political and Constitutional History; External Relations (General, The Indian Empire, The Colonial Empire, Foreign Countries); The Armed Forces; The Legal System; The Churches; Economic History; Social History; Intellectual and Cultural History; Local History; Wales; Scotland; and Ireland. A total of 10,829 entries current through 1970 are descriptively and evaluatively annotated. The main body is followed by a massive and elaborate index of persons, places, and subjects.

This work is chronologically the most recent in the authoritative series of bibliographies of British history which includes volumes by Graves (F–25), Read (F–30), Davies (F–32), Par-

gellis (F–38), and Brown and Christie (F–40). Comparable bibliographies do not exist for the period from 1915 on, but the bibliographical handbook by Havighurst (F–45), though less amply annotated, is a strong and available alternative.

F–45 **Havighurst, Alfred F. *Modern England, 1901–1970.*** Cambridge: Cambridge University Press, 1976. Z2020.H38

Another volume in the series of bibliographical handbooks for the advanced scholar sponsored by the Conference on British Studies, this work contains 2,502 serially numbered entries current to 1 January 1974. It is disposed into the usual fourteen chapters, with subdivisions and an index (see F–27).

VII. AMERICAN (AND CANADIAN) HISTORY

See also section S.

F–50 **Beers, Henry Putney. *Bibliographies in American History: Guide to Materials for Research.*** Rev. ed. New York: H. W. Wilson, 1942. Z1236.A1 B4

A comprehensive but unannotated and now rather out-of-date list of more than 11,000 bibliographies published separately or as parts of other works. No limitations on language or origin of the bibliography are set. Serially numbered entries are disposed into fifteen chapters: General Aids; Colonial Period, Revolution, Confederation; The United States; Diplomatic History; Economic History; Education; Political Science, Constitutional, Legal History; Army and Navy; Races; Religious History; Social, Cultural, Scientific History; Biography and Genealogy; Territories, Possessions, Dependencies; States; Cartography. A brief list of addenda is followed by an extensive author-subject index.

This work is continued by Beers' *Bibliographies in American History, 1942–1978: Guide to Materials for Research*, 2 vols. (Woodbridge, Conn.: Research Publications, 1982) [Z1236.B39], which supplement the original work, adding nearly 11,800 primarily bibliographic works, or works which describe or list archival or manuscript collections or offer similar research support. Volume 2 concludes with an index of main entries and subjects.

F–51 **Freidel, Frank, et al. *Harvard Guide to American History.*** Rev. ed. 2 vols. Cambridge: Harvard University Press, 1974. Z1236.F77 1974

A standard, classified selective bibliography, current to July 1970, of research materials, prepared by boards of distinguished scholars. The present guide was preceded by a series of comparable works, the first of which was published in 1897; the immediately preceding *Guide*, compiled by Oscar Handlin et al., was published in 1954 [Z1236.H27]. The focus of both guides is on political, social, constitutional, and economic history. Entries are generally cited with short titles and in sheer lists, preceded or followed by a commentary. There is an emphasis on books that may be regarded as starting points for research into any aspect of American history. The 1954 guide has not been entirely replaced because it includes printed collections of primary source materials for each topic. But the 1974 should be used for its greater currency in all other areas.

Entries in volume 1 are topically classified and subclassified: cited items tend to be general in scope and not confined to one period of American history (see volume 2 for these). Part 1 treats Research Methods and Materials (sections on Research,

Writing, and Publication; Care and Editing of Manuscripts; Materials of History; Aids to Historical Research; Printed Public Documents; Unpublished Primary Sources; Microform Materials; and Printed Historical Works). Part 2 concerns Biographies and Personal Records: here are listed standard biographies and bibliographies of all persons of historical consequence. Part 3 treats both Comprehensive and Area (Regional) Histories; part 4 concerns Histories of Special Subjects (sections on Physical Environment, Government, Law, Polititcs, Economic History, Demography and Social Structure, Immigration and Ethnicity, Social Ills and Reform, Social Manners and Customs, Education, Religion, Intellectual History, Literature, Communication, The Arts, and Pure and Applied Sciences).

Entries in volume 2 are classified by period, with each chronological segment elaborately subclassified into general sections and then such particular subsections as are appropriate. The volume concludes with elaborate and extensive indexes of names and of subjects.

F–52 **Basler, Roy P., et al. *Guide to the Study of the United States of America: Representative Books Reflecting the Development of American Life and Thought.*** Washington, D.C.: Library of Congress, 1960. Supplement: 1956–1965. Washington, D.C.: Library of Congress, 1976.   Z1215.U53

A topically arranged, annotated bibliography of 6,487 serially numbered titles disposed into thirty-two chapters. These treat Literature (1607–1955); Language; Literary History and Criticism; Biography and Autobiography; Periodicals and Journalism; Geography; The American Indian; General History; Diplomatic History and Foreign Relations; Military History and the Armed Forces; Intellectual History; Local History: Regions, States, Cities; Travel and Travelers; Population, Immigration, and Minorities; Society; Communications; Science and Technology; Medicine and Public Health; Entertainment; Sports and Recreation; Education; Philosophy and Psychology; Religion; Folklore, Folk Music, Folk Art; Music; Art and Architecture; Land and Agriculture; Economic Life; Constitution and Government; Law and Justice; Politics, Parties, Elections; and Books and Libraries. An appendix presents a series of 190 selected readings in American studies which synthesize works in various academic and scholarly disciplines concerned with the study of the United States.

Annotations of 100 words' average length aim to clarify the cited work's contribution to understanding; in addition, related works are frequently mentioned and evaluated. There is an extensive index of authors, subjects, and titles. The *Supplement* is identical in purpose and structure with the original volume. The 2,943 serially numbered entries treat (with rare exceptions) works published 1956–1965. For works published after 1965 the *Harvard Guide* (F–51) can provide some help; the current serial bibliographies *Writings on American History* (F–53) and *America, History and Life* (F–54), should also be consulted, along with the various reviews of research and related aids published regularly in the interdisciplinary quarterly *American Studies* (S–13).

F–53 ***Writings on American History [1902–1903, 1906–1940, 1947–1961].*** 48 vols. Princeton [later Washington, D.C.]: Carnegie Institute; later the American Historical Association, 1904–1973.   Z1236.L331

An annual, elaborately classified bibliography of books and articles including descriptive annotations and references to book reviews. From 1906 through 1935 the history of Latin America, Canada, the West Indies, and the Pacific Islands was included; from 1936 through 1940 Canada was included; since 1941, coverage has been limited to United States history. Entries are serially numbered. A list of analyzed periodicals precedes the author-title-subject index of each volume. These have been partially cumulated and partially supple-

mented in the author, subject, and (occasionally) title *Index to the "Writings on American History," 1902–40* (Washington, D.C.: American Historical Association, 1956). The time lag of publication became so severe in the early 1970s that the series was ended with the bibliography for 1961 (not published until 1973).

The following decade is covered, though less adequately, in the four-volume work *Writings on American History, 1962–73: A Subject Bibliography of Articles* (Millwood, N.Y.: Kraus-Thomson, 1976) [Z1236.L331]. This bibliography is based on the "Recently Published Articles" section of the *American Historical Review* (see F–6), expanded to include more than 33,000 citations from 510 journals. Volume 1 presents articles dealing primarily with general topics (Bibliography, Historiography, Methodology, and Source Guides), with United States history in general, or with large periods (subdivided into sections on Colonial History, and the occasionally overlapping periods 1763–1789, 1789–1828, 1828–1860, 1861–1877, 1865–1896, 1876–1917, 1917-1932, 1933–1945, and the post-World War II period). Volume 2 lists articles concerned with a particular geographical region. Volumes 3 and 4 present articles on relatively broad topics (e.g., Black History, Transportation, Visual Arts). Also in volume 4 is a comprehensive index of authors, but no subject index. A total of 86,099 entries are filed under chronological, geographical, and subject classifications as warranted by their scope.

The annual serial bibliography resumes with articles published 1973/74 under the title *Writings on American History [1973/74–]: A Subject Bibliography of Articles* (Millwood, N.Y.: Kraus Thomson, 1974–). Entries are gathered from the lists in *RPA* (F–6), expanded through the consultation of additional periodicals. Some 400 journals are analyzed from the annual for 1974/75 on, and dissertations are included in the bibliography. Publication is within a year of the date of coverage: volumes treat publications from June of one year through June of the next and are published before the end of that second year. Arrangement of the annual volumes is parallel to that used in the retrospective cumulation for 1962–1973. Major subject headings include Economic History, Historical Geography, Cultural and Intellectual History, Social History, Oral History, Quantitative Studies, and Genealogy. Each volume concludes with an index of authors. Coverage may be supplemented by *America, History and Life* (F–54), and the more general serial bibliographies of historical studies.

F–54 ***America, History and Life: A Guide to Periodical Literature [AHL].*** Vol. 1– [1964–]. Santa Barbara, Calif.: ABC-Clio, 1964–.   Z1236.A48

Published quarterly, the July, December, and March issues present signed abstracts (about 1,400 per issue) of books, articles, reviews, parts of composite volumes, and dissertations on United States and Canadian life, history, ethnography, and related subjects. About 2,000 journals worldwide are currently surveyed. Beginning in 1974 the work is issued in four parts. Part A, Article Abstracts, appears three times a year with subject and author indexes in each issue. Part B, published twice a year, indexes book reviews alphabetically by reviewed author, with an index of reviewers; some 130 key reviewing journals are analyzed. Part C, American History Bibliography, is an annual list of articles from part A, reviewed books from part B, and dissertations, in a classification system identical with that used in part A. Part D, finally, is an annual index volume with indexes of subjects, authors, and reviewers.

Arrangement of the abstract issues (since 1974, part A) is by broad geographical and subject headings: North America; Canada; United States History to 1945; United States History after 1945; Regional, State, and Local United States History; and a general section on History (Historiography and Methodology), The Humanities, and The Social Sciences. The annual cumulated index (since 1974, part D) is of authors, names of persons and places, and subjects. Cumulative subject and author indexes covering volumes 1–5 (1964–1969) and 6–10 (1969–1973) have been published. The complete data base is available for computer-aided searching through the Lockheed/DIALOG system.

F–55 **Books about Early America: A Selected Bibliography.** 4th ed. Williamsburg, Va.: Institute of Early American History and Culture, 1970.   Z1237.I58 1970

A selective bibliography, disposed into twenty-four chapters, covering American history to 1815. The first chapters treat surveys and reference books. Chapters 3 through 8 are chronologically arranged: Discovery and Exploration, 985–1620; The Seventeenth Century, 1607–1710; The Eighteenth Century, 1689–1776; Colonial Policy and Administration, 1607–1763; The Revolutionary Era, 1763–1788; and The Young Republic, 1789–1815. Chapter 9 is concerned with other European New World colonies. The remaining chapters are topically organized, as follows: Education; Thought; Law and Jurisprudence; Religion; Science and Medicine; Culture (including Architecture, Sculpture and Painting, Folk Arts and Crafts, Literature, Theater and Music); Books, Journalism, and Printing; Economic Development; Social History; The Negro in Early America; The Indian in Early America; The Frontier; Historical Geography; Biographies and Autobiographies of Principal Men; Diaries, Journals, Letters, and Travel Accounts. Entries are occasionally annotated. An index of authors concludes the volume.

A supplement, *Books about Early America, 1970–1975* (Williamsburg, 1976) [Z1237.I58 1976] adds more than 200 titles. The supplement is divided into the same topical areas as the main work, but the divisions are grouped differently. Because of the high degree of selectivity, this difference proves only slightly inconvenient.

The Library of Congress, which is the largest repository of Americana in the world, has recently published *Revolutionary America, 1763–1789: A Bibliography*, comp. Ronald M. Gebhart, 2 vols. (Washington, D.C., 1984) [Z1238.G43 1984], containing more than 14,810 entries listing more than 20,000 titles in LC collections. Nearly half the entries are annotated, and they are arranged in twelve chronological and topical chapters treating Research Aids including Bibliographies, Guides to Eighteenth-Century Imprints and Manuscript Collections, Maps, Atlases, and Geographical Aids; General Studies of the Period, including Local Histories; Works on Great Britain and the Empire; and The Economic, Social, and Intellectual Life of Revolutionary America, among other matters. An extensive index of persons and places concludes the work.

F–56 **Goldentree Bibliographies in American History.** Arthur S. Link, general editor.   LC numbers vary

A series of bibliographies of varying quality designed for the use of graduate students, consisting of classified but unannotated lists of selected works on particular fields of American history. Published to date are the following volumes:

Vaughan, Alden T. *American Colonies in the Seventeenth Century* (New York, 1971).   Z1237.V38
Greene, Jack P. *American Colonies in the Eighteenth Century, 1689–1763* (New York, 1969).   Z1237.G74
Shy, John. *American Revolution* (New York, 1973).   Z1238.S45
Ferguson, E. James. *Confederation, Constitution, and Early National Period, 1781–1816* (Northbrook, Ill., 1975).   Z1238.F46

Remini, Robert V., and Edwin A. Miles. *Era of Good Feelings and the Age of Jackson, 1816–1841* (Arlington Heights, Ill., 1979).   Z1240.5.R45
Fehrenbacker, Don E. *Manifest Destiny and the Coming of the Civil War, 1840–1861* (New York, 1970).   Z1236.F34
Donald, David. *Nation in Crisis, 1861–1877* (New York, 1969).   Z1242.D57
DeSantis, Vincent P. *Gilded Age, 1877–1896* (New York, 1973).   Z1242.8.D4
Link, Arthur S., and William Leary, Jr. *Progressive Era and the Great War, 1896–1920* (New York, 1969).   Z1244.L56
Burke, Robert E., and Richard Lowitt. *Twenties and the New Deal, 1920–1940* (Northbrook, Ill., 1981).   Z1244.B87
Cronon, E. David, and Theodore B. Rosenof. *Second World War and the Atomic Age, 1940–1973* (Northbrook, Ill., 1975).   Z1245.C76
Green, Fletcher Melvin. *Old South* (Northbrook Ill., 1980).   Z1251.S7 G69 1980
Paul, Rodman W. *Frontier and the American West* (Northbrook, Ill., 1977).   Z1251.W5 P38
Grob, Gerald N. *American Social History before 1860* (New York, 1970).   Z1361.C6 G7
Bremner, Robert H. *American Social History since 1860* (New York, 1971).   Z1361.C6 B7
Graebner, Norman A. *American Diplomatic History before 1900* (Northbrook, Ill., 1978).   Z6465.U567 1978
Fowler, Winton B. *American Diplomatic History since 1890* (Northbrook, Ill., 1975).   Z6465.U5 F68
Taylor, George R. *American Economic History before 1860* (New York, 1969).   Z7165.U5 T37
Kirkland, Edward C. *American Economic History since 1860* (New York, 1971).   Z7165.U5 K53
Mason, Alpheus T., and D. Grier Stephenson. *American Constitutional Development* (Northbrook, Ill., 1977).   KF4546.M38
Burr, Nelson R. *Religion in American Life* (New York, 1971).   Z7757.U5 B8
Herbst, Jurgen. *History of American Education* (Northbrook, Ill., 1973).   Z5815.U5 H47

F–57 **Adams, James Truslow, and R. V. Coleman. *Dictionary of American History [DAH]*.** 3d rev. ed. Compiled by Harold W. Chase et al. 8 vols. New York: Charles Scribner's Sons, 1976.   E174.D52 1976

Originally published in 1940 and conceived of as a companion to the *Dictionary of American Biography* (G–35), the first six-volume edition of this work contained some 6,425 articles written by more than 1,000 contributors. In 1961 a supplementary volume was published, with articles concerning American history during the period 1940–1960. The present edition is a complete revision, with some 7,200 entries contributed by more than 800 specialists. In each of its versions this work has been an encyclopedic dictionary treating all aspects of American history except biography. Articles are signed, with bibliographies appended. An elaborate analytical index (volume 8) includes every reference in the text; the headwords of articles are given in boldface type. Index entries include dates for personal names and events, identification of place-names, and identification of vocation or profession for each person cited. Abundant cross-references are also included.

For pertinent illustrations see James T. Adams et al., *Album of American History*, 5 vols. plus index (New York: Scribner's, 1944–1961) [E178.5.A48]. For a historical atlas designed to supplement the *Dictionary* see James T. Adams, *Atlas of American History* (New York: Scribner's, 1943) [G1201.S1 A2 1943], recently revised by Kenneth T. Jackson to accompany the new edition of the *Dictionary* (New York: Scribner's, 1978) [G1201.S1 J3 1978].

A one-volume epitome of the second edition of Adams's *Dictionary* was published as the *Concise Dictionary of American History*, ed. Thomas C. Cochran and Wayne Andrews (New York: Scribner's, 1962) [E174.A45]. A group of some 110 contributors chose, regrouped, and epitomized articles from the original volumes and the 1961 supplement, creating a work of some 7,000 articles, including some longer ones on essential or broad topics. An extended index also refers users to related subjects.

F–58   Morris, Richard B., and Jeffrey B. Morris, eds.   *Encyclopedia of American History.* 6th ed.   New York: Harper and Row, 1982.   E174.5.E52 1982

A one-volume encyclopedia of essential facts organized chronologically from 1763 and topically into three sections. The first, a historical chronology, presents a chronological narrative of specific events in United States history. The second part, a topical chronology, narrates the history of particular topics such as constitutional development, population and immigration, American expansion, the history of the American economy, and science and invention. The third part presents biographical sketches of some 400 persons notable in American history. There is an index of subjects and names.

Another useful one-volume work is *Encyclopedia of American History*, comp. Dean Albertson et al. (Guilford, Conn.: Dushkin, 1973) [E174.E52], which has a series of some 1,000 entries prepared by fifty-six contributors. Articles of more than 250 words are signed. There are abundant cross-references, and also some twelve "Subject Maps" relating schematically the many individual articles in the work which touch on such broad subjects as "American Wars" or "Blacks in the United States" or "The Frontier in American History." There are also some twenty articles known as "Item Guides" which enumerate the various articles in the work that treat such subjects as "Abolitionism." A ten-part classified bibliography concludes the work; there is no index.

F–59   *Oxford Companion to American History*, Edited by Thomas H. Johnson.   New York: Oxford University Press, 1966.
E174.J6

This work, designed as a sister volume to the *Oxford Companion to American Literature* (S–40), provides brief responses to queries arising from reading American history. There are more than 4,700 articles on persons, events, and places associated with American history, as well as discussions of social, political, and labor movements, the accounts of travelers, and the history of American art, science, commerce, literature, education, and law. References to important figures and events in sports and entertainment will also be found. Appended is a text of the Constitution. The work is without an index; longer articles generally include brief bibliographies.

F–60   Some Standard Reference Histories of the United States.

The most comprehensive history currently available is *American Nation: A History*, ed. Albert Bushnell Hart, 28 vols. (New York: Harper, 1904–1916) [E178.A54]. This work is to be replaced, more or less, by the forty projected volumes of *New American Nation Series*, ed. H. S. Commager and R. B. Morris (New York: Harper, 1954), many volumes of which have been published to date [LC numbers vary].

Of the shorter standard histories the best-known is Samuel Eliot Morison, Henry Steele Commager, and William E.

Leuchtenburg, *Growth of the American Republic*, 7th ed., 2 vols. (New York: Oxford University Press, 1980) [E178 .M85 1980], a 1,900-page work that embraces economic, social, literary, spiritual, political, and military history from pre-Columbian times through the 1970s. An extended classified bibliography and an index of authors, titles, and subjects, along with a variety of statistical and factual appendixes, will be found at the end of the second volume. An abbreviated version of the sixth edition, *Concise History of the American Republic* (New York: Oxford University Press, 1977) [E178.M83 1977], is about half as long as the original work. Morison has also written *Oxford History of the American People* (New York: Oxford University Press, 1965) [E178.M855], a personal history to the end of the Kennedy administration which concludes with the words and music to Rodgers and Hammerstein's "Camelot."

Another standard one-volume history is that by Richard Hofstadter et al., *United States: The History of a Republic*, 2d ed. (Englewood Cliffs, N.J.: Prentice-Hall, 1967).

A last, relatively brief, reference history for modern American history is the text by T. Harry Williams, Richard N. Current, and Frank Freidel, *History of the United States since 1865*, 3d ed., 2 vols. (New York: Alfred A. Knopf, 1969) [E178.1.W7282]. Each chapter has a short bibliographical essay; a general bibliography and an index of persons, places, and subjects conclude the second volume. An unusual and useful feature is the series of entries on *Where Historians Disagree*, in which cruxes of interpretation are identified and the differing positions of leading proponents of each alternative view are explicated.

VIII.   CHRONOLOGICAL ANCILLAE— GENERAL

F–65   Cheney, C. R.   *Handbook of Dates for Students of English History.* London: Royal Historical Society, 1945.   Rev. ed. Folkestone: Dawsons, 1970.   DA34.C5

This work is a revision of the section on reckonings of time in the 1939 first edition of Powicke's *Handbook of British Chronology* (G–16). It begins with a select, classified bibliography of approximately 100 items. Both the bibliography and the various sections of the text proper are designed to assist students in establishing dates based on each of the various systems of reckoning current in England at one time or another. Sections on the rulers to England begin the main text, with lists of rulers of 1154, regnal years 1154, and exchequer years. A list of popes is followed by a section on saints' days and festivals used in dating. A detailed discussion of legal chronology and the history of the four legal terms is next. A section on the Roman calendars follows, and then a series of calendars showing the dates of all the movable feasts based on all possible dates of Easter from 22 March to 25 April. A table giving the English calendar for A.D. 1752 and a chronological table of Easter days from A.D. 500 to 2000 conclude the volume. There is a brief index of subjects.

See also John J. Bond's *Handy-book of Rules and Tables for Verifying Dates of Historical Events, and of Public and Private Documents, Giving Tables of Regnal Years of English Sovereigns . . . 1066–1889*, 4th ed. (London: Bell, 1889) [CE11.B7 1889].

F–66 Carruth, Gorton, et al. *Encyclopedia of American Facts and Dates.* 7th ed. with a Supplement of the 70s. New York: Crowell, 1979.   E174.5.C3 1979

Chronologically arranged from A.D. 986 to 1965, information is in four parallel columns, treating concurrent events in the areas of (1) Politics and Government, War, Disasters, and Vital Statistics; (2) Books, Painting, Drama, Architecture, and Sculpture; (3) Science, Industry, Economics, Education, Religion, and Philosophy; and (4) Sports, Fashion, Popular Entertainment, Folklore, and Society. An interesting feature of this work is the initial brief narrative summary of each year's events given in each column. An elaborate, cross-referenced index covers all names, titles, and events cited, identifying the appropriate year and column of the entry. The *Supplement of the 70s* treats material from 1970 through 1977; it is separately indexed.

F–67 *Haydn's Dictionary of Dates and Universal Information Relating to All Ages and Nations.* Edited by Benjamin Vincent. 25th ed. London: Ward, Locke, 1910.   D9.H45

The first edition of this unique work was published in 1841. The contents of the successive editions vary, though certain principles of inclusion generally hold, namely that arrangement is *topical* and coverage includes historical, political, ecclesiastical, legal, social, commercial, scientific, literary, artistic, educational and other movements and occurrences. This information is disposed in articles varying in length from one sentence to many pages; the articles are alphabetical by a main entry term or phrase that is generally the name of the person, organization, place, or subject at the center of interest. There are, for example, articles on countries, continents, offices and holders, places, events, and battles. Dates are arranged under the main entry within the body of the article. An index refers to the main entry terms of articles.

F–68 Keller, Helen Rex. *Dictionary of Dates.* 2 vols. New York: Macmillan, 1934.   D9.K4

A *geographically* and *chronologically* organized digest of historical events from earliest times through 1930. The two volumes treat the Old World and the New World, respectively. The first, based on Haydn's *Dictionary of Dates* (F–67), has articles on the major countries, wars, and international gatherings of Europe, Africa, Asia, Australasia, and Oceania. Volume 2 treats similarly North America, the West Indies, Central America, South America, and the Arctic and Antarctic regions. For each country a general discussion of history is followed by a detailed chronology within which events are given by their exact day when possible.

F–69 Little, Charles E. *Cyclopedia of Classified Dates, with an Exhaustive Index, for the Use of Students of History and for All Persons Who Desire Speedy Access to the Facts and Events Which Relate to the Histories of the Various Countries of the World, from the Earliest Recorded Dates.* New York: Funk and Wagnalls, 1900.   D9.L7

A *geographically* and *topically* organized handbook, this work is organized alphabetically by country. Within that structure, history is treated topically under the subheadings: Army-Navy, Art-Science-Nature [Exploration], Births-Deaths, Church, Letters, Society, State, and Miscellaneous. Every two facing pages treat one country for a specified period indicated in the headline. An exceptionally full index of almost 300 triple-column small-print pages attempts to cite every name and subject mentioned in the main body.

F–70 *Everyman's Dictionary of Dates.* 6th ed. Revised by Aubrey Butler. New York: E. P. Dutton; London: J. M. Dent, 1971.   D9.D5 1971

The first edition of this standard work was published in 1911. It is topically arranged, with three types of articles: short entries on particulars; narratives of the histories of countries; and classified entries listing wars, earthquakes, and other types of recurring events. A list of the longer entries and an extremely useful introductory description of the various predominant secular and religious calendars precede the main body of the work. Treated are dates associated with countries, national institutions, and dynasties; cities, provinces, local institutions, and families; the arts, sciences, philosophy, religion, and invention; and many miscellaneous topics. A slightly greater prominence is given to dates associated with Britain, and current topics are included. Though there are cross-references, there is no index.

F–71 *Who Was When? A Dictionary of Contemporaries.* Edited by Miriam Allen de Ford. 2d ed. New York: H. W. Wilson, 1940.   CT103.D4 1940

A chronology from 500 B.C. to A.D. 1938 of contemporaries, arranged in twelve parallel columns. Beside the time period indicated in the first column are listed persons living at that time who distinguished themselves in eleven fields of endeavor, each assigned to one of the remaining columns. The fields are labeled as follows: Government and Law; Military and Naval Affairs; Industry, Commerce, Economics, Finance, Invention, and Labor; Travel and Exploration; Philosophy and Religion; Science and Medicine; Education, Scholarship, and History; Literature; Painting and Sculpture; Music; and Miscellaneous.

F–72 Grun, Bernard. *Timetables of History: A Horizontal Linkage of People and Events.* New, updated ed. New York: Simon and Schuster, 1979.   D11.G78 1979

An English translation, with revisions designed both to update and to increase the Anglo-American emphasis of Werner Stein's *Kulturfahrplan: Die wichtigsten Daten der Kulturgeschichte von Anbeginn bis 1973* (Munich, 1974) [D11.S823], originally published with the title *Kleiner Kulturfahrplan*, 6 vols. (Berlin: Herbig, 1946–1951) [D11.S82]. Both Stein and Grun present in parallel columns on facing pages the events and activities occurring throughout the world in particular years or periods from 5000 B.C. to A.D. 1974. Material is placed in one of seven realms: A. History and Politics; B. Literature and Theatre; C. Religion, Philosophy, and Learning; D. The Visual Arts; E. Music; F. Science, Technology and [Economic] Growth; and G. Daily Life. Stein has a statistical appendix, which Grun has omitted. A detailed index of names, titles, and subjects concludes the volume.

A similar work is Sigfrid Henry Steinberg's *Historical Tables: 58 B.C.–A.D. 1978, 8th ed. (London: Macmillan, 1979) [D11.S83 1979]. There are usually six columns presented on facing pages, with the three columns on the left concerning political relations of the major powers and those on the right treating ecclesiastical history, constitutional and economic history, and cultural life, respectively. Steinberg gives some emphasis to British and United States history.

F–73 Mayer, Alfred. *Annals of European Civilization 1501-1900.* London: Cassell, 1949.   D11.M3

This work presumes a knowledge of political and economic history and presents both a chronological and a synchronic conspectus of European cultural history from the Renaissance to the twentieth century. After the introduction and indexes of names (with dates) and places, the first main section presents cultural events in chronological sequence. Each year's information is subdivided into the various European regions in which events occurred (British Isles, Low Countries, Northern Europe, Central Europe, Latin Europe, and Slavonic Europe); cited are the country, the intellectual field of endeavor, the name of the person or group involved, and, in the case of works, the title of the production.

This chronology is followed by a second, quite distinctive section in which the events of the first part are rearranged chronologically within the intellectual field of endeavor in which they participate, thus permitting an overview, a summary history, of each civilized art and science. The fields treated include Schools, Societies, Universities, and Academies; Aesthetics and Poetics; Archaeology; Architecture; Astronomy; Biology, Botany, and Zoology; Chemistry and Physics; Church, Religious Life, and Theology; Colonization, Discoveries, and Travels; Economics, Politics, and Sociology; History (i.e., Historiography); History of Art; Jurisprudence; Libraries and Museums; Literature (Classical—dates of the Renaissance *editiones principes* of classical authors, Belgian, Czech, Danish, Dutch, English, French, German, Hungarian, Italian, Neo-Latin, Norwegian, Polish, Portuguese, Russian, Spanish, and Swedish); Mathematics; Medicine; Music; Newspapers and Periodicals; Painting; Pedagogics; Philology; Philosophy; Sculpture; and Theatre. In the fields where national distinctions matter, summaries are subdivided by nations. Further, cultural events in America and elsewhere are treated for the periods during which those places were European colonies.

This work is written throughout from an English perspective. A later version, *400 Jahre europäischer Kulturgemeinschaft in Übersichten 1500–1900* (Munich: Ernst Reinhardt Verlag, 1959) [D11.M34], shifts the perspective to a western European one but retains the fundamental structure of the English version. Added are a valuable series of tables under the title "Der Wechsel der Generationen" listing figures central to the history of European civilization who were alive during 1500, 1525, 1550, 1575, and so on for every twenty-fifth year through 1900. The overviews of cultural fields include occurrences through about 1949 and are often more fully elaborated than those in the earlier English edition.

F–74 **Mellersch, H. E. L. *Chronology of the Ancient World, 10,000 B.C. to A.D. 799.*** London: Barrie and Jenkins, 1976.   CB311.M4

The most recently published of a series of chronological handbooks which includes those by Storey (F–75), Williams (F–76), and Williams (F–77). Each set of facing pages presents a series of seven columns. At the extreme left, dates are given. These may be as rough as a millennium, a century, a decade, or a year; in this volume they are rarely more precise than that. In the remaining six columns, labeled A-F, are found descriptions of important events in the realms of A—Politics, Law, and Economics; B—Science and Discovery; C—Religion and Philosophy; D—The Arts; E—Literature, and F—Biography (births and deaths of famous persons). An elaborate index with notes for use concludes the volume. In addition to a number of major general headings and general subjects under which many references are arranged, the index terms include persons, places, and specific subjects. There are also abundant cross-references. This volume and the others in this series are generally regarded as the most satisfactory chronologies available.

F–75 **Storey, R. L. *Chronology of the Medieval World, 800–1491.*** New York: David McKay, 1973.

D118.S855 1973

Arranged in a series of parallel columns across facing pages, this volume is preceded in the series of similarly conceived chronologies by the work of Mellersch (F–74) and followed

by the two works of Williams (F–76 and F–77). At the extreme left are entered dates—years, months, occasionally even particular days. The remaining space on the left-hand pages is used to describe events in political history, using the code A to identify events occurring in the first quarter of a year, B for those of the second quarter, C for the third, and D for the fourth quarter of the year. E designates events that cannot be dated to a particular quarter. The right-hand pages present additional columns, F-L, that identify events in the realms of F—Law and Politics, G—Economics, Science, Technology and Discovery; H—Religion and Education; J—Art, Architecture, and Music; K—Literature, Philosophy, and Scholarship; and L—Biography (births and deaths of famous persons). The volume concludes with an analytical index to persons, places, subjects, titles, and works of art cited.

F–76 **Williams, Neville. *Chronology of the Expanding World, 1492–1762.*** New York: David McKay, 1969.   D11.5 W48

This volume, covering the period 1492–1762, has the same structure and arrangement as does Storey's *Chronology of the Medieval World* (F–75). The left-hand pages give dates and cite events in political history according to the A-E system used also by Storey. The right-hand pages cite additional events in the realms of F—Politics, Economics, Law and Education; G—Science, Technology, and Discovery; H— Philosophy, Religion, and Scholarship; J—Art, Sculpture, Fine Arts, Architecture; K—Music; L—Literature Including Drama; and M—Biography (Births and Deaths of Notabilities). The index, like Storey's, treats persons, places, subjects, titles, and works of art cited. This work is followed by Williams's earlier publication treating the period 1763–1965 (F–77).

F–77 **Williams, Neville. *Chronology of the Modern World, 1763 to the Present Time [i.e., 1965].*** London: Barrie and Rockliff, 1965.   D11.5.W5

This volume has the same structure and arrangement as the work of Williams covering the period 1492–1762, save that the coding is more elaborate to reflect the greater elaboration in records. Letters A-M designate events in political history occurring during the particular months January-December; N designates events that cannot be assigned to a particular month. Events in other realms are designated as follows: O—Politics, Economics, Law, and Education; P—Science, Technology, and Discovery; Q—Scholarship; R—Philosophy and Religion; S—Art, Sculpture, Fine Arts, and Architecture; T—Music; U—Literature (Excluding Plays); V—The Press; W—Drama and Entertainment (Including Film and Television); X—Sport; Y—Statistics; and Z—Biography (Births and Deaths of Notabilities). The analytical index treats persons, places, subjects, titles, and works of art cited.

IX. CHRONOLOGICAL ANCILLAE— LITERARY

See also handbooks such as Holman (L–12); the various Oxford Companions (e.g., M–31, S–31); and chronologies in the *OHEL* (M–31), the *LHUS* (S–31), and other standard histories.

F–80 *Répertoire chronologique des littératures modernes.* Edited by Paul van Tieghem. Paris: E. Droz, 1935–1937.
Z6519.I61

Prepared by an international committee of scholars under the auspices of the Commission internationale d'histoire littéraire moderne, this volume is arranged by year, from 1455 through 1900. For each year, general events of literary importance (e.g., the beginning of printing) are listed. Then follow lists for each of the thirty-two modern literatures covered. Events in the lives of prominent authors are cited, as are general cultural events, but the emphasis is distinctly on the citation of authors and titles of works performed or published, followed by a brief genre description in parentheses and, for those performed, indication (where applicable) of the date of publication. Translations of major works are indicated. Titles are listed in the original language, with a French translation given when the original is not in German, English, Spanish, or Italian. A brief list of additions and corrections is followed by an index of authors and the titles of anonymous and periodical works.

Adolf Spemann's *Vergleichende Zeittafel der Weltliteratur, vom Mittelalter bis zur Neuzeit (1150–1939)* (Stuttgart: Engelhornverlag, 1951) [PN554.S63] is a comparable though less elaborate chronology. It does include the period 1150–1455, however, though briefly, and it also covers 1900–1939 very extensively. It concludes with an index of all cited authors with the titles and dates of their works.

F–83 **Brett-James, Antony.** *Triple Stream: Four Centuries of English, French, and German Literature, 1531–1930.* Cambridge: Bowes and Bowes, 1953.
PN524.B8

Five parallel columns present an annual chronology from 1531 through 1930. For each year are listed (1) the names of authors born that year, (2) authors who died, and the titles and authors of works published in (3) English, (4) French, and (5) German, in Great Britain, France, Germany, Belgium, Austria, or Switzerland. Included are important children's books, certain reference books, some distinguished translations, and various otherwise influential books and literary journals. There are nine separate indexes: three treating titles published 1531–1900 in English, French, and German; three treating similarly titles published 1901–1930; and three treating English, French, and German authors. Some dates are inaccurate; thus all dates should be verified in another source.

F–85 *Annals of English [and American] Literature 1475–1950: The Principal Publications of Each Year Together with an Alphabetical Index of Authors with Their Works.* [Original edition by J. C. Ghosh.] 2d ed. [Revised by R. W. Chapman et al.] Oxford: Clarendon Press, 1961.
Z2011.A5

Originally published in 1935, this volume is arranged by year. Under each year are two parallel columns giving the principal works of English and American literature published that year and listing events of the year which had a bearing on the development of English literature (including the births and deaths of authors, important "nonliterary" publications, and the publication of important works of foreign literature).

Works of English literature are listed by the author's surname (with birth date in parentheses), title, and an indication whether the work is prose (P), verse (V), tragedy (T), comedy (C), or drama (D). The index of authors (and titles of periodical and anonymous works) provides for each author his given name(s), his dates, and, in chronological order, the titles and dates of works cited. A new edition of this work is in preparation.

John O. Stark's *Almanac of British and American Literature* (Littleton, Colo.: Libraries Unlimited, 1979) [PR87.S7] presents a calendar of months and days, listing for each day notable events in British and American literary history with the year of their occurrence through 1977. Thus, on 9 October 1849, Poe published "Annabel Lee." On the same date in 1900, Conrad's *Lord Jim* [PZ3.C764L. 1920] was published. And on that very day in 1967, William Styron's *Confessions of Nat Turner* [PZ4.5938C] was scheduled for publication. Some 2,500 entries cite births, deaths, and publications. Indexes to some 600 cited authors giving all the dates associated with them and to the titles of works with their dates of citation conclude the volume.

Another recent volume by Samuel J. Rogal, *Chronological Outline of British Literature* (Westport, Conn.: Greenwood, 1980) [PR87.R57], is organized by year, citing births, deaths, and works published. Genres of works are identified. Coverage is from A.D. 516 through 1979. An index of authors and of titles of anonymous works concludes the volume. Reviewers note errors sufficient to require verification of entries in other sources.

F–86 **Ludwig, Richard M., and Clifford A. Nault, Jr., eds.** *Annals of American Literature, 1602–1983.* New York: Oxford University Press, 1986.
PS94.L83

This long needed work is modeled on the *Annals of English Literature 1475–1950* (F–85). It also lists each year from 1602 to 1983, with two parallel columns. The left hand column includes all the works of major writers and selected minor works, and those works of minor authors which were influential. Entries give the author's name, date of birth, title, and genre designation (F—fiction, NF—non-fiction, D—drama, V—poetry). Excluded as authors are screen and radio writers and musical and opera librettists. The right hand column lists events of social and cultural history, foundation dates of newspapers and periodicals, birth and death dates of authors, and publication dates of major works of foreign literature. The volume concludes with an index of authors, some titles, and an index of titles with the dates under which they are cited.

Another new work also designed to fill the need for a modern chronology of American literature is Samuel J. Rogal, *Chronological Outline of American Literature* (Westport, Conn.: Greenwood, 1987) [PS92.R67 1987]. It is organized in seven chapters which record dates of The Sixteenth Century, The Seventeenth Century, The Eighteenth Century, The Nineteenth Century: 1800–1850, The Nineteenth Century: 1851–1899, The Twentieth Century: 1900–1940, and The Twentieth Century: 1941–1986. Rogal lists the birth and death dates of literary figures, important historical facts, and the authors and titles of works published each year. The chronology is complemented by an introduction, a list of references, and an index of authors and events.

F–87 **Whitcomb, Selden L.** *Chronological Outlines of American Literature.* New York: Macmillan, 1894.
PS94.W4

The main part of this guide is arranged in six parallel columns on facing pages. The work lists dates from 1603 through 1894; names of authors (with dates) and works published; birth and death dates; events in British literary history; events in the history of foreign literatures; and historical events that have a bearing on the history of American literature. Part 2 presents the names and dates of all authors cited and a chronological list of the titles of their works. It is supplemented but not replaced for modern American literary history by the more recent *Chronology* of Waterman (F–88), which is, however, much less thorough in its treatment.

F–88 **Waterman, Arthur E.** *Chronology of American Literary History.* Columbus, Ohio: Charles E. Merrill, 1970.

PS94.W3

Arranged in parallel columns, this work lists dates from 1000 through 1969. At the tops and bottoms of pages are indicated the historical and literary period terms designating the years enumerated. The first column lists the titles of literary works published and other major events in United States literary history. Works are listed with the author's last name and (where there are many) in the order of poetry, fiction, drama (by date of first performance), essays, and miscellaneous works. Other literary events follow the list of works. The second column cites births and deaths of important people which occurred that year. Noteworthy events in United States history occupy the third column. Major literary works and events are listed in the fourth column. The last column cites world historical events that bear on the development of American literary history. There is no index.

For more complete information the user is referred to standard encyclopedias, the *Oxford Companion to American Literature* (S–40), or standard textbooks.

X.   TOPOGRAPHICAL ANCILLAE—GENERAL

F–90 **Brewer, James G.** *Literature of Geography: A Guide to Its Organization and Use.* 2d ed. London: Bingley; Hamden, Conn.: Linnet Books, 1978.   Z6001.B74 1978

Originally published in 1973, this work has chapters on the scope, structure, and use of geographical literature and on its organization in libraries. These are followed by bibliographic essays on Geographical Bibliographies and Reference Works; Periodicals; Monographs, Textbooks, and Collections; Cartobibliography; Sources of Statistics; Government and International Organizations' Publications; The History of Geography and Geographical Thought; Geographical Techniques and Methodology; Physical Geography; Human Geography; and Regional Geography. Sample pages illustrate the most important works. There is an index of personal and corporate authors and of titles of serials and periodicals, as well as broad subject terms.

A briefer but less current guide is Charles S. Minto's *How to Find Out in Geography: A Guide to Current Books in English* (Oxford and New York: Pergamon, 1966) [Z6001.M55 1966]. See also Chauncey D. Harris, *Bibliography and Reference Works for Research in Geography* (Chicago: Dept. of Geography, University of Chicago, 1967) [Z6001.A1 H3]. Another such guide is Tom L. Martinson's *Introduction to Library Research in Geography: An Instruction Manual and Short Bibliography* (Metuchen, N.J.: Scarecrow, 1972) [Z6001.M36]. See also the more elaborate work of Clara Beatrice Lock, *Geography and Cartography: A Reference Handbook*, 3d ed., rev. and enl. (London: Bingley, 1976) [G63.L6 1976].

The oldest of these guides, published in 1947, is the one sponsored by the American Geographical Society, *Aids to Geographical Research: Bibliographies, Periodicals, Atlases, Gazetteers, and Other Reference Books*, by John Kirtland Wright and Elizabeth T. Platt, 2d ed. (New York: Columbia University Press, 1947) [Z6001.A1 W9]. The work by Harris cited above is designed to supplement this volume.

The standard serial bibliography in the field is the *Bibliographie géographique internationale* [1891–] (Paris: A. Colin, 1894–) [Z6001.B57], which annually lists books, articles, and maps that have been published. It is divided into a general and a regional part, both of which have subsections on the various fields of human geography.

For cartography the most comprehensive bibliography is the annual *Bibliographia Cartographica: Internationale Dokumentation kartographischen Schrifttums / International Documentation of Cartographical Literature / Documentation internationale de la littérature cartographique* (Munich: Saur, 1974–) [Z6021.B48], prepared by the Staatsbibliothek preussischer Kulturbesitz in cooperation with the Deutschen Gesellschaft für Kartographie. It lists books and articles in a classified arrangement.

A new, six volume work, *History of Cartography* is now in production. *Volume 1: Cartography in Prehistoric, Ancient, and Medieval Europe and the Mediterranean*, edited by J. B. Harley and David Woodward, has appeared (Chicago: University of Chicago Press, 1987) [GA201.H53 1987].

F–91 **British Museum.** *Catalogue of Printed Maps, Charts, and Plans.* Photolithographic edition complete to 1964. 15 vols. London: British Museum, 1967.   Z6028.B863 1967

This catalog records the inventory of printed maps, atlases, globes, and related materials acquired through 1964 in the Map Room and other facilities of the British Museum. Entries are arranged alphabetically under the name of the place or area mentioned in the title or represented. Added entries cite names of persons associated with the design, printing, and publication of the item. Entries under a heading are arranged chronologically. Corrections and additions were published in London, 1968.

A *Ten Year Supplement, 1964–1974* has been published (London, 1978) [Z6028.B855 1978], and further decennial supplements are projected. Among other major collections of similar materials to which access is possible through printed catalogs, the most important include the *Dictionary Catalog* of the New York Public Library's Map Division, 10 vols. (Boston: G. K. Hall, 1970); and the *Research Catalogue of the American Geographical Society*, 15 vols. (Boston: G. K. Hall, 1962) [Z6009.A48], updated through the periodical *Current Geographical Publications: Additions to the "Research Catalogue" of the American Geographical Society* (New York: The Society, 1938–) [Z6009.A47].

Another important reference tool based on the collections of the American Geographical Society is its *Index to Maps in Books and Periodicals*, 10 vols. (Boston: G. K. Hall, 1968) [Z6028.A5], *First Supplement* (Boston: G. K. Hall, 1971), which presents altogether some 200,000 entries.

F–92 **United States Library of Congress, Map Division.** *List of Geographical Atlases in the Library of Congress, with Bibliographical Notes.* 8 vols. Washington, D.C.: Library of Congress, 1909–1974.   Z6028.U562

A serially numbered list of authors of some 18,435 atlases now held by the Geography and Map Division of the library. Volumes 1–4 by Philip Lee Philips record the 5,324 atlases held by the library in 1920. Volumes 1 and 2 are indexed in volume 2; volumes 3 and 4 each have their own index. Volumes 5 to 8 supplement the original series; all are compiled by Clara Egli LeGear. Volume 5, with its own index, enumerates the 2,326 world atlases acquired 1920–1955 (1958); volume 6 lists the 2,647 atlases of Europe, Asia, Africa, Oceania, the polar regions, and the oceans which were acquired 1920–1960 (1963). Volume 7 lists the 8,181 atlases of the Western Hemisphere published before 1968 and acquired 1920–1969 (1973). Volume 8 provides an index of authors and place-names, subjects, and map authors, engravers, etc., for volume 7. Similar indexes are provided for each of the earlier volumes. Entries give full bibliographical information and notes on contents.

F–93 Bartholomew (John) and Son, Ltd. *Times Atlas of the World.* Revised Comprehensive Edition. 6th ed., rev. London: The Times, 1980.   G1021.B3 1980

Generally regarded as the finest single atlas of the world, this work, first published in 1967, is divided into three sections. The first section contains forty pages of preliminary materials, including lists of the states, territories, and principal islands of the world; tables of geographical comparisons; discussion of the resources of the world with maps; discussions of the universe, the earth, space flight, and satellites; and lunar charts and maps. The main 244-page central section of the work consists of 123 plates of maps.

The final, 227-page index section is a gazetteer of some 210,000 place-names. It is preceded by an international glossary of geographical terms and their English equivalents and a list of geographical terms.

Also published by *The Times*, London, is the *Index-Gazetteer of the World* (London, 1965) [G103.T5], which identifies some 345,000 geographical locations with coordinates of latitude and longitude. The basis of this *Index-Gazetteer* was the five-volume Mid-Century Edition (1955–1959) of *"The Times" Atlas of the World* (predecessor of the Comprehensive Edition), and map references to the 198,000 locations of the *Atlas* are given in the gazetteer. The major English-language world gazetteer is, however, the *Columbia Lippincott Gazetteer of the World*, ed. Leon E. Settzer (New York: Columbia University Press, 1962) [G103.L7], which lists in one alphabet the names of 130,000 countries, regions, provinces, states, counties, cities, towns, islands, lakes, mountains, deserts, seas, rivers, canals, dams, peninsulas, and capes of the world and, for each of these physical features, provides information about variant spellings and pronunciations of its name, and, as pertinent, population, geographic and political location, altitude, trade, industry, agriculture, mineral and other natural resources, irrigation works, river lengths, communications, history, cultural institutions and monuments, battles, and other facts. A shorter and less informative work is *Webster's New Geographical Dictionary: A Dictionary of Names and Places with Geographical and Historical Information and Pronunciations* (Springfield, Mass.: G. and C. Merriam, 1972) [G103.W45 1972]. It has about 47,000 names and gives special emphasis to places in the English-speaking world.

Other important world atlases are *New International Atlas* (Chicago: Rand McNally, 1980) [G1019.R355]; *Britannica World Atlas International* (Chicago, 1961) [G1019.E58]; *New York Times Atlas of the World* (New York: Quadrangle, 1972) [G1019.N498]; and the National Geographic *Atlas of the World*, 5th ed. (Washington, D.C.: National Geographic Society, 1981) [G1019.N28 1981].

F–94 Shepherd, William R. *Historical Atlas.* 9th ed., rev. and updated. New York: Barnes and Noble, 1964.
                    G1030.S4 1963

Covering all periods and continents from ancient Egypt (ca. 2000 B.C.) to 1929, this easy-to-use work contains 226 maps arranged chronologically, with no supplemental texts. Major emphasis is on political history. Characteristic maps are those titled "The Expansion of Europe, 1600–1700" and "Campaigns of the American Revolution, 1775–1781."

As these titles make clear, some maps illustrate dynamic and some static conditions; annotations on the maps themselves clarify the representations. An extensive index of names with some 25,000 entries is valuable in itself and has the further value of including classical and medieval place-names with cross-references to modern forms. There is a separate section

of eight maps with a separate index for the period 1929–1955.

A similar aid is *Muir's Historical Atlas: Ancient, Medieval and Modern*, 10th ed., ed. R. F. Traharne and Harold Fullard (New York: Barnes and Noble, 1963) [G1030.M838], the most recent version of the pioneering work in historical geography of Ramsay Muir, who first demonstrated the importance of historical geography to the study of history.

F–95 Rand McNally and Co. *Atlas of World History.* Edited by Robert R. Palmer. Chicago, 1965.   G1030.R3 1965

Compiled by six experts, this volume presents 120 maps concerned with the political, economic, and social history of the world. The maps are arranged chronologically, with intervening pages of commentary. A bibliography refers to further discussion of points made in the commentary. Statistical tables appended to the main work give estimates of population, by country and city; mortality, disease, and migration figures; and statistics on commodity production and on transportation for various periods. Cultural data are not given, nor is the written text indexed. The index gives place-names, ethnic and state names, explorers' routes, and names found in the annotation of the maps.

F–98 Meer, Frederic van der. *Atlas of Western Civilization.* English version by T. A. Birrell. 2d ed., rev. Princeton, N.J.: Van Nostrand, 1960.   G1030.M42 1960

Originally published in Amsterdam in 1954, this work offers fifty-two maps and a text that together with 977 illustrations provides a running commentary on the maps. The maps themselves present an epoch or a particular aspect of Western culture, emphasizing the cultural centers, frontiers, points of exchange, and the pattern of intellectual currents found. An introduction presents the organizing principle of the work, the notion of *translatio studii*, the progress of Western Civilization. The volume is disposed into four main sections, treating The Three Roots of Western Culture (Greece, Rome, and Christianity); Medieval Christendom; National Civilizations and their Expansion; and The Progress from a European to an Atlantic World. The first illustrations are of heads on Greek coins; the last is of the United Nations headquarters in New York. An extended index treats the maps, text, illustrations, place-names, personal names, and historical concepts found in the work.

Companion volumes include A. A. M. van der Heyden and H. H. Scullard, *Atlas of the Classical World* (London: Nelson, 1959) [DE29.H463]; L. H. Grollenberg, *Atlas of the Bible* (London: Nelson, 1956) [BS620.G752]; and Frederic van der Meer and Christine Mohrmann, *Atlas of the Early Christian World* (London: Nelson, 1958) [G1046.E4 M6].

XI. TOPOGRAPHICAL ANCILLAE— BRITISH AND IRISH

F–100 Anderson, John. *Book of British Topography: A Classified Catalogue of the Topographical Works in the Library of the British Museum Relating to Great Britain and Ireland.* London: Satchell, 1881.   Z2023.A54

The nearly 14,000 entries of this old but still most comprehensive catalog give author, title, place of publication, date, and format of each work. Entries are designed for ease of cross-reference to an earlier version of the *British Museum General Catalogue* (B–41). They are disposed into more than 150 sections, beginning with Catalogs and General Topography (divided into subheadings such as Antiquities, Directories, Ecclesiastical Topography, Rivers, Schools,

Views, and Watering Places) and continuing with works on the individual counties of England, Wales, Scotland, and Ireland. Works on London are further subdivided, as are general works on Wales, Scotland, and Ireland. A brief addendum is followed by an index of place-names and subjects.

See also Walter V. Daniell and F. J. Nield, *Manual of British Topography* (London, 1909), and the early bibliography of William Upcott, a *Bibliographical Account of the Principal Works Relating to English Topography*, 3 vols. (London, 1818), which gives detailed analyses of the contents of some 5,000 works.

F–101 Humphreys, Arthur L. *Handbook to County Bibliography: Being a Bibliography of Bibliographies Relating to the Counties and Towns of Great Britain and Ireland.* London: For the author, 1917.   Z2001.A1H84

Arranged alphabetically by county, this work enumerates systematic bibliographies, sourcebooks, indexes, and related works that form the basis of bibliographical control of the topography of Great Britain and Ireland. By virtue of their topographical interest, bibliographies of ballads, broadsides, chapbooks, newspapers, maps, and portraits are included, as are bibliographies of local "garlands," accounts of parochial documents, and calendars of local documents (excluding wills). Addenda follow the main body and are arranged as it is. An appendix of general works follows, giving only a few leading works and attempting to focus on the less known. It is divided into sections on England, Scotland, Ireland, and Wales. An elaborate index of names and subjects concludes the volume.

For local history see Charles Gross, *Bibliography of British Municipal History Including Guilds and Parliamentary Representation* (London: Longmans, Green, 1897) [Z7164.L8 G8], which was reprinted in 1966 by Leicester University Press with an evaluative introduction by Geoffrey H. Martin. Martin, along with S. McIntyre, is working on a continuation of Gross, *Bibliography of British and Irish Municipal History*, vol. 1, *General Works* (Leicester: University Press, 1972–) [Z2033.M26], which will cite works from the earliest times to 1960.

F–102 *Victoria History of the Counties of England.* H. A. Doubleday and W. Page [now R. B. Pugh et al.], general editors. London: Constable [then St. Catherine Press; and now Oxford University Press for the Institute of Historical Research], 1900–.   LC numbers vary

The best available account of this monumental project, the goal of which is to narrate the history of all the English counties based upon original research, is Ralph B. Pugh's *Victoria History of the Counties of England: General Introduction* (London: Oxford University Press, 1970) [DA670.A1 P83]. Pugh gives a detailed account of the origin and progress of the *Victoria History*, which was originally to include some 160 volumes of history along with additional volumes concerning the genealogy of the principal families of each county. Included in the *Introduction* is a list of all volumes published to the end of 1970 with enumerations of the contents of each, including the authors of individual chapters. The volume concludes with an index of the titles of individual articles in each volume of each county history through 1970 and an index of their authors.

The volumes treating a particular county are of two kinds. The first two or three contain general articles treating Natural Features; Flora and Fauna; Pre-Roman, Roman, and Post-Roman Antiquities; the Domesday Survey; Political, Ecclesiastical, Social, and Economic History; Architecture, The Arts, Industries, Biography, Folklore, and Sport. Subsequent volumes treat the topography and history of individual parishes and boroughs, grouped by hundreds. Numerous il-

lustrations, maps, and references to primary and secondary sources enrich each volume. Though the work has been criticized for adherence to the positivism of Victorian historical scholarship, general agreement is that it has developed over the years and kept pace, more or less, with conceptual and methodological changes in historical scholarship. From the point of view of the literary student, it remains an invaluable source, in part because of the very abundance of minute detail about county life which has been criticized from other perspectives.

Of the counties of England only Northumberland and Westmoreland are without any volumes in the series. Numbers and dates of the available county volumes are as follows (see the *General Introduction* for details):

Bedfordshire. 3 vols. (1904–1912) plus index (1914).
DA670.B3 V6

Berkshire. 4 vols. (1906–1924) plus index (1927).
DA670.B4 V6

Buckinghamshire. 4 vols. (1905–1927) plus index (1928).
DA670.B9 V6

Cambridgeshire and the Isle of Ely. 5 vols. (1938–1973) plus index to vols. 1–4 (1960).   DA670.C2 V5

Cheshire. Vol. 2 (1979) only.   DA670.C6 H52

Cornwall. Vol. 1 (1906) and parts of vol. 2 (1956) only.
DA670.C8 V5

Cumberland. Vols. 1–2 (1901–1905) only.   DA670.C9 V6

Derbyshire. Vols. 1–2 (1905–1907) only.   DA670.D42 V5

Devonshire. Vol. 1 (1906) only.   DA670.D5 V5

Dorset. Vols. 2 (1908) and 3 with index to both (1968).
DA670.D7 V6

Durham. 3 vols. (1905–1928).   DA670.D9 V6

Essex. Vols. 1–2 (1903–1907), vol. 3 with index to vols. 1–3 (1963), vols. 4–6 (1956–73).   DA670.E7 V6
Bibliography supplement (1959).   DA 670.E7 V62

Gloucestershire. Vols. 2 (1907), 6 (1965), 8 (1968), 10 (1972), and 11 (1976) only. Vol. 2: DA670.G5 V6; Vols. 6 ff.   DA670.G5 H5

Hampshire and the Isle of Wight. 5 vols. (1900–1912) plus index (1914).   DA670.H2 V6

Herefordshire. Vol. 1 (1908) only.   DA670.H4 V6

Hertfordshire. 4 vols (1902–1914) plus index (1923)
DA670.H5V6
Genealogical vol. (1907).   DA670.H5 V7

Huntingtonshire. 3 vols. (1926–1936) plus index (1938).
DA670.H8 V5

Kent. 3 vols. (1908–1932).   DA670.K3 V6

Lancashire. Vols. 1–2 with index to vols. 1–2 (1906–1908), vols. 3–5 with index to vols. 3–5 (1907–1911), vols. 6–7 with index to vols. 6–7 (1911–1912), vol. 8 (1914).   DA670.L2 V5

Leicestershire. Vol. 1 (1907), vols. 2–3 with index to 1–3 (1954–1955), vols. 4–5 (1958–1964). DA670.L5 V5

Lincolnshire. Vol. 2 (1906) only.   DA670.L7 V6

London, including London within the Bars, Westminster, and Southwark. Vol. 1 (1909) only.   DA677.V6

Middlesex. Vol. 1 (1969), vols. 2–3 with index to vols. 2–3 (1911–1962), vol. 4 (1971).
Vols. 1–3: DA670.M6 V6
Vol. 4: DA670 .M6 H55

Norfolk. Vols. 1–2 (1901–1906) only.   DA670.N6 V6

Northamptonshire. 4 vols. (1902–1937).   DA670.N7 V6
Genealogical volume (1906).   DA670.N7 V7

Northumberland. None yet published.

Nottinghamshire. Vols. 1–2 (1906–1910) only.
DA670.N9 V5

Oxfordshire. Vol. 1 (1939), vol. 2 (1907), vol. 3 (1954), vols. 5–10 (1957–1972).   DA670.O9 V6

Rutland. 2 vols. (1908–1935) plus index (1936).   DA670.R9 V6

Shropshire. Vol. 1 (1908), vol. 2 with index to vols. 1–2 (1973), vol. 8 (1968).   DA670.S4 V6

Somerset. Vols. 1–2 (1906–1911) only.   DA670.S5 V5

Staffordshire. Vol. 1 (1908), vol. 2 with index to vols. 1–2 (1967), vols. 3–5 (1958–1970), vol. 8 (1963).   DA670.S7 V6

Suffolk. Vols. 1 and 2 (1907–1911) only.   DA670.S9 V6

Surrey. 4 vols. (1902–1912), plus index (1914).   DA670.S96 V6

Sussex. Vols. 1–2 (1905–1907), vols. 3–4 (1935–1953), vol. 7 (1940), vol. 9 (1937).   DA670.S98 V6

Warwickshire. Vols. 1–2 (1904–1908), vols. 3–6 (1945–1951), index to vols. 1–6 (1955), vols. 7–8 (1964–1969).   DA670.W3 V64

Westmoreland. None yet published.

Wiltshire. 9 vols. (1953–1970).   DA670.W7 V5

Worcestershire. 4 vols. (1901–1924) plus index (1926).   DA670.W9 V6

Yorkshire. 3 vols. (1907–1913) plus index (1925).   DA670.Y6 V6

Yorkshire, East Riding. Vols. 1–2 (1969–1974) only.   DA670.Y6 H5

Yorkshire, North Riding. 2 vols. (1914–1923) plus index (1925).   DA670.Y6 V63

Yorkshire, The City of York. 1 vol. (1961).   DA690.Y6 H65

F–103 **Stephens, W. B. *Sources for English Local History*.** 2d ed. Cambridge: Cambridge University Press, 1981.   Z2023.S8 1981

First published in 1973 and reprinted with amendments in 1975, this volume is widely regarded as the best introduction to published and unpublished research materials, including bibliographies, guides, texts, and calendars. It is in the form of a discursive text with extensive footnotes, divided into nine chapters, as follows: 1. Introduction (Published and Unpublished Sources); 2. Population and Social Structure; 3. Local Government and Politics (The Manor, Parish, Town, County, Local Politics); 4. Poor Relief, Charities, Prices, and Wages; 5. Industry, Trade, and Communications; 6. Agriculture (to 1750, from 1750); 7. Education (elementary, secondary, adult); 8. Religion (The Church, Protestant Nonconformity, Catholic Nonconformity); and 9. Houses, Housing, and Health.

F–104 **Richardson, John. *Local Historian's Encyclopedia*.** New Barret, Herts.: Historical Publications, 1974.   DA34.R53

A handbook of information of use to students of local history, this work is disposed into eighteen sections, as follows: A—Land and Agriculture (Measurement, Field Names and Features, Commons and Enclosures, Tenants and Tenures, The Transfer and Inheritance of Land, Agricultural History, Farm Houses and Buildings, and Miscellaneous); B—The Local Community and its Administration (Types of Area and Administration, Local Officials, Classes of Society, Manor Customs and Procedures, Borough Charters, Local Government Franchise); C—Taxes, Services, Rents, Rates, and Other Dues (Local, Ecclesiastical, and National); D— Archives, Documents, and Printed Records (General Terms, Parish Records and Registration, Nonparochial Registers and Records, County and Quarter Sessions Records, Civil Records, State Records, Army and Navy Records, Maps and Map Makers, County Record Offices, Societies and Periodicals, National

Societies and Periodicals, Specialist Libraries, The Calendar, Regnal Years, Latin Terms); E— Archaeology (Terms, Methods, Artefacts, Industrial Archaeology); F—Education (Legislation, Types of Schools, Foundations of Schools and Universities); G—Social Welfare (The Treatment of the Poor, Hospitals, Charities and Philanthropic Societies, Miscellaneous, Municipal Housing); H—Law and Order (The Development of the Police, Prisons, Judicial Authorities, Judicial Officials, General); J—Public Utilities and Services (Fire, Post Office, Water, Cemeteries, Gas, Electricity, Public Libraries); K—Transport (Roads, Railways, Canals, Road Transport); L—Religion (Church of England Administration, Religious Sects, Miscellaneous Terms); M—The Local Militia; N—Architecture (General Terms, Church Architecture, Castle Architecture, Building Materials); O—Place-names; P—Coins and Tokens (Coins, Mints, Numismatic Terms); Q—Heraldry (General, Heraldic Terms); R—Trade, Commerce and Industry (City of London Livery Companies, Fairs and Markets, Public Houses and Brewing, Old Names for Trades and Occupations, Legislation on Employment and Wages); S—Bibliography (Classified by Section). An index of names, terms, and subjects concludes this very useful volume.

An introductory pamphlet, *Discovering Local History*, by Daniel Iredale, 2d ed. (Aylesbury, Bucks.: Shive Publications, 1977) [DA1.I68 1977], can be recommended for research guidance. The Historical Association Pamphlet (no. 69) edited by Frederick G. Emmison and F. W. Kuhlicke, *English Local History Handlist* (London, 1965) [Z2016.H5], provides a convenient bibliographical guide supplementing the older works of Anderson (F–100) and Humphreys (F–101). See also (F–10) the journals *Local Historian* (1952–) and *History* (1962–).

F–105 **Ekwall, Eilert, *Concise Oxford Dictionary of English Place-Names*.** 4th ed. Oxford: Clarendon Press, 1960.   DA645.E38

An alphabetical listing of about 15,000 English place-names, primarily names still in use of cities, towns, and villages. Each entry, by the modern form of the name, gives the location by county of the town, lists early forms of the name if available, and provides some references to sources. The book includes an excellent introduction on etymology and its value in the study of the history of towns and of languages. Entries are compressed by the use of many abbreviations.

For more detailed information see the ongoing *Survey of English Place-Names* of the English Place-Name Society, vol. 1– (Cambridge: Cambridge University Press, 1924–) [DA645.A4], to be completed in fifty volumes. Within the county volume(s), names are arranged by Hundreds (the ancient Saxon administrative division of the counties). For place-names of Ireland see Patrick W. Joyce, *Origin and History of Irish Names of Places*, 3 vols. (London and New York: Longmans, 1898–1913) [DA920.J893]. For those of Scotland see James B. Johnston, *Place-Names of Scotland*, 3d ed., enl. (London: Murray, 1934) [DA869.J72].

F–106 ***Atlas of Britain and Northern Ireland*.** Planned and directed by D. P. Bickmore and M. A. Shaw. Edited by G. E. Blackman et al.   G1810.O85

Some 200 pages treat the physical characteristics (geology, coasts, climate, water, vegetation, and forestry) of the whole United Kingdom and its regions; the economic features (agriculture and fisheries, industry) of both Britain and Northern Ireland and the various regions; and the demographic patterns (including demography and communications) of the whole and the regions. Counties, it should be noted, are not separately treated, nor are cultural features, except indirectly. The maps themselves refer to the National (or, in the case of

Northern Ireland, to the Irish) Grid system, in which every 100 square kilometers are identified with a unique letter, and reference is made from the southwestern corner of the 100-square-kilometer square by citing the distance east (easting) and north (northing) from that corner to a particular locality. A twenty-four page gazetteer refers readers to locations using this grid system.

For more elaborate, relatively current gazetteer information see Bartholomew's *Survey Gazetteer of the British Isles,* 9th ed. (Edinburgh: Bartholomew, 1972) [DA640.B], in which are listed in a single alphabet all towns, villages, and hamlets, as well as county seats, shooting lodges, deer forests, fishing lochs, streams, grouse moors, and other localities of note. For more detailed information about localities one may consult, in addition to local histories (see F–103), the four works of Samuel Lewis: a *Topographical Dictionary of England,* 2d ed., 4 vols (London: S. Lewis, 1833) [DA625.L676]; a *Topographical Dictionary of Ireland,* 1st ed., 2 vols. plus atlas (London: S. Lewis, 1837) [DA975.L67]; a *Topographical Dictionary of Scotland,* 2 vols. plus atlas (London: S. Lewis, 1846-1851) [DA865.L67]; and a *Topographical Dictionary of Wales,* 1st ed., 2 vols. (London: S. Lewis, 1833) [DA734.L47].

For earlier maps see the bibliography by G. R. Crone, *Early Maps of the British Isles, A.D. 1000–A.D. 1579, with Introduction and Notes* (London: Royal Geographic Society, 1961) [G1807.R6 1961], and R. W. Shirley's *Early Printed Maps of the British Isles, 1477–1640* (London: Map Collectors' Circle, 1900) [Z6003.M3 no. 97]. There is also a bibliography and finding list of *Large-Scale County Maps of the British Isles, 1596–1850: A Union List,* by Elizabeth M. Rodger, 2d ed. (Oxford: Bodleian Library, 1972) [Z6027.G709 1972]. For county maps see Raleigh Ashlin Skelton, *County Atlases of the British Isles, 1579–1850: A Bibliography,* vol. 1– (London: Carta Press, 1978–) [Z6027.G7 S55], based on and partly superseding Thomas Chubb's *Printed Maps in the Atlases of Great Britain and Ireland: A Bibliography 1577–1870* (London: Homeland Association, 1927) [Z6027.G7 C5]. A bibliography of travelers' accounts is Sir Herbert George Fordham's *Road-Books and Itineraries of Great Britain, 1570 to 1850: A Catalogue with an Introduction and a Bibliography,* 2d ed. (Cambridge: Cambridge University Press, 1924) [Z6027.G7 F62 1924].

For London maps, see Frederick Crace, *Catalogue of Maps, Plans, and Views of London, Westminster, and Southwark* (London: Spottiswoode, 1878) [Z6027.L84 C8], along with the fifty-seven portfolios, eighteen rollers, and four volumes of maps which constitute the collection reported on in the catalog. See also James L. Howgego, *Printed Maps of London circa 1553–1850,* 2d ed. (London: Dawson, 1978) [Z6027 .G7 D3], and Ralph Hyde, *Printed Maps of Victorian London, 1851–1900* (London: Dawson, 1975) [Z6027 .G7 H9].

There are, of course, numerous other catalogs and bibliographies relating to the historical cartography of Great Britain and Ireland. An excellent source for these and other works of historical cartography is the *Guide to the History of Cartography: An Annotated List of References on the History of Maps and Mapmaking,* comp. Walter W. Ristow (Washington, D.C.: Library of Congress, 1973) [Z6021.R57].

F–107 **Falkus, Malcolm, and John Gillingham, gen. eds.** *Historical Atlas of Britain.* New York: Continuum, 1981.
G1812.21.S1 H5 1981

This volume presents a series of 200 original maps and numerous diagrams treating British history from 4000 B.C. to the present. Included are such topics as military history; voyages of exploration and expansion; migration patterns; the growth of settlements, towns, and cities; and all manner of social, political, economic, cultural, and religious changes. Maps are organized both chronologically and thematically; each topic is separately treated, illustrated by appropriate maps, diagrams, and paintings and photographs of persons, places, and events. A text by thirty-seven contributing scholars accompanies the maps, diagrams, and pictorial illustrations.

XII. LITERARY TOPOGRAPHY—BRITISH AND IRISH

F–110 **Oxford Literary Guide to the British Isles.** Edited by Dorothy Eagle and Helen Carnell. Oxford: Clarendon Press, 1977.   PR109.E18

Primarily an alphabetical dictionary of selected place-names with literary associations in Britain and Ireland, this work includes names of cities, towns, villages, buildings, houses, castles, schools, inns, and districts—whether or not they can still be seen. Fictitious names of real places are entered as cross-references. Entries give counties, references to the grid location on the series of specially drawn outline maps which are appended, a brief geographical description, and a discussion of the place's connections with authors and works of English literature. Notes add opening hours for those places that are otherwise closed to the public. The main section is followed by an alphabetical index of over 900 authors (excluding those still living), the entries to which present a short geographical biography keyed to the page and column numbers of the main body. In the absence of full cross-referencing or a complete index, some ingenuity must be used for place-names that are not main entries. For example, "Strawberry Hill" is found under the district "Twickenham," which is found under the main heading "London." An illustrated edition, revised by Dorothy Eagle, was published in 1981 [PR109.E18 1981].

A more discursive presentation of literary homes and haunts is the volume by David Daiches and John Flower, *Literary Landscapes of the British Isles: A Narrative Atlas* (New York: Paddington Press, 1979) [PR109.D34].

F–111 **Hardwick, John Michael.** *Literary Atlas and Gazetteer of the British Isles.* Cartography by Alan G. Hodgkiss. Detroit: Gale Research Co., 1973.   PR109.H25 1973

Arranged according to the British National Grid reference system described on page 8, a total of thirty-two reference maps (with the exception of the map of London) are marked with numbered dots locating places of literary significance. Some 4,500 entries, alphabetically arranged by locality for each county, relate to the numbered dots on the various maps. Each note gives the place-name, the literary figure and his dates, and a brief explanation of the relation between person and place. The table of contents lists the counties of England, Scotland and Wales, respectively, in alphabetical order and identifies the map(s) on which that county and the entries concerning its localities may be found. The volume concludes with one index to personal names arranged alphabetically and another done geographically by county.

A relatively new work by Lois H. Fisher, *Literary Gazetteer of England* (New York: McGraw-Hill, 1980) [PR109.F5], has entries for more than 1,200 places. Entries describe local literary connections for more than 500 authors and their works from the medieval period through 1950. There are several hundred illustrations. An earlier work, *Literary England: Photographs of Places Made Memorable in English Literature,* by David E. Scherman (New York: Random House, 1944) [PR109.S35], contains some fifty plates of photographs.

F–112 **Goode, Clement Tyson, and Edgar Finley Shannon.** *Atlas of English Literature.* New York and London: Century Co., 1925.   PR109.G6

The main body of this work is disposed into nine sections, treating respectively the Anglo-Saxon Period, the Middle English Period, the Elizabethan and Puritan Periods, Restoration and Eighteenth Century Literature, the Nineteenth Century, Scotland, Ireland, and Italy in Relation to English Literature. Each section has an outline map followed by a list of writers (with dates) and the places associated with their lives (keyed to the grid system of the pertinent map). For the Anglo-Saxon period there is a separate list of places in Anglo-Saxon literature. For the map of Italy the listing is of English writers who visited there and the places associated with them. The London map is accompanied by a general list of places of literary interest. The volume concludes with an index of places (and of all writers' names associated with them) and an index of writers.

F–113 **Briscoe, John D'Auby, et al.** *Mapbook of English Literature.* New York: Henry Holt, 1936.   PR109.B7

A total of sixteen outline maps with annotation directly on the map present the geographical background of English literature. The first nine maps present three groups of three maps each, two of England and one of London, covering these three periods: pre–1660, 1660–1800, and 1800–1935. The first map in each group is biographical, noting birthplaces, residences, and places where books were written. The second map notes places featured in plays, novels, or poems. The London maps contain both kinds of information for the authors and works of their periods. Map 10 presents the environs of London, 1800–1935; map 11, the Lake Country; and map 12, Wessex: The Hardy Country. A list of the colleges of Oxford and Cambridge and the principal writers who studied at each is followed by maps 13 of Oxford and 14 of Cambridge. Map 15 notes places in western and central continental Europe featured in English literature, and map 16 treats Ireland.

An elaborate index includes authors and places; all but anonymous works are listed under authors' names. There are special lists of prisons, schools, taverns, theaters, the districts of London, and the counties of England, Ireland, Scotland, and Wales.

XIII. TOPOGRAPHICAL ANCILLAE— AMERICAN AND CANADIAN

F–115 **Kane, Joseph N.** *American Counties: Origin of Names, Dates of Creation and Organization, Area, Population, Historical Data, and Published Sources.* 3d ed. Metuchen, N.J.: Scarecrow Press, 1972.   E180.K3 1972

Disposed into nine chapters. The first is on the origin of county names. Chapter 2 lists the counties alphabetically with the state, date of establishment, area, population 1970, 1960, and 1950, the name of the county seat, nicknames for the county, the origin of the name, and a bibliography of works on the county. Chapter 3 lists the counties by state, giving the number of counties in each state, the county names, the county seats, dates of creation, and the relevant statutes. Chapter 4 lists the counties chronologically, by date of creation to 1949. Chapter 5 lists the counties whose names have changed, giving the present name, date of creation, and relevant statute, along with the old name, date of creation, and earlier statute. Chapter 6 lists the county seats alphabetically with the name of the county given in parentheses. Chapter 7 enumerates persons for whom counties have been named. Chapter 8 lists independent cities. Chapter 9 lists Alaska boroughs. For information about the counties see also E. Kay Kirkham's *Counties of the United States and Their Genealogical Value* (Salt Lake City, 1965) and *Counties of the United States, Their Derivation and Census Schedules: A Verified*

and Corrected Listing That Shows Parent County, County Seat, and Census Information for Each County (Salt Lake City: Kay Publishing Co., 1961) [E180.K5].

For additional bibliographical information see Clarence S. Peterson's *Consolidated Bibliography of County Histories in Fifty States in 1961, 1935–1961*, 2d ed. (Baltimore: Genealogical Publishing Co., 1973) [Z1250.P47 1973], which lists some 4,000 county histories and remains the most comprehensive bibliography in spite of numerous omissions and inaccuracies. See also Peterson's two volumes on local history: *Bibliography of Local Histories in the Atlantic States* (Baltimore: Genealogical Publishing Co., 1966) [Z1251.A8 P4 vol. 1] and *Bibliography of Local Histories of Thirty-Five States beyond the Atlantic States* (Baltimore: Genealogical Publishing Co., 1967) [Z1251.A8 P4 vol. 2]. There are many libraries with massive local-history collections. The two most extensive for which printed catalogs exist are those of the Library of Congress and the New York Public Library. See Marion J. Kaminkow, ed., *United States Local Histories in the Library of Congress: A Bibliography*, 4 vols. (Baltimore: Magna Carta Book Co., 1975) [Z1250.U59 1975], and both the *Dictionary Catalog of the Local History and Genealogy Division, the Research Libraries of the New York Public Library*, 18 vols. (Boston: G. K. Hall, 1974) [Z881.N59 1974], and the *United States Local History Catalog*, 2 vols. (Boston: G. K. Hall, 1974) [Z881.N59 1974a], which supplements it. The latter is a modified shelflist arranged alphabetically by state and then by locality.

F–116 **Sealock, Richard B., and Paulina A. Seely.** *Bibliography of Place-Name Literature: United States and Canada.* 2d ed. Chicago: American Library Association, 1967.   Z6824.S4 1967

This work, the first edition of which appeared in 1948, presents a comprehensive bibliography of books and articles dealing with particular types of names (e.g., Spanish, French, Indian) or names of particular regions (e.g., Western states, names in the Yosemite Valley). Its 3,599 serially numbered entries are arranged alphabetically by state or province, then alphabetically by author, or, in the case of anonymous works, by title. There is an author index and a subject index that includes specific place-names, broad categories of names (e.g., river, mountain), foreign-language names, and types of names. Biennial supplements have appeared since the first edition of this work in *Names: Journal of the American Name Society* (Potsdam, N.Y.: The Society, 1952–) [P769.N3].

Though there is no comprehensive United States gazetteer, Ayer's *Directory of Periodicals* (D–103) has extensive gazetteer information for each locality that publishes a newspaper; George R. Stewart, *American Place-Names: A Concise and Selective Dictionary for the Continental United States of America* (New York: Oxford University Press, 1970) [E155.S79], will prove generally useful for those localities included among the 12,000 entries, in which are given the meaning and derivation of the place-name, the date and occasion of its naming, and, where possible, an account of the person who named the locality and his or her motives for choosing that particular name.

F–117 **Felt, Thomas E.** *Researching, Writing, and Publishing Local History.* Nashville: American Association for State and Local History, 1976.   D13.F387

This work begins with a discursive text treating in three sections researching, writing, and publishing. An annotated bibliography disposed into the same three sections follows, and an index.

Other guides to research in American local history include Enid T. Thompson's *Local History Collections* (Nashville:

American Association for State and Local History, 1978) [Z688.L8 T48].

F-118   *National Atlas of the United States of America.* Washington, D.C.: United States Geological Survey, 1970.

G1209.U57 1970

A total of 765 maps treat the physical features (landforms, geophysical forces, geology, marine features, soils, climate, water), historical evolution, economic activities (fishing and forestry, agriculture, mineral and energy resources, manufacturing, business, transportation), sociocultural conditions, administrative subdivisions, and place in world affairs of the United States. The work is divided into two parts, the first with general reference maps and the second with the special subjects already enumerated. Maps are annotated with references to additional sources of information about the data they reflect. There is an index to map subjects and an index of 41,000 place-names with map location, population, and latitude and longitude given.

For historical cartography of the United States the best source is the bibliography compiled by Clara Egli LeGear, *United States Atlases: A List of National, State, County, City and Regional Atlases in the Library of Congress* (New York: Arno Press, 1971) [Z881.U5 1971at].

F-119   **Paullin, Charles O.** *Atlas of the Historical Geography of the United States.* Washington, D.C.: Carnegie Institution, 1932.

G1201.S1 P3 1932

Authoritative and comprehensive, this atlas covers American history from earliest times to about 1930. Part 1 provides the descriptive text and explanation for each map; a detailed index accompanies it. Part 2 contains 688 maps, chronologically arranged under the following major headings: The Natural Environment; Cartography (historical geography) 1492–1867; Indians 1567–1930; Explorations in the West and Southwest 1535–1852; Lands 1603–1930; Settlement, Population, and Towns 1650–1790; States, Territories, and Cities 1790–1930; Population 1790–1930; Colleges, Universities, and Churches 1775–1890; Boundaries 1607–1927; Political Parties and Opinion 1788–1930; Political, Social, and Educational Reforms 1775–1931; Industries and Transportation 1620–1931; Foreign Commerce 1701–1929; Distribution of Wealth 1799–1928; Plans of Cities 1775–1803; Military History 1689–1919; Possessions and Territorial Claims of the United States; also Certain Military Operations and Grounds Formerly Frequented (ca. 1815–1860) by American Whalers.

Two other, more recent historical atlases may be mentioned, *American Heritage Pictorial Atlas of United States History* (New York: American Heritage, 1966) [G1201.S1 A4], and Clifford L. and Elizabeth H. Lord, *Historical Atlas of the United States*, rev. ed. (New York: Henry Holt, 1953) [Z1201.S1 L6 1953]. The latter is organized into chronological sections of general maps, maps of the colonial period, maps of the 1775–1865 period, and maps of the 1865–1950 period. The former has 210 new maps, many in color, which present the geographic, political, economic, social, and cultural history of the United States. See also the *Atlas of American History* by James T. Adams (New York: Scribner's, 1943) [G1201.S1 A2], designed to accompany Adams's *Dictionary of American History* (F-57).

XIV. LITERARY TOPOGRAPHY— AMERICAN

F-120   **Ehrlich, Eugene, and Gorton Carruth.** *Oxford Illustrated Literary Guide to the United States.* New York: Oxford University Press, 1982.

PS141.E74

This literary gazetteer presents information on the homes, workplaces, and other localities associated with 1,527 American writers. A total of 1,586 places (hamlets, villages, towns, and cities) are arranged in five main regional sections: New England, the Middle Atlantic, the South, the Midwest, and the Far West. Within the entry on a particular place are mentioned associated authors, addresses of their houses, titles of works written there, and so on. There are extensive and well-reproduced illustrations on nearly every page, pertinent quotations from literary works, and a number of maps. Two indexes, of places and of authors, conclude the volume.

Though reviewers have noted omissions and occasional errors, this work remains the first comprehensive guide of its kind. It will no doubt be corrected and enlarged in an eventual second, revised edition.

F-121   **Bartholomew, John George, comp.** *Literary and Historical Atlas of North and South America.* Rev. and enl. ed. Everyman's Library, no. 553. London: J. M. Dent; New York: E. P. Dutton, 1931. G1101.S1 B3 or Ac1.E8 no. 533

In addition to a series of maps of North and South America, this volume presents an index of "Contributors to the Literature of the United States" giving name, dates, and some brief description of the individual's accomplishments, and citing the localities with which the individual was associated along with their latitudes and longitudes. Also included are a map of the Concord, Massachusetts Neighborhood; one on Virginia in American Fiction; and a "Gazetteer of Towns and Places in North and South America Having a Literary and Historic Interest," which gives place-names together with latitudes, longitudes, and a brief characterization of the literary or historical interest of each place. The volume concludes with an index of place-names, with latitudes and longitudes as well as page numbers where each place is mentioned.

F-123   *Literary Tour Guide to the United States: Northeast,* by Emilie C. Harting. New York: William Morrow, 1978.

PS144.N65 H3

Literary Tour Guide to the United States: West and Midwest, by Rita Stein. New York: William Morrow, 1979.

PS144.W47 S75

Literary Tour Guide to the United States: South and Southwest, by Rita Stein. New York: William Morrow, 1979.

PS144.S67 S75

These three companion volumes are each arranged alphabetically by state and then literary locality within the regions covered. The entry for each locality is a discursive treatment of literary monuments found there, giving addresses, hours of opening, special features, and descriptions of each monument's significance for American literary history. An index of authors, literary works, and names of monuments concludes each volume. The index to the Northeast volume is inferior to those of the other two. A brief section of photographic illustrations is bound into the middle of each volume. The volumes are meant to guide the tourist and should not be taken as scholarly treatments. They are, however, the best available general works on American literary places, an atlas of American literary history remaining a desideratum.

Other works that can supplement this series are David E. Scherman and Rosemarie Redlich, *Literary America: A Chronicle of American Writers from 1607–1952 with 173*

Photographs of the American Scene That Inspired Them (New York: Random House, 1952) [PS141.S35], and the volume by Van Wyck Brooks and Otto L. Bettman, *Our Literary Heritage: A Pictorial History of the Writer in America* (1956). The most recent of such volumes is Marcella Thum's *Exploring Literary America* (New York: Atheneum, 1979)

[PS141.T5]. It has photographically illustrated chapters on various authors arranged in the chronological order of their dates of birth, each chapter discussing its author's associations with places. A geographical index, author-title index, and subject (including author-as-subject) index conclude the volume.

BIOGRAPHY AND BIOGRAPHICAL REFERENCES

For biographies and biographical information concerning authors see also the dictionaries of authors, literary encyclopedias, and literary handbooks cited in sections L, M, N, O, P, Q, R, S, T, U, and W. For scholars see also the directories cited in section Z.II. General and special encyclopedias cited in section A.V and A.VI and periodical and newspaper indexes cited in section D are also sources of biographical information, as are book reviews (see section E.VI).

I. INDEXES, BIBLIOGRAPHIES, AND GENERAL WORKS

G–1 **Slocum, Robert B., ed.** *Biographical Dictionaries and Related Works. An International Bibliography of Collective Biographies, Biobibliographies, Collections of Epitaphs, Selected Genealogical Works, Dictionaries of Anonyms and Pseudonyms, Historical and Specialized Dictionaries, Biographical Materials in Government Manuals, Bibliographies of Biography, Biographical Indexes, and Selected Portrait Catalogs.* Detroit: Gale Research Co., 1967. Supplement. Detroit: Gale Research Co., 1972.
Z5301.S55

A list of more than 4,800 serially numbered items arranged analytically, with the bibliography of items including universal biography first, followed by national and area biography alphabetical by country or area, followed in turn by vocational biography with subheadings by field of endeavor. Within classifications, entries are arranged alphabetically by author, or by title if anonymous. Full bibliographical information is given, including descriptive annotation. A table of contents guides users to the pertinent sections of the work, as do the detailed author, title, and subject indexes that conclude the volume. A number of important qualifications on the accuracy and completeness of this work are discussed in the prefatory materials, which should be consulted by anyone attempting a definitive compilation.

The *Supplement* follows the scope and arrangement of the original volume, with some 3,400 new entries. These include corrections of entries in the original work as well as references to new editions of some items first cited there. There are cross-references to the original entries wherever pertinent.

G–2 **Hyamson, Albert M.** *Dictionary of Universal Biography of All Ages and of All Peoples.* 2d ed., rev. London: Routledge and Kegan Paul, 1951.
CT103.H9 1951

An index to articles appearing in twenty-three major collective biographies, this work, first published in 1916, identifies locations for more than 100,000 biographies of individuals. Arranged alphabetically by biographical subject, entries give a brief description designed to aid identification (including dates) and then use a code to indicate which collected biographies include material on an individual.

An earlier index, analyzing over forty major nineteenth-century collective biographies, is that by Lawrence B. Phillips, the *Dictionary of Biographical Reference Containing over One Hundred Thousand Names, Together with a Classed Index of the Biographical Literature of Europe and America*, new ed., corr. and augm. with supplement to date by Frank Weitenkampf, 3d ed. (London: Sampson Low, 1889) [CT103.P5].

G–3 **Riches, Phyllis.** *Analytical Bibliography of Universal Collected Biography, Comprising Books Published in the English Tongue in Great Britain and Ireland, America, and the British Dominions.* London: The Library Association, 1934.
Z5301.R53

An index of English-language biographies and short lives, appearing in more than 3,000 relatively obscure volumes of collective biography. A bibliography of the items analyzed appears in part 2 of this work. Part 1, the analytical index, lists more than 56,000 biographical subjects alphabetically, with dates and occupations, and indicates the books in which their biographies appear. This is followed by part 2, the bibliography, which is followed in turn by a chronological index ordering the subjects by the centuries in which they lived, a subject index arranging them under profession or trade, and an author-subject index of the biographical dictionaries analyzed.

Because of the relatively obscure sources used and the aim of completeness through 1933, this volume remains an excellent guide to "hidden" biographies of minor figures.

G–4 **Arnim, Max.** *Internationale Personalbibliographie, 1800–1943.* 2d ed. 2 vols. Leipzig [later Stuttgart]: Hiersemann, 1944–1952.
Z8001.A1 A72

An index, first published in 1936, to bibliographies of works by individuals as found in books, periodicals, biographical dictionaries, and composite volumes such as festschriften. Though international in scope, the work has German emphasis. It is ordered alphabetically by author and gives the person's name, profession, date of death, and then references to bibliographies of the author's works wherever located. It is particularly valuable for locating "hidden" bibliographies of individuals; since these are often appended to biographies, the work is also an index to collected biographies.

A third volume, edited by G. Bock and F. Hodes, covers the period 1944–1959, and was published in 1963. It also contains a supplement to volumes 1–3. Together the three volumes of the second edition include more than 90,000 authors.

G–5 *IBN: Index Bio-bibliographicus Notorum Hominum.* Edited by Jean-Pierre Lobies, François-Pierre Lobies, et al. Osnabrück: Biblio Verlag, 1973–.   Z5301.L7

This massive new biobibliographical index is to be published in five parts. Part A will be the Allgemeine Einführung / General Introduction and is not yet published. Part B, the Liste der ausgewerteten bio-bibliographischen Werke / List of the Evaluated Bio-bibliographical Works, was published in one volume in 1973 and is described below. Part C, the Corpus Alphabeticum, is in progress and is described below. Part D, a supplement, is not yet in progress, and part E, the Gesamtregister der Verweisungen / General Index of References, is not yet published.

Part B, the list of evaluated works, enumerates all of the works of collected biography which are being analyzed. The primary list is taken from Slocum (G–1) and follows Slocum's numeration. A second series presents additional titles especially numbered from 5,000 on. This second series is to be continued by the irregular publication of fascicles enumerating additional analyzed works. Entries both in the primary list and in the second series present bibliographical information on the work and give the call numbers at the Bibliothèque nationale, British Museum, and Library of Congress. There is an index of authors and subjects at the end of the volume; cumulated indexes will be published later.

Part C, the alphabetical list of persons, is being published in six sections: a General section, and one each for Arabian, Armenian, Indian, Japanese, and Chinese persons. To date, sixteen volumes (1974–1979) of the General section have been published (A–Bernstein, Peteru). Entries give the name of the person as cited in the biographical reference work, dates, and a brief description of occupation or profession. There are cross-references from variant forms of a person's name and to various forms of a name, which may or may not be relevant to a particular search.

G–6 *Biography Index: A Cumulative Index to Biographical Material in Books and Magazines [1946–] [BI].* Vol. 1–. New York: H. W. Wilson, 1947–.   Z5301.B5

A quarterly name index to English-language biographical materials in some 1,700 periodicals, in current works of collective biography, and in separately published biographies and autobiographies. Also covered are obituaries, diaries, memoirs, journals, letters, genealogies, and other sources of biographical materials, such as biographical prefaces or chapters in otherwise nonbiographical publications. The quarterly issues are cumulated annually and triennially. Each issue and cumulation has a main body that lists entries alphabetically by the name of the subject, with dates, profession or occupation, nationality (unless American), location of the biography, and notation of a portrait or illustration. A second section indexes the biographical subjects by profession or occupation, with subdivisions by nationality in the case of large groups such as authors. A checklist of the composite books analyzed is also included.

Entries since July 1984 may be searched on WILSONLINE (see Z–78).

G–8 *Chambers' Biographical Dictionary.* Rev. ed. Edited by J. O. Thorne and T. C. Collcott. Edinburgh: Chambers, 1969. Paperbound ed. 2 vols. Edinburgh: Chambers, 1975. New ed., 1984.   CT103.C4 1984

More than 15,000 short biographies of persons of all countries are arranged alphabetically by subject. Entries often include references to biographical sources and are composed with an eye to factual accuracy and readability. An extensive subject index at the end of volume 2 lists individuals by occupational categories and other headings such as nicknames. The subject category "Literature and Drama" lists the titles of works with references to authors. The work is preceded by a brief supplementary section at the beginning of volume 1. The original edition of this work appeared in 1897.

Among other one-volume general biographical dictionaries, see *Webster's Biographical Dictionary: A Dictionary of Names of Noteworthy Persons with Pronunciations and Concise Biographies* (Springfield, Mass.: Merriam, 1972) [CT103.W4], the first edition of which appeared in 1943. This work is frequently revised; the current edition gives more than 40,000 brief biographies including dates, citizenship, profession, and career summary. Appended tables list holders of major offices in the United States, Britain, and the British Empire, and the rulers of most other countries of the world.

G–9 *Biographie universelle ancienne et moderne: ou, Historie, par ordre alphabétique, de la vie publique et privée de tous les hommes qui sont fait remarquer. . . .* Compiled by Joseph-François Michaud and Louis-Gabriel Michaud. New ed. 45 vols. Paris: Mme C. Desplaces, 1843–1865.
CT143.M52

This is the most important and the most generally useful of all the large nineteenth-century dictionaries of universal biography. The second edition presents numerous revisions of articles originally published among the eighty-four volumes of the first edition (1811–1857). Entries, signed with initials of contributors, include bibliographies (titles translated into French) and are quite long and detailed. They are written from a mid–nineteenth-century French perspective, however, and thus will not be found very useful for, say, English romantic authors unless, like Byron, they have a reputation in continental Europe. This same limitation on perspective also affects the names chosen for inclusion in the first place: Keats, for example, is not included. But for figures of French or continental-European reputation in the late eighteenth-century or earlier, Michaud is among the sources to be checked for biographical information.

The rival publication compiled by M. le Dr. [Jean-Chrétien-Ferdinand] Hoefer was published by the firm of Firmin-Didot frères under the title *Nouvelle biographie universelle ancienne et moderne*, later changed under the pressure of a lawsuit by Michaud's publisher to *Nouvelle biographie général depuis les temps plus reculés jusqûá nos jours, avec les renseignements bibliographiques et l'indication des sources à consulter* [CT143.H5]. A total of forty-six volumes were published 1853–1866. Though less satisfactory than Michaud from most points of view, Hoefer does include more names, especially of living persons and minor figures in the first half of the alphabet, A-M, and cites titles in their original language of publication.

Another universal biographical dictionary of particular interest to scholars is Christian Gottlieb Jöcher's *Allgemeines Gelehrten-Lexikon, darinne die Gelehrten aller Stände sowohl männ- als weiblichen Geschlechts, welche vom Anfange der Welt bis auf jetzige Zeit gelebt, und sich der gelehrten Welt bekannt gemacht, nach ihrer Geburt, Leben, merckwürdigen Geschichten, Absterben und Schriften aus den glaubwürdigsten Scribenten in alphabetischer Ordnung beschrieben werden*, 4 vols. (Leipzig: Gleditsch, 1750–1751)

[Z1010.J63], with seven volumes of *Fortsetzung und Ergänzugen* (Leipzig [and other places], 1784–1897). The original work contains biographical sketches of learned persons living before 1750. The continuation and supplemental volumes also treat persons of later date but remain an incomplete alphabet, A-Romuleus. Bibliographies and references to source materials are found throughout but are more extensive in the continuation volumes.

II. BRITISH BIOGRAPHY

G–10 **Dictionary of National Biography [DNB].** Edited by Sir Leslie Stephen and Sir Sidney Lee. 63 vols. London: Smith Elder, 1885–1901. Reprint (63 vols. in 21). London: Oxford University Press, 1921–1922.   DA28.D47 1921

The *DNB* was originally conceived and published by George M. Smith of Cornhill, London. Smith's aim was to provide a biographical record of those men and women deceased before 22 January 1901 of the "British and Irish race," including foreigners who had settled in England and colonials (including Americans of the colonial period) who had distinguished themselves "in any walk of life," from the beginning of recorded history to the end of the nineteenth century. The first edition listed 29,120 biographies, prepared by 653 contributors. Entries are alphabetical by surname; they vary from short paragraphs to the forty-page entry on Shakespeare. Dates of birth and death and details of education and achievements are always included, and each entry is signed with the initials of the contributing author. A list of manuscript and printed sources is provided and often constitutes an adequate bibliography for preliminary investigation. But information is sometimes inaccurate and often incomplete. Dates, particularly, need verification in additional sources. Note the published additions and corrections discussed below. The first volume lists contributors so that initials can be identified; it also includes an account of the *DNB*'s origin. The last volume of the original series includes a list of eminent persons not dead at the time of publication and thus excluded from the work (e.g., Robert Browning). Each volume contains an index giving names with dates and the page numbers of their biographies.

After the original series a *First Supplement: Additional Names* was published (London, 1901; reprint, London, 1959–1960) originally in three volumes, then in one (numbered volume 22 to follow the numeration of the reprinted original series). It covered those 1,000 persons who should have been included in the original series but were not, either because they died before 21 January 1901 but after the volume in which their entry belonged was published, or because they were accidentally omitted. The supplement has its own index. In addition, the indexes of the original series were adjusted in the twenty-two-volume reprinting so that each page of each index to each volume notes the names of persons treated in the first *Supplement*.

Further supplements have been published at roughly ten-year intervals; these are collectively known as the *Twentieth Century Dictionary of National Biography* because they each include persons of note who died during the ten or so years of the twentieth-century since the previous supplement was published. Published to date are the *Second Supplement*, covering persons who died between 22 January 1901 and 31 December 1911 (London, 1912); the *Third Supplement*, 1912-1921 (1927); the *Fourth Supplement*, 1922–1930 (1937); the *Fifth Supplement*, 1931–1940 (1949); the *Sixth Supplement*, 1941–1950 (1959); the *Seventh Supplement*, 1951–1960 (1971); and the *Eighth Supplement*, 1961–1970 (1981). Each supplement's index cumulates the names of all persons in the *Twentieth Century DNB*; their dates indicate in which volume their biographies are found.

A *Concise Dictionary of National Biography*, presenting an epitome (about one-fourteenth) of the whole work, has been published [DA28.D56]. Part 1, covering the scope of the original series and first supplement, was published in 1903, with a second edition in 1906 and numerous reprints since then; in 1961 a second part was published, giving a one-volume epitome of the *Twentieth Century DNB* through 1950. This latter has been replaced by the *Concise DNB 1901–1970* (1982) [DA28.D56 1982]. Also published is a two-volume *Compact Edition* (1975) [DA28.C64], which includes the original series and all supplemental volumes through 1960, along with an extremely useful single general index to the entire *DNB*.

In addition to the corrections noted in the single volume of *Errata* published in 1904, addenda and corrigenda to *DNB* articles have been discovered in the course of contemporary research; these have been published in the *Bulletin of the Institute of Historical Research* since 1923 [D1.L65]. A single volume, *Corrections and Additions to the Dictionary of National Biography Cumulated from the Bulletin of the Institute of Historical Research, University of London*, was published by G. K. Hall (Boston, 1966) [DA28.L65]. Some 1,300 emendations published 1923–1963 are arranged in a single alphabet by surname of subject; reference is made to the volume, page, column, and line of the entry being corrected. Further corrections and additions continue to be published in the *Bulletin*.

More than 4,000 Welsh persons of note, 400–1940, are treated in the *Dictionary of Welsh Biography down to 1940*, ed. Sir John Edward Lloyd, under the auspices of the Honourable Society of Cymmrodorion (Oxford: Blackwell, 1959) [DA710 .A1 B913], the Welsh original of which is *Y Bywgrafiadur Cymreig hyd 1940* (London, 1953) [DA710.A1 B9]. For the Irish see Alfred J. Webb, *Compendium of Irish Biography, Comprising Sketches of Distinguished Irishmen, and of Eminent Persons Connected with Ireland by Office or by Their Writings* (Dublin: M. H. Gill and Son, 1878) [DA916.W3]. See also the more recent but less complete work of John S. Crone, *Concise Dictionary of Irish Biography*, rev. and enl. ed. (Dublin: Talbot; and New York: Longmans, 1937) [DA916.C7]. The best source for the Scots is Robert Chambers, *Biographical Dictionary of Eminent Scotsmen*, new ed., revised and continued by Thomas Thomson, 3 vols. (Edinburgh: Blackie and Son, 1870) [CT813.C5 1870]. See also Joseph Irving's *Book of Scotsmen Eminent for Achievements in Arms and Arts* (Paisley: A. Gardner, 1881) [CT813.I7], and William Anderson's *Scottish Nation*, 3 vols. (Edinburgh: Fullarton, 1878–1880) [CT813.A6].

G–11 **Boase, Frederick. *Modern English Biography, Containing Many Thousand Concise Memoirs of Persons Who Have Died since the Year 1850, with an Index of the Most Interesting Matter.*** 3 vols. Truro: Netherton and Worth, 1892–1901. Supplement. 3 vols. Truro: Netherton and Worth, 1908–1921.   CT773.B612

Each volume in both the original and supplemental series of this biographical dictionary, which supplements the *DNB* (G–10) for minor figures of the nineteenth-century, contains an elaborate index to all the facts included in the articles, from pseudonyms to names of persons, places, organizations, or topics with which the biographical subjects were associated. Altogether more than 40,000 biographies are presented.

For pre-nineteenth-century English figures not included in the *DNB* the best sources of biographical information are genealogical reference works (G–13 through G–23) and biographical registers of schools, colleges, and universities (G–25 through G–29). Additional help may be gathered from Sir William Musgrave, *Obituary Prior to 1800 (As Far As Relates to England, Scotland, and Ireland)*, ed. Sir George T.

Armytage, 6 vols. (London, 1899–1901) [CS410.H3 vol. 44–49], which is an index of pre–nineteenth-century obituaries containing some ninety collected works. Brief entries give name, brief description, date of death, place of residence, and source. This work may be supplemented by Robert Henry Farrar, *Index to the Biographical and Obituary Notices in the Gentleman's Magazine, 1731–1780* (London, 1886–1891) [AI3.I4 vol. 15] and the new *Index to Biographies of Englishmen, 1000–1485, Found in Dissertations and Theses*, comp. Jerome V. Reel (Westport, Conn.: Greenwood, 1975) [Z5305.G7 R43].

G–12 *British Biographical Archive [BBA]*. Ed. by Paul Sieveking. Microfiche ed. with 4 vol. index. New York: K. G. Saur, Inc., 1984–1987.   CT101.B74 1984 Guide

This series of approximately 1,200 microfiche, with a four-volume, hard-copy index, presents a single alphabetical listing of the entries in 324 original English language biographical dictionaries and other source volumes published between 1601 and 1926. A total of approximately 450,000 entries treat approximately 200,000 individuals. The *DNB* (G–10) is not included, but where a *DNB* entry for an individual exists, there is a notation in the *Archive* for the user's information. Included are persons from England, Scotland, Wales, Ireland, all British colonies to the date of their independence or home rule, and persons generally associated with Britain but not of British birth. Coverage is from the period of Roman Britain through the early twentieth-century. The index volumes are computer-generated, and include a complete bibliography of all of the source works.

G–14 **Filby, P. William.** *American and British Genealogy and Heraldry: A Selected List of Books.* 3d ed. Boston: New England Historic Genealogy Society, 1983. Z5311.F55 1983

A selective, critical, annotated bibliography (the first edition of which appeared in 1970) of 9,773 serially numbered sources of genealogical and heraldic information, current to the fall of 1981. Entries are disposed in twelve main sections, treating the United States in general, its regions, and then works on individual states; Latin America in general, and then individual countries; Canada in general, then individual provinces; England; Ireland; Scotland; Wales; British Island Areas; British Dominions and Former Dominions; the Non-English-Speaking World; Heraldry; and Chivalry. Each section is subdivided into such headings as Bibliographies, Record Guides and Offices, Periodicals and Series, Biographies, Registers, Vital Statistics, Wills, Topography, Names, Manuals, Peerages, Baronetages, Knightages, Gentry, and Religions. Annotations describe the contents, arrangement, and use of each item and compare one tool with other similar works. The volume concludes with a detailed author-title-subject index. A supplement covering 1982–1985 was published in 1987.

Two other reference works with a similar focus on the reference library are Richard A. M. Harvey, *Genealogy for Librarians* (London: Bingley, 1983) [CS9.H35 1983] and the edition by Raymond S. Wright III, *Syllables, Genealogy and Local History Reference Services*, based on a conference sponsored by the Reference and Adult Services Division of the ALA (Chicago: ALA, 1981) [CS47.S9].

G–15 **Wagner, Sir Anthony Richard.** *English Genealogy*, 3d ed., rev. and enl. Chichester: Phillimore, 1983.
CS414.W3 1983

Though not a basic handbook, this volume by the Garter King of Arms and the premier genealogist in England is valuable to the literary scholar precisely because it places genealogical research in a comprehensive framework of the study of English social history and the history of English families. Chapters treat The Roots of English Society, Anglo-Saxon, Viking, Celtic, and French; The English and Norman Background; The Social Framework From Barons to Peers to Recusants and Dissenters; The Rise and Fall of Prominent Families; Strangers in England; and English Settlers. The last three chapters, 8–10, concern the genealogical aspects of biographical research, treating The Records, The Study and Literature of Genealogy, and The Practice of Genealogy. There is an index of names, titles, and subjects.

Further developments of the author's thought will be found in the collection *Pedigree and Progress: Essays in the Genealogical Interpretation of History* (London: Phillimore, 1975) [CS4.W33].

Of the basic handbooks the most professional is that by David E. Gardner and Frank Smith, *Genealogical Research in England and Wales*, 3 vols. [vol. 1, 7th ed. (Salt Lake City: Bookcraft Publishers, 1967); vol. 2, 4th ed. (1970); vol. 3, 2d ed. (1966)] [CS414.G3]. Among its contents are detailed accounts of the present whereabouts of genealogical records, both in general and by individual county. Also highly regarded is the volume by Gerald K. S. Hamilton-Edwards, *In Search of British Ancestry*, 3d ed. (Baltimore: Genealogical Publishing Co., 1974) [CS9.H27 1974]. More elementary are Anthony J. Camp, *Genealogy for Beginners*, 3d ed., rev. (Chichester: Phillimore, 1976) [CS16.W55 1976], and the fifth edition of the Society of Genealogists' invaluable *Genealogists' Handbook*, rev. Peter Spufford and Anthony J. Camp (London: The Society, 1969) [CS414.S6 1969]. For Scottish genealogy see Gerald K. S. Hamilton-Edwards, *In Search of Scottish Ancestry*, 2d ed. (Baltimore: Genealogical Publishing Co., 1984) [CS463.H35 1984]; for Irish see Margaret Dickson Falley, *Irish and Scotch-Irish Ancestral Research: A Guide to the Genealogical Records, Methods and Sources in Ireland*, 2 vols. (Strasburg, Va.: Privately printed, 1961–1962) [CS483.F32].

There are several major genealogical collections with published catalogs that serve as bibliographies of the field. See Marion J. Kaminkow, *Genealogies in the Library of Congress: A Bibliography of Family Histories of America and Great Britain* (Baltimore: Magna Carta Book Co., 1972) [Z5319.U53] with its 20,000 entries and more than 25,000 cross-references. A *Supplement*, 1972–1976, also edited by Kaminkow, was published in 1977 [Z5319.U53 suppl.]. See also the catalog of the Local History and Genealogy Collection of the New York Public Library (see F–115), and the *Index* to the massive collection of the Newberry Library (see B–16).

G–16 **Powicke, Sir F. Maurice, and E. B. Fryde, eds.** *Handbook of British Chronology*. 3d ed. by E. B. Fryde, et al. London: Royal Historical Society, 1986.   DA34.P6 1986

A standard work that includes lists of The Independent Rulers of England, Wales, Scotland, and the Isle of Man; English Officers of State from Chief Justicians, 1102–1265, to Ministers of Defence, 1940–1959; Officers of State in Scotland; Officers of State in the Channel Islands; Archbishops and Bishops of England, Wales, Scotland; Archbishops and Bishops of Ireland; Dukes, Marquesses, and Earls (England, Ireland, and Scotland); English and British Parliaments and Related Assemblies to 1832; and Provincial and National Councils of the Church in England to 1536.

Sources of information are cited; there is also a bibliographic guide to some 261 pre–1800 lists of English officeholders. Within the bibliography, lists are classified by office and then chronologically. The original edition of Powicke, published in 1939, included a section on the reckoning of time published separately by C. R. Cheney as a *Handbook of Dates for Students of English History* (F–65).

G–17 **Haydn, Joseph, and Horace Ockerby.** *Book of Dignities, Containing Lists of the Official Personages of the British Empire, Civil, Diplomatic, Heraldic, Judicial, Ecclesiastical, Municipal, Naval, and Military, from the Earliest Periods to the Present Time; Together with the Sovereigns and Rulers of the World, from the Foundation of Their Respective States; the Orders of Knighthood of the United Kingdom and India, etc., etc.* 3d ed. London: W. H. Allen, 1894.   DA34.H32

These invaluable lists are divided into seventeen parts, as follows: I—Royal (by continent and country); II—Diplomatic (Ambassadors, Envoys Extraordinary, Ministers Plenipotentiary, etc. from Great Britain and the United Kingdom of Great Britain and Ireland, from 1760 on to Foreign States); III—Political and Official (Cabinet Officers, Officers of State, Officers of the Household, etc.); IV—Political and Official (Cabinet Officers, Officers of State, Officers of the Household, etc.); V—Lord-Lieutenants of Counties, Governors and Constables of Castles, etc.; VI—Heraldic (Earl-Marshals, Kings of Arms, Heralds, and Pursuivants); VII—Legal (Judges and Other Legal Dignitaries, by Court); VIII—Ecclesiastical (Archbishops, Bishops, and Deans of England and Wales); IX—London (Officers); X—Scotland (subtopics parallel to those in parts I-VII); XI—Ireland (subtopics parallel); XII—India (subtopics parallel); XIII—The Colonies (Governors and Bishops); XIV—Orders of Knighthood; XV—Naval Lists; XVI—Military Lists; and XVII—Miscellaneous. Names in the detailed index are given under the actual style or title of the official at the date of his appointment; references are made to each title represented in the volume.

G–18 **Burke, John.** *Burke's Genealogical and Heraldic History of the Peerage, Baronetage, and Knightage.* London: Burke's Peerage, 1826–. [Title, publisher, frequency, and contents vary.]   CS420.B85

An account of the lineage of currently living nobility, this work appeared every few years from 1826 through a 105th edition in 1970. To trace a noble line, one edition for each decade or so is needed. Complete from 1700 to date, early editions tended to rely on some information supplied by families which has been found inaccurate. Also, Burke traces male lineage fully, providing little information on sons who died young or without issue; daughters are named without dates of birth or death and without reference to their issue.

The main body, divided into sections on the Peerage and Baronetage, then the Lords Spiritual, then the Knightage, presents an alphabetically arranged list of titles, with entries then in chronological order by each holder. Entries include a biography of the nobleman, a table of his offspring, a genealogical history of his family, and a description of his arms, motto, and seat. Among the varying contents of preliminary and appended matter have been descriptive accounts of the history of the peerage, royal lineages, tables of precedence, rolls of the lords spiritual and temporal, lists of foreign titles conferred on British subjects, surnames of peers and peerages, lists of British orders of knighthood, and lists of seats and mansions. There are tables of contents but no indexes; some cross-references among entries aid users.

As titles were dropped from listing in the *Peerage*, they were included in the two editions of *Genealogical and Heraldic History of the Extinct and Dormant Baronetcies of England, Ireland, and Scotland* (London, 1838; 2d ed., 1844, reprinted 1977) [CS424.B5 1977] or in *Genealogical and Heraldic History of the Dormant, Abeyant, Forfeited, and Extinct Peerages of the British Empire,* five editions (London, 1831–1883) [CS424.B88]. The latter publication has been continued by Leslie G. Pine's *New Extinct Peerage, 1884–1971: Containing Extinct, Abeyant, Dormant and Suspended Peerages with Genealogies and Arms* (Baltimore: Genealogical Publishing Co., 1972) [CS422.P56].

G–19 **Burke, John, and Sir John Bernard Burke.** *Burke's Genealogical and Heraldic History of the Landed Gentry of Great Britain and Ireland.* 18th ed. 3 vols. London: Burke's Peerage, 1965–1972.   CS425.B8

Originally published in four volumes, the first three with the title *Genealogical and Heraldic History of the Commoners of Great Britain and Ireland* (London, 1833–1835), and reissued in 1837 with a fourth volume titled *Genealogical and Heraldic History of the Landed Gentry,* this work presented the lineage of untitled men of property. The second edition appeared with the current title in 1850–1853, and new editions have been issued regularly since then. All should be consulted in tracing lineage, for contents have varied. After the ninth edition (1898), Irish families were omitted, as the new *Burke's Genealogical and Heraldic History of the Landed Gentry of Ireland* [CS490.B8] made its first appearance; its most recent edition, the fourth, was published in London in 1958. The sixteenth edition of *Burke's Landed Gentry* (1939) is prized for including the lineage of some 1,600 prominent American families of British origin.

Two other related publications should be mentioned: George Ormerod's *Index to the Pedigrees in Burke's Commoners,* ed. J. R. Magrath (Oxford, 1907), and the two-volume *Genealogical and Heraldic History of the Colonial Gentry* (London, 1891–1895) [CS425.B72].

Among other publications of Burke's Peerage, those on the seats of the nobility and gentry are of interest to literary scholars. The earliest is Sir John Bernard Burke's *Visitation of the Seats and Arms of the Noblemen and Gentlemen of Great Britain,* 4 vols. in 2 series (London: Hurst and Blackett, 1852–1855) [CS419.B88], with engravings of houses and arms, pedigrees, and indexes of seats and owners. The most recent related publication is *Burke's Guide to Country Houses,* the first volume of which concerns Ireland and was edited by Mark Bence-Jones (London: Burke's Peerage, 1978) [NA7620.B86].

G–20 *Burke's Family Index.* Edited by Hugh J. Montgomery-Massingberd. London: Burke's Peerage, 1976.

Z5035.G7B87

The Family Index presents a comprehensive listing of all the families that have appeared in Burke's publications through 1976, including all editions and all reprints of editions. Under entries arranged alphabetically by the family's name will be found reference to the most complete and up-to-date version of that family's narrative pedigree. Codes are used for the titles of each of Burke's series and years of issues or reissues. A "Guide to the Reader" is preceded by "A Bibliography of Burke's 1826–1976," in which all editions, reissues, and reprints of each of Burke's series are enumerated.

G–21 **C[okayne], G. E.** *Complete Baronetage.* 5 vols. and Index. Exeter: W. Pollard, 1900–1909.   CS424.C68

The standard work on the baronetage, Cokayne covers English Baronetcies, 1611–1800; Irish, 1619–1800; and Scottish, 1625–1707. The entries present the fullest accounts available; the index volume also contains an appendix.

G–22 **C[okayne], G. E.** *Complete Peerage of England, Scotland, Ireland, Great Britain, and the United Kingdom, Extant, Extinct, or Dormant.* New ed., rev. and much enl. Edited by the Hon. Vicary Gibbs [and others]. 13 vols. in 14. London: St. Catherine Press, 1910–1959.

CS421.C71 1910–59

The previous edition in eight volumes was published in 1887–1898. This work is known for its concise and precise articles, giving particulars of the parentage, birth, honors, orders, offices, public services, politics, marriage, death, and burial of every holder of a peerage. Well-documented articles include pedigrees and cite authorities. Volume 13 contains peerage creations and promotions from 22 January 1901 to 31 December 1938. Corrections and additions are published in *Genealogists' Magazine* [CS410.S61] and *American Genealogist* [CS42.A55].

G-23 **Debrett's Peerage, Baronetage, Knightage, and Companionage [title varies].** London: Kelly's Directories, 1713-.
CS420.D32

This annual directory is concerned with the lineage of living nobility. One issue of Debrett in every decade is, therefore, needed to trace a family. In contrast with Burke's, however, Debrett contains the birth dates of daughters and the names of their surviving children, thus making it possible to trace a female collateral line.

G-24 **Lodge, Edmund. Peerage, Baronetage, Knightage, and Companionage of the British Empire [title varies].** London: Hurst & Blackett, 1832-1919.

In contrast with Burke's, Lodge includes the birth dates of daughters; like Debrett, this work is concerned with the lineage of living titleholders, and the dead are included only to clarify present-day relationships.

G-25 **Gabriel, Astrik Ladislas. Summary Bibliography of the History of the Universities of Great Britain and Ireland up to 1800, Covering Publications between 1900 and 1968.** Notre Dame, Ind.: Medieval Institute, University of Notre Dame, 1974.
Z5815.G5 G3

Prepared in collaboration with the International Commission for the History of Universities, this volume enumerates a total of 1,514 publications including many rich in biographical information. Entries are disposed into six sections. The sections list works on the history of education in Europe, in England, the history of English universities, Scottish universities and colleges, Welsh universities, and Irish colleges, respectively. Indexes of authors and of subjects conclude the work.

G-26 **Raven-Hart, Hester E., and Marjorie Johnston. "Bibliography of the Registers (Printed) of the Universities, Inns of Court, Colleges, and Schools of Great Britain and Ireland."** *Bulletin of the Institute of Historical Research* 9 (1932): 19-30, 65-83, 154-170; 10 (1933): 109-113.
D1.L65

Part I lists registers of universities, inns of court, colleges, and other similar institutions. The list is alphabetical by university or inn. Colleges within universities are listed under the parent institution. Following the name of the institution is a list of the relevant publications. Part II lists school registers alphabetically by school names. The last segment in volume 10 consists of "Addenda and Corrigenda" arranged to correspond to the two parts. The list is generally limited to schools now operating.
Phyllis M. Jacobs has produced a more recent bibliography, "Registers of the Universities, Colleges, and Schools of Great Britain and Ireland: A List," *Bulletin of the Institute of Historical Research* 37 (1964): 185-232 [D1.L65], which was also published separately (London: Athlone Press, 1964) [Z5815.G5 J33].
A further aid in tracing the education of persons educated in Britain is P. J. Wallis, "Histories of Old Schools: A Preliminary List for England and Wales," *British Journal of Educational Studies* 14 (1965): 48-89, 224-265; 15 (1966): 74-82, published as *Histories of Old Schools: A Revised List for Eng-*

land and Wales (Newcastle-upon-Tyne University, Department of Education, 1966) [Z5815.G5 W3].

G-27 **Alumni Cantabrigenses: A Biographical List of All Known Students, Graduates, and Holders of Office at the University of Cambridge from the Earliest Times to 1900.** Edited by John Venn and J. A. Venn. 10 vols. Cambridge: Cambridge University Press, 1922-1954.
LF124.A2

Part I in four volumes (1922-1944) treats persons associated with Cambridge from about 1250 through 1751. Entries are alphabetical by surname, followed by abbreviated first name, date and place of birth, and name of father. Then follows the college of matriculation; social status within the college (e.g., sizer, pensioner, etc.); term and year of matriculation; degree earned and year awarded; further degrees and years of receipt; and special additional information. Part II in six volumes (1940-1954) covers the same information in a similar arrangement for persons associated with Cambridge, 1752-1900. The information incorporated in Venn is derived from official lists and other sources; a revision is now in progress.
For the earliest years of the university see Alfred B. Emden, *Biographical Register of the University of Cambridge to A.D. 1500* (Cambridge: Cambridge University Press, 1963) [LF113.E4]. This work is also arranged alphabetically by the most common spelling of last names. As available, further information includes particulars of birth, place of origin, parentage; records of licenses to study and details of college membership and offices held; then ecclesiastical affiliations; then ecclesiastical and secular employment; finally, date of death, place of burial, and details of testamentary provisions.
For a convenient bibliography of works on the history of the university and its colleges see Gabriel (G-25), items 295-534.

G-28 **Alumni Oxonienses: The Members of the University of Oxford [1500-1886].** Edited by Joseph Foster. 8 vols. Oxford: Parker, 1887-1892.
LF524.B3 1891

The first four volumes cover the period 1500-1714; the second four treat members of the university 1715-1886. Entries in each part are alphabetical by surname and include initials, name of father, birthplace, year of birth, name of college in which the member matriculated, year of matriculation, degree(s) and year(s) of receipt. The work is supplemented for 1880-1892 by Foster's *Oxford Men and Their Colleges* (Oxford: J. Parker, 1893) [LF525.F7].
Alfred B. Emden, *Biographical Register of the University of Oxford to A.D. 1500*, 3 vols. (Oxford: Clarendon Press, 1957-1959) [LF525.E5], presents for the early period of Oxford history a much more detailed biographical record than that found in Foster. Entries are alphabetical by the most general spelling of the surname, followed by variant spellings. Then follow particulars of birth date and place; parentage; licenses to study and particulars of membership in colleges and offices held; then particulars of ecclesiastical affiliation; then an account of ecclesiastical work and an account of secular accomplishments, including a list of works authored. Two lists of additions and corrections appeared in the *Bodleian Library Record* 6 (1961): 668-688; 7 (1964): 149-174 [Z792.O94]. An additional volume, *Biographical Register of the University of Oxford, A.D. 1501-1540*, was also published by Emden (Oxford: Clarendon Press, 1974) [LF525.E52].
For a convenient bibliography of works concerning the history of Oxford University and its colleges see Gabriel (G-25), items 535-1336. See also E. H. Cordeaux and D. H. Merry, *Bibliography of Printed Works Relating to the University of Oxford* (Oxford: Clarendon Press, 1968) [Z5055.G7093].

G–29 *Alumni Dublinenses: A Register of the Students, Graduates, Professors, and Provosts of Trinity College in the University of Dublin, 1593–1860.* Edited by George D. Burtchaell and T. U. Sadleir. New ed. Dublin: Thom, 1935.   LF904.A2 A31593 1860

A revision of the 1924 volume by the same authors, this work presents the most complete college record extant, supplying in entries arranged alphabetically by surname the name of the father, county of origin, birth date, date of matriculation, and degree(s) received for each person listed. A *Catalogue of Graduates of the University of Dublin*, issued irregularly since 1928, covers more contemporary students; volume 6 (1955) covers matriculations 1931–1952 [LF908.A2].

For Scottish universities individual records must be used. For Aberdeen University see Peter J. Anderson, *Officers and Graduates of University and King's College, Aberdeen, 1495–1860* (Aberdeen: For the New Spalding Club, 1893) [DA750.N5 vol. 11], and Theodore Watt, *Roll of the Graduates 1901–25, with Supplement, 1860–1900* (Aberdeen: Aberdeen University Press, 1935) [LF968.A2 1925]. For Edinburgh see David Laing, *Catalogue of the Graduates. . . since Its Foundations* [1587–1858] (Edinburgh, 1858), and the *Alphabetical List of Graduates of the University of Edinburgh from 1859 to 1888* (Edinburgh: J. Thin, 1889) [LF1038.A2 1889]. For Glasgow University see William I. Addison, *Matriculation Albums of the University of Glasgow from 1728 to 1858* (Glasgow: J. Maclehose and Sons, 1913) [LF1074.A2 1858], and *Roll of Graduates, 1727–1898, with Short Biographical Notes* (Glasgow: J. Maclehose and Sons, 1898) [LF1078.A2 1897]. For St. Andrews see James M. Anderson, *Early Records: . . . The Graduation Roll, 1413–1579, and the Matriculation Roll, 1478–1579*, Publications of the Scottish History Society, 3d ser., vol. 8 (Edinburgh: T. and A. Constable, 1926) [DA75.525 3d ser. vol. 8], and his *Matriculation Roll, 1747–1897* (Edinburgh: W. Blackwood and Sons, 1905) [LF1108.A4 1905].

G–32 **Matthews, William.** *British Diaries: An Annotated Bibliography of British Diaries Written between 1442 and 1942.* Berkeley and Los Angeles: University of California Press, 1950.   Z5305.G7 M3

A bibliography of published and unpublished diaries or diary extracts written by citizens of the United Kingdom wherever they reside and by foreigners writing English diaries published in England. Diaries are understood by the compiler to be personal, day-by-day records of what interested the diarist, written soon after the events occurred. Thus travel narratives that are not daily records are excluded, as are chronicles, commonplace books, ships' logs, reminiscences, autobiographies, minutes, accounts, muster rolls, memoirs, parliamentary diaries, and explorers' journals. Entries with brief description (including chief subjects, places, and persons dealt with, and manuscript location) are arranged chronologically. A chronological index of diaries extending over more than ten years precedes the main body. The volume ends with an index of names, anonymous diarists being excluded from the index though not from the main work.

Supplementing Matthews is John Stuart Batts, *British Manuscript Diaries of the Nineteenth Century: An Annotated Listing* (Totowa, N.J.: Rowman and Littlefield, 1976) [Z6611.B6 B38 1976]. This work contains over 3,000 diaries started after 1800, listed chronologically. Included are some already listed in Matthews, with or without additional information, and many here are listed for the first time. Entries give descriptions of the writer, the diary's content, and its location. An appendix lists nineteenth-century diaries the dates of which have not been precisely determined. There are indexes of diarists and of broad subjects, including places,

people, professions, and events. For American diaries see the companion bibliography by Matthews (G–46).

See also Jane DuPree Begos, *Annotated Bibliography of Published Women's Diaries* (Pound Ridge, N.Y.: Begos, 1977) [Z7963.B6 B44].

G–33 **Matthews, William.** *British Autobiographies: An Annotated Bibliography of British Autobiographies Published or Written before 1951.* Berkeley and Los Angeles: University of California Press, 1955.   Z2027.A9 M3

Entries on 6,654 autobiographies by native or naturalized Englishmen are arranged alphabetically, unless anonymous (in which case by title). Title, date, and brief descriptive annotations are given for each entry. A subject index to professions and occupations, places and regions, reminiscences, wars, and general events concludes the volume.

III.   AMERICAN BIOGRAPHY

G–35 *Dictionary of American Biography [DAB].* Edited by Allen Johnson and Dumas Malone. 20 vols. and Index. New York: Scribner's, 1928–1937. 6 Supplements [to the ends of 1935, 1940, 1945, 1950, 1955, and 1960 respectively]. New York: Charles Scribner's Sons, 1944, 1958, 1973, 1975, 1977, 1980.   E176.D563

This authoritative American national biographical dictionary was prepared under the auspices of the American Council of Learned Societies. The original volumes and supplements provide more than 15,000 long biographical articles on prominent but deceased Americans from colonial times to the present and on prominent foreigners who have resided in what is now the United States. Articles are signed and have bibliographies appended. They treat ancestry, parentage, education, and achievements, and range in length from 500 to 16,500 words. Articles are of uneven quality, and some incorrect dates make it advisable to verify them all. The original index volume is in six parts: biographical subjects, contributors, biographical subjects by state or country and city of birth, by schools or colleges attended, by occupation or profession, and an index to topics and subjects treated which includes titles of literary works. The supplements cover prominent Americans who died during the five-year period each covers; an index to all persons included in the first three supplements appears at the end of the third. The American Council of Learned Societies and Oxford University Press have announced plans for a new twenty-volume encyclopedia of American biography to be published in 1996 as a revision and updating of the *DAB*.

A précis of the larger work is provided in the *Concise Dictionary of American Biography [CDAB]*, 2d ed. (New York: Scribner's, 1977) [E176.D564 1977], which is an epitome of the original and first three supplements.

Since prominent women are not fully represented in the *DAB*, scholars may need to consult the similarly authoritative 1,359 entries in *Notable American Women, 1607–1950: A Biographical Dictionary*, ed. Edward T. James and Janet W. James, 3 vols. (Cambridge: Belknap Press of Harvard University, 1971) [CT3260 .N57], which was prepared under the auspices of Radcliffe College. A fourth volume, *Notable American Women: The Modern Period: A Biographical Dictionary*, ed. Barbara Sicherman and Carol Hurd Green (Cambridge: Harvard University Press, 1980) [CT3260 .N573], adds the biographies of 442 women whose deaths occurred between 1951 and the end of 1975.

A similar lack of representation of black Americans has led to a number of recent biographical reference works. The most extensive is the *Dictionary of American Negro Biography*, ed. Rayford W. Logan and Michael R. Winston (New York: Norton, 1982) [E185.96.D53 1982]. It has more than 700 signed entries written by specialists, with bibliographical references, all concerned with persons who died before 1970.

Now in course of publication is the comparable authoritative *Dictionary of Canadian Biography [DCB]* (Toronto: University of Toronto Press, 1966–) [F1005.D49], which will also run to a length of twenty volumes plus an index. Unlike the *DAB*, however, the *DCB* is arranged chronologically, with names alphabetical within their chronological place in the series. This work is being published simultaneously in English- and French-language editions.

G–36 Dargan, Marion. *Guide to American Biography.* Part 1, 1607–1815. Part 2, 1815–1933. Alburquerque: University of New Mexico Press, 1949–1952.   Z5305.U5 D32

A selective annotated bibliographical guide to biographical works on representative Americans, 1607–1933. For each outstanding person discussed (a total of 559 individuals) are listed original sources (including autobiographies, diaries, and letters); full-length biographies; entries in collective biographies; relevant books on history; works on special aspects of the individual's life; and cross-references to contemporaries whose lives are not readily seen to be related to the life of the subject person. Both parts are arranged in sections for each generation: 1607–1660, 1660–1715, 1715–1760, 1760–1815, 1815–1850, 1850–1901, and 1901–1933, with subsections for each of the leading states or regions. Individuals are then listed alphabetically. Each part has its own "Checklist of Books Cited Frequently." An index by occupations and an index of persons conclude each part.

G–37 *National Cyclopaedia of American Biography.* New York: James T. White, 1892–. Current Series. New York: James T. White, 1930–.   E176.N27

Though its articles are shorter and less scholarly than the ones in the *DAB*, the *National Cyclopaedia* is the most comprehensive collection of American biographies in any one source. The emphasis is on persons born after 1850 who hold or held high positions in government, professional, financial, industrial, or religious circles. Articles are unsigned, are derived from questionnaires, interviews, and information supplied by families, and generally include full name, field of work, birth date, parentage and ancestry, education, career history, honors and awards, organization memberships, religious and political affiliations, preferred recreation, date of marriage, children, and a portrait. It is published in both a Permanent Series and a Current Series. All volumes are arranged in rough chronological, rather than alphabetical, order, and each has an alphabetical index of the biographical subjects included. The volumes of the Permanent Series, containing biographies of deceased Americans, extended to volume 62 (1984). Volumes of the Current Series provide biographies of living Americans which are much fuller than the accounts in the biennial volumes of *Who's Who in America* (G–57). The Current Series was published every other year; volume 0 appeared in 1982. Beginning with volume N63 (1984), the two series have been combined, and subsequent volumes will treat both living and deceased individuals.

An index to volumes 1–52 and A–K was published in 1971; a revised Index, published in 1975, covers volumes 1–55 and A-L. The revised index brings together the names of biographical subjects in all volumes published through 1974, altogether more than 60,000 biographies in seventy-one volumes. Also indexed are professional subject headings such as "poetry" and "drama," under which are listed the names of

poets and dramatists whose biographies are included. Photographs are generally provided.

An old but still useful work (based in part upon the *National Cyclopaedia*) is *White's Conspectus of American Biography: A Tabulated Record of American History and Biography*, 2d ed., rev. and enl. (New York: James T. White, 1937) [E176.N28], which presents a list of important Americans in a chronological and classified arrangement so that the series of holders of particular offices, for example, may be identified. The revised edition of the *Conspectus* serves also as a subject index to the biographies in the *National Cyclopaedia* as of 1936.

G–38 *Appleton's Cyclopaedia of American Biography.* Edited by J. G. Wilson and John Fiske. 7 vols. New York: D. Appleton, 1888–1900. Reprinted with excisions under the title *Cyclopaedia of American Biography*. 6 vols. New York: Press Association Compilers, 1915.   E176.A666

Bibliographies of deceased Americans include native and adopted United States citizens and eminent citizens of Canada, Mexico, and other countries of the Americas, as well as foreigners closely connected with American history. Detailed but unsigned articles with portraits and facsimiles of autographs are arranged alphabetically by surname; family members are arranged chronologically rather than alphabetically by first names. This work must be used with caution: Margaret C. Schindler, in "Fictitious Biography," *AHR* 42 (1937): 680–690, has established that it contains an undetermined number of ghost biographies. See also Curtis D. MacDougall, *Hoaxes* (New York: Dover, 1958), 234 ff. [AG243 .M3 1958].

Among other nineteenth-century works of collected biography often recommended, see William Allen's *American Biographical Dictionary, Containing an Account of the Lives, Characters and Writing of the Most Eminent Persons Deceased in America from Its First Settlement*, 3d ed. (Boston: J. P. Jewett, 1857) [E176.A435], first published in 1809 and especially valuable, as all such early collections are, for its inclusion of many names since dropped from standard biographical dictionaries.

G–39 *American Biographical Archive [ABA].* Edited by Gerry Easter. Microfiche ed. with 4 vol. index. New York: K. G. Saur, Inc., 1986–.   CT211.A43 Guide 1987

This series of approximately 1,750 microfiche, with a hardcopy, four volume index presents a single alphabetical listing of the entries in 367 original English-language biographical dictionaries and other source volumes published from 1702 to 1920. Included are persons from the American colonies, the United States, and persons generally associated with America but not of American birth. Coverage is from the earliest period of American history through the early twentieth century. Where an individual has been treated in more than one source, the several biographical entries are reproduced in chronological order of their original publication. The index volumes are computer-generated, and include a complete bibliography of all of the source works.

G–42 Greenwood, Val D. *Researcher's Guide to American Genealogy.* 4th ed. Baltimore: Genealogical Publishing Co., 1973.   CS47.G73

This work is generally regarded as the definitive text on the subject of American genealogy; it includes a chapter on Canadian research as well. Other frequently recommended works include the guide published by the American Society of Genealogists, *Genealogical Research: Methods and Sources*, vol. 1, ed. Milton Rubincam and Jean Stephenson, 6th printing (Washington, D.C., 1966), and vol. 2, ed. Kenn

Stryker-Rodda, 2d printing (Washington, D.C., 1973) [CS16.A5]. Also recommended, as a particularly excellent introductory work, is Gilbert H. Doane's *Searching for Your Ancestors: The How and Why of Genealogy*, 5th ed. (Minneapolis: University of Minnesota Press, 1980) [CS16 .D6 1980]. Finally, the Newberry Library, one of the national centers of genealogical research, has published *Genealogy Beginner's Manual*, by Rick J. Ashton et al. (Chicago: Newberry Library, 1977) [CS16.A85 1977]. Further titles may be located in Filby (G–14).

G–45 **Chamberlain, Joshua L. *Universities and Their Sons . . . with Biographical Sketches and Portraits of Alumni and Recipients of Honorary Degrees.*** 5 vols. Boston: R. Herndon, 1898–1900.   LA225.C44

Chamberlain includes selected graduates of Harvard, Yale, Princeton, and Columbia.

Harvard graduates are systematically identified in the Massachusetts Historical Society's *Sibley's Harvard Graduates: Biographical Sketches of Those Who Attended Harvard College* [title varies], vol. 1–, 1642– (Boston: Massachusetts Historical Society, 1873–) [LD2139.S5].

Yale graduates will be found in Franklin B. Dexter's *Biographical Sketches of the Graduates of Yale College*, 6 vols. (New York: Holt, 1885–1912) [LD6323.D5], covering 1701–1815; *Biographical Notices . . . Including Those Graduated in Classes Later Than 1815* (New Haven, 1913), covering 1815–1884; and *Obituary Record of Graduates . . . 1859–1951* (New Haven, 1860–1951).

Princeton graduates are treated in the three volumes so far published of an ongoing retrospective series: *Princetonians, 1748–1768: A Biographical Dictionary*, by James McLachlan (Princeton, N.J.: Princeton University Press, 1976) [LD4601.M32]; *Princetonians, 1769–1775 . . .* , by Richard A. Harrison (1980) [LD4501.H37]; and *Princetonians, 1776–1783 . . .* also by Harrison (1981) [LD4601.H38].

G–46 **Matthews, William. *American Diaries: An Annotated Bibliography of American Diaries Written Prior to the Year 1861.*** University of California Publications in English, no. 16. Berkeley, 1945.   Z5305.U5 M3

A chronologically arranged annotated bibliography of published diaries written in English in America between 1629 and 1861. Entries give diarists, their dates, and their occupations. Annotations describe contents, including chief subjects, places, and persons discussed. Particularly interesting diaries are identified as such. There is an index to names but not to events and other subject matters.

This work is supplemented by Matthews's *American Diaries in Manuscript, 1580–1954: A Descriptive Bibliography* (Athens: University of Georgia Press, 1974) [Z5305.U5 M32], which enumerates 5,022 unpublished American diaries in some 350 libraries. It, too, is arranged chronologically. Entries cite diarists and time span of the diaries, describe contents, and identify the location of both the diary and any copies. An index to diarists concludes the volume.

Matthews has also compiled *Canadian Diaries and Autobiographies* (Berkeley and Los Angeles: University of California Press, 1950) [Z5305.C3 M3], covering both British and French Canadians and both published and unpublished works. See also Jane DuPree Begos, *Annotated Bibliography of Published Women's Diaries* (Pound Ridge, N.Y.: Begos, 1977) [Z7963.B6 B44], and Joyce D. Goodfriend, *Published Diaries and Letters of American Women: An Annotated Bibliography* (Boston: G. K. Hall, 1987) [Z5305.U5 G66 1987].

G–47 **Kaplan, Louis. *Bibliography of American Autobiographies.*** Madison: University of Wisconsin Press, 1961.
Z1224.K3

A bibliography of 6,377 autobiographies written by Americans from colonial days through 1945 arranged alphabetically by author with anonymous works listed by title. An extensive index to biographical subjects and to occupations, regions, and other subject features concludes the volume.

See also Richard G. Lillard, *American Life in Autobiography: A Descriptive Guide* (Stanford: Stanford University Press, 1956) [Z5301.L66], which is limited to twentieth-century works or reprintings of earlier works. It is arranged alphabetically by occupation or profession. Each entry gives the name of the author, birth and death dates, information on editions and reprintings, and an annotation on style and reader interest. There is a general index.

This volume is updated by Mary Louise Briscoe, ed., *American Autobiography, 1945–1980: A Bibliography* (Madison: University of Wisconsin Press, 1982) [Z5305.U5 A47 1982], which includes annotated entries for a wide range of modern autobiographies, including works by women, blacks, and representatives of diverse ethnic groups.

IV.   CONTEMPORARY BIOGRAPHY

For contemporary authors see also the various handbooks in section R, particularly those of Kunitz and Haycroft (R–21), Millett (R–8), and Harte and Riley (R–23).

G–50 ***Biographical Dictionaries Master Index [BDMI].*** 3 vols. Detroit: Gale Research Co., 1975–1977.   Z5305.U5 B56

A guide, supplemented twice [supplement 1 (1979); supplement 2 (1980)], to more than 725,000 biographies in fifty-three current biographical dictionaries including general, national and area, and vocational dictionaries. Stress is on American and English-language sources and persons. Entries give the subject's name, dates, and sources of current biographical information. Names are derived directly from the analyzed sources and are not edited into conformity; thus the same individual may appear under as many different entries as there are different ways of naming him. With some care, however, consultation of this index will prove a timesaving first step in the study of current biography. An eight-volume "second edition" has the title *Biography and Genealogy Master Index: A Consolidated Index to More Than 3,200,000 Biographical Sketches in over 300 Current and Retrospective Biographical Dictionaries*, ed. Miranda C. Herbert and Barbara McNeil (Detroit: Gale, 1980) [Z5305.U5 B57 1980]. A three-volume *Supplement* was published in 1982 and a two-volume *Supplement* in 1983. The "second edition" was republished in 1985.

An earlier index to current collected biography is that by Helen Hefling and Eva Richards, *Index to Contemporary Biography and Criticism*, rev. and ed. by Helen Hefling and Jesse W. Dyde (Boston: Faxon, 1934) [Z5301.H46], which analyzes 420 collections of biographical and critical material on persons born after 1850. A distinctive feature of this index is its exclusion of the most common biographical dictionaries (such as *Who's Who*, G–56); it is thus valuable for tracing more obscure citations.

G–55 ***Current Biography.*** New York: H. W. Wilson, 1940–.
CT100.C8

An average of 300–350 short biographical articles on currently newsworthy persons of all countries are published each year in monthly issues (except August), with annual and decennial cumulations. Entries normally include full name, date of birth, occupation, reason for prominence, address, a biographical sketch of several pages, a portrait, and references to additional sources of information. An index in each issue cumulates references to all entries for all issues of the year; each annual volume has an index that covers all persons included during the preceding decade. There is a separately published index, *Current Biography: Cumulative Index, 1940–70* (1973). In contrast with the entries for current biography in *Who's Who* (G–56) and related works, those in *Current Biography* are derived entirely from the research of the editorial staff rather than from data supplied by the biographical subjects.

A primary source for current biography of recently deceased persons is the obituary column. See the *New York Times Obituary Index, 1858–1968* (New York, 1969) [CT213.N47], which is, however, limited to the 353,000 names written about in the obituary columns. Those whose obituaries were located elsewhere in the paper must be found through the personal-name index to the general *New York Times Index* (D–23). Another *New York Times* publication of value to the student of current biography is the *New York Times Biographical Edition* [from 1974: *Service*]: *A Compilation of Current Biographical Information of General Interest*, vol. 1– (Ann Arbor, Mich.: University Microfilms 1970–) [CT120.N45], a weekly (monthly since 1974) reprinting of biographical articles from the *New York Times* with an index that cumulates every month and quarter and an annual cumulation of the entire work.

G–56 ***Who's Who: An Annual Biographical Dictionary, with Which Is Incorporated "Men and Women of the Time."*** London: Black, 1849–. DA28.W6

From 1849 to 1896 the work bearing this title was a list of British nobility and government officials; in 1897, the "First Year of New Issue," it became a current biographical dictionary of persons of merit. To be included, an individual must be a living British subject (there are a few exceptions permitted). Emphasis is on persons in government and public administration. Entries, using information supplied and updated by the biographical subjects themselves, are brief: they ordinarily include the subject's occupation, parentage, birth date, education, awards and titles, marriages, children, offices, publications, avocations, club memberships, address, and telephone number. For authors, works and their dates are cited; films and plays and their dates are cited for actors. Cross-references are provided to other family members whose biographies are found in the volume. Each year each subject is invited to correct and update the entry; thus information is quite current.

Among the volumes of collected biography, current and retrospective, which have developed from this original, see *Who's Who in America* (G–57) and the *International Who's Who* (G–58). There is also a retrospective series *Who Was Who: A Companion to "Who's Who" Containing the Biographies of Those Who Died during the Period [years]* (London: Black, 1929–) [DA28.W65], in which revised volumes are available for persons who died 1897–1915 (5th rev. ed., 1967), 1916–1928 (4th rev. ed., 1967), 1929–1940 (2d rev. ed., 1967), and decennial volumes for those who died 1941–1950 (1952), 1951–1960 (1961), and 1961–1970 (1972).

G–57 ***Who's Who in America: A Biographical Dictionary of Notable Living Men and Women.*** Chicago: A. N. Marquis, 1899–. E663.W56

A work parallel in every respect to the original *Who's Who* (G–56), except that subjects are residents of the United States or are outstanding foreigners. It is published biennially and lists some 66,000 living persons who have achieved prominence in government, the arts, science, business, or sports. Works and dates are cited for authors, composers, and artists.

This work also has a companion series for deceased persons, *Who Was Who in America: A Companion Biographical Reference Work to "Who's Who in America"* (Chicago: Marquis, 1942–) [E176.W64]. Published to date are volumes treating persons who died 1897–1942 (1943), 1943–1950 (1950), 1951–1960 (1960), 1961–1968 (1968), and 1969–1973 (1973). The last two volumes have cumulative indexes. There is also a single retrospective volume, *Who Was Who in America: Historical Volume, 1607–1896*, rev. ed. (Chicago: Marquis, 1967) [E176.W64 1967], which summarizes the lives of some 13,450 leading Americans of the period before *Who's Who in America* began publication.

G–58 ***International Who's Who.*** London: Europa Publications, 1935–. CT120.I5

This annual is parallel in every respect to the original *Who's Who* (G–56) save that it contains between 8,000 and 14,000 entries each year. Biographies are concise, based on questionnaires sent to selected subjects, and include name, title, dates, nationality, education, profession, career, present positions, achievements, publications, address, and telephone number.

V. SOUTH AMERICAN AND CONTINENTAL BIOGRAPHY

G–60 ***Allgemeine deutsche Biographie.*** Edited by the Historische Kommission bei der Königlichen [Bayerischen] Akademie der Wissenschaften. 56 vols. Leipzig: Duncker und Humblot, 1875–1912. CT1053.A5

This is the German equivalent of the *DNB*. The volumes include long, signed articles, with bibliographies, on German persons of note who died before the end of the nineteenth-century. The arrangement is alphabetical, with additions and corrections to articles often listed at the end of each volume. The fifty-sixth volume is a general register and index to the full set. Because of additions and corrections it should be consulted first to locate all materials pertaining to an individual. The *Neue deutsche Biographie* (G–61) will supplement this work, but is not intended to replace it.

G–61 ***Neue deutsche Biographie.*** Edited by the Hostorische Kommission bei der Bayerischen Akademie der Wissenschaften. Vol. 1–. Berlin: Duncker und Humblot, 1953–. CT1053.N4

This work is not meant to supersede the *Allgemeine deutsche Biographie* (G–60), but it does include many of the names from the older work. It also adds names of persons who have died since 1900 and before 1953, along with additions and corrections to the older work. It refers to articles in the previous work when no updating is required. The articles are relatively brief, are signed, and have good bibliographies of both primary and secondary works appended. Each volume has an index and lists of additions and corrections to past (i.e., previously published) volumes in the series.

G–62 *Deutsches Biographisches Archiv: Eine Kumulation aus 254 der wichtigsten biographischen Nachschlage werke für den deutschen Bereich bis zum Ausgang des neunzehnten Jahrhunderts.* Ed. by Bernhard Fabian. Microfiche ed. with 4 vol. index. New York: K. G. Saur, Inc., 1984–1986.

This series of 1,340 microfiche, with a four-volume, hardcopy index presents a single alphabet listing of the entries in 254 original German biographical dictionaries and other reference works published between 1700 and 1910. There are a total of approximately 400,000 entries which treat some 225,000 individuals. Entries are arranged alphabetically by the surname of the biographical subject, and then chronologically by the date of the reference work in which the biographical entry originally appeared. The index volumes are computer-generated and include a complete bibliography of all of the source works.

G–64 *Scandinavian Biographical Archive.* Microfiche ed. with 4 vol. index. New York: K. G. Saur, Inc., 1988–.

G–65 *Dictionnaire de biographie française.* Edited by M. Jules Balteau et al. Vol. 1–. Paris: Letouzey, 1929–. CT143.D5

This work, to be completed in twenty volumes, presents lengthy, authoritative, signed articles, with bibliographies appended. Included are outstanding inhabitants of France and her dependent territories and foreigners important in French history. No living persons are included. Until this French dictionary of national biography is complete, users will need to consult a variety of other sources. Though universal in scope, both Michaud (G–9) and Hoefer (see G–9) have a predominance of French individuals. For contemporary persons see the *Dictionnaire biographique français contemporain*, 2d ed. (Paris: Agence internationale de documentation contemporaine, 1954) [DC406 .D5], and its two *Supplements* (1955–1956), and the *Nouveau dictionnaire national des contemporains*, 4th ed. (Paris: Edition du Nouveau dictionnaire national des contemporains, 1966) [DC412 .N58]. There is also a *Who's Who in France / Qui est qui en France*, [date]: *Dictionnaire biographique des principales personnalités de France, des départements et territoires français d'Outre-Mer, des états africains d'expression française, de la République Malgache, de la principauté de Monaco, des français vivant à l'étranger et des étrangers notables résidant en France*, which has been published in Paris (Lafitte) biennially since 1953 [DC705.A1 W46].

G–66 *Archives Biographiques Françaises.* Microfiche ed. with 4 vol. index. New York: K. G. Saur, Inc., 1988–.

This work which will be published in approximately 1200 fiche, will contain a single alphabetical cumulation of biographical entries from approximately 180 biographical reference works published from 1647 through 1919, treating a total of some 150,000 individuals from the first century through 1914. Covered are persons born in France; those of French extraction born abroad, but returning to France or a French colony; French speakers and those of French ancestry living in Belgium, Luxembourg, or Switzerland; expatriates who lived in France for ten years or more or made a notable contribution during a shorter period of residence; colonials of French extraction born in or before the year preceding independence, and those holding office under French administration; and Canadians of French extraction. Multiple entries for the same individual are arranged chronologically in order of publication of the original source works. The index volumes are computer-generated and include a complete bibliography of all of the source volumes.

G–68 *Archivo Biografico de España, Portugal e Iberoamerica: una Compilacíon de 300 abras biográficas las más importantes y representativas, editadas entre el siglo XVII y los inicias del sigla XX.* Ed. by Victor Herrero Mediavilla and L. Rosa Aguayo Nayle. Microfiche ed. with 4 vol. Index. New York: K. G. Saur, Inc., 1986–.   CT1344.A73 1986

This series of approximately 1,500 microfiche, with a four-volume, hard-copy index presents a single alphabet listing of the entries in more than 600 volumes of 304 original biographical dictionaries and encyclopedias treating persons from South and Central America, Portugal, and Spain published between 1700 and 1920. Approximately half of the material pertains to Spain and Portugal, the Balearic and Canary Islands. The remaining material collected on a total of twenty-one Latin American countries is the first biographical cumulation for this part of the world. In addition, Portuguese provinces in Asia and Africa are also covered. There are entries on a total of approximately 300,000 individuals. In Spanish and Portuguese, the entries are arranged alphabetically by the surname of the biographical subject, and then chronologically by the date of the reference work in which the biographical entry originally appeared. Variant spellings of names and alternative names are cross-referenced. The index volumes are computer-generated and include a complete bibliography of all of the source works.

G–70 *Dizionario biografico degli Italiani.* Alberto M. Ghisalberti, general editor. Vol. 1–. Rome: Istituto della Enciclopedia Italiana fondata da Giovanni Treccani, 1960–.
CT1123.D5

This work, the Italian dictionary of national biography, is scheduled to be completed in some forty volumes. Long, authoritative, signed articles with bibliographies appended treat Italians from the fifth through the twentieth century, excluding living persons.

An important additional resource is Mario Emilio Cosenza, *Biographical and Bibliographical Dictionary of the Italian Humanists and of the World of Classical Scholarship in Italy, 1300–1800*, 2d ed., rev. and enl., 5 vols. (Boston: G. K. Hall, 1962) [Z7128.H9 C6], with a supplemental vol. 6 (1967). Cosenza has also compiled a *Checklist of Non-Italian Humanists, 1300–1800* (Boston: G. K. Hall, 1969) [PA83.C6 1969].

G–71 *Archivo Biografico Italiano.* Microfiche ed. with 4 vol. Index. New York: K. G. Saur, Inc., 1986–.

This work, consisting of approximately 1400 fiche, cumulates entries in 321 Italian biographical and reference works published between 1646 and 1931. A total of some 200,000 entries treat individuals from ancient classical philosophers to persons of the early 20th century. All regions of Italy are covered, along with persons from Dalmatia, Savoy, Malta, and Istria, as well as Sicily and Sardinia. Entries are arranged alphabetically, and where more than one source treats an individual, the several texts are arranged chronologically by the publication date of the original source volume. The computer-generated index volumes include a complete bibliography of all of the source works.

VI. ANCILLAE TO BIOGRAPHICAL STUDY

Portraits of authors will be found in numerous handbooks and dictionaries of literary biography including Kunitz and Haycroft (M–55, M–56, R–21, and S–27); *Chambers's Cyclopaedia of English Literature* (M–46); Fleischman's *Encyclopedia of World Literature in the Twentieth Century*; Herzberg's *Reader's Encyclopedia of American Literature* (S–41); and *McGraw-Hill Encyclopedia of World Drama* (U–22).

G–80 **A.L.A. Portrait Index: Index to Portraits Contained in Printed Books and Periodicals.** Edited by William Coolidge Lane and Nina E. Browne. Washington, D.C.: Government Printing Office, 1906.   N7620.A2

More than 120,000 portraits of about 40,000 persons are located in 6,216 volumes that represent 1,181 different titles. Brief entries are arranged alphabetically by surname and give the subject's dates, profession, the source of the portrait, name of artist, and name of engraver. Photographs are asterisked. There is a list of sourcebooks that contain more than five portraits each. The index is current to about 1904; it is indispensable for portraits of the nineteenth century and earlier but is weak on portraits of Americans, for which see the *Dictionary of American Portraits* (G–87).

G–81 **Singer, Hans W. Allgemeiner Bildniskatalog.** 14 vols. Leipzig: Karl W. Hiersemann, 1930–1936.   N7575.S56

These volumes contain an index to some 140,000 engraved portraits of all persons, countries, and times, as found in seventeen extensive German collections. Entries are arranged alphabetically by portrait subjects. A list of sources will be found in volume 1, a general index in volume 14.

A supplementary *Neuer Bildniskatalog*, 5 vols. (Leipzig: Hiersemann, 1937–1938) [N7575.S56], adds nearly 40,000 portrait paintings, sculptures, and photographs of nearly 20,000 persons of all countries and times. Entries give brief biographical descriptions and dates; they are arranged by surname and then by serially numbered portrait under the name of the subject. The fifth volume contains an index of occupations and professions and an index of artists.

For engraved British portraits see also the British Museum, Department of Prints and Drawings, *Catalogue of Engraved British Portraits in the Department*, 6 vols. (London: British Museum, 1908–1925) [NE265.L8 A5 1908], arranged alphabetically by sitter in volumes 1–4, with groups in volume 5 and a supplement and index in volume 6.

G–85 **Ormond, Richard, and Malcolm Rogers, gen. eds. Dictionary of British Portraiture.** 4 vols. New York: Oxford University Press, 1979–1982.   N7598.O5 1979

This work presents in compact form a handbook on portraits of famous British persons which are accessible to public view. The four volumes treat *Middle Ages to the Early Georgians: Historical Figures Born before 1700*; *The Late Georgians and Early Victorians: Historical Figures Born between 1700 and 1800*; *The Victorians: Historical Figures Born between 1800 and 1860*; and *The Twentieth Century: Historical Figures Born before 1900*. The first and fourth volumes were compiled by Adrianna Davies, the second and third by Elaine Kilmurray. Volumes 3 and 4 are forthcoming. Entries in each volume are alphabetical by the surname of the sitter and give the sitter's forenames, dates, and profession or occupation. There follows a list of all known portraits in the public domain, with a code signifying the category of medium. When there is more than one portrait available, they are listed

by medium, then chronologically, then alphabetically by the name of the artist. For each portrait are given the name of the artist, the date, size, other distinguishing features, medium, and location. There are no illustrations. The categories of media include painting, drawing, miniature, manuscript, silhouette, group portraits, sculpture, tapestry, stained-glass window, print, caricature, and photography.

G–86 **London. National Portrait Gallery. Concise Catalogue, 1856–1969.** Edited by Maureen Hill. London: Her Majesty's Stationery Office, 1970.   N7598.L58 1970

Alphabetical by the name of the portrayed subject, this volume is an index to the collection of the National Portrait Gallery. Entries specify the sitter's dates and occupation; the material support of paintings and the medium of drawings; and the size, artist, pose, and date of acquisition for each item in the collection. An appendix lists the names of sitters portrayed in a group or a collection of portraits. Under the appendix of unknown sitters are placed those portraits which contemporary research has shown are not of persons traditionally identified. An index of artists concludes the volume.

A supplement, *Concise Catalogue, 1970–76*, compiled by K. K. Yung (London, 1978) [N1090.A53], includes all acquisitions to December 1976. It is arranged into sections on single and double portraits, group portraits, and portrait collections, and gives information comparable to that found in the basic volume. An index of artists concludes the supplement.

The National Portrait Gallery is also publishing a series of elaborate *catalogues raisonnés* of portraits from individual periods. These volumes are arranged alphabetically by the name of the sitter and give a brief biographical account based on the entry in the *Concise DNB* (see G–10). Following this, each portrait in the National Portrait Gallery is discussed, in chronological order. Given are the accession number, artist, date, medium, size, and transcripts of signatures and other markings. A description of the portrait follows with an account of its history, condition, and available secondary literature. Then comes an account of the portrait's iconography, discussing relations to other portraits, other known images of the subject, and the like. These volumes end with indexes of owners and collections; artists; engravers, etchers, and lithographers; and photographers. To date, the following have been published:

Roy Strong, *Tudor and Jacobean Portraits*, 2 vols. (London: HMSO, 1969).   N7598.S7

David Piper, *Seventeenth Century Portraits in the National Portrait Gallery, 1625–1714* (Cambridge, 1963).

N1090.A598

John F, Kerslake, *Early Georgian Portraits* [1714–1760], 2 vols. (London; HMSO, 1977).   N7598.K43

Richard Walker, *Regency Portraits* [1790–1830], 2 vols. (London: National Portrait Gallery, 1985). ND1314.4

Richard Ormond, *Early Victorian Portraits* [1830–1860], 2 vols. (London: HMSO, 1974).   N7592.5.L66 1974

Planned volumes include *Mid–Georgian Portraits* [1760–1789], *Late Victorian Portraits* [1860–1890], *Edwardian Portraits* [1890–1910], and at least two volumes of modern portraits.

G–87 **Dictionary of American Portraits: 4045 Pictures of Important Americans from Earliest Times to the Beginning of the Twentieth Century.** Compiled by Hayward and Blanche Cirker et al. New York: Dover, 1967.   N7593.C53

This work includes a reproduction of what scholarship considers the most accurate portrait of each of 4,045 Americans and foreigners who lived on the American continent or contributed to American life in some vital way before 1905. The only exception to this terminal date is for presidents, vice presidents, chief justices, first ladies and White House hostesses. The portraits are arranged alphabetically under the best-known name of the subject; they are printed six to a page and are identified by the name, dates, and a brief phrase about the profession or vocation of their subjects. Reference is made to articles in the *DAB* (G–35) or in *Webster's Biographical Dictionary* (see G–8). A supplement lists notable persons selected for inclusion in this dictionary but for whom no available and authentic portrait could be located. A list of sources, a bibliography of published sources on American portraits, and an index of variant names are appended. The index is disposed into twenty-seven occupational and vocational classes; names are listed under all relevant categories, which include such divisions as Actors and Actresses, Poets, Playwrights, Authors: Fiction, and Authors: Non-Fiction.

Also useful for American portraits is the National Portrait Gallery's *Permanent Collection Illustrated Checklist*, comp. Linda T. Neumaier (Washington, D.C., 1978) [N857.8 .A66 1978], which, replacing the list of 1975, enumerates the more than 1,300 portraits now held by the NPG. Entries are in alphabetical order by the name of the sitter, with dates, a black-and-white photograph of the portrait, and a brief biographical designation; the name of the artist, printmaker, or photographer; the medium, measurements, and a brief description of the actual artwork; and the accession number. Group portraits are listed after the main catalog alphabetically by title; notable persons in groups are cross-referenced in the main catalog. The work concludes with an index of artists, printmakers, and photographers, and a list of their subjects.

Another important source is the two-volume *Catalogue of American Portraits in the New York Historical Society* (New Haven, 1974) [N7593.N5 1974] with its partly illustrated account of the 2,420 portraits held by the society.

ARCHIVES AND MANUSCRIPTS

See also entries in section B on general library resources as well as for discussions of holdings and resources of individual research libraries. See entries in section E. IV. For the role of manuscripts in the history of learning, see entries in K–98. And for the study of manuscripts in analytic bibliography and textual criticism, see section Y; see section Y also for works on collecting manuscripts and for works on the role of manuscripts in the history of libraries and librarianship.

I. GENERAL GUIDES TO THE LOCATION, STUDY, AND USE OF ARCHIVES AND MANUSCRIPTS

H–1 **Thorpe, James.** *Use of Manuscripts in Literary Research: Problems of Access and Literary Property Rights.* 2d ed. New York: *Modern Language Association*, 1979.
Z692.M28 T47 1979

This pamphlet, first published in 1974, was sponsored by the Committee on Research Activities of the MLA. It is disposed into three sections, treating Preliminaries, Access to Manuscripts, and Literary Property Rights, respectively. The topics covered in the first section include Locating Manuscripts, Research from a Distance, Visiting a Library, and Private Collections. The middle section on access is divided into discussions of The General Situation, Admittance, Regulations, Aids, Photocopies, and Permission to Publish. The section on Literary Property Rights, revised in the second edition to reflect the new (1976) United States copyright law, has the following subdivisions: Basic Facts, Copyright, Ownership of Copyrights, Unpublished Letters, Transfer of Literary Rights, Infringement of Literary Rights, Literary Rights in Other Countries, and International Copyright.

For a similarly helpful though rather dated treatment of procedures concerning the discovery of, and access to, manuscripts in booksellers' hands (and in private collections), see James M. Osborne's "The Search for English Literary Documents," in the *English Institute Annual* for 1939 (New York: Columbia University Press, 1940) [PE1010.E5].

H–2 **Madan, Falconer.** *Books in Manuscript: A Short Introduction to Their Study and Use, with a Chapter on Records and an Appendix.* 2d ed., rev. and corr. London: K. Paul, Trench, Trubner, 1920. Z105.M17

This somewhat out-of-date introduction to manuscripts treats

The Materials for Writing and The Forms of Manuscript Books, The History of Writing, Scribes and Scribal Conventions, Illumination, Scribal Errors and Their Analysis, Famous Manuscript Libraries, Famous Manuscripts, and concludes with a chapter on Public and Private Records. Three appendixes present a list of the published guides and catalogs of libraries holding 5,000 or more manuscripts (in 1920); a list of the chief manuscript catalogs of the British Museum, the Bodleian, and the Cambridge University Library; and a classified bibliography of aids for manuscript study. There are eight facsimiles and an index.

H–3 **Haselden, Reginald B.** *Scientific Aids for the Study of Manuscripts.* Oxford: Oxford University Press for the Bibliography Society, 1934. Z105.H34

This account of modern methods of studying manuscripts contains nine chapters: an Introduction; a chapter on the Care and Handling of Manuscripts; one on Light and Color; a fourth chapter on The Use of Illuminants and Light Filters; a fifth on Microscopes and Magnifiers; a sixth on Use of the Ultraviolet Lamp and Fluorescence; a seventh on Photography; an eighth on Measuring Instruments and The Analysis of Handwriting; and a ninth giving Samples of Problems and Their Solutions, including the treatment of palimpsests, deleted passages, and charred or faded pages. The work concludes with an index. There are a number of diagrams and sixteen collotype illustrations.

H–4 **Brooks, Philip C.** *Research in Archives: The Use of Unpublished Primary Sources.* Chicago: University of Chicago Press, 1969. D16.B87 1969

This discursive manual for users of archives is modeled on Max Bär's *Leitfaden für Archivbenutzer* (Leipzig: S. Hirzel, 1896) [CD955.B2], though its examples are drawn from the use of American historical archives. The seven chapters cover The Nature and Characteristics of Archives and Private Papers; The Types of Reference Works Available to Aid in Finding Primary Sources; The Relationship between Researchers and Archivists; The Nature of Limitations that can be imposed on Access to and Use of Archives; Note-taking and Copying; topics such as Authorship, Dating, and Authenticity Associated with the Criticism of Modern Unpublished Sources; and a discussion of Contemporary Developments in Archival Administration and Records Management. The volume concludes with a selected classified bibliography and an index of authors, titles, and subjects.

Though not designed as a manual, more elaborate bibliographies will be found in Frank B. Evans, *Modern Archives and*

Manuscripts: A Select Bibliography (Chicago: Society of American Archivists, 1975) [Z5140.E87], which focuses on United States archival theory and practice. It is divided into four parts and thirty-three chapters. Part I treats archives administration, with chapters on general bibliographical aids and the history of archives administration, among other topics. Part II surveys archival functions, with chapters listing works concerned with various archival activities from appraisal to preservation, and various archival specialties from cartographic collections to archives of oral history. Part III treats the archives of governments and organizations with chapters citing works on federal, state, business, university, and church archives and records. Part IV treats international archival developments, focusing on the archives of international organizations. Commentaries identify basic readings in each area and refer to supplementary works. There are indexes of subjects and authors.

Two introductions to archives refer particularly to British records. They are Frederick George Emmison's *Introduction to Archives* (London: Phillimore, 1978) [CD1043.3.E47 1978] and David Iredale's *Enjoying Archives: What They Are, Where to Find Them, How to Use Them* (London: David and Charles, 1973) [CD1041.I73]. Emmison briefly treats the main groups of British archives, the chief repositories, the nature and location of archives relating to places, the nature and location of archives relating to persons, and matters concerning public access to and use of such materials. Iredale has fourteen chapters, as follows: Research Methods, National Archives, Family Muniment Room, Cathedral, Parish Chest, Municipal Muniment Room, Company Safe, Solicitor's Office, Newspaper Office, Various Repositories, County Record Office, Some Records in the County Record Office, Palaeography, and Handwriting in England. Appendixes enumerate some record repositories in England and Wales and the names of some national record societies. A classified bibliography and index of subjects, authors, and a few titles conclude the volume.

H–5 Bordin, Ruth B., and Robert M. Waner. *Modern Manuscript Library.* New York: Scarecrow Press, 1966.
                                    Z110.C7 B6

This concise, well-organized volume contains nine chapters, each ending with a bibliography of suggested readings. The chapters are as follows: 1, Who Should Collect and What Should Be Collected; 2, How to Collect; 3, Processing a Collection; 4, Preparing Finding Aids (Calendars, Inventories, and Catalogs); 5, Problems with Contemporary Papers; 6, Administering the Library; 7, A Publications Program; 8, The Library and the Researcher; 9, The Library and the General Public. There is a further bibliography at the end of the volume, six appendixes illustrating various forms to use in manuscript administration, and a general index.

The Society of American Archivists has published a Basic Manual Series, *Archives and Manuscripts* (Chicago, 1977), each volume in which contains a selected bibliography. The authors and subtitles are as follows: David B. Gracy, *Arrangement and Description* [Z695.2.G73]; Maynard J. Brichford, *Appraisal and Accessioning* [CD950.B68]; John A. Fleckner, *Surveys* [CD950.F457]; Timothy Walch, *Security* [CD986.W34]; Sue E. Holbert, *Reference and Access* (including sections on finding aids, research, and copyright) [CD950.H64]. A classic British text with similar topics is Hilary Jenkinson's *Manual of Archive Administration* (Oxford: Clarendon Press, 1922) [HC56.C35 no. 4].

H–7 Martin, Charles Trice. *Record Interpreter: A Collection of Abbreviations, Latin Words, and Names Used in English Historical Manuscripts and Records.* 2d ed. London: Stevens, 1910.   Z111.M22

The original edition of this work (1892) was an amplification of the appendix to the ninth edition of Andrew Wright's *Court-Hand Restored; or, The Student's Assistant in Reading*

Old Deeds, Charters, Records, etc. (1879), one of the principal works of English paleography, originally published in 1772 (10th ed.; London: Stevens and Sons, 1912) [Z113.W95 1912]. Ten sections present abbreviations of Latin words used in English records; abbreviations of French words found in English records; a glossary of Latin words found in records and other English manuscripts but not occurring in classical authors; a list of Latin names of places in Great Britain and Ireland; the Latin names of bishoprics in England; in Scotland; and in Ireland; the Latin forms of English surnames; a list of Latin forenames with their English equivalents; and a number of additional lists, including addenda and corrigenda. Though there are a number of other works that can supplement *Record Interpreter*, from dictionaries to paleographical handbooks, no single volume brings together more that is helpful for the user of medieval and early modern English manuscripts and records.

There are, however, some briefer works of more limited scope which may be of use. See, for example, Frederick G. Emmison, *How to Read Local Archives, 1550–1700*, 2d ed. (London: Historical Association, 1967) [Z115.E5 E5], and K. C. Newton, *Medieval Local Records: A Reading Aid* (London: Historical Association, 1971) [Z113.N5]. For further help with Latin texts see Latham, *Revised Medieval Latin Word-List* (I–69).

H–8 Some Journals Concerned with the Administration, Study, and Use of Archives and Manuscripts Collections.

AA *American Archivist.* Vol. 1– Cedar Rapids, Iowa, etc.: Society of American Archivists. 1943–. 4/yr. Includes the annual bibliography "Writings on Archives, Current Records, and Historical Manuscripts" (see H–83). Index to vols. 1–20 (1938–1957).   CD3020.A45

Archives *Archives: The Journal of the British Records Association.* Vol. 1–. London: The Association, 1949–. 2/yr. Includes the important series of surveys of record office holdings, "Local Archives of Great Britain."   CD1.B7

Archivum: Revue internationale des archives. Vol. 1–. Paris: Presses universitaires de France, 1951–. 1/yr.   CD1.A18

CRL *College and Research Libraries.* Vol. 1–. Fulton, Mo., etc.: Association of College and Research Libraries, 1939–. 4/yr. 1939–1955; 6/yr. 1956–. Indexes to vols. 1–10 (1939–1940) with vol. 11; 11–15 (1950–1954) with vol. 16; 16–20 (1955–1959) with vol. 21.   Z671.C6

English Manuscript Studies 1100–1700. Vol. 1–. Oxford: Basil Blackwell, 1988–. 1/yr. Reviews.

Genealogist's Magazine. London: Society of Genealogists. 1925–. 4/yr.   CS410.S61

Journal of the Society of Archivists. [former title 1947–1954: *Bulletin of the Society of Archivists 1–14*]. Vol. 1–. London: The Society, 1947–. 2/yr.   CD23.S6 A3

Manuscripta. Vol. 1–. St. Louis: St. Louis University Library, 1957–. 3/yr. Reviews.   Z6602.M3

MSS *Manuscripts.* [former title 1948–1953: *Autograph Collectors Journal*]. Vol. 1–. Newton, Mass.: Manuscript Society, 1948–. 4/yr. Reviews. Index to vols. 1–11.   Z41.A3 A925

Scriptorium: Revue international des études relatives aux manuscrits / International Review of Manuscript Studies. Vol. 1–. Antwerp and Brussels: Standard Boekhandel, 1946/47–. 2/yr. Includes reviews, important international bibliographies, and a "Bulletin codicologique," giving a serially numbered, signed, annotated bibliography of contributions to manuscript studies, including facsimile editions.   Z108.S35

Year's Work in Archives. Vol. 1–. London: British Records Association, 1934–. 1/yr.   CD1040.Y4

Work concerning archives and manuscripts collections will also be found in history journals (F–10), in classical and modern philological and literary journals (L–57), and in the publications of major libraries (B–20 ff.).

H–9 **Weil, Gerald E., ed. *International Directory of Manuscripts Collections, Libraries, Private Collections, Repositories and Archives / Répertoire des bibliothèques, collections, dépôts de manuscrits et archives dans le monde.*** Paris: Berger-Lerault, 1978–.   Z6602.I57

When complete, this new directory will make it possible to locate particular manuscripts by institutions (from its address, present or past, place-name, or title), by language, or by catalog reference. The directory is under the sponsorship of the Centre d'analyse et de traitement automatique de la Bible et des traditions écrites at the University of Nancy. It will appear in two volumes, each with three parts. Volume 1 will cover manuscript collections in Europe; volume 2 will cover those outside Europe. The first part of each volume will present locations of collections in alphabetical order by country, town, and the name of the library, repository, private collection, or archive in question. Also in part 1 will be an alphabetical index of repository names, an index of all private collections treated, and an alphabetical index of all town names. The second part of each volume will present linguistic and documentary information on the manuscript collections. This will include identification of the languages of the manuscripts; a list of collections of incunabula, epigraphica, numismatics, musical manuscripts, and prints; a comparative glossary of terms; and addenda to part 1. Finally, part 3 of each volume will give a catalog of catalogs, listing for each country, town, and library, repository, private collection, or archive the titles and bibliographical details of all catalogs describing its manuscript holdings.

Published to date is part 1 of volume 1, which includes 3,209 European institutions reporting manuscript holdings. The work presents a list of institutions, an alphabetical index of institutional names, an alphabetical index of private collections, a record of cross-references, and a list of place-names (toponyms) with equivalents in German, English, Spanish, French, Italian, Dutch, and Portuguese, as warranted. Entries include an elaborate system of cross-references from alternative toponyms, including references from old place-names to current ones that are the result of political changes, and references from old locations to the new locations of transferred collections. The preface and introduction give details about the system of reference used and should be consulted. They and the work throughout are in English and French; in addition, there are synopses of the introduction in German, Spanish, Italian, Dutch, Portuguese, and Russian. It should be noted that the information in this first edition of part 1 is based on unverified responses to questionnaires returned by participating institutions.

II.   BRITISH REPOSITORIES

H–10 **Skeat, T. C. *Catalogues of the Manuscript Collections in the British Museum.*** Rev. ed. London: British Museum, 1962.   Z6621.B844 1962

First published in the *Journal of Documentation* 7 (1951): 18–60, this remains the most elaborate account of the various published and unpublished catalogs that enumerate and describe the vast manuscript holdings of the British Library. It is disposed into twenty-three sections, as follows: Introduction; the Collections of the Department of Manuscripts; Sloane and Additional Manuscripts, Arundel, Ashley, Burney, Cotton, Egerton, Hargrave, Harley, King's, Lansdowne, Royal, Stowe, and Yates Thompson Manuscripts; Charters and Rolls; Papyri; Greek Ostraca (potsherds with writing); Seals; Manuscript Facsimiles; Microfilms; Manuscripts on Permanent Loan; and a final section treating special catalogs of subjects, countries, and the famous 106-volume unpublished class (subject) slip index of the manuscripts collections.

British Library: Guide to the Catalogues and Indexes of the Department of Manuscripts, comp. M. A. E. Nickson (London: The Department, 1978) [Z6621.B8376B74 1978], provides a quick reference aid for students using or planning to use the collections. All the catalogs are briefly cited, without the abundance of detail regarding the collections found in the Skeat volume. Only the 1978 guide will give information about the several reference tools found or published since 1962 (see B–40).

H–11 **An Overview of Published Catalogs and Indexes of British Library Manuscript Collections Often Consulted by Students of English and American Language and Literature (see B–40).**

1. Sloane MSS 1–4100. 2 vols. with Index. 1782. Index. 1904.   Z6621.B85 S6
2. Cotton MSS. 1 vol. 1802.   Z6621.B85 C8
3. Harleian MSS 1–7639. 4 vols. 1808–1812.   Z6621.B85 H3
4. Old Royal Collections. 4 vols. with Index [with King's Collection]. 1921.   Z6621.B843
5. Lansdowne MSS 1–1245. 1 vol. 1819.   Z6621.B85 L3
6. Hargrave MSS 1–5141. 1 vol. 1818.   Z6621.B85 H2
7. Burney MSS 1–524. 1 vol. in 3 parts with Index [with Arundel MSS]. 1834–1840.   Z6621.B84 1834
8. King's or New Royal 1–446. 4 vols. with Index [with Old Royal MSS]. 1921.
9. Egerton MSS. With the additional MSS (no. 13 below).
10. Arundel MSS #1–550. 1 vol. in 3 parts with Index [with Burney MSS]. 1834–1840.   Z6621.B84 1834
11. Ashburnham MSS. 1 vol.
12. Stowe MSS 1–1085. 2 vols. with Index. 1895–1896.   Z6621.B85 A8
13. Additional MSS 1–4100. Same as Sloane MSS (no. 1 above).
14. #4101–5017. *Additions 1756–1782,* with Index. 1 vol. 1977.   Z6621.B837 B74
15. #5018–10018 and Egerton 1–606. *Additions 1783–1835,* with Index. 1 vol. 1849.   Z6621.B841 35a
16. #10019–11748 and Eg. 607–888. *Additions 1836–1840,* with Index. 1 vol. 1843.   Z6621. B842
17. #11749–15667 and Eg. 889–1139. *Additions 1841–1845,* with Index. 1 vol. 1850.   Z6621.B842
18. #15668–17277 and Eg. 1140–1149. *Additions 1846-1847,* with Index. 1 vol. 1864.   Z6621.B842

19. #17378–19719 and Eg. 1150–1636. *Additions 1848-1853*, with Index. 1 vol. 1868.　　　Z6621.B842

20. #19720–29909 and Eg. 1637–2399. *Additions 1854-1875*, with Index. 3 vols. 1875–1880.　Z6621.B842

21. #29910–31896 and Eg. 2400–2600. *Additions 1876-1881*, with Index. 1 vol. 1882.　　Z6621.B842

22. #31897–33344 and Eg. 2601–2678. *Additions 1882-1887*, with Index. 1 vol. 1889.　　Z6621.B842

23. #33345–34526 and Eg. 2679–2790. *Additions 1888-1893*, with Index. 1 vol. 1894.　　Z6621.B842

24. #34527–36297 and Eg. 2791–2826. *Additions 1849-1899*, with Index. 1 vol. 1901.　　Z6621.B842

25. #36298–37232 and Eg. 2827–2861. *Additions 1900-1905*, with Index. 1 vol. 1907.　　Z6621.B842

26. #37233–38091 and Eg. 2862–2889. *Additions 1906-1910*, with Index. 1 vol. 1912.　　Z6621.B842

27. #38092–39255 and Eg. 2890–2909. *Additions 1911-1915*, with Index. 1 vol. 1925.　　Z6621.B842

28. #39256–40015 and Eg. 2910–3030. *Additions 1916-1920*, with Index. 1 vol. 1933.　　Z6621.B842

29. #40016–41295 and Eg. 3031–3038. *Additions 1921-1925*, with Index. 1 vol. 1950.　　Z6621.B842

30. #41296–42181 and Eg. 3039–3048. *Additions 1926–1930*, with Index. 1 vol. 1959.　Z6621.B842

31. #42182–42864 and #43039–44085 and Eg. 3049–3135. *Additions 1931–1935*, with Index. 1 vol. 1967.
　　　　　　　　　　　　　　Z6621.B842

32. #42865–43038. *Lord Chamberlain's Plays, 1824–1851*, with Indexes. 1 vol. 1964.　　Z6621.B842

33. #44086–44835. *Gladstone Papers*, and #44836–46172 and Eg. 3135–3319. *Additions 1936–1945*, with Index. 1 vol. 1970.　　　　Z6621.B842

34. #46173–47458 and Eg. 3320–3675. [Looseleaf] 1946-1950.

35. #47459–48988 and Eg. 3676–3724. "Handlist" 1951-1955.

36. #48989–50483 and Eg. 3725–3764. "Handlist" 1956-1960.

37. #40584–53708 and Eg. 3765–3776. "Rough Register" 1961–1965. 1974.　　CD1042.A2 L56 vol. 7

38. #53709–56485 and Eg. 3777–3783. "Rough Register" 1966–1970. 1975.　　CD1042.A2 L56 vol. 8

39. #56486–59651 and Eg. 3784–3795. "Rough Register" 1971–1975. 1977.　　CD1042.A2 L56 vol. 10

40. #59652– and Eg. 3796–. "Rough Register" 1976–1980. 1 vol. 1982.　　Z6621.B837 B74 1982

41. *Index of Manuscripts in the British Library*. 10 vols. Cambridge. Eng.: Chadwyck-Healey, 1984–1985.
　　　　　　　　　　　Z921.L553 B74 1984

This *Index* is the first published which consolidates the names of persons and places found in more than thirty separate catalogs. More than one million entries include references to all collections acquired by the British Library to 1950.

See also the *British Museum Quarterly* (1926–) [AM101.B832] for descriptions of recent manuscript acquisitions. Many of the most important manuscripts have been microfilmed. See, among other reference aids, the *Register of Microfilms and Other Photocopies in the Department of Manuscripts, British Library* (London, 1976) [CD1042.A2 L56 vol. 9], which identifies 841 microfilms of manuscripts held and 299 films of manuscripts that have been exported from Britain since 1973.

Harvester Microform is publishing multiple series of *British Literary Manuscripts From the British Library*, London. *Series One: The English Renaissance: Literature from the Tudor Period to the Restoration* is published in six parts on a total of 109 reels [PR1121.B68 1986]. *Series Two: The Eighteenth Century* is published in several parts, two of which will be available in 1988.

H–12　**Madan, Falconer, et al.** ***Summary Catalogue of Western Manuscripts in the Bodleian Library, Oxford.*** 7 vols. in 8. Oxford: Clarendon Press, 1895–1953.　　Z6621.O94

Volume 1 gives a historical introduction and conspectus of shelfmarks. Volume 2 in two parts treats collections received before 1660 and miscellaneous manuscripts acquired in the nineteenth century. Volume 3 treats eighteenth-century acquisitions; Volumes 4 and 5 treat nineteenth-century additions; and volume 6 treats acquisitions of 1890–1904 and 1905–1915. Volume 7 is an index. In all, there are some 37,299 entries.

In addition to those descriptions found in the *Summary Catalogue*, see the more detailed accounts of the older manuscript collections in the Quarto Catalogues: *Catalogi Codicum Manuscriptorum Bibliothecae Bodleianae*, parts 1–14 (Oxford: Oxford University Press, 1858–1918) [Z6621.0942]. See also the Crum *First-Line Index of Poetical Manuscripts* (T–10), the catalog of O. Pächt and J. J. G. Alexander, *Illuminated Manuscripts in the Bodleian Library, Oxford*, 3 vols. (Oxford: Clarendon Press, 1966–1973) [ND2897.093 0936 1966]; and A. G. Watson's *Catalogue of Dated and Datable Manuscripts c. 435–1600 in Oxford Libraries*, 2 vols. (Oxford: Clarendon Press, 1984) [Z6620.G7 W37 1984]. Harvester Microform is publishing multiple series of *British Literary Manuscripts from the Bodleian Library, Oxford. Series One: The English Renaissance, c. 1500-c. 1700* is being published in several parts, the first two of which reproduce important poetry manuscripts.

A brief guide by H. H. E. Craster, *Western Manuscripts of the Bodleian Library*, was published in the series Helps for Students of History (London: SPCK, 1921) [Z6621.O96 W5].

For manuscripts in Oxford colleges see Paul Morgan's guide (B–49).

H–13　**Hardwick, Charles, and H. R. Luard.** ***Catalogue of the [Western] Manscripts Preserved in the Library of the University of Cambridge.*** 5 vols. plus Index. Cambridge: Cambridge University Press, 1856–1867.　　Z6621.C17 1856

These volumes contain descriptions of all Western manuscripts in the "two-letter classes" and additional manuscripts through B337. Arranged by shelf mark, descriptions include material, size, pages, columns, lines, style of hand(s), probable age, traces of original ownership and provenance, present condition, and whether published or collated. Contents notes follow. The subject matters of the manuscript classes are as follows: Anglo-Saxon and Early English Literature; Classical; Heraldic; Historical; Legal; Musical; Scientific, Medical, etc.; and Theological. This early catalog is supplemented by *Catalogue of Adversaria and Printed Books Containing Manuscript Notes Preserved in the Library of the University of Cambridge* (Cambridge: Cambridge University Press, 1864) [Z6621.C17 1864] which contains descriptions, notes, and an index of authors and annotators.

For acquisitions since the mid-nineteenth century see A. E. B. Owen, *Summary Guide to Accessions of Western Manuscripts (Other Than Medieval) since 1867* (Cambridge: Cambridge University Press, 1966) [Z6621.C173], which contains brief descriptions of some 4,500 of the nearly 7,700 additional manuscripts acquired through 1964, along with indexes of subject headings and personal names. A fuller catalog of accessions since 1867 is in preparation.

Manuscripts preserved in Cambridge colleges are included in the guide by A. N. L. Munby (B–51). A *Catalogue of Irish Manuscripts in Cambridge Libraries* has been prepared by Padraig DeBrun (Cambridge: Cambridge University Press,

1986) [Z6621.C193 I753 1986]. Harvester Microforms is publishing multiple series of *British Literary Manuscripts from Cambridge University Library*. *Series One: The Medieval Age, c. 1150–1500* [Z6611.L7 B68], and *Series Two: The English Renaissance, c. 1500-c. 1700* are available.

H–14 Some Other Catalogs of Important Manuscript Collections in British and Irish Repositories.

Aberdeen, Aberdeen University Library. *Catalogue of the Mediaeval Manuscripts in the University Library, Aberdeen*. Edited by M. R. James. Aberdeen, 1932.
Z6621.A13

Aberystwyth. National Library of Wales. *Handlist of Manuscripts. . ., 1940–1942 [annual].*

Dublin. Trinity College. *Catalogue of the Manuscripts in the Library ..., Edited by T. K. Abbott*. Dublin, 1900.
Z6621.D84

Edinburgh. Edinburgh University Library. *Index to Manuscripts*. 2 vols. Boston: G. K. Hall, 1964.
Z6621.E232

Edinburgh. National Library of Scotland. *Catalogue of Manuscripts Acquired since 1925*. 4 vols. Edinburgh, 1938–1980.
Z6621.E192

Edinburgh. NLS. *Summary Catalogue of the Advocates Manuscripts*. Edinburgh, 1970.
Z6621.E193 S36

Edinburgh. NLS. *Accessions of Manuscripts 1959–1964*. Edinburgh, 1964.
Z6621.S36

Edinburgh. NLS. *Accessions of Manuscripts 1965–1970*. Edinburgh, 1971.

Edinburgh, NLS. *British Literary Manuscripts from the National Library of Scotland Microform Series. Part 1: Medieval and Renaissance Literature, c. 1300-c. 1700. Part 2: Eighteenth Century Literary Manuscripts. Parts 3–4: Nineteenth Century Manuscripts*. Each part has a separately published inventory and descriptive catalog volume. 3 vols. (Brighton: Harvester Press, Microform Publications Ltd., 1986-1987) [PR9.B7 1986].

London. Lambeth Palace. *Catalogue of Manuscripts #1–1906*. Cambridge: Cambridge University Press, 1930–1932.
Z6621.L82J 1930

London. Lambeth Palace. *Catalogue of Manuscripts #1907–2340*. London: Oxford University Press, 1976.
Z6621.L8194

London. University College Library. *Manuscript Collection in the Library of University College, London*. London, 1978.
Z6621.L84515 1978

London. University of London. *Catalogue of the Manuscripts and Autograph Letters in the University Library*. Edited by R. A. Rye. London: University of London Press, 1921.
Z6621.L84

London. Victoria and Albert Museum. *Forster and Dyce Manuscript Collections*. Microform series in four parts. Part I: *Sixteenth and Seventeenth Century Manuscripts*; Part 2: *Eighteenth Century Manuscripts*; Part 3: *Nineteenth Century Manuscripts, Section A*; Part 4: *Nineteenth Century Manuscripts, Section B*. Each part has a separately published Descriptive Catalogue volume. Brighton: Harvester Press, Microform Publications Ltd., 1987.

Manchester. The John Rylands University Library of Manchester. *Handlist of English Manuscripts*. Edited by Moses Tyson. Manchester: Manchester University Press, 1929. *Supplements*. Manchester: Manchester University Press, 1935, 1951.
Z6621.M26 E5

Manchester. The John Rylands University Library. *Handlist of Additions to the Collection of English Manuscripts . . . 1952–1970*. Manchester: The Library, 1977.
Z6621.J693 E54

See also relevant sections of Robert B. Downs, *British Library Resources* (B–5).

H–15 Ker, Neil R. *Medieval Manuscripts in British Libraries.* 3 vols. Oxford: Clarendon Press, 1969–.
Z6620.G7 K4

This work lists manuscripts preserved in British repositories which were written before 1500 in Latin or a Western language either by reference to an existing catalog or by a new description. Descriptions are arranged alphabetically by the locality and then the institution in which the manuscript may be found. Within institutional listings the individual manuscripts are numbered either using the institution's own system or one provided by the compiler. Entries begin with a heading citing the date, place of origin, and provenance of the manuscript; this is followed by reference to an acceptable description already published or a more detailed description, including a short title, a list of the contents and, for each item contained, information about it (including bibliographical references). The descriptions conclude with the number of leaves and other codicological details about the manuscript, a discussion of its history, and information about its provenance.

The first volume, published in 1969, includes London institutions; volume 2, published in 1976, treats institutions located in places from Abbotsford to Keele, along with a brief addendum to volume 1; the third and final volume will conclude the alphabet of place-names. Excluded entirely are manuscripts in the British Library, the National Library of Scotland, the National Library of Wales, the Bodleian, and the Cambridge University Library, on the grounds that other catalogs are available (see H–10 ff.). Manuscripts in Anglo-Saxon are also excluded; see Ker's earlier catalog of those (H–10). The preface to volume 1 should be consulted before use, as should the amplifications of it which are prefaced to volume 2.

H–19 Born, Lester K., comp. *British Manuscripts Projects: A Checklist of the Microfilms Prepared in England and Wales for the American Council of Learned Societies, 1941–1945.* Washington, D.C.: Library of Congress, 1955.
Z6620.G7 U5

This checklist records the contents of 2,652 reels of microfilm which reproduce nearly 5,000,000 pages from rare and choice manuscripts preserved in England and Wales. The filming was done during World War II to preserve a record of the manuscripts that were, of course, in danger of destruction. Entries are alphabetical by repository, then collection name, and then in the numerical sequence of the manuscripts. Each entry gives the accepted designation of the manuscript by depository and manuscript name and number, a concise enumeration of its contents, and the number of the reel that contains the reproduction, as well as an indication of the manuscript's position on the reel. An index of personal names and place-names concludes the checklist.

III. AMERICAN REPOSITORIES

H–20 United States National Historical Publications Commission. *Guide to Archives and Manuscripts in the United States.* Edited by Philip M. Hamer. New Haven: Yale University Press, 1961.
CD3022.A45

This guide is intended to assist in locating groups of archives or manuscripts. It gives the location of approximately 20,000 collections, including the papers of some 7,600 prominent persons as well as those of numerous businesses and social and political organizations. The holdings of 1,300 repositories in the fifty states, the District of Columbia, Puerto Rico, and the Canal Zone are included; the repositories surveyed are listed alphabetically by state or district, then alphabetically by city or town. The address and director's name is given. The contents of collections exceeding a minimum of fifty items are then inventoried. For each such collection, summary descriptions are given about its approximate size, its major subjects, and prominent persons associated with it. Prominence is defined as citation in standard biographical references such as the *DAB* (G–35) or *Who's Who* (G–56). For each collection of personal papers, the information given includes place of residence, dates, and quantities of papers held. At the end of each repository's entry are listed available published guides or catalogs to individual collections. An index to all proper names and to subjects mentioned in the entries concludes the volume; the index, though thorough, is not a detailed subject analysis of the collections described. This guide has been succeeded, but not replaced, by the more recent *Directory of Archives and Manuscript Repositories* (H–21).

H–21 **National Historical Publications and Records Commission [NHPRC].** *Directory of Archives and Manuscript Repositories*. Washington, D.C.: NHPRC, 1978.

CD3020.U54 1978

This directory, which succeeds Hamer (H–20) but does not entirely replace it, presents information on about 3,250 libraries, historical societies, government agencies, and other United States institutions reporting holdings of documents, photographs, architectural drawings, oral history records, and other sources of value to historical inquiry. Entries are arranged alphabetically by state, town, and the name of the reporting repository. Each entry gives the name, address, telephone number, and hours of the repository. Information is provided as to the availability of copying facilities, rules of access to holdings, and acquisitions policy. Holdings are described in general terms (volume, inclusive dates, brief summaries of collection character), and published bibliographical reference works are cited. The volume concludes with an index to subjects and proper names as well as an index to institutions by type (including corporate archives, religious archives, and state historical societies). It should be noted that approximately 75 percent of the institutions reported on are not in the Hamer Guide (H–20), and about 84 percent are not in the *NUCMC* (H–22), which makes this work the most comprehensive of all available sources. It is, however, also the most general in its descriptions of actual records.

Further information about the work of the NHPRC is available from the commission's quarterly newsletter, *Annotation* (1973–) [E171.A73], and from the various papers included in Leslie W. Dunlap and Fred Shelley, eds., *Publication of American Historical Manuscripts* (Iowa City: University of Iowa Libraries, 1976) [Z286.H5 P83], which presents the proceedings of a conference of the NHPRC held at the University of Iowa. Of particular note is the fact that the directory does not report all of the information communicated to the NHPRC by contributing repositories. It includes information submitted before about mid–1977 but not the detailed descriptions of individual collections which were submitted. These descriptions have, however, been retained and computerized by the NHPRC and currently may be made available to researchers in the form of detailed reports on the archives and manuscripts of a particular institution, locality, or state. Inquiries about such reports should be directed to the Guide Staff, National Historical Publications and Records Commission, National Archives, Washington, DC 20408. Eventually, collection-level descriptions will be included in a planned multivolume *Guide to Historical Source Materials in the United States*, which will cover more than 100,000 collections and which will be made available in both hard-copy and microform editions.

H–22 *National Union Catalog of Manuscript Collections (NUCMC) [1959–]: Based on Reports from American Repositories of Manuscripts [1959–].* Ann Arbor, Mich. [place varies], 1962–.   Z6620.U5 N3

The volumes of this catalog present brief, serially numbered descriptions of more than 37,600 manuscript collections of fifty items or more in some 900 reporting American repositories. All together, these numbered collection reports are indexed by approximately 382,000 references to topics and to personal, family, corporate, and geographical names. Each volume presents reports received in the year or two prior to its publication; thus all volumes and all indexes must be checked since a collection's inclusion in a particular volume is determined only by the date on which it was reported.

Included are any large collections of papers from a common source, whether an individual, family, corporate entity, or subject matter. Also included are public and quasi-public collections and private manuscripts on deposit in public repositories. Small groups of items are excluded, as are public records located where one would expect to find them, and collections of photographic and other forms of manuscript reproductions. To date, the following volumes have been published: 1959–1961; 1962 with a cumulative index, 1959–1962; 1963–1964; 1965; 1966 with a cumulative of index, 1963–1966; 1967; 1968; 1969 with a cumulative index 1967–1969; 1970; 1971; 1972; 1973–1974 with a cumulative index 1970–1974. From 1975 on, publication has been in five-year cycles. There are four annual volumes (e.g., 1975, 1976, 1977, 1978), each with an index that cumulates all references of prior volumes in the cycle up to a final cumulative index every fifth year (e.g., 1979 with a cumulative index 1975–1979).

Although descriptions vary with respect to completeness and detail, each entry includes the title of the collection, its inclusive dates, its location, and its scope. Many include physical descriptions and information about other published or unpublished descriptions of the collection. Under scope, many descriptions enumerate the types and groupings of records, the subjects they concern, the persons associated with them, and any special features likely to be of research interest. Biographical data are often supplied. Arrangement in each volume is sequential by arrival of the repository's report; access by index is therefore essential. Indexes of names, subjects, and repositories are included in each volume published; they are cumulated as indicated above. The difficulty of using all the separate indexes has been somewhat alleviated by an *Index to Personal Names in the National Union Catalog of Manuscript Collections, 1959–1984* which has been published by Chadwyck-Healey (Cambridge, Eng., 1986) [Z6620.U5 I53 1987]. The most recent volume includes a geographical guide to all reporting repositories, 1959–1976, giving the state, locality, and *NUCMC* volumes in which reports of its collections are found. Also included is a general guide to repositories which arranges them by type (e.g., colleges and universities, museums, historical societies, etc.) and by subject areas. A list of contributing libraries gives their addresses and the entry numbers where their collections are described.

A work designed, among other things, to supplement the *NUCMC* for manuscript sources relating to black Americans is Wilber Schatz, *Directory of Afro-American Resources* (New York: Bowker, 1970) [Z1361.N39 R3], which provides references to 5,365 collections in 2,108 institutions.

For manuscripts in Canadian repositories see the *Union List of Manuscripts in Canadian Repositories/Catalogue collectif des manuscrits des archives canadiennes*, ed. E. Grace Maurice, rev. ed., 2 vols. (Ottawa: Public Archives, 1975) [CD3622.A2 U54 1975], reporting on holdings in 171 institutions. Sequentially numbered entries are arranged by repository, and then collection number. Main headings are the name of the individuals or bodies that received, created, or accumulated the papers. There is an index of persons, bodies, places, and selected subjects. A first supplement (1976) adds some 5,000 entries covering collections at sixty additional repositories; a second supplement (1979) adds 3,000 further entries from sixty-six repositories.

H–23 United States. Library of Congress. Manuscript Division. *Manuscripts on Microfilm: A Checklist of the Holdings in the Manuscript Division.* Compiled by Richard B. Bickel. Washington, D.C.: Library of Congress, 1975.
Z6621.U572 1975

Since the Library of Congress has one of the largest collections in the world of microfilmed manuscripts, this checklist is an important resource, particularly since these microfilms can generally be duplicated. Entries give the name and dates of the collections, a description of the material and the dates it spans, the location of the manuscript originals, the Library of Congress shelf number, the collection number in the *National Union Catalog of Manuscript Collections* (H–22), and the number of reels.

A series of important articles on various aspects of the microfilmed manuscript collection will be found in the *Quarterly Journal of the Library of Congress*, vol. 24 (July 1967), titled "Manuscripts on Microfilm: A Symposium." Of the many microfilmed manuscript collections held by the LC, the most important for students of English and American literature are the *British Manuscripts Project* (H–19) and the massive holdings of foreign manuscript materials relative to American history (see H–50). LC manuscript accessions are reported and described in annual accessions lists, *Library of Congress Acquistions: Manuscript Division* [1979–] (Washington, D.C.: The Library, 1981–) [Z733.L735 L48a]. For other aids to the use of Library of Congress manuscript holdings, see B–23.

H–24 *Guide to Literary Manuscripts in the Huntington Library.* San Marino, Calif.: Huntington Library, 1979.
Z6621.H527 H46 1979

The second of four new guides to the manuscript collections of the Huntington Library, this volume lists approximately 125,000 pieces by more than 1,000 authors. Excluded are manuscripts by authors who died before 1600; these are included in the *Guide to Medieval and Renaissance Manuscripts in the Huntington Library* (H–29). For inclusion in this guide an author must be identified as a literary figure in at least one standard biographical dictionary. Entries are alphabetical by author. Under each author are listed five categories of manuscript materials: verse (alphabetical by title or first line); prose; letters (the total number held and inclusive dates); documents (including checks, bills, wills, and the like); and other materials (such as annotations, marginalia, and the like). The volume concludes with a list of the twenty-eight-volume collection of commonplace books held by the Huntington, an alphabetical list of authors whose work is in the collection of Larpent Plays (see B–20), and a list of unidentified items.

This work replaces the earlier articles by Herbert C. Schulz, "American Literary Manuscripts in the Huntington Library," *HLQ* 22 (1959): 209–250, and "English Literary Manuscripts in the Huntington Library," *HLQ* 31 (1968): 251–302. In addition to the *Guide to Medieval and Renaissance Manuscripts* cited above, the complete series of five volumes includes a *Guide to American Historical Manuscripts* (H–52) and a *Guide to British Historical Manuscripts* (H–44). For general information on the Huntington collections see B–20.

H–25 *Catalog of Manuscripts of the Folger Shakespeare Library, Washington, D.C.* 3 vols. Boston: G. K. Hall, 1971.
Z6621.F6

A photographic reproduction of nearly 50,000 catalog cards with author, title, and subject analysis of the Folger's extensive collection of Renaissance and dramatic manuscript materials. For general information on the Folger collections see B–22. Publication of a *First Supplement* volume has been announced by G. K. Hall.

H–27 Some Other Guides and Catalogs of Important Manuscript Collections in American Repositories.

CtY
Beinecke Rare Books and Manuscript Library: A Guide to Its Collections. New Haven: Yale University Library, 1974. Z733.Y18 1974
Catalogue of Medieval and Renaissance Manuscripts in the Beinecke Rare Book and Manuscript Library, Yale University. Binghamton, N.Y.: Medieval and Renaissance Texts and Studies, 1984–.

MB
American Literary Manuscripts in the Boston Public Library. Boston: Boston Public Library, 1973.
Z6611.L7 B67 1973

MB
English Literary Manuscripts in the Boston Public Library: A Check List. Boston: Boston Public Library, 1966. Z6611.L7 B67 1966

MH
Catalogue of Manuscripts in the Houghton Library, Harvard University. 8 vols. Cambridge, Eng.: Chadwyck-Healey, 1986. Z6621.H5913 1986

MdHi
Manuscript Collections of the Maryland Historical Society. Baltimore: Maryland Historical Society, 1968. Z6623.M37

MWA
Catalogue of the Manuscript Collections of the American Antiquarian Society. 4 vols. Boston: G. K. Hall, 1979. Z1361.C6A43 1979

MWH
Catalog of Manuscripts in the Massachusetts Historical Society. 7 vols. Boston: G. K. Hall, 1969. Supplement. 2 vols. 1980. Z1295.M39 1969

MiU-C
Guide to the Manuscript Collections in the William L. Clements Library. Compiled by William S. Ewing. 3d ed. Boston: G.K. Hall, 1978.
Z6621.M63 M5 1978

MiU-C
Author/Title Catalog of Americana, 1493–1860, in the William L. Clements Library, University of Michigan. 7 vols. Boston: G. K. Hall, 1970.
Z1236.M53

MoSW
Guide to the Modern Literary Manuscripts in the Special Collections of the Washington University Libraries. St. Louis: Washington University Libraries, 1985. Z6611.L7 W37 1985.

NN
New York Public Library. *Dictionary Catalog of the Manuscript Division.* 2 vols. Boston: G. K. Hall, 1967. Z6621.N56

NN
New York Public Library. *Dictionary Catalog of the Berg Collection.* 5 vols. plus Supplement. Boston: G. K. Hall, 1969–1975. Z2011.N55

NNC
Manuscript Collections in the Columbia University Libraries: A Descriptive List. New York, 1959.
Z6621.N48

NNPM
Major Acquistions of the Pierpont Morgan Library, 1924–1974. Vol. 1; *Medieval and Renaissance Manuscripts.* Vol. 3; *Autograph Letters and Manuscripts.* New York, 1974.
Vol. 1: ND2920.P53 1974
Vol. 3: Z6621.P6512

NjP
Manuscript Collections of the Princeton University Library: An Introductory Survey. Compiled by

Alexander P. Clark. Princeton: Princeton University Library, 1958.   Z6621.P9 C6

WHi   *Guide to the Manuscripts of the Wisconsin Historical Society.* Madison, Wisc.: State Historical Society, 1944.   Z6621.W77

See also the many relevant entries in Robert B. Downs, *American Library Resources* and its *Supplements* (B–8).

H–28   **de Ricci, Seymour, and William J. Wilson. *Census of Medieval and Renaissance Manuscripts in the United States and Canada.*** 3 vols. New York: H. W. Wilson, 1935–1940. Supplement by W. H. Bond. New York: Bibliographical Society of America, 1962.   Z6620.U5 R5

This survey of manuscript holdings was performed under the auspices of the American Council of Learned Societies. Questionnaires and personal visits to public and private owners gathered information on all Western manuscripts written before about 1600 and held in the United States and Canada. Entries are ordered alphabetically by state, locality, and collection name. Individual manuscripts are then numbered, unless the local numeration was adequate. For each manuscript (or group of letters, charters, or deeds) reported on, a complete bibliographical description is provided, which includes authors and titles, incipits (as appropriate), physical description, details of current ownership and provenance, and references in the scholarly literature. Some 6,000 items are covered. A list of errata and addenda to the first two volumes is presented on pages 2239–2343 of volume 2. Volume 3 contains the indexes, which include a General Index of Names, Titles, and Headings; Scribes, Illuminators, and Cartographers; Gregory Numbers for Greek New Testament Manuscripts; Present Owners; and Previous Owners.

The *Supplement* was originated by C. W. Faye and continued and edited by Bond. It is limited to Western manuscripts written before 1600 and is arranged in parallel to the original volumes. For each manuscript the manuscript number or shelf mark is given, along with names of authors and titles of works included, and incipits. A physical description follows, including material, foliation or pagination, dimensions, origins, date, scribe, decoration, and binding. Provenance is then discussed and references to relevant scholarly literature are cited. After some pages of addenda the *Supplement* concludes with seven indexes and a concordance interrelating its contents with that of the original *Census* by corresponding pages and item numbers. The indexes include a general index supplementary to that in volume 3, as well as individual indexes of scribes, illuminators, cartographers, incipits, present owners, and former owners.

Also compiled by de Ricci in the same format "A Handlist of Latin Classical Manuscripts in American Libraries," *Philological Quarterly* 1 (April 1922): 100–108.

H–29   ***Guide to Medieval and Renaissance Manuscripts in the Huntington Library.*** By Consuelo Wager Dutschke with the assistance of Richard H. Rouse, et al. 2 vols. San Marino, Calif.: Huntington Library, 1988.   Z6621.H527.H46 1988

This work is the fourth and final guide to the manuscripts of the Huntington Library, sponsored in part by the National Endowment for the Humanities. The guide contains full descriptive entries for the more than 350 medieval and Renaissance codices at the Huntington, including information about the text of each volume, its physical description including detailed descriptions of art and illumination, its provenance, and relevant bibliography. An extensive collection of photographic plates of selected texts, miniatures, and decorations are included in volume 2.

This work will expand and update the Huntington Library entry in de Ricci's *Census of Medieval and Renaissance Manuscripts in the United States and Canada* (H–28).

IV.   THE MANUSCRIPT BOOK

H–30   **Ivy, G. S. "The Bibliography of the Manuscript-Book." In Francis Wormald and G. E. Wright, eds., *English Library before 1700,*** pp. 32–65. London: Athlone Press, 1958.   Z791.W7

Based on a lecture given in 1952, this chapter presents a general account of how the medieval manuscript-book was produced and of the features that distinguish it from a printed book. After an introductory segment the chapter is disposed into sections concerning makeup, scribal practice, and correction and decoration. There are four illustrations and extensive notes.

H–33   **Kristeller, Paul Oskar. *Latin Manuscript Books before 1600: A List of Printed Catalogues and Unpublished Inventories of Extant Collections.*** 3d ed. New York: Fordham University Press, 1965.   Z6601.A1 K7 1965

First published in *Traditio* 6 (1948): 227–317, and 9 (1953): 393–418, this work was originally compiled as an aid to the *Catalogus Translationum et Commentariorum* (I–115), though it has independent value as the most extensive bibliography available (ca. 4,000 items) of catalogs and inventories of pre–1600 Western manuscripts. It is divided into three main sections: (A) a list of works giving bibliographical or statistical treatments concerning libraries and their manuscript collections, arranged alphabetically by author or title; (B) a list of works describing manuscripts located in more than one city, arranged alphabetically by author or title; and (C) an enumeration of printed catalogs and handwritten inventories of manuscript collections in individual repositories, listed alphabetically by city name, and including cross-references to the pertinent sections of more general works cited in parts A and B. There follows supplementary material to each of the three sections, arranged in the same format as the original enumerations. Entries record the number of manuscripts included in a list. Catalogues and inventories concerning private collections and public archives are generally excluded.

With the publication under the direction of F. Edward Cranz of a *Microfilm Corpus of the Indexes to Printed Catalogues of Latin Manuscripts before 1600 A.D.* (New London, Conn.: Connecticut College Bookstore, 1982–), it is now possible to search all the indexes cited in Kristeller without consulting the individual volumes.

H–34   **Richardson, Ernest Cushing. *Union World Catalog of Manuscript Books: Preliminary Studies in Method. III. A List of Printed Catalogs of Manuscript Books.*** New York: H. W. Wilson, 1935.   Z6601.A1 R4

This volume, Richardson's third study preliminary to a World Catalog, is arranged alphabetically under the locality whose manuscripts the catalog describes. Under localities the works are listed alphabetically by author. Though valuable, this bibliography is incomplete, frequently inaccurate, and must be checked against other authorities.

V.   ENGLISH STUDIES—MANUSCRIPTS

H–40   **Ker, Neil R. *Catalogue of Manuscripts Containing Anglo-Saxon.*** Oxford: Clarendon Press, 1957. Z6605.A56 K4

The alphabetical arrangement of the entries follows first the name of the collector or locality of the repository and then the names of the manuscripts. An extensive introduction in seven sections treats the following topics: Humfrey Wanley and the First Catalog of Anglo-Saxon Texts (1705); The Scope and Method of the Present Catalog; Methods of Manuscript Description Followed; Notes on the Paleography and History of the Principal Manuscripts; Scribes and Scriptoria; a discussion of Manuscripts and Parts of Manuscripts Datable within Close Limits; and a discussion of Fragments. Lists of addenda and corrigenda are followed by the catalog proper. It contains entries for 402 serially numbered manuscripts (plus ten additional manuscripts that are lost or untraced). Each entry gives the dates of the manuscript as precisely as can be determined. Contents are itemized, the number of leaves is given, and all titles found in the manuscript are cited. The catalog proper is followed by an appendix of Manuscripts Containing Anglo-Saxon Written by Foreign Scribes; a Bibliography of Related Works; a Table of Aelfric's *Sermones Catholici*; and three indexes, of the contents of the manuscripts, of paleographical and historical information, and of owners and former owners. The index of contents treats anonymous works under generic headings, such as folklore; homilies . . . and lives of saints; poetry; proverbs, maxims, and apothegms; and glosses.

A supplement also compiled by N. R. Ker is published in *Anglo-Saxon England* 5 (1976): 121–131 [DA152.2 .A75]. Further "Addenda and Corrigenda" are provided by Mary Blockley in *Notes and Queries* N.S. 29 (1982): 1–3. For illuminated manuscripts, see further Thomas H. Ohlgren, ed. *Insular and Anglo-Saxon Illuminated Manuscripts: An Iconographic Catalogue, c. A. D. 625 to 1100* (New York: Garland, 1986) [ND3128.045 1986]. A supplement is scheduled in 1988. Latin manuscripts are cataloged in Helmut Gneuss, "Preliminary List of Manuscripts Written or Owned in England up to 1100," *Anglo-Saxon England* 9 (1981): 1–60. A revision of this list is scheduled for publication in 1988, also in *Anglo-Saxon England*.

H–42 **Ward, H. L. D., and J. A. Herbert, eds.** *Catalogue of Romances in the Department of Manuscripts.* 3 vols. London: British Museum, 1883–1910.   Z6621.B87 R7

Organized by romance types and titles, this catalog of prose and verse romances and related works preserved in manuscript in the British Library provides detailed descriptions of each manuscript. An index of manuscripts placed at the front of each volume provides access by manuscript name. For each romance treated, the catalog provides a description, a summary of the tale, a discussion of different versions, a list of other manuscripts in which it is found, discussion of its authorship and provenance, and bibliographical references to printed texts and to commentaries. Though out of date, the work remains standard. It must, however, be supplemented for current information by the relevant volumes of Wells (N–30) and Severs (N–32).

H–43 **Gudat-Figge, Gisela.** *Catalogue of Manuscripts Containing Middle English Romances.* Munich: W. Fink, 1976.
        Z6611.L7 G83 1976

The volume, originally presented as a Bonn doctoral thesis in 1973, begins with a general two-part introduction to romance manuscripts as artifacts. It covers production methods, contents, and formats, as well as the literary-historical context of the romances and the provenance of the manuscripts that record them. The catalog proper follows, with an introduction discussing procedures and arrangement. Manuscripts are then enumerated alphabetically by locality, collection, and repository. Holdings of twenty-seven repositories are reported. The ninety-nine serially numbered entries give the current name of the manuscript and other names by which it has been known, its date, material and size, number of folios and collation, outward appearance, origin, format, contents, miscella-

neous information, and references to other descriptions. There are three indexes. The first is of shelf marks and the names of manuscripts described or referred to. The second is of titles of romances described or referred to. The third is of personal names, including scribes, owners, and others, but excluding names of famous collectors now used as part of the manuscript's offical shelf mark (e.g., Cotton, Harley).

H–44 *Guide to British Historical Manuscripts in the Huntington Library.* San Marino, Calif.: Huntington Library, 1982.
        DA32.5.H46 1982

This work is part of a multiyear project to provide current guides to the manuscript holdings of the Huntington Library. This volume contains descriptions of each collection in the field of British history; all together, some 450,000 pieces are discussed. Major collections include the Stowe, Ellesmere, Hastings, and Battle Abbey papers. Within the description of each collection, each class of papers is separately described, with reference made to names and other significant particulars including dates, subject matter, and the like. Items are given brief physical descriptions. An extensive dictionary index of persons, places, and subjects concludes the volume.

The other guides in this series are a *Guide to Literary Manuscripts* (H–24), a *Guide to American Historical Manuscripts* (H–52), and a *Guide to Medieval and Renaissance Manuscripts* (H–29). For general information on the library see B–20.

H–45 **Stratford, Jenny, ed.** *Arts Council Collection of Modern Literary Manuscripts 1963–1972: A Catalogue.* London: Turret Books, 1974.   Z661.L7 S77

This catalog describes some 200 volumes of modern literary manuscripts purchased by the Arts Council and located in various British repositories, chiefly the British Library. An appendix lists manuscripts acquired 1972–1974. An index of names concludes the volume.

H–48 **Beal, Peter, comp.** *Index of [English] Literary Manuscripts. Volume I, 1450–1625.* 2 parts. London: Mansell; New York: R. R. Bowker, 1980. *Volume II, 1625–1700. Part 1, A–K.* 1987. *Volume III, 1700–1800. Part 1, A–F.* 1988. Comp. by Margaret M. Smith with Penny Boumelha. *Volume IV, 1800–1900. Part 1, A–G.* Comp. by Barbara Rosenbaum and Pamela White. 1982.   Z6611.L7 I5

These are the first of a series of volumes being prepared under the general editorship of John Horden at the Institute of Bibliography and Textual Criticism, Leeds University, which together will list, describe, and locate more than 40,000 literary texts and other manuscript materials related to some 300 major British writers who flourished between 1450 and 1900. The last volume published will be a detailed index of titles, first lines, names, and repositories. The series should be complete in 1990.

The first volume, in two parts, records the manuscripts of seventy-two Renaissance writers including Andrews, Bacon, Campion, Donne, Jonson, Marlowe, Raleigh, Shakespeare, Spenser, and Wyatt who were selected on the basis of their inclusion in the *Concise Cambridge Bibliography of English Literature* (M–10). Volume 2, part 1 includes Browne, Bunyan, Congreve, Dryden, Herrick, and Hobbes. Volume 3, part 1 records the manuscripts of twenty-one authors, including Addison, Blake, Burke, Burns, Chatterton, Cowper, Defoe, and Fielding. Volume 4, part 1 includes twenty-three nineteenth-century writers, among them Arnold, Austen, the Brontes, Browning, Byron, Coleridge, DeQuincy, Dickens, and George Eliot. The series of entries on each author is preceded by an introduction of variable length which includes an account of existing manuscripts, work that has been or is now being done on them, and other matters of interest to students. Discussion of autograph manuscripts of poems, novels, plays, and other literary works as well as notebooks, diaries, journals, corrected proof sheets, and marginalia is followed by an account of existing material of biographical interest, including wills and letters written to the author. Reference is made throughout to published texts.

The index proper uses a flexible system of letters and decimal numbers to identify each entry. A separate entry is found for each manuscript text (both autograph and scribal) of each separable work; thus almost one-fourth of the entries in volume 1, part 1 are devoted to the "manuscripts" of Donne's poems, which by this system number nearly 4,000. The entries are divided into the following categories for each author: Verse, Prose, Dramatic Works, Diaries and Notebooks, Marginalia in Printed Books and Manuscripts, and Miscellaneous; within each section entries are arranged alphabetically. Each is in four parts; the separate work is identified, the manuscript containing it is described (its hand or hands, date, variant title, state of completeness, provenance, and location are given), scholarly use of the text is reported (both original publication and subsequent authoritative editions), and a shelf mark with folio numbers is given. The volumes include a number of facsimiles of selected manuscripts.

The work has been criticized on two grounds. First, reviewers have questioned the value of recording every contemporary transcript. Second, the disassembling of manuscript volumes of poems, for example, makes it difficult to judge the quality of the "manuscript" of a particular work, since its quality depends on the quality of the full manuscript volume in which it is found. The final index volume will, apparently, reassemble the manuscript volumes analyzed in the index proper, and this will somewhat alleviate the problem by making it easier to visualize the complete contents and structure of whole manuscript volumes. In spite of these criticisms, however, the publication of this work has been widely celebrated, for it brings together in one place a vast amount of information from widely disparate sources.

Volume 2, Part 2 is scheduled to appear in November 1988; Volume 3, Part 2 is expected in May 1989; Volume 3, Part 3 is anticipated in early 1990; and Volume 4, Parts 2 and 3 are expected by February 1990, with the Index Volume 5 by the end of 1990.

VI.   AMERICAN STUDIES— MANUSCRIPTS

H–50   **Raimo, John W., comp.   *Guide to Manuscripts Relating to America in Great Britain and Ireland.*** Rev. ed. Westport, Conn.: Meckler, 1979.   Z1236.C74 1979

Sponsored by the British Association for American Studies, this volume is more than half again as long as its predecessor, originally published in 1961 under the editorship of Bernard R. Crick and Miriam Alman. The work lists by county, locality, repository, and collection-name manuscript materials in Great Britain, Northern Ireland, and the Republic of Ireland (Eire) relating to the history and literature—both construed in the widest possible sense—of the American colonies and the United States. Canadian material has also been included. Not recorded are materials already located in Charles McLean Andrews, *Guide to the Materials for American History, to 1873, in the Public Record Office of Great Britain*, 2 vols. (Washington, D.C., 1912–1914) [AC32.A5 no. 90A]; in Charles Mclean Andrews and Frances C. Davenport, *Guide to the Manuscript Materials for the History of the United States to 1783, in the British Museum, in Minor London Archives, and in the Libraries of Oxford and Cambridge* (Washington, D.C., 1908) [Z1237.A56]: or in Charles O. Paullin and Frederick C. Paxton, *Guide to the Materials in London Ar-*

chives for the History of the United States since 1783 (Washington, D.C., 1914) [AS32.A5 no. 90B]; all of which are volumes in the *Guides to Manuscript Materials for the History of the United States* series published by the Carnegie Institution in twenty-three volumes, 1906–1943 (see Sheehy, A–20, item DB 35, for a full list). In addition to further clarifying the scope and method of the volume, Raimo's introduction contains many helpful hints for the scholar considering a visit to British manuscript repositories. The volume concludes with an extensive, elaborate dictionary index of subjects and names of persons and places.

Complementing this work is Peter Snow's compilation *United States: A Guide to Library Holdings in the United Kingdom* (Westport, Conn.: Meckler, 1982) [Z1215.S64 1982], the result of a survey to establish the locations of printed, microform, and audiovisual materials. Holdings of more than 350 libraries are described, with a detailed index of subjects concluding the work.

There are comparable guides to manuscripts relating to America in other foreign repositories, such as Waldo G. Leland's two-volume *Guide to Materials for American History in the Libraries and Archives of Paris* (Washington, D.C.: Carnegie Institution, 1932–1943) [CD1198.U6 L4]. See the bibliography of such guides in the Library of Congress publication *Manuscripts on Microfilm* (H–23).

H–51   **Robbins, J. Albert, et al.   *American Literary Manuscripts [ALM]: A Checklist of Holdings in Academic, Historical, and Public Libraries, Museums, and Authors' Homes in the United States.*** 2d ed.   Athens: University of Georgia Press, 1977.   Z6620.U5 M6 1977

Sponsored by the American Literature Section of the Modern Language Association of America, this finding list by author is a complete revision of the 1960 first edition. The manuscripts reported held by some 600 libraries and other repositories are recorded; holdings of private persons and dealers are not listed. A total of 2,750 American authors are listed alphabetically, with birth and death dates and pseudonyms. Repositories holding manuscript materials relating to each author are then listed, using NUC symbols. For each repository the classes of materials held and item count in the class are given. The following symbols are used to identify the categories of material: MS—manuscripts (including original typescripts); J—journals or diaries; L—letters, postcards, telegrams, cablegrams; C—correspondence addressed to the author; D—other documents; MG—marginalia; PR—galley or page proofs; R—audio recording; M—memorabilia; REF—numbers of the reference works that treat manuscript holdings of the author, keyed to the list at the end of the volume. There follow two appendixes, the first citing cross-references and the second enumerating a list of authors for whom no holdings were reported.

The *Checklist* may be supplemented by Raimo (H–50) and by George Hendrick's "Checklist of American Literary Manuscripts in Australia, Canada, India, Israel, Japan, and New Zealand," *BB* 29 (1972): 84–86, 92, as well as by his "Checklist of American Literary Manuscripts in Continental Libraries," *BB* 25 (1967): 49–58. A general discussion by John C. Broderick, "American Literary Manuscripts: An Essay Review," *Resources for American Literary Study* 6 (1976): 70–78, provides further guidance.

H–52   ***Guide to American Historical Manuscripts in the Huntington Library.*** San Marino, Calif.: Huntington Library, 1979.   Z1236.H46 1979

The work is part of a multiyear project to provide current guides to the manuscript holdings of the Huntington Library. This volume presents a descriptive entry for each Huntington collection in the field of American history that contains forty or more pieces and was processed before September 1975. Entries contain the name, with birth and death dates, of the collection's originator or central figure; details as to the size of the collection and range of dates for items in it; a biographical sketch of the central figure; a brief description of the subject matter; a list of all significant persons associated with the collection if there are five or more letters, manuscripts, or documents concerning such persons; a brief physical description of the items; a review of the collection's provenance; and a bibliography of any further descriptions of the collection. The volume is concluded by an extended dictionary index of persons, places, and subjects.

The other volumes in this series are a *Guide to Literary Manuscripts* (H–24), a *Guide to Medieval and Renaissance Manuscripts* (H–29), and a *Guide to British Historical Manuscripts* (H–44). For general information on the Huntington Library see B–20.

H–53   **Katz, Joseph, gen. ed.**   ***Calendars of American Literary Manuscripts [CALM].***   Columbus: Ohio State University Press, 1967–.   LC numbers vary

Each volume in this series presents a descriptive inventory of all the known manuscripts of a single American author. Entries are given in a classified alphanumeric order and include seven sections. The citation (heading) gives the title of the manuscript, the type of manuscript, the number of written sides, the writing medium, the purpose, the location symbol, and the call number. There follow transcripts of the title and the first line. Entries next present the collation, including the number of leaves, color, substance, paper type, dimensions, pagination, and details about physical condition. The date follows, either conjectural or specific. Contents are next specified, including the type of manuscript, the number of stanzas and lines included, and the relation of the text presented to various published versions. Finally, notes are added to supplement the description, as appropriate. Following the main body of classified entries are such additional features as a checklist of unlocated manuscripts, a table of cross-references, a table of paper types, a list of addenda, and indexes of names and titles and of repositories. Not all such elements are found in each volume, but most are. Further addenda to each volume were published in *Proof: The Yearbook of American Bibliographical and Textual Studies*, 1971–1975 (see Y–5). To date, the following volumes have appeared: the *Literary Manuscripts of Hart Crane*, ed. Kenneth A. Lohf (1967) [Z8198.1.L6]; the *Literary Manuscripts of Upton Sinclair*, ed. Ronald Gottesman and Charles L. P. Silet (1973) [Z8819.5.G66]; and the *Literary Manuscripts of Henry David Thoreau*, ed. William L. Howarth (1974) [Z8873.H6].

H–54   **Cripe, Helen, and Diane Campbell.**   ***American Manuscripts 1763–1815: An Index to Documents Described in Auction Records and Dealers' Catalogues.***   Wilmington, Del.: Scholarly Resources, 1977.   Z1237.C89

This volume, under the sponsorship of the American Antiquarian Society, presents 32,483 serially numbered entries in chronological order for 1763 through 1815. In the chronology, undated or partly dated items follow those of more precise date: entries are thus in the order 9 October 1785, before October 1785, before [1785] (brackets indicating the conjectural dating in 1785). The chronological index is followed by a name index, presenting an alphabetical list of all individual and corporate names. Those associated with correspondence are further identified as S (sender) or R (receiver). Auction catalogs are identified by reference to their number in McKay (Y–63). An index of dealers' catalogs lists all of the 12,896 catalogs consulted. It should be noted that the manuscript materials here enumerated are those appearing in American auction records and dealers' catalogs; the materials need not

be of American origin nor pertain to American subject matter, though they generally do. Ephemera are excluded, but every effort has been made to include all items of potential value to historical research.

H–55   **Young, William C.** ***American Theatrical Arts: A Guide to Manuscript and Special Collections in the United States and Canada.***   Chicago: American Library Association, 1971.   Z6935.Y68

This volume presents entries describing the holdings of 138 repositories holding manuscript and primary collections on drama, drama criticism, and theater, including vaudeville and the circus. The introduction presents a list of the repositories whose holdings are described, with their *NUC* symbols. The volume is in two parts. The first is arranged alphabetically by states and then provinces. Within state and province, numbered entries are then given alphabetically by institutions, using the *NUC* symbols. Within each institutional entry, collections are identified by names and are also numbered. The second part, an index to the collections, persons, and subjects, has entries keyed to institution and collection numbers in the first part. An interesting feature is the grouping of persons under professional/occupational classes, including actors and actresses, authors, choreographers, composers, conductors, costume designers, critics, dancers, directors, entrepreneurs, impresarios, lighting designers, lyricists, opera singers, producers, singers, and teachers. There are also general entries for playbills, posters, and theaters.

VII.   BRITISH ARCHIVES

H–60   **Historical Manuscripts Commission.**   ***Record Repositories in Great Britain: A Geographical Directory.***   6th ed. London: H. M. Stationery Office, 1979.   CD1040.G73 1979

This edition of a standard guide first published in 1964 takes account of the substantial changes introduced by the reorganization of local administrative units in England and Wales in 1974 and in Scotland in 1975. Its aim is to list all repositories that regularly provide for public access and that preserve substantial collections of records. Repository types included are national record offices and libraries (government and parliamentary archives, and national libraries and museums); local record offices and libraries, as well as county and city record offices; university libraries, as well as those of colleges and other societies and educational institutions; and, finally, special libraries and archives, including those of nationalized industries, public utilities, and the archives of banking and other businesses. Entries are arranged under the current name of the county in which they are located in England, Wales, Scotland, Northern Ireland, Isle of Man, and the Channel Islands. Individual entries identify the name of the repository, its address, telephone, special archival jurisdictions (manorial and tithe records, ecclesiastical records, etc.), presiding officer, hours of opening, access restrictions, copying facilities, and a bibliography of printed guides or indexes to holdings. The introduction provides a brief summary of the kinds of repositories found in Great Britain. The main body is followed by a section entitled, "Other Useful Addresses," describing major organizations that aid the search for specific record materials; a bibliography of current reference works; and an index.

Among more specialized guides to British repositories may be noted Dorothy Mary Owen, *Records of the Established Church of England, Excluding Parochial Records* (London: British Records Association, 1970) [CD1041.O95], with a supplement published in *Archives* 10 (1971–1972): 53–56, and C. Kitching, *Central Records of the Church of England:*

A Report and Survey Presented to the Pilgrim and Radcliffe Trustees (London: CIO Publishing, 1976) [CD1069.L72 K57]. For parochial records see William E. Tate, *Parish Chest: A Study of the Records of Parochial Administration in England*, 3d ed. (Cambridge: Cambridge University Press, 1969) [CD1068.A2 T43 1969], and J. A. Tallis, *Original Parish Registers in Record Offices and Libraries* (Matlock: "Local Population Studies" for the Cambridge Group for the History of Population and Social Structure, 1974) [CD1068.A2 T27].

For county records see Frederick G. Emmison and Irving Gray, *County Records (Quarter Sessions, Petty Sessions, Clerk of the Peace and Lieutenancy)* (London: Historical Association, 1967) [CD1064.E6 1967], with its appendix on "Printed Catalogues and Transcripts of County Records."

H–61 Great Britain. Historical Manuscripts Commission. *Guide to the Reports [1870–1911] on Collections of Manuscripts of Private Families, Corporations, and Institutions in Great Britain and Ireland.* 2 vols. in 3. London: H. M. Stationery Office, 1914–1938.   DA25.M25

The first part of this guide presents a *Topographical Index* to the Reports of the Royal Commission on Historical Manuscripts which were published from 1870, the year after the Commission's first appointment, through 1911. The volume begins with a number of lists: of reports published but not otherwise referred to in the volume; of reports referred to; of short titles of reports referred to; and (at the end of the volume) a chronological index to the reports, giving exact dates of issue and other descriptive information. Between the opening's three lists and the chronological index occurs the topographical index proper, presenting an alphabetical list of places covered by the reports.

The second part of the guide, in two volumes, presents an index of persons mentioned in the reports. The first of those volumes, published in 1935, treats A-Lever; the second, published in 1938, concludes the alphabet of names and presents a list of addenda and corrigenda and some explanatory notes. It should be noted that the index to persons cites references to peers and bishops under their family names. These guides are continued by the *Guide to the Reports of the Royal Commission on Historical Manuscripts, 1911–1957*, part I, *Index of Places*, ed. A. S. C. Hall (London: H.M.S.O., 1973) [DA25.M1 G73 1973], and part II, *Index of Persons*, ed. A. S. C. Hall, 1 vol. in 3 (London: H.M.S.O., 1966) [DA25 .M1 G73 1966].

Her Majesty's Stationery Office publishes a frequently revised bibliographical aid, known as Sectional List 17, which enumerates the *Publications of the Royal Commission on Historical Manuscripts* and indicates their availability and current price. Recent activities of the commission may be followed in the annual *Reports of the Secretary to the Commissioners*, 1968/69–1978/79, and in the annual list of *Accessions to Repositories and Reports Added to the National Register of Archives* (1958–) [CD1042.A2 G74a].

H–62 The National Register of Archives.

The National Register of Archives, housed at Quality House, Quality Court, Chancery Lane, London, is a computerized index of persons cited in the reports of the Historical Manuscripts Commission. Also incorporated are references to other published and unpublished reports of archival holdings which have been analyzed, including such items as the guides to manuscripts held by the Boston Public Library and Lambeth Palace Library, to give some indication of the range of additional sources incorporated. Publications of the National Register of Archives include the *Bulletin*, nos. 1–9 (1948–1957), and the annual *List of Accessions to Repositories* (1958–) (see H–61).

In the absence of a published version of the National Register of Archives, students may find Philip Hepworth's *Select Biographical Sources: The Library Association Manuscript Survey* (London, 1971) [Z6616.A2 H4] of some value. It presents the results of a 1970 survey of manuscripts relating to persons which was undertaken by the Library Association. Given are the name, dates, and profession of each person cited, followed by the type of manuscript materials preserved (letters, proof copy, journals, and notebooks) and their location. But much more information is available from the National Register of Archives, which should be consulted by mail when undertaking any complete search for archival materials associated with a particular individual and preserved in British repositories.

H–65 *National Inventory of Documentary Sources in the United Kingdom.* Microfiche series. Cambridge, Eng.: Chadwyck-Healey, 1985–.   CD1040.N37

This series reproduces unpublished finding aids to archives and manuscript collections in the United Kingdom, accompanied by a machine readable names and subject index. Included are finding aids to the holdings of County Record Offices, university and public libraries, learned societies, professional institutions, museums, galleries, and private collections.

H–70 Galbraith, V. H. *Introduction to the Use of the [British] Public Records.* 2d ed. Oxford: Clarendon Press, 1954.
                    CD1043.G3

This volume, originally published in 1934, presents the substance of five lectures given at Oxford to graduate students beginning original research. Its aim is to give a simple, practical description of the chief classes of public records and of their interrelationships, as well as of the interrelationships of the various branches of the government charged with the administration of these records. The five chapters are as follows: 1, Introductory; 2, The Secretariat in the Middle Ages; the Records of the Chancery, the Privy Seal, and the Signet; 3, The Exchequer and the Legal Records; 4, The Transition to Modern Times; and 5, The Approach to Research. There are four appendixes: an invaluable list of books and references; rules and regulations made by the master of the rolls regarding public use of the public records; regulations regarding the opening of departmental records for scholarly research; and a list of places approved by the master of the rolls for the deposit of manorial records. The volume concludes with a brief index.

For more detailed discussion of certain particulars see Galbraith's *Studies in the Public Records* (London: T. Nelson, 1948) [CD1043.G32]. Other usefully brief accounts are the discussion of the Public Record Office of Hilary Jenkinson in the first edition of Raymond Irwin, the *Libraries of London* (see B–44), pp. 55–91, and the special report prepared by the Virginia Colonial Records Project on the *British Public Record Office* (Richmond: Virginia State Library, 1960) [CD3560.V53 no. 25/28].

H–71 Great Britain. Public Record Office. *Guide to the Contents of the Public Record Office.* Revised, to 1960, from the Guide by the Late M. S. Giuseppi. 2 vols. London: H.M. Stationery Office, 1963. Vol. 3, Documents Transferred 1960–1966. London: H.M. Stationery Office, 1969.
                    CS1043.A553

Volumes 1 and 2 deal with Legal Records and with State Papers and Departmental Records respectively. Both report on records transferred to the P. R. O. up to 31 August 1960. Both replace the earlier two-volume *Guide to the Manuscripts Preserved in the Public Record Office* by M. S. Giuseppi

(London: H.M.S.O., 1923–1924) [CD1043.A55], though they preserve its structure. Volume 1 presents a general introduction that includes a brief history of the P. R. O. and an account of the basic structure of the records. Records are divided into groups according to the courts or departments from which they have emanated; these groups are then further divided into classes, each of which has a distinctive name and a class number. Some records are made into artificial groups and artificial classes for the convenience of the record keepers. Classes are then divided chronologically, topographically, or alphabetically in serially numbered units or pieces (which may be individual rolls, or volumes, or bundles, or boxes), and these units may then be further numbered to indicate actual individual documents. The introduction also defines the various sorts of published and unpublished works that provide access to the records. Published works include numerical and descriptive lists of the items in particular classes; calendars that summarize the essential contents of items in a class; transcripts that attempt to reproduce faithfully the text of records in a class (with abbreviations expanded); indexes of persons or places or (rarely) subjects that appear in a class of records; and catalogs listing and describing miscellaneous collections of documents brought together for various purposes (e.g., display, a special subject interest, etc.). Unpublished aids include card indexes and manuscript lists and indexes that are found in the two main student reading rooms of the P. R. O.

Following the introduction, volume 1 enumerates and describes the various classes of legal records preserved, along with the available published and unpublished aids to their use. Treated are records of the King's Court (*Curia Regis*) and its administrative, financial, and judicial branches; the Chancery; the Exchequer; the Courts of Common Law; and other similar record groups. The volume concludes with a key to the dating system using regnal years, a list of abbreviations, a glossary, a brief index of persons and places, and a full index of subjects.

Volume 2 presents a similarly detailed enumeration of the various groups and classes of state papers and archives of government departments, along with the available published and unpublished aids to their use. It concludes with a key to regnal years, a list of abbreviations, and indexes of persons and places and of subjects.

Volume 3 supplements both of the earlier volumes, with corrigenda and addenda, including accessions through 1966. Accessions since 1960 are also recorded in the *Annual Report of the Keeper of the Public Records* (beginning with the second, for 1960) [JN329.P75 A3]. A useful aid for the student seeking access to the P. R. O. through published sources is the bibliographical pamphlet published by H.M. Stationery Office, Sectional List 24, *British National Archives* (H–72).

H–72 Great Britain. H.M. Stationery Office. *Government Publications: Sectional List No. 24* **[revised to 1 January 1980]: British National Archives.** London: H.M. Stationery Office, 1980.

A useful aid for the student, this frequently revised bibliographical guide identifies all H.M.S.O.-published works, listing current prices if the work is still in print or available through a reprint house. Contents are disposed into fourteen sections as follows: I. P.R.O. Calendars, Guides, etc.; II. P.R.O. Lists and Indexes; IIa. P.R.O. Lists and Indexes, Supplementary Series; III. P.R.O. Privy Council Registers; IV. *Rerum Britannicarum Medii Aevi Scriptores*; or, Chronicles and Memorials of Great Britain and Ireland during the Middle Ages; V. Publications of the Record Commissioners, etc.; VI. Works in Facsimile; VII. Micro-opaque Cards; VIII. Microfilms; IX. House of Lords Record Office Publications; X. Miscellaneous Publications; XI. Ireland; XII. Northern Ireland; XIII. Scotland. The pamphlet concludes with an index of persons, titles, and subjects.

H–75 Mullins, Edward Lindsay Carson. *Texts and Calendars: An Analytical Guide to Serial Publications [held in the library of the Royal Historical Society].* London: Royal Historical Society, 1958. Z2016.M8

This volume presents an analytical guide to Royal Historical Society library holdings of published texts and calendars of documents and other records relating to English and Welsh history which were issued in general collections and/or in series by a public body or a private society before the end of March 1957. Excluded are parish records publications and sources relating to the history of Scotland or Ireland. Included are works of reference, guides, and aids to historical research; enumeration of published texts and calendars; and some individual works that are included by the compiler though they are not part of a general collection or series.

The work is disposed into six parts. Part 1 enumerates the texts and calendars published by official bodies such as Record Commissioners, Commissions on Chronicles and Memorials, and Commissions on Historical Monuments. Part 2 is similarly comprehensive for the publications of national societies, such as the British Academy, the Caxton Society, the English Place-Name Society, and the Navy-Records. Part 3 presents the text and calendar publications of English local societies, such as the Buckinghamshire Record Society, the Kent Archaeological Society Records Branch, and the Bradford Historical and Antiquarian Society. Part 4 presents the publications of Welsh local societies such as the Historical Society of the Church in Wales and the South Wales and Monmouth Record Society. Part 5 enumerates addenda to the main body, and part 6 is an index of place-names and titles. Entries (numbered consecutively in each part) are given under the author's name or a short title; analytical notes describe the documentary contents of the volumes, the mode of presentation, the language, and so on.

A partial supplement to Mullins for Scottish publications is the *Handlist of Scottish and Welsh Record Publications*, ed. Peter Gouldesbrough, A. P. Kup, and Idwal Lewis (London: British Records Association, 1954) [CD1040.B71 no. 4], which presents a classified list of publications by forty-six Scottish and Welsh societies.

H–76 Mullins, Edward Lindsay Carson. *Guide to the Historical and Archaeological Publications of Societies in England and Wales, 1901–1933.* London: University of London, Athlone Press, 1968. Z5055.G6 M8

This volume, compiled for the Institute of Historical Research, includes the publications of more than 400 local and national societies relating to the history and archaeology of England, Wales, the Isle of Man, and the Channel Islands. There are 6,560 serially numbered entries followed by an elaborate analytical index of nearly 300 pages. A parallel enumeration for publications after 1933 is found in *Writings on British History* (F–15), from which publications of societies had been excluded (in the volumes for 1900–1933).

Additional guides to society publications include Robert Somerville, *Handlist of Record Publications* [by sixty-four English societies] (London: British Records Association 1951) [CD1040.B71 no. 3], which is concerned primarily with societies publishing from medieval records; and the recent volume by Joyce Youings, *Local Record Sources in Print and in Progress* (London: Historical Association, 1972) [Z2023 .Y68], which surveys recent and forthcoming publications related to record sources for English and Welsh local historical records. See also Sara E. Harcup, *Historical, Archaeological, and Kindred Societies in the British Isles: A List*, rev. ed. (London: University of London, 1968) [AS118 .H34 1968], published for the Institute of Historical Research.

VIII. AMERICAN ARCHIVES

H-80 Some Guides for Research in American Archives.

Among the most general aids for archival research in the United States is Ray Allen Billington's *Guides to American History Manuscript Collections in Libraries of the United States* (New York: P. Smith, 1952) [Z1236.B5], originally published in the *Mississippi Valley Historical Review* 38 (December 1951): 467–496, which surveys both union and individual guides to federal and state depositories, university and public libraries, historical societies, and private libraries.

Published inventories of state, county, and municipal records are listed in Sargent B. Child and Dorothy P. Holmes, *Check List of Historical Records Survey Publications*, rev. ed., (Washington, D.C.: Federal Works Agency, Work Projects Administration, Division of Service Projects, 1943; reprinted Baltimore, Md.: Genealogical Publications Company, 1969) [Z1223.Z7 C52].

The American Association for State and Local History publishes the biennial *Directory of Historical Societies and Agencies in the United States and Canada* (1966–) [E172.A538]. The Society of American Archivists has published a series of directories, including the *Directory of State and Provincial Archivists* (Chicago, 1968); the *Directory of State [and Provincial] Archives* (Austin, Tex., 1975) [CD3000.D57]; a directory of *College and University Archives in the United States and Canada* (Chicago, 1972) [CD3050.S6324]; the *Directory of Business Archives in the United States and Canada* (Chicago, 1975–) [no LC number]; and the *Directory of Religious Archivists and Historians in America* (Denver, Colo., 1963–) [no LC number]. There is also the *Directory of Genealogical Societies in the U.S.A. and Canada, with an Appended List of Independent Genealogical Periodicals*, by Mary Keysor Meyer, 6th ed. (Mt. Airy, Md.: Meyer, 1986) [CS44.M45 1986].

For municipal records see also E. Kay Kirkham, a *Handy Guide to Record-Searching in the Larger Cities of the United States* (Logan, Utah: Everton, 1974) [Z5305.U5 K57], as well as Houston Gwynne Jones, *Local Government Records: An Introduction to Their Management, Presentation, and Use* (Nashville: American Association for State and Local History, 1980) [CD3024.J66]. For religious archives see Kirkham, a *Survey of American Church Records*, 2d ed., 2 vols. (Salt Lake City, 1978) [CD3065.K5 1978]; for all archives see the reports in Hamer (H–20), the NHPRC Guide (H–21), and the *NUCMC* (H–22).

H-82 *National Inventory of Documentary Sources in the United States.* Microfiche series in four parts. Part 1. *Federal Records*; Part 2. *Manuscript Division, Library of Congress*; Part 3. *State Archives, State Libraries and State Historical Societies*; Part 4. *Academic and Research Libraries and other Repositories.* Cambridge, Eng.: Chadwyck-Healey, 1984–.
CD3050.N258 1984

This extensive microfiche collection reproduces published and unpublished finding aids, registers, indexes, and guides to selected archives and manuscript collections in the United States. Part 1 includes finding aids to the National Archives, the Smithsonian Institution Archives, and the seven Presidential Libraries. Part 3 includes State Archives, State Libraries, and State Historical Societies. The first two parts are published already, with an updating service available; the third and fourth parts are open-ended series, with continual additions.

H-83 "Writings on Archives, Historical Manuscripts, and Current Records: [1943–]." *American Archivist*. Cedar Rapids, Iowa [place varies]: Society of American Archivists, 1943–.
CD3020.A45

The title of this annual bibliography have varied over the years, as have its divisions. Currently, entries are disposed into nine sections, as follows: I. General Literature (bibliographies, general studies, manuals, and terminologies); II. Management of Current Records; III. Repositories: History, Organization, and Activities (United States, U.S. State and Local, Canada, Others); IV. Preservation, Restoration, and Storage of Records and Historical Manuscripts; V. Appraisal and Disposition of Manuscripts; VI. Arrangement and Description of Records and Manuscripts; VII. Use of Archives and Historical Manuscripts; VIII. Historical Editing and Documentary Publication; IX. Training and Professional Development. The bibliography is currently published about two years after the publication date of its citations.

H-85 U.S. National Archives and Records Service. *Guide to the National Archives of the United States.* Washington, D.C.: U. S. Government Printing Office, 1974.
CD3023.U54 1974

This massive guide, which includes information of all official records of the U.S. government accessioned by the National Archives as of 30 June 1970, supersedes the earlier guides of 1940 and 1948. The introduction treats the history of the National Archives, the organization of the guide, and the use of the records. It makes clear that record group is the basic term of reference in the national archives, being defined as a body of organizationally and functionally related records, generally those of a bureau or independent agency. At the end of the introduction is a chart showing the time span covered by each of the 409 record groups described in this guide. The descriptions are not in numerical order but rather are in organizational and chronological order within six major divisions. The six parts of the guide treat the following categories of records: 1, United States Government—General; 2, Records of the Legislative Branch; 3, Records of the Judicial Branch; 4, Records of the Executive Branch (subdivided into sections on Records of Presidential Agencies, Records of Executive Departments, and Records of Independent Agencies); 5, Records of or Relating to Other Governments; and 6, Other Holdings. Within each part of a subsection are described all of the record groups that belong within it, generally arranged in the order of creation of the agency or bureau from which the record group emanated.

The entry for each record group consists of a general description of the group and an annotated list of the commissions, committees, agencies, and other administrative units placed in the group. Annotation of the subgroups includes the types of record series and files available (reports, office files, correspondence, minutes of meetings, etc.), the years spanned, and a brief history of the administrative unit itself.

Three appendixes treat procedures for the public use of records, provide suggestions for citing records in print, and list the record groups in numerical order with reference to the pages in which each is described. The concluding index is limited to the names and functions of organizational units and to broad subjects mentioned in the text of the guide.

A briefer guide, *Your Government's Records in the National Archives* (Washington, D.C.: GPO, 1950) [CD3023.A46 1950], is available, as are a series of *Preliminary Inventories*, nos. 1–153 (1941–1963), which list records of particular agencies in more detail. Among more specialized reference aids see the serially published *Catalog of National Archives Microfilm Publications* (Washington, D.C., 1974) [CD3027.M514] and such works as the *American Indian* (1972), *Black Studies* (1973), and the *Guide to Genealogical Records* (1964). Current information about National Archives activity and publications may be gathered from *Prologue: The Journal of the National Archives*, published three times a year (Washington, D.C., 1969–) [CD3020.P75].

IX. PALEOGRAPHY

H–90 **Braswell, Laurel Nichols. *Western Manuscripts from Classical Antiquity to the Renaissance: A Handbook.*** New York: Garland, 1981.   Z105.B73 1981

This bibliography presents more than 2,000 annotated entries concerning the study of paleography. Entries are divided into sections on bibliographies, collections of primary sources, indexes of incipits and first lines, general studies of paleography, reference works, studies of scripts, works on papyrology, and guides to archives, to library holdings, and to the study of textual criticism.

H–93 **Hector, Leonard Charles. *Handwriting of English Documents.*** 2d ed. rev., London: Edward Arnold, 1966.
                                                 Z115.E5 H4 1966

Originally published in 1958, this work focuses on the hands written in England for administrative, legal, or business purposes since the Norman Conquest. A general introduction is followed by six chapters marked by the clarity and succinctness of their presentations. Chapter 1 treats the equipment of the writers, including surfaces, paper, formats, pens, and inks. Chapter 2 discusses the equipment of the reader, treating the languages used, with special focus on Medieval Latin and Anglo-Norman French. Chapter 3, on abbreviations, describes the medieval system, the methods of abbreviation, the types of abbreviation found in various records types, the abbreviation of proper names, and practices specific to Anglo-Norman, English, and postmedieval texts. Chapter 4 discusses scribal conventions and expedients. Chapter 5 offers a history of English handwriting from the conquest to 1500, and chapter 6 continues the history since 1500. A total of thirty-six plates present fifty-six facsimile illustrations of documents, with transcripts. A "table of confusibilia" (showing the possible identification of forms often mistaken on first impression), a classified bibliography, and an index conclude the volume.

H–94 **Denholm-Young, Noël. *Handwriting in England and Wales.*** 2d ed. Cardiff: University of Wales Press, 1964.
                                                 Z115.E5 D4 1964

A useful general treatment, originally published in 1954, with much detail and background information, though lacking the precision of Hector's presentation (H–93). Of the thirty-one plates of facsimiles, six are fully transcribed. The work is in eight chapters, as follows: 1, The History of Palaeography, How to Begin, Terminology, Handwriting in the West to c. A.D. 800, Old English Hands to c. A.D. 1200, Accents; 2, The Caroline Minuscule to the Development of the Gothic Script; 3, The Gothic Script; 4, Court Hands, Handwriting in Wales; 5, Localization, the Production of Manuscripts; 6, Abbreviations; 7, The Secretary Hand and the Coming of Italic; 8, Punctuation, Numerals, Mathematical Symbols, Musical Palaeography, Dating, How to Describe a Manuscript, Rules for Transmission. There are abundant footnotes and endnotes, and the volume concludes with a classified bibliography.

H–95 **Grieve, Hilda E. P. *Examples of English Handwriting, 1150–1750, with Transcripts and Translations.*** Part I, From Essex Parish Records. Part II, From Other Essex Archives. Essex Record Office Publications, no. 21. Chelmsford, 1954.   Z115.E G7 or
                                            DA670.E7 A17 no. 21

This compilation brings together a total of twenty-eight plates with full transcriptions, notes, and (when needed) translations, illustrating the history of English handwriting from local Essex documents. Accompanying the plates and transcriptions are illustrations of the alphabets of secretary hand and court hand, notes on the scripts by R. W. Hunt and on the abbreviations by N. R. Ker, and a short list of books for detailed study and reference.

H–96 **Thompson, Sir Edward Maunde. "The History of English Handwriting, A.D. 700–1400."** *Transactions of the Bibliographical Society* 5 (1898–1900): 109–142, 213–253.
                                                 Z671.L69

This survey remains valuable despite its date. Its author, formerly the Director and Principal Librarian of the British Museum, was a distinguished paleographer; his *Introduction to Greek and Latin Palaeography* (Oxford: Clarendon Press, 1912) [Z114.T472] remains the standard work in the field. This survey is complemented by Thompson's illustrated article, "Handwriting," in *Shakespeare's England*, ed. C. T. Onions et al., 2 vols. (Oxford: Clarendon Press, 1916), 1:284–310 [PR2910.S 1917], which carries the story into the seventeenth century. See also E. A. Lowe, "Handwriting," in *Legacy of the Middle Ages*, ed. C. G. Crump and E. F. Jacob (Oxford: Clarendon Press, 1926) [D113.5.C7].

H–100 **Bishop, Terence Alan Martyn. *English Caroline Minuscule [950–1100].*** Oxford: Clarendon Press, 1971.
                                                 Z115.E5 B57

This volume in the series of Oxford Palaeographical Handbooks provides an introduction and select bibliography, followed by twenty-four plates with twenty-eight facsimiles illustrating texts using the English Caroline minuscule hand. Facing each plate is a transcription and discussion of its text, including treatment of materials, script, related specimens, and bibliographical information. The transcribed facsimiles are followed by an index of manuscripts represented, identified by place, repository, and shelf number.

H–101 **Johnson, Charles, and Hilary Jenkinson. *English Court Hand, A.D. 1066 to 1500, Illustrated Chiefly from the Public Records.*** 2 vols. Oxford: Clarendon Press, 1915.
                                                 Z115.E J54

The two volumes of this standard work present its two parts: text and illustrations. The second volume contains both an atlas and forty-four plates offering a total of eighty-one documentary illustrations. The text in volume 1 presents an introduction giving a general sketch of the history of English court hand; an account of the system of abbreviations; hints on transcribing; a classified summary bibliography; and an account of the various classes of documents prepared with this hand. This is followed by an elaborate account of court hand, involving a history of each individual letter, and chapters treating the runes used, the ordinary abbreviations, the special abbreviations, conjoined letters, numerals, punctuation, punctuation marks, insertion, deletion, and finally a list of plates, a classified list of documents illustrated, and transcripts of the illustrated texts. The detailed chapters present an invaluable series of drawings illustrating the development of individual letters and other matters.

One may also wish to consult Jenkinson's *Palaeography and the Practical Study of Court Hand* (Cambridge: Cambridge University Press, 1915) [Z113.J36].

H–102 Parkes, Malcolm Beckwith. *English Cursive Book Hands 1250–1500.* Oxford: Clarendon Press, 1969.   Z115.E5 P37

A volume in the series of Oxford Palaeographical Handbooks, this work contains an introductory brief account of the origin and development of the major scripts in relation to the history of later medieval book production. This is followed by twenty-four plates with a total of fifty facsimile illustrations, each faced with detailed notes presenting criteria for the hand's classification and dating and a transcription.

H–103 Wright, Cyril Ernest. *English Vernacular Hands from the Twelfth to the Fifteenth Centuries.* Oxford: Clarendon Press, 1960.   Z115.E5 W7

A volume in the series of Oxford Palaeographical Handbooks, this work presents an introduction to the vernacular manuscript tradition and to vernacular handwriting, along with a select bibliography, followed by twenty-four plates of facsimile illustrations each conjoined with an introduction and description and a full transcription.

H–105 Jenkinson, Hilary. "Elizabethan Handwritings: A Preliminary Sketch." *The Library,* 4th ser., 3 (1922): 1–34.

This brief article presents a text, twelve plates, and transcriptions, giving a history and description of twenty-six different Elizabethan hands, including text, exchequer, chancery, legal, bastard secretary, general set hands, pipe roll, secretary and general free, as well as Italic. Other brief treatments include Muriel St. Clare Byrne, "Elizabethan Handwriting for Beginners," *RES* 1 (1925): 198–209, and the article on "Handwriting" in *Shakespeare's England* by Sir Edward Maunde Thompson (see H–91).

H–106 Dawson, Giles E., and Laetitia Kennedy-Skipton. *Elizabethan Handwriting, 1500–1650: A Manual.* New York: W. W. Norton, 1966.   Z115.E5 D38 1966

This volume, now the standard work on the secretary hand, consists of an introduction in five sections and a series of fifty-four plates with facsimiles, transcriptions, and commentaries. The introduction treats the survival of manuscripts; the handwriting of the Tudor and Stuart ages; historical development of the secretary hand; the mechanics of writing; some letters of the secretary hand, spelling, punctuation, abbreviation and contraction; and editorial principles and methods of study. A classified bibliography and an index conclude the volume.
Earlier volume-length treatments include Samuel A. Tannenbaum's the *Handwriting of the Renaissance: Being the Development and Characteristics of the Script of Shakespeare's Time* (New York: Columbia University Press, 1930) [Z113.T17] and Cyril B. Judge, *Specimens of Sixteenth Century English Handwriting Taken from Contemporary Public and Private Records* (Cambridge, Mass.: Harvard University Press, 1935) [Z113.J91]. For humanistic cursive scripts, also used in Elizabethan England, see Alfred Fairbank and Berthold Wolpe, *Renaissance Handwriting: An Anthology of Italic Scripts* (London: Faber and Faber, 1960) [Z115.I8 F3].

H–108 Whalley, Joyce Irene. *English Handwriting, 1540–1853: An Illustrated Survey Based on Material in the National Art Library, Victoria and Albert Museum.* London: H. M. Stationery Office,, 1969.   Z43.W5 1969

After a historical introduction, a brief survey of calligraphic material in the National Art Library, a bibliography of English calligraphic manuscripts in the National Art Library, a short-title catalog of English writing-books published before 1800 in the National Art Library, and a brief bibliography of further readings, there is a list of 100 illustrations, followed by 90 plates, each with descriptive annotation. The volume ends with a glossary of hands taken from Jenkinson's *Later Court Hands* (H–109) and a brief index.
The authoritative bibliography of English writing-books of this period is by Ambrose Heal, *English Writing-Masters and Their Copy-Books, 1570–1800: A Biographical Dictionary and a Bibliography, with an Introduction on the Development of Handwriting* by Stanley Morison (Cambridge: Cambridge University Press, 1931) [Z43.A2 H4]. Heal contains eighty-nine plates of illustrations; his bibliography includes some 1,315 serially numbered entries. There are appendixes on writing schools, engravers of copybooks, and booksellers' imprints; lists of addenda and errata; and an index of authors, titles, and subjects.

H–109 Jenkinson, Hilary. *Later Court Hands in England from the 15th to the 17th Century, Illustrated from the Common Paper of the Scriveners' Company of London, the English Writing Masters, and the Public Records.* 2 parts. Cambridge: Cambridge University Press, 1927.

Z115.E5 J57

Part I of this work contains an introduction surveying the documents, forms, materials, languages, and teaching of handwriting in the English Renaissance period. Letter forms of the fifteenth century, runes, and abbreviations are discussed, and then each of the leading hands is described at length, with sections on the bastard hands, set hands, free hands, the secretary hands, the Italic/Roman hands, mixed hands, special set hands, and text hands. Further sections treat personal marks, paragraphs and signatures, symbols and ciphers, numerals, and punctuation. A bibliography is followed by a list of archives preserving documents from this period, a chronology, and twenty sample alphabets. The portfolio of illustrations which constitutes part II provides forty-four facsimiles and transcriptions, and an index.

H–110 Petti, Anthony G. *English Literary Hands from Chaucer to Dryden.* Cambridge: Harvard University Press, 1977.

Z115.E5 P47

This work presents an introduction and sixty-seven plates. The introduction discusses the survival of literary manuscripts, the materials used in their production, and the terminology of their description, and presents a history of literary scripts. The plates offer facsimiles of manuscript texts written by fifty-two identified writers or their scribes. Each is accompanied by a transcription, a discussion of the hand, and an account of the sources and availability of other manuscripts by that author (or scribe). The work is concluded by a selected, classified bibliography and an index of authors, titles, and subjects.
An earlier, similarly conceived volume is W. W. Greg's *English Literary Autograph, 1550–1650* (London: Oxford University Press, 1932) [Z42.G82], which presents 100 plates illustrating the hands of 130 English authors at work during the century it covers. Of the plates, thirty each are given to illustrating the hands of dramatists, poets, and prose writers, and ten additional plates, illustrating a miscellaneous group of writers, are given in an appendix. They are arranged in each

part in rough chronological order. Introductions, transcriptions, and some paleographical notes accompany each plate.

H–111 **Croft, Peter John. *Autograph Poetry in the English Language: Facsimiles of Original Manuscripts from the Fourteenth to the Twentieth Century.*** 2 vols. New York: McGraw-Hill; London: Cassell, 1973.   PR1174.C75 1973

The two volumes are chronologically ordered. Volume 1 presents 146 plates illustrating autograph poetry from William Herbert to Robert Burns; volume 2 presents 197 plates illustrating autograph poetry from Robert Bloomfield to Dylan Thomas. An introduction, commentary, and transcript accompany each illustration. Volume 1 has a table of manuscript locations; indexes to all authors represented in the two volumes are located at the end of each volume.

H–115 **Some Other References of Use to Students of British Paleography.**

Schulz, H. C. "The Teaching of Handwriting in Tudor and Stuart Times." *HLQ* 6 (1943): 381–425.

Simpson, Grant G. *Scottish Handwriting, 1150–1650: An Introduction to the Reading of Documents.* Edinburgh, 1973.   Z115.S3 S55

H–120 **Kirkham, E. Kay. *Handwriting of American Records for a Period of 300 Years.*** Logan, Utah: Everton, 1973.
Z43.K55

This work, intended primarily for the use of genealogical researchers, treats American handwriting from the seventeenth through the nineteenth centuries. It is disposed into eight chapters. These cover The Use and Abuse of Original Records and Manuscripts; The History of Writing; Techniques to Use in Reading; The American Alphabet through 300 Years (with illustrations); Abbreviations, Contractions, etc. (with il-

lustrations); Numbers and Dates (with illustrations); Handwriting Examples from American Census Documents; and a discussion of Some Problem Areas. Two appendixes describe foreign alphabets and present a glossary of legal words, terms, and phrases.

Researchers may also wish to consult Kirkham's earlier work, *How to Read the Handwriting and Records of Early America* (Salt Lake City: Kay, 1961) [Z113.K5].

A recent overview of the early period is provided by Laetitia Yeandle in "The Evolution of Handwriting in the English-Speaking Colonies of North America," *American Archivist* 43 (1980): 294–311 [CD3020.A45].

H–123 **Cahoon, Herbert, Thomas V. Lange, and Charles Ryskamp, eds. *American Literary Autographs from Washington Irving to Henry James.*** New York: Dover, 1977.
Z43.2.A9 C34

This volume presents in ninety-eight plates illustrations from autographic American literary manuscripts held by the Pierpont Morgan Library. A checklist of American Literary Autographs in the Pierpont Morgan and an alphabetical list of authors conclude the work.

H–125 **Some Other References of Use to Students of American Paleography.**

Nash, Ray. *American Penmanship 1800–1850: A History of Writing and a Bibliography of Copybooks from Jankins to Spencer.* Worcester, Mass.: American Antiquarian Society, 1969.   Z43.A2 N26

———. *American Writing Masters and Copybooks: History and Bibliography through Colonial Times.* Boston: Colonial Society of Massachusetts, 1959.
Z43.A2 N28

LANGUAGE, LINGUISTICS, AND PHILOLOGY

I. BIBLIOGRAPHIES—LANGUAGE AND LINGUISTICS

Many of the general bibliographies of literature include extensive bibliographies of language and linguistics. See, for example, the *MLA International Bibliography* (L–50), the MHRA *Year's Work in Modern Language Studies* (L–52), the MHRA *Annual Bibliography of English Language and Literature* (M–21), and the *Year's Work in English Studies* (M–22). See also the leading bibliographies of national literatures. Many pertinent entries will be found in section X.IV, Rhetoric, Communications, and Discourse Theory; in section X.V, Style and Stylistics; and in section X.VI, Composition and the Teaching of Writing.

I–1 **Schmitter, Peter, et al.** *Bibliographie zur Linguistik: nach Themenkreisen.* 3d ed. Münster: Institut für allgemeine Sprachwissenschaft der Westfälischen Wilhelms-Universität, 1984.   Z7001.S33

Intended as a handy guide for students at the Institute for General Linguistics, this work provides an excellent selected bibliography of linguistic bibliographies, listing approximately 440 titles in the field. Bibliographies treating single regions or single languages are omitted; bibliographies of single linguists or schools of linguistics are included only when their subject is of the first importance. Entries are disposed into a systematic classification that moves from bibliographies of bibliographies to general bibliographies (of linguistics and of English, German, classical, Romance, and Slavic philology), then to special bibliographies of fields and subjects within the domain of linguistics (e.g., phonetics and phonology, morphology, grammar and syntax, generative transformational grammar, tagmemics, semantics, psycholinguistics, etc.), and finally to special bibliographies concerned with single authors and schools. An appendix describes the rules followed in constructing the bibliographic form of each entry. There is no index.

See also the bibliography by Hans-Dieter Kreuder, *Studienbibliographie Linguistik*, mit einem Anhang zur Sprechwissenschaft von Lothan Berger. 2d ed. (Wiesbaden: Steiner, 1982) [Z7001.K74] which offers a classified listing of German and English books and articles, some briefly annotated, and an author index.

I–2 **Allen, Harold B.** *Linguistics and English Linguistics* [A Goldentree Bibliography]. 2d ed. Arlington Heights, Ill.: AHM, 1977.   Z7001.A4 1977

This selective bibliography enumerates primarily twentieth-century works, with special emphasis on those published in 1922 or later. Excluded are publications in languages other than English, unpublished doctoral dissertations cited in *Dissertation Abstracts* (E–6), and articles in festschriften, proceedings, and other composite volumes. The 3,000 serially numbered entries, which give minimal bibliographical information, are classified according to eight major subject divisions: Bibliographies; Dictionaries and Glossaries; Collections of Festschriften; Miscellaneous Collections; Linguistics; English Linguistics; Special Topics; and Reading and Linguistics. The last four of these subject divisions are further classified into subtopics that are fully displayed in the table of contents. Essential items are indicated with an asterisk; critical review articles, reviews, and reviewing notices are listed in angular brackets within the entry for the reviewed item. Some cross-referencing is done. An author index concludes the volume.

I–3 **Rice, Frank, and Allene Guss, eds.** *Information Sources in Linguistics: A Bibliographical Handbook.* Washington, D.C.: Center for Applied Linguistics, 1965.   Z7001.R5

This brief, out-of-date student guide attempts to cover all the major traditional fields in linguistics, most major theoretical approaches to linguistic analysis, and most major fields of linguistics and related disciplines. Languages and groups of languages are covered only under the rubrics Language Families and Language Areas. Articles, festschriften, and monographic series published outside the United States are generally excluded except when judged indispensable. Arrangement of the 537 serially numbered entries is by subject within the following chapters: 1.1, General Works of Linguistics; 1.2, Terminology; 1.3, Phonetics and Phonemics; 1.4, Morphology and Syntax; 1.5, Semantics; 1.6, Lexicography and Lexicology; 1.7, Linguistic Geography and Dialectology; 1.8, Scripts, Writing Systems, Orthographies; 2.1, General Works on Linguistics and Related Disciplines; 2.2, Anthropological Linguistics; 2.3, Sociolinguistics; 2.4, Psycholinguistics (Including Child Language); 2.5, Mathematical and Computational Linguistics; 3.1, General Works in Applied Linguistics; 3.2, Language Teaching; 3.3, Translation; 3.4, Stylistics; 4, Abstracts; 5, Classification Systems; 6, Manpower. Within chapters entries are arranged—as warranted—under the following divisions: Bibliographies; Periodicals; Monographs; Congresses and Proceedings; Maps, Atlases, Handbooks;

Histories and Surveys; Theory and Method. An author index concludes this slim but exceptionally well designed guide.

The *Dictionary Catalog of the Library of the Center for Applied Linguistics*, 4 vols. (Boston: G. K. Hall, 1974) [Z7004.A6 C46 1974], presents the opposite bibliographical extreme, an unselected, alphabetically classified list of all titles in this large special collection, in the form of some 52,500 photolithographically reproduced catalog cards.

I-4 **Wawrzyszko, Aleksandra K.** *Bibliography of General Linguistics, English and American.* Hamden, Conn.: Archon, 1971.   Z7001.W35

A well-annotated advanced student bibliographical guide focusing on works in general linguistics published in the mid- and late 1960s. The 344 serially numbered entries are disposed into the following sections: Abbreviations, Directories; Bibliographies, Abstracts, Indexes; Current Bibliographies; Dictionaries and Glossaries; Encyclopedias of Linguistics; Theory and Philosophy of Language and Methodology of Linguistics; History of Linguistics; Grammars; History of Language and Historical Linguistics; Phonetics; Phonology; Morphology; Syntax; Semantics; Stylistics; Psycholinguistics; Sociolinguistics; Computational Linguistics; Translation; Study and Teaching; and a large section describing Linguistics Periodicals and Series Publications. The useful volume concludes with an author index and an index of periodicals and series titles.

I-5 **Gazdar, Gerald, Ewan Klein, and Geoffrey K. Pullum.** *Bibliography of Contemporary Linguistic Research.* New York: Garland, 1978.   Z7001.G38

This volume focuses on articles and short notes published since 1970, excluding those that appeared in the journal *Linguistics*. The 500 serially numbered entries give the author, date of publication, article title, journal name, and page numbers. There are indexes of languages and topics and a subject index that takes as terms elements naming general constraints on grammars; grammatical rules; problem areas in linguistic description; and particular lines of research or schools of thought. This work provides a way to secure a convenient overview bibliography on a particular topic in current research; it does not aim at completeness of coverage.

I-6 **Verschueren, Jef.** *Pragmatics: An Annotated Bibliography.* Amsterdam: John Benjamins, 1978. Z7004.P73 V47

This bibliography covers such topics as speech act theory, presuppositions, implicature, frame analysis, and the wide variety of other matters that concern the use and extralinguistic functions of language and the relations between such uses and functions and the structure of language. After a preface and list of abbreviations an unnumbered bibliography is presented with well-annotated entries listed alphabetically by author and chronologically beneath authors. The volume concludes with an index of subjects and one of languages. Supplements appear in the *Journal of Pragmatics*, vol. 2– (Amsterdam: North-Holland Publishing, 1978–) [P99.4 P72 J68].

I-7 ***Bibliographie linguistique de l'année [1939–] et complément des années précédentes / Linguistic Bibliography for the Year [1939–] and Supplement for Previous Years.*** Utrecht and Antwerp: Spectrum, 1949–.   Z7001.P4

Sponsored by the Permanent International Committee of Linguists, this annual bibliography lists books, articles, and reviews. It is international in scope with entries in their original languages; those in the rarer languages are accompanied by a translation into French or English. Entries are serially numbered and arranged alphabetically by author within the subcategory of the classified subject arrangement into which they fall. The entire bibliography is arranged in two main

sections: (1) General Linguistics and Related Fields and (2) Works on Language Families; the section on General Linguistics is preceded by a List of Analyzed Periodicals and a brief section on General Works (Bibliography, Reviews of Periodicals, Congresses, Festschriften and Miscellanies, and Biographical Works). The main subcategories in the first main section are as follows: Bibliography and General; Phonetics and Phonology; Grammar; Historical Linguistics; Linguistic Geography and Dialectology; Vocabulary; Script, Orthography; Stylistics; Prosody, Metre, and Versification; Translation; Mathematical Linguistics; Psycholinguistics; Sociolinguistics; Nonverbal Communication; and Onomastics. The subcategories in the section on language families are the names of the various families of languages (Indo-European, Asiatic and Mediterranean, etc.). The work is concluded by an index of authors, including authors of reviews whose names are given in the entries where the reviews are cited.

Volumes 1 and 2, published in 1949–1950, treated publications of 1939–1947; the annual volumes are now published some three to four years after the year covered; the 1982 volume was published in 1985.

In addition to the *Quarterly Check-List of Linguistics* (I–8), the *Bibliographie unselbständiger Literatur—Linguistik* (I–9), and the *Bulletin signalétique 524: Sciences du langage* (I–10), there are a number of other serial bibliographies that supplement and complement the annual *Linguistic Bibliography*. For anthropological linguistics see the quarterly *Abstracts in Anthropology*, vol. 1–. (Westport, Conn.: Greenwood, 1970–) [GN1.A15]; for computational linguistics see the quarterly *Language and Automation: An International Reference Publication*, No. 1– (Washington, D.C.: Center for Applied Linguistics, 1970–) [Z7004.L3 L35]; for general and applied linguistics, particularly in reference to pedagogy, see the quarterly *Language–Teaching Abstracts*, retitled *Language Teaching and Linguistics: Abstracts*, vol. 1– (London: Cambridge University Press, 1968–) [PB35.L32]; and for general language behavior and psycholinguistics see the quarterly *L.L.B.A.: Language and Language Behavior Abstracts*, vol. 1– (San Diego, Calif.: Sociological Abstracts, 1967–) [Z7001.L15]. The *MLA International Bibliography* has extensive coverage of linguistics (L–20), as do the MHRA bibliographies, the *Year's Work in Modern Language Studies* (L–22) and the *Annual Bibliography on English Language and Literature* (M–21), and the English Association's *Year's Work in English Studies* (M–22). Finally, linguistics is covered in all of the general bibliographical tools, from the *Bibliographical Index* (A–2) to the various current periodical indexes, dissertation indexes, and indexes to composite works.

I-8 ***Quarterly Check-List of Linguistics: An International Index of Current Books, Monographs, Brochures, and Separates.*** Darien, Conn.: American Bibliographical Service, 1958–1972.   Z7003.Q35

This quarterly checklist presented some 250–400 serially numbered entries describing current, separately published works in linguistics and related fields. Unclassified entries give author, editor, or translator; title and subtitle (with annotation to clarify, as needed); number of volumes; author of the introduction, foreword, or preface; series name; date of publication; size; pagination; presence of illustrations or bibliography; binding; publisher; and address. An index of authors, editors, and translators and a directory of publishers' addresses conclude each annual volume.

I-9 ***Bibliographie linguistischer Literatur: Bibliographie zur allgemeinen Linguistik und zur anglistischen, germanistischen, und romanistischen Linguistik [BLL]*** Vol. 1–, 1971/75–. Frankfurt am Main: Klostermann, 1976–.
                                                     Z7001.F7 1976

Published by the Stadt- und Universitätsbibliothek in Frankfurt, this quarterly catalog, the first three volumes of which were titled *Bibliographie unselbständiger Literatur— Linguistik [BUL-L]*, presents approximately 13,500 titles in the field of linguistics located in periodicals, proceedings, or composite volumes and thus not bibliographically independent. Lists of analyzed periodicals, proceedings, and composite volumes precede the bibliographical portion. Serially numbered entries are disposed into sections on General Linguistics, Germanistics, English, General Romance, French, Italian, Spanish, Portuguese, Romanian, and Rhaeto-Romanic. Each section is divided into Formal, Systematic, and Language History portions. The formal part cites bibliographies and other works; the systematic part is arranged by subjects from Phonetics to Rhetoric; the language history portion is arranged by historical periods and other sociohistorical categories. An individual article may be cited in up to four different places within this arrangement. A subject-author index concludes the volume.

A related publication of the Frankfurt Stadt- und Universitätsbibliothek is *Current Contents Linguistic / Inhaltsverzeichnisse linguistischer Fachzeitschriften [CCL]* [1974–] (Frankfurt, 1975–) [Z7003.F7 1976], which reprints the tables of contents of journals, proceedings, composite volumes, and working papers in the field of linguistics which are received by the Frankfurt library.

I–10 ***Bulletin signalétique 524: Sciences du langage.*** Paris: Centre national de la recherche scientifique [CNRS], 1947–.
P2.B84

One of the bibliographical series published by the Centre de documentation: Sciences humaines, this volume analyzes books, periodicals, proceedings, miscellanies, and other composite volumes in the field of linguistics, in quarterly issues, cumulated annually. Serially numbered entries are arranged alphabetically within a classification of eighteen topics, as follows: 1. Biology of Language; 2. Pathology of Language; 3. Psycholinguistics; 4. Sociolinguistics and Ethnolinguistics; 5. Comparison and Classification of Languages; 6. Diachronics; 7. History of Linguistics; 8. Epistemology and Methodology; 9. Philosophy of Language and Logic; 10. Linguistic Theories; 11. Descriptive Studies; 12. Linguistics and Mathematics; 13. Semiotics and Communication; 14. Literary Semiotics; 15. Applied Linguistics; 16. Congresses of Linguistics and Current Professional Activities [including works in progress]; 17. Biographies and Necrologies of Linguists; 18. Bibliographies. There are annual indexes of subjects, languages, and authors, along with a list of the periodicals (and composite volumes) analyzed.

I–11 ***American Speech: A Quarterly of Linguistic Usage.*** Vol. 1–. Tuscaloosa: University of Alabama Press for the American Dialect Society, 1925/26–.
PE2801.A6

This journal, the production of the American Dialect Society, included a current bibliography in each quarterly issue. This bibliography consisted of briefly annotated alphabetically arranged entries. They were in two sections: "Present-day English" and either "Phonetics" (in the first and third quarter) or "General and Historical Studies" (in the second and fourth). Each section had its own compiler(s).

Since the bibliography has been discontinued, most though not all issues have carried a list of books "Briefly Noted" after the fuller reviews. Currently, there is also a section titled "Bibliographical Department" which carries notices of bibliographical interest.

I–12 **Alston, R. C.** ***Bibliography of the English Language from the Invention of Printing to the Year 1800: A Systematic Record of Writings on English, and on Other Languages in English, Based on the Collections of the Principal Libraries of the World.*** Bradford and Leeds: Arnold [publisher varies], 1965–.
Z2015.A1 A4

This extraordinary series is projected to include some twenty volumes. Each volume contains a briefly annotated checklist of items, locating copies and giving bibliographical notes and references. Entries within the scope of each volume are arranged chronologically, then alphabetically by author. To date the following volumes have been published:

1. *English Grammars Written in English and English Grammars Written in Latin by Native Speakers* (Leeds, 1965).
2. *Polyglot Dictionaries and Grammars: Treatises on English Written for Speakers of French, German, Dutch, Danish, Swedish, Portuguese, Italian, Hungarian, Persian, Bengali, and Russian* (Bradford, 1967).
3. Part 1. *Old English, Middle English, Early Modern English, Miscellaneous Works; Vocabulary* (Leeds, 1970).
   Part 2. *Punctuation, Concordances, Origin of Language, Theory of Grammar* (Leeds, 1971).
4. *Spelling Books* (Leeds, 1967).
5. *English Dictionary* (Leeds, 1966).
6. *Rhetoric, Style, Elocution, Prosody, Rhyme, Pronunciation, Spelling Reform* (Leeds, 1969).
7. *Logic, Philosophy, Epistemology, Universal Language* (Bradford, 1967).
8. *Treatises on Short-hand* (Leeds, 1966).
9. *Non-Standard English; English Dialects; Scottish Dialects; Cant and Vulgar English* (Leeds, 1971). Supplement (1973).
10. *Place and Personal Names* (Leeds, 1972).
    Supplement: Additions and Corrections, vols. 1–10. List of Libraries, Cumulative Index (Leeds, 1973).

Projected volumes are to cover (11) Education; Teaching of Language; Surdomutism; (12) Romance Languages; (13) Germanic Languages; (14) Other Languages; (15) Latin Language 1500–1650; (16) Latin Language 1651–1800; Greek Language; (17) Vocabulary of Science, Technology, Arts, Crafts, Sports, Pastimes; (18) Periodical Literature; Essay Material; (19) Material in Manuscript; and (20) Indexes.

I–13 **Kennedy, Arthur Garfield.** ***Bibliography of Writings on the English Language from the Beginning of Printing to the End of 1922.*** Cambridge: Harvard University Press, 1927.
Z2015.A1 K3

This inclusive index to the history of the study of the English language is now out of date and must be supplemented by Allen (I–2) and other, more recent bibliographies. It is nevertheless still regarded as an essential tool. The aim of the work is to include materials on the scientific study of English as a language rather than studies on English literary style and the art of expression. It is divided into ten chapters, as follows: General Collections, General and Historical Writings, English Palaeography, English and Other Languages, Anglo-Saxon or Old English, Middle English, Modern English, Recent Tendencies in English, History of the Study of the English Language, Theory and Method of the Study and Teaching of English. Each chapter includes three grades of subclassification: most general works, general topic headings, and specific topic headings. A chronological arrangement is used for the 13,402 individual entries. The volume concludes with a subject index and an index of authors and reviewers.

See the additions and corrections by Arvid Gabrielson, *Studia Neophilologica* 2 (1929): 117–168. A continuation of Kennedy, covering the period from 1923 to 1973, is now in progress.

I–14 **Brenni, Vito J. *American English: A Bibliography*.** Philadelphia: University of Pennsylvania Press, 1964.

Z1231.D5 B7

A serially numbered, annotated bibliography of 1,496 books and articles published through 1961 concerning English as spoken and written in the United States. Sections cover General and Historical works on American English; Spelling; Pronunciation; Grammar, Syntax, and Usage; Dialects; Slang; Loanwords; Dictionaries; and Miscellaneous References. There is a detailed index of authors, titles, and subjects.

This volume may be supplemented in part by the newer work of Ila W. Brasch and Walter M. Brasch, *Comprehensive Annotated Bibliography of American Black English* (Baton Rouge: Louisiana State University Press, 1974) [Z1234.D5 B7]. For Canadian English see Dieter Bahr, *Bibliography of Writings on the English Language in Canada from 1857 to 1976* (Heidelberg: Winter, 1977) [Z1379.B34], which updates Walter S. Avis, *Bibliography of Writings on Canadian English (1857-1965)* (Toronto: W. J. Gage, 1965) [Z1379.A85].

I–15 **Scholarly Journals in Language, Linguistics, and Philology.**

American Journal of Philology. Vol. 1–. Baltimore: Johns Hopkins University Press, 1880–. 4/yr. Reviews. Indexes to vols. 1–10 in vol. 10; 11–20 in vol. 20; 21–30 in vol. 30; 31–40 in vol. 40; 41–60 in vol. 60; 61–75 in vol. 75; and 75–90 in vol. 90. P1.A5

AS *American Speech: A Quarterly of Linguistic Usage*. Vol. 1–. Tuscaloosa: University of Alabama Press for the American Dialect Society, 1925/26–. 4/yr. Reviews. Contained bibliographies during 1925–1968 on present-day speech, phonetics, and general and historical studies. PE2801.A6

ALing *Analecta Linguistica: Information Bulletin of Linguistics*. *Vol. 1–*. Budapest: Akademiai Kiado, 1971–. 2/yr. Notes. Current Contents. Bibliographies. Z7003.A5

AnL *Anthropological Linguistics*. Vol. 1–. Bloomington: Indiana University, Department of Anthropology, 1959–. 4/yr. Reviews. No LC number

ArL *Archivum Linguisticum: A Review of Comparative Philology and Comparative Linguistics*. Vols. 1–17. London: Mansell, 1949–1965. New Series, vols. 1–11. 1970–1980. 1–2/yr. Reviews. P1.A73

BSLP *Bulletin de la Société de linguistique de Paris*. Vol. 1–. Paris: CNRS, 1865–. 1/yr. Reviews. P12.S45

CJL *Canadian Journal of Linguistics / La révue canadienne de linguistique*. Vol. 1–. Toronto: Canadian Linguistic Association, 1954–. 2/yr. Reviews. No LC number

Dictionaries: Journal of the Dictionary Society of North America. Vol. 1–. Terre Haute, Ind.: Dictionary Society, 1979–. 1/yr. Reviews. P327.D53

ESP *English for Specific Purposes: An International Journal*. Vol. 1–. Oxford and New York: Pergamon Press, 1981–. 3/yr. Reviews. PE1128.A2 E76

English Today: The International Review of the English Language. Vol. 1–. New York: Cambridge University Press, 1985–. 4/yr. Reviews. PE1001.E37

ETC *ETC: A Review of General Semantics*. New York: International Society for General Semantics, 1943–.

4/yr. Reviews. B840.E85

FoLi *Folia Linguistica [from 1980: Historica]: Acta Societatis Linguisticae Europaeae*. Vol. 1–. Vienna: Societas Linguistica Europaea, 1967–1979; The Hague: Mouton, 1980–. 2/yr. Reviews. P140.F64

FL *Foundations of Language: International Journal of Language and Philosophy*. Vols. 1–14. Dordrecht, Holland: D. Reidel, 1965–1976. 4–6/yr. Reviews. P1.A1 F6

GL *General Linguistics*. Vol. 1–. University Park, Pa.: Penn State University Press, 1955–. 4/yr. Reviews. Since 1970, the annual MLA Linguistics Bibliography (see L–20) has been published as a special supplement to *GL*. No LC number

General Semantics Bulletin. No. 1/2–. Lakeville, Conn.: Institute of General Semantics, 1949/50–. Annual. Index to nos. 1–37 (1949–1970) in 1 vol. B820.G4

Glossa *Glossa: An International Journal of Linguistics*. Vol. 1–. Burnaby, B.C.: Dept. of Modern Languages, Simon Fraser University, 1967–. No LC number

IncL *Incorporated Linguist*. Vol. 1–. London: Institute of Linguistics, 1962–. 4/yr. Reviews. P1.I5

IJAL *International Journal of [Native] American Linguistics*. Vol. 1–. Bloomington: Indiana University Press, 1917–. 4/yr. and supplements. Reviews. Index to vols. 1–10 in vol. 11. PM101.I5

IJPs *International Journal of Psycholinguistics*. 8 vols. The Hague: Mouton, 1972–1981. 2–4/yr. No LC number

IJSL *International Journal of the Sociology of Language*. Vol. 1–. Berlin: de Gruyter, 1974–. 3–6/yr. Reviews. P40.I57

IRAL *International Review of Applied Linguistics in Language Teaching / Révue internationale de linguistique appliquée enseignement des langues / Internationale Zeitschrift für angewandte Linguistik in der Spracherziehung*. Vol. 1–. Heidelberg: Julius Groos Verlag, 1963–. 4/yr. Reviews. No LC number

JEngL *Journal of English Linguistics*. Vol. 1–. Bellingham, Wash.: Western Washington University, 1967–. 1/yr. Reviews. PE1001.J65

JL *Journal of Linguistics*. Vol. 1–. Cambridge: Cambridge University Press, 1964–. 2/yr. Reviews. P1.J65

JLS *Journal of Literary Semantics*. Vol. 1–. Heidelberg: Julius Groos Verlag, 1972–. 3/yr. Reviews. PN54.J68

Journal of Pragmatics: An Interdisciplinary Quarterly of Language Studies. Vol. 1–. Amsterdam: North-Holland Publishing, 1977–. 4/yr. Reviews. Bibliography [see I–6]. P99.4.P72 J68

JPsyR *Journal of Psycholinguistic Research*. Vol. 1–. New York: Plenum, 1971–. 4–6/yr. Reviews. P106.J68

Language: Journal of the Linguistic Society of America. Vol. 1–. Baltimore: The Society, 1925–. 4/yr. plus supplements. Reviews. Index to vols. 1–40 (1925–1964) in 1 vol. P1.L3

L & S *Language and Speech*. Vol. 1–. Middlesex, England: Kingston Press Services, 1958–. 4/yr. P1.L32

Lang & S *Language and Style: An International Journal*.

Vol. 1–. Carbondale: Southern Illinois University Press, 1968–. 4/yr. Reviews.   PN203.L35

LSoc   *Language in Society.* Vol. 1–. Cambridge: Cambridge University Press, 1972–. 2–4/yr. Reviews.   P41.L34

LL   *Language Learning: A Journal of Applied Linguistics.* Vol. 1–. Ann Arbor, Mich.: Research Club in Language Learning, 1948–. 2–4/yr. Reviews. Index to vols. 1–10 (1948–1960) in 1 vol., vols. 11–20 (1961–1970) in 1 vol.   P1.L33

Lingua: International Review of General Linguistics / Révue international de linguistique générale. Vol. 1–. Amersterdam: North-Holland Publishing, 1947–. 4–9/yr. Reviews. Index to vols. 1–10 (1947–1961) in 1 vol.; 11–20 (1962–1968) in 1 vol.; 21–30 (1968–1972) in 1 vol.; and 31–40 (1973–1976) in 1 vol.   P9.L47

LingA   *Linguistic Analysis.* Vol. 1–. Amsterdam: Elsevier North Holland, 1975–. 4–8/yr. Reviews.   P123.L49

LingI   *Linguistic Inquiry.* Vol. 1–. Cambridge: MIT Press, 1970–. 4/yr.   P1.L48

Linguistics: An Interdisciplinary Journal of the Language Sciences. no. 1–. Berlin: de Gruyter, 1963–. 6–12/yr. Reviews. Annotated bibliography. Index to nos. 1–50 (1963–1969) issued as no. 51.   P1.A125

Ling & P   *Linguistics and Philosophy: An International Journal.* Vol. 1–. Dordrecht, Holland: D. Reidel, 1977–. 4/yr. Reviews.   P1.A1 L513

Names: Journal of the American Name Society. Vol. 1–. Potsdam, N.Y.: American Name Society, 1953–. 4/yr. Reviews. Annual "Bibliography of Personal Names." Also biennial bibliography of "Place Name Literature, United States and Canada."   P769.N3

Onoma: Bibliographical and Information Bulletin / Bulletin d'information et de bibliographie. Vol. 1–. Louvain: Editions Peeters, 1950–. 3/yr. Reviews. Annual "Bibliographia Onomastica."   P323.O6

Orbis: Bulletin internationale de documentation linguistique. Vol. 1–. Louvain: Centre international de dialectologie générale, 1952–. 2/yr. Bibliography. Reviews.   P2.O7

QJS   *Quarterly Journal of Speech.* Vol. 1–. Falls Church, Va: Speech Communication Association, 1915–. 4/yr. Reviews. Index (see X–104).   No LC number

Semiotica: Journal of the International Association for Semiotic Studies / Revue de l'Association internationale de semiotique. Vol. 1–. Berlin: de Gruyter, 1969–. 10/yr. Reviews. Bibliographies.   B828.S45

SM   *Speech Monographs.* Vol. 1–. Falls Church, Va.: Speech Communication Association, 1934–. 4/yr. Reviews. Bibliography (see X–103). Index to vols. 1–26 (1934–1959) with vol. 27.   PN4077.S6

SLang   *Studies in Language: International Journal Sponsored by the Foundation "Foundations of Language."* Vol. 1–. Amsterdam: John Benjamins, 1977–. 3/yr. Reviews.   No LC number

Style. Vol. 1–. Fayetteville: University of Arkansas, 1967–. 4/yr. Reviews. Bibliography (see X–136).   PE1.S89

Text: An Interdisciplinary Journal for the Study of Discourse. The Hague: Mouton, 1981–. 4/yr. Bibliographic surveys.   No LC number

Theoretical Linguistics. Vol. 1–. Berlin: de Gruyter, 1974–. 4/yr.   P1.T5

TPS   *Transactions of the Philological Society.* Vol. 1–. Oxford: Blackwell, 1842–. 1/yr. Index to vols. for 1917–1966 in 1 vol.   P11.P6

Verbatim: The Language Quarterly. Vol. 1–. Essex, Conn.: Verbatim, 1974–. 4/yr. Reviews. Cumulative index to vols. 1–6.   P1.V472

VLang   *Visible Language: The Quarterly Concerned with All That Is Involved in Our Being Literate.* Vol. 1–. Cleveland, Ohio: Press of Case Western Reserve University, 1967–. 4/yr. Reviews.   Z119.J88

WL   *Women and Language.* Vol. 1–. Urbana: University of Illinois, 1976–. 3/yr. Reviews. Research in Progress.   P120.W66 W65

Word Study. 45 vols. Springfield, Mass.: G. & C. Merriam, 1925–1970. Irregular.   PE1.W6

Lists of periodicals specializing in linguistics are available in the various current bibliographies. In addition, see T. Ulving, *Periodica Philologica Abbreviata: A List of Initial Abbreviations of Periodicals in Philology and Related Subjects* (Stockholm: Almqvist and Wiksell, 1963) [Z6945.A2 U5513], with its approximately 3,300 entries, and the *Liste mondiale des pèriodiques specialisés-linguistique / World List of Specialized Periodicals-Linguistics* (Paris and the Hague: UNESCO, 1971) [Z7003.M34], in which some 540 periodicals, arranged by country of publication, are described in three-paragraph entries treating editorial information, practical information (publisher, periodicity, and indexing), and contents description, respectively.

For work on linguistics and literature see also entries on the linguistic analysis of poetry (T–53, T–58), on prosody and prosodic theory (T–60 ff.), on the linguistic analysis of drama (U–67), on the language of fiction (W–27), and on prose style (W–127); and works in literary theory (X–1 ff.) in rhetoric and rhetorical theory (X–100 ff.), and in style and stylistics (X–130 ff.).

I–16   **Some Frequently Recommended Works in Linguistics.**

Aitchison, Jean. *Articulate Mammal: An Introduction to Psycholinguistics.* 2d ed. New York: Universe Books, 1983.   P37.A37 1983

Akmajian, Adrian, et al. *Linguistics: An Introduction to Language and Communication.* 2d ed. Cambridge: MIT Press, 1984.   P121.A4384 1984

Allport, A., et al. *Language Perception and Production: Relationships Between Listening, Speaking, Reading and Writing.* London: Academic Press, 1987.   BF637.C45 L36

Bach, Emmon. *Introduction to Transformational Grammars.* New York: Holt, Rinehart, and Winston, 1964.   P123.U5

Baldi, Philip. *Introduction to the Indo-European Languages.* Carbondale: Southern Illinois University Press, 1983.   P561.B3 1983

Bloomfield, Leonard. *Language.* New York: H. Holt, 1933.   P121.B5

———. *Linguistic Aspects of Science.* Chicago: University of Chicago Press, 1939.   Q121.I5 vol. 4 no. 4

Bolinger, Dwight L. *Aspects of Language.* 3d ed. New York: Harcourt Brace Jovanovich, 1981.   P106.B59 1981

Brown, Gillian, and George Yule. *Discourse Analysis.* Cambridge: Cambridge University Press, 1983.   P302.B76 1983

Brown, Roger. *Words and Things.* Glencoe, Ill.: Free Press, 1958.   P105.B77

————, ed. *Psycholinguistics*. New York: Free Press, 1970.
    BF455.B73 1970

Carroll, John B. *Study of Language: A Survey of Linguistics and Related Disciplines in America*. Cambridge: Harvard University Press, 1953.   P121.C35

Chafe, Wallace L. *Meaning and the Structure of Language*. Chicago: University of Chicago Press, 1970.
    P121.C423

Chomsky, Noam. *Aspects of the Theory of Syntax*. Cambridge: MIT Press, 1965.   P291.C4

————. *Language and Mind*, 2d ed. New York: Harcourt Brace Jovanovich, 1972.   P106.C52 1972

————. *Reflections on Language*. New York: Pantheon, 1975.   P106.C54 1975

————. *Rules and Representations*. New York: Columbia University Press, 1980.   P106.C544

————. *Syntactic Structures*. The Hague: Mouton, 1968.
    P291.C5 1968

Clark, Herbert H., and Eve V. Clark. *Psychology and Language: An Introduction to Psycholinguistics*. New York: Harcourt Brace Jovanovich, 1977. BF455.C59

Clark, Virginia P., et al., eds. *Language: Introductory Readings*. 4th ed. New York: St. Martin's Press, 1985.   P25.C555 1985

Comrie, Bernard. *Language Universals and Linguistic Typology: Syntax and Morphology*. Chicago: University of Chicago Press, 1981.   P204.C6

Couthard, Richard M. *Introduction to Discourse Analysis*. London: Longman, 1977.   P302.C68

Crystal, David. *First Dictionary of Linguistics and Phonetics*. London: André Deutsch, 1981.   P29.C7

————. *Linguistics*. Baltimore: Penguin, 1971   P121.C68

Dillon, George L. *Introduction to Contemporary Linguistic Semantics*. Englewood Cliffs, N.J.: Prentice-Hall, 1977.   P325.D54

Dittmar, Norbert. *Sociolinguistics. A Critical Survey of Theory and Application*. London: Edward Arnold, 1976.   P40.D513

Dressler, Wolfgang U., ed. *Current Trends in Textlinguistics*. Berlin: de Gruyter, 1978.   P302.C8

Ducrot, O., and T. Todorov. *Encyclopedic Dictionary of the Sciences of Language*. Translation by Catherine Porter of *Dictionnaire encyclopédique des sciences du langage* (Paris: Seuil, 1972). Baltimore: Johns Hopkins University Press, 1979.   P29.D813

Fillmore, Charles J. "The Case for Case," in E. Bach and R. T. Harms, *Universals in Linguistic Theory*. pp. 1–88. New York: Holt, Rinehart and Winston, 1968.
    P123.U5

Firth, John R. *Papers in Linguistics, 1934–1951*. London: Oxford University Press, 1957.   P27.F5

————. *Selected Papers of J. R. Firth 1952–1959*. Edited by F. R. Palmer. London: Longman, 1968.
    P27.F52 1968

Fletcher, Paul, and Michael Garman, eds. *Language Acquisition*. Cambridge: Cambridge University Press, 1979.
    LB1139.L3 L323

Fodor, Jerry A., and Jerrold J. Katz. *Structure of Language: Readings in the Philosophy of Language*. Englewood Cliffs, N.J.: Prentice-Hall, 1964.   P121.F6

Fowler, Roger. *Understanding Language*. London: Routledge and Kegan Paul, 1974.   P121.F63

Frank, Francine, and Frank Anshen. *Language and the Sexes*. Albany, N.Y.: SUNY Press, 1984.
    PE2808.F73 1984

Fromkin, Victoria, and Robert Rodman. *Introduction to Language*. 3d ed. New York: Holt, Rinehart and Winston, 1983.   P106.F75 1983

Giglioli, Pier Paolo, ed. *Language and Social Context: Selected Readings*. Harmondsworth: Penguin, 1972.
    P41.G54

Gleason, Henry A. *Introduction to Descriptive Linguistics*. 2d ed. New York: Holt, Rinehart and Winston, 1961.
    PE1135.G59 1961

Gordon, W. Terence. *Semantics: A Bibliography, 1965–78*. Metuchen, N.J.: Scarecrow, 1980.   Z7004.S4 G67

Greenberg, Joseph H. *Anthropological Linguistics: An Introduction*. New York: Random House, 1968.
    P121.G74

Hall, Edward G. *Silent Language*. Garden City, N.Y.: Doubleday, 1959.   HM258.H3

Halliday, M. A. K. *Exploration in the Function of Language*. London: Edward Arnold, 1973.   P27.H25

————. *System and Function in Language: Selected Papers*. Edited by G. R. Cress. London: Oxford University Press, 1976.   P149.H34

————, and R. Hason. *Cohesion in English*. London: Longman, 1976.   PE1421.H34

Harris, Zellig. *Methods in Structural Linguistics*. Chicago: University of Chicago Press, 1951.   P121.H35

Hill, Archibald A. *Introduction to Linguistic Structures: From Sound to Sentence in English*. New York: Harcourt Brace Jovanovich, 1958.   PE1105.H5

Hockett, Charles F. *Course in Modern Linguistics*. New York: Macmillan, 1958.   P121.H63

Hoenigswald, Henry M. *Language Change and Linguistic Reconstruction*. Chicago: University of Chicago Press, 1960.   P123.H55

Jakobson, Roman, and Morris Halle. *Fundamentals of Language*. 2d ed. The Hague: Mouton, 1971.
    P217.J28 1971

————. *Selected Writings*. 2d expanded ed. 5 vols. The Hague: Mouton, 1971–.   P27.J343

Jespersen, Otto. *Language: Its Nature, Development, and Origin*. London: Allen and Unwin, 1922.   P105.J45

————. *Philosophy of Grammar*. London: Allen and Unwin, 1924.   P201.J55

Joos, Martin, ed. *Readings in Linguistics*. 2d ed. New York: American Council of Learned Societies, 1958.
    P25.J6 1958

Kempson, Ruth M. *Presupposition and the Delimitation of Semantics*. Cambridge: Cambridge University Press, 1975.   P325.K44

Koerner, E. F. K. *Western Histories of Linguistic Thought: An Annotated Bibliography, 1822–=1976*. Amsterdam: John Benjamins, 1978. Annotated entries, chronologically arranged.   Z7004.H56 K64

Labov, William. *Sociolinguistic Patterns*. Philadelphia: University of Pennsylvania Press, 1973.   P41.L26 1973

Lado, Robert. *Linguistics across Cultures: Applied Linguistics for Language Teachers*. Ann Arbor: University of Michigan Press, 1957.   P53.L3

Lehmann, Winfred P. *Historical Linguistics: An Introduction*. 2d ed. New York: Holt, Rinehart and Winston, 1973.   P121.L45 1973

————. *Syntactic Typology: Studies in the Phenomenology of Language*. Austin: University of Texas Press, 1978.
    P204.S9

Lightfoot, David. *Principles of Diachronic Syntax*. Cambridge: Cambridge University Press, 1979. P291.L48

Lyons, John. *Introduction to Theoretical Linguistics.* Cambridge: Cambridge University Press, 1968.   P106.L9

———. *Language and Linguistics: An Introduction.* Cambridge: Cambridge University Press, 1981.
P121.L9 1981

———. *New Horizons in Linguistics.* Harmondsworth: Penguin, 1970.   P25.L95

———. *Semantics.* 2 vols. Cambridge: Cambridge University Press, 1977.   P325.L96

Martinet, André. *Elements of General Linguistics.* Chicago: University of Chicago Press, 1964.
P121.M3133 1964

Matthews, Peter H. *Generative Grammar and Linguistic Competence.* London: Allen and Unwin, 1979.
P158.M37

———. *Morphology: An Introduction to the Theory of Word Structure.* Cambridge: Cambridge University Press, 1974.   P241.M3

———. *Syntax.* Cambridge: Cambridge University Press, 1981.   PE1361.M37

Nida, Eugene A. *Morphology: The Descriptive Analysis of Words.* 2d ed. Ann Arbor: University of Michigan Press, 1949.   P25.M47 vol. 2 1949

Pedersen, Holger. *Linguistic Science in the Nineteenth Century.* Translation of *Sprogvidenskaben det nittende aarhundrede* (Copenhagen: Gyldendal Nordisk forlag, 1924). Cambridge: Harvard University Press, 1931. Reprinted with the title *Discovery of Language.* Bloomington: Indiana University Press, 1962.
P75.P44 1962

Pike, Kenneth. *Language in Relation to a Unified Theory of the Structure of Human Behavior.* The Hague: Mouton, 1971.   P123.P49 1971

Postal, Paul. *On Raising: One Rule of English Grammar and Its Implications.* Cambridge: MIT Press, 1974.
PE1380.P6

Robins, R. H. *General Linguistics: An Introductory Survey.* 3d ed. London: Longmans, 1980.   P121.R6 1980

———. *Short History of Linguistics.* 2d ed. London: Longmans, 1979.   P61.R6 1979

Sampson, Geoffrey. *Schools of Linguistics.* Stanford: Stanford University Press, 1980.   P77.S35

Sapir, Edward. *Language: Introduction to the Study of Speech.* New York: Harcourt, Brace 1921.   P105.S2

Saussure, Ferdinand de. *Course in General Linguistics.* Rev. ed. Translation by Wade Baskin of *Cours de linguistique générale,* ed. Charles Bally. London: Fontana, 1974.   P121.S363 1974

Schmalstieg, William R. *Indo-European Linguistics: A New Synthesis.* University Park: Pennsylvania State University Press, 1980.   P575.S35

Searle, John R. *Speech Act Theory and Pragmatics.* Dordrecht, Holland: D. Reidel, 1980.   P95.55.S63

Sebeok, Thomas A., ed. *Current Trends in Linguistics.* 14 vols. in 17. The Hague: Mouton, 1963–1976. Vol. 1, Soviet and East European Linguistics [includes an important general bibliography of linguistics] (1963). Vol. 2, Linguistics in East Asia and Southeast Asia (1967). Vol. 3, Theoretical Foundations (1966). Vol. 4, Ibero-American and Caribbean Linguistics (1968). Vol. 5, Linguistics in South Asia (1969). Vol. 6, Linguistics in Southwest Asia and North Africa (1970). Vol. 7, Linguistics in Sub-Saharan Africa (1971). Vol. 8, Linguistics in Oceania, 2 vols. (1971). Vol. 9, Linguistics in Western Europe, 3 vols. (1972). Vol. 10, Linguistics in North America, 2 vols. (1973). Vol. 11, Diachronic, Area, and Typological Linguistics (1973). Vol. 12,

Linguistics and Adjacent Arts and Sciences, 4 vols. (1974). Vol. 13, Historiography of Linguistics, 2 vols. (1975). Vol. 14, Indexes (1976).   P25.S4

Sturtevant, Edgar H. *Introduction to Linguistic Science.* New Haven: Yale University Press, 1947.
P121.S815

Traugott, Elizabeth Closs, and Mary Louise Pratt. *Linguistics for Students of Literature.* New York: Harcourt Brace Jovanovich, 1980.   P123.T67

Trubetzkoy, N. S. *Principles of Phonology.* Translation by Christiane A. M. Baltaxe of *Grundzuge der Phonologie.* Berkeley and Los Angeles: University of California Press, 1969.   P217.T72

Ullmann, Stephen. *Semantics: An Introduction to the Science of Meaning.* New York: Barnes and Noble, 1962.
P325.U52

Van Dijk, Teun A. *Studies in the Pragmatics of Discourse.* Amsterdam: Mouton, 1981.   P302.D473 1981

———. *Text and Context: Explorations in the Semantics and Pragmatics of Discourse.* London: Longman, 1980.   P302.D5 1980

———, ed. *Pragmatics of Language and Literature.* Amsterdam: North-Holland Publishing, 1976.   P302.P7

Whorf, Benjamin L. *Language, Thought, and Reality.* Edited by John B. Carroll. Cambridge: MIT Press, 1957.   P27.W53

I–17 **Some Frequently Recommended Works on the History, Character, and Teaching of the English Language.**

Allen, Harold B., ed. *Teaching English as a Second Language: A Book of Readings.* New York: McGraw-Hill, 1965.   PE1128.A2 A38

Bailey, Richard W., and Manfred Görlach, eds. *English as a World Language.* Ann Arbor: University of Michigan Press, 1982.   PE1700.E5 1982

Baugh, Albert C., and Thomas Cable. *History of the English Language.* 3d ed. Englewood Cliffs, N.J.: Prentice Hall, 1978.   PE1075.B3 1978

Bloomfield, Morton W., and Leonard Newmark. *Linguistic Introduction to the History of English.* New York: Knopf, 1963.   PE1075.B5

Bolton, Whitney F. *Language of 1984: Orwell's English and Ours.* Nashville: University of Tennessee Press, 1984.
PR6029.R8 Z558 1984

———. *Short History of Literary English.* 2d ed. London: Edward Arnold, 1972.   PE1075.B64 1972

Bryant, Margard M. *Modern English and Its Heritage.* 2d ed. New York: Macmillan, 1962.
PE1072.B75 1962

Campbell, A. *Old English Grammar.* Oxford: Clarendon Press, 1959.   PE131.C3

Cook, Albert B. *Introduction to the English Language: Structure and History.* New York: Ronald Press, 1969.   PE1075.C6

Dillard, J. L. *All-American English: A History of the English Language in America.* New York: Random House, 1975.   PE2809.D54

———. *Black English: Its History and Usage in the United States.* New York: Random House, 1972.
PE3102.N4 D5

Finocchiaro, Mary. *English as a Second Language: From Theory to Practice.* New York: Regents Publishing Co., 1964.   PE1128.A2 F5

Francis, Winthrop Nelson. *English Language, an Introduction: Background for Writing.* New York: W. W. Norton, 1965.   PE1072.F68 1965

—————. *Structure of American English.* New York: Ronald Press, 1958.   PE2811.F67

Galinsky, Hans. *Das amerikanische Englisch: Seine innere Entwicklung und internationale Ansstrahlung.* Darmstadt: Wissenschaftliche Buchgesellschaft, 1979.   PE2888.G29

—————. *Amerikanisches und britisches Englisch.* Munich: Hueber, 1975.   PE2888.G3

—————. *Die Sprache des Amerikaners: Eine Einführung in die Hauptunterschiede zwischen amerikanischem und britischem Englisch der Gegenwart.* 2 vols. Heidelberg: Kerle, 1951–1952.   PE2813.G3

Gleason, H. A., Jr. *Linguistics and English Grammar.* New York: Holt, Rinehart and Winston, 1965.   PE1111.G575

Goldstein, Wallace L. *Teaching English as a Second Language: An Annotated Bibliography.* New York: Garland, 1975. (See Z–134.)

Jespersen, Otto. *Essentials of English Grammar.* New York: H. Holt, 1933.   PE1105.J4

—————. *Growth and Structure of the English Language,* 10th ed. Chicago: University of Chicago Press, 1982.   PE1075.J4 1982

—————. *Modern English Grammar on Historical Principles.* 7 vols. Heidelberg: C. Winter, 1909–1949.   PE1101.J5

Joos, Martin. *English Verb.* 2d ed. Madison: University of Wisconsin Press, 1968.   PE1271.J6 1968

Kittredge, George Lyman, and Frank E. Farley. *Advanced English Grammar.* Boston: Ginn, 1913.   PE1111.K8

Krapp, George Philip. *English Language in America.* 2 vols. New York: Appleton Century Crofts, 1925.   PE2808.K7

Kurath, Hans. *Handbook of the Linguistic Geography of New England.* 2d ed. with a new introduction, word index, etc. by Audrey R. Duckert. New York: AMS Press, 1973.   PE2902.K78 1973

—————, ed. *Linguistic Atlas of New England.* Providence, R.I.: Brown University Press, 1939–1943.   PE2902.K8

Lass, R., ed. *Approaches to Historical English Linguistics: An Anthology.* New York: Holt, Rinehart and Winston, 1969.   PE1075.L33

Mencken, H. L. *American Language: The Fourth Edition . . . and the Two Supplements.* Abridged and edited by Raven I. McDavid, Jr. New York: Alfred A. Knopf, 1963.   PE2808.M4 1963

Michael, Ian. *English Grammatical Categories and the Tradition to 1800.* Cambridge : Cambridge University Press, 1970.   PE1098.M5

Mitchell, Bruce. *Old English Syntax.* 2 vols. Oxford: Clarendon Press, 1985.   PE213.M5

Nida, Eugene A. *Synoposis of English Syntax.* 3d ed. The Hague: Mouton, 1973.   PE1365.N5 1973

Partridge, Eric. *Slang To-Day and Yesterday, with a Short Historical Sketch and Vocabularies of English, American, and Australian Slang.* 4th ed. New York: Barnes and Noble, 1970.   PE3711.P3 1970

Pyles, Thomas, and John Algeo. *Origins and Development of the English Language.* 3d ed. New York: Harcourt Brace and Jovanovich, 1982.   PE1075.P9 1982

Quirk, Randolph. *Essays on the English Language, Medieval and Modern.* Bloomington: Indiana University Press, 1968.   PE1072.Q49

—————, et al. *Grammar of Contemporary English.* London: Longman, 1972.   PE1106.G67

Robertson, Stuart. *Development of Modern English.* 2d ed. Revised by Frederic G. Cassidy. New York: Prentice-Hall, 1954.   PE1075.R57 1954

Samuels, Michael L. *Linguistic Evolution, With Special Reference to English.* Cambridge: Cambridge University Press, 1972.   P123.S26

Scheurweghs, Gustave. *Analytical Bibliography of Writings on Modern English Morphology and Syntax, 1877–1960.* 4 vols. Louvain: Nauwelaerts, 1963–1968.   Z2015.A1S33

Sledd, James. *Short Introduction to English Grammar.* Chicago: Scott, Foresman, 1959.   PE1111.S487

Stagberg, Norman C. *Introductory English Grammar.* 3d ed. New York: Holt, Rinehart and Winston, 1977.   PE1112.S7 1977

Starnes, D. T., and Gertrude E. Noyes. *English Dictionary from Cawdrey to Johnson, 1604–1755.* Chapel Hill: University of North Carolina Press, 1946.   PE1611 .S68

Strang, Barbara M. H. *History of English.* London: Methuen, 1970.   PE1075 .S85

Sweet, Henry. *New English Grammar, Logical and Historical.* 2 vols. Part 1, *Introduction, Phonology.* Part 2, *Syntax.* Oxford: Clarendon Press, 1891–1898.   PE1101.S8 1892

Thomas, Owen. *Transformational Grammar and the Teacher of English.* New York: Holt, Rinehart and Winston, 1974.   PE1106.T47 1974

Trager, George L., and Henry Lee Smith, Jr. *Outline of English Structure.* Rev. ed. Washington, D.C.: ACLS, 1957.   P1.S931 no.3 1957

Traugott, Elizabeth C. *History of English Syntax: A Transformational Approach to the History of English Sentence Structure.* New York: Holt, Rinehart and Winston, 1972.   PE1361.T7

Visser, F. Th. *Historical Syntax of the English Language.* 3 parts in 4 vols. Leiden: E. J. Brill, 1963–1973.   PE1361.V5

Wells, J. C. *Accents of English.* 3 vols. Vol. 1, *Introduction.* Vol. 2, *British Isles.* Vol. 3, *Beyond the British Isles.* Cambridge: Cambridge Press, 1982.   PE1711. W4

II. BIBLIOGRAPHIES—DICTIONARIES

Each issue of the annual *Cahiers de lexicologie* (Paris: Didier, 1958–) [P327.C3] has a "Bibliographie des lexicales," which lists new works of significant lexicographical value.

I-20 **Brewer, Annie M. *Dictionaries, Encyclopedias, and Other Word-Related Books: A Classed Guide to Dictionaries, Encyclopedias, and Similar Works, Based on Library of Congress Catalog Cards, and Arranged according to the Library of Congress Classification System, Including Compilations of Acronyms, Americanisms, Colloquialisms, Etymologies, Glossaries, Idioms and Expressions, Orthography, Provincialisms, Slang, Terms and Phrases, and Vocabularies in English and All Other Languages.* 2d ed. 2 vols. Detroit: Gale Research Co., 1979.   AE5.B75 1979**

The first edition (1975) included LC cards issued from 1966 through 1974; this second edition adds cards from 1975 through 1978/79, along with cards for all dictionaries, encyclopedias, and word-related books in the LC Main Reading Room reference collection, without regard to their issue date. Some 25,000 titles are covered. Volume 1 treats English and polyglot books (i.e., concerning English words or English and other words); volume 2 treats non-English books (i.e., books concerning non-English words). Arrangement in each volume is parallel to the LC subject arrangement, as revealed by the LC call numbers, according to which the individual cards are organized. The only exception is the K section (Law), which is alphabetically arranged by main entry. The photographically reduced cards are presented in three columns. A keyword index identifies the LC call number under which to search for materials in a given subject area. A late-arrivals section and a group of unclassified cards conclude the work.

I-21 **Zischka, Gert A.** *Index Lexicorum: Bibliographie der lexikalischen Nachschlagewerke.* Vienna: Verlag Hollinek, 1959.   Z1035.Z5

This excellent bibliography of dictionaries and other word-related books is disposed into twenty-one sections as follows: (1) Encyclopedias and Conversational Dictionaries; (2) Religion; (3) Philosophy and Psychology; (4) Pedagogy; (5) Books and Printing; (6) History and Ancillae; (7) Biography; (8) Folklore; (9) Geography; (10) Art History; (11) Classical Architecture; (12) Literature, Author Dictionaries, and Dictionaries of Scholars; (13) General Linguistics; (14) Music, Theatre and Dance; (15) Law and Politics; (16) Economics; (17) Medicine; (18) Natural Science; (19) Technology and Mathematics; (20) Agriculture, Forestry, Horticulture, Home Economics; (21) Varia. Briefly annotated entries are arranged within each section by language; in addition, works generally regarded as standard or of special value are indicated by asterisks. A single index of authors, keywords, and subjects concludes the volume.

I-22 **Collison, Robert Lewis.** *Dictionaries of English and Foreign Languages: A Bibliographical Guide to Both General and Technical Dictionaries with Historical and Explanatory Notes and References.* 2d ed. New York: Hafner, 1971.   Z7004.D5 C6 1971

The 1955 first edition of this guide did not include English-language dictionaries. Included in this volume are bilingual and monolingual dictionaries of English and foreign languages. Historically interesting dictionaries, dictionaries likely to be of use to current translators, historical dictionaries that display earlier states of a language, and etymological dictionaries are covered. The work consists of a discursive introduction followed by classified lists of dictionaries: full bibliographical details and some comments are given for each dictionary cited. The chapters are as follows: Introduction; French; German, Dutch, and Afrikaans; Italian; Spanish, Basque, and Portuguese; Russian; Dictionaries of the Scandinavian Languages; Greek (Ancient and Modern) and Latin; Languages of the Baltic, the Balkans, and Central Europe; Languages of Africa; Languages of the Near and the Middle East; Languages of Asia and the Pacific; The English Language to 1753; The Modern English Dictionary; The Celtic Languages; and Dictionaries of Comparative Philology. The appendixes present a list of technical dictionaries, a list of specialized subject dictionaries, and a general bibliography. The volume concludes with an index of authors, subjects, languages, dialects, titles, and subtitles.

A more detailed review of the English dictionary is that by Mitford M. Mathews, *Survey of English Dictionaries* (London: Oxford University Press, 1933) [Z2015.D6 M4].

I-23 **Whittaker, Kenneth.** *Dictionaries.* Sydney, Australia: James Bennett, 1966.   Z7004.D5 W5 1966

This brief and rather elementary guide presents an introduction and seven chapters concerned respectively with Defining Dictionaries, using Dictionaries, describing Dictionaries for General Use, Dictionaries for Special Purposes, Foreign Lan-

guage Dictionaries, Dictionaries for Special Subject Interests, and Childrens' Dictionaries. There are two indexes: of authors (with some titles) and of subjects.

I-24 **Walford, A. J., and J. E. E. Screen, ed.** *Guide to Foreign Language Courses and Dictionaries.* 3d ed., rev. and enl. Westport, Conn.: Greenwood, 1977.   Z7004.G7 W3 1977

The guide was first published in 1964, with a second edition in 1967, both under the title *Guide to Foreign Language Grammars and Dictionaries.* All editions have presented discursive critical treatments of available resources for English speakers wanting access to foreign-language materials. The recent edition includes audiovisual aids, grammars, and general and special dictionaries. Each of the chapters is written by an authority. The twenty-four chapters treat materials for the following languages: French, Italian, Spanish, Portuguese, German, Dutch, Scandinavian, Russian, Ukrainian, Byelorussian, Bulgarian, Macedonian, Serbo-Croatian, Slovene, Czech, Slovak, Polish, Rumanian, Modern Greek, Finnish, Hungarian, Arabic, Japanese, and Chinese. The volume concludes with an index of authors, titles, and subjects.

I-25 *International Bibliography of Dictionaries / Fachwörterbücher und Lexika: Ein internationales Verzeichnis.* Edited by Helga Lengenfelder. 5th ed., rev. New York: R. R. Bowker; Munich: Verlag Dokumentation, 1972.
                                     Z7004.D5 I55

This is a seriously incomplete subject bibliography, first published in 1960, of currently available dictionaries. Serially numbered entries give authors, editors, and compilers; title; languages treated; date and place of publication and name of publisher; and cost. They are disposed into ten main sections, which are further divided into about 120 individual subject categories. Entries in each subject category are further subdivided into multilanguage and single-language groups. The main sections are: 1) Humanities, Social Sciences, Arts; 2) Law and Government; 3) Economics, Trade; 4) Natural Sciences; 5) Medicine; 6) Earth Sciences, Meteorology, Oceanography; 7) Agriculture, Forestry; 8) Applied Sciences, Technology; 9) Transportation, Communications; 10) Industry, Raw Materials, etc. Subcategories of the first section are as follows: (1) Antiquity, Archaeology, and Classical Philology; (2) Architecture, Fine Arts, and Applied Arts; (3) Book Trade and Librarianship, Documentation; (4) Film and Photography; (5) History, Ethnology, History of Culture (Genealogy, Heraldry, Hunting, Fashion, Numismatics, Travels); (6) Mass Media, TV and Journalism; (7) Music, Theatre, and Dance; (8) Education, Educational Technology, and Braille; (9) Philosophy; (10) Psychology; (11) Sociology, Criminology, Sexology; (12) Sports, Games; (13) Linguistics, Literature (further subdivided as follows: a. General Dictionaries, Dialects; b. Special Languages, Languages of Professions; c. Linguistics; d. Literary Languages; e. Literature; f. History of Languages, Synonyms; g. Translation Techniques, Bibliographies of Dictionaries, Abbreviations); (14) Theology. In spite of this massive range, fewer than 5,000 titles are listed. There is a useful subject index of additional fields and cross-references to the given structure, as well as an index of authors and editors and a directory of publishers and other suppliers, with addresses. A more complete new edition would be welcome.

I-26 **Library of Congress.** *Foreign Language–English Dictionaries.* 2 vols. Washington, D.C.: Library of Congress, 1955.
                                     Z7004.D5 U52

This revision of the original edition of 1942 presents lists of bi- or multilingual dictionaries that include English as one language. Volume 1, *Special Subject Dictionaries with Emphasis on Science and Technology*, presents 1,524 serially numbered entries arranged by subject category, then by language, with polyglot dictionaries last. Not always accurate entries present bibliographical information on the title, describe its contents, and give the LC call number. Volume 2, *General Dictionaries*, presents 1,465 entries arranged alphabetically by the name of the individual language, dialect, or language group. Both volumes list their bibliographical sources. Entries give locations in the Library of Congress or one or two other libraries.

I–27 **Zaunmüller, Wolfram.** *Bibliographisches Handbuch der Sprachwörterbücher: Ein internationales Verzeichnis von 5600 Wörterbüchern der Jahre 1460–1958 für mehr als 500 Sprachen und Dialekte / An Annotated Bibliography of Language Dictionaries / Bibliographie critique des dictionnaires linguistiques.* Stuttgart: Hiersemann, 1958.
Z7004.D5 Z3 1958

The more than 5,600 entries are arranged alphabetically by the name of the (first) language they include for more than 400 living and dead languages and more than 100 dialectical variants of them. Emphasis is on dictionaries that include European languages. Within each language the order of entries is as follows: (1) academic dictionaries or other single-language general dictionaries published since 1850; (2) bi- or multilingual general dictionaries; (3) usage, pronunciation, and name dictionaries; (4) synonym, antonym, homonym, etc. dictionaries; (5) dictionaries of professional jargon and slang; (6) foreign word and phrase books; (7) dialect dictionaries and dictionaries of the language of single authors; (8) etymological dictionaries; (9) historical dictionaries; (10) important dictionaries published or prepared before 1850. Entries are briefly annotated. There are indexes of languages (by continent) and of persons.

III. DICTIONARIES—ENGLISH

I–30 **Wall, C. Edward, and Edward Przebienda, comps.** *Words and Phrases Index: A Guide to Antedatings, Key Words, New Compounds, New Meanings, and Other Published Scholarship Supplementing the 'OED', the Dictionary of American English and Other Major Dictionaries of the English Language.* 4 vols. Ann Arbor, Mich.: Pierian Press, 1969–1970. PE1689.W3

This important reference tool serves as an index to more than 185,000 notes, articles, and other sources of information which supplement or complement the discussions of individual words and phrases found in the major general dictionaries of English and American English. Entries are alphabetical, with compound words entered as if they were single words and phrases entered under their first word other than an article.

All four volumes must be used, as they each index a different series of source publications or index that series differently. Volume 1 indexes word and phrase information appearing in *American Notes and Queries*, vols. 1–5 (1962–1966/67); *American Speech*, vols. 1–41 (1925–1966); the *Britannica Book of the Year*, 1945–1967; and *Notes and Queries*, vols. 148–211 (1925–1966). Volume 2 presents the same set of entries found in volume 1 but arranged under keyword cross-references. Volume 3 includes further materials from *American Notes and Queries*; *College English*, vols. 1–29 (1939/40–1967/68); *Dialect Notes*, vols. 1–60 (1890/96–1920/39); and *Publications of the American Dialect Society*, issues 1–47 (1944–1967). Volume 4 presents the same set of

entries found in volume 3 but arranged under keyword cross-references, adding also entries from *California Folklore Quarterly*, vols. 1–6 (1942–1947) and *Western Folklore*, vols. 7–26 (1948–1967). It should be understood that more recent issues of these sources as well as many additional sources will yield further additions and corrections to the entries of the standard dictionaries. In particular, the literary scholar will find that many additions and corrections to the accounts of particular words and phrases given in standard dictionaries appear in notes, articles, and books concerned more generally with the text or texts in which such words are found.

I–31 **Klein, Ernest.** *Comprehensive Etymological Dictionary of the English Language Dealing with the Origin of Words and Their Sense Development, Thus Illustrating the History of Civilization and Culture.* 2 vols. Amsterdam and New York: Elsevier, 1966–1967, 1-vol. ed. 1971.
PE1580.K47

About 45,000 entries present the latest conclusions of scholarship regarding the origins and cognates of English words. The full range of Indo-European cognates is traced, including relations with the Semitic languages. The volume's ambition, in the words of its author, is "to give the history of human civilization and culture condensed in the etymological data of words." Entries identify the part of speech, the direct origins, and the cognates of each word; cross-references point to interesting comparisons.

This work is the most comprehensive and elaborate available etymological dictionary; for inquiries of limited scope the *Oxford Dictionary of English Etymology* (I–32) should be consulted.

I–32 **Onions, Charles T., et al.** *Oxford Dictionary of English Etymology.* London: Oxford University Press, 1966.
PE1580.O5

The etymologies of some 24,000 English words are presented in the main entries of this standard work, while another 14,000 are treated subordinately. Information is given regarding the origin of each word, the date of its entry into English, and the history of its subsequent development and changes of meaning. Unlike Klein's *Comprehensive Etymological Dictionary* (I–31), this work does not attempt to point out all cognates of every word. Klein is also to be preferred for scientific and technical words and many proper names.

An earlier work, still standard for its 12,000 entries, is W. W. Skeat's *Etymological Dictionary of the English Language*, 4th ed. (Oxford: Clarendon Press, 1910) [PE1580.S5 1910], originally published 1878–1882, a concise edition of which was published in 1911 (rev. 1958).

I–33 *The Oxford English Dictionary [OED]: Being a Corrected Re-issue with an Introduction, Supplement, and Bibliography of a New English Dictionary on Historical Principles, Founded Mainly on the Materials Collected by the Philological Society.* Edited by James A. H. Murray et al. 13 vols. Oxford: Clarendon Press, 1933. PE1625.N53 1933

The *New English Dictionary on Historical Principles [NED]*, 10 vols. (Oxford: Clarendon Press, 1888–1928) [PE1625.N53 1888] and this reissue were created to "furnish an adequate account of the meaning, origin, and history of English words now in general use, or known to have been in use at any time during the last seven hundred years. It endeavours to (1) show with regard to each individual word, when, how, in what shape, and with what signification it became English; what development of form and meaning it has since received; which of its uses have in the course of time become obsolete, and which still survive; what new uses have since arisen, by what processes and when; (2) to illustrate these facts by a series of quotations ranging from the first known occurrence of the word to the latest, or down to the present day; the word being thus made to exhibit its own history and meaning; and (3) to treat the etymology of each word strictly on the basis of historical fact; and in accordance with the methods and results of modern philological science." The preface and section of "General Explanations" set forth the principles, methods, and techniques employed by the compilers, with their rationales. Two classes of entries are used, arranged under the modern or most usual British spelling of the word. Main Words, exhibited in Main Articles, comprise all single words, radical or derivative, and all compound words that from their meaning, history, or importance require treatment in separate articles. Subordinate Words, exhibited in Subordinate Articles (in smaller type), include such variant and obsolete forms of Main Words and additional words of bad formation, doubtful existence, or alleged use as were thought proper to record. Entries give the usual modern British spelling, pronunciation, part of speech, specification of semantic field, usage status (if peculiar), earlier spellings, and inflections. This is followed by a discussion of morphology (including etymology, phonetic changes, and other notes on the history of the word's form). Definitions in chronological order follow, with obsolete or otherwise remarkable senses indicated with illustrative quotations beginning with the first instance of the word used in a particular sense and continuing at intervals of about 100 years. Each of the almost 2,000,000 illustrations is identified as to author, source, and date. The *Supplement*, volume 13, adds new words and senses noted between about 1880 and 1930; additions and emendations; a list of spurious words; and a full bibliography of works consulted. The main dictionary, supplement, and additions and emendations should be checked for early or recent meanings or uses.

The *OED*, monument to scholarship though it is, has not gone without criticism, particularly for its lack of reliability on citations of first usages of words in print. See in this and other connections the recent volume by Jurgen Schafer, *Documentation in the OED* (Oxford: Oxford University Press, 1980) [PE1625.N53 S3].

The entire work was reissued in a photographically reduced *Compact Edition*, 2 vols., with a magnifying glass (Oxford: Clarendon Press, 1971) [PE1625.N53 1971]. *Supplement to the Oxford English Dictionary*, ed. R. W. Burchfield [PE1625.N53 1933 Suppl.], which supersedes the original 1933 *Supplement* (vol. 13), records new words and changes in form and usage which have occurred since the late nineteenth century. Volume 1, A-G, appeared in 1972; volume 2, H-N, in 1976; volume 3, O-Scz in 1980; volume 4, Se-Z, in 1986. Reference to some further additions and corrections may be found through the use of the *Words and Phrases Index* (I–30).

An authorized two-volume abridgment of the *OED* with some 163,000 words was first published in 1933 as the *Shorter Oxford English Dictionary on Historical Principles [SOED]*, by William Little et al., ed. C. T. Onions, with revised etymologies by G. W. S. Friedrichsen and revised addenda from the *Supplement* materials (Oxford: Clarendon Press, 1973) [PE1625.L53 1973]. Those who depend on the *OED*, as all students of the history of English language and literature do, will find the excellent biography by K. M. Elisabeth Murray, *Caught in the Web of Words: James Murray and the Oxford English Dictionary* (New Haven: Yale University Press, 1977) [PE64.M8 M78], especially valuable.

An international project sponsored by Oxford University Press, the British Government, IBM Corporation, the University of Waterloo (Ontario), and International Computaprint Corporation in Fort Washington, Pennsylvania, is now under way to produce a *New Oxford English Dictionary* both on-line and in hard copy. It is expected that the seventeen-volume *New OED* will be available in 1987 and that the database will be available for on-line searching by 1989. In 1988, Bowker Electronic Publishing announced the availability of the origin-

al 12 volume *OED* database on CD-ROM. Using the database, it is possible now to search the *OED* using singly or in combination any of the following fields for every entry: the lemma, the etymotogy, the definition, the label (part of speech, mode of speech, subject category), the quote date, the quote author, the quote work, or the quote text.

I–34 **Fowler, H. W.** *Dictionary of Modern English Usage.* 2d ed., rev. and enl. Revised by Sir Ernest Gowers. Oxford: Oxford University Press, 1965. PE1628.F65 1965

Originally published in 1926, this standard and widely known guide has made its author's name a household word (in literate circles). Entries are often more like short learned essays and treat questions of word choice predominantly, though there are many articles on matters of grammar, syntax, spelling, or pronunciation. Though flexible and generally governed by common sense, Fowler's stance is unmistakably both personal and prescriptive rather than descriptive; his reader is constantly being urged with almost moral fervor to see and to avoid certain good and bad expressions or habits of expression. Bad examples predominate. An enumeration of the entry titles of the first dozen articles (omitting the four cross-references that occur among them) will illustrate the scope of the work: (1) a, an; (2) a-, an-; (3) abdomen; (4) abetter, -or; (5) abide; (6) -able, -ible; (7) ablutions; (8) aborigines; (9) above; (10) absolute construction; (11) absolute possessives; (12) abstractitis. Because article titles are sometimes rather enigmatic, Sir Ernest Gowers has introduced a "Classified Guide" that lists certain article titles, briefly describing their contents, in four classes as they concern usage (including points of grammar, syntax, style, or diction); word formation, spelling, and inflection; pronunciation; or punctuation and typography. A further aid is J. Arthur Greenwood's keyword index, *Find It in Fowler: An Alphabetical Index to the Second Edition (1965) of H. W. Fowler's 'Modern English Usage'* . . . (Princeton, N.J.: Wolfhart Book Co., 1969) [PE1628.F65 1965a Index].

An adaptation for American usage by Margaret Nicholson (I–51) is based on the original edition.

I–35 **Jones, Daniel.** *Everyman's English Pronouncing Dictionary, Containing over 58,000 Words in International Phonetic Transcription.* 13th ed. Edited by A. Gimson. London: J. M. Dent, 1967. Reprinted, with corrections, 1972. PE1137.J55

This standard work, first published in 1917, contains about 44,000 words and nearly 15,000 proper names and abbreviations. It includes a glossary of phonetic terms and a bibliography of works on English pronunciation. The standard treatment of early modern English pronunciation is Eric John Dobson's *English Pronunciation, 1500–1700*, 2d ed., 2 vols. (Oxford: Clarendon Press, 1968) [PE1137.D58 1968].

I–36 **Toller, T. Northcote, ed.** *Anglo-Saxon Dictionary Based on the Manuscript Collections of the Late Joseph Bosworth [Bosworth & Toller].* Oxford: Clarendon Press, 1882–1898, with a Supplement, 1908–1921. 3 parts in 4. 2 vols. Enlarged Addenda and Corrigenda to the "Supplement" by Alistair Campbell. Oxford: Clarendon Press, 1972. PE279.B5

The original and supplemental volumes contain together about 60,000 entries treating the words of the Anglo-Saxons in use before A.D. 1100. Entries give the inflected forms, designate the part of speech, provide a definition, and present identified illustrative quotations. The *Supplement*, which both corrects and adds to the main work, must be consulted, as must the recently published volume of *Enlarged Addenda*.

A new *Dictionary of Old English [DOE]*, sponsored by the Centre for Medieval Studies at the University of Toronto (under the editorship of Christopher Ball and Angus Cameron), has been in production since 1969. Planning for this new work began formally with a conference in March 1969. The proceedings were published as *Computers and Old English Concordances*, ed. Angus Cameron, Roberta Frank, and John Leyerle (Toronto: University of Toronto Press, 1970) [PR171.C6]. The proceedings of a second conference, held in September 1970, have also been published: *Plan for the Dictionary of Old English*, ed. Roberta Frank and Angus Cameron (Toronto: University of Toronto Press, 1973) [PE273.P5]. This volume includes "The Dictionary of Old English Conference," by Roberta Frank; "Guide to the Editing and Preparation of Texts for the Dictionary of Old English," by Helmut Gneuss; "A List of Old English Texts," by Angus Cameron; "Computational Aids to Dictionary Compilation," by Richard L. Venezky; and "Some Specimen Entries for the Dictionary of Old English," by C. J. E. Ball and Angus Cameron. Cameron's list of texts cites the authoritative manuscripts, facsimiles, and scholarly editions for each work. It is divided into six sections, treating poetry, prose (subdivided into twenty-eight parts by type of text), interlinear glosses, glossaries, runic inscriptions, and inscriptions in the Latin alphabet; appended is an index of the printed editions of Anglo-Saxon texts. Also available is the listing, "Short Titles of Old English Texts," by Bruce Mitchell, Christopher Ball, and Angus Cameron, in *Anglo-Saxon England* 4 (1975): 207–221; "Addenda and Corrigenda," in *Anglo-Saxon England* 8 (1979): 331–333. Most recently, Angus Cameron et al. have published *Old English Word Studies: A Preliminary Author and Word Index* (Toronto: University of Toronto Press, 1983) [Z2015.S4 C35 1983].

Editing, checking, and preparing the texts and concording each text are now in progress; in due course an alphabetical slip index will be prepared and the actual editing of the *Dictionary of Old English* can begin. Ten-year supplements to the *DOE* are planned. Periodic reports on the status of the *DOE* will be found in the *Old English Newsletter* (N–22). Additional information may be obtained from The Editors, Dictionary of Old English, Centre for Medieval Studies, University of Toronto, Toronto M5S 1A1, Canada.

I–37 Clark-Hall, John Richard. *Concise Anglo-Saxon Dictionary*. 4th ed., with a Supplement by Herbert D. Meritt. Cambridge: Cambridge University Press, 1960.

PE279.H3 1961

First published in 1894, this dictionary includes only 40,000 words but covers the language up to A.D. 1200, thus treating a significant number of twelfth-century words that are excluded from Bosworth and Toller (I–36). The supplement treats some 1,700 words.

Other important dictionaries of Old English include Henry Sweet, *Student's Dictionary of Anglo-Saxon* (Oxford: Oxford University Press, 1896) [PE279.S8]; Christian M. W. Grein with F. Holthausen, *Sprachschatz der angelsächsischen Dichter*, rev. ed., ed. J. T. Köhler (Heidelberg: C. Winter, 1912) [PE281.L5 G7 1912]; F. Holthausen, *Altenglisches etymologisches Wörterbuch*, 2d ed. with revised bibliography by H. C. Matthes (Heidelberg: C. Winter, 1963) [PE263.H6 1963]; and F. Holthausen with Jess B. Bessinger, Jr., *Short Dictionary of Anglo-Saxon Poetry in a Normalized Early West-Saxon Orthography* (Toronto: University of Toronto Press, 1960) [PE279.B4].

I–38 Kurath, Hans, Sherman M. Kuhn, John Reidy, et al., eds. *Middle English Dictionary [MED]*. Ann Arbor: University of Michigan Press, 1952–.

PE679.M54

This work, still in progress, is the definitive authority on Middle English. To date, fasicles covering A-P have been published; the complete work in some sixty-five fasicles is expected to run to more than 10,000 pages. Each entry gives a brief etymology of the word, its various forms, and its various meanings. A total of up to ten examples of the word used in context are cited, with quotations given in the chronological order of manuscript dates; presumed dates of actual composition are given in parentheses.

Users should consult the *Plan and Bibliography*, published in 1954. There the history of the *MED* is set forth; its plan and methods are described by Hans Kurath, with maps identifying the scheme of dialect areas being used; and a bibliography by Margaret S. Ogden, Charles E. Palmer, and Richard L. McKelvey is given. The bibliography, which enumerates preferred manuscripts and editions for each text and version of a text, is arranged in two sections, one of dated short titles for texts generally known thus, and the other with incipits by means of which untitled texts are identified. The *Plan and Bibliography: Supplement I* (1984) updates the bibliography. A more recent account of the methodology of the *MED* was published by Sherman M. Kuhn, "On the Making of the *Middle English Dictionary*," *Dictionaries: Journal of the Dictionary Society of America* 4 (1982): 14–41. Until the *MED* is completed, students will have to consult the *Middle-English Dictionary* of Francis Henry Stratmann (I–39).

I–39 Stratmann, Francis Henry. *Middle-English Dictionary, Containing Words Used by English Writers from the Twelfth to the Fifteenth Century*. New ed. Re-arranged, revised, and enlarged by Henry Bradley. Oxford: Clarendon Press, 1891.

PE679.S7

This single volume, originally published in 1867, presents some 17,000 entries giving brief definitions, some sources, and some contextualizing illustrations of usage. Entries cite words, part of speech, etymology, a definition, and an illustrative quotation. For all parts of the alphabet covered by the newer and vastly more complete and accurate *Middle English Dictionary* (I–38), that work should be preferred; when it is completed, it will replace Stratmann entirely.

I–40 Skeat, Walter W. *Glossary of Tudor and Stuart Words, Especially from the Dramatists*. Edited with additions by A. L. Mayhew. Oxford: Clarendon Press, 1914.   PE1667.S5

A glossary of some 7,000 words giving definitions and references to their place in texts, particularly of the drama. A bibliography of references concludes the volume.

There are two other guides to the vocabulary of the Renaissance period: Robert Nares, *Glossary or Collection of Words, Names and Allusions to Customs, Proverbs, etc. Which Have Been Thought to Require Illustration in the Works of English Authors, Particularly Shakespeare and His Contemporaries*, rev. and enl. ed., ed. James O. Halliwell [-Phillips] and Thomas Wright, 2 vols. (London: G. Routledge, 1905) [PE1667.N3], and James Halliwell-Phillips, *Dictionary of Archaic and Provincial Words, Obsolete Phrases, and Ancient Customs, from the XIVth Century; Supplement* by T. L. O. Davies, 7th ed., 2 vols. in 1 (London: G. Routledge and Sons, 1924) [PE1667.H3 1924]. The first of these was originally published in 1822 and contains both definitions and identified illustrations; the second was originally published in 1847 and includes some 35,000 archaic and provincial words with definitions and identified illustrations.

I-41 **Wright, Joseph.** *English Dialect Dictionary: Being the Complete Vocabulary of All Dialect Words Still in Use, or Known to Have Been in Use during the Last Two Hundred Years; Founded on the Publications of the English Dialect Society and on a Large Amount of Material Never Before Printed.* 6 vols. London: Henry Frowde, 1898–1905.

PE1776.W8

This dictionary includes the complete vocabulary of all English dialect words in use during the eighteenth and nineteenth centuries in England, Scotland, Ireland, and Wales. Some 100,000 dialect words and phrases are discussed. Entries present each dialect word, its part of speech, the geographical region over which each word extends, quotations and references to sources from which each quotation has been obtained, exact pronunciation according to a distinctive phonetic scheme, etymology, and definitions. Volume 1 contains a preface, select bibliographical list, pronunciation key, list of abbreviations, and a list of the countries with abbreviations used in reference to them. Volume 6 contains a supplemental list of words not treated in the main body for various reasons, a bibliography of the principal books, manuscripts, and other sources quoted in the dictionary, and a 187-page *English Dialect Grammar* (which was also separately published in 1905) treating the English dialects of England, Scotland, Ireland, and Wales.

I-42 **Partridge, Eric.** *Dictionary of Slang and Unconventional English: Colloquialisms and Catch-Phrases, Solecisms and Catachreses, Nicknames and Vulgarisms [Partridge].* Edited by Paul Beale. 8th ed. New York: Macmillan, 1984.

PE3721.P3 1984

This work, designed as a companion to the *OED*, presents both the original dictionary of 1937 and a revised supplement to it. It is a dictionary of linguistically unconventional English words and phrases, that is, of all English other than standard and dialectical, including both British and American words. Like the *OED*, this dictionary is historical in nature, citing the approximate dates of use for each of its 65,000 entries, though specific attested usages for each term and each sense of each term are not always identified. References are made, however, to citations in other dictionaries. The work is useful for locating the meaning and often the origin of slang, cant, and other forms of unconventional English; whenever the literal meaning of a word or phrase seems unclear or inappropriate, and whenever it is suspected that a non-literal meaning is intended, consultation of Partridge is indicated.

There are a variety of dictionaries concerned with the slang of specific groups. Bibliographies of such dictionaries include listings in the standard bibliographical guides (A–20, A–21, A–22, A–23, A–24) and in both Brewer (I–20), and Zischka (I–21). See also William J. Burke's annotated bibliography, *Literature of Slang* (New York: New York Public Library, 1939) [Z2015.S6 B9]. The best source for help with current slang is the journal *Current Slang: A Quarterly Glossary of Slang Expressions Presently in Use* (1966–).

John S. Farmer and W. E. Henley, *Slang and Its Analogues, Past and Present: Historical and Comparative Dictionary*, 7 vols. (London: Printed for subscribers only, 1890–1904) [PE3721.F4], is the standard reference work, on which Partridge also depends. Entries for more than 100,000 words include also German, French, Italian, and Spanish synonyms.

I-43 **Partridge, Eric.** *Dictionary of the Underworld, British and American: Being the Vocabularies of Crooks, Criminals, Racketeers, Beggars and Tramps, Convicts, the Commercial Underworld, the Drug Traffic, the White Slave Traffic, Spies.* 3d ed. London: Routledge and Kegan Paul, 1968.

PE3726.P3 1968

The first edition of this specialized slang dictionary was published in 1949. This work, like Partridge's more general dictionary (I–42), presents not only some 25,000 terms and definitions but also an overview of historical development, with dated quotations illustrating usage.

IV. DICTIONARIES—AMERICAN

I-45 **Craigie, Sir William A., and James R. Hulbert.** *Dictionary of American English on Historical Principles [DAE].* 4 vols. Chicago: University of Chicago Press, 1938–1944.

PE2835.C72

This dictionary of words with a distinctly American usage and/or origin includes materials from colonial times through the end of the nineteenth century. Entries list the word, give variant spellings, rarely give etymologies, and by means of symbols indicate whether the word or one of its senses was found in England before 1600, whether the word or sense clearly originated in the United States, or whether its origin cannot be determined. Definitions are accompanied by dated, identified, chronologically arranged quotations. In general, the format and character of entries reflect the format and character of the *OED* (I–33), on which this work was modeled. Volume 1 has an introduction to American English, which should be supplemented by more recent sources (see entries in I–17). Volume 4 includes a bibliography of sources for illustrative quotations. The project to create such a supplement to the *OED* was outlined in Craigie's "The Historical Dictionary of American English," *English Journal* 15 (1926): 13–23. Joseph A. Weingarten compiled a volume of *Supplementary Notes to the Dictionary of American English* (New York, 1948), which includes additional quotations for about 700 entries, some antedating those in the original volumes.

I-46 **Mathews, Mitford M., ed.** *Dictionary of Americanisms on Historical Principles.* 2 vols. Chicago: University of Chicago Press, 1951.

PE2835.D5

This dictionary includes only terms with an American origin or with a distinct sense first given them in American usage. There are some 50,000 entries. Many words recorded in the *DAE* (I–45) are not recorded here; others, including twentieth-century words, are found here but not in the *DAE*. In general, both dictionaries should be used together.

Entries give definitions with chronologically arranged quotations illustrating changes in meaning. Entries on words that have United States origins include pronunciation and etymologies. An abridgment, *Americanisms: A Dictionary of Selected Americanisms on Historical Principles* (Chicago: University of Chicago Press, 1966) [PE2835.D52], gives about 1,000 entries of special interest.

There is a similarly conceived and constructed work on Canadian English, *Dictionary of Canadianisms on Historical Principles*, ed. Walter S. Avis (Toronto: W. J. Gage, 1967) [PE3237.B7 or PE3243.D5], and an abridgment, *Concise Dictionary of Canadianisms* (Toronto: Gage Educational Publishers, 1973) [PE3243.C6].

I–47 *Webster's New International Dictionary of the English Language.* 2d ed. William Allan Neilson, editor in chief. Springfield, Mass.: G. and C. Merriam, 1934.

PE1625.W3 1934

This conventional and prescriptive dictionary prepared by 209 special editors contains some 600,000 entries, including large numbers of obsolete and rare words and proper names of persons and places. Entries give the American and alternate spellings of each word, the pronunciation (as determined by cultivated use), the part of speech, inflection, area of special use, etymology, definitions (in chronological order), and status (obsolete, colloquial, etc.) of each word. Additional notes and cross-references are often added, along with extensive lists of synonyms and antonyms. At the foot of each page is a second alphabetical series of additional entries, including obsolete and rare words and proverbs, as indicated. There are appendixes on abbreviations, signs and symbols, forms of address, a pronouncing gazetteer (of some 36,000 place-names), and a pronouncing biographical dictionary with some 13,000 entries.

I–48 *Webster's Third New International Dictionary of the English Language.* Unabridged. Philip B. Gove, editor in chief. Springfield, Mass.: Merriam-Webster, 1961.   PE1625.W36

An extensive unabridged dictionary of modern English which has become the most controversial reference book of its time because unlike its predecessor, *Webster's Second* [I–47], it does not prescribe correct usage and instead describes current usage in an almost democratic fashion. There are some 450,000 entries. Obsolete and rare words and proverbs are omitted, along with most proper names, in contrast with the practice in *Webster's Second*, which therefore has one-fourth more entries. Of the material included in *Webster's Third*, some 100,000 items are words or meanings never before included in a Webster's unabridged dictionary. Entries give American spelling and syllabification with cross-references from British spellings to the main entry of the word. American pronunciation is given, along with part of speech, inflections, capitalization, etymology, and usage status. Archaic or slang words are identified as such but "colloquial" is not differentiated from standard English. In general, usage information is less stressed and less rigorously assertive than in any former dictionary. Definitions are arranged in chronological order of developing meanings. The more than 200,000 citations illustrating current usage are more likely to come from popular culture than from the literary canon. Cross-references to other entries and lists of synonyms conclude entries. *9000 Words: A Supplement to Webster's Third New International Dictionary* (Springfield, Mass.: Merriam-Webster, 1983) [PE1630.A16 1983] adds 9,000 words and meanings that have come into use since about 1960.

The controversy surrounding the publication of this work may be followed in J. H. Sledd and W. R. Ebbitt, *Dictionaries and That Dictionary: A Casebook on the Aims of Lexicographers and the Targets of Reviewers* (Chicago: Scott, Foresman, 1962) [PE1625.W37 S4]. The moderate conclusion is that both *Webster's Second* and *Webster's Third* have value, depending on what you want to know about a word, a meaning, or a usage.

I–49 *American Heritage Dictionary of the English Language.* Edited by William Morris. Boston: American Heritage and Houghton Mifflin, 1969.   PE1625.A54

Generally regarded as the best of the recent one-volume English dictionaries, the *American Heritage* treats both British and American usage. The 155,000 entries include both personal names and place-names. They are quite readable and include usage labels with reports given of the attitudes held toward particular locutions by a specially formed panel of writers and other respected users of the language. The work is illustrated and includes among the preliminaries seven essays on the English language by distinguished scholars, as well as a long appendix on Indo-European roots. The usage survey employed in preparing this dictionary is analyzed by Albert H. Marckwardt in "Lexicographical Method and the Usage Survey," in *Lexicography and Dialect Geography: Festgabe for Hans Kurath*, ed. Harald Scholler and John Reidy (Wiesbaden: F. Steiner, 1973) [P327.L43], pp. 134–146, and both more extensively and more critically in Thomas J. Creswell, *Usage in Dictionaries and Dictionaries of Usage* (University: University of Alabama Press, 1975) [PE1702.A5 vols. 63–64].

The other well-regarded one-volume recent dictionary is the *Random House Dictionary of the English Language*, 2d ed., unabridged (New York: Random House, 1987) [PE1625.R3 1987]. It, too, is moderately prescriptive in the notes and comments on usage following some entries.

I–50 **Ehrlich, Eugene, et al.** *Oxford American Dictionary.* New York: Oxford University Press, 1980.   PE2835.O9

A one-volume inventory of current American English containing brief, readable definitions, a guide to pronunciation which does not use phonetic transcription, and usage notes. Distinctively American technical terms and other special vocabulary are included, with derivations of common words and phrases.

I–51 **Nicholson, Margaret.** *Dictionary of American-English Usage, Based on Fowler's Modern English Usage.* New York: Oxford University Press, 1957.   PE2835.N5

An adaptation of the 1926 classic guide to English usage by Fowler (I–34) with American variations, shortened articles, and omission of those that were more academic or had become less pertinent to usage in the late 1950s. The approximately 6,000 entries give American spellings and pronunciations. A list of general articles precedes the dictionary proper. These articles include such topics as Absolute Construction, Hackneyed Phrases, Malaprops, Superfluous Words, Vulgarization, and Worn-out Humor.

I–52 **Follett, Wilson.** *Modern American Usage: A Guide.* Edited and completed by Jacques Barzun et al. New York: Hill and Wang, 1966.   PE2835.F6

An American "Fowler" (I–34), this is generally considered the most successful guide to current American usage. A discussion of general points is followed by entries on words and phrases, giving recommended usage.

For additional information see also Margaret M. Bryant, ed., *Current American Usage* (New York: Funk and Wagnalls, 1962) [PE2835.B67]; Bergen Evans and Cornelia Evans, *Dictionary of Contemporary American Usage* (New York: Random House, 1957) [PE2835.B67]; and Roy H. Copperud, *American Usage and Style: The Consensus* (New York: Van Nostrand Reinhold, 1980) [PE1460.C648], which gathers opinion on disputed points from all the leading dictionaries and guides.

I–53 **Kenyon, John Samuel, and Thomas Albert Knott.** *Pronouncing Dictionary of American English.* 2d ed. Springfield, Mass.: G. and C. Merriam, 1949.

PE1137.K37 1949

This standard work, first published in 1944, gives the pronunciation using IPA of the colloquial speech of educated Americans, with regional variants. Proper names are included, with an emphasis on American personal names and place-names. Some literary, scientific, and geographic terms frequently seen in print are also included.

I-54 Wentworth, Harold. *American Dialect Dictionary*. New York: Thomas Y. Crowell, 1944. PE 2835.W4

Some 13,000 American dialect words—vocabulary, phrasal, semantic, phonological, and morphological variations—are included, particularly localisms, regionalisms, provincialisms, folk speech, urban speech, and dialect of the New England and Southern regions which deviates from General Northern or Western American English. Entries give definitions, geographical area of use, and illustrative quotations. Additions and corrections to this work and elaborations of it will be found in the *Publications of the American Dialect Society* (Greensboro, N.C., 1944–) [PE1702.A5].

I-55 Wentworth, Harold, and Stuart Berg Flexner. *Dictionary of American Slang*. 2d, supplemented ed. New York: Crowell, 1975. PE3729.V5 W4 1966

Originally published in 1960, this standard dictionary of slang terms used in the United States includes colloquialisms, cant, jargon, argot, and idioms in popular novels and the movies. More than 10,000 terms are identified, dated, and quoted in context when possible, and sources are identified. There are over 60,000 illustrative quotations. Some etymologies are given. Appended are word lists, including affixes; shortened forms; reduplications; rhyming terms and rhyming slang; back slang and pig Latin; onomatopoeia; blend words, corruptions, redundancies, omnibus terms, nonce and nonsense words; nicknames, place-names, and group names; children's bathroom vocabulary; synonyms for "drunk"; expressions concerning sex and food; and synthetic fad expressions. There is a select bibliography. The supplement adds some 2,500 entries and an updated bibliography. A revised edition edited by Robert L. Chapman, *New Dictionary of American Slang* was published by Harper & Row in 1986 [PE2846.C46 1986].

Two other dictionaries of American slang may be recommended. Lester V. Berrey and Melvin Van Den Bark, *American Thesaurus of Slang: A Complete Reference Book of Colloquial Speech*, 2d ed. (New York: Crowell, 1952) [PE3729.A5 B4 1953], is divided into two parts, presenting general slang and the slang of special groups. Within the two parts some 100,000 terms are presented in an elaborate subject-category arrangement. There is also a 370-page single-alphabet index of words and subject categories. Joseph A. Weingarten, *American Dictionary of Slang and Colloquial Speech* (New York, 1954) [PE3721.W4], is arranged along the same lines as Wentworth and Flexner. Note, too, that Partridge (I-42) includes some American slang.

There are, in addition, dictionaries treating the slang of a special group or discourse community. See, for example, Clarence Major, *Dictionary of Afro-American Slang* (New York: International Publishers, 1970) [PE3727.N4 M3], or H. E. Golden et al., *Dictionary of American Underworld Lingo* (New York: Twayne, 1957) [PE3726.D5].

V. DICTIONARIES—SCOTTISH

I-58 Scottish Dictionaries.

The standard dictionary of the Scottish language after 1700 is the *Scottish National Dictionary, Designed Partly on Regional Lines and Partly on Historical Principles, and Containing All the Scottish Words Known to Be in Use since c. 1700*, ed.

William Grant and David D. Murison, 10 vols. (Edinburgh: Scottish National Dictionary Association, 1931–1976) [PE2106.S4], which treats both written and spoken Scots, giving variant spellings, grammatical function, status, pronunciation, illustrative quotations, and exact references to sources, along with etymology if known.

The *Scottish National Dictionary* is complemented by Sir William Alexander Craigie, *Dictionary of the Older Scottish Tongue from the Twelfth Century to the End of the Seventeenth* (Chicago: University of Chicago Press; and London: Oxford University Press, 1937–) [PE2116.C7], of which four volumes, covering A-Pn, have been published to date. This work treats the full vocabulary of 1600 and words not common in English usage to 1700; entries include variant forms, etymology, and chronologically ordered meanings with illustrative quotations.

A shorter, less elaborate, but handy work is *Scots Dialect Dictionary, Comprising the Words in Use from the Latter Part of the Seventeenth Century to the Present Day* (Edinburgh: Chambers, 1911) [PE2106.W2], ed. A. Warrack, with an introduction and dialect map by W. Grant, the most recent issue of which appeared in 1965. It contains 25,000–30,000 words, giving only word function and definitions.

See also J. S. Woolley, *Bibliography for Scottish Linguistic Studies* (Edinburgh; J. Thin, 1954) [Z2059.D5 W66].

VI. DICTIONARIES—FOREIGN LANGUAGE

I-60 Liddell, Henry George, and Robert Scott. *Greek-English Lexicon*. 9th ed. Revised by H. Stuart Jones and R. McKenzie. 2 vols. Oxford: Clarendon Press, 1925–1940. A Supplement Designed for Use in Conjunction with Liddell and Scott. Edited by E. A. Barber et al. Oxford: Clarendon Press, 1968. PA445.E5 L6 1968

Originally published in 1843, this is the standard and authoritative Ancient Greek–Modern English dictionary. About 10,000 entries cover the Greek language to about A.D. 600 but omit Byzantine and Patristic Greek. For the former see E. A. Sophocles, *Greek Lexicon of the Roman and Byzantine Periods (from 146 B.C. to A.D. 1100)*, 3d "memorial" ed. (New York: Scribner's, 1900) [PA1125.S7]. For the latter see G. W. H. Lampe, *Patristic Greek Lexicon* (Oxford: Clarendon Press, 1961–1968) [PA681.P3]. See also Charles du Fresne, Sieur du Cange, *Glossarium ad Scriptores Mediae et Infimae Graecitatis*, 2 vols. (Lyons: Anisson, Posuel, et Rigaud, 1688) [PA1125.D8], frequently reprinted, which is parallel in its structure and value to du Cange's better-known glossary of Medieval Latin (see I-69).

I-65 Lewis, Charlton T., and Charles Short. *Latin Dictionary Founded on Andrews' Edition [1850] of Freund's Latin Dictionary*. New ed. Oxford: Clarendon Press, 1907. Often reprinted, most recently in 1962. PA2265.E5 A7 1962

With some 60,000 entries, including personal names and place-names, this has since its first presentation in 1879 been the standard Latin-English dictionary, though the *Oxford Latin Dictionary* (I-66) is now regarded as standard. It contains many identified illustrative citations from classical authors and includes a bibliography of authors and works quoted. Entries must be corrected by reference to A. Ernout and P. J. A. Meillet, *Dictionnaire étymologique de la langue latine: Histoire des mots*, 4th ed., 2 vols. in 1 (Paris: C. Klincksieck, 1954–1960) [PA2342.E7 1960].

The best modern Latin-English/English-Latin dictionary is *Cassell's New Latin Dictionary*, ed. D. P. Simpson, 4th ed.

(London: Cassell, 1966) [PA2365.L3C3 1966], which has about 30,000 entries, including place-names and personal names.

I–66 ***Oxford Latin Dictionary [OLD].*** Edited by P. G. W. Glare. Oxford University Press, 1968–1982. PA2365.E509 1982

This new, independent dictionary contains some 80,000 words, making it approximately one-third longer than Lewis and Short (I–65). It treats the Latin language to the end of the second century A.D. and is based on the principles and practices of the *Oxford English Dictionary* (I–2). Many identified quotations arranged in chronological order illustrate the development of different meanings for each word. The 40,000 entries in A. Souter, *Glossary of Later Latin, to 600 A.D.* (Oxford: Clarendon Press, 1949) [PA2308.S6], serves as the link between the *OLD* and the various dictionaries and glossaries of Medieval Latin (see I–69).

I–67 ***Thesaurus Linguae Latinae, Editus Auctoritate et Consilio Academiarum Quinque Germanicarum Berolinensis, Gottingensis, Lipsiensis, Monacensis, Vindobonensis.*** Leipzig: B. G. Teubner, 1900–. PA2361.T4

This massive thesaurus, still in production, will serve to index and illustrate all use of Latin to A.D. 150. It is now being edited by the Wissenschaftliche Thesaurus-Kommission in Munich. A record is given, with representative quotations from each author, of every word in the text of each Latin author down to the Antonines, with a selection of important passages from the works of all writers to the seventh century. The sources are identified in the *Index Librorum Scriptorum Inscriptionum ex Quibus Exempla Adferuntur* (Leipzig: Teubner, 1904) [PA2361.T4 index], with a *Supplementum* (1958) and a first *Addendum* (1963). A side series, being published more or less simultaneously, is the *Supplementum: Nomina Propria* (*Onomasticon*) (Leipzig: Teubner, 1907–) [PA2361.T4 Add.], which will provide a comparable index and record of all proper names.

Articles growing out of work on the *Thesaurus* have been published in the journals *Philologus: Zeitschrift für klassische Philologie* (1889–) [PA3.P5] and *Museum Helveticum: Schweizerische Zeitschrift für klassische Altertumswissenschaft* (1946–) [PA3.M73]. They are being reprinted in the series *Beiträge aus der Thesaurus-Arbeit* (Leiden: Brill, 1979–) [PA2320.B44].

I–69 **Latham, Ronald E., ed. *Revised Medieval Latin Word-List from British and Irish Sources.*** London: Oxford University Press, 1965. PA2891.B3 1965

This work, based on J. H. Baxter and C. Johnson, eds., *Medieval Latin Word List* (London: Oxford University Press, 1934) [PA2891.B3], is indispensable for reading medieval British and Irish documents. It records approximately 40,000 entry terms with modern English equivalents and dated illustrative quotations.

The standard dictionary of Medieval Latin is that originated by Charles du Fresne, Sieur du Cange, *Glossarium Mediae et Infimae Latinitatis* . . . , first published in three volumes in 1678 but used in the *Editio Nova, Aucta Pluribus Verbis Aliorum Scriptorum*, ed. Leopold Favre, 10 vols. in 11 (Niort: Faure, 1883–1887) [PA2889.D8], to which there is a one-volume *Petit supplément* (*au Dictionnaire de du Cange*) by Charles Schmidt (Strassburg, 1906) [PA2893.F7 S37]. There is a *Novum Glossarium Mediae Latinitatis ab Anno DCCC Usque ad Annum MCC* being prepared by the International Union of Academies under the editorship of F. Blatt (Copenhagen: Munksgaard, 1957–) which will supplement du Cange. The *Index Scriptorum Novus Mediae Latinitatis* was

published in 1973 [Z6517.I52]. For British sources the new *Dictionary of Medieval Latin from British Sources*, ed. Ronald E. Latham, fasc. 1– (London: Oxford University Press, 1975–) [PA2891.L28], will replace du Cange. It will include classical Latin used by British authors, postclassical words and usages, and words with Anglo-Saxon, Anglo-Norman, and other vernacular flavor. Most Irish and certain Welsh sources are excluded. A project for Medieval Latin similar to that of the *Thesaurus Linguae Latinae* (I–67) is being cosponsored and published by the Bayerische Akademie der Wissenschaften and the Deutsche Akademie der Wissenschaften zu Berlin, the *Mittellateinisches Wörterbuch bis zum ausgehenden 13. Jahrhundert; in Gemeinschaft mit den Akademien der Wissenschaften zu Göttingen, Heidelberg, Leipzig, Mainz, Wien, und der Schweizerischen Geisteswissenschaftlichen Gesellschaft* (Munich: Beck, 1959–) [PA2893.G3 M48 1959]. An *Abkurzungs-und Quellenverzeichnis* was published in 1959, along with the first parts of the dictionary.

For Renaissance Latin see the bibliography in *Renaissance Dictionaries, English-Latin and Latin-English*, by D. T. Starnes (Austin: University of Texas Press, 1954) [PA2353.S7].

I–70 **Mansion, J. E., comp. *Harrap's New Standard French and English Dictionary.*** Revised and enlarged by R. P. L. Ledesert and Margaret Ledesert. 4 vols. Part 1, French-English, 2 vols. Part 2, English-French, 2 vols. London: Harrap, 1972–1980. PC2640.H317

This is the leading French-English/English-French dictionary. Part 1 of this work lists more than 100,000 headwords, representing the vocabulary of modern spoken and written French, including colloquialisms, slang, scientific terms, words from Canadian, Swiss, and Belgian French, "franglais," and some obsolete literary and technical terms. Similarly, the English-French part, with its more than 125,000 headwords, includes the English of the British Isles, Australia, New Zealand, North America, and South Africa. Obsolete and archaic words, literary words, and obsolescent words are included, as are colloquialisms, slang words and expressions, and frequently used vulgarisms. A broad selection of compound words is given, and proper names are included if their form is different in French. This dictionary, now the standard work, is based upon and replaces *Harrap's Standard French and English Dictionary*, in two parts (1934–1939) [PC2640.H3].

Also available is *Harrap's New Shorter French and English Dictionary*, rev. and enl. (London: Harrap, 1979) [PC2640.H32 1979], with some 41,000 words in the French-English part and some 56,000 words in the English-French section. Another frequently recommended one-volume French-English/English-French is the *New Cassell's French Dictionary*, ed. Denis Girard et al. (New York: Funk and Wagnalls, 1962) [PC2640.C3 1962].

The most authoritative and massive French-language dictionary is that of Emile Littré, *Dictionnaire de la langue française*, complete ed., 7 vols. (Paris: J. Pauvert, 1956–1958) [PC2625.L63], originally published in 1863–1872. For further references to French-language dictionaries see the bibliography by R. M. Klaar, *French Dictionaries* (London: CILT, 1976) [Z2175.D6 K58], with its extended descriptions of thirty-seven bilingual French-and-English dictionaries and sixty monolingual French dictionaries.

I–75 **Velázquez de la Cadena, Mariano, Edward Gray, and Juan L. Iribas, eds.** *Revised Velázquez Spanish and English Dictionary.* Newly revised by Ida Navarro Hinojosa et al. 2 vols. in 1. Chicago: Follett, 1960. PC4640.V5

Originally published in 1852 under the title *Pronouncing Dictionary of the Spanish and English Languages*, this frequently revised work has remained standard. This, its most current revision, includes new terms and idiomatic expressions, treating usage in Spanish America and English America as well as Britain and Spain. Many geographical and proper names are included.

Also highly esteemed is the *Collins Spanish-English English-Spanish Dictionary*, compiled by Colin Smith in collaboration with M. Bermejo Marcos and E. Chang-Rodriguez (London: Collins, 1971) [PC4640.S595].

I–76 *Cassell's Spanish-English, English-Spanish Dictionary / Diccionario Español-Inglés, Inglés-Español.* Revised by Anthony Gooch and Angel Garcia de Paredes. London: Cassell, 1978. PE4640.C35 1978

This dictionary, first published in 1959, includes both Castilian and Latin American usage, and both British and American English. Examples of use, with appropriate contexts, are given; regional and idiomatic usage is indicated.

Another well-regarded one-volume dictionary is that compiled by Carlos Castillo and Otto Ferdinand Bond, *University of Chicago Spanish Dictionary: A New Concise Spanish-English and English-Spanish Dictionary of Words and Phrases Basic to the Written and Spoken Languages of Today* (Chicago: University of Chicago Press, 1948) [PC4640.U5]. The standard authority for current Spanish usage is the *Diccionario de la lengua española*, 19th ed. (1970) [PC4625.A3 1970], by the Real Academia Española, first published in six vols. in 1726–1739 [PC4625.A3 1970]. The standard historical dictionary of the Spanish language, under the sponsorship of the Spanish Academy, is the *Diccionario historico de la lengua española*, 18th ed. (Madrid: Libreria y casa Hernando, 1960–) [PC4625.A35 1960], still in progress. For additional references see M. Fabbri, *Bibliography of Hispanic Dictionaries: Catalan, Galician, Spanish, Spanish in Latin America and the Philippines* [with an appended bibliography of Basque dictionaries] (Imola: Galeati, 1979) [Z2695.D6 F32 1979].

I–80 **Reynolds, Barbara.** *Cambridge Italian Dictionary.* 2 vols. Italian-English and English-Italian. Cambridge: Cambridge University Press, 1962–1981. PC1640.R4

This work supersedes Alfred Hoare's *Italian Dictionary*, 2d ed. (Cambridge: Cambridge University Press, 1925) [PC1640.H6 1925], as the standard work for English speakers. The 50,000 entry words include obsolete and obsolescent words for readers of Italian literature present and past, along with a selection of specialist terms and proper names. Also available is the *Concise Cambridge Italian Dictionary* (Cambridge: Cambridge University Press, 1975) [PC1640.R44], which contains some 42,000 of the most frequently used words.

I–81 **Macchi, Valdimiro, ed.** *Sansoni-Harrap Standard Italian and English Dictionary.* 2 parts in 4 vols. Part 1, Italian-English, 2 vols. Part 2, English-Italian, 2 vols. Florence: Sansoni; London: Harrap, 1970–1976. PC1640.I5

This is the largest and most comprehensive Italian-English/English-Italian dictionary with some 320,000 entries, including words in everyday use, neologisms, regionalisms, words from classical and modern Italian literature, and some technical vocabulary. Both British and American English are given.

The standard authority on the Italian language is Niccolo Tommaseo et al., *Dizionario della lingua italiana*, 4 vols. in 8 (Turin: Unione tipografico, 1861–1879) [PC1625.T6 1861]. This is gradually being replaced by Salvatore Battaglia, *Grande dizionario della lingua italiana* (Turin: Unione tipografico, 1961–) [PC1625.B3].

I–85 **Springer, Otto, ed.** *Langenscheidts [neu Muret-Sanders] enzyklopädisches Wörterbuch der englischen und deutschen Sprache / Langenscheidt's [New Muret-Sanders] Encyclopaedic Dictionary of the English and German Languages.* Rev. ed. based on the original work by Edward Muret and Daniel Sanders. 4 vols. Berlin: Langenscheidt, 1962–1975. PF3640.L257

The original Muret-Sanders English and German dictionary was published in four volumes (Berlin, 1891–1901). This new work is in two parts, as follows: part 1, English-German, 2 vols. (1962–1963); part 2, German-English, 2 vols. (1974–1975). A total of approximately 380,000 entry words are included, 180,000 in part 1 and 200,000 in part 2. The vocabulary of special subjects, simple phrases, and many idioms are found in the four volumes. Words from both American and British English are recorded, as are the regional vocabularies of the German Democratic Republic, Austria, and Switzerland.

Langenscheidt's Concise German Dictionary, new ed. (1933) [PF3640.L24], compiled by Heinz Messinger and Werner Rüdenberg and based upon the more encyclopedic work, presents about 150,000 entry terms in two parts, German-English and English-German.

The standard historical dictionary of the German language is that of Jakob and Wilhelm Grimm, *Deutsches Wörterbuch*, 32 vols. (Leipzig: Hirzel, 1854–1961) [PF3625.G7]; *Quellenverzeichnis*, 2d ed. (1965–1971) [PF3625.G72]. A second edition of this monumental work is being prepared by the Deutsche Akademie der Wissenschaften zu Berlin in cooperation with the Akademie der Wissenschaften zu Göttingen. See also the recently published *Geschichte des Deutschen Wörterbuches, 1838–1863: Dokumente zu den Lexikographen Grimm*, ed. Alan Kirkness (Stuttgart: Hirzel, 1980) [PF3617.G75 G47 1980].

I–86 *Oxford-Harrap Standard German and English Dictionary.* Part 1, German-English. Vols. 1–3 edited by Trevor Jones. Vols. 4–5 edited by John Pheby. London: Harrap, 1963–1947; Oxford: Clarendon Press, 1980–. PF3640.H3 1977

The first three volumes have the title *Harrap's Standard German and English Dictionary* and are meant to parallel the *Standard French and English Dictionary* (I–70). Part 1, German-English, will include approximately 100,000 entry words when completed and treats both general vocabulary and scientific terms, including both Austrian and Swiss vocabularies. It presents extensive information about each word's stylistic level with examples of usage, including proverbial and idiomatic uses, and definitions. In general, American words are given only when the British English term would be misleading or unintelligible in America. Part 2, English-German, will begin appearing in the mid-1980s.

For additional references to German dictionaries see Peter Kuhn, *Deutsche Wörterbücher: Eine systematische Bibliographie* (Tübingen: Niemeyer, 1978) [Z2235.D6 K83 1978].

I–89 **Rosten, Leo C.** *Joys of Yiddish: A Relaxed Lexicon of Yiddish, Hebrew, and Yinglish Words Often Encountered in English.* New York: McGraw-Hill, 1968. PN6231.J5 R67

For further detail see the more complete, scholarly dictionaries of Yiddish: Alexander Harkavy, *English-Yidisher Weterbuch / English-Yiddish Dictionary*, 22d ed. (New York: Hebrew Publishing Co., 1940) [PJ5117.H5 1940]; Uriel Weinreich, *Modern English-Yiddish, Yiddish-English Dictionary* (New York: Yivo Institute for Jewish Research and McGraw-Hill, 1968) [PJ5117.W4]; and the *Great Dictionary of the Yiddish Language* (*Groyser Verterbukh fun der Yidischer Shprakh*), ed. J. A. Joffe and Y. Mark, vol. 1– (New York, 1961–), to be completed in eight volumes [PJ5117.G7].

I–90 **Wheeler, Marcus.** *Oxford Russian-English Dictionary.* B. O. Unbegaun, general editor. Oxford: Clarendon Press, 1972. Reprinted with corrections, 1978.   PG2640.W5

There are approximately 70,000 headwords in this general-purpose dictionary of written and spoken Russian, designed primarily for the use of English speakers. Entries indicate the pattern of declension and conjugation for nouns and verbs and give idioms and examples of usage.

Also recommended are V. K. Miuller, ed., *Anglo-russkii Slovar' / English-Russian Dictionary*, 7th ed., rev. (Moscow, 1969); 14th ed., newly rev. (New York: Dutton, 1973) [PG2640.M8 1973b]; and the companion volume edited by A. I. Smirnitskii et al., *Russko-Angliiskii Slovar'* (Russian-English Dictionary); (Moscow, 1969); 11th ed. (New York: Dutton, 1981) [PG2640.R844 1981]. The former contains some 70,000 entries; the latter has about 50,000 entries.

VII. TRANSLATION—BIBLIOGRAPHIES AND GUIDES

For additional bibliographies and guides to translation see works on General and Comparative Literature (section L.I) and the *MLA International Bibliography* (L–50), among many other sources.

I–100 **Olmsted, Hugh M.** *Translations and Translating: A Selected Bibliography of Bibliographies, Indexes, and Guides.* Binghamton, N.Y.: Center for Translation and Intercultural Communication, SUNY-Binghamton, 1975.
Z7004.T72 O45

This "preliminary version" (which has not been updated) provides a basic listing that excludes general bibliographical references, bibliographies on translations of single writers, works on the professional or legal aspects of translating, and translated works or individual works about translating. Included are (1) bibliographies of works on translation; (2) guides to translations; (3) works listing translated journals; (4) works listing translations from the press, including material on current events and politics; (5) major serial bibliographies of technical translations; and (6) a miscellaneous section that includes retrospective bibliographies of translations and bibliographies of literary or general translations. This last section is arranged alphabetically by "source" language: subdivisions first list bibliographies of translations from English and then bibliographies of translations into English.

I–101 **Bausch, Karl Richard, Josef Klegraf, and Wolfram Wilss.** *Science of Translation: An Analytical Bibliography (1962–1969).* Tübinger Beiträge zur Linguistik, no 21. Tübingen, 1970.   Z7004.T72 B37

The original volume of this bibliography was designed to supplement the bibliography in Eugene A. Nida, *Toward a Science of Translating* (Leiden: Brill, 1964), pp. 265–320 [P306.N5]. It is divided into two parts. The first contains 902 serially numbered entries referring to books and articles published 1962–1969 arranged alphabetically by author, with reviews cited after the work reviewed. The second part indexes the entries by subject, language, and reviewer.

A second volume with the same title presents a bibliography of publications of 1970–1971 and a supplement for the period 1962–1969. Entries continue the serial numeration of the original volume. The first part lists some 400 works published 1970–1971 and some 400 additional works published 1962–1969. These lists are followed by corrigenda and a list of reviewed works (gathering all entries from both volumes which cite reviews). Part 2 presents indexes parallel to those found in the original volume. A third volume is in preparation.

I–102 **Van Hoof, Henri.** *Internationale Bibliographie der Übersetzung / International Bibliography of Translation.* Pullach bei Munich: Verlag Dokumentation, 1973.
Z7004.T72 H66

This bibliography of more than 4,600 titles comprises materials published before July 1971. It is divided into three parts. The first, a bibliography of translations, is in eight sections, as follows: General; History of Translation; Theory of Translation; Study-Education of Translators; Profession of Translation; Typology of Translation (subdivided into Religious, Literary and Technical-Scientific texts, with literary texts further subdivided into genres); Machine Translation; and Bibliography. The second part lists organizations of translators alphabetically by country; the third part lists journals specializing in translation theory and practice. There are indexes of authors and journals. The work is marred by numerous slight errors and must be used with caution.

I–103 **Congrat-Butlar, Stefan, ed.** *Translation and Translators: An International Directory and Guide.* New York: R. R. Bowker, 1979.   P305.A2 C6

This professional guide and directory has eight sections treating Recent History of Translating; Translating Associations and Centers; Awards, Fellowships, Grants, and Prizes; Training and Access to the Profession; Professional Guidelines; Journals and Books; a Register of Translators and Interpreters by agency and by type of material, including second classifications by language; and a List of Agencies, Enterprises, and Publishers that employ translators and interpreters. There is an index of names, titles, and subjects.

I–104 *Index Translationum / Répertoire international des Traductions / International Bibliography of Translations / Repertorio internacional de traducciones.* Nos. 1–31 (1932–1940) issued by the International Institute of Intellectual Cooperation. New series, vol. 1–. (1948–), issued by UNESCO.   Z6514.T7 I38

Coverage has varied over the years. The volume for 1975 lists 47,232 translated books published in sixty-eight states. Entries are grouped under the French name of the country in which they were published, and are arranged in a system based on the Universal decimal classification, except that the works in UDC category 4 (Languages) are interfiled in category 8 (Literature). Numbered entries give the original author, title of the translation, the name of the translator, the place, publisher, and year of publication, the original language, and the title of the original work (if the translated title is different). There is an alphabetical list of original authors and anonymous works at the end of the annual volume. Through volume 6 (1954) there were also indexes of translators and of publishers.

Translations published 1948–1968 in seven countries where English is among the primary languages (i.e., Australia, Canada, New Zealand, the Republic of Ireland, South Africa, the United Kingdom, and the United States) have been cumulated in two volumes, *Cumulative Index to English Translations, 1948–1968* (Boston: G. K. Hall, 1973) [Z6514 .T7C8]. Entries have been taken over *without change* from the *Index Translationum*, new series, vols. 1–21, and merged into one alphabet by author or first keyword of the title, thus producing a work with various sorts of errors and some erratic entries. There are no cross-references.

Because the *Index Translationum* is published with a time lag of several years, the monthly card serial *Chartotheca Translationum Alphabetica* (I–105) should be consulted for very current work. In addition, for medieval texts see the "Bibliography of Editions and Translations in Progress of Medieval Texts" in *Speculum*, vol. 43– (1973–). From 1952 through 1967 the *Yearbook of Comparative and General Literature* (L–2) contained a section "Reviews of Recent Translations." From 1961 through 1971 the *Yearbook* included an annual "List of Translations" [1960–1970]. Current bibliographies of translations will be located through *Bibliographic Index* (A–2).

Among important closed bibliographies that cite literary translations into English, see Howard-Hill (M–1) and the *New Cambridge Bibliography of English Literature* (M–11), which also cites translations from English.

I–105 ***Chartotheca Translationum Alphabetica / Internationale Bibliographie der Übersetzungen auf Karteikarten / International Bibliography of Translations on Index Cards / Réportoire international des traductions sur fiches mobiles.*** Frankfurt: Bentz, 1954–[in annual vols. from 1961–].
Z6514.T7 C48

This annual compilation is a photographic reproduction of files of index cards issued monthly, preceded by an introduction specifying both the source languages and the translation languages included in that year's compilation. In general, these volumes are limited to original sources in the European languages and translations into the European languages, but the actual limits for any particular year should be checked. Entries give the name of the author, the original language, the language of the translator, the original title, place of publication, publisher, edition and year of publication, price, the name of the translator, title of the translation, place of publication, edition and year of publication, and price. In addition to the annual volume there are five-year cumulations treating translations published 1954–1960, 1961–1965, and 1966–1970.

I–106 **Scholarly Journals in Translation Theory and Practice.**

Babel   *Babel: Revue internationale de traduction / International Journal of Translation.* Vol. 1–. Bonn-Gerlingen: Federation of Translation, 1955–. 4/yr. Reviews. "International Bibliography on Translation" [after 1971: "and Applied Linguistics"].
PN241.A1 B15

Delos   *Delos: A Journal on and of Translation.* Vols. 1–3. Austin, Tex.: National Translation Center, 1968–1970. 4/yr. 2d Ser. Vol. 1–. College Park: The University of Maryland and the Center for World Literature, 1988–. 2/yr.   PN241.A1 D4

IncL   *Incorporated Linguist: The Journal of the Institute of Linguistics.* Vol. 1–. London: The Institute, 1962–. 4/yr. Reviews. Each issue carries a list of translations in progress and titles of recent translations.   P1.I5

Meta   *Meta: Journal des traducteurs / Translators' Journal.* Vol. 1–. Montreal: Presses de l'Université de Montréal, 1956–. 4/yr. Reviews. Bibliography.
No LC number

Paintbrush: A Journal of Poetry, Translations, and Letters. Vol. 1–. Laramie, Wyo.: Ishtar Publications, 1974–. 2/yr. Reviews.   PN6099.6.P33

Translation: The Journal of Literary Translation. New York Translation Center, Columbia University, 1973–. 2/yr.   PN241.T7

TRev   *Translation Review.* Vol. 1–. Richardson: Tex.: University of Texas at Dallas, Center for Writing and Translation, 1978–. 3/yr. Reviews. Bibliography. Lists of translations in progress.
PN241.A1T7

See also the journals in Comparative Literature (L–9), which often include material on the theory and practice of literary translation and lists of recent translations.

I–107 **Some Frequently Recommended Works on Translation Theory and Practice.**

Adams, Robert Martin. *Proteus: His Lies, His Truth: Discussions of Literary Translations.* New York: W. W. Norton, 1973.   PN241.A32

Arrowsmith, William, and Roger Shattuck, eds. *Craft and Context of Translation: A Critical Symposium.* Austin: University of Texas Press, 1961; Garden City, N.Y.: Doubleday, 1964.   PN241.A74 1964

Bates, Ernest Stuart. *Modern Translation.* London: Oxford University Press, 1936.   PN241.B7

Beckman, J., and J. Callow. *Translating the Word of God.* Grand Rapids, Mich.: Zondervan, 1974. BS449.B43

Brislin, R. W., ed. *Translation: Applications and Research.* New York: Gardner Press, 1976.   P306.T7

Brower, Reuben A. *Mirror on Mirror: Translation, Imitation, Parody.* Cambridge: Harvard University Press, 1974.   PN886.B7

———, ed. *On Translation.* Cambridge: Harvard University Press, 1959; New York: Oxford University Press, 1966. Includes seventeen essays, among which is Bayard Quincy Morgan's "A Critical Bibliography of Works on Translation, 46 B.C.–1958."   PN241.B7

Catford, J. C. *Linguistic Theory of Translation.* London: Oxford University Press, 1965.   P306.C33 1965

Crandell, T. Ellen, ed. *Translators and Translating.* SUNY-Binghamton, 1974.   PN241.A49 1974

DeBeaugrande, Robert. *Factors in a Theory of Poetic Translating.* Assen: Van Gorcum, 1978.   PN241.D35

Friar, Kimon. "On Translation," *Comparative Literature Studies*, 8 (1971): 197–213.

Fuller, Frederick. *Translator's Handbook.* University Park: Pennsylvania State University Press, 1984.
P306.F8 1984

Guenthner, F., and M. Guenthner-Reutter, eds. *Meaning and Translation.* New York: New York University Press, 1978.   P306.2.M4 1978b

Holmes, James S., ed. *Nature of Translation: Essays on the Theory and Practice of Literary Translation.* The Hague: Mouton, 1970.   PN241.I54 1968

Holmes, J. S., José Lambert, and Raymond Vanden Broeck, eds. *Literature and Translation: New Perspectives in Literary Studies: With a Basic Bibliography of Books on Translation Studies.* Louvain, Acco, 1978.

PN241.L57

International Conference on Translation as an Art. *Nature of Translation.* The Hague: Mouton, 1970.   PN241.I54

Jacobsen, Eric. *Translation: A Traditional Craft.* Copenhagen, 1958.

Lefevere, Andre. *Translating Literature: The German Tradition from Luther to Rosenzweig.* Assen: Van Gorcum, 1977.   PN241.L35

———. *Translating Poetry: Seven Strategies and a Blueprint.* Assen: Van Gorcum, 1975.   PN241.L36

———, and José Lambert. *Littérature Comparée, Traduction Littéraire, théorie de la littérature.* Paris: Minard, 1979.

Levy, Jiri. *Literary Translation: The Theory and the Practice.* Translation of the Czech *Umeni Prekladv* (Prague: Panorama, 1969; 2d ed., 1983). Amsterdam: Van Gorcum, 1977.   PN241.L4315 1977

Literature and Translation. Louvain: Acco, 1978.

PN241.L57

Mounin, Georges. *Les Problèmes théoretiques de la traduction.* Paris: Gallimard, 1963.   P306.M66 1963

———. *Linguistique et traduction.* Brussels: Dessart et Mandaga, 1976.   P306.M65

Nida, Eugene A. *Toward a Science of Translating, with Special Reference to Principles and Procedures Involved in Bible Translating.* Leiden: E. J. Brill, 1964. Includes an important bibliography, pp. 265–320.

P306.N5

Nida, Eugene A., and Charles R. Taber. *Theory and Practice of Translation.* Leiden: E. J. Brill, 1969.

BS450.N55

Popovic, Anton. *Dictionary for the Analysis of Literary Translation.* Edmonton: Department of Comparative Literature, University of Alberta, 1975.   PN241.P567

Radice, William, and Barbara Reynolds, eds. *Translator's Art: Essays in Honour of Betty Radice.* Harmondsworth: Penguin Books, 1987.   P306.T747 1987

Reiss, Katharina. *Text typ und Übersetzungsmethode.* Kronberg: Scriptor Verlag, 1976.   P306.R44

Rose, Marilyn Gaddis, ed. *Translation in the Humanities.* SUNY-Binghamton, 1977.   P306.T74

———, ed. *Translation Spectrum: Essays in Theory and Practice.* Albany: State University of New York Press, 1981. Includes eighteen essays, among which is the bibliographical "Translation Sources in the Humanities and the Social Sciences," by Michael Jasenas.   P306.T743

Savory, Theodore Horace. *Art of Translation.* 2d ed. London: Jonathan Cape, 1968.   PN241.S25 1968

Selver, P. *Art of Translating Poetry.* London: Baker, 1966.

PN241.S4 1966

Steiner, George. *After Babel: Aspects of Language and Translation.* New York: Oxford University Press, 1975.

Steiner, T. R. *English Translation Theory, 1650–1800.* Assen: Van Gorcum, 1975.   PN241.S74 1975

Zuber, Ortrun. *Languages of Theatre: Problems in the Translation and Transposition of Drama.* Oxford: Pergamon Press, 1980.   PN1661.L28 1980

I–108 ***Literatures of the World in English Translation: A Bibliography.*** 5 vols. New York: Frederick Ungar, 1967–.

LC numbers vary

This massive bibliographical undertaking was originally conceived as part of a guide to comparative and world literatures planned by the National Council of Teachers of English. It retains this original character, particularly in the background sections of each volume which serve as handy guides to major works concerning the literatures from which English translations are subsequently cited. These volumes attempt to record all significant English translations of length, even early ones, of the world's literature, broadly defined to include works of belles lettres, literary history and criticism, and greater works in the history of human thought, including works in history, philosophy, theology, law, and natural science. Throughout, the most important translations are indicated by an asterisk. In addition, arrangement is generally chronological, making convenient the study of an author's English reception over time by reference to the history of translations. Five volumes are planned, each of which is described in greater detail in its own entry:

Vol. 1, *Greek and Latin Literatures.* Edited by George B. Parks and Ruth Z. Temple. 1968. (See I–120.)

Vol. 2, *Slavic Literatures.* Compiled by Richard C. Lewansky et al. 1967. (See I–150.)

Vol. 3, *Romance Literatures.* Edited by George B. Parks and Ruth Z. Temple. 1970. (See I–130.)

Vol. 4, *Celtic, Germanic and Other Literatures of Europe* [not published].

Vol. 5, *Literatures of Asia and Africa* [not published].

VIII. TRANSLATION OF MEDIEVAL TEXTS

See also reference works in Medieval History (F.III) and in Medieval Studies (section N, passim).

I–110 **Farrar, Clarissa P., and Austin B. Evans. *Bibliography of English Translations from Medieval Sources.*** New York: Columbia University Press, 1946.   Z6517.F3

This volume offers an annotated bibliography of English versions produced before 1943 of important writings from the fourth through the fifteenth century in Europe, western Asia, and North Africa, arranged alphabetically by medieval authors. Some 4,000 entries give information for each medieval text on the existence of English translations and their quality and provide an account of their relationships with one another. There is an author-title-subject index.

This work is continued by Mary Anne Heyward Ferguson, *Bibliography of English Translations from Medieval Sources, 1943–1967* (New York: Columbia University Press, 1974) [Z2617.F47]. The later volume includes Talmudic materials, Aesop, and material related to the Dead Sea Scrolls, in addition to all of the matters treated in the earlier bibliography. It adds some 1,980 entries. The index is also more elaborate in its subject categories.

For translations from medieval sources since 1973, see the bibliographical listings in *Speculum* (N–7) and also the entries under the category "translations" in the *International Medieval Bibliography* (F–23).

I–115 **Kristeller, Paul Oskar [now F. Edward Cranz], Editor in chief.** *Catalogus Translationum et Commentariorum: Medieval and Renaissance Latin Translations and Commentaries: Annotated Lists and Guides.* Vol. 1–. Washington, D.C.: Catholic University of America Press, 1960–.
Z7016.K84

This work is sponsored by a consortium of learned societies, including the International Union of Academies/Union académique internationale, which includes the ACLS, MLA, the Medieval Academy of America, British Academy, Académie des inscriptions et belles-lettres, Accademia nazionale dei Lincei, the Union accademica nazionale, and the Consiglio nazionale delle accademie. This massive longterm project, concerned with the appropriation, utilization, and transmission of the literature and intellectual heritage of Greek and Latin antiquity, aims to describe the Latin translations of the works of ancient Greek authors written before A.D. 600 and the Latin commentaries on ancient Latin and Greek authors composed prior to the year 1600. Excluded are commentaries on the Bible and on legal and canonistic texts. After preliminaries, each volume includes bibliographies prepared by individual scholars on a series of classical authors, arranged randomly, according to their completion. The bibliography on a single author begins with a list of and brief introduction to his works. Then follows a chronological list of translations and commentaries. For each is given the name of the translator or commentator; the date, place, and circumstances of the translation or commentary; a list of all manuscript copies and printed editions of the translation or commentary, with bibliographical information; the *incipit* and *explicit* of the various sections of the work; and finally a bio-bibliographical note on the translator or commentator. The treatment includes a *fortuna* outlining the influences of the author and his various works. An index of translators and commentators is also provided.

Among the authors covered to date may be mentioned, in volume 1 (1960), Juvenal and the Hermetic philosophers; in volume 2 (1971), Aeschylus, pseudo-Longinus (On the Sublime), Strabo, Theophrastus, Livy, and Lucretius; and in volume 3 (1977), Priscian, Caesar, Persius, and Petronius. Also in volume 3 are addenda and corrigenda and cumulative indexes for volumes 1–3. Volume 4 (1980), edited by F. E. Cranz, includes Martial, Pliny, and Varro. Volume 5 (1984), edited by Cranz, includes Valerius Maximus; volume 6 (1986), also edited by Cranz, includes Tacitus.

IX. TRANSLATION OF WORLD LITERATURES, ANCIENT AND MODERN

Most literary bibliographies devote sections to translations of texts and to the availability of foreign works in translation. See, for example, the *New Cambridge Bibliography of English Literature* (M–11), where both translations of English texts and translations of texts into English are treated extensively.

I–120 **Greek and Latin Literatures.** Vol. 1 of *Literatures of the World in English Translation: A Bibliography.* Edited by George B. Parks and Ruth Z. Temple. New York: Frederick Ungar, 1968.
Z7018.T7 E85

This volume, which covers English translations (through 1965) of both ancient and modern Greek and Latin literatures, is divided into four main parts. Part I is a general reference section introductory to the whole series (see I–108). It has the following subdivisions: History and Theory of Translation; Collective Bibliographies of English Translations; Collective Histories of Literature; Collections of Translations

from Several Languages. Part II is an introductory section concerning Greek and Roman literature. It is subdivided as follows: Background: General Reference, History, Mythology, and Cultural Aspects and Influences; Bibliography; Literary Studies; Influences on Later Literature; Collections of Translations; and Collections of Translations of Christian Literature.

Part III is concerned with Greek Literature. It has three divisions, concerned with ancient, Byzantine, and modern Greek literature respectively. The Ancient Greek section is subdivided as follows: Background: History, Greek Thought, and Art and Archaelogy; Bibliography; Literary Studies; Collections; Individual Authors (grouped alphabetically under the headings Early and Classical Periods to 323 B.C.; Pagan Authors of the Hellenistic and Graeco-Roman Eras to A.D. 330; and Greek Christian Literature to A.D. 300). The Byzantine section is subdivided as follows: Backgrounds; Bibliography; Literary Studies; Collections; Individual Authors to A.D. 900, first Non-Christian and Secular, then Christian Authors; Individual Authors, to A.D. 1453. Finally, the Modern Greek section is subdivided as follows: Background; Literary Studies; Collections; Individual Authors.

Part IV is concerned with Latin Literature and is similarly divided into three main sections on Latin Literature to A.D. 450, Medieval Latin Literature A.D. 450–1450, and Neo-Latin Literature from A.D. 1450. The Classical Latin section is subdivided as follows: Background, Literary Studies, Collections; Individual Authors of the Republican Era (to 30 B.C.); Individual Authors of the Literature of the Empire (30 B.C. to A.D. 450), first Pagan, then Christian. The Medieval Latin section is subdivided thus: Background; Bibliography; Literary Studies; Collections; Individual Authors and Works A.D. 450 to A.D. 1000; Individual Authors A.D. 1000 to A.D. 1450. Finally, the section on Neo-Latin Literature is subdivided into portions on Literary Studies, Bibliography, Collections and Individual Authors. Only those translations of Latin works by English authors are listed which were published after the original author's death.

Within each author entry, collected, then selected, and then individual works are listed, alphabetically, by the title of the English translation. Multiple translations of the same work are listed in chronological order. The work concludes with a brief list of addenda, and lists of anonymous works attributed to translated authors, titles of anonymous works, and anthologies.

I–130 **Romance Literatures.** Vol. 3 of *Literatures of the World in English Translation: A Bibliography.* Edited by George B. Parks and Ruth Z. Temple. 1 vol. in 2 parts. New York: Frederick Ungar, 1970.
Z7033.T7 E56

Part I of this volume treats English translations from Catalan, Italian, Portuguese and Brazilian, Provençal, Romanian, Spanish, and Spanish-American literatures. It is preceded by a general reference section that repeats and expands upon the introductory reference section to the whole series (see I–108) found in the volume on *Greek and Latin Literatures* (I–120). The remainder of the volume is given to listings for each literature, always subdivided into sections on general background, bibliography, literary studies, collections of translations, and individual authors. The section on Spanish-American literatures is further subdivided into sections on colonial literature and then the literature produced in each Central and South American country, alphabetically by country. The volume concludes with an index of translated authors and the titles of anonymous works.

Part II of this volume treats English translation (through 1968) of French literature. It is divided into two main sections on French Literature of France and French Literature of Other Countries. The first main section is subdivided into general works (Background, Bibliography, Literary Studies, Collections) and works on medieval French literature and

French literature of the sixteenth, seventeenth, eighteenth, nineteenth, and twentieth centuries. Each period's entries are further subdivided into sections on Background, Bibliography, Literary Studies, Collections and Individual Works. The second, much briefer section treating French Literature of Other Countries is divided by country or geographical area, with subsections on Belgium, Switzerland, Canada, Louisiana, West Indies, and Africa. Sections are contributed by authorities on these various literatures. The volume concludes with an index of translated authors and the titles of anonymous works.

For French, see Forrest Bowe, *French Literature in Early American Translation: A Bibliographical Survey of Books and Pamphlets Printed in the United States from 1668 through 1820* (New York: Garland, 1977) [Z1215.B66].

For Spanish but not Spanish-American literature, Robert S. Rudder, *Literature of Spain in English Translation* (New York: Ungar, 1975) [Z2694.T7 R83], supersedes the Spanish section of Parks. It is arranged chronologically by periods and lists translated books as well as translations appearing in periodicals and anthologies. Literature is broadly defined. Addenda, a list of frequently cited anthologies, and indexes of authors and anonymous works conclude the volume. See, for early translation, A. F. Allison's *English Translations from the Spanish and Portuguese to the Year 1700: An Annotated Catalogue of the Extant Printed Versions (Excluding Dramatic Adaptations)* (London: Dawson, 1974) [Z2694 .T7 A38].

For Latin American literature see also the more recent work of Bradley A. Shaw, *Latin American Literature in English Translation: An Annotated Bibliography* (New York: New York University Press, 1976) [Z1609.T7 S47], and Juan R. Freudenthal and Patricia M. Freudenthal, *Index to Anthologies of Latin American Literature in English Translation* (Boston: G. K. Hall, 1977). [Z1609.T7 F74]. See also Claude L. Hulet, *Latin American Poetry in English Translation: A Bibliography* (Washington, D.C.: Pan American Union, 1965) [Z1609.P6 H8], and *Latin American Prose in English Translation: A Bibliography* (Washington, D.C.: Pan American Union, 1964) [Z1601.H764], as well as Suzanne J. Levine, *Latin America: Fiction & Poetry in Translation* (New York: Center for Inter-American Relations, 1970) [Z1609.T7 L45].

I–141 **Morgan, Bayard Quincy.** *Critical Bibliography of German Literature in English Translation, 1481–1927.* 2d ed. With a Supplement Embracing the Years 1928–1935. Stanford: Stanford University Press, 1938.   Z2234.T7 M8 1938

This bibliography, based on a work originally published in 1922, lists all English translations of German literature of importance with critical evaluations. Consecutively numbered entries are arranged alphabetically by authors and include information regarding reprints and new editions, along with brief annotations as to the quality of the translations. Also included are bibliographies of translations and collections of translated works. There is an index of translators. There have been two further supplements that follow the format and numbering of the original volume. The first is by Morgan, *Supplement Embracing the Years 1928–1955* (New York, 1965) [Z2234.T7 M8 suppl.]. The second is by F. Smith Murray, *Selected Bibliography of German Literature in English Translation 1956–1960: A Second Supplement to Bayard Quincy Morgan's A Critical Bibliography of German Literature in English Translation* (Metuchen, N.J.: Scarecrow, 1972) [Z2234.T7 S6]. A recent, selective bibliography is by Patrick O'Neill, *German Literature in English Translation: A Select Bibliography* (Toronto: University of Toronto Press, 1981) [Z2234.T7 O5], which is arranged by period, then alphabetically by author. There are indexes of authors and of translations.

For more recent translations see the bibliographic series *Translations from the German,* ed. Richard Monnig (Göttingen: Vandenhoeck und Ruprecht, 1968–) [Z2221 .T73], including the volume on *English, 1948–1964,* 2d rev. ed. (1968). See also the current *Bibliographie der übersetzungen deutschsprachiger Werke,* published quarterly (Leipzig: Verlag für Buch- und Bibliothekswesen, 1954–) [Z2234.T7 B5].

For translations from Flemish, see Prosper Arents, *De Vlaamse Schrijvers im Let* Engels vertaald, 1481–1949 (Gent: Erasmus, 1950 [Z2424.F5 A7] and *Flemish Writers Translated (1830–1931): Bibliographical Essay* (The Hague: Nijhoff, 1931) [Z2414.T7 A6].

For translations from the Danish see Elias Bredsdorff, *Danish Literature in English Translation, with a Special Hans Christian Andersen Supplement: A Bibliography* (Copenhagen: Munksgaard, 1950) [Z2574.T7 B4], supplemented by Carol L. Schroeder, *Bibliography of Danish Literature in English Translation, 1950–1980 . . .* (Copenhagen: Det Danske Selskab, 1982) [Z2574.T7 S37].

For modern Icelandic literature, see Phillip Marshall Mitchell and Kenneth H. Ober, *Bibliography of Modern Icelandic Literature in Translation.* (Ithaca: Cornell University Press, 1975) [Z2551.M57].

For recent Yiddish literature see Dina Abramowicz, *Yiddish Literature in English Translation: Books Published 1945-1967,* 2d ed. (New York: Yivo Institute for Jewish Research, 1968) [Z7070.A2 1969].

I–150 **Slavic Literatures.** Vol. 2 of *Literatures of the World in English Translation: A Bibliography.* Compiled by Richard C. Lewanski. New York: New York Public Library and Frederick Ungar, 1967.   Z7041.L59

The volume differs somewhat from others in the series (see I–108) in that it is based upon a bibliography that was already in preparation at the New York Public Library; it therefore has less of the character of a general bibliographical guide to the Slavic literatures and is more nearly a bibliography of translations. Also, though the term *belles lettres* is broadly interpreted, there is not an attempt to include in this volume translations of important works in the humanities generally. Used throughout is the system of Cyrillic alphabet transliteration adopted by the New York Public Library. The intent is to list all translations (through 1960) into English from any Slavic language whether they were separately published or published in an anthology or periodical. A section on general anthologies of translations from more than one language is given first. Anthologies are numbered. Anthologized texts in them are then cross-referenced from citations found under the names of individual translated authors. The volume is further subdivided into sections treating the following literatures: Belorussian, Bulgarian, Croatian, Czech, Kashubian, Lusatian, Macedonian, Polish, Russian, Serbian, Slovak, Slovenian, and Ukranian. Each subsection lists anthologies with a description of their contents numbered for easy cross-reference. Then follows a list of individual authors with collected and then single works. Titles included in the collected works are not listed separately, but all translations of a title can be found using the index. Anonymous works are then listed after the list of authors. The volume concludes with two indexes, of individual authors and titles, and of compilers and titles of anthologies.

A more recent but more narrowly defined bibliography is Maurice B. Line, *Bibliography of Russian Literature in English Translation to 1900 (Excluding Periodicals)* (London: Library Association, 1963) [Z2504.T8 L6]. This volume was published in a combined edition, *Bibliography of Russian Literature in English Translation to 1945,* (Totowa, N.J.: Rowman and Littlefield, 1972) [Z2504.T8 B53] along with Amrei Ettlinger and Joan M. Gladstone, *Russian Literature, Theatre and Art: A Bibliography of Works in English Published*

1900–1945 (London: Hutchinson, 1947) [Z2501.E8].

For Soviet literature see George Gibian, *Soviet Russian Literature in English: A Checklist Bibliography: A Selective* [annotated] *Bibliography of Soviet Russian Literary Works in English and of Articles and Books in English about Soviet Russian Literature* (Ithaca, N.Y.: Cornell University Press, 1967) [Z2504.T8 G5].

For Czech and Slovak literature see George J. Kouton, *Czech and Slovak Literature in English: A Bibliography* 2d ed. (Washington, D.C.: Library of Congress, 1984) [Z2138.L5 K68 1988].

For Hungarian literature see Magda Czigany, *Hungarian Literature in English Translation Published in Great Britain 1830–1968* (London: Szepsi Csombor Literary Circle, 1969) [Z2148.T7 C9].

For Polish literature see Marion E. Coleman, *Polish Literature in English Translation: A Bibliography* (Cheshire, Conn.: Cherry Hill Books, 1963) [Z2528.T7 C6]; J. W. Hoskins, *Polish Books in English, 1945–1971* (Washington, D.C.: Library of Congress, 1974) [Z2528.L5 H37]; Kirkley S. Coulter, *Polish Literature Recently Translated* (Falls Church, Va.: Quarterly Review of Polish Heritage, 1977) [Z2528.L5 C68]; J. J. Maciusko, *Polish Short Story in English: A Guide and Critical Bibliography* (Detroit: Wayne State University Press, 1968) [Z2528.T7 M33]; and B. Taborski, *Polish Plays in English Translations: A Bibliography* (New York: Polish Institute of Arts and Sciences in America, 1968) [Z2528.L5 T3].

For Yugoslav literature see Vasa D. Mihailovich and Mateja Matejic, *Yugoslav Literature in English: A Bibliography of Translations and Criticism (1821–1975)* (Cambridge, Mass.: Slavica Publishers, 1976) [Z2958.L5 Y83].

I–161 Guides to Translations of Asian and African Literatures.

African

National Book League (Great Britain). *Creative Writing from Black Africa (Sub-Sahara): Checklist [of translations]*. London: National Book League, 1971.
Z2011.N28

Chinese

Davidson, Martha. *List of Published Translations from Chinese into English, French, and German*. Part 1, Literature Exclusive of Poetry. Ann Arbor, Mich.: Edwards, 1952–1958. Part 2, Poetry. New Haven: Far Eastern Publications, Yale University, 1957.
Z7059.D38

Gibbs, Donald A. *Bibliography of Studies and Translations of Modern Chinese Literature, 1918–1942*. Cambridge: Harvard University Press, 1975.
Z3108.L5 G52

Tung-Li, Yuan, comp. *China in Western Literature*. New Haven: Far Eastern Publications, Yale University, 1958.
Z3101.Y8

Hebrew

Goell, Ychai. *Bibliography of Modern Hebrew Literature in English Translation*, Jerusalem: Israeli Universities Press, 1968.
Z7070.G57

———. *Bibliography of Modern Hebrew Literature in Translation*. Tel Aviv: Institute for the Translation of Hebrew Literature, 1975.
Z7070.G58

Goldberg, Isaac, comp. *Bibliography of Modern Hebrew Literature in Translation*. No. 1–, 1972/76–. Tel Aviv: Institute for the Translation of Hebrew Literature, 1979–. [2/yr. updates Goell above.] Z7070.B52

Japanese

Inada, Hide Ikehara. *Bibliography of Translations from the Japanese into Western Languages from the 16th Century to 1912*. Tokyo: Sophia University, 1979.
Z3308.T7 I5

International House Library. *Modern Japanese Literature in Translation: A Bibliography*. Tokyo: Kodansha International, 1978. Z3308.L5 K66 1979

Kokusai Bunka Kaikan, Tokyo. Toshoshitsu. *Modern Japanese Literature in Translation: A Bibliography*. Tokyo: Kodansha International, 1979. Z3308.L5 K66

Nihon Pen Kurabu [PEN Club]. *Japanese Literature in Western Languages: A Bibliography*. 2d ed. Tokyo, 1961. Supplement 1964. Z3308.L5 N68

Southeast Asian

Jenner, Philip N. *Southeast Asian Literature in Translation: A Preliminary Bibliography*. Honolulu: University Press of Hawaii, 1973. D53.A2 A82 no.9

LITERARY MATERIALS AND CONTEXTS

I. FOLKLORE

Folklore is also treated extensively in the *MLA International Bibliography* (L–50), in the MHRA *Annual Bibliography* (M–21), and in *American Literary Scholarship* (S–14). See also material on Children's Literature in section L.XVI and on verse and prose narratives in sections T and W. Many of the reference works in comparative and general literature and many of the standard bibliographies of national literatures include folklore sections (see section L, *passim*). Works on ethnic and regional literature in sections M and S are also likely to be pertinent sources.

K–1 **Aarne, Anti.** *Types of the Folk-Tale: A Classification and Bibliography.* Translated, revised, and enlarged by Stith Thompson. Helsinki: FF Communications, 1961.

GR40.A1513

This work, published originally as *Verzeichnis der Märchentypen* (1910) and translated by Thompson originally in 1928, presents the standard typology and bibliography of oral folktales. It was compiled to establish a uniform system of reference to the plots (i.e., "types") found in all Indo-European folklore and particularly in the folktale. With catchword title variations, true comparison of tales across national boundaries was impossible; through a uniform typology, systematic comparison is not only possible but encouraged. The type index in its original format was divided into three groups of plots, (1) animal tales such as the story of the hare and the tortoise, (2) "regular" folktales including wonder tales and fairy tales such as Cinderella, and (3) jokes and anecdotes such as the numskull story. The 1961 revised translation adds another group, (4) formula tales, which rely on a strict pattern of delivery for effect, such as the cumulative effect of the House That Jack Built. Entries are numbered sequentially and give a brief descriptive phrase that becomes the name of the type. The type entry enumerates a bibliography of sources, identifies the languages and geographical regions in which the type is found, and then presents a complete narrative of the tale with its constituent motifs cross-referenced to the *Motif-Index* (K–2) in such a fashion that one unfamiliar with it would be able to identify the type. Variant forms of the type are also identified, and some cross-references to other types are given. An index to themes at the end of the volume provides access to the types according to key notions, such as "abandonment on an island."

K–2 **Thompson, Stith.** *Motif-Index of Folk-Literature: A Classification of Narrative Elements in Folktales, Ballads, Myths, Fables, and Mediaeval Romances, Exempla, Fabliaux, Jest-Books, and Local Legends.* Rev. and enl. ed. 6 vols. Bloomington: Indiana University Press, 1955–1958.

GR67.T52

Designed for use with Aarne's type index (K–1), this work, the first edition of which was published 1932–1936, is an attempt "to reduce the traditional narrative material of the whole earth to order" by means of a "classification of single motifs." Motifs are "details out of which the full-fledged narratives are composed." The story of Cinderella, for example, is a "full-fledged narrative" or a "type," while the discovery of a true owner by fitting a slipper is a "motif." In this work motifs dealing with one subject are handled together, irrespective of their literary form or place of origin, thus making possible a uniform and universal classification. Specifically excluded from consideration are superstitions, customs, religious beliefs, riddles, and proverbs, for all of which other reference tools are available.

The included material is arranged under twenty-three grand divisions progressing from the mythological and supernatural toward the realistic and naturalistic. Thus chapter A has to do with the creation and nature of the world and with creators, gods, and demigods; B with fantastic animals; Q with rewards and punishments; T with sex and marriage; X with humorous incidents. Within the grand divisions, arrangement is by tens or groups of ten. The first ten subheadings deal with the general ideas of the chapter, and particular ideas are taken up in succeeding divisions. Within these divisions a similar arrangement of particular motifs is followed, with the first number referring to the general concept and subsequent numbers to specific variations. For example, E deals with "The Dead," E200 with "Malevolent Return from the Dead," and E225 specifically with "Ghost of Murdered Child Returns." Entries include a description of the action, characters, and attendant circumstances of the action in the motif. Cross-references to other headings under which the motif might also be classified and to other narrative elements to which it is related are given. Versions of the motif (listed by continent or country of origin) and special studies of the motif or remarkable lists of its variant forms are also enumerated. The last volume provides an extremely detailed subject index to the entire work.

Through the joint use of the Aarne type index (K–1), which in its revised form includes reference to "motif" numbers in the text of the "type," and the Thompson motif index, it is possible to establish a network of narratives that are related to each other, thus permitting comparative analysis. Both Gerald Bordman's *Motif-Index of the English Metrical Romances*

(K–5) and Ernest W. Baughman's *Type and Motif Index of the Folk-Tales of England and North America* (K–4) correct and supplement this work, with a focus on materials likely to be of special interest to students of English and American literature.

K–4 Baughman, Ernest Warren. *Type and Motif-Index of the Folk-Tales of England and North America.* Indiana University Folklore Series, no. 20. The Hague: Mouton, 1966.
GR67.B3

This index, the revision of a 1953 doctoral dissertation, is limited to English-language tales, excluding Indian, Negro, and Celtic materials. In all, 371 types and 1,652 variants are identified, along with 1,211 complete motifs and 11,431 variants. All are numbered according to the system in the Aarne type index (K–1) and the Thompson motif index (K–2). New motifs are numbered accordingly with an asterisk to indicate their newness. There are an introduction and a bibliography. The introduction presents data on the frequency and distribution of the tales and discusses the relations between English and North American folktales, including relations between versions and questions of direct borrowing. By virtue of the method of numbering, a student interested in locating English or North American folktales of a particular type or that use a particular motif will need to know its Aarne/Thompson index number.

K–5 Bordman, Gerald. *Motif-Index of the English Metrical Romances.* Folklore Fellows Communications, no. 190. Helsinki: FF Communications, 1963. GR1.F55 vols. 79–80

This work is designed to fill a gap in Thompson's motif index (K–2) that resulted from his use of summaries in Wells's *Manual of Writings in Middle English* (N–30) rather than his own direct examination of the English metrical romances. Bordman's index is, however, designed to fit in with Thompson's and uses his numeration; new listings are identified by asterisks. Excluded are prose romances and such metrical romances as are contained in other works (e.g., Chaucer, Gower). The motif-index proper is followed by an alphabetical index to motifs (by keywords).

A convenient finding tool, designed to assist users in locating texts of English language folktales is D. L. Ashliman, *Guide to Folktales in the English Language: Based on the Aarne-Thompson Classification System* (Westport, Conn.: Greenwood, 1987) [Z5983.F17 A83 1987]. Disposed into six main sections, treating Animal Tales, Magic Tales, Religious Tales, Romantic Tales, Anecdotes, and the Grimms' Tales, the work is preceded by an Introduction and concludes with a Bibliography of Secondary Literature, a Bibliography of Folktale Collections, and an Index. Entries in each main section present capsule plots, followed by titles and bibliographic data of published variants.

K–6 Cleveland Public Library, John G. White Department. *Catalog of Folklore and Folk Songs.* 2 vols. Boston: G. K. Hall, 1964.
Z5985.C5

These volumes reproduce the approximately 25,000 cards of titles in the Folklore and Folk Song portion of the John G. White collection, bequeathed to the Cleveland Public Library by White, a Cleveland attorney, in 1928. The collection itself numbers over 110,000 individual volumes. The cards are arranged under some 150 subject headings, treating the Folklore, Folk Tales, Folk Sayings, and Folk Songs of all countries and all times.

K–7 Diehl, Katharine Smith. *Religions, Mythologies, Folklores: An Annotated Bibliography.* 2d ed. New Brunswick, N.J.: Scarecrow Press, 1962.
Z7751.D54 1962

Originally published in 1956 with 1,240 serially numbered, annotated entries, the second edition has 2,388 items disposed into six chapters, as follows: 1, Universal Religious Knowledge; 2, Fine Arts; 3, Folklore; 4, Religions, Exclusive of Judaism and Christianity; 5, The Judaeo-Christian Tradition; and 6, Journals. Each section begins with general reference books and bibliographies and continues with individual items. Annotations are primarily descriptive. There is an author-title index.

K–8 Bonser, Wilfrid. *Bibliography of Folklore As Contained in the First Eighty Years of the Publication of the Folklore Society [i.e., 1878–1957].* Publications of the Folklore Society, no. 121. London, 1961.
Z5981.B6

This work with its 2,626 serially numbered entries classifies the contents of the Folklore Society's publications into twelve major subject areas and a total of 218 numbered subtopics. The major areas are as follows: A. General Topics; B. Folklore of the British Isles (subclassified by county); C. Folklore of Other Countries and Races (subclassified by continent); D. Mankind; E. Human Activities; F. Natural History; G. Natural Phenomena; K. Calendar Customs (both movable feasts and fixed days); L. Religious Folklore and the Supernatural; M. Miscellaneous Aspects of Folklore; N. Narrative Folklore; and P. Folklore in Literature and Art. References to reviews are included. The volume ends with an index of authors; an index to places in the British Isles; an index of foreign countries, races, and tribes; and an index of subjects.

A second volume compiled by Bonser is titled *Bibliography of Folklore for 1958–1967: Being a Subject Index to Volumes 69–78 of the Journal "Folklore"* (London: Folklore Society, 1969) [Z5981.B62]; it supplements the original index, adding 832 serially numbered entries in a parallel classification.

K–9 Haywood, Charles. *Bibliography of North American Folklore and Folksong.* 2d. ed. 2 vols. New York: Dover, 1961.
Z5984.U5 H32

This work, originally published in 1951, has been criticized for its casual character and the many gaps and errors it contains. It continues to be regarded as useful, though it must be used with caution. The first volume treats the American people north of Mexico, exclusive of American Indians and Eskimos, including Canada. It is divided into five parts, treating general folklore, regional folklore, ethnic folklore, occupational folklore, and miscellaneous materials. Primary and secondary materials are included, and the individual parts are elaborately subclassified. Music, both sheet and recorded, is also included. The second volume treats the American Indians north of Mexico, including the Eskimos. A first part covers general bibliography; the second part presents bibliographies of the folklore of the various cultural areas. There is a comprehensive author-title-subject index to both volumes, as well as an index supplement giving the names of composers, arrangers, and performers.

K–10 Flanagan, Cathleen C., and John T. Flanagan. *American Folklore: A Bibliography, 1950–1974.* Metuchen, N.J.: Scarecrow Press, 1977.
Z5984.V6 F55

This work contains 3,639 entries, many of which are evaluatively annotated. It cites primarily work done on United States folklore, with some attention to the folklore of Canada, Mexico, and the Caribbean. Entries are disposed into sixteen sections, as follows: 1, List of Magazines and Abbreviations;

2, Festschriften, Symposia, and Collections; 3, Bibliographies, Dictionaries, and Archives; 4, Folklore: Study and Teaching; 5, General Folklore; 6, Ballads and Songs; 7, Tales and Narrative Material; 8, Legends; 9, Myth and Mythology; 10, Beliefs, Customs, Superstitions, Cures; 11, Folk Heroes; 12, Folklore in Literature; 13, Proverbs, Riddles, Wellerisms, Limericks; 14, Speech, Names, Cries, etc.; 15, Minor Genres; 16, Obituaries [of prominent folklorists]. There is an author index.

K–11 **"Annual Bibliography of Folklore [1954–1962]."** *Journal of American Folklore*, **vols. 68–76.** Austin, Tex.: American Folklore Society, 1955–1963. GR1.J8

This well-organized, annual, international bibliography, published in the supplemental Bibliographical and Special Series of the *JAF*, contained between 700 and 1,400 items in each annual listing. Entries were arranged according to the following scheme: A. General Folklore; B. Material Culture; C. Customs; D. Belief and Superstitions; E. Linguistic Folklore; F. Prose Narratives; G. Folklore and Folk Poetry; H. Music; I. Dance; J. Games; K. Drama; L. Folklore and Literature; M. Peripheral Materials. Brief explanatory annotations and cross-references to related items are given. The last of these annual bibliographies, for 1963 and 1964, appeared in volumes 2 and 3 of the new work, *Abstracts of Folklore Studies* (K–12).

The predecessor of the "Annual Bibliography" was the quarterly enumeration "Folklore in Periodical Literature" that appeared in each number of the *JAF* from 1949 through 1953. Prior to it, the journal contained for various periods a combination of current-contents lists (1888–1902); lists of books received (1888–1954); bibliographical notes and reviews (passim); and in 1910 and 1911, an analyzed bibliography of "Periodical Literature."

The annual supplement to *JAF* also from its inception carried a "Work in Progress" account, listing (by author) books, monographs, articles, field studies, and dissertations, identified as to folklore type, with titles, institutional affiliations, and a detailed "Cross-Index by Subject."

K–12 *Abstracts of Folklore Studies.* Vols. 1–13. Richmond, Va., and Austin, Tex.: American Folklore Society, 1963–1975. GR1.A52

This quarterly series of informational abstracts of articles in folklore or related studies drawn from an international range of journals is organized alphabetically by the name of the journal in which the abstracted article appeared. The quarterly issues were cumulated into annual volumes with a name-subject-title index. The second and third volumes contain the annual bibliography of folklore studies from *JAF* (K–11); from 1971 on, these abstracts are complemented by the folklore portion of the *MLA International Bibliography* (L–50). Publication ceased with volume 13, which contains abstracts of articles published in 1974–1975.

K–14 **"Folklore Bibliography for 1937–72."** *Southern Folklore Quarterly*, **vols. 2–37 (1938–1973).** GR1.S65

This annual international bibliography of folklore and related studies appeared 1938–1964 in the March issue of *SFQ*, in the June issue 1965–1968, and in the September issue 1969-1973. It is classified using a genre approach and is limited to the folklore of the several American and Luso-Hispanic cultures. The main divisions are as follows: A. General Folklore (Scholars, Research Materials and Methods; Related Subjects, Miscellaneous; Texts and Studies); B. Prose Narrative; C. Song—Game—Dance; D. Drama; F. Ritual—Festival; H. Belief and Practice; M. Material Culture; S. Speech; V. Proverbs; W. Riddles. Over the years the scope of this Western Hemisphere folklore bibliography has become progressively

narrow, while its size has grown. The last annual bibliography to appear in *SFQ* covered publications for 1972.

Since 1973 a number of separate volumes have been published, compiled by Merle E. Simmons, which carry on the scope and structure of the *SFQ* bibliography. The first two, *Folklore Bibliography for 1973* and *Folklore Bibliography for 1974*, were published as volumes 28 and 29 of the *Indiana Folklore Institute Monograph Series* (Bloomington, 1974, 1975) [Z5981.S53]. Each carries 1,200 serially numbered, generally annotated entries (including some for material published in 1971 and 1972). A continuing series of annuals, *Folklore Bibliography for* [1975–] (Philadelphia: Institute for the Study of Human Issues, 1979–) [Z5981.S54], contain about 1,200 serially numbered items (including some for previous years).

K–15 *Internationale volkskundliche Bibliographie / International Folklore and Folklife Bibliography / Bibliographie internationale des arts et traditions populaires* [1939/41–], issued by the Commission internationale des arts et tradition populaires under the auspices of the Conseil international de la philosophie et des sciences humaines. Basel: Krebs; Bonn: Rudolf Habelt, 1949–. [Title etc. varies.] Z5982.I523

Sponsored by the Société internationale d'ethnologie et de folklore and prepared by Robert Wildhaber and an international group of collaborators, this is the standard scholarly bibliography in the field. It appears biennially; the volume for 1981–1982 appeared in 1986. It continues the *Volkskundliche Bibliographie*, 14 vols., which treated publications 1917–1937/38 (Berlin: de Gruyter, 1919–1957) [Z5982.V92] in a classified arrangement with author and subject indexes.

Serially numbered and occasionally annotated entries are disposed under an elaborate classification, the main components of which are as follows: I. Folklore and Folklife in General (A. Bibliography; B. Reports on Folklore Research; C. History, Principles, and Methodology of Folklore; D. Summary and Miscellaneous Articles on Geographical or Ethnographical Units); II. Settlement; III. Buildings; IV. Objects; V. Signs; VI. Technology, Arts and Crafts, Industries; VII. Characteristics and Types of Peoples; VIII. Costume, Adornment; IX. Food; X. Manners and Customs, Festivals, Pastimes; XI. Social Traditions, Folk Law; XII. Popular Beliefs (A. Bibliography, B. General Articles, C. Summary and Miscellaneous Articles, D. Mythology and Ritual, E. Omens, F. Magic and Countermagic, G. Monographs); XIII. Folk Medicine; XIV. Popular Science; XV. Folk-Literature in General; XVI. Popular Poetry (by language areas); XVII. Music and Dance. XVIII. Fairy Tales, Folktales, Myths, Legends (A. Bibliography, B. General, C. Fairy Tales—General, Themes and Motifs, Texts, D. Anecdotes, Tall Tales, Fables—General, Themes and Motifs, Texts, E. Myths and Legends—General, Themes and Motifs, Texts, F. Christian Legends—General, Themes and Motifs, Texts); XIX. Folk Drama; XX. Other Folk Literature; XXI. Popular Speech (A. General and Miscellaneous, B. Riddles, C. Proverbs and Sayings, D. Witticisms and Jests, Nicknames, E. Cries and Formulae, F. Speech Attributed to Animals and Objects, G. Vernacular and Slang).

The volumes conclude with a list of analyzed periodicals, an index of authors' names, and a subject index. The list of periodicals includes those new to the bibliography or those with changed titles. The subject index uses German terms, with some terms from other languages; subject terms are either keywords from entry titles or are supplied by a contributing bibliographer. Each biennial volume includes a supplement of entries missed in the preceding volume. It should be noted that articles dealing with pure archaelology, monumentology, city planning, linguistics and dialectology, onomastics, museum science, and restoration are deliberately excluded.

An additional bibliography, published in East Germany, complements the *International Folklore Bibliography* for Eastern European publications: *Demos: Internationale ethnographische und folkloristische Informationen* (Berlin: Akademie der Wissenschaften der DDR, 1960–) [Z5112.D38]. Published quarterly, this unclassified but annotated bibliography includes books and articles. There are annual indexes of authors, book reviewers, and periodical titles.

K–17   **Funk and Wagnalls' Standard Dictionary of Folklore, Mythology and Legend.** Edited by Maria Leach and Jerome Fried. 2 vols. New York: Funk and Wagnalls, 1949–1950. Issued in 1 vol. with corr. New York, 1972.   GR35.F8

This comprehensive, encyclopedic dictionary generally contains short, initialed articles of definition, summary, and description. There are some longer, signed articles, with bibliographies appended. Treated are references to gods, folk heroes, culture heroes, tricksters, and numskulls; the folklore of animals, birds, plants, insects, stones, gems, minerals, and stars; dances, ballads, and folksongs; festivals and rituals; food customs and their significances; games and children's rhymes, riddles, and tongue twisters; diviners and "lookmen"; witches, witchcraft, omens, magic charms, and spells; supernatural impregnations and the supernatural beings of folk belief and story, including demons, ogres, fairies, elves, guardian spirits, werewolves, vampires, and zombies. Greek mythology is deemphasized. The intialed articles are keyed to the list of contributors, in which each author's credentials are also given. There is an index of authors, titles, and topics; motifs are numbered using the Thompson *Motif-Index* (K–2). There is a list of important survey articles on the fields of folklore, mythology, and legend at the beginning of each volume. The one-volume edition of 1972 adds a "Key to countries, regions, cultures, culture areas, peoples, tribes, and ethnic groups."

An often-recommended alternative for American materials is Majorie Tallman, *Dictionary of American Folklore* (New York: Philosophical Library, 1960) [GR105.T3].

K–18   **Brewer, Ebenezer Cobham.** *Dictionary of Phrase and Fable, Giving the Derivation, Source, or Origin of Common Phrases, Allusions, and Words That Have a Tale to Tell.* Classic [12th rev.] Edition, with an introduction by Alix Gudefin. New York: Avenel Books, 1978.   PN43.B65 1978

This work, first published in 1870, and published in a New and Enlarged Edition in 1894, has remained a standard source of information on the origins and meanings of words and expressions in common use. Its author referred to it as a "Treasury of Literary Bric-à-brac." Some sense of its range may be gathered from the dozen entries following that for "Bric-à-brac": "Brick," as in "A regular Brick"; "Brick-and-mortar Franchise"; "Brickdusts"; "Brick-tea"; "Bride"; "Bride Cake"; "Bride or Wedding Favours"; "Bride of Abydos"; "Bride of Lammermoor"; "Bride of the Sea"; "Bridegroom"; and "Bridegroom's Men." There are altogether more than 17,000 main entries, with frequent illustrative quotations, and cross-references. Sources of information are generally indicated with short titles. There are some longer articles, giving such miscellaneous information as Cambridge, Oxford, and American college colors; dying sayings; gender-words; kingly titles; long words; the most renowned misers; owners' names for their swords; and a list of the waters at continental spas with indication of the disorders for which they were reputed helpful in the nineteenth century.

K–19   **Robbins, Rossell Hope.** *Encyclopedia of Witchcraft and Demonology.* New York: Crown, 1959.   BF1503.R6

This elaborately illustrated, scholarly encyclopedia treats the history of witchcraft proper as a Western European and theological phenomenon from its fifteenth-century beginnings through its peak in the 1600s to its ending in the eighteenth

century. Names, places, events, and terminology constitute the entry terms. The volume concludes with classification by subject of a select bibliography of 1,140 items.

Many of the entries cited here are also found in the well-illustrated and elaborately annotated more recent work of Robbins, *Witchcraft: An Introduction to the Literature of Witchcraft: Being the Preface and Introduction to the "Catalogue of the Witchcraft Collection in Cornell University Library"* (Millwood, N.Y.: KTO Press, 1978) [Z6878 .W8 R63].

K–20   **Briggs, Katherine M., ed.** *Dictionary of British Folk-Tales in the English Language, Incorporating the F. J. Norton Collection.* 2 parts in 4 vols. London: Routledge; Bloomington: Indiana University Press, 1970–1971.

GR141.B68

This standard record of indigenous British folktales is divided into two parts, each taking up two volumes. Part A, Folk Narratives, presents the texts of some 850 folk fictions. Volume 1 contains Fables and Exempla and Fairy Tales; Volume 2 contains Jocular Tales, Novelle, and Nursery Tales. Part B, Folk Legends, presents the texts of some 1,200 legends, tales (once) thought to be true accounts. Volume 1 of this part contains legends about Black Dogs, Bogies, Devils, Dragons, Fairies, Ghosts, and Giants; Volume 2 presents Historical Traditions, Local Legends, Origin Myths, Saints Legends, Legends of the Supernatural, of Witches, and Miscellaneous Legends. The first volume of each part contains an introduction, a list of books quoted, an index of tale types in numerical order, and an index to story titles. Entries for each tale or legend give either the tale or a summary of it, discuss its source, identify its type and its motifs (using Aarne and Thompson numbers), provide cross-references to related tales, and give such notes as are warranted.

Another important reference work in the study of British folklore is William Carew Hazlitt's *Faiths and Folklore in the British Isles*, 2 vols. (London, 1905) [DA110.H38], itself a revision of John Brand, *Popular Antiquities of Great Britain, Comprising Notices of the Moveable and Immoveable Feasts, Customs, Superstitions and Amusements Past and Present*, 3 vols. (London: J. R. Smith, 1870) [DA110.B82 1870].

K–21   **Child, Francis James.** *English and Scottish Popular Ballads.* 10 parts in 5 vols. Cambridge: Harvard University Press, 1882–1898. Often reprinted, most recently in 3 vols. New York: Cooper Square, 1962.   PR1181.C5 1962

This standard and authoritative work on English and Scottish balladry and its continental relationships contains a total of 305 ballads in all extant versions. The original five volumes each have two parts, treating ballads as follows: part 1: ballads 1–28; 2: 29–53; 3: 54–82; 4: 83–113; 5: 114–155; 6: 156–188; 7: 189–225; 8: 226–265; 9: 266–305; 10: appendixes and indexes. Each volume includes a set of additions and corrections. Volume 5 contains the following elements: additions and corrections; a glossary; a list of sources of texts; an index of published airs; a list of ballad airs taken from manuscripts; an index of ballad titles; a list of titles of collections briefly cited in the work; an index of matters (i.e., *Stoff*) and literature; a bibliography; and a list of corrigenda. The Child entry on any individual ballad contains all the versions of the ballad, with elaborate annotation identifying relationships between the versions.

An important complementary work is Bertrand Harris Bronson's *Traditional Tunes of the Child Ballads with Their Texts, according to the Extant Records of Great Britain and America*, 4 vols. (Princeton: N.J.: Princeton University Press, 1959–1972) [ML3650.B82]. Bronson presents the tunes and variants to Child Ballads 1–299, excluding texts without tunes. Numbered variants are grouped into tune families, then tunes are given without texts. The headnote gives the tune's musical history in the English-speaking world and describes its recorded tradition. The tune's mode and range are identified. Addenda to the entire work are found in volume 4, along with the following indexes: a bibliography of works referred to or drawn from (including printed collections, periodicals, manuscripts, and sound recordings); an index of sources including authors, editors, collectors, and titles (references by volume number, Child number, and variant number to specific items); an index of tunes and ballads quoted, giving an alphabetical list of cited ballads and tune titles, including variants (reference to volume, Child number, and variant number); an index of singers, by county of origin, alphabetical by name, with the state or shire given (reference by volume number, Child number, and variant number); a geographical index referring to variants recorded in a particular county, shire, or state; an index of works and titles referred to in headnotes and footnotes; an index of persons (other than singers), including recording operators, transcribers, noters, transmitters, annotators, etc. An abridgment with general introduction has been published by Bronson, *Singing Tradition of Child's Popular Ballads* (Princeton, N.J.: Princeton University Press, 1976) [ML3650.B82 1976], which treats the 299 ballads, gives a bibliography of printed collections, periodicals, and manuscripts, and provides an index of tune and ballad titles.

K–23 Scholarly Journals in Folklore Studies.

Abstracts of Popular Culture: A Quarterly Publication of International Popular Phenomena. Vol. 1–. Bowling Green, Ohio: Popular Culture Press, 1975–. 4/yr., then 2/yr.   Z7164.S66 A27

Arts et traditions populaires. Vol. 1–. Paris: Presses universitaires de France, 1955–. 4/yr.   DC1.A7

Deutsches Jahrbuch für Volkskunde. Vol. 1–. East Berlin, 1955–. 1/yr.   GR165.D4

Fabula: Zeitschrift für Erzählforschung; Journal of Folktale Studies; Revue d'etudes sur le conte populaire. Vol. 1–. Berlin: de Gryter, 1957–. 3/yr. Reviews.   GR1.F25

FF *Folklore Forum: A Communication for Students of Folklore.* Bloomington, Ind.: Folklore Forum Society, 1968–. 6/yr. 1968–1976; 4/yr. 1976–.   GR1.F564

FFC *Folklore Fellows, FF Communications.* Vol. 1–. Helsinki: Suomaliainen Tiedeakatemia, 1911–. Irregular. Volumes include important monographs and bibliographies (see K–1, K–2, for examples). They are indexed, as follows: Index to vols. 1–81, numbers 1–195 (1910–1964). Helsinki, 1964.   GR1.F55

Folklore *Folk-Lore: A Quarterly Review of Myth, Tradition, Institution, and Custom* [former title 1883–1890: *Folklore Journal*; 1878–1882: *Folklore Record*]. Vol. 1–. London: English Folklore Society, 1878–. Reviews. Indexes by Bronser (K–8).   GR1.F5

JAF *Journal of American Folklore.* Vol. 1–. Austin, Tex.: American Folklore Society, 1888–. 4/yr. Location of an important annual bibliography, vols. 62–76 (1949–1963), see K–11. Contains an annual list of "Work in Progress," from vol. 60– (1947–). *Analytical Index* [to vols. 1–70], by Tristram P. Coffin, including notes, texts, and reviews, was published in Philadelphia, 1958.   GR1.J8

JFI *Journal of the Folklore Institute.* [former title 1951–1963: *Midwest Folklore*; 1942–1950: *Hoosier Folklore Bulletin*]. Vol. 1–. The Hague: Mouton, 1964–. 3/yr.   GR1.I5

JPC *Journal of Popular Culture.* Vol. 1–. Bowling Green, Ohio: Bowling Green University Press, 1967–. 4/yr. Reviews.   AP2.J8325

NYFQ *New York Folklore Quarterly.* Vol. 1–. Ithaca, N.Y.: Cornell University Press, 1945–.   GR1.N473

SFQ *Southern Folklore Quarterly.* Vol. 1–. Gainesville, Fla.: 1937–. Location of an important annual bibliography, 1938–1974 (see K–14). Reviews.   GR1.S65

WF *Western Folklore* [former title 1942–1946: *California Folklore Quarterly*]. Vol. 1–. Berkeley: University of California Press, 1942–. Index to vols. 1–25 (1942–1966) in 1 vol.   GR1.C26

ZfV *Zeitschrift für Volkskunde* [former title 1891–1928: *Zeitschrift des Vereins für Volkskunde*]. Vol. 1–. Berlin [and Stuttgart]: 1891–.

K–24 Some Frequently Recommended Works in Folklore.

General

Brunvand, Jan Harold. *Folklore: A Study and Research Guide.* New York: St. Martin's, 1976.   Z5981.B78

Cocchiara, Giuseppe. *History of Folklore in Europe.* Translation by John N. McDaniel of *Storia del folklore in Europa* (Turin: Einaudi, 1952). Philadelphia, Pa.: Institute for the Study of Human Issues, 1981.   GR135.C613

Dorson, Richard M., ed. *Folklore and Folklife: An Introduction.* Chicago: University of Chicago Press, 1972. Annotated bibliographies of selected readings at the end of each chapter.   GR65.D57

Dundes, Alan. *Study of Folklore.* Englewood Cliffs, N.J.: Prentice-Hall, 1965. Thirty-four articles with bibliographical footnotes and a brief general bibliographical essay at the end.   GR45.D8

Edmonson, Munro S. *Lore: Introduction to the Science of Folklore and Literature.* New York: Holt, Rinehart and Winston, 1971.   PN871.E3

Jones, Steven Swann. *Folklore and Literature in the United States: An Annotated Bibliography of Studies of Folklore in American Literature.* New York: Garland, 1983.   Z1225.J66 1984

Krappe, Alexander Haggerty. *Science of Folk-Lore.* New York: L. MacVeagh, Dial Press, 1930. With bibliographical notes covering the whole field.   GR65.K7

Peuckert, Will-Erich, and Otto Lauffer. *Volkskunde: Quellen und Forschungen seit 1930.* Bern: Francke, 1951.   GR45.P45

British and Irish Lore

Hazlitt, W. Carew. *Faiths and Folklore: A Dictionary of National Beliefs, Superstitions and Popular Customs, Past and Current, with Their Classical and Foreign Analogues, Described and Illustrated, Forming a New Edition of "The Popular Antiquities of Great Britain" by [John] Brand and [Henry] Ellis, Largely Extended, Corrected, Brought Down to the Present Time, and Now First Alphabetically Arranged.* 2 vols. London, 1905.   DA110.H38

O'Suilleabhain, Sean. *Handbook of Irish Folklore.* Dublin: Educational Society of Ireland, 1942.   GR65.O78

American Lore

Brewer, J. Mason. *American Negro Folklore.* Chicago: Quadrangle, 1968.   GR103.B66

Brunvand, Jan Harold. *Study of American Folklore: An Introduction.* 2d ed. New York: W. W. Norton, 1978.   GR105.B7 1978

Dorson, Richard M. *American Folklore*. Chicago: University of Chicago Press, 1959.

Hughes, Langston, and Arna W. Bontemps, eds. *Book of Negro Folklore*. New York: Dodd, Mead, 1958.
GR103.H74

Rosenberg, Bruce A. *Art of the American Folk Preacher*. New York: Oxford University Press, 1970.
BV4209.U6 R67

Ullom, Judith C. *Folklore of the North American Indians: An Annotated Bibliography*. Washington, D.C.: Library of Congress, 1969.
Z1209.U4

Wildhaber, Robert. "A Bibliographic Introduction to American Folklife." *New York Folklore Quarterly* 21 (December 1965): 259–302.
GR1.N473

Folk Music: The Ballad, Folksongs

Brunnings, Florence E. *Folk Song Index: A Comprehensive Guide to the Florence E. Brunnings Collection*. New York: Garland, 1981.
ML128.F75 B83 1981

Coffin, Tristram P. *British Traditional Ballad in North America*. Rev. ed. Publications of the American Folklore Society, Bibliographical and Special Series, Philadelphia, 1963.
ML3553.C6 1963

Fowler, David C. *Literary History of the Popular Ballad*. Durham, N.C.: Duke University Press, 1968.
PR507.F6

Friedman, Albert B. *Ballad Revival: Studies in the Influence of Popular or Sophisticated Poetry*. Chicago: University of Chicago Press, 1961.
PR507.F85 1961

Gerould, Gordon H. *Ballad of Tradition*. New York: Oxford University Press, 1932.
PN1376.G4

Gummere, Francis B. *Popular Ballad*. New York: Dover, 1959.
PN1376.G8 1959

Henry, Melliger E. *Bibliography for the Study of American Folksongs with Many Titles of Folk-Songs . . . from Other Lands*. London: Mitre Press, 1937.
ML120.U5 H5

Hodgart, Matthew J. C. *Ballads*. 2d ed. New York: Hillary House, 1962.
PR507.H7 1962

Hustvedt, Siguard B. *Ballad Books and Ballad Men*. Cambridge: Harvard University Press, 1930. PN1376.H78

Leach, MacEdward, and Tristram P. Coffin. *Critics and the Ballad*. Carbondale: Southern Illinois University Press, 1961.
PS476.L4

Rollins, Hyder E. *Analytical Index to the Ballad Entries (1557–1709) in the Registers of the Company of Stationers of London*. Chapel Hill: University of North Carolina Press, 1924.
Z2014.B2 L8

Vaughan Williams Memorial Library, London. *Vaughan Williams Memorial Library Catalogue of the English Folk Dance and Song Society*. London: Mansell, 1973.
ML136.L8 V4

Wilgus, D. K. *Anglo-American Folksong Scholarship since 1898*. New Brunswick, N.J.: Rutgers University Press, 1959.
ML3553.W48

Folk Narrative; Folktales; Folk Epic

Anderson, George K. *Legend of the Wandering Jew*. Providence, R.I.: Brown University Press, 1965.
GR75.W3 A5

Briggs, Katherine M. *Fairies in Tradition and Literature*. London: Routledge and Kegan Paul, 1967.
GR550.B685

Cook, Elizabeth. *Ordinary and the Fabulous: An Introduction to Myths, Legends, and Fairy Tales for Teachers and Storytellers*. 2d ed. Cambridge: Cambridge University Press, 1976.
Z1037.C767 1976

Eastman, Mary H. *Index to Fairy Tales, Myths, and Legends*. 2d ed., rev. and enl. Boston: F. W. Faxon, 1926. Supplements 1937, 1952, etc. See also Ireland below.
Z5983.F17 E2

Encyclopädie des Märchens: Handwörterbuch zur historischen und vergleichenden Erzählforschung. Edited by Kurt Ranke. Vol. 1–. Berlin: de Gruyter, 1975–.
GR72.E58

Grimm, Jakob L. K. *Anmerkungen zu den Kinder- und Hausmärchen der Brüder Grimm*. New ed. Edited by Johannes Bolte and Georg Polivka. 5 vols. Leipizig: Dieterische Verlagsbuchhandlung, 1913–1932.
PT921.B6

Ireland, Norma O. *Index to Fairy Tales, 1949–1972, Including Folklore, Legends, and Myths in Collections*. Boston: F. W. Faxon, 1973. Fourth Supplement, 1973–1977 (1979). See also Eastman above.
Z5983.F17 I73

Jolles, André. *Einfache Formen: Legende, Sage, Mythe, Rätsel, Spruch, Kasus, Memorabile, Märchen, Witz*. 4th ed. Tubingen: Niemeyer, 1972.   PN45.J6 1972

Lord, Albert B. *Singer of Tales*. Cambridge: Harvard University Press, 1960.   PN1303.L62

Lüthi, Max. *Once upon a Time: On the Nature of Fairy Tales*. Translation by Lee Chadeayne and Paul Gottwald of *Es war Einmal: Vom Wesen des Volksmärchens* (Göttingen: Vandenhoeck und Ruprecht, 1962). New York: Ungar, 1970.
PN3437.L7813

———. *European Folktale: Form and Nature*. Translation by John D. Niles of *Das europäische Volksmärchen* (3d ed. (Bern: Francke, 1968). Philadelphia: Institute for the Study of Human Issues, 1982.
GR135.L8313 1982

———. *Volksmärchen und Volkssage: Zwei Grundformen erzählender Dichtung*. 3d ed. Bern: Francke, 1975.
PN3437.L8

Mayer, Fanny Hagin, ed. and tr. *Yanagita Kunio Guide to the Japanese Folktale*. Bloomington: Indiana University Press, 1986.   GR340.N52213 1986

O'Sulleabhain, Sean, and R. Th. Christiansen. *Types of the Irish Folk-Tale*. FF Communications, no. 188. Helsinki, 1963.   GR1.F55 no. 188

Propp, Vladimar. *Morphology of the Folktale*. Translation by Laurence Scott of the Russian *Morfologiia skazki*. 2d ed. Revised and edited by Louis A. Wagner. Bloomington: Indiana University Press, 1968.
GR550.P7613 1968

Thompson, Stith. *Folktale*. New York: Dryden Press, 1946.
PN1001.T5

Vries, Jan de. *Heroic Song and Heroic Legend*. New York: Oxford University Press, 1963.   PN1303.V713

Ward, Donald, ed and tr. *German Legends of the Brothers Grimm*. 2 vols. Philadelphia: Institute for the Study of Human Issues, 1981.   PT915.G513 1981

Yassif, Eli. *Jewish Folklore: An Annotated Bibliography*. New York: Garland, 1986.   Z6374.F6 Y37 1986

Proverbs and Proverbial Expressions: Riddles and Folk Speech [see also K–50 ff.].

Permiakov, Grigorii L'vovich. *From Proverb to Folk-Tale: Notes on the General Theory of Clichés*. Translation by Y. N. Filippov from the Russian (1968). Moscow: Nauka, 1979.   GR40.P4213

Taylor, Archer. *Bibliography of Riddles*. FF Communications, no. 126. Helsinki, 1939.   GR1.F55 no. 126

Festivals and Celebrations

Banks, Mary Macleod. *British Calendar Customs: Orkney and Shetland.* London: Folk-Lore Society, 1946.
GR145.O7 B3

————. *British Calendar Customs: Scotland.* 3 vols. London: Folk-Lore Society, 1937–1941. GT4845.B3

Chambers, Robert. *Book of Days: A Miscellany of Popular Antiquities in Connection with the Calendar, including Anecdote, Biography, and History, Curiosities of Literature, and Oddities of Human Life and Character.* 2 vols. Philadelphia: Lippincott, 1899.
DA110.C52

Douglas, George W. *American Book of Days: A Compendium of Information about Holidays, Festivals, Notable Anniversaries, and Christian and Jewish Holy Days, with Notes on Other American Anniversaries Worthy of Remembrance.* Revised by Helen Douglas Compton. New York: H. W. Wilson, 1948.
GT4803.D6

Gregory, Ruth W. *Anniversaries and Holidays: A Calendar of Days and How to Observe Them.* 4th ed. Chicago: American Library Association, 1983.
GT3930.G74 1983

Walsh, William Shepard. *Curiosities of Popular Customs and of Rites, Ceremonies, Observances, and Miscellaneous Antiquities.* Philadelphia: Lippincott, 1898.
GT31.W2

Wright, Arthur R. *British Calendar Customs: England.* Edited by T. E. Lones. 3 vols. London: Folk-Lore Society, 1936–1940. GT4843.W7

Recreation and Games

Callois, Roger. *Man, Play, and Games.* Translated by Meyer Barash of *Les jeux et les hommes* (Paris: Gallimard, 1958). Glencoe, Ill.: Free Press, 1961. CB151.C273

Gomme, Lady Alice B. *Traditional Games of England, Scotland, and Ireland with Tunes, Singing-Rhymes, and Methods of Playing.* 2 vols. London: D. Nutt, 1894–1898. GR141.G5

Huizinga, Johann. *Homo Ludens: A Study of the Play Element in Culture.* London: Routledge and Kegan Paul, 1949. GR151.H815

Strutt, Joseph. *Sports and Pastimes of the People of England from the Earliest Period, Including the Rural and Domestic Recreations, May Games, Mummeries, Pageants, Processions, and Pompous Speeches. . . .* A new edition, much enlarged and corrected by J. Charles Cox. London: T. Tegg, 1903 [originally published 1801]. GV75.S9 1903

Folk Beliefs

Bächtold-Stäubli, Hans. *Handwörterbuch des deutschen Aberglaubens.* 10 vols. Berlin: de Gruyter, 1927–1942. GR166.B25

Radford, Edwin, and M. A. Radford. *Encyclopedia of [English] Superstitions.* Edited and revised by Christina Hole. London: Hutchinson, 1961. BFA75.R3 1961

Thorndike, Lynn. *History of Magic and Experimental Science.* 8 vols. New York: MacMillan, 1923–1958.
Q125.T52

II. MYTHOLOGY

K–25 **Smith, Ron. *Mythologies of the World: A Guide to Sources.*** Urbana, Ill.: NCTE, 1981. Z7836.S63

This 346-page guide consists of twenty-nine bibliographic essays disposed into seven sections and an appendix. The first section, on Worldwide Mythologies, includes a subdivision on Prehistoric Mythologies. The subsequent sections treat respectively West Asian (Mesopotamian, Hittite, Canaanite, Persian, Biblical, and Islamic), South and East Asian (Indian, Chinese, Japanese), European (Greek and Roman, Etruscan, Celtic, Norse/Teutonic, Arthurian, and Other Ancient and Medieval), American Indian (North, Middle, South), African (Ancient Egyptian, Later African), and Oceanic mythologies. The appendix discusses Contemporary Mythology—mainly American.

Each geographically bounded bibliographical essay treats collections of myths; general studies of myth analysis and interpretation; specialized works on religion, on the historical/cultural background, on archaeology, on art and architecture, and even on language and its translation, as relevant. Commentary is both descriptive and evaluative, with sources compared with one another, as appropriate.

The omission of any index at all is a severe limitation on the usefulness of this valuable work.

K–26 **MacCulloch, John A., and Louis H. Gray, eds. *Mythology of All Races.*** 13 vols. New York: Cooper Square, 1916–1922. BL25.M8

Each volume—or half-volume, in the case of volumes 3, 6, 7, 8, and 12—except the last in this massive series presents a monographic account of the mythology of a particular race by a noted authority, as follows: vol. 1, Greek and Roman; vol. 2, Eddic; vol. 3, Celtic and Slavic; vol. 4, Finno-Ugric and Siberian; vol. 5, Semitic; vol. 6, Indian and Iranian; vol. 7, Armenian and African; vol. 8, Chinese and Japanese; vol. 9, Oceanic; vol. 10, North American; vol. 11, Latin American; vol. 12, Egypt and the Far East. Each volume or half-volume has its own detailed table of contents, list of illustrations, elaborate notes, and extensive, classified bibliography. Volume 13 is an elaborate comprehensive subject and name index to the entire work.

K–27 ***New Larousse Encyclopedia of Mythology.*** Introduction by Robert Graves. Translated by Richard Aldington and Delano Ames. New ed. New York: G. P. Putnam's Sons, 1968.
BL311.L33

This work, a translation with supplemental revisions of the *Larousse mythologie générale,* ed. Felix Guirand (Paris: Larousse, 1935) [BL310.L453], was originally published in 1959. Amply illustrated articles are arranged by cultures, with entries on each culture authored by experts. The sections are as follows: Prehistoric, Egyptian, Assyrio-Babylonian, Phoenician, Greek, Roman, Celtic, Teutonic, Slavonic, Finno-Ugric, Ancient Persian, Indian, Chinese, Japanese, North and South American, Oceanic, and Black African mythologies. There is a bibliography arranged by cultural sections, followed by an index of names, subjects, and key terms.

K–28 **Oswalt, Sabine G. *Concise Encyclopedia of Greek and Roman Mythology.*** London: Collins, 1969. BL303.O83

This English edition of a 1965 Larousse publication is arranged alphabetically by the name of the mythological person, place, or thing. The text refers to all related terms in bold-face type. Multiple traditions are described in chronological order from early to late accounts and are numbered. There are some illustrations from the art of classical antiquity. At the end of this extremely handy volume is a list of classical sources used; genealogies of the original gods, the descendants of Prometheus, the descendants of Io, the family of Cadmus, and the family of Tantalus; and maps of ancient Italy and ancient Greece.

K–29 Tripp, Edward. *Crowell's Handbook of Classical Mythology.* New York: Crowell, 1970.   BL303.T75 1970

This volume presents a retelling of classical myths with reference to original sources in an alphabetical arrangement with cross-references. Designed as a companion for reading, the work makes reference to original texts as found in the Loeb Classical Library (L–46). There is a pronouncing index at the end of the volume.

A similarly designed work, concerned only with Greek mythology, is Robert Graves, *Greek Myths*, 4th ed. 2 vols. (Baltimore: Penguin, 1965) [BL781.G65 1965]. A total of 171 sections recount in roughly chronological order the myths of Greek antiquity, with source references and a commentary focused on anthropological, archaeological, and comparative-religious aspects of each narrative. The commentary must be regarded as highly idiosyncratic, as it has been rejected by most classicists, archaeologists, and mythographers. But the summaries and citations of sources are useful, as is the index of names and terms at the end of volume 2 which refers to the serially numbered sections.

Other sources which may be consulted with profit include William Smith, ed., *Dictionary of Greek and Roman Biography and Mythology*, 3 vols. (London: J. Murray, 1890; reprint, New York: AMS Press, 1967) [DE5.S75 1967]; Pierre Grimal, *Dictionary of Classical Mythology*, trans. by A. R. Maxwell-Hyslop of *Dictionnaire de la mythologie grecque et romaine* (Paris: Presses universitaires de France, 1951) [BL715.G7] (Oxford and New York: Basil Blackwell, 1985) [BL715.G713 1986]; and the new *Lexicon Iconographicum Mythologiae Classicae* [*LIMC*], in progress (Zurich: Artemis Verlag, 1981–) [N7760.L49 1981].

K–30 Roscher, Wilhelm. *Ausführliches Lexikon der griechischen und römischen Mythologie.* 6 vols. plus 4 supplementary vols. Leipzig: B. G. Teubner, 1884–1937.   BL715.R7

This is the most comprehensive scholarly work on classical mythology, with extensive, signed articles containing primary and secondary bibliographies and many illustrations. The contents are as follows: vol. 1, pt. 1, Aba-Evan (1884–1886); vol. 1, pt. 2, Euxistratos-Hysiris (1886–1890); vol. 2, pt. 1, Iada-Kyzikos (1890–1894); vol. 2, pt. 2, Laas-Myton (1894–1897); vol. 3, pt. 1, Nabaiothes-Pasicharea (1897–1902); vol. 3, pt. 2, Pasikrateid–Pyxios (1902–1909); vol. 4, Q-S (1910–1915); vol. 5, T (1916–1924); vol. 6, ed. Konrat Ziegler, U-Z and supplement (1924–1937).

K–31 Hunger, Herbert. *Lexikon der griechischen und römischen Mythologie mit Hinweisen auf das Fortwirken antiker Stoffe und Motive in der bildenken Kunst, Literatur und Musik des Abendlandes bis zur Gegenwart.* 6th ed., rev. and enl. Vienna: Hollinek, 1959.   BL303.H8 1969

Originally published in 1953, this work is unique in presenting for each entry three kinds of information: mythographic (designated M), religious-historical (designated R), and subsequent realization in the arts, "Nachwirkung" (designated N). Hunger provides an exceptionally convenient resource for comparative studies by enumerating the sculptures, vases, paintings, dramas, poems, novels, symphonies, oratorios, cantatas, and operas concerned with or employing a particular figure or event of classical mythology and by referring also to secondary literature discussing the "Nachwirkung" of that figure or event. The volume concludes with two bibliographies, of literature on Greek and Roman mythol-

ogy and religious history, and of major works on the continued artistic use to the present of materials from classical mythology.

K–32 Haussig, Hans-Wilhelm, ed. *Wörterbuch der Mythologie.* 7 vols. planned. Stuttgart: Klett-Cotta, 1961–.
                                                    BL303.W63 1965

This massive scholarly treatment of the mythologies of the world is being published in some thirty-four fascicles; to date, about half of them have appeared. The finished work will be disposed into seven volumes according to the following cultural and regional division: vol. 1, Myths of the Near East; vol. 2, Myths of Old Europe; vol. 3, Classical Greek and Roman Mythology; vol. 4, Myths of the Caucasian and Iranian Peoples; vol. 5, Myths of the Indian Subcontinent; vol. 6, Myths of East, Southeast, and Northern Asia; and vol. 7, Myths of Old America. Within volumes are subdivisions for particular cultural groups, each subdivision written by one or several specialists. Elaborate introductory materials are followed by a dictionary arrangement of information on the persons and places of the individual mythology being treated. Each volume will be separately indexed.

K–33 Edwardes, Marian, and Lewis Spence. *Dictionary of Non-Classical Mythology.* Rev. and enl. ed. Edited by Netta Peacock and J. K. Moorhead. London: J. M. Dent, 1929.
                                                    BL303.E25

This dictionary from A [the god] through Zuma begins with a list of chief authorities from which the relatively brief entries have been derived. Appended are a number of plates with illustrations of deities, temples, and religious symbols. A new edition, by Egerton Sykes, was published with the same title in 1962 [BL303.S9]. It follows, but updates, the entries of the 1929 version.

K–34 Some Frequently Recommended Works on Mythology (see also works in Stoff- und Motivgeschichte, K–80 ff.).

Boswell, Jeanetta. *"Past Ruined Ilion—" : A Bibliography of English and American Literature Based on Greco-Roman Mythology.* Metuchen, N.J.: Scarecrow Press, 1982.   Z2011.B67 1982

Bush, Douglas. *Mythology and the Renaissance Tradition in English Poetry.* Rev. ed. New York: W. W. Norton, 1957.   PR508.M9 B8 1957

———. *Mythology and the Romantic Tradition in English Poetry.* Cambridge: Harvard University Press, 1937.   PR508.M9 B85

———. *Pagan Myth and Christian Tradition in English Poetry.* Philadelphia: American Philosophical Society, 1968.   AC1.J39 1967

Campbell, Joseph. *Hero with a Thousand Faces.* 2d ed. Princeton, N.J.: Princeton University Press, 1968.
                                                    BL313.C28 1968

———. *Historical Atlas of World Mythology.* Vol. 1–. New York: Harper and Row, 1983–.
                                                    BL311.C26 1983

———. *Masks of God.* 4 vols., *Primitive, Oriental, Occidental, and Creative Mythology.* New York: Viking, 1959–1968.   BL311.C272

Cassirer, Ernst. *Language and Myth.* Translation by Suzanne K. Langer of *Sprache und Mythos*, Studien der Bibliothek Warburg, no. 6) (Leipzig and Berlin: Teubner, 1925), New York: Harper, 1946. P105.C32

———. *Philosophy of Symbolic Forms.* 3 vols. Translation by Ralph Manheim of *Die Philosophie der symbolischen Formen* (Berlin: B. Cassirer, 1923–1929). New

Haven: Yale University Press, 1955. See vol. 2, *Mythical Thought.*   B3216.C33 P5 1955

Chase, Richard. *Quest for Myth.* Baton Rouge: Louisiana State University Press, 1949.   BL313.C47 1949a

Dumézil, Georges. *Mythe et épopée.* 3 vols. Paris: Gallimard, 1968–1974.   BL660.D815

Éliade, Mircea. *Birth and Rebirth: The Religious Meanings of Initiation in Human Culture.* Translation by Willard R. Trask of *Naissances mystiques* (Paris: Gallimard, 1959). New York: Harper, 1958.   BL615.E4

———. *History of Religious Ideas.* Vol. 1: *From the Stone Age to Eleusinian Mysteries,* Vol. 2: *From Gautama Buddha to the Triumph of Christianity,* Vol. 3: *From Muhammad to the Age of Reforms.* Chicago: University of Chicago Press, 1978–1982.

———. *Myth and Reality.* Translated by Willard R. Trask. New York: Harper and Row, 1963.   BL304.E413

———. *Myth of the Eternal Return.* Translation by Willard R. Trask of *Le mythe de l'éternel retour: Archétypes et répétition* (Paris: Gallimard, 1949). New York: Pantheon, 1954.   BD701.E38 1954

———. *Myths, Dreams, and Mysteries.* Translation by Philip Mairet of *Mythes, rêves et mystéres* (Paris: Gallimard, 1957). New York: Harper, 1960.   BL311.E413

Feder, Lillian. *Ancient Myth in Modern Poetry.* Princeton: Princeton University Press, 1971.
PN56.M94 F43 1971

Feldman, Burton, and Robert D. Richardson, eds. *Rise of Modern Mythology, 1680–1860.* Bloomington: Indiana University Press, 1972.   BL311.F43

Frazer, Sir James G. *Golden Bough: A Study in Magic and Religion.* 3d ed. 12 vols. London: Macmillan, 1907–1915. Reprinted in 13 vols. including *Aftermath.* London, 1955. Excellent indexes.   BL310.F7

———. *Aftermath: A Supplement to the Golden Bough.* London: Macmillan, 1936.   BL310.F715

———. *New Golden Bough: A New Abridgment of the Classic Work.* Edited by Theodor H. Gaster. New York: Criterion, 1959.   BL310.F72

Fromm, Erich. *Forgotten Language: An Introduction to the Understanding of Dreams, Fairy Tales, and Myths.* New York: Rinehart, 1951.   BF1078.F84

Frye, Northrop. *Fables of Identity: Studies in Poetic Mythology.* New York: Harcourt, Brace, 1963.   PR503.F7

———. "Myth and Myth Criticism: An Introductory Bibliography" [see X–31].

Gayley, Charles M. *Classic Myths in English Literature and in Art.* Boston: Ginn and Co., 1911.   BL721.G3 1911

Graves, Robert. *White Goddess: A Historical Grammar of Poetic Myth.* Amended and enl. ed. London: Faber and Faber, 1952.   PN1077.G7 1952

Grimal, Pierre, ed. *Larousse World Mythology.* Translated by Patricia Beardsworth. New York: G. P. Putnam's Sons, 1965.   BL311.G683 1965

Hamburger, Käte. *From Sophocles to Sartre: Figures from Greek Tragedy, Classical and Modern.* Translation by Helen Sebba of *Von Sophokles zu Sartre: Griechische Drammenfiguren antik und modern.* New York: Ungar, 1969.   PN1711.H313

Hamilton, Edith. *Mythology.* New York: Grosset and Dunlap, 1942.   BL310.H3

Jung, Carl G., and Karl Kerenyi. *Introduction to Mythology: Essays on a Science of Mythology.* Translation by R. R. C. Hull of *Einfuhrüng in das Wesen der Mythologie,* 4th ed. (Zurich: Rheinverlag, 1951). New York: Pantheon, 1948.   BL313.J83

Kirk, G. S. *Myth: Its Meaning and Functions in Ancient and Other Cultures.* Berkeley, Los Angeles, London: University of California Press, 1970.   BL311.K55 1970

Kitagawa, Joseph M., et al. *Myths and Symbols: Studies in Honor of Mircea Éliade.* Chicago: University of Chicago Press, 1969.   BL25.M85

Kleinstück, Johannes. *Mythos und Symbol in englischer Dichtung.* Stuttgart: Kohlhammer, 1964.   PR504.K55

Law, Helen H. *Bibliography of Greek Myth in English Poetry.* New York: Service Bureau for Classical Teachers, 1932.   Z7836.L41

Levi-Straus, Claude. *Mythologiques.* 4 vols. Paris: Plon, 1964–1971.   F2519.3.R3 L48

Levy, Gertrude R. *Sword from the Rock.* London: Faber, 1953.   PN1303.L4 1953

McCune, Marjorie W., et al. *Binding of Proteus: Perspectives on Myth and the Literary Process.* Lewisburg, Pa.: Bucknell University Press, 1980.   PN56.M94 B5

McPeek, James A. S. *Selected Bibliography of Myth in Literature,* issued with Kathleen Raine, *On the Mythological,* as a CEA Chap Book: A Supplement to the *CEA Critic,* vol. 32, no. 1 (October 1969). Fullerton, Calif.: College English Association, 1969. Five sections treat General Reference Works; Myth: Its Meaning and Tradition; The Bible: Texts and Critical Studies; Classical Literature: Texts and Critical Studies; Works on Selected Myths.   BL304.R33

Maranda, Pierre. *Mythology: Selected Readings.* Harmondsworth: Penguin, 1972.   BL315.M37

Murray, Henry A., ed. *Myth and Mythmaking.* New York: Braziller, 1960.   BL311.M85

Norton, Dan L., and Peter S. Rushton. *Classical Myths in English Literature.* New York: Rinehart, 1952.
BL313.N6

Olson, Alan M., ed. *Myth, Symbol, and Reality.* Notre Dame, Ind.: University of Notre Dame Press, 1980.
BL304.M87

Olson, Paul A., ed. *Uses of Myth: Papers Relating to the Anglo-American Seminar on the Teaching of English [Dartmouth, 1966].* Champaign, Ill.: NCTE, 1968.
LB1631.U8

Prescott, Frederick C. *Poetry and Myth.* New York: Macmillan, 1927.   PN1077.P7

Raglan, FitzRoy Richard Somerset, Baron. *Hero: A Study in Tradition, Myth, and Drama.* London: Methuen, 1937.   BL325.H46 R3

Richardson, Robert D. *Myth and Literature in the American Renaissance.* Bloomington: Indiana University Press, 1978.   PS217.M93 R5

Righter, William. *Myth and Literature.* London: Routledge and Kegan Paul, 1975.   PN56.M94 R5

Ruthven, K. K. *Myth.* London: Methuen, 1976.
PN56.M94 R8 1976

Sebeok, Thomas A., ed. *Myth: A Symposium.* Bloomington: Indiana University Press, 1958.   BL310.S37

Seznec, Jean. *Survival of the Pagan Gods: The Mythological Tradition and Its Place in Renaissance Humanism and Arts.* Translation by Barbara F. Sessions of *La survivance des dieux antiques* (London: Warburg Institute, 1939). New York: Pantheon Books, 1953.
BL313.S52

Slote, Bernice, ed. *Myth and Symbol: Critical Approaches and Applications.* Lincoln: University of Nebraska Press, 1963.   PN501.S55

Starnes, D. T., and Ernest W. Talbert. *Classical Myth and Legend in Renaissance Dictionaries: A Study of Renaissance Dictionaries in Their Relation to the Classical Learning of Contemporary English Writers.* Chap-

el Hill: University of North Carolina Press, 1955.
PR428.C6 S7

Vickery, John B. *Myths and Texts: Strategies of Incorporation and Displacement.* Baton Rouge: Louisiana State University Press, 1983.   PN56.M95 V5 1983

————, ed. *Myth and Literature: Contemporary Theory and Practice.* Lincoln: University of Nebraska Press, 1966. Extensive bibliography.   PN56.M94 V5

Vries, Jan de. *Forschungsgeschichte der Mythologie.* Freiburg: Karl Alber, 1961.   BL304.V7

Weisinger, Herbert. *Agony and the Triumph: Papers on the Use and Abuse of Myth.* East Lansing: Michigan State University Press, 1964.   PN710.W45

White, John J. *Mythology in the Modern Novel: A Study of Prefigurative Techniques.* Princeton, N.J.: Princeton University Press, 1971.   PN3351.W5

III. THE BIBLE

Note that both the British Museum's *General Catalogue of Printed Books* (B–41) and the *National Union Catalog* (B–12, B–13) have multiple volumes listing holdings of and about the Bible.

K–35 **Marrow, Stanley B. *Basic Tools of Biblical Exegesis: A Student's Manual.*** Rome: Biblical Institute Press, 1976.
Z7770.M33 1976

First published in 1971 with the title *Biblical Methodology: A Student's Manual of Basic Tools*, this short but extremely useful guide contains 215 serially numbered, descriptively and evaluatively annotated entries, disposed into eight sections, as follows: Bibliographical Sources, Texts and Versions, Grammars, Lexica, Dictionaries, Concordances, Apocrypha and Pseudepigrapha, and Subsidiary Material. A list of periodicals in the field of Bible study is appended.

The most comprehensive bibliography of publications in the field of Bible study is the *Elenchus Bibliographicus Biblicus*, published by the Pontifical Biblical Institute since 1920. The first forty-eight years of bibliographies (through those of 1968) appeared quarterly in *Biblica* with an annual subject index [BS410.B7]. Since then, the *Elenchus* has been separately published [Z7770.E63]. It is edited in Latin, with entries in the original languages, and uses a detailed classification scheme (currently there are 22 major sections). Books, articles, reviews, dissertations, and items in composite volumes are cited; there are indexes of authors, subjects, and Scripture texts.

Another annual bibliography is the *Internationale Zeitschriftenschau für Bibelwissenschaft und Grenzgebiete / International Review of Biblical Studies*, Vol. 1– (Stuttgart [then Düsseldorf]: Verlag Katholisches Bibelwerk, 1952) [Z7770.I57], which presents abstracts, usually in German, of articles in periodicals and composite volumes. Some 2,000 abstracts drawing from more than 400 journals are arranged topically, with an author index.

In addition to these more specialized bibliographies, students should consult the appropriate entries in *L'année philologique* (L–17) and other bibliographies and guides to the study of classical antiquity (L–10 ff.).

There are also many relevant entries in the more general works on religion and the history of religion. See, for example, John G. Barrow's annotated, comprehensive *Bibliography of Bibliographies in Religion* (Ann Arbor, Mich., 1955) [Z7751.B33]. And see Shirley J. Case et al., *Bibliographical Guide to the History of Christianity* (Chicago: University of Chicago Press, 1931) [Z7777.C33]. Additional titles are cited and described in the standard general reference guides (A–20 ff.).

K–36 **Society for Old Testament Study. *Booklist.*** London: The Society, 1946–.   LC numbers vary

The annual volumes carry extensive signed reviews of work in the field arranged in a classified format. These lists have been gathered together as follows: H. H. Rowley, ed., *Eleven Years of Bible Bibliography: The Book Lists of the Society for Old Testament Study, 1946–1956* (Indian Hills, Colo., 1957) [Z7770.S6]; G. W. Anderson, ed., *Decade of Bible Bibliography: The Book Lists of the Society for Old Testament Study, 1957–1966* (Oxford, 1967) [Z7772.A1 S66]; and Peter R. Ackroyd, ed., *Society for Old Testament Study Bible Bibliography 1967–1973* (Oxford, 1974) [Z7772.A1 S64].

K–37 **Hurd, John Coolidge, Jr., comp. *Bibliography of New Testament Bibliographies.*** New York: Seabury Press, 1966.
Z7772.L1 H8

This classified, annotated bibliography of bibliographies contains more than 1,000 entries, arranged into the categories of selective book lists both general and special; historical and chronological surveys; comprehensive (research) bibliographies on the whole New Testament, on individual books or sections, on special subjects, and on related areas of study; and biographical and bibliographical studies of noted New Testament scholars.

Current material is recorded in *New Testament Abstracts: A Record of Current Literature* (Cambridge, Mass.: Western School of Theology, 1956–) [BS410.N35]. The triannual issues present classified abstracts of books and articles; there are annual indexes of book authors and titles, of authors and titles, of authors of articles, of book reviews, and of biblical texts.

K–38 ***New Oxford Annotated Bible with the Apocrypha, Revised Standard Version Containing the Second Edition of the New Testament and an Expanded Edition of the Apocrypha.*** Edited by Herbert G. May and Bruce M. Metzger. New York: Oxford University Press, 1977.   BS191.A1 N4

This work, designed as an ecumenical study Bible, contains the text of all books held to be canonical by Protestant, Roman Catholic, and Eastern Orthodox traditions. The text is that of the Revised Standard Version, Old Testament Section (1952); New Testament Section, Second Edition (1971); and Apocrypha (1957); with the Third and Fourth Books of the Maccabees and Psalm 151 (1977). Among the study aids are introductions, page-by-page annotations, and a series of informative essays by distinguished authorities on "The Number and Sequence of the Books of the Bible"; "How to Read the Bible with Understanding"; "Modern Approaches to Biblical Study"; "Characteristics of Hebrew Poetry"; "Literary Forms in the Gospels"; "Survey of the Geography, History and Archaeology of the Bible Lands"; "Measures and Weights in the Bible"; "Chronological Tables of Rulers"; and "English Versions of the Bible: The Tyndale–King James Tradition." There are two separate indexes, to annotations of the Old and New Testaments and to annotations of the Apocrypha. Following the Apocrypha are a series of twelve colored maps based on the *Oxford Bible Atlas*, and an index to them.

K–39 ***Cambridge History of the Bible.*** 3 vols. Cambridge: Cambridge University Press, 1963–1970.   BS445.C26

In a format similar to that of the other standard Cambridge histories (see F–12, F–13, F–14, F–20), these volumes are complete in themselves; they are divided into sections written by individual scholars, with authoritative accounts, extensive selected classified bibliographies, and full indexes. The aim of this history is to give an account of the text and versions, textual transmission, circulation, authority, exegesis, and place of the Bible in the West (i.e., Europe and America). Volume 1 (1970), *From the Beginnings to Jerome*, was edited by P. R. Ackroyd and C. F. Evans; volume 2 (1969), *West from the Fathers to Jerome*, by G. W. H. Lampe; and volume 3 (1963), *West from the Reformation to the Present Day*, by S. L. Greenslade. Volume 3 contains two bibliographical appendixes, "Aids to the Study of the Bible, A Selective Historical Account of the Major Grammars, Lexicons, Concordances, Dictionaries and Encyclopedias, and Atlases," and "Commentaries: A Historical Note."

K–40 Buttrick, George Arthur. *Interpreter's Dictionary of the Bible: An Illustrated Encyclopedia Identifying and Explaining All Proper Names and Significant Terms and Subjects in the Holy Scriptures, Including the Apocrypha, with Attention to Archaeological Discoveries and Researches into the Life and Faith of Ancient Times.* 4 vols. New York: Abingdon Press, 1962.   BS440.I63

This work presents authoritative, signed articles with bibliographies appended, and includes both general articles and those more specific. Alphabetically arranged, entries give the name or term, its pronunciation, its Hebrew, Aramaic, or Greek original, its root meaning, variant forms in the text of the Bible, a list of places where it is found in the text, a short definition, and then a more elaborate article. There are some illustrations, colored maps, and frequent cross-references to aid users.

A *Supplementary Volume*, ed. Keith Crim et al. (Nashville: Abingdon, 1976) [BS440.I63 1976] follows the scope and format of the original work, in recent printings of which entries have been asterisked to indicate that additional material will be found in the *Supplement*.

K–41 Hastings, James, ed. *Dictionary of the Bible.* Rev. ed. Edited by Frederick C. Grant and H. H. Rowley. New York: Charles Scribner's Sons, 1963.   BS440.H5 1963

This standard one-volume dictionary was originally published in 1913. Initials following articles refer to the group of authorities who contributed to the original and revised editions. Both editions are based on the text of the *Revised Standard Version* of the Bible. There are color maps and abundant cross-references to aid users.

Hastings also edited the more massive five-volume *Dictionary of the Bible, Dealing with Its Language, Literature, and Contents, Including Biblical Theology* (Edinburgh, 1898–1904) [BS440.H5 1898], with extensive, signed articles by scholars. This older work has not been updated.

Another useful one-volume work is the *Oxford Dictionary of the Christian Church*, ed. F. L. Cross and Elizabeth A. Livingstone, 2d ed. (London: Oxford University Press, 1974) [BR95.O8 1974], with more than 6,000 articles, some two-thirds of which have bibliographies appended. A *Concise* version was published in 1977 [BR95.O8 1977].

K–42 Herbert, Arthur Sumner. *Historical Catalogue of Printed Editions of the English Bible: 1525–1961.* Revised and Expanded from the Edition of T. H. Darlow and H. F. Moule, 1903. London: British and Foreign Bible Society, 1968.   Z7771.E5 H47 1968

This work revises and brings up to date the first volume of Darlow and Moule's *Historical Catalogue of the Printed Editions of Holy Scripture in the Library of the British and Foreign Bible Society*, 2 vols. in 4 (London: Bible House, 1903–1911) [Z7770.B73], which was and remains the most important bibliography of the printed Bible. The first vol-

ume, treating English Bibles, was arranged chronologically; the new revised edition contains 2,331 serially numbered entries with bibliographical descriptions and up to ten location citations (five in the United Kingdom and five in the United States). There are two appendixes, one of commentaries with new translations and one listing Bible versions in English provincial dialects. There are indexes of translators, revisers, and editors; of printers and publishers; of places of printing and publication; and a general index. The remaining volumes of the original catalog are arranged alphabetically by language and then chronologically, giving bibliographical descriptions of polyglot Bibles and those in languages other than English. Altogether the catalog has almost 10,000 entries.

K–44 Some Frequently Recommended Works on the History of the English Bible and on the Bible in Literary History.

Alter, Robert. *Art of Biblical Narrative*. New York: Basic Books, 1981.   BS1171.2.A45

Avni, Abraham A. "The Influence of the Bible on European Literature: A Review of Research from 1955 to 1965." *YCGL* 19 (1970): 39–57.

Bailey, Lloyd R., ed. *Word of God: A Guide to English Versions of the Bible*. Atlanta, Ga.: John Knox Press, 1982.   BS196.W67 1982

Barr, James. *Holy Scripture: Canon, Authority, Criticism*. Oxford: Clarendon Press, 1983.   BS465.B35 1983

Berlin, Adele. *Poetics and Interpretation of Biblical Narrative*. Sheffield: Almond Press, 1983.   BS5535.B39 1983

Bruce, Frederick F. *History of the Bible in English, from the Earliest Versions*. 3d ed. New York: Oxford University Press, 1978.   BS455.B74 1978

Butterworth, Charles C. *Literary Lineage of King James' Bible, 1340–1611*. Philadelphia: University of Pennsylvania Press, 1941–.   BS455.B8

Daiches, David. *King James Version of the English Bible*. Chicago: University of Chicago Press, 1941.   BS455.D26

Frye, Northrop. *Great Code: The Bible and Literature*. New York: Harcourt Brace Jovanovich, 1982. PN56.B5F7

Hammond, Gerald. *Making of the English Bible*. Manchester: Carcanet New Press, 1982.   BS186.H35 1982

Henn, T. R. *[English] Bible as Literature*. New York: Oxford University Press, 1970.   BS535.H45

Hills, Margaret Thorndike. *English Bible in America; A Bibliography of the Bible and the New Testament Published in America: 1777–1957*. New York: American Bible Society, 1962.   Z771.A5 H5 1962

Jobling, David. *Sense of Biblical Narrative: Structural Analyses in the Hebrew Bible*. 2d ed. Sheffield: JSOT Press, Department of Biblical Studies, University of Sheffield, 1986.   BS1325.2.J56 1986

Kugel, James L. *Idea of Biblical Poetry: Parallelism and its History*. New Haven: Yale University Press, 1981.   BS1405.2.K83

Leach, Edmund, and D. Alan Aycock. *Structuralist Interpretations of Biblical Myth*. Cambridge: Cambridge University Press, 1983.   BS540.L35 1983

Robinson, H. W., ed. *Bible in Its Ancient and English Versions*. Oxford: Clarendon Press, 1940.   BS445.R66

Schneidau, Herbert. *Sacred Discontent: The Bible and Western Literature*. Berkeley, Los Angeles, London: University of California Press, 1977. BS511.2.S36 1977

———. *Sacred Discontent: The Bible and Western Tradition*. Baton Rouge: Louisiana State University Press, 1976.   BS511.2.S36 1976

Schwarz, Werner. *Principles and Problems of Biblical Translation*. Cambridge: Cambridge University Press, 1955.   BS450.S3

Sternberg, Meir. *Poetics of Biblical Narrative: Ideological Literature and the Drama of Reading*. Bloomington: Indiana University Press, 1985.   BS535.S725 1985

Trible, Phyllis. *Texts of Terror: Literary-Feminist Readings of Biblical Narratives*. Philadelphia: Fortress Press, 1984.   BS575.T74 1984

K–45 **Strong, James. *Exhaustive Concordance of the Bible: Showing Every Word of the Text of the Common English Version of the Canonical Books, and Every Occurrence of Each Word in Regular Order Together with a Comparative Concordance of the Authorized and Revised Versions, Including the American Variations; Also Brief Dictionaries of the Hebrew and Greek Words of the Original, with References to the English Words.*** New York: Abingdon Press, 1955.   BS425.S8 1955

This most extensive concordance of the English Bible was first published in 1894. There are approximately 400,000 entries. The work was prepared in five sections: 1. Main Concordance by Keyword; 2. Appendix with 47 Common Words; 3. Comparative Concordance of the *Revised Standard Version* (1881) and the *American Standard Version* (1901); 4. A Dictionary of Hebrew and Chaldee Old Testament Roots Keyed to the Main Concordance; and 5. A Dictionary of Greek New Testament Roots Keyed to the Main Concordance. In this edition these sections are maintained but have been slightly revised to incorporate needed corrections.

The classic concordance to the King James version of the English Bible is that by Alexander Cruden, *Cruden's Complete Concordance to the Old and New Testaments*, issued in many editions since its original publication in 1737. It contains some 225,000 entries and an appendix of proper names. Among the most recent editions is that by C. H. Irwin et al. (Toronto: Welch, 1977) [BS425.C8 1977].

The standard concordance to the *Revised Standard Version* is compiled by J. W. Ellison, *Nelson's Complete Concordance of the Revised Standard Version Bible* (New York, 1957) [BS425.E4 1957]. See also the *Oxford Concise Concordance to the Revised Standard Version*, comp. Bruce M. Metzger (New York: Oxford University Press, 1962) [BS425.M4].

For the Roman Catholic Bible the standard concordance is by N. W. Thompson and Raymond Stock, *Complete Concordance to the Bible (Douay Version)* (St. Louis: B. Herder, 1945) [BS425.T45 1945].

K–46 **Gottcent, John H. *Bible as Literature: A Selective Bibliography.*** Boston: G. K. Hall, 1979.   Z7770.G68

This valuable annotated bibliography with entries in an alphanumeric order is disposed into an introduction and eight chapters. The chapters are as follows: 1, Editions and Translations; 2, General Reference Works; 3, The Bible as a Whole; 4, The Old Testament as a Whole; 5, The Old Testament: Individual Books; 6, The Apocrypha; 7, The New Testament as a Whole; and 8, The New Testament: Individual Books. The chapter on editions and translations is subdivided into lists for the complete Bible, texts for literary study, works on the style of the English Bible, and works on the history of Bible translation. The chapter on general reference works is subdivided into sections on Bibliographical Sources, Useful Journals, Works Treating the Archaeological Background, Atlases and Other Works on the Geographical Background, Dictionaries and Encyclopedias, Word Books, Concordances, Commentaries and Handbooks, and Miscellaneous Reference Books. There is an index of authors, titles, and subjects.

K–47 ***Literary Guide to the Bible.*** Edited by Robert Alter and Frank Kermode. Cambridge, Mass.: Belknap Press of Harvard University Press, 1987.   BS511.2.L58

This volume provides a series of authoritative, discursive essays on the literary aspects of each of the books or groups of books of the *Old Testament* and the *New Testament*. The essays, written by an international team of biblical and literary scholars, treat the structures, themes, narrative techniques, and poetic forms of the book or books which are their subject, using all of the resources of contemporary literary and textual criticism and theory. Most essays conclude with notes and suggested further readings.

The editors together contribute a General Introduction, while Alter has an Introduction to the Old Testament, and Kermode an Introduction to the New Testament. In addition, a series of General Essays follow those on the books of the Bible. Their topics are "The Hebrew Bible and Canaanite Literature," "The New Testament and Greco-Roman Writing," "Fishing for Men on the Edge of the Wilderness," "The Canon," "The Characteristics of Ancient Hebrew Poetry," "Midrash and Allegory," and "English Translations of the Bible." This important new reference work ends with a Glossary of Biblical and Literary Terms and an Index to Literary Topics.

IV.   PROVERBS

K–50 **Stevenson, Burton E. *Home Book of Proverbs, Maxims and Familiar Phrases.*** New York: Macmillan, 1948.
PN6405.S8

This work aims to present the sources of proverbs, maxims, and familiar phrases in English and American use. It is arranged by topics and subtopics. Under the subtopic, numbered individual entries are arranged in chronological order, with Greek and Latin expressions given in English (the original in parentheses). For each entry, the source author, text, book, and line numbers (as appropriate) are given, along with the date of the edition from which the quoted expression is taken. The volume concludes with an index of keywords.

K–51 **Stephens, Thomas A. *Proverb Literature: A Bibliography of Works Relating to Proverbs.*** Edited by Wilfrid Bonser. London: William Glaisher, 1930.   Z7191.S83

This somewhat out-of-date work contains 4,004 briefly annotated entries, moving from general works to works by language and country (Latin, Greek, Jewish, Gypsy, English . . .) and then to works treating local materials. At the end, works of a nonregional kind are enumerated. The book concludes with an index of authors, compilers, etc. This work can be updated by reference to the *Sprichwörterbibliographie* of Moll (K–52), who imitates Stephens's structure and arrangement.

A valuable, brief, also somewhat out-of-date bibliography is that by Archer Taylor, "An Introductory Bibliography for the Study of Proverbs" *MP* 30 (1932): 195–210.

K–52 **Moll, Otto E. *Sprichwörterbibliographie.*** Frankfurt am Main: Klostermann, 1958.   Z7191.M6

This work contains a total of more than 9,051 serially numbered entries. It begins with a 251-item bibliography of proverb bibliographies, followed by general works on the history, psychology, form, and use of proverbs. Entries are arranged in a total of twenty sections, further divided into forty-five groups. Within each group, entries are in chronological order. The sections move from general to specific, from polyglot collections to single-language collections, to works treating the proverb literature of ancient peoples and languages, to works on the proverb literature of the Romance languages; and so on through each group of peoples or languages. Section 20 has additional works that deal with the proverb literature of a certain subject, type, or area. Dialect dictionaries are included in their appropriate sections. The work concludes with an author index.

Moll is supplemented by J. Werner, "Sprichwortliteratur," *Zeitschrift für Volkskunde* 57 (1961): 118–132; and 58 (1962): 114–129; and by "Bibliographie" (treating 306 works published 1955–1975) in Wolfgang Mieder, ed., *Ergebnisse der Sprichwörterforschung* (Bern, 1978) [PN6401.E73]

K–53 Wilson, F. P. "English Proverbs and Dictionaries of Proverbs." *The Library,* 4th ser., 26 (1945): 51–75.
Z671.L69

This essay on the study of proverbs cites earlier collections, discusses the problem of defining the proverb, and surveys the early history of the collecting and study of proverbs in England from 1640 to 1670.

K–54 *Oxford Dictionary of English Proverbs.* Compiled by William George Smith. 3d ed. Revised by F. P. Wilson. Oxford: Clarendon Press, 1970.   PN6421.O9 1970

The first edition of this standard work was published in 1935. Proverbs are arranged alphabetically by the first significant word of the standard form of each, with the part of the proverb preceding that word transferred to the intermediate or concluding part of the citation. There are some 14,000 main entries, in which each proverb is followed by quotations illustrating its history, arranged in chronological order, with dated references to sources. Cross-references from every other important word in a proverb send the user to the first important word, under which the citation is found. A list of sources precedes the dictionary proper, as does an introduction that briefly surveys the history of the study of proverbs and changing attitudes taken toward them. There are also cross-references to Tilley (K–56), as appropriate.

K–55 Whiting, Bartlett Jere, with the collaboration of Helen Wescott Whiting. *Proverbs, Sentences, and Proverbial Phrases from English Writings Mainly before 1500.* Cambridge: Harvard University Press, 1968.   PN6083.W45

Some 10,000 proverbs, sententiae, and proverbial phrases are arranged in alphabetical order by a boldface keyword of the standard form of the proverb. The keyword is the first important noun, verb, or adjunct. Each proverb is numbered in alphanumeric order. Illustrative dated quotations with bibliographical references and references to works with later examples of the proverb's use complete each entry. There are cross-references from other important words in the proverb. The volume concludes with an index of important words and an index of proper nouns in the standard forms and in the illustrative quotations.

K–56 Tilley, Morris Palmer. *Dictionary of the Proverbs in England in the Sixteenth and Seventeenth Centuries: A Collection of Proverbs Found in English Literature and the Dictionaries of the Period.* Ann Arbor: University of Michigan Press, 1950.   PN6420.T5

Proverbs are cited alphabetically by a keyword (the first substantive) in the standard form of the proverb. Entries are numbered in alphanumeric order and present dated illustrative quotations of the proverb's use, with bibliographical references. There are approximately 11,780 proverbs cited. The volume concludes with a bibliography of proverb collections and works cited, a separate index to Shakespearian quotations in the text, and an index of keywords.

K–57 Whiting, Bartlett Jere. *Early American Proverbs and Proverbial Phrases.* Cambridge: Harvard University Press, 1977.   PN6426.T28

This dictionary treats proverbs found in America before about 1820. After an introduction and bibliography of references, proverbs are listed alphabetically by keywords of the standard form of the proverb, that is, the first important noun, verb, or adjunct. Each entry is numbered in alphanumeric order with dated illustrative quotations arranged in chronological order. Later uses of the proverb are noted by references to the Oxford Dictionary (K–54), Whiting and Whiting (K–55), Tilley (K–56), and Taylor and Whiting (K–58). There are a series of appendixes, of which appendix C on "Proverb, Proverbial, and Proverbially" is especially recommended. The volume concludes with indexes of important words and of proper nouns.

K–58 Taylor, Archer, and Bartlett Jere Whiting. *Dictionary of American Proverbs and Proverbial Phrases, 1820–1880.* Cambridge: Harvard University Press, 1958.   PN6426.T28

After an introduction and bibliography of texts and reference works, proverbs and proverbial phrases are arranged alphabetically by keyword in their standard form. The keyword is the first important noun, verb, or adjunct. Entries give dated illustrative quotations in chronological order.

K–59 DeCaro, F. A., and W. K. McNeil. *American Proverb Literature: A Bibliography.* Folklore Forum, Bibliographical and Special Series, no. 6, Bloomington, Ind., 1971.
GR1F564 Bibl. and Spec. Ser.

This bibliography contains 374 annotated entries, preceded by an introduction on the study of American proverbs.

K–60 Mieder, Wolfgang. *Proverbs in Literature: An International Bibliography.* Bern: Peter Lang, 1978.
Z6514.P76 M53

This bibliography's 1,166 serially numbered entries are disposed into two parts, a general section (items 1–135) and then a section arranged alphabetically by the name of the literary author (with dates) whose use of proverb material has been studied. Studies are listed alphabetically by their authors. Cross-reference is made in entries to citations in Stephens/Bonser (K–51) and Moll (K–52). An index of scholars concludes the volume.

See also Mieder's articles, "The Essence of Literary Proverb Studies," *Proverbium* 23 (1974), 888–894, and "The Proverb and Anglo-American Literature," *SFQ* 38 (1974): 49–62, the latter of which enumerates 147 works dealing with the proverb in English and American literature.

K–61 Mieder, Wolfgang. *International Bibliography of Explanatory Essays on Individual Proverbs and Proverbial Expressions.* Bern: Herbert Lang, 1977.   Z7191.M54 1977

This first attempt at an international bibliography of these materials analyzes 237 journals, bibliographies, and books, seeking articles on individual proverbs. Excluded are articles that appeared in *Notes and Queries*, which has its own index (see Z–58). Entries are arranged alphabetically by keyword, using the terms identified as such in the major proverb collections. There are some 2,000 keywords, under which are arranged numbered entries citing articles on proverbs associated with that keyword. There is, regrettably, no index.

V.   QUOTATIONS

K–65 *Oxford Dictionary of Quotations.* 3d ed. Compiled by Richard T. Brain et al. New York: Oxford University Press, 1979.   PN6081.O9 1979

This edition drops about one-third of the quotations cited in the first (1941) and second (1953) editions, on the grounds that they were found no longer popular by the majority of those on the revising board. Nursery rhymes have been excluded, as have snatches of popular songs and the citation of advertisements, slogans, and other media catchphrases. Titles of books, films, and plays have also been excised. Among the newly included quotations are passages from the works of authors since World War II, from memorable texts in the political and social life of the last twenty-five years, and from works of foreign writers neglected in earlier editions but now better known to the English-speaking world. Also included are quotations apparently omitted on the grounds of indelicacy in former editions but now found tolerable.

The more than 17,000 quotations included are numbered on each page and are ordered under the alphabetically arranged names of their authors by the titles of the works from which they come. Source works are identified briefly. Both authors' dates and the dates of publication or performance of their works are given, as are cross-references. Subheadings are used for the titles of Dickens novels, books of the Bible (in canonical order, followed by the Vulgate), and for the titles of Shakespeare's plays and poems. The computer-generated index, which occupies about one-third of the volume, contains some 70,000 entries. Keywords are followed by phrases in which the keyword is employed. Both keywords and phrases are in strict alphabetical order, the little words *a, an, the, oh, O, but, and, for, as* having been dropped. References show the author's name (in abbreviated form), with the page and quotation number following. There is a separate index of Greek words.

K–66 *Familiar Quotations: A Collection of Passages, Phrases, and Proverbs Traced to Their Sources in Ancient and Modern Literature.* Compiled by John Bartlett. 15th and 125th Anniversary Edition, Completely Revised. Edited by Emily Morison Beck et al. Boston: Little, Brown, 1980.
                                                            PN6081.B27 1980

The work, first published in 1855 in a compilation by John Bartlett, has long been a standard source. This edition contains more than 119,000 index entries to quotations from more than 2,600 authors. The quotations themselves are arranged chronologically by author, and within the citations from one author, in the chronological order of his works. Quotations are numbered on each page. Footnotes identify the edition of a source from which a text or translated text is cited, refer to related quotations, give the foreign original if it is in a familiar language, provide background information, or present cross-references to related quotations. There is a section of anonymous quotations at the end of the main section, arranged in roughly chronological order. The last third of the volume contains a very full index of keywords and phrases, keyed to the pages and location numbers of the citation. An index of authors precedes the main body.

K–67 Stevenson, Burton E. ***Home Book of Quotations, Classical and Modern.*** 10th ed. New York: Dodd, Mead, 1967.
                                                            PN6081.S73 1967

First published in 1934, this massive dictionary contains some 43,000 quotations, arranged alphabetically by subject, then alphabetically by author. Important subjects are subdivided into sections of quotations that define, discuss, praise, or criticize the subject term. Major subjects are further divided. The index of subjects which precedes the main body identifies the various subheadings for each. There are also cross-references to related subjects and to entries in the first and second appendixes, where additional, related quotations are given. In the first appendix, reference is made to pages in the original; in the second, there is a second series of subject headings. The index of authors cites names of all persons quoted, with dates and a brief designation of nationality and occupation. If the work contains 150 or fewer quotations from an author, reference is made to all of the quotations by page and quotation number. If more than 150 quotations are cited, such reference is not given (with few exceptions). The index of authors is followed by an index of authors of added quotations. The volume concludes with an index and concordance to keywords, referring to quotations by page and location number. The added quotations are treated in a supplementary index and concordance.

K–68 Evans, Bergen. ***Dictionary of Quotations.*** New York: Delacorte, 1968.   PN6081.E9

This work is arranged in three sections. The topical index lists topics and makes cross-references to further related topics; it serves as a table of contents for the main body, which consists of the quotations themselves arranged under the various topics and notions specified in the topical index. This is followed by an author index listing the page numbers for each quotation cited from each author's works. Finally, there is a detailed subject index citing each quotation under every one of its keywords and such general subjects as it illustrates. There are a variety of notes interspersed among the quotations which clarify or otherwise comment on them.

K–69 Some Frequently Recommended Works on Proverbs, Sententiae and Quotations.

Apperson, G. L. *English Proverbs and Proverbial Phrases: A Historical Dictionary.* London: J. M. Dent, 1929. Additions and corrections by B. J. Whiting in *JAF* 61 (1948): 44–48.   PN6421.A7

Auden, W. K., and Louis Kronenberger, eds. *Viking Book of Aphorisms: A Personal Selection.* New York: Viking, 1966.   PN6271.V5

Büchmann, Georg. *Geflügelte Worte.* Newly revised and edited by Hanns Martin Elster. 32d ed. Berlin: Haude und Spener, 1972.   PN6090.B8 1972

Fumagalli, Giuseppe. *Chi l'ha detto? Tesoro di citazioni italiane e straniere, di origine letteraria e storica.* 9th ed. Milano: U. Hoepli, 1946.   PN6080.F8 1946

Guerlac, O. G. *Les citations françaises: Recueil de passages célèbres, phrases familières, mots historiques, avec l'indication exacte de la source.* 4th ed. Paris: A. Colin, 1953.   PN6086.G8 1953

Lean's Collectanea. Collections by Vincent Stuckey Lean of Proverbs (English and Foreign), Folklore and Superstitions. . . . 4 vols. in 5. Bristol: Public Libraries, 1902–1904.   Z921.B853

Mieder, Wolfgang, and Alan Dundes, eds. *Wisdom of Mary: Essays on the Proverb.* New York: Garland, 1981.
                                                            PN6481.W57

Proverbium: Bulletin d'informations sur les recherches pare-miologiques. Vol. 1– Helsinki: Suomalaisen Kirjalli-suuden Seura / Société de littérature finnoise, 1963—.
PN6401.P76

Rörich, Lutz, and Wolfgang Mieder. *Sprichwort.* Stuttgart: Metzler, 1977.   PN6401.R6

Sarasino, Ernesto. *Flores Sententiarum: Raccolta di 5000 sentenze, proverbi e motti latini di uso quotidano in ordine per materie, con le fonti indicate, schiarimenti e la traduzione italiana.* Milan, 1956.

Singer, S. *Sprichwörter des Mittelalters.* 3 vols. Bern: H. Lang, 1944–1947.   PN6401.S5

Taylor, Archer. *Proverb.* Cambridge: Harvard University Press, 1931. Reprinted with *Index to the Proverb.* Hatboro, Pa.: Folklore Association, 1962.
GR1.F55 no. 113 or PN6401.T3

————. *Selected Writings on Proverbs.* Edited by Wolfgang Mieder. FF Communications, no. 216. Helsinki, 1975. Includes Taylor's still valuable article, "An Introductory Bibliography for the Study of Proverbs," originally published in *MP* 30 (1932): 195–210.
GR1.F55 no. 216

VI. SYMBOLS

K–70 Lurker, Manfred, et al. *Bibliographie zur Symbolkunde.*
3 vols. Baden-Baden: Heitz, 1964–1968.   Z7660.L8

This work contains a total of 11,466 serially numbered entries, descriptively annotated, of works on or related to the study of symbols published in the late nineteenth and twentieth centuries. Volume 1 contains the following sections: Bibliographies; Periodicals (by discipline); Dictionaries and Lexica; The Concept, Philosophical Underpinnings, and History of Symbols; a Selection from the Literature of the 16th through 18th Centuries; Ethnology, Religion, and Mythology; Oriental Studies; Folklore and Cultural History; Christian Liturgy, Bible Study, and Judaic Symbolism; Art History; Archaeology, Prehistory; Literature; Music; Legal History; Psychology and Psychotherapy. Volume 2 cites works concerned with symbols themselves, arranged in sections from Cosmic Powers, to Letters and Names, to Those who Carry Symbols. Volume 3 presents a Supplement to volumes 1 and 2, following their structure. In addition, it contains a list of introductory works in the theological and dogmatic study of symbols, a list of addenda and corrigenda, and indexes of authors and of subjects. The work is being continued by an annual serial bibliography (K–71).

K–71 Lurker, Manfred, ed. *Bibliographie zur Symbolik, Ikonographie und Mythologie: Internationales Referateorgan.* Vol. 1–. Baden-Baden: Heitz [later Koerner], 1968–.   Z7836.B5

This annual bibliography of articles with initialed descriptive abstracts in German, English, French, or Italian surveys the disciplines of prehistory, archaeology, classical studies, oriental studies, ethnology, American studies, folklore, the history of medicine, the history of law, literature, music, art history, liturgical studies, religion, theology, psychology, psychiatry, sociology, and philosophy. The aim is to cite all items published during the year (or during the previous three years if not already cited) which pertain to the study of symbols. An average of 550 entries appear each year. There are extensive indexes of topics and authors and a list of contributors. Each annual also contains a bibliographical essay on some aspect of the subject of symbol study.

K–72 Chevalier, Jean, and Alain Gheerbrant. *Dictionnaire des symboles: Mythes, rêves, coutumes, gestes, formes, figures, couleurs, nombres.* Paris: Robert Laffont, 1969.
GR35.C47

This dictionary contains some 1,200 long, illustrated articles, initialed by contributors and with coded references to a bibliography of sources at the end.

Two other French-language dictionaries may be mentioned: the older volume by M. P. Verneuil, *Dictionnaire des symboles, emblèmes et attributs* (Paris: Henri Laurens, 1897) [AZ108.V47], and the more recent Catholic dictionary by Olivier Beigbeder, *Lexique des symboles* (Paris: Zodiaque, 1969) [N6280.B37].

K–73 Jobes, Gertrude. *Dictionary of Mythology, Folklore, and Symbols.* 3 vols. New York: Scarecrow Press, 1961–1962.
GR35.J6

This work attempts to cover the myth, folklore, folk sayings, and symbols of all countries and times with a focus on symbols and symbolic features of myth and lore. For gods, entries include their genealogy, function, explanations of their activities and behavior, attributes or emblems, how they are depicted in art, and other deities to which they are parallel. For symbols, entries discuss (as appropriate) their universal and popular symbolism, significance in dreams, significance in freemasonry, heraldic significance, etymology of their names, give cognates or comparisons, and enumerate their mythological and religious significances alphabetically by culture. There is an index of some 22,000 items in two parts. The first cites deities and mythological characters by fields of interest, grouping together, for example, all references to the Abandoned Child (by name, culture, sex), the False Informer, the Fertility Figure, the Healer/Medicine Man. The second part of the index enumerates all entries that share the same mythological affiliation, attributes, or nature, grouping together, for example, all animals, dragons, dwarfs, giants, monsters, mountains, and water creatures.

K–74 Cirlot, Juan Eduardo. *Dictionary of Symbols.* Translated from the Spanish by Jack Sage. 2d ed. London: Routledge and Kegan Paul, 1971.   BF1623.S9 C513 1971

The original English translation of the *Diccionario de simbolos tradicionales* (1958) was published in 1962 [BF1629.S9 C5]. The dictionary proper is preceded by a long and valuable introduction to symbols and symbolism. Although longer articles treat such subjects as architecture, color, cross, graphics, mandala, numbers, serpent, and zodiac, most entries are brief and make reference to the numbered bibliography of principal sources at the end, to which an additional bibliography is appended. There are thirty-two plates of photographic illustration; some line drawings in the text; cross-references; and an index of names, subjects, attributes, and the like.

K–75 de Vries, Ad. *Dictionary of Symbols and Imagery.* Amsterdam: North-Holland Publishing Co., 1974.   BL600.V74

Symbols and images drawn from Western civilization are listed alphabetically by name. Following the name are a numbered series of meanings, each beginning with a contextualizing phrase (e.g., "in heraldry"). There are numerous cross-references.

K–76 Cooper, J. C. *Illustrated Encyclopedia of Traditional Symbols.* New York: Thames and Hudson, 1978.
BL603.C66

This work contains short articles, a glossary, and an unannotated bibliography of some 500 works. It is rich in non-Western symbols, but articles are not documented. It should be used in conjunction with other dictionaries, which it supplements by its valuable illustrations.

K–77 **Hall, James.** *Dictionary of Subjects and Symbols in Art.* Rev. ed. New York: Harper and Row, 1979.
N7560.H34 1979

This non-illustrated dictionary, originally published in 1974, is concerned with the Western use of Christian and classical themes. Entries in a single alphabetical sequence include descriptions of persons and personifications, with "attributes" and themes; titles of pictures; and objects, especially their "attributes." There are many cross-references. In addition, there are general articles on widely used types, such as "hunter" and "pilgrim," and on popular situations and activities, such as "prayer," "repast," and "judgment." There is a supplementary index of ideas, beliefs, social and religious customs, and additional "attributes." There are also notes on the typology of the Old Testament, the names of gods and goddesses, and the impresa; there is a list of sources (excepting books of the Bible), and a selected bibliography of iconographical studies and reference books.

K–79 **Some Frequently Recommended Works on Symbols, Iconography, and Literary Symbolism.**

Allen, Don Cameron. *Mysteriously Meant: The Rediscovery of Pagan Symbolism and Allegorical Interpretation in the Renaissance.* Baltimore: Johns Hopkins University Press, 1970.   PA57.A4

Anderson, David L., et al. *Symbolism: A Bibliography of Symbolism as an International and Multi-Disciplinary Movement.* New York: NYO Press, 1975.
Z5936.S9 A52

Balakian, Anna, ed. *Symbolist Movement in the Literature of European Languages.* Budapest: Akademiai Kiado, 1982.   PN761.S95 1982

Bayley, H. *Lost Language of Symbolism: An Inquiry into the Origin of Certain Letters, Words, Names, Fairy-Tales, Folklore, and Mythologies.* 2 vols. London: Williams and Norgate, 1911.   CB475.B3

Beebe, Maurice, ed. *Literary Symbolism.* San Francisco, Calif.: Wadsworth, 1960.   PN56.S9 B4

Bowra, Cecil Maurice. *Heritage of Symbolism.* London: Macmillan, 1943.   PN1271.B6

Bullinger, E. W. *Number in Scripture: Its Supernatural Design and Spiritual Significance.* 3d ed., rev. London: Eyre and Spottiswoode, 1913.   BS534.B83 1913

Cahiers internationaux de symbolisme. Vol. 1–. Mons: Centre interdisciplinaire d'études philosophique de l'Université de Mons, 1963.   BF458.C3

Cassirer, Ernst. *Philosophy of Symbolic Forms.* 3 vols. Vol. 1, *Language*, Vol. 2, *Mythical Thought*, Vol. 3, *Phenomenology of Knowledge.* Translated by Ralph Manheim of *Die Philosophie der symbolischen Formen* (Berlin: B. Cassirer, 1923–1929). New Haven: Yale University Press, 1953–1957. B3216.C33 P513

Chydenius, Johan. *Theory of Medieval Symbolism.* Helsinki: Finska Vetenskaps Societeten, 1960.
P9.F5 t. 27 no. 2

Clébert, Jean-Paul. *Bestiaire fabuleux.* Paris: Éditions Albin Michel, 1971.

Daly, Peter M., ed. *European Emblem: Toward an Index Emblematicus.* Waterloo, Ont.: Wilfrid Laurier University Press, 1980.   Z1021.3.E94

———, ed. *English Emblem and the Continental Tradition.* New York: AMS Press, 1988. Z1021.3.E54 1988

———, with Virginia W. Callahan. *Andreas Alciatus: Index Emblematicus.* Vol. I *Latin Emblems: Indexes and Lists*; Vol. II *Emblems in Translation.* Toronto: University of Toronto Press, 1985.   PN6349.A4 1985

Diehl, Huston. *Index of Icons in English Emblem Books 1500–1700.* Norman: University of Oklahoma Press, 1986.   Z1021.3.D53 1986

Dunbar, Helen Flanders. *Symbolism in Mediaeval Thought and Its Consummation in the Divine Comedy.* New Haven: Yale University Press, 1929.
PQ4406.D8 1929a

Eaton, R. M. *Symbolism and Truth: An Introduction to the Theory of Knowledge.* Cambridge: Harvard University Press, 1925.   BD161.E2

Éliade, Mircea. *Images and Symbols: Studies in Religious Symbolism.* Translation of *Images et symboles: Essais sur le symbolisme magico-religieux* (Paris: Gallimard, 1952). London: Harvill, 1961. BL600.E413 1961a

Emblematica: An Interdisciplinary Journal for Emblem Studies. Vol. 1–. New York: AMS Press, 1986–. 2/yr. Reviews. Research Reports. Notes and Queries. Bibliographies. [Supplementing the enumerations in Henkel, below].   CR1.E42

Feidelson, Charles. *Symbolism and American Literature.* Chicago: University of Chicago Press, 1953.
PS201.F4

Ferguson, George W. *Signs and Symbols in Christian Art with Illustrations from Paintings of the Renaissance.* 2d ed. London: Zwemmer, 1955.   N7830.F37

Foss, Martin. *Symbol and Metaphor in Human Experience.* Princeton, N.J.: Princeton University Press, 1949.
BF458.F6

Freeman, Rosemary. *English Emblem Books.* London: Chatto and Windus, 1948.   PR535.E5 F7

Gadamer, Hans-Georg. *Die Aktualität des Schönen—Kunst als Spiel, Symbol, und Fest.* Stuttgart: Reclam, 1977.
BH39.G26

Henkel, Arthur, and Albrecht Schöne. *Emblemata: Handbuch zur Sinnbildkunst des XVI und XVII Jahrhunderts.* 2d ed. Stuttgart: Metzler, 1976. [Bibliographies supplemented by the serial enumerations in *Emblematica*, above.]   N7740.H53 1976

Hopper, Vincent F. *Medieval Number Symbolism.* New York: Columbia University Press, 1938.
BF1623.P9 H53 1938a

International Journal of Symbology [IJSym]. Atlanta, Ga.: International Society for the Study of Symbols, 1968–. 3/yr.   BF458.I62

Kahler, Erich. "The Nature of the Symbol." In Rollo May, ed., *Symbolism in Religion and Literature.* pp. 50–73. New York: Braziller, 1960.   BL600.M35

Kirschbaum, S., et al., eds. *Lexikon der christlichen Ikonographie.* 8 vols. Freiburg: Herder, 1968–1976.
BV150.L4

Knights, L. C., and B. Cottle, eds. *Metaphor and Symbol.* London: Butterworth, 1960.

Krawitz, Harry. *Post-Symbolist Bibliography.* Metuchen, N.J.: Scarecrow Press, 1973. (See R–35.)
Z6520.S9 K7

Langer, Susan K. *Philosophy in a New Key: A Study in the Symbolism of Reason, Rite and Art.* Cambridge: Harvard University Press, 1942.   BF458.L3

Lehner, Ernst. *Symbols, Signs, and Signets.* Cleveland, Ohio: World Publishing Co., 1950.   AZ108.L4

Levin, Harry. *Symbolism and Fiction.* Charlottesville: University of Virginia Press, 1956.   PN3491.L4

Lurker, Manfred, ed. *Wörterbuch der Symbolik.* 2d ed. Stuttgart: Kroner, 1983.   BL600.W64 1983

Male, Emile. *Gothic Image*. Translation by Dora Nussey of *L'art religieux der XllIe siećle en France* (Paris: A. Colin, 1902). London: Collins, 1961.

    N7949.M313 1961

Panofsky, Erwin. *Meaning in the Visual Arts*. Garden City, N.J.: Doubleday, 1955.   N7445.P22

————. *Studies in Iconology: Humanistic Themes in the Art of the Renaissance*. London: Oxford University Press, 1939.   N6370.P3

Peyre, Henri. *What Is Symbolism?* Translation by Emmett Parker, with addenda, of *Qu'est-ce que le symbolisme?* (Paris: Presses universitaires de France, 1974). University: University of Alabama Press, 1980.

    PQ439.P413

Praz, Mario. *Bibliography of Emblem Books*. London, 1947.

Réau, Louis. *Iconographie de l'art chrétien*. 3 vols. in 6. Vol. 1, *Introduction générale*. Vol. 2, *Iconographie de la Bible*, 2 parts (*Ancien Testament, Nouveau Testament*). Vol. 3, *Iconographie des saints*, 3 parts. Paris: Presses universitaires de France, 1955–1959.

    No LC number

Rehder, H. *Literary Symbolism: A Symposium*. Austin: University of Texas Press, 1965.   PT107.R37

Schlesinger, Max. *Geschichte des Symbols*. Berlin: L. Simion, 1912.   BF458.S5

Senior, John. *Way Down and Out: The Occult in Symbolist Literature*. Ithaca, N.Y.: Cornell University Press, 1959.   PN56.S9 S4

Strelka, Joseph, ed. *Perspectives in Literary Symbolism*. University Park: Pennsylvania State University Press, 1968.   PN56.S9 P4

Tindall, William York. *Literary Symbol*. New York: Columbia University Press, 1955.   PN56.S9 T5

Todorov, Tzvetan. *Theories of the Symbol*. Translation by Catherine Porter of *Theories du symbole* (Paris: Editions du Seuil, 1977). Ithaca, N.Y.: Cornell University Press, 1982.   P99.T613 1982

Urban, W. M. *Language and Reality: The Philosophy of Language and the Principles of Symbolism*. London: Allen and Unwin, 1939.   P105.U7

Wheelwright, Philip. *Burning Fountain: A Study in the Language of Symbolism*. Bloomington: Indiana University Press, 1954.   P105.W57

Whittick, A. *Symbols, Signs, and Their Meaning*. Part 3, pp. 129–298: "Encyclopedic Dictionary: Traditional and Familiar Symbols, Their Origin, Meaning, and History." London: L. Hill, 1960.   N7740.W52

Wind, Edgar. *Pagan Mysteries in the Renaissance*. Rev. and enl. ed. New York: W. W. Norton, 1968.

    N6915.W53 1968

VII. STOFF- UND MOTIVGESCHICHTE (CHARACTERS, THEMES, MOTIFS)

See also Baldensperger (L–1), the *Yearbook of Comparative and General Literature* (L–2), the *MLA International Bibliography* (L–50) and many entries in section X.I, X.II, and X.III.

K–80 **Magill, Frank N. *[Masterplots] Cyclopedia of Literary Characters*. New York: Harper, 1963.**   PN44.M31 1963

This handy work makes reference to about 16,000 characters from some 1,300 literary works of all countries and periods. Arranged by the title of the literary work, entries give lists of characters arranged in the order of their importance and a brief plot summary with character roles indicated. The volume is concluded with an author index and an index of characters.

Additional dictionaries of literary characters include Benet (L–23); Bompiani, vol. 8, *Personnaggi*, and its French-language parallel, *Dictionnaire des personnages littéraires et dramatiques* (L–25); Sharp and Sharp (U–24); and all of the Oxford Companions (L–42, L–71, L–91, L–111, M–40, S–40, and U–21). For English literature see also Freeman (M–48).

Historical characters and events that are incorporated as fictive elements in literary works are treated in Georg Schneider, *Die Schlusselliteratur*, 3 vols. (Stuttgart: Hiersemann, 1951–1953) [Z1026.S4]. The first volume includes indexes of authors and of historical persons. Volumes 2 and 3 treat works of German fiction and drama and non-German works respectively.

K–85 **Frenzel, Elisabeth. *Stoffe der Weltliteratur: Ein Lexikon dichtungsgeschichtlicher Längsschnitte*. 4th rev. ed. Stuttgart: Kröner Verlag, 1976.**   PN56.4.F7 1976

This volume presents a dictionary of the subject matters of world literature, those major themes and figures that constitute the material for literary works. The names of literary, historical, and mythological figures constitute main entries. Articles trace the subject's appearances and roles in world literature from classical antiquity and folk literature to the twentieth century. Uses of the figure are characterized, and differences among them are specified. Most articles conclude with brief reading lists. The work is meant to be used in conjunction with Frenzel's *Motive der Weltliteratur* (K–86).

K–86 **Frenzel, Elisabeth. *Motive der Weltliteratur: Ein Lexikon dichtungsgeschichtlicher Längsschitte*. 2d ed., rev. and enl. Stuttgart: Kröner, 1980.**   PN43.F7 1980

This work, a companion to Frenzel's *Stoffe der Weltliteratur* (K–85), presents a dictionary of articles on those basic, impersonal situations (e.g., father-son conflict), settings (e.g., arcadia), activities (e.g., revenge), and character types (e.g., the amazon, the beggar, the doppelgänger, the picaro) that are found throughout the history of world literature. Articles describe the motif, discuss works that employ it, and compare its appearances and uses at different moments in literary history. Brief bibliographies of secondary sources are appended. There are "see" cross-references from names of motifs to articles where they are considered, and there is an index of authors and titles.

K–89 **Some Frequently Recommended Works on Stoff- und Motivgeschichte.**

Anderson, George K. *Legend of the Wandering Jew*. Providence, R.I.: Brown University Press, 1965.

    GR75.W3 A5

Bauerhorst, Kurt. *Bibliographie der Stoff- und Motivgeschichte der deutschen Literatur*. Berlin: de Gruyter, 1932.   Z2231.B34

Bisanz, Adam J., and Raymond Trousson. *Elemente der Literatur: Beiträge zur Stoff-, Motiv- und Themenforschung*. [Festgabe für] Elisabeth Frenzel zum 65. Geburtstag. 2 vols. Stuttgart: Kröner, 1980.

    PN45.E47

Blackman, Murray. *Guide to Jewish Themes in American Fiction, 1940–1980*. Metuchen, N.J.: Scarecrow Press, 1981.   Z1231.F4 B52

Crane, Thomas F. "Medieval Sermon-Books and Stories and Their Study since 1883." *Proceedings of the American Philosophical Society* 56 (1917): 369–402.

Dédéyan, Charles. *La thème de Faust dans la littérature européenne.* 4 vols. in 6. Paris: Lettres modernes, 1954–1967.   PN57.F3 D4

de Rougement, Denis. *Love in the Western World.* Translation by Montgomery Belgion of *L'amour dans le Occident,* rev. ed. (Paris: Plon, 1972) Rev. and enl. ed. Princeton N.J.: Princeton University Press, 1983.   HQ21.R86 1983

Dinter, Annegret. *Der Pygmalion-Stoff in der europaischen Literatur: Rezeptionsgeschichte einer Ovid-Fabel.* Heidelberg: C. Winter, 1979.   PN57.P86 D5 1979

Drake, Dana B. *Don Quijote in World Literature: A Selective Annotated Bibliography.* New York: Garland, 1979.   Z8158.D694

———, and Frederick Vina. *Don Quijote (1894–1970): A Selective Annotated Bibliography, Extended to 1979.* Lincoln, Nebr.: Society of Spanish and Spanish-American Studies, 1984.

Frenzel, Elisabeth. *Stoff-, Motiv, und Symbolforschung.* 4th ed., rev. and enl. Stuttgart: Metzler, 1978.   PN874.F73 1978

———. *Stoff- und Motivgeschichte.* 2d rev. ed. Berlin: Erich Schmidt, 1974 (with extensive, classified bibliography).   PN874.F75 1974

Galinsky, Hans. *Naturae Cursus: Der Weg einer antiken kosmologischen Metapher von der Alten in die Neue Welt: Ein Beitrag zu einer historischen Metaphorik der Weltliteratur.* Heidelberg: C. Winter, 1968.   PN228.M4 G3

Heinzel, Erwin. *Lexikon der Kulturgeschichte in Literatur, Kunst und Musik, mit Bibliographie und Ikonographie.* Vienna: Hollinek, 1962.   CT143.H4

———. *Lexikon historischer Ereignisse und Personen in Kunst, Literatur und Musik.* Vienna: Hollinek, 1956.   D9.H48

Henning, H., ed. *Faust-Bibliographie.* 3 vols. Berlin: Aufbau-Verlag, 1966–1976.   Z6514.C5 F343

Levin, Harry. "Thematics and Criticism." In Peter Demetz, ed., *Disciplines of Criticism.* pp. 125–145. New Haven: Yale University Press, 1968.   PN36.W4

Marcan, Peter. *Poetry Themes: A Bibliographical Index to Subject Anthologies.* See T–25.

Modder, Montagu Frank. *Jew in the Literature of English.* Philadelphia: Jewish Publication Society of American, 1939.   PR151.J5 M6

Moog-Grunewald, Maria. *Metamorphosen der Metamorphosen: Rezeptionsarten der Ovidianische Verwandlungsgeschichten in Italien und Frankreich im 16. und 17. Jahrhunderts.* Heidelberg: C. Winter, 1979.   PA6519.M9 M58 1979

Poschl, Victor. *Bibliographie zur antiken Bildersprache.* Revised by Helga Gärtner and Waltraut Keyke. Heidelberg: C. Winter, 1964.   Z7016.P6

Rosenberg, Edgar. *From Shylock to Svengali: Jewish Stereotypes in English Fiction.* Stanford: Stanford University Press, 1960.   PR151.J5 R6

Schmitt, Franz Anselm. *Stoff- und Motivgeschichte der deutschen Literatur: Eine Bibliographie, begrundet von Kurt Bauerhorst.* 3d ed., rev. Berlin: de Gruyter, 1976. Some 37,000 titles, including many themes treated in other European national literatures.   Z2231.S35 1976

Singer, A. E. *Don Juan Theme, Versions and Criticism: A Bibliography.* Morgantown: West Virginia University, 1965. Supplements in the West Virginia University Bulletin: Philological Papers, nos. 15, 17, 20, 23, and 26 (Morgantown: West Virginia University, 1966–80).   Z6514.C5 J87 1965

Sola-Solé, Joseph M., and George E. Gingras, eds. *Tirso's Don Juan: The Metamorphosis of a Theme.* Washington, D.C.: Catholic University of America Press, 1988.   PQ6434.B83 T57 1988

Stanford, W. B. *Ulysses Theme: A Study in the Adaptability of a Traditional Hero.* 2d ed. New York: Barnes and Noble, 1964.   PN57.O3S8 1964

Trousson, Raymond. *Un problème de littérature comparée: Les études de thèmes: Éssai de methodologie.* Paris: Minard, 1965.   PN873.T76

Urdang, Laurence, ed. *Allusions: Cultural, Literary, Biblical, and Historical: A Thematic Dictionary.* Detroit: Gale Research Co., 1982.   PN43.A4 1982

Wais, Kurt. *Das Vater-Sohn Motiv in der Dichtung bis 1800.* Berlin and Leipzig: 1931.

Weinstein, Leo. *Metamorphoses of Don Juan.* Stanford: Stanford University Press, 1959.   PN57.D7 W4 1959

Weir, Robert F., ed. *Death in Literature [an anthology].* New York: Columbia University Press, 1980.   PN6071.D4 D43 1980

Wilpert, Gero von. *Sachwörterbuch der Literatur.* 6th ed. Stuttgart: Kroner, 1979.   PN41.W5 1979

VIII. GUIDES TO HISTORICAL CONTEXTS

K–90 **Some Frequently Recommended Studies in Social and Cultural History, English and American.**

England—General

Briggs, Asa. *Social History of England.* New York: Viking Press, 1984.   HN398.E5 B74 1984

Quennell, Marjorie, and C. H. B. Quennell. *History of Everyday Things in England.* 5 vols. London: Batsford, 1937–1968.   DA110.Q43

Traill, H. Duff, ed. *Social England: A Record of the Progress of the People in Religion, Laws, Learning, Arts, Industry, Commerce, Science, Literature, and Manners, from the Earliest Times to the Present Day.* 6 vols. London: Cassell, 1894–1898. Illustrated edition. 6 vols. London: Cassell, 1901–1904.   DA30.T77 1894 and DA30.T77 1901

Trevelyan, G. M. *English Social History. A Survey of Six Centuries, Chaucer to Queen Victoria.* 3d ed. London: Longmans, 1942.   DA32.T7487

———. *Illustrated English Social History.* 4 vols. London: Longmans, 1949–1952.   DA32.T749

Wright, T. *Homes of Other Days: A History of Domestic Manners and Sentiments in England.* London: Trubner, 1871.   DA110.W84

Medieval

Ackerman, Robert W. *Backgrounds to Medieval English Literature.* New York: Random House, 1966.   PR255.A3

Bateson, M. *Medieval England, 1066–1350.* London: T. F. Unwin, 1903.   DA175.B32

Blair, Peter Hunter. *Introduction to Anglo-Saxon England.* 2d ed. Cambridge: Cambridge University Press, 1977.   DA152.2.B55 1977

Bloch, Marc. *Feudal Society.* Translation of *La société feodal* (Paris: A. Michel, 1939). Chicago: University of Chicago Press, 1961. D131.B513 1961

Brewer, Derek S. *Chaucer in His Time.* London: Nelson, 1963. PR1906.5.B7

Brooke, Christopher N. L. *London, 800–1216.* Berkeley, Los Angeles, London: University of California Press, 1975. HC258.L6 B76

Chadwick, Dorothy. *Social Life in the Days of Piers Plowman.* Cambridge: Cambridge University Press, 1922. PR2015.C5

Chadwick, H. M. *Studies on Anglo-Saxon Institutions.* Cambridge: Cambridge University Press, 1905. DA152.C43

Coulton, G. C. *Chaucer and His England.* With a New Bibliography by T. W. Craik. London: Methuen, 1963. PR1905.C58 1963

———. *Medieval Panorama: The English Scene from Conquest to Reformation.* Cambridge: Cambridge University Press, 1938. DA185.C85

Green, A. S. *Town Life in the Fifteenth Century.* 2 vols. London, 1894.

Jusserand, Jean A. A. J. *English Wayfaring Life in the Middle Ages.* Translation by Lucy T. Smith of *Les Anglais au moyen age* (Paris: Hachette, 1893). 5th ed. London: Benn, 1950. DA185.J9

Knowles, David. *Religious Orders in England.* 3 vols. Cambridge: Cambridge University Press, 1948–1959. BX2592.K583

Mead, W. E. *English Medieval Feast.* London: G. Allen and Unwin, 1931. GT2850.M4

Myers, Alec R. *England in the Middle Ages, 1307–1536.* Harmondsworth: Penguin, 1952. DA30.P4 vol. 4

Poole, Austin Lane, ed. *Medieval England.* 2d ed. 2 vols. Oxford: Clarendon Press, 1958. DA130.P65 1958

Power, Eileen. *Medieval People.* 10th rev. ed. London: Methuen, 1963. D127.P6 1963

Rickert, Edith, comp. *Chaucer's World.* Edited by Clare C. Olson and Martin M. Crow. New York: Columbia University Press, 1948. DA220.R5

Robertson, D. W., Jr. *Chaucer's London.* New York: Wiley, 1968. DA680.R6

Salzman, L. F. *English Life in the Middle Ages.* London: Oxford University Press, 1926. DA185.S25

Schlauch, Margaret. *English Medieval Literature and Its Social Foundations.* Warsaw: Państwowe Wydawnnaukowe, 1956. PR173.S33

Stenton, D. M. *English Society in the Early Middle Ages (1066–1307).* 2d ed. Harmondsworth: Penguin, 1959. DA30.P4 vol. 3 1959

Thompson, A. Hamilton. *English Clergy and Their Organization in the Later Middle Ages.* Oxford: Clarendon Press, 1947. BR750.T5

Thrupp, Sylvia L. *Merchant Class of Medieval London (1306–1500).* Chicago: University of Chicago Press, 1948. HF3510.L8 T4

Whitelock, Dorothy. *Beginnings of English Society.* London: Penguin Books, 1952, 1959. DA30.P4 vol. 2

Wilson, David M. *Anglo-Saxons.* Rev. ed. Harmondsworth: Penguin, 1971. DA155.W5 1971

Renaissance

Ashley, Maurice Percy. *England in the Seventeenth Century, 1603–1714.* London: Penguin Books, 1956. DA30.P4 vol. 6

Bradbrook, Muriel C. *Rise of the Common Player: A Study of Actor and Society in Shakespeare's England.* London: Chatto and Windus, 1962. PN2589.B7 1962

Byrne, Muriel St. Clare. *Elizabethan Home.* London, 1930.

———. *Elizabethan Life in Town and Country.* 7th ed., rev. London: Methuen, 1954. DA355.B8 1954

Coate, M. *Social Life in Stuart England.* London: Methuen, 1924. DA380.C6

Elliot, Margaret M., and Dorothy Hartley. *Life and Work of the People of England: The Seventeenth Century.* London: B. T. Batsford, 1926. DA110.H35

Hall, Hubert S. *Society in the Elizabethan Age.* 2d ed. London: S. Sonnenschein, Lowry and Co., 1887. DA355.H176

Hill, Christopher, and M. Dell. *Good Old Cause: The English Revolution of 1640–60.* London: Lawrence and Wishart, 1949. HN385.H57 H5

Onions, C. T., et al. *Shakespeare's England: An Account of the Life and Manners of His Age.* 2 vols. Oxford: Clarendon Press, 1917. PR2910.S5 1917

Rowse, A. L. *Elizabethan Renaissance.* Vol. 1, *Life of the Society.* Vol. 2, *Cultural Achievement.* London: Macmillan, 1971–1972. DA356.R65

———. *England of Elizabeth: The Structure of Society.* London: Macmillan, 1950. DA356.R65

Stone, Lawrence. *Crisis of the Aristocracy, 1558–1641.* Oxford: Clarendon Press, 1965. DA356.S8

Wilson, J. Dover. *Life in Shakespeare's England: A Book of Elizabethan Prose.* Cambridge: Cambridge University Press, 1913. PR1293.W5

Wright, Louis B. *Middle-Class Culture in Elizabethan England.* Chapel Hill: University of North Carolina Press, 1935. PR421.W7

Youings, Joyce A. *Sixteenth-Century England.* Pelican Social History of Britain. London: A. Lane, 1984. HN398.E5 Y68 1984

Restoration and Eighteenth Century

Allen, R. J. *Clubs of Augustan London.* Cambridge: Harvard University Press, 1933. DA682.A4

Ashton, J. *Social Life in the Reign of Queen Anne.* New ed. London: Chatto and Windus, 1897. DA495.A83

George, M. Dorothy. *London Life in the Eighteenth Century.* London: Kegan Paul, 1925. HN398.L7 G4

Greene, Donald J. *Age of Exuberance: Backgrounds to Eighteenth-Century English Literature.* New York: Random House, 1970. DA380.G7 1970

Humphreys, A. R. *Augustan World.* London: Methuen, 1954. DA485.H85

Mathias, Peter. *Transformation of England: Essays in the Economic and Social History of England in the Eighteenth Century.* London: Methuen, 1979. HC254.5.M37

Porter, Ray. *English Society in the Eighteenth Century.* Pelican Social History of Britain. London: A. Lane, 1982. HN398.E5 P67 1982

Rude, George F. E. *Hanoverian London, 1714–1808.* London: Secker and Warburg, 1971. DA677.H56 vol. 6

Schwartz, Richard B. *Daily Life in Johnson's London.* Madison: University of Wisconsin Press, 1983. DA682.S38 1983

Stephen, Leslie. *English Literature and Society in the Eighteenth Century.* London: Duckworth, 1904. PR443.S8

Stone, Lawrence. *Family, Sex, and Marriage in England, 1500–1800*. London: Weidenfeld and Nicolson, 1977.
HQ615.S76

Turberville, A. S. *English Men and Manners in the Eighteenth Century*. Oxford: Clarendon Press, 1929.
DA485.T75

———, ed. *Johnson's England: An Account of the Life and Manners of His Age*. 2 vols. Rev. ed. Oxford: Clarendon Press, 1952.   DA485.T77 1952

Williams, Kathleen, ed. *Backgrounds to 18th Century Literature*. Scranton, Pa.: Chandler, 1971.   PR442.W5

Nineteenth Century

Altick, Richard D. *Victorian People and Ideas: A Companion for the Modern Reader of Victorian Literature*. New York: W. W. Norton, 1973. DA533.A55 1973

Briggs, Asa. *Age of Improvement, 1783–1867*. London: Longmans, Green, 1965.   DA530.B68

———. Victorian People: *Some Reassessments of People, Institutions, and Events, 1851–1867*. London: Oldhams, 1954.   DA560.B84

Buckley, Jerome Hamilton. *Victorian Temper*. Cambridge: Harvard University Press, 1951.   PR461.B75

Clark, George K. *Making of Victorian England*. Cambridge: Harvard University Press, 1962.   DA533.K55

Gay, Peter. *Bourgeois Experience: Victoria to Freud*. Vol. 1, *Education of the Senses*. London: Oxford University Press, 1984–.   BF692.G36 1984

Halevie, Elie. *History of the English People in the Nineteenth Century*. Translation by E. I. Watkin and D. A. Barker of *Histoire du peuple anglaise au XIXᵉ siècle* (Paris, 1913–1946). 6 vols. in 7. 2d rev. ed. New York: Barnes and Noble, 1949–1952. DA530.H443

Levine, Richard, ed. *Backgrounds to Victorian Literature*. San Francisco: Chandler, 1967.   PR463.L57

Perkin, Harold J. *Origins of Modern English Society, 1780–1880*. London: Routledge and K. Paul, 1969.
HN385.P46

Reed, John R. *Victorian Conventions*. Athens: Ohio University Press, 1975.   PR468.S6 R4

Sheppard, Francis H. W. *London, 1808–1870*. Berkeley, Los Angeles, London: University of California Press, 1971.   HC258.L6 S5 1971

Thomson, David. *England in the Nineteenth Century*. Harmondsworth: Penguin Books, 1950. DA30.P4 vol. 8

Williams, Raymond. *Culture and Society 1780–1950*. New York: Columbia University Press, 1958.
DA533.W6 1958

Wingfield Stratford, Esme C. *Victorian Sunset*. London: G. Routledge and Sons, 1932.   DA550.W78

Young, G. M. *Portrait of an Age: Victorian England*. 2d ed. Annotated by George K. Clark. New York: Oxford University Press, 1977.   DA550.Y6 1977

———, ed. *Early Victorian England, 1830–1865*. 2 vols. Oxford: Clarendon Press, 1934.   DA533.E3

Twentieth Century

Bradbury, Malcolm. *Social Context of Modern English Literature*. New York: Schocken, 1971.   PR471.B67

Cecil, Robert. *Life in Edwardian England*. New York: G. P. Putnam's Sons, 1969.   DA566.4.C36 1969

Hynes, Samuel. *Edwardian Turn of Mind*. Princeton, N.J.: Princeton University Press, 1968.   DA570.H9

Martin, Christopher. *Edwardians*. London: Wayland, 1974.
HN385.M297 1974

———. *English Life in the First World War*. London: Wayland, 1974.   D546.M3

Marwick, Arthur. *British Society since 1945*. Pelican Social History of Britain. London: A. Lane, 1982.
HN385.5.M364 1982

———. *Deluge: British Society and the First World War*. Boston: Little, Brown, 1966.   DA577.M37

Nowell-Smith, Simon H., ed. *Edwardian England, 1901–1914*. London: Oxford University Press, 1964.
DA566.4.N6 1964

Stevenson, John. *British Society, 1914–45*. Pelican Social History of Britain. London: A. Lane, 1984.
HN385.S7665 1984

America-General

Boorstin, Daniel J. *Americans*. 3 vols. Vol. 1, *Colonial Experience (1958)*, Vol. 2, *National Experience (1965)*, Vol. 3, *Democratic Experience (1973)*. New York: Random House, 1958–1973.   E188.B72

Ditzion, Sidney Herbert. *Marriage, Morals, and Sex in America: A History of Ideas*. New York: Bookman Association, 1953.   HQ535.D5

Dulles, Foster Rhea. *America Learns to Play: A History of Popular Recreation, 1607–1940*. New York: Appleton, 1940.   E161.D85

Furnas, J. C. *Americans: A Social History of the United States, 1587–1914*. New York: G. P. Putnam's Sons, 1969.   HN57.F86

Langdon, William Chauncy. *Everyday Things in American Life*. 2 vols. New York: Charles Scribner's Sons, 1937–1941.   E161.L32

Lerner, Max. *America as a Civilization: Life and Thought in the United States Today*. New York: Simon and Schuster, 1957.   E169.1.L532

Lynes, Russell. *Domesticated Americans*. New York: Harper and Row, 1963.   E161.L9

Mitterling, Philip I. *United States Cultural History: A Guide to Information Sources*. Detroit: Gale Research Co., 1980.   Z1361.C6 M57

Rourke, Constance. *Roots of American Culture and Other Essays*. Edited by Van Wyck Brooks. New York: Harcourt, Brace and World, 1942.   E169.R78

Schlesinger, Arthur M., and Dixon R. Fox, eds. *History of American Life*. 13 vols. New York: Macmillan, 1927–1948. Vol. 1, *Coming of the White Man, 1492–1848*, by Herbert Ingram Priestley. Vol. 2, *First Americans, 1607–1690*, by Thomas Jefferson Wertenbaker. Vol. 3, *Provincial Society, 1690–1763*, by James Truslow Adams. Vol. 4, *Revolutionary Generation, 1763–1790*, by Evarts Boutell Greene. Vol. 5, *Completion of Independence, 1790–1830*, by John Allen Krout and Dixon Ryan Fox. Vol. 6, *Rise of the Common Man, 1830–1850*, by Carl Russell Fish. Vol. 7, *Irrepressible Conflict, 1850–1865*, by Arthur Charles Cole. Vol. 8, *Emergence of Modern America, 1865–1878*, by Allan Nevins. Vol. 9, *Nationalizing of Business, 1878–1898*, by Ida M. Tarbell. Vol. 10, *Rise of the City, 1878–1898*, by Arthur Meier Schlesinger. Vol. 11, *Quest for Social Justice, 1898–1914*, by Harold Underwood Faulkner. Vol. 12, *Great Crusade and After, 1914–1928*, by Preston William Slosson. Vol. 13, *Age of the Great Depression, 1929–1941*, by Dixon Wecter.
LC numbers vary

Smith, Bradford. *Why We Behave Like Americans*. Philadelphia: Lippincott, 1957.

Stewart, George R. *American Ways of Life*. Garden City, N.Y.: Doubleday, 1954.   E169.1.S84

Tingley, Donald Fred. *Social History of the United States: A Guide to Information Sources*. Detroit: Gale Research Co., 1979.   Z7165.U5 T5

Wecter, Dixon. *Hero in America: A Chronicle of Hero-Worship*. New York: Charles Scribner's Sons, 1941.
E176.W4

———. *Saga of American Society: A Record of Social Aspiration, 1607–1937.* New York: Charles Scribner's Sons, 1937. E161.W43

Wright, Louis B. *Cultural Life of the American Colonies, 1607–1763.* New York: Harper, 1957. E162.W89

National, 1776–1870

Jones, Howard Mumford. *Revolution and Romanticism.* Cambridge: Belknap Press of Harvard University Press, 1974. CB411.J66

Nye, Russell B. *Cultural Life of the New Nation, 1776–1830.* New York: Harper, 1960. E169.1.N9

Tyler, Alice (Felt). *Freedom's Ferment: Phases of American Social History to 1860.* Minneapolis: University of Minnesota Press, 1944. BR516.T9

Later Nineteenth Century, 1870–1914

Jones, Howard Mumford. *Age of Energy: Varieties of American Experience, 1865–1915.* New York: Viking, 1971. E169.1.J6435 1971

Ziff, Larzer. *American 1890's: Life and Times of a Lost Generation.* New York: Viking, 1966. PS214.Z5

Twentieth Century

Allen, Frederick Lewis. *Big Change: America Transforms Itself, 1900–1950.* New York: Harper, 1952.
E161.1.A47

Cohn, David Lewis. *Good Old Days: A History of American Morals and Manners as Seen through the Sears, Roebuck Catalogs, 1905 to the Present.* New York: Simon and Schuster, 1940. E161.C68

Lapp, Ralph Eugene. *New Priesthood: The Scientific Elite and the Uses of Power.* New York: Harper, 1965.
Q127.U6 L3

Mayo, Elton. *Social Problems of an Industrial Civilization.* Boston: Harvard Graduate School of Business Administration, 1945. HD6331.M32

Morris, Lloyd. *Not So Long Ago [before motion pictures, the automobile, and the radio].* New York: Random House, 1949. E169.1.M83

———. *Postscript to Yesterday: America—The Last Fifty Years.* New York: Random House, 1947. E741.M65

K–91 Some Frequently Recommended Works on Costume and Courtesy—General, English, and American.

Costume

Colas, René. *Bibliographie générale du costume et de la mode: Description des suites, recueils, séries, révues et livres français et étrangers relatifs au costume civil, militaire, et religieux, aux modes, aux coiffures, et aux divers accessoires de l'habillement, avec une table méthodique et un index alphabetique.* 2 vols. Paris, 1933. Z5691.C682

Cunnington, C. W., with Phillis Emily Cunnington. *Handbook of English Costume in the Sixteenth-Nineteenth Century.* 4 vols. London: Faber and Faber, 1954–1959. GT730.C87

Hiler, Hilaire, and Hiler, Meyer. *Bibliography of Costume: A Dictionary Catalogue of About Eight Thousand Books and Periodicals.* Edited by Helen Grant Cushing. New York: H. W. Wilson, 1939. Z5691.H64

Planché, James R. *Cyclopaedia of Costume; or, Dictionary of Dress from the Commencement of the Christian Era to the Accession of George the Third.* 2 vols. London: Chatto and Windus, 1876–1879. GT510.P5

Planché, James R. *History of British Costume, from the Earliest Period to the Close of the Eighteenth Century.* 3d ed. London: G. Bell and Sons, 1874.
GT730.P5 1874

Courtesy and Etiquette

Bobbitt, Mary Reed. *Bibliography of Etiquette Books Published in America before 1900.* New York: New York Public Library, 1947. Z5877.B6

Helzel, Virgil B., comp. *Check List of Courtesy Books in the Newberry Library.* Chicago: Newberry Library, 1942.
Z5873.N5

Kelso, Ruth. *Doctrine for the Lady of the Renaissance.* Urbana: University of Illinois Press, 1956. Bibliography, pp. 326–462. HQ1148.K4

———. *Doctrine of the English Gentleman in the Sixteenth Century, with a Bibliographical List of Treatises on the Gentleman and Related Subjects Published in Europe to 1625.* Urbana: University of Illinois Press, 1929. HT647.K4 1929

Mason, John E. *Gentlefolk in the Making: Studies in the History of English Courtesy Literature and Related Topics from 1531 to 1774.* Philadelphia: University of Pennsylvania Press, 1935. BJ1547.M3 1935

Noyes, Gertrude E. *Bibliography of Courtesy and Conduct Books in Seventeenth-Century England.* New Haven: Yale University Press, 1937. Z5877.N95

Post, Elizabeth L. *New Emily Post's Etiquette.* New York: Funk and Wagnalls, 1975. BJ1853.P6 1975

Schlesinger, Arthur. *Learning How to Behave: A Historical Study of American Etiquette Books.* New York: Macmillan, 1946. E161.S25

K–92 Some Frequently Recommended Works on the History of Taste and Related Problems, English and American.

(See also X–65 ff., Literature and Society; and Z–26, Aids for Locating Contemporary Reviews.)

General

Duncan, Hugh Dalziel. *Language and Literature in Society: A Sociological Essay on Theory and Method in the Interpretation of Literary Symbols with a Bibliographical Guide to the Sociology of Literature.* Chicago: University of Chicago Press, 1953. (See X–65.)
PN51.D8

Hauser, Arnold. *Social History of Art and Literature.* 2 vols. New York: Alfred A. Knopf, 1951.
N72.H353 1951a

Schücking, Levin. *Sociology of Literary Taste.* Translation by Brian Battershaw of *Die Soziologie der literarischen Geschmacksbildung,* 3d ed. (Bern, 1961). Chicago: University of Chicago Press, 1966.
PN45.S262 1966

England—General

Ebisch, Walther, and Levin L. Schücking, "Bibliographie zur Geschichte des literarischen Geschmacks in England." *Anglia* 63 (1939): 1–64.

Saunders, J. W. *Profession of English Letters.* London: Routledge and Kegan Paul, 1964. PR401.S36

Medieval

Auerbach, Erich. *Literary Language and Its Public in Late Latin Antiquity and in the Middle Ages.* Translation of *Literatursprache und Publikum in der lateinischen Spätantike und in Mittelalter* (Bern: Francke, 1958). New York: Bollingen, 1965. PA8027.A813

Bennett, H. S. *Author and His Public in the Fourteenth and Fifteenth Centuries.* Oxford, 1938.

Holzknecht, Karl J. *Literary Patronage in the Middle Ages.* Philadelphia, 1923. PN682.P3 H6

Whitelock, Dorothy. *Audience of Beowulf.* 2d ed. Oxford: Clarendon Press, 1958. PR1587.A8 W5 1958

Renaissance and Elizabethan

Bennett, H. S. *English Books and Readers, 1475 to 1557: Being a Study of the History of the Book Trade from Caxton to the Incorporation of the Stationers' Company.* 2d ed. Cambridge: Cambridge University Press, 1969.   Z151.B4 1969

———. *English Books and Readers, 1558 to 1603: Being a Study of the History of the Book Trade.* Cambridge: Cambridge University Press, 1965.   Z151.3.B4

———. *English Books and Readers, 1603 to 1640: Being a Study of the History of the Book Trade in the Reigns of James I and Charles I.* Cambridge: Cambridge University Press, 1970.   Z151.4.B45

———. *Shakespeare's Audience.* London: H. Milford, 1944.   PR2900.B4

Buxton, John. *Elizabethan Taste.* London: Macmillan, 1963.   N6765.B87 1963

Harbage, Alfred. *Shakespeare's Audience.* New York: Columbia University Press, 1941.   PR3091.H36

Miller, Edwin H. *Professional Writer in Elizabethan England: A Study of Non-Dramatic Literature.* Cambridge: Harvard University Press, 1959.
PR428.A5 M5

Sheavyn, Phoebe A. B. *Literary Profession in the Elizabethan Age.* 2d ed. Revised by J. W. Saunders. Manchester: Manchester University Press, 1967.
PR428.A8 S5 1967

Seventeenth and Eighteenth Centuries

Allen, B. Sprague. *Tides in English Taste (1619–1800): A Background for the Study of Literature.* 2 vols. Cambridge: Harvard University Press, 1937.   N6766.A4

Bate, Walter Jackson. *From Classic to Romantic: Premises of Taste in Eighteenth Century England.* Cambridge: Harvard University Press, 1946.   BH221.G7 B36

Beljame, Alexandre. *Men of Letters and the English Public.* Translation with new notes by Bonamy Dobrée of *Le public et les hommes des lettres en Angleterre au XVIIIᵉ siécle, 1660–1744,* 2d ed. (Paris: Hachette et cie, 1897). London: K. Paul, Trench, Trubner, 1948.
PR448.S6 B42

Collins, A. S. *Authorship in the Days of Johnson, 1726–1780.* London: R. Holden, 1927.   PN151.C6

Hughes, Leo. *Drama's Patrons: A Study of the Eighteenth-Century London Audience.* Austin: University of Texas Press, 1971.   PN2596.L6 H8

Knights, L. C. *Drama and Society in the Age of Jonson.* London: Chatto and Windus, 1937.   PR655.K6

Loftis, John. *Comedy and Society from Congreve to Fielding.* Stanford, Calif.: Stanford University Press, 1959.
PR714.S6 L6

———. *Politics of Drama in Augustan England.* Oxford: Clarendon Press, 1963.   PR714.P6 L6

Ogden, H. V. S., and Margaret S. Ogden. *English Taste in Landscape in the Seventeenth Century.* Ann Arbor: University of Michigan Press, 1956.   BH301.L303

Pedicord, Harry William. *Theatrical Public in the Time of Garrick.* New York: King's Crown Press, 1954.
PN2596.L6 P4

Nineteenth and Twentieth Centuries

Altick, Richard D. *English Common Reader: A Social History of the Mass Reading Public, 1800–1900.* Chicago: University of Chicago Press, 1957.   Z1003.A57

Clark, Sir Kenneth M. *Gothic Revival: An Essay in the History of Taste.* 3d ed. London: Murray, 1962.
NA610.C5 1962

Collins, A. S. *Profession of Letters: A Study of the Relation of Author to Patron, Publishers, and Public,*

1780–1832. London: G. Routledge and Sons, 1928.
PN151.C62

Cruse, Amy. *Englishman and His Books in the Early Nineteenth Century.* London: G. G. Harrap, 1930.
PR456.C7

———. *Victorians and Their Reading.* Boston: Houghton Mifflin, 1935.   PR461.C7

———. *After the Victorians.* London: G. Allen and Unwin, 1938.   PR461.C67

Ellegård, Alvar. *Readership of the Periodical Press in Mid-Victorian Britain.* Gothenburg: University of Gothenburg Press, 1957.   AS284.G6 vol. 63, no. 3

Ford, George H. *Dickens and His Readers.* Princeton, N.J.: Princeton University Press, 1955.   PR4588.F6

Gross, John. *Rise and Fall of the Man of Letters: English Literary Life since 1800.* London: Weidenfeld and Nicolson, 1969.   PR63.G7 1969

James, Louis. *Fiction for the Working Man, 1830–1850.* New York: Oxford University Press, 1963.
PR878.L3 J3

Leavis, Q. D. *Fiction and the Reading Public.* London: Chatto and Windus, 1932.   PR821.L4

Webb, R. K. *British Working Class Reader, 1790–1858.* London: G. Allen and Unwin, 1955.   HD8389.W42

America

Charvat, William. *Literary Publishing in America, 1790–1850.* Philadelphia: University of Pennsylvania Press, 1959.   PN155.C5

———. *Profession of Authorship in America, 1800–1870: The Papers of William Charvat.* Edited by Matthew J. Bruccoli. Columbus: Ohio State University Press, 1968.   PS88.C47

Hackett, Alice Payne, and James Henry Burke. *Eighty Years of Best Sellers, 1895–1975.* New York: R. R. Bowker, 1977.   Z1033.B3 H342

Hart, James D. *Popular Book: A History of America's Literary Taste.* New York: Oxford University Press, 1950.
Z1003.H328

Lynes, Russell. *Tastemakers.* New York: Harper, 1954.
E169.1.L95

Mott, Frank Luther. *Golden Multitudes: The Story of Best Sellers in the United States.* New York: Macmillan, 1947.   Z1033.B3 M6

Nye, Russell B. *Unembarrassed Muse: The Popular Arts in America.* New York: Dial Press, 1970.   E169.1.N92

K–95 Some Frequently Recommended Studies in Intellectual History and the History of Ideas.

Bibliographical

Tobey, Jeremy L. *History of Ideas: A Bibliographical Introduction.* 2 vols. Santa Barbara, Calif.: ABC-Clio, 1975–1977. Vol. 1, *Classical Antiquity.* Vol. 2, *Medieval and Early Modern Europe.* (See X–55.)
Z7125.T58

History of Ideas News Letter. Vols. 1–6 (1954–1960). Semiannual bibliography of books and articles in intellectual history, from some sixty journals.   AS30.H5

Journal of the History of Ideas: A Quarterly Devoted to Cultural and Intellectual History. Philadelphia: 1940–. Reviews.   CB3.J6

Meier, Hans, Richard Newald, and Edgar Wind, eds. *Bibliography of the Survival of the Classics.* 2 vols. London: Warburg Institute, 1934–1938.   Z5579.W251

General

Barnes, Harry Elmer, et al. *Intellectual and Cultural History of the Western World*. 3d rev. ed. 3 vols. New York: Dover, 1965.   CB53.B36 1965

Brinton, Crane. *Ideas and Men: The Story of Western Thought*. 2d ed. Englewood Cliffs, N.J.: Prentice-Hall, 1963.   CB245.B73 1963

Heer, Friedrich. *Intellectual History of Europe*. Translation by J. Steinberg of *Europäische Geistesgeschichte*. 2 vols. Garden City, N.Y.: Doubleday, 1966.   B82.H413 1966a

Pelikan, Jaroslav. *Christian Tradition: A History of the Development of Doctrine*. 5 vols. Chicago: University of Chicago Press, 1971–.   BT21.2.P42

Randall, John Herman, Jr. *Making of the Modern Mind: A Survey of the Intellectual Background of the Present Age*. Rev. ed. Boston: Houghton Mifflin, 1940.   CB57.R32 1940

From Classical Antiquity to Modern Europe

Baker, Herschel. *Dignity of Man: A Study in the Idea of Human Dignity in Classical Antiquity, the Middle Ages, and the Renaissance*. Cambridge: Harvard University Press, 1947.   BD431.B24

Boas, George. *Vox Populi: Essays in the History of an Idea*. Baltimore: Johns Hopkins University Press, 1969.   BD175.B6

Bolgar, R. R. *Classical Heritage and Its Beneficiaries: From the Carolingian Age to the End of the Renaissance*. Cambridge: Cambridge University Press, 1954.   CB245.B63

Curtius, Ernst R. *European Literature and the Latin Middle Ages*. Translation by Willard Trask of *Europäische Literatur und lateinisches Mittelalter*, 2d ed. (Bern: Francke, 1954). New York: Pantheon, 1953.   PN674.C82

Glacken, Clarence J. *Traces on the Rhodian Shore: Nature and Culture in Western Thought from Ancient Times to the End of the Eighteenth Century*. Berkeley and Los Angeles: University of California Press, 1967.   GF31.G6

Highet, Gilbert. *Classical Tradition: Greek and Roman Influences on Western Literature*. London: Oxford University Press, 1949.   PN883.H5

Lovejoy, Arthur O. *Great Chain of Being*. Cambridge: Harvard University Press, 1936.   B105.C5 L6

Patrides, C. A. *Grand Design of God: The Literary Form of the Christian View of History*. London: Routledge and Kegan Paul, 1972.   BR115.H5 P28 1972

Spitzer, Leo. *Classical and Christian Ideas of World Harmony: Prolegomena to an Interpretation of the Word "Stimmung."* Edited by Anna Granville Hatcher. Baltimore: Johns Hopkins University Press, 1965.   PN56.H3 S6 1963

Thorndike, Lynn. *History of Magic and Experimental Science During the First Thirteen Centuries of our Era*. 8 vols. New York: Macmillan, 1923–1958. Q125.T52

From Classical Antiquity to Medieval Europe

Bundy, Murray W. *Theory of Imagination in Classical and Medieval Thought*. Urbana: University of Illinois Press, 1927.   BF408.B85

Cassidy, Frank. *Molders of the Medieval Mind: The Influence of the Fathers of the Church on the Medieval Schoolmen*. St. Louis: B. Herder, 1944.   LA96.C3

Chadwick, Henry. *Early Christian Thought and the Classical Tradition: Studies in Justin, Clement, and Origen*. Oxford: Clarendon Press, 1966.   BR67.C43 1966a

Cochrane, Charles Morris. *Christianity and Classical Culture: A Study of Thought and Action from Augustus to Augustine*. Rev. and corr. ed. London: Oxford University Press, 1944.   BR170.C6 1944

Marrou, Henri-Irenée. *Saint Augustin et la fin de la culture antique*. 2 parts. Paris: Éditions de Boccard, 1937–1939.   BR1720.A9 M32 1937

Newald, Richard. *Nachleben des antiken Geistes im Abendland bis zum Beginn des Humanismus*. Tübingen: Niemeyer, 1960.

The Middle Ages

Artz, Frederick B. *Mind of the Middle Ages, 500–1500: An Historical Survey*. 3d ed., rev. New York: Alfred A. Knopf, 1965.   CB351.A56 1965

Boas, George. *Essays on Primitivism and Related Ideas in the Middle Ages*. Baltimore: Johns Hopkins University Press, 1948.   CB353.B6

Carlyle, Robert W., and Alexander J. Carlyle. *History of Medieval Political Theory in the West*. 6 vols. London: W. Blackwood, 1903–1936.   JA82.C3

Gierke, Otto von. *Political Theories of the Middle Ages*. Boston: Beacon Press, 1958.   JA82.G4 1958

Gilson, Etienne H. *History of Christian Philosophy in the Middle Ages*. New York: Random House, 1955.   B72.G48

———. *Spirit of Medieval Philosophy*. Translation by A. H. C. Downes of *L'esprit de la philosophie medievale*. London: Sheed and Ward, 1936.   B721.G433 1936

Harrison, Frederick. *Medieval Man and His Notions*. London: J. Murray, 1947.   DA185.H3

Haskins, Charles H. *Renaissance of the Twelfth Century*. Cambridge: Harvard University Press, 1927.   PA8035.H3

Howard, Donald R. *Three Temptations: Medieval Man in Search of the World*. Princeton, N.J.: Princeton University Press, 1966.   PR365.H6

Huizinga, Johan. *Waning of the Middle Ages: A Study of the Forms of Life, Thought and Art in France and the Netherlands in the Fourteenth and Fifteenth Centuries*. London: Edward Arnold, 1924.   DC33.2.H83

Kantorowicz, Ernst H. *King's Two Bodies: A Study in Medieval Political Theology*. Princeton, N.J.: Princeton University Press, 1957.   JC385.K25

Knowles, David. *Evolution of Medieval Thought*. New York: Vintage, 1962.   B721.K6

Laistner, M. L. W. *Thought and Letters in Western Europe, A.D. 500–900*. 2d ed. Ithaca, N.Y.: Cornell University Press, 1957.   CB351.L27 1957

Leff, Gordon. *Medieval Thought: St. Augustine to Ockham*. Harmondsworth: Penguin, 1958.   B721.L4

LeGoff, Jacques. *Les intellectuels au moyen âge*. Paris: Editions du Seuil, 1955.   DC33.2.L43

Morris, Colin. *Discovery of the Individual, 1050–1200*. New York: Harper and Row, 1972.   B824.M65 1927b

Patch, Howard R. *Tradition of Boethius: A Study of His Importance in Medieval Culture*. New York: Oxford University Press, 1935.   B659.Z7 P3

Poole, Reginald. *Illustrations of the History of Medieval Thought and Learning*. 2d ed. London: SPCK, 1920.   B721.P6 1920

Schaller, Heinrich. *Die Weltanschauung des Mittelalters*. Berlin: R. Oldenbourg, 1934.   CB351.S4

Southern, R. W. *Medieval Humanism and Other Studies.* Oxford: B. Blackwell, 1970.   .   CB353.SC5

Taylor, Henry O. *Medieval Mind: A History of the Development of Thought and Emotion in the Middle Ages.* 5th ed. 2 vols. Cambridge: Harvard University Press, 1959.   CB351.T3 1959

Ullman, Walter. *History of Political Thought: The Middle Ages.* Harmondsworth: Penguin, 1965.   JA82.U4

Vossler, Karl. *Medieval Culture: An Introduction to Dante and His Times.* 2 vols. New York: Harcourt, Brace, 1929.   PQ4390.V82

Wenzel, Siegfried. *Sin of Sloth: Acedia in Medieval Thought and Literature.* Chapel Hill: University of North Carolina Press, 1967.   BV4627.S65 W43

Wulf, Maurice de. *History of Mediaeval Philosophy.* 3d English ed. 2 vols. London: Longmans, Green, 1935.   B721.W93 1935

Medieval and Renaissance

Bugge, J. *Virginitas: An Essay in the History of a Medieval Ideal.* The Hague: Nijhoff, 1975.   BV4647.C5 B84

Gossman, Elizabeth. *Antiqui und Moderni um Mittelalter: Eine geschichtliche Standortbestimmung.* Munich: Schöningh, 1974.   CB353.G6

Lewis, C. S. *Allegory of Love: A Study in Medieval Tradition.* Rev. ed. Oxford: Clarendon Press, 1939.   PN600.L4

———. *Discarded Image: An Introduction to Medieval and Renaissance Literature.* Cambridge: Cambridge University Press, 1964.   PN671.L4

Zimmerman, A., ed. *Antiqui und Moderni: Traditionsbewusstsein und Fortschrittsbewusstsein im späten Mittelalter.* Berlin: de Gruyter, 1974.   B738.T5 K63 1972

Renaissance and the Renaissance in England

Allen, John W. *History of Political Thought in the Sixteenth Century.* Rev. ed. London: Methuen, 1957.   JA83.A6 1957

Babb, Lawrence. *Elizabethan Malady.* East Lansing: Michigan State University Press, 1951.   PR658.M37 B3

Bamborough, J. B. *Little World of Man.* New York: Longmans, Green, 1952.   BF98.B2

Baumer, Franklin Le Van. *Early Tudor Theory of Kingship.* New Haven: Yale University Press, 1940.   JN338.B3 1940

Bolgar, R. R., ed. *Classical Influences on European Culture, A.D. 1500–1700.* Cambridge: Cambridge University Press, 1976.   CB401.C64

Caspari, Fritz. *Humanism and the Social Order in England.* Chicago: University of Chicago Press, 1954.   B778.C35

Cassirer, Ernst. *Individual and the Cosmos in Renaissance Philosophy.* New York: Barnes and Noble, 1964.   B775.C313

Cassirer, Ernst, Paul O. Kristeller, and John H. Randall, Jr. *Renaissance Philosophy of Man.* Chicago: University of Chicago Press, 1948.   B775.C32

Craig, Hardin. *Enchanted Glass: The Elizabethan Mind in Literature.* New York: Oxford University Press, 1936.   PR421.C67

———. *New Lamps for Old: A Sequel to "The Enchanted Glass."* Oxford: Blackwell, 1960.   BD161.C68

Elton, W. R., with Gisela Schlesinger. *Shakespeare's World: Renaissance Intellectual Contexts: A Selective Annotated Guide, 1966–71.* New York: Garland, 1979. 2,835 serially numbered entries.   Z8813.E38

Haydn, Hiram. *Counter-Renaissance.* New York: Charles Scribner's Sons, 1950   CB369.H3

Heninger, S. K. *Touches of Sweet Harmony: Pythagorean Cosmology and Renaissance Poetics.* San Marino, Calif.: Huntington Library, 1974.   B243.H46

Koyré, Alexandre. *From the Closed World to the Infinite Universe.* Baltimore: Johns Hopkins University Press, 1968.   BD511.K67

Kristeller, Paul O. *Renaissance Thought: The Classic, Scholastic, and Humanistic Strains.* New York: Harper and Row, 1961.

———. *Renaissance Thought and Its Sources.* Edited by Michael Mooney. New York: Columbia University Press, 1979.   B775.K73

———. *Renaissance Thought II: Papers on Humanism and the Arts.* New York: Harper and Row, 1965.   CB361.K69

———. *Studies in Renaissance Thought and Letters.* Rome: Edizioni di Storia e letteratura, 1956.   CB361.K7

Levin, Harry. *Myth of the Golden Age in the Renaissance.* Bloomington: Indiana University Press, 1969.   PN721.L4

Morris, Christopher. *Political Thought in England: From Tyndale to Hooker.* London: Oxford University Press, 1953.   JA84.G7 M6

Quinones, Richard J. *Renaissance Discovery of Time.* Cambridge: Harvard University Press, 1972.   PN721.Q5

Shumaker, Wayne. *Occult Sciences in the Renaissance: A Study in Intellectual Patterns.* Berkeley, Los Angeles, London: University of California Press, 1972.   BF1429.S58

Spencer, Theodore. *Shakespeare and the Nature of Man.* 2d ed. New York: Macmillan, 1949.   PR2976.S65 1949

Taylor, Archer. *Renaissance Guides to Books: An Inventory and Some Conclusions.* Berkeley and Los Angeles: University of California Press, 1945.   Z1002.T34

Tillyard, E. M. W. *Elizabethan World Picture: A Study of the Idea of Order in the Age of Shakespeare, Donne and Milton.* London: Chatto and Windus, 1943.   PR428.P5 T5

Tonelli, Giorgio. *Short-Title List of Subject Dictionaries of the Sixteenth, Seventeenth, and Eighteenth Centuries as Aids to the History of Ideas.* London: Warburg Institute, 1971.   Z5848.T65

Tussner, F. S. *Tudor History and the Historians.* New York: Basic Books, 1970.   DA315.F88

Yates, Frances A. *Art of Memory.* Chicago: University of Chicago Press, 1966.   BF381.Y3 1966a

———. *Giordano Bruno and the Hermetic Tradition.* Chicago: University of Chicago Press, 1964.   B783.27 Y3

———. *Theatre of the World.* Chicago: University of Chicago Press, 1969.   PN2589.Y3

The Seventeenth Century in Europe and England

Baker, Herschel C. *Wars of Truth: Studies in the Decay of Christian Humanism in the Earlier Seventeenth Century.* Cambridge: Harvard University Press, 1952.   BD431.B242

Bredvold, Louis I. *Intellectual Milieu of John Dryden.* Ann Arbor: University of Michigan Press, 1934.   PR3423.B7

Burtt, E. A. *Metaphysical Foundations of Modern Science: A Historical and Critical Essay.* Rev. ed. London: Routledge and Kegan Paul, 1950.   B67.B8

Bury, J. B. *Idea of Progress: An Inquiry into Its Origins and Growth.* London: Macmillan, 1920.   CB67.B8

Clark, G. N. *Seventeenth Century.* 2d ed. Oxford: Clarendon Press, 1947.   CB401.C6 1947

Gierke, Otto Friedrich von. *Natural Law and the Theory of Society, 1500–1800.* 2 vols. Cambridge: Cambridge University Press, 1934.   JA83.G5

Hazard, Paul. *European Mind, 1680–1715.* Translation by J. Lewis May of *La crise de la conscience européenne (1680–1715)* (Paris: Boivin, 1935). London: Hollis and Carter, 1953.   D273.5.H32

Hill, Christopher. *Intellectual Origins of the English Revolution.* Oxford: Clarendon Press, 1965.   DA380.H48

Hunter, Michael. *Science and Society in Restoration England.* Cambridge: Cambridge University Press, 1981.   Q127.G4 H85

Jones, Richard Foster. *Ancients and Moderns: A Study of the Rise of the Scientific Movement in Seventeenth-Century England.* 2d ed. St. Louis: Washington University, 1961.   Q127.G4 J6 1961

Levi, Anthony. *French Moralists: The Theory of the Passions, 1585–1649.* Oxford: Clarendon Press, 1964.   BJ702.L4

Mazzeo, Joseph A., ed. *Reason and the Imagination: Studies in the History of Ideas, 1600–1800.* New York: Columbia University Press, 1962.   CB411.M3

Merton, Robert K. *On the Shoulders of Giants: A Shandean Postscript.* Boston: Free Press, 1965.   PS3525.E7173 O5

Pocock, J. G. A. *Ancient Constitution and the Feudal Law: English Historical Thought in the Seventeenth Century.* Cambridge: Cambridge University Press, 1957.   JN191.P6

Shapiro, Barbara. *Probability and Certainty in Seventeenth Century England.* Princeton, N.J.: Princeton University Press, 1983.   DA380.S53

Stimson, Dorothy. *Scientists and Amateurs: A History of the Royal Society.*   Q41.L85 S7

Wade, Ira O. *Intellectual Origins of the French Enlightenment.* Princeton N.J.: Princeton University Press, 1971.   B1925.E5 W3

Walker, D. P. *Decline of Hell: Seventeenth Century Discussions of Eternal Torment.* Chicago: Chicago University Press, 1964.   BT836.2.W3

Webster, Charles, ed. *Intellectual Revolution of the Seventeenth Century.* London: Routledge and Kegan Paul, 1974.   DA380.I58 1974

Willey, Basil. *English Moralists.* New York: Norton, 1964.   BJ602.W64 1964

———. *Seventeenth Century Background: Studies in the Thought of the Age in Relation to Poetry and Religion.* New York: Columbia University Press, 1935.   B1131.W5

The Eighteenth Century in Europe and England

Becker, Carl L. *Heavenly City of the Eighteenth Century Philosophers.* New Haven: Yale University Press, 1932.   B802.B4

Bryson, G. *Man and Society: Scottish Inquiry of the Eighteenth Century.* Princeton, N.J.: Princeton University Press, 1945.   B1402.S6 B7

Cassirer, Ernst. *Philosophy of the Enlightenment.* Translation by Fritz C. A. Koelin and James P. Pettegrove of *Die Philosophie der Aufklärung* (Tübingen: Mohr, 1932). Princeton: Princeton University Press, 1951.   B802.C34

Gay, Peter. *Enlightenment: An Interpretation.* 2 vols. New York: Columbia University Press, 1966–1969. Vol. 1, *Rise of Modern Paganism.* Vol. 2, *Science of Freedom.*   B802.G3

Hazard, Paul. *European Thought in the Eighteenth Century from Montesquieu to Lessing.* Translation by J. Lewis May of *La pensée européene au xviiie siècle: De Montesquieu à Lessing* (Paris: A. Fayard, 1946). New Haven: Yale University Press, 1954.   B802.H313

Himmelfarb, Gertrude. *Idea of Poverty: England in the Early Industrial Age.* New York: Alfred A. Knopf, 1984.   HV4086.A3 H55 1984

Johnson, James William. *Formation of English Neo-Classical Thought.* Princeton N.J.: Princeton University Press, 1967.   PR441.J6

Klingender, Francis D. *Art and the Industrial Revolution.* London: N. Carrington, 1947.   N8218.K55

Lovejoy, A. O. *Essays in the History of Ideas.* Baltimore: Johns Hopkins University Press, 1948.   B945.L583 E7

Nicholson, Marjorie Hope. *Breaking of the Circle: Studies in the Effect of the "New Science" upon Seventeenth Century Poetry.* Rev. ed. New York: Columbia University Press, 1960.   PR545.S3 N5 1960

———. *Mountain Gloom and Mountain Glory: The Development of the Aesthetics of the Infinite.* Ithaca, N.Y.: Cornell University Press, 1959.   PR508.N3 N5

———. *Newton Demands the Muse: Newton's "Optics" and the Eighteenth Century Poets.* Princeton, N.J.: Princeton University Press, 1946.   PR565.O6 N5

Rostvig, Maren-Sofie. *Happy Man: Studies in the Metamorphosis of a Classical Ideal.* 2 vols. Oxford: Clarendon Press, 1954–1958.   PR545.H3 R6

Selby-Bigge, L. A. *British Moralists.* 2 vols. Oxford: Clarendon Press, 1897.   BJ601.S4

Sheriff, John K. *Good-Natured Man: The Evolution of a Moral Ideal, 1660–1800.* University: University of Alabama Press, 1982.   PR449.E83 S5 1982

Stephen, Leslie. *History of English Thought in the Eighteenth Century.* 2 vols. London: Murray, 1876.   B1301.S8 1876

Trawick, Leonard M., ed. *Backgrounds of Romanticism: English Philosophical Prose of the Eighteenth Century.* Bloomington: Indiana University Press, 1967.   B1300.T7

Tucker, Susie I. *Enthusiasm: A Study in Semantic Change.* Cambridge: Cambridge University Press, 1972.   PE1599.E5789 E6

Tuveson, Ernest Lee. *Imagination as a Means of Grace: Locke and the Aesthetics of Romanticism.* Berkeley and Los Angeles: University of California Press, 1960.   B1297.T8

Willey, Basil. *Eighteenth Century Background: Studies on the Idea of Nature in the Period.* London: Chatto and Windus, 1940.   B1303.W5

The Nineteenth Century

Barzun, Jacques. *Darwin, Marx, Wagner: Critique of a Heritage.* Boston: Little, Brown, 1941.   CT105.B33

Brentlinger, Patrick. *Spirit of Reform: British Literature and Politics, 1832–1867.* Cambridge: Harvard University Press, 1977.   PR469.P6 B65

Brinton, Crane. *English Political Thought in the Nineteenth Century*. 2d ed. Cambridge: Cambridge University Press, 1949. JA84.G7 B67 1949

Buckley, Jerome. *Triumph of Time: A Study of the Victorian Concepts of Time, History, Progress, and Decadence*. Cambridge: Belknap Press of Harvard University Press, 1966. PR731.B8

Burrow, John W. *Evolution and Society: A Study in Victorian Social Theory*. London: Cambridge University Press, 1966. HM106.B8

Culler, A. Dwight. *Imperial Intellect: A Study of Newman's Educational Ideal*. New Haven: Yale University Press, 1955. LB675.N45 C8

Harris, Wendell V. *Omnipresent Debate: Empiricism and Transcendentalism in Nineteenth Century Prose*. De-kalb: Northern Illinois University Press, 1981. PR778.P55 H3 1981

Himmelfarb, Gertrude. *Victorian Minds*. New York: Alfred A. Knopf, 1968. PR468.T458

Holloway, John. *Victorian Sage: Studies in Argument*. London: Macmillan, 1953. PR463.H6

Houghton, Walter F. *Victorian Frame of Mind, 1830–1870*. New Haven: Yale University Press, 1957. DA533.H85

Kroeber, Karl, ed. *Backgrounds to British Romantic Literature*. San Francisco: Chandler, 1968. PR447.K7

Mandelbaum, Maurice H. *History, Man, and Reason: A Study in Nineteenth–Century Thought*. Baltimore: Johns Hopkins University Press, 1971. B803.M34

Marcus, Steven. *Other Victorians: A Study of Sexuality and Pornography in Mid–Nineteenth–Century England*. New York: Basic Books, 1966. PR468.P6 M3

Merz, John T. *History of European Thought in the Nineteenth Century*. 4 vols. Edinburgh: Blackwood, 1912–1928. B803.M52

Paradis, James, and Thomas Postlewaite, eds. *Victorian Science and Victorian Values: Literary Perspectives*. Annals of the New York Academy of Sciences, vol. 360. New York, 1981. Q11.N5 vol. 360

Reardon, Bernard M. *Religious Thought in the Nineteenth Century*. Cambridge: Cambridge University Press, 1966. BR477.R4

Routh, H. V. *Towards the Twentieth Century: Essays in the Spiritual History of the Nineteenth Century*. New York: Macmillan, 1937. PR451.R72 1937

Schneewind, J. B. *Backgrounds of English Victorian Literature*. New York: Random House, 1970. DA550.S33

Somervell, D. C. *English Thought in the Nineteenth Century*. 4th ed. London: Methuen, 1929. DA533.S65

Willey, Basil. *Nineteenth Century Studies: Coleridge to Matthew Arnold*. London: Chatto and Windus, 1949. B1561.W52

————. *More Nineteenth Century Studies: A Group of Honest Doubters*. London: Chatto and Windus, 1956. B1561.W5 1956a

The Twentieth Century

Ackroyd, Peter. *Notes for a New Culture: An Essay on Modernism*. London: Vision Press, 1976. PN56.M54 A3

Brinton, Crane. *Shaping of the Modern Mind*. Englewood Cliffs, N.J.: Prentice-Hall, 1963. CB245.B73 1963A

Colum, Mary. *From These Roots: The Ideas That Have Made Modern Literature*. New York: Columbia University Press, 1944. PN701.C6 1944

Cox, C. B., and A. E. Dyson, eds. *Twentieth Century Mind: History, Ideas, and Literature in Britain*. 3 vols. London: Oxford University Press, 1972. DA566.4.C68

Ellman, Richard, and Charles Feidelman, Jr., eds. *Modern Tradition: Backgrounds of Modern Literature*. New York: Oxford University Press, 1965. PN49.E5

Foster, John Burt, Jr. *Heirs to Dionysus*. Princeton, N.J.: Princeton University Press, 1981. PN771.F59

Gibbons, Tom. *Rooms in the Darwin Hotel*. Nedlands, Western Australia: University of Australia Press, 1973. PR76.G53

Heller, Erich. *Disinherited Mind: Essays in Modern German Literature and Thought*. Expanded ed. New York: Harcourt Brace Jovanovich, 1975. PT343.H47 1975

Hoffman, Frederick J. *Freudianism and the Literary Mind*. 2d ed. Baton Rouge: Louisiana State University Press, 1957. PN49.H6 1957

Howe, Irving, ed. *Idea of the Modern in Literature and the Arts*. New York: Horizon, 1968. PN771.H5895

Hynes, Samuel. *Edwardian Turn of Mind*. Princeton, N.J.: Princeton University Press, 1968. DA570.H9

Kampf, Louis. *On Modernism: The Prospects for Literature and Freedom*. Cambridge: MIT Press, 1967. AZ361.K3

Kenner, Hugh. *Pound Era*. Berkeley, Los Angeles, London: University of California Press, 1971. PS3531.O82 Z712

Nicholson, Norman. *[Ideas of] Man and [Modern] Literature*. London: SCM Press, 1943. PR479.M3 N5

Sears, Sallie, and Georgiana W. Lord, eds. *Discontinuous Universe: Selected Writings in Contemporary Consciousness*. New York: Basic Books, 1972. AC8.S4283

Whitehead, Alfred North. *Science and the Modern World*. Cambridge: Cambridge University Press, 1930. Q175.W65 1930

America: General

Ahlstrom, Sydney. *Religious History of the American People*. New Haven: Yale University Press, 1972. Comprehensive bibliography. BR515.A4

Cargill, Oscar. *Intellectual America: Ideas on the March*. New York: Macmillan, 1941. PS88.C37

Cohen, Morris R. *American Thought: A Critical Sketch*. Edited by Felix S. Cohen. Glencoe, Ill.: Free Press, 1954. B851.C6

Curti, Merle E. *Growth of American Thought*. 3d ed. New York: Harper and Row, 1964. E169.1.C87 1964

Egbert, Donald Drew, and Stow Persons, eds. *Socialism and American Life*. Vol. 2, *Bibliography, Descriptive and Critical*, by T. D. Seymour Bassett. Princeton, N.J.: Princeton University Press, 1952. HX83.E45

Hartz, Louis. *Liberal Tradition in America: An Interpretation of American Political Thought since the Revolution*. New York: Harcourt, Brace, 1955. E175.9.H37

Hofstadter, Richard. *Anti-Intellectualism in American Life*. New York: Alfred A. Knopf, 1963. E169.1.H74

Horton, Rod W., and Herbert W. Edwards. *Backgrounds of American Literary Thought*. 3d ed. Englewood Cliffs, N.J.: Prentice-Hall, 1974. PS88.H6 1974

Jones, Howard Mumford. *Pursuit of Happiness*. Cambridge: Harvard University Press, 1953. BJ1481.J65

Marty, Martin E. *Pilgrims in Their Own Land: 500 Years of Religion in America.* Boston: Little, Brown, 1984.
BR515.M324 1984

Parrington, Vernon Louis. *Main Currents in American Thought: An Interpretation of American Literature from the Beginnings to 1920.* 3 vols. New York: Harcourt, Brace, 1927–1930. Vol. 1, *Colonial Mind, 1620–1800.* Vol. 2, *Romantic Revolution in America, 1800–1860.* Vol. 3, *Beginning of Critical Realism in America, 1860–1920.* PS88.P33

Perry, Lewis. *Intellectual Life in America: A History.* New York: F. Watts, 1984. E169.1.P446 1984

Persons, Stow, ed. *Evolutionary Thought in America.* New Haven: Yale University Press, 1950. B818.P4

Riley, Isaac Woodbridge. *American Thought from Puritanism to Pragmatism.* 2d ed. New York: Holt, 1923.
B851.R5 1923

Rossiter, Clinton L. *Conservatism in America: The Thankless Persuasion.* 2d ed. New York: Alfred A. Knopf, 1962. JK31.R58 1962a

Schneider, Herbert W. *History of American Philosophy.* 2d ed. New York: Columbia University Press, 1963.
B851.S4 1963

Skotheim, Robert Allen. *American Intellectual Histories and Historians.* Princeton, N.J.: Princeton University Press, 1966. E175.45.S5

Smith, James Ward, and A. Leland Jamison, eds. *Religion in American Life.* 4 vols. Princeton, N.J.: Princeton University Press, 1961. Vol. 1, *Shaping of American Religion.* Vol. 2, *Religious Perspectives in American Culture.* Vol. 3, *Religious Thought and Economic Society* (not yet published). Vol. 4, in 2 parts, *Critical Bibliography of Religion in American Life,* comp. Nelson R. Burr. BR515.S6

Sweet, William W. *Story of Religion in America.* 2d ed. New York: Harper, 1950. BR515.S82 1950

Ward, John William. *Red, White, and Blue: Men, Books, and Ideas in American Culture.* New York: Oxford University Press, 1969. E178.6.W3

Whittemore, Robert Clifton. *Makers of the American Mind: Three Centuries of American Thought and Thinkers.* New York: William Morrow, 1964. B851.W48

Seventeenth and Eighteenth Centuries

Gummere, Richard M. *American Colonial Mind and the Classical Tradition.* Cambridge: Harvard University Press, 1963. E162.G88

Miller, Perry. *New England Mind.* Vol. 1, *Seventeenth Century.* New York: Macmillan, 1939. F7.M56

———. *New England Mind.* Vol. 2, *From Colony to Province.* Cambridge: Harvard University Press, 1953.
F7.M54

———. *Orthodoxy in Massachusetts.* Cambridge: Harvard University Press, 1933. BR520.M57

Miller, Perry, and Thomas H. Johnson. *Puritans.* Rev. ed. 2 vols. New York: American Book Co., 1963.
PS530.M5

Morison, Samuel Eliot. *Intellectual Life of Colonial New England.* Ithaca, N.Y.: Cornell University Press, 1956. Original 1936 title: *Puritan Pronaos: Studies in the Intellectual Life of New England in the Seventeenth Century.* F7.M82 1956

Schneider, Herbert W. *Puritan Mind.* Ann Arbor: University of Michigan Press, 1958. BX9321.S4 1958

Nineteenth and Twentieth Centuries

Cash, Wilbur J. *Mind of the South.* New York: Alfred A. Knopf, 1941. F209.C3 1941

Commager, Henry Steele. *American Mind: An Interpretation of American Thought and Character since the 1880's.* New Haven: Yale University Press, 1950.
E169.1.C673

Degler, Carl N. *Out of Our Past: The Forces That Shaped Modern America.* New York: Harper, 1959.
E178.D37

Gabriel, Ralph Henry. *Course of American Democratic Thought: An Intellectual History since 1815.* 2d ed. New York: Ronald, 1956. E169.1.G23 1956

Hofstadter, Richard. *Social Darwinism in American Thought, 1860–1915.* Rev. ed. Boston: Beacon Press, 1955. HM22.U5 H6 1955

Matthiessen, F. O. *American Renaissance: Art and Expression in the Age of Emerson and Whitman.* New York: Oxford University Press, 1941. PS201.M3

Trilling, Lionel. *Freud and the Crisis of Our Culture.* Boston: Beacon Press, 1955. BF173.F85 T7

K–98 Some Frequently Recommended Studies in the History of Learning, including Education, Scholarship, and Librarianship.

See also sections on schools and universities in section G (G–25 to G–29 and G–45) and many of the entries in section B on libraries, H on manuscripts, Y on the history of the book and of libraries, and Z on the history of English studies and related matters.

Bibliographical

Brickman, William W. *Guide to Research in Educational History.* New York: New York University Bookstore, 1949. LA9.B7

Powell, John P. *Philosophy of Education: A Select Bibliography.* 2d ed. rev., Manchester: University of Manchester Press, 1970. Z5811.P64 1970

———. *Universities and University Education: A Select Bibliography.* 2 vols. Slough, Bucks: National Foundation for Educational Research in England and Wales, 1966–1971. Vol. 1, covering through 1964. Vol. 2, covering 1965–1970 and Supplement to vol. 1. Z5814.U7 P65

History of Education Quarterly. Vol. 1–. New York: New York University, 1961–. 4/yr. "Annual Bibliography." L11.H67

General Reference

Adamson, John William. *Short History of Education.* Cambridge: Cambridge University Press, 1919.
LA631.A3

Bowen, James. *History of Western Education.* 4 vols. New York: St. Martin's Press, 1972–. LA11.B622

Collison, Robert L. *Encyclopedias: Their History throughout the Ages: A Bibliographical Guide with Extensive Historical Notes to the General Encyclopedias Issued throughout the World from 350 B. C. to the Present Day.* 2d ed. New York: Hafner, 1966. AE1.C6 1966

Jöcher, Christian Gottlieb. *Allgemeines Gelehrten-Lexikon.* 4 vols. Leipzig, 1750–1751. Z1010.J63

History of Classical Scholarship

Bolgar, R. R. *Classical Heritage and Its Beneficiaries.* Cambridge: Cambridge University Press, 1954.
CB245.B63

Grafton, Anthony. "The Origins of Scholarship." *The American Scholar*: 48 (Spring 1979), 236–261.

Kenney, E. J. *Classical Text: Aspects of Editing in the Age of the Printed Book*. Berkeley, Los Angeles, London: University of California Press, 1974.   P47.K45

Momigliano, Arnaldo. *Contributo alla storia degli studi classici*. 2 vols. Rome: Edizioni di storia e letteratura, 1955–1960.   PA27.M65

Pfeiffer, Rudolf. *History of Classical Scholarship from the Beginnings to the End of the Hellenistic Age*. Oxford: Clarendon Press, 1968.   AZ301.P4

———. *History of Classical Scholarship from 1300 to 1850*. Oxford: Clarendon Press, 1976.   AZ201.P43

Platnauer, M., ed. *Fifty Years of Classical Scholarship*. Oxford: Blackwell, 1954.   PA3001.P4

Reynolds, Leighton D., and Nigel G. Wilson. *Scribes and Scholars: A Guide to the Transmission of Greek and Latin Literature*. London: Oxford University Press, 1968.   Z40.R4

Sandys, John E. *History of Classical Scholarship*. 3 vols. Cambridge: Cambridge University Press, 1903–1908. 3d ed. of vol. 1 only, 1921. Vol. 1, *From the Sixth Century B.C. to the End of the Middle Ages*. Vol. 2, *From the Revival of Learning to the End of the Eighteenth Century (in Italy, France, England, and the Netherlands)*. Vol. 3, *Eighteenth Century in Germany and the Nineteenth Century in Europe and the United States of America*.   PA51.S3

Willison, Ian R. *On the History of Libraries and Scholarship*. Washington, D.C.: Library of Congress Center for the Book, 1980.   Z721.W7

Education and Learning in Classical Antiquity

Clark, D. *Rhetoric in Graeco-Roman Education*. New York: Columbia University Press, 1957.   PA3265.C55

Clark, M. *Higher Education in the Ancient World*. Albuquerque: University of New Mexico Press, 1971.   LA71.C55 1971b

Gwynn, Aubrey O. *Roman Education from Cicero to Quintilian*. Oxford: Clarendon Press, 1926.   LA81.G8

Jaeger, Werner. *Paideia: The Ideals of Greek Culture*. Translated by Gilbert Highet from the German. 3 vols. Oxford: Blackwell, 1939–1944.   DF77.J273

Marrou, Henri Irénée. *History of Education in Antiquity*. Translation by George Lamb of *Histoire de l'éducation dans l'antiquité*, 3d. ed. (Paris: Éditions du Seuil, 1955). Toronto: Mentor, 1964. LA31.M32

Rauschen, Gerhard. *Das griechisch-römische Schulwesens zur Zeit des ausgehenden Heidentums*. Bonn, 1900.

Medieval Education and Learning

Alexander, J. J. G., and M. T. Gibson, eds. *Medieval Learning and Literature: Essays Presented to Richard William Hunt*. Oxford: Clarendon Press, 1976.   AZ603.M4

Baldwin, John W. *Scholastic Culture of the Middle Ages, 1000–1300*. Lexington, Mass.: D. C. Heath, 1971.   AZ321.B34

Daly, Lowrie John. *Medieval University 1200–1400*. New York: Sheed and Ward, 1961.   LA177.D3

Gabriel, Astrik L. *Garlandia: Studies in the History of the Medieval University*. Frankfurt: Knecht, 1969.   LA177.G3

Graves, F. P. *History of Education during the Middle Ages and the Transition to Modern Times*. New York: Macmillan, 1910.   LA96.G7

Haskins, Charles Homer. *Rise of Universities*. New York: H. Holt, 1923.   LA177.H3

Ijsewijn, Jozef, and Jacques Paquet, eds. *Universities in the Late Middle Ages*. Louvain: Louvain University Press, 1978.   LA631.3.V54

Koch, J., ed. *Artes Liberales: Von der antiken Bildung zur Wissenschaft des Mittelalters*. Leiden: E. J. Brill, 1959.   LA98.K6 1955aa

Leclerq, Jean. *Love of Learning and the Desire for God: A Study of Monastic Culture*. Translation by Catherine Marsh of *L'amour des lettres et le desir de Dieu: Initiation aux auteurs monastiques du moyen âge*, 3d ed. (Paris, 1957). New York: Fordham University Press, 1982.   BX2470.L413 1982

Leff, Gordon. *Paris and Oxford Universities in the Thirteenth and Fourteenth Centuries: An Institutional and Intellectual History*. New York: Wiley, 1968.   LA91.L4

Paetow, Louis J. *Arts Course at Medieval Universities, with Special Reference to Grammar and Rhetoric*. Champaigne: University of Illinois, 1910.   LA177.P28

Rait, Robert S. *Life in the Medieval Cambridge University*. Cambridge: Cambridge University Press, 1912.   LA177.R22

Rashdall, Hastings. *Universities of Europe in the Middle Ages*. New ed. Edited by F. M. Powicke and A. B. Emden. 3 vols. Oxford: Clarendon Press, 1936.   LA177.R25 1936

Thompson, James Westfall. *Medieval Library*. Chicago: University of Chicago Press, 1939.   Z723.T47

Thorndike, Lynn. *University Records and Life in the Middle Ages*. New York: Columbia University Press, 1944.   LA627.T45

Verger, J. *Les universités au moyen âge*. Paris: Presses universitaires de France, 1973.   LA177.V47

Renaissance Education and Learning

Harbison, E. H. *Christian Scholar in the Age of the Reformation*. New York: Charles Scribner's Sons, 1956.   AZ341.H3

Müller, G. *Bildung und Erziehung im Humanismus der italienischen Renaissance: Grundlagen, Motive, Quellen*. Wiesbaden: F. Steiner, 1969.   DG445.M8

Spargo, John W. "Some Reference Books of the Sixteenth and Seventeenth Centuries: A Finding List." *PBSA* 31 (1937): 133–175.

Taylor, Archer. *Renaissance Guides to Books. An Inventory and Some Conclusions*. Berkeley: University of California Press, 1945.   Z1002.T34

Tonelli, Giorgio. *Short-Title List of Subject Dictionaries of the Sixteenth, Seventeenth, and Eighteenth Centuries*. London: Warburg Institute, 1971.   Z5848.T65

Weiss, Roberto. *Renaissance Discovery of Classical Antiquity*. Oxford: Basil Blackwell, 1969.   DG431.W4

Woodward, W. H. *Studies in Education during the Age of the Renaissance, 1400–1600*. Cambridge: Cambridge University Press, 1906.   LA106.W7

Education and Learning in England

Armytage, Walter H. G. *Four Hundred Years of English Education*. 2d ed. Cambridge: Cambridge University Press, 1970.   LA631.A7 1970

Clarke, M. L. *Classical Education in Britain*. Cambridge: Cambridge University Press, 1959.   LA631.7.C54 1959

Higson, C. W. J. *Sources for the History of Education: A List of Materials (Including School Books) Contained in the Libraries of the Institutes and Schools of Education.* . . . London: Library Association, 1967. Z5811.H5

Lawson, John, and Harold Silver. *Special History of Education in England.* London: Methuen, 1973. LA631.L36 1973

Medieval Education in England

Allison, Thomas. *Pioneers of English Learning.* Oxford: Blackwell, 1932. LA98.A44

Kerr, Neil R. *Medieval Libraries of Great Britain: A List of Surviving Books.* 2d ed. London: Royal Historical Society, 1964. Z723.K47 1964

Leach, Arthur F. *Schools of Medieval England.* London: Methuen, 1915. LA634.L4

McMahon, Clara P. *Education in Fifteenth Century England.* Baltimore: Johns Hopkins University Press, 1947. LA631.3.M25 1947a

Orme, Nicholas. *English Schools in the Middle Ages.* London: Methuen, 1973. LA631.3.O75

Parry, A. W. *Education in England in the Middle Ages.* London: W. B. Clive, 1920. LA631.3.P37

Streeter, Barnett H. *Chained Library: A Survey of Four Centuries in the Evolution of the English Library.* London: Macmillan, 1931. Z791.S91

Wormald, Francis, and Cyril E. Wright, eds. *English Library before 1700: Studies in Its History.* London: University of London, Athlone Press, 1958. Z791.W7

Renaissance Education in England

Baldwin, T. W. *William Shakespeare's Petty School.* Urbana: University of Illinois Press, 1943. PR2903.B3

————. *William Shakespeare's Small Latine and Lesse Greek.* 2 vols. Urbana: University of Illinois Press, 1944.

Brown, J. Howard. *Elizabethan School Days: An Account of the English Grammar Schools in the Second Half of the Sixteenth Century.* Oxford: Clarendon Press, 1933. LA631.4.B7

Charlton, Kenneth. *Education in Renaissance England: Studies in Social History.* Edited by Harold Perkin. London: Routledge and Kegan Paul, 1965. LA631.4.C5

Clark, Donald L. *John Milton at St. Paul's School: A Study of Ancient Rhetoric in English Renaissance Education.* New York: Columbia University Press, 1948. PR3582.C5

Clarke, Martin L. *Classical Education in Britain, 1500–1900.* Cambridge: Cambridge University Press, 1959. LA631.7.C54 1959

Curtis, Mark. *Oxford and Cambridge in Transition, 1558–1642: An Essay on Changing Relations between the English Universities and English Society.* Oxford: Clarendon Press, 1959. LA636.4.C8

Gathorne-Hardy, Jonathan. *Public School Phenomenon, 598–1977.* London: Hodder and Stoughton, 1977. LA631.G38

Jayne, Sears. *Library Catalogues of the English Renaissance.* Berkeley and Los Angeles: University of California Press, 1956. Z921.A1 J3

Kearney, Hugh. *Scholars and Gentlemen: Universities and Society in Pre-Industrial Britain, 1500–1700.* London: Faber and Faber, 1970. LA627.K4

Mulder, John R. *Temple of the Mind: Education and Literary Task in Seventeenth Century England.* New York: Pegasus, 1969. LA116.M84

Partridge, A. C. *Landmarks in the History of English Scholarship, 1500–1700.* Cape Town, South Africa: Nasou, 1974. AZ614.P37

Simon, Joan. *Education and Society in Tudor England.* Cambridge: Cambridge University Press, 1966. LA636.4.S5

Thompson, Craig R. *Schools in Tudor England.* Washington, D.C.: Folger Shakespeare Library, 1958. LA631.4.T5

Wallis, P. J. *Histories of Old Schools: A Revised List for England and Wales.* Newcastle upon Tyne: University of Newcastle upon Tyne, Department of Education, 1966. Z5815.G5 W3

Watson, Foster. *English Grammar Schools to 1660: Their Curriculum and Practice.* London: F. Cass, 1908. LA635.W3

————. *English Writers on Education, 1480–1603: A Source Book.* Gainesville, Fla.: Scholars' Facsimiles. Z5815.G5 W35 1967

————. *Old Grammar Schools.* Cambridge: Cambridge University Press, 1916. LA634.W3

Restoration and Eighteenth Century Education in England

Adams, Eleanor N. *Old English Scholarship in England from 1566–1800.* New Haven: Yale University Press, 1917. PE51.A3

Braver, George C., Jr. *Education of a Gentleman: Theories of Gentlemanly Education in England, 1660–1775.* New York: Bookman Associates, 1959. LC4945.G7 B7

Douglas, David C. *English Scholars, 1660–1730.* 2d ed., rev. London: Eyre and Spottiswoode, 1951. DA3.A1 D6 1951

Evans, Joan. *History of the Society of Antiquaries.* Oxford: Oxford University Press, 1956. DA20.S624

Foucault, Michel. *Order of Things: An Archaeology of the Human Sciences.* Translation of *Les mots et les choses: Une archéologie des sciences humaines* (Paris: Gallimard, 1966). New York: Pantheon Books, 1971. AZ101.F6913 1971

Hans, N. *New Trends in Education in the Eighteenth Century.* London: Routledge and K. Paul, 1951. LA121.H35

Law, Alexander. *Education in Edinburgh in the Eighteenth Century.* London: University of London Press, 1965. LA659.E3 L3

Vincent, W. A. L. *Grammar Schools: Their Continuing Tradition, 1660–1714.* London: Murray, 1969. LA634.V5

Walsh, S. Patrick. *Anglo-American General Encyclopedias: A Historical Bibliography, 1703–1967.* New York: R. R. Bowker, 1968. 419 annotated entries. Z5849.E5 W3

Later Eighteenth, Nineteenth, and Twentieth Centuries Education in England

Aarsleff, Hans. *Study of Language in England, 1780–1860.* Princeton, N.J.: Princeton University Press, 1967. P81.G7 A62

Barnard, Howard C. *Short History of English Education from 1760 to 1944.* 2d ed. London: University of London Press, 1961. LA681.B25 1961

Kelly, Thomas. *Early Public Libraries*. London: Library Association, 1966.   Z791.K37

Knights, Ben. *Idea of the Clerisy in the Nineteenth Century*. Cambridge: Cambridge University Press, 1978.   PR778.S47 K5

Oldman, Cecil B., et al. *English Libraries, 1800–1850*. London: H. K. Lewis, 1958.   Z791.L8515

Palmer, David John. *Rise of English Studies: An Account of the Study of English Language and Literature from Its Origins to the Making of the Oxford English School*. London: For the University of Hull, Oxford University Press, 1965.   PE68.G5 P3 1967

Reed, John R. *Public Schools in British Literature*. Syracuse, N.J.: Syracuse University Press, 1965.

Silver, Harold, and S. John Teague. *History of the British Universities, 1800–1969, Excluding Oxford and Cambridge: A Bibliography*. London: Society for Research into Higher Education, 1971.   Z5815.G5 S55

Simon, Brian. *Studies in the History of Education, 1780–1870*. London: Lawrence and Wishart, 1960.   LA631.7.S5

Steeves, Harrison Ross. *Learned Societies and English Literary Scholarship in Great Britain and the United States*. New York: Columbia University Press, 1913.   PN22.A2 S8

Truscot, Bruce. *Redbrick University*. London: Faber and Faber, 1943.   LA639.T7

Walsh, William. *Use of Imagination: Educational Thought and the Literary Mind*. New York: Barnes and Noble, 1960.   PR149.I45 W3 1961

Ward, William R. *Victorian Oxford*. London: F. Cass, 1965.   LF509.W3

American

Butts, Robert Freeman, and Lawrence A. Cremin. *History of Education in American Culture*. New York: Holt, 1953.   LA205.B88

Carpenter, Charles H. *History of American School Books*. Philadelphia: University of Pennsylvania Press, 1963.   LT23.C3 1963

Cordasco, Francesco. *Bibliography of American Educational History: An Annotated and Classified Guide*. New York: AMS Press, 1975.   Z5815.U5 B5

————, et al. *History of American Education: A Guide to Information Sources*. Detroit: Gale Research Co., 1979. 2,495 items in a sheer list with indexes of names and of subjects.   LA212.H57

Cremin, Laurence A. *Traditions of American Education*. New York: Basic Books, 1977.   LA205.C67

————. *American Education: The Colonial Experience, 1607–1783*. New York: Harper and Row, 1970.   LA215.C73 1970

————. *American Education: The National Experience, 1783–1876*. New York: Harper and Row, 1980.   LA215.C74 1980

————. *American Education: The Metropolitan Experience, 1876–1976*. Forthcoming.

Curti, Merle, ed. *American Scholarship in the Twentieth Century*. Cambridge: Harvard University Press, 1953.   AZ505.C8

DeVane, William Clyde. *Higher Education in Twentieth-Century America*. Cambridge: Harvard University Press, 1965.   LA226.D4

Hofstadter, Richard, and Wilson Smith, eds. *American Higher Education: A Documentary History*. 2 vols. Chicago: University of Chicago Press, 1961.   LA226.H53 1961

Knight, Edgar W. *Education in the United States*. 3d rev. ed. Boston: Ginn, 1951.   LA205.K6 1951

Rudolph, Frederick. *American College and University: A History*. New York: Alfred A. Knopf, 1962.   LA226.R72

————. *Curriculum: A History of the American Undergraduate Course of Study since 1636*. San Francisco: Jossey-Bass, 1977.   LB2361.5.R8

Sedlack, Michael W., and Timothy Walch, eds. *American Educational History: A Guide to Information Sources*. Detroit: Gale Research Co., 1981.   LA205.S42

Thomas, Russell Brown. *Search for a Common Learning: General Education, 1800–1960*. New York: McGraw-Hill, 1962.   LC1011.T53

Veysey, Laurence R. *Emergence of the American University*. Chicago: University of Chicago Press, 1965.   LA226.V47

LITERATURE

I. GENERAL AND COMPARATIVE LITERATURE

Most literary bibliographies have sections devoted to questions of general and comparative literature. See, in particular, the *MLA International Bibliography* (L–50), the MHRA's *Year's Work in Modern Language Studies* (L–52), Klapp (L–73), Rancoeur (L–74), the *NCBEL* (M–11), the MHRA *Annual Bibliography of English Language and Literature* (M–21), section M.IX and following on Commonwealth Literature and World Literature Written in English, and bibliographies in *Twentieth-Century Literature* (R–16) and the *Journal of Modern Literature* (R–17). See further materials in section F, History (especially F.III on Medieval Studies); section I, Language, Linguistics, and Philology (especially I.VI, Dictionaries, and I.VII through I.IX, Translation); section K, Literary Materials and Contexts; sections T, U, and W on genre studies; and section X, Theory, Rhetoric, and Composition.

L–1 **Baldensperger, Ferdinand, and Werner P. Friedrich.** *Bibliography of Comparative Literature.* Chapel Hill: University of North Carolina Press, 1950. Reprint. New York: Russell and Russell, 1960, with a revised section on Scandinavian contributions.   Z6514.C7 B3

This bibliography contains more than 30,000 entries covering books, articles, and some dissertations in the field of comparative literature. The governing principle of inclusion is that the cited work must relate to the phenomenon of influence, whether general, of a national literature, of an author, of a work, or of a particular theme or motif. Organization throughout is from the general to the particular, from influence of a country to influence of an author or a work. Entries concerned with influence *on* an individual are placed at the end of sections. The entries are elaborately classified into four main books, each of which is divided into parts, chapters, and further subsections.

Book I treats Generalities, Intermediaries, Thematology, and Literary Genres. Its seven parts are as follows (the number of chapters in each follows in parentheses): I–1, Comparative Literature, World Literature, European Literature (5); I–2, Literature and Politics (5); I–3, Literature and the Arts and Sciences (5); I–4, Intermediaries (8); I–5, Comparisons, Sources, Imitations (3); I–6, Literary Themes—Stoffgeschichte (11); I–7, Literary and Semi-literary Genres and Forms (4).

Book II treats The Orient, Antiquity (Greece, Rome), Judaism, Early Christianity, Mohammedanism, and Their Contributions. It is divided into five parts, as follows: II–1, The Orient (10); II–2, Classical Antiquity (6); II–3, Greek Contributions (17); II–4, Latin Contributions (11); II–5, Hebraism and Christianity (6).

Book III is divided into three parts, as follows: III–1, Modern Christianity (4); III–2, Literary Currents (8); and III–3, International Literary Relations, Collective Influences upon Continents, Nations, and Individuals (14).

Book IV treats The Modern World, and is organized into thirteen parts, as follows: IV–1, Celtic and Arthurian Contributions (10); IV–2, Provençal Contributions (3); IV–3, Italian Contributions (17); IV–4, Spanish Contributions (12); IV–5, Portuguese Contributions (4); IV–6, Dutch and Belgian Contributions (7); IV–7, French Contributions (25); IV–8, English Contributions (16); IV–9, Swiss Contributions (6); IV–10, German Contributions (14); IV–11, North and South American Contributions (11); IV–12, Scandinavian Contributions (5); and IV–13, East European Contributions (9).

A detailed table of contents substitutes, but not satisfactorily, for the absence of an index. One must, therefore, be inventive and energetic in searching out all the places where relevant entries might be cited. Entries within the smallest subsection are at times arranged chronologically for those published before 1900 and then alphabetically by the name of the scholar; most often they are in alphabetical order by the name of the scholar. Those sections that treat the influence of individual literary authors are arranged alphabetically by the name of the author influencing or being influenced; that name is printed in boldface type within the cited title of the article or book.

Although it has been criticized for weakness in the treatment of Slavic languages and literatures and for weakness in the treatment of main genres, this is the standard and indispensable closed bibliography in the field. It is supplemented by the annual bibliographies in the *Yearbook of Comparative and General Literature* (L–2) and in the comparative and general literature portions of the *MLA International Bibliography* (L–50). It is complemented by the comparative and general literature portions of standard closed bibliographies treating each of the major national literatures. For supplementation in relatively obscure nineteenth-century materials, see the forerunner of this bibliography, Louis Paul Betz, *La littérature comparée: Essai bibliographique*, 2d ed., enl. with index by Ferdinand Baldensperger (Strasbourg: Trübner, 1904) [Z6514.C7 B6], with its 5,969 unannotated, classified entries.

L–2 ***Annual Bibliography [of Comparative and General Literature 1949/51–1970]: Yearbook of Comparative and General Literatures.*** Vols. 1–9. Chapel Hill, N.C., 1952-1960, Vols. 10–19. Bloomington, Ind., 1961–1971.

PN851.Y4

Published in collaboration with the Comparative Literature Committee of NCTE, the American Comparative Literature Association, and the Comparative Literature Section of the MLA, this annual bibliography was designed to be a continuing supplement to Baldensperger and Friedrich (L–1). The principles of inclusion and organization were taken from the parent work—particularly the limitation to genuinely and explicitly comparative studies—save for the additional enumeration of new translations into English of important foreign works of literature. Books, articles, and dissertations are included. Volumes 1–9 are organized into four major sections, as follows: A. Generalities, Intermediaries, Thematology and Literary Genres (subdivisions include Comparative Literature, World Literature, European Literature; Literature and Politics; Literature and the Arts and Sciences; Intermediaries; Comparisons, Similarities, Contrasts, Sources; Literary Themes; and Literary and Semi-literary Genres and Forms); B. Orient, Antiquity, Judaism, Islam; C. Aspects of Western Culture; D. The Modern World. General studies are followed in each relevant instance by studies treating individual authors whose names, in titles, are given in boldfaced large type. The structure was changed for volumes 10–19, in which entries were disposed into eight major sections, as follows: I. Comparative, World and General Literature; II. Translations, Translators, Correspondents, Travelers, and other Intermediaries; III. Themes, Motifs, and Topoi; IV. Literary Genres, Types, Forms and Techniques; V. Epochs, Currents and Movements; VI. The Bible, Classical Antiquity; Arab Influences, larger Geographical and Linguistic Units; VII. Individual Countries; VIII. Individual Authors.

The work was discontinued in 1972; for citations from 1970 on, see the Comparative and General Literature sections of the *MLA International Bibliography* (L–50), the Ancillary Studies and General Literature sections of the MHRA *Year's Work in Modern Language Studies* (L–52), as well as citations in the general and comparative literature sections of the various serial bibliographies treating one or several national literatures. Though lacking a formal bibliography, each volume of the *Yearbook of Comparative and General Literature* does contain bibliographical essays and reviews and thus continues to be an important if not indispensable source.

L–3 **UNESCO.** *Bibliographie générale de littérature comparée [1949/50–1957/58].* 5 vols. Paris: Boivin, 1950-1959.

Z6514.C7 B4

Each of these five biennial volumes, meant to supplement Baldensperger and Friedrich (L–1), reprints two years' worth of the quarterly bibliographies published in each issue of the *Revue de littérature comparée* (Paris: Boivin, 1921–) [PN851.R4]. For the period of the *Revue* beginning through 1948, and from 1958 through the first quarter of 1960, the original issues of the *Revue* must be directly consulted. These bibliographies list books, articles, reviews, and parts of volumes in broad subject categories including such divisions as bibliographies, theory, style, literary influences, current movements, intermediaries, genres, themes, and types. Entries drawn from Romance-language journals predominate. Each issue's detailed author-subject index must be consulted.

L–4 **General Guides to the Study of Comparative Literatures.**

Brandt-Corstius, Jan. *Introduction to the Comparative Study of Literature.* New York: Random House, 1968.

PN871.B7

Clements, Robert J. *Comparative Literature as Academic Discipline: A Statement of Principles, Praxis, Standards.* New York: MLA, 1978.   PN865.C57

Dyserinck, M. *Komparatistik: Eine Einführung.* Bonn: Bouvier, 1977.   PN865.D9

Gifford, Henry. *Comparative Literature: Concepts of Literature.* London: Routledge and Kegan Paul, 1969.

PN871.G5 1969

Jeune, Simon. *Littérature générale et littérature comparée: Essai d'orientation.* Paris: Lettres moderns, 1968.

PN873.J4

Jost, François. *Introduction to Comparative Literature.* New York: Bobbs-Merrill, 1974.   PN871.J6

Pichois, Claude, and André-Marie Rousseau. *La littérature comparée.* Paris: Armand Colin, 1967. Important bibliography, pp. 182–209, "Conseils pratiques."

PN873.P5

Prawer, S. S. *Comparative Literature Studies: An Introduction.* London: Duckworth; New York: Barnes and Noble, 1973.   PN871.P7

Rudiger, Horst. *Komparatistik: Aufgaben und Methoden.* Stuttgart: Kohlhammer, 1973.   PN865.R8

Stallknecht, Newton, and Horst Franz, eds. *Comparative Literature: Method and Perspective.* 2d ed. Carbondale: Southern Illinois University Press, 1971. Contains important annotated bibliographies.

PN871.S75 1971

Van Tieghem, Paul. *La littérature comparée.* 4th ed. Paris: Colin, 1951.   PN873.V3 1951

Weisstein, Ulrich. *Comparative Literature and Literary Theory.* Translation by William Riggan of *Einführung in die vergleichende Literaturwissenschaft* (Stuttgart: Kohlhammer, 1968). Bloomington: Indiana University Press, 1973. Contains an important bibliography of more than 400 items.   PN874.W4 1974

Wellek, René, and Austin Warren. *Theory of Literature.* 3d ed. New York: Harcourt, Brace, 1956. Topically arranged bibliographical notes and bibliography (See X–4).   PN45.W36 1956

L–5 **"Revue des revues"** in *Canadian Review of Comparative Literature / Revue canadienne de la littérature comparée.* Vol. 1–. Toronto: University of Toronto Press, 1974–.

PN851.C35

The third issue each year of this triannual and then quarterly *Review*, sponsored by the Canadian Comparative Literature Association, contains a series of numbered abstracts of current articles from the leading journals in comparative literature and literary theory. A list of the journals surveyed precedes each annual enumeration. The informational abstracts in either French or English are arranged in three groups: (1) literary history and relationships; (2) literary theory and the methodology of literary scholarship; and (3) literature and the other arts. Though not complete, the "Revue" is an extremely convenient way of keeping abreast of the most important periodical literature in the field. There is an author index.

This journal also carries an annual "Preliminary Bibliography of Comparative Canadian Literature (English-Canadian and French-Canadian)" from 1976 on. Books, articles, and dissertations are included.

L–6 *Bulletin signalétique 523: Histoire et sciences de la littérature: Révue trimestrielle.* Vol. 1–. Paris: Centre national de la recherche scientifique (CNRS), 1947–.

Z6513.B82

This quarterly index has developed gradually over the years. From 1947–1955 it was titled *Bulletin analytique*; from 1956–1960, *Bulletin signalétique: Philosophie, sciences humaines*; and from 1961–1968, *Bulletin C (19–24): Sciences humaines*. Currently it is a quarterly index and French-language abstracting service for more than 1,200 periodicals and other works (including festschriften, dissertations, and congress proceedings). Entries provide both complete bibliographical information and an informational abstract. More than 6,900 such abstracts are done each year. The serially numbered entries are disposed into an elaborate classification consisting of three main parts, Généralités, Science de la littérature, and Historie de la littérature. The first part is further divided into sections treating bibliographies, archives, and libraries; institutes, societies, and universities; colloquia; and editions and manuscripts. The second part is divided into four sections. The first is on general topics and methodology; the second includes the theory of literature (with subdivisions on general topics, theories of the literary work, aesthetics, theories of language and writing, and theories of genres). The third part contains sections on theoretical studies of literature and its relations to philosophy and ideology, history, sociology, science and technology, psychology and psychoanalysis, and ethnology and folklore. The fourth section is on comparative literature, with subdivisions on general topics; methodology; themes, symbols, and myths; literary relations; influences; and comparative studies concerned with individual works.

The third and final part of the classification, on literary history, is disposed into six sections treating general topics, periodization and related problems, classical literature, occidental literature, African literature, and literature of French-language island cultures. Editors refer users to the *Abstracta islamica* (L–150) and the *Revue bibliographique de sinologie* (L–164) for citations on Near or Far Eastern studies. Both the section on classical literature and that on occidental literature are further subdivided. The former is subdivided into general topics, the Near East, Egypt, Greece, Rome, and Byzantium. The latter is divided into nine subsections: general topics, the Romance domain, the Celtic domain, the Anglo-Saxon domain, the Germanic domain, the Scandinavian domain, the Slavic domain, Soviet but non-Slavic literatures, and a miscellaneous section. Each of these sections is then further divided into general, various national, and miscellaneous subsections.

Each quarterly issue also includes a list of indexed periodicals, an index of subjects and concepts, and an index of authors of abstracted articles. Both indexes are cumulated annually. Because the *Bulletin* is produced using a computerized data base, special individualized searches are available for order by interested researchers.

L–7 *LLINQUA: Language and Literature Index Quarterly.* Aachen: Cobra Verlag, 1980–.

Z7003.L35

This quarterly index to articles and book reviews analyzes some 500 periodicals. Entries are alphabetical by author or reviewer. Each issue contains an index of authors of reviewed books and an elaborate subject index that includes both authors and literary works as subjects.

L–8 Ruttkowski, Wolfgang. *Bibliographie der Gattungspoetik für den Studenten der Literaturwissenschaft / Bibliography of the Poetics of Literary Genres for the Student of Literature / Bibliographie de la poétique des genres littéraires pour l'étudiant de la littérature.* Munich: Max Hueber Verlag, 1973.

Z6511.R86

A short-title list of more than 3,000 books, dissertations, and articles in English, French, and German published, generally, during the period 1940–1970 which concern literary genre. The work is disposed into three parts. The first two present, respectively, a list of literary dictionaries that contain articles on genres and a list of works on literary genres in general. The third, main part enumerates works on individual literary genres, grouped into some 140 sections from Acrostic to Zauberspruch/Gebet. Actually, there are more than 800 genre terms treated in the volume, and the trilingual index of genres identifies which of the 140 sections contains materials on a particular genre, subgenre, or alternative genre name. There is also an index of authors.

See also Klaus W. von Hempfer, "Bibliographie zur Gattungspoetik (1): Allgemeine Gattungstheorie (1890–1971)," *ZFSL* 82 (1972): 53–66; as well as the notes and bibliography to Alastair Fowler, *Kinds of Literature: An Introduction to the Theory of Genres and Modes* (Cambridge: Harvard University Press, 1982) [PN45.5.F6]. Both the *ABELL* (M–21) and the *MLAIB* (L–50) cover the bibliography of genres and genre studies, perhaps most conveniently in the post 1980 "Genres and Literary Forms" section of the *MLAIB*.

L–9 **Scholarly Journals in Comparative and General Literature.**

Arcadia   *Arcadia: Zeitschrift für vergleichende Literaturwissenschaft.* Vol. 1–. Berlin: de Gruyter, 1966–. 3/yr. Reviews.   PN851.A7

CCrit   *Comparative Criticism: A Yearbook.* Vol. 1–. Cambridge: Cambridge University Press for the British Comparative Literature Association, 1979–. 1/yr. Reviews. "Bibliography of Comparative Literature in Britain [1975–]."   PN863.C58

CL   *Comparative Literature: Official Journal of the American Comparative Literature Association.* Vol. 1–. Eugene: University of Oregon, 1949–. 4/yr. Reviews. Cumulative index to vols. 1–15 (1949–1963).   PN851.C595

CLS   *Comparative Literature Studies.* Vol. 1–. Urbana: University of Illinois Press, 1964–. 4/yr. Reviews.   PN851.C63

East-West Center Review. Vol. 1–. Honolulu: East-West Center, 1964–.   AS9.E2

Genre   *Genre.* Vol. 1–. Norman: University of Oklahoma Press, 1968–. 4/yr. Reviews.   PN80.G4

Literature East and West: The Journal of the Conference on Oriental-Western Literary Relations of the MLA. Austin: University of Texas Press, 1954–. 4/yr. Reviews.   PN2.L67

Mosaic   *Mosaic: A Journal for the Comparative Study of Literature and Ideas.* Vol. 1–. Winnipeg: University of Manitoba Press, 1967–. 4/yr.   No LC number

Neohelicon: Acta Comparationis Litterarum Universarum. Vol. 1–. Budapest: Akademiai Kiado, 1973–. 4/yr.   PN851.N46

OL   *Orbis Litterarum: An International Review of Literary Studies / Revue international d'études littéraires.* Vol. 1–. Copenhagen: Munksgaard, 1943–. 4/yr. Reviews.   PN1.O7

RNL   *Review of National Literatures.* Vol. 1–. Whitestone, N.Y.: Council on National Literatures, 1970–. 1/yr. Reviews.   PN2.R44

RL   *Revue de littérature comparée*. Paris: Librairie M. Didier, 1921–1940, 1946–. 6/yr. Bibliographies. Reviews. Index cumulates every ten years; two vol. cumulation 1921–1950.   **PN851.R4**

RLMC   *Rivista di letterature moderne e comparate*. Vol. 1–. Florence: Sansoni, 1947–. 4/yr. Reviews. Contains the "Bibliografia delle pubblicazioni italiane [1945–]." 1946–.   **PN5.R5**

YCGL   *Yearbook of Comparative and General Literature*. Chapel Hill, N.C.: then Bloomington: Indiana University Press, 1952–. 1/yr. Reviews. Annual bibliography (see L–2).   **PN851.Y4**

YCC   *Yearbook of Comparative Criticism*. University Park: Pennsylvania State University Press, 1968–. Annual special number.   **LC numbers vary**

For a more detailed discussion of these and other periodicals see A. O. Aldridge et al., "International and New Periodicals in Comparative Literature," *YCGL* 17 (1968): 122–135. Note that many journals limited to periods or national literatures contain articles of importance to students of comparative and general literature. In particular, see the lists of scholarly journals in the fields of classical languages and literatures (L–48), modern languages and literatures (L–57), Romance languages and literatures (L–63), Germanic languages and literatures (L–108), Slavic and East European studies (L–128), African studies (L–138), Asian studies (L–148), Children's literature (L–179), Women's studies (L–189), English literature (M–25), Commonwealth literature (M–108), contemporary literature (R–18), American literature (S–18), poetry and poetics (T–8), drama (U–18), prose fiction (W–8), and literary theory and criticism (X–13).

L–10   **Some Frequently Recommended Works on Comparative, General, and World Literature.**

Aldridge, Alfred Owen, ed. *Comparative Literature: Matter and Method*. Urbana: University of Illinois Press, 1969.   **PN863.A6**

Bodmer, Martin. *Eine Bibliothek der Weltliteratur*. Zurich: Atlantis, 1947.   **Z989.B6A3**

————. *Variationen zum Thema Weltliteratur*. Frankfurt: Suhrkamp, 1956.   **PN514.B58**

Chadwick, H. M., and N. K. Chadwick. *Growth of Literature*. 3 vols. Cambridge: Cambridge University Press, 1932–1940.   **PN523.C5**

Friedrich, Werner P., ed. *Comparative Literature [Proceedings of the Second Congress of the International Comparative Literature Association]*. 2 vols. Chapel Hill: University of North Carolina Press, 1959.   **PN863 .I54**

Friedrich, Werner P., and David M. Malone. *Outline of Comparative Literature from Dante Alighieri to Eugene O'Neill*. Chapel Hill: University of North Carolina Press, 1954.   **PN871. F7**

Guérard, Albert L. *Preface to World Literature*: New York: Holt, 1940.   **PN523.G77**

Jost, François, ed. *Proceedings of the Fourth Congress of the International Comparative Literature Association, Fribourg, 1964*. 2 vols. The Hague: Mouton, 1966.   **PN863.I53**

Lausberg, H. *Handbuch der literarischen Rhetorik: Eine Grundlegung der Literaturwissenschaften*. (See X–60.)

McCormick, John O., ed. *Syllabus of Comparative Literature, Compiled by the Faculty of Comparative Literature, Livingston College, Rutgers University*. 2d ed. Metuchen, N.J.: Scarecrow Press, 1972.   **Z6511.L57**

Nichols, Stephen G., Jr., and Richard B. Vowles, eds. *Comparatists at Work: Studies in Comparative Literature*. Waltham, Mass.: Blaisdell, 1968.   **PN863.N5**

Prampolini, G. *Storia universale della letteratura*. 2d ed., rev. and enl. 7 vols. Turin: Unione tipografico-editrice torinese, 1948–1953.   **PN563.P712**

Proceedings of the Fifth Congress of the International Comparative Literature Association, Belgrade, 1967. Amsterdam: Swets and Zeitlinger, 1969.   **PN863.I52**

Queneau, Raymond, ed. *Histoire des littératures*. 2 vols. Paris: Encyclopédie de la Pléiade, 1955–1956.   **PN543.Q4**

Wais, Kurt K. T. *Beiträge zur vergleichenden Literaturgeschichte*. Tübingen: Niemeyer, 1972.   **PN863.B27**

————. *Europäische Literatur im Vergleich*. Tübingen: Niemeyer, 1983.   **PN874.W3 1983**

————. *Forschungsprobleme der vergleichende Literaturgeschichte*. 2 vols. Tübingen: Niemeyer, 1951–1958.   **PN863.F66**

Wehrli, Max. *Allgemeine Literaturwissenschaft*. 2d ed. Munich: Francke, 1969.   **PN441.W4 1969**

II.   GENERAL LITERARY DICTIONARIES, TERMINOLOGIES, AND SIMILAR REFERENCES

Dictionaries and companions devoted to one genre, one period, or, indeed, one author (see M–60 and S–50) may also prove more generally useful. See, for example, the *Handbook of Elizabethan and Stuart Literature* (O–16); handbooks and encyclopedias of modern world literature (R–25, R–27, R–28, and R–29); Deutsch, *Poetry Handbook* (T–50), Shapiro and Beum, *Prosody Handbook* (T–65); theater handbooks, reader's encyclopedias, and dictionaries (U–20 through U–27); film handbooks and encyclopedias (U–100 through U–109); various fiction handbooks (e.g., W–96, W–105); and handbooks of rhetoric and rhetorical terms (X–110, X–111, X–112, and X–117).

L–11   **Shipley, Joseph T., ed. *Dictionary of World Literary Terms: Criticism, Forms, Techniques*. Rev. ed. Boston: Writer, 1970.   PN41.S5 1970**

Originally published as the *Dictionary of World Literature* (New York, 1943), this work is a standard reference for definitions of literary terms, including terms of literary criticism and literary history. Names of literary forms and techniques and of literary schools and movements predominate. There are also historical surveys of literary criticism in England, America, France, Germany, Italy, Spain, Greece, Russia, as well as in Greco-Roman antiquity and in the medieval world. Many entries are signed by the 266 contributors; many articles have short bibliographies appended.

The work is in three parts. The first is a glossary of literary terms and is generally regarded as the most useful section. The second section contains the surveys of criticism. The third is a listing of critics and their works from countries not included in the surveys of part 2, listed by country and then in chronological order.

Somewhat differently conceived is Roger Fowler, ed., *Dictionary of Modern Critical Terms* (London: Routledge and Kegan Paul, 1973) [PN41.F6], which contains longish essays by some twenty-seven contributors on frequently encountered terms. Its goal is to display the potential uses of the term by offering extended essays in definition with comments on works that use the term and lists of readings pertinent to its study. It thus serves more nearly as an introduction to the study of modern critical terminology than as an authority for correct definitions, an intention which it declines as suspect. Essays are initialed and often have bibliographies appended.

John A. Cuddon's *Dictionary of Literary Terms* (London: André Deutsch, 1977) [PN41.C83] differs from both Shipley and Fowler in that relatively brief entries are all prepared by the compiler. The range of terms is extremely broad and includes technical terms; forms; genres; technicalities; groups, schools, and movements; well-known phrases; -isms; motifs or themes; personalities; and modes, attitudes and styles. A distinctive feature is the frequent indication of a term's etymology. Abundant illustrations and examples and extensive cross-references make this a convenient reference source. There are no bibliographies appended.

L–12 **Holman, C. Hugh, and William Harmon, eds. *Handbook to Literature: Based on the Original by William Flint Thrall and Addison Hibbard.*** 5th ed., rev. New York: Macmillan, 1986.   PN41.H6 1986

Originally published by Thrall and Hibbard in 1936, this handbook has become a standard guide to the terminology associated with the study of English and American literature. This edition is revised and updated to include the terminology of the most recent movements in literary and film criticism. Approximately 1,560 terms are included. Omitted are articles on individual authors and on individual literary works. Instead, entries cover critical and historical terms; rhetorical terms; genres, forms, and types; common allusions; styles; schools; literary movements; and leading literary periodicals and associations. Entries are relatively brief, running from a sentence to a few pages in length, and in this edition many now do include bibliographical guidance.

The following ten entry terms indicate the range of terms covered: Alazon, Allegory, Almanac, American Academy of Arts and Letters, Amerind Literature, Ana, Anathema, Ancients and Moderns, Angry Young Men, Anticlimax.

Appended to the dictionary of terms is a chronological "Outline of Literary History, English and American," giving dates and events of English literary history from the period of Celtic and Roman Britain (to A.D. 428) through 1979; from 1607 on, a parallel column presents the events of American literary history. The volume concludes with appendixes listing winners of Nobel and Pulitzer prizes. Another new feature of this edition is an Index of Proper Names, especially helpful because entry terms do not include personal names.

L–13 **Abrams, Meyer H. *Glossary of Literary Terms.*** 4th ed., rev. New York: Holt, Rinehart and Winston, 1981.
                                        PN44.5.A2 1981

Based on the original glossary of Dan S. Norton and Peters Rushton (1941), this glossary has become a standard undergraduate introduction to literary terms. It consists of essay definitions of major or general terms, arranged in alphabetical order, with less general minor terms included in the discussion. Examples and illustrations assist in the introduction; for further development, reference is made to a selected bibliography of standard treatments. The fourth edition adds recently current terminology (e.g., structuralism, speech-action theory, hermeneutics), incorporates revision of earlier essays, and presents updated and expanded bibliographies. The handy volume ends with an index to terms which incorporates a pronunciation guide.

Another valuable introductory glossary is that by Lee T. Lemon, *Glossary for the Study of English* (New York: Oxford University Press, 1971) [PN44.5.L4]. It is arranged topically, with terms presented and discussed in relation to one an-

other in the contexts of short essays in definition, themselves set within longer discursive chapters on fields within or relevant to English studies. The chapters are as follows: Literary Types; Elements of Narrative; Versification and Stanza Forms; Logical and Rhetorical Terms; A Brief Linguistics Lexicon; Of Books and Bookmaking; General Literary Terms; and Literary Groups, Periods, Movements, and Styles. An alphabetical index of terms permits dictionary access, but the distinctive feature of this glossary is that the common senses of a term are given within a framework that identifies the conceptual distinctions for the sake of which the terminological distinctions exist. It is thus a particularly valuable aid for the beginning student because it works against the tendency to memorize a set of terms and definitions rather than learn to use and distinguish a set of interrelated concepts.

There are dozens of other dictionaries of literary terms designed for the use of undergraduate students. Among those that are generally cited are *Dictionary of Literary, Dramatic, and Cinematic Terms* by Sylvan Barnet, Morton Berman, and William Burto, 2d ed. (Boston: Little, Brown, 1971) [PN44.5.B3]; *Literary Terms: A Dictionary*, rev. and enl. ed., ed. K. Beckson and A. Ganz (New York: Farrar, Strauss, 1975) [PN41.B33]; A. Lazarus et al., *Modern English: A Glossary of Literature and Language* (New York: Grosset and Dunlap, 1971) [PN43.M77]; *Literary Criticism: A Glossary of Major Terms* by Patrick Murray (New York: Longman, 1978) [PN43.M77]; and *Dictionary of Literary Terms* by Harry Shaw (New York: McGraw-Hill, 1972) [PN44.5.S46]. Barnet, Berman, and Burto includes cinematic terms; Beckson and Ganz have an appendix arranging the 1,000 terms by subject areas; Lazarus et al. includes terms in rhetoric and language, with specific references; Murray is very selective, while Shaw's more than 2,000 entries include terms from journalism, television, film, and the stage.

L–14 **Ruttkowski, Wolfgang, and R. E. Blake. *Glossary of Literary Terms in English, German, and French, with Greek and Latin Derivations of Terms for the Student of General and Comparative Literature.*** Bern: Francke, 1969.
                                        PN44.5.R8

Trilingual tables of some 780 of the most important terms in each of the three languages, with some Italian and Spanish terms included. Arrangement is in five sections: (1) metrics, meter, versification, prosody; (2) style and rhetoric; (3) structure/technique; (4) genre/kind/type; (5) periods/movements. Entries give antonyms, synonyms, and subordinate terms. They may supply etymologies for Greek and Latin roots. There are abundant cross-references and indexes in German, English, and French.

Another multilingual dictionary of terms is the *Liberal Arts Dictionary in English, French, German and Spanish*, ed. Mario A. Pei and Frank Gaynor (New York: Philosophical Library, 1952) [PB333.P4], which contains definitions of literary, artistic, and philosophical terms with reference to corresponding terms in the other languages. There is a full index of foreign-language terms. A third such polyglot dictionary is by Saad Elkhadem, *York Dictionary of English–French–German-Spanish Literary Terms and Their Origin* (Fredericton, New Brunswick: York Press, 1976) [PN41.E4].

For Russian terminology see Anthony W. Mlikotin, *Dictionary of Russian Literary Terminology and an English-Russian Glossary of Literary Terms* (Los Angeles: University of Southern California, 1968) [PN44.5.M55] which has a preface surveying the difficulties of relating the Russian and Anglo-American critical traditions, followed by a dictionary of articles on the major terms of Russian literary criticism. This is followed by a glossary of English terms and reference to the Russian term or terms that refer to more or less comparable entities.

There are, of course, a large number of foreign-language dictionaries and handbooks of literary terminology. Among the most frequently recommended are the French works *Lexique de la terminologie linguistique, français, allemand, anglais, italien* by Jules Marouzeau, 3d ed. (Paris: Geuthner, 1951) [P152.M3 1951]; the *Dictionnaire de poétique et de rhétorique* by Henri Morier (Paris: Presses universitaires de France, 1961) [PN1021.M6]; and the *Dictionnaire international des termes littéraires* published by the Association internationale de litterature comparée (Paris: Mouton, 1973) [PN44.5.E8]. In Italian see the *Dizionario di termini della critica letteraria, con l' aggiunta di termini della metrica, della stilistica e della retorica classicistica* by R. Berardi (Florence: Le Monnier, 1968) [PC1691.B4 1968]. In German see the *Sachwörterbuch der Literatur* by Gero von Wilpert, 6th ed., rev. and enl. (Stuggart: Kroner, 1979) [PN41.W5 1979], and Egon Werlich, *Wörterbuch der Textinterpretation* (Dortmund: Lensing, 1969) [PE1129.G3 W45].

L–15 Guide to the Study of Individual Literary Terms.

A plausible first step in studying a single literary term is to look it up in a number of standard dictionaries of literature and in both literary and general encyclopedias, such as the *Dictionary of World Literary Terms* (L–11), the *Princeton Encyclopedia of Poetry and Poetics* (L–21), *Cassell's Encyclopedia of World Literature* (L–20), the *Encyclopaedia Britannica* (A–40), the *New Catholic Encyclopedia* (A–65), and the *Encyclopedia of the Social Sciences* (A–60). Such consultation will provide both orientation and the beginnings of a working bibliography.

The *MLA International Bibliography* (L–50) uses some literary terms in its system of classification, as does the annual bibliography in the *Yearbook of Comparative and General Literature* (L–2). Checking these will extend the bibliography into current work.

For historical information about English terms, consult the *OED* (I–33); many terms are treated in historical or systematic context in various works on the history and theory of literary criticism (see section X).

There are several enumerative bibliographies of articles defining individual literary terms. Edward D. Seeber, "On Defining Terms," in Stallknecht and Frenz, *Comparative Literature: Method and Perspective* (see L–4), pp. 58–83, includes the following terms in his bibliography: baroque, burlesque, catharsis, classicism, conceit, creative, enthusiasm, expressionism, fancy, futurism, genius, gothic, grotesque, idea, imagination, imitation, impressionism, influence, invention, mannerism, metaphysical poets, myth, natural goodness, naturalism, nature, novel, originality, parody, pastiche, picaresque, picturesque, Pre-Raphaelitism, progress, realism, reason, relativism, rococo, satire, sense, situation, stream of consciousness, sublime, surrealism, symbol, taste, travesty, *ut pictura poesis*, virtue, vorticism, and wit.

A similar bibliography, "Key Terms and Concepts," is included in Bateson and Meserole's *Guide to English and American Literature* (A–13). The terms cited there include: classicism, courtesy, culture, dissociation of sensibility, gothic, grotesque, image, imagination, irony, nature, novelty, picturesque, plenitude, primitivism, realism, romanticism, sentimental, simplicity, sincerity, sublime, and wit.

In addition, the *Critical Idiom Series* published by Methuen has provided since 1969 a number of useful monographs on key terms and concepts. To date, volumes have been published on the following terms: The Absurd; Aestheticism; Allegory; The Ballad; Biography; Burlesque; Classicism; Comedy; Comedy of Manners; The Conceit; Dada and Surrealism; Drama and the Dramatic; Dramatic Monologue; The Epic; Expressionism; Farce; Genre; The Grotesque; Irony and the Ironic; Melodrama; Metaphor; Metre, Rhyme and Free Verse; Modern Verse Drama; Modernism; Myth Naturalism; The Ode; Pastoral; The Picaresque; Plot; Primitivism; Realism; Rhetoric; The Romance; Romanticism; Satire; The Short Story; The Sonnet; The Stanza; Symbolism; and Tragedy.

Among other works that focus exclusively or predominantly on the definition of several important literary terms, see the following:

Crane, R. S. *Idea of the Humanities and Other Essays Critical and Historical.* 2 vols. Chicago: University of Chicago Press, 1967. Ancients and moderns, the man of feeling, progress. PN50.C7

————, ed. *Critics and Criticism.* Chicago: University of Chicago Press, 1957. New Criticism, Imitation, Plot. PN81.C8 1957

Hipple, Walter J. *Beautiful, the Sublime, and the Picturesque in Eighteenth-Century British Aesthetic Theory.* Carbondale: Southern Illinois University Press, 1957. BH221.G72 H5

Levin, Harry. *Gates of Horn: A Study of Five French Realists.* New York: Oxford University Press, 1963. Realism, romance. PQ637.R4 L4

————. *Perspectives of Criticism.* Cambridge: Harvard University Press, 1950. Convention. PN85.L47

Lewis, C. S. *Studies in Words.* Cambridge: Cambridge University Press, 1960. Conscious, nature, sense, simple, wit. PE1585.L4

Lovejoy, A. O. *Essays in the History of Ideas.* Baltimore: Johns Hopkins University Press, 1948. Classicism, gothic, nature, romanticism. B945.L583 E7

Smith, Logan P. *Four Words: Romantic, Originality, Creative, Genius.* Oxford: Clarendon Press, 1924. PE1011.S6 no. xvii

Wellek, René. *Concepts of Criticism.* New Haven: Yale University Press, 1963. Baroque, realism, romanticism. PN85.W38

————. *Discriminations: Further Concepts of Criticism.* New Haven: Yale University Press, 1970. Classicism, symbolism. PN81.W36

Williamson, George. *Seventeenth Century Contexts.* London: Faber and Faber, 1960. Enthusiasm, mutability, strong lines, wit. PR543.W5 1960

Wood, Theodore E. B. *Word 'Sublime' and Its Context, 1650–1760.* The Hague: Mouton, 1972. BH301.S7 W66

L–20 *Cassell's Encyclopedia of World Literature.* John Buchanan Brown, general editor. 2d ed., rev. and enl., 3 vols. London: Cassell; New York: William Morrow, 1973. PN41.C3 1973

Originally published in 1953 in two volumes, this work, treating some eighty literatures of the world, has been prepared by more than 250 contributors. It is in three sections. Volume 1 contains 555 long signed articles on the histories of the individual national literatures of the world and on general literary subjects including terms, genres, schools, movements, themes, and topics. Bibliographies of standard works are appended. Volumes 2 and 3 contain some 9,000 initialed biographical articles with assessments of an author's significance and bibliographies of primary and secondary works.

Among other major encyclopedias of world literature is the *Lexikon der Weltliteratur*, ed. Gero von Wilpert, 2d ed., rev. and enl., 2 vols. (Stuttgart: Kroner, 1975–) [PN41.W8 1975]. Volume 1, first published in 1963, is the *Biographisch-bibliographisches Handwörterbuch nach Autoren und anonymen Werken* and contains brief biographies by about fifty-six contributors of some 10,000 authors, with primary bibliographies and brief secondary bibliographies. Volume 2, published in 1968 (second edition in preparation), treats about 4,000 *Hauptwerke der Weltliteratur in Charakteristiken und Kurzinterpretationen*. It is arranged by titles and gives the author and date of the work, a summary and/or a description, and a secondary bibliography. There is an index of authors whose works are cited.

Another frequently cited, distinctively organized encyclopedia of world literature is Hans Wilhelm Eppelsheimer, *Handbuch der Weltliteratur von den Anfängen bis zur Gegenwart*, 3d ed., rev. and enl., 2 vols. (Frankfurt: Klostermann, 1960) [PN551.E66 1960]. This work, first published in 1937, emphasizes western European literature, presenting brief biographies and selected bibliographies. It is arranged by broad geographical and chronological divisions, as follows: East Asia, India, the Ancient Near East, Islam, Greece and Rome, the Middle Ages, Europe (further divided by century and country). Within each of these divisions a brief introduction to the literature of that time and place is given, followed by bibliographical essays, biographical sketches of leading authors, and lists of editions, translations, and important criticism of their works. Specially recommended items are starred. The volume concludes with two valuable bibliographical appendixes, the first on general and national literatures, the second on forms, motifs, types, and genres. There is an index of authors and titles of anonymous works.

The most frequently cited French-language encyclopedia of world literature is that by Philippe van Tieghem and P. Josserand, *Dictionnaire des littératures*, 3 vols. (Paris: Presses universitaires de France, 1968) [PN41.V26], with more than 20,000 articles on authors, anonymous works, terms, themes, genres, literary schools and movements, and the national literatures of the world. There are brief bibliographies appended to the articles, and there is a more extensive, general bibliography at the end of volume 3, along with an author index.

Among earlier encyclopedias the ones most likely to be consulted with profit are Erich Frauwallner et al., *Die Weltliteratur: Biographisches, literarhistorisches, und bibliographisches Lexicon in Übersichten und Stichwörtern*, 3 vols. (Vienna: Hollinek, 1951–1954) [PN41.W4]; *Ergänzungsbänd* 1–2 (1968–1970); Gustave Louis Vapereau, *Dictionnaire universel des littératures contenant: I. Des notices sur les écrivains de tous les temps et de tous le pays; II. La théorie et l'historique des différents genres de poésie et de prose; III. La bibliographie générale et particulière . . .*, 2d ed. (Paris: Hachette, 1876) [PN41.V3]; and Johann Georg Theodor Grässe, *Lehrbuch einer allgemeinen Literärgeschichte aller bekannten Völker der Welt, von der ältesten bis auf die neueste Zeit*, 4 vols. in 11 (Dresden and Leipzig: Arnoldische Buchhandlung, 1837–1859) [PN553.G7].

For encyclopedic dictionaries treating the world literature of particular periods or genres, see the entries for that period or genre.

L–21 *Princeton Encyclopedia of Poetry and Poetics.* Edited by Alex Preminger, Frank J. Warnke, and O. B. Hardison, Jr. 2d ed., rev. and enl. Princeton, N.J.: Princeton University Press, 1974.   PN1021.E5 1974

This work, first published in 1965, contains some 1,000 signed authoritative articles by some 240 contributors. Articles range in length from a few sentences to more than 20,000 words and treat poetic schools, terms, movements, and national literatures. The category of poetry and poetics is understood to include the history of poetics, its techniques, poetics and criticism, and poetry in its relations to other aspects of culture. No articles are included which treat individual authors or works. The 1975 edition adds an 84-page supplement that includes both additional entries and added materials for some existing entries.

L–22 **Shipley, Joseph T.** *Encyclopedia of Literature.* 2 vols. New York: Philosophical Library, 1946.   PN41.S52

This work, complementing Shipley's *Dictionary of World Literature* (L–11), presents in the first volume a series of histories surveying the national literatures of the world, alphabetically by country, with bibliographies of literary histories appended. Volume 2 includes a biographical dictionary of world authors.

Another volume containing specialist surveys of world literatures is the *World through Literature*, ed. Charlton Laird (New York: Appleton-Century-Crofts, 1951) [PN501.L3], which includes bibliographies (often with descriptive annotation) appended to each survey of a national or regional body of literature.

A more recent comprehensive and authoritative work is the volume edited by Wolfgang von Einsiedel, *Die Literatur der Welt in ihrer mündlichen und schriftlichen Überlieferung* (Zurich: Kindler, 1964) [PN593.E45]. Some seventy contributors present concise signed articles with appended bibliographies surveying 150 oral and written literatures of all times and places. Less known literatures are more fully treated, making this volume the source for the most adequate available surveys of such obscure literatures as Sorb, Romany, and Eskimo.

L–23 **Bénet, William Rose.** *Reader's Encyclopedia: An Encyclopedia of World Literature and the Arts.* 2d ed. New York: Crowell, 1965.   PN41.B4 1965

First published in 1948 with a 1955 supplement, this work is designed as a companion to reading, and features some 25,000 brief articles on topics likely to be inquired about in the course of reading world literature. Modeled, with respect to scope, on Brewer's *Dictionary of Phrase and Fable* (K–18), Bénet contains information on authors, major works, notable figures including artists, philosophers, and musicians, literary terms, historical events, allusions of all sorts, plots, characters, and various other items somehow associated with the literatures of all nations and periods or with one or more of the ancillary fields of aesthetics, science, philosophy, economics, and politics. There are summaries of texts, plots, and arguments. A particular use of the work results from its inclusion of articles on a disproportionately large number of minor American writers.

Another reader's encyclopedia is the *Reader's Companion to World Literature*, ed. Calvin S. Brown, 2d ed., rev. Lillian Horstein et al. (New York: New American Library, 1973) [PN41.R4 1973], originally published in 1956. It is a pocketbook companion for undergraduate readers. Entries are primarily on major authors and works of world literature, with additional entries on literary types and terms, mythological figures, and literary periods and movements. Biographical articles treat minor works and refer to entries on major works. There is no index.

L–24 *Penguin Companion to Literature.* 4 vols. Harmondsworth, England: Penguin, 1969–1971.   LC numbers vary

This work is conceived as a set of four independent reader's companions, as follows:

Vol. 1. *Penguin Companion to Literature: Britain and the Commonwealth [including French Canada]*. Edited by David Daiches (1971).   PN849.C5 P4

Vol. 2. *Penguin Companion to European Literature*. Edited by Anthony K. Thorlby (1964).   PN41.P43 1971

Vol. 3. *Penguin Companion to United States and Latin American Literature*. Edited by Malcolm Bradbury, Eric Mottram, and Jean Franco (1971).   PN843.P4

Vol. 4. *Penguin Companion to Classical and Byzantine, Oriental and African Literatures*. Edited by Donald R. Dudley [classical and Byzantine] and David M. Lang [Oriental and African] (1971).   PA31.P4

While some of the initialed articles treat movements, anonymous works, genres and types, and period terms, the majority are about authors. Thus this is more nearly a biobibliography of world literature. Major works are briefly described and available editions and translations are cited, along with selected works of criticism in brief one- or two-paragraph appended bibliographies. Volume 2 ends with a convenient guide to entries by language and country. All authors writing in each language are listed in chronological order. Entries give author's birth and death dates and nonliterary profession or literary specialization.

L–25 ***Dizionario letterario Bompiani delle opere e dei personnaggi di tutti i tempi e di tutte le letterature.*** 9 vols. Milan: Bompiani, 1947–1952.   PN41.D5

The first seven volumes of this work consist of long, signed articles on works of literature, art, and music of all times and places. Entries are arranged alphabetically by the Italian form of their title followed by the original title in brackets. In addition, the first half of volume 1 contains fifty-eight long essays on chief intellectual and literary movements. Regular articles give brief histories of the works, summarize them, critically estimate their significance, and present bibliographies of editions, critical studies, adaptations, and important translations. There are brief biographical notes provided in entries, but no separate author articles. The work is elaborately illustrated.

Volume 8, *Personnaggi*, is a list of characters from the literature of all times and places in alphabetical order by the Italian form of their names. Characters are described, the works enumerated in which they appear, and their significance discussed. Volume 9 presents chronological tables of all literatures and a full index of titles in their original language, with the Italian equivalent given. Volume 9 also contains an index of authors and illustrators with the Italian form of the name given when that differs from the original. A two-volume supplement, *Appendice*, was published 1964–1966; it is arranged in parallel with the original *Dizionario* and adds some 25,000 entries on twentieth-century works. The complementary *Dizionario letterario Bompiani degli autori* (L–27) provides comparably full and authoritative articles on authors of all times and places. Bompiani has been translated into French (see below), German (see below), Hebrew, Portuguese, Serbo-Croatian, and Spanish.

For contemporary literature (that is, literature from about 1870 to 1960), there is a parallel publication designed to supplement Bompiani, the five-volume *Dizionario universale della letteratura contemporanea* (Milan: Mondadori, 1959–1963) [PN41.D53]. This work includes long, elaborately illustrated, signed articles on titles, authors, literary movements, and national literatures. Very full primary and secondary bibliographies are included. The fifth volume includes chronological tables for 1870–1961 and indexes to authors, titles, translations, foreign works not translated into Italian, and literary surveys by country or period.

A French-language text, based upon the original Bompiani but abridged, was published in 1958: *Dictionnaire des oeuvres de tous les temps et de tous les pays: Littérature, philosophie, musique, sciences*, ed. Robert Laffont and Valentino Bompiani, 5 vols. (Paris: Société d'éditions de dictionnaires et encyclopédies [SEDE], 1952–1968) [AE25.O52]. The work omits the first volume's articles on literary and intellectual movements and the eighth volume's dictionary of

characters but is otherwise based on the Italian original, though it differs in format and arrangement. There are over 20,000 entries for works, under the French form of their titles. A *Supplement* volume, consisting of addenda and an author index, was published in 1959. In the same series SEDE published a one-volume *Dictionnaire des oeuvres contemporaines de tous les temps et de tous les pays* (1967) [AG25 .D524], which is based on the title entries in the *Dizionario universale della letteratura contemporanea* for works of authors who died after 1955 or who were born after 1910. It has no author index. In addition, a French-languageage version of the *Personnaggi* volume was published as the *Dictionnaire des personnages littéraires et dramatiques de tous les temps et tous les pays: Poésie, théâtre, roman, musique*, ed. Robert Laffont and Valentino Bompiani (1960) [PN41.D485]. This elaborately illustrated volume contains cross-references to the *Dictionnaire des oeuvres*. In addition, a one-volume abridgment of the full series was published: Pierre Clarac, ed., *Laffont-Bompiani Dictionnaire universel des lettres* (1961) [PN41 .D488].

The German-language *Kindlers Literatur Lexikon*, 2d ed., ed. Wolfgang von Einsiedel et al., 12 vols. (Zurich: Kindler Verlag, 1971) [PN44.K54 1971], was also inspired by the *Dizionario*, though it is a new work rather than a German translation/adaptation. But the editors had access to and made use of both the original and the Laffont-Bompiani series. Initialed entries are by the title of the work only, usually in the original language, and give a brief history, a précis of the plot, and a bibliography of editions, critical works, adaptations, and translations. Works of both Eastern and Western literature are included, with an emphasis on the contemporary. The first volume includes an appendix of some 130 general articles on the literatures of individual countries, areas, and languages. Each volume contains indexes of authors with dates and titles of their works and of anonymous titles, collected works, and generic entry-terms. Volume 12 in the 1971 edition contains a *Supplement* and a series of general indexes of authors and works; of anonymous works, collective works, and generic entry-terms; titles in German with reference to the original form under which they are entered in the dictionary proper; and an index to the general articles in volume 1. The general indexes incorporate supplement entries.

L–27 ***Dizionario letterario Bompiani degli autori di tutti i tempi e di tutte le letterature.*** 3 vols. Milan: Bompiani, 1956-1957.   Z1010.D5

This work provides a companion set to the *Dizionario . . . delle opere e dei personaggi* (L–25). Biographical and critical sketches are presented for some 6,000 authors of all places and times. Bibliographies include only important primary works. There are abundant illustrations. A two-volume *Appendice* was published 1964–1966.

The French-language series includes a translation/adaptation under the title *Dictionnaire biographique des auteurs de tous les temps et de tous les pays*, ed. Robert Laffont and Valentino Bompiani, 2d ed., 2 vols. (Paris: SEDE, 1964) [PN41.D48]. It includes extensive cross–references to the *Dictionnaire des oeuvres* (see L–25).

L–29 ***Neues Handbuch der Literaturwissenschaft.*** Ed. Klaus von See. 23 vols. Frankfurt and then Wiesbaden: Akademische Verlagsgesellschaft [later AULA Verlag], 1972–.
     PN553.N48

This multivolume handbook is designed to replace the *Handbuch der Literaturwissenschaft* published in Berlin, 1923–1943 [PN553.H3]. Like its predecessor, this handbook has been produced by a group of specialists in each of the major literatures of the world. Individual volumes are discursive histories of the literature that is their subject, with chronologies, names and titles of literary works, maps and illustrations, and bibliographies, generally both at the ends of chapters and at the end of each volume.

Individual volumes and their authors are as follows:

Vol. 1. Rollig, Wolfgang, *Altorientalische Literaturen* (1978).

Vol. 2. Vogt, Ernst. *Griechische Literatur* (1981).

Vol. 3. Fuhrmann, Manfred. *Romische Literatur* (1974).

Vol. 4. In preparation.

Vol. 5. In preparation.

Vol. 6. Von See, Klaus. *Europäisches Frühmittelalter* (1985).

Vol. 7. Krauss, Henning. *Europäisches Hochmittelalter* (1981).

Vol. 8. Erzgräber, Willi. *Europäisches Spätmittelalter* (1978).

Vols. 9–10. Buck, August. *Renaissance und Barock* (1972–).

Vols. 11–13. Hinck, Walter. *Europäische Aufklärung* (1974–1984).

Vols. 14–16. Heitmann, Klaus. *Europäische Romantik* (1982–1985).

Vol. 17. Lauer, Reinhard. *Europäische Realismus* (1980).

Vols. 18–19. Kreuzer, Helmut. *Jahrhundertende, Jahrhundertwende* (1976–).

Vol. 20. Koebner, Thomas. *Zwischen den Weltkriegen* (1983).

Vols. 21–22. Hermand, Jost. *Literatur nach 1945.* Vol. 1: *Politische und regionale Aspekte*, Vol. 2: *Themen und Genres* (1979).

Vol. 23. Debon, Günther. *Ostasiatische Literaturen* (1984).

L–30 **Havlice, Patricia Pate. *Index to Literary Biography.*** 2 vols. Metuchen, N.J.: Scarecrow Press, 1975.   Z6511.H38

Indexed are some fifty leading biographical dictionaries, both English–language and foreign. About 68,000 authors are cited, with real name, pseudonyms, dates, nationality, and type or writing specialization (e.g., nonfiction, journalism, fiction, poetry, essays, juveniles, criticism, plays, translations). Codes are then given to the biographical dictionaries with articles about that author. The work is thus a quick reference to readily available biographical information on authors of world literature. There are no cross-references from real names to pseudonyms and the reverse.

An earlier index is that by Richard E. Combs, *Authors: Critical and Biographical References: A Guide to 4,700 Critical and Biographical Passages in Books* (Metuchen, N.J.: Scarecrow, 1971) [PN524.C58], which analyzes nearly 500 books for references to more than 1,400 authors. The list of books is uneven, with a bias toward works citing modern authors and novelists.

L–31 **Author Biographies Master Index [ABMI]: A Consolidated Guide to Biographical Information Concerning Authors Living and Dead As It Appears in a Selection of the Principal Biographical Dictionaries Devoted to Authors, Poets, Journalists, and Other Literary Figures.** Edited by Dennis LaBeau. 2 vols. Detroit: Gale Research Co., 1978.
No LC number

This index is parallel in structure but not in content to the *Biographical Dictionaries Master Index* (G–2). It directs users to entries in some 140 English-language biographical dictionaries specializing in authors and writers of all times and places. More than 416,000 references to some 238,000 authors are cited. Some standardization of spelling has occurred in the editorial process, but alternate spellings of an author's name should be checked.

L–33 **Patterson, Margaret C. *Author Newsletters and Journals: An International Annotated Bibliography of Serial Publications Concerned with the Life and Works of Individual Authors.*** Detroit: Gale Research Co., 1979.
Z6513.P37

This annotated guide treats 1,129 serials that publish bibliographies, biographical information, criticism, textual studies, reviews, and related scholarship on the life and works of a single author. The titles enumerated treat a total of 435 authors from twenty-eight countries.

The main body, authors and their periodicals, lists authors alphabetically by name with cross-references from pseudonyms. Under each author, periodicals are listed alphabetically and numbered. For each author entry, birth and death dates, nationality, and areas of interest are given. For each cited periodical, the more recent title is the main entry, with earlier titles given. Further information includes standard abbreviations of the title, the editor's, the sponsor's, and publisher's name and address, the date of first publication, frequency, price, approximate number of pages, circulation figures, and the latest issue examined. Further annotation includes the character of a periodical's contents, language if not English, availability of reprints, indexing information, and information on alternate titles.

The main body is followed by an addendum of titles located after the guide was in press. The volume concludes with a title index preceded by a series of seven valuable appendixes: Countries and Their Authors (listing also the number of periodicals cited for each); Centuries and Their Authors; Sponsoring Institutions (with all societies and *Gesellschaften* grouped under the generic heads "Societies" and "Gesellschaften"); Indexing and Abstracting Services, Annual and Quarterly Bibliographies (listing forty-two services and then listing for each the author periodicals which they regularly analyze); Publishers (with addresses); a Glossary of Foreign Terms; and a List of Sources Consulted with their abbreviations. All in all, this volume is a splendidly conceived and extremely well executed attempt to fill a significant bibliographical gap; it is a primary reference for the serious bibliographical study of an author.

The work has been updated by two supplements in *Serials Review* 8.4 (1982): 61–72; 10.1 (1984): 51–59.

III. CLASSICAL STUDIES

See also section F, History; section N, Medieval; section I.VIII, Translation of Medieval Texts; the *Greek and Latin Literatures . . . in English Translation* (I–120); many entries in section K, Literary Materials and Contexts; the *Penguin Companion to Classical, Oriental and African Literatures* (L–24); section O.VI, Neo-Latin Studies; section X.II, the History of Literary Criticism and Literary Theory; and entries in section Y.II on textual criticism.

L–40 **McGuire, Martin R. P. *Introduction to Classical Scholarship: Syllabus and Bibliographical Guide.*** New, rev. ed. Washington, D.C.: Catholic University of America Press, 1961.   Z7016.M25 1961

This student's guide is divided into four parts, beginning with a discursive introduction to classical scholarship which includes discussion of the history, scope, and definition of the field and cites relevant readings. Part II is concerned with the main divisions of classical scholarship and discursively introduces each, citing relevant readings. The divisions specified are as follows: 1. Bibliography; 2. History of Classical Scholarship; 3. Criticism and Hermeneutics; 4. The History of Greek and Latin Literature; 5. Language and Style: Grammar, Lexicography, Rhetoric and Poetics, Metrics and Prose

Rhythm; 6. Music and Dancing; 7. Greek and Latin Epigraphy; 8. Papyrology and Greek and Latin Palaeography; 9. Ancient Geography and Topography; 10. Political and Cultural History of Antiquity; 11. Greek and Roman Law; 12. Chronology; 13. Metrology and Numismatics; 14. Archaeology and the Plastic and Graphic Arts; 15. Religion, Mythology and Magic; 16. Philosophy; 17. The Sciences, Mathematics, Medicine, and Technology. Part III concerns preprofessional matters anticipating a career of teaching and research. The discussion is in four parts, treating philological training, postdoctoral study, teaching, and postdoctoral research respectively, with readings cited. The final part of this guide is a Select Bibliography of Ancient History and of Greek and Latin Literature, including the Early History and Literature of Christianity. It is divided into seven sections, presenting sheer lists of titles in the following categories: 1. Bibliography, Periodicals, General Reference Works; 2. General Ancient History, Prehistory, and the History of the Near East; 3. Select Bibliography of Greek History; 4. Select Bibliography of Greek Literature, Philosophy, and Science; 5. Select Bibliography of Roman History; 6. Select Bibliography of Latin Literature; and 7. The Early History and Literature of Christianity.

Though somewhat out of date, this slim volume remains a model student bibliographical guide.

L–41 **von Pauly, August Friedrich. *Paulys Real–Encyclopädie der klassischen Altertumswissenschaft [R-E].*** Neue Bearbeitung begonnen von Georg Wissowa. Stuttgart: Metzler, 1894–1976.   DE5.P33

The basic scholarly reference work in the field of classical studies, this massive encyclopedia provides comprehensive, signed articles with biographies appended on all aspects of classical civilization, including history, geography, archaeology, and literature. It was published in two main series, the first (A-Q) with twenty-four volumes (in 32 parts) and the second (R-Z) with 10 volumes (in 18 parts). In addition, 15 supplementary volumes have been published from 1903 to date, as well as a series of "Sonderausgaben" on special topics extracted from the *R-E* itself. The work in its entirety presents thousands of columns with densely packed information on all aspects of classical antiquity.

A revised, concise edition in five volumes, *Der kleine Pauly: Lexikon der Antike auf der Grundlage von Pauly's Realencyclopädie* was edited by Konrat Ziegler et al. (Stuttgart: Druckenmüller, 1964–1975) [DE5.K5]. It contains signed articles by ninety-nine contributors which condense information to approximately 20 percent of that found in the original work.

The best sources in English of similar kinds of information are Leonard Whibley, ed., *Companion to Greek Studies*, 4th ed., rev. (Cambridge: Cambridge University Press, 1905) [DF77.W5 1931], and J. E. Sandys, *Companion to Latin Studies*, 3d ed. (Cambridge: Cambridge University Press, 1921) [DG77.S3 1921], as well as the two volumes by Herbert Jennings Rose, *Handbook of Greek Literature from Homer to the Age of Lucian*, 4th ed. (London: Methuen, 1950) [PA3052.R6 1950], and *Handbook of Latin Literature from the Earliest Times to the Death of St. Augustine* 3d ed. (London: Methuen, 1954) [PA6003.R6], and particularly the *Oxford Classical Dictionary* (L–42).

Two French-language reference works are to be recommended. L. Laurand's *Manuel des études grecques et latines*, new ed., rev. A. Lauras, 2 vols. (Paris: Picard, 1955–1957) [PA93.L3 1955] includes concise, systematically arranged articles with bibliographies on all aspects of classical antiquity. And for information on customs, daily life, and social and cultural history, excluding literature, see C. Daremberg and E. Saglio, *Dictionnaire des antiquités grecques et romaines, d'après les textes et les monuments, contenant l'explication des termes qui se rapportent aux moeurs, aux institutions, à la*

religion . . . et en général à la vie publique et privée des anciens, 6 vols. (Paris: Hachette, 1873–1919) [D15.D18]. The work has signed articles and indexes of authors, Greek words, Latin words, and subjects in the sixth, index volume.

Another German-language reference work of major importance is the three-volume *Einleitung in die Altertumswissenschaft*, ed. A. Gercke and E. Norden, 2d ed. (Leipzig: Teubner, 1912–1914) [PA91.G42]. Volume 1, concerned with the history of classical philology and related topics, contains 11 parts; parts 1–10 have appeared in a third edition (1921–1927). Volume 2 treats topics in private life, the arts, religion, science, and philosophy; its parts 1–6 have appeared in a fourth edition (1930–1933). Volume 3, finally, concerns history and public antiquities; parts 2, 3, and 5 were published in a third edition (1932–1933).

Finally, there is the *Handbuch der klassischen Altertumswissenschaft*, ed. Iwan von Müller, 9 vols. in 31 (Munich: Beck, 1892–1920) [PA25.H25]; the revised edition, titled *Handbuch der Altertumswissenschaft*, under the general direction first of W. Otto and then H. Bengtson, has been in course of publication since 1923 [PA25 .H24]. To date there are some forty volumes, divided into twelve sections, as follows: I. Introductory and Auxiliary Disciplines (including the history of scholarship, criticism, and hermeneutics); II. Greek and Latin Grammar; III. History and Geography; IV. Politics, Society, Private Life, Military History, and Theater; V. Philosophy, Mathematics, Science, Religion, and Magic; VI. Archaeology; VII. the History of Greek Literature; VIII. the History of Roman Literature; IX. the Classical Tradition; X. the History of Law in Antiquity; XI. (open); and XII. a Handbook on Byzantine Civilization. Most volumes in this series have gone through numerous editions and remain the standard references on their subjects. Thus Wilhelm Schmid and Otto Stählin's *Geschichte der griechischen Literatur*, volume 7 in the *Handbuch*, 3 vols. (Munich: Beck, 1929–1940) [PA25 .H24 Abt. 7, T.1], is the standard authority on Greek literary history, as Martin Schanz, *Geschichte der römischen Literatur bis zum Gesetzgebungswerk des Kaisers Justinian . . .*, 4th ed. rev. and enl. by Carl Hosius, volume 8 in the *Handbuch*, 2 vols. (Munich: Beck, 1927–1935), is the standard authority on Roman literary history.

A new work, the *Cambridge History of Classical Literature*, is now in production. Volume 2, *Latin Literature*, ed. by E. J. Kenney, was the first to be published (Cambridge: Cambridge University Press, 1982) [PA6003.L3]. It consists of chapters written by contributing scholars. An "Appendix of Authors and Works" includes biographical, bio-bibliographical, and bibliographical information. A five-volume paperback edition of this volume has also been issued. Volume 1, *Greek Literature*, ed. by P. E. Easterling and B. M. W. Knox, appeared in 1985 [PA3052.G73 1985]. A paperback edition of this volume is also being issued.

L–42 ***Oxford Classical Dictionary [OCD].*** 2d ed. Edited by Nicholas G. L. Hammond and Howard H. Scullard. Oxford: Clarendon Press, 1970.   DE5.O9

Originally edited by Max Cary et al. (Oxford, 1949), this massive volume features extensive initialed scholarly articles with bibliographies appended which treat all aspects of classical civilization from ancient Greece to the death of the emperor Constantine in 337. Included are names of mythological and legendary persons and places, accounts of the lives of historical persons and peoples, and discussions of the festivals, customs, arts, and crafts of classical antiquity. Places of legendary, historical, or archaeological interest are described. There are many articles on literary forms and on writers and their works. Christian persons and terms are less fully covered than those of pagan antiquity; for them, the *OCD* can be supplemented by reference to the various Bible dictionaries and dictionaries of church history (see K–39, K–40, and K–41).

The dictionary proper is followed by an appended General Bibliography and an index of names mentioned in articles but not themselves entry terms. There is also an index to the initials which identifies the names of the 350 or so contributing authorities.

The earlier but, for rapid reference, still useful *Oxford Companion to Classical Literature [OCCL]*, ed. by Paul Harvey (Oxford: Clarendon Press. 1937) [DE5.H3], deals with the literatures of classical antiquity in themselves and not in their relations to medieval or modern literature. There are entries on authors, titles, persons, forms and types, allusions, and miscellaneous background topics of interest to readers of classical literature. There is a pronunciation guide among the volume's preliminaries, along with a list of general articles; at the end appears a chronology of classical literature, a table of weights and measures, and a series of plates of illustrations and maps. More extensive, though older, with over 10,000 entries and 1,500 illustrations, is *Harper's Dictionary of Classical Literature and Antiquities*, ed. H. T. Peck, 2d ed. (New York: Harper, 1897) [DE5.P36], which is, however, limited to the state of knowledge of classical antiquity at the end of the nineteenth century.

L–43 Hadas, Moses. *Ancilla to Classical Reading.* New York: Columbia University Press, 1954.   PA3001.H3

A book of general information concerning matters ancillary to reading in classical literature, this work is divided into two parts, "Production, Reception, and Preservation" and "Literary Gossip." The first contains chapters on technical, sociological, economic, ideological, and academic aspects of classical literary culture. The second is divided into chapters and sections covering the major authors of classical literature in chronological order, with various items of information about them as persons of their own time and place spoke of them. The volume concludes with a series of bibliographical notes and an index that includes brief biographical identifications and dates.

L–44 *Everyman's Classical Dictionary 800 B.C.–A.D. 337.* Compiled by John Warrington. 3d ed., rev. London: J. M. Dent, 1978.   DE5.W33 1978

This compact volume, first published in 1961, presents brief articles on subjects associated with the study of pagan Greece and Rome from the late eighth century B.C. to the death of Constantine. There are extensive entries on matters of geography and topography; on races and tribes; on Greek history and institutions; on Greek literature; on Greek legend, mythology, and religion; on Roman history and institutions; on Latin literature; on Roman legend, mythology, and religion; on philosophy and science; on art and architecture; and on classical sport, entertainment, and domestic life. Entries give aids to pronunciation and are abundantly cross-referenced. With the exception of the major mythology legends, which are told at length, the preference has been to increase the number, brevity, and particular detail of articles in preference to encyclopedic treatments. The volume begins with a list of modern place-names with ancient equivalents, a brief enumeration of the chief philosophical schools of antiquity and their most distinguished members, genealogical tables of the Julian and Claudian imperial houses, a systematic select general bibliography, and a list of entries disposed into the above-mentioned classes. Some reviewers regard it as less reliable than the *Oxford Companion to Classical Literature* (see L–42), though it is more up to date.

L–45 *New Century Classical Handbook.* Edited by Catherine B. Avery. New York: Appleton-Century-Crofts, 1962.   DE5.N4

Designed for the general reader, this handbook presents about 6,000 unsigned articles on classical culture to A.D. 68, including primarily topics in literature and the arts. There are articles on mythological and legendary figures, gods and heroes; on dramatists, poets, sculptors, painters, potters, philosophers, generals, statesmen, and politicians; on places including rivers, mountains, shrines; on ancient works of art, ruins, and monuments. A valuable feature is the summaries of major works of Greek and Latin literature. Literary terms are, however, excluded, as are bibliographies and exact references to texts. There are many cross-references, a pronunciation guide, and illustrations.

Selections from the *Handbook* were published in 1972 in a series of compact volumes, as follows: *New Century Handbook of Greek Literature* [PA31.N4]; *New Century Handbook of Greek Art and Architecture* [N5633.N39]; *New Century Handbook of Greek Mythology and Legend* [BL782.N45]; *New Century Handbook of Classical Geography* [DE25.N48]; and *New Century Handbook of Leaders of the Classical World* [D55.N48].

Two other handbooks for the general reader and student may be mentioned. The first, Lillian Feder, *Crowell's Handbook of Classical Literature* (New York: Crowell, 1964) [PA31.F4], has a dictionary arrangement of articles on places, persons (authors and characters), genres, themes, allusions, and summaries of works, which includes but with less emphasis both Greek literature of the Hellenistic period and Latin literature of the Silver Age. The second, Herbert Jennings Rose, *Outlines of Classical Literature for Students of English* (London: Methuen, 1959) [PA3001.R6 1959], consists of a series of discursive essays on those aspects of classical literature that have had effect on writers in English. An introduction is followed by seven chapters, treating Homer, Epic and the Troy-Saga; Elegiac, Iambic and Lyric Poetry; Attic Drama; the Development of Prose; the Alexandrian and Roman Periods; the Golden Age of Rome; and the Silver Age and After. An extremely brief bibliography is followed by an index of names, subjects, and terms.

L–46 *Loeb Classical Library.* London: Heinemann; Cambridge: Harvard University Press, 1912–.   LC numbers vary

Founded in 1912 by James Loeb, the Loeb Classical Library is the standard series of texts and English translations of Greek and Latin literature. Epic, lyric poetry, drama, history, travel, philosophy, oratory, science, mathematics, and theology—all genres and subjects treated by major and minor authors of classical antiquity are represented in compact volumes with original text and English translation on facing pages. Most volumes include helpful introductions, a brief biography of the author, textual and explanatory notes, and various appendixes and indexes, including a selected bibliography for further reference. To date, 471 volumes have been published, 168 treating Latin texts and 303 treating Greek. The Latin volumes are bound in red, the Greek in green. There are multiple volumes for most authors: the works of Cicero, for example, occupy twenty-eight volumes; those of Plutarch fill twenty-seven; those of Aristotle take twenty-three; and Augustine's works are in ten volumes. There are a number of miscellaneous volumes, including ones for Minor Latin Poets, Remains of Old Latin, Greek Elegy and Iambus, Greek Bucolic Poets, Greek Lyric, Minor Attic Orators, and Greek Mathematical Works. Because of their wide availability, the Loeb texts are standard references for quotations of classical texts; because the translations are literal, they are valuable aids for students with "little Latin and less Greek."

L–47 ***L'année philologique: Bibliographie critique et analytique de l'antiquité gréco-latine [1924/26–].*** Paris: Société d'édition 'Les belles lettres,' 1928–.   Z7016.M35A

This standard annual bibliography presents the most complete coverage of current literature in the field of classical studies, including books, articles, and dissertations. More than 12,000 briefly annotated, serially numbered items are listed per year. The bibliography is in two parts. The first part, *Auteurs et textes*, is disposed into sections on each major author and text, arranged in alphabetical order. The second part, *Matières et disciplines*, a classification of entries by subject headings, includes the broad headings 1. literary history; 2. linguistics and philology; 3. textual history; 4. antiquities; 5. history; 6. law; 7. philosophy; 8. sciences, technics, and trades; 9. classical studies; and 10. miscellaneous. The annual bibliography concludes with five valuable indexes, of collective (i.e., generic) headings used in the bibliography's first part; of Greek and Latin names; of geographical names; of humanists (that is, post-medieval students of antiquity writing on classical authors and texts); and of contemporary scholars whose work is cited.

For citations of works published prior to 1924, see Wilhelm Engelmann and E. Preuss, *Bibliotheca Scriptorum Classicorum*, covering publications 1700–1878, vol. 1, *Scriptores Graeci*; vol. 2, *Scriptores Latini*, 8th ed. (Leipzig: Engelmann, 1880–1882) [Z7016.E58 1880]; Rudolf Klussmann, *Bibliotheca Scriptorum Classicorum et Graecorum et Latinorum*, covering publications 1878–1896, 2 vols. in 4 (Leipzig: O. R. Reisland, 1909–1913) [Z7016.E592]; Scarlat Lambrino, *Bibliographie de l'antiquité classique, 1896-1914*, part I, *Auteurs et textes*; part II, *Matières et disciplines*, 2 vols. (Paris: Société d'édition "Les belles lettres," 1951–1968) [Z7016.L3]; and J. Marouzeau, *Dix années de bibliographie classique: Bibliographie critique et analytique de l'antiquité gréco-latine pour la periode 1914–1924*, part I, *Auteurs et textes*; part II, *Matières et disciplines*, 2 vols. (Paris: Société d'édition "Les belles lettres," 1927–1928) [Z7016.M35].

There are two other important serial bibliographies in classical studies, both produced in the form of bibliographic essays. The earlier is Bursian's *Jahresbericht über die Fortschritte der klassischen Altertumswissenschaft* [1873–1955], 65 vols. (Berlin and Leipzig: O. R. Reisland, 1875–1956) [PA3.J3]. This work is continued by the current annual, *Lustrum: Internationale Forschungsberichte aus dem Bereich des klassischen Altertums* [1956–] (Göttingen: Vandenhoeck und Ruprecht, 1957– [PA3.L8]. The second, now defunct, is the *Year's Work in Classical Studies* [1906–1947] (London, 1907–1950) [PA11.C7], with chapters written by specialists in each field. Neither of these is as comprehensive as *L'année philologique* or its predecessors; both, however, provide evaluative commentary unavailable in the more comprehensive works.

In addition, there were two now defunct checklists published by the American Bibliographical Service in Darien, Conn.: the *International Guide to Classical Studies: A Continuous Guide to Periodical Literature* (1961–1978) [Z7016.I5], a quarterly author list for 1960–1973, with cumulated annual author and subject indexes, and the *Quarterly Checklist of Classical Studies: An International Index of Current Books, Monographs, Brochures, and Separates* (1958–1978) [Z7016.Q35], an author list for publications 1958–1977, with an annual index of authors, editors, and translators.

For a closed and selective checklist of twentieth-century English-language criticism of classical authors and texts, see the compilation by Thomas Gwinup and Fidelia Dickinson, *Greek and Roman Authors: A Checklist of Criticism* (Metuchen, N. J.: Scarecrow, 1973) [Z7016.G9].

An additional resource is the cumulations in five volumes of the sixty-six comprehensive, selective bibliographical surveys listing, summarizing, and evaluating recent scholarship which were originally published from 1953 to 1971 in *Classical World*, the journal of the Classical Association of the Atlantic States. The volumes and their subject areas are as follows: *Classical World Bibliography of Greek Drama and Poetry* (New York: Garland, 1977) [Z7023.D7 C58 1977], including surveys of scholarship on Aeschylus, Aristophanes, Euripides, Homer, Menander, Sophocles, and Greek lyric poetry; *Classical World Bibliography of Greek and Roman History* (New York: Garland, 1977) [Z6207.G7 C58], including surveys of work on Alexander the Great, Herodotus, Josephus, Julian, Livy, Philo, Judaeus, Tacitus, and Thucydides; *Classical World Bibliography of Philosophy, Religion, and Rhetoric* (New York: Garland, 1977) [Z7129.G7 C58 1977], including surveys on Aristotle, Cicero, Epicurus, Lucretius, Plato, Seneca's prose, Hellenistic philosophy, the Pre-Socratics, rhetoric, and Roman religion; *Classical World Bibliography of Vergil* (New York: Garland, 1977) [Z8932 .C58 1977], surveying works published between 1940 and 1973; and *Classical World Bibliography of Roman Drama and Poetry and Ancient Fiction* (New York: Garland, 1977) [Z7026.C53], including surveys of recent work on Apuleius, Catullus, Horace, Ovid, Petronius, Plautus, Terence, the novel, prose fiction, and satire.

A relatively new work by A. H. M. Kessels and W. J. Verdenius, *Concise Bibliography of Greek Language and Literature* (Apeldoorn: Administratief Centrum, 1979), presents a classified arrangement of topics, along with sections on individual authors and schools. Editions of classical texts are listed, along with secondary materials. There is a limited index.

L–48 Scholarly Journals in Classical Studies.

American Classical Review. Vol. 1–. New York: CUNY, 1971–. 4/yr. Reviews. Annual list of "North American Doctoral Dissertations in Progress."   Z7016.A46

AJP *American Journal of Philology.* Vol. 1–. Baltimore: Johns Hopkins University Press, 1880–. 4/yr. Reviews.   P1.A5

CJ *Classical Journal.* Vol. 1–. Menosha, Wis., [place varies], 1905–.   PA1.C4

CP *Classical Philology: A Quarterly Journal Devoted to Research in the Languages, Literatures, History and Life of Classical Antiquity.* Vol. 1–. Chicago: University of Chicago Press, 1906–. 4/yr.   PA1.C5

CQ *Classical Quarterly.* Vol. 1–. London: D. Nutt [then John Murray], 1907–.   PA1.C6

CR *Classical Review.* London: D. Nutt; then Oxford: Clarendon Press, 1887–. 3/yr.   PA1.C7

GL *Glotta: Zeitschrift für griechische und lateinische Sprache.* Vol. 1–. Göttingen: Vandenhoeck und Ruprecht, 1909–.   PA3.G5

Gn *Gnomon: Kritische Zeitschrift für die gesamte klassische Altertumswissenschaft.* Vol. 1–. Munich: C. H. Beck, 1925–. 8/yr. Reviews. "Bibliographische Beilage" in every other issue.   PA3.G6

G&R *Greece and Rome.* Vol. 1–. Oxford: Clarendon Press, 1931–. 3/yr. Reviews.   DE1.G7

HSCP *Harvard Studies in Classical Philology.* Vol. 1–. Cambridge: Harvard University Press, 1890–. Index to vols. 1–50 (1890–1939) in vol. 52.   PA25.H3

Hermes *Hermes: Zeitschrift für klassische Philologie.* Vol. 1–. Wiesbaden: Steiner, 1866–. 4/yr.   AP30.H6

JHS   *Journal of Hellenic Studies*. Vol. 1–. London: Society for the Promotion of Hellenic Studies, 1880–. Bibliography. Reviews.   DF10.J8

JRS   *Journal of Roman Studies*. Vol. 1–. London: Society for the Promotion of Roman Studies, 1911–. Bibliography. Reviews. Indexes to vols. 1–20 in vol. 20, part 2; to vols. 21–40 in 1 vol.   DG11.J7

REA   *Revue des études anciennes*. Vol. 1–. Bordeaux: Feret et fils, 1899–. 4/yr.   PA12.R4

REG   *Revue des études grecques*. Vol. 1–. Paris: Société d'édition "Les belles lettres," 1888–. Bibliography. Reviews.   DF10.R4

REL   *Revue des études latines*. Vol. 1–. Paris: E. Champion, 1923–. 3/yr. Reviews.   PA2002.R4

         Revue de philologie, de littérature et d'histoire anciennes. Vol. 1–. Paris: 1845–1847; new ser., 1877–1926; 3d ser., 1927–. Bibliographies. Reviews.   PA2.R4

         Revue biblique. Vol. 1–. Paris: L'École pratique d'études bibliques. 1892–.   BS410.R3

TAPA   *Transactions of the American Philological Association*. 1869–.   P11.A5

For a more elaborate list of periodicals see Joyce E. Southan, *Survey of Classical Periodicals: Union Catalogue of Periodicals Relevant to Classical Studies in Certain British Libraries* (London: Institute of Classical Studies, London University, 1962) [Z2260.S67].

L–49 Some Frequently Recommended Works in Classical Studies. (See also K–95, Intellectual History, and K–98, History of Scholarship.)

General

Bengsten, Hermann. *Introduction to Ancient History*. Berkeley and Los Angeles: University of California Press, 1970.   Z6202.B413

Bieber, Margarete. *History of the Greek and Roman Theater*. Princeton, N. J.: Princeton University Press, 1961.   PA3201.B52 1961

Brown, Huntington. "The Classical Tradition in English Literature: A Bibliography." *Harvard Studies and Notes in Philology and Literature* 18 (1935): 7–46.   PN35.H4

Harsh, P. W. *Handbook of Classical Drama*. Stanford: Stanford University Press, 1944.   PA3024.H3

Hathorn, R. Y. *Handbook of Classical Drama*. New York: Crowell, 1967.   PA3024.H35 1967b

Highet, Gilbert. *Classical Tradition: Greek and Roman Influences on Western Literature*. Oxford: Oxford University Press, 1949. Reprinted with corrections, 1953. Contains important bibliographies.   PN883.H5 1953

Moss, Joseph William. *Manual of Classical Bibliography, Comprising a Copious Detail of the Various Editions of the Greek and Latin Classics, and of the Critical and Philological Works Published in Illustration of Them, with an Account of the Principal Translations*. 2 vols. London: W. Simpkin and R. Marshall, 1825.   Z7016.M91

Pickard-Cambridge, A. W. *Dithyramb, Tragedy, and Comedy*. 2d ed. Oxford: Clarendon Press, 1962.   PA3131.P5 1962

Smith, R. W., et al. *Ancient Greek and Roman Rhetoricians: A Biographical Dictionary*. Compiled for the Speech Association of America. Edited by Donald C. Bryant. Columbia, Mo.: Artcraft Press, 1968.   PA83.A5

Snell, Bruno. *Discovery of the Mind: The Greek Origins of European Thought*. Translation by Thomas G. Rosenmeyer of *Die Entdeckung des Geistes* (Hamburg: Claaszen und Goverts, 1946). Cambridge: Harvard University Press, 1953.   B181.S513

Thomson, J. A. K. *Classical Background of English Literature*. London: G. Allen and Unwin, 1948.   PR127.T5

Greek Studies

Bowra, C. M. *Greek Lyric Poetry from Alcman to Simonides*. 2d ed. Oxford: Clarendon Press, 1961.   PA3019.B6 1961

Croiset, Alfred, and Maurice Croiset. *Histoire de la littérature grecque*. 3d ed. 5 vols. Paris: Thorin, 1914–1947.   PA3055.C8 1914

Defradas, Jean. *Guide de l'étudiant helléniste*. Paris: Presses universitaires de France, 1968.   PA240.F8 D4

Dodds, Eric Robertson. *Greeks and the Irrational*. Berkeley and Los Angeles: University of California Press, 1951.   BF1421.D6

Ferguson, J. *Companion to Greek Tragedy*. Austin: University of Texas Press, 1972.   PA3131.F4

Finley, M. I. *World of Odysseus*. 2d ed. London: Chatto and Windus, 1977.   PA4037.F48 1977

Hadas, Moses. *Hellenistic Culture: Fusion and Diffusion*. New York: Columbia University Press, 1959.   DF77.H3

———. *History of Greek Literature*. New York: Columbia University Press, 1950.   PA3052.H3 1950

Kitto, H. D. F. *Greek Tragedy: A Literary Study*. London: Methuen, 1968.   PA3131.K5 1968

Lesky, Albin. *History of Greek Literature*. Translation of *Geschichte der griechischen Literatur*, 2d ed. (Bern: Francke, 1963). London: Methuen, 1966.   PA3057.L413 1966

Murray, Gilbert. *Euripides and His Age*. London: Oxford University Press, 1946.   PA3978.M8 1946

Rissenfeld, Harald, and Blenda Rissenfeld. *Repertorium Lexicographicum Graecum: A Catalogue of Indexes and Dictionaries to Greek Authors*. Stockholm: Almqvist and Wiksell, 1954.   Z7021.R5

Thomson, George D. *Greek Language*. Cambridge, Eng.: W. Heffer, 1960.   PA227.T5

Whitman, Cedric H. *Homer and the Heroic Tradition*. Cambridge: Harvard University Press, 1958.   PA4037.W66

Roman Studies

Beare, William. *Roman Stage: A Short History of Latin Drama in the Time of the Republic*. 3d ed. New York: Barnes and Noble, 1965.   PA6067.B4 1965

Duff, J. W. *Literary History of Rome from the Origins to the Close of the Golden Age*. 3d ed. Revised by A. M. Duff. London: Benn, 1953.   PA6003.D8 1953

———. *Literary History of Rome in the Silver Age*. 3d ed. New York: Barnes and Noble, 1964.   PA6042.D8 1964

Faider, Paul. *Répertoire des éditions de scolies et commentaires d'auteurs latins*. Paris: Société d'édition "Les belles lettres," 1931.   Z7028.S4 F2

———. *Répertoire des indexes et lexiques d'auteurs latins*. Paris: Société d'édition "Les belles lettres," 1926.   Z7028.D6 F2

Fraenkel, E. *Horace*. Oxford: Clarendon Press, 1957.
PA6411.F67

Frank, Tenney. *Life and Literature in the Roman Republic*. Berkeley: University of California Press, 1930.
PA6011.F7

Hadas, Moses. *History of Latin Literature*. New York: Columbia University Press, 1952.   PA6004.H3

Herescu, N. *Bibliographie de la littérature latine*. Paris: Société d'édition "Les belles lettres," 1943.
Z7026.H4

Martinband, James H. *Dictionary of Latin Literature*. New York: Philosophical Library, 1956.   PA31.M3

Palmer, L. R. *Latin Language*. London: Faber and Faber, 1954.   PA2071.P26 1954

Rostagni, A. *Storia della letteratura latina*. 2d ed., rev. 2 vols. Turin: Unione Tipografico, 1954–1955.
PA6008.R6

Teuffel, Wilhelm S. *Teuffel's History of Roman Literature*. Authorized translation from the 5th German edition, rev. and enlarged by Ludwig Schwabe. 2 vols. London: G. Bell, 1891–1893.   PA6007.T55 1891

IV. MODERN LANGUAGES AND LITERATURES

See also the works of literary chronology (F–80 and F–83).

L–50 *MLA International Bibliography of Books and Articles on the Modern Languages and Literatures [MLAIB]*. New York: Modern Language Association of America, 1969–.
Z7006.M64

This work is the single most important annual, classified, unannotated bibliography of books, monographs, essays, and articles by scholars and critics of all nations on the language and postclassical literature of all nations. Because *Dissertation Abstracts International* (E–7) is among the serial publications indexed here, the MLA bibliography also includes most American and some foreign doctoral dissertations. Reviews are excluded, as are textbooks and most primary texts of literary works. The work's aim is a selectively comprehensive coverage of secondary literature.

The history of the MLA bibliography involves a progressive expansion of scope. Its predecessor was the series of *Literature and Language Bibliographies from* [i.e., published in] *the American Year Book, 1910–19*, cumulated with an index by Arnold N. Rzepecki (Ann Arbor, Mich.: Pierian Press, 1970) [Z7001.L57]. From 1922 through 1955 the MLA bibliography was appended to the June issue of *PMLA*; titled "American Bibliography," it included the work of only American scholars and critics. From 1956 through 1962 it was titled "Annual Bibliography" and included the work of scholars and critics of all nationalities. From 1963 through 1968 it had its current title but was published as a separate issue of *PMLA*. Since 1969 it has been separately published in three volumes, independently of the journal. (From 1969 through 1972 it was in four volumes.) As of 1982 it has been published in five volumes.

Volume 1 during the period 1969–1981 included the following parts: 1, General Literature and Related Topics (Esthetics; Literary Criticism and Theory; Literature—General and Comparative; Themes and Types; Bibliographical; Miscellaneous). 2, English (General; Australia, Canada, etc.; Themes, Types, and Special Topics; Old English; Middle English; Renaissance and Elizabethan; 17th Century; 18th Century; 19th Century; 20th Century). 3, American Litera-

ture (General; 17th and 18th Centuries; 19th Century 1800–1870; 19th Century 1870–1900; 20th Century). 4, Medieval and Neo-Latin (General: Medieval Latin; Neo-Latin). 5, Celtic (General; Bibliography; Bretan; Cornish; Gaulish; Irish Gaelic; Manx; Scottish Gaelic; Welsh). 6, Folklore (General; Prose Narrative; Gnomic; Folk Poetry; Games and Toys; Dramatic Folklore; Music and Dance; Customs, Beliefs, and Symbolism; Material Culture).

Volume 2 included the following sections: General Romance; French (General and Miscellaneous, French-Canadian, Medieval, 16th Century, 17th Century, 18th Century, 19th Century, 20th Century); Italian (General and Miscellaneous; Dante; 13th and 14th Centuries; 15th, 16th, and 17th Centuries; 18th and 19th Centuries, 20th Century); Spanish Literature (General and Miscellaneous; Literature in Spanish America—Before 1930, After 1930; Literature before 1500; Literature from 1500 to 1700; 18th and 19th Centuries; 20th Century); Portuguese and Brazilian Literature (Portuguese; Brazilian); Romanian Literature (General and Miscellaneous, Literature); General Germanic Literature (General; Yiddish Literature); German Literature (General and Miscellaneous; Themes, Types, and Special Topics; Literature before 1500; 16th and 17th Centuries; 18th and Early 19th Centuries; 19th and Early 20th Centuries; 20th Century Literature; Americana Germanica); Netherlandic Literature (General and Miscellaneous; Frisian; Literature before 1500; 16th and 17th Centuries; 18th and Early 19th Centuries; 19th and Early 20th Centuries; 20th Century; Afrikaans); Scandinavian Literatures (General and Miscellaneous; Literatures to 1500; Danish and Faroese Literature; Icelandic Literature; Norwegian Literature; Swedish Literature); Modern Greek Literature (General and Miscellaneous; Folklore; Medieval Literature in the Vernacular; Literature 1453–1669; 1670–1830; 1831–1880; 1881–1922; after 1922); Oriental Literatures (General and Miscellaneous; Bibliography; East-West Relations; Near- and Middle-Eastern Literatures; Central Asian; South Asian; Southeast Asian; East Asian); African Literatures (General and Miscellaneous; Bibliography; Folklore; Literature); East European Literatures (General and Miscellaneous; Baltic and Balto-Slavic; East Slavic Literatures; Russian; West Slavic Literatures; Polish; South Slavic Literatures; Non-Indo-European Literatures; Folklore—Indo-European and Non-Indo-European; Albanian).

Volume 3, the linguistics bibliography, was divided into three parts, as follows: 1, General Linguistics (Generalities; Mathematical and Computational Linguistics; Information and Communication Theory; Stylistics; Psycholinguistics; Socio- and Ethnolinguistics; Language Interaction; Dialectology; Animal Communication). 2, Theoretical and Descriptive Linguistics (Phonology; Prosody—Suprasegmentals; Writing Systems; Lexis; Grammar; Semantics; Philosophy of Language). 3, Comparative and Historical Linguistics (Comparative; Diachronics; Indo-European Studies); Indo-European Linguistics (A. Italic; B. Baltic and Slavic; C. Germanic Including English; D. Hellenic; E. Indic; F. Iranian; G. Celtic; H. Tocharian; J. Albanian and Others; K. Armenian; L. Anatolian); Asiatic Linguistics; African Linguistics; Afro-Asiatic Linguistics; Linguistics of Australasia and Oceania; American Indian Linguistics; and Composite and Derivative Languages and Other Communicative Behavior.

Volume 4, published only 1969–1972, was the Annual Bibliography of Books and Articles on Pedagogy in foreign Languages, prepared in conjunction with ACTFL, the American Council on the Teaching of Foreign Languages. It was disposed into the following major sections: General; Linguistics (General, Phonology, Grammar, Vocabulary, Semantics, Stylistics, Philosophy of Language, Travel); Culture; Teaching of Foreign Literature; Curriculum Problems and Development (from Elementary to Graduate Education); Physiology and Psychology of Language Teaching; Teacher Education and Certification; Methods; Equipment; and Testing. See Z–135 for more information about this bibliography.

Within major headings were subdivisions, moving from general to specific terms (general treatments, bibliography, genres, authors, individual works).

Individual entries appeared only once, in the most appropriate division or subdivision, with cross-references from other plausible locations. They were serially numbered (since 1957), and cross-references were made at the end of sections and subsections to other relevant entry numbers. Brief annotations were used only when necessary to clarify a reference. Each volume was preceded by a master list of indexed serials with their abbreviations. Detailed information about the indexed serials may be gathered from the biennial *Directory of Periodicals* published by the MLA (see Z–100).

Since 1964 there has been an index of secondary authors at the end of each volume. It should be noted that since 1957 the bibliography has begun with a list of festschriften and other collections, numbered F–1, F–2, etc., and that the contents of these volumes are analyzed and indexed along with books, articles, and dissertations, in appropriate sections and subsections.

From 1970 through 1975 the MLA also sponsored an abstracting service (see L–51), and entries in the bibliography for which abstracts were published are indicated by asterisks after their serial number.

Since 1978 the bibliography database has also been available for on-line computer searching, through the Lockheed DIALOG Service, and since 1986 on WILSON LINE and by subscription on CD-Rom through WILSON DISK. The file now (1988) includes materials from 1968 through 1987; it thus presents the only currently available multiyear cumulation. By the end of this decade, retrospective coverage through 1921 will be completed and available for retrieval.

By virtue of a developing series of more complex "supercoded descriptors," it is possible to search out materials within rather specific fields of interest. These descriptors include the following: Subject, Author, Work, or Folk Work; Genre (e.g., essay, drama, novel); Group (e.g., women, Russians); Literary Sources (e.g., history, Bible, Marxism, myth); Place or Time Period (e.g., Wales, 1950–1980, Renaissance); Literary Process (e.g., creative process, textual revision, communication); Literary Technique (e.g., characterization, point-of-view, metaphor); Literary Theme, Motif, or Character (e.g., the quest, prodigal son, Theseus); Literary Influence (e.g., painting, literary movement, name of an influential work); Performance Medium (e.g., theater, film); Scholar; Scholarly Theory, Discipline, Type (e.g., speech act theory, reception study); Scholarly Tool (e.g., tape recorder, computer); Subject Classification (all terms from the subject index); Specific Language; Specific Literature.

Beginning in September 1982 with the publication of the 1981 *MLA International Bibliography*, the printed text has the greater specificity and flexibility that had formerly been available only through the computer terminal. The annual bibliography henceforth appears in five volumes, each with a more detailed system of classification and an extremely useful context-preserving subject index. The five volumes have the following coverage: volume 1, British, American, Australian, English-Canadian, New Zealand, and English-Caribbean Literatures; volume 2, European, Asian, African, and South American (including Latin American and French-Caribbean) Literatures; volume 3, Linguistics (further subdivided by topics, Language, History of Linguistics, Theory of Linguistics, Area Linguistics, Comparative Linguistics, Diachronic Linguistics, Language Interaction, Mathematical Linguistics, Paralinguistics, Psycholinguistics, Sociolinguistics, Topics of Professional Interest, by features, Dialectology, Grammar, Lexicology, Morphology, Onomastics, Phonetics, Syntax, Translation, Writing Systems, and by Specific Languages); volume 4, General Literature and Related Topics (further subdivided into nine sections, General Literature, Literary Movements, Bibliographical Studies, Criticism, Literary Theory, Genres, Literary Forms, Professional Topics, Themes); and

volume 5, Folklore (General Studies, History and Study of Folklore, Folk Literature, Ethnomusicology, Folk Belief Systems, Folk Rituals, and Material Culture, and then by types, genres, and geographical areas).

Each volume's classified section presents entries under a revised system of topics. National literatures are classified chronologically, generically, and to the level of individual works by a subject author so that, for example, all studies of Pope's *Essay on Man* appear together. The linguistics volume is classified to the level of minor linguistic aspects within individual languages. The General Literature and Related Topics volume is classified by names of schools of criticism and similarly particular topics. The folklore volume is classified first by broad folklore type (e.g., Rituals) and then by specific types (e.g., Rite of Passage) and places. Each entry, in addition to the usual bibliographical information, also contains a string of descriptive terms used to describe that item in the subject index. By reading the series of descriptive terms as if they constituted the keywords of a descriptive abstract, a user is able to judge the probable relevance of the item.

These descriptors, in alphabetical order, provide the terms for the context-preserving subject index in each of the five volumes. In this index all items appear together which have any particular word in the string of descriptors associated with them. Each entry includes all the other descriptors assigned to the item. The indexes have several other functions besides providing subject access to the classified entries. Using them makes possible the location of subject authors within the classified section; they also lead users to a variety of broader, narrower, and related subject terms. In addition, they provide access to topics that do not fit within the classification by period, author, and work, such as the influence of a particular text or author on another. Finally, the cross-references in the classified section have been eliminated, and instead cross-references to alternative subject terms appear in the index under subject or concept.

For students of English and American literature the *MLA International Bibliography* supplements the entries of the *NCBEL* (M–11), the *LHUS* (S–10), and all closed bibliographies, and it complements the entries of the MHRA *Annual Bibliography* (M–21), the *Year's Work in English Studies* (M–22), all general serial indexes, and all current bibliographies limited to one genre or period. It is difficult to imagine any bibliographical search in English studies which would not turn to this bibliography in due course.

L–51 **MLA Abstracts of Articles in Scholarly Journals [1970–1975].** New York: MLA, 1973–1977.   P1.M64

Published in five annual volumes, this regrettably short-lived abstracting service included a very limited selection of abstracts of articles cited in the *International Bibliography* (L–50), identified by their serial entry numbers. The volumes were organized to parallel the structure of the *International Bibliography*, volumes 1–3. The abstracts themselves were generally prepared by the author of the article cited and were descriptive summaries of about 200 words in length.

L–52 **Modern Humanities Research Association. Year's Work in Modern Language Studies by a Number of Scholars [YWMLS].** Vol. 1–. [1929/30–]. London: Oxford University Press, 1931–1940; Cambridge: Cambridge University Press, 1951–1963; Cambridge: Modern Humanities Research Association, 1964—.   PB1.Y45

This annual guide contains bibliographical essays on the year's work in each of the European and Latin-American languages and literatures. The essays selectively describe and evaluate books and major articles published during the year; their quality varies from compiler to compiler. Coverage and arrangement have varied over the years. Currently there are six major parts subdivided as follows: 1, General Linguistics; 2, Latin (Medieval Latin, Neo-Latin); 3, Romance Languages (Romance Linguistics, French Studies, Occitan, Spanish, Catalan, Portuguese, Latin-American, Italian, Rumanian, Romansh); 4, Celtic Languages (Common Celtic and Gaulish, Welsh Studies, Bretan and Cornish, Irish, Scottish Gaelic); 5, Germanic Languages (German Studies, Dutch, Danish, Norwegian, Swedish); 6, Slavonic Studies (Czech, Slovak, Polish, Russian, Ukrainian, Byelorussian, and Serbo-Croat Studies).

Within these divisions there is further partition into chronological periods from medieval to modern and from general studies to those more specialized. The volume concludes with a guide to abbreviations and an index of names (of both authors and scholars) and, since 1968, an excellent index of subjects, including themes and types. Note that volume 2 (1951) contains bibliographic essays surveying the scholarship of 1940–1949.

L–54 Magnus, Laurie. *Dictionary of European Literature, Designed as a Companion to English Studies.* 2d impression, rev. with addenda. London: George Routledge and Sons, 1927.   PN41.M3

This volume, concerned with European literature from the twelfth to the twentieth centuries, contains articles on movements and topics that cross over boundaries of period and national literature; surveys of the literary histories of each national literature; biographical and critical sketches of major and minor authors (with minimal bibliographical information); and definitions of some literary terms. Authors living in 1925 are excluded except for Thomas Hardy and Georg Brandes. There are abundant cross-references and some ten pages of addenda. For authors of the late nineteenth century, entries in the *Columbia Dictionary* (L–55) are much to be preferred; nevertheless this remains the most substantial comprehensive dictionary of postmedieval European literature.

L–55 *Columbia Dictionary of Modern European Literature.* 2d ed., rev. and enl. Jean Albert Bede and William Edgerton, general editors. New York: Columbia University Press, 1980.   PN41.C6

Originally edited by Horatio Smith (New York, 1947), this new edition contains articles prepared by approximately 500 contributors on 1,853 individual writers as well as on thirty-three national literatures. Philosophers and critics, as well as poets, dramatists, and novelists, are included. Treated are authors important to Modern European literature, including some later-nineteenth-century figures whose work the editors judge of continuing importance in the twentieth century. Individual author articles give dates, basic biographical information, a critical discussion of principal works, and a brief bibliography. There are cross-references from survey articles to the principal authors of a national literature as well as to other authors whose work has importantly influenced that literature. Titles are translated into English; when an English translation of a work has been published, the title and date of the translation are given. Articles are initialed; contributors are identified in a list at the beginning of the volume.

L–56 Kunitz, Stanley J., and Vineta Colby, eds. *European Authors, 1000–1900: A Biographical Dictionary of European Literature.* New York: H. W. Wilson, 1967.   PN451.K8

This volume contains biographies of 967 continental writers from thirty-one different national literatures who were born after 1000 or who died before 1925. Written for the general reader, these biographies present signed articles with brief bibliographies of primary and a few secondary works. Trans-

lations into English are cited when they are available. 309 of the articles are accompanied by portraits of their subjects.

Other available dictionaries of European authors include William N. Hargreaves-Mawdsley, *Everyman's Dictionary of European Writers* (London, 1968) [PN451.H3], the companion to David C. Browning's *Everyman's Dictionary of Literary Biography, American and English* (M–51). It contains more than 2,000 brief biographies of non-English authors since the tenth century from twenty European countries, with standard editions and English translations of their major works listed. For obscure European writers of the nineteenth century the best source is Angelo de Gubernatis, *Dictionnaire international des écrivains du jour*, 3 vols. (Florence: L. Niccolai, 1890–1891) [Z1010.G91].

Other Wilson Authors volumes include works on *American Authors 1600–1900* (S–27); *British Authors Before 1800* (M–55); *British Authors of the Nineteenth Century* (M–56); *Twentieth Century Authors* and *Twentieth Century Authors: First Supplement* (R–21); *World Authors 1970–1975* (R–21); and *World Authors 1975–1980* (R–21). A revised *Index to the Wilson Authors Series* was published in 1986 [PN451.I5 1986] and includes access to the more than 8,600 authors treated in one of the ten volumes of the series.

L–57 Scholarly Journals in the Modern European Languages and Literatures.

Archiv   *Archiv für das Studium der neueren Sprachen und Literaturen [Herrig's Archiv].* Vol. 1–. Berlin: Erich Schmidt Verlag, 1848–. 2/yr. Reviews. Bibliographies [from 1948 to 1961 annual enumerations of studies on English and American Language and Literature]. Indexes to volumes 1–50 (1874), 51–100 (1900),101–10 (n.d.), 111–20 (n.d.), 121–30 (1913).   PB3.A5

DVLG   *Deutsche Vierteljahresschrift für Literaturwissenschaft und Geistesgeschichte.* Vol. 1–. Stuttgart: J. B. Metzlersche Verlags-Buchhandlung, 1923– [place and publisher vary]. 4/yr. Reviews. PN4.D4

FMLS   *Forum for Modern Language Studies.* Vol. 1–. Edinburgh: Scottish Academic Press, 1965–. 4/yr.   PB1.F63

GRM   *Germanisch-Romanische Monatsschrift.* 31 vols. Heidelberg: Carl Winter Universitätsverlag, 1909-1943, Neue Folge, vol. 1–, 1950/51–. 4/yr. Reviews. Index to vols. 1–41 (1909–1960) published 1964.   PB3.G3

Literaturblatt für germanische und romanische philologie. 65 vols. Leipzig: O. R. Reisland, 1880–1944. Bibliographies. Reviews. Indexes.   Z7037.L7

MLJ   *Modern Language Journal.* Vol. 1–. Madison: University of Wisconsin Press, 1916–. 4/yr. Reviews. Annual list of "American Doctoral Degrees Granted in Foreign languages [1925–]," giving names and titles of dissertations.   PB1.M47

MLN   *MLN [Modern Languages Notes].* Vol 1–. Baltimore: Johns Hopkins University Press, 1886–. 5/yr. Formerly included all modern European literatures; now issues treat Italian (January), Hispanic (March), German (April), French (September), and Comparative Literature (including poetics and literary theory) (December) respectively. Reviews. Current bibliography of books on prose fiction before 1800, 1927–1945. Surveys by Kemp Malone of linguistic studies at intervals. Indexes to vols. 1–50 and 51–60.   PB1.M6

MLQ   *Modern Language Quarterly.* Vol. 1–. Seattle: University of Washington, 1940–. 4/yr. Reviews.

"Bibliography of Critical Arthurian Literature" in vols. 1–24 (1940–1963) (see N–56). PB1.M642

MLR *Modern Language Review*. Vol. 1–. Cambridge: Modern Humanities Research Association, 1918–. 4/yr. Reviews. Cumulative indexes to vols. 1–10, 11–20, 21–30, 31–50, and 51–60. PB1.M65

MLS *Modern Language Studies: Journal of the Northeast Modern Language Association*. Vol. 1–. Kingston, R. I.: NEMLA, 1970–. 4/yr. Reviews. PB1.M67

MP *Modern Philology: A Journal Devoted to Research in Medieval and Modern Literature*. Vol. 1–. Chicago: University of Chicago Press, 1903/4–. 4/yr. Reviews. Current Bibliography of Victorian Studies, 1932–1957 (see Q–38). PB1.M7

Neophil *Neophilologus: A Quarterly Devoted to the Study of the Modern and Medieval Languages and Literature, Including General Linguistics, Literary Theory and Comparative Literature*. Vol. 1–. Groningen: Wolters-Noordhoff, 1916–. 4/yr. PB5.N4

NS *Die neueren Sprachen*. Vol. 1–. Frankfurt, 1952–. 6/yr. Reviews. No LC number

NM *Neuphilologische Mitteilungen / Bulletin de la Société néophilologique / Bulletin of the Modern Language Society*. Vol. 1–. Helsinki: Modern Language Society, 1889–. 4/yr. Reviews. Includes, since 1964, bibliographies and work-in-progress listings on Old English, Middle English, and Chaucer studies (see N–25, N–40, and N–47), as well as bibliography of Finnish theses and work in progress on modern languages and literatures. PB10.N415

PLL *Papers on Language and Literature: Journal of the Midwest Modern Language Association*. Vol. 1–. Edwardsville: Southern Illinois University, 1965–. 4/yr. Reviews. Cumulative index to vols. 1–6 in vol. 6, 1–15 (n. d.), 16–20 in vol. 20 (1984). PR1.P3

PQ *Philological Quarterly*. Vol. 1–. Iowa City: University of Iowa Press, 1922–. 4/yr. Reviews. Contained the eighteenth-century annual bibliography 1926–1970 (see P–5) and the Romantic bibliography 1950–1964 (see Q–25). Now contains bibliographical reviews of eighteenth-century studies. Cumulative index to vols. 1–25 (1950). P1.P55

PMLA *PMLA [Publications of the Modern Language Association of America]*. Vol. 1–. New York: MLA, 1884/85–. 6/yr. Reviews. The *International Bibliography* (see L–50). From 1950 through 1960, "Research in Progress in the Modern Humanities" appeared in the bibliography numbers; it noted books and American doctoral dissertations. Professional Notes and Comments. Directory and Program [of the annual meeting] issues. A history of the journal by John H. Fisher, "Remembrance and Reflection: *PMLA* 1884–1982" was published in *PMLA* 99 (1984): 398–407. PB6.M6

RLV *Revue des langues vivantes / Tijdschrift voor levendetalen*. Vol. 1–. Brussels: Librairie Marcel Didier, 1934–. 6/yr. Reviews. PN9.R45

SAB *South Atlantic Bulletin: Journal of the South Atlantic Modern Language Association*. Vol. 1–. 1935–. Reviews. PB1.S6

SN *Studia Neophilologica: A Journal of Germanic and Romance Languages and Literature*. Vol. 1–. Stockholm: Almqvist and Wiksell, 1928–. 2/yr. Reviews. PB5.S7

SP *Studies in Philology*. Vol. 1–. Chapel Hill: University of North Carolina Press, 1906–. 5/yr. Bibliography of Renaissance Studies, 1926–1970 (see O–5). Cumulative Index to vols. 1–50. P25.S8

Symposium: A Quarterly Journal in Modern Foreign Literatures. Syracuse: Syracuse University Press, 1946–. 4/yr. Reviews. Bibliography on Literature and Science from 1951 on (see X–86). PB1.S9

TSLL *Texas Studies in Literature and Language: A Journal of the Humanities*. Vol. 1–. Austin: University of Texas Press, 1911–. 4/yr. Annual index. AS30.T4

UTQ *University of Toronto Quarterly: A Canadian Journal of the Humanities*. Vol. 1–. Toronto: University of Toronto Press, 1931–. 4/yr. Reviews. AP5.U58

See also the lists of journals in Comparative Literature (L–8) and the *MLA Directory of Periodicals: A Guide to Journals and Series in Languages and Literatures* (Z–100).

L–59 **Some Frequently Recommended Works on Modern European Languages and Literatures.**

Auerbach, Erich. *Mimesis: The Representation of Reality in Western Literature*. Translation by Willard Trask of *Mimesis: Dargestellte Wirklichkeit in der abendlandischen Literatur* (Bern: A. Francke, 1946). Princeton, N.J.: Princeton University Press, 1953. PN56.R3 A83

———. *Scenes from the Drama of European Literature*. Foreword by Paolo Valesio. Minneapolis: University of Minnesota Press, 1984. PN710.A83 1984

Curtius, Ernst Robert. *European Literature and the Latin Middle Ages*. Translation by Willard Trask of *Europäische Literatur und lateinische Mittelalter* (Bern: A. Francke, 1948). New York: Pantheon, 1953. PN674.C82

Kranz, G. *Europas christliche Literatur von 500 bis 1500*. Munich: Schöningh, 1968. PN674.K7

———. *Europas christliche Literatur von 1500 bis Heute*. 2d ed. Munich: Schöningh, 1968. PN704.K7 1968

Marill, René. *L'aventure intellectuelle du XXe siècle: Panorama des littératures européennes, 1900–1959*. 4th ed., rev. and enl. Paris: A. Michel, 1969. PN773.M3 1969

Van Tieghem, Paul. *Le romantisme dans la littérature européenne*. Paris: A. Michel, 1940. PN603.V26

V. ROMANCE LANGUAGES AND LITERATURES

See also Palfrey et al. (A–19); pertinent works in section I on Language, Linguistics, and Philology; the *MLA International Bibliography* (L–50); the MHRA *Year's Work in Modern Language Studies* (L–52); and works on General and Comparative Literature (L–1 ff.).

L–60 ***Romanische Bibliographie / Bibliographie romane / Romance Bibliography [1961/62–]***. Tübingen: Niemeyer, 1965–. Z7032.Z45

This work continues the coverage of the *Bibliographie* [for 1875–1960] published annually or biennially (since 1878) as a *Supplementheft* to the *Zeitschrift für romanische Philologie*. The volume for 1940–1950 was published in 1957; that for

1951–1955 in 1960 in two volumes; and that for 1956–1960 in 1964 in two volumes. In its current form the bibliography is published biennially in three or four volumes and treats publications on all the Romance languages and literatures. Included are articles, collected volumes, proceedings, festschriften, reviews, and titles of monographs that have been reviewed. There has been a six- to seven-year time lag in publication, but efforts are under way to reduce this considerably. As of 1971–1972, French literature is excluded and users are referred to the Klapp bibliography (L–73). Entries are classified and numbered accordingly; users should become acquainted with the system, which assigns digits by language, by chronological coverage, and by the type of scholarly project cited (bibliography, literary history, anthology, etc.).

The first volume in each biennial group includes a list of general bibliographies consulted and lists of journals, research institute reports, congress proceedings, collected volumes, and festschriften analyzed. A key to abbreviations of journal names is followed by indexes of authors, of reviewed authors, and of subjects. The second volume treats Romance linguistics and philology, with sections devoted to general linguistics and then to Latin, general Romance, and the various Romance languages in turn. The third volume is similarly disposed into sections on general and comparative literature, Romance literature, and then the individual literatures of the Romance language communities. Sections are elaborately subdivided into chronological periods and then individual authors and works.

Entries present bibliographical information only, with cross-references and occasional clarifying annotations. The most recently published bibliography covers publications of 1971 and 1972 and appeared in 1980, but volumes for 1973/74 and 1975/76 are either in press or soon to be. Nevertheless, for more current Romance bibliography, students must turn either to more general sources, such as the *MLA International Bibliography* (L–50) and the MHRA *Year's Work in Modern Language Studies* (L–52), or to the more specialized bibliographies of national languages and literatures (L–70 ff.). East European and Soviet scholarship in the field will be found in the *Bibliographie der in den sozialistischen Ländern erschienenen Arbeiten zur Romanistik aus dem Jahre* [1958–], prepared by the Deutsche Staatsbibliothek, Berlin, and published in the *Beiträge zur romanischen Philologie*, vol. 1–. (Berlin: Verlag Rütten und Loening, 1961–) [PC3.B4]. For scholarship of the period 1890–1912 a more elaborate review of research is available in the *Kritischer Jahresbericht über die Fortschritte der romanischen Philologie, 1890–1912*, 13 vols. (Erlangen, 1892–1915) [Z7032.K92].

L–61 **Auerbach, Eric.** *Introduction to Romance Languages and Literature: Latin, French, Spanish, Provençal, Italian.* New York: Capricorn, 1961.   PC41.A813 1961

This work is divided into four parts. The first discusses philology and its variant forms; the second treats the origins of the Romance languages. Part 3 presents general doctrines regarding literary epochs (the Middle Ages, the Renaissance, and Modern Times). The fourth part is a bibliographical guide that is more selective than Palfrey (A–19). The guide is in three parts: Linguistics (covering Latin, Romance, French, Provençal, Italian, Spanish, Portuguese, Rumanian, Sardinian, and Rhaetian-Romansh); Literature (similarly divided); and a third part enumerating periodicals treating the Romance languages and literatures. The volume concludes with a detailed index of authors, titles, and subjects.

L–63 **Scholarly Journals in the Romance Languages and Literatures.**

BRP	*Beiträge zur romanischen Philologie.* Vol. 1–. [East] Berlin: Verlag Rütten und Loening. 1961–. 2/yr. Reviews. PC3.B4
CRLN	*Comparative Romance Linguistics Newsletter.* Vol. 1– [1950–]. Rochester, N. Y.: University of Rochester; now Carbondale: Southern Illinois University Press, 1951–. 2/yr. Bibliography of books, articles, reviews, dissertations. PC1.C65
CN	*Cultura neolatina.* Vol. 1–. Modena: Istituto di filologia romanza, Università di Roma, 1941–. 3/yr. [now 4/yr.]. Reviews. PC4.C8
LR	*Les lettres romanes.* Vol. 1–. Korbeek-Lo, Belgium: Fondation universitaire de Belgique, Ministère de l'education nationale, 1947–. 4/yr. Reviews. PC2.L4
	Revue des langues romanes. Vol. 1–. Montpellier: Centre d'études occitanes de l'Université de Montpellier, 1870–. 2/yr. Reviews. Annual "Bibliographie des études romanes en Amerique du Nord," 1968–, listing books on languages and literatures classified by country and period. PC2.R4
RLiR	*Revue de linguistique romane.* Strasbourg: Société de linguistique romane, 1925–. 2/yr. Reviews. Bibliographies. PC2.R35
RomN	*Romance Notes.* Chapel Hill: Department of Romance Languages, University of North Carolina, 1959–. 3/yr. Reviews. PC1.R58
RPh	*Romance Philology.* Vol. 1–. Berkeley: University of California Press, 1947–. 4/yr. Reviews. Bibliographic Index to vols. 1–25 by Mark G. Littlefield. Berkeley, Los Angeles, London: University of California Press, 1974. PC1.R6
Romania	*Romania: Revue trimestrielle consacrée à l'étude des langues et des littératures romanes.* Vol. 1–. Paris: Société des amis de la Romania, 1872–. 4/yr. Reviews. Bibliography of current articles. Indexes 1872–1901, 1901–1934. PC2.R6
RR	*Romanic Review.* Vol. 1–. New York: Department of Romance Languages, Columbia University, 1909–. 4/yr. Reviews. Annual "Anglo-French and Franco-American Studies: A Current Bibliography," vols. 29–39 (1938–1948). PC1.R7
RF	*Romanische Forschungen: Vierteljahresschrift für romanische Sprachen und Literaturen.* Vol. 1–. Erlangen and Frankfurt: Klostermann, 1888–1942, 1950–. 4/yr. Reviews. Bibliographical survey of philological studies. PC3.R5
RJ	*Romanistisches Jahrbuch.* Vol. 1–. Berlin: de Gruyter, 1947–. 1/yr. Reviews. Annual list of West German and Austrian Habilitations-Schriften and dissertations on Romance languages and literatures [1945–]. Hamburg, 1947–. 1/yr. Reviews. PC3.R73
VR	*Vox Romanica: Annales Helvetici Explorandis Linguis Romanicis Destinati.* Vol. 1–. Bern: Francke, 1936–. 1/yr. Reviews. PC1.A1 V6
ZRP	*Zeitschrift für romanische Philologie.* Halle [later Tübingen]: Niemeyer, 1877–1913, 1924–1944, 1949–. 4/yr., then 3 double issues/yr. Reviews. Bibliographical supplement (see L–30). PC3.Z5

For a more elaborate enumeration see the *Union List of Periodicals in the Romance Languages and Literatures in British National, University, and Special Libraries* (London: University of London Library, 1964) [Z7032.L6].

L–64 Some Frequently Recommended Works on the Romance Languages and Literatures.

Bal, Willy, and Jean Germain. *Guide bibliographique de linguistique romane*. Louvain, 1978.　Z7031.B34

Braet, Herman, and J. Lambert. *Encyclopédie des études littéraires romanes: Répertoire bibliographique*. Ghent: Wetenschapplijke vitgeverij en boekhandel, 1971.　Z6514.C7B7

Elcock, W. D. *Romance Languages*. New and rev. ed. London: Faber and Faber, 1975.　PC43.E55 1975

Flasche, Hans. *Romance Languages and Literatures as Presented in German Doctoral Dissertations, 1885–1950*. Charlottesville: Bibliographical Society of the University of Virginia, 1958.　Z7031.F55

Gauger, Hans-Martin, et al. *Einführung in die romanische Sprachwissenschaft*. Darmstadt: Wissenschaftliche Buchgesellschaft, 1981.　PC25.G38 1981

Glanville, P. *Romance Linguistics and the Romance Languages: A Bibliography of Bibliographies*. London: Grant and Cutler, 1977.　Z7031.A1 B33

Gröber, Gustav, ed. *Grundriss der romanischen Philologie*. 2 vols. in 4. Strassburg: Trübner, 1897–1906. Neue Folge, part I. 3 vols. Berlin: de Gruyter, 1933–1938.　PC41.G7

Hatzfeld, Helmut A. *Bibliografía crítica de la nueva estilística, aplicada a las literaturas románicas*. Madrid: Gredos, 1955.　Z7031 .H379

　Supplemented by Hatzfeld and Yves Le Hir, *Essai de bibliographie critique de stylistique français et romane (1955–1960)* (Paris: Presses universitaires de France, 1961) [Z7031.H33]. There is also a supplement (Chapel Hill: University of North Carolina Press, 1966), covering the period 1953–1965, of the more selective English version, *Critical Bibliography of the New Stylistics Applied to the Romance Literatures* (Chapel Hill: University of North Carolina Press, 1953) [Z6514.S8 H35], which itself covered the period 1900–1952. See X–133.

Iordan, Iorgu. *Introduction to Romance Linguistics: Its Schools and Scholars*. Rev. with a *Supplement Thirty Years On*, by R. Posner. Oxford: Blackwell, 1970.　PC25.I63 1970

Mourin, Louis, and Jacques Pohl. *Bibliographie de linguistique romane*. 4th ed., rev. and enl. Brussels: Presses universitaires de Bruxelles, 1971.　Z7031.M68

Posner, Rebecca. *Romance Languages: A Linguistic Introduction*. Garden City, N. Y.: Doubleday, 1966.　PC43.P6

Renzi, Lorenzo. *Introduzione alla filologia romanza*. Padua: Libreria editrice universitaria Patròn, 1973; Bologna: Il Mulino, 1976.　PC43.R4

Rohlfs, Gerhart. *Einführung in das Studium der romanische Philologie*. 2 vols. Heidelberg: C. Winter, 1966.　PC41.R6 1966

Rohr, Ruprecht. *Einführung in das Studium der Romanistik*. 3d ed. rev., Berlin: Erich Schmidt, 1980.　PC53.R6 1980

VI.　FRENCH LANGUAGE AND LITERATURE

See also Palfrey (A–19); pertinent works in section I on Language, Linguistics, and Philology; the *MLA International Bibliography* (L–50); the MHRA *Year's Work in Modern Language Studies* (L–52); and works on General and Comparative Literature (section L.I). See also the *International Medieval Bibliography* (F–23); the *Bibliographie internationale de l'humanisme et de la Renaissance* (O–3); the *Eighteenth Century: A Current Bibliography* (P–5); and the bibliography of *The Romantic Movement* (Q–25). Among many pertinent works in section R, see especially the bibliographies in *Journal of Modern Literature* (R–17), *Twentieth Century Literature* (R–16), and *Modern Drama* (R–44).

L–70 Osburn, Charles B. *Research and Reference Guide to French Studies*. 2d ed. Metuchen, N. J.: Scarecrow Press, 1981.　Z2175.A208 1981

This elaborately classified but generally unannotated guide, first published in 1969 followed by a supplement in 1972, is disposed into twelve parts, as follows: 1, General Sources; 2, Dissertations and Theses; 3, French Literature; 4, Scholars and Critics; 5, French Language; 6, Romance Philology; 7, French Language and Literature outside France; 8, Provençal and Southern France; 9, Medieval and Later Latin; 10, Comparative Literature and Travel; 11, General Language and Literature; 12, Related Areas. The volume concludes with cumulative author and subject indexes.

Osburn has also edited *Present State of French Studies: A Collection of Research Reviews* (Metuchen, N. J.: Scarecrow, 1971) [PQ51.O8] with forty-eight essays by recognized authorities surveying the state of scholarship and criticism in individual fields of French studies. Appended are a series of supplementary bibliographical essays that update the references in the main essays and a bibliography of additional reviews of research published elsewhere.

A less comprehensive, more recent, exceptionally well annotated guide is the volume by Fernande Bassan, Paul F. Breed, and Donald C. Spinelli, *Annotated Bibliography of French Language and Literature*, 2d, rev. printing, with additions and corrections (New York: Garland, 1977) [Z2175.A2 B38]. It contains 1,592 serially numbered entries disposed into three parts and a total of twenty chapters. Part 1 is devoted to General Bibliographies and Reference Works, with chapters on Bibliographies of Bibliographies, International General Bibliographies, National and Trade Bibliographies, Reference Works, Catalogs of Books and Manuscripts of Main Libraries, Periodicals, Ph.D. Dissertations and Theses, Encyclopedias and Dictionaries, Biographical Dictionaries, and Main Publishers and Collections (Reprints, Microforms, etc.). Part 2 contains two chapters devoted to the French Language, the first giving Bibliographies and General Studies, the second subdivided into sections for studies on various aspects of the language. Part 3, concerned with French Literature, contains eight chapters, as follows: Surveys, Anthologies, and General Studies of the Literature of France; Medieval Language and Literature; Literature of the sixteenth, seventeenth, eighteenth, nineteenth, and twentieth centuries; and a last chapter concerned with Literature of French Expression Outside of France. The volume concludes with an author/title index.

Among other guides available to the student, the most recent and best is the pamphlet by Richard Kempton, *French Literature: An Annotated Guide to Selected Bibliographies* (New York: MLA, 1981) [Z2171.A1 C34 1981]. The earlier volume by Denis Mahaffey, *Concise Bibliography of French Literature* (New York: Bowker, 1975) [Z2171.M33], has been adversely reviewed and should be avoided. Robert K.

Baker's *Introduction to Library Research in French Literature* (Boulder, Colo.: Westview Press, 1978) [Z2171.B34] is elementary.

The leading French-language annotated guide is by Pierre Langlois and André Mareuil, *Guide bibliographique des études littéraires*, 3d ed., rev. and corr. (Paris: Hachette, 1965) [Z2171.L17 1965], which is limited in scope but has a handy, selective list of the most important editions and critical studies of French authors. It also provides general bibliography, including sections on genres, on literary periods, on literary criticism and literary theory, and the like. Also recommended is Emile Bouvier and Pierre Jourda, *Guide de l'étudiant en littérature française*, 6th ed., rev. and enl. (Paris: Presses universitaires de France, 1968) [PQ51.B6 1968], which discusses methods of explication, writing literary history, and the like and includes an appended annotated bibliography of selected secondary works concerning periods, genres, and literary movements. The newest guide is Bernard Beugnot and J. M. Moureaux, *Manuel bibliographique des études littéraires; les bases de l'histoire littéraire, les voies nouvelles de l'analyse critique* (Paris: Nathan, 1982) [Z6511.B48 1982], which treats basic tools, principal areas of research, and new trends including the study of French literature outside of France.

A highly recommended guide covering publications to 1954 is the volume by Carlo Cordié, *Avviamento allo studio della lingua e della letteratura francese* (Milan: Marzorati, 1955) [Z2171.C67], which consists of Italian-language bibliographical essays concerning general works of reference, each of the periods of French literature, and the history of French literature in general. It has both name and subject indexes.

For French-Canadian literature see Gérard Tougas, *Checklist of Printed Materials Relating to French-Canadian Literature 1763–1968 / Liste de référence d'imprimés relatifs à la littérature canadienne-française*, 2d ed. (Vancouver: University of British Columbia Press, 1973) [Z1377.F8 B72 1973]. See also the bibliographies of Canadian/English literature which also cite French-Canadian work (section M.XII).

L–71 *Oxford Companion to French Literature [OCFL]*. Edited by Paul Harvey and J. E. Hazeltine. Oxford: Clarendon Press, 1959. Corrected reprint. 1961.   PQ41.H3

This volume presents some 6,000 entries surveying topics of interest to the reader of pre–World War II French literature. There are articles on authors, works, critics, historians, savants, statesmen, philosophers, scientists, and literary figures; allusions to matters historical, geographical, social, economic, and political; literary terms and forms; and other topics of reader reference. No bibliographies of secondary references are included in the individual articles, but a bibliography of works about French literature and culture for the beginning student is appended, along with a series of maps.

An abridged and revised version edited by Joyce M. H. Reid has the title *Concise Oxford Dictionary of French Literature* (New York, 1976) [PQ41.B7]. It combines and condenses articles from the *Companion*, expands others, and adds some new articles. Another single volume, similar in scope, is Sidney David Braun, ed., *Dictionary of French Literature* (New York: Philosophical Library, 1958) [PQ41.B7].

A new title of value to the student of French literature is Sandra Dolbrow's *Dictionary of Modern French Literature: From the Age of Reason through Realism* (Westport, Conn.: Greenwood, 1986) [PQ41.D65 1986]. This dictionary covers the period 1715–1880. Writers and major works constitute the majority of the alphabetically arranged entries, but there are also entries for literary and philosophical movements and for literary terms. Bibliographical references are to recent scholarship (1980–1985). A companion volume extending coverage to post-modernism is planned, and cross-references to it are found throughout this work.

In contrast with these single-volume works the resource for detailed reference is the *Dictionnaire des lettres françaises*, ed. Cardinal Georges Grente, 7 vols. (Paris: Arthème Fayard, 1951–1973) [PQ41.D53], which presents an encyclopedic treatment of persons, academies, universities, and literary titles, forms, themes, and topics in signed articles with extensive primary and secondary bibliographies appended. Volumes treat the Middle Ages and the sixteenth, seventeenth, and nineteenth centuries. Each begins with a general survey of the period and a general bibliography. French-language dictionaries of contemporary literature include Pierre de Boisdeffre, ed., *Dictionnaire de la littérature contemporaine*, 3d ed. (Paris, 1967) [PQ305.B54], and André Bourin and Jean Rousselot, *Dictionnaire de la littérature française contemporaine*, new ed., rev. and corr. (Paris: Larousse, 1971) [PQ41.B6 1971]. The Italian *Dizionario critico della letteratura francese*, ed. Franco Simone, 2 vols. (Turin: Unione Tipografico-Editrice Torinese, 1972) [PQ41.S55] is also highly recommended, particularly for its critical evaluations of the work of major and minor authors. Articles are signed and have extensive bibliographies appended.

Two other sources of supplementary information may be mentioned: John B. Pemberton, *How to Find Out about France: A Guide to Sources of Information* (Oxford: Pergamon, 1966) [Z2161.P4 1966], and Donald Charlton, *France: A Companion to French Studies*, 2d ed. (London: Methuen, 1979) [DC33.F666 1979]. Both include considerable sections treating French literature.

L–72 Cabeen, David C., and Jules Brody, gen. eds. [later Richard A. Brooks]. *Critical Bibliography of French Literature*. Syracuse, N. Y.: Syracuse University Press, 1947–.
Z2171.C74 1947

This ongoing, multivolume series of closed, selective, evaluatively annotated bibliographies of works concerning French literature is regarded as absolutely indispensable for specialists and advanced students. Cited are editions, bibliographies, and critical studies whether in the form of books, articles, or dissertations. Reviews are included, too. Each volume has been compiled in chapters, each by a specialist; each volume covers a particular period of French literary history. Volumes vary in quality; they each conclude with a name and subject index. For titles of materials published after the closing dates of these essentially closed period bibliographies, the various serial bibliographies must be used, including Klapp (L–73), Rancoeur (L–74), the *Romance Bibliography* (L–60), *MLA* (L–50), and the *Year's Work* (L–52).

The individual volumes published to date are as follows:

Vol. 1. *Medieval Period*, ed. Urban T. Holmes, Jr., 2d enl. ed. (1952) with entries to 1951 disposed into seventeen chapters by specialists. The consensus seems to be that the bibliography of Bossuat is preferable (see below).

Vol. 2. *Sixteenth Century*, ed. Alexander H. Schultz (1956) with eighteen chapters, each by a specialist. Rev. ed. by Raymond C. LaCharité (1985).

Vol. 3. *Seventeenth Century*, ed. Nathan Edelman (1961), with fourteen chapters, each by a specialist, covering publications to March 1959. *Supplement.*, ed. H. Gaston Hall (1983).

Vol. 4. *Eighteenth Century*, ed. George R. Havens and Donald F. Bond (1951). *Supplement*, ed. Richard A. Brooks (1968), with eleven chapters, each by a specialist, the Supplement covering publications until about 1966.

Vol. 5. *Nineteenth Century.* In progress.

Vol. 6. *Twentieth Century*, ed. Douglas W. Alden and Richard A. Brooks. 3 vols. (1980). Part 1, *General Subjects and the Novel to 1940.* Part 2, *Poetry, Theatre, Essay and Criticism before 1940.* Part 3, *Writing since 1940 and an Index to the Whole.* In all there are forty chapters, each by a specialist, with cut off dates for citations varying from 1973 to 1977. An index of authors and subjects for all three volumes appears at the end of volume 3.

There are several other closed bibliographies of French literature which should be used either in conjunction with Cabeen and Brody or in preference to it. They are as follows:

1. Robert Bossuat, *Manuel bibliographique de la littérature française du moyenâge* (Melun: Librairie d'Argence, 1951) [Z2172.B7]. Supplement [1949–1953] with Jacques Monfrin (Paris, 1955); 2d Supplement [1954–1960] (Paris, 1961). Annotated guide in two sections on Old and Middle French language and literature, with a total of 8,073 books, articles, dissertations, and reviews cited. Neither Latin nor Provençal literature is covered. There are indexes of literary authors and titles and of scholars and editors.

2. Alexandre Cioranesco [sic] with V.-L. Saulnier, *Bibliographie de la littérature française du seizième siècle* (Paris: Klincksieck, 1959) [Z2172.C5]. Cites 22,000 books, articles, and dissertations published by 1950. Unannotated entries are either listed under generalities or within an author bibliography. There is an index of authors and subjects.

3. Alexandre Cioranescu, *Bibliographie de la littérature française du dix-septième siècle*, 3 vols. (Paris: CNRS, 1965–1967) [Z2172.C52]. Listed are 67,000 books, articles, and dissertations treating literature of the period 1601–1715, published before 1962. Unannotated entries are listed in a section on generalities or in the relevant author section. There are four indexes, of authors and scholars, artists and musicians, pseudonyms, and subjects.

4. Alexandre Cioranescu, *Bibliographie de la littérature française du dix-huitième siècle*, 3 vols. (Paris: CNRS, 1969–1970) [Z2172.C48]. Cited are 67,000 books, articles, and dissertations treating the period 1701–1815 which were published before 1961. The structure of these volumes corresponds to that found in the seventeenth-century bibliography cited above.

5. Talvart, Hector, Joseph Place, and Georges Place, *Bibliographie des auteurs modernes de langue française (1801–)*, 22 vols. (A-Morgan) as of 1980 (Paris: Éditions de la chronique des lettres françaises, 1928–) [Z2171.T16]. Contains short biographies with exhaustive lists of primary and secondary works, current to the date of publication of the individual volume. Volumes 16–17 present a title index of works cited in volumes 1–15, along with an index of names and pseudonyms of authors and collaborators.

6. Hugo Paul Thieme, *Bibliographie de la littérature française de 1800 à 1930*, 3d ed., 3 vols. (Paris: Droz, 1933) [Z2171.T43]. Supplemented by S. Dreher and M. Rolli, *Bibliographie de la littérature française, 1930-1939 (Complément à la Bibliographie de H. P. Thieme)*, 2 vols. (Geneva: Droz, 1948-1949) [Z2171.D73]. Further supplemented by Marguerite Drevet, *Bibliographie de la littérature française 1940-1949 (Complément à la Bibliographie de H. P. Thieme)*, 2 vols. (Geneva: Droz, 1954-1955) [Z2171.D73]. Thieme cites books and articles by and about French authors of the nineteenth and ear-

ly twentieth centuries; his third volume cites works concerned with French civilization. The supplements are of the author sections only and do not add titles to the bibliography in Thieme's volume 3.

L–73 **Bibliographie der französischen Literaturwissenschaft / Bibliographie d'histoire littéraire française.** Edited by Otto Klapp. Vol. 1– [1956/58–]. Frankfurt: Klostermann, 1960–. Z2171.B56

This annual (biennial before 1969) serial bibliography is regarded as the finest available reference for current studies in French language and literature. It indexes books, periodicals, festschriften, theses, and long or important reviews concerned with French language and literature, excluding Provençal but including literature of French expression outside France. Collected and individual critical texts are included, along with works of history and criticism. French-language materials predominate. More than 600 periodicals are analyzed; they are listed in each annual volume with identification of the volumes, years, and issues studied. From volume 7 on, entries are serially numbered. From the beginning they are in a classified arrangement, by century, with general categories preceding those that are more specific. Each annual volume includes an *Index nominum* of scholars and an *Index rerum* of subjects, including literary authors-as-subjects.

A *Supplement zu den Banden I-VI* (1956–1968) edited by Friedrich-Albert Klapp was published in 1970; it includes a subject index and a one-volume cumulated index of scholars cited in volumes 1–4.

L–74 **Bibliographie de la littérature française du moyenâge à nos jours.** Compiled by René Rancoeur [1966–]. Paris: A. Colin, 1967–. Z2171.B54

This annual serial bibliography is a continuation of the *Bibliographie littérature* published from 1953 through 1961, and the succeeding *Bibliographie de la littérature française moderne [XVIᵉ-XXᵉ siècles]* [Z2171.B55], published from 1962 through 1965. It is cumulated from the bibliographies appearing in each quarterly issue of the *Revue d'histoire littéraire de la France* (see below). The annual volume, with the quarterly issues of the *Revue*, constitute the most current bibliography available of French literary studies.

The bimonthly unannotated "Bibliographie" in the *Revue d'histoire littéraire de la France* has been published since 1894. Until 1961 these quarterly bibliographies were assembled in an annual volume; from 1961 on they have been cumulated. From 1894 through 1922, articles were cited from French journals only; from 1923, arrangement has been by period and subject; from 1936 on, books have been added, regularly appearing along with dissertations since 1949. Currently, books are distinguished by an asterisk from article citations. There has been an index of authors since the beginning; since 1967 a subject index has also been included. Listings exclude living authors and the medieval period, and are otherwise less complete than the bound volumes.

Entries in the bound volumes have been serially numbered since 1967. They are now disposed into a section on generalities, and then sections on individual periods of French literary history, subdivided into general and specific categories. Coverage has varied; until 1961, literature of the fifteenth through twentieth century was covered, though twentieth-century coverage was very selective; from 1962 on, the twentieth century has been more fully covered; and from 1966 on, medieval literature has also been included. Monographs, dissertations, articles, and a few reviews are included; more than 600 periodicals are currently analyzed. There are indexes of authors and subjects.

Another serial publication of importance is the *Répertoire analytique de littérature française [RALF]*, published since January 1970 six times a year by the Centre Nationale du Recherche Scientifique [CNRS] and the Faculté des lettres et sciences humaines de l'Université de Bordeaux [Z2171.R42]. Each issue contains special subject bibliographies, articles on the present state of studies within a particular specialty, news items, descriptive reviews of recent publications, and accounts of work in progress. A similar publication, sponsored by the Centre de recherche pour un trésor de la langue française in Nancy and published six times a year since October 1969, is the *Bulletin analytique de linguistique française* (Paris: Didier, 1970–) [Z2175.A2 B85]. It contains a briefly annotated, classified bibliography of books, articles, and dissertations, with an author index that is cumulated annually.

L–75 **"Rassegna bibliografia"** [di studi francesi] in *Studi francesi*, vol. 1– [1955–]. Turin: Società editrice internazionale, 1957–.   PQ5.S75

Each of three yearly issues contains a series of bibliographical essays treating books and articles on French language and literature for each of the periods. The essays are signed, written in Italian, French, or English, and present evaluative bibliographies generally regarded as of equal or greater value compared with those of similar character appearing in the relevant portions of the *Year's Work in Modern Language Studies* (L–52). There is an annual index for each volume and a ten-year index covering the thirty issues for 1957–1966.

L–76 *Anglo-French and Franco-American Studies: A Current Bibliography.* Romanic Review. 1938–1948.   PC1.R7

Books, articles, and reviews are cited which treat literary relations between France and America from the sixteenth century to the present. The bibliography has two main sections that are indicated by the title. Within these sections are divisions for bibliographies and general studies, historical background, languages, French-English influences, and English-French influences. Entries are descriptively annotated.

L–78 **Scholarly Journals in French Studies.**

Billot, Mary M. "French Language and Literature Periodicals: An Annotated Select List of Current Serial Publications." *International Library Review* 1, no. 2 (April 1969): 283–304.

Fiber, Louise A. "A Selected Guide to 91 United States and Canadian Journals in the Field of French Language and Literature." *French Review* 47 (1974): 1128–1141.

AJFS   *Australian Journal of French Studies.* Vol. 1–. Clayton, Victoria: Monash University, 1964–. 3/yr. Reviews. Current bibliography of Anglo-Norman Studies.   PQ1.A8

ECr   *L'ésprit créateur: A Critical Quarterly of French Literature.* Vol. 1–. Lawrence: University of Kansas, Department of French, 1961–. 4/yr. Reviews.   PQ1.E78

EF   *Études françaises.* Vol. 1–. Montreal: Presses de l'Université de Montréal, 1965–. 4/yr.   No LC number

Études litteraires. Vol. 1–. Quebec: Presses de l'Université Laval, 1968–. 3/yr. Reviews.   PQ2.E83

FM   *Le français moderne: Revue de linguistique française.* Vol. 1–. Paris: Centre national de la recherche scientifique, 1933–. 4/yr. Reviews.   PC2002.F81

FR   *French Review: Journal of the American Association of Teachers of French.* Vol. 1–. Champaign, Ill.: AATF, 1927–. 6/yr. Reviews. Annual bibliography of North American "Dissertations in Progress [1963–]."   PC2001.F75

FS   *French Studies: A Quarterly Review.* Vol. 1–. Oxford: B. Blackwell, 1947–. 4/yr. Reviews.   PQ1.F85

Oeuvres et critiques: Revue internationale détude de la reception critique des oeuvres littéraires françaises. Vol. 1–. Paris: Place, 1976–. 2/yr. Contains a series of bibliographies on research in seventeenth-century French literature.   PQ2.O35

RHL   *Revue d'histoire littéraire de la France.* Vol. 1–. Paris: Librairie Armand Colin, 1894–. 6/yr. Reviews. Bibliographies in each issue (see L–74).

La revue des lettres modernes: Histoire des idées et des littératures. Paris: Minard, 1954–. Irreg. Bibliographies of editions, books, and articles on modern authors.   PN3.R4

SFr   *Studi francesi.* Vol. 1–. Turin: Società editrice internazionale, 1957–. 3/yr. Reviews. Bibliographical essays.   PQ5.S75

ZFSL   *Zeitschrift für französische Sprache und Literatur.* Vol. 1–. Wiesbaden: Franz Steiner Verlag, 1879–. Reviews.   PC2003.Z5

L–79 **Some Frequently Recommended Works on French Language and Literature.**

Bibliographical Works

Bibliographie annuelle de l'histoire de France du cinquième siècle à 1945; [Année 1955–]. Paris: CNRS, 1956–. Includes a bibliography of French literature in the section "Histoire de la civilisation." A supplement for 1953/54 was published in 1964.   Z2176.B5

Giraud, Jeanne. *Manuel de bibliographie littéraire pour les XVIe, XVIIe et XVIIIe siècles français, 1921–1935.* Paris: Vrin, 1939. *Supplément 1936–1945.* Paris: Nizet, 1956, *Supplément 1946–1955.* Paris: Nizet, 1970. Supplements Lanson, below, for the periods specified.   Z2171.G5

Lanson, Gustave. *Manual bibliographique de la littérature française moderne (XVIe, XVIIe, VIIIe et XIXe siècles).* New ed., rev. and corr. Paris: Hachette, 1931. An early standard bibliography, comprehensive in scope but selective with limited bibliographic information supplied, supplemented for 1921–1955 by Giraud, above.   Z2171.L22 1931

Martin, Robert, and Eveline Martin. *Guide bibliographique de linguistique française.* Paris: Klincksieck, 1973.   Z2175.A2 M37

MLA. *French 17: An Annual Bibliography of French Seventeenth Century Studies.* [Formerly French III Section. *Bibliography of French Seventeenth Century Studies.*] Bloomington, Ind. [place varies], 1952/53–. Very current listing of books, articles, reviews, and dissertations.   Z2172.M6

MLA. French V Section. *Bibliography of French Eighteenth Century Studies.* New York, 1950–1955.

MLA. French VI. Bibliography Committee. *French VI Bibliography: Critical and Biographical References for the Study of 19th Century French Literature* [covering books, articles, reviews, and dissertations, 1954–1967]. 2 vols. in 7 parts. New York: French Institute and the MLA, 1955–1969. For the late nineteenth century see also MLA French VII/XX, below.   Z2173.F72

MLA. *French XX Bibliography: Critical and Biographical References for French Literature since 1885.* [Formerly *French VII Bibliography*, 20 numbers in 4 volumes, New York: Stechert-Hafner, 1949–1968.] Vol. 5–. New York: French Institute and the MLA, 1969–. Cites materials from popular journals and newspapers in addition to scholarly books and articles. Indexes have been published for vols. 1–2 (1965), 3–4 (1969), and 5 (1974). Z2171.F7

"Recent Books on French History." *French Historical Studies.* Vol. 1–. Columbus, Ohio: Society for French Historical Studies, 1958–. Place of publication varies. Very current. DC1.F69

Société Rencesvals. *Bulletin bibliographique pour l'étude des épopées romanes.* Paris: Nizet, 1958–.

Taylor, Robert A. *La littérature occitane du moyen âge: Bibliographie selective et critique.* Toronto: University of Toronto Press, 1977. Annotated entries emphasize work on Provençal literature since 1950. Z7033.P8 T38

Historical and Special Studies

Abraham, Pierre, and Roland Desné, gen. eds. *Manuel d'histoire littéraire de la France.* 6 vols. Paris: Éditions sociales, 1965–1973. PQ101.M3

Adam, Antoine. *Histoire de la littérature française au XVIIe siècle.* 5 vols. Paris: Domat Montchrestien, 1948–1962. PQ241.A3

————, et al. *Littérature française.* 2 vols. Paris: Larousse, 1967–1968. Updates and generally replaces Bedier-Hazard, below. PQ101.A3

Baldner, Ralph W. *Bibliography of Seventeenth-Century French Prose Fiction.* New York: MLA, 1967. Z2174.B3

Bédier, Joseph. *Les legendes epiques: Recherches sur la formation des chansons de geste . . .* 3d ed., rev. and corr. 4 vols. Paris: Champion, 1926–1929. PQ201.B4 1926

Bédier, Joseph, and Paul Hazard. *Littérature française.* New ed., rev. and enl. by Pierre Martino. 2 vols. Paris: Larousse, 1948–1949. Generally replaced by Adam et al., above. PQ101.H52

Bray, René. *La préciosité et les précieux de Thibaut de Champagne à Jean Giroudoux.* Paris: Albin Michel, 1948. PQ245.B73

Bremer, Clarence D. *Bibliographical List of Plays in the French Language, 1700–1789.* Berkeley: University of California Press, 1947. Z2174.D7 B7

Brereton, Geoffrey. *Short History of French Literature.* 2d ed. London: Penguin, 1976. PQ119.B7 1976

Brunot, Ferdinand. *Histoire de la langue française, des origines à nos jours.* New ed. 13 vols. Paris: A. Colin, 1966–1972. PC2075.B72

Calvet, Jean, ed. *Histoire de la littérature française.* New ed. 10 vols. Paris: Del Duca, 1955–1964. PQ101.H66 1955

Cazamian, Louis F. *History of French Literature.* Oxford: Oxford University Press, 1955. PQ103.C3

Clarke, A. F. B. *Boileau and the French Classical Critics in England (1660–1830).* Paris: E. Champion, 1925. PQ1723.C6

Clouard, Henri. *Histoire de la littérature française du symbolisme à nos jours.* New ed. 2 vols. Paris: A. Michel, 1956–1962. PQ296.C4 1956

Cohen, Gustave. *La vie littéraire en France au moyen âge.* Paris: Tallandier, 1949. PQ151.C6

Cruickshank, John, ed. *French Literature and Its Background.* 6 vols. London: Oxford University Press, 1969–1970. PQ103.C7

Engler, Winfried. *French Novel from Eighteen Hundred to the Present.* New York: Ungar, 1969. PQ631.E5213 1969

Fowlie, Wallace. *French Critic, 1549–1967.* Carbondale: Southern Illinois University Press, 1968. PN99.F8 F6

Guth, Paul. *Histoire de la littérature française.* 2 vols. Paris: Fayard, 1967. PQ101.G8

Hicks, Benjamin E. *Plots and Characters in Classic French Fiction.* Hamden, Conn.: Archon, 1981. PQ631.H5 1981

Histoire littéraire de la France: Ouvrage commencé par les religieux bénédictins de la Congrégation de Saint-Maure, et continué par des membres de l'Institut [de France]. New ed. 41 vols. Paris, 1865–1981. Volumes 15, 23, and 32 are index volumes. PQ101.A2 H6

Holmes, Urban T. *History of Old French Literature from the Origins to 1300.* Rev. ed. New York: Russell and Russell, 1962. PQ156.H6 1962

Jasinski, René. *Histoire de la littérature française.* New ed. 2 vols. Paris: Nizet, 1965. PQ116.J3

Jeanroy, Alfred. *Les origines de la poésie lyrique en France au moyen âge.* 4th ed. Paris: H. Champion, 1969. PQ211.J4 1969

Jones, S. Paul. *List of French Prose Fiction from 1700 to 1750.* New York: H. W. Wilson, 1939. Z2174.F4 J7 1939

Lanson, Gustave. *Histoire de la littérature française, remaniée et completée pour la période 1850–1950 par Paul Tuffrau.* Paris: Hachette, 1953. PQ101.L3

Le Gentil, Pierre. *La littérature française du moyen âge.* Paris: A. Colin, 1968. PQ151.L4 1968

Literary History of France. 6 vols. London: Benn, 1967–1974. Includes the *Middle Ages*, by John H. Fox; *Renaissance France*, by Ian D. McFarlane; the *Seventeenth Century*, by Philip John Yarrow; the *Eighteenth Century*, by Robert Niklaus; the *Nineteenth Century*, by Patrick E. Charvet; and the *Twentieth Century*, by Patrick E. Charvet. PQ103.L5

Malignon, Jean. *Dictionnaire des écrivains française.* Paris: Éditions du seuil, 1971. PQ41.M3

Nathan, Jacques, and Raymond Basch, eds. *Encyclopédie de la littérature française.* Paris: Fernand Nathan, 1952. PQ116.N3

Neubert, Fritz. *Geschichte der französischen Literatur.* Tübigen: Niemeyer, 1949.

Nitze, William, and E. Preston Dargan. *History of French Literature, from the Earliest Times to the Present.* 3d ed. New York: H. Holt, 1938. PQ119.N5 1938

Pichois, Claude, gen. ed. *Littérature française.* 16 vols. Paris: Arthaud, 1968–1979. PQ101.P56

Roger, Jacques, and Jean-Claude Payen. *Histoire de la littérature française.* 2 vols. Paris: A. Colin, 1969–1970. PQ101.R74

Theisen, Josef. *Geschichte der französischen Literatur.* 5th ed. Stuttgart: Kohlhammer, 1978. PQ105.T4 1978

Thibaudet, Albert. *Histoire de la littérature française de 1789 à nos jours.* Paris: Stock, 1936. PQ281.T5

Van Tieghem, Paul. *Les influences étrangères sur la littérature française (1550–1880)*. 2d ed. Paris: Presses universitaires de France, 1967.

PQ143.A2 V4 1967

———. *Petite histoire des grandes doctrines littéraires en France de la Pléiade au surréalisme*. Paris: Presses universitaires de France, 1946.   PQ226.V3

Vier, Jacques. *Histoire de la littérature française, XVIᵉ-XVIIᵉ siècles*. 2d ed. Paris: A. Colin, 1967.

PQ226.V48 1967

———. *Histoire de la littérature française, XVIIIᵉ siècle*. 2 vols. Paris: A. Colin, 1965–1970.   PQ261.V47

Voretzsch, Carl. *Einführung in das Studium der altfranzösischen Literatur in Anschluss an die Einführung in das Studium der altfranzösischen Sprache*. 3d ed. Halle: Niemeyer, 1925.

PQ151.V7 1925

Wicks, C. Beaumont. *Parisian Stage [1800–1900]: Alphabetical Indexes of Plays and Authors*. 5 vols. University: University of Alabama Press, 1950–1979.

PN2636.P3 W5

Belgium

Charlier, Gustave, and Joseph Hanse. *Histoire illustrée des lettres françaises de Belgique*. Brussels: Renaissance du livre, 1958.   PQ3814.C5

French Africa

(see also entries for African literature, section L.XII)

Baratte, Eno Belinga, Thérèse, et al. *Bibliographie des auteurs africains de langue française*. 4th ed. Paris: Fernand Nathan, 1979.

Déjeux, Jean. *Dictionnaire des auteurs maghrebins de langue française*. Paris: Karthala, 1984.

PQ3988.5.N6 D43 1984

French Canada

(see also entries for Canadian Literature, section M.XII)

Barbeau, Victor, and André Fortier. *Dictionnaire bibliographique du Canada français*. Montreal: Académie canadienne-française, 1974.   Z1365.B3

Brunet, Berthelot. *Histoire de la littérature canadienne-française*. Montreal: Editions de l'arbre, 1946.

PQ3901.B7

Cotnam, Jacques. *Contemporary Québec: An Analytical Bibliography*. Toronto: McClelland and Stewart, 1973.   Z1392.Q3 C68

Grandpré, Pierre de. *Histoire de la littérature française de Québec*. 4 vols. Montreal: Beauchemin, 1965–1967.

PQ3917.G7

Hamel, Reginald, John Hare, and Paul Wyczynski. *Dictionnaire pratique des auteurs québécois*. Montreal: Fides, 1976.   PQ3904.H3

Roy, Camille. *Histoire de la littérature canadienne française*. 21st ed. Montreal: Beauchemin, 1959.

PQ3901.R6 1959

Tougas, Gerard. *Histoire de la littérature canadienne-française*. 4th ed. Paris: Presses universitaires de France, 1967. Also published in English as *History of French-Canadian Literature*. Translated by Alta Lind Cook. 2d ed. Toronto: Ryerson Press, 1966.

PQ3901.R6

VII. ITALIAN LANGUAGE AND LITERATURE

See also Palfrey (A–19); pertinent works in section I on Language, Linguistics, and Philology; the *MLA International Bibliography* (L–50); the MHRA *Year's Work in Modern Language Studies* (L–52); works on General and Comparative Literature (section L.I); and works in Classical Studies (section L.II). See also the *International Medieval Bibliography* (F–23), the *Bibliographie internationale de l'humanisme et de la Renaissance* (O–3); the *Eighteenth Century: A Current Bibliography* (P–5); and the bibliography of the *Romantic Movement* (Q–25). Among many pertinent works in section R see especially the bibliographies in the *Journal of Modern Literature* (R–17), *Twentieth Century Literature* (R–16), and *Modern Drama* (R–44).

L–80 **Puppo, Mario. *Manuale critico-bibliografico per lo studio della letterature italiana*.** 13th ed., rev. Turin: Società editrice internazionale, 1980.   PQ4037.P8 1980

The table of contents summarizes the extensive scope of this most up-to-date student bibliographical guide first published in 1954. It consists of a series of discursive essays followed by bibliographies of works referred to or otherwise relevant. The work is disposed into five main sections, as follows: I. Critical orientation and general bibliography, including reviews, collections, literary history, encyclopedias, and dictionaries of Italian literature; II. Methodology, both philological and critical, including textual criticism, aesthetics, and the history of criticism and literary history; III. Stylistics and linguistics, including grammar, the history of the Italian language, and similar topics; IV. The major literary periods and minor writers; V. The major authors. The volume concludes with an appended glossary of philological and critical terms and an index of names, the table of contents serving in lieu of an analytical index of subjects.

Four other guides are often recommended. The first, Renzo Frattarolo, *Introduzione bibliografica alla letteratura italiana* (Rome: Edizioni dell'Ateneo, 1963) [Z2351.F7], consists of bibliographical essays with notes and additional enumerations of titles appended, treating introductory and general bibliography; encyclopedias, encyclopedic dictionaries, and biographical dictionaries; literary history; philology and linguistics; editions of the classics and collections of poetry; reviews and periodicals. The second, Walter Binni, *Introduzione ai problemi critici della letteratura italiana* (Messina: G. D. D'Anna, 1967) [Z2351.B5], is divided into two parts, the first concerned with general works and the second with literary movements and major figures (minor figures are discussed in the context of their literary movements). Cited throughout are bibliographies, editions, and prominent secondary works. The volume concludes with an index of names and an analytical table of contents. The third is Guido Mazzoni, *Avviamento allo studio critico delle lettere italiane*, 5th ed., rev. and enl., ed. Carmine Jannacó (Florence: Sansoni, 1971) [Z2351.M47 1971], which is divided into sections on manuscripts; books and printing; libraries; reference works and periodicals; literary history; poets and poetics; vocabulary, grammar, rhetoric, and metrics; and bibliographies. And the fourth is Felice del Beccaro, *Guida allo studio della letteratura italiana* (Milan: Mursia, 1975) [Z2354.C8 B4], which is divided into a general section followed by chapters of the literature of each century, including subsections on major authors. Material is presented in essay form, with an index of names.

The one English-language reference work likely to be helpful in this context is F. S. Stych, *How to Find Out about Italy* (Oxford: Pergamon Press, 1970) [Z2356.S76 1970], which contains evaluative discussions of reference works on libraries, archives, manuscripts, rare books, encyclopedias, newspapers, societies, literature, the fine arts, the social sciences, language, applied science, technology, and natural science.

L–81 Bondanella, Peter, and Julia Conway Bondanella, eds. *Dictionary of Italian Literature.* Westport, Conn.: Greenwood Press, 1979.   PQ4006.D45

This work contains some 362 signed articles on major and minor Italian writers from the twelfth century to the present; on metrics, poetic forms and genres; and on literary and critical schools, periods, problems, and movements. Articles are prepared by the two editors or one of thirty-five contributors, and each includes an appended bibliography. The first of two appendixes is a chronology with four columns enumerating events in Italian literature; world literature; political theory, history, and religion; and philosophy, science, and the arts. The second appendix is a classification of the articles by subject matter or chronological period. The volume concludes with "Reference Aids: A Selected List."

The most distinguished dictionary of Italian literature is the three-volume *Dizionario critico della letteratura italiana*, ed. Vittore Branca (Turin: Unione tipografico-editrice torinese, 1974) [PQ4057.D59]. It contains signed articles on authors and terms, with bibliographies of editions and secondary studies appended. The third volume concludes with an index of names. Other Italian dictionaries include Giuseppe Petronio, ed., *Dizionario enciclopedico della letteratura italiana*, 6 vols. (Bari: Laterza, 1966–1970) [PQ4006.D5], with short articles on authors, and some on titles, genres, and characters, all with appended bibliographies. For authors see also Bruno Cordati and Mario Farina, eds., *DAI: Dizionario degli autori italiani* (Florence: D'Anna, 1974) [PQ4057.D3], and Enzo Ronconi, ed., *Dizionario generale degli autori italiani contemporanei*, 2 vols. (Florence: Vallecchi, 1974) [PQ4113.D58].

L–82 *Ornamenti culturali: Letteratura italiana.* 19 vols. Milan: Marzorati, 1956–1974.   LC numbers vary

This massive collection of monographs by various contributors on the periods and authors of Italian literature presents biographical or biobibliographical essays followed by extensive critical bibliographies. The nineteen volumes are divided as follows: two volumes treat literary periods [PQ4037.L43], two treat major authors [PQ4037.L455], four treat minor authors [PQ4037.L46], six are on contemporary writers [PQ4087.L44], and five are on literary critics from De Sanctis to the present [PQ4027.L4].

The other important multivolume work of scholarly orientation is Atillio Momigliano, ed., *Problemi ed orientamenti critici di lingua e di letteratura italiana*, 2d ed., rev. and enl., 5 vols. in 7 (Milan: Marzorati, 1948–1960) [LC numbers vary]. The five volumes, with many contributors writing in each, treat the following subject matters: bibliography [Z1001.N92]; literary theory and technique [PN45.T4]; problems and currents in Italian literary history; Italy's literary relations with other major literatures; and the history of aesthetics.

Also published by Marzorati is the three-volume *Notizie introduttive e sussidi bibliografici*, 3d ed. (Milan, 1965) [Z1001.N92 1965]. Volume 1 treats generalities, volume 2 major and minor writers and literary movements, and volume 3 contains the indexes.

For students of the Italian language the standard closed bibliography is Robert Anderson Hall, *Bibliografia della linguistica italiana*, 2d rev. ed., 3 vols. (Florence: Sansoni, 1958) [Z2355.A2 H315], with its citations of some 6,900 items published since 1860, disposed into sections on the history of Italian, the description of Italian, Italian dialectology, and the history of Italian linguistics. There are indexes of authors, titles, regions, dialects, words, and general subjects.

L–83 Prezzolini, Giuseppe. *Repertorio bibliografico della storia e della critica della letteratura italiana dal 1902 al 1942.* 4 vols. Rome: Edizioni Roma, 1936–1946.   Z2351.P93

This work forms the basis for the current serial bibliography of Italian literature. Volumes 1 and 2 treat selected works published 1902–1932; volumes 3 and 4 cover publications 1933–1942. Sponsored by the Council on Research in the Humanities in Columbia University, this bibliography includes monographs, articles, and reviews. Entries are in chronological order by their subject, including authors as subjects, and are presented in the form of bibliographical essays. There are also a series of general articles, listed at the ends of volumes 2 and 4, on such generic subjects as children's literature, political literature, religious literature, etc. There are additions and an index of scholars' names at the ends of volumes 2 and 4.

This series has been continued under the editorship of Umberto Bosco, with entries arranged by scholarly author and indexed by subject, under the title *Repertorio bibliografico della letteratura italiana a cura della facoltà di magistero di Roma* (Florence: Sansoni, 1953–) [Z2341.R4]. Because it is so far behind, it is more nearly a retrospective than a current bibliography. Listed are monographs, articles, and reviews; some 500 journals are analyzed for materials. Entries are curiously arranged into three series. The first group contains monographs and articles arranged in alphabetical order by the names of the scholars and literary authors with whom they are associated or the titles of collected volumes. A second series contains articles signed with initials or pseudonyms. A third series is alphabetical by article title and contains anonymous articles. There are relatively few cross-references, and though there is a subject index, it does not overcome the difficulty of using this work.

A further serial bibliography, more selective but much more current than the *Repertorio*, is the evaluative bibliographic essay *Rassegna bibliografica* [della letteratura italiana], which appears in each of the two or three issues per year of *Rassegna della letteratura italiana*. Parallel in character to the French *Rassegna* (see L–75), this work cites books, articles, and reviews. It is arranged by periods and authors, with signed, often lengthy bibliographic essays by recognized authorities. There is an annual index of titles, arranged by centuries, then literary figures, then alphabetically by names of scholars.

L–88 Scholarly Journals in Italian Studies.

GSLI   *Giornale storico della letteratura italiana.* Vol. 1–. Turin: Loescher, 1883–. Reviews. Systematic index to vols. 1–100.   PQ4001.G5

IMU   *Italia medioevale e umanistica.* Vol. 1–. Padua: Antenore, 1958–. 1/yr.   PA9.I8

Italica   *Italica.* Vol. 1–. Chicago: Northwestern University Press [publisher varies] for the American Association of Teachers of Italian, 1924–. 4/yr. Annual "Bibliography of Italian Studies in America [1923–]," including books, articles, and reviews published in North America or by North American scholars.   PC1068.U6 I8

IS   *Italian Studies.* Cambridge: Society for Italian Studies, 1937–. 1/yr. Reviews. Bibliography of books and articles published in Great Britain.   DG401.I85

IRLI   *Italianistica: Rivista di letteratura italiana.* Vol. 1–. Milan: Marzorati, 1972–. Reviews. Bibliographies.   PQ4001.I78

LI   *Lettere italiane*. Vol. 1–. Florence: Leo S. Olsch-ki, 1949–. 4/yr. Reviews. Quarterly "Rassegna," a bibliographical essay on recent criticism.
PQ4001.L47

RLI   *Rassegna della letteratura italiana*. Vol. 1–. Florence: Licosa, 1883–1948, 1953–. 2–3/yr. Reviews. Annual classified bibliography for Italian literature [see L–83].   PQ4001.R3

REI   *Revue des études italiennes*. Vol. 1–. Paris: Société d'études italiennes, 1936–. 4/yr. Reviews.
PQ4001.R47

L–89   Some Frequently Recommended Works on Italian Studies.

Bibliographical Works

D'Ancona, Alessandro, and Orazio Bacci. *Manuale della letteratura italiana*. Revised and annotated by Mario Sterzi. 3 vols. in 4. Florence, 1932–1934.
PQ4010.A6 1932

Ferrari, Luigi. *Onomasticon: Repertorio bibliografico degli scrittori italiani dal 1501 al 1850*. Milan: Hoepli, 1947.   Z2350.F4

Fucilla, Joseph G. *Universal Author Repertoire of Italian Essay Literature [1821–1938]*. New York: Vanni, 1941.   Z6511.F8

———. *Saggistica letteraria italiana: Bibliografia per soggetti, 1938–1952*. Florence: Sansoni, 1956.
Z2354.E7 F8

Mazzamuto, Pietro. *Rassegna bibliografico-critica della letteratura italiana*. 3d ed., rev. Florence: Le Monnier, 1956.   PQ4037.M35 1956

Santini, Emilio. *Strumenti dell'arte critica: Introduzione allo studio della letteratura italiana*. 2d ed. Palermo: G. B. Palumbo, 1948.   Z2351.S3 1948

Historical and Special Studies

Avery, Catherine, ed. *New Century Italian Renaissance Encyclopedia*. New York: Appleton-Century-Crofts, 1972.   DG537.8.A1 N48

Binni, Walter, and Natalino Spageno. *Storia letteraria della regione d'italia*. Florence: Sansoni, 1968.
PQ4037.B5

Cecchi, Emilio, and Natalino Sapegno, eds. *Storia della letteratura italiana*. 9 vols. Milan: Garzanti, 1965–1969.   PQ4037.C4

Corrigan, Beatrice, ed. *Italian Poets and English Critics, 1755–1859*. Chicago: University of Chicago Press, 1969.   PQ4094.C6

Cosenza, Mario Emilio. *Biographical and Bibliographical Dictionary of the Italian Humanists and of the World of Classical Scholarship in Italy, 1300–1800*. 2d ed., rev. and enl. 6 vols. Boston: G. K. Hall, 1962–1967.   Z7128.H9 C6

Croce, Benedetto. *La letteratura della nuova Italia*. 3d ed. 6 vols. Bari: Laterza, 1947–1954.   PQ4085.C76

De Sanctis, Francesco. *History of Italian Literature*. Translation by Joan Redfern of *Storia della letteratura italiana, a cura di Benedetto Croce*, 6th ed., 2 vols. (Bari: Laterza, 1958). 2 vols. New York: Basic Books, 1960.   PQ4037.D413 1960

Donadoni, Eugenio. *History of Italian Literature*. 2 vols. New York: New York University Press, 1969.
PQ4037.D613 1969

Flora, Francesco. *Storia della letteratura italiana*. 6th ed. 5 vols. Milan: Mondadori, 1972.   PQ4037.F63 1972

Gardner, E. G. *Italy: A Companion to Italian Studies*. London: Methuen, 1934.   DG441.G3

Gaspary, Adolph. *History of Italian Literature to the Death of Dante*. London: G. Bell, 1901.   PQ4040.G35

Migliorini, Bruno. *Italian Language*. Rev. ed. Translation by T. Gwynfor Griffith of *Storia della lingua italiana* (Florence: Sansoni, 1960). London: Faber and Faber, 1966.   PC1075.M513 1966a

Momigliano, Atillio, ed. *Problemi ed orientamenti critici di linguae di letteratura italiana*. 5 vols. in 7. Milan: C. Marzorati, 1948–1961.   PQ4005.M655

Palgen, R. *Geschichte der italienischen Literatur*. Bonn: Athenäum-Verlag, 1949.   PQ4044.P3

Sansone, Mario. *La letteratura italiana*. 3 vols. Bari: Laterza, 1956–1957.   PQ4005.C7

Storia letteraria d'Italia, scritta da una società di professori. 3d ed. 10 vols. Milan: F. Vallardi, 1942–. This series, first published 1880–1913 is under a program of continual revision.   PQ4037.S82

Vossler, K. *Italienische literaturgeschichte*. 2d ed. Leipzig: G. J. Göschen, 1908.   PQ4044.V7

Whitfield, John Humphreys. *Short History of Italian Literature*. Harmondsworth: Penguin Books, 1960.
PQ4043.W5

Wilkins, Ernest Hatch. *History of Italian Literature*. Rev. ed. Edited by Thomas G. Bergin. Cambridge: Harvard University Press, 1974.   PQ4038.W5 1974

VIII. HISPANIC, HISPANIC-AMERICAN, AND PORTUGUESE LANGUAGES AND LITERATURES

See also Palfrey (A–19); pertinent works in section I on Language, Linguistics, and Philology; the *MLA International Bibliography* (L–50); the MHRA *Year's Work in Modern Language Studies* (L–52); and works on General and Comparative Literature (section L.I). For Latin American authors writing in English see section M; for Spanish-American authors see also section S. See also the *International Medieval Bibliography* (F–23); the *Bibliographie de l'humanisme et de la Renaissance* (O–3); the *Eighteenth Century: A Current Bibliography* (P–5); and the bibliography of the *Romantic Movement* (Q–25). Among the many pertinent works in section R, see especially the bibliographies in the *Journal of Modern Literature* (R–17), *Twentieth Century Literature* (R–16), and *Modern Drama* (R–44).

L–90   Bleznick, Donald W.   *Sourcebook for Hispanic Literature and Language: A Selected, Annotated Guide to Spanish and Spanish-American and Chicano Bibliography, Literature, Linguistics, Journals and Other Source Materials.* Metuchen, N. J.: Scarecrow Press, 1983.
Z2695.A2 B55 1983

This briefly annotated guide, originally published in 1974, contains serially numbered entries disposed into sixteen sections, as follows: Aims and Methods of Research; General Bibliographic Guides and References; Style Guides; Bibliographies of Hispanic Literature; Literary Dictionaries and Encyclopedias; Histories of Hispanic Literatures; Histories of Spanish Literature; Histories of Spanish-American Literature; Anthologies; Books on Metrics; Literature in Translation; Bibliographies in Linguistics; Scholarly Periodicals [an extensive listing of 100 journals]; Libraries; Guides to Dissertations; and Other Useful References in the Hispanic Field. There are two further sections listing selected publishers and selected book dealers respectively. The index is of names and titles. Most sections are divided into separate subsections for Spain and Spanish America.

A second, more recent reference guide is David Williams Foster and Virginia Ramos Foster, *Manual of Hispanic Bibliography*, 2d ed., rev. and exp. (New York: Garland, 1977) [Z2691.A1 F68 1977], originally published by the University of Washington Press in 1970. This work contains over 1,000 serially numbered, well-annotated entries on primary and secondary reference sources for Spanish and Spanish-American literature. Language and linguistics are deliberately excluded. Included are national bibliographies, guides to theses, indexes of periodicals, and other general works, as well as specifically literary reference tools.

A recent addition to these is the small volume by Hensley C. Woodbridge, *Spanish and Spanish-American Literature: An Annotated Guide to Selected Bibliographies* (New York: MLA, 1983) [Z2691.A1 W66 1983], which treats bibliographies, dictionaries and lexicons, and encyclopedias published since 1950 on various genres and on the literatures of specific countries.

L–91 *Oxford Companion to Spanish Literature [OCSL].* Edited by Philip Ward. Oxford: Clarendon Press, 1978.
PQ6006.O95

This work serves as a companion for readers of literature written in Spanish. Most articles are on authors, including any persons who may be said to have contributed to Spanish literary life. Portuguese writers are excluded, but Basque, Catalan, and Galician authors are included, as are Spanish writers of Central and South America. Titles are included, with summaries of important works; also included are articles on some literary and prosodic terms and on institutions important in the history of Spanish literature. Massive amounts of bibliographical information are given in the articles.

The most distinguished dictionary of Spanish literature is the *Diccionario de la literatura española*, ed. Germán Bleiberg and Julián Marías, 4th ed., corrected and augmented (Madrid: Revista de Occidente, 1972) [PQ6006.D5 1972]. Originally published in 1949, this work contains initialed articles on literary terms, genres, and movements, as well as on Spanish and Spanish-American authors and works. Bibliographies are included. There is an index of titles and a two-column chronology of dates in Spanish and Spanish-American literary history and their relation to events in political and cultural history. There is a bibliographical appendix, an appendix on Catalan literature, one on Galician literature, a short paleographical appendix with twenty-four plates and transcriptions, and a series of literary maps.

A third dictionary is Maxim Newmark's *Dictionary of Spanish Literature* (New York: Philosophical Library, 1956) [PQ6006.N4], which treats both Spanish and Spanish-American authors, terms, and other references. Another useful resource is P. E. Russell, ed., *Spain: A Companion to Spanish Studies*, new ed. (London: Methuen, 1976) [DP48.R87 1976], first published in 1929. Of the twelve chapters, each with a bibliography, chapters 6–10 concern Spanish and Spanish-American literature.

L–92 **Simón Díaz, José.** *Manuel de bibliografía de la literatura española.* 3d ed., rev., corr., and enl. Madrid: Gredos, 1980.
Z2691.S54 1980

This work was originally published in 1963; the 1966 edition includes a supplement of 100 pages covering works published during the years 1962–1964. A second supplement covering 1965–1970, was published in 1974. There are general sections on genres and periods of Spanish literature, followed by studies on all aspects of the literature arranged by periods, then authors. Bibliographies, editions, and biographies are listed for major and minor writers. This edition has nearly

27,000 serially numbered, unannotated entries in six sections: Generalities, Middle Ages, Golden Age, Eighteenth, Nineteenth, and Twentieth Centuries. Cited editions include complete works, selected works, single works, anthologies, and letters. There are indexes of names and subjects.

The *Manuel* is regarded as the best single-volume bibliography of Spanish literature; it is kept current by the "Informacíon bibliografíca literatura castellana" in the *Revista de literatura* (Madrid, 1952–) [PN6.R48], which is edited by Simón Díaz. Before 1960 this serial bibliography included non-Spanish titles published in Spain; since then, only Spanish titles published in Spain and Latin America are cited. Two double issues per year are published. They are arranged by centuries and authors, there is no index, and there are no cross-references. Entries have been continuously numbered since the publication's beginning.

Titles from the "Informacíon bibliografíca" are transferred subsequently into the multivolume *Bibliografía de la literatura hispánica* by Simón Díaz, 13 vols. to date, plus supplements (Madrid: Consejo superior de investigaciones científicas, Instituto "Miguel de Cervantes" de filologia hispanica, 1958–1984; 2d ed., corr. and enl., 1960– [Z2691 .S5]). A comprehensive bibliography of all the Hispanic literatures, this work cites books, articles, theses, and even lectures, as well as some reviews. Locations in Spanish libraries are often noted. Each volume concludes with comprehensive indexes.

Volume 1 (2d ed., 1960) contains 4,506 serially numbered entries concerned with the history of Castilian literature, collections of texts, anthologies, monographs, comparative literature, and Catalan, Galician, and Basque literatures (with parallel subdivisions). Entries are annotated and give locations of copies. The volume ends with indexes of authors and of libraries. Volume 2 (1951) contains bibliographies of bibliographies, biographies, and biobibliographies; catalogs of libraries, of periodicals, of archives; indexes to periodical publications; general and partial bibliographies of Castilian literature; and bibliographies of ancillary subjects; there are parallel sections for Catalan and Basque literature. Volume 3, in two parts (2d ed., 1963–1965), contains 6,778 serially numbered entries treating medieval literature. Arrangement is into general sections followed by sections on particular authors. There are indexes of names, of first lines, and of libraries. Volume 4 (2d ed., 1972) is the first of a series of volumes treating the Golden Age of Spanish literature. It contains 2,662 serially numbered entries, beginning with general sections and moving on to extensive bibliographies of individual authors. The volume concludes with indexes of names, first lines of poems, first lines of plays, of titles of dramas, and of subjects. Volumes 5 through 13 continue the bibliography of Golden Age authors, volume 13 covering through Llusas. These volumes are continuously being revised, rewritten, or supplemented; collectively they constitute the fullest bibliography available for the literatures of Spain and Spanish America.

L–93 **"Bibliografía [de filogía hispánica]"** in *Nueva revista de filología hispánica [1946–].* Vol. 1–. Mexico City, 1947–.
PC4008.N84

This bibliography, which is confined to peninsular Spanish and Portuguese language and literature, was originally published in the *Revista de filología hispánica* (Buenos Aires: Universidad nacional, 1939–1946) [PQ6001.R453]. Each double issue includes a bibliography of monographs, articles, reviews, and dissertations arranged in three parts. The first part treats generalities, including intellectual and cultural history and general and comparative literature. The second part contains entries on linguistics (general, Romance, and Hispanic). Part three focuses on Catalan, Portuguese, and Spanish literature. It is organized from general to specific topics, then by periods, with sections on individual authors given in roughly the chronological order of their birth. This arrangement is difficult to use, especially because there is no index, though there are some cross-references. There is, however, a detailed table of contents.

A similar difficulty exists with the quarterly "Bibliografía hispánica" published in the *Revista hispánica moderna*, 1934/35– [PQ6001.R47]. The relationship between this serial bibliography and the one cited above has varied; from 1939 through 1948 and from 1956 through 1966, this bibliography only cited works on Hispano-American literature, while the other treated materials on the literatures of the Iberian Peninsula. Since 1967 both European and American Hispanic literature has been cited. This bibliography is also in three sections. The first, on generalities, was until 1967 especially strong in its treatment of works in ancillary fields. Part 2 is on linguistics; part 3 on literature, with entries ordered by literary genres, then by national literatures, and then by authors in roughly chronological order. Titles are serially numbered, but there is neither an index nor any cross-referencing.

The consensus is that neither of these bibliographies should be used except to extend a search begun with the *MLA International Bibliography* (L–50) and the *Romance Bibliography* (L–60).

L–94   Some Frequently Recommended Works on Spanish (and Portuguese) Languages and Literatures.

Bibliographical Works

Arnaud, Emile, and Vicente Tusón. *Guide de bibliographie hispanique.* Toulouse: Privat-Didier, 1967. Some annotation.   Z2681.A75

Bibliographical Index for Spanish and Spanish American Studies in the United States. New York: Anaya–Las Americas, Spanish Book Center, 1974.
Z2691.A55 1974

Delk, Lois J., and James N. Greer. *Spanish Language and Literature in the Publications of American Universities: A Bibliography.* Austin, Tex., 1952.
Z2695.A1 D4

Fitzmaurice-Kelly, James. *Spanish Bibliography.* London: Oxford University Press, 1925.   Z2691.F557

Foulché-Delbosc, Raymond, and Louis Barrau-Dihigo. *Manuel de l'hispanisant.* 2 vols. New York: G. P. Putnam's Sons for the Hispanic Society of America, 1920–1925. Includes materials on Portugal as well as Spain.   Z2681.A1F7

Grismer, Raymond L. *Bibliography of the Drama of Spain and Spanish America.* 2 vols. Minneapolis: Burgess-Beckwith, 1968–1969.   PQ6100.G72

Hispanic Society of America. *Catalogue of the Library.* 10 vols. Boston: G. K. Hall, 1962.
Z2707.C55 H57 1962

Laurenti, Joseph L. *Bibliografía de la literatura picaresca: Desde sus orígenes hasta el presente / A Bibliography of Picaresque Literature from its Origins to the Present.* Metuchen, N.J.: Scarecrow Press, 1973. (See W–61.)   Z5917.P5 L35

McCready, Warren T. *Bibliografía temática de estudios [1850–1950] sobre el teatro español antiguo.* Toronto: University of Toronto Press, 1966.
Z2694.D7 M18

Rohlfs, Gerhard. *Manual de filología hispánica: Guía bibliográfica, crítica y metódica.* Bogotá: Instituto Caro y Cuervo, 1957. Includes Spanish-American and Portuguese sections.   Z2695.A1 R6

Serís, Homero. *Bibliografía de la lingüística española.* Bogotá: Instituto Caro y Cuervo, 1964. Z2695.A1 S4

———. *Manual de bibliografía de la literatura española.* 2 parts. Syracuse, N. Y.: Centro de estudios hispánicos, 1948–1954. Includes 8,779 items.
Z2691.S47

Stubbings, H. V. *Renaissance Spain in Its Literary Relations with England and France: A Critical Bibliography.* Nashville, Tenn.: Vanderbilt University Press, 1969.
Z6514.C7 S78

Historical and Special Studies

Alborg, Juan Luis. *Historia de la literatura española.* 5 vols. planned. Madrid: Gredos, 1966–.
PQ6032.A45

Brenan, Gerald. *Literature of the Spanish People, from Roman Times to the Present Day.* 2d ed. Cambridge: Cambridge University Press, 1953.   PQ6033.B7

Brown, Reginald F. *La novela española, 1700–1850.* Madrid: Dirección general de archivos y bibliotecas, 1953.   PQ6144.B7

Cejador y Frauca, Julio. *Historia de la lengua y literatura castellana, comprendidos los autores hispano-americanos.* 14 vols. in 7. Madrid: Revista de archivos, bibliotecas, y museos, 1915–1922. 2d ed., vols. 1–4, 1927–1935. 3d ed., vol. 1, 1932–1933.
PC4051.C4

Chandler, Richard E., and Kessel Schwartz. *New History of Spanish Literature.* Baton Rouge: Louisiana State University Press, 1961.   PQ6633.C45

del Río, Angel. *Historia de la literatura española.* 2d ed. 2 vols. New York: Holt, Rinehart and Winston, 1963.
PQ6037.R45

Díaz-Plaja, Guillermo, ed. *Historia general de las literaturas hispánicas.* 7 vols. Barcelona: Vergara, 1949–1968. Sections by specialists cover not only Spanish literature in Spain, America, the Philippines, and elsewhere, but also Arab, Catalan, Hebrew, and Latin literatures that have flourished in Spain.
PQ6032.D5

Díez Borque, Jose Maria, gen. ed. *Historia de la literatura española.* Vol. 1–. Madrid: Taurus, 1980–.
PQ6032.D53 1980

Díez-Echarri, Emiliano, and José Mariá Roca Franguesa. *Historia general de la literatura española e hispano-americana.* 2d ed. Madrid: Aguilar, 1966.
PQ6032.D54 1966

Enciclopedia lingüística hispánica. 6 vols. planned. Edited by M. Alvar et al. Madrid: Consejo superior de investigaciones científicas, 1960–.   PC45.E5

Fitzmaurice-Kelly, James. *History of Spanish Literature.* Rev. ed. New York: G. E. Stechert, 1926. 4th ed. New York, 1968.   PQ6033.F6 1968

Ford, Jeremiah D. M. *Main Currents of Spanish Literature.* 2d ed. New York: Holt, 1931.   PQ6033.F75 1931

García López, Jóse. *Historia de la literatura española.* 12th ed. Barcelona: Vincens-Vives, 1968.
PQ6032.G3 1968

Giese, W. *Geschichte der spanischen und portuguiesischen Literatur.* Bonn: Athenäum-verlag, 1949.
PQ6035.G5

González López, Emilio. *Historia de la literatura española.* 2 vols. New York: Las Americas, 1962–1965.
PQ6057.G6

Literary History of Spain. 6 vols. London: Benn, 1971–1972. Includes *Middle Ages*, by A. D. Deyermond; *Golden Age: Prose and Poetry—the Sixteenth and Seventeenth Centuries*, by R. O. Jones; *Golden Age: Drama, 1492–1700*, by Edward M. Wilson and Duncan Moir; *Eighteenth Century*, by Nigel Glendinning; *Nineteenth Century*, by Donald L. Shaw; and

Twentieth Century, by G. G. Brown. Associated with the series are volumes on *Catalan Literature* by A. Terry and on *Spanish-American Literature* by J. Franco. LC numbers vary

Mérimée, Ernest. *History of Spanish Literature*. Enlarged translation by S. Griswold Morley of *Précis d'histoire de la literature espagnole* (Santiago de Chile: Imp. "La Ilustracion," 1911). New York: Holt, 1930.
PQ6034.M42

Northrup, George T., and Nicholson B. Adams. *Introduction to Spanish Literature*. 3d rev. ed. Chicago: University of Chicago Press, 1960. PQ6037.N6 1960

Pattison, Walter Thomas, and Donald W. Bleznick. *Representative Spanish Authors*. 3d ed. 2 vols. New York: Oxford University Press, 1971. PQ6172.P324

Stamm, James R. *Short History of Spanish Literature*. Rev. ed. New York: New York University Press, 1979.
PQ6033.S7 1979

Ticknor, G. *History of Spanish Literature*. 3 vols. 1849. Reprint. New York: Ungar, 1965.
PQ6033.T5 1965b

Valbuena-Prat, Angel. *Historia de la literatura española*. 8th ed., corr. and enl. 4 vols. Barcelona: Gustavo Gili, 1968. Associated with this history as volume 5 is Angel Valbuena Briones, *Literatura hispanoamericana*, 4th ed., 1969. PQ6032.V3

Portuguese Literature (including Brazilian)

Bell, A. F. G. *Portuguese Literature*. Oxford: Clarendon Press, 1922. PQ9011.B4

Brinches, Victor Manuel Fernandes. *Dicionário bio-bibliográfico lusobrasileiro*. Rio de Janeiro: Editoria Fundo de cultura, 1965. Sections on Portuguese and Brazilian authors, living and deceased. PQ9027.B7

Coelho, Jacinto do Prado. *Dicionário de literatura portuguesa, literatura brasileira, e literatura galega, estilistica literária*. 3d ed. Porto: Livraria Figueirinhas, 1978.
PQ9006.C65 1978

da Costa Pimpao, Alvaro Julio. *História da literatura portuguêsa*. Coimbra: Edicoes Quadrante, 1949–.
PQ9011.C62

Le Gentil, G. *La littérature portugaise*. Paris: A. Colin, 1935. PQ9012.I4

Moisés, Massaud, et al. *Bibliografia da literatura portuguêsa*. Sao Paulo: Ed. Saraiva, Ed. da Universidade, 1968. Bibliographic guide by period and genre. Z2721.M63

Paiva Boléo, Manuel de. *Introdução ao estudo da filologia portuguesa*. Lisbon: Revista de Portugal, 1946.
PC5038.P6 P3

Saraiva, António José, and Óscar Lopes. *História da literatura portuguêsa*. 11th ed. Pôrto: Pôrto Editôra, 1979.
PQ9012.S3 1979

L–95 **Scholarly Journals in Hispanic and Hispanic-American Studies.** (See also Latin American materials in reference works on West Indian studies, M.XV.)

Anales de la literatura española contemporánea. Vol. 1–. Lincoln, Neb.: Society of Spanish and Spanish-American Studies, 1975–. 1/yr.
PQ6144.A53

BH *Bulletin hispanique: Annales de la Faculté des lettres de Bordeaux*. Vol. 1–. Bordeaux: Éditions Bière, 1899–. 4/yr. Reviews. Bibliographies. Indexes for 1899–1928, 1929–1948, 1949–1958.
PQ6001.B8

BHS *Bulletin of Hispanic Studies* [former title: *Bulletin of Spanish Studies*]. Vol. 1–. Liverpool: University of Liverpool, 1923–. 4/yr. Reviews. Index to vols. 1–30 in vol. 30. PC4008.B8

Bulletin of the Comediantes. Vol. 1–. Los Angeles:

University of Southern California, 1948–. 2/yr. Reviews. Annual (1950–) "Bibliography of Publications on the Comedia," containing books, articles, reviews, and dissertations on Golden Age Spanish drama. From vol. 26 (1974–) on, covers North American publications in addition to non–North American. Index to vols. 1–22 with vol. 23 (1971).
PQ6098.C64a

Chasqui: Revista de literatura latinoamericana. Vol. 1–. Williamsburg, Va.: College of William and Mary, 1971–. 3/yr. Reviews. Bibliographical lists of current criticism in each issue.
PQ7081.A1 C48

Cuadernos hispano-americanos. Vol. 1–. Madrid: Ediciones Cultura Hispanica, 1950–. AP63.C6697

Hispania *Hispania: A Journal Devoted to the Interests of the Teaching of Spanish and Portuguese*. Stanford, Calif. [place varies]: American Association of Teachers of Spanish and Portuguese, 1918–. 4–6/yr. Reviews. Bibliographies of Spanish-American studies and of dissertations in progress and completed [1935–]. Since 1978 a section "Research Tools in Progress" reports on bibliographies, editions, concordances, and other aids. Index to vols. 1–40 in one vol. and cumulative index every ten years.
PC4001.H7

Hispanic Issues. Vol. 1–. Minneapolis, Minn.: The Prisman Institute, 1987–. 2/yr.

HR *Hispanic Review: A Quarterly Journal Devoted to Research in the Hispanic Languages and Literatures*. Vol. 1–. Philadelphia: Department of Romance Languages, University of Pennsylvania, 1933–. 4/yr. Reviews. Index to vols. 1–25 (1933–1957) published as a supplement to vol. 25 (1958). PQ6001.H5

LALR *Latin American Literary Review*. Vol. 1–. Pittsburgh: Carnegie-Mellon University, 1972–. 2/yr.
PQ7081.A1 L35

Mundo nuevo: Revista de estudios latinoamericanos. Vol. 1–. Caracas: Universidad Simón Bolívar, Instituto de altos estudios de America Latina, 1978–. 4/yr. Reviews. F1401.M86

NRFH *Nueva revista de filología hispánica [former title 1939–1946: Revista de filología hispánica]*. Vol. 1–. Buenos Aires and New York City, 1939–1946. Mexico City: Colegio de México, Centro de estudios lingüísticos y literarios, 1947–. 4/yr. 1939–1946, 2/yr. 1947–. Reviews. Bibliographies. (See L–93.) PC4008.N84

Revista de dialectología y tradiciones populares. Vol. 1–. Madrid: Consejo superior de investigaciones cientificas, 1944–. 4/yr. Reviews. Annual bibliography of books and articles [1948–] on linguistics, dialectology, folklore, music, and religion in Spain and Spanish America. GR1.R293

REH *Revista de estudios hispánicos*. Vol. 1–. University: University of Alabama, Department of Romance Languages, 1967–. 3/yr. Reviews and "Revista de revistas." PQ6001.R432

Revista de estudios hispánicos. Vol. 1–. Rio Piedras: Universidad de Puerto Rico, Facultad de humanidades, 1971–. 4/yr. Reviews. PC4001.R48

RFE *Revista de filología española*. Madrid: Consejo superior de investigaciones cientificas, Instituto "Miguel de Cervantes," 1914–1937, 1941–. 4/yr. Reviews. Annual bibliography on Spanish linguistics and Spanish and Spanish-American literature [1913–]. Indexes to vols. 1–46 (1914–1963) in vol. 47 (1964). See also Alice M. Pollin and Raquel Kersten, *Guia para la consulta de la 'RFE' 1914–1960* (New York: New York University Press, 1964).   PQ6001.R45

RL   *Revista de literatura* [former title 1942–1946: *Cuadernos de literatura contemporánea*; 1947- 1950: *Cuadernos de literatura: Revista general de las letras*]. Vol. 1–. Madrid: Consejo superior de investigaciones cientificas, 1942–. 4/yr. Reviews. Bibliographies.   PN6.R48

RHM   *Revista Hispánia moderna: Columbia University Hispanic Studies*. Vol. 1–. New York: Columbia University Press, 1934–. 3/yr. Reviews. "Bibliografía hispano-americana" in each issue. (See L–93.)   PQ6001.R47

Revista ibero-americana. Vol. 1–. Pittsburgh: Instituto internacional de literatura ibero-americana, 1939. 2–4/yr. Reviews.   PQ7081.A1 R4

RIB   *Revista interamericana de bibliografía: Organo de estudios humanisticos / Inter-American Review of Bibliography: Journal of Humanistic Studies*. Washington, D.C.: OAS, 1951–. 4/yr. Reviews. Bibliography in each issue of books on Latin America acquired by the OAS and other libraries, organized by subject. Index to vols. 1–15 (1951–1965) in vol. 15.   Z1007.R4317

For additional information see David S. Zubatsky, "A Bibliography of Cumulative Indexes to Spanish Language and Literary Reviews of the Nineteenth and Twentieth Centuries," *Hispania* 51 (1968): 622–628.

L–96   Foster, David William, and Virginia Ramos Foster, eds. *Manual of Hispanic American Bibliography*. 2d ed., rev. and exp. New York: Garland, 1977.   Z2691.A1 F68 1977

This work contains well-annotated entries disposed into thirty-three sections that are in turn organized into four parts as follows: 1, General Bibliographies Including General Romance Bibliography; 2, Bibliographies of Spanish Literature; 3, Bibliographies of Spanish-American Literature; and 4, Spanish-American National Bibliographies. Among the bibliographical materials included in parts 2 and 3 are General Bibliographies; Period Bibliographies; Guides to Spanish and Spanish-American Libraries and Special Collections; Guides to Spanish and Spanish-American Periodicals and Periodical Literature; and Guides to Theses and Dissertations on Spanish-American Topics. Entries are serially numbered within each of the thirty-three sections and are descriptively and evaluatively annotated by one of the authors or one of four other contributors. The volume concludes with indexes of authors and of short titles.

Also compiled by Foster is the two-volume bibliography, *Modern Latin American Literature* (New York: Ungar, 1975) [PQ7081.F63 1975], which contains fully annotated bibliographies of 137 authors.

L–97   Rela, Walter. *Guía bibliográfica de la literatura hispanoamericana desde el siglo XIX hasta 1970*. Buenos Aires: Casa Pardo, 1971.   Z1609.L7 R44

This bibliography contains 6,023 serially numbered, unannotated entries, arranged in sections by the type of reference work involved. Sections include general, national (Argentina to Venezuela), and personal bibliographies; general and national literary histories; historical and critical works on apects of the various national literatures; historical and critical treatments of the works of individual writers; general and national anthologies; anthologies of the works of individual authors; collective biographies; literary dictionaries; individual biogra-

phies; and a miscellaneous section. National sections are subdivided by countries in alphabetical order. Individual sections are not subdivided by literary author but are in alphabetical order by the name of the scholar or critic. Access to bibliographies, historical and critical studies, and biographies of individual literary authors is through the index of names which concludes the volume. Entries cite authors, titles, place, publisher, date, and pagination.

Rela has also published a supplement, *Spanish American Literature: A Selected Bibliography / Literatura hispanoamericana: Bibliografía selecta, 1970–1980* (East Lansing: Michigan State University, Department of Romance and Classical Languages, 1982) [Z1609.L7 R45 1982].

In addition to Rela's guides the most important bibliography of Latin American literature is the unfinished work of Luis Alberto Sánchez, *Repertorio bibliográfico de la literatura latino-americana*, 3 vols. published (Santiago de Chile [place varies], 1955–1962) [Z1609.L753]. Each volume is elaborately classified into five parts, treating critical histories and anthologies; general and national bibliographies of literature and linguistics; genres; general and national subjects; and translations. Within these parts, annotated entries are further classified into general and individual sections, with monographs, periodical articles, and anthologies separately listed, and with indexes of names. Volume 1 (1955) treats Central America and Argentina with a total of some 1,100 entries. Volume 2 (1957) treats Bolivia and Brazil with a comparable number of entries. Volume 3 (1962) covers Chile and Columbia and contains a similar number of entries. The three together contain 3,356 entries; no further volumes were published.

L–98   Carrera Andrade, Jorge, coord. *Bibliografía general de la literatura latinoamericana*. Paris: UNESCO, 1972.   Z1609.L7 B5

An annotated bibliography covering colonial (by Guillermo Loman Villena and Luis Jaime Cisneros), nineteenth-century (by Julio Ortega), and twentieth-century (by Horatio Jorge Becco) Spanish-American literature. Included are bibliographies of bibliographies (general, monographic, periodical, and regional); critical studies (general and regional); literary histories; collections of essays; theater; proceedings of literary congresses; and various miscellaneous items. A total of 3,125 serially numbered entries are included. There is an index of names.

Additional bibliographical support will be found in Shasta M. Bryant, *Selective Bibliography of Bibliographies of Hispanic American Literature*, 2d ed., greatly expanded and revised (Austin: Institute of Latin American Studies, University of Texas, 1976) [Z1609.L7 B77 1976], which cites and describes but does not classify 662 general and special bibliographies. It includes an index of authors and a few broad subjects. See also Julio A. Leguizamón, *Bibliografía general de la literatura hispanoamericana* (Buenos Aires: Reunidas, 1954) [Z1609.L7 L4 1954], which cites both anthologies of and critical studies about Latin American literature of all countries and genres, with some 3,000 unannotated entries and an author index. In addition see Jóse Manuel Topete, *Working Bibliography of Latin American Literature* (St. Augustine, Fla.: Inter-American Bibliographical Association, etc., 1952) [Z1609.L7 T65], which is arranged by country, with entries disposed into an elaborate subject classification including histories, anthologies, bibliographies, criticism, and translations. The volume concludes with an index of authors.

L–99 **Handbook of Latin American Studies.** Vols. 1–13. Cambridge: Harvard University Press, 1936–1950, Vol. 14–. Gainesville: University of Florida Press, 1951–. Publisher varies. Z1605.H26

This important annual bibliography, sponsored by the Latin American Studies Association and compiled since 1944 by the Hispanic Division of the Library of Congress, cites the best books and articles published on all aspects of Latin America. It is classified into chapters on major disciplines, including literature, each compiled by a specialist contributing editor. Since 1964, works in the humanities are treated in the Handbooks of even-numbered years, while the social-science disciplines are covered in those published in odd-numbered years. The social sciences treated include anthropology, economics, education, geography, government and politics, international relations, and sociology; the humanities volumes cover the disciplines of art, film, folklore, history, language, literature, music, and philosophy. More than 6,000 monographs and articles from some 400 journals are cited; serially numbered entries are divided by language, all are annotated, and there are abundant cross-references. The sections on Latin American literature are divided into periods (colonial period, nineteenth, and twentieth century) and then into genres and national literatures. Brazilian, Spanish-American, and French West Indian literatures are all included. There are author and subject indexes concluding each volume. In addition, there is a cumulative *Author Index* for volumes 1–28 (1936–1966) published in 1968; a cumulative *Subject Index* is in preparation.

Another serial publication is the new *Bibliographic Guide to Latin American Studies* published annually by G. K. Hall (Boston, 1979–) [Z1610.B52], which presents books, serials, and other separate publications [for 1978–] cataloged by the Library of Congress and the New York Public Library. Entries are arranged in author, title, and subject lists.

L–100 **Flores, Angel. Bibliografía de escritores hispanoamericanos / A Bibliography of Spanish American Writers, 1609–1974.** New York: Gordion Press, 1975.
Z1609.L7 F55

This work is the most current and authoritative available biobibliographical dictionary. Information for each of some 200 author entries includes a biographical sketch, a critical estimate, an enumeration (as appropriate) of principal and some other editions, anthologies, and reference works, and a select bibliography of secondary works.

The extensive number of entries in the earlier index of Raymond L. Grismer may also be consulted with profit, especially for minor figures: *Reference Index to 12,000 Spanish American Authors: A Guide to the Literature of Spanish America* (New York: Wilson, 1939) [Z1601.G86]. Grismer's entries give pseudonyms, dates, nationality, and a brief discursive treatment of each author's "life and works." Readers are referred to the 129 biographical dictionaries and other reference sources analyzed for more detailed information.

For contemporary Latin American authors see the dictionary by David William Foster, *Dictionary of Contemporary Latin American Authors* (Tempe: Center for Latin American Studies, Arizona State University, 1975) [PQ7081.3.F6]. It contains entries for about 250 living authors with bibliographical sketches, critical estimates, and primary bibliographies.

The most elaborate biobibliographical effort for Latin American authors was that undertaken by the Pan-American Union in Washington, D.C., in the *Diccionario de la literatura latinoamericana* [PQ7081.P27], of which six volumes were published, 1958–1963. Individual volumes treat the authors of one or several national literatures, giving in signed articles biographies, primary and secondary bibliographies, and (at the end) a bibliography of national bibliographies. The individual volumes published are as follows: vol. 1, *Bolivia* (1958); vol. 2, *Chile* (1958); vol. 3, *Columbia* (1959); vol.

4, 2 parts, *Argentina* (1960–1961); vol. 5, *Ecuador* (1962); vol. 6, *Central America*: part 1, *Costa Rica, El Salvador, and Guatamala* (1963); part 2, *Honduras, Nicaragua, and Panama* (1963).

L–101 **Some Frequently Recommended Works on Latin American Languages and Literatures.**

Bibliographical

Anderson, Robert Roland. *Spanish American Modernism: A Selected Bibliography.* Tucson: University of Arizona Press, 1970. Z1609.L7 A66

Ayala Poveda, Fernando. *Manual de literatura Colombiana.* Bogotá: Educar Editores, 1984. PQ8161.A9

Barriga López, Franklin, and Leonardo Barriga López. *Diccionario de la literatura ecuatoriana.* 2d ed., rev. and enl. 5 vols. Quito: Editorial Casa de la Cultura Ecuatoriana, 1980. PQ8201.B35

Becco, Horacio Jorge. *Fuentes para el estudio de la literatura Venezolana.* 2 vols. Caracas: Ediciones Centauro, 1978. Z1921.B4

Foster, David William. *Argentine Literature: A Research Guide.* 2d ed., rev. and exp. New York: Garland, 1982. Z1621.F66 1982

———. *Chilean Literature: A Working Bibliography of Secondary Sources.* Boston: G. K. Hall, 1978.
Z1711.F67

———. *Cuban Literature: A Research Guide.* New York: Garland, 1985. Z1521.F694 1985

———. *Mexican Literature: A Bibliography of Secondary Sources.* Metuchen, N. J.: Scarecrow, 1981.
Z1421.F63

———. *Peruvian Literature: A Bibliography of Secondary Sources.* Westport, Conn.: Greenwood, 1981.
Z1861.F67 1981

———. *Puerto Rican Literature: A Bibliography of Secondary Sources.* Westport, Conn.: Greenwood, 1982.
Z1557.L56 F67 1982

———. *Twentieth Century Spanish-American Novel: A Bibliographic Guide.* Metuchen, N. J.: Scarecrow, 1975.
Z1609.F4 F68

Gropp, Arthur E. *Bibliography of Latin American Bibliographies.* Metuchen, N. J.: Scarecrow, 1968. Three Supplements: 1971, 1979, and 1982.
Z1601.A2 G76 1968

Hebbelwaite, F. P. *Bibliographic Guide to the Spanish American Theatre.* Washington, D.C.: Pan-American Union, 1969. Z1609.D7 H42

Jackson, Richard L. *Afro-Spanish American Author: An Annotated Bibliography of Criticism.* New York: Garland, 1980. Z1609.L7 J32

Maratos, Daniel C., and Marnesba D. Hill. *Escritores de la Diaspora Cubana: Manual Bibliographico / Cuban Exile Writers: A Bibliographic Handbook.* Metuchen, N. J.: Scarecrow, 1986. Z1520.M37 1986

Matos, Antonio. *Guía a las resenas de y sobre Hispano-América / A Guide to Reviews of Books from and about Hispanic America.* Rio Piedras, Puerto Rico, 1965. Supplements: 1973, 1976. Z1035.A1 G84

Ortega, José, and Adolfo Caceres Romero. *Diccionario de la literatura boliviana.* La Paz: Editorial Los Amigos del Libro, 1977. Z1650.O77

Rolando, Carlos A. *Las bellas letras en el Ecuador.* Guayaquil: Impr. i Talleres municipales, 1944. Z1771.R75

Rela, Walter. *Fuentes para el estudio de la literatura uruguya, 1835–1968.* Montevideo: Ediciones de la Banda Oriental, 1969. Z1891.R42

Sable, Martin H. *Guide to Latin American Studies.* 2 vols. Los Angeles: Latin American Center, University of California, 1967. 5,000 items annotated.

Zubatsky, David S. *Latin American Literary Authors: An Annotated Guide to Bibliographies.* Metuchen, N. J.: Scarecrow, 1986.   Z1609.L7 Z82 1986

Historical and Special Studies

Anderson-Imbert, Enrique. *Spanish American Literature: A History.* 2d ed. Detroit: Wayne State University Press, 1969.   PQ7081.A5634

Delpar, Helen, ed. *Encyclopedia of Latin America.* New York: McGraw-Hill, 1974.   F1406.E52

Englekirk, John E., et al. *Outline History of Spanish American Literature.* 3d ed. New York: Appleton-Century-Crofts, 1965.   PQ7081.I5 1965

Franco, Jean. *Introduction to Spanish American Literature.* Cambridge: Cambridge University Press, 1969.
                PQ7081.F64

————. *Modern Culture of Latin America: Society and the Artist.* Harmondsworth: Penguin Books, 1970.
                F1408.3.F84 1970

Hamilton, Carlos Depassier. *Historia de la literatura hispanoamericana.* 2d ed., corr. and enl. Madrid: Ediciones y publicaciones españolas, 1966.
                PQ7081.H3 1966

Lequizamon, Julio A. *Historia de la literatura hispanoamericana.* 2 vols. Buenos Aires: Reunidas, 1945.
                PQ7081.L4

Sanchez, Luis Alberto. *Historia comparada de las literaturas americanas.* 4 vols. Buenos Aires: Editorial Losada, 1973–1976.   PN843.S26 1976

Schwartz, Kessel. *New History of Spanish American Fiction.* 2 vols. Coral Gables, Fla.: University of Miami Press, 1972.   PQ7081.S34

Torres-Rioseco, Arturo. *Epic of Latin American Literature.* 3d ed. Berkeley and Los Angeles: University of California Press, 1967.   PQ7081.T73 1967

Brazilian Literature

(see also L–94 under Portuguese Literature)

Bosi, Alfredo. *Historia concisa de literatura brasileira.* 3d ed. São Paulo: Editoria Cultrix, 1981.
                PQ9511.B6 1981

Coutinho, Afrânio Dos Santos. *A literatura no Brasil.* 6 vols. 2d ed., rev. Rio de Janeiro: Editoria Sul Americana, 1968–1972.   PQ9511.C66

————. *Introduction to Literature in Brazil.* Rio de Janeiro: Livraria São Jose, 1959. Translation by Gregory Rabassa of *Introducao a literatura no Brasil* (Rio de Janeiro: Livraria São Jose, 1959). New York: Columbia University Press, 1969.   PQ9511.C6313

Hulet, Claude L. *Brazilian Literature.* 3 vols. Washington, D.C.: Georgetown University Press, 1974.
                PQ9635.H8

Topete, J. M. *Working Bibliography of Brazilian Literature.* Gainesville: University of Florida Press, 1957.
                Z1681.T6

IX. GERMANIC LANGUAGES AND LITERATURES

See also Hansel (A–18); pertinent works in section I on Language, Linguistics, and Philology; the *MLA International Bibliography* (L–50); the MHRA *Year's Work in Modern Language Studies* (L–52); and many works on English language and literature which attend to its Germanic origins and character (see sections M and N particularly).

L–105 **Hoops, Johannes. *Reallexikon der germanischen Altertumskunde.*** 4 vols. Strassburg and Berlin: Trübner, 1911–1919. 2d ed. Revised and enlarged by H. Beck, Jan Kuhn, et al. Berlin: de Gruyter, 1968–.   DD51.H6

This encyclopedia deals with the life and culture of the Germanic tribes from their origins to the end of the Old High German, Old Low German, and Old English periods. For northern tribes, life of the twelfth century is included. The encyclopedia consists of long, signed articles, divided into subsections, each of which has an extensive bibliography. The work is valuable as a background to Old English studies and as a bibliographical supplement to virtually all medieval studies.

The second edition, to be in eight volumes, is virtually a new work [DD51.R42]. It also has signed articles with bibliography; the old articles have been drastically rewritten and updated, and there are many new entries.

L–106 **Paul, Hermann, ed. *Grundriss der germanischen Philologie.*** 3d ed., rev. and enl. 6 vols. Strassburg: Trübner, 1911–1916.   PD71.P3

This introduction to the fundamentals of Germanic philology, first published 1891–1893, consists of a series of chapters by recognized authorities of the late nineteenth and early twentieth century on a vast range of topics relevant to Germanic studies as then conceived. The work includes treatments of the concept and purpose of Germanic philology, the history of Germanic philology, methodology, paleography (2 chapters), history of language (12 chapters), and mythology. Also covered are literary history (13 chapters) and metrics (4 chapters). There are chapters on economics, law, military practice, mythology, customs (2 chapters), art (2 chapters), the heroic sagas, and the ethnography of the Germanic tribes. There is an index of subjects at the end of the last volume. A new edition is being published in a series of monographs, thus losing the character of a handbook; the individual volumes are listed in Hansel (A–18).

There is also a single-volume *Handbuch der germanischen Philologie bis 1500* by F. Stroh (Berlin: de Gruyter, 1952) [PD71.S3]. It is arranged in three parts treating respectively the concept of Germanic philology, the history of Germanic philology, and the subject matters of literature, religion, ethics, manners, customs, law, art, and settlement practices.

More up to date yet is the *Kurzer Grundriss der germanischen Philologie bis 1500*, ed. Ludwig Erich Schmitt, to be completed in three volumes (Berlin: de Gruyter, 1970–) [PD71.S3]. Volume 1, history of the language, was published in 1970; volume 2, literary history, in 1971. Volume 3, to treat material culture and cultural history, is in preparation. Volumes consist of well-organized, extremely reliable individual essays on each of the Germanic languages in volume 1, and on the histories of the genres of each of the national literatures in volume 2.

L–107 *Jahresbericht über die Erscheinungen auf dem Gebiete der germanischen Philologie.* Edited by the Gesellschaft für deutsche Philologie. Vols. 1–42 [1879–1920]. Berlin: Calvary, 1880–1923.   Z7037.J25

This annotated bibliography of books, pamphlets, articles, and dissertations treats work on the Germanic literatures to the end of the Middle Ages. An extensive bibliographical review is followed by a classified enumerative bibliography. Entries are disposed by language (English philology, including Old and Middle English literature, is included), then by period and region. Author-reviewer and subject indexes are provided in each annual volume. Coverage varies: volume 41 includes works on the Germanic literatures to 1770; volume 42 continues coverage to 1832.

The original series was continued by a *Neue Folge*, vols. 1–15 [1921–1935] (Berlin: de Gruyter, 1924–1939). Coverage in the continuation is of Germanic literatures to 1700; annotations vary from brief descriptions to extended reviews. The series is further continued in the retrospective *Neue Folge*, vols. 16–19 [1936–1939] in one volume, edited by the Deutsche Akademie der Wissenschaften zu Berlin (Berlin: de Gruyter, 1954). This volume is divided into two parts, a "Sprachlich-sachlicher Teil" and a "Literatur-historischer Teil" and gives but little annotation.

This "philological" series was complemented by the *Jahresberichte für neuere deutsche Literaturgeschichte* and its sequels (see L–117).

L–108 **Scholarly Journals in the Germanic Languages and Literatures.**

APS   *Acta Philologica Scandinavica / Tidsskrift for Nordisk Sprogforskning / Journal of Scandinavian Philology.* Vol. 1–. Copenhagen: Munksgaard, 1926–. 2/yr. Annual Bibliography of Scandinavian Philology [1925–] with summaries of books, articles, and dissertations. Supplemented [1970–] with sheer lists of current books and articles in the "Bulletin of Scandinavian Philology."   PD1503.A3

AGR   *American German Review.* Vol. 1–. Cherry Hill, N. J.: American Association of Teachers of German, 1928–. 4/yr. Reviews. Bibliography 1968–1970. "Bibliography Americana Germanica [1967–1969]." (See L–118.)   E183.8.G3A6

BDP   *Beiträge zur deutschen Philologie.* Giessen: Wilhelm Schmitz, 1954–.   LC numbers vary

BGDSL   *Beiträge zur Geschichte der deutschen Sprache und Literatur.* Vol. 1–. Halle (Salle): Niemeyer, 1873–1954; Tübingen: Niemeyer, 1955–. 3/yr. Reviews. Includes much material on Old English.   PF3003.B52

Bibliographie van de Nederlandse taal- en literaturwetenschap. Vol. 1–. Antwerp: Archief en Museum voor het Vlaamse Culturleven, 1970–. l/yr. Bibliography of books and articles on Dutch language and literature.   Z2435.B58

Dutch Studies: An Annual Review of the Language, Literature, and Life of the Low Countries. Vol. 1–. The Hague: Nijhoff, 1974–. l/yr. Bibliography of "Publications on Dutch Language and Literature in Languages Other Than Dutch."   PF1.D85

EG   *Études germaniques: Revue trimestrielle.* Vol. 1–. Paris: Société des études germaniques, 1946–. 4/yr. Reviews.   DD1.E8

GL&L   *German Life and Letters: A Quarterly Review.* Vol. 1–. Oxford: Basil Blackwell, 1936–. 4/yr.   AP4.G43

GQ   *German Quarterly.* Vol. 1–. Appleton, Wis. [place varies]: American Association of Teachers of German, 1928–. 4/yr. Reviews. Annual Bibliogra-

phy of "Americanica Germanica." Index to vols. 1–10.   PF3001.G3

German Studies Review. Vol. 1–. Tempe: Arizona State University for the German Studies Association, 1978–. 3/yr. Reviews.   D1.G382

GR   *Germanic Review: Devoted to Studies Dealing with the Germanic Languages and Literatures.* Vol. 1–. New York: Department of Germanic Languages, Columbia University, 1926–. 4/yr. Reviews. Contains "German Literature of the Nineteenth Century: 1830–1880: A Current Bibliography."   PD1.G4

Germanistik: Internationales Referatenorgan mit bibliographischen Hinweisen (see L–116).

IF   *Indogermanische Forschungen: Zeitschrift für Indogermanistik und allgemeine Sprachwissenschaft.* Vol. 1–. Berlin: de Gruyter, 1891–. Originally 3/yr., now 1/yr.   P501.I4

Indogermanisches Jahrbuch. Vols. 1–55. Strassburg [place varies]: Trübner, 1914–1955. Bibliography of Indo-European linguistics, 1912–1948.   Z7049.A718

JEGP   *Journal of English and Germanic Philology: A Quarterly Devoted to the English, German, and Scandinavian Languages and Literatures.* Urbana: University of Illinois Press, 1897–. 4/yr. Reviews. Bibliographies (see L–118). Index to vols. 1–50 published as a Supplement to vol. 61 (1962).   PD1.J7

Kratylos: Kritisches Berichts- und Rezensionsorgan für indogermanische und allgemeine Sprachwissenschaft. Vol. 1–. Wiesbaden: Harrassowitz, 1956.   P501.K7

MAL   *Modern Austrian Literature.* Binghamton, N. Y.: SUNY, 1961–. 4/yr. Reviews.   PT3810.I52

Monatshefte für deutschen Unterricht, deutsche Sprache und Literatur. Vol. 1–. Madison: University of Wisconsin, Department of German, 1899–. 4–8/yr. Reviews. Annual lists of dissertations in progress and completed.   PF3003.M6

ScanR   *[American-]Scandinavian Review.* Vol. 1–. New York: American-Scandinavian Foundation, 1913–. 4/yr. Reviews.   AP2.A457

SS   *Scandinavian Studies [and Notes].* Vol. 1–. Menasha, Wis., [place varies]: Society for the Advancement of Scandinavian Study, 1911–. 4/yr. Reviews. Annual bibliography of North American articles on Scandinavian literature, 1947–1972, in vols. 20–45 (1948–1973).   PD1505.S6

Scan   *Scandinavica: An International Journal of Scandinavian Studies.* Vol. 1–. London: Academic Press, 1962–. 2/yr. Reviews.   PT7001.S25

WB   *Weimarer Beiträge: Zeitschrift für Literaturwissenschaft, Ásthetik und Kulturtheorie.* Vol. 1–. Weimar: Aufbau Verlag, 1955–. 12/yr. Reviews. Contains the annual "International Bibliographie zur deutschen Klassik, 1750–1850," published separately since 1964/65 by the Nationale Forschungs- und Gedenkstätten der klassischen deutschen Literatur in Weimar.   PT3.W38

Wolfenbütteler Barock-Nachrichten. Vol. 1–. Hamburg: Hauswedell, 1974–. 4/yr. Quarterly bibliography of books, articles, reviews, and German dissertations on German baroque culture.   Z2232.W65

Yiddish. Vol. 1–. New York: Queen's College Press, 1973–. 4/yr. Reviews.   PJ5120.A385

ZDA   *Zeitschrift für deutsches Altertum* [from vol. 19 on, "und deutsche Literatur"]. Vol. 1–. Leipzig, 1841–1853; Berlin: Weidmann, 1857–1947; Wiesbaden: Franz Steiner, 1948/50–. 4/yr. Reviews.   PF3003. Z42

ZDP	*Zeitschrift für deutsche Philologie.* Berlin [place varies]: Erich Schmidt Verlag, 1869–. 4/yr. Reviews. PF3003.Z35
ZGL	*Zeitschrift für germanistische Linguistik.* Vol. 1–. Berlin: de Gruyter, 1973–. 3/yr. Reviews. PF3003.Z45

See also the entries on journals in Comparative Literature (L–9) and Modern European Languages and Literatures (L–57), as well as Carl Dietsch, *Bibliographie der germanistischen Zeitschriften* (Leipzig: Hiersemann, 1927) [Z7036.L6] and the *Union List of Periodicals Dealing with Germanic Languages and Literatures in the University* (London: Institute of Germanic Languages and Literatures, London University, 1956) [Z7036.L6].

L–109   Some Frequently Recommended Works on the Germanic Languages and Literatures.

General

Loewenthal, Fritz. *Bibliographisches Handbuch zur deutschen Philologie.* Halle: Niemeyer, 1932.
Z7036.L82

Netherlandic (Dutch/Flemish)

Brachin, Pierre. *La littérature néerlandaise.* Paris: A. Colin, 1962.   PT5062.B7

Lagerwey, Walter. *Guide to Dutch Studies: A Bibliography of Textual Materials for the Study of Dutch Language, Literature, Civilization.* Grand Rapids, Mich.: 1961.
Z2431.L3

Meijer, Reinder P. *Literature of the Low Countries: A Short History of Dutch Literature in the Netherlands and Belgium.* Assen: Van Gorcum, 1971.   PT5061.M4

Wabeke, Bertus H. *Guide to Dutch Bibliographies.* Washington, D. C.: Library of Congress, 1951.
Z2416.U6 1951c

Scandinavian—General

"American Scandinavian Bibliography for [1947–]," *Scandinavian Studies,* 1948–.

Blankkner, F. *History of the Scandinavian Literatures: A Survey of the Literatures of Norway, Sweden, Denmark, Iceland and Finland from Their Origins to the Present Day, Including Scandinavian-American Authors and Selected Bibliographies.* New York: Dial Press, 1938.   PT7063.B5

Budd, John. *Eight Scandinavian Novelists: Criticism and Reviews in English.* Westport, Conn.: Greenwood, 1981.   Z2559.F52 B82

Friese, Wilhelm. *Nordische Literaturen im 20. Jahrhundert.* Stuttgart: Kroner, 1971.   PT7078.F7

Hangen, Einer Ingvald. *Bibliography of Scandinavian Languages and Linguistics, 1900–1970.* Oslo: Universitetsforlaget, 1974.   Z2555.H38 1974

Rossel, Sven Hakon. *History of Scandinavian Literature, 1870–1980.* Trans. by Anne C. Ulmer of *Skandinavische Literatur, 1870–1970* (Stuttgart: W. Kohlhammer, 1973), with extension to 1980. Minneapolis: University of Minnesota Press, 1982.   PT7065.R6

Danish

Denmark: Literature, Language, History, Society, Education, Arts: A Select Bibliography. Copenhagen: Royal Library, 1966.   Z2561.C6

Mitchell, Philip M. *Bibliographical Guide to Danish Literature.* Copenhagen: Munksgaard, 1951.   Z2571.M5

———. *History of Danish Literature.* 2d ed. New York: Kraus-Thomson, 1971.   PT7663.M5 1971

Munch-Petersen, Erland. *Guide to Danish Bibliography.* Copenhagen: Royal School of Librarianship, 1965.
Z2561.A1 M8

Ober, Kenneth H. *Contributions in Dutch, English, Faroese, German, Icelandic, Italian, and Slavic Languages to Danish Literary History, 1925–1970: A Provisional Bibliography.* Copenhagen: Koneglige Bibliotek, 1976.   Z2574.C8 O2

Gothic

Bennett, William H. *Introduction to the Gothic Language.* New York: MLA, 1980.   PD1123.B4 1980

Icelandic/Old Norse

Bekker-Nielsen, Hans. *Old Norse-Icelandic Studies: A Select Bibliography.* Toronto: University of Toronto Press, 1967.   Z2556.B4

Bibliography of Old Norse-Icelandic Studies [1963–]. Copenhagen: Munksgaard [now the Royal Library], 1964–.
Z2556.B5

Einarsson, Stefán. *History of Icelandic Literature.* Baltimore: Johns Hopkins University Press for the American Scandinavian Foundation, 1957.   PT7150.E4

Hermannsson, Halldor. *Bibliography of the Icelandic Sagas and Minor Tales.* Ithaca, N.Y.: Cornell University Press, 1908.   Z2556.C65

———. *Old Icelandic Literature: A Bibliographical Essay.* Ithaca, N. Y.: Cornell University Press, 1933.
PT7103.I7 vol. 23

Hollander, Lee Milton. *Bibliography of Skaldic Studies.* Copenhagen: Munksgaard, 1958.   Z2555.H6

Norwegian

Beyer, Harald. *History of Norwegian Literature.* New York: New York University Press for the American Scandinavian Foundation, 1956.   PT8360.B42

Bryan, George B. *Ibsen Companion: A Dictionary-Guide to the Life, Works, and Critical Reception of Henrik Ibsen.* Westport, Conn.: Greenwood, 1984.
PT8887.B79

Jorgenson, Theodore. *History of Norwegian Literature.* New York: Macmillan, 1933.   PT8363.J6

Lescoffier, Jean. *Histoire de la littérature norvégienne.* Paris: Société d'édition "Les belles lettres," 1952.
PT8364.L4

Schneider, Hermann. *Geschichte der norwegischen und isländischen Literatur.* Bonn: Universitäts-Verlag, 1948.   PT8365.S3

Swedish

Gustafson, Alrik. *History of Swedish Literature.* Minneapolis: University of Minnesota Press for the American Scandinavian Foundation, 1961. Bibliography published separately as *Bibliographical Guide to Swedish Literature.* Stockholm, 1962.   PT9263.G9 1961

Holm, Ingvar, and Magnus von Platen. *La littérature suédoise.* Stockholm: Institut suédois, 1957.
PT9264.H6

Yiddish

Liptzin, Sol. *Flowering of Yiddish Literature.* New York: T. Yoseloff, 1963.   PJ5120.L55

Madison, Charles. *Yiddish Literature: Its Scope and Major Writers.* New York: Ungar, 1968. PJ5120.M2

Samuel, Maurice. *In Praise of Yiddish.* New York: Cowles Book Co., 1971. PJ5113.S2 1971

Weinreich, Uriel, and Beatrice Weinreich. *Yiddish Language and Folklore: A Selective Bibliography for Research.* The Hague: Mouton, 1959. Z7070.W4

X. GERMAN LANGUAGE AND LITERATURES

See also Hansel (A–18); pertinent works in section I on Language, Linguistics, and Philology; the *MLA International Bibliography* (L–50); the MHRA *Year's Work in Modern Language Studies* (L–52); works on General and Comparative Literature; and many works on English literature particularly of the Anglo-Saxon period (sections N.I and N.II). See also the *International Medieval Bibliography* (F–23); the *Bibliographie internationale de l'humanisme et de la Renaissance* (O–3); the *Eighteenth Century: A Current Bibliography* (P–5); and the bibliography of the *Romantic Movement* (Q–25). And among many pertinent works in section R, see especially the bibliographies in the *Journal of Modern Literature* (R–17), *Twentieth Century Literature* (R–16), and *Modern Drama* (R–44).

L–110 **Faulhaber, Uwe K., and Penrith B. Goff. *German Literature: An Annotated Reference Guide.*** New York: Garland, 1979. Z2231.F38

This well-conceived student bibliographical guide contains 2,046 briefly annotated entries disposed into thirteen chapters, as follows: 1, Bibliographies of Bibliographies; 2, General and National Bibliographies; 3, Bibliographies of German Literature; 4, Dissertations: Abstracts, Bibliographies, Indexes; 5, Biography and Bio-Bibliography; 6, Literary Criticism, Methodology, Theory; 7, History of German Literature; 8, The Genres of German Literature; 9, Collections of Interpretations, Critical Summaries, Digests, and Plot Outlines; 10, General and Comparative Literature; 11, Literature in Translation and Literary Relations; 12, Literary Newspapers, Journals, Periodicals, and Yearbooks; 13, Related Fields: Checklist of Information Sources on German Art, Music, Philosophy, History, Geography, Folklore, Philology, Language Teaching. The volume concludes with an author-title-subject index.

Another relatively recent English-language student bibliographical guide is L. M. Newman, *German Language and Literature: Select Bibliography* (London: Institute for Germanic Studies, London University, 1966) [Z2235.A2 L6]. It has 302 serially numbered and annotated entries disposed into seven sections as follows: 1, Research methods; 2, German language and literature; 3, German literature (no works on individual forms or authors); 4, German language; 5, Germanic subjects; 6, All subjects; 7, Related subjects. There are indexes of names, titles, and subjects.

Another new guide is by Larry L. Richardson, *Introduction to Library Research in German Studies: Language, Literature, and Civilization* (Boulder, Colo.: Westview Press, 1984) [Z2235.A2 R5], which includes annotations to about 250 sources, among them a special section on computer-assisted searches.

L–111 **Oxford Companion to German Literature [OCGL].** Edited by Henry Garland and Mary Garland. 2d ed. London: Oxford University Press, 1986. PT41.G3 1986

In a structure parallel to that of the other Oxford Companions, this volume, the first edition of which was published in 1976, contains articles of information likely to be of use to a reader of German literature from A.D. 800 to the 1970's, including the German literature of Austria and Switzerland. There are biographical articles, synopses of works, first lines, articles on literary genres, forms, techniques, movements, styles, and on social, political, and cultural background topics likely to be alluded to in works of German literature.

The best introductory handbook in German is Paul Merker and Wolfgang Stammler, *Reallexikon der deutschen Literaturgeschichte*, 2d ed., rev. and enl. by Werner Kohlschmidt et al., 4 vols. (Berlin: de Gruyter, 1958–) [PT41 .R4 1958]. The first edition of this standard work, published in four volumes 1925–1931, has been mostly replaced by the second edition. This work contains long, signed, encyclopedic articles on literary terminology, forms, genres, types, techniques, epochs, movements, and themes. Authoritative definitions, historical surveys, and carefully selected primary and secondary bibliographies make this work valuable for the beginner and specialist alike. There are no biographical articles included; for them, see the massive work edited by Kosch (L–119), among other sources.

More elaborate articles meant to serve as an introduction to the study of German philology will be found in *Deutsche Philologie im Aufriss*, 2d rev. ed., ed. Wolfgang Stammler, 3 vols. (Berlin: Schmidt, 1957–1962) [PF3025.S83], and *Register* (1969), compiled by Maria-Lioba Lechner et al. This work contains eighty-six articles on German studies, disposed into five main parts treating respectively Methodology; The History of the German Language and its Dialects; German Literary History by Genre, along with German Literary Relations, German Literature and the Other Arts, and Contributions by German Authors to World Literature; Cultural History and the History of Religion; and Folklore. Articles are arranged into subsections within these five parts and contain comprehensive selected bibliographies. Access to all the information contained in this handbook is greatly facilitated by the index volume.

Another frequently recommended encyclopedic dictionary is Wolfgang Kayser, ed., *Kleines literarisches Lexikon*, 4th ed., rev. and enl. by Horst Rudiger et al., 3 vols. (Bern and Munich: Francke, 1969) [Z1010.K584]. Volume 1 treats authors through the nineteenth century; volume 2, authors of the twentieth century; volume 3 has articles on literary genres and themes. Altogether there are some 1,000 signed articles by about twenty-seven contributors. See also the Italian *Dizionario critico della letteratura tedesca*, ed. Sergio Lupi, 2 vols. (Turin: Unione tipografico, 1976) [PT41.D58].

A useful guide is Jethro Bithell, *Germany: A Companion to German Studies*, 5th ed., rev. (London: Methuen, 1955) [DD61.B56].

L–112 **Arnold, Robert Franz. *Allgemeine Bücherkunde zur neueren deutschen Literaturgeschichte.*** 4th ed. Revised by Herbert Jacob. Berlin: de Gruyter, 1966. Z1035.3.A8 1966

This standard work, originally published in 1910, presents a series of bibliographical essays that record resources available to compile a bibliography of literature on any subject within the field of postmedieval German literature, along with a bibliography of general works on the history of modern German literature and a survey of general biographical and bibliographical sources and basic handbooks in related disciplines. The work is disposed into a total of 102 sections, within six parts treating Basic Literary Reference Tools, World Literature, German Literature, Biography, Bibliography, and Ancillary Fields respectively. Each section is organized chronologically, with early reference works (seventeenth-century histories of world or German literature, for example) finding their place in the enumeration. Thus this work is also an excellent guide to the history of German Studies. There are indexes of authors and editors and of subjects.

Other German-language bibliographical guides include Hansel's *Bücherkunde für Germanisten* (A–18) and Paul Raabe's *Einführung in die Bücherkunde zur deutschen Literaturwissenschaft* (see A–18). For East German publications see the introductory handbook by Wolfgang Friedrich, *Einführung in die Bibliographie zur deutschen Literaturwissenschaft* (Halle: Niemeyer, 1967) [Z2231.F87].

L–113 **Goedeke, Karl.** ***Grundriss zur Geschichte der deutschen Dichtung: Aus den Quellen.*** 2d, completely revised ed. Vols. 1–13. Düsseldorf and Dresden: Ehlermann, 1884–1953. Continuation, vols. 14, 15 (vols. 16–18 are still in preparation). Berlin: Akademie Verlag, 1959–1966.

PT85.G7

This is the most complete bibliography of German literature, covering the beginnings to 1830. Individual volumes treat the primary and secondary bibliography of major and minor authors, or groups of writers. Volume 5 (1893), for example, treats Schiller and his contemporaries; volume 9 (1910) treats regional novelists; and volume 14 (1959) treats northeast German authors. There are exhaustive enumerations of editions, treatises, historical, biographical, and critical articles on authors or groups of authors. Each volume has a detailed index. Because the scope and structure of this work has changed over the years, its character must be studied carefully before full use. See both the outline of contents in Faulhaber (L–110) and the more detailed *Index zu Goedeke* by Hartmut Rambaldo (Nendeln, Liechtenstein: Kraus-Thomson, 1975), which is based on the second edition cited above, along with the third revised edition of volume 4 on Goethe (parts 1–4, Dresden: Ehlermann, 1910–1916; part 5, Berlin: Akademie Verlag, 1960), and on part of volume 1 of the new project, *Goedeke's Grundriss zur Geschichte der deutschen Dichtung, Neue Folge, Fortführung von 1830 bis 1880*, edited by the Deutsche Akademie der Wissenschaften zu Berlin (Berlin: Akademie Verlag, 1955–) [PT85.G73]. The *Neue Folge* will include some 10,000 German authors of the period 1830–1880. Volume 1 treats A-Aysslinger.

A side product of the Goedeke series is the short pocket version by Leopold Hirschberg, *Der Taschengoedeke* (1924) [Z2231.H66], which lists some 50,000 titles by author, chronologically, with dates of first editions. It has fourteen different indexes. A reprint in two volumes was published in 1970 (Munich: DTV) [Z2231.H67 1970].

Goedeke is updated in a number of different ways. There is, to begin with, the volume by Josef Körner, *Bibliographisches Handbuch des deutschen Schrifttums*, 3d ed., rev. and enl. (Bern: Francke, 1949) [Z2231.K6], which emphasizes German literature from 1830 through 1948. It is divided into four parts. A general division including histories of literature, related fields, and bibliography of bibliography is followed by three chronological divisions, before Goethe, the Goethe period, and after Goethe. These divisions are further ordered by subject into literary periods, directions, movements, and so on. The table of contents details the elaborate organization, while the subject and author-as-subject indexes provide additional access to the entries.

The Körner volume is inadequately supplemented by Otto Olzien, *Bibliographie zur deutschen Literaturgeschichte* (Stuttgart: Metzler, 1953) [Z2231.O4], and his *Nachträge 1953–54 mit Engänzungen und Berichtigungen* (1955). This work begins with a small general bibliography on sources for the history of German literature, then proceeds to cite works primarily published 1948–1952 (in the *Nachträge* to 1954) on the various periods of German literature and on individual au-

thors. Articles, collected volumes, and dissertations are cited, along with books. There are, however, more than the usual number of errors in citations.

L–114 **Handbuch der deutschen Literaturgeschichte.** 2. Abteilung. Bibliographien. Paul Stapf, general editor. Bern and Munich: Francke, 1969–.

LC numbers vary

This series of handy individual monographs accompanying a parallel series of historical and critical introductions to the periods of German literature, *Erste Abteilung* [PT3.H35] presents bibliographies that revise, enlarge, and update those in the parallel sections of Körner, emphasizing publications 1950–1965/67. Each volume contains indexes of authors and subjects. The individual bibliographies are as follows:

1. Kratz, Henry. *Frühesmittelalter: Vor- und Frühgeschichte des deutschen Schrifttums (1970).*
   Z7036.K7
2. Batts, Michael. *Hohes Mittelalter (1969).* Z2232.B38
3. Jones, George F. *Spätes Mittelalter (1300–1450) (1971).* Z2232.J65
4. Engel, James E. *Renaissance, Humanismus, Reformation (1969).* Z2232.E53
5. Merkel, Ingrid. *Barock (1971).* Z2232.M4
6. Grotegut, Eugene K., and G. F. Leneaux. *Das Zeitalter der Aufklärung (1974).* Z2232.G76
7. Not yet published: to cover the "Goethezeit."
8. Osborne, John. *Romantik (1971).* Z2233.O8
9. Cowen, Roy C. *Neuzehntes Jahrhundert (1830–80) (1970).* Z2233.C68
10. Goff, Penrith. *Wilheliminisches Zeitalter (1971).*
    Z2233.G63
11. Pickar, Gertrud B. *Deutsches Schrifttum zwischen den beiden Weltkreigen (1918–1945)* (1974). Z2233.P52
12. Glenn, Jerry. *Deutsches Schrifttum der Gegenwart (ab 1945)* (1971). Z2233.3.G54

The other recent bibliographical enterprise that updates Körner et al. is the new *Internationale Bibliographie zur Geschichte der deutschen Literatur von den Anfängen bis zur Gegenwart*, ed. Günther Albrecht and Günther Dahlke, 4 vols. in 6 (East Berlin: Volk und Wissen; Berlin: Volk und Wissen, 1969–1984) [Z2231.A4]. This bibliography, designed to accompany the eleven-volume *Geschichte der deutschen Literatur von den Anfängen bis zur Gegenwart* [PT85.G47], compiled by East German, Soviet, Bulgarian, Yugoslavian, Polish, Rumanian, Czechoslovakian, and Hungarian scholars, is especially important for its inclusion of books and articles published through 1974 in Socialist countries and not generally cited in Western bibliographies. The work's structure is as follows: Vol. 1, *Von den Anfängen bis 1789* (1969); Vol. 2/pt. 1 *Von 1789 bis zur Gegenwart* (1971); Vol. 2/pt. 2, *Von 1789 bis zur Gegenwart*; *Personal-Bibliographie zur deutschen literatur des 20. Jahrhunderts*; *Bibliographien zur deutschsprachigen Literatur Österreichs und der Schweiz dieses Zeitraums*; *Nachträge zur Gesamtbibliographie* (1972); Vol. 3, *Sachregister*; *Personen-Werk Register* (1977); Vol. 4, pts. 1 and 2, *Zehnjahres-Ergänzungsband*; *Berichtzeitraum: 1965 bis 1974* (1984). Within the individual parts, arrangement is by periods and forms. There is a detailed table of contents at the end of each volume. Because of an elaborate system of abbreviations, this excellent bibliography is somewhat difficult to use.

L–115 ***Bibliographie der deutschen Literaturwissenschaft.*** Edited by Hanns W. Eppelsheimer. Vols. 1–8 (1945–1968). Frankfurt: Klostermann, 1957–1969. Continued under the title *Bibliographie der deutschen Sprach- und Literaturwissenschaft*. Edited by Clemens Köttelwesch (from 1983, Bernhard Kossmann). Vol. 9– (1969–). Frankfurt: Klostermann, 1970–. Z2231.B5

Originally published biennially; appearing annually from volume 9 (1969) on,, this is the leading serial bibliography for German literature. Citations are of Western-language materials, including French, English, Russian, Polish, Italian, and Dutch. Cited are books, pamphlets, festschriften and other composite volumes, articles, dissertations, and reviews. Bibliographies, reviews of research, editions, letters, and biographies are included. Entries are unannotated. The work is divided into large subject areas, within which further arrangement is either alphabetical or chronological. General sections on language and comparative or world literature are followed by sections on German language and literature and then on the periods (subdivided by genres and other subject areas) of German literature. It should be noted that within period divisions there are two lists of authors, first major and then minor figures. A detailed table of contents clarifies the bibliography's organization, while subject and authors indexes further facilitate access.

The annual and biennial bibliographies from 1945 through 1969 (1972) have been cumulated in two volumes: Clemens Köttelwesch, ed., *Bibliographisches Handbuch der deutschen Literaturwissenschaft 1945–1969* [Z2231.K63], vol. 1, *Von den Anfangen bis zur Romantik* (Frankfurt: Klostermann, 1973); and *Bibliographisches Handbuch der deutschen Literaturwissenschaft 1945–1972*, vol. 2, *Von 1830 bis zur Gegenwart* (1976). Subject arrangement is comparable to that in the annual and biennial bibliographies; the last volume contains author, subject, and title indexes. About 200,000 monographs, articles, reviews, and sections of composite volumes are cited.

L–116 ***Germanistik: Internationales Referatenorgan mit bibliographischen Hinweisen.*** Edited by Tilman Kroner. Vol. 1–. Tübingen: Niemeyer, 1960–. Z2235.A2G4

Published quarterly, with an annual cumulation, this work presents an international bibliography of materials on German language and literature, including books, sections of composite volumes (symposia, conference proceedings, festschriften), periodical articles, and dissertations. Monographs, studies, and editions are briefly reviewed; most entries, though not all, are annotated. The work is arranged chronologically in thirty-three sections with some 1,700 to 2,000 serially numbered items in a year. The fourth number of each annual volume contains author and indexes, along with a list of editions in progress or newly published. This work is the most current available serial bibliography for German language and literature and supplements Köttelwesch both by virtue of its annotation and because it is more current.

For more complete coverage of current titles published in the German Democratic Republic, see the publication of the Zentralinstitut für Literaturgeschichte of the Deutsche Akademie der Wissenschaften zu Berlin, *Referatendienst zur Germanistischen Literaturwissenschaft: Literaturwissenschaftliche Information und Dokumentation*, vol. 1– (1969–) [PN4.R4], published bimonthly from 1970 through 1974 and quarterly from 1975 on. This presents a selective review of the latest books and significant journal articles in a subject arrangement treating German literary history from the fifteenth through the twentieth century. There are indexes of authors of books, of articles, and of reviews.

L–117 ***Jahresberichte für neuere deutsche Literaturgeschichte.*** Vols. 1–26, pt. 1 (1890–1915). Stuttgart, Berlin-Steglitz [place varies]: Behr, 1892–1919. Z2231.J25

A comprehensive survey of monographs, critical editions, articles, and dissertations on German literature from the mid-fifteenth century to the present. Coverage varies and complements that in the *Jahresbericht für deutsche Philologie* (L–107). Vols. 1–12 (1890–1901) are organized as reviews of research on a variety of subjects, with bibliographical information recorded in footnotes; volumes 13–26 (1902–1915) are in two parts, an enumerative bibliography and a review of research with cross-references to the bibliography. Each volume contains indexes of authors and subjects.

The series was continued by *Jahresbericht über die wissenschaftliche Erscheinungen auf dem Gebiet der neueren deutschen Literatur* [Z2231.J26], edited by the Literaturarchiv-Gesellschaft in Berlin, *Neue Folge*, vols. 1–15 (1921–1935) (Berlin and Leipzig: de Gruyter, 1924–1939). Entries, some annotated, are in an arrangement of broad subject categories. There are indexes of authors-reviewers and subjects. This series was continued retrospectively for volumes 16–19 (1936–1939) in a single volume by the Deutsche Akademie der Wissenschaften zu Berlin (Berlin: de Gruyter, 1956).

In 1960 appeared the first volume of the retrospective *Jahresbericht für deutsche Sprache und Literatur* [Z2231.A2 J3], which combines elements covered in the philological series with those found in the annual reviews of research in literary history. Edited by the East Berlin Institut für deutsche Sprache und Literatur of the Deutsche Akademie der Wissenschaften zu Berlin, under the direction of Gerhart Marx, this work has been published in two five-year cumulative volumes: vol. 1 for the years 1940–1945 (Berlin: Akademie-Verlag, 1960) and vol. 2 for the years 1946–1950 (1966). Each volume is in four sections: A—General, treating German Philology, Bibliography, and so on; B—Linguistics; C—Literary Studies; and D—Supplements. Arrangement within sections is in further subject and period subdivisions. Monographs, articles, and dissertations are enumerated, with frequent descriptive annotations. There are indexes of authors-reviewers, titles, and subjects. This very full, scholarly work overlaps the West German *Bibliographie der deutschen Sprach- und Literaturwissenschaft* (L–115); it is less current, but for coverage including Eastern European materials, both should be used.

L–118 **"Anglo-German Literary Bibliography [1933–1969]."** Compiled by L. Price et al. *JEGP: Journal of English and Germanic Philology*, vols. 34–69. Urbana: University of Illinois, 1935–1970. PD1.J7

This annual bibliography began publication under the title "Anglo-German Bibliography," in *JEGP*, vol. 34 (1935); it ran through vol. 40 (1941). For 1942–1944 it was published in the *American German Review* only (see below) and then returned to *JEGP*. Covering American-German cultural relations in the widest sense, this bibliography presented an author list of current books (with reviews cited) and periodical articles.

Another bibliography, including books, articles, and dissertations, was carried 1941–1966 in the *American German Review* (Philadelphia: National Carl Schutz Foundation, 1940/46–) [E183.8.G3 A6]; for 1967–1969 it was continued under the title "Bibliography Americana Germanica" in vols. 41–43 of the *German Quarterly* (Cherry Hill, N. J.: American Association of Teachers of German, 1968–1970) [PF3001 .G3].

L–119 **Kosch, Wilhelm.** *Deutsches Literatur-Lexikon: Biographisch-bibliographisches Handbuch.* 3d ed. Revised by Bruno Berger and Heinz Rupp. 9 vols. in 10. Bern and Munich: Francke, 1966–1984.   Z2231.K663

This handbook, first published in two volumes, 1927–1930, contains authoritative articles on German authors in the widest sense, including theologians, philosophers, and historians. Articles include comprehensive primary and secondary bibliographies. Swiss and Austrian authors are also included. The earlier editions contained articles also on terminology, themes, motifs, forms, genres, types, movements, styles, and titles of German literature.

The less comprehensive, less reliable second edition in four volumes, with the title *Deutsches Literatur-Lexikon: Biographisches und bibliographisches Handbuch* (Bern: Francke, 1947–1958) [Z2230.K862], can be used, as can the single volume derived from it, *Deutsches Literatur-Lexikon*, ed. Bruno Berger (Bern: Francke, 1963) [Z2231.K66].

For contemporary literature the best handbook is Hermann Kunisch, *Handbuch der deutschen Gegenwartsliteratur*, 2d rev. and enl. ed., 3 vols. (Munich: Nymphenburger Verlagshandlung, 1968–1970) [PT155.K82], originally published in 1965. Volumes 1 and 2 contain biobibliographies of authors. Volume 2 also contains a series of general articles on such umbrella topics as Expressionism, Exile literature, the Third Reich, and Literature of the German Democratic Republic, along with an index of proper names. Author articles contain biographical summaries and primary bibliographies. Volume 3, ed. H. Wiesler et al., has the title *Bibliographie der Personal-bibliographien zur deutschen Gegenwartsliteratur* [Z2221.A1 W54] and presents bibliographies for some 500 authors and scholars, including primary and secondary works, archival materials, and surveys of research. There are indexes of authors, editors, and translators.

For bibliographies of authors see also Johannes Hansel, *Personalbibliographie zur deutschen Literaturgeschichte, Studienausgabe*, 2d rev. ed., ed. Carl Paschek (Berlin: Schmidt, 1974) [Z1002.H24 1974], which gives bibliographies for some 1,500 German authors including primary and secondary publications, manuscript and archive information, and reviews of research and societies devoted to the author. It is meant to serve as a companion to Hansel's *Bücherkunde für Germanisten* (A–18). An additional source of reliable biographical sketches for some 2,000 authors is Gero von Wilpert's *Deutsches Dichterlexikon: Biographisch-bibliographisches Handwörterbuch zur deutschen Literaturgeschichte*, 2d ed. (Stuttgart: Kröner, 1976) [Z2234.P7 W5 1976]. For authors of East Germany see also Günther Albrecht et al., *Deutsches Schriftsteller Lexikon von den Anfängen bis zur Gegenwart*, 4th enl. and rev. ed. (Weimar: Volksverlag, 1963) [PT41.A4 1963].

L–120 **Some Frequently Recommended Works on the German Language and Literatures.**

Bibliographical

Batts, Michael S. *Bibliography of German Literature: An Historical and Critical Survey.* Bern: Peter Lang, 1978.   Z2231.A1 B37

Fromm, Hans. *Germanistische Bibliographie seit 1945: Theorie und Kritik.* Stuttgart: Metzler, 1960. Z2235.F7

"German Literature of the 19th Century, 1830–1880: A Current Bibliography." *Germanic Review*, 1953–1960. From 1949 through 1952 this bibliography, sponsored by the MLA German VI Group, appeared in *Modern Language Forum*.

Henning, H., and S. Seifert, eds. *International Bibliographie zur deutschen Klassik, 1750–1850.* Weimar: National Forschungs- und Gedenkstätten der klassischen deutschen Literatur, 1960–.   Z2233.I6

Prohl, Jürgen. *Elemente und Formen der Personalbibliographien zur deutschen Literaturgeschichte.* Bonn: Bouvier, 1979.   Z2231.A1 P76

Raabe, Paul. *Einführung in die Quellenkunde zur neueren deutschen Literaturgeschichte.* 2d ed. Stuttgart: Metzler, 1966.   Z2231.R24 1966

———. *Quellen repertorium zur neueren deutschen Literaturgeschichte.* 2d ed. Stuttgart: Metzler, 1966.
                                                Z2231.R25 1966

———, ed. *Index Expressionismus: Bibliographie der Beiträge in der Zeitschriften und Jahrbüchern des literarischen Expressionismus, 1910–1925.* 18 vols. Nendeln, Liechtenstein: Kraus-Thomson, 1972.
                                                Z5936.E9 R3

Sternfeld, W., and E. Tiedemann. *Deutsche Exilliteratur, 1933–1945: Eine Bio-bibliographie.* 2d rev. and enl. ed. Heidelberg: Lambert Schneider, 1970. Z2233.S7

Widmann, Hans. *Bibliographien zum deutschen Schrifttum des Jahre 1939–1950.* Tübingen: Niemeyer, 1951.
                                                Z1002.W5

Wilpert, Gero von, and Adolf Gühring. *Erstausgaben deutscher Dichtung: Eine Bibliographie zur deutschen Literatur 1600–1960.* Stuttgart: Kröner, 1967.
                                                Z2231.W74

Historical and Special Studies

Bartels, Adolf. *Handbuch zur Geschichte der deutschen Literatur.* 2d ed. Leipzig: E. Avenarius, 1909.
                                                PT96.B3 1909

Bennett, Edwin K. *History of the German Novelle.* Revised by E. M. Waidson. Cambridge: Cambridge University Press, 1961.   PT747.S6 B4 1961

Blackall, Eric. *Emergence of German as a Literary Language, 1700–1775.* 2d ed. Ithaca, N. Y.: Cornell University Press, 1978.   PF3083.B6 1978

Brummer, Franz. *Lexikon der deutschen Literatur und Prosaisten vom Beginn des 19. Jahrhunderts zur Gegenwart.* 8 vols. in 4. Nendeln, Liechtenstein: Kraus, 1975.   Z2230.B894 1975

Burger, Heinz Otto, ed. *Annalen der deutschen Literatur: Eine Gemeinschaft zahlreichen Fachgelehrter.* 2d ed. Stuttgart: Metzler, 1961–1971.   PT85.B8 1971

Closs, August. *Genius of the German Lyric: An Historical Survey of Its Formal and Metaphysical Values.* 2d ed. Philadelphia: Dufour, 1962.   PT571.C6 1962

de Boor, Helmut, Anton Wilhelm, and Richard Newald, gen. eds. *Geschichte der deutschen Literatur, von den Anfängen bis zur Gegenwart.* 7 vols. in 10 to date. Munich: Beck, 1949–1983.   PT85.B64

Ehrismann, Gustav. *Geschichte der deutschen Literatur bis zum Ausgang des Mittelalters.* 2 parts in 4 vols. Munich: Beck, 1918–1935.   PF3071.M4

Franke, Konraal. *Die Literatur der Deutschen Demokratischen Republik.* Vol. 2 of *Kindlers Literaturgeschichte der Gegenwart.* Rev. ed. Munich: Kindler, 1974.
                                                PT3716.F7 1974

Frenzel, Herbert Alfred, and Elizabeth Frenzel. *Daten deutscher Dichtung: Chronologischer Abriss der deutschen Literaturgeschichte von den Anfängen bis zur Gegenwart.* 6th ed. 2 vols. Cologne: Kiepenheuer und Witsch, 1971.   PT103.F72

Friedrich, Werner P., et al. *History of German Literature.* 2d ed. New York: Barnes and Noble, 1961.
PT99.F7 1961

Galinsky, Hans. *Amerikanisch-deutsche Sprach- und Literaturbeziehungen: Systematische Übersicht und Forschungsbericht 1945–1970.* Frankfurt: Athenäum Verlag, 1972.
PT123.U6 G3

Gebhardt, Bruno. *Handbuch der deutschen Geschichte.* 8th ed. Revised by Herbert Grundmann. 4 vols. Stuttgart: Union Deutsche Verlagsgesellschaft, 1954–1960.
DD90.G32

Hill, C., and R. Ley. *Drama of German Expressionism.* Chapel Hill: University of North Carolina Press, 1960.
PD25.N6 no. 28

Introductions to German Literature. 4 vols. New York: Barnes and Noble; London: Barrie and Rockcliff; Cressett Press, 1967–1970. Includes *Literature in Medieval Germany,* by P. Salmon; *German Literature in the Sixteenth and Seventeenth Centuries,* by R. Pascal; *German Literature in the Eighteenth and Nineteenth Centuries,* by E. L. Stahl and W. E. Yuill; and *Twentieth-Century German Literature,* by A. Closs.
PT91.I5

Jungandreas, Wolfgang. *Geschichte der deutschen und der englischen Sprache.* 3 vols. Göttingen: Vandenhoeck und Ruprecht, 1946–.
PD75.J8

Lederer, Herbert. *Handbook of East German Drama 1945–1985 / DDR Drama Handbuch.* Berne: Peter Lang, 1987.

Martini, Fritz. *Deutsche Literaturgeschichte von den Anfangen bis zur Gegenwart.* 18th ed. Stuttgart: Kröner, 1984.
PT85.D37 1984

Northcott, Kenneth J., and R. T. Llewellyn, gen. eds. *Literary History of German.* 8 vols. London: Croom Helm, 1975–.
PT35.L57

Pasley, Malcolm, ed. *Germany: A Companion to German Studies.* London: Methuen, 1982. DD61.G42 1982

Petry, Karl. *Handbuch zur deutschen Literaturgeschichte.* 2 vols. Cologne: B. Pick, 1949. PT85.P4

Pochmann, Henry A. *German Culture in America: Philosophical and Literary Influences, 1600–1900.* Madison: University of Wisconsin Press, 1957.
Z1361.G37P6

Price, Lawrence M. *English-German Literary Influences: Bibliography and Survey.* 2 parts. University of California Publications in Modern Philology, vol. 9. Berkeley, 1919.
PB13.C3 vol. 9.

Radler, Rudolf, ed. *Die deutschsprachige Sachliteratur.* Zurich: Kindler, 1978.
Z1035.3.D53

Ritchie, James M., ed. *Periods in German Literature.* 2 vols. London: Wolff, 1966–1969. PT107.R5

Robertson, J. G. *History of German Literature.* 6th ed. Edited by Dorothy Reich et al. Edinburgh: Blackwood, 1970.
PT91.R7 1970

Schmitt, Fritz. *Deutsche Literaturgeschichte in Tabellen.* 3 vols. Bonn: Athenaeum, 1949–1952. PT103.S4

Stammler, Wolfgang, Karl Langosch, et al. *Die deutsche Literatur des Mittelalters: Verfasserlexikon.* 5 vols. Berlin: de Gruyter, 1931–1955.
Z2230.S78

Vogt, Friedrich H. T., and Max Koch. *Geschichte der deutschen Literatur von den ältesten Zeiten bis zur Gegenwart.* 5th ed. Revised and enlarged by Willi Koch. 3 vols. Leipzig: Bibliographisches Institut, 1934–1938.
PT85.V7 1934

Waidson, H. M. *Modern German Novel: A Mid-Twentieth Century Survey.* London: Oxford University Press, 1959.
PT772.W3

Wegner, Matthias. *Exil und Literatur: Deutsche Schriftsteller im Ausland, 1933–1945.* 2d ed. rev. and enl. Frankfurt: Athenäum Verlag, 1968.
PT405.W34 1968

Austria

Bamberger, Richard, and Franz Meier-Bruck. *Österreich Lexikon.* 2 vols. Vienna: Österreichischer Bundesverlag, 1966.
DB14.O48

Giebisch, Hans, and Gustav Gugitz, eds. *Bio-bibliographischer Literatur-Lexikon Österreichs: Von den Anfängen bis zur Gegenwart.* Vienna: Hollinek, 1964.
Z2110.G48

————, et al. *Kleines österreichisches Literaturlexikon.* Vienna: Hollinek, 1948. Z2110.G5

Spiel, Hilde. *Die zeitgenossische Literatur Österreichs.* Vol. 3 of *Kindlers Literaturgeschichte der Gegenwart.* Zurich: Kindler, 1976. PT3811.Z4

Stock, K. F., et al. *Personalbibliographien österreichischer Dichter und Schriftsteller von den Anfängen bis zur Gegenwart: Mit Auswahl einschlägigen Bibliographien, Nachschlagewerke, Sammelbiographien, Literaturgeschichten, und Anthologien.* Pullach bei Munich: Dokumentation, 1972.
Z2111.A1 S76

Ungar, Frederick, ed. *Handbook of Austrian Literature.* New York: Ungar, 1973. PT155.U5

Switzerland

Calgari, Guido. *Four Literatures of Switzerland.* London: Adam Books, 1963. PN849.S9 C29

Gsteiger, Manfred, ed. *Kindlers Literaturgeschichte der Gegenwart: Die zeitgenossischen Literaturen der Schweiz: Autoren, Werke, Themen, Tendenzen seit 1945.* Vol. 4. Zurich and Munich: Kindler, 1974.
PN849.S9 Z4

XI. RUSSIAN AND OTHER SLAVIC LANGUAGES AND LITERATURES

See also relevant entries in section I on Language, Linguistics, and Philology; the *MLA International Bibliography* (L–50); the MHRA *Year's Work in Modern Languages and Literatures* (L–52); and works in General and Comparative Literature.

L–121 **Zenkovsky, Serge A., and David L. Armbruster. *Guide to Bibliographies of Russian Literature.*** Nashville, Tenn.: Vanderbilt University Press, 1970. Z2501.A1 Z4

This guide consists of 320 serially numbered, unannotated entries classified into two main sections enumerating General and Literary Bibliography respectively. The section on General Bibliography contains chapters on General Matters; on Periodicals and Periodical Indexes; on Libraries, Private Collections, Trade Catalogs, and Memoirs; on Biobibliography, Biography, and Pseudonyms; on Selective Bibliography; Dissertations; and Encyclopedias. The section on Literary Bibliography lists both period and subject bibliographies, the first in seven subsections (General, Old Russian to 1700, 1700–1800, 1800–1900, 1890–1917, Since 1917 Published in Russia, Since 1917 Published Abroad); and the second in nine (Poetry, Drama, Prose, Literary Criticism and History, Periodicals and Almanacs, Biobibliography and Pseudonyms, Literary Encyclopedias, Literary Archives, and Bibliographies in English). Abundant cross-references and an index of authors, editors, and compilers facilitate the use of this handy volume.

A less comprehensive but more recent reference is John Simon Gabriel Simmons, *Russian Bibliography, Libraries, and Archives* (Oxford: For the Author, 1973) [Z2491.A1 S54], items 494–607, which concern literary bibliography. The highly selective listing includes bibliographies of bibliographies, guides, works on methodology and historiography, literary encyclopedias and biographical dictionaries, biobibliographies, general and special retrospective and current bibliographies, and bibliographies on special periods and topics (including comparative literature, theater, children's literature, and folklore).

The most comprehensive non-Russian-language guide to Slavic literary bibliographies is the German-language work of Günther Wytrzens, *Bibliographische Einführung in das Studium der slavischen Literaturen* (Frankfurt am Main: Klostermann, 1972) [Z7041.W9], citing over 5,000 items in a total of 106 sections. Outstanding items are asterisked. Sections 1–22 cover Literary Theory and Literary History (including sections on the history of each Slavic literature); 23–32 treat Ancillary and Related Disciplines (from Versification to the History of Slavic Studies); 33–100 treat Bibliography; and 101–106 are Supplements. There is an index of names. A supplement, also by Wytrzens, *Bibliographie der literaturwissenschaftlichen Slawistik, 1970–1980* was published (Frankfurt am Main: Klostermann, 1982) [Z7041.W89] adding another 5,000 items similarly arranged and also covering all the Slavic literatures.

Complementing the *Bibliographische Einführung* is Wytrzens's more recent *Bibliographie der russischen Autoren und anonymen Werke* (Frankfurt: Klostermann, 1975) [Z2501 .W95], containing biobibliographies in eight sections: Old Russian (Old East Slavic) Authors and Anonyma; Authors and Anonyma translated into Old Russian; Russian Literature of the Eighteenth Century; of the Period 1800–1890; of the Period 1890–1917 including also Émigré Literature; and Russian Soviet Literature. Individual works are identified as to their type (reference, bibliography, review of research, edition, etc.). There is an index of authors and titles. A supplement for the period 1975–1980 was published (Frankfurt am Main: Klostermann, 1982) [Z2501.W952 1982].

Also available is the single volume by Annemarie Hille, *Bibliographische Einführung in das Studium der slawischen Philologie* (Halle [Saale]: Niemeyer, 1959) [Z7041.H5], which presents a range of reference works, bibliographies, and historical and critical works on both the Slavic languages and the Slavic literatures, and the more recent volume by Günther Wyrtzens, *Bibliographische Einführung in das Studium der slavischen Literaturen* (Frankfurt: Klostermann, 1972) [Z7041.W9].

L–122 Auty, Robert, and Dimitri Obolensky, eds. *Introduction to Russian Language and Literature.* Cambridge: Cambridge University Press, 1977.   PG2051.I5

This volume contains ten chapters by specialists with classified, discursive guides to further reading appended to each. The chapters treat the Russian Language, Russian Writing and Printing, Early Russian Literature (1000–1300), Literature in the Muscovite Period (1300–1700), The Age of Classicism (1700–1820), From the Golden Age to the Silver Age (1820–1917), Literature in the Soviet Period (1917–1975), The Early Theater, The Nineteenth- and Early-Twentieth-Century Theater, and The Soviet Theater respectively.

Wider in scope and earlier in date is the *Handbook of Slavic Studies*, ed. Leon I. Strakhovsky (Cambridge: Harvard University Press, 1949) [DK32.S86] with chapters on the history of each of the Slavic countries. Chapters 18–24 deal with

Russian, Polish, Czech and Slovak, Balkan Slav, Lusatian, and Soviet Russian literatures.

For the Slavic languages see Reginald George Arthur de Bray, *Guide to the Slavonic Languages*, rev. ed. (London: Dent, 1969) [PG53.D4], originally published in 1951. Each language is treated separately and described in detail with illustrations from its literature. The volume concludes with a full bibliography of grammars, dictionaries, and other reference aids. The detailed table of contents does not compensate for the lack of an index.

L–123 Horecky, Paul, ed. *Russia and the Soviet Union: A Bibliographic Guide to Western Language Publications.* Chicago: University of Chicago Press, 1965.   Z2491.H64

This volume contains a total of 1,960 serially numbered entries, with brief descriptive and evaluative annotations, of works in the major Western languages (emphasis on English) to the beginning of 1964. The entries are divided into nine major sections, as follows: 1, General Reference Aids and Bibliographies; 2, General and Descriptive Works; 3, The Land; 4, The People: Ethnic and Demographic Features; 5, The Nations: Civilizations and Politics; 6, History; 7, The State; 8, The Economic and Social Structure; and 9, The Intellectual and Cultural Life. Section 9 is subdivided into sections on Language (Bibliography, The Modern Russian Language, History of the Russian Language, Onomastics, and Dialectology); Literature (Prior to the 19th Century—Bibliography, Historical and Critical Studies, Anthologies, Texts and Translations—and 19th and 20th Centuries—Survey Studies, Histories of Literature, Reference Works, and General Bibliographies, Anthologies, and Translations of Works of Individual Authors and Works about Them); Folklore; History of Thought and Culture; Religion; Education and Research; The Fine Arts; Music; Theater and Cinema. This excellent bibliography, produced by a series of contributors and consultants, concludes with an index of names, titles, and principal subject headings.

Horecky has also compiled *Basic Russian Publications; An Annotated Bibliography on Russia and the Soviet Union* (Chicago: University of Chicago Press, 1962) [Z2491.H6].

An earlier but still valuable bibliographical guide, similarly though more broadly conceived, is Robert Joseph Kerner, *Slavic Europe: A Selected Bibliography in the Western European Languages: Comprising History, Languages, and Literatures* (Cambridge: Harvard University Press, 1918) [Z2041.K37]. It contains a total of 4,521 serially numbered, occasionally annotated entries, citing both major and less important works, with massive cross-referencing. Arrangement is by nationality, as follows: 1, The Slavs (history, languages, literatures); 2, The Russians (history—subdivided by domain and period; language; Great Russian literature—subdivided into generalities, genres, periods, and authors); 3, The Poles (history, language, literature); 4, The Slavs in the German Empire (subdivided by individual communities); 5, The Bohemians and the Slovaks (history, language, literature); and 6, The Southern Slavs (subdivided by individual communities, with subsections for each on history, language, and literature). The volume concludes with an index of authors.

L–124 Terras, Victor, ed. *Handbook of Russian Literature.* New Haven: Yale University Press, 1985.   PG2940.H29

This significant volume presents a single alphabet listing of signed articles on major and minor Russian authors, scholars, critics, literary movements and schools, leading journals, literary organizations and prizes, literary genres and themes, and technical terms, as well as articles on relations with other literatures, both foreign and intra-slavic. A total of 106 contributors have authored nearly 1,000 articles, nearly all of which conclude with both primary and secondary bibliographies, though their character and extent vary from contributor to contributor. There is also a separate entry titled "Bibliography of Russian Literature," and there is a bibliography at the end of the *Handbook* which includes about 300 items divided into the following categories: General Bibliographic Works and Serials; Comprehensive Bibliographic Works and Serials Covering Russian Literature; Archives and Libraries; Bibliographic Works and Serials Arranged by Periods; Anthologies of Russian Literature; History of Russian Literature; Literary Theory and Criticism; Encyclopedias and Dictionaries of Literature. Access is enhanced not only by cross-references, but also by an index of nearly 2,000 names, terms, and topics.

L–125 **Harkins, William E.** *Dictionary of Russian Literature.* New York: Philosophical Library, 1956.   PG2940.H3

This dictionary treats matters concerned with Great Russian literature, literary criticism, journalism, philosophy, and related subjects. Major and minor authors, historical schools, and genres constitute the article headings; titles and dates of major works are given in the author entries, along with biographical information and a critical summary of the author's career. There are no articles on individual literary works, nor are bibliographies included in the articles. There are a significant number of factual inaccuracies, and the work must be used with caution.

L–126 **[Bibliographical Survey]** *Revue des études slaves.* Paris: Institut d'études slaves de l'Université de Paris, 1921–.
      PG1.R4

Each annual volume of the *Revue* contains an extensive bibliographical survey article on books and articles in Russian and other languages on the following subjects: Russian language, literature, history, religion, art, and bibliography.

English-language materials concerning Russian studies were included in the serial bibliography published in the *Russian Review*, 1942–1959. These annual bibliographies have been conveniently cumulated in Thomas Schultheiss, ed., *Russian Studies 1941-1958: A Cumulation of the Annual Bibliographies from the Russian Review* (Ann Arbor, Mich.: Pierian Press, 1972) [Z2491.R94].

English-language materials, including books and articles published outside the Soviet Union and Eastern Europe, are listed in the annual "American Bibliography of Russian [later Slavic] and East European Studies for [1956–]" published in the *Russian [later Slavic] and East European Journal* (Bloomington: Indiana University Press, 1957–) [Z2483. A65]. Entries are arranged by subject and by country. There is an index of authors and editors. The annual bibliography for 1977 and a combined bibliography for 1978–1979 have been separately published. It is now compiled by the European Division of the Library of Congress.

The annual *European Bibliography of Soviet, East European and Slavonic Studies* [formerly (1971–1974) titled, among other absorbed separate publications, *East European and Slavonic Studies in Britain*] (Glasgow: University of Glasgow, 1971–) [Z2483.E94], includes books, articles, reviews, and newspaper articles published in Great Britain, arranged by country and subject, including individual writers as subjects. There is an index of authors. In addition, see the new *Bibliographic Guide to Soviet and East European Studies* (Boston: G. K. Hall, 1978–) [Z2483.B48], which lists by author, title, and subject all books, serials, and other separates cataloged by the Library of Congress and the New York Public Library.

A convenient if not easily available index is that compiled by Garth M. Terry, *Subject and Name Index to Articles on the Slavonic and East European Languages and Literatures, Music and Theatre, Libraries and the Press, Contained in English-Language Journals, 1920-1975* (Nottingham: Notting-

ham University Library, 1976) [Z7041.T47]. It contains 4,841 serially numbered items, arranged by subject, with a name index.

L–127 **Modern Encyclopedia of Russian and Soviet Literature.** Ed. by Harry B. Weber. 7 vols. to date. Gulf Breeze, Fla.: Academic International Press, 1977–1984. PG2940.M6

This work includes writers and their works, but also treats aspects of Russian and Soviet cultural life which affect literature. Thus literary criticism, past literary scholarship, selected linguistic problems, dramatic literature, literary genres, movements, and journals, and folklore are also treated. Russian and other Soviet literatures, their literary traditions and their literary history, are all covered. Articles are often translated from older reference works, or are compilations of material from several works, but their origins are not identified. There are also numerous signed articles prepared by specialists. Longer articles include bibliographies. Volume 1 through 7 treat Abaginskii to Fonvizin.

An earlier work by Valentine Snow, *Russian Writers: A Bio-Bibliographical Dictionary from the Age of Catherine II to the October Revolution of 1917* (New York: International Book Service, 1946) [Z2500.S6], is a guide for general readers, treating briefly the biographies of some 200 authors. Bibliographies of their most important works are included in the biographical sketch, along with brief descriptions of those works. For inclusion, a writer must have been known before October 1917; a second volume, treating authors who came to prominence after that date, was never published. The short work concludes with an index of authors. It should be used with caution because of numerous inaccuracies.

L–128 **Scholarly Journals in Slavic and East European Studies.**

IJSLP   *International Journal of Slavic Linguistics and Poetics.* Vol. 1–. The Hague: Mouton, 1959–. Irreg. Reviews.   PG1.I5

Revue des études slaves. Vol. 1–. Paris: Institut d'études slaves, Université de Paris, 1921–. 1/yr. Bibliography (see L–126).   PG1.R4

Rocznik slawistyczny / Revue slavistique. Vol. 1–. Warsaw: Ossolineum, 1908–. 1/yr. Annual bibliography of books, articles, and reviews on all Slavic languages and literatures in vols. 1–49 (1908–1972). Currently individual bibliographies on specific subjects are a regular feature.   PG1.R6

RLJ   *Russian Language Journal.* Vol. 1–. East Lansing: Michigan State University, 1947–. 3/yr. Reviews.   PG2003.V2

Russian Linguistics: International Journal for the Study of the Russian Language [RusLing]. Vol. 1–. Dordrecht: D. Reidel, 1974–. 4/yr. Reviews.   PG2001.R85

RusL   *Russian Literature.* Vol. 1–. Amsterdam: North-Holland Publishing Co., 1971–. 4/yr. Reviews.   PG2900.A1 R9

RLT   *Russian Literature Tri-quarterly.* Vol. 1–. Ann Arbor, Mich.: Ardis, 1971–. 3/yr. Reviews.   PG2901.R86

RusR   *Russian Review: An American Quarterly Devoted to Russia Past and Present.* Vol. 1–. Hanover, N. H.: Hoover Institution, Stanford University, 1941–. 4/yr. Annual bibliography (see L–126). Cumulative index to vols. 1–20 (1941–1961) compiled by Virginia L. Close (1962).   DK1.R82

SEEJ   *Slavic and East European Journal.* Vol. 1–. Madison, Wis.; Bloomington, Ind.; American Association of Slavic and East European Languages, 1957–.

4/yr. Reviews. Annual bibliography (see L–126).
PG38.U6A5

SlavR *Slavic Review: American Quarterly of Soviet and East European Studies* [former title: *American Slavic and East European Review*]. Vol. 1–. Seattle, Wash. [place varies]: American Association for the Advancement of Slavic Studies, 1941–. 4/yr. Reviews. Annual list of "Doctoral Dissertations on Russia, the Soviet Union, and Eastern Europe Accepted by American, Canadian, and British Universities [1960–]" from vol. 23 (1964). D377.A1A5

SEER *Slavonic and East European Review.* Vol. 1–. London: School of Slavonic and East European Studies, University of London, 1922–. 2/yr. then 4/yr. Reviews. D377.A1S65

SovL *Soviet Literature.* Vol. 1–. Moscow: Writers' Union of the USSR, 1946–. 12/yr. Reviews.
PG2900.S72

WSl *Die Welt der Slaven: Halbjahresschrift für Slavistik.* Vol. 1–. Munich: Harrassowitz, 1955–. 4/yr. Reviews. PG1.W4

ZSP *Zeitschrift für slavische Philologie.* Vol. 1–. Leipzig and Cologne: Market und Petters, 1924–. 2/yr. Reviews. PG1.Z4

ZS *Zeitschrift für Slawistik.* Vol. 1–. East Berlin: Institut fur Slawistik, Akademie der Wissenschaften der DDR and National Kommittee der Slawisten der DDR, 1956–. 6/yr. Reviews. PG1.Z43

L–129 **Some Frequently Recommended Works on Russian, Other Slavic, and Other Eastern European Languages and Literatures.**

Russian

Alexandrova, Vera [pseud. of Vera A. Schwarz]. *History of Soviet Literature.* Garden City, N.Y.: Doubleday, 1963. PG3022.A413

Berdyaev, Nicholas. *Russian Idea.* Boston: Beacon, 1962.

Berry, Thomas Edwin. *Plots and Characters in Major Russian Fiction.* 2 vols. Hamden, Conn.: Archon, 1977–1978. Vol. 1, *Pushkin, Lermontov, Turgenev, Tolstoi.* Vol. 2, *Gogol, Goncharov, Dostoevskii.*
PG3095.B4

Blair, Katherine Hunter. *Review of Soviet Literature.* London: Ampersand, 1967. PG3022.B5

Brown, Edward J. *Russian Literature since the Revolution.* Rev. and enl. ed. Cambridge: Harvard University Press, 1982. PG3022.B7 1982

Chizhevsky, Dimitri. *Comparative History of Slavic Literatures.* Nashville, Tenn.: Vanderbilt University Press, 1971. PG501.C513

———. *History of Russian Literature from the Eleventh Century to the End of the Baroque.* The Hague: Mouton, 1960.

———. *Outline of Comparative Slavic Literatures.* Boston: American Academy of Arts and Sciences, 1952.
PG502.C35

Cross, Anthony Glenn, and Gerald Stanton Smith. *Eighteenth Century Russian Literature, Culture and Thought: A Bibliography of English-Language Scholarship and Translations.* Newtonville: Oriental Research Partners, 1984. Z2502.C76 1984

Duwel, W., et al., eds. *Geschichte der klassischen russischen Literatur.* Berlin and Weimar: Aufbauverlag, 1965. PG3014.D8

Erlich, Victor. *Russian Formalism: History, Doctrine.* 3d ed. New Haven: Yale University Press, 1981.
PG3026.F6 E7 1981

Foster, Ludmilla A. *Bibliography of Russian Émigré Literature, 1918- 1968.* 2 vols. Boston: G. K. Hall, 1970.
Z2513.F66

Great Soviet Encyclopedia. A. M. Prokhorov, editor in chief. 3d ed. 31 vols. New York: Macmillan, 1970–1979.
AE5.G68

Holthusen, Johannes. *Twentieth-Century Russian Literature: A Critical Study.* New York: Ungar, 1972.
PG3019.H613

Jünger, Harri. *Literatures of the Soviet Peoples: A Historical and Biographical Survey.* New York: Ungar, 1970.
PN849.R9 J813

Lo Gatto, E. *Histoire de la littérature russe des origines à nos jours.* Brussels: Desclée de Brouwer, 1965.
PG2954.L614

McGraw-Hill Encyclopedia of Russia and the Soviet Union. Edited by Michael T. Florinsky. New York: McGraw-Hill, 1961. DK14.M26

Masaryk, Thomas G. *Spirit of Russia: Studies in History, Literature and Philosophy.* 2d ed. 2 vols. New York: Macmillan, 1955. DK32.M4 1955

Mirsky, Dimitri S. *History of Russian Literature, Comprising "A History of Russian Literature from Its Beginnings to 1900" (1945) and "Contemporary Russian Literature" (1927).* New York: Vintage, 1958.
PG2951.M5

Simmons, Ernest J. *English Literature and Culture in Russia (1553–1840).* Cambridge: Harvard University Press, 1935. PR129.R8 S5

———. *Outline of Modern Russian Literature, 1800–1940.* Ithaca, N. Y.: Cornell University Press, 1943.
PG3017.S5 1943

Slonim, Marc. *Epic of Russian Literature from Its Origins through Tolstoy.* New York: Oxford University Press, 1950. PG2951.S5

———. *Modern Russian Literature from Chekhov to the Present.* New York: Oxford University Press, 1953.
PG3011.S538

———. *Outline of Russian Literature.* New York: Oxford University Press, 1958. A condensed version of the previous two works. P2951.S53

Stankiewicz, Edward, and Dean S. Worth. *Selected Bibliography of Slavic Linguistics.* 2 vols. The Hague: Mouton, 1966–1970. Z7041.S82

Struve, Gleb. *Russian Literature under Lenin and Stalin: 1917–1953.* Norman: University of Oklahoma Press, 1971. PG3022.S82

———. *Soviet Russian Literature, 1917–1950.* Norman: University of Oklahoma Press, 1951. PG3022.S82

Unbegaun, Boris O. *Russian Grammar.* Oxford: Clarendon Press, 1967. PG2111.U453 1968

———, and J. S. G. Simmons. *Bibliographical Guide to the Russian Language.* Oxford: Clarendon Press, 1953.
Z2505.U5

Wall, Josephine. *Soviet Dissident Literature: A Critical Guide.* Boston: G. K. Hall, 1983. Z2511.U5 W64

Yarmolinsky, A. *Literature under Communism.* Bloomington: Indiana University Press, 1960. DK268.3.Y3

Baltic (general)

Devoto, Giacomo. *Le letterature dei paesi baltici.* Florence: Sansoni, 1969. PH302.D4 1969

Rubulis, Aleksis. *Baltic Literature.* Notre Dame, Ind.: Notre Dame University Press, 1970. PH302.R8

Estonian

Jänes, Henno. *Geschichte der estnischen Literatur.* Stockholm: Almqvist and Wiksell, 1965. PH631.J26

Magi, Arvo. *Estonian Literature: An Outline.* Stockholm: Baltic Humanitarian Association, 1968. PH631.M313

Mallene, Endel. *Estonian Literature in the Early 1970's: Authors, Books, and Trends of Development.* Tallinn: Eesti Raamat, 1978. PH632.M33

Nirk, Endell. *Estonian Literature: Historical Survey with Bio-Bibliographical Appendix.* Tallinn: Eesti Raamat, 1970. PH631.N5

Oras, Ants, and Bernard Kangro. *Estonian Literature in Exile.* Lund: Eesti kirjanike kooperatiiv, 1967. PH632.O67

Latvian

Andrups, Janis, and Vitauts Kalve. *Latvian Literature.* Stockholm: M. Goppers, 1954. PG9005.A713

Ekmanis, Rolfs. *Latvian Literature under the Soviets, 1940–1975.* Belmont, Mass.: Nordland Publishing Co., 1978. PG9005.E4

Bulgarian

Manning, Clarence A., and Roman Smal-Stocki. *History of Modern Bulgarian Literature.* New York: Bookman Associates, 1960. PG1008.M3

Czech

Harkins, W. E., and K. Šimončič. *Czech and Slovak Literature, with a Bibliography on Lusatian Language by Clarence A. Manning.* New York: Department of Slavic Languages, Columbia University, 1950. PG5001.H35

Jelinek, Hanus. *Histoire de la littérature tchèque.* 4th ed. 3 vols. Paris: Éd. de Sagittaire, 1930–1935. PG5001.J4

Meriggi, Bruno. *Storia della letteratura ceca e slovacca.* Milan: Nuova accademia editrice, 1958. PG5001.M47

Polish

Herman, M. *Histoire de la littérature polonaise, des origines à 1961.* Paris: Nizet, 1963. PG7012.H4

Kridl, Manfred. *Survey of Polish Literature and Culture.* New York: Columbia University Press, 1956. PG7012.K713

Krzyzanowski, Julian. *History of Polish Literature.* Translation by Doris Ronowicz of *Dzieje Literatury Polskiej od Poczatkow do Czasow Najnowszych,* 2d ed. (Warsaw: Panstwowe Wydawn, 1972). Warsaw: PWN-Polish Scientific Publishers, 1978. With bibliography and bibliography of "Polish Literature in English Translations." PG7012.K7713 1978

Milosz, Czeslaw. *History of Polish Literature.* 2d ed. Berkeley, Los Angeles, London: University of California Press, 1983. PG7012.M48 1983

Ukrainian

Chyzhevskyi, Dmytro. *History of Ukrainian Literature from the 11th to the End of the 19th Century.* Littleton, Colo.: Ukrainian Academic Press, 1975. PG3905.C513

Yugoslav

Barac, Antun. *History of Yugoslav Literature.* Belgrade: Committee for Foreign Cultural Relations of Yugoslavia, 1955. PG561.B313

Cronia, Arturo. *Storia della letteratura serbo-croata.* Milan: Nuova accademia editrice, 1956. PG1401.C7

Meriggi, Bruno. *Storia della letteratura slovena.* Milan: Nuova accademia editrice, 1961. PG1900.M4

Slodnjak, Anton. *Geschichte der slowenischen Literatur.* Berlin: de Gruyter, 1958. PG1900.S5

Trogrančić, Franjo. *Storia della letteratura croata.* Rome: Editrice Studium, 1953. PG1601.T7

Non-Slavic Eastern Europe

Albanian

Bihiku, Koco. *History of Albanian Literature.* Tiranë: "8 nentori" Publishing House, 1980. PG9603.B49 1980

Elsie, Robert. *Dictionary of Albanian Literature.* Westport, Conn.: Greenwood, 1986. PG9602.E47 1986

Mann, S. E. *Albanian Literature: An Outline of Prose, Poetry and Drama.* London: Quaritch, 1955. PG9603.M3

Finnish

Ahokas, Jaako. *History of Finnish Literature.* Bloomington: Indiana University for the American-Scandinavian Foundation, 1973. PH301.A35

Modern Greek

Keeley, Edmund, and Peter Bien, eds. *Modern Greek Writers.* Princeton: Princeton University Press, 1972. PA5225.M6

Hungarian

Czigány, Lóránt. *Oxford History of Hungarian Literature from the Earliest Times to the Present.* Oxford: Clarendon Press, 1984. PH3012.C94

Klaniczay, Tibor, et al. *History of Hungarian Literature.* London: Collet's, 1964. PH3012.K513 1964a

Tezla, Albert. *Introductory Bibliography to the Study of Hungarian Literature.* Cambridge: Harvard University Press, 1964. Z2148.L5 T4

———. *Hungarian Authors: A Bibliographical Handbook.* Cambridge: Harvard University Press, 1970. Z2148.L5 T39

Rumanian

Fischer-Gallati, Stephan A. *Rumania: A Bibliographic Guide.* Washington, D. C.: Library of Congress, Slavic and Central European Division, 1963. Z2921.F53 1963

Schröder, Klaus-Henning. *Einführung in das Studium des rumänischen Sprachwissenschaft und Literaturgeschichte.* Berlin: E. Schmidt, 1967. PC625.S3

XII. AFRICAN LANGUAGES AND LITERATURES

See also section M.X for Commonwealth English Literature from African Countries. And see relevant materials from section I on Language, Linguistics, and Philology. And see also the *MLA International Bibliography* (L–50), as well as works on General and Comparative Literature in section L.I, and the entries on French language African literature in section L.VI.

L–130 **Zell, Hans M., et al., eds.** *New Reader's Guide to African Literature.* 2d ed., rev. and exp. New York: Africana Publishing Co., 1983.   PN849.A35 Z44 1983

This volume enumerates 3,091 English, French, and Portuguese works by Black African authors, south of the Sahara, arranged by language, country, and then alphabetically by author, with a bibliography of secondary materials included. There are additional sections at the beginning of the volume enumerating Bibliographies and Reference Materials, Critical Works, Anthologies, Children's Books, Some Articles on African Literature, and Periodicals and Magazines. These lists are followed by biographies of fifty-two leading Black African authors, with pictures and lists of works, a list of essential addresses, and an index.

L–132 **Herdeck, Donald E., ed.** *African Authors: A Companion to Black African Writing.* Vol. 1, 1300–1973. Rockville, Md.: Black Orpheus, 1973.   PL8010.H38

This well-reviewed work presents biobibliographical sketches with photographs and critical estimates of 594 Black African authors writing in English, French, and a total of thirty-seven vernacular languages. Some 2,000 works are enumerated and discussed. Authors are mainly from sub-Sahara Africa, with the exception of those from Malagasy and Mauritius. There are cross-references from pseudonyms. A number of appendixes group authors by periods, genres, countries of origin, and languages. There is also a list of publishers, journals, and bookshops specializing in Africana.

Another biobibliographical guide is Janheinz Jahn et al., *Who's Who in African Literature: Biographies, Works, Commentaries* (Tübingen: Horst Erdmann Verlag for the Deutsche Afrika Gesellschaft, 1972) [PL8010.J33]. Nearly 450 modern authors of sub-Saharan Africa writing in African and European languages are included, with biographies and primary and secondary bibliographies. There are two appendixes grouping authors by languages and countries, and there are indexes of languages and countries. This work is intended to serve as a companion to Jahn and Dressler's *Bibliography of Creative African Writing* (L–133), to which the user is referred for bibliographical details.

L–133 **Jahn, Janheinz, and Claus Peter Dressler.** *Bibliography of Creative African Writing.* Millwood, N. Y.: Kraus-Thomson, 1973.   Z3508.L5 J28 1973

This work, first published in 1971, is a revised and enlarged version of Jahn's earlier compilation (see below) but is limited to African writers only. The approximately 2,500 entries present titles of works written by sub-Saharan African authors in European or African languages (except Arabic). If the original is in an African language, the title is given also in English, French, and German. If works have been translated, the translated title and details of publication are given. Reviews, critiques, and other secondary treatment of an author or his works are also cited. Entries are arranged into five main sections: General, West African, Central African, Eastern African, and Austral-African. Arrangement within sections begins with secondary literature, followed by anthologies, and then individual works, alphabetically by author. A section on forgeries and a set of addenda follow the main body, to which are appended lists of books in African languages, translations, books classified by countries, and an index. The introduction and notes are given in English, French, and German. There is general agreement that this work and its predecessor are the most authoritative bibliographies of African writing currently available.

Jahn's first bibliography, a ground-breaking work in the field of African literary studies, was published in German as *Die neoafrikanische Literatur: Gesamtbibliographie von den*

Anfängen bis zur Gegenwart (Düsseldorf: Diedrichs, 1965) [Z3508.L5 J3], and in English as *Bibliography of Neo-African Literature from Africa, America, and the Caribbean* (New York: Praeger, 1965) [Z3508.L5 J3]. A total of 3,566 serially numbered unannotated entries list by author or editor the works of literature written by African authors and authors of African descent writing in America and the Caribbean. Arrangement is into three main sections, listing General Anthologies, Work from Africa, and Work of America and the Caribbean respectively. The section on Africa is subdivided into General Anthologies and Authors of Western, Central, Eastern, and Southern Africa; the section on America is subdivided into General Anthologies and Authors of the Antilles and Guianas, Latin America, and North America. Cited works include published books, performed plays, and completed manuscripts; translations are listed after the originals. Cited works are classified as to genre, including the following categories: autobiographical novel, biography, novel, diary, essays, children's books, letters, poetry, story, tale, speeches, plays, treatise.

The original 1965 bibliography was supplemented by additions and corrections supplied by Bernth Lindfors in the *African Studies Bulletin* (September 1968): 129–148, and by the first half of Pál Páricsy, *New Bibliography of African Literature* (Budapest: Center for Afro-Asian Research of the Hungarian Academy of Sciences, 1969) [Z3508.L5 P37], where 361 entries are enumerated. The second half of Páricsy's work lists 377 items published during the period 1965–1969. For works of African authors the 1971 or 1973 bibliography should be used; the 1965 volume and supplements remain valuable for the sections on American and Caribbean authors.

L–134 *International African Bibliography / Bibliographie internationale africain: Current Books, Articles and Papers in African Studies [for 1971–].* Vol. 1–. London: School of Oriental and African Studies, University of London [since vol. 3, published by Mansell for the School of Oriental and African Studies], 1971–.   No LC number

Previously titled the "Bibliography of Current Publications" in *Africa: Journal of the International African Institute* (London: Oxford University Press, 1928–1970) [PL8000.I6], this separate bibliography, published quarterly, covers the whole of the African continent apart from Egypt. Though it concentrates on publications related to the arts and humanities, some publications in the social and natural sciences are cited. Monographs, pamphlets, proceedings, articles, and new periodical titles are included; excluded are works of fiction, textbooks, theses, government publications, and audiovisual materials. Entries are arranged geographically, with a section on Africa in general followed by regional headings that are further subdivided into countries and subjects, then ethnic groupings and languages. There is an author index.

The quarterly issues for 1971–1972, along with those in the *Africa* quarterly bibliography (1928–1970), have been brought together in the *Cumulative Bibliography of African Studies*, 5 vols. (Boston: G. K. Hall, 1973) [Z3509.I57 1973]. The Author catalog in two volumes has some 57,000 entries; the classified subject catalog in three volumes has about 76,500 entries. A second quinquennial *Cumulative Bibliography of African Studies*, for 1973–1978, ed. J. D. Pearson, 2 vols. (Boston: G. K. Hall, 1981) [Z3509 .I57 1981], contains some 20,000 entries, of which 3,000 are added entries omitted in the quarterly issues.

Another serial bibliography, *African Abstracts: Quarterly Review of Articles Appearing in Current Periodicals*, vols. 1–23 (London: International African Institute, 1950–1972) [DT1.I553], presented abstracts of articles in leading European, African, and American journals; each volume included a detailed analytical index.

A third serial bibliography in African studies is available, the *Current Bibliography on African Affairs*, published for the African Bibliographical Center in Washington, D.C. (Farmingdale, N.Y.: Baywood, 1962–) [Z3501.C87]. Frequency and scope of this work have varied; now published quarterly, the work is in four parts: Features, Book Reviews, Bibliographical Section, and Author Index. The Bibliographical Section is further divided into General Subjects (General, African Heritage Studies, Apartheid, The Arts, Education, History and Archaeology, Literature, Music and Dance, Philosophy and Religion, Politics, Society and Culture, and Women, among other topics) and Regional Studies (Central, East, North, Southern, South, and West Africa, and Western Sahara).

The serial bibliography for sub-Saharan Africa is the *Bibliographie ethnographique de l'Afrique sud-saharienne* [1925/30–], published annually by the Koninklijk Museum vor Midden-Africa, Tervuren, Belgium, 1932– [Z5113.T33].

The Library of Congress indexes periodical literature on sub-Saharan Africa. The cards for 1900–1970 were published in *Africa South of the Sahara: Index to Periodical Literature, 1900–1970*, 4 vols. (Boston: G. K. Hall, 1971) [Z3503.U47]. A *First Supplement* (1973) covered materials of 1971–1972. A *Second Supplement* (1982) covered materials of 1972–1976.

L–135 **Taylor, A. V. *African Studies Research: A Brief Guide to Selected Bibliographies and Other Sources for African Studies.*** Bloomington: Indiana University Press, 1964.

This bibliography is in five sections: basic bibliographies and general reference works; special bibliographies; lists of standard works by countries; lists of standard works by subjects; and a guide to archives and special collections of Africana.

Another valuable, more recently completed bibliographical guide is that compiled by Peter Duignan and Helen Conover, *Guide to Research Works on Sub-Saharan Africa* (Stanford, Calif.: Hoover Institution, 1971) [Z3501.D78]. This work presents a classified listing of 3,127 annotated entries concerned with both general and subject bibliography for sub-Saharan Africa, its regions and its countries. Included works were published through about 1969. The volume is in four parts; a guide to research organizations, libraries and archives, and the Africana book trade; a bibliography for Africa in general; a guide to subject bibliography; and a guide to regional and area bibliography. There is an elaborate analytical index of authors, titles, subjects, and places. See also Conover's *Africa South of the Sahara: A Selected Annotated List of Writings* (Washington, D. C.: Library of Congress, 1963) [Z3501.U49], with more than 3,000 entries.

L–138 **Scholarly Journals in African Studies.**

AfricaM *Africa*. Vol. 1–. Madrid: Instituto de estudios africanos, Consejo superior de investigaciones cientificas, 1942. 12/yr. Reviews. DT37.A1 A4

AfricaL *Africa: Journal of the International African Institute / Revue de l'Institut africain international*. Vol. 1–. London: International African Institute, 1928–. 4/yr. Reviews. PL8000.I6

Africa *Africa: Rivista trimestrale di studi e documentazione dell'Istituto italo-africano*. Vol. 1–. Rome: Istituto italo-africano, 1946–. 4/yr. Reviews. DT1.A843

Afr-T *Africa-Tervuren*. Vol. 1–. Tervuren, Belgium: Musée royal de l'Afrique centrale, 1955–. 4/yr. DT1.A219

AfrLS *African Language Studies*. Vol. 1–. London: School of Oriental and African Studies, University of London, 1960–. 1/yr. PL8003.A34

African Languages / Langues africaines. Vol. 1–. London: International African Institute, 1975–. 4/yr. Reviews. PL8000.A28

ALT *African Literature Today: A Journal of Explanatory Criticism* [former title 1965–1967: *Bulletin of the Association for African Literature in English*]. Vol. 1–. London: Heinemann, 1964–. 2/yr. Reviews. Current Bibliography of New African Literature. PL8010.A4

AfrS *African Studies: The Bi-annual Multi-disciplinary Journal of the African Studies Institute, University of Witwatersrand [former title 1921–1941: Bantu Studies]*. Vol. 1–. Johannesburg: Witwatersrand University Press, 1921–. 2/yr. Reviews. DT764.B2 B3

AfrSR *African Studies Review* [former title 1957–1969: *African Studies Bulletin*]. Vol. 1–. Waltham, Mass.: African Studies Association, Brandeis University, 1957–. 3/yr. Notes, bibliographies, bibliographical essays. DT1.A2293

AfrLJ *Africana [1971–1973: Africana Library] Journal: A Bibliographic and Review Quarterly*. New York: Africana Publishing Co., 1971–. 4/yr. Reviews. Bibliography of books on aspects of Africa, with author and subject indexes. Supplements Zell, L–130. Z3503.A37

Ba Shiru: A Journal of African Languages and Literatures. Vol. 1–. Madison: University of Wisconsin African Studies Program, 1970–. 2/yr. Reviews. No LC number

BSOAS *Bulletin of the School of Oriental and African Studies*. Vol. 1–. London: University of London, 1917–. 3/yr. Reviews. PJ3.L6

Conch *Conch: A Sociological Journal of African Cultures and Literatures*. Vol. 1–. Buffalo, N. Y.: Conch Magazine, 1969–. 2/yr. Reviews. GR350.C65

CRevB *Conch Review of Books: A Literary Supplement on Africa*. Vol. 1–. Buffalo, N. Y.: Conch Magazine, 1973–. 4/yr. Reviews. Bibliographies. Z3501.C66

Journal des africanistes [former title 1931–1975: *Journal de la Société des africanistes*]. Vol. 1–. Paris: Société des africanistes, 1931–. 2/yr. Reviews. Annual bibliography of primarily French books and articles. DT1.S65

Journal of African Languages. 11 vols. London: Macmillan, 1962–1972. 4/yr. PL8000.J6

JCL *Journal of Commonwealth Literature*. Vol. 1–. London: Oxford University Press, 1965–. Reviews. Bibliographies. (See M–100.) PR1.J67

Journal of the New African Literature and the Arts. Vol. 1–.

PA *Présence africaine: Revue culturelle du monde noir*. Vol. 1–. Paris: Editions du Seuil, 1947–. 4/yr. Reviews. Index of authors and subjects, 1947–1976 in 1 vol. GN645.P74

RAL *Research in African Literatures*. Austin: Department of English, University of Texas, 1970–. 3/yr. Reviews. Surveys. Bibliographies (including an annual list of North American dissertations on African literature). Discographies. Filmographies. Conference notes. Sponsored by the African Literature Committee of the African Studies Association and the African Literatures Seminar of the MLA. PL8010.R46

For additional titles see Helen F. Conover, comp., *Serials for African Studies* (Washington, D.C.: Library of Congress,

1961) [Z3503.U48]; Peter Duignan and Kenneth M. Glazier, *Checklist of Serials for African Studies* (Stanford, Calif.: Hoover Institution, 1963) [Z3503.D8]; and the *Liste mondiale des périodiques specialisés: Études africaines / World List of Specialized Periodicals: African Studies* (The Hague: Mouton, 1970) [Z3503.M32]. See also *Sub-Saharan Africa: A Guide to Serials* (Washington, D.C.: Library of Congress, 1970) [Z3503.U49].

L–139 Some Frequently Recommended Works in African Studies. (See also works on African Literature in English, M–110 ff.)

Baker, Houston A. *Reading Black: Essays in the Criticism of African, Caribbean, and Black American Literature.* Ithaca, N. Y.: Cornell University, Africana Studies and Research Center, 1976.   PN841.R4

Beier, Ulli, ed. *Introduction to African Literature: An Anthology of Critical Writings from "Black Orpheus."* New ed. London: Longman, 1979. PL8010.B4 1979

Cartey, Wilfred G. O. *Whispers from a Continent: Writings from Contemporary Black Africa.* New York: Random House, 1969.   PL8010.C3

Dathorne, Oscar Ronald. *Black Mind: A History of African Literature.* Minneapolis: University of Minnesota Press, 1974.   PL8010.D37

East, N. B. *African Theatre: A Checklist of Critical Materials.* New York: Africana, 1970.   Z3508.T4 E3

Jahn, Janheinz. *History of Neo-African Literature: Writing in Two Continents.* London: Faber, 1968.
          PL8010.J313

————, and John Ramsaran. *Approaches to African Literature: Non-English Writings.* Ibadan, Nigeria: Ibadan University Press, 1959.   PL8010.A6

Kesteloot, Lilyan. *Black Writers in French: A Literary History of Negritude.* Philadelphia: Temple University Press, 1974.   PQ3897.K3913 1974

Legum, Colin, ed. *Africa: A Handbook to the Continent.* Rev. and enl. ed. New York: Praeger, 1966.
          DT30.L38

Moore, Gerald. *Seven African Writers.* London: Oxford University Press, 1962.   PL8010.M6

Murphy, John D., and Harry Goff. *Bibliography of African Languages and Linguistics.* Washington, D.C.: Catholic University of America Press, 1969.   Z7106.M8

Pieterse, Cosmo, and Donald Munro, eds. *Protest and Conflict in African Literature.* London: Heinemann, 1969.
          PL8010.P7 1969

Povey, J. F. *Four African Literatures: Xhosa, Sotho, Zulu, Amharic.* Berkeley, Los Angeles, London: University of California Press, 1971.   PL8010.G4

Ramsaran, John. *New Approaches to African Literature: A Guide to Negro-African Writing and Related Studies.* 2d ed. Ibadan, Nigeria: Ibadan University Press, 1970. Bibliography.   Z3508.L5 R3 1970

Rosenthal, Eric. *Encyclopedia of Southern Africa.* 5th ed. London: Frederick Warne, 1970.   DT752.R59

Unesco General History of Africa. Prepared by the International Scientific Committee for the Drafting of a General History of Africa. 8 vols. London: Heinemann; Berkeley and Los Angeles: University of California Press, 1981–.   DT20.G45 1981

Vol. 1. *Methodology and African Prehistory.* Ed. J. Ki-Zerbo. (1981).

Vol. 2. *Ancient Civilizations of Africa.* Ed. G. Mokhtar. (1981).

Vol. 3. *Africa from the Seventh to Eleventh Century.* Ed. M. El Fasi.

Vol. 4. *Africa from the Twelfth to Sixteenth Century.* Ed. D. T. Niane. (1984).

Vol. 5. *Africa form the Sixteenth to Eighteenth Century.* Ed. B. A. Ogot.

Vol. 6. *Nineteenth Century until 1880.* Ed. J. F. A. Ajayi.

Vol. 7. *Africa under Colonial Domination, 1880–1935.* Ed. A. A. Boahen. (1985).

Vol. 8. *Africa since 1935.* Ed. A. A. Mazrui.

Wauthier, Claude. *Literature and Thought of Modern Africa.* Translation by Shirley Kay of *L'Afrique des Africains* (Paris: Editions du Seuil, 1964). London: Pall Mall, 1966.   DT21.W313 1966

XIII. ORIENTAL LANGUAGES AND LITERATURES

See also section M.XIII for Commonwealth English Literature from India. And see also the *MLA International Bibliography* (L–50) and on General and Comparative Literature in section L.I.

L–140 Lang, David M., gen. ed. *Guide to Eastern Literatures.* New York: Praeger; London: Weidenfeld and Nicolson, 1971.   PJ307.L3 1971

This volume contains fifteen chapters, each with sections by individual scholars treating the historical background, main trends in literary history, periods and genres, and individual writers of the national literature or literatures under discussion. Each chapter includes a general bibliography with descriptive annotations and, in discussions of individual authors and their works, reference to some translations and critical works. The chapters are as follows: Arabic, Jewish, Persian (Old Iranian, Classical, and Modern), Turkish, Armenian and Georgian, Ethiopic, Indian and Pakistani, Sinhalese, Indonesian and Malaysian, Chinese, Tibetan, Mongolian, Korean, Burmese, and Japanese. The volume concludes with an index of authors, titles, and subjects. Reviewers regard the treatments as somewhat uneven.

L–141 De Bary, William Theodore, and Ainslie T. Embree, eds. *Guide to Oriental Classics.* 2d ed. New York: Columbia University Press, 1975.   Z7046.C65 1975

Prepared by the staff of the Oriental Studies Program in Columbia College, this guide was first published in 1964. There is an introduction, followed by four main sections treating classics of the Islamic, Indian, Chinese, and Japanese traditions respectively. Each section begins with a briefly annotated bibliography of general works (basic bibliographies and references, standard works on literature, and leading works in ancillary fields including thought, religion and philosophy, history and geography). There follow sections on each of the major works of the literature, citing complete and selected translations and important secondary works and presenting a list of topics for the reflection and discussion of new readers.

L–142 Ceadel, Eric B., ed. *Literatures of the East: An Appreciation.* London: John Murray, 1953; New York: Grove, 1959.   PJ307.C4

This volume presents revised versions of public lectures delivered in the University of Cambridge in 1952 by members of the Faculty of Oriental Languages. Texts and bibliographies are cited in course. After an introduction there are seven chapters, as follows: 1, Ancient Hebrew Literature; 2, Arabic

Literature; 3, Iranian Literature; 4, Persian Literature; 5, Ancient Indian Literature; 6, Chinese Literature; and 7, Japanese Literature.

A much more elaborate, though somewhat dated, review of eastern literatures, including the literatures of Eastern Europe, is the monographic series *Die Literaturen des Ostens in Einzeldarstellungen* (Leipzig, 1901–1930) [LC numbers vary]. The ten volumes published treat the following national literatures: 1, Polish; 2, Russian; 3, Hungarian, Rumanian; 4, Byzantine and Modern Greek, Turkish; 5, Czech and Old South Slavic; 6, Persian, Arabic; 7, Old Hebrew, and Christian literature of the Orient; 8, Chinese; 9, Indian; 10, Japanese.

L–143 **Prušek, Jaroslav, gen. ed.** *Dictionary of Oriental Literatures.* 3 vols. New York: Basic Books; London: George Allen and Unwin, 1974.   PJ31.D5

This three-volume dictionary, intended for the educated but nonspecialist reader, was prepared under the auspices of the Oriental Institute in Prague with the collaboration of an international board of advisory editors and an international community of some 150 scholarly contributors. The 2,000 articles are signed with initials and generally include brief bibliographies. Each volume includes the national literatures of one large region of the Orient. Volume 1, *East Asia*, includes Chinese, Japanese, Korean, Mongolian, and Tibetan. Volume 2, *South and South-East Asia*, includes the ancient and modern literature of India, Pakistan, and Bangladesh (including Ancient Indian, Assamese, Baluchi, Bengali, Gujarati, Hindi, Indian literature in English, Indo-Persian, Kannada, Kashmiri, Maithili, Malayalam, Marathi, Oriya, Punjabi, Pashto, Rajasthani, Sindhi, Tamil, Telugu, and Urdu); Nepalese; Sinhalese; Burmese; Cambodian; Javanese; Malay and Indonesian; Philippines; Thai; and Vietnamese. Volume 3, *West Asia and North Africa*, includes the literature of the ancient Near East (Akkadian, Aramaic, Assyrian, Babylonian, Carthaginian, Coptic, Egyptian, Hebrew, Hittite, Mandaic, Ancient and Middle Persian, Phoenician, Sumerian, Syriac, and Ugaritic); the Arab countries (classical Arabic, Algerian, Egyptian, Iraqi, Jordanian, Lebanese, Moroccan, Palestinian, Sudanese, Syrian, Tunisian); Turkey (Turkish, Turkic, Kurdish, and Armenian); Iran (Ancient and Middle Persian, New Persian, Jewish-Persian, Kurdish, and Armenian); Afghanistan (Pashto and Dari); and the Soviet East (Abkhazian, Armenian, Arai, Azerbaijan, Chukot, Circassian, Darg, Georgian, Kazakh, Kirghiz, Kurdish, Lezgian, Ossetian, Tatar, Tajik, Turkic, Turkmen, Uzbek, and Yakut). Each volume begins with a list of contributors identifying the initials and concludes with a list of national literatures, enumerating the entry terms in alphabetical order for all entries concerning authors, works, or technical terms associated with that literature. Volume 1 also has a chronological table. The majority of entries treat authors, with brief biography, description and evaluation of works, their reception and importance, and reference to translations and important secondary works.

For a more elaborate and scholarly treatment see B. Spuler et al., *Handbuch der Orientalistik* (Leiden: Brill, 1952–) [LC numbers vary], with eight volumes treating the Near and Middle East, and multiple volumes treating India; Indonesia, Malaysia, and the Philippines; China; Japan; and Art and Archaeology of the Orient.

L–144 **"Bibliography of Asian Studies"** in *Journal of Asian Studies.* Ann Arbor, Mich.: Association for Asian Studies, 1957–.   Z3001.B49

This annual bibliography lists without annotation books, periodicals, and articles in European languages about the history and life of the twenty-five countries and regions of Asia. Items are arranged within geographical divisions by disciplines. The subdivisions include Periodicals; General and

Miscellaneous; Bibliography; History; Geography, Description and Travel; Economics; Social Sciences; Politics and Government; Education, Study and Teaching; Arts, Language and Literature. There are indexes of authors.

Originally published 1936–1940 as the "Bulletin of Far Eastern Bibliography" and 1941–1956 as "Far Eastern Bibliography" in the journal *Far Eastern Quarterly*, this serial bibliography appeared as a special issue of the *Journal of Asian Studies* from 1957 through 1968. Since 1969 it has been published separately. The issues from 1941 through 1965 have been brought together in the *Cumulative Bibliography of Asian Studies: Author Bibliography* and *Subject Bibliography*, 1941–1965, 8 vols. (Boston: G. K. Hall, 1970) [Z3001 .C93]. A total of 107,000 entries are found in the author volumes; about 100,000 entries are in the subject volumes. Similarly, the issues from 1966 through 1970 were brought together in a *Cumulative Bibliography . . . 1966-1970: Author Bibliography* and *Subject Bibliography*, 8 vols. (Boston: G. K. Hall, 1972) [Z3001.C95]. Approximately the same number of entries is found in the second cumulation as in the first. Further quinquennial cumulations are planned.

The earliest serial bibliography of Oriental studies is the twenty-six-volume *Orientalische Bibliographie*, 1887–1911, 1926 (Berlin: Reuther, 1888–1922, 1928)[Z7046.O7]. Also published since the late nineteenth century is the *Orientalische Literaturzeitung: Monatsschrift für die Wissenschaft vom ganzen Orient und seinen Beziehungen zu den Angrenzenden Kulturkreisen* (Berlin: Deutsche Akademie der Wissenschaften zu Berlin, 1898–) [PJ5.O6]. Treating both monographic and serial publications in German only is the quarterly, partially annotated *Asien-Bibliographie*, vol. 1– [1949–]. (Bad Wildungen: Asien-Bücherei, 1949) [Z3001 .A84]. More extensive in coverage is the *Bibliographia Asiatica* published since 1953 by the same organization but including periodical articles in English, French, and German [Z3001.B48]. A far less satisfactory serial bibliography was the *Quarterly Checklist of Oriental Studies* (Darien, Conn.: American Bibliographic Service, 1959–1978) [Z3001.O34] which offered sheer lists of published monographs, with an annual index of authors, translators, and editors.

L–145 **Birnbaum, Eleazar.** *Books on Asia, from the Near East to the Far East: A Guide for the General Reader.* Toronto: University of Toronto Press, 1971.   Z3001.B54

This guide lists about 2,000 items with descriptive and evaluative annotations addressed to the general reader. It is generally regarded as the best of the available guides. G. Raymond Nunn, *Asia: Reference Works: A Select Annotated Guide*, rev. ed. (London: Mansell, 1980) [Z3001.N79 1980], enumerates with descriptive and evaluative annotations more than 1,550 books and periodicals but excludes Soviet Asia from its coverage. Arrangement is by region, country, and type of work. Current, Western-language works are emphasized. A discussion of the full range of resources available in the mid–1960s may be found in J. D. Pearson's *Oriental and Asian Bibliography: An Introduction with Some Reference to Africa* (Hamden, Conn.: Archon, 1966) [Z7046.P4].

L–148 **Scholarly Journals in Asian Studies.**

> *Asian and African Studies.* Vol. 1–. Bratislava: Department of Oriental Studies, Slovak Academy of Sciences, 1965–. 1/yr.   DS1.A4733
>
> *AAS* *Asian and African Studies.* Vol. 1–. Jerusalem: Jerusalem Academic Press, 1965–. 1–3/yr.   DS1.A4734
>
> *BSOAS* *Bulletin of the School of Oriental (and African) Studies.* Vol. 1–. London: University of London, 1917–. 3/yr. Reviews.   PJ3.L6

ChinaQ   *China Quarterly: An International Journal for the Study of China.* Vol. 1–. London: School of Oriental and African Studies, University of London, 1960–. 4/yr. Reviews.   DS701.C472

ChinL   *Chinese Literature.* Vol. 1–. Peking: Foreign Languages Press, 1951–. 2–12/yr.   DS777.55.C45

Chinese Literature: Essays, Articles, and Reviews. Madison, Wis.: Coda Press, 1979–. 2/yr. Reviews. Bibliographic essay on "Recent Publications on Chinese Literature."   PL2250.C533

East and West. Vol. 1–. Rome: Istituto italiano per il Medio ed Estremo Oriente, 1950–. 4/yr.   AP37.E22

HJAS   *Harvard Journal of Asiatic Studies.* Cambridge: Harvard-Yenching Institute, 1936–. 2/yr. Reviews.   DS501.H3

IndL   *Indian Literature.* New Delhi: Sahitya Akademi, 1957–. 6/yr. Reviews. Irregular bibliographical survey of all twenty-two literary languages of India, including Indo-English.   AP8.I395

JapQ   *Japan Quarterly.* Vol. 1–. Tokyo: Asahi Shinbunsha, 1954–. 4/yr. Reviews.   DS801.J274

JAsiat   *Journal asiatique.* Vol. 1–. Paris: Société asiatique and CNRS, 1822–. 4/yr. Reviews. Indexes 1828–1842, 1843–1862, 1863–1872, and every ten years thereafter.   PJ4.J5

JArabL   *Journal of Arabic Literature.* Vol. 1–. Leiden: Brill, 1970–. 1/yr. Reviews. Bibliography of "Recent Publications (1973–)."   PJ7501.J63

Journal of Asian and African Studies. Vol. 1–. Leiden: Brill, 1966–. 4/yr.   DT1.J66

JASt   *Journal of Asian Studies* [former title: *Far Eastern Quarterly*]. Vol. 1–. Ann Arbor, Mich.: Association for Asian Studies, 1941/42–. 4/yr. Reviews. "Bibliography of Asian Studies" (L–144).   DS501.F274

JJS   *Journal of Japanese Studies.* Vol. 1–. Seattle: University of Seattle, Society for Japanese Studies, 1974–. 2/yr. Reviews.   DS801.J7

JKS   *Journal of Korean Studies.* Seattle: Korean Studies Society, 1969–. 2/yr.   DS901.J63

JSoAL   *Journal of South Asian Literature* [former title: *Mahfil: A Quarterly of South Asian Literature*]. East Lansing: Asian Studies Center, Michigan State University, 1963–. 4/yr. Reviews.   PK1501.M34

JAOS   *Journal of the American Oriental Society.* Baltimore [place varies]: American Oriental Society, 1849–. 4/yr. Reviews. Indexes for vols. 1–20 in vol. 21, vols. 21–60 (1955).   PJ2.A6

JBRS   *Journal of the Burma Research Society.* Vol. 1–. Rangoon: Burma Research Society, 1911–.   DS527.B85a

JRAS   *Journal of the Royal Asiatic Society of Great Britain and Ireland.* Vol. 1–. London: Royal Asiatic Society, 1834–. 2/yr. Reviews.   AS122.L72

LE & W   *Literature East and West.* Vol. 1–. New Paltz, N.Y. [place varies]: Conference on Oriental-Western Literary Relations of the MLA, 1954–. 4/yr. Reviews.   PN2.L67

Middle East Journal. Washington, D.C.: Middle East Institute, 1946–. 4/yr. Reviews. Bibliography (see L–151).   DS1.M5

MIO   *Mitteilungen des Instituts für Orientforschung.* Vol. 1–. East Berlin: Deutsche Akademie der Wissenschaften zu Berlin, 1953–.   PJ5.A5 A25

MN   *Monumenta Nipponica: Studies in Japanese Culture.* Vol. 1–. Tokyo: Sophia University, 1938–. 4/yr. Reviews.   DS821.A1 M6

Muséon   *Le Muséon: Revue d'études orientales.* Vol. 1–. Louvain: Société des lettres et des sciences, 1882–. 2/yr. Reviews.   AS242.L63

Orientalia. Vol. 1–. Rome: Pontificium Institutum Biblicum, 1920–. 4/yr. Reviews.   PJ6.O7

Proof Texts: A Journal of Jewish Literary History. Vol. 1–. Baltimore: Johns Hopkins University Press, 1981–. 3/yr.   PJ5001.P76

Revue des études islamiques. Vol. 1–. Paris: Geuthner, 1927–. 2/yr. Reviews. Bibliography (see L–151).   BP1.R53

TPA   *T'oung Pao: Revue internationale de sinologie: Archives concernant l'histoire, les langues, la géographie, l'ethnographie et les arts de l'Asie orientale.* Leiden: Centre national français de la recherche scientifique and Organisation néerlandaise pour le développement de la recherche pure, 1890–. 5/yr. Reviews. Index to vols. 1–47 (Leiden, 1953).   DS501.T45

TASJ   *Transactions of the Asiatic Society of Japan.* Yokahama: The Society, 1872–. Irreg.   AS552.Y8

THJCS   *T'sing-hua [Tsing Hua] Journal of Chinese Studies.*, Vol. 1–. T'sing-hua University, 1956–. 2/yr. Reviews.   AS455.A1 C5

WLT   *World Literature Today* [former title 1927–1976: *Books Abroad: An International Literary Quarterly*]. Vol. 1–. Norman: University of Oklahoma Press, 1927–. 4/yr. Reviews.   Z1007.B717

ZDMG   *Zeitschrift der Deutschen morgenländischen Gesellschaft.* Giessen: Deutsche morgenländische Gesellschaft, 1846–. 2/yr. Reviews. General index to vols. 1–100 (Wiesbaden, 1955).   PJ5.D4

For additional information see F. Ljunggren and M. Hamdy, *Annotated Guide to Journals Dealing with the Middle East and North Africa* (Cairo: American University in Cairo Press, 1964) [Z3013.L655].

L–149 **Some Frequently Recommended Works in Asian (Oriental) Studies.**

Botto, O., ed. *Storia della letteratura d'Oriente: La letteratura antiche e moderne di tutti i paesi orientali.* 4 vols. Milan: Villardi, 1969.   PJ307.B65

Lach, Donald F. *Asia in the Making of Europe.* 2 vols. in 5. Chicago: University of Chicago Press, 1965–1977.   CB203.L32

Philips, C. H., ed. *Handbook of Oriental History.* London: Royal Historical Society, 1951.   DS33.1.L6

Wilber, Donald Newton, ed. *Nations of Asia.* New York: Hart, 1966.   DS33.W5

Wint, Guy. *Asia: A Handbook.* New York: Praeger, 1966.   DS5.W5

XIV. NEAR EASTERN LANGUAGES AND LITERATURES

L–150 **Hopwood, Derek, and Diana Grimwood-Jones, eds. *Middle East and Islam: A Bibliographical Introduction.* Zug, Switzerland: Interdocumentation, 1972.   Z3013.M48**

Sections contributed by specialists treat Islamic history, Islamic law, anthropology of the Middle East, and political science.

Also valuable is the *Introduction to the History of the Muslim East: A Bibliographical Guide* (Berkeley and Los Angeles: University of California Press, 1965) [Z3013.S314], an English translation of Jean Sauvaget, *Introduction à l'histoire de l'Orient musulman: Elémente de bibliographie*, completed by Claude Cahen, 2d ed. (Paris: Librairie A. Maisonneuve, 1961).

L–151 **Index Islamicus: A Catalogue of Articles on Islamic Subjects in Periodicals and Other Collective Publications 1906–1955.** Compiled by J. D. Pearson et al. Cambridge: Cambridge University Press, 1958.   Z7835.M6 L6

This work exhaustively indexes some 26,000 items contained in some 10,000 volumes of more than 500 periodicals, along with analyzed entries from some 120 festschriften and seventy volumes of proceedings and other composite volumes. The entire field of Islamic studies is covered, including both the Near and the Middle East and Islamic culture in other countries. Entries are disposed into an elaborate subject arrangement, the main sections of which are as follows: General Works and Bibliography; Religion and Theology; Law; Philosophy and Science; Art; Geography; Ethnology and History; Language; Literature; and Education. There is an author index.

To date, four supplements have been published: *First Supplement, 1956–1960* (1962); *Second Supplement, 1961-1965* (1967); *Third Supplement, 1966–1970* (1972); and *Fourth Supplement, 1971–1975* (1977). Since 1977, *Quarterly Index Islamicus: Current Books, Articles, and Papers on Islamic Studies*, ed. J. D. Pearson, has appeared (London: Mansell, 1977–) [Z3013.Q34].

The other major serial bibliographies of Islamic Studies are the "Abstracta Islamica," published in connection with the *Revue des études islamiques*, vol. 1– (Paris: Geuthner, 1927–) [BP1.R53], which lists books, articles, and reviews and has an index of authors, and the "Bibliography of Periodical Literature," which lists only articles and appears in *Middle East Journal* (Washington, D. C.: Middle East Institute, 1947–) [DS1.M5]. A cumulation of these *Articles on the Middle East, 1947–1971 . . . from the Middle East Journal*, ed. Peter M. Rossi et al., was published in 4 vols. (Ann Arbor, Mich.: Pierian, 1980) [Z3013.A76].

L–153 **Some Frequently Recommended Works in Near Eastern Studies.**

General

Atiyeh, George Nicholas. *Contemporary Middle East, 1948–1973*. Boston, G. K. Hall, 1975.   Z3013.A85

Encyclopedia of Islam (see A–53).

Hospers, J. H., ed. *Basic Bibliography for the Study of Semitic Languages*. Vol. 1–. Leiden: Brill, 1973–.   Z7049.S5 B35

LaSor, William Sanford. *Basic Semitic Bibliography, Annotated*. Wheaton, Ill.: Van Kampen Press, 1950.   Z7049.S5 L3

Middle East: A Handbook. Edited by Michael Adams. New York: Praeger, 1971.   DS44.A3

Pfannmuller, Gustav. *Handbuch der Islam-Literatur*. Berlin: de Gruyter, 1923.   Z7835.M6 P5

Arabic (including Arabic Palestine)

Altoma, Salih J. *Modern Arabic Literature: A Bibliography of Articles, Books, Dissertations, and Translations in English*. Bloomington: Indiana University, Asian Studies Research Institute, 1975.

Arberry, A. J. *Arabic Poetry: A Primer for Students*. Cambridge: Cambridge University Press, 1965.   PJ7692.E3 A7

Blachère, R. *Histoire de la littérature arabe des origines à la fin du XVe siècle de J.-C.* 3 vols. Paris: A. Maisonneuve, 1952–.   PF7510.B6

Brockelmann, Carl. *Geschichte der arabischen Literatur*. 2d ed. Leiden: Brill, 1943–1949. Also 3 vols. supplementary to the 1st ed. (1898–1902). Leiden: Brill, 1937–1942. The 2d ed. is designed to incorporate the supplementary volumes.   PJ7510.B7 1943

Cambridge History of Arabic Literature. In progress. Vol. 1: *Arabic Literature to the End of the Umayyad Period*, ed. by A. F. L. Beeston, et al. Cambridge: Cambridge University Press, 1983–.   PJ7510.A8 1983

Chauvin, Victor. *Bibliographie des ouvrages arabes ou relatifs aux Arabes, publiés dans l'Europe chrétienne de 1810 à 1885*. 12 parts in 5 vols. Liège: Vaillant-Carmanne, 1892–1922.   Z7052.C511

Gibb, Hamilton Alexander R. *Arabic Literature: An Introduction*. 2d ed., rev. London: Oxford University Press, 1963.   PJ7510.G5

Huart, Clément Imbault. *History of Arabic Literature*. New York: D. Appleton, 1903.   PJ7510.H83 1903

Nicholson, Reynold A. *Literary History of the Arabs*. 2d ed. Cambridge: Cambridge University Press, 1930.   PJ7510.N5

Ronart, Stephan, and Nancy Ronart. *Concise Encyclopedia of Arabic Civilization*. 2 vols. (Arab East; Arab West). New York: Praeger, 1960–1966.   DT173.R6

Sezgín, Fuat. *Geschichte des arabischen Schrifttums*. 9 vols. to date. Leiden: Brill, 1967–.   Z7052.S44

Armenian

Lang, David M. *Armenia: Cradle of Civilization*. 3d ed. corr. London: Allen and Unwin, 1980.   DS175.L35

Coptic

Kammerer, Winifred. *Coptic Bibliography*. Ann Arbor: University of Michigan Press, 1950.   Z7061.K3

Wilson, R. McL. *Future of Coptic Studies*. Leiden: Brill, 1978.   PJ2015.F88

Hebrew

(including Israel, Judaic Palestine and Jewish in general)

Alexander, Yonah. *Israel: Selected, Annotated and Illustrated Bibliography*. Gilbertsville, N.Y.: Victor Buday, 1968.   Z3476.A43

Brisman, Shimeon. *Jewish Research Literature*. Vol. 1–, *History and Guide to Judaic Bibliography*. Cincinnati, Ohio: Hebrew Union College Press, 1977.   Z6366.B8 1971

Encyclopedia Judaica (see A–51).

Klausner, J. G. *History of Modern Hebrew Literature, 1785–1932*. Translated from the Hebrew by Herbert Danby. Westport, Conn.: Greenwood, 1972.   PJ5017.K513 1972

Shunami, Shlomo. *Bibliography of Jewish Bibliographies*. 2d ed. enl. Jerusalem: Magnes Press, Hebrew University, 1965.   Z7070.A1 S5

Strack, Hermann L. *Introduction to the Talmud and Midrash*. Philadelphia: Jewish Publication Society of America, 1931.   BM503.5.S73

Thomsen, Peter. *Die Palästina-Literatur: Eine internationale Bibliographie in systematischer Ordnung mit Autoren und Sachregister*. 7 vols. to date. Leipzig: Hinrichs, 1911–1970.   Z3476.T42

Waxman, Meyer. *History of Jewish Literature.* 3d ed. 5 vols. in 6. New York: Yoseloff, 1960. PJ5008.W323

Zinberg, Israel. *History of Jewish Literature.* Translation by Bernard Martin of *Di geshikhte fun der literatur bay Yidn* (1929–1937). 12 vols. Cleveland, Ohio: Press of Case Western Reserve University, 1972–1979. PJ5008.Z5313

Iranian (and Persian)

Arberry, A. J. *Classical Persian Literature.* London: Allen and Unwin, 1958. PK6406.A7

Browne, E. G. *Literary History of Persia.* 4 vols. Cambridge: Cambridge University Press, 1906–1924. Reprint 1953–1956. PK6097.B7

Cambridge History of Iran. Edited by A. J. Arberry et al. 8 vols. planned. Cambridge: Cambridge University Press, 1968–. DS272.C34

Elwell-Sutton, Laurence Paul. *Guide to Iranian Area Study.* Washington, D. C.: Council of Learned Societies, 1952. DS254.5.E4

Farzaad, Masuud. *Main Currents in Persian Literature.* London, 1965.

Kamshad, H. *Modern Persian Prose Literature.* Cambridge: Cambridge University Press, 1966. PK6423.K3

Levy, Reuben. *Introduction to Persian Literature.* New York: Columbia University Press, 1969. PK6406.L38

Pearson, J. D. *Bibliography of Pre-Islamic Persia.* London: Mansell, 1975. Z3366.P36

Ricks, Thomas, Thomas Gouttierre, and Denis Egan. *Persian Studies: A Selected Bibliography of Works in English.* Bloomington: Indiana University Press, 1969. Z3001.R5

Rypka, Jan, et al. *History of Iranian Literature.* Revised and enlarged by Karl Jahn. Translated from the German by P. Van Popta-Hope. Dordrecht: D. Reidel, 1968. PK6097.R913

Storey, Charles Ambrose. *Persian Literature: A Bio-Bibliographical Survey.* 5 parts. London: Luzac, 1927-1971. Z7085.S88

Wilson, Sir Arnold Talbot. *Bibliography of Persia.* Oxford: Clarendon Press, 1930. Z3366.W74

Syriac

Wright, William. *Short History of Syriac Literature.* London: Black, 1894. PJ5601.W7

Turkish

Bombaci, A. *Historie de la littérature turque.* Paris: Klincksieck, 1968. PL205.B614 1968

Hofman, H. F. *Turkish Literature: A Bio-Bibliographical Survey.* 6 vols. in 2. Leiden: Brill, 1969. Z7101.J3 H6

Loewenthal, Rudolf. *Turkic Languages and Literatures of Central Asia: A Bibliography.* The Hague: Mouton, 1957. Z7049.U5 C4 no. 1

XV. FAR EASTERN LANGUAGES AND LITERATURES

L–155 **Mahar, J. Michael. *India: A Critical Bibliography.*** Tucson: University of Arizona Press, 1964. Z3201.M3

A total of 2,023 descriptively annotated entries present a selected, graded list of primarily book-length English-language works published after 1940 which aid the academic study of traditional and modern India. Entries are grouped into nine

main sections, all of which are further subdivided into general and particular subcategories. The main sections are India—General (introductory works, bibliographies, journals); Land and People (including languages); History; Political Patterns; Economic Patterns; Social Patterns; Religion and Philosophy; Intellectual and Aesthetic Patterns (literature, further subdivided into Sanskrit, the regional literatures, and modern Indian literature); Education. The volume concludes with an index of authors and some anonymous titles.

Among other single-volume closed bibliographies may be mentioned George M. Moraes, *Bibliography of Indological Studies* (Bombay: Examiner Press, 1945–) [Z3206.M6].

L–156 **Index Indo-Asiaticus.** Vol. 1–. Calcutta: Center for Asian Documentation, 1978–. G. Chaudhuri, 1968–1977. Z3001.I426

This quarterly serial bibliography contains a current index of recent articles, an index to the files of one or more periodicals, and a cumulative index of all writings in a particular discipline. The disciplines covered include archaeology, art, epigraphy, ethnology, geography, folklore, history, languages, literatures, linguistics, numismatics, philosophy, and religion. Coverage focuses on works treating the Indian subcontinent, but materials on ancient Asia in general are sometimes included.

Another serial bibliography concerned with Indian studies was the *International Guide to Indic Studies*, vols. 1–9, published by the American Bibliographic Service (Darien, Conn.: 1963–1972) [no LC number].

L–157 **Kesavan, B. S., et al. *National Bibliography of Indian Literature, 1901–1953.*** 4 vols. New Delhi: Sahitya Akademi, 1962–1974. Z3201.N3

This massive bibliography, prepared by the Indian Academy of Letters, presents publications 1901–1953 in sixteen contemporary Indian languages in all fields of the *sciences humaines*. The bibliography for each language is prepared by noted authorities and classified into eight categories, as follows: General Works (bibliographies, general encyclopedias, dictionaries); Philosophy and Religion; Social Sciences (education, sociology, economics, politics); Linguistics; Arts; Literature (subdivisions include general histories, anthologies, and general criticism; poetry; drama; fiction; essays; letters; humor and satire; miscellaneous); History, Biography (including autobiography), and Travel; and Miscellaneous. Each volume contains the bibliographies for four languages, as follows: vol. 1, Assamese, Bengali, English, and Gujarati; vol. 2, Hindi, Kannada, Kashmiri, Malayalam; vol. 3, Marathi, Oriya, Punjabi, Sanskrit; vol. 4, Sindhi, Tamil, Telugu, and Urdu. Each volume is preceded by a table indicating the schemes of transliteration employed, and each ends with an index of authors and titles.

L–158 **Sahitya Akademi. *Who's Who of Indian Writers, 1983.*** New Delhi: Sahitya Akademi, 1983. PK2908.W49

Prepared by the Indian National Academy of Letters and first published in 1961, this volume presents brief biographical accounts (facts plus a short-title list of works) of nearly 6,000 living writers in twenty-two Indian literary languages, including English.

L–159 **Some Frequently Recommended Works in Indian (Classical and Modern), Sinhalese, and Pakistani Studies.** (See also M–159.)

Ajwani, Lalsing H. *History of Sindhi Literature.* 2d ed. New Delhi: Sahitya Akademi, 1977. PK2788.A7 1977

Ali, Abdullah Yusuf. *Cultural History of India during the British Period.* Bombay: D. B. Taraporevgla Sons, 1940.   DS463.A56

Banerji, Sures Chandra. *Companion to Sanskrit Literature: Spanning a Period of over Three Thousand Years, Containing Brief Accounts of Authors, Works, Characters, Technical Terms, Geographical Names, Myths, Legends, and Twelve Appendices.* Delhi: Motilal Banarsidass, 1971.   PD414.B3

Barua, Birinchi Kumar. *History of Assamese Literature.* New Delhi: Sahitya Akademi, 1964.
PK1560.B313 1964

Basham, Aruther L. *Wonder That Was India: A Survey of the Culture of the Indian Sub-continent before the Coming of the Muslims.* 2d ed. New York: Hawthorne, 1963.
DS425.B33 1963

Bausani, Alessandro. *Storia della letteratura del Pakistan.* Milan: Nuova accademia editrice, 1958.   PK2903.B3

Bhattacharya, Sachchindanda. *Dictionary of Indian History.* Calcutta: University of Calcutta, 1967.   DS433.B48

Cambridge History of India. 5 vols. Cambridge: Cambridge University Press, 1922–1937. Supplemental Volume, *Indus Civilization.* 3d ed. 1968. Vol. 1, *Ancient India.* Vol. 2, never published. Vol. 3, *Turks and Afghans.* Vol. 4, *Mughil Period.* Vol. 5, *British India 1497–1858.* Vol. 6, *Indian Empire, 1858–1918.*   DS436.C22

Chaitanya, Krishna. *History of Malayalam Literature.* New Delhi: Orient Longman, 1971.   PL4718.K675

———. *New History of Sanskrit Literature.* 2d ed. New Delhi: Manohar Book Service, 1977.
PK2903.K66 1977

Chatterji, S. K. *Languages and Literatures of Modern India.* Calcutta: Bengal Publishers, 1963.   PK1508.C45

Chenchiah, Pandippedi, and M. Bhujanga Rao. *History of Telugu Literature.* Bombay: Oxford University Press, 1928.   PL4780.C5

Clark, T. W., ed. *Novel in India: Its Birth and Development.* Berkeley, Los Angeles, London: University of California Press, 1970.   PK5423.N6

Dasgupta, S. C., comp. *Bengali Language and Literature.* Calcutta: National Library, 1964.

Dasgupta, Surendra Nath. *History of Indian Philosophy.* 5 vols. Cambridge: Cambridge University Press, 1922–1955.   B131.D3

Dasgupta, Surendra Nath, and Sushil Kumer De. *History of Sanskrit Literature.* Vol. 1, *Classical Period.* 2d ed. Calcutta: University of Calcutta, 1962.   PK2903.D32

De, Sushil Kumar. *History of Sanskrit Poetics.* 2d ed., rev. 2 vols. in 1. Calcutta: K. L. Mukhopadhyay, 1960.
PK871.D42

———. *Sanskrit Poetics as a Study of Aesthetic.* Berkeley and Los Angeles: University of California Press, 1963.   PK2916.D4

DeBary, William Theodore, et al. *Sources of Indian Tradition.* New York: Columbia University Press, 1958.
DS423.D33

Dhingra, Baldoon. *Dictionary of Indian Aesthetics.* Delhi: Radha Krishna Prakashan, 1974.

Dimock, Edward C., Jr., et al. *Literatures of India: An Introduction.* Chicago: University of Chicago Press, 1974.   PK2903.L48

Dowson, John. *Classical Dictionary of Hindu Mythology and Religion, Geography, History, and Literature.* London: Trubner and Co., 1879.   BL1105.D6

Garagi, Balwanta. *Theatre in India.* New York: Theatre Arts Books, 1962.   PN2881.G3

George, K. M. *Survey of Malayalam Literature.* Bombay: Asia Publishing House, 1968.   PL4718.G37 1968

Godakumbura, Charles E. *Literature of Sri Lanka.* Rev. ed. Colombo: Dept. of Cultural Affairs, Sri Lanka, 1976.
PR2850.G6 1976

Gode, Parashuram Krishna. *Studies in Indian Literary History.* 3 vols. Bombay: Singhi Jain Sastri Sikshapith, 1953–1956.   PK2903.G58

Gonda, Jan, gen. ed. *History of Indian Literature.* 10 vols. in 22. Wiesbaden: Harrassowitz, 1973–. [LC numbers vary]. Vol. 1. Gonda, Jan. *Ritual Sutras* (1977) [BL1126.46.G66]. Gonda, Jan. *Vedic Literature* (1975) [BL115.G597]. Vol. 2. Gonda, Jan. *Medieval Religious Literature in Sanskrit* (1977) [BL1147.G66]. Vol. 3. *Classical Sanscrit Literature* [not yet published]. Vol. 4. Derrett, John D. M. *Dharmasastra and Juridical Literature* (1973). Sternbach, Ludwik. *Subhasita, Gnomic and Didactic Literature* (1974) [PN6307.S2569]. Vol. 5. Scharfe, Hartmut. *Grammatical Literature* (1977) [PK121.S3]. Vogel, Claus. *Indian Lexicography* (1979) [PK171.V6]. Gerow, Edwin. *Indian Poetics* (1977) [PK2916.G4]. Vol. 6. Hulin, Michel. *Samkhya Literature* (1978) [B132.S3 H84]. Matilal, Bimal Krishna. *Nyaya-Vaisesika* (1977) [B132.N8 M34]. Nijenhuis, Emmie te. *Musicological Literature* (1977) [ML338.N55]. Pingree, David Edwin. *Jyotihsastra* (1981) [QB18.P55]. Vol. 7. Schimmel, Annemaire. *Islamic Literatures of India* (1973) [PK2905.S36]. Ruegg, David S. *Literature of the Madhyamaka School of Philosophy in India* (1981) [BQ7457.R84 1981]. Vol. 8. MacGregor, Ronald Stuart. *Hindi Literature of the Nineteenth and Early Twentieth Centuries* (1974) [PK2037.M32]. Schimmel, Annemarie. *Classical Urdu Literature from the Beginning to Iqbal* (1975) [PK2155.S38]. Schimmel, Annemarie. *Sindhi Literature* (1974) [PK2788.S34]. Gaeffke, Hans P. T. *Hindi Literature in the Twentieth Century.* (1978) [PK2038.G28]. Vol. 9. Zbavitel, Dusan. *Bengali Literature* (1976) [PK1701.Z2]. Tulpule, Shankar Gopal. *Classical Marathi Literature* (1979) [PK2401.T84]. Sarma, Satyendranath. *Assamese Literature* (1976) [PK1560.S317]. Vol. 10. Hart, George L. *Relation between Tamil and Classical Sanskrit Literature* (1976) [PL4758.O5.H37]. Zvelebil, Kamil. *Tamil Literature* (1974) [PL4758.Z93 1974].

Goonetileke, H. A. I. *Bibliography of Ceylon.* 2 vols. Zug, Switzerland: Interdocumentation, 1970.   Z3211.G65

Gowan, Herbert Henry. *History of Indian Literature from Vedic Times to the Present Day.* New York: Columbia University Press, 1931.   PK2903.G6

Jesudasan, C., and H. Jesudasan. *History of Tamil Literature.* Calcutta: YMCA Publishing House, 1961.
PL4758.J4

Jhaveri, Mansukhlal. *History of Gujarati Literature.* New Delhi: Sahitya Akademi, 1978.   PK1850.J54

Jindal, K. B. *History of Hindi Literature.* Allahabad: Kitab Mahal, 1955.

Keay, F. E. *History of Hindi Literature.* 3d ed. Calcutta: YMCA Publishing House, 1960.   PK2031.K4 1960

Keith, Arthur Berriedale. *History of Sanskrit Literature.* Oxford: Clarendon Press, 1928.   PK2903.K45

―――. *Sanskrit Drama: Its Origin, Development, Theory, and Practice.* Oxford: Clarendon Press, 1924.
PK2931.K4

Kosambi, D. D. *Ancient India: A History of Its Culture and Civilization.* New York: Pantheon Books, 1966.
DS425.K58 1966

Law, Bimala Churn. *History of Pali Literature.* 2 vols. London: Kegan Paul, Trench, Trubner, 1933.
PK4503.L3

Macdonnell, Arthur A. *History of Sanskrit Literature.* New York: Appleton, 1900.   PK2903.M3

Mansinha, Mayadhar. *History of Oriya Literature.* New Delhi: Sahitya Akademi, 1962.   PK2570.M3

Mishra, Jayakanta. *History of Maithili Literature.* New Delhi: Sahitya Akademi, 1976.   PK1818.M54

Mugali, R. S. *History of Kannada Literature.* New Delhi: Sahitya Akademi, 1975.   PL4650.M78

Parameswaran Nair, P. K. *History of Malayalam Literature.* 2d ed. New Delhi: Sahitya Akademi, 1978.
PL4718.P3413 1978

Raju, Poolla Tirupati. *Telugu Literature (Andhra Literature).* Bombay: International Book House, 1944.
PL4780.R3

Renou, Louis. *Indian Literature.* New York: Walker Books, 1966.   PK2903.R543

―――, et al. *Classical India and Vedic India.* 2 vols. Calcutta: Gupta, 1957.   DS425.R453

Rice, Edward P. *History of Kanarese [Kannada] Literature.* Calcutta: YMCA Press, 1921.   PL4650.R5 1921

Roadarmel, Gordon C. *Bibliography of English Source Materials for the Study of Modern Hindi Literature.* Berkeley: University of California Center for South and Southeast Asia Studies, 1969.   Z3208.L5 R6

Sadiq, Mohammed. *History of Urdu Literature.* London: Oxford University Press, 1964.   PK2155.S25

Sahitya Akademi. *Contemporary Indian Literature: A Symposium.* 2d ed. New Delhi: Sahitya Akademi, 1959.
PK2903.S29 1959

Saksena, Ram Babu. *History of Urdu Literature.* Allahabad: Ram Narain Lal, 1940.   PK2031.S3 1940

Sen, Sukumar. *History of Bengali Literature.* New Delhi: Sahitya Akademi, 1960.   PK1701.S483

Shastr, Gaurinath B. *Concise History of Classical Sanskrit Literature.* 2d ed. London: Oxford University Press, 1961.   PK2903.S5 1960

Shivanath. *History of Dogri Literature.* New Delhi: Sahitya Akademi, 1976.   PK2647.5.S56

Spear, Thomas George Percival. *History of India.* Vol. 2, *1526–The Present.* Harmondsworth: Penguin, 1965.
DS436.T37

Thapar, Romila. *History of India.* Vol. 1, *To 1526.* Harmondsworth: Penguin, 1966.   DS436.T372

Wickramasinghe, Martin. *Sinhalese Literature.* Colombo: M. D. Gunasena, 1950.   PK2850.W55

Winternitz, Moriz. *History of Indian Literature.* Translation by S. Ketkar and H. Kohn of *Geschichte der indianischen Literatur,* 3 vols. (Leipzig, 1905–1922). 3d ed. 3 vols. in 5 parts. Calcutta: University of Calcutta, 1959–1967. The English edition was extensively revised by the author from the original German.
PK2903.W622

Yusuf, Ali A. *Cultural History of India during the British Period.* Bombay: D. B. Taraporevala Sons, 1940.
DS463.A56

L–161   **Anderson, George L.   *Asian Literature in English: A Guide to Information Sources.*** Detroit: Gale Research Co., 1981.   Z3001.A655

This volume presents a guide to English translations of the literatures of East Asia and to English scholarship and criticism on these literatures. A total of 2,224 serially numbered, frequently annotated entries are disposed into sixteen chapters, as follows: 1, Far East (bibliography and reference, anthologies, literary history and criticism, periodicals); 2, China (bibliography, reference, sections on anthologies and history and criticism of each major genre, comparative studies, and a number of sections on modern Chinese literatures with subdivisions parallel to those for traditional literature); 3, Japan (similarly subdivided); 4, Korea; 5, Southeast Asia; 6, Burma; 7, Cambodia; 8, Indonesia; 9, Laos; 10, Malaya and Singapore; 11, Thailand (Siam); 12, Vietnam; 13, Mongolia; 14, Tibet; 15, Turkic and Other Literatures of Central Asia; 16, Central Asia—Periodicals. There is an unusually large number of typographical errors; entries should probably be checked against other authorities. The volume concludes with an index of authors, editors, translators, corporate authors, and titles of anonymous works.

L–162   **Cordier, Henri.   *Bibliotheca Sinica: Dictionnaire bibliographique des ouvrages relatifs à l'Empire chinois.*** 2d ed., rev., corr., and enl. 4 vols. Paris: Guilmoto, 1904–1908. Supplément. Paris: Geuthner, 1922–1924. Author Index to the original and supplement. New York: Columbia University Libraries, 1953.   Z3108.C8

This standard bibliography contains some 50,000 entries in the main work plus an additional 20,000 in the supplement. Volumes 1–3 contain works on China proper; volume 3, part 2 contains works concerning foreigners in China. Volume 4 contains three parts concerning relations of foreigners with the Chinese; the Chinese abroad; and countries tributary to China. Cordier is further supplemented by Tung-Li Yüan, comp., *China in Western Literature: A Continuation of Cordier's Bibliotheca Sinica* (New Haven: Yale University Far Eastern Publications, 1958) [Z3101.Y8]. The 15,000 entries cover all books in English, French, and German treating China which were published during the period 1921–1957. The unannotated entries are elaborately classified into some twenty-eight major sections, of which section 15 is on language and 16 on literature. Other sections include bibliography and reference, geography and travel, history, biography, philosopy, religion, archaeology, and regions. There are two appendixes, of serial publications and of addenda, and there is an index of names.

These two works are further supplemented by John Lust, *Index Sinicus: A Catalogue of Articles Relating to China in Periodicals and Other Collective Publications, 1920-1955* (Cambridge: Heffer, 1964) [Z3101.L8]. This work contains 19,734 serially numbered unannotated entries citing articles published in Western languages, arranged in a series of twenty-seven subject and area classes.

In contrast with these works is the highly selective volume by Charles O. Hucker, *China: A Critical Bibliography* (Tucson: University of Arizona Press, 1962) [Z3101.H8], which is an excellent guide to the literature. See also the recent volume by C. H. Lowe, *Notable Books on Chinese Studies* (Taipei: China Printing, 1978) [Z3106.L8].

L–163   ***Revue bibliographique de sinologie.*** Vol. 1– [1955–]. Paris: Mouton, 1957–.   Z7059.R4

This irregularly published serial bibliography includes abstracts of Western and Eastern-language articles and notices of books in the fields of Chinese history, sociology, anthropology, art, language and literature, and philosophy. Entries are systematically arranged and well indexed.

The school of Oriental and African Studies, London University, publishes a *Monthly List of Periodical Articles on the Far East and South East Asia*, 1956– [Z3221.L6].

L–164 **Bailey, Roger B.** *Guide to Chinese Poetry and Drama.* Boston: G. K. Hall, 1973.   Z3108.L5 B34

This small volume, one of those in the new Asian Literature Bibliography Series, consists of an annotated bibliography of 112 serially numbered English-language items with descriptive and explanatory essays following. The Poetry section is divided into five parts after the introduction: General Anthologies, Pre-T'ang Poetry, T'ang Poetry, Post-T'ang Poetry, and General References; the Drama section is not subdivided after its introduction.

Further Chinese-literature volumes in the Asian Literature Bibliography Series are the *Guide to Chinese Prose*, comp. Jordan D. Paper, 2d ed. (Boston: G. K. Hall, 1984) [Z3108.L5 P34 1984]; and the two volumes edited by Winston L. Y. Yang and Nathan K. Mao: *Classical Chinese Fiction: A Guide to Its Study and Appreciation: Essays and Bibliographies* (Boston: G. K. Hall, 1978) [Z3108.L5 Y29], and *Modern Chinese Fiction: A Guide to Its Study and Appreciation: Essays and Bibliographies* (Boston: G. K. Hall, 1980) [Z3108.L5 Y293].

Another often-recommended brief bibliographical guide for Chinese literature is Tien-yi Li, *History of Chinese Literature: A Selected Bibliography*, rev. ed. (New Haven: Yale University Far Eastern Publications, 1968) [Z3108.L5 L5], which presents in eleven sections unannotated entries on some 300 books in Chinese, English, French, German, and Japanese.

L–165 *Indiana Companion to Traditional Chinese Literature.* Ed. by William H. Nienhauser, Jr., et al. Bloomington: Indiana University Press, 1986.   Z3108.L5 I53 1986

This volume has been widely hailed as an indispensable reference work for students of Chinese literature, surpassing all others both in size and in quality. Approximately 170 contributors from 12 different nations were involved in completing this volume, which is in two parts. Part I, Essays, presents surveys of Buddhist Literature, Drama, Fiction, Literary Criticism, Poetry, Popular Literature, Prose, Rhetoric, Taoist Literature, and Women's Literature. Part II, Entries, presents a dictionary arrangement of entries on an Oxford Companion model. Authors, titles, movements, societies, technical terms are all treated. Both the essays and the entries append bibliographies, and are signed. In addition to extensive cross-references, the volume concludes with indexes of names, titles, and subjects.

L–166 **Fukuda, Naomi.** *Bibliography of Reference Works for Japanese Studies.* Ann Arbor: Center for Japanese Studies, University of Michigan, 1979.   Z3306.B48

This selective, annotated bibliography presents entries in twelve alphanumeric sections treating General Works; Philosophy and Religion; Fine Arts; Language; Literature; History; Biography; Geography; and other subjects in Japanese studies. The volume concludes with title index.

See also the *Selected List of Books and Articles on Japan in English, French, and German* by Hugh Borton et al., rev. and enl. ed. (Cambridge: Harvard University Press for the Harvard-Yenching Institute, 1954) [Z3306.B67]. More recent is the work of Bernard S. Silberman, *Japan and Korea: A Critical Bibliography* (Tucson: University of Arizona Press, 1962) [Z3301.S55], which enumerates, classifies, and describes primarily book-length works in Western languages, particularly English, published since 1940.

The most detailed bibliography of Western-language works is the *Bibliography of the Japanese Empire, 1477-1926*, 4 vols. (Leiden: Brill [publisher varies], 1885–1928), originally compiled by Friedrich von Wenckstern [Z3301.W471]. It was continued as the *Bibliographie von Japan, 1927-37*, in four additional volumes (Leipzig: Hiersemann, 1931–1940) [Z3301.W472].

L–167 **Miner, Earl.** *Princeton Companion to Classical Japanese Literature.* Princeton: Princeton University Press, 1986.   PL726.1.M495 1985

This splendid volume is designed to be an indispensable *vade mecum* for any student of Japanese literature. It is disposed into ten parts, as follows: 1, A Brief Literary History (essays on periods); 2, Chronologies (works, events, in tabular form); 3, Major Authors and Works (entries in dictionary format); 4, Literary Terms (entries in dictionary format); 5, Theaters (essays, diagrams, photographs); 6, Collections, Kinds, Criticism; Buddhism and Confucianism; Dictionaries (essays and enumerations); 7, Time, Directions, Related Symbolism, and Annual Celebrations (essays, enumerations, diagrams); 8, Geography, Maps, Poetic Place Names (essays, enumerations, diagram); 9, Ranks, Offices, and Certain Incumbents (essays, tables, enumerations); 10, Architecture; Clothing, Armor, and Arms; Illustrated Popular Books and Other Genre Representations (diagrams, enumerations, illustrations, photographs). The volume concludes with a list of principal immediate sources and with an index of authors and titles referred to in parts one, three, and six.

A relatively recent closed bibliography by Yasuhiro Yoshizaki, *Studies in Japanese Literature and Language: A Bibliography of English Materials* (Tokyo: Nichigai Associates, 1979) [Z7072.Y67], is in three sections: Studies in Japanese Literature; Studies in Japanese Language; and Materials for Further Information. Entries are in a classified arrangement in each section. Books, periodical articles, and dissertations are included. There is an index of names and titles.

There is also a new, annual bibliography of *Research in Japanese Literature 1977–* (Tokyo: Kokubungaku Kenkyu Shiyokan, 1978–) [Z7072.K56] which presents both a classified bibliography and a yearbook, and concludes with an author index.

L–168 **Pronko, Leonard C.** *Guide to Japanese Drama.* Boston: G. K. Hall, 1973.   Z3308.L5 P76

This small volume, part of the new Asian Literature Bibliography Series, contains a bibliography of some seventy-five English-language works on Japanese drama with long annotations, preceded by an introductory essay on theater in Japan. The volume concludes with a chronology, a list of further readings, and an index of authors, editors, translators, and titles.

Additional titles treating Japanese literature in this new series are J. Thomas Rimer and Robert E. Morrell, *Guide to Japanese Poetry* 2d ed. (Boston: G. K. Hall, 1984) [Z3308.L5 R54 1984], which contains a historical sketch and bibliographical outline, followed by some 140 annotated, chronologically arranged entries; and Alfred H. Marks and Barry D. Bort, *Guide to Japanese Prose* 2d ed. (Boston: G. K. Hall, 1984) [Z3308.L5 M37 1984], which includes brief plot summaries and critical comments on leading works of fiction and nonfiction, in two sections on Pre-Meiji Literature (Beginnings to 1867) and Meiji Literature and after (1867 to the present).

See also the *Biographical Dictionary of Japanese Literature*, ed. Sen'ichi Hisamatsu (Tokyo: Kodansha International, 1976) [PL723.B5].

L–169 Some Frequently Recommended Works in Far Eastern Studies.

Chinese

Birch, Cyril, ed. *Studies in Chinese Literary Genres*. Berkeley, Los Angeles, London: University of California Press, 1974. PL2253.S8

Bishop, John L., ed. *Studies in Chinese Literature*. Cambridge: Harvard University Press, 1965. PL2272.5.B5

Chen Shou-yi. *Chinese Literature: A Historical Introduction*. New York: Ronald Press, 1961. PL2265.C45

Chou, Shu-jen. *Brief History of Chinese Fiction*. New ed. Peking: Foreign Language Press, 1959. PL2415.C513

Couling, Samuel. *Encyclopedia Sinica*. Shanghai: Kelly and Walsh, 1917. DS733.C7

De Bary, William Theodore, et al., eds. *Sources of Chinese Tradition*. 2 vols. New York: Columbia University Press, 1965. DS703.D4

Dolby, William. *History of Chinese Drama*. New York: Harper and Row, 1976. PL2357.D6b

Giles, Herbert A. *History of Chinese Literature, with a Continuation by Liu Wu-chi*. New York: D. Appleton, 1901. PL2265.G5

Hightower, James R. *Topics in Chinese Literature: Outlines and Bibliographies*. Rev. ed. Cambridge: Harvard University Press, 1953. PL2909.H5 1953

Hsia, Chih-Tsing. *Classic Chinese Novel. A Critical Introduction*. 2d ed. New York: Columbia University Press, 1980. PL2415.H8 1980

———. *History of Modern Chinese Fiction [1917–1957]*. 2d ed. New Haven: Yale University Press, 1971. PL2442.H8 1971

Hucker, Charles O. *China's Imperial Past: An Introduction to Chinese History and Culture*. Stanford: Stanford University Press, 1975. DS721.H724

Li, Tien-yi. *Chinese Fiction: A Bibliography of Books and Articles in Chinese and English*. New Haven: Far Eastern Publications, Yale University, 1968. Z3108.L5 L4

Liu, James J. Y. *Art of Chinese Poetry*. 2d ed. Chicago: University of Chicago Press, 1966. PL2307.L57 1962a

———. *Chinese Theories of Literature*. Chicago: University of Chicago Press, 1975. PN99.C5 L58

Liu, Wu-Chi. *Introduction to Chinese Literature*. Bloomington: University of Indiana Press, 1966. PL2265.L5

Prušek, J. *Chinese History and Literature: A Collection of Studies*. Prague: Academia; Dordrecht: D. Reidel, 1970. PL2445.P7

———. *Lyrical and the Epic: Studies of Modern Chinese Literature*. Edited by Leo Ou-fan Lee. Bloomington: Indiana University Press, 1980. PL2302.P7

Rickett, Adele A., ed. *Chinese Approaches to Literature from Confucius to Liang Chi-i-Ch'ao*. Princeton, N.J.: Princeton University Press, 1978. PL2272.5.C5327

Scott, A. C. *Art and Literature in Twentieth Century China*. New n York: Anchor, 1963.

———. *Classical Theatre of China*. London: Allen and Unwin, 1957. PN2871.S4

Watson, Burton. *Chinese Lyricism*. New York: Columbia University Press, 1971. PL2307.W4

———. *Early Chinese Literature*. New York: Columbia University Press, 1962. PL2280.W3

Wu, Yuan-li. *China: A Handbook*. New York: Praeger, 1973. DS706.W8

Yang, Winston L. Y., and Teresa S. Yang. *Bibliography of the Chinese Language*. New York: American Association of Teachers of Chinese Language and Culture, 1966. Z7059.Y3

Japanese

Arnott, Peter D. *Theatres of Japan*. New York: St. Martin's Press, 1969. PN2921.A73

Aston, William G. *History of Japanese Literature*. New York: Appleton Century, 1899. PL855.A8 1899

Bershihand, Roger. *Japanese Literature*. New York: Walker and Co., 1965. PL717.B413

Bonneau, Georges. *Bibliographie de la littérature japonaise contemporaine*. Paris: Geuthner; Tokyo: Mitsukushi, 1938. Z7072.B72

Bowers, Faubion. *Japanese Theatre*. New York: Hermitage Books, 1952. PN2921.B6

Brower, Robert, and Earl Miner. *Japanese Court Poetry*. Stanford: Stanford University Press, 1961. PL865.B7

Cordier, Henri. *Bibliotheca Japonica: Dictionnaire bibliographique des ouvrages relatifs à l'Empire japonais rangée par ordre chronologique jusqu'à 1870, suivi d'un appendice renfermant la liste alphabétique des principaux ouvrages parus de 1870 à 1912*. Paris: Leroux, 1912. Z3301.C7

Ernst, Earle. *Kabuki Theatre*. Oxford: Oxford University Press, 1956. PN2921.E7

Hibbett, Howard. *Floating World in Japanese Fiction*. New York: Oxford University Press, 1959. PL873.H5

Hisamatsu, Seníchi. *Biographical Dictionary of Japanese Literature*. Tokyo: Kodansha International, 1976. PL723.B5

Inoura, Yohinobu, and Toshio Kawatake. *History of Japanese Theatre*. 2 vols. Tokyo: Kokusai Bunka Shikoka, 1971. Vol. 1, by Inoura, treats Noh and Kyōgen. Vol. 2, by Kawatake, treats Bunraku and Kabuki. PN2921.H55

Introduction to Classic Japanese Literature. Tokyo: Kokusai Bunka Shinkokai Publications, 1948. PL855.K6

Introduction to Contemporary Japanese Literature. Tokyo: Kokusai Bunka Shinkokai Publications, 1939. PL740.6.K6

Itasaka, Gen, editor in chief. *Kodansha Encyclopedia of Japan*. 9 vols. Tokyo: Kodansha International, 1983. DS805.K633 1983

Japan: Its Land, People, and Culture. Rev. ed. Tokyo: Printing Bureau, 1964. DS806.A54

Kato, Shuichi. *History of Japanese Literature*. 3 vols. Tokyo: Kodansha International, 1979–1983. PL716.K2413

Keene, Donald. *Dawn to the West: Japanese Literature of the Modern Era*. 2 vols. New York: Holt, Rinehart and Winston, 1984. Vol. 1, *Fiction*; vol. 2, *Poetry, Drama, Criticism*. PL726.55.K39 1984

———. *Japanese Literature: An Introduction for Western Readers*. London: John Murray, 1953. PL855.K4

———. *World within Walls: Japanese Literature of the Pre-Modern Era, 1600–1867*. New York: Holt, Rinehart and Winston, 1976. PL726.35.K4

Konishi, Jinichi. *History of Japanese Literature*. 4 vols. Princeton, N. J.: Princeton University Press, 1984–. PL717.K6213 1984

Martins Janeira, Armando. *Japanese and Western Literature: A Comparative Study.* Rutland, Vt.: Charles E. Tuttle, 1970. PL720.5.M3

Miller, Roy Andrew. *Japanese Language.* Chicago: University of Chicago Press, 1967. P1523.M493

Miner, Earl R. *Introduction to Japanese Court Poetry.* Stanford: Stanford University Press, 1968. PL733.2.M5

——. *Japanese Tradition in British and American Literature.* Princeton, N. J.: Princeton University Press, 1958. PR129.J3 M5

Putzar, Edward. *Japanese Literature: A Historical Outline.* Tucson: University of Arizona Press, 1973. PL717.P8

Rimer, J. Thomas. *Toward a Modern Japanese Theatre.* Princeton, N. J.: Princeton University Press, 1974. PL832.I8 Z85

——. *Modern Japanese Fiction and Its Traditions.* Princeton, N. J.: Princeton University Press, 1978. PL747.55.R55

Sansom, George. *Japan: A Short Cultural History.* Rev. ed. New York: Appleton, 1943. DS821.S3 1943a

Ueda, Makado. *Literary and Art Theories in Japan.* Cleveland, Ohio: Western Reserve University Press, 1967. PL708.U33

Other Far Eastern Literatures

Indochina (Laos, Thailand, Vietnam)

Cordier, Henri. *Bibliotheca Indosinica: Dictionnaire bibliographique des ouvrages relatifs à la péninsule indochinoise.* 4 vols. Paris: Imprimé national Leroux, 1912–1932. Index. 1932. Z3221.C78

Boudet, Paul, and Remy Bourgeois. *Bibliographie de l'Indochine française, 1913–34.* 4 vols. Hanoi: Imprimerie d'Extrême Orient, 1929–1934. Continuation of Cordier. Z3226.B68

Hall, Daniel G. E. *History of Southeast Asia.* 3d ed. New York: St. Martin's Press, 1968. DS511.H15 1968

Jemer, Philip N. *Southeast Asian Literatures in Translation: A Preliminary Bibliography.* Honolulu: University of Hawaii Press, 1973. DS3.A2 A82 no. 9

Tregonning, Kennedy G. *South East Asia: A Critical Bibliography.* Tucson: University of Arizona Press, 1969. Z3221.T7

Indonesia

Teeuw, A. *Modern Indonesian Literature.* 2d ed. The Hague: Nijhoff, 1979. PL5080.T4 1979

Vlekke, Bernard H. M. *Nusantara: A History of Indonesia.* Rev. ed. The Hague: W. Van Hoeve, 1959. DS634.V55 1959

Korea

Korea: Its People and Culture. Seoul: Kakwon-Sa, 1970. DS904.K59

Lee, Peter H. *Korean Literature: Topics and Themes.* Tucson: University of Arizona Press, 1965. PL950.L4

Malaya and Singapore

Winstedt, Sir Richard O. *History of Classical Malay Literature.* Rev. ed. Oxford: Oxford University Press, 1969. PL5130.W5 1969

——. *Malays: A Cultural History.* Revised and updated by Tham Seong Chee. Singapore: G. Brash, 1981. DS523.4.M35 W57 1981

Mongolia and Central Asia

Gerasimovich, L. K. *History of Modern Mongolian Literature, 1921–64.* Bloomington: Indiana University Press, 1970. DS798.M575 no. 6

Heissig, Walther. *Geschichte der mongolischen Literatur.* 2 vols. Wiesbaden: Harrassowitz, 1972. PL410.H4

Rupen, Robert Arthur. *Mongols of the Twentieth Century.* 2 vols. Bloomington: Indiana University Press, 1964. DS798.R8

Sanders, Alan J. J. *People's Republic of Mongolia: A General Reference Guide.* New York: Oxford University Press, 1968. DS798.S33

Oceania (Melanesia, Micronesia, Papua New Guinea, and Polynesia)

Klieneberger, H. R. *Bibliography of Oceanic Linguistics.* London: Oxford University Press, 1957. Z7111.K5

Thailand

Graham, W. A. *Siam.* 2 vols. London: Alexander Moring, 1924. DS565.G8 1924

Tibet

Chaudhuri, Sibadas. *Bibliography of Tibetan Studies.* Calcutta: Asiatic Society, 1971. Z3107.T5 C46

Snellgrove, David, and Hugh Richardson. *Cultural History of Tibet.* London: Weidenfeld and Nicolson, 1968. DS786.S6

Stein, R. A. *Tibetan Civilization.* Translated by J. E. Stapleton Driver. London: Faber and Faber, 1972. D7786.S7713

XVI. CHILDREN'S LITERATURE

See also many relevant entries in section K.I, Folklore; the Children's Literature sections in the *MLA International* Bibliography (L–50); in the MHRA *Annual Bibliography on English Language and Literature* (M–21); and in both the *CBEL* (M–10) and the *NCBEL* (M–11). And see pertinent materials in general bibliographies of nineteenth- and twentieth-century English and American literature.

L–170 **Haviland, Virginia, ed. *Children's Literature: A Guide to Reference Sources.*** Washington, D. C.: Library of Congress, 1966. Z1037.A1 H35

This guide, compiled by the Head of the Children's Literature Center at the Library of Congress, is far and away the most important research tool in the field of children's literature. It presents an elaborate, annotated reference bibliography, including books, dissertations, articles, pamphlets, newspapers, recordings, and catalogs. Omitted, regrettably, are citations of books and articles that treat works of children's literature as works of literature simply—that is, without a primary emphasis on their special status. Thus most of the major scholarship on such texts as *Pilgrim's Progress, Gulliver's Travels,* or the works of Kipling or Stevenson or Twain is not cited. As a result, this work must be supplemented by general bibliographies for studies of individual authors and works.

The work is organized into eight major divisions. These are History and Criticism (including studies, reviewing, criticism, and awards); Authorship; Illustration; Bibliography (including general lists and catalogs, special bibliographies, and bibliographies of sources); Books and Children (including reading guidance; storytelling; folktales, myths, and legends; nursery rhymes; poetry and children; and children's magazines); The Library and Children's Books; International Studies; and National Studies. The 1,073 serially numbered entries include LC call numbers (or location symbols of items not held by the Library of Congress) and give considerable descriptive and evaluative annotation. Descriptions include analytical entries for significant parts of general works; evaluations indicate the relative importance and value of an item as well as its use and interest. There are abundant cross-references. The guide concludes with a directory of professional associations and agencies that publish cited items and an index of authors, titles, and subjects.

The *First Supplement* (Washington, D. C., 1972) adds 746 entries for publications chiefly from 1966–1969. Two new subsections are also included, one in the History and Criticism division on the publishing and promotion of children's books and one in the Books and Children section on Teaching Children's Literature. Abundant cross-references occur, both to the original guide and to other entries in the supplement. Otherwise the supplement follows the structure of the original volume exactly.

The *Second Supplement* (Washington, D. C., 1977) treats chiefly publications of 1970–1974, adding 929 entries. A subsection on Research in Children's Literature is added after the Teaching section; also added is a section on the selection of nonprint materials. The entire International Studies section is rearranged, and in the National division a new section on French Canada has been added. There are cross references both to the original guide and to the first supplement; in every other respect the structure of the volume is parallel to that of the earlier ones.

A *Third Supplement* was published in 1982, covering publications chiefly from the five years 1975–1979, adding more than 700 books and articles.

Among the multitude of other works in this field by Virginia Haviland may be mentioned the annotated selection guide, *Best of Children's Books 1964-1978, Including 1979 Addenda* (Washington, D. C., 1981) [Z1037.H358 1981], a selection of some 1,000 titles from the annual LC guides, arranged by type of work, with full bibliographical information, and the valuable anthology, *Children and Literature: Views and Reviews* (Glenview, Ill.: Scott, Foresman, 1973) [PN1009 .A1 H27], which includes a selection disposed into twelve chapters treating articles written before the twentieth century, classics, children's reading interests and needs, writers, illustrations, children's literature and fantasy, poetry, fiction and realism, history and fact, international children's literature, criticism and reviewing, and awards.

Another less comprehensive but still useful aid is Alec Ellis, *How to Find Out about Children's Literature*, 3d ed. (Oxford: Pergamon, 1973) [PN1009.A1 E43 1973], which includes lists of organizations, keys to book selection, and annotated bibliographies of works related to the history of children's literature. There are chapters discussing schoolbooks and information books, Commonwealth literature, American literature, translations, retellings, purpose in children's reading, and reading and children's development.

L–171 *Oxford Companion to Children's Literature.* Compiled by Humphrey Carpenter and Mari Prichard. London: Oxford University Press, 1984.   PN1008.5.C37 1984

This ready-reference guide presents more than 2,000 entries in a dictionary arrangement of which some 900 are biographies of authors, illustrators, printers, publishers, educators, scholars, and philosophers of education. The definition of literature is broad enough to include film, television, radio, comics, and dime novels. Traditional and popular genres are treated in articles, as are sketches of the children's literatures of various countries. Titles, characters, periodicals, awards— all are included. There is, however, a British bias, and a number of important American authors and critics are left either undiscussed or less fully discussed than their British counterparts.

Another guide, the *Penguin Companion to Children's Literature*, is in preparation; it will include articles by contributing specialists.

L–172 **Pellowski, Anne.** *World of Children's Literature.* New York: R. R. Bowker, 1968.   Z1037.P37

This massive and ambitious bibliography contains 4,496 serially numbered entries on monographs, series, and multivolume works that represent the development of children's literature in some 126 countries. An attempt is made to include works concerned with the history and criticism of children's literature, public and school library work with children, national book clubs, subjects related to children's literature (such as folklore), the reading interests of children, criteria for or techniques of writing or illustrating children's books, national bibliographies of children's literature, and special exhibits. Also included are selected monographs and series that list recommended books for children, anthologize children's literature, or present biographies of authors of children's literature. Entries give full bibliographical description and are generally annotated with respect to scope, completeness, and other descriptive categories. Symbols locate items in one of twenty-one libraries. The entries are arranged in eight large geographical areas, subdivided in turn into eighty area groups, and then into country listings. Within the citations from a particular country, entries are alphabetical by author. The volume begins with a list of abbreviations, identification of library symbols, an introductory essay (similar discursive introductions precede each of the various area and country sections of the work), and an initial section of sixty-three items that are international in scope. The volume ends with an exhaustive index.

L–173 **Bingham, Jane, and Grayce Scholt.** *Fifteen Centuries of Children's Literature: An Annotated Chronology of British and American Works in Historical Context.* Westport, Conn.: Greenwood Press, 1980.   Z1037.A1 B582

This volume contains a convenient, single annotated chronological listing of significant or representative books written for, used with, or appropriated by British or American children from about A.D. 523 to 1945. The listing is in six sections: Anglo-Saxon, from ca. 523 to 1099; Middle English, 1100–1499; Renaissance to Restoration, 1500–1659; Restoration to American Independence, 1660–1799; Nineteenth Century, 1800–1899; and Earlier Twentieth Century, 1900–1945. Each of the six sections begins with a brief introduction, treating the historical background, the history of books, and the history of attitudes toward and treatment of children during the period in question.

The 735 main entries present a descriptive annotation of the work's contents followed by facts, additional works by the author, and publication information judged to be relevant to the main citation. The work is not meant to be bibliographically accurate, and the descriptive annotation of contents is emphatically not of scholarly value.

The chronology is supplemented by a series of appendixes: American Periodicals for Children: A Chronological Checklist (by date of publication); British Periodicals for Children (similar in scope and structure); Facsimiles and Reprints of Books Included in the Chronology (with a key to cited publishers). There are also a bibliography of secondary sources cited; an index of authors, illustrators, translators, and early publishers; and an index of the approximately 9,700 cited titles arranged chronologically by the date the book was first used by English-speaking children, then alphabetically by author, or by title in the case of anonymous works. A supplement or revised edition is hoped for.

L–174 **Rahn, Suzanne.** *Children's Literature: An Annotated Bibliography of the History and Criticism.* New York: Garland, 1981.   Z1037.R15 1981

A total of 1,328 serially numbered descriptively and evaluatively annotated entries are disposed into four main parts. The first cites works concerned with the Aims and Definitions of the study of children's literature. Part 2 treats historical studies and is divided into sections citing general histories and then special historical studies. Part 3 describes works on the various genres of children's literature and is subdivided into sections on each, from Adolescent Novels, Animal Stories, and "Bad Boy" Novels to Nonsense, Nursery Rhymes, Retellings of Folk Literature, Science Fiction, and Sports Fiction. Part 4, finally, enumerates studies of authors and is divided into biobibliographical treatments of individual authors and then groups of authors. An appendix cites the leading scholarly journals in children's literature for further reading; the volume concludes with an index of names.

L–175 **Hendrickson, Linnea.** *Children's Literature: A Guide to the Criticism.* Boston: G. K. Hall, 1987. Z2014.5.H46 1987

This annotated bibliography brings together significant critical analyses of children's literature from all disciplines. Treated are classics of children's literature, as well as criticism of 20th century works. The first section enumerates criticism focused on a particular author or illustrator. The second section, Subjects, Themes, and Genres, covers such diverse topics as the role of the critic and the history of fairy tales. The volume concludes with an index of critics and an index of topics.

L–176 **Darton, Frederick J. Harvey.** *Children's Books in England: Five Centuries of Social Life.* 3d ed. Edited by Brian Alderson. Cambridge: Cambridge University Press, 1982.
PN1009.A1 D35 1982

First published in 1932, and in a revised edition by Kathleen Lines in 1958, Darton's is the standard authority on the history of children's literature in England from Caxton's translation of *Aesop's Fables* to the work of Stevenson and Kipling. Chapters are arranged chronologically with bibliographies of chief works at the ends of each. Each edition has added both supplements to the individual chapter bibliographies and a separate list of books on contemporary children's literature. The third edition has also an appendix of new material on the study of children's literature. A preliminary sketch of this history is available as chapter 16 in volume 11 of the *Cambridge History of English Literature* (M–32), pp. 407–430.
Among other often-recommended titles concerned with the history of children's literature in England are Louise F. Field, *Child and His Book: Some Account of the History and Progress of Children's Literature in England*, 2d ed. (London: Wells, Gardner, Darton and Co., 1895) [Z1037.F45]; Percy H. Muir, *English Children's Books, 1600 to 1900* (New York: Praeger, 1954) [PN1009.A1 M8 1954]; Elva S. Smith, *History of Children's Literature: A Syllabus with Selected Bibliographies*, rev. and enl. ed., ed. Margaret Hodges (Chicago: American Library Association, 1980) [Z2014.5.S57]; Mary F. Thwaite, *From Primer to Pleasure in Reading: An Introduction to the History of Children's Books in England from the Invention of Printing to 1914, with an Outline of Some Developments in Other Countries*, 2d ed. (London: Library Association, 1972) [PN1009.A1 T5 1972]; and John Rowe Townsend, *Written for Children: An Outline of English-Language Children's Literature*, rev. ed. (Harmondsworth: Penguin, 1974) [PN1009.A1 T6 1974]. The Smith volume includes period outline syllabi and lists of primary and secondary sources from Anglo-Saxon times to the late nineteenth century. The Thwaite work includes a chronological list of important works in children's literature from the period 1479–1800 and a massive annotated bibliography of 342 items concerned with English children's literature from that period.

L–177 **Meigs, Cornelia L., et al.** *Critical History of Children's Literature: A Survey of Children's Books in English from the Earliest Times to the Present.* Rev. ed. New York: Macmillan, 1969.   PN1009.A1 M4 1969

Originally published in 1953, this only slightly revised work continues to have a strong American bias with a concomitant nostalgic and sentimental treatment of childhood. Nevertheless, it offers a fairly complete chronicle history of American children's literature and its English and European antecedents. It is divided into four parts, as follows: 1, Roots in the Past up to 1840, by Cornelia Meigs (with 14 chapters); 2, Widening Horizons 1840–1890, by Anne Thaxter Eaton (with 11 chapters); 3, A Rightful Heritage 1890–1920, by Elizabeth Nesbill (with 12 chapters); 4, Golden Years and Time of Tumult 1920–1967, by Ruth Hill Viguers (with 13 chapters). There are bibliographies appended to each chapter, and the large volume concludes with an extensive index of authors and titles.
Among other recommended titles for the history of American children's literature are D'Alte Aldridge Welch, *Bibliography of American Children's Books Printed Prior to 1821* (Barre, Mass.: American Antiquarian Society and Barre Publishers, 1972) [Z1232.W44 1972]; William Sloane, *Children's Books in England and America in the 17th Century: A History and Checklist* (New York: King's Crown Press, Columbia University, 1955) [Z1037.S62]; Monica Kiefer, *American Children through Their Books, 1700–1835* (Philadelphia: University of Pennsylvania Press, 1948) [PN1009.A1 K5 1948]; and Alice M. Jordan, *From Rollo to Tom Sawyer and Other Papers* [on nineteenth-century American children's literature] (Boston: Horn Book, 1948) [PN1009.A1 J6].
For greater detail on the history of American children's literature, see the valuable essay by R. Gordon Kelly, "American Children's Literature: An Historiographical Review," *American Literary Realism* 6 (1973): 89–107 [PS1.A65]. See also his discussion of children's literature in volume 1 of the *Handbook of American Popular Culture* (S–48), pp. 49–76.

L–178 ***Phaedrus: A Journal of Children's Literature Research.*** Vol. 1–. Madison, N. J.: Fairleigh Dickinson University Press [then Boston: Phaedrus, Inc.], 1973–.   Z1037.A1 P5

This thrice-yearly journal has become the leading international reference for current scholarly research in children's literature. Issues present such invaluable aids as annotated lists of selected dissertations arranged alphabetically by title; lists of periodical articles arranged by subject; lists of antiquarian and new booksellers' catalogs having bibliographical value; lists of recent bibliographies, catalogs, and studies in the field of children's literature; and lists of new and continuing periodicals in the field. Special surveys treat various national children's literatures and other topics of concern. In addition, the journal serves the function of a professional newsletter for the International Research Society for Children's Literature, giving information about upcoming publications, symbols, and other events of concern to the active scholar. There is an index to volumes 1–5.

L–179 **Scholarly Journals in Children's Literature.**

Beiträge zur Kinder- und Jugendliteratur. No. 1–. Berlin: Kinderbuchverlag, 1962–. 4/yr.
No LC number

Bookbird: Literature for Children and Young People. Vienna: International Institute for Children's, Juvenile, and Popular Literature, 1957–. 4/yr. Includes reviews, lists of recommended books, bibliographies. PN1009.A1 B6

CCL *Canadian Children's Literature / Littérature canadienne pour la jeunesse*. Guelph, Ont.: Canadian Children's Press, 1975–. 4/yr. Reviews. Annual and special bibliographies. PN1009.A1 C317

CBRI *Children's Book Review Index*. Detroit: Gale Research Co., 1975–. 3/yr. with annual cumulation entitled *Children's Literature Review: Excerpts from Reviews, Criticism, and Commentary on Books for Children and Young People*. Entries duplicate those found in *Book Review Index* (E–74). Z1037.A1 C475

Child L *Children's Literature: An International Journal*. Annual of the MLA Seminar on Children's Literature and the Children's Literature Association. Storrs, Conn.: Department of English, University of Connecticut, 1972–. 1/yr. Reviews. Index of vols. 1–5 in vol. 6. PN1009.A1 C514

Children's Literature Abstracts. Birmingham, England: International Federation of Library Associations, 1973–. 4/yr. Comprehensive bibliography with brief descriptive abstracts and annual indexes of authors and subjects. Z1037.C5446

Children's Literature Association Quarterly. Vol. 1–. Winnipeg: The Association, 1975–. 4/yr. PN1008.2.C48

Children's Literature in Education: An International Quarterly. New York: APS Publications, 1970–. 3/yr. from 1970 to 1976, 4/yr. since. Includes bibliographical surveys. Z1037.A1 C5

Children's Literature Review. Vol. 1–. Detroit: Gale Research Co., 1976–. 1/yr. PN1009.A1 C5139

Horn Book Magazine. Vol. 1–. Boston, Mass., 1924–. 4/yr. 1924–1974, 6/yr. since. Reviews. Bibliographies. Extra issues. Z1037.A1 A15

L & U *Lion and the Unicorn: A Critical Journal of Children's Literature*. Vol. 1–. Brooklyn, N. Y.: Department of English, Brooklyn College, 1977–. 2/yr. Theme-centered. Reviews. PN1009.A1 L54

Phaedrus: An International Journal of Children's Literature Research [Phaedrus]. [see L–178].

SLJ *School Library Journal*. Vol. 1–. New York: Bowker, 1953–. 9/yr. Z675.S3 S29115

Signal: Approaches to Children's Literature. Vol. 1–. Gloucester, England, 1970–. 3/yr. Includes a reprint series. PN1009.A1 S39

Wilson Library Bulletin. Vol. 1–. New York: H. W. Wilson, 1914–. Z1217.W75

L–180 **Some Frequently Recommended Works on Children's Literature.**

Barry, Florence V. *Century [the Eighteenth] of Children's Books*. London: Methuen, 1922. Z10037.A1 B28

Bingham, Jane M., ed. *Writers for Children: Critical Studies of the Major Authors since the Seventeenth Century*. New York: Scribners, 1987. PN1009.A1 W73 1987

Coveney, Peter. *Image of Childhood; The Individual and Society: A Study of the Theme in English Literature*. Rev. ed. Harmondsworth: Penguin, 1967. PR151.C5C6 1967

Doderer, Klaus, editor in chief. *Lexikon der Kinder- und Jugendliteratur; Personen—Länder—und Sachartikel zu Geschichte und Gegenwart der Kinder- und Jugendliteratur in drei Bänden und einem Ergänzugs- und Registerband*. 4 vols. Basel: Verlag Dokumentation, 1975–. PN1008.5.L4

Egoff, Sheila A., G. T. Stubbs, and L. F. Ashley, eds. *Only Connect: Readings in Children's Literature*. 2d ed. New York: Oxford University Press, 1969. PN1009.A1 E28 1980

Field, Carolyn W., ed. *Subject Collections in Children's Literature*. New York: Bowker, 1969. Z688.C47 F5

Grade, Arnold. *Guide to Early [American] Juvenile Literature*. Columbus, Ohio: Charles E. Merrill, 1970. PN1009.A1 G65

Haas, Gerhard, ed. *Kinder- und Jugendliteratur: Zur Typologie und Funktion einer literarischen Gattung*. Stuttgart: Reclam, 1974. PN1009.A1 K517

Haviland, Virginia. *Children's Books of International Interest*. Chicago: American Library Association, 1978. Z1037.H37 1978

Hazard, Paul. *Books, Children, and Men*. Translation by Marguerite Mitchell of *Les livres, les enfants et les hommes* (Paris: Flammarion, 1932). Boston: Horn Book, 1944. PN1009.A1 H33

Hürlimann, Bettina. *Three Centuries of Children's Books in Europe*. Translation with additions and revisions by Brian Alterson of *Europäische Kinderbücher in drei Jahrhunderten*, 2d ed. (Zurich: Atlantis, 1963). London: Oxford University Press, 1967. PN1009.A1 H813 1967

Jan, Isabelle. *On Children's Literature*. Translation by Catherine Storr of *Essai sur la littérature enfantine*, 2d ed. (Paris, 1973). London: Allen Lane, 1973. PN1009.A1 J313 1973

Kuhn, Reinhard. *Corruption in Paradise: The Child in Western Literature*. Hanover, N. H.: University Press of New England for Brown University Press, 1982. PN56.5.C48 K83 1982

Lurie, Alison, and Justin G. Schiller, eds. *Classics of Children's Literature, 1621–1932*. 73 vols. planned. New York: Garland, 1975–. LC number varies

MacDonald, Ruth K. *Literature for Children in England and America from 1646–1774*. Troy, N.Y.: Whitston Publishing Co., 1982. PR990.M32 1982

St. John, Judith, comp. *Osborne Collection of Early Children's Books, 1566–1910: A Catalogue*. Toronto: Public Library, 1958. Z1038.T6 T67 1958

Sarkissian, Adele, ed. *Children's Authors and Illustrators: An Index to Biographical Dictionaries*. 2d ed. Detroit: Gale Research Co., 1978. Z1037.A1 L2

Scudder, Horace. *Childhood in Literature and Art, with Some Observations on Literature for Children: A Study*. Boston: Houghton Mifflin, 1894. NX652.C48 S38 1894

Smith, James Steel. *Critical Approach to Children's Literature*. New York: McGraw-Hill, 1967. PN1009.A1 S58

Wolgast, Heinrich. *Das Elend unserer Jugendliteratur: Ein Beitrag zur kunstlerischen Erziehung der Jugend*. 7th ed. Worms: Ernst Wunderlich, 1950. PN1009.G3 W6 1950

On Literature for and about Adolescents

Bakerman, Jane, and Mary Jean DeMarr. *Adolescent Female Portraits in the American Novel, 1961–1981*. New York: Garland, 1983.   Z1231.F4 B354 1983

Carlsen, G. Robert. *Books and the Teenage Reader*. 2d rev. ed. New York: Harper and Row, 1980.
          Z1037.A1 C34 1980

DeJovine, F. Anthony. *Young Hero in American Fiction: A Motif for Teaching Literature*. New York: Appleton-Century-Crofts, 1971.   PS374.Y6 D4

Donelson, Ken, ed. *Adolescent Literature, Adolescent Reading and the English Class*. Arizona English Bulletin, vol. 14, no. 3 (Spring 1972). Bibliography, pp. 136–156.   Z1037.A1 A102

———. *Adolescent Literature Revisited after Four Years*. Arizona English Bulletin, vol. 18, no. 3 (Spring 1976). Bibliography, pp. 231–248.
          Z1037.A1 A102 1976

Kiell, Norman. *Adolescent through Fiction: A Psychological Approach*. New York: International Universities Press, 1959.   HQ796.K448

Lenz, Millicent, and Ramona M. Mahood. *Young Adult Literature: Background and Criticisms*. Chicago: American Library Association, 1980.   PN1009.A1 Y59

Moss, Robert F. *Rudyard Kipling and the Fiction of Adolescence*. New York: St. Martin's, 1982.
          PR4858.A33 M6 1982

O'Brien, Justin. *Novel of Adolescence in France: The Study of a Literary Theme*. New York: Columbia University Press, 1937.   PQ637.Y6 O2

Probst, Robert E. *Adolescent Literature: Response and Analysis*. Columbus, Ohio: Merrill, 1984.
          PN59.P7 1984

Schwartz, Sheila. *Teaching Adolescent Literature: A Humanistic Approach*. Rochelle Park, N. J.: Hayden Book Co., 1979.   PN1009.A1 S353

Spacks, Patricia Meyer. *Adolescent Idea: Myths of Youth and the Adult Imagination*. New York: Basic Books, 1981.   PR830.A36 S66

Varlejs, Jana, ed. *Young Adult Literature in the Seventies: A Selection of Readings*. Metuchen, N. J.: Scarecrow, 1978.   Z1037.A1 Y68

Witham, W. Tasker. *Adolescent in the American Novel, 1920–1960*. New York: Ungar, 1964.   PS374.Y6 W5

XVII. WOMEN'S STUDIES

Almost every section contains references useful to scholarship in women's studies. For women and literature see among many other resources the *MLA International Bibliography* (L–50).

L–181 **Stineman, Esther. *Women's Studies: A Recommended Core Bibliography*.** Littleton, Colo.: Libraries Unlimited, 1979.   Z7961.S75

This elaborately annotated bibliography of 1,763 serially numbered entries is disposed into twenty-six chapters. Treated are both primary and secondary works; entries include author, title, place, publisher, and date of publication, price, ISBN, and both descriptive and evaluative commentary, including reference to other, related works. Of the twenty-six chapters, those likely to be of most interest to students of English and American language and literature are the chapters on autobiography, biography, diaries, memoirs, letters; on fine arts, photography, film, music; on history; on languages and linguistics; the six chapters on literature (anthologies, drama, essays, fiction, history and criticism, poetry); the four chapters on reference works (audiovisuals, bibliographies, biographical materials, general); and the chapters on religion and philosophy, and on periodicals. The volume concludes with author, title, and subject indexes.

A supplement, *Women's Studies: A Recommended Core Bibliography 1980–1985* was published in 1987, edited by Catherine R. Loeb, Susan E Searing, and Esther Stineman [Z7963.F44 L63 1987].

L–182 **Ballou, Patricia K. *Women: A Bibliography of Bibliographies*.** Boston: G. K. Hall and Co., 1980.   Z7961.A1 B34

This work enumerates 557 bibliographies concerned with women or with topics traditionally associated with women. Included are lists, essays, reviews, catalogs, and guides to primary resources, whether published as books, pamphlets, articles, or in microform. All items were published between 1970 and 1979. Virtually all of the serially numbered entries include descriptive and evaluative annotation. They are organized into four main sections, as follows: General and Interdisciplinary; Publications of One Type or Format (bibliographies of reference books, government documents, special periodical issues, dissertations, women's movement publications, library catalogs, guides to archives and manuscript collections, biographies/autobiographies/diaries, and oral history); Geographical Subjects (subdivided by country, region, state); Topical Subjects (history, literature, mass media, fine arts, music, philosophy, religion, education, economics, political science, anthropology, sociology, psychology, health and reproduction, sports). The volume concludes with an index of personal names.

L–183 **Williamson, Jane. *New Feminist Scholarship: A Guide to Bibliographies*.** Old Westbury, N. Y.: Feminist Press, 1979.   Z7161.A1 W54

This volume cites 391 English-language bibliographies, reference lists, and reviews of literature on women's studies. More than half of the serially numbered entries are descriptively annotated, with occasional evaluations. They are disposed into thirty topical areas from Art and Music to Minority and Ethnic Women, Rape, Reference Sources, and Work. There is a section on Literature with eighteen items described. The volume concludes with indexes of authors and titles and a list of publishers' addresses.

L–184 **Ritchie, Maureen. *Women's Studies: A Checklist of Bibliographies*.** London: Mansell, 1980.   Z7961.A1 R57

A total of 452 entries plus an additional 37 appended are restricted to works in the English language published through August 1979. Entries are in subject groups and subgroups, and give author, title, publication date, number of pages, price, ISBN, bibliographical notes on series, and (if problematic) name and address of publishers. Subject groups include General, Area Studies, the Arts (subdivided), History, Language, and Literature. The slim volume concludes with author and keyword indexes.

L–185 **Humm, Maggie. *Annotated Critical Bibliography of Feminist Criticism*.** Boston: G. K. Hall, 1987
          Z7963.F44 H85 1987

This volume provides a guide to the most important feminist writings in every discipline, listing and describing over 900 English-language books and articles published in the United

States and Britain from 1950 through 1985, along with some seminal earlier works. Entries are chronologically arranged within eight subject areas: Feminist Theory; Literary Criticism; Sociology, Political Science and Economics; The Arts; Psychology; History; Anthropology; and Education. Considerable annotations highlight recurring issues and trace the development of feminist theory within each discipline.

L–186 **Women Studies Abstracts.** Vol. 1–. Rush, N. Y.: Rush Publishing Co., 1972–.   Z7962.W65

This standard source for citations to current research is published quarterly. Each issue includes abstracts of more than 200 articles, a list of current books and articles not abstracted, and often both book reviews and a bibliographic essay. It is arranged with tables of contents for recent issues of the leading journals in women's studies and special issues of other journals preceding the body of abstracts and other citations, which are arranged in nineteen subject categories. Following the main body is an enumeration of recent reviews of books on women and various indexes. There is an annual cumulated index to authors and subjects of abstracted articles and book reviews, but the indexing is not entirely reliable.

From 1972 through 1975 there was an annual, interdisciplinary, classified, and partly annotated bibliography published by the Women's Center at Barnard College, with the title *Women's Work and Women's Studies* [Z7961.W64]. The three published volumes covered the year's work for 1971, 1972, and 1973/74, listing completed works, research in progress, and organizations.

From 1983, there is a quarterly international abstracting service with a slight British bias, *Studies on Women Abstracts*, vol. 1– (Abingdon, Oxfordshire, England: Carfax, 1983–) [HQ1180.S78], which is in separate book and article sections, arranged by author and by periodical title, respectively. The last quarterly issue each year includes the annual author and subject index.

L–187 **Resources for Feminist Research / Documentation sur la recherche feministe** [former title: **Canadian Newsletter of Research on Women / Recherches sur la femme: Bulletin d'information canadien**]. Vol. 1–. Toronto: Ontario Institute for Studies in Education, Department of Sociology, 1972–. 3–4/yr.   HQ1101.R47

This quarterly publication, international in scope, cites research in progress, theses, and current bibliographies, updates information on current periodicals and other available resources, includes book reviews and conference reports, and is meant to serve as a general guide to current research in all aspects of women's studies. Occasional special numbers have also been published.

L–188 **Feminist Periodicals: A Current Listing of Contents.** Madison, Wisc.: Office of the Women's Studies Librarian-at-Large, University of Wisconsin System, 1981–.

This quarterly periodical includes both bibliographic and descriptive iinformation on periodicals and copies of contents pages. See also the new annual review, *Women's Annual: The Year in Review*, 1980– (Boston: G. K. Hall, 1981–) [HQ1402.W65], a yearly collection of essays reviewing developments in each field of women's studies research (e.g. domestic life, education, politics and law, popular culture, psychology, religion, work), with extensive appended bibliographies.

L–189 **Scholarly Journals in Women's Studies.**

Female Studies. Vol. 1–. Old Westbury, N. Y.: Feminist Press, 1970–. 1/yr. Volumes are titled individually.   No LC number

Feminist Forum: A Newsletter [former title, 1981 only: *Women's Studies International Quarterly Forum*]. Oxford: Pergamon, 1981–. 4/yr.
HQ1101.W776

FS   *Feminist Studies.* Vol. 1–. College Park: University of Maryland, Women's Studies Program, 1972–. 3–4/yr.   HQ1101.F18

Feminist Review. Vol. 1–. London: Feminist Review, 1979–.   HQ1154.F4465

Feministische Studien. Vol. 1–. Weinheim: Beltz, 1982–. 2/yr.   No LC number

Genders. Vol. 1–. Austin: University of Texas Press in cooperation with the University of Colorado at Boulder, 1988–. 3/yr.

JWSL   *Journal of Women's Studies in Literature.* Vol. 1–. Montreal: Eden Press, 1979–. 4/yr.
No LC number

Legacy: A Journal of Nineteenth-Century American Women Writers. Vol. 1–. Amherst: University of Massachusetts Press, 1984–. 2/yr. Reviews. Bibliographies.   PS149.L43

RFI   *Regionalism and the Female Imagination.* Vol. 1–. University Park: Pennsylvania State University Press, 1975–. 3/yr. Reviews.   No LC number

Resources for Feminist Research (see L–187).

Signs   *Signs: Journal of Women in Culture and Society.* Vol. 1–. Chicago: University of Chicago Press, 1975–. 4/yr. Reviews. Important review essays. "New Scholarship" bibliographical essays. Most distinguished in the field.   HQ1101.S5

Trivia: A Journal of Ideas. Vol. 1–. North Amherst, Mass.: Trivia, 1982–. 3/yr. Reviews.
HQ1402.T75

TSWL   *Tulsa Studies in Women's Literature.* Vol. 1–. Tulsa: University of Tulsa, 1982–. 2/yr. Reviews.
PN471.T84

University of Michigan Papers on Women's Studies. Vols. 1–5. Ann Arbor: Women's Studies Program, 1974–1978.   HQ1180.M5

Women and Language News. Vol. 1–. Stanford: Stanford University, Department of Linguistics, 1976–.   No LC number

W & L   *Women and Literature: A Journal of Women Writers and Literary Treatment of Women* [former title 1972–1974: *Mary Wollstonecraft Newsletter*]. Vol. 1–. New York: Holmes and Meier, 1973–. 1–4/yr. Reviews. Bibliography (see L–197).
PN481.W65

Women's Review of Books. Vol. 1–. Wellesley, Mass.: Wellesley College Center for Research on Women, 1983–. 12/yr.   HQ1101.W768

WS   *Women's Studies: An Interdisciplinary Journal.* Vol. 1–. New York: Gordon and Breach Science Publishers, 1972–. 3/yr. Reviews. HQ1101.W77

Women Studies Abstracts (see L–186).

Women's Studies International Forum [former title 1978–1981: *Women's Studies International Quarterly*]. Vol. 1–. Oxford: Pergamon, 1978–. 4/yr.
HQ1101.W775

Women's Studies Quarterly [former title 1972–1981: *Women's Studies Newsletter*]. Vol. 1–. Old Westbury, N. Y.: Feminist Press, 1972–81. 4/yr.
HQ1101.W68

L–190 **Some Frequently Recommended Works in Women's Studies.**

Bibliographical

Brewer, Joan Scherer, ed. *Sex and the Modern Jewish Woman: An Annotated Bibliography.* Fresh Meadows, N. Y.: Biblio Press, 1987.

Cantor, Aviva. *Bibliography on the Jewish Woman; A Comprehensive and Annotated Listing of Works Published, 1900–1978.* Fresh Meadows, N.Y.: Biblio Press, 1979.　Z7964.J4 C36

Conway, Jill K., Linda Kealey, and Janet E. Schulte. *Female Experience in Eighteenth- and Nineteenth Century America: A Guide to the History of American Women.* New York: Garland, 1982.　Z7961.C64

Fishburn, Katherine. *Women in Popular Culture: A Reference Guide.* 1982.　HQ1426.F685

Frey, Linda, et al. *Women in Western European History: A Select Chronological, Geographical and Topical Bibliography.* 2 vols. Vol. 1, *From Antiquity to the French Revolution.* Vol. 2, *Nineteenth and Twentieth Centuries.* Westport, Conn.: Greenwood, 1982–1984.　Z7961.F74 1982

Goodwater, Leanna. *Women in Antiquity: An Annotated Bibliography.* Metuchen, N.J.: Scarecrow, 1975.　Z7961.G66

Jacobs, Sue-Ellen. *Women in Perspective: A Guide for Cross-Cultured Studies.* Urbana: University of Illinois Press, 1974.　Z7961.J33

Jarrand, Mary E. W., and Phyllis R. Randall. *Women Speaking; An Annotated Bibliography of Verbal and Nonverbal Communication, 1970–1980.* New York: Garland, 1982.　HQ1426.J37

Leonard, Eugenie Andruss, Sophie Hutchinson Drinker, and Miriam Young Holden. *American Woman in Colonial and Revolutionary Times, 1565–1800: A Syllabus with Bibliography.* Philadelphia: University of Pennsylvania Press, 1962.　Z7964.U49 L4

Loytved, Dagmar. *Bibliographic Guide to Women's Studies.* 2 vols. Berlin: John F. Kennedy-Institut für Nordamerikastudien, Freie Universität Berlin, 1976.　Z7965.L69

Oakes, Elizabeth H. *Guide to Social Science Resources in Women's Studies.* Santa Barbara, Calif.: ABC-Clio, 1978.　Z7961.O23

Stansburg, Sherry. "A Bibliography of Feminist Criticism." *Canadian Newsletter of Research on Women* 6 (1977): 84–114. Sullivan, Kaye. *Films for, by, and about Women.* Metuchen, N. J.: Scarecrow, 1980.　PN1995.9.W6 S95

Thorne, Barrie, and Nancy Henley. *Language and Sex: Difference and Dominance.* Rowley, Mass.: Newberry House, 1975. Includes "Sex Differences in Language, Speech, and Nonverbal Communication," pp. 204–305.　P96.S48 L3

Weitz, Margaret Collins. *Femmes: Recent Writings on French Women.* Boston: G. K. Hall, 1985.　Z7964.F8 W44

General

Beauvoir, Simone de. *Second Sex.* Trans. and ed. by H. M. Parshley. New York: Knopf, 1953.　HQ1208.B352

Bowles, Gloria, and Renate Duelli-Klein, eds. *Theories of Women's Studies.* London: Routledge and Kegan Paul, 1983.　HQ1180.T48 1983

Browne, Alice. *Eighteenth Century Feminist Mind.* Detroit: Wayne State University Press, 1987.　HQ1599.E5 B76 1987

Cameron, Deborah. *Women and Linguistic Theory.* London: Macmillan, 1985.

Chodorow, Nancy. *Reproduction of Mothering: Psychoanalysis and the Sociology of Gender.* Berkeley and Los Angeles: University of California Press, 1978.　HQ759.C56

Daly, M. *Beyond God the Father: Toward a Philosophy of Women's Liberation.* Boston: Beacon Press, 1973.　HQ1154.D3

Douglas, Ann. *Feminization of American Culture.* New York: Knopf, 1977.　PS152.D6 1977

Du Bois, Ellen Carol, et al. *Feminist Scholarship: Kindling in the Groves of Academe.* Urbana: University of Illinois Press, 1986.　HQ1181.U5 F46 1986

Eisenstein, Hester. *Contemporary Feminist Thought.* Boston: G. K. Hall, 1983.　HQ1426.E39 1983

Ellman, Mary. *Thinking about Women.* New York: Harcourt Brace Jovanovich, 1968.　PN56.S5 E4

Fadermann, Lillian. *Surpassing the Love of Men: Romantic Friendship and Love Between Women from the Renaissance to the Present.* New York: Morrow, 1981.　HQ75.5.F33 1981

Friedan, Betty. *Feminine Mystique.* New York: Dell, 1963.　HQ1420.F7

Fritz, Paul S., and Richard Morton, eds. *Women in the Eighteenth Century and Other Essays.* Toronto: S. Stevens, 1976.　NX180.F4 W64

Gallup, Jane. *Daughter's Seduction: Feminism and Psychoanalysis.* Ithaca: Cornell University Press, 1982.　BF175.G33 1982

Gilligan, Carol. *In a Different Voice: Psychological Theory and Women's Development.* Cambridge: Harvard University Press, 1982.　HQ1206.G58

Greer, Germaine. *Female Eunuch.* New York: McGraw Hill, 1971.　HQ1206.G77 1971

Heilbrun, Carolyn C. *Reinventing Womanhood.* New York: Norton, 1979.　HQ1206.H43 1979

————. *Toward a Recognition of Androgyny.* New York: Knopf, 1973.　PN56.S52 H4

Hull, Gloria T., Patricia Bell Scott, and Barbara Smith. *But Some of Us Are Brave: Black Women's Studies.* Old Westbury, N. Y.: Feminist Press, 1982.　E185.86.A4 1982.

Jardine, Alice, and Paul Smith, eds. *Men in Feminism.* New York: Methuen, 1987.　HQ1154.M439

Keohane, Nannerl, Michelle Z. Rosaldo, and Barbara Gelpi. *Feminist Theory: A Critique of Ideology.* Chicago: University of Chicago Press, 1982. Originally published in *Signs.*　HQ1426.F474 1982

Kimball, Gayle, ed. *Women's Culture: The Women's Renaissance of the Seventies.* Metuchen, N. J.: Scarecrow, 1981.　HQ1426.W6634

Lakoff, Robin. *Language and Women's Place.* New York: Harper and Row, 1975.　HQ1206.L36 1975

Levin, Carole, and Jeanie Watson, eds. *Ambiguous Realities: Women in the Middle Ages and Renaissance*. Detroit: Wayne State University Press, 1987.
PN56.5 W64 1987

McConnell-Ginet, Sally, et al. *Women and Language in Literature and Society*. New York: Praeger, 1980.
HQ1206.W872

Maggio, Rosalie. *Nonsexist Word Finder: A Dictionary of Gender-Free Usage*. Phoenix, Ariz.: Oryx Press, 1987.
PE1689.M23 1987

Marks, Elaine, and Isabelle de Courtivron, eds. *New French Feminisms: An Anthology*. Amherst: University of Massachusetts Press, 1980.
HQ1617.N43

Matheson, Gwen. *Women in the Canadian Mosaic*. Toronto: Peter Martin, 1976.
HQ1453.W62

Millett, Kate. *Sexual Politics*. Garden City, N. Y.: Doubleday, 1970.
HQ1154.M5

Mitchell, Juliet. *Psychoanalysis and Feminism: Freud, Reich, Laing, and Women*. New York: Pantheon, 1974.
HQ1206.M56

———, and Jacqueline Rose, eds. *Feminine Sexuality: Jacques Lacan and the École Freudienne*. New York: W. W. Norton, 1982.
HQ21.L15213 1982

Pomeroy, Sarah B. *Goddesses, Whores, Wives and Slaves: Women in Classical Antiquity*. New York: Schocken, 1975.
HQ1134.P64

Rogers, Katherine M. *Feminism in Eighteenth-Century England*. Champaign: University of Illinois Press, 1982.
HQ1599.E5 R63 1982

Smith, Hilda. *Reason's Disciples: Seventeenth-Century English Feminists*. Urbana: University of Illinois Press, 1982.
HQ1599.E5 S62 1982

Stanley, Liz, and Sue Wise. *Breaking Out: Feminist Consciousness and Feminist Research*. London: Routledge and Kegan Paul, 1983.
HQ1154.S64 1983

Taylor, Barbara. *Eve and the New Jerusalem: Socialism and Feminism in the Nineteenth Century*. New York: Pantheon, 1983.
HQ1206.T33 1983

XVIII. WOMEN AND LITERATURE

L–191 **Todd, Janet M., ed. *Bibliography of Women and Literature*.** New York: Holmes and Meier, 1987.
Z2014.W65 B5 1987

Not yet published.

L–192 **Women and Literature Collective. *Women and Literature: An Annotated Bibliography of Women Writers*.** 3d ed. Cambridge, Mass., 1976.
Z5917.W6 S46

Originally published in 1973 by the then-named Sense and Sensibility Collective, this bibliography now includes 819 citations arranged by country, then chronologically by author. More than half of the entries are concerned with American and British authors, but writers of sixteen other countries, regions, or continents are also covered. Entries are carefully annotated from a uniformly feminist perspective. Brief biographical sketches are provided for major authors, but no attempt is made to provide complete primary bibliographies. There are sections for anthologies and for works of literary history and criticism, but the volume is predominantly a bibliography of primary works. It concludes with indexes of authors and of subjects.

L–193 **Myers, Carol Fairbanks. *Women in Literature: Criticism of the Seventies*.** Metuchen, N. J.: Scarecrow Press, 1976.
Z6514.C5 W643

This volume is arranged alphabetically by scholarly author, with unclassified, unannotated citations to "criticism," including interviews, book reviews, discussions of female characters, and all sorts of other items published between January of 1970 and the spring of 1975. At the end are gathered general works not limited to a single author or character. There is an index of critics and editors.

A sequel, by Carol Fairbanks, *More Women in Literature: Criticism of the Seventies*, was published in 1979 and includes items published 1970–1977 [Z6514.C5 W6432].

L–194 **Howe, Florence, and Deborah S. Rosenfelt. *Women Writers in Britain and the United States*.** [A Goldentree Bibliography.] In preparation.

L–195 **Schwartz, Nada Lacey. *Articles on Women Writers 1960–1975: A Bibliography*.** Santa Barbara, Calif.: ABC-Clio, 1977.
Z2013.5.W6 S37

A bibliography of popular and scholarly articles cited in twenty-one serial bibliographies and in *Dissertation Abstracts International*. Articles concern more than 600 English-speaking women writers from the Middle Ages to the present. Entries give author name, pseudonym, birth and death dates, and country. There follow citations to articles in three divisions, first bibliographical, then biographical and critical works, and then articles on individual works. A list of the twenty-one sources consulted is provided, as is an index of authors of articles. This careful compilation is particularly valuable as a starting point for locating materials on obscure writers.

A sequel, *Articles on Women Writers: V. 2: 1976–1984: A Bibliography*, was published in 1986.

L–197 **"[1974–] Bibliography of Literature in English by and about Women, 600–1960." *Women and Literature: A Journal of Women Writers and Literary Treatment of Women*,** vols. 3– (1975–).
PN481.W65

This annual bibliography began in the fall of 1975 with an issue titled "1974 Bibliography of Women in British and American Literature: 1660–1900." Nearly 200 journals were indexed in this original list, which was, however, limited to British and American women writers and to the period 1660–1900. The bibliography in subsequent years has been expanded both geographically to all English-speaking writers and chronologically back to 600 and forward to 1960. The number of journals indexed has increased steadily and now includes more than 400. Book reviews are cited. Occasionally annotated entries are arranged according to a unique decimal classification system whereby each book, dissertation, review, or article cited is assigned a number from 0 to 10 depending on the period and country of origin of the material it treats (0—general, 1—Great Britain 600–1600, 6—United States 1800–1900, 9—English-speaking writers) and a decimal from .0 to .9 depending on the literary genre with which it is concerned (.0—general, .4—women essayists, .7—male authors). Thus when entries are arranged in numerical order, all those concerned with works produced in Great Britain 1660–1800 by and for children will be located at 2.9 and following. The bibliography now appears about two years after the works it covers, the volume for 1978 having been published in the Winter 1980 issue of *Women and Literature*.

L-199 Some Frequently Recommended Works on Women and Literature.

Bibliographical

Addis, Patricia K. *Through a Woman's I: An Annotated Bibliography of American Women's Autobiographical Writings, 1946–1976.* Metuchen, N.J.: Scarecrow, 1983.   Z7963.B6 A32

Alcaron, Norma, and Sylvia Kossner. *Bibliography of Hispanic Women Writers.* Bloomington, Ind.: Chicano-Riqueño Studies, 1980.   Z1609.L7 A45

Batchelder, Eleanor. *Plays by Women: A Bibliography.* New York: Womanbooks, 1977.

Cortina, Lynn Ellen Rice. *Spanish-American Women Writers: A Bibliographical Research Checklist.* New York: Garland, 1983.   Z1609.L7 C66 1983

Coven, Brenda. *American Women Dramatists of the Twentieth Century.* Metuchen, N. J.: Scarecrow, 1982.   Z1231.D7 C68 1982

Daims, Diva, and Janet Grimes. *Toward a Feminist Tradition: An Annotated Bibliography of Novels in English by Women, 1891–1920.* New York: Garland, 1982.   Z2013.5.W6.D34 1982

Galerstein, Carolyn L., and Kathleen McNerney, eds. *Women Writers of Spain: An Annotated Bio-Bibliographical Guide.* Westport, Conn.: Greenwood, 1986.   Z2693.5.W6 W65 1986

Gelfand, Elissa D., and Virginia Thorndike Hules. *French Feminist Criticism: Women, Language and Literature: An Annotated Bibliography.* New York: Garland, 1985.   HQ1386.G44 1985

Goodfriend, Joyce D. *Published Diaries and Letters of American Women: An Annotated Bibliography.* Boston: G. K. Hall, 1987.   CT3260.G66 1987

Jacobus, Mary, ed. *Women Writing and Writing about Women.* London: Croom Helm in Association with the Oxford Women's Studies Committee, 1979.   PN481.W66 1979

Kaplan, Sydney Janet, "Review Essay: Literary Criticism." *Signs* 4 (1979): 514–527.   HQ1101.S5

Kolodny, Annette. "Review Essay: Literary Criticism." *Signs* 2 (1976): 404–421.   HQ1101.S5

Kowalski, Rosemary Ribich. *Women and Film: A Bibliography.* Metuchen, N. J.: Scarecrow, 1976.   Z5784.M9 K68

Kramer, Cheris, et al. "Review Essay: Perspectives on Language and Communication." *Signs* 3 (1978): 638–651.   HQ1101.S5

Marks, Elaine. "Review Essay: Women and Literature in France." *Signs* 3 (1978): 833–842.   HQ1101.S5

Messer-Davidow, Ellen, and Joan E. Hartman. *Women in Print I: Opportunities for Women's Studies Research in Language and Literature.* New York: MLA, 1982.   PN481.W656 1982

————. *Women in Print II: Opportunites for Women's Studies Publication in Language and Literature.* New York: MLA, 1982.   PN481.W656 1982

Palmegiano, E. M. *Women and British Periodicals, 1832–67: A Bibliography.* New York: Garland, 1976.   Z7962.P29

Reardon, Jean, and Kristine Thorsen. *Poetry by American Women, 1900–1975: A Bibliography.* Metuchen, N. J.: Scarecrow, 1979.   Z1229.W8 R4

Resnick, Margery, and Isabelle de Courtivron. *Women Writers in Translation: An Annotated Bibliography, 1945–1982.* New York: Garland, 1984.   Z7963.A8 R47 1984

Showalter, Elaine. "Review Essay: Literary Criticism." *Signs* 1 (1975): 435–460.   HQ1101.S5

Sweeney, Patricia, ed. *Women in Southern Literature: An Index.* Westport, Conn.: Greenwood, 1986.   PS261.W64 1986

General

Abel, Elizabeth, ed. *Writing and Sexual Difference.* Chicago: University of Chicago Press, 1982. Originally a special issue of *Critical Inquiry.*   PN481.W75 1982

Baym, Nina. *Women's Fiction: A Guide to Novels by and about Women in America, 1820–1870.* Ithaca, N. Y.: Cornell University Press, 1978.   PS149.B38

Benstock, Shari, ed. *Feminist Issues in Literary Scholarship.* Bloomington: Indiana University Press, 1987.   PN98.W64 F37 1987

Brown, Cheryl L., and Karen Olson, eds. *Feminist Criticism: Essays on Theory, Poetry, and Prose.* Metuchen, N. J.: Scarecrow, 1978.   PS147.F4

Brownstein, Rachel M. *Becoming a Heroine: Reading about Women in Novels.* New York: Viking, 1982.   PR830.H4 B76 1982

Cornillon, Susan Koppelman, comp. *Images of Women in Fiction: Feminist Perspectives.* Rev. ed. Bowling Green, Ohio: Bowling Green University Popular Press, 1973.   PN3411.C6 1973

Diamond, Arlyn, and Lee R. Edwards, eds. *Authority of Experience: Essays in Feminist Criticism.* Amherst: University of Massachusetts Press, 1977.   PR151.W6 A9

Donovan, Josephine, ed. *Feminist Literary Criticism: Explorations in Theory.* Lexington: University Press of Kentucky, 1975.   PN98.W64 F4

Eagleton, Mary, ed. *Feminist Literary Theory: A Reader.* Oxford: Blackwell, 1986.   PR65.W6

Ferguson, Mary Anne. *Images of Women in Literature.* 3d ed. Boston: Houghton Mifflin, 1981.   PN6071.W7 F4 1981

Fetterley, Judith. *Resisting Reader: A Feminist Approach to American Fiction.* Bloomington: Indiana University Press, 1978.   PS374.W6 F4

Flynn, Elizabeth A., and Patrocinio P. Schweickart, eds. *Gender and Reading: Essays on Readers, Texts, and Contexts.* Baltimore: Johns Hopkins University Press, 1986. [Includes "A Selected Annotated Bibliography."]   Z1039.W65 G46 1986

Garvin, Harry R., ed. *Women, Literature, Criticism.* Bucknell Review (Lewisburg, Pa.), vol. 24, no. 1 (1978).   AP2.B887 v. 24 no. 1

Greene, Gayle, and Coppelia Kahn, eds. *Making a Difference: Feminist Literary Criticism.* New York: Methuen, 1985.   PN98.W64 M35 1985

Hardwick, Elizabeth. *Seduction and Betrayal: Women and Literature.* New York: Random House, 1974.   PN471.H3 1974

Hoffman, Lenore, and Margo Culley, eds. *Women's Personal Narratives: Essays in Criticism and Pedagogy.* New York: MLA, 1985.   PS42.W65 1985

Hoffman, Lenore, and Deborah Rosenfelt, eds. *Teaching Women's Literature from a Regional Perspective.* New York: MLA, 1982.   PS42.T4 1982

Homans, Margaret. *Women Writers and Poetic Identity.* Princeton, N. J.: Princeton University Press, 1980.
PR589.W6 H6 1980

Humm, Maggie. *Feminist Criticism: Women as Contemporary Critics.* New York: St. Martin's Press, 1986.
PN98.W64 H86 1986

Jelinek, Estelle C. *Tradition of Women's Autobiography: From Antiquity to the Present.* Boston: G. K. Hall, 1986.
CT25.J45 1986

Kolodny, Annette. *Land before Her: Fantasy and Experience of the American Frontiers, 1630–1860.* Chapel Hill: University of North Carolina Press, 1984.
E179.5.K64 1984

———. *Lay of the Land: Metaphor as Experience and History in American Life and Letters.* Chapel Hill: University of North Carolina Press, 1975.   PS88.K65

———. "Some Notes on Defining a 'Feminist Literary Criticism'." *CI* (1975): 75–92, and the reply by William W. Morgan, ibid., 807–816.

Lawrence, Margaret. *School of Femininity: A Book for and about Women As They Are Interpreted through Feminine Writers of Yesterday and Today.* New York: F. A. Stokes, 1936.   PR830.W62 L38

MacCarthy, Bridget G. *Women Writers: Their Contribution to the English Novel, 1621–1744.* London: University of London Press, 1944.   PR113.M3

———. *Later Women Novelists, 1744–1818.* Vol. 2 of *Female Pen.* Cork, Ireland: Cork University Press, 1947.   PR111.M22

Marting, Diane E., ed. *Women Writers of Spanish America: An Annotated Bibliography.* New York: Greenwood Press, 1987.   Z1609.L7 W63 1987

Miller, Nancy K., ed. *Poetics of Gender.* New York: Columbia University Press, 1986.   PN481.P64 1986

Moers, Ellen. *Literary Women.* Garden City, N.Y.: Doubleday, 1976.   PN471.M63

Moi, Toril. *Sexual / Textual Politics.* London: Methuen, 1985.   PN98.W64

Mora, Gabriela, and Karen S. Van Hooft, eds. *Theory and Practice of Feminist Literary Criticism.* Ypsilanti, Mich.: Bilingual Press, 1982.   PN98.W64 T47

Ostriker, Alicia Suskin. *Stealing the Language: The Emergence of Women's Poetry in America.* Boston: Beacon Press, 1986.   PS147.O8 1986

Rogers, Katherine M. *Troublesome Helpmate: A History of Misogyny in Literature.* Seattle: University of Washington Press, 1966.   PN56.W6 R6

Ruthven, K. K. *Feminist Literary Studies: An Introduction.* Cambridge: Cambridge University Press, 1984.
PR77.R88 1984

Shockley, Ann Allen. *Afro-American Women Writers 1746–1933: An Anthology and Critical Guide.* Boston: G. K. Hall, 1988.   PS508.N3 A36 1988

Showalter, Elaine. *Female Malady: Women, Madness, and Culture 1830–1980.* New York: Pantheon, 1985.
RC451.4.W6 S56 1986

———. *Literature of Their Own: British Women Novelists from Bronte to Lessing.* Princeton, N. J.: Princeton University Press, 1977.   PR115.S5

———, ed. *New Feminist Criticism: Essays on Women, Literature and Theory.* New York: Pantheon, 1986. Includes a classified bibliography.
PN98.W64 N48 1985

———, ed. *Women's Liberation and Literature.* New York: Harcourt Brace Jovanovich, 1971.   HQ1121.S54

Spacks, Patricia Meyer. *Female Imagination: A Literary and Psychological Investigation of Women's Writing.* New York: Knopf, 1972.   PR115.S6

Squier, Susan M., ed. *Women Writers and the City: Essays in Feminist Literary Criticism.* Knoxville: University of Tennessee Press, 1984.   PR830.C53 W66 1984

Sternberg, Janet, ed. *Writer on Her Work: Contemporary Women Writers Reflect on Their Art and Their Situation.* New York: Norton, 1980.   PS151.W7 1980

Stimpson, Catherine R. *Where the Meanings Are: Feminism and Cultural Spaces.* New York: Routledge, 1988.
PN98.W64 S75 1988

Todd, Janet. *Feminist Literary History.* New York: Routledge, 1988.   PN98.W64 T63 1988

———. *Women's Friendship in Literature.* New York: Columbia University Press, 1980.   PR858.W6 T6

Toth, Emily. *Regionalism and the Female Imagination: A Collection of Essays.* New York: Human Sciences Press, 1984.   PS152.R4 1984

Weedon, Chris. *Feminist Prctice and Poststructuralist Theory.* Oxford: Blackwell, 1987.   HQ1154.W42 1987

Williams, Merryn. *Women in the English Novel, 1800–1900.* New York: St. Martin's Press, 1984.
PR830.W6 W54 1984

XIX. WOMEN AND BRITISH LITERATURE

L–200 **Kanner, Barbara, ed. *Women of England from Anglo-Saxon Times to the Present: Interpretive Bibliographical Essays.* Hamden, Conn.: Archon, 1979.   HQ1599.E5 W65**

An introduction and eleven chapters, each by a different authority, discuss the history of women in England from Anglo-Saxon society (2 chapters), Norman and Plantagenet England (2 chapters), the Age of Transition 1485–1714, the eighteenth century (2 chapters), and the Victorian period (2 chapters), through the earlier twentieth century (2 chapters). Each chapter has extensive notes and a lengthy bibliography. The focus throughout is on historical source materials, including records and documents, literary texts, unwritten sources, and secondary sources of all types.

L–202 **Backscheider, Paula R., Felicity Nussbaum, and Philip B. Anderson. *Annotated Bibliography of Twentieth-Century Critical Studies of Women and Literature, 1660–1800.* New York: Garland, 1977.   Z2012.B13**

A total of 1,568 numbered entries treat, first, general books and articles on the Restoration and eighteenth century, including literary criticism, social history, biography, and art history. A second section, on literature, is arranged by genre. Finally, there are primary and secondary bibliographies of some sixty-five Restoration and eighteenth-century women writers. Some entries are annotated. The volume concludes with an index to Restoration and eighteenth-century women and an index to authors of books and articles.

For women authors before 1660, see Patricia Gartenberg and Nena Whittemore, "Checklist of English Women in Print, 1475–1640," *BB* 34 (1977): 1–13; Norma Greco and Ronaele Novotny, "Bibliography of Women in the English Renaissance," *University of Michigan Papers in Women's Studies* 1 (1974): 29–57 [HQ1101.M53]; Elizabeth Hageman, "Images of Women in Renaissance Literature: A Selected Bibliography of Scholarship," *Women Studies Newsletter* 5 (1977):

15–19; and Susan Schibanoff, "Images of Women in Medieval Literature: A Selected Bibliography," *Women Studies Newsletter* 4 (1976): 10–11.

XX. WOMEN AND AMERICAN LITERATURE

L–205 **Hinding, Andrea, ed. *Women's History Sources: A Guide to Archives and Manuscript Collections in the United States.*** 2 vols. New York: R. R. Bowker, 1979.
Z7964.U49 W64

These volumes cite more than 18,000 collections in some 1,600 repositories. Entries, arranged by locality, give the collection title, a physical description (types of items, dates spanned), information about access and bibliographical control, and a concise description of the collection's contents.

Other primary reference works for the history of American women include Cynthia E. Harrison, ed., *Women in American History: A Bibliography* (Santa Barbara, Calif.: ABC-Clio, 1979) [Z7962.H37], a set of abstracts drawn from the data base of *America: History and Life* (F–54); Barbara Haber, *Women in America: A Guide to Books, 1963-1975, with an Appendix on Books Published 1976–1979* (Urbana: University of Illinois Press, 1981) [Z7964.U49 H3 1981]; Gerda Lerner, *Bibliography in the History of American Women*, 3d ed., rev. (Bronxville, N. Y.: Sarah Lawrence College, 1978) [Z7961.L4 1978]; and Virginia P. Terris, *Women in America: A Guide to Information Sources* (Detroit: Gale, 1980) [Z7964.V49 T45]. This last work contains 2,495 serially numbered items dispersed into chapters on General References; Role, Image, Status; History; Women's Movement; Education; Sociology; Employment; Health, Mental Health, and Sexuality; Women in the Arts; and Biographies and Autobiographies; along with a series of useful appendixes listing centers, collections, organizations, and so on.

L–206 **Mainiero, Lina, ed. *American Women Writers: A Critical Reference Guide from Colonial Times to the Present.*** 4 vols. New York: Ungar, 1979–1982.   PS147.A4

These volumes present signed biographical and critical essays on more than 1,500 American women writers. Selected for inclusion are not only writers of the first rank but also representative authors of popular literature and children's literature. Essays conclude with comprehensive primary bibliographies and selected bibliographies of secondary works. Reviewers have noted many factual errors and some dubious critical judgments, and so this work should be used with caution. An abridged edition in two volumes, edited by Langdon Lynne Faust, has been published (New York: Ungar, 1983) [PS147.A42 1983].

L–207 **White, Barbara A. *American Women Writers: An Annotated Bibliography of Criticism.*** New York: Garland, 1977.
Z1229.W8 W45

This work treats general works of criticism through 1975; for works on individual writers, other bibliographies (including Myers, L–193) must be consulted. The 413 entries are divided into ten chapters, as follows: Biography; Criticism on Specific Groups of Female Writers; Specific Topics (Genres and Themes); Feminine Sensibility; The Problems of Women Writers; Phallic Criticism—Discriminatory Treatment of Women Writers; Feminist Criticism; and Miscellaneous. There is no subject index, but there is an index of critics and editors.

L–208 **Duke, Maurice, Jackson R. Bryer, and M. Thomas Inge, eds. *American Women Writers: Bibliographical Essays.*** Westport, Conn.: Greenwood, 1983.   Z1229.W8 A44 1983

This volume presents a total of twenty-four bibliographical essays by specialists on leading women writers including Anne Bradstreet, Djuana Barnes, Pearl Buck, Kate Chopin, Ellen Glasgow, Carson McCullers, Margaret Mitchell, Marianne Moore, Anais Nin, Sylvia Plath, Katherine Anne Porter, Anne Sexton, and Edith Wharton. Essays include sections on bibliography, editions, manuscripts, biography, criticism, and further study.

ENGLISH LITERATURE

I.   BIBLIOGRAPHIES

M-1 Howard-Hill, Trevor H. *Bibliography of British Literary Bibliographies [BBLB].* Oxford: Clarendon Press, 1969.

Z2011.A1 H68

This is the first in a multivolume series, the *Index to British Literary Bibliography.* For the most part a list of true bibliographies, this volume attempts to record all publications in English which list and describe British literary works written from 1475 to the present. The bibliographies cited were published, with few exceptions, after 1890. Generally excluded are catalogs of manuscripts and of letters, list of specifically non-English incunabula or booksellers' catalogs, library accession lists, theses, exhibition catalogs of less than ten pages, library catalogs of general literature, auction and sale catalogs, and retrospective catalogs of private English libraries. Shakespeare is excluded for separate treatment (see below).

There are seven sections. The first includes general bibliographies and Bibliographies of and Guides to British Literature. The second lists General and Period Bibliographies. The third enumerates Regional Bibliographies for England, Wales, Scotland, and Ireland. The fourth section records bibliographies relating to Presses and Printing. The fifth section lists bibliographies pertaining to Forms and Genres alphabetically from "Almanacs and Prognostications" through "Ballads," "Poetry," and "Proverbs," to "Unfinished Books." The sixth section lists subject bibliographies alphabetically from "Alchemy" through "Rhetoric" to "Witchcraft." The last section lists author bibliographies alphabetically by author, and includes bibliographies of primary works, of secondary works, and those which combine both sorts.

Entries giving author, shortened title, and collation are briefly but helpfully annotated and are arranged chronologically. Reviews are indicated. The index is organized by author, title, and subject and includes the names of major collectors whose books are in public collections. There are occasional cross-references.

This is the first volume of a series titled *Index to British Literary Bibliography*, which will cover books, parts of books, and periodicals written in England which contribute to the bibliographical and textual examination of "literary" material dating from the establishment of printing in England to the 1960s. The second volume of the series, published in 1971, is titled *Shakespearian Bibliography and Textual Criticism: A Bibliography* (O-42) [Z2011.A1 H68 vol. 2]. It contains a "Supplement" to volume 1 on pages 179–322 which corresponds to the structure and arrangement of the original volume. A revised and enlarged second edition of volume 1 was published in 1986; it incorporates entries from the "Supple-

ment" in volume 2 and additional titles of items published through 1969.

The third volume of the *Index* will treat bibliographical materials published before 1890 and is not expected to appear for some years. Volumes 4 and 5, published in 1979, carry the title *British Bibliography and Textual Criticism: A Bibliography* (Y-1) [Z2011.A1 H68 vols. 4, 5] and enumerate works concerned with the production and transmission of texts. The fifth volume also contains, under Shakespeare, a supplement to the second volume on *Shakespearian Bibliography and Textual Criticism.*

All four volumes that have appeared to date have been indexed in volume 6, *British Literary Bibliography and Textual Criticism, 1890–1969: An Index* (Oxford, 1980) [Z2011.A1 H68 vol. 6], which incorporates entries from volume 5's Shakespeare supplement as if they occurred in volume 2. This volume has an author-title index and a separate subject index. Users should first consult the introduction to its elaborate structure; once it is understood, however, the redundancy principle on which the index is constructed makes it easy to locate materials quickly. Though this entire work has been criticized for an undue complexity of organization, it is an invaluable resource and amply repays the effort required to learn how to use it with ease.

Planned volumes 7 and 8 will treat *British Literary Bibliography, 1970–1979* and *Dissertations on British Literary Bibliography to 1980*, respectively. Also planned are an index to all volumes and decennial supplements. Howard-Hill's article, "Index to British Literary Bibliography," in *TEXT: Transactions of the Society for Textual Scholarship* 2 (1985): 1–12, clarifies changes in principles of inclusion and other alterations which have been introduced into this monumental bibliographical effort since its earlier days.

M-2 Northup, Clark S., et al. *Register of Bibliographies of the English Language and Literature, with Contributions by Joseph Quincy Adams and Andrew Keogh.* New Haven: Yale University Press, 1925.

Z2011.N87

This work presents a closed bibliography of bibliographies on both the language and the literature of the English-speaking peoples current to 1 October 1924, though the majority of items are from 1922 or earlier. Language and literature are defined so broadly as to make this almost a general bibliography of bibliographies. Both separately published works and those in books and periodicals are included. Entries include the author, title, publisher, date, and collation. There are notes and many references to reviews. Arrangement of the more than 12,000 entries is alphabetical in two sections: General, and then Individual Authors and Topics. There are occasional descriptive annotations. A large section of additions and corrections is followed by a detailed author-title index. This volume is continued by Van Patten (M–3).

M–3 Van Patten, Nathan. *Index to Bibliographies and Bibliographical Contributions Relating to the Work of American and British Authors, 1923–1932.* Stanford: Stanford University Press, 1934.   Z1225.A1 V2

Designed as a sequel to Northup (M–2), this volume includes books, articles, notes, catalogs, facsimiles, and reviews but is limited to strictly enumerative and descriptive bibliograpies. Entries are grouped by subject author, alphabetically, and are given in alphabetical order by the author or compiler of the bibliography or bibliographical contribution. In the case where there are many entries for a single subject author, they are arranged in a general list followed by those pertaining to each subject work, arranged alphabetically by the work's title. There are numerous cross-references. At the end is a list of general and comprehensive bibliographies the contents of some of which are analyzed in the main body of the work. The work concludes with an index of authors and compilers giving a short title or brief identification of the work or author under which their compilation appears.

M–5 Wright, Andrew H. *Reader's Guide to English and American Literature.* Glenview, Ill.: Scott, Foresman, 1970.   Z2011.W73

This highly selective guide treats reference works, the most reliable editions, biographies, and standard critical works for some 250 leading English and American authors. Books only are cited. A general section for English Literature (including Guides to Literary Study; Serial Bibliographies; Reference Works; Political, Social and Intellectual History; Language; Folklore; Poetry; Drama; Fiction; and Criticism) is followed by sections on Old English, Middle English, the Sixteenth Century, the Earlier Seventeenth Century, the Restoration and Eighteenth Century; the Romantic Period; the Victorian Period (1830–1890); the Early Modern Period (1890–1920); and the Recent Past (1920–1960). Within each period section, divisions include Bibliography; Literary History; Political, Social, and Intellectual History; Collections; the Genres; and then the leading authors in chronological order. The American Literature portion is similarly arranged with a general section (similarly subdivided) followed by period divisions for Colonial and Revolutionary America, the Nineteenth Century, and the Twentieth Century, each of which is further subdivided as are the periods of English literature. The work concludes with citation of some works important in the study of general, classical, and modern European history and literature; some further important reference works; leading dictionaries; and some works on cultural and intellectual history. There is an index of authors.

M–6 McPherson, David C., and Robert L. Montgomery, Jr. *Student's Guide to British and American Literature: A List of Significant Works, with Special Sections on Linguistics and Criticism.* Austin: Department of English, University of Texas, 1967.   Z2011.M2

This slim volume presents select reading lists of primary and supplementary readings, the latter of which are divided into lists of primary and secondary works. After a preface and a list of major bibliographies, histories, and guides to British and American literature, the work is disposed into eleven sections, as follows: English Literature to 1500; English Literature 1500–1660; 1660–1800; 1800–1900; 1900–Present; American Literature, Beginning to 1800; 1800–1860; 1860–1920; 1920–Present; English Language and Linguistics; Literary Criticism. Within each section are subdivisions for genres and major authors, and within the subsections are primary and supplementary reading lists.

M–7 *Bibliography for English Undergraduate Concentrators.* Selected and compiled by Members of the Tutorial Board and of the Department of English and American Literature and Language . . . Harvard University. Edited by Kevin P. VanAnglen. 4th ed. Cambridge: Harvard College, 1981.   Z2011.B52 1983

This guide refers students to both the principal and related primary and secondary readings for the major periods of English and American literary history. It is disposed into seven sections: 1, English Literature from the Beginnings to 1500; 2, From 1500 to 1660; 3, From 1660 to 1790; 4, From 1790 to 1890; 5, American Literature to 1890; 6, English and American Literature from 1890 to the Present; 7, General Historical and Critical Books. These sections are further classified into subperiods, major genres, and major authors. Lists give first the principal primary readings within a subheading and then related primary and secondary readings.

M–8 Some Additional Guides to Reference Works for Students of English Literature.

In addition to Altick and Wright (A–10), Bond (A–11), Kennedy (A–12), Bateson and Meserole (A–13), Patterson (A–14), Kehler (A–15), and Schweik and Riesner (A–16), there are a number of other guides available, some of which have distinct and noteworthy features.

Of these, the most valuable is Inglis Freeman Bell and Jennifer A. Gallup, *Reference Guide to English, American and Canadian Literature: An Annotated Checklist of Bibliographical and Other Material* (Vancouver: University of British Columbia Press, 1971) [Z2011.B42]. The 569 annotated entries are disposed into two sections treating General Materials (Bibliographies, Indexes and Annual Surveys, Book Reviews, Indexes to Collections, Biography, Handbooks, Dictionaries, Literary Histories and Critical Surveys, Auxiliary Subjects) and individual authors. In addition to a glossary, there are indexes of authors and of authors-as-subjects. In addition to its high-quality annotations this volume is useful for its inclusion of materials on Canadian literature.

Differently conceived is James Thompson's *English Studies: A Guide for Librarians to the Sources and Their Organization*, 2d ed. (London: Bingley, 1971) [Z688.E6 T48 1971]. Originally published in 1968 as the *Librarian and English Literature*, the volume contains fifteen chapters of discursive commentary on standard reference works and on the selection, cataloging, classification, and exploitation of an English literature collection.

M–10 *Cambridge Bibliography of English Literature [CBEL].* Edited by F. W. Bateson. With Supplement: A.D. 600–1900. Edited by George Watson. 5 vols. Cambridge: Cambridge University Press, 1940–1957.   Z2011.B28

The *Cambridge Bibliography*, begun as a modernization of the bibliographies appended to individual chapters of the *Cambridge History of English Literature* (M–32), records the titles and editions of writings in English or Latin, in book form, which possess some literary interest, by authors born in the British Empire who were established before 1900, along with bibliographies and relevant biographical and critical material published through the mid–1930s. The bibliography excludes the literature of the United States but includes brief sections on Welsh, Gaelic, and Celtic material and also includes bibliographies of Commonwealth English literature. Selection of materials for inclusion was entrusted to a group of specialist editors, under the direction of the general editor.

The contents of the individual volumes should be studied through their tables of contents, though a more detailed account of each will be found in the individual entries devoted to it below, as follows: volume 1: Anglo-Saxon, A.D. 600–1100 (see N–10); Middle English, A.D. 1100–1500 (see N–10); Renaissance to Restoration, 1500–1660 (see O–10); volume 2: Restoration to Romantic Revival, 1660–1800 (see P–10); volume 3: Nineteenth Century (see Q–10). Volume 4 is an extensive subject, author-as-subject, and title index (for periodicals and anonymous books) to the whole work. The *Supplement* volume covers all sections of the work and includes secondary material published through 1955. It is not indexed.

An introductory section in volume 1 lists works such as general bibliographies, histories, dictionaries, and works on the English language which belong to no one historical section. Each of the historical sections begins with an introductory portion containing items of intellectual, social, and political background. Subsequent to this are divisions by the major forms, Poetry, Drama, and Fiction, along with sections for such broad classes as Prose, Periodicals, History, Philosophy, and Education. Entries are then grouped by individual authors or topics, with bibliographies listed first, followed by primary materials (including collected editions and, for separate works, all editions and translations published within fifty years of the date of the first, along with reference to important or convenient modern editions). Only English-language biographical and critical material is listed, but this is arranged chronologically. The only disturbance to this convenient arrangement, which allows an immediate overview of the history of an author's reception, is that all works by a secondary author are cited immediately after the first one.

Concise Cambridge Bibliography of English Literature 600–1950 [CCBEL] was edited by George Watson (2d ed. with corrections and additions; Cambridge, 1965) [Z2011.W3]. From the *CBEL*, its *Supplement*, and files treating the first half of the twentieth century, he selected the primary works and a handful of standard secondary works for some 400 "major" writers. There is a general introductory section covering Bibliographies, General Literary History and Criticism, and the like, followed by six sections covering Old English, Middle English, Renaissance, Restoration and Eighteenth Century, Nineteenth Century, and Twentieth Century respectively.

Although much of the material in the *CBEL* has been incorporated in the *NCBEL* (M–11), the earlier work must still be consulted for all those classes of materials excluded from the new work. These include "background" works, older works of scholarship judged no longer up to date by the compiling bibliographers of the *NCBEL*, and all materials associated with Commonwealth English literature.

M–11 **New Cambridge Bibliography of English Literature [NCBEL].** Edited by George Watson and I. R. Willison. 5 vols. Cambridge: Cambridge University Press, 1969–1977.
Z2011.N45

The *New Cambridge Bibliography* is the result of a general revision of the original 1940 volumes of the *CBEL* (M–10), into which the 1957 *Supplement* entries have been integrated and to which an additional volume on the twentieth century has been added. New secondary material through the mid–1960s has been added, with some titles dated in the early 1970s. The *NCBEL* includes only authors active before 1950 and born or mainly resident in the British Isles (thus T. S. Eliot and Auden are included; Pound is not), excluding Celtic literature. Selection of both primary and secondary materials for inclusion has been entrusted to a group of more than 200 bibliographical authorities working under the general editors. Lists of contributors with initials are in the front matter of each volume.

The contents of the individual volumes may be viewed best from their individual tables of contents, though each is more closely described in its own entry below as follows: volume 1, to 1660 (see N–11 and O–11), published in 1974; volume 2, 1660–1800 (see P–11), published in 1971; volume 3, 1800–1900 (see Q–11), published in 1969; and volume 4,

1900–1950, ed. I. R. Willison (see R–11), published in 1972. General exclusions include parts of books (in the secondary bibliographies), superceded studies, insignificant notes, encyclopedia articles, ephemeral publications and unpublished dissertations. The Index volume, compiled by J. D. Pickles, was published in 1977.

General arrangement of each volume is by author and subject under the basic forms Poetry, Drama, and Novel. There are also large General sections, and sections on Prose and Periodicals. Though much background material included in the *CBEL* has been omitted, there are still representative bibliographies of works in history, theology, philosophy, scholarship; and science; representative ephemeral literature (pamphlets of political, religious, and literary controversy); and representative works in such literary side-paths as law, letter writing, oratory, sport, and travel literature. There are also extensive treatments of pre–1500 manuscripts; the history of printing and publishing; and newspaper and magazine publishing. Entries are ordered chronologically with primary materials first and secondary following, under each author or subject heading; bibliographical aids are listed regularly at the beginning of each author or subject grouping. Author listings are divided into bibliographies, collections, primary works, and secondary material. Editions and translations follow the entry for a primary work. Secondary material is not classified by works treated, however, so that the entire listing for an author must be scanned when searching for materials on only one work. Titles are short and omissions are not indicated. The arrangement in chronological order is disturbed only in the case of secondary authors, where all entries by an individual are listed after the first one and thus out of overall chronological order. In spite of this unfortunate practice, it is still possible to use the generally chronological arrangement to apprehend both a primary author's career and his critical and scholarly reception.

Each individual volume has a separate author-subject index; the final Index volume has a more complete index including all main subordinate headings from the four bibliographical volumes. It contains all primary authors (including those cited in sections devoted to minor figures); names of foreign authors cited in sections on literary relations; many general subject entries; titles of newspapers and periodicals with names of their publishers, proprietors, and editors; titles of important anonymous works; pseudonyms; both maiden and married names of women; personal titles; and a comprehensive system of cross-references.

For bibliographies of the English literatures of India, Canada, South Africa, Australia, and New Zealand, the original *CBEL* must be used, since they have been omitted from the new version. Also eliminated are the sections on social and historical background, though many titles from those sections have been introduced under different headings. With its faults and shortcomings, including those more specifically enumerated in the entries on its individual volumes, the *NCBEL* is still the resource of first resort for full primary and secondary bibliographies of major and minor authors and major and minor subjects associated with the study of English literature. It is an indispensable reference tool of the first importance.

A one-volume abstract, the *Shorter New Cambridge Bibliography of English Literature*, ed. George Watson, was published in 1981 [Z2011.S417 1981]. The primary sections listing an author's work have been generally retained; secondary listings have been reduced to a few major works of biography and criticism; both primary and secondary material on writers who are not "literary" has been cut extensively; and whole sections (such as "Book Production and Distribution," "Literary Relations with the Continent," "Travel," "Sport," "Education," and "Newspapers and Magazines") have been omitted. The effect is to narrow the scope of "English Literature" to the traditional canon of mainstream writers of imaginative literature.

M–15 **Dobrée, Bonamy, ed.** *Introductions to English Literature*. 5 vols. London: Cressett Press, 1938–1940. 3d ed. London: Cressett Press, 1961–1966.

PR83.I615 [vol. 5: PR471.M8]

The intention of this series is to provide beginning students with both orientation and bibliographical guidance. Each of the volumes contains, therefore, both a discursive introductory treatment of leading topics associated with the history of English literature during its period and a classified, annotated, selective primary and secondary bibliography. The goal of the series is to reveal the historical (social, political, economic, intellectual, and artistic) contexts of literature. The bibliographies are therefore particularly rich in reference to such matters.

The volumes in the series are described more particularly in individual entries (see N–12, O–12, P–13, Q–30, and R–12). They reflect an infrequent periodization of English literary history, based upon changes in the primary audiences for whom the majority of texts were composed, as follows: The Beginnings to 1509; The Renaissance, 1510–1688; Augustans and Romantics, 1689–1830; The Victorians and After, 1831–1914; The Present Age.

M–21 **Modern Humanities Research Association.** *Annual Bibliography of English Language and Literature [ABELL]*. [1920–]. Vol. 1–. Cambridge: Cambridge University Press, 1921–.

Z2011.M69

The British equivalent of the Modern Language Association, the Modern Humanities Research Association publishes this *Annual Bibliography* as counterpart to the English portion of the *MLA International Bibliography* (L–50). This is a universal, serial, unannotated but classified bibliography of books, articles, essays in festschriften and other composite volumes, dissertations, and (an important and distinctive feature) reviews, pertaining to English, American, and Commonwealth language and literature, along with English folklore, bibliography, and other ancillary studies. Materials are not segregated into national groups. The twenty sections into which they are divided, each with an individual section editor, are as follows: Bibliography; Biography; Academies, Learned Societies, Miscellanies; Language, General; The Sounds of Speech; Dictionaries and Grammars; Vocabulary; Syntax; Orthography, Punctuation, Handwriting; Ancillary Studies; Literature, General; Language, Literature, and the Computer; Old English; Middle English; Fifteenth Century; Sixteenth; Seventeenth; Eighteenth; Nineteenth; Twentieth. Individual Sections move from general to particular subsections (those in the period sections, for example, are divided thus: Anthologies; Literary History and Criticism; Social History; Documents, Historical Biography; Individual Authors). Entries are serially numbered and extensively cross-referenced. Reviews are cited immediately under the entry for the book reviewed (short-title entries being used in subsequent years when additional reviews appear).

Each volume concludes with a selective index of authors, editors, compilers, and translators of works cited; a selective index of anonymous works cited; and a selective index of works in facsimile.

Because this work analyzes a somewhat different series of journals from that analyzed in the *MLA International Bibliography* (a list of journals covered, with abbreviations, appears in each volume) and because it cites reviews, it should always be used in conjunction with the *MLA Bibliography*. In addition, for the period prior to 1956 when MLA cited only work by American scholars, the MHRA *Bibliography* is the only comprehensive source for British and Continental scholarship. All current comparisons between the two bibliographies conclude by recommending that the scholar always consult both, though the *MLA Bibliography* is published considerably sooner.

For more current citations than those found here or in *MLA*, see the *Humanities Index* (D–16), the *British Humanities Index* (D–17), the *American Humanities Index* (D–18), the *Arts and Humanities Citation Index* (D–19), and the *Essay and General Literature Index* (E–81), all of which are less reliable and less complete but appear with greater frequency and more promptly after the publication date of cited work.

M–22 *Year's Work in English Studies [YWES]*. [1919–.] London: For the English Association by Oxford University Press, 1921–.

PE58.E6

This annual selective critical survey of studies in English and (since 1954) American language and literature consists of a series of descriptive and evaluative bibliographical essays on various author, subject, period, and genre subdivisions, written by individual scholars. The scope and quality of the essays varies from year to year and compiler to compiler. American literature has been included since 1954 (volume 35), African, Caribbean and Canadian literature in English were added in 1982 (volume 63), and Australian, New Zealand, and Indian literature in English were added in volume 64 (for 1983). Books and articles are treated. Footnotes provide bibliographical data for works discussed in the essays.

Currently, volumes include eighteen sections, as follows: 1, Literary History and Criticism: General Works; 2, English Language; 3, Old English Literature; 4, Middle English Literature Excluding Chaucer; 5, Middle English: Chaucer; 6, The Earlier Sixteenth Century; 7, Shakespeare; 8, English Drama 1550–1660, Excluding Shakespeare; 9, The Later Sixteenth Century, Excluding Drama; 10, The Earlier Seventeenth Century, Excluding Drama; 11, Milton; 12, The Later Seventeenth Century; 13, The Eighteenth Century; 14, The Nineteenth Century, Romantic Period; 15, The Nineteenth Century, Victorian Period; 16, The Twentieth Century; 17, American Literature to 1900; 18, American Literature, Twentieth Century. Sections are subdivided for convenience of reference into various genre and author sections. Indexes by authors, authors-as-subjects, titles, and subjects complete the annual volumes. While these surveys are helpful reviews, they should not be relied upon either as providing authoritative selected bibliographies or as presenting consensus judgments about the value of studies discussed.

M–23 *Abstracts of English Studies: An Official Publication of the National Council of Teachers of English [AES]*. Vol. 1–. Champagne, Ill.: NCTE, 1958–1980; Calgary: University of Calgary, 1980–.

PE25.A16

Ten issues a year (four a year since 1980) present serially numbered brief informational abstracts summarizing periodical articles on English and American literature, on world literature in English and related languages, and on the English language. Organization has varied from an arrangement in volumes 1–12 by journal in a "current contents" format to the present arrangement in four parts, General, English, American, and World Literature in English and Related Languages. The general part has four sections: I. General Studies (Aesthetics, Bibliographies, Comparative Literature, Education, Literary Theory, Literature and Society, Literature and the Other Arts, Prosody, Research Methods and Resources, Rhetoric, Schools and Creeds, Theory of Criticism, Translation, Women's Studies); II. Bibliography (Analytical, Descriptive, Editing, History of Printing and Publishing); III. Language (History, Linguistics, Theoretical Studies); and IV. Themes and Types (Characters, Plot Patterns, Subjects, Myth, Drama, Fiction, Poetry, Prose, Humor and Satire, Film, Folklore, Travel Literature). The English part has ten sections: I. Particularism and Regionalism (Wales, Scotland, Northern Ireland, Jewish, etc.); II-IV (equivalent to General II-IV); V. Medieval to 1485; VI. Renaissance to 1660; VII. Restoration and Eighteenth Century; VIII. Romantic; IX. Victorian; and X. Modern. The American part is in eight sections: I. Particularism and Regionalism (Black, Jewish, Southern, etc.); II-IV (equivalent to General II-IV); V. Seventeenth and Eighteenth Centuries; VI. Nineteenth Century, 1800–1870; VII. Nineteenth Century, 1870–1900; and VIII. Twentieth Century. The fourth part, on World Literature in English and Related Languages, is arranged by continent or country. Anglo-Irish literature written after 1900 is included in this part. In period subcategories further division groups individual entries by authors, by titles of anonymous works, and by such rubrics as Studies of Characters, Plot Patterns, Subject, Drama, Fiction, Poetry, Prose, and general topics associated with that particular period.

Journals covered have varied extremely from issue to issue, making use of the work quite frustrating. Current issues cover more than 1,500 journals, with more than 3,000 articles abstracted annually. Many covered journals are relatively obscure, making *Abstracts* a source of information on some items that might otherwise pass unnoticed. There is a limited subject and name index in each individual issue. The annual index is somewhat fuller, also including names of scholars and additional subject subcategories.

As an often informative supplement to other sources of current bibliographical information, *Abstracts* is valuable; because of its variability in coverage, however, it cannot serve as a fundamental source of bibliographical control.

M–24 *Literary Criticism Register: A Monthly Listing of Studies in English & American Literature [LCR].* Vol. 1–. DeLand, Fla.: Literary Criticism Register, 1983–. Z2011.L76

The purpose of *LCR* is to provide timely access to current scholarship through monthly listings. Citations include current articles in recent issues of journals, as well as current books and dissertations. Current contents of more than 300 covered journals are listed, with each listed article assigned a serial number, as is each item in the other listings of each issue. A list of journals treated in a monthly issue precedes the citations of current contents. The recent-books listing is taken from current issues of the *American Book Publishing Record* (see C–29), and titles are grouped into the general categories of Bibliographies, General and Comparative American Literature, and English Literature. Similar categories are used to group listings of recent dissertation titles taken from current issues of *Dissertation Abstracts International* (E–7). At the conclusion of all monthly listings are found subject and author indexes, keyed to the serial numbers used in that issue. Serial numeration of entries continues through the year, and the subject and author indexes are cumulated semiannually and annually.

M–25 **Scholarly Journals in English and American Literature.**

Anglia *Anglia: Zeitschrift für englische Philologie.* Vol. 1–. Tübingen: Niemeyer, 1878–. 2 double issues/yr. Reviews. Cumulative indexes to vols. 1–50 (in vol. 54) and 51–75 (1961). See also the *Beiblatt zur Anglia*, published 1890–1944, with additional reviews and bibliographical essays. From 1969 on, see also the annual *English and American Studies in German: Summaries of Theses and Monographs: A Supplement to Anglia* (E–22). PE3.A6

ArielE *Ariel: A Review of International English Literature.* Vol. 1–. Calgary, Alberta: University of Calgary, 1970–. 4/yr. Reviews. PR1.R352

British Studies Monitor. Vol. 1–. Brunswick, Me.: Bowdoin College, 1969–. Reviews. DA4.B75

CLAJ *CLA Journal: Official Quarterly Publication of the College Language Association.* Vol. 1–. Atlanta: Morehouse College, 1957–. 4/yr. Reviews. P1.A1 C22

DQR *Dutch Quarterly Review of Anglo-American Letters.* Vol. 1–. Amsterdam: Rodopi, 1971–. 4/yr. Reviews. Bibliographic essay on recent studies in every issue. PE9.D87

ELH *ELH: A Journal of English Literary History.* Baltimore: Johns Hopkins University Press, 1934–. 4/yr. Published "The Romantic Movement: A Selective and Critical Bibliography for 1936 [–1948]" (see Q–25). PR1.E5

Englische Studien: Organ für englische Philologie. Vols. 1–76. Leipzig [and Heilbrun], 1877–1939. Reviews. Indexes to volumes for 1877–1898 (1902) and 1899–1917 (1924).

English *English: Journal of the English Association.* Vol. 1–. London: Oxford University Press, 1935–. 3/yr. Reviews PE11.E5

ELN *English Language Notes.* Vol. 1–. Boulder: University of Colorado, 1963–. 4/yr. Reviews. Published "The Romantic Movement: A Selective and Critical Bibliography for 1964 [- 1978]" (see Q–25). PE1.E53

ES *English Studies [Amsterdam]: A Journal of English Language and Literature.* Vol. 1–. Lisse: Swets en Zeitlinger, 1919–. 6/yr. Reviews. Annual bibliography: 2–4 essays titled "Current Literature," from 1925 on, discuss both creative writing and criticism, literary history, and literary biography. Cumulative index to vols. 1–40 (1960). PE1.E55

ESA *English Studies in Africa* (see M–118).

E&S *Essays and Studies by Members of the English Association.* Vol. 1–. London: The English Association, 1910–. 1/yr. PR13.E4

EA *Études anglaises: Grande Bretagne, États-Unis.* Vol. 1–. Paris: Librairie Didier, 1937–1940, 1952–. 4/yr. Reviews. The "Révue des Révues" gives contents of journals received. The "Chronique" prints summaries of French university theses and dissertations and lists proceedings and contents of collections of essays published by learned societies and research centers in France. PR1.E8

RES *Review of English Studies: A Quarterly Journal of English Literature and the English Language.* Vol. 1–. Oxford: Clarendon Press, 1925–. 4/yr. Reviews. A "Summary of Periodical Literature" lists contents of journals received. PR1.R4

SEL *SEL: Studies in English Literature, 1500–1900.* Vol. 1–. Houston, Tex.: Rice University, 1961–. 4/yr. Bibliographical reviews of studies in the English Renaissance, Elizabethan and Jacobean drama, the Restoration and eighteenth century, and the nineteenth century. (see O–7, O–32, P–4, and Q–5). PR1.S82

YES *Yearbook of English Studies.* Vol. 1–. Cambridge: Modern Humanities Research Association, 1971–. 1/yr. Reviews. PE1.Y43

ZAA *Zeitschrift für Anglistik und Amerikanistik.* Leipzig: VEB Verlag Enzyklopädie, 1953–. 4/yr. Reviews. 2 annual enumerative bibliographies. PR1.Z4

See also the Gerstenberger and Hentrick *Directory of Periodicals Publishing Articles on English and American Literature and Language* (Z–45). Many articles on English and American literature will also be found in journals of general and comparative literature (see L–9), journals on the modern languages and literatures (see L–57), and in journals on the Germanic languages and literatures (see L–108).

II.   LITERARY HISTORIES

For chronological ancillae (including the *Annals of English Literature*) to English literary history see F–80 ff.; for topographical ancillae (including various guides to literary England) see F–110 ff.

M–30   **Baugh, Albert C., ed.   *Literary History of England.* 4** vols. 2d ed., rev. New York: Meredith Appleton, 1967.
PR83.B3 1967

This work, first published in 1948, is a comprehensive history of the pre–World War II literature of England which succeeds in being both authoritative and readable, generally speaking. It is in four Books, which are published both together in one volume and separately:

Book I.   *Middle Ages (to 1500)*, by Kemp Malone and Albert Baugh;

Book II.   *Renaissance (1500–1660)*, by Tucker Brooke and Matthias A. Shaaber;

Book III.   *Restoration and Eighteenth Century (1660–1789)*, by George Sherburn and Donald F. Bond;

Book IV.   *Nineteenth Century and After (1789–1939)*, by Samuel Chew and Richard Altick.

Anglo-Scottish and Anglo-Irish literature are included; literature of the United States and Commonwealth English literature are excluded. Some medieval Latin and French writers in England are treated.

The text is supplied with excellent footnotes drawing attention to standard editions and important bibliographical and critical books and articles on authors and subjects. Footnotes, as well as the entries in the bibliographical supplements at the end of each book, are sometimes briefly annotated.

The revised edition retains the text of the original but is made more current through the creation of Bibliographical Supplements (current to the mid–1960s) for each Book. The supplemented pages of the text show an asterisk beside the page number, referring readers to additional materials cited in the supplement. Each Book has a table of contents and an author-subject index to both the text and the Bibliographical Supplement.

In most contexts Baugh remains the literary history of first resort for students of English literature; it is unquestionably the one most often cited.

M–31   ***Oxford History of English Literature [OHEL].*** 12 vols. in 15 planned. Edited by F. P. Wilson and Bonamy Dobrée. Oxford: Clarendon Press, 1945–.   LC numbers vary

This work, still in progress, is intended to provide a comprehensive survey of English literary history from the beginning to the twentieth century in a series of fifteen volumes by individual authors working independently, each of whom is assigned a period of roughly fifty years. The only uniformity among the volumes is their division into a narrative portion, followed by an extended chronology, followed by an extensive primary and secondary bibliography. The individual volumes published or scheduled for publication are as follows:

Vol. 1, pt. 1. *English Literature before the Norman Conquest.* In preparation.

Vol. 1, pt. 2. *Middle English Literature.*, by J. A. W. Bennett, edited and completed by Douglas Gray, 1986.
PR255.B45 1986

Vol. 2, pt. 1. *Chaucer and the Fifteenth Century*, by Henry Stanley Bennett. 1947; corrected ed., 1948.
PR255.B43

Vol. 2, pt. 2. *English Literature at the Close of the Middle Ages*, by Edmund K. Chambers. 1945.   PR291.C5

Vol. 3. *English Literature in the Sixteenth Century* (Excluding Drama), by C. S. Lewis, 1954.   PR411.L4

Vol. 4, pt. 1. *English Drama, 1485–1585*, by Frank P. Wilson and George K. Hunter. 1968.   PR641.W58

Vol. 4, pt. 2. *English Drama, c. 1586–1642.* In preparation.

Vol. 5. *English Literature in the Earlier Seventeenth Century, 1600–1660*, by Douglas Bush. 2d ed. rev. 1962.
PR431.B8 1962

Vol. 6. *English Literature of the Late Seventeenth Century*, by James Sutherland. 1969.   PR437.S9 1969

Vol. 7. *English Literature in the Early Eighteenth Century, 1700–1740*, by Bonamy Dobrée. 1959.   PR445.D6

Vol. 8. *English Literature in the Mid-Eighteenth Century*, by John Butt, ed. and completed by Geoffrey Carnall, 1979.   PR441.B83 1979

Vol. 9. *English Literature, 1789–1815*, by W. L. Renwick. 1963.   PR447.R4 1963

Vol. 10. *English Literature, 1815–1832*, by Ian Jack. 1963.
PR457.J24

Vol. 11. *English Literature, 1832–1890: Excluding the Novel*, by Paul Turner. 1989.   No LC number yet

Vol. 12. *Eight Modern Writers.* J. I. M. Stewart. 1963.
PR461.S8

Vol. 13. *English Literature, 1890–1945.* In preparation.

The narrative components of most volumes treat the historical context of the literature of their period, including intellectual, economic, political, religious, and social history. The developments in each of the major forms of literature as well as the literary careers of major and minor authors are treated at length. Because of their variability, however, individual volumes have received extremely varied critical receptions. In particular, volumes 3 and 5 have been universally well received, volume 9 has been very adversely reviewed, and volume 10 has been accorded a rather cool reception.

The extended, elaborate chronologies present a more detailed conspectus of concurrent literary and historical events than will be found in the more general chronologies (see F–65 ff.). The extensive bibliographies are divided into sections treating General Bibliography and Works of Reference, General Collections and Anthologies, General Literary Histories and Criticism, Special Literary Studies, Background Studies, and sections on major and minor individual authors. The entries are both descriptively and evaluatively annotated and are particularly valuable in the case of minor figures for which few other bibliographical aids are available. Each volume concludes with a full author-title-subject index.

M–32   ***Cambridge History of English Literature [CHEL].*** Edited by Adolphus W. Ward and Alfred R. Waller. 15 vols. Cambridge: Cambridge University Press, 1907–1916. Reprinted without bibliographies, 1932–1933.   PR83.C22

This work presents a comprehensive account of English literature to the end of the nineteenth century. Included are Anglo-Irish and Commonwealth English literature; American literature is excluded. The definition of literature is very broad and the work treats a variety of allied subjects, including the literatures of science, philosophy, politics, and economics; parliamentary eloquence; scholarship and the works of schools, universities, and libraries; the pamphlet literature of religious and political controversy; newspapers and magazines; printing and bookselling; books dealing with precepts, manners, and social life; domestic letters; street songs; travel accounts; and records of sports events. The fourteen volumes are disposed into between fourteen and twenty chapters each, with each chapter written by a single scholar whose goal is to present a coherent and continuous narrative of one certain chronological or generic movement. The volumes are ordered by periods, as follows:

Vol. 1. *From the Beginnings to the Cycles of Romance.*

Vol. 2. *End of the Middle Ages.*

Vol. 3. *Renaissance and Reformation.*

Vol. 4. *Prose and Poetry: Sir Thomas North to Michael Drayton.*

Vol. 5. *Drama to 1642, part 1.*

Vol. 6. *Drama to 1642, part 2.*

Vol. 7. *Cavalier and Puritan.*

Vol. 8. *Age of Dryden.*

Vol. 9. *From Steele and Addison to Pope and Swift.*

Vol. 10. *Age of Johnson.*

Vol. 11. *Period of the French Revolution.*

Vol. 12. *Nineteenth Century, part 1.*

Vol. 13. *Nineteenth Century, part 2.*

Vol. 14. *Nineteenth Century, part 3.*

Vol. 15. *General Index.*

At the end of each volume there is a bibliography arranged by chapter headings and subheadings and then by bibliographical subcategories such as collected editions, separate works, correspondence, biography, and criticism. The volume bibliographies are followed by chronologies of important events and publications. Finally, each volume has an index of names with birth and death dates.

The last volume presents a general index to the whole work which is indispensable, particularly given the unexpected locations of chapters on certain topics. For example, the chapter on all Scottish poetry before Burns is located in volume 9; the chapter on the literature of travel from 1700 to 1900 will be found in volume 14. An overview of these arrangements will be found prefaced to the index volume in the form of a list of contents for the entire history, giving chapter titles and the names of the responsible scholars. A list of corrections and additions precedes the index proper.

Though now quite out of date, the *CHEL* still remains valuable for its treatment of minor and out-of-the-way topics and authors, many of which have been neglected in more recent histories. And the work's broadly inclusive definition of literature renders it more nearly a history of English civilization than a history of English literature narrowly defined. Though the bibliographies were so out of date as to be omitted in the 1932–1933 reprinting, they are indexed in Northup (M–2) and remain useful precisely because they treat a number of authors and topics on which more recent bibliographies are difficult to find. There are slight variations between the different editions of *CHEL*; the English edition is preferred.

M–33 Sampson, George. *Concise Cambridge History of English Literature, with Additional Chapters on the Literature of the United States of America and the Mid-Twentieth Century of the English-Speaking World by R. C. Churchill [CCHEL].* 3d ed. Cambridge: Cambridge University Press, 1969. PR85.S34 1969

Originally published in 1941, this work is based on the *CHEL* (M–32), with one chapter given to each of the *CHEL* volumes. Texts follow the order of the original work and sometimes even the wording, though this volume has been favorably reviewed for having its own stylistic integrity. The third edition introduces many additions and changes in the last chapters of the original, along with a series of additional chapters on American literature and on twentieth-century British and Commonwealth literature.

M–34 *[Sphere] History of Literature in the English Language.* 11 vols. London: Barrie and Jenkins, 1969–.
LC numbers vary

Each volume in this history to 1960 of English, Commonwealth, and American literature and language is under the direction of a single editor; it consists of a series of essays on individual authors, groups of authors, literary movements, and other relevant topics. Each essay is written by a specialist, and extended footnotes along with primary and secondary selected bibliographies are appended to each. Each volume also includes a chronology and an index.

The individual volumes and their editors and publication dates are as follows:

Vol. 1. *Middle Ages.* Edited by Whitney F. Bolton. Rev. ed. 1986. PR166.B6 1986

Vol. 2. *English Poetry and Prose, 1540–1674.* Edited by Christopher B. Ricks. Rev. ed. 1986.
PR533.E5 1986

Vol. 3. *English Drama to 1710.* Edited by Christopher B. Ricks. 1971. PR625.R5

Vol. 4. *Dryden to Johnson.* Edited by Roger H. Lonsdale. Rev. ed. 1986. PR437.L6 1986

Vol. 5. *Romantics* (in preparation).

Vol. 6. *Victorians.* Edited by Arthur Pollard. 1970.
PR463.P6 1970

Vol. 7. *Twentieth Century.* Edited by Bernard Bergonzi. 1970. PR473.B4 1970

Vol. 8. *American Literature to 1900.* Edited by Marcus Cunliffe. Rev. ed. 1986. PS88.C8 1986

Vol. 9. *American Literature since 1900.* Edited by Marcus Cunliffe. 1975. PS221.A65

Vol. 10. *English Language.* Edited by Whitney F. Bolton. 1975. PE1072.E55

Vol. 11. *Commonwealth Literature* (in preparation).

M–35 *Longman Literature in English Series.* Edited by David Carroll and Michael Wheeler. London and New York: Longman, 1985–. LC numbers vary

The volumes of this series are meant to serve as critical introductions to the major genres of English literature in their historical contexts from Anglo-Saxon times to the present. In addition to covering all periods of English and American literature, the series includes volumes on criticism and literary theory and on intellectual and cultural contexts. The individual volumes published to date include chronologies and both general bibliographies and individual author biobibliographies.

Volumes planned (and published) in the series are as follows:

English Literature before Chaucer. By Michael Swanton. 1987. PR166.S96 1987

English Literature in the Age of Chaucer.

English Medieval Romance. By W. R. J. Barron. 1987.
PR321.B37 1987

English Poetry of the Sixteenth Century. By Gary Waller. 1986. PR531.W33 1986

English Poetry of the Seventeenth Century. By George Parfitt. 1985. PR541.P3 1985

English Poetry of the Eighteenth Century, 1700–1789.

English Poetry of the Romantic Period, 1789–1830. By J. R. Watson. 1985. PR590.W33 1985

English Poetry of the Victorian Period, 1830–1890. By Bernard Richards. 1988. PR591.R5 1988

English Poetry of the Early Modern Period, 1890–1940.

English Poetry since 1940.

English Drama before Shakespeare.

English Drama: Shakespeare to the Restoration, 1590–1660. By Alexander Leggatt. 1988.   PR651.L44 1988

English Drama: Restoration and the Eighteenth Century, 1660–1789. By Richard W. Bevis. 1988.
PR691.B48 1988

English Drama: Romantic and Victorian, 1789–1890.

English Drama of the Early Modern Period, 1890–1940.

English Drama since 1940.

English Fiction of the Eighteenth Century, 1700–1789. By Clive T. Probyn. 1987.   PR851.P76

English Fiction of the Romantic Period, 1789–1830. By Gary Kelly. 1988.   PR868.R73.K45 1988

English Fiction of the Victorian Period, 1830–1890. By Michael Wheeler. 1985.   PR871.W49 1985

English Fiction of the Early Modern Period, 1890–1940. By Douglas Hewitt. 1988.   No LC number yet

English Prose of the Renaissance, 1550–1700.

English Prose of the Eighteenth Century.

English Prose of the Nineteenth Century.

Criticism and Literary Theory from Sidney to Johnson.

Criticism and Literary Theory from Wordsworth to Arnold.

Criticism and Literary Theory from 1890 to the Present.

Sixteenth Century: The Intellectual and Cultural Context of English Literature, 1500–1599.

Seventeenth Century: The Intellectual and Cultural Context of English Literature, 1600–1699. By Graham Parry. 1989.   PR438.S63 P37 1989

Eighteenth Century: The Intellectual and Cultural Context of English Literature, 1700–1789. By James Sambrook. 1986.   PR441.S33

Romantic Period: The Intellectual and Cultural Context of English Literature, 1789–1830.

Victorian Period: The Intellectual and Cultural Context of English Literature, 1830–1890.

Twentieth Century: The Intellectual and Cultural Context of English Literature, 1890 to the Present.

American Literature before 1889.

American Poetry of the Twentieth Century.

American Drama of the Twentieth Century.

American Fiction, 1865–1940. By Brian Lee. 1987.
PS377.L44 1987

American Fiction since 1940.

Twentieth-Century America.

Irish Literature since 1800.

Scottish Literature since 1700.

Australian Literature.

Indian Literature in English.

Southern African Literature in English.

African Literature in English: East and West.

Caribbean Literature in English.

Canadian Literature in English. By W. J. Keith. 1985.
PR9184.3.K4 1985

M–36 **Craig, Hardin, ed. *History of English Literature.*** 4 vols. New York: Oxford University Press, 1950. Reprinted with a new preface in two [later four] volumes. New York: Collier Books, 1962.   PR85.C682

Each volume in this history is organized as a sustained narrative covering backgrounds, movements, groups of writers, and individual writers. Each volume is meant to stand on its own, though there was close collaboration among the four au-

thors, according to the editor. Bibliographies are included in each volume, though neither in text nor in bibliographical reference is this history designed to be primarily a scholarly resource. On the contrary, narrative interest and readability are preferred to copiousness or meticulousness of detail. The individual volumes are as follows:

Vol. 1. Anderson, George K. *Old and Middle English Literature from the Beginnings to 1483.*

Vol. 2. Craig, Hardin. *Literature of the English Renaissance, 1485–1660.*

Vol. 3. Bredvold, Louis. *Literature of the Restoration and Eighteenth Century, 1660–1798.*

Vol. 4. Beach, Joseph W. *Literature of the Nineteenth and Early Twentieth Centuries.*

A fifth volume, never published, was to have covered English Literature of the Twentieth Century.

M–37 **Legouis, Emile, and Louis Cazamian. *History of English Literature, 650–1914.*** Translation by Helen Douglas Irvine and W. D. MacInnes of *Histoire de la littérature anglaise* (Paris: Hachette, 1924). New rev. ed. London: Macmillan, 1964.   PR93.L43 1964

This relatively brief history of English literature, first translated in 1916–1927, and again in 1934 by V. F. Boyson and J. Coulson (Oxford), is organized as a single continuous narrative emphasizing literary movements and tendencies rather than the developing work of individual authors. Footnotes present both biographical sketches of authors and cite relevant primary and secondary material. The volume ends with an index to authors and titles of anonymous works.

A new edition contains an additional Book VIII, Modern Times, on the period 1914 to the 1960s prepared by Raymond Las Vergnas, with bibliographies by Donald Davie and Pierre Legouis (London: Dent, 1965) [PR93.L43 1971].

M–38 **Some Other Histories of English Literature.**

Albert, Edward. *History of English Literature.* 5th ed. Edited by J. A. Stone. London: Harrap, 1979.
PR85.A45 1979

Daiches, David. *Critical History of English Literature.* 2d ed. 2 vols. New York: Ronald Press, 1970. For reading, not reference.   PR83.D29

Day, Martin S. *History of English Literature: A College Course Guide.* 3 vols. Garden City, N.Y.: Doubleday, 1963–1964.   PR83.D35

Evans, Sir Ifor. *Short History of English Literature.* 2d ed. London: Penguin, 1963. 5 chapters on poetry, 3 on drama, 3 on the novel, and 2 on prose.
PR85. E8 1963

Fowler, Alastair. *History of English Literature.* Harvard University Press, 1987.   PR83.F65 1987

Garnett, Richard, and Edmund Gosse. *English Literature: An Illustrated Record.* 4 vols. London: Heinemann, 1903. New ed. with a chapter by John Erskine on the literature of 1902–1922. New York: Macmillan, 1923. Reprint (4 vols. in 2). New York: Macmillan, 1935. Illustrations, some in color, including illuminations and portraits, taken chiefly from contemporary prints.   PR83.G3 1923

Quennell, Peter. *History of English Literature—Illustrated.* New York: Meridian, 1973.   PR83.Q4 1973

Saintsbury, George. *Short History of English Literature.* London: Macmillan, 1929. 11 books, with interchapters, written from a later-nineteenth-century historiographical perspective: e.g., book 10: "The Triumph of Romance."   PR85.S3 1929

Schirmer, Walter P. *Geschichte der englischen und amerikanischen Literatur von den Anfängen bis zur Gegenwart.* 5th ed. Revised by Arno Esch. Tübingen: Niemeyer, 1968. Standard German survey, with extensive bibliography.   PR95.S392 1968

Standop, Ewald, and Edgar Mertner. *Englische Literaturgeschichte.* 3d ed., rev. and enl. Heidelberg: Quelle und Meyer, 1976. Survey focused on major work of major authors.   PR95.S8 1976

Taine, Hippolyte Adolphe. *History of English Literature.* Translation by H. Van Laun of *Histoire de la littérature anglaise*, 4 vols. (Paris: Hachette, 1863–1864). Rev. ed. 3 vols. London: Colonial Press, 1908.   PR93.T4 1908A

Tibble, Anne. *Story of English Literature. A Critical Survey.* London: Owen, 1970.   PR83.T5

M–39 **Ford, Boris, ed. *New Pelican Guide to English Literature.*** Rev. and exp. ed. 9 vols. in 10. Harmondsworth: Penguin, 1982–1988.   PR83.N49 1982

This is a substantially revised third edition of a work first published in 1954–1961 and revised in 1961–1963. Each period volume of this historically organized critical guide contains four sorts of materials, disposed into a number of chapters, each written by an individual authority. These are (1) an account of the social, cultural, and intellectual context of literature in the period; (2) a survey of the literature of the period; (3) essays discussing the careers of some of the chief writers in each period, as well as some of the leading movements, genres and other topics of concern to students of the period; and (4) a bibliography citing primary works, biographies, and general critical works. The dates of individual essays are not given, but many are reprinted from the earlier editions and are thus rather out of date. The individual volumes are as follows:

Vol. 1, part 1. *Medieval Literature: Chaucer and the Alliterative Tradition.* 1983.

Vol. 1, part 2. *Medieval Literature: The European Inheritance.* 1983.

Vol. 2. *Age of Shakespeare.* 1982.

Vol. 3. *From Donne to Marvell.* 1982.

Vol. 4. *From Dryden to Johnson.* 1982.

Vol. 5. *From Blake to Byron.* 1982.

Vol. 6. *From Dickens to Hardy.* 1982.

Vol. 7. *From James to Eliot.* 1983.

Vol. 8. *Present.* 1983.

Vol. 9. *Literature of the United States.* 1988.

In addition, see *Guide for Readers to the New Pelican Guide to English Literature.* 1984 [Z2011.G85 1984], which contains biobibliographical appendixes updating those found in volumes 1–8.

III. HANDBOOKS AND READER'S ENCYCLOPEDIAS

See also the handbooks in section L and references there to additional ones in various other sections.

M–40 ***Oxford Companion to English Literature [OCEL].*** 5th ed. By Margaret Drabble. Oxford: Oxford University Press, 1985.   PR19.D73 1985

A ready-reference tool intended primarily for the British user with queries arising from reading in English literature. The dictionary arrangement of some 9,000 entries includes English (with some American and European) authors born before 1940, with brief biographies, works, and dates; titles with generic and thematic descriptions and, for major works, plot summaries; fictive and historical character sketches; references to literary terms, societies, movements, periods, prizes, theories, periodicals, places and topics; and allusions to proper names of persons and places. There are extensive cross-references and brief bibliographical notes for major authors. Appendixes concluding the volume treat censorship (of literature, journalism, and the theater) from the sixteenth century to the present; the history of the English Copyright Law; and the calendar (Julian, Gregorian, saints' days and church feasts, regnal years of the English monarchs).

An abridgment by Dorothy Eagle of her 4th edition (1967) revision of Sir Paul Harvey's original work, *Concise Oxford Dictionary of English Literature*, 2d ed. (London, 1970) [PR19.C65 1970], contains some additional articles on literary periods and subjects as well as more articles on contemporary English and American writers.

For references and allusions not found here, consult companions, encyclopedias, and handbooks pertinent to the subject field (e.g., American history), type of reference (e.g., quotation, literary term, French author), literary period (e.g., medieval), or genre (e.g., drama).

M–41 ***Cambridge Guide to English Literature.*** Compiled and edited by Michael Stapleton. Cambridge: Cambridge University Press, 1983.   PR85.C28 1983

A ready-reference, alphabetically arranged companion, wide in scope—treating British, American, Irish, South African, White Commonwealth, West Indian, African, and Indian authors—but adversely reviewed and to be used with caution. See the review by Claude Rawson in *TLS*, 20 May 1983, p. 508.

A new edition, *Cambridge Guide to Literature in English*, edited by Ian Ousby, is scheduled for 1989 publication [PR85.C29 1988].

M–42 ***New Century Handbook of English Literature.*** Edited by Clarence L. Barnhart with the assistance of William D. Halsey. Rev. ed. New York: Appleton-Century-Crofts, 1967.   PR19.N4 1967

Originally published in 1956 and not very much revised, this American work presents a dictionary arrangement of some 14,000 entries treating authors (with brief biographies and primary bibliographies) and titles (with brief summaries) of English, Irish, Anglo-American, and Commonwealth literature. There are also entries on literary characters, mythological allusions, genres, and other literary terms (with quotations illustrating usage). Intended for the use of American readers, this work indicates British pronunciations and in general assumes an audience needing some ready-reference help with allusions to British and Continental history and geography. Articles tend to be longer than those in the *Oxford Companion* (M–40).

M–43 *Webster's New World Companion to English and American Literature.* Edited by Arthur Pollard. New York: World, 1973.   PR19.W4 1973

This work, prepared by eighty-nine contributors for the use of the general reader, contains brief biographies of some 1,100 authors (some living) along with brief articles on national literatures, literary genres, and literary movements. An appendix of secondary bibliographies for the articles is arranged in alphabetical order at the end of the volume. A list of contributors, with initials, precedes the main body of the text.

M–44 Gillie, Christopher. *Longman Companion to English Literature.* 2d ed. London: Longman, 1978.   PR19.G54 1977

First published in 1972, this companion is intended for readers studying English literature both in Britain and, particularly, elsewhere. There is, thus, an emphasis on information likely to be needed by foreign readers. The work is arranged in two sections, the first containing seven omnibus essays, the second containing a series of brief articles in a dictionary arrangement. The seven essays are each outlined at their beginning and are carefully divided into sections so that readers need not be obligated to read entire texts. Their subjects are: Political History and Institutions of England 1066 to the Present Day; Society and the Arts; Religion, Philosophy, and Myth: 1350 to the Present Day; Narrative Literature from Romance to the Novel: 1350 to the Present Day; Drama in Britain; Poetic Form since 1350; and the History of English Critical Thought. Terms in the essays are asterisked if informative articles appear on them in the second portion of the *Companion*. These articles treat authors, titles, and topics with emphasis and space devoted to those prominent in scholastic circles during the last fifty years or so. Biographical articles give facts; those on works summarize contents; all give brief secondary bibliographies. Matters associated with American and Commonwealth English literature are treated only when they are authors, works, or topics central also to the British tradition of English literature. There are some illustrations, some maps, and a guide to pronunciation.

M–46 *Chambers's Cyclopaedia of English Literature: A History Critical and Biographical of Authors in the English Tongue from the Earliest Times till the Present Day with Specimens of Their Writings.* Edited by David Patrick. Revised by J. Liddell Geddie. 3 vols. Philadelphia: J. B. Lippincott, 1922–1938.   PR83.C4 1938

This work, originally compiled by Robert Chambers (1802–1871), began with an 1841 plan to publish a chronological conspectus of the history of English literature broadly conceived, constructed, in part, by means of extracts from works, accompanied by biographical and critical articles. A first edition in two volumes appeared in 1844, a second in 1858, a third edition revised by Carruthers in 1876, a fourth in 1888. The most current version is based on the new edition in three volumes by David Patrick which was published in 1901 and subsequently revised by J. L. Geddie. Articles, many signed, were contributed by authorities and include many facsimiles and portraits, as well as appended notes and bibliographies, along with massive numbers of illustrative extracts from the literary works discussed. The three volumes treat the seventh through the seventeenth centuries, the eighteenth century, and the nineteenth and twentieth centuries respectively. At the end of volume 1 is a general index of names, titles, and topics covering the contents of all three volumes; the third volume, revised and expanded by Geddie and J. C. Smith, includes Commonwealth literature and the literature of the United States from Cotton Mather to Eugene O'Neill. For current (as of 1938) nineteenth- and twentieth-century au-

thors, there are three lists with brief descriptions of them and their works: of male authors from Britain and the Commonwealth, of female authors from Britain and the Commonwealth, and of American authors male and female.

M–48 Freeman, William. *Dictionary of Fictional Characters [in English Literature].* 3d ed. Revised by Fred Urquhart. Author and Title Indexes by J. M. F. Leaper. London: J. M. Dent, 1973.   PR19.F7

This helpful work gives names and brief descriptions of some 25,000 characters in some 2,500 works of about 500 British, Commonwealth, and American authors over six centuries. Articles also give titles of the work(s) in which the characters appear, the genres of those works, the names of their authors, and dates of publication of production. The works of John Gay and of Gilbert and Sullivan are not analyzed. The index of authors gives titles and page numbers on which articles concerning characters from those works will be found. The index of titles gives the names of their authors.

IV. BIOBIBLIOGRAPHIES

M–50 Allibone, Samuel Austin. *Critical Dictionary of English Literature and British and American Authors Living and Deceased from the Earliest Accounts to the Latter Half of the Nineteenth Century; Containing over 45,000 Articles (Authors) with 40 Indexes of Subjects.* 3 vols. Philadelphia: Lippincott, 1858–1871. *Supplement . . . Containing 37,000 Articles (Authors), and Enumerating over 93,000 Titles,* by John Foster Kirk. 2 vols. Philadelphia: Lippincott, 1891.   Z2010.A44 1858

This work is arranged as a dictionary of English and American authors from A.D. 500 until A.D. 1850 (1888, in case of the supplement). Entries give biographical information, primary bibliographies, long excerpts from contemporary critical reviews (with sources cited), and a wide variety of miscellaneous information. This includes bibliophilic data on sales and prices of rare items, whereabouts of manuscripts, and a careful record of variant spellings of names. Pseudonyms are identified by cross-reference to actual names.

In addition to abundant cross-references, there are indexes to some forty major subjects, with several hundred subdivisions under which are listed the names of all authors who have contributed to the literature of the subject. Following the preface to volume 1 is an "Introduction to Literary History, with Chronology of Prominent Authors and Their Works." There are three charts, of minor authors to A.D. 1199; of principal British authors with birth and death dates and the most significant work of the author or his major genre; and of the reigns of English sovereigns to Victoria.

The Supplement continues coverage until 1888; volume 1 covers A-O and cites work published from 1850 on, unless already mentioned in the original work; volume 2 begins with citations from about 1870 and continues to 1888. The Supplement follows Allibone's arrangement, except that it excludes cross-references, does not cite sources of critical review extracts, and lacks both author and subject indexes. Both the original work and the supplement must be consulted.

Although information in Allibone must be verified in more accurate and current bibliographical sources, this dictionary remains an invaluable source of information on minor figures. Altogether the original volumes and supplement provide information on some 83,000 authors and list some 433,000 titles. In addition, Allibone presents a convenient starting place for study of contemporary reception, as well as a contribution to the record of the provenance of rare books.

M–51 **Browning, David Clayton.** *Everyman's Dictionary of Literary Biography: English and American [DLB].* 3d ed. rev. with Supplement. London: J. M. Dent, 1969. PR19.B7

A biographical dictionary originally compiled in 1958 with entries on about 2,300 English and American authors, including contemporaries, some 650 entries being new to this edition. Biographies are brief and include citation of important primary works, but there are no secondary bibliographies. There are cross-references from pseudonyms to given names.
  For Europeans see the companion *Everyman's Dictionary of European Writers* (L–26).

M–52 **Myers, Robin.** *Dictionary of Literature in the English Language from Chaucer to 1940.* 2 vols. Oxford: Pergamon Press, 1970. Z2010.M9

This dictionary contains in volume 1 bibliographical and biographical details concerning some 3,500 authors writing in English over 600 years. Also treated are important English literary journals and periodicals. Authors include poets, dramatists, novelists, plus selected writers of popular and semi-literary kinds such as the detective story and the romantic novel. Distinguished writers who were scientists, historians, economists, lawyers, and statesmen are also included. Articles give an author's full name and title, dates, a biographical note, a bibliography, and a list of sources. First editions of separately published works are then listed in their chronological order. The sequence of entries begins generally with collected or complete works followed by separately published works divided into generic categories. A list of studies and critical works follows. The volume concludes with a select handlist of general reference works consulted and a geographical index to authors cited, arranged in chronological order by each country represented. The countries with English writers represented in this volume are as follows: America, Australia, Belgium, Canada, Ceylon, China, England, France, Germany, Holland, Hungary, India, Ireland, Israel, Italy, Jamaica, Japan, New Zealand, Norway, Pakistan, Persia, Rhodesia, Scotland, South Africa, Spain, and Wales. The second volume consists of a valuable title-and-author index to the 50–60,000 titles cited in volume 1, making this work a handy reference when seeking the author of a known title.

M–53 *British Writers: Edited under the Auspices of the British Council.* Edited by Ian Scott-Kilvert. 8 vols. New York: Scribner's, 1979–. PR85.B688

Originally published in pamphlet form in the series *Writers and Their Work*, no. 1– (1950–), these critical biographical articles of 10–15,000 words on British writers are here cumulated in seven volumes with an eighth index volume. The articles have been revised and brought up to date; articles conclude with brief, annotated, current bibliographies of primary and secondary works. The volumes are chronological with volume 1 treating authors of the late fourteenth through the sixteenth centuries, volume 2 the seventeenth century, volume 3 the eighteenth, and so on. There are also some general articles on the English Bible, the Metaphysical Poets, the Cavalier Poets, The Restoration Court Poets, the Gothic Novel, the World War I Poets, and the World War II Poets.

M–54 **Vinson, James, ed.** *Great Writers of the English Language.* 3 vols. New York: St. Martin's Press, 1979. P106.G9

These three volumes, intended for use by broad general audiences, treat Poets, Novelists and Prose Writers, and Dramatists, respectively. They bring together biographies, bibliographies, and critical essays on some 1,200 writers (500 poets, 500 novelists and prose stylists, 200 dramatists) in English. Biographies are brief; primary bibliographies are exhaustive and are categorized by genre. A further reading section cites important biographical and critical studies. Critical essays are signed by one of the approximately 400 contributing scholar-critics.
  Contemporary writers are treated in the four volumes of Vinson's *Contemporary Writers* Series (see R–33, R–43, R–52, and R–62).

M–55 **Kunitz, Stanley, and Howard Haycroft.** *British Authors before 1800: A Bibliographical Dictionary.* New York: H. W. Wilson, 1952. PR105.K9

Short (300–1500 words) popular biographies of some 650 authors are followed by very brief primary and secondary bibliographies. There are some 220 portraits of authors. This work is intended for the general readers, as are its companion volumes, *British Authors of the Nineteenth Century, 1000–1900* (M–56), *American Authors, 1600–1900* (S–27), and *Twentieth Century Authors* (R–21).

M–56 **Kunitz, Stanley J., and Howard Haycroft, eds.** *British Authors of the Nineteenth Century.* New York: H. W. Wilson, 1936. PR451.K8

Provides short (100–2500 words) biographies of more than 1,000 nineteenth-century British authors, including authors of the Commonwealth, with brief primary and secondary bibliographies. Some 350 articles are illustrated with pictures of their subjects. This work is popular in character and intended for the use of general audiences, as are its companion volumes, *British Authors before 1800* (M–55), *European Authors, 1000–1900* (L–56), *American Authors, 1600–1900* (S–27), and *Twentieth Century Authors* (R–21).

M–58 *Dictionary of Literary Biography [DLB].* Detroit: Gale Research Co., 1978–. LC number varies

The volumes in this continuing series present critical biobibliographies of English, American, and Commonwealth writers grouped by period, genre, or movement. Volumes are well edited by authorities and contain individual articles by specialists. To each article is appended both a list of primary works and a bibliography of scholarship and criticism. Volumes are illustrated with portraits and other photographs. In addition to the individual volumes cited below, *Dictionary of Literary Biography Yearbooks* are published annually (1981–) and contain updatings and expansions of articles on authors treated in previously published volumes of the *DLB*, along with material on additional writers not included in previously published volumes.
  The following volumes published to date treat groups of English and Irish authors:

Elizabethan Dramatists, Edited by Fredson Bowers (vol. 62; 1987). PR651.E48 1987
Jacobean and Caroline Dramatists. Edited by Fredson Bowers (vol. 58; 1987). PR671.J33 1987
Restoration and Eighteenth Century Dramatists, First Series. Edited by Paula R. Backschneider (vol. 80; 1989). PR701.R4 1989

British Novelists, 1660–1800. 2 vols. Edited by Martin C. Battestin (vol. 39; 1985).   PR851.B7 1985

Victorian Poets before 1850. Edited by William E. Fredeman and Ira B. Nadel (vol. 32; 1984).   PR591.V53 1984

Victorian Poets after 1850. Edited by William E. Fredeman and Ira B. Nadel (vol. 35; 1985).   PR591.V5 1985

Victorian Novelists before 1885. Edited by Ira B. Nadel and William E. Fredeman (vol. 21; 1983).   PR871.V55 1983

Victorian Novelists after 1885. Edited by Ira B. Nadel and William E. Fredeman (vol. 18; 1983).   PR871.V54 1983

Victorian Prose Writers before 1867. Edited by William B. Thesing (vol. 55; 1987).   PR781.V53 1987

Victorian Prose Writers after 1867. Edited by William B. Thesing (vol. 57; 1987).   PR781.V52 1987

British Poets, 1880–1914. Edited by Donald E. Stanford (vol. 19; 1983).   PR581.B7 1983

British Poets, 1914–1945. Edited by Donald E. Stanford (vol. 20; 1983).   PR610.B7 1983

Poets of Great Britain and Ireland, 1945–1960. Edited by Vincent B. Sherry, Jr. (vol. 27; 1984).   PR610.P56 1984

Poets of Great Britain and Ireland since 1960. 2 vols. Edited by Vincent B. Sherry, Jr. (vol. 40; 1985).   PR611.P58 1985

British Novelists, 1890–1929: Traditionalists. Edited by Thomas F. Staley (vol. 34; 1985).   PR881.B724 1985

British Novelists, 1890–1929: Modernists. Edited by Thomas F. Staley (vol. 36; 1985).   PR861.B73 1985

Modern British Dramatists, 1900–1945. 2 vols. Edited by Stanley Weintraub (vol. 10; 1982).   PR623.M63 1982

British Dramatists since World War II. 2 vols. Edited by Stanley Weintraub (vol. 13; 1982).   PR106.B74 1982

British Novelists, 1930–1959. 2 vols. Edited by Bernard Oldsey (vol. 15; 1983).   PR881.B725 1983

British Novelists since 1960. 2 vols. Edited by Jay L. Halio (vol. 14; 1983).   PR881.B73 1983

British Mystery Writers, 1860–1919. Edited by Bernard Benstock and Thomas F. Staley (vol 70; 1988).   PR830.D4 B75 1988

British Mystery Writers, 1920–1939. Edited by Bernard Nedstock and Thomas F. Staley (vol 77; 1988).   PR888.D4 B7 1988

The following volumes treat groups of American authors:

American Colonial Writers, 1606–1734. Edited by Emory Elliott (vol. 24; 1984).   PS185.A39 1984

American Colonial Writers, 1735–1781. Edited by Emory Elliott (vol. 31; 1984).   PS193.A38 1984

American Writers of the Early Republic. Edited by Emory Elliott (vol. 37; 1985).   PS208.A44 1985

American Humorists, 1800–1950. 2 vols. Edited by Stanley Trachtenberg (vol. 11; 1982).   PS430.A44 1982

Antebellum Writers in New York and the South. Edited by Joel Myerson (vol. 3; 1979).   PS128.A5

American Renaissance in New England. Edited by Joel Myerson (vol. 1; 1978).   PS243.A54

American Realists and Naturalists. Edited by Donald Pizer and Earl N. Harbert (vol. 12; 1982). PS201.A46 1982

American Poets, 1880–1945, First Series. Edited by Peter Quartermain (vol. 45; 1986).   PS129.A545 1986

American Poets, 1880–1945, Second Series. Edited by Peter Quartermain (vol. 48; 1986).   PS129.A545 1986

American Poets, 1880–1945, Third Series. 2 vols. Edited by Peter Quartermain (vol. 54; 1987). PS324.A44 1987

American Novelists, 1910–1945. 3 vols. Edited by James J. Martine (vol. 9; 1981)   PS129.A53

American Short Story Writers before 1880. Edited by Bobby Ellen Kimbel (vol. 74; 1988).

American Short Story Writers, 1880–1910. Edited by Bobby Ellen Kimbel (vol. 78; 1988).   PS374.S5 A39 1988

American Writers in Paris, 1920–1939. Edited by Karen Lane Rood (vol. 4; 1980).   PS129.A57

Twentieth-Century American Dramatists. 2 vols. Edited by John MacNicholas (vol. 7; 1981).   PS351.T9

American Poets since World War II. 2 vols. Edited by Donald J. Greiner (vol. 5; 1980).   PS323.5.A5

American Novelists since World War II. Edited by Jeffrey Helterman and Richard Layman (vol. 2; 1978).   PS379.A554

American Novelists since World War II. Second Series. Edited by James E. Kibler, Jr. (vol. 6; 1980).   PS379.A554 1980

Twentieth-Century American Science Fiction Writers. 2 vols. Edited by David Cowart and Thomas L. Wymer (vol. 8; 1981).   PS374.S35 T88

Twentieth-Century American-Jewish Fiction Writers. Edited by Daniel Walden (vol. 28; 1984).   PS153.J4 T84 1984

Afro-American Writers before the Harlem Renaissance. Edited by Trudier Harris (vol. 50; 1986).   PS153.N5 A393 1986

Afro-American Writers from the Harlem Renaissance to 1940. Edited by Trudier Harris (vol. 51; 1987).   PS153.N5 A396 1987

Afro-American Writers, 1940–1955. Edited by Trudier Harris (vol. 76; 1988).   PS153.N5 A386 1988

Afro-American Writers after 1955. Edited by Thadious M. Davis and Trudier Harris (vol. 38; 1985).   PS153.N5 A39 1985

Afro-American Poets since 1955. Edited by Trudier Harris (vol 41; 1985).   PS153.N5 A38 1985

Afro-American Fiction Writers after 1955. Edited by Thadious M. Davis and Trudier Harris (vol. 33; 1984).   PS153.N5 A34 1984

Beats, Literary Bohemians in Postwar America. 2 vols. Edited by Ann Charters (vol. 16; 1983).   PS228.B6 B47 1983

Chicano Writers, First Series. (vol. 82; 1988).

American Screenwriters, First Series. Edited by Robert E. Morsberger et al. (vol. 26; 1984).   PN1998.A2 A585 1984

American Screenwriters, Second Series. Edited by Randall Clark (vol. 44; 1986).   PN1998.A2 A586 1986

American Writers for Children before 1900. Edited by Glenn E. Estes (vol. 42; 1985).   PS490.A44 1985

American Writers for Children, 1900–1960. Edited by John Cech (vol. 22; 1983).   PS490.A43 1983

American Writers for Children since 1960: Fiction. Edited by Glenn E. Estes (vol. 52; 1986).   PS374.C454 A4 1986

American Writers for Children since 1960: Poets, Illustrators and Nonfiction Authors. Edited by Glenn E. Estes (vol. 61; 1987).   PS490.A45 1987

American Newspaper Journalists, 1690–1872. Edited by Perry J. Ashley (vol. 43; 1985).   PN4871.A48 1985

American Newspaper Journalists, 1873–1900. Edited by Perry J. Ashley (vol. 23; 1983).   PN4871.A49 1983

American Newspaper Journalists, 1901–1925. Edited by Perry J. Ashley (vol. 25; 1984).   PN4871.A5 1984

American Newspaper Journalists, 1926–1950. Edited by Perry J. Ashley (vol. 29; 1984).   PN4871.A52 1984

American Magazine Journalists, 1741–1850. Edited by Sam G. Riley (vol. 73; 1988).   PN4871.A47 1988

American Magazine Journalists, 1850–1900. Edited by Sam G. Riley (vol. 79; 1988).   PN4871.A474 1988

American Historians, 1607–1865. Edited by Clyde N. Wilson (vol. 30; 1984). E175.45.A48 1984

American Historians, 1866–1912. Edited by Clyde N. Wilson (vol. 47; 1986). E175.45.A483

Twentieth Century American Historians. Edited by Clyde N. Wilson (vol. 17; 1983). E175.45.T85 1983

American Literary Publishing Houses, 1638–1899. Edited by Peter Dzwonkoski (vol. 49; 1986). Z479.A448 1986

American Literary Publishing Houses, 1900–1980: Trade and Paperback. Edited by Peter Dzwonkoski (vol. 46; 1986). Z479.A45 1986

American Literary Critics and Scholars, 1800–1850. Edited by John W. Rathbun and Monica M. Grecu (vol. 59; 1987). PS74.A44 1987

American Literary Critics and Scholars, 1850–1880. Edited by John W. Rathbun and Monica M. Grecu (vol. 64; 1988). PS74.A45 1988

American Literary Critics and Scholars, 1880–1900. Edited by John H. Rathbun and Monica M. Grecu (vol. 71; 1988). PS74.A46 1988

Modern American Critics, 1920–1955. Edited by Gregory S. Jay (vol. 63; 1988). PS78.M58 1988

Modern American Critics since 1955. Edited by Gregory S. Jay (vol. 67; 1988). PS78.M59 1988

Canadian Writers, 1920–1959, First Series. Edited by W. H. New (vol. 68; 1988). PR9186.2.C34 1988

Canadian Writers since 1960, First Series. Edited by W. H. New (vol. 53; 1986). PR9186.2.C36 1986

Canadian Writers since 1960, Second Series. Edited by W. H. New (vol. 60; 1987). PR9186.2.C363 1987

V. GUIDES TO INDIVIDUAL AUTHORS

M–60 Guide to Major-Author Reference Works.

The following entries present information about author newsletters and journals; primary and secondary bibliographies; handbooks, indexes, and guides; standard editions; concordances; and biographies for the study of forty-four major English and Irish authors. The following writers are included:

Arnold	Hopkins
Auden	Johnson
Austen	Jonson
Bacon	Joyce
The Beowulf poet	Keats
Blake	Lawrence
Boswell	Malory
The Brontës	Mill
Browning	Milton
Byron	Pope
Carlyle	Ruskin
Chaucer	Scott
Coleridge	Shakespeare
Conrad	Shaw
Dickens	Shelley
Donne	Spenser
Dryden	Swift
Eliot, George	Tennyson
Eliot, T. S.	Woolf
Fielding	Wordsworth
Hardy	Yeats

There are, of course, separate journals, bibliographies, and other reference aids for many other English authors. For journals see Patterson, *Author Newsletters and Journals* (L–33); for bibliographies see the series of individual author bibliographies published by Gale Research, by Garland, by G. K. Hall (Reference Guide Series) by Northern Illinois University Press, by the Scarecrow Press (Author Bibliographies Series) and by the University of Pittsburgh Press, to mention only the most prominent.

ARNOLD (1822–1888)

Journal

Arnoldian: A Review of Mid-Victorian Culture [former title: *Arnold Newsletter*, 1973–1975]. Vol. 1–. Annapolis, Md.: U.S. Naval Academy, 1973–. 2–3/yr. Reviews. Annual Bibliographic Essay.
PR4023.A14

Bibliographies

Smart, Thomas Burnett. *Bibliography of Matthew Arnold.* London: J. Davy, 1892. Z8044.5.S63

Tollers, Vincent L. *Bibliography of Matthew Arnold, 1932–1970.* University Park: Pennsylvania State University Press, 1974. Z8044.5.T64

Handbook

Tinker, C. B., and H. F. Lowry. *Poetry of Matthew Arnold: A Commentary.* New York: Oxford University Press, 1940. PR4024.T5

Editions

Allott, Miriam, ed. *Poems of Matthew Arnold.* Edited by Kenneth Allott. 2d ed. Longman's Annotated English Poets. London: Longman's, 1979.
PR4021.A45 1979

Super, R. H. *Complete Prose Works of Matthew Arnold.* 11 vols. Ann Arbor: University of Michigan Press, 1960–1977. PR4021.S8

Concordance

Parrish, Stephen M., ed. *Concordance to the Poems of Matthew Arnold.* Ithaca, N. Y.: Cornell University Press, 1959. Based on the variorum edition by C. B. Tinker and H. F. Lowry (Oxford University Press, 1950). PR4023.A3 P3

Biography

Honan, Park. *Matthew Arnold: A Life.* New York: McGraw-Hill, 1981. PR4023.H6

AUDEN (1907–1973)

Bibliographies

Bloomfield, B. C., and Edward Mendelson. *W. H. Auden: A Bibliography, 1924–1969.* 2d ed. [3d ed. in progress]. Charlottesville: University Press of Virginia, 1972. Primary and Secondary.
Z8057.55.B5

Gingerich, Martin F. *W. H. Auden: A Reference Guide.* Boston: G. K. Hall, 1977. Z8047.55.G55

Handbook

Fuller, John. *Reader's Guide to W. H. Auden.* New York: Farrar, Straus and Giroux, 1970.
PR6001.U4 Z69 1970

Editions

Mendelson, Edward, ed. *Complete Works of W. H. Auden.* 8 vols. planned. Vol. 1 *Plays and Other Dramatic Writings, 1928–1938* [by Auden and Christopher Isherwood]. Princeton: Princeton University Press, 1988.

———. *Collected Poems of Auden.* New York: Random House, 1976. PR6001.U4 A17 1976

———. *Early Auden.* New York: Viking Press, 1981. PR6001.U4 Z758 1981

———. *English Auden.* New York: Random House, 1977. PR3501.U55 A6 1977

Biography

Osborne, Charles. *W. H. Auden: The Life of a Poet.* New York: Harcourt Brace Jovanovich, 1979. PS3501.U55 Z83

AUSTEN (1775–1817)

Journal

Jane Austen Newsletter. Vol. 1–. 1980–. No LC number

Bibliographies

Chapman, Robert W. *Jane Austen: A Critical Bibliography.* 3d ed. Oxford: Clarendon Press, 1969. Primary and secondary. Z8084.C47

Gilson, David. *Bibliography of Jane Austen.* Oxford: Clarendon Press, 1982. Z8048.G54 1982

Roth, Barry, and Joel Weinsheimer. *Annotated Bibliography of Jane Austen Studies, 1952–1972.* Charlottesville: University Press of Virginia, 1974. Z8048.R67

Roth, Barry. *Annotated Bibliography of Jane Austen Studies, 1973–83.* Charlottesville: University Press of Virginia, 1985. Z8048.R68 1985

Handbooks

Apperson, G. L. *Jane Austen Dictionary.* London: C. Palmer, 1932. PR4036.H29

Grey, J. David, et al. *Jane Austen Companion; with a Dictionary of Jane Austen's Life and Works.* New York: Macmillan, 1986. PR4036.J35 1986

Halperin, John, and Janet Kunert. *Plots and Characters in the Fiction of Jane Austen, the Brontës, and George Eliot.* Hamden, Conn.: Shoestring, 1976. PR825.H11

Hardwick, John M. D. *Guide to Jane Austen.* New York: Scribner, 1973. PR4036.H29

Leeming, Glenda. *Who's Who in Jane Austen and the Brontës.* London: Elm Tree Books, 1974. PR4037.L4

Pinion, F. B. *Jane Austen Companion: A Critical Survey and Reference Book.* London: Macmillan, 1973. PR4036.P53

Edition

Chapman, R. W., ed. *Novels of Jane Austen.* Text Based on Collation of the Early Editions. 3d ed. rev. 5 vols. Oxford: Clarendon Press, 1933, 1965. Plus Vol. 6, *Minor Works,* ed. B. C. Southam, 1954. PZ3.A93

Concordance

De Rose, Peter L., and S. W. McGuire. *Concordance to the Works of Jane Austen.* 3 vols. New York: Garland, 1982. Based on the Chapman edition. PR4036.A24 1982

Biography

Rees, Joan. *Jane Austen: Woman and Writer.* New York: St. Martin's Press, 1976. PR4036.R4

BACON (1561–1626)

Journal

Baconiana: The Journal of the Francis Bacon Society. Vol. 1–. London: The Society, 1892–. Irreg. Reviews. PR2941.A3

Bibliography

Gibson, Reginald Walker. *Francis Bacon: A Bibliography of His Works and Baconiana to the Year 1750.* Oxford: Scrivener Press, 1950. Supplement, 1959. Z8061.2.G5

Handbook

Gundry, W. G. C. *Francis Bacon: A Map of Days, A Guide to His Homes and Haunts.* London: The Bacon Society, 1946. B1199.H6 G8

Edition

Spedding, James, et al., eds. *Works of Francis Bacon.* 15 vols. Boston: Brown and Taggard, 1860–1864. B1153 1860

Concordances

Davies, David W., and Elizabeth S. Wrigley. *Concordance to the Essays of Francis Bacon.* Detroit: Gale, 1973. Computer-compiled. Based on the Spedding edition, vol. 6. B1151.D38

Fattori, Marta. *Lessico del Novum Organum di Francesco Bacone.* 2 vols. Rome: Edizioni dell'Ateneo e Bizzarri, 1980. B1169.F37

Biography

Sturt, Mary. *Francis Bacon: A Biography.* London: K. Paul, Trench, Trubner, 1932. B1197.586 1932

BEOWULF (8th century)

Bibliographies

Fry, Donald K. *Beowulf and the Fight at Finnsburgh; A Bibliography.* Charlottesville: University Press of Virginia, 1969. Primary and secondary. Z2012.F83

Short, Douglas D. *Beowulf Scholarship: An Annotated Bibliography.* New York: Garland, 1980. Z2012.S53

Editions

Klaeber, Friederich, ed. *Beowulf and the Fight at Finnsburgh.* 3d ed. Boston: Heath, 1936. Supplements 1941, 1950. PR1580.K5 1950

Stevick, Robert D. *Beowulf: An Edition with Manuscript Spacing Notation and Graphotactic Analyses.* New York: Garland, 1975. PR1580.S8 1975

Concordances

Bessinger, Jess B., Jr. *Concordance to the Anglo-Saxon Poetic Records.* Ithaca, N. Y.: Cornell University Press, 1978. Computer-compiled. Based on the *Anglo-Saxon Poetic Records,* 6 vols. (New York, 1931–1953). PR1506.B47 1978

———. *Concordance to Beowulf.* Ithaca, N. Y.: Cornell University Press, 1969. Computer-compiled. Based on *Anglo-Saxon Poetic Records,* vol. 4, *Beowulf and Judith.* PR1585.A2 B4

Cook, Albert S. *Concordance to Beowulf.* Halle: Niemeyer, 1911. Based on A. J. Wyatt text, 2d ed. (Cambridge: Cambridge University Press, 1898). PR1585.A2 C6

BLAKE (1757–1827)

Journals

Blake: An Illustrated Quarterly [former title: *Blake Newsletter, 1967–1977*]. Vol. 1–. Albuquerque: University of New Mexico, 1967–. 4/yr. Reviews. Bibliography: "A Checklist of Recent Blake Scholarship." PR4147.B47

Blake Studies. Vol. 1–. Normal: Illinois State University, 1968–. 2/yr. Reviews. Bibliographical Notices. PR4147.B48

Bibliographies

Bentley, G. E., Jr. *Blake Books: Annotated Catalogues of William Blake's Writing in Illuminated Printing, in Conventional Typography, and in Manuscript, and Reprints Thereof; Reproductions of His Designs; Books with His Engravings; Catalogues; Books He Owned; and Scholarly and Critical Works about Him*. Oxford: Clarendon Press, 1977. 2d ed. of *A Blake Bibliography (1964)*. Z8103.B4 1977

Natoli, Joseph P. *Twentieth-Century Blake Criticism: Northrop Frye to the Present*. New York: Garland, 1982. Z8103.N37 1982

Handbook

Damon, S. Foster. *Blake Dictionary: The Ideas and Symbols of William Blake*. Providence, R.I.: Brown University Press, 1965. Reprinted with a New Index by Morris Brown. Boulder, Colo.: Shambala Publications, 1979. Has been adversely criticized for disproportionate emphases. PR4114.A24

Editions

Bentley, G. E., Jr., ed. *William Blake's Writings*. 2 vols. Oxford: Clarendon Press, 1978. PR4141.B46

Erdman, David V., ed. *Complete Poetry and Prose of William Blake, with Commentary by Harold Bloom*. Newly rev. ed. Garden City, N. Y.: Doubleday, 1981. PR4141.E7 1981

———, ed. *Illuminated Blake*. Garden City, N. Y.: Anchor Press, 1974. NE642.B5 E72

Keynes, Sir Geoffrey, ed. *Complete Writings of William Blake, with All Variant Readings*. New ed. London: Oxford University Press, 1966. PR4141.K42 1966

Stevenson, W. H., ed. *Poems of William Blake*. Text by David V. Erdman. Longman's Annotated English Poets. Harlow: Longman, 1971. PR4141.S8

Concordance

Erdman, David V., et al. *Concordance to the Writings of William Blake*. 2 vols. Ithaca, N. Y.: Cornell University Press, 1968. Computer-compiled. Based on Keynes edition (London, 1957). PR4146.A25

Biographies

Bentley, G. E., Jr. *Blake Records*. Oxford: Clarendon Press, 1969. PR4146.B37

———. *Blake Records Supplement: Being New Materials Relating to the Life of William Blake Discovered since the Publication of Blake Records*. Oxford: Clarendon Press, 1988. PR4146.B374 1988

Wilson, Mona. *Life of William Blake*. New York: Cooper Square, 1969. PR4146.W5

BOSWELL (1740–1795)

Journal

JNL *Johnsonian Newsletter* (see P–9).

Bibliographies

Brown, Anthony E. *Boswellian Studies: A Bibliography*. 2d ed., rev. Hamden, Conn.: Archon Books, 1972. Z8110.2.B75 1972

Pottle, F. A. *Literary Career of James Boswell, Esq*. Oxford: Clarendon Press, 1929. Z8110.2.P87

Handbook

Smith-Dampier, John Lucius. *Who's Who in Boswell*. Oxford: Blackwell, 1935. PR3533.B756

Editions

Hill, G. B., ed. *Boswell's Life of Johnson, Together with Boswell's Journal of a Tour to the Hebrides and Johnson's Diary of a Journey into North Wales*. Rev. ed. by L. F. Powell. 6 vols. Oxford: Clarendon Press, 1934–1964. PR3533.B6 1934

Pottle, Frederick A., et al., eds. *Yale Edition of the Private Papers of James Boswell*. 25 vols. planned. New York: McGraw-Hill, 1950–.
LC number varies

———, eds. *Research Edition of the Private Papers of James Boswell*. 40 vols. planned. New York: McGraw-Hill, 1966–. LC number varies

Biographies

Pottle, Frederick A. *James Boswell: The Earlier Years, 1740–1769*. New York: McGraw-Hill, 1966. PR3325.P62

Brady, Frank. *James Boswell: The Later Years, 1769–1795*. New York: McGraw-Hill, 1984. PR3325.B72 1984

THE BRONTËS (Charlotte, 1816–1855; Emily, 1818–1848; Anne, 1820–1849)

Journal

BST *Brontë Society, Transactions*. Vol. 1–. Haworth, Yorkshire: The Society, 1895–. 1/yr. Reviews. Bibliography: "A Brontë Reading List." Analytical subject-author index to vols. 1–15, 1895–1967. PR4168.A4

Bibliographies

Alexander, Christine. *Bibliography of the Manuscripts of Charlotte Brontë*. Westport, Conn.: Meckler for the Brontë Society, 1982. Z6616.B8286 A4 1982

Barclay, J. M. *Emily Brontë Criticism, 1900–1982: An Annotated Checklist*. Westport, Conn.: Meckler, 1983. Update of *Emily Brontë Criticism, 1900–1968* (1974). Z8121.98.B38

Crump, R. W. *Charlotte and Emily Brontë: A Reference Guide*. Vol. 1, 1846–1915; vol. 2, 1916–1954; vol. 3, 1955–1983. Boston: G. K. Hall, 1982–1986. Z8122.C78 1982

Passel, Anne. *Charlotte and Emily Brontë: An Annotated Bibliography*. New York: Garland, 1979. Z8122.P37

Wise, T. J. *Bibliography of the Writings in Prose and Verse of the Members of the Brontë Family*. London: Privately printed, 1917. Z8122.W68

Yablon, G. Anthony, and John R. Turner. *Brontë Bibliography*. Westport, Conn.: Meckler Books, 1978. Z8122.Y3

Handbooks

Evans, Barbara Lloyd. *Scribner Companion to the Brontës*. New York: Scribner, 1982. PR4169.E835

Halperin, John, and Janet Kunert. *Plots and Characters in the Fiction of Jane Austen, the Brontës, and George Eliot*. Hamden, Conn.: Shoestring, 1976. PR825.H3

Leeming, Glenda. *Who's Who in Jane Austen and the Brontës*. London: Elm Tree Books, 1974. PR4037.L4

Pinion, F. B. *Brontë Companion: Literary Assessment, Background, and Reference*. London: Macmillan, 1975. PR4168.P5

Editions

Jack, Ian, et al., eds. [editors vary]. *Clarendon Edition of the Novels of the Brontës*. Oxford: Clarendon Press, 1969–. LC numbers vary

Neufeldt, Victor A., ed. *Poems of Charlotte Brontë: A New Text and Commentary*. New York: Garland, 1985. PR4166.N48 1985

Wise, T. J., and J. A. Symington, eds. *Shakespeare Head Brontë*. 19 vols. Oxford: B. Blackwell, 1931–1938. PR4165.A2 1931

Concordances

Sabol, C. Ruth, and Todd K. Bender. *Concordance to Brontë's Jane Eyre*. New York: Garland, 1981. Based on 2d British ed. (1848). PR4167.J5 S2 1981

———. *Concordance to Brontë's Wuthering Heights*. New York: Garland, 1984. PR4172.W73 S25 1984

Biographies

Gerin, Winifred. *Anne Brontë*. New ed. London: Allen Lane, 1976. PR4163.G4 1976

———. *Branwell Brontë*. London: T. Nelson, 1961. PR4174.B2 G4

———. *Charlotte Brontë: The Evolution of Genius*. Oxford: Clarendon Press, 1967. PR4168.G4

———. *Emily Brontë: A Biography*. Oxford: Clarendon Press, 1971. PR4173.G4

Hanson, Laurence, and E. N. Hanson. *Four Brontës: The Lives and Works of Charlotte, Branwell, Emily, and Anne Brontë*. Rev. ed. Hamden, Conn.: Archon, 1967. PR4168.H25 1967

BROWNING (1812–1889)

Journals

BIS   *Browning Institute Studies*. New York: Browning Institute, 1973–. 1/yr. Review-essay. Annual Bibliography: "Robert and Elizabeth Barrett Browning: An Annotated Bibliography." PR4229.B77a

SBHC   *Studies in Browning and His Circle: A Journal of Criticism, History and Bibliography* [former title: *Browning Newsletter*, nos. 1–9, 1968–1972]. Vol. 1–. Waco, Tex.: Armstrong Browning Library, Baylor University, 1973–. 4/yr. Reviews. Bibliography: "Checklist of Publications." PR4229.S7

Bibliographies

Broughton, Leslie N., et al. *Robert Browning: A Bibliography, 1830–1950*. Ithaca, N. Y.: Cornell University Press, 1953. Primary and secondary. Z8124.5.B7

Peterson, William S. *Robert and Elizabeth Barrett Browning: An Annotated Bibliography, 1951–1970*. New York: Browning Institute, 1974. Z8124.5.P48

Wise, Thomas J. *Complete Bibliography of the Writings in Prose and Verse of Robert Browning*. London: Privately printed, 1897. Z8124.5.W52

Handbooks

Berdoe, Edward. *Browning Cyclopaedia: A Guide to the Study of the Works of Robert Browning, with Copious Explanatory Notes and References on All Difficult Passages*. 2d ed. London: Allen and Unwin, 1897. PR4230.B4

Crowell, Norton B. *Reader's Guide to Robert Browning*. Albuquerque: University of New Mexico Press, 1972. PR4238.C76

DeVane, William C. *Browning Handbook*. 2d ed. New York: Appleton-Century-Crofts, 1955. PR4231.D45 1955

Orr, Alexandra L. *Handbook to the Works of Robert Browning*, by Mrs. Sutherland Orr. 6th ed. London: Bell, 1982. PR4238.O7

Editions

Complete Poetic and Dramatic Works of Robert Browning. Cambridge Edition. Boston: Houghton Mifflin, 1895. PR4200.E95

Altick, Richard, ed. *Ring and the Book*. Harmondsworth: Penguin, 1971. PR4219.A2 A4 1971

Collins, Thomas J., and Richard J. Shroyer, eds. *Plays of Robert Browning*. New York: Garland, 1988. PR4203.C57 1988

Kenyon, F. G., ed. *Works of Robert Browning*. Centenary Edition. 10 vols. London: Smith, Elder, 1912. PR4200.F12

King, Roma A., Jr., et al., eds. *Complete Works of Robert Browning*. 14 vols. planned. Athens: Ohio University Press, 1969–. PR4201.K5 1969

Jack, Ian, and Rowena Fowler, eds. *Poetical Works of Robert Browning*. 3 vols. Oxford: Clarendon Press, 1983–1988. PR4203.J3 1983

Pettigrew, John, ed. *Robert Browning, The Poems*. Edition supplemented and completed by Thomas J. Collins. 2 vols. New Haven: Yale University Press, 1981. PR4202.P44 1981

Concordances

Broughton, Leslie N., and Benjamin F. Stelter. *Concordance to the Poems of Robert Browning*. 4 vols. New York: Stechert-Hafner, 1924–1925. Based on the New Globe edition. PR4245.B7 1970

Collins, Thomas J., and Richard J. Shroyer, comps. *Concordance to the Works of Robert Browning*. 2 vols. New York: Garland, 1989. Based on the Altick, Collins and Pettigrew, and Collins and Shroyer editions; computer-generated.

Biography

Griffen, W. H., and H. C. Minchin. *Life of Robert Browning with Notices of His Writings, His Family, and His Friends*. London: Methuen, 1938. PR4231.G7

BYRON (1788–1824)

Journal

Byron Journal. Vol. 1–. London: Byron House and the Byron Society, 1973–. 1/yr. Reviews. Bibliographical notes. PR4379.B78

Bibliographies

Santucho, Oscar José. *George Gordon, Lord Byron: A Comprehensive Bibliography of Secondary Materials in English, 1807–1973, with a Critical Review of Research, by Clement Tyson Goode, Jr.* Metuchen, N. J.: Scarecrow, 1977.   Z8139.S27

Randolph, Francis Lewis. *Studies for a Byron Bibliography.* Lititz, Pa.: Sutter House, 1979.
Z8139.R35

Wise, Thomas James. *Bibliography of the Writings in Verse and Prose of George Gordon Noel, Baron Byron.* 2 vols. London: Dawsons, 1932–1933.
Z8139.W81 1932

Editions

Coleridge, Ernest Hartley, and R. E. Prothero, eds. *Works of Lord Byron.* 13 vols. London: John Murray, 1898–1904.   PR4351.C5 1966

McGann, Jerome J. *Complete Poetical Works of Lord Byron.* 7 vols. planned. Oxford: Clarendon Press, 1980–.   PR4351.M27

Steffan, Truman Guy, and Willis W. Pratt, eds. *Don Juan: A Variorum Edition.* 2d ed. 4 vols. Austin: University of Texas Press, 1971.
PR4359.A1 1971

Concordances

Hagelman, Charles W., Jr., and Robert J. Branes. *Concordance to Byron's Don Juan.* Ithaca, N. Y.: Cornell University Press, 1967. Computer-compiled. Based on the variorum edition of *Don Juan* (Austin, Tex., 1956).   PR4359.H3

Young, Ione Dodson. *Concordance to the Poetry of Byron.* 4 vols. Austin, Tex.: Pemberton Press, 1965. Based on the Cambridge edition, ed. Paul Elmer More (Boston: Houghton Mifflin, 1905).
PR4395.Y6

Biography

Marchand, Leslie A. *Byron: A Portrait.* New York: Knopf, 1970.   PR4381.M3317

CARLYLE (1795–1881)

Journal

Carlyle Newsletter. Vol. 1–. Edinburgh: Department of English Literature, University of Edinburgh, 1979–. 1/yr. Bibliography: "Carlyle Bibliography [year]."   No LC number

Bibliographies

Dyer, Isaac W. *Bibliography of Carlyle's Writings and Ana.* Portland, Me.: Southworth Press, 1928.
Z8147.D98

Tarr, R. L. *Thomas Carlyle: A Bibliography of English-Language Criticism, 1824–1974.* Charlottesville: University Press of Virginia for the Bibliographical Society of the University of Virginia, 1976.   Z8147.T37

Handbooks

General Index to the People's Edition [1871–1874] of Thomas Carlyle's Works. London: Chapman and Hall, 1874.   PR4432.P4

Ralli, Augustus. *Guide to Carlyle.* 2 vols. London: G. Allen and Unwin, 1920.   PR4433.R3

Edition

Traill, Henry Duff, ed. *Centenary Edition of the Works of Thomas Carlyle.* 30 vols. plus 1-vol. Supplement. New York: Scribner's, 1896–1901.
PR4420.E96

Biography

Froude, J. A. *Thomas Carlyle: A History.* 2 vols. London: Longmans, Green, 1882–1884.
PR4435.F75

CHAUCER (c. 1343–1400)

Journals

Chaucer Review (see N–47).

Studies in the Age of Chaucer. Vol. 1–. Norman, Okla.: New Chaucer Society, 1979–.   PR1901.S8

Bibliographies

Baird (see N–45).

Baird-Lange and Schnuttgen (see N–45).

Baugh (see N–45).

Crawford (see N–45).

Fisher and Allen (see N–45).

Griffith (see N–45).

Hammond (see N–45).

Leyerle and Quick (see N–45).

Peck (see N–45).

Spurgeon (see N–45).

Handbooks

Bowden, Muriel A. *Reader's Guide to Geoffrey Chaucer.* New York: Farrar, Strauss, 1964.
PR1924.B6

Davis, Norman, et al. *Chaucer Glossary.* Oxford: Clarendon Press, 1979.   PR1941.C5

Dillon, Bert. *Chaucer Dictionary: Proper Names and Allusions, Excluding Place Names.* Boston: G. K. Hall, 1974.   PR1903.D5

Fleay, Frederick G. *Guide to Chaucer and Spenser.* London: Collins, 1877.   PR1927.F5

French, Robert Dudley. *Chaucer Handbook,* 2d ed. New York: Crofts, 1947.   PR1905.F7 1947

Magoun, F. P., Jr. *Chaucer Gazetteer.* Chicago: University of Chicago Press, 1961.   PR1941.M3

Ross, Thomas Wynne. *Chaucer's Bawdy.* New York: Dutton, 1972.   PR1903.R6

Rowland, Beryl. *Companion to Chaucer Studies.* Rev. ed. London: Oxford University Press, 1979.
PR1924.R68 1979

Scott, Arthur Finley. *Who's Who in Chaucer.* London: Elm Tree Books, 1974.   PR1903.S3

Skeat, W. W. *Glossarial Index to the Works of Geoffrey Chaucer.* Oxford: Clarendon Press, 1899.
PR1941.S5

Editions

Manley, John M., and Edith Rickert, eds. *Text of the Canterbury Tales Studied on the Basis of All Known Manuscripts.* 8 vols. Chicago: University of Chicago Press, 1940.   PR1874.M35

Robinson, Fred N., ed. *Works of Geoffrey Chaucer.* 2d ed., rev. Boston: Houghton Mifflin, 1957.
PR1851.R6

Ruggiers, Paul G., ed. *Variorum Edition of the Works of Geoffrey Chaucer.* 25 vols. in 40 fascicles planned. Norman: University of Oklahoma Press, 1979–.   LC numbers vary

Concordance

Tatlock, J. S. P., and A. G. Kennedy. *Concordance to the Complete Works of Geoffrey Chaucer and the Romaunt of the Rose.* Washington, D. C.:

Carnegie Institution, 1927. Based on the Globe edition, 1898. PR1941.T3 1927

Biographies

Crow, Martin M., and Clair C. Olson, eds. *Chaucer Life-Records*. Oxford: Clarendon Press, 1966. PR1905.C7 1966

Howard, Donald R. *Chaucer: His Life, His Works, His World*. New York: Dutton, 1987.

COLERIDGE (1772–1834)

Journal

WC *Wordsworth Circle*. Vol. 1–. Washington, D. C.: Heldref Publications, 1970–. 4/yr. Reviews. Bibliography: "Coleridge Scholarship: An Annual Register." PR1.W67

Bibliographies

Haven, Richard, et al. *Samuel Taylor Coleridge: An Annotated Bibliography of Criticism and Scholarship*. Vol. 1, 1793–1899. Boston: G. K. Hall, 1976. Z8182.H26

Caskey, Jefferson D., and Melinda M. Stapper. *Samuel Taylor Coleridge: A Selective Bibliography of Criticism, 1935–1977*. Westport, Conn.: Greenwood, 1978. Z8182.C37

Crawford, Walter B., and Edward S. Lauterbach, eds. *Samuel Taylor Coleridge: An Annotated Bibliography of Scholarship*. Vol. 2, 1900–1939 with additional entries for 1795–1899. Boston: G. K. Hall, 1983. Z8182.H26

Milton, Mary Lee Taylor. *Poetry of Samuel Taylor Coleridge: An Annotated Bibliography of Criticism, 1935–1970*. New York: Garland, 1981. Z8182.M54

Wise, Thomas J. *Bibliography of the Writings in Prose and Verse of Samuel Taylor Coleridge*. London: For the Bibliographical Society, 1913. Z8182.W81

———. *Coleridgeiana: Being a Supplement to the Bibliography of Coleridge*. London: For the Bibliographical Society, 1919. Z8182.W57 suppl.

Editions

Coburn, Kathleen, ed. *Collected Works of Samuel Taylor Coleridge*. 24 vols. planned. Princeton, N.J.: Princeton University Press, 1969–. PR4470.F69

Coleridge, Ernest Hartley, ed. *Complete Poetical Works of Samuel Taylor Coleridge, Including Poems and Versions of Poems Now Published for the First Time, with Textual and Bibliographical Notes*. 2 vols. Oxford: Clarendon Press, 1912. PR4471.C4

Concordance

Logan, Sister Eugenia. *Concordance to the Poetry of Samuel Taylor Coleridge*. Saint Mary-of-the-Woods, Ind.: Privately printed, 1940. Based on the E. H. Coleridge edition, 2 vols. (Oxford University Press, 1912). PR4482.L6

Biography

Doughty, Oswald. *Perturbed Spirit: The Life and Person of Samuel Taylor Coleridge*. Rutherford, N.J.: Fairleigh Dickinson University Press, 1981. PR4483.D6 1981

CONRAD (1857–1924)

Journal

Conradiana: A Journal of Joseph Conrad [Conradiana]. Vol. 1–. Lubbock: Texas Tech University, 1968–. 3/yr. Reviews. Annual "Conrad Bibliography: A Continuing Checklist." PR6005.04.Z5812

Bibliographies

Lohf, Kenneth A., and Eugena P. Sheehy. *Joseph Conrad at Mid-Century: Editions and Studies, 1895–1955*. Minneapolis: University of Minnesota Press, 1957. Z8189.7.L6

Teets, Bruce E., and Helmut E. Gerber. *Joseph Conrad: An Annotated Bibliography of Writings about Him*. De Kalb: Northern Illinois University Press, 1972. Z8189.7.T4

Wise, Thomas James. *Bibliography of the Writings of Joseph Conrad, 1895–1920*. 2d ed. London: Privately printed, 1921. Z8189.7.W8

———. *Conrad Library: A Catalogue of Printed Books, Manuscripts, and Autograph Letters by Joseph Conrad*. London: Privately printed, 1928. Z8189.7.W83

Handbooks

Karl, Frederick R. *Reader's Guide to Joseph Conrad*. Rev. ed. New York: Farrar, Straus and Giroux, 1969. PR6005.04 Z76

Page, Norman. *Conrad Companion*. New York: St. Martin's Press, 1986. PR6005.04 Z78478 1986

Editions

Collected "Memorial Edition" of the Works of Joseph Conrad. 21 vols. Garden City, N. Y.: Doubleday, Page, 1925. PR6005.04 1925

"Uniform Edition" of the Works of Joseph Conrad. 22 vols. London: J. M. Dent, 1923–1938. PR6005.04 1923

Collected Edition of the Works of Joseph Conrad. 24 vols. London: J. M. Dent, 1946–1958. Rev. ed., 1974–. LC numbers vary

Concordances

Bender, Todd K., et al. *Conrad Concordances*. 20 vols. planned. New York: Garland, 1975–. Computer-compiled. By 1988, concordances had been published to *Almayer's Folly*; *The Arrow of Gold*; *Heart of Darkness*; *The Inheritors*; *Lord Jim*; *The Mirror of the Sea*; *The Nigger of the Narcissus*; *Nostromo*; *Outcast of the Islands*; *The Rescue*; *Romance*; *The Rover*; *The Secret Agent*; *A Set of Six*; *The Shadow Line*; *Tales of Hearsay*; *Tales of Unrest*; *Typhoon and Other Stories*; *Under Western Eyes*; *Victory*; *Within the Tides*; and *Youth*. PR6005.04

Biography

Karl, Fredrick R. *Joseph Conrad, The Three Lives, A Biography*. New York: McGraw-Hill, 1979. PR6005.04 Z759

DICKENS (1812–1870)

Journals

DSA *Dickens Studies Annual* [former title: *Dickens Studies: A Journal of Modern Research and Criticism*, 1965–1969, 3/yr.]. Vol. 1–. Carbondale: Southern Illinois University Press, 1970–. 1/yr. Reviews. PR4579.D49

Dickens Quarterly [former title: *Dickens Studies Newsletter*, 1970–1983]. Vol. 1–. Louisville, Ky.: Dickens Society, University of Louisville, 1970–.

4/yr. Reviews. Bibliography: "The Dickens Checklist." PR4579.D495

Dickensian: A Magazine for Dickens Lovers [Dickensian]. Vol. 1–. London: Dickens Fellowship, Dickens House, 1905–. 3/yr. Reviews. Annual Bibliographical Survey: "Year's Work in Dickens Studies." Index: Frank T. Dunn, *Cumulative Analytical Index to "The Dickensian," 1905–1974* (Hassocks, Sussex, 1976). PR4579.D5
Index: PR4580.D8

Bibliographies

Churchill, R. C. *Bibliography of Dickensian Criticism, 1836–1975.* New York: Garland, 1975.
Z8230.C47

Cohn, Alan M., and K. K. Collins. *Cumulated Dickens Checklist, 1970–1979.* Troy, N. Y.: Whitston Publishing, 1982. Z8230.C64 1982

De Vries, Duane, ed. *Garland Dickens Bibliographies.* 7 vols. to date (1988). New York: Garland, 1981–. LC numbers vary

Fenstermaker, John J. *Charles Dickens, 1940–1975: Analytical Subject Index to Periodical Criticism of the Novels and Christmas Books.* Boston: G. K. Hall, 1979. Z8230.F46

Ford, George H., and Lauriat Lane, Jr. *Dickens Critics.* Ithaca, N. Y.: Cornell University Press, 1961. PR4588.F63

Gold, Joseph. *Stature of Dickens: A Centenary Bibliography.* Toronto: University of Toronto Press for the University of Manitoba Press, 1971. Z8230.G65

Hatton, Thomas, and Arthur H. Clearer. *Bibliography of the Periodical Works of Charles Dickens. Bibliographical, Analytical, and Statistical.* London: Chapman and Hall, 1933. Z8230.H36

Handbooks

Bentley, Nicolas, Michael Slater, and Nina Burgis. *Dickens Index.* Oxford: Oxford University Press, 1988. PR4580.B46 1988

Greaves, John. *Who's Who in Dickens.* London: Elm Tree Books, 1972. PR4589.G75

Hardwick, Michael, and Mollie Hardwick. *Charles Dickens Encyclopedia.* Reading, Berks.: Osprey, 1973. PR4595.H28

Hayward, A. L. *Dickens Encyclopaedia: An Alphabetical Dictionary of References to Every Character and Place Mentioned in the Works of Fiction, with Explanatory Notes on Obscure Allusions and Phrases.* London: Routledge, 1924. PR4595.H3

Hobsbaum, Phillip. *Reader's Guide to Charles Dickens.* London: Thames and Hudson, 1972. PR4588.H54 1972

Lohrli, Anne. *Household Words...Table of Contents....* Princeton, N.J.: Princeton University Press, 1973. PN5130.H6 L6

London Transport Executive. *London of Charles Dickens.* London: London Transport, 1970. PR4584.L6

Page, Norman. *Dickens Companion.* New York: Schocken Books, 1984. PR4588.P33 1984

Shatto, Susan, ed. *Dickens Companions.* 4 vols. to date (1988). Boston: Allen and Unwin, 1986–. LC numbers vary

Williams, Mary. *Dickens Concordance: Being a Compendium of Names and Characters and Principal Places Mentioned in All the Works of Charles Dickens.* London: F. Griffiths, 1907. PR4595.W5

Editions

Butt, John, and Kathleen Tillotson, eds. [editors of individual vols. vary]. *Clarendon Dickens.* Oxford: Clarendon Press, 1966– LC numbers vary
New Oxford Illustrated Dickens. 21 vols. London: Oxford University Press, 1947–1959.
LC numbers vary

Storey, Graham, Kathleen Tillotson, and Nina Burgis, eds. *Letters of Charles Dickens.* The Pilgrim Edition. 12 vols. planned. Oxford: Oxford University Press, 1965–. PR4581.A3 H6

Biographies

Forster, John. *Life of Charles Dickens.* 3 vols. London: Chapman and Hall, 1872–1874. Frequently reprinted in 2 vols. (London: J. M. Dent).
PR4581.F7 1872

Johnson, Edgar. *Charles Dickens: His Tragedy and Triumph.* New ed. 2 vols. Boston: Little, Brown, 1965. PR4581.J6 1965

DONNE (1592–1631)

Journal

John Donne Journal: *Studies in the Age of Donne.* Vol. 1–. Raleigh: North Carolina State University, 1982–. 2/yr. Reviews. Bibliographical notices.
No LC number

Bibliographies

Keynes, Sir Geoffrey. *Bibliography of Dr. John Donne.* 4th ed. Oxford: Clarendon Press, 1973. Primary. Z8237.K38 1973

Roberts, John R. *John Donne: An Annotated Bibliography of Modern Criticism, 1912–1967.* Columbia: University of Missouri Press, 1973. Z8237.R6

———. *John Donne: An Annotated Bibliography of Modern Criticism, 1968–1978.* Columbia: University of Missouri Press, 1982. Z8237.R63 1982

Handbooks

Reeves, Troy D. *Annotated Index to the Sermons of John Donne.* 2 vols. Vol. 1, *Index to the Scriptures.* Vol. 2, *Index to Proper Names.* Salzburg: Institut für Anglistik und Amerikanistik, Universität Salzburg, 1979–. BX5133.D623 R44 1979

Williamson, George. *Reader's Guide to the Metaphysical Poets: John Donne, George Herbert, Richard Crashaw, Abraham Cowley, Henry Vaughan, Andrew Marvell.* London: Thames and Hudson, 1968. American edition under the title *Six Metaphysical Poets: A Reader's Guide.* New York: Farrar, Straus and Giroux, 1967. PR541.W54

Editions

Gardner, Helen, ed. *John Donne: The Divine Poems.* 2d ed. Oxford: Clarendon Press, 1978.
PR2246.G26 1978

———, ed. *John Donne: The Elegies and the Songs and Sonnets.* Oxford: Clarendon Press, 1965. PR2246.G27

Grierson, H. J. C., ed. *Poems of John Donne.* Rev. ed. 2 vols. London: Oxford University Press, 1929. PR2245.A5G6

Manley, Frank, ed. *John Donne: The Anniversaries.* Baltimore: Johns Hopkins University Press, 1963. PR2247.A5 1963

Milgate, W. *John Donne: The Satires, Epigrams, and Verse Letters.* Oxford: Clarendon Press, 1967.
PR2246.M5

————. *John Donne: The Epithalamions, Anniversaries, and Epicedes.* Oxford: Clarendon Press, 1978.   PR2246.M48

Potter, George R., and Evelyn Simpson, eds. *Sermons of John Donne.* 10 vols. Berkeley and Los Angeles: University of California Press, 1953–1962.
BX5133.D61 P68 1953

Concordance

Combs, Homer C., and Zay Rusk Sullens. *Concordance to the English Poems of John Donne.* Chicago: Packard, 1940. Based on the rev. ed. of H. J. C. Grierson (Oxford, 1929).   PR2248.A3 1940

Biography

Bald, R. C. *John Donne: A Life.* New York: Oxford University Press, 1970.   PR2248.B35

DRYDEN (1631–1700)

Journal

Scriblerian and the Kit-Cats (P–8).

Bibliographies

Hall, James M. *John Dryden: A Reference Guide.* Boston: G. K. Hall, 1984.   Z8244.H34 1984

Latt, D. J., and Samuel Holt Monk. *John Dryden: A Survey and Bibliography of Critical Studies, 1895–1974.* Minneapolis: University of Minnesota Press, 1976.   Z8244.M6

Zamonski, J. A. *Annotated Bibliography of John Dryden: Texts and Studies, 1949–1973.* New York: Garland, 1975.   Z8244.Z35

Handbooks

Aden, John M. *Critical Opinions of John Dryden: A Dictionary.* Nashville: Vanderbilt University Press, 1963.   PR3422.A7

Jensen, H. J. *Glossary of John Dryden's Critical Terms.* Minneapolis: University of Minnesota Press, 1969.   PR3422.J4

Edition

Hooker, E. N., et al., eds. *California Edition of the Works of John Dryden.* 21 vols. planned. Berkeley and Los Angeles: University of California Press, 1956–.   PR3410.F56

Concordance

Montgomery, Guy, comp. *Concordance to the Poetical Works of John Dryden.* Berkeley and Los Angeles: University of California Press, 1957. Based on the Cambridge edition, revised and enlarged by George R. Noyes (Boston, 1950).
PR3422.M6 1957

Biographies

Ward, Charles E. *Life of John Dryden.* Chapel Hill: University of North Carolina Press, 1961.
PR3423.W3

Winn, James A. *John Dryden and His World.* New Haven: Yale University Press, 1987.
PR3423.W5 1987

ELIOT, GEORGE (1819–1880)

Journal

GEFR *George Eliot Fellowship Review.* Vol. 1–. Coventry: George Eliot Fellowship, 1970–. 1/yr. Reviews.   PR4679.G46

Bibliographies

Fulmer, Constance M. *George Eliot: A Reference Guide.* Boston: G. K. Hall, 1977.   Z8259.F84

Haight, Gordon S. *Century of George Eliot Criticism.* Boston: Houghton Mifflin, 1965.
PR4688.H25

Muir, Percival Horace. *Bibliography of the First Editions of Books by George Eliot (Mary Ann Evans), 1819–1880.* London: The Bookman's Journal, 1927.   Z2013.B58

Handbooks

Halperin, John, and Janet Kunert. *Plots and Characters in the Fiction of Jane Austen, the Brontës, and George Eliot.* Hamden, Conn.: Shoestring, 1976.   PR825.H3

Hartnoll, Phyllis. *Who's Who in George Eliot.* New York: Taplinger, 1977.   PR4689.H3

Mudge, Isadore G., and M. E. Sears. *George Eliot Dictionary: The Characters and Scenes of the Novels, Stories, and Poems Alphabetically Arranged.* London: G. Routledge, 1924.   PR4695.M8

Pinion, F. B., ed. *George Eliot Companion: Literary Achievement and Modern Significance.* New York: Barnes and Noble, 1981.   PR4688.P5

————, ed. *George Eliot Miscellany: A Supplement to Her Novels, with Commentary and Notes.* Totowa, N. J.: Barnes and Noble, 1982.
PR4653.P5 1982

Editions

Haight, Gordon S., et al., eds. [editors vary]. *Clarendon Edition of the Novels of George Eliot.* Oxford: Clarendon Press, 1980–. LC numbers vary

Writings of George Eliot. 25 vols. Boston: Houghton Mifflin, 1907–1908.   PR4650.F70

Biography

Haight, Gordon S. *George Eliot: A Biography.* New York: Oxford University Press, 1968.
PR4681.H27

ELIOT, T. S. (1888–1965)

Journal

YER *Yeats-Eliot Review: A Journal of Criticism and Scholarship.* [former titles: *T. S. Eliot Review*, vols. 2–4, 1975–1977; *T. S. Eliot Newsletter*, vol. 1 only, 1974]. Vol. 5–. Edmonton: University of Alberta, 1978–. 2/yr. Reviews. "Bibliographical Update." List of Dissertations Completed. Work in Progress.
No LC number

Bibliographies

Gallup, D. *T. S. Eliot: A Bibliography.* New ed. London: Faber and Faber, 1969. Addenda, *PBSA* 70 (1976).   Z8260.5.G16 1969

Martin, Mildred. *Half-Century of Eliot Criticism: An Annotated Bibliography of Books and Articles in English, 1916–1965.* Lewisburg, Pa.: Bucknell University Press, 1972.   Z8260.5.M3

Ricks, Beatrice. *T. S. Eliot: A Bibliography of Secondary Works.* Metuchen, N. J.: Scarecrow Press, 1980.   Z8260.5.R5

Handbooks

Southam, B. C. *Student's Guide to the Selected Poems of T. S. Eliot.* New ed. London: Faber and Faber, 1974.   PS3509.L43 Z869 1974

Williamson, George. *Reader's Guide to T. S. Eliot. A Poem-by-Poem Analysis.* 2d ed. London: Thames and Hudson, 1967.   PS3509.L43 Z898 1967

Editions

Complete Poems and Plays of T. S. Eliot. London: Faber and Faber, 1969.   PS3509.L43 1969

Eliot, Valerie, ed. *T. S. Eliot, The Wasteland: A Facsimile and Transcript of the Original Drafts Including the Annotations of Ezra Pound.* New York: Harcourt Brace Jovanovich, 1971.
PS3509.L43 W3 1971

Biography

Bergonzi, Bernard. *T. S. Eliot.* London: Macmillan, 1978.   PS3509.L43 Z643

FIELDING (1707–1754)

Bibliographies

Hahn, George. *Henry Fielding: An Annotated Bibliography.* Metuchen, N. J.: Scarecrow Press, 1979.
Z8293.72.H33

Morrissey, LeRoy J. *Henry Fielding: A Reference Guide.* Boston: G. K. Hall, 1980.   Z8293.72.M67

Stoler, John A. *Henry Fielding: An Annotated Bibliography of Twentieth Century Criticism.* New York: Garland, 1980.   Z8293.72.S76

Handbook

Johnson, Clifford R. *Plots and Characters in the Fiction of Eighteenth-Century English Authors.* Vol. 2, *Henry Fielding, Tobias Smollett, Laurence Sterne, Samuel Johnson, and Oliver Goldsmith.* Hamden, Conn.: Archon, 1978.
PR858.P53 J64 1977

Edition

Coley, William B., et al., eds. *Wesleyan Edition of the Works of Henry Fielding.* 10 vols. planned. Middletown, Conn.: Wesleyan University Press, 1967–.   LC numbers vary

Biography

Cross, Wilber L. *History of Henry Fielding.* 3 vols. New Haven: Yale University Press, 1918.
PR3456.C8

HARDY (1840–1928)

Journals

Thomas Hardy Annual. No. 1–. Atlantic Highlands, N.J.: Humanities Press, 1983–.
PR4752.A37

THY   *Thomas Hardy Year Book.* Vol. 1–. [Place of publication varies.] Oxford: Blackwell and Mott, 1970–. 1/yr. Reviews. Bibliography: "Thomas Hardy: A Bibliography."   PR4752.A4

Bibliographies

Gerber, Helmut E., and W. Eugene Davis. *Thomas Hardy: An Annotated Bibliography of Writings about Him.* 2 vols. Vol. 1, *1871–1969.* Vol. 2, *Supplement and Writings of 1970–78.* De Kalb: Northern Illinois University Press, 1973–1983.
Z8386.5.G47

Purdy, Richard L. *Thomas Hardy: A Bibliographical Study.* London: Oxford University Press, 1954. Corrected reissue. Oxford: Clarendon Press, 1968.
Z8386.5.P8 1968

Handbooks

Bailey, James O. *Poetry of Thomas Hardy: A Handbook and Commentary.* Chapel Hill: University of North Carolina Press, 1970.   PR4753.B27

Hurst, Allen. *Hardy: An Illustrated Dictionary.* London: Kaye and Ward, 1980.   PR4752.H8 1980

Leeming, Glenda. *Who's Who in Thomas Hardy.* New York: Taplinger, 1975.   PR4752.L4

Pinion, F. B. *Hardy Companion: A Guide to the Works of Thomas Hardy and Their Background.* London: Macmillan, 1968.   PR4752.P5

Saxelby, F. O. *Thomas Hardy Dictionary: The Characters and Scenes of the Novels and Poems.* London: Routledge, 1911.   PR4752.A27

Editions

Collected Poems of Thomas Hardy. 2d ed. London: Macmillan, 1932.   PR4741.F26

Wessex Library Edition of the Works of Thomas Hardy in Prose and Verse, with Prefaces and Notes. Rev. ed. 21 vols. London: Macmillan, 1912–1914.   PR4740.F12

Furbank, P. N., et al., eds. [editors vary]. *New Wessex Edition of the Works of Thomas Hardy.* London: Macmillan, 1974–.   LC number varies

Gibson, James, ed. *Variorum Edition of the Complete Poems of Thomas Hardy.* New York: Macmillan, 1979.   PR4741.G5 1979

Biographies

Millgate, Michael. *Thomas Hardy: A Biography.* New York: Random House, 1982.
PR4753.M54 1982

————, ed. *Life and Works of Thomas Hardy* [an autobiography]. Athens: University of Georgia Press, 1985.   PR4753.A28 1985

HOPKINS (1844–1889)

Journal

HQ   *Hopkins Quarterly: A Journal Devoted to Critical and Scholarly Inquiry into the Life and Works of Gerard Manley Hopkins.* Vol. 1–. Guelph, Ontario: University of Guelph, 1974–. Reviews. Annual Bibliography: "Hopkins and His Circle: A Bibliography for [year]."   PR4803.H44 Z649

Bibliographies

Cohen, Edward H. *Works and Criticism of Gerard Manley Hopkins: A Comprehensive Bibliography.* Washington, D. C.: Catholic University of America Press, 1969. Primary and secondary. Z8415.6.C63

Dunne, Tom. *Gerard Manley Hopkins: A Comprehensive Bibliography.* Oxford: Clarendon Press, 1976.   Z8415.6.D85

Handbooks

McChesney, Donald. *Hopkins Commentary: An Explanatory Commentary on the Main Poems.* London: University of London Press, 1968.
PR4803.H44 Z713

Weyland, Norman, ed. *Immortal Diamond: Studies in G. M. Hopkins.* London: Sheed and Ward, 1949.
PR4803.H44 Z65

Editions

Devlin, Christopher, ed. *Sermons and Devotional Writings of Gerard Manley Hopkins.* New York: Oxford University Press, 1959.
PR4803.H44 A16 1959

Gardner, W. H., and N. H. MacKenzie. *Poems of Gerard Manley Hopkins.* 4th ed. Oxford: Oxford University Press, 1967.   PR4803.H44 A17 1967

House, Humphrey, ed. *Journals and Papers of Gerard Manley Hopkins.* New York: Oxford University Press, 1959.   PR4803.H44 A12 1959

Concordances

Borrello, Alfred. *Concordance to the Poetry in English of Gerard Manley Hopkins*. Metuchen, N. J.: Scarecrow Press, 1969. Computer-compiled. Based on the Oxford edition of the poems, ed. W. H. Gardner and N. H. MacKenzie, 4th ed. (1967). Caution: Poem citation and line numbering is off.
PR4803.H44 Z49

Dilligan, Robert J., and Todd K. Bender. *Concordance to the English Poetry of Gerard Manley Hopkins*. Madison: University of Wisconsin Press, 1970. Computer-compiled. Based on the Oxford editon of the poems, ed. W. H. Gardner and N. H. Mackenzie, 4th ed. (1967).   PR4803.H44 Z49 1970

Biography

None is regarded as standard.

JOHNSON (1709–1784)

Journals

Johnson Society. *Transactions*. Lichfield: Johnson Society, 1948–. Irreg. Reviews.   No LC number

JNL   *Johnsonian Newsletter* (see P–9).

NRam   *New Rambler: Journal of the Johnson Society of London*. Broadmead, Kent: The Society, 1941–. 2/yr. Reviews.   PR3532.A16

Bibliographies

Clifford, James L., and Donald J. Greene. *Samuel Johnson. A Survey and Bibliography of Critical Studies*. Minneapolis: University of Minnesota Press, 1970.   Z8455.8.C62

Courtney, William P. *Bibliography of Samuel Johnson*. Revised by David Nichol Smith. Oxford: Clarendon Press, 1915.   Z8455.8.C68

Fleeman, J. D. *Preliminary Handlist of Documents and Manuscripts of Samuel Johnson*. Oxford: Bibliographical Society, 1967.   Z8455.8.F55

Greene, Donald, and John A. Vance. *Bibliography of Johnsonian Studies, 1970–1985*. Victoria, B.C.: ELS Monograph Series, no. 39, 1987.
Z8455.8.G74 1987

Handbooks

Johnson, Clifford R. *Plots and Characters in the Fiction of Eighteenth Century English Authors*. Vol. 2, *Henry Fielding, Tobias Smollett, Laurence Sterne, Samuel Johnson, and Oliver Goldsmith*. Hamden, Conn.: Archon, 1978.
PR858.P53 J64 1977

Struble, Mildred C. *Johnson Handbook*. New York: F. S. Crofts, 1933.   PR3533.S76

Edition

Hazen, Allen T., and John H. Middendorf, eds. [editors vary]. *Yale Edition of the Works of Samuel Johnson*. 14 vols. planned. New Haven: Yale University Press, 1958–.   PR3521.Y3

Concordance

Naugle, Helen H. *Concordance to the Poems of Samuel Johnson*. Ithaca, N. Y.: Cornell University Press, 1973. Computer-compiled. Based on the edition by Nichol Smith and McAdam (Oxford: Clarendon, 1941) but includes additional poems and readings from the Yale edition.   PS3522.N3 1973

Biographies

Bate, W. Jackson. *Samuel Johnson*. New York: Harcourt Brace Jovanovich, 1975.   PR3533.B334

Clifford, James L. *Young Sam Johnson*. New York: McGraw-Hill, 1955.   PR3533.C6 1955

———. *Dictionary Johnson*. New York: McGraw-Hill, 1979.   PR3533.C58

JONSON (1572–1637)

Bibliographies

Brock, D. Heyward, and James M. Welsh. *Ben Jonson: A Quadricentennial Bibliography*. Metuchen, N. J.: Scarecrow Press, 1974.   Z8456.6.B75

Judkins, David C. *Non-Dramatic Works of Ben Jonson: A Reference Guide*. Boston: G. K. Hall, 1982.   Z8456.6.J83 1982

Lehrman, Walter D., et al. *Plays of Ben Jonson: A Reference Guide*. Boston: G. K. Hall, 1980.
Z8456.6.L43

Handbooks

Bradley, Jesse F., and Joseph Quincy Adams, eds. *Jonson Allusion Book*. New Haven: Yale University Press, 1922.   PR2636.B7

Brock, D. Heyward. *Ben Jonson Companion*. Bloomington: Indiana University Press, 1983.
PR2630.B7

Chalfont, Franc. *Ben Jonson's London: A Jacobean Place Name Dictionary*. Athens: University of Georgia Press, 1978.   PR2645.C4354

Editions

Herford, C. H., Percy Simpson, and Evelyn Simpson, eds. *Works of Ben Jonson*. 11 vols. Oxford: Clarendon Press, 1925–1952.   PR2601.H4

Hunter, William B., Jr. *Complete Poetry of Ben Jonson*. Edited with an introduction, notes, and variants. New York: W. W. Norton, 1963.
PR2625.A2 1963

Kernan, Alvin B., and R. B. Young, eds. *Yale Ben Jonson*. 8 vols. New Haven: Yale University Press, 1962–.   LC numbers vary

Concordances

Bates, Steven L., and Sidney D. Orr. *Concordance to the Poems of Ben Jonson*. Athens: Ohio University Press, 1978. Computer-compiled. Based on vol. 8 of the Herford and Simpson edition of the *Works* (Oxford, 1925–1952).   PR2645.B3

DiCesare, Mario A., and Ephim Fogel. *Concordance to the Poems of Ben Jonson*. Ithaca, N. Y.: Cornell University Press, 1978. Computer-compiled. Based on vol. 8 of the Herford and Simpson edition of the *Works* (Oxford, 1925–1952).
PR2645.D5

Biographies

Chute, Marchette. *Ben Jonson of Westminster*. New York: Dutton, 1953.   PR2631.C53

Herford and Simpson. Vol. 1 of *Works of Ben Jonson* (see above).

JOYCE (1882–1941)

Journals

JJQ   *James Joyce Quarterly*. Vol. 1–. Tulsa, Okla.: University of Tulsa, 1963–. 4/yr. Reviews. Bibliography, "Current JJ Checklist." PR6019.O9.Z637

AWN   *Wake Newslitter* [sic]. Vol. 1–. Colchester: University of Essex, Department of Literature, 1962–. 6/yr.   PR6019.O9.F594

Bibliographies

Deming, Robert H. *Bibliography of James Joyce Studies*. 2d ed., rev. and enl. Boston: G. K. Hall, 1977.   Z8458.1.D4 1977

Rice, Thomas Jackson. *James Joyce: A Guide to Research*. New York: Garland, 1982.
Z8458.1.R5 1982

Slocum, John J., and Herbert Cahoon. *Bibliography of James Joyce, 1882–1941*. London: Hart-Davis, 1953.   Z8458.1.555

State University of New York at Buffalo. *Complete James Joyce Catalog*. Boston: G. K. Hall, 1986.
No LC number

Handbooks

Benstock, Shari, and Bernard Benstock. *Who's He When He's at Home: A James Joyce Directory*. Urbana: University of Illinois Press, 1980.
PR6019.O9.Z5259

Blamires, Harry. *Bloomsday Book: A Guide through Joyce's Ulysses*. London: Methuen, 1966.
PR6019.O9.U626

Bonheim, Helmut. *Lexicon of the German in Finnegan's Wake*. Berkeley and Los Angeles: University of California Press, 1967.   PR6019.O9.F545

Bowen, Zack R., and James F. Carens, eds. *Companion to Joyce Studies*. Westport, Conn.: Greenwood, 1984.   PR6019.O9.Z52717 1983

Campbell, Joseph, and Henry Morton Robinson. *Skeleton Key to Finnegan's Wake*. New York: Harcourt, Brace, 1944.   PR6019.O9.F57

Glasheen, Adaline. *Third Census of Finnegan's Wake: An Index of the Characters and Their Roles*. Revised and expanded from the *Second Census* (1963). Berkeley, Los Angeles, London: University of California Press, 1977. PR6019.O9.F59 1977

Hodgart, Matthew. *James Joyce: A Student's Guide*. London: Routledge and Kegan Paul, 1978.
PR6019.O9.Z585 1978

MacNicholas, John. *James Joyce's Exiles: A Textual Companion*. New York: Garland, 1979.
PR6019.O9.E954

McHugh, Roland. *Annotations to Finnegan's Wake*. Baltimore: Johns Hopkins University Press, 1980.   PR6019.O9.F59357

Mink, Lewis O. *Finnegan's Wake Gazetteer*. Bloomington: Indiana University Press, 1978.
PR6019.O9.F593615

O'Hehir, Brendan. *Gaelic Lexicon for Finnegan's Wake and Glossary for Joyce's Other Works*. Berkeley and Los Angeles: University of California Press, 1967.   PR6019.O9.47

O'Hehir, Brendan, and John M. Dillon, eds. *Classical Lexicon for Finnegan's Wake: A Glossary of the Greek and Latin in the Major Works of Joyce*. Berkeley, Los Angeles, London: University of California Press, 1979.   PR6019.O9.Z58

Thornton, Weldon. *Allusions in Ulysses: An Annotated List*. Chapel Hill: University of North Carolina Press, 1961.   PR6019.O9.U49

Tindall, William York. *Reader's Guide to Finnegan's Wake*. New York: Farrar, Straus and Giroux, 1969.   PR6019.O9.F938

————. *Reader's Guide to James Joyce*. New York: Noonday, 1959.   PR6019.O9.Z833

Editions

Anderson, Chester, ed. *Portrait of the Artist as a Young Man: Text, Criticism, and Notes*. New York: Viking, 1968.   PZ3.J853 P23

Gabler, Hans Walter, ed. *Ulysses: A Critical and Synoptic Edition*. 3 vols. New York: Garland, 1984.   PR6019.O9.U4 1984

————. *Ulysses: The Corrected Text*. New York: Random House, 1986.   PR6019.O9.U4 1986

Joyce, James. *Ulysses. A Facsimile of the Manuscript*. 3 vols. Charlottesville: University Press of Virginia, 1975.   No LC number

Scholes, Robert, and Richard Ellman, eds. *Dubliners*. New York: Viking, 1967.   PZ3.J853 Du4

Concordances

Anderson, Chester G. *Word Index to James Joyce's Stephen Hero*. Ridgefield, Conn.: Ridgebury Press, 1958.   PR6019.O9.P643

Bauerle, Ruth. *Word List to James Joyce's Exiles*. New York: Garland, 1980. Penguin Text.
PR6019.O9.E929 1981

Doyle, Paul A. *Concordance to the Collected Poems of James Joyce*. New York: Scarecrow Press, 1966.   PR6019.O9.Z49 1966

Fuger, Wilhelm. *Concordance to James Joyce's Dubliners*. New York: Olms, 1980.
PR6019.O9.O855 1980

Hancock, Leslie. *Word Index to James Joyce's Portrait of the Artist*. Carbondale: Southern Illinois University Press, 1967.   PR6019.O9.P6444

Hanley, Miles L. *Word Index to James Joyce's Ulysses*. Rev. ed. Madison: University of Wisconsin Press, 1962.   PR6019.O9.U66

Hart, Clive A. *Concordance to Finnegan's Wake*. Minneapolis: University of Minnesota Press, 1963.
PR6019.O9.F592

Lane, Gary, ed. *Word Index to James Joyce's Dubliners*. New York: Haskell House, 1972.
PR6019.O9.D855 1972

Steppe, Wolfhard. *Handlist to James Joyce's Ulysses: A Complete Alphabetical Index to the Critical Reading Text* [of Gabler]. New York: Garland, 1985.   PR6019.O9.U725 1985

Biography

Ellmann, Richard. *James Joyce*. New and rev. ed. New York: Oxford University Press, 1982.
PR6019.O9.Z5332 1982

KEATS (1795–1821)

Journals

KSMB   *Keats-Shelley Memorial Bulletin, Rome* [title varies slightly]. Vol. 1–. London: Keats-Shelley Memorial Association, 1910–. 1/yr. Reviews. Bibliographies. *Bibliographical Index, I–XX, 1910–69* (London: Dawson, 1972).   PR4836.A15

KSJ   *Keats-Shelley Journal* (see Q–26).

Bibliographies

MacGillivray, James R. *Keats: A Bibliography and Reference Guide, with an Essay on Keats' Reputation*. 2d ed. Toronto: University of Toronto Press, 1968.   Z8461.M3 1968

Rhodes, Jack Wright. *Keats' Major Odes: An Annotated Bibliography of the Criticism*. Westport, Conn.: Greenwood Press, 1984. Z8461.R48 1984

Editions

Allott, Miriam, ed. *Poems of John Keats.* Longman's Annotated English Poets. London: Longmans, 1970.   PR4831.A4

Garrod, H. W. *Poetical Works of John Keats.* 2d ed. London: Oxford University Press, 1958.
PR4830.F58

Stillinger, Jack, ed. *Poems of John Keats.* Cambridge: Belknap Press of Harvard University Press, 1978.   PR4831.S75 1978

Concordances

Baldwin, Dane L., et al. *Concordance to the Poems of John Keats.* Washington, D. C.: Carnegie Institution, 1917. Based on H. Buxton Forman, ed. (Oxford, 1910, 1914).   PR4836.A3

Becker, Michael G., Robert J. Dilligan, and Todd K. Bender. *Concordance to the Poems of John Keats.* New York: Garland, 1981. Computer-compiled. Based on the Stillinger edition (1978).
PR4836.A3 1981

Biography

Brown, Charles A. *Life of John Keats.* London: Oxford University Press, 1937.   PR4836.B76

LAWRENCE (1885–1930)

Journal

DHLR   *D. H. Lawrence Review.* Vol. 1–. Fayetteville: University of Arkansas, 1968–. 3/yr. Annual "Checklist of D. H. Lawrence Criticism and Scholarship." Volumes from 1977 on include a copy of *Newsletter—the D. H. Lawrence Society*, no. 1–.
PR6023.A93 Z6234

Bibliographies

Cowan, James C. *D. H. Lawrence: An Annotated Bibliography of Writings about Him.* 2 vols. Vol. 1, 1909–1960. Vol. 3, 1961–1975. De Kalb: Northern Illinois University Press, 1982–1985.
Z8490.5.C68 1982

Phillips, Jill M. *D. H. Lawrence: A Review of the Biographies and Literary Criticism: A Critically Annotated Bibliography.* New York: Gordon Press, 1978.   PR6023.A93 Z7693

Rice, Thomas Jackson. *D. H. Lawrence: A Guide to Research.* New York: Garland, 1983.
Z8490.5.R5 1983

Roberts, Warren. *Bibliography of D. H. Lawrence.* 2d ed. Cambridge: Cambridge University Press, 1982.   Z8490.5.R6 1982

Sagar, Keith. *D. H. Lawrence: Calendar of His Works, with a Checklist of the Manuscripts of D. H. Lawrence by Lindeth Vasey.* Manchester: Manchester University Press; Austin: University of Texas Press, 1979.   PR6023.A93 Z862

Stoll, John E. *D. H. Lawrence: A Bibliography, 1911–1975.* Troy, N. Y.: Whitston Publishing, 1977.   Z8490.5.S86

Tedlock, E. W. *Frieda Lawrence Collection of Lawrence Manuscripts: A Descriptive Bibliography.* Albuquerque: University of New Mexico Press, 1948.   Z6616.L4 L3

Handbooks

Hobsbaum, Philip. *Reader's Guide to D. H. Lawrence.* London: Thames and Hudson, 1981.
PR6023.A93 Z63137

Holderness, Graham. *Who's Who in D. H. Lawrence.* London: Elm Tree Books, 1976.
PR6023.A93 Z49 1976

Pinion, F. B. *D. H. Lawrence Companion: Life, Thought, and Works.* London: Macmillan, 1978.
PR6023.A93 Z695 1978

Sager, Keith. *D. H. Lawrence Handbook.* Manchester: Manchester University Press, 1982.
PR6023.A93 Z538 1982

Editions

Phoenix Edition of the Works of D. H. Lawrence. 26 vols. London: Heinemann, 1954–1972.
LC number varies

deSola Pinto, Vivian, and Warren Roberts, eds. *Complete Poems of D. H. Lawrence.* 3d ed. 2 vols. London: Heinemann, 1972.
PR6023.A93 A17 1972

Boulton, James T., et al., eds. [editors vary]. *Cambridge Edition of the Letters and Works of D. H. Lawrence.* Cambridge: Cambridge University Press, 1979–.   LC number varies

Concordances

Garcia, Reloy, and James Karabatsos. *Concordance to the Poetry of D. H. Lawrence.* Lincoln: University of Nebraska Press, 1970. Based on *Complete Poems*, ed. deSola Pinto and Roberts.
PR6023.A93 Z49

————. *Concordance to the Short Fiction of D. H. Lawrence.* Lincoln: University of Nebraska Press, 1972. Based mainly on *Complete Short Stories* (Viking, 1961) and *Four Short Novels* (Viking, 1965).
PR6023.A93 Z49 1972

Biography

Moore, Harry T. *Intelligent Heart: The Story of D. H. Lawrence.* New York: Grove Press, 1962.
PR6023.A93 Z685 1962

MALORY (fl. c. 1470)

Bibliography

Life, Page West. *Sir Thomas Malory and the Morte D'Arthur: A Survey of Scholarship and Annotated Bibliography.* Charlottesville: University Press of Virginia for the Bibliographical Society, 1980.
Z8545.5.L53

Handbook

Dillon, Bert. *Malory Handbook.* Boston: G. K. Hall, 1978.   PR2045.D5

Edition

Vinaver, Eugene, ed. *Works of Sir Thomas Malory.* 2d ed. 3 vols. Oxford: Clarendon Press, 1968.
PR2041.V5 1968

Concordance

Kato, Tomomi. *Concordance to the Works of Sir Thomas Malory.* Tokyo: University of Tokyo Press, 1974. Based on the 2d ed. by Vinaver of the *Works* (Oxford, 1967).   PR2045.K37

Biography

Hicks, Edward. *Sir Thomas Malory: His Turbulent Career: A Biography.* Cambridge: Harvard University Press, 1928.   PR2045.H5

MILL (1806–1873)

Journal

Mill News Letter. Vol. 1–. Toronto: University of Toronto Press in association with Victoria College, 1965–. 2/yr. Reviews. Bibliographies.
No LC number

Bibliographies

Laine, Michael. *Bibliography of Works on John Stuart Mill*. Toronto: University of Toronto Press, 1982. Z8574.8.L34 1982

MacMinn, Ney, et al., eds. *Bibliography of the Published Writings of John Stuart Mill*. Evanston, Ill.: Northwestern University Press, 1945.
Z8574.8 M5

Edition

Priestley, F. E. L., ed. *Collected Edition of the Works of John Stuart Mill*. 25 vols. planned. Toronto: University of Toronto Press, 1963–.
B1602.A2 1963

Biography

Packe, Michael St. John. *Life of John Stuart Mill*. London: Secker and Warburg, 1954.
B1606.P3 1954

MILTON (1608–1674)

Journals

Milton Quarterly [former title: *Milton Newsletter*, 1967–1969]. Vol. 1–. Athens: Ohio University, 1967–. 4/yr. Reviews. Bibliography, Abstracts, Dissertations, Works in progress. PR3579.M48

Milton Studies. Vol. 1–. Pittsburgh: University of Pittsburgh Press, 1969–. PR3579.M5

Bibliographies

Fletcher, Harris F. *Contributions to a Milton Bibliography, 1800–1930, Being a List of Addenda to Stevens . . .* Urbana: University of Illinois Press, 1931. Z8578.S84 F5

Hanford, James Holly (see O–28).

Huckabay, Calvin. *John Milton: An Annotated Bibliography, 1929–1968*. Rev. ed. Pittsburgh: Duquesne University Press, 1969. Z8578.H82

Patrides, C. A. *Annotated Critical Bibliography of John Milton*. New York: St. Martin's Press, 1987.
Z8578.P37 1987

Shawcross, John T. *Milton: A Bibliography for the Years 1624–1700*. Binghamton, N. Y.: Medieval and Renaissance Texts and Studies, 1984.
Z8578.S52 1984

Stevens, David Harrison. *Reference Guide to Milton, from 1800 to the Present Day*. Chicago: University of Chicago Press, 1930. Z8578.S84

Thompson, Elbert. *John Milton: Topical Bibliography*. New Haven: Yale University Press, 1916.
Z8578.T68

Handbooks

Hanford, James Holly, and James C. Taafee. *Milton Handbook*. 5th ed. New York: Appleton-Century-Crofts, 1970. PR3588.H2 1970

Hunter, William B., Jr. ed. *Milton Encyclopedia*. 8 vols. Lewisburg, Pa.: Bucknell University Press, 1978–1980. PR3580.M5

LeComte, Edward S. *Milton Dictionary*. New York: Philosophical Library, 1961. PR3580.L4

Nicholson, Marjorie Hope. *John Milton: A Reader's Guide to His Poetry*. New York: Farrar, Straus and Giroux, 1963. PR3588.N5

Pecheux, M. Christopher. *Milton, A Topographical Guide*. Washington, D. C.: University Press of America, 1981. PR3584.P4

Editions

Hughes, Merritt Y., ed. *Variorum Commentary on the Poems of John Milton*. 6 vols. in 9 planned. New York: Columbia University Press, 1970–.
PR3595.V3

Patterson, Frank Allen, ed. *Columbia Edition of the Works of Milton*. 18 vols. in 21. New York: Columbia University Press, 1931–1938. Index in 2 vols. by Patterson and French R. Fogle. 1940.
PR3550.F31

Wolfe, Don M., ed. *Complete Prose Works of John Milton*. 8 vols. in 9 planned. New Haven: Yale University Press, 1953–1982. PR3569.W6

Concordances

Bradshaw, John. *Concordance to the Poetical Works of John Milton*. London: S. Sonnenschein; New York: Macmillan, 1894. PR3595.B7

Cleveland, Charles Dexter. *Complete Concordance to the Poetical Works of John Milton*. London: S. Low, Son, and Marston, 1867. PR3595.C55

Cooper, Lane. *Concordance to the Latin, Greek, and Italian Poems of John Milton*. Halle: Niemeyer, 1923. PR3595.C6

Hudson, Gladys W. *Paradise Lost: A Concordance*. Detroit: Gale, 1970. Based on the 2d ed. in 3 vols. (1674). PR3562.H8 1970

Ingram, William, and Kathleen Swaim, eds. *Concordance to Milton's English Poetry*. Oxford: Clarendon, 1972. Computer-compiled. Based on various early editions of each work, with apparently authorized variants included. PR3595.I55

Sterne, Laurence, and Harold Kollmeier, eds. *Concordance to the English Prose of John Milton*. Binghamton, N. Y.: Medieval and Renaissance Texts and Studies, 1985. Based upon the Wolfe edition of the complete prose works. PR3592.P757 1985

Biography

Parker, William Riley. *Milton: A Biography*. Oxford: Clarendon Press, 1968. PR3581.P27

POPE (1688–1744)

Journal

Scriblerian and the Kit-Cats (see P–8).

Bibliographies

Griffith, R. H. *Alexander Pope: A Bibliography*. 2 vols. Austin: University of Texas Press, 1922-1927. Primary. Z8704.G78

Lopez, Cecilia L. *Alexander Pope: An Annotated Bibliography, 1945–1967*. Gainesville: University of Florida Press, 1970. Z8704.L65 1970

Tobin, James E. *Alexander Pope: A List of Critical Studies from 1895 to 1944*. New York: Cosmopolitan Science and Art Service Co., 1945. Z8704.T6

Editions

Butt, John, ed. *Twickenham Edition of the Poems of Alexander Pope*. 11 vols. in 12. London: Oxford University Press; New Haven: Yale University Press, 1939–1969. PR3621.B82

Ault, Norman, ed. *Prose Works of Alexander Pope*. Vol. 1, *Earlier Works*. Oxford: Basil Blackwell, 1936. No more published. PR3621.A8 1936

Cowler, Rosemary, ed. *Prose Works of Alexander Pope*. Vol. 2, *Major Works, 1725–1744*. Hamden, Conn.: Shoestring, 1986.   PR3622.C69 1986

Steeves, Edna L., ed. *Art of Sinking in Poetry*. New York: King's Crown Press, 1952.
PR3631.P4 1952

Concordances

Abbott, Edwin. *Concordance to the Works of Alexander Pope*. London: Chapman and Hall, 1875. Based on the Warburton edition (1751).
PR3632.A73

Bedford, Emmett G., and Robert J. Dilligan. *Concordance to the Poems of Alexander Pope*. 2 vols. Detroit: Gale, 1974. Computer-compiled. Based on the Twickenham edition.   PR3622.B4

Biographies

Sherburn, George. *Early Career of Alexander Pope*. Oxford: Clarendon Press, 1934.
PR3633.S45

Mack, Maynard. *Alexander Pope: A Life*. New York: Norton, 1985.   PR3633.M27 1985

———. *Garden and the City: Retirement and Politics in the Later Poetry of Pope, 1731–1743*. Toronto: University of Toronto Press, 1969.
PR3633.M33

RUSKIN (1819–1900)

Bibliographies

Beetz, Kirk H. *John Ruskin: A Bibliography, 1900–1974*. Metuchen, N. J.: Scarecrow Press, 1976.   Z8765.B43

Cook, E. T., and A. D. O. Wedderburn. Bibliography in vol. 38 of *Works of Ruskin* (see below).

Wise, T. J., and J. P. A. Smart. *Complete Bibliography of the Writings in Prose and Verse of John Ruskin, with a List of the More Important Ruskiniana*. 2 vols. London: Privately printed, 1891–1893.   Z8765.W81

Edition

Cook, Sir Edward T., and Alexander D. O. Wedderburn, eds. *Works of John Ruskin*. 39 vols. London: G. Allen, 1903–1912.   PR5251.C6

Biographies

Abse, Joan. *John Ruskin, the Passionate Moralist*. London: Quartet Books, 1980.   PR5263.A54

Hunt, John Dixon. *Wider Sea: A Life of Ruskin*. New York: Viking, 1982.   PR5263.H86 1982

Lutyens, Mary. *Millais and the Ruskins*. London: Murray, 1967.   PR5263.L8

———. *Ruskins and the Grays*. London: Murray, 1972.   PR5263.L83

SCOTT (1771–1832)

Bibliographies

Corson, J. C. *Bibliography of Sir Walter Scott: A Classified and Annotated List of Books and Articles Relating to His Life and Works, 1797–1940*. Edinburgh: Oliver and Boyd, 1943.   Z8802.C75

Rubenstein, Jill. *Sir Walter Scott: A Reference Guide*. Boston: G. K. Hall, 1978.   Z8802.R82

Handbooks

Bradley, Philip. *Index to the Waverly Novels*. Metuchen, N. J.: Scarecrow Press, 1975.   PR5331.B7

Burr, Allston. *Sir Walter Scott: An Index Placing the Short Poems in His Novels and in His Long Poems and Dramas*. Cambridge: Harvard University Press, 1936.   PR5331.B8 1936

Husband, Margaret Fair Anderson. *Dictionary of the Characters in the Waverly Novels of Sir Walter Scott*. London: G. Routledge, 1910.   PR5331.H8

Editions

Lang, Andrew, ed. *Complete Poetical Works*. 6 vols. Boston: Estes and Co., 1900.   PR5305.F00

———. *Waverley Novels*. Edition de grand luxe. 48 vols. Boston: Estes and Lauriat, 1892–1894.
LC numbers vary

Biography

Lockhart, J. G. *Memoirs of the Life of Sir Walter Scott*. 1837–1838. Cambridge Edition. 5 vols. Boston: Houghton Mifflin, 1902.   PR5332.L6 1902

SHAKESPEARE (1564–1616)

Journals

Deutsche Shakespeare Gesellschaft West. Jahrbuch (see O–54).

Shakespeare Jahrbuch (see O–54).

Shakespeare Newsletter (see O–53).

Shakespeare Quarterly (see O–50).

Shakespeare Studies (see O–52).

Shakespeare Survey (see O–51).

Shakespearian Research Opportunities (see O–58).

Bibliographies

(See O–40 ff.)

Bate, John. *How to Find Out about Shakespeare*. Oxford: Pergamon Press, 1968.   Z8811.R35

Handbooks

Alden (see O–59).

Andrews, John F. (see O–59).

Barnet (see O–59).

Brooke (see O–59).

Brown (see O–59).

Campbell, O. J., and Edward G. Quinn (see O–59).

Chambers, E. K. (see O–59).

Clark (see O–59).

Halliday, F. E. (see O–59).

Harbage (see O–59).

Martin and Harrier (see O–59).

Parrott (see O–59).

Shabert, Ina (see O–59).

Wain (see O–59).

Wright and Lamar (see O–59).

Zesmer (see O–59).

Editions

Arden Shakespeare (see O–59).

Craig and Bevington, eds. (see O–59).

Harbage, ed. (see O–59).

New Arden Shakespeare (see O–59).

New Cambridge Shakespeare (see O–59).

New Clarendon Shakespeare (see O–59).

New Penguin Shakespeare (see O–59).

New Variorum Shakespeare (see O–59).

Oxford Old Spelling Edition (see O–59).

Riverside Shakespeare (see O–59).

Variorum Edition of Shakespeare (see O–59).

Concordances

Howard-Hill, T. H. (see O–55).

Spevack, Marvin (see O–55).

Biographies

Chambers, Sir Edmond K. *William Shakespeare: A Study of Facts and Problems.* 2 vols. Oxford: Clarendon Press, 1930.   PR2894.C44

Schoenbaum, Samuel. *Shakespeare: A Documentary Life.* Oxford: Clarendon Press, 1975.
PR2893.S3

————. *Shakespeare's Lives.* Oxford: Clarendon Press, 1970.   PR2894.S3

SHAW (1856–1950)

Journals

Independent Shavian: Journal of the New York Shavians, Inc. Vol. 1–. New York: New York Shavians, 1962–. 3/yr. Reviews.   PR5366.A136

ShawR   *Shaw: The Annual of Bernard Shaw Studies* [former titles: *Shaw Review,* 1957–1980; *Shaw Bulletin,* 1951–1956]. University Park: Pennsylvania State University Press, 1951–. 1/yr. Reviews. Bibliography: "A Continuing Checklist of Shaviana."
PR5366.A15

Shavian: The Journal of the Shaw Society. Vol. 1–. London: The Shaw Society. 1953–. 2–3/yr. Reviews. Bibliographies.   No LC number

Bibliographies

Laurence, Dan H. *Bibliography of Bernard Shaw.* 2 vols. Oxford: Clarendon Press, 1983.
Z8814.5.L35

Wearing, J. P., Elsie B. Adams, and Donald C. Haberman, comps. and eds. *G. B. Shaw: An Annotated Bibliography of Writings about Him.* 3 vols. Vol. 1: 1871–1930; Vol. 2, 1931–1956; vol. 3, 1957–1978. De Kalb: Northern Illinois University Press, 1986.   Z8814.5 W4 1986

Handbooks

Broad, C. Lewis, and Violet M. Broad. *Dictionary to the Plays and Novels of Bernard Shaw, with Bibliography of His Works and of the Literature concerning Him, with a Record of the Principal Shavian Play Productions.* London: A. and C. Black, 1929.
PR5366.H36 1975

Hardwick, Michael, and Molly Hardwick. *Bernard Shaw Companion.* New York: St. Martin's Press, 1973.   PR5367.H35 1974

Hartnoll, Phyllis. *Who's Who in Shaw.* New York: Taplinger, 1975.   PR5366.H36 1975

Kozelba, Paula. *Glossary to the Plays of Bernard Shaw.* New York: Teachers' College, Columbia University, 1959.   PR5366.A25

Purdom, Charles B. *Guide to the Plays of Bernard Shaw.* London: Methuen, 1963.   PR5367.P8 1963

Wagenknecht, Edward C. *Guide to Bernard Shaw.* New York: D. Appleton and Co., 1929.
PR5367.W3

Editions

Works of Bernard Shaw. 36 vols. London: Constable, 1930–1950.   LC numbers vary

Laurence, Dan H. *Shaw's Music: The Complete Musical Criticism in Three Volumes.* London: Max Reinhart, The Bodley Head, 1981.
ML60.S5175 1981b

————, ed. *Bodley Head Bernard Shaw: Collected Plays with Their Prefaces.* 7 vols. London: Max Reinhart, The Bodley Head, 1970–1975.
PR5360.F70

Concordance

Bevan, E. Dean. *Concordance to the Plays and Prefaces of Bernard Shaw.* 10 vols. Detroit: Gale, 1971. Computer-compiled. Based on the Constable edition, 1930–1938. KWIC format.   PR5366.A22

Biography

Henderson, Archibald. *George Bernard Shaw: Man of the Century.* New York: Appleton-Century-Crofts, 1956.   PR5366.H43

SHELLEY (1792–1822)

Journals

KSMB   *Keats-Shelley Memorial Bulletin, Rome* [title varies slightly]. Vol. 1–. London: Keats-Shelley Memorial Association, 1910–. 1/yr. Reviews. Bibliographies. *Bibliographical Index, I-XX, 1910- 69* (London: Dawson, 1972).   PR4836.A15

KSJ   *Keats-Shelley Journal* (see Q–26).

Bibliographies

Dunbar, Clement. *Bibliography of Shelley Studies, 1823–1950.* New York: Garland, 1976. Z8815.D85

Forman, Harry Buxton. *Shelley Library: An Essay in Bibliography: I. Shelley's Own Books, Pamphlets, and Broadsides, Posthumous Separate Issues, and Posthumous Books Wholly or Mainly by Him.* London: Reeves and Turner, 1886.
PR5428.L6 4th ser. no. 1

Handbook

Ellis, Frederick S. *Alphabetical Table of Contents of Shelley's Political Works. Shelley Society Publications,* 4th ser., no. 6. London: Reeves and Turner, 1888.   PR5428.L6 4th ser. no. 6

Editions

Ingpen, Roger, and Walter E. Peck, eds. *Complete Works of Percy Bysshe Shelley.* 10 vols. London: For the Julian Editions by E. Benn, 1926–1930.
PR5400.F26

Rogers, Neville, et al., eds. *Complete Poetical Works of Percy Bysshe Shelley.* 4 vols. planned. Oxford: Clarendon, 1972–.   PR5402 1972

Concordance

Ellis, Frederick S. *Lexical Concordance to the Poetical Works of Percy Bysshe Shelley: An Attempt to Classify Every Word Found Therein according to Its Signification.* London: Quaritch, 1892. Based on the Forman edition.   PR5430.E5

Biography

Holmes, Richard. *Shelley: The Pursuit.* New York: Dutton, 1975.   PR5431.H65 1975

SPENSER (c. 1552–1599)

Journals

Spenser Newsletter. Vol. 1–. Albany: State University of New York at Albany, 1968–. 3/yr. Reviews. Bibliographical notices.   No LC number

Spenser Studies: A Renaissance Poetry Annual. Vol. 1–. Pittsburgh: University of Pittsburgh Press, 1980–. 1/yr.   PR2362.A45

Bibliographies

Atkinson, Dorothy F. *Edmund Spenser: A Bibliographical Supplement.* Baltimore: Johns Hopkins University Press, 1937.   Z8830.8.C3E8

Carpenter, Frederick Ives. *Reference Guide to Edmund Spenser.* Chicago: University of Chicago Press, 1923. Rev. ed. Edited by Dorothy F. (Atkinson) Evans. Chicago: University of Chicago Press, 1967.   Z8830.8.C3E8 1967

McNeir, Waldo F., and Foster Provost. *Edmund Spenser: An Annotated Bibliography, 1937–1972.* 2d ed. Pittsburgh: Duquesne University Press, 1975.   Z8830.8.M33 1975

Sipple, William L., with the assistance of Bernard J. Vondersmith. *Edmund Spenser, 1900–1936: A Reference Guide.* Boston: G. K. Hall, 1984.
                                 Z8830.8.S58 1984

Handbooks

Fleay, Frederick G. *Guide to Chaucer and Spenser.* London: Collins, 1877.   PR1927.F5

Hamilton, A. C., ed. *Spenser Encyclopedia.* Toronto: University of Toronto Press, forthcoming.

Jones, H. S. V. *Spenser Handbook.* New York: Crofts, 1930.   PR2363.J6

Whitman, C. H. *Subject-Index to the Poems of Edmund Spenser.* New Haven: Yale University Press, 1918.   PR2362.W5

Editions

Greenlaw, Edwin, et al., eds. *Works of Edmund Spenser: A Variorum Edition.* 10 vols. Baltimore: Johns Hopkins University Press, 1932–1957.
                                 PR2351.G65

Smith, James C., and Ernest de Selincourt, eds. *Poetical Works of Edmund Spenser.* 3 vols. Oxford: Clarendon Press, 1910.   PR2350 1909

Concordances

Bjorvand, Einer. *Concordance to Spenser's Fowre Hymnes.* Oslo: Universitetsforlaget, 1973.
                                 PR2360.F63 B5 1973

Donow, Herbert J. *Concordance to the Sonnet Sequences of Daniel, Drayton, Shakespeare, Sidney, and Spenser.* Carbondale: Southern Illinois University Press, 1969.   PR1175.8.D6

Osgood, Charles G. *Concordance to the Poems of Edmund Spenser.* Washington, D. C.: Carnegie Institution, 1915. Based on the Globe edition of Morris (London, 1869) and the Cambridge edition of Dodge (Boston, 1908) and including variants of the Smith and de Selincourt edition (Oxford, 1910).
                                 PR2362.07

Biography

Judson, Alexander C. *Life of Edmund Spenser.* Baltimore: Johns Hopkins University Press, 1966.
                                 PR2351.G65 1966 vol. 11

SWIFT (1667–1745)

Journal

Scriblerian and the Kit-Cats (see P–8).

Bibliographies

Landa, Louis A., and James E. Tobin. *Jonathan Swift: A List of Critical Studies Published from 1895 to 1945.* New York: Cosmopolitan Science and Art Service Co., 1945.   Z8856.L18

Rodino, Richard H. *Swift Studies, 1965–1980: An Annotated Bibliography.* New York: Garland, 1984.
                                 Z8856.R6 1984

Stathis, James J. *Bibliography of Swift Studies, 1945–1965.* Nashville: Vanderbilt University Press, 1967.   Z8856.S8

Teerink, Herman. *Bibliography of the Writings of Jonathan Swift.* 2d ed., rev. and corr. Edited by by Arthur H. Scouten. Philadelphia: University of Pennsylvania Press, 1963.   Z8856.T26 1963

Vieth, David M. *Swift's Poetry, 1900–1980: An Annotated Bibliography of Studies, with a Critical Introduction.* New York: Garland, 1982.
                                 Z8856.V54 1982

Voigt, Milton. *Swift and the Twentieth Century.* Detroit: Wayne State University Press, 1964.
                                 PR3726.V6

Handbook

Johnson, Clifford R. *Plots and Characters in the Fiction of Eighteenth-Century English Authors.* Vol. 1, *Jonathan Swift, Daniel Defoe, and Samuel Richardson.* Hamden, Conn.: Archon, 1977.
                                 PR858.P53 J64 1977

Editions

Davis, Herbert, ed. *Prose Works of Jonathan Swift.* 15 vols. Oxford: B. H. Blackwell, 1939–1968.
                                 PR3721.D3

Guthkelch, A. C., and David Nichol Smith, eds. *Tale of a Tub, to Which Is Added the Battle of the Books and the Mechanical Operation of the Spirit. . .etc. . . ., with an Introduction and Notes Historical and Explanatory.* 2d ed. Oxford: Clarendon Press, 1958.   PR3724.T3 1958

Williams, Harold, ed. *Journal to Stella.* 2 vols. Oxford: Clarendon Press, 1948. PR3726.A65 1948

———, ed. *Poems of Jonathan Swift.* 2d ed. 3 vols. Oxford: Clarendon Press, 1958. PR3721.W5

Concordances

Kelling, Harold D., and Cathy L. Preston. *KWIC Concordance to Jonathan Swift's A Tale of a Tub, The Battle of the Books, and A Discourse concerning the Mechanical Operation of the Spirit, A Fragment.* New York: Garland, 1984. Computer-compiled. Based on the edition of Guthkelch and Nichol-Smith (1958).   PR3728.L33 K44 1984

Shinagel, Michael A. *Concordance to the Poems of Jonathan Swift.* Ithaca, N. Y.: Cornell University Press, 1972. Computer-compiled. Based on the 2d ed. by Harold Williams of the *Poems* (1958).
                                 PR3726.S45 1972

Biography

Ehrenpreis, Irvin. *Swift: The Man, His Works, and His Age.* 3 vols. Cambridge: Harvard University Press, 1962–1983.   PR3726.E37

TENNYSON (1809–1892)

Journal

Tennyson Research Bulletin. Vol. 1–. London: Tennyson Research Centre, 1967–. 1/yr. Reviews. Bibliographical notes.   PR5579.T43

Bibliographies

Beetz, Kirk H. *Tennyson: A Bibliography, 1827–1982*. Metuchen, N. J.: Scarecrow Press, 1984.   Z8866.B43 1984

Tennyson, Charles, and Christine Fall, eds. *Alfred Tennyson: An Annotated Bibliography*. Athens: University of Georgia Press, 1967.   Z8866.T38

Wise, T. J. *Bibliography of the Writings of Alfred, Lord Tennyson*. 2 vols. London: Privately printed, 1908. Primary.   Z8866.W57

Handbooks

Baker, Arthur E. *Tennyson Dictionary*. London: Routledge and Sons, 1916.   PR5580.B4

Luce, Morton. *Handbook to the Works of Alfred, Lord Tennyson*. Rev. ed. London: G. Bell and Sons, 1914.   PR5588.L75

Marshall, George O. *Tennyson Handbook*. New York: Twayne, 1963.   PR5588.M3

Editions

Pfordresher, John, ed. *Variorum Edition of Tennyson's Idylls of the King*. New York: Columbia University Press, 1973.   PR5558.A1 1973

Ricks, Christopher, ed. *Poems of Tennyson*. Longman's Annotated English Poets. Harlow: Longmans, 1969.   PR5550.F69

Shatto, Susan, and Marion Shaw, eds. *In Memoriam/Tennyson*. Oxford: Clarendon Press, 1982.   PR5562.A1 1982

Concordances

Baker, Arthur E. *Concordance to the Poetical and Dramatic Works of Alfred, Lord Tennyson*. London: Kegan Paul, Trench, Trubner, 1914. Based on the Macmillan complete edition. Criticized as somewhat unreliable.   PR5580.B3

Brightwell, Danile B. *Concordance to the Entire Works of Alfred Tennyson*. London: E. Moxon, 1869.   PR5595.B8

Biographies

Martin, Robert B. *Tennyson: The Unquiet Heart*. Oxford: Clarendon Press, 1980.   PR5581.M3 1980

Tennyson, Sir Charles. *Alfred Tennyson, by His Grandson*. New York: Macmillan, 1949.
PR5581.T38

WOOLF (1882–1941)

Journal

VWQ   *Virginia Woolf Quarterly*. Vol. 1–. San Diego, Calif.: San Diego State University Press, 1972–. 4/yr. Reviews. Bibliographies.   PR6045.O72 Z894

Bibliographies

Kirkpatrick, B. J. *Bibliography of Virginia Woolf*. 3d ed. Oxford: Clarendon Press, 1980.
Z8984.2.K5 1980

Majumdar, Robin. *Virginia Woolf: An Annotated Bibliography of Criticism, 1915–1974*. New York: Garland, 1976.   Z8984.2.M33

Handbook

Steele, Elizabeth. *Virginia Woolf's Literary Sources and Allusions: A Guide to the Essays*. New York: Garland, 1983.   Z8984.2.S74 1983

Editions

Uniform Edition of the Works of Virginia Woolf. 17 vols. London: Hogarth, 1929–1955.
LC numbers vary

McNellie, Andrew, ed. *Essays of Virginia Woolf*. Vol. 1, *1904–1912*. San Diego: Harcourt Brace Jovanovich, 1986.   PR6045.O72 A6 1986

Woolf, Leonard, ed. *Collected Essays of Virginia Woolf*. 4 vols. London: Hogarth, 1966.
PR6045.O73 A16 1966

Concordances

Haule, James M., and Philip H. Smith, Jr., eds. *Concordances to the Novels of Virginia Woolf*. A text-fiche series including more than 80 microfiche and 9 printed guides. Oxford: Microforms International, 1981–.

Biography

Bell, Quentin. *Virginia Woolf: A Biography*. London: Hogarth, 1972.   PR6045.O72 2545

WORDSWORTH (1770–1850)

Journal

WC   *Wordsworth Circle*. Vol. 1–. Washington, D. C.: Heldref Publications, 1970–. 4/yr. Reviews. Bibliography: "Wordsworth Scholarship: An Annual Register."   PR1.W67

Bibliographies

Bauer, Neil S. *William Wordsworth: A Reference Guide to British Criticism, 1793–1899*. Boston: G. K. Hall, 1978.   Z8985.B38

Healey, G. H. *Cornell Wordsworth Collection. A Catalogue*. Ithaca, N. Y.: Cornell University Press, 1957. Primary and secondary.   Z8985.C65

Hearn, Ronald B., et al. *Wordsworth Criticism since 1952: A Bibliography*. Salzburg: Institut für englische Sprache und Literatur, Universität Salzburg, 1978.   Z8985.W9

Henley, Elton F., and David H. Stam. *Wordsworthian Criticism 1945–1964*. Rev. ed. New York: New York Public Library, 1965.   Z8985.H4 1965

Jones, Mark, and Karl Kroeber. *Wordsworth Scholarship and Criticism, 1973–1984: An Annotated Bibliography, with Selected Criticism, 1809–1972*. New York: Garland, 1985.
Z8985.J66 1985

Logan, James V. *Wordsworthian Criticism [1850–1944]: A Guide and Bibliography*. Columbus: Ohio State University Press, 1947. Rev. ed. 1961.   PR5887.3.L6 1961

Stam, David H. *Wordsworthian Criticism 1964–1973: An Annotated Bibliography, Including Additions to Wordsworthian Criticism 1945–1964*. New York: New York Public Library and Readex Books, 1974.   Z8985.S8

Handbooks

Pinion, F. B. *Wordsworth Companion: Survey and Assessment*. New York: Free Press, 1984.
PR5888.P5x 1984

Tutin, J. R. *Wordsworth Dictionary of Persons and Places, with the Familiar Quotations from His Works, Including Full Index and a Chronologically Arranged List of His Best Poems*. Hull: For the author, 1891. Bound with: Tutin., J. R. *Index to the Animal and Vegetable Kingdoms of Wordsworth*. Hull: For the author, 1892. Reprint. New York: Johnson Reprint, 1967.   PR5880.T8 1967

Editions

Abrams, M. H., Jonathan Wordsworth, and Stephen Gill, eds. *Prelude, 1799, 1805, 1850: Authoritative Texts, Context and Reception: Recent Critical Essays.* New York: Norton, 1979.
PR5864.A2 W6 1979

Brett, R. L., and A. R. Jones, eds. *Lyrical Ballads [by] Wordsworth and Coleridge; the Text of the 1798 Edition with the Additional 1800 Poems and the Prefaces.* New York: Barnes and Noble, 1963.
PR5869.L9 1963

de Selincourt, Ernest, and Helen Darbishire, eds. *Poetical Works of William Wordsworth, Edited from the Manuscripts, with Textual and Critical Notes.* Rev. ed. 5 vols. Oxford: Clarendon Press, 1952–1959.
PR5850.F40

——, ed. *Prelude.* Rev. ed. by Helen Darbishire. Oxford: Clarendon, 1959.
PR5864.A2 D4 1959

Parrish, Stephen M. *Cornell Wordsworth.* 11 vols. planned. Ithaca, N. Y.: Cornell University Press, 1977–.
LC numbers vary

Smyser, Jane Worthinton, and W. J. B. Owen, eds. *Prose Works of William Wordsworth.* 3 vols. Oxford: Clarendon Press, 1974.   PR5851.09 1974

Concordance

Cooper, Lane, ed. *Wordsworth Concordance.* London: Smith Elder, 1911. Based on Hutchinson edition (Oxford, 1907).   PR5880.C6

Biographies

Davies, Hunter. *William Wordsworth: A Biography.* London: Weidenfeld and Nicolson, 1980.
PR5881.D34 1980

Moorman, Mary (Trevelyan). *William Wordsworth: A Biography.* 2 vols. Oxford: Clarendon Press, 1957–1965.   PR5881.M6

Reed, Mark L. *Wordsworth.* 3 vols. planned. Vol. 1, *Chronology of the Early Years, 1720–1799.* Vol. 2, *Chronology of the Middle Years, 1800–1815.* Cambridge: Harvard University Press, 1967–1975.   PR5881.R43

YEATS (1865–1939)

Journal

YER   *Yeats-Eliot Review: A Journal of Criticism and Scholarship* [former titles: *T. S. Eliot Review*, vols. 2–4, 1975–1977; *T. S. Eliot Newsletter*, vol. 1 only, 1974]. Vol. 5–. Edmondton: University of Alberta, 1978–. 2/yr. Reviews. Bibliographical update. List of dissertations completed. Work in progress.   PS3509.L43 Z96

Bibliographies

Cross, K. G. W., and R. T. Dunlop. *Bibliography of Yeats Criticism, 1887–1965.* London: Macmillan, 1971.   Z8992.C76

Jochum, K. P. S. *W. B. Yeats: A Classified Bibliography of Criticism, Including Additions to Allan Wade's Bibliography of the Writings of W. B. Yeats and a Section on the Irish Literary and Dramatic Revival.* Urbana: University of Illinois Press, 1978.
Z8992.J59 1978

Saul, George B. *Prolegomena to the Study of Yeats' Plays.* Philadelphia: University of Pennsylvania Press, 1958.   Z8992.S29

——. *Prolegomena to the Study of Yeats' Poems.* Philadelphia: University of Pennsylvania Press, 1957.   Z8992.S3

Stoll, John E. *Great Deluge: A Yeats Bibliography.* Troy, N. Y.: Whitston, 1971.   Z8992.S74

Wade, Allan. *Bibliography of the Writings of W. B. Yeats.* 3d ed. Revised and edited by Russell K. Alspach. London: Hart-Davis, 1968.   Z8992.W14

Handbooks

Jeffares, A. Norman. *New Commentary on the Poems of W. B. Yeats.* Stanford: Stanford University Press, 1984.   PR5907.J39 1984

——, and A. S. Knowland. *Commentary on the Collected Plays of W. B. Yeats.* Stanford: Stanford University Press, 1975.   PR5909.D7 J4

McGarry, James P. *Place Names in the Writings of William Butler Yeats.* Edited with additional material by Edward Malins. Toronto: Macmillan of Canada, 1976.   PR5906.A27 1976

Taylor, Richard. *Reader's Guide to the Plays of W. B. Yeats.* New York: St. Martin's Press, 1983.
PR5908.D7 T38 1983

Unterecker, John. *Reader's Guide to William Butler Yeats.* New York: Noonday, 1959.
PR5907.U5

Editions

Allt, Peter, and Russell K. Alspach, eds. *Variorum Edition of the Poems of W. B. Yeats.* 2d ed. London: Macmillan, 1966.   PR5900.A3 1966

Alspach, Russell K., ed. *Variorum Edition of the Plays of W. B. Yeats.* New York: Macmillan, 1966.
PR5900.A4

Finneran, Richard J., ed. *Poems of W. B. Yeats: A New Edition.* New York: Macmillan, 1983.
PR5900.A3 1983

Frayne, John P., and Colton Johnson. *Uncollected Prose by William Butler Yeats, 1887–1939.* New York: Columbia University Press, 1976.
PR5900.A5

Concordances

Domville, Eric, ed. *Concordance to the Plays of W. B. Yeats.* 2 vols. Ithaca, N. Y.: Cornell University Press, 1972. Computer-compiled. Based on the variorum edition by R. K. Alspach (1966).
PR5901.A24

Parrish, Stephen M., and James A. Painter. *Concordance to the Poems of W. B. Yeats.* Ithaca, N. Y.: Cornell University Press, 1963. Computer-compiled. Based on the variorum edition by Allt and Alspach (1957).   PR5907.P35

Biographies

Mikhail, E. H., ed. *W. B. Yeats: Interviews and Recollections.* 2 vols. London: Macmillan, 1977.
PR5906.W2 1977b

Tuohy, Frank. *Yeats.* London: Macmillan, 1976.
PR5906.T8 1976b

VI. SCOTTISH LITERATURE AND SCOTTISH STUDIES

M–70   **Lloyd, D. M., ed.** *Reader's Guide to Scotland: A Bibliography.* London: National Book League, 1968.   Z2051.N37

This guide by the Keeper of Printed Books in the National Library of Scotland is a discursive commentary on primarily up-to-date works in print, divided into twelve sections, which are themselves further subdivided. The sections treat Scotland in General; its History; Tourism; Arts and Crafts; Language and Literature; Philosophy; Education; Law; Administration; Agriculture, Industry and Commerce; Food and Drink; and Sports. An appendix lists some supplementary titles published too late for inclusion or otherwise overlooked. There is an index of personal names.

The section on Scottish Language and Literature is subdivided as follows: Scottish Language, Scottish Place Names; Literature, General; Literature before 1700 (with further divisions of individual authors here and in the subsequent sections); Literature after 1700; 1850–1920; 1920 to the Present; Gaelic Literature.

M–72   **Aitken, William R., ed.** *Scottish Literature in English and Scots: A Guide to Information Sources.* Detroit: Gale Research Co., 1982.   Z2057.A35 1982

A total of 3,956 serially numbered entries are disposed into six sections. Section 1, General Works, has subdivisions for Bibliographies and Reference Works; Literary History and Criticism; Current Scottish Literary Periodicals; Anthologies; Language; Dictionaries; Collective Biography; Background Studies; and Societies and Organizations. The second section treats Medieval and Renaissance Scots Literature with subsections on Bibliographies, Literary History and Criticism, Anthologies, Background Studies, and Printing and Publishing, followed by bibliographies of thirty-six Individual Authors and Anonymous Works.

Similar arrangements characterize section 3, 1600–1800, with general subsections for Bibliographies, Literary History and Criticism, Anthologies, Background Studies, Printing and Publishing, and Periodicals, followed by bibliographies for individual authors; section 4, 1800–1900, with general subsections followed by bibliographies of individual authors; and section 5, 1900, with general subsections followed by bibliographies of individual authors. The sixth and last section treats Popular and Folk Literature with appropriate subdivisions for texts, general studies, and the various genres of folk literature.

Some entries are briefly annotated, often with an evaluative remark. A chronological rather than alphabetical arrangement is used in the general section, and the author sections are organized in the chronological order of authors' birth dates. The author bibliographies themselves begin with a brief biographical and critical notice, followed by a primary bibliography in chronological order, subdivided if necessary to include individual works, collections and selections, and letters. A selective secondary bibliography follows, including as appropriate chronologically arranged sections for biography and criticism, bibliography, and reference works. The volume concludes with indexes of authors, titles, and subjects.

M–73   **Royle, Trevor.** *Companion to Scottish Literature.* Detroit: Gale Research Co., 1983.   PR8506.R69 1983

This volume, published in England under the title *Macmillan Companion to Scottish Literature*, is a dictionary consisting of primarily biographical articles on writers born before 1950 writing in English, Scots, and Scots Gaelic. Authors include poets, dramatists, and novelists, along with men of letters, essayists, historians, philosophers, divines, diarists, and others noted for literary excellence. Relatively brief biographies are followed by lists of major works and works of reference. In addition to biographical articles, the dictionary includes entries on major literary works, institutions, literary movements, historical persons and events significant to Scottish literary history, printed ephemera, and publishing history. The dictionary is preceded by a brief bibliography of sources consulted in its preparation.

M–74   **Daiches, David, ed.** *Companion to Scottish Culture.* London: Edward Arnold, 1981.   DA772.C63 1981

This well-illustrated volume contains more than 300 articles (some of considerable length) in a dictionary arrangement. Subjects range from the Scottish Enlightenment to children's street games to marriage customs, eating habits, and from literary movements and institutions to authors and genres. A bibliography of books and articles in a topical arrangement and an index conclude the work.

M–75   *Annual Bibliography of Scottish Literature [1969–].* Supplement 1– to the *Bibliotheck: A Scottish Journal of Bibliography and Allied Topics.* Aberdeen: Scottish Group of the University, College, and Research Sections of the Library Association, 1970–.   Z2057.A65

This work, carried as part of the *Bibliotheck* 1956–1968 and now separately published, lists books, articles, essays, and reviews in the field of Scottish literature. It is arranged in four sections, with serially numbered entries in each. The sections are as follows: A. General Bibliographical and Reference Materials; B. General Literary Criticism, Including Anthologies and Collections; C. Individual Authors (Medieval and Renaissance; 1660–1800; 19th Century; 20th Century); and D. Ballads and Folk Literature. There are some cross-references. Indexes of authors as subjects and of scholars, editors, and compilers conclude each annual list.

For more complete treatment of Scottish Gaelic literature, users are referred to the *Bibliotheca Celtica*. For critical commentary on current publications, see "The Year's Work in Scottish Literary Studies" (M–76).

M–76   "**The Year's Work in Scottish Literary and Linguistic Studies [1973–].**" Annual supplement to the *Scottish Literary Journal: A Review of Studies in Scottish Languages and Literature.* Aberdeen: Association for Scottish Literary Studies, 1974–.   PR8514.S3 suppl.

Originally titled "The Year's Work in Scottish Literature" and published annually from 1970 through 1974 in *Scottish Literary News*, this annual set of bibliographical essays provides descriptive and evaluative commentary on selected materials cited in the annual bibliography published as a supplement to the *Bibliotheck* (M–75). The signed essays currently treat work on Language, Folk Literature, Medieval to 1650, 1650–1800, 19th Century, and 20th Century Literature. In its original format the year's work in language was not surveyed.

The annual supplement (1976–) also includes a bibliography of "Current Scottish Prose and Verse [1974–]."

An earlier, still valuable bibliographical review is R. H. Carnie's "The Bibliography of Scottish Literature, 1957–1967: A Survey," *Forum for Modern Language Studies* 3 (1967): 263–275 [PB1.F63].

M–77   "**Scottish Studies in [1956–]: An Annual Bibliography.**" *Scottish Studies,* vol. 1–. Edinburgh: University of Edinburgh, 1957–.   AS121.S35

This bibliography presents briefly annotated citations of works concerned with Scottish traditional life and arts, excluding written literature, art, architecture, and archaeology; political and institutional history; biographies of well-known individuals; Scottish topography and travel literature; and reprints. The classification of entries varies but includes such rubrics as Dialect and Names; Biography and Reminiscences; Clan and Family History; Local Life, History, and Geography; Material Culture: Farming, Fishing, Crafts, and Industries; Communications, Navigation, and Trade; Social Life and Custom; Traditional Music, Song, and Verse; Traditional Tales and History; Proverbs and Riddles; and Beliefs.

M–78 Scholarly Journals in Scottish Literature and Scottish Studies.

> *Bibliothek Bibliotheck: A Scottish Journal of Bibliography and Allied Topics.* Vol. 1–. Glasgow: Library Association, University, College and Research Section, Scottish Group, 1956–. 3/yr. Reviews. Annual Bibliography (see M–75).   Z1007.B6

> *Scottish Historical Review.* Vol. 1–. Aberdeen: Aberdeen University Press, 1903–. 2–4/yr. Reviews. Annual Bibliography. Index to vols. 1–12 (1918), 13–25 (1933).   DA750.S21

> *Scottish Literary Journal* [former title: *Scottish Literary News*, 1970–1974]. Vol. 1–. Aberdeen: Association for Scottish Literary Studies, 1974–. 2/yr. Reviews. Annual Bibliography (see M–76).   PR8514.S3

> ScS *Scottish Studies: The Journal of the School of Scottish Studies.* Vol. 1–. Edinburgh: University of Edinburgh, 1957–. 1/yr. Reviews. Annual Bibliography (see M–77).   AS121.S35

> SSL *Studies in Scottish Literature.* Vol. 1–. Columbia: University of South Carolina, English Department, 1963–. 1/yr. Reviews.   PR8500.S82

M–79 Some Frequently Recommended Works on Scottish Literature and Scottish Studies.

Aitken, A. J., and Tom McArthur, eds. *Languages of Scotland.* Edinburgh: W. and R. Chambers, 1979.   P381.S35 L3 1979

Craig, D. *Scottish Literature and the Scottish People, 1680–1930.* London: Chatto and Windus, 1961.   PR8511.L7 1961

Daiches, David. *Paradox of Scottish Culture: The Eighteenth Century Experience.* London: Oxford University Press, 1964.   DA812.D3

———, ed. *Companion to Scottish Culture.* London: Edward Arnold, 1981.   DA772.C63 1981

Geddie, William. *Bibliography of Middle Scots Poets, with an Introduction on the History of Their Reputations.* Edinburgh: Blackwood, 1912.   PR8633.S4

Glen, Duncan. *Hugh Macdiarmid (Christopher Murray Grieve) and the Scottish Renaissance.* Edinburgh: W. and R. Chambers, 1964.   PR6013.R735 Z68

———, ed. *Bibliography of Scottish Poets from Stevenson to 1974.* Preston, Lancs: Akros Publications, 1974.   Z2059.P6 G58

Handley Taylor, Geoffrey. *Scottish Authors Today: Being a Checklist of Authors Born in Scotland Together with Brief Particulars of Authors Born Elsewhere Who Are Currently Working or Residing in Scotland—An Assemblage of More Than 700 Authors. . . .* London: Eddison Press, 1972.   Z2057.H35

Hart, Francis R. *Scottish Novel: A Critical Survey.* Cambridge: Harvard University Press, 1978. PR8597.H37

Henderson, T. F. *Scottish Vernacular Literature: A Succinct History.* London: D. Nutt, 1898.   PR8511.H4

Kinsley, James, ed. *Scottish Poetry: A Critical Survey.* London: Cassell, 1955.   PR8561.K5

Lindsay, Maurice John. *History of Scottish Literature* (with a classified, select bibliography). London: Hale, 1977.   PR8511.L5

MacKenzie, A. M. *Historical Survey of Scottish Literature to 1714.* London: A. Maclehose, 1933. PR8511.M25

Millar, John H. *Literary History of Scotland.* London: T. F. Unwin, 1903.   PR8561.M5

Mitchison, Rosalind. *History of Scotland.* 2d ed. London: Methuen, 1982.   DA760.M58 1982

New History of Scotland. 8 vols. London: Edward Arnold, 1981–.

> Vol. 1. Smyth, Alfred P. *Warlords and Holy Men: Scotland, A. D. 80–1000* (1984).
> DA777.S68 1984

> Vol. 2. Barrow, G. W. S. *Kingship and Unity: Scotland, 1000–1306* (1984).   DA788.B37

> Vol. 3. Grant, Alexander. *Independence and Nationhood: Scotland, 1306–1469* (1984).
> DA783.G72 1984

> Vol. 4. Not yet published.

> Vol. 5. Mitchison, Rosalind. *Lordship to Patronage: Scotland, 1603–1745* (1983). DA800.M56 1983

> Vol. 6. Lenman, Bruce. *Integration, Enlightenment, and Industrialization: Scotland, 1746–1832* (1981).   DA809.L46 1981

> Vol. 7. Checkland, S. G. *Industry and Ethos: Scotland, 1832–1914* (1984).   DA815.C44 1984

> Vol. 8. Harvie, Christopher T. *No Gods and Precious Few Heroes: Scotland, 1914–1980* (1981).
> DA821.H33 1981

Smith, G. Gregory. *Scottish Literature: Character and Influence.* London: Macmillan, 1919.   PR8511.S6

Spiers, John N. *Scots Literary Tradition: An Essay in Criticism.* 2d rev. ed. London: Chatto and Windus, 1962.
PR8561.S65

Thomson, Derick. *Introduction to Gaelic Poetry.* London: Gollancz, 1974.   PB1607.T5 1974b

Webster, Bruce. *Scotland from the Eleventh Century to 1603.* Cambridge: Cambridge University Press, 1975.
DA774.8.W4

Wittig, Kurt H. *Scottish Tradition in Literature.* Edinburgh: Oliver Boyd, 1958.   PR8511.W5

Woolley, John S. *Bibliography for Scottish Linguistic Studies.* Edinburgh: James Thin for the Linguistic Survey of Scotland, University of Edinburgh, 1954.
No LC number

VII. ANGLO-IRISH LITERATURE AND IRISH STUDIES

M–80 Eager, Alan R. *Guide to Irish Bibliographical Material: Being a Bibliography of Irish Bibliographies and Some Sources of Information.* 2d ed., rev. and enl. London: Library Association, 1980.   Z2031.E16 1980

Originally published in 1964, this work in its much revised and enlarged form presents a bibliography of 9,517 serially numbered bibliographies and reference sources concerning Irish studies. Included are separately published works as well as items in books and periodicals and studies in manuscript form. The occasionally annotated entries are classified by subject in a scheme roughly based on the Dewey decimal classification. The main sections are as follows: General Works, Philosophy, Religion, Sociology, Philology, Science, Useful Arts, Fine Arts, Literature, Geography and Travel, Biography and History. A brief supplement is followed by an author index and an elaborate subject index.

M–81 **Brown, Stephen J., S.J.** *Guide to Books on Ireland. Part 1. Prose Literature, Poetry, Music, and Plays.* Dublin: Figgis, 1912.   Z2031.B86

This bibliographical guide, of which no more parts were published, presents annotated entries on books in English on Irish literature. Both primary and secondary works are included and are arranged in sections listing works of authors in general collections, of prose works, of poetry, of music, and of Irish plays by titles and by subjects. Though an old work, the consensus is that Brown's *Guide* remains a key resource for assembling bibliographies of nineteenth- and early-twentieth-century Anglo-Irish literature.

Brown also compiled *Ireland in Fiction: A Guide to Irish Novels, Tales, Romances, and Folklore*, new ed. (Dublin and London: Maunsel, 1919) [Z2039.F488]. This annotated bibliography, first published in 1916, is arranged by author, with brief biographical notes and synopses of the 1,713 works of fiction cited. An appendix presents an annotated bibliography of reference works consulted and a classified index to the fiction with such categories as fiction in periodicals, historical fiction, legends, and Catholic clerical life. There is an index of titles and subjects.

M–82 **Finneran, Richard J., ed.** *Anglo-Irish Literature: A Review of Research.* New York: Modern Language Association, 1976.   PR8713.A5

This work contains a series of eleven extended bibliographical essays by specialists treating work on writers of Anglo-Irish background published through 1974, with some items published in 1975 included. The eleven sections are as follows: 1, General Works (Richard M. Kain); 2, Nineteenth Century Writers (James F. Kilroy); 3, Oscar Wilde (Ian Fletcher and John Stokes); 4, George Moore (Helmut E. Gerber); 5, Bernard Shaw (Stanley Weintraub); 6, W. B. Yeats (Richard J. Finneran); 7, J. M. Synge (Weldon Thornton); 8, James Joyce (Thomas F. Staley); 9, Four Revival Figures: Lady Gregory, AE [i.e., George W. Russell], Oliver St. John Gogarty, and James Stephens (James F. Carens); 10, Sean O'Casey (David Krause); and 11, The Modern Drama (Robert Hogan, Bonnie R. Scott, and Gorgon Henderson). More than 500 pages in length, the volume concludes with an index of authors.

A supplement, *Recent Research on Anglo-Irish Writers* (New York: Modern Language Association, 1983) [PR8712.R4 1983] extends coverage through 1980. The section on General Works is by Maurice Harmon; in addition, there are new chapters on Modern Fiction (Diane Tolomeo) and Modern Poetry (Mary M. Fitzgerald). The editor indicates in the preface that there will be further supplements in due course.

M–83 **"Bibliography Bulletin."** *Irish University Review: A Journal of Irish Studies,* vol. 2–. Dublin: University College, 1971–.   PR8700.I73

This annual bibliography of Irish studies is produced by the Bibliography Subcommittee of the International Association for the Study of Anglo-Irish Literature [IASAIL]. In the first few volumes were presented a number of current and retrospective bibliographies concerned with Irish studies over various periods of time in various countries. Starting with the bibliography for 1973 published in volume 6 (1976), a uniform system of entries for work from scholars in all countries was established and a single classification. There are now two main classes, the first treating general books and articles (including bibliographies, festschriften, and anthologies), the second work on individual authors, including citation of both primary works (new editions etc.) and secondary works. Each annual bibliography ends with a comprehensive author index.

M–84 **"Annual Bibliography."** *Journal of Irish Literature,* vol. 1–. Newark, Del.: Proscenium Press, 1972–.   PR8800.J68

M–85 **"The Year's Work in Anglo-Irish Literature [1975–]."** *Études irlandaises: Revue française d'histoire, civilisation et littérature de l'Irlande.* New series, vol. 1–. Villeneuve d'Ascq: Université de Lille III, 1976–.   DA925.E86

This work, published under the auspices of the Centre d'études et de recherches irlandaises, presents a descriptively annotated listing in two sections of work on Anglo-Irish literature. The first section, on General Studies, is followed by a section of individual authors which is further subdivided into authors of the eighteenth, nineteenth, and twentieth centuries. Abbreviations identify the genre of the work cited, from ant[hology] to p[oetry] and e.c. [étude critique]. In addition to this bibliography the journal includes bibliographical notes and articles on current professional activities in the field of Irish studies, as well as an annotated bibliography titled "Histoire, politique, institutions irlandaises [year]," the entries of which are disposed into eight categories, as follows: 1, Bibliographies; 2, Generalities; 3, Archaeology and Antiquities; 4, History (from the origins to 1916; the contemporary period); 5, Economics; 6, Institutions; 7, Miscellaneous; and 8, Northern Ireland. In addition, there are numerous reviews of new works in Irish studies and reviews of reviews, citing current contents in a number of other Irish studies periodicals.

M–86 **Harmon, Maurice.** *Modern Irish Literature, 1800–1967: A Reader's Guide.* Dublin: Dolmen Press, 1967.   Z2037.H3

This work is an introduction to Anglo-Irish literature in four parts, with bibliographies, which presents an introduction to Irish writing in English arranged to highlight certain literary themes and literary movements. The parts are: 1, Irish Literature 1800–1900; 2, Irish Literature, 1890–1920; 3, Post-Revolutionary Irish Literature; and 4, Irish History and Culture: Selected Bibliography. There is no index.

Harmon has also published *Select Bibliography for the Study of Anglo-Irish Literature and Its Backgrounds* (Port Credit, Ont.: P. D. Meany, 1977) [Z2037.H32].

M–87 **McKenna, Brian.** *Irish Literature, 1800–1875: A Guide to Information Sources.* Detroit: Gale Research Co., 1978.   Z2037.M235

This bibliographical guide is divided into two parts, the first on Background and Research, with subsections citing Anthologies; Periodicals; Bibliography, Biography, and Criticism; and four supplementary sections on "Current Awareness," Irish Literature and Antiquities, Irish History, and Irish Songs and Folklore. The second part presents complete primary and selective secondary bibliographies for 114 individual authors. Cited works are unnumbered and are treated as components in a series of discursive essays. There are indexes of authors, titles, and subjects.

M–88 **Kersnowski, F. L., et al.** *Bibliography of Modern Irish and Anglo-Irish Literature.* San Antonio, Tex.: Trinity University Press, 1977.   Z2037.K47

After a brief introduction this work presents bibliographies for a total of sixty-one authors from 1880 to the present. For each author are listed standard bibliographies, bibliographies of criticism, collected works, individual works by genres, and important works of biography and criticism. In the absence of the second McKenna volume (see M–87) this remains the best available closed bibliography exclusively concerned with modern Irish and Anglo-Irish authors.

M–89 Hogan, Robert, editor in chief. *Dictionary of Irish Literature.* Westport, Conn.: Greenwood Press, 1979.

PR8706.D5 1979

Available outside the United States under the title *Macmillan Dictionary of Irish Literature,* the bulk of this work treats Irish writing in English, though the main body is preceded by a survey of "Gaelic Literature" written by Seamus O'Neill. Articles signed by contributors vary in length from twenty-five words to about 10,000 and present biographical and critical essays on some 500 Irish writers writing in English. There are also general articles on such topics as folklore, and the genres; articles on major historians, political writers, editors, orators, and of letters; as well as on various theaters, presses, journals, and literary organizations, groups, and movements. Many articles have primary and secondary bibliographies appended. After the main body is a chronology of historical and literary events from A.D. 432, the date of St. Patrick's mission, to the present. This is followed by a classified general bibliography of best books on Ireland in general and on its geography, climate, history, economics, architecture, customs, and especially on its literature. The volume concludes with an index of names, titles, and subjects.

Among other dictionaries may be mentioned the frequently cited *Dictionary of Irish Writers* by Brian Talbot Cleeve, 3 vols. (Cork: Mercier Press, 1967–1971) [PR8727.C5], the first volume of which treats some 500 fiction writers including novelists, dramatists, poets, and short-story writers in English; the second volume treats 300 nonfiction authors, historians, biographers, scientists; the third treats Gaelic authors. Entries should be verified by recourse to other sources of information. See also David James O'Donoghue's *Poets of Ireland: A Biographical and Bibliographical Dictionary* (Dublin: Hodges Figgis, 1912) [Z2037.O26].

M–93 Scholarly Journals in Anglo-Irish Literature, Irish Studies, and Celtic Studies.

Anglo-Irish Studies. Vol. 1–4. Buckinghamshire, England: Alpha Academic, 1975–1979. 1/yr.

No LC number

CJIS   *Canadian Journal of Irish Studies: Official Journal of the Canadian Association for Irish Studies.* Vol. 1–. Vancouver: University of British Columbia, 1975–. 2/yr. Reviews.   No LC number

DM   *Dublin Magazine* [former title: *Dubliner*]. Vol. 1–. Dublin: Dun Laoghaire Co., 1923–. 4/yr. Reviews.   PR8844.D8

Éire   *Eire-Ireland: A Journal of Irish Studies.* Vol. 1–. Published by the Irish American Cultural Institute. St. Paul, Minn.: College of St. Thomas, 1965–. 4/yr. Reviews.   No LC number

EI   *Études irlandaises: Revue française d'histoire, civilisation et littérature de l'Irlande.* Vol. 1–. Lille: Université de Lille, Centre d'études et de recherches irlandaises, 1972–. 1/yr. Reviews. Bibliography: Year's Work in Irish Studies (M–85).   DA925.E86

Hermathena: A Dublin University Review [Hermathena]. Trinity College. Vol. 1–. Dublin: Hodges Figgis, 1873–. 1 or 2/yr. Reviews.   AS121.H5

IHS   *Irish Historical Studies.* Vol. 1–. Dublin: Hodges, Figgis, for the Irish Historical Society and the Ulster Society for Irish Historical Studies, 1938–. 2/yr. Reviews. Bibliographies: "Writings on Irish History [year]" and "Research on Irish History in Irish Universities."   DA900.I63

Irish Studies. Vol. 1–. Cambridge: Cambridge University Press, 1980–. 1/yr.   No LC number

IUR   *Irish University Review: A Journal of Irish Studies.*

Vol. 1–. Dublin: University College, 1970–. 2/yr. Reviews. Bibliographical Bulletin of the International Association for the Study of Anglo-Irish Literature (M–83).   PR8700.I73

JIL   *Journal of Irish Literature.* Vol. 1–. Newark, Del.: Proscenium Press, 1972–. 3/yr. Reviews.

PR8830.J68

JJQ   *James Joyce Quarterly* (see M–60).

ShawR   *Shaw Review* (see M–60).

SH   *Studia Hibernica.* Vol. 1–. Drumcondra, Dublin: St. Patrick's College, 1960–. 1/yr. Reviews.

PB1201.S88

YER   *Yeats-Eliot Review* (see M–60).

Celtic Studies

Bibliotheca Celtica (see B–53).

Celtica   *Celtica.* Vol. 1–. Dublin: Dublin Institute for Advanced Studies, 1946–. Irregular. Reviews.

PB1001.C63

EC   *Études celtiques* [former title: *Revue celtique, 1870–1934*]. Vol. 1–. Paris: Societe d'édition "Les belles lettres," 1936–. 1/yr. Reviews. "Periodiques" presents a list of French articles on Celtic studies, with abstracts.   PB1001.E8

Lochlann: A Review of Celtic Studies. 6 vols. Oslo: Universitetsforlaget, 1958–1974. 2/yr. Reviews.

PB1001.L625

StC   *Studia Celtica.* Vol. 1–. Aberstwyth: University of Wales, Board of Celtic Studies, 1966–. 1–2/yr. Reviews.   PB1001.S73

ZCP   *Zeitschrift für celtische Philologie.* Vol. 1–. Tübingen: Niemeyer, 1896–. 2/yr. Reviews.

PB1001.Z5

See also Royal Irish Academy, Committee for the Study of Anglo-Irish Language and Literature, *Irish and Anglo-Irish Periodicals* (Dublin: Royal Irish Academy, 1970) [Z6956.I7 R67 1970], and R. P. Holzapfel, a *Survey of Irish Literary Periodicals from 1900 to the Present Day* (M.Litt. thesis, Trinity College, Dublin, 1963 / 64).

M–94 Some Frequently Recommended Works on Anglo-Irish Literature, Irish Studies, and Celtic Studies.

Best, Richard. *Bibliography of Irish Philology and Manuscript Literature: Publications 1913–1941.* Dublin: Institute for Advanced Studies, 1942. Celtic literature.   Z2037.D83 B4

————. *Bibliography of Irish Philology and of Irish Printed Literature.* Dublin: National Library of Ireland, 1913. Celtic literature.   Z2037.D81

Bieler, Ludwig. *Ireland, Harbinger of the Middle Ages.* Translation of *Irland: Wegbereiter des Mittelalters* (Olten: U. Graf, 1961). London: Oxford University Press, 1963.   BR794.B513 1963

Boyd, Ernest. *Ireland's Literary Renaissance.* New rev. ed. Dublin: Allen Figgis, 1968.   PR8750.B6

Bromwich, Rachel. *Medieval Celtic Literature: A Select Bibliography.* Toronto: University of Toronto Press, 1974.   Z7011.B76

Brown, Malcolm. *Politics of Irish Literature: From Thomas Davis to W. B. Yeats.* Seattle: University of Washington Press, 1972.   DA950.B76 1972

Deane, Seamus. *Short History of Irish Literature.* University of Notre Dame Press, 1986.   PR8711.D42 1986

Dillon, Myles. *Early Irish Literature*. Chicago: University of Chicago Press, 1948. Celtic literature.
PB1327.D5

Ellis-Fermor, Una. *Irish Dramatic Movement*. 2d ed. London: Methuen, 1954. PR8789.E6 1954

Encyclopedia of Ireland. Dublin: Figgis, 1968. DA979.E5

Fallis, Richard. *Irish Renaissance*. Syracuse, N. Y.: Syracuse University Press, 1977. PR8750.F34

Flower, Robin. *Irish Tradition*. Oxford: Clarendon Press, 1947. PB1322.F5

Gill History of Ireland. 11 vols. London and Dublin: Gill, 1972–. In progress.

Vol. 1. MacNiocaill, G. *Ireland before the Vikings* (1972). DA932.4.M33

Vol. 2. Not yet published.

Vol. 3. Dolley, Reginald H. M. *Anglo-Norman Ireland, c. 1100–1318* (1972). DA933.D64

Vol. 4. Nicholls, Kenneth. *Gaelic and Gaelicised Ireland in the Middle Ages* (1972). DA933.N5

Vol. 5. Watt, John A. *Church in Medieval Ireland* (1972). BR794.W353

Vol. 6. Lydon, James F. *Ireland in the Later Middle Ages* (1972). DA933.L89

Vol. 7. MacCurtain, Margaret. *Tudor and Stuart Ireland* (1972). DA935.M22

Vol. 8. Johnston, Edith Mary. *Ireland in the Eighteenth Century* (1974). DA947.J63

Vol. 9. O'Tuathaigh, Gearoid. *Ireland before the Famine, 1798–1848* (1972). DA950.2.O88

Vol. 10. Lee, Joseph. *Modernization of Irish Society, 1848–1918* (1973). DA951.L295

Vol. 11. Murphy, John A. *Ireland in the Twentieth Century* (1975). DA959.M87

Gwynn, Stephen L. *Irish Literature and Drama in the English Language: A Short History*. New York: Nelson, 1936. PR8711.G8

Hayes, Richard J. *Sources for the History of Irish Civilization*. 9 vols. Boston: G. K. Hall, 1970. Z2034.H35

Hogan, Robert. *After the Irish Renaissance: A Critical History of the Irish Drama since the Plough and the Stars*. Minneapolis: University of Minnesota Press, 1967.
PR8789.H6

Hogan, Robert, and James Kilroy. *Modern Irish Drama: A Documentary History*. Dublin: Dolmen Press, 1975–.
PR8789.H62

Vol. 1. *Irish Literary Theatre, 1899–1901*.

Vol. 2. *Laying the Foundations, 1902–1904*.

Vol. 3. *Abbey Theatre: the Years of Synge, 1905–1909*.

Howarth, Herbert. *Irish Writers, 1880–1940*. New York: Hill and Wang, 1959. PR8753.H6 1959

Hughes, Kathleen. *Early Christian Ireland: Introduction to the Sources*. Cambridge: Cambridge University Press, 1972. DA908.H831 1972

Hull, Eleanor. *Text Book of Irish Literature*. 2 vols. Dublin: Gill, 1904–1908. The standard textbook on Irish Gaelic literature. PB1306.H75

Hyde, Douglas. *History of Ireland from Earliest Times to the Present Day*. New ed. with introduction by Brian Ó'Cuív. New York: Barnes and Noble, 1967. Originally published in 1899. The standard history with bibliographical notes. Irish Gaelic literature is included. PB1306.H8 1967

Jeffares, A. Norman. *Anglo-Irish Literature*. New York: Schocken Books, 1982. PR8711.J4 1982

Kersnowski, Frank. *Outsiders: Poets of Contemporary Ireland*. Fort Worth: Texas Christian University, 1975.
PR8771.K4

Kiely, Benedict. *Modern Irish Fiction*. Dublin: Golden Eagle, 1950. PR8797.K5

King, Kimball. *Ten Modern Irish Playwrights: A Comprehensive Annotated Bibliography*. New York: Garland, 1978. Z2039.D7 K56

Law, Hugh Alexander. *Anglo-Irish Literature*. Dublin: Talbot Press, 1926, 1976. PR8711.L3

Loftus, Richard J. *Nationalism in Modern Anglo-Irish Poetry*. Madison: University of Wisconsin Press, 1964.
PR8771.L6

MacDonagh, Thomas. *Literature in Ireland: Studies Irish and Anglo-Irish*. London: T. Fisher Unwin, 1916.
PR8711.M5

Maxwell, D. E. S. *Critical History of Modern Irish Drama, 1891–1980*. Cambridge: Cambridge University Press, 1984. PR8789.M39 1984

Mercier, Vivian. *Irish Comic Tradition*. Oxford: Clarendon Press, 1962. PB1307.M45

Mikhail, E. H. *Bibliography of Modern Irish Drama, 1899–1970*. London: Macmillan, 1972.
Z2039.D7 M53 1972

———. *Dissertations on Anglo-Irish Drama: A Bibliography of Studies 1870–1970*. London: Macmillan, 1973.
Z2039.D7 M54 1973b

Moody, T. W., F. X. Martin, and F. J. Byrne, eds. *New History of Ireland*. 9 vols. planned. Oxford: Clarendon Press, 1976–. DA912.N48

Vol. 3. *Early Modern Ireland, 1534–1691* (1976).

Vol. 8. *Chronology of Irish History to 1976* (1982).

Vol. 9. *Maps, Genealogies, Lists* (1984).

Morris, Lloyd R. *Celtic Dawn: A Survey of the Renascence in Ireland, 1889–1916*. New York: Macmillan, 1917.
PR8750.M6

O'Connor, Frank [Michael O'Donovan]. *Short History of Irish Literature*. New York: Capricorn Books, 1967. Published in London by Macmillan, 1967, under the title *Backward Look: A Survey of Irish Literature*. Includes Irish Gaelic literature. PB1306.O3 1967

Ó'Cuív, Brian, ed. *View of the Irish Language*. Dublin: Stationery Office, 1969. PB1213.V5

O'Driscoll, Robert, ed. *Theatre and Nationalism in Twentieth-Century Ireland*. Toronto: University of Toronto Press, 1971. PR8789.T5

O'Farachain, Roibeard. *Course of Irish Verse in English*. New York: Sheed and Ward, 1947. PR8765.O3

O'Mahony, M. *Progress Guide to Anglo-Irish Plays*. Dublin: Progress House, 1960. Synopses of more than 500 plays. Z2039.D705 1960

Power, Patrick C. *Literary History of Ireland*. Cork: Mercier Press, 1969. PR8711.P6

———. *Story of Anglo-Irish Poetry, 1800–1922*. Cork: Mercier Press, 1967. PR8765.P6

Rafroidi, Patrick. *Irish Literature in English: The Romantic Period (1789–1850)*. Translation of *L'Irlande et le romantisme* (Paris: Éditions universitaires, 1972). 2 vols. Gerrards Cross, Bucks: C. Smythe, 1980.
PR8750.R313 1980

Rafroidi, Patrick, Raymond Popot, and William Parker, eds. *Aspects of the Irish Theatre*. Paris: Éditions universitaires, 1972. PR8783.R3

Royal Irish Academy. Committee for the Study of Anglo-Irish Language and Literature. *Handlist of Work in Progress*. No. 1–. Dublin, 1969–. Z2037.R68

———. *Handlist of Theses [on Anglo-Irish Literature] Completed but Not Published*. No. 1–. Dublin, 1973–. Z2037.R68a

Warner, Alan. *Guide to Anglo-Irish Literature*. Dublin: Gill; New York: St. Martin's, 1981.   PR8711.W37 1981

White, Terence de Vere. *Anglo-Irish*. London: Gollancz, 1972.   DA916.W47

VIII. ANGLO-WELSH LITERATURE AND WELSH STUDIES

M–95   Jones, Brynmor. *Bibliography of Anglo-Welsh Literature, 1900–1965.* Llandysul, Swansea: Wales and Monmouthshire Branch of the Library Association, 1970.   Z2013.3.J64

This bibliography of 1,942 primary and secondary works is in three parts. The first treats twentieth-century Anglo-Welsh literature, giving primary bibliographies of anthologies and individual authors. The second part lists bibliographies and critical works including both dissertations and some unpublished sources, both on Anglo-Welsh literature in general and on individual authors. The third part is concerned with Anglo-Welsh children's literature. There are bibliographical notes and notes on locations. The volume concludes with regional and general indexes.

M–96   Stephens, Meic, compiler and ed. *Oxford Companion to the Literature of Wales.* Oxford: Oxford University Press, 1986.   PB2202.O94 1986

This volume, commissioned by Yr Academi Gymreig, The Welsh Academy, spans the period from the days of King Arthur to contemporary Welsh nationalism. Nearly 3,000 entries treat the principal genres of Welsh poetry, myth, legend, folklore, as well as literary associations, events, movements, and institutions, along with biographical articles on major figures of Welsh literary history. Bibliographies are appended to certain articles.

M–98   Scholarly Journals in Anglo-Welsh Literature and Welsh Studies.

AWR   Anglo-Welsh Review. Vol. 1–. Tenby, Dyfed, Wales: H. G. Walters, 1949–. 3/yr. Reviews.   PR8901.A52

Welsh History Review. Vol. 1–. Cardiff: University of Wales Press, 1960–. 4/yr. Reviews.   DA700.W68

Welsh Review: A Quarterly Journal about Wales, Its People, and Their Activities. Vol. 1–. Cardiff, 1949–. 4/yr.   DA700.W485

M–99   Some Frequently Recommended Works on Anglo-Welsh Literature and Welsh Studies.

Adams, Sam. *Triskel One: Essays on Welsh and Anglo-Welsh Literature.* Llandybie: C. Davies, 1971.   PR2207.A3

Ballinger, John, and James Ifano Jones. *[Author] Catalogue of Printed Literature in the Welsh Department [of the Cardiff Free Public Library].* Cardiff, 1898.   Z2089.C26

Bell, H. Idris. *Development of Welsh Poetry.* Oxford: Clarendon Press, 1936.   PB2227.B4

Dictionary of Welsh Biography (see G–10).

Garlick, Raymond. *Introduction to Anglo-Welsh Literature.* Cardiff: University of Wales Press, 1970. PR8911.G3

Griffith, Wyn. *Welsh.* London: Pelican, 1950.

Handley-Taylor, Geoffrey. *Authors of Wales Today: Being a Checklist of Authors Born in Wales, Together with Brief Particulars of Authors Born Elsewhere Who Are Currently Working or Residing in Wales—An Assemblage of More Than 600 Authors.* London: Eddison Press, 1972.   Z2077.H35

Jack, R. I. *Medieval Wales.* Cambridge: Cambridge University Press, 1972.   Z2081.J3

Jarman, A. O. H., and Gwilym R. Hughes, eds. *Guide to Welsh Literature.* 6 vols. planned. Swansea: C. Davies, 1975–. Gaelic literature.   PB2206.G8

Jones, Glyn. *Dragon Has Two Tongues: Essays on Anglo-Welsh Writers and Writing.* London: Dent, 1968.   PR8916.J6

Jones, Gwyn. *First Forty Years.* Cardiff: University of Wales Press, 1957.   PR8923.J6

Lewis, Sanders. *Is There an Anglo-Welsh Literature?* Cardiff, 1939.   PR8923.J6

Lloyd, J. E. *History of Wales from the Earliest Times to the Edwardian Conquest.* 3d ed. 2 vols. London: Longmans, Green, 1939.   DA715.L8 1939

Parry, Thomas. *History of Welsh Literature.* Translated from the Welsh by H. Idris Bell. Oxford: Clarendon Press, 1955. Gaelic literature.   PB2206.P33

Roderick, A. J., ed. *Wales through the Ages.* 2 vols. Llandybie, Carmarthenshire: C. Davies, 1959–1960.   DA714.R6

Williams, David. *History of Modern Wales.* London: Murray, 1950.   DA720.W48

IX. COMMONWEALTH LITERATURE AND WORLD LITERATURE WRITTEN IN ENGLISH

Note that many reference works on English literature also treat Commonwealth writers. See, in particular, such works as the *CBEL* (M–10), the *ABELL* (M–21), *AES* (M–23), and most of the handbooks, reader's encyclopedias, and biobibliographies (M–40 ff.), but especially the Longman *Companion* (M–44) and Myers (M–52). See also some references in section L.XII. on African Languages and Literatures.

M–100   New, William H. *Critical Writings on Commonwealth Literatures: A Selective Bibliography to 1970, with a List of Theses and Dissertations.* University Park: Pennsylvania State University Press, 1975.   Z2000.9.N48

This work enumerates separately published books and articles from 800 periodicals. Items offer criticism of the literature of Africa, Australia, Canada, New Zealand, South and Southeast Asia, and the West Indies. A total of 6,576 serially numbered, unannotated entries are divided into ten major sections, as follows: Master List of Periodicals, Commonwealth Literature in General, Africa (East and West), Australia, Canada, New Zealand, South Africa and Rhodesia, South Asia (India and Pakistan, Ceylon), Southeast Asia (Malaysia, Singapore, Phillipines), West Indies. These are followed by a supplement listing theses and dissertations in parallel sections. The volume concludes with an index of critics, editors, and translators.

M–101 "Annual Bibliography of Commonwealth Literature [1964–]." *Journal of Commonwealth Literature.* Nos. 1–10 (equivalent to vols. 1–5). London: Heinemann Educational Books for the University of Leeds, 1965–1969. Vol. 6–. London: Oxford University Press, 1971–.

PR1.J67

This annual bibliography covers both creative and critical writing concerned with literature of countries associated with the British Commonwealth of Nations. The current sections, each compiled by an authority, are as follows: Commonwealth—General; Africa—General; East and Central Africa; Southern Africa; West Africa; Australia; Canada; Ceylon; India; Malaysia and Singapore; New Zealand; Pakistan; The West Indies; and an appendix on South Africa. An introductory brief essay pointing out items the compiler judges especially worthy of notice is followed by an enumerative bibliography (with some annotation) of books and articles. This is generally divided into sections on bibliography, poetry, drama, fiction, anthologies, nonfiction, translations, criticism (individual authors, general studies), and current journals.

This bibliography may be somewhat supplemented by reference to the *Index to Commonwealth Little Magazines* (see D–28) and by entries in the *MLA International Bibliography* (L–50). This is, however, the most comprehensive source available for current bibliography of and about Commonwealth literature.

M–108 Scholarly Journals in Commonwealth Literature and in World Literature Written in English.

ACLALSB ACLALS Bulletin. Vol. 1–. Association of Commonwealth Literature and Language Studies, University of Mysore, India, 1965–. 2/yr. Reviews.
PR9080.A15

ArielE Ariel: A Review of International English Literature. Vol. 1–. University of Calgary, 1970–. 4/yr. Reviews.
PR1.R352

CES Commonwealth: Essays and Studies. Vol. 1–. Paris: Société française d'études du commonwealth, 1974–75. 1/yr. Reviews.
PN849.C5 C65

Commonwealth Newsletter. Vol. 1–. Aarhus, Denmark: Department of English, University of Aarhus; then Dangaroo Press, 1979–. 2/yr. No LC number

JCL Journal of Commonwealth Literature. Vol. 1–. Oxford: Hans Zell, 1965–. 3/yr. Reviews. Bibliography (see M–101).
PR1.J67

Powre above Powres. Vol. 1–. Mysore, India: Centre for Commonwealth Literature and Research, University of Mysore, 1977–.
PR9080.P6

WLWE World Literature Written in English [former titles: *CBCL Newsletter, Conference on British Commonwealth Literature,* 1962–1966; then *WLWE Newsletter,* 1966–1978]. Vol. 1–. Place varies. Now published at the University of Guelph, Ontario, 1979–. 2/yr. Reviews. Bibliographies. PR1.W65

For additional bibliographical aid see Ronald Warwick, comp. and ed., *Commonwealth Literature Periodicals: A Bibliography, Including Periodicals of Former Commonwealth Countries, with Locations in the United Kingdom* (London: Mansell, 1979) [Z2000.9.W37].

M–109 Some Frequently Recommended Works on Commonwealth Literature and on World Literature written in English.

Bradbrook, Muriel C. *Literature in Action: Studies in Continental and Commonwealth Society.* London: Chatto and Windus, 1972. PN51.B67 1972

Flint, John E. *Books on the British Empire and Commonwealth: A Guide for Students.* London: Oxford University Press, 1968. Z2021.C7 F56

Fiedler, Leslie A., and Houston A. Baker, Jr., eds. *English Literature: Opening Up the Canon.* Selected Papers from the English Institute, 1979, n.s. 4. Baltimore: Johns Hopkins University Press, 1981.
PR9080.E54 1981

Goodwin, Kenneth, ed. *National Identity: Papers Delivered at the Commonwealth Literature Conference, University of Queensland, 9th–15th August, 1968.* London and Melbourne: Heinemann, 1970.
PR849.C5 N3 1968

Hill, W. *Overseas Empire in Fiction: An Annotated Bibliography.* London: H. Milford, 1930. Z2014.F4 H6

Jones, Joseph J. *Terranglia: The Case for English as World-Literature.* New York: Twayne, 1965.
PR471.J65

Journal of General Education, Winter 1977. Special issue on World Literature in English. L11.J775

King, Bruce. *Literatures of the World in English.* London: Routledge and Kegan Paul, 1974. PR9080.K5

———. *New English Literatures—Cultural Nationalism in a Changing World.* New York: St. Martin's, 1980.
PR9080.K53 1980

Kosok, Heinz, and Horst Priessnitz, eds. *Literaturen in englischer Sprache: Ein Überblick über englischsprachige National-Literaturen ausserhalb Englands.* Bonn: Bouvier, 1977. PR9080.5.L5

McDowell, Robert E., and Judith H. McDowell. *Asian/Pacific Literatures in English: Bibliographies [Sri Lanka, the Philippines, Malaysia/Singapore Region, Aboriginals in Australian Literature, Papua New Guinea, Hong Kong].* Washington, D.C.: Three Continents Press, 1978. Z3008.L58 A8

McIntyre, W. David. *Commonwealth of Nations: Origins and Impact 1869–1971.* Minneapolis: University of Minnesota Press, 1977. DA16.M234

McLeod, Alan L., ed. *Commonwealth Pen: An Introduction to the Literature of the British Commonwealth.* Ithaca, N. Y.: Cornell University Press, 1961. PR9080.M3

Mannoni, M. *Prospero and Caliban: The Psychology of Colonization.* Translation of *Psychologie de la colonisation* (Paris: Éditions du Seuil, 1950). New York: Praeger, 1964. DT469.M264 M313 1964

Moore, Gerald. *Chosen Tongue: English Writing in the Tropical World.* London: Longmans, 1969.
PR9320.5.M6

Narasimhaiah, C. D., ed. *Awakened Conscience: Studies in Commonwealth Literature.* New Delhi: Sterling, 1978. PR9080.A9

———, ed. *Commonwealth Literature: A Handbook of Select Reading Lists.* Delhi: Oxford University Press, 1976. Z2000.9.C65

New, William H. *Among Worlds: An Introduction to Modern Commonwealth and South African Fiction.* Erin, Ontario: Porcepic, 1975. PR9084.N4

Niven, Alastair, ed. *Commonwealth Writer Overseas: Themes of Exile and Expatriation.* Brussels: Marcel Didier, 1976. PR9080.A2

Perren, G. E., and Michael F. Holloway. *Language and Communication in the Commonwealth.* London: H. M. Stationery Office, 1965. P381.C6 P4

Press, John, ed. *Commonwealth Literature: Unity and Diversity in a Common Culture: Extracts from the Proceedings of a Conference Held . . . 9–12 September 1964, under the Auspices of the University of Leeds.* London: Heinemann, 1965. PE13.C6

Riemenschneider, Dieter, ed. *History and Historiography of Commonwealth Literature.* Tübingen: G. Narr, 1983.
PR9080.A515 H57 1983

Robertson, Robert T. *Handbook to the Study of British Commonwealth Literature in English.* Blacksburg, Va., 1968.   Z2010.R65

Rooney, D. D. *Story of the Commonwealth.* New York: Pergamon, 1967.   DA16.R57 1967

Rutherford, Anna, ed. *Commonwealth: Proceedings of the Conference on Commonwealth Literature, Aarhus University, 26–30 April 1971.* Aarhus: Akademisk Boghandel, 1972.   PR9080.C6 1971

Srinvasa Iyengar, K. R. *Two Cheers for the Commonwealth: Talks on Literature and Education.* London: Asia, 1970.   PR99.S69

Times Literary Supplement. Language in Common. Special Number for August 10, 1962. Reprinted for the National Council of Teachers of English. London: *The Times*, 1963.   PR99.T57

Tyler, Priscilla. *Writers on the Other Side of the Horizon: A Guide to Developing Literatures of the World.* Champaign, Ill.: NCTE, 1964.   PR473.T9

Walsh, William. *Manifold Voice. Studies in Commonwealth Literature.* London: Chatto and Windus, 1970.   PR9080.W31 1970

———. *Commonwealth Literature.* London: Oxford University Press, 1973.   PR9080.W28

———. *Readings in Commonwealth Literature.* Oxford: Clarendon Press, 1973.   PR9080.W34 1973

Williamson, James A., and D. G. Southgate. *Notebook of Commonwealth History.* London: Macmillan, 1967.   DA16.W73 1967

X.   AFRICA

See also references in section L.XII on African Languages and Literatures.

M–110 Lindfors, Bernth. *Black African Literature in English: A Guide to Information Sources.* Detroit: Gale Research Co., 1979.   Z3508.L5 L56

This guide contains 3,305 serially numbered, rarely annotated entries, disposed into two parts. Part 1 treats genre and topical studies and reference sources; a total of twenty-six subdivisions include such classifications as Bibliography, Biography, Fiction, Drama, Poetry, Audience, Research, Conferences, and Festivals. Part 2 treats individual authors, presenting both primary and secondary bibliographies. There are four indexes, of authors, titles, subjects, and places.

A supplement, *Black African Literature in English: 1977–1981*, was published by Lindsfors (New York: Africana, 1986) [Z3508.L5 L56 Suppl.], adding nearly 400 pages of additional material.

A less comprehensive, earlier work that is still valuable is Barbara Abrash, *Black African Literature in English since 1952:, Works and Criticism* (New York: Johnson Reprint, 1967) [Z3508.L5 A25]. 463 serially numbered entries enumerate creative works and selected relevant criticism in books and articles. There is also a list of literary magazines publishing Black African literature in English and an author index.

M–115 Adey, David, et al. *Companion to South African English Literature.* Craighall, South Africa: Ad Donker, 1986.   PR9350.2.C66 1986

M–118 Scholarly Journals in African Literature Written in English.

ALT   *African Literature Today.* Vol. 1–. London: Heinemann, 1968–. 1/yr. Reviews. Bibliography.   PL8010.A4

BO   *Black Orpheus: Journal of African and Afro-American Literature.* Vol. 1–. Lagos, Nigeria: University of Lagos, Bookshop, 1957–. 2/yr. Reviews.   PL8000.B6

ESA   *English Studies in Africa: A Journal of the Humanities.* Vol. 1–. Johannesburg, South Africa: Witwatersrand University Press, 1957–. 2/yr. Annual "Select Bibliography: Books and Articles on English Language and Literature Published or Written in South Africa."   PR1.Eɔ

RAL   *Research in African Literatures.* Austin: African and Afro-American Research Center, University of Texas, 1970–. 3/yr. Reviews. Surveys. Bibliographies. Discographies. Filmographies. Conference notes.   PL8010.R46

SBL   *Studies in Black Literature.* 8 vols. Fredericksburg, Va.: Department of English, Mary Washington College, 1970–1977. 3/yr.   PS153.N5 S88

M–119 Some Frequently Recommended Works on African Literature Written in English and Related African Studies.

Baldwin, Claudia. *Nigerian Literature: A Bibliography of Criticism, 1952–1976.* Boston: G. K. Hall, 1988.   PR9387.B34

Beeton, Douglas Ridley, ed. *Pilot Bibliography of South African English Literature from the Beginnings to 1971.* Pretoria: Subject Reference Department of the Library, University of South Africa, 1976.   Z3608.L5 S68 1976

———, and H. E. T. Dorner *Dictionary of English Usage in Southern Africa.* Cape Town: Oxford University Press, 1975.   PE3451.B36 D5

Beier, Ulli, ed. *Introduction to African Literature: An Anthology of Critical Writing on African and Afro-American Literature and Oral Tradition.* London: Longmans, 1967.   PL8010.B4 1967b

Clark, John Pepper. *Example of Shakespeare: Critical Essays in African Literature.* Evanston, Ill.: Northwestern University Press, 1971.   PR9798.C6

Dabydeen, David, ed. *Black Presence in English Literature.* Manchester: Manchester University Press, 1985.   PR409.B53 B55 1985

Dathorne, O. R. *African Literature in the Twentieth Century.* London: Heinemann, 1975.   PL8010.D37 1975

———. *Black Mind: A History of African Literature.* Minneapolis: University of Minnesota Press, 1974.   PL8010.D37

Gleason, J. I. *This Africa: Novels by West Africans in English and French.* Evanston, Ill.: Northwestern University Press, 1965.   PQ3984.G4 1965

Heywood, Christopher, ed. *Perspectives on African Literature: Selections from the Proceedings of the Conference on African Literature Held at the University of Ife, 1968.* London: Heinemann, 1971.   PL8010.C6 1968b

Jan Mohamed, Abdul R. *Manichean Aesthetics: The Politics of Literature in Colonial Africa.* Amherst: University of Massachusetts Press, 1983.   PR9344.J36

Killam, G. D. *Africa in English Fiction, 1894–1939.* Ibadan: Ibadan University Press, 1968. PR878.A4 K5

King, Bruce, ed. *Introduction to Nigerian Literature.* New York: Africana, 1972. PR9898.N5 I5 1972

Laurence, Margaret. *Long Drums and Cannons: Nigerian Dramatists and Novelists, 1952–1966.* London: Macmillan, 1968. PR9898.N5 L3

Lindfors, Bernth. *Early Nigerian Literature.* New York: Africana, 1982. PR9387.L5 1982

Miller, G. M., and H. Sergeant. *Critical Survey of South African Poetry in English.* Cape Town: Balkema, 1957. PR9826.M5

Moore, Gerald. *Chosen Tongue: English Writing in the Tropical World.* Harlow: Longmans, 1969. PR9320.5.M6

Musiker, R. "South African English Literature: Bibliographical and Biographical Resources and Problems." *English Studies in Africa* 13 (1970): 265–273. PR1.E6

Nathan, M. *South African Literature: A General Survey.* Cape Town: Juta, 1925. PR9806.N3

Pettman, Charles. *Africanderisms: A Glossary of South African Colloquial Words and Phrases.* London: Longman, Green, 1913. PE3401.P4

Pieterse, C., and D. Munro, eds. *Protest and Conflict in African Literature.* London: Heinemann, 1969. PL8010.P7 1969

Roscoe, Adrian A. *Mother in Gold: A Study in West African Literature.* Cambridge: Cambridge University Press, 1971. PR9898.W4R6

Snyman, J. P. L. *Achievement of the South African Novel in English (1880–1930): A Critical Study.* Potchefstroom: Potchefstroom University of Christian Higher Education, 1951. Includes a bibliography.

Spencer, John, ed. *English Language in West Africa.* London: Longmans, 1971. PE3441.S6

Tibble, Anne, ed. *African-English Literature: A Short Survey and Anthology of Prose and Poetry up to 1965.* London: P. Owen, 1966. No LC number

Wilson, Monica, and Leonard Thompson, eds. *Oxford History of South Africa.* 2 vols. New York: Oxford University Press, 1969–1971. Vol. 1, To 1870. Vol. 2, 1870–1966. DT766.W762

XI. AUSTRALIA

M–120 **Lock, Fred, and Alan Lawson. *Australian Literature: A Reference Guide.*** 2d ed., rev. and enl. Melbourne: Oxford University Press, 1980. Z4011.L6

This comprehensive bibliographical guide for students of Australian literature, first published in 1977, contains a total of 417 well-annotated entries, including citations of many general reference works that contain material on Australian literature. The work is divided into seven sections as follows: I. Bibliographical Aids; II. Other Reference Sources; III. Authors (bibliographies of forty Australian authors from the sixteenth through the twentieth centuries); IV. Periodicals (twenty-four current literary periodicals); V. Library Resources (descriptions of special collections in the chief Australian libraries); VI. Literary Studies; VII. Organizations. The volume concludes with an author index and an index of titles and subjects.

For a more general bibliography of bibliographies see the standard work of Dietrich H. Borchardt, *Australian Bibliography: A Guide to Printed Sources of Information,* 3d ed., rewritten and considerably enlarged (Rushcutter's Bay, N.S.W.: Pergamon Press, 1976) [Z4011.B65 1975]. One may also consult with profit the bibliographical appendixes by L. T. Hergenham in both the first (1964) and the second (1976) editions of Geoffrey Dutton's *Literature of Australia* [PR9609.6.D8 1976].

M–121 **Johnston, Kevin W. Grahame, comp. *Annals of Australian Literature.*** Melbourne and London: Oxford University Press, 1970. Z4021.J8

This now somewhat out-of-date but still well-regarded volume presents a chronology from 1789 through 1968, listing the principal publications and notable literary events of each date. Main entries note genres, series, editions, pseudonyms, and collaborations. The author index lists books by and about authors, with dates, and also lists major periodicals. For more recent secondary literature see the annual bibliographies in *Australian Literary Studies* (M–127) and the *Journal of Commonwealth Literature* (M–101).

M–122 **Andrews, Barry G., and William H. Wilde. *Australian Literature to 1900: A Guide to Information Sources.*** Detroit: Gale Research Co., 1980. Z4021.A54

This bibliographical guide presents a total of 1,576 serially numbered, generally annotated entries citing works concerned with Australian literature from the arrival of the First Fleet at Botany Bay in January 1788 through the end of the nineteenth century. Entries are arranged in a total of seventy-seven sections in three parts. Part 1, General Bibliography, contains six sections, as follows: 1, Bibliography and Bibliographical Guides; 2, Reference Works; 3, Literary History and Criticism; 4, Australian English; 5, Nineteenth Century Journals; 6, Anthologies. Part 2, presenting bibliographies on Individual Authors, contains sections 7 through 72. Part 3, concerning selected nonfiction prose, has five sections, as follows: 73, Exploration; 74, Transportation; 75, Travel and Exploration; 76, History and Biography; 77, Literary and Theatrical Reminiscences. Indexes of names and of titles conclude the volume.

M–123 **Jaffa, Herbert C. *Modern Australian Poetry, 1920–1970: A Guide to Information Sources.*** Detroit: Gale Research Co., 1979. Z4024.P7 J34

This work contains a series of elaborately annotated entries that are unnumbered and together resemble a set of bibliographical essays on the subjects of the ten sections into which the volume is divided. These are as follows: 1, Bibliographical Aids and Reference Material; 2, Major Books; 3, Major Anthologies; 4, Major Articles; 5, Individual Poets (bibliographical discussions for 6 major and 20 minor writers); 6, The Jindyworobak Poets (8 writers); 7, The Angry Penguins (2 writers); 8, The Expatriate Poets (4 writers); 9, Other Poets (5 writers); and 10, The Younger Poets (16 writers). A general index concludes the volume.

M–124 **Day, A. Grove. *Modern Australian Prose, 1901–1975: A Guide to Information Sources.*** Detroit: Gale Research Co., 1980. Z4011.D38

This volume contains a total of 2,463 serially numbered, partially annotated entries, divided into eleven sections in four parts. Part 1, General Bibliography: Prose and Criticism, contains six sections, as follows: 1, Bibliographies and Bibliographical Guides; 2, Reference Works (history, biography, culture and society, libraries and the book trade); 3, Literary History and Criticism; 4, Australian English; 5, Twentieth Century Serials; 6, Anthologies. Part 2 presents individual bibliographies for fifty-four authors of Fiction. Part 3, Selected Non-Fiction, contains three sections on Travel and Description; Biography and Essays; and Special Topics (military and naval literature; aboriginals). Part 4 contains a bibliography on modern Australian drama. In addition to many cross-references, there are indexes of authors, titles, and subjects.

M–125 **Wilde, William H., Joy Hooten, and Barry Andrews, compilers. *Oxford Companion to Australian Literature.*** Melbourne and New York: Oxford University Press, 1985.
PR9600.2.W55 1985

This volume covers the history and cultural context of Australian literature from the first settlement in 1788 to the present. More than 3,000 entries cover such contextual subjects as Aboriginal culture, transportation, exploration, gold discoveries, bushranging, and the outback ethos, as well as the most important authors and works of Australian poetry, drama, fiction, journals, diaries, biographies, and autobiographies.

Another new volume from Oxford is the *Oxford Literary Guide to Australia*, edited by Peter Pierce (Melbourne and New York: Oxford University Press, 1988) [no LC number yet]. The *Guide* discusses the places of Australian literature, treating writers, publishers, booksellers, patrons of literature, and important gathering places. Numerous black and white photographs, some color photographs, and eight maps help users visualize localities.

M–126 **Miller, Edmund Morris, ed. *Australian Literature, from Its Beginnings to 1935: A Descriptive and Bibliographical Survey of Books by Australian Authors in Poetry, Drama, Fiction, Criticism, and Anthology, with Subsidiary Entries to 1938.*** 2 vols. Melbourne: Melbourne University Press in association with Oxford University Press, 1940. Facsimile reprint with corrections, Sydney: Sydney University Press, 1975.
Z4021.M5

This work is the standard, comprehensive primary and secondary bibliography of Australian literature. It is arranged in fifteen chapters as follows: 1, Introduction; 2, Poets and Poetry: New South Wales; 3, Poets and Poetry: Victoria; 4, Poets and Poetry: Queensland; 5, Poets and Poetry: South Australia; 6, Poets and Poetry: Western Australia; 7, Poets and Poetry: Tasmania. Each of these sections contains a discursive treatment of biographical, critical, and historical works, as well as primary entries; materials are generally arranged in chronological order. Chapter 8 contains a Bibliography of Poetry 1810–1935, with additions for the period 1936–1938. Chapter 9 presents a discursive Historical Introduction to Australian Drama; chapter 10 presents a Bibliography of Drama 1835–1935, with additions for 1936–1938. Chapter 11 presents a discursive Introduction to Novelists and Novels 1829–1899; while chapter 12 continues for the period 1900–1935. Chapter 13 presents a Bibliography of Fiction 1829–1935, with additions for 1936–1938. Chapter 14 gives a Historical Introduction to Australian Criticism; chapter 15 presents a Bibliography of Literary Criticism 1833–1935, with additions for 1936–1938, divided into six subsections: Essays and Reviews; Criticism of English Literature; Criticism of Australian Literature; Criticism of the Classical Literatures Including Philology and Translation; Criticism of the Modern Literatures Including Philology and Translation; and a section on Anthologies and Miscellanies. An appendix presents an alphabetical list of "Non-Australian Authors of Novels Associated with Australia." There are three indexes; a subject index to fiction; an index of subjects and names as subjects; and a general index of Australian authors, including

pseudonyms and titles of anonymous works. Given the strange arrangement, it is fortunate that the general index includes author entries, and access to work by or about a particular author is through the index.

An abridgment that updates the work to 1950 but differs significantly from it should be consulted along with the original: E. Morris Miller, *Australian Literature: A Bibliography to 1938, Extended to 1950 with an Historical Outline and Descriptive Commentaries* by Frederick T. Macartney (Sydney: Angus and Robertson, 1956) [Z4021.M5 1956]. All entries concerning one author are here placed under a single heading, and there are lists of authors by genre to facilitate access from that perspective. But much of the biographical, descriptive, and critical material in the original is here omitted. This edition lacks an index. Also by Miller and Macartney is an abstract of both works, *Historical Outline of Australian Literature* (Sydney: Angus and Robertson, 1957) [no LC number].

M–127 **"Annual Bibliography of Studies in Australian Literature."** *Australian Literary Studies*, vol. 1–. St. Lucia: University of Queensland Press, 1964–.
PR9400.A86

This annual bibliography of critical and scholarly books and articles on Australian authors, works, and subjects is divided into two sections, the first citing general materials (with references to reviews) and the second citing materials on individual authors. Since 1968 this bibliography has been prepared by the staff of the Fryer Library at the University of Queensland; it may be supplemented, particularly for contemporary creative writing by Australians, by the Australian portion of the "Annual Bibliography of Commonwealth Literature" (M–101).

Also published in *Australian Literary Studies* is the irregular list of "Research in Progress in Australian Literature," which will be found in volumes 2–8 and then every two years or so. Entries are by institution and give author, title, and genre (M.A. or Ph.D. thesis). Appended to each list is an enumeration of some non-University research in progress.

M–128 **Scholarly Journals in Australian Literature.**

ALS   *Australian Literary Studies.* St. Lucia: University of Queensland Press, 1963–. 2/yr. Reviews. Annual Bibliography (see M–127).
PR9400.A86

Meanjin   *Meanjin Quarterly.* Melbourne: Meanjin Company in association with the University of Melbourne, 1940–. 4/yr. Reviews.
No LC number

Southerly   *Southerly: A Review of Australian Literature.* Surry Hills, N. S. W.: Wentworth Press, 1939–. 4/yr. Reviews.
AP7.S6

For additional titles see *Australian Literary Periodicals: A Bibliography* (Canberra: National Library of Australia, 1971) [no LC number].

M–129 **Some Frequently Recommended Works on Australian Literature.**

Allen, H. C. *Bush and Backwoods: A Comparison of the Frontier in Australia and the United States.* East Lansing: Michigan State University Press, 1959.
E179.5.A44 1959

Australian Encyclopaedia. 3d ed. 6 vols. Sydney: Grolier Society of Australia, 1977.
DU90.A82 1977

Baker, Sidney J. *Dictionary of Australian Slang.* South Yarra, Victoria, 1982. Originally published as part of the *Drum: Australian Character and Slang* (Sydney: Currawong, 1959).
PE3601.Z5 B3 1982

————. *Australian Language: An Examination of the English Language and English Speech As Used in Australia from Convict Days to the Present, with Special Ref-*

erence to the Growth of Indigenous Idiom and Its Use by Australian Writers. 2d ed. Sydney: Currawong, 1966. PE3601.B3

Barnes, Richard J., ed. *Writer in Australia: A Collection of Literary Documents, 1856 to 1964.* Melbourne and New York: Oxford University Press, 1969.
PR9411.B3 1969

Bennett, Bruce, et al. *Western Australian Literature: A Bibliography.* Melbourne: Longman Cheshire, 1981.
Z4438.L5 B46 1981

Blake, Leslie J. *Australian Writers.* Adelaide: Rigby, 1968.
Z4021.B55

Buckley, V. *Essays in Poetry, Mainly Australian.* Carlton: Melbourne University Press, 1957. PR9471.B8

Cuthbert, Eleanora I. *Index of Australian and New Zealand Poetry.* New York: Scarecrow Press, 1963.
Z4024.P7 C8

Dutton, Geoffrey, ed. *Literature of Australia.* Rev. ed. Harmondsworth: Penguin, 1976. Bibliographical Appendix by L. T. Hergenham, pp. 463–514.
PR9414.D8

————, comp. *Modern Australian Writing.* London: Collins, 1966. PR9535.D8

Evans, John Keith. *Creative Writing in Australia: A Selective Survey.* 5th ed. Melbourne: Georgian House, 1966. PR9412.E9

Fredrich, Werner P. *Australia in Western Imaginative Prose Writings, 1600–1960: An Anthology and a History of Literature.* Chapel Hill: University of North Carolina Press, 1967. PN56.3.A9 F7

Green, Henry Mackenzie. *History of Australian Literature Pure and Applied: A Critical Review of All Forms of Literature Produced in Australia from the First Books Published after the Arrival of the First Fleet until 1950, with Short Accounts of Later Publications up to 1960.* 2d ed. 2 vols. Sydney: Angus and Robertson, 1971. PR9411.G7 1971

Hadgraft, Cecil. *Australian Literature: A Critical Account to 1955.* London: Heinemann, 1960. PR9411.H3

Heseltine, Harry. *Uncertain Self: Essays in Australian Literature and Criticism.* London: Oxford University Press, 1987. PR9604.6.H47 1986

Hope, A. D. *Australian Literature.* Parkville, Victoria: Melbourne University Press, 1963. PR9453.H6

Ingamells, Rex. *Handbook of Australian Letters.* Melbourne: Jindyworobak, 1949. PR9413.I4

Kramer, Leonie. *Oxford History of Australian Literature.* London: Oxford University Press, 1981.
PR9604.3.O9 1981

McAuley, James P. *Personal Element in Australian Poetry.* Sydney: Angus and Robertson, 1970.
DU80.F69 no.3

————. *Map of Australian Verse.* Melbourne: Oxford University Press, 1975. PR9610.5.M3

Moore, Tom Inglis. *Social Pattern in Australian Literature.* Sydney: Angus and Robertson, 1971.
PR9422.S6 M6 1971

Morris, Edward Ellis. *Austral English: A Dictionary of Australasian Words, Phrases, and Usages.* London: Macmillan, 1898. Historical Dictionary. PE3601.M8

Pike, Douglas, et al. *Australian Dictionary of Biography.* 9 vols. to date (1983). Melbourne: Melbourne University Press, 1966–. DU82.A9

Ramson, William S. *Australian English: An Historical Study of the Vocabulary, 1788–1898.* Canberra: Australian National University Press, 1966. PE3601.R3

————. *Australian National Dictionary.* London: Oxford University Press, 1988. No LC number yet

————. *English Transported: Essays on Australasian English.* Canberra: Australian National University Press, 1970. Includes a partly annotated classified bibliography by David Blair. PE3601.R33

Rees, Leslie. *Making of Australian Drama: A Historical and Critical Survey from the 1830s to the 1960s.* 2 vols. Cremorne, New South Wales: Angus and Robertson, 1973–1978. PR9616.6.R4 1973

Roderick, C. *Australian Novel.* Sydney: W. Brooks and Co., 1945. PR9576.R6

Roderick, Colin A. *Suckled by a Wolf; or, The Nature of Australian Literature.* Sydney: Angus and Robertson, 1968. PR9416.R6

Ross, Robert L. *Australian Literary Criticism, 1945–1988: An Annotated Bibliography.* New York: Garland, 1988. Z4024.C8 R67 1988

Serle, Geoffrey. *From Deserts the Prophets Come: The Creative Spirit in Australia, 1788–1972.* Melbourne: Heinemann, 1973. NX590.A1 S47

Serle, Percival. *Bibliography of Australasian Poetry and Verse: Australia and New Zealand.* Melbourne: Melbourne University Press, 1925. Z4011.S48

Sharp, Andrew. *Discovery of Australia.* Oxford: Clarendon Press, 1963. DU97.S5 1963

Shaw, A. G. L. *Convicts and the Colonies: A Study of Penal Transportation from Great Britain and Ireland to Australia and Other Parts of the British Empire.* 3d ed. Melbourne: Melbourne University Press, 1977.
HV8950.A8 S5 1977

————. *Story of Australia.* 4th ed., rev. London: Faber, 1972. DU112.S5 1972

Shaw, John. *Australian Encyclopedia.* Sydney: Collins, 1985. No LC number

Turner, George W. *English Language in Australia and New Zealand.* 2d ed. London: Longmans, 1972.
PE3601.T8 1972

Wallace-Crabbe, Chris, ed. *Australian Nationalists: Modern Critical Essays.* Melbourne: Oxford University Press, 1971. PR9450.W3

Wilkes, Gerald A. *Australian Literature: A Conspectus.* Sydney: Angus and Robertson, 1969.
DU80.F69 no. 2

————, and John C. Reid, eds. *Literatures of the British Commonwealth: Australia and New Zealand.* University Park: Pennsylvania State University Press, 1971.
PR9412.W5

Wood, G. Arnold. *Discovery of Australia.* Revised by J. C. Beaglehole. 2d ed. Melbourne: Macmillan of Australia, 1969. DU98.1.W6 1969

Wright, Judith. *Preoccupations in Australian Poetry.* Melbourne: Oxford University Press, 1965. PR9461.W7

XII. CANADA

See also L–70 ff. for francophone Canadian literature.

M–130 **Rhodenizer, Vernon Blair.** *Canadian Literature in English.* Montreal: Quality Press, 1965.   Z1375.R5

This massive work contains twenty sections of bibliographical essays and enumerative bibliographies with running commentaries. The sections are as follows: 1, Literature in General; 2, The Indians in Literature; 3, The Literature of Travel; 4, The Outdoors; 5, Outdoors-Indoors; 6, The Nature Writers; 7, Scientific Literature; 8, The Literature of Affairs; 9, Philosophical and Religious Literature; 10, Juvenile Literature; 11, Autobiography; 12, Biography; 13, History; 14, Creative Non-Fiction; 15, Fiction; 16, Drama; 17, Poetry; 18, The Essay; 19, Humor and Satire; 20, Criticism.

The lack of an index to the original work is supplied by Lois Mary Thierman, *Index to Vernon Blair Rhodenizer's Canadian Literature in English* (Edmonton, Alberta: La Survivance Printing Co., 1969) [no LC number]. The author index designates also those pages that include biographical information on an author; the title index indicates those titles that were not independently verified by the compiler; the subject index is very brief. The index volume concludes with a list of errata.

M–131 **Watters, Reginald.** *Checklist of Canadian Literature and Background Materials, 1628–1960: In Two Parts: First, a Comprehensive List of the Books Which Constitute Canadian Literature Written in English; and Second, a Selective List of Other Books by Canadian Authors Which Reveal the Backgrounds of That Literature.* 2d ed., rev. and enl. Toronto: University of Toronto Press, 1972.
                                          Z1375.W 1972

Originally published in 1959 and covering materials of the period 1628–1950, this checklist presents in the first part an inventory of all known separately published titles (about 16,000) by some 7,000 English-speaking Canadian authors. This part is classified into four sections treating Poetry (Chapbooks, Individual Works, Collections, and Anthologies), Poetry and Prose (Mixed Anthologies and Books with Both Forms), Fiction (Novels, Collected Short Stories, Anthologies, and Works of Juvenile Literature), and Drama (Stage and Radio Plays). Within each section, works are arranged alphabetically by author and then alphabetically by title. Entries give the earliest imprint of a title and indicate locations.

The second part presents a selection of works by Canadians in the fields of Biography (including Memoirs, Genealogy, Autobiography, Reminiscences, Letters, and Diaries); Essays and Speeches; Local History and Description; Religion and Morality; Social History; Scholarship; and Travel and Description. The volume concludes with an index of anonymous titles and an index of names, initials, and pseudonyms.

This work can be supplemented by reference to citations in Raymond Tanghe, *Bibliography of Canadian Bibliographies*, 2d ed., ed. Douglas Lochhead (Toronto: University of Toronto Press, 1972) [Z1365.A1 T3 1972], and by Watters and Bell, *On Canadian Literature* (M–136).

M–132 **Gnarowski, Michael.** *Concise Bibliography of English-Canadian Literature.* Rev. ed. Toronto: McClelland and Stewart, 1978.   Z1375.G53 1978

This brief work, first published in 1973, is designed as a concise and ready-reference checklist of bibliographies on 118 English-Canadian authors. Cited are the first or earliest edi-

tions of works, classified by genre, with biographical and selected critical studies also enumerated. Arrangement of titles is in chronological order.

M–135 **Lecker, Robert, and Jack David.** *Annotated Bibliography of Canada's Major Authors.* Vol. 1–. Downsview, Ontario: ECW, 1979–; Boston: G. K. Hall, 1980–.
                                          Z1375.A56

In ten projected volumes this work will present a comprehensive annotated bibliography of all works by and about major (and some minor) English and French Canadian authors of the nineteenth and twentieth centuries. The bibliography for each author is by a specialist compiler; for each, entries are in two parts. Part 1 is a chronologically arranged bibliography of works by the author, disposed into two sections: A. Books and Manuscripts (with locations cited); and B. Contributions to Books, Periodicals, and Anthologies; Poems, Short Stories, Articles, Reviews, Letters; Audio-visual Material; Miscellaneous Works and Contributions. Part 2 is an alphabetically arranged selected bibliography of works on the author, also disposed into two sections: C. Books, Articles, Sections of Books, Theses and Dissertations, Interviews, Audio-visual Material, Awards and Honors; and D. Selected Book Reviews. Both principles of selection and cut-off dates are obscure and vary from compilation to compilation.

Entries are numbered within each section, and descriptively annotated. Brief introductions to each author are written by the compiler, reviewing both the primary work and its critical reception. To date, six volumes have been published, treating the following authors: vol. 1 (1980), Margaret Atwood (prose), Margaret Laurence, Hugh MacLennan, Mordecai Richler, and Gabrielle Roy; vol. 2 (1981), Margaret Atwood (poetry), Leonard Cohen, Archibald Lampman, E. J. Pratt, and Al Purdy; vol. 3 (1981), Ernest Buckler, Robertson Davies, Raymond Knister, W. O. Mitchell, and Sinclair Ross; vol. 4 (1983), Earle Birney, Dorothy Livesay, F. R. Scott, and A. J. M. Smith; vol. 5 (1984), Morley Callaghan, Mavis Gallant, Hugh Hood, Alice Munro, and Ethel Wilson; vol. 6 (1985), Margaret Avison, John Newlove, Michael Ondaatje, P. K. Page, Miriam Waddington, and Phyllis Webb; vol. 7 (1987), Marian Engel, Anne Hébert, Robert Kroetsch, Stephen Leacock, and Thomas Raddall.

M–136 **Watters, Reginald E., and Inglis Freeman Bell, eds.** *On Canadian Literature, 1806–1960: A Checklist of Articles, Books, and Theses on English-Canadian Literature, Its Authors, and Language.* Toronto: University of Toronto Press, 1966.   Z1375.W33

This closed retrospective bibliography includes biographical, critical, and scholarly works but excludes reviews and standard reference works. The bibliography is in two parts, the first on Canadian literature in general, and the second on individual authors. Part 1 is disposed into fourteen sections, as follows: General Bibliographies; Canadian Culture and Background; Canadian English; Language and Linguistics; Canadian Literature—General; Drama and Theatre; Fiction; Poetry; Literary Criticism; Literary History; Regionalism; Songs, Folksongs, and Folklore; Journalism, Publishing, and Periodicals; Libraries and Reading; Censorship and Copyright. Entries are sometimes briefly annotated with descriptive notes. The second part lists authors alphabetically and then cites all biographical and critical materials alphabetically by its authors. There is, regrettably, no index.

For work after 1960 this bibliography must be supplemented for belles lettres by the annual bibliography in *Canadian Literature* (M–143) and for language and linguistics by the annual bibliography in the *Canadian Journal of Linguistics* (see M–143).

M–137 **Moyles, R. G., ed.** *English-Canadian Literature to 1900: A Guide to Information Sources.* Detroit: Gale Research Co., 1976. Z1375.M68

This work is disposed into seven chapters that contain unnumbered but annotated entries, generally in alphabetical order. The chapters are as follows: 1, General Reference Guides; 2, Literary Histories and Criticism; 3, Anthologies; 4, Major Authors (12 are listed); 5, Minor Authors (36); 6, Literature of Exploration, Travel, and Description; and 7, Selected 19th Century Journals. Within chapters 4 and 5, which constitute the bulk of the volume, author bibliographies include citation of primary sources (manuscripts, collections, bibliographies, works) and citation of secondary materials. The volume concludes with indexes by author and by title.

M–140 **Stevens, Peter, ed.** *Modern English-Canadian Poetry: A Guide to Information Sources.* Detroit: Gale Research Co., 1978. Z1377.P7 S79

The unnumbered, annotated entries in this volume are disposed into eight chapters, as follows: 1, Introduction; 2, Reference Sources; 3, Literary Histories, General and Critical Studies; 4, Major Anthologies; 5, Periodicals; 6, The Beginnings: 1900–1940 (with primary and secondary bibliographies for 21 poets); 7, Poetic Renaissance: The 1940's and Beyond (23 poets); and 8, Contemporary Poetry: The 1960's and '70's (16 poets). The volume concludes with author, title, and subject indexes.

M–141 **Fee, Margery, and Ruth Cawker.** *Canadian Fiction: An Annotated Bibliography.* Toronto: P. Martin Associates, 1976. Z1377.F4 F4

This work aims to list every novel, short-story collection, critical, or biographical study by or about Canadian novelists published before 1975. There are brief descriptive annotations.

M–142 **Hoy, Helen, ed.** *Modern English-Canadian Prose: A Guide to Information Sources.* Detroit: Gale Research Co., 1983. Z1377.F4 H69 1983

This volume treats twentieth-century Canadian prose, written in English, through 1979–1981. The total of 5,259 serially numbered, occasionally briefly annotated entries are disposed into three main sections, as follows: Reference Sources (bibliographies and general reference works; biographical references; indexes to serial publications, anthologies, and collections; indexes to theses; manuscripts and special collections); Literary History, Criticism, and Theory (monographs and then articles); and Individual Author Guides. The third section, which occupies the largest part of the book, offers very brief biographical sketches followed by enumerations of primary material in chronological order (divided into lists for fiction and nonfiction monographs, short works, and manuscripts) and then of secondary material (bibliographies, criticism, and book reviews). A total of sixty-eight writers of fiction and ten nonfiction prose writers are treated. The volume concludes with indexes of authors, titles, and subjects.

M–143 **"Canadian Literature: A Checklist [1959–70]."** *Canadian Literature / Littérature canadienne: A Quarterly of Criticism and Review,* nos. 7–48. Vancouver: University of British Columbia Press, 1960–1971. PR9100.C25

This annual, unannotated bibliography contains three listings, mainly of books. The first treats English Canadian Literature. Its general section has the following subheadings: Collections, Fiction, Poetry, Drama, Essays, Humour, Biog-

raphy, Bibliography, Books and Reading, Periodicals, and Literary History and Criticism. This is followed by sections citing current work on individual authors. The second listing is of theses, first those in English and then those in French. Entries give author, title, degree, granting institution, and name of supervisor. Finally, the third list, on Littérature canadienne-française, has the same subheadings as the first. For complete bibliographical control it is wise to supplement Canadian listings in the *MLA International Bibliography* (L–50) and in the annual bibliography on Commonwealth Literature (M–101) with this serial bibliography.

The lists of 1959–1963 have been emended and cumulated by Inglis F. Bell and Susan W. Port, *Canadian Literature: Littérature canadienne: 1959–1963. A Checklist of Creative and Critical Writings: A Canadian Literature Supplement* (Vancouver: Publications Center, University of British Columbia, 1966) [Z1375.B4]. Regular five-year cumulations are planned.

For a bibliographical review on work about Canadian literature see the annual selective critical bibliography, "Letters in Canada [1935–]," published in the July issue of the *University of Toronto Quarterly: A Canadian Journal of the Humanities* [AP5.U58] from 1936 on. Essays treat work on Poetry, Fiction, The Humanities (with subdivisions), Social Studies (with subdivisions), Livres en français, and Publications in Other Languages. From 1966 on, there is an author index to books reviewed in the essays.

M–144 **"Canadian Literature: An Annotated Bibliography / Littérature canadienne: Une bibliographie avec commentaire."** *Journal of Canadian Fiction,* vol. 1–. Montreal: Bellrock Press, 1972–. 4/yr. No LC number

This is an annual, classified bibliography of books, articles, reviews, and dissertations on French and English Canadian literature. Creative writing, critical works, historical scholarship, and reviews of books, films, and theater are all included. An index of names concludes the bibliography.

M–145 *Oxford Companion to Canadian History and Literature.* Edited by Norah Story. Toronto: Oxford University Press, 1967. PR9106.S7 1967

This volume, in parallel to the other Oxford companions, is meant to serve as a ready-reference source for readers of Canadian history or literature written in English or French. There are broad survey articles on poetry, drama, and fiction in English and in French; on periods of literary history; on authors and works. There are also biographical articles on historically important persons, and articles on places, topics, and events in Canadian history. Separate articles survey the history and literature of the individual provinces. There are five maps and a series of five appendixes listing the governors of New France, of British North America, the Governors General of Canada, the Prime Ministers, and the recipients of Governor General's Awards. There are cross-references from names of authors cited in bibliographies and an alphabetical list of titles referred to in the text.

A *Supplement to the Oxford Companion to Canadian History and Literature* edited by William Toye was published in 1973 [PR9180.2.T6 1973]. It both updates entries in the original *Companion* and introduces a variety of new articles by thirty-seven contributors on books appearing between 1967 and 1972, on literary forms, and on writers.

For general reference purposes see H. C. Campbell, *How to Find Out about Canada* (Oxford: Pergamon Press, 1967) [Z1365.C18 1967], which contains sections on General Bibliography, Philosophy and Religion, Social and Political Structure, Economics and Business, Language, Literature, Science and Technology, Medicine, Art, Architecture, Music, Biography, History, and Sport, along with an index of subjects, authors, and titles.

Two other reference guides are Douglas Lochhead's *Bibliography of Canadian Bibliographies*, 2d ed., rev. and enl. (Toronto: University of Toronto Press, 1972) [Z1365.A1L6 1972], and Dorothy E. Ryder's *Canadian Reference Sources: A Selective Guide*, 2d ed. (Ottawa: Canadian Library Association, 1981) [Z1365.R8 1981], which is comparable in character to Sheehy (A–20) or Walford (A–21) and includes sections giving full bibliographical information and extended annotation on general reference works, works in history and allied subjects, in the humanities, in the sciences, in the social sciences, and in law. It has an author-title index along with a brief subject index.

M–146 **Toye, William, ed. *Oxford Companion to Canadian Literature*.** Toronto and New York: Oxford University Press, 1983.   PR9180.2.O94 1983

In contrast to the earlier Oxford companion (see M–145), this volume focuses exclusively on Canadian literature, treating English literature primarily, but also a substantial number of entries on French-Canadian writing. Entries treat the full history of Canadian literature, including biographical articles on novelists, poets, dramatists, and other writers; surveys of periods of fiction, poetry, and drama; and miscellaneous articles on such topics as crime fiction, children's drama, criticism, expatriate writers, foreign writers in Canada, humor and satire.

Oxford is also publishing a sort of companion volume, compiled by Albert Moritz and Theresa Moritz, the *Oxford Illustrated Literary Guide to Canada* (Toronto and New York: Oxford University Press, 1988) [no LC number yet], which tours some 500 locations, noting writers' homes and haunts. Some 300 black and white photographs complement the anecdotal text. A related reference work is John R. Colombo's *Canadian Literary Landmarks* (Willowdale, Ontario: Hounslow Press, 1984) [PR9187.C65 1984].

M–147 **Sylvestre, Guy, Brandon Conron, and Carl F. Klinck, eds. *Canadian Writers: Écrivains canadiens: A Biographical Dictionary*.** New ed., rev. and enl. Toronto: Ryerson, 1966.   PR9127.S9

This dictionary gives biographical sketches in English and French for some 300 English and French Canadian authors, along with bibliographies of secondary works concerning them. The work concludes with a chronological table citing publication dates, a brief general bibliography, and an index of titles mentioned in the text.

Another biobibliographical reference work for Canadian writers is *Authors and Areas of Canada* by Joseph J. Jones and Johanna Jones (Austin, Tex.: Stack-Vaughn Co., 1970) [PR9127.J6], which contains a literary map of Canada with authors' names entered on it; a series of articles on thirty-five representative authors giving brief biographies with portraits and lists of selected readings; a reference bibliography for Canadian literature; a reference bibliography for world literature written in English; and a list of suggestions for further reading.

The *Macmillan Dictionary of Canadian Biography*, 3d ed., rev. William Stewart Wallace (Toronto: Macmillan, 1963) [F1005.D5] contains a large number of biographies of Canadian authors. See also the *Dictionary of Canadian Biography* (G–35).

M–148 **Scholarly Journals in Canadian Literature in English.**

CanL   *Canadian Literature: A Quarterly of Criticism and Review*. Vol. 1–. Vancouver: University of British Columbia, 1959–. 4/yr. Reviews. Bibliography (see M–143).   PR9100.C25

JCF   *Journal of Canadian Fiction*. Vol. 1–. Montreal: Journal of the Canadian Fiction Association, 1972–. 4/yr. Reviews. Annual Bibliography after 1972 (see M–144).   No LC number

JCP   *Journal of Canadian Poetry*. Vols. 1–3; n.s. vol. 1–. Ontario: Borealis Press, 1978–1982; 1986–. 2/yr. then 1/yr. Reviews.
                                         PR9190.25.J68a

SCL   *Studies in Canadian Literature*. Vol. 1–. Fredericton: University of New Brunswick, 1976–. 2/yr.
                                         No LC number

M–149 **Some Frequently Recommended Works on Canadian Literature in English.**

Atwood, Margaret. *Survival: A Thematic Guide to Canadian Literature*. Toronto: Anansi, 1972.   PR9184.3.A8

Avis, Walter S. *Bibliography of Writings on Canadian English (1857–1965)*. Toronto: W. J. Gage, 1965.
                                         Z1379.A85

Brown, Edward K. *On Canadian Poetry*. Toronto: Ryerson Press, 1943.   PR9165.B7

Cappon, Paul, ed. *In Our House: Social Perspectives on Canadian Literature*. Toronto: McClelland and Stewart, 1978.   PR9185.2.I6

Dictionary of Canadian Biography (see G–35).

Dictionary of Canadian English (see I–46).

Frye, Northrup. *Bush Garden: Essays on the Canadian Imagination*. Toronto: Anansi, 1971.   PR9153.F7

Jones, Douglas G. *Butterfly on Rock: A Study of Themes and Images in Canadian Literature*. Toronto: University of Toronto Press, 1970.   PR9111.J6

Klinck, Carl Frederick, et al. *Literary History of Canada: Canadian Literature in English*. 2d ed., rev. and enl. Toronto: University of Toronto Press, 1976. Contains more than 40 essays by 30 specialists, treating literature broadly conceived.   PR9111.K4

Mandel, Eli, ed. *Contexts of Canadian Criticism: A Collection of Critical Essays*. Chicago: University of Chicago Press, 1971.   PR9114.M3 1971

Marshall, Tom. *Harsh and Lovely Land: The Major Canadian Poets and the Making of a Canadian Tradition*. Vancouver: University of British Columbia Press, 1979.   PR9190.25.M37

Matthews, William. *Canadian Diaries and Autobiographies* (see G–46).

Moss, John G. *Reader's Guide to the Canadian Novel*. Toronto: McClelland and Stewart, 1981.
                                         PR9192.2.M62 1981

Pacey, William C. Desmond. *Creative Writing in Canada: A Short History of English-Canadian Literature*. Rev. and enl. ed. Toronto: Ryerson Press, 1961.
                                         PR9111.P3

Rome, David. *Jews in Canadian Literature: A Bibliography*. 2 vols. Montreal: Canadian Jewish Congress and the Jewish Public Library, 1962.   Z6373.C3 R58

Roy, Camille. *Histoire de la littérature canadienne française*. 8th ed. Montreal: Beauchemin, 1940.
                                         PQ3901.R6 1940

Smith, A. J. M. *Towards a View of Canadian Letters: Selected Critical Essays 1928–1971*. Vancouver: University of British Columbia Press, 1973.
PR9189.6.S6

Staines, David, ed. *Canadian Imagination: Dimensions of a Literary Culture*. Cambridge: Harvard University Press, 1977.
PR9184.6.C35

Wallace, W. S. *Dictionary of North American Authors Deceased before 1950*. Toronto: Ryerson Press, 1951. Cites some 25,000 references in 78 biographical dictionaries.
PS128.W3

Waterson, Elizabeth. *Survey: A Short History of Canadian Literature*. Toronto: Methuen, 1973. Substantial reading lists appended to each of 11 chapters.

Wilson, Edmund. *O Canada: An American's Notes on Canadian Culture*. New York: Farrar, Straus, Giroux, 1965.
PR9153.W5

Woodcock, George. *Odysseus Ever Returning: Essays on Canadian Writers and Writings*. Toronto: McClelland and Stewart, 1970.
PR9153.W6

XIII. INDIA

See also L–140 ff.

M–150 **Singh, Amritjit, Rajiva Verma, and Irene M. Joshi, eds. *Indian Literature in English, 1827–1979: A Guide to Information Sources*.** Detroit: Gale Research Co., 1981.
Z3208.L5 S56

This not-much-annotated bibliography of creative writing in English by Indians includes both primary and secondary works. Entries are unnumbered and divided into two parts: general, and individual authors. Part 1 is in 4 sections: Backgrounds (Philosophy, Religion and the Arts, History, Sociology and Politics); Reference Works; Criticism and Literary History (general and by genre); Anthologies (general and by genre). Part 2 lists authors and their works in four sections: Poetry, Drama, Fiction, and Selected Prose. There are two appendixes, the first listing relevant journals, the second listing Indian publishers. The work concludes with a primary author (i.e., author-as-subject) index, an author index, and a title index.

M–151 **Alphonso-Karkala, John, and Leena Karkala. *Bibliography of Indo-English Literature: A Checklist of Works by Indian Authors in English, 1800–1966*.** Bombay: Nirmala Sadanad Publishers, 1974.
Z3815.B5

This bibliography of writings by Indian authors in English excludes English translations from other Indian languages; it is disposed into three parts, an introduction, followed by a checklist and then a series of author indexes. The checklist of Indo-English works is classified into the following divisions: Poetry; Poetry Anthologies; Drama; Fiction; Biography and Autobiography; Criticism; Essays; Prose (Fine Arts, History and Politics, Philosophy and Religion, Travel); Bibliography; and Reference (Survey, Biographical, General). The indexes are to Indian pseudonyms; to Indian names with multiple English spellings; to Indo-English authors; and to Indian authors cited in the divisions for anthologies, bibliography, and reference works.

M–152 **Jain, Sushil Kumar. *Indian Literature in English: An Annotated Bibliography*.** 3 vols. London: The author, 1964. New ed. 3 vols. Regina, Saskatchewan, 1965–1967.
Z3208.L5 J32

The three parts of this checklist treat Poetry, Drama, and Fiction respectively. Works included are written by Indians in English or translated by Indians into English from a modern Indian language. Entries are arranged in alphabetical, serially numbered author lists. Part 1 treats Poetry. Part 2, Drama, presents an author list, an addendum, and a further list of "Classical Indian Drama in English Translation." Part 3, Fiction, contains 435 serially numbered entries along with a personal memoir by the compiler regarding the history of this bibliographical project.

A more recent compilation is Jain's *Indian Literature in English: A Select Reading List* (Windsor, Ontario: University of Windsor Library, 1972–73?) [Z3208.L5 J319]. This volume contains only monographs published since 1900. It is in two parts. The first contains three sections: A. Reference Works and Bibliographies, Current Bibliographies; B. General Histories, Critical Studies, Indian Influences on Foreign Literatures, Theses, and Miscellaneous; and C. Current Literary Periodicals, Book Trade Tools, Semi-literary and Popular Journals. Part two is divided into five sections and contains primary and secondary works of and concerning Indian English A. Poetry, B. Drama, C. Short Stories, D. Novels, and E. Autobiographies. Appended are reprints of several bibliographical contributions by Jain on Indian Historical Fiction in English, Indian Autobiographies, and Trends in the Bibliography of Modern Indian Literature.

M–153 **Central Institute of English and Foreign Languages, Hyderabad. *Bibliography of Indian English*.** Hyderabad, 1972.
Z3208.L5 C36

This bibliography, prepared in July 1972, lists publications from 1827 to 1970 in two parts, the first presenting a primary and secondary bibliography of 1,847 serially numbered unannotated entries on Indian English literature. The second, much briefer, presents a bibliography on the Indian English language. The first part is divided into nine sections, as follows: Bibliographies; General Criticism (Books, Periodical Literature, Unpublished Literature, Unpublished Dissertations); Poetry; Drama; Fiction; Addenda; an Index; a list of English Language Dailies Published in India; and a list of Periodicals Pertaining to Indian English Literature. Part 2 is divided into six sections, as follows: Dictionaries; General Discussions; Phonology (General and Comparative); Syntax, Lexis, Usage and Registers; Contrastive Syntactic Analysis and Translation; and Borrowings.

M–154 ***BEPI: A Bibliography of English Publications in India*.** Vol. 1–. Delhi: D. K. F. Trust, 1976–.
Z3201.B18

An integrated author-title-subject index to scholarly and significant publications of the year.

M–158 **Scholarly Journals in Anglo-Indian Literature.**

Indian Journal of English Studies. Vol. 1–. Bombay: Orient Longmans, 1960–. 1/yr.
PR1.I55

IndLing *India Linguistics: Journal of the Linguistic Society of India*. Vol. 1–. Calcutta: Linguistic Society of India, 1931–. 4/yr. Reviews.
No LC number

IndL *Indian Literature*. Vol. 1–. New Delhi: Sahitya Akademi, 1957–. 6/yr. Reviews.
AP8.I39

Journal of Indian Writing in English. Vol. 1–. Gulbarga: Postgraduate Center, Karnataka State University, 1973. 2/yr.
PR9480.J64

JSoAL   *Journal of South Asian Literature* [former title: *Mah-fil*]. Vol. 1–. East Lansing: Asian Studies Centre, Michigan State University, 1963–. 4/yr. Reviews.
PK1501.M34

LHY   *Literary Half-Yearly*. Vol. 1–. Mysore: University of Mysore, 1960–. 2/yr. Reviews.   AP8.L5

OJES   *Journal of English Studies*. Vol. 1–. Hyderbad: Osmania Department of English, Osmania University, 1962–. 1/yr. Reviews.   PR1.O75

Quest   *Quest*. Vol. 1–. Bombay: S. Singh for the Indian Committee for Cultural Freedom, 1955–. 4–6/yr.
AP8.Q4

M–159 Some Frequently Recommended Works on Anglo-Indian and Indo-English Literature.

Alphonso-Karkala, John B. *Indo-English Literature in the Nineteenth Century*. Mysore: University of Mysore Literary Half-Yearly, 1970.   PR9722.A4 1970

Asvatthanarayana Reddi, G. *Indian Writing in English and Its Audience*. Bareilly: Prakash Book Depot, 1979.
PR9490.25.A8

Basham, A. L., ed. *Cultural History of India*. Oxford: Clarendon Press, 1975.   DS423.C86

Butter, P. *English in India*. Belfast: The Queen's University of Belfast, 1960.   AS122.B4 A3 no.9

Derrett, M. E. *Modern Indian Novel in English*. Brussels: Université Libre de Bruxelles, 1966.   PR9737.D4

George, Robert Esmonde Gordon [Robert Sencourt, pseud.]. *India in English Literature*. London: Simpkin Kurt Co., 1925.   PR149.I6 S4

Gokak, V. K. *English in India: Its Present and Future*. Bombay: Asia Publishing House, 1964.
No LC number

———. *Studies in Indo-Anglian Poetry*. Bombay, 1972.
No LC number

Gopaul, B. *Indian Writing in English: Critical Studies*. Reduit, Mauritus: University Press, 1983.
PR9489.6.G66 1983

Gupta, Brijen K. *India in English Fiction, 1800–1970: An Annotated Bibliography*. Metuchen, N. J.: Scarecrow, 1973.   Z2014.F5 G86

Lal, P. *Concept of an Indian Literature: Six Essays*. Calcutta: Writer's Workshop, 1968.   PK2903.L28

———, ed. *Modern Indian Poetry in English*. Calcutta: Writer's Workshop, 1969.   PR9764.L3

McCutchion, David. *Indian Writing in English: Critical Essays*. Calcutta: Writer's Workshop, 1973.
PR9708.M3

Melwani, Murli Das. *Themes in Indo-Anglian Literature*. Bareilly: Prakash Book Depot, 1976.
PR9484.6.M4 1976

Mokashi-Punekar, S. *Indo-Anglian Creed and Allied Essays*. Calcutta: Writer's Workshop, 1972.   PE3501.M6

Moorhouse, Geoffrey. *India Britannica*. New York: Harper and Row, 1983.   DS463.M73 1983

Mukherjee, Meenakshi. *Twice-born Fiction: Themes and Techniques of the Indian Novel in English*. 2d ed. New Delhi: Arnold-Heinemann, 1974.   PR9737.M8

Naik, M. K., S. K. Desai, and G. S. Amur, eds. *Critical Essays on Indian Writing in English*. 2d ed. Dharwar: Karhnatak University, 1972.   PR9484.6.C7 1972

Naik, M. K., and Mokashi-Punekar, S., eds. *Perspectives on Indian Drama in English*. Delhi: Oxford University Press, 1976.   PR9491.2.P47

Narasimhaiah, C. D. *Indian Writing in English*. Bombay, 1962.   No LC number

———. *Swan and the Eagle*. Simla: Indian Institute of Advanced Studies, 1969.   PR9709.N3

———, ed. *Fiction and the Reading Public in India*. Mysore: University of Mysore, 1967.   PR9735.S4 1965

Oaten, Edward Farley. *Sketch of Anglo-Indian Literature*. London: Kegan Paul, Trench, Trubner and Co., 1908.
No LC number

Raju, Anand Kumar. *Indian Writing in English: A Concise Bibliography of Secondary Sources*. Bombay: Ivon Publishing Home, 1981.   Z3208.L5 R34 1981

Rao, G. Subha. *Indian Words in English: A Study in Indo-British Cultural and Linguistic Relations*. Oxford: Oxford University Press, 1954.   PE3501.R3

Riemenschneider, Dieter. *Der moderne englischsprachige Roman Indiens*. Darmstadt: Thesen-Verlag, 1974.
PR9492.2.R5 1974

Sharma, K. K., ed. *Indo-English Literature: A Collection of Critical Essays*. Ghaziabad: Vimal Prakanshan, 1977.
PR9484.6.I56

Singh, Bhupal. *Survey of Anglo-Indian Fiction*. London: Oxford University Press, 1934. Contains an elaborate bibliography of more than 350 authors.
PR830.A5 S5

Sinha, R. C. P. *Indian Autobiographies in English*. New Delhi: S. Chand, 1978.   CT25.S55 1978

Speight, E. E. *Indian Masters of English*. London: Longmans, Green, 1934.   PR9779.S6

Spencer, Dorothy M. *Indian Fiction in English: An Annotated Bibliography*. Philadelphia: University of Pennsylvania, 1960.   Z3208.L5 S6

Srinivasa Iyengar, K. R. *Indian Contribution to English Literature*. Bombay: Karnatak, 1945.   PR9706.S68

———. *Indian Writing in English*. 3d ed. with a postscript chapter on the seventies and after, in collaboration with Prema Nandakumar. New Delhi: Sterling, 1983.
PR9484.3.S7 1983

———. *Indo-Anglian Literature*. Bombay: P.E.N. Books, International Book House, 1943.   PR9706.S7

———. *Literature and Authorship in India*. London: Allen and Unwin, 1943.   PK2903.S76

———. *Study of Indian Writing in English*. Bombay: Popular Book Depot, 1959.   No LC number

———. *Two Cheers for the Commonwealth: Talks on Literature and Education*. Bombay: Asia Publishing House, 1970.   PR99.S69

Venkateswaran, Khyamala. *Indian Fiction in English: A Bibliography*. Mysore: University of Mysore, 1970.
No LC number

Verghese, C. Paul. *Problems of the Indian Creative Writer in English*. Bombay: Somaiya Publications, 1971.
PR9706.V4

Wadia, A. R. *Future of English in India*. Bombay: Asia Publishing House, 1954.   PE3501.W3

Whiteworth, George Clifford. *Anglo-Indian Dictionary: A Glossary of Indian Terms Used in English and of Such English or Non-Indian Terms As Have Obtained Special Meanings in India*. London: Kegan Paul, Trench and Co., 1885.   PE3502.I6 W47

Williams, Haydn Moore. *Indo-Anglian Literature—1800–1970: A Survey*. Madras: Orient Longman, 1976.   PR9489.2.W5

Yule, Henry, and Arthur C. Burnell. *Dictionary of Indian English*. Edited by G. B. T. Kurian. Madras: Indian Universities Press, 1966.   PE3501.Y76

————. *Hobson-Jobson: A Glossary of Colloquial Anglo-Indian Words and Phrases, and of Kindred Terms, Etymological, Historical, Geographical, and Discursive.* New ed. Edited by William Crooke. London: J. Murray, 1886. PE3501.Y78

XIV. NEW ZEALAND AND THE SOUTH PACIFIC

M–160 **Thomson, J. E. P.** *New Zealand Literature to 1977: A Guide to Information Sources.* Detroit: Gale Research Co., 1980. Z4111.T45

The unnumbered but annotated entries are disposed into seven chapters as follows: 1, Bibliographies and Other Works of Reference; 2, Literary Histories and Criticism; 3, Anthologies; 4, Individual Authors (a short biographical sketch, followed by primary works classified by genre, followed by secondary works for a total of 31 important authors); 5, Other Authors; 6, Periodicals; 7, Non-Fiction Prose. The volume concludes with indexes of authors and titles.

For additional reference see the preliminary editions of the *Bibliography of New Zealand Bibliographies* (Wellington: New Zealand Library Association, 1967) [Z4101.A1 N4]. Also useful are T. M. Hocken's *Bibliography of the Literature Relating to New Zealand* (Wellington: J. Mackay, 1909) [Z4101.H7] and A. H. Johnstone's *Supplement to Hocken's Bibliography of New Zealand Literature* (1951) [No LC number]. The *New Zealand National Bibliography to the Year 1960*, ed. A. G. Bagnall (Wellington: A. R. Shearer, 1970–1980) [Z4101.B28], has been compiled in four volumes, the first volume in two parts covering publications to 1889, the subsequent three treating publications 1890–1960.

M–168 **Scholarly Journals in New Zealand Literature and the Other English Literatures of the South Pacific [excluding Australia]; [including Fiji, Malaysia, New Hebrides, Papua, New Guinea, Philippines, the Solomon Islands, Western Samoa].**

Islands: A New Zealand Quarterly of Arts and Letters. Vol. 1–. Torbay, Auckland, 1972–. 4/yr. No LC number

JPS *Journal of the Polynesian Society: A Quarterly Study of the Peoples of the Pacific Area.* Vol. 1–. Auckland, New Zealand: Polynesian Society, 1892–. 4/yr. Reviews. GN2.P7

Landfall *Landfall: A New Zealand Quarterly.* Vol. 1–. Christchurch: Caxton Press, 1947–. 4/yr. Reviews. AP7.L35

Mana [former title: *Mana Review*]: *A South Pacific Journal of Language and Literature.* Vol. 1–. Suva, Fiji: Mana Publications, 1976–. PR9645.M36

PQM *Pacific [Moana] Quarterly: An International Review of Arts and Ideas.* Vol. 1–. Hamilton, New Zealand: Outrigger Publisher, 1976–. 4/yr. Reviews. PN1.N48

M–169 **Some Frequently Recommended Works on New Zealand Literature and the Other English Literatures of the South Pacific (excluding Australia).**

Annals of New Zealand Literature: Being a Preliminary List of New Zealand Authors and Their Works. [Wellington]: New Zealand Authors' Week Committee, 1936. Z4104.N54

Baker, Sidney S. *New Zealand Slang: A Dictionary of Colloquialisms, the First Comprehensive Survey Yet Made of Indigenous English Speech in This Country—From the Argot of Whaling Days to Children's Slang in the Twentieth Century.* Christchurch: Whitcombe and Tombs, 1945.

Beaglehole, J. C. *Discovery of New Zealand.* 2d ed. London: Oxford University Press, 1961. DU410.B4 1961

Curnow, Wystan, ed. *Essays in New Zealand Literature.* Auckland: Heinemann Educational Books, 1973. PR9624.6.C8

Leland, Louis S., Jr. *Personal Kiwi-Yankee Dictionary.* Gretna: Pelican Publishing Co., 1984. PE3602.Z5 L44 1984

McCormick, E. H. *Letters and Art in New Zealand.* Wellington: Department of Internal Affairs, 1940. DU400.N35 vol.10

————. *New Zealand Literature: A Survey.* London: Oxford University Press, 1959. PR9606.M3

McLintock, A. H., ed. *Encyclopedia of New Zealand.* 3 vols. Wellington: Government Printer, 1966. DU405.E5

Manuel, Esperanza V., and Resil B. Majares. *Philippine Literature in English.* Cebu City: E. Q. Cornejo, 1973. PR9550.5.P5

Mulgan, Alan. *Literature and Authorship in New Zealand.* London: Allen and Unwin, 1943. PR9606.M8

New Zealand Writing: A Selective List of Poetry, Prose Fiction and Criticism in Print, 1967. Wellington: University Book Shop, 1967. Z4111.N48

Oliver, W. H. *Story of New Zealand.* London: Faber and Faber, 1963. DV420.O45

Park, Iris M. *New Zealand Periodicals of Literary Interest.* Wellington: Library School, National Library Service, 1962. MLCS 84/128(Z)

Ransom, W. S. [see above, under Australia].

Reid, J. C. "New Zealand Literature." In C. A. Wilkes and J. C. Reid, *Literature of Australia and New Zealand*, pp. 155–233. University Park: Pennsylvania State University Press, 1970. PR9412.W5

Sinclair, Keith. *History of New Zealand.* Harmondsworth: Penguin Books, 1959. DU420.S53

Smith, Bernard. *European Vision and the South Pacific, 1768–1850: A Study in the History of Art and Ideas.* Oxford: Clarendon Press, 1960. N7410.S6

Smith, E. M. *History of New Zealand Fiction from 1862 to the Present Time, with Some Account of Its Relation to the National Life and Character.* Wellington: Reed, 1939. No LC number

Stevens, Joan. *New Zealand Novel: 1860–1960.* Rev. ed. Wellington: Reed, 1966. PR9635.S7 1966

Tiffin, Chris, comp. *South Pacific Images.* Queensland: Department of English, University of Queensland, for the South Pacific Association for Commonwealth Literature and Language Studies, 1978. Contains reading lists. PR9080.S6

Wilkes, Gerald A., and J. C. Reid. *[Literature of] Australia and New Zealand.* University Park: Pennsylvania State University Press, 1970. PR9412.W5

Yapes, Leopoldo Y. *Philippine Literature in English, 1898–1957: A Bibliographical Survey.* Quezon City: University of the Philippines, 1958. Z3298.L5 Y3

XV. WEST INDIES

See also L–90 ff.

M–172 **Allis, Jeannette B.** *West Indian Literature: An Index to Criticism, 1930–1975.* Boston: G. K. Hall, 1981.
Z1502.B5 A38

This volume begins with a list of the periodicals and newspapers indexed which identifies the volumes and years analyzed in each case. The closing date is generally 1975, though some journals are indexed through 1977. There is also a brief list of composite volumes that were analyzed. The main body is in three parts, indexing authors, critics, and general articles respectively. The author index (giving birthplace and dates) first lists general treatments, then treatments of specific works (in chronological order by date of publication), then other primary works for which there are no secondary citations. Entries in the index of critics are arranged in chronological order and include reviews. Works discussed are identified if they are not evident from the article titles. Finally, the index of general articles is also arranged chronologically and is annotated with brief descriptive abstracts. An appendix lists books on West Indian literature.

M–173 **Carnegie, Jeniphier R.** *Critics on West Indian Literature: A Selected Bibliography.* Mona, St. Augustine, Trinidad: University of the West Indies, 1979.   Z1501.C37

After a brief introduction, serially numbered secondary bibliographies of twelve leading authors are presented, arranged alphabetically by author or, if anonymous, by title. The authors treated include E. K. Brathwaite, T. W. Harris, George Lamming, Roger Mais, V. S. Naipaul, V. S. Reid, and J. Phys. A general section follows listing fifteen bibliographies and indexes followed by nearly 200 general works on West Indian literature.

M–174 **Hughes, Michael.** *Companion to West Indian Literature.* London: Collins, 1979.   Z1502.B5 H83

An alphabetically arranged guide to 106 English writers and twenty-two important literary journals. For authors the articles contain biographical sketches followed by complete primary and selected secondary bibliographies. Journal articles review the history of the journal and indicate secondary works concerning it.

M–175 **Herdeck, Donald E., et al.** *Caribbean Writers: A Bio-bibliographical–Critical Encyclopedia.* Washington, D. C.: Three Continents Press, 1979.   PN849.C3 C3

This work treats some 2,000 writers and more than 15,000 works written in English, Dutch, French, Spanish, or a Creole language. The four main sections treat Anglophone Literature from the Caribbean; Francophone Literature from the Caribbean; Literatures of the Netherlands Antilles and Surinam; and Spanish Language Literature from the Caribbean, respectively. Each section includes essays on the literatures of the areas or countries included, followed by lists of writers. For each are given dates, a brief biography, a bibliography of primary works, and a bibliography of secondary works. This latter is classified if the number of entries warrants it.

M–176 **Dance, Daryl Cumber, ed.** *Fifty Caribbean Writers: A Bio-Bibliographical Critical Sourcebook.* Westport, Conn.: Greenwood Press, 1986.   PR9205.A52 F54 1986

This volume presents guides prepared by authoritative contributors to the lives and works of fifty writers from 1700 to the present who were either born or lived in the Caribbean region and whose works have a regional character. Both major new writers and important authors from the past are among the selected group. Entries provide a short biography followed by a detailed analysis of major works and themes and a summary of critical reception. A primary bibliography and selected secondary bibliography follow the entry.

M–178 **Scholarly Journals in West Indian Literature in English.**

BIM *BIM.* Vol. 1–. Trinidad, Barbados: Coles Printery, 1942–. Irreg. Index, 1942–1972, by Richard W. Sander (Trinidad, 1973); also in *JCL* 11 (1976): 1–41.   PR9230.45.B542

Caribbean Quarterly. Vol. 1–. Kingston, Jamaica: University of the West Indies, 1949–. 4/yr.
F1601.C3

Caribbean Studies. Vol. 1–. Rio Piedras: University of Puerto Rico, Institute of Caribbean Studies, 1961–. 4/yr. Reviews. "Current Bibliography" in each issue; two issues annually are devoted to the islands and two for the countries bordering the Carribean.   No LC number

Kyk-Over-Al. Vols. 1–15. Georgetown, British Guyana: British Guyana Writers' Association, 1945–1961. Irreg.   F1601.S26

SAVACOU: A Journal of the Caribbean Artists Movement [SAVACOU]. Vol. 1–. Kingston, Jamaica: University of the West Indies, Mona, 1970–. 2/yr.   F1601.S26

M–179 **Some Frequently Recommended Works on West Indian Literature in English [Barbados, Guyana, Jamaica, St. Lucia, Trinidad, and Tobago].**

Baker, Houston A. *Reading Black: Essays in the Criticism of African, Caribbean, and Black American Literature.* Ithaca, N. Y.: Cornell University Press, 1976.
PN841.R4

Baugh, Edward. *West Indian Poetry 1900–1970: A Study in Cultural Decolonisation.* Kingston, Jamaica: Savacou Publications, 1971.   PR9212.B3

————, ed. *Critics on Caribbean Literature.* London: George Allen and Unwin, 1978.   PR9210.C7

Brathwaite, Edward. *Roots: Essays.* Havana: Casa de las Americas, 1986.   PR9205.B73 1986

Cassidy, Frederic G., and Robert B. LePage, eds. *Dictionary of Jamaican English.* 2d ed. Cambridge: Cambridge University Press, 1980.   PE3313.Z5 C3 1980

Coulthard, G. R. *Race and Colour in Caribbean Literature.* London: Institute of Race Relations, 1962.
PR849.C3 C63 1962

Dathorne, O. R. *Dark Ancestor: The Literature of the Black Man in the Caribbean.* Baton Rouge: Louisiana State University Press, 1981.   PN849.C3 D37

Gilkes, Michael. *Racial Identity and Individual Consciousness in the Caribbean Novel.* Georgetown, Guyana: Ministry of Information and Culture, National History and Arts Council, 1975.   PR9320.9.M5 268

————. *West Indian Novel.* Boston: Twayne, 1981.
PR9214.G5

Griffiths, Gareth. *Double Exile: African and West Indian Writing Between Two Cultures*. London: Boyars, 1978. PR9080.G7

Harris, Wilson. *Tradition, the Writer, and Society: Critical Essays*. London: New Beacon Press, 1967.
PR6058.A692 T7

Holm, John A. *Dictionary of Bahamian English*. Cold Sprint, N. Y.: Lexik House, 1982.
PE3311.25.H64 1982

James, C. L. R. *Beyond a Boundary*. London: Stanley Paul, 1963. GV928.W47 J35

James, Louis, ed. *Island In Between: Essays on West Indian Literature*. London: Oxford University Press, 1968.
PR9320.5.J3

Jones, Joseph J., and Johanna Jones. *Authors and Areas of the West Indies*. Austin, Tex.: Steck-Vaughn Co., 1970. PR9320.J6

King, Bruce, ed. *West Indian Literature*. London: Macmillan, 1979. PR9210.W 1979

Knowles, Roberta, and Erika Smilowitz. *Critical Approaches to West Indian Literature*. Charlotte Amalie: Humanities Division, College of the Virgin Islands, 1981. PR9210.A515 1981

Lamming, George. *Pleasures of Exile*. London: M. Joseph, 1960. PR6023.A518 P5

Lewis, Gordon K. *Growth of the Modern West Indies*. London: MacGibbon and Kee, 1968. F2131.L48

Livingston, James T., ed. *Caribbean Rhythms: The Emerging English Literature of the West Indies*. New York: Washington Square Press, 1974. PR9215.C37

McWatt, Mark A., ed. *West Indian Literature and Its Social Context*. St. Michael, Barbados: Department of English, University of the West Indies, Cave Hill, 1985.
PR9210.A515 C66 1985

Merriman, Stella E. *Commonwealth Caribbean Writers: A Bibliography*. Georgetown: Guyana Public Library, 1970. Z1502.B5 M44

Moore, Gerald. *Chosen Tongue: English Writing in the Tropical World*. New York: Harper and Row, 1970.
PR9210.5.M6 1970

Ngugi Wa Thiong 'O. *Homecoming. Essays on African and Caribbean Literature, Culture, and Politics*. London: Heinemann, 1972. PR9340.N4

Ramchand, Kenneth. *Introduction to the Study of West Indian Literature*. Kingston, Jamaica: Nelson Caribbean, 1976. PR9210.R35

———. *West Indian Novel and Its Background*. 2d ed. London: Heinemann, 1983. PR9324.R3 1983

Soakana, Amon Saba. *Colonial Legacy in Caribbean Literature*. Vol. 1–. London: Karnak House, 1987–.
PN849.C3 S23 1987.

Sertima, Ivan van. *Caribbean Writers: Critical Essays*. London: New Beacon Books, 1968. PR9320.V3

Taylor, Patrick. *Narrative of Liberation: Perspectives on Afro-Caribbean Literature, Popular Culture, and Politics*. Ithaca, N. Y.: Cornell University Press, 1989.
F1609.5.T39 1989

MEDIEVAL LITERATURE

See also works in section F.III, Medieval History, and other pertinent entries in section F; in section G, Biography and Biographical References; in section H on the study of manuscripts and paleography; and in section I on Anglo-Saxon and Middle English. See also numerous references in sections K, L, and M, including the *MLA International Bibliography* (L–50), the MHRA *Annual Bibliography of English Language and Literature* (M–21), and the *Year's Work in English Studies* (M–22). See additional references on medieval poetry and poetics in section T, on medieval drama and theater in section U, and on medieval prose and prose fiction in section W. See also references on medieval literary and rhetorical theory in section X.

I. GENERAL

N–1 **Rouse, Richard H. *Serial Bibliographies for Medieval Studies.*** Berkeley and Los Angeles: University of California Press, 1969.   Z6302.R66

This work, published through the Center for Medieval and Renaissance Studies, UCLA, describes 283 bibliographies containing material of interest to students of the Middle Ages. Entries are disposed into eleven divisions and thirty-two subdivisions, within which they are listed alphabetically by title. The excellent descriptive annotations treat the bibliography's coverage, organization, and unique features. An asterisk indicates an exceptional degree of thoroughness. The division of entries is as follows: I. General Bibliography; II. National and Regional Bibliographies; III. Byzantine, Islamic, and Judaic Studies; IV. Archival and Auxiliary Studies; V. Art and Archaeology; VI. Ecclesiastical History; VII. Economic, Social, and Institutional History; VIII. Intellectual History; IX. Literature and Language (A. General, B. Germanic, C. Latin, D. Romance, E. Slavic); X. Music; XI. Science, Technology, and Medicine. The volume concludes with indexes of authors and editors. For serial bibliographies in the field of medieval literature, see also the more recent guide by Wortman (A–9).

N–2 **Crosby, Everett U., C. Julian Bishko, and Robert L. Kellogg. *Medieval Studies: A Bibliographical Guide*.** New York: Garland, 1983.   Z5579.5.C76

This massive volume offers an annotated, selective bibliography of books and monographs on all aspects of medieval studies from 200 A.D. to 1500. Included are the major collections of sources and the secondary literature which the compilers consider of basic importance for students of the history and culture of the western European Middle Ages, Byzantium, and medieval Islamic civilization. About 9,000 entries are classified into 138 sections covering reference works, the arts, sciences, social sciences, religion, laws, languages, literatures, numismatics, and heraldry. These broader subjects are subdivided into sections on specific geographical areas, and each is then further subdivided as appropriate to the subject in question. The brief annotations are both descriptive and evaluative, and nearly every entry is annotated. In addition to the detailed table of contents, there are two indexes of authors and editors and of topics.

N–3 **Powell, James M. M., ed. *Medieval Studies: An Introduction.*** Syracuse: Syracuse University Press, 1976.
D116.M4

This volume contains a series of ten introductory essays orienting the serious undergraduate or graduate beginner to various methodological and subject fields of medieval studies. The chapters and authors are as follows: Latin Palaeography (James J. John); Diplomatics (Leonard E. Boyce); Numismatics (Philip Grierson); Prosopography (George Beech); Computer-Assisted Analysis of the Statistical Documents of Medieval Society (David Herliky); Medieval Chronology; Theory and Practice (R. Dean Ware); Medieval English Literature (Paul Theiner); Latin Philosophies of the Middle Ages (Edward A. Synan); Tradition and Innovation in Medieval Art (Wayne Dyres); and Medieval Music in Perspective (Theodore Karp). Each chapter concludes with an enumerative bibliography of standard works for further consultation. There is an index of names, authors, titles, and subjects.
The editor intends in a subsequent volume to present further introductions to other fields.

N–4 ***Lexikon des Mittelalters.*** Edited by Robert Auty. 5 volumes planned. Munich: Artemis-Verlag, 1977. D101.5.L49

This dictionary of the history and culture of the European Middle Ages from about 300 A.D. to 1500 is being published in parts. It is through volume 3.8 as of 1986. Entries range from brief definitions and identifications to signed lengthy articles by scholars from around the world. There are entries treating individuals, literary forms and genres, material culture, places, and events. Most conclude with brief bibliographies.
Less scholarly but broader in scope is the planned 12 volume *Dictionary of the Middle Ages* edited by Joseph R. Strayer (New York: Scribner's, 1982–1989) [D114.D5]. These volumes cover the Latin West, the Slavic World, Asia Minor, the

lands of the caliphate in the East, and the Muslim-Christian areas of North Africa from ca. 500 A.D. to 1500. The 5,000 entries treat intellectual history, ecclesiastical history, political history, literary history, material culture, and geography, and range in length from 100 word brief identifications and definitions to 10,000 word articles by primarily North American scholars. Places, persons, works of art, events, literary forms and genres, national literatures, and other topics are treated. Most entries conclude with brief bibliographies which are generally and regrettably confined to English language references. There are numerous cross-references, and an *Interim Index* (1985) to volumes 1–5 which will eventually be replaced by a comprehensive index.

Two one-volume dictionaries of the Middle Ages are the *Dictionary of Medieval Civilization* by Joseph Dahmus (New York: Macmillan, 1984) [CB351.D24 1984] which presents short definitions and identifications but lacks both bibliographies and an index, and the *Illustrated Encyclopedia of Medieval Civilization* by Arveh Grabois (New York: Mayflower Books; Jerusalem: Jerusalem Publishing House, 1980) [CB353.G7 1980] which includes longer articles, including some which survey a field, short bibliographies, and both a chronology and an index.

-

N–5 Fisher, John H., ed. *Medieval Literatures of Western Europe: A Review of Research, Mainly 1930–1960.* New York: For the MLA, 1966.   PN671.F5

Though not current, the surveys of scholarship presented in this volume are still regarded as authoritative for the period covered. The work is intended for graduate students and others not specializing in the field, and its aim is to point out fundamental tools and fundamentally important research in medieval studies. Bibliographical reviews are presented by language: Medieval Latin (Albert C. Friend), Old English (George K. Anderson), Middle English to 1400 (Robert W. Ackerman), Medieval French (Charles A. Knudsun and Jean Misrahi), Medieval German (W. T. H. Jackson), Old Norse (Paul Schach), Medieval Italian (Vincent Luciani), Medieval Spanish (John E. Eller), Medieval Catalan (Joan Ruiz i Calonja and Josep Roca i Pons), Medieval Portuguese (Thomas R. Hart), and Medieval Celtic (Charles Donahue). Each essay discusses books and articles with respect to content and value, is divided into appropriate subject categories, and is sometimes subdivided. The essay on Middle English Literature, for example, is divided into twelve sections, from "Bibliographies" and "General Treatments" to "Mysticism," "Lyric and Other Poetry," and "Chaucer." Subdivisions in the section on "The Romance" included "General Works," "The Non-Arthurian Romances," and "The Arthuriana." There is an index of names including both authors of secondary works cited and medieval authors as subjects.

More limited in scope, though more current, is the volume of bibliographical review essays, *Present State of Scholarship in Fourteenth-Century Literature*, ed. Thomas D. Cooke (Columbia: University of Missouri Press, 1982) [PN681.P73 1982], with essays on each of the six major literatures of the century, English, French, German, Italian, Spanish and Portuguese. Extensive bibliographies present work published *since* 1962.

N–6 *Progress of Medieval and Renaissance Studies in the United States and Canada: Bulletin.* Nos. 1–25. Boulder: University of Colorado, 1923–1960.   Z6203.P96

From 1923 through 1942 this report of research in progress included only medieval studies; thereafter Renaissance studies were also included. The bulletins were annual to 1932, biennial thereafter. They included a "List of Active Medieval and Renaissance Scholars" giving current publications, fields of specialization, and related information; and a list of "Doctoral

Dissertations" completed and in progress, with institutional affiliations of authors, in lists arranged by broad fields of interest (English Language and Literature, Romance Language and Literature, etc.). A very useful list was of "Papers Read at Meetings of Learned Societies." "Books in Press" was the last of the listings.

Since 1960 there has been no comparable single listing, though the equivalent information can be more or less fully compiled by combining information for medieval studies from reports of work in progress in *Neuphilologische Mitteilungen* (N–25, N–40, and N–47) along with notes and announcements in *Speculum* (N–7), the *Old English Newsletter* (N–22), the *Chaucer Review* (N–47), and the *Bulletin bibliographique de la société internationale arthurienne* (N–57). For Renaissance studies a similar compilation is possible using information in *Seventeenth Century News* (O–9), *Research Opportunities in Renaissance Drama* (O–33), and the *Shakespeare Newsletter* (O–53).

N–7 "Bibliography of Editions and Translations [of Medieval Texts] in Progress." *Speculum: A Journal of Medieval Studies*, vol. 48–. 1973–.   PN661.S6

Originally prepared in response to a 1972 questionnaire, this list gives the name of the medieval author, the title of the work being edited or translated, a brief description of its contents, the century and language of its composition, the type of edition being prepared (or the language into which it is being translated), and the name and address of the project director. Only the first entry for a project carries complete information on it; subsequent entries are cross-referenced to the original entry and give only the current status of the project and the estimated date of completion. This list is meant to be used in conjunction with several other listings being published by the University of Erlangen-Nürnberg, the Centre d'études supérieures de civilisation médiévale, the Institut de recherche et d'histoire des textes, and the annual list in the Bulletin of the Société internationale pour l'étude de la philosophie médiévale (see N–18).

From 1937 through 1972, *Speculum* vols. 9–47 included a "Bibliography of American Periodical Literature" in each issue. Entries were classified into a few general subject areas (e.g., bibliography and textual studies, Chaucer, education and the fine arts, history, language, literature, medicine, philosophy, theology and law, science). Books have been covered through the extensive series of reviews in each issue, along with the list of books received, both of which features continue after the suspension of the bibliography of articles.

N–10 *Cambridge Bibliography of English Literature [CBEL].* Vol. 1, 600–1600, pp. 1–316. Edited by F. W. Bateson. Cambridge: Cambridge University Press, 1941.
                    Z2011.B3 1941 vol. 1

This portion of the first volume of the *CBEL* (see M–10) is divided into three parts: General Introduction (pages 1–52); The Anglo-Saxon Period to 1100 (pages 53–110); and The Middle English Period 1100–1500 (pages 113–314). The General Introduction has four main sections: I. Bibliographies; II. Histories and Anthologies; III. Prosody and Prose Rhythm; and IV. Language (General, Dictionaries, Syntax, Vocabulary, Old English Phonology and Grammar, Middle English Phonology and Grammar, Modern English Phonology, Place and Personal Names).

The Anglo-Saxon Period (to 1100) bibliography is in two sections, treating Old English Literature and Writings in Latin. The Old English section has subdivisions for General Works, Poetry, and Prose; the Latin section has subdivisions for General Works, British Celtic Writers, Irish Writers of the first and second period, and Anglo-Saxon Writers of the first and second period.

The bibliography of the Middle English Period (110–1500) is in six sections, as follows: I. Introduction (Bibliographies, Surveys, Anthologies, and Dictionaries; The Political Background; The Social Background; Education); 2. Middle English Literature (The Middle English Romances; Middle English Literature to 1400; Chaucer); 3. The Fifteenth Century (The English Chaucerians; Middle Scots Writers; English Prose of the fifteenth Century; Miscellaneous and Anonymous Verse and Prose of the fifteenth Century); 4. Songs and Ballads (Songs and Lyrics, The Ballads); 5. The Medieval Drama; and 6. Writings in Latin. Throughout, general studies are followed by works of or on specific periods, genres, forms, and authors.

The *Supplement* (1957) covers each of the major headings enumerated; added entries for this period are on pages 1–168. This volume and the section of the supplement pertaining to it have been almost but not entirely replaced by the first volume of the *NCBEL* (N–11).

N–11 *New Cambridge Bibliography of English Literature [NCBEL].* Vol. 1. 600–1600, cols. 1–806. Edited by George Watson. Cambridge: Cambridge University Press, 1974. Z2011.N45 vol. 1

This portion of the first volume of the *NCBEL* (see M–11), with entries current to 1972 or so, is divided into three parts: General Introduction (cols. 1–186); The Old English Period to 1100 (cols. 187–356); and the Middle English Period, 1100–1500 (cols. 357–806). Preceding the general section is a list of the fifty-six contributors to volume 1 with the initials used to indicate the bibliographies contributed by each. The General Introduction has four main sections: I. Bibliographies; II. Histories (general, Scottish, Irish, of genres) and Anthologies; III. Prosody and Prose Rhythm (subsections by periods); and IV. Language (A. General Works, B. Phonology and Morphology, C. Syntax, D. Vocabulary and Word Formation, and E. Place and Personal Names).

The Old English Period bibliography is in two main sections, treating Old English Literature and Writings in Latin respectively. The Old English portion is divided into a section on general works (Bibliographies, Histories, Anthologies, General Studies, Ancillary Studies) and then large sections on Poetry and Prose, both of which have general bibliographies followed by bibliographies of individual authors and works. The Poetry section has subdivisions for Dictionaries, Collections, Manuscript Studies, General Criticism, and Individual Poems and Authors, The Prose section is divided into subsections on Collections, General Criticism, Major Translators of Kind Alfred's Reign, Major Writers of the Later Period, Other Religious Prose, Chronicles, Laws and Charters, and Secular Prose. The Latin portion has six subsections, treating General Works, British Celtic Writers, Irish Writers, and Anglo-Saxon Writers, each grouped into earlier and later periods. Within sections general studies are followed by bibliographies on individual authors.

The Middle English part has six sections: Introduction; Middle English Literature (Middle English Romances, Literature to 1400, Chaucer, and Education); The Fifteenth Century (The English Chaucerians, Middle Scots Poets, English Prose; Miscellaneous and Anonymous Verse and Prose); Songs and Ballads; Medieval Drama; and Writings in Latin. Throughout, the arrangement has general sections followed by bibliographies of individual authors and works. A limited index at the end of the volume includes some names and titles from this portion of the volume. A more complete index is found in the *NCBEL Index*, vol. 5 (1977).

Because this is the last volume of the *NCBEL* to appear, it is the most current. Its reception has been generally favorable. Among the reviews see *TLS*, 11 December 1969, p. 1432, and the letter of F. W. Bateson in *TLS*, 18 December 1969, p. 1472, as well as the review in *ARBA* 7 (1976): 607–608, and that by Fred G. Robinson, *Anglia* 97 (1979): 511–517.

N–12 **Renwick, W. L., and H. Orton.** *Beginnings of English Literature to Skelton, 1509.* 3d ed. Revised by Martyn F. Wakelyn. *Introductions to English Literature*, edited by Bonamy Dobree, vol. 1. London: Cressett Press, 1966. PR83.I615 vol. 1

Originally published in 1939, this volume, along with the others in the series (see M–15, O–12, P–12, Q–30, and R–12), contains both a discursive introduction to Anglo-Saxon, Middle-English, and early Renaissance literature and a student's bibliographical guide. The guide, more detailed than those in other volumes of the series, contains both discussions of works and trends and lists of both primary and secondary works. It is organized into the following categories: General Bibliographies of Old and Middle English Language and Literature; The Old English Period—People, Institutions, Language; Old English Literature—General; Old English Literature—Poetry; Old English Literature—Prose; Middle English Period—People, Institutions, Language; Middle English Literature—General; Middle English Period—Individual Authors and Texts; Middle English Period—Other Texts; Scottish Literature; The Arts. There are extensive subdivisions for both general topics and particular authors and texts. The bibliographies on particular texts list bibliographies, manuscript sources, facsimiles, editions, translations, concordances, and critical discussions. Similar treatment is given to authors and their works. The volume ends with an index to names, titles, and subjects.

N–15 **Greenfield, Stanley B.** "Old English and Middle-English Bibliographical Guides." In David M. Zesmer, *Guide to English Literature from Beowulf through Chaucer and Medieval Drama*, pp. 287–381. New York: Barnes and Noble, 1961. PR166.Z4

These highly selective, extensively annotated guides emphasize recent studies and current scholarly thought and controversy. Foreign-language publications are excluded. Items suitable for the general reader and those that summarize and review scholarship are given prominence. A total of 356 items are included.

The first guide, covering Old English language and literature, is divided into sections on Historical and Linguistic Backgrounds; Anglo-Saxon Literary Culture; Beowulf and the Heroic Tradition; Elegiac, Caedmonian, and Cynewulfian Verse; Prose and Miscellaneous Poetry. The Middle English guide is divided into sections on General Studies; Historical and Linguistic Studies, Literary Surveys, and Studies in Prosody and Style; Romance; Prose; Lyrics and Folk Ballads; The Alliterative Revival; Debates, Didactic Poems, Satire, Mannyng and Gower; Chaucer—General; Chaucer—The Canterbury Tales; Fifteenth Century Chaucerians; and Medieval Drama. The volume index includes items in the two bibliographical guides.

N–16 **Matthews, William, ed.** *Old and Middle English Literature.* [A Goldentree Bibliography.] New York: Appleton-Century-Crofts, 1968. Z2012.M32

This highly selective guide to primarily British and American scholarship from about 1935 through 1965 in the more important areas of English literature and culture before 1525 excludes unpublished dissertations, most literary histories, short notes, and most older works. The Old English part is disposed into the following divisions: Texts, Reference and General Works, General Background, Poetics, Literary Background, Language, Anglo-Latin, Literary Themes and Modes, Scop Poetry, Beowulf, Elegiac Poems, Caedmonian Poems, Cynewulf and Cynewulfian Poems, Other Poetry, Charms, etc., The Anglo-Saxon Chronicle, King Alfred, Aelfric, Wulfstan, and Other Prose. The Middle English part has the following divisions: Texts; Reference; Manuscripts, Printing, Patrons; General Background; Anglo-Latin; Anglo-French; Language; Metrics, Rhetoric, Style; Literary Themes and Modes; English Chronicles; Moral Instruction, Proverbs, Sermons; Religious Narratives; Fabliaux, Animal Stories, Satires; Debates and Dialogues; Lyrics; Ballads; Romances; Breton Lays; Arthurian Romances; Malory; The Gawain Poet; Chaucer; Gower; Piers Plowman; Fifteenth-Century English Poets; Religious Prose; Secular Prose; Scottish Poetry and Prose; Miracle Plays; and Morality Plays. Under the headings there is further classification into texts and then commentary, as necessary. An index of modern authors and an index of medieval authors and anonymous writings conclude this handbook.

N–17 Beale, Walter H. *Old and Middle English Poetry to 1500: A Guide to Information Sources.* Detroit: Gale Research Co., 1976.   Z2014.P7B34

This descriptively and evaluatively annotated bibliography of work on English poetry to about 1500 aims to be complete with regard to primary works and selective, but extensive and representative, with regard to the listing of editions and criticism. The first book, treating Old English poetry, contains a total of 411 serially numbered entries in two parts. The first part has the following sections: Bibliographies and Surveys of Scholarship; Collections; Historical and Cultural Background; Literary History and General Criticism; Anthologies of Criticism and Festschriften; Literary Topics, Themes, and Traditions; Poetics, Rhetoric, Style; and Language (Bibliographies, Grammar and Phonology, Dictionaries and Concordances). The second part, listing Texts and Commentaries, is organized by poetic genre.

The second book, treating Middle English poetry, contains 918 serially numbered entries similarly disposed into two parts. The first part has sections parallel to those used for Old English works, save the addition of a section on Literary Transmission, Manuscripts, and Printed Books. The second part lists Texts and Commentaries and is similarly organized by the genres of Middle English poetry. The volume concludes with indexes of medieval authors and titles, subjects, and names of modern editors and commentators.

N–18 Scholarly Journals in Medieval Studies.

AnBol   *Analecta Bollandiana.* Vol. 1–. Brussels: Société des Bollandistes, 1882–. 2/yr. Reviews. Bibliography.   BX4655.A3

ASE   *Anglo-Saxon England.* Vol. 1–. Cambridge: Cambridge University Press, 1972–. 1/yr. Bibliography [see N–24]. Cumulative quinquennial indexes in each fifth volume.   DA152.2.A75

AnM   *Annuale Mediaevale.* Vol. 1–. Pittsburgh: Duquesne University, 1960–. 1/yr.   D111.A55

ALMA   *Archivum Latinitatis Medii Aevi (Bulletin Du Cange).* Vol. 1–. Brussels: International Union of Academies, 1924–. 1/yr. Reviews.   PA2801.B8

Bibliography of Old Norse–Icelandic Studies [1963–]. Vol. 1–. Copenhagen: The Royal Library, 1964–. Covers books, articles, and reviews, with a subject index.   Z2556.B5

Bibliothèque de l'École des chartes: Revue d'érudition consacrée spécialement a l'étude du moyen âge. Vol. 1–. Paris: M. Didier, 1839/40–. Reviews. Bibliography. Index, 1839–1909.   D111.B5

BHR   *Bibliothèque d'humanisme et Renaissance.* Vol. 1–. Paris [then Geneva]: Association d'humanisme et Renaissance, 1933–. 3/yr. Reviews. Bibliography (see O–3).   CB361.B5

Bulletin de philosophie médiévale. Vol. 1–. Louvain: Société internationale pour l'étude de la philosophie médiévale, 1959–. 1/yr. Reviews. Bibliography: list of new editions and translations of medieval texts.   B721.I57a

CCM   *Cahiers de civilisation médiévale: X^e-XIIe siècles.* Vol. 1–. Poitiers: Centre d'études supérieures de civilisation médiévale, 1958–. 4/yr. Reviews. Annual Bibliography (see F–24).   CB3.C3

ChauR   *Chaucer Review: A Journal of Medieval Studies and Literary Criticism.* Vol. 1–. University Park: Pennsylvania State University Press, 1966–. 4/yr. Annual Bibliography (see N–47).   PR1901.C5

Comitatus *Comitatus: A Journal of Medieval and Renaissance Studies.* Vol. 1–. Los Angeles: English Medieval Club, Center for Medieval and Renaissance Studies, UCLA, 1970–. 1/yr. Reviews.   PR251.C65

DAEM   *Deutsches Archiv für Erforschung des Mittelalters.* Vol. 1–. Marburg: Simons, 1937–. 2/yr. Reviews. Bibliography.   DD126.A1D4

Envoi: A Review Journal of Medieval Literature. Vol. 1–. New York: AMS Press, 1988–. 2/yr. Review essays and reviews.   No LC number

Exemplaria: A Journal of Theory in Medieval and Renaissance Studies. Vol. 1–. Binghampton: State University of New York, Medieval and Renaissance Texts & Studies, 1989–. 2/yr.   No LC number

JMRS   *Journal of Medieval and Renaissance Studies.* Vol. 1–. Durham, N.C.: Duke University, 1971–. 2/yr. Reviews.   CB351.J78

MS   *Mediaeval Studies.* Vol. 1–. Toronto: Pontifical Institute of Mediaeval Studies, 1939–. 1/yr. Cumulative index to vols. 1–25.   D111.M44

Mediaevalia: A Journal of Mediaeval Studies. Vol. 1–. Binghamton, N. Y.: Center for Medieval and Early Renaissance Studies, SUNY, 1975–. 1/yr.   CB351.M38

Medieval and Renaissance Drama in England [exclusive of Shakespeare]: *An Annual Gathering of Research, Criticism, and Reviews.* Vol. 1–. New York: AMS Press, 1984–. 1/yr. Reviews.   PR621.M65

Medieval and Renaissance Studies. Vol. 1–. London: Warburg Institute, 1941–.   D2.M36

Medieval and Renaissance Studies: Proceedings of the Southeastern Institute of Medieval and Renaissance Studies. Vol. 1–. Durham, N.C.: Duke University Press, 1966–. 1/yr.   CB361.M42

Medieval Archaeology. Vol. 1–. London: Society for Medieval Archaeology, 1957–. Reviews. Bibliography.   D111.M46

Medieval English Theatre. Vol. 1–. Lancaster, Eng.: University of Lancaster, 1979–. 2/yr.   No LC number

M & H   *Medievalia et Humanistica: An American Journal for the Middle Ages and Renaissance.* Vol. 1–. Boulder: University of Colorado, 1943–1966. New Series, with the subtitle Studies in Medieval and Renaissance Culture. Cambridge: Cambridge University Press, 1970–. 1/yr. Reviews.   D111.M5

MAE   *Medium Aevum.* Journal of the Society for the Study of Mediaeval Languages and Literature. Vol. 1–. Oxford: Blackwell, 1932–. 2/yr. Reviews. *General Index to Volumes I–XXV, 1932–1957 (1958).*   PB1.M4

MA   *Le moyen âge: Revue trimestrielle d'histoire et de philologie.* Vol. 1–. Brussels: Fondation universitaire de Belgique and CNRS, 1888–. 4/yr. Reviews. Bibliography.   D111.M9

NM   *Neuphilologische Mitteilungen.* Vol. 1–. Helsinki: Modern Language Society, 1899–. 4/yr. Reviews. Annual bibliographies (see N–25, N–40, and N–47).   PB10.N415

OENews *Old English Newsletter.* Vol. 1–. Binghamton, N.Y.: Center for Medieval and Early Renaissance Studies, SUNY, 1967–. 2/yr. Reviews. Bibliography (see N–22). A supplementary series, *Subsidia*, has been published irregularly since 1978.   No LC number

RB   *Revue bénédictine.* Vol. 1–. Maredsous, Belgium: Abbaye de Maredsous, 1884–. 2–4/yr. Reviews. Bibliographies.   BX3001.R4

Speculum *Speculum: A Journal of Mediaeval Studies.* Vol. 1–. Cambridge: Medieval Academy of America, 1926–. 4/yr. Reviews. Bibliographies (see N–7).   PN661.S6

SMed   *Studi Medievali.* Vol. 1–. Spoleto: Centro italiano di studi sull' alto medioevo. Series 1, 1904–1913; series 2, 1928–1953; series 3, 1960–. 2/yr. Reviews.   PN661.S83

Studies in Medieval and Renaissance History. Vol. 1–. Lincoln: University of Nebraska Press, 1964–.   D119.S

SMC   *Studies in Medieval Culture.* Vol. 1–. Kalamazoo: Western Michigan University Medieval Institute, 1964–. 1/yr.   CB351.S83

Studies in the Age of Chaucer: The Yearbook of the New Chaucer Society. Vol. 1–. Norman, Okla.: The Society, 1979–. Reviews. Annual Bibliography.   PR1901.S88

Traditio *Traditio: Studies in Ancient and Medieval History, Thought, and Religion.* Vol. 1–. New York: Fordham University Press, 1943–. 1/yr. Reviews. Bibliography.   D111.T7

See the article on Medieval Journals in *TLS*, 6 June 1980, p. 647, and the annotated list by Christopher Kleinhenz, "Medieval Journals and Publication Series in North America," in *Medieval Studies in North America: Past, Present, and Future*, ed. by Francis G. Gentry and Christopher Kleinhenz (Kalamazoo, Mich.: Medieval Institute, 1982) [CB351.M394 1982].

N–19 Some Frequently Recommended Works in Medieval Studies.

For additional frequently recommended works on general medieval history see section F; for works on social, intellectual, and educational history of the medieval period see K–90, K–95, and K–98 respectively. For works on the history of taste and related topics see K–92. For works on the other medieval literatures of the world see appropriate portions of section L; for works on medieval Scottish, Irish, and Welsh literature see appropriate portions of section M. For works on medieval poetry generally, see also section T; for medieval drama see also section U; for medieval prose see also section W; and for medieval literary theory and criticism see also section X. For frequently recommended works in Anglo-Saxon studies see N–29; for frequently recommended works in Middle English studies, see N–49.

Ackerman, Robert W. *Backgrounds to Medieval English Literature.* New York: Random House, 1966.   PR255.A3

Alston, Robert C., et al. *English Language and Medieval English Literature: A Select Reading List for Students.* Leeds: University of Leeds School of English, 1966.

Anderson, George K. *Old and Middle English Literature, from the Beginnings to 1485.* Vol. 1 of Hardin Craig's History (see M–36).

Auerbach, Eric. *Literary Language and Its Public in Late Latin Antiquity and in the Middle Ages.* Translated by R. Manheim. Princeton, N.J.: Princeton University Press, 1965.   PA8027.A813

Benham, Allen R. *English Literature from Widsith to the Death of Chaucer: A Source Book.* New Haven: Yale University Press, 1916.   PR255.B4

Bethurum, Dorothy, ed. *Critical Approaches to Medieval Literature.* New York: Columbia University Press, 1960.   PN681.B4

Bolton, Whitney F., ed. *Middle Ages.* Vol. 1 of the Sphere History, 1970 (see M–34).

Bromwich, Rachel. *Medieval Celtic Literature: A Select Bibliography.* Toronto: University of Toronto Press, 1974.   Z7011.B76

Chaytor, H. J. *From Script to Print: An Introduction to Medieval Vernacular Literature.* Cambridge: Heffer, 1950.   PN671.C5

Constable, Giles. *Medieval Monasticism: A Select Bibliography.* Toronto: University of Toronto Press, 1976.   Z7839.C8

Curtius, E. R. *European Literature and the Latin Middle Ages.* Translated by Willard Trask. New York: Pantheon, 1953.   PN674.C82

Goldschmidt, E. P. *Medieval Texts and Their First Appearance in Print.* London: Oxford University Press for the Bibliographical Society, 1943.   Z6517.G6

Gransden, Antonia. *Historical Writing in England, ca. 550–1307.* Ithaca, N.Y.: Cornell University Press, 1974.   DA1.G75 1974

Jackson, W. T. H. *Medieval Literature: A History and a Guide.* New York: Collier, 1960.   PN671.J33

Ker, W. P. *Epic and Romance: Essays on Medieval Literature.* 2d ed. London: Macmillan, 1908.   PN671.K44 1908

Malone, Kemp, and Albert C. Baugh. *Middle Ages.* Part 1, *Old English Period (to 1100)*, by Malone. Part 2, *Middle English Period (1100–1500)*, by Baugh. Vol. 1 in Baugh et al., *History of English Literature*, 2d ed., 1967 (see M–30).

Mandel, Jerome, and Bruce A. Rosenberg. *Medieval Literature and Folklore Studies: Essays in Honor of Francis Lee Utley.* New Brunswick, N.J.: Rutgers University Press, 1970.   PN681.M42

Panofsky, Erwin. *Gothic Architecture and Scholasticism.* New York: World Publishing Co., 1957.   NA440.P23 1957

Pearsall, Derek. *Old English and Middle English Poetry.* Vol. 1 of the Routledge History of English Poetry (see T–43).

Ullman, Walter. *Law and Politics in the Middle Ages.* Cambridge: Cambridge University Press, 1975.

Wilson, Richard M. *Lost Literature of Medieval England.* 2d ed. London: Methuen, 1970.   PR255.W5 1970

II.　ANGLO-SAXON

See also the references to Anglo-Saxon and early medieval history in section F. And see also the various dictionaries of Old English in section I.

N–20　**Greenfield, Stanley B., and Fred C. Robinson.** *Bibliography of Publications on Old English Literature to the End of 1972.* Toronto: University of Toronto Press, 1980.

Z2012.G83

This splendid bibliography contains a total of 6,550 serially numbered entries treating all works on Old English Literature with the exception of doctoral dissertations in typescript and purely linguistic studies. The intention is to list every book, monograph, article, note, or review in print from the invention of printing to 1972. The bibliography is based on the collection of entries begun by Kemp Malone in the 1930s, and its completion represents the first attempt at an exhaustive bibliography since 1885. Entries are in a classified arrangement of subject divisions, within which they are presented in chronological order. Brief annotations clarify the significance of a work and its place in ongoing scholarly discussion. Reviews of books are cited. The arrangement is in three parts. Part 1, General Works in Old English Literature, includes 872 entries in the following subdivisions: Bibliographies; Dictionaries; Concordances, Glosses, and Frequency Word Lists; Manuscripts; Modern Collections; Collections of Essays; Studies in Historical, Linguistic, and Cultural Subjects; Histories and Surveys of Literature; Studies of Themes and Topics; Special Vocabulary and Semantic Field Studies; Textual Criticism; Studies of Style and Language; Studies of Scholars and Scholarship. Part 2, Old English Poetry, contains the vast bulk of entries, over 4,250. They are disposed into the following subdivisions: Discussions of the Corpus of Poetry; Themes and Topics; Textual Criticism; Style and Language; Prosodic Studies; Studies of Problems in Translation; and (by far the most extensive section) Studies of Individual Poems, Authors, and Genres. Part 3, Old English Prose, contains more than 1,300 entries, disposed into the following divisions: Surveys, Studies of Topics and Miscellaneous Studies; Studies in Style and Language; and (again the vast majority) Studies of Individual Authors, Works, and Genres. Entries are extensively cross referenced, and the volume concludes with an index of authors and reviewers and a detailed index of subjects. A supplement covering 1973–1982 is in preparation by Carl T. Berkhout. See his essay, "Research on Early Old English Literary Prose, 1973–1982," in *Studies in Earlier Old English Prose*, ed. Paul E. Szarmach (Albany: State University of New York Press, 1986) 401–409 [PR221.S78 1986]. For a bibliographic essay addressing sources for Anglo-Saxon research not included in Greenfield and Robinson, see E. G. Stanley, "The Scholarly Recovery of the Significance of Anglo-Saxon Records in Prose and Verse: A New Bibliography," *Anglo-Saxon England* 9 (1981): 223–262. For a review of literary histories, see Daniel G. Calder, "Histories and Surveys of Old English Literature: A Chronological Review," *Anglo-Saxon England* 10 (1982): 201–244. And for desiderata, see Fred G. Robinson, "Anglo-Saxon Studies: Present State and Future Prospects," *Mediaevalia* 1 (1975): 62–77.

N–21　**Robinson, Fred C.** *Old English Literature: A Select Bibliography.* Toronto: University of Toronto Press, 1970.

Z2012.R6

This highly selective, annotated bibliography concerns all aspects of Old English literary scholarship to 1968. Exam-

ples of the best and most recent scholarship are chosen for each area of interest. Entries are in five sections, as follows: 1, Text (Collective editions, Facsimile editions, Collected translations in prose); 2, Literary History, Criticism, and Versification (Comprehensive critical-historical surveys, Stylistic studies, Studies of special aspects of form and content, Versification; 3, Individual Writers and Monuments (Poetry, Prose); 4, Fundamental Reference Works (Bibliographies, Dictionaries, Concordances, Biblical quotations, and Grammars); 5, Guide to Ancillary Subjects (General bibliography, Anglo-Latin, Archaeology, Art and Architecture, Early English Libraries, Historical Geography, History, Paleography, Religion, Magic and Mythology, Runology).

Serially numbered entries are annotated with descriptions of contents, summaries of conclusions, and indications of several important reviews of the cited item. There is an author index. A new edition of this guide is in progress. Robinson has also prepared a brief interim review of research, "Anglo-Saxon Studies: Present State and Future Prospects," *Mediaevalia*, 1 (1975): 62–77.

An earlier, selective, annotated bibliography is that by Arthur H. Heusinkveld and Edwin J. Bashe, *Bibliographical Guide to Old English: A Selective Bibliography of the Language, Literature and History of the Anglo-Saxons* (Iowa City: University of Iowa Press, 1931) [Z2012.A1 H5]. Entries are disposed into twelve chapters; indexes of Old English works and of modern authors conclude the volume.

N–22　**"Old English Bibliography" and "The Year's Work in Old English Studies."** *Old English Newsletter,* vol. 1–. Binghamton, N.Y.: Center for Medieval and Renaissance Studies, SUNY, 1967–.

PE101.O44

The "Old English Bibliography" published in the second number each year of the *Old English Newsletter* is a classified list of books, articles, dissertations, reprints, and reviews. Not limited to literature, the listing includes all aspects of Anglo-Saxon civilization. International in scope, this is the most detailed bibliography in the field. The classification has varied; a typical breakdown is as follows: I. Miscellaneous and General Literary; II. Linguistics; III. Historical and Cultural; IV. Beowulf; V. Other Old English Poems; VI. Old English Prose and Anglo-Latin Subjects; VII. Palaeography, Illumination; VIII. Reviews (by author, title, and reviewer); IX. Work Forthcoming and in Progress; X. Addenda. There is no index published.

"The Year's Work in Old English Studies," also published in the second number each year, is an extended bibliographical essay that summarizes and evaluates the significant work of the year. It is arranged in eight classified sections, as follows: General, Language, Literature, Anglo-Latin and Ecclesiastical Works, Manuscripts and Illumination, History and Culture, Onomastics, and Archaeology and Numismatics. Contributors' initials identify authors.

N–24　**Clemoes, Peter, et al., eds.** **"Bibliography [of Anglo-Saxon Studies] for 1971–."** *Anglo-Saxon England,* vol. 1–. Cambridge: Cambridge University Press, 1972–.

DA152.2.A75

This classified listing of books, articles, and significant reviews published in any branch of Anglo-Saxon studies during the year is organized in ten sections, as follows: 1, General and Miscellaneous; 2, Old English Language; 3, Old English Literature (general, poetry, prose); 4, Anglo-Latin, Liturgy and Other Latin Ecclesiastical Texts; 5, Palaeography, Diplomatic and Illumination; 6, History; 7, Numismatics; 8, Onomastics; 9, Archaeology (general; towns and other major settlements, rural settlements, agriculture, and the countryside; pagan cemeteries and Sutton Hoo; churches, monastic sites, and Christian cemeteries; ships and seafaring; sculpture on bone, stone, and wood; metalwork and other minor objects; inscriptions; pottery and glass; musical instruments); 10, Reviews (alphabetically by the reviewed author, then the name of the reviewer and citation). There are occasional explanatory annotations and some cross-references. Work excluded in a previous year is cited subsequently, with an asterisk; the citation includes the year of publication.

N–25 **"Old English Research in Progress [1964–]."** *Neuphilologische Mitteilungen,* vol. 66–. Helsinki: Modern Language Society, 1965–. PB10.N415

Organization of the list is alphabetical by subject (including author-as-subject) treated. Entered is the name of the researcher, the tentative title of the project, an indication of its form (a—article, essay, lecture, or chapter; b—book or monograph; asterisk before the author's name—doctoral dissertation); and its current status (IP—in progress; C—completed). Projects are not repeated once they have been listed; there is a list of lapsed projects at the conclusion of the year's enumeration.

For North American scholarship during the period 1923–1960 one may consult the annual *Progress of Medieval and Renaissance Studies in the United States and Canada* (N–6).

N–27 **Quinn, Karen J., and Kenneth P. Quinn.** *Manual of Old English Prose.* New York: Garland, 1988. PR221.Q5 1988

This work is arranged in five parts, and includes books, articles, and dissertations, but not reviews. The first, Manuscripts, lists all manuscripts containing Old English prose, arranged in the order established by Ker's catalogue. Part two, Texts, lists all Old English prose texts except legal documents and works by Wulfstan and Aelfric. Part three, Editions, lists all editions of the texts in part two, except student readers and primers. Part four, Criticism, lists all scholarship and criticism on the texts in part two. Part five, Indexes, includes indexes of Modern Title, Manuscript Title, First Line, and Subject of Homilies. Most entries are annotated; they are complemented by extensive cross references.

N–29 **Some Frequently Recommended Works in Anglo-Saxon Studies.**

For additional works see entries in N–19 as well as many pertinent titles cited in K–90, K–92, K–95, and K–98.

Amos, Ashley Crandell. *Linguistic Means of Determining the Dates of Old English Literary Texts.* Cambridge: Mediaeval Academy of America, 1980. PR179.C45 A47 1980

Anderson, George K. *Literature of the Anglo-Saxons.* Rev. ed. Princeton, N.J.: University Press, 1966. PR173.A5

Anglo-Saxon Poetic Records: A Collective Edition. 6 vols. New York: Columbia University Press, 1931–1953. PR1580.D6

Barney, Stephen A. *Word-Hoard: An Introduction to Old English Vocabulary.* New Haven: Yale University Press, 1977. PE274.B3

Bartlett, Adeline C. *Larger Rhetorical Patterns in Anglo-Saxon Poetry.* New York: Columbia University Press, 1935. PR203.B3 1935

Bessinger, Jess B., Jr., ed. *Concordance to the Anglo-Saxon Poetic Records.* Ithaca: Cornell University Press, 1978. [Based on Krapp and Dobbie, eds. *Anglo Saxon Poetic Records* (1931–1953).] PR1506.B47

————, and Stanley J. Kahrl, eds. *Essential Articles for the Study of Old English Poetry.* Hamden, Conn.: Archon, 1968. PR176.B4

Blair, Peter. *Introduction to Anglo-Saxon England.* 2d ed. Cambridge: Cambridge University Press, 1977. DA152.2.B55 1977

Brodeur, Arthur G. *Art of Beowulf.* Berkeley and Los Angeles: University of California Press, 1959. PR1585.B68

Chadwick, Hector M. *Heroic Age.* Cambridge: Cambridge University Press, 1912. PN1303.C6

Chambers, R. W. *Beowulf: An Introduction to the Study of the Poem with a Discussion of the Stories of Offa and Finn.* 3d ed. Revised with a supplement by C. L. Wrenn. Cambridge: Cambridge University Press, 1959. PR1585.C

————. *England before the Norman Conquest.* London: Longmans, Green, 1926. DA135.C47

Creed, Robert P., ed. *Old English Poetry: Fifteen Essays.* Providence, R.I.: Brown University Press, 1967. PR201.C7

Duckett, Eleanor S. *Alcuin, Friend of Charlemagne: His World and His Work.* New York: Macmillan, 1951.

————. *Alfred the Great.* Chicago: University of Chicago Press, 1956. DA153.D85

————. *Anglo-Saxon Saints and Scholars.* New York: Macmillan, 1947. BR754.A1D8

Early English Manuscripts in Facsimile. Vol. 1–. Copenhagen: Rosenkilde and Bagger, 1951–. LC numbers vary

Early English Text Society. Publications. Vol. 1–. Oxford: Oxford University Press, 1864–. PR1119.A2

Elliott, Ralph W. V. *Runes: An Introduction.* 2d corr. printing with bibliography. Manchester: Manchester University Press, 1963. PD2013.E4

Fry, Donald K. *Norse Sagas Translated into English: A Bibliography.* New York: AMS Press, 1981. Z2556.F78

————, ed. *Beowulf Poet: A Collection of Critical Essays.* Englewood Cliffs, N.J.: Prentice-Hall, 1968. PR1585.F7

Garmonsway, George N., and Jacqueline Simpson, trans. *Beowulf and Its Analogues.* London: Dent, 1968. PR1583.G28

Gradon, Pamela. *Form and Style in Early English Literature.* London: Methuen, 1971. PR166.G7

Greenfield, Stanley B. *Interpretation of Old English Poems.* Boston: Routledge and Kegan Paul, 1972. PR201.G7

————, and Daniel G. Calder. *New Critical History of Old English Literature, with a Survey of the Anglo-Latin Background,* by Michael Lapidge. New York: New York University Press, 1986. PR173.G73 1986

Haymes, Edward. *Bibliography of Studies Relating to Parry's and Lord's Oral Theory.* Cambridge: Harvard University Press, 1973. See T–73.

Hodgkin, R. H. *History of the Anglo Saxons.* 3d ed. 2 vols. London: Oxford University Press, 1952. DA152.H62

Huppé, Bernard F. *Doctrine and Poetry: Augustine's Influence on Old English Poetry.* Albany: SUNY Press, 1959. PR182.H8

Irving, E. B., Jr. *Reading of Beowulf.* New Haven: Yale University Press, 1968. PR1585.I7

Kennedy, Charles. *Earliest English Poetry: A Critical Survey of the Poetry Written before the Norman Conquest, with Illustrative Translations.* London: Oxford University Press, 1943. PR201.K4

Ker, W. P. *Dark Ages*. New York: C. Scribner's Sons, 1904.   PN671.K4

Krapp, George Philip, and Elliott Van Kirk Dobie, eds. *Anglo Saxon Poetic Records: A Collective Edition*. 6 vols. New York: Columbia University Press, 1931–1953.   PR1502.A7

Lawrence, William W. *Beowulf and Epic Tradition*. Cambridge: Harvard University Press, 1928.   PR1585.L3

Magoun, Francis P., Jr. "The Sutton-Hoo Ship Burial: A Chronological Bibliography." *Speculum* 29 (1954): 116–124; "Part Two" by Jess B. Bessinger, Jr., *Speculum* 33 (1958): 515–522.

Mayr-Harting, Henry. *Coming of Christianity to Anglo-Saxon England*. London: B. T. Batsford, 1972.
                                               BR749.M42

Morrell, Minnie C. *Manual of Old English Biblical Material*. Knoxville: University of Tennessee Press, 1965.
                                               BS132.M6

Ogilvy, Jack David Angus. *Books Known to the English, 597–1066*. Cambridge, Mass.: Mediaeval Academy of America, 1967.   Z6002.O35

Quirk, Randolph, and C. L. Wrenn. *Old English Grammar*. 2d ed. New York: Holt, Rinehart and Winston, 1958.
                                               PE131.Q5 1958

Sisam, K. *Structure of Beowulf*. Oxford: Clarendon Press, 1965.   PR1585.S5

———. *Studies in the History of Old English Literature*. Oxford: Clarendon Press, 1953. Reprinted with corrections. 1962.   PR181.S5

Stanley, E. G. *Continuations and Beginnings: Studies in Old English Literature*. London: Nelson, 1966.
                                               PR171.S7

Stenton, Frank M. *Anglo-Saxon England*. 2d ed., rev. Oxford: Oxford University Press, 1947.
                                               DA152.S74 1947

Tolkien, J. R. R. *Beowulf: The Monsters and the Critics*. London: Oxford University Press, 1959. Originally published 1936.   PR1585.T6

Whitelock, Dorothy. *Changing Currents in Anglo-Saxon Studies: An Inaugural Lecture*. Cambridge: Cambridge University Press, 1958.   CB216.W5

Wilson, D. M. *Anglo-Saxons*. New York: Praeger, 1960.
                                               DA155.W5

Wrenn, C. L. *Study of Old English Literature*. London: Harrap, 1967.   PR173.W75

III.   MIDDLE ENGLISH

See also the references to high and late medieval history in section F. And see the *Dictionary of Middle English* in section I.

N–30 **Wells, John E. *Manual of Writings in Middle English, 1050–1400*.** New Haven: Yale University Press, 1916. Nine Supplements, 1919–1951.   PR255.W4

This work, originally a Ph.D. dissertation, remains an indispensable tool for students of Middle English. All extant writings pertaining to works composed in English during the period 1050–1400 are included. The volume of Tucker and Benham (N–31) supplements Wells for works of the fifteenth century. As updated, it is the most extensive bibliography of Middle English literature available. The work is divided into two parts, a discursive manual and a bibliography.

The text of the first part is generally arranged by genre, with each Middle English work in the genre listed chronologically to facilitate a comparative and historical approach. Each work is assigned a number for easy reference. For each work listed, the probable date, manuscripts, form and extent, dialect, sources, language, and other features are discussed. For longer works the entry concludes with an abstract of the work and a consensus assessment of its value, formed by a summary of scholarly and critical opinion.

The second part, "Bibliographic Notes," gives citations of editions and other scholarship relating to each text. These citations, though unannotated, are classified, and items are keyed by "Wells number" to the reference to them in the first part. The index serves to cross-reference the text.

Supplements, paged continuously with the original volume, are keyed in to the basic work and to each other through the use of the "Wells number." Supplements include new information, revisions of old information, and additions and corrections to bibliographical notes. Supplement 8 (1941) includes an index to Supplements 1–8. The whole *Manual* will be updated and generally replaced by Severs and Hartung (N–32).

N–31 **Tucker, Lena Lucile, and Allen Rogers Benham. *Bibliography of Fifteenth Century Literature, with Special Reference to the History of English Culture*.** Seattle: University of Washington Press, 1928.   Z2012.T89

This annotated bibliography is meant to supplement the coverage of Wells's *Manual* (N–30) for fifteenth-century literature. Entries are disposed into seven sections as follows: I. Bibliography; II. Political Background; III. Social and Economic Background; IV. Cultural Background; V. Linguistic Background; VI. Literature (General Texts, General Discussion, Drama, Individual Authors, Anonymous Works); and VII. An Appendix of Some References on the Beginnings of the Sixteenth Century. The volume concludes with an index of authors, anonymous titles, and subjects.

N–32 **Severs, J. Burke, and Albert E. Hartung, et al. *Manual of Writings in Middle English, 1050–1500*.** New Haven: Connecticut Academy of Arts and Sciences, 1967–.
                                   PR255.M3 or PR255.S4

Based upon Wells's *Manual* (N–30), this multivolume work has been prepared by members of the Middle English Group of the Modern Language Association of America. When complete in ten volumes, it will replace Wells for most purposes. The intention, that is, is a complete revision and enlargement of Wells. The individual volumes treat genres or groups of genres. All have the same two-part structure initiated by Wells. The first part describes Middle English texts and summarizes and evaluates books, book reviews, and articles that treat them, aiming to present proportionately and authoritatively the consensus of scholarly judgment and investigation about each. For each entry, information on manuscripts, date of composition, dialect, sources, form, and content is presented, followed by the summary of pertinent scholarship and criticism. The second part provides an analytical, unannotated, bibliography on each work, divided into chronologically arranged sections on manuscripts, editions, selections, modernizations and abstracts, textual matters, language, versification, date, authorship, sources and literary relations, other scholarly problems, literary criticism, general references, and bibliographies. This bibliography aims at completeness through 1955 and at the inclusion of all important studies from 1955 through the cutoff date for the individual volume. Each volume ends with its own indexes of Middle English works, authors, modern works, printers, and subjects. To date, seven volumes of the projected ten have been published. A master index will complete the project.

Volume 1, edited by Severs (1967), treats Romances. It is divided into a general section followed by ten sections on the different subgenres of romances.

Volume 2, edited by Severs (1970), contains the following parts: II. The *Pearl* Poet; III. Wyclyf and His Followers; IV. Translations and Paraphrases of the Bible, and Commentaries; V. Saints' Legends; and VI. Instructions for Religious.

Volume 3, edited by Albert E. Hartung (1972), contains the following parts: VII. Dialogues, Debates, and Catechisms (edited by Francis Lee Utley); VIII. Thomas Hoccleve (edited by William Matthews); and IX. Malory and Caxton (edited by Robert H. Wilson).

Volume 4, edited by Albert E. Hartung (1973), contains the following parts: X. Middle Scots Writers and XI. The Chaucerian Aprocrypha.

Volume 5, edited by Albert E. Hartung (1975), contains the following parts: XII. Dramatic Pieces, divided into sections on Miracles, Mysteries, Moralities, and Folk Drama, and XIII. Poems Dealing with Contemporary Conditions.

Volume 6, edited by Albert E. Hartung (1979), contains the following parts: XIV. Carols, XV. Ballads, and XVI. John Lydgate.

Volume 7, edited by Albert E. Hartung (1986), contains the following parts: XVII. John Gower (edited by John H. Fisher, et al.), XVIII. *Piers Plowman* (edited by Anne Middleton), XIX. Travel and Geographical Writings (edited by Christian K. Zacher), XX. Works of Religious and Philosophical Instruction (edited by Robert R. Raymo).

The last three projected volumes, still in progress, will contain the following parts: Tales; Chronicles; Homilies; Proverbs, Precepts, and Monitory Pieces; Science, Information, and Documents; Letters; Legal Writings; Rolle and His Followers; Lyrics; and Undistributed Prose.

N–33 Simms, Norman Toby. *Ritual and Rhetoric: Intellectual and Ceremonial Backgrounds to Middle English Literature: A Critical Survey of Relevant Scholarship.* Norwood, Pa.: Norwood Editions, 1973. Z2012.S55

This volume presents a total of 1,481 serially numbered articles describing works on ritual and rhetoric pertinent to the Middle English period. The two parts are divided into the following sections: Ritual: General Studies, Audiences, The Court, The Church, Monasteries, Schools, The City, and History; Rhetoric: General Themes, Inventio, Disposition, Elocutio, Genres, Drama, Related Literature, Thought, Aesthetics, Education, Art, and Reference Books and Aids.

N–35 Brown, Carleton. *Register of Middle English Religious and Didactic Verse.* 2 vols. Oxford University Press for the Bibliographical Society, 1916–1920. Z2012.B87

Manuscripts containing verse rather than printed texts have been taken as the basis in compiling this register. Only religious and didactic verse is included, excluding (1) chronicle histories and political pieces, (2) romances, (3) secular lyrics, (4) charms, (5) alchemical poems, and (6) dramatic texts. The chronological limits are approximately 1200 to 1400 (dates of composition). Volume 1 contains a list of all known manuscript material arranged in the order of the manuscript repositories in which it is preserved. There are thirteen chapters on the Bodleian, Oxford Colleges, Cambridge University Library, Cambridge Colleges, the Fitzwilliam Museum, the British Museum, Other Library Repositories, Cathedral Libraries, Various College and Public Libraries, Manuscripts in Private Hands, Repositories in Scotland, in Ireland, and in America or on the Continent. Volume 2 is an index of subjects and titles added to a main index of first lines. Each first-line listing enumerates the manuscripts in which the verse is contained, listing locations and notes as to significant variation in various manuscripts. References to printed texts

are also made. A list of addenda and corrigenda is given. The second volume, though not the first, is superseded by Brown and Robbins (N–36), which is supplemented in turn by Robbins and Cutler (N–37).

N–36 Brown, Carleton, and Rossell Hope Robbins. *Index of Middle English Verse.* New York: Columbia University Press for the Index Society, 1943. Z2012.B86

Based on the *Register of Middle English Religious and Didactic Verse* (N–35), this index replaces volume 2 of that work. It contains 4,365 first-line entries from some 2,000 manuscripts, compared with the 2,273 entries from 1,100 manuscripts in the *Register*. Old entries have been expanded and new entries of materials found since 1916 have been added, as have entries for secular verse. The index is alphabetical according to first lines. Entries give the title, the contents, and the poetic form of the composition, list manuscripts containing it, and list published editions of it. Appendixes include a conversion table to the *Register* entries, manuscript numbers from the Bodleian *Summary Catalogue of Western Manuscripts* (H–12), and a list of manuscripts in private possession. A subject-and-title index is found at the end of the volume. The *Index* also includes a special section of acephalous fragments of verse. Additions and corrections were printed in *Speculum* 20 (1945): 105–111, and in *Neuphilologische Mitteilungen* 49 (1948): 126–133. The *Supplement to the Index of Middle English Verse* (N–37) updates and corrects the *Index*, and Ringer (see N–37) extends its coverage to work composed before 1500.

N–37 Robbins, Rossell Hope, and John L. Cutler. *Supplement to the Index of Middle English Verse.* Lexington: University of Kentucky Press, 1965. Z2012.B862

The *Supplement* updates the *Index of Middle English Verse* (N–36) to 1965, expanding about 2,300 of the original entries and adding about 1,500 more. Old entry numbers and decimals are used to preserve the original numeration which is the standard reference form for Middle English verse. The current situation of the manuscripts is described, additions and corrections to the information in the *Index* is given, and locations of manuscripts in private hands are updated. Further, the cataloging of those manuscripts unavailable in 1943 because of the war is here completed, with first lines, description of contents and poetic form, and lists of manuscripts and of printed editions given for each new entry. Appendixes include a conversion table for the acephalic fragments renumbered from the *Index* and put into the main sequence; *Summary Catalogue* numbers of Bodleian manuscripts; the present locations of some 500 moved manuscripts; a list of the 147 Middle English poems preserved in eight or more manuscripts; and corrigenda to the original subject-and-title index. In the *Supplement* there is not strict adherence to the period 1200–1500 for the date of the manuscripts included. The *Supplement* has its own subject-and-title indexes. For a complete survey of Middle English verse the 1916 *Register* (N–35), the 1943 *Index*, and the 1965 *Supplement* must be checked.

Also pertinent is the supplement by William Ringler, "A Bibliography and First-Line Index of English Verse Printed through 1500: A Supplement to Brown and Robbins' *Index of Middle English Verse*," *PBSA* 49 (1955): 153–180, which identifies by first lines the Middle English verse published in early printed books. See also Robbins, "Middle English Lyrics: Handlist of New Texts," *Anglia* 83 (1965): 35–47; and "The Middle English Carol Corpus: Some Additions," *MLN* 74 (1959): 198–208. Further additions and corrections include articles by Linne R. Mooney in *Anglia* 99 (1981): 394–398; by Ralph Hanna III in *PBSA* 74 (1980): 234–258; and by Siegfried Wenzel in *Anglia* 92 (1974): 55–78.

N–38 **Edwards, A. S. G., et al.** *Index of Middle English Prose.* In progress since 1977.

The production of an *Index of Middle English Prose*, meant to complement the *Index of Middle English Verse* (N–36), was formally begun at a conference on "Problems in Middle English Prose" held at Emmanuel College, Cambridge, 22–23 July 1978, the proceedings of which were published as *Middle English Prose: Essays on Bibliographical Problems*, ed. A. S. G. Edwards and Derek Pearsall (New York: Garland, 1981) [PR275.T45 M5 1981]. The papers include opening remarks by Rossell Hope Robbins, among the most active proposers of this *Index*, as well as two essays describing the project, "Towards an *Index of Middle English Prose*" by A. S. G. Edwards and "Editorial Technique in the *Index of Middle English Prose*" by R. E. Lewis. Five additional papers discuss problems associated with one or another particular group of Middle English prose texts.

The stages of the project are three. The first, already completed, is an *Index of Printed Middle English Prose* edited by Robert E. Lewis, N. F. Blake, and A. S. G. Edwards (New York: Garland, 1985) [Z2014.P795 L49 1985]. The second stage, to which there will be between fifty and 100 contributing editors, will consist of a series of bibliographical handlists of prose items (printed and not) by manuscript and/or manuscript collection. Finally, in some twenty years, an actual first-line *Index* will be produced.

The first-stage *Index of Printed Middle English Prose* has entries with four elements. The first line of the actual Middle English text (omitting titles, tables of contents, and prefatory materials) from the first listed edition of that text provides the alphabetically arranged main entry. Following the first line are indications of the author, title, genre, and date of composition of the text that it begins. Following this is a numbered list of all editions and all manuscripts. Notes of additional useful information make up the fourth and final element.

Several second-stage handlists have appeared to date: *Handlist I: A Handlist of Manuscripts Containing Middle English Prose in the Henry E. Huntington Library*, by Ralph Hanna III (Cambridge: D.S. Brewer, 1984) [Z6621.H5273 M534 1984]; *Handlist II: A Handlist of Manuscripts Containing Middle English Prose in the John Rylands University Library of Manchester and Chetham's Library, Manchester*, by G. A. Lester (Cambridge: D. S. Brewer, 1984) [Z6605.E5 L47 1985]; and *Handlist III: A Handlist of Manuscripts Containing Middle English Prose in the Digby Collection, Bodleian Library, Oxford*, by Patrick J. Horner (Cambridge: D. S. Brewer, 1986) [Z6621.B663.M55 1986]. Organized by shelf-marks, entries include the incipit and explicit for each item, physical description, and pertinent references to other manuscripts, reference works, and scholarship. *Handlist IV: A Handlist of Douce Manuscripts Containing Middle English Prose in the Bodleian Library, Oxford*, by Laurel Braswell (Cambridge: D. S. Brewer, 1987) [Z6621.B663 M53 1987]; *Handlist V: A Handlist of Manuscripts Containing Middle English Prose in the Additional Collections (10001–12000), British Library, London*, by Peter Brown *and in the Additional Collection (12001–14000), British Library, London*, by Elton D. Higgs (Cambridge: D. S. Brewer, 1988) [Z6621.B85 E53 1988]; *Handlist VI: A Handlist of Manuscripts Containing Middle English Prose in Yorkshire Libraries and Archives*, by O. S. Pickering (Cambridge: D. S. Brewer, 1989) [Z6605.E5 P5 1989]; and *Handlist VII: A Handlist of Manuscripts Containing Middle English Prose in Parisian Libraries*, by James Simpson (Cambridge: D. S. Brewer, 1989) [Z6605.E5 S57 1989].

N–40 **"Middle English Research in Progress [1963–]."** *Neuphilologische Mitteilungen,* vol. 65–. Helsinki: Modern Language Society, 1964–.   PB10.N415

This annual listing is classified by the name of the subject, text, or author studied. Excluded from citation are late Tudor studies, books and articles already in proof or print, short or minor projects, and reviews. Textbooks and collected anthologies are included, as are dissertations in progress (which are identified by an asterisk and for which sponsoring institutions and, since 1978/79, names of directors are given). Studies previously entered are repeated on occasion.

N–42 **Severs, J. Burke, ed.** *Recent Middle English Scholarship and Criticism: Survey and Desiderata.* Pittsburgh: Duquesne University Press, 1971.   PR255.R4

This volume contains four reviews of research, as follows: *Piers Plowman* (David Fowler); *Sir Gawain and the Green Knight* (Donald R. Howard); Middle English Romances (Lillian Herlands Horstein); and Chaucer's *Canterbury Tales* (Helaine Newstead). The first essay takes up with the work published since Morton W. Bloomfield's "Present State of *Piers Plowman* Studies," *Speculum* 14 (1939): 215–232. The second takes up with Bloomfield's article "*Sir Gawain and the Green Knight*: An Appraisal," *PMLA* 76 (1961): 7–19. The third essay surveys material published since volume 1, *Romances*, of a *Manual of the Writings in Middle English 1050-1500* (N–32) went to press. The fourth focuses on trends in materials published since Albert Baugh's review, "Fifty Years of Chaucer Scholarship," *Speculum* 26 (1951): 659–672.

N–45 **Baugh, Albert C.** *Chaucer.* [A Goldentree Bibliography.] New York: Appleton-Century-Crofts, 1968.   Z8164.B33

This bibliography emphasizes work published in the twentieth century. Excluded are school editions, short articles on minor points, popular and semipopular books and articles, and dissertations not available in the printed form. Some 2,500 entries are unannotated, but works of special importance are designated with an asterisk. The entries are classified into fairly narrow groupings that move from general to particular. They include Bibliographies and Surveys of Scholarship; Societies and Journals; Reference Works; Life; Literary, Political, and Social Environment; Collective Editions; Comprehensive and General Criticism; Language and Versification; Sources and Influences; and then sections on each of the Major Poems (with subheadings for Editions, Modernizations, general and specific Criticism), on each of the Canterbury Tales, and on the Short Poems and the Lost and Apocryphal Works. The volume concludes with an index of names.

The most recent selective bibliographies are by John Leyerle and Anne Quick, *Chaucer: A Bibliographical Introduction* (Toronto: University of Toronto Press, 1986) [Z8164.L49 1986], and John H. Fisher and Mark Allen, *Essential Chaucer: An Annotated Bibliography of Major Modern Studies* (Boston: G. K. Hall, 1987) [Z8164.A43 1987]. The standard closed bibliographies of Chaucer studies are as follows: Carolyn F. E. Spurgeon, *Five Hundred Years of Chaucer Criticism and Allusion, 1357-1900*, 3 vols. (Cambridge: Cambridge University Press, 1925) [PR1924.A2 1925]; Eleanor P. Hammond, *Chaucer: A Bibliographical Manual* (New York: Macmillan, 1908) [Z8164.H29]; Dudley D. Griffith, *Bibliography of Chaucer, 1903-1953* (Seattle: University of Washington Press, 1955) [Z8164.G85 1955]; W. R. Crawford, *Bibliography of Chaucer, 1954-1963* (Seattle: University of Washington Press, 1967) [Z8164.C79]; Lorrayne Y. Baird, *Bibliography of Chaucer 1964-1973* (Boston: G. K. Hall, 1977) [Z8164.B27]; Lorrayne Y. Baird-Lange and Hildegard Schnuttgen, *Chaucer Bibliography, 1974-1985* (Hamden,

Conn.: Archon, 1988) [Z8164.B274 1988]; Russell A. Peck, *Chaucer's Lyrics and Anelida and Arcite: An Annotated Bibliography, 1900–1980* (Toronto: University of Toronto Press, 1983) [Z8164.P42 1983]; and Peck's forthcoming volume, *Chaucer's Romaunt of the Rose and Boece, Treatise on the Astrolabe, Equatorie of the Planetis, Lost Works, and Chaucerian Apocrypha: Annotated Bibliography, 1900–1985* (Toronto: University of Toronto Press, 1988) [PR1905.Z99 P43x 1988]. This series is supplemented by the annual bibliographies now appearing in the *Chaucer Review* and *Studies in the Age of Chaucer* (see N–47). See also the bibliographical reviews cited in Severs (N–42).

N–47 "Chaucer Research in Progress [1968–]." *Neuphilologische Mitteilungen*, vol. 70–. Helsinki: Modern Language Society, 1969–. PB10.N415

This annual list of work in progress is classified into sections on Bibliography, Editions and Translations, General Studies, *Canterbury Tales*, Individual Tales, *Troilus and Criseyde*, Other Works, and Prosody and Language. As in the other research-in-progress listings (N–25, N–40), authors and titles are identified as to whether the work is a book, an article, or a doctoral dissertation (in which case sponsoring institution and the name of director are given), and whether in progress or completed.

Since 1967 has appeared the extensive annual unannotated listing of primarily American "Chaucer Research [1966–]" in the *Chaucer Review: Journal of Medieval Studies and Literary Criticism*, vol. 1– (University Park: Pennsylvania State University Press, 1967–). Prepared previously as a mimeographed list, it was distributed at the annual meetings of the MLA Chaucer section, which sponsors this printed bibliography. Entries are in four categories: I. Current Research (books, articles, dissertations and theses); II. Completed Projects (books, articles, dissertations and theses); III. Desiderata; and IV. Publications—Books—Articles.

And since 1979 see the annual annotated Chaucer bibliography in *Studies in the Age of Chaucer: The Yearbook of the New Chaucer Society* (Norman, Okla.: The Society, 1979–) [PR1901.S88].

N–49 Some Frequently Recommended Works in Middle English Studies.

See also entries listed in N–19, as well as many pertinent titles in K–90, K–92, K–95, and K–98.

Ackerman, Robert W. *Index of the Arthurian Names in Middle English*. Stanford: Stanford University Press, 1952. PE1660.A23

Baldwin, Charles S. *Three Medieval Centuries of Literature in England, 1100–1400*. Boston: Little, Brown, 1932. PR255.B3

Bennett, H. S. *Chaucer and the Fifteenth Century*. Vol. 2, part 1 of the *Oxford History of English Literature*. 1947. (See M–31.)

Bennett, J. A. W. *Middle English Literature*, edited and completed by Douglas Gray. Vol. 1, part 2 of the *Oxford History of English Literature*. 1986. (See M–31.)

Billings, Anne Hunt. *Guide to the Middle English Metrical Romances, Dealing with English and Germanic Legends, and with the Cycles of Charlemagne and of Arthur*. New York: Holt, 1901. PR321.B6

Booker, John Manning. *Middle English Bibliography: Dates, Dialects, and Sources of the XII, XIII, and XIV Century Monuments and Manuscripts Exclusive of the Works of Wyclif, Gower, and Chaucer, and the Documents in the London Dialect*. 1912. Z2012.B75

Bronson, Bertrand H. *In Search of Chaucer*. Toronto: University of Toronto Press, 1960. PR1924.B76

Bruce, James D. *Evolution of Arthurian Romance* (see N–55).

Brunner, Karl. *Outline of Middle English Grammar*. Translated by G. Johnston of *Abriss der mittelenglischen Grammatik*, 5th ed. Cambridge: Harvard University Press, 1963. PE531.B713

Bryan, William F., and G. Dempster, eds. *Sources and Analogues of Chaucer's Canterbury Tales*. Chicago: University of Chicago Press, 1941. PR1912.A2B7

Burrow, J. A. *Ricardian Poetry: Chaucer, Gower, Langland, and the Gawain Poet*. New Haven: Yale University Press, 1971. PR311.B8

Chambers, Edmund K. *Arthur of Britain*. London: Sidgwick and Jackson, 1927. PN686.A7 C5

——. *English Literature at the Close of the Middle Ages*. Vol. 2, part 2 of the *Oxford History of English Literature*. 1945. Reprinted with corrections. 1947. (See M–31.)

——. *Mediaeval Stage*. 2 vols. Oxford: Oxford University Press, 1903. PN2152.C4

Chambers, Edmund K., and F. Sidgwick. *Early English Lyrics: Amorous, Divine, Moral and Trivial*. London: Sidgwick and Jackson, 1926. PR1203.C6

Coghill, Nevill. *Poet Chaucer* London: Oxford University Press, 1949. PR1905.C55

Colaianne, A. J. *Piers Plowman: An Annotated Bibliography of Editions and Criticism, 1550–1977*. New York: Garland, 1978. Z8482.4.C64

Coulton, George C. *Chaucer and His England*. 7th ed. London: Methuen, 1946. Reprinted with a new Bibliography. London: Methuen, 1963. PR1905.C58 1963

Craig, Hardin. *English Religious Drama of the Middle Ages*. Oxford: Clarendon Press, 1955. PR641.C7

Curry, Walter C. *Chaucer and the Mediaeval Sciences*. Rev. ed. New York: Barnes and Noble, 1960. PR1933.S3 C8

Denny, N., ed. *Medieval Drama*. London: Edward Arnold, 1973. PR641.D4

Elton, G. R. *England, 1200–1640: The Sources of History*. Cambridge: Cambridge University Press, 1969. DA176.E4

Everett, Dorothy. *Essays on Middle English Literature*. Edited by Patricia Kean. Oxford: Clarendon Press, 1955. PR255.E9

Field, P. J. C. *Romance and Chronicle: A Study of Malory's Prose Style*. Bloomington: Indiana University Press, 1971. PR2048.F45 R7

Ford, Boris. *Medieval Literature: Chaucer and the Alliterative Tradition*. Vol. 1, pt. 1 of the *New Pelican Guide to English Literature* (see M–39).

——. *Medieval Literature: The European Inheritance*. Vol. 1, pt. 2 of the *New Pelican Guide to English Literature* (see M–39).

Frank, Robert W., Jr. *Piers Plowman and the Scheme of Salvation: An Interpretation of Dowel, Dobet, and Dobest*. New Haven: Yale University Press, 1957. PR2015.F7

Gardner, J., ed. *Complete Works of the Gawain Poet in a Modern English Version with a Critical Introduction*. Chicago: University of Chicago Press, 1965. PR1203.C68

Geddie, William. *Bibliography of Middle Scots Poets, with an Introduction on the History of Their Reputations.* Edinburgh: W. Blackwood and Sons, 1912.
PR8633.S4

Haidu, Peter, ed. *Approaches to Medieval Romance.* Yale French Studies, no. 51. New Haven: Yale University Press, 1974.   DC1.Y3 no. 51

Hardison, O. B. *Christian Rite and Christian Drama in the Middle Ages: Essays in the Origin and Early History of Modern Drama.* Baltimore: Johns Hopkins University Press, 1965.   BX1970.H28

Howard, Donald R. *Idea of the Canterbury Tales.* Baltimore: Johns Hopkins University Press, 1976.
PR1874.H65

Kane, George. *Middle English Literature: A Critical Study of the Romances, the Religious Lyrics, Piers Plowman.* London: University of London, Athlone Press, 1951.   PR255.K3

———, ed. *Piers the Plowman.* London: University of London, Athlone Press, 1960.   PR2010.K3

Ker, W. P. *English Literature, Medieval.* London: Oxford University Press, 1912.   PR255.K4

Kittredge, George L. *Chaucer and His Poetry.* Cambridge: Harvard University Press, 1915.   PR1924.K5

Kolve, V. A. *Play Called Corpus Christi.* Stanford: Stanford University Press, 1966.   PR643.G7 K6

Kottler, B., and Alan M. Markman. *Concordance to Five Middle English Poems: Cleanness, St. Erkenwald, Sir Gawain and the Green Knight, Patience, Pearl.* Pittsburgh: University of Pittsburgh Press, 1966.
PR265.K6

Leech, C., and T. W. Crain, eds. *Revels History of Drama in English.* Vol. 1, *Medieval Drama* (see U–72).

Legge, M. Dominica. *Anglo-Norman Literature and Its Background.* Oxford: Clarendon Press, 1963.
PR281.L4

Lewis, C. S. *Allegory of Love: A Study in Medieval Tradition.* Rev. ed. Oxford: Clarendon Press, 1939.
PN688.L4

Loomis, Roger Sherman. *Development of Arthurian Romance.* London: Hutchinson, 1963.   PN685.L62

———, ed. *Arthurian Literature in the Middle Ages: A Collaborative History.* Oxford: Clarendon Press, 1959.
PN57.A6L6

Lumiansky, Robert M. *Of Sondry Folk: The Dramatic Principle in the Canterbury Tales.* Austin: University of Texas Press, 1955.   PR1874.L8

Morris, Lynn K. *Chaucer Source and Analogue Criticism: A Cross-Referenced Guide.* New York: Garland, 1984.
Z8164.M67 1984

Muscatine, Charles. *Chaucer and the French Tradition: A Study in Style and Meaning.* Berkeley and Los Angeles: University of California Press, 1957.   PR1912.A3

Mustanoja, T. F. *Middle English Syntax.* I. Parts of Speech. Helsinki, 1960.

Oliver, Raymond. *Poems without Names: The English Lyric, 1200–1500.* Berkeley, Los Angeles, London: University of California Press, 1970.   PR351.O5

Owst, Gerald R. *Literature and Pulpit in Medieval England: A Neglected Chapter in the History of English Letters and of the English People.* Cambridge: Cambridge University Press, 1933.   PR275.O8

Peter, John D. *Compliant and Satire in Early English Literature.* Oxford: Clarendon Press, 1956.   PR931.P4

Potter, Lois, ed. *Revels History of Drama in English.* Volume 1, *Medieval Drama.* London: Methuen, 1983.
PR625.R44

Potter, R. *English Morality Play: Origins, History, and Influence of a Dramatic Tradition.* London: Routledge and Kegan Paul, 1975.   PR643.M7 P6 1975

Robertson, D. W., Jr. *Preface to Chaucer: Studies in Medieval Perspective.* Princeton, N.J.: Princeton University Press, 1962.   PR1924.P58

Root, Robert K. *Poetry of Chaucer: A Guide to Its Study and Appreciation.* Rev. ed. Boston: Houghton Mifflin, 1922.   PR1924.R6 1922

Rose, Donald M., ed. *New Perspectives in Chaucer Criticism.* Norman, Okla.: Pilgrim Press, 1981.
PR1924.N37 1981

Russell, Josiah C. *Dictionary of Writers of Thirteenth Century England.* London: Longmans, Green, 1936.
D1.L65

Schoeck, Richard J., and Jerome Taylor, eds. *Chaucer Criticism.* Vol. 2, *Troilus and Criseyde and the Minor Poems.* Notre Dame, Ind.: University of Notre Dame Press, 1961.   PR1924.S37

Skeat, Walter W., ed. *Vision of William concerning Piers the Plowman, in Three Parallel Texts.* 2 vols. Oxford: Clarendon Press, 1886.   PR2011.S5

Spearing, A. C. *Medieval Dream Poetry.* Cambridge: Cambridge University Press, 1976.   PR317.D7S6

Speirs, John A. *Medieval English Poetry: The Non-Chaucerian Tradition.* London: Faber and Faber, 1957.
PR311.S7 1957

Spence, Lewis. *Dictionary of Medieval Romance and Romance Writers.* London: Routledge, 1913.   PN669.S6

Tatlock, John S. P. *Mind and Art of Chaucer.* New York: Syracuse University Press, 1950.   PR1905.T3

Utley, Francis L. *Crooked Rib: An Analytic Index to the Argument about Women in English and Scots Literature to the End of the Year 1568.* Columbus: Ohio State University, 1944.   Z2014.W8 U8

Vasta, E., ed. *Middle English Survey: Critical Essays.* Notre Dame, Ind.: University of Notre Dame Press, 1965.
PR251.V3

Vinaver, Eugène. *Malory.* Oxford: Clarendon Press, 1929.
PR2045.V5

———. *Rise of Romance.* Oxford: Clarendon Press, 1971.
PQ207.V5

Wagenknecht, Edward. *Chaucer: Modern Essays in Criticism.* New York: Oxford University Press, 1959.
PR1924.W3

Wickham, Glynne. *Early English Stages, 1300 to 1660.* 4 vols. 2d ed. London: Routledge; New York: Columbia University Press, 1980–.   PN2587.W53 1980

Wilson, Richard M. *Early Middle English Literature [1066–1300].* 3d ed. London: Methuen, 1968.
PR281.W5 1968

Woolf, Rosemary. *English Mystery Plays.* Berkeley, Los Angeles, London: University of California Press, 1972.   PR643.M8 W66 1972

———. *English Religious Lyric in the Middle Ages.* Oxford: Clarendon Press, 1968.   PR311.W6

Wright, Joseph. *Elementary Middle English Grammar.* 2d ed. Oxford: Oxford University Press, 1928.
PE535.W7

Young, Earl. *Drama of the Medieval Church.* 2 vols. Oxford: Clarendon Press, 1951.   PN1751.Y6

IV. DRAMA AND THEATER

See also section U.

N–50 Stratman, Carl J. *Bibliography of Medieval Drama.* 2d ed., rev. and enl. 2 vols. New York: Ungar, 1972.

Z5782.A2 S8 1972

Originally published in 1954, this new edition contains a total of 9,105 serially numbered, unannotated entries treating books and articles, but not reviews, as well as individual and collected editions. Entries are disposed into eleven sections, as follows: I. General Studies; II. Festschriften (analysis follows the entry, with relevant articles cited); III. Liturgical Latin Drama (collections, individual plays, studies); IV. English Drama (bibliography, collections of plays, general studies, mystery and miracle plays, morality plays and interludes, folk drama). The second volume continues with quite selective sections on Continental drama (which are intended as an aid to students of the English drama). These include V. Byzantine Drama; VI. French Drama; VII. German Drama; VIII. Italian Drama; IX. Low Countries Drama; X. Spanish Drama; and XI. Addenda (keyed in by item numbers).

Within sections, subsections are arranged in order from general to particular subjects; within subsections, entries are generally in chronological order. They give the author, title, place, publisher, date, major pagination, note a bibliography if it is important, and give a library symbol, using *NUC* abbreviations for North American locations but also giving British locations (BM—British Museum; O—Bodleian; C—Cambridge; Dyce—Victoria and Albert Museum, etc.). To find locations of periodical files, users are referred to the *ULS* (D–91) and *NST* (D–92). In lieu of cross-references, entries are multiple, with the same work cited in a number of different locations if necessary. The volume concludes with a detailed index.

To update Stratman, users are referred to the Medieval Supplement published in *Research Opportunities in Renaissance Drama* from 1967 on (see O–33).

N–51 Houle, Peter D. *English Morality and Related Drama: A Bibliographical Survey.* Hamden, Conn.: Archon, 1972.

PR643.M7 H6

This work is divided into fifty-nine numbered sections giving bibliographical essays on each of fifty-nine morality plays, in the alphabetical order of their titles. Essays for each play discuss editions, enumerate the dramatis personae, give the length, summarize the main theme and place of the play in the canon (with cross-references to related plays), and provide a selected bibliography of pertinent critical studies.

These sections are followed by six appendixes treating general, thematic, and formal topics, including staging. A general bibliography and an index of characters concludes the volume.

N–52 Penninger, Frieda Elaine. *English Drama to 1660 (Excluding Shakespeare): A Guide to Information Sources.* Detroit: Gale Research Co., 1976.   Z2014.D7 P46

This bibliography of primary and secondary sources omits most periodical articles. Entries are annotated, but unnumbered, and are disposed into two parts, as follows: part 1, General Works; Bibliographies; Editions; Availability and Prices; Festschriften and Other Collections; General Literary Histories; General Studies of Drama; Studies of Medieval Drama; Studies of Tudor and Stuart Drama; Playlists, Records of Early Publications; Contemporary and Other Early Records, Allusions, etc.; The Theatre and Stagecraft; Biographical Notes and Studies: Collective. The second part contains bibliographies for a total of thirty-four individual authors and

anonymous works. The volume concludes with an index of authors, editors, compilers, anonymous titles, and a few topics.

N–53 Caldwell, Harry B., and David L. Middleton. *English Tragedy, 1370–1600: Fifty Years of Criticism.* San Antonio, Tex.: Trinity University Press, 1971.   Z2014.D763

This work contains 816 serially numbered entries and is arranged in two main parts treating nondramatic verse tragedy of the *De Casibus* tradition and dramatic tragedy (exclusive of Marlowe and Shakespeare) respectively. Each part is chronologically arranged by author or title, and citations are given to relevant criticism that appeared from 1919 to 1969. A third part treats general studies, including critical work on Senecan influence and a series of sections on primary works peripheral to the material of the two main sections. An appendix titled "Works in Need of Further Scholarship" is divided into nondramatic and dramatic tragedy and focuses on works that had received virtually no critical attention as of 1970. Indexes for primary and secondary authors conclude the volume.

N–54 *Records of Early English Drama [REED].* 6 vols. planned. Toronto: University of Toronto Press, 1979–.

LC numbers vary

These volumes present segments of the surviving performance records of early (pre–1642) drama, including transcripts of the unedited or badly edited records themselves, and an elaborate apparatus of appendixes, translations, notes, glossaries, and indexes. Included are civic, guild, and ecclesiastical records, wills, and antiquarians' compilations. Each volume begins with a general introduction to the city, its dramatic activities, and the nature of available records. Chronologically arranged transcriptions follow. To date, the following volumes have appeared:

York. Edited by Alexandra F. Johnston and Margaret Rogerson. 2 vols. 1979.   PN2596.Y6 Y6

Chester. Edited by Lawrence M. Clopper. 1979.
                                PN2596.C48 C4

Coventry. Edited by R. W. Ingram. 1981.
                                PN2596.C68 C6 1981

Newcastle upon Tyne. Edited by J. J. Anderson. 1982.
                                PN2596.N4 N48 1982

Norwich 1540–1642. Edited by David Galloway. 1984.
                                PN2596.N6.N67 1984

Cumberland/Westmoreland/Gloucestershire. Edited by Audrey Douglas and Peter Greenfield. 1986.
                                PN2589.C86 1986

News of the project may be found in the *Records of Early English Drama Newsletter [REEDN]* published twice yearly by the University of Toronto Press, 1976– [PR G41.R43], along with an annual "Annotated Bibliography of Printed Records of Early British Drama and Minstrelsy."

An important complement to *REED* is Ian Lancashire's *Dramatic Texts and Records of Britain: A Chronological Topography to 1558* (Toronto: University of Toronto Press, 1984) [Z2014.D7 L36]. This calendar and finding list identifies references to texts and other records of dramatic presentations or shows, playing places, playwrights, visits of acting troupes, official acts of control over playing, and other evidence relating to plays and their production. Entries are organized chronologically under sites, which are grouped into separate sections for England, Wales, Scotland, and Ireland. Entries briefly summarize a record and refer to the most reliable printed editions or manuscript sources. A chronological list of published and unpublished dramatic works is included, with references to editions and important scholarship. This massive compendium is completed by five indexes. The first, of playing companies, is broken into two subindexes, of places and of patrons and players. The second index is of playwrights. The third is of playing places and buildings. The fourth is a chronological index giving dates and entry numbers. The last is a general index of places, persons, and subjects. This compendium is continued by the "Annotated Bibliography" in the *REED Newsletter* which is cited above.

V. EPIC AND ROMANCE

See also section T and section W.

N–55 **Parry, John J., and Margaret Schlauch.** *Bibliography of Arthurian Critical Literature for the Years 1922–1929.* New York: Modern Language Association, 1931.

Z8045.M69

This volume, sponsored by the Arthurian Group of the MLA, is meant to supplement the "Select Bibliography of Arthurian Critical Literature" that appears as chapter 7 in volume 2 of James D. Bruce, *Evolution of Arthurian Romance from the Beginnings Down to the Year 1300* (Göttingen and Baltimore, 1923–1924; 2d ed., 1928) [PN685.B7 1928]. The total of 686 serially numbered entries are arranged alphabetically by author and include both books and articles; reviews are cited in conjunction with the books reviewed. Included are texts, translations, and critical studies as well as studies of subjects related to the Arthurian materials. There are some cross-references.

Annual mimeographed lists were cumulated in a second volume, compiled by the same authors with the title *Bibliography of Arthurian Critical Literature for the Years 1930–1935* (New York, 1936) [Z8045.M69]. It includes 1,088 additional entries, serially numbered from 687 to 1774. Citations include works published 1922–1929 but omitted from the first volume as well as reviews of works cited in the first volume. These appear in the alphabet under the name of the reviewed author and are assigned the serial number given in the first citation of the work. Both volumes conclude with an index of authors, titles, and subjects. They are supplemented by the annual bibliographies appearing in *MLQ* (N–56).

The bibliographical entries from Parry and Schlauch, from *MLQ* (see N–56), from the *Bibliographical Bulletin of the International Arthurian Society* (N–57), from *Arthuriana*, and from J. D. Bruce's *Evolution of Arthurian Romance* (Göttingen: Vandenhoeck and Ruprecht, 1923) [PN685.B7] have been merged by computer into the *Arthurian Bibliography*, by Cedric Edward Pickford and Rex Last, 2 vols. (Cambridge: D. S. Brewer, 1981–1983) [Z8045.P53 1983]. Volume 1 lists entries by author, with full citation and reference to the original bibliographic source; volume 2 includes a list of corrections and a subject index. A third volume, *Arthurian Bibliography III: Supplement, 1979–1983*, edited by Rex Last (Cambridge: D.S. Brewer, 1986) is to be followed by an updated edition which will correct various inconsistencies in this initial compilation.

N–56 **"A Bibliography of Critical Arthurian Literature for the Year [1936–1962]."** *Modern Language Quarterly*, vols. 1–24. 1940–1963.   PB1.M642

Volume 1 of *MLQ* contains "A Bibliography . . . for the Years 1936–1939" prepared by John J. Parry and Margaret Schlauch, with entries numbered from 1774 to 2279, thus supplementing their separately published bibliography, volumes 1 and 2 (N–55). Scope here is narrowed to exclude reference

to short reviews and to books and articles more remotely connected with Arthurian studies. As in the original volumes, reviews are cited under the names of the reviewed authors. Entries often have descriptive or explanatory notes. An index of authors, titles, and subjects concludes the listing. Serial numeration continues from year to year; the final bibliography, published in 1963 and treating material published in 1962, includes items 5136 through 5328.

This bibliography has been replaced by the annual *Bibliographical Bulletin of the International Arthurian Society* (N–57). Both it and the *Bibliographical Bulletin* are part of the Pickford and Last *Arthurian Bibliography* (N–55).

N–57 **Frappier, Jean, et al.** *Bulletin bibliographique de la Société internationale arthurienne / Bibliographical Bulletin of the International Arthurian Society.* No. 1– [for 1939–1948–]. Paris, 1949–.   Z8045.I5

For the first dozen years this bibliography appeared alongside the *MLQ* bibliography (N–56). Unlike that, this work includes books, articles, dissertations, and reviews on medieval Arthurian materials (the Matter of Britain). It is classified into sections on scholarship produced by the various national branches of the society (Germany and Austria; United States and Canada; Denmark; Spain; Portugal and Brazil; France; Great Britain; Ireland;; taly; Netherlands; Switzerland; Sweden; and Miscellaneous). Each national bibliography is subdivided into genres of scholarly work as follows: I. Texts, Translations, and Adaptations; II. Critical and Historical Studies; III. Reviews; and IV. Doctoral Dissertations. Entries have detailed annotations, including signed informative abstracts in the language of the cited item and cross-references to related work in the scholarly literature. Items are serially numbered in each annual volume. Each volume has an index of authors and one of subjects (including works and authors) which is keyed to item numbers. Languages of the bibliography are English, French, and German. Also reported in most issues of the Bulletin is "Work in Progress" in the field of medieval Arthurian studies. Entries from the *Bulletin* are included in the Pickford and Last *Arthurian Bibliography* (N–55).

A related serial bibliography is the *Bulletin bibliographique pour l'étude des épopées romanes* (Paris: Nizet, 1958–) [PQ201.S66a] sponsored by the Société Rencesvals, which treats scholarship on medieval epic and romance, with a special emphasis on the Matter of France. In addition, *Olifant: A Publication of the Société Rencesvals, American-Canadian Branch* (Winnipeg: The Society, 1973–) [PN689.O57] carries a quarterly checklist of books, articles, reviews, and North American dissertations on the medieval romance. An earlier, mimeographed list appeared 1966–1972. Finally, *Encomia* (Philadelphia: International Courtly Literature Society, 1975–) [PN661.E5] is a partially annotated annual bibliography of books, articles, and reviews.

For postmedieval Arthurian materials see the bibliography by Clark S. Northup and J. Parry, "The Arthurian Legends: Modern Retellings of the Old Stories: An Annotated Bibliography," *JEGP* 43 (1944): 173–221; with a "Supplement" by Paul A. Brown, *JEGP* 49 (1950): 208–216.

N–58 *Arthurian Encyclopedia.* Edited by Norris J. Lacy. New York: Garland, 1984.   DA152.5.A7 A78 1986

This large work contains over 650 entries by a total of ninety-four Arthurian scholars from around the world. It is comprehensive and treats the entire 1,500 years of Arthurian legend and Arthurian fact, including all forms in which Arthurian materials are found: history, chronicle, art, archaeology, folklore, mythology, music, film, and television. There are signed entries on Arthurian characters, themes, motifs, works, authors, artists, and critics, and on Arthurian legend in

English, German, Old Norse, Dutch, Latin, French, Italian, Spanish, Portuguese, Welsh, Hebrew, Yiddish, and other languages. In addition to numerous illustrations, there are both brief bibliographies appended to each entry, and a general bibliography. A topical list of entries and extensive cross-references facilitate access.

Lacy, along with Geoffrey Ashe, has also produced a briefer reference work, the *Arthurian Handbook* (New York: Garland, 1988) [PN685.L3 1988], which summarizes a variety of Arthurian subjects, including Origins (history, archaeology, folklore, and legend), Early Arthurian Literature, Modern Arthurian Literature, and The Arts (painting and sculpture, decorative arts, music, film, television, and radio). A lengthy glossary of Arthurian characters, motifs, and places is a particularly helpful feature.

VI. PROSE, PROSE FICTION, CRITICISM, AND RHETORIC

See also section W and section X.

N–60 **Heninger, S. K.** *English Prose, Prose Fiction, and Criticism to 1660.: A Guide to Information Sources.* Detroit: Gale Research Co., 1975.   Z2014.P795 H45

This well-reviewed guide contains a total of 778 serially numbered primary works of prose, prose fiction, or criticism disposed into twelve generic sections, as follows: I. General; II. Religious Writings; III. Historical Writings; IV. Travel Literature; V. Scientific and Technical Writings; VI. Ephemeral and Polemical Writings; VII. Essays; VIII. Narrative Fiction; IX. Literary Criticism; X. Writings on Education; XI. Translations; and XII. Translations of the Bible. Each section has an introduction that includes a list of general works on the genre. Then follow the serially numbered primary works, organized by their dates of composition or publication, thus making possible a historical perspective on the development of the genre. Following the citation of primary works are lists of the best modern editions, of bibliographies and bibliographical studies, and of scholarly and critical treatments, which are also arranged in chronological order. There are occasional annotations and a detailed index of names, but not of titles nor of subjects.

N–62 **Edwards, A. S. G., ed.** *Middle English Prose: A Critical Guide to Major Authors and Genres.* New Brunswick, N.J.: Rutgers University Press, 1984.   PR255.M52 1984

This volume presents a series of bibliographic essays surveying scholarship, identifying desiderata, and enumerating (in appended primary and secondary bibliographies) significant work in the study of Middle English prose. A total of eighteen chapters treat the following subject matters: 1, *Ancrene Wisse*, the Katherine Group, and the *Wohunge Group*; 2, Richard Rolle and Related Works; 3, *Cloud of Unknowing* and Walter Hilton's *Scale of Perfection*; 4, Nicholas Love; 5, Julian of Norwich; 6, Margery Kempe; 7, Mandeville; 8, John Trevisa; 9, Minor Devotional Writings; 10, Sermon Literature; 11, Historical Prose; 12, Wycliffite Prose; 13, The Romances; 14, Chaucer; 15, Medical Prose; 16, Utilitarian and Scientific Prose; 17, William Caxton; and 18, Works of Religious Instruction. The volume ends with an index of authors and titles.

Malory was excluded on the grounds that there are recent bibliographies including the volume by Page West Life (see M–60).

N–65 **Jolliffe, P. S.** *Check-list of Middle English Prose Writings of Spiritual Guidance.* Toronto: Pontifical Institute of Mediaeval Studies, 1974.   Z2014.P795 J64

This bibliography lists manuscripts in public and semipublic depositories in Great Britain and Dublin of texts composed in the fourteenth and fifteenth centuries. The checklist is classified into fifteen sections under such rubrics as Prose Tracts, Treatises, Handbooks of Pastoral Intention (confession, spiritual guidance). Within classes, texts are listed alphabetically by their incipit(s), with authors, titles, and other information, including manuscript location given. After the checklist proper is an alphabetical list of all incipits; a list of all cited manuscripts; an alphabetical list of all titles and authors mentioned in the checklist; and a list of acephalous texts cited in the checklist. The volume concludes with a bibliography for further reference.

VII. MEDIEVAL LATIN

See also section L.II and section O.VI.

N–70 **McGuire, Martin R. P., and Hermigild Dressler.** *Introduction to Medieval Latin Studies: A Syllabus and Bibliographical Guide.* 2d ed. Washington, D.C.: Catholic University of America Press, 1977.   PA2816.M24 1977

This work, originally published in 1964, is parallel in character to McGuire's *Introduction to Classical Scholarship* (L–40). It is in two main parts, a syllabus and a select bibliography, and the goal of both is to present the beginning student with a comprehensive and current guide to the field. The syllabus is divided into sixteen chapters with numerous subsections; topics are outlined and brief bibliographies are appended; the select bibliography, disposed into twenty-one sections, is more comprehensive than the chapter bibliographies and includes all the works cited in the syllabus along with others.

The syllabus, after an introductory chapter, covers the periods of Latin use from classical antiquity through the twelfth-century Renaissance in chapters 2–9. Chapter 10 treats the knowledge of Greek in the West during this period, while chapter 11 concerns the study and knowledge of other foreign languages. Chapter 12 concerns medieval rhetoric and poetic, chapter 13 is on knowledge and influence of ancient pagan and Christian authors in the West, and chapter 14 is on the development of the vernacular languages and literatures in the West. Chapter 15 discusses the history of Medieval Latin literature; chapter 16 deals with the history of Latin handwriting during the Middle Ages.

The select bibliographies are as follows: 1, Collections of Sources and Related Works; 2, Bibliographical Guides and Works for General Backgrounds; 3, Dictionaries, Glossaries, etc.; 4, Encyclopedias, etc.; 5, Medieval Latin Literature, Historical and Generic Studies; 6, Grammar, Grammatical and Linguistic Theory, and Related Areas; 7, Medieval Rhetoric and Poetic; 8, the Medieval Artes: Metrica, Rithmica, Dictaminis, Praedicandi; 9, Medieval Education; 10, Medieval Political and Cultural History; 11, Vernacular Languages and Literatures in Western Europe to ca. 1200 (General, English, French, German, Celtic, Norse, etc.); 12, Medieval Philosophy and Theology; 13, Scripture and Exegesis; 14, Art and Architecture; 15, Aesthetics; 16, Music; 17, The Sciences, Mathematics and Medicine; 18, The Patristic and Medieval Book; 19, Medieval Libraries and Catalogues; 20, Palaeography and Diplomatics; 21, Periodicals for Medieval Latin Studies.

The volume concludes with three indexes, of ancient and Medieval Latin authors and works; of modern authors; and of subjects. As is true of McGuire's *Introduction to Classical Studies*, this Introduction is a model of what a student bibliographical guide can be. While intended for the student of Medieval Latin, much in the volume will be of value to the student of any branch of medieval culture.

N–79   Some Frequently Recommended Works in Medieval Latin Studies.

Baxter, J. H., Charles Johnson, and J. F. Willard. "An Index of British and Irish Latin Writers, 400–1520." *Bulletin du Cange* 7 (1932): 110–219.

Bolton, Whitney F. *History of Anglo-Latin Literature, 597–1066.* Vol. 1, 597–740. Princeton, N.J.: Princeton University Press, 1967. Vol. 2, 741–1066. In preparation.   PA8045.E5 B6

Brunholzl, Franz. *Geschichte der lateinischen Literatur des Mittelalters.* Munich: Fink, 1975–.   PA8015.B7

de Ghellinck, J. *Littérature latine au moyen âge.* 2 vols. Paris: Bloud et Gay, 1939.   PA8035.G5

Hélin, Maurice. *History of Medieval Latin Literature.* Rev. ed. Translation by Jean Chapman Snow of *Littérature d'Occident: Histoire des lettres latines du moyen âge* (Brussels, 1943). New York: W. Salloch, 1949.   PA8035.H42

de Labriolle, Pierre C. *History and Literature of Christianity from Tertullian to Boethius.* Translation of *Histoire de la littérature latine chrétienne,* 3d ed., rev. and enl., 2 vols. (Paris, 1947). London: Kegan Paul, 1924.   BR67.L32

Manitius, Max. *Geschichte der lateinischen Literatur des Mittelalters.* 3 vols. Munich: Beck, 1911–1931.   PA25.H24 Abt. 9 t. 2

Mann, Wolfgang. *Lateinische Dichtung in England vom Ausgang des Frühhumanismus bis zum Regierungsantritt Elizabeths.* Halle: Niemeyer, 1939.   PA8051.M3

Norberg, Dag L. *Manuel pratique de latin médiéval.* Paris: A. Picard, 1968.   PA2813.N6

Owst, G. *Literature and Pulpit in Medieval England.* 2d rev. ed. New York: Barnes and Noble, 1961.   PR275.08 1961

Raby, Frederic J. E. A. *History of Christian-Latin Poetry from the Beginnings to the Close of the Middle Ages.* 2d ed. Oxford: Clarendon Press, 1953.   PA8056.R3 1953

———. *History of Secular Latin Poetry in the Middle Ages.* 2d ed. 2 vols. Oxford: Clarendon Press, 1957.   PA8051.R3 1957

Strecker, Karl. *Introduction to Medieval Latin.* English translation and revision by Robert B. Palmer of *Einführung in das Mittellatein* (Berlin, 1928). Berlin: Weidmann, 1957.   PA2816.S72

Wright, F., and T. Sinclair. *History of Later Latin Literature from the Middle of the Fourth to the End of the Seventeenth Century.* London: G. Routledge and Sons, 1931.   PA8015.W7 1931

LITERATURE OF THE RENAISSANCE AND EARLIER SEVENTEENTH CENTURY

See also works in section C.II, British National Bibliography; in section F, History; in section G, Biography; in section H, Manuscripts and Paleography; and in section I on Language, Linguistics, and Philology. See also numerous references in sections K, L, and M, including the *MLA International Bibliography* (L–50), the MHRA *Annual Bibliography of English Language and Literature* (M–21), and the *Year's Work in English Studies* (M–22). See additional references on Renaissance poetry and poetics in section T, drama and theater in section U, and prose and prose fiction in section W. See also references on Renaissance literary and rhetorical theory in section X and on Renaissance printing, publishing, and bookselling in section Y.

I. GENERAL

O–2 **Jones, William M., ed.** *Present State of Scholarship in Sixteenth Century Literature.* Columbia: University of Missouri Press, 1978.   PN731.P7

The bibliographical essays collected in this volume represent a series of lectures presented under the auspices of the Committee for Medieval and Renaissance Studies of the Graduate School of the University of Missouri in 1976/77. Each essay includes bibliographical footnotes and is followed by a somewhat classified, selected bibliography. The literatures treated are as follows: Italian (Beatrice M. Corrigan and Bonner Mitchell); French (Doland A. Stone, Jr.); Spanish (Theodore S. Beardsley); English (Richard J. Schoeck); German (Eli Sobel); and Neo-Latin (Laurence V. Ryan).

Among other recent reviews of research on English Renaissance literature are the following, arranged chronologically:

Tuve, Rosemond. "A Critical Survey of Scholarship in the Field of English Literature of the Renaissance." *SP* 40 (1943): 204–255.

Levin, Harry. "English Literature of the Renaissance." In Tinsley Helton, ed., *Renaissance: A Reconsideration of the Theories and Interpretations of the Age.* Madison: University of Wisconsin Press, 1961.
                    CB361.S93 1959a

Bateson, F. W. "Work in Progress II: Renaissance Literature." *Essays in Criticism* 13 (1963): 117–131.

Barker, Arthur E. "An Apology for the Study of Renaissance." In Carroll Camden, ed., *Literary Views:*

Critical and Historical Essays, pp. 15–43. Chicago: University of Chicago Press, 1964.

Hamilton, A. C. "The Modern Study of Renaissance English Literature: A Critical Survey." *MLQ* 26 (1965): 150–183.

Summers, Joseph H. "Notes on Recent Studies in English Literature of the Earlier 17th Century." *MLQ* 26 (1965): 135–149.

Levin, Richard. *New Readings vs. Old Plays: Recent Trends in the Reinterpretation of English Renaissance Drama.* Chicago: University of Chicago Press, 1979.
                    PR651.L48

O–3 *Bibliographie internationale de l'humanisme et de la Renaissance [BIHR].* Geneva: Fédération international des sociétés et instituts pour l'étude de la Renaissance. Vol. 1– [Travaux parus en 1965–]. Geneva: Droz, 1966–.
                    Z6207.R4 B5

This annual bibliography lists books and articles from all countries where Renaissance studies are pursued. For purposes of this work, Renaissance studies are broadly defined to include studies in fifteenth- and sixteenth-century literature, philosophy, history, religion, and the arts; the humane disciplines of economics, political science, and the law; and Renaissance explorations in science and technology. The bibliography is in two serially numbered lists, alphabetically arranged by author: the first, of books, is prepared by the Renaissance Society of America; the second, of articles, is prepared by a consortium of editors. Supplemental lists of articles missed in previous years are appended. An index of names of persons and places and of subjects cited in titles concludes the volume; it is keyed to item numbers. More recently, sheer lists have been classified into two parts, treating I. Persons and Anonymous Works and II. Subjects. The Subjects section is subdivided into Generalities; History (further divided); Religion and Religious, Philosophical, Political, and Legal Ideas; Literature, including Pedagogy, Grammar and Linguistics, Theatre, History of the Book and Libraries; the Arts; and Science and Technology. Subdivisions are into geographical units. Indexes of historical persons and authors conclude the bibliographies.

From 1956 through 1965 this bibliography appeared annually under the title "Bibliographie des articles relatifs à l'histoire de l'humanisme et de la Renaissance" in the *Bibliothèque de humanisme et Renaissance*, vols. 20–27. Unlike the more recent separate publication, these bibliographies were of articles only and were not indexed. The 1965 separate *Bibliographie* includes a supplement to these lists.

For a useful discussion of problems encountered in establishing bibliographic control of this period, see John B. Dillon, "Renaissance Bibliography in the Electronic Age: Recent Work on a Computer-Produced Annual Bibliography of Studies on Early Modern Europe," *Collection Development* 6.12 (1984): 217–226.

O–5 **"Recent Literature of the Renaissance."** *Studies in Philology*, **vols. 14–66.** Chapel Hill: University of North Carolina Press, 1917–1969.   P25.S8

This now defunct annual bibliography included books, articles, and dissertations, along with important book reviews. Its scope before 1939 was the English Renaissance; after that, it covered the European Renaissance in general. Entries, many of which are accompanied by extensive descriptive and evaluative annotation, have been differently classified over the years. Originally there were seven sections limited to English literature, as follows: Drama, Shakespeare, Spenser, Other Writers and Books, Milton, General Works, History and Criticism, and Continental Influences. After 1940 the divisions expanded as follows: General Works of the Renaissance; English (with the same seven subdivisions as above); French; Germanic; Italian; Neo-Latin; Spanish and Portuguese. Subdivisions include general sections and sections for major authors. After 1941 an index of proper names was attached. In its last years this bibliography became one of the most extensive ever assembled with 300–400 pages of citations, though without the elaborate annotations of earlier years. Expense and the existence of other bibliographies covering parts of the field brought it to an end; unfortunately, it has never been cumulated, nor has its scope and quality been replaced.

O–6 *Quarterly Check-List of Renaissance Studies: An International Index of Current Books, Monographs, Brochures, and Separates.* Vols. 1–17. Darien, Conn.: American Bibliographical Service, 1959–1975.   Z6207.R4 Q34

In a format parallel to the *Quarterly Check-List of Medieval Studies* (F–23), this work is a sheer author list. Renaissance studies include history, religion, philosophy, arts, and sciences. Studies of literature are selectively included. The list is alphabetical, by author, and entries include basic bibliographical information. A directory of publishers is in each quarterly issue; a cumulated subject index is in the fourth quarterly issue, as is an author-editor-translator index.

Students interested in the early Renaissance will find some pertinent materials in the still current *Check-List of Medieval Studies* cited above. Other sheer lists of Renaissance studies publications include the listing of "Renaissance Books" in each issue of *Renaissance Quarterly* (see O–18) under the rubrics Fine Arts, History, Literature, Philosophy, Religion, and Science.

O–7 **"Recent Studies in the English Renaissance."** *SEL*, Winter Issue, vol. 1–. 1961–.   PR1.S82

These annual bibliographical essays by established scholars in the field offer descriptive and evaluative comment on recent work, normally of the previous year. Emphases are chosen by the individual authors. To date, the following essays have appeared:

Vol. 1 (1961), pp. 121–157. By Arthur E. Barker.
Vol. 2 (1962), pp. 119–150. By Sears Jayne.
Vol. 3 (1963), pp. 119–150. By Arthur E. Barker.
Vol. 4 (1964), pp. 163–194. By Walter J. Ong, S.J.

Vol. 5 (1965), pp. 175–203. By Hugh N. MacLean.
Vol. 6 (1966), pp. 159–192. By Ernest Sirluck.
Vol. 7 (1967), pp. 153–189. By Howard Schultz.
Vol. 8 (1968), pp. 151–185. By Kathleen Williams.
Vol. 9 (1969), pp. 169–197. By A. C. Hamilton.
Vol. 10 (1970), pp. 215–250. By Richard J. Schoeck.
Vol. 11 (1971), pp. 345–375. By French Fogle.
Vol. 12 (1972), pp. 183–222. By Stanley E. Fish.
Vol. 13 (1973), pp. 163–197. By John T. Shawcross.
Vol. 14 (1974), pp. 139–175. By Barbara K. Lewalski.
Vol. 15 (1975), pp. 169–202. By Walter R. Davis.
Vol. 16 (1976), pp. 157–175. By Thomas P. Roche, Jr.
Vol. 17 (1977), pp. 149–174. By Stewart A. Baker.
Vol. 18 (1978), pp. 169–197. By S. K. Heninger, Jr.
Vol. 19 (1979), pp. 143–169. By Joseph A. Wittreich.
Vol. 20 (1980), pp. 153–180. By Annabel Patterson.
Vol. 21 (1981), pp. 161–188. By Susan Snyder.
Vol. 22 (1982), pp. 157–192. By Patrick Cullen.
Vol. 23 (1983), pp. 145–176. By George K. Hunter.
Vol. 24 (1984), pp. 157–199. By Jonathan Goldberg.
Vol. 25 (1985), pp. 183–248. By Gordon Braden.
Vol. 26 (1986), pp. 145–199. By Richard Helgerson.
Vol. 27 (1987), pp. 141–176. By A. Leigh Deneef.
Vol. 28 (1988), pp. 149–196. By Donald Cheney.
Vol. 29 (1989), pp. 157–199. By Judith H. Anderson.

O–8 **"Recent Studies in the English Renaissance."** *English Literary Renaissance,* vol. 1–. Amherst: University of Massachusetts, 1971–.   PR1.E43

In a format parallel to Logan and Smith's series of "Recent Studies" volumes (see O–35 ff.), most issues of *ELR* include a bibliographical article summarizing recent scholarship (i.e., from ca. 1945 until a few years before publication) on one or several authors of the English Renaissance. The articles combine sheer listing aiming at a reasonable completeness with a topically organized descriptive and evaluative bibliographical review of research. The quality of coverage varies with the individual contributors; most include discussion of biographical and general works, editions, canon and text, special topics, and the current state of scholarship on an author. They are available for purchase separately. To date, the following articles have been published:

Vol. 1 (1971) John Skelton; Sir Thomas Wyatt and the Earl of Surrey; Robert Burton and Isaac Walton (1945–1969);
Vol. 2 (1972) Sir Philip Sidney (1945–1969); Sir Thomas Browne; Fulke Greville;
Vol. 3 (1973) George Gascoigne; Robert Herrick;
Vol. 4 (1974) Thomas Traherne; Henry Vaughan; Thomas Campion; Sir John Davies;
Vol. 5 (1975) Andrew Marvell; The Corpus Christi Mystery Plays;
Vol. 6 (1976) George Herbert; Thomas Elyot; Abraham Cowley;
Vol. 7 (1977) The Cavalier Poets (Carew, Suckling, Lovelace, Waller), Christopher Marlowe;
Vol. 8 (1978) Early Tudor Drama (*Gorboduc, Ralph Roister Doister, Gammer Gurton's Needle*, and *Cambises*); Sir Philip Sidney (1970–1977); John Rastell;
Vol. 9 (1979) Richard Crashaw; *Mirror for Magistrates*; Sir Thomas More;

Vol. 10 (1980) Roger Ascham;

Vol. 11 (1981) Lancelot Andrewes; John Foxe; Thomas Nashe;

Vol. 12 (1982) John Webster (1972–1980);

Vol. 13 (1983) John Heywood; Robert Southwell; the 1611 "Authorized Version" of the Bible;

Vol. 14 (1984) Thomas Middleton (1971–1981); Women Writers, 1485–1603; Mary Sidney, Countess of Pembroke;

Vol. 15 (1985) Literature and Painting in the English Renaissance; Sir Walter Raleigh;

Vol. 16 (1986) Poetry and Music of the English Renaissance; the English Emblem;

Vol. 17 (1987) John Bale; Robert Burton and Izaac Walton (1970–1985); Francis Bacon;

Vol. 18 (1988) Women Writers of the English Seventeenth Century (1604–1674); Christopher Marlowe (1977–1986); George Herbert (1974–1986).

O–9 *Seventeenth Century News.* Vol. 1–. University Park: Pennsylvania State University Press, 1942–.   PR1.S47

This newsletter includes reviews, summaries of conference papers, initialed short notices of recent books, and a classified selection of abstracts of recent articles. Since 1954 it has included a separate section, "Neo-Latin News" with similar contents in Neo-Latin studies (see O–71). The classification has separate sections for Milton, Donne, Dryden, and Jonson, and both general and individual-author sections for Poetry, Drama, and Prose.

O–10 *Cambridge Bibliography of English Literature.* Vol. 1, *600–1600*, pp. 317–912. Edited by F. W. Bateson. Cambridge: Cambridge University Press, 1941.
                                        Z2011.B3 1941 vol. 1

This portion of volume 1 is in seven main parts. Part 1, the Introduction, has six divisions: Bibliographies, Collections of Documents, Literary Histories, and Special Studies; Literary Relations with the Continent; Book Production and Distribution; Education; The Social Background; The Political Background. Part 2, The Poetry, has ten: General Introduction; The Tudor Poets; The Elizabethan Sonneteers; Minor Tudor Verse; The Jacobean and Caroline Poets; John Milton; Minor Jacobean and Caroline Verse, 1603–1660; Emblem Books; Epigrammatists and Formal Satirists; and Song Books. Part 3, The Drama, has twelve divisions: General Introduction; Theatres and Actors; The Puritan Attack upon the Stage; The Moralities; The Early Comedies; The Early Tragedies; The Later Elizabethan Dramatists; The Minor Elizabethan Drama, 1580–1603; William Shakespeare; The Jacobean and Caroline Dramatists; The Minor Jacobean and Caroline Drama, 1603–1660; and University Plays, 1500–1642.

Part 4 concerns Religious Prose: Controversial and Devotional, and has eight divisions: Humanists and Reformers; The English Bible; The Prayer Book; Versions of the Psalms; Sermons and Devotional Writings: Fisher to Donne; Richard Hooker; The Marprelate Controversy; and the Caroline Divines. Part 5, on Popular and Miscellaneous Prose, has seven divisions: Pamphleteers and Miscellaneous Writers; Minor Popular Literature; Character-Books and Essays; Prose Fiction; News-Sheets and News-Books; Books of Travel; and Translations into English. Part 6 concerns works of History, Philosophy, Science, and Other Forms of Learning and is in seven sections: Historians, Biographers, and Antiquaries; Economists and Political Theorists; Legal Writers; Scholars and Scholarship; Literary Criticism; Bacon, Hobbes, and Other Philosophical Writers; Science and Pseudo-Science. Part 7, finally, concerns Scot-

tish Literature and is in three sections: General; Poetry and Drama; Prose.

Pages 171–357 of the *Supplement* (1957) provide additions to each section of this bibliography. This portion of volume 1 of the *CBEL* and the *Supplement* pertaining to it have been largely but not entirely replaced by the parallel portion of the *NCBEL* (O–11). The entire first volume but not the supplement is indexed in the *CBEL Index*, which is volume 4 (1941) of the *CBEL*.

O–11 *New Cambridge Bibliography of English Literature.* Vol. 1, *600–1600*, cols. 807–2476. Edited by George Watson. Cambridge: Cambridge University Press, 1974.
                                        Z2011.N45 vol. 1

This portion of the first volume of the *NCBEL* (see M–11), with entries current to 1972 or so, is in seven main parts. Part 1, the Introduction, has three divisions: General Works; Literary Relations with the Continent; and Book Production and Distribution. Part 2, Poetry, has ten divisions: Introduction; Tudor Poetry; The Elizabethan Sonnet; Minor Tudor Poetry; Jacobean and Caroline Poetry; John Milton; Minor Jacobean and Caroline Poetry; 1603–60; Emblem Books; Epigrams and Formal Satire; and Song Books. Part 3, Drama, has twelve divisions: Introduction; Theatres and Actors; The Puritan Attack on the Stage; Moralities; The Early Comedies; The Early Tragedies; Later Elizabethan Drama; Minor Elizabethan Drama, 1580–1603; William Shakespeare; Jacobean and Caroline Drama; Minor Jacobean and Caroline Drama, 1603–60; and University Plays, 1500–1642.

Part 4, Religion, is in eight sections: Humanists and Reformers; The English Bible; The Prayer Book; Versions of the Psalms; Sermons and Devotional Writings; Richard Hooker; The Marprelate Controversy; and The Caroline Divines, 1620–60. Part 5, on Popular and Miscellaneous Prose, has seven sections: Pamphleteers and Miscellaneous Writers; Minor Popular Literature; Character-Books and Essays; Prose Fiction; News-Sheets and News-Books; Travel; and Translations into English. Part 6 treats History, Philosophy, Science, and Other Forms of Learning in nine divisions: Historians, Biographers, and Antiquaries; Letters, Diaries, Autobiographies, and Biographies; Economics and Politics; Law; Scholarship; Literary Criticism; Philosophy; Science and Education. Finally, part 7, on Scottish Literature, has three sections: Introduction; Poetry and Drama; and Prose. A limited index concludes the volume; more complete analysis is in the *NCBEL Index*, which is volume 5 (1977) of the *NCBEL*.

Arrangement here, as in the other parts of the *CBEL* and *NCBEL*, moves from general subsections to primary and secondary bibliographies for individual authors. Note that the fifty-six contributors are listed prior to the first part of this volume and that their contributions are signed with initials. Reviews of all of volume 1 of the *NCBEL* have been generally favorable. Among them see the comments of L. S. Thompson in *PBSA* 71 (1977): 237. See also those cited above at N–11.

O–12 de Sola Pinto, Vivian. *English Renaissance, 1510–1688, with a Chapter on Literature and Music by Bruce Pattison. Introductions to English Literature*, edited by Bonamy Dobrée, vol. 2. 3d ed., rev. London: Cressett Press, 1966.
                                        PR83.I615 vol. 2

In parallel to the other volumes in this series (see M–15, N–12, P–12, Q–30, and R–12), this work, originally published in 1938, contains both a discursive introduction (1, Renaissance and Reformation; 2, The Elizabethans; 3, The Seventeenth Century; 4, Literature and Music) and a Students' Guide to Reading. The bibliographical guide, in the form of bibliographical essays, contains both primary and secondary sources. It is disposed into three larger divisions (Renaissance and Reformation; the Elizabethans; the Seventeenth Century) and twenty individual sections, as follows: The Humanists; The New Poetry up to the Accession of Elizabeth (1558); The Protestant Reformers; Early Elizabethan Poetry; The Translators; Chronicles, Antiquarian Works, and Voyages; Later Elizabethan Poetry; Tudor Drama up to Shakespeare; Elizabethan Secular Prose; William Shakespeare; Elizabethan Divines; Philosophical Writers; Metaphysical Poetry; The Later Drama up to the Civil War; Secular Prose of the Seventeenth Century; Religious Prose of the Seventeenth Century; Poetry from Carew to Oldham; John Milton; Restoration Drama; John Dryden. There are considerable numbers of subdivisions for subtopics and for individual authors (works, biography and criticism). The volume concludes with an index to proper names in the introduction and to names of authors and titles treated as primary entries in the students' guide.

O-13 **Lievsay, John L.** *Sixteenth Century: Skelton through Hooker.* [A Goldentree Bibliography.] New York: Appleton-Century-Crofts, 1968.   Z2012.L5

This highly selective closed bibliography of essentially twentieth-century books and articles on English Renaissance nondramatic literature and Renaissance culture is designed for the use of beginning graduate students. Items are not much annotated; those of special importance are asterisked. The eleven divisions include Background Studies; Series Publications; General Collections; Period Literary Histories; *Festschriften*; Anthologies; Bibles, Prayer Books, and Primers; Anonymous and Pseudonymous Authors and Works; Translations; and then, alphabetically by author, individual author bibliographies. Token recognition only is given to Scottish and Irish writers of the period, and those authors (Milton, Shakespeare) with separate bibliographies in the series (O–28, O–43) are generally omitted, as are authors primarily of the seventeenth century who are treated in the companion bibliography by Arthur Barker (O–14). Author bibliographies include bibliography and other reference works, collected editions, selections, individual works, and then a listing of biography, criticism, articles, and notes. There is some cross-referencing and an author index.

O-14 **Barker, Arthur E.** *Seventeenth Century: Bacon through Marvell.* [A Goldentree Bibliography.] Arlington Heights, Ill.: AHM Publishing, 1979.   Z2012.B27

This highly selective classified sheer list intended for the beginning graduate student cites works published primarily during the period 1935–1975. Excluded are materials found in the sixteenth-, late-seventeenth-, and eighteenth-century volumes of this series (see O–13, P–14, and P–16) or in the volumes on Shakespeare and Milton (see O–28 and O–43) and on the drama (see O–30). The classification of the 2,391 serially numbered entries is into five main parts, as follows: Aids to Research: Bibliographies, Guides, Surveys; Anthologies; Literary History and Criticism (General, Poetry, Prose); Backgrounds (Intellectual and Aesthetic, Scientific, Social and Political, Religious); and Individual Authors (subcategories for each include Editions, Bibliographies and Concordances, General Studies, and Specific Studies). The volume concludes with an index of names.

O-15 **Tannenbaum, Samuel Aaron, and Dorothy R. Tannenbaum.** *Elizabethan Bibliographies.* 41 parts, with Supplements. New York: The author, 1937–1950. Reprint (10 vols.). Port Washington, N. Y.: Kennikat, 1967. Z2012.T3

Containing primary and secondary materials, but neither complete nor entirely accurate, the original series of these bibliographies was published in 41 parts as follows: 1. Marlowe (with supplements 1 and 2); 2. Jonson (with supplement); 3. Beaumont and Fletcher (with supplement); 4. Massinger; 5.

Chapman; 6. Thomas Heywood; 7. Dekker (with supplement); 8. Greene (with supplement); 9. Shakespere—Macbeth; 10. Shakespere—Sonnets; 11. Lodge; 12. Lyly; 13. Middleton; 14. Marston; 15. Peele; 16. Shakespere—King Lear; 17. Shakespere—Merchant of Venice; 18. Kyd; 19. Webster; 20. Ford; 21. Nashe; 22. Drayton; 23. Sidney; 24. Montaigne; 25. Daniel; 26. Gascoigne; 27. Anthony Mundy; 28. Shakespere—Othello; 29. Shakespere—Troilus and Cressida; 30–32. Marie Stuart—Vols. 1–3; 33. Tourneur; 34. Shirley; 35. Herbert; 36. John Heywood; 37. Ascham; 38. Thomas Randolph; 39. Nicholas Breton; 40. Herrick; 41. Shakespere—Romeo and Juliet. Each part contained author, title, and subject indexes.

In the ten-volume format, supplements were incorporated and the authors arranged in alphabetical order, as follows: I. Ascham to Chapman; II. Daniel to Gascoigne; III. Greene to Thomas Heywood; IV. Jonson to Lodge; V. Lyly to Marston; VI. Massinger to Thomas Randolph; VII-VIII. Shakespere; IX. Shakespere to Sidney; X. Marie Stuart to Webster.

These bibliographies are further supplemented by those edited by Charles A. Pennel: *Elizabethan Bibliographies: Supplements* (London: Nether Press, 1967–) [Z2012.E38]. These bibliographies are also intended for the advanced student. They aim for completeness excepting brief mentions, anthology texts, M.A. theses, and Ph.D. dissertations not completed in England or America. They take up wherever the original volume ended. Works are listed within subdivisions chronologically, then alphabetically; editions are listed under the name of the author; reviews are cited. Entries are serially numbered, with some annotations, and subdivisions tend to move from general and bibliographical sections to those citing studies of individual works. The series includes some authors not treated by Tannenbaum.

Numbers published to date, with their authors, are as follows: 1. Webster and Middleton, 1939–65 (Dennis G. Donovan, 1967); 2. Tourneur, 1945–65, Heywood, 1938–65; and Dekker, 1945–65 (Dennis G. Donovan, 1967); 3. Jonson, 1947–65; Herrick, 1949–65; Randolph, 1949–65 (George Guffey, 1968); 4. Chapman and Marston (Charles Pennel and William P. Williams); 5. The University Wits: Lyly, 1939–65; Greene, 1945–65; Peele, 1939–65; Nashe, 1941–65; and Lodge, 1939–65 (Robert C. Johnson, 1967); 6. Marlowe, 1946–65 (Robert C. Johnson, 1967); 7. Sidney, Daniel, Drayton (George Guffey); 8. Beaumont and Fletcher, Massinger, Ford and Shirley, 1937–65 (Charles Pennell and William P. Williams, 1968); 9. Minor Elizabethans: Ascham, Mundy, Gascoigne, Kyd, and John Heywood (Robert C. Johnson, 1968); 10. Burton, 1924–66 and Browne, 1924–66 (Dennis G. Donovan); 11. Traherne and the Oxford and Cambridge Neo-Platonists, 1900–66 (George Guffey, 1969); 12. Marvell, 1927–1967 (Dennis G. Donovan); Intellectual Backgrounds of the English Renaissance (Rolf Soellner); 14. Jeremy Taylor (William P. Williams); 15. Bacon (J. K. Houck); 16. Skelton and the English and Scottish Chaucerians (William J. Brondell); 17. Sir Walter Raleigh (Humphrey Tonkin); 18. John Evelyn, 1920–68; Samuel Pepys, 1933–68 (Dennis G. Donovan, 1970).

O-16 **Ruoff, James E.** *Crowell's Handbook of Elizabethan and Stuart Literature.* New York: Crowell, 1975.

PR19.R8 1975

This dictionary handbook, published in Britain with the title, *Macmillan's Handbook of Elizabethan and Stuart Literature*, presents relatively brief articles on authors, works, genres, movements, and terms associated with English Literature 1558–1660 and with the Elizabethan, Jacobean, Stuart, and Commonwealth periods. For authors it provides dates, biographical summaries, and bibliographies. For works it gives titles, summaries, and notices of standard editions and major critical studies. Bibliographies are generally in chronological order. This work has been favorably reviewed, but users are cautioned to verify factual information with additional references. See reviews by Warren W. Wooden, *LRN* 3 (1978): 135–137 and by J. Max Patrick, *SCN* 35 (1977): 26–27.

O–17 **Hazlitt, W. Carew.** *Handbook to the Popular, Poetical, and Dramatic Literature of Great Britain, from the Invention of Printing to the Restoration.* London: John Russell Smith, 1867. Z2012.H3 1967

This volume presents a 700-page, double-column, small-print listing of persons, places, titles, and subjects pertinent to English Renaissance literature. Entries are in a single alphabet, with anonymous works entered either under the rubric "plays, anonymous," or, if a topographically identifiable broadside ballad, under the county with which it is associated, or under its title in the alphabetical sequence. Entries of works include brief bibliographical descriptions and notes, including bibliophilic annotations about provenance, cost, and related matters. A set of additions, A-Z, concludes the original volume.

Further additions were published in six volumes under the title *Bibliographical Collections and Notes on Early English Literature, 1474–1700* (London: Bernard Quaritch, 1876-1903) [Z2012.H31 1876]. Each volume is parallel in contents and arrangement to the original work. The volumes are designated first series (1876), second series (1882), third series (1887), supplement to the third series (1889), second supplement to the third series (1892), and fourth series (1903). In total there are more than 2,200 additional pages of entries in these volumes.

Both the first four supplemental volumes (first, second, third series, and supplement to third series) and the original work are indexed by G. J. Gray, *General Index to Hazlitt's Handbook and His Bibliographical Collections (1867–1889)* (London: Bernard Quaritch, 1893) [Z2012.G8]. The index gives a single alphabetical sequence containing all titles (including those of anonymous and pseudonymous works), authors, booksellers, printers, subjects, and persons-as-subjects (of epitaphs, dedications, etc.) cited in any of the source volumes. In addition, it contains and indexes its own appendix of further additions to the *Handbook* and supplements.

O–18 **Scholarly Journals in Renaissance Studies.** (See also the journals specializing in Milton and Shakespeare in sections O–58 and M–60.)

Archiv für Reformationsgeschichte. Vol. 1–. Gütersloh: C. Bertelsmann, 1906–. BR300.A6

BHR   *Bibliothèque d'humanisme et Renaissance.* Vol. 1–. Paris [later Geneva]: Association d'humanisme et Renaissance, 1933–. 3/yr. Reviews. Bibliography (see O–3). CB361.B5

Cahiers élizabéthaines. Vol. 1–. Centre d'études et de recherches élizabéthaines, Université Paul Valéry, 1972–. 2/yr. Reviews.

ELR   *English Literary Renaissance.* Vol. 1–. Amherst: University of Massachusetts, 1970–. 3/yr. Reviews. Bibliography (see O–8). PR1.E43

Moreana: A Bilingual Quarterly. Vol. 1–. Angiers, France: The Association Amici Thomae Morio, 1963–. PR2322.M66

RMS   *Renaissance and Modern Studies.* Vol. 1–. Nottingham: University of Nottingham Press, 1957–. 1/yr. AS121.R4

Ren & R   *Renaissance and Reformation / Renaissance et Réforme.* vol. 1–5. Toronto: Canadian Society for Renaissance Studies, 1964–1969; vols. 6–12: University of Toronto Press, 1970–1976. 3/yr. N.s., vol. 1– [o.s., vol. 13–], 1977–. 2/yr. Reviews. CB359.R4

RenD   *Renaissance Drama* [former title: *Research Opportunities in Renaissance Drama (RORD)*, 1955–1963]. Vols. 1–9. 1955–1967. N.s., vol. 1–. 1968–. 1/yr. The volumes of the new series are each organized around a particular theme or topic (Intellectual Contexts, Drama and the Other Arts, Comedy, Tragedy, Dramatic Technique). PN1785.R4

RenQ   *Renaissance Quarterly* [former title: *Renaissance News*, 1948–1966]. Vol. 1–. New York: Renaissance Society of America, 1948–. 4/yr. Reviews. Bibliography (see O–6). CB361.R45

SCN   *Seventeenth-Century News* [incorporating *Neo-Latin News*]. Vol. 1–. University Park: Pennsylvania State University Press, 1942–. 4/yr. Reviews. Bibliography (see O–9). PR1.S47

Spenser Studies: A Renaissance Poetry Annual (see M–60).

SEL   *SEL: Studies in English Literature, 1500–1900.* Vol. 1–. Houston: Rice University Press, 1961–. 4/yr. Issues 1 and 2 are devoted to Renaissance Literature and Elizabethan and Jacobean Drama. Bibliographical Essays (see O–7 and O–32). PR1.S82

S Ren   *Studies in the Renaissance.* Vols. 1–21. New York: Renaissance Society of America, 1954–1974. Reviews. Index to vols. 1–10 (1954–1963) in 1 vol., and vols. 11–21 (1964–1974) in 1 vol. From 1975, essays of similar nature and extent are found in the 4th issue of *Renaissance Quarterly.* D223.S8

O–19 **Some Frequently Recommended Works in Renaissance Studies.**

For additional frequently recommended works on general Renaissance history see section F; for works on social, intellectual, and educational history of the Renaissance see K–90, K–95, and K–98, respectively. For works on the history of taste see K–92. For works on Renaissance literatures of the world see appropriate portions of section L; for works on Renaissance Scottish, Irish, and Welsh Literature see appropriate portions of section M. For works on Renaissance poetry generally, see also section T; for Renaissance drama see also section U, for Renaissance prose and prose fiction see also section W, and for Renaissance literary theory and criticism see also section X.

Alpers, Paul J., ed. *Elizabethan Poetry: Modern Essays in Criticism.* New York: Oxford University Press, 1968. PR533.A65 1968

Bennett, Josephine W. *Evolution of "The Faerie Queene."* Chicago: University of Chicago Press, 1960. PR2358.B4 1960

Bevington, David M. *From Mankind to Marlowe: Growth of Structure in the Popular Drama of Tudor England.* Cambridge: Harvard University Press, 1962. PR646.B4 1962

———. *Tudor Drama and Politics.* Cambridge: Harvard University Press, 1968. PR649.P6 B4

Bluestone, Max, and Norman Rabkin. *Shakespeare's Contemporaries: Modern Studies in English Renaissance Drama.* 2d ed. Englewood Cliffs, N. J.: Prentice-Hall, 1970. PR653.B52 1970

Brooke, Tucker, and Matthias A. Shaaber. *Renaissance (1500–1660)*. Vol. 2 of Baugh, *Literary History of England* (see M–30).

Bush, Douglas. *English Literature in the Earlier Seventeenth Century, 1600–1660*. Vol. 5 of the *Oxford History of English Literature* (see M–31).

Charlton, H. B. *Senecan Tradition in Renaissance Tragedy*. Manchester: Manchester University Press, 1946. Original essay published in 1921.   PN1899.S4 C4

Craig, Hardin. *Literature of the English Renaissance, 1485–1660*. Vol. 2 of Craig, *History of English Literature* (see M–36).

Danby, John F. *Poets on Fortune's Hill: Studies in Sidney, Shakespeare, Beaumont and Fletcher*. London: Faber and Faber, 1952.   PR535.S6 D3 1952

Davis, Walker R. *Sidney's Arcadia*. New Haven: Yale University Press, 1965.   PR2342.A6 D35

Dollimore, Jonathan. *Radical Tragedy*. Chicago: University of Chicago Press, 1984.   PR658.T7 D6 1984

———, and Alan Sinfield, eds. *Political Shakespeare: New Essays in Cultural Materialism*. Ithaca: Cornell University Press, 1985.   PR3017.P59 1985

Doran, Madeleine. *Endeavors of Art: A Study of Form in Elizabethan Drama*. Madison: University of Wisconsin Press, 1954.   PR651.D67

Dubrow, Heather, and Richard Strier, eds. *Historical Renaissance*. Chicago: University of Chicago Press, 1988.   PR418.S64 H57 1988

Ferguson, Margaret W., Maureen Quilligan, and Nancy J. Vickers, eds. *Rewriting the Renaissance: The Discourses of Sexual Difference in Early Modern Europe*. Chicago: University of Chicago Press, 1986.   HQ1075.5.E85 R48 1986

Fish, Stanley. *John Skelton's Poetry*. New Haven: Yale University Press, 1965.   PR2348.F5

———. *Self-Consuming Artifacts: The Experience of Seventeenth-Century Literature*. Berkeley, Los Angeles, London: University of California Press, 1972.   PN741.F5

———. *Seventeenth-Century Prose: Modern Essays in Criticism*. New York: Oxford University Press, 1971.   PR796.F5 1971

Ford, Boris, ed. *Age of Shakespeare*. Vol. 2 in the *New Pelican Guide to English Literature* (see M–39).

———, ed. *From Donne to Marvell*. Vol. 3 in the *New Pelican Guide to English Literature* (see M–39).

Frank, Joseph. *Hobbled Pegasus: A Descriptive Bibliography of Minor English Poetry, 1641–60*. Albuquerque: University of New Mexico Press, 1968. Z2014.P7 F7

Garvin, Katherine, ed. *Great Tudors*. London: I. Nicholson and Watson, 1935.   DA317.G3

Goldberg, Jonathan. *James I and the Politics of Literature: Jonson, Shakespeare, Donne, and Their Contemporaries*. Baltimore: Johns Hopkins University Press, 1983.   PR658.P65 G64 1983

Greene, Thomas M. *Light in Troy: Imitation and Discovery in Renaissance Poetry*. New Haven: Yale University Press, 1982.   - PN223.G7

Grierson, Herbert J. C. *Cross Currents in English Literature of the Seventeenth Century; or, The World, the Flesh and the Spirit: Their Actions and Reactions*. London: Chatto and Windus, 1929.   PR431.G7

Grundy, Joan. *Spenserian Poets: A Study in Elizabethan and Jacobean Poetry*. London: Edward Arnold, 1969.   PR534.G7

Haller, William. *Rise of Puritanism, 1570–1643*. New York: Columbia University Press, 1938.   BX9334.H3

Hamilton, A. C., ed. *Essential Articles for the Study of Edmund Spenser*. Hamden, Conn.: Archon, 1972.   PR2358.H277

Helgerson, Richard. *Self-Crowned Laureates: Spenser, Jonson, Milton, and the Literary System*. Berkeley, Los Angeles, London: University of California Press, 1983.   PR531.H4

Hughes, Philip. *Reformation in England*. 5th ed. 3 vols. in 1. London: Macmillan, 1963.   BR375.H752

Javitch, Daniel. *Poetry and Courtliness in Renaissance England*. Princeton, N. J.: Princeton University Press, 1978.   PR535.C6 J2

Kaufmann, Ralph J., ed. *Elizabethan Drama: Modern Essays in Criticism*. New York: Oxford University Press, 1961.   PR653.K3

Keach, William. *Elizabethan Erotic Narrative: Irony and Pathos in the Ovidian Poetry of Shakespeare, Marlowe, and Their Contemporaries*. New Brunswick, N. J.: Rutgers University Press, 1977.   PR539.N3 K4

Keast, William R., ed. *Seventeenth-Century English Poetry: Modern Essays in Criticism*. 2d ed. New York: Oxford University Press, 1971.   PR543.K4 1971

Levin, Harry T. *Myth of the Golden Age in the Renaissance*. Bloomington: Indiana University Press, 1969.   PN721.L4

———. *Overreacher: A Study of Christopher Marlowe*. Cambridge: Harvard University Press, 1952.   PR2673.L4

Lewalski, Barbara. *Protestant Poetics and the Seventeenth-Century Religious Lyric*. Princeton, N. J.: Princeton University Press, 1979.   PR545.R4 L48

Lewis, C. S. *English Literature in the Sixteenth Century (Excluding Drama)*. Vol. 3 of the *Oxford History of English Literature* (see M–31).

Mahood, Moris Maureen. *Poetry and Humanism*. New Haven: Yale University Press, 1950.   PR549.R4 M3 1950a

Martz, Louis L. *Poetry of Meditation: A Study in English Religious Literature of the Seventeenth Century*. 2d ed. New Haven: Yale University Press, 1962.   PR549.R4 M32 1962

Matthiessen, F. O. *Translation: An Elizabethan Art*. Cambridge: Harvard University Press, 1931.   PR428.T7 M3

Miner, Earl R. *Cavalier Mode from Jonson to Cotton*. Princeton, N. J.: Princeton University Press, 1971.   PR541.M48

———. *Metaphysical Mode from Donne to Cowley*. Princeton, N. J.: Princeton University Press, 1969.   PR541.M5

———. *Restoration Mode from Milton to Dryden*. Princeton, N. J.: Princeton University Press, 1974.   PR541.M52.

Morgues, Odette. *Metaphysical, Baroque, and Precieux Poetry*. Oxford: Clarendon Press, 1953.   PR129.F8 M6

Muir, Kenneth. *Introduction to Elizabethan Literature*. New York: Random House, 1967.   PR424.M8

Nelson, Lowry, Jr. *Baroque Lyric Poetry*. New Haven: Yale University Press, 1961.   PN1356.N4

Norbrook, David. *Poetry and Politics of the English Renaissance*. London: Routledge and Kegan Paul, 1984.   PR535.H5 N67 1984

Ornstein, Robert. *Moral Vision of Jacobean Tragedy*. Madison: University of Wisconsin Press, 1960.   PR658.T7 O7

Parker, Patricia A. *Literary Fat Ladies: Rhetoric, Gender, Property*. Berkeley: Univeristy of California Press, 1987. PN56.5.W64 P37 1987

——, and David Quint, eds. *Literary Theory / Renaissance Texts*. Balitmore: Johns Hopkins University Press, 1986. PN721.L58 1986

Patterson, Annabel. *Censorship and Interpretation: The Conditions of Writing and Reading in Early Modern England*. Madison: University of Wisconsin Press, 1984. Z658.G7 P37 1984

Richmond, Hugh M. *School of Love: The Evolution of the Stuart Love Lyric*. London, 1964.

Ricks, Christopher, ed. *English Drama to 1710*. Vol. 3 in the *[Sphere] History of Literature in the English Language* (see M–34).

——, ed. *English Poetry and Prose, 1540–1674*. Vol. 2 in the *[Sphere] History of Literature in the English Language* (see M–34).

Rose, Mark. *Heroic Love: Studies in Sidney and Spenser*. Cambridge: Harvard University Press, 1968. PR2343.R6

Salzman, Paul. *English Prose Fiction, 1558–1700: A Critical History*. Oxford: Clarendon Press, 1985. PR836.S24

Schweitzer, Frederick M., and Harry E. Wedeck. *Dictionary of the Renaissance*. New York: Philosophical Library, 1967. CB361.S45

Sharp, Robert L. *From Donne to Dryden: The Revolt against Metaphysical Poetry*. Chapel Hill: University of North Carolina Press, 1940. PR541.S5

Sharpe, Kevin, and Steven N. Zwicker, eds. *Politics of Discourse: The Literature and History of Seventeenth-Century England*. Berkeley: University of California Press, 1987. PR438.P65 P64 1987

Sloan, Thomas O., and R. B. Waddington, eds. *Rhetoric of Renaissance Poetry from Wyatt to Milton*. Berkeley, Los Angeles, London: University of California Press, 1974. PR533.S5

Smuts, R. Malcolm. *Court Culture and the Origins of a Royalist Tradition in Early Stuart England*. Philadelphia: University of Pennsylvania Press, 1987. DA390.S68 1987

Southall, Raymond. *Courtly Maker*. Oxford: Blackwell, 1964. PR2403.S6

Stevens, David. *English Renaissance Theatre History: A Reference Guide*. Boston: G. K. Hall, 1982. Z2014.D7.S78

Tuve, Rosemund. *Allegorical Imagery: Some Medieval Books and Their Posterity*. Princeton, N. J.: Princeton University Press, 1966. PN731.T8

——. *Elizabethan and Metaphysical Imagery: Renaissance Poetics and Twentieth-Century Critics*. Chicago: University of Chicago Press, 1947. PR535.F5 T8

Waith, Eugene M. *Herculean Hero in Marlowe, Chapman, Shakespeare, and Dryden*. New York: Columbia University Press, 1962. PR658.T7 W3 1962

——. *Ideas of Greatness: Heroic Drama in England*. New York: Columbia University Press, 1971. PR691.W3

Wallerstein, Ruth C. *Studies in Seventeenth Century Poetic*. Madison: University of Wisconsin Press, 1950. PR529.E4 W3

Webber, Joan. *Eloquent "I": Style and Self in Seventeenth-Century Prose*. Madison: University of Wisconsin Press, 1968. PR679.W4

Wedgwood, Cecily Veronica. *Poetry and Politics under the Stuarts*. Cambridge: Cambridge University Press, 1960. PR545.P6 W4

——. *Seventeenth-Century English Literature*. 2d ed. London: Oxford University Press, 1970. PR431.W4 1970

Whigham, Frank. *Ambition and Privilege: The Social Tropes of Elizabethan Courtesy Literature*. Berkeley: University of California Press, 1984. PR428.C64 W5 1984

White, Helen C. *Metaphysical Poets: A Study in Religious Experience*. New York: Macmillan, 1936. PR549.R4 W5

Williamson, George. *Donne Tradition*. Cambridge: Harvard University Press, 1930. PR541.W5

——. *Proper Wit of Poetry*. London: Faber and Faber, 1961. PR545.H8 W5

Wilson, Frank P. *Elizabethan and Jacobean*. Oxford: Clarendon Press, 1945. PR421.W5

——. *English Drama, 1485–1585*. Vol. 4, pt. 1 of the *Oxford History of English Literature* (see M–31).

——. *Seventeenth Century Prose: Five Lectures*. Berkeley and Los Angeles: University of California Press, 1960. PR679.W55

Zocca, Louis R. *Elizabethan Narrative Poetry*. New Brunswick, N. J.: Rutgers University Press, 1950. PR535.N3 Z6

II. POETRY

See also section T.

O–21 **Case, Arthur E.** *Bibliography of English Poetical Miscellanies, 1521–1750*. Oxford: For the Bibliographical Society, 1935. Z2014.P7 C3

A closed bibliography of some 480 anthologies of poetry, both original and translated, by British subjects in any language or country. Excluded are the collected poems of a single writer, or work ascribed to a single author but written by several; hymnbooks; and songbooks containing music. The survey is based on the holdings primarily of the British Museum, the Bodleian, Yale, and Harvard. Serially numbered entries are arranged chronologically, the determining factor being the date of the earliest known edition. Following the formal bibliographical description of the first edition, all other editions and/or issues down to 1750 are presented. Descriptive data consist of a quasi-facsimile title-page transcription, a collation, and location of the volume. Short annotations follow. Four indexes are keyed to the entry serial numbers: 1. Index of Titles; 2. Chronological Index of Books Not in Their Normal Chronological Position in the Bibliography; 3. Index of Authors or Other Persons Mentioned in Title Pages, Dedications, or Prefaces; and 4. Index of Printers and Publishers. "A Finding List of English Poetical Miscellanies, 1700–1748 in Selected American Libraries," by Richard C. Boys, *ELH* 7 (1940): 144–162, is a kind of supplement. A few volumes not in Case have been added, making the total of described anthologies about 500. Locations in fourteen major American research libraries are noted.

O–22 **Williams, Franklin B., Jr.** *Index of Dedications and Commendatory Verses in English Books before 1641*. London: The Bibliographical Society, 1962. PN171.D4 W55

This volume presents an enumeration by name of contributors of commendatory verses and recipients of dedications, authorial epistles, and other preliminary materials. These materials are indexed by personal names, institutions, and geographical names, and by anonymous title. Entries identify the work in question by *STC* number and give a source of biographical information about the person addressed. A bibliography of works concludes the volume.

O–25 Spencer, Theodore. "A Bibliography of Studies in Metaphysical Poetry, 1912–1938." In Theodore Spencer and Mark Van Doren, *Studies in Metaphysical Poetry: Two Essays and a Bibliography*. New York: Columbia University Press, 1939.   Z2014.P7 S6

This bibliography, preceded by Spencer's essay, "Recent Scholarship in Metaphysical Poetry" and Van Doren's "Seventeenth Century Poets and Twentieth Century Critics," lists scholarship and criticism on the metaphysical poets from the 1912 publication of Herbert J. C. Grierson's edition of Donne (Oxford: Clarendon) to 1938. The 540 serially numbered entries are divided into sections treating general studies and then studies of the twelve "metaphysical" poets: Carew, Cleveland, Cowley, Crashaw, Donne, Lord Herbert of Cherbury, Herbert, King, Marvell, Katherine Philips, Traherne, and Vaughan. Within sections, entries are grouped by year in chronological order, and within years, in alphabetical order by the name of the cited author. An index of modern authors concludes the volume.

The volume is continued by the compilation of Lloyd E. Berry, *Bibliography of Studies in Metaphysical Poetry, 1939–1960* (Madison: University of Wisconsin Press, 1964) [Z2014.P7 B4]. Its total of 1,147 serially numbered entries are arranged in a format identical with that of the earlier bibliography. Unlike the earlier work, however, not even important reviews are cited; users are referred instead to the annual bibliography in *SP* (O–5).

See also the recent work of William McCarron and Robert Shenk, *Lesser Metaphysical Poets: A Bibliography, 1961–1980* (San Antonio, Tex.: Trinity University Press, 1983) [Z2014.P7 M36 1983], which provides an unannotated checklist of 621 items on the following poets: Carew, Cleveland, Cowley, Crashaw, Edward Hubert, King, Philips, Traherne, and Vanshaw. Entries include books, articles, and dissertations; initial editions, revised editions and some anthologies are also cited, as is a list of general studies.

O–28 Hanford, James Holly, and William A. McQueen. *Milton*. [A Goldentree Bibliography.] 2d ed. Arlington Heights, Ill.: AHM Publishing Corp., 1979.
                                                    Z8578.H35 1979

This selective bibliography designed for the use of beginning graduate students was first published in 1966. The second edition contains more than 1,650 serially numbered entries that occasionally provide brief descriptive annotation. Excluded are school editions, short articles on minor points, popular and semipopular books and articles, and unpublished doctoral dissertations. Entries are classified into twelve sections, as follows: Bibliography and Reference Works; Useful Background Studies; Editions Published in Milton's Lifetime; Facsimiles of Editions Published in Milton's Lifetime; Collected Editions; Important Editions of Individual Works; Biographies; Biographical Studies; Collections of Essays; General Criticism and Interpretation; Studies of Individual Works; Special Topics (Text, Language, Prosody, Fame and Influence, etc.). The volume concludes with an index of names.

III. DRAMA AND THEATER

See also section U, and see Penninger, *English Drama to 1660* (N–52).

O–30 Ribner, Irving, and Clifford C. Huffman. *Tudor and Stuart Drama*. 2d ed. [A Goldentree Bibliography.] Arlington Heights, Ill.: AHM Publishing Corp., 1978.
                                                    Z2014.D7 R5 1978

This highly selective bibliography, first published in 1966, is designed for the beginning graduate student. Emphasized are studies published 1920–1975. Excluded are general studies unless they deal significantly and specifically with major playwrights and their plays; articles subsequently incorporated into books; selections of plays for classroom use; collections of previously published essays; anonymous plays; and unpublished material. The 2,274 serially numbered entries are disposed into eight sections, as follows: Basic Works of Reference, Textual and Historical; Anthologies and Reprint Series; Bibliographical Guides; The Printing and Publication of Plays; Dramatic Companies, Theatres, Conditions of Performance; Critical and Historical Studies (collections, general studies, genres); The Major Dramatists (21); and Masques; Pageants and Folk Drama. The volume concludes with an index of names.

O–31 Greg, W. W. *Bibliography of the English Printed Drama to the Restoration*. 4 vols. London: Oxford University Press for the Bibliographical Society, 1939–1959.   Z2014.D7 G78

This extended and elaborate descriptive bibliography aims to give the student all essential bibliographical information about printed plays from the earliest known publications to plays known to have been written before the end of 1642 (when the theaters closed on 2 September) and printed before the end of 1700, along with those written after 1642 but printed before the beginning of 1660 (the year of the Restoration on 29 May).

Volumes 1 and 2 contain chronologically arranged descriptions of printed individual plays both in separate editions and in collections. Entries give reference to Stationers' Register notations; quasi-facsimile transcriptions of title pages, collations, and detailed annotations are given. Locations of copies are listed, and notable variants in individual copies are identified. Volume 1 gives extracts of pertinent materials from the records of the Stationers' Company (C–6) and lists extant plays to 1616; volume 2 lists extant plays from 1617 to 1689; Latin plays; and lost plays.

Volume 3 contains a list of collections of plays, with bibliographical descriptions of the anthology volume, arranged alphabetically by author. Also in volume 3 is an appendix of such sources as advertisements in newspapers, prefaces, lists of actors, lists of publications, lists of authors, private collections, and early play catalogs. Also in volume 3 are a general index, lists of stationers, authors, dedicatees, incipits of prologues and epilogues, acting company performances, producers, licensers, printers, and a list of all persons and titles mentioned in either descriptions of plays or editorial comments, and a subject index. Volume 4 contains a 200-page introduction not only to the aims and methods of this bibliography but also to theoretical and critical matters associated with the study of the drama. There is an index to the introduction. Also in the last volume are additions and corrections to the list of plays, corrections to the record of copies (giving new or different locations of copies of editions), and an index of titles.

Based upon Greg is *Index of Characters in English Printed Drama to the Restoration* by Thomas L. Berger and William C. Bradford (Englewood, Col.: Microcard Editions Books,

1975) [PR1265.3.B4]. Titles are recorded under character names; ambiguities result from characters with generic names—the Lady, the Melancholic, the Tyrant, the Attendant—and this work should be used as a finding aid rather than an exhaustive authority. The index proper is followed by a bibliography of modern studies of character types.

O–32 **"Recent Studies in Elizabethan and Jacobean Drama."** *SEL*, Spring issue, 1961–.   PR1.S82

These annual bibliographical essays by established scholars offer descriptive and evaluative comments on recent work, normally of the previous year. Emphases are chosen by the individual authors. To date, the following essays have appeared:

Vol. 1 (1961), pp. 119–128. By Frank Kermode [Shake-speare and Jacobean drama].

Vol. 2 (1962), pp. 241–254. By Kenneth Muir.

Vol. 3 (1963), pp. 269–285. By Clifford Leech.

Vol. 4 (1964), pp. 325–349. By Eugene M. Waith.

Vol. 5 (1965), pp. 383–402. By Paul A. Jorgensen.

Vol. 6 (1966), pp. 357–379. By Jonas A. Barish.

Vol. 7 (1967), pp. 351–376. By M. A. Shaaber.

Vol. 8 (1968), pp. 365–390. By Cyrus Hoy.

Vol. 9 (1969), pp. 351–378. By Mark Eccles.

Vol. 10 (1970), pp. 425–438. By Douglas Cole.

Vol. 11 (1971), pp. 377–399. By Alvin Kernan [with head-note précis].

Vol. 12 (1972), pp. 391–428. By Roy Battenhouse.

Vol. 13 (1973), pp. 374–406. By Mark Eccles [with head-note].

Vol. 14 (1974), pp. 297–314. By Maurice Charney.

Vol. 15 (1975), pp. 339–362. By Norman Rabkin.

Vol. 16 (1976), pp. 333–348. By David Young.

Vol. 17 (1977), pp. 333–357. By Robert Y. Turner.

Vol. 18 (1978), pp. 361–418. By Arthur F. Kinney.

Vol. 19 (1979), pp. 327–354. By Bernard P. McElroy, Jr.

Vol. 20 (1980), pp. 345–365. By Robert Ornstien.

Vol. 21 (1981), pp. 333–368. By Alexander Leggatt.

Vol. 22 (1982), pp. 331–369. By J. L. Styan.

Vol. 23 (1983), pp. 329–365. By Lawrence Danson.

Vol. 24 (1984), pp. 373–406. By Richard Wheeler.

Vol. 25 (1985), pp. 439–489. By Sidney Homan.

Vol. 26 (1986), pp. 345–402. By Charles Frey.

Vol. 27 (1987), pp. 321–379. By Jean E. Howard.

Vol. 28 (1988), pp. 331–389. By Jill L. Levenson.

Vol. 29 (1989), pp. 357–408. By J. L. Simmons.

O–33 *Research Opportunities in Renaissance Drama [RORD]* [1955–]. Vol. 1–. New Orleans: University of New Orleans [place varies], 1956–.   PR621.M75a

This annual report of the MLA Conference on Research Opportunities in Renaissance Drama has had a somewhat complicated publication history. The issues covering 1955–1961 (published 1956–1964) were titled *Opportunities for Research in Renaissance Drama*. Those published from 1964 on were issued as supplements to the journal *Renaissance Drama*. Currently, the volumes are separately published. They include reviews, summaries of research opportunities, a census of productions of Renaissance plays, checklists of plays and other bibliographical aids on authors and topics, summaries of current research projects, reports on collections of documents, and discussion of texts and articles relevant to the teaching of

Renaissance Drama. From vol. 10 (1967) on, a "Medieval Supplement" prepared by Stanley J. Kahrl has been included. An index to the "Current Projects" list was prepared by Christopher J. Thaiss, "An Index to Volumes I-XVI of *RORD*," and published in vol. 17 (1974): 34–44.

O–34 **Salomon, Brownell.** *Critical Analyses in English Renaissance Drama: A Bibliographical Guide.* 2d ed. New York: Garland, 1985.   Z2014.D7 S24 1985

Originally published in 1979, this volume aims to refer users to the best modern English-language analytical studies of every play, masque, pageant, and entertainment written between 1580 and 1642. Cited studies exclude unpublished theses and doctoral dissertations. Major works are identified by asterisks. The descriptively annotated entries are divided into five sections, as follows: Critical Theory; Concordances and Word Indexes; Dramatists, 1580–1642, Excluding Shakespeare; Anonymous Plays; Masques, Entertainments, Pageants. There is an index of modern authors and an analytical subject index using large headings such as allegory, costume, emblems, figures, gesture, parody, rhetorical devices, and sound effects.

O–35 **Logan, Terence P., and Denzell S. Smith, eds.** *Predecessors of Shakespeare: A Survey and Bibliography of Recent Studies in English Renaissance Drama.* Lincoln: University of Nebraska Press, 1973.   Z2014.D7 L83

This volume, part of a large project to review recent studies in English Renaissance drama, contains analytical and descriptive bibliographical essays by authorities, and an enumerative bibliography of studies drawn from thirteen leading scholarly journals, 1923–1968, on which the bibliographical essays are based. Each essay contains a general section treating biography and general studies of an author's plays and works; a section on criticism of individual plays; and a section on the canon, dates, and editions. There are cross-references. This volume contains essays on dramatists writing 1580–1592, Marlowe, Greene, Kyd, Nashe, Lyly, Peele, Lodge, anonymous plays, and other minor dramatists. A list of contributors and an index of persons and plays conclude the work.

For earlier Renaissance drama, see D. Jerry White, *Early English Drama, Everyman to 1580: A Reference Guide* (Boston: G. K. Hall, 1986) [Z2014.D7 W48], which presents editions and studies published from the late seventeenth century through 1982 of plays from ca. 1495 to 1580 by British authors. Excluded are studies of folk drama, pageants, entertainments, masques, and John Skelton. Entries are arranged chronologically in sections on Bibliographies, Collections, General Studies, and Authors / Translators / Anonymous Works. There are indexes of authors, scholars, anonymous works, and subjects.

O–36 **Logan, Terence P., and Denzell S. Smith, eds.** *Popular School: A Survey and Bibliography of Recent Studies in English Renaissance Drama.* Lincoln: University of Nebraska Press, 1975.   Z2014.D7 L82

This volume, like its predecessor, *Predecessors of Shakespeare* (O–35), is part of a larger project surveying research on English Renaissance Drama. Its bibliographical essays and enumerative bibliographies survey the contents of twelve scholarly journals from 1925 through 1971 or so. Dramatists writing for the open-air public theaters rather than the private theaters between 1593 and 1616 are treated, with essays and bibliographies on Dekker, Middleton, Webster, Thomas Heywood, Anthony Munday, Drayton, anonymous plays, and other dramatists. The structure of the volume parallels that of the earlier work in the series.

O–37 **Logan, Terence P., and Denzell S. Smith, eds. *New Intellectuals: A Survey and Bibliography of Recent Studies in English Renaissance Drama.*** Lincoln: University of Nebraska Press, 1977.   Z2014.D7 N29

This volume, the third in a series surveying research on English Renaissance drama (see O–35, O–36), contains bibliographical essays and enumerative bibliographies treating studies 1923–1974 found in twelve leading scholarly journals of the work of Jonson, Chapman, Marston, Tourneur, Daniel, anonymous plays, and other minor dramatists writing for private theaters during the period 1593–1616. The volume is identical in arrangement with its predecessors.

O–38 **Logan, Terence P., and Denzell S. Smith, eds. *Later Jacobean and Caroline Dramatists: A Survey and Bibliography of Recent Studies in English Renaissance Drama.*** Lincoln: University of Nebraska Press, 1978.   Z2014.D7 L816

This volume, the fourth and last in the series reviewing scholarship on English Renaissance drama (see O–35, O–36, and O–37), treats the work of dramatists writing 1616–1642. Coverage is of scholarship from 1923 through 1976. It is designed to supplement treatment in E. K. Chambers, *Elizabethan Stage* (U–74), and in Gerald E. Bentley, *Jacobean and Caroline Stage*, 1941– (U–75). Bibliographical essays and enumerative bibliographies treat Beaumont and Fletcher, Massinger, Ford, Shirley, Richard Brome, Davenant, anonymous plays, and other minor dramatists. The structure of this volume is identical with that of its predecessors.
  Mark J. Lidman's *Studies in Jacobean Drama, 1973–1984: An Annotated Bibliography* (New York: Garland, 1986) [Z2014.D7 L5 1986] updates Logan and Smith's coverage of English language work on Chapman, Dekker, Heywood, Tourneur, Marston, Middleton, Webster, Massinger, Ford, Brome, and Shirley.

O–39 **Bergeron, David H. *Twentieth-Century Criticism of English Masques, Pageants, and Entertainments: 1558–1642, with a Supplement on the Folk-Play and Related Forms by Henry B. Caldwell.*** San Antonio, Tex.: Trinity University Press, 1972.   Z2014.D7 B44

This checklist contains 416 serially numbered entries disposed into four sections. All cited items are critical articles or books in English published since 1900. The sections are: I. General Works (including works in which there are parts on the masque, pageant, or entertainment); II. Jonson (and Inigo Jones); III. Milton's *Comus*; IV. Other Writers. The Supplement contains 103 separately numbered entries. A brief introduction reviews this research and identifies some desiderata. The volume concludes with indexes of authors and of subjects.

IV. SHAKESPEARE

See also section T and section U.

O–40 **Wells, Stanley, ed. *Shakespeare: Select Bibliographical Guides.*** London: Oxford University Press, 1973.
Z8811.W44

This selective guide to Shakespeare scholarship and criticism up to about 1969 is planned as a companion to the volume on the rest of English drama also edited by Wells (see U–20). It consists of seventeen chapters, each consisting of a bibliographical essay followed by a list of references for each work cited in the text. The chapters and their authors are as follows: The Study of Shakespeare (Stanley Wells); Shakespeare's Text (Norman Sanders); Shakespeare in the Theatre (Michael Jamieson); The Sonnets and Other Poems (J. M. Nosworthy); The Early Comedies (D. J. Palmer); The Middle Comedies (Gamini Salgado); The Problem Comedies: *Troilus and Cressida, All's Well That Ends Well*, and *Measure for Measure* (John Wilders); The Late Comedies (Philip Edwards); *Titus Andronicus* and *Romeo and Juliet* (G. R. Hibbard); *Hamlet* (John Jump); *Othello* (Robert Hapgood); *King Lear* (Kenneth Muir); *Macbeth* (R. A. Foakes); *Julius Caesar* and *Antony and Cleopatra* (T. J. B. Spencer); *Coreolanus* and *Timon of Athens* (Maurice Charney); The English History Plays (A. R. Humphreys); *Henry VIII, The Two Noble Kinsmen*, and the Apocryphal Plays (G. R. Proudfoot). Notes on contributors conclude the volume; there is no index.

O–41 **McManaway, James G., and Jeanne Addison Roberts. *Selective Bibliography of Shakespeare: Editions, Textual Studies, Commentary.*** Charlottesville: University Press of Virginia for the Folger Shakespeare Library, 1975.
Z8811.M23

This volume contains 4,519 serially numbered unannotated entries that present an overview of primarily English-language scholarship and criticism on Shakespeare from the 1930 publication of E. K. Chambers, *William Shakespeare: A Study of Facts and Problems*, 2 vols. (Oxford: Clarendon Press, 1930) [PR2894.C44] through 1970. Entries are disposed into eleven main sections, as follows: General Reference Works; Bibliographies—Enumerative; Dictionaries and Concordances; Textual Studies and Critical Bibliography; Shakespearean Publications; Shakespeare Collections; Biography; Works (Canon, Chronology, Editions, Adaptations, Promptbooks, Translations); Individual Works (with subsections for Editions, Textual Commentary, and Commentary, as warranted); General Commentary (Collections of Essays, Comprehensive Essays, Comedies, History Plays, Tragedies, Problem Plays, Roman Plays, Romances); Special Topics (Sources, Background, Stage History, Audience, Allusions, Reputation and Influence, Music, Recordings, Illustrations, Authorship). The volume concludes with an Index of Authors, Editors, and Translators.
  For more extensive treatments, users are referred to the more complete bibliographies of Jaggard (O–46), Ebisch and Schücking (O–47), and Smith (O–48), and to the various current serial bibliographies (O–50 ff.).

O–42 **Payne, Waveney R. N. *Shakespeare Bibliography.*** London: Library Association, 1969.   Z8811.P35

This highly selective list of 576 serially numbered briefly annotated entries, prepared by the Librarian of the Birmingham Shakespeare Library, is organized in eight main sections, as follows: Reference Works; The Text; Literary Criticism; Philosophy and Knowledge of Shakespeare; Special Groups of the Plays; The Separate Plays and Poems (with subsections for each); Stage History and Production; Biographical Appendix. The list concludes with an index of authors.

Another selective bibliography of Shakespeeare has appeared more recently, compiled by Larry S. Campion, *Essential Shakespeare: An Annotated Bibliography of Major Modern Studies* (Boston: G. K. Hall, 1986) [Z8811.C53 1986]. Covering the period 1900–1984, this volume presents descriptive and evaluative annotations for approximately one thousand entries. They are disposed into two main divisions: General Studies and Shakespeare's Individual Works. The former is further divided into the following broad categories: Reference Works, Biographies, Dating and Textual Studies, Language and Style, the Stage, Film, and Thematic and Topical Studies. The latter is divided into sections on Poems and Sonnets, Histories, Comedies (including the Dark Comedies), Tragedies (including the Roman plays), and Romances. Chapters on individual works include Reference Material, Editions, Textual Studies, and Criticism.

O–43 **Bevington, David.** *Shakespeare.* [A Goldentree Bibliography.] Arlington Heights, Ill.: AHM Publishing Co., 1978.
Z8811.B47 1978

This selected bibliography, designed for the use of graduate students, contains 4,689 serially numbered entries. Its focus is on the present state of Shakespeare studies, items having been selected on the grounds that the compiler judged them unsafe to ignore in any work on that particular topic of Shakespeare studies. Most items have been published since 1930, and the cutoff date is February 1977. Those items judged absolutely indispensable are designated with an asterisk. Entries are divided into two parts, general and individual works. The first part is in twelve sections, as follows: The Study of Shakespeare (Bibliographies, Periodicals, and Annual Bibliographies; Handbooks, Study Guides, Companions; Dictionaries, Concordances, and Other Reference Works; Modern Editions of Shakespeare's Sources; Commentary on Shakespeare and his Sources); Shakespeare's Life (Biography, Shakespeare's Life and Artistic Achievements; The Authorship Question); Social, Political, and Intellectual Backgrounds; Collected Editions; Textual Criticism; Style and Language; Shakespeare and His Stage; The History of Shakespeare Production on Stage and in Film; The History of Shakespeare Criticism, His Reputation and Influence; General Criticism Relating to Shakespeare's Works as a Whole; Studies in the Chronology and Development of Shakespeare's Art; and Studies in Genres. The second part, on the individual works, is subdivided variously, with such headings as Textual Criticism and Sources; Collections of Essays; General Studies; Character Studies; Studies in Dramatic Structure; Staging and Stage History; Language and Imagery. There are numerous cross-references; occasional annotations expand titles as necessary. The work concludes with an index of authors.

O–44 **Bergeron, David M., and Geraldo U. de Sousa.** *Shakespeare: A Study and Research Guide.* 2d ed. rev. Lawrence: University Press of Kansa, 1987. Z8811.B44 1987

This guide, first published in 1975, is designed for the beginning student or general reader. It offers an introduction to the state and character of current Shakespearean scholarship, the most useful research aids, and the method of preparing a research paper. The first of its three chapters reviews the state of Shakespearean scholarship; the second surveys in bibliographical essay form indispensable reference works and other aids to research; and the third introduces the research paper. The second, central chapter is disposed into eight sections, as follows: Bibliography and Reference Guides; Literary Histories; Editions; Studies in the Genres; Studies of Groups and Movements; Interdisciplinary Studies; Journals; and Biographical Studies. There is no index.

O–45 **Howard-Hill, Trevor H.** *Shakespearean Bibliography and Textual Criticism: A Bibliography.* Vol. 2 of the *Index to British Literary Bibliography.* Oxford: Clarendon Press, 1971. Z2011.A1 H68

This volume presents a total of 1,981 serially numbered entries, including general bibliographies of and guides to the Shakespearean literature; works that enumerate editions of Shakespeare's works or study them as physical objects; and those that study Shakespearean texts as transmitted semiotic systems. Gathered here are all those entries on Shakespeare which are excluded from Howard-Hill's *Bibliography of British Literary Bibliographies* (M–1) and from his *British Bibliography and Textual Criticism* (Y–1). Excluded from citation are catalogs of manuscripts, letters, library accession lists, theses, brief exhibition catalogs, booksellers' catalogs, and auction and sales catalogs. There are notes on the contents of cited entries and references to reviews. The bibliography concludes with an index of authors, compilers, editors, and publishers; subjects (including authors) and works (with reference by act and scene if citations are limited in that way).

The volume also contains, pp. 179–322, a separate *Supplement* to volume 1 of the *Index to British Literary Bibliography* (see M–1). A supplement to *Shakespearean Bibliography* containing ninety-five new items appears in Howard-Hill's *British Bibliography and Textual Criticism*, vol. 5 of the *Index to British Literary Bibliography* (Oxford, 1979), pp. 374–388 (see Y–1).

O–46 **Jaggard, William.** *Shakespeare Bibliography: A Dictionary of Every Known Issue of the Writings of Our National Poet and of Recorded Opinion Thereon in the English Language, with Historical Introduction, Facsimiles, Portraits, and Other Illustrations.* Stratford-on-Avon: Shakespeare Head Press, 1911. Z8811.J21

This 700-page, double-column, small-print volume contains more than 36,000 entries, arranged in a single alphabet, including names of authors, printers, engravers, publishers, artists, scholars and critics, actors, actresses, places, plays, characters, titles, and miscellaneous subjects associated with Shakespearean bibliography. Only English-language materials are cited. Entries give short titles, place and date of publication, format, a location symbol, and descriptive annotations (analyzing the contents of composite volumes and so on). Appended is a second alphabet of "Aftermath" containing additions and corrections to the main list. There are occasional inaccuracies.

As might be expected, this bibliography is invaluable for its citation of editions and issues and for its records toward the history of Shakespeare reception; for criticism and scholarship it is drastically out of date. A more recent compilation that supplements it is Henrietta C. Bartlett and Alfred W. Pollard, *Census of Shakespeare's Plays in Quarto, 1594–1709*, rev. and extended (New Haven: Yale University Press, 1939) [Z8811.B28].

O–47 **Ebisch, F. Walther, and Levin L. Schücking, eds.** *Shakespeare Bibliography.* Oxford: Clarendon Press, 1931.
Z8811.E18

This selective bibliography containing publications through 1929 is elaborately classified into two main parts, A. General, and B. The Works of Shakespeare Examined Individually. Part A contains fourteen sections, as follows: I. Shakespeare Bibliography; II. Elizabethan Literature; III. Shakespeare's Life; IV. Shakespeare's Personality; V. Text; Transmission and Emendation; VI. Shakespeare's Sources, Literary Influences, and Cultural Relations; VII. The Art of Shakespeare, Part I: Language, Vocabulary, Prosody, and Style; VIII. The Art of Shakespeare, Part II: Shakespeare's Dramatic Art; IX. Shakespeare's Stage and the Production of His Plays; X. Literary Taste in Shakespeare's Time; XI. Aesthetic Criticism of Shakespeare; XII. Shakespeare's Influence through the Centuries; XIII. Civilization in Shakespeare's England; XIV. The Shakespeare-Bacon Controversy and Similar Theories. Part B is in four sections, as follows: I. Chronology of the Dramas; II. The Individual Dramas; III. Shakespeare's Poems; IV. The Shakespeare Apocrypha. Entries cite reviews and are frequently annotated. The volume concludes with an index of authors.

A *Supplement for the Years 1930–1935* (Oxford: Clarendon Press, 1937) [Z8811.E18 suppl.] is parallel in contents and structure to the original volume. It includes publications of 1930 through 1935 as well as pre–1930 additions missed in the original compilation. There is a strong German-language bias in both the original and the supplement.

O–48   **Smith, Bordon Ross.   *Classified Shakespeare Bibliography, 1936–1958.*** University Park: Pennsylvania State University Press, 1963.   Z8811.S64

The classes in this bibliography are generally continued from those used in the Ebisch and Schücking volumes (O–47). Added are categories for Surveys of Scholarship; Comparisons with Other Writers; Shakespeare and the Modern Stage; and Other Aspects of Shakespeare's Influence through the Centuries. Many new subdivisions are also added. The bibliography of studies of Elizabethan literature in general is omitted. Serially numbered entries total more than 20,000. An elaborate table of contents enumerates all the subclasses under each main heading and keys them in to the Ebisch and Schücking categories. There is relatively sparse annotation, but entries do list reviews. This bibliography is difficult to use for beginners, who are advised to consult a multiplicity of possible classes and subclasses as the only way to compensate for the lack of a detailed index.

O–49   ***Shakespeare Bibliography: The Catalogue of the Birmingham Shakespeare Library.*** Compiled and edited by Waveney R. N. Payne Fredrick. 7 vols. London: Mansell, 1971.   Z8813.B5

This work is in two parts. Volumes 1–3, Accessions pre–1932, reproduce entries in the original guard-book catalog; volumes 4–7, Accessions post–1931, reproduce cards in the modern card catalog of what is one of the largest collections of Shakespeare in the world. Both catalogs must be checked, as must the indexes to each. Volumes 1–2 and 4–6 contain English editions and English Shakespeareana; volumes 3 and 7 each contain foreign editions and Shakespeareana as well as an index of editors, translators, illustrators, and series. Many entries analyze Shakespearean matter in periodicals and composite volumes, thus making these catalogs serve as Shakespearean indexes to a vast range of miscellaneous materials.

The other major published catalog is that of the Folger Shakespeare Library, *Catalog of the Shakespeare Collection*, 2 vols. (Boston: G. K. Hall, 1972) [Z8811.F65]. Volume 1 covers, in chronological order, the editions of Shakespeare's plays, both collected and individual. Volume 2 is a subject catalog with sixteen main headings, including one containing all works with Shakespeare as the first word of the title.

O–50   **"Shakespeare: An Annotated [since 1965: World] Bibliography for [1949–]."** *Shakespeare Quarterly*, vol. 1–. Washington, D.C.: Folger Shakespeare Library [place varies], 1950–.   PR2885.S63

This annual, noncumulated, annotated bibliography is under the sponsorship of the Shakespeare Association of America through a committee of correspondents. Collated with the *MLA Annual Bibliography* (L–50), this work has varied in size and structure since its inception, though the general tendency has been toward greater inclusiveness (particularly of foreign and of non-Shakespearean but related studies) and greater precision. The 1977 bibliography contains 2,184 entries listed alphabetically by author under the following head-

ings: (1) Annuals, Bibliographies, Festschriften, and Surveys; (2) Editions and Translations, Selections and Adaptations; (3) Books; (4) Dissertations; (5) Articles, Including Selections from or References to Works not Devoted Exclusively to Shakespeare or even Germane to the Study of Elizabethan Drama Narrowly Considered; (6) Reviews of Current Stage and Screen Productions—Surveys, Individual Performances; (7) Reviews of Books Recorded in Previous Annual Bibliographies—Annuals, etc., Editions, etc., Books. It is concluded by indexes to Shakespeare's works, to topics (keyword index), and to names.

Prior to 1950 this journal was titled *Bulletin of the Shakespeare Association of America* [PR2887.N5], and the bibliography ran from 1925 through 1949 under various titles, including "Annual Bibliography of Shakespeariana," "Classified Index of Shakespeariana in the Periodicals of [year]," and "Shakespeare and His Contemporaries (A Classified Bibliography for [year])." In early years only American periodical literature was included; later other English-language periodicals were added. Only in the last volume were entries annotated.

An important new project, Harrison T. Meserole's *Cumulative Shakespeare Bibliography*, will cumulate and extend all the serial and closed Shakespeare bibliographies from 1900–1979 in both printed bibliographies for 1900–1957 and 1958–1979, and in a database which will permit customized searches. See Harrison T. Meserole and John B. Smith, "The Cumulative Shakespeare Bibliography: A Product of Project Planning in the Humanities," *Perspectives in Computing*, 1.2 (1981): 4–11.

O–51   **"The Year's Contributions to Shakespearian Study"** [1947–]. *Shakespeare Survey*, vol. 1–. Cambridge: Cambridge University Press, 1948–.   PR2888.C3

This annual review contains three bibliographical essays by authorities treating (1) Critical Studies; (2) Shakespeare's Life, Times, and Stage; and (3) Textual Studies. A selection of the preceding year's books and articles are described and evaluated, often in considerable detail. There are bibliographical footnotes, but there is no index.

O–52   **"Significant Articles, Monographs, and Reviews."** *Shakespeare Studies*, vol. 1–. Cincinnati, Ohio: University of Cincinnati, 1965–.   PR2885.S64

With a different title the first two years, this annual survey contains an enumeration of "Significant Articles" with a brief critical annotation, a list of important reviews, and a briefly annotated enumeration of "Ancillary Studies," primarily monographs.

O–53   **"Review of Periodicals" and "Dissertation Digest."** *Shakespeare Newsletter,* vol. 1–. Washington, D.C. [place varies]: Shakespeare Association of America, 1951–.
PR2885.S48

Each bimonthly issue of the *Newsletter* contains abstracts of recent articles under the rubric "Review of Periodicals"; abstracts of recently completed dissertations; and a variety of other bibliographical notes, including reference to work in progress.

"Shakespearean Work in Progress" is also a regular feature of the annual *Shakespearean Research and Opportunities*: Report of the MLA Conference, published irregularly since 1965 [PR2885.S8]. This publication was temporarily suspended in 1979. Since issue 3 (1967) this report also includes "Shakespeare and Renaissance Intellectual Contexts: A Selective, Annotated List." These have been cumulated in W. R. Elton and Giselle Neuschloss, *Shakespeare's World: Renais-*

sance Intellectual Contexts: A Selective, Annotated Guide, 1966–71 (New York: Garland, 1979) [Z8813.E38].

O–54 **"Shakespeare-Bibliographie für [1865–1963] mit Nachträgen aus früheren Jahren."** *Shakespeare Jahrbuch*, vols. 1–100. Weimar and Leipzig: Deutsche Shakespeare-Gesellschaft, 1865–1964. With continuations as described below. PR2889.D4

This, the oldest serial bibliography of Shakespeare studies in existence, has now split into two separate productions. From 1965 on, the "Shakespeare-Bibliographie" has been published in the *Jahrbuch* of the Heidelberg *Deutsche Shakespeare Gesellschaft, West*, vol. 1– (Quelle und Meyer, 1964–) [PR2889.D42]. Books, articles, dissertations, and reviews are included. Entries are in five sections treating I. Bibliographies and Periodicals; II. Collected and Selected Editions; III. Excerpts from Several Works, Anthologies, Quotations; IV. Editions of Single Works; and V. Other Works about Shakespeare. A detailed index concludes the annual listing.

Meanwhile, the Weimar bibliography resumed in vol. 103 of the *Shakespeare Jahrbuch* (Böhlau 1965–) [PR2889.D4] with the "Shakespeare-Bibliographie für 1964–65." Thus, there are now two annual bibliographies being produced in Germany; that in Weimar is particularly strong in eastern European publications; the Heidelberg volume is valuable for its somewhat fuller coverage of Western Europe. Both complement the bibliography in *Shakespeare Quarterly* (O–50) and contain about 10 percent more entries.

O–55 **Spevack, Marvin.** *Complete and Systematic Concordance to the Works of Shakespeare.* 6 vols. Hildesheim: Georg Olms, 1968–1970. PR2892.S6

This computer-generated concordance is based upon the modern-spelling edition of G. Blakemore Evans in the *Riverside Shakespeare* (Boston: Houghton Mifflin, 1974) [PR2754.E9 1974]. It consists of a series of interlocking concordances to the individual plays, to the poems (both singly and together), and to the complete works. Volume 1 presents drama and character concordances to the folio comedies; volume 2 gives drama and character concordances to the folio histories and to the nondramatic works; volume 3 presents drama and character concordances to the folio tragedies and to *Pericles, The Two Noble Kinsmen,* and *Sir Thomas More.* Volumes 4–6 present a complete concordance to the works. Each of the individual drama concordances begins with general statistical information including the total number of speeches, of lines, and of words in verse, in prose, and in mixed contexts, and the total number of different words in the play. Then follows an alphabetical list of the words in the play, with indications for each word of its frequency within the drama, its relative frequency, and its location by act, scene, and line reference. The context (verse or prose) is noted. The character concordances follow the individual drama concordances and list the names of each character (including such rubrics as "Song" or "Servant 1" or "All") followed by an alphabetical list of the words spoken by that character, along with indications of frequency, relative frequency, and location by act, scene, and line reference. The percentage of the total number of speeches, lines, and words assigned to each character is indicated.

The complete concordance in volumes 4–6 lists every occurrence of every word, giving for each word a line of statistical information including total frequency in Shakespeare's works, relative frequency, and total number of appearances in verse and prose passages. Each occurrence of the word is then indicated, with a full line, meaningful context and an act, scene, line reference.

Throughout the six volumes, homographs are asterisked, referring users to the appendix on them at the end of volume 6.

A total of five appendixes are provided, as follows: A, Word Frequency, giving the total vocabulary in the descending order of frequency; B, Reverse Word Index, giving the total vocabulary spelled backwards to facilitate consideration of rhymes and similar concerns; C, Hyphenated Words (listed in order of their first, second, and then third elements); D, Homographs (with brief explanations of the relevant semantic or grammatical distinctions); E, a Conversion Table giving act, scene, and line number references for every twenty lines of a through-numbered text of each play. Following the appendixes is a list of corrigenda to the entire work.

Volumes 4–6 in a slightly abbreviated form constitute the contents of the one-volume *Harvard Concordance to Shakespeare* (Cambridge: Belknap Press of Harvard University Press, 1973) [PR2892.S62].

In contrast with the Spevack concordances, the thirty-seven volumes of the *Oxford Shakespeare Concordances* edited by T. H. Howard-Hill (Oxford: Clarendon Press, 1969–1973) [LC number varies] are each based on the copy text chosen for the forthcoming Oxford old-spelling Shakespeare edition. Every word in each play is listed, with frequency count, line number, and reference lines given.

See also John Bartlett's *New and Complete Concordance or Verbal Index to Words, Phrases, and Passages in the Dramatic Works of Shakespeare with a Supplementary Concordance to the Poems* (London: Macmillan, 1894) [PR2892.B34], which is based on the text of the Globe edition of 1891. For purposes of identification only, one may also find useful Burgon Egbert Stevenson's *Home Book of Shakespeare Quotations, Being Also a Concordance and a Glossary of the Unique Words and Phrases in the Plays and Poems* (New York: Scribner, 1937) [PR2892.S63].

O–58 **Scholarly Journals in Shakespeare Studies.**

SAB *Shakespeare Association Bulletin.* See *Shakespeare Quarterly.* PR2887.N5

ShJ *Shakespeare-Jahrbuch.* Vols. 1–99. Berlin: G. Reimer; then Heidelberg: Quelle und Meyer, 1865–1964. Since 1965 the journal has been split into two series: the first is published in Weimar: [ShJE] Böhlau, for the Deutsche Shakespeare-Gesellschaft [East], 1964–; and the second in Heidelberg: [ShJW] Quelle und Meyer, for the Deutsche Shakespeare Gesellschaft [West], 1964–. Each contains an annual bibliography (see O–54). Index to vols. 1–99 by Marianne Rohde (Heidelberg: Quelle und Meyer, 1964).
PR2889.D4 [Original and East]
PR2889.D42 [West]

ShN *Shakespeare Newsletter.* Washington, D.C. [place varies]: Shakespeare Association of America, 1951–. 6/yr. Reviews. Bibliography (see O–53).
PR2885.S48

SFNL *Shakespeare on Film Newsletter.* Vol. 1–. Burlington: University of Vermont, 1976–. 2/yr.
No LC number

SQ *Shakespeare Quarterly.* Washington, D.C.: Folger Shakespeare Library, 1950–. 4/yr. Reviews. Bibliography (see O–50). Cumulative Index to vols. 1–15 (1950–1964) by Martin Seymour Smith (New York: AMS, 1969). Formerly the *Shakespeare Association Bulletin*, vols. 1–24. New York: The Shakespeare Association of America, 1924–1949.
PR2885.S63

ShStud *Shakespeare Studies* (Tokyo). Vol. 1–. Tokyo: Shakespeare Society of Japan, Department of English, University of Tokyo, 1962–. Reviews.
PR2889.S54

ShakS *Shakespeare Studies: An Annual Gathering of Research, Criticism, and Reviews.* Vol. 1–. Colum-

bia: University of South Carolina Press, 1965–. 1/yr. Reviews. Bibliography (see O–52).
PR2885.S64

ShS   *Shakespeare Survey.* Vol. 1–. Cambridge: Cambridge University Press, 1948–. 1/yr. Bibliography (see O–51). Cumulative indexes to vols. 1–10 in vol. 10 and to vols. 11–20 in vol. 21.   PR2888.C3

SRO   *Shakespearean Research and Opportunities* [former title: *Shakespearean Research Opportunities*]. Riverside, Calif., and then New York: Report of the MLA Conference, 1965–. 1/yr. Bibliography (see O–53).   PR2885.S8

O–59 Some Frequently Recommended Bibliographies, Editions, Handbooks, Guides, and Other Reference Works in Shakespeare Studies.

Alden, Raymond Macdonald. *Shakespeare Handbook.* Revised and enlarged by O. J. Campbell. New York: F. S. Crofts, 1932.   PR2894.A6

Allen, Michael J. B., and Kenneth Muir, eds. *Shakespeare's Plays in Quarto: A Facsimile Edition of Copies Primarily from the Henry E. Huntington Library.* Berkeley, Los Angeles, London: University of California Press, 1981.   PR2750.C8 1981

Andrews, John F. *William Shakespeare: His World, His Work, His Influence.* 3 vols. New York: Scribner's, 1985.   PR2976.W5354 1985

THE ARDEN SHAKESPEARE

Craig, W. J., then Robert H. Case, ed. *Arden Edition of the Works of William Shakespeare.* 39 vols. London: Methuen, 1904–1924.   PR2753.C8 1904

Ellis-Fermor, Una, then Harold F. Brooks and Harold Jenkins, eds. *New Arden Edition of the Works of William Shakespeare, 1951–.* Individual editors for each title.
PR2753.C8

Bate, John. *How to Find Out about Shakespeare.* Oxford: Pergamon, 1968.   PR3112.Z99 R35

Berman, Ronald S. *Reader's Guide to Shakespeare's Plays.* Rev. ed. Chicago: Scott, Foresman, 1973. Text, editions, sources, criticism, and staging of each play.
Z8811.B45

Brooke, Tucker. *Shakespeare of Stratford: A Handbook for Students.* 1926.   PR2893.B7

Brown, John Russell. *Discovering Shakespeare: A New Guide to the Plays.* New York: Columbia University Press, 1981.   PR3091.B68 1981

Bullough, Geoffrey. *Narrative and Dramatic Sources of Shakespeare.* 8 vols. New York: Columbia University Press, 1957–1974.   PR2952.B8

Campbell, James Oscar, and Edward G. Quinn, eds. *Reader's Encyclopedia of Shakespeare.* New York: Crowell, 1966. Published under the title *Shakespeare Encyclopaedia.* London: Methuen, 1966. A-Z with appendixes on chronology, document transcripts, and a thirty-page selected bibliography.   PR2892.C3

Chambers, Edmund K. *William Shakespeare: A Study of Facts and Problems.* 2 vols. Oxford: Clarendon Press, 1930. Index by Beatrice White, to this and to Chambers's *Elizabethan Stage,* 4 vols. (Oxford: Clarendon Press, 1923). London: Oxford University Press, 1934.   PR2894.C44

Charney, Maurice. *How to Read Shakespeare.* New York: McGraw-Hill, 1971.   PR2987.C47

Clark, Sandra, ed. *Hutchinson Shakespeare Dictionary: An A-Z Guide to Shakespeare's Plays.* London: Hutchinson, 1986.   PR2892.H88 1986

Craig, Hardin, and David Bevington, eds. *Complete Works of Shakespeare.* 3d ed. Glenview, Ill.: Scott Foresman, 1980.   PR2754.C7 1980

Fox, Levi, ed. *Shakespeare Handbook.* Boston: G. K. Hall, 1987.   PR2976.S3374 1987

Frye, Robert M. *Shakespeare: The Art of the Dramatist.* Boston: Houghton Mifflin, 1970.   PR2893.F4

Granville-Barker, Harley. *More Prefaces to Shakespeare.* Edited by Edward M. Moore. Princeton, N. J.: Princeton University Press, 1974.
PR2976.G668 1974

———. *Prefaces to Shakespeare.* 2 vols. London: Sidgwick and Jackson, 1927–1947. 2 vols. Reprint. Princeton, N. J.: Princeton University Press, 1946–1947.   PR2976.G67

Granville-Barker, Harley, and G. B. Harrison. *Companion to Shakespeare Studies.* Cambridge: Cambridge University Press, 1934.   PR2894.G7

Halliday, Frank Ernest. *Shakespeare Companion, 1564-1964.* 2d ed. London: Duckworth, 1964. PR2892.H3

Harbage, Alfred. *William Shakespeare: A Reader's Guide.* New York: Farrar, Strauss. 1963, 1971.
PR2976.H32

———, ed. *Complete Works of William Shakespeare.* Baltimore: Penguin Books, 1969. One-volume editions of works issued in separate volumes 1956–1967, each with its own editor.   PR2754.H33 1969

Hinman, Charlton. *Printing and Proof-Reading of the First Folio of Shakespeare.* 2 vols. Oxford: Clarendon Press, 1963.   Z8813.H5

Hosely, Richard, Richard Knowles, and Ruth McQueen. *Shakespeare Variorum Handbook: A Manual of Editorial Practice.* New York: MLA, 1971.   PR3071.M65

Luce, Morton. *Handbook to the Works of William Shakespeare.* London: G. Bell, 1907.   PR2976.L8

McLean, Andrew M. *Shakespeare: Annotated Bibliographies and Media Guide for Teachers.* Urbana, Ill.: NCTE, 1980.   Z8813.M32

Martin, Michael R., and Richard C. Harrier. *Concise Encyclopedic Guide to Shakespeare.* New York: Horizon, 1971. Includes glossary of critics, scholars, and actors; modern productions, list of composers of music based on Shakespeare; discography.   PR2892.M39

Muir, Kenneth, and S. Schoenbaum, eds. *New Companion to Shakespeare Studies.* Cambridge: Cambridge University Press, 1971.   PR2890.M8

NEW ARDEN SHAKESPEARE (see THE ARDEN SHAKESPEARE)

THE NEW CAMBRIDGE SHAKESPEARE

Wilson, J. Dover, and Arthur T. Quiller-Couch, eds. *New Cambridge Edition of the Works of William Shakespeare.* 39 vols. Cambridge: Cambridge University Press, 1921–1963. Paperbound edition, 1968–. One play per volume; various editors.   PR2753.Q3

NEW CLARENDON EDITION

Houghton, R. E. C., ed. *New Clarendon Shakespeare.* Oxford: Clarendon Press, 1938–. One play per volume; various editors.   LC numbers vary

NEW PENGUIN SHAKESPEARE

Spencer, Terence J. B., ed. *New Penguin Shakespeare*. Harmondsworth: Penguin, 1967–. One play per volume; various editors.   LC numbers vary

NEW VARIORUM EDITION (see VARIORUM EDITION)

Onions, Charles Talbot. *Shakespeare Glossary*. 2d ed., rev. Oxford: Clarendon Press, 1919.   PR2892.O6

ORIGINAL-SPELLING EDITION

Wells, Stanley, and Gary Taylor, eds. *William Shakespeare: The Complete Works: Original-Spelling Edition*. Oxford: Oxford University Press, 1987.
PR2754.W45 1986

OXFORD COMPLETE SHAKESPEARE

Wells, Stanley, and Gary Taylor, eds. *William Shakespeare: The Complete Works*. Oxford: Clarendon Press, 1986.
PR2754.W45 1986b

OXFORD [OLD-SPELLING EDITION OF] SHAKESPEARE

Muir, Kenneth, ed. *Oxford Shakespeare Press, 1982–*. One play per volume; various editors.   LC numbers vary

Parrott, Thomas Marc. *William Shakespeare: A Handbook*. Rev. ed. New York: Scribner, 1955.
PR2894.P3 1955

Quinn, Edward, James Ruoff, and Joseph Grennen, eds. *Major Shakespearean Tragedies: A Critical Bibliography*. New York: Free Press, 1973.   Z8812.Q5

RIVERSIDE SHAKESPEARE

Evans, G. Blakemore, ed. *Riverside Shakespeare*. Boston: Houghton Mifflin, 1974.   PR2754.E9 1974

Schoenbaum, Samuel. *Shakespeare, the Globe, and the World*. New York: Oxford University Press, 1979.
PR2933.F64 S3

———. *Shakespeare's Lives*. Oxford: Clarendon Press, 1970.   PR2894.S3

———. *William Shakespeare: A Documentary Life*. Oxford: Clarendon and Scolar Press, 1975. Compact Edition. Oxford: Clarendon Press, 1975.
PR2893.S3 1975b and PR2893.S3

Shabert, Ina, ed. *Shakespear-Handbuch: Die Zeit—Der Mensch—Das Werk—Die Nachwelt*. Stuttgart, 1972.

Shattuck, Charles Harlen. *Shakespeare Promptbooks: A Descriptive Catalogue*. Urbana: University of Illinois Press, 1965.   PR3091.S4

VARIORUM EDITION OF SHAKESPEARE

Furness, Horace H., and H. H. Furness, Jr., eds. *Variorum Edition of Shakespeare*. Philadelphia: Lippincott, 1871–1928. Hyder E. Rollins, then James G. McManaway, ed. *New Variorum Edition of the Works of William Shakespeare*. New York: The Modern Language Association, 1929–. One play per volume; various editiors.   PR2753.F5

Velz, John W. *Shakespeare and the Classical Tradition: A Critical Guide to Commentary, 1660–1960*. Minneapolis: University of Minnesota Press, 1968.
Z8811.V4 1968

Wells, Stanley W. *Shakespeare: A Reading Guide*. London: Oxford University Press, 1969.   Z8811.W43

———, and Gary Taylor, et al. *William Shakespeare: A Textual Companion*. Oxford: Clarendon Press, 1987.
PR3071.W44 1987

Wilson, F. P. *Shakespeare and the New Bibliography*. Revised and edited by Helen Gardner. Oxford: Clarendon Press, 1970.   Z8813.W75

Wright, Louis B., and Virginia A. LaMar. *Folger Guide to Shakespeare*. New York: Washington Square Press, 1969.   PR2987.W7

Zesmer, David M. *Guide to Shakespeare*. New York: Barnes and Noble, 1976.   PR2976.Z46 1976

V.   PROSE AND PROSE FICTION

See also section W.

O–61 **Harner, James L. *English Renaissance Prose Fiction, 1500–1660: An Annotated Bibliography of Criticism***. Boston: G. K. Hall, 1978.   Z2014.F4 H37

A total of 3,236 annotated entries present editions and studies published 1800–1976 of prose fiction originally written in English, or translated into English, or printed in England from 1500–1660. Entries include doctoral dissertations; reprints and later editions are excluded unless of special importance. The entries are disposed into four main sections, treating Bibliographies; Anthologies; General Studies; and finally Authors, Translators, or Titles (of anonymous works). The last section, by far the largest, cites—under the author or title—bibliographies, editions, and studies of each individual work or group of works.

A supplement, *English Renaissance Prose Fiction, 1500-1660: An Annotate Bibliography of Criticism (1976- 1983)* was published by G. K. Hall in 1985 [Z2014.F4 H37 1985]. Both volumes are indexed by persons, anonymous works, and subjects, but the supplement is more fully indexed than the original volume.

O–65 **O'Dell, Sterg. *Chronological List of Prose Fiction in English Printed in England and Other Countries, 1475–1640***. Cambridge: Massachusetts Institute of Technology Press, 1954.   Z2014.F5033

Compiled from Esdaile (W–14), the *Short Title Catalogue* (C–5), and several other published sources, this list is arranged in chronological order from the date of the first volume printed in 1475. Prose fiction is defined as "imaginative narrative not in verse." An introduction on prose fiction in Elizabethan England precedes the list.

O–67 **Mish, Charles C. *English Prose Fiction, 1600–1700: A Chronological Checklist***. 2d ed., rev. Charlottesville: Bibliographical Society of the University of Virginia, 1967.
Z2014.F4 M58 1967

Originally published in mimeographed form in 1952, this checklist is basically a chronological rearrangement of the seventeenth century material in Esdaile (W–14), with a number of added entries. Entries are listed alphabetically by author or title catchword under each year; undated works are assigned a date in brackets. Entries include shortened title, name of publisher, and reference to *STC* (C–5) or Wing (C–7) numbers, or to catalogs or other sources of information about the work. Finally, there is a statement about editions unless there was only one.

VI. NEO-LATIN STUDIES

See also section L.II. and section N.VII.

O–70 **Ijsewijn, Jozef.** *Companion to Neo-Latin Studies.* Amsterdam: North-Holland, 1977.   PA8020.I37

This volume presents a compendium of basic factual and bibliographic information on Neo-Latin literature in Europe and America from fourteenth-century Italian humanism to the present. A survey of Neo-Latin literature around the world along with a survey of Neo-Latin studies and an anthology of characteristic texts are also presented. Bibliographical entries are classified by subject and/or area and are presented at the end of the paragraph, section, or chapter on that subject or area. Most such bibliographies are in two parts, "general" and "authors: editions and monographs."

The chapters are as follows: 1, Classical, Mediaeval, and Neo-Latin; 2, Bibliographical Aids; 3, A Historical Survey of Neo-Latin Literature; 4, Texts and Editions; 5, Language and Style; 6, Prosody and Metrics; 7, Literary Forms and Genres; 8, Scholarly and Scientific Works in Neo-Latin; 9, A Historical Survey of Neo-Latin Studies; and 10, An Anthology of Neo-Latin Texts from Petrarch to Herman Weller (1878-1956). The volume concludes with an index of names.

O–71 **"Instrumentum Bibliographicum."** *Humanistica Lovaniensia: Journal of Neo-Latin Studies,* vol. 23–. Louvain: Louvain University Press [publisher varies], 1974–.
          PA8001.H8

This annual classified bibliography includes books, articles, dissertations, and reviews on Neo-Latin studies. It is classified into six main sections, as follows: 1. General; 2. Poetry (General, Authors); 3. Theatre (General, Authors); 4. Prose (General, Authors); 5. Inscriptions; 6. Work in Progress. Entries within sections are alphabetical according to the name of the Neo-Latin author being edited or commented upon. In addition, the journal carries a variety of miscellaneous bibliographical lists and notes, including "Neo Latina Recens Edita" and "Opera Quae Parantur."

Another source of serial bibliography for Neo-Latin studies is the "Neo-Latin News," vol. 1–, no. 1– (1954–), published as a quarterly supplement to *Seventeenth Century News* (O–9) from vol. 12, no. 2 on. It contains short reviews, bibliographical notices, and descriptive abstracts of recent publications.

In addition, there is a separate section on "Neo-Latin" in the annual *Year's Work in Modern Language Studies* (L–52).

O–72 **Reviews of Research in Neo-Latin Studies.**

The most recent reviews have been published biennially by R. Desmed under the title "Chronique neo-latine," in *Latomus,* from volume 29 (1970) on [PA2002.L3]. Earlier reviews include W. L. Grant, "Scholarship in the Renaissance: Neo-Latin Studies," *Renaissance News* 16 (1963): 102–106; and Don Cameron Allen, "Latin Literature, Renaissance Studies," *MLQ* 2 (1941): 403–420.

O–78 **Scholarly Journals in Neo-Latin Studies.**

Humanistica Lovaniensia: Journal of Neo-Latin Studies. Vol. 1–. Louvain: Louvain University Press. Reviews. Bibliography (see O–71).   PA8001.H8

Latomus: Revue d'études latines. Brussels: Librairie Falk fils, 1937–. 4/yr. Reviews. Bibliographical reviews (see O–72).   PR2002.L3
Neo-Latin News. Vol. 1–. University Park: Pennsylvania State University, 1954–. 4/yr. Reviews. Bibliography (see O–71). Published as a supplement to *Seventeenth Century News,* vol. 12–.   PR1.S47

A list of periodicals carrying articles in Neo-Latin studies was published by René Hoven, "Les études neo-latines dans le monde," in *Les études classiques* 42 (1974): 163–172.

O–79 **Some Frequently Recommended Works on Neo-Latin Literature** (see also N–79).

Bradner, Leicester. *Musae Anglicanae: A History of Anglo-Latin Poetry, 1500–1925.* New York: Modern Language Association, 1940. See also Bradner's supplementary checklist published in the *Library,* 5th ser., 22 (1967): 93–103.   PA8052.B7

Grant, W. Leonard. *Neo-Latin Literature and the Pastoral.* Chapel Hill: University of North Carolina Press, 1965.
          PA8027.G7

International Congress of Neo-Latin Studies, 1st. *Acta Conventus Neo- Latini Lovaniensis: Proceedings of the First International Congress of Neo-Latin Studies.* Louvain: Louvain University Press, 1973.
          PA2901.I5 1971

———, 2nd. *Acta Conventus Neo-Latini Amstelodamensis.* Munich: Fink, 1979.   PA8002.I57 1973

———, 3rd. *Acta Conventus Neo-Latini Turonensis.* Paris: J. Vrin, 1980.   PA8002.I57 1976

———, 4th. *Acta Conventus Neo-Latini Bononiensis.* Binghamton, N. Y.: Center for Medieval and Early Renaissance Studies, 1985.   PA8002.I57 1979

———, 5th. *Acta Conventus Neo-Latini Sanctandriani.* Binghamton, N. Y.: Medieval and Renaissance Texts and Studies, 1986.   PA8002.I57 1982

———, 6th. *Acta Conventus Neo-Latini Guelpherbytana.* Binghamton, N. Y.: Center for Medieval and Early Renaissance Studies, 1988.   PA8002.I57 1985

Laurens, Pierre, and Claudie Balavoire, eds. and trs. *Musae Reduces: Anthologie de la poésie latine dans l'Europe de la Renaissance: Textes choisis.* 2 vols. Leiden: Brill, 1975.   PA8174.M8

Myers, Weldon T. *Relations of Latin and English as Living Languages in England during the Age of Milton.* Dayton, Va.: Ruebush-Elkins, 1966.   PA2847.E5 M8

Nichols, Fred J., ed. and trans. *Anthology of Neo-Latin Poetry.* New Haven: Yale University Press, 1979.
          PA8164.A5

Van Tieghem, P. *La littérature latine de la Renaissance: Étude d'histoire littéraire européenne.* 2d ed. Paris: Droz, 1966.   PA8040.V3 1966

Wright, F. A., and T. A. Sinclair. *History of Later Latin Literature from the Middle of the Fourth to the End of the Seventeenth Century.* London: Macmillan, 1931.
          PA8015.W7 1931a

LITERATURE OF THE RESTORATION AND EIGHTEENTH CENTURY

See also works in section C.II, British National Bibliography; in section D on Early Periodicals; in section F, History; in section G, Biography; in section H, Manuscripts, Archives, and Paleography; and in section I on Language, Linguistics, and Philology. See also numerous references in sections K, L, and M, including the *MLA International Bibliography* (L–50), the MHRA *Annual Bibliography of English Language and Literature* (M–21), and the *Year's Work in English Studies* (M–22). See additional references on restoration and eighteenth-century poetry and poetics in section T, drama and theater in section U, and prose and prose fiction in section W. See also references on restoration and eighteenth-century literary and rhetorical theory in section X and on restoration and eighteenth-century printing, publishing, and bookselling in section Y.

I.   GENERAL

P–3 Surveys of Recent Scholarship in the Period of the Restoration and Eighteenth Century.

After ending its part in the publication of the annual eighteenth century current bibliography (P–5), *Philological Quarterly* for several years published one issue that contained a series of review essays on recent scholarship. The annual issues and their contents are as follows:

Vol. 55 (1976): "Studies in English Drama, 1660–1800," pp. 451–488, by Robert D. Hume; "Studies in Restoration Literature," pp. 489–506, by Phillip Harth; "Studies in Eighteenth Century Fiction," pp. 507–532, by J. Paul Hunter; "Studies in Augustan Literature," pp. 533–552, by William Kupersmith; "Literary Criticism and Intellectual Foregrounds," pp. 553–566, by Paul K. Alkon; and "The Age of Johnson in 1975," pp. 567–583, by Carey McIntosh.

Vol. 56 (1977): "Studies in Restoration Literature," pp. 427–437, by Philip Harth; "Studies in English Drama, 1660–1800," pp. 438–469, by Robert D. Hume; "Augustan Studies in 1976," pp. 470–497, by William Kupersmith; "Studies in Eighteenth-Century Fiction, 1976," pp. 498–539, by J. Paul Hunter; and "Political Consciousness in the Age of Johnson: A Review Article," pp. 540–553, by Carey McIntosh.

Vol. 57 (1978): "Studies in Restoration Literature," pp. 415–436, by Dustin Griffin; "Studies in English Drama, 1660–1800," pp. 437–472, by Robert D. Hume; "Augustan Studies," pp. 473–492, by William Kupersmith; "Fiction and Its Discontents," pp. 493–526, by J. Paul Hunter; and "The Age of Johnson in 1977," pp. 527–544, by Felicity A. Nussbaum.

Vol. 58 (1979): "Restoration Studies in 1978," pp. 377–402, by Dustin Griffin; "Studies in Restoration and Eighteenth-Century Drama, 1978," pp. 403–428, by Judith Milhous; "Studies in Eighteenth-Century Fiction, 1978," pp. 429–468, by Susan Staves; and "The Age of Johnson in 1978," pp. 469–500, by Robert E. Kelley.

In addition to these reviews, there are a number of single review essays that might be noted. These include:

Brückman, Patricia C. "Exuberant Mixtures: Some Recent Studies in the Eighteenth Century." *UTQ* 46 (1976/77): 83–91.

Clifford, James L. "The Eighteenth Century." *MLQ* 26 (1965): 111–134.

———. "The Eighteenth Century." In Lewis Leary, ed., *Contemporary Literary Scholarship*, pp. 83–108. New York: Appleton-Century-Crofts, 1958 [PR77.N3].

Hume, Robert D. "English Drama and Theatre, 1660–1800: New Directions in Research." *Theatre Survey* 23.1 (1982): 71–100.

P–4 "Recent Studies in Restoration and 18th Century Literature." *SEL*, Summer issue, 1961–.   PR1.S82

These annual bibliographical essays comment on recent work, normally of the previous year, with emphases chosen by their individual authors. To date, the following essays have been prepared:

Vol. 1 (1961), pp. 115–141. By Donald J. Greene.
Vol. 2 (1962), pp. 359–384. By William Frost.
Vol. 3 (1963), pp. 433–447. By Robert Halsband.
Vol. 4 (1964), pp. 497–517. By Patricia M. Spacks.
Vol. 5 (1965), pp. 553–574. By Martin Price.
Vol. 6 (1966), pp. 599–628. By Frederick W. Hilles.

Vol. 7 (1967), pp. 531–558. By Ronald H. Paulson.

Vol. 8 (1968), pp. 551–572. By Frank Brady.

Vol. 9 (1969), pp. 539–571. By Henry Knight Miller.

Vol. 10 (1970), pp. 605–636. By Marshall Waingrow.

Vol. 11 (1971), pp. 563–593. By W. B. Coley (with an abstract).

Vol. 12 (1972), pp. 567–590. By Robert Rodgers and Richard N. Ramsey (with an abstract).

Vol. 13 (1973), pp. 550–573. By William Frost (with an abstract).

Vol. 14 (1974), pp. 458–475. By Calhoun Winton.

Vol. 15 (1975), pp. 505–527. By Paul Fussell.

Vol. 16 (1976), pp. 517–544. By Ronald Paulson.

Vol. 17 (1977), pp. 531–569. By Leo Braudy.

Vol. 18 (1978), pp. 553–593. By G. S. Rousseau.

Vol. 19 (1979), pp. 533–563. By Eric Rothstein.

Vol. 20 (1980), pp. 517–552. By J. Paul Hunter.

Vol. 21 (1981), pp. 513–539. By Richard B. Schwartz.

Vol. 22 (1982), pp. 531–558. By Maximilian Novak.

Vol. 23 (1983), pp. 495–527. By Ronald Paulson.

Vol. 24 (1984), pp. 583–604. By Morris R. Brownell.

Vol. 25 (1985), pp. 671–717. By Howard D. Weinbrot.

Vol. 26 (1986), pp. 537–587. By Paul J. Korshin.

Vol. 27 (1987), pp. 503–553. By Robert Folkenflick.

Vol. 28 (1988), pp. 513–557. By Robert D. Hume.

P–5 **"English Literature: 1660–1800—A Current Bibliography [for 1925–1969]."** New title: **"The Eighteenth Century: A Current Bibliography 1970–."** *Philological Quarterly*, vols. 1–49. Iowa City: University of Iowa, 1926–1972.

P1.P55

This, the oldest annual serial bibliography in English studies, was founded by R. S. Crane and published in the pages of *PQ*, or as a separate issue (1970–1974), until its publication was assumed by the American Society for Eighteenth Century Studies in 1975. The original annual bibliographies were designed to include the "more significant" work done in the preceding year. Entries were originally grouped into four sections: I. Bibliographical Aids; II. General Studies; III. Studies of Authors; and IV. Studies Relating to the Political and Social Environment. Within sections, entries are arranged alphabetically by author and give complete bibliographical information along with descriptive and evaluative annotation and reference to reviews. In the case of important or methodologically interesting works, there are often full-length signed reviews presented in the pages of the bibliography. In subsequent years the number of sections increased to six, with the addition of a section on Continental Backgrounds and one on Philosophy, Science, and Religion.

The annual bibliographies for 1925–1969 are cumulated in six volumes under the title *English Literature, 1660–1800: A Bibliography of Modern Studies* (Princeton, N. J.: Princeton University Press, 1950–1972) [Z2011.E62]. The cumulations reprint the annual issues without change, save that continuous pagination is introduced to facilitate indexing. Volumes 1 and 2 contain the annual bibliographies 1925–1950 and are indexed at the end of volume 2. Volumes 3 and 4 reprint those for 1951–1960 and are indexed at the end of volume 4; volumes 5 and 6 contain 1961–1969 and are indexed at the end of volume 6.

When the bibliography came under the sponsorship of the ASECS in 1971, its scope widened to include all of eighteenth-century studies, and its title, *Eighteenth Century: A Current Bibliography*, reflects the changed scope. The sections are now six: 1. Printing and Bibliographical Studies; 2. Historical, Social, and Economic Studies; 3. Philosophy, Science, and Religion; 4. The Fine Arts; 5. Literary Studies; 6. Individual Authors. Studies concerned with any part or all of Europe are included, and authors include the significant writers of England, France, Germany, Spain, Italy, Russia, and Eastern Europe. The volumes for 1971–1974 were published as single bound issues of *Philological Quarterly*, volumes 50–54. With the volume for 1975, known as New Series, volume 1, sponsorship and publishing responsibility shifted gradually first to the ASECS and then to AMS Press in New York, which now publishes the annual volume [Z5579.6.E36]. The volumes covering from 1970 on have not been cumulated, but each has a full index comparable to those in the cumulations for 1925–1950, 1951–1960, and 1961–1970. Currently the bibliography contains some 5,000 entries, about half of which are critically annotated. Volumes now appear three to five years after the year of coverage, but there is hope that this delay may be reduced. A full account of this important and influential bibliography by Donald Greene, "'More Than a Necessary Chore': *The Eighteenth-Century Current Bibliography* in Retrospect and Prospect," was published in *ECS* 10 (1976): 94–110.

P–7 **"Some Current Publications."** *Restoration: Studies in English Literary Culture, 1660–1700*, vol. 1–. Knoxville: University of Tennessee, 1977–.   PR437.R47

Since it began publication, this semiannual journal has included in each issue a classified, descriptively annotated bibliography prepared by various compilers of recent studies, "Some Current Publications." Classes have changed; currently there are seven: Individuals (alphabetically by name); Bibliography, Compilations, and Anthologies; Drama; Nondramatic Literature; History, Pedagogy, Philosophy, Politics, Religion, and Science; The Colonies; The Sister Arts. Entries are given alphabetically by author in each section. Included are books, articles, and dissertations. There are numerous cross-references. The quality of the bibliography varies from one contributor to another.

In addition to the enumerative bibliography, *Restoration* carries occasional review essays under the rubric "Essential Studies of Restoration [Drama etc.]." The journal also includes notes and announcements, some of bibliographical interest.

P–8 **"Recent Articles," "Foreign Reviews," "Book Reviews," and "Books Briefly Noted."** *Scriblerian* [after 1971: *and the Kit-Cats*], vol. 1–. Philadelphia: Temple University, 1968–.   PR445.S3

Since it began publication, this semiannual news journal has included classified bibliographies of recent articles with signed descriptive and evaluative annotation; reviews by foreign correspondent editors of "Scriblerian" studies by scholars neither British nor American; and both extended signed reviews and briefer signed accounts of books on late-seventeenth- and early-eighteenth-century English literature and related fields. Subdivisions in a 1981 "recent articles" section include Gay, Pope, Swift, the Kit-Cats, Dryden, Rochester, Defoe and the Early Novelists, Miscellaneous, History, Philosophy. The intention of the editors is that every book, article, paper, or other item about any of the Scriblerians be noted. Since 1971 similar completeness of coverage has been attempted for the Kit-Cats and since 1972 for Dryden.

All of the bibliographical materials are classified and their authors indexed in the quinquennial bibliographies and indexes to volumes 1–5 (1968–1973), 6–10 (1973–1978), and 11–15 (1978–1983). The index to volumes 1–5 is in two parts, the first citing all materials on Individual Authors; History; Anthologies; Collections of Essays; Essays on the Drama; Miscellaneous; and Societies. Part 2 is an index of scholars' names. The Bibliography and Index for 1973–1978 contains a total of 1,342 serially numbered articles, classified into sections on Anthologies, The Arts, Bibliographies, The City, Critical Theory, Drama, Errata, Essay Collections, Genre and Theme Studies, History, Letters, Meetings, Miscellaneous, Studies of Poetry, Satire-Irony-Comedy, and lists of items on Individual Authors. These are followed by an index of scholars' names. The Bibliography and Index for 1979–1983 is in production.

P–9 **"Some New Books," "Recent Articles," etc.** *Johnsonian Newsletter,* vol. 1–. New York: Columbia University, 1940–.   No LC number

Each issue of this, the oldest newsletter or journal dedicated to a single author, has from its inception included enumerations with descriptive and evaluative reviews of new books on Johnsonian studies. Included have been most studies of mid- and later-eighteenth-century English literature and culture, lists of recent articles on Boswell and Johnson, on various other important figures of the mid and later eighteenth century, and on miscellaneous topics related to Johnsonian studies. In addition, there are numerous notes, announcements, and queries of bibliographical interest.

P–10 **Cambridge Bibliography of English Literature.** Vol. 2, 1660–1800. Edited by F. W. Bateson. Cambridge: Cambridge University Press, 1941.   Z2011.B3 1941 vol.2

This bibliography is in seven main parts. The first part, Introduction, has eight sections: Bibliographies, Literary Histories, and Special Studies; Literary Theory; Literary Relations with the Continent; Medieval Influences; Book Production and Distribution; Education, 1660–1800; The Social Background; and The Political Background. Part 2, The Poetry, has eight divisions: Recent Criticism: Surveys and Special Studies; Miscellanies, Anthologies and Collections of Poetry; The Restoration Poets; Minor Verse, 1660–1700; The Early Eighteenth-Century Poets; Minor Verse, 1700–1750; The Later Eighteenth-Century Poets; and Minor Verse, 1750–1800. Part 3, The Drama, has nine divisions: General Introduction; Theatres and Actors; The Restoration Dramatists; Minor Restoration Drama, 1660–1700; The Early Eighteenth-Century Dramatists; Minor Drama, 1700–1750; The Later Eighteenth Century Dramatists; Minor Drama, 1750–1800; and Adaptations and Translations, 1660–1800.

Part 4, Prose Fiction, is in four sections: Recent Criticism; The Principal Novelists; Minor Fiction and Translations; and Children's Books. Part 5, Miscellaneous Prose, has seven divisions: Essayists and Pamphleteers; Periodical Publications—Dialogue Papers, the Periodical Essays, Magazines and Reviews, the Newspaper; Books of Travel; Translations into English; The Literature of Sport; Diarists and Letter-Writers; Religious Prose: Devotional and Controversial. The sixth part concerns History, Philosophy, Science, and Other Forms of Learning and has six sections: Historians, Biographers, and Antiquaries; Literary Historians and Antiquaries; Classical and Oriental Scholars; The Philosophers; The Literature of Science; and Legal Literature. Part 7, finally, is on Scottish Literature and has three sections: General Introduction; Poetry and Drama; and Prose.

Additional materials for most of these sections will be found in the *Supplement* (1957), pages 361–516. This volume and its supplement have been almost but not entirely replaced by the corresponding volume of the *NCBEL* (P–11). The original volume, though not the supplement, is indexed in the *CBEL Index,* which is volume 4 (1941) of the *CBEL.*

P–11 **New Cambridge Bibliography of English Literature.** Vol. 2, 1660–1800. Edited by George Watson. Cambridge: Cambridge University Press, 1971.   Z2011.N45 vol.2

This volume of the *NCBEL* (M–11), the second to be published (with entries current to 1968 or so), is in six main parts. The first, Introduction, has five sections: General Works; Literary Theory; Literary Relations with the Continent; Medieval Influences; Book Production and Distribution. Part 2, Poetry, is in eight sections: Histories and Surveys; Miscellanies, Anthologies, and Collections of Poetry; Restoration Poetry; Minor Poetry 1660–1700; Early Eighteenth-Century Poetry; Minor Poetry 1700–1750; Later Eighteenth-Century Poetry; Minor Poetry 1750–1800. Part 3, Drama, is in nine sections: General Introduction; Theatres and Actors; Restoration Drama; Minor Restoration Drama 1660–1700; Early Eighteenth-Century Drama; Minor Drama 1700–1750; Later Eighteenth-Century Drama; Minor Drama 1750–1800; and Adaptations and Translations.

The novel is treated in part 4, in four sections: General Works; The Principal Novelists; Minor Fiction; and Children's Books. There are fourteen divisions in part 5, Prose: Essayists and Pamphleteers; Periodical Publications; Travel; Translations into English; Sport; Letters, Diaries, Autobiographies and Memoirs; Religion; History; Literary Studies; Classical and Oriental Studies; Philosophy; Science; Law; and Education. Finally, there are three sections in part 6, Scottish Literature: General Introduction; Poetry and Drama; Prose. A limited index concludes the volume; a more complete index will be found in the *NCBEL Index,* which is volume 5 (1977) of the *NCBEL.* Here, as in the other volumes, a list of contributors following the preface identifies the initials of, in this case, a total of fifty-two contributing bibliographers.

Reception of this volume has been mixed. Basic criticism has been of the inconsistencies and inaccuracies that make this standard and fundamental work more imperfect than a work of its standing should be. See Eric Rothstein's review, *MP* 71 (1973): 176–186. See also the review by George Rousseau in *SBHT* 17 (1976): 149–151.

P–12 **Dyson, H. V. D., and John Butt.** *Augustans and Romantics, 1689–1830, with Chapters on Art, Economics, and Philosophy* by Geoffrey Webb, F. J. Fisher, and H. A. Hodges. 3rd rev. ed. *Introductions to English Literature,* edited by Bonamy Dobrée, vol. 3. London: Cressett Press, 1961.   PR83.I615 vol.3

Like the other volumes in this series (see M–15, N–12, O–12, Q–30, and R–12), this work, first published in 1940, contains both a discursive account (Introduction: Augustans; The Age of Johnson and the Close of the Eighteenth Century; Romantics; British Philosophy, 1689–1830; Eighteenth Century Art; The Economic Backgrounds of Eighteenth Century Literature) and a primary and secondary bibliography. The bibliography, done in the form of bibliographical essays, is classified as follows: Poetry; Imitation and Parody; Criticism; The Novel; Philosophy; Political and Economic Thought; Historians; Political Pamphleteers; Journalism; Biography; Autobiography and Memoirs; Travel; Diaries; Letters; Drama; The Blue Stockings. Subdivisions treat authors' works and biography and criticism. There is an index of names, anonymous titles, and a few subjects.

P–13 **Averley, G., et al.** *Eighteenth-Century British Books: A Subject Catalogue Extracted from the British Museum General Catalogue of Printed Books.* 4 vols. London: Dawson, 1979.   Z1016.B75 1979

To compile this work, the editors assigned up to three three-digit subject codes based on the Dewey decimal classification system to each eighteenth-century work cited in a main entry or cross-reference of the British Museum General Catalogue (B–41). Entries give the author, an epithet, and dates; the subject code, along with a code indicating the date of the first edition; and an enumeration of all editions, formats, places of publication, translations, and other related information found in the *General Catalogue*. The four volumes are arranged in subject order, as follows: vol. 1: Generalities 000–099; Philosophy 100–199; Religion 200–299; vol. 2: Social Sciences 300–399; Pure Sciences 500–599; Technology 600–699; The Arts 700–799; vol. 3: Language 400–499; Literature 800–899; and vol. 4: Geography and History 900–999. With cross-references and multiple classifications, it is estimated that the four volumes contain more than 200,000 entries.

Though this work has some utility, there being limited general-subject access to eighteenth-century books apart from the subject portion of Watt's *Bibliotheca Britannica* (A–30), its utility is drastically limited by the limits of the three-digit code, which are often considerable. Thus, for example, 821 is English poetry and 942 is English history. In cases of broad subjects such as these with thousands of entries under them, entries are arranged chronologically by year of first edition and then alphabetically by author or title within that year. Those published before 1701 or after 1800 are listed in two sections preceding the list for 1701 and following the list for 1800. The greatest utility will be found in locating works on subjects about which relatively little was written, or in locating works on broad subjects published in a particular year or within a limited number of years.

P–14 **Bond, Donald F.** *Age of Dryden.* [A Goldentree Bibliography.] New York: Appleton-Century-Crofts, 1970.
                                                    Z2012.B74

This closed, selective bibliography designed for the use of the graduate student covers the period of the Restoration, 1660–1700. Emphasis is on the recent works; the closing date is 1967/68. Entries are rarely annotated, though works of special importance are marked with an asterisk. There are thirteen divisions, as follows: Bibliography and Surveys of Scholarship; Surveys and Reference Works; Historical Background; Social and Cultural Background; Literary Criticism; John Dryden; Poetry (Bibliography, Collections, General Studies, Individual Poets); Drama (similar subdivisions); Fine Arts; Philosophy; Religion; Science; Miscellaneous Prose Writers. In the last four sections there are bibliographies of individual authors in addition to general works. Within divisions, entries are in alphabetical order. There are indexes of authors and of subjects.

P–15 **Lund, Roger D.** *Restoration and Early Eighteenth-Century English Literature, 1660–1740: A Selected Bibliography of Resource Materials.* New York: MLA, 1980.
                                                    Z2012.L88

This bibliography is a highly selective, briefly annotated guide to 380 current periodicals, bibliographies, concordances, and other reference resources published through 1978 for English literature 1660–1740 which are readily available. The entries are disposed into fifteen sections, as follows: Current Journals and Newsletters; Annual Bibliographies; General Bibliographies; Poetry; Drama; Fiction; Literary Criticism and Language Study; Translation; Publishing and Bookselling; Newspapers and Periodicals; Art and Music; History, Biography, and Autobiography; Religious Literature; Miscellaneous Bibliographies; and Individual Authors (bibliographies and concordances only). Coverage is uneven, and there are errors of omission.

P–16 **Bond, Donald F.** *Eighteenth Century.* [A Goldentree Bibliography.] Northbrook, Ill.: AHM Publishing, 1975.
                                                    Z2013.B63

This closed, selective bibliography is designed for the use of graduate students. The total of 2,916 serially numbered entries exclude the works of eighteenth-century novelists, which are to be treated in another bibliography in the Goldentree series. Blake is treated in the Romantic bibliography (Q–21); and because of the availability of full-length bibliographies for each, primary works of Pope, Swift, and Johnson are treated more casually. The entries are disposed in two parts, the first containing general matters, the second primary and secondary bibliographies on individual authors, major and minor. The divisions of part 1 are as follows: Bibliographies and Surveys of Scholarship; Collected Studies; Histories of Literature and General Studies; The Question of Nomenclature; Backgrounds; Romanticism and Related Ideas; Poetry; Drama; Literary Criticism; Periodicals; The Writing of History; Biography and Autobiography; Satire; Humor; Rhetoric and Oratory; Letter Writing; Language and Prose Style. Part 2 treats a total of more than 100 authors. Entries of special importance are designated with an asterisk. Subject and author indexes conclude the volume.

P–17 **Tobin, James E.** *Eighteenth Century English Literature and Its Cultural Backgrounds: A Bibliography.* New York: Fordham University Press, 1939.   Z2013.T62

This checklist, useful but not authoritative, presents an odd and incomplete, selective, unannotated but classified bibliography of primary and secondary materials disposed into two parts, The Cultural and Critical Background and Bibliographies of Individual Authors. Part 1 is disposed into ten sections, as follows: I. Historical Background (History, Politics, and Economics); II. Social Thought (Travel Books and Foreign Society, Taste, Philosophy, Religion and Science, Sociology, Education); III. Memoirs, Diaries, and Anecdotes; IV. Criticism; V. Poetry; VI. Prose; VII. Journalism; VIII. Drama; IX. Extra-National Relations; X. Further Bibliographical Aids. Asterisks identify those works that contain additional bibliographical materials. The volume concludes with an index. Additions were published by Donald F. Bond, *Library Quarterly* 10 (1940): 446–450.

Waldo Sumner Glock's *Eighteenth-Century English Literary Studies: A Bibliography* (Metuchen: Scarecrow, 1984) [Z2012.G56 1984] is an 850-page compilation of books and articles published 1925–1980 on twenty-five authors. Entries are culled from *ECCB* (P–5), *MLAIB* (L–50), *ABELL* (M–21), and *YWES* (M–22), and are selectively annotated.

Another earlier compilation of some use is Francesco Cordasco's *Register of Eighteenth Century Bibliographies and References: A Chronological Quarter-Century Survey Relating to English Literature, Booksellers, Newspapers, Periodicals, Printing and Publishing, Aesthetics, Art and Music, Economics, History and Science; A Preliminary Contribution* (Chicago: V. Giorgio, 1950) [Z1002.C78], which contains 523 serially numbered items disposed into two parts, one on General References and Bibliographies, the other citing Bibliographies and Bibliographical Aids for Eighteenth Century Studies published 1926–1948. The entries are arranged in sheer lists, alphabetically by author. Two appendixes cite reference works for anonyma and pseudonyma and bibliographies of bibliographies. There is a subject index as well as an author-title index.

Many of Cordasco's other relevant bibliographies were gathered together under the title *Eighteenth Century Bibliographies: Handlists of Critical Studies Relating to Smollett* [2 lists, 1770–1924 and 1925–1945]; *Richardson* [1896–1946]; *Sterne* [1895–1946]; *Fielding* [1895–1946]; *Dibdin* [primary and secondary]; *Eighteenth Century Medicine* [list of medical references and bibliographies published in the eighteenth century]; *Eighteenth Century Novel* [General Histories and articles of the last twenty-five years, e.g., 1925–1950]; *Godwin* [to 1947]; *Gibbon* [to 1947]; *Young* [to 1947]; *and Burke* [to 1947]; *to Which Is Added John P. Anderson's* [primary] *Bibliography of Smollett* (Metuchen, N. J.: Scarecrow Press, 1970) [Z2013.C67].

P–18 **Scholarly Journals in Restoration and Eighteenth-Century Studies.**

Age of Johnson. Vol. 1–. New York: AMS Press, 1987–. 1/yr. Reviews.   PR3532.A15

British Journal for Eighteenth Century Studies. Vol. 1–. Durham, England: British Society for Eighteenth Century Studies, 1978–. 4/yr.   No LC number

Dix-huitième siècle. Vol. 1–. Oxford: Voltaire Foundation for the Société française d'étude du dix-huitième siècle, 1969–.   CB411.D57

ECT&I *Eighteenth Century: Theory and Interpretation* [former titles: vols. 1–8, *Burke Newsletter*; vols. 9–17, *Studies in Burke and His Time*]. Vol. 1–. Lubbock: Texas Tech University [place varies], 1959–. 3/yr. Reviews.   DA506.B9 B86

ECF *Eighteenth-Century Fiction.* Vol. 1–. Downsview, Ont.: University of Toronto Press, 1988–. 4/yr. Reviews.   No LC number

ECLife *Eighteenth Century Life.* Vol. 1–. Williamsburg, Va.: William and Mary College for the East Central American Society for Eighteenth Century Studies, 1974–. [Originally published 4/yr by the University of Pittsburgh, School for International Studies.] 3/yr. Reviews. Bibliography: "Abstracts of Recent Dissertations" [1980–].   HN1.E42

ECS *Eighteenth-Century Studies: An Interdisciplinary Journal.* Vol. 1–. Davis: University of California for the American Society for Eighteenth Century Studies, 1967–. 4/yr. Reviews. Cumulative Index to vols. 1–20 published 1988.   NX452.E54

EnlE *Enlightenment Essays.* Vol. 1–. Chicago: University of Illinois, Chicago Circle, Department of English, 1970–. 4/yr.   No LC number

Etudes sur le XVIIIᵉ siècle. Vol. 1–. Brussels: Groupe d'étude du XVIIIᵉ siècle of the Université libre de Bruxelles, 1974–.   No LC number

JNL *Johnsonian Newsletter.* Vol. 1–. New York: Columbia University, 1940–. Reviews. Bibliographical notes (see P–9).   No LC number

Locke Newsletter. Vol. 1–. York, England: Department of Philosophy, University of York, 1970–. 1/yr. Reviews. Bibliography.   B1250.L6

NRam *New Rambler: Journal of the Johnson Society of London.* Vol. 1–. London: The Society, 1941–. 2/yr. Reviews.   PR3532.A16

Restoration: Studies in English Literary Culture 1660–1700 [*Restoration*]. Vol. 1–. Knoxville: University of Tennessee, 1977–. 2/yr. Reviews. Bibliography (see P–7).   PR437.R47

RECTR *Restoration and Eighteenth Century Theatre Research.* Vols. 1–15. Chicago: Loyola University, 1962–1977. New series vol. 1–. Chicago: Loyola University, 1986–. 2/yr. Reviews. Bibliography (see P–30).   PN2592.R46

Scriblerian and the Kit-Kats [former title: *Scriblerian: A Newsletter Devoted to Pope, Swift, and Their Circle*] [*Scriblerian*]. Vol. 1–. Philadelphia: Temple University, 1968–. 2/yr. Reviews. Bibliogra-

phy (see P–8). Cumulative indexes to vols. 1–5 (1968–1973), 6–10 (1973–1978), and 11–15 (1974–1983).   PR445.S3

SCN *Seventeenth Century News.* Vol. 1–. University Park: Pennsylvania State University Press, 1942–. 4/yr. Reviews. Bibliography (see O–9).   PR1.S47

SEL *SEL: Studies in English Literature, 1500–1900.* Vol. 1–. Houston, Tex.: Rice University, 1961–. 4/yr. Summer issue is devoted to Restoration and Eighteenth-Century Literature (see P–4).   PR1.SE2

SECC *Studies in Eighteenth Century Culture.* Vol. 1–. Madison: University of Wisconsin Press for the American Society for Eighteenth Century Studies, 1972–. 1/yr.   CB411.S8

Studies in the Eighteenth Century. Vol. 1–. New York: AMS, 1980–.   No LC number

SVEC *Studies on Voltaire and the Eighteenth Century.* Vol. 1–. Oxford: The Taylor Institution, 1955–. Irregular. A Summary Index by Martin Smith (1983).   LC numbers vary

P–19 **Some Frequently Recommended Works in Restoration and Eighteenth-Century Studies.**

For additional frequently recommended works on Restoration and eighteenth-century history generally, see section F; for works on social, intellectual, and educational history of the Restoration and eighteenth-century period, see K–90, K–95, and K–98, respectively. For works on the history of taste see K–92. For works on colonial American literature see section S. For works on the later-seventeenth- and eighteenth-century literatures of the world see appropriate portions of section L; for works on Restoration and eighteenth-century Scottish, Irish, Welsh, and world literature written in English, see appropriate portions of section M. For works on Restoration and eighteenth-century poetry generally, see section T; for Restoration and eighteenth-century drama see also section U; for Restoration and eighteenth-century prose and prose fiction see also section W; and for Restoration and eighteenth-century literary theory and criticism see also section X.

Allison, Alexander Ward. *Toward an Augustan Poetic.* Louisville: University of Kentucky Press, 1962.   PR3754.A4

Anderson, Howard, and John S. Shea, eds. *Studies in Criticism and Aesthetics, 1660–1800: Essays in Honor of Samuel Holt Monk.* Minneapolis: University of Minnesota Press, 1967.   PR73.A5

Bender, John. *Imagining the Penitentiary: Fiction and the Architecture of Mind in Eighteenth-Century England.* Chicago: University of Chicago Press, 1987.   PR858.P7B4 1987

Bond, Donald F., ed. *Spectator.* 5 vols. Oxford: Clarendon Press, 1965.   PR1365.S7 1965

———. *Tatler.* Oxford: Clarendon Press, 1985–.   PR1369.T2 1985

Bond, Richmond. *English Burlesque Poetry, 1700–1750.* Cambridge: Harvard University Press, 1932.   PR559.B8 B6

Bond, W. H., ed. *Eighteenth Century Essays in Honor of Donald F. Hyde.* New York: Grolier Club, 1970.   PR442.E4

Boys, Richard C. *Studies in the Augustan Age: Essays Collected in Honor of Arthur Ellicott Case.* New York: Gordian, 1966.   PR442.B6

Bredvold, Louis. *Literature of the Restoration and Eighteenth Century, 1660–1798*. Vol. 3 of Craig, *History of English Literature* (see M–36).

British Museum. *Thomason Collection: Catalogue of the Pamphlets, Books, Newspapers, and Manuscripts Relating to the Civil War, the Commonwealth and Restoration*. Collected by G. Thomason, 1640–1661. Edited by G. K. Fortescue. 2 vols. London: The Museum, 1908.   Z2018.B85

Bronson, Bertrand. *Facets of the Enlightenment*. Berkeley and Los Angeles: University of California Press, 1968.   PR442.B7

———. *Johnson Agonistes and Other Essays*. Cambridge: Cambridge University Press, 1946.
PR3533.B85 1946

Brower, Reuben. *Alexander Pope: The Poetry of Allusion*. London: Oxford University Press, 1969.   PR3634.B7

Butt, John. *Augustan Age*. 3d ed. London: Hutchinson's University Library, 1965.   PR441.B8

———. *English Literature in the Mid-Eighteenth Century*. Edited and completed by Geoffrey Carnall. Vol. 8 of the *Oxford History of English Literature* (see M–31).

Camden, Carroll, ed. *Restoration and Eighteenth-Century Literature: Essays in Honor of Alan Dougald McKillop*. Chicago: University of Chicago Press, 1963.
PR442.C3

Castle, Terry. *Masquerade and Civilization: The Carnivalesque in Eighteenth-Century English Culture and Fiction*. Stanford, Calif.: Stanford University Press, 1986.   PR858.M37 C36 1986

Clifford, James L., and Louis A. Landa. *Pope and His Contemporaries: Essays Presented to George Sherburn*. Oxford: Clarendon Press, 1949.   PR442.C6

Clifford, James L., ed. *Eighteenth Century English Literature: Modern Essays in Criticism*. New York: Oxford University Press, 1959.   PR442.C58

Critical Review; or, Annals of Literature. 144 vols. London, 1756–1817.   AP4.C9

Damrosch, Leopold, Jr., ed. *Modern Essays on Eighteenth-Century Literature*. Oxford: Oxford University Press, 1987.   PR442.M57 1988

Dobrée, Bonamy. *English Literature in the Early Eighteenth Century, 1700–1740*. Vol. 7 of the *Oxford History of English Literature* (see M–31).

Doody, Margaret Anne. *Daring Muse: Augustan Poetry Reconsidered*. Cambridge: Cambridge University Press, 1985.   PR561.D6 1985

Ehrenpreis, Irvin. *Acts of Implication: Suggestion and Covert Meaning in the Works of Dryden, Swift, Pope, and Austen*. Berkeley, Los Angeles, London: University of California Press, 1981.   PR442.E38 1980

———. *Swift: The Man, His Works, and The Age*. 3 vols. Cambridge: Harvard University Press, 1962–1983.
PR3726.E37

Elton, Oliver. *Survey of English Literature, 1730–1780*. 2 vols. London: Macmillan, 1928.   PR441.E6

Erskine-Hill, Howard. *Social Milieu of Alexander Pope: Lives, Example, and the Poetic Response*. New Haven: Yale University Press, 1975.   PR3633.E7

Folkenflick, Robert, ed. *English Hero, 1660–1800*. Newark: University of Delaware Press, 1982.
PR449.H45 E5 1982

Ford, Boris, ed. *From Dryden to Johnson*. Vol. 4 in the *New Pelican Guide to English Literature* (see M–39).

Fussell, Paul. *Rhetorical World of Augustan Humanism*. Oxford: Clarendon Press, 1965.   PR561.F8

Gentleman's Magazine. London, 1731–1907. General Indexes, 1731–1786 in 2 vols. (1818); 1787–1818 in 2 vols. (1821); and a number of special indexes.
AP4.G3

Griffin, Dustin H. *Regaining Paradise: Milton and the Eighteenth Century*. Cambridge: Cambridge University Press, 1986.   PR3588.G75 1986

Hagstrum, Jean. *Eros and Vision: The Restoration to Romanticism*. Evanston, Ill.: Northwestern University Press, 1989.   PR442.H34 1989

———. *Sex and Sensibility: Ideal and Erotic Love from Milton to Mozart*. Chicago: University of Chicago Press, 1980.   PR409.L67 H3

Havens, Raymond D. *Influence of Milton on English Poetry*. Baltimore: Johns Hopkins University Press, 1922.
PR3588.H3

Hilles, Frederick W., ed. *Age of Johnson*. New Haven: Yale University Press, 1949.   PR442.T5

Hilles, Frederick W., and Harold Bloom, eds. *From Sensibility to Romanticism*. New York: Oxford University Press, 1965.   PR571.H5

Hume, Robert D. *Development of English Drama in the Late Seventeenth Century*. Oxford: Clarendon Press, 1976.
PR691.H8

———. *Rakish Stage: Studies in English Drama, 1660–1800*. Carbondale: Southern Illinois University Press, 1983.   PR708.C6 H8 1983

———, ed. *London Theatre World, 1660–1800*. Carbondale: Southern Illinois University Press, 1980.
PN2592.L64

Hunt, John Dixon. *Figure in the Landscape: Poetry, Painting, and Gardening during the Eighteenth Century*. Baltimore: Johns Hopkins University Press, 1976.   PR555.A34 H8

Jones, R. F., ed. *Seventeenth Century: Studies in the History of English Thought and Literaure from Bacon to Pope*. Stanford: Stanford University Press, 1951.   PR433.J6

Korshin, Paul J. ed. *Proceedings of the Modern Language Association Neoclassicism Conferences, 1967–68, with a Selected Bibliography 1920–68*. New York: AMS, 1970.   PR445.P7

Lewis, W. S., et al., eds. *Yale Edition of Horace Walpole's Correspondence*. 48 vols. in 49. New Haven: Yale University Press, 1937–1983.   DA483.WZ A12

London Magazine: or, Gentleman's Monthly Intelligencer. London, 1732–1785.

Lonsdale, Roger, ed. *Dryden to Johnson*. Vol. 4 in *The [Sphere] History of Literature in the English Language* (see M–34).

Lord, George de F., et al., eds. *Poems on Affairs of State: Augustan Satirical Verse, 1660–1714*. 7 vols. New Haven: Yale University Press, 1963–1975.
PR1195.H5 P62

Mack, Maynard. *Collected in Himself: Essays Critical, Biographical, and Bibliographical on Pope and Some of His Contemporaries*. Newark: University of Delaware Press, 1982.   PR3633.M28 1982

———. *Essential Articles for the Study of Alexander Pope*. 2d ed., rev. and enl. Hamden, Conn.: Archon, 1968.
PR3633.M3

———. *Garden and the City: Retirement and Politics in the Later Poetry of Pope, 1731–1743*. Toronto: University of Toronto Press, 1969.   PR3633.M33

Mack, Maynard, and James A. Winn, eds. *Pope: Recent Essays by Several Hands*. Hamden, Conn.: Archon, 1980.   PR3634.P66

MacLean, Kenneth. *John Locke and English Literature of the Eighteenth Century*. New Haven: Yale University Press, 1936. B1294.M2

McKillop, Alan D. *English Literature from Dryden to Burns*. New York: Appleton-Century-Crofts, 1948. Biobibliographies of major figures. PR404.M3

Messenger, Ann. *His and Hers: Essays in Restoration and Eighteenth-Century Literature*. Lexington: University Press of Kentucky, 1986. PR448.W65 M47 1986

Milhous, Judith, and Robert D. Hume. *Producible Interpretation: Eight English Plays, 1675–1787*. Carbondale: Southern Illinois University Press, 1985. PR691.M55 1985

Miller, Henry Knight, Eric Rothstein, and G. S. Rousseau, eds. *Augustan Milieu: Essays Presented to Lewis A. Landa*. London: Oxford University Press, 1970. PR442.A9

Miner, Earl, ed. *Restoration Dramatists*. Englewood Cliffs, N. J.: Prentice-Hall, 1966. PR693.M5 1966

Monthly Review: A Periodical Work, Giving an Account, with Proper Abstracts of, and Extracts from, the New Books, Pamphlets, etc., As They Come Out. London, 1749–1845. General Indexes 1749–1784 in 2 vols. (1786); 1749–1789 (1934); 1790–1815 (1955). AP4.M88

Nichols, John. *Illustrations of the Literary History of the Eighteenth Century, Consisting of Authentic Memoirs and Original Letters of Eminent Persons, and Intended as a Sequel to the Literary Anecdotes*. 8 vols. London: Nichols, Son, and Bentley, 1817–1858. PR443.N42

———. *Literary Anecdotes of the Eighteenth Century; Comprising Biographical Memoirs of William Bowyer, Printer, . . .and Many of His Learned Friends; an Incidental View of the Progress and Advancement of Literature in This Kingdom during the Last Century; and Biographical Anecdotes of a Considerable Number of Eminent Writers and Ingenious Artists; with a Very Copious Index*. 9 vols. London: Nichols, 1812–1816. PR453.N5

Nussbaum, Felicity. *Brink of All We Hate: English Satires on Women, 1660–1750*. Lexington: University Press of Kentucky, 1984. PR449.W65 N87 1984

———, and Laura Brown, eds. *New Eighteenth Century: Theory, Politics, English Literature*. New York: Methuen, 1987. PR442.N48 1987

Paulson, Ronald. *Satire and the Novel in Eighteenth Century England*. New Haven: Yale University Press, 1967. PR858.S3 P3

Pollak, Ellen. *Poetics of Sexual Myth: Gender and Ideology in the Verse of Swift and Pope*. Chicago: University of Chicago Press, 1985. PR565.S48 P64 1985

Rawson, Claude. *Order from Confusion Sprung: Studies in Eighteenth-Century Literature from Swift to Cowper*. London: Allen and Unwin, 1985. PR442.R36 1985

Rogers, Pat. *Grub Street: Studies in a Subculture*. London: Methuen, 1972. PR935.R6

Rothstein, Eric. *Restoration and Eighteenth Century Poetry*. Boston: Routledge and Kegan Paul, 1981. PR502.R58

Schilling, Bernard N. *Essential Articles for the Study of English Augustan Backgrounds*. Hamden, Conn.: Archon, 1961. PR437.S35

Schwartz, Richard B., ed. *Theory and Tradition in Eighteenth-Century Studies*. Carbondale: Southern Illinois University Press, 1990. PR442.T44 1990

Scots Magazine, Containing a General View of the Religion, Politics, Entertainment, in Great Britain. 97 vols. Edinburgh: Sands, Brymer, Murray, and Cochran, 1739–1826. AP3.S35

Sherbo, Arthur. *Studies in the Eighteenth Century Novel*. East Lansing: Michigan State University Press, 1969. PR823.S55

Sherburn, George, and Donald F. Bond. *Restoration and Eighteenth Century (1660–1789)*. Vol. 3 in Baugh, *Literary History of England* (see M–30).

Spacks, Patricia Meyer. *Insistence of Horror: Aspects of the Supernatural in Eighteenth-Century Poetry*. Cambridge: Harvard University Press, 1962. PR555.S8 S65

Spector, Robert D. *Essays on the English Eighteenth Century Novel*. Bloomington: Indiana University Press, 1965. PR853.S6

Stephen, Leslie. *English Literature and Society in the Eighteenth Century*. London: Duckworth and Co., 1904. PR443.S8

Sutherland, James. *English Literature of the Late Seventeenth Century*. Vol. 6 in the *Oxford History of English Literature* (see M–31).

Swedenberg, H. T., Jr., ed. *Essential Articles for the Study of John Dryden*. Hamden, Conn.: Archon, 1966. PR3422.A4

Tillotson, Geoffrey. *On the Poetry of Pope*. 2d ed. Oxford: Clarendon Press, 1950. PR3634.T5 1950

Todd, Janet. *Sensibility: An Introduction*. London: Methuen, 1986. PR449.S4 T63 1986

Wasserman, Earl R., ed. *Aspects of the Eighteenth Century*. Baltimore: Johns Hopkins University Press, 1965. CB411.W3

Watt, Ian. *Rise of the Novel: Studies in Defoe, Richardson, and Fielding*. Berkeley: University of California Press, 1957. PR851.W3

Weinbrot, Howard. *Alexander Pope and the Traditions of Formal Verse Satire*. Princeton, N. J.: Princeton University Press, 1982. PR3634.W4 1982

———. *Augustus Caesar in Augustan England: The Decline of a Classical Norm*. Princeton, N.J.: Princeton University Press, 1978. PR445.W4

———. *Eighteenth-Century Satire: Essays on Text and Context from Dryden to Peter Pindar*. Cambridge: Cambridge University Press, 1988. PR935.W39 1988

———. *Formal Strain: Studies in Augustan Imitation and Satire*. Princeton, N. J.: Princeton University Press, 1969. PR935.W4

Williams, Joan M., ed. *Novel and Romance, 1700–1800: A Documentary Record*. New York: Barnes and Noble, 1970. PR852.W5

Wilson, John Harold. *Preface to Restoration Drama*. Boston: Houghton Mifflin, 1965. PR2592.W52

II.   POETRY

See also section T.

P–20   **Foxon, David F.   *English Verse 1701–1750: A Catalogue of Separately Printed Poems with Notes on Contemporary Collected Editions.* 2 vols. London: Cambridge University Press, 1975.**   Z2014.P7 F69

This work presents a short-title catalog of all separately published verse in English and in all other languages printed in the British Isles from 1701 through 1750. Translated and versified works are treated as if they were original. Excluded are multiauthor collections and miscellanies. Also excluded are ephemera such as popular broadside ballads, slipsongs, chapbooks, and the like, unless they are by major authors or make significant reference to contemporary events. Excluded, too, are engraved sheets of songs with music or political cartoons, oratorios and opera libretti, and works in both prose and verse if the prose precedes and is not an introduction to the verse.

Main entries, which are assigned an alphanumeric code, are given under the author or the first word of the title of an anonymous work, with cross-references from titles, initials, and pseudonyms. Under the author are listed, first, collected works and then separate works in alphabetical order. There are cross-references to the titles of attributed and supposed works. The contents of the individual entry for collected works are the title, the imprint, collation, and the location of copies in up to two British and two American libraries. For single works the entry gives the title, the imprint, the collation, a bibliographical note, the first line, notes on authorship and subject matter, and the location of copies in up to five British and five United States libraries. Where there are multiple issues and editions, they are listed chronologically, with authorized editions preceding unauthorized editions at the place of original publication, and with reprints elsewhere following unauthorized editions.

The second volume contains a series of six indexes, as follows: an index of first lines, a chronological index, an index of imprints, an index of bibliographical notabilia, an index of descriptive epithets, and a subject index. It is estimated that the volume contains some 10,000 entries.

P–25   **Mell, Donald C.   *English Poetry, 1660–1800: A Guide to Information Sources.* Detroit: Gale Research Co., 1982.**   Z2014.P7 M44 1982

This volume contains a total of 2,264 entries with trenchant, informative abstracts. They are disposed into two parts. The first, in four sections, treats General Bibliography; English Literature, 1660–1800—Reference Materials; English Literature, 1660–1800: Background Resources; and English Poetry: 1660–1800: Literary Studies. The second part contains primary and secondary bibliographies for a total of thiry-one Restoration and eighteenth-century poets. The individual bibliographies contain six parts: 1, Important or Standard Editions and Collected Works; 2, Standard Editions of Correspondence, Diaries, and Journals; 3, Separately Published Bibliographies and Embedded Bibliographies; 4, Collections of Articles, Essays, and Festschriften Devoted Exclusively or Primarily to the Poet; 5, Books and Essays of Biographical Interest; and 6, Critical Studies. Entries in all of these sections are arranged alphabetically save the first two, which are in chronological order. The volume concludes with a combined author-title index.

III.   DRAMA AND THEATER

See also section U.

P–30   **Stratman, Carl J., David G. Spencer, and Mary Elizabeth Devine, eds.   *Restoration and Eighteenth Century Theatre Research: A Bibliographical Guide, 1900–1968.* Carbondale: Southern Illinois University Press, 1971.**   Z2014.D7 S854

This primarily retrospective bibliography was prepared by a group of contributing editors, each of whom completed a five-year segment. The total of 6,560 serially numbered entries concern works on the drama and theater, including studies and editions of plays, and the work of Shakespeare and other pre-Restoration dramatists when these are aspects of eighteenth-century theater. A total of 780 subject headings are arranged A-Z; entries beneath subjects are in chronological order. Headings include 432 names of actors, musicians, playwrights, scene painters, stage managers, and other persons of the theater. The remaining 348 headings are extremely diverse, including such rubrics as Audience, Cities, Marriage, Methodism, Negro, and Taste. Entries are annotated. Among the large subject headings are such general topics as Bibliography, General History, Periodicals, Theatres, and the various genres. Under author headings, the subdivisions include Letters, Collected Works, Collected Poems, Collected Plays, Individual Plays, Biography and Criticism.

The volume is designed to complement the current annual bibliographies in *Restoration and Eighteenth Century Theatre Research* (P–31).

P–31   **"Restoration and Eighteenth Century Theatre Research Bibliography for [1961–1975]." *Restoration and Eighteenth Century Theatre Research,* vol. 1–15. Chicago: Loyola University, 1962–1976.**   PN2592.R46

This annual bibliography included several hundred serially numbered, briefly annotated items, including books, articles, and dissertations. Entries are arranged under the same vast array of subject headings, both names and topics, used for the Stratman *Bibliography* (P–30). There are abundant cross-references and an index of authors.

The annual bibliographies for 1961–1967 have been cumulated under the title *Restoration and Eighteenth Century Theatre Research Bibliography*, *1961-1968*, ed. Carl J. Stratman, comp. Edmund A. Napieralski (1961–1968) and Jean E. Westbrook (1961–1966) (Troy, N. Y.: Whitston, 1969) [Z2014.D7 S853]. The cumulation contains a total of 1,186 serially numbered, annotated entries. Further cumulations were planned.

Publication of *RECTR* resumed with New Series volume 1 (1986), where the resumption of the annual bibliography is announced, along with a project to put a comprehensive bibliography of *Restoration and Eighteenth Century Theatre Research* into computerized form.

P–32   **Link, Frederick M.   *English Drama, 1660–1800: A Guide to Information Sources.* Detroit: Gale Research Co., 1976.**   Z2014.D7 L55

This guide, current to 1973 or 1974, presents a series of bibliographical essays on books and articles concerned with the drama in England, 1660–1800. Reviews, theses, dissertations, and manuscript materials are generally omitted from discussion. The essays are in two main parts, General Bibliography and Individual Authors. The first part contains eight sections, with essays on I. Bibliography and Reference Works; II. Collections of Theatrical Pieces; III. Playhouses and Playgoers; IV. Theatrical Biography; V. Dramatic Theory; VI. Dramatic History; VII. Literary Criticism and Scholarship; and VIII. Antecedents and Influences. Part 2 presents bibliographical essays on primary and secondary works for individual authors. The volume concludes with indexes of names and play titles.

P–33 **Woodward, Gertrude L., and James G. McManaway.** *Check List of English Plays, 1641–1700.* Chicago: Newberry Library, 1945.   Z2014.D7 W6

This work records, with minimum annotation, 1,340 plays and masques printed in English in Britain and other countries in the years 1641–1700 inclusive. The list is complete for the designated years and includes translations, classical plays, moral and literary pieces, and royal and civic pageants. Generally, untranslated classical Greek and Latin plays are excluded, as are political and critical dialogues. The lists are arranged alphabetically by author, with cross-references to translators and adapters. Anonymous plays are listed under their titles. The initial list was compiled from bibliographies and printed catalogs and supplemented by an inventory of the holdings of fifteen research libraries. Locations of copies in American libraries are indicated.

Supplement to the Woodward and McManaway Checklist of English Plays 1641-1700 by Fredson Bowers (Charlottesville: Bibliographical Society of the University of Virginia, 1949) [No LC number] corrects omissions.

P–35 **Highfill, Philip H., Jr., Kalman A. Burnim, and Edward A. Langhans, eds.** *Biographical Dictionary of Actors, Actresses, Musicians, Dancers, Managers, and Other Stage Personnel in London, 1660–1800.* 16 vols. planned. Carbondale: Southern Illinois University Press, 1973–.
                                          PN2597.H5

This work, when completed, will contain biographical notices of more than 8,500 persons associated with the theaters and other places of public entertainment in London and its environs during the Restoration and the eighteenth century. The ideal entry gives the date and place of birth, christening, marriage, death, and burial; inclusive dates and places of residence and career; information about an individual's spouses and children; information about first and last public appearance; about involvements in notable theatrical occurrences; about "lines" of character; assessments of professional worth; salaries; pseudonyms; offices, associations, liaisons, and clubs; honors; and creative contributions to the theater. Articles range in length from a brief paragraph to more than 100 pages on David Garrick. To date, twelve volumes have been published, as follows: 1, Abaco to Belfille; 2, Belfort to Byzand; 3, Cabanel to Cory; 4, Corye to Dynion; 5, Eagen to Garrett; 6, Garrick to Gyngell; 7, Habgood to Houbert; 8, Hough to Keyse; 9, Kickill to Machin; 10, McIntosh to Nash; 11, Naso to Penkethman; and 12, Pennell to Provost.

IV. PROSE FICTION

See also section W.

P–40 **Beasley, Jerry C.** *English Fiction, 1660–1800: A Guide to Information Sources.* Detroit: Gale Research Co., 1978.
                                          Z2014.F5 B42

This guide is disposed into two parts, general bibliography and individual authors, with a total of 1,475 serially numbered, annotated entries. The entries in part 1 are divided as follows: Background (General Reference Works, English Lit-

erature 1660–1800: General History and Criticism); The English Novel: General Histories and Critical Surveys; The Novel as Genre: Selected Studies in Form and Technique; English Fiction, 1660–1800: History and Criticism; Checklists and Other Bibliographical Resources; Special Resources (Serials, Reprint Series and Selected Modern Editions); Selected Background Readings. Those in part 2 give primary and secondary bibliographies of twenty-nine individual authors. Subdivisions under each author include Principal Works; Collected, Selected, Specialized, and Important Individual Editions; Letters; Bibliographies; Biographies; and Critical Studies and Commentaries. Entries for primary works are given in chronological order; those for secondary works are in alphabetical order by authors' names. The guide ends with an index to authors and works.

An attempt to index scholarship to 1984 by topic is found in H. George Hahn and Carl Behm III, *Eighteenth-Century British Novel and Its Background: An Annotated Bibliography and Guide to Topics* (Metuchen: Scarecrow, 1985) [Z2014.F4 H33 1985], but it is not very successful. It contains an index of subjects, themes, and critical issues; bibliographies and surveys of criticism; lists of studies of eighteenth century life; and inadequately annotated bibliographies of major and minor novelists.

P–44 **McBurney, William Harlin.** *Check List of English Prose Fiction, 1700–1739.* Cambridge: Harvard University Press, 1960.   Z2014.F4 M3

Compiled from Esdaile (W–14), the *Cambridge Bibliography of English Literature* (M–10), and C. N. Greenough's unpublished Harvard card catalog, "English Prose Fiction, 1470–1832," this checklist is arranged in chronological order. Works included must be in prose, fictional, "of a certain extent," by a native author, and first published in England between 1700 and 1739. Translations into English are included. Serially numbered entries include title, printers and booksellers mentioned on the title page, pagination, format, price, and the library call number of at least one extant copy. Translations are listed at the end of each year's entries, and their entries include names of author and translator, original title, and date of original publication. There is an appendix of dubious or unauthenticated titles, a bibliography, and an index of all items.

P–45 **Beasley, Jerry C.** *Check List of Prose Fiction Published in England 1740–1749.* Charlottesville: University Press of Virginia for the Bibliographical Society of the University of Virginia, 1972.   Z2014.F4 B37

All English-language novels, including both native works and foreign fiction in translation, are included in this continuation of the McBurney checklist (P–44). Excluded are works of magazine fiction, brief chapbooks, character sketches, jestbooks, and dialogues. Novels and works calling themselves such, and narrative fiction with such titles as "history," "life," "voyage," are included, along with collections of letters with a narrative line. Entries are organized chronologically by the earliest date of a work's appearance and are alphabetical under the year. Entries are serially numbered, and modern reprints are designated with an asterisk. Entries include short titles, booksellers, pagination, format, price, and location of at least one extant copy in an American library. For translations, which are listed at the end of each year's chronology, the author, translator, original title, and original date are included. Subsequent editions and reissues are listed, with brief descriptive annotations. The volume concludes with a bibliography of secondary sources consulted and an index to names and titles.

P–47 **Orr, Leonard.** *Catalog Checklist of English Prose Fiction 1750–1800.* Troy, N. Y.: Whitston, 1979.   Z2014.F4 O77

This work, which has been very adversely reviewed, lists chronologically almost 1,200 novels published in the second half of the eighteenth century. Entries are compiled from the published catalogs of a dozen research libraries; announcements, advertisements, and reviews in a number of eighteenth-century periodicals; and a number of bibliographies. There are two essays included, the first presenting an introductory overview of the mid- and late-eighteenth-century novel, the second tracing changes in the reading public during this period. Author and title indexes follow the chronological listing. The volume should be used with caution, if at all.

P–48 **Spector, Robert Donald.** *English Gothic: A Bibliographic Guide to Writers from Horace Walpole to Mary Shelley.* Westport, Conn.: Greenwood, 1984.   PR830.T3

This volume presents a bibliographic survey of English language publications on gothic fiction and its most important authors. An introduction discusses the definition and history of the genre. The first chapter treats bibliographies; studies of genre, influence, and critical reception; and work on minor writers. The remaining four chapters treat biographies, editions, and studies of the following pairs of authors: Walpole and Reeve, Charlotte Smith and Radcliffe, Lewis and Beckford, and Maturin and Mary Shelley. The work is indexed by subject and author. Though highly selective, this volume provides extensive evaluations of important studies and thus serves as a useful starting point for research. The McNutt bibliography (P–49) is less selective, but is only complete through 1971.

P–49 **McNutt, Dan J.** *Eighteenth-Century Gothic Novel: An Annotated Bibliography of Criticism and Selected Texts.* New York: Garland, 1975.   Z2014.F5 M3 1975

This bibliography of English works published to 1971 (with some of later date) on the Eighteenth-Century Gothic Novel is disposed into thirteen sections, as follows: I. Bibliographies and Research Guides; II. Aesthetic Background; III. Literary Background; IV. Psychological, Social, and Scientific Background; V. Eighteenth-Century Gothic, in General Studies; VI. Studies Devoted to Eighteenth-Century Gothic; VII. The Gothic Legacy; VIII–XIII. Bibliographies for Horace Walpole, Clara Reeve, Charlotte Smith, Ann Radcliffe, Matthew Gregory Lewis, and William Beckford (with subdivisions for Texts, Bibliographies, Full-length Studies, Articles, Notices in General Works, and Early Reviews). Entries are numbered and include brief descriptive annotations. The volume concludes with an appendix of selected foreign-language works in a classification parallel to that of the main body, and an index of authors.

V.   PROSE AND CRITICISM

See also section W and section X.

P–50 **Draper, John W.** *Eighteenth-Century English Aesthetics: A Bibliography.* Heidelberg: Carl Winter, 1931.   Z5870.D76

This bibliography of eighteenth-century works is disposed into five parts, as follows: I. General Works on Aesthetics; II. Architecture and Gardening; III. Pictorial and Plastic Arts; IV. Literature and Drama; V. Music, Including Opera. Unnumbered entries are often annotated. An appendix lists modern commentary on eighteenth-century aesthetics. There is no index.

Supplements were published by William D. Templeman, *MP* 30 (1933): 309–316; R. D. Havens, *MLN* 47 (1932): 118–120; R. S. Crane, *MP* 29 (1931): 251–252; and F. T. Wood, *ES* 66 (1931): 279–281.

LITERATURE OF THE NINETEENTH CENTURY

See also works in section C.II, British National Bibliography; in section D on Nineteenth-Century Periodicals and Newspapers; in section F on History; in section G on Biography; in section H on Manuscripts and Archives; and in section I on Language, Linguistics, and Philology. See also numerous references in sections K, L, and M, including the *MLA International Bibliography* (L–50), the MHRA *Annual Bibliography of English Language and Literature* (M–21), and the *Year's Work in English Studies* (M–22). See additional references on nineteenth century poetry and poetics in section T, on drama and theater in section U, and on prose and prose fiction in section W. See also references on Nineteenth-Century Literary and Rhetorical Theory in section X, and on Nineteenth-Century Printing and Publishing in section Y.

I. GENERAL

Q–5 **"Recent Studies in Nineteenth Century English Literature."** *SEL*, Fall issue, vol. 1– 1961–. PR1.S82

These annual bibliographical essays offer descriptive and evaluative comment on recent work, normally of the previous year. Emphases are chosen by the individual authors. To date, the following essays have been prepared:

Vol. 1 (1961), pp. 149–166. By G. Robert Strange.

Vol. 2 (1962), pp. 509–528. By Jack Stillinger.

Vol. 3 (1963), pp. 595–611. By Morse Peckham.

Vol. 4 (1964), pp. 663–685. By R. H. Super.

Vol. 5 (1965), pp. 735–748. By Richard H. Fogle [Romanticism].

Vol. 6 (1966), pp. 753–782. By Geoffrey Hartman.

Vol. 7 (1967), pp. 741–766. By Edward Bosletter.

Vol. 8 (1968), pp. 725–749. By Carol Woodring.

Vol. 9 (1969), pp. 737–753. By J. Hillis Miller. Continued in vol. 10 (1970), pp. 183–214.

Vol. 10 (1970), pp. 817–829. By Harold Bloom.

Vol. 11 (1971), pp. 763–782. By A. Dwight Culler.

Vol. 12 (1972), pp. 801–824. By U. C. Knoepflmacher.

Vol. 13 (1973), pp. 701–729. By Gerhard Joseph.

Vol. 14 (1974), pp. 637–668. By Stuart Curran.

Vol. 15 (1975), pp. 671–694. By John E. Jordan.

Vol. 16 (1976), pp. 693–727. By Thomas McFarland.

Vol. 17 (1977), pp. 739–759. By Jerome J. McGann.

Vol. 18 (1978), pp. 727–765. By Carl Dawson.

Vol. 19 (1979), pp. 721–755. By Karl Kroeber.

Vol. 20 (1980), pp. 713–748. By G. B. Tennyson.

Vol. 21 (1981), pp. 703–738. By Stuart M. Sperry.

Vol. 22 (1982), pp. 707–747. By Frances Ferguson.

Vol. 23 (1983), pp. 685–722. By John E. Jordan.

Vol. 24 (1984), pp. 769–806. By Nina Auerbach.

Vol. 25 (1985), pp. 885–945. By Donald H. Reiman.

Vol. 26 (1986), pp. 777–824. By Gerald Monsman.

Vol. 27 (1987), pp. 683–729. By Peter J. and Sylvia Manning.

Vol. 28 (1988), pp. 713–756. By David G. Riede.

Q–10 **Cambridge Bibliography of English Literature.** Vol. 3, 1800–1900. Edited by F. W. Bateson. Cambridge: Cambridge University Press, 1941. Z2011.B3 1941 vol. 3.

This bibliography is in seven main parts. The first, an Introduction, has six sections: Bibliographies, Literary Histories and Special Studies, Prose-Selections, and Literary Memoirs and Reminiscences; Literary Relations with the Continent; The Intellectual Background; Book Production and Distribution; Education; and The Political and Social Background. Part 2, The Poetry, is in seven sections: Surveys, Critical Studies and Anthologies; The Early Nineteenth Century Poets; Minor Verse, 1800–1835; The Mid-Nineteenth Century Poets; Minor Verse, 1835–1870; The Later Nineteenth Century Poets; and Minor Verse, 1870–1900. Part 3, Prose Fiction, has eight parts: Bibliographies, Histories, and Critical Studies; The Early Nineteenth Century Novelists; Minor Fiction, 1800–1835; The Mid-Nineteenth Century Novelists; Minor Fiction, 1835–1870; The Later Nineteenth Century Novelists; Minor Fiction, 1870–1900; Children's Books. The Drama is treated in the very brief part 4 in four sections: General Introduction, The Early Nineteenth Century Drama, 1800–1835; The Mid-Nineteenth Century Drama; and The Late Nineteenth Century Drama.

Part 5 concerns Critical and Miscellaneous Prose and has nine sections: The Early Nineteenth Century Essayists; Minor Critics and Essayists, 1800–1835; The Mid-Nineteenth Century Essayists; Minor Critics and Essayists, 1835–1870; The Late Nineteenth Century Critics and Miscellaneous Writers; Minor Critics and Essayists, 1870–1900; The Literature of Sport; Newspapers and Magazines; Writings on Religion. Part 6, Philosophy, History, Science and Other Forms of Learning, has eight sections: Philosophy; History, Biography, and Archaeology; The Literature of Science; Economics and

Political Theory; Writers on Law; Books on Travel; Classical, Biblical, and Oriental Scholarship; and English Scholarship. Finally, part 7 concerns The Literatures of the Dominions and has five sections: Anglo-Irish Literature; Anglo-Indian Literature; English-Canadian Literature (1769–1900); English-South African Literature (1789–1914); and The Literature of Australia and New Zealand (1819–1914).

Added entries for this volume will be found on pages 519–710 of the *Supplement* (1957). The volume and its supplement are almost, but not entirely, replaced by the corresponding volume of the *NCBEL* (Q–11). The original volume but not its supplement is indexed in the *CBEL Index*, which is volume 4 (1941) of the *CBEL*.

Q–11 *New Cambridge Bibliography of English Literature [NCBEL].* Vol. 3, 1800–1900. Edited by George Watson. Cambridge: Cambridge University Press, 1969.
Z2011.N45 vol. 3

This volume of the *NCBEL* (M–11), the first to be published, is current through 1965 or so. Entries are in six main parts. Part 1, Introduction, contains three sections: General Works; Book Production and Distribution; and Literary Relations with the Continent. Part 2, Poetry, is in seven sections: General Works; Early Nineteenth Century Poetry; Minor Poetry 1800–1835; Mid-Nineteenth Century Poetry; Minor Poetry 1835–1870; Late-Nineteenth Century Poetry; and Minor Poetry 1870–1900. Part 3, The Novel, is in eight divisions: General Works; The Early Nineteenth Century Novel; Minor Fiction 1800–1835; The Mid-Nineteenth Century Novel; Minor Fiction 1835–1870; The Late Nineteenth Century Novel; Minor Fiction 1870–1900; and Children's Books.

Part 4, on the Drama, has four sections: General Introduction; The Early Nineteenth Century Drama; The Mid-Nineteenth Century Drama; The Late Nineteenth Century Drama. Prose is treated in part 5, in fifteen sections: General Works; Early Nineteenth Century Prose; Minor Prose 1800–1835; Mid-Nineteenth Century Prose; Minor Prose 1835–1870; Late Nineteenth Century Prose; Minor Prose 1870–1900; History; Philosophy; Religion; English Studies; Travel; Sport; Education; and Newspapers and Magazines. Finally, Anglo-Irish Literature, part 6, is in five sections: Gaelic Sources; General Works; Poets; Yeats and Synge; and Dramatists. A limited index concludes the volume; a more complete index is available in *NCBEL*, volume 5, which is the *Index* (1977). For greater detail see "An Index to the *NCBEL*, Volume III" by John Townsend West III (*Dissertation Abstracts International* 36 [1973]: 2861A). The list of fifty-five contributors at the end of the preface identifies the initials with which contributed bibliographies are signed.

This volume, though welcomed by the scholarly community, has been criticized for errors in titles and dates, omissions, and uneven treatment of minor authors. It must, therefore, be used with due caution and supplemented with other bibliographies.

Q–18 **Scholarly Journals in Nineteenth-Century Studies.**

DSA *Dickens Studies Annual: Essays on Victorian Fiction.* Vol. 1–. Carbondale: Southern Illinois University, 1970–1978; New York: AMS Press, 1979–. 1/yr. Bibliographical essays. PR4579.D49

ELT *English Literature in Transition, 1880–1920* (see R–18). PR1.E55

KSJ *Keats-Shelley Journal: Keats, Shelley, Byron, Hunt, and Their Circles.* Vol. 1–. Cambridge: Harvard University for the Keats-Shelley Association of America, 1952–. 1/yr. Reviews. Bibliography (see Q–26). Cumulative index to vols. 1–9 in vol. 10. PR4836.A145

KSMB *Keats-Shelley Memorial, Rome. Bulletin.* Vol. 1–. London: Keats-Shelley Memorial Association, 1910–. 1/yr. PR 4836.A15

NCF *Nineteenth Century Fiction* [former title: *Trollopian: A Journal of Victorian Fiction, 1945–1949*]. Vol. 1–. Berkeley: University of California Press, 1945–. 4/yr. Reviews. Bibliographical essay: "Recent Books." Index to vols. 1–30 (1945–1975), compiled by G. B. and Elizabeth J. Tennyson (Berkeley, 1977). PR873.T76

NCTR *Nineteenth Century Theatre Research.* Vol. 1–. Tucson: University of Arizona, 1973–. 2/yr. Reviews. Bibliography (see Q–62). PN1851.N55

RPP *Romanticism Past and Present* [former title: *Milton and the Romantics, 1975–1980*]. Vol. 1–. Boston: Northeastern University, 1975–. 1/yr. then 2/yr. PR3579.M47

SIR *Studies in Romanticism.* Vol. 1–. Boston: Boston University, 1961–. 4/yr. Reviews. PN751.S8

Victorian: Newsletter of the Victorian Society in America. Philadelphia: The Society, 1981–. 10/yr. No LC number

VN *Victorian Newsletter.* Vol. 1–. New York: CUNY, 1952–. 2/yr. Reviews. Bibliography "Recent Publication: A Selected List" (see Q–38). PR1.V48

VPR *Victorian Periodicals Review* [former title: *Victorian Periodicals Newsletter, 1967–1978*]. Vol. 1–. Toronto: Research Society for Victorian Periodicals, 1967–. 4/yr. Reviews. Bibliography (see Q–48). PN5124.P4 V52

VP *Victorian Poetry: A Critical Journal of Victorian Literature.* Vol. 1–. Morgantown: West Virginia University, 1963–. 4/yr. Reviews. Bibliography (see Q–39). PR500.V5

VS *Victorian Studies: A Quarterly Journal of the Humanities, Arts, and Sciences.* Vol. 1–. Bloomington: Indiana University, Program for Victorian Studies, 1957–. 4/yr. Reviews. Bibliography (see Q–38). PR1.V5

VIJ *Victorians Institute Journal.* Vol. 1–. Norfolk, Va.: Victorians Institute, Old Dominion University, 1972–. 1/yr. AS36.V45

WC *Wordsworth Circle.* Vol. 1–. Philadelphia: Temple University, 1970–. 4/yr. Reviews. Bibliographical notices. PR1.W67

Q–19 **Some Frequently Recommended Works in Nineteenth Century Studies.**

For additional frequently recommended works on nineteenth-century history generally, see section F; for works on social, intellectual, and educational history of the nineteenth century see K–90, K–95, and K–98, respectively. For studies in the history of taste see K–92. For works on nineteenth-century American literature see section S. For works on the other nineteenth-century literatures of the world, see appropriate portions of section L; for works on nineteenth-century Scottish, Irish, Welsh, Commonwealth, and world literature written in English, see appropriate portions of section M. For works on nineteenth-century poetry generally, see also section T; for nineteenth-century drama see also section U; for nineteenth-century prose and prose fiction see also section W; and for nineteenth-century literary theory and criticism see also section X. And for frequently recommended works on romanticism see Q–29; for those in Victorian studies see Q–49.

Ball, Patricia M. *Central Self: A Study in Romantic and Victorian Imagination*. London: Athlone Press, 1968.
PR590.B25

Beach, Joseph Warren. *Concept of Nature in Nineteenth Century English Poetry*. New York: Macmillan, 1936.
PR585.N3 B4

———. *Literature of the Nineteenth and Early Twentieth Centuries, 1798 to World War I*. Vol. 4 of Craig's *History of English Literature* (see M–36).

Chew, Samuel, and Richard D. Altick. *Nineteenth Century and After (1789–1939)*. Vol. 4 of Baugh, *Literary History of England* (see M–30).

Gilbert, Sandra, and Susan Gubar, *Madwoman in the Attic: The Woman Writer and the Nineteenth-Century Imagination*. New Haven: Yale University Press, 1979.
PR115.G5

Ryals, Clyde de L., ed. *Nineteenth Century Literary Perspectives: Essays in Honor of Lionel Stevenson*. Durham, N.C.: Duke University Press, 1974.
PR453.N53

Woodring, Carl. *Nature Into Art: Cultural Transformations in Nineteenth-Century Britain*. Cambridge: Harvard University Press, 1989.
PR468.A76 W6 1989

II. THE ROMANTIC MOVEMENT

Q–20 **Bernbaum, Ernest. *Guide through the Romantic Movement*.** 2d ed., rev. and enl. New York: Ronald Press Co., 1949.
PR447.B55 1949.

This generally superseded guide for college and graduate students studying the romantic movement (originally published in 1929) was designed as the introductory volume to Bernbaum's multivolume *Anthology of Romanticism* [PR1105.B4 1948]. It is divided into chapters on broader subjects (such as The Pre-Romantic Movement, and The Imagination) and chapters on individual authors. Each chapter is followed by its own selected bibliography. These are divided into those entries considered "Of First Importance" and those "For the Advanced Student." Both primary and secondary sources are given for authors. Following the chapter titled "The Romantic Movement" is a general bibliography that is, highly selective. The entries are divided into such sections as History, Criticism, and Anthologies. The work also contains a chronological table of the chief romantic works and a one-page index of major authors and topics.

Q–21 **Fogle, Richard Harter. *Romantic Poets and Prose Writers*.** [A Goldentree Bibliography.] New York: Appleton-Century-Crofts, 1967.
Z2013.F6

This selected bibliography is prepared as a guide for the beginning graduate student. Major works and topics are covered, with emphasis on secondary works published in the twentieth century. The first pages contain general works on backgrounds, historical, intellectual, social; literary and aesthetic foregrounds; and bibliographies, journals, and surveys of scholarship. The remainder of the text is devoted to sections on each of fourteen authors: Blake, Byron, Coleridge, DeQuincey, Hazlitt, Hunt, Keats, Lamb, Landor, Moore, Scott, Shelley, Southey, and Wordsworth. Each author section has the subcategories: Editions, Biography, Criticism, Individual Work, Bibliography, Concordance, and Survey of Scholarship. An author index is included. Items of special importance are asterisked.

Q–22 **Reiman, Donald H. *English Romantic Poetry, 1800–1835: A Guide to Information Sources*.** Detroit: Gale Research Co., 1979.
Z2014.P7 R46

This excellent guide is disposed into eight chapters, as follows: 1, General and Background Studies (Social, Economic, and Political Background; Intellectual and Artistic Background; Literary Background); 2, The Romantic Movement; 3, Wordsworth; 4, Coleridge; 5, Byron; 6, Shelley; 7, Keats; 8, Secondary and Minor Poets (a total of twelve). Subdivisions for each of the major poets are A. Concordances, Bibliographies, and Studies of Reputation and Influence; B. Editions; C. Biographical Sources and Studies; and D. Criticism. The unnumbered entries include extensive descriptive and evaluative annotation. In addition, special symbols are used to designate three sorts of works: those of major significance; those that contain important scholarship; and those that are good, popular introductions for beginners. There are detailed indexes of authors, titles, and subjects.

Q–23 **Jordan, Frank, ed. *English Romantic Poets: A Review of Research and Criticism*.** 4th ed., rev. New York: Modern Language Association, 1985.
PR590.J6 1985

This volume is an updated version (current to 1980–81) of the guides published by Raysor et al. in 1950 and 1956, and by Jordan et al. in 1972. The purpose is to furnish help to the graduate student as he or she begins the specialized study of the field. There are a total of seven chapters in this edition, each in the form of an elaborate bibliographical essay by one or several specialists. The chapters are as follows: 1, The Romantic Movement in England (Frank Jordan); 2, Blake (Mary Lynn Johnson); 3, Wordsworth (Karl Kroeber); 4, Coleridge (Max F. Schulz); 5, Byron (John Clubbe); 6, Shelley (Stuart Curran); 7, Keats (Jack Stillinger). The first chapter has subdivisions treating Bibliographies; Historics and Guides, Backgrounds and Introductions, General Studies; Natural Supernaturalism and Romantic Irony; Earlier Controversies; Romantic Consciousness and Romantic Self; Romanticism and Criticism; Romantic Imagination, Romantic Will, and Romantic Sublime; Romantic Religion, Romantic Myth, and Romantic Occult; Romanticism and Science; Romanticism, Politics, and Society; Romantic Philosophy and Romantic Psychology; Romanticism and Language; Romantic Images and Themes; Romantic Forms and Modes; Romantic Literature and the Other Arts; English Romanticism Abroad; and Romanticism Past, Present, and Future. Subsequent essays are divided into sections discussing such matters as bibliographies; editions, concordances, manuscripts; biographies and biographical studies, criticism, reputation and influence, and special topics appropriate to the particular author. There is a detailed index of authors, titles, and subjects.

Q–24 **Houtchens, Carolyn Washburn, and Lawrence Huston Houtchens, eds. *English Romantic Poets and Essayists: A Review of Research and Criticism*.** 2d ed. New York: Modern Language Association, 1968.
PR590.H6 1968

This volume, originally published in 1957, is designed as a companion to *English Romantic Poets: A Review of Research* (Q–23). It contains bibliographical reviews by specialists on eleven additional authors of the earlier nineteenth century. The chapters are as follows: 1, Blake (Northrop Frye and Martin K. Nurmi); 2, Lamb (George L. Barnett and Stuart M. Tave); 3, Hazlitt (Elisabeth W. Schneider); 4, Scott (James T. Hillhouse and Alexander Welsh); 5, Southey (Kenneth Curry); 6, Thomas Campbell (Hoover H. Jordan); 7, Thomas Moore (Hoover H. Jordan); 8, Walter Savage Landor (R. H. Super); 9, Leigh Hunt (Carolyn W. Houtchens and Lawrence H. Houtchens); 10, Thomas De Quincey (John E. Jordan); and 11, Carlyle (Carlisle Moore). The essays are subdivided, generally, into sections treating bibliographies, edition, biographies and biographical studies, criticism, and such special topics as are appropriate to the individual author. Indexes of authors and subjects conclude the volume.

Q–25 **"The Romantic Movement: A Selective and Critical Bibliography for 1936–1948."** Published in *ELH*, vols. 4–16 (1937–1949): for 1949–1963 in *PQ*, vols. 29–43 (1950–1964); and for 1964–1978 in *ELN*, vols. 3–17 (1965–1979). Now separately published with the title *Romantic Movement: A Selective and Critical Bibliography for [1979–].* New York: AMS Press, 1982–.   Z6514.R6 R64

This current, annual bibliography was begun in imitation of the eighteenth-century annual bibliography (P–5). This work, like that one, has varied in scope, arrangement, and precision of coverage over the years. Not only has the editorship changed, but the bibliography's focus, purpose, and principles of inclusion have varied. Some years are better annotated than others, with both descriptive and evaluative comments and occasional lengthy, signed reviews. Some enumerations include both books and articles, some include articles only. Reviews have always been included, though they have been listed with varying degrees of completeness. The bibliography now covers the romantic movement in England (1789–1937), as well as in each of the European countries where it was significant (France, Germany, Italy, Portugal, Spain). Entries are divided by country, then by listings of studies of general, social, political, and religious contexts; studies in criticism and aesthetics; and studies of individual authors.

A cumulation, the *Romantic Movement Bibliography, 1936–1970*, ed. David B. Erdman, A. C. Elkins, Jr., and L. J. Forstner, was published in seven volumes (Ann Arbor, Mich.: Pierian Press, 1973) [Z6514.R6 R65]. It reprints the annual bibliographies in six volumes and adds an index volume with indexes by authors, main entries, and reviewers; persons as subjects; and topics.

Q–26 **"Current Bibliography [of Keats, Shelley, Byron, Hunt, etc., 1950–]."** *Keats-Shelley Journal,* vol. 1–. New York: Keats-Shelley Association of America, 1952–. Since 1968 the Bibliography has been a separately issued number of the journal.   PR4836.A145

This annual bibliography (biennial after 1971) aims to present a complete listing of current books and articles on Keats, Shelley, Byron, Hunt, and their circles. Dissertations, new editions of poems, reprints, selections, translations, even phonographic records from 1958 through 1972—all are included, with the exception of textbooks. Any work containing a substantial reference to one of the figures is included. In the first two bibliographies, research in progress was also cited, but in subsequent years listing has been limited to published works. A degree of arbitrariness with respect to the limits of the "circles" of the four primary authors has been unavoidable. Thus works concerning William Godwin, Thomas Hood, Thomas Love Peacock, Mary Wollstonecraft, Mary Shelley, and William Hazlitt have been treated fully; in contrast, Thomas Moore has been included only with respect to materials relevant to Byron, and Carlyle has been excluded entirely. Serially numbered entries are annotated with references given both to abstracts and to book reviews. Entries are classified into a general section followed by sections on each author and his circle (subdivided into primary and secondary listings) and, from volume 6 on, a separate list of phonograph recordings. There are abundant cross-references and annual indexes of authors.

Two comprehensively indexed cumulated reprints have been published: volumes 1–12, *Keats, Shelley, Byron, Hunt and Their Circles: A Bibliography: July 1, 1950 to June 30, 1962,* ed. David Bonnell Green and Edwin Graves Wilson (Lincoln: University of Nebraska Press, 1964) [Z2013.K4] with 4,690 entries; and volumes 13–25, *Keats, Shelley, Byron, Hunt and Their Circles: A Bibliography: July 1, 1962 to December 31, 1974,* ed. Robert A. Hartley (Lincoln: University of Nebraska Press, 1978) [Z2013.K42] with 6,285 entries. Both cumulations (after brief introductions) simply reprint the annual bibliographies. The index, primarily of names, is a cumulation of the individual annual indexes, with volume numbers inserted to facilitate reference to the items that retain the serial numeration of their original citation.

Q–29 **Some Frequently Recommended Works on Romanticism** (see also Q–19).

Abrams, Meyer H. *Correspondent Breeze: Essays on English Romanticism.* New York: Norton, 1984.
              PR457.A2 1984

———. *Mirror and the Lamp: Romantic Theory and the Critical Tradition.* New York: Oxford University Press, 1953.   PN769.R7 A2

———. *Natural Supernaturalism: Tradition and Revolution in Romantic Literature.* New York: Norton, 1971.
              PN603.A3

———, ed. *English Romantic Poets: Modern Essays in Criticism.* New York: Oxford University Press, 1960.
              PR590.A2

Aers, David, Jonathan Cook, and David Porter, eds. *Romanticism and Ideology: Studies in English Writing, 1765–1830.* Boston: Routledge & Kegan Paul, 1981.
              PR447.A37 1981

Auden, W. H. *Enchafèd Flood; or, The Romantic Iconography of the Sea.* New York: Random House, 1950.
              PN56.S4 A8 1950

Babbitt, Irving. *Rousseau and Romanticism.* Boston: Houghton Mifflin, 1919.   PN603.B3

Bloom, Harold. *Visionary Company: A Reading of English Romantic Poetry.* Rev. and enl. ed. Ithaca, N.Y.: Cornell University Press, 1971.   PR590.B39 1971

———. *Romanticism and Consciousness: Essays in Criticism.* New York: Norton, 1970.   PR590.B387

Bowra, C. M. *Romantic Imagination.* London: Oxford University Press, 1950.   PR590.B6 1950

Butler, Marilyn. *Romantics, Rebels, and Reactionaries: English Literature and Its Background, 1760–1830.* Oxford: Oxford University Press, 1982. PR447.B8 1982

Cooke, Michael. *Romantic Will.* New Haven: Yale University Press, 1976.   PR590.C6

Donohue, Joseph W., Jr. *Dramatic Character in the English Romantic Age.* Princeton: Princeton University Press, 1970.   PR719.C47 D6

Elton, Oliver. *Survey of English Literature, 1780–1830.* 2 vols. London: Edward Arnold, 1912.   PR447.E5

Engell, James. *Creative Imagination: Enlightenment to Romanticism.* Cambridge: Harvard University Press, 1981.   B105.I49 E53

Fletcher, Richard. *English Romantic Drama 1795–1843; A Critical History.* New York: Exposition Press, 1966.
              PR716.F55

Ford, Boris, ed. *From Blake to Byron.* Vol. 5 in *New Pelican Guide to English Literature* (see M–39).

Frye, Northrop. *Study of English Romanticism.* New York: Random House, 1968.   PR447.F7

———, ed. *Romanticism Reconsidered: Selected Papers from the English Institute.* New York: Columbia University Press, 1963.   PN603.E5

Furst, Lilian R. *Romanticism in Perspective: A Comparative Study of Aspects of the Romantic Movements in England, France, and Germany.* 2d ed. London: Macmillan, 1979.　　PN603.F8 1979

Gaull, Marilyn. *English Romanticism: The Human Context.* New York: W. W. Norton, 1988.　PR590.G38

Gérard, Albert. *English Romantic Poetry: Ethos, Structure, and Symbol in Coleridge, Wordsworth, Shelley and Keats.* Berkeley and Los Angeles: University of California Press, 1968.　　PR5888.G4

———. *L'idée romantique de la poésie en Angleterre: Études sur la théorie de la poésie chez Coleridge, Wordsworth, Keats, et Shelley.* Paris: Les belles lettres, 1955.　　PR590.G4

Gleckner, Robert F., and Gerald E. Enscoe, eds. *Romanticism: Points of View.* 2d ed. Englewood Cliffs, N.J.: Prentice-Hall, 1970.　　PR146.G5 1970

Heller, Erich. *Artist's Journey into the Interior, and Other Essays.* New York: Random House, 1965.　　PT343.H45

———. *Disinherited Mind: Essays in Modern German Literature and Thought.* Expanded ed. New York: Harcourt Brace Jovanovich, 1975.　PT343.H47 1975

Honour, Hugh. *Romanticism.* London: Allen Lane, 1979.　　N6465.R6 H66

Hough, Graham. *Romantic Poets.* 2d ed. London: Hutchinson University Library, 1957.　　PR590.H57

Jack, Ian. *English Literature 1815–1832.* Vol. 10 in the *Oxford History of English Literature* (see M–31).

Jackson, J. R. de J. *Poetry of the Romantic Period.* Vol. 4 in the *Routledge History of English Poetry, 1980.* (See T–43.)

James, D. G. *Romantic Comedy.* New York: Oxford University Press, 1948.　　PR457.J3

Jones, Howard Mumford. *Revolution and Romanticism.* Cambridge: Belknap Press of Harvard University Press, 1974.　　CB411.J66

Kiely, Robert J. *Romantic Novel in England.* Cambridge: Harvard University Press, 1972.　PR858.R73 K5

Kroeber, Karl. *Romantic Narrative Art.* Madison: University of Wisconsin Press, 1960.

———, ed. *Images of Romanticism: Verbal and Visual Affinities.* New Haven: Yale University Press, 1978.　　NX543.I52

McGann, Jerome J. *Romantic Ideology: A Critical Investigation.* Chicago: University of Chicago Press, 1983.　　PR590.M34 1983

Mellor, Anne K., ed. *Romanticism and Feminism.* Bloomington: Indiana University Press, 1988.　　PR469.F44 R66 1988

Peckham, Morse. *Triumph of Romanticism: Collected Essays.* Columbia: University of South Carolina Press, 1970.　　PN603.P4

Praz, Mario. *Romantic Agony.* Translation by Angus Davidson of *La carne, la morte e il diavolo nella letteratura romantica* (Milan: Editrice "La Cultura," 1930). 2d ed. London: Oxford University Press, 1951.　　PN56.R7 P72 1951

Rajan, Tilottama. *Dark Interpreter: The Discourse of Romanticism.* Ithaca, N.Y.: Cornell University Press, 1980.　　PR590.R27 1980

Reiman, Donald H. *Romantic Texts and Contexts.* Columbia: University of Missouri Press, 1987.　　PR457.R45 1987

Schenk, H. G. *Mind of the European Romantics: An Essay in Cultural History.* London: Constable, 1966.　　AZ604.S3

Siskin, Clifford. *Historicity of Romantic Discourse.* New York: Oxford University Press, 1988.　　PR468.H57 1988

Smith, Olivia. *Politics of Language, 1791–1819.* Oxford: Clarendon Press, 1984.　　P40.45.G7 S65 1984

Thorlby, Anthony, ed. *Romantic Movement.* London: Longmans, 1966.　　CB417.T58

Thorpe, C. D., Carlos Baker, and Bennett Weaver, eds. *Major English Romantic Poets: A Symposium in Reappraisal.* Carbondale: Southern Illinois University Press, 1957.　　PR590.T5 1957

Wellek, René. "Romanticism Re-examined." In S. G. Nichols, ed., *Concepts of Criticism.* New Haven: Yale University Press, 1963.　　PN85.W38

Woodring, Carl. *Politics in English Romantic Poetry.* Cambridge: Harvard University Press, 1970.　PR590.W57

III.　THE VICTORIANS

Q–30 **Batho, Edith C., and Bonamy Dobrée.** *Victorians and After, 1830–1914, with a Chapter on the Economic Background* **by Guy Chapman. 3d rev. ed.** *Introductions to English Literature,* **edited by Bonamy Dobrée,** vol. 4. London: Cresset Press, 1962.　　PR85.I615 vol. 4

In parallel to the other volumes in this series (see M–15, N–12, O–12, P–12, and R–12), this work, first published in 1938, contains both a discursive introduction (1. The Background, 1830–1914; 2. Poetry; 3. Fiction; 4. General Prose Writers; 5. Drama; 6. Conclusion; 7. The Economic Background) and a bibliography. The bibliography is classified as follows: the Background; General Reading; Biography and Autobiography; History; Travel; Science; Theology; Philosophy; Poetry; Drama; Words and Short Stories; Children's Books; Criticism and Essays; Nonsense and Parody, Humorous and Light Verse; and Sport. Both the discursive-essay and sheer-list formats are used; under authors, there are sheer lists of primary works by genre followed by brief essays on selected scholarship (editions, bibliographies, biographies, critical works). An index of names concludes the volume.

Q–33 **Chaudhuri, Brahma, ed.** *Annual Bibliography of Victorian Studies,* 1977–. Edmonton, Alberta: LITIR Database, 1980–.　　Z2019.A64 1977

This annual, computerized current bibliography analyzes the contents of both general and specialized journals containing materials on the period 1830–1914. A list of journals precedes the bibliography proper. Currently, only English-language materials are included in the data base. Both articles and reviews are cited. In addition, books and dissertations are analyzed. There are duplicate entries under any subject heading that applies. The serially numbered entries, which are unannotated except to expand titles, are disposed into seven major sections, as follows: General and Reference Works; Fine Arts; Philosophy and Religion; History; Social Science; Science and Technology; and Language and Literature. The latter category is subdivided into sections for individual Victorian authors. The annual volume ends with four indexes, of subjects, authors, titles, and names of reviewers.

The intention of the publishers is to create retrospective bibliographies for publications of the years from 1970 through 1976, and to prepare five-year cumulative indexes to the series. A *Cumulative Bibliography of Victorian Studies: 1976–1980* was published in 1982. Another cumulation, designated as a *Comprehensive Bibliography of Victorian Stud-*

ies, 1970–1984 was announced for 1985 publication in three volumes (1970–1974, 1975–1979, and 1980–1984). The data base is available for computerized searches.

Q–35 **Madden, Lionel.** *How to Find Out about the Victorian Period: A Guide to Sources of Information.* Oxford: Pergamon Press, 1970.   Z2019.M34 1970

This discursive guide to the Victorian period in Britain contains fourteen chapters, as follows: 1, Introductory; 2, General Guides to the Literature; 3, Victorian Periodicals and Newspapers; 4, Guides to Special Collections and Source Materials; 5, Philosophy; 6, The Christian Church; 7, Social and Economic Life and Thought; 8, Education; 9, Science; 10, The Visual Arts; 11, Music Literature; 12, English Literature; 13, History; 14, General Biographical Works. Chapters cite reference works, give both descriptive and evaluative commentary, and include illustrative pages from works of primary importance. An index of subjects of topics concludes the volume.

An additional general-reference tool that updates chapter 4 of the Madden guide is the more recent work of Richard Storey and Lionel Madden, *Primary Sources for Victorian Studies: A Guide to the Location and Use of Unpublished Materials* (London: Phillimore, 1977) [Z2019.S86]. Also a discursive guide, this slim volume is divided into nine sections, as follows: The Research Student and His Materials; The Historical Manuscripts Commission and the National Register of Archives; National Repositories; Local Repositories; General Published Guides; Guides to Collections Outside Britain; Some Special Subject Interests; Organization and Description of Materials; and Some Practical Hints. These are followed by a list of reference notes to the chapters, some addenda, and an index of subjects.

Q–37 **Buckley, Jerome H.** *Victorian Poets and Prose Writers.* **[A Goldentree Bibliography.]** 2d ed. Arlington Heights, Ill.: AHM Publishing, 1978.   Z2013.B8 1978

This guide for beginning graduate students of Victorian literature enumerates important (almost exclusively English-language) works published after 1940. Entries are disposed into the following sections: Social and Political Background; General Studies in Intellectual and Literary History; Anthologies of Victorian Poetry and Prose; and Individual Authors. The latter section offers selective primary and secondary bibliographies for thirty-one Victorian poets and prose writers, including all major figures and many minor ones. Writers of fiction are excluded and are to be found in another volume of the Goldentree series (see Q–73). Also excluded are theses and dissertations and most secondary material of the late nineteenth and early twentieth centuries. Works of particular significance are designated with an asterisk. There is an index of authors.

Q–38 **"Victorian Bibliography for [1932–1956]."** *Modern Philology*, vols. 30–54 (1933–1957). For 1957– in *Victorian Studies*, vol. 1– (1958–).   (1) PB1.M7 / (2) PR1.V5

The current annual bibliography of studies in Victorian literature began in imitation of the eighteenth-century annual bibliography (P–5). Like its original, the scope and arrangement of this bibliography has varied over the years. It is prepared under the auspices of the Victorian Literature section of the MLA. Books, articles, reviews, and dissertations are included. After 1942, entries are occasionally annotated and list book reviews. In the early years of the bibliography, they were disposed into four sections, as follows: Bibliographical Materials; Economic, Political, Religious, and Social Environment; Movements of Ideas and Literary Forms; and Individual Authors. A section on Continental Material was soon added. When the bibliography moved to *Victorian Studies* in

1958, it became more inclusive. Entries are now in six sections, as follows: Bibliographical Material; Histories, Biographies, Autobiographies, and Historical Documents; Economic, Educational, Political, Religious, Scientific, and Social Environment; Fine Arts, Music, Photography, Architecture, City Planning, Performing Arts; Literary History, Literary Forms, Literary Ideas; Individual Authors.

Four cumulations have been published to date. *Bibliographies of Studies in Victorian Literature for the Thirteen Years 1932–1944*, ed. William D. Templeman (Urbana: University of Illinois Press, 1945) [Z2013.B589], cumulates the annual bibliographies and adds an index of Victorian authors. *Bibliographies of Studies in Victorian Literature for the Ten Years 1945–1954*, ed. Austin Wright (Urbana, 1956) [Z2013.B5], has a more elaborate index, including literary authors, names of scholars, other Victorian figures mentioned in the articles, and certain topics. The third cumulation, *Bibliographies of Studies in Victorian Literature for the Ten Years 1955–1965*, ed. Robert C. Slack (Urbana, 1967) [Z2013.B59], contains some 7,900 entries, not counting book reviews. The reprinted annual bibliographies are continuously paginated to facilitate reference. The index, keyed to the continuous pagination, is comparable in complexity to that in the second cumulation. The most recent cumulation, *Bibliographies of Studies in Victorian Literature for the Ten Years 1965–1974*, ed. Ronald E. Freeman (New York: AMS Press, 1981) [Z2013.B592], contains some 18,000 entries. The annual bibliographies are continuously paginated, and the index keyed to the pagination is more elaborate than that of any previous cumulation, including names of scholars, Victorians, periodicals, organizations, societies, theaters, places, and both general and specific subjects. Further decennial cumulations are planned.

For the most current citations see "Recent Publications: A Selected List" in each issue of the *Victorian Newsletter*, vol. 1– (New York: New York University, 1952–) [PR1.V48]. The list of books and articles is in two sections, General (with further divisions) and Individual Authors. Items are annotated and book reviews are listed.

Q–39 **"Guide to the Year's Work in Victorian Poetry [1962–]."** *Victorian Poetry: A Critical Journal of Victorian Literature*, vol. 1–. Morgantown: West Virginia University, 1963–.   PR500.V5

This selective, critical survey of books and articles began as a single bibliographical review essay; in its second year it expanded to three sections, treating Monographs and Special Publications; Arnold, Browning, and Tennyson; and Other Poets, A-Z. Composed by Richard C. Tobias, the annual essays have had various limits. The 1968 essay, for example, is on studies of Victorian prose; that for 1970 features work on the Victorian essayists. The last of Tobias's reviews is for 1971.

In 1974, *Victorian Poetry* published a Special Issue of volume 12 with the imprecise title *Guide to the Year's Work in Victorian Poetry and Prose: 1972*, which is designed as a supplement to the research guides by Faverty (Q–40) and De-Laura (Q–42) and is thus meant to cumulate and supplement the materials in the annual reviews from 1962 through 1972 or so and to link the research guides with subsequent annual guides to Victorian poetry and prose, now conceived as a series of continuing supplements to the research guides. The contents of this special issue are as follows: General Materials (Richard C. Tobias); Arnold (John P. Farrell); Browning (Roma A. King, Jr.); The Carlyles (G. B. Tennyson); Clough (Michael Timko); The Critics (Wendell V. Harris); Fitzgerald and Other Mid-Victorian Poets (Michael S. Helfand); Hardy (Frank R. Giordano, Jr.); Hopkins (John Pick); The Poets of the Nineties (Lionel Stevenson); The Pre-Raphaelites (William E. Fredeman); Ruskin (Francis Townsend); Swinburne (Robert A. Greenberg); and Tennyson (Dan Tannacito).

The annual reviews from 1974 on have the title "Guide to the Year's Work in Victorian Poetry and Prose" and continue to present a series of review essays by specialists. Reviewers have changed in some cases from the group responsible for the Special Issue. The 1975 guide, for example, has reviews of Elizabeth Barrett Browning (Gardner B. Taplin); Robert Browning (Thomas J. Collins); Hopkins (Howard W. Fulweiler); Poets of the Nineties (Benjamin Franklin Fisher IV); and Tennyson (Joseph Sendry).

Q–40 **Faverty, Frederic E., ed.** *Victorian Poets: A Guide to Research.* 2d ed. Cambridge: Harvard University Press, 1968.
PR593.F3 1968

This guide, first published in 1956, provides a series of bibliographical review essays by specialists, covering publications on the Victorian poets and related subjects through the end of 1966. The individual chapters are as follows: 1, General Materials (Jerome Buckley); 2, Tennyson (E. D. H. Johnson); 3, Browning (Park Honan); 4, Elizabeth Barrett Browning (Michael Timko); 5, Fitzgerald (Michael Timko); 6, Clough (Michael Timko); 7, Arnold (Frederic E. Faverty); 8, Swinburne (Clyde K. Hyder); 9, The Pre-Raphaelites (William E. Fredeman); 10, Hopkins (John Pick); 11, The Later Victorian Poets (Lionel Stevenson). The general section has the following subdivisions: Bibliographies; Anthologies; Background Studies; General Histories of Victorian Poetry; The Romantic Tradition; The Content of Victorian Poetry; and The Form of Victorian Poetry. The essays on individuals or groups of authors have different subdivisions, but all include bibliographies, editions, biography and biographical studies, influences, general and special critical studies, and discussions of the scholarship on individual poems. The volume concludes with an author index. It is continuously supplemented by the annual bibliographical review essays in *Victorian Poetry* (Q–39).

Q–42 **DeLaura, David J., ed.** *Victorian Prose: A Guide to Research.* New York: Modern Language Association, 1973.
PR785.D4

This work is a companion to the other guides to research in Victorian studies edited by Faverty (Q–40), Stevenson (Q–43), Ford (Q–44) and Vann and VanArsdel (Q–47). Coverage of the bibliographical essays in this volume extends through 1971 with some materials from 1972 included. The volume consists of thirteen bibliographical review essays by specialists. The chapters are as follows: General Materials (David J. DeLaura); Macaulay (John Clive and Thomas Pinney); The Carlyles (G. B. Tennyson); Newman (Martin J. Svaglic and Charles Stephen Dessain); Mill (John M. Robson); Ruskin (Francis G. Townsend); Arnold (David J. DeLaura); Pater (Lawrence Evans); The Oxford Movement (Howard W. Fulweiler); The Victorian Churches (Richard Helmstadter); The Critics (Wendell V. Harris); and The Unbelievers (John W. Bicknell). The section on general materials has the following subdivisions: Bibliography; Anthologies; The Traditions of Victorian Prose; The Themes of Victorian Prose; and The Art of Victorian Prose. Essays on individual authors and groups of authors have various subdivisions but generally include Manuscripts and Bibliography; Editions; Biography and Biographical Studies; and Criticism (both general and specific). But there are also sections describing the state of research on such specific topics as "Newman as Literary Artist," "Arnold and the Classics," and "Christian Socialism." The volume concludes with an index of authors. It is supplemented by the annual bibliographical review essays in *Victorian Poetry* (Q–39).

Q–43 **Stevenson, Lionel, ed.** *Victorian Fiction: A Guide to Research.* Cambridge: Harvard University Press, 1964.
PR873.S8

This work, designed as a companion volume to the guide to research on Victorian Poetry (Q–40), consists of twelve bibliographical essays, each by a different authority, surveying the scholarship and criticism published on Victorian fiction through 1962. The chapters are as follows: 1, General Materials (Bradford A. Booth); 2, Benjamin Disraeli and Edward Bulwer-Lytton (Curtis Dahl); 3, Dickens (Ada Nisbet); 4, Thackeray (Lionel Stevenson); 5, Trollope (Donald Smalley); 6, The Brontës (Mildred G. Christian); 7, Mrs. Gaskell and Charles Kingsley (James D. Barry); 8, Wilkie Collins (Robert Ashley) and Charles Reade (Wayne Burns); 9, George Eliot (W. J. Harvey); 10, Meredith (C. L. Cline); 11, Hardy (George S. Fayen, Jr.); 12, George Moore and George Gissing (Jacob Korg). The General Materials chapter has the following subdivisions: Bibliographies, Histories, Essays and Interpretations, Studies in Forms and Types, Studies in Technique, and Special Studies. Subdivisions for individual authors or pairs of authors include sections on Bibliography; Biography and Biographical Studies; Criticism; and topics specific to individual writers. An index of authors concludes the volume. All of the essays in this volume are supplemented by those in Ford's *Victorian Fiction: A Second Guide to Research* (Q–44).

Q–44 **Ford, George H.** *Victorian Fiction: A Second Guide to Research.* New York: Modern Language Association, 1978.
PR871.V5 1978

This volume, designed to complement, not replace, the earlier guide edited by Stevenson (Q–43), treats scholarship from 1963 through 1974, with some items of 1975. Also included are significant items published before 1963 which were omitted by compilers of the earlier guide. The guide consists of eighteen bibliographical essays, each by an authority, surveying scholarship and criticism. The chapters are as follows: General Materials (Richard D. Altick); Benjamin Disraeli (Curtis Dahl); Edward Bulwer-Lytton (Curtis Dahl); Dickens (Philip Collins); Thackeray (Robert A. Colby); Trollope (Ruth A. Roberts); The Brontës (Herbert J. Rosengarten); Elizabeth Gaskell (James D. Barry); Charles Kingsley (James D. Barry); Wilkie Collins (Robert Ashley); Charles Reade (Wayne Burns); George Eliot (U. C. Knoepflmacher); Meredith (Gilliam Beer); Samuel Butler (Daniel F. Howard); Hardy (Michael Millgate); Robert Louis Stevenson (Robert Kiely); George Moore (Jacob Korg); and George Gissing (Jacob Korg). The General Materials Chapter includes the following subdivisions: Bibliography, Historical Materials, Theoretical Studies, General Criticism, and Studies of Special Aspects. Individual chapters have various subdivisions that generally include such rubrics as bibliography, editions, letters; biography; general criticism; studies of special aspects; studies of individual works. An index of authors concludes the volume. This volume is supplemented by the annual "Guide to the Year's Work in Victorian Poetry and Prose" (Q–39).

Q–45 **Vann, J. Don.** *Victorian Novels in Serial.* New York: Modern Language Association, 1985.   Z2014.F4 V36 1985

This small volume presents a general introduction to serialization, followed by an identification of the parts of a novel included in each installment, thus allowing modern readers to know the dates when each part of a novel first was published and to duplicate the reading experience of Victorian readers.

The body of the work is arranged alphabetically by author and includes all authors cited in Stevenson's *Victorian Fiction* (Q–43) and in Ford's *Victorian Fiction: A Second Guide* (Q–44), with the addition of William Harrison Ainsworth and

Frederick Marryat, and excluding those who never published in serial (the Brontës, Disraeli, Gissing, Samuel Butler, and George Moore). Beneath the author's name are listed chronologically all of his or her serially published works, with the name of the periodical in which the work was published followed by columns identifying the part number, date of publication, and chapter numbers in the full volume edition(s) which that part includes. Notes identify the date(s) of publication in volume(s) and modern editions which identify serial parts. The work concludes with brief Notes on Periodicals and a Selected Bibliography.

Q–47 **Vann, J. Don, and Rosemary T. VanArsdel, eds.** *Victorian Periodicals: A Guide to Research.* New York: Modern Language Association, 1978.   PN5124.P4 V5

This volume is designed to guide researchers who want to work with Victorian periodicals but are unaware of the resources. It is disposed into eight chapters that address the chief problems encountered in using Victorian periodicals. The chapters and their individual authors are as follows: 1, The Rationale—Why Read Victorian Periodicals (John S. North); 2, The Bibliographic Control of Victorian Periodicals (Scott Bennett); 3, Finding Lists for Victorian Periodicals (J. Don Vann and Rosemary T. VanArsdel); 4, Biographical Resources (William H. Scheuerle); 5, General Histories of the Press (Joanne Shattock); 6, Histories and Studies of Individual Periodicals (Lionel Madden and Diana Dixon); 7, The Identification of Authors: The Great Victorian Enigma (Mary Ruth Hiller); and 8, Circulation and the Stamp Tax (John H. Wiener). An index of authors and titles concludes the volume. For accounts of more recent work in this field see the annual checklist in the *Victorian Periodicals Newsletter* (Q–48) as well as the various bibliographical notices in each issue.

Q–48 **"Victorian Periodicals [1971/72–]: A Checklist of Scholarship and Criticism."** *Victorian Periodicals Review* [former title: *Victorian Periodicals Newsletter, 1968–1978*], vol. 6–. Toronto: Research Society for Victorian Periodicals, 1973–.   PN5124.P4 V52

This annual bibliography began with a listing of books, articles, and important reviews, published in 1971/72, pertaining to all aspects of the study of Victorian periodicals, thus continuing the work of Madden and Dixon, the *Nineteenth Century Periodical Press in Britain: A Bibliography of Modern Studies* (D–57). The bibliography is a sheer list, annotated only to clarify titles, alphabetically arranged by author, and serially numbered. Indexes of names, periodical titles, and subjects conclude each year's enumeration.

Q–49 **Some Frequently Recommended Works in Victorian Studies.**

Altholz, Josef L., ed. *Mind and Art of Victorian England.* Minneapolis: University of Minnesota Press, 1976.
          NX543.A1 M55 1976
Altick, Richard D. *Victorian People and Ideas: A Companion for the Modern Reader of Victorian Literature.* New York: W. W. Norton, 1973.   DA533.A55 1973
———. *Writers, Readers, and Occasions: Selected Essays on Victorian Literature and Life.* Columbus: Ohio State University Press, 1989.   PR463.A48 1989
Armstrong, Isobel, ed. *Major Victorian Poets: Reconsiderations.* London: Routledge and Kegan Paul, 1969.   PR593.A75
Baker, Joseph E., ed. *Reinterpretation of Victorian Literature.* Princeton N.J.: Princeton University Press, 1950.   PR732.B3

Buckler, William E. *Victorian Imagination: Essays in Aesthetic Exploration.* New York: New York University Press, 1980.   PR463.B8
Buckley, Jerome H., ed. *Worlds of Victorian Fiction.* Cambridge: Harvard University Press, 1975.   PR873.W6
Cooke, John D., and Lionel Stevenson. *English Literature of the Victorian Period.* New York: Appleton-Century-Crofts, 1949. Biobibliographies of major figures.
          PR461.C6
DeLaura, David J. *Hebrew and Hellene in Victorian England: Newman, Arnold, and Pater.* Austin: University of Texas Press, 1969.   PR461.D4
Eisen, Sydney, and Bernard V. Lightman, eds. *Victorian Science and Religion: A Bibliography with Emphasis on Evolution, Belief, and Unbelief, Comprised of Works Published from c. 1900–1975.* Hamden, Conn.: Archon, 1984.   Z5320.E57 1984
Elton, Oliver. *Survey of English Literature 1830–1880.* 2 vols. London: Edward Arnold, 1932.   PR451.E53
Ford, Boris, ed. *From Dickens to Hardy.* Vol. 6 in *New Pelican Guide to English Literature* (see M–39).
Hough, Graham. *Last Romantics.* London: Duckworth, 1949.   PR468.R65 H6
Kaplan, Fred. *Sacred Tears: Sentimentality in Victorian Literature.* Princeton, N.J.: Princeton University Press, 1987.   PR468.S46K36 1987
Kincaid, James R., and Albert J. Kuhn, eds. *Victorian Literature and Society: Essays Presented to Richard D. Altick.* Columbus: Ohio State University Press, 1984.
          PR463.V53 1984
Knoepflmacher, U. C. *Religious Humanism and the Victorian Novel: George Eliot, Walter Pater, and Samuel Butler.* Princeton, N.J.: Princeton University Press, 1965.
Levine, Richard A., ed. *Victorian Experience: The Poets.* Athens: Ohio University Press, 1982.   PR593.V48
———, ed. *Victorian Experience: The Novelists.* Athens: Ohio University Press, 1976.   PR783.V5
———, ed. *Victorian Experience: The Prose Writers.* Athens: Ohio University Press, 1982.
          PR781.V5 1982
McGann, Jerome, J., ed. *Victorian Connections.* Charlottesville: University Press of Virginia, 1989.
          PR468.H57V53 1989
McMurtry, Jo. *Victorian Life and Victorian Fiction: A Companion for the American Reader.* Hamden, Conn: Archon, 1979.   PR872.M2
Miller, J. Hillis. *Disappearance of God: Five Nineteenth Century Writers.* Cambridge: Belknap Press of Harvard University Press, 1963.   PR469.R4 M5
Mitchell, Sally. *Victorian Britain: An Encyclopedia.* New York: Garland, 1989.   DA550.V53 1988
Parrott, Thomas M., and Robert B. Martin. *Companion to Victorian Literature.* New York: Scribner's, 1955.
          PR461.P3
Pollard, Arthur, ed. *Victorians.* Vol. 6 of the *[Sphere] History of Literature in the English Language* (see M–34).
Praz, Mario. *Hero in Eclipse in Victorian Fiction.* Translation by Angus Davidson of *La crisi del'eroe nel romanzo vittoriano* (Florence: Sansoni, 1952). New York: Oxford University Press, 1956.   PR871.P712
Preyer, Robert O., ed. *Victorian Literature: Selected Essays.* New York: Harper and Row, 1967.   PR461.P7
Sussman, Herbert L. *Victorians and the Machine: The Literary Response to Technology.* Cambridge: Harvard University Press, 1968.   PR468.T458

Thesing, William. *London Muse: Victorian Poetic Responses to the City.* Athens: University of Georgia Press, 1982. PR595.L64 T4 1982

Thomson, Patricia. *Victorian Heroine: A Changing Ideal, 1837–1873.* London: Oxford University Press, 1957. PR878.W6 T5

Tillotson, Geoffrey. *View of Victorian Literature.* Oxford: Clarendon Press, 1978. PR461.T5

Turner, Paul. *English Literature, 1832–1890: Excluding the Novel.* Vol. 11, pt. 1 in the *Oxford History of English Literature* (see M–31).

Watt, Ian, ed. *Victorian Novel: Modern Essays in Criticism.* New York: Oxford University Press, 1971. PR873.W3 1971

Wright, Austin, ed. *Victorian Literature: Modern Essays in Criticism.* New York: Oxford University Press, 1961. PR463.W7

IV. POETRY

See also section T.

Q–52 Jackson, J. R. de J. *Annals of English Verse, 1770–1835: A Preliminary Survey of the Volumes Published.* New York: Garland, 1985. Z2039.P6 J32

This work presents a chronological listing of volumes of poems and verse drama published in the United Kingdom in English. Excluded are books of hymns, songs not intended to be read, annuals, reprints of pre–1770 works, volumes of fewer than eight pages, and stage adaptations of plays, operas, textbooks, and foreign works in foreign languages. Entries are alphabetical by title under the year of publication. They include a short title, the name of the editor or translator, publication information, edition number if other than the first edition, format, number of volumes, pagination for single volume works, price, author, and the source of the citation (generally the *CBEL* (M–10), *NCBEL* (M–11), British Museum *General Catalogue of Printed Books* (B–41), and the *National Union Catalog, Pre–56 Imprints* (C–12). There are indexes of authors and of titles of anonymous works.

Q–55 Fredeman, William E. *Pre-Raphaelitism: A Bibliocritical Study.* Cambridge: Harvard University Press, 1965. Z5948.P9 F7

This work is divided into two main parts, one of commentary containing "A Survey of Pre-Raphaelite Scholarship" and the other an elaborately classified 100-section enumerative bibliography. The survey includes both a definition of Pre-Raphaelitism and an examination of shifting attitudes toward the movement. The primary and secondary bibliography, generally current to early 1964 (though the official cutoff date is 1962), is divided into four parts and a number of subdivisions treating I. Sources for Bibliography and Provenance (Bibliographical Sources, Descriptions of Collections, Exhibitions of Separate Artists, General Exhibitions, Sales, Notices); II. Bibliography of Individual Figures (Dante Gabriel Rossetti, Other Pre-Raphaelite Brothers, Associates, and Later Pre-Raphaelites, Minor Figures); III. Bibliography of the Pre-Raphaelite Movement (General Discussions, Primary Works and Studies of Specific Aspects of Pre-Raphaelitism, Other Works); and IV. Bibliography of Pre-Raphaelite Illustrations (References, Joint Illustrations, Books and Periodicals Illustrated by Separate Artists). Entries, nearly half of which are descriptively and evaluatively annotated, are numbered serially within the sections in which they are found.

Each of the 100 sections contains an introduction, as does each of the four main parts. These introductions provide orientation to background materials, special problems, critical commentaries, and individual biographies. Those items referred to in the opening survey of scholarship are generally unannotated, though cross-reference is made to citation there. A brief section of additions is followed by an elaborate index of authors, anonymous titles, and subjects which, along with the abundant cross-references found throughout, is keyed to section and item numbers of individual entries.

V. DRAMA AND THEATER

See also section U.

Q–60 Conolly, Leonard W., and J. P. Wearing, eds. *English Drama and Theatre, 1800–1900: A Guide to Information Sources.* Detroit: Gale Research Co., 1978. Z2014.D7 C72

A total of 3,234 serially numbered entries, often annotated, describe books, articles, and dissertations concerned with nineteenth-century English drama and theater. The entries are in ten chapters and are arranged throughout in chronological rather than alphabetical order. The chapters are as follows: 1, Contemporary Works of History and Criticism 1800–1900; 2, Modern Works of History and Criticism 1901–1974; 3, Individual Authors (total of 110; with the following subheadings: Collected Works; Acted Plays; Unacted Plays; Bibliographies; Biographies; Critical Studies; Journals and Newsletters); 4, Bibliographies and Reference Works; 5, Anthologies of Plays; 6, The Theatres; 7, Acting and Management; 8, The Critics; 9, Stage Design, Scenic Art, and Costume; and 10, Periodicals. The volume concludes with a general index of authors and titles.

Q–62 "Nineteenth-Century Theatre Research: A Bibliography For 1972–." *Nineteenth-Century Theatre Research,* vol. 1–. Tucson: University of Arizona Department of English [place varies], 1973–. PN1851.N55

These annual bibliographies of books, articles, and dissertations contain serially numbered entries arranged under subject headings, including names of authors, theaters, performers; topics from censorship to pantomime; and general categories such as American Theatre and Reference and Bibliography. There are cross-references to assist users both to find current subject headings and to locate articles that treat several subjects.

A newsletter accompanying the journal since 1977 lists both works in progress and supplemental entries to the annual bibliography.

VI. PROSE FICTION

See also section W.

Q–73 Watt, Ian, ed. *British Novel: Scott through Hardy.* [A Goldentree Bibliography.] Northbrook, Ill.: AHM Publishing Co., 1973. Z2014.F5 W37

This volume, designed as a guide to scholarship in Victorian fiction for graduate students, includes selective coverage of primary and secondary materials concerning major authors and topics of novelists whose major works were published after 1817 and before 1890. Emphasis is on works published in the twentieth century; general literary histories, short notes and explications, and largely superseded older studies are omitted. A total of 1,804 serially numbered entries are disposed into seven major divisions, as follows: Bibliographies, Journals, and Surveys of Scholarship; Literary Histories; General Critical Studies and Collections; Special Topics (Historical, Social, and Intellectual Background); Publishing, Authorship, and the Reading Public; Genres, Schools, Influences, and Subjects; Individual Novelists (a total of eighty-four, with subdivisions listing Major Novels, Bibliographical and Reference Works, Textual Studies, Biographical and General Studies, and Critical Studies); and Minor and Occasional Novelists. Especially recommended entries are designated with an asterisk. An index of names concludes the work. There is a sequel to this volume in the same series (R–50) and a complementary volume on the nineteenth-century American novel (S–80).

Q–76 **Sadleir, Michael. *XIX Century Fiction: A Bibliographical Record Based on His Own Collection.*** 2 vols. Berkeley and Los Angeles: University of California Press, 1951.
Z2014.F4 S16 1951

This bibliography is based upon (though not limited to) the Sadleir collection now at UCLA, much of which has been microfilmed. The text is in three parts. The first, in volume 1, presents an alphabet of authors, describing their first and certain subsequent editions. Any novelist who wrote within the limits of the nineteenth-century is included; any who published fiction before 1800 is excluded (except Maria Edgeworth); and any who published also in the twentieth century may be included. Entries for each novel include title and subtitles word for word; size and format; author or anonymous author (if attributable); date on title page or information for such a date; condition of the book; half titles or preliminary leaves before the title page; provenance (sales and dates); inscription or autograph (if any) with the date. In addition, standard bibliographies are noted, brief biographies of little-known authors are given, and other notes of bibliographical interest are appended.

The second part, in volume 2, includes the yellowback collection, citing authors, titles, and series headings for works issued in noncloth bindings. Descriptions are parallel to those found in part 1. Also in volume 2 is the third part, enumerating published series by keyword in series title. First editions and reprints of each series are noted, so that the continued reputation of an author can be gauged.

The volumes are illustrated; they conclude with two indexes, of authors and of titles.

Q–77 **Wolff, Robert Lee. *Nineteenth-Century Fiction: A Bibliographical Catalogue Based on the Collection Formed by Robert Lee Wolff.*** 5 vols. New York: Garland, 1981–1986.
Z2014.F4 W64 1982

This catalog includes first editions, original manuscripts, periodicals, yellowbacks and other reprints, and autograph letters associated with the authors of nineteenth-century English fiction. Serially numbered entries, alphabetically arranged by author, contain full bibliographical descriptions, including collations, along with brief discussions of such questions as authorship, composition, publication history, provenance, sources, influences, and other matters of scholarly interest. Autograph letters are reproduced in full or in excerpts; presentation inscriptions are transcribed; and pages are profusely illustrated. For the third of the Wolff collection which duplicates materials in the Sadleir collection, the Sadleir number is cited (see Q–76). Coverage of individual volumes is as follows: 1, A-C; 2, D-K; 3, L-P; 4, Q-Z; 5, anonymous and pseudonymous works, periodicals, and indexes of themes, of illustrations, and of titles.

VII. PROSE AND CRITICISM

See also section W and section X.

Q–80 **Wilson, Harris W., and Diane Long Hoeveler. *English Prose and Criticism in the Nineteenth Century: A Guide to Information Sources.*** Detroit: Gale Research Co., 1979.
Z2014.P795 W54

Unnumbered entries, many with mediocre annotations, are disposed into four sections, as follows: 1, Basic Surveys and Reference Works (bibliographies, literary histories, anthologies); 2, Background (literary and cultural); 3, Individual Authors, thirty-four individuals listed by field (Critical, Philosophical, Polemical; Aesthetic; Historical; Journalistic; Religious; Scientific; Travel), with subheadings listing Principal Prose Works, Collected Works, Letters, Biographies, Critical Studies, and Bibliographies; and 4, Nineteenth Century Periodicals; Guides and Studies. This volume concludes with author, title, and subject indexes. It has been adversely reviewed.

LITERATURE OF THE TWENTIETH CENTURY

See also many pertinent references in section L, section M, and section S. See works in section C on National Bibliography, in section D on Periodicals and Newspapers, in section F on Modern History, in section G on Modern Biography, and in section H on Archives and Manuscripts. See additional references on modern poetry and poetics in section T, on modern drama and theater in section U, and on modern prose and prose fiction in section W. See also references on modern Literary and Rhetorical Theory in section X, and on modern Printing and Publishing in section Y.

I. AGE OF TRANSITION

See also materials in section Q.III which treat authors of this period.

R–1 **Lauterbach, Edward S., and W. Eugene Davis. *Transitional Age. British Literature, 1880–1920.*** Troy, N.Y.: Whitston Publishing Co., 1973. Z2013.L38

This work is divided into two parts. The first contains four essays surveying significant developments in British fiction (including the novel, the short story, and other forms), poetry, drama, and nonfictional prose between 1880 and 1920.

Part 2 contains selective bibliographies of primary and secondary works for more than 170 major and minor authors prominent during those forty years. Among authors excluded on chronological and ideological grounds are Meredith, Morris, and Joyce; among those included, although outside the chronological limits, are Pater, Yeats, Lawrence, Shaw, Maugham, and Forster. Author bibliographies include, for primary works, standard editions, collected works, letters, journals, and other autobiographical materials. The secondary entries are in two sections, treating bibliographical references and then important biographical and critical sources. The bibliographies end with a brief account of the author's place in and contribution to the literary scene during this period.

Included in alphabetical order among the author bibliographies are a number of brief articles in defining of pertinent literary terms (such as Celtic Renaissance, Decadence, and Fin de Siècle). The volume ends with an index of names and terms.

R–2 **"Bibliography, News, and Notes," *English Literature in Transition, 1880–1920* [*ELT*],** vols. 1–18. Tempe: Arizona State University Department of English [location varies], vols. 1957–1975. PR1.E55

Formerly titled *English Fiction in Transition [EFT]*, this journal, since its beginning, carried bibliographical notices of books, articles, and reviews alphabetically by author, with descriptive abstracts of books and long reviews, lists of "Books Received," and other notes of bibliographical value. In addition, a number of substantial author bibliographies have been published in *ELT*, taking the form of unabstracted listings. Coverage is limited to works treating authors on whom the editors have published a bibliography (either selective or comprehensive) or on whom a major bibliographical project is in progress. After volume 18 (1975) the "bibliography, news, and notes" feature was dropped in favor of occasional supplements to previously published author bibliographies. The "Books Received" section continues to the present, as do reviews of important books in the field.

II. GENERAL BIBLIOGRAPHIES AND GUIDES

R–4 **Mellown, Elgin W. *Descriptive Catalogue of the Bibliographies of Twentieth Century British Poets, Novelists, and Dramatists.*** 2d ed., rev. and enl. Troy, N.Y.: Whitston Publishing Co., 1978. Z2011.A1 M43 1978

This bibliography of bibliographies includes both separately published bibliographies and those published in books and articles. It begins with a list of general bibliographies that include twentieth-century British authors, and then proceeds alphabetically by literary author to cite individual author bibliographies of primary works, of first editions, of books, of secondary works, and of selected secondary works. Coverage is limited to authors born after 1840 who published the major portion of their *oeuvre* after 1890. Entries for each bibliography identify its scope (limited to primary works, to secondary, to first editions, etc.), its principles of arrangement (chronological, by form of publication, by genre), the character of its entries (whether they include title-page transcriptions, collations, etc.), and an evaluation of it. The work concludes with an index of names excluding both principal entries and the authors of general bibliographies, but including all others.

R–5 **Temple, Ruth Z., and Martin Tucker.** *Twentieth Century British Literature: A Reference Guide and Bibliography.* New York: Frederick Ungar, 1968.   Z2013.3.T4

This work is in two parts. The first is a briefly annotated reference guide to twentieth-century literature including a bibliography of bibliographies (general reference works, bibliographies of English literature, special reference guides, genre bibliographies, author bibliographies, and annual bibliographies); a section of sources for biographical study; a list of reference books; a list of journals treating modern English literature and one of those carrying bibliographies of contemporary writers; a section on modern history; a list of general histories of modern literature; a list of special studies of modern literature; a section on autobiographies, diaries, memoirs, and reminiscences; lists of essay collections; and then for criticism, drama, the novel, and modern poetry, bibliographies of histories and of works of theory and special studies.

The second part presents bibliographies for approximately 400 English, Welsh, and Commonwealth authors who lived in the British Isles. The author bibliographies include all primary works except those privately printed and ephemera. These are listed chronologically with a code identifying the genre of the work. A brief secondary bibliography is also included.

R–8 **Millett, Fred B.** *Contemporary British Literature. Critical Survey and 232 Author Bibliographies.* 3d rev. ed. New York: Harcourt Brace and Co., 1935.   PR471.M5 1935

This work is based on a 1928 second edition by John M. Manly and Edith Rickert of their work originally published in 1921. The critical survey contains eight sections, treating Background, The Novel, The Short Story, Drama, Poetry, Essay and Travel, Biography, and Criticism. This is followed by an alphabetical list of 232 authors born after 1850, giving for each a brief biographical sketch, the titles and dates of all primary works, arranged by genre, and a brief secondary bibliography of selected books and articles, including contemporary reviews. The work also includes a select bibliography of contemporary social, political, and literary history. Though citations end with works published in 1934, this bibliography remains useful, among other things for the series of indexes that classify the authors as biographers and historians, critics, dramatists, essayists, novelists and short story writers, philosophers, poets, and travelers.

A work parallel in content and arrangement to Millet's is by Mark Longaker and Edwin C. Bolles, *Contemporary English Literature* (New York: Appleton-Century-Crofts, 1953) [PR85.L7].

R–11 *New Cambridge Bibliography of English Literature [NCBEL].* Vol. 4, 1900–1950. Edited by I. R. Willison. Cambridge: Cambridge University Press, 1972.
Z2011.N45 vol.4.

This volume, the only one of those in the *NCBEL* (M–11) not preceded by an original volume of the *CBEL* (M–10), is nevertheless designed according to the same principles of inclusion and organization which govern the other volumes in both series. Entries, current through 1969, are in six main parts. Part 1, Introduction, has two sections: General Works, and Book Production and Distribution. Part 2, Poetry, has two sections: General Works and Individual Poets. Part 3, The Novel, has three parts: General Works, Individual Novelists, and Children's Books.

Part 4, Drama, has two sections: General Works and Individual Dramatists. Part 5, Prose, is in four sections: Critics and Literary Scholars, Essayists and Humorists; Historians, Autobiographers, Writers on Politics, Society, Economics, etc.; Philosophers, Theologians, Writers on Natural Science and

on Psychology; and Writers on Travel, the Countryside, and Sport. Part 6, finally, treats Newspapers and Magazines. A limited index at the end of the volume is complemented by a more complete index in the *NCBEL*, vol. 5, *Index* (1977). A detailed index to part 2, Poetry, was prepared by James Edward Tennyson (see *Dissertation Abstracts International* 36:2858A–2859A). The list of thirty contributors following the preface identifies the initials of contributing bibliographers.

Reviews of this volume have been mixed. See the attack by Christopher Ricks in *Listener* and T. A. Birrell's "Notes on *NCBEL* IV" in *Neophilologus* 59:306–315, as well as the more moderate treatment by L. S. Thompson in *PBSA* 71 (1977): 236–237.

R–12 **Daiches, David.** *Present Age in British Literature.* *Introductions to English Literature*, edited by Bonamy Dobree, vol. 5. Bloomington: Indiana University Press, 1958.
PR471.D3

This work is a substantially new volume that replaces the original volume by Edwin Muir, *Present Age, after 1920* (London: Cressett Press, 1939) [PR83.I6 vol. 5], though the original title is retained in the British edition also published by Cressett. Like the other volumes in this series (see M–15, N–12, O–12, P–12, Q–30), this work also is in two sections, a text and a bibliography. The text is in five chapters: 1, General Background; 2, Poetry; 3, Fiction; 4, Criticism and General Prose; and 5, Drama. The bibliography is divided into the genres, as follows: Poetry (Yeats, Georgians and Others, Eliot and Others, Auden and Others, The Younger Generation, The Scottish Renaissance); Fiction (Older Generation, Age of Experiment, The 30's and After); Drama; and General Prose (History and Biography, Criticism and Scholarship, Philosophy and Science, Travel, Politics and Economics). For each author, titles and dates are given for primary works and selected secondary works. The volume concludes with an index of names.

R–13 **Somer, John, and Barbara Eck Cooper.** *American and British Literature 1945–1975: An Annotated Bibliography of Contemporary Scholarship.* Lawrence: Regents Press of Kansas, 1980.   Z1227.S65

This volume, which excludes primary works, secondary works on a single author, dissertations, and articles and essays, contains more than 1,500 alphanumerically arranged entries disposed into two parts. The first part gives descriptively annotated entries for books about contemporary literature. It is in six sections: A. General Studies; B. Drama; C. Fiction and Prose; D. Poetry; E. Critical Theory; and F. Studies Published after 1975 (this section is not annotated). Annotations give the thesis or purpose of the work, a description of its special features, and a list of the contemporary writers it treats. The second part presents unannotated lists of ancillary works in four sections: G. Collections of Abstracts, Summaries, and Excerpts; H. Bibliographies and Indexes; I. Biographical Guides and Directories; J. Handbooks and Guides. The volume ends with an index of authors and subjects.

R–15 **Pownall, David E.** *Articles on Twentieth Century Literature: An Annotated Bibliography 1954 to 1970: An Expanded Cumulation of "Current Bibliography" in the Journal Twentieth Century Literature, Volume One to Volume Sixteen, 1955 to 1970.* 7 vols. New York: Kraus Thomson, 1973–1980.   Z6519.P66

This work includes nearly 24,000 entries taken from the annual bibliographies in *TCL* (see R–16), compiled, indexed, verified, regularized, corrected, and supplemented by the author to include, among others, the articles published in *TCL* itself. Articles cited exclude book reviews, review articles, popular journalism, and elementary articles on teaching. Annotations summarize the contents of cited works, stating their premises or conclusion, thus serving as informative abstracts. Entries are in two sections, on literary and general topics. Entries are alphabetically arranged by author for general works and for studies treating several works; those concerned with a single work are then arranged alphabetically by the title of that work. The entries are serially numbered in an alphanumeric pattern, and the index refers to the serial numeration.

R–16 **"Current Bibliography [of Twentieth-Century Literature, 1954–]."** *Twentieth Century Literature: A Scholarly and Critical Journal [TCL]*, vol. 1–. Hempstead, N.Y.: Hofstra University Press, 1955–. PN2.T8

The aim of this list is to provide a bibliography of current critical literature appearing in both American and foreign periodicals. It is published in each quarterly issue except those that are special issues devoted to a single author or topic. Articles appearing in *TCL* are excluded. Each entry is annotated with an initialed informational abstract. Entries are arranged alphabetically by subject, including authors-as-subjects. Reviews are excluded, and no index is provided. For listings through 1970 the expanded cumulation of Pownall (R–15) should be used. Because of its quarterly appearance this bibliography is the most current for studies of twentieth-century literature.

R–17 **"[1970–] Annual Review Number."** *Journal of Modern Literature [JML]*, vol. 1–. Philadelphia: Temple University, 1970–. PN2.J6

This descriptively and evaluatively annotated list of studies written in English contains brief signed reviews of important books. It is divided into two sections, the first with entries disposed into ten general subjects, the second with entries for individual authors on whom at least one book or several dissertations and articles were published during the covered year. The general part is divided into the following sections: 1. Reference and Bibliography; 2. Literary History; 3. Themes and Movements; 4. Regional, National, and Ethnic Literatures; 5. Comparative Studies–Two or More Authors; 6. Criticism of Modern Literature Generally; 7. Criticism of Fiction; 8. Criticism of Poetry; 9. Criticism of Drama; 10. Criticism of Film and/as Literature–History and Criticism. The sections under both the general subjects and the individual author entries are as follows: A. [Primary] Books and reviews of them; B. Secondary Books; C. Dissertations (listing institutions, dates, and advisors); D. Symposia and Special Numbers [of Journals]; E. Articles; and F. Miscellaneous. The annual review numbers conclude with an index of authors-as-subjects and authors.

R–18 **Scholarly Journals in Modern Studies.**

Boundary 2: A Journal of Post-Modern Literature. Vol. 1–. Binghamton: State University of New York, Department of English, 1972–. 3/yr. Reviews. PN2.B68

ConL *Contemporary Literature* [former title: *Wisconsin Studies in Contemporary Literature*, 1960–1967]. Vol. 1–. Madison: University of Wisconsin Press, 1960–. 4/yr. Reviews. PN2.W55

Crit *Critique: Studies in Modern Fiction.* Vol. 1–. Atlanta: Georgia Institute of Technology, 1956–. 3/yr. Cumulative indexes for vols. 1–10 in vol. 10 and vols. 11–12 in vol. 12. PN3503.C7

ELT *English Literature in Transition, 1880–1920* [former title: *English Fiction in Transition*, 1957–1962]. Vol. 1–. Tempe: Arizona State University, 1957–. Reviews. Bibliography (see R–2). Cumulative index to vols. 1–15 (1957–1972). PR1.E55

JML *Journal of Modern Literature.* Vol. 1–. Philadelphia: Temple University, 1970–. 5/yr. Reviews. Bibliography (see R–17). PN2.J6

MD *Modern Drama: A Journal Devoted to the Drama since Ibsen.* Vol. 1–. Toronto: University of Toronto, Graduate Center for the Study of Drama, 1958–. 4/yr. Reviews. Bibliography (see R–44). Analytical index to vols. 1–13 (1958–1971) by David F. Holden (Toronto: Hakkert, 1972). PN1861.M55

MFS *Modern Fiction Studies.* Vol. 1–. Lafayette, Ind.: Purdue University, Department of English, 1955–. 4/yr. Reviews. Bibliography (see R–59). PS379.M55

Modern Poetry Studies. Buffalo, N.Y.: Media Study, 1969–. 6/yr. then 3/yr. Reviews. PS301.M58

NConL *Notes on Contemporary Literature [post–1940].* Vol. 1–. Carrollton: West Georgia College, 1971–. 5/yr. No LC number

Review of Contemporary Fiction. Vol. 1–. Elmwood Park, Ill.: The Review of Contemporary Fiction, 1981–. 2/yr. then 3/yr. Reviews. PN3503.R45

STCL *Studies in Twentieth Century Literature.* Vol. 1–. Lincoln: University of Nebraska, 1976–. 2/yr. PN771.S78

TDR *tdr: the drama review* [former title: *Tulane Drama Review*]. Vol. 1–. New York: New York University School of Arts, 1955–. 4/yr. Reviews. PN2000.D68

TCL *Twentieth Century Literature: A Scholarly and Critical Journal.* Vol. 1–. Hempstead, N.Y.: Hofstra University, 1955–. 4/yr. Reviews. Bibliography (see R–16). PN2.T8

R–19 **Some Frequently Recommended Works on Modern Literature.**

For additional frequently recommended works on general modern history see section F; for works on social, intellectual, and educational history of the modern period see K–90, K–95, and K–98, respectively. For works on the history of taste, see K–92. For works on modern American literature, see section S. For works on the other modern literatures of the world see appropriate portions of section L; for works on modern Scottish, Irish, Welsh, Commonwealth, and world literature written in English, see appropriate portions of section M. For works on modern poetry generally, see section T; for modern drama and film see section U; for modern prose and prose fiction see section W; and for modern literary theory and criticism see section X.

Aldridge, John W., ed. *Critiques and Essays on Modern Fiction, 1920–1951.* New York: Ronald Press, 1952. Includes Robert W. Stallman, "A Selected Bibliography of Criticism of Modern Fiction," pp. 553–610.

Alvarez, Alfred. *Shaping Spirit: Studies in Modern English and American Poets.* London: Chatto and Windus, 1958. PR603.A4

Baker, Houston A. *Modernism and the Harlem Renaissance.* Chicago: University of Chicago Press, 1987.
PS153.N5 B25 1987

Beach, Joseph Warren. *Twentieth-Century Novel: Studies in Technique.* New York: Appleton-Century-Crofts, 1932.
PN3503.B4

Benstock, Shari. *Women of the Left Bank: Paris, 1900–1940.* Austin: University of Texas Press, 1986.
PS151.B46 1986

Bergonzi, Bernard. *Heroes' Twilight: A Study of the Literature of the Great War.* 2d ed. London: Macmillan, 1980.
PR478.E8 B4

———. *Myth of Modernism and Twentieth Century Literature.* New York: St. Martin's Press, 1986.
PR473.B397 1986

———. *Turn of the Century: Essays on Victorian and Modern English Literature.* New York: Barnes and Noble, 1973.
PR463.B4 1973

———, ed. *Twentieth Century.* Vol. 7 in the *[Sphere] History of Literature in the English Language* (see M–34).

Berthoff, Warner. *Literature without Qualities.* Berkeley, Los Angeles, London: University of California Press, 1979.
PS225.B4

Bornstein, George. *Transformations of Romanticism in Yeats, Eliot, and Stevens.* Chicago: University of Chicago Press, 1976.
PS324.B69

Brack, O. M., Jr., ed. *Twilight of Dawn: Studies in English Literature in Transition.* Tucson: University of Arizona Press, 1987.
PR464.T85 1987

Bradbury, Malcolm, and James McFarlane, eds. *Modernism 1890–1930.* Pelican Guide to European Literature. Middlesex: Penguin, 1974.
PN56.M54 M6

Brooks, Cleanth. *Modern Poetry and the Tradition.* Chapel Hill: University of North Carolina Press, 1939.
PN1136.B75

Connolly, Cyril. *Modern Movement: One Hundred Key Books from England, France, and America, 1880–1950.* New York: Atheneum, 1966.   Z6519.C6

Cunningham, Valentine. *British Writers of the Thirties.* Oxford: Oxford University Press, 1988.
PR478.S57 C86 1988

Daiches, David. *Present Age in British Literature.* Vol. 5 of Dobree, *Introductions to English Literature* (see M–15).

Davies, Alistair. *Annotated Critical Bibliography of Modernism.* Sussex: Harvester Press, 1982.
Z2014.M6 D38 1982

Dennison, Sally. *Alternative Literary Publishing: Five Modern Histories.* Iowa City: University of Iowa Press, 1984.
Z231.5.L5 D47 1984

Dodsworth, Martin, ed. *Survival of Poetry: A Contemporary Survey.* London: Faber and Faber, 1970.   PR611.D6

Donoghue, Denis. *Ordinary Universe: Soundings in Modern Literature.* London: Faber, 1968.   PR471.D6

Ellmann, Richard. *Eminent Domain: Yeats among Wilde, Joyce, Pound, Eliot, and Auden.* London: Oxford University Press, 1965.   PR5906.E38

———. *James Joyce.* New and rev. ed. New York: Oxford University Press, 1982.   PR6019.09 Z5332 1982

Evans, B. Ifor. *English Literature between the Wars.* London: Methuen, 1948.   PR478.I5 E9

Faulkner, Peter. *Modernism.* London: Methuen, 1977.
PR478.M6 F3

Ford, Boris, ed. *From James to Eliot.* Vol. 7 in the *New Pelican Guide to English Literature* (see M–39).

———, ed. *The Present.* Vol. 8 in the *New Pelican Guide to English Literature* (see M–39).

Fraser, G. S. *Modern Writer and His World.* 3d ed. rev. Baltimore: Penguin Books, 1964.   PR471.F72

Fussell, Paul. *Great War and Modern Memory.* New York: Oxford University Press, 1975.   PR478.E8 F8

Gilbert, Sandra M., and Susan Gubar. *No Man's Land: The Place of the Woman Writer in the Twentieth Century.* 2 vols. New Haven: Yale University Press, 1988–.
PR116.G5 1988

Hall, James. *Tragic Comedians: Seven Modern British Novelists.* Bloomington: Indiana University Press, 1963.
PR881.H3

Hamburger, Michael. *Truth of Poetry: Tensions in Modern Poetry from Baudelaire to the 1960's.* London: Weidenfeld and Nicolson, 1969.   PN1261.H35 1969

Hassan, Ihab Habib. *Dismemberment of Orpheus: Toward a Postmodern Literature.* 2d ed. Madison: University of Wisconsin Press, 1982.   PN771.H33 1982

———. *Postmodern Turn: Essays in Postmodern Thory and Culture.* Columbus: Ohio State University Press, 1987.   PN771.H346 1987

Hewison, Robert. *Under Siege: Literary Life in London, 1939–45.* New York: Oxford University Press, 1977.
PR478.W67 H4 1977

Hoare, Dorothy M. *Some Studies in the Modern Novel.* London: Chatto and Windus, 1938.   PR883.H6

Hoffman, Frederic J. *Mortal No: Death and the Modern Imagination.* Princeton, N.J.: Princeton University Press, 1964.   PN771.H57

Hynes, Samuel. *Auden Generation: Literature and Politics in England in the 1930's.* London: Bodley Head, 1976.   PR479.P6 H9 1976

Johnstone, J. K. *Bloomsbury Group: A Study of E. M. Forster, Lytton Strachey, Virginia Woolf, and Their Circle.* New York: Noonday, 1963.   PR478.B46 J6

Josipovici, Gabriel D. *Lessons of Modernism and Other Essays.* London: Macmillan, 1977.
PR6060.064 L4 1977b

———. *World and the Book: A Study of Modern Fiction.* London: Macmillan, 1971.   PN3451.J6

Kenner, Hugh. *Colder Eye: The Modern Irish Writers.* New York: Knopf, 1983.

———. *Homemade World: The American Modernist Writers,* New York: Knopf, 1975.   PS221.K4

———. *Pound Era: The Age of Ezra Pound, T. S. Eliot, James Joyce, and Wyndham Lewis.* Berkeley, Los Angeles, London: University of California Press, 1971.
PS3531.082 Z712

———. *Sinking Island: The Modern English Writers.* New York: Knopf, 1988.   PR478.M6 K4 1988

Langbaum, Robert. *Mysteries of Identity: A Theme in Modern Literature.* New York: Oxford University Press, 1977.   PR469.I33 L3

Leavis, F. R. *New Bearings in English Poetry: A Study of the Contemporary Situation.* Rev. ed. New York: Stewart, 1950.   PR601.L4

Levenson, Michael H. *Genealogy of Modernism: A Study of English Literary Doctrine, 1908–1922.* Cambridge: Cambridge University Press, 1984.
PR478.M6 L4 1984

Lewis, R. W. B. *Picaresque Saint: Representative Figures in Contemporary Fiction.* Philadelphia: Lippincott, 1959. PN3503.L4

Lodge, David. *Modes of Modern Writing.* London: Edward Arnold, 1977. PN203.L58

Meisel, Perry. *Myth of The Modern: A Study in British Literature and Criticism after 1850.* New Haven: Yale University Press, 1987. PR478.M6 M4 1987

Miller, J. Hillis. *Poets of Reality: Six Twentieth Century Writers.* Cambridge: Harvard University Press, 1965. PR601.M5

Morrison, Blake. *Movement: English Poetry and Fiction of the Fifties.* Oxford: Oxford University Press, 1980. PR601.M64 1980

Mowat, Charles Loch. *Great Britain since 1914: The Sources of History: Studies in the Uses of Historical Evidence.* Ithaca, N.Y.: Cornell University Press, 1971. Z2020.M63

O'Connor, William Van. *New University Wits and the End of Modernism.* Carbondale: Southern Illinois University Press, 1963. PR471.O3

————, ed. *Forms of Modern Fiction.* Minneapolis: University of Minnesota Press, 1948. PN3355.M5

O'Faolain, Sean. *Vanishing Hero: Studies of the Hero in the Modern Novel.* New York: Grosset and Dunlap, 1958. PR888.H403 1958

Paz, Ottavio. *Children of the Mire: Modern Poetry from Romanticism to the Avant Garde.* Cambridge: Harvard University Press, 1974. PN1161.P3

Pinsky, Robert. *Situation of Poetry: Contemporary Poetry and Its Traditions.* Princeton, N.J.: Princeton University Press, 1976. PS325.P5

Pritchett, V. S. *Living Novel and Later Appreciations.* New York: Random House, 1964. PN3324.P7 1964

Robson, W. W. *Modern English Literature.* New York: Oxford University Press, 1970. PR471.R6

Rosenthal, Macha Louis. *Modern Poets: A Critical Introduction.* New York: Oxford University Press, 1960. PR601.R6

Schorer, Mark, ed. *Modern British Fiction: Essays in Criticism.* New York: Oxford University Press, 1961. PR883.S3 1961

Scott-James, Rolfe Arnold. *Fifty Years of English Literature, 1900–1950, with a Postscript, 1951–55.* London: Longman's, Green, 1957. PR471.S35 1957

Shapiro, Charles, ed. *Contemporary British Novelists.* Carbondale: Southern Illinois University Press, 1965. PR883.S5

Sinfield, Alan. *Literature, Politics, and Culture in Postwar Britain.* Berkeley: University of California Press, 1989. PR478.P64S5 1989

Spears, Monroe. *Dionysus and the City: Modernism in Twentieth-Century Poetry.* New York: Oxford University Press, 1970. PS323.5.S65

Stewart, J. I. M. *Eight Modern Writers [Hardy, James, Shaw, Conrad, Kipling, Yeats, Joyce, and Lawrence].* Vol. 12 in the *Oxford History of English Literature* (see M–31).

Sultan, Stanley. *Eliot, Joyce, and Company.* New York: Oxford University Press, 1987. PR748.M6 S8 1987

Swinnerton, Frank. *Georgian Scene: A Literary Panorama.* New York: Farrar and Rinehart, 1934. PR471.S8

Symons, Julian. *Makers of the New: The Revolution in Literature, 1914–1939.* New York: Random House, 1987. PR478.M6 S96 1987

Taylor, A. J. P. *English History, 1914–1945.* Oxford: Clarendon Press, 1965.

Tichi, Cecilia. *Shifting Gears: Technology, Literature, Culture in Modernist America.* Chapel Hill: University of North Carolina Press, 1987. PS228.T42 T5 1987

Tindall, William York. *Forces in Modern British Literature 1885–1956.* Rev. ed. New York: Knopf, 1956. PR471.T5 1956

Trachtenberg, Stanley, ed. *Postmodern Movement: A Handbook of Contemporary Innovation in the Arts.* Westport, Conn.: Greenwood Press, 1985. NX456.5.P66 1985

Vendler, Helen. *Part of Nature, Part of Us: Modern American Poets.* Cambridge: Harvard University Press, 1980. PS323.5.V4

Wilson, Edmund. *Axel's Castle: A Study in the Imaginative Literature of 1870–1930.* New York: Scribner's, 1931. PN771.W55

Zabel, Morton D. *Craft and Character: Texts, Methods, and Vocation in Modern Fiction.* New York: Viking, 1957. PR823.Z3

III. BIOBIBLIOGRAPHIES AND HANDBOOKS

R–21 **Kunitz, Stanley J., and Howard Haycroft.** *Twentieth Century Authors: A Biographical Dictionary of Modern Literature.* New York: H. W. Wilson, 1942. PN771.K86

The popularly written biographical sketches in this volume treat 1,850 authors of all nations whose work is known to English-speaking readers. Articles include a biographical sketch, a survey of the author's critical reception, and brief primary and secondary bibliographies; most are illustrated by a portrait.

A *First Supplement* by Kunitz and Vineta Colby was published in 1955. It adds some 700 additional subjects and updates both the biographies and the bibliographies of the original volume, listing all 2,550 names, with reference to the original article if no new information is added.

A further supplement by John Wakeman and Stanley J. Kunitz with the title, *World Authors, 1950–1970: A Companion Volume to "Twentieth Century Authors,"* was published in 1975 [PN451.W3]. It contains about 950 entries for those authors who secured prominence between 1950 and 1970. Format is the same as the original and *First Supplement,* though entries are somewhat longer and there is a larger proportion of writers who are not English or American. An additional volume edited by Wakeman and published in 1980, *World Authors 1970–1975* [PN451.W667], adds 348 biobibliographies. And *World Authors, 1975–1980,* edited by Vineta Colby [PN451.W672 1985] adds 379 additional writers who came into prominence in the 1970s.

These volumes form the twentieth-century component to a series that includes *European Authors 1000–1900* (L–56), *British Authors before 1800* (M–55), *British Authors of the Nineteenth Century* (M–56), and *American Authors 1700–1900* (S–27). An *Index to the Wilson Author Series,* rev. ed. (New York, 1986) [PN451.I5 1986] provides a quick check to determine whether an individual is treated among the 7,500 biobibliographies found in these volumes.

R–23 ***Contemporary Authors: A Bio-Bibliographical Guide to Current Authors and Their Works[CA].*** Edited by James M. Ethridge et al. Vol. 1–. Detroit: Gale Research Co., 1962–.   Z1224.C6 vol.1–

Issued semiannually, the current volumes of this continuing series contain a cumulative index to all preceding volumes. Living writers of all countries are included; entries give brief biographies and primary and secondary bibliographies. The original plan was that biographies of deceased or retired writers would be removed from the current volumes and reprinted in *Contemporary Authors: Permanent Series[CAP]*, vol. 1– (1975–) [Z1010.C65]; entries so treated were to continue to be indexed in the regular cumulating indexes. In fact, only two such volumes were published, in 1975 and in 1978.

In addition to removing deceased or retired writers, the plan was to have a system of continuous, complete revision, and *Contemporary Authors: First Revision[CAR]* began publication in 1967 [Z1224.C59]. A total of forty-four volumes in eleven were published 1967–1979. A further set of revisions including only articles requiring significant change began to be published in 1980 with the title *Contemporary Authors: New Revision[CANR]* [Z1224.C58]. In 1980 a *Cumulative Index* was published which covers volumes 1–100 of the original series, the forty-four volumes of the *First Revision*, the two volumes of the *Permanent Series*, the first volume of the *New Revision*, and entries in the related series *Contemporary Literary Criticism* (see R–62). A total of 61,000 entries appear in these volumes. Beginning with volume 101 (1981), the title of new volumes in the original series reads *Contemporary Authors: A Bio-Bibliographical Guide to Current Writers in Fiction, General Non-Fiction, Poetry, Journalism, Drama, Motion Pictures, Television and Other Fields*. From volume 101 on, all volumes must be consulted.

Yet another series, *Contemporary Authors: Autobiography Series*, began in 1984 [PN453.C63] with volumes containing autobiographies by authors treated elsewhere in these works.

A further series, *Contemporary Authors: Bibliographical Series*, began in 1986 [Z6519.C64]. These volumes treat groups of authors defined by nationality or genre, and offer primary and secondary bibliographies, along with a bibliographical essay. Volume 1, for example, treats ten *American Novelists*; Volume 2 treats eleven *American Poets*.

R–25 **Ward, A. C. *Longman Companion to Twentieth Century Literature.*** 3d ed. Revised by Maurice Hussey. London: Longmans, 1981.   PN771.W28 1981

Originally published in 1970, this work treats primarily English writers of the twentieth-century, though it also includes Commonwealth and American writers and non-English-language writers with international reputations whose works are available in English. Articles present biographical and bibliographical entries on major and minor authors; identifications of pseudonyms; plot summaries of important works; descriptions of characters and identification of works in which they appear; and articles on such topics as literary genres, terms, topics, and allusions. There are also articles on censorship, copyright, literary societies, and literary organizations, and on such questions as contemporary procedures for the preparation and publication of manuscripts. Though bibliographies are included, they are brief.

R–27 **Klein, Leonard S., gen. ed. *Encyclopedia of World Literature in the 20th Century.*** 2d rev. ed. 4 vols. in 5. New York: Ungar, 1981–1984.   PN771.E5 1981

An enlarged and updated edition of Wolfgang Bernard Fleischmann's *Lexikon der Weltliteratur im 20. Jahrhundert*, 2d ed., 2 vols. (Freiburg: Herder, 1960–1961) [PN774.L43], originally published in 3 vols. (New York: Un-

gar, 1967–1971) [PN774.L433], this completely revised and much enlarged new edition presents some 1,700 articles that, with something of an Anglo-American focus, survey 150 national literatures of the world, numerous literary movements, the history of ideas, literary criticism, the major genres, and those lesser genres that have become prominent in the twentieth-century, along with biobibliographical articles on twentieth-century authors including those now living. Entries on authors consist of a headnote with vital statistics, a critical assessment of the author's work, a listing of further works not cited in the main part of the article, a chronologically arranged bibliography of biographical and critical works, and frequently an illustrative portrait. All articles are signed by the more than 750 contributors to the work. An index to contributors begins each volume and includes a list of the articles contributed by each. The fifth *Index* volume gives authors, titles, and subjects in single alphabet with subheadings and abundant cross-references. The only other reference work for twentieth-century literature which is as comprehensive as this one is the five-volume *Dizionario universale della letteratura contemporanea* (see L–25).

R–28 **Grigson, Geoffrey, ed. *Concise Encyclopedia of Modern World Literature.*** New York: Hawthorn Books, 1963.
PN41.C64

This handy volume includes unsigned surveys of national literatures and of the major genres of literature in the twentieth-century, as well as biobibliographies of major and minor authors, both those writing in the English language and those whose work is available in English. There are many illustrative portraits. The work concludes with indexes of authors and titles.

A more recent brief volume is Harry Blamires, ed. *Guide to Twentieth Century Literature in English* (London: Methuen, 1983) [PR471.G78 1983] which treats the English literatures of the following places: Australia, Canada, The Caribbean, The Gambia, Ghana, India, Ireland, Kenya, New Zealand, Nigeria, Pakistan, Southern Africa, Sri Lanka, Uganda, and the United Kingdom. More than 500 brief author entries are listed alphabetically by country. Biographical details, career summaries, and separate descriptions of major works comprise the articles which are signed by one of the four contributors to the work.

R–29 **Ivask, Ivar, and Gero von Wilpert, eds. *World Literature since 1945: Critical Surveys of the Contemporary Literatures of Europe and the Americas.*** New York: Ungar; Stuttgart: Kröner, 1973.   PN771.I9

This volume contains a total of twenty-eight articles by noted scholars surveying the literature of one American or European country or region from the time of World War II through the early 1970s. Articles describe and follow trends, treating authors (with dates) and their works (with a translated title and date of first publication). Appended to each article is a list of published English translations of works cited. For those literatures not widely translated into English, the appendix enumerates available anthologies. Each article concludes with a secondary bibliography.

IV. POETRY

See also section S.VI and section T.

R–30 **Altieri, Charles F. *Modern Poetry.* [A Goldentree Bibliography.]** Arlington Heights, Ill.: AHM Publishing Co., 1979.   Z1231.P7 A45

A total of more than 1,788 serially numbered entries treat English and American poetry and poets prominent before the 1970s. There is an emphasis on recent criticism through the end of 1974, with the addition of some important matter from 1975–1978, the period during which publication of this bibliography was delayed. Entries are disposed into eight main sections, as follows: General Bibliographies and Literary Histories; Social, Intellectual, and Artistic Contexts; General Studies of Modern Poetry; General Studies of Post-Modern Poetry, 1950–1970; Special Topics and Movements in Modern and Post-Modern Poetry and Poetics; Anthologies of Interviews and Critical Essays; Important Literary Magazines of the Period and Bibliographic Guides; Specific Works by and about the Poets. The last section includes bibliographies for a total of fifty-six poets with the following subdivisions: Works of Poetry; Other Relevant Primary Materials; Biography, Bibliography, and Other Reference Materials; Collections of Critical Essays; Critical Books and Essays. Throughout, asterisks designate entries of particular significance.

R–31 **Anderson, Emily Ann. *English Poetry, 1900–1950: A Guide to Information Sources.*** Detroit: Gale Research Co., 1982.   Z2014.P7 A54 1982

This guide contains three parts, with entries descriptively and evaluatively annotated throughout. Part 1 treats General Aids under the following headings: Autobiographies and Diaries, Bibliographies, Bibliographies of Bibliographies, Bibliographical Manuals, Serial Bibliographies, Biographies, Serial Biographies, Companions, Dictionaries, Encyclopedias, Guides, Handbooks, and Indexes. Part 2 contains a set of entries meant to serve as background readings. The third part presents bibliographies for a total of twenty-one modern English poets. The individual bibliographies are in nine sections, presenting Principal Works of Poetry and Selected Other Writings; Primary Bibliographies; Checklists of Criticism; Autobiographies; Biographies; Letters; Dictionaries, Companions, and Yearbooks; Periodicals Devoted to the Author; and a Selected Checklist of Criticism. The work concludes with indexes of authors, of titles, and of subjects.

R–33 **Vinson, James, and Daniel Kirkpatrick, eds. *Contemporary Poets.*** 4th ed., rev.. London and New York: St. Martin's Press, 1985.   Z2014.P7 C62 1985

Originally published in 1970, with a second edition in 1975, and a third in 1980, this volume includes biobibliographies of some 850 living contemporary poets of all countries. Entries give brief biographies, a list of primary materials, a list of other bibliographies and reference lists, and a bibliography of critical works which authors themselves consider relevant to understanding their work. Appendixes include a treatment of major postwar poets who have died, explanatory notes on recent poetic movements, and a selected list of anthologies published since 1960 which include contemporary poetry in English.

R–35 **Krawitz, Henry. *Post-Symbolist Bibliography.*** Metuchen, N.J.: Scarecrow Press, 1973.   Z6520.S9 K7

This bibliography is designed to explore the impact of symbolist aesthetics after the symbolist movement proper. The 4,141 serially numbered annotated entries are disposed into four sections, treating International Studies (books and articles written from a supranational perspective); National Studies (limited to authors of one country); Comparative Studies (involving two or more individual figures and questions of influence); and a long section on studies of nineteen individual authors from Bely to Yeats and including Eliot and Stevens. Emphasis throughout is on criticism written 1950–1970 in English, French, German, Spanish, and Italian.

R–37 **Woolmer, J. Howard. *Catalogue of the Imagist Poets, with Essays by Wallace Martin and Ian Fletcher.*** New York: AMS Press, 1981.   Z2014.P7 C33 1981

Originally published in a limited edition in 1966, this bibliophile's catalog of books and periodicals pertaining to the imagist movement contains a list of some 267 items, described with prices, preceded by two essays on imagism and followed by an addendum listing other books and periodicals not in the catalog but necessary for a full imagist collection.

V. DRAMA AND THEATER

See also section S. VII and section U.

R–40 **Carpenter, Charles A. *Modern Drama Scholarship and Criticism, 1966–1980: An International Bibliography.*** Toronto: University of Toronto Press, 1986.   Z5781.C37 1986

This essentially unannotated, selected bibliography treats work published 1966–1980 in over 1,600 journals on world drama since Ibsen. An Index of Playwrights precedes the bibliography proper, along with an Introduction, a Guide to Format, and a list of Abbreviations.

The body of the work includes 27,300 entries arranged in fourteen sections with alphabetically arranged, numbered entries, as follows: u: Unclassified Books (works analyzed for citations that do not themselves deal primarily with drama); A: World Drama; B: American Drama; C: British and Irish Drama; D: Canadian Drama; E: Hispanic Drama (Spanish, Portuguese, Brazilian, Spanish American); F: French Drama; G: Italian Drama; H: Germanic Drama (German, Austrian, and Swiss; Dutch and Flemish); J: Scandinavian Drama; K: Eastern European Drama (Balkan, Baltic, Czech, Hungarian, Polish, Russian and Soviet); L: African and West Indian Drama; M: Australiasian Drama (Australia, New Zealand, Philippine); and N: Asian Drama (Arab and Near East, Chinese, Indian, Israeli, Japanese, Southeast Asian).

Each major section is further classified into such headings as the following for World Drama: Bibliography; Other Reference Works: Collections of Essays: General and Miscellaneous: Contemporary Theory (especially Structuralism and Semiotics); Religion, Myth, and Legend in Modern Drama; Modern Tragedy and Comedy; Naturalism and Expressionism; Poetic, Symbolic, and Surrealist Drama; Theatre of the Absurd, Theatre of Cruelty, Theatre of Ritual; Political Drama; Modern Theatre. The first four categories are found at the beginning of most sections; additional categories are as appropriate to the material being covered. For example, the additional headings for American Drama are To the 1930s, The 1930s and World War II, Postwar, Since the 1960s, Afro-American Drama and Theatre, Chicano Drama and Theatre, American Theatre, and a long section on Playwrights (listed alphabetically, with primary bibliographies followed by lists of secondary works).

An index of Names concludes this massive work, which is updated by the annual bibliography appearing in *Modern Drama* (R–44).

R–41 **Carpenter, Charles A. *Modern British Drama*.** [A Goldentree Bibliography.] Arlington Heights, Ill.: AHM Publishing Co., 1979.   Z2014.D7 C35

A total of 2,342 serially numbered entries are disposed into nine main sections, as follows: Bibliographies, Modern Drama (Reference Works, Collections of Essays, Reviews, and Interviews); Anthologies of Modern British Plays; Modern English Drama (to the 1890's, 1890's to 1930's, 1930's to 1950's, 1950's to 1970s); Theatre in England since the 1860's; Modern Scottish and Welsh Drama and Theatre; Modern Irish Drama (1890's to 1920's, 1920's to 1970s); Theatre in Ireland since the 1890's; and Individual British Dramatists. The last section includes bibliographies for a total of fifty-four dramatists, with subdivisions treating Editions and Modern Writings; Bibliographies and Reference Materials; and Scholarly, Critical, and Expository Works. Important items are throughout designated by an asterisk. The volume ends with an index of names. Bibliographies are updated by reference to the annual lists of *Modern Drama* (R–44).

R–42 **King, Kimball. *Twenty Modern British Playwrights: A Bibliography, 1956–1976*.** New York: Garland, 1977.
                                                         Z2014.D7 K47

The volume presents for each of twenty playwrights from John Arden to Charles Wood a brief biographical and critical introduction, followed by classified bibliographies of primary and secondary sources. Classes of the former include Stage Plays by title, with production and publication data; Film Scripts; Television Plays, Radio Plays; Poetry; Works of Fiction; Non-Fiction; and Interviews. Secondary bibliographies list bibliographical works, works of criticism, dissertations, and reviews, with descriptive abstracts for each cited work. The volume concludes with an index of authors, including interviewers and other persons cited.

Related volumes by King are parallel in structure to this one; see *Ten Modern Irish Playwrights: A Comprehensive Annotated Bibliography* (New York: Garland, 1970) [Z2039.D7 K56] and *Ten Modern American Playwrights: An Annotated Bibliography* (New York: Garland, 1982) [Z1231.D7 K56 1982].

R–43 **Kirkpatrick, D. L., and James Vinson eds. *Contemporary Dramatists*.** 4th ed. Chicago: St. James Press, 1988.
                                                         PR106.V5 1988

Unlike other volumes in this series (see R–33, R–52, and R–62), this one, first published in 1970, with a second edition in 1977 and a third in 1982, is limited to 300 living contemporary dramatists in England, Canada, and the United States. Entries give a brief biography, a list of primary works with dates of first productions in London and New York, and brief references to critical works. Manuscript locations are often given, as are comments by the dramatist and signed critical comments.

Separate supplements include one listing 184 playwrights under the rubrics: Screenwriters, Radio Writers, Television Writers, Musical Librettists, and The Theatre of Mixed Means. Another supplement outlines the history and work of important contemporary theater collectives such as La Mama, The Negro Ensemble, The Women's Theatre Group, and The San Francisco Mime Troupe. An appendix treats important playwrights who have died since 1950 but are still regarded as contemporary. A title index of all plays cited concludes the volume.

R–44 **"Modern Drama Studies: An Annual Bibliography [1959–]." *Modern Drama [MD]*.** Vol. 3–. Lawrence: University of Kansas, 1960–.   PN1861.M55

From 1960 through 1968 (vols. 3–11) the *Modern Drama Journal* contained Robert Shedd's "Modern Drama: A Selective Bibliography of Works Published in English, 1959 [–1967]." These bibliographies covered work on playwrights alive after 1900 plus a few others, but only English-language materials in a limited number of journals were cited. Beginning with volume 17 (1974), the bibliography was reinstated under the editorship of Charles Carpenter. The number of journals covered has been expanded, and important foreign-language works are included. Serially numbered entries are now divided into general and national sections, as follows: A. General; B. American; C. British; D. Commonwealth; E. Spanish (and Portuguese); F. French; G. Italian; H. Germanic; J. Scandinavian; K. Eastern Europe (Russian and others); L. Asian. Topics, playwrights, and important persons other than performers are included in the classification system.

R–45 **Adelman, Irving, and Rita Dworkin. *Modern Drama: A Checklist of Critical Literature on Twentieth Century Plays*.** Metuchen, N.J.: Scarecrow Press, 1967.   Z5781.A35

This bibliography is arranged alphabetically by the names of dramatists. Under each, a list of general books and articles is followed by an enumeration of the titles of individual plays, under which relevant studies are listed alphabetically by their authors. Basic bibliographical information is given for each critical book or article cited. At the end of the volume is a list of the books and composite volumes analyzed by the compilers.

R–46 **Breed, Paul F., and Florence M. Sniderman, eds. *Dramatic Criticism Index: A Bibliography of Commentaries on Playwrights From Ibsen to the Avant-Garde*.** Detroit: Gale Research Co., 1972.   Z5781.B8

With nearly 12,000 entries this volume indexes commentary on more than 300 contemporary American and foreign playwrights found in some 630 composite volumes and some 200 periodicals. Entries are grouped by playwrights into general sections and then sections of commentary on individual plays. Citations are alphabetically arranged within their sections. Foreign play titles are given in English (with the original title in parentheses), unless there was no English translation. The volume concludes with two massive indexes, of play titles and of critics; there is also a list of the composite volumes analyzed in the work.

R–47 **Mikhail, E. H. *English Drama, 1900–1950: A Guide to Information Sources*.** Detroit: Gale Research Co., 1977.
                                                         Z2014.D7 M545

The 2,054 serially numbered entries in this volume are disposed into five chapters treating Bibliographies, Reference Works, Critical Books and Essays, Periodical Articles, and Individual Dramatists, respectively. The first four chapters are divided into both general and special sections. The bulk of the volume consists of chronologically arranged bibliographies of primary and secondary sources for each of the seventy-nine individual modern British and Irish dramatists treated in chapter 5. Most entries are briefly annotated. The volume ends with indexes of authors, titles, and subjects. The latter is helpful in sorting out titles on special topics from the mixed lists in chapters 1–4.

A second volume by Mikhail, *Contemporary British Drama, 1950–1976: An Annotated Critical Bibliography* (London: Macmillan, 1976) [Z2014.D7 M55 1976], is divided into four sections, on Bibliographies, Reference Works, Books, and Periodical Articles. Entries are alphabetically arranged and have brief descriptive annotation. There are no indexes.

R–48 **Anderson, Michael, et al. *Crowell's Handbook of Contemporary Drama.*** New York: Thomas Y. Crowell, 1971.
PN1861.C7

This work is a guide to written drama, not the theater, since the Spanish Civil War. Both factual information and critical appraisals of plays and playwrights are included. Though articles are not signed, the contributors and their fields of expertise are listed. Entries include articles on playwrights, plays, terms, and the various contemporary national dramas. There is no index.

See also the *Concise Encyclopedia of Modern Drama*, ed. S. Melchinger (New York: Horizon, 1964) [PN1861.M4], which offers brief articles on theories, themes, ideas, modern production and acting methods, and both a bibliography and a chronology of first performances.

R–49 **Matlaw, Myron. *Modern World Drama: An Encyclopedia.*** New York: E. P. Dutton, 1972.
PN1851.M36

This well-illustrated encyclopedia includes primarily articles on the major dramatists born or living in the twentieth-century, with biographies, lists of works, discussion of critical reception, and a brief critical bibliography of secondary materials. There are also articles on major works of twentieth-century drama, with notes on the first production and on publication, and with a synopsis; long articles on the dramas of various national literatures; and articles on technical terms, including movements and other developments in the modern drama. There is a marked emphasis throughout on Western-language materials. The work concludes with two indexes, a general index and a very useful index of character names.

A useful supplement to Matlaw is the production guide by Siegfried Kienzle, *Modern World Theatre: A Guide to Productions in Europe and the United States since 1945* (New York: Ungar, 1970) [PN6112.5.K513], which is arranged alphabetically by dramatist and lists translations.

VI. PROSE FICTION

See also section S.VIII and section W.

R–50 **Wiley, Paul L. *British Novel: Conrad to the Present.*** [A Goldentree Bibliography.] Northbrook, Ill.: AHM Publishing, 1973.
Z2014.F55 W54

This guide covers work on the English novel and novelists from about 1890 through 1950. Both recent and older works of scholarship are included, and selection is meant to be of a representative set of viewpoints. Numbered entries are disposed into ten main sections, as follows: Bibliographies; Reference Works; Literary Histories; Histories of the Novel; Period Studies of the Novel; Studies of Theory; Studies of Form and Narrative; Studies of Genre and Theme; Collections of Studies: Twentieth-Century Novel; and British Novelists. The last section contains primary and secondary bibliographies for a total of forty-four modern novelists. These individual bibliographies are divided into subsections for texts,

bibliographies, critical and biographical books, and critical essays. Works of special importance are designated by an asterisk. The volume ends with an index of names. There is a volume in the same series covering the nineteenth-century novel (Q–73) and a complementary volume on the modern American novel (S–81).

R–51 **Bufkin, E. C. *Twentieth-Century Novel in English: A Checklist.*** Athens: University of Georgia Press, 1967.
Z2014.F5 B93

This work aims to present a complete list (through 1966) of novels written by more than 400 writers in English, regardless of nationality, who have published the greater part of their work in the twentieth century. For purposes of inclusion a novel is defined as a separately published work of narrative prose fiction of any length. It must have been published in book form and not subsequently included in a collected volume. For each novel, information includes the title, place, and publication data of the first English edition for English authors, and of the first American edition for Americans. Reference is made to reissues and revised editions with new titles. Literature for juveniles is omitted unless it has been appropriated by adult readers. Awards are noted, including National Book Awards and Pulitzer Prizes, among others.

R–52 **Kirkpatrick, D. L., and James Vinson eds. *Contemporary Novelists.*** 4th ed., rev. New York: St. Martin's Press, 1986.
PR883.V55 1986

Originally published in 1972, with a second edition in 1977 and a third in 1981, this work presents biobibliographies of some 600 living novelists of all countries. Entries give brief biographies, lists of primary materials, and signed critical commentary. Information on published bibliographies and locations of manuscript sources is given, along with comments by the authors themselves. An appendix cites important postwar novelists who have recently died but are still regarded as essentially contemporary. A title index of novels named in the work concludes the volume.

R–53 **Rice, Thomas Jackson. *English Fiction, 1900–1950: General Bibliography and Individual Authors: Aldington to Huxley: A Guide to Information Sources.*** 2 vols. Detroit: Gale Research Co., 1979–1983.
Z2014.F4 R5

These excellently organized, exceptionally well done volumes are in two sections, treating general and then individual author bibliographies. All together the work contains some 25,061 serially numbered, annotated entries. The general bibliography has entries disposed into eight sections, as follows: 1. Bibliography (1.1 Primary Bibliographies; 1.2 Annual Secondary Bibliographies; 1.3 General Selective Bibliographies; 1.4 Bibliographies of Modern English Literature, the Novel, and Fiction Criticism; 1.5 Bibliographies of Bibliographies; 1.6 Book Review Indexes); 2. Literary History (2.1 General; 2.2 History of the Novel; 2.3 Ideological Backgrounds, Periods, Special Themes and Literary Groups); 3. Critical Studies of Modern English Fiction; 4. Theory of Fiction; 5. Studies of the Short Story; 6. Studies of Major Types (6.1 Crime Fiction; 6.2 Political Fiction; 6.3 Religious Fiction; 6.4 Science Fiction, Fantasy, and Utopian Fiction); 7. Histories and Memoirs (7.1 Histories, 7.2 Memoirs, Reminiscences, and Biographies); 8. Related Arts: Art, Film, and Music. Entries under individual authors are also well classified, as follows: 1. Primary Bibliographies (1.1 Fiction; 1.2 Miscellaneous; 1.3 Collected and Selected Editions; 1.4 Letters; 1.5 Concordance); and 2. Secondary Bibliographies (2.1 Bibliographies; 2.2 Biographies, Memoirs, Reminiscences, Interviews; 2.3 Book-Length Critical Studies and Essay Collections; 2.4 General Critical Articles or Chapters in Books; 2.5 Studies of Individual Works).

Volume 1 contains the general section and the first fifteen individual author bibliographies. Volume 2 contains twenty additional individual author bibliographies. Both volumes conclude with indexes of authors; volume 1 also has indexes of titles and subjects. Throughout, works of special importance are designated with an asterisk.

R–55 **Stanton, Robert J.** *Bibliography of Modern British Novelists.* 2 vols. Troy, N.Y.: Whitston Publishing Co., 1978.
Z2014.F5 S8

The first part of this bibliography presents a total of 347 books and articles that refer to two or more of the total of seventeen modern novelists treated in this bibliography. The seventeen authors are Amis, Bowen, Drabble, Golding, Hartley, Hughes, Lehmann, Lessing, and Moore in volume 1; and Murdoch, Naipaul, Powell, Rhys, Sillitoe, Snow, Spark, and Wilson in volume 2. For each, primary works are enumerated according to genre, giving titles, editions (place, publisher, date, title changes), and translations (translator, place, publisher, date, title of the translation) in chronological order. Entries are serially numbered. The primary bibliography is followed by general secondary works and then by secondary works that treat individual novels. Asterisks refer users to the addendum in which are enumerated articles located too late for placement at their proper place in the bibliography.

R–56 **Adelman, Irving, and Rita Dworkin.** *Contemporary Novel: A Checklist of Critical Literature on the British and American Novel since 1945.* Metuchen, N.J.: Scarecrow Press, 1972.
Z1231.F4 A34

The novelists treated in this volume were all writing after 1945, achieving their most significant recognition after 1945 (e.g., Faulkner), or publishing major works after 1945 (e.g., Hemingway). Lists identify the journals and the composite volumes that were analyzed. Included criticism was published before 1970. Unannotated entries are arranged by novelist, with general works given first and then studies of individual novels listed under their titles.

R–57 **Drescher, Horst W., and Bernd Kahrmann.** *Contemporary English Novel: An Annotated Bibliography of Secondary Sources.* Frankfurt: Athenaeum Verlag, 1973.
Z2014.F5 D74

This work is divided into three sections: I. Bibliographies and Reference Works; II. General Studies; and III. Individual Authors. No authors who were prominent before World War II are included. Entries under each author include all novels published before 1972 with their dates, bibliographies, anonymous works, and secondary works published in 1954 or more recently. Entries are unnumbered and descriptively annotated. There is an index of author's names. The particular value of this bibliography is its inclusion of numerous secondary works by European scholars and critics.

R–58 **Cassis, A. F.** *Twentieth-Century English Novel: An Annotated Bibliography of General Criticism.* New York: Garland, 1977.
Z2014.F5 C35

This bibliography includes criticism published from 1900 to 1972 on the English novel. General studies are included; studies of only one writer are generally excluded. A total of 2,832 serially numbered entries are classified as follows: 1. Bibliographies and Checklists; 2. Criticism (A. Books, B. Ar-

ticles); and 3. Dissertations. Entries include descriptive annotations. The volume concludes with an index of novelists and an index of selected topics and themes. This latter index uses fairly broad technical terms but is nevertheless an extremely useful and distinctive feature.

R–59 **"Recent Books on Modern Fiction."** *Modern Fiction Studies [MFS],* vol. 1–. Lafayette, Ind.: Purdue University, Department of English, 1955–.
PS379.M55

Originally (vols. 1–14) titled *Modern Fiction Newsletter,* this journal carried biennial bibliographical essays covering English-language scholarship on general topics and individual authors. After volume 15 (1969) the title changed to "Recent Books." The format has always been to present long review essays comparing related titles. These reviews are now classified into those treating Continental, British, American, and General topics and novelists. Those issues that do not carry this series of reviews are dedicated to a single author; in these special issues will often be found essay-reviews and checklists for work of or about the subject author. Access to this material is simplified by using the *Cumulative Index* of *MFS,* vols. 1–20 (1955–1975) compiled by Teddie McFerrin and Carla Cooper (West Lafayette, Ind.: Purdue Research Foundation, 1975) [PS379.M553 C6].

VII. PROSE AND CRITICISM

See also section S.IX, section W, and section X.

R–60 **Brown, Christopher C., and William B. Thesing.** *English Prose and Criticism, 1900–1950: A Guide to Information Sources.* Detroit: Gale Research Co., 1983.
Z2014.P795 B76 1983

This bibliography of primary and secondary works of nonfictional prose is current through 1980. Briefly annotated, unnumbered entries are disposed into two major sections. The first, Generic and Period Studies, is in six subsections, treating Bibliographies, Literary Histories, Studies of Biography and Autobiography, Essay and Prose Style, Literary Criticism, and Travel Writing, respectively. The second and larger section presents primary and secondary bibliographies for a total of thirty-seven authors. Entries for each author are in five categories: Published Non-fictional Prose, Works Edited by Others, Bibliographies (both primary and secondary), Biographies and Biographical Studies, and Criticism. Almost all entries are descriptively annotated, and some have evaluative indications. The volume concludes with indexes of authors and of titles.

R–62 **Borklund, Elmer, ed.** *Contemporary Literary Critics.* 2d ed. Detroit: Gale Research Co., 1982.
PS78.B56 1982

Biobibliographies are presented in this volume for more than 150 living literary critics writing in English. Both reviewer-critics and academic critics are included. An analysis of each critic's work by the editor, including liberal quotations, citations of the opinions of others, and a description and evaluation of his chief attitudes, is an important feature of the volume.

AMERICAN LITERATURE

Note that many reference works on English literature also treat American literature. See, therefore, section M and sections O through R, passim. See also section L.XVII–L.XX for works on American Women's studies.

I. BIBLIOGRAPHIES AND GUIDES

Other major bibliographies that include American literature are the *MLA International Bibliography* (L–50), the MHRA *Annual Bibliography of English Language and Literature* (M–21), the *Year's Work in English Studies* (M–22), and *Abstracts of English Studies* (M–23). See also *McNamee's Dissertations in English and American Literature* (E–20), Howard's *Theses in American Literature* (E–26), and Woodress's *Dissertations in American Literature* (E–35), as well as the numerous bibliographies and guides for the study of American history (F–50 and following).

S–1 Nilon, Charles E. *Bibliography of Bibliographies in American Literature.* New York: R. R. Bowker, 1970.
Z1225.A1 N5

This generally unannotated bibliography of bibliographies includes both separately published and embedded bibliographies, listings at the ends of historical and critical studies, and bibliographical studies. It was compiled primarily from secondary sources. There are four parts. Part 1 lists basic American bibliographies, Library of Congress and National Union catalogs, other basic bibliographies, and general bibliographies. Part 2 lists author bibliographies by century and, within centuries, alphabetically by subject author. Part 3 contains general bibliographies on American literary history and criticism and then divisions for the genres of drama, fiction, and poetry. The ancillary bibliographies of part 4 are listed under their subject areas, as follows: Almanacs, Annuals, Chap Books, Gift Books; Biographies, Diaries, Genealogies; Children's Literature; Cinema; Dissertations; Education; Folklore, Legend, Myth; Foreign Criticism of American Literature; History: Social, Economic, Political, Legal; Humor, Satire; Indian Language, Literature; Language; Linguistics; Libraries: Catalogs, Guides; Manuscripts; Music; Negro; Periodicals, Journalism, Serials; Printing and Publishing; Book Collections, Americana; Imprints; Presses; Regionalism; Regions; States; Religion, Theology, Philosophy; Science; Themes and Types; Translations; and Travels. There are no cross-references in the volume, but it concludes with an elaborate and detailed index of authors, compilers, titles, and authors-as-subjects.

S–2 Koster, Donald N. *American Literature and Language: A Guide to Information Sources.* Detroit: Gale Research Co., 1982.
Z1225.K68 1982

This highly selective guide contains 1,885 serially numbered entries with brief descriptive annotations. Recent scholarship (after 1950) is featured, and the selection is eccentric, with an unmistakable bias in favor of reference works published by Gale. The first part, treating literature, has a brief section on General Aids (Bibliographies, Checklists, Indexes and Reference Guides; Biographical Reference Aids; General Histories; Literary Histories; and General Critical Studies), followed by individual author bibliographies. The second part, treating the American language, is not further subdivided. There are indexes of authors, titles, and subjects.

In addition to Koster, there are a number of other relevant bibliographical guides in Gale's American Studies series. These include guides by Frank Cassara to *History of the United States of America* (1977) [Z1236.C33]; by Ernest R. Sandeen and Frederick Hale to *American Religion and Philosophy* (1978) [Z7757.U5 S25]; by Larry Landrum to *American Popular Culture* (1982) [Z1361.C6 L28 1982]; by Charles D. Peavy to *Afro-American Literature and Culture since World War II* (see S–129); by Virginia R. Terris to *Women in America* (1980) [Z7964.U49 T45]; and by Ira Bruce Nadel to *Jewish Writers of North America* (see S–137).

S–3 Gohdes, Clarence. *Bibliographical Guide to the Study of the Literature of the U.S.A.* 4th ed., rev. and enl. Durham, N.C.: Duke University Press, 1976.
Z1225.G6 1976

This excellent guide, first published in 1959, is topically organized to aid the professional scholar in the study of American literature and ancillary fields. More than 1,400 entries, briefly annotated, are numbered within each of thirty-five topical headings. General bibliographic and methodological sections are followed by sections on general American history, intellectual, religious, and artistic history, and then headings on genres, periods, themes, regions, ethnic literature, and the reception of American literature. There is an appendix citing standard biographical studies of 100 American authors. There are two indexes, by subject and by author, editor, or compiler.

S–4 **Leary, Lewis, and John Auchard.** *American Literature: A Study and Research Guide.* New York: St. Martin's Press, 1976.   Z1225.L47

Though this brief guide is intended as an aid to undergraduate students, more advanced students will find much of it valuable since it presents the winnowing effort of one of the leading authorities on American literary scholarship (see S–13). The work is divided into eleven chapters, the first presenting an essay on the history of the study and teaching of American literature, and the last providing an essay on writing the research paper. The intermediate chapters offer essentially bibliographical essays emphasizing recent work in the categories of literary histories, studies in genre, foreign influences and influence abroad, language, types and schools of criticism, periodicals, bibliographical guides, biographical sources, and major writers. The long chapter on major American writers is divided into sections on each of the twenty-eight authors treated from Bryant to Whitman. An index of authors, scholars, and critics concludes the volume.

S–5 **Kolb, Harold H., Jr.** *Field Guide to the Study of American Literature.* Charlottesville: University Press of Virginia, 1976.   Z1225.K65

This volume, an expansion of earlier mimeographed versions, is intended as an introduction to the most significant works for students of American literature. It offers sufficient annotation for each entry to indicate contents and directions for use. The 373 serially numbered entries are disposed into six sections on Bibliography, Literary History and Criticism, Reference Works, Editions and Series, Anthologies, and Journals. Within each section, entries are arranged alphabetically by author or title. There are cross-references to entry numbers, and a combined index of authors, subjects, and genres concludes the volume.

S–6 **Davis, Richard Beale.** *American Literature through Bryant: 1585–1830.* [A Goldentree Bibliography.] New York: Appleton-Century-Crofts, 1969.   Z1225.D3

This student bibliographical guide begins with a series of general sections: (General Reference and Literary History, General Bibliography, General Anthologies, Periodicals and Newspapers, and Commentaries on Periodicals and Newspapers). These are followed by three major divisions on The Colonial Period to 1763; The Revolutionary Period, 1763–1790; and The Early National Period, 1790–1830. Within these divisions materials are arranged into sections on Bibliography; Anthologies; Historical and Cultural Background; Literary History, Criticism, and General Biography; Major Figures (alphabetically arranged with subsections under each for Texts, Bibliography, Biographical and Critical Books, and Biographical and Critical Essays); and Lesser Figures (in alphabetical order with cited material in the same order as that used for major figures, though not formally subdivided). In sum, listings are given for nearly fifty major and more than seventy-five minor figures. Unlike many volumes in the Goldentree series, this one does not use asterisks to distinguish especially significant works. An index of names concludes the guide. The bibliography is to be supplemented by the separate Goldentree Bibliographies on the American drama (S–70), on the American novel (S–80, S–81), and on Afro-American writers (S–120).
A second volume by Harry Hayden Clarke, *American Literature: Poe through Garland* [A Goldentree Bibliography] (New York: Appleton-Century Crofts, 1971) [Z1227. 58], deals with American authors (except minor novelists and dramatists) whose work reached a peak between 1830 and 1914. When dealing with major novelists, this work emphasizes contributions to the short story, literary theory and criticism,

social or travel commentary, history, and letters, since other matters are dealt with in another guide within the same series (see below). This guide is disposed into sections on Bibliographies and Reference Works; Backgrounds; Literary History; twenty-one Major American Writers (Exclusive of Novelists and Dramatists) which is subdivided into listings of Texts, Bibliographies, Biographies, and Critical Studies; and twenty-three Lesser Writers. Unlike many volumes in the Goldentree series, this one does not use asterisks to distinguish especially significant works. It is concluded by an index of names.
This work is to be supplemented by the separate Goldentree Bibliographies on the American drama (S–70), on the American novel (S–80, S–81), and on Afro-American writers (S–120).

S–7 **Callow, James T., and Robert J. Reilly.** *Guide to American Literature from Its Beginnings through Walt Whitman: Summaries, Interpretations, and Annotated Bibliography.* New York: Barnes and Noble, 1976.   PS92.C33

This volume and its companion are each divided into two parts: the first presents outline history with sketches of representative writers and works, while the second offers an annotated bibliography to complement the outline and sketches. The first part of this volume is divided into sixteen chapters covering the Earliest American Writing; Puritans and Non-Puritans in New England; Later Puritans; Diarists; Essayists, Statesmen, and Propagandists; Neoclassic Poets; Preromantics; Early Fiction and Drama; The Knickerbockers; The Transcendentalists; Hawthorne, Poe, and Melville; New England Poets; Humorists, Wits, and Informal Essayists; Writers in the Civil War; Walt Whitman; and a helpful last chapter on Compiling and Updating Your Own Bibliography. The second part is divided into a section on General Bibliography (GB), which cites any work referred to in short form at least twice in the Chapter-by-Chapter Bibliographies that follow it. These annotated bibliographies are designed to supplement and document the outlines and sketches of the first part, and they follow its structure of sections and subsections. The volume concludes with an index of literary and historical authors, the titles of their works, and selected subjects. The first part of the comparison volume, *Guide to American Literature from Emily Dickinson to the Present: Summaries, Interpretations, and Annotated Bibliography* (New York: Barnes and Noble Books, 1977) [PS203.C27] is divided into thirteen chapters covering Emily Dickinson; American Humorists, 1850–1900; Local Color; Social Critics; Literary Realists; Naturalism; Social Protest and Realism; The Modern Temper; Modern Poets; Modern Novelists and Short-Story Writers; Modern Dramatists; Modern Literary Criticism; and a helpful last chapter on Compiling and Updating Your Own Bibliography. The second part is identical in character and structure with that of the companion volume described above.

S–8 **Jones, Howard Mumford, and Richard M. Ludwig.** *Guide to American Literature and Its Background since 1890.* 4th ed., rev. and enl. Cambridge: Harvard University Press, 1972.   Z1225.J65 1972

Originally published in 1953, this guide, updated to about 1970, is in two main parts. The first, Backgrounds of American Literature since 1890, is a very selective compilation of secondary titles, some with annotation, treating the context of American literature and its general study. It is in six divisions, as follows: I. General Guides; II. General Reference Works; III. General Histories; IV. Special Aspects (Social and Economic History, International Affairs, Education, Science and Technology, General Intellectual History, The Fine Arts, The Popular Arts); V. Literary History (A. General Works, B. General Reference Works, C. Literary Histories of

Special Scope, D. Special Themes, E. The English Language in America, F. Fiction, G. Poetry, H. Drama, I. General Prose and Criticism, J. Biography, K. Magazines, and L. American Publishing); and VI. A Critical List of Magazines (both historical and current). A final section VII presents a summary of the Chief Historical Events 1890–1971, subdivided by presidential terms.

Part 2, Reading Lists of American Literature since 1890, presents a syllabus of primary works of American literature after 1890 disposed into fifty-two sections, from "The Genteel Tradition" through sections on historical periods, movements, and the major genres of twentieth-century American Literature. Brief introductions to each section are followed by lists of authors with dates, and titles of pertinent readings. The guide concludes with an index of authors.

S–9 **Havlice, Patricia P.** *Index to American Author Bibliographies.* Metuchen, N.J.: Scarecrow Press, 1971.

Z1225.H37

This index, which supplements Nilon (S–1), is of author bibliographies and bibliographical studies published in periodicals. Both American citizens and those foreign authors who were professionally active in America are included. The work is arranged alphabetically by some 1,200 subject authors, with dates. A total of 2,225 bibliographical entries are given under their subject author; when there is more than one entry for an author, the entries are listed alphabetically by compiler. An index of compilers concludes the volume.

S–10 **Spiller, Robert E., Willard Thorp, Thomas H. Jensen, Henry Seidel Canby, and Richard M. Ludwig, eds.** *Literary History of the United States: Bibliography.* 4th ed., rev. 2 vols. New York: Macmillan, 1974.   PS88.L522

Originally published in 1948 in three volumes, with a second edition in 1953, a 268-page bibliographical supplement published in 1959, and a second bibliographical supplement of 366 pages published in 1972, this work remains the standard history of American literature and is described as such below (S–31). It is also a standard discursive bibliography of American literature.

Presented in the second volume of the fourth edition, then, is a corrected reprint of the 790-page bibliography first published in 1948, along with the bibliographical supplements of 1959 and 1972, along with a new index to the whole. The original bibliography, done in discursive form, is in four main parts. Part 1 is a Guide to Resources and treats Bibliographical Centers (arranged by geographical regions), Publisher Catalogues and Directories, Union Lists and Special Collections, Guides to Professional Studies and Bibliographies, Registries of Publication, Dictionaries and Digests, and Sources for Cultural History. The second part, Bibliographies: Literature and Culture, is subdivided as follows: Definition, History, and Criticism; Colonial Period to 1760; Forming of the Republic, 1760–1820; Mid 19th Century; Late 19th Century; 20th Century; Civilization in the United States; The American Language; Songs and Ballads; Folk Tales and Humor; Indian Lore and Antiquities; Popular Literature (Best Sellers, Juvenile Literature, Hymns and Hymn Writing, Oratory and the Lyceum, Almanacs and Chapbooks). Part 2 has many subtopics, including the recurrent, distinctive topic Instruments of Culture and Literary Production, treating libraries and reading journals and magazines, and the publishing scene.

The third part, Bibliographies: Movements and Influences, is subdivided as follows: Chronicles of the Frontier: Literature of Travel and Westward Migration; Mingling of Tongues; Writing Other Than English; Regionalism and Local Color; Science and Social Criticism; The Machine Age and the Literature of Exposure; Slavery and Conflict; Transcendentalism and Utopian Ventures; Bohemia; Escapism and Aestheticism;

and American Writers and Books Abroad. The fourth and final part presents a total of 207 individual author bibliographies, including Primary Works, Collected Editions, Biographical and Critical Works, Primary Manuscript Sources, and Bibliographies. A subject-and-title index, including author-as-subject, concludes the volume.

The bibliographical supplement of 1959 cites works published 1948–1958 and includes bibliographies for sixteen additional authors; the supplement of 1972 adds works published 1958–1970 as well as those overlooked in the earlier compilations and also adds bibliographies for sixteen new authors. Both supplements continue the discursive form of the original bibliography. Each is indexed by author. For works published after 1970 the annual *American Literary Scholarship* (S–14) provides a similarly discursive bibliography. Both the *Articles on American Literature* (S–12) and the American Literature sections of the *MLA International Bibliography* (L–50) provide further classified, but unannotated, supplemental lists.

S–11 ***Bibliography of United States Literature [BUSL].*** Edited by Matthew J. Bruccoli. In preparation.

This long-awaited multi-volume primary and secondary bibliography of American literature is scheduled to begin publication in 1990 in a joint venture by the New York firm Facts on File and the Bruccoli Clark Layman company of Columbia, S.C. Some sixteen volumes are planned, and are to be published at the rate of one every six months. Individual volumes will treat periods and genres: the first four volumes will cover American fiction in chronological order, with Volume I going to 1865; Volume II, 1866–1918; Volume III, 1919–1946; and Volume IV, 1947–1980. Subsequent volumes will also be organized by genre and period, including volumes on poetry, drama, and nonfiction, as well as two volumes on the American language and folklore, including the ethnic influences on American literature.

There will be two types of entries treating either authors or backgrounds. Author bibliographies, by far the more numerous, will include biographical information, critical assessments, and some samples, along with full primary and secondary bibliographies prepared by individual contributors. Sample entries give a brief summary of the author's reception followed by sections on Bibliographies and Catalogues; Books (by the author, in chronological order); Letters, Diaries, Notebooks; Other (works); Editions and Collections; Manuscripts and Archives; Concordance; Biographies (Books, Book Sections and Articles); and then Critical Studies (Books, Collections of Essays, Special Journals, Book Sections and Articles). Background entries cover intellectual studies in the humanities, literary histories, general critical works, and scholarship in the fields of publishing, librarianship, and book collecting.

S–12 ***Articles on American Literature, 1900–1950.*** Compiled by Lewis Leary. Durham, N.C.: Duke University Press, 1954.

Z1225.L49

This volume cumulates and reclassifies the quarterly checklists of "Articles on American Literature Appearing in Current Periodicals" in *American Literature* from 1929 on, along with the "American Bibliography" in the *MLA Annual Bibliography* (see L–50), both supplemented with additional listings culled by the compiler from some sixty journals 1900–1929. It expands upon and revises the earlier cumulation by Leary published in 1947 with the title *Articles on American Literature Appearing in Current Periodicals, 1920–1945* [Z1225.L48]. A total of some 17,000 items are cited.

The original listings in *American Literature* continue to be published. Briefly annotated entries are disposed into five sections: I. 1607–1800; II. 1800–1870; III. 1870–1920; IV.

1920– [present]; V. General (including regional and ethnic studies). Also included in *AL* as a regular quarterly feature is the listing of "Research in Progress," which includes both doctoral theses and other works in preparation.

Articles from 1950 through 1975 are cumulated in two supplemental volumes. The first, edited by Leary, with Carolyn Bartholet and Catherine Ross, covers the period 1950–1967, was published in 1967, and contains some 20,000 items [Z1225.L492]. The second, edited by Leary with John Auchard, covers the period 1968–1975, was published in 1979, and contains some 27,000 entries [Z1225.L493]. Both supplemental volumes and the original take the form of sheer listings under a number of rubrics. Those for the second supplement are as follows: American Authors (alphabetical by subject author); American Literature (Aims and Methods, Bibliography; Biography and Autobiography; Ethnic Groups); Fiction; Foreign Influences and Estimates; Frontier; Humor; Language and Style; Libraries and Literary Collections; Literary Criticism; Literary History; Literary Societies; Literary Trends and Attitudes; Newspapers and Periodicals; Philosophy and Philosophical Trends; Poetry; Printing, Publishing, Bookselling; Regionalism; Religion; Science; Social and Political Aspects; Theatre; Women. Within each rubric entries are alphabetical by subject, including authors as subjects. The supplemental volumes include also entries omitted from previous compilations; thus all three volumes should be used together. Entries that are bibliographical are designated by an asterisk. There are no cross-references; instead, entries are repeated under several headings as necessary. There is no index.

S–13 *Articles on American Studies, 1954–1968: A Cumulation of the Annual Bibliographies from American Quarterly.* Edited by Hennig Cohen. 2 vols. Ann Arbor, Mich.: Pierian Press, 1972.   Z1361.C6 A44

This volume reprints the annual bibliographies of *American Quarterly* with a series of indexes. The articles are serially numbered to 1,960 (a total of 2,350 entries had appeared) and unnumbered after that. They are arranged in categories after the annual lists for 1954/1955, as follows: Art and Architecture; Economics; Education; Folklore; History and Political Science; Language; Law; Literature [and Drama, and Librarianship]; Mass Culture; Music; Philosophy; Psychiatry and Psychology; Public Address; Religion; Science and Technology; Sociology and Anthropology.

The three indexes in this cumulation are by author, joint author, or main entry (some 9,500 citations); by subjects: personal names (some 5,000 citations including names and nicknames of persons, characters, and folk heroes cited in the titles and annotations of the original bibliographies); and by general subject categories. There is a key to subject categories and symbols.

The annual lists continue to appear in *American Quarterly* through 1975 (volume 25). In addition, there are lists from 1956 of "American Studies Dissertations" (see E–36) and from 1958 on "Writings on the Theory and Teaching of American Studies." There is also, from 1968, an "Annual Review of Books" in the form of a bibliographical essay. Since 1975, bibliographic articles summarizing work on various aspects of American studies appear regularly, in lieu of an annual bibliography.

The *Jahrbuch für Amerikastudien*, vols. 1–18 (Heidelberg, 1956–1973) [E169.1.J33], featured an annual bibliography of American studies under the title "Deutsche amerikanistische Veröffentlichungen [1956–1971]." Serially numbered entries, drawn from the German National Bibliography (C–65) and the *IBZ* (D–13), are rarely annotated and are listed under the following headings: I. Allgemeines, Bibliographien, Wörterbücher; II. Sprache und Literatur; III. Geschichte, Staat und Gesellschaft; IV. Wirtschaft, Arbeit und Verkehr;

V. Recht, Gesetz und Verwaltung; VI. Erd- und Völkerkunde; VII. Bildungswesen; VIII. Kunstschaffen; IX. Philosophie, Psychologie und Religion; and X. Reiseberichte, Verschiedenes. Since volume 19 (1974) the journal, renamed *Amerikastudien / American Studies* and published half-yearly (Stuttgart: Metzler) [E169.12.J33], continues unchanged the annual bibliography in the second issue each year.

S–14 *American Literary Scholarship: An Annual.* Edited by James Woodress and J. Albert Robbins. Durham, N.C.: Duke University Press, 1965–.   PS3.A47

Similar in style to the *Year's Work in English Studies* (M–22), this annual review features selective, critical bibliographical essays by authorities on various topics of American literary study. It is in two parts, the first treating major authors and the second treating periods, genres, and various themes and topics. The original volume treated work of the year 1963 (along with materials of 1961 and 1962). The *Annual* is normally published two years after the work its essays describe. The separate essays in recent years have treated the following topics: in part 1: 1. Emerson, Thoreau and Transcendentalism; 2. Hawthorne; 3. Poe; 4. Melville; 5. Whitman and Dickinson; 6. Mark Twain; 7. Henry James; 8. Pound and Eliot; 9. Faulkner; 10. Fitzgerald and Hemingway; and in part 2, 11. Literature to 1800; 12. 19th Century Literature; 13. Fiction: 1900 to the 1930s; 14. Fiction: The 1930s to the 1950s; 15. Fiction: The 1950s to the Present; 16. Poetry: 1900 to the 1930s; 17. Poetry: The 1930s to the Present; 18. Drama; 19. Black Literature; 20. Themes, Topics, Criticism; 21. Foreign Scholarship (French, German, Italian, Japanese, Scandinavian); 22. Bibliographical Addendum / General Reference Works. There are appropriate subdivisions in each section. The annual volumes conclude with an author index and a subject index that includes both authors-as-subjects and titles.

S–15 *Resources for American Literary Study.* Vol. 1–. College Park: University of Maryland, 1971–.   Z1225.R46

This semiannual journal publishes annotated and evaluative checklists of critical and biographical scholarship on significant works of major American authors and on the total work of minor authors; evaluative bibliographical essays on major authors, works, genres, trends, and periods; informative accounts or catalogs of collections of research materials, particularly recent acquisitions; and finally, edited texts of correspondence and other documents of interest to American literary or cultural historians. Bibliographical reviews, book reviews, and news and notes features are also found in each issue.

S–16 *American Studies: An Annotated Bibliography.* Edited by Jack Salzman on behalf of the American Studies Association. 3 vols. New York: Cambridge University Press, 1986.
                    Z1361.C6 A436 1986

This bibliography, with full descriptive annotation is limited to books written 1900–1983. It is a massive expansion with more than double the number of entries of a four-volume 1982 bibliography, *American Studies: An Annotated Bibliography of Works on the Civilization of the United States* prepared by the American Studies Association for the United States Information Agency, then called the International Communication Agency.

This work includes more than 6,500 entries alphanumerically disposed into eleven fields of American Studies, as follows: Anthropology and Folklore (A-F); Art and Architecture

(A–A); History (H); Literature (L) in volume 1; and Music (M); Political Science (PS); Popular Culture (PC); Psychology (PSY); Religion (R); Science, Technology, and Medicine (STM); and Sociology (SOC) in volume 2.

Each of the eleven sections was prepared by a group of contributors and begins with a preface which refers users to other reference sources pertinent to the study of the field. Each section is appropriately classified for entries in that field. The Literature section, for example, is classified as follows: I. General Surveys, II. Colonial Period, III. Nineteenth Century, IV. Twentieth Century, and V. Themes. The third volume, *Indexes*, contains separate author, title, and subject indexes, the last with numerous cross references.

A useful collection of bibliographical essays will be found in Robert H. Walker, ed. *American Studies: Topics and Sources* (Westport, Conn.: Greenwood Press, 1976) [E175 .8.A582] which prints a series of twenty-one essays originally published in *American Studies International* or scheduled to appear there. The essays provide bibliographical reviews, enumerations, and discussions on various topics associated with American studies, arranged in three main parts, as follows: I. American Studies and Traditional Topics (e.g., Cultural History; Religious History; 19th-Century Literature; The Presidency; Labor); II. New Accents for American Studies (e.g., Ecology; Black Studies; Popular Culture; Women's Studies); and III. General Resources for Teaching and Research. An index of titles is followed by a general bibliography and an author index to all works cited in the individual essays.

A further volume, *Sources for American Studies*, ed. Jefferson B. Kellogg and Robert H. Walker (1983) [E175.S58 1983], both updates and expands upon the original essays. The expansions take the form of new essays on Afro-American Studies, Architectural History, Detective Fiction, Economic History, Folklore, Foreign Policy, Historiography, Immigration History, Journalism, Study of the American Language, Military History, Music, the National Character, Philosophy, Poetry, and the Supreme Court. The updates, prepared by the original authors, provide added coverage into the early 1980s.

S–17 Selected Reviews of Research in American Literature and American Studies (in chronological order).

Leisy, Ernest. "Materials for Investigations in American Literature," *SP* 23 (1926); 90–115.

Link, Franz H. *Amerikanische Literatur geschichtsschreibung: Ein Forschungsbericht*. Stuttgart, 1963.

Tanselle, G. Thomas. "The Historiography of American Literary Publishing," *SB* 18 (1965); 3–39.

Thorp, Willard. "Exodus: Four Decades of American Literary Scholarship," *MLQ* 26 (1965): 40–61.

Flanagan, John T. "American Literary Bibliography in the Twentieth Century," *Library Trends* 15 (1966/67): 550–572. Reprinted in Robert B. Downs and Francis B. Jenkins, eds., *Bibliography: Current State and Future Trends* (Y–19).

Tanselle, G. Thomas. "The Descriptive Bibliography of American Authors." *SB* 21 (1968): 1–24.

———. "The State of Reference Bibliography in American Literature." *RALS* 1 (1971): 3–16.

Riewald, J. G. "The Translational Reception of American Literature in Europe. 1800–1900: A Review of Research." *ES* 60 (1979): 562–602.

See *ALS* (S–14) and *RALS* (S–15), *passim*.

S–18 Scholarly Journals in American Literature and American Studies.

AHumor *American Humor: An Interdisciplinary Newsletter*. Vol. 1–. College Park, Md.: American Humor Studies Association, 1974–. 2/yr. Reviews.
PS438.A53

AICRJ *American Indian Culture and Research Journal*. Vol. 1–. Los Angeles: American Indian Studies Center, UCLA, 1974–. 4/yr. E75.A5124

AIQ *American Indian Quarterly: A Journal of Anthropology, History, and Literature*. Vol. 1–. Hurst, Tex.: Society for American Indian Studies and Research, 1974–1979. Berkeley: Native American Studies Program, University of California, 1980–. 4/yr. Reviews. E75.A547

ALH *American Literary History*. Vol. 1–. Oxford: Oxford University Press, 1989–. 4/yr. Reviews.
No LC number

ALR *American Literary Realism, 1870–1910*. Vol. 1–. Arlington: University of Texas at Arlington, 1967–. 4/yr. Reviews. Bibliographical studies. Cumulative index to vols. 1–10 in vol. 10. PS1.A65

AmLS *American Literary Scholarship: An Annual* (S–14).

AL *American Literature: A Journal of Literary History, Criticism, and Bibliography*. Vol. 1–. Durham, N.C.: Duke University Press, 1929–. 4/yr. Reviews. Annual Bibliography, annual "Research in Progress" (see S–12). Indexed by author, subject, and author-as-subject with a separate index of book reviews, in Thomas F. Marshall, *Analytical Index to American Literature (Volumes I-XXX March 1929-January 1959)* (Durham, N.C.: Duke University Press, 1963). PS1.A6

AN&Q *American Notes and Queries* (see Z–58).

American Poetry. Vol. 1–. Albuquerque: University of New Mexico Press, 1983–. 4/yr. Reviews.

AQ *American Quarterly*. Vol. 1–. Philadelphia: University of Pennsylvania Press, 1949–. 5/yr. Reviews. Bibliography (see S–13). Analyzed Index to vols. 1–25 by Thomas F. Marshall and Nancy Walker. AP2.A3985

AS *American Speech: A Quarterly of Linguistic Usage* (see I–15).

Amer S *American Studies*. Vol. 1–. Lawrence: University of Kansas for the Midcontinent American Studies Association, 1971–. 2/yr. Reviews.
No LC number

ATQ *American Transcendental Quarterly: A Journal of New England Writers*. Vol. 1–. Kingston: University of Rhode Island, 1969–. 4/yr. Reviews. Bibliography: "Current Bibliography on Ralph Waldo Emerson," 1972–. PS243.A55

AmST *Amerikastudien / American Studies* [former title: *Jahrbuch für Amerikastudien 1956–1937*, vols. 1–18]. Vol. 1–. Frankfurt: Deutsche Gesellschaft für Amerikastudien, 1956–. 1/ then 2/yr. Reviews. Bibliography (see S–13). E169.12.J33

AJAS *Australian Journal of American Studies*. Vol. 1–. Sydney: Australian and New Zealand American Studies Association, 1981–. 1/yr. Reviews.
E169.1.A443

BALF *Black American Literature Forum*. Vol. 1–. Terre Haute: Indiana State University, 1967–. Reviews.
E185.5.N35

Canadian Review of American Studies. Vol. 1–. Downsview, Ontario: Canadian Association of American Studies, 1970–.   No LC number

CLAJ   *College Language Association Journal.* Vol. 1–. Baltimore, Md.: College Language Association, 1957–. 4/yr. Reviews. Bibliographical notes, bibliography (see S–137).   P1.A1 C22

EAL   *Early American Literature.* Vol. 1–. Amherst: University of Massachusetts, 1966–. 3/yr. Reviews. "Work in Progress." "Dissertations in Progress."
PS271.W46

ESQ   *ESQ: A Journal of the American Renaissance* [former title: *Emerson Society Quarterly.* 1955–1968, vols. 1–17]. Pullman: Washington State University, 1955–. Reviews. Bibliographical notices.
PS1629.E6

JAC   *Journal of American Culture.* Vol. 1–. Bowling Green, Ohio: Bowling Green State University, 1978–. 4/yr. Reviews. Bibliography: "Technology in American Culture: Recent Publications [1980–]."   E169.1.J7

JAF   *Journal of American Folklore* (see K–11).

JAH   *Journal of American History* (see F–10).

JAmS   *Journal of American Studies.* Vol. 1–. Cambridge: Cambridge University Press, for the British Association of American Studies, 1967–. 3/yr. Reviews.
E151.J6

JEGP   *Journal of English and Germanic Philology* (see L–118).

JES   *Journal of Ethnic Studies.* Vol. 1–. Bellingham: Western Washington University, 1973–. 4/yr.
E184.A1 J68

MELUS   *MELUS: Multi-Ethnic Literature of the United States.* Vol. 1–. Commerce: East Texas State University, 1976–. 4/yr. Reviews.   PN843.M18

Midamerica: The Yearbook of the Society for the Study of Midwestern Literature [Midamerica]. Vol. 1–. East Lansing: Michigan State University, 1974–. Bibliography (see S–111).   No LC number

MissQ   *Mississippi Quarterly: The Journal of Southern Culture.* Vol. 1–. State College: Mississippi State University, 1947–. 4/yr. Reviews. Annual bibliography "A Checklist of Scholarship on Southern Literature" (see S–103).   AS30.M58 A2

NEQ   *New England Quarterly: A Historical Review of New England Life and Letters.* Vol. 1–. Brunswick, Me.: Colonial Society of Massachusetts, 1928–. 4/yr. Reviews. Annual Bibliography (see S–101). Index to vols. 1–20.   F1.N62

Obsidian   *Obsidian: Black Literature in Review.* Vol. 1–. Fredonia: State University of New York—Fredonia, 1975–. 3/yr. Reviews. Annual Bibliography (see S–118).   PR1110.B503

Proof   *Proof: The Yearbook of American Bibliographical and Textual Studies* (see Y–5).

Prospects: The Annual of American Cultural Studies. Vol. 1–. New York: Burt Franklin, 1975–. 1/yr.   E169.1.P898

RALS   *Resources for American Literary Study* (see S–15).

SLJ   *Southern Literary Journal.* Vol. 1–. Chapel Hill: University of North Carolina, 1968–. 2/yr. Reviews.   PS261.S527

SoR   *Southern Review.* Vol. 1–. Baton Rouge: Louisiana State University, 1935–. 4/yr. Reviews.
AP2.S8555

SoSt   *Southern Studies: An Interdisciplinary Journal of the South.* Vol. 1–. Natchitoches, La.: Northwestern State University, 1961–. 4/yr. Reviews.
F366.L935

SWAL   *Southwestern American Literature.* Vol. 1–. Denton: North Texas State University, 1972–. 3/yr. Reviews.

SA   *Studi americani.* Vol. 1–. Rome: Edizioni di storia e letteratura, 1955–. 1/yr.   PS1.S8

SAF   *Studies in American Fiction.* Vol. 1–. Boston, Northeast University, 1973–. 2/yr. Reviews.
PS370.S87

StAH   *Studies in American Humor.* San Marcos: Southwest Texas State University, 1975–. 3/yr. Reviews.
PS430.S88

SAIL   *Studies in American Indian Literature* [former title: *Newsletter of the Association for Study of American Indian Literatures 1977–1979,* vols. 1–3]. Vol. 4–. New York: Columbia University, Department of English, 1980–. 4/yr. Reviews. Bibliographical Notices.   No LC number

SAJL   *Studies in American Jewish Literature.* Vol. 1–. University Park: Pennsylvania State University, 1975–. 2/yr. Reviews.   PS153.J4 S78

SBL   *Studies in Black Literature.* Vol. 1–. Fredericksburg, Va.: Mary Washington College, 1970–. 3/yr.
PS153.N5 S88

Studies in the American Renaissance. Vol. 1–. Boston: G. K. Hall, 1977–. 1/yr. Reviews. Bibliographies.   PS201.S86

WAL   *Western American Literature.* Vol. 1–. Logan: Utah State University, for the Western American Literature Association, 1966–. 4/yr. Reviews. "Annual Bibliography of Studies in Western American Literature" (see S–117).   PS501.E2

A full list of current journals in the fields of American literature and American studies is found in the March issue of *American Literature.* See also the listing in the *American Historical Review* (F–54). Further, see the compilation by Cathy Deering, *Union Catalogue of United States Studies Periodicals in the United Kingdom* (1982).

S–19   **Some Frequently Recommended Works on American Literature and American Studies.**

For frequently recommended works on Local and Regional American Literature, see S–119; for Afro-American Literature, see S–139; for Native American Literature, see S–149; for American Jewish Literature, see S–159; for Chicano Literature, see S–169; and for Asian-American Literature, see S–179. For additional frequently recommended works on American history generally, see section F; for works on American social, intellectual, and educational history, see K–90, K–95, and K–98 respectively. Important work on American literature is often included in studies of British literature. See, therefore, entries in sections P–19, Q–19, Q–29, Q–49, and R–19 for additional treatments of colonial, nineteenth-century, and modern American literature. Work on Canadian literature written in English will be found in section M (M–130 and following); work on French-Canadian literature in section L (L–70 and following); and work on Latin American literature in section L (L–90 and following). For work on American Women's studies and on Women and American Literature, see also Section L (L–182 and following). For works on American poetry generally, see also section T; for American drama and film see also section U, for American prose and prose fiction see also section W, and for American literary theory and criticism see also section X.

Aldridge, A. Owen. *Early American Literature: A Comparatist Approach*. Princeton, N.J.: Princeton University Press, 1982.   PS185.A38 1982

Baym, Nina. *Woman's Fiction: A Guide to Novels by and about Women in America, 1820–1870*. Ithaca, N.Y.: Cornell University Press, 1978.   PS149.B38

Bell, Michael D. *Development of American Romance: The Sacrifice of Relation*. Chicago: University of Chicago Press, 1980.   PS377.B4

Bercovitch, Sacvan, *American Jeremiad*. Madison: University of Wisconsin Press, 1978.   PS362.B43

———. *Puritan Origins of the American Self*. New Haven: Yale University Press, 1975.   F7.B48

———, and Myra Jehlen, eds. *Ideology and Classic American Literature*. New York: Cambridge University Press, 1986.   PS217.P64 I36 1986

Berthoff, Warner. *Ferment of Realism: American Literature, 1884–1919*. New York: Free Press, 1965.   PS214.B4

———. *Literature Without Qualities: American Writing Since 1945*. Berkeley: University of California Press, 1979.   PS225.B4

Bewley, Marius. *Eccentric Design: Form in the Classic American Novel*. New York: Columbia University Press, 1959.   PS371.B4

Bigsby, C. W. E. *Critical Introduction to Twentieth-Century American Drama*. 3 vols. New York: Cambridge University Press, 1982–1985.   PS351.B483 1982

Breitwieser, Mitchell R. *Cotton Mather and Benjamin Franklin*. New York: Cambridge University Press, 1984.   F67.M43 B74 1984

Brodhead, Richard H. *School of Hawthorne*. New York: Oxford University Press, 1986.   PS377.B68 1986

Cady, Edwin H. *Light of Common Day: Realism in American Fiction*. Bloomington: Indiana University Press, 1971.   PS374.R37 C3

Carton, Evan. *Rhetoric of American Romance: Dialectic and Identity in Emerson, and Dickinson, Poe, and Hawthorne*. Baltimore: Johns Hopkins University Press, 1985.   PS217.R6 C3 1985

Chase, Richard V. *American Novel and Its Tradition* (see S–86).

Cowie, Alexander *Rise of the American Novel* (see S–86).

Cunliffe, Marcus. *Literature of the United States* (see S–32).

Daly, Robert. *God's Altar: The World and the Flesh in Puritan Poetry*. Berkeley: University of California Press, 1978.   PS312.D3

Davidson, Cathy N. *Revolution and the Word: The Rise of the Novel in America*. New York: Oxford University Press, 1986.   PS374.S67 D38 1986

DiPietro, Robert J., and Edward Ifkovic, eds. *Ethnic Perspectives in American Literature: Selected Essays on the European Contribution*. New York: MLA, 1983.   PN843.E8 1983

Douglas, Ann. *Feminization of American Culture*. New York: Knopf, 1977.   PS152.D6 1977

Elliott, Emory. *Revolutionary Writers: Literature and Authority in the New Republic*. New York: Oxford University Press, 1982.   PS193.E4 1982

Feidelson, Charles, Jr. *Symbolism and American Literature*. Chicago: University of Chicago Press, 1953.   PS201.F4

Fiedler, Leslie. *Love and Death in the American Novel*. Rev. ed. New York: Stein and Day, 1966.   PS374.L6 F5 1966

Fliegelman, Jay. *Prodigals and Pilgrims: The American Revolution Against Patriarchal Authority, 1750–1800*. New York: Cambridge University Press, 1982.   E163.F58 1982

Fussell, Edwin. *Frontier: American Literature and the American West*. Princeton, N.J.: Princeton University Press, 1965.   PS169.W4 F8

Gilmore, Michael T. *American Romanticism and the Marketplace*. Chicago: University of Chicago Press, 1985.   PS217.R6 G54 1985

Girgus, Sam B. *Law of the Heart: Individualism and the Modern Self in American Literature*. Austin: University of Texas Press, 1979.   PS169.I53 G5

Grimsted, David. *Melodrama Unveiled: American Theater and Culture 1800–1950*. Chicago: University of Chicago Press, 1968.   PN1918.U5 G7

Hassan, Ihab. *Contemporary American Literature, 1945–1972: An Introduction*. New York: Ungar, 1973.   PS221.H36

Hoffman, Daniel, ed. *Harvard Guide to Contemporary American Writing*. Cambridge: Harvard University Press, 1979.   PS221.H357

Howard, Leon. *Literature and the American Tradition*. New York: Doubleday, 1960.   PS88.H65

Hughes, Glenn. *History of the American Theatre, 1700–1950*. New York: S. French, 1951.   PN2221.H76

Inglehart, Babette F., and Anthony R. Mangione. *Image of Pluralism in American Literature: An Annotated Bibliography on the American Experience of European Ethnic Groups*. New York: Institute of Pluralism and Group Identity of the American Jewish Committee, 1974.   Z1225.I53

Irwin, John T. *American Hieroglyphics: The Symbol of the Egyptian Hieroglyphics in the American Renaissance*. New Haven: Yale University Press, 1980.   PS217.H54I7

Jehlen, Myra. *American Incarnation: The Individual, The Nation, and The Continent*. Cambridge: Harvard University Press, 1986.   E169.1.J435 1986

Karcher, Carolyn L. *Shadow Over the Promised Land: Slavery, Race, and Violence in Melville's America*. Baton Rouge: Louisiana State University Press, 1980.   PS2388.P6 K37

Kaul, A. N. *American Vision: Actual and Ideal Society in Nineteenth Century Fiction*. New Haven: Yale University Press, 1963.   PS374.S7 K3 1963

Kazin, Alfred. *Bright Book of Life: American Novelists and Storytellers from Hemingway to Mailer*. Boston: Little, Brown, 1973.   PS379.K25 1973

———. *On Native Grounds: An Interpretation of Modern American Prose Literature*. New York: Reynall and Hitchcock, 1942.   PS379.K3

Klein, Marcus. *Foreigners: The Making of American Literature, 1900–1940*. Chicago: University of Chicago Press, 1981.   PS223.K5

Kolb, Harold. *Illusion of Life: American Realism as a Literary Form*. Charlottesville: University Press of Virginia, 1970.   PS214.K63

Kolodny, Annette. *Land Before Her: Fantasy and Experience of the American Frontiers, 1630–1860*. Chapel Hill: University of North Carolina Press, 1984.   E179.5.K64 1984

———. *Lay of the Land: Metaphor as Experience and History in American Life and Letters*. Chapel Hill: University of North Carolina Press, 1975.   P588.K65

Kronick, Joseph G. *American Poetics of History: From Emerson to the Moderns.* Baton Rouge: Louisiana State University Press, 1984.   PS169.H5 K7 1984

Lawrence, D. H. *Studies in Classic American Literature.* New York: Seltzer, 1923.   PS121.L3

Leary, Lewis. *Soundings: Some Early American Writers.* Athens: University of Georgia Press, 1975. PS193.L4

Levin, Harry. *Power of Blackness: Hawthorne, Poe, Melville.* New York: Knopf, 1958.   PS1888.L4

Lewis, R. W. B. *American Adam: Innocence, Tradition, and Tragedy in the Nineteenth Century.* Chicago: University of Chicago Press, 1955.   PS201.L4

McWilliams, John P. *Hawthorne, Melville, and the American Character.* New York: Cambridge University Press, 1984.   PS217.N38 M38 1984

Martin, Jay. *Harvests of Change: American Literature 1865–1914.* Englewood Cliffs, N.J.: Prentice-Hall, 1967.   PS214.M35

Marx, Leo. *Machine in the Garden: Technology and the Pastoral Ideal.* New York: Oxford University Press, 1964.   E169.1.M35

Matthiessen, F. O. *American Renaissance: Art and Expression in the Age of Emerson and Whitman.* New York: Oxford University Press, 1941.   PS261.M3

Mazzaro, Jerome. *Post-Modern American Poetry.* Urbana: University of Illinois Press, 1980.   PS323.5 .M39

Michaels, Walter Benn. *Gold Standard and the Logic of Naturalism: American Literature at the Turn of the Century.* Berkeley: University of California Press, 1987.   PS374.N29 M5 1987

Moses, Montrose J. *Representative American Dramas.* 2d ed. Boston: Little, Brown, 1933. Bibliography.   PS634.M6

Pease, Donald E. *Visionary Compacts: American Renaissance Writings in Cultural Context.* Madison: University of Wisconsin Press, 1987.   PS211.P38 1987

Pizer, Donald. *Realism and Naturalism in Nineteenth-Century American Literature.* Rev. ed. Carbondale: Southern Illinois University Press, 1984.   PS214.P5 1984

Poirier, Richard. *World Elsewhere: The Place of Style in American Literature.* New York: Oxford University Press, 1966.   PS88.P6

Quinn, Arthur H. *History of the American Drama* (see S–76).

Stauffer, Donald B. *Short History of American Poetry.* New York: Dutton, 1974.   PS303.S67

Straumann, Heinrich. *American Literature in the Twentieth Century.* 3d ed. New York: Harper and Row, 1965.   PS221.S8 1965

Sundquist, Eric J. *Home as Found: Authority and Genealogy in Nineteenth-Century American Literature.* Baltimore: Johns Hopkins University Press, 1979.   PS217.F35 S8

———, ed. *American Realism: New Essays.* Baltimore: Johns Hopkins University Press, 1982.   PS374.R37 A37 1982

Tate, Allen. *Sixty American Poets, 1896–1944.* Rev. ed. Washington, D.C.: Library of Congress, 1954. Bibliographies.   Z1231.P7 U55 1954

Thorp, Willard. *American Writing in the Twentieth Century.* Cambridge: Harvard University Press, 1960.   PS221.T48

Todorov, Tzvetan. *Conquest of America: The Question of the Other.* New York: Harper and Row, 1984.   E123.T6313 1984

Tompkins, Jane. *Sensational Designs: The Cultural Work of American Fiction, 1790–1860.* New York: Oxford University Press, 1985.   PS374.S7 T66 1985

Tyler, Moses Coit. *History of American Literature during the Colonial Period.* Rev. ed. 2 vols. New York: G. P. Putnam's Sons, 1897.   PS185.T8 1897

———. *Literary History of the American Revolution.* 2 vols. New York: G. P. Putnam's Sons, 1897.   PS185.T82

Vendler, Helen. *Part of Nature, Part of Us: Modern American Poet.* Cambridge: Harvard University Press, 1980.   PS323.5.V4

Voss, Arthur. *American Short Story: A Critical Survey.* Norman: University of Oklahoma Press, 1973.   PS374.S5 V6

Wagenknecht, Edward. *Cavalcade of the American Novel: From the Birth of the Nation to the Middle of the Twentieth Century.* New York: Holt, 1952.   PS371 .W3

Waggoner, Hyatt H. *American Poets from the Puritans to the Present.* Rev. ed. Baton Rouge: Louisiana State University Press, 1984.   PS303.W3 1984

Walcutt, C. C. *American Literary Naturalism: A Divided Stream.* Minneapolis: University of Minnesota Press, 1956.   PS379.W28

Walker, Cheryl. *Nightingale's Burden: Women Poets and American Culture Before 1900.* Bloomington: Indiana University Press, 1982.   PS147.W27 1982

Wilson, Edmund. *Patriotic Gore: Studies in the Literature of the American Civil War.* New York: Oxford University Press, 1962.   PS211.W5

Wolf, Bryan Jay. *Romantic Revision: Culture and Consciousness in Nineteenth-Century American Painting and Literature.* Chicago: University of Chicago Press, 1982.   ND210.5.R6 W6 1982

Ziff, Larzer. *American 1890s: Life and Times of a Lost Generation.* New York: Viking Press, 1966.   PS214.Z5

II. BIOBIBLIOGRAPHIES AND REVIEWS OF RESEARCH

Among other biobibliographies and dictionaries of literary biography see, for American authors, Allibone's *Critical Dictionary* (M–50), *Everyman's Dictionary* (M–51), Myers's *Dictionary* (M–52), Kunitz and Haycroft's *Twentieth Century Authors* (R–21), and both *Contemporary Authors* (R–23) and the volumes by Vinson et al., *Contemporary Poets* (R–33), *Contemporary Dramatists* (R–43), *Contemporary Novelists* (R–52), and *Contemporary Literary Critics* (R–62).

S–20 **Woodress, James, et al. *Eight American Authors: A Review of Research and Criticism.*** Rev. ed. New York: W. W. Norton, 1971.   PS201.E4 1971

This series of bibliographical essays first appeared in 1956 under the editorship of Floyd Stovall, who also wrote the chapter on Emerson. It was reissued with a Bibliographical Supplement by J. Chesley Mathews in 1963 [PS201 .S8 1963]. The other contributors to that widely imitated volume were Jay B. Hubbell on Poe, Walter Blair on Hawthorne, Lewis Leary on Thoreau, Stanley Williams on Melville, Willard Thorp on Whitman, Harry Hayden Clark on Twain, and Robert Spiller on James. The present greatly expanded volume, which reviews scholarship published through 1969, has been carried out under the sponsorship of the American Literature Section of the Modern Language Association and has attempted to consider, though not necessarily to discuss, all the available biobibliographical and critical material on the eight authors. The same contributors prepared this revised edition, except for the new essays by Nathalia Wright on Melville, Roger Asselineau on Whitman, and Robert L. Gale on Henry James.

Each of the bibliographical essays is divided into sections on bibliography, editions, biography, and criticism, with some also including separate sections on manuscripts, studies of the author's ideas, dissertations, fame and influence, and periodicals devoted exclusively to the author. The volume concludes with notes on the contributors and an index combining authors and their works with the names of scholars and critics whose research is discussed.

S–21 **Rees, Robert A., and Earl N. Harbert, eds. *Fifteen American Authors before 1900: Bibliographic Essays on Research and Criticism.* Rev. ed. Madison: University of Wisconsin Press, 1984.** PS55.F53 1984

This volume, one of the series initiated by the success of *Eight American Authors* (S–20), was originally published in 1971 with essays by Earl N. Harbert on Adams, James E. Rocks on Bryant, James Franklin Beard on Cooper, Donald Pizer on Stephen Crane, James Woodress on Dickinson, Everett H. Emerson on Edwards, Bruce Granger on Franklin, Barry Menikoff on Holmes, George Fortenberry on Howells, Henry A. Pochmann on Irving, Richard Dilworth Rust on Longfellow, Robert A. Rees on J. R. Lowell, William B. Pillingham on Norris, Norman S. Grabo on Taylor, and Karl Keller on Whittier. In addition, there were essays by C. Hugh Holman on "Literature of the Old South" and Louis D. Rubin, Jr. on "Literature of the New South." Each author essay is divided into sections on Bibliography, Editions, Manuscripts and Letters, Biography and Criticism; the regional essays are divided for the Old South into sections on Bibliography, Texts, and General and Special Studies, and for the New, into sections on Bibliography and Scholarship. The essays are selective and evaluative and do not refer to all materials considered, though contributors reviewed all available materials on their authors published through 1969. The volume concludes with notes on the contributors and an index of authors, scholars, and critics.

This revised edition excludes the essays on the Old and New South but includes updated essays by the original contributors. In addition, there are chapters on William Dean Howells by David J. Nordloh and on Washington Irving by James W. Tuttleton. Entries contain reference to materials published through the 1970s, with some references to work of the early 1980s.

S–22 **Bryer, Jackson R., ed. *Sixteen Modern American Authors: A Survey of Research and Criticism.* Rev. ed. Durham, N.C.: Duke University Press, 1974.** PS221.B7 1974

This volume, prepared to complement the original *Eight American Authors* (S–20), was published originally as *Fifteen Modern American Authors* (Durham, N.C., 1969) [PS221.B7] with essays by Walter B. Rideout on Sherwood Anderson, Bernice Slote on Cather, Brom Weber on Hart Crane, Robert H. Elias on Dreiser, Richard M. Ludwig on T. S. Eliot, James B. Meriwether on Faulkner, Jackson R. Bryer on Fitzgerald, Reginald L. Cook on Frost, Frederick J. Hoffman on Hemingway, John Henry Raleigh on O'Neill, John Espey on Pound, Ellsworth Barnard on Robinson, Warren

French on Steinbeck, Joseph N. Riddel on Stevens, and C. Hugh Holman on Thomas Wolfe. The revised edition, dedicated to the memory of Frederick J. Hoffman (as was the original volume), adds an essay on William Carlos Williams by Linda W. Wagner and supplements by each contributor covering work through 1971 (with some 1972 and 1973 items), the Hemingway supplement having been contributed by Melvin J. Friedman.

The essays and the supplements appended to each are divided into sections on Bibliography, Editions, Manuscripts and Letters, Biography, and Criticism. Though comprehensive, the essays and supplements do not refer to all materials surveyed but instead are selective and evaluative reviews. The volume concludes with notes on contributors and a detailed index to the sixteen authors and their works, as well as other literary and historical figures cited, and the scholars and critics whose research is discussed.

A supplement, *Sixteen Modern American Authors: Volume 2, A Survey of Research and Criticism Since 1972*, is scheduled for publication (Durham, N.C.: Duke University Press, 1989) [PS221.S625 1989]. Articles in the new volume do not incorporate either the original or the supplemental materials of the revised edition. The contributors remain the same except as follows: James B. Woodress on Cather; James L. W. West III on Dreiser; Stuart McDougal on T. S. Eliot; Philip Cohen, David Krause, and Karl Zender on Faulkner; Bruce Stark on Hemingway; and Richard S. Kennedy on Wolfe.

S–23 **Emerson, Everett, ed. *Major Writers of Early American Literature.* Madison: University of Wisconsin Press, 1972.** PS185.E4

This volume presents fresh critical appraisals by recognized authorities, summarizing and extending current research and criticism of the work of eight early American authors. Each essay has a bibliography appended, with divisions for editions and scholarship and criticism. The authors are as follows: William Bradford (by David Levin); Anne Bradstreet (by Ann Stanford); Edward Taylor (by Donald E. Stanford); Cotton Mather (by Sacvan Bercovitch); William Byrd (by Richard Beale Davis); Jonathan Edwards (by Daniel B. Shea, Jr.); Benjamin Franklin (by J. A. Leo Lemay); Philip Freneau (by Lewis Leary); and Charles Brockden Brown (by Donald A. Ringe). The volume concludes with an index of names.

S–24 **Myerson, Joel, ed. *Transcendentalists: A Review of Research and Criticism.* New York: Modern Language Association, 1984.** Z7128.T7 T7 1984

This first comprehensive bibliography of American Transcendentalism is current through 1981, with additional material provided by some contributors. Its forty-four essays are disposed into three sections. The first contains five general essays by noted authorities surveying The Transcendentalist Movement, Transcendentalism; The Times; Unitarianism and Transcendentalism; Transcendentalist Communities and Transcendentalist Periodicals.

The second section deals with twenty-eight individual transcendentalists in essays which treat Bibliographies, Manuscripts, Editions, Biography, and Criticism. For some figures such as Emerson and Thoreau there are further sections concerning Sources, Thought (Philosophy, Aesthetics, Nature, Science, Religion, Social and Political Reform, Specific Ideas), Writings (Literary Expression, Lectures, Poetry, Individual Works), and Influence.

The third section contains essays on eleven figures (including Dickinson, Hawthorne, Melville, Poe, and Whitman) who represent The Contemporary Reaction to transcendentalism, influencing the movement, influenced by it, or reacting against it.

The volume concludes with a bibliography of all works cited, brief notices about the thirty contributors, and an index of names and some titles.

S–25 **Blanck, Jacob.** *Bibliography of American Literature.* 10 vols. planned. Vol. 1–. New Haven: Yale University Press, 1955–   Z1225.B55

A selective, meticulously compiled descriptive bibliography of the first editions of approximately 300 American writers from the period of the Revolution to 1930, excluding any author living after 1930. Only writers whose work is primarily of literary or belletristic interest are included; omitted in general are historians, travel writers, authors of children's literature, scientific and medical texts, textbooks, and sermons. For each included author, cited information is arranged chronologically, beginning with first editions of all books, pamphlets, broadsides, and books containing the first appearance of any work by the author. Next are cited variant issues or states, reprints, and subsequent editions that might be confused with first editions or that incorporate significant textual changes. Not cited are the author's publications in periodicals and newspapers, later editions without textual or bibliographical interest, translations, and volumes of correspondence.

For each book cited, a quasi-facsimile title-page transcription is given, along with the imprint, pagination, collation, and a description of the binding, wrapper, color, insets, cover title, binder's title, and headlines, along with a location of one copy. A selected list of biographical, bibliographical, and critical works concerning the author concludes each listing. Each volume contains an index of initials, pseudonyms, and anonyms.

Published to date are volumes 1, Adams to Byrne (1955); 2, Cable to Dwight (1957); 3, Eggleston to Harte (1959); 4, Hawthorne to Ingraham (1963); 5, Irving to Longfellow (1969); 6, Longstreet to Parsons (1973); 7, Paulding to Stockton (1983), edited and completed by Virginia L. Smyers and Michael Winship.

For those authors not yet covered by Blanck see Merle DeVore Johnson, *American First Editions*, 4th ed., rev. and enl. Jacob Blanck (1942) [Z1231.F5 J6]. For prerevolutionary authors see Evans (C–22); for the work of authors living after 1930 see, among other sources, Millet (S–28), and works on contemporary literature including Kunitz (R–21), *Contemporary Authors* (R–23), *Contemporary Poets* (R–33), *Contemporary Dramatists* (R–43), *Contemporary Novelists* (R–52), and bibliographies of contemporary American literature confined to one genre such as those located at S–65, S–66, S–74, S–75, S–76, S–83, and S–84.

S–26 **Levernier, James A., and Douglas R. Wilmes, eds.** *American Writers before 1800: A Biographical and Critical Dictionary.* 3 vols. Westport, Conn.: Greenwood, 1983.   PS185.A4 1983

Biographical, bibliographical, and critical discussion by some 250 contributing specialists is presented for a total of 786 writers residing permanently or temporarily in the colonies or the United States or residing elsewhere but contributing significantly to early American culture. Emphasis has been placed throughout on less-known figures. Entries begin with a chronologically arranged primary bibliography of published and important unpublished works. A biographical summary follows, stressing the social context of the writer's development. The third segment of each entry offers a critique of the author's work in the form of a summary and an evaluation in terms of intellectual, religious, social, and/or political significance. Entries conclude with a bibliography of suggested further reading and the name and academic affiliation of the contributing specialist.

Appendixes index the writers chronologically by date of birth, geographically by place of birth, and geographically by primary place(s) of residence. A fourth appendix presents a chronology of cultural, political, and literary events.

S–27 **Kunitz, Stanley J., and Howard Haycroft.** *American Authors, 1600–1900: A Bibliographical Dictionary of American Literature.* New York: H. W. Wilson, 1938.   PS21.K8

This volume, one in a series (see L–56, M–55, M–56, and R–21), contains brief (150 to 2,500 words) biographical sketches of approximately 1,300 major and minor American authors, including educators, statesmen, orators, jurists, and clergymen, whose works are of some literary interest. Sketches include a list of principal works with original dates of publication and end with a list of biographical and critical sources. More than one-fourth of the entries include portraits of their subjects.

A more extensive range of authors will be found in Oscar Fay Adams, *Dictionary of American Authors*, 5th ed., rev. and enl. (Boston: Houghton Mifflin, 1905) [Z1124.A22], where more than 6,000 writers are treated. The state where they were born, their dates, and a brief sketch of their career are given, along with a list of main titles, including dates and often publishers.

S–28 **Millett, Fred B.** *Contemporary American Authors. A Critical Survey and 219 Bio-Bibliographies.* New York: Harcourt, Brace, 1940.   PS221.M5

This volume has a dual purpose: to give a systematic survey of American literature of the period 1900–1940 (under the headings Backgrounds, The Novel, The Short Story, Drama and Theatre, Poetry, Literary Journalism, Biography and Autobiography, and Criticism) and to present biobibliographies for 219 authors. The biographies give relatively full sketches. Bibliographies cite first editions of all separately published works up to 1 January 1939, including works edited, compiled, translated, or illustrated by the author. There follow lists of books and articles about the author. Appended are lists of standard works of contemporary social, political, and literary history and a list of recommended titles by genre. The work concludes with an index of authors by types (autobiographers, biographers, critics, dramatists, essayists, historians, humorists, novelists, philosophers, poets, short story writers, travelers, and writers of children's books); abbreviations of standard secondary works cited; periodicals with their authors; and authors' names, including those treated in Millet's companion volume, *Contemporary British Literature* (see R–8).

S–29 *American Writers: A Collection of Literary Biographies.* Leonard Ungar, editor in chief. New York: Scribner, 1974–1981.   PS129.A55

This work presents, in the first four volumes, a revised and updated gathering of the ninety-seven *Pamphlets on American Writers* published by the University of Minnesota Press 1959–1972. Each of these pamphlets contains both an account of the subject author's life and a critical discussion of his work and place in literary history. The biographies are signed and have appended a classified, selected bibliography of primary works, bibliographies, and critical and biographical studies. Two *Supplements*, each in two volumes, add specially commissioned articles on fifty-nine additional American authors. The total of 156 critical essays are fully indexed by names and subjects in the *Index* found at the end of volume 8.

III. LITERARY HISTORIES

For chronological ancillae to American literary history see also *Annals of English Literature* (F–85); Whitcomb, *Chronological Outlines of American Literature* (F–87); and Waterman, *Chronology of American Literary History* (F–88). For topographical ancillae see the *Oxford Illustrated Literary Guide to the United States* (F–120).

S–30 **Columbia Literary History of the United States.** Gen. ed. Emory Elliott. New York: Columbia University Press, 1988.
PS92.C64 1988

This 1,263 page volume presents the first major history of American literature to be published since the *Literary History of the United States* (S–31) was published in 1948. It is organized into five large parts, each with its own associate editor, and each disposed into sections and then individual essays prepared by a total of seventy-four contributors and editors, chosen in part to represent the complex variety of contemporary perspectives on the field. Reviewers note the volume's inclusion of authors, movements, genres, and groups whose writing had traditionally been excluded from consideration, from the Native American cave narratives with which the volume opens to the experimentalists writing in the late 20th century with which it closes. Also recognized has been the work's effort to present the history of American Literature understood as a more crowded, contentious, and contradictory field of study than traditional treatments would suggest.

Part One, Beginnings to 1810, is divided into four sections and fifteen essays, as follows: I. A Key into the Languages of America (The Native Voice, The Literature of Discovery and Exploration, English Literature at the American Moment, The Puritan Vision of the New World); II. The Prose and Poetry of Colonial America (History and Chronicle, Sermons and Theological Writings, Biography and Autobiography, The Poetry of Colonial America); III. America in Transition (From Cotton Mather to Benjamin Franklin; Jonathan Edwards, Charles Chauncy, and the Great Awakening; Thomas Jefferson and the Writing of the South); IV. The Literature of the New Republic (The American Revolution as a Literary Event, Poetry in the Early Republic, Charles Brockden Brown and Early American Fiction, Towards a National Literature).

Part Two, 1810–1865, is divided into four sections and fifteen essays, as follows: I. The Age in Perspective (Idealism and Independence); II. Cultural Diversity and Literary Forms (Washington Irving and the Knickerbocker Group, James Fenimore Cooper and the Writers of the Frontier, Edgar Allan Poe and the Writers of the Old South, William Cullen Bryant and the Fireside Poets, The Rise of the Woman Author, Forms of Regional Humor, A New Nation's Drama); III. Intellectual Movements and Social Change (Social Discourse and Nonfictional Prose, The Transcendentalists); IV. The American Renaissance (Ralph Waldo Emerson, Henry David Thoreau, Nathaniel Hawthorne, Herman Melville, Walt Whitman).

Part Three, 1865–1910, is also divided into four sections with eleven essays, as follows: I. Signs of the Times (Literature and Culture, Culture and Consciousness); II. Genre Deliberations (Realism and Regionalism, Naturalism and the Languages of Determinism); III. Literary Diversities (Literature of the Populace, Immigrants and Other Americans, Women Writers and the New Woman); IV. Major Voices (Emily Dickinson, Mark Twain, Henry Adams, Henry James).

Part Four, 1910–1945, contains four sections and sixteen essays, as follows: I. Contexts and Backgrounds (The Emergence of Modernism, Intellectual Life and Public Discourse, Literary Scenes and Literary Movements); II. Regionalism, Ethnicity, and Gender: Comparative Literary Cultures (Regionalism: A Diminished Thing, Afro-American Literature, Mexican American Literature, Asian American Literature, Women Writers Between the Wars); III. Fiction (The Diversity of American Fiction; Ernest Hemingway, F. Scott Fitzgerald, and Gertrude Stein; William Faulkner); IV. Poetry and Criticism (The Diversity of American Poetry, Robert Frost, Ezra Pound and T. S. Eliot, William Carlos Williams and Wallace Stevens, Literary Criticism).

The fifth and last part, 1945 to the Present, contains three sections and nine essays, as follows: I. The Postwar Era (Culture, Power, and Society; The New Philosophy; Literature as Radical Statement); II. Forms and Genres (Poetry, Twentieth-Century Drama, Neorealist Fiction, Self-Reflexive Fiction); III. The Present (The Fictions of the Present, The Avant-Garde and Experimental Writing).

The volume begins with a General Introduction which clarifies the principles used in the construction of this work, and concludes with notes on contributors, and a full index of authors, titles, and subjects, with extensive cross-references.

Because there has been no effort to edit the volume's essays into a single, coherent narrative, an author or movement may be treated in more than one essay, within a number of different contexts, and from a variety of competing perspectives. For this reason, the editors advise use of the index to locate all the essays relevant to a particular line of inquiry.

S–31 **Spiller, Robert E., et al. *Literary History of the United States.*** 4th ed., rev. 2 vols. New York: Macmillan, 1974.
PS88.L522 1974

This work served as the standard history of American literature for exactly four decades. Originally published in three volumes in 1948, the *LHUS* consisted of eighty-one essays on literary contexts, movements, groups, and major authors (i.e., Edwards, Franklin, Irving, Cooper, Poe, Emerson, Thoreau, Hawthorne, Melville, Whitman, Howells, Lanier, Dickinson, Twain, James, Adams, E. A. Robinson, Dreiser, and O'Neill) prepared by a total of fifty-six collaborators. Transitions between sections were supplied by the editors. Throughout, the work was conceived as a history of the United States seen by way of a study of its literature, and literature was defined broadly as the record of a people's experience. Thus this work was concerned to document the interaction of literature with the history of ideas and with general historical trends, as a view of its major divisions will reveal.

A second, revised edition appeared in 1953, a third edition in 3 vols. in 1963–1972, with two new chapters added: "The End of an Era," and "Postscript." This fourth edition includes a new chapter on Emily Dickinson and drops the new chapters of the third edition in favor of three new essays on post–World War II developments. The chapters are divided into eleven main parts as follows: I. The Colonies (1–8); II. The Republic (9–15); III. The Democracy (16–23); IV. Literary Fulfillment (24–29); V. Crisis (30–37); VI. Expansion (38–47); VII. The Sections (48–56); VIII. The Continental Nation (57–65); IX. The United States (66–73); X. A World Literature (74–81); XI. Postscript (82–84). The individual chapters are not signed, but at the end there is a table of authors, identifying the sections for which each was responsible. The history is followed by a highly selective bibliography for the general reader arranged by chapters and citing works referred to and used as sources. An excellent author-title index to all persons and works cited concludes the volume. The second volume contains the standard closed bibliography of American literature discussed above (see S–10).

S–32 **Cunliffe, Marcus.** *Literature of the United States.* 4th ed. New York: Penguin Books, 1986.   PS92.C8 1986

This is generally regarded as the best short history of American literature by a single author. It is organized in fifteen chapters, each focused on a group of authors or a genre and moving chronologically from the colonial to the post–World War II period. The volume is organized to display certain leading themes in American literature, expressive of a distinctly American character and experience. A brief list of further readings, both general and specific to the topics of the individual chapters, a brief chronology of American history, and an index of names, titles, and some subjects conclude the compact volume.

Professor Cunliffe is also the editor of the two volumes *American Literature to 1900* and *American Literature since 1900* in the *Sphere History of English Literature* (M–34).

The other recommended one-volume history is Robert E. Spiller's *Cycle of American Literature* (New York: Macmillan, 1955) [PS88.S6], which is derived from the *LHUS* (S–31) and organized according to a controversial theory of cyclical development.

S–33 **Quinn, Arthur Hobson, et al.** *Literature of the American People: An Historical and Critical Survey.* New York: Appleton-Century-Crofts, 1951.   PS88.Q5

This volume, largely superseded by the *LHUS* (S–31), is in four parts, each written by an authority. Part 1, "The Colonial and Revolutionary Period," is by Kenneth B. Murdock; part 2, by A. H. Quinn treats the "Establishment of a National Culture"; part 3, "The Later Nineteenth Century," is by Clarence Gohdes; part 4, by George F. Whicher, covers "The Twentieth Century" to mid-century. Of these, the third part remains the most valuable. Selective bibliographies for each part are appended, as is an author-title-subject index.

S–34 **Trent, William P., et al.** *Cambridge History of American Literature.* 4 vols. Cambridge: Cambridge University Press, 1917–1921.   PS88.C3

Although now much out of date, this collaborative history of literature in the broadest possible sense is still recommended for the thoroughness of its coverage of the colonial and revolutionary periods and for its inclusion of such topics as the literature of travelers and explorers, historians, publicists, and orators, newspapers, magazines, children's literature, oral literature, and non-English-language American literature. Each chapter is by a specialist and is keyed to a detailed primary and secondary bibliography at the end of volumes 1, 2, and 4. These very full bibliographies are valuable for older, less cited works. Because of their thorough indexes, at the ends of volumes 1, 2, and 4, occasional use of the volumes for particular, out-of-the-way topics is quite convenient.

S–35 *[New] Cambridge History of American Literature.* Gen. ed. Sacvan Bercovitch. In preparation.

The project for a major new five-volume history of American Literature is described by its general editor, Sacvan Bercovitch, in his essay, "America as Canon and Context: Literary History in a Time of Dissensus." *AL* 58 (1986): 99–107. Making an ordering principle of the dissent which characterizes contemporary discourse about "literature," "history," and "American," and thus about "American literary history," the project will present American Literature through a multiplicity of young, professional solo voices. The twenty-two contributors are tenured specialists with diverse views and interests, all under the age of forty-five, and open to other, conflicting views and interests. They have been given a deliberately open invitation to produce their individual texts free of any effort to unify or coordinate their perspectives. The resulting work is thus expected to integrate these voices only in giving them place, not by harmonizing them. The exception, one might add, would include such harmonies as emerge from the contributors' shared generational perspective and acknowledged success as Americanists in the current academic marketplace.

S–36 **Jones, Howard Mumford.** *Theory of American Literature.* 2d ed., rev. Ithaca, N.Y.: Cornell University Press, 1965.   PS31.J6 1965

This reissue, with a new concluding chapter and a revised bibliography, presents a volume substantially the same as the original work of 1948, which can best be described as a history of American literary historiography. In a series of six extensively documented chapters, Jones critically reviews the ideas that governed the making of histories of American literature from the late eighteenth century through the 1940s. The new concluding chapter, Postscript 1965, takes up developments of the fifties and early sixties. A short-title list of works on the history and philosophy of American literature is followed by an index of authors, titles, and subjects.

To this volume may be added a number of other, more recent studies which interrogate the definition of American Literature and the body of writings which constitute its subject matter. These include the following works:

Bercovitch, Sacvan, "Problem of Ideology in American Literary History." *CI* 12 (1986): 631–653.

————, ed. *Reconstructing American Literary History.* Cambridge: Cambridge University Press, 1986.
          PS92.R4 1986

Carafiol, Peter. "Constraints of History: Revision and Revolution in American Literary Studies," *CE* 50 (1988): 605–622.

————. "The New Orthodoxy: Ideology and the Institution of American Literary History," *AL* 59 (1987): 626–638.

Colacurcio, Michael. "Does American Literature Have a History?" *Early American Literature* 13 (1978): 110–131.

Hubbel, Jay B. *Who Are the Major American Writers? A Study of the Changing Literary Canon.* Durham, N.C.: Duke University Press, 1972.   PS62.H8

Kartiganer, Donald M., and Malcolm A. Griffith, comps. *Theories of American Literature.* New York: Macmillan, 1971.   PS121.K3 1972

Lauter, Paul. *Reconstructing American Literature: Courses, Syllabi, Issues.* Old Westbury, N.Y.: Feminist Press, 1983.   PS41.R4 1983

Reising, Russell, *Unusable Past: Theory and the Study of American Literature.* New York: Methuen, 1986.
          PS25.R44 1986

Ruland, Richard. *Rediscovery of American Literature: Premises of Critical Taste, 1900–1940.* Cambridge: Harvard University Press, 1967.   PS221.R8

Spencer, Benjamin P. *Quest for Nationality.* Syracuse: Syracuse University Press, 1957.   No LC number

Spengemann, William C. *Mirror for Americanists: Reflections on the Idea of American Literature.* Hanover, N.H.: University Press of New England, 1989.
          PS25.S64 1989

S–38 **Some Other Histories of American Literature.**

> Clark, Harry Hayden, ed. *Transitions in American Literary History*. Durham, N.C.: Duke University Press, 1953.
> PS88.C6

> Lüdeke, Henry. *Geschichte der amerikanischen Literatur*. 2d rev. and enl. ed. Bern: Francke, 1963.
> PS106.L8 1963

> Parrington, Vernon Louis. *Main Currents in American Thought: An Interpretation of American Literature from the Beginnings to 1920*. 3 vols. New York: Harcourt, Brace, 1927–1930. PS88.P3

> Pattee, Fred Lewis. [*Literary History of the American People* in 4 vols., viz.] *First Century of American Literature 1770–1870* (New York: Appleton, Century, 1935) [PS88.P35]; *Development of the American Short Story: An Historical Survey* (New York: Harper, 1923) [PS374.S5 P3 1923]; *History of American Literature since 1870* (New York: Century, 1915) [PS214.P3]; and *New American Literature, 1890–1930* (New York: Century, 1930) [PS221.P3].

> Wilson, Edmund. *Shock of Recognition: The Development of Literature in the United States Recorded by the Men Who Made It*. 2 vols. Rev. ed. New York: Farrer, Straus, and Cudahy, 1955. PS55.W 1955

> Young, Thomas D., and Ronald E. Fine. *American Literature: A Critical Survey*. 2 vols. New York: American Book Co., 1968. PS58.Y6

IV. HANDBOOKS AND READER'S ENCYCLOPEDIAS

Among other handbooks and encyclopedias that treat American literature, see volume 3 of the *Penguin Companion to Literature* (L–24) and *Webster's New World Companion to English and American Literature* (M–43).

S–40 *Oxford Companion to American Literature*. Edited by James D. Hart. 5th ed., rev. and enl. New York: Oxford University Press, 1982. PS21.H3 1982

This 1,000-page volume, the first edition of which was published in 1941, is meant to serve as a ready reference for students and all readers of American literature. In a dictionary arrangement will be found short biographies and bibliographies of authors; titles of important novels, stories, essays, poems, and plays, with summaries; definitions of literary terms; historical outlines of literary schools and movements; descriptions of literary characters; explanations of allusions; and information on literary societies, magazines, newspapers, anthologies, cooperative publications, awards, book collectors, printers, publishers, and other persons of note on the literary scene. An appended chronology from 1577 presents events in literary and social history in parallel columns.

S–41 **Herzberg, Max J., et al.** *Reader's Encyclopedia of American Literature*. New York: Crowell, 1962. PS21.R4

This 1,300-page volume, which treats both United States and Canadian literature, includes biographical sketches of authors, with bibliographies; articles on novels, poems, essays, and plays; on the various genres; on the schools and movements of American writing; and entries on magazines, editors, statesmen, famous characters, folk heroes, and historical events. It is generally thought equal to the *Oxford Companion* (S–40), though it is perhaps somewhat broader in scope and is sometimes more penetrating in treatment, particularly in the long, signed articles on major topics. There are occasional portraits and genealogies, and an appendix on literary terms.

S–42 **Burke, W. J., and Will D. Howe.** *American Authors and Books, 1640–1940.* Revised by Irving Weiss and Anne Weiss. 3d rev. ed. New York: Crown, 1972.
Z1224.B87 1972

Originally published in 1943 and revised in 1962, this bio-bibliographical dictionary is less critical than the author entries in the *Oxford Companion* (S–40) or Herzberg (S–41) but is more comprehensive. The various editions may be consulted with profit, for minor figures not listed in the third may appear in the first. Entries include authors, especially the obscure and neglected, as well as a variety of other persons including editors, publishers, booksellers, librarians, printers, book collectors, presidents, heroes, and famous characters. There are also subject headings treating aspects of the writing, illustrating, editing, publishing, reviewing, collecting, selling, and preservation of American books, as well as newspapers and magazines. Titles, characters, magazines, newspapers, publishing firms and bookstores, book clubs, place-names, genres, themes, topics, subjects, bibliographical and literary terms are also included. Articles are brief and descriptive and include bibliographical references in the text. There are some cross-references. Earlier editions tend to include more articles on "book people" as opposed to authors.

S–43 **Salzman, Jack, ed.** *Cambridge Handbook of American Literature*. Cambridge and New York: Cambridge University Press, 1986. PS21.C36 1986

This compact volume was prepared by the staff of Columbia University's Center for American Culture Studies. It contains some 750 unsigned entries on writers, works, and movements of American literature. The volume is more inclusive of women and minority writers than earlier handbooks have been, with considerable space devoted to writers and works who remain unmentioned, for example, in the most recent edition of the *Oxford Companion* (S–40). Articles range in length from a paragraph to several pages, and include primary but not secondary bibliographies. A double-columned Chronology of American history and Chronology of American literature follow the entries, and are followed in turn by a classified select bibliography of the most important critical and historical studies from the mid–1930s to the end of 1983, excepting books on only one author.

S–45 **Duyckinck, Evert A., and George L. Duyckinck, eds.** *Cyclopedia of American Literature: Embracing Personal and Critical Notices of Authors, and Selections from Their Writings, from the Earliest Period to the Present Day; with Portraits, Autographs, and Other Illustrations.* Rev. ed. 2 vols. Philadelphia: William Rutter and Co., 1875.
PS85.D7

Originally published in 1855, this work is arranged in chronological order; access to specific information therefore depends on use of the index of names, titles, organizations, and subjects which concludes the second volume. Excerpts and illustrations are interspersed in biographical articles that identify works, summarize current critical opinion, and provide anecdotes. A special value of this work is that those mid-nineteenth-century authors treated were apparently invited to revise or even compose their own biographies. There is an abundance of contemporary, out-of-the-way information on minor figures.

S–48 **Inge, M. Thomas, ed.** *Handbook of American Popular Culture.* 3 vols. Westport, Conn.: Greenwood Press, 1979–1981.   E169.1.H2643

This work is disposed into various chapters, by specialists, which present chronological surveys of their respective fields, and then bibliographical essays on such matters as pertinent reference works, research collections, history and criticism, and periodicals used by students of that field. Chapters also have selective sheer-list bibliographies. The chapters are as follows. In volume 1: Animation; The Automobile; Children's Literature; Comic Art; Detective and Mystery Novels; Film; Gothic Novels; Popular Music; The Pulps; Radio; Science Fiction; Sports; Stage Entertainment; Television, and The Western. In volume 2: Advertising; Best Sellers; Circus and Outdoor Entertainments; Death in Popular Culture; Editorial Cartoons; Foodways; Games and Toys; Historical Fiction; Occult and the Supernatural; Photography as Popular Culture; Popular Architecture; Popular Religion and Theories of Self-Help; Romantic Fiction; Verse and Popular Poetry; Women in Popular Culture. In volume 3: Almanacs; Debate and Public Address; Illustration; Jazz; Leisure Vehicles, Pleasure Boats, and Aircraft; Magazines; Magic and Magicians; Medicine and the Physician in Popular Culture; Minorities in Popular Culture; Newspapers; Physical Fitness; Pornography; Propaganda; Records and the Recording Industry; Regionalism in Popular Culture; Science in Popular Culture; Stamp and Coin Collecting; Trains and Railroading. At the end of each volume is an index of proper names; concluding volume 3 is a subject index to all three volumes.

V.   INDIVIDUAL AUTHORS

S–50 **Guide to Major-Author Reference Works.**

The following entries present information about author newsletters and journals; primary and secondary bibliographies; handbooks, indexes, and guides; standard editions; concordances; and biographies for twenty-five major Arican authors. The following writers are included:

Cooper	Irving
Crane	James
Dickinson	Melville
Dreiser	O'Neill
Edwards	Poe
Emerson	Pound
Faulkner	Stevens
Fitzgerald	Taylor
Franklin	Thoreau
Frost	Twain
Hawthorne	Whitman
Hemingway	Williams
Howells	

COOPER (1789–1851)

Bibliography

Spiller, Robert E., and Philip C. Blackburn. *Descriptive Bibliography of the Writings of James Fenimore Cooper.* New York: R. R. Bowker, 1934.   Z8191.7.S85

Handbooks

Summerlin, Mitchell Eugene. *Dictionary to the Novels of James Fenimore Cooper.* Greenwood, Fla.: Penkevill, 1987.   No LC number

Walker, Warren S. *Plots and Characters in the Fiction of James Fenimore Cooper.* Hamden, Conn.: Archon Books, 1978.   PS1441.W3 1978

Editions

Beard, James Franklin, ed. *Works of James Fenimore Cooper.* 48 vols. planned. Albany, N.Y.: State University of New York Press, 1980–. [CEAA approved edition]   LC numbers vary
Cooper's Novels. *People's Edition Illustrated by F. O. C. Darley.* 32 vols. New York: W. A. Townsend, 1858–1861.   LC numbers vary

CRANE S. (1871–1900)

Journal

SCraN *Stephen Crane Newsletter.* Vols. 1–5. Columbia: University of South Carolina, 1966–1970. 4/yr. Reviews. Bibliography: "Quarterly Checklist."
                     No LC number

Bibliographies

Gross, Theodore L., and Stanley Wertheim. *Hawthorne, Melville, Stephen Crane: A Critical Bibliography.* New York: Free Press, 1971.   Z1225.G76
Hudspeth, Robert. *Bibliography of Stephen Crane Scholarship: 1893–1969.* Syracuse, N.Y.: Syracuse University Press, 1970.   Z8198.2.H8
Stallman, R. W. *Stephen Crane: A Critical Bibliography.* Ames: Iowa State University Press, 1972.
                   Z8198.2.S76

Edition

Bowers, Fredson, ed. *University of Virginia Edition of the Works of Stephen Crane.* 10 vols. Charlottesville: University Press of Virginia, 1969–1975. [CEAA approved edition]   PS1449.C85 1969

Concordances

Baron, Herman. *Concordance to the Poems of Stephen Crane.* Edited by Joseph Katz. Boston: G. K. Hall, 1974.   PS1449.C85 Z49 1974
Crosland, Andrew T. *Concordance to the Complete Poetry of Stephen Crane.* Foreword by T. H. Howard-Hill. Detroit: Gale Research, 1975.
                 PS1449.C85 Z49 1975

Biography

Stallman, R. W. *Stephen Crane.* New York: Braziller, 1968.   PS1449.C85 Z9

DICKINSON (1830–1886)

Journal

Dickinson Studies [former title: *Emily Dickinson Bulletin,* nos. 1–33, 1968–1978]. No. 34–. Brentwood, Md.: Higginson Press for the Emily Dickinson Society, 1978–. 2/yr. Reviews. "Emily Dickinson Annual Bibliography." Index 1968–1974.
                  Z8230.5.E44

Bibliographies

Buckingham, Willis J., ed. *Emily Dickinson: An Annotated Bibliography; Writings, Scholarship, Criticism, and Ana, 1850–1968.* Bloomington: Indiana University Press, 1970.   Z8230.5.B8 1970
Clendenning, Sheila T. *Emily Dickinson: A Bibliography: 1850–1966.* Kent, Ohio: Kent State University Press, 1968.   Z8230.5.C55

Myerson, Joel. *Emily Dickinson: A Descriptive Bibliography*. Pittsburgh: University of Pittsburgh Press, 1984.   Z8230.5.M96 1984

Handbook

Duchac, Joseph. *Poems of Emily Dickinson: An Annotated Guide to Commentary Published in English, 1890–1977*. Boston: G. K. Hall, 1979.
PS1541.Z5 D8

Editions

Franklin, R. W., ed. *Manuscript Books of Emily Dickinson*. 2 vols. Cambridge: Belknap Press of Harvard University Press, 1981. PS1541.A1 1981

————. *Master Letters of Emily Dickinson*. Amherst, Mass.: Amherst College Press, 1986.
PS1541.Z5 A4 1986

Johnson, Thomas H., ed. *Poems of Emily Dickinson, Including Variant Readings Critically Compared with All Known Manuscripts*. 3 vols. Cambridge: Belknap Press of Harvard University Press, 1955. PS1541.A1 1955

————, and Theodora Ward, eds. *Letters of Emily Dickinson*. Cambridge: Belknap Press of Harvard University Press, 1958. No LC number

Concordance

Rosenbaum, Stanford P. *Concordance to the Poems of Emily Dickinson*. Ithaca, N.Y.: Cornell University Press, 1964. Computer-compiled.
PS1541.Z49 R6

Biography

Sewall, Richard. *Life of Emily Dickinson*. New York: Farrar, Strauss and Giroux, 1974.
PS1541.Z5 S42

DREISER (1871–1945)

Journal

DreiN   *Dreiser Newsletter*. Vol. 1–. Terre Haute: Indiana State University English Department, 1970–. 2/yr. Reviews. Bibliography. PS3507.R55 Z5893

Bibliographies

Atkinson, Hugh C. *Theodore Dreiser: A Checklist*. Kent, Ohio: Kent State University Press, 1971.
Z8241.7.A92

Boswell, Jeanetta. *Theodore Dreiser and the Critics, 1911–1982: A Bibliography with Selective Annotations*. Metuchen, N.J.: Scarecrow, 1986.
Z8241.7.B67 1986

Pizer, Donald, et al. *Theodore Dreiser: A Primary and Secondary Bibliography*. Boston: G. K. Hall, 1975. Z8241.7.P58

Handbook

Gerber, Philip L. *Plots and Characters in the Fiction of Theodore Dreiser*. Hamden, Conn.: Archon, 1977. PS3507.R55 Z6358

Edition

Berkey, John C., James L. W. West III, et al. *Pennsylvania Edition of the Works of Theodore Dreiser*. Philadelphia: University of Pennsylvania Press, 1981–. LC numbers vary

Biography

Swanberg, W. A. *Dreiser*. New York: Scribner, 1965. PS3507.R55 Z84

EDWARDS (1703–1758)

Bibliographies

Johnson, Thomas L. *Printed Writings of Jonathan Edwards, 1703–1758: A Bibliography*. Princeton, N.J.: Princeton University Press, 1940.
Z8255.5.J69

Lesser, M. X. *Jonathan Edwards: A Reference Guide*. Boston: G. K. Hall, 1981. Z8255.5.L47

Edition

Miller, Perry, and John E. Smith, eds. *Works of Jonathan Edwards*. 10 vols. planned. New Haven: Yale University Press, 1957–. BX7117.E3 1957

Biography

Winslow, Ola Elizabeth. *Jonathan Edwards, 1703–1758*. New York: Macmillan, 1940.
BX7260.E3 W5 1940

ELIOT, T. S. (1880–1965): see M–60.

EMERSON (1803–1882)

Journal

ESQ   *ESQ: A Journal of the American Renaissance* [former title: *Emerson Society Quarterly*, nos. 1–65, 1955–1968]. Vol. 18–. Pullman: Washington State University Press, 1969–. 4/yr. Reviews. "Current Bibliography on Ralph Waldo Emerson," 1955–1972. Now in *American Transcendental Quarterly* (see S–18). PS1629.E6

Bibliographies

Boswell, Jeanetta. *Ralph Waldo Emerson and the Critics: A Checklist of Criticism, 1900–1977*. Metuchen, N.J.: Scarecrow, 1979. Z8265.B64

Bryer, Jackson R., and Robert A. Rees. *Checklist of Emerson Criticism 1951–1961, with Detailed Index*. Hartford, Conn.: Transcendental Books, 1964.
Z8265.B7

Cooke, George Willis. *Bibliography of Ralph Waldo Emerson*. Boston: Houghton Mifflin, 1908.
Z8265.C65

Myerson, Joel. *Ralph Waldo Emerson: A Descriptive Bibliography*. Pittsburgh: University of Pittsburgh Press, 1982. Z8265.M94 1982

Sowder, William J. *Emerson's Reviewers and Commentators; A Biographical and Bibliographical Analysis of Nineteenth-Century Periodical Criticism, with a Detailed Index*. Hartford, Conn.: Transcendental Books, 1968. Z8265.S6

Handbooks

Cameron, Kenneth W. *Emerson Index; or, Names, Exempla, Sententiae, Symbols, Words and Motifs in Selected Notebooks of Ralph Waldo Emerson*. Hartford, Conn.: Transcendental Books, 1958.
PS1630.C3

Carpenter, Frederick Ives. *Emerson Handbook*. New York: Hendricks House, 1953. PS1631.C34

Editions

Emerson, Edward Waldo, ed. *Centenary Edition of the Works of Ralph Waldo Emerson*. 12 vols. Boston: Houghton Mifflin, 1903–1921. PS1600.F79

Ferguson, Alfred R., ed. *Collected Works of Ralph Waldo Emerson*. 12 vols. planned. Cambridge: Belknap Press of Harvard University Press, 1959–. [CEAA approved edition] PS1600.F71

Concordances

Cameron, Kenneth W. *Index-Concordances to Emerson's Sermons.* 2 vols. Hartford, Conn.: Transcendental Books, 1963.   BX9843.E487 S47

Hubbell, George S. *Concordance of the Poems of Ralph Waldo Emerson.* New York: H. W. Wilson, 1932.   PS1645.H8

Ihrig, Mary Alice. *Emerson's Transcendental Vocabulary: A Concordance.* New York: Garland, 1982. Based on vols. 1–7 of the Centenary ed. (Houghton Mifflin, 1903–1904).   PS1645.I5 1982

Irey, Eugene F. *Concordance to Five Essays of Ralph Waldo Emerson.* New York: Garland, 1981. Based on the Centenary ed. (Houghton Mifflin, 1903).   PS1645.I73 1981

Biography

Rusk, Ralph L. *Life of Ralph Waldo Emerson.* New York: C. Scribner's Sons, 1949.   PS1631.R78

FAULKNER (1897–1962)

Journals

Faulkner Journal. Vol. 1–. Ada, Ohio: Ohio Northern University, 1985–. 2/yr.
PS3511.A86 Z4584

Faulkner Studies: An Annual of Research, Criticism, and Reviews. Vol. 1–. Coral Gables, Fla.: University of Miami, Department of English, 1980–. 1/yr. Reviews. Bibliography.   No LC number

Bibliographies

Bassett, John. *William Faulkner: An Annotated Checklist of Criticism.* New York: David Lewis, 1972.   Z8288.B38

————. *Faulkner: An Annotated Checklist of Recent Criticism.* Kent, Ohio: Kent State University Press, 1983.   Z8288.B38 1983

McHaney, Thomas L. *William Faulkner: A Reference Guide.* Boston: G. K. Hall, 1976.   Z8288.M22

Meriwether, James B. *William Faulkner: A Checklist.* Princeton, N.J.: Princeton University Press, 1957.   Z8288.M4

————. *Literary Career of William Faulkner: A Bibliographical Study.* Princeton, N.J.: Princeton University Press, 1961. "Authorized Reissue." Columbia: University of South Carolina Press, 1971.   Z8288.M37 1971

Ricks, Beatrice. *William Faulkner: A Bibliography of Secondary Works.* Metuchen, N.J.: Scarecrow, 1981.   Z8288.R53

Handbooks

Brown, Calvin S. *Glossary of Faulkner's South.* New Haven: Yale University Press, 1976.
PS3511.A86 Z49 1976

Cox, Leland H., ed. *William Faulkner: Biographical and Reference Guide: A Guide to His Life and Career; with a Checklist of His Works, a Concise Biography, and a Critical Introduction to Each of His Novels.* Detroit: Gale, 1982.
PS3511.A86 Z773 1982

————, ed. *William Faulkner; Critical Collection: A Guide to Critical Studies with Statements by Faulkner and Evaluative Essays on His Works.* Detroit: Gale, 1982.   PS3511.A86 Z985695 1982

Dasher, Thomas E. *William Faulkner's Characters: An Index to the Published and Unpublished Fiction.* New York: Garland, 1981.
PS3511.A86 Z7816 1981

Kirk, Robert W., and Marvin Klotz. *Faulkner's People: A Complete Guide and Index to the Characters in the Fiction of William Faulkner.* Berkeley and Los Angeles: University of California Press, 1963.   PS3511.A86 Z87

Volpe, Edmond L., ed. *Reader's Guide to William Faulkner.* New York: Farrar, Straus, 1964.
PS3511.A86 Z983

Editions

In the absence of a collected edition, use the volumes of individual works published in New York by Random House, 1930–.   LC number varies

Blotner, Joseph, ed. *Uncollected Stories of William Faulkner.* New York: Random House, 1979.
PZ3.F272 U1 1979

Concordances

Capps, Jack L., et al. *Faulkner Concordances.* Ann Arbor, Mich.: University Microfilms International, for the Faulkner Concordance Advisory Board, West Point, New York, 1977–. By 1984 concordances had been published to the following texts: *As I Lay Dying; Light in August; Go Down, Moses; Intruder in the Dust; The Sound and the Fury; Requiem for a Nun;* and *The Wild Palms.*
LC number varies

Biography

Blotner, Joseph L. *Faulkner: A Biography.* 2 vols. New York: Random House, 1974.
PS3511.A86 Z63

FITZGERALD (1896–1940)

Journal

FHA   *Fitzgerald/Hemingway Annual* [former title: *Fitzgerald Newsletter,* nos. 1–40, 1958–1968]. Vols. 1–11. Detroit: Gale, 1969–1979. 1/yr. Reviews. Bibliography.   PS3511.I9 Z617

Bibliographies

Bruccoli, Matthew J. *F. Scott Fitzgerald, A Descriptive Bibliography.* Pittsburgh: University of Pittsburgh Press, 1972. Supplement. Pittsburgh: University of Pittsburgh Press, 1980.   Z8301.2 B69

Bryer, Jackson R. *Critical Reputation of F. Scott Fitzgerald: A Bibliographical Study.* Hamden, Conn.: Archon, 1967. Supplement 1 through 1981. Hamden, Conn.: Archon, 1984.   PS3511.I9 Z57
Z8301.2.B74 1967 suppl.

Stanley, Linda. *Foreign Critical Reputation of F. Scott Fitzgerald: An Analysis and Annotated Bibliography.* Westport, Conn.: Greenwood, 1980.
PS3511.I9 Z865

Edition

Bodley Head Scott Fitzgerald. 6 vols. London: Bodley Head, 1958–1963.   PS3511.I9 A6 1960

Concordance

Crosland, Andrew T. *Concordance to F. Scott Fitzgerald's The Great Gatsby.* Detroit: Gale, 1974. Based on the 1925 first edition.
PS3511.I9 G833

Biography

Mizener, Arthur. *Far Side of Paradise.* Rev. ed. Boston: Houghton Mifflin, 1965.
PS3511.I9 Z7 1965

FRANKLIN (1706–1790)

Bibliographies

Buxbaum, Melvin H. *Benjamin Franklin: A Reference Guide.* 2 vols. Vol. 1 1721–1906, vol. 2 1907–1983. Boston: G. K. Hall, 1983–1988.
Z8313.B89 1983.

Ford, Paul L. *Franklin Bibliography: A List of Books Written by or Relating to Benjamin Franklin.* Brooklyn, N.Y.: P. L. Ford, 1889. Z8313.F69

Handbook

MacLaurin, Lois M. *Franklin's Vocabulary.* Garden City, N.Y.: Doubleday, 1928. PS751.M27

Edition

Labaree, Leonard W., et al., eds. *Papers of Benjamin Franklin.* 25 vols. planned. New Haven: Yale University Press, 1959–. E302.F82 1959

Concordance

Barbour, Frances M. *Concordance to the Sayings in Franklin's Poor Richard.* Detroit: Gale, 1974.
PS749.B3

Biography

Van Doren, Carl. *Benjamin Franklin.* New York: Viking, 1938. E302.6.F8 V32

FROST (1874–1963)

Bibliographies

Greiner, Donald J. *Robert Frost: The Poet and His Critics, [1913–1947].* Chicago: American Library Association, 1974. PS3511.R94 Z73

Lentricchia, Frank, and Melissa Christensen. *Robert Frost: A Bibliography, 1913–1974.* Metuchen, N.J.: Scarecrow Press, 1976. Z8317.78.L45

Van Egmond, Peter. *Critical Reception of Robert Frost: An Annotated Bibliography of Secondary Comment.* Boston: G. K. Hall, 1974.
Z8317.78.V35

Handbook

Porter, James L. *Robert Frost Handbook.* University Park: Pennsylvania State University Press, 1980.
PS3511.R94 Z88

Edition

Lathem, Edward Connery, ed. *Poetry of Robert Frost.* New York: Holt, Rinehart and Winston, 1969. PS3511.R94 1969

Concordance

Lathem, Edward Connery. *Concordance to the Poetry of Robert Frost.* New York: Holt Information Systems, 1971. Based on the Lathem ed. (1969); Computer-compiled; severely reviewed for incompleteness. PS3511.R94 Z49 1971

Biography

Thompson, Lawrance. *Robert Frost.* 3 vols. New York: Holt, Rinehart and Winston, 1966.
PS3511.R94 Z953

HAWTHORNE (1804–1864)

Journals

NHJ   *Nathaniel Hawthorne Journal.* Vol. 1–. Detroit: Gale, 1971–. 1/yr. Reviews. Bibliography: "Checklist." PS1879.N36

Nathaniel Hawthorne Society Newsletter. Vol. 1– Brunswick, Me.: Nathaniel Hawthorne Society, Bowdoin College, 1975–. 2/yr. No LC number

Bibliographies

Browne, Nina E. *Bibliography of Nathaniel Hawthorne.* Boston: Houghton Mifflin, 1908. Primary.
Z8393.B85

Boswell, Jeanetta. *Nathaniel Hawthorne and the Critics: A Checklist of Criticism, 1900–1978.* Metuchen, N.J.: Scarecrow, 1982. Z8393.B67 1982

Clark, C. E. Frazer, Jr. *Nathaniel Hawthorne: A Descriptive Bibliography.* Pittsburgh: University of Pittsburgh Press, 1978. Z8393.C56

Gross, Theodore L., and Stanley Wertheim. *Hawthorne, Melville, and Stephen Crane: A Critical Bibliography.* New York: Free Press, 1971.
Z1225.G76

Jones, Buford. *Checklist of Hawthorne Criticism, 1951–1966.* Hartford, Conn.: Transcendental Books, 1967. Z8393.J6

Ricks, Beatrice, et al. *Nathaniel Hawthorne: A Reference Bibliography, 1900–1971, with Selected Nineteenth Century Materials.* Boston: G. K. Hall, 1972. Z8393.R53

Handbooks

Cameron, Kenneth W. *Hawthorne Index to Themes, Motifs, Topics, Archetypes, Sources, and Key Words Dealt with in Recent Criticism.* Hartford, Conn.: Transcendental Books, 1968. PS1880.C3

Cohen, Benjamin B. *Merrill Guide to Nathaniel Hawthorne.* Columbus, Ohio: Merrill, 1970.
PS1888.C6

Gale, Robert L. *Plots and Characters in the Fiction and Sketches of Nathaniel Hawthorne.* Hamden, Conn.: Archon, 1968. PS1891.G3

Newman, Lea B. V. *Reader's Guide to the Short Stories of Nathaniel Hawthorne.* Boston: G. K. Hall, 1979. PS1888.N4

O'Connor, Evangeline Maria. *Analytical Index to the Works of Nathaniel Hawthorne.* Boston: Houghton Mifflin, 1882. PS1880.O4

Edition

Charvat, William, et al., eds. *Centenary Edition of the Works of Nathaniel Hawthorne.* 20 vols. to date. Columbus: Ohio State University Press, 1962–. [CEAA approved edition] PS1850.F63

Concordance

Byers, John R., and James J. Owen. *Concordance to the Five Novels of Nathaniel Hawthorne.* 2 vols. New York: Garland, 1979. PS1895.B9 1979

Biographies

Stewart, Randall. *Nathaniel Hawthorne: A Biography.* New Haven: Yale University Press, 1948.
PS1881.S67

Turner, Arlin. *Nathaniel Hawthorne: A Biography.* New York: Oxford University Press, 1980.
PS1881.T79

HEMINGWAY (1899–1961)

Journals

FHA   *Fitzgerald/Hemingway Annual.* Vols. 1–11. Detroit: Gale, 1969–1979. 1/yr. Reviews. Bibliography. PS3511.I9 Z617

Hemingway Newsletter: Publication of the Hemingway Society. Vol. 1–. Ada: Ohio Northern University, 1981–. 2/yr. No LC number

Hemingway Review. Vol. 1–. Ada: Ohio Northern University, 1981–. 2/yr. Reviews.

PS3515.E37 Z6194

Bibliographies

Hanneman, Audre. *Ernest Hemingway: A Comprehensive Bibliography*. Princeton, N.J.: Princeton University Press, 1967. Supplement, 1973.

Z8396.3.H45

Wagner, Linda Welshimer. *Ernest Hemingway: A Reference Guide*. Boston: G. K. Hall, 1977.

Z8396.3.W33

Young, Philip, and Charles W. Mann. *Hemingway Manuscripts: An Inventory*. University Park: Pennsylvania State University Press, 1969.   Z8396.3.Y6

Handbooks

Smith, Paul. *Reader's Guide to the Short Stories of Ernest Hemingway*. Boston: G. K. Hall, 1989.

PS3515.E37 Z864 1989

Waldhorn, Arthur. *Reader's Guide to Ernest Hemingway*. New York: Farrar, Straus and Giroux, 1972.   PS3515.E37 Z92

White, William. *Merrill Guide to Ernest Hemingway*. Columbus, Ohio: Merrill, 1969.

PS3515.E37 Z947

Edition

In the absence of a collected edition, use the volumes of individual works published in New York: Scribner's, 1926–.   LC numbers vary

Biographies

Baker, Carlos. *Ernest Hemingway: A Life Story*. New York: Scribner, 1969.

PS3515.E37 Z575 1969

Griffin, Peter. *Along with Youth: Hemingway, The Early Years*. New York: Oxford University Press, 1985.   PS3515.E37 Z6114 1985

Meyers, Jeffrey. *Hemingway: A Biography*. New York: Harper and Row, 1985.

PS3515.E37 Z7418 1985

HOWELLS (1837–1920)

Bibliographies

Brenni, Vito J. *William Dean Howells: A Bibliography*. Metuchen, N.J.: Scarecrow, 1973.

Z8420.25.B74

Eichelberger, Clayton L. *Published Comment on William Dean Howells through 1920: A Research Bibliography*. Boston: G. K. Hall, 1976.

Z8420.25.E38

Gibson, William M., and George Arms. *Bibliography of William Dean Howells*. New York: New York Public Library, 1948. Reprinted with an Additional Note, 1971.   Z8420.25.G5 1971

Handbook

Carrington, George C., Jr., and Idiko de Papp Carrington. *Plots and Characters in the Fiction of William Dean Howells*. Hamden, Conn.: Archon, 1976.

PS2037.P54 C3

Edition

Cady, Edwin, et al., eds. *Selected Edition of the Works of William Dean Howells*. 39 vols. Bloomington: Indiana University Press, 1968–. [CEAA approved edition]   PS2020.F68

Biography

Lynn, Kenneth S. *William Dean Howells: An American Life*. New York: Harcourt Brace Jovanovich, 1971.   PS2033.L9

IRVING (1783–1859)

Bibliographies

Springer, Haskell S. *Washington Irving: A Reference Guide*. Boston: G. K. Hall, 1976.

Z8439.7.S65

Williams, Stanley T., and Mary Allen Edge. *Bibliography of the Writings of Washington Irving: A Checklist*. New York: Oxford University Press, 1936.   Z8439.7.W73 1936

Editions

Pochmann, Henry A., et al., eds. *Complete Works of Washington Irving*. 28 vols. planned [18 vols. *Works*; 4 vols. *Letters*; 5 vols. *Journals*; 1 vol. *Bibliography*]. Madison: University of Wisconsin Press; and New York: Twayne Publishers, 1969–. [CEAA approved edition]   LC numbers vary

Works of Washington Irving. Author's revised edition. 21 vols. New York: Putnam, 1848–1860.

LC numbers vary

Biography

Williams, Stanley T. *Life of Washington Irving*. 2 vols. New York: Oxford University Press, 1935.

PS2081.W45

JAMES (1843–1916)

Journal

Henry James Review. Vol. 1–. Baton Rouge: Louisiana State University Press, 1979–. 3/yr. Reviews. Annual bibliographic review.   PS2124.H46

Bibliographies

Bradbury, Nicola. *Annotated Critical Bibliography of Henry James*. New York: St. Martin's Press, 1987.   Z8447.B73 1987

Budd, John. *Henry James: A Bibliography of Criticism, 1975–1981*. Westport, Conn.: Greenwood Press, 1983.   Z8447.B82 1983

Edel, Leon, and Dan H. Laurence. *Bibliography of Henry James*. 3d ed., rev. Oxford: Clarendon Press, 1982.   Z8447.E3 1982

McColgan, Kristin Pruitt. *Henry James, 1917–1959: A Reference Guide*. Boston: G. K. Hall, 1979.   Z8447.M32

Ricks, Beatrice. *Henry James: A Bibliography of Secondary Works*. Metuchen, N.J.: Scarecrow Press, 1975.   Z8447.R5

Scura, Dorothy McInnis. *Henry James, 1960–1974: A Reference Guide*. Boston: G. K. Hall, 1979.

Z8447.S38

Taylor, Linda J. *Henry James, 1866–1916: A Reference Guide*. Boston: G. K. Hall, 1982.

Z8447.T39 1982

Handbooks

Cargill, Oscar. *Novels of Henry James*. New York: Macmillan, 1961.   PS2124.C25

Franklin, Rosemary F. *Index to Henry James' Prefaces to the New York Edition*. Charlottesville: Bibliographical Society of the University of Virginia, 1966.   PS2122.F7

Gale, Robert L. *Plots and Characters in the Fiction of Henry James*. Hamden, Conn.: Archon, 1965.
PS2124.G32

Leeming, Glenda. *Who's Who in Henry James*. New York: Taplinger Publishing Co., 1976.
PS2122.L4

Powers, Lyall H. *Merrill Guide to Henry James*. Columbus, Ohio: Merrill, 1969.   PS2123.P6

Putt, S. Gorley. *Henry James: A Reader's Guide*. Ithaca, N.Y.: Cornell University Press, 1966.
PS2123.P8

Stafford, William T. *Name, Title, and Place Index to the Critical Writings of Henry James*. Englewood, Colo.: Microcard Editions Books, 1975. PS2122.S8

Edition

"New York Edition" of the Novels and Tales of Henry James. 26 vols.   New York: Scribner's, 1907–1917.   PS2110.F07

Concordances

Bender, Todd K., et al. *Concordances to the Works of Henry James*. New York: Garland, 1984–.
LC numbers vary

Biography

Edel, Leon. *Henry James*. 5 vols. Philadelphia: Lippincott, 1953–1972. Vol. 1, *Untried Years, 1843–1870* (1953) [PS2123.E385 1953]. Vol. 2, *Conquest of London, 1870–1881* (1962) [PS2123.E36 1962]. Vol. 3, *Middle Years, 1882–1895* (1962) [PS2123.E375 1962]. Vol. 4, *Treacherous Years, 1895–1901* (1969) [PS2123.E38 1969]. Vol. 5, *Master, 1901–1916* (1972) [PS2123 .E37].

MELVILLE (1819–1891)

Journal

MSEX *Melville Society Extracts* [former title: *Extracts—Melville Society: An Occasional Newsletter*, nos. 1–33, 1969–1978]. No. 1–. Glassboro, N.J.: Glassboro State College, Melville Society of America, 1969–. 4/yr. Reviews. Bibliographies.
No LC number

Bibliographies

Boswell, Jeanetta. *Herman Melville and the Critics: A Checklist of Criticism, 1900–1978*. Metuchen, N.J.: Scarecrow, 1981.   Z8562.58.B67

Gross, Theodore L., and Stanley Wertheim. *Hawthorne, Melville, and Stephen Crane: A Critical Bibliography*. New York: Free Press, 1971.
Z1225.G76

Higgins, Brian. *Herman Melville: An Annotated Bibliography*. 2 vols. Vol. 1, 1846–1930. Vol. 2, (with the title *Herman Melville: A Reference Guide, 1931–1960*). Boston: G. K. Hall, 1979–1987.
Z8562.58.H53

Phelps, Leland R. *Herman Melville's Foreign Reputation: A Research Guide*. Boston: G. K. Hall, 1983.   Z8562.58.P47 1983

Ricks, Beatrice, and Joseph D. Adams. *Herman Melville: A Reference Bibliography, 1900–1972, with Selected Nineteenth-Century Materials*. Boston: G. K. Hall, 1973.   Z8562.58.R53

Handbooks

Bryant, John, ed. *Companion to Melville Studies*. Westport, Conn.: Greenwood, 1986.
PS2386.C66 1986

Coffler, Gail H. *Melville's Classical Allusions: A Comprehensive Index and Glossary*. Westport, Conn.: Greenwood, 1985.   PS2388.G73 C63 1985

Gale, Robert L. *Plots and Characters in the Fiction and Narrative Poetry of Herman Melville*. Hamden, Conn.: Archon, 1969.   PS2387.G3

Gidmark, Jill B. *Melville Sea Dictionary: A Glossed Concordance and Analysis of the Sea Language in Melville's Nautical Novels*. Westport, Conn.: Greenwood, 1982.   PS2388.L33 G5 1982

Maeno, Shigeru. *Melville Dictionary*. Tokyo: Kaibunsha, 1976.   PS2386.A23

Miller, James E., Jr. *Reader's Guide to Herman Melville*. New York: Farrar, Straus and Cudahy, 1962.   PS2387.M5

Newman, Lea Bertani Vozar. *Reader's Guide to the Short Stories of Herman Melville*. Boston: G. K. Hall, 1986.   PS2387.N5 1986

Edition

Hayford, Harrison, et al. *Northwestern-Newberry Edition of the Writings of Herman Melville*. 16 vols. planned. Chicago: Northwestern University Press, 1968–. [CEAA approved edition]   PS2380.F68

Concordances

Cohen, Hennig, et al. *Concordance to Melville*. Ann Arbor, Mich.: University Microfilms International, then New York: Garland, for the Melville Society, 1978–. By 1989, concordances had been published to *Clarel, A Poem and Pilgrimage in the Holy Land; Pierre, or, the Ambiguities; The Confidence Man: His Masquerade;* and to *Moby Dick*. The Irey concordance should be used in preference to the latter.   LC numbers vary

Irey, Eugene F. *Concordance to Herman Melville's Moby Dick*. 2 vols. New York: Garland, 1982.
PS2384.M619 I7 1982

Biographies

Leyda, Jay. *Melville Log: A Documentary of Herman Melville, 1819–1891*. 2 vols. New York: Harcourt, Brace, 1951.   PS2386.L4

Miller, Edwin Haviland. *Melville*. New York: Braziller, 1975.   PS2386.M49

Sealts, Merton M. *Early Lives of Melville*. Madison: University of Wisconsin Press, 1974.
PS2386.S38

O'NEILL (1888–1953)

Journal

Eugene O'Neill Newsletter. Vol. 1–. Boston: Suffolk University, Department of English, 1977–. 3/yr. Reviews. Bibliography.   No LC number

Bibliographies

Atkinson, J. M. *Eugene O'Neill: A Descriptive Bibliography*. Pittsburgh, Pa.: University of Pittsburgh Press, 1974.   Z8644.5.A74

Miller, Jordan Y. *Eugene O'Neill and the American Critic: A Bibliographical Checklist*. 2d ed., rev. Hamden, Conn.: Archon, 1974. Z8644.5.M5 1974

Sanborn, Ralph, and Barrett Clark. *Bibliography of the Works of Eugene O'Neill*. New York: Random House, 1931. Reprint 1965.   Z8644.5.S19

Smith, Madeline, and Richard Eaton. *Eugene O'Neill: An Annotated Bibliography, 1973–1985*. New York: Garland, 1988.   Z8644.5.S6 1988

Handbook

Ranald, Margaret Loftus. *Eugene O'Neill Companion*. Westport, Conn.: Greenwood Press, 1984.
PS3529.N5 Z792 1984

Edition

Plays of Eugene O'Neill. [The Wilderness Edition.] 12 vols. New York: Charles Scribner's Sons, 1934–1935.   PS3529.N5 1934

Concordance

Reaver, J. Russell. *O'Neill Concordance.* 3 vols. Detroit: Gale, 1969.   PS3529.N5 Z793

Biography

Gelb, Arthur, and Barbara Gelb. *O'Neill.* New York: Harper and Row, 1962.   PS3529.N5 2653

POE (1809–1849)

Journal

PoeS   *Poe Studies* [former title: *Poe Newsletter*, vols. 1–3, 1968–1970]. Vol. 4–. Pullman: Washington State University Press, 1971–. 2/yr. Reviews. "Current Poe Bibliography."   PS2631.P63

Bibliographies

Dameron, J. Lasley, and Irby B. Cauthen, Jr. *Edgar Allan Poe: A Bibliography of Criticism, 1827–1967.* Charlottesville: University Press of Virginia, 1974.   Z8699.D34

Heartman, D. F., and J. R. Canny. *Bibliography of First Printings of the Writings of Edgar Allan Poe, Together with a Record of First and Contemporary Later Printings of His Contributions to Annuals, Anthologies, Periodicals, and Newspapers Issued during His Lifetime . . . .* Rev. ed. Hattiesburg, Mich.: The Book Farm, 1943.   Z8699.H44 1943

Hyneman, Esther F. *Edgar Allan Poe: An Annotated Bibliography of Books and Articles in English, 1827–1973.* Boston: G. K. Hall, 1973.   Z8699.H94

Phillips, Leona Rasmussen. *Edgar Allan Poe: An Annotated Bibliography [with Filmography].* New York: Gordon Press, 1978.   Z8699.P48

Handbooks

Deas, Michael J. *Portraits and Daguerreotypes of Edgar Allan Poe.* Charlottesville: University Press of Virginia, 1989.   PS2635.D4 1989

Gale, Robert L. *Plots and Characters in the Fiction and Poetry of Edgar Allan Poe.* Hamden, Conn.: Archon, 1970.   PS2641.G3

Pollin, Burton R. *Dictionary of Names and Titles in Poe's Collected Works.* New York: Da Capo Press, 1968.   PS2630.P6

Editions

Harrison, James A., ed. *Complete Works of Edgar Allan Poe.* [The Virginia Edition.] 17 vols. New York: T. Y. Crowell, 1902.   PS2601.H3

Mabbott, Thomas O., ed. *Collected Works of Edgar Allan Poe.* 6 vols. Cambridge: Belknap Press of Harvard University Press, 1969–.   PS2600.F69

Peithman, Stephen, ed. *Annotated Tales of Edgar Allan Poe with an Introduction, Notes, and Bibliography.* Garden City, N.Y.: Doubleday, 1981.
PS2612.A1 1981

Stovall, Floyd, ed. *Poems of Edgar Allan Poe, Edited with an Introduction, Variant Readings, and Textual Notes.* Charlottesville: University Press of Virginia, 1965.   PS2605.A1 1965a

Concordances

Booth, Bradford A., and Claude E. Jones. *Concordance of the Poetical Works of Edgar Allan Poe.* Baltimore: Johns Hopkins University Press, 1941.
PS2645.B6

Dameron, J. Lasley, and Louis Charles Stagg. *Index to Poe's Critical Vocabulary.* Hartford, Conn.: Transcendental Books, 1966.   PS2645.D3

Pollin, Burton Ralph. *Word Index to Poe's Fiction.* New York: Gordian Press, 1982.
PS2645.P63 1982

Biographies

Quinn, Arthur H. *Edgar Allan Poe: A Critical Biography.* New York: Appleton-Century Co., 1941.
PS2631.Q5

Thomas, Dwight, and David K. Jackson. *Poe Log: A Documentary Life of Edgar Allan Poe, 1809–1849.* Boston: G. K. Hall, 1987.
PS2631.T47 1987

POUND (1885–1972)

Journal

Paideuma   *Paideuma: A Journal Devoted to Ezra Pound Scholarship.* Vol. 1–. Orono: University of Maine at Orono, 1972–. 3/yr. Reviews. Bibliography.
PS3531.O82 Z7855

Bibliographies

Gallup, Donald. *Ezra Pound: A Bibliography.* Charlottesville: University Press of Virginia for the Bibliographical Society of the University of Virginia and St. Paul's Bibliographies, 1983. Rev. ed. of *Bibliography of Ezra Pound* (1963). Additions and corrections in *Paideuma* 12 (1983); 117–130.
Z8709.3.G3 1983

Ricks, Beatrice. *Ezra Pound: A Bibliography of Secondary Works.* Metuchen, N.J.: Scarecrow, 1986.   Z8709.3.R53 1986

Handbooks

Brooke-Rose, Christine. *ZBC of Ezra Pound.* Berkeley, Los Angeles, London: University of California Press, 1971.   PS3531.O82 Z55

Brooker, Peter. *Student's Guide to the Selected Poems of Ezra Pound.* London: Faber and Faber, 1979.   PS3531.O82 Z5513

Edwards, John Hamilton, and William W. Vasse. *Annotated Index to the Cantos of Ezra Pound. Cantos I–LXXXIV.* Berkeley, Los Angeles, London: University of California Press, 1980.
PS3531.O82 Z597

Frould, Christine. *Guide to Ezra Pound's Selected Poems.* New York: New Directions, 1983.
PS3531.O82 Z632 1983

Henault, Marie. *Merrill Guide to Ezra Pound.* Columbus, Ohio: Merrill, 1970.   PS3531.O82 Z642

Kearns, George. *Guide for Ezra Pound's Selected Cantos.* New Brunswick, N.J.: Rutgers University Press, 1980.   PS3531.O82 C294

Rosenthal, Macha. *Primer of Ezra Pound.* New York: Macmillan, 1960.   PS3531.O82 Z795

Ruthven, K. K. *Guide to Ezra Pound's "Personae," 1926.* Berkeley and Los Angeles: University of California Press, 1969.   PS3531.O82 P476

Terrell, Carroll F. *Companion to the Cantos of Ezra Pound.* 2 vols. Berkeley, Los Angeles, London: University of California Press, 1980–.
PS3531.O8 C289

Editions

Personae: The Collected Poems. New York: New Directions, 1950.   PS3531.O82 P4 1950

Cantos of Ezra Pound [I-CXVII, CXX]. New York: New Directions, 1971.   PS3531.O82 C24 1972

Cantos of Ezra Pound. Revised collected edition. London: Faber, 1975. I-CIX, drafts and fragments of CX-CXVII.   PS3531.O82 C29 1975

Concordances

Dillingham, Robert, James W. Parins, and Todd K. Bender. *Concordance to Ezra Pound's Cantos.* New York: Garland, 1981.

PS3531.O82 C259 1981

Lane, Gary, ed. *Concordance to Personae: The Shorter Poems of Ezra Pound.* New York: Haskell House, 1972.   PS3531.O82 P429 1972

Biography

Stock, Noel. *Life of Ezra Pound.* New York: Pantheon, 1970.   PS3531.O82 Z839

STEVENS (1879–1955)

Journal

WSJour *Wallace Stevens Journal: A Publication of the Wallace Stevens Society.* Vol. 1–. Northridge: California State University, Department of English, 1977–. 4/yr.; from 1983, 2/yr. Reviews. "Current Bibliography."   No LC number

Bibliographies

Edelstein, J. M. *Wallace Stevens: A Descriptive Bibliography.* Pittsburgh: University of Pittsburgh Press, 1973.   Z8842.7.E35

Morse, Samuel French, et al. *Wallace Stevens Checklist and Bibliography of Stevens Criticism.* Denver, Colo.: Swallow, 1963.   Z8842.7.M63

Handbook

Sukenick, Ronald. *Wallace Stevens: Musing the Obscure: Readings, an Interpretation, and a Guide to the Collected Poetry.* New York: New York University Press, 1967.   PS3537.T4753 Z768

Editions

Collected Poems of Wallace Stevens [First Collected Edition]. New York: Knopf, 1954.

PS3537.T4753 1954

Morse, Samuel French, ed. *Opus Posthumous.* [Poems, Plays, Prose.] New York: Knopf, 1957.

PS3537.T4753 A6 1957

Concordance

Walsh, Thomas F. *Concordance to the Poetry of Wallace Stevens.* University Park: Pennsylvania State University Press, 1963.   PS3537.T4753 Z9

Biography

Stevens, Holly Bright. *Souvenirs and Prophecies: The Young Wallace Stevens.* New York: Knopf, 1977.   PS3537.T4753 Z7673 1977

TAYLOR (1645?–1729)

Bibliography

Gefvert, Constance J. *Edward Taylor: An Annotated Bibliography, 1668–1970.* Kent, Ohio: Kent State University Press, 1971.   Z8861.4.G44

Editions

Johnson, Thomas H. *Poetical Works of Edward Taylor.* New York: Rockland Editions, 1939.

PS850.T2 1939

Stanford, Donald E., ed. *Poems of Edward Taylor.* New Haven: Yale University Press, 1960.

PS850 .T2 A6 1960

Concordance

Russell, Gene. *Concordance to the Poems of Edward Taylor.* Washington, D.C.: Microcard Editions, 1973.   PS850.T2 Z49 1973

Biography

Terry, John T. *Rev. Edward Taylor, 1642–1729.* New York: The DeVinne Press, 1892.

BX7260.T28 T4

THOREAU (1817–1862)

Journals

TQ *Thoreau Quarterly* [former title: *Thoreau Journal Quarterly, vols. 1–13, 1968–1981*]. Vol. 14–. Minneapolis: University of Minnesota, 1982–.

PS3053.T5

TSB *Thoreau Society Bulletin.* Vol. 1–. Genesco: Thoreau Society, State University of New York, Genesco, 1941–. 4/yr. Reviews. Bibliographies.

PS3053.A23

Bibliographies

Advena, Jean Cameron. *Bibliography of the Thoreau Society Bulletin Bibliographies, 1941–1969: A Cumulation and Index.* Edited by Walter Harding. Troy, N.Y.: Whitston Publishing, 1971.   Z8873.A3

Allen, Francis Henry. *Bibliography of Henry David Thoreau.* Boston: Houghton Mifflin, 1908.

Z8873.A44

Borst, Raymond R. *Henry David Thoreau: A Descriptive Bibliography.* Pittsburgh: University of Pittsburgh Press, 1982.   Z8873.B66

———. *Henry David Thoreau: A Reference Guide, 1835–1899.* Boston: G. K. Hall, 1987.

Z8873.B664 1987

Boswell, Jeanetta, and Sarah Crouch. *Henry David Thoreau and the Critics: A Checklist of Criticism, 1900–1978.* Metuchen, N.J.: Scarecrow, 1981.

Z8873.B67

Handbooks

Harding, Walter, and Michael Meyer. *New Thoreau Handbook.* New York: New York University Press, 1980.   PS3053.H32 1980

Stowell, Robert F. *Thoreau Gazetteer.* Rev. ed. Revised by William L. Howarth. Princeton, N.J.: Princeton University Press, 1970. PS3052.S7 1970

Editions

Bode, Carl. *Collected Poems of Henry David Thoreau.* Enl. ed. Baltimore: Johns Hopkins University Press, 1964.   PS3041.B6 1964

Scudder, H. E., et al., eds. *Walden Edition of the Writings of Henry David Thoreau.* 20 vols. Boston: Houghton Mifflin, 1906.   PS3040.F82

Witherell, Elizabeth Hall, et al., eds. *Writings of Henry David Thoreau.* 25 vols. planned. Princeton, N.J.: Princeton University Press, 1971–. [CEAA approved edition]   LC numbers vary

Concordances

Karabatsos, James. *Word-Index to A Week on the Concord and Merrimack Rivers*. Hartford, Conn.: Transcendental Books, 1971.   F72.M7 T534 1971

Sherwin, J. Stephen, and Richard C. Reynolds. *Word Index to Walden, with Textual Notes*. Hartford, Conn.: Emerson Society, 1969. Based on the Modern Library ed. (1950).   PS3048.S53 1969

Biographies

Harding, Walter R. *Days of Henry Thoreau*. New York: Knopf, 1965.   PS3053.H3

Salt, H. S. *Life of Henry D. Thoreau*. Rev. ed. London: W. Scott, 1896.   PS3053.S3 1896

TWAIN (1835–1910)

Journal

MTJ   *Mark Twain Journal* [former title: *Mark Twain Quarterly*, vols. 1–9, 1936–1953]. Vol. 9–. St. Louis, Mo.: Mark Twain Memorial Association, 1954–. 4/yr. Reviews.

Bibliographies

Asselineau, Roger. *Literary Reputation of Mark Twain from 1910 to 1950: A Critical Essay and a Bibliography*. Paris: Didier, 1954.
PS1338.A8 1954a

Johnson, Merle De Vore. *Bibliography of the Works of Mark Twain, Samuel Langhorne Clemens: A List of First Editions in Book Form and of First Printings in Periodicals and Occasional Publications of His Varied Literary Activities*. Rev. and enl. ed. New York: Harper, 1935.   Z8176.J8 1935

Rodney, Robert M., ed. *Mark Twain International: A Bibliography and Interpretation of His Worldwide Popularity*. Westport, Conn.: Greenwood, 1982.
Z8176.R62 1982

Tenney, Thomas Asa. *Mark Twain: A Reference Guide*. Boston: G. K. Hall, 1977.   Z8176.T45

Handbooks

Gale, Robert L. *Plots and Characters in the Works of Mark Twain*. 2 vols. Hamden, Conn.: Archon, 1973.   PS1341.G3

Long, E. Hudson, and J. R. LeMaster. *New Mark Twain Handbook*. New York: Garland, 1985.
PS1331.L6

Ramsay, Robert L., and Frances G. Emberson. *Mark Twain Lexicon*. Columbia: University of Missouri, 1938.   PS1345.R3

Wilson, James D. *Reader's Guide to the Short Stories of Mark Twain*. Boston: G. K. Hall, 1987.
PS1338.W5 1987

Editions

Baender, Paul, et al. [editors vary]. *Works of Mark Twain*. 24 vols. planned. Berkeley, Los Angeles, London: University of California Press for the Iowa Center for Textual Studies, 1972–. [CEAA approved edition]   PS1300.F72

Mark Twain Papers. [Editors vary.] Berkeley and Los Angeles: University of California Press, 1967–.
LC numbers vary

Biographies

Emerson, Everett. *Authentic Mark Twain: A Literary Biography of Samuel L. Clemens*. Philadelphia: University of Pennsylvania Press, 1984.
PS1331.E47 1984

Paine, Albert Bigelow. *Mark Twain: A Biography*. 3 vols. New York: Harper, 1912. PS1331.P3 1912

WHITMAN (1819–1892)

Journal

WWR   *Walt Whitman Review* [former title: *Walt Whitman Newsletter*, vols. 1–4, 1955–1958]. Vol. 5–. Detroit: Wayne State University Press, 1955–. 4/yr. Reviews. "Whitman: A Current Bibliography." Cinquennial cumulative index.   PS3229.W39

Bibliographies

Boswell, Jeanetta. *Walt Whitman and the Critics: A Checklist of Criticism, 1900–1978*. Metuchen, N.J.: Scarecrow, 1980.   Z8971.5.B65

Giantvalley, Scott. *Walt Whitman, 1838–1939: A Reference Guide*. Boston: G. K. Hall, 1981.
Z8981.5.G5 1981

Kummings, Donald D. *Walt Whitman, 1940–1975: A Reference Guide*. Boston: G. K. Hall, 1982.
Z8981.5.K85 1982

Walt Whitman: Catalog Based upon the Collections of the Library of Congress, with Notes on Whitman Collections and Collectors by Charles E. Feinberg. Washington D.C.: Library of Congress, 1955.
Z89711.5.U62

White, William. *Bibliography*. In the *Collected Writings* (below).

Handbooks

Allen, Gay Wilson. *New Walt Whitman Handbook*. Rev. ed. New York: New York University Press, 1980.   PS3231.A7 1980

———. *Reader's Guide to Walt Whitman*. New York: Farrar, Straus and Giroux, 1970.
PS3231.A687

Edition

Allen, Gay Wilson, Sculley Bradley, et al., eds. *Collected Writings of Walt Whitman*. 18 vols. New York: New York University Press, 1961–. [CEAA approved edition]   LC numbers vary

Concordance

Eby, Harold Edwin. *Concordance of Walt Whitman's Leaves of Grass and Selected Prose Writings*. 5 vols. Seattle: University of Washington Press, 1949–1954.   PS3245.E2

Biographies

Allen, Gay Wilson. *Solitary Singer: A Critical Biography of Walt Whitman*. Rev. issue. New York: New York University Press, 1967.
PS3231.A69 1967

Asselineau, Roger. *Evolution of Walt Whitman*. 2 vols. Cambridge: Belknap Press of Harvard University Press, 1960–1962.   PS3231.A833

WILLIAMS (1883–1963)

Journal

WCWN   *William Carlos Williams Review* [former title: *William Carlos Williams Newsletter*, vols. 1–5, 1975–1979]. Vol. 1–. Middletown: Capitol Campus, Pennsylvania State University, 1975–. 2/yr. Reviews. Bibliography.   PS3545.I544 Z957

Bibliographies

Wagner, Linda W. *William Carlos Williams: A Reference Guide*. Boston: G. K. Hall, 1978.
                                                Z8976.44.W27

Wallace, Emily Mitchell. *Bibliography of William Carlos Williams*. Middletown, Conn.: Wesleyan University Press, 1968.   Z8976.44.W3

Handbook

Engles, John. *Merrill Guide to William Carlos Williams*. Columbus, Ohio: Merrill, 1969.
                                           PS3545.I544 Z5875

Editions

Collected Earlier Poems. New York: New Directions, 1951.   PS3545.I544 A17 1951

Collected Later Poems. Rev. ed. New York: New Directions, 1963.   PS3545.I544 A17 1963

Biography

Whittemore, Reed. *William Carlos Williams, Poet from Jersey*. Boston: Houghton Mifflin, 1975.
                                            PS3545.I544 Z95

S–55 *Library of America*. New York: The Library of America, 1982–.   LC numbers vary

This widely celebrated series is intended to present the collected works of America's foremost authors in uniform hardcover editions of between 1,000 and 1,600 pages, with text selected for their authoritativeness by the volume's editor. To date, the following volumes have been published, at the rate of six to eight volumes annually:

Adams, Henry. Vol. I. *Novels, Mont Saint Michel, The Education*. Ed. by Ernest Samuels and Jayne N. Samuels.

———. Vol. II. *History of the United States during the Administrations of Thomas Jefferson*. Ed. by Earl N. Harbert.

———. Vol. III. *History of the United States during the Administrations of James Madison*. Ed. by Earl N. Harbert.

Cather, Willa. *Early Novels and Stories*. Ed. by Sharon O'Brien.

Cooper, James Fenimore. *The Leatherstocking Tales*. Ed. by Blake Nevius. 2 vols.

Crane, Stephen. *Prose and Poetry*. Ed. by J. C. Levenson.

Dreiser, Theodore. *Sister Carrie, Jennie Gerhardt, Twelve Men*. Ed. by Richard Lehan.

DuBois, W. E. B. *Writings*. Ed. by Nathan I. Huggins.

Emerson, Ralph Waldo. Vol. I. *Essays and Lectures*. Ed. by Joel Porte.

———. Vol. II. *Poetry and Essays*. Ed. by Harold Bloom.

Faulkner, William. *Novels 1930–1935*. Ed. by Joseph Blotner and Noel Polk.

Franklin, Benjamin. *Writings*. Ed. by J. A. Leo Lemay.

Hawthorne, Nathaniel. Vol. I *Tales and Sketches*. Ed. by Roy Harvey Pearce.

———. Vol. II. *Novels*. Ed. by Millicent Bell.

Howells, William Dean. Vol. I. *Novels 1875–1886*. Ed. by Edwin H. Cady.

———. Vol. II. *Novels 1886–1888*. Ed. by Edwin H. Cady.

Irving, Washington. Vol. I. *History, Tales and Sketches*. Ed. by James W. Tuttleton.

James, Henry. Vol. I. *Novels 1871–1880*. Ed. by William T. Stafford.

———. Vols. II and III. *Literary Criticism*. Ed. Leon Edel and Mark Wilson.

———. Vol. IV. *Novels 1881–1886*. Ed. by William T. Stafford.

———. Vol. V. *Novels 1886–1890*. Ed. by William T. Stafford.

James, William. *Writings 1902–1910*. Ed. by Bruce Kuklick.

Jefferson, Thomas. *Writings*. Ed. by Merrill D. Peterson.

Lincoln, Abraham. *Speeches and Writings 1832–1858*. Ed. by Don E. Fehrenbacher.

———. *Speeches and Writings 1859–1865*. Ed. by Don E. Fehrenbacher.

London, Jack. Vol. I. *Novels and Stories*. Ed. by Donald Pizer.

———. Vol. II. *Novels and Social Writings*. Ed. by Donald Pizer.

Melville, Herman. Vol. I. *Typee, Omoo, Mardi*. Ed. by G. Thomas Tanselle.

———. Vol. II. *Redburn, White-Jacket, Moby-Dick*. Ed. by G. Thomas Tanselle.

———. Vol. III. *Pierre, Israel Porter, The Confidence Man, Tales and Billy Budd*. Ed. by Harrison Hayford.

Norris, Frank. *Novels and Essays*. Ed. by Donald Pizer.

O'Connor, Flannery. *Collected Works*. Ed. by Sally Fitzgerald.

O'Neill, Eugene. *Complete Plays*. Ed. by Travis Bogard. 3 vols.

Parkman, Francis. *France and England in North America*. Ed. by David Levin. 2 vols.

Poe, Edgar Allan. Vol. I. *Poetry and Tales*. Ed. by Patrick F. Quinn.

———. Vol. II. *Essays and Reviews*. Ed. by G. R. Thompson.

Stowe, Harriet Beecher. *Three Novels*. Ed. by Kathryn Kish Sklar.

Thoreau, Henry David. *A Week, Walden, Maine Woods, Cape Cod*. Ed. by Robert F. Sayre.

Twain, Mark. Vol. I. *Mississippi Writings*. Ed. by Guy Cardwell.

———. Vol. II. *The Innocents Abroad and Roughing It*. Ed. by Guy Cardwell.

———. Vol. III. *Tales and Sketches*. Ed. by Louis J. Budd.

Wharton, Edith. *Novels*. Ed. by R. W. B. Lewis.

Whitman, Walt. *Complete Poetry and Selected Prose*. Ed. by Justin Kaplan.

VI.   POETRY

See also materials on contemporary American poetry in section R and on American poetry generally in section T, passim.

S–63 **Gingerich, Martin E.** *Contemporary Poetry in America and England, 1950–1975: A Guide to Information Sources.* Detroit: Gale Research Co., 1983.
                                            Z1231.P7 G56 1983

This volume contains a total of 1,637 serially numbered entries disposed into eight chapters, as follows: Bibliographies and Reference Works; Studies in Contemporary Culture and Sociology; Studies in General Aesthetics and Poetic Theory; General Studies of Poetry and Poets; General Studies of American Poets and Literature; General Studies of English Poets and Literature; Studies of Two or More Poets; and Individual Poets. The last, longest chapter presents individual bibliographies for a total of 131 contemporary English, American (i.e., United States), and Welsh poets, excluding Canadian, Irish, and Scottish Poets, and Black American Poets, all of whom are treated in other volumes in the "Guide to Information Sources" series. The individual bibliographies are divided into sections listing poems, bibliographies, critical books, journals devoted to the author, and critical articles. Indexes of authors and of titles conclude the volume.

S–64 *Crowell's Handbook of Contemporary American Poetry.* Edited by Karl Malkoff. New York: Crowell, 1973.
PS323.5.M3

This volume concerns American poets whose first commercially published book appeared in 1940 or later. The introduction presents a short history of contemporary American poetry in nine sections, as follows: Contexts; From Imagism to Projectivism; Three Major Poems; Beat Poetry; The New York Poets; The Confessional Poets; The New Black Poetry; Deep Imagism; and The Formal Poets. The main body offers a dictionary arrangement of articles on about seventy poets, schools, and movements. Entries are biographical or historical and critical in character and have selected bibliographies of primary and secondary sources appended.

S–65 **Davis, Lloyd, and Robert Irwin.** *Contemporary American Poetry: A Checklist.* Metuchen, N.J.: Scarecrow Press, 1975.
Z1231.P7 D38

This sheer list contains 3,381 serially numbered items arranged chronologically under the names of authors from Walter Abish to Paul Zweig. Cited are separately published volumes of postmodern poetry of the fifties and sixties, along with the works of poets born after 1900 who were still publishing after 1950. The cutoff date for inclusion is the end of 1973. Excluded are vanity press publications, collaborations, translations, light verse, children's books, broadsides, reprints, and similar items. The volume concludes with a title index.
A second volume, *Contemporary American Poetry: A Checklist. Second Series, 1973–1983.* (Metuchen, N.J.: Scarecrow, 1985) [Z1231.P7 D38 1985] continues the original work through the end of 1983.

S–66 **Gershator, Phyllis.** *Bibliographic Guide to the Literature of Contemporary American Poetry, 1970–1975.* Metuchen, N.J.: Scarecrow Press, 1976.
Z1231.P7 G47

This guide is in four sections and treats work concerned with North American poetry from 1970 through 1975. The first section presents a bibliographical essay on available reference works. The second section lists the literature on contemporary American poetry, citing critical and other works but excluding those that treat individual poets. Entries in the second section are accompanied by descriptive and evaluative commentary. The third and fourth sections list anthologies and textbooks respectively, both with descriptive annotations. Three indexes complete the volume, the first of which is a topical guide listing references to such matters as Afro-American poetry, Juvenile poetry, Women poets, and so on. This is followed by indexes of authors and of titles.

S–67 **Wegelin, Oscar.** *Early American Poetry: A Compilation of the Titles of Volumes of Verse and Broadsides by Writers Born or Residing in North America, North of the Mexican Border.* 2d ed., rev. and enl. 2 vols. in 1. New York: Peter Smith, 1930.
Z1231.P7 W4

This work lists a total of 1,379 titles alphabetically by author, after which is a separate list by title for anonymous works. The list is in two sections, one for 1650–1799 and the other for 1800–1820. Entries give full title-page descriptions, formats, and some locations.
The Wegelin compilation is supplemented by Roger E. Stoddard, *Catalogue of Books and Pamphlets Unrecorded in Oscar Wegelin's Early American Poetry, 1650–1820* (Providence, R.I.: Friends of the Library of Brown University, 1969) [Z1231.P7 S75]. This work describes and locates 261 items either not recorded or not fully described in the original compilation. Many of them are located in the Harris Collection at Brown, for which see the *Dictionary Catalog of the Harris Collection of American Poetry and Plays*, 13 vols. (Boston: G. K. Hall, 1972) [Z1231.P7 B72].

S–68 **Scheick, William, and JoElla Doggett.** *Seventeenth Century American Poetry: A Reference Guide.* Boston: G. K. Hall, 1977.
Z1227.S3

This volume is an annotated bibliography of secondary criticism on sixty colonial poets. Sections on each poet are divided into subsections as follows: A. Books, B. Shorter writings (including sections from books and articles), C. Dissertations. Within subsections, entries are arranged chronologically. In addition to the sixty sections on individual poets, there are four sections divided into the same subsections and following the same chronological arrangement which treat the following topics: General and Thematic Studies, Literary Influences and Aesthetics; The Bay Psalm Book, Psalm-Singing, and other Church Music; Broadsides, Ballads, and Anonymous Verse; and Elegies. The volume ends with an Index of Authors, Poets, and Selected Topics.

VII.   DRAMA AND THEATER

See also materials on contemporary American drama and theater in section R and on American drama and theater in general in section U, passim.

S–70 **Long, E. Hudson.** *American Drama from Its Beginnings to the Present.* [A Goldentree Bibliography.] New York: Appleton-Century-Crofts, 1970.
Z1231.D7 L64

This student bibliographical guide includes sections on (general) Reference Works; American Literary History; Bibliographies of the American Drama; Anthologies of the American Drama; Histories of the American Drama; Histories of the American Theatre; Accounts of Actors and Producers; Studies of Technique; Special Theatrical Groups; Special Studies of the American Drama (by Periods, Regions, Genre, and Theme or Subject); and, finally, a long section on twenty-six Major American Dramatists, and one on twenty-six Lesser Dramatists, both alphabetically ordered. Under each author are found (sometimes) a few primary references to editions and the like, and then an alphabetical list of critical books and articles. Asterisks indicate works of special importance. Other annotations, in square brackets, refer to paperback publishers and briefly describe ambiguous titles. There are cross-references and an index of authors. While this guide is highly selective, there is an effort to cover major works and topics with emphasis on scholarship of the twentieth century.

S–71 **Ryan, Pat M.** *American Drama Bibliography: A Checklist of Publications in English.* Fort Wayne, Ind.: Fort Wayne Public Library, 1969.　　　D1231.D7 R92

This sheer-list bibliography of American plays and playwrights is divided into three sections, treating works of history and reference, general background, and individual authors. English-language books, articles, and pamphlets are listed; excluded are unpublished theses, editions of individual plays, and articles in standard reference works. Pageants, film, radio, and television plays are not cited. There are no annotations, but an asterisk designates entries that contain extensive bibliography, and stars indicate that the bibliography is annotated. There is no index.

S–72 **Eddleman, Floyd Eugene, comp.** *American Drama Criticism: Interpretations 1890–1977.* 2d ed. Hamden, Conn.: Shoe String Press, 1979.　　　Z1231.D7 P3 1979

This volume replaces the first edition, *American Drama Criticism: Interpretations, 1890–1965 Inclusive, of American Drama since the First Play Produced in America,* comp. Helen H. Palmer and Jane Anne Dyson (Hamden, Conn.: Shoe String Press, 1967) [D1231.D7 P32], along with its *Supplement I* by the same compilers (1970) and its *Supplement II*, compiled by Floyd Eugene Eddleman (1976). Entries list criticism published between 1890 and 1977 (with some earlier) as monographs or in books or periodicals of all plays performed in America and written by United States citizens (or by Canadians or Caribbean dramatists whose works have been or are being performed in the United States). Interviews, bibliographical studies, and author bibliographies are excluded.

New to this edition are an index of critics and an index of adapted authors and works, in addition to a list of books indexed, a list of journals indexed, an index of titles, and an index of playwrights with their dates noted. Entries are arranged alphabetically by author or title under the title of the play being interpreted. The plays with their dates of first production are listed alphabetically under the alphabetically arranged names of their playwrights. The intention is to update this volume with supplements.

A *Supplement One* to the second edition was published in 1984 [Z1231.D7 P3 1979 suppl.]. It brings the coverage of the work down to 1982 but primarily adds items missed in the second edition. A new feature is the addition of a general category immediately after the name of the playwright and prior to the first play title. A *Second Supplement* is scheduled to appear in 1989. This work may be further supplemented by the following additional lists: Adelman, *Modern Drama* (R–45); Breed, *Dramatic Criticism Index* (R–46); Coleman and Tyler (U–53); and Salem (U–58).

S–73 **Meserve, Walter J.** *American Drama to 1900: A Guide to Information Sources.* Detroit: Gale Research Co., 1980.　　　Z1231.D7 M45

This volume contains a total of 1,494 annotated entries divided into two sections. The first, containing critical, historical, and reference resources, has the following divisions: Bibliographies and Checklists, Indexes, Library and Microreproduction Collections, Anthologies and Collected Plays, Histories, History and Criticism. There are numerous subdivisions. The second section contains a total of thirty-four bibliographies of individual dramatists, giving both primary and secondary sources. There are many cross-references, and the volume concludes with author, title, and subject indexes.

S–74 **Harris, Richard H.** *Modern Drama in America and England, 1950–1970: A Guide to Information Sources.* Detroit: Gale Research Co., 1982.　　　Z1231.D7 H36 1982

This guide is in two parts. The first is a descriptively annotated, unnumbered reading list of secondary sources. The second is a collection of individual bibliographies for 255 contemporary playwrights. The individual bibliographies list only titles published between 1950 and 1975, irrespective of their performance date, citing bibliographies, selected nondramatic writing, and pertinent criticism, with other subdivisions as appropriate. The volume ends with author, title, and subject indexes.

S–75 **Kolin, Philip C., ed.** *American Playwrights Since 1945: A Research Survey of Scholarship, Criticism, and Performance.* Westport, Conn.: Greenwood Press, 1989.　　　Z1231.D7 A53 1989

This volume provides bio-bibliographical essays by specialists on forty American playwrights whose works have shaped and influenced the American stage. Included are Albee, Baldwin, Baraka, Hansberry, Kopit, Mamet, McCullers, Miller, Rabe, Shepard, Simon, Sondheim, Williams, and twenty-seven others. Each essay provides information on the playwright's reputation and achievements; a primary bibliography; a production history of where, when, how often, and how well the playwright's works were performed; an identification and evaluation of secondary materials (including bibliographies, biographies, influence studies, general works, and analyses of individual plays); and suggestions of *desiderata* for future research. The volume concludes with an index.

An earlier work which may still be of use is Kimball King's *Ten Modern American Playwrights; An Annotated Bibliography* (New York: Garland, 1982) [Z1231.D7 K56 1982] in which brief biographical sketches precede the primary and secondary bibliographies for the following contemporary authors: Edward Albee, Amiri Baraka, Ed Bullins, Jack Gelber, Arthur Kopit, David Mamet, David Rabe, Sam Shepard, Neil Simon, and Lanford Wilson. Primary sources with annotations are disposed into the following categories: I. Stage: II. Film; III. Miscellaneous and Unpublished Writings; IV. Non-fiction; V. Translations (listed by play); VI. Interviews. Secondary sources are listed in three sections: I. Criticism, with descriptive and evaluative annotations; II. Dissertations; and III. Reviews and Announcements (listed by play). The volume concludes with an index of authors of secondary sources including interviewers, critics, and reviewers.

S–76 **Quinn, Arthur Hobson.** *History of the American Drama from the Beginning to the Civil War.* 2d ed. New York: Harper and Bros., 1943　　　PS332.Q5

———. *History of the American Drama from the Civil War to the Present Day.* Rev. ed. New York: Harper and Bros., 1927.　　　PS332.Q55

These volumes present what remains the outdated but standard history of the American drama through the 1920s. Emphasis is on the drama as staged, and the volumes thus include much material on the American theater.

Both volumes have extensive bibliographies. That in volume 1 is in two parts, the first containing bibliographic essays on bibliographies and checklists of plays, collections, histories of the drama and the stage, libraries of importance for research, and essays citing references for each chapter of the text. The second part is a list by title of American plays 1665–1860, with places and dates of first production and first publications, when available. The bibliography in volume 2 is also in two parts, the first giving general lists of historical and critical works, bibliographies, biographies, works on actors and managers, and anthologies. The second part lists plays by author, with dates of publication and place and date of first production. For major playwrights, the list is followed by a selected secondary bibliography.

S–77 **Wegelin, Oscar.** *Early American Plays 1714–1830: A Compilation of the Titles of Plays and Dramatic Poems Written by Authors Born in or Residing in North America Previous to 1830.* 2d ed., rev. New York: Literary Collector Press, 1905.   Z1231.D7 W41

Originally published in 1900, this bibliography provides three lists identifying anonymous plays alphabetically by title, plays alphabetically by author, and plays in manuscript. Entries give title, title-page transcription, format, pagination, and a brief biographical sketch of the author. There is an index to titles of published plays.

Based on Wegelin is Frank P. Hill's *American Plays Printed 1714–1830: A Bibliographical Record* (Stanford: Stanford University Press, 1934) [Z1231.D7 H6], which is expanded beyond Wegelin by a 1918 typescript list of plays in the collection of F. W. Atkinson. This author list gives names and dates, titles of plays, dates of publication, formats, and locations of copies in ten American libraries. Anonymous plays are listed by title. The work concludes with a title index and a chronology.

For American plays after 1830 see Robert F. Roden, *Later American Plays, 1831–1900: Being a Compilation of the Titles of Plays of American Authors Published and Performed in America since 1831* (New York: Dunlap Society, 1900) [Z1231.D7 W5]. It is generally agreed, however, that the best record is the U.S. Copyright Office's *Dramatic Compositions Copyrighted in the United States, 1870–1916,* 2 vols. (Washington, D.C.: G.P.O., 1918) [Z5781.U55], which provides a title list of some 60,000 published and manuscript plays submitted for copyright between 1817 and 1916. There is an index of authors, editors, translators, and pseudonyms.

S–78 **Stratman, Carl J.** *Bibliography of the American Theatre, Excluding New York City.* Chicago: Loyola University Press, 1965.   Z1231.D7 S8

This bibliography, designed to support study of the development of the American theater and stage outside New York City, is arranged by state and city. A total of 3,856 numbered entries include theses and dissertations but exclude both general histories and general critical studies, newspaper articles, manuscripts, and materials on the movies, radio, or television. Within the listing for each city, materials are arranged in chronological order, with undated items in a miscellaneous group at the end. Annotations identify the subject matter of the cited item, and locations of copies are given. Included are materials on such topics as the legitimate theater, the arena theater, open air theaters, childrens's theater, college and university theater, community theater, little theater, masques, minstrels, ballet, puppet shows, variety shows, vaudeville, lighting, scenery, Chinese theater in the United States, and Shakespeare in the American theater. An index of proper names and of subjects concludes this volume.

A related reference work is Stratman's *American Theatrical Periodicals, 1798–1967: A Bibliographical Guide* (Durham, N.C.: Duke University Press, 1970) [Z6935.S75], which lists in chronological order 685 periodicals published in 122 cities and 31 states.

For the theater and stage in New York City see Clarence Gohdes, "The Theatre in New York: A Tentative Checklist," *BNYPL* 69 (1965): 232–246; Carl J. Stratman, "The Theatre in New York: Addenda," *BNYPL* 70 (1966): 389–407; and Stratman, "The New York Stage: A Checklist of Unpublished Dissertations and Theses," *BB* 24 (1963): 41–44.

S–79 **Wilmeth, Don B.** *American Stage to World War I: A Guide to Information Sources.* Detroit: Gale Research Co., 1978.   Z1231.D7 W55

This guide presents a total of 1,480 annotated entries in thirteen sections, as follows: General References, Dictionaries, and Biographical Guides; Bibliographies; Indexes; General Histories, Surveys, and Regional Studies; State and Local Histories; General Sources on Actors and Acting on the American Stage; Individuals in the American Theatre (including international artists); Scenery, Architecture, and Lighting; Foreign Language Theatre in America; Paratheatrical Forms (circus, burlesque, Wild West shows, etc.); Theatre Collections: Guides and Descriptions; Suspended Periodicals and Serials; Current Periodicals and Serials. The volume concludes with indexes of author, title, and subject.

VIII. PROSE FICTION

See also materials on contemporary American fiction in section R and on American fiction in general in section W, passim.

S–80 **Holman, C. Hugh, with Janis Richardi.** *American Novel through Henry James.* [A Goldentree Bibliography.] 2d ed. Northbrook, Ill.: AHM Publishing Corp., 1979.
                                    Z1231.F4 H64 1979

This student bibliography is divided into ten sections covering Bibliographies, Reference Works, American Literary History, American Publishing and Bookselling, the Novel as a Form, Histories of the American Novel, Special Studies of the American Novel (by period, genre, and by theme and subject), Collections of Studies of the American Novel, Major American Novelists, and Lesser American Novelists. A total of more than 3,100 entries are occasionally briefly annotated. Those for individual novelists are generally arranged in the subcategories of Texts, Bibliography, Biographical and Critical Books, and Critical Essays. Twenty-one major and twenty-one minor American novelists are included in the enumerations of the last two sections. Works of special importance are designated throughout by an asterisk; an index of names concludes the work. This work and its sequel in the same series (S–81) complement the other Goldentree bibliographies of American literature in the series (see S–6, S–70, and S–120) as well as the other Goldentree bibliographies of the novel (see Q–73 and R–50).

S–81 **Nevius, Blake.** *American Novel: Sinclair Lewis to the Present.* [A Goldentree Bibliography.] New York: Appleton-Century-Crofts, 1970.   Z1231.F4 N4

This student bibliography is divided into eight sections, covering Bibliographies, Reference Works, American Literary History, The Novel as a Form, Histories of the American Novel, Special Studies of the American Novel (by period and by theme and subject), Collections of Studies of the American Novel, and Contemporary American Novelists. Entries are occasionally briefly annotated. Those for the individual novelists are arranged in the subcategories of Texts, Bibliography, Biographical and Critical Books, Biographical and Critical Essays. Enumerations are given for forty-eight novelists. Unlike many of the volumes in the Goldentree series, this one does not use asterisks to designate items of special significance. An index of names concludes the work. Along with its predecessor in the same series (S–80), this bibliography complements the other Goldentree bibliographies of American literature (see S–6, S–70, and S–120) as well as the other Goldentree bibliographies of the novel (see Q–73 and R–50).

S–82 Kirby, David K. *American Fiction to 1900: A Guide to Information Sources.* Detroit: Gale Research Co., 1975.
Z1231.F4 K57

This volume contains a total of 1,430 serially numbered entries with primarily descriptive but some evaluative annotation. The entries are divided into two parts. The first, General Aids, contains sections on Handbooks and other Reference Works; Bibliographies and Checklists of both Primary and Secondary Literature; Periodicals and Serials; and General Critical Studies. The second part contains Bibliographies for a total of forty-one individual authors, citing for each Principal Works, Collected Works, Letters, Primary and Secondary Bibliographies, Checklists, Journals, Biographies, and Important Critical Studies. The work concludes with an index of authors, editors, translators, and titles.

S–83 Woodress, James. *American Fiction, 1900–1950: A Guide to Information Sources.* Detroit: Gale Research Co., 1974.
Z1231.F4 W64

This work, which lists materials published through 1972, is in two parts, the first of which contains general bibliography in four sections: 1. Background Source Material (Reference Works, Bibliographies of American Literature and Fiction, Literary History and Criticism of the 19th and 20th Centuries, Literary History and Criticism of the 20th Century, Special Topics); 2. Specialized Source Material—the Novel (General History and Criticism, 20th Century History and Criticism, Technique and Structure, Types, Characters, Themes and Motifs, Regionalism: the South, the Negro, Bestsellers, Foreign Reception, Essay Collections of Criticism); 3. Special Source Material—the Short Story; and 4. Special Source Material—Interviews with Authors. These sections all contain brief descriptive annotations of entries, with some evaluative comments.

Part 2, sections 5–48, contains bibliographical essays on each of forty-four authors. The essays include brief biographical sketches followed by discussion of Bibliography and Manuscripts, Works of Fiction, Editions and Reprints, Biographical Studies, and Critical Studies. The volume concludes with an index of authors and critics.

S–84 Rosa, Alfred F., and Paul A. Eschholz, eds. *Contemporary Fiction in America and England, 1950–1970: A Guide to Information Sources.* Detroit: Gale Research Co., 1976.
Z1231.F4 R57

This work is disposed into three parts. The first enumerates Studies and Reference Works Concerned with Contemporary Fiction. Literary Histories, Reference Works, Bibliographies, and Studies and Collections are listed, and each entry is descriptively annotated. The second part lists Journals Concerned with Contemporary Fiction. The third gives primary and secondary bibliographies for a total of 136 authors, eighty American and fifty-six British. These bibliographies are subdivided as follows: A. Novels (listed chronologically by date of publication); B. Short Story Collections; C. Bibliographies of Articles and Books; D. Critical Books; E. Special Issues of a Journal Devoted to the Author; F. Critical Articles. The volume has been adversely reviewed and should be used with caution.

S–85 Wright, Lyle H. *American Fiction: A Contribution Toward a Bibliography.* 3 vols. *American Fiction 1774–1850.* 2d rev. ed. San Marino, Calif.: Huntington Library, 1969. *American Fiction 1851–1875*, with additions and corrections appended. San Marino: Huntington, 1965. *American Fiction 1876–1900.* San Marino: Huntington, 1966.
Z1231.F4 L68

This bibliography of all American editions of prose fiction by Americans includes novels, romances, tales, short stories, fictitious biographies, travels, sketches, allegories, tractlike tales, and other similar prose works. Omitted are annuals, gift books, works of juvenile fiction, folklore, anthologies, collections of anecdotes, and periodicals. Over 11,000 entries are alphabetical under the author's name, or by title when the author is unknown. Entries give title, imprint, pagination, illustrations, and some library locations. A chronological index in volume 1 notes the first or earliest listed edition of each cited work; a title index in each volume lists titles of all entries in the main body of the volume.

S–86 Quinn, Arthur H. *American Fiction: An Historical and Critical Survey.* New York: Appleton-Century, 1936.
PS371.Q5

This is one of the earliest attempts to write the history of American fiction. It treats both the novel and the short story from the late eighteenth century to the 1930s and includes a bibliography of nearly fifty pages, as well as a convenient author-title index.

Other frequently recommended histories of American fiction include the first full-length history by Carl Van Doren, *American Novel, 1789–1939*, rev. and enl. ed. (New York: Macmillan, 1940) [PS371.V3], originally published in 1921, which concentrates attention on Cooper, Hawthorne, Howells, Twain, and James. More recent are Alexander Cowie's *Rise of the American Novel* (New York: American Book Co., 1948) [PS371.C73], which treats the novel by way of extended discussion of representative writers through the later nineteenth century, with a final chapter indicating the main lines of twentieth-century development, and Richard Chase's *American Novel and Its Tradition* (Garden City, N.Y.: Doubleday, 1957) [PS371.C5], which focuses on the tradition of romance in the American novel, with chapters on Charles Brockden Brown, Cooper, Hawthorne, Melville, James, Twain, Norris, and Faulkner.

S–87 Gerstenberger, Donna, and George Hendrick. *American Novel: A Checklist of Twentieth-Century Criticism.* 2 vols. Vol. 1, 1789–1959. 2d ed. Denver, Colo.: Swallow, 1969. Vol. 2, 1960–1968. Chicago: Swallow, 1970.
Z1231.F4 G4

These checklists of books, chapters and sections of books, and articles are each divided into two parts. The first treats criticisms of individual authors and their works, citing treatments of individual novels, general studies, and bibliographies. The second part, on the novel as a genre, cites general studies by century and then works that cover the genre in general. The second volume includes some pre–1960 articles omitted from the first volume. Short fiction is generally not treated in these volumes, with the exception of *Billy Budd* and *Go Down, Moses*. For criticism of other short fiction see the checklist by Weixlmann (S–89).

S–88 Eichelberger, Clayton L., et al. *Guide to Critical Reviews of United States Fiction, 1870–1910.* 2 vols. Metuchen, N.J.: Scarecrow Press, 1971–1974.
Z1225.E35

An index to reviews published in one of twenty-nine periodicals of some 5,500 fictional sketches, short stories, and novels published 1870–1930. Excluded are travel sketches, biography, and juvenile fiction. A special effort has been made to include reference to commentary on minor works and the works of minor authors. Entries are arranged by writer and then by work. An appendix lists reviews of anonymous and pseudonymous works that may be by an American author. The volume ends with an index of titles.

Volume 2 lists about 9,000 additional notices culled from ten additional periodicals. Both volumes must therefore be used in compiling a bibliography on a particular author or title.

S–89 **Weixlmann, Joseph. *American Short Fiction Criticism and Scholarship, 1959–1977: A Checklist.*** Athens: Ohio University Press, 1982.   Z1231.F4 W43

A total of 6,946 serially numbered entries list critical and scholarly material found in books, chapters and sections of books, and articles published between 1959 and 1977 on the work of more than 500 American writers of short fiction. This work thus updates for American short fiction the bibliography of Thurston et al., *Short Fiction Criticism 1928–1958* (W–50). The typographically well-designed bibliography is divided into two sections, the first listing general matters (general studies of the eighteenth and nineteenth centuries; general studies of the twentieth century; general studies; and general bibliographies). The second section presents author bibliographies with subdivisions for each short-fiction title, general studies, bibliography, and interviews. The work concludes with a list of the indexed serial publications.

IX.   PROSE AND CRITICISM

See also materials on American literary journals and little magazines in section D; on contemporary American prose and criticism in section R; on American prose in general in section W; and on American criticism in general in section X.

S–92 **Yannella, Donald. American Prose to 1820: A Guide to Information Sources.** Detroit: Gale Research Co., 1979.
                    Z1231.P8 Y36

A total of 2,957 serially numbered entries that are both descriptively and evaluatively annotated are disposed into five sections. The first, General References and Special Studies, is subdivided as follows: Literary and Cultural Studies, Printing and Publishing, Anthologies and Collections, Bibliographies and Checklists, Genre and Rhetoric, Period Criticism, Periodicals and Newspapers, Black Slave Narratives, and Indian Captivity Narratives. The second and third sections treat works concerning the Colonial Period and the Revolutionary and Early National Period respectively. The fourth section presents bibliographies for a total of eighty-three principal authors, listing unnumbered primary works, editions, and secondary sources under the categories of Bibliography, and Biography and Criticism. The fifth section presents material on additional, minor authors. The volume's index combines authors, titles, and subjects.

S–93 **Partridge, Elinore Hughes. *American Prose and Criticism, 1820–1900: A Guide to Information Sources.*** Detroit: Gale Research Co., 1983.   Z1231.P8 P37 1983

This volume is disposed into three main parts. The first, General Guides, has the following sections: Bibliographies and Reference Works; Periodicals and Annual Bibliographies; Cultural, Historical and Literary Studies; and Anthologies. The second part, on Prose, is in six sections, as follows: Liter-

ary Theory and Criticism; Autobiographies, Memoirs, and Diaries; Essay and Sketch; Travel and Description; Writings in Education, Religion, Philosophy, and Science; and the Literature of History and Politics. Within each section are divisions listing representative primary works and then various classes of secondary works. The third and final part contains bibliographies for a total of forty-five individual authors, divided into sections listing Principal Prose Works; Letters and Journals; Later Editions, Selections, and Reprints; Bibliographies; Biography and Criticism; and Related General Studies. Most of the unnumbered entries are very well annotated with both descriptive and evaluative comments. An index of authors, titles, and some subject headings concludes the volume.

S–94 **Brier, Peter A., and Anthony Arthur, eds. *American Prose and Criticism, 1900–1950: A Guide to Information Sources.*** Detroit: Gale Research Co., 1981.   Z1231.P8 B74

This volume is in two halves, the first, on prose, compiled by Arthur, and the second, by Brier, on criticism. Entries are unnumbered and not very well annotated. The prose half is in two parts, General Bibliographical Aids (Handbooks, Bibliographies and Checklists, Studies and Texts on Intellectual Backgrounds, Rhetorical Studies, Anthologies, Serial Studies) and Individual Authors. For the individual authors (fifteen entertainers, fifteen teachers, and eight reporters are included), entries give Principal Works, Collected Works, Coauthored Works, Bibliographies, Letters, Biographies, Memoirs, and Critical Works. Annotation is primarily descriptive and very brief.

The half on American criticism contains an introduction to the schools of criticism (Expressionism and Impressionism, The New Humanism, Literal and Radical Criticism, The New Criticism and the Neo-Aristotelians, Psychological and Myth Criticism, and Beyond 1950). The entries are in three parts. The first, General Bibliographical Aids, includes Bibliographies of Criticism, General Histories of Criticism, Specialized Histories and Studies of Major Schools and Movements, and Literary Histories of Significance to Literary Criticism. The second lists collections of critical essays. The third contains bibliographies of twelve major critics, citing Bibliographies, Critical Works, Representative Secondary Sources, and Resources for Further Research. The volume concludes with author, title, and subject indexes.

X.   LOCAL AND REGIONAL LITERATURE

Note that *Abstracts of English Studies* (M–23) has a special section on Regional Studies.

S–100 **Gohdes, Clarence. *Literature and Theatre of the States and Regions of the U.S.A.: An Historical Bibliography.*** Durham, N.C.: Duke University Press, 1967.   Z1225.G63

The bibliography lists monographs, anthologies, pamphlets, chapters in books, and articles pertinent to the study of regional and local literature and theater from colonial times to the present. Arranged by the names of the fifty states, the dependencies (Canal Zone, District of Columbia, Puerto Rico, and the Virgin Islands), and the principal regions (Middle West, New England, Northwest, South, Southwest, and West) are items referring to literature and (separately) to the theater. Individual entries are alphabetical by author, editor, or compiler. Appendixes list materials on "Western" film and fiction, on regionalism in general, and on regional theater.

S–101 **"A Bibliography of New England [1917–1965]."** *New England Quarterly*, vols. 1–39. Brunswick, Me.: Colonial Society of Massachusetts, 1928–1966.   F1.N62

Originally titled "Articles on the History of New England in Periodical Publications . . . Including Bound Volumes of Historical Societies That Publish No Serials," this annual sheer-list bibliography on all aspects of New England was classified into ten or eleven categories. In recent years entries, listed alphabetically by author, appeared under the following categories: General, Colonial Period, Revolutionary War, National Period, Maritime History, Religious History, Educational History, Fine Arts and Architecture, Household and Minor Arts, Literature. With volume 40 (1967) publication was suspended and users were referred to the *MLA International Bibliography* (L–50) and the bibliographies in *American Literature* (S–12), the *American Historical Review* (F–53), and *American Quarterly* (S–13).

S–102 **Rubin, Louis D.** *Bibliographic Guide to the Study of Southern Literature, with an Appendix Containing Sixty-eight Additional Writers of the Colonial South by J. A. Leo Lemay.* Baton Rouge: Louisiana State University Press, 1969.   Z1225.R8

This volume contains a series of selective checklists, each with a brief introduction, prepared by more than 100 individual compilers. It is in two parts, the first treating a total of twenty-three general topics and themes (e.g., the Civil War, southwestern humorists) and the second providing bibliographies for a total of 135 individual authors. With the sixty-eight treated in the appendix, a total of 203 authors are included. The section on each topic or author begins with a signed, brief bibliographic essay discussing the available scholarship and pointing up desiderata. This is followed by a sheer list of secondary works. Throughout, cited items with extensive bibliographical material are identified by an asterisk.

S–103 **Williams, Jerry T., ed.** *Southern Literature 1968–1975: A Checklist of Scholarship Compiled by the Committee on Bibliography of the Society for the Study of Southern Literature.* Boston: G. K. Hall, 1978.   Z1225.S63 1978

This volume, which forms a continuation to Rubin's *Bibliographic Guide* (S–102), is a conflation and supplemented edition of the annual bibliographies appearing since 1968 in the spring issues of the *Mississippi Quarterly: The Journal of Southern Culture* under the title "A Checklist of Scholarship on Southern Literature" [AS30.M58 A2]. Both the annual checklists and the Williams compilation are arranged in five divisions, as follows: I. Colonial (1607–1800); II. Antebellum (1800–1865); III. Postbellum (1865–1920); IV. Contemporary (1920–1973); and V. General. Entries are arranged alphabetically by author, with a Miscellaneous section under each of the first four divisions. Entries have brief descriptive annotations that attempt to state the thesis of the item. The cumulation includes some entries added from periodicals not analyzed in the annual lists, provides some cross-referencing, and concludes with an index of names.

The annual lists, prepared by the Committee on Bibliography of the Society for the Study of Southern Literature, continue to appear in the volumes of the *Mississippi Quarterly*; another cumulated volume will be published in due course.

O. B. Emerson and Marion C. Michael have compiled a revised edition of *Southern Literary Culture: A Bibliography of Masters' and Doctors' Theses* (University: University of Alabama Press, 1979) [Z1251.S7 C3 1979], the original edition of which was published in 1955.

S–104 *History of Southern Literature.* Gen. ed. Louis D. Rubin, Jr. Baton Rouge: Louisiana State University Press, 1985.   PS261.H53 1985

This volume is comprised of four major sections, each edited by a different scholar and containing about a dozen essays by specialists on various authors and topics in southern literature. The first section, edited by Lewis P. Simpson, treats Southern writing from 1607–1860; the second, edited by Rayburn S. Moore, treats literature from 1860–1920; the third, edited by Thomas Daniel Young, treats the Southern Renaissance of 1920–1950; and the fourth, edited by Rubin, treats the work of writers who matured after 1950, from Welty to Ammons. The volume closes with an appendix by M. Thomas Inge, titled "The Study of Southern Literature," with a bibliographical essay treating major works of scholarship in the field.

S–105 **Bain, Robert, Joseph M. Flora, and Louis D. Rubin, Jr., eds.** *Southern Writers: A Biographical Dictionary.* Baton Rouge: Louisiana State University Press, 1979.   PS261.S59

This dictionary consists of short (1–3 pages) biographical articles by scholars on 379 authors born in, living in, writing about, or in some other way associated with the South. For those writers covered in Bain and Flora's later volumes (S–106, S–107), this dictionary has been superseded.

S–106 **Bain, Robert, and Joseph M. Flora.** *Fifty Southern Writers Before 1900: A Bio-Bibliographical Sourcebook.* Westport, Conn.: Greenwood, 1987.   PS261.F543 1987

This volume contains essays by specialists on the lives, works, and critical reception of fifty writers living in or associated with the history of Southern literature. Each essay contains a biographical sketch, a discussion of the author's major themes, an assessment of scholarship on the author's works, a chronological list of primary works, and a bibliography of selected criticism. The volume begins with an Introduction and concludes with an Index of names, titles, and subjects, and notes on contributors. A companion volume (S–107) treats fifty writers *after* 1900.

S–107 **Flora, Joseph M.** *Fifty Southern Writers After 1900: A Bio-Bibliographical Sourcebook.* Westpost, Conn.: Greenwood, 1987.   PS261.F54 1987

This volume contains essays by specialists on the lives, works, and critical reception of fifty writers living in or associated with the history of Southern literature. Each essay contains a biographical sketch, a discussion of the author's major themes, an assessment of scholarship on the author's works, a chronological list of primary works, and a bibliography of selected criticism. The volume begins with an Introduction and concludes with an Index of names, titles, and subjects, and notes on contributors. A companion volume (S–106) treats fifty writers *before* 1900.

S–110 **Nemanic, Gerald.** *Bibliographical Guide to Midwestern Literature.* Iowa City: University of Iowa Press, 1981.   Z1251.W5 B52

This work contains materials published through 1976 on the literature of Illinois, Indiana, Iowa, Michigan, Minnesota, Missouri, Ohio, and Wisconsin, as well as parts of Kansas, Nebraska, North Dakota and South Dakota. Treated also are the social, cultural, and historical contexts of that literature. The work, consisting primarily of classified sheer lists, was prepared by nearly 100 contributors, whose contributions are signed. It is divided into two parts. The first, Subject Bibliographies, begins with bibliographies on the literature and language of the midwest, the pre-frontier and frontier periods, and the individual states. Throughout, lists are subdivided into sections on anthologies and bibliographies. The next subject area, History and Society, has fifteen subdivisions from General, to Utopian Communities, and Intellectual Life. Additional subject bibliographies include Folklore (subdivided), Personal Narratives, Architecture and Graphics, Chicago, Black Literature, Indians, and Literary Periodicals. The second part presents individual bibliographies for a total of 120 authors. For inclusion an author must have written literary works, and these works must in some sense concern midwestern culture. Two appendixes, A and B, add lists of 101 additional midwestern writers and 101 additional fictional narratives concerning some aspect of midwestern culture. There is, regrettably, no index.

S–111 **"Annual Bibliography of Studies in Midwestern Literature [1971–]."** *Midamerica: Yearbook of the Society for the Study of Midwestern Literature*, vol. 1–. East Lansing: Center for the Study of Midwestern Literature, Michigan State University, 1973–.   PS251.M53

This annual bibliography lists American books and articles. Arrangement is by general topics and by individual midwestern authors' names.

Another serial bibliography is published in the biennial *Great Lakes Review: A Journal of Midwest Culture*, vol. 1–. (Mt. Pleasant: Central Michigan University, 1974–) [PS273.G73]. It lists both creative writing and academic studies. Entries are arranged under various topics including such rubrics as Architecture, Ethnic Studies, Fiction, Folklore, Guidebooks, Indians, Language, Literary Studies, Poetry, Personal Narrative, and Social Sciences. In addition to these listings, the journal also publishes closed retrospective bibliographies that treat one particular subject matter.

S–114 **Anderson, John Q., Edwin W. Gaston, Jr., James W. Lee, et al., eds.** *Southwestern American Literature: A Bibliography.* Chicago: Swallow Press, 1980.
                                                          Z1251.S8 A52

This is the first major effort to list primary and secondary bibliography for the literature of New Mexico, Arizona, Oklahoma, and Texas. It is divided into three parts, and consists of sheer lists, signed by the various contributors. Part I, General Topics, is divided into sections on The Land, The People, The Work, The Art, and The Ethos, each of which is appropriately subdivided. Part II, The Literature, is divided into sections on each of the genres. Part III, which occupies half the volume, treats Individual Authors, giving both primary and secondary bibliographies for each.

S–115 **Etulain, Richard W.** *Bibliographical Guide to the Study of Western American Literature.* Lincoln: University of Nebraska Press, 1982.   Z1251.W5 E8 1982

Based in part on Etulain's earlier volume, *Western American Literature: A Bibliography of Interpretive Books and Articles* (Vermillion, S.D.: Dakota Press, 1972) [Z1225.E8], this work contains a total of 5,030 serially numbered entries. They are disposed into four general sections and an extensive section of works on Individual Authors. The general sections treat Bibliographies, Anthologies, General Works, and Special Topics (Local Color and Regionalism, Popular Western Literature, Western Film, Indian Literature and Indians in Western Literature, Mexican-American Literature and Chicanos in Western Literature, The Beats, and Canadian Western Literature). The section on Individual Authors contains secondary bibliographies for a total of more than 350 writers. An index of names concludes this work.

S–116 **Erisman, Fred, and Richard W. Etulain, eds.** *Fifty Western Writers: A Bio-bibliographical Sourcebook.* Westport, Conn.: Greenwood Press, 1982.   PS271.F5 1982

This research and reference guide presents narrative introductions by contributing specialists to the work of fifty leading Western authors from Willa Cather and Bret Harte to Robinson Jeffers, Ken Kesey, and Theodore Roethke. Entries provide a biography, a critical analysis of the author's leading themes and ideas, and a review of research.

S–117 **"Annual Bibliography of Studies in Western American Literature."** *Western American Literature*, vol. 1–. Logan: Utah State University for the Western American Literature Association, 1967–.   PS271.W46

Books and articles are listed alphabetically by the last name of the literary author or topic with which a given item is associated. Topics include the rubrics Bibliography, General, and Midwest, among others. Native American Writers are also treated. In addition to the annual bibliography, there is a section given to listing "Research in Western American Literature," divided into one part listing completed theses and dissertations and another listing works in progress.

S–118 *Literary History of the American West.* Sponsored by the Western Literature Association. Eds. J. Golden Taylor and Thomas J. Lyon, et al. Fort Worth: Texas Christian University, 1987.   PS271.L58 1987

This 1,353 page volume was produced by the Western Literature Association and some seventy contributors specializing in the major writers of the American West, the various regional literatures and historical periods, a wide range of genres and literary methods, and literatures written—or spoken—in languages other than English. The work is divided into three parts, and each is further divided into sections. These sections are in turn divided into chapters written by specialists. Each part and section begin with an introduction by the editor.

Part One: Encountering the West, is divided into four sections, as follows: Oral Traditions, The Written Donnée of Western Literature, Beginnings of Genres in the West, and Beginnings of Literary Historiography. Part Two: Settled In: Many Wests, is also in four sections: The Far West, The Southwest, The Midwest, and The Rocky Mountains. Part Three: Rediscovering the West, is in two sections, as follows: Earth Tones: Ethnic Expression in American Literature, and Present Trends. The chapters within these sections are signed and many conclude with notes and selected bibliographies for further research.

The volume begins with a Chronology by Richard W. Etulain, and concludes with an Epilogue: The Development of Western Literary Criticism by Martin Bucco; a bibliography of 126 Major Reference Sources on the West by George F. Day; a list of contributors; and an Index of names and some subjects.

S–119 **Some Frequently Recommended Works on Local and Regional American Literature.**

New England

Brooks, Van Wyck. *Flowering of New England.* New York: Dutton, 1952.   PS243.B7 1952

————. *New England: Indian Summer, 1865–1915.* New York: Dutton, 1950.   PS243.B72 1950

Buell, Lawrence. *New England Literary Culture from Revolution Through Renaissance.* New York: Cambridge University Press, 1986.   PS243.B84 1986

Clark, Edward. *Black Writers in New England: a Bibliography, with Biographical Notes, of Books by and about Afro-American Writers Associated with New England.* Boston: National Park Service, 1985.
Z1229.N39 C57 1985

Donovan, Josephine. *New England Local Color Literature: A Women's Tradition.* New York: Ungar, 1983.
PS243.D66 1983

Jantz, Harold S. "The First Century of New England Verse," *Proceedings of the American Antiquarian Society* 53 (1954): 219–508. Bibliography of 164 pre–1701 writers.
E172.A34

Lowance, Mason I., Jr. *Language of Canaan: Metaphor and Symbol in New England from the Puritans to the Transcendentalists.* Cambridge: Harvard University Press, 1980.
PS243.L6

Simpson, Lewis P. *Man of Letters in New England and the South: Essays on the History of the Literary Vocation in America.* Baton Rouge: Louisiana State University Press, 1973.
PS243.S48

Westbrook, Perry D. *Literary History of New England.* Bethlehem: Lehigh University Press, 1988.
PS243.W42 1988

The South

Gray, Richard J. *Writing the South: Ideas of an American Region.* New York: Cambridge University Press, 1986.
F209.G724 1986

Gwin, Minrose. *Black and White Women of the Old South: The Peculiar Sisterhood in American Literature.* Knoxville: University of Tennessee Press, 1985.
PS261.G85 1985

Hubbell, Jay B. *South in American Literature, 1607–1900.* Durham, N.C.: Duke University Press, 1954. Bibliography.
PS261.H78

O'Brien, Michael. *Rethinking the South: Essays in Intellectual History.* Baltimore: Johns Hopkins University Press, 1988.
F212.O24 1988

Rubin, Louis D., Jr. *Edge of the Swamp: A Study in the Literature and Society of the Old South.* Baton Rouge: Louisiana State University Press, 1989.
PS261.R59 1989

———. *Gallery of Southerners.* Baton Rouge: Louisiana State University Press, 1982.
PS261.R64 1982

———. *Writer in the South: Studies in Literary Community.* Athens: University of Georgia Press, 1972.
PS261.R69

———, ed. *American South: Portrait of a Culture.* Baton Rouge: Louisiana State University Press, 1980.
F209.5.A47

———, and C. Hugh Holman, eds. *Southern Literary Study: Problems and Possibilities.* Chapel Hill: University of North Carolina Press, 1965. PS261.S528

Simpson, Lewis P. *Dispossessed Garden: Pastoral and History in Southern Literature.* Athens: University of Georgia Press, 1975.
PS261.S467

Sweeney, Patricia, comp. *Women in Southern Literature: An Index.* Westport, Conn.: Greenwood Press, 1986.
PS261.W64 1986

The Midwest

Bredahl, A. Carl, Jr. *New Ground: Western American Narrative and the Literary Canon.* Chapel Hill: University of North Carolina Press, 1989. PS271.B74 1989

Rusk, Ralph Leslie. *Literature of the Middle Western Frontier.* 2 vols. New York: Ungar, 1962.
PS273.R8 1962

The Southwest

Lensink, Judy Nolte, ed. *Old Southwest/New Southwest: Essays on a Region and Its Literature.* Tucson: University of Arizona Press for the Tucson Public Library, 1987.
PS277.O4 1987

Major, Mabel, Rebecca W. Smith, and T. M. Pearce. *Southwest Heritage: A Literary History with Bibliography.* 3d rev. ed. Albuquerque: University of New Mexico Press, 1972.
PS277.M3 1972

Pilkington, William T. *My Blood's Country: Studies in Southwestern Literature.* Fort Worth: Texas Christian University Press, 1973.
PS277.P5

Powell, Lawrence Clark. *Southwest Classics: The Creative Literature of the Arid Lands: Essays on the Books and Their Writers.* Los Angeles: W. Ritchie Press, 1974.
PS277.P63

The West

Fender, Stephen. *Plotting the Golden West: American Literature and the Rhetoric of the California Trail.* New York: Cambridge University Press, 1981. PS271.F4

Haslam, Gerald W., ed. *Western Writing.* Albuquerque: University of New Mexico Press, 1974. PS271.H3

Simonson, Harold P. *Beyond the Frontier: Writers, Western Regionalism, and a Sense of Place.* Fort Worth: Texas Christian University, 1989. PS271.S5 1989

Smith, Henry Nash. *Virgin Land: The American West as Symbol and Myth.* Cambridge: Harvard University Press, 1950.
F591.S65 1950

XI. ETHNIC AMERICAN LANGUAGES AND LITERATURES

The *MLA International Bibliography* (L–50) is a major source for current bibliography on studies of all ethnic American literatures. See also relevant entries in section L for non-English-language American literatures and in section M for other American literatures in English.

S–120 **Turner, Darwin T. *Afro-American Writers.*** [A Goldentree Bibliography.] New York: Appleton-Century-Crofts, 1970.
Z1361.N39 T78

This student bibliographical guide represents a milestone in the bibliography of Afro-American authors. It is divided into four parts: Aids to Research (including Bibliographies; Guides to Collections; Encyclopedias, Handbooks, and Other Reference Works; and Periodicals Significant to the Study of Literature by Afro-Americans); Backgrounds (including Significant Autobiographies and Collections of Essays by Afro-Americans; Slave Narratives; Historical, Social, and Intellectual Backgrounds; Art, Journalism, Music, and Theatre); Literary History and Criticism (including Anthologies, General History and Criticism, Drama, Fiction, Poetry, and Folklore); and Afro-American Writers, with bibliographies of some 135 authors disposed into subsections listing primary works and works of autobiography, biography, and criticism. An appendix of Selected Criticism of Africans and Afro-Americans as Characters follows the author bibliographies. Throughout, asterisks are used to designate both primary and secondary works of major significance. The volume is concluded by an index of names and a supplement of recently published materials that came to the compiler's attention after the manuscript was prepared for publication. The supplement is organized to parallel the classifications of the main work.

This work has been further supplemented by Carol Myers, "A Selected Bibliography of Recent Afro-American Writers," *CLA Journal* 16 (1973): 377–382.

S–121 **Fisher, Dexter, and Robert B. Stepto, eds. *Afro-American Literature: The Reconstruction of Instruction.*** New York: MLA, 1979.   PS153.N5 A35

This volume contains a series of papers presented at a seminar held under the auspices of the MLA's Commission on Minority Groups and the Study of Literature. The fourteen essays and course designs it contains treat issues in Afro-American literary history; black figurative language; Afro-American literature and folklore; theories of how to approach diverse literary texts; and designs for survey, genre, and interdisciplinary courses in Afro-American literature.

S–122 **Miller, Elizabeth W., ed. *Negro in America: A Bibliography.*** 2d ed. Revised and enlarged by Mary L. Fisher. Cambridge: Harvard University Press, 1970.
Z1361.N39 M5 1970

Originally published in 1966, this standard work contains a total of twenty-one chapters listing occasionally annotated entries citing works on all aspects of American Negro life. The first sections are as follows: 1. General Background; 2. History; 3. Demography; 4. Definition and Description; 5. Biography and Letters; 6. Folklore and Literature; 7. Theatre, Dance and the Arts; 8. The Negro in Literature and the Arts; 9. Music. These are followed by sections treating various aspects of economic and social history and circumstance. Chapter 21 is titled a Guide to Further Research.

A major source of bibliography on the American Negro is the *Dictionary Catalog of the Schomburg Collection of Negro Literature and History*, 9 vols. (Boston: G. K. Hall, 1962) [Z881.N592 S35]. It presents author, title, and subject lists of books and monographs. Two supplements were published: the first in two volumes (1967) and the second in four (1972). A continuing supplement is the annual *Bibliographic Guide to Black Studies* (Boston: G. K. Hall, 1976–) [Z1361.N39 S373a], which presents author, title, and subject entries for all relevant books and monographs cataloged (1975–) by the Library of Congress and the New York Public Library. G. K. Hall also publishes the annual *Index to Periodical Articles by and about Blacks* (1950–) [AI3.O4], an author-subject index to some fifty black American periodicals.

S–124 **Inge, M. Thomas, Maurice Duke, and Jackon R. Bryer, eds. *Black American Writers: Bibliographical Essays.*** 2 vols. New York; St. Martin's Press, 1978.   PS153.N5 B55

These volumes present a series of bibliographical essays by specialists which give an overview and appraisal of the primary and secondary bibliography on black American writers. Volume 1 covers the beginnings through the Harlem Renaissance and Langston Hughes, in six sections: 1. Early Writers (by Jerome Klinkowitz); 2. Slave Narratives (by Ruth Miller and Peter J. Katopes); 3. The Polemicists (by W. Burghardt Turner); 4. Modern Beginnings (by Ruth Miller and Peter J. Katopes); 5. The Harlem Renaissance (by Ruth Miller and Peter J. Katopes); and 6. Langston Hughes (by Blyden Jackson). Treated are Bibliographies, Editions, Manuscripts and Letters, Biographies and Biographical Studies, and Selected Criticism.

The second volume presents essays on the bibliography of Richard Wright (by John M. Reily); Ralph Ellison (by Joanne Giza); James Baldwin (by Daryl Dance); and Amiri Baraka/Leroi Jones (by Letitia Dace). Both volumes conclude with indexes of names of both authors and critics.

See also Geraldine O. Matthews and the African-American Materials Project Staff, comps., *Black American Writers, 1773–1949: A Bibliography and Union List* (Boston: G. K. Hall, 1975) [Z1361.N39 M35], which catalogs the names of some 1,600 black American writers with up to three of their monographs listed and indications for about 60 percent of locations in some sixty-five southern libraries where the works can be found. The work is arranged by topics, including such rubrics as Hairstyling, Language, Literature, Philosophy, and Religion. An author index concludes the volume. Within topics, entries are by author, and then by title.

The extremely and admittedly imperfect two-volume work, *Black American Writers Past and Present: A Biographical and Bibliographical Dictionary* (Metuchen, N.J.: Scarecrow, 1975) [Z1229.N39 R87], complements and extends the work of Matthews, including some 2,000 writers from the early eighteenth century through roughly 1973. Where possible, entries have a biographical statement, a primary bibliography of published books, and a selected bibliography of secondary sources of biography and criticism, along with a concluding section termed "interjections," in which are quoted statements by the authors themselves identifying their ideas, theories, impressions, and philosophies. Although it must be used with caution, this is to date the most complete biobibliography of black American authors available.

S–125 **French, William P., et al. *Afro-American Poetry and Drama, 1760–1975: A Guide to Information Sources.*** Detroit: Gale Research Co., 1979.   Z1229.N39 A37

This volume is in two halves, the first on Afro-American Poetry, 1760–1975, by William P. French, Michael J. Fabre, and Amritjit Singh, and the second on Afro-American Drama, 1850–1975, by Geneviève E. Fabre. The Poetry half is in two parts, treating General Studies (Bibliographies and Reference Works, Critical Studies, and Anthologies) and Individual Authors (alphabetical within the chronological groupings 1760–1900, 1901–1945, and 1946–1975). Unnumbered entries are often annotated. Entries under individual poets are divided, when appropriate, into sections on Published Works, Bibliographies, and Biography and Criticism.

The Drama half is similarly organized with General Studies (Library Resources, Periodicals, Bibliographies, Play Collections, and Critical Studies) followed by Bibliographies of Individual Authors (alphabetically, but grouped 1850–1900, 1901–1950, 1951–1975). In the general studies section are some chronological subdivisions; author bibliographies are in sections listing Published Plays, Unpublished Plays, Collected Plays, Biography and Criticism. Indexes of authors, titles, and subjects conclude the volume.

S–126 **Porter, Dorothy B. *North American Negro Poets: A Bibliographical Checklist of Their Writings, 1760–1944.*** Hattiesburg, Miss.: The Book Farm, 1945.   Z1361.N39 P6

This volume, an expansion of a *Bibliographical Checklist of American Negro Poetry* by Arthur A. Schomburg (New York, 1916), lists books, pamphlets, anthologies, and a few broadsides alphabetically by author. Entries give title, publication information, pagination, and some locations.

S–129 **Hatch, James V. *Black Image on the American Stage: A Bibliography of Plays and Musicals 1770–1970.*** New York: DBS Publishers, 1970.   Z5784.N4 H35

This chronologically arranged volume lists under year alphabetically by author more than 2,000 entries for plays, musicals, revues, and operas either by black authors or with a least one black character, or on a black theme. It concludes with a bibliography of related works, an author index, and an index of titles.

See also the volume edited by Hatch and Omanii Abdullah, *Black Playwrights, 1823–1977: An Annotated Bibliography of Plays* (New York: Bowker, 1977) [Z1231.D7 H37], which lists by author more than 2,700 plays, most with brief plot summaries. A "Selected Bibliography of Anthologies Containing Scripts by Black Playwrights" and a title index conclude the volume.

S–132 Margolies, Edward, and David Bakish. *Afro-American Fiction, 1853–1976: A Guide to Information Sources.* Detroit: Gale Research Co., 1979.   Z1229.N39 M37

This volume contains 1,173 serially numbered, partially annotated entries disposed into four chapters, as follows: 1, a checklist of works alphabetically arranged by author; 2, short story collections (by individuals, anthologies); 3, secondary sources on a total of fifteen major Afro-American novelists (subdivided into sections listing Bibliographies and Critical Studies); and 4, Bibliographies and General Studies. An appendix presents a chronological bibliography of Afro-American fiction, 1853–1976. There are some cross-references. Author, title, and subject indexes conclude the volume.

This volume may be complemented with material from Carol Fairbanks and Eugene A. Engeldinger, eds., *Black American Fiction: A Bibliography* (Metuchen, N.J.: Scarecrow Press, 1978) [Z1229.N39 F34]. The main part of this work is an alphabetical list of authors with bibliography, grouped into the sections: Novels, Short Fiction, Biography and Criticism, and Reviews (by title). A general bibliography concludes the volume. Entries are not annotated.

S–135 Peavy, Charles D. *Afro-American Literature and Culture since World War II: A Guide to Information Sources.* Detroit: Gale Research Co., 1979.   Z1229.N39 P4

This bibliography is in two parts. The first lists works under a total of twenty-eight subject headings, including Bibliographies, Black Aesthetic, Black Speech, Black Studies, Drama, Folklore, Movies, Novels, Poetry, Prison Writing, Theater, and Women. The second presents bibliographies for a total of fifty-six authors. Entries are descriptively annotated. The volume concludes with indexes of authors, titles, and subjects.

S–137 "An Annual Bibliography of Afro-American Literature [1975–1976], with Selected Bibliographies of African and Caribbean Literature." *CLA Journal.* vols. 20–21 (1976–1978).   P1.A1 C22

This short-lived, comprehensive bibliography was divided into nine sections, with annotations to clarify titles of otherwise sheerly listed entries. The divisions were as follows: Anthologies and Collections; Autobiographies and Biographies; Bibliographies, Indexes, and Checklists; Drama (published plays, criticism and history, individual playwrights); Fiction (novels and collections of short stories, criticism and history, individual novelists); Folklore; General Literary Criticism and History; Poetry (publications, criticism and history, individual poets); and Miscellaneous. This bibliography was followed by two others, on African and Caribbean literature respectively, divided into the same categories.

Another serial bibliography was titled "Studies in Afro-American Literature: An Annual Annotated Bibliography [1974–1976]," published in *Obsidian: Black Literature in Review*, vols. 1–3 (Fredonia: State University of New York–Fredonia, 1975–1977) [PR1110.B503]. Entries included only secondary works and only works published in the United States. Entries were numbered and were descriptively annotated with initialed informative abstracts. They were divided into from seven to nine sections, as follows: [Bibliogra-

phies, Reports on Scholarly Events], Interviews, General Studies, Studies in Poetry, in Fiction, in Drama, in Narratives and Autobiographies, Studies of Individual Authors.

S–138 Miller, Wayne Charles, with Faye Nell Vowell and Gary K. Crist, et al. *Comprehensive Bibliography for the Study of American Minorities.* 2 vols. New York: New York University Press, 1976.   Z1361.E4 M529

This classified, briefly annotated bibliography contains approximately 29,300 entries. Most citations are books, with articles and pamphlets cited where insufficient material is available for a particular ethnic group. Historical-bibliographical essays precede each group of citations. These have been reprinted as the *Handbook of American Minorities* (New York: New York University Press, 1976) [Z1361.E4 M53].

This bibliography is continued by the annual serial publication, *Minorities in America: The Annual Bibliography, [1976–]* (University Park: Pennsylvania State University Press, 1985–) [Z1361.E4 M57]. Each annual volume contains about 7,500 entries for works dealing with the life and culture of forty-one ethnic minorities ranging from Arab-Americans to Yugoslav-Americans, including both indigenous peoples and immigrants. Within each group, entries are arranged by subject area (including such rubrics as Biography, Economics, Education and Language, History, Literature and the Arts, Politics and Law, Religion, Sociology, and Women), with such subdivisions as are warranted. Entries include summaries of books and monographs, and abstracts of other materials.

S–139 Some Frequently Recommended Works on Afro-American Literature and Afro-American Studies.

Baker, Houston A., Jr. *Afro-American Poetics: Revisions of Harlem and the Black Aesthetic.* Madison: University of Wisconsin Press, 1988.   PS153.N5 B22 1988

——. *Blues, Ideology and Afro-American Literature: A Vernacular Theory.* Chicago: University of Chicago Press, 1984.   PS159.N5 B23 1984

——. *Journey Back: Issues in Black Literature and Criticism.* Chicago: University of Chicago Press, 1980.
PS153.N5 B24

——. *Modernism and the Harlem Renaissance.* Chicago: University of Chicago Press, 1987.
PS153.N5 B25 1987

——, and Patricia Redmond, eds. *Afro-American Literary Study in the 1990s.* Chicago: University of Chicago Press, 1989.   PS153.N5 A345 1989

Bone, Robert. *Down Home: A History of Afro-American Short Fiction, from its Beginnings to the End of the Harlem Renaissance.* New York: Putnam, 1975.
PS374.S5 B6

——. *Negro Novel in America.* Rev. ed. New Haven: Yale University Press, 1965.   PS153.N5 B5

Bruce, Dickson, D., Jr. *Black American Writing from the Nadir: The Evolution of a Literary Tradition, 1877–1915.* Baton Rouge: Louisiana State University Press, 1989.   PS153.N5 B77 1989

Carby, Hazel V. *Reconstructing Womanhood: The Emergence of the Afro-American Woman Novelist.* New York: Oxford University Press, 1987.
PS153.N5 C37 1987

Chapman, Dorothy Hilton, comp. *Index to Poetry by Black American Women.* Westport, Conn.: Greenwood, 1986.   Z1229.N39 C45 1986

Christian, Barbara. *Black Feminist Criticism: Perspectives on Black Women Writers.* New York: Pergamon Press, 1985.   PS153.N5 C47 1985

———. *Black Women Novelists: The Development of a Tradition, 1892–1976.* Westport, Conn.: Greenwood Press, 1980.   PS374.N4 C5

Davis, Arthur. *From the Dark Tower: Afro-American Writers (1900–1960).* Washington, D.C.: Howard University Press, 1974. Bibliography.   PS153.N5 D33

Dixon, Melvin. *Ride Out the Wilderness: Geography and Identity in Afro-American Literature.* Urbana: University of Illinois Press, 1987.   PS153.N5 D58 1987

Gates, Henry Louis. *Figures in Black: Words, Signs, and the "Racial" Self.* New York: Oxford University Press, 1987.   PS153.N5 G27 1987

———. *Signifying Monkey: A Theory of Afro-American Literary Criticism.* New York: Oxford University Press, 1988.   PS153.N5 G28 1988

———, ed. *Black Literature and Literary Theory.* New York: Methuen, 1984.   PS153.N5 B555 1984

———, ed. *"Race," Writing, and Difference.* Chicago: University of Chicago Press, 1986.

PN56.R18 R3 1986

Glenn, Robert W. *Black Rhetoric: A Guide to Afro-American Communication.* Metuchen, N.J.: Scarecrow, 1976.   Z1361.N39 G55

Hogue, W. Lawrence. *Discourse and the Other: The Production of the Afro-American Text.* Durham, N.C.: Duke University Press, 1986.   PS153.N5 H6 1986

Huggins, Nathan Irvin. *Harlem Renaissance.* New York: Oxford University Press, 1971.   NX512.3.N5 H8

Jackson, Blyden. *History of Afro-American Literature.* Vol. 1. *The Long Beginning, 1746–1895.* Baton Rouge: Louisiana State University Press, 1989–.

PS153.N5 J33 1989

———. *Waiting Years: Essays on American Negro Literature.* Baton Rouge: Louisiana State University Press, 1976.   PS153.N5 J34

Kellner, Bruce, ed. *Harlem Renaissance: An Historical Dictionary for the Era.* Westport, Conn.: Greenwood, 1984.   NX511.N4 H37 1984

Low, W. Augustus, and Virgil A. Clift, eds. *Encyclopedia of Black America.* New York: McGraw-Hill, 1981.

E185.E55

McDowell, Deborah E., and Arnold Rampersad, eds. *Slavery and the Literary Imagination.* Baltimore: Johns Hopkins University Press, 1989.

PS217.S55 S55 1989

Perry, Margaret. *Harlem Renaissance: An Annotated Bibliography and Commentary.* New York: Garland, 1982.

Z5956.A47 P47 1987

Pryse, Marjorie, and Hortense J. Spillers. *Conjuring: Black Women, Fiction, and Literary Tradition.* Bloomington: Indiana University Press, 1985.

PS153.N5 C63 1985

Rosenblatt, Roger. *Black Fiction.* Cambridge: Harvard University Press, 1974.   PS374.N4 R6

Shockley, Ann Allen. *Afro-American Women Writers, 1746–1933: An Anthology and Critical Guide.* Boston: G. K. Hall, 1988.   PS508.N3 A36 1988

Smith, Dwight La Vern. *Afro-American History: A Bibliography.* 2 vols. Santa Barbara, Calif.: ABC-Clio, 1974–1981.   Z1361.N39 S53 1974

Southgate, Robert L. *Black Plots and Black Characters: A Handbook for Afro-American Literature.* Syracuse, N.Y.: Gaylord Publications, 1979.   PS153.N5 S65

Stepto, Robert B. *From Behind the Veil: A Study of Afro-American Narrative.* Urbana: University of Illinois Press, 1979.   PS366.A35 S7

Wagner, Jean. *Black Poets of the United States: from Laurence Dunbar to Langston Hughes.* Urbana: University of Illinois Press, 1973.   PS153.N5 W313

Wall, Cheryl, ed. *Changing Our Own Words: Essays on Criticism, Theory, and Writing by Black Women.* New Brunswick: Rutgers University Press, 1989.

PS153.N5 C44 1989

Whitlow, Roger. *Black American Literature: A Critical History with a 1,520 Title Bibliography of Works Written by and about Black Americans.* Rev. ed. Chicago: Nelson-Hall, 1976.   PS153.N5 W45 1976

Willis, Susan. *Specifying: Black Women Writing the American Experience.* Madison: University of Wisconsin Press, 1987.   PS153.N5 W56 1987

Yancy, Preston M., comp. *Afro-American Short Story: A Comprehensive, Annotated Index with Selected Commentaries.* Westport, Conn.: Greenwood Press, 1986.

Z1229.N39 Y36 1986

S–140 **Marken, Jack W. *American Indian: Language and Literature.*** [A Goldentree Bibliography.] Arlington Heights, Ill.: AHM Publishing Co., 1978.   Z7118.M27

This student bibliographical guide contains a total of 3,695 serially numbered entries disposed into a total of sixteen sections, the first of which are as follows: I. Bibliography; II. Autobiography; III. General Literature (with subdivisions); and IV. General Language (with subdivisions). The remaining sections treat the various regions, as follows: The Northwest Coast, Oregon and the Washington Seaboard, California, Southern California, The Plateau, The Plains, The Midwest, The Northeast, The Southeast and Gulf, The Southwest, Western Canada, and Eastern Canada. Each of these regional sections is subdivided into entries on literature and on language. Throughout, important works are designated by an asterisk. An index of names and subjects concludes this guide.

S–141 **Stensland, Anna Lee, with Aune M. Fadum. *Literature by and about the American Indian: An Annotated Bibliography.*** 2d ed. Urbana, Ill.: NCTE, 1979. Z1209.S73 1979

First published in 1973, this bibliography is focused on teaching in grades K–12, though it includes material of interest to adult readers and to readers with scholarly interests. It is disposed into two sections. The first presents discursive treatments of Teaching the Literature of the American Indian (themes, stereotypes, references), Teaching Aids (curriculum planning, basic library sources), and Bibliographies of Selected American Indian Authors. The second part presents an annotated bibliography of nearly 800 titles, disposed into seven sections, as follows: Myth, Legend, Oratory, and Poetry; Fiction; Biography and Autobiography; History; Traditional Life and Culture; Modern Life and Problems; and Music, Arts, and Crafts. Sections are further divided into works appropriate for Elementary, Junior High, and Senior High and Adult use. Annotations give brief summaries, evaluations, and occasional citations from reviews. A directory of publishers and index of authors and of titles conclude the work.

S–142 Jacobson, Angeline, comp. *Contemporary Native American Literature: A Selected and Partially Annotated Bibliography.* Metuchen, N.J.: Scarecrow Press, 1977.

Z1229.I52 J32

This volume contains a total of 2,024 entries, many of them descriptively and evaluatively annotated, which treat the literature of the Eskimo, Canadian, and Mexican tribal writers, and American Indians. It is divided into twelve chapters, as follows: Introduction; Poets and Their Poetry (alphabetical by author); Native American Spiritual Heritage (including a selection of traditional narratives); Autobiography, Biography, Letters, and Personal Narratives; Fiction; Present-Day Realities (interviews, letters, stories, and other prose); Humor and Satire; Collections Analyzed; Sources—Bibliographies and Indexes; Periodicals Analyzed; Title and First Line Index to Single Poems; Author Index.

S–143 Allen, Paula Gunn. *Studies in American Indian Literature: Critical Essays and Course Designs.* New York: MLA, 1983.

PS153.I52 S8 1983

After an introduction on the study and teaching of American Indian literature, this volume is disposed into five sections treating distinct types of courses about particular topics in American Indian literature. The section topics are Oral Literature; Personal Narrative, Autobiography, and Intermediate Literature (i.e., between oral and written); American Indian Women's Literature; Modern and Contemporary American Indian Literature; and the Indian in American Literature. Each section includes general critical essays on the topic and at least three designs of courses that treat the topic or aspects of it from distinct perspectives.

These topical sections are followed by a section on resources which begins with a discursive bibliographical guide by A. LaVonne Brown Ruoff, "American Indian Literature: A Guide to Anthologies, Texts, and Research," which is disposed into sections discussing Teaching Aids, Bibliographies, and Handbooks; General Anthologies; Oral Literatures (Chants, Ceremonies, Rituals; Narratives: Anthologies and Texts; Narratives: Criticism; Songs: Anthologies and Texts; Songs: Criticism; Ritual Oratory); Philosophies and Religions; Personal Narratives: Oral and Written; Speeches: Oral and Written; and Written Literature: Prose, Fiction, Poetry, and Drama. A list, briefly annotated, of selected periodicals follows, and this is followed by a list of periodical special issues devoted to an aspect of American Indian literature. A list of selected presses publishing work by and about American Indian authors follows and then a bibliography of all works cited in the entire volume. An elaborate index of writers' names, tribal names, titles of literary works, subjects, and topics concludes the volume. Alternate names and tribal affiliations are identified in parentheses after the writer's name.

S–144 Hirschfelder, Arlene B., ed. *American Indian and Eskimo Authors: A Comprehensive Bibliography.* New York: Association of Indian Affairs, 1973.

Z1209.H55

The work is a greatly expanded revision of Hirschfelder's 1970 *American Indian Authors: A Representative Bibliography* [Z7118.H55]. It contains about 400 titles of works written or narrated by about 300 Indian and Eskimo authors from more than 100 tribes. Most are primary works, though some secondary studies and a number of anthologies are included. The volume begins with a tribal index, which is followed by an alphabetical author list giving authors, titles, publication information, cost, and brief descriptive annotation for each entry; the work concludes with a list of cited publishers.

S–145 Littlefield, Daniel F., and James W. Parins. *Biobibliography of Native American Writers, 1772–1924.* Metuchen, N.J.: Scarecrow Press, 1981.

Z1209.2.U5 L57

This work excludes Canadian Indian authors. In Part I of this guide, American Indian authors are listed in alphabetical order with a tribal designation given after the author's name. In Part II are listed authors known only by pseudonyms. In both parts, authors' works are listed in chronological order. Entries are numbered and lettered to designate a genre category according to the following system: A[ddress], C[ollections and Compilations], D[rama], E[dition], F[iction], L[etter], M[yths or Legends], N[onfiction Prose], P[oetry], S[ermon], and T[ranslation into English]. Part III presents biographical notes on the various authors. It is followed by indexes of writers' tribal affiliations and of subjects.

A supplement, *Biobibliography of Native American Writers, 1772–1924. A Supplement* (Metuchen, N.J.: Scarecrow Press, 1985) [Z1209.2.U5 L57 Suppl.] has been published.

S–147 Hirschfelder, Arlene B., Mary Gloyne Byler, and Michael A. Dorris. *Guide to Research on North American Indians.* Chicago: American Library Association, 1983.

Z1209.2.N67 H57 1983

This guide cites and describes some 1,100 English-language books, articles, and government documents in twenty-seven fields of study that concern North American Indians. The twenty-seven chapters are arranged in four parts as follows: Part I, Introductory Material (1, General Sources; 2, General Studies); Part II, History and Historical Sources (3, Geography and Cartography; 4, Archaeology and Prehistory; 5, Descriptive Narratives; 6, Autobiographies and Biographies; . . . 10, Histories); Part III, Economic and Social Aspects (11, Population and Demography; . . . 20, Language); Part IV, Religion, Arts, and Literature (21, Religion and Philosophy; 22, Music and Dance; 23, Education; 24, Arts; 25, Science; 26, Law; and 27, Literature). Chapters begin with a bibliographic essay tracing the main lines of scholarly inquiry and keyed to the bibliographies that follow. Those lists cite books treating the topic generally, works treating the topic across several geographic areas, and bibliographies on the topic. The volume concludes with an index of authors and titles and an index of subjects (including authors).

A current index is the irregularly published *Index to Literature on the American Indian* (San Francisco: Indian Historian Press, 1970–) [Z1209.I53], which offers author and subject analysis of both scholarly and popular periodicals on a wide range of topics. Books and articles on or by Native Americans are cited.

S–149 Some Frequently Recommended Works on Native American Literature.

Allen, Paula Gunn. *Sacred Hoop: Recovering the Feminine in American Indian Traditions.* Boston: Beacon Press, 1986.   E98.W8 A44 1986

Baker, Houston A., ed. *Three American Literatures: Essays in Chicano, Native American, and Asian American Literature for Teachers of American Literature.* New York: MLA, 1982.   PS153.M56 T5 1982

Bright, William. *American Indian Linguistics and Literature.* New York: Mouton, 1984.   PM206.B74 1984

Colonnese, Tom, and Louis D. Owens. *American Indian Novelists: An Annotated Critical Bibliography.* New York: Garland, 1985.   Z1229.I52 C65 1985

Haslam, Gerald W. *Forgotten Pages of American Literature.* Boston: Houghton Mifflin, 1970.   PS508.I5 H3

Krupat, Arnold. *Voice in the Margin: Native American Literature and the Canon.* Berkeley: University of California Press, 1989.　PS153.I52 K78 1989

Larson, Charles R. *American Indian Fiction.* Albuquerque: University of New Mexico Press, 1978.
PS153.I52 L3

Prucha, Francis Paul. *Bibliographical Guide to the History of Indian-White Relations in the United States.* Chicago: University of Chicago Press, 1977.
Z1209.2.U5 P67

Rock, Roger O., comp. *Native American in American Literature: A Selectively Annotated Bibliography.* Westport, Conn.: Greenwood Press, 1985.
Z1229.I52 R64 1985

Smith, Dwight L. *Indians of the United States and Canada: A Bibliography.* 2 vols. Santa Barbara: ABC-Clio, 1974–1983.　Z1209.N67 I52

Swann, Brian, and Arnold Krupat, eds. *Recovering the Word: Essays on Native American Literature.* Berkeley: University of California Press, 1987.
PS153.I52 R43 1987

Wiget, Andrew. *Native American Literature.* Boston: Twayne Publishers, 1985.　PM155.W54 1985

————, ed. *Critical Essays on Native American Literature.* Boston: G. K. Hall, 1985.　PM156.C75 1985

S–150　**Nadel, Ira Bruce.　*Jewish Writers of North America: A Guide to Information Sources.*** Detroit: Gale Research Co., 1981.　Z1229.J4 N32

A total of 3,291 numbered entries are divided into four parts. Within each part, works on American and Canadian writers are treated separately. Entries are occasionally annotated. Part 1, General Reference Guides, is subdivided as follows: Bibliographies, Biographical References; Indexes to Periodicals and General Source Materials; Research Catalogs, Manuscript Collections, and Special Libraries; Literary History; Literary Criticism; Anthologies. Part 2, Poets, presents bibliographies for a total of twenty-four American and fifteen Canadian poets. Part 3, Novelists and Short Story Writers, presents bibliographies for forty-seven Americans and thirteen Canadians. Part 4 presents individual bibliographies for fifteen American and eight Canadian Jewish dramatists. Throughout, primary works are chronologically arranged and secondary works are listed alphabetically. There are two appendixes, the first on Yiddish literature in three sections treating Reference Guides, History and Criticism in English, and Anthologies. The second appendix presents checklists of additional poets, novelists and short story writers, and dramatists. The volume concludes with indexes of authors, titles, and subjects.

For current material on Jewish writing in North America see the *Jewish Book Annual* (New York: Jewish Book Council, 1942–) [PN60672.J4], which reviews books and presents selective, annotated bibliographies of Current Fiction, Non-Fiction, Juvenile Literature, Yiddish Literature, Israeli Literature, and so on. See also the quarterly *Index to Jewish Periodicals* (Cleveland Heights, Ohio: Index to Jewish Periodicals, 1963–) [Z6367.I5], which analyzes some fifty general-interest and scholarly English-language periodicals by author and subject.

S–151　**Fried, Lewis, Editor-in-Chief.　*Handbook of American-Jewish Literature: An Analytical Guide to Topics, Themes, and Sources.*** Hamden, Conn.: Greenwood Press, 1988.　PS153.J4 H365 1988

This volume contains a total of eighteen essays with bibliographies appended by a total of seventeen contributors and the

Editor-in-Chief. The essays treat the following topics: In the Beginning, American-Jewish Fiction 1880–1930; American-Jewish Fiction 1930–1945; American-Jewish Fiction Since 1945; The Greening of American-Jewish Drama; American-Jewish Poetry; An Overview; American Yiddish Literary Criticism; A Question of Tradition: Women Poets in Yiddish; Makers of a Modern American-Jewish Theology: Zionist Ideology in America; American-Jewish Autobiography, 1912 to the Present; Images of America in American-Jewish Fiction; Eastern Europe in American-Jewish Writing; Shadows of Identity; German-Jewish and American-Jewish Literature—A Comparative Study; Fictions of the Holocaust; The Holocaust and its Historiography; The Major Texts; American Jewish Fiction; The Germanic Reception; and Guide to European Bibiliography.

The volume ends with a bibliography of Selected Reference Materials and Resources; an index of names, titles, and subjects; and notes on contributors and advisors.

S–159　**Some Frequently Recommended Works on American-Jewish Literature.**

Chametzky, Jules. *Our Decentralized Literature: Cultural Mediations in Selected Jewish and Southern Writers.* Amherst: University of Massachusetts Press, 1986.
PS153.J4 C45 1986

Dembo, L. S. *Monological Jew: A Literary Study.* Madison: University of Wisconsin Press, 1988.
PS153.J4 D46 1988

Guttman, Allen. *Jewish Writer in America: Assimilation and the Crisis of Identity.* New York: Oxford University Press, 1971.　PS153.J4 G8

Harap, Louis. *Creative Awakening: The Jewish Presence in Twentieth-Century American Literature, 1900–1940s.* Westport, Conn.: Greenwood Press, 1987.
PS173.J4 H29 1987

————. *Dramatic Encounters: The Jewish Presence in Twentieth-Century American Drama, Poetry, and Humor, and the Black-Jewish Literary Relationship.* Westport, Conn.: Greenwood Press, 1987.
PS173.J4 H294 1987

————. *Image of the Jew in American Literature: From Early Republic to Mass Immigration.* Philadelphia: Jewish Publication Society of America, 1974.
PS173.J4 H3

————. *In the Mainstream: The Jewish Presence in Twentieth Century American Literature, 1950s–1980s.* Westport, Conn.: Greenwood Press, 1987.
PS153.J4 H37 1987

Link, Franz, ed. *Jewish Life and Suffering as Mirrored in English and American Literature / Judisches Leben und Leiden im Spiegel der englischen und amerikanischen Literatur.* Paderborn: F. Schoningh, 1987.
PS173.J4 J49 1987

Liptzin, Solomon. *Jew in American Literature.* New York: Block, 1966.　PS173.J4 L5

Schechner, Mark. *After the Revolution: Studies in the Contemporary Jewish American Imagination.* Bloomington: Indiana University Press, 1987.
PS153.J4 S48 1987

S–160　**Martinez, Julio A., and Francisco A. Lomeli, eds.　*Chicano Literature: A Reference Guide.*** Westport, Conn.: Greenwood Press, 1985.　PS153.M4 C46

This volume is an alphabetical guide to Chicano authors since 1848, with signed articles to which selective primary and secondary bibliographies are appended. In addition to authors, there are articles on the Chicano Novel, Chicano Poetry, Chicano Theatre, the Chicana in Chicano Literature, Chicano Literature from 1942 to the Present, Chicano Literary Criticism, Chicano Children's Literature, Chicano Philosophy, Hispanic-Mexican Literature in the Southwest, and Mexican-American Literature.

To this dictionary guide are added an appendix on several non-Chicano authors of importance in Chicano studies, a Chronology of Chicano Literature, a Glossary, and a Bibliography of General Works. An index of names, selected titles, and selected subjects, and a set of notes on contributors conclude the volume.

S–161 **Eger, Ernestina.** *Bibliography of Criticism of Contemporary Chicano Literature.* Berkeley: Chicano Studies Library Publications, University of California, 1982.

Z1229.M48 E36 1982

This 295-page work has served as the standard guide to critical studies on Chicano literature.

S–162 **Tatum, Charles M.** *Selected and Annotated Bibliography of Chicano Studies.* 2d ed. Lincoln: University of Nebraska, Department of Modern Languages and Literatures, Society of Spanish and Spanish-American Studies, 1979.

Z1361.M4 T36 1979

Originally published in 1976, this descriptively and evaluatively annotated bibliography presents a total of 526 serially numbered entries. They are disposed into the following categories: Bibliographies; Background and General Interest Materials; General Readers and Anthologies; Art; Audio-Visual Materials; The Chicana; Folklore; Journals, Magazines, Newsletters, and Newspapers; Language Instruction and Linguistics; Literature (Anthologies, Bibliographies, General Criticism, Criticism of Drama, Criticism of Poetry, Criticism of Prose, Drama, Novel, Poetry, and Short Fiction); and Music. A list of useful addresses is followed by an appendix describing four courses in Chicano studies: an Introduction, a course in Chicano History; one in Chicano Literature; and one on La Chicana. The volume concludes with an index of names.

S–169 **Some Frequently Recommended Works on Chicano Literature and Chicano Studies.** (See also related works on Hispanic American Literature in section L (L–90 and following.)

Baker, Houston A., Jr. ed. *Three American Literatures: Essays in Chicano, Native American, and Asian American Literature for Teachers of American Literature.* New York: MLA, 1982. PS153.M56 T5 1982

Bruce-Novoa, Juan. *Chicano Authors: Inquiry by Interview.* Austin: University of Texas Press,1980.

PS153.M4 B7

———. *Chicano Poetry: A Response to Chaos.* Austin: University of Texas Press, 1982. PS153.M4 B73 1982

Candelaria, Cordelia. *Chicano Poetry: A Critical Introduction.* Westport, Conn.: Greenwood Press, 1986.

PS153.M4 C27 1986

Chicano Studies Periodical Index. Berkeley: University of California, Chicano Studies Library, 1978–.

Durán, Livie I., and H. Russell Bernard. *Introduction to Chicano Studies: A Reader.* 2d ed. New York: Macmillan, 1982. E184.M5 D85 1982

Herrera-Sobek, Maria, ed. *Beyond Stereotypes: The Critical Analysis of Chicana Literature.* Binghamton, N.Y.: Bilingual Press,1985. PS153.M4 B49 1985

Huerta, Jorge. *Chicano Theatre: Themes and Forms.* Ypsilanti, Mich.: Bilingual Press/Editorial Bilingüe, 1982.

PN2270.M48 H83 1982

Jiménez, Francisco. *Identification and Analysis of Chicano Literature.* New York: Bilingual Press/Editorial Bilingüe, 1979. PS153.M4 I33 1979

Leal, Luis, et al. *Decade of Chicano Literature, (1970–1979): Critical Essays and Bibliography.* Santa Barbara, Calif.: Editorial La Causa, 1982.

PS153.M4 D4 1982

Lomeli, Francisco A., adn Donaldo W. Urioste. *Chicano Perspectives in Literature: A Critical and Annotated Bibliography.* Albuquerque, N.M.: Pajarito Publications, 1976. Z1229.M48 L65

Meier, Matt S., and Feliciano Rivera. *Dictionary of Mexican-American History.* Westport, Conn.: Greenwood Press, 1981. E184.M5 M453

Robinson, Cecil. *Mexico and the Hispanic Southwest in American Literature.* Tucson: University of Arizona Press, 1977. PS173.M4 R6 1977

Rocard, Marcienne. *Children of the Sun: Mexican-Americans in the Literature of the United States.* Translation by Edward G. Brown, Jr. of *Les fils du soleil.* Tucson: University of Arizona Press, 1989.

PS173.M39 R613 1989

Shirley, Carl R., and Paula W. Shirley. *Understanding Chicano Literature.* Columbia: University of South Carolina Press, 1988. PS153.M4 S55 1988

Sommers, Joseph, and Thomás Ybarra-Frausto. *Modern Chicano Writers: A Collection of Critical Essays.* Englewood Cliffs, N.J.: Prentice-Hall, 1979.

PS153.M4 M6

Tatum, Charles M. *Chicano Literature.* Boston: Twayne Publishers, 1982. PS173.M39 T36 1982

S–170 **Cheung, King-Kok, and Stan Yogi.** *Asian American Literature: An Annotated Bibliography.* New York: MLA, 1988. Z1229.A75 C47 1988

This volume contains 3,395 generally unannotated, numbered entries of primary English language works of Asian-American literature and of secondary works in English concerning the literature of Asian-American writers in the United States and Canada. The bibliography is classified into seven sections, as follows: Bibliographical and Reference Works; Anthologies; Journals and Periodicals; Primary Sources; Secondary Sources; Literature by Non-Asians about Asians and Asian Americans; Selected Books; and Background Sources; Selected Works.

The section on Primary Sources is further divided as follows: Chinese American Literature, Japanese American Literature, Filipino American Literature, Korean American Literature, South Asian American Literature, Vietnamese and Other Southeast Asian American Literature, Literature for Children and Young Adults: Selected Books, with each subsection except the last further divided into enumerations for Prose, Poetry, and Drama. Within each division authors are listed alphabetically, with cross-references from other forms of their names.

The section on Secondary Sources is further divided as follows: General Criticism, Chinese American Literature, Japanese American Literature, Filipino American Literature, Korean American Literature, and South Asian American Literature, with each subsection further divided into enumerations of Books, Theses, and Dissertations; Articles; Interviews; Profiles; and Commentary.

The volume begins with explanatory notes which include the

criteria for making judgments of ethnic categories and ends with four indexes—of creative writers; authors of secondary materials; reviewers; and editors, translators, and illustrators.

S–179 Some Frequently Recommended Works on Asian-American Literature.

Amerasia Journal. Vol. 1–. Los Angeles: UCLA Asian American Studies Center, 1971–. 4/yr, then 2/yr. Annual bibliography.   E184.O6 A44

Baker, Houston A., Jr. ed. *Three American Literatures: Essays in Chicano, Native American, and Asian American Literature for Teachers of American Literature*. New York: MLA, 1982.   PS153.M56 T5 1982

Chin, Frank, et al., eds. *Aiiieeee! An Anthology of Asian American Writers*. Washington, D.C.: Howard University Press, 1974.   PS508.A8 A4

Kim, Elaine H. *Asian American Literature: An Introduction to the Writings and Their Social Context*. Philadelphia: Temple University Press, 1982.
PS153.A84 K55 1982

Vassanji, M. G., ed. *Meeting of Streams: South Asian Canadian Literature*. Toronto: TSAR Publications, 1985.
PR9188.2.S66 M44 1985

Wu, William F. *Yellow Peril: Chinese Americans in American Fiction 1850–1940*. Hamden, Conn.: Archon, 1982.   PS374.C46 W8

POETRY AND VERSIFICATION

See also works concerning poetry and versification in section L, Comparative and World Literature; section M, English Literature; section N, Medieval; section O, Renaissance; section P, Restoration and Eighteenth Century; section Q, Nineteenth Century; section R, Twentieth Century; and section S, American Literature.

I. BIBLIOGRAPHIES, BIBLIOGRAPHICAL GUIDES, AND BIOBIBLIOGRAPHIES

Bibliographies and guides limited to the poets of one literary period will generally be found in the poetry subsection of that period (i.e., N–17, O.II, P.II, Q.II, Q.III, and R.IV). Similarly, most of the bibliographies concerning American poets and poetry are found in section S.VI.

T–1 **Dyson, A. E., ed. *English Poetry: Select Bibliographical Guides.*** London: Oxford University Press, 1971.

Z2014.P7 E53

This volume consists of bibliographical essays by specialists citing, describing, and evaluating scholarship up to about 1970 on each of twenty major English poets. The poets and their bibliographers are as follows: Chaucer (J. A. Burrow); Spenser (Peter Bayley); Donne (W. Milgate); Herbert (Margaret Bottrall); Milton (Douglas Bush); Marvell (D. I. B. Smith); Dryden (James Kinsley); Pope (Geoffrey Tillotson); Blake (David V. Erdman); Wordsworth (J. C. Maxwell and S. C. Gill); Coleridge (John Beer); Byron (John Jump); Shelley (R. B. Woodings); Keats (Robert Gittings); Tennyson (John Dixon Hunt); Browning (Ian Jack); Arnold (James Bertram); Hopkins (Graham Storey); Yeats (Jon Stallworthy); and Eliot (Anne Ridler). Bibliographical essays treat texts, critical studies and commentary, biographies and letters, bibliographies, and background reading for each author. The discursive portion is followed by a similarly subdivided list of references, giving full citations for each item cited, along with additional works. Unhappily, there is no index.

T–5 **Spender, Stephen, and Donald Hall, eds. *Concise Encyclopedia of English and American Poets and Poetry.*** New York: Hawthorne Books, 1963. PR19.S6

Containing primarily biographical articles, this volume also includes thirty-two general articles on the national poetry of Commonwealth countries, on genres, schools, movements, and a few technical terms. Longer articles are signed with initials, and at the end of the volume is a key to the initials which presents biobibliographies of the various contributing scholars. Biographical articles give brief accounts of subjects' lives, devoting most of their extent to critical assessment. Major primary, but not secondary, works are cited in the articles. An appendix lists primary and secondary further readings for each article. There are numerous portraits of poets, some cross-references, and two indexes, of poets and of names, subjects, and terms.

T–8 **Scholarly Journals Concerned Exclusively or Primarily with English or American Poetry and Verse.**

APR   *American Poetry Review.* Vol. 1–. Philadelphia: Temple University, 1972–. 6/yr. Reviews.
PS580.A44

CP   *Concerning Poetry.* Vol. 1–. Bellingham: Western Washington State College, 1968–. 2/yr. Reviews.
PS301.C64

ConP   *Contemporary Poetry: A Journal of Criticism.* Vol. 1–. Bryn Mawr, Pa.: Bryn Mawr College, 1973–. 4/yr. Reviews. PS301.C68

Expl.   *Explicator.* Vol. 1–. Washington, D.C.: Heldref Publications, 1942–. 4/yr. Bibliography (see T–31). PR1.E9

FDP   *Four Decades of Poetry, 1890–1930.* Vol. 1–. Toronto: University of Toronto Press, 1976–. 2/yr. Reviews. PN1042

LOP   *Language of Poems.* Vol. 1–. Columbia: University of South Carolina, 1972–. Irr., usually 3/yr.
No LC number

MPS   *Modern Poetry Studies.* Buffalo, N.Y.: Modern Poetry Studies, 1970–. 3/yr. Reviews. PS301.M58

Parnassus: Poetry in Review. New York: Poetry in Review Foundation, 1972–. 2/yr. Reviews.
PN6099.6.P36

Poet and Critic. Vol. 1–. Ames: Iowa State University, 1967–.   No LC number

Poetry. Vol. 1–. Chicago: Modern Poetry Association, 1912–. 12/yr. Reviews.   PS301.P6

II.   VERSE AND SONG INDEXES

See also N–35, N–36, N–37, O–22, P–20, among other indexes limited to the verse of one literary period.

T–10 **Crum, Margaret, ed. *First Line Index of English Poetry, 1500–1800, in Manuscripts of the Bodleian Library, Oxford.*** 2 vols. Oxford: Clarendon Press, 1969. Z2014.P7 F5

This work, begun in card index form in 1932, is designed to make the Bodleian's extensive holdings in poetical manuscripts more widely accessible. More than 23,000 poems are included; excluded are manuscripts acquired after April 1961, for which only a card index is available. Entries are in alphabetical order by the first line and are sequentially numbered in an alphanumeric system. Entries give the first line of the poem in modernized spelling, cross-references to variant forms of the first line, the last line of the usual version of the poem, the author's name, the poem's title, and other information derived from the manuscript. After editorial notes (chiefly referring to printed versions of the poem), the entry concludes with a list of all the Bodleian manuscripts in which the poem is found. In the list autograph manuscripts are given a line of their own, while others are enumerated in alphabetical and numerical order by Bodleian shelf mark. Five indexes complete the second volume: 1, an index of Bodleian manuscripts by shelf marks (*Summary Catalogue* number is given in brackets [see H–12]); 2, an index of authors; 3, an index of names mentioned; 4, an index of original authors of works translated, paraphrased, or imitated (with an index of the Psalms); 5, an index of references to composers of tunes and settings named or quoted.

T–18 ***Index of American Periodical Verse.*** Metuchen, N.J.: Scarecrow Press, 1971–.   Z1231.P7 I47

This annual author-title index analyzes some 200 North American periodicals, including both popular and little magazines, for current poetry. Some 4,000 contemporary poets are included.

See also the three retrospective indexes published by Scarecrow, *Contemporary American Poetry: A Checklist*, compiled by Lloyd M. Davis and Robert Irwin (1975) [Z1231.P7 D38], which treats some 1,100 poets of the 1950s and 1960s, *Contemporary American Poetry: A Checklist: Second Series, 1973–1983*, also by Davis (1985) [Z1231.P7 D38 1985], and *Contemporary Poets in American Anthologies 1960–1977* compiled by Kirby Congdon (1978) [Z1231.P7 C65], which analyzes several hundred anthologies. Other indexes of current poetry include almost all the general periodical indexes, such as the *Reader's Guide* (D–15), the *American Humanities Index* (D–18), and the *British Humanities Index* (D–17), as well as the current indexes to little magazines (D–27).

III.   ANTHOLOGIES AND COLLECTIONS—BIBLIOGRAPHIES AND INDEXES

T–20 ***Granger's Index to Poetry.*** 8th ed. Edited by William James Smith and William F. Bernhardt. New York: Columbia University Press, 1986.   PN1022.G7 1986

Each edition of this Index provides first-line, author, title, and subject indexes to collected volumes of poetry published during a definite period. This edition indexes a total of 405 anthologies published between 1970 and 1985. A total of more than 50,000 poems are indexed. More than 5,000 subject categories are used.

Because each edition keeps some anthologies, adds others, and drops many, all of them are potentially significant for research. The original edition by Edith Granger was published in 1904; the second in 1918; a supplement for anthologies published in 1919–1928 in 1929. The third in 1940 was followed by a supplement for 1938–1944 in 1953; the fourth edition in 1953 by a supplement for 1951–1955 publications in 1957. The fifth edition (1962) was followed in 1967 by a supplement on anthologies published 1960–1965. The sixth edition (1973) indexed work in 514 anthologies published before the end of 1970. It was supplemented in 1978 with analysis of some 115 new anthologies published 1970–1977. The seventh edition (1982) indexed works in 248 anthologies published 1970–1981.

It should be noted that the first three editions also indexed prose selections and that the fourth, fifth, and sixth editions combine the title and first-line indexes. An extremely handy reference aid is the *Compilation of Works Listed in Granger's Index to Poetry, 1904–1978: A Cumulative and Complete Listing by Granger Symbol, Title, and Author of Over 1500 Works Analyzed and Indexed in Granger's Index to Poetry from the First Edition of 1904 to the Edition of 1978*, prepared by the Editorial Board of the Granger Book Company (Great Neck, N.Y.: The Company 1980) [Z7156.A1 C64], which includes a table of the eleven editions and supplements published through 1978, and for each anthology lists all editions and indexes in which its contents were analyzed.

T–21 ***Poetry Index Annual: A Title, Author, First Line, and Subject Index to Poetry in Anthologies [1981–].*** Great Neck, N.Y.: Poetry Index, 1982–.   PN1022.P63

This annual aims to index all English language anthologies published during the year preceding the year of issue. Its coverage is more extensive than *Granger's Index* (T–20), especially with regard to publications from small presses. It is useful for identifying poems on subjects, or poems by lesser-known writers. Issues are not cumulative.

T–22 **Hoffman, Herbert H. *Hoffman's Index to Poetry: European and Latin American Poetry in Anthologies.*** Metuchen, N.J.: Scarecrow Press, 1985.

This massive volume indexes about 14,000 poems from about 100 anthologies by author, title, and first line. Included are English translation from European and Latin American poems.

T–23 ***Chicorel, Marietta, ed. Chicorel Index to Poetry in Anthologies and Collections in Print.*** 4 vols. New York: Chicorel, 1974.   PN1022.C55

These volumes, which constitute volumes 5, 5A, 5B, and 5C of the *Chicorel Index*, analyze more than 1,000 anthologies and collections, including collections of the works of single poets. It is a single alphabetical index of authors, editors, translators, adapters, titles, first lines, and collection titles. Complete bibliographic information is found only under the main, author entry. A list of the titles of analyzed collections is appended, but no information about principles for selection is provided. Volume 5C has an index of general subjects (e.g., satirical poetry, women's poetry, religious poetry).

The second edition, published 1975–1977, adds anthologies published in 1974 and removes collection titles to a separate index of analyzed works.

T–24 ***Chicorel Index to Poetry in Anthologies and Collections: Retrospective Index to Out-of-Print Titles.*** 4 vols. New York: Chicorel, 1975.   PN1022.C54

These volumes, which constitute volumes 6, 6A, 6B, and 6C of the *Chicorel Index*, analyze collections that have gone out of print since about 1967. The arrangement of the volumes is identical with that of the in-print index (T–23).

T–25 **Marcan, Peter.** ***Poetry Themes: A Bibliographical Index to Subject Anthologies and Related Criticism in the English Language, 1875–1975.*** Hamden, Conn.: Linnet, 1977.   PN1022.M3

A total of 1,964 serially numbered entries classify anthologies and related studies and criticism, including theses and dissertations, in an elaborate universal classification, the main divisions of which are as follows: The World of Knowledge, Religion, The Human Life Cycle, Customs and Manners, Work, Education, The Arts, Topography, History, Science and The Natural World. Each subclassified section includes a list of anthologies and a bibliography of works about poetry on that subject or theme. This extremely useful volume concludes with an index of authors and compilers.

T–26 **Chapman, Dorothy.** ***Index to Black Poetry.*** Boston: G. K. Hall, 1974.   PS153.N5 C45

Originally titled *Black Poetry Index*, this volume analyzes a total of ninety-four books and thirty-three anthologies. It consists of three separate indexes, of first lines and titles, of subjects, and of authors. Poems by a total of about 5,000 black poets are cited.

T–27 **Bruncken, Herbert.** ***Subject Index to Poetry: A Guide for Adult Readers.*** Chicago: American Library Association, 1940.   PN1021.B7

This volume's subject analysis is particularly strong in its citation of minor American verse of the nineteenth and earlier twentieth centuries. A total of 215 anthologies are analyzed by subject matter, topic, or idea. Categories include names of persons and places, fields of interest, activities, classes and groups of people, things, attitudes, states of mind, and aspects of civilization.

In addition to this subject index, subject access to single poems is aided by the subject analyses in Granger (T–20), and the subject/topic arrangements of several dictionaries of quotations (see especially Stevenson, K–67, and Evans, K–68).

T–28 **Sears, Minnie E., and Phyllis Crawford.** ***Song Index: An Index to More Than 12,000 Songs in 177 Song Collections Comprising 262 Volumes.*** New York: H. W. Wilson, 1926.   ML128.S3 S3

Songs (that is, poems that have been set to music) are indexed in this volume, which includes many poems not in Granger (T–20), particularly English translations of foreign songs. Entries give titles, first lines, authors' names, and composers' names in one alphabet. Full bibliographical information is given under the song title, with cross-references from other entries, including variant, alternate, and translated titles.

A *Supplement: An Index to More Than 7,000 Songs in 104 Song Collections Comprising 124 Volumes* (New York: Wilson, 1934) [ML128.S3 S31 1966], identically arranged, has been reprinted with the original index in a single volume (Hamden, Conn.: Archon, 1966).

A partial continuation of Sears is Robert Leigh's *Index to Song Books: A Title Index to over 11,000 Copies of Almost 6,800 Songs in 111 Song Books Published* [in the United States] *between 1933 and 1962* (New York: Da Capo, 1964) [ML128.S3 L45], that is limited to those collections that contain both words and music (i.e., "songbooks"). A volume that complements both Sears and Leigh is Desiree De Charms and Paul F. Breed's *Songs in Collections: An Index* (Detroit: Gale, 1966) [ML128.S3 D37], which indexes a total of 9,493 songs in 411 collections, in a main index of titles, first lines, and authors, as well as in a series of separate sections for composed songs, anonymous and folk songs, carols, and sea chanties.

IV. INDEXES OF EXPLICATION AND CHECKLISTS OF CRITICISM

T–30 **Kuntz, Joseph M., and Nancy C. Martinez.** ***Poetry Explication: A Checklist of Interpretation since 1925 of British and American Poems Past and Present.*** 3d ed. Boston: G. K. Hall, 1980.   Z2014.P7K8 1980

This volume indexes some 12,000 explications of poems less than 500 lines in length which appeared 1925–1962 in any of the analyzed books and literary periodicals, a list of which is appended to the volume. Omitted are articles of criticism concerned with parts rather than the whole of the work, paraphrase and metrical analysis not concerned with the total effect, and commentary exclusively concerned with sources and circumstances of a poem's composition. When uncertainty arose about particular cases, they were included. Arrangement is alphabetical by poet, then by title, and then by author of the explication. Earlier editions are entirely replaced by this volume, which is, in turn, supplemented by the annual checklist of explications published in the *Explicator* (T–31).

T–31 **"A Check List of Explication for 1943–."** *Explicator.* vol. 1– (1942–).   PR1.E9

Unless otherwise noted, this annual checklist, limited to English explications of works of English and American literature, includes items that appeared in the previous year, in selected journals and books, though not in the *Explicator*, which is separately indexed. Included are explications of short and long poems, plays, and both fictive and nonfictive prose; only items of unquestioned explicatory merit and substance are included, though nothing is omitted because of brevity or concern with minor subjects. Arrangement is alphabetical by author and then by author of the explication. The work(s) treated, unless clear from the title, are given in brackets at the end of the citation. Because of its highly selective character, this work should be used as a guide to some explications of merit rather than as an exhaustive bibliography of all explications. For such coverage, all current bibliographies treating a particular work must be consulted.

T–32 Walcott, Charles C., and J. Edwin Whitesell, eds. *Explicator Cyclopedia.* 3 vols. Chicago: Quadrangle Books, 1966–1968. PR401.E9

These three volumes reprint abstracts of the best explications published in the first twenty volumes of the *Explicator* (1942–1962). Volume 1 treats Modern Poetry; volume 2 treats Traditional Poetry, Medieval to Late Victorian; and volume 3 treats Explications of Prose, both fiction and nonfiction. Volumes are arranged alphabetically by author, then title, with abstracts of articles explicating individual works then given in alphabetical order by the names of their authors.

T–34 Cline, Gloria Stark, and Jeffrey A. Baker, comps. *Index to Criticisms of British and American Poetry.* Metuchen, N.J.: Scarecrow Press, 1973. PR89.C5

This index to 2,862 works of criticism, emphasizing interpretations published 1960–1970 in some thirty journals and a few books, treats a total of 1,510 poems by 285 different English and American poets of all periods. It is in two parts. Part 1, arranged by literary author, contains brief references first to the authors of works of general criticism about a poet and then references to authors of criticism of individual poems. Part 2, the main index, cites critical works in a single alphabetical list by the name of the critic. A bibliography of books (collections of criticism) and journals analyzed and an index of titles cited conclude the volume.

T–35 Alexander, Harriet S. *American and British Poetry: A Guide to the Criticism, 1925–1978.* Athens, Ohio: Swallow Press, 1984. Z1231.P7 A44 1984

This work includes criticism of poems of up to 1,000 lines in length. It has about 20,000 entries citing both articles and sections of books and including both explications and longer critical studies.

V. HISTORIES OF ENGLISH OR AMERICAN POETRY

T–40 Courthope, W. J. *History of English Poetry.* 6 vols. London: Macmillan, 1895–1910. PR502.C8

This massive work treats the history of poetry (including dramatic poetry) from the Middle Ages through the romantic movement as an aspect of the history of culture, focusing on political and intellectual currents and their impact on poetry. Each volume includes a detailed table of contents. A cumulative general index of authors and titles concludes volume 6.

T–43 Foakes, R. A., ed. *Routledge History of English Poetry.* London: Routledge and Kegan Paul, 1977–. PR502.R58

This first major history since that of Courthope (T–40) is planned to occupy six volumes, each by a specialist author. Each volume will follow the emphases and argument developed by its author, though all will be characterized by a more intensive focus on the history of poetry (its composition, character, and reception) than on the place of poetry in a general history of culture. Each will also provide bibliographical and chronological support for its text. The individual volumes are as follows:

Vol. 1. *Old English and Middle English Poetry*, by Derek A. Pearsall (1977). This volume has a special focus on matters of provenance and audience. It contains two massive appendixes, the first on technical terms (mainly metrical) and the second providing a chronological table from 410 to 1557 (Tottel's *Songes and Sonettes*) in which historical events, the composition date of poems, and the dates of important manuscripts of poetry are indicated.

Vol. 2. Not yet published.

Vol. 3. *Restoration and Eighteenth-Century Poetry, 1660–1780*, by Eric Rothstein (1981), is divided into three sections treating poetry of the Restoration, the early eighteenth century, and the later eighteenth century respectively, with two appendixes, the first a chronology listing with commentary and bibliography the major poems of each year, and the second listing the poets laureate.

Vol. 4. *Poetry of the Romantic Period*, by James Robert de Jager Jackson (1980), focuses on the contemporary conventions and traditions in which the major poets wrote, and provides an appended Chronological Table that cites additional works with brief commentaries.

Vol. 5. Not yet published.

Vol. 6. Not yet published.

T–45 Bush, Douglas. *English Poetry: The Main Currents from Chaucer to the Present.* London: Oxford University Press, 1952. PR502.B88

One of the two most frequently recommended single-volume histories of English poetry, this work is disposed into six chapters, from the Middle Ages to the modern period. Beginning with Chaucer, and generally concentrating on main figures, the history has as its leading theme the interplay of convention and revolt in generating continuity and difference within the context of a world progressively thought less and less divinely ordained and more and more an endless natural order. The volume is without notes or bibliography; it concludes with an index of names.

The other often-recommended single-volume history is Herbert J. Grierson and James C. Smith, *Critical History of English Poetry*, 2d rev. ed. (London: Chatto and Windus, 1947) [PR502.G76 1947], originally published in 1944. Also recommended are the more recent volumes by F. W. Bateson, *English Poetry and the English Language*, 3d ed. (Oxford: Clarendon Press, 1973) [PR502.B3 1973], and *English Poetry: A Critical Introduction*, 2d ed. (London: Longmans, 1966) [PR502.B29]; the volume by T. R. Barnes, *English Verse: Voice and Movement from Wyatt to Yeats* (Cambridge: Cambridge University Press, 1967) [PR401.B3]; and the recent volume by G. S. Fraser, *Short History of English Poetry* (Totowa, N.J.: Barnes and Noble, 1981) [PR502 .F7 1981].

T–46 Pearce, Roy Harvey. *Continuity of American Poetry.* Princeton, N.J.: Princeton University Press, 1961. PS303.P4

Regarded as the best general review of the theory and history of American poetry, this volume argues for the centrality of Walt Whitman in the development of American poetry. An alternate perspective, arguing for the centrality of Ralph Waldo Emerson, is put forward by Hyatt H. Waggoner in *American Poets, from the Puritans to the Present Day*, rev. ed. (Baton Rouge: Louisiana State University Press, 1984) [PS303.W3 1984]. Other recommended one-volume surveys of American poetry are Henry W. Wells, *American Way of Poetry* (New York: Columbia University Press, 1943) [PS303.W4]; Donald B. Stauffer, *Short History of American Poetry* (New York: Dutton, 1974) [PS303.S67]; and Albert Gelphi, *Tenth Muse: The Psyche of the American Poet* (Cambridge: Harvard University Press, 1975) [PS303.G4].

T–47 **Perkins, David.** *History of Modern Poetry.* 2 vols. Vol. 1. *From the 1890's to the High Modernist Mode.* Vol. 2. *Modernism and After.* Cambridge: Harvard University Press, 1976–87.   PR610.P4

This history traces developments in modern poetry as they are related to changing theories, audiences, critical premises and procedures, and developments in the other arts, as well as to changes in social, political, and intellectual history. The first volume treats poetry to the mid–1920s, considering some 130 major and minor poets on both sides of the Atlantic. Volume 2, covers poetry from the 1920s to the present, considering some 160 American and British Poets. There is a detailed table of contents at the beginning and brief general indexes at the ends of each volume. No footnotes or bibliography are provided.

T–48 **Fairchild, Hoxie Neale.** *Religious Trends in English Poetry.* 6 vols. New York: Columbia University Press, 1939–1968.   PR508.R4 F3

This massive history of religious thought and feeling in post-Renaissance English poetry is divided into the following volumes:

Vol. 1. *1700–1740, Protestantism and the Cult of Sentiment.*

Vol. 2. *1740–1780, Religious Sentimentalism in the Age of Johnson.*

Vol. 3. *1780–1830, Romantic Faith.*

Vol. 4. *1830–1880, Christianity and Romanticism in the Victorian Era.*

Vol. 5. *1880–1920, Gods of a Changing Poetry.*

Vol. 6. *1920–1965, Valley of Dry Bones.*

T–49 **Some Frequently Recommended Histories of Poetry over One or Several Periods of English or American Literary History.**

Old English

Kennedy, Charles W. *Earliest English Poetry: A Critical Survey of the Poetry Written before the Norman Conquest.* New York: Oxford University Press, 1943.   PR201.K4

Renaissance

Berdan, John M. *Early Tudor Poetry, 1485–1547.* New York: Macmillan, 1920.   PR521.B4

Bush, Douglas. *Mythology and the Renaissance Tradition in English Poetry.* Rev. ed. New York: Norton, 1963.   PR508.M9 B8 1963

Peterson, Douglas L. *English Lyric from Wyatt to Donne: A History of the Plain and Eloquent Styles.* Princeton, N.J.: Princeton University Press, 1967.   PR529.L894

Smith, Hallet. *Elizabethan Poetry: A Study in Conventions, Meaning, and Expression.* Cambridge: Harvard University Press, 1952.   PR531.S6

Restoration

Hamilton, K. G. *Two Harmonies: Poetry and Prose in the Seventeenth Century.* Oxford: Oxford University Press, 1963.   PR541.H3

Miner, Earl. *Metaphysical Mode from Donne to Dryden.* Princeton, N.J.: Princeton University Press, 1969.   PR541.M49

Colonial American

Otis, William B. *American Verse, 1625–1807: A History.* New York: Moffatt, Yard, 1909.   PS312.O7

Eighteenth Century

Sutherland, James. *Preface to Eighteenth Century Poetry.* Oxford: Oxford University Press, 1948. Reprint, with additions, 1962.   PR551.S8 1962

Thorpe, Peter. *Eighteenth Century English Poetry.* Chicago: Nelson-Hall, 1975. Excellent bibliography.   PR551.T45 1975

Romantic

Bush, Douglas. *Mythology and the Romantic Tradition in English Poetry.* Cambridge: Harvard University Press, 1934. Reissued with a new preface, 1969.   PR508.M9 B85 1969

Gérard, Albert. *English Romantic Poetry: Ethos, Structure, and Symbol in Coleridge, Wordsworth, Shelley, and Keats.* Berkeley and Los Angeles: University of California Press, 1968.   PR5888.G4

Grierson, H. J. C. *Lyrical Poetry from Blake to Hardy.* New York: Harcourt, Brace, 1929.   PR589.L8 G68

Victorian

Ifor, Evans B. *English Poetry in the Later Nineteenth Century.* 2d ed. London: Methuen, 1966.   PR591.E8 1966a

Pinto, Vivian de Sola. *Crisis in English Poetry, 1880–1940.* 5th ed. London: Hutchinson, 1967.   PR601.P57 1967

Modern

Bailey, John. *Romantic Survival: A Study in Poetic Evolution.* London: Chatto and Windus, 1969.   PR590.B27 1969

Bowra, C. M. *Background of Modern Poetry.* Oxford: Clarendon Press, 1946.   PR584.B6

Davie, Donald. *Thomas Hardy and British Poetry.* Oxford: Oxford University Press, 1972.   PR4754.D3

Deutsch, Babette. *Poetry in Our Time: A Critical Survey of Poetry in the English-Speaking World, 1900–1960.* 2d ed. Garden City, N.Y.: Doubleday, 1963.   PR601.D43 1963

Hughes, Glen. *Imagism and the Imagists.* Stanford: Stanford University Press, 1931.   PR605.I6 H8

Kermode, Frank. *Romantic Image.* New York: Viking, 1964.   PN1111.K4 1963

Maxwell, D. E. S. *Poets of the Thirties.* London: Routledge and Kegan Paul, 1969.   PR610.M3 1969

Press, John. *Map of Modern English Verse.* London: Oxford University Press, 1969.   PR604.P7

Rosenthal, M. L. *Modern Poets. A Critical Introduction.* New York: Oxford University Press, 1960.   PR601.R6

————. *New Poets: American and British Poetry since World War Two.* New York: Oxford University Press, 1967.   PS326.R6

Thwaite, Anthony. *Twentieth-Century English Poetry: An Introduction.* New York: Barnes and Noble, 1978.   PR601.T56 1978

Modern American

Gregory, Horace, and Marya Zaturenska. *History of American Poetry, 1900–1940.* New York: Harcourt, Brace, 1946.   PS324.G7 1946

VI.   THE LANGUAGE OF POETRY

See also section X.V, Style and Stylistics, as well as many references in section I, Language, Linguistics, and Philology.

T–50   Deutsch, Babette.   *Poetry Handbook: A Dictionary of Terms.* 4th ed.   New York: Funk and Wagnalls, 1974.
PN44.5.D4 1974b

This volume contains brief definitions, with illustrations from English poetry, of terms used in the description of poetry.   There are extensive cross-references and an appended index of poets cited.

For prosodic terms see also the handbook of Beum and Shapiro (T–65).   Poetic terms are also treated in the standard handbooks of literary terms, in particular the *Princeton Handbook of Poetic Terms* (T–52), *Princeton Encyclopedia of Poetry and Poetics* (L–21), the Shipley *Dictionary of World Literary Terms* (L–11), and the Abrams *Glossary of Literary Terms* (L–13).   Among the most extensive dictionaries of this sort is the *Dictionnaire de poétique et de rhétorique* by Henri Morier, 3d ed. (Paris: Presses universitaires de France, 1981) [PN1021.M6 1981], which, though centered on French-language material, is in many regards applicable to the study of English poetry.

T–52   *Princeton Handbook of Poetic Terms.* Ed. by Alex Preminger; Frank J. Warnke and O. B. Hardison, Jr., Associate Editors; with a select reading list by T. V. F. Brogan.   Princeton: Princeton University Press, 1986.
PN1042.P75 1986

This work is a selection of 462 entries from the original and revised versions of the *Princeton Encyclopedia of Poetry and Poetics* (L–21), with an emphasis on prosodic and poetic terms.   Twenty-nine articles are new or totally rewritten, many more have been revised and updated, and many left as they were in the original work.   The preface gives some account of the entries which fall into these categories.

The reading list by T. V. F. Brogan, "Poetic Genres, Modes, and Forms: A Select Reading List," supplements the bibliographies appended to entries by offering a general reading list with references for the more common forms, which also lists the best and most recent work on the topics covered.

T–53   Leech, Geoffrey N.   *Linguistic Guide to English Poetry.* London: Longmans, 1969.   PR508.L3 L4

This introduction to stylistics regarded as the study of the poet's language is in twelve chapters, as follows: 1, Poetry and the Language of Past and Present; 2, The Creative Use of Language; 3, Varieties of Poetic License; 4, Foregrounding and Interpretation; 5, Verbal Repetition; 6, Patterns of Sound; 7, Metre; 8, The Irrational in Poetry; 9, Figurative Language; 10, Honest Deceptions; 11, Implications of Context; 12, Ambiguity and Indeterminacy.   Bibliographical notes, suggestions for further reading, and a general index conclude this volume.

T–58   Some Frequently Recommended Works on the Language of Poetry.

Diction

Arthos, John.   *Language of Natural Description in Eighteenth Century Poetry.*   Ann Arbor: University of Michigan Press, 1949.   PR555.L3 A7

Barfield, Owen.   *Poetic Diction: A Study in Meaning.* 3d ed.   Middletown, Conn.: Wesleyan University Press, 1973.   PN1031.B3 1973

Davie, Donald.   *Purity of Diction in English Verse.*   New ed.   New York: Schocken Books, 1967.
PR555.L3 D3 1967

Easthope, Antony.   *Poetry as Discourse.*   London: Methuen, 1983.   PR508.D57 E2 1983

Empson, William.   *Structure of Complex Words.*   London: Chatto and Windus, 1951.   PE1585.E6 1951a

Groom, Bernard.   *Diction of Poetry from Spenser to Bridges.*   Toronto: University of Toronto Press, 1955.
PR508.D5 G7

Hungerland, Isabel P. C.   *Poetic Discourse.*   Berkeley and Los Angeles: University of California Press, 1958.
PN1031.H74

Levin, Samuel R.   *Linguistic Structures in Poetry.*   The Hague: Mouton, 1962.

Miles, Josephine.   *Continuity of Poetic Language: The Primary Language of Poetry, 1540's–1940's.*   Berkeley: University of California Press, 1948–1951.
PE1541.M48

————.   *Eras and Modes in English Poetry.*   2d ed.   Berkeley and Los Angeles: University of California Press, 1964.   PR502.M48

————.   *Major Adjectives in English Poetry from Wyatt to Auden.*   Berkeley: University of California Press, 1946.   PR508.V6 M5

————.   *Poetry and Change: Donne, Milton, Wordsworth, and the Equilibrium of the Present.*   Berkeley, Los Angeles, London: University of California Press, 1974.
PR502.M49

————.   *Renaissance, Eighteenth Century, and Modern Language in English Poetry: A Tabular View.*   Berkeley and Los Angeles: University of California Press, 1960.   PR508.L3 M5

Nowottny, Winifred.   *Language Poets Use.*   London: Athlone Press, 1962.   PN1031.N6

Partridge, Eric.   *Shakespeare's Bawdy: A Literary and Psychological Essay and a Comprehensive Glossary.*   New ed.   London: Routledge and Kegan Paul, 1955.
PR2892.P27 1955

Pottle, Frederick A.   *Idiom of Poetry.*   Rev. ed.   Ithaca, N.Y.: Cornell University Press, 1946.   PN1055.P6

Quayle, Thomas.   *Poetic Diction: A Study of Eighteenth Century Verse.*   London: Methuen, 1924.   PR555.L3 Q3

Rubel, Veré L.   *Poetic Diction in the English Renaissance from Skelton through Spenser.*   New York: MLA, 1941.   PR525.L3 R82

Wimsatt, W. K., Jr.   *Philosophic Words: A Study of Style and Meaning in the "Rambler" and "Dictionary" of Samuel Johnson.*   New Haven: Yale University Press, 1948.   PR3538.W48

Wyld, H. C.   *Some Aspects of the Diction of English Poetry.*   Oxford: Blackwell, 1933.   PR508.L3 W9

Grammar

Berry, Francis.   *Poet's Grammar: Person, Time, and Mood in Poetry.*   London: Routledge and Kegan Paul, 1958.
PR502.B43

Jakobson, Roman.   *Poetry of Grammar and Grammar of Poetry.*   Ed. by Stephen Rudy.   Vol. 3 of his *Selected Writings.*   2d ed.   The Hague: Mouton, 1981.
P27.J332 1962 vol. 3

Syntax

Baker, William E. *Syntax in English Poetry, 1870–1930.*
    Berkeley and Los Angeles: University of California
    Press, 1967.   PR595.L3 B3

Davie, Donald. *Articulate Energy: An Enquiry into the Syntax of English Poetry.* 2d ed. London: Routledge and
    Kegan Paul, 1976.   PR508.S95 D3 1976

Redin, Mats Algot. *Word-Order in English Verse from Pope
    to Sassoon.* Uppsala: Almqvist and Wiksell, 1925.

**T–59 Some Frequently Recommended Guides to the Reading of
Poetry.**

Boulton, Marjorie. *Anatomy of Poetry.* London: Routledge
    and Kegan Paul, 1953.   PN1042.B6

Brooks, Cleanth, and Robert Penn Warren. *Understanding
    Poetry.* 3d ed. New York: Holt, Rinehart and Winston, 1960.   PR1109.B676 1960

Ciardi, John, and Miller Williams. *How Does a Poem
    Mean?* 2d ed. Boston: Houghton Mifflin, 1975.
                                              PS586.C53 1975

Eastman, Max. *Enjoyment of Poetry.* One-vol. ed. New
    York: Scribner, 1951.   PN1031.E32

Graves, Robert. *On English Poetry: Being an Irregular Approach to This Art.* London: Heinemann, 1922.
                                              PR502.G7 1922a

Hill, Archibald A. *Constituent and Pattern in Poetry.* Austin: University of Texas Press, 1976.   PR1042.H46

Lewis, C. Day. *Poetic Image.* London: J. Cape, 1947.
                                              PN1042.D39

Pound, Ezra. *ABC of Reading.* Norfolk, Conn.: New Directions, 1951.   PN59.P6

Roberts, Philip D. *How Poetry Works: The Elements of English Poetry.* Harmondsworth, Eng.: Penguin, 1986.
                                              PR508.V45 R6 1986

Rosenblatt, Louise. *Reader, the Text, and the Poem.* Carbondale: Southern Illinois University Press, 1978.
                                              PN45.R587

Rosenheim, Edward W., Jr. *What Happens in Literature: A
    Student's Guide to Poetry, Drama, and Fiction.* Chicago: University of Chicago Press, 1960.   PN45.R6

Scholes, Robert. *Elements of Poetry.* New York: Oxford
    University Press, 1969.   PN1042.S3

Stauffer, Donald A. *Nature of Poetry.* New York: Norton,
    1946.   PN1031.S78

Williams, John. *Reading Poetry: A Contextual Introduction.*
    London: Edward Arnold, 1985.   PR502.W56 1985

Wright, George T. *Poet in the Poem: The Personae of Eliot,
    Yeats, and Pound.* Berkeley and Los Angeles: University of California Press, 1960.   PS3509.L43 Z95

VII. PROSODY AND VERSIFICATION

**T–60 Brogan, T. V. F. *English Versification, 1570–1980: A
Reference Guide with a Global Appendix.*** Baltimore: Johns
Hopkins University Press, 1981.   Z2015.V37 B76

This magnificent bibliography, the aim of which is to list all
known studies of English versification from the Renaissance
to the present and all major studies of the versification of any
language, is organized by theoretical subject. It contains
more than 6,000 entries that, except in the appendixes, include synoptic, interpretative, contextualizing, and evaluative
annotations. The entries are alphanumerically designated in
fourteen categories, grouped into two main parts and an appendix. Part I, Modern English Verse (since Wyatt), contains nine sections as follows: A. Primary Reference Works
(Histories, Collections of Essays, Earlier Bibliographies); B.
General Studies; C. Sound; D. Rhythm; E. Meter; F. Syntax
and Grammar; G. Stanza Structures; H. Visual (Typographic)
Structures; I. The Poem in Performance. Part II, Early English Verse (to Skelton), contains two sections: J. Old English;
K. Middle English. There are three appendixes: L. Global
Versification (subdivided into General and Comparative Studies and then Studies on the Versification of Individual Language Groups); M. Classical Versification; N. Poetry and
Music (as metrical analogues).

Because each study is entered only once, a system of extensive and systematic cross-references is used. An annotated
list of works consulted, an index of poets and poems, and an
index of scholarly authors conclude this massive volume.

**T–61 Omond, Thomas Stewart. *English Metrists: Being a
Sketch of English Prosodical Criticism from Elizabethan
Times to the Present Day.*** Oxford: Clarendon Press, 1921.
                                              PE1515.O4

This volume contains references only to work written in English on English metrics, but it remains the most extensive history of critical theory on verse structure, containing a discursive amplified commentary particularly on the work of theorists and historians of the eighteenth and ninteenth centuries.
It is organized in two parts, the first treating all those materials
concerned with quantitative metrics and the second treating
those concerned with accentual/syllabic metrics.

Other essentially historical surveys of English prosody include the following frequently recommended works:

Alden, Raymond M., ed. *English Verse: Specimens Illustrating Its Principles and History.* New York: Henry
    Holt, 1903.   PE1505.A3

Hamer, Enid. *Metres of English Poetry.* 4th ed. London:
    Methuen, 1930.   PE1505.H3

Ing, Catherine. *Elizabethan Lyrics: A Study in the Development of English Metres and Their Relation to Poetic
    Effect.* London: Chatto and Windus, 1951.
                                              PR525.N415 1951

Kaluza, Max. *Short History of English Versification.* London: G. Allen, 1911.   PE1505.K33

Lewis, Charlton M. *Foreign Sources of Modern English
    Versification.* New Haven: Yale University Press,
    1898.   PE1505.L55 1898a

Saintsbury, George. *History of English Prosody from the
    12th Century to the Present Day.* 2d ed. 3 vols.
    London: Macmillan, 1923.   PE1505.S163
    Also published in a one-volume abridged format under
    the title *Historical Manual of English Prosody* (London: Macmillan, 1910).   PE1505.S18

Schipper, Jakob. *Englische Metrik in historischer und systematischer Entwicklung dargestellt.* 2 vols. in 3.
    Bonn, 1881–1888. A one-volume abridgment, *Grundriss der englischen Metrik* (Vienna: W. Braunmuller,
    1895) [PE1509.S3], was translated into English with
    the title *History of English Versification* (Oxford:
    Clarendon Press, 1910).   PE1505.S3

Tarlinskaja, Marina. *English Verse: Theory and History.*
    The Hague: Mouton, 1976.   PE1505.T3613

Thompson, John. *Founding of English Metre.* New York:
    Columbia University Press, 1961.   PE1505.T46 1961

Wyld, H. C. K. *Studies in English Rhymes from Surrey to
    Pope: A Chapter in the History of English.* London,
    1923.   PE1517.W8

For a historical treatment of American versification see Gay
Wilson Allen, *American Prosody* (New York: American
Book Co., 1935) [PS303.A5 1934].

T–62 **Wimsatt, W. K., ed.** *Versification: Major Language Types.* New York: New York University Press for the Modern Language Association, 1972.   PN1942.W52

This volume consists of sixteen essays, each written by a specialist, on versification in general, on the versification system of one language group, or on an aspect of English versification. The articles are primarily historical and focus on exposition of the systems actually employed by poets. The essays and their specialist authors are as follows: Elements of Versification (John Lotz); Classical Chinese (Hans H. Frankel); Japanese (Robert H. Brower); Biblical Hebrew (Perry B. Yoder); Classical Greek and Latin (A. Thomas Cole); Slavic (Edward Stankiewicz); Uralic (John Lotz); Germanic (W. P. Lehmann); Celtic (Charles W. Dunn); Italian (A. Bartlett Giamatti); Spanish (Lowry Nelson, Jr.); French (Jacqueline Flescher); English I: Historical (Paul Fussell, Jr.); English II: Bibliographical (Rae Ann Nager); English III: The Iambic Pentameter (Morris Halle and Samuel Jay Keyser); and Verse and Music (Monroe C. Beardsley). Each essay concludes with bibliographical notes and a selected bibliography of further readings. Brief biobibliographies of each scholar are provided.

The bibliographical essay by Rae Ann Nager (English II: Bibliography) contains a total of 126 annotated entries, divided into four main parts, with subsections, as follows: I. Bibliographical Guides; II. Theoretical and Analytical Studies; III. Special Aspects (Phonology, Linguistics and Verse, Verse and Music, Prose Rhythm); IV. Historical Studies (General History, Old English, Middle English, Renaissance, Milton, 18th Century, and 1800 to the Present). This bibliography is supplemented by Nager's "Selective Bibliography of Recent Work on English Prosody," *Style* 11 (1977); 136–170, which contains 285 entries citing work published 1968–1976.

T–63 **Brogan, T. V. F.** *Verseform: A Comparative Bibliography.* Baltimore: Johns Hopkins University Press, 1988.   Z7156.V6 B76 1988

T–64 **Di Cristo, Albert.** *Soixante et dix ans de recherches en prosodie (Bibliographie alphabétique, thématique, et chronologique).* Aix-en-Provence: Université de Provence and the CNRS, 1975.   Z7004.P5 D52

This volume presents a sheer alphabetical list of 4,390 numbered items concerned with linguistic prosody, followed by an index of the periodicals examined.

T–65 **Shapiro, Karl and Robert Beum.** *Prosody Handbook.* New York: Harper and Row, 1965.   PN1042.S57

This work contains a total of nineteen chapters treating aspects of prosody from the smallest to the largest elements. The chapters are as follows: Prosody as a Study; Poetry and Verse; Syllables; Color, Stress, Quantity, Pitch; The Foot; The Line; Accentual and Syllabic Verse; Meter and Rhythm; The Uses of Meter; Tempo; Rhyme; The Uses of Rhyme; The Stanza; Stanza Forms; The Sonnet; Blank Verse; Free Verse; Classical Prosody; Prosody and Period (synopsis by periods of significant developments in the history of English prosody); Scansions and Comments. In addition, this volume contains an extensive glossary and a chronologically arranged bibliography.

Another useful handbook for students of English verse is Joseph Malof's *Manual of English Meters* (Bloomington: Indiana University Press, 1970) [PE1505.M3 1970], which contains seven chapters, as follows: Basic Terms and Symbols; Foot-Verse (Syllabic-stress Verse); Simple Stress Verse; Stress Verse; The Native Meters; Syllabic Verse; Free Verse; Using the Scansion. There are six appendixes; common stan-

zas; a checklist of rhymes; a glossary; a list of suggested readings; a key to quoted poems; and a short summary of metrical forms. The volume concludes with a general index.

To these manuals may be added the recent work of John Hollander, *Rhyme's Reason* (New Haven: Yale University Press, 1981) [PE1505.H6], which follows the example of Pope's *Essay on Criticism* in simultaneously presenting, discussing, and illustrating terms and techniques of English prosody.

T–67 **Turco, Lewis,** *New Book of Forms: A Handbook of Poetics.* Hanover, N.H.: University Press of New England, 1986.   PN1042.T78 1986

This volume is an expanded revision of Turco's *Book of Forms* (1968). It is organized in two main parts. Part I, A Handbook of Poetics, discusses four levels of poetic structure (Typographic, Sonic, Sensory, and Ideational). Part II begins with a Form-Finder Index, and then presents an alphabetical compilation of over 300 verse forms described in prose and (where necessary) with a schematic diagram. Many entries are followed with illustrative examples of poems by poets from different periods. An analytical outline of topics covered, an index of authors and titles, and an index of terms conclude the work.

T–68 **Williams, Miller.** *Patterns of Poetry: An Encyclopedia of Forms.* Baton Rouge: Louisiana State University Press, 1986.   PN1042.W514 1986

This volume begins with a section of Notes on the Elements of Poetic Forms, followed by seven chapters on poetic forms of increasing complexity, as follows: 1. Fully Defined Traditional Stanza Patterns; 2. Loosely Defined Traditional Stanza Patterns; 3. Traditional Poems of Set Length; 4. Traditional Poems of Indefinite Length; 5. Nonspecific Forms and Formal Elements; 6. Variations on the Stanzas; 7. Variations on the Poems. For each pattern or poem type, a definition and historical discussion is followed by a schematic diagram and one or more illustrations from English poetry or poetry translated into English.

There are three appendixes. The first enumerates Additional Poems in the Various Patterns. Appendix B treats Some Applications of Certain Devices of Structural Linguistics to Poetry; Appendix C treats Some Observations on the Line. A Glossary of Additional Useful Terms, a Selected Bibliography, and an Index of Authors, Titles, and Terms conclude this compact and useful volume.

T–69 **Some Frequently Recommended Works on Prosody.**

Abercrombie, Lascelles. *Theory of Poetry.* London and New York: Harcourt, Brace, 1926.   PN1031.A25 1926

Baum, Paull Franklin. *Principles of English Versification.* Cambridge: Harvard University Press, 1922.   PE1505.B25

Berry, Francis. *Poetry and the Physical Voice.* London: Routledge and Kegan Paul, 1962.   PR504.B44 1962

Brower, Reuben A. *Forms of Lyric: Selected Papers from the English Institute [1968 and 1969].* New York: Columbia University Press, 1970.   PR509.L8 E5

Chatman, Seymour. *Theory of Meter.* The Hague: Mouton, 1965.   PE1505.C4

Crystal, David. *English Tone of Voice: Essays in Intonation, Prosody and Paralanguage.* London: Edward Arnold, 1975. Extensive bibliography.   PE1139.7.C7

———. *Prosodic Systems and Intonation in English.* Cambridge: Cambridge University Press, 1969.   PE1139.5.C7

Crystal, David, and Randolph Quirk. *Systems of Prosodic and Paralinguistic Features in English.* The Hague: Mouton, 1964.   PE1133.C7

DeFord, Sara, and Clarinda H. Lott. *Forms of Verse.* New York: Appleton–Century–Crofts, 1971.   PE1505.D4

Diller, Hans-Jurgen. *Metrik und Verslehre.* Dusseldorf: A Bagel, 1978.   PE1505.D55 1978

Epstein, Edmund L., and Terence Hawkes. *Linguistics and English Prosody.* Buffalo, N.Y.: Studies in Linguistics, 1959.   P1.S872 no. 7

Fraser, George S. *Metre, Rhyme, and Free Verse.* London: Methuen, 1970.   PE1505.F7 1970

Frye, Northrop, ed. *Sound and Poetry: English Institute Essays, 1956.* New York: Columbia University Press, 1957.   PE1010.E5

Fussell, Paul. *Poetic Meter and Poetic Form.* Rev. ed. New York: Random House, 1979. Brief bibliography.
                    PE1505.F78 1979

————. *Theories of Prosody in Eighteenth-Century England.* New London, Conn.: Shoe String, 1954.
                    PE1505.F8

Gross, Harvey. *Sound and Form in Modern Poetry: A Study of Prosody from Thomas Hardy to Robert Lowell.* Ann Arbor: University of Michigan Press, 1964.
                    PE1505.G7

————. *Structure of Verse: Modern Essays on Prosody.* Rev. ed. New York: Ecco Press, 1979. Selected bibliography.   PN1042.G7 1979

Halle, Morris, and Samuel J. Keyser. *English Stress: Its Form, Its Growth, and Its Role in Verse.* New York: Harper, 1971.   PE1139.H27

McAuley, James. *Versification.* East Lansing: Michigan State University Press, 1966.   PE1509.M15

Nabokov, Vladimir. *Notes on Prosody: From the Commentary to His Translation of Pushkin's Eugene Onegin.* Princeton N.J.: Princeton University Press, 1965.   PG2531.I3 N3

Russom, Geoffrey. *Old English Meter and Linguistic Theory.* Cambridge: Cambridge University Press, 1987.   PE257.R87 1987

Smith, Barbara Herrnstein. *Poetic Closure: A Study of How Poems End.* Chicago: University of Chicago Press, 1968.   PN1042.S65

Wesling, Donald. *Chances of Rhyme: Device and Modernity.* Berkeley, Los Angeles, London: University of California Press, 1980. PN1059.R5W4

Young, George. *English Prosody on Inductive Lines.* London, 1928.   PE1505.Y6

VIII. SPECIAL SUBJECTS— BIBLIOGRAPHIES AND INDEXES

For bibliographies of works on the various forms and genres of poetry, see also the works on comparative and general literature in section L.

T–70   **Coleman, Arthur.   *Epic and Romance Criticism.*** 2 vols. Vol. 1, ***Checklist of Interpretations, 1940–1972, of English and American Epics and Metrical Romances.*** Vol. 2, ***Checklist of Interpretations, 1940–1973, of Classical and Continental Epics and Metrical Romances.*** Searingtown, N.Y.: Watermill, 1973–1974.   Z7156.E6 C64

A total of some 20,000 citations are arranged alphabetically in the two volumes by the title of the English or American, or classical or Continental epic or metrical romance in question. Primary works cited include epics, metrical romances, mock epics, and epiclike poems (such as *Howl, Patterson, Wasteland,* and *Wreck of the Deutschland*). Included are English-language interpretations of these works published in monographs, festschriften, pamphlets, and periodicals. There are no indexes of authors or of critics. Though this work must be used with caution, reviewers having found it often careless and unreliable, it does provide a convenient means of access to criticism of major long poems.

For much more adequate bibliography of work on specifically Arthurian materials, see the bibliography of Parry and Schlauch and related works (N–55).

T–73   **Haymes, Edward R.   *Bibliography of Studies Relating to Parry's and Lord's Oral Theory.*** Cambridge: Harvard University Press, 1973.   Z7156.E6 H39

This sheer-list, alphabetically organized bibliography includes more than 500 items concerned with the exposition or elaboration of Parry and Lord's theory of oral composition. Included are numerous works on the oral composition of Anglo-Saxon poetry. There is no index.

More recent is the volume by John Miles Foley, *Oral-Formulaic Theory and Research: An Introduction and Annotated Bibliography* (New York: Garland, 1985) [GR44.072.F65 1985], which treats dozens of ancient, medieval, and modern literatures. More than 1,400 items published through 1981 are separately indexed for the poetry of each national literature.

T–76   **Julian, John.   *Dictionary of Hymnology, Setting Forth the Origin and History of Christian Hymns of All Ages and Nations.*** 2d ed. rev. with a new Supplement. London: J. Murray, 1908.   BV305.J8

First published in 1892, this work remains the standard guide to hymnology. It contains biographical articles on authors and translators as well as articles on the hymns of nations and denominations and on terms. Articles are signed and include bibliographies. The dictionary proper is followed by a polyglot cross-reference index to first lines, and an index of authors and translators. There follow two alphabetically arranged appendixes, the first of late articles and the second of additions and corrections to articles in the main dictionary. The supplement follows with its own articles, and this is followed by first-line and author indexes to the appendixes and supplement. A revision of this work by L. H. Bunn has been announced.

For early English hymnody, Julian can be supplemented by reference to E. D. Parks's listing of *Early English Hymns* (Metuchen, N.J.: Scarecrow, 1972) [BV305.P37]. For authors see also R. W. Thompson, *Who's Who of Hymn Writers* (London: Epworth, 1967) [BV325.T5].

T–78   **Diehl, Katherine Smith.   *Hymns and Tunes: An Index.*** Metuchen, N.J.: Scarecrow, 1966.   BV305.D5 1966

This volume indexes songs found in seventy-eight primarily English-language hymnals in use by North American and British Judeo-Christian denominations. The work is in two parts: the hymns (listing them by first lines, variant first lines, and by authors) and the tunes (listing them by names, variants, and by a systematic index to the melodies).

A sort of subject index to hymns is the *Judson Concordance to Hymns* by Thomas Bruce McDormand and Frederic S. Crossman (Valley Forge, Pa.: Judson, 1965) [BV305.M5], which indexes 2,342 hymns by keyword.

T–80　**Donow, Herbert S.** *Sonnet in England and America: A Bibliography of Criticism.* Westport, Conn.: Greenwood Press, 1982.　　　　Z2014.S6 D66 1982

This volume includes a total of 4,191 briefly annotated entries on works of history and criticism published before mid–1981 on the sonnet. They are disposed into four major sections, as follows: I. The Sonnet: A General Overview; II. The Sonnet in the Renaissance (anthologies, general criticism, authors A to Z); III. Shakespeare; IV. The Sonnet Revival (anthologies, general criticism, authors A-Z). There are numerous cross-references and three indexes, of contributors (i.e., scholarly authors), of poets, and of subjects.

T–89　**Some Frequently Recommended Histories and Studies of One or Several of the Poetic Kinds in England or America.**

The Ballad (see K–21)

The Collection

Fraistat, Neil. *Poem and the Book: Interpreting Collections of Romantic Poetry.* Chapel Hill: University of North Carolina Press, 1985.

———, ed. *Poems in Their Place: The Inter-textuality and Order of Poetic Collections.* Chapel Hill: University of North Carolina Press, 1986. PN1059.E35 P6 1986

Concrete Poetry

McLuhan, Marshall. *Verbi-Voco-Visual Explorations.* New York: Something Else Press, 1967.

Newell, Kenneth B. *Pattern Poetry: A Historical Critique from the Alexandrian Greeks to Dylan Thomas.* Boston: Marlborough House, 1976. PN1059.C64 N4

Solt, Mary E., and Willis Barnstone, eds. *Concrete Poetry: A World View.* Bloomington: Indiana University Press, 1969.　　　　PN6110.C77 S6

Dramatic Monologue

Carleton, Frances B. *Dramatic Monologue: Vox Humana.* Salzburg: Institut für englische Sprache und Literatur, University of Salzburg, 1977.　PR509.M6 C3 1977

Langbaum, Robert. *Poetry of Experience: The Dramatic Monologue in Modern Literary Tradition.* 2d ed. New York: Norton, 1963.　　PR509.M6 L3 1963

Mermin, Dorothy. *Audience in the Poem.* New Brunswick, N.J.: Rutgers University Press, 1983.

PR599.M6 M47

Sinfield, Alan. *Dramatic Monologue.* London: Methuen, 1977.　　　　PN1530.S5

The Elegy

Draper, John W. *Funeral Elegy and the Rise of English Romanticism.* New York: New York University Press, 1929.　　　　PR508.E5 D7

Harrison, Thomas P., and H. J. Leon, eds. *Pastoral Elegy: An Anthology.* Austin: University of Texas Press, 1939.　　　　PN6110.C8 H3

Lambert, Ellen Zetzel. *Placing Sorrow: A Study of the Pastoral Elegy Convention from Theocritus to Milton.* Chapel Hill: University of North Carolina Press, 1976.

PN1389.L3

Pigman, G. W., III. *Grief and English Renaissance Elegy.* Cambridge: Cambridge University Press, 1985.

PR539.E45 P53 1985

Potts, Abbie F. *Elegiac Mode: Poetic Form in Wordsworth and Other Elegists.* Ithaca, N.Y.: Cornell University Press, 1967.　　　　PR508.E5 P6

Sacks, Peter M. *English Elegy: Studies in the Genre from Spenser to Yeats.* Baltimore: Johns Hopkins University Press, 1985.　PR509.E4 S23 1985

Sickels, Eleanor M. *Gloomy Egoist: Moods and Themes of Melancholy from Gray to Keats.* New York: Columbia University Press, 1932.　　PR508.M4S5

The Epic

Bowra, Cecil M. *From Vergil to Milton:* London: Macmillan, 1945.　　　　PN 1303.B65

———. *Heroic Poetry.* London: Macmillan, 1952.

PN1303.B67

Forster, D. M. *Fortunes of Epic Poetry: A Study in English and American Criticism, 1750–1950.* Washington, D.C.: Catholic University Press, 1962.　PN1303.F6

Giametti, A. Bartlett. *Earthly Paradise and the Renaissance Epic.* Princeton N.J.: Princeton University Press, 1966.

Greene, Thomas M. *Descent from Heaven: A Study in Epic Continuity.* New Haven: Yale University Press, 1963.

PN1303.G7

Lewis, C. S. *Preface to Paradise Lost.* Rev. and enl. London: Oxford University Press, 1960.

PR3562.L4 1960

Lord, Albert B. *Singer of Tales.* Cambridge: Harvard University Press, 1960.　　PN1303.L62

Merchant, Paul. *Epic.* London: Methuen, 1971.

PN56.E65 M4

Tillyard, E. M. W. *English Epic and Its Background.* London: Chatto and Windus, 1954.　PR125.T5 1954

The Epigram

Hamilton, George R. *English Verse Epigrams.* Writers and Their Work, vol. 188. London: Longmans, 1965.

PR509.E73 H3

Hudson, Hoyt H. *Epigram in the English Renaissance.* Princeton N.J.: Princeton University Press, 1947.

PN6279.H8

Whipple, Thomas K. *Martial and the English Epigram from Sir Thomas Wyatt to Ben Jonson. University of California Publications in Modern Philology,* vol. 10, no. 4. Berkeley, 1925. Reprint. New York: Phaeton Press, 1970.　　　　PR509.E73 W5 1970

The Fragment

Levinson, Marjorie. *Romantic Fragment Poem: A Critique of a Form.* Chapel Hill: University of North Carolina Press, 1986.　　　　PR590.L43 1986

The Georgic

Chalker, John. *English Georgic: A Study in the Development of a Form.* London: Routledge and Kegan Paul, 1969.

PR509.D5 C5 1969b

Durling, Dwight L. *Georgic Tradition in English Poetry.* New York: Columbia University Press, 1935.

PR509.D5 D8 1935a

Low, Anthony. *Georgic Revolution.* Princeton: Princeton University Press, 1985.　PR546.P3 L68 1985

The Heroic Couplet

Brown, W. C. *Triumph of Form: A Study of the Later Masters of the Heroic Couplet.* Chapel Hill: University of North Carolina Press, 1948.

PR509.H4 B4

Piper, William Bowman. *Heroic Couplet.* Cleveland, Ohio: Case Western Reserve University Press, 1969.

PR509.H4 P5

The Hymn

Benson, Louis F. *English Hymn.* New York: Hodder and Stoughton, 1915.　　　　BV312.B4

Foote, Henry W. *Three Centuries of American Hymnody.* Cambridge: Harvard University Press, 1940.
ML3111.F6 T4

Manning, B. L. *Hymns of Wesley and Watts.* London: Epworth Press, 1942. BV312.M24

Pollard, Arthur. *English Hymns.* London: Longmans, Green, 1960. BV312.P6

Reeves, Jeremiah Bascom. *Hymn as Literature.* New York: Century Co., 1924. BV312.R4

The Mock Heroic

Broich, Ulrich. *Rise and Fall of the Mock-Heroic Poem.* Tr. from the German by David Henry Wilson. Cambridge: Cambridge University Press, 1990.
PR559.M63 B7613 1990

Occasional Poetry

Hardison, O. B., Jr. *Enduring Monument.* Chapel Hill: University of North Carolina Press, 1962. PN88.H34

The Ode

Engler, Bernard. *Amerikanische Ode: Gattungsgesch-ichtliche Untersuchungen.* Paderborn: W. Schoningh, 1985. PS309.O33 E5 1985

Fry, Paul H. *Poet's Calling in the English Ode.* New Haven: Yale University Press, 1980. PR509.O3 F7 1980

Heath-Stubbs, John F. *Ode.* London: Oxford University Press, 1969. PR509.O3 H4

Jump, John. *Ode.* London: Methuen, 1974.
PR509.O3 J8 1974

Maddison, Carol. *Apollo and the Nine: A History of the Ode.* Baltimore: Johns Hopkins University Press, 1960.
PN1371.M3

Schlüter, Karl. *Die englische Ode: Studien zu ihrer Entstehung unter dem Einfluss der antiken Hymne.* Bonn: H. Bouvier, 1964. PR509.O3 S3

Schuster, George N. *English Ode from Milton to Keats.* New York: Columbia University Press, 1940.
PR509.O3 S55

Shafer, Robert. *English Ode to 1660: An Essay in Literary History.* Princeton N.J.: Princeton University Press, 1918. PR509.O3 S5

Williams, Anne. *Prophetic Strain: The Greater Lyric in the Eighteenth Century.* Chicago: University of Chicago Press, 1984. PR551.W48 1984

The Pastoral

Cody, Richard. *Landscape of the Mind.* Oxford: Clarendon Press, 1969. PQ4639.A3 C6

Cooper, Helen. *Pastoral: Medieval into Renaissance.* Ipswich: D. S. Brewer, 1978. PR539.P366 1977

Empson, William. *Some Versions of Pastoral.* London: Chatto and Windus, 1935. PR149.P3 E6

Ettin, Andrew V. *Literature and the Pastoral.* New Haven: Yale University Press, 1984. PN56.P3 E87 1984

Greg, W. W. *Pastoral Poetry and Pastoral Drama.* London: A. H. Bullen, 1906. PR509.P3 G7

Halperin, D. M. *Before Pastoral: Theocritus and the Ancient Tradition of Bucolic Poetry.* New Haven: Yale University Press, 1983. PA4444.H33 1983

Heath-Stubbs, John F. *Pastoral.* London: Oxford University Press, 1969. PN1421.H4

Lincoln, Eleanor Terry, ed. *Pastoral and Romance: Modern Essays in Criticism.* Englewood Cliffs, N.J.: Prentice-Hall, 1969. PN56.P3 L5

Marinelli, Peter V. *Pastoral.* London: Methuen, 1971.
PN56.P3 M3

Patterson, Annabel. *Pastoral and Ideology: Virgil to Valery.* Berkeley and Los Angeles: University of California Press, 1987. PA6804.B7 P38 1987

Poggioli, Renato. *Oaten Flute: Essays on Pastoral Poetry and the Pastoral Ideal.* Cambridge: Harvard University Press, 1975. PN1421.P6 1975

Rosenmeyer, Thomas G. *Green Cabinet: Theocritus and the European Pastoral Lyric.* Berkeley, Los Angeles, London: University of California Press, 1970.
PA4444.R6

Sambrook, James. *English Pastoral Poetry.* Boston: Twayne, 1983. PR509.P3 S35 1983

Shore, David R. *Spenser and the Poetics of Pastoral: A Study of the World of Colin Clout.* Kingston, Ont.: McGill-Queen's University Press, 1985.
PR2367.P34 S56 1985

Toliver, Harold E. *Pastoral Forms and Attitudes.* Berkeley, Los Angeles, London: University of California Press, 1971. PR408.P3 T6

The Song

Day, C. L., and E. B. Murrie. *English Song-Books, 1651–1702. A Bibliography [with finding list].* London: University of London Press, 1940.
ML120.G7 D31

Stevens, Denis W., ed. *History of Song.* London: Hutchinson, 1960. ML2800.S8

The Sonnet

Booth, Stephen. *Essay on Shakespeare's Sonnets.* New Haven: Yale University Press, 1969. PR2848.B65

Cruttwell, Patrick. *English Sonnet.* London: Longmans, 1966. PR509.S7 C83

John, L. C. *Elizabethan Sonnet Sequences.* New York: Columbia University Press, 1938.
PR539.S7 J6 1938a

Lever, Julius W. *Elizabethan Love Sonnet.* 2d ed. London: Methuen, 1966. PR539.S7 L4 1966

Mönch, Walter. *Das Sonett: Gestalt und Geschichte.* Heidelberg, 1956. Extended bibliography.

Schlutter, Hans-Jurgen. *Sonett.* Stuttgart: Metzler, 1979.
PN1514.S34

Sterner, Lewis G. *Sonnet in American Literature.* Philadelphia, 1930. PS309.S6 S7 1930

Tomlinson, Charles. *Sonnet: Its Origin, Structure, and Place in Poetry.* London: J. Murray, 1874.
PN1514.T7

The Verse Satire (see W–150 ff.).

The Villanelle

McFarland, Ronald E. *Villanelle: The Evolution of a Poetic Form.* Moscos: University of Idaho Press, 1987.
PR509.V54 M36 1987

THE PERFORMING ARTS—
THEATER, DRAMA, AND FILM

See also works concerning the performing arts, theater, drama, and film, in section L, Comparative and World Literature; section M, English Literature; section N, Medieval; section O, Renaissance; section P, Restoration and Eighteenth Century; section Q, Nineteenth Century; section R, Twentieth Century; and section S, American Literature. And see many pertinent entries in section X, Literary Theory, and section Y, Bibliography and Textual Criticism.

I. PERFORMING ARTS AND THEATER BIBLIOGRAPHIES

Bibliographies and guides limited to the drama and theater of one period of English literary history will generally be found in the drama and theater subsection of that period (i.e., N.IV, O.III and O.IV, P.III, Q.V, R.V). Similarly, most of the bibliographies concerned with American drama and theater will be found in section S.VII. See also Litto's bibliography of dissertations (E–40) and the serial bibliographies of the MLA (L–50), the MHRA (M–21), *Research Opportunities in Renaissance Drama* (O–33), *Restoration and Eighteenth Century Theatre Research* (P–31), *Nineteenth Century Theatre Research* (Q–62), and *Modern Drama* (R–44).

U–1 Baker, Blanche M. *Theatre and Allied Arts: A Guide to Books Dealing with the History, Criticism, and Technic of the Drama and Theatre and Related Arts and Crafts.* New York: H. W. Wilson, 1952.   Z5781.B18

A complete revision and enlargement of the author's *Dramatic Bibliography* (New York: Wilson, 1933) [Z5781A.B16], this volume cites primarily English-language materials published between 1885 and 1948. It includes a selection of about 6,000 books (doctoral theses omitted) of interest to professional and amateur artists and craftsmen, actors, drama students, and librarians as well as playgoers and general readers. Included are works concerned with dance, music, and puppetry; excluded are works concerned exclusively with film, radio, television, and grand opera. There are three main parts: 1. Drama, Theatre, and Actors (Inclusive General Histories, Drama and Theater, Theatres, Actors); 2. Stagecraft and Al-

lied Arts of the Theatre (Playwriting and Dramatization, Production, Scenic Art, Costume, Make-up, Acting, Dance, Music, Marionettes and Puppets); 3. Miscellaneous Reference Material (Reference Guides, Indexes, Play Lists, Directories, Periodicals, etc.). Each part contains geographical or subject divisions that are further subdivided, often chronologically. Main entries within subdivisions are alphabetical by author and give standard bibliographical information; most are descriptively annotated. There are abundant cross-references at the ends of sections. The author index includes cross-references for pseudonyms, joint authors, and editors. There is a detailed subject index.

U–2 Whalon, Marion K. *Performing Arts Research: A Guide to Information Sources.* Detroit: Gale Research Co., 1976.   Z6935.W5

This well-ordered guide, current to about 1973, includes dance, music, opera, film, costume, circus, and the drama. Entries are disposed into seven sections, as follows: I. Guides (listing basic references in theater arts, dance, costume, visual arts, music, aesthetics, literature, rhetoric, general reference, and periodicals); II. Dictionaries, Encyclopedias, and Handbooks; III. Directories; IV. Play Indexes and Finding Lists; V. Sources for Reviews of Plays and Motion Pictures; VI. Bibliographies, Indexes, and Abstracts; and VII. Illustrative and Audiovisual Sources (including reference sources for many classes of theatrical ephemera). Entries within sections are subdivided as appropriate and are descriptively and evaluatively annotated. There are numerous cross-references. The volume begins with a brief essay on "Problems of Research in Theatre Arts" and concludes with a detailed index of authors, titles, and subjects.

The Whalon work is the first volume in Gale's Performing Arts Information Guide Series. Additional volumes published include the following:

Vol. 2. Stoddard, Richard. *Stage Scenery, Machinery, and Lighting* (1977).   Z5784.S8 S79

Vol. 3. Parker, David L. *Guide to Dance in Film* (1978).   GV1779.P37

Vol. 4. Wilmeth, Don B. *American Stage to World War I* (1978).   Z1231.D7 W55

Vol. 5. Stoddard, Richard. *Theatre and Cinema Architecture* (1978).   Z5784.S8 S82

Vol. 6. Kesler, Jackson. *Theatrical Costume* (1979).
                                              Z5691.K47

Vol. 7. Wilmeth, Don B. *American and English Popular Entertainment* (see U–4).

Vol. 8. Archer, Stephen M. *American Actors and Actresses* (1983).   Z5784.M9 A7 1983

Additional planned volumes include guides to the *American Stage from World War I to the 1970's*; *Business of the Theatre, Films, and Broadcasting*; and *Law of the Theatre, Films, and Broadcasting.*

Another useful reference work for Performing Arts study from Gale is Steven R. Wasserman, ed., the *Lively Arts Information Directory: A Guide to the Fields of Music, Dance, Theatre, Film, Radio, and Television for the United States and Canada, Covering National, International, State, and Regional Organizations, Government Grant Sources, Foundations, Consultants, Special Libraries, Research and Information Centers, Education Programs, Journals and Periodicals, Festivals and Awards* (Detroit: Gale, 1982) [PN2289.L55 1982].

U–3   **Schoolcraft, Ralph N.   *Performing Arts Books in Print: An Annual Bibliography.*** New York: Drama Book Specialists, 1973.   Z6935.S34

This annotated guide describes approximately 12,000 books in print in the United States in 1970–1971. Primarily English-language works are included, and no plays or collections of plays are cited, with the exception of Shakespeare's work. Included are books on the theater, the drama, the technical arts of the theater, film, television, radio, the mass media, and related popular arts. The main list is current to 1970, while a supplemental list includes materials in print in 1971 and some earlier, omitted items. This guide replaces the earlier volume by A. E. Santaniello, *Theatre Books in Print*, originally published in 1963 with a second edition in 1966 [Z5781.S2 1966].

Schoolcraft is supplemented by the quarterly *Annotated Bibliography of New Publications in the Performing Arts*, published by the Drama Bookshop in New York since 1970 [Z6935.S34 suppl.]. Books are listed in large classes, such as Books on Theatre and Drama, or Mass Media and Popular Arts, with subdivisions under such headings as General Reference Works, Shakespeare, Costume, or The Actor and His Craft. There is a detailed table of contents but no index.

Other lists of current publications include the "[1964–] Publications of Recently Produced Plays" and the limited "Selected List of Other Plays Published in [1964–]" that appear in the *Burns Mantle Yearbook* (see U–40).

U–4   **Wilmeth, Don B.   *American and English Popular Entertainment: A Guide to Information Sources.*** Detroit: Gale Research Co., 1980.   Z7511.W53

This volume in the Performing Arts Information Guide Series (see U–2) is in three parts. Part 1 concerns General Sources in Popular Entertainment. Part 2, Popular Entertainment Forms: Predominantly American, is in six chapters, treating The Circus and Wild West Exhibitions, Outdoor Amusements, Variety Shows, Optical and Mechanical Entertainments, Early Musical Theatre and Reviews, and Major Sources on Principal English Forms. Part 3, Popular Theatre: English and American, includes General Sources for both the United States and Britain, a chapter on Major Genres and Forms, one on Native American Types from the Yankee to Toby, one on American Small Town and Provincial Operations, and a final chapter on the American Showboat. Three appendixes list selected periodicals and serials, collections and museums, and concerned organizations. Author, title, and subject indexes conclude the volume.

U–5   **Cheshire, David F.   *Theatre: History, Criticism, and Reference.*** Hamden, Conn.: Archon, 1967.   Z5781.C48 1967

This discursive bibliographical guide provides a running commentary on standard works in theater arts. The volume is in six chapters, as follows: 1, General Reference Works (encyclopedias, biographical dictionaries, dictionaries, bibliographies, catalogs, guides, annuals, periodicals); 2, Theater History (books, current periodicals); 3, Dramatic Criticism (books, current periodicals); 4, Theater Biographies and Autobiographies; 5, Drama Theory; and 6, Current Periodicals of the Theater World. The work concludes with an author-title-subject index.

U–6   **Bailey, Claudia Jean.   *Guide to Reference and Bibliography for Theatre Research.*** 2nd ed. Columbus: Publications Committee, Ohio State University Libraries, 1983.
                                              Z5781.B15 1983

This student bibliographical guide, first published in 1971, has more than 650 serially numbered entries in two parts, the first citing and briefly describing general reference works and the second treating works on theater and drama. The second part is in ten sections, as follows: A. Reference Guides; B. Bibliographies; C. Special Collections and Libraries; D. Theory and Criticism; E. Dissertations and Theses; F. Indexes of Periodicals and of Plays and Characters; G. Illustrations and Designs, Portraits, Stage Scenery and Costume; H. Biographical Sources; I. Encyclopedias and Dictionaries; and J. Annuals and Directories. Annotations are descriptive and very brief. A short appendix lists a few sources for fine-arts and music reference. The work concludes with an author-title index.

U–7   **Hunter, Frederick J.   *Drama Bibliography: Short-Title Guide to Extended Reading in Dramatic Art for the English-Speaking Audience and Students in Theatre.*** Boston: G. K. Hall, 1971.   Z5871.H84

This volume, with a strong emphasis on the theater, seeks to extend the amount of sheer bibliographical information available in Baker (U–1) to 1970 or so, for the use of researchers and performers. Entries are in sheer lists and are disposed into eight sections, as follows: Reference Works; Periodicals; Drama Literature from the Greek and Roman Period to The Present; Selected Sources in Theater History; Biography and Autobiography; Techniques of Theater; Theory and Criticism of Dramatic Art; and The World of Dance. There is an index of persons at the end.

U–8   **American Educational Theatre Association.   *Bibliography on Theatre and Drama in American Colleges and Universities, 1937–1947.* Speech Monographs**, vol. 16, no. 3. New York: AETA, 1949.   Z5781.A48

This volume, the first of a series sponsored by the AETA, contains 2,522 entries including books, articles, published original plays and designs, theses, and dissertations. Entries are classified by subject. The list concludes with an author index.

It is continued by the AETA *Theatre Arts Publications in the United States* [and Canada], *1947-1952*, ed. William W. Melnitz (Washington, D.C.: AETA, 1959) [Z5781.M5], which includes 4,063 books and articles published in the United States and Canada, excluding theses and dissertations, on the theater, film, and television. Entries are arranged by subject. There is an author index.

The series is continued by the AETA's *Theatre Arts Publications Available in the United States* [and Canada], *1953-1957*, ed. Roger M. Busfield, Jr. (Washington, D.C.: AETA, 1964) [Z5781.A52], which contains 8,089 publications, including some foreign works available in the United States but also excluding theses and dissertations. Entries are arranged by subject. The volume concludes with an author index.

A further continuation, edited by Bernard F. Dukore, is *Bibliography of Theatre Arts Publications in English, 1963* (Washington, D.C.: AETA, 1965) [Z5781.A48]. The 1,771 numbered entries are in a sheer alphabetical author list, with a detailed subject index. Annual bibliographies were planned, but this is the only one that was published.

Doctoral dissertations, excluded from these bibliographies, are treated in the annual "Doctoral Projects in Progress in Theatre Arts [1953–]" published in the *Educational Theatre Journal* (1953–1978), renamed the *Theatre Journal* (1979–) [PN3171.E38]. Author, title, sponsoring institution, faculty supervisor, and expected date of completion are given; projects are classified. Section I, The Drama, has the subdivisions A. Individual Dramatists; B. Dramaturgy; C. Dramatic Types; D. Technique and Dramaturgy; E. Dramatic Theories and Theorists; F. Dramatic Critics and Criticism.

U–9 *Performing Arts Resources.* Vol. 1–. New York: Theatre Library Association, 1974–.   Z6935.P46

This annual volume presents information on research materials for theater, film, television, and popular entertainment. Articles describing and evaluating current reference guides, indexes, bibliographies, and catalogs of various collections are found along with descriptions of theater archives, surveys of research materials in particular localities, and guides to the current state of research in specific fields of performing arts research.

U–10 Arnott, James F., and John W. Robinson. *English Theatrical Literature, 1559–1900: A Bibliography Incorporating Robert W. Lowe's "A Bibliographical Account of English Theatrical Literature" Published in 1888.* London: Society for Theatre Research, 1970.   Z2014.D7 A74

This volume retains, but extends, all entries in Lowe and, like its original, focuses on the theater as contrasted with the drama (i.e. the play texts). Therefore, no plays or play criticisms are cited. Instead the volume presents a descriptively annotated bibliography of works concerning the theater of the British Isles, including Scotland and Ireland. Work published in Britain as well as American and other foreign items and editions are noted. The 4,506 serially numbered entries are classified by subject into fourteen sections, including Bibliography; Government Regulation of the Theatre; The Morality of the Theatre; The Arts of the Theatre; General History; The London Theatre; The Theatre out of London; A National Theatre; Opera; Irregular Forms; Pantomimes, Music Hall, etc.; The Amateur Theatre; Biography; Theory and Criticism; and Periodicals. There are numerous subdivisions. Under headings, arrangement is chronological. The work concludes with three indexes: of authors, of short titles, and places of publication (excluding London).

U–11 Lowenberg, Alfred. *Theatre of the British Isles, Excluding London: A Bibliography.* London: For the Society for Theatre Research, 1950.   Z2014.D7 L8

This bibliography, which supplements Arnott and Robinson for provincial theater and for the twentieth century, cites books, periodicals, and pamphlets. It is arranged geographically and alphabetically by place-name, then chronologically. An author index concludes the work.

U–12 Brockett, Oscar G., Samuel L. Becker, and Donald C. Bryant. *Bibliographical Guide to Research in Speech and Dramatic Art.* Chicago: Scott, Foresman, 1963. Z1002.B87

This well-designed student guide is in three parts. The first cites general references. The second concerns guides and reference sources in speech and dramatic art and has six sections: General Guides; Communication Research; Radio, Television, Film; Rhetoric and Public Address; Speech Science, Speech Pathology, and Audiology; and Theatre and Drama. The third contains references to ancillary fields including not only Literature and Fine Arts but also works in Education, History and Politics, the Social Sciences, and Law. There are a total of twenty-one sections, A-U, within which are appropriate subdivisions moving from the general to the specific. Entries are numbered serially, and most have brief descriptive annotations. There is a detailed table of contents that does not quite compensate for the lack of an index.

U–13 *Speech Communication Abstracts* [title 1974, *Theatre/Drama and Speech Index*]. 7 vols. Pleasant Hill, Calif.: Theatre/Drama and Speech Information Center, 1974–1980.
                    No LC number

This triannual abstracting service, which was cumulated annually, combined two series, *Theatre/Drama Abstracts*, which analyzed approximately sixty journals, and *Speech Communication Abstracts*, which analyzed another thirty. Arrangement in both was topical, with author and subject indexes to each.

There are a number of other bibliographical aids that result from the academic association of speech and theater arts. Most of these will be found in section X. They include the various lists, abstracts, and indexes of graduate theses in *Speech Monographs* (X–103); the *Index to Journals in Communication Studies* (X–104); and the *Bibliographic Annual of Speech Communication* (X–105).

U–14 Trussler, Simon, comp. "Current Bibliography." *Theatre Quarterly,* vols. 1–3. London: TQ Publications, 1971–1973. Thereafter in *Theatrefacts: International Theatre Reference*, vols. 1–4 London: TQ Publications, 1974–1977.   PN2001.T435

This comprehensive serial bibliography in each issue of *Theatre Quarterly* and then in each of the eight annual issues of *Theatrefacts* aims to record all books on all aspects of the drama and theater, including all the performing arts. Entries are often annotated and are keyed to an elegantly simple yet complete classification system designed by the compiler which consists of twenty-six categories, as follows: A. Reference Works and Miscellaneous; B. Conceptual Studies; C. Associations and Origins of Drama and Theatre; D. History of Drama and Theatre; E. Ancient and Classical Drama and Theatre; F. British; G. European; H. American; I. Asian; J. African; K. Dramatic Theory; L. Dramatic Form; M. Dramatic Craftsmanship/Playwriting; N. Theatrical Craftsmanship; O. Ethics and Organization of the Theatre; P. Forms of Theatre and Staging; Q. Stagecraft: Production and Design; R. Acting; S. The Play in Performance: Production Records; T. The Play in Performance: Reviews and Retrospective Studies; U. Theatrical Biographies and Memoirs; V. Musical Theatre: Opera; W. Musical Theatre: Ballet, Dance; X. Circus, Puppetry, etc.; Y. Cinematic and Allied Arts; Z. Broadcasting and Television.

The intention is to cumulate these bibliographies into a *Bibliography of Drama and Theatre* to be published in due course as a complementary volume to the *Oxford Companion to the Theatre* (see U–21). Trussler's classification system is described in the *Theatre Quarterly*, vol. 2 (1971), and in a revised form it is the subject of his monograph *Classification for the Performing Arts* (London: Commission for a British The- atre Institute, 1974) [Z697.P44 T78].

Theatre Quarterly has also included numerous other biblio- graphical and reference materials, such as the 1976 and 1977 "Bibliography of Theatrical Craftsmanship." *Theatrefacts* is primarily a reference source, with a "Theatre Checklist," an "International Theatrelog," and a "British Theatrelog" regu- larly featured along with the current bibliography.

U–15 *International Bibliography of Theatre: [1982–] [IBT].* Vol. 1–. Brooklyn, N.Y.: Theatre Research Data Center, Brooklyn College, City University of New York, 1985–.

Z6935.I53

This annual bibliography is sponsored by the American Soci- ety for Theatre Research and the International Association of Libraries and Museums of the Performing Arts, in coopera- tion with the International Federation for Theater Research. More than sixty contributors participated in the bibliography for 1982. Theater books, book articles, dissertations, journal articles, and miscellaneous theater documents are included. Writings are on any aspect of theater significant to research, without historical, cultural, or geographical limitations. Re- prints are generally excluded, as is purely literary scholarship. Playtexts are excluded unless they are published with signifi- cant introductory materials. Reviews are generally excluded.

Entries are classified using a taxonomy of the theater devel- oped for the *IBT* and fully explained in the "Guide for Users." The first levels of classification are as follows: Theatre in General, Dance, Dance-Drama, Media, Mime, Mixed Enter- tainment, Music-Drama, and Puppetry. The major subtopics indicating the focus of an entry are as follows: Administra- tion, Audience, Basic Theatrical Documents, Design/tech- nology, Institutions, Performance/production, Performance spaces, Plays/librettos/scripts, Reference materials, Relation to other fields, Research/historiography, Theory/criticism, and Training.

Each entry is numbered and gives full bibliographical infor- mation, including an English translation of non-English titles. There are three additional items of information appended to each entry: content geography and dates (country, city, and date[s] under discussion in the entry), document treatment (identifies the type of scholarly approach, such as biblio- graphical, biographical, critical, empirical, historical, techni- cal, textual, etc.), and a brief precis of content.

There are three indexes. An elaborate subject index, which is a primary means of access to the major aspects of the docu- ments cited in the classification, uses subject terms including names of persons, names of institutions, forms and genres of theater, elements of the theater arts, titles of plays, and the like. Each citation in the subject index gives the subtopic that identifies the major focus of the entry and both the brief precis and the entry number. A geographical-chronological index is arranged alphabetically by country, then by year (date is of the material treated in the entry), then by the subtopic which iden- tifies the major focus of the item; it gives both the brief precis and the entry number of the item. Finally, there is an index of document authors arranged alphabetically and giving entry numbers to the authored documents.

U–16 **"Bibliographie."** *Revue d'histoire du théâtre,* vol. 1–. Paris: Société d'histoire du théâtre, 1948/49–.   PN2003.R38

This bibliography focuses on the theater rather than the dra- ma, but excludes stagecraft. It indexes monographs and more than 180 journals, emphasizing European publications. Scope and arrangement have varied over the years. The bib- liography appeared in each quarterly issue 1948–1965 and has appeared annually since then. Currently, about 4,000 serially numbered entries each year are classified into sixteen sec-

tions, as follows: I. Bibliographies et répertoires; II. Cata- logues; III. Généralités; IV. Théâtres et troupes; V. Le comédien; VI. Biographies; VII. Histoire de la littérature dra- matique (subdivided by country); VIII. Relations interna- tionales et littérature comparée; IX. Théâtre non- professionnel; X. Théâtre pour la jeunesse et pour l'enfance; XI. Pantomime, cirque, et music-hall, marionnettes, ombres, etc.; XII. Rapports du théâtre avec les autres arts ou tech- niques; XIII. La langue dramatique; XIV. Théoriciens et cri- tiques dramatiques; XV. Études sur la littérature dramatique; XVI. Varia. There is no index.

U–17 *Theatre Documentation.* Vol. 1–. New York: Theatre Li- brary Association, 1969–.   PN1560.T398

This journal publishes bibliographies, indexes, accounts of theater and film reference collections, and other materials of use for research in theater arts. A regular listing of scholarly work in progress is another feature. Work in progress is also listed in each issue of the *Theatre Journal*, where entries give name, project title, a short description defining project limits, publisher if known, and a contemplated date of completion.

U–18 **Scholarly Journals in Drama, Theater, and Theater Histo- ry.**

BBT   *Bulletin of Black Theatre: Newsletter of the AETA Black Theatre Project.* No. 1–. Washington, D.C.: American Theatre Association, 1971–. Irreg.

CTR   *Canadian Theatre Review.* Vol. 1–. Downsview, Ont.: York University, Faculty of Fine Arts, 1974–. 4/yr. Reviews.   PN2004.C35

CompD   *Comparative Drama.* Vol. 1–. Kalamazoo: West- ern Michigan University, 1967–. 4/yr. Reviews. Annual Index.   PN1601.C66

Drama   *Drama: The Quarterly Theatre Review.* Vol. 1–. London: British Drama League, 1946–. 4/yr. Re- views. Subject index 1946–1954 in 1 vol.
PN2001.D64

Drama Review (see TDR: The Drama Review).

DramS   *Drama Survey.* Vol. 1–. Minneapolis, 1962–.
PN1601.D65

ETJ   *Educational Theatre Journal (see Theatre Journal).*

International Theatre Annual. No. 1–. New York: Grove Press, 1956–. 1/yr.   PN2012.I6

KSGT   *Kleine Schriften der Gesellschaft für Theater- geschichte.* Vol. 1–. Berlin: Gesellschaft für Thea- tergeschichte, 1902–.

LATR   *Latin-American Theatre Review.* Vol. 1–. Law- rence: Center for Latin American Studies, Universi- ty of Kansas, 1967–. 2/yr. Reviews.
PN2309.L37

MuK   *Maske und Kothurn: Vierteljahres Schrift für Thea- terwissenschaft.* Weimar: Böhlau; Vienna: Institut für Theaterwissenschaft, University of Vienna, 1955–. 4/yr. Reviews. Annual bibliography of German books and articles, with an emphasis on German theater and German productions of foreign drama.   PN2004.M36

MD   *Modern Drama.* Vol. 1–. Toronto: University of Toronto Press, 1958–. 4/yr. Reviews. Bibliogra- phy (see R–44).   PN1861.M55

NCTR   *Nineteenth Century Theatre Research.* Vol. 1–. Tucson: University of Arizona, 1973–. 2/yr. Re- views. Bibliography (see Q–62).   PN1851.N55

PAR   *Performing Arts Resources.* Vol. 1–. New York: Theatre Library Association, 1974–. 1/yr. (see U–9).   Z6935.P46

Players   *Players: Magazine of American Theatre.* Vol. 1–. DeKalb, Ill.: National Collegiate Players, Northern Illinois University, 1924–. 6/yr.

REEDN   *Records of Early English Drama Newsletter.* Vol. 1–. Toronto: University of Toronto, Erindale College, 1976–. 2/yr.   No LC number

RenD   *Renaissance Drama.* Vol. 1–. Evanston, Ill.: Northwestern University Press, 1964–. Reviews.   PN1785.R4

RORD   *Research Opportunities in Renaissance Drama.* Vol. 1–. New Orleans, La.: University of New Orleans, 1956–. 1/yr. Reviews. Bibliographical notices (see O–33).   PR621.M75a

RECTR   *Restoration and Eighteenth Century Theatre Research.* Vol. 1–. Chicago: Loyola University of Chicago, 1962–. 2/yr. Reviews. Bibliography (see P–31).   PN2592.R46

Rht   *Revue d'histoire du théâtre.* Vol. 1–. Paris: Société d'histoire du théâtre, 1933–. 4/yr. Reviews. Bibliography (see U–16).   PN2003.R38

SGT   *Schriften der Gesellschaft für Theatergeschichte.* Vol. 1–. Berlin: Gesellschaft für Theatergeschichte, 1902–.   LC numbers vary

   Speech and Drama. Vol. 1–. Loughborough, Leics: Society of Teachers of Speech and Drama, 1951–.   PN4071.S73

TDR   *TDR: The Drama Review* [former title: *Tulane Drama Review*]. Vol. 1–. New York University School of Arts, 1955–. Reviews. Annual list, "Books and Theatre: A Bibliography."   PN2000.D68

Theatre   *Theatre* [former title: *Yale/Theatre* 1968–1977]. Vol. 1–. New Haven: Yale School of Drama, 1968–. 3–4/yr. Reviews.   PN2000.Y34

TA   *Theatre Annual: A Publication of Information and Research in the Arts and History of the Theatre.* Vol. 1–. Hiram, Ohio: Theatre Library Association, 1942–. 1/yr.   PN2012.T5

TArts   *Theatre Arts Monthly.* Vols. 1–47. New York: Theatre Arts, 1919–1964. 12/yr. Reviews.

   Theatre Documentation. Vol. 1–. New York: Theatre Library Association, 1968–. Bibliography (see U–17).   PN1560.T398

   Theatre History Studies. Vol. 1–. Grand Forks: University of North Dakota Press, 1981–. 1/yr.   PN2000.T49

   Theatre Journal [former title: *Educational Theatre Journal, 1949–1978*]. Vol. 1–. Baltimore: Johns Hopkins University Press for the University and College Theater Association, 1949–. 4/yr. Reviews. "Doctoral Projects in Progress in Theatre Arts (1953–)," "Scholarly Works in Progress (1974–)."   PN3171.E38

TN   *Theatre Notebook: A Journal of the History and Technique of the British Theatre* [early subtitle: *Quarterly of Notes and Research*]. Vol. 1–. London: Society for Theatre Research, 1945–. 3–4/yr. Reviews. Annual index.   PN2001.T43

TQ   *Theatre Quarterly.* Vol. 1–. London: TQ Publications, 1971–. 4/yr. Reviews. Bibliography (see U–14).   PN2001.T435

ThR   *Theatre Research International* [Former title, *Theater Research/Recherches Théâtres*, 1958–1974]. Vol. 1–. Oxford: Oxford University Press for the International Federation for Theatre Research, 1975–. 3/yr. Reviews. Annual index.   PN2001.T436

TheatreS   *Theatre Studies.* Vol. 1–. Columbus: Ohio State University Theatre Research Institute, 1955–. 1/yr. Reviews. Includes Reviews of Research and Dissertations in Progress.   PN1620.D45 A3

ThS   *Theatre Survey: The American Journal of Theatre History.* Vol. 1–. Albany: State University of New York at Albany and the American Society for Theatre Research, 1960–. 2/yr. Reviews. Cumulative index to vols. 1–20 in vol. 20 (1979).   PN2000.T716

   Theatrefacts: International Theatre Reference. Vol. 1–. London: TQ Publications, 1974–. Reviews. Checklists (see U–14).   No LC number

   Yale/Theatre (see *Theatre*).

For aids in locating and studying theatrical periodicals see Carl J. Stratman, *American Theatrical Periodicals 1798-1967: A Bibliographical Guide* (Durham, N.C.: Duke University Press, 1970) [Z6935.S75] and *Britain's Theatrical Periodicals, 1720-1967: A Bibliography*, 2d ed. (New York: New York Public Library, 1972) [Z6935.S76 1972], originally published in 1962 under the title *Bibliography of British Dramatic Periodicals 1720-1960.*

U–19   **Some Frequently Recommended General Works on the Performing Arts, the Theater, and the Drama.** (See also U–67 and U–68.)

Abel, Lionel. *Metatheater: A New View of Dramatic Form.* New York: Hill and Wang, 1964.   PN1623.A35

Altick, Richard D. *Shows of London.* Cambridge: Harvard University Press, 1978.   T395.5.G7 A45

Bentley, Eric. *In Search of Theatre.* New York: Knopf, 1953.   PN2189.B4

Brownstein, Oscar Lee, and Darlene M. Daubert. *Analytic Sourcebook of Concepts in Dramatic Theory.* Westport, Conn.: Greenwood, 1981.   Z5781.B84

Burns, Elizabeth. *Theatricality: A Study of Convention in the Theatre and in Social Life.* London: Longman, 1972.   PN2049.B87

Calderwood, James L., and Harold E. Toliver, eds. *Perspectives on Drama.* New York: Oxford University Press, 1968.   PN1621.C3

Clark, Barnett H., ed. *European Theories of the Drama, with a Supplement on American Drama: An Anthology of Dramatic Theory and Criticism from Aristotle to the Present Day, in a Series of Selected Texts, with Commentaries, Biographies, and Bibliographies.* 2d ed. Revised by Henry Popkin. New York: Crown, 1962.   PN1661.C55 1955

Ellis-Fermor, Una. *Frontiers of Drama.* With an introduction by Allardyce Nicoll and a bibliography by Harold Brooks. 2d ed. London: Methuen, 1964.   PN1623.E6 1964

Ferguson, Francis. *Idea of a Theater: A Study of Ten Plays: The Art of Drama in Changing Perspective.* Princeton, N.J.: Princeton University Press, 1949.   PN1661.F4

Hunninger, B. *Origin of the Theatre: An Essay.* The Hague: M. Nijhoff, 1955.   PN1737.H8

Nicoll, Allardyce. *Theatre and Dramatic Theory.* London: Harrap, 1962.   PN1631.N42

———. *Theory of Drama.* New rev. and enl. ed. of *Introduction to Dramatic Theory* (1923). London: G. G. Harrap, 1931.   PN1631.N4 1931

Peacock, Ronald. *Art of the Drama.* London: Routledge and Kegan Paul, 1957.   PN1631.P37 1957

Southern, Richard. *Open Stage and the Modern Theatre in Research and Practice*. London: Faber and Faber, 1959.   PN2081.O6 S6 1959

Vowles, Richard B. *Dramatic Theory: A Bibliography* [books and articles 1930–1956]. New York: New York Public Library, 1956.   Z5781.V6

II. HANDBOOKS AND READER'S ENCYCLOPEDIAS

In addition to the general handbooks and reader's encyclopedias cited in section L.II, section M.III, and section S.IV, see also the handbooks of modern literature in section R.III.

U–20 *Enciclopedia dello spettacolo.* 9 vols. Rome: Maschere, 1954–1964.   PN1625.E7

This massive and lavishly illustrated encyclopedia of the performing arts treats theater, opera, ballet, vaudeville, film, television, radio, the circus, and allied arts. Long, signed articles with superior bibliographies appended have been prepared by an international board of contributing specialists. Biographical articles treat performers, authors, composers, directors, designers, and other theatrical personnel. There are articles on organizations and acting companies, on important places in performing arts history, on types of entertainment, on dramatic themes, and on historical and technical subjects.

An *Aggiornamento 1955-65* (Rome: Unione editoriale, 1966) adds new articles, primarily of contemporary biography. The *Indice repertorio* (Rome: Unione editoriale, 1968) presents a general alphabetical list of some 145,000 titles of plays and other productions mentioned in the main work and the *Aggiornamento*, giving the art form, author, and date for each. It is preceded by an index of Greek-language titles cited in the encyclopedia.

U–21 **Hartnoll, Phyllis. *Oxford Companion to the Theatre.*** 4th ed. London: Oxford University Press, 1983.
                                                                PN2035.H3 1983

This work was originally published in 1951, with a second edition in 1957, and a completely revised third edition in 1967. This edition's more than 3,500 entries are current to the end of 1981, with focus on the theaters of England, America, and France. Articles treat all aspects of theater but do emphasize theater as opposed to drama. For the opposite emphasis see Gassner and Quinn's *Reader's Encyclopedia* (U–23). There are numerous long, signed articles surveying the theater of individual nations and broad topics such as incidental music and trick work. The cinema is, however, excluded. In addition, there are biographical articles on playwrights (under which individual plays are cited and described), actors, actresses, producers, directors, designers, and other theater personnel. Other articles treat sets, costumes, acting companies, stage terms, and other technical aspects of the theater. Though not emphasized, there are articles on dramatic characters, genres, and the history of dramatic criticism. Appendixes include a list of contributors, a select bibliography of books on the theater, and a set of illustrations with notes.

The work has been published in a condensed edition as *Concise Oxford Companion to the Theatre* (London: Oxford University Press, 1972) [PN2035.C63]. Oxford has also published the *Oxford Companion to American Theater*, compiled by Gerald Bordman (New York: Oxford University Press, 1984) [PN2220.B6 1984] which has comparable coverage to the Hartnoll volume, but because of its narrower scope, this work is able in its approximately 3,000 entries to treat more ephemeral figures and productions, including many often neglected aspects of the nineteenth-century American theater. A *Concise Oxford Companion to the American Theatre* (New York: Oxford University Press, 1987) [PN2220.B6 1987] cuts approximately forty percent of the entries in the original volume.

Another smaller volume is John Russel Taylor's *Dictionary of the Theatre*, 2d ed., rev. (Harmondsworth, Middlesex: Penguin, 1970) [PN1625.T3 1970], which emphasizes the contemporary theater, but includes plays, actors, playwrights, theater terms, and much that the inquiring student might find useful. Yet another guide is William Packard, et al., eds., *Facts on File Dictionary of the Theatre* (New York: Facts on File, 1988) [PN2035.F27 1988].

U–22 ***McGraw-Hill Encyclopedia of World Drama.*** 2d ed. Stanley Hochman, ed. 5 vols. New York: McGraw-Hill, 1984.
                                                                PN1625.M3 1984

Although this massive encyclopedia prepared by nearly 100 contributing editors includes articles on various genres and terms, the majority of its articles are on individual playwrights of all times and places. The original four volume edition of 1972 has been expanded upon, particularly with regard to African, Asian, and Latin American drama. Articles on major playwrights give brief biographies, general critical surveys of their works, synopses of the major plays, lists of all plays written, and extended primary and secondary bibliographies. Those for minor playwrights give a succinct account of their lives and works. There are many illustrations including portraits and scenes from plays. Volume 5 includes a glossary of dramatic terms, forms, movements, and styles based on Jack A. Vaughn's *Drama A to Z: A Handbook* (New York: Ungar, 1978) [PN1625.V3]. An index of playrights, play titles (with foreign titles given in both their original and English versions), dramatic genres, historical periods and theaters concludes the volume, along with an alphabetical playtitle list keyed to the author entries.

U–23 **Gassner, John, and Edward Quinn, eds. *Reader's Encyclopedia of World Drama.*** New York: Crowell, 1969.
                                                                PN1625.G3

In contrast with the *Oxford Companion to the Theatre* (U–21), this reader's companion treats drama rather than theater, excluding actors, playhouses, and technical aspects of the theater. Instead, it features articles on the drama of all times and places, with articles on plays giving summaries and critical analyses as well as biographical and critical articles on dramatists. There are, in addition, survey articles on national dramas, on various genres, movements, and terms, and on the historical contexts of the drama. Each article is signed with initials of one of the ninety-five specialist contributors. The work concludes with an appendix of "Basic Documents on Dramatic Theory" from Aristotle to Dürrenmatt.

U–24 **Sharp, Harold S., and Marjorie Z. Sharp. *Index to Characters in the Performing Arts.*** 4 parts in 6 vols. New York: Scarecrow Press, 1966–1973.   PN1579.S45

This dictionary of major and minor characters is intended to include works of all times and places. Part I, Non-Musical Plays, is an alphabetical listing of 30,000 characters and occupies volumes 1 and 2. Character names, including both proper names and type names (e.g., shrew, old man) are listed alphabetically; the character is briefly described, including function, and identified by the author, year, and a short-title production code that refers to the list of productions at the end of the second volume. There, each of the 3,600 analyzed productions is described in detail, giving the full title, the production type, the number of acts, and the author. There are cross-references from first and middle character names and from titles (e.g., King of Bohemia).

Part II, Operas and Musical Productions, occupies volumes 3 and 4. Productions include ballad operas, operettas, musical comedies, and plays in which music is introduced. Approximately 20,000 characters are listed in these volumes, taken from more than 2,500 productions that range from the folk plays of the thirteenth century to the 1965/66 Broadway season. Volume 4 contains the list of productions analyzed in these volumes with the five-letter citation symbol used in the index, followed by full production details.

Part III, Ballet, occupies volume 5 of the series and similarly identifies and describes some 3,000 characters from 818 ballets. The ballets are each given a five-letter citation symbol, and at the end of the volume, in the alphabetical order of their citation symbols, full production information is given.

Part IV, finally, treats Radio and Television production to about 1955 for radio and to 1972 for television, listing some 20,000 characters found in some 2,500 productions. Characters and production names are listed in a single alphabet with cross-references from all the subordinate characters to the main entry.

U–25 **Esslin, Martin.** *Encyclopedia of World Theater.* New York: Scribner, 1977.   PN2035.E52 1977

This volume is a translation and adaptation of *Friedrichs Theaterlexikon* by Karl Gröning and Werner Kliess (Velber bei Hannover: Friedrich Verlag, 1969) [PN2035.G75], to which additional materials on the American and British theater have been added. The volume does, however, retain its original international flavor. Brief articles, primarily biographical, frequently have current bibliographies appended. There are also articles on theater history, movements, and terminology. And there are numerous high-quality illustrations. There are many cross-references within articles, and the encyclopedia concludes with an index of play titles.

U–26 *International Dictionary of Theatre Language.* Ed. Joel Trapido. Westport, Conn.: Greenwood, 1985.
          PN2035.I5 1985

This 1,032 page dictionary contains about 10,000 English language and about 5,000 foreign language terms used both in the past and currently in connection with the drama and theater throughout the world. The foreign language terms are only those used in the English-speaking world. There are brief definitions which cite works in the accompanying bibliography where more complete discussions will be found. The prefatory materials include "A Brief History of Theatre Glossaries and Dictionaries."

An earlier and more compact work is by Walter P. Bowman and Robert H. Ball, *Theatre Language: A Dictionary of Terms in English of the Drama and Stage from Medieval to Modern Times* (New York: Theatre Arts, 1961) [PN2035.B6]. It contains definitions of some 5,000 terms derived from usage in the American and British theater. Both slang and technical terms are included, but for the most part, opera and ballet terms are excluded. Earlier still is Wilfred Granville's *Dictionary of Theatrical Terms* (London: Deutsch, 1952), published in the United States under the title *Theatre Dictionary: British and American Terms in the Drama, Opera, and Ballet* (New York: Oxford University Press, 1952) [PN2035 .G7 1952], which contains theater slang but not technical terms. About 3,000 terms are defined. For many of the most frequently used terms see also Barnet, Berman, and Burto's *Dictionary of Literary, Dramatic and Cinematic Terms*, 2d ed. (L–13).

U–27 **Lounsbury, Warren C.** *Theatre Backstage from A to Z.* Rev. ed. Seattle: University of Washington Press, 1972.
          PN2035.L6 1972

Originally published in 1959, this volume treats all of the technical aspects of play production in a dictionary form. Only technical terms are given, but they are discussed in considerable detail.

The standard polyglot dictionary of technical terms is Kenneth Rae and Richard Southern, *International Vocabulary of Technical Theatre Terms in Eight Languages / Lexique international de termes techniques de théâtre en huit langues* (New York: Theatre Arts, 1964) [PN2035.R3], which gives American, Dutch, English, French, German, Italian, Spanish, and Swedish terms. It is in two parts, the first a numbered alphabetical list of 637 terms in English (with American variants indicated) with equivalent terms in other languages, and the second a series of alphabetical indexes in the other languages. Another polyglot dictionary, which includes jargon, is Karen R. M. Band-Kuzmany, *Glossary of the Theatre, in English, French, Italian, and German* (Amsterdam: Elsevier, 1969) [PN2035.B3], which has, however, been criticized for some inaccuracies.

U–28 **Bryan, George B., comp.** *Stage Lives: A Bibliography and Index to Theatrical Biographies in English.* Westport, Conn.: Greenwood Press, 1985.   Z5781.S78 1985

This volume is divided into two parts. The first, a Bibliography of Biographies enumerates three types of biographies, as follows: A. Collective Theatrical Biographies (a total of 126 items, descriptively annotated); B. Other Collective Biographies (a total of twenty-eight items, with descriptive annotation); and C. Individual Biographies and Autobiographies (a total of 2,597 items). Part two, Index of Biographees lists names of persons from 534 to the present whose life was connected to the living theater and whose biography appears in one of the items in part one. Entries in the index give dates, a brief identifying statement, and the alpha-numeric entry number (with pages) where the biography can be found.

An unusual feature of this volume is the Appendix, titled Necrological annals, which lists theater people who died each year from 1700 to 1984. Persons who died before 1700 are included in lists of biographees from classical and medieval times, the sixteenth century, and the seventeenth century.

U–29 **Wearing, J. P.** *American and British Theatrical Biography: A Directory.* Metuchen, N.J.: Scarecrow Press, 1979.
          PN2285.W42

This volume analyzes the contents of some 175 dictionaries of theatrical biography and other biographical sources. For each person listed, entries cite the name, dates of birth and death, nationality, and theatrical occupation, along with codes referring to the source(s) of biographical information. More than 50,000 persons are listed, along with all the standard sources of theatrical biography. These include such frequently recommended sources as the following titles:

Adams, William D. *Dictionary of the Drama: A Guide to the Plays, Playwrights, Players, and Playhouses of the United Kingdom and America from the Earliest Times to the Present.* London: Chatto and Windus, 1904. Only volume 1, A-G, was published.   PR623.A3

Baker, David E., et al. *Biographia Dramatica: A Companion to the Playhouse* [to 1764 by D. E. Baker; to 1782 by Isaac Reed; to 1811 by Stephen Jones]. 3 vols. in 4. London: Longmans, 1812.   Z2014.D7 B167

Fleay, Frederick G. *Biographical Chronicle of the English Drama, 1559–1642.* 2 vols. London: Reeves and Turner, 1891. Many inaccuracies.   PR651.F5

Highfill, Philip, et al. *Biographical Dictionary of Actors, Actresses, Musicians, Dancers, Managers and Other Stage Personnel in London, 1660–1800* (see P–35).   PN2597.H5

Langbaine, Gerard. *Lives and Characters of the English Dramatick Poets.* Continued by C. Gildon. London: For T. Leigh and W. Turner, 1969.   Z2014.D7 L23

Nungezer, Edwin. *Dictionary of Actors and of the Persons Associated with the Public Representation of Plays in England before 1642.* New Haven: Yale University Press, 1929.   PN2597.N8

Rigdon, Walker, ed. *Biographical Encyclopedia and Who's Who of the American Theatre.* New York: J. H. Heineman, 1966.   PN2285.R5

Who's Who in the Theatre: A Biographical Record of the Contemporary Stage. 15th ed. London: Pitman, 1972.   PN2012.W5

III.   CATALOGS OF MAJOR THEATER AND DRAMA COLLECTIONS

See also Young's *American Theatrical Arts: A Guide to Manuscripts and Special Collections in the United States and Canada* (H–55).

U–30 **New York Public Library.** *Catalog of the Theatre and Drama Collections.* 51 vols. Boston: G. K. Hall, 1967–1976.   Z5785.N56 1967

These fifty-one volumes are in four groups: Part I (A) is a six-volume author listing of the Drama Collection, including editions for some 120,000 Western-language plays (including translations), along with Western-language translations from Slavic, Hebrew, and Oriental languages. Both separately published works and plays in anthologies and periodicals are included.

Part I (B) is a six-volume re-listing of the Drama Collection by country of origin.

Part II is a volume listing of the Theatre Collection, citing more than 23,500 books on the theater, including stage history, biography, criticism, acting, and stage management. There are approximately 121,000 entries, since each work is given under author, title, subject, and other secondary headings.

Part III is a thirty-volume catalog of the Theatre Collection's nonbook materials and includes such materials as reviews, playbills, and promptbooks.

There are three series of supplements. The first three-volume *Supplement* (Boston: G. K. Hall, 1973) continues Parts I (A) and I (B) and Part II through the end of 1971. The second supplement, *Dictionary Catalog of the Theatre and Drama Collections, 1974* (Boston: G. K. Hall, 1976) [Z5785.N56 1967 Suppl.2], contains information on additions to the collections made between January 1972 and September 1974. The third and continuing series of supplements takes the form of an annual *Bibliographic Guide to Theatre Arts* [1975—] (Boston: G. K. Hall, 1976–) [Z6935.N46a], listing by author, title, and subject theater material cataloged during the preceding year by the New York Public Library combined with material cataloged by the Library of Congress.

Other catalogs of major American drama and theater collections include the *Catalogue of the Larpent Plays in the Huntington Library,* comp. Dougald Macmillan (B–20) [Z2014.D7 H525]; the thirteen-volume *Dictionary Catalog of the Harris Collection of American Poetry and Plays in the*

Brown University Library (S–67) [Z1231.P7 B72]; and the *Catalogues of the Allen A. Brown Collection of Books Relating to the Stage* (Boston: Public Library, 1919) [Z5785.B72].

U–32 **British Drama League.** *Player's Library: The Catalogue of the Library of the British Drama League.* 2d ed. London: Faber and Faber, 1950.   Z2014.D7 B8

This catalog of the largest special collection in Britain supersedes the library's first catalog of 1930 and its 1934 supplement. The work is arranged as an alphabetical author catalog of approximately 15,000 plays. Entries give play titles, types, the number of acts, the scene settings, costume requirements, and publication information. Both separately published plays and those in anthologies are cited. A bibliography of books on the theater, organized by subject according to the Dewey classification, is followed by an index of play titles and an author index to the theater book bibliography.

There have been three supplements to date, published in 1951, 1954, and 1956, respectively. The third supplement has a special section of plays in French; otherwise the supplements are arranged in parallel to the original volume, with theater book lists following lists of plays. There are also important collections of nonbook theater materials at the League, including collections of promptbooks, periodicals, press cuttings, playbills, and the like, for which no published catalog is yet available.

U–33 **Angotti, Vincent L.** *Source Materials in the Field of Theatre: An Annotated Bibliography and Subject Index to the Microfilm Collection.* Ann Arbor, Mich.: University Microfilms, 1967.   Z5781.A57

A bibliography arranged alphabetically by author of the microfilmed monographs, manuscripts, journals, and diaries related to the theater held by various libraries and available on microfilm. English-, French-, German-, Italian-, and Latin-language materials are included. Entries give author, titles, publishers, pagination, and a descriptive annotation. The volume concludes with a subject index.

U–34 **Young, William C.** *Documents of American Theater History.* 4 vols. to date. Chicago: American Library Association; New York: *The New Yorker,* 1973–.   NA6830.Y68

These volumes bring together a chronologically arranged anthology of primary and secondary sources for those interested in the American theater. Diaries, letters, journals, autobiographies, newspaper articles and reviews, magazine articles, playbills, publicity materials, and architectural descriptions are included in verbatim transcription. The volumes and their subjects are as follows:

Vol. 1. *Famous American Playhouses, 1716–1899* (1973).

Vol. 2. *Famous American Playhouses, 1900–1971* (1973).

Vols. 3–4. *Famous Actors and Actresses on the American Stage* (1975).

Throughout, New York theater is treated separately from regional theater. Each volume has indexes by theater name, by location, and by personal name.

IV. ANNALS, CHECKLISTS, AND INDEXES TO PLAYS IN ANTHOLOGIES AND COLLECTIONS

For recorded drama see section E.IX; for filmed drama see section E.X and material on film and literature in section U.VIII below.

U–35 Harbage, Alfred. *Annals of English Drama 975–1700: An Analytical Record of All Plays, Extant or Lost, Chronologically Arranged and Indexed by Authors, Titles, Dramatic Companies, etc.* Rev. ed. Revised by Samuel Schoenbaum. London: Methuen, 1964.   Z2014 .D7 H25 1964

This volume, originally published in 1940, is arranged in compact, tabular form, as a chronological list by century and year and, within each year, alphabetically by playwright's name. Included are plays in Latin, French, and English, lost or extant, acted or not, published or not, translated, adapted, or original, devised in England or by Englishmen abroad. Entries give in seven columns the author (noting questions of attribution); the title (and alternate titles); the date of a play's first performance (or an approximation); the type of play (mask, tragedy, comedy, etc.); the auspices under which it was acted; the date of its first edition (or an approximation); and the date of the most recent modern edition. The chronology proper is followed by lists of extant plays of uncertain date and therefore not placed in the chronology, and of lost plays similarly excluded. Appended is a list of extant play manuscripts with locations and catalog numbers. There are indexes of English playwrights; titles of foreign plays adapted or translated; of dramatic companies; and of theaters, each of which is briefly described.

There are two supplements: *Supplement to the Revised Edition*, ed. Schoenbaum (Evanston: Northwestern University Press, 1966), and *Second Supplement to the Revised Edition*, also ed. Schoenbaum (Evanston, Ill.: Northwestern University Press, 1970). A third edition of the *Annals* is now in preparation.

For plays after 1700 see *Egerton's Theatrical Remembrancer, Containing a Complete List of All the Dramatic Performances in the English Language, Their Several Editions, Dates, and Sizes, and the Theatres Where They Were Originally Performed . . . to the End of the Year* [1787] *to Which Are Added Notitia Dramatica: Being a Chronological Account of Events Relative to the English Stage* (London: For T. and J. Egerton, 1788) [Z2014.D7 E2], which is continued to the end of the eighteenth century by W. C. Oulton, *Barker's Continuation of Egerton's Theatrical Remembrancer* (London: Barker, 1801) [Z2014.D7 B38].

U–36 Stratman, Carl J. *Dramatic Play Lists, 1591–1963.* New York: New York Public Library, 1966.   Z2014.D7 S85 1966

This reprint of articles in *BNYPL* 70 (1966): 71–85, 169–88, presents a descriptive catalog of printed play lists, giving the titles in chronological order with bibliographical information and extended descriptive and evaluative annotations. The work is indexed by author and by title.

U–37 Bergquist, George W. *Three Centuries of English and American Plays, A Checklist; England: 1500–1800, United States: 1714–1830.* New York: Readex Microprint, 1963.   Z2014.D7 B45 1963

This checklist provides a single alphabetical list of authors and titles for the Microprint edition of 5,500 English and American plays in various editions and manuscripts which was published under the title *Three Centuries of English and American Plays* (see E–50). A total of 5,350 British and 250 American plays are included. Entries give the title and publication information and, where possible, cite standard reference sources, including Greg (O–31), Woodward and McManaway (P–33), or Wegelin and Hill (S–77).

U–38 Thompson, Laurence S. *Nineteenth and Twentieth Century Drama: A Selective Bibliography of English Language Works.* Nos. 1–3029. Boston: G. K. Hall, 1975.   Z2014.D7 T5

This alphabetical author index, with anonymous works listed by title, consists of 3,029 post–1800 English-language plays and anthologies containing plays and other works for the stage which have been microfilmed by General Microfilm Company, Cambridge, Mass. Included are classic plays, monologues, children's plays, school drama, vaudeville, and various other entertainments. The author list, called the "Drama File," is followed by a series of eight indexes, as follows: Titles, Subjects, Editors, Authors and Joint Authors, Translators, Pseudonyms, Illustrators, and Composers.

U–39 Eldredge, H. J., comp. *"The Stage" Cyclopedia: A Bibliography of Plays by Reginald Clarence [pseud.]: An Alphabetical List of Plays and Other Stage Pieces of Which Any Record Can Be Found since the Commencement of the English Stage, together with Descriptions, Authors' Names, Dates and Places of Production, and Other Useful Information, Comprising in All Nearly 50,000 Plays and Extending over a Period of Upwards of 500 Years.* London: "The Stage," 1909.   Z2014.D7 E4

This volume contains in one alphabet a list of authors and titles of plays, operas, oratorios, sketches, and other stage pieces recorded in any way through September 1909.

U–40 Odell, George C. D. *Annals of the New York Stage.* 15 vols. New York: Columbia University Press, 1927–1949.   PN2277.N504

This detailed chronological history of the theater in New York from 1699 to 1894 gives authors, titles, and accounts of productions. The volumes (which are each separately indexed) and their years of coverage are as follows: vol. 1, to 1798; vol. 2, 1798–1821; vol. 3, 1821–1834; vol. 4, 1834–1843; vol. 5, 1843–1850; vol. 6, 1850–1857; vol. 7, 1857–1865; vol. 8, 1865–1870; vol. 9, 1870–1875; vol. 10, 1875–1879; vol. 11, 1879–1882; vol. 12, 1882–1885; vol. 13, 1885–1888; vol. 14, 1888–1891; and vol. 15, 1891–1894. There is a separately published *Index to the Portraits in Odell's Annals of the New York Stage . . .* (New York: American Society for Theatre Research, 1963).

For a chronology of the New York stage after 1894, see *Best Plays, 1894–99–*(New York: Dodd, Mead, 1899–), the title of which varies (e.g., *Burns Mantle Best Plays, Burns Mantle Yearbook,* etc.) [no LC number].

There are similar compilations for the London and Paris stages For London, see *Best Plays,* which includes an annual survey of "The London Scene."

For Paris from 1800 to 1900 see Charles B. Wicks, *Parisian Stage: Alphabetical Indexes of Plays and Authors,* 5 vols. (University: University of Alabama Press, 1975–1979) [PN2636.P3 W5].

U–43 Firkins, Ina Ten Eyck. *Index to Plays, 1800–1926.* New York: H. W. Wilson, 1927.   Z5781.A1 F5

This volume indexes by author and then by subject and title a total of 7,872 English plays by 2,203 authors. Periodicals, collections, and anthologies published 1800–1926 are analyzed, and separately published editions are also identified. Under authors are listed first separately published plays, then collected works, then works found in composite editions, and finally works located in periodicals and magazines. Entries often include details about setting, characterization, and the like, as well as bibliographical information. The title/subject index refers to the author entry for full information. The subject index is incomplete and meant to be merely suggestive of a number of plays on a given subject. There are two appendixes, a list of books by one author containing two or more plays, and an index of composite collections.

A *Supplement* analyzing publications 1927–1934 was published in 1935 and adds 3,284 additional plays by 1,335 to the original work. It is arranged in parallel to the original volume.

U–44 **Samples, Gordon. *Drama Scholars' Index to Plays and Filmscripts: A Guide to Plays and Filmscripts in Selected Anthologies, Series, and Periodicals.*** 3 vols. Metuchen, N.J.: Scarecrow Press, 1974–1986.   Z5781.S17

These volumes index a total of some 1,550 anthologies and collections, about 128 publishers' series, and about 128 periodicals through 1983, emphasizing the analysis of works not covered in other available indexes, including eighteenth- and nineteenth-century anthologies and collections and foreign-language periodicals. Entries are in a single alphabetical list of authors, of original authors (for translated works), of historical characters, and of titles. Main entries are given under the author, with cross-references from other entries. Appended to volume 1 is a list of analyzed collections and a list of analyzed periodicals and publishers' series. At the end of volume 2 is found an author list of anthologies in volume 2 as well as title lists to anthologies and collections, publishers' series, and periodical titles indexed in both volumes. Similar lists conclude volume 3.

U–45 **Connor, Billie M., and Helene G. Mochedlover. *Ottemiller's Index to Plays in Collections: An Author and Title Index to Plays Appearing in Collections Published between 1900 and 1985.*** 7th ed., rev. and enl. Metuchen, N.J.: Scarecrow Press, 1988.   Z5781.O8 1988

Originally published in 1943, this work, now in its seventh edition, indexes a total of 6,548 plays by 2,555 authors in 1,350 collections published in England or the United States. Main entries are in alphabetical order by author and give name, dates, play title, date of first production, a list of variant titles, and a code referring to the appended list of collections analyzed. Anonymous plays are listed alphabetically by title under the entry Anonymous. Foreign plays are listed under both original and English titles, with cross-references to main author entries. The volume concludes with an Author Index, a List of Collections and Key to Symbols, and a Title Index.

U–46 **Keller, Dean H. *Index to Plays in Periodicals.*** Rev. and exp. ed. Metuchen, N.J.: Scarecrow Press, 1979.
            Z5781.K43 1979

Originally published in 1971, with a supplement in 1973, this work provides an author index to 9,562 plays in 267 periodicals. Entries give author, dates, title, and a brief description, and cite the periodical in which the play is published. The volume ends with a title index.

See also Charlotte A. Patterson, *Plays in Periodicals: An Index to English Language Scripts in Twentieth Century Journals* (Boston: G. K. Hall, 1970) [Z5781.P3], which indexes by title about 4,000 plays in ninety-seven periodicals published 1900–1968. Entries give title, author, translator,

adapter, length, size and mix of cast, and the periodical in which the script is published. There is a separate index of authors and a "cast analysis" index that gives the number of males, females, children, and extras called for in production.

U–47 **Thomson, Ruth G. *Index to Full Length Plays, 1895 to [1944].*** 2 vols. Boston: Faxon, 1946–1956.   Z5781.T5

These volumes together index 1,902 published plays in English alphabetically by title. Information includes author, translator, number of acts, characters, sets, and subject matter, along with publication data. There are author and subject indexes. The first volume treats 562 plays of 1895–1925 and was published in 1956; the second treats 1,340 plays of 1926–1944 and was published in 1946. Both volumes are continued by Norma O. Ireland, *Index to Full Length Plays 1944 to 1964* (Boston: Faxon, 1965) [Z5781.T52], which adds 798 English-language plays in a single-alphabet author-title-subject index.

U–48 ***Play Index: 1949–.*** New York: H. W. Wilson, 1953–.
            Z5781.P53

The volumes of this continuing index to published plays are in four parts. Part I lists each play by author, title, and subject in a single alphabet. The main author entry includes the title, a brief synopsis, the number of acts and scenes, the cast size and number of sets, noting also required dance or music. Title and subject entries refer to main entries. Sources of adapted plays are given, with cross-references from the sources to the adaptations. Subject entries include specific subjects and genre and type headings. This is the sole index of its type to provide subject access to plays.

Part II is a "Cast Analysis" index and cites plays under an elaborate series of divisions. Part III lists the collections and publishers' series analyzed, with publication details. Part IV is a directory of publishers and distributors.

To date, the following volumes of the *Index* have appeared: 1949–1952, listing 2,616 plays (1953); 1953–1960, listing 4,592 plays (1963); 1961–1967, listing 4,793 plays (1968); 1968–1971, listing 3,848 plays (1973); and 1973–1977, listing 3,878 plays (1978).

U–49 **Chicorel, Marietta, ed. *Chicorel Theater Index to Plays in Anthologies, Periodicals, Discs, and Tapes.*** 2 vols. New York: Chicorel, 1970–1971.   Z5781.C485

These volumes, the first and second of the *Chicorel Index Series*, include some 2,000 plays in over 550 collections in print and in current periodicals. The index provides in a single alphabet periodical titles, play titles, authors, translators, adapters, and editors of scripts.

A companion volume, *Chicorel Theater Index to Plays in Anthologies, Periodicals, and Discs in England*, volume 3 in the *Chicorel Index Series*, was published in 1972 [Z5781.C486].

Subsequent volumes separate the index of periodicals from that of anthologies and collections. The *Chicorel Theater Index to Plays in Periodicals*, volume 8 in the *Chicorel Index Series*, was published in 1973 and provides an analysis of plays in 159 periodicals [Z5781.C487]. The *Chicorel Theater Index to Plays in Anthologies and Collections, 1970-1976*, volume 25 in the *Chicorel Index Series*, was published in 1977 and updates the original volumes [Z5781.C4846]. All of the now out-of-print Chicorel Indexes are available in Microform through Microforms International.

V.   BIBLIOGRAPHIES AND CHECKLISTS OF CRITICISM

See also the bibliographies of drama criticism in the drama and theater subsections of the individual periods of English literature and of section S.   See also the treatment of poetic drama in section T, and note that the checklists of explication cited there (T–31, T–32) include dramatic texts as well.

U–50 **Wells, Stanley, ed.   *English Drama (Excluding Shakespeare): Select Bibliographical Guides.*** London: Oxford University Press, 1975.   Z2014.D7 E44

This volume consists of a series of bibliographical essays that together constitute a bibliographical guide to the history of English drama.   There are seventeen chapters, each of which presents a survey of its subject and then a classified list of references mentioned in the text.   The chapters and their authors are as follows: The Study of Drama (Peter Thomson); Medieval Drama (John Leyerle); Tudor and Early Elizabethan Drama (T. W. Craik); Marlowe (D. J. Palmer); Jonson and Chapman (J. B. Bamborough); Marston, Middleton, and Massinger (S. Schoenbaum); Beaumont and Fletcher, Heywood, and Dekker (Michael Taylor); Webster, Tourneur, and Ford (Inga-Stina Ewbank); The Court Masque (K. M. Lea); Davenant, Dryden, Lee and Otway (H. Neville Davies); Etherege, Shadwell, Wycherley, Congreve, Vanbrugh, and Farquhar (John Barnard); Gay, Goldsmith, Sheridan, and Other Eighteenth-Century Dramatists (Cecil Price); Nineteenth-Century Drama (Michael R. Booth); Shaw (Margery M. Morgan); The Irish School (Ann Saddlemyer); English Drama 1900–1945 (Allardyce Nicoll); and English Drama since 1945 (John Russell Brown).   Notes on the contributors and a brief index of dramatists and anonymous plays conclude the volume.   The Shakespeare companion volume is listed at O–40.   For more recent bibliographical essays on the English drama, see the *Year's Work in English Studies* (M–21).

U–53 **Coleman, Arthur, and Gary R. Tyler.   *Drama Criticism: A Checklist of Interpretation since 1940.*** Vol. 1, English and American Plays.   Denver, Colo.: Swallow, 1966.
No LC number

This work, which aims at inclusiveness, indexes the contents of some 1,050 periodicals and 1,500 books for criticism published between 1940 and 1964 of American and British plays (including Irish, Canadian, Australian, and New Zealand drama).   Excluded are dissertations, monographs, and books on only one dramatist which can easily be located in a library catalog.   Also excluded are dramatic poems and studies focused exclusively on questions of source, genesis, milieu, or staging.   Entries are in two lists.   The first, treating plays other than Shakespeare's, is arranged alphabetically by author, then by play title and then by authors of criticism.   The second list, on the plays of Shakespeare, is alphabetical by play title and then alphabetical by critic.   The volume concludes with three bibliographies; the first a list of books containing drama criticism cited in the volume; the second, of books studied but not cited; and the third, of books published before 1940 which were not studied but which might yield additional materials.

Volume 2, *Checklist of Interpretation since 1940 of Classical and Continental Plays* (Denver, Colo.: Swallow, 1969) [No LC number] is similarly limited in coverage and similarly arranged.   Criticism published 1940–1968 in over 1,000 journals and numerous books and monographs is included.

U–54 **Palmer, Helen, and A. J. Dyson.   *European Drama Criticism, 1900–1975.*** 2d ed.   Hamden, Conn.: Shoe String Press, 1977.   Z5781.P2 1977

Originally published in 1968, this volume contains criticism published through 1975 located in more than 700 journals and more than 950 books and monographs on the plays of dramatists from Aeschylus to modern times.   Shakespeare is excluded, but other English playwrights are not.   Entries are alphabetically arranged by author, then by play title, and then by critic.   A list of books indexed, a list of journals analyzed, and an author-title index to playwrights and plays conclude the volume, which is designed as a companion to the volume of *American Drama Criticism* originally compiled by the same authors (S–72).

U–55 ***Cumulated Dramatic Index, 1909–1949.*** 2 vols.   Boston: F. W. Faxon, 1965.   Z5781.C8

These volumes reproduce in a single alphabet all entries in the original forty-one volumes of the *Dramatic Index* published as Part II of the *Annual Magazine Subject Index*, 1909–1952 (see D–14).   These annual listings are themselves cumulations of the quarterly lists with the title "Dramatic Index for [1909–], Covering Articles and Illustrations concerning the Stage and Its Players in the Periodicals of America and England," published in volumes 6–21 of the *Bulletin of Bibliography and Magazine Notes*, 1909–1949 (see A–7).   In that form the lists constituted a subject index to some 150 English-language periodicals concerned with drama and the theater.   Plays, play synopses, reviews, articles on actors, portraits, scholarly articles–all drama- and theater-related material appearing in the analyzed periodicals is here recorded.   In the *Cumulated Dramatic Index* all these entries are arranged alphabetically by subject, titles, playwrights, and famous characters.   Three appendixes conclude volume 2: an author list of the more than 6,500 books analyzed; a title list of some 24,000 plays published separately, in collections, or in periodicals; and an author list of some 20,000 published play texts.

U–57 **Samples, Gordon.   *How to Locate Reviews of Plays and Films: A Bibliography of Criticism from the Beginning to the Present.*** Metuchen, N.J.: Scarecrow Press, 1976.
Z5781.S19

This extremely useful finding aid, an expansion and revision of a brief pamphlet guide originally published in 1971, provides an annotated bibliography of sources of reviews and references to reviews.   It is in two parts, the first treating plays and the second, film.   Both are organized into chronologically arranged subsections.   Those of Part I are as follows: 1. A Chronology of Study Guides (listing manuals on the theater in chronological order of the period of theater history they cover); 2. Review Indexing Services; 3. Newspaper Indexes; 4. Dramatic Criticism Checklists; 5. Collected Reviews of Individual Critics; 6. Leading Theatre Periodicals; 7. Leading Reference Guides; 8. Play Synopses and Production Controlling Agencies.   This part ends with an index of authors and titles.

The subsections of Part II, on Film Reviews, follow the same divisions for the first six sections, and then continue as follows: 7. Documentary and Factual Films; 8. Special Effects and Animated Films; 9. Leading Reference Guides; 10. Representative Film Distributors' Catalogs; and 11. Sources for Stills.   An index of authors and titles also concludes this half of the volume.

U–58 **Salem, James M.** *Guide to Critical Reviews [of plays].* 4 parts in 5 vols. Metuchen, N.J.: Scarecrow Press, 1966-1971. 2d ed. 3 vols. 1973–1979. Part I, ***American Drama 1909–1969.*** Part II, ***Musical 1909–1974.*** Part III, ***Foreign Drama, 1909–1977.*** Plus Part IV, ***Screenplay, Supplement One, 1963 to 1980*** (1982). 3d ed. Vol. 1–. 1984–.
LC numbers vary

The original edition of this guide [Z5782.S34] presents four lists of critical reviews of modern plays found in newspapers (especially the *New York Times*) and magazines, arranged alphabetically by play author, with anonymous works listed by title. The four lists treat the following texts: I. American Drama, 1909–1969 (O'Neill to Albee); II. The Broadway Musical from 1920 to 1965 (Rogers and Hart to Lerner and Lowe); III. British and Continental Drama from Ibsen to Pinter 1909–1966; and IV. The Screenplay. Entries give authors, titles, dates of the first American performance between 1909 and 1966, and a list of reviews of *that* performance. Each part has its own author and title indexes.

The second edition of Parts I, II, and III [Z5781.S16 1973] involves extensions of coverage in Part II to 1974 and in Part III to 1977; the supplement to Part IV extends that portion's dates to 1980 [Z5784.M9 S24 1982]. The first volume of the third edition, finally, brings the coverage of Part I, American Drama, forward to 1982 [Z5781.S16 1984].

U–59 ***New York Times Directory of the Theatre.*** New York: The Times, 1973.
Z6935.N48 1973

This misleadingly titled volume is actually a title and personal-name index to all theater reviews in the *New York Times* from 1920 through 1970, along with lists of *New York Times* theater critics, theater awards, and reprints of *Times* articles on the awards.

A related and convenient reference is the collection of reprints of *Times* reviews edited by Bernard Beckerman and Howard Siegman, *On Stage: Selected Theatre Reviews from the New York Times, 1920-1970* (New York: The Times, 1973) [PN2277.N5 B4], which contains also indexes to authors of plays reviewed and to their titles.

A more extensive compilation is the weekly *New York Theatre Critics' Reviews* (1940–) [PN2000.N76], which compiles reviews of all New York productions from six newspapers, two weekly news-magazines, and two broadcast network review services. There are two indexes, one of titles and one of persons, including authors, producers, directors, composers and lyricists, set designers, choreographers, costume designers, and cast.

VI. BIBLIOGRAPHIES AND CHECKLISTS CONCERNING PARTICULAR DRAMATIC GENRES

U–60 **Mikhail, E. H.** ***Comedy and Tragedy: A Bibliography of Critical Studies.*** Troy, N.Y.: Whitston Publishing Co., 1972.
Z5784.C6 M55

This small volume lists first books and then articles on first comedy and then tragedy. Unnumbered and unannotated entries include monographs, dissertations, theses, articles in little magazines, and articles in newspapers; they were culled from some twenty-five standard reference sources. There is no index.

U–61 **Evans, James E.** ***Comedy: An Annotated Bibliography of Theory and Practice.*** Metuchen, N.J.: Scarecrow, 1987.
Z5784.C6 E94 1987

With a cut-off date of 1984 and an emphasis on works since 1900, this bibliography lists 3,106 works concerned with the theory and practice of comedy. Serially numbered entries are divided into four parts, as follows: I. Comic Theory Before 1900 (Classical and Medieval, Renaissance, Neoclassical, Nineteenth Century); II. Comic Theory After 1900; III. Comic Literature (arranged by nationality, with a section of entries concerned with Comic Film and Other Media); and IV. Related Subjects (Farce, The Tragic, Parody and Burlesque; Satire; Irony; The Fool and Other Comic Types; The Grotesque; Caricature; Humor; Laughter; and Jokes). Entries are briefly annotated. There are numerous cross references at the ends of sections. The volume concludes with an Author Index and a Subject Index which includes writers as subjects.

U–62 **Stratman, Carl J., ed.** ***Bibliography of English Printed Tragedy, 1565–1900.*** Carbondale: Southern Illinois University Press, 1966.
Z2014.D7 S8

This volume includes a total of 1,483 individual extant tragedies (as identified by the work's title page or in its introduction or preface) the first editions of which were printed in England, Scotland, or Ireland between 1565 and 1900, along with notes of various editions of each and locations. Of these, 1,380 are by a total of 769 authors and 103 are anonymous. Excluded are the tragedies of Shakespeare, literal translations of plays from other languages, translations into other languages, and one-act plays unless they are by an author who also has full-length plays. They are arranged in alphabetical order by author, then title, or, for the anonymous tragedies, by title. After collected works are listed individual tragedies. Editions are listed in chronological order. Serially numbered entries give author, complete title, imprint, pagination, symbols for library locations, and notes and commentary (including standard numbers for *STC* entries, Stationers' Register, attribution authority, and notes about the presence or absence of stage history) as appropriate. The bibliography proper is followed by an analysis of 285 anthologies and collections containing tragedies; a chronological table giving dates, titles, and authors; and a title index including cross-references from alternate titles and subtitles. Appended is a list of extant manuscript tragedies 1565–1900 citing locations and catalog numbers. The appendix is followed by a list of addenda and corrigenda.

U–67 **Some Frequently Recommended Works on the Language and Elements of Drama.**

Barish, Jonas. *Ben Jonson and the Language of Prose Comedy.* Cambridge: Harvard University Press, 1960.
PR2644.B3

Bentley, Eric. *Life of the Drama.* New York: Atheneum, 1964.
PN1631.N42

Esslin, Martin. *Anatomy of Drama.* London: T. Smith, 1976.
PN1631.E8

Kennedy, Andrew K. *Six Dramatists in Search of a Language: Shaw, Eliot, Beckett, Pinter, Osborne, Arden: Studies in Dramatic Language.* Cambridge: Cambridge University Press, 1975.
PR739.L3 K4

Koskenniemi, Inna. *Studies in the Vocabulary of English Drama, 1550–1600.* Turku: Turun Yliopisto, 1962.
AS262.T84 A3 osa. 84

Prior, Moody E. *Language of Tragedy.* New York: Columbia University Press, 1948.
PR633.P7

Styan, John L. *Elements of Drama*. Cambridge: Cambridge University Press, 1960.   PN1655.S75

Williams, Raymond. *Drama in Performance*. London: F. Muller, 1954.   PN1731.W5

U–68 **Some Frequently Recommended Works on Reading Drama.**

Altenbernd, Lynn. *Handbook for the Study of Drama*. New York: Macmillan, 1966.   PN1701.A5

Ball, David. *Backwards and Forwards: A Technical Manual for Reading Plays*. Carbondale: Southern Illinois University Press, 1983.   PN1661.B34 1983

Boulton, Marjorie. *Anatomy of Drama*. London: Routledge and Kegan Paul, 1960.   PN1661.B6

Brooks, Cleanth, and Robert Heilman. *Understanding Drama*. New York: Holt, Rinehart and Winston, 1960.   PN1657.B7 1960

Dawson, S. W. *Drama and the Dramatic*. London: Methuen, 1970.   PN1631.D3

Drew, Elizabeth. *Discovering Drama*. New York: Norton, 1937.   PN1655.D7

Rosenheim, Edward W., Jr. *What Happens in Literature: A Student's Guide to Poetry, Drama, Fiction*. Chicago: University of Chicago Press, 1960.   PN45.R6

Scholes, Robert, and Carl H. Klaus. *Elements of Drama*. New York: Oxford University Press, 1970.   PN4500.S25

Styan, John L. *Dramatic Experience: A Guide to the Reading of Plays*. Cambridge: Cambridge University Press, 1965.   PN1701.S8

Wells, Stanley. *Literature and Drama with Special Reference to Shakespeare and His Contemporaries*. London: Routledge and Kegan Paul, 1970.   PR625.W4

Whitman, Robert F. *Play-readers' Handbook*. Indianapolis: Bobbs-Merrill, 1966.   PN1657.W45

U–69 **Some Frequently Recommended Works on Particular Dramatic Genres.**

Absurd

Esslin, Martin. *Theatre of the Absurd*. 3d ed. London: Methuen, 1974.   PN1861.E8 1974

Ballad Opera

Gagey, Edmund McAdoo. *Ballad Opera*. New York: Columbia University Press, 1937.   ML1731.3.G13 B17

Bourgeois Drama (see also Tragicomedy)

Nolte, Fred O. *Early Middle Class Drama, 1696–1774*. Lancaster, Pa.: Lancaster Press, 1935.   PN1841.N6

Szondi, Peter. *Die Theorie des bürgerlichen Trauerspiels im 18. Jahrhundert: Der Kaufmann, der Hausvater, und der Hofmeister*. Frankfurt: Suhrkamp, 1973.   PN1897.S95

Burlesque Drama

Clinton-Baddeley, V. C. *Burlesque Tradition in the English Theatre after 1660*. London: Methuen, 1952.   PR635.B8 C5

Comedy

Barber, C. L. *Shakespeare's Festive Comedy: A Study in Dramatic Form and Its Relation to Social Custom*. Princeton N.J.: Princeton University Press, 1959.   PR2981.B3

Charnie, Maurice. *Comedy High and Low: An Introduction to the Experience of Comedy*. New York: Oxford University Press, 1978.   PN1922.C5

Cook, Albert. *Dark Voyage and the Golden Mean: A Philosophy of Comedy*. New York: W. W. Norton, 1966.   PN1922.C6 1966

Donaldson, Ian. *World Upside Down: Comedy from Jonson to Fielding*. Oxford: Clarendon Press, 1970.   PR631.D6

Frye, Northrup. *Natural Perspective: The Development of Shakespearean Comedy and Romance*. New York: Columbia University Press, 1965.   PR2981.F7

Fujimura, Thomas H. *Restoration Comedy of Wit*. Princeton, N.J.: Princeton University Press, 1952.   PR698.C6 F8

Heck, Thomas F. *Commedia dell'Arte: A Guide to the Primary and Secondary Literature*. New York: Garland, 1988.   Z2354.D7 H37 1988

Heilman, Robert B. *Ways of the World: Comedy and Society*. Seattle: University of Washington Press, 1978.   PN1922.H44

Holland, Norman. *First Modern Comedies: The Significance of Etheredge, Wycherly, and Congreve*. Cambridge: Harvard University Press, 1959.   PR3432.H6

Hoy, Cyrus. *Hyacinth Room: An Investigation into the Nature of Comedy, Tragedy, and Tragicomedy*. New York: Knopf, 1964.   PN1631.H6

Kronenberger, Louis. *Thread of Laughter: Chapters on English Stage Comedy from Jonson to Maugham*. New York: Knopf, 1952.   PR631.K7

Lauter, Paul, ed. *Theories of Comedy*. Garden City, N.Y.: Doubleday, 1964.   PN1922.L3

Lever, Katherine. *Art of Greek Comedy*. London: Methuen, 1956.   PA3161.L4

McCollom, William G. *Divine Average: A View of Comedy*. Cleveland, Ohio: Press of Case Western Reserve University, 1971.   PN1922.M28

Merchant, W. Moelwyn. *Comedy*. London: Methuen, 1972.   PN1922.M38

Meredith, George. *Essay on Comedy and the Uses of the Comic Spirit*. 2d ed. London: A. Constable and Co., 1898.   PN1921.M4 1898

Monro, David H. *Argument of Laughter*. Carlton: Melbourne University Press, 1955.   BF575.L3 M6

Muir, Kenneth. *Comedy of Manners*. London: Hutchinson, 1970.   PR691.M8 1970

Olson, Elder. *Theory of Comedy*. Bloomington: Indiana University Press, 1968.   PN1922.O4 1968

Parrot, Thomas M. *Shakespearean Comedy*. New York: Oxford University Press, 1949.   PR2981.P3

Partridge, Edward B. *Broken Compass: A Study of the Major Comedies of Ben Jonson*. New York: Columbia University Press, 1958.   PR2638.P3 1958

Perry, Henry Jon Eyck. *Masters of Dramatic Comedy and Their Social Themes*. Cambridge: Harvard University Press, 1939.   PN1929.S6 P4

Potts, L. J. *Comedy*. London: Hutchinson's University Library, 1966.   PR932.P6 1966

Rodway, Allan. *English Comedy: Its Role and Nature from Chaucer to the Present Day*. Berkeley, Los Angeles, London: University of California Press, 1975.   PR149.C65 R6

Sharma, R. C. *Themes and Conventions in the Comedy of Manners*. New York: Asia Publishing House, 1965.   PR698.C6 S5 1965

Sypher, Wylie, ed. *Comedy*. Garden City, N.Y.: Doubleday, 1956.   PN1922.S9

Thorndike, Ashley H. *English Comedy*. New York: Macmillan, 1929.   PR631.T5

Whitman, Cedric H. *Aristophanes and the Comic Hero*. Cambridge: Harvard University Press, 1964.   PA25.M3 vol. 19

Wimsatt, William K., ed. *English Stage Comedy*. English Institute Essays, 1954. New York: Columbia University Press, 1955.   PE1010.E5

————, ed. *Idea of Comedy: Essays in Prose and Verse, Ben Jonson to George Meredith*. Englewood Cliffs, N.J.: Prentice-Hall, 1969.   PR631.W47

Farce

Bermel, Albert. *Farce: A History from Aristophanes to Woody Allen*. New York: Simon and Schuster, 1982.   PN1942.B4 1982

Davis, Jessica M. *Farce*. London: Methuen, 1978.   PN1942.D3 1978

Hughes, Leo. *Century of Farce*. Princeton, N.J.: Princeton University Press, 1956.   PR698.F35 H77

History Play

Lindenberger, Herbert. *Historical Drama: The Relation of Literature and Reality*. Chicago: University of Chicago Press, 1975.   PN1872.L5

Ornstein, Robert. *Kingdom for a Stage: The Achievement of Shakespeare's History Plays*. Cambridge: Harvard University Press, 1972.   PR2982.O7

Ribner, Irving. *English History Play in the Age of Shakespeare*. Rev. ed. London: Methuen, 1965.   PR658.H5 R5

Saccio, Peter. *Shakespeare's English Kings: History, Chronicle, and Drama*. New York: Oxford University Press, 1977.   PR2982.S2

Tetzeli von Rosador, Kurt. *Das englische Geschichtsdrama seit Shaw*. Heidelberg: Winter, 1976.   PR635.H5 T4

Tillyard, E. M. W. *Shakespeare's History Plays*. London: Chatto and Windus, 1944.   PR2982.T5

Masque

Nicoll, Allardyce. *Stuart Masques and the Renaissance Stage*. New York: Harcourt, Brace, 1938.   PR658.M3 N5 1938

Welsford, Enid. *Court Masque*. Cambridge: Cambridge University Press, 1927.   PN2582.C6 W4

Melodrama

Heilman, Robert B. *Tragedy and Melodrama: Versions of Experience*. Seattle: University of Washington Press, 1968.   PN1892.H38

Rahill, Frank. *World of Melodrama*. University Park: Pennsylvania State University Press, 1967.   PN1912.R3

Taylor, John Russell. *Rise and Fall of the Well-made Play*. New York: Hill and Wang, 1967.   PR731.T3 1967b

Miracle Play

See N–49 and U–80.

Morality Play

See N–49 and U–80.

Pastoral Drama

Greg, W. W. *Pastoral Poetry and Pastoral Drama*. London: A. H. Bullen, 1906.   PR509.P3 G7

Sentimental Drama

Bernbaum, Ernest. *Drama of Sensibility: A Sketch of the History of English Sentimental Comedy and Domestic Tragedy, 1696–1780*. Boston: Ginn and Co., 1915.   PR701.B4

Sherbo, Arthur. *English Sentimental Drama*. East Lansing: Michigan State University Press, 1957.   PR635.S4 S5 1957

Tragedy

Abel, Lionel, ed. *Moderns on Tragedy: An Anthology of Modern and Relevant Opinions on the Substance and Meaning of Tragedy*. New York: Fawcett, 1967.   PN1892.A2

Bradley, A. C. *Shakespearean Tragedy*. 2d ed. London: Macmillan, 1929.   PR2983.B7 1929

Brereton, Geoffrey. *Principles of Tragedy: A Radical Examination of the Tragic Concept in Life and Literature*. Coral Gables, Fla.: University of Miami Press, 1968.   PN1892.B68

Brooks, Cleanth, ed. *Tragic Themes in Western Literature*. New Haven: Yale University Press, 1955.   PN1892.B7

Ferguson, John. *Companion to Greek Tragedy*. Austin: University of Texas Press, 1972.   PA3131.F4

Green, André. *Tragic Effect: The Oedipus Complex in Tragedy*. Translation by Alan Sheridan of *Un OEil en trop, le complexe d'OEdipe dans la tragédie* (Paris: Editions de minuit, 1969). Cambridge: Cambridge University Press, 1979.   PN1899.O3 G713

Henn, Thomas R. *Harvest of Tragedy*. London: Methuen, 1956.   PN1892.H4

Kaufmann, Walter. *Tragedy and Philosophy*. New York: Doubleday, 1968.   PN1892.K3

Kerr, Walter. *Tragedy and Comedy*. New York: Simon and Schuster, 1967.   PN1675.K4

Kitto, H. D. F. *Greek Tragedy: A Literary Study*. 2d ed., rev. London: Methuen, 1950.   PA3131.K5

Krook, Dorothea. *Elements of Tragedy*. New Haven: Yale University Press, 1969.   PN1892.K7

Lattimore, Richmond. *Story Patterns in Greek Tragedy*. Ann Arbor: University of Michigan Press, 1964.   PA3133.L3

Leech, Clifford. *Tragedy*. London: Methuen, 1969.   PN1892.L44

Lenson, David. *Achilles' Choice: Examples of Modern Tragedy*. Princeton, N.J.: Princeton University Press, 1975.   PN1892.L46

Lucas, F. L. *Tragedy: Serious Drama in Relation to Aristotle's Poetics*. Rev. and enl. ed. London: Hogarth Press, 1957.   PN1892.L8 1957

Mandel, Oscar. *Definition of Tragedy*. New York: New York University Press, 1961.   PN1892.M33

Michel, Laurence. *Thing Contained: Theory of the Tragic*. Bloomington: Indiana University Press, 1970.   PR149.T7 M5

Michel, Laurence, and Richard B. Sewall, eds. *Tragedy: Modern Essays in Criticism*. Englewood Cliffs, N.J.: Prentice-Hall, 1963.   PN1892.M5

Mueller, Martin. *Children of Oedipus and Other Essays on the Imitation of Greek Tragedy, 1550–1800*. Toronto: University of Toronto Press, 1980.   PN1899.G74 M8

Muller, Herbert J. *Spirit of Tragedy*. New York: Knopf, 1956.   PN1892.M7

Olson, Elder. *Tragedy and the Theory of Drama*. Detroit: Wayne State University Press, 1961.   PN1655.O55

Pickard-Cambridge, A. W. *Dithyramb, Tragedy and Comedy*. Oxford: Clarendon Press, 1927.   PA3131.P5

Quinlan, Michael A. *Poetic Justice in the Drama: The History of an Ethical Principle in Literary Criticism*. Notre

Dame, Ind.: University of Notre Dame Press, 1912.
PN1675.Q6

Scott, Nathan A., Jr. ed. *Tragic Vision and the Christian Faith*. New York, 1957. No LC number

Sewall, Richard B. *Vision of Tragedy*. New ed., enl. New Haven: Yale University Press, 1980.
PN1892.S43 1980

Steiner, George. *Death of Tragedy*. New York: Knopf, 1961. PN1892.S7

Terzakis, Angelos. *Homage to the Tragic Muse*. Boston: Houghton Mifflin, 1978. PN1892.T4713

Vickers, Brian. *Comparative Tragedy*. Vol. 1, *Towards Greek Tragedy: Drama, Myth, Society*. London: Longman, 1973. PN1892.V45 vol. 1

Von Szeliski, John. *Tragedy and Fear: Why Modern Tragic Drama Fails*. Chapel Hill: University of North Carolina Press, 1971. PS336.T7

Weisinger, Herbert. *Tragedy and the Paradox of the Fortunate Fall*. East Lansing: Michigan State University Press, 1953. BH301.T7W4 1953

Williams, Raymond. *Modern Tragedy: Essays on the Idea of Tragedy in Life and in the Drama, and on Modern Tragic Writing from Ibsen to Tennessee Williams*. Stanford: Stanford University Press, 1966.
PN1897.W5

Tragicomedy (see also Bourgeois Drama)

Guthrie, Karl S. *Modern Tragi-comedy: An Investigation into the Nature of the Genre*. New York: Random House, 1966. PN1907.G8

Herrick, Marvin. *Tragicomedy: Its Origin and Development in Italy, France, and England*. Urbana: University of Illinois Press, 1955. PN1902.H4

Styan, John L. *Dark Comedy: The Development of Modern Comic Tragedy*. 2d ed. Cambridge: Cambridge University Press, 1968. PN1861.S75 1968

Waith, Eugene. *Pattern of Tragicomedy in Beaumont and Fletcher*. New Haven: Yale University Press, 1952.
PR2434.W285

Verse Drama

Browne, E. Martin. *Verse in the Modern Theatre*. Cardiff: University of Wales Press, 1963. PR738.B7

Donoghue, Denis. *Third Voice: Modern British and American Verse Drama*. Princeton, N.J.: Princeton University Press, 1959. PR736.D6

Hinchcliff, Arnold P. *Modern Verse Drama*. London: Methuen, 1977. PR635.V4 H55

VII. HISTORIES OF THE DRAMA AND THE THEATER

See also Quinn's *History of the American Drama* (S–76).

U–70 **Kindermann, Heinz. *Theatergeschichte Europas.*** 10 vols. Salzburg: Muller, 1957–1974. PN2570.K55

This work is a comprehensive history of European theater (including the theater of England) from its beginnings to the present. The individual volumes are as follows:

Vol. 1. *Das Theater der Antike und des Mittelalters* (1957).

Vol. 2. *Das Theater der Renaissance* (1959).

Vol. 3. *Das Theater der Barockzeit* (1959).

Vols. 4–5. *Von der Anfklärung zur Romantik* (1961–62).

Vol. 6. *Romantik* (1964).

Vol. 7. *Realismus* (1965).

Vols. 8–10. *Naturalismus und Impressionismus* (1968–74).

Each volume is fully documented and includes a chronological table, illustrations, a classified bibliography keyed to chapters, an index of places, an index of playwrights and titles, and a detailed subject index.

Earlier multivolume histories of drama include Karl Mantzius, *History of Theatrical Art in Ancient and Modern Times*, translation by Louise von Cossel of *Skuespilkunstens historie* (Copenhagen, 1897–1916), 6 vols. (London: Duckworth, 1903–1921) [PN2104.M3], which covers the theater from classical antiquity to the later nineteenth century and has extensive bibliographies in each volume. Another is by L. Dubech et al., *Histoire générale illustrée du théâtre*, 5 vols. (Paris: Librairie de France, 1931–1934) [PN2103.D8], the individual volumes of which are extensively illustrated and contain indexes of authors, actors, play titles, and character types, all of which are cumulated in the index to volume 5. The individual volumes are as follows:

Vol. 1. *Le théâtre grecque / Le théâtre latin (1931)*.

Vol. 2. *Le théâtre des miracles et des mystères. Le théâtre profane au moyen âge; Le théâtre espagnol; Le théâtre italien (1931)*.

Vol. 3. *Le théâtre anglais; Le théâtre français (1932)*.

Vol. 4. *Le théâtre français [18th century]; Le théâtre européen au XVIIIe siècle (1933)*.

Vol. 5. *Le théâtre français [19th and 20th centuries]; Le théâtre européen (1934)*.

Single-volume surveys of the theater include Glynne Wickham, *History of the Theatre*. Cambridge: Cambridge University Press, 1985 [PN2101.W52 1985]; Patt: P. Gillespie and Kenneth Cameron. *Western Theatre: Revolution and Revival*. New York: Macmillan, 1984 [PN2101. G53 1984]; Margot Berthold, *History of World Theater* (New York: Ungar, 1972) [PN2104.B413]; Oscar G. Brockett, *History of the Theater*, 4th ed. (Boston: Allyn and Bacon, 1982) [PN2101.B68 1982]; Sheldon Cheney, *Theatre: Three Thousand Years of Drama, Acting, and Stagecraft*, rev. and enl. ed. (New York: Longmans, Green, 1952) [PN2101 .C5 1952]; and George Freedley and John A. Reeves, *History of The Theatre*, 3d ed., rev. (New York: Crown, 1968) [PN2101.F7 1955]. A massive single-volume survey is Guy Dumur et al., *Histoire des spectacles* (Paris: Gallimard, 1965) [PN2103.H5], which covers in two sections by specialists developments in all the performing arts from ancient to modern times, in the Orient and Occident, and ends with a massive chronology to 1960 and detailed indexes of names (125 pages long) and works.

See also two important volumes by Allardyce Nicoll, *Development of the Theatre: A Study of Theatrical Art from the Beginnings to the Present Day*, 5th ed., rev. (New York: Harcourt, Brace and World, 1966) [PN2101.N5], and *Masks, Mimes and Miracles: Studies in the Popular Art* (New York: Harcourt, Brace, 1931) [PN2071.G4 N5], which has a special emphasis on the *commedia dell'arte*.

U–71 **Nicoll, Allardyce. *History of English Drama, 1660–1900.*** Rev. ed. 6 vols. Cambridge: Cambridge University Press, 1952–1959. PR625.N52 1952

This is the standard history of post-Renaissance English drama. Treated are the history of the English theater, its audience, actors, stages, acting companies, and the like; the history of English tragedy, its types, sources, and the like; and the history of English comedy including its types and sources. There are, in addition, numerous appendixes, including materials on the history of the playhouse, and ephemeral documents illustrating the history of the stage (e.g., lists of plays, playbills, tickets, royal orders). Each volume but the last also includes a handlist of plays from its period arranged alphabetically under the playwright's name. The entry for each play includes its title, type, theater, month and year of performance, date of separate editions, and dating evidence. And each volume but the last also includes an index of persons and subjects. The individual volumes are as follows:

Vol. 1. *Restoration Drama, 1660–1700* (1923; 4th ed., 1955).
Vol. 2. *Early Eighteenth Century Drama* (1925; 3d ed., 1955).
Vol. 3. *Late Eighteenth Century Drama, 1750–1800* (1927; 2d ed., 1952).
Vol. 4. *Early Nineteenth Century Drama, 1800–1850* (1930; 2d ed., 1955).
Vol. 5. *Late Nineteenth Century Drama, 1850–1900* (1946; 2d ed., 1959).
Vol. 6. *Short-Title Alphabetical Catalogue of Plays Produced or Printed in England from 1660 to 1900* (1959).

The second and subsequent editions of individual volumes have their supplementary notes added to chapters and generally gathered at the end of the volumes for publishing convenience. Thus both the original text and supplemental pages must be consulted in any particular inquiry. The sixth volume presents a complete title index to the first five volumes and indicates for each play the author (when known) and the date of the original production, publication, or submission to the Lord Chamberlain's office for review, whichever is earliest. In contrast with their inclusion on the handlists of individual volumes, Italian operas, French and Italian comedies presented in London, and similar items are not in the *Short-Title Catalogue*. Subtitles of plays are entered in the alphabetical sequence with cross-references to the main title entry. Volume and page references are given to the play's discussion in the history. Those entries not included in the original handlists are marked with a plus sign. Adaptations and translations are cited under the names of the authors concerned in adapting and translating.

This history is supplemented for the early twentieth century by Nicoll's *English Drama, 1900-1930: The Beginning of the Modern Period* (Cambridge: Cambridge University Press, 1973) [PR721.N45], which contains a 600-page "Handlist of English Plays 1900–1930" arranged alphabetically by author and giving the play title, dramatic kind, date of licensing, date and place of first performance, and the name of the sponsoring person or organization.

Among numerous other volumes, Nicoll has also produced a single-volume survey, *British Drama: An Historical Survey from the Beginnings to the Present Time*, 6th ed., rev. J. C. Trewin (London: Harrap, 1978) [PR625.N5 1978].

U–72 Revels History of Drama in English. 8 vols. London: Methuen, 1976–1983.   PR625.R44

This new illustrated history spans the development of English-language drama from medieval times to the present. Each volume has its own team of authors and each is self-contained, covering the social background, the theater history, the stage and stagecraft, the actors and companies, and the plays themselves. Each volume also contains a bibliography, an index of names, titles, and subjects, and a chronological table including historical events, theatrical events, literary events, first performances, and authors' births and deaths. But each team of authors has been free to construct its own narrative and to divide responsibility for chapters as needed.

The individual volumes and their authors are as follows:

Vol. 1. *Medieval Drama*, by A. C. Cawley, David Mills, Peter McDonald, and Marion Jones, ed. Lois Potter (1982).
Vol. 2. *1500–1576*, by T. W. Craik, Norman Sanders, Richard Southern, and Lois Potter (1980).
Vol. 3. *1576–1613*, by J. Leeds Barroll, Alexander Leggatt, Richard Hosley, and Alvin Kernan (1975).
Vol. 4. *1613–1660*, by Philip Edwards, Gerard Eades Bentley, Kathleen McLuskie, and Lois Potter (1982).
Vol. 5. *1660–1750*, by John Loftis, Richard Southern, Marion Jones, and A. H. Scouten (1978).
Vol. 6. *1750–1880*, by Michael R. Booth, Richard Southern, Frederick and Lise-Lone Marker, and Robertson Davies (1975).
Vol. 7. *1880 to the Present Day*, by Hugh Hunt, Kenneth Richards, and John Russell Taylor (1979).
Vol. 8. *American Drama*, by Travis Bogard, Richard Moody, and Walter J. Meserve (1977).

Different volumes have been differently received. In particular, volumes 6, 7, and 8 have been very well reviewed, whereas volumes 2, 3, and 5 have been greeted less enthusiastically.

U–73 Chambers, E. K. *Medieval Stage.* 2 vols. Oxford: Clarendon Press, 1903.   PN2152.C4

This pioneer history of the medieval theater from the end of Roman civilization to the Tudor period contains four main parts, treating minstrelsy, folk drama, religious drama, and the interludes respectively. There are extensive bibliographies and a total of twenty-four appendixes that contain various sorts of documentation including transcriptions of original documents. The second volume concludes with an elaborate subject index.

A more recent volume concerning the stage in England is A. H. Nelson, *Medieval English Stage: Corpus Christi Pageants and Plays* (Chicago: University of Chicago Press, 1974) [PR643.C7 N4], with bibliography, detailed index, and transcriptions of original documents. Further treatment of the theater in the English Middle Ages will be found in Glynne Wickham, *Early English Stages, 1300-1600*, 4 vols. vol. 1, *1300 to 1576*, 2d ed. (London: Routledge and Kegan Paul, 1980) [PN2587.W532 1980]; in sections of Karl Young, *Drama of the Medieval Church*, 2 vols. (Oxford: Clarendon, 1933) [PN1751.Y6], and in the chapter on staging in Hardin Craig, *English Religious Drama of the Middle Ages* (Oxford: Clarendon, 1955) [PR641.C7].

U–74 Chambers, E. K. *Elizabethan Stage.* 4 vols. Oxford: Clarendon Press, 1923. Corrected reprint, 1951.
                    PN2589.C4

These volumes present an authoritative account of theater in England during the period 1558–1616. Each of the four volumes covers a particular aspect of the theater from the court and its influence (volume 1), to the acting companies and the individual actors in them (volume 2), and finally to the individual playing companies, their playwrights and their plays (volumes 3 and 4). Throughout all volumes are extensive bibliographical headnotes, footnotes, lists of sources, and various checklists of persons and plays. The fourth volume also contains a series of thirteen appendixes on such matters as court calendars, documents of criticism, a list of academic plays, a list of lost plays, and a list of extant manuscript plays. In addition, volume 4 contains selective indexes of plays, persons, places, and subjects. A more extensive index was prepared for the Shakespeare Association by Beatrice White (Oxford: Clarendon Press, 1934) [PR2894.C442 1934a] which analyzes both this work and Chambers's *William Shakespeare: A Study of Facts and Problems*, 2 vols. (Oxford: Clarendon Press, 1930) [PR2894.C442].

Other more recent works include C. W. Hodges, *Globe Restored*, 2d ed. (London: Oxford University Press, 1968) [PR2920.H6 1968] and A. Gurr, *Shakespearean Stage, 1574-1642*, 2d ed. (Cambridge: Cambridge University Press, 1980) [PN2589.G8 1980]. For more recent studies see David Stevens, *English Renaissance Theatre History: A Reference Guide* (Boston: G. K. Hall, 1982) [Z2014. D7 S78 1982].

U–75 Bentley, Gerald Eades. *Jacobean and Caroline Stage.* 7 vols. Oxford: Clarendon Press, 1941–1968.   PN2592.B4

These volumes continue the Chambers histories of the medieval and Renaissance English theater (U–63, U–64) from 1616 to 1642 and the closing of the theaters. Volumes 1 and 2 treat the London dramatic companies, including biographies of actors. Volumes 3–5 treat playwrights and plays in alphabetical order, citing dates, manuscripts, modern editions, secondary materials to 1950, entries in the Stationers' Register, and other contemporary records and references. Volume 6 treats the theater buildings, public, private, and court, with a detailed history and bibliography. The seventh and last volume contains a number of appendixes, a chronological table of Jacobean and Caroline theatrical affairs, and a full analytical index of more than 250 pages. Throughout are an abundance of bibliographical aids, charts, lists, and other research materials.

For more recent studies, see David Stevens, *English Renaissance Theatre History: A Reference Guide* (Boston: G. K. Hall, 1982) [Z2014.D7 S78 1982].

U–76 Harbage, Alfred. *Cavalier Drama: A Historical and Critical Supplement to the Study of the Elizabethan and Restoration Stage.* New York: Modern Language Association, 1936.   PR678.C3 H3

This volume supplements the theater histories of Chambers (U–73, U–74) and Bentley (U–75) for Cavalier theater from 1626 to 1669. The work is in two parts. The first is a summary of trends of general interest, and the second is a description of the body of materials about which the conclusions of the first part summary are made. The second part includes material on courtier playwrights, amateurs of town and the university, professional playwrights, plays on the civil wars, Caroline and commonwealth private theater, closet drama, and the last of the cavalier playwrights. Biographical data and synopses of plays are followed by a chronological list of plays from 1626 to 1669 giving the author's name, title, date of first performance, dramatic type, name of the professional company of the first performance, and date of the earliest known publication. Limited secondary bibliography is found in the volume, but users are referred to Volume 1 of the *CBEL* (M–10, O–10) for primary bibliography.

See also Leslie Hotson, *Commonwealth and Restoration Stage* (Cambridge: Harvard University Press, 1928) [PN2592.H6].

U–77 *London Stage, 1660–1800. A Calendar of Plays, Entertainments, and Afterpieces, Together with Casts, Box-Receipts, and Contemporary Comment Compiled from the Playbills, Newspapers, and Theatrical Diaries of the Period.* 5 parts in 11 vols. Carbondale: Southern Illinois University Press, 1960–1968.   PN2592.L6

This work is literally an annotated calendar of theatrical events in London between 1660 and 1800. Listings are given on a daily basis for each month of each season. Included in each daily listing is the title of any play being performed, its cast, notations about singers and dancers in the production, the name of the theater, and indication of whether the performance was specially sponsored. Prologues and epilogues are quoted, afterpieces and other associated entertainments are described, and contemporary comment about the performance is quoted. Cast lists, if identical, are not repeated, but instead cross-references are given to the first listing. The calendar is divided into five parts, as follows:

Part 1. *1660–1700*, by William Van Lennep, 1 vol. (1965).

Part 2. *1770–1729*, by Emmet L. Avery, 2 vols. (1960).

Part 3. *1729–1747*, by Arthur H. Scouten, 2 vols. (1961).

Part 4. *1747–1776*, by George W. Stone, Jr., 3 vols. (1962).

Part 5. *1776–1800*, by C. Beecher Hogan, 3 vols. (1968).

Each volume includes a lengthy critical introduction to the London stage of its period. These introductions have been separately published in a paperback edition (1968). Each volume also includes an index of playwrights, plays, and cast members.

The content of these volumes has been computerized as "The London Stage Information Bank" at Lawrence University, Appleton, Wisconsin. Using it, scholars are able to search for such combinations of information as a full list of all roles performed by a particular actor. The process of computerizing these materials is described by Ben Ross Schneider, Jr. in *Travels in Computerland; or, Incompatibilities and Interfaces: A Full and True Account of the Implementation of the London Stage Information Bank* (Reading, Mass.: Addison-Wesley, 1975) [QA76.S3588]. And with this computerized data bank a 939-page *Index to The London Stage, 1660–1880* was compiled by Schneider (1979) [PN2592.L6353].

A separate guide to Shakespeare performance in eighteenth-century London has been published by Charles Beecher Hogan, *Shakespeare in the Theatre, 1701-1800*, 2 vols. (Oxford: Oxford University Press, 1952–1957) [PR3097.H6], the first volume recording performance to 1750, and the second from 1751. Each volume is in two parts, the first a chronological list of performances, and the second, an alphabetical list of plays giving complete casts for every performance. Appended to each volume is information on Shakespeare's popularity in the theater, the order of popularity of the plays, and a list of the London theaters in use. Each volume is indexed by actors with dates and parts performed and by characters (with names of all actors who played the part).

See also the chronologically arranged miscellaneous material in J. Genest, *Some Account of the English Stage, from the Restoration in 1660 to 1830*, 10 vols. (Bath: Carrington, 1832) [PN2581.G4], with an account of the Irish stage, additions, corrections, and an index in volume 10.

U–78 *London Stage, 1800–1900.* In preparation.

Under the leadership of James Ellis and Joseph W. Donohue, general editors, an effort is under way to create a calendar of the nineteenth-century London theater parallel to that already available for the eighteenth century (U–77).

The first volume of this project to appear is the *Adelphi Calendar Project, 1806–1850: Sans Pareil Theatre, 1806–1819/Adelphi Theatre, 1819–1850*. Eds. Alfred L. Nelson and Gilvert B. Cross (New York: Greenwood Press, 1989) [PN2596.L7 A56 1989].

A currently available work that assembles some of this material is Diana Howard, *London Theatres and Music Halls, 1850-1950* (London: Library Association, 1970) [PN2596.L6 H595], which contains a directory of 910 theaters, music halls, and pleasure gardens in London during this period, with information listed and reference to locations of archival materials; a bibliography of bibliographies, a calendar of official records, a listing of local newspapers and theatrical periodicals, and a list of works on the history of the theater; and a directory of collections and index of buildings.

U–79   **Wearing, J. P. *London Stage, 1890–1899: A Calendar of Plays and Players.*** 2 vols. Metuchen, N.J.: Scarecrow Press, 1976.   PN2596.L6 W37

This is the first in a series of calendars published over the years by J. P. Wearing. Remaining include the *London Stage, 1900–1909*, 2 vols. (Scarecrow, 1981) [PN2596.L6 W38]; the *London Stage, 1910–1919*, 2 vols. (Scarecrow, 1982) [PN2596.L6 W383]; and the *London Stage, 1920-1929*, 3 vols. (Scarecrow, 1984) [PN2596.L6 W384 1984].

Each volume provides a day-by-day chronicle of productions in the legitimate theaters of central London, the Old Vic, and the Lyric. Plays, operas, and ballets are included; variety and cinematic programs are not. For each listed production, the entry includes play title, genre, number of acts, author, theater, date and length of run, performers, production staff, and references to reviews. Indexes of titles and of personal names are keyed to a serial numbering system used throughout which identifies the year and number of each production (e.g., 15.75 refers to the 75th production in 1915).

The volumes for 1890–1899 list 3,026 productions at thirty theaters; those for 1900–1909 list 2,973 productions at thirty-five theaters for a total of 95,810 performances. The volumes for 1910–1919 list 3,278 productions at thirty-nine theaters for a total of 122,300 performances; those for 1920–1929 list 3,980 productions at fifty-one theaters for a total of more than 164,000 performances. Additional volumes are expected.

U–80   **Some Frequently Recommended Works on the History of Drama and Theater over One or Several Periods of English or American Literary History.**

English—General

Bradbrook, Muriel C. *English Dramatic Form: A History of Its Development.* London: Chatto and Windus, 1965.   PR625.B68 1965

Burton, Ernest Jones. *British Theatre.* London: Jenkins, 1960. Extensive appendixes and bibliograhical aids.   PN2581.B8

Downer, Alan S. *British Drama: A Handbook and Brief Chronicle.* New York: Appleton–Century–Crofts, 1950.   PR625.D55

Roberts, Peter. *Theatre in Britain.* 2d ed. London: Pitman, 1975.   PN2595.R6 1975

Stamm, Rudolf. *Geschichte des englischen Theaters.* Bern: Francke, 1951.   PN2581.S8

Ward, Sir Adolphus William. *History of English Dramatic Literature to the Death of Queen Anne.* New rev. ed. 3 vols. London: Macmillan, 1899.   PR625.W32

Medieval

Polter, Robert. *English Morality Play: Origins, History, and Influence of a Dramatic Tradition.* Boston: Routledge and Kegan Paul, 1975.   PR643.M7 P6 1975

Rossiter, A. P. *English Drama from Early Times to the Elizabethans.* London: Hutchinson, 1950.   PR641.R6 1950

Taylor, J., and A. H. Nelson, eds. *Medieval English Drama: Essays Critical and Contextual.* Chicago: University of Chicago Press, 1972.   PR641.T3

Woolf, Rosemary. *English Mystery Plays.* London: Routledge and Kegan Paul, 1972.   PR643.M8 W66 1972

Renaissance

Bevington, David. *From Mankind to Marlowe: Growth of Structure in Popular Drama of Tudor England.* Cambridge: Harvard University Press, 1962.   PR646.B4 1962

Boas, Frederick S. *Introduction to Stuart Drama.* Oxford: Clarendon Press, 1946.   No LC number

———. *Introduction to Tudor Drama.* Oxford: Clarendon Press, 1933.   PR646.B6

Bowers, Fredson. *Elizabethan Revenge Tragedy, 1587–1642.* Princeton, N.J.: Princeton University Press, 1940.   PR658.T7 B6

Bradbrook, M. C. *Growth and Structure of Elizabethan Comedy.* London: Chatto and Windus, 1955.   PR658.C63 B7

———. *Living Monument: Shakespeare and the Theatre of His Time.* Cambridge: Cambridge University Press, 1976.   PR3095.B66

———. *Rise of the Common Player: A Study of Actor and Society in Shakespeare's England.* London: Chatto and Windus, 1962.   PN2589.B7 1962

———. *Shakespeare and Elizabethan Poetry: A Study of His Earlier Work in Relation to the Poetry of the Time.* London: Chatto and Windus, 1951.   PR2976.B59

———. *Shakespeare the Craftsman.* London: Chatto and Windus, 1969.   PR2976.B57 1969b

———. *Themes and Conventions of Elizabethan Tragedy.* 2d ed. Cambridge: Cambridge University Press, 1980.   PR658.T7 B7 1980

Clemen, Wolfgang. *English Tragedy before Shakespeare: The Development of Dramatic Speech.* Translation by T. S. Dorsch of *Tragödie vor Shakespeare.* London: Methuen, 1967.   PR658.T7 C513 1967

Cope, Jackson I. *Theatre and the Drama: From Metaphor to Form in Renaissance Drama.* Baltimore: Johns Hopkins University Press, 1973.   PN1791.C6

Ellis-Fermor, Una. *Jacobean Drama: An Interpretation.* London: Methuen, 1965. 5th rev. ed.   PR651.E5 1965

Farnham, Willard. *Medieval Heritage of Elizabethan Tragedy.* Berkeley: University of California Press, 1936.   PR658.T7 F3

Harbage, Alfred B. *Shakespeare and the Rival Traditions.* New York: Macmillan, 1952.   PN2589.H3

Levin, Richard. *Multiple Plot in English Renaissance Drama.* Chicago: University of Chicago Press, 1971.   PR658.P6 L4

Lucas, F. L. *Seneca and Elizabethan Tragedy.* Cambridge: Cambridge University Press, 1922.   PR6675.L8

Reed, A. W. *Early Tudor Drama.* London: Methuen, 1926.   PR646.R45

Ribner, Irving. *Jacobean Tragedy: The Quest for Moral Order.* London: Methuen, 1962.   PR658.T7 R5

Simpson, Percy. *Studies in Elizabethen Drama.* Oxford: Clarendon Press, 1955.   PR654.S5

Stevens, David. *English Renaissance Theatre History: A Reference Guide.* Boston: G. K. Hall, 1982.   Z2014.D7 S78 1982

Ure, Peter. *Elizabethan and Jacobean Drama: Critical Essays.* Edited by J. C. Maxwell. Liverpool: Liverpool University Press, 1974.   PR653.U7 1974b

Wilson, F. P. *English Drama, 1485–1585.* Ed. G. K. Hunter. Vol. 4 of the *Oxford History of English Literature* (see M–31).

Restoration and Eighteenth Century

Bateson, F. W. *English Comic Drama, 1700–1750.* London: Oxford University Press, 1929.   PR714.C6 B3

Bevis, Richard. *Laughing Tradition: Stage Comedy in Garrick's Day*. Athens: University of Georgia Press, 1980.   PR708.C6 B4 1980

Boas, Frederick S. *Introduction to Eighteenth Century Drama, 1700–1780*. Oxford: Clarendon Press, 1953.   PR703.B6

Brown, Laura. *English Dramatic Form, 1600–1760: An Essay in Generic History*. New Haven: Yale University Press, 1981.   PR691.B7

Hume, Robert D. *Development of English Drama in the Late Seventeenth Century*. Oxford: Clarendon Press, 1976.   PR691.H8

———, ed. *London Theatre World, 1660–1800*. Carbondale: Southern Illinois University Press, 1980.   PN2592.L64

Loftis, John. *Comedy and Society from Congreve to Fielding*. Stanford: Stanford University Press, 1959.   PR714.S6 L6

———. *Politics of Drama in Augustan England*. London: Oxford University Press, 1963.   PR714.P6 L6

———. *Restoration Drama: Modern Essays in Criticism*. New York: Oxford University Press, 1966.   PR693.L6

Miner, Earl, ed. *Restoration Dramatists: A Collection of Critical Essays*. Englewood Cliffs, N.J.: Prentice-Hall, 1966.   PR693.M5

Nicoll, Allardyce. *Garrick Stage: Theatres and Audience in the Eighteenth Century*. Edited by Sybil Rosenfeld. Athens: University of Georgia Press, 1980.   PN2593.N5 1980

Rothstein, Eric. *Restoration Tragedy: Form and the Process of Change*. Madison: University of Wisconsin Press, 1967.   PR691.R6

Summers, Montague. *Restoration Theatre*. London: Routledge, 1934.   PN2592.S86

Nineteenth Century

Booth, Michael. *English Melodrama*. London: Jenkins, 1965.   PR728.M4 B6

Donohue, Joseph. *Dramatic Character in the English Romantic Age*. Princeton, N.J.: Princeton University Press, 1970.   PR719.C47 D6

Reynolds, Ernest. *Early Victorian Drama, 1830–1870*. Cambridge: Cambridge University Press, 1936.   PR731.R4

Rowell, George. *Victorian Theatre: A Survey* [1792–1914]. London: Oxford University Press, 1956. Bibliography.   PN2594.R65

American—General

Brown, Thomas Allston. *History of the American Stage, Containing Biographical Sketches of Nearly Every Member of the Profession That Has Appeared on the American Stage, from 1733 to 1870*. New York: Dick and Fitzgerald, 1870.   PN2285.B75

Hughes, Glenn. *History of the American Theatre, 1700–1950*. New York: French, 1951.   PN2221.H76

Mayorga, Margaret C. *Short History of the American Drama: Commentaries on Plays Prior to 1920*. New York: Dodd, Mead, 1932. Bibliography.   PN332.M3

Meserve, Walter J. *Outline History of American Drama*. Totowa, N.J.: Littlefield, Adams, 1965.   PS332.M4

Moses, Montrose J. *American Dramatist*. Boston: Little, Brown, 1925.   PS332.M6 1925

Quinn (see S–76).

Colonial

Rankin, Hugh F. *Theatre in Colonial America*. Chapel Hill: University of North Carolina Press, 1965. PN2237.R3

Nineteenth Century

Grimstead, David. *Melodrama Unveiled: American Theatre and Culture, 1800–1850*. Chicago: University of Chicago Press, 1968.   PN1918.U5 G7

Moody, Richard. *America Takes the Stage: Romanticism in American Drama and Theatre, 1750–1900*. Bloomington: Indiana University Press, 1955.   AS36.I385 no. 34

Modern and Contemporary English and American

Armstrong, William A., ed. *Experimental Drama*. London: G. Bell and Sons, 1963.   PR737.A75

Bentley, Eric. *Playwright as Thinker: A Study of Drama in Modern Times*. Amended ed. Cleveland: Meridian, 1955.   PN1851.B4 1955

Bernstein, Samuel. *Strands Entwined: A New Direction in American Drama*. Boston: Northeastern University Press, 1980.   PS351.B4

Bigsby, C. W. E. *Confrontation and Commitment: A Study of Contemporary American Drama, 1959–1966*. Columbia: University of Missouri Press, 1968.   PS351.B48

———, ed. *Contemporary English Drama*. London: Edward Arnold, 1981.   PR737.C66

Bogard, Travis, and William I. Oliver, eds. *Modern Drama: Essays in Criticism*. New York: Oxford University Press, 1965.   PN1851.B6

Brown, John Russell. *American Theatre*. London: Edward Arnold, 1967.   PR737.A6

———. *Contemporary Theatre*. London: Edmund Arnold, 1962.   PR737.C6

———, ed. *Modern British Dramatists: A Collection of Critical Essays*. Englewood Cliffs, N.J.: Prentice-Hall, 1968.   PR737.B7

———, ed. *Modern British Dramatists: New Perspectives*. Englewood Cliffs, N.J.: Prentice-Hall, 1984.   PR737.M58 1984

Brustein, Robert. *Theatre of Revolt: An Approach to Modern Drama*. Boston: Little, Brown, 1964.   PN2189.B7

Downer, Alan S. *Fifty Years of American Drama, 1900–1950*. Chicago: Regnery, 1951.   PS351.D6

Gassner, John. *Directions in Modern Theatre and Drama*. New York: Holt, Rinehart and Winston, 1965.   PN2189.G3 1965

———. *Theatre in Our Times: A Survey of the Men, Materials, and Movements of the Modern Drama*. New York: Crown, 1954.   PN1655.G3

Golden, Joseph. *Death of Tinker Bell: The American Theatre in the Twentieth Century*. Syracuse, N.Y.: Syracuse University Press, 1967.   PN2266.G63

Hinchliffe, Arnold P. *British Theatre, 1950–1970*. Totowa, N.J.: Rowman and Littlefield, 1974.   PN2595.H5

Kernan, Alvin, ed. *Modern American Theatre: A Collection of Critical Essays*. Englewood Cliffs, N.J.: Prentice-Hall, 1967.   PN2266.K38

Krutch, Joseph Wood. *American Drama since 1918: An Informal History*. Rev. ed. New York: Braziller, 1957.   PS351.K7 1957

Reynolds, Ernest R. *Modern English Drama: A Survey of the Theatre from 1900*. Rev. ed. London: G. G. Harrap, 1950.   PR736.R4

Taylor, John Russell. *Anger and After: A Guide to the New British Drama*. Rev. ed. London: Methuen, 1969.   PR736.T3 1969

———. *Second Wave*. New York: Hill and Wang, 1971.   PR736.T34

Weales, Gerald. *American Drama Since World War II*. New York: Harcourt, Brace and World, 1962.   PS351.W4

————. *Jumping Office: American Drama in the 1960s*. New York: Macmillan, 1969.   PS351.W43 1969

Williams, Raymond. *Drama From Ibsen to Brecht*. 2d rev. ed. Harmondsworth: Penguin, 1973.
PN1851.W5 1973

Worth, Katherine J. *Revolutions in Modern English Drama*. London: Bell, 1973.   PR736.W6

VIII.   FILM—BIBLIOGRAPHIES AND GUIDES

Note the inclusion of film in the *MLA International Bibliography* (L–50), in the *Journal of Modern Literature* (R–17), and in most of the general periodical indexes where reviews and other materials are cited under various headings including cinema, film, motion pictures, and moving pictures.

U–83 **Fisher, Kim N.** *On the Screen: A Film, Television, and Video Research Guide.* Littleton, Co.: Libraries Unlimited, Inc., 1986.   Z5784.M9 F535 1986

This bibliography of reference works includes a total of 731 serially numbered, descriptively and evaluatively annotated entries, disposed into a total of fourteen chapters. Many chapters have subdivisions for works concerning the various media individually and in combination. The chapters are as follows: 1. Bibliographic Guides; 2. Dictionaries and Encyclopedias; 3. Indexes, Abstracts, and Databases; 4. Biographies; 5. Credits; 6. Film Reviews and Television Programming; 7. Catalogs; 8. Directories and Yearbooks; 9. Filmographies and Videographies; 10. Bibliographies; 11. Handbooks and Miscellaneous Sources; 12. Core Periodicals; 13. Research Centers and Archives; and 14. Societies and Associations. An Appendix listing Database Service Suppliers and both an Author/Title and a Subject Index conclude the volume.

U–85 **Sheahan, Eileen.** *Moving Pictures: An Annotated Guide to Selected Film Literature with Suggestions for the Study of Film.* Cranbury, N.J.: A. S. Barnes and Co., 1979.
Z5784.M9 S5 1979

The most current (to mid 1977) and helpful of all the general student guides, this work is disposed into ten sections, as follows: A. Guides and Handbooks; B. Dictionaries and Encyclopedias; C. Annuals and Directories; D. Bibliographies and Catalogs (subheadings for Comprehensive and Serial Bibliographies of Books on Motion Pictures, Catalogs of Books, Book Reviews, and National Bibliographies); E. Film Lists and Sources (subheadings for International Filmographies, National Filmographies, Lists of Films of Individuals, Film Catalogs, Film Scripts, Literary Sources and Film Adaptations, and Plot Summaries); F. Film Histories (subheadings for International Histories, National Histories, Genre Studies and Partial Histories, and Basic Studies of Theory and Technique); G. Biography; H. Film Reviews and Criticism; I. Periodicals (subheadings for Film Periodicals, Periodical Lists, Film and General Periodical Indexes, and Periodical Location Aids); J. Dissertations.

The 374 serially numbered entries, descriptively and evaluatively annotated, are arranged in sections or subsections alphabetically by author or title. Introductory comments discuss the relationship among various works cited in each section; there are extensive cross-references. A subject index and an author and title index conclude this first-rate guide.

Another student guide is the German volume *Wie finde ich film - und theaterwissenschaftliche Literatur?* by Frank Heidtmann and Paul S. Ulrich (Berlin: Berlin-Verlag, 1978) [Z5784.M9 H38].

U–86 **Bukalski, Peter J.** *Film Research: A Critical Bibliography with Annotations and Essay.* Boston: G. K. Hall, 1972.
Z5784.M9 B897

A brief description of fifty "essential works" is followed by a list of some 3,000 other film books classified as follows: Film History, Theory, Criticism; Production and Technology; Genre; Sociology and Economics; National Cinema; Scripts; Particular Films; Personalities, Biographies, and [individual] Filmographies; Education; Film-related Works; Careers in Film; Bibliographies, Guides, and Indexes; Selected Works in Foreign Languages. Entries are partially annotated. Lists of film periodicals and of sources for film rental and purchase are also included. There is no index.

U–87 **Gottesman, Ronald, and Harry M. Geduld.** *Guidebook to Film: An Eleven-in-One Reference.* New York: Holt, Rinehart and Winston, 1972.   Z5784.M9 G66

This dated but still valuable eleven-part reference guide includes (1) an elaborately classified and annotated list of standard books and periodicals; (2) a list of United States theses on film, 1916–1969; (3) a directory by continent of film museums and archives; (4) a list of film courses and schools; (5) a list of United States film equipment and supply sources; (6) a list of United States film distributors for film rental and purchase; (7) lists of bookstores, publishers, and sources of stills; (8) a list of film organizations and series including the major studios; (9) a list of film festivals and contests; (10) chronologies of important United States film awards; and (11) a glossary of film terms and abbreviations.

More current versions of some of these lists may be obtained through the continuously updated series of pamphlets published by the American Film Institute (AFI) under the series title "Factfiles." The titles currently available include "Film and Television Periodicals in English"; "Careers in Film and Television"; "Film/Video Festivals and Awards"; "Guide to Classroom Use of Film"; "Women and Film/Television"; "Independent Film and Video"; "Movie and TV Nostalgia"; "Film Music"; "Animation"; "Third World Cinema"; "Film/Television: A Research Guide"; and "Film/Television: Grants, Scholarships, Special Programs."

U–88 **Manchel, Frank.** *Film Study: A Resource Guide.* Rutherford, N.J.: Fairleigh Dickinson University Press, 1973.
Z5784.M9 M34

An excellent discursive introduction to the teaching of film, this work also presents in essay format extended recommendations of films and books and articles on film, with appended bibliographies. Lists of reliable film critics, periodicals, and distributors of 16mm and 8mm film are included, as is a glossary of film terms. Indexes of article titles, book titles, authors of articles, authors of books, film personalities, film titles, and subjects conclude the volume.

U–89 **Armour, Robert A.** *Film: A Reference Guide.* Westport, Conn.: Greenwood Press, 1980.   PN1993.45.A75

This volume presents a series of discursive bibliographic essays on the study of American film. The eleven chapters are as follows: History of Film; Production; Film Criticism; Film and Related Arts; Film and Society; Major Artists; Major Films; The International Influence on American Film; Reference Works and Periodicals; A Selected Chronology of American Film; and a Guide to Research Collections. To each chapter is appended a bibliography of references discussed. The work concludes with indexes of authors and of subjects.

U–90 **Vincent, Carl, Riccardo Redi, and Franco Venturini.** *Bibliografia generale del cinema / Bibliographie général du cinéma/General Bibliography of Motion Pictures.* Rome: Ateneo, 1973.   Z5784.M9 V5 1972

This selective, general bibliography of the literature of film from its beginnings to about 1952 emphasizes foreign-language works. Entries are divided into eleven subject categories including General Works; Film History; Aesthetics and Criticism; Film Technique; Social and Moral Problems; Legal and Economic Problems; The Cinema and Science; Sixteen Millimeter and Amateurs' Films; Documentation (i.e., reference works) and Anthologies; Subjects and Screenplays; and an unclassified, Miscellaneous section. Entries are descriptively annotated by listing the contents of chapters. Introductory materials are in Italian, French, and English. The volume concludes with an index of names and a table of contents showing the subclassifications of the various sections.

U–91 **Mitry, Jean.** *Bibliographie internationale du cinéma et de la télévision.* 7 vols. to date. Paris: Institut des hautes études cinématographiques [IDHEC], 1966–.
Z5784.M9 M55

This is the most extensive and ambitious bibliography of film literature in existence. Part 1, *France et pays de langue française*, is in four volumes: 1, *Ouvrages de référence et histoire du cinéma*; 2, *Histoire du cinéma*; 3, *Esthétique et technique*; 4, *Administration, législation, exploitation, biographies*. Volume 4 also contains an index of authors.
Part 2, *Italie*, is in two volumes: 1, *Bibliographie, histoire du cinéma, sociologie*; 2, *Esthétique, technique, administration, manifestations, biographies*. Part 3, *Espagne, Portugal et pays de langue espagnole et portugaise*, is in one volume.
Additional volumes are planned to treat the film of England, Germany, Hungary, and German-speaking countries; Sweden, Denmark, and Scandinavian countries; and the Soviet Union, Poland, Czechoslovakia, and Yugoslavia.
A similarly comprehensive international filmography, *Filmographie universelle*, is also in process at the Institut des hautes études cinématographiques (1963–) [PN1993 .5.A1 M5]. Twenty-six volumes have been published to date: vol. 1, *Index historique des techniques et industries du film* (1963); vols. 2–4, *Primitifs et précurseurs, 1895-1915* (1964–1965); vol. 5, *L'école européenne, 1910-1925* (1965); vols. 6–11, *L'école americaine, 1910-1925* (1966–1969); vol. 12, *Les serials en Amerique et en Europe, 1908–30* (1970); vols. 13–16, *Etats-Unis, 1915–35* (1970- 1972); vols. 17–19, *Etats-Unis 1920–45* (1979–1980); vols. 20–21, *Russie, 1910–25* (1980–1981); vol. 22, *Russie, 1925–50* (1981); vols. 23–24, *France, 1910–25* (1981); vol. 25, *Nouvelle école française, 1919–40* (1982); and vol. 26, *L'Ecole France, 1925–50* (1982).
A new series under the editorship of Hans-Peter Manz, *Internationale Filmbibliographie 1979-80 / Bibliographie internationale du cinéma / International Motion-Picture Bibliography*, has recently begun publication (Munich: Filmland Presse, 1981–) [Z5784.M9 M36 1981].

U–92 **Monaco, James, and Susan Schenker.** *Books about Film: A Bibliographical Checklist.* 3d rev. ed. New York: Zoetrope, 1976.   Z5984.M9 M50 1976

This bibliography, designed for student use, was first published by AFI in 1971. It is one of the most compact available and is divided into fifteen chapters, each with a brief in-

troduction and an essentially unannotated selective list of readily available standard works. The chapters cover the following topics: Historical and Theoretical Surveys and Texts; Film Techniques; Classical Critics and Critical Attitudes; Contemporary Critics; Anthologies of Criticism and Interviews; National Cinemas; Area Studies (Genres, Studies of Film and . . .); Filmmakers; Individual Films; The New Criticism: Semiotics and Dialectics; Television and Media; Reference Guides; Scripts; Magazines and Journals; a Bibliographical Note (Listing Publishers Specializing in Film Books; Important Series of Film Books; and Major Cinema Bookshops).
A companion to this work is Monaco's "Film: How and Where to Find Out What You Want to Know," originally published in *Take One* (1975) and available with an update including 1976 publications. It is disposed into five main sections: Film Lists and Encyclopedias; Film Book Bibliographies; Guides to Periodical Literature; Miscellaneous Guides; and a long section on Journals and Magazines. Entries in the first four sections include descriptive and evaluative annotation; the journal entries include publishers' addresses and costs.

U–93 **Bowles, Stephen E.** *Approach to Film Study: A Selected Booklist.* New York: Revisionist Press, 1974.
Z5784.M9 B63

This brief guide is notable for its effort to present a systematic classification of film literature. Entries are presented in alphabetically arranged sheer lists under the following headings (or one of the three levels of subheadings beneath them): I. General Reference Sources; II. General Introductory Books; III. Film History; IV. Film Classifications; V. Film Theory and Aesthetics; VI. Film Criticism; VII. Film Personalities; VIII. Individual Films; IX. Film Making; X. Film Teaching and Education; XI. Film Periodicals; and XII. Addenda. There is no index.

U–94 *Film Index: A Bibliography.* Vol. I, *Film As Art.* New York: Museum of Modern Art Film Library and the H. W. Wilson Co., 1941.   Z5784.M9 W75

This volume, prepared by workers in the Writer's Program of the New York City Work Project Administration (WPA), presents an annotated, classified bibliography of some 8,600 English-language entries. Cited are some 700 books, 3,000 magazine and journal articles, and 4,300 film reviews found in the film collections of the Museum of Modern Art, the New York Public Library, and other New York City libraries. In part 1, descriptively annotated entries are divided into several dozen subject categories. The work concludes with an index of names and titles; the latter includes some 4,300 films grouped into three lists: Fictional, Factual, and Miscellaneous. Projected volumes on the film industry and film society were never published.
Other early film bibliographies include the following works: Frances Christeson, *Guide to the Literature of the Motion Picture* (Los Angeles: University of Southern California, 1938) [Z5784.M9 C5]; M. Jackson Wrigley and Eric Leyland, *Cinema: Historical, Technical, and Bibliographical: A Survey for Librarians and Students* (London: Grafton, 1939) [PN1994.W7]; *Moving Pictures in the United States and Foreign Countries: A Selected List of Recent Writings*, prepared by the Library of Congress Division of Bibliography, 2d ed. (Washington, D.C.: GPO, 1940) [Z5784.M9 U67]; and the *Reader's Guide to Books on the Cinema* (London: Library Association, 1953) [Z1035.L7 no. 21].

U–95 **Rehrauer, George. *Macmillan Film Bibliography: A Critical Guide to the Literature of the Motion Picture.*** 2 vols. New York: Macmillan, 1982.   Z5784.M9 R423 1982

The original of this bibliography was published in 1972 under the title *Cinema Booklist* (Metuchen, N.J.: Scarecrow) [Z5784.M9 R42], with *Supplement Number 1* following in 1974 and *Supplement Number 2* in 1977. The present two-volume work is a cumulation and expansion of the earlier volumes. It presents in volume 1 a total of 6,762 serially numbered, alphabetically arranged titles of English-language books on the cinema, including reference works, histories, biographies, critical studies, scripts, and other works of interest to students of film. Entries, called "reviews," include author and publishing information along with a substantial descriptive and often evaluative annotation.

Volume 2 presents extensive indexes keyed to the "review" number of volume 1. The subject index is a guide to persons, film titles, and general topics. For films, index entries give the title, release date, principal actors, director, and the list of titles of works in volume 1 which treat the film. General topics are at various levels of abstraction from "Apes in films" to History (with such subheadings as American film, general; American film, silent; American film, sound; Canadian; Horror films; International film; and Technology, inventions, etc.). The author index lists authors of works listed in volume 1; the script index lists scripts alphabetically by movie title, with the director's name in parentheses below the title.

Another bibliography of monographs is A. R. Dyment, *Literature of the Film: A Bibliographical Guide to the Film as Art and Entertainment, 1936–1970* (London: White Lion, 1975) [Z5784.M9 D9], which contains 1,303 generally annotated entries for monographs. It is disposed into nine sections on film, history, aesthetics and criticism, personalities, techniques, the film industry, and the like.

U–96 **Ellis, Jack C., Charles Derry, and Sharon Kern. *Film Book Bibliography, 1940–1975.*** Metuchen, N.J.: Scarecrow Press, 1979.   Z5784.M9 E44

This work, designed to complement the *Film Index* (U–94) and the *New Film Index* (U–122), presents a subject index to books, monographs, and dissertations on film published in English from 1940 to 1975. A total of 5,442 serially numbered, occasionally annotated entries are disposed into ten sections, as follows: I. Reference; II. Film Technique and Technology; III. Film Industry; IV. Film History; V. Film Classifications; VI. Biography, Analysis, and Interviews; VII. Individual Films; VIII. Film Theory and Criticism; IX. Film and Society; X. Film and Education. The complete structure of the volume is indicated in the detailed table of contents. Most subdivisions begin with a descriptive headnote. Arrangement within subsections is chronological except section 6, which is alphabetical by subject person, and section 7, which is alphabetical by film title. This well-designed volume concludes with indexes of names as authors or subjects and of titles.

U–97 **Ross, Harris. *Film as Literature, Literature as Film: An Introduction to and Bibliography of Film's Relationship to Literature.*** Westport, Conn.: Greenwood Press, 1987.   Z5784.M9 R66 1987

This volume cites 2,449 serially numbered articles and books published from 1908 to 1985 on the relationship between film and literature. After an introduction on the relations between literature and film (A. Camera Eye, Narrator's Voice; B. Time; C. Space), entries are disposed into a series of seventeen chapters, as follows: 1. Literature and Film: General Studies; 2. Language and Film: Linguistic Approaches to Film; 3. Prose Fiction and Film: General Studies;

4. Drama and Film: General Studies; 5. Poetry and Film: General Studies; 6. Adaptation: General Studies and Anthologies; 7. Writers and the Film Industry; 8. Literary Figures of the United States; 9. Literary Figures of the United Kingdom; 10. William Shakespeare and Film; 11. Literary Figures of Classical Literature; 12. Literary Figures of Europe; 13. Literary Figures of Latin America; 14. Literary Figures of Asia and Africa; 15. Scripts by Literary Figures, Scripts of Adaptations; 16. Literature/Film in the Classroom; and 17. Research Tools. An Author Index and Subject Index including titles conclude the volume.

An earlier work is Jeffrey Egan Welch's *Literature and Film: An Annotated Bibliography, 1900–1977* (New York: Garland, 1981) [Z5784.M9 W37] which cites a total of 1,235 serially numbered items. Excluded are reviews, bibliographies and filmographies, screenplays, and interviews. Included items are arranged in two lists, one of books and articles with descriptively annotated entries and the other of dissertations, without annotation. Both lists are organized chronologically by year of publication and alphabetically by author within the year. An Appendix lists authors of literary works and the film(s) related to that work, with names of directors, screenwriters, producers, release dates, and reference to the entry numbers which address that particular literature/film relation.

U–98 **Some Frequently Recommended Works on Literature and Film.**

Bibliographical

Note that the annual "Bibliography on Relations of Literature and the Other Arts" (X–35) includes Literature and Film from 1973–1975.

Daniel, Wendell. "A Researcher's Guide and Selected Checklist to Film as Literature and Language." *Journal of Modern Literature* 3 (1973): 323–350. Annotated bibliography in seven sections.

De Marco, Norman. "Bibliography of Books on Literature and Film." *Style* 9 (1975): 593–607.

Goodwin, James. "Literature and Film: A Review of Criticism." *Quarterly Review of Film Studies* 4 (1979): 227–246.

Manvell, Roger. *Shakespeare and the Film.* Rev. and updated. South Brunswick, N.J.: A. S. Barnes, 1979. Includes a filmography and selected bibliography.
    PR3093.M3 1979

———. "Shakespeare on Film, with an Index of Films: 1929–1971," *Films in Review* 24 (1973): 132–163.

Parker, Barry M. *Folger Shakespeare Filmography.* Washington, D.C.: Folger Shakespeare Library, 1979.
    PR3093.P3

Ross, Harris. "A Select Bibliography of the Relations of Literature and Film," *Style* 9 (1975): 564–592.

Wicks, Ulrich. "Literature/Film: A Bibliography," *Literature/Film Quarterly* 6 (1978): 135–143.

General

Armes, Roy. *Ambiguous Image: Narrative Style in Modern European Cinema.* Bloomington: Indiana University Press, 1976.   PN1993.5.E8 A7

Beja, Morris. *Film and Literature: An Introduction.* New York: Longman, 1979.   PN1995.3.B4

Bluestone, George. *Novels into Film.* Baltimore: Johns Hopkins University Press, 1957. Bibliography.
    PN1997.85.B5

Boyum, Joy Gould. *Double Exposure: Fiction into Film.* New York: New American Library, 1985.
    PN1997.85.B69 1985b

Cohen, Keith. *Film and Fiction.* New Haven: Yale University Press, 1979.   PN1995.3.C6

Conger, Syndy M., and Janice R. Welsch, eds. *Narrative Strategies: Original Essays on Film and Prose Fiction.* Macomb: Western Illinois University, 1980.   PN1997.85.N3

Enser, A. G. S. *Filmed Books and Plays: A List of Books and Plays from Which Films Have Been Made, 1928–1974* (see E–110).

Estermann, Alfred. *Die Verfilmung literarischer Werke.* Bonn: Bouvier, 1965.   PN1997.85.E8 1965

Fell, John L. *Film and the Narrative Tradition.* Norman: University of Oklahoma Press, 1974.   PN1993.5.U6 F4 1974

Giddings, Robert., et al. *Screening the Novel: The Theory and Practice of Literary Dramatization.* New York: St. Martin's Press, 1989.   PN1995.3.G53 1989

Harrington, John, ed. *Film and/as Literature.* Englewood Cliffs, N.J.: Prentice-Hall, 1977.   PN1995.3.H3

Hurt, James. *Focus on Film and Theatre.* Englewood Cliffs, N.J.: Prentice-Hall, 1974.   PN1995.H87

Jinks, William. *Celluloid Literature: Film in the Humanities.* Riverside, N.J.: Glencoe, 1971.   PN1994.J5

Jorgens, Jack J. *Shakespeare on Film.* Bloomington: Indiana University Press, 1977.   PR3093.J6

Jost, François. *L'il-camera; entre film et roman.* Lyon: Presses Universitaires de Lyon, 1987.   PN1995.3.J67 1987

Kawin, Bruce F. *Telling It Again and Again: Repetition in Literature and Film.* Ithaca, N.Y.: Cornell University Press, 1972.   PN56.R45 K3

Klein, Michael, and William Parker, eds. *English Novel and the Movies.* New York: Ungar, 1981.   PN1997.85.E53 1981

McConnell, Frank D. *Spoken Seen: Film and the Romantic Imagination.* Baltimore: Johns Hopkins University Press, 1975.   PN1995.M22

———. *Story Telling and Mythmaking.* New York: Oxford University Press, 1979.   PN1995.3.M26

Marcus, Fred H. *Short Story/Short Film.* Englewood Cliffs, N.J.: Prentice-Hall, 1977.   PN1997.85.M27

———, ed. *Film and Literature: Contrasts in Media.* Scranton, Pa.: Chandler, 1971.   PN1994.M3294

Miller, Gabriel. *Screening the Novel: Rediscovered American Fiction in Film.* New York: Ungar, 1979.   PN1997.85.M5

Morris, Peter. *Shakespeare on Film.* Ottawa: Canadian Film Institute, 1972.   PR3093.M6

Murray, Edward. *Cinematic Imagination: Writers and the Motion Pictures.* New York: Ungar, 1972.   PN1995.3.M8

Nicoll, Allardyce. *Film and Theatre.* New York: Crowell, 1937.   PN1994.N5 1937a

Paech, Joachim. *Literatur und Film.* Stuttgart: J. B. Metzler, 1988.   PN1995.3.P34 1988

Peary, Gerald, and Roger Shatzkin, eds. *Classic American Novel and the Movies.* New York: Ungar, 1977.   PN1997.85.C55

———, eds. *Modern American Novel and the Movies.* New York: Ungar, 1978.   PN1997.85.M64

Richardson, Robert. *Literature and Film.* Bloomington: Indiana University Press, 1969.   PN1995.3.R5

Sheridan, Marion C., et al. *Motion Picture and the Teaching of English.* New York: Appleton-Century-Crofts, 1965.   PN1994.N32

Spiegel, Alan. *Fiction and the Camera Eye: Visual Consciousness in Film and the Modern Novel.* Charlottesville: University Press of Virginia, 1976.   PN3491.S65

Thiery, Herman. *Dictionnaire filmographique de la littérature mondiale / Filmographic Dictionary of World Literature* (E–112).

Wagner, Geoffrey. *Novel and the Cinema.* Rutherford, N.J.: Fairleigh Dickinson University Press, 1975.   PN1997.85.W33

Winston, Douglas G. *Screenplay as Literature.* Rutherford, N.J.: Fairleigh Dickinson University Press, 1973.   PN1996.W555

U–99 **Some Frequently Recommended Works on Film History, Theory, and Criticism.**

Andrew, J. Dudley. *Major Film Theories: An Introduction.* New York: Oxford University Press, 1976.   PN1995.A5

Arijon, Daniel. *Grammar of the Film Language.* New York: Hastings House, 1976.   TR850.A8 1976

Armes, Roy. *Films and Realty: An Historical Survey.* Harmondsworth, England: Penguin, 1974.   PN19935.A1 A74

Arnheim, Rudolf. *Film as Art.* Berkeley and Los Angeles: University of California Press, 1960.   PN1994.A67

Barnouw, Erik. *Documentary: A History of the Non-Fiction Film.* London: Oxford University Press, 1976.   PN1995.9.D6 B37

Bazin, André. *What Is Cinema?* Selected and translated by Hugh Gray from *Qu'est-ce que le cinema*? 4 vols. (Paris: Editions du Cerf, 1958–1962). 2 vols. Berkeley and Los Angeles: University of California Press, 1967–1971.   PN1994.B35

Braudy, Leo. *World in a Frame: What We See in Films.* Garden City, N.Y.: Anchor Press, 1976.   PN1995.B72

Brownlow, Kevin. *Parade's Gone By.* New York: Ballantine, 1968.   PN1993.5.U6 B7

Cavell, Stanley. *World Viewed: Reflections on the Ontology of Film.* Enl. ed. Cambridge: Harvard University Press, 1979.   PN1995.C42 1979

Cowie, Peter, ed. *Concise History of the Cinema.* 2 vols. New York: A. S. Barnes, 1970.   PN1993.5.A1 C76

Deslandes, Jacques. *Histoire comparée du cinéma.* 5 vols. Tournai: Casterman, 1966–. Bibliographies.

Eisenstein, Sergei. *Film Form: Essays in Film Theory.* Edited and translated by Jay Leyda. New York: Harcourt, Brace and World, 1949.   PN1995.E5

———. *Film Sense.* Edited and translated by Jay Leyda. New York: Harcourt, Brace and World, 1942.   PN1995.E52

Fielding, Raymond, ed. *Technological History of Motion Pictures and Television.* Berkeley and Los Angeles: University of California Press, 1967.   TR848.F5

Giannetti, Louis. *Understanding Movies.* 3d ed. Englewood Cliffs, N.J.: Prentice-Hall, 1982.   PN1994.G47 1982

Huss, Roy, and Norman Silverstein. *Film Experience: Elements of Motion Picture Art.* New York: Harper and Row, 1968.   PN1995.9.P7 H8

Jacobs, Lewis. *Rise of the American Film: A Critical History, with an Essay "Experimental Cinema in America, 1921–1947."* New ed. New York: Teachers College Press, Columbia University, 1968.   PN1993.5.U6 J2 1968

Jarvis, Ian C. *Movies and Society.* New York: Basic Books, 1970.   PN1995.9.S6 J3 1970

Jeanne, René, and Charles Ford. *Histoire encyclopédique du cinéma.* 5 vols. Paris: Laffont, 1947–1962.
PN1993.5.A1 J43

Kaminsky, Stuart M. *American Film Genres: Approaches to a Critical Theory of Popular Film.* Dayton, Ohio: Pflaum Publishers, 1974.   PN1993.5.U6 K34

Knight, Arthur. *Liveliest Art: A Panoramic History of the Movies.* Rev. ed. New York: Macmillan, 1978.
PN1993.5.A1 K6 1978

Kracauer, Siegfried. *Theory of Film: The Redemption of Physical Reality.* New York: Oxford University Press, 1960.   PN1994.K7

Lingren, Ernest. *Art of the Film.* 2d ed. London: George Allen and Unwin, 1963.   PN1995.L47 1963

Low, Rachel, and A. Roger Manvell. *History of the British Film [1896–1939].* 4 vols. to date. London: Allen and Unwin, 1948–1979.   PN1993.5.G7 L6

McCann, Richard Dyer, ed. *Film: A Montage of Theories.* New York: Dutton, 1966.   PN1944.M312

McLuhan, H. Marshall. *Understanding Media: The Extensions of Man.* New York: McGraw-Hill, 1964.
P90.M26

Mast, Gerald. *Comic Mind: Comedy and the Movies.* 2d ed. Chicago: University of Chicago Press, 1979.
PN1995.9.C55 M38 1979

———. *Film/Cinema/Movie: A Theory of Experience.* New York: Harper and Row, 1977.   PN1995.M37 1977

———. *Short History of the Movies.* 3d ed. Indianapolis: Bobbs-Merrill, 1981.   PN1993.5.A1 M39 1981

Mast, Gerald, and Marshall Cohen, eds. *Film Theory and Criticism: Introductory Readings.* 2d ed. New York: Oxford University Press, 1979. PN1994.M364 1979

Metz, Christian. *Film Language: A Semiotics of the Cinema.* Translation by Michael Taylor of *Essais sur la signification au cinéma* (Paris: Klincksieck, 1968). New York: Oxford University Press, 1974.
PN1995.M4513

Mitry, Jean. *Ésthetique et psychologie du cinéma.* 2 vols. Paris: Éditions universitaires, 1963. PN1995.5.M53

———. *Histoire du cinéma, art et industrie [1895–1950].* 5 vols. Paris: Éditions universitaires, 1967–1980.
PN1993.5.A1 M53

———. *Histoire du cinéma muet, 1895–1930.* 3 vols. Paris: Éditions universitaires, 1972–1973.
No LC number

Monaco, James. *How to Read a Film: The Art, Technology, Language History, and Theory of Film and Media.* Rev. ed. New York: Oxford University Press, 1982.
PN1994.M59 1981

Perkins, V. F. *Film as Film: Understanding and Judging Movies.* Baltimore: Penguin, 1972.   PN1994.P394

Reisz, Karel. *Technique of Film Editing.* 2d enl. ed. New York: Amphoto/Hastings House, 1968.
PN1996.R43 1968

Rhode, Eric. *History of the Cinema: From Its Origins to 1970.* London: Allen Lane, 1976. PN1993.5.A1 R46

Robinson, David. *History of World Cinema.* New York: Stein and Day, 1973.   PN1993.5.A1 R56 1973

Rotha, Paul. *Film till Now: A Survey of World Cinema.* With an additional section by Richard Griffith. 4th ed. London: Spring Books, 1967.
PN1993.5.A1 R69 1967

———, et al. *Documentary Film: The Use of the Film Medium to Interpret Creatively and in Social Terms the Life of the People As It Exists in Reality.* 3d ed.,

rev. and enl. London: Faber, 1952.
PN1995.9.D6 R68 1952

Sadoul, Georges. *Histoire du cinéma mondial des origines à nos jours.* 9th ed. Paris: Flammarion, 1972.
PN1993.5.A1 S3 1972

———. *Histoire générale du cinéma.* 6 vols. Rev. ed. Paris: Editions Denoël, 1973–1975.
PN1993.5.A1 S345

Sklar, Robert. *Movie-Made American: A Social History of American Movies.* New York: Random House, 1975.
PN1993.5.U6 S53

Solomon, Stanley J. *Beyond Formula: American Film Genres.* New York: Harcourt Brace Jovanovich, 1976.   PN1993.5.U6 S57

Spottiswoode, Raymond R. *Film and Its Techniques.* Berkeley and Los Angeles: University of California Press, 1951.   PN1995.9.D6 S6

———. *Grammar of the Film.* Berkeley: University of California Press, 1935.   PN1994.S65 1935

Stam, Robert. *Subversive Pleasures: Bakhtin, Cultural Criticism, and Film.* Baltimore: Johns Hopkins University Press, 1989.   PN1995.3.S73 1989

Stephenson, Ralph, and Jean R. Debrix. *Cinema as Art.* 2d ed. Harmondsworth: Penguin, 1976.
PN1995.9.P7 S7 1976

Talbot, Daniel, ed. *Film: An Anthology.* Berkeley and Los Angeles: University of California Press, 1959.
PN1994.T27

Taylor, John Russell. *Cinema Eye, Cinema Ear.* New York: Hill and Wang, 1964.   PN1998.A2 T38

Tudor, Andrew. *Theories of Film.* New York: Viking, 1974.
PN1995.T78 1974

Wollen, Peter. *Signs and Meaning in the Cinema.* 3d ed. Bloomington: Indiana University Press, 1972.
PN1995.W64 1972

IX. FILM—HANDBOOKS AND ENCYCLOPEDIAS

See also the *Encyclopedia dello spettacolo* (U–20).

U–100 **Cawkwell, Tim, and John M. Smith. *World Encyclopedia of Film.*** New York: World, 1972.   PN1993.43.C3

This volume, regarded as the best of the film encyclopedias, contains long, informative essays by thirty-four contributors on various aspects of film history, along with some 2,000 shorter biographical articles on directors, actors, writers, cameramen, set designers, and other personnel. At the end is an index of films which lists some 22,000 works with complete credits for each.

U–101 **Halliwell, Leslie. *Filmgoer's Companion.*** 6th ed. New York: Hill and Wang, 1977.   PN1993.H3 1977

The sixth edition of this popular encyclopedia, the first edition of which appeared in 1965, includes more than 10,000 entries on a variety of topics from persons to subjects, techniques, specific films, film genres, film industry organizations, and other matters of interest to the general moviegoer. There are numerous illustrations and several appendixes, including lists films, fictional characters, themes, title changes, and film books.

Another popular encyclopedia is by Ephraim Katz, *Film Encyclopedia*: *The Most Comprehensive Encyclopedia of World Cinema in a Single Volume* (New York: Crowell, 1979) [PN1993.45.K34 1979], which contains some 7,000 entries, primarily biographical. There are entries for stars, feature players, many minor actors, screenwriters, composers, designers, art directors, and cinematographers. There are also articles on studios, film centers, national cinemas, technical terms and equipment, film events, and film organization. But the strength of the volume is in its short biographical pieces on film people.

U–102 **Manvell, Roger, and Lewis Jacobs.** *International Encyclopedia of Film.* New York: Crown, 1972.   PN1993.45.I5

Although there are only 1,280 entries, this is a very well-received, well-illustrated encyclopedia. Articles are longer and more detailed than those found, for example, in Halliwell (U–101). International in scope, there are articles on persons, technical terms, general topics, and national film histories. A chronological outline of film history at the end is followed by a select bibliography of about 500 items, an index of title changes, an index of some 6,500 film titles, and an index of names.

U–103 **Bawden, Lizz-Anne, ed.** *Oxford Companion to Film.* New York: Oxford University Press, 1976.   PN1993.45.O9

Three thousand entries treat some 700 films, biographies of artists, critics, and film personnel, film genres and movements, film versions of literary classics, and technical terms and processes. The focus throughout is sociological and political, relating film as an art form and technological achievement to political and social phenomena. The volume's reception has been mixed.

U–104 **Boussinot, Roger.** *L'encyclopédie du cinéma.* 2 vols. Paris: Bordas, 1967–1970.   PN1993.45.B6

Volume 1, *Oeuvres, écoles, réalisateurs, acteurs,* of this international encyclopedia contains primarily articles on individual films and biographical articles on film personalities. There are some terms and technical topics treated, and there are brief national film histories included. Volume 2, *L'encyclopédie du cinéma par l'image,* contains more than 3,000 illustrations. A planned but unpublished third volume was to have treated the immediately contemporary cinema.

U–105 *Filmlexikon degli autori e delle opere.* 9 vols. Rome: Bianco e nero, 1958–74.   PN1998.A2 E53

The first seven volumes of this well-illustrated comprehensive work treat "Autori" of the world cinema, including directors, producers, story- and scriptwriters, actors, actresses, cameramen, composers, art directors, and costume designers. Biographies, filmographies, and, for major figures, bibliographies are included in the detailed, signed articles. Titles are given in the original language and in Italian. Volumes 8 and 9 are a supplement, *Aggiornamenti,* covering 1958–1971. There was to have been a second part, treating "Opere," which would have included films, film terms, biographies of historians and critics, and an index of film titles, but it was never published.

U–106 **Bessay, Maurice, and Jean-Louis Chardans.** *Dictionnaire du cinéma et de la télévision.* 5 vols. Paris: Jean-Jacques Pauvert, 1965–1975.   PN1993.45.B4

This general, well-illustrated international dictionary is valuable primarily for its extended articles in volumes 1–4 on technical terms and on aspects of the history and technique of the cinema. There are biographical articles as well, giving brief biographies and chronological lists of films. Television history, technique, and biography is less thoroughly treated. The fifth and final volume is a filmography, listing by title all films cited.

U–107 **Thomson, David.** *Biographical Dictionary of the Cinema.* 2d ed., rev. London: Secker and Warburg, 1975.
PN1998.A2 T55 1975

This work presents long articles on nearly 900 selected film personalities including directors, producers, actresses, and actors. Articles present in discursive form a combination of biographies, critiques, and filmography, all written in an entirely personal style. Indeed, this work is more nearly a monographic critique of "film people" in dictionary arrangement than it is a biographical reference work, for which most of the general encyclopedias of film are more useful, if less interesting.

Useful indexes to published but buried biographical materials are found in Mel Schuster's two volumes, *Motion Picture Directors: A Bibliography of Magazine and Periodical Articles, 1900-1972* (Metuchen, N.J.: Scarecrow, 1973) [Z5784.M9 S34] and *Motion Picture Performers: A Bibliography of Magazine and Periodical Articles, 1900-1969* (Metuchen, N.J.: Scarecrow, 1971) [Z5784.M9 S35].

U–108 **Sadoul, Georges.** *Dictionary of Film Makers.* Translation and revision by Peter Morris of *Dictionnaire des cinéastes* (Paris, 1965). Berkeley, Los Angeles, London: University of California Press, 1972.   PN1993.45.S313

This illustrated, selective international bibliographical dictionary, a companion to Sadoul's *Dictionary of Films* (U–112), contains brief articles on more than 1,000 directors, scriptwriters, cinematographers, art directors, composers, producers, inventors, scenarists, photographers, and designers. Excluded are actors and actresses.

Among other biographical dictionaries see the highly selective French *Dictionnaire du cinéma,* ed. Raymond Bellour and Jean-Jacques Brochier (Paris: Éditions universitaires, 1966) [PN1998.A2 D55], which provides long signed biographies of 273 directors, producers, and scriptwriters by thirty-nine contributors, with a series of introductory essays on film history and an index of names cited.

U–109 **Geduld, Harry M., and Ronald Gottesman.** *Illustrated Glossary of Film Terms.* New York: Holt, Rinehart and Winston, 1973.   PN1993.45.G38

This dictionary of technical film production vocabulary for laymen and beginning film students provides definitions that avoid highly technical jargon, along with both line drawings and photographs. Also useful is James Monaco's *Standard Glossary for Film Criticism,* 2d ed. (New York: Zoetrope, 1975) [PN1993.45.M64 1975], which collects terms likely to be useful to critics from the various glossaries of filmmaking and presents definitions for the technically uninitiated.

Much more technical is Raymond Spottiswoode, ed., *Focal Encyclopedia of Film and Television Techniques* (New York: Focal, 1969) [TR847.F62], which presents 1,600 long, signed articles by 107 specialists, along with many unsigned shorter articles on all technical aspects of film and television production. Articles are illustrated, and there is a detailed subject index with about 10,000 entries. Another encyclopedic guide is Eli L. Levitan, *Alphabetical Guide to Motion Picture, Television, and Videotape Production* (New York: McGraw-Hill, 1970) [TR847.L47]. This volume, too, is extensively illustrated and concludes with a detailed subject index.

Polyglot dictionaries include the volume by W. E. Clason, *Elsevier's Dictionary of Cinema, Sound, and Music in Six Languages* (Amsterdam: Elsevier, 1956) [TR847.E4], which presents a total of 3,213 numbered English-language terms and definitions with equivalents in Dutch, French, German, Italian, and Spanish. Appendixes present alphabetical lists of terms in each of the other five languages, with cross-references to their English equivalents. Also available is the sixth edition of *Vocabulaire du cinéma / Film Vocabulary / Film Woordenlijst*, ed. S. I. Van Nooten (The Hague: Netherlands Information Service, 1973) [PN1993 .45.V6 1973], which treats 900 terms in French, English, Dutch, Italian, German, Spanish, and Danish.

X.   FILM—FILMOGRAPHIES, CHECKLISTS, AND CATALOGS

See also the checklists and guides to films from literary works in section E.X.

U–110   **Halliwell, Leslie. *Halliwell's Film Guide.*** 2d ed.   New York: Scribner, 1980.   PN1993.45.H27 1980

This volume presents an account of some 9,500 films including silent and sound films, English and foreign films. Films are alphabetical by title, with foreign films in their original titles. Entries include credits, ratings, dates, a brief synopsis, brief quotations from critics, and notation of awards, using a system of abbreviations for compactness. There is an alphabetical index of alternate titles and an index of English-language titles of foreign films.

U–111   ***Film Buff's Checklist of Motion Pictures (1912–1979).*** Hollywood, Calif.: Hollywood Film Archive, 1979.
                                                PN1998.F52

Originally published as *Film Buff's Bible of Motion Pictures (1915-1972)* by D. Richard Baer (Hollywood: Hollywood Film Archive, 1972) [PN1998.B25], this edition cites some 19,000 films alphabetically by title. Included are silent films, short films, and television films. Information given includes the year, distributor, length, country of origin, cast, and a rating of its quality from 1 to 10 in lieu of any critical annotations.
In this connection see also the title list of sound films prepared by Richard Dimmitt, *Title Guide to the Talkies, 1927-1963*, and its sequel by Andrew Aros, *Title Guide to the Talkies 1964 through 1974* (E–111).

U–112   **Sadoul, Georges. *Dictionary of Films.*** Translation and revision by Peter Morris of *Dictionnaire des films* (Paris, 1965). Berkeley, Los Angeles, London: University of California Press, 1972.   PN1993.45.S3213

This volume, a companion to Sadoul's *Dictionary of Film Makers* (U–108), presents a selective list of some 1,300 films from the beginning of motion pictures through the 1960s. Films are listed alphabetically by their original-language title, with cross-references from alternate titles under which they were released. Entries give country of origin, date, major credits, the cast, a brief plot summary, running time, and a brief account of the film's critical reception. There is no index.

U–113   **McCarty, Clifford. *Published Screenplays: A Checklist.*** Kent, Ohio: Kent State University Press, 1971.
                                                Z5784.M9 M3

This volume presents a list of 388 English-language screenplays alphabetically by title. Entries give the producing organization, date, director, author of the screenplay, source (when pertinent), and bibliographical information on the book or periodical in which a complete text is published. The work concludes with indexes of names and titles.

U–114   ***American Film Institute Catalog of Motion Pictures Produced in the United States from 1893 to 1970.*** 19 vols. planned.   New York: R. R. Bowker, 1971–.   PN1998.A57

These volumes will provide complete physical descriptions, production credits, cast credits, brief summaries, sources of the screenplay, and other pertinent information for all feature films, short films, and newsreels produced in the United States. To date, the following volumes have been published: *Feature Films, 1921–30* in 2 vols.; and *Feature Films, 1961–70* in 2 vols. In each case the second volume includes an index of credits and a subject index.

U–115   **Library of Congress. *Catalog of Copyright Entries: Cumulative Series: Motion Pictures [1894–1969].*** 5 vols. Washington, D.C.: Library of Congress, 1951–1971.
                                        (v. 1) PN1998.W25
                                        (v. 2–5) PN1998.U6152

Each volume presents an alphabetical title list of films registered for copyright during the dates of its coverage, as follows:

Vol. 1. *1894–1912* by Howard L. Walls (1953).
Vol. 2. *1912–1939* (1951).
Vol. 3. *1940–1949* (1953).
Vol. 4. *1950–1959* (1960).
Vol. 5. *1960–1969* (1971).

Entries give screenplay author, producer, distributor, cast, director, date, number of reels, and, in some cases, a summary. Volumes 2–5 conclude with indexes of persons and organizations.

U–116   **Library of Congress. *Library of Congress Catalog: Motion Pictures and Filmstrips: A Cumulative List of Works Represented by Library of Congress Printed Cards, 1953 [–1972].*** 9 vols. Ann Arbor, Mich.: Edwards, 1958–1973.
                                                Z881.U49 A25

There are four different listings of motion pictures cataloged by the Library of Congress (see B–12, B–13) as follows:

1953–1957, published as vol. 28 of the *National Union Catalog*.

1958–1962, published as vols. 53 and 54 of the *NUC*.

1963–1967, 2 vols. published with the *NUC* but not numbered.

1968–1972, 4 vols. published with the *NUC* but not numbered.

In each, films are listed alphabetically by title, and entries give the producer, director, screenplay author, and a brief summary. Each series has a subject index. These lists were preceded by volume 24, *Films*, of the *Library of Congress Author Catalog*, 1948–1952, and were continued by the new series *Films and Other Materials for Projection* [1972–], published since 1974. Three quarterly issues and an annual cumulation were further gathered in seven volumes appended to the quinquennial cumulation of 1973–1977. From 1978 through 1982, quarterly issues were cumulated in annual volumes; in 1979 the title changed to *Audiovisual Materials*. From 1983 on, this catalog has been produced in COM microfiche in cumulating quarterly issues.

U–117 **Gifford, Denis.** *British Film Catalogue, 1895–1970: A Guide to Entertainment Films.* 2 vols. Newton Abbot: David and Charles, 1973. PN1993.5.G7 G5

This is a complete list of most films produced in Britain since the invention of the film. Excluded are documentaries; films produced through cooperative arrangements with studios elsewhere are included. Volume 1 lists silent and volume 2 sound films. 14,161 numbered films are chronologically arranged by month, year, and date of production. Entries include title, director, studio, release date, distributor, cast and characters, footage or running time, whether silent or sound, the color system used, awards received, story source, and a brief plot summary. There are illustrations and an index to titles cited.

U–118 *Monthly Film Bulletin.* Vol. 1–. London: British Film Institute, 1934–. LB1044.B66

This listing of British feature films and foreign feature films released in Britain, as well as new short films, identifies the title, date, distributor, producer, cast, and running time of each film released. Extended critical comments are provided for feature films. An annual index of titles accompanies the last issue of the year.
British National Film Catalogue: A Record of British and Foreign Films Which Have Recently Been Made Available in Great Britain . . . Classified by Subject, with Alphabetical Indexes under Subject and Title, Distributors, Production Sponsors, and Technicians, 21 vols. (London: British Film Institute, 1963–1983) [PN1998.A1B75] provides a quarterly (formerly a bimonthly) account of nonfeature films (also feature films before 1969) in two lists, one of nonfictional films listed by Universal decimal classification, and the other of fictional films alphabetically by title. Entries give running time, distributor, information about color versus black-and-white, sound or silent, and the cast. There are production, subject, and title indexes in each issue; the lists are cumulated annually.

XI. FILM—INDEXES AND CHECKLISTS OF FILM LITERATURE

For current reviews see also general periodical and newspaper indexes in section D under such headings as motion picture reviews and moving picture reviews.

U–121 **Gerlach, John C., and Lana Gerlach.** *Critical Index: A Bibliography of Articles on Film in English, 1946–1973, arranged by Names and Topics.* New York: Teachers College Press, Columbia University, 1974. Z5784.M9 G47

This computer-compiled index to twenty-two British and American film and general periodicals is in two parts. The first is an index by names of the director, producer, actor, critic, or screenwriter. The second uses an arrangement of numbered subject headings, the major divisions of which are as follows: Economics, 100; History, 200; Criticism, 300; Society, 400; Technique, 500; Education and Scholarship, 600; and Miscellaneous, 700. These subjects are then further divided and subdivided, in a pattern similar to that of the Dewey system, and individual entries are then given under the appropriate subject number. The volume concludes with indexes to authors of articles and to film titles.

U–122 **McCann, Richard D., and Edward S. Perry.** *New Film Index: A Bibliography of Magazine Articles in English, 1930–1970.* New York: Dutton, 1975. Z5784.M9 M29 1975

This volume, designed as a sequel to *Film Index* (U–94), contains some 12,000 references to articles on film in thirty-eight English-language periodicals. Reviews are not cited. Briefly annotated entries are disposed into subject categories, with nine main divisions and a total of 278 subdivisions. Under each category, entries are in chronological order. The nine main parts are as follows: 1. Introductory and Reference; 2. Motion Picture Arts and Crafts; 3. Film Theory and Criticism; 4. Film History; 5. Biography (here entries are alphabetical by subject); 6. Motion Picture Industry; 7. Film and Society; 8. Non-Fiction Films; 9. Case Histories of Film Making (here entries are alphabetical by film title). There is a personal name index to the *Index*.

U–123 *International Index to Film Periodicals: An Annotated Guide [1972–].* Vol. 1–. New York: R. R. Bowker, 1973–. Z5784.M9 I49

This index, prepared by the twenty-four different members of the International Federation of Film Archives (FIAF), now contains some 9,000 entries annually taken from a total of eighty journals published in twenty-one different countries. Articles and reviews are both cited; entries are annotated and divided into a total of eleven main sections with hundreds of subdivisions. The main sections are as follows: 1. General Reference Material; 2. Institutions, Festivals, Conferences; 3. Film Industry: Economics, Production; 4. Film Industry: Distribution, Exhibition; 5. Society and Cinema; 6. Film Education; 7. Aesthetics, Theory, Criticism; 8. History of the Cinema; 9. Reviews and Studies of Individual Films; 10. Biography; 11. Miscellaneous. The annual volumes conclude with indexes of directors, script authors, and subjects.

U–124 *Film Literature Index: A Quarterly Author-Subject Index to the International Literature of Film.* Vol. 1–. Albany, N.Y.: Filmdex, Inc., 1973–. Z5784.M9 F45

This index, the widest-ranging of available indexes, analyzes some 300 film periodicals along with some 125 English-language general-interest magazines. Quarterly issues are cumulated annually. Entries are in a single alphabet that includes authors, subjects, and individual film titles. The more than 1,000 subject headings are taken from a series of film glossaries and related tools. Titles include both the original title and the title of the film in its American release. Directors, date of first showing, and country of origin are included in the citation. In addition to geographical subheadings, there are general subheadings: bibliographies, filmographies, history, study and teaching, techniques, and theory. Articles on festivals are all listed under the general heading Festivals; book reviews under the heading Book Reviews. There are extensive cross-references from the names of actors, actresses, cinematographers, composers, distributing organizations, exhibiting organizations, industry entities, screenwriters, and television industry entities. Lists in the annual volume of all cross-references to persons or entities of each of these kinds make it possible to determine immediately whether there have been entries pertaining to that individual person or organization.

U–125 ***Chicorel Index to Film Literature.*** Edited by Marietta Chicorel. New York: Chicorel, 1975.   Z5784.M9 C48

These volumes constitute volumes 22 and 22A of the Chicorel Index Series. They analyze the contents of some 3,000 books. About 15,000 entries are disposed under about 150 subject headings such as "Actors and Acting," "Cinema Verité," "Hollywood," "Literature and Film," "Newsreels," "Screenplays," "Violence in Film," and "Youth Appeal Films." A total of some 3,000 books were analyzed and are listed.

U–126 **Bowles, Stephen E., ed. *Index to Critical Film Reviews in British and American Film Periodicals, Together with: Index to Critical Reviews of Books about Film, 1930–1972.*** 3 vols. in 2. New York: Burt Franklin, 1975.   Z5784.M9 B64

A total of thirty-one professional and scholarly English-language periodicals are analyzed for film and film-book reviews published from 1930 through 1972. Main entry in the film-review section is the most frequently used title of a film, with cross-references from other titles, both English and foreign. Serially numbered entries include the name of the reviewer, the length of the review, and an indication of whether the review lists production credits. The index to critical reviews of film books is arranged by title, giving authors and bibliographical information as well as the names of the reviewed films, film reviewers, authors of books reviewed, book reviewers, and subjects of books reviewed.

U–127 ***New York Times Film Reviews, 1913–1968.*** 6 vols. New York: Arno Press, 1970.   PN1995.N4

These volumes provide reprints of the total of 16,000 reviews that appeared in the pages of the *Times* during these fifty-five years. Volume 6 includes an appendix of omissions, lists of film awards, a selection of some 2,000 portraits, and an index of titles, persons, and corporations, with reference to the date and page of the newspaper. Biennial supplements are being published starting with a volume for 1969–1970 published in 1971, and following that schedule to the present. The index volume, volume 6, has been reprinted as the *New York Times Directory of the Film* (New York: Arno, 1971), save that the award list has been updated to include 1970. The *New York Times Index* (D–23) is the source for citations to reviews after 1968.

Another major series of reprinted reviews was published by Garland, *Variety Film Reviews, 1907–1980*, in 15 vols. [PN1995.V34 1983]. A total of more than 40,000 reviews are reprinted in chronological order. Separately published is volume 16, *Title Index to Variety Film Reviews, 1907-1980*. A four-volume *Credit Index* with more than 800,000 entries is in preparation.

The *Film Review Digest Annual* (Millwood, N.Y.: Kraus-Thomson Organization, 1976–) [PN1995.F465] provides excerpts from English-language reviews of feature-length films, 1975–.

U–129 **Scholarly Journals in Film Studies.**

Bianco e nero. Vol. 1–. Rome: Centro sperimentale di cinematografia, 1937–. 6/yr. Reviews. Annual Index to subjects, writers, films, and directors.

Cahiers du cinéma. No. 1–. Paris: Éditions de l'etoile, 1951–. 12/yr. Reviews. Filmographies.

Indexes to nos. 1–50 (1951–1955) in 1 vol., to nos. 51–100 (1955–1959) in 1 vol., and to nos. 193–206 (1967–1968) in 1 vol.   PN1993.C25

Cinema Journal. Vol. 1–. Evanston, Ill.: Northwestern University for the Society for Cinema Studies, 1962–. 4/yr. Reviews.   PN1993.S62

Critical Inquiry (see X–13).

Diacritics (see X–13).

FC   *Film Comment.* Vol. 1–. New York: Film Society of Lincoln Center, 1962–. 4–6/yr. Filmographies. Annual index.   PN1993.F438

FC   *Film Criticism.* Vol. 1–. Edinboro, Pa.: Edinboro State College, 1976–. 3/yr. Reviews.
          PN1993.F4183

Film Journal. Virginia: Hollins College, 17–. 2–4/yr. Reviews.   PN1993.F613

FQ   *Film Quarterly* [former titles: *Hollywood Quarterly*, 1945–1951; *Quarterly of Film, Radio, and Television*, 1951–1957]. Vol. 1–. Berkeley: University of California Press, 1945–. 4/yr. Reviews. Annual Index.   PN1993.H457

Film Review. Vol. 1–. London: W. H. Allen, 1969–. 1/yr. Reviews. Bibliographic notices.
          PN1993.F624

FG   *International Film Guide.* Vol. 1–. London: Yoseloff Tantivy Press, 1964–. 1/yr. Reviews. Filmographies. Bibliographical notices. No LC number

JUFVA *Journal of the University Film [after 1982: and Video] Association.* Vol. 1–. Philadelphia [place varies]: University Film [and Video] Association, Temple University, 1948––. 4/yr. Reviews. Bibliographical Contributions. Annotated List of Books Received.   PN1993.U63

LFQ   *Literature/Film Quarterly.* Vol. 1–. Salisbury, Md.: Salisbury State College, 1973–. 4/yr. Reviews. Bibliographies.   PN1995.3.L57

QRFS *Quarterly Review of Film Studies.* Vol. 1–. Pleasantville, N.Y.: Redgrave Publishing, 1976–. 4/yr. Reviews. Bibliographical notices.   PN1994.Q34

Screen *Screen.* Vol. 1–. London: Society for Education in Film and Television, 1969–. 4/yr. PN1993.S2372

S & S *Sight and Sound.* Vol. 1–. London: British Film Institute, 1932–. 4/yr. Reviews. Annual Index.
          PN1993.S56

For additional English-language titles see Adam Reilly, *Current Film Periodicals in English* (New York: Educational Film Library Association, 1972) [Z5784.M9 R43 1972]. For an international list see the *Répertoire mondial des périodiques cinématographiques / World List of Film Periodicals and Series*, 2d ed. (Brussels: Cinémathèque de Belgique, 1960) [Z5784.M9 B88]. Originally published in 1955, this work lists 769 titles by country and then alphabetically. Entries give address, date, frequency, and brief descriptions in French and English. There are indexes by author and subject. A more recent list is Gillian Barrett, *Periodical Holdings* [of the] *British Film Institute* (London: The Institute, 1974) [No LC number], which is a title arrangement of the approximately 800 current and ceased periodicals held by the Institute, with a country-title-date index.

PROSE FICTION AND NONFICTIONAL PROSE

See also works concerning prose fiction and nonfictional prose in section L, Comparative and World Literature; section M, English Literature; section N, Medieval; section O, Renaissance; section P, Restoration and Eighteenth Century; section Q, Nineteenth Century; section R, Twentieth Century; and section S, American Literature.

I. BIBLIOGRAPHIES—PROSE FICTION

Bibliographies and guides limited to the writers of one literary period will generally be found in the prose fiction subsection of that period (i.e., N.VI, O.V, P.IV, Q.VI, R.VI). Similarly, most of the bibliographies concerning American writers and American prose fiction are found in section S.VIII.

W–1 **Dyson, A. E., ed.** *English Novel: Select Bibliographical Guides.* London: Oxford University Press, 1974.
Z2014.F5 D94

This volume contains a total of twenty bibliographical essays on the major English novelists, each written by a specialist. Generally the essays are divided into sections on Texts, Critical Studies and Commentary, Biography and Letters, Bibliographies, and Background Reading. The essays are followed by classified lists of references to works cited. The novelists included are as follows: Bunyan (Roger Sharrock); Defoe (Maximilian E. Novak); Swift (Louis A. Landa); Richardson (John Carroll); Fielding (Martin C. Battestin); Sterne (Duncan Isles); Smollett (Lewis M. Knapp); Scott (W. E. K. Anderson); Jane Austen (B. C. Southam); Thackeray (Arthur Pollard); Dickens (Michael Slater); Trollope (Bradford A. Booth); the Brontës (Miriam Allott); George Eliot (Jerome Beaty); Hardy (F. B. Pinion); James (S. Gorley Putt); Conrad (J. A. V. Chapple); Forster (Malcolm Bradbury); Lawrence (Mark Spilka); and Joyce (A. Walton Litz).
To supplement these essays, see the annual reviews in *Year's Work in English Studies* (M–22).

W–3 **Souvage, Jacques.** *Introduction to the Study of the Novel, with Special Reference to the English Novel.* Gent: Story, 1965.
PN3331.S65

The first part of this work is a discursive, elementary overview of opinions on topics in the theory of the novel, disposed into thirty chapters. This is followed by a valuable 140-page "Systematic Bibliography for the Study of the Novel," which

is in fourteen sections. Entries are alphanumerically designated and are in sheer lists under each section head, as follows: A. Bibliographies of the Novel, Checklists, Catalogues, Reference Works; B. Periodicals Devoted to the Novel; C. The Philosophy and Sociology of the Novel; D. The Novel as a Literary Genre, Its Relation to Other Genres, Trends in the History of the Novel; E. The Theory of the Novel, Criticism and History of Criticism, Study of the Novel and its Critical Vocabulary, Treatises on the Novel; F. The History of the Novel, General Surveys and Materials up to ca. 1880, Critical-Historical Studies; G. The Modern and the Contemporary Novel; H. The Comparative Study of the Novel; I. Studies of Special Topics; J. Form and Structure in the Novel, Time in the Novel; K. Technique, Narrative Technique, Character and Characterization in the Novel; L. The Novel in the Making, The Psychology of the Novel; M. Tone and Feeling in the Novel, Style in the Novel; N. General Studies of Individual Novelists. There are numerous cross-references, addenda numbered to fit into their appropriate place in the lists, and an index of authors and titles.

W–4 **Cotton, Gerald B., and Hilda Mary McGill.** *Fiction Guides: General: British and American.* London: Clive Bingley, 1967.
Z5916.C77 1967

This discursive bibliographical guide to secondary work on English-language fiction is disposed into eleven chapters, as follows: 1, Comprehensive Guides; 2, The Novel–Some General Studies; 3, British and Some General Fiction: Histories, Surveys, etc.; 4, American Fiction; 5, Subject Guides, Sequels; 6, Historical Fiction; 7, Regional Fiction; 8, Thrillers; 9, Science Fiction and Fantasy; 10, Humor and Satire; 11, Short Stories. There are, in addition, six appendixes treating general reference works as follows: 1, Guides to Research; 2, Indexes to Reviews, Criticisms, Digests; 3, Bibliographies, Series, Pseudonyms; 4, Tracing Tools, Trade and Library Catalogues; 5, Dictionaries of World and European Literature, English and American Literature, Literary Theory, and Fictional Characters; and 6, Biographical Reference Works. A postscript identifies additional references overlooked in the main body and appendixes. The work concludes with an index of authors and titles. A subject index is lacking.

W–5 *Studies in the Novel [SNNTS].* Vol. 1–. Denton: North Texas State University, 1969–.
PN3311.S82

There is no current general annual bibliography of studies in prose fiction. Quarterly issues of *Studies in the Novel* do, however, carry original bibliographical checklists, supplements to existing bibliographies, and indexes by special topics.

In addition, the general numbers of *Modern Fiction Studies* (R–59) contain checklists of new books, while those issues devoted to single writers include a "selected checklist of criticism" on the subject author.

"A Selective and Critical Bibliography of Studies in Prose Fiction for the year [1948–1951]" appeared annually in *JEGP* from 1949 to 1952. It was a numbered listing, with brief annotations, arranged alphabetically by author, but was discontinued with users being referred to the annual *MLA Bibliography* (L–50).

W–7 Rosenberg, Betty. *Genreflecting: A Guide to Reading Interests in Genre Fiction.* Littleton, Colo.: Libraries Unlimited.   PS374.P63 R67 1982

This rather breezy guide is in seven sections, as follows: The Common Reader, Libraries, and Publishing; The Western; The Thriller; The Romance; Science Fiction; Fantasy; and Horror. Each section has a combination of discursive essays, lists, and annotated entries treating both primary and secondary bibliography. Each of the six genre sections has two main divisions, into Themes and Types (listing subgenres and leading primary works under each) and Topics (including such subdivisions as Anthologies, Bibliographies, Biographies, Encyclopedias, History and Criticism, Film, Magazines, Scholarly Journals, Awards, and Specialist Publishers). Annotations tend to be descriptive and rather brief, with evaluative remarks, if any, on questions of tone. The work concludes with an index of genre fiction authors followed by an author-title index to secondary materials.

W–8 Scholarly Journals in Prose Fiction Studies.

ArmD   *Armchair Detective: A Quarterly Journal Devoted to the Appreciation of Mystery, Detective, and Suspense Fiction.* Vol. 1–. New York: The Armchair Detective, Inc., 1967–. 4/yr. Reviews. Bibliography (see W–92).   PR830.D4 A75

Crit   *Critique: Studies in Modern Fiction.* Vol. 1–. Atlanta: Georgia Institute of Technology, 1956–. 3–4/yr. Index to vols. 1–10 (1956–1968) in 1 vol.   PN3503.C7

Extrapolation: A Journal of Science Fiction and Fantasy. Vol. 1–. Kent, Ohio: Kent State University Press, 1959–. 2–4/yr. Reviews. Bibliography (see W–113). Index to vols. 1–10 (1959–1969) with vol. 10.   PN3448.S45 E92

IFR   *International Fiction Review.* Vol. 1–. Fredericton: University of New Brunswick, 1974–. 2/yr. Reviews.   No LC number

JCF   *Journal of Canadian Fiction.* Vol. 1–. Montreal: Journal of the Canadian Fiction Association, 1972–. 4/yr. Reviews. Bibliography.   No LC number

JNT   *Journal of Narrative Technique.* Vol. 1–. Ypsilanti: Eastern Michigan University, 1971–. 4/yr. Reviews. Index to vols. 1–10 in Vol. 10; index to vols. 11–14 in Vol. 14.   PE1425.J68

JSSE   *Journal of the Short Story in English / Les Cahiers de la nouvelle.* Angers: Presse de l'Université d'Angers, 1983–. 2/yr.   PN3373.C33

MFS   *Modern Fiction Studies.* Vol. 1–. West Lafayette, Ind.: Purdue University, 1955–. 4/yr. Reviews. Bibliography (see R–59). Index by Brooke K. Horvath, *Cumulative Index to Modern Fiction Studies (1955–1884), Volumes 1–30* (West Lafayette, Ind.: Modern Fiction Studies, 1985).   PS379.M55

MDAC   *Mystery and Detection Annual.* Vol. 1–. Beverly Hills, Calif.: 1972–. 1/yr. Reviews.

NCF   *Nineteenth Century Fiction* [former title: *Trollopian*]. Vol. 1–. Berkeley: University of California Press, 1945–. 4/yr. Reviews. Cumulative Index by G. B. Tennyson to vols. 1–30 (1945–1976) (Berkeley, Los Angeles, London: University of California Press, 1977).   PR873.T762

Novel   *Novel: A Forum on Fiction.* Vol. 1–. Providence, R.I.: Brown University Press, 1967–. 3/yr. Reviews. Cumulative Index to vols. 1–5 in Vol. 5.   PN3311.N65

SFS   *Science Fiction Studies.* Vol. 1–. Montreal: McGill University, Department of English, 1973–. 3/yr. Reviews. Index to vols. 1–10 in Vol. 10.   PN3448.S45 S34

SAF   *Studies in American Fiction.* Vol. 1–. Boston: Northeastern University, Department of English, 1973–. 2/yr. Reviews.   PS370.S87

SSF   *Studies in Short Fiction.* Vol. 1–. Newberry, S.C.: Newberry College, 1963–. 4/yr. Reviews. Bibliography (see W–52). Cumulative Index to vols. 1–10 in vol. 12; index to vols. 1–20 in Vol. 22.   PN3311.S8

SNNTS   *Studies in the Novel.* Vol. 1–. Denton: North Texas State University, 1969–. 4/yr. Reviews. Bibliographical Notes (see W–5).   PN3311.S82

W–9 Some Frequently Recommended Works on Narratology, the History of Narrative, and the Theory of the Novel.

Aldridge, John W., ed. *Critiques and Essays on Modern Fiction, 1920–1951.* New York: Ronald Press, 1952. Extended bibliography.   PN3355.A8

Allott, Miriam, ed. *Novelists on the Novel.* New York: Columbia University Press, 1959.   PN3321.A4

Alter, Robert. *Partial Magic: The Novel as a Self-Conscious Genre.* Berkeley and Los Angeles: University of California Press, 1975.   PN3340.A4

Bal, Mieke. *Narratology: Introduction to the Theory of Narrative.* Trans. by Christine Van Boheemen of *Theorie van Vertellen en Verhalen.* 2d ed. (Muiderberg: Lovtinho, 1980). Toronto: Toronto University Press, 1985.   PN212.B313 1985

Bentley, Phyllis. *Some Observations on the Art of Narrative.* London: Home and Van Thal, 1946.   PN3383.N35 B4

Bloomfield, Morton W. *Interpretation of Narrative: Theory and Practice.* Cambridge: Harvard University Press, 1970.   PR14.I75

Booth, Wayne C. *Rhetoric of Fiction.* 2d ed. Chicago: University of Chicago Press, 1983. Extensive, classified, indexed bibliography, with supplement by James Phelan for works 1961–1982, together citing some 765 items.   PN3355.B597 1983

Brooks, Peter. *Reading for the Plot: Design and Intention in Narrative.* New York: Knopf, 1984.   PN3378.B76 1984

Brown, Edward K. *Rhythm in the Novel.* Toronto: University of Toronto Press, 1950.   PN3383.R5 B7

Calderwood, James L., and Harold E. Toliver, eds. *Perspectives on Fiction.* New York: Oxford University Press, 1968.   PN3354.C27

Caserio, Robert L. *Plot, Story, and the Novel: From Dickens and Poe to the Modern Period.* Princeton, N.J.: Princeton University Press, 1979.   PR826.C3

Chatman, Seymour. *Story and Discourse: Narrative Structure in Fiction and Film.* Ithaca, N.Y.: Cornell University Press, 1978.   NX650.N37 C45

Cohn, Dorrit. *Transparent Minds: Narrative Modes for Presenting Consciousness in Fiction.* Princton, N.J.: Princeton University Press, 1978.   PN3448.P8 C6

Davis, Robert Murray. *Novel: Modern Essays in Criticism.* Englewood Cliffs, N.J.: Prentice-Hall, 1969.   PN3354.D27 1969

Docherty, Thomas. *Reading (Absent) Character: Towards a Theory of Characterization in Fiction.* Oxford: Clarendon, 1983.   PN3383.C4 D6 1983

Ermarth, Elizabeth Deeds. *Realism and Consensus in the English Novel.* Princeton, N.J.: Princeton University Press, 1983.   PR830.R4 E75 1983

Forster, E. M. *Aspects of the Novel.* London: Edward Arnold, 1927.   PN3353.F6

Friedman, Norman. *Form and Meaning in Fiction.* Athens: University of Georgia Press, 1975.   PN3353.F7

Genette, Gérard. *Narrative Discourse: An Essay in Method.* Translation by Jane E. Lewin of *Discours du récit* from *Figures, essais III* (Paris: Seuil, 1972). Ithaca, N.Y.: Cornell University Press, 1980.   PQ2631.R63 A791713

Halperin, John, ed. *Theory of the Novel: New Essays.* New York: Oxford University Press, 1974. Selected annotated bibliography.   PN3331.H33

Hardy, Barbara. *Appropriate Form: An Essay on the Novel.* London: Athlone Press, 1964.   PN3335.H3

———. *Tellers and Listeners: The Narrative Imagination.* London: Athlone Press, 1975.   PN3451.H3

Harvey, William J. *Character and the Novel.* Ithaca, N.Y.: Cornell University Press, 1965.   PN218.H3

Haubrichs, Wolfgang, ed. *Erzählforschung: Theorien, Modelle und Methoden der Narrativik, mit einer Auswahlbibliographie zur Erzählforschung.* 3 vols. Göttingen: Vandenhoeck und Ruprecht, 1976–1978. Extensive bibliographies.   P302.E7

Hoffman, Michael J., and Patrick Murphy, eds. *Essentials of the Theory of Fiction.* Durham, N.C.: Duke University Press, 1984.   PN3331.E87 1988

Holloway, John. *Narrative and Structure: Exploratory Essays.* Cambridge: Cambridge University Press, 1979.   PN212.H6

James, Henry. *Art of the Novel: Critical Prefaces.* Edited by R. P. Blackmur. New York: Scribner's, 1934.   PS2112.A31934

Jameson, Frederic. *Political Unconscious: Narrative as a Socially Symbolic Act.* Ithaca: N.Y.: Cornell University Press, 1981.   PN81.J29

Jones, Peter H. *Philosophy and the Novel.* Oxford: Clarendon Press, 1975.   PN3347.J6

Kahler, Erich. *Inward Turn of Narrative.* Translation by Richard and Clara Winston of *Die Verinnerung des Erzählens,* rev. ed. (Munich, 1970). Princeton, N.J.: Princeton University Press, 1973.   PN3331.K3 1970

Kermode, Frank. *Sense of an Ending: Studies in the Theory of Fiction.* New York: Oxford University Press, 1967.   PN45.K44

Kumar, Shiv, and Keith McKean, eds. *Critical Approaches to Fiction.* New York: McGraw-Hill, 1965.   PN3354.K8

Lämmert, Eberhard. *Bauformen des Erzählens.* Stuttgart: Metzler, 1955. Bbibliography.   PN3355.L3

Lanser, Susan S. *Narrative Act: Point of View in Prose Fiction.* Princeton, N.J.: Princeton University Press, 1981.   PN3383.P64 L3

Liddell, Robert. *Some Principles of Fiction.* London, 1953. Reprinted together with *Treatise on the Novel* (1947) in *Robert Liddell on the Novel,* edited by Wayne Booth. Chicago: University of Chicago Press, 1969.   PN3353.L49

Lubbock, Percy. *Craft of Fiction.* London: Jonathan Cape, 1921. 2d ed. London: Cape, 1954; New York: Viking, 1957.   PN3355.L8 1957

Lukács, Georg. *Theory of the Novel: An Historical–Philosophical Essay on the Forms of Great Epic Literature.* Translation by Anna Bostock of *Die Theorie des Romans* (Berlin: Paul Cassirer, 1920). Cambridge: MIT Press, 1971.   PN3331.L813

McKeon, Zahva Karl. *Novels and Arguments: Inventing Rhetorical Criticism.* Chicago: University of Chicago Press, 1982.   PN3335. M38 1982

Martin, Wallace. *Recent Theories of Narrative.* Ithaca, N.Y.: Cornell University Press, 1986. (Classified bibliography, pp. 212–238.)   PN212.M37 1986

Mendilow, A. A. *Time and the Novel.* London: Peter Nevill, 1952.   PN3355.M4

Miller, D. A. *Narrative and Its Discontents: Problems of Closure in the Traditional Novel.* Princeton, N.J.: Princeton University Press, 1981.   PN3383.N35 M54

Miller, J. Hillis, ed. *Aspects of Narrative. Selected Papers from the English Institute, 1969–1970.* New York: Columbia University Press, 1971.   PN3321.E5

Miller, James E., Jr. *Myth and Method: Modern Theories of Fiction.* Lincoln: University of Nebraska Press, 1960.   PN3331.M5

Mitchell, W. J. T., ed. *On Narrative.* Chicago: University of Chicago Press, 1981. Articles from *Critical Inquiry,* vol. 7 (1980/81).   P302.O6

Muir, Edwin. *Structure of the Novel.* London: Hogarth Press, 1928.   PN3358.M8

O'Connor, William Van, ed. *Forms of Modern Fiction: Essays Collected in Honor of Joseph Warren Beach.* Minneapolis: University of Minnesota Press, 1948.   PN3355.M5

Pavel, Thomas G. *Fictional Worlds.* Cambridge: Harvard University Press, 1986.   PN3331.P36 1986

Prado, C. G. *Making Believe: Philosophical Reflections on Fiction.* Westport, Conn.: Greenwood Press, 1984.   PN49.P7 1984

Prince, Gerald. *Dictionary of Narratology.* Lincoln: University of Nebraska Press, 1987.   P302.7.P75 1987

———. *Narratology: The Form and Functioning of Narrative.* Berlin: Mouton, 1982.   P302.P75 1982

Pritchett, V. S. *Living Novel and Later Appreciations.* Rev. and exp. ed. New York: Random House, 1964.   PN3324.P7 1964

Rimmon-Kenan, Shlomith. *Narrative Fiction: Contemporary Poetics.* London: Methuen, 1983.   PN3383.N35

Robert, Marthe. *Origins of the Novel*. Translation by Sacha Rabinovitch of *Roman des origines et origines du roman* (Paris: Ed. Bernard Grasset, 1972). Bloomington: Indiana University Press, 1980.
PN3353.R613 1980

Roberts, Thomas J. *When Is Something Fiction?* Carbondale: Southern Illinois University Press, 1972.
PN3331.R6

Rubin, Louis D., Jr. *Teller in the Tale*. Seattle: University of Washington Press, 1967. PN3331.R8

Sale, Roger, ed. *Discussion of the Novel*. Boston: D. C. Heath, 1960. PN3321.S3

Scholes, Robert. *Fabulation and Metafiction*. Urbana: University of Illinois Press, 1979. PN3503.S32

————, ed. *Approaches to the Novel: Materials for a Poetics*. Rev. ed. San Francisco: Chandler, 1966.
PN3321.S35 1966

Scholes, Robert, and Robert Kellogg. *Nature of Narrative*. New York: Oxford University Press, 1966.
PN3451.S3 1966

Schorer, Mark. *World We Imagine: Selected Essays*. New York: Farrar, Straus and Giroux, 1968. PS379.S39

————, ed. *Modern British Fiction*. New York: Oxford University Press, 1961. PR883.S3 1961

————, ed. *Society and Self in the Novel*. New York: Columbia University Press, 1955. PE1010.E5 1955

Stanzel, Franz K. *Narrative Situations in the Novel: Tom Jones, Moby Dick, The Ambassadors, Ulysses*. Translation by J. P. Pusack of *Die typischen Erzählsituationen im Roman* (Vienna, 1955). Bloomington: Indiana University Press, 1971.
PN3331.S89413

————. *Theory of Narrative*. Translation by Charlotte Goedsche of *Theorie des Erzählens* (Göttingen: Vandenhoeck und Ruprecht, 1979). Cambridge: Cambridge University Press, 1984.
PN3383.N35 S813 1984

————. *Typische Formen des Romans*. Göttingen: Vandenhoeck und Ruprecht, 1964. PN3331.S89

Stevick, Philip. *Chapter in Fiction: Theories of Narrative Division*. Syracuse, N.Y.: Syracuse University Press, 1970.

————, ed. *Theory of the Novel*. New York: Free Press, 1967. Selected bibliography. PN3331.S9

Tillyard, E. M. W. *Epic Strain in the English Novel*. London: Chatto and Windus, 1958. PR830.E6T5

Todorov, Tzvetan. *Poetics of Prose*. Ithaca, N.Y.: Cornell University Press, 1977. PN218.T613

Toliver, Harold. *Animate Illusions: Explorations of Narrative Structure*. Lincoln: University of Nebraska Press, 1974. PN3335.T6

Torgovnick, Marianna. *Closure in the Novel*. Princeton, N.J.: Princeton University Press, 1981. PN3378.T6

Uspenskii, Boris. *Poetics of Composition: The Structure of the Artistic Text and Typology of Compositional Form*. Translation by Valentina Zavarin and Susan Wittig of *Poetika Kompozitsii*. Berkeley, Los Angeles, London: University of California Press, 1973.
NX 200.U613

Valdes, Mario J., and Owen J. Miller, eds. *Interpretation of Narrative*. Toronto: University of Toronto Press, 1979. PN80.5.I5 1976

Van Ghent, Dorothy. *English Novel: Form and Function*. New York: Harper, 1953. PR821.V3

Walcutt, Charles C. *Man's Changing Mask: Modes and Methods of Characterization in Fiction*. Minneapolis: University of Minnesota Press, 1966. PN218.W3

Wilson, Colin. *Craft of the Novel*. London: Gollancz, 1975. PN3491.W5

Wright, Austin M. *Formal Principle in the Novel*. Ithaca, N.Y.: Cornell University Press, 1982.
PN3365.W7 1982

II. CHECKLISTS OF PROSE FICTION

Checklists of prose fiction limited to the fiction of one period are generally found in the Prose Fiction subsection of that period (i.e., N.VI, O.V, P.IV, Q.VI, R.VI). Similarly, checklists of American prose fiction are found in S.VIII.

W–10 **Wright, R. Glenn, ed. *Author Bibliography of English Language Fiction in the Library of Congress through 1950.*** 8 vols. Boston: G. K. Hall, 1975. Z5918.W74

These volumes present an author index totaling 121,000 entries to all works in the Library of Congress's PZ3 (fiction) section. Arranged by countries (United States, Great Britain and all Commonwealth countries past and present), authors are then listed alphabetically under the country with which each is identified. Under authors, entries are alphabetical by title. Appended is an index of pseudonyms (vol. 7) and a list of authors of works translated into English with an index of translators (vol. 8).

A second eight-volume series, Wright's *Chronological Bibliography of English Language Fiction in the Library of Congress through 1950* (Boston: G. K. Hall, 1974) [Z5918.W75], presents some 131,000 entries in chronological order by the year of publication of all works in the PZ3 category. Again, the first division is by country, then by year, and then alphabetically by author and then by title. Appended are lists of translated foreign authors, an index of translators, and an index of pseudonyms.

A third and final series, in nine volumes, is Wright's *Title Bibliography of English Language Fiction in the Library of Congress through 1950* (Boston: G. K. Hall, 1976) [Z5918.W753]. Here about 133,000 entries provide a title index to all works in the library's PZ3 section. Appended is a complete list by title of works translated into English, an index of translators, and an index of pseudonyms.

W–14 **Esdaile, Arundel. *List of English Tales and Prose Romances Printed before 1740.*** London: For the Bibliographical Society, 1912. Z2014.F4 E8

This work is divided into two parts, the first treating original and subsequent editions of works published 1475–1642, and the second those published 1643–1739. Each part is arranged alphabetically by author or, for anonymous works, by title or catchword title. Both native works and English translations of foreign works are included. Entries give author, title, place and publisher, date of publication, and format. In addition, locations are given or a reference to the source of the citation is provided.

The contents of Esdaile have been subjected to a chronological treatment in the checklists by O'Dell for the period 1475–1640 (O–65); by Mish for the period 1600–1700 (O–67); and by McBurney for the period 1700–1739 (P–44).

W–15 Block, Andre W., ed. *English Novel, 1740–1850: A Catalogue Including Prose Romances, Short Stories, and Translations of Foreign Fiction.* Rev. ed. London: Dawsons, 1961.   Z2014.F4 B6 1961

Originally published in 1939 as a continuation of the Esdaile bibliography (W–14), this incomplete and unreliable checklist remains nevertheless valuable if used with caution. Entries are alphabetical by the name of the author or the translator or, if anonymous, by title. Entries locate copies or identify the bibliographical source of the citation. The work's values include its citations of English translations of foreign fiction and the fact that it is the only English fiction checklist for the period 1800–1850. Chronological treatment of its contents for the period 1740–1749 will be found in the Beasley checklist (P–45), and for the period 1750–1800 in the Orr checklist (P–47). The volume ends with a title index.

III. HANDBOOKS, GUIDES, AND INDEXES

For works on prose style and stylistics see also section X.V as well as many references in section I, Language, Linguistics, and Philology.

W–20 Yaakov, Juliette. *Fiction Catalogue.* 11th ed. New York: H. W. Wilson, 1986.   Z5916.H17 1986

This volume, the most recent edition of a work that first appeared in 1908, presents a critically annotated bibliography of more than 5,000 selected titles, including analytical entries for more than 2,250 composite volumes. Entries in Part I are arranged alphabetically by author and give full bibliographical information along with a brief annotation providing both a plot summary and quotations from a few reviews. Recent and available editions are noted. The most important feature of the volume is, however, the detailed subject index in Part II, which follows the index of titles and concludes the volume. Subject headings are at about the same level of specificity found in the Wilson indexes generally, which is to say, highly specific, and thus this index is both current and useful when one is searching for works concerned with very specific subjects. It is supplemented annually, with new editions every five years.

W–22 Baker, Ernest A., and James Packman. *Guide to the Best Fiction English and American Including Translations from Foreign Languages.* New and enl. ed. London: Routledge, 1932.   Z5916.B18

This work, in a markedly different format, was originally published in 1903, with a second edition in 1913. The earlier editions were divided into national lists with chronological subgroupings, whereas this edition is a single alphabetical list of authors and uses the index for access to national and chronologically defined groups of works. In addition, this edition does not attempt to cover historical fiction to the same extent, given the availability of Baker's separately published guide (W–80). Entries give authors, identify pseudonyms, give the English title (and, for translations, the original title in parentheses), and the date of the first edition. A brief summary description follows, with a list of important editions. The volume concludes with its most important feature, a detailed index of authors, titles, subjects, historical names and allusions, places, characters, some forms, and plot types.

The oldest subject guide to fiction is Zella Allen Dixon's *Comprehensive Subject Index to Universal Prose Fiction* (New York: Dodd, Mead, 1897) [Z5916.O62], which contains relatively narrow headings for specific persons, places, events, and activities and thus may complement more recent indexes in the context of a specific search.

W–23 Olbrich, W. *Der Romanführer.* 15 vols. Stuttgart: Hiersemann, 1950–1971.   PN3326.R6

These volumes present summaries of novels and short stories from around the world, with notes on characters, setting, and other details. Entries are arranged by country and then alphabetically by author. The volumes are as follows:

Vols. 1–2. *Der Inhalt der deutsche Romane und Novellen vom Barok bis zum Naturalismus* (1950–1951).

Vols. 3–5. *Der Inhalt der deutsche Romane und Novellen der Gegenwart* (1952–1954).

Vol. 6. *Der Inhalt der französische, italienische, spanische und portugiesische Romane und Novellen von den Anfängen bis zum Beginn des 20. Jahrhunderts* (1955).

Vol. 7. *Der Inhalt der englische, nordamerikanische, flämische und holländische Romane und Novellen von den Anfängen bis zum Beginn des 20. Jahrhunderts* (1956).

Vol. 8. *Der Inhalt der nordische, slawische, ungarische und romänische Romane und Novellen von den Anfängen bis zum Beginn des 20. Jahrhunderts* (1957).

Vols. 9–12. *Die Inhalt der ausländischen Romane der Gegenwart* (1958–1961).

Vol. 13. *Die Inhalt der deutschen Romane und Novellen aus dem Jahrzehnt 1954 bis 1963* (1964).

Vol. 14. *Die Inhalt der ausländischen Romane und Novellen aus dem Jahrzehnt 1957 bis 1966* (1969).

Vol. 15. *Register zu Bände 1–15* (1971).

In addition to the author, title, and type indexes in volume 15, each volume has its own author and title indexes, volumes 5 and 14 have cumulated author and title indexes for all volumes that precede them, and volumes 6 and 12 have cumulated subject indexes for the volumes that precede them. A revised second edition was begun in 1960 [PN3326.R62].

W–25 Cotton, Gerald B., and Alan Glencross. *Cumulated Fiction Index, 1945–1960: A Guide to More Than 25,000 Works of Fiction, Including Short Story Collections, Anthologies, Omnibus Volumes, Extracts and Condensed Books, Mainly Available between January 1945 and February 1960, Arranged under 3,000 Subject Headings with Numerous References. . . .* London: Association of Assistant Librarians, 1960.   Z5916.F52

This index contains authors and short titles for fictional works, listed under a system of headings that includes persons, places, countries, historical periods, animals, events; abstract themes (good and evil, jealousy, love); types (detective story, horror story); forms and techniques (experimental novel, first person narrative), and others that do not as easily fall into categories. A long introduction will prove useful reading for anyone interested in a systematic search of this index. With the extensive system of cross-references, however, it is unlikely that even a novice user will fail to locate relevant headings.

A continuation by Raymond F. Smith, *Cumulated Fiction Index, 1960–1969* (London: Association of Assistant Librarians, 1970) [No LC number], adds some 18,000 works, both those newly available during the specified period and those previously available but not cited. A further continuation by Raymond F. Smith and A. J. Gordon, *Cumulated Fiction Index, 1970–1974* (London: Association of Assistant Librarians, 1975) [No LC number], adds a further 20,000 works. Annual volumes supplement this continuation and will be superseded in turn.

W-26   Leech, Geoffrey N., and Michael H. Short. *Style in Fiction: A Linguistic Introduction to English Fictional Prose.* London: Longman, 1981.   PR826.L4

This volume is in ten sections disposed into two parts. Part 1, Approaches and Methods, treats 1. Style and Choice; 2. Style, Text, and Frequency; 3. A Method Of Analysis and Some Examples; and 4. Levels of Style. Part 2, Aspects of Style, treats 5. Language and the Fictional World; 6. Mind Style; 7. The Rhetoric of Text; 8. Discourse and Discourse Situation; 9. Conversation in the Novel; and 10. Speech and Thought Presentation. The volume concludes with a brief bibliographical essay "For Further Reading," a formal bibliography of relevant works, an index of works discussed, and a general index.

W-27   Some Frequently Recommended Works on the Linguistic Analysis of Fictional Discourse.

Banfield, Ann. *Unspeakable Sentences. Narration and Representation in the Language of Fiction.* London: Routledge and Kegan Paul, 1982.   P302.B35 1982

Bronzwaer, W. J. M. *Tense in the Novel: An Investigation of Some Potentialities of Linguistic Criticism.* Groningen: Wolters-Noordhoff, 1970.   P47.B7 1971

Fowler, Roger. *Linguistics and the Novel.* London: Methuen, 1977.   P302.F6

Kroeber, Karl. *Styles in Fictional Structure: The Art of Jane Austen, Charlotte Brontë, George Eliot.* Princeton, N.J.: Princeton University Press, 1971.   PR861.K7

Leistner, Detlef B. *Autor, Erzähltext, Leser: Sprachhandlungstheoretische Überlegungen zur Sprachverwendung in Erzähltexten.* Erlangen: Palm and Enke, 1975.
                                   PN3383.N35 L4 1975

Lodge, David. *Language of Fiction: Essays in Criticism and Verbal Analysis of the English Novel.* London: Routledge and Kegan Paul, 1966.   PR821.L6 1966

Martin, Harold C., ed. *Style in Prose Fiction: English Institute Essays, 1958.* New York: Columbia University Press, 1959. Bibliography.   PE1010.E5

Page, Norman. *Speech in the English Novel.* London: Longmans, 1973.   PR830.L35 P3

Pascal, Roy. *Dual Voice: Free Indirect Speech and Its Functions in the Nineteenth-Century European Novel.* Manchester: Manchester University Press, 1977.
                                   PN3383.F74 P36

Phelan, James. *Worlds from Words: A Theory of Language in Fiction.* Chicago: University of Chicago Press, 1981.   PN3331.P5

Prince, Gerald. *Grammar of Stories: An Introduction.* The Hague: Mouton, 1973.   PN45.P68

Russell, John. *Style in Modern British Fiction: Studies in Joyce, Lawrence, Foster, Lewis, and Green.* Baltimore: Johns Hopkins University Press, 1978.
                                   PR881.R8

Smitten, Jeffrey R., and Ann Daghistany, eds. *Spatial Form in Narrative.* Ithaca, N.Y.: Cornell University Press, 1981.   PN3383.N35 S64

Sternberg, Meir. *Expositional Modes and Temporal Ordering in Fiction.* Baltimore: Johns Hopkins University Press, 1978.   PN3383.E958

Ullman, Stephen. *Style in the French Novel.* 2d ed. Oxford: Blackwell, 1964. Bibliography.
                                   PQ635.U4 1964

Weinrich, Harald. *Tempus: Besprochene und erzählte Welt.* 2d ed., rev. Stuttgart: Kohlhammer, 1971.
                                   P281.W4 1971

W-28   Some Frequently Recommended Works on Reading Fiction.

Allen, Walter. *Reading a Novel.* Rev. ed. London: Phoenix House, 1963.   PN3354.A4

Altenbernd, Lynn. *Handbook for the Study of Fiction.* New York: Macmillan, 1966.   PN3385.A5

Boulton, Marjorie. *Anatomy of the Novel.* London: Routledge and Kegan Paul, 1975.   PN3365.B65

Brooks, Cleanth, and Robert Penn Warren, eds. *Understanding Fiction.* 2d ed. New York: F. S. Crofts and Co., 1943.   PN335.B7

Burgess, Anthony. *Novel Now: A Student's Guide to Contemporary Fiction.* New ed. London: Faber and Faber, 1971. Bibliographical lists.
                                   PN3503.B78 1971

Dillon, George L. *Language Processing and the Reading of Literature.* Bloomington: Indiana University Press, 1978.   P302.D54 1978

Gerould, Gordon Hall. *How to Read Fiction.* Princeton, N.J.: Princeton University Press, 1937.   PN3355.G4

Gordon, Caroline. *How to Read a Novel.* New York: Viking Press, 1957.   PN3385.G6

Gregor, Ian, ed. *Reading the Victorian Novel: Detail into Form.* New York: Barnes and Noble, 1980.
                                   PR874.R4 1980

Henkle, Roger B. *Reading the Novel: An Introduction to the Techniques of Interpreting Fiction.* New York: Harper and Row, 1977.   PN3365.H46

Hugo, Howard E. *Aspects of Fiction: A Handbook.* Boston: Little, Brown, 1962.   PN3321.H8

Iser, Wolfgang. *Implied Reader: Patterns of Communication in Prose Fiction from Bunyan to Beckett.* Translation of *Der implizite Leser.* Munich: Fink, 1972. Baltimore: Johns Hopkins University Press, 1974.
                                   PN3491.I813

————. *Act of Reading.* Translation of *Der Akt des Lesens.* Munich: Fink, 1976. Baltimore: Johns Hopkins University Press, 1978.   PN83.I813

Leggett, H. W. *Idea in Fiction.* London: Allen and Unwin, 1934.   PN3365.L4

Lever, Katherine. *Novel and the Reader.* London: Methuen, 1961.   PN3491.L36

Mailloux, Steven. *Interpretive Conventions: The Reader in the Study of American Fiction.* Ithaca, N.Y.: Cornell University Press, 1982.   PN98.R38M6 1982

Preston, John. *Created Self: The Reader's Role in Eighteenth-Century Fiction.* London: Heinemann, 1970.
                                   PR851.P7 1970

Rosenheim, Edward W., Jr. *What Happens in Literature: A Student's Guide to Poetry, Drama, and Fiction.* Chicago: University of Chicago Press, 1960.   PN45.R6

Ruthrof, Horst. *Reader's Construction of Narrative.* London: Routledge and Kegan Paul, 1981.   PN212.R87

Saks, Sheldon. *Fiction and the Shape of Belief: A Study of Henry Fielding with Glances at Swift, Johnson and Richardson.* Berkeley and Los Angeles: University of California Press, 1967.   PR3457.S3

Savage, Arthur W. *How to Analyze the Short Story*. Boston: Branden Press, 1971. PN3385.S3

Scholes, Robert. *Elements of Fiction*. New York: Oxford University Press, 1968. PN3354.S33

Wilson, Anne D. *Traditional Romance and Tale: How Stories Mean*. Ipswich: D. S. Brewer, 1976. GR74.W54 1976

W–29 Some Guides to Novels on Special Subjects or in Special Forms. (See also the various sections on Genre Fiction, W–60 ff.)

Bibliographical

Hartman, Donald K., and Jerome Drost. *Themes and Settings in Fiction: A Bibliography of Bibliographies*. New York: Greenwood Press, 1988. Z5916.H28 1988

Special Subjects

Bentley, Phyllis. *English Regional Novel*. London: G. Allen and Unwin, 1941. PR868.R45 B4

Bernard, Harry. *Le roman regionaliste aux Etats-Unis, 1913–1940*. Montreal: Fides, 1949. Bibliography. PS379.B45

Blotner, Joseph. *Political Novel*. Garden City, N.Y.: Doubleday, 1955. PN3448.P6 B6

———. *American Political Novel, 1900–1960*. Austin: University of Texas Press, 1966. PS374.P6 B55

Burns, Grant. *Sports Pages: A Critical Bibliography of Twentieth-Century American Novels and Stories Featuring Baseball, Basketball, Football, and Other Athletic Pursuits*. Metuchen, N.J.: Scarecrow, 1987. Z1231.S66 1987

Drew, Bernard A., et al. *Western Series and Sequels: A Reference Guide*. New York: Garland, 1986. Z1251.W5 D74 1986

Howe, Susanne. *Novels of Empire*. New York: Columbia University Press, 1950. PN3448.I5 H6

Kramer, John E. *American College Novel: An Annotated Bibliography*. New York: Garland, 1981. Z1231.F4 K7 1981

LeClaire, Lucien. *General Analytical Bibliography of the Regional Novelists of the British Isles, 1800–1950*. Paris: Clermont-Ferrand, 1954. Primary bibliographies, index of authors by place-name and by region. Z2014.F4 L4 1954

———. *Le roman regionaliste dans les Îles Britanniques, 1800–1850*. Paris: Clermont-Ferrand, 1953. PR830.R45 L4

Menendez, Albert J. *Catholic Novel: An Annotated Bibliography*. New York: Garland, 1988. Z5917.C47 M46 1988

———. *Civil War Novels: An Annotated Bibliography*. New York: Garland, 1986. Z1231.F4 M46 1986

Milne, Gordon. *American Political Novel*. Norman: University of Oklahoma Press, 1966. PS374.P6 M5

Proctor, M. R. *English University Novel*. Berkeley and Los Angeles: University of California Press, 1957. PR830.U5 P7

Proper, C. B. A. *Social Elements in English Prose Fiction between 1770 and 1832*. Amsterdam: H. J. Paris, 1929. PR830.S6 P7

Speare, M. E. *Political Novel: Its Development in England and America*. New York: Oxford University Press, 1924. PR868.P6 S62

Wise, Suzanne. *Sports Fiction for Adults: An Annotated Bibliography of Novels, Plays, Short Stories, and Poetry with Sporting Settings*. New York: Garland, 1986. Z2014.S63 W57 1986

Special Forms

Altman, Janet G. *Epistolarity: Approaches to a Form*. Columbus: Ohio State University Press, 1982. PN3448.E6 A4 1982

Black, Frank G. *Epistolary Novel in the Late Eighteenth Century: A Descriptive and Bibliographical Study*. Eugene: University of Oregon Press, 1940. P25.O7 no. 2

Buckley, Jerome H. *Season of Youth: The Bildungsroman from Dickens to Golding*. Cambridge: Harvard University Press, 1974. PR830.A8 B8

Day, Robert Adams. *Told in Letters: Epistolary Fiction before Richardson*. Ann Arbor: University of Michigan Press, 1966. PR821.D3

Edel, Leon. *Psychological Novel, 1900–1950*. Rev. ed. London: Hart-Davis, 1961. PN3448.P8 E3 1961

Friedman, Melvin J. *Stream of Consciousness: A Study in Literary Method*. New Haven: Yale University Press, 1955. PN3448.P8 F7

Gardner, Frank M. *Sequels, Incorporating Aldred and Parker's "Sequel Stories."* 5th ed. London: Association of Assistant Librarians, 1967. Z5916.G3

Goldsmith, Elizabeth C., ed. *Writing the Female Voice: Essays on Epistolary Literature*. Boston: Northeastern University Press, 1989. PN6131.W75 1989

Humphrey, Robert. *Stream of Consciousness in the Modern Novel*. Berkeley and Los Angeles: University of California Press, 1954. PN3377.5.S77 H8

Husband, Janet. *Sequels, An Annotated Guide to Novels in Series*. Chicago: American Library Association, 1982. Z5917.S44 H87 1982

Hutcheon, Linda. *Narcissistic Narrative: The Metafictional Paradox*. Waterloo, Ont.: Wilfried Laurier University Press, 1980. PN3503.H8

Kerr, Elizabeth. *Bibliography of the Sequence Novel*. Minneapolis: University of Minnesota Press, 1950. Z5917.S45 K4

McCafferty, Larry, ed. *Postmodern Fiction: A Bio-bibliographical Guide*. New York: Greenwood Press, 1986. PN3503.P594 1986

Mayo, Robert D. *English Novel in the Magazines, 1740–1815, with a Catalogue of 1,375 Magazine Novels and Novelettes*. Evanston, Ill.: Northwestern University Press, 1962. PR851.M37

Romberg, Bertil. *Studies in the Narrative Technique of the First-Person Novel*. Stockholm: Almqvist and Wiksell, 1962. PN3365.R613 1962

Rose, Margaret. *Parody/Metafiction: An Analysis of Parody as a Critical Mirror to the Writing and Reception of Fiction*. London: Croom Helm 1979. PN6149.P3 R6

Singer, Godfrey F. *Epistolary Novel: Its Origin, Development, Decline, and Residuary Influence*. Philadelphia: University of Pennsylvania Press, 1933. PN3448.E6 S5 1933

Smitten, Jeffrey, and Ann Daghistany, eds. *Spatial Form in Narrative*. Ithaca: Cornell University Press, 1982. PN3383.N35 S64

Steinberg, Günter. *Erlebte Rede: Ihre Eigenart und ihre Formen in neuer deutscher, französischer, und englischer Erzählliteratur*. 2 vols. Göttingen: Kümmerle, 1971. PN3383.I5 S7 1971

Sternberg, Meir. *Expositional Modes and Temporal Ordering in Fiction.* Baltimore: Johns Hopkins University Press, 1978.   PN3383.E9 S8

Waugh, Patricia. *Metafiction: The Theory and Practice of Self-Conscious Fiction.* London: Methuen, 1984.
PN3335.W38 1984

Wurzbaugh, Natascha. *Novel in Letters: Epistolary Fiction in the Early English Novel, 1678–1740.* Coral Gables, Fla.: University of Miami Press, 1969.
P21.W97 no. 3

IV. CHECKLISTS OF CRITICISM

See also the checklists of explications in section T (T–31 and T–32).

W–30 **Bell, Inglis F., and Donald Baird, comps. *English Novel, 1578–1956: A Checklist of Twentieth Century Criticisms.*** Denver, Colo.: Swallow, 1959.   Z2014.F5 B44

This volume selectively indexes critical work published in the twentieth century on seventy-two authors of prose fiction from Lily's *Euphues* to the mid-twentieth-century work of Graham Greene. Some 2,000 monographs and the files of more than 100 periodicals were searched. Plot summaries and eulogistic commentaries on authors are excluded. Entries are listed in alphabetical order by the critic's name under the relevant title; titles in turn are listed alphabetically under the names of their authors. A list of analyzed and cited books and periodicals is appended. This volume is supplemented by Palmer and Dyson (W–32).

W–31 **Dunn, Richard J., ed. *English Novel: Twentieth Century Criticism.* Vol. 1, *Defoe through Hardy.*** Chicago: Swallow, 1976.   Z2014.F4 D86

This volume which lists books, parts of books, and articles is in two parts: the first is arranged alphabetically by the forty-five individual authors who are covered. It lists criticisms of individual works, general studies of the novelist, and bibliographies of the novelist's work. The second part cites general studies on the English novel. The work concludes with a bibliography of sources.
A second volume, *English Novel: Twentieth Century Criticism, vol. 2, Twentieth Century Authors*, compiled by Paul Schlueter, and June Schlueter was published in 1982 [Z2014.F4 E53]. It is similarly organized, with more than 7,500 entries, and treats some eighty-three British novelists. Criticism through 1975 is included.

W–32 **Palmer, Helen H., and Anne Jane Dyson. *English Novel Explication: Criticisms to 1972.*** Hamden, Conn.: Shoe String, 1973.   Z2014.F5 P26 1973

This volume is designed to supplement Bell and Baird (W–30). It covers some 4,800 items of criticism written from 1958 through 1972 on English novels from the Renaissance to the mid-twentieth century. Entries are alphabetical by critic, under the alphabetically arranged individual titles of an author's works. The volume concludes with an index of critics and novel titles.
Three supplements have been published (see W–33).

W–33 **Abernethy, Peter L., Christian J. W. Kloesel, and Jeffrey R. Smitten. *English Novel Explication. Supplement I.*** Hamden, Conn.: Shoe String, 1976. Z2014.F5 P26 Suppl.

This volume supplements Palmer and Dyson, (W–32), itself a supplement to Bell and Baird (W–30). It covers primarily works of novel explication published 1972–1974, with a broad definition of novel and a broader definition of explication than that found in the original volume. Book reviews, dissertations, and explications of short novels cited in Walker's bibliography (W–51) are excluded. English novelists are defined as those born in England, Scotland, Ireland, Wales, and the Commonwealth, who lived a significant part of their life in one or several of those places. Explications are listed alphabetically by critic under the alphabetically arranged titles of works that in turn are listed under their alphabetically arranged authors. A section of explications of anonymous titles follows the main author list. Works of explication are often cited with brief titles, and the user is referred to the List of Books Indexed for full citations. The work concludes with an index of authors and titles.
Kloesel and Smitten edited *Supplement II* (1981) in this continuing series. This volume follows the same pattern as that already described, except that it covers work published 1975–1979. Kloesel alone edited *Supplement III* covering explications 1980–1985, which was published in 1986.

W–35 **Bonheim, Helmut. *English Novel before Richardson: A Checklist of Texts and Criticisms to 1970.*** Metuchen, N.J.: Scarecrow Press, 1971.   Z2014.F4 B65

This volume provides a convenient supplement to existing bibliographies for early English prose fiction (romances, novellas, picaresque tales, among other types). Prominent figures are excluded (Bunyan) or treated less fully (Defoe) than are neglected authors. It is arranged in three parts. The first is an alphabetically arranged list of twenty-six authors of prose narratives from Aphra Behn to Sir Philip Sidney, citing texts and criticism. The second part lists anthologies, bibliographies, and checklists concerned with texts and criticism. The second part lists anthologies, bibliographies, and checklists concerned with texts and criticism of the novel before Richardson. The third part contains bibliographies on a series of related subjects, including autobiography; biography; the character; conduct and courtesy books; the literature of roguery; satire; translations; travel literature; utopian fiction; and women and literature. Throughout, entries are in sheer lists, with cross-references. There is an index of authors, critics, and occasional titles.

W–37 **Kearney, Elizabeth I., and Louise S. Fitzgerald. *Continental Novel: A Checklist of Criticism in English 1900–1966.*** Metuchen, N.J.: Scarecrow Press, 1968.
Z5916.K4

This work is arranged in sections for each of the covered national or regional groups, as follows: The French Novel; The Spanish and Portuguese Novel; The Italian Novel; The German Novel; The Scandinavian Novel; and The Russian and East European Novel. Most titles are translated; Spanish titles are generally given under their Spanish name, with a frequently used English translation cited, if there is one. Short fiction, travel fiction, and autobiographical fiction is included if it is referred to in the criticism as a novel or novella. National sections are subdivided alphabetically by novelists, then by title, and then entries for criticism are listed under the pertinent novel alphabetically by name of the critic.
A supplement, *Continental Novel: A Checklist of Criticism in English, 1967–1980*, was compiled by Louise S. Fitzgerald and Elizabeth I. Kearney (1983) [Z5916.F57 1983]. It is ar-

ranged in parallel to the original volume. A new volume compiled by Harriet Semmes Alexander, *English Language Criticism on the Foreign Novel*, is scheduled for 1989 publication by Swallow Press, Ohio State University Press [Z5916.A39 1989].

V.   HISTORIES OF THE NOVEL

W–40   **Baker, Ernest A.   *History of the English Novel.* 10 vols.** London: Witherby, 1924–1939.   PR821.B32

These volumes present the standard history of the English novel from narratives of the Middle Ages to 1930. Basic biographical information on major and minor authors, descriptions of works, discussions of relationships between writers and their public, and between writers—all these topics find their places in a series now valued less for its critical judgments than for the massive quantity of information that can be found in its pages. Each volume has its own brief reading and reference list; its own index of subjects, authors, and titles; and its own chronological scope, as follows:

Vol. 1. *Age of Romance: From the Beginnings to the Renaissance.*

Vol. 2. *Elizabethan Age and After.*

Vol. 3. *Later Romance and the Establishment of Realism [including Bunyan, Defoe, and Swift].*

Vol. 4. *Intellectual Realism: From Richardson to Sterne.*

Vol. 5. *Novels of Sentiment and the Gothic Romance.*

Vol. 6. *Edgeworth, Austen, Scott.*

Vol. 7. *Age of Dickens and Thackeray.*

Vol. 8. *From the Brontës to Meredith: Romanticism in the English Novel.*

Vol. 9. *Day before Yesterday [including Hardy, Gissing, George Moore, and Henry James].*

Vol. 10. *Yesterday [including Conrad, Kipling, Arnold Bennett, Galsworthy, and D. H. Lawrence].*

An additional volume, *Yesterday and After*, by Lionel Stevenson (New York: Barnes and Noble, 1967) [PS881.S7], was prepared to complete the history through the 1950s. It treats H. G. Wells, Maugham, Ford, Forster, C. S. Lewis, Joyce, and Graham Greene, among others.

W–41   **Allen, Walter.   *English Novel.*** London: Phoenix House, 1954.   PR821.A4

Generally thought the best one-volume history of the English novel, this work is addressed to the general reader, though it is of value to the specialist. There are seven chapters, as follows: The Beginnings; The 18th Century; The 19th Century—The First Generation; The Early Victorians; The Later Victorians; The Novel from 1881 to 1914; 1914 and After. The work concludes with an index of names and titles.

W–42   **Stevenson, Lionel.   *English Novel: A Panorama.*** Boston: Houghton Mifflin, 1960.   PR821.S7

This frequently recommended historical survey begins with an introduction on the definition of the novel. It is then disposed into seventeen chronological chapters beginning with Pastoral and Picaresque and then treating The Precursors of the Novel in three chapters; The Eighteenth-Century Novel in three more; The Nineteenth-Century Novel in nine chapters;

and concluding with two chapters, "The Anatomy of Society" treating the novel from 1895 through 1915, and "Exploring the Psyche" treating the novel since 1915. A twenty-three-page classified bibliography keyed to the chapters follows, citing both general works and leading works on each of the novelists discussed. A handy chronological summary follows the bibliography, listing authors by their year of birth, and beneath each author, titles of novels in chronological order. An index of names, some titles, and some subjects concludes the volume.

W–43   **Kettle, Arnold.   *Introduction to the English Novel.* 2 vols.** London: Hutchinson University Library, 1950–1951.

PR821.K4

These two volumes, the first to George Eliot, the second from Henry James to the present day, present a Marxist but not especially doctrinaire approach to the history of the English novel, with a stress on relations between the development of English society and its fiction. Each volume focuses on major writers. A second edition of the first volume was published in 1967 [PR821.K42].

W–49   **Some Frequently Recommended Works on the History of Narrative Fiction over One or Several Periods of Literary History.**

General

Dunlop, John C.   *History of Prose Fiction: Being a Critical Account of the Most Celebrated Prose Works of Fiction, from the Earliest Greek Romances to the Novels of the Present Day.* New ed. Revised by Henry Wilson.   2 vols.   London: G. Bell and Sons, 1896.
PN3451.D6 1896

Grossvogel, David I.   *Limits of the Novel: Evolution of a Form from Chaucer to Robbe-Grillet.* Ithaca, N.Y.: Cornell University Press, 1968.   PN3451.G87 L7

Reed, Walter L.   *Exemplary History of the Novel: The Quixotic versus the Picaresque.* Chicago: University of Chicago Press, 1981.   PN3491.R43

Wagenknecht, Edward C.   *Calvacade of the English Novel from Elizabeth to George VI [1943].* Reprint, with supplemental bibliographies.   New York: Holt, 1954.
PR821.W25

Ancient

Heiserman, Arthur.   *Novel before the Novel: Essays and Discussions about the Beginnings of Prose Fiction in the West.* Chicago: University of Chicago Press, 1977.
PA3040.H38 1977

Perry, Ben Edwin.   *Ancient Romances.* Berkeley and Los Angeles: University of California Press, 1967.
PA3040.P4

Medieval

Vinaver, Eugène.   *Rise of Romance.* Oxford: Clarendon Press, 1971.   PN671.V5

Renaissance

Crane, Ronald S.   *Vogue of Medieval Chivalric Romance during the English Renaissance.* Menosha, Wisc.: George Banta Publishing Co., 1919.   PR418.R7C7

Davis, Walter R.   *Idea and Act in Elizabethan Fiction.* Princeton, N.J.: Princeton University Press, 1969.
PR836.D3

Jusserand, Jean J.   *English Novel in the Time of Shakespeare.* Translated by Elizabeth Lee. Rev. and enl. ed. London: Unwin, 1908.   PR836.J7 1908

Salzman, Paul. *English Prose Fiction, 1558–1700: A Critical History*. Oxford: Clarendon Press, 1984.
PR836.S24 1984

Schlauch, Margaret. *Antecedents of the English Novel, 1400–1600 (from Chaucer to Deloney)*. London: Oxford University Press, 1963.   PR833.S3

Wolff, Samuel L. *Greek Romances in Elizabethan Fiction*. New York: Columbia University Press, 1912.
PR839.G7 W6

Seventeenth Century

Davis, Lennard J. *Factual Fictions: The Origins of the English Novel*. New York: Columbia University Press, 1983.   PR851.D3 1983

Haviland, Thomas P. *Roman de Longue Haleine on English Soil: A Study of the Manner, Form and Content of the French Heroic Romance in Translation, and of Those English Productions Which Fall within the Class, with Some Account of the Popularity of Both and of Their Influence on the Modern English Novel in Its Earliest Years*. Philadelphia, Pa.: 1931.   PN3448.H4 H3

McKeon, Michael. *Origins of the English Novel, 1600-1740*. Baltimore: Johns Hopkins University Press, 1987.   PR841.M3 1987

Mish, Charles. "English Short Fiction in the Seventeenth Century." *SSF* 6 (1969): 233–330.

Morgan, Charlotte. *Rise of the Novel of Manners: A Study of English Prose Fiction between 1600 and 1740*. New York: Columbia University Press, 1911.   PR841.M6

Richetti, John. *Popular Fiction before Richardson*. New York: Oxford University Press, 1969.   PR851.R5

Tieje, Arthur J. *Theory of Characterization in Prose Fiction Prior to 1740*. Minneapolis: University of Minnesota Press, 1916.   PN3383.C4 T5

Eighteenth Century

Beasley, Jerry C. *Novels of the 1740s*. Athens: University of Georgia Press, 1982.   PR851.B4 1982

Brissenden, R. F. *Virtue in Distress: Studies in the Novel of Sentiment from Richardson to Sade*. London: Macmillan, 1974.   PN3495.B74

Foster, James R. *History of the Pre-romantic Novel in England*. New York: MLA, 1949.   PR858.R6 F6

Greiner, W. *Studien zur Entstehung der englischen Romantheorie an der Wende zum 18. Jahrhundert*. Tübingen: Niemeyer, 1969.   PN3335.G7

Karl, Frederick R. *Adversary Literature: The English Novel in the Eighteenth Century: A Study in Genre*. New York: Farrar, Straus and Giroux, 1974.
PR851.K3 1975

McKillop, Alan Dugald. *Early Masters of English Fiction*. Lawrence: University Press of Kansas, 1956.
PR851.M33

Tompkins, J. M. S. *Popular Novel in England, 1770–1800*. London: Constable and Co., 1932.   PR854.T6

Watt, Ian. *Rise of the Novel: Studies in Defoe, Richardson, and Fielding*. Berkeley and Los Angeles: University of California Press, 1957.   PR851.W3

Wright, W. F. *Sensibility in English Prose Fiction, 1760–1814*. Urbana: University of Illinois Press, 1937.   PR858.S4 W7

Nineteenth Century

Cazamian, Louis F. *Social Novel in England, 1830–1850*. Translation by Marin Fido of *Le roman social en Angleterre 1830–1850*. Boston: Routledge and Kegan Paul, 1973.   PR871.C213 1973

Cazamian, Madeline Louis. *Le roman et les idées en Angleterre [1860–1914]*. 3 vols. Strasbourg: Librairie Istra, 1923–1955.   PR871.C3

Cecil, Lord David. *Early Victorian Novelists*. Rev. ed. under the title, *Victorian Novelists: Essays in Revaluation*. Chicago: University of Chicago Press, 1958.
PR873.C4

Coustillas, Pierre, et al. *Le roman anglais au XIXᵉ siècle*. Paris: Presses universitaires de France, 1978.
PR861.C64

Karl, Frederick R. *Age of Fiction: The Nineteenth Century British Novel*. New York: Farrar, Straus and Giroux, 1964.   PR861.K3

Myers, Walter L. *Later Realism: A Study of Characterization in the British Novel*. Chicago: University of Chicago Press, 1927.   PR830.R4 M8

Polhemus, Robert M. *Comic Faith: The Great Tradition from Austen to Joyce*. Chicago: University of Chicago Press, 1980.   PR868.C63 P6

Rathburn, R. C., and Marten Steinmann, eds. *From Jane Austin to Joseph Conrad*. Minneapolis: University of Minnesota Press, 1958.   PR863.R3

Tillotson, Kathleen. *Novels of the Eighteen-Forties*. Oxford: Clarendon Press, 1954.   PR871.T5

Williams, Raymond. *English Novel from Dickens to Lawrence*. New York: Oxford University Press, 1970
PR871.W5

American

Chase, Richard. *American Novel and Its Tradition* (see S–86).

Cowie, Alexander. *Rise of the American Novel* (see S–86).

Maxwell, D. E. S. *American Fiction: The Intellectual Background*. London: Routledge and Kegan Paul, 1963.

Petter, Henri. *Early American Novel*. Columbus: Ohio State University Press, 1971.   PS375.P4

Quinn, Arthur H. *American Fiction: An Historical and Critical Survey* (see S–86).

Stegner, Wallace, ed. *American Novel from James Fenimore Cooper to William Faulkner*. New York: Basic Books, 1965.   PS371.S73

Wagenknecht, Edward C. *Cavalcade of the American Novel, from the Birth of the Nation to the Middle of the Twentieth Century*. New York: Holt, 1952. Bibliography.
PS371.W3

Modern

Allen, Walter. *Tradition and Dream: The English and American Novel from the Twenties to Our Time*. London: Phoenix House, 1964. American title: *Modern Novel in Britain and the United States*. New York: Dutton, 1964.   PR881.A4 1964

Daiches, David. *Novel and the Modern World*. Rev. ed. Chicago: University of Chicago Press, 1965.
PR881.D3 1965

Friedman, Alan. *Turn of the Novel: The Transition to Modern Fiction*. London: Oxford University Press, 1966.
PR881.F78

Frierson, William C. *English Novel in Transition, 1885-1940*. Norman: University of Oklahoma Press, 1942.
PR881.F8

Hardy, John Edward. *Man in the Modern Novel*. Seattle: University of Washington Press, 1964.   PR881.H35

Hoffman, Frederick J. *Modern Novel in America, 1900-1950*. Chicago: Regnery, 1951.   PS379.H6

Johnstone, Richard. *Will to Believe: Novelists of the 1930's.* New York: Oxford University Press, 1982.
PR888.B44 J64 1982

Karl, Frederick R. *Reader's Guide to the Contemporary English Novel.* Rev. ed. New York: Farrar, Straus and Giroux, 1972.
PR881.K25 1972

McCormick, John. *Catastrophe and Imagination: An Interpretation of the Recent English and American Novel.* London: Longmans, Green, 1957.   PR881.M25

Simon, Irène. *Formes du roman anglais de Dickens à Joyce.* Liège: Faculté de philosophie et lettres, 1949.
PR821.S5

West, Paul. *Modern Novel.* Vol. 1, *England and France.* 2d ed. London: Hutchinson University Press, 1965.
PN3448.P8 W4 1965

Zabel, Morton D. *Craft and Character: Texts, Method, and Vocation in Modern Fiction.* New York: Viking, 1957.   PR823.Z3

Contemporary

Bradbury, Malcolm. *Possibilities: Essays on the State of the Novel.* London: Oxford University Press, 1973.
PR821.B7

Bradbury, Malcolm, and David Palmer, eds. *Contemporary English Novel.* New York: Holmes and Meier, 1980.
PR883.C6 1980

Tanner, Tony. *City of Words: American Fiction, 1950-1970.* New York: Harper and Row, 1971.   PS379.T3

VI.   SHORT FICTION

W–50 **Thurston, Jarvis A.   *Short Fiction Criticism: A Checklist of Interpretation since 1925 of Stories and Novelettes (American, British, Continental), 1800–1958.*** Denver, Colo.: Swallow, 1960.   Z5917.S5 T5

This volume contains the results of searching more than 200 periodicals and numerous anthologies and collected volumes (including collections devoted to individual authors) for work of criticism. Only English-language critical work is included, and it is cited alphabetically by critic under the title of the alphabetically arranged works of individual short-fiction authors. A list of sources consulted is appended, but there is no index.

This volume is replaced for American short fiction by the more recent work of Weixlmann (S–89).

W–51 **Walker, Warren S., comp.   *Twentieth-Century Short Story Explication: Interpretations 1900–1975 of Short Fiction since 1800.*** 3d ed. Hamden, Conn.: Shoe String Press, 1977.   Z5917.S5 W33 1977

This work, originally published in 1961, with a second edition in 1967 and supplements in 1970 and in 1973, has established itself as a standard reference. It excludes source studies, biographical work, and background studies. Explications in books, monographs, and periodicals are cited for a total of 850 short-story authors of all countries. Entries are arranged alphabetically by critic under the alphabetically arranged titles of individual short-story authors. The work concludes with an index to short-story authors. This edition has been criticized for a variety of typographical errors and for the practice of giving full citations only the first time an article is cited in connection with the work of a particular short-story author. In the case of an author of many stories, such a citation system is cumbersome.

A *Supplement to the Third Edition, with Check Lists of Books and Journals Used* was published in 1980. *Supplement II* was published in 1984.

W–52 **"Annual Bibliography of Short Fiction [1963—]." *Studies in Short Fiction,*** vol. 1–. Newberry, S.C.: Newberry College, 1964–.   PN3311.S8

This bibliography of books and articles provides a checklist of explications of short fiction of all countries. Entries are alphabetical by short-fiction author, then title, and then alphabetical by critic. Coverage is almost entirely of American criticism, and there is also a predominance of nineteenth-century American short-fiction authors. Nonetheless, this annual bibliography serves as a continuing supplement to Thurston (W–50), Walker (W–51), and, for American works, Weixlmann (S–89).

W–53 **Powell, David.   *Bibliography of Books of the Short Story.*** Troy, N.Y.: Whitston Publishing Co., 1978.   No LC number

This volume, international in scope, contains some 1,700 entries describing books concerned with the short story. Entries are in five sections, as follows: short-story collections, listed alphabetically by author for some 200 authors; a cross-index for short-story authors and their critics and a bibliography of book-length works of criticism; a bibliography of collections and anthologies containing the short stories of more than one author; a bibliography of mixed-genre anthologies containing short stories; and a bibliography of books on the history, theory, and criticism of the short story. The volume has been praised for the meticulous accuracy of its citations and blamed for the absence of articulated principles of selection and for its limitation to book-length studies.

W–54 **Magill, Frank N., ed.   *Critical Survey of Short Fiction.*** 7 vols. Englewood Cliffs, N.J.: Salem Press, 1981.
PN3321.C7

The first volumes in this massive and comprehensive reference guide to the short story consist of some fifty essays that treat the precursors and development of the genre from fables, ballads, and tales of rogues; its national, regional, and ethnic evolutions; special subgenres such as the detective, horror, and science fiction story; technical matters such as devices, narrative voice, and point of view; and similar broad general topics. Volumes 3–6 present articles on 261 authors with primary bibliographies, brief discussions of the author's work in other forms, sources and influences, characteristics, a brief biographical account, and an analysis of the author's short stories in general, along with a more detailed critique of key works. Articles conclude with a bibliography of works about the author and the author's work. Volume 7 contains brief statements by 390 current writers of short fiction about themselves and their work. An index of authors concludes volume 7.

W–55 **Cook, Dorothy E., and Isabel S. Monro.   *Short Story Index: An Index to 60,000 Stories in 4,320 Collections [SSI].*** New York: H. W. Wilson, 1953.   Z5917.S5 C6

The basic list contains a combined author-title-subject index to some 60,000 stories in a total of 4,320 collections. Seven supplements have been published to date, covering 1950–1954 (1956), 1955–1958 (1960), 1959–1963 (1965), 1964–1968 (1969), 1969–1973 (1974), 1974–1978 (1979), and 1979–1983 (1984). Together they add a total of more than 68,000 additional stories in more than 4,800 further collections. Thus the complete, supplemented index provides author, title, and subject access to more than 128,000 stories in more than 9,000 collections. In addition, annual volumes published since 1984 add an average 4,300 stories in an average of 245 collections each year.

There are a number of more specialized story indexes. For science fiction see Marilyn Fletcher, *Science Fiction Story Index, 1950–1979* (Chicago: American Library Association, 1981) [Z5917.S36 S5 1979], a revision of the 1971 index by Frederick Siemon. See also William Contento, *Index to Science Fiction Anthologies and Collections* (Boston: G. K. Hall, 1978) [Z1231.F4 C65] and Marshall B. Tymn et al., *Index to Stories in Thematic Anthologies of Science Fiction* (Boston: G. K. Hall, 1978) [Z5917.S36 I53].

For horror stories see Frederick Siemon, *Ghost Story Index: An Author-Title Index to More Than 2,000 Stories of Ghosts, Horrors, and the Macabre Appearing in 190 Books and Anthologies* (San Jose, Calif.: Library Research Associates, 1967) [Z6514.G5 S5].

W–56 **Chicorel, Marietta.** ***Chicorel Index to Short Stories in Anthologies and Collections.*** 4 vols. New York: Chicorel, 1974.   Z5917.S5 C44

These volumes, constituting numbers 12, 12A, 12B, and 12C of the *Chicorel Index*, analyze about 1,500 anthologies and collections alphabetically by authors, titles, and collection titles. The fourth volume, 12C, has an index of broad subject terms including countries, periods, and types (mystery, folktale, etc.), as well as a list of the collections analyzed.

These volumes are updated by serially published supplemental volumes, the first of which appeared in 1977.

W–57 ***Best [American] Short Stories . . . and the Yearbook of the American Short Story.*** Vol. 1–. Boston: Houghton Mifflin, 1915–. 1/yr.   PZ1.B446235

Coverage has varied over the years; in general, this annual has been a source for lists of stories, anthologies, and (in some years) criticism.

An *Index to Best American Short Stories and O. Henry Prize Stories* by Ray Lewis White has been published (Boston: G. K. Hall, 1988) [Z1231.F4 W52 1988].

W–59 **Some Frequently Recommended Works on Short Fiction.**

Allen, Walter. *Short Story in English.* London: Oxford University Press, 1981.   PR829.A47

Aycock, Wendell M., ed. *Teller and the Tale: Aspects of the Short Story.* Lubbock: Texas Tech University Press, 1982.   PN3373.C65 1982

Bates, Herbert E. *Modern Short Story: A Critical Survey.* London: T. Nelson, 1941.   PN3372.B24

Bayley, John. *Short Story: Henry James to Elizabeth Bowen.* New York: St. Martin's Press, 1988.
                                                      PN3373.B28 1988

Beachcroft, Thomas O. *Modest Art: A Survey of the Short Story in English.* London: Oxford University Press, 1968.   PR829.B42 1968

Bonheim, Helmut. *Narrative Modes.* Cambridge: D. S. Brewer, 1982.   PN3373.B64 1983

Canby, Henry Seidel, and Alfred Dashiell. *Study of the Short Story.* Rev. ed. New York: Henry Holt, 1935.
                                                      PN3357.C33 1935

Clements, Robert J., and Joseph Gibaldi. *Anatomy of the Novella: The European Tale Collection from Boccaccio and Chaucer to Cervantes.* New York: New York University Press, 1977.   PN692.C55

Conant, M. P. *Oriental Tale in England in the Eighteenth Century.* New York: Columbia University Press, 1908.   PR851.C6

Current-Garcia, Eugene, and Walton R. Patrick, eds. *What Is the Short Story?* Rev. ed. Glenview, Ill.: Scott, Foresman, 1974.   PN3373.C8 1974

Grabo, Carl. *Art of the Short Story.* New York: Scribner's, 1913.   PN3373.G7

Hanson, Clare. *Short Stories and Short Fictions, 1880-1980.* New York: St. Martin's Press, 1985.
                                                      PR829.H34 1985

——, ed. *Re-reading the Short Story.* New York: St. Martin's Press, 1989.   PN3373.R5 1989

Ingram, Forrest L., S. J. *Representative Short Story Cycles of the 20th Century: Studies in a Literary Genre.* The Hague: Mouton, 1971.   PN3503.I5

Lohafer, Susan. *Coming to Terms with the Short Story.* Baton Rouge: Louisiana State University Press, 1983.
                                                      PN3373.L56 1983

——, and Jo Ellyn Clarey, eds. *Short Story Theory at a Crossroads.* Baton Rouge: Louisiana State University Press, 1989.   PN3373.S395 1989

Lubbers, Klaus. *Typologie der Short Stroy.* Darmstadt: Wissenschaftliche Buchgesellschaft, 1977.
                                                      PS374.S5 L8

Mann, Susan Garland. *Short Story Cycle: A Genre Companion and Reference Guide.* New York: Greenwood Press, 1989.   PS374.S5 M36 1989

May, Charles E., ed. *Short Story Theories.* Athens: Ohio University Press, 1976.   PN3373.S39

O'Brien, Edward J. H. *Advance of the American Short Story.* Rev. ed. New York: Dodd, Mead, 1931.
                                                      PS374.S503 1931

O'Connor, Frank [pseud. of Michael O'Donovan]. *Lonely Voice: A Study of the Short Story.* Cleveland: World, 1963.   PN3373.O36

O'Faolain, Sean. *Short Story.* London: Collins, 1948.
                                                      PN3373.O37 1948

Papinchak, Robert Allen. *Beginnings, Middles, and Ends: A Study of the American Short Story.* Madison: University of Wisconsin Press, 1972.

Pattee, Fred Lewis. *Development of the American Short Story: An Historical Survey.* New York: Harper, 1923.
                                                      PS374.S5 P3

Peden, Margaret Sayers, ed. *Latin American Short Story: A Critical History.* Boston: Twayne, 1983.
                                                      PQ7082.S5 L35 1983

Peden, William. *American Short Story: Continuity and Change, 1940–1975.* 2d ed. Boston: Houghton Mifflin, 1975.   PS374.S5 P4

Reid, Ian. *Short Story.* New York: Barnes and Noble, 1977.   PN3373.R38 1977

Shaw, Valerie. *Short Story: A Critical Introduction.* New York: Longman, 1983.   PN3373.S384 1983

Springer, Mary Doyle. *Forms of the Modern Novella.* Chicago: University of Chicago Press, 1975.
                                                      PN3503.S66

Stevick, Philip. *American Short Story, 1900–1945: A Critical History.* Boston: Twayne, 1984.
                                                      PS374.S5 A366 1984

Stone, Wilfrid, Nancy Huddleston Parker, and Robert Hoopes. *Short Story: An Introduction.* New York: McGraw-Hill, 1976.   PN6014.S4

Swales, Martin. *German Novelle*. Princeton, N.J.: Princeton University Press, 1977. PT763.S86

Voss, Arthur. *American Short Story: A Critical Survey*. Norman: University of Oklahoma Press, 1973. PS374.S5 V6

Ward, Alfred C. *Aspects of the Modern Short Story,: English and American*. London: University of London Press, 1924. PN3373.W34

Weaver, Gordon, ed. *American Short Story, 1945–1980: A Critical History*. Boston: Twayne, 1983. PS374.S5 A37 1983

West, Ray B., Jr. *Short Story in America, 1900–1950*. Rev. ed. Chicago: Regnery, 1956 PS374.S5 W4

Wright, Austin M. *American Short Story in the Twenties*. Chicago: University of Chicago Press, 1961. PS379.W7

VII. THE PICARESQUE

W–60 Wicks, Ulrich. *Picaresque Narrative, Picaresque Fictions: A Theory and Research Guide*. New York: Greenwood Press, 1989. PN3428.W53 1989

This work is an elaborate expansion and extension of Wick's earlier treatment, "Picaro, Picaresque: The Picaresque in Literary Scholarship," *Genre* 2 (1972): 153–192, and "A Picaresque Bibliography," *Genre* 2 (1972): 193–216 [PN80.G4]. This volume is divided into two parts, "A Theory of Picaresque Narrative" followed by "A Guide to Basic Picaresque Fictions."

Part I is divided into four chapters, as follows: Chapter 1, The Picaresque Genre; Chapter 2, The Picaresque Genre in Literary Scholarship; Chapter 3, The Picaresque Mode; Chapter 4, The Nature of Picaresque Narrative. This part concludes with a selective bibliography, "Basic Studies in Picaresque Novel/Works Cited," which lists bibliographies, critical anthologies and collections, and books and articles on the genre.

Part II provides brief discussions of sixty-four representative fictions from Kafka's *Amerika* to Woody Allen's film *Zelig*. Essays review scholarship on the work and evaluate the strengths and weaknesses. Each discussion is followed by a suggested Edition(s) section, and a brief selective bibliography of books and articles devoted to the work. As an addendum to Part II, Wicks presents a "Chronology of Basic Picaresques," a list of dates and works that begins in prehistory with archetypal myths and ends with McInerey's 1984 novel *Bright Lights, Big City*. The index includes items from the bibliographies only if they have also been mentioned in one of the essays.

W–61 Laurenti, Joseph L. *Bibliografía de la literatura picaresca desde sus orígenes hasta el presente / A Bibliography of Picaresque Literature from Its Origins to the Present*. Metuchen, N.J.: Scarecrow Press, 1973. Z5917.P5 L35

This volume contains a total of twenty-seven sections with 2,439 serially numbered entries arranged in chronological order. The first six sections are general, as follows: 1. Bibliografías; 2. Antologías (by language); 3. Colecciones amplias y selecciones (by language), 4. Estudios y conceptos sobre la etimología de "pícaro"; 5. Generalidades; 6. Influencias y relaciones con otras literaturas y géneros literarios. Sections 7–25 present bibliographies of individual texts from *Lazarillo de Tormes* (1554) until the mid-eighteenth century. The bibliographies identify bibliographies, editions, translations (by language) and studies and commentaries. Section 26 is a miscellany, and section 27 an index of bibliographical sources. The volume concludes with an index of names.

This original volume was reprinted by the AMS Press in 1981, along with a *Supplemento/Supplement* also compiled by Laurenti [Z5917.P5.L35 Suppl.]. The supplement carries on coverage from 1973 to 1978, adding more than 850 entries to the material provided in the first volume.

W–69 Some Frequently Recommended Works on the Picaresque.

Alter, Robert. *Rogue's Progress: Studies in the Picaresque Novel*. Cambridge: Harvard University Press, 1964. PN3428.A4

Bjornson, Richard. *Picaresque Hero in European Fiction*. Madison: University of Wisconsin Press, 1977. PN3428.B5

Blackburn, Alexander. *Myth of the Picaro*. Chapel Hill: University of North Carolina Press, 1979. PN3428.B53

Chandler, Frank W. *Literature of Roguery*. 2 vols. Boston: Houghton Mifflin, 1907. PN3430.G6 C5

———. *Romances of Roguery: An Episode in the History of the Novel*. Part I, *Picaresque Novel in Spain*. New York: Macmillan for Columbia University Press, 1899. PN3428.C5

Gondebeaud, Louis. *Le roman "picaresque" anglais, 1650–1730*. Lille: Universite de Lille III, 1979. PR844.P52 G6

Heidenreich, Helmut, ed. *Pikarische Welt: Schriften zum europäischen Schelmenroman*. Darmstadt: Wissenschaftliche Buchgesellschaft, 1969. "Bibliographie zur Pikaresken Literatur," pp. 479–501. PN3428 .H4

Lewis, R. W. B. *Picaresque Saint: Representative Figures in Contemporary Fiction*. Philadelphia: Lippincott, 1959. PN3503.L4

Miller, Stuart. *Picaresque Novel*. Cleveland: Press of Case Western Reserve University, 1967. PN3428.M5

Monteser, Frederick. *Picaresque Element in Western Literature*. University: University of Alabama Press, 1975. PN3428.M6

Parker, Alexander A. *Literature and the Delinquent: The Picaresque Novel in Spain and Europe, 1599–1753*. Edinburgh: Edinburgh University Press, 1967. PN3428.P3

Sieber, Harry. *Picaresque*. London: Methuen, 1977. PN3428.S5

Whitbourne, Christine J., ed. *Knaves and Swindlers: Essays on the Picaresque Novel in Europe*. London: Oxford University Press, 1974. PN3428.K5

VIII. GOTHIC FICTION

W–70 **Tymn, Marshall B., ed.** *Horror Literature: A Core Collection and Reference Guide.* New York: R. R. Bowker, 1981.   Z2014.H67 H67

This volume consists of twelve chapters by authorities giving primary and secondary bibliographies on the history and study of gothic, horror, and supernatural literature. The first part, Fiction, contains the following chapters: 1, The Gothic Romance, 1762–1820; 2, The Residual Gothic Impulse, 1824–1873; 3, Psychological, Antiquarian, and Cosmic Horror, 1872–1919; 4, The Modern Masters, 1920–1980; and 5, The Horror Pulps, 1933–1940. Each discursive chapter is accompanied by a descriptively and critically annotated bibliography of primary works, generally in alphabetical order by author, with entries numbered sequentially within the chapter list. A total of more than 1,100 entries are found in these five bibliographies. Part 2, Poetry, contains a chapter on supernatural verse in English in jaunty, essay form with a total of sixty-four entries describing original volumes, anthologies, and related items. Part 3, Reference Sources, contains six chapters treating Biography, Autobiography and Bibliography; Criticism, Indexes, and General Reference Works; Periodicals; Societies and Organizations; Awards; and Research Collections, respectively. These, too, are annotated as appropriate with descriptive and evaluative comments. The volume concludes with a Core Collection Checklist, a directory of publishers, and an author-title index.

W–71 **Fisher, Benjamin Franklin, IV.** *Gothic's Gothic: Study Aids to the Tradition of the Tale of Terror.* New York: Garland, 1988.   Z5917.G66 F57 1988

This annotated bibliography includes a total of 2,600 books, dissertations, articles, introductions to editions, and reviews from the late eighteenth century through 1977. The work is divided into two parts, Authors and Subjects. In the first more than one hundred British, American, and German writers are arranged chronologically in the order in which their works began to be noticed. The annotated entries for secondary works are arranged alphabetically by critic under each subject author. A broad range of subjects constitutes the main divisions of the second part. Included are such traditional topics as Germanism, Orientalism, Vampires, Doppelgangers, Faust, Demonism and Witchcraft, the Wandering Jew, and the Flying Dutchman; as well as entries for British and American Gothic drama; for gift books and literary annuals; for the Minerva Press; one on the Sublime and the Picturesque, and one on the Grotesque. In addition, there are entries for related genres, including Ghost Stories and Supernatural Fiction, Detective and Mystery Writing, Science Fiction, and Fantasy.

The volume concludes with three indexes. The first lists authors, artists, and subjects. The second and third indexes treat titles and critics, respectively. The entire volume is meant to be supplemented by the annual bibliographies in *Gothic* (W–74).

W–72 **Frank, Frederick S.** *Guide to the Gothic: An Annotated Bibliography of Criticism.* Metuchen, N. J.: Scarecrow Press, 1984.   Z5917.G66 F7

This volume contains more than 2,500 serially numbered, often annotated entries, classified into eight sections, as follows: Previous Guides to the Gothic; English Gothic (General Histories, Definitions, and Theories; individual authors in chronological order); American Gothic (General Histories and Critical Studies; individual authors in chronological order); French Gothic; German Gothic; Other National Gothics; Spe-

cial Subject Areas (including The Gothic Revival; Parodies; Victorian Gothic; The Double; The Legend of the Wandering Jew; The Vampire and Vampirism; Special Collections of Gothic Literature; Selected Criticism on Gothic Films). Three indexes (journals; critics; authors, artists, and actors) conclude the volume.

W–73 **Frank Frederick S.** *Gothic Fiction: A Master List of Twentieth-Century Criticism and Research.* Westport, Conn.: Meckler, 1988.   Z5917.G66 F69 1988

This volume, which cumulates and culminates Frank's earlier checklists in the *Bulletin of Bibliography* (1973, 1978), presents a total of 2,491 entries, including books, articles, and dissertations, in thirteen sections, as follows: I. English Gothic Fiction: Primary and Secondary Bibliographies, Special Collections, Research and Reference Works; II. English Gothic Fiction: Literary Histories, Theories and Formal Definitions, Genre Studies; III. English Gothic Fiction: Individual Author Studies; IV. English Gothic Fiction: Special Subject Areas; V. American Gothic Fiction: General Histories, Critical Surveys, Definitions of Genre; VI. American Gothic Fiction: Individual Author Studies; VII. The French Gothic Novel or Roman Noir; VIII. The German Gothic Novel or Schauerroman; IX. Other National Gothics and Comparative Gothicism; X. Special Gothic Themes: The Evil Eye, Spontaneous Combustion, Science Fiction Gothic, Prominent Gothicists, Writing the Gothic Novel; XI. The Wandering Jew and the Double Figure; XII. Werewolfery and Vampirism; XIII. The Gothic Film: A Selective Listing. Addenda are followed by an Index of Critics and an Index of Authors and Artists.

W–74 **"The [1978–] Bibliography of Gothic Studies,"** *Gothic,* vol. 1–. Baton Rouge, La.: Gothic Press, 1979–.
    PR830.T3 G67

This annual bibliography includes books, articles, doctoral dissertations, and masters' theses related to any phase of Gothicism. Entries are descriptively annotated and disposed into three categories: Bibliography and Textual Studies; General Studies or Broad Considerations of Gothic Themes Involving Many Writers; and Individual Authors and Comparative Studies [of a few authors]. Unfortunately, the last section is not subdivided by subject author, requiring a search of the entire list to locate materials on a single author of interest. Foreign-language titles are followed by an English translation.

W–75 **Spector, Robert D.** *English Gothic: A Bibliographic Guide to Writers from Horace Walpole to Mary Shelley.* Westport, Conn.: Greenwood, 1984.   Z2014.H67 S66 1984

This well-received volume consists of an introduction and five chapters that discuss in discursive essay form research on The Gothic, Gothicism, and Gothicists; The Beginnings; Horace Walpole and Clara Reeve; Sentimental Gothicism: Charlotte Smith and Ann Radcliffe; Schauer-Romantik: Matthew Gregory Lewis and William Beckford; and The Inheritors: Charles Robert Maturin and Mary Shelley. The essays are followed by reference lists that enumerate books and articles referred to in the essays.

W–76 **Frank, Frederick S.** *First Gothics: A Critical Guide to the English Gothic Novel.* New York: Garland, 1987.
    Z2014.H67 F7 1987

This volume lists in alphabetical order by title, summarizes, evaluates, and classifies five hundred serially numbered English gothic titles originally published between 1762 and 1832. Entries cite modern editions and reprints, as well as criticism of the work. Entries are alphabetized and extensively cross-referenced. Three appendixes add a Glossary of Gothic Terms; a Selected Bibliography of Critical Sources on the English Gothic Novel; and an Annual Chronology of the First Gothics 1753–1832 which lists all titles published each year, with reference to the item number under which the title is discussed. The item number is used for reference also in the Index of Gothic Authors, the Index of Gothic Titles, and the Index of Critics which complete the volume.

W–79 **Some Frequently Recommended Works on Gothic Fiction.**

Birkhead, Edith. *Tale of Terror: A Study of the Gothic Romance.* London: Constable, 1921.   PN3435.B5

Blakey, Dorothy. *Minerva Press, 1790–1820.* London: Oxford University Press, 1939.   Z232.M66 B6

Briggs, Julia. *Night Visitors: The Rise and Fall of the English Ghost Story.* London: Faber, 1977.
　　　　　　　　　　　　　　　　　　　PR830.G45 B7

Day, William Patrick. *In the Circles of Fear and Desire: A Study of Gothic Fantasy.* Chicago: University of Chicago Press, 1985.   PR830.T3 D39 1985

Graham, Kenneth W., ed. *Gothic Fictions: Prohibition / Transgression.* New York: AMS Press, 1989.
　　　　　　　　　　　　　　　　　　　PR830.T3 G68 1989

Haggerty, George E. *Gothic Fiction / Gothic Form.* University Park: Pennsylvania State University Press, 1989.
　　　　　　　　　　　　　　　　　　　PR830.T3 H25 1989

Hennessy, Brandan. *Gothic Novel.* Harlow: Longmans for the British Council, 1978.   PR830.T3 H4

Howells, Coral Ann. *Love, Mystery, and Misery: Feeling in Gothic Fiction.* London: Athlone Press, 1978.
　　　　　　　　　　　　　　　　　　　PR858.T3 H6

Klein, Jürgen. *Der Gotische Roman und die Ästhetik des Bösen.* Darmstadt: Wissenschaftliche Buchgesellschaft, 1975.   PN3435.K6 1975

Lévy, Maurice. *Le roman "gothique" anglais 1764–1824.* Toulouse: Association des publications de la faculté des lettres et sciences humaines, 1968. Extensive chronological bibliography.   PR830.T3 L4

MacAndrew, Elizabeth. *Gothic Tradition in Fiction.* New York: Columbia University Press, 1979. PN3435.M3

McNutt, Dan. *Eighteenth-Century Gothic Novel: An Annotated Bibliography of Criticism and Selected Texts.* New York: Garland, 1975 (see P–48).   Z2014.F5M3

Mise, Raymond W. *Gothic Heroine and the Nature of the Gothic Novel.* New York: Arno Press, 1980.
　　　　　　　　　　　　　　　　　　　PR830.T3 M5 1980

Punter, David. *Literature of Terror: A History of Gothic Fictions from 1765 to the Present Day.* London: Longman, 1980.   PR408.G68 P8 1980

Radcliffe, Elsa J. *Gothic Novels of the Twentieth Century: An Annotated Bibliography.* Metuchen, N.J.: Scarecrow Press, 1979. 1,973 entries.   Z1231.F4 R32

Railo, Eino. *Haunted Castle: A Study of the Elements of English Romanticism.* London: Routledge and Kegan Paul, 1927.   PR146.R3

Scarborough, Dorothy. *Supernatural in Modern English Fiction.* New York: Putnam, 1917.   PR147.S3

Sedgwick, Eve Kosofsky. *Coherence of Gothic Conventions.* New York: Arno Press, 1980.   PR868.T3 S35

Sullivan, Jack. *Elegant Nightmares: The English Ghost Story from LeFanu to Blackwood.* Athens: Ohio University Press, 1978.   PR830.G45 S9

Summers, Montague. *Gothic Bibliography.* London: Fortune Press, 1941. Use with caution.   Z2014.F4 S9

――――. *Gothic Quest: A History of the Gothic Novel.* London: Fortune Press, 1938.   PR830.T3 S9

Thompson, G. R., ed. *Gothic Imagination: Essays in Dark Romanticism.* Pullman: Washington State University Press, 1974.   PR146.T5

Tracy, Ann Blaisdell. *Gothic Novel, 1790–1830: Plot Summaries and Index to Motifs.* Lexington: University Press of Kentucky, 1981.   PR868.T3 T7

Varma, Devendra. *Gothic Flame: Being a History of the Gothic Novel in England: Its Origins, Efflorescence, Disintegration, and Residuary Influence.* London: A. Barker, 1957.   PR830.T3 V3

Varnade, S. L. *Haunted Presence: The Numinous in Gothic Fiction.* Tuscaloosa: University of Alabama Press, 1987.   PR830.S85 V37 1987

Watt, William W. *Shilling Shockers of the Gothic School: A Study of Chapbook Gothic Romances.* Cambridge: Harvard University Press, 1932.   PR838.G6 W3

IX. HISTORICAL FICTION

See also references to historical fiction in many of the bibliographies and guides of section F, History.

W–80 **Baker, Ernest A. *Guide to Historical Fiction.*** London: Routledge, 1914.   Z5917.H6 B2

Originally published in two volumes in 1907 under the title *History in Fiction*, this volume presents an annotated bibliography of historical fiction primarily in the English language, arranged by the country and then the historical period in which the novel is set. Medieval romances, novels of manners, and avowedly historical fictions are all included. Annotations indicate settings and characters and summarize plots. Juvenile fiction is identified. The volume concludes with an elaborate index to authors and titles and to historical names, places, events, and allusions.

An earlier, related work that has a more current revision is Jonathan Nield, *Guide to the Best Historical Novels and Tales*, first published in 1902, the fifth and last edition of which was published in 1929 (London: Mathews) [Z5917.H6 N6]. It contains a total of 2,392 serially numbered entries arranged into large sections by historical periods, and within period in rough chronological order of the historical events narrated. There is a supplementary list of semi-historical fiction and a bibliography of works consulted. The volume ends with three indexes: of authors (giving all titles in chronological order of date of publication), of titles, and of subjects (historical persons, places, and events).

W–85 **McGarry, Daniel D., and Sarah H. White. *World Historical Fiction Guide: An Annotated, Chronological, Geographical, and Topical List of Selected Historical Novels.*** 2d ed. Metuchen, N.J.: Scarecrow Press, 1973.
　　　　　　　　　　　　　　　　　　　Z5917.H6 M3 1973

Originally published with a narrower geographical focus in 1963, this volume presents a selective bibliography of English language historical fiction, defined as fiction that refers to actual past customs, conditions, identifiable persons, or events, including those contemporary with the writer (e.g., Dickens). The work is organized in three main sections, Antiquity to ca. 400 A.D.; The Middle Ages and Early Renaissance, ca. 400 to 1500; and The Modern World, ca. 1500–1900. Within these sections, which are further subdivided into periods and countries, a total of 6,455 serially numbered entries provide author, title, publication date, and a description of the historical time and place of the novel. The work concludes with an index of authors and titles but not of historical subjects, for which the detailed table of contents is the sole means of access.

W–88 Gerhard Stein, Virginia Brokaw. *Dickinson's American Historical Fiction*. 5th ed. Metuchen, N.J.: Scarecrow Press, 1986.   Z1231.F4 D47 1986

Originally published in 1958, the second part of this volume contains a checklist of more than 2,700 annotated entries describing twentieth-century American historical fiction through 1984 with some earlier works, in the form of a list classified by historical period and place. The volume concludes with an author-title index and a detailed subject index.

Other bibliographies of American historical fiction include Jack W. Vanderhoof, *Bibliography of Novels Related to American Frontier and Colonial History* (Troy, N.Y.: Whitston, 1971) [Z1231.F4 V3]; the list of novels in Robert A. Lively, *Fiction Fights the Civil War* (Chapel Hill: University of North Carolina Press, 1957) [PS374.H5 L5]; and the thematically arranged volume *America in Fiction: An Annotated List of Novels That Interpret Aspects of Life in the United States, Canada, and Mexico* by Otis W. Coan and Richard G. Lillard, 5th ed. (Palo Alto, Calif.: Pacific Books, 1967) [Z1361.C6 C6], originally published in 1941. See the guide at W–29 for some additional titles.

W–89 Some Frequently Recommended Works on the Historical Novel.

Butterfield, Herbert. *Historical Novel: An Essay*. Cambridge: Cambridge University Press, 1924.
                                        PN3441.B8

Cam, Helen. *Historical Novels*. London: Historical Association, 1961.   PN3441.C3

Cowart, David. *History and the Contemporary Novel*. Carbondale: Southern Illinois University Press, 1989.
                                        PN3343.C68 1989

Feuchtwanger, Leon. *House of Desdemona; or, The Laurels and Limitations of Historical Fiction*. Translation by Harold A. Basilius of *Das Haus der Desdemona* (Rudolstadt: Greifenverlag, 1961). Detroit: Wayne State University Press, 1963.   PN3441.F413

Fleishman, Avrom. *English Historical Novel: Walter Scott to Virginia Woolf*. Baltimore: Johns Hopkins University Press, 1971.   PR868.H5 F5

Hager, Phillip E., and Desmond Taylor. *Novels of World War I: An Annotated Bibliography*. New York: Garland, 1981.   Z5917.W33 H33 1981

Henderson, Harry B., III. *Versions of the Past: The Historical Imagination in American Fiction*. New York: Oxford University Press, 1974.   PS374.H5 H46

Leisy, Ernst F. *American Historical Novel*. Norman: University of Oklahoma Press, 1950.   PS374.H5 L4

Levin, David. *In Defense of Historical Literature: Essays on American History, Autobiography, Drama, and Fiction*. New York: Hill and Wang, 1967. PS169.H5 L4

Lúkacs, Georg. *Historical Novel*. Translation by Hannah and Stanley Mitchell of *Der historische Roman* (Berlin: Aufbau Verlag, 1955). Boston: Beacon Press, 1963.   PN3441.L813

Manzoni, Alessandro. *On the Historical Novel*. Translation by Sandra Bermann of *Del romanzo storico*. Lincoln: University of Nebraska Press, 1984.
                                        PN3441.M313 1984

Marriott, Sir John. *English History in English Fiction*. London: Blackie and Son, 1940.   PR830.H5 M3

Nélod, Gilles. *Panorama du roman historique*. Paris: SODI, 1969.   PN3441.N4

Phillips, William, et al. *American History in the Novel, 1585–1900*. Jefferson City, Mo.: Lincoln University, 1956.

Saintsbury, George. *Historical Novel*. London: Dent, 1895.
                                        PN3441.S25

Sheppard, Alfred T. *Art and Practice of Historical Fiction*. London: H. Toulmin, 1930.   PN3441.S5 1930

X. DETECTIVE FICTION

W–90 Breen, Jon L. *What about Murder? A Guide to Books about Mystery and Detective Fiction*. Metuchen, N.J.: Scarecrow Press, 1981.   Z5917.D5 B73

This excellent reference guide contains extended descriptive and evaluative annotations for a total of 239 works. It is divided into seven sections, as follows: General Histories; Reference Books (including encyclopedias, dictionaries, bibliographies); Special Subjects (particular aspects, groupings, or theories of the genre); Collected Essays and Reviews; Technical Manuals; Coffee-Table Books (large-size, illustrated books); and Works on Individual Authors. An addendum is followed by an index combining authors, titles, series, major subjects, and authors-as-subjects.

W–91 Hubin, Allen J. *Crime Fiction, 1749–1980*. New York: Garland, 1984.   Z2014.F4 H82 1984

This work, which both updates and extends Hubin's *Bibliography of Crime Fiction, 1749–1975* (San Diego: University Extension, University of California, San Diego, 1979), is now the most extensive and authoritative bibliography of primary works of crime fiction available. It includes more than 65,000 English language novels, plays, and short-story collections. There are three sections: an author index, followed by title and series indexes. The author index gives titles, publishers, and dates of publication, identifying series and series characters as needed. Works published under pseudonyms are listed under the pseudonym and cross-referenced to both the author's true name and any other pseudonyms he or she used. The title index refers to authors' names; the series index lists series titles and series characters and refers back to the author index. Hubin has also published the *1981–1985 Supplement to Crime Fiction, 1749–1980* (New York: Garland, 1988) [Z2014.F4 H82 1984 Suppl.]. It adds 6,900 new titles plus additional information on 4,300 previously cited titles.

For all but a few purposes the Hubin bibliography supersedes that by Orden A. Hagen, *Who Done It? A Guide to Detective, Mystery and Suspense Fiction* (New York: Bowker, 1969) [Z5917.D5 H3], especially its first part, a comprehensive bibliography of mystery fiction, 1841–1967, which Hubin used as the basis of his own list. The second part of Hagen, a bibliographical guide to mystery fiction, does continue to have value. It contains the following items: a subject guide to mysteries, a guide to the mystery novel on the screen, a listing of mystery plays, a list of mysteries set in different countries, a directory of series characters, a bibliography of anthologies and collections, a bibliography of secondary sources, and a variety of additional miscellaneous information.

Hagen must, however, be used with caution, for it has been discovered to contain numerous errors of omission and commission, corrections to it being published as a regular feature of *Armchair Detective* since its publication in 1969.

W–92 **Barzun, Jacques, and Wendell H. Taylor.** *Catalogue of Crime.* New York: Harper and Row, 1971.
Z5917.D5 B37 1971

This extensively annotated bibliography of mystery and detective fiction contains a total of 3,476 serially numbered entries. Though material published after 1960 is slighted and though it is thought somewhat eccentric, most reviewers find this volume particularly valuable for its commentary. The entries are divided into six sections, as follows: I. Novels of Detection, Crime, Mystery, and Espionage; II. Short Stories, Collections, Anthologies, Magazines, Parodies, and Plays; III. Studies and Histories of the Genre, Lives of Writers, and the Literature of *Edwin Drood*; IV. True Crime: Trials, Narratives of Cases, Criminology and Police Science, Espionage and Cryptography; V. The Literature of Sherlock Holmes: Studies and Annotations of the Tales, Non-Fiction Parodies, and Critical Pastiches; and VI. Ghost Stories, Studies and Reports of the Supernatural, Psychical Research, and E.S.P. There is an extremely useful index that includes authors and titles, along with boldface rubrics for settings and various categories of detective fiction.

The issues of *Armchair Detective: A Quarterly Journal Devoted to the Appreciation of Mystery, Detective and Suspense Fiction*, vol. 1– (New York: The Armchair Detective, Inc., 1967–) [PR830.D4 A75] contain bibliographies on new books and articles that provide a continuing supplement to the Barzun and Taylor bibliography. There is an Index to vols. 1–10 available, published in 1979. The other journal in this field is *Clues: A Journal of Detection*, vol. 1– (Bowling Green, Ohio: Bowling Green University Popular Press, 1980–) [PN3448.D4.C6], which appears twice yearly.

W–93 **Johnson, Timothy W., and Julia Johnson.** *Crime Fiction Criticism: An Annotated Bibliography.* New York: Garland, 1981.
Z5917.D5 J63 1981

A total of 1,810 serially numbered entries with descriptive, summarizing annotations are disposed into two sections. The first, General Works, is divided into subsections for Reference Works, Books, Dissertations, and Articles and Parts of Books. The second has bibliographies of criticism for more than 250 authors. Throughout, arrangement within divisions is alphabetical. The volume ends with an index of authors.

W–94 **Melvin, David S., and Ann Skene Melvin.** *Crime, Detective, Espionage, Mystery, and Thriller Fiction and Film: A Comprehensive Bibliography of Critical Writing through 1979.* Westport, Conn.: Greenwood Press, 1980.
Z5917.D5 S55

This volume contains a total of 1,628 alphabetically arranged entries providing a sheer list of English-language books and articles about the types of fiction and film enumerated in the title, except that Holmesiana are omitted. An appendix lists a selection of materials in other languages, with entries grouped alphabetically under the language in which they are written. The work concludes with a title index and a fairly detailed subject index.

W–95 **Albert, Walter.** *Detective and Mystery Fiction: An International Bibliography of Secondary Sources.* Madison: Ind.: Brownstone, 1985.
Z5917.D5

This 781-page classified bibliography incorporates the author's bibliographies in *Armchair Detective* through 1983, excluding work on Sherlock Holmes. The curiously arranged work is in four sections, as follows: Bibliographies, Encyclopedias, and Checklists (numbered A–1 to A–182); General Reference Works: Historical and Critical—Part A: Books (numbered B–1 to B–451); Part B: Articles (numbered C–1 to C–886); Dime Novels, Juvenile Series, and Pulps—Part A: Dime Novels and Juvenile; Part B: Pulps (numbered continuously D–1 to D–503); and individual Authors (numbered E–1 to E–3167). Entries are then arranged alphabetically by the name of the critic. Descriptive and evaluative annotations by one of the volume's twenty-two contributors increase this volume's usefulness, as do its cross references to standard reference works for further information on individual authors. The work concludes with an index of critics, authors, series characters, magazines, and publishers.

W–96 **Steinbrunner, Chris, and Otto Penzler, eds.** *Encyclopedia of Mystery and Detection.* New York: McGraw-Hill, 1976.
P96.D4 E5 1976

This volume contains primarily biobibliographical articles on major and minor authors of detective fiction and on persons associated with related stage, screen, radio, and television scripts. There are articles, too, on fictitious detectives and other major characters and on some general topics (e.g., locked-room mysteries, scientific detectives, sinister orientals).

Otto Penzler, Chris Steinbrunner, and Marvin Lachman also edited the *Detectionary: A Biographical Dictionary of Leading Characters in Detective and Mystery Fiction, Including Famous and Little-Known Sleuths, Their Helpers, Rogues, Both Heroic and Sinister, and Some of Their Most Memorable Adventures, As Recounted in Novels, Short Stories, and Films*, rev. and updated ed. (Woodstock, N.Y.: Overlook Press, 1977) [PN3448.D4 D4 1977]. It is in four sections, the first on Detectives, with biographies. The second section, Rogues and Helpers, has articles on criminals, villains, aides, and secondary detectives. A third section has summaries of selected Cases. And the fourth section, on Movies lists films and especially film series under the name of the detective or the movie title.

W–97 **Reilly, John M.** *Twentieth-Century Crime and Mystery Writers.* London: Macmillan, 1980.
PR888.D4 T8

This volume provides extended biobibliographies for 614 English-language writers of crime and mystery fiction. Signed essays vary in length and in quality but do include biographical, critical, and bibliographical information. There are two appendixes, the first providing biobibliographical articles on nine nineteenth-century writers, and the other giving similar treatment to sixteen foreign authors whose works are available in English translation and significantly influenced English mystery writing.

W–99 **Some Frequently Recommended Works on Detective Fiction.**

Becker, Jens-Peter. *Sherlock Holmes & Co.: Essays zur englischen und amerikanischen Detektivliteratur.* Munich: Goldmann, 1975.
PR830.D4 B4

Boileau, Pierre, and Thomas Narcejac. *Le roman policier.* Paris: Payof, 1964.   PN3448.D4

Buchloh, Paul G., and Jens-Peter Becker, eds. *Der Detektiverzahlung auf der Spur: Essays zur Form und Wertung der englischen Detektivliteratur.* 2d ed. rev. and enl. Darmstadt: Wissenschaftliche Buchgesellschaft, 1978.   PR830.D4 B8 1978

Caillois, Roger. *Le roman policier.* Buenos Aires: Editions des lettres françaises, 1941.   PN3448.D4 C3

Champigny, Robert. *What Will Have Happened: A Philosophical and Technical Essay on Mystery Stories.* Bloomington: Indiana University Press, 1977.
     PN3377.5.D4 C5 1977

Conrad, Horst. *Die literarische Angst: Das Schreckliche in Schauerromantik und Detektivgeschichte.* Düsseldorf: Bertelsmann, 1974.

Cook, Micheal L., and Stephen T. Miller. *Mystery, Detective, and Espionage Fiction: A Checklist of Fiction in U. S. Pulp Magazines, 1915–1974.* New York: Garland, 1988.   Z1231.D47 C66 1988

Grossvogel, David I. *Mystery and Its Fictions: From Oedipus to Agatha Christie.* Baltimore: Johns Hopkins University Press, 1979.   PN49.G727

Harper, Ralph. *World of the Thriller.* Cleveland: Press of Case Western Reserve University, 1969.
     PN3448.D4 H25

Haycroft, Howard. *Murder for Pleasure: The Life and Times of the Detective Story.* New ed. New York: Appleton-Century, 1968.   PN830.D4 H3

————, ed. *Art of the Mystery Story: A Collection of Critical Essays.* New York: Simon and Schuster, 1946.
     PN3448.D4 H28

Marsch, Edgar. *Die Kriminalerzählung: Theorie, Geschichte, Analyse.* 2d ed., rev. and enl. Munich: Winkler, 1983.   PN3448.D4 M35 1983

Menendez, Albert J. *Subject is Murder: A Selective Subject Guide to Mystery Fiction.* New York: Garland, 1986.
     Z1231.D47 M46 1986

Merry, Bruce. *Anatomy of the Spy Thriller.* Montreal: McGill-Queen's University Press, 1977.
     PR830.S65 M4

Murch, A. E. *Development of the Detective Novel.* London: Owen, 1958. New York: Philosophical Library.
     PN3448.D4 M78

Narcejac, Thomas. *Esthétique du roman policier.* Paris: Le Portulan, 1947.   PN3448.D4 N3

Nusser, Peter. *Der Kriminalroman.* Stuttgart: Metzler, 1980.   PN3448.D4 N8 1980

Oleksiw, Susan. *Reader's Guide to the Classic British Mystery.* Boston: G. K. Hall, 1988.   PR888.D4 O4 1988

Ousby, Ian. *Bloodhounds of Heaven: The Detective in English Fiction from Godwin to Doyle.* Cambridge: Harvard University Press, 1976.   PR868.D4 09

Routley, Erik. *Puritan Pleasures of the Detective Story.* London: Gollancz, 1972.   PR830.D4 R6

Schulz-Buschhaus, Ulrich, ed. *Formen und Idealogien des Kriminalromans: Ein gattungsgeschichtlich Essay.* Frankfurt: Athenaeum, 1975.   PN3448.D4 S3

Smith, Myron J., Jr. *Cloak-and-Dagger Bibliography: An Annotated Guide to Spy Fiction, 1937–1975.* Metuchen, N.J.: Scarecrow Press, 1976.   Z2014.F5 S62

Stewart, R.F. *. . . And Always a Detective: Chapters on the History of Detective Fiction.* London: David and Charles, 1980.

Symons, Julian. *Bloody Murder: From the Detective Story to the Crime Novel: A History.* London: Faber and Faber, 1972.   PN3448.D4 S87

Thomson, H. D. *Masters of Mystery: A Study of the Detective Story.* London: W. Collins Sons and Co., 1931.
     PN3448.D4 T5 1931

Vogt, Jochen. *Der Kriminalroman.* 2 vols. Munich, 1971.
     PN3448.D4 V6

de Vries, P. H. *Poe and After: The Detective Story Investigated.* Amsterdam: Bakker, 1956.

Watson, Colin. *Snobbery with Violence: Crime Stories and Their Audience.* London: Eyre and Spottiswoode, 1971.   PR830.D4 W3

Wells, Carolyn. *Technique of the Mystery Story.* Rev. ed. Springfield, Mass.: The Home Correspondence School, 1929.   PN3365.W4 1929

Winks, Robin W. *Modus Operandi: An Excursion into Detective Fiction.* Boston: D. R. Godine, 1982.
     PN3448.D4 W5 1982

————, ed. *Detective Fiction: A Collection of Critical Essays.* Englewood Cliffs, N.J.: Prentice-Hall, 1980. Bibliography.   PN3448.D4 D43

Wölcken, Fritz. *Der literarische Mord: Eine Untersuchung über die englische und amerikanische Detektivliteratur.* Nuremberg: Nest, 1953.
     PR1309.D4 W6 1953

Zmegac, Viktor, ed. *Der wohltemperierte Mord: Zur Theorie und Geschichte des Detektivromans.* Frankfurt-am-Main: Athenaeum-Verlag, 1971.   PN3448.D4 Z4

XI. FANTASY, UTOPIAN FICTION, AND SCIENCE FICTION

W–100 **Tymn, Marshall B., Roger C. Schlobin, and L. W. Currey.** *Research Guide to Science Fiction Studies: An Annotated Checklist of Primary and Secondary Sources for Fantasy and Science Fiction.* New York: Garland, 1977.
     Z5917.S36 T93

This descriptively and evaluatively annotated guide contains a total of 403 serially numbered entries on books and journals published in the United States and England through 1976. Articles are excluded. Entries are disposed into six main sections, as follows: Preliminary Sources (General, Science Fiction); Sources for Primary Materials (General, Science Fiction); Sources for Secondary Materials Including Book and Film Reviews (General, Science Fiction); Author Studies and Bibliographies (Collective, Individual); Periodicals (Science Fiction and Fantasy Journals and Magazines, Special Issues of Other Journals); and Sources for Acquisition (Directories, Book Dealers). Appended is a Checklist of Doctoral Dissertations in Science Fiction and Fantasy compiled by Douglas R. Justus. The volume concludes with indexes of authors and of titles.

W–101 **Briney, Robert E., and Edward Wood.** *Science Fiction Bibliographies: An Annotated Bibliography of Bibliographical Works in Science Fiction and Fantasy Fiction.* Chicago: Advent, 1972.   Z5917.S36 B75

This volume describes about 100 separately published bibliographies, indexes, and checklists, with an emphasis on English-language references. Entries are in four sections, as follows: Magazine Indexes; Individual Author Bibliographies;

General Indexes and Checklists; and Foreign-Language Bibliographies. The work concludes with an author-title index.

W–102 **Barron, Neil, ed.** *Anatomy of Wonder: A Critical Guide to Science Fiction.* 3d ed. New York: R. R. Bowker, 1981.
Z5917.S36 A52 1987

This work, the first and second editions of which were published in 1976 and 1981 respectively, is in sixteen sections, each done by a specialist. Sections include both discussion and selected annotated bibliographies pertaining to their topics. There are two main parts, treating the literature (with more than 2,000 works cited) and research aids (more than 600 items) respectively. Sections in Part I are as follows: The Emergence of Science Fiction: Beginnings to 1920's; Science Fiction between the Wars; The Early Modern Period: 1938–1963; The Modern Period: 1964–1986; Children's Science Fiction; and Foreign Language Science Fiction (subdivided for German, French, Russian, Japanese, Italian, Danish, Swedish, Norwegian, Dutch, Belgian, Romanian, Yugoslav, and Hebrew). Sections in Part II are as follows: Selection, Acquisition, and Cataloging of Science Fiction; Indexes and Bibliographies; History and Criticism; Autobiography, Biography, and Author Studies; Science Fiction on Film and Television; Science Fiction Illustration; Classroom Aids; Science Fiction Magazines; Library and Private Collections of Science Fiction and Fantasy; and a Core Collection Checklist. This useful volume concludes with author and title indexes.

W–103 **Bleiler, Everett F., ed.** *Checklist of Fantastic Literature: A Bibliography of Fantasy, Weird, and Science Fiction Books Published in the English Language.* Rev. ed. Glen Rock, N.J.: Firebell Books, 1978.   Z5917.F3 B55 1978

Originally published in 1948 with about 5,300 titles, this author list of primary literature includes some 5,600 titles, making it the most comprehensive available. Its distinctive feature is a system of ninety subject categories that identify the type of work being cited. Categories (coded, with tables inside both the front and back covers) include such rubrics as Ideal Societies, Extraterrestrial Cultures, Imaginary Wars, Space Travel, Time Travel, Visitors from Other Worlds or Times, Journeys into the Past, Changes in Size, Future History, Drugs, and Lost Continents. Main entries are in an author list, giving title, publication information, pagination, and subject category. A title list refers to authors.

W–104 **Day, Bradford M.** *Supplemental Checklist of Fantastic Literature.* Denver: Science Fiction and Fantasy Publications, 1963.   Z5917.F3 D35

Designed to supplement Bleiler (W–103), this volume contains information on about 2,800 titles, with stress on British and American publications 1949–1961. Entries are alphabetical by author, with a short-title index that refers back to authors' names.

W–105 **Tuck, Donald H.** *Encyclopedia of Science Fiction and Fantasy: A Bibliographic Survey of the Fields of Science Fiction, Fantasy, and Weird Fiction through 1968.* 3 vols. Chicago: Advent, 1974–1982.   Z5917.S36 T83

This work, said to be a sort of supplement to Bleiler (W–103), is actually the third edition of Tuck's *Handbook of Science Fiction and Fantasy,* originally published in Hobart, Tasmania in 1954, with a second edition in two volumes in 1959. This edition presents biobibliographies of authors, editors, and translators, A-L in volume 1, and M-Z, along with a title list, in volume 2. The contents of collected volumes by

an author are enumerated along with separately published works. The third volume presents checklists of magazines; paperback series; pseudonyms; connected stories, series, and sequels; and general works on science fiction and fantasy. Supplements are planned every five years or so.

For more than 600 twentieth-century authors see also Curtis S. Smith, *Twentieth Century Science Fiction Writers* (New York: St. Martin's Press, 1981) [PS374.S35 T89], which provides short biographies; a complete, classified list of primary and secondary works; information on any bibliographies available on the author; a brief, signed critical essay by one of 150 contributors; and often comments by authors on their own work.

W–106 **Reginald, Robert.** *Science Fiction and Fantasy Literature: A Checklist, 1700–1974, with Contemporary Science Fiction Authors II.* 2 vols. Detroit: Gale Research Co., 1979.   Z5917.S36 R42

This work presents a checklist of some 15,884 English-language first-edition books and pamphlets, including about 2,000 retitled works. Volume 2 provides a total of 1,443 biographical sketches of Science Fiction writers. Volume 1 is arranged alphabetically by author, and within an author bibliography, alphabetically by title. Works in series are identified with the name of the series and number of the work's place. A series of five indexes complete the volume: an author index, along with an addendum to the author checklist; a title index with reference back to authors' names; a series index, giving the actual or an arbitrary title of the series, numbering the individual works that make up the actual series (or that have characters and setting in common and thus constitute an artificial series); an awards index (with lists of conventions, officers, awards, and related matters); and an Ace and Belmont Doubles Index, listing all volumes in both series.

Volume 2, *Contemporary Science Fiction Authors II,* is the second edition of a work first published in 1970 under the title *Stella Nova: The Contemporary Science Fiction Authors,* then in 1975 as *Contemporary Science Fiction Authors, First Edition.* Entries give name and vital statistics, education, details of the author's career, honors and awards, avocations and interests, and comments by the author. Entries are supplied by authors in response to questionnaires. Also in volume 2 is a "Pictoral History of Science Fiction and Fantasy Publishing," with reproductions of cover work.

A series of related works have been published or announced by the Borgo Press in San Bernardino, Calif. These include the *Science Fiction Price Guide* (1985) [Z5917.S36 R4213]; *To Be Continued . . .: An Annotated Bibliography of Science Fiction and Fantasy Series and Sequels* (1985) [Z5917 .S36 R43]; and *X, Y, and Z: A List of Those Books Examined in the Course of Compiling "Science Fiction and Fantasy Literature, A Checklist, 1700–1974" . . . Which Were Judged to Fall outside the Genre of Fantastic Literature: An Anti-Bibliography* (1980) [Z5917.F3 R43].

W–107 **Schlobin, Roger C.** *Literature of Fantasy: A Comprehensive, Annotated Bibliography of Modern Fantasy Fiction.* New York: Garland, 1979.   Z2014.F4 S33

This work begins with an essay on the nature and origins of this genre, followed by a total of 1,249 serially numbered selected items published from the mid-nineteenth century (1837) to early 1979. The work is in two sections. In the first, novels, collections, and bibliographies are listed alphabetically by author. Novel entries are annotated with plot summaries; lists of contents are given for collections. The second section lists anthologies alphabetically by editor, with lists of contents in each entry. The volume has an author index that includes pseudonyms and joint authors, and a full title index.

W–108   **Hall, Hal W., comp.** *Science Fiction Book Review Index [SFBRI].* Bryan, Texas: SFBRI, 1970–.   Z5917.S36 S19

This index lists works reviewed in science fiction and some other magazines alphabetically by the fiction author, with a title index. These listings have been cumulated and augmented (including retrospective coverage) in Hall's *Science Fiction Book Review Index, 1923–1973* (Detroit: Gale, 1975) [Z5917.S36 H35]; *Science Fiction Book Review Index, 1974–1979* (Detroit: Gale, 1981) [Z5917.S36 H36]; and *Science Fiction and Fantasy Book Review Index, 1980–1984* (Detroit: Gale, 1985) [Z5917.S35 H36 1985].

W–109   **Hall, Hal W., ed.** *Science Fiction and Fantasy Reference Index, 1878–1985: An International Author and Subject Index to History and Criticism.* 2 vols. Detroit, Mich.: Gale Research Co., 1987.   Z5917.S36 S297 1987

This volume cumulates selections from the first two volumes, and all entries in the third volume of *Science Fiction Book Review Index [SFBRI]* (W–108), along with additional titles from 1985. It presents a comprehensive index to secondary works in English on science fiction and fantasy. There are approximately 42,000 author and subject entries which treat more than 19,000 books, articles, essays, news reports, and audiovisual items. Most entries date from 1945 to 1985. Volume 1 contains the author entries, along with a list of sources; volume 2 contains the subject index, along with a Thesaurus of Science Fiction and Fantasy Indexing Terms. The annual *SFBRI* from 1986 will serve as a supplement to this volume.

W–110   **Nicholls, Peter, ed.** *Science Fiction Encyclopedia.* Garden City, N.Y.: Doubleday, 1979.   PN3448.S45 S29

This volume has more than 2,800 signed articles on themes, major and minor authors, films and television programs, magazines, illustrators, editors, critics, pseudonyms, series, anthologies, comics, terminology, awards, and other topics relevant to the study of Science Fiction. Articles are long and contain extended bibliographies.

Other encyclopedias include Pierre Versins, *Encyclopédie de l'utopie des voyages extraordinaires et de la science fiction* (Paris: L'age d'homme, 1972) [No LC number] with articles on terms and names, and with extensive illustrations.

W–111   **Gunn, James, ed.** *New Encyclopedia of Science Fiction.* New York: Viking, 1988.   PN3433.4.N48 1988

This concise, illustrated encyclopedia was prepared by more than 100 contributors. Author entries treat writers, artists and illustrators, actors, and directors. Film entries are given alphabetically by title. Signed essay entries treat broad subjects such as Agents, Alien Worlds, Children's Science Fiction, Evolution, France, Germany, Literary Conventions, Scholarship, Space Opera, The Two Cultures Debate, Utopias and Dystopias, War, and Women. There is a list of all essay topics among the volume's preliminaries.

W–112   **Clareson, Thomas D.** *Science Fiction Criticism [to 1971]: An Annotated Checklist.* Kent, Ohio: Kent State University Press, 1972.   Z5917.S36 C55

This volume lists approximately 800 English-language books and articles in a total of nine sections, as follows: General Studies; Literary Studies; Book Reviews; The Visual Arts; Futurology, Utopia, and Dystopia; Classroom and Library; Publishing; Specialist Bibliographies, Checklists, and Indexes; and The Contemporary Scene. It concludes with an author index to the entries, and an index of authors mentioned in the annotations.

This bibliography is continued by Marshall Tymn's annotated "Checklist of American Critical Works in Science Fiction: 1972–1973," published in the December 1975 issue of *Extrapolation* and, for publications after 1973, in the annual bibliography in *Extrapolation* (W–113).

W–113   **"The Year's Scholarship in Science Fiction and Fantasy [1972–]."** *Extrapolation: A Journal of Science Fiction and Fantasy,* vol. 17–. Kent, Ohio: Kent State University Press, 1975–.   PN3448.S45 E92

This annual bibliography lists books, arts, dissertations, and educational films, primarily published in the United States. Annotated entries are disposed into four categories: General; Reference and Bibliography; Teaching and Visual Aids; and Individual Authors.

The annual bibliographies for 1973–1975, along with Tymn's checklist of 1972–1973 publications (see W–112), have been cumulated in the *Year's Scholarship in Science Fiction and Fantasy, 1972–1975,* by Marshall B. Tymn and Roger C. Schlobin (Kent, Ohio: Kent State University Press, 1979) [Z5917.S36 T95]. All American scholarship, selected British scholarship, books, monographs, articles, doctoral dissertations, and published theses are included, with brief summary annotations. A name and a title index conclude the volume, keyed to the overelaborate "access code" used in lieu of serial numeration.

Tymn and Schlobin also cumulated the *Year's Scholarship in Science Fiction and Fantasy, 1976–1979* (Kent, Ohio: Kent State University Press, 1982) [Z5917.S36 T96 1979]. The bibliographies for 1980–1982 were dropped by *Extrapolation,* but published separately as the *Year's Scholarship in Science Fiction, Fantasy, and Horror Literature* 1980 [–1982], ed. Marshall B. Tymn (Kent, Ohio: Kent State University Press, 1983–1984) [Z5633.S34 Y42 1983]. Bibliographies have been published for *Extrapolation* for 1983 and subsequent years, without annotation from 1984 on.

W–117   **Sargent, Lyman Tower.** *British and American Utopian Literature 1516–1985: An Annotated, Chronological Bibliography.* New York: Garland, 1988.   Z2014.U84 S27

This chronologically arranged bibliography is an expanded and augmented version of Sargent's *British and American Utopian Literature, 1516–1975: An Annotated Bibliography* (Boston: G. K. Hall, 1979) [Z2014.V84 S27]. It includes works from More's *Utopia* to 1985, and is prefaced with a careful essay defining the genre. More than 4,000 works of utopian literature are included, more than half of which were published in the twentieth century, and most of which are written by Americans. Entries with complete publication data are briefly annotated and give the location of copies. The chronological list of primary works is followed by an extensive bibliography of secondary works on utopian literature, and an author and title index to the primary list.

Sargent's work may be supplemented for European fiction by Glenn Negley's *Utopian Literature: A Bibliography, With a Supplementary Listing of Works Influential in Utopian Thought* (Lawrence: Regent's Press of Kansas, 1977) [Z7164.U8 M43]. It may be complemented by reference to the catalog of the *Utopia Collection of the Duke University Library* compiled by Glenn Negley (Durham, N.C.: Duke University Press, 1965) [Z7164.U8 D8], which gives both an author list and a chronology.

W–118 **Clarke, Ignatius F.** *Tale of the Future from the Beginning to the Present Day: A Checklist of Those Satires, Ideal States, Imaginary Wars and Invasions, Political Warnings and Forecasts, Interplanetary Voyages and Scientific Romances—All Located in an Imaginary Future Period—That Have Been Published in the United Kingdom between 1644 and 1970.* 2d ed. London: Library Association, 1972.   Z5917.S36 C56

Originally published in 1961 and including some 1,200 titles, the second edition contains a total of 2,300 chronologically arranged items, giving bibliographical information and a not always accurate one-sentence summary comment. Translations from foreign languages are included.

W–119 **Some Frequently Recommended Works on Fantasy, Utopian Fiction, and Science Fiction.**

Aldiss, Brian W. *Billion Year Spree: The History of Science Fiction.* London: Weidenfeld and Nicolson, 1973.
PR830.S35 A38

Amis, Kingsley. *New Maps of Hell: A Survey of Science Fiction.* New York: Harcourt, Brace, 1960.
PR830.S35 A4

Bailey, Joseph O. *Pilgrims through Space and Time: Trends and Patterns in Scientific and Utopian Fiction.* New York: Argus, 1947. Extensive bibliography.
PN3448.S45 B27

Berneri, Marie L. *Journey through Utopia.* London: Routledge, 1950.   HX806.B4

Bretnor, Reginald, ed. *Modern Science Fiction: Its Meaning and Its Future.* 2d ed. Chicago: Advent Publishers, 1979.   PN3448.S45 B65 1979

Carter, Lin. *Imaginary Worlds: The Art of Fantasy.* New York: Ballantine, 1973.

Clareson, Thomas D., ed. *Many Futures, Many Worlds: Theme and Form in Science Fiction.* Kent, Ohio: Kent State University Press, 1977.   PN3448.S45 M3

———, ed. *SF: The Other Side of Realism: Essays on Modern Fantasy and Science Fiction.* Bowling Green, Ohio: Bowling Green University Popular Press, 1971.
PN3448.S45 C5

Clarke, I. F. *Voices Prophesying War, 1773–1984.* London: Oxford University Press, 1966.   D445.C6

Contento, William. *Index to Science Fiction Anthologies and Collections.* 2 vols. Boston: G. K. Hall, 1978–1984.   Z1231.F4 C65

Cottrill, Tim, et al. *Science Fiction and Fantasy Series and Sequels: A Bibliography.* Vol. 1: Books. New York: Garland, 1986.   Z5917.S36 C67 1986

Davenport, Basil, et al. *Science Fiction Novel: Imagination and Social Criticism.* Chicago: Advent Publishers, 1959.   PN3448.S45 S33

Elliott, Robert C. *Shape of Utopia: Studies in a Literary Genre.* Chicago: University of Chicago Press, 1970.
PN56.U8 E5

Gerber, Richard. *Utopian Fantasy: A Study of English Utopian Fiction since the End of the Nineteenth Century.* 2d ed. New York: McGraw-Hill, 1973. Bibliography.   PR888.U7 G4 1973

Gove, Philip B. *Imaginary Voyage in Prose Fiction: A History of Its Criticism and a Guide for Its Study, with an Annotated List of 215 Imaginary Voyages from 1700 to 1800.* New York: Columbia University Press, 1941. Detailed bibliography with full annotations.
PN3432.G6

Gunn, James. *Alternate Worlds: The Illustrated History of Science Fiction.* Englewood Cliffs, N.J.: Prentice-Hall, 1975.   PN3448.S45 G8

Hillegas, Mark R. *Future as Nightmare: H. G. Wells and the Anti-Utopians.* New York: Oxford University Press, 1967.   PR5777.H5

Irwin, W. R. *Game of the Impossible: A Rhetoric of Fantasy.* Urbana: University of Illinois Press, 1976.
PR830.F317

Ketterer, David. *New Worlds for Old: The Apocalyptic Imagination, Science Fiction, and American Literature.* Bloomington: Indiana University Press, 1974.
PS374.S35 K4

LeGuin, Ursula K. *Language of the Night: Essays on Fantasy and Science Fiction.* New York: Putnam, 1979.
PN3435.L4

Locke, George A. *Voyages in Space: A Bibliography of Interplanetary Fiction, 1801–1914.* London: Ferrett Fantasy, 1975.   Z5917.S36 L63 1975

Lovecraft, H. P. *Supernatural Horror in Literature.* New York: Ben Abramson, 1945.   PN3435.L64

Manguel, Alberto, and Gianni Guadalupi. *Dictionary of Imaginary Places.* London: Macmillan, 1980.
GR650.M36 1980

Manlove, C. N. *Modern Fantasy: Five Studies.* Cambridge: Cambridge University Press, 1975. PR830.F3 M3

Nicholson, Marjorie Hope. *Voyages to the Moon.* New York: Macmillan, 1948.   PN56.V6 N5

Parrinder, Patrick. *Science Fiction: Its Criticism and Teaching.* London: Methuen, 1980. PR830.S35 P3 1980

Philmus, Robert M. *Into the Unknown: The Evolution of Science Fiction from Francis Goodwin to H. G. Wells.* Berkeley, Los Angeles, London: University of California Press, 1970.   PR830.S35 P5

Post, J. B. *Atlas of Fantasy.* Rev. ed. New York: Ballantine, 1979.   G3122.P6 1979

Rabkin, Eric S. *Fantastic in Literature.* Princeton, N.J.: Princeton University Press, 1975.   PN56.F34 R3

———, et al., eds. *End of the World.* Carbondale: Southern Illinois University Press, 1983.
PN3433.6.E6 1983

Rose, Mark, ed. *Science Fiction: A Collection of Critical Essays.* Englewood Cliffs, N.J.: Prentice-Hall, 1976.
PN3448.S45 S27

Scholes, Robert. *Structural Fabulation: An Essay on the Fiction of the Future.* Notre Dame, Ind.: University of Notre Dame Press, 1975.   PR830.S35 S3

Scholes, Robert, and Eric S. Rabkin, eds. *Science Fiction: History, Science, Vision.* New York: Oxford University Press, 1977.   PN3448.S45 S26

Slusser, George E., et al., eds. *Coordinates: Placing Science Fiction and Fantasy.* Carbondale: Southern Illinois University Press, 1983.   PN3433.2.C66 1983

Suvin, Darko. *Metamorphoses of Science Fiction: On the Poetics and History of a Literary Genre.* New Haven: Yale University Press, 1979.   PN3448.S45 S897

Todorov, Tzvetan. *Fantastic: A Structural Approach to a Literary Genre.* Translation by Richard Howard of *Introduction à la littérature fantastique* (Paris: Editions du Seuil, 1976). Cleveland, Ohio: Press of Case Western Reserve University, 1973.   PN3435.T613

Walsh, Chad. *From Utopia to Nightmare.* New York: Harper and Row, 1962.   HX806.W2

Wolfe, Gary K.   *Critical Terms for Science Fiction and Fantasy: A Glossary and Guide to Scholarship.* New York: Greenwood Press, 1986.   PN3435.W64 1986

————.   *Known and the Unknown: The Iconography of Science Fiction.* Kent, Ohio: Kent State University Press, 1979.   PS374.S35 W6

XII. NONFICTIONAL PROSE

Bibliographies of nonfictional prose limited to the prose of one period will generally be found in the Prose and Criticism subsection of that period (i.e., N.VI, O.V, P.V, Q.VII, R.VII). Similarly, bibliographies of American nonfictional prose will be found in section S.IX.

W–120   **Some Frequently Recommended Works on the Relation between Fiction and Nonfictional Prose.**

Berger, Morroe.   *Real and Imagined Worlds: The Novel and Social Science.* Cambridge: Harvard University Press, 1977.   PN3344.B4

Braudy, Leo.   *Narrative Form in History and Fiction: Hume, Fielding, and Gibbon.* Princeton, N.J.: Princeton University Press, 1970.   D13.B684

Bremner, Robert H., ed.   *Essays on History and Literature.* Columbus: Ohio State University Press, 1966.   D13.B69

Canary, Robert H., and Henry Kozicki, eds.   *Writing of History: Literary Form and Historical Understanding.* Madison: University of Wisconsin Press, 1978.   D13.2.W74

Davis, Lennard J.   *Factual Fictions: The Origins of the English Novel.* New York: Columbia University Press, 1983.   PR851.D3 1983

Fletcher, Angus, ed.   *Literature of Fact: Selected Papers from the English Institute [1974 and 1975].* New York: Columbia University Press, 1976.   PN50.E5 1976

Hellman, John.   *Fables of Fact: The New Journalism as New Fiction.* Urbana: University of Illinois Press, 1981.   PR369.H44

Hollowell, John.   *Fact and Fiction: The New Journalism and the Nonfiction Novel.* Chapel Hill: University of North Carolina Press, 1977.   PS374.N6 H6 1977

Neff, Emery.   *Poetry of History: The Contribution of Literature and Literary Scholarship to the Writing of History since Voltaire.* New York: Columbia University Press, 1947.   D13.N35 1979

Nelson, William K.   *Fact or Fiction: The Dilemma of the Renaissance Storyteller.* Cambridge: Harvard University Press, 1973.   PN3329.N4

Rader, Ralph.   "Literary Form in Factual Narrative: The Example of Boswell's Johnson." In *Essays in Eighteenth-Century Biography,* edited by Philip B. Daghlian, pp. 3–42. Bloomington: Indiana University Press, 1968.   CT.21.E8

Said, Edward W., ed.   *Factual Fictions: Studies in the Origin of the English Novel: Literature and Society. Selected Papers from the English Institute, 1978.* Baltimore: Johns Hopkins University Press, 1980.   PR99.E67 1980

Schulze, Leonard, and Walter Werzels, eds.   *Literature and History.* Lanham, Md.: University Press of America, 1983.   PN50.L57

Siebenschuh, William R.   *Fictional Techniques and Factual Works.* Athens: University of Georgia Press, 1983.   PR751.S5 1983

Stephens, Lester D., ed.   *Historiography: A Bibliography.* Metuchen, N.J.: Scarecrow, 1975. 2,293 briefly annotated entries.   Z6208.H5 S73

Weber, Ronald.   *Literature of Fact: Literary Nonfiction in American Writing.* Athens: Ohio University Press, 1980.   PS369.W4

White, Hayden.   *Content of the Form: Narrative Discourse and Historical Representation.* Baltimore: Johns Hopkins University Press, 1987.   D13.W564 1987

————.   *Metahistory: The Historical Imagination in Nineteenth-Century Europe.* Baltimore: Johns Hopkins University Press, 1973.   D13.W565

————.   *Tropics of Discourse: Essays in Cultural Criticism.* Baltimore: Johns Hopkins University Press, 1978.   P13.W566

Winterowd, W. Ross.   *Rhetoric of the "Other" Literature.* Carbondale: Southern Illinois University Press, 1990.   PS366.R44 W56 1990

Zavarzadeh, Masud.   *Mythopoeic Reality: The Postwar American Nonfiction Novel.* Urbana: University of Illinois Press, 1976.   PS374.N6Z3

W–126   *Prose Studies* [former title: *Prose Studies, 1800–1900,* vols. 1–3]. Vol. 1–. London: Frank Cass, 1977–.   PR750.P76

This triannual journal contains articles on all aspects of nonfictional English prose, originally of the nineteenth century (which is still the emphasis) but now of all periods. It also carries a serial bibliography on "Nineteenth-Century Non-Fictional Prose: A Bibliography of Work," listing books and articles on English and American writers and on literary aspects of nonfictional prose.

W–127   **Some Frequently Recommended Works on Prose Stylistics, Including the Study of Prose Rhythm.** (See also section X.X, Style and Stylistics.)

Baum, Paul Franklin.   *Other Harmony of Prose: An Essay in English Prose Rhythm.* Durham, N.C.: Duke University Press, 1952.   PE1559.B3

Bennett, James R., ed.   *Prose Style: A Historical Approach through Studies.* San Francisco: Chandler Publishing Co., 1972. Bibliography.   PE1421.B38 1972

Brown, Huntington.   *Prose Styles: Five Primary Types.* Minneapolis: University of Minnesota Press, 1966.   PN203.B73

Burton, S. H.   *Criticism of Prose.* London: Longman, 1973.   PN3355.B8

Clark, A. C.   *Prose-Rhythm in English.* Oxford: Oxford University Press, 1913.   PE1561.C5

Classé, André.   *Rhythm of English Prose.* Oxford: Oxford University Press, 1939.   PE1561.C54

Croll, Morris W.   *Style, Rhetoric and Rhythm: Essays by Morris W. Croll.* Edited by J. Max Patrick et al. Princeton, N.J.: Princeton University Press, 1965.   PN203.C76

Dobrée, Bonamy. *Modern Prose Style*. 2d. ed. Oxford: Clarendon Press, 1964. PE1403.D6 1964

Miles, Josephine. *Style and Proportion: The Language of Prose and Poetry*. Boston: Little, Brown, 1967. PE1421.M5

Patterson, W. M. *Rhythm of Prose: An Experimental Investigation of Individual Differences in the Sense of Rhythm*. New York: Columbia University Press, 1916. PE1561.P3

Read, Herbert. *English Prose Style*. New rev. ed. London: Bell, 1952. PE1421.R35 1952

Saintsbury, George. *History of English Prose Rhythm*. London: Macmillan, 1922. PE1561.S3 1922

Scott, John H. *Rhythmic Prose*. Iowa City: University of Iowa Press, 1925. PE1561.S35

Tempest, N. R. *Rhythm of English Prose*. Cambridge: Cambridge University Press, 1939. PE1561.T4

W–128 Some Frequently Recommended Works on Reading English Prose.

Boulton, Marjorie. *Anatomy of Prose*. London: Routledge and Kegan Paul, 1954. PN3355.B63

Cluett, Robert. *Prose Style and Critical Reading*. New York: Teachers College Press, 1976. PE1421.C57

Graves, Robert, and Alan Hodge. *Reader over Your Shoulder: A Handbook for Writers of English Prose*. London: J. Cape, 1947. PR751.G7

Lanham, Richard. *Analyzing Prose*. New York: Scribner's, 1983. PE1421.L295 1983

Scholes, Robert, and Carl H. Klaus. *Elements of Writing*. New York: Oxford University Press, 1972. LB1631.S265

W–129 Some Frequently Recommended Works on the History of English Prose.

General

Francis, J. H. *From Caxton to Carlyle: A Study of the Development of Language, Composition and Style in English Prose*. Cambridge: Cambridge University Press, 1957. PR1285.F68

Gordon, Ian A. *Movement of English Prose*. London: Longman, 1966. PR751.G6

Sutherland, James. *On English Prose*. Toronto: University of Toronto Press, 1957. PR753.S8

Thomson, James A. K. *Classical Influences on English Prose*. London: Allen and Unwin, 1956. PR127.T55

Medieval

Chambers, R. W. *On the Continuity of English Prose from Alfred to More and His School*. Oxford: Oxford University Press, 1932. PR767.C5

Workman, Samuel K. *Fifteenth Century Translation as an Influence on English Prose*. Princeton, N.J.: Princeton University Press, 1940. PR297.W6 1940

Renaissance

Crane, William G. *Wit and Rhetoric in the Renaissance: The Formal Basis of Elizabethan Prose Style*. New York: Columbia University Press, 1937. PR428.W5 C7 1937

Krapp, George P. *Rise of English Literary Prose*. Oxford: Oxford University Press, 1915. PR767.K7

Seventeenth Century

Fish, Stanley, ed. *Seventeenth-Century Prose: Modern Essays in Criticism*. New York: Oxford University Press, 1971. PR769.F5

Hamilton, K. G. *Two Harmonies: Poetry and Prose in the Seventeenth Century*. Oxford: Clarendon Press, 1963. PR541.H3

Webber, Joan. *Eloquent "I": Style and Self in Seventeenth-Century Prose*. Madison: University of Wisconsin Press, 1968. PR769.W4

Williamson, George. *Senecan Amble: A Study in Prose Form from Bacon to Collier*. Chicago: University of Chicago Press, 1951. PR769.W5

Wilson, Frank P. *Seventeenth Century Prose: Five Lectures*. Berkeley and Los Angeles: University of California Press, 1960. PR769.W55

Eighteenth Century

Adolph, Robert. *Rise of Modern Prose Style*. Cambridge: MIT Press, 1968. PR769.A3

Lannering, Jan. *Studies in the Prose Style of Joseph Addison*. Uppsala: Lundeqvist; Cambridge: Harvard University Press, 1951. PR3308.S8 L3

Tucker, Susie I. *Protean Shape: A Study in Eighteenth-Century Vocabulary and Usage*. London: Athlone Press, 1967. PE1083.T8

Wimsatt, W. K. *Prose Style of Samuel Johnson*. New Haven: Yale University Press, 1941. PR3538.W5

Nineteenth Century

Allott, Kenneth. *Victorian Prose, 1830–1880*. Harmondsworth: Penguin, 1956.

Brownell, William C. *American Prose Masters*. New York: Scribner's, 1909. PS645.P7

Levine, George L., and William Madden, eds. *Art of Victorian Prose*. New York: Oxford University Press, 1968. PR783.L4

Wright, Raymond, ed. *Prose of the Romantic Period*. Harmondsworth: Penguin, 1956.

Modern

Gibson, Walker. *Tough, Sweet and Stuffy: An Essay on Modern Prose Styles*. Bloomington: Indiana University Press, 1966. PE1427.G5

Joos, Martin. *Five Clocks*. New York: Harcourt, Brace and World, 1967. PE1421.J65 1967

Lodge, David. *Modes of Modern Writing*. Ithaca, N.Y.: Cornell University Press, 1977. PN203.L58

XIII. THE SERMON, THE CHARACTER, AND THE ESSAY

W–130 Some Frequently Recommended Works on the English and American Sermon.

Blench, J. W. *Preaching in England in the Late Fifteenth and Sixteenth Centuries: A Study of English Sermons, 1450–c1600*. Oxford, 1964. BV4208.G7 B55

Charland, Thomas M. *Artes Praedicandi: Contribution à l'histoire de la rhétorique au moyen âge.* Paris: J. Vrin, 1936.   BV4207.C5

English Sermon: An Anthology. 3 vols. Cheadle: Carcanet Press, 1976.
    Vol. 1. 1550–1650,
    Vol. 2. 1650–1750,
    Vol. 3. 1750–1850.   BX5133.A1 E53

Herr, A. F. *Elizabethan Sermon: A Survey and a Bibliography.* Philadelphia, 1940.   BV4208.G7 H4 1940

Maclure, Millar. *Paul's Cross Sermons, 1534–1642.* Toronto: University of Toronto Press, 1958.
                                                        BV4208.E5 M2

Mitchell, William F. *English Pulpit Oratory from Andrewes to Tillotson: A Study of Its Literary Aspects.* London, 1932. Bibliography.   BV4208.G7 M5

Owst, Gerald R. *Literature and Pulpit in Medieval England: A Neglected Chapter in the History of English Letters of the English People.* Rev. ed. Oxford: Clarendon Press, 1961.   PR275.O8 1961

——. *Preaching in Medieval England.* Cambridge: Cambridge University Press, 1926.   BV4208.G7 O8

Pfander, H. G. *Popular Sermon of the Medieval Friar in England.* New York, 1937.   BV4208.G7 P5 1937

Pollard, Arthur. *English Sermons.* London: Longmans, Green, 1963.   BV4288.G7 P6

Richardson, Caroline F. *English Preachers and Preaching, 1640–1670.* New York: Macmillan, 1928.
                                                        BX5175.R5 1928

Smyth, C. *Art of Preaching: A Practical Survey of Preaching in the Church of England, 747–1939.* London: SPCK, 1940.   BV4208.G7 S55

W–132 Some Frequently Recommended Works on the Character in English. (See also work in the history of biography, W–149.)

Bibliographical

Greenough, Chester Noyes. *Bibliography of the Theophrastan Character in English, with Several Portrait Characters.* Prepared for publication by J. Milton French. Cambridge: Harvard University Press, 1947.
                                                        Z2014. C5 G8

Murphy, Gwendolen. *Bibliography of English Character-Books, 1608–1700.* London: Oxford University Press, 1925.   Z2014.C5 M9

General

Boyce, Benjamin. *Character-Sketches in Pope's Poems.* Durham, N.C.: Duke University Press, 1962.
                                                        PR3634.B65 1962

——. *Polemic Character 1640–1661: A Chapter in English Literary History.* Lincoln: University of Nebraska Press, 1955.   PR149.C37 B58

——. *Theophrastan Character in England to 1642.* Cambridge: Harvard University Press, 1947.
                                                        PR149.9.C37 B6

Smith, Nichol D. *Characters from the Histories and Memoirs of the Seventeenth Century.* Oxford: Clarendon Press, 1918.   DA377.S7

Smeed, J. W. *Theophrastan "Character": The History of a Literary Genre.* Oxford: Clarendon Press, 1985.
                                                        PN56.4.S64 1985

W–134 Some Frequently Recommended Works on the English and American Essay.

Bryan, William F., and Ronald S. Crane, eds. *English Familiar Essay.* Boston: Ginn and Co., 1916.
                                                        PR1363.B7

Christadler, Martin. *Geshichte des amerikanischen Essays 1720–1820.* Heidelberg, 1967.

Conway, Adaline M. *Essay in American Literature.* New York: The Faculty of the Graduate School, New York University, 1914.   PS420.C6

Davis, William H. *English Essayists: A Reader's Handbook.* Boston: R. G. Badger, 1916.   PR921.D16

Dobrée, Bonamy. *English Essayists.* London: Collins, 1946.
                                                        PR922.D6

Eleanore, Sister Mary. *Literary Essay in English.* Boston: Ginn, 1923.   PR921.E5

Good, Graham. *Observing Self: Rediscovering the Essay.* London: Routledge, 1988.   PR921.G66 1988

Law, Marie H. *English Familiar Essay in the Early Nineteenth Century: The Elements, Old and New, Which Went into Its Making, As Exemplified in the Writings of Hunt, Hazlitt, and Lamb.* Philadelphia, 1934.
                                                        PR926.L3 1932

MacDonald, Wilbert L. *Beginnings of the English Essay.* Toronto: University of Toronto, 1914.   PR921.M3

Marr, George S. *Periodical Essays of the Eighteenth Century with Illustrative Extracts from the Rarer Periodicals.* New York, 1923.   PR925.M3

Scholes, Robert, and Carl H. Klaus. *Elements of the Essay.* New York: Oxford University Press, 1969.
                                                        PN4500.S25

Thompson, Elbert N. S. *Seventeenth-Century English Essay.* Iowa City: University of Iowa Press, 1926. PR924.T5

——. *Style of the English Essay.* Iowa City: University of Iowa Press, 1925.

Walker, Hugh. *English Essay and Essayists.* London: Dent, 1915.   PR921.W25

Watson, Melvin R. *Magazine Serials and the Essay Tradition, 1746–1820.* Baton Rouge: Louisiana State University Press, 1956.   PR925.W28

Weber, Horst, ed. *Englische Essay: Analysen.* Darmstadt: Wissenschaftliche Buchgesellschaft, 1975. Bibliography.   PR921.E54

Wylie, Laura J. *English Essay.* Boston: Houghton Mifflin, 1916.   PR921.W9

XIV. TRAVEL LITERATURE

See also topographical ancillae to historical study cited in sections F.X, F.XI, F.XII, F.XIII, and F.XIV.

W–135 Cox, Edward Godfrey. *Reference Guide to the Literature of Travel, Including Voyages, Geographical Descriptions, Adventures, Shipwrecks and Expeditions.* 3 vols. Seattle: University of Washington Press, 1935–1949.
                                                        Z6011.C87

This work includes in a classified and chronological arrangement all travel books published in Great Britain, all English translations of foreign works, and all Continental translations of English works from the earliest days to 1800. Classification is geographical by destination, with volume 1 treating travels to the Old World (1935); volume 2, travels to the New World (1938); and volume 3, travels in England (1949). Entries generally include extended descriptive annotation, with additional information, including reference to critical comments, names of persons associated with the travel book, and all sorts of further biographical and bibliographical notation. Volumes 2 and 3 both conclude with an annotated list of general reference works and bibliographies useful to the student of travel literature. Volume 2 contains an index to personal names in both volumes 1 and 2; volume 3 has its own index of personal names.

W–139 **Some Frequently Recommended Works on English and American Travel Literature.**

Adams, Percy G. *Travel Literature and the Evolution of the Novel.* Lexington: University of Kentucky Press, 1983. PN3432.A32

————. *Travelers and Travel Liars, 1660–1800.* Berkeley and Los Angeles: University of California Press, 1962. G560.A3

————, ed. *Travel Literature Through the Ages: An Anthology.* New York: Garland, 1988. G463.T782 1988

Arthos, John. *Milton and the Italian Cities.* New York: Barnes and Noble, 1968. PR3592.I8 A7 1968

Cawley, Robert Ralston. *Unpathed Waters: Studies in the Influence of the Voyagers on Elizabethan Literature.* Princeton, N.J.: Princeton University Press, 1940. PR421.C3

Conrad, Peter. *Imagining America.* London: Oxford University Press, 1980. PR129.U5 C6 1980

Frantz, Ray W. *English Traveller and the Movement of Ideas, 1660–1732.* Lincoln: University of Nebraska Press, 1934. G490.F7

Fussell, Paul. *Abroad: British Literary Traveling between the Wars.* London: Oxford University Press, 1980. PR479.T72 F8 1980

Hibbert, Christopher. *Grand Tour.* New York: Putnam, 1969. D907.H56 1969

Howard, Clare M. *English Travellers of the Renaissance.* London: John Lane, 1914. DA185.H72 1914

Jusserand, Jean J. *English Wayfaring Life in the Middle Ages (XIVth Century).* Translation by Lucy Toulmin Smith of *Les Anglais au moyen âge,* 4th ed. London: Unwin, 1892. DA185.J9 1892

Keith, W. J. *Rural Tradition: A Study of the Non-Fiction Prose Writers of the English Countryside.* Toronto: University of Toronto Press, 1974. PR756.C6 K4

Morrison, Helen. *Golden Age of Travel: Literary Impressions of the Grand Tour.* New York: Twayne, 1951. D907.M65

Newton, Arthur Percival, ed. *Travel and Travellers in the Middle Ages.* London: Kegan Paul, 1929. G89.N4

Parkes, Joan. *Travel in England in the Seventeenth Century.* London: Oxford University Press, 1925. DA380.P3

Parks, George B. *English Traveler to Italy.* Vol. 1, *Middle Ages (to 1525).* Stanford: Stanford University Press, 1954.

Penrose, Boies. *Travel and Discovery in the Renaissance, 1420–1620.* Cambridge: Harvard University Press, 1955. G95.P45 1955

Sells, Arthur L. *Paradise of Travelers: The Italian Influence on Englishmen of the Seventeenth Century.* Bloomington: Indiana University Press, 1964. DA47.9.I8 S4

Spencer, T. J. B. *Fair Greece, Sad Relic: Literary Philhellenism from Shakespeare to Byron.* London: Weidenfeld and Nicolson, 1954. PR129.G856

Stoye, John W. *English Travelers Abroad, 1604–1667.* London: Cape, 1952. D915.S86

Trease, G. *Grand Tour.* New York: Holt, Rinehart and Winston, 1967. G156.T7

XV. LIFE WRITING

See section G, Biography, *passim*, but especially G–32, G–33, G–46, and G–47.

W–141 **"Current Bibliography on Life-Writing [1977–78–]."** *Biography: An Interdisciplinary Quarterly,* vol. 1–. Honolulu: University of Hawaii Press, 1978–. CT100.B54

This annual listing is alphabetical by author and identifies British and American books and articles on biography, autobiography, the literature of fact, historiography, oral history, and a variety of other topics related to life writing. Most entries have a brief descriptive annotation.

W–145 **Winslow, Donald J. *Life-Writing: A Glossary of Terms in Biography, Autobiography, and Related Forms.* Hono-**lulu: University Press of Hawaii, 1980. CT21.W56

This glossary, originally published in a series of articles in *Biography,* emphasizes British and American terms. More than 200 entries make reference both to primary works and to scholarship. There are numerous cross-references but no index. The volume concludes with a selected bibliography of general works concerned with life writing.

W–149 **Some Frequently Recommended Works on the History and Theory of Biography, Including Autobiography, Diaries, Journals, and Letters.** (See also bibliographies at G–32, G–33, G–46, and G–47.)

Aaron, Daniel, ed. *Studies in Biography.* Cambridge: Harvard University Press, 1978. CT21.S85

Altick, Richard D. *Lives and Letters: A History of Literary Biography in England and America.* New York: Knopf, 1965. CT31.A4

Altman, Janet Gurkin. *Epistolarity: Approaches to a Form.* Columbus: Ohio State University Press, 1982. PN3448.E6 A4 1982

Benstock, Shari, ed. *Private Self: Theory and Practice of Women's Autobiographical Writings.* Chapel Hill: University of North Carolina Press, 1988. PR756.A9 P75 1988

Blasing, Motlu Konuk. *Art of Life: Studies in American Autobiographical Literature.* Austin: University of Texas Press, 1977. PS169.A95 B5

Blodgett, Harriet. *Centuries of Female Days: Englishwomen's Private Diaries.* New Brunswick, N.J.: Rutgers University Press, 1988. PR908.B56 1988

Bowen, Catherine D. *Biography: The Craft and the Calling.* Boston: Little, Brown, 1969. CT21.B564

Browning, John, ed. *Biography in the Eighteenth Century.* New York: Garland, 1980. CT21.B47

Bruss, Elizabeth. *Autobiographical Acts: The Changing Situation of a Literary Genre.* Baltimore: Johns Hopkins University Press, 1976.   PR756.A9 B7

Clifford, James L. *Biography as an Art: Selected Criticism, 1560–1960.* New York: Oxford University Press, 1962.   CT21.C55

———. *From Puzzles to Portraits: Problems of a Literary Biographer.* Chapel Hill: University of North Carolina Press, 1970.   CT21.C553

Cockshut, A. O. J. *Truth to Life: The Art of Biography in the Nineteenth Century.* London: Colliers, 1974.   CT21.C58

Cooley, Thomas. *Educated Lives: The Rise of Modern Autobiography in America.* Columbus: Ohio State University Press, 1976.   PS169.A95 C6

Couser, G. Thomas. *American Autobiography: The Prophetic Mode.* Amherst: University of Massachusetts Press, 1979.   CT34.U6 C68

Culley, Margo, ed. *Day at a Time: The Diary Literature of American Women from 1764 to the Present.* New York: Feminist Press of the City University of New York, 1985.   CT3260.D395 1985

Daghlian, Philip B., ed. *Essays in Eighteenth-Century Biography.* Bloomingdale: Indiana University Press, 1968.   CT21.E8

Delany, Paul. *British Autobiography in the Seventeenth Century.* London: Routledge and Kegan Paul, 1969. Bibliography.   CT77.D4

Drew, Elizabeth. *Literature of Gossip: Nine English Letter Writers.* New York: Norton, 1964.   PR911.D7

Edel, Leon. *Literary Biography.* Toronto: University of Toronto Press, 1957.   CT21.E3

———. *Writing Lives: Principia Biographica.* New York: Norton, 1984.   CT21.E33 1984

Ellmann, Richard. *Golden Codgers: Biographical Speculations.* New York: Oxford University Press, 1973.   CT21.E44

———. *Literary Biography.* London: Oxford University Press, 1971.   CT21.E45

Epstein, William H. *Recognizing Biography.* Philadelphia: University of Pennsylvania Press, 1987.   PR756.B56 E67 1987

Fleishman, Avrom. *Figures of Autobiography.* Berkeley and Los Angeles: University of California Press, 1983.   PR756.A9 F5 1983

Fothergill, Robert A. *Private Chronicles: A Study of English Diaries.* London: Oxford University Press, 1974.   PR908.F6

Franklin, Penelope, ed. *Private Pages: Diaries of American Women, 1830s–1970s.* New York: Ballantine Books, 1986.   CT3260.P75 1986

Garraty, John A. *Nature of Biography.* New York: Knopf, 1957. Extensive bibliography.   CT21.G3

Gittings, Robert. *Nature of Biography.* Seattle: University of Washington Press, 1978.   CT21.G5

Goodfriend, Joyce D. *Published Diaries and Letters of American Women: An Annotated Bibliography.* Boston: G. K. Hall, 1987.   Z5305.U5 G66 1987

Havlice, Patricia Pate. *And So to Bed: A Bibliography of Diaries Published in English.* Metuchen, N. J.: Scarecrow Press, 1987.   Z5301.H38 1987

Hinz, Evelyn, ed. *DATA and ACTA: Aspects of Life-Writing.* Winnipeg: University of Manitoba, 1987.   CT21.D38 1987

Hoffman, William J. *Life Writing: A Guide to Family Journals and Personal Memoirs.* New York: St. Martin's Press, 1982.   CS16.H62 1982

Huff, Cynthia Anne. *British Women's Diaries: A Descriptive Bibliography of Selected Nineteenth-Century Women's Manuscript Diaries.* New York: AMS Press, 1985.   Z7964.G6 H84 1985

Irving, William H. *Providence of Wit in the English Letter Writers.* Durham, N. C.: Duke University Press, 1955.   PR911.I7

Johnson, Edgar. *One Mighty Torrent: The Drama of Biography.* 2d ed. New York: Macmillan, 1955.   CT34.G7 J6

Jones, Charles W. *Saints' Lives and Chronicles in Early England.* Ithaca, N. Y.: Cornell University Press, 1947.   BX4662.J6

Kagle, Steven E. *American Diary Literature, 1620–1799.* Boston: Twayne, 1979.   PS409.K3

———. *Early Nineteenth-Century American Diary Literature.* Boston: Twayne, 1986.   PS409.K33 1986

———. *Late Nineteenth-Century American Diary Literature.* Boston: Twayne, 1988.   PS409.K33 1988

Kendall, Paul M. *Art of Biography.* New York: Norton, 1965.   CT21.K4

Longacre, Mark. *Contemporary Biography.* Philadelphia: University of Pennsylvania Press, 1934.   CT21.L6

———. *English Biography in the Eighteenth Century.* Philadelphia: University of Pennsylvania Press, 1931.   CT34.G7 L6

Mallon, Thomas. *Book of One's Own: People and Their Diaries.* New York: Tickner and Fields, 1984.   PN4390.M34 1984

Matthews, William, and Ralph Rader. *Autobiography, Biography, and the Novel.* Los Angeles: William Andrews Clark Memorial Library, University of California, 1973.   PR403.M33

Maurois, André. *Aspects of Biography.* Cambridge: Cambridge University Press, 1929.   CT21.M3

Meyers, Jeffrey, ed. *Craft of Literary Biography.* New York: Schocken Books, 1985.   CT21.C69 1985

Misch, Georg. *Geschichte der Antobiographie.* 3d ed. 8 vols. Bern, 1949–1969.   CT25.M513

Morris, John N. *Versions of The Self: Studies in English Autobiography from John Bunyan to John Stuart Mill.* New York: Basic Books, 1966.   CT25.M6

Nadel, Ira Bruce. *Biography: Fiction, Fact, and Form.* New York: St. Martin's Press, 1984.   CT21.N3 1984

Nicholson, Harold. *Development of English Biography.* London: Hogarth Press, 1927.   CT21.N5 1927

O'Brien, Kate. *English Diaries and Journals.* London: Collins, 1943.   PR908.O2

Olney, James. *Autobiography: Essays Theoretical and Critical.* Princeton, N.J.: Princeton University Press, 1980.   CT25.A95

———. *Metaphors of Self: The Meaning of Autobiography.* Princeton, N.J.: Princeton University Press, 1972.   CT25.O44

———. *Studies in Autobiography.* New York: Oxford University Press, 1988.   P5366.A88 S84 1988

O'Neill, Edward H. *Biography by Americans, 1658–1936: A Subject Bibliography.* Philadelphia: University of Pennsylvania Press, 1939. Locates copies.   Z5301.O58

———. *History of American Biography, 1800–1935*. Philadelphia: University of Pennsylvania Press, 1935. Bibliography.   CT34.U6 05

Pachter, Marc, ed. *Telling Lives: The Biographer's Art*. Washington, D. C.: New Republic Books, 1979.
                              CT21.T44

Pascal, Roy. *Design and Truth in Autobiography*. Cambridge: Harvard University Press, 1960.   CT25.P37

Ponsonby, Arthur. *English Diaries: A Review of English Diaries from the Sixteenth to the Twentieth Century, with an Introduction on Diary Writing*. London: Methuen, 1923.   PR908.P6

———. *More English Diaries: Further Reviews of Diaries from the Sixteenth to the Nineteenth Century, with an Introduction on Diary Reading*. London: Methuen, 1927.   PR908.P62

———. *Scottish and Irish Diaries*. London: Methuen, 1927.   PR908.P7

Reed, Joseph W. *English Biography in the Early Nineteenth Century, 1801–1838*. New Haven: Yale University Press, 1966.   CT81.R4

Robertson, Jean L. *Art of Letter Writing: An Essay on the Handbooks Published in England during the Sixteenth and Seventeenth Centuries*. Liverpool: Liverpool University Press, 1942.   Z2014.L4 R6

Saintsbury, George. *Letter Book: Selected with an Introduction on the History and Art of Letter Writing*. London: Bell, 1922.   PR1342.S25

Schuster, Max Lincoln. *Treasury of the World's Great Letters from Ancient Days to Our Own Time*. New York: Simon and Schuster, 1940.   PN6131.S35 1940c

Shea, Daniel B., Jr. *Spiritual Autobiography in Early America*. Princeton, N.J.: Princeton University Press, 1968.
                              BR520.S5

Shelston, Alan. *Biography*. London: Methuen, 1977.
                              CT21.S44

Shumaker, Wayne. *English Autobiography: Its Emergence, Materials, and Form*. Berkeley and Los Angeles: University of California Press, 1954.   CT34.G7 S5

Smith, Sidonie. *Poetics of Women's Autobiography: Marginality and the Fictions of Self-Representation*. Bloomington: Indiana University Press, 1987.
                              PR756.A9S65 1987

Smith, Valerie. *Self-Discovery and Authority in Afro-American Narrative*. Cambridge: Harvard University Press, 1987.   PS153.N5 S63 1987

Spacks, Patricia M. *Imagining a Self: Autobiography and Novel in Eighteenth Century England*. Cambridge: Harvard University Press, 1976.   PR858.I3 S6

Spengemann, William C. *Forms of Autobiography: Episodes in the History of a Literary Genre*. New Haven: Yale University Press, 1980.   CT25.S63 1980

Stauffer, Donald A. *Art of Biography in Eighteenth Century England*. 2 vols. Princeton, N.J.: Princeton University Press, 1941. Vol. 2, *Annotated Bibliographical Supplement*.   CT34.G7 S67

———. *English Biography before 1700*. Cambridge: Harvard University Press, 1930. Extensive, partly annotated bibliography.   CT34.G7 S7

Weintraub, Karl J. *Value of the Individual: Self and Circumstance in Autobiography*. Chicago: University of Chicago Press, 1978.   CT25.W37

Whittemore, Reed. *Pure Lives: The Early Biographers*. Baltimore: Johns Hopkins University Press, 1988.
                              CT21.W5 1988

———. *Whole Lives: Shapers of Modern Biography*. Baltimore: Johns Hopkins University Press, 1989.
                              CT21.W52 1989

XVI. HUMOR AND SATIRE

W–150   **Brummack, Jürgen. "Zu Begriff und Theorie der Satire."** *DVLG* 45 (1971), Sonderheft Forschungsreferate, pp. 275–377.   PR4.D4

This bibliographical review is disposed into two parts, both with extensive bibliographical footnotes. Part I, on the history of the concept of satire, is in four sections: satire as an historical genre, natural form, or philosophical genre; early humanist commentary on Roman verse satire; the influence of Aristotle's *Poetics* on the theory of satire; and comic versus tragic satire and satire as the poetry of the satiric impulse. Part II surveys research under eight headings: 1. an introductory survey of work done, with an identification of fundamental problems and issues; 2. works on the question of definition; 3. works on the question of limiting the genre and setting it off from other literary kinds; 4. works on theory; 5. works on form; 6. introductions to satire; 7. works on the typology of satire; and 8. works on modern satire. There is no index.

W–151   **"[1963—] Bibliography: Criticism, Scholarship, Satire."** *Satire Newsletter*. vol. 1–. Oneonta, N.Y.: State University College, 1963–.   PN169.S35

This bibliography, appearing in each semiannual issue, contains citations of books and articles which are arranged in thirteen sections, as follows: Criticism and Theory; Classical Literature; American Literature; French Literature; German Literature; Spanish and Italian Literatures; Scandinavian, Russian, and East European Literatures; Novels; Non-fiction; Art; Recordings; and Miscellaneous. Publication of the bibliographies was suspended in 1966.

Current journals treating satire include the annuals, *Satire Jahrbuch*, vol 1– (Cologne: Satire Verlag, 1978–) [no LC number] and *Studies in Contemporary Satire*, vol. 1– (Sharon, Pa.: Pennsylvania State University, Shenango Valley College, 1974–) [PN6149.S2578].

W–153   **Kirk, Eugene P. *Menippean Satire: An Annotated Catalogue of Texts and Criticism*.** New York: Garland, 1980.
                              Z6514.S38 K57

This guide is meant to include all primary works up to 1660 and all relevant secondary works through the 1970s. A total of 969 extensively annotated entries are disposed into thirteen sections, as follows: 1. Ancient Parodic Menippean Satire; 2. Educational or Didascalic Menippean Satire, from Antiquity up to the Late Middle Ages; 3. The Paradoxical Encomium in Antiquity; 4. Menippean Satire at Byzantium; 5. Some Major Renaissance Editions of the Significant Classical Menippean Satires; 6. Menippean Satire during the Early 16th Century; 7. Dornavius' *Amphitheatre* and Other Renaissance Anthologies of *Satyrae* and Paradoxical Encomia; 8. Menippean Satire and the Jesuits; 9. Menippean Satire and the New Science; 10. Other Renaissance *Menippeae*, Including Banquets; 11. Menippean Satire in the English Renaissance; 12. Menippean Satire during the Puritan Interlude; 13. Criticism of Menippean Satire. An index of authors, titles, and selected subjects concludes the volume.

W–157 **Some Frequently Recommended Works on English and American Humor.** (See also U–69, "Comedy.")

American Humor: An Interdisciplinary Newsletter. Vol. 1–. Richmond, Va.: American Humor Studies Association, 1974–. 2/yr. Reviews. Annual Bibliography: "Criticism on American Humor: An Annotated Checklist."   PS438.A53

Ashton, John. *Chap-Books of the Eighteenth Century.* London: Chatto and Windus, 1882.   PR972.A7

Bier, Jesse. *Rise and Fall of American Humor.* New York: Holt, Rinehart and Winston, 1968.   PS430.B47

Blair, Walter. *Horse Sense in American Humor from Benjamin Franklin to Ogden Nash.* Chicago: University of Chicago Press, 1942.   PS430.B5

Blair, Walter, and Hamlin Hill. *America's Humor, from Poor Richard to Doonesbury.* New York: Oxford University Press, 1978.   PS430.B495

Brack, O. M., ed. *American Humor: Essays Presented to John C. Gerber.* Scottsdale, Ariz.: Arete Publications, 1977.   PS430.A43

Cazamian, Louis. *Development of English Humor. Parts I and II.* Durham, N.C.: Duke University Press, 1952.   PR931.C3

Chapman, Anthony, and Hugh C. Foot, eds. *International Conference of Humor and Laughter.* Cardiff, Wales, 1976. Proceedings published with the title, *It's a Funny Thing, Humor.* New York: Pergamon, 1977.   PN6149.P515 1976

Clark, William Bedford, and W. Craig Turner, eds. *Critical Essays on American Humor.* Boston: G. K. Hall, 1984.   PS430.C7 1984

Cohen, Sarah Blacker, ed. *Comic Relief: Humor in Contemporary American Literature.* Urbana: University of Illinois Press, 1978.   PS438.C6 1978

Eastman, Max. *Sense of Humor.* New York, 1921.   PN6147.E3

Esar, Evan. *Humor of Humor: The Art and Techniques of Popular Comedy.* New York: Horizon Press, 1952.   PN6153.E652

Gale, Steven H., ed. *Encyclopedia of American Humorists.* Vol. 1. New York: Garland, 1988. PS430.E53 1988

Goldstein, Jeffrey H., and Paul E. McGhee, eds. *Psychology of Humor: Theoretical Perspectives and Empirical Issues.* New York: Academic Press, 1972.   PN6149.P5 G55

Hauck, Richard Boyd. *Cheerful Nihilism: Confidence and "The Absurd" in American Humorous Fiction.* Bloomington: Indiana University Press, 1971.   PS430.H27

Humor: International Journal of Humor Research. Vol. 1–. Berlin: Mouton de Gruyter, 1988–. 4/yr.   No LC number

Inge, M. Thomas, ed. *Frontier Humorists: Critical Views.* Hamden, Conn.: Archon, 1975.   PS430.F7

Levin, Harry, ed. *Veins of Humor.* Cambridge: Harvard University Press, 1972.   PR932.L4

McGhee, Paul E. *Humor: Its Origin and Development.* San Francisco: W. H. Freeman, 1979.   BF723.H85 M32

————, and Jeffrey H. Goldstein, eds. *Handbook of Humor Research.* 2 vols. New York: Springer-Verlag, 1983.   BF575.L3 H36 1983

Mintz, Lawrence E., ed. *Humor in America: A Research Guide to Genres and Topics.* New York: Greenwood Press, 1988.   PS430.H86 1988

Neuburg, Victor E. *Chapbooks: A Guide to Reference Material on English, Scottish, and American Chapbook Literature of the Eighteenth and Nineteenth Centuries.* 2d ed. London: Woburn Press, 1972.   Z6514.P7 N4 1972

Nicholson, Harold. *English Sense of Humor and Other Essays.* London: Constable, 1956.   PR6027.I4 E5

Pochestov, Georgii Georgievich. *Language and Humor: A Collection of Linguistically Based Jokes, Anecdotes, etc., Topically Arranged, with an Introductory Essay on the Linguistic Foundations of Humor.* Kiev: Vysca skola, 1974.   PN6175.P59

Priestly, John Boynton. *English Humor.* London: Heinemann, 1976.   PR931.P74

Rourke, Constance. *American Humor: A Study of the National Character.* New York: Harcourt, Brace, 1931.   PS430.R6

Rubin, Louis, Jr., ed. *Comic Imagination in American Literature.* New Brunswick, N.J.: Rutgers University Press, 1973.   PS430.R8

Schechter, William. *History of Negro Humor in America.* New York: Fleet Press, 1970.   E185.86.S29

Schmitz, Neil. *Of Huck and Alice: Humorous Writing in American Literature.* Minneapolis: University of Minnesota Press, 1983.   PS430.S35 1983

Schulz, Ernest. *Die englischer Schwankbücher bis 1607.* Berlin, 1912.

Studies in American Humor. Vol. 1–. San Marcos: Southwest Texas State University, 1974–. 3/yr.   PS430.S88

Tave, Stuart M. *Amiable Humorist: A Study in the Comic Theory and Criticism of the Eighteenth and Early Nineteenth Centuries.* Chicago: University of Chicago Press, 1960.   PR935.T3

Wallace, Ronald. *God Be With the Clown: Humor in American Poetry.* Columbia: University of Missouri Press, 1984.   PS309.H85 W3 1984

Wilson, F. P. "The English Jestbooks of the Sixteenth and Early Seventeenth Centuries." *HLQ* 2 (1939): 121–58.

World Humor and Irony Membership Serial Yearbook [WHIMSY]: Proceedings of the [First–] International Humor Conference. Tempe, Ariz.: W.H.I.M., English Department, Arizona State University, 1981–. 1/yr.   No LC number

Yates, Norris W. *American Humorist: Conscience of the Twentieth Century.* Ames: Iowa State University Press, 1964.   PS438.Y3

W–158 **Some Frequently Recommended Works on Irony.**

Booth, Wayne. *Rhetoric of Irony.* Chicago: University of Chicago Press, 1974. Bibliography. PN56.I65 B66

Conrad, Peter. *Shandyism: The Character of Romantic Irony.* Oxford: Blackwell, 1978.   PR3714.T73 C6 1978

Dyson, A. E. *Crazy Fabric: Essays in Irony.* London: Macmillan, 1965.   PR149.I7 D9

Enright, D. J. *Alluring Problem: An Essay on Irony.* Oxford: Oxford University Press, 1986.   PN56.I65 E57 1986

Japp, Uwe. *Theorie der Ironie.* Frankfurt am Main: Klostermann, 1983.   BH301.I7 J34 1983

Kierkegaard, Soren. *Concept of Irony, with Continual Reference to Socrates.* Translation with an introduction and notes by Lee M. Capel. New York: Octagon Books, 1983.   B4373.O4 E52 1983

Knox, Norman D. *Word "Irony" and Its Context, 1500–1755*. Durham, N.C.: Duke University Press, 1961. PE1599.I7 K55

Muecke, Douglas C. *Compass of Irony*. London: Methuen, 1969. PN56.I65 M8

———. *Irony and the Ironic*. 2d ed. London: Methuen, 1982. BH301.I7 M8 1982

Sedgewick, Garnett G. *Of Irony, Especially in Drama*. 2d ed. Toronto: University of Toronto Press, 1948. PN1680.S4 1948

States, Bert O. *Irony and Drama: A Poetics*. Ithaca, N.Y.: Cornell University Press, 1971. PN1680.S7

Strohschneider-Kohrs, Ingrid. *Die romantische Ironie in Theorie und Gestaltung*. Tübingen: Niemeyer, 1960. PT363.I7 S7

Thomson, James A. K. *Irony: An Historical Introduction*. London: G. Allen and Unwin, 1926. PA3014.I7 T5

Turner, Francis McD. *Element of Irony in English Literature: An Essay*. Cambridge: Cambridge University Press, 1926. PR931.T8

W–159 **Some Frequently Recommended Works on the History and Theory of Satire.**

Alden, Raymond M. *Rise of Formal Satire in England under Classical Influence*. Philadelphia: The University, 1899. PR931.A5

Anderson, William S., ed. *Essays on Roman Satire*. Princeton, N.J.: Princeton University Press, 1982. PA6056.A56

Bloom, Edward A., and Lillian D. Bloom. *Satire's Persuasive Voice*. Ithaca, N.Y.: Cornell University Press, 1979. PN6149.S2 B57

Coffey, Michael. *Roman Satire*. New York: Barnes and Noble, 1976. PA6056.C6

Elliott, Robert C. *Power of Satire: Magic, Ritual, Art*. Princeton, N.J.: Princeton University Press, 1960. PN6149.S2 E37

Guilhamet, Leon. *Satire of the Transformation of Genre*. Philadelphia: University of Pennsylvania Press, 1987. PR931.G85 1987

Highet, Gilbert. *Anatomy of Satire*. Princeton, N.J.: Princeton University Press, 1962. PN6149.S2 H5

Hodgart, Matthew J. *Satire*. New York: McGraw-Hill, 1969. PN6149.S2 H6

Hopkins, Kenneth. *Portraits in Satire*. London: Barrie Books, 1958. PR935.H6

Jack, Ian. *Augustan Satire: Intention and Idiom in English Poetry, 1660 to 1750*. Oxford: Clarendon Press, 1952. PR565.L3 J3

Kernan, Alvin B. *Cankered Muse: Satire of the English Renaissance*. New Haven: Yale University Press, 1959. PR933.K4

———. *Plot of Satire*. New Haven: Yale University Press, 1965. PN6147.K4

Leyburn, Ellen. *Satiric Allegory: Mirror of Man*. New Haven: Yale University Press, 1956. PR921.L46

Nichols, John W. *Insinuation: The Tactics of English Satire*. The Hague: Mouton, 1971. PR931.N48 I5

Nokes, David. *Raillery and Rage: A Study of Eighteenth Century Satire*. New York: St. Martin's Press, 1987. PR935.N64 1987

Paulson, Ronald. *Fictions of Satire*. Baltimore: Johns Hopkins University Press, 1967. PN6149.S2 P33

———, ed. *Satire: Modern Essays in Criticism*. Englewood Cliffs, N.J.: Prentice-Hall, 1971. PN6149.S2 P35

Peter, John. *Complaint and Satire in Early English Literature*. Oxford: Clarendon Press, 1956. PR931.P4

Petro, Peter. *Modern Satire: Four Studies*. Berlin: Mouton, 1982. PN6149.S2 P47 1982

Rawson, Claude, ed. *English Satire and the Satiric Tradition*. Oxford: B. Blackwell, 1984. PR932.E54 1984

Rosenheim, Edward W., Jr. *Swift and the Satirist's Art*. Chicago: University of Chicago Press, 1963. PR3727.R6

Sutherland, James. *English Satire*. Cambridge: Cambridge University Press, 1958. PR931.S8

Walker, Hugh. *English Satire and Satirists*. London: Dent, 1925. PR931.W3

Weinbrot, Howard D. *Eighteenth-Century Satire: Essays on Text and Context from Dryden to Peter Pindar*. Cambridge: Cambridge University Press, 1988. PR935.W39 1988

Worcester, David. *Art of Satire*. Cambridge: Harvard University Press, 1940. PN6149.S2 W6

THEORY, RHETORIC, AND COMPOSITION

I. LITERARY CRITICISM AND LITERARY THEORY BEFORE CA. 1950

Works pertinent to the study of literary criticism and literary theory will be found in virtually every section. See especially section I on Language, Linguistics, and Philology; section K on Literary Materials and Contexts; and section L on Comparative and World Literature. For references in textual criticism see also section Y; for works on literary research methodology see section Z.

X–1 Hall, Vernon, comp. *Literary Criticism: Plato through Johnson.* [A Goldentree Bibliography.] New York: Appleton-Century-Crofts, 1970. Z6514.C97 H3

This guide to literary criticism from Plato through Johnson is highly selective and is designed to serve the needs of the novice scholar. Asterisks mark out especially important works, further to guide the beginner. The bibliography is arranged chronologically by period and alphabetically by critic within his period. The periods are those conventional to the history of criticism: Classical, Medieval, Renaissance, and "Later Criticism through Johnson." An opening section contains selected collections of critical essays followed by general works. The period sections start with lists of general works, followed by fairly full listings of individual critics of the period with primary works followed by a list of secondary works. An index to authors concludes the volume.

Because many of the seminal works of literary criticism are in foreign languages, this bibliography is necessarily more international in scope than many other manuals of its kind. Nevertheless, it is compiled with a bias toward publications in English, and whenever an English translation of a foreign work is available, that is listed rather than a standard edition of the original. Omitted entirely are unpublished dissertations, almost all literary histories, and short notes and explications unless of unusual significance. Although not specified, the closing date for the volume is approximately 1967.

X–3 Stallman, Robert W., ed. "Bibliography 1920–1950: Topical Checklists of Selected Readings [in Modern Criticism]." In the *Critic's Notebook,* pp. 255–293. Minneapolis: University of Minnesota Press, 1950. PN81.S66

The *Critic's Notebook* collects and connects statements of critics writing between 1920 and 1950 on the major theoretical questions then being deliberated. Quotations are arranged in

eight chapters, with subdivisions, and the checklists of readings in the bibliographical appendix are divided according to the same topics. The chapters and selected subdivisions are as follows: 1, The Nature and Function of Criticism (Kinds of Criticism; The Boundaries of Criticism; Scholarship and Criticism); 2, Life and Art (Theories of "Pure Poetry"); 3, Form; 4, The Problem of Meaning (What the Poem Means: The Language of Poetry; What the Poem Means: Obscurity in Poetry; How Meaning Is Said: Symbolism); 5, The Concept of the "Objective Correlative" (Art as the Expression of Emotion); 6, The Problem of the Personal Element; 7, The Problem of Belief in Poetry (Myth in Poetry); 8, The Problem of Intentions. The checklists are arranged in alphabetical order under each of the various topics and subtopics.

X–4 Wellek, René, and Austin Warren. *Theory of Literature.* 3d ed. New York: Harcourt, Brace and World, 1962. PN45.W36 1962

Originally published in 1942, with a second edition in 1956, this work has probably been more influential than any other in setting the course of literary study in the mid-twentieth century. It combines a New-Critical focus on the literary work as such with an extensive introduction to Continental *Literaturwissenschaft.* The volume is organized into four parts, as follows: I. Definitions and Distinctions (Literature and Literary Study; The Nature of Literature; The Function of Literature; Literary Theory, Criticism, and History; General, Comparative, and National Literature); II. Preliminary Operations (The Ordering and Establishing of Evidence); III. The Extrinsic Approach to the Study of Literature (Literature and Biography; Literature and Psychology; Literature and Society; Literature and Ideas; Literature and the Other Arts); and IV. The Intrinsic Study of Literature (The Mode of Existence of a Literary Work of Art; Euphony, Rhythm, and Metre; Style and Stylistics; Image, Metaphor, Symbol, Myth; the Nature and Modes of Narrative Fiction; Literary Genres; Evaluation; Literary History). A forty-page bibliography organized according to the chapters of the book is particularly valuable for its inclusion of pertinent nineteenth- and early twentieth-century materials.

The third edition, substantially unchanged from the second, can be supplemented by additional discussion and bibliography in Wellek's two volumes of essays, *Concepts of Criticism,* ed. Stephen G. Nichols, Jr. (New Haven: Yale University Press, 1963) [PN85.W38] and *Discriminations: Further Concepts of Criticism* (New Haven: Yale University Press, 1970) [PN81.W36], as well as by his *History of Modern Criticism, 1750–1950* (see X–9).

A number of more recent volumes are comparably designed

as general introductions to the theory and methodology of literary study, with extensive reference bibliographies. In particular, see Wolfgang Kayser, *Das sprachliche Kunstwerk: Eine Einführung in die Literaturwissenschaft*, 2d ed. enl. (Bern: Francke, 1951) [PN45.K35 1951], and Joseph Strekla, *Methodologie der Literaturwissenschaft* (Tübingen: Niemeyer, 1978) [PN441.S745], as well as the several general guides to the study of comparative literature (L–4).

X–5 **Wimsatt, William K. "A List of Books and Articles Relating to Assignments in English 170" [Theories of Poetry].** Available from the Secretary, Department of English, Yale University for $3.00.   No LC number

This 129-page single-spaced, typed, mimeographed bibliography is divided into twenty-six chapters that cover the history of literary theory and literary criticism from classical antiquity to the contemporary scene. The chapters are generally defined by key theorists and the central theoretical problems with which they are associated. Both books and articles are cited, with 1970 an approximate cutoff date. With over 4,000 items, this is the most comprehensive bibliography of its subject currently available. It is to be hoped that one of the late Professor Wimsatt's students or colleagues will transform this already valuable work into a more permanent form, with much needed indexes and the inclusion of materials from the 1970s.

X–6 **Wimsatt, William K., and Cleanth Brooks.** *Literary Criticism: A Short History.* New York: Alfred A. Knopf, 1957.   PN86.W5

This massive work is the standard single-volume history of literary criticism. It is an argumentative history in that its authors do have an organizing thesis, but it can also be read for its abundant information about historical particulars. The critical thought of Greek and Roman antiquity and of the Renaissance, Augustan, Romantic, Victorian, and twentieth-century English and American periods is featured, but consideration is also given to the thought of the Middle Ages and to major lines of critical thought in Italy, France, Germany, and Russia. Extensive bibliographical information is provided in footnotes. An important review of this volume, that points up the somewhat distorting effect that its thesis has on its presentation of historical particulars, is by Robert Marsh, "The 'Fallacy' of Universal Intention," *MP* 55 (1958): 263–275.

X–7 **Atkins and Saintsbury. Histories of Literary Criticism.**

Atkins, J. W. H. *Literary Criticism in Antiquity: A Sketch of Its Development.* 2 vols. Cambridge: Cambridge University Press, 1934.   PA3013.A8

———. *English Literary Criticism: The Medieval Phase.* Cambridge: Cambridge University Press, 1943.
PN99.G7 A8

———. *English Literary Criticism: The Renaissance.* 2d ed. London: Methuen, 1951.   PN99.G7 A83

———. *English Literary Criticism: 17th and 18th Centuries.* London: Methuen, 1951.   PN99.G7 A78

For this last volume see the important review by R. S. Crane, "On Writing the History of Criticism in England, 1650–1800," *UTQ* 22 (1953): 376–391; reprinted in *Idea of the Humanities*, 2 vols. (Chicago: University of Chicago Press, 1967), vol. 2: pp. 157–175 [PN50.C7].

Saintsbury, George. *History of Criticism and Literary Taste in Europe.* 4th and 5th eds. Edinburgh: Blackwood, 1922–1934.   PN86.S3

———. *History of English Criticism: Being the English Chapters of "A History of Criticism and Literary Taste in Europe," Revised, Adapted, and Supplemented.* Edinburgh, 1911.   PR63.S3

X–8 **Baldwin and Howell. Histories of Rhetoric and Poetic.**

Baldwin, Charles Sears. *Ancient Rhetoric and Poetic.* New York: Macmillan, 1924.   PA3265.B3

———. *Medieval Rhetoric and Poetic (to 1400): Interpreted from Representative Works.* New York: Macmillan, 1928.   PN671.B3

———. *Renaissance Literary Theory and Practice.* Edited with an introduction by Donald Lemen Clark. New York: Columbia University Press, 1939.   PN721.B3

Howell, Wilbur Samuel. *Logic and Rhetoric in England, 1500–1700.* Princeton, N.J.: Princeton University Press, 1956.   BC38.H6

———. *Eighteenth-Century British Logic and Rhetoric.* Princeton, N.J.: Princeton University Press, 1971.
BC38.H59

X–9 **Welleck, René.** *History of Modern Criticism, 1750–1950.* 6 vols. New Haven: Yale University Press, 1955–1986.
PN86.W4

This comprehensive account of modern literary criticism emphasizes literary theory but also deals with the history of literary taste. Topics in aesthetics, poetics, literary history, and practical criticism all find their place within the scope of this work. The individual volumes are as follows:

Vol. 1. *Later Eighteenth Century (1955).*

Vol. 2. *Romantic Age (1955).*

Vol. 3. *Age of Transition (1966).*

Vol. 4. *Later Nineteenth Century (1966).*

Vol. 5. *English Criticism, 1900–1950 (1986).*

Vol. 6. *American Criticism, 1900–1950 (1986).*

The first two volumes consider the thought of England and Scotland, France, Germany, and Italy, touching only slightly on other countries. Volumes 3 and 4 do include the thought of Spain, Russia, and the United States. Each volume has an extensive section of bibliographies and notes, keyed to the divisions of the text; a chronological table of works; an index of names; and an index of topics and terms.

X–10 **Guide to Historical Collections of Critical Essays.**

General

Adams, Hazard, ed. *Critical Theory since Plato.* New York: Harcourt, Brace, Jovanovich, 1971.   BH39.A23

Allen, Gay Wilson, and Harry Hayden Clark, eds. *Literary Criticism: Pope to Croce.* Detroit: Wayne State University Press, 1962.   PN86.A5 1962

Bate, Walter Jackson, ed. *Criticism: The Major Texts.* Enl. ed. New York: Harcourt, Brace, Jovanovich, 1970.
PN86.B3 1970

Gilbert, Allan H., ed. *Literary Criticism: Plato to Dryden.* Detroit: Wayne State University Press, 1962.
PN1035.G5 1962

Schorer, Mark, Josephine Miles, and Gordon McKenzie, eds. *Criticism: The Foundations of Modern Literary Judgment.* New York: Harcourt, Brace and World, 1958.
PN81.S23 1958

Trilling, Lionel, ed. *Literary Criticism: An Introductory Reader*. New York: Holt, Rinehart and Winston, 1970. PN85.T7

Classical Antiquity

Russell, D. A., and M. Winterbottom, eds. *Ancient Literary Criticism: The Principal Texts in New Translations*. Oxford: Clarendon, 1972. PA3013.R8

Renaissance and After

Elledge, Scott, ed. *Eighteenth-Century Critical Essays*. 2 vols. Ithaca, N.Y.: Cornell University Press, 1961. PR74.E4

Elledge, Scott, and Donald Schier, eds. *Continental Model: Selected French Critical Essays of the Seventeenth Century, in English Translation*. Rev. ed. Ithaca, N.Y.: Cornell University Press, 1970. PN99.F82 E55 1970

Hardison, O. B., Jr., ed. *English Literary Criticism: The Renaissance*. New York: Appleton-Century-Crofts, 1963. PR70.H3 1963

Hoffman, Daniel G., and Samuel Hynes, eds. *English Literary Criticism: Romantic and Victorian*. New York: Appleton-Century-Crofts, 1963. PR76.H6 1963

Hudson, Derek, ed. *English Critical Essays: Twentieth-Century. Second Series*. Oxford: Oxford University Press, 1958. PR67.H8

Hynes, Samuel, ed. *English Literary Criticism: Restoration and Eighteenth Century*. New York: Appleton-Century-Crofts, 1963. PR76.H6

Jones, Edmund, ed. *English Critical Essays: Sixteenth, Seventeenth, and Eighteenth Centuries*. Oxford: Oxford University Press, 1924.

————, ed. *English Critical Essays: Nineteenth Century*. Oxford: Oxford University Press, 1916. PR503.J6

Jones, Phyllis M., ed. *English Critical Essays: Twentieth-Century. First Series*. Oxford: Oxford University Press, 1933. PR67.J65

Lipking, Lawrence, and A. Walton Litz, eds. *Modern Literary Criticism 1900–1970*. New York: Atheneum, 1972. PN94.L48

Lodge, David, ed. *20th Century Literary Criticism: A Reader*. London: Longman, 1972. PN94.L6

Ridler, Anne, ed. *Shakespeare Criticism 1919–1935*. Oxford: Oxford University Press, 1936. PR2976.R48

————, ed. *Shakespeare Criticism 1935–1960*. Oxford: Oxford University Press, 1963. PR2976.R482 1963

Sigworth, Oliver F., ed. *Criticism and Aesthetics, 1660–1800*. San Francisco: Rinehart Press, 1971. PN99.G72 S5

Smith, Gregory, G. ed. *Elizabethan Critical Essays*. 2 vols. Oxford: Oxford University Press, 1904. PR70.S6

Smith, Nichol D., ed. *Eighteenth-Century Essays on Shakespeare*. 2d ed. Oxford: Clarendon Press, 1963. PR2975.S6 1963

Spingarn, J. E., ed. *Critical Essays of the Seventeenth Century*. 3 vols. Oxford: Clarendon Press, 1908-1909. PR72.S7

Sutton, Walter, and Richard Foster, eds. *Modern Criticism: Theory and Practice*. New York: Odyssey Press, 1963. PN81.S8

Weinberg, Bernard, ed. *Critical Prefaces of the French Renaissance*. Evanston, Ill.: Northwestern University Press, 1950. PQ84.W4 1950

American

Beaver, Harold, ed. *American Critical Essays. [Second Series.]* Oxford: Oxford University Press, 1959. For First Series see under Foerster. PS121.B45

Brown, Clarence A., ed. *Achievement of American Criticism: Representative Selections from Three Hundred Years of American Criticism*. New York: Ronald Press, 1954. PN99.U5 B7

Foerster, Norman, ed. *American Critical Essays. [First Series.]* Oxford: Oxford University Press, 1930. For Second Series see under Beaver. PN501.F6

Hoffman, Daniel G. *American Poetry and Poetics: Poems and Critical Documents from the Puritans to Robert Frost*. Garden City, N.Y.: Doubleday Anchor, 1962. PS583.H55

Stallman, Robert. *Critiques and Essays in Criticism, 1920–1948: Representing the Achievement of Modern British and American Critics*. New York: Ronald Press, 1949. PN81.S67

West, Ray B., ed. *Essays in Modern Literary Criticism*. New York: Rinehart, 1952. PN85.W4

Zabel, Morton D., ed. *Literary Opinion in America: Essays Illustrating the Status, Methods, and Problems of Criticism in the United States in the Twentieth Century*. 2 vols. 3d ed., rev. New York: Harper and Row, 1962. PN771.Z2

Modern Continental

Gras, Vernon W., ed. *European Literary Theory and Practice from Existential Phenomenology to Structuralism*. New York: Delta, 1973. PN94.G7

Hardison, O. B., Jr. *Modern Continental Literary Criticism*. New York: Appleton-Century-Crofts, 1962. PN501.H27

Lang, Bevel, and Forrest Williams, eds. *Marxism and Art: Writings in Aesthetics and Criticism*. New York: McKay, 1972. HX521.L34

Polletta, Gregory T., ed. *Issues in Contemporary Literary Criticism*. Boston: Little, Brown, 1973. PN94.P6 1973

Simon, John K., ed. *Modern French Criticism: From Proust and Valery to Structuralism*. Chicago: University of Chicago Press, 1972. PN99.F82 S55

Solomon, Maynard, ed. *Marxism and Art: Essays Classic and Contemporary*. New York: Knopf, 1974. HX521.S63 1974

Many valuable series of collections of critical essays are published, of which the most important are the volumes of the *Critical Heritage Series* (London: Routledge and Kegan Paul) [LC numbers vary], which exhibit the history of an author's critical reception; *Twentieth Century Views* (Englewood Cliffs, N.J.: Prentice-Hall) [LC numbers vary], which display the range of contemporary criticism of an author (a *Reader's Index to . . . Volumes 1-100* was published in 1973); and *Modern Essays in Criticism* (London: Oxford University Press) [LC numbers vary], which collect a series of essays on the English literature of a period, a genre, or a genre within a period.

There are many series of "Casebooks," presenting one or several primary texts of English or American literature around which are gathered a range of secondary materials; of these, the most important are the *Norton Critical Editions* (New York: W. W. Norton) and the *Crowell Literary Casebooks* (New York: Thomas Y. Crowell). Collections of essays about a single major work will be found in the series *Twentieth Century Interpretations* (Englewood Cliffs, N.J.: Prentice-Hall).

X-11 **Some Frequently Recommended Works on the History of Literary Criticism and Literary Theory before the Twentieth Century.** (See also entries in X-119.)

Abrams, Meyer H. *Mirror and the Lamp: Romantic Theory and the Critical Tradition*. New York: Oxford University Press, 1953.   PN769.R7 A2

Baldick, Chris. *Social Mission of English Criticism, 1848-1932*. Oxford: Clarendon Press, 1987.
                    PR63.B35 1987

Bate, Walter Jackson. *Burden of the Past and the English Poet*. Cambridge: Belknap Press of Harvard University Press, 1970.   PR99.B19

————. *From Classic to Romantic: Premises of Taste in Eighteenth-Century England*. Cambridge: Harvard University Press, 1946.   BH221.G7 1953

Baym, Max I. *History of Literary Aesthetics in America*. New York: Ungar, 1973.   PS88.B3

Beardsley, Monroe C. *Aesthetics from Classical Greece to the Present: A Short History*. New York: Macmillan, 1966.   BH81.B4

Bosker, Aisso. *Literary Criticism in the Age of Johnson*. 2d ed. Groningen: J. B. Wolters, 1953.   PR73.B6 1953

Elioseff, Lee Andrew. *Cultural Milieu of Addison's Literary Criticism*. Austin: University of Texas Press, 1963.
                    PR3307.E5

Engell, James. *Forming the Critical Mind: Dryden to Coleridge*. Cambridge: Harvard University Press, 1989.
                    PR73.E54 1989

Foerster, Donald M. *Fortunes of Epic Poetry: A Study in English and American Criticism, 1750-1950*. Washington, D.C.: Catholic University of America Press, 1962.   PN1303.F6

Foerster, Norman. *American Criticism: A Study in Literary Theory from Poe to the Present*. Boston: Houghton Mifflin, 1928.   PS62.F6

Fowlie, Wallace. *French Critic, 1549-1967*. Carbondale: Southern Illinois University Press, 1968. PN99.F8 F6

Grube, G. M. A. *Greek and Roman Critics*. Toronto: University of Toronto Press, 1965.   PA3013.G7

Hall, Vernon. *Short History of Literary Criticism*. New York: New York University Press, 1963.   PN86.H3

Hardison, O. B., Jr. *Enduring Monument: A Study of the Idea of Praise in Renaissance Literary Theory and Practice*. Chapel Hill: University of North Carolina Press, 1962.   PN88.H34

Hathaway, Baxter. *Age of Criticism: The Late Renaissance in Italy*. Ithaca, N.Y.: Cornell University Press, 1962.
                    PN99.I82 H3

————. *Marvels and Commonplaces: Renaissance Literary Criticism*. New York: Random House, 1968. Bibliography; Biographical Glossary.   PN88.H37

Hipple, Walter J. *Beautiful, the Sublime, and the Picturesque in Eighteenth-Century British Aesthetic Theory*. Carbondale: Southern Illinois University Press, 1957.   BH221.G72 H5

Hohendahl, Peter Uwe, ed. *History of German Literary Criticism*. Lincoln: University of Nebraska Press, 1988.
                    PT47.G4713 1988

Lipking, Lawrence. *Ordering of the Arts in Eighteenth-Century England*. Princeton, N.J.: Princeton University Press, 1970.   NX543.L56

McKenzie, Gordon. *Critical Responsiveness: A Study of the Psychological Current in Later Eighteenth-Century Criticism*. Berkeley: University of California Press, 1949.   PR73.M23

Marks, Emerson R. *Poetics of Reason: English Neoclassical Criticism*. New York: Random House, 1968.
                    PR445.M28

Maurocordato, Alexandre. *La critique classique en Angleterre de la Restauration á la mord de Joseph Addison*. Paris: Didier, 1964.   PR437.M3

Monk, Samuel Holt. *Sublime: A Study of Critical Theories in XVIII-Century England*. New ed. Ann Arbor: University of Michigan Press, 1960. BH301.S7 M6 1960

Parks, Edd Winfield. *Ante-bellum Southern Literary Critics*. Athens: University of Georgia Press, 1962.
                    PN99.U52 P3

Pritchard, John P. *Criticism in America: An Account of the Development of Critical Techniques from the Early Period of the Republic to the Middle Years of the Twentieth Century*. Norman: University of Oklahoma Press, 1956.   PN99.U5 P67

————. *Return to the Fountains: Some Classical Sources of American Criticism*. Durham, N.C.: Duke University Press, 1942.   PN99.U5 P7

Selden, Raman. *Theory of Criticism: From Plato to the Present*. London: Longmans, 1988.

Spingarn, Joel E. *History of Literary Criticism in the Renaissance*. 2d ed. New York: Columbia University Press, 1908.   PN88.S6 1908

Stovall, Floyd, ed. *Development of American Literary Criticism*. Chapel Hill: University of North Carolina Press, 1955.   PN99.U5 S75

Tillotson, Geoffrey. *Criticism and the Nineteenth Century*. London: University of London, Athlone Press, 1951.
                    PR463.T5

Warren, Alba, Jr. *English Poetic Theory, 1825-1865*. Princeton, N.J.: Princeton University Press, 1950.
                    PN1031.W27

Watson, George C. *Literary Critics: A Study of English Descriptive Criticism*. Hardmondsworth: Penguin, 1962.
                    PR63.W3

Weinberg, Bernard. *History of Literary Criticism in the Italian Renaissance*. 2 vols. Chicago: University of Chicago Press, 1961. Bibliography.   PQ4027.W4

————. *Rise of English Literary History*. Chapel Hill: University of North Carolina Press, 1941.   PR401.W4

White, Harold O. *Plagiarism and Imitation during the English Renaissance: A Study in Critical Distinctions*. Cambridge: Harvard University Press, 1935.
                    PR419.P6 W5

X-13 **Scholarly Journals in Literary Theory and Literary Criticism.**

American Journal of Semiotics. Vol. 1-. Cambridge, Mass.: Schenkman Publishing Co., 1981-. 4/yr.   P99.A46

Boundary 2. Vol. 1-. Binghamton, N.Y.: Department of English, General Literature, and Rhetoric, SUNY, 1971-. 3/yr.   PN2.B68

BJA   *British Journal of Aesthetics*. Vol. 1-. London: For the Society by Routledge and Kegan Paul, 1960-.
                    BH1.B7

BLS   *Bulletin of Literary Semiotics*. [See *Semiotic Scene*.]

Cambridge Quarterly. Vol. 1-. Cambridge: Cambridge University Press.   AS121.C3

Centrum: Working Papers of the Minnesota Center for Advanced Studies in Language, Style, and Literary Theory. Vol. 1-. Minneapolis: University of Minnesota, 1973-. 2/yr. Reviews.   P301.C45

Comparative Criticism: A Yearbook. Vol. 1–. Cambridge: Cambridge University Press, 1980–. 1/yr.   PN863.C58

Critical Inquiry. Vol. 1–. Chicago: University of Chicago Press, 1974–. 4/yr. Reviews.   NX1.C64

Critical Quarterly Vol. 1–. Hull: Critical Quarterly, 1959–. 4/yr.   AP4.C887

Critical Survey: The Journal of the Critical Quarterly Society. 1962–. 2/yr.   PN2.C7

Critical Texts: A Review of Theory and Criticism. Vol. 1–. New York: Department of English, Columbia University, 1982–. 3/yr. Reviews.   No LC number

Criticism: A Quarterly for Literature and the Arts. Vol. 1–. Detroit: Wayne State University Press, 1958–.   AS30.W3 A2

Cultural Critique: An International Journal of Cultural Studies. Vol. 1–. Minneapolis: University of Minnesota Press, 1985–. 3/yr.   No LC number

Diacritics *Diacritics: A Review of Contemporary Criticism.* Vol. 1–. Baltimore: Johns Hopkins University Press, 1971–. 4/yr. Reviews.   PN80.D5

Discourse: Journal for Theoretical Studies in Media and Culture. Vol. 1–. Bloomington: Indiana University Press, 1978–. 2/yr. Reviews.   P87.D57

EIE *English Institute: Selected Papers* [title varies]. New York: Columbia University Press, 1939–. 1/yr.   LC numbers vary

L'esprit créateur. Vol. 1–. Lawrence, Kans.: L'esprit créateur, 1961–. 4/yr.   No LC number

EIC *Essays in Criticism.* Vol. 1–. Oxford: Oxford University Press, 1951–. 4/yr. Reviews.   PR1.E75

Études littéraires. Vol. 1–. Quebec: Presses de l'Université Laval, 1968–. 3/yr. Reviews.   PQ2.E83

Genders. Vol. 1–. Austin: University of Texas Press, 1988–. 3/yr.   No LC number

Genre *Genre: A Quarterly Devoted to Generic Criticism.* Vol. 1–. Norman: University of Oklahoma, 1968–. 4/yr.   PN80.G4

Glyph *Glyph: Johns Hopkins Textual Studies.* Vol. 1–. Baltimore: Johns Hopkins University Press, 1977–. 2/yr.   PN2.G58

Journal of Aesthetic Education. Vol. 1–. Urbana: University of Illinois Press, 1966–.   N1.J58

JAAC *Journal of Aesthetics and Art Criticism.* Vol. 1–. Philadelphia: Temple University, 1941–. 4/yr.   N1.J6

New Formations. Vol. 1–. London: Methuen, 1987–. 3/yr.   No LC number

NLH *New Literary History: A Journal of Theory and Interpretation.* Vol. 1–. Baltimore: Johns Hopkins University Press, 1968–. 3/yr.   PR1.N44

NRF *Nouvelle revue française.* Vol. 1–. Paris, 1909–1943, 1953–.   AC20.N6

PTL *PTL: A Journal for Descriptive Poetics and Theory of Literature.* 4 Vols. Amsterdam: North-Holland, 1976–1979. 3/yr. Reviews. Bibliographical Notes.   No LC number

Paragraph: The Journal of the Modern Critical Theory Group. Vol. 1–. Oxford: Oxford University Press, 1983–. 2 then 3/yr.   No LC number

Poetica *Poetica: Zeitschrift für Sprach- und Literaturwissenschaft.* Vol. 1–. Amsterdam: Verlag B. R. Grüner, 1967–.   P3.P6

Poetics: International Review for the Theory of Literature. Vol. 1–. Amsterdam: North-Holland, 1971–. 4/yr. Reviews. Bibliographical Notes.   PN45.P58

Poetics Today: A Central Interim Final Quarterly for Theory of Literature and Related Fields. Vol. 1–. Durham, N.C.: Duke University Press for the Porter Institute for Poetics and Semiotics, 1979–. 4/yr. Reviews.   No LC number

Poétique *Poétique: Revue de théorie et d'analyse littéraires.* Vol. 1–. Paris: Seuil, 1970–. 4/yr.   PN3.P64

Reader: Essays in Reader-Oriented Theory, Criticism, and Pedagogy. Vol. 1–. Houghton: Department of Humanities, Michigan Technological University, 1986–.   No LC number

Revue des sciences humaines. Vol. 1–. Paris, 1927–1931, 1933–.

Semiotic Scene [former title: *Bulletin of Literary Semiotics*, 1975–1976]. Vol. 1–. Medford, Mass.: Tufts University, Semiotic Society of America, 1977–. Reviews. Bibliographical Notices.   No LC number

Semiotica. Vol. 1–. The Hague: Mouton, 1969–. 4–17/yr. Reviews.   B820.S45

Sociocriticism/Sociocritique. Vol. 1–. Montpellier: Université Paul Valéry, 1985–. 2/yr.

Structuralist Research Information. No. 1–. Nashville, Tenn.: Vanderbilt University, 1978–. Irreg. Reviews. Annotated lists of books, articles, and dissertations.

Structuralist Review: A Journal of Theory, Criticism, and Pedagogy. Vol. 1–. New York: Queens College Press, 1978–. 3/yr. Reviews. Annual bibliography of structuralist theory and criticism.   No LC number

Studies in the Literary Imagination. Vol. 1–. Atlanta: Department of English, Georgia State University, 1968. 2/yr.   PR1.S84

Sub-stance: A Review of Theory and Literary Criticism. Vol. 1–. Madison: University of Wisconsin, Department of French and Italian, 1971–. 3/yr. Reviews.   PN2.S82

Textual Practice. Vol. 1–. London: Methuen, 1986–. 3/yr.   No LC number

Yale Journal of Criticism. Vol. 1–. New Haven: Yale University Press, 1987–. 2/yr. Review essays.   PN2.Y34

Yearbook of Comparative Criticism. Vol. 1–. University Park: Pennsylvania State University Press, 1968–. 1/yr.   No LC number

Zeitschrift für Literaturwissenschaft und Linguistik. 3 vols. Frankfurt: Athenäum, 1971–1973.   P3.Z36

X–14 Some Frequently Recommended Works on Modern Literary Criticism and Literary Theory before ca. 1950, including Russian Formalism, Anglo-American New Criticism, and Related Theoretical Perspectives.

Auerbach, Erich. *Mimesis: The Representation of Reality in Western Literature.* Princeton, N.J.: Princeton University Press, 1953.   PN56.R3 A83

Bagwell, J. Timothy. *American Formalism and the Problem of Interpretation.* Houston, Texas: Rice University Press, 1986.   PN98.N4 B34 1986

Bann, Stephen, and John E. Bowlt. *Russian Formalism.* Edinburgh: Scottish Academic Press, 1973.   PG3026.F6 B3 1973b

Battersby, James L. *Elder Olson: An Annotated Bibliography*. New York: Garland, 1983.   Z8643.72.B37 1983

Beardsley, Monroe C. *Possibility of Criticism*. Detroit: Wayne State University Press, 1970. PN81.B39 1970

Blackmuir, R. P. *New Criticism in the United States*. Tokyo: Kenkyusha, 1959.   PN98.N4 B5 1959

Brooks, Cleanth. *Well Wrought Urn; Studies in the Structure of Poetry*. Harcourt, Brace and World, 1947.   PR502.B7

Burke, Kenneth. *Language as Symbolic Action*. Berkeley and Los Angeles: University of California Press, 1966.

——. *Philosophy of Literary Form: Studies in Symbolic Action*. 3d ed. Berkeley, Los Angeles, London: University of California Press, 1974.   PN511.B795 1974

Cain, William E. *F. O. Matthiessen and the Politics of Criticism*. Madison: University of Wisconsin Press, 1988.   PS29.M35 C35 1988

Crane, Ronald S. *Languages of Criticism and the Structure of Poetry*. Toronto: University of Toronto Press, 1953.

——, ed. *Critics and Criticism, Ancient and Modern*. Chicago: University of Chicago Press, 1952.   PN81.C8

Daiches, David. *Critical Approaches to Literature*. Englewood Cliffs, N.J.: Prentice-Hall, 1956.   PN81.D3

Day, Frank. *Sir William Empson: An Annotated Bibliography*. New York: Garland, 1984.   Z8265.6.D38 1984

Eggers, Walter, and Sigrid Mayer. *Ernst Cassirer: An Annotated Bibliography*. New York: Garland, 1988.   Z8153.45.E37 1988

Eliot, T.S. *Sacred Wood*. London: Faber, 1920.   PN511.E44 1920

——. *Selected Essays*. 3d ed. London: Faber and Faber, 1951.   PN511.E443 1951

Empson, William. *Seven Types of Ambiguity*. 3d ed. London: Chatto and Windus, 1953.   PN1031.E5 1953

Ehrlich, Viktor. *Russian Formalism: History-Doctrine*. 2d. ed. The Hague: Mouton, 1965. PG3026.F6 E7 1965

Fekete, John. *Critical Twilight: Explorations in the Ideology of Anglo-American Theory from Eliot to McLuhan*. Boston: Routledge and Kegan Paul, 1977.   PN99.U52 F4

Fubini, Mario. *Critica e poesia: Saggi e discorsi di teoria letteraria*. 2d ed., rev. and enl. Bari: Laterza, 1966. Contains the study, "Genesi e storia dei generi letterari," translated by Ursula Vogt as *Entstehung und Geschichte der literarischen Gattungen* (Tübingen: Niemeyer, 1971). With bibliography. PN45.5.F815

Gardner, Helen. *Business of Criticism*. Oxford: Clarendon Press, 1959.   PN85.G33

Hyman, Stanley Edgar. *Armed Vision: A Study in the Methods of Modern Literary Criticism*. New York: Knopf, 1948. The 1955 abridged edition omits the bibliography.   PN94.H9

——. *Poetry and Criticism: Four Revolutions in Literary Taste*. New York: Atheneum, 1961.   PN86.H9

Kinsch, Maurice, John Kimber, and William Baker, *F. R. and Q. D. Leavis: An Annotated Bibliography*. New York: Garland, 1989.   Z8494.2.K56 1989

Krieger, Murray. *New Apologists for Poetry*. Bloomington: Indiana University Press, 1963.   PN1031.K7 1963

Langer, Suzanne K. *Feeling and Form: A Theory of Art*. New York: Scribners, 1957.   BF458.L29

——. *Philosophy in a New Key*. Cambridge: Harvard University Press, 1942.   BF458.L3 1957

Leavis, F. R. *Common Pursuit*. London: Chatto and Windus, 1952.   PR99.L35

——. *Revaluation: Tradition and Development in English Poetry*. London: Chatto and Windus, 1936.   PR503.L4

Lemon, Lee T. *Partial Critics*. New York: Oxford University Press, 1965.   PN94.L4

Lemon, Lee T., and Marion J. Reis, eds. *Russian Formalist Criticism*. Lincoln: University of Nebraska Press, 1965.   PN501.R87

Levenson, Michael H. *Genealogy of Modernism: A Study of English Literary Doctrine, 1908–1922*. Cambridge: Cambridge University Press, 1984.   PR478.M6 L4 1984

Levin, Harry. *Contexts of Criticism*. Cambridge: Harvard University Press, 1957.   PN511.L36

Luthe, Rudolf. *New Criticism und idealistische Kunstphilosophie*. Bonn: Bouvier, 1985.   PN98.N4 L8

Matejka, Ladislav, and Kristina Pomorska, eds. *Readings in Russian Poetics: Formalist and Structuralist Views*. Cambridge: MIT Press, 1971.   PN441.M34

Norris, Christopher. *William Empson and the Philosophy of Literary Criticism*. London: Athlone Press, 1978.   PR6009.M7 Z79

O'Connor, William Van. *Age of Criticism, 1900–1950*. Chicago: Regnery, 1952. Selected bibliography of bibliographies.   PN99.U52O3

Oppel, Horst. *Methodenlehre der Literaturwissenschaft*. Berlin, 1957.

Orwell, George. *Shooting an Elephant and Other Essays*. London: Secker and Warburg, 1950.   PR6029.R8 S5

Ransom, John Crowe. *New Criticism*. Norfolk, Conn.: New Directions, 1941.   PN1031.R3

——. *World's Body*. New York: Scribners, 1938.   PN1136.R3

Reichert, John. *Making Sense of Literature*. Chicago: University of Chicago Press, 1977.   PN81.R36

Richards, I. A. *Practical Criticism: A Study of Literary Judgement*. London: Kegan Paul, 1929. PN1031.R48

——. *Principles of Literary Criticism*. New York: Harcourt, Brace, 1924.   PN81.R5

Rueckert, William H., ed. *Critical Responses to Kenneth Burke, 1924–1966*. Minneapolis: University of Minnesota Press, 1969.   PS3503.U6134 Z84

Sherwood, John C. *R. S. Crane: An Annotated Bibliography*. New York: Garland, 1984.   Z8198.17.S5 1984

Shusterman, Richard. *T. S. Eliot and the Philosophy of Criticism*. New York: Columbia University Press, 1988.   PS3509.L43 Z8649 1988

Simons, Herbert W., and Trevor Melia, eds. *Legacy of Kenneth Burke*. Madison: University of Wisconsin Press, 1989.   PN75.B8 L44 1989

Staiger, Emil. *Grundbegriffe der Poetik*. 6th ed. Zurich: Atlantis Verlag, 1946.   PN1044.S7

Steiner, Peter. *Russian Formalism: A Metapoetics*. Ithaca, N.Y.: Cornell University Press, 1984.   PN98.F6 S73 1984

Sutton, Walter. *Modern American Criticism*. Englewood Cliffs, N.J.: Prentice-Hall, 1963.   PN99.U5S8

Thompson, Ewa M. *Russian Formalism and Anglo-American New Criticism*. The Hague: Mouton, 1971.   PG3026.F6 T5 1971

Trilling, Lionel. *Liberal Imagination: Essays on Literature and Society.* New York, 1950.   PS3593.R56 L5

Wehrli, Max. *Allgemeine Literaturwissenschaft.* 2d rev. ed. Bern: Francke, 1969.   PN441.W4 1969

Weimann, Robert. *"New Criticism" und die Entwicklung bürgerlicher Literaturwissenschaft: Geschichte und Kritik autonomen Interpretations-methoden.* 2d ed., rev. and enl. Munich: Beck, 1962. Bibliography.   PN94.W4 1962

Wilson, Daniel J. *Arthur O. Lovejoy: An Annotated Bibliography.* New York: Garland, 1982.   Z8520.94.W54 1982

Wilson, Edmund. *Axel's Castle: A Study in the Imaginative Literature of 1870–1930.* New York: Scribner's, 1931.   PN771.W55

Wimsatt, W. K. *Day of the Leopards: Essays in Defense of Poems.* New Haven: Yale University Press, 1976.   PN1031.W516 1976

———. *Hateful Contraries: Studies in Literature and Criticism.* Lexington: University of Kentucky Press, 1965.   PN85.W49

———. *Verbal Icon: Studies in the Meaning of Poetry.* Lexington: University of Kentucky Press, 1954.   PN1031.W517

Young, Thomas D. *John Crowe Ransom: An Annotated Bibliography.* New York: Garland, 1982.   Z8733.18.Y68 1982

Zitner, Sheldon P., James D. Kissane, and M. M. Liberman, eds. *Practice of Criticism.* Chicago: Scott, Foresman, 1966.   PN86.Z5

II. LITERARY CRITICISM AND LITERARY THEORY AFTER CA. 1950

Works on Marxist theory and on critical theory will be found in section X.III., as will works on literature and psychology, and on relations between literature and other arts and sciences.

See also the history of rhetoric and rhetorical theory in section X.IV. And see pertinent works on the history of criticism and theory in section L, Comparative and World Literature, on feminist theory in section L, in each of the individual period sections N through R, and in section S, American Literature.

X–15 **Some Frequently Recommended General Works on Contemporary Literary Theory.** [See also L–199 for works on feminist literary criticism and literary theory; X–19 for works on structuralism and semiotics; X–24 for works on hermeneutics, reception theory, and reader-response criticism; X–28 for works on deconstruction and post-structuralism; X–64 for works on psychology, psychoanalysis, and literary theory and criticism; and X–74 for works on Marxist literary criticism and literary theory.]

Adams, Hazard. *Interests of Criticism: An Introduction to Literary Theory.* New York: Harcourt, Brace and World, 1969.   PN81.A36

———, and Leroy Searle, eds. *Critical Theory Since 1965.* Tallahassee: Florida State University Press, 1986.   PN94.C75 1986

Berman, Art. *From the New Criticism to Deconstruction: The Reception of Structuralism and Post-Structuralism.* Urbana: University of Illinois Press, 1988.   PN98.S7 B47 1988

Bloomfield, Morton W., ed. *In Search of Literary Theory.* Ithaca, N.Y.: Cornell University Press, 1972.   PN85.I5

Booth, Wayne. *Critical Understanding: The Power and Limits of Pluralism.* Chicago: University of Chicago Press, 1979.   PN81.B58

Brady, Frank, John Palmer, and Martin Price, eds. *Literary Theory and Structure: Essays in Honor of William K. Wimsatt.* New Haven: Yale University Press, 1973.   PR14.L48

Bruss, Elizabeth W. *Beautiful Theories: The Spectacle of Discourse in Contemporary Criticism.* Baltimore: Johns Hopkins University Press, 1982.   PN99.U5 B77 1982

Cane, William E. *Crisis in Criticism: Theory, Literature, and Reform in English Studies.* Baltimore: Johns Hopkins University Press, 1984.   PN94.C3 1984

Chiavi, Joseph. *Aesthetics of Modernism.* London: Vision Press, 1970.   NX456.C5

Davis, Robert Con, and Ronald Schliefer, eds. *Contemporary Literary Criticism: Literary and Cultural Studies.* 2d ed. New York: Longman, 1989.   PN94.C67 1989

de Beaugrande, Robert. *Critical Discourse: A Survey of Literary Theorists.* Norwood, N.J.: Ablex, 1987.   PN94.D3 1987

Dembo, L. S., ed. *Criticism: Speculative and Analytical Essays.* Madison: University of Wisconsin Press, 1968.   PN85.D4

Demetz, Peter, et al. *Disciplines of Criticism: Essays in Literary Theory, Interpretation, and History.* New Haven: Yale University Press, 1968.   PN36.W4

Denham, Robert D. *Northrop Frye: An Annotated Bibliography of Primary and Secondary Sources.* Toronto: University of Toronto Press, 1987.   Z6519.D45 1987

———. *Northrop Frye and Critical Method.* University Park: Pennsylvania State University Press, 1978.   PN81.D39

Ellis, John M. *Theory of Literary Criticism: A Logical Analysis.* Berkeley, Los Angeles, London: University of California Press, 1974.   PN81.E4

Fokkema, D. W., and Elrud Kunne-Ibsch. *Theories of Literature in the Twentieth Century: Structuralism, Marxism, Aesthetics of Reception, Semiotics.* New York: St. Martin's, 1977.   PN441.F6

Frye, Northrop. *Anatomy of Criticism.* Princeton, N.J.: Princeton University Press, 1957.   PN81.F75

Graff, Gerald. *Literature against Itself: Literary Ideas in Modern Society.* Chicago: University of Chicago Press, 1977.   PN51.G68

Guillén, Claudio. *Literature as System: Essays toward the Theory of Literary History.* Princeton, N.J.: Princeton University Press, 1971.   PN441.G78

Harland, Richard. *Superstructuralism: The Philosophy of Structuralism and Post-Structuralism.* New York: Methuen, 1987.   B841.4.H37 1987

Hartman, Geoffrey H. *Beyond Formalism.* New Haven: Yale University Press, 1970.   PN710.H32

———. *Fate of Reading and Other Essays.* Chicago: University of Chicago Press, 1975.   PN441.H35

Hernadi, Paul. *Beyond Genre: New Directions in Literary Classification.* Ithaca, N.Y.: Cornell University Press, 1972.   PN81.H4

———. *What Is Criticism?* Bloomington: Indiana University Press, 1981.   PN85.W47

————. *What Is Literature?* Bloomington: Indiana University Press, 1978.   PN45.W46 1978

Hobsbaum, Philip. *Theory of Criticism*. Bloomington: Indiana University Press, 1970.   PN81.H52 1970

Jefferson, Ann, and David Robey, eds. *Modern Literary Theory: A Comparative Introduction*. 2d ed. London: Batsford, 1986.   PN94.M6 1986

Krieger, Murray. *Theory of Criticism: A Tradition and Its System*. Baltimore: Johns Hopkins University Press, 1976.   PN81.K714

————. *Words about Words: Criticism, and the Literary Text*. Baltimore: Johns Hopkins University Press, 1988.   PN85.K67 1988

Lambropoulos, Vassilis, and David Neal Miller, eds. *Twentieth-Century Literary Theory: An Introductory Anthology*. Albany: State University of New York Press, 1987.   PN45.T94 1986

Latimer, Dan. *Contemporary Literary Theory*. New York: Harcourt, Brace Jovanovich, 1989.   PN94.C66 1989

Leitch, Vincent B. *American Literary Criticism from the Thirties to the Eighties*. New York: Columbia University Press, 1988.   PS78.L4 1988

Lentriccia, Frank. *After the New Criticism*. Chicago: University of Chicago Press, 1980.   PN94.L43

Lodge, David, ed. *Modern Criticism and Theory*. London: Longman, 1988.

Merquior, J. G. *From Prague to Paris: A Critique of Structuralist and Post-Structuralist Thought*. London: Verso, 1986.   B841.4.M47 1986

Moore, Arthur K. *Contestable Concepts of Literary Theory*. Baton Rouge: Louisiana State University Press, 1973.   PN37.M6

Natoli, Joseph, ed. *Tracing Literary Theory*. Urbana: University of Illinois Press, 1987.   PN94.T73 1987

Nelson, Cary, ed. *Theory in the Classroom*. Urbana: University of Illinois Press, 1986.   LB2331.T44 1986

Newton, K. M. *Twentieth-Century Literary Theory: A Reader*. New York: St. Martin's Press, 1988.   PN94.T87 1988

Newton-de Molina, ed. *On Literary Intention: Critical Essays*. Edinburgh: Edinburgh University Press, 1976.   PN85.O56

Pratt, Mary Louise. *Toward a Speech Act Theory of Literary Discourse*. Bloomington: Indiana University Press, 1977.   P302.P74

Richter, David H. *Critical Tradition: Classic Texts and Contemporary Trends*. New York: St. Martin's Press, 1989.

Ruthven, K. K. *Critical Assumptions*. Cambridge: Cambridge University Press, 1979.   PN81.R8

Scott, Wilbur S., ed. *Five Approaches of Literary Criticism: An Arrangement of Contemporary Critical Essays*. New York: Collier Books, 1962.   PN94.S28

Selden, Raman. *Reader's Guide to Contemporary Literary Theory*. 2d ed. Lexington: University Press of Kentucky, 1989.   PN94.S45 1989

Smith, Barbara Herrnstein. *On the Margins of Discourse: The Relation of Literature to Language*. Chicago: University of Chicago Press, 1978.   PN54.S6

Sparshott, F. E. *Concept of Criticism*. Oxford: Clarendon Press, 1967.   PN81.S575

————. *Structure of Aesthetics*. Toronto: University of Toronto Press, 1963.   BH201.S53

Staton, Shirley F. *Literary Theories in Praxis*. Philadelphia: University of Pennsylvania Press, 1987.   PN94.L487 1987

Sturrock, J., ed. *Structuralism and Since: from Levi-Strauss to Derrida*. Oxford: Oxford University Press, 1979.   B841.4.S853

Todorov, Tzvetan. *Introduction to Poetics*. Translation by Richard Howard of *Poétique* (Paris: Editions du Seuil, 1973). Minneapolis: University of Minnesota, 1981.   PN1043.T613

————. *Literature and Its Theorists*. Ithaca, N.Y.: Cornell University Press, 1987.   PN94.T613 1987

Uitti, Karl. *Linguistics and Literary Theory*. Englewood Cliffs, N.J.: Prentice-Hall, 1969.   P33.U4

Watson, George. *Discipline of English: A Guide to Critical Theory and Practice*. London: Macmillan, 1978.   PR21.W3 1978

X–16 **Miller, Joan M., comp. *French Structuralism: A Multidisciplinary Bibliography, with a Checklist of Sources for Louis Althusser, Roland Barthes, Jacques Derrida, Michel Foucault, Lucien Goldmann, Jacques Lacan, and an Update of Works on Claude Lévi-Strauss.*** New York: Garland, 1981.   Z7128.S7 M54

This bibliography covers primarily work published during the period 1968–1978. It thus extends Josue V. Harari's *Structuralists and Structuralism: A Selected Bibliography of French Contemporary Thought (1969-1970)*, published by *Diacritics* (Ithaca, N.Y.: Cornell University Press, 1971) [Z7128.S7 H33]. This is particularly so for Miller's Part I, which cites general and introductory works. Her Part II, providing primary, secondary, and review sources for each of the authors named in the title, is preceded only in the case of Levi-Strauss by an earlier compilation, that of François and Claire Lapointe, *Claude Lévi-Strauss and His Critics: An International Bibliography (1950-1976)*, published in 1977 by Garland [Z8504.35.L36], to which the Miller bibliography is a supplement. Part III is a bibliography of Structuralism as Applied to Various Disciplines. Entries are presented under the following thirteen disciplines: Aesthetics / Art and Music; Anthropology; Cinema; Language and Literature / Literary Analysis; Linguistics; Literary Criticism; Marxism; Philosophy; Poetics; Psychoanalysis/ Psychology; Religion/ Scripture/Theology; Semiotics; and Social Science. The total of 5,300 serially numbered entries in this volume are occasionally given descriptive annotation. The volume concludes with an author and a subject index.

X–17 **Eschbach, Achim, and Viktória Eschbach-Szabó, comps. *Bibliography of Semiotics, 1975–1985.*** 2 vols. Philadelphia: J. Benjamins Publishing Co., 1986.
                    Z7004.S43 E76 1986

This work incorporates and replaces the earlier bibliographies by Eschbach: *Zeichen, Text, Bedeutung: Bibliographie zu Theorie und Praxis der Semiotik* (Munich: Fink, 1974) [Z7004.S43 E78], and *Semiotik-Bibliographie* (Frankfurt: Autoren- und Verlagsgesellschaft Syndikat, 1976) [Z7004. S43 E77]. A total of 10,839 citations are listed alphabetically by author's name. The volume concludes with indexes of reviews, and subjects and names.

For a more detailed treatment of Soviet semiotics, see the bibliography by Karl Eimermacher and Serge Shishkoff, *Subject Bibliography of Soviet Semiotics: The Moscow-Tartu School* (Ann Arbor: Department of Slavic Languages and Literatures, University of Michigan, 1977) [Z7004.S43 E44].

X–18 Culler, Jonathan. *Structuralist Poetics: Structuralism, Linguistics, and the Study of Literature.* Ithaca, N.Y.: Cornell University Press, 1975.   PN98.S7 C8

This work remains the standard introduction to structuralism and literary criticism and literary theory. It consists of eleven chapters disposed in three parts. Part 1, Structuralism and Linguistic Models, has chapters on The Linguistic Foundation (in de Saussure), The Development of a Method (in Lévi-Strauss), Jakobson's Poetic Analyses, Greimas and Structural Semantics, and Linguistic Metaphors in Criticism. Part 2, Poetics, summarizes the principles of structuralist thought in chapters on Literary Competence, Convention and Naturalization, Poetics of the Lyric, and Poetics of the Novel. Part 3, Perspectives, looks "Beyond" Structuralism, and then presents a Conclusion: Structuralism and the Qualities of Literature. In addition to notes, there is a useful twenty-page sheer list bibliography.

X–19 Some Frequently Recommended Works on Czech and French Structuralism and Semiotics.

Barthes, Roland. *Critical Essays.* Translation by Richard Howard of *Essais critiques* (Paris: du Seuil, 1964). Evanston, Ill.: Northwestern University Press, 1972.   PN710.B2713

————. *Elements of Semiology.* London: Jonathan Cape, 1967.   P123.B3813

————. *Writing Degree Zero.* London: Jonathan Cape, 1967.   PN203.B313

Boon, James A. *From Symbolism to Structuralism: Lévi-Strauss in a Literary Tradition.* New York: Harper and Row, 1972.   GN21.L4 B66

Broekman, Jan M. *Structuralism: Moscow, Prague, Paris.* Dordrecht: D. Reidel, 1974.   B841.4.B7613 1974

Caws, Peter. *Structuralism: The Art of the Intelligible.* Atlantic Highlands, N.J.: Humanities Press International, 1988.   B841.4.C39 1988

Culler, Jonathan. *Ferdinand de Saussure.* Rev. ed. Ithaca: Cornell University Press, 1986.   P85.518 C8 1986

————. *Pursuit of Signs: Semiotics, Literature, Deconstruction.* Ithaca, N.Y.: Cornell University Press, 1981.   PN98.S46 C84

Doubrovsky, Serge. *New Criticism in France.* Chicago: University of Chicago Press, 1973.   PN81.D613

Eco, Umberto. *Theory of Semiotics.* Bloomington: Indiana University Press, 1979.   P99.E3

Ehrmann, Jacques, ed. *Structuralism.* New York: Doubleday, Anchor Books, 1970.   B841.4.E34

Elam, Keir. *Semiotics in Theatre and Drama.* London: Methuen, 1980.   PN1633.S45 E4 1980

Freedman, Sanford, and Carole Anne Taylor. *Roland Barthes: A Bibliographical Reader's Guide.* New York: Garland, 1983.   Z8076.77.F73 1983

Galan, F. W. *Historic Structures: The Prague School Project, 1928–1946.* Austin: University of Texas Press, 1984.   PN98.S7 G34 1984

Gardner, Howard. *Quest for Mind: Piaget, Lévi-Strauss, and the Structuralist Movement.* New York: Random House, 1972.   B841.4.G37 1972

Garvin, Paul L. *A Prague School Reader on Esthetics, Literary Structure and Style.* Washington, D.C.: Georgetown University Press, 1964.   P121.G32

Greimas, A. J., and J. Courtes. *Semiotics and Language: An Analytical Dictionary.* Bloomington: Indiana University Press, 1982.   P99.G6913 1982

Hawkes, Terence. *Structuralism and Semiotics.* Berkeley, Los Angeles, London: University of California Press, 1977. Extended, annotated Bibliography.   P146.H3

Innis, Robert E. *Semiotics: An Introductory Anthology.* Bloomington: Indiana University Press, 1985.   P99.S3873 1985

Jakobson, Roman. *Language in Literature.* Edited by Krystyna Pomorska and Stephen Rudy. Cambridge: Belknap Press of Harvard University Press, 1987.   PN54.J35 1987

————. *Questions de poétique.* Paris: du Seuil, 1973.   PN1136.J34

————. *Verbal Art, Verbal Sign, Verbal Time.* Edited by Krystyna Romorska and Stephen Rudy. Minneapolis: University of Minnesota Press, 1985.   P49.J35 1985

Jakobson, Roman, and Morris Halle. *Fundamentals of Language.* 2d rev. ed. The Hague: Mouton, 1971.   P217.J28 1971

Jameson, Frederic. *Prison-House of Language: A Critical Account of Structuralism and Russian Formalism.* Princeton, N.J.: Princeton University Press, 1972. Bibliography.   P123.J34

Kurzweil, Edith. *Age of Structuralism: Lévi-Strauss to Foucault.* New York: Columbia University Press, 1980.   B2424.S75 K87

Lane, Michael, ed. *Structuralism: A Reader.* London: Jonathan Cape, 1970.   B841.4.L3

Lotman, Yuri M. *Analysis of the Poetic Text.* Ed. and trans. by D. Barton Johnson. Ann Arbor: Ardis, 1976.   PN1047.L5713

Mukarovsky, Jan. *Aesthetic Function: Norm and Value as Social Facts.* Ann Arbor: University of Michigan Press, 1979.   PN45.M6713 1979

————. *Word and Verbal Art: Selected Essays.* Translated and edited by John Burbank and Peter Steiner. New Haven: Yale University Press, 1977.   PN37.M79

Pettit, Philip. *Concept of Structuralism: A Critical Analysis.* Berkeley and Los Angeles: University of California Press, 1975.   P123.P46

Piaget, Jean. *Structuralism.* New York: Basic Books, 1970.   B841.4.P513

Riffaterre, Michael. *Semiotics of Poetry.* Bloomington: Indiana University Press, 1978.   P99.R5

Robey, David, ed. *Structuralism: An Introduction.* Oxford: Clarendon Press, 1973.   B841.4.S85

Schmid, Herta, and Aloysius van Kesteren, eds. *Semiotics of Drama and Theatre: New Perspectives in the Theory of Drama and Theatre.* Amsterdam: J. Benjamins, 1984.   PN1633.S45 S47 1984

Scholes, Robert. *Semiotics and Interpretation.* New Haven: Yale University Press, 1982.   PN98.S46 S3 1982

————. *Structuralism in Literature: An Introduction.* New Haven: Yale University Press, 1974. Annotated bibliography.   PN98.S753

Sebeok, Thomas A., ed. *Encyclopedia Dictionary of Semiotics.* 3 vols. Berlin: Mouton de Gruyter, 1986.   P99.E65 1986

Sheriff, John K. *Fate of Meaning: Charles Peirce, Structuralism, and Literature.* Princeton: Princeton University Press, 1989.   PN81.S43 1989

Shukman, Ann. *Literature and Semiotics: A Study of the Writings of Yuri M. Lotman.* Amsterdam: North-Holland Publishing Co., 1977.   PN98.S7 S5

Silverman, Kaja. *Subject of Semiotics.* New York: Oxford University Press.   P99.S52 1983

Steiner, Peter, ed. *Prague School: Selected Writings, 1929–1946*. Austin: University of Texas Press, 1982.
P147.P7 1982

Tavor Bannet, Eve. *Structuralism and the Logic of Dissent: Barthes, Derrida, Foucault, Lacan*. Urbana: University of Illinois Press, 1989.   PN98.S7 T37 1989

Tejera, V. *Semiotics from Peirce to Barthes: A Conceptual Introduction to the Study of Communication, Interpretation, and Expression*. Leiden: E.J. Brill, 1988.
P99.T39 1988

Wellek, René. *Literary Theory and Aesthetics of the Prague School*. Ann Arbor: University of Michigan Press, 1969.   PN72.P7 W4

X–20 **Cohen, Ralph, ed. *New Literary History International Bibliography of Literary Theory and Criticism [for 1984–1985]*.** Baltimore: Johns Hopkins University Press, 1988.   Z6514.C97 C65 1988

This annual bibliography is disposed into thirty-two sections, categorized by the language, country, and year of publication of the works enumerated. Works in a total of twenty languages are cited, and they are enumerated under such topics as deconstruction, feminism, hermeneutics, semiotics, and structuralism. There is an alphabetical index by author.

X–21 **Orr, Leonard. *Research in Critical Theory Since 1965: A Classified Bibliography*.** New York: Greenwood, 1989.
Z5514.C97 O77 1989

This volume enumerates a total of 5,523 books, articles, and dissertations published during the period 1965–1987. It is classified in twelve sections as follows: A. Structuralism; B. Semiotics (excluding Narrative Semiotics); C. Narratology, Narrative Text-Grammar, Narrative Semiotics; D. Psychological Criticism; E. Sociological Criticism, Literature and Society; F. Marxist Criticism, Literature and Politics; G. Feminist Criticism, Gender Criticism; H. Reader-Response Criticism; I. Reception Aesthetics; J. Phenomenological Criticism; K. Hermeneutics; and L. Deconstruction, Post-Structuralist Criticism, Post-Deconstruction Criticism. Each chapter has its own index, all twelve of which are grouped together into a Classified Index of Subjects and Major Theories. In addition, a General Index and an Author Index further facilitate access to the contents of the volume.

Orr is now preparing a *Dictionary of Critical Theory* and a *Handbook of Critical Theory*, both of which are scheduled for publication by Greenwood Press when they are completed.

X–23 **Tompkins, Jane, ed. *Reader-Response Criticism: From Formalism to Post-structuralism*.** Baltimore, Md.: Johns Hopkins University Press, 1980.   PN98.R38 R4

This standard anthology of major articles in reader-response criticism (including works by Gibson, Prince, Riffaterre, Poulet, Iser, Fish, Culler, Holland, Bleich, and Benn Michaels) begins with an excellent "Introduction to Reader-Response Criticism" and concludes with a survey review, "The Reader in History: The Changing Shape of Literary Response." A forty-page annotated bibliography in two parts, Theoretical and Applied, concludes this useful volume.

X–24 **Some Frequently Recommended Works on Phenomenology, Hermeneutics, Reception Theory, and Reader-Response Criticism.**

Armstrong, Paul, B. *Conflicting Readerings: Variety and Validity in Interpretation*. Chapel Hill: University of North Carolina Press, 1990.   PN98.R38 A76 1990

Bleich, David. *Subjective Criticism*. Baltimore: Johns Hopkins University Press, 1978.   P51.B55

Caws, Mary Ann, ed. *Textual Analysis: Some Readers Reading*. New York: MLA, 1986.   PN710.T467 1986

Davis, Walter A. *Act of Interpretation*. Chicago: University of Chicago Press, 1978.   PN81.D377

Eco, Umberto. *Role of the Reader: Explorations in the Semiotics of Texts*. Bloomington: Indiana University Press, 1979.   P99.E28

Falk, Eugene H. *Poetics of Roman Ingarden*. Chapel Hill: University of North Carolina Press, 1981.
B4691.J534 F34

Fish, Stanley. *Is There a Text in This Class? The Authority of Interpretive Communities*. Cambridge: Harvard University Press, 1980.   PN81.F56

——. *Self-Consuming Artifacts: The Experience of Seventeenth-Century Literature*. Berkeley and Los Angeles: University of California Press, 1972.
PN741.F5

——. *Surprised by Sin: The Reader in* Paradise Lost. Berkeley and Los Angeles: University of California Press, 1967.   P$3562.F5 1967

Freund, Elizabeth. *Return of the Reader: Reader-Response Criticism*. New York: Methuen, 1987.
PN98.R38 F7 1987

Hirsch, E. D., Jr. *Aims of Interpretation*. Chicago: University of Chicago Press, 1976.   PN81.H49

——. *Validity in Interpretation*. New Haven: Yale University Press, 1967.   PN81.H5

Holland, Norman. *Five Readers Reading*. New Haven: Yale University Press, 1975.   PN49.H65

Holub, Robert C. *Reception Theory: A Critical Introduction*. London: Methuen, 1984.   PT80.H64 1984

Howard, Roy J. *Three Faces of Hermeneutics: An Introduction to Current Theories of Understanding*. Berkeley and Los Angeles: University of California Press, 1982.   BD241.H73

Hoy, David Couzens. *Critical Circle: Literature, History, and Philosophical Hermeneutics*. Berkeley, Los Angeles, London: University of California Press, 1978.
BD241.H74

Ihde, Don. *Hermeneutic Phenomenology: The Philosophy of Paul Ricoeur*. Evanston, Ill.: Northwestern University Press, 1971.   B2430.R554 I43

Ingarden, Roman. *Cognition of the Literary Work of Art*. Translation by Ruth Ann Crowley and Kenneth R. Olson of *Vom Erkennen des literarischen Kunstwerks* (1937). Evanston, Ill.: Northwestern University Press, 1973.   PN45.I513

——. *Literary Work of Art: An Investigation on the Borderline of Ontology, Logic, and the Theory of Literature*. Translation by George Grabowicz of *Das literarische Kunstwerk*, 3d ed. (Tübingen: Niemeyer, 1965). Evanston, Ill.: Northwestern University Press, 1973.   PN49.I613

Iser, Wolfgang. *Act of Reading: A Theory of Aesthetic Response*. Translation of *Der Akt des Lesens* (Munich: Fink, 1976). Baltimore: Johns Hopkins University Press, 1978.   PN83.I813

——. *Implied Reader: Patterns of Communication in Prose Fiction from Bunyan to Beckett*. Translation of *Der implizite Leser* (Munich: Fink, 1972). Baltimore: Johns Hopkins University Press, 1974. PN3491.I813

Jauss, Hans Robert. *Aesthetic Experience and Literary Hermeneutics*. Minneapolis: University of Minnesota Press, 1982.   PN45.J313 1982

———. *Literaturgeschichte als Provokation.* Frankfurt: Suhrkamp, 1970. PN441.J3

———. *Toward an Aesthetic of Reception.* Minneapolis: University of Minnesota Press, 1982. PN98.R38 J38 1982

Lawall, Sarah, N. *Critics of Consciousness: The Existential Structures of Literature.* Cambridge: Harvard University Press, 1968. PN99.F83 L3

Magliola, Robert R. *Phenomenology and Literature.* West Lafayette, Ind.: Purdue University Press, 1977. PN49.M375

Mailloux, Steven. *Interpretive Conventions: The Reader in the Study of American Fiction.* Ithaca: Cornell University Press, 1982. PN98.R38 M3 1982

Newton, K. M. *In Defense of Literary Interpretation: Theory and Practice.* New York: St. Martin's, 1986. PN81.N44 1986

Palmer, Richard E. *Hermeneutics: Interpretation Theory in Schleiermacher, Dilthey, Heidegger, and Gadamer.* Evanston, Ill.: Northwestern University Press, 1969. BD241.P32

Ray, William. *Literary Meaning: From Phenomenology to Deconstruction.* Oxford: Clarendon Press, 1984. PN94.R33 1984

Ricoeur, Paul. *Hermeneutics and the Human Sciences: Essays on Language, Action and Interpretation.* Cambridge: Cambridge University Press, 1981. BD241.R484

———. *Interpretation Theory: Discourse and the Surplus of Meaning.* Fort Worth: Texas Christian University Press, 1976. P302.R5

Rosenblatt, Louise. *Reader: The Text, The Poem.* Carbondale: Southern Illinois University Press, 1978. PN45.R587

Seung, T. K. *Semiotics and Thematics in Hermeneutics.* New York: Columbia University Press, 1982. P99.S443 1982

———. *Structuralism and Hermeneutics.* New York: Columbia University Press, 1982. B841.4.S45

Singleton, Charles, ed. *Interpretation: Theory and Practice.* Baltimore: Johns Hopkins University Press, 1969. BD241.I54

Slatoff, Walter. *With Respect to Readers: Dimensions of Literary Response.* Ithaca, N.Y.: Cornell University Press, 1970. PN61.S58

Spanos, William V., et al., eds. *Question of Textuality: Strategies of Reading in Contemporary American Criticism.* Bloomington: Indiana University Press, 1982. PN99.U5 Q4 1984

———, ed. *Martin Heidegger and the Question of Literature: Toward a Postmodern Literary Hermeneutics.* Bloomington: Indiana University Press, 1979. B3279.YH49 M285

Suleiman, Susan, and Inge Crosman, eds. *Reader in the Text: Essays on Audience and Interpretation.* Princeton, N.J.: Princeton University Press, 1980. Excellent bibliography. PN83.R4

Warning, Rainer, ed. *Rezeptionsästhetik: Theorie und Praxis.* Munich: Fink, 1975. PN45.R474

X-27 **Eagleton, Terry.** *Literary Theory: An Introduction.* Minneapolis: University of Minnesota Press, 1983. PN94.E2 1983

This standard history of contemporary theory from a Marxist perspective is disposed into five chapters, preceded by an Introduction: What is Literature? and a Conclusion: Political Criticism. The chapters treat the Rise of English; Phenomenology, Hermeneutics, Reception Theory; Structuralism and Semiotics; Post-Structuralism; and Psychoanalysis. A classified, sheer list bibliography of eight pages concludes the volume.

X-28 **Some Frequently Recommended Works on Deconstruction and Poststructuralism.**

Arac, Jonathan, ed. *Postmodernism and Politics.* Minneapolis: University of Minnesota Press,1986. PN98.P64 P67 1986

———, et al., eds. *Yale Critics: Deconstruction in America.* Minneapolis: University of Minnesota Press, 1983. PN98.D43 Y34 1983

Atkins, G. Douglas. *Reading Deconstruction: Deconstructive Reading.* Lexington: University Press of Kentucky, 1983. PN98.D43 A84 1983

———, and Michael Johnson, eds. *Writing and Reading Differently: Deconstruction and the Teaching of Composition and Literature.* Lawrence: University of Kansas Press, 1985. PE66.Q74 1985

Barthes, Roland. *Pleasure of the Text.* New York: Hill and Wang, 1975. PN45.B2813 1975

———. *S/Z.* Translation by Richard Miller of *S/Z* (Paris: du Seuil, 1970). New York: Hill and Wang, 1974. P99.B313 1974

Belsey, Catherine. *Critical Practice.* London: Methuen, 1980. PN81.B395

Bloom, Harold. *Anxiety of Influence: A Theory of Poetry.* London: Oxford University Press, 1973. PN1031.B53

———. *Map of Misreading.* New York: Oxford University Press, 1975. PR504.B56

———, et al. *Deconstruction and Criticism.* New York: Seabury Press, 1979. PN94.D4

Clark, Michael. *Jacques Lacan: An Annotated Bibliography.* 2 vols. New York: Garland, 1988. Z8469.39.C58 1988

———. *Michel Foucault: An Annotated Bibliography. Tool Kit for a New Age.* New York: Garland, 1983. Z8310.8.C57 1983

Cousins, Mark, and Athar Hussein. *Michel Foucault.* New York: St. Martin's, 1984. B2430.F724 C68 1984

Coward, Rosalind, and John Ellis. *Language and Materialism: Developments in Semiology and the Theory of the Subject.* London: Routledge and Kegan Paul, 1977. P99.C65

Culler, Jonathan. *On Deconstruction: Theory and Criticism after Structuralism.* London: Routledge and Kegan Paul, 1983. PN98.D43 C8 1982

———. *Theory and Criticism after Structuralism.* Ithaca, N.Y.: Cornell University Press, 1982. Bibliography with brief annotations. PN98.D43 C8

Deleuze, Gilles, and Felix Guattari. *Anti-Oedipus: Capitalism and Schizophrenia.* New York: Viking Press, 1977. RC455.D42213

de Man, Paul. *Allegories of Reading: Figural Language in Rousseau, Nietzsche, Rilke, and Proust.* New Haven: Yale University Press, 1979. PQ145.D45

———. *Blindness and Insight: Essays in the Rhetoric of Contemporary Criticism.* 2d ed., rev. Minneapolis: University of Minnesota Press, 1971. PN85.M28 1983

———. *Critical Writings: 1953-1978.* Ed. by Lindsay Waters. Minneapolis: University of Minnesota Press, 1989. PN75.D45 A25 1989

———. *Resistance to Theory*. Minneapolis: University of Minnesota Press, 1986.   PN85.D374 1986

Derrida, Jacques. *Of Grammatology*. Translation by Gayatri C. Spivak of *La grammatologie*. Baltimore: Johns Hopkins University Press, 1976.   P105.D5313 1976

———. *Speech and Phenomena, and Other Essays on Husserl's Theory of Signs*. Evanston: Northwestern University Press, 1973.   B3279.H94 D382

———. *Writing and Difference*. Chicago: University of Chicago Press, 1978.   B2430.D482 E5 1978

Dew, Peter. *Logics of Disintegration: Post-structuralist Thought and the Claims of Critical Theory*. London: Verso, 1987.   B841.4.D49 1987

Dreyfus, Hubert, and Paul Rabinow. *Michel Foucault: Beyond Structuralism and Hermeneutics*. Brighton, Eng.: Harvester Press, 1982.   B2430.F724 D73 1982

Ellis, John M. *Against Deconstruction*. Princeton: Princeton University Press, 1989.   PN98.D43 E45 1989

Felperin, Howard. *Beyond Deconstruction: The Uses and Abuses of Literary Theory*. Oxford: Clarendon Press, 1985.   PN94.F45 1985

Foucault, Michel. *Language, Counter-Memory, Practice, Selected Essays and Interviews*. Ed. D. F. Bouchard. Ithaca, N.Y.: Cornell University Press, 1977.   P106.F67

Gasché, Rodolphe. *Tain of the Mirror: Derrida and the Philosophy of Reflection*. Cambridge: Harvard University Press, 1986.   B2430.D494 G37

Goodheart, Eugene. *Skeptic Disposition in Contemporary Criticism*. Princeton: Princeton University Press, 1984.   PN98.D43 G66 1984

Handelman, Susan A. *Slayers of Moses: The Emergence of Rabbinic Interpretation in Modern Literary Theory*. Albany: State University of New York Press, 1982.   BM496.5.H34 1982

Harari, Josué, ed. *Textual Strategies: Perspectives in Post-structuralist Criticism*. Ithaca, N.Y.: Cornell University Press, 1979.   PN94.T4

Hartman, Geoffrey H. *Criticism in the Wilderness*. Baltimore: Johns Hopkins University Press, 1980.   PN94.H34

———. *Saving the Text: Literature/Derrida/Philosophy*. Baltimore: Johns Hopkins University Press, 1981.   PN81.J56 1981

Johnson, Barbara. *Critical Difference: Essays in the Contemporary Rhetoric of Reading*. Baltimore: Johns Hopkins University Press, 1980.   PN85.J5 1981

———. *World of Difference*. Baltimore: Johns Hopkins University Press, 1987.   PN85.J5 1987

Kristeva, Julia. *Desire in Language: A Semiotic Approach to Literature and Art*. Edited by Leon S. Rondiez. New York: Columbia University Press, 1980.   PN98.S46 K7413

———. *Revolution in Poetic Language*. Translation by Margaret Waller of *Revolution du langage poétique* (Paris: du Seuil, 1974). New York: Columbia University Press, 1984.   PN54.K75 1984

LaCapra, Dominick. *Soundings in Critical Theory*. Ithaca: Cornell University Press, 1989.   PN94.L35 1989

Leitch, Vincent B. *Deconstructive Criticism: An Advanced Introduction*. New York: Columbia University Press, 1983.   PN98.D43 L4 1983

Lyotard, Jean François. *Postmodern Condition: A Report on Knowledge*. Minneapolis: University of Minnesota Press, 1984.   BD162.L913 1984

McGann, Jerome J. *Social Values and Poetic Acts: The Historical Judgment of Literary Work*. Cambridge: Harvard University Press, 1988.   PN81.M49 1988

———, ed. *Historical Studies and Literary Criticism*. Madison: University of Wisconsin Press, 1985.   PN98.H57 H57 1985

Macksey, Richard, and Eugenio Donato, eds. *Structuralist Controversy: The Languages of Criticism and the Sciences of Man*. Baltimore: Johns Hopkins University Press, 1970.   B841.4.L33

Magliola, Robert R. *Derrida on the Mend*. West Lafayette, Ind.: Purdue University Press, 1984.   B2430.D484 M34 1984

Merrell, Floyd. *Deconstruction Reframed*. West Lafayette, Ind.: Purdue University Press, 1984.   PN98.D43 M47 1985

Moi, Toril, ed. *Kristeva Reader*. New York: Columbia University Press, 1986.   P99.K687 1986

Norris, Christopher. *Deconstruction: Theory and Practice*. London: Methuen, 1982.   PN98.D43 N6 1982

———. *Deconstructive Turn: Essays in the Rhetoric of Philosophy*. London: Methuen, 1983.   PN98.D43 N62 1984

———. *Derrida*. Cambridge: Harvard University Press, 1987.   B2430.D434 N66 1987

———. *Paul deMan: Deconstruction and the Critique of Aesthetic Ideology*. New York: Routledge, 1988.   PN98.D43 N63 1988

Rabinow, Paul, ed. *Foucault Reader*. New York: Pantheon Books, 1984.   B2430.F721 1984

Ryan, Michael. *Marxism and Deconstruction: A Critical Articulation*. Baltimore: Johns Hopkins University Press, 1982.   HX73.R9 1982

Said, Edward. *Beginnings: Intention and Method*. New York: Basic Books, 1975.   PN441.S3

———. *World, the Text, and the Critic*. Cambridge: Harvard University Press, 1983.   PN81.S223 1983

Sarup, Madan. *Introductory Guide to Post-Structuralism and Postmodernism*. Athens: University of Georgia Press, 1989.   B841.4.S26 1989

Scholes, Robert. *Textual Power: Literary Theory and the Teaching of English*. New Haven: Yale University Press, 1985.   PN94.S25 1985

Smith, Barbara Herrnstein. *Contingencies of Value: Alternative Perspectives for Critical Theory*. Cambridge: Harvard University Press, 1988.   PN45.S4794 1988

Taylor, Mark C. *Deconstruction in Context*. Chicago: University of Chicago Press, 1986.   B29.D365 1986

Waters, Lindsay, and Wlad Godzich, eds. *Reading deMan Reading*. Minneapolis: University of Minnesota Press, 1989.   PN75.D45 R43 1989

Young, Robert, ed. *Untying the Text: A Post-Structuralist Reader*. London: Routledge and Kegan Paul, 1981.   PN45.U5

X–29 Guide to Collections of Excerpts from Modern Criticism.

The earliest guide to opinions, primarily of nineteenth-century critics, was edited by Charles Wells Moulton, the *Library of Literary Criticism of English and American Authors*, 8 vols. (Buffalo, N.Y.: Moulton, 1901–1905) [PR83.M73]. This work, reprinted with additions and revisions by Martin Tucker, 4 vols. (New York: Ungar, 1966) [PR83.M73 1966], is arranged chronologically for English and American authors from 680 to 1904. Biographical notes are followed by quotations from a variety of critics. The original eighth volume and the reprinted fourth volume contain indexes of authors and critics.

Martin Tucker also edited *Critical Temper: A Survey of Modern Criticism in English and American Literature from the Beginnings to the Twentieth Century*, 3 vols. (New York: Ungar, 1969–1979) [PR85.C77]. These volumes were designed to supplement Moulton with twentieth-century critical commentary on authors to 1900. Also chronologically arranged by period (vol. 1, From Old English to Shakespeare; vol. 2, From Milton to Romantic Literature; vol. 3, Victorian Literature and American Literature), this series concludes with an index to literary authors and to critics whose judgments are quoted.

These two works have been extended and expanded as the Ungar series a *Library of Literary Criticism*, to include multivolume gatherings of contemporary critical commentary on various literatures. The subtitles of the volumes published to date are as follows:

Hebrew Bible in Literary Criticism. Edited by Alex Preminger and Edward L. Greenstein. New York: Ungar, 1986.   BS1171.2.H43 1986

Major Modern Dramatists. Edited by Rita Stein and Friedhelm Rickert. 2 vols. New York: Ungar, 1984-1986.   PN1861.M27 1984

Modern American Literature. Edited by Dorothy N. Curley. 4th enl. ed. 4 vols. New York: Ungar, 1969–1976. Vol. 5, Second Supplement to the 4th ed. Compiled by Paul Schlueter and June Schlueter. 1985.
                                        PS221.C8 1969

Modern Arabic Literature. Edited by Roger Allen. New York: Ungar, 1987.   PJ7538.M58 1987

Modern Black Writers. Edited by Michael Popkin. New York: Ungar, 1978.   PN841.M58

Modern British Literature. Edited by Ruth Z. Temple and Martin Tucker. 5 vols. New York: Ungar, 1966–1985.   PR473.T4

Modern Commonwealth Literature. Edited by John H. Ferres and Martin Tucker. New York: Ungar, 1977.
                                        PR9080.M6

Modern French Literature. Edited by Debra Popkin and Michael Popkin. 2 vols. New York: Ungar, 1977.
                                        PQ306.M57

Modern German Literature. Edited by Agnes Domandi Langdon. 2 vols. New York: Ungar, 1972.   PT401.D6

Modern Irish Literature. Edited by Denis Lane and Carol McCrory Lane. New York: Ungar, 1988.
                                        PR8753.L36 1988

Modern Latin American Literature. Edited by David W. Foster. 2 vols. New York: Ungar, 1975–.
                                        PQ7081.F63 1975

Modern Slavic Literature. Edited by Vasa D. Mihailovich. 2 vols. New York: Ungar, 1972–1976.   PG501.M518

New Testament in Literary Criticism. Edited by Leland Ryken. New York: Ungar, 1984. BS2361.2.N38 1984

Also published is an *Index Guide to Modern American Literature and Modern British Literature* (New York: Ungar, 1988) [PS221.C83 I53 1988] which indexes the five volumes of *Modern American Literature* and the five volumes of *Modern British Literature*.

A competing but less valuable set of five continuing multivolume series is being published by Gale Research in Detroit. Each volume in each series contains for each literary author a biographical and bibliographical notice, including a list of the author's principal works, followed by excerpts from the critical literature (contemporary to current) and a checklist of additional sources of critical commentary. The following series are now in publication:

Literature Criticism from 1400 to 1800. Edited by Dennis Poupard. Vol. 1–. Detroit: Gale, 1984–.
                                        PN86.L53 1984

Shakespearean Criticism. Edited by Laurie L. Harris. Vol. 1–. Detroit: Gale, 1984–.   PR2965.S43 1984

Nineteenth-Century Literature Criticism. Edited by Laurie L. Harris. Vol. 1–. Detroit: Gale, 1981–. PN761.N56

Twentieth-Century Literature Criticism [authors, 1900–1960]. Edited by Sharon K. Hall. Vol. 1–. Detroit: Gale, 1978–.   PN771.G27

Contemporary Literary Criticism [authors living or deceased after 1959]. Edited by Sharon R. Gunton. Vol. 1–. Detroit: Gale, 1973–.   PN771.C59

III. LITERATURE AND THE OTHER ARTS AND SCIENCES

In addition to the materials found in this division, see many references in section F for History and Literature and for Geography and Literature, and in section G for Biography and Literature. See entries in section I for Linguistics and Literature (along with entries in X.IV and X.V below). See section K.I for Folklore and Literature; section K.II for Myth and Literature; and section K.VIII for Social, Cultural and Intellectual History and Literature. In addition, see sections U.VIII-XI for film and literature.

X–30 **Barricelli, Jean-Pierre, and Joseph Gibaldi, eds.** *Interrelations of Literature*. New York: MLA, 1982.
                                        PN45.8.I56 1982

This volume provides an introduction to various arts and sciences in relation to which literature is studied. Each essay, written by a noted scholar, examines the relation between literature and the discipline in question; provides a historical overview of its study, with a review of leading scholarship; and considers selected methodologies, issues, and prospects for research. Brief basic bibliographies are appended to each essay. The individual disciplines and the scholars responsible for their introduction are as follows: Literature and Linguistics (Jonathan Culler); Literature and Philosophy (Thomas McFarland); Literature and Religion (Giles Gunn); Literature and Myth (John B. Vickery); Literature and Folklore (Bruce A. Rosenberg); Literature and Sociology (Priscilla B. P. Clark); Literature and Politics (Matei Calinescu); Literature and Law (Richard Weisberg and Jean-Pierre Barricelli); Literature and Science (George Slusser and George Guffey); Literature and Psychology (Murray M. Schwartz and David Willburn); Literature and Music (Steven P. Scher); Literature and the Visual Arts (Ulrich Weisstein); Literature and Film (Gerland Mast). A glossary and an index of names conclude the volume.

X–31 **Thorpe, James, ed.** *Relations of Literary Study: Essays on Interdisciplinary Contributions*. New York: Modern Language Association of America, 1967.   PN45.R39

This volume contains a series of introductory essays on interdisciplinary literary studies designed to complement the earlier MLA pamphlet on the *Aims and Methods of Scholarship in Modern Languages and Literatures* (see Z–19). Included are chapters on "Literature and History" by Rosalie L. Colie; "Literature and Myth" by Northrop Frye, with "Myth and Myth Criticism: An Introductory Bibliography" appended; "Literature and Biography" by Leon Edel, with a "Bibliographical Note" appended; "Literature and Psychology" by

Frederick L. Crews; "Literature and Sociology" by Leo Lowenthal, with a bibliographical survey appended; "Literature and Religion" by J. Hillis Miller; and "Literature and Music" by Bertrand H. Bronson, with a supplemental bibliography appended.

X–32 **"Selective Current Bibliography for Aesthetics and Related Fields [1941–1972]." in the** *Journal of Aesthetics and Art Criticism [JAAC]*, **vols.** 4–31. Philadelphia: American Society for Aesthetics, 1945–1973.　　　　N1.J6

This unannotated international bibliography includes books and articles, with some analysis of composite volumes. Entries are of materials concerned with the theoretical study of the arts. They are disposed into various categories according to their primary field of interest. The categories have varied over the years, but include such headings as the following: Architecture; Art Education; Cultural History; General Aesthetics; Literature; Music; Musicology; Motion Pictures and Photography; Museums; Philosophy and General Theory of Art; Psychology of Art; The Visual Arts.

X–33 **Hammond, William A., ed.** *Bibliography of Aesthetics and of the Philosophy of the Fine Arts, from 1900 to 1932.* Rev. and enl. ed. New York: Longmans, 1934.　　Z5069.H3

This work, originally published as a supplement to the 1933 *Philosophical Review*, contains a total of 2,191 serially numbered, briefly annotated entries disposed into seventeen categories, as follows: I. Reference Works; II. Systematic and General Works; III. History of Aesthetic Theories; IV. Painting and the Graphic Arts; V. Sculpture; VI. Architecture; VII. Civic Art; VIII. Poetry and the Aesthetics of Literature (with subdivisions by genre); IX. Music; X. Color; XI. Design and Decorative Art; XII. Style (subdivisions for the various period styles); XIII. Origins of Art and Primitive Art; XIV. Symbolism; XV. Art and Psychology; XVI. Art and Morality; and XVII. Art and Religion. There is an index of authors.

X–34 **Erdman, David.** *Literature and the Other Arts: A Select Bibliography, 1952-[1967].* New York: AMS Press, 1968.　　　　Z6511.M628

This volume partly cumulates the briefly annotated, annual bibliographies of secondary materials on the relations between literature and music and between literature and the visual arts. Prepared by MLA General Topics Group IX during the period 1953–1966, entries are in three categories: Theory and General, Music and Literature, and Visual Arts and Literature. A single cumulation for the period 1952–1958 (to which an index of authors is appended) is followed by annual lists for 1959 to and including 1967.

X–35 **"A Bibliography on Relations of Literature and the Other Arts [1973–1975]."** *Hartford Studies in Literature,* **vols.** 6–8. West Hartford, Conn.: University of Hartford, 1974–1976.　　　　PN2.H3

This comprehensive, international bibliography, sponsored by the MLA Division on Literature and the Other Arts, includes books and articles on the theory and methodology of comparative studies and on relations between literature and music, literature and art, and literature and film.

Since 1978 this bibliography has been published separately by the Department of German, Dartmouth College, Hanover, N.H., with the title *Bibliography on Relations of Literature and the Other Arts* [1976–] [No LC number].

X–38 **Scholarly Journals in Literature and the Other Arts and Sciences.**

General

BUR 　*Bucknell Review.* Vol. 1–. Lewisburg, Pa.: Bucknell University Press, 1941–. 2/yr.
　　　　　　　　　　　　　　　No LC number

Daedalus *Daedalus: Journal of the American Academy of Arts and Sciences.* Vol. 1–. Boston: American Academy of Arts and Sciences, 1958–. 4/yr.
　　　　　　　　　　　　　　　No LC number

　　Empirical Studies of the Arts. Vol. 1–. Farmingdale, N.Y.: Baywood Publishing Co., 1983. 2/yr. Reviews. Research in Progress.

　　Hartford Studies in Literature. Vol. 1–. West Hartford, Conn.: University of Hartford, 1968–. 3/yr. Annual Bibliography on Literature and the Other Arts. (X–35)　　　　PN2.H3

　　Mosaic: A Journal for the Interdisciplinary Study of Literature. Vol. 1–. Winnipeg: University of Manitoba, 1967–.　　　　PN2.M68

　　Representations. Vol. 1–. Berkeley, Los Angeles, London: University of California Press, 1983–. 4/yr.　　　　NX1.R46

Soundings *Soundings: A Journal of Interdisciplinary Studies.* Vol. 1–. Nashville: Vanderbilt University Press, 1968–. 4/yr. Reviews.　　　　BV1460.C6

Note that numerous other journals in English and American literature in period or in genre studies are also hospitable to interdisciplinary studies.

Art and Art History

Dada 　*Dada/Surrealism.* Vol. 1–. New York: Queen's College Press, 1971–. 1/yr. "A Selective Bibliography of Works on Dada/Surrealism Published in North America."　　　　NX600.D3 D34

JAAC 　*Journal of Aesthetics and Art Criticism.* Vol. 1–. Philadelphia: American Society for Aesthetics, 1941–. 4/yr. Reviews. Annual "Selective Current Bibliography for Aesthetics and Related Fields" X–32.　　　　N1J6

JWCI 　*Journal of the Warburg and Courtauld Institutes.* Vol. 1–. London: University of London, 1937–. 1/yr.　　　　AS122.L8515

　　Word and Image: A Journal of Verbal/Visual Inquiry. Vol. 1–. London: Taylor & Francis, 1985–. 4/yr.　　　　NX1.W64

Religion

C&L 　*Christianity and Literature.* Vol. 1–. Grand Rapids, Mich.: Calvin College for the Conference on Christianity and Literature, 1951–. 4/yr. Reviews. Annual Bibliography (X–52).　　　　PN49.C49

Cithara *Cithara: Essays in the Judeo-Christian Tradition.* Vol. 1–. New York: St. Bonaventure University. 1961–. 2/yr. Reviews.　　　　No LC number

　　Clio (see History).

　　Literature and Theology. Vol. 1–. Oxford: Oxford University Press, 1987–. 4/yr. Reviews.
　　　　　　　　　　　　　　　No LC number

　　Renascence: Essays on Values in Literature [Renascence]. Milwaukee, Wisc.: Marquette University, 1948–. 4/yr. Reviews.　　　　PN2.R4

Thought *Thought: A Review of Culture and Ideas.* Vol. 1–. New York: Fordham University Press, 1926–. 4/yr. Reviews.　　　　AP2.T333

Philosophy

Clio (see History).

JHI   *Journal of the History of Ideas.* Vol. 1–. Baltimore: Johns Hopkins University Press, 1940–. 4/yr.   B1.J75

P&L   *Philosophy and Literature.* Vol. 1–. Baltimore: Johns Hopkins University Press, 1976–. 2/yr. Reviews.   PN2.P5

Psychology

AI   *American Imago: A Psychoanalytic Journal for Culture, Literature, Science, and the Arts.* Vol. 1–. Detroit: Wayne State University Press, 1939–. 4/yr. Reviews.   No LC number

Gradiva   *Gradiva: A Journal of Contemporary Theory and Practice.* Vol. 1–. Stony Brook, N.Y.: SUNY Stony Brook, 1976–. 4/yr. Reviews.   PN80.G7

L&P   *Literature and Psychology.* Vol. 1–. Teaneck, N.J.: Fairleigh Dickinson University Press, 1950–. 4/yr. Reviews. Annual bibliography (X–61).   PN49.L5

Psychiatry: Journal for the Study of Interpersonal Processes [Psychiatry]. Vol. 1–. Washington, D.C.: William Alanson White Psychiatric Foundation, 1938–. 4/yr. Reviews.   RC321.P93

Psychoanalytic Study of Literature. Vol. 1–. Hillsdale, N.J.: Analytic Press, 1975–. 4/yr.   PN56.P92 P74

Politics

L&I   *Literature and Ideology.* Vol. 1–. Montreal, 1965–.   No LC number

New Left Review. Vol. 1–. London: New Left Review, Ltd., 1960–. 6/yr.   HX3.N36

Praxis   *Praxis: A Journal of Radical Perspectives on the Arts.* Goleta, Calif.: Praxis, 1975–. 3/yr.

S&S   *Science and Society: An Independent Journal of Marxism.* New York, 1976–.   No LC number

History

Clio   *Clio: An Interdisciplinary Journal of Literature, History, and the Philosophy of History.* Vol. 1–. Ypsilanti: Eastern Michigan University Press, 1971–. 3–4/yr. Reviews. Bibliography: "Relations of Literature and Science" (X–87).   No LC number

Historical Methods [former title: *Historical Methods Newsletter,* 1967–1977.]. Vol. 1–. Washington, D.C.: Heldref, 1967–. 4/yr.   H1.H525

History and Theory: Studies in the Philosophy of History. Vol. 1–. Middletown, Conn.: Wesleyan University Press, 1960–. 4/yr. Index to vols. 1–5 in vol. 5 and vols. 6–10 in vol. 10.   D1.H8173

Journal of Interdisciplinary History. Vol. 1–. Cambridge: Massachusetts Institute of Technology, 1970–. 4/yr.   D1.J59

L&H   *Literature and History: A Journal for the Humanities.* Vol. 1–. London: Thames Polytechnic, 1975–. 2/yr. Review essays and reviews.   AS122.T45 A25

Science

Clio (see History).

Isis   *An International Review Devoted to the History of Science and Its Cultural Influences.* Vol. 1–. Washington, D.C.: History of Science Society, 1913–. 5/yr. Reviews. Annual "Critical Bibliography of the History of Science and its Cultural Influences" (X–88).   Q1.I7

Medicine

Bulletin of the History of Medicine. Vol. 1–. Baltimore: Johns Hopkins University Press, 1933–. 4/yr. Reviews. Bibliography (see X–91).   R11.B93

Journal of the History of Medicine and Allied Sciences. Vol. 1–. New York: Schuman, 1946–.   R131.A1 J6

Literature and Medicine. Vol. 1–. Baltimore: Johns Hopkins University Press, 1983–. 1/yr.   PN56.M38 L57

Technology

Technology and Culture: The International Quarterly of the Society for the History of Technology. Vol. 1–. Chicago: University of Chicago Press, 1959–. 4/yr. Reviews. Annual "Current Bibliography in the History of Technology" (X–95).   T1.T27

Transactions of the Newcomen Society for the Study of the History of Engineering and Technology. Vol. 1–. London: The Society, 1920/21–. Reviews. Annual "Analytical Bibliography of the History of Engineering and Applied Science." General Index for vols. 1–32 (1920–1960).   T1.N47

X–39   **Some Frequently Recommended Works on Literature and the Other Arts and Sciences in General.**

General

Giovannini, Giovanni. "Method in the Study of Literature and Its Relations to the Other Fine Arts." *JAAC* 8 (1950): 185–194.

Greene, Theodor Meyer. *Arts and the Art of Criticism.* 3d ed. Princeton, N.J.: Princeton University Press, 1947.   N66.G74

Malek, James S. *Arts Compared: An Aspect of Eighteenth Century British Aesthetics.* Detroit: Wayne State University Press, 1974.   BH221.G73 M33

Munro, Thomas. *Arts and Their Interrelationships: An Outline of Comparative Aesthetics.* Rev. and enl. ed. Cleveland: Case Western Reserve University Press, 1967.   N7425.M9 1967

Scher, Steven P., and Ulrich Weisstein, eds. *Literature and the Other Arts.* Vol. 3 of *Proceedings of the IXth Congress of the International Comparative Literature Association.* Innsbruck: AMOE: Institut für Sprachwissenschaft der Universität Innsbruck, 1981.   PN858.I572 1979 vol. 3

Souriau, Etienne. *La correspondance des arts: Eléments d'esthétique comparée.* Paris: Flammarion, 1947.   N70.S7

Weiss, Paul. *Nine Basic Arts.* Carbondale: Southern Illinois University Press, 1961.   N66.W32

Literature and Several Arts

Jensen, H. James. *Muses Concord: Literature, Music, and the Visual Arts in the Baroque Age.* Bloomington: Indiana University Press, 1976.   NX45.1.5.B3 J46 1976

Studing, Richard, and Elizabeth Kruz. *Mannerism in Art, Literature, and Music: A Bibliography.* San Antonio, Tex.: Trinity University Press, 1979. Z5936.M34 S85

X–40   ***RILM Abstracts: Répertoire internationale de la littérature musicale / International Repertory of Music Literature.*** New York: International RILM Center, 1967–.   ML1.I83

This quarterly, international comprehensive collection of informative abstracts (about 4,000 yearly) includes books, reviews, articles, dissertations, catalogs, and various other publications. Abstracts are classified into the following divisions: Reference and Research Materials; Historical Musicology; Enthnomusicology; Instruments and Voice; Performance Practice; Theory, Analysis, and Composition; Pedagogy; Music and the Other Arts; Music and Related Disciplines; and Music and Liturgy. Each issue concludes with an author index; there is also an annual subject index. (A quinquennial cumulation with some 45,000 entries was issued in 1975 for coverage 1967–1971.)

Also available is the monthly *Music Index: A Subject-Author Guide to Current Music Periodical Literature* (Detroit: Information Coordinators, 1949–) [ML118.M84], which provides a detailed alphabetical author-subject index to articles on classical, popular, jazz, folk, and ethnic music, on musicology, and on music performance. Reviews of books, performances, and recordings are listed. Some 350 periodicals, both United States and foreign, are analyzed.

X–44 Some Frequently Recommended Works on Literature and Music. (See also Ballads in section K and Prosody in section T.)

Aronson, Alex. *Music and the Novel.* Totowa, N.J.: Rowman and Littlefield, 1980.   PN3503.A76

Barry, Kevin. *Language, Music, and the Sign: A Study in Aesthetics, Poetics, and Poetic Practice from Collins to Coleridge.* Cambridge: Cambridge University Press, 1987.   ML3849.B28 1987

Bowen, Zuck. *Musical Allusions in the Works of James Joyce: Early Poetry through Ulysses.* Albany: State University of New York Press, 1974. ML80.J75 B7

Brown, Calvin S. *Music and Literature: A Comparison of the Arts.* Athens: University of Georgia Press, 1948.   ML3849.B84

———. "Musico-Literary Research in the Last Two Decades." *YCGL* 19 (1970): 5–27.

———. "The Relations between Music and Literature as a Field of Study." *Comparative Literature* 22 (1970): 97–102.

———. *Tunes into Words: Musical Compositions as Subjects of Poetry.* Athens: University of Georgia Press, 1953.   ML3894.B842

Caldwell, John, et al., eds. *Well-enchanting Skill: Music, Poetry, and Drama in the Culture of the Renaissance. Essays in Honour of F. W. Sternfeld.* Oxford: Clarendon Press, 1989.   ML55.S832 1989

Clinton-Baddeley, V. C. *Words for Music.* Cambridge: Cambridge University Press, 1941. ML3849.C63 W6

Cluck, Nancy Anne, ed. *Literature and Music: Essays on Form.* Provo, Utah: Brigham Young University Press, 1981.   PN56.M87 L5 1981

Cooke, Deryck. *Language of Music.* London: Oxford University Press, 1959.   ML3000.C75

Erskine, John. *Elizabethan Lyric.* New York: Macmillan, 1903.   PR539.L8 E8

Finney, Gretchen. *Musical Backgrounds for English Literature, 1580–1650.* New Brunswick, N.J.: Rutgers University Press, 1962.   ML3849.F55

Friedrich, Martin. *Text und Ton: Wechselbeziehungen zwischen Dichtung und Musik.* Hohengehren: Schneider, 1973.   ML3849.F865T5

Furness, Raymond. *Wagner and Literature.* New York: St. Martin's Press, 1982.   ML410.W13 F95 1982

Gagey, Edward M. *Ballad Opera.* New York: Columbia University Press, 1937.   ML1731.3.G13 B17

Groos, Arthur, and Roger Parker, eds. *Reading Opera.* Princeton, N.J.: Princeton University Press, 1988.   ML2110.R4 1988

Harris, Ellen T. *Handel and the Pastoral Tradition.* London: Oxford University Press, 1980.   ML410.H13 H28

Hartnoll, Phyllis, ed. *Shakespeare in Music: Essays by John Stevens and Others.* New Wmrk: St. Martin's Press, 1967.   ML80.S5 H37 1967

Hertz, David Michael. *Tuning of the Word: The Musico-Literary Poetics of the Symbolist Movement.* Carbondale: Southern Illinois University Press, 1987.   ML3849.H39 1987

Hollander, John. *Untuning of the Sky: Ideas of Music in English Poetry, 1500–1700.* Princeton, N.J.: University Press, 1961.   ML3849.H54

Johnson, Paula. *Form and Transformation in Music and Poetry of the English Renaissance.* New Haven: Yale University Press, 1972.   ML286.2.J6

Jorgens, Elise Bickford. *Well-tun'd Word.* Minneapolis: University of Minnesota Press, 1982.   ML3849.J67

Knapp, Bettina L. *Music, Archetype, and the Writer: A Jungian View.* University Park: Pennsylvania State University Press, 1988.   PN56.M87 K6 1988

Kramer, Lawrence. *Music and Poetry: The Nineteenth Century and After.* Berkeley, Los Angeles, London: University of California Press, 1984. ML3849.K7 1984

Maynard, Winifred. *Elizabethan Lyric Poetry and Its Music.* Oxford: Clarendon Press, 1986.   ML79.M4 1986

Mellers, Wilfrid. *Harmonious Meeting: A Study of the Relationship between English Music, Poetry, and Theatre c. 1600–1900.* London: Dobson, 1965. ML3849.M5

Meyer, Leonard. *Music, the Arts, and Ideas.* Chicago: University of Chicago Press, 1967.   ML3800.M633

Meyers, Robert Manson. *Handel, Dryden, and Milton: Being a Series of Observations on the Poems of Dryden and Milton, As Alter'd and Adapted by Various Hands, and Set to Music by Mr. Handel.* London: Bowes and Bowes, 1956.   ML410.H13 M968

Orgel, Stephen. *Jonsonian Masque.* Cambridge: Harvard University Press, 1965.   PR2642.M37 O7 1965

Orrey, Leslie. *Programme Music: A Brief Survey from the Sixteenth Century to the Present.* London: Davis-Poynter, 1975.   ML3300.O77

Pattison, Bruce. *Music and Poetry of the English Renaissance.* London: Methuen, 1948.   ML286.2.P3

Petri, Horst. *Literatur und Musik: Form- und Strukturparallelen.* Göttingen: Sachse und Pohl, 1964.   ML3849.P42

Phillips, James E., and Bertrand H. Bronson. *Music and Literature in England in the Seventeenth and Eighteenth Centuries.* Los Angeles: William Andrews Clark Memorial Library, University of California, 1953.

Rempel, W. John, and Ursula M. Rempel, eds. *Music and Literature.* Winnipeg: University of Manitoba, 1985.   ML3849.M92 1985

Scher, Steven P. *Verbal Music in German Literature.* New Haven: Yale University Press, 1968.   ML3849.S29

———, ed. *Literatur und Musik: Ein Handbuch zur Theorie und Praxis eines komparatistischen Grenzgebietes.* Berlin: Schmidt, 1984. Bibliography.   ML3849.L56 1984

Schmidgall, Gary. *Literature as Opera.* New York: Oxford University Press, 1977.   ML3858.S37

Staiger, Emil. *Musik und Dichtung.* Zurich: Atlantis Verlag, 1980.   ML79.S7 1980

Steiner, Wendy. *Sign in Music and Literature.* Austin: University of Texas Press, 1981.   NX180.S46 S53

Sternfeld, Frederick W. *Music in Shakespearean Tragedy.* London: Routledge and Kegan Paul, 1963.   ML80.S5 S8

Stevens, John E. *Words and Music in the Middle Ages: Song, Narrative, Dance, and Drama, 1050–1350.* Cambridge: Cambridge University Press, 1986.   ML172.S86 1986

Unger, Hans-Heinrich. *Die Beziehunger zwischen Musik und Rhetorik im 16.–18. Jahrhundert.* Hildesheim: G. Olms, 1969. ML80.A2 U54

Wallace, Robert K. *Jane Austen and Mozart: Classical Equilibrium in Fiction and Music.* Athens: University of Georgia Press, 1983. PR4037.W32 1983

Winn, James Anderson. *Unsuspected Eloquence: A History of the Relations between Poetry and Music.* New Haven: Yale University Press, 1981. ML3849.W58

X–45 **RILA: *Répertoire internationale de la littérature de l'art / International Repertory of the Literature of Art.*** Williamstown, Mass.: College Art Association, 1975–. Z5937.R16

This semi-annual bibliography provides abstracts of books, articles, reviews, festschriften, conference proceedings, exhibition catalogs, museum publications, and dissertations in all the fields of art and art history except those of classical antiquity and pre-Columbian America. Entries are arranged in seven major categories: Reference Works; General Works; Medieval Art; Renaissance, Baroque and Rococo Art; Neo-Classicism and Modern Art; Modern Art; and Collections and Exhibitions. Within the period categories are subdivisions for Miscellanea, Architecture, Sculpture, Pictorial Arts, Decorative Arts, and Artists, Architects [and Photographers]. Each issue concludes with an author and a subject index. A *Cumulative Index* to volumes 1–5 was published in 1982.

Also available is the *Art Index: A Quarterly Author and Subject Index to Publications in the Fields of Archaeology, Architecture, Art History, Arts and Crafts, City Planning, Fine Arts, Graphic Arts, Industrial Design, Interior Design, Landscape Design, Photography and Films, and Related Subjects* (New York: Wilson, 1929–) [Z5937.A78]. The annual cumulations number some 60,000 entries. Approximately 150 American and European periodicals are analyzed with respect to both general and specific subjects in art and aesthetics. Arrangement in both the quarterly issues and the annual cumulation is a single alphabet of authors and subjects.

X–49 **Some Frequently Recommended Works on Literature and the Visual Arts.** (See also Symbols, section K.)

Bender, John B. *Spenser and Literary Pictorialism.* Princeton, N.J.: Princeton University Press, 1972. PR2364.B38

Binyon, *Lawrence. Landscape in English Art and Poetry.* London: Cobden-Sanderson, 1931. ND1340.B5

Faust, Wolfgang. *Bilden werden Worte: Zum Verhält-nis von bildender Kunst und Literatur im 20. Jahrhundert oder vom Anfang der Kunst im Ende der Kunste.* Munich: C. Hanser, 1977. NX456.F38

Frank, Joseph. *Widening Gyre: Crisis and Mastery in Modern Literature.* New Brunswick, N.J.: Rutgers University Press, 1963. Contains "Spatial Form in Modern Literature," pp. 3–62. PN771.F7

Frankl, Paul. *Gothic: Literary Sources and Interpretations through Eight Centuries.* Princeton, N.J.: Princeton University Press, 1960. NA440.F7

Frye, Roland Muschat. *Milton's Imagery and the Visual Arts: Iconographic Tradition in the Epic Poems.* Princeton, N.J.: Princeton University Press, 1978. PR3592.A66 F78

Gilman, Ernest B. *Curious Perspective: Literary and Pictorial Wit in the Seventeenth Century.* New Haven: Yale University Press, 1978. PR438.P47 G5

Hagstrum, Jean. *Sister Arts: The Tradition of Literary Pictorialism and English Poetry from Dryden to Gray.* Chicago: University of Chicago Press, 1958. PR445.H3

Hatzfeld, Helmut. *Literature through Art: A New Approach to French Literature.* New York: Oxford University Press, 1952. PQ142.H3

Heffernan, James A. W., ed. *Space, Time, Image, Sign: Essays on Literature and the Visual Arts.* New York: P. Lang, 1987.

Hermand, Jost. *Literaturwissenschaft und Kunstwissenschaft: Methodologische Wechselbeziehungen seit 1900.* 2d ed. Stuttgart: Metzler, 1965. PT47.H4 1971

Higgins, Ian, ed. *Literature and the Plastic Arts, 1880-1930.* New York: Barnes and Noble, 1973. NX454.H53

Huddleston, Eugene L., and Douglas A. Noverr. *Relationship of Painting and Literature: A Guide to Information Sources.* Detroit: Gale, 1978. Z5069.H84

Hussey, Christopher. *Picturesque: Studies in a Point of View.* London: G. P. Putnam's Sons, 1927. BH301.L3 H8

Jack, Ian. *Keats and the Mirror of Art.* Oxford: Oxford University Press, 1967. PR4837.J26

Kayser, Wolfgang. *Grotesque in Art and Literature.* Translation by Ulrich Weisstein of *Das Groteske in Malerei und Dichtung* (Oldenburg, 1957). Bloomington: Indiana University Press, 1963. N8217.G8 K33

Larrabee, Stephen. *English Bards and Grecian Marbles: The Relationship between Sculpture and Poetry.* New York: Columbia University Press, 1943. PR508.A7 L3

Lee, Rensselaer W. *"Ut Pictura Poesis*: The Humanistic Theory of Painting." *Art Bulletin* 22 (1940): 197–269. Reprinted with a preface and 32 illustrations. New York: Norton, 1967. ND1263.L4

Manwaring, Elizabeth W. *Italian Landscape in Eighteenth Century England.* New York: Oxford University Press, 1925. BH301.L3 M3

Meyers, Jeffrey. *Painting and the Novel.* Manchester: Manchester University Press, 1975. PN3342.M4 1975

Park, Roy. *"Ut pictura poesis*: The Nineteenth Century Aftermath." *JAAC* 28 (1969): 155–164.

Paulson, Ronald. *Book and Painting: Shakespeare, Milton, and the Bible.* Knoxville: University of Tennessee Press, 1982. N6766.P36 1982

Pickering, F. P. *Literature and Art in the Middle Ages.* Translation of *Literatur und darstellende Kunst im Mittelalter.* Coral Gables, Fla.: University of Miami Press, 1970. PN674.P513

Praz, Mario. *Mnemosyne: The Parallel between Literature and the Visual Arts.* Princeton, N.J.: Princeton University Press, 1967. PN53.P7

Pugh, Simon, ed. *Reading Landscape: Country, City, Capital.* Manchester: Manchester University Press, 1990. N8205.R4 1990

Rogers, Franklin R. *Painting and Poetry: Form, Metaphor, and the Language of Literature.* Lewisburg, Pa.: Bucknell University Press, 1985. N66.R64 1985

Smith, Warren H. *Architecture in English Fiction.* New Haven: Yale University Press, 1934. PR830.A7 S6

Steiner, Wendy. *Colors of Rhetoric: Problems in the Relationship between Modern Literature and Painting.* Chicago: University of Chicago Press, 1982. PN53.S74 1982

———. *Pictures of Romance: Form against Context in Painting and Literature.* Chicago: University of Chicago Press, 1988. PN53.S75 1988

Sypher, Wylie. *Four Stages of Renaissance Style: Transformations in Art and Literature, 1400–1700.* New York: Doubleday, 1955. N6370.S95

———. *Rococo to Cubism in Art and Literature*. New York: Random House, 1960.   N6350.S9

Tinker, Chauncey Brewster. *Painter and Poet: Studies in the Literary Relations of English Painting*. Cambridge: Harvard University Press, 1938.   ND466.T5

Weisstein, Ulrich, ed. *Expressionism as an International Literary Phenomenon: 21 Essays and a Bibliography*. Paris: Didier, 1973.   NX600.E9 W44

X–50 Griffin, Ernest G. *Bibliography of Literature and Religion*. Edmonton: University of Alberta, 1969.

No LC number

This bibliography of recent books and articles is arranged by author. The listing is preceded by twenty-one broad subjects such as Literature and Belief and Religious Typology and Symbolism in Literature.

Although narrower in scope, the volume by George Boyd and Lois A. Boyd, *Religion in Contemporary Fiction: A Checklist* (San Antonio, Tex.: Trinity University Press, 1973) [Z5917.M6 B69], actually contains many general studies in its total of 884 serially numbered entries. The bibliography is preceded by a useful list of journals cited. It is in three main parts, with subdivisions as follows: I. Religion in Contemporary Fiction (A. General Criticism and Studies; B. Criticism concerning Theological Motifs and Themes; C. Criticism concerning Selected Topics in Religion; D. Criticism concerning the Relation of Religion to the Work of Individual Authors); II. Religion, Literature, and the Arts; Materials Relating to the Study of Religion and Fiction; and III. Earlier Bibliographies on Religion and Literature. A series of appendixes add entries discovered while the volume was in press; an index of primary and secondary authors concludes the volume.

X–51 Ruland, Vernon, S. J. *Horizons of Criticism: An Assessment of Religious-Literary Options*. Chicago: American Library Association, 1975.   PN49.R8

This highly personal bibliographical survey is disposed into fifteen chapters in three parts. Part 1, Religious-Literary Criticism, contains three chapters: 1, An Overview of Religious-Literary Criticism; 2, Key Critics and Texts; 3, Themes and Fallacies in Religious-Literary Criticism. Part 2, Religious Aspects of Literary Criticism, contains six chapters; 4, The Literary Symbol: An Inclusive Theory; 5, Autotelist Criticism; 6, Humanist Semiotic Criticism; 7, Ortho-Cultural Criticism; 8, Psycho-Mythic Criticism; 9, Two New Religious-Literary Scenarios. Part 3, Literary Aspects of Religious Thought, also has six chapters: 10, Toward a Functional Religious Humanism; 11, Autotelist Religious Thought; 12, Humanist Semiotic Religious Thought; 13, Ortho-Cultural Religious Thought; 14, Psycho-Mythic Religious Thought; 15, Conclusion: A Theology of the Religious-Literary Experience. These chapters, in the form of discursive essays, are followed by an alphabetically arranged bibliography of works concerning the interrelations of religion and literature. An index of names, titles, and subjects concludes the volume.

Several serial bibliographies also can be of considerable use in the search for work concerning interrelations of religion and literature. See, in particular, the annual *International Bibliography of the History of Religions / Bibliographie internationale de l'histoire des religions* (Leiden: Brill, 1954–) [Z7833.I53]; the bibliography in the *Révue d'histoire ecclésiastique* (Louvain: Université Catholique de Louvain, 1900–) [BX940.R5]; the quarterly *Bulletin signalétique 527: Sciences religieuses* (Paris: CNRS, 1948–) [Z7751.B85]; and the annual *Elenchus Bibliographicus Biblicus* (see K–35).

X–52 "Bibliography." *Christianity and Literature*, vol. 9–. Grand Rapids, Mich.: Calvin College, Department of English, 1960–.   PN49.C49

Each quarterly issue of this journal of the Conference on Christianity and Literature contains a serially numbered set of initialed abstracts of pertinent books and articles. The journals analyzed are listed at the beginning of each quarterly bibliography, and the entries are numbered in one continuous series since the first bibliography. Currently, about 400 abstracts a year are presented, arranged alphabetically by author under broad chronological headings (General, Ancient and Medieval to 1500, each century thereafter).

Beginning with an index to the bibliography in volume 25 (1975/76), an annual subject index to entries has been a feature of the journal. The index is classified into eight sections: I. Bibliography; II. Linguistics; III. Literature (A. Criticism; B. Teaching and Learning; C. Tempers, Types, Techniques; D. Relation to Other Disciplines; E. Specific Nations and Cultures); IV. Religious Concepts (specified); V. Symbols and Types (specified); VI. Authors and Works; VII. Judeo-Christian Influences (A. The Bible; B. Christian Writers and Movements; C. Denominations and Sects; D. Miscellaneous); and VIII. Other Religions. Reference is to the serial number of each relevant entry. A retrospective index to volumes 9–24 is now in progress.

X–54 Some Frequently Recommended Works on Literature and Religion. (See also section K, Mythology, and The Bible.)

Abrams, Meyer H. *Natural Supernaturalism: Tradition and Revolution in Romantic Literature*. New York: Norton, 1971.   PN603.A3

———, ed. *Literature and Belief: English Institute Essays, 1957*. New York: Columbia University Press, 1958.
PE1010.E5

Ahlstrom, Sidney E. *Religious History of the American People*. New Haven: Yale University Press, 1972. Extensive bibliography.   BR515.A4 1972

Andreach, Robert J. *Slain and Resurrected God: Conrad, Ford, and the Christian Myth*. New York: New York University Press, 1970.   PR6005.O4.Z547

———. *Studies in Structure*. New York: Fordham University Press, 1964.

Baden, Hans Jürgen. *Poesie und Theologie*. Hamburg: Agentur des Rauhen Hauses, 1971.   PT405.B23

Bowman, Mary Ann, comp. *Western Mysticism: A Guide to the Basic Works*. Chicago: ALA, 1978.   Z7819.B68

Buckley, Vincent. *Poetry and the Sacred*. London: Chatto and Windus, 1968.   PR508.R4 B8

Burke, Kenneth. *Rhetoric of Religion: Studies in Logology*. Boston: Beacon Press, 1961.   BL65.L2 B8

Burr, Nelson R. *Religion in American Life*. New York: Appleton-Century-Crofts, 1971. A bibliography with a section on "Religion in Literature."   Z7757.U5 B8

Daly, Robert. *God's Altar: The World and the Flesh in Puritan Poetry*. Berkeley, Los Angeles, London: University of California Press, 1978.   PS312.D3

De Rougement, Denis. *Love in the Western World*. Translation by Montgomery Belgion of *L'amour et l'Occident*. Rev. and aug. ed. with a new postscript. Princeton, N.J.: Princeton University Press, 1983.
HQ21.R86 1983

Driver, Tom F. *Romantic Quest and Modern Query: A History of the Modern Theatre*. New York: Delacorte, 1970.   PN1655.D75

Fairchild, Hoxie N. *Religious Trends in English Poetry* (see T–48).

Gardner, Helen. *Religion and Literature*. New York: Oxford University Press, 1971.   PN49.G34

Gilby, Thomas. *Poetic Experience: An Introduction to Thomist Aesthetic.* London: Sheed and Ward, 1934.
BX1395.E7 no. 13

Glicksberg, Charles. *Literature and Religion: A Study in Conflict.* Dallas: Southern Methodist University Press, 1960.
PN49.G54

Gunn, Giles. *Interpretation of Otherness: Literature, Religion, and the American Imagination.* New York: Oxford University Press, 1979.
PS166.G8

Gunn, Giles B., ed. *Literature and Religion.* New York: Harper and Row, 1971.
PN49.G76 1971

Heller, Erich. *Disinherited Mind: Essays in Modern German Literature and Thought.* 4th ed. New York: Harcourt, Brace, 1975.
PT343.H47 1975

Hoffman, Frederick J. *Imagination's New Beginning: Theology and Modern Literature.* Notre Dame, Ind.: University of Notre Dame Press, 1967.
PN49.H62

Hopper, Stanley Romaine, ed. *Spiritual Problems in Contemporary Literature.* New York: Institute for Religions and Social Studies, Harper and Row, 1952.
PN49.I64 1957

Jarrett-Kerr, Martin. *Studies in Literature and Belief.* London: Rockcliff, 1954.
PN49.J37

Lewis, R. W. B. *Trials of the Word: Essays in American Literature and the Humanistic Tradition.* New Haven: Yale University Press, 1965.

Maritain, Jacques. *Art and Scholasticism, with Other Essays.* Translated by J. F. Scanlan. 2d ed. New York: Scribner's, 1943.
N61.M3 1943

———. *Creative Intuition in Art and Poetry.* New York: Pantheon, 1953.
BF408.M25 1953

———, and Raissa Maritain. *Situation of Poetry: Four Essays on the Relations between Poetry, Mysticism, Magic, and Knowledge.* New York: Philosophical Library, 1955.
PN1136.313

Martz, Louis L. *Poetry of Meditation: A Study in English Religious Literature of the Seventeenth Century.* 2d ed. New Haven: Yale University Press, 1962.
PR549.R4 M3 1962

Miller, J. Hillis. *Disappearance of God: Five Nineteenth-Century Writers.* Cambridge: Harvard University Press, 1963.
PR469.R4 M5

Murdock, Kenneth. *Literature and Theology in Colonial New England.* Cambridge: Harvard University Press, 1949.
PS195.R4 M8

Panichas, George A. *Mansions of the Spirit: Essays in Literature and Religion.* New York: Hawthorn, 1967.
PN49.P28 1967

Patrides, C. A. *Milton and the Christian Tradition.* Baltimore: Johns Hopkins University Press, 1966.
PR3592.R4 P3

Reynolds, David S. *Faith in Fiction: The Emergence of Religious Literature in America.* Cambridge: Harvard University Press, 1981. Bibliography; chronology of fiction.
PS374.R47 R49

Rooney, William J. *"Problem of Poetry and Belief" in Contemporary Criticism.* Washington, D.C.: Catholic University of America Press, 1949.
PN1077.R6

Sacks, Sheldon. *Fiction and the Shape of Belief: A Study of Henry Fielding with Glances at Swift, Johnson, and Richardson.* Berkeley and Los Angeles: University of California Press, 1966.
PR3457.S3

Scott, Nathan A., Jr. *Broken Center: Studies in the Theological Horizons of Modern Literature.* New Haven: Yale University Press, 1966.
PN49.S325

———. *Modern Literature and the Religious Frontier.* New York: Harper and Bros., 1958.
PN1077.S39

———. *Negative Capability: Studies in the New Literature and the Religious Situation.* New Haven: Yale University Press, 1969.
PN771.S33

———. *Rehearsals of Discomposure: Alienation and Reconciliation in Modern Literature.* New York: Columbia University Press, 1952.
PN49.S33

———. *Wild Prayer of Longing: Poetry and the Sacred.* New Haven: Yale University Press, 1971.
BL65.C8 S36 1971

———, ed. *New Orpheus: Essays toward a Christian Poetic.* New York: Sheed and Ward, 1964.
PN49.S328

Strelka, Joseph P., ed. *Anagogic Qualities of Literature.* University Park: Pennsylvania State University Press, 1971.
PN49.A5

Tennyson, G. B., and Edward E. Ericson, Jr., eds. *Religion and Modern Literature: Essays in Theory and Criticism.* Grand Rapids, Mich.: Eerdmans, 1975.
PN49.T37

White, Helen C. *Metaphysical Poets: A Study in Religious Experience.* New York: Macmillan, 1936.
PR549.R4 W5

Wilder, Amos. *New Voice: Religion, Literature, Hermeneutics.* New York: Herder and Herder, 1969.
PN49.W48

———. *Theology and Modern Literature.* Cambridge: Harvard University Press, 1958.
PN49.W5

Woodhouse, A. S. P. *Poet and His Faith: Religion and Poetry in England from Spenser to Eliot and Auden.* Chicago: University of Chicago Press, 1965.
PR508.R4 W6

Wright, T. R. *Theology and Literature.* Oxford: B. Blackwell, 1988.
PN49.W73 1988

Ziolkowski, Theodore. *Fictional Transfigurations of Jesus.* Princeton, N.J.: Princeton University Press, 1972.
PN3503.245

X–55 **Tobey, Jeremy L. *History of Ideas: A Bibliographical Introduction.*** 2 vols. Santa Barbara, Calif.: ABC-Clio, 1975–1977.
Z7125.T58

These two volumes treat Classical Antiquity and Medieval and Early Modern Europe respectively. Both volumes present discursive bibliographical essays. The first is in five chapters: Introduction, Ancient Philosophy, Ancient Science, Ancient Aesthetics, and Ancient Religion, with numerous subdivisions for specific disciplines, periods, national groups, and individual thinkers. The second volume is also in five chapters: Introduction, Philosophy, Science, Religion, and Aesthetics. Both conclude with an index listing all periodicals cited and a second index listing all cited authors and titles.

X–56 ***Bibliographie de la philosophie / Bibliography of Philosophy.*** Vol. 1–. Paris: Vrin, 1937–.
Z7127.B5

This quarterly annotated bibliography of books is arranged by broad subjects within the discipline of philosophy, including such headings as Semantics, Aesthetics, The Philosophy of History and The History of Philosophy. The last issue of each year contains indexes of authors, subjects, and publishers.

For a bibliography of articles see the quarterly *Bulletin signalétique 519: Philosophie* (Paris: CNRS, 1948–) [Z7751.F7118], which briefly summarizes articles and provides author and subject indexes that are cumulated annually.

X–57 ***Philosopher's Index: An International Index to Philosophical Periodicals.*** Vol. 1–. Bowling Green, Ohio: Bowling Green State University, Philosophy Documentation Center, 1966–. 4/yr with an annual cumulation.
Z7127.P47

This work presents a classified subject and author index to books, articles, anthologies, abstracts, and book reviews, from 1940 to the present. It is available online through DIALOG.

Two retrospective sets have been published: *Philosopher's Index: A Retrospective Index to United States Publications from 1940*, 3 vols. (1978) [Z7127.P474] and *Philosopher's Index: A Retrospective Index to Non-United States English Language Publications from 1940*, 3 vols. (1980) [Z7127.P473]. In both, the subject index occupies the first two volumes, and the author index occupies the third.

X–59 **Some Frequently Recommended Works on Literature and Philosophy.** (See, especially, K–95, Guide to Works on Intellectual History and the History of Ideas.)

Cain, William E., ed. *Philosophical Approaches to Literature: New Essays on Nineteenth- and Twentieth-Century Texts.* Lewisburg, Penna.: Bucknell University Press, 1984. PR409.P48 P54 1984

Crane, Ronald S. "Literature, Philosophy, and the History of Ideas." *MP* 52 (1954): 73–83.

Gilson, Étienne. *Les idées et les lettres.* Paris, 1932.

Hook, Sidney, ed. *Art and Philosophy.* New York: New York University Press, 1966. N70.N395 1964

Hospers, John. *Meaning and Truth in the Arts.* Chapel Hill: University of North Carolina Press, 1946. N70.H74 1946

Kuhns, Richard. *Structures of Experience: Essays on the Affinity between Philosophy and Literature.* New York: Basic Books, 1971. B66.K84

Marshall, Donald G., ed. *Literature as Philosophy / Philosophy as Literature.* Iowa City: University of Iowa Press, 1987. PN49.L52 1987

Nicholson, Marjorie. "The History of Literature and the History of Thought." *English Institute Annual, 1939*, pp. 56–89. New York: Columbia University Press, 1940. PE1010.E5

Strelka, Joseph P., ed. *Literary Criticism and Philosophy.* Vol. 10 of the *Yearbook of Comparative Criticism.* University Park: Pennsylvania State University Press, 1983. PN85.L573 1983

Weitz, Morris. *Hamlet and the Philosophy of Criticism.* Chicago: University of Chicago Press, 1964. PR2807.W38

———. *Philosophy in Literature: Shakespeare, Voltaire, Tolstoy, and Proust.* Detroit: Wayne State University Press, 1963. PN49.W38

Wellek, René. *Confrontations: Studies in the Intellectual and Literary Relations between Germany, England, and the United States during the Nineteenth Century.* Princeton, N.J.: Princeton University Press, 1965. B803.W37

———. *Immanuel Kant in England, 1793–1838.* Princeton, N.J.: Princeton University Press, 1931. B2798.W5

X–60 **Kiell, Norman. *Psychoanalysis, Psychology, and Literature: A Bibliography.* 2d ed. 2 vols. Metuchen, N.J.: Scarecrow Press, 1982.** Z6511.K5 1982

This work was first published in 1963 and contained 4,460 serially numbered, unannotated entries citing books, monographs, and articles, primarily of the twentieth century, on all aspects of the interrelations of psychology and literature. The present two-volume second edition is nearly five times as large, with a total of 19,674 serially numbered entries.

The scope and arrangement of both editions is similar, with all schools of psychology and psychological thought represented. Entries are arranged by genre, with general, theoretical, and methodological treatments appearing in section 2, under Criticism. The fourteen chapters are as follows: 1, Autobiography, Biography, Diaries, Letters; 2, Criticism: Literary, Psychoanalytical, Psychological; 3, Drama; 4, Fairy Tales and Fables; 5, Fiction; 6, Film; 7, Folklore and Folktales; 8, Myths and Legends; 9, Poetry; 10, Scriptures; 11, Technical Studies; 12, Therapy; 13, Wit, Humor, and Jokes;

14, Ancillary. Within sections, entries are alphabetical by author.

Volume 2 contains indexes of authors, of titles, and of subjects, including literary works as subjects. This bibliography is supplemented by the annual lists in *Literature and Psychology* (X–61).

Kiell has also prepared a related volume, *Psychiatry and Psychology in the Visual Arts and Aesthetics: A Bibliography* (Madison: University of Wisconsin Press, 1965) [Z5931.K5].

A recent work which to an extent complements Kiell is the volume by Joseph Natoli and Frederick L. Rusch, *Psychocriticism: An Annotated Bibliography* (Westport, Conn.: Greenwood, 1984) [Z6514.P78 P89 1984]. This work presents an annotated bibliography of books and articles largely culled from Kiell but presented because they represent the systematic use of a specific method of psychological analysis or apply the doctrines of a specific school of psychology. Within this narrow scope, the work enumerates and describes several thousand studies. Entries are distributed into chapters by period, beginning with a chapter of general studies and essay collections and continuing with chapters on "psycho-criticism" of literary works from classical antiquity to the twentieth century. While the selection is limited and the annotations are sometimes rather uninformative, the volume can be used with caution to complement Kiell. Indexes of subjects and authors facilitate that use.

X–61 **"Bibliography for [1951–1970]." *Literature and Psychology*, vols. 1–23. Teaneck, N.J.: Fairleigh Dickinson University Press, 1951–1973.** PN49.L5

This bibliography, published prior to 1964 in each issue and then once a year, took the form most recently of an annotated current contents list of relevant studies from some 200 analyzed periodicals. Numbered entries provided informative abstracts of articles.

Current monthly issues of *Psychological Abstracts* (Washington, D.C.: American Psychological Association, 1927–) [BF1.P65] contain abstracts of books and articles, as well as references to dissertations and some unpublished papers, in a classified arrangement. Headings for students of literature and psychology include Autobiography, Biography, Drama, Literature, Poetry, and Prose. Each issue contains an author and subject index, both of which are cumulated semiannually.

X–62 **Meurs, Joseph van. *Jungian Literary Criticism, 1920–1980: An Annotated, Critical Bibliography of Works in English (with a Selection of Titles after 1980).* Metuchen, N.J.: Scarecrow, 1988.** Z6514.P78 M48 1988

This exhaustive bibliography is devoted to books and articles which use Jungian psychology as a tool in the interpretation of literary texts written in English. Works of particular significance are marked with asterisks. The bibliography proper is preceded with an evaluative, historical survey of seminal works and the current state of scholarship in the field. The bibliography is arranged alphabetically. By design, entries frequently begin with phrases that indicate the author's estimate of the work. Meurs also includes both briefly annotated entries on work published after 1980 and unannotated citations of doctoral dissertations. Author and subject indexes conclude the volume.

X–63 ***Psychological Abstracts: Nonevaluative Summaries of the World's Literature in Psychology and Related Disciplines.*** Arlington, Va.: American Psychological Association, 1927–. 12/yr with annual expanded cumulated author and subject indexes. BF1.P65

This work is disposed into classified sections, including (in recent years) Language and Speech, and Literature and Art headings. It is easiest to locate materials through the subject index which is best used in conjunction with current edition of the *Thesaurus of Psychological Index Terms.* In addition to the annual cumulations, there are also triennial and larger cumulations. *Psychological Abstracts* is part of the PsycINFO database; abstracts since 1967 can be searched through BRS and DIALOG.

X–64 **Some Frequently Recommended Works on Literature and Psychology.** (See also K–25 ff. on myth; X–24, on reader-response criticism; and X–94, Literature and Medicine.)

Basler, Roy P. *Sex, Symbolism, and Psychology in Literature.* New Brunswick, N.J.: Rutgers University Press, 1948.   PN49.B17.

Benvenuto, Bice, and Roger Kennedy. *Works of Jacques Lacan: An Introduction.* London: Free Association Books, 1986.   BF173.L15 B46 1986

Berman, Jeffrey. *Talking Cure: Literary Representations of Psychoanalysis.* New York: New York University Press, 1985.   PS228.P74 B47 1985

Bodkin, Maud. *Archetypal Patterns in Poetry: Psychological Studies of Imagination.* London: Oxford University Press, 1934.   PN1031.B63

Brooks, Peter. *Reading for the Plot.* New York: Knopf, 1984.   PN3378.B76 1984

Crews, Frederick C. *Out of My System.* New York: Oxford University Press, 1975.   PN56.P92 C7

———. *Sins of the Father: Hawthorne's Psychological Themes.* New York: Oxford University Press, 1966.   PS1881.C7

———, ed. *Psychoanalysis and Literary Process.* Cambridge: Winthrop, 1970.   PR14.P76

Davis, Robert Con, ed. *Lacan and Narration: The Psychoanalytic Difference in Narrative Theory.* Baltimore: Johns Hopkins University Press, 1984.
                    PN212.L3 1984

Edel, Leon. *Henry James.* 5 vols. Philadelphia: Lippincott, 1953–1972.   PS2123.E385 1953

———. *Modern Psychological Novel.* New York: Grosset and Dunlap, 1955.   PN3348.P8 E3 1964

Ehrenzweig, Anton. *Hidden Order of Art: A Study in the Psychology of Artistic Imagination.* Berkeley and Los Angeles: University of California Press, 1967.
                    N71.E5 1967

Faber, M. D. *Design Within: Psychonalytic Approaches to Shakespeare.* New York: Science House, 1970.
                    PR3001.F3

Felman, Shoshana. *Jacques Lacan and the Adventure of Insight: Psychoanalysis in Contemporary Culture.* Cambridge: Harvard University Press, 1987.
                    PN98.P75 F45 1987

———, ed. *Literature and Psychoanalysis: The Question of Reading—Otherwise.* Baltimore: Johns Hopkins University Press, 1982.   PN56.P92 L5 1982

Fraiberg, Louis B. *Psychoanalysis and American Literary Criticism.* Detroit, 1960.   PS78.F7

Gallop, Jane. *Reading Lacan.* Ithaca, N.Y.: Cornell University Press, 1985.   BF173.L15 G34 1985

Gay, Peter. *Freud Reader.* New York: W. W. Norton, 1989.
                    BF173.F6255 1989

Hartman, Geoffrey, ed. *Psychoanalysis and the Question of the Text. Selected Papers from the English Institute,* n.s., no. 2 (1976/77). Baltimore: Johns Hopkins University Press, 1978.   BF175.E53 1978

Hoffman, Frederick J. *Freudianism and the Literary Mind.* Baton Rouge: Louisiana State University Press, 1957.
                    PN49.H6 1957

Holland, Norman N. *Dynamics of Literary Response.* New York: Oxford University Press, 1968.   PN49.H64

———. *Poems in Persons: An Introduction to the Psychoanalysis of Literature.* New York: Norton, 1973.
                    PN56.P92 H6

———. *Psychoanalysis and Shakespeare.* New York: McGraw-Hill, 1966.   PR2976.H55

Kallich, Martin. *Association of Ideas and Critical Theory in Eighteenth Century England: A History of a Psychological Method in English Criticism.* The Hague: Mouton, 1970.   PN99.G72 K3

Kaplan, Morton, and Robert Kloss. *Unspoken Motive: A Guide to Psychoanalytic Literary Criticism.* New York: Free Press, 1973.   PN98.P75 K3

Kris, Ernst. *Psychoanalytic Explorations in Art.* New York: International Universities Press, 1952.   N70.K84

Kurzweil, Edith, and William Phillips, eds. *Literature and Psychoanalysis.* New York: Columbia University Press, 1983.   PN56.P92 L49 1983

Lacan, Jacques. *Ecrits: A Selection.* Translated by Alan Sheridan. New York: Norton, 1977.
                    BF173.L14213 1977

———. *Four Fundamental Concepts of Psychoanalysis.* New York: Norton, 1978.   BF173.L146 Z13

———. *Language of the Self: The Function of Language Psychoanalysis.* Tran. with Notes and Commentary by Anthony Wilder. Baltimore; Johns Hopkins University Press, 1968.   BF175.L213

Laplanche, Jean, and Jean Baptiste Pontalis. *Language of Psycho-analysis.* London: Hogarth Press, 1973.
                    RC437.L313 1973

Lesser, Simon O. *Fiction and the Unconscious.* Boston: Beacon Press, 1957.   PN3331.L4

Lindauer, Martin S. *Psychological Study of Literature: Limitations, Possibilities, and Accomplishments.* Chicago: Nelson-Hall, 1973. Bibliography.   PN49.L49

Lindner, Robert, ed. *Explorations in Psychoanalysis.* New York: Julian Press, 1953.   BF173.R44 L5

Lucas, F. L. *Literature and Psychology.* London: Cassell, 1951.   PN45.L67

MacCabe, Colin, ed. *Talking Cure: Essays in Psychoanalysis and Language.* New York: St. Martin's Press, 1981.   RC489.P73 T34 1981

MacCannell, Juliet F. *Figuring Lacan.* Lincoln: University of Nebraska Press, 1986.   PN98.P75 M3 1986

Mahony, Patrick. *Psychoanalysis and Discourse.* London: Tavistock Publications, 1987.   RC489.P73 M34 1987

Malin, Irving, ed. *Psychoanalysis and American Fiction.* New York: Dutton, 1965.   PS371.M26

Manheim, Leonard, and Eleanor Manheim, eds. *Hidden Patterns: Studies in Psychoanalytic Criticism.* New York: Macmillan, 1966.   PN81.M465

Mollinger, Robert N. *Psychoanalysis and Literature: An Introduction.* Chicago: Nelson-Hall, 1981.   PS88.M57

Morrison, Claudia C. *Freud and the Critic: The Early Use of Depth Psychology in Literary Criticism.* Chapel Hill: University of North Carolina Press, 1968.   PS78.M6

Nagele, Rainer. *Reading After Freud.* New York: Columbia University Press, 1987.   PT129.N34 1987

Phillips, William, ed. *Art and Psychoanalysis.* New York: Criterion, 1957.   PN501.P5

Punter, David. *Hidden Script: Writing and the Unconscious.* London: Routledge and Kegan Paul, 1985.
                    PR471.P8 1985

Ragland-Sullivan, Ellie. *Jacques Lacon and the Philosophy of Psychoanalysis.* Urbana: University of Illinois Press, 1986.   BF173.L15 R34 1986

Rimmon-Kenan, Shlomith, ed. *Discourse in Psychoanalysis and Literature.* London: Methuen, 1987.
                    PN56.P92 D57

Rogers, Robert R. *Metaphor: A Psychoanalytic View.* Berkeley, Los Angeles, London: University of California Press, 1978.   PN228.M4 R6

———. *Psychoanalytic Study of the Double in Literature*. Detroit: Wayne State University Press, 1970.
PN56.D67 R6

Roland, Alan, ed. *Psychoanalysis, Creativity, and Literature: A French-American Inquiry*. New York: Columbia University Press, 1978.   RC506.P77

Ruitenbeck, Hendrick M., ed. *Psychoanalysis and Literature*. New York: Dutton, 1964.   PN501.R8

Schneiderman, Stuart. *Jacques Lacan: The Death of an Intellectual Hero*. Cambridge: Harvard University Press, 1983.   BF109.L28 S36 1983

Schwartz, Murray M., and Coppelia Kahn, eds. *Representing Shakespeare: New Psychoanalytic Essays*. Baltimore: Johns Hopkins University Press, 1980. Bibliography.   PR2976.R4

Skura, Meredith Anne. *Literary Use of the Psychoanalytic Process*. New Haven: Yale University Press, 1981.
PN98.P75 S58

Smith, Joseph H., ed. *Literary Freud: Mechanisms of Defense and the Poetic Will*. New Haven: Yale University Press, 1980.   RC321.P943 vol. 4

———, and William Kerrigan, eds. *Interpreting Lacan*. New Haven: Yale University Press, 1983.
RC321.P943 vol. 6

———, eds. *Taking Chances: Derrida, Psychoanalysis, and Literature*. Baltimore: Johns Hopkins University Press, 1984.   RC321.P943 vol. 7

Strelka, Joseph P., ed. *Literary Criticism and Psychology*. University Park: Pennsylvania State University Press, 1976.   PN98.P75 L5

Tennenhouse, Leonard, ed. *Practice of Psychoanalytic Criticism*. Detroit: Wayne State University Press, 1976.
PN98.P75 P67

Turkle, Sherry. *Psychoanalytical Politics: Freud's French Revolution*. New York: Basic Books, 1978.
BF175.T87

Urban, Bernd, ed. *Psychoanalyse und Literaturwissenschaft: Texte zur Geschichte ihrer Beziehungen*. Tübingen: Niemeyer, 1973.   PN56.P92 U7

———, and Winfried Kudszus, eds. *Psychoanalytische und Psychopathologische Literaturinterpretation*. Darmstadt: Wissenschaftliche Buchgesellschaft, 1981.
PN56.P92 P75

Vowles, Richard B. "Psychology and Drama: A Selected Checklist." *Wisconsin Studies in Contemporary Literature* 3 (1962): 35–48.

Wright, Elizabeth. *Psychoanalytic Criticism: Theory in Practice*. London: Methuen, 1984.
PN56.P92 W75 1984

X–65 **Duncan, Hugh Dalziel. *Language and Literature in Society: A Sociological Essay on Theory and Method in the Interpretation of Literary Symbols with a Bibliographical Guide to the Sociology of Literature*.** Chicago: University of Chicago Press, 1953.   PN51.D8

The bibliography in Duncan's standard work in the field of interrelations of literature and society occupies some seventy pages and is organized to reveal the author's theory of literature as a social institution. It is in three main divisions. The first, Language and Literature in Society, has the following sections: A. General Observations on the Structure and Function of Symbolic Action; B. Meaning and Metaphor: The Resources of Language; C. Function of Literature in Society; D. Psychological Conceptions of Literature; E. Literature Considered as Myth; F. Literature as Humor: Laughter and Social Adaptation. The second division, The Structure of Literature as Social Institution, has the following sections (most with national subdivisions, as appropriate): A. Authors; B. Associations of Writers; C. Critics; D. Publics; E. Publications; F. Publishing; G. Distribution. The third and final part, Literary Perspective of Society, has the following

sections: A. General Treatments of the Nature of Literary Perspectives; B. Societies As Depicted in Literature (with subdivisions for various actual and utopian societies); C. Social Types As Depicted (with subdivisions for general and special types, such as The Jew, The Negro, or The Gentleman); D. Social Institutions As Depicted (Family, Science, Economics, War, Religion, Values, Political Institutions); and E. Social Structure As Depicted (General; Elites, Aristocracy, Upper Classes; Middle Classes; Workers, Farmers, Proletariats). Entries are unannotated and are arranged alphabetically within their subdivision. The index to the entire volume includes the bibliography.

X–66 **Marshall, Thomas F., ed. *Literature and Society, 1950-[1965]: A Selective Bibliography*.** 3 vols. Coral Gables, Fla.: University of Miami Press, 1956–1967.   Z6511.M6

These volumes continue the uncumulated annual mimeographed bibliographies entitled "Relations of Literature and Society" compiled by the MLA General Topics Group V from 1938 to 1946. The volumes treat the periods 1950–1955, 1956–1960, and 1961–1965 respectively. Both the original annual lists and the quinquennial published bibliographies present alphabetically organized, serially numbered listings first of books and then of articles, both with brief annotations. Included are works that focus on the social provenance and status of writers, the social content of literary works, or the audience and social influence of the writing. The quinquennial volumes conclude with an index of subjects and selected authors and scholars.

X–67 ***Bulletin signalétique 521: Sociologie, ethnologie*.** Paris: CNRS, 1948–.   LC number varies

This quarterly classified bibliography treats both books and articles under such headings as The Sociology of Art and Literature and The Sociology of Communications and the Mass Media. Indexes of authors and subjects cumulate annually.

Abstracts of current articles will be found in *Sociological Abstracts* (San Diego, Calif.: Sociological Abstracts, 1952–) [HM1.S67], which appears quarterly, with an annual subject index. Abstracts are classified under general headings including History, Theory, and Methodology; areas of sociological study including Organizations, The Family, and The Arts; and such special topics as Feminism, Marxism, and The Sociology of Knowledge. Indexes of authors and subjects conclude each issue. Abstracts since 1963 can be searched online through BRS and DIALOG.

X–68 ***International Bibliography of Social and Cultural Anthropology / Bibliographie internationale d'anthropologie sociale et culturelle*.** Vol. 1–. Paris: UNESCO; London: Tavistock, 1955–.   Z7161.I593

This is one of four annual bibliographies begun in the 1950s under the auspices of UNESCO with the general title, *International Bibliography of the Social Sciences*. The others treat Sociology, Political Science, and Economics. Entries totaling more than 7,000 annually are serially numbered and disposed in alphabetical order under subject classifications. The elaborate classification (which goes to three levels of subdivision) is as follows: A. General Studies; B. Material and Methods; C. Morphological Foundations; D. Ethnographic Studies of Peoples and Communities; E. Social Organization and Relationships; F. Religion, Magic, and Witchcraft; G. Problems of Knowledge, Arts and Sciences, Folk Traditions (G.4, Artistic and Literary Expression); H. Studies of Culture and Personality, "National Character"; I. Problems of Acculturation and Social Change, Contact Situations; J. Applied Anthropology (J.28, Language and Writing). An index of authors and an elaborate subject index conclude each year's bibliography.

X–69 Some Frequently Recommended Works on Literature and Sociology. Including the Critical Theory of the Frankfurt School, and on Literature and Anthropology. (See also works on the history of taste, K–92 and on Marxist theory in X–74.)

Albrecht, Milton C., et al., eds. *Sociology of Art and Literature: A Reader*. New York: Praeger, 1970.
NR650.S6 A4

Bock, Philip K. *Shakespeare and Elizabethan Culture: An Anthropological View*. New York: Schocken Books, 1984.   PR2198.B6 1984

Burger, Peter, ed. *Seminar: Literatur und Kunstsoziologie*. Frankfurt: Suhrkamp, 1978.   BH41.S44

Burns, Elizabeth, and Tom Burns, eds. *Sociology of Literature and Drama*. Harmondsworth, England: Penguin, 1973.   PN51.B87

Clark, Priscilla B. P. *Battle of the Bourgeois: The Novel in France, 1789–1848*. Paris: Didier, 1973.   PQ655.C55

Cros, Edmond. *Theory and Practice of Sociocriticism*. Minneapolis: University of Minnesota Press, 1988.
PN98.S6 C7413 1987

Connerton, Paul. *Tragedy of Enlightenment: An Essay on the Frankfurt School*. Cambridge: Cambridge University Press, 1980.   HM24.C653

Daiches, David. *Literature and Society*. London, 1938.
PR83.D3

Dennis, Philip A., and Wendell Aycock, eds. *Literature and Anthropology*. Lubbock: Texas Tech University Press, 1989.   PN51.L5738 1989

Dubois, Jacques. *L'institution de la littérature: Introduction à une sociologie*. Paris: Nathan, 1978.   PQ283.D8

Duncan, Hugh Dalziel. *Language and Literature in Society*. Chicago: University of Chicago Press, 1953. Bibliography (see X–65).   PN51.D8

Escarpit, Robert. *Sociology of Literature*. Translation of *Sociologie de la littérature* (Paris: Presses universitaires de France, 1958). London: Frank Cass, 1971.
PN51.E813 1971

Fay, Brian. *Critical Social Science: Liberation and Its Limits*. Ithaca: Cornell University Press, 1987.
H61.F35 1987

Frye, Northrop. *Critical Path: An Essay in the Social Context of Literature*. Bloomington: Indiana University Press, 1974.   PN81.F754

Geuss, Raymond. *Idea of Critical Theory*. Cambridge: Cambridge University Press, 1981.
HM22.G8 H274 1981

Gillian, Rose. *Melanchology Science: An Introduction to the Thought of Theodor W. Adorno*. New York: Columbia University Press, 1978.   HM22.G3 A37 1978

Glicksberg, Charles F. *Literature and Society*. The Hague: Martinus Nijhoff, 1972.   PN51.G5

Goldmann, Lucien. *Toward a Sociology of the Novel*. Translation by Alan Sheridan of *Pour une sociologie du roman*. London: Tavistock, 1975.
PN3344.G613 1975

Guérard, Albert. *Literature and Society*. Boston: Lathrop, Lee, and Shapherd, 1935. Bibliography.   PN51.G8

Hall, Jonathan, and Akbar Abbas, eds. *Literature and Anthropology*. Hong Kong: Hong Kong University Press, 1986.   PN51.L5733 1986

Harris, Ronald W. *Romanticism and the Social Order, 1780–1830*. New York: Barnes and Noble, 1969.
PA485.H325 1969

Held, David. *Introduction to Critical Theory*. Berkeley and Los Angeles: The University of California Press, 1980.   HM24.H457

Jay, Martin. *Adorno*. Cambridge: Harvard University Press, 1984.   HM22.G3 A33 1984

———. *Dialectical Imagination: A History of the Frankfurt School*. Boston: Little, Brown, 1973.   H62.J37

Knights, L. C. *Drama and Society in the Age of Jonson*. London: Chatto and Windus, 1937.   PR655.K6

Laurenson, Diana T., ed. *Sociology of Literature: Applied Studies*. Keele: University of Keele, 1978.
HM15.S545 no. 26

Laurenson, Diana T., and Alan Swingewood. *Sociology of Literature*. New York: Schocken, 1972. Select bibliography.   PN51.L35 1972b

Lentricchia, Frank. *Criticism and Social Change*. Chicago: University of Chicago Press, 1983.   PN81.L42 1983

Lowenthal, Leo. *Literature and the Image of Man: Sociological Studies of the European Drama and Novel, 1600–1900*. Boston: Beacon Press, 1957.
PN511.L69

———. *Literature, Popular Culture, and Society*. Englewood Cliffs, N.J.: Spectrum, 1961.   PN51.L6

Muir, Edwin. *Essays on Literature and Society*. Enl. and rev. ed. Cambridge: Harvard University Press, 1965.
PR99.M85 1965

Orr, John. *Tragic Realism and Modern Society: Studies in the Sociology of the Modern Novel*. Pittsburgh: University of Pittsburgh Press, 1977.   PN3499.O7

Plekhanov, Georgi V. *Art and Social Life*. New enl. ed. London: Lawrence and Wishart, 1953.   N72.P57

Poyatos, Fernando, ed. *Literary Anthropology: A New Interdisciplinary Approach to People, Signs, and Literature*. Amsterdam: J. Benjamins, 1988.
PN51.L56 1988

Read, Herbert E. *Art and Society*. 4th ed. London: Faber, 1967.   N72.S6 R4

Rideout, Walter B. *Radical Novel in the United States, 1900–1954: Some Interrelations of Literature and Society*. Cambridge: Harvard University Press, 1956.
PS379.R5

Rockwell, Joan. *Fact in Fiction: The Use of Literature in the Systematic Study of Society*. London: Routledge and Kegan Paul, 1974.   PN51.R65

Roderick, Rick. *Habermas and the Foundations of Critical Theory*. New York: St. Martin's Press, 1986.
HM22.G3 H347 1986

Rosengren, Karl Erik. *Sociological Aspects of the Literary System*. Stockholm: Naturloch Kultur, 1968.
PN51.R73

Routh, Jane, and Janet Wolff, eds. *Sociology of Literature: Theoretical Approaches*. Keele: University of Keele, 1977.   HM15.S545 no. 25

Said, Edward, ed. *Literature and Society: Selected Papers from the English Institute*, n.s. no. 3 (1978). Baltimore: Johns Hopkins University Press, 1980.
PR99.E67 1980

Salusinszky, Imre. *Criticism in Society: Interviews....* New York: Methuen, 1987.   PN98.S6 S25 1987

Sammons, Jeffrey L. *Literary Sociology and Practical Criticism: An Inquiry*. Bloomington: Indiana University Press, 1977. Extensive, classified bibliography.
PN98.S6 S3

Seymour-Smith, Charlotte, ed. *Dictionary of Anthropology*. Boston: G. K. Hall, 1987.   GN11.D48 1986

Strelka, Joseph P. ed. *Literary Criticism and Sociology*. University Park: Pennsylvania State University Press, 1973.   PN98.S6 S8

Tarr, Zoltan. *Frankfurt School*. New York: Wiley, 1977.
HM24.T27

Thomson, George. *Aeschylus and Athens: A Study in the Social Origins of the Drama*. 3d ed. New York: Haskell House, 1967.   PA3829.T5 1967b

Tinker, Chauncey B. *Salon and English Letters: Chapters on the Interrelations of Literature and Society in the Age of Johnson.* New York: Macmillan, 1915.
PR448.S3 T5

Tomars, Adolph Siegfried. *Introduction to the Sociology of Art.* Mexico City, 1940.   N72.T6

Watt, Ian. *Rise of the Novel.* Berkeley and Los Angeles: University of California Press, 1957.   PR851.W3

Wilson, Robert N., ed. *Arts in Society.* Englewood Cliffs, N.J.: Prentice-Hall, 1964.   NX180.S6 W54

X–70   Baxandall, Lee. *Marxism and Aesthetics: A Selective Annotated Bibliography; Books and Articles in the English Language.* New York: Humanities Press, 1968.   Z5069.B38

This work is regarded as the definitive international bibliography of material related to Marxist thought about art and the arts. Its policy is to be inclusive rather than exclusive, entering any doubtfully relevant items. Articles and essays are included both when they offer an intrinsically valuable contribution to Marxist aesthetic theory in general or a Marxist response to a particular writer, artist, or artwork, and when they are of historical interest.

Unfortunately, the arrangement of the volume is confusing and cumbersome. Entries are organized by the nationality or language grouping of their author (who can be a subject author as well as a critic).

A total of sixty-three Roman-numeraled sections divide the author lists into national groups, though some of the national groups have extra lists associated with them. These include those for the United States and the Soviet Union, which are subdivided; a set of seven appendixes to major national author lists which contain critiques of national aesthetic theory and practice; and a set of three chronological listings (for China, the United States, and the Soviet Union) which cite works that had a role in official or semiofficial party congresses, debates, or cultural programs. Finally, the last three lists cite non-Marxist but related works, including important works on the sociology of literature and art; works on non-Marxist artists; and supplemental bibliographies of Marxist and non-Marxist but related works. To these lists are added a series of topic/subject indexes, which list author and Roman-numeral section numbers for any entries that pertain to that topic. There are both a general topic/subject index, which precedes the first author list, and further such topic/subject indexes preceding the major national lists.

X–71   Bullock, Chris, and David Peck. *Guide to Marxist Literary Criticism.* Bloomington: Indiana University Press, 1980.
Z2014.C8 B84

This volume brings together books in English on English, Canadian, and United States literature. All entries either are by Marxists or significantly employ Marxist thought in their approach to literary works. Entries are numbered serially within each of the fifteen sections, in alphabetical order by critic, and in chronological order if there is more than one work by a critic. The sections are as follows: 1. Bibliographical Tools; 2. General Collections; 3. Journals; 4. Marxist Criticism; General; 5. Literary Genres: Drama; 6. Literary Genres: Fiction; 7. Literary Genres: Poetry; 8. National Lists: British (with period subdivisions); 9. National Lists: United States (with period subdivisions); 10. National Lists: English Canadian (with period subdivisions); 11. Individual Authors; 12. Teaching English; 13. Language, Linguistics, and Literacy; 14. Literature and Society (many non-Marxist works, marked NM, included because of their relevance to a study of Marxist thought about literature); 15. Appendix: A Reading List on Mass Culture (subdivided into the various media). The work concludes with two indexes, the first of critics who authored three or more items cited, and the second of topics about which there are three or more cited items.

X–72   Bottomore, Tom, ed. *Dictionary of Marxist Thought.* Cambridge: Harvard University Press, 1983. HX17.D5 1983

This volume brings together the work of eighty-one contributors whose articles are signed and include bibliographies. The entries treat all of the basic concepts of Marxism, with cross-references to other, related concepts in the dictionary. There are biographical entries for leading figures in the history of Marxist thought. In addition, there is an index of persons and subjects at the end of the work, along with a bibliography of all the writings of Marx and Engels mentioned in the text and of all other works referred to in the articles.

X–74   Some Frequently Recommended Works on Marxist Approaches to Literature. (See also material on Russian formalism in X–14, on contemporary theory in general in X–15, on deconstruction and post-structuralism in X–28, on literature and sociology in X–69, on literature and politics in X–78, and on literature and history in X–84.)

Anderson, Perry. *In the Tracks of Historical Materialism.* Chicago: University of Chicago Press, 1984.
B809.8.A599 1984

Arvon, Henri. *Marxist Aesthetics.* Ithaca, N.Y.: Cornell University Press, 1973.   HX523.A7613

Bakhtin, Mikhail. *Diologic Imagination: Four Essays.* Austin: University of Texas Press, 1981. PN3331.B2513

———. *Problems of Dostoevsky's Poetics.* Minneapolis: University of Minnesota Press, 1984.
PG3328.Z6 B2413 1984

———. *Rabelais and His World.* Bloomington: Indiana University Press, 1984.   PQ1694.B313 1984

———. *Speech Genres and Other Late Essays.* Edited by Caryl Emerson and Michael Holquist. Austin: University of Texas Press, 1986.   P49.B2813 1986

Benjamin, Walter. *Illuminations.* New York: Harcourt, Brace and World, 1968.   PN514.B3623

Benton, Ted. *Rise and Fall of Structural Marxism.* New York: St. Martin's Press, 1984.
B2430.A474 B45 1984

Buck-Morss, Susan. *Origin of Negative Dialectics.* New York: Free Press, 1977.   B3199.A34 B8

Clark, Katarina, and Michael Holquist. *Mikhail Bakhtin.* Cambridge: Harvard University Press, 1984.
PG2947.B3 C58 1984

Craig, David, ed. *Marxists on Literature.* Harmondsworth: Penguin, 1975.   PN501.M3

Demetz, Peter. *Marx, Engels, and the Poets: Origins of Marxist Literary Criticism.* Rev. ed. Translation by Jeffrey L. Sammons of *Marx, Engels, und die Dichter: Zur Grundlagenforschung des Marxismus* (Stuttgart: Deutsche Verlags-Anstalt, 1959). Chicago: University of Chicago Press, 1967.
PN98.C6 D413

Dowling, William C. *Jameson, Althusser, Marx: An Introduction to the Political Unconscious.* Ithaca: Cornell University Press, 1984.   PN81.J293 D6 1984

Eagleton, Terry. *Criticism and Ideology.* London: New Left Books, 1976.   PN98.C6 E2

———. *Marxism and Literary Criticism.* London: Methuen, 1976.   PN.C6 E23

———. *Significance of Theory.* Oxford: Blackwell, 1989.
PN94.E23 1989

———. *Walter Benjamin, or Towards a Revolutionary Criticism.* London: Verso, 1981.   PN75.B43 E17 1981

Feenberg, Andrew. *Lukács, Marx, and the Sources of Critical Theory.* Totowa, N. J.: Rowman and Littlefield, 1981.   B4815.L84 F43

Frow, John. *Marxism and Literary History.* Oxford: Blackwell, 1986.   P302.5.F76 1986

Goldstein, Philip. *Politics of Literary Theory: An Introduction to Marxist Criticism.* Tallahassee: Florida State University Press, 1990. PN98.C6 G6 1990

Heller, Agnes. *Lukács Reappraised.* New York: Columbia University Press, 1983. B4815.L84 L883 1983

James, C. Vaughan. *Soviet Socialist Realism: Origins and Theory.* New York: St. Martin's, 1973. PG3026.S58 J3

Jameson, Frederic. *Ideologies of Theory (Essays 1971–1986). Volume 1: Situations of Theory; Volume 2: Syntax of History.* Minneapolis: University of Minnesota Press, 1988–. PN94.J36 1988

———. *Marxism and Form: Twentieth Century Dialectical Theories of Literature.* Princeton, N.J.: Princeton University Press, 1972. PN98.C6 J3 1972

———. *Political Unconscious: Narrative as a Socially Symbolic Act.* Ithaca, N.Y.: Cornell University Press, 1980. PN81.J29

Jay, Martin. *Marxism and Totality: The Adventures of a Concept from Lukacs to Habermas.* Berkeley and Los Angeles: University of California Press, 1984. HX533.J39 1984

Kellner, Douglas, ed. *Postmodernism/Jameson/Critique.* Washington, D.C.: Maisonneuve Press, 1989. PN98.C6 P67 1989

Kettle, Arnold. *Literature and Liberation: Selected Essays.* Edited by Graham Martin and W. R. Owens. Manchester: Manchester University Press, 1988. PR99.K434 1988

Laing, Dave. *Marxist Theory of Art: An Introductory Survey.* Hassocks, Sussex: Harvester Press, 1978. HX521.L32 1978

Lukács, Georg. *History and Class Consciousness.* Cambridge: MIT Press, 1971. HX260.H8 L783

———. *Schriften zur Literatursoziologie.* Edited by Peter E. Ludz. 3d ed. Neuwied: Luchterhand, 1968. Bibliography. PN51.L83 1968

———. *Soul and Form.* Cambridge: MIT Press, 1974. PN45.L713 1974

———. *Writer and Critic and Other Essays.* New York: Grosset and Dunlap, 1971. PN37.L8 1971

Macherey, Pierre. *Theory of Literary Production.* London: Routledge and Kegan Paul, 1978. PN45.M31713

Nelson, Cary, and Lawrence Grossberg, eds. *Marxism and the Interpretation of Culture.* Urbana: University of Illinois Press, 1988. HX523.M3755 1988

Siegel, Holger. *Sowietische Literarturtheorie (1917–1940): Von der historisch-materialistischen zur marxistisch-leninistischen Literaturtheorie.* Stuttgart: Metzler, 1981. PG2949.S53

Slaughter, Cliff. *Marxism, Ideology, and Literature.* London: Macmillan, 1980. HX531.S58 1980

Smith, Steven. *Reading Althusser: An Essay on Structural Marxism.* Ithaca: Cornell University Press, 1984. B2430.A474 S65 1984

Todorov, Tzvetan. *Mikhail Bakhtin: The Dialogical Principle.* Minneapolis: University of Minnesota, 1984. PG2947.B3 T613 1984

Voloshinov, V. N. *Marxism and the Philosophy of Language.* New York: Seminar Books, 1973. B809.8.V59413 1973

Weimann, Robert. *Structure and Society in Literary History: Studies in the History and Theory of Historical Criticism.* Charlottesville: University Press of Virginia, 1976. PN441.W45

Williams, Raymond. *Culture and Society, 1780–1950.* New York: Columbia University Press, 1958. DA533.W6 1958

———. *Marxism and Literature.* London: Oxford University Press, 1977. HX531.W47

———. *Politics and Letters: Interviews with New Left Review.* London: New Left Books, 1979. No LC number

———. *Politics of Modernism: Against the New Conformists.* New York: Verso, 1989. NX456.5.M64 W5 1989

———. *Problems in Materialism and Culture: Selected Essays.* London: New Left Books, 1980. HX523.W54 1980

Wolff, Janet. *Social Production of Art.* New York: St. Martin's, 1981. NX180.S6 W64 1981

X–76 **International Political Science Abstracts / Documentation politique internationale.** Vol. 1–. Paris: International Political Science Association, 1951–. JA36.I5

Annual volumes present about 5,000 informative abstracts of books and articles in political science, prepared by the International Political Science Association and the International Studies Conference. Entries are disposed into six main divisions, as follows: I. Political Science: Methods and Theory; II. Political Thinkers and Ideas; III. Government and Administrative Institutions (A. Central; B. State, Regional and Local); IV. Political Process: Public Opinion, Attitudes, Parties, Forces, Groups, and Elections; V. International Relations (A. International Law, Organization and Administration; B. Foreign Policy and International Relations); and VI. National and Area Studies. A list of periodicals analyzed and a subject index conclude each volume.

X–77 **Walker, David M. Oxford Companion to Law.** New York: Oxford University Press, 1980. K48.W34

This volume contains several thousand entries on every aspect of law from ancient Greek and Roman civilization to the present. Entries treat topics in legal history and philosophy, comparative law, international law, and the main legal systems of the Western legal tradition. Appendixes give Lists of Holders of Various Offices, and a Bibliographical Note.

X–78 **Some Frequently Recommended Works on Literature and Politics, including the New Historicism.** [See also works on Marxist Theory in X–74.]

Adereth, Maxwell. *Commitment in Modern French Literature.* London: Gollancz, 1967. PQ305.A3 1968

Barker, Francis, et al., eds. *Literature, Politics, and Theory.* London: Methuen, 1986. PN710.L58 1986

Blotner, Joseph L. *Modern American Political Novel, 1900–1960.* Austin: University of Texas Press, 1966. PS374.P6 B55

———. *Political Novel.* Garden City, N.Y.: Doubleday, 1955. PN3448.P6 B6

Bowra, C. M. *Poetry and Politics, 1900–1960.* Cambridge: Cambridge University Press, 1966. PN1081.B6

Boyers, Robert. *Atrocity and Amnesia: The Political Novel Since 1945.* New York: Oxford University Press, 1985. PN3448.P6 B68 1985

Bradbrook, Muriel C. *Literature in Action: Studies in Continental and Commonwealth Society.* London: Chatto and Windus, 1972. PN51.B67 1972

Brantlinger, Patrick. *Spirit of Reform: British Literature and Politics, 1832–1867.* Cambridge: Harvard University Press, 1977. PR469.P6 B65

Brinton, C. Crane. *Political Ideas of the English Romanticists.* London: Oxford University Press, 1926. PR457.B7

Chace, William M. *Political Identities of Ezra Pound and T. S. Eliot.* Stanford: Stanford University Press, 1973.
PS3531.O82 Z553

———. *Lionel Trilling, Criticism and Politics.* Stanford: Stanford University Press, 1980.   PS3539.R5628

Cole, G. D. H. *Politics and Literature.* London: Hogarth Press, 1929.   PR149.P6 C6 1929

Dollimore, Jonathan, and Alan Sinfield, eds. *Political Shakespeare: New Essays in Cultural Materialism.* Ithaca: Cornell University Press, 1985.
PR3817.P59 1985

Edwards, Thomas R. *Imagination and Power: A Study of Poetry on Public Themes.* New York: Oxford University Press, 1971.   PR428.P6 E3

Egbert, Donald Drew. *Social Radicalism and the Arts: Western Europe: A Cultural History from the French Revolution to 1968.* New York: Knopf, 1970. HX521.E34

Flower, J. E., J. A. Morris, and E. E. Williams. *Writers and Politics in Modern Britain, France, and Germany.* New York: Holmes and Meier, 1977.   PN51.F55

Foulkes, A. Peter. *Literature and Propaganda.* London: Methuen, 1983.   PN51.F66 1983

Goldberg, Jonathan. *James I and the Politics of Literature.* Baltimore: Johns Hopkins University Press, 1983.
PR658.P65 G64

Green, Philip, and Michael Walzer, eds. *Political Imagination in Literature: A Reader.* New York: Free Press, 1969.   PN6071.P57 G7 1969

Holland, Henry M., Jr. *Politics through Literature.* Englewood Cliffs, N.J.: Prentice-Hall, 1968.
PN6071.P57 H6

Hoskins, Katharine B. *Today the Struggle: Literature and Politics in England during the Spanish Civil War.* Austin: University of Texas Press, 1969.
PR478.S6 H6

Howe, Irving. *Politics and the Novel.* New York: Horizon, 1957.   PN3448.P6 H6

———. *World More Attractive: A View of Modern Literature and Politics.* New York: Horizon Press, 1963.
PN771.H6

Hynes, Samuel. *Auden Generation: Literature and Politics in England in the 1930s.* London: Bodley Head, 1976.
PR479.P6 H9 1976b

LaCapra, Dominick. *History, Politics, and the Novel.* Ithaca, N.Y.: Cornell University Press, 1987.
PN3343.L33 1987

Lequer, Walter, and George L. Mosse, eds. *Literature and Politics in the Twentieth Century.* Totowa, N.J.: Rowman and Littlefield, 1977.   PN51.L574 1967

Lucas, John, ed. *Literature and Politics in the Nineteenth Century.* London: Methuen, 1971.   PR469.P6 L8

Mauder, John. *Writer and Commitment.* London: Secker and Warburg, 1961.   PR471.M27

Norbrook, David. *Poetry and Politics in the English Renaissance.* London: Routledge and Kegan Paul, 1984.
PR535.H5 N67 1984

O'Brien, Conor Cruise. *Writers and Politics.* New York: Pantheon, 1965.   PR6065.B67 W7

Ohmann, Richard M. *Politics of Letters.* Middletown, Conn.: Wesleyan University Press, 1987.
PS228.P6 O36 1987

Panichas, George A., ed. *Politics of Twentieth Century Novelists.* New York: Crowell, 1974.   PN3503.P3 1974

Patterson, Lee, ed. *Literary Practice and Social Change in Britain, 1380–1530.* Berkeley and Los Angeles: University of California Press, 1989.
PR275.S63 L5 1989

Patterson, Mark R. *Authority, Autonomy, and Representation in American Literature, 1776–1865.* Princeton: Princeton University Press, 1988.
PS217.P64 P38 1988

Rahv, Philip. *Essays on Literature and Politics, 1932–1972.* Boston: Houghton, Mifflin, 1978. PN710.R327 1978

Raskin, Jonah. *Mythology of Imperialism: Rudyard Kipling, Joseph Conrad, E. M. Forster, D. H. Lawrence, and Joyce Cary.* New York: Random House, 1971.
PR471.R3

Rühle, Jürgen. *Literature and Revolution: A Critical Study of the Writer and Communism in the Twentieth Century.* New York: Praeger, 1969.   PN51.R813

Sharpe, Kevin, and Steven N. Zwicker, eds. *Politics of Discourse: The Literature and History of Seventeenth-Century England.* Berkeley and Los Angeles: University of California Press, 1987. PR438.P65 P64 1987

Sperber, Murray, comp. *Literature and Politics.* Rochelle Park, N.J.: Hayden, 1979.   PN6071.P57 L5

Stallybrass, Peter, and Allan White. *Politics and Poetics of Transgression.* Ithaca: Cornell University Press, 1986.
PN51.S666

Stein, Peter, ed. *Theorie der politischen Dichtung.* Munich: Nymphenburger, 1973.   PN51.S68

Tennenhouse, Leonard. *Power on Display: The Politics of Shakespeare's Genres.* New York: Methuen, 1986.
PR3817.T46 1986

Veeser, H. Aram, ed. *New Historicism.* New York: Routledge, 1989.   D16.9.N38 1989

Von Hallberg, Robert, ed. *Politics and Poetic Value.* Chicago: University of Chicago Press, 1987.
PN1881.P65 1987

Watson, George. *Politics and Literature in Modern Britain.* London: Macmillan, 1977.   PR479.P6 W3 1977b

Whigham, Frank. *Ambition and Privilege: The Social Tropes of Elizabethan Courtesy Theory.* Berkeley and Los Angeles: University of California Press, 1984.
PR428.C64 W5 1984

White, George A., and Charles Newman, eds. *Literature in Revolution.* New York: Holt, Rinehart and Winston, 1972.   PN51.W45 1972

Wilson, Edmund. *Letters on Literature and Politics, 1912–1972.* Selected and edited by Elena Wilson. New York: Farrar, Strauss and Giroux, 1977.
PS3545.I6254 Z54 1977

Winegarten, Renée. *Writers and Revolution: The Fatal Lure of Action.* New York: New Viewpoint–Watts, 1974.
PN51.W57 1975

Woodcock, George. *Writer and Politics.* London: Porcupine Press, 1948.   PR6045.O638 W7

Woodring, Carl. *Politics in English Romantic Poetry.* Cambridge: Harvard University Press, 1970. PR590.W57

———. *Politics in the Poetry of Coleridge.* Madison: University of Wisconsin Press, 1961.   PR4487.P6 W6

X–79 **Some Frequently Recommended Works on Literature and Law.**

Alford, John A., and Dennis P. Seniff. *Literature and Law in the Middle Ages: A Bibliography of Scholarship.* New York: Garland, 1984.   No LC number

Bloch, R. Howard. *Medieval French Literature and Law.* Berkeley and Los Angeles, London: University of California Press, 1977.   PQ158.B55

Davis, David B. *Homicide in American Fiction, 1798–1860.* Ithaca, N.Y.: Cornell University Press, 1957.
PS374.H6 D3

Eden, Kathy. *Poetic and Legal Fiction in the Aristotelian Tradition.* Princeton: Princeton University Press, 1986.   PN1040.A53 E3 1986

Ferguson, Robert A. *Law and Letters in American Culture.* Cambridge: Harvard University Press, 1984.
PS217.L37 F47 1984

Frank, Jerome. *Law and the Modern Mind*. 6th ed. New York, 1949.

Gest, John Marshall, *Lawyer in Literature*. Boston: Boston Book Company, 1913.   PN56.L33 G47

Goodrich, Peter. *Legal Discourse: Studies in Linguistics, Rhetoric and Legal Analysis*. New York: St. Martin's, 1987.   K213.G67 1987

Green, Adwin W. *Inns of Court and Early English Drama*. New Haven: Yale University Press, 1931.
             KD502.G73 1931

Holdsworth, William S. *Charles Dickens as a Legal Historian*. New Haven: Yale University Press, 1928.
             PR4589.H6

Jackson, Bernard. *Semiotics and Legal Theory*. London: Routledge and Kegan Paul, 1985.   K213.J32 1985

Levinson, Sanford, and Steven Mailloux, eds. *Interpreting Law and Literature*. Evanston, Ill.: Northwestern University Press, 1988.   KF4550.A2 I53 1988

London, Ephraim, ed. *World of Law*. 2 vols. Vol. 1. *Literature and Law*. Vol. 2. *Law as Literature*. New York: Simon, 1960.   PN6071 .L33 L6

Manheim, Leonard F., ed. *Hartford Studies in Literature*, vol. 9, nos. 2–3, Special Issue on Literature and Law.
             PN2.H3

Mellinkoff, David. *Language of the Law*. Boston: Little, Brown, 1963.

———. *Legal Writing: Sense and Nonsense*. New York: Scribner, 1982.   KF250. M44 1981b

Phillips, Owen Hood. *Shakespeare and the Lawyers*. London: Methuen, 1972.   PR328.P65

Posner, Richard A. *Law and Literature: A Misunderstood Relation*. Cambridge: Harvard University Press, 1988.   K290.P67 1988

Smith, Carl S., John P. McWilliams, and Maxwell Bloomfield. *Law and American Literature: A Collection of Essays*. New York: Knopf, 1983.
             PS169.L37 S64 1983

Suretsky, Harold. "Search for a Theory: An Annotated Bibliography of Writings on the Relation of Law to Literature and the Humanities." *Rutgers Law Review*, 32 (1979): 727–740.

Thomas, Brook. *Cross-examinations of Law and Literature: Cooper, Hawthorne, Stowe, and Melville*. Cambridge: Cambridge University Press, 1987.
             PS374.L34 T56 1987

White, James Boyd. *Heracles' Bow: Essays on the Rhetoric and Poetics of the Law*. Madison: University of Wisconsin Press, 1985.   K230.W5 H47 1985

———. *Legal Imagination: Studies in the Nature of Legal Thought and Expression*. Boston: Little, Brown, 1973.   KF250.W45

———. *When Words Lose Their Meaning: Constitutions and Reconstitutions of Language, Character and Community*. Chicago: University of Chicago Press, 1984.   P106.W574 1984

X–84 **Some Frequently Recommended Works on Literature and History.** (See also section F, History; section W.IX, on Historical Fiction, and W–120 on Relations between Fictional and Non-fictional Prose.)

Bremner, Robert H., ed. *Essays on History and Literature*. Columbus: Ohio State University Press, 1966.
             D13.B69

Damon, Philip, ed. *Literary Criticism and Historical Understanding: Selected Papers from the English Institute*. New York: Columbia University Press, 1967.
             PN81.D35

Delfau, Gerard. *Histoire, littérature*. Paris: du Seuil, 1977.
             PN86.D4

Henderson, Harry B. *Versions of the Past: The Historical Imagination in American Fiction*. New York: Oxford University Press, 1974.   PS374.H5 H46

Levin, David. *In Defense of Historical Literature: Essays on American History, Autobiography, Drama, and Fiction*. New York, 1967.   PS169.H5 L4

McRobbie, Kenneth, ed. *Chaos and Form: History and Literature: Ideas and Relationships*. Winnipeg: University of Manitoba Press, 1972.   PN695.M3

Strout, Cushing. *Veracious Imagination: Essays on American History, Literature, and Biography*. Middletown, Conn.: Wesleyan University Press, 1981.
             PS169.H5 S85

Toliver, Harold E. *Past That Poets Make*. Cambridge: Harvard University Press, 1981.   PN1080.T6

Watson, George. *Study of Literature: A New Rationale of Literary History*. London: Allen Lane, 1968.
             PN81.W3

X–85 **Schatzberg, Walter, Robert A. Waite, and Jonathan K. Johnson, eds. *Relations of Literature and Science: An Annotated Bibliography of Scholarship, 1880–1980*. New York: MLA, 1987.**   Z6511.R44 1987

This volume contains 2,548 annotated entries, divided into eight major sections, each of which is subdivided into two parts. The first, General section is subdivided into a section on Interactions of Literature and Science and another on Surveys of Literature and Science. The remaining seven sections are divided into sections on Studies and Surveys, and Individual Authors: they treat Antiquity, the Middle Ages, Renaissance, Seventeenth Century, Eighteenth Century, Nineteenth Century, and Twentieth Century. The volume concludes with an author and a subject index.

X–86 **Dudley, Fred A., ed. *Relations of Literature and Science: A Selected Bibliography, 1930–1967*. Ann Arbor, Mich.: University Microfilms, 1968.**   Z6511.D8

This volume brings together the annual bibliographies of books and articles, "Relations of Literature and Science: Selected Bibliography for [1950–1966]," published in *Symposium: A Quarterly Journal in Modern Foreign Literatures*, vols. 5–21 (1951–1967), supplementing them with additional titles from the period 1930–1950. The sheer list is in five sections: I. General Studies; II. Antiquity and the Middle Ages; III. Renaissance; IV. Seventeenth and Eighteenth Centuries; V. Nineteenth and Twentieth Centuries. The compilation concludes with an index of scholars, translators, editors, and critics.

X–87 **"Relations of Literature and Science: A Bibliography of Scholarship [1972—]." *Clio: An Interdisciplinary Journal of Literature, History, and the Philosophy of History*, vol. 4–. Fort Wayne: Indiana University—Purdue University, 1974–.**   No LC number

This annual bibliography continues the bibliography of studies 1930–1967 prepared by Fred Dudley (X–86). It presents a list of books and articles classified in a system parallel to that used in the Dudley volume, with general studies followed by studies concerned with classical antiquity, the Middle Ages, the Renaissance, and each subsequent century.

X–88 **Whitrow, Magda. *Isis Cumulative Bibliography: A Bibliography of the History of Science Formed from Isis Critical Bibliographies, 1–90, 1913–1965*. 4 vols. in 5. London: Mansell, 1971–1981.**   Z7405.H612

This bibliography cumulates the classified, international "Critical Bibliography of the History of Science and Its Cultural Influences" published annually in *Isis: An International Review Devoted to the History of Science and Its Cultural Influences* (Washington, D.C.: History of Science Society, 1913–). Books and articles are treated, and are disposed into three series: Volumes 1 and 2, *Personalities and Institutions*, list materials that deal with the life and work of an individual, his publications, and the history and publications of institutions and societies. Volume 3, *Subjects*, lists studies of topics in the history of science, including theories, concepts, and mechanisms. Vol. 4, *Periods and Civilizations*, contains works on the history of science, medicine, and technology relating to specific periods and civilizations. Separate indexes of book reviews and of authors and subjects conclude each volume of the cumulation, as they do each of the annual bibliographies.

A second cumulation, edited by John Neu, is now in progress, *Isis Cumulative Bibliography 1966-1975: A Bibliography of the History of Science Formed from Isis Critical Bibliographies 91-100, Indexing Literature Published from 1965 through 1974.* Volume 1, *Personalities and Institutions*, was published in 1980 [Z7405 .H612 suppl.].

The annual bibliographies, which have been published as a supplement to *Isis* since volume 58 (1969), must be used for studies of subjects, periods, and civilizations until the new cumulation is completed, and for all work after 1974.

X–89 **Some Frequently Recommended Works on Literature and Science.** (See also section W.XI, Science Fiction.)

Backscheider, Paula R., ed. *Probability, Time, and Space in Eighteenth-Century Literature.* New York: AMS Press, 1979.   PR442.P68

Bush, Douglas. *Science and English Poetry: An Historical Sketch.* London: Oxford University Press, 1950.
                                              PR508.S3 B8

Chapple, J. A. V. *Science and Literature in the Nineteenth Century.* Houndmills, Hampshire: Macmillan, 1986.
                                          PR468.S34 C43 1986

Crum, Ralph B. *Scientific Thought in Poetry.* New York: Columbia University Press, 1931.   PN1059.S3 C7

Evans, B. Ifor. *Literature and Science.* London: George Allen and Unwin, 1954.   PR149.S4 E9

Garvin, Harry R., ed. *Science and Literature.* Lewisburg, Pa.: Bucknell University Press, 1982.
                                          AP2.B887 vol. 27 no. 2

Grabo, Norman. *Newton among Poets: Shelley's Use of Science in* Prometheus Unbound. Chapel Hill: University of North Carolina Press, 1930.   PR5416.G7

Jeffries, A. Norman. *Language, Literature, and Science.* Cambridge: Leeds University Press, 1959. PN55.J4

Jennings, Edward M., ed. *Science and Literature: New Lenses for Criticism.* Garden City, N.Y.: Doubleday, 1970.   P47.J4

Johnson, Francis R. *Astronomical Thought in Renaissance England.* Baltimore: Johns Hopkins University Press, 1937.   QB33.G7 J6

Jones, William Powell. *Rhetoric of Science: A Study of Scientific Ideas and Imagery in Eighteenth-Century English Poetry.* Berkeley and Los Angeles: University of California Press, 1966.

Kuhn, Thomas. *Structure of Scientific Revolutions.* Chicago: University of Chicago Press, 1962.
                                          Q121.I5 vol. 2 no. 2

Levine, George. *Darwin and the Novelists: Patterns of Science in Victorian Fiction.* Cambridge: Harvard University Press, 1988.   PR878.S34 L4 1988

————, ed. *One Culture: Essays in Science and Literature.* Madison: University of Wisconsin Press, 1987.
                                          PR438.S35 O54 1987

Levy, Hyman, and Helen Spalding. *Literature for an Age of Science.* London: Methuen, 1952.   PN55.L4

Nadeau, Robert. *Readings from the New Book on Nature: Physics and Metaphysics in the Modern Novel.* Amherst: University of Massachusetts Press, 1981.
                                              PS374.P45 N3

Nicholson, Marjorie Hope. *Breaking of the Circle: Studies in the Effect of the "New Science" on Seventeenth-Century Poetry.* Rev. ed. New York: Columbia University Press, 1960.   PR545.S3 N5 1960

————. *Mountain Gloom and Mountain Glory: The Development of the Aesthetics of the Infinite.* Ithaca, N.Y.: Cornell University Press, 1959.   PR508.N3 N5

————. *Newton Demands the Muse: Newton's Optics and the Eighteenth-Century Poets.* Princeton, N.J.: Princeton University Press, 1956.   PR565.O6 N5

————. *Science and Imagination.* Ithaca, N.Y.: Cornell University Press 1956.   PR149.S4 N5

Peterfreund, Stuart, ed. *Literature and Science.* Boston: Northeastern University Press, 1990.   PN55.L5 1990

Whitehead, Alfred North. *Science and the Modern World.* New York: Macmillan, 1925.   Q171.W55 1925

X–90 **Trautman, Joanne, and Carol Pollard, comps.** *Literature and Medicine: An Annotated Bibliography.* Rev. ed. Pittsburgh, Pa.: University of Pittsburgh Press, 1982.
                                          Z6514.M43 T7 1982

Originally published in 1975, this bibliography of primary works of interest in the study of literature and medicine is in two parts. The first is a chronologically subdivided sequence of primary entries, giving author, title, and a lengthy descriptive annotation that highlights the medically interesting features of the cited text. These entries are in seven subdivisions as follows: Classical, Medieval, Renaissance, 18th Century, 19th Century, 20th Century, and Added Entries for the Revised Edition. Each entry also identifies which of thirty-nine topics the particular text is associated with. The second part lists the thirty-nine topics, which range from Abortion, Adolescence, The Body, Death, Disease and Health, Drugs, and Dying, to Madness, Nurses, Plague, Science and Poetry, Sexuality, Suicide, Surgery, Women as Healers, and Women as Patients. Beneath each topic is a list of the authors, titles, and period subdivisions of all entries from the first part which pertain.

X–91 ***Bibliography of the History of Medicine*** [1964–]. Vol. 1–. Bethesda, Md.: United States National Library of Medicine, 1965–.   Z6660.B582

This annual, comprehensive bibliography of books and articles, cumulated quinquennially, is in two sections. Section 1 treats studies on individuals and is arranged alphabetically by the name of the individual as subject; section 2 treats other subjects, including literature and medicine. Each volume concludes with an index of authors.

This bibliography was preceded by a "Bibliography of the History of Medicine in the United States and Canada [for 1939–1965]," in the *Bulletin of the History of Medicine*, vols. 8–40 (Baltimore: Johns Hopkins University Press, 1940–1966) [R11.B93]. All but the last few of these annual bibliographies are cumulated in Genevieve Miller's *Bibliography of the History of Medicine of the United States and Canada, 1939-1960* (Baltimore: Johns Hopkins University Press, 1964) [Z6661.U5 M52].

X–92 **Walton, Sir John, Paul R. Beeson, and Sir Ronald Bodley Scott, eds.** *Oxford Companion to Medicine.* 2 vols. London: Oxford University Press, 1986.   R121.O88 1986

This work contains more than 10,000 alphabetically arranged entries, ranging from extended essays to brief definitions. Entries present definitions of common medical terms; treat the historical development and current state of each of the major medical disciplines; discuss the academic, educational, and administrative structure of the medical profession, and its relation to government and the law; and include numerous biographies of those who have made significant contributions to medicine.

Volume 2 ends with two appendixes, the first on medical and related qualifications, listing abbreviations of medical degrees, medical association memberships, and the like. The second lists standard abbreviation for various diseases, tests, and equipment.

X–94   **Some Frequently Recommended Works on Literature and Medicine.**

Abrams, Meyer H. *Milk of Paradise*. Cambridge: Harvard University Press, 1934.   PR468.O6 A3

Anderson, Charles M. *Richard Selzer and the Rhetoric of Surgery*. Carbondale: Southern Illinois University Press, 1989.   PS3469.E585 Z54 1989

Angyal, Andrew J. *Lewis Thomas*. Boston: Twayne, 1989.   PS3570.H566 Z54 1989

Biasin, Gian-Paolo. *Literary Diseases: Theme and Metaphor in the Italian Novel*. Austin: University of Texas Press, 1975.   PQ4053.D5 B5

Byrd, Max. *Visits to Bedlam: Madness and Literature in the Eighteenth Century*. Columbus: University of South Carolina Press, 1974.   PR449.M4 B4

Ceccio, Joseph, ed. *Medicine in Literature*. London: Longman's, 1978.   PN6071.M38 M4

Claire, William, ed. *Physician as Writer*. Baltimore: Johns Hopkins University Press, 1985.   PS508.P58 P48 1985

Fiedler, Leslie. *Freaks*. New York: Simon and Schuster, 1978.   GT6730.F53

Goellnicht, Donald C. *Poet-Physician: Keats and Medical Science*. Pittsburgh, Penna.: University of Pittsburgh Press, 1984.   PR4838.M4 G63 1984

Hayter, Alethea. *Opium and the Romantic Imagination*. Berkeley, Los Angeles, London: University of California Press, 1970.   PN751.H3

Jones, Anne Hudson, ed. *Images of Healers*. Baltimore: Johns Hopkins University Press, 1985.   P96.H42 I5 1985

Ober, William B., M.D. *Boswell's Clap and Other Essays: Medical Analyses of Literary Men's Afflictions*. Carbondale: Southern Illinois University Press, 1979.   R703.O23

————. *Bottoms Up!: A Pathologist's Essays on Medicine and the Humanities*. Carbondale: Southern Illinois University Press, 1987.   R702.O24 1987

Peschel, Richard E., and Enid Rhodes Peschel. *When a Doctor Hates a Patient and Other Chapters in a Young Physician's Life*. Berkeley and Los Angeles: University of California Press, 1986.   R737.P42137 1986

Peschel, Enid Rhodes, ed. *Medicine and Literature*. New York: Neale Watson Academic Publications, 1980   PN56.M38 M4

Sena, John F. *Bibliography of Melancholy, 1660–1800*. London: Nether Press, 1977.   Z7204.E5 S4

Sontag, Susan. *Illness as Metaphor*. New York: Farrar, Strauss and Giroux, 1978.   PN56.T82 S6 1978

Trautmann, Joanne. *Healing Arts in Dialogue: Medicine and Literature*. Carbondale: Southern Illinois University Press, 1981.   PN56.M38 H4

X–95   **"Current Bibliography in the History of Technology [1962–]."** *Technology and Culture: The International Quarterly of the Society for the History of Technology*, vol. 4–. Chicago: University of Chicago Press, 1964–.   T1.T27

This annual bibliography of books and articles is disposed into chronological periods, with items arranged by subject within each period. Most entries are briefly annotated. An author index concludes each annual bibliography and is complemented by a biennial subject index. On occasion, specialized bibliographies are included in *Technology and Culture*.

An annual, annotated list of books and articles, "Technology in American Culture: Recent Publications [1980–]," is a regular feature of the *Journal of American Culture*, vol. 4–, (Bowling Green, Ohio: Bowling Green State University Popular Press, 1981–) [E169.1J7].

X–98   **Blackburn, David, and Geoffrey Holister, eds.** *G. K. Hall Encyclopedia of Modern Technology*. Boston: G. K. Hall, 1987.   T47.G18 1987

This volume with 480 black and white and full color illustrations surveys hundreds of modern technologies from nuclear power to microchips and compact discs. An extensive glossary, an index, and numerous cross-references extend the usefulness of this work.

X–99   **Some Frequently Recommended Works on Literature and Technology.** (See also Section W.XI, Science Fiction.)

Daumas, Maurice, ed. *History of Technology and Invention: Progress through the Ages*. Translation by Eileen B. Hennessey of *Histoire générale des techniques*, 5 vols. (Paris: Presses universitaires de France, 1962–1979). 3 vols. New York: Crown, 1969–.   T15.D2613

Ferguson, Eugene S. *Bibliography of the History of Technology*. Cambridge: Society for the History of Technology and MIT Press, 1968.   Z7914.H5 F4

Marx, Leo. *Machine in the Garden: Technology and the Pastoral Ideal in America*. New York: Oxford University Press, 1964.   E169.1.M35

————. *Pilot and the Passenger: Essays on Literature, Technology, and Culture in the United States*. New York: Oxford University Press, 1988.   PS121.M28 1988

Segeberg, Harro. *Literarische Technik-Bilder: Studien zum Verhältnis von Technik-und Literaturgeschichte im 19. und frühen 20. Jahrhundert*. Tübingen: M. Niemeyer, 1987.   PT395.S4 1987

————. *Technik in der Literatur: Ein Forschungsbericht und zwölf Aufsätze*. Frankfort: Suhrkamp, 1987.   PT395.T44 1987

Singer, Charles Joseph, et al. *History of Technology*. 5 vols. Oxford: Clarendon, 1954–1958. Reprinted with corrections. 1965.   T15.S53 1965

Slade, Joseph W., and Judith Yaross Lee, eds. *Beyond Two Cultures: Essays on Science, Technology, and Literature*. Ames: Iowa State University Press, 1989.   PN55.B49 1989

Steinman, Lisa M. *Made in America: Science, Technology, and American Modernist Poets*. New Haven: Yale University Press, 1987.   PS324.S67 1987

Sussman, Herbert L. *Victorians and the Machine: The Literary Response to Technology*. Cambridge: Harvard University Press, 1968.   PR468.T4 S8

Sypher, Wylie. *Literature and Technology: The Alien Vision*. New York: Random House, 1968.   PN55.S9

Tichi, Cecelia. *Shifting Gears: Technology, Literature, Culture in Modernist America*. Chapel Hill: University of North Carolina Press, 1987.   PS228.T42 T5 1987

IV. RHETORIC, COMMUNICATIONS, AND DISCOURSE THEORY

See also Brockett et al., *Bibliographic Guide to Research in Speech and Dramatic Art* (U–12).

X–100 **Horner, Winifred, ed. *Present State of Scholarship in Historical and Contemporary Rhetoric.*** Columbia: University of Missouri Press, 1983.   PN183.P7 1983

This set of six bibliographical essays, each written by a specialist, provides an overview of primary works, authors, and rhetorical issues of the period surveyed with special attention given to editions and translations and relevant scholarship. Essays also identify desiderata for future work. The essays and their authors are as follows:

1. *Classical Period* (Richard L. Enos).
2. *Medieval Period* (James J. Murphy).
3. *Renaissance* (Don Paul Abbott).
4. *Eighteenth Century* (Winifred Bryan Horner).
5. *Nineteenth Century* (Donald Stewart).
6. *Twentieth Century* (James L. Kinneavy).

Aside from the first chapter, authors exclude discussion of Continental rhetoric except as it impinges on British or American thought.

X–101 **Alston, R. C., and J. L. Rosier. "Rhetoric and Style: A Bibliographical Guide."** *Leeds Studies in English*, n.s. 1 (1967): 137–159.   PE10.L4

This brief, selective bibliography of leading books and articles is in five sections, as follows: I. The Classical Rhetorical Heritage (primary treatises, secondary critical works); II. The Medieval Tradition (primary treatises, pulpit rhetoric, secondary critical works); III. The Renaissance Tradition (treatises—other than English, treatises in English, and Latin treatises printed in England, secondary critical works); IV. The Teaching of Rhetoric in the Schools of Renaissance England (contemporary treatises, modern secondary works); and V. Stylistics (theories of style, stylostatistics, diction, metaphor, prose rhythm, prose style, prosody, poetic language).

X–102 **Cleary, James W., and Frederick W. Haberman. *Rhetoric and Public Address: A Bibliography, 1947–1961.*** Madison: The University of Wisconsin Press, 1964. Z6514.S7 C5

Based on the annual "Bibliography of Rhetoric and Public Address" published in the *Quarterly Journal of Speech*, 1947–1951, and in *Speech Monographs*, 1952–1961, this work consists of a main section of 8,035 serially numbered, briefly annotated entries arranged alphabetically by author. Of these, 4,363 are articles and monographs; 2,753 are books; and 919 are doctoral theses. To this main section are added a historically and geographically classified list of practitioners and theorists of rhetoric and public address who appear as subjects in the index; an index of reviewers cited in entries for books in the main section; and a detailed subject and person-as-subject index of more than eighty double-column pages. A brief but lucid preface and two lists of the approximately 650 journals searched to compile the bibliography complete the volume. For more recent materials see the annual "Bibliographies of Rhetoric and Public Address" in *Speech Monographs* (X–103) from 1962 through 1969.

X–103 **"Bibliography of Rhetoric and Public Address [1962–1968]."** *Speech Monographs*, vols. 29–36. Falls Church, Va.: Speech Communication Association, 1962–1969.
PN4077.S6

The annual bibliographies began in *Speech Monographs*

with the listing for 1950 in volume 18 (1951). Prior to that, they were published in the *Quarterly Journal of Speech* (1947–1951). The bibliographies through 1961 were cumulated in Cleary and Haberman (X–102). Those from 1962 through 1968 have not been cumulated. The bibliography for 1969 is the first in the separately published *Bibliographic Annual in Speech Communication* (X–105).

Also transferred to the *Bibliographic Annual* were the three other listings appearing annually in *Speech Monographs*. The first, "Abstracts of Theses in the Field of Speech [1945–1968]," published in volumes 13–36 (1946–1969), gives abstracts of both M.A. and doctoral theses. The second, "Doctoral Dissertations in Speech: Work in Progress [1950–1968]," appeared in volumes 18–36 (1951–1969) and listed by subject theses in progress, identifying titles, authors, and institutions. Previously reported projects are not repeated. The third, "Graduate Theses: An Index to Graduate Work in Speech," was published in volumes 2–36 (1935–1969). A retrospective list in volume 2 covered work of the years 1902–1934. Thereafter indexes were annual. Both M.A. and doctoral theses are included in three sections: a sheer list by author, a list by granting institutions, and a detailed subject index.

X–104 **Matlon, Ronald J., and Irene R. Matlon. *Index to Journals in Communication Studies.*** Annandale, Va.: Speech Communication Association, 1981.   Z5630.M37

This volume presents tables of contents along with a subject index and an index of contributors to a total of thirteen journals in communications, rhetoric, and speech from the date of their inception through 1979 (in all but four cases). Articles in each journal are numbered serially. The indexed journals are as follows: *Quarterly Journal of Speech* (1915–1974), entries 1–2674; *Speech Monographs* (1934–1979), entries M1-M955; *Speech Teacher* (1952–1979), entries T1 - T1018; *Southern Speech Communication Journal* (1935–1979), entries S1 - S987; *Western Journal of Speech Communication* (1937–1979), entries W1 - W894; *Central States Speech Journal* (1949–1979), entries C1 - C581; *Today's Speech* (1953–1979), entries E1 - E814; *Association of Departments and Administrators in Speech Communication Bulletin* (1972–1979), entries A1 - A60; *Philosophy and Rhetoric* (1968–1979), entries P1 - P92; *Journal of Communication* (1951–1979), entries N1 - N652; *Journalism Quarterly* (1924–1975), entries J1 - J2210; *Journal of Broadcasting* (1956–1975), entries B1 - B623; and *Journal of the American Forensic Association* (1964–1975), entries F1 - F166. Entries in the indexes are to the distinct entry numbers.

X–105 ***Bibliographic Annual of Speech Communication: An Annual Volume Devoted to Maintaining a Record of Graduate Work in Speech Communications, Providing Abstracts of Doctoral Dissertations, and Making Available Specialized Bibliographies [1969–1974].*** 6 vols. Falls Church, Va.: Speech Communication Association, 1970-1975.   Z5630.B48

The annual "Selected Bibliography of Rhetoric and Public Address [1967–1974]," "Abstracts of Doctoral Dissertations [1969–1974]," and "Graduate Theses and Dissertations: An Index of Graduate Work in Speech [1969–1974]" were all included in these annual volumes, along with "Studies in Mass Communication: A Selected Bibliography [1972–1974]." The series was unfortunately discontinued in 1975 because of high costs; it has not been replaced.

Among sources that may provide current supplementation see the *Communication Yearbook* (New Brunswick, N.J.: International Communication Association, 1977) [P87.C5974], which offers bibliographical reviews on information systems; interpersonal, mass, organizational, intercultural, political, instructional, and health communications; and both subject and author indexes. See also the quarterly *Communication Abstracts: An International Information Service* (Beverly Hills, Calif.: Sage, 1978-) [P87.C59733], which analyzes about eighty English-language journals, presents a classified set of abstracts, and provides both author and subject indexes.

X–106 **"Current Bibliography of Books on Rhetoric."** *Rhetoric Society Quarterly*, vol. 1–. St. Cloud, Minn.: St. Cloud State University for the Rhetoric Society of America, 1968–.
PN171.4.R6

Since volume 6 (1976) each issue of *RSQ* has contained a sheer listing of books and articles now disposed into eight categories, as follows: I. Basic Rhetorical Research; II. Metarhetorical Research; III. Pedagogical Research; IV. Rhetorical Criticism; V. Reading Research; VI. Rhetorical History; VII. Miscellany of Research Related to Rhetoric; VIII. Professional and Technical Writing. During the years prior to 1976, the journal, then the *Rhetoric Society Newsletter*, contained such a bibliography from time to time.

Most issues of *RSQ* have included bibliographies on special topics in rhetorical history or theory. Recent volumes, for example, contain such special bibliographies as the following: "A Bibliography of the Rhetoric of Conversation in England, 1600–1800"; "A Bibliography: The Rhetoric and Sermons of St. Augustine"; "Imitation Theory and Teaching Writing: An Annotated Bibliography"; "The Ethics of Rhetoric: A Bibliography"; "A Bibliography for the Study of Aristotle's Rhetoric"; "A Decade of Research on Aristotle's *Rhetoric*: 1970–1980"; "Recent Work in Paragraph Analysis: A Bibliography"; and "Written Texts and Contexts of Situation and Culture: A Bibliography." A bibliography of all bibliographies published in *RSQ* through 1981 was published in vol. 11 (1981), pp. 269–270.

See also the *Classical World Bibliography of Rhetoric* published in 1978 (New York: Garland) [Z7129.C7 C58 1978].

X–110 **Lausberg, Heinrich.** *Handbuch der literarischen Rhetorik: Eine Grundlegung der Literaturwissenschaft.* 2d ed., enl. by an appendix. 2 vols. Munich: Hueber, 1973.
PA181.L3 1973

These volumes, originally published in 1960, present a lengthy and authoritative, discursive treatment of the system of classical rhetoric arranged in a series of 1,326 numbered paragraphs. The first, main volume contains the exposition, while the second volume contains the indexes and appendix. The table of contents presents a detailed eight-level outline of the system, with three main parts: the definition and place of rhetoric; rhetoric in itself; and poetics. Subdivisions upon subdivisions locate each aspect of the art in relation to all others. The second volume contains a list of abbreviations and bibliography, and a glossary of terms, Latin, Greek, and French, as well as an appendix with some seventy-five paragraphs of additions and corrections.

X–111 **Lanham, Richard A.** *Handlist of Rhetorical Terms: A Guide for Students of English Literature.* Berkeley and Los Angeles: University of California Press, 1968.
PE1445.A2 L3

This handy volume contains an alphabetically arranged list of Greek, Latin, and English rhetorical terms, for each of which a pronunciation guide, definition, and often an example are provided. To this list are appended a classification of the terms according to the divisions of classical rhetorical theory; a classification of the terms by the type of linguistic or semantic action they refer to (e.g., omission, repetition); a list of terms especially useful in literary criticism with short definitions; a brief chronology of some important dates in the history of rhetoric; and a brief bibliography of primary and secondary books cited.

X–112 **Woodson, Linda.** *Handbook of Modern Rhetorical Terms.* Urbana, Ill.: NCTE, 1979.
PN172.W6

This annotated alphabetical list contains some 400 terms of the new rhetoric, chosen from textbooks, theoretical, and pedagogical studies primarily of the twentieth century. Annotations include a definition, quoted when possible from the text of the term's originator, bibliographic references to the term's first or principal use, and quotations illustrating the term's use in context. An appendix lists the terms by subject category, bringing together, for example, all terms concerned with invention, with arrangement, with style, and all terms taken from communications and speech act theory, linguistics, philosophy, or psychology. An index of cited authors concludes the *Handbook*.

X–113 **Shibles, Warren.** *Metaphor: An Annotated Bibliography and History.* Whitewater, Wis.: Language Press, 1971.
Z7004.M4 S5

This volume is meant to contain reference to all books and articles in all major languages and fields concerned with metaphor and related terms such as simile, archetype, or analogy. Some 1,800 entries, most with informative abstracts giving an account of the work's ideas about metaphor, are arranged in an alphabetical list by author. There are two indexes: The first cites general terms and names. The second is a subject index to ideas about metaphor. Because of the detailed, informative annotation, the author claims that the volume also makes possible a view of the history of ideas about metaphor.

X–114 **Horner, Winifred Bryan, ed.** *Historical Rhetoric: An Annotated Bibliography of Sources in English.* Boston: G. K. Hall, 1980.
Z7004.R5 H57

This volume brings together English books and articles, both primary and secondary, available for the study of the history of rhetoric from classical antiquity through the nineteenth century. A total of 777 entries are disposed into five sections and numbered consecutively in each section. They are descriptively and evaluatively annotated by the section's compiler, who also provides a brief introduction. The individual sections and their compilers are as follows: 1. The Classical Period (Richard Enos); 2. The Middle Ages (Luke Reinsma); 3. The Renaissance (Charles Stanford); 4. The Eighteenth Century (Winifred Bryan Horner); and 5. The Nineteenth Century (Donald C. Stewart). In addition to abundant cross-references, the volume concludes with an index of authors, titles of primary works, and subjects, though regrettably, few rhetorical terms are included.

X–115 **Murphy, James J.** *Medieval Rhetoric: A Select Bibliography.* Toronto: University of Toronto Press, 1971.
Z7004.R5 M87

This volume contains some 500 titles that are carefully annotated with both descriptive and particularly evaluative comments. The entries are numbered within each of eight sections, as follows: I. Background Works; II. The Transitional Period; III. Transmission of Classical Rhetorical Traditions; IV. Grammar (*Ars Grammatica*); V. The Art of Letter-Writing (*Ars Dictaminis*); VI. The Art of Preaching (*Ars Praedicandi*): VII. The University Disputation; VIII. Miscellany. An appendix presents a Basic Library for the study of medieval rhetoric. In addition to extensive cross-referencing in the annotations themselves, the volume concludes with an index of authors, editors, and scholars.

X–116 **Murphy, James J. *Renaissance Rhetoric: A Short-Title Catalogue of Works on Rhetorical Theory from the Beginning of Printing [ca. 1455] to A.D. 1700, with Special Attention to the Holdings of the Bodleian Library, Oxford: With a Select Basic Bibliography of Works on Renaissance Rhetoric.*** New York: Garland, 1981.

Z7004.R5 M873 1981

This work is divided into the two parts indicated in its subtitle. A brief introduction is followed by a list of the location codes and abbreviations for cited standard secondary sources. The Short-Title Catalogue is arranged alphabetically by author, with a total of 867 serially numbered entries. Dates and aliases are given for each author. More than 3,000 short titles of rhetorical treatises are then arranged in chronological order beneath the name of their author. Works cited under authors such as Aristotle are presented in a more elaborate classification including collected works, two or more works, editions of the *Rhetorica*, and then lists of commentaries, vernacular translations, and epitomes. Entries give places and dates of publication and codes indicating a library location or, where no extant copy has been found, a standard source for the reference.

The thirty-page highly select bibliography is unannotated but classified into seven sections: Bibliographies and Bibliographic Surveys, Ancient and Medieval Backgrounds, General Studies, Special Subjects, Rhetoric in Education, Countries and Geographical Regions, and Individual Authors. It is followed by the volume's three special indexes: of aliases, of English works or works published in Britain, and of preaching manuals.

X–117 **Sonnino, Lee Ann. *Handbook to Sixteenth-Century Rhetoric.*** London: Routledge and Kegan Paul, 1968.

PN227.S6

After an introduction this volume presents a series of lists with detailed definitions and contemporary examples of terms used in sixteenth-century rhetorical treatises. There are four such lists that occupy the body of this work. The first presents the Latin names for the figures or colors of rhetoric. Greek equivalents are given in parentheses, and other equivalent terms in italics. Definitions from authorities follow, and then examples taken from texts cited by the authorities. The second list presents those figures with Greek names only, following them with similar treatments of definition and example. Style terms follow, similarly defined, and the last list gives genre terms.

A bibliographical section follows, with four enumerations: A Checklist of Rhetorical Textbooks in Use in Sixteenth-Century Schools and Universities; A Critical Bibliography with Descriptive and Evaluative Annotations of Important Renaissance Texts; Rhetorical Treatises Written in English; and The Texts Used in Compiling This Handbook. A series of charts detailing the major systems for dividing the material of traditional rhetoric follows the bibliographies, and these are followed by four indexes: a descriptive index of tropes and schemes; an index of Greek terms and the Latin terms under which they will be found; an index of Latin terms; and an index of Italian terms (with just two items: *canzone* and *sonetto*).

A new *Dictionary of Literary-Rhetorical Conventions of the English Renaissance* by Marjorie Donker and George M. Muldrow (Westport, Conn.: Greenwood, 1982) [PR531 .D6 1982] contains long essays defining in Renaissance terms and from Renaissance contexts a total of sixty-eight genres, verse forms, metrical forms, and other verbal and linguistic conventions from Acrostic to Vulgar Language. Entries cite extensively from contemporary writers and are followed by extensive bibliographies. Appendixes list modern literary terms and their Renaissance equivalents, and present a subject index to the sixty-eight terms. The volume concludes with a general subject index.

Another research aid is the relatively new 450-page bibliography by Heinrich F. Plett, *Englische Rhetorik und Poetik, 1479–1660: Eine systematische Bibliography* (Opladen: Westdeutscherverlag, 1985) [T7.F65 Nr. 3201].

X–118 **Houlette, Forrest. *Nineteenth-Century Rhetoric: An Enumerative Bibliography.*** New York: Garland, 1989.

Z2015.R5 H68 1989

This volume includes English-language articles, books, and individual chapters on rhetoric, composition, grammar, writing, and the teaching of English which were published between 1800 and 1920. Articles are enumerated alphabetically by author, but the subject index facilitates access. Sources of citations are given, as are lists of publishers and journals cited.

X–119 **Some Frequently Recommended Works on the History of Rhetoric and Rhetorical Theory and on Relations of Rhetoric and Poetics.** (See also entries in X–11 and X–129, X–139, and X–164.)

Baldwin, T. W. *William Shakespeare's Small Latine and Lesse Greeke.* 2 vols. Champaign: University of Illinois Press, 1944.

Benson, Thomas W. *American Rhetoric: Context and Criticism.* Carbondale: Southern Illinois University Press, 1989.   PE2827.A44 1989

———, and Michael H. Prosser, eds. *Readings in Classical Rhetoric.* Bloomington: Indiana University Press, 1972.   PA3637.R5 B4 1972

Berlin, James A. *Rhetoric and Reality: Writing Instruction in American Colleges, 1900–1985.* Carbondale: Southern Illinois University Press, 1987.

PE1405.U6 B466 1987

———. *Writing Instruction in Nineteenth-Century American Colleges.* Carbondale: Southern Illinois University Press, 1984.   PE1405.U6 B47 1984

Bryant, Donald C., ed. *Ancient Greek and Roman Rhetoricians: A Biographical Dictionary.* Columbia, Mo.: Artscraft Press, 1968.   PA83.A5

Caplan, Harry. *Of Eloquence: Studies in Ancient and Medieval Rhetoric.* Ithaca, N.Y.: Cornell University Press, 1970.   PA6083.C3

Clark, Donald Lemen. *John Milton at St. Paul's School: A Study of Ancient Rhetoric in English Renaissance Education.* New York: Columbia University Press, 1948.

PR3582.C5

———. *Rhetoric and Poetry in the Renaissance: A Study of Rhetorical Terms in English Renaissance Literary Criticism.* New York: Columbia University Press, 1922.   PN1035.C5

———. *Rhetoric in Greco-Roman Education.* New York: Columbia University Press, 1957.   PA3265.C55

Clarke, Martin L. *Rhetoric at Rome: A Historical Survey.* London: Cohen and West, 1953.   PA6083.C6

Connors, Robert J., Lisa S. Ede, and Andrea A. Lunsford, eds. *Essays on Classical Rhetoric and Modern Discourse.* Carbondale: Southern Illinois University Press, 1984.   PN175.E8 1984

Cooper, Lane, ed. *Rhetoric of Aristotle: An Expanded Translation with Supplementary Examples for Students of Composition and Public Speaking.* New York: Appleton-Century-Crofts, 1932.

PN173.A7 C6

Corbett, Edward P. J. *Classical Rhetoric for the Modern Student.* 2d ed. New York: Oxford University Press, 1971.   PN175.C57 1971

———. *Rhetorical Analyses of Literary Works*. New York: Oxford University Press, 1969. Extensive bibliography. PR14.C6

Covino, William A. *Art of Wondering: A Revisionist Return to the History of Rhetoric*. Portsmouth, N.H.: Boynton/Cook, 1988. PN183.C68 1988

Crocker, Lionel, and Paul A. Carmack. *Readings in Rhetoric*. Springfield, Ill.: Charles C. Thomas, 1965.

Dixon, Peter. *Rhetoric*. London: Methuen, 1971. PN175.D55

Enos, Richard Leo. *Literate Mode of Cicero's Legal Rhetoric*. Carbondale: Southern Illinois University Press, 1988. KJA190.E56 1988

Erickson, Keith V., ed. *Aristotle's Rhetoric: Five Centuries of Philological Research*. Metuchen, N.J.: Scarecrow, 1975. Supplement, 1970–1980, in *Rhetoric Society Quarterly* 12 (1982): 62–66. Z8044.E74

Golden, James L., Goodwin F. Berquist, and William E. Coleman, eds. *Rhetoric of Western Thought*. 3d ed. Dubuque, Iowa: Kendall/Hunt, 1983. PN183.G6 1983

Golden, James L., and Edward P. J. Corbett. *Rhetoric of Blair, Campbell and Whately*. New York: Holt, Rinehart and Winston, 1968. PE1402.G6

Havelock, Eric A. *Preface to Plato*. Cambridge: Belknap Press of Harvard University Press, 1963. B393.P6 H33

Herrick, Marvin. *Fusion of Horatian and Aristotelian Literary Criticism, 1531–1555*. Urbana: University of Illinois Press, 1946. PN88.H4

Howell, Wilbur Samuel. *Poetics, Rhetoric, and Logic: Studies in the Basic Disciplines of Criticism*. Ithaca, N.Y.: Cornell University Press, 1975. PN86.H6

Howes, Raymond F. *Historical Studies of Rhetoric and Rhetoricians*. Ithaca, N.Y.: Cornell University Press, 1961. PN4021.H6

Ijsseling, Samuel. *Rhetoric and Philosophy in Conflict: An Historical Survey*. The Hague: Nijhoff, 1976. PN179.I513

Joseph, Sister Miriam. See Miriam Joseph.

Kennedy, George. *Art of Persuasion in Greece*. Princeton, N.J.: Princeton University Press, 1963. PA3265.K4

———. *Art of Rhetoric in the Roman World, 300 B.C.–A.D. 300*. Princeton, N.J.: Princeton University Press, 1972. PA6085.K4

———. *Classical Rhetoric and Its Christian and Secular Tradition from Ancient to Modern Times*. Chapel Hill: University of North Carolina Press, 1980. Bibliography. PN183.K4

Kennedy, William J. *Rhetorical Norms in Renaissance Literature*. New Haven: Yale University Press, 1978. PN721.K4

Lanham, Richard A. *Motives of Eloquence: Literary Rhetoric in the Renaissance*. New Haven: Yale University Press, 1976. PN88.L3

McKeon, Richard. "Rhetoric in the Middle Ages." *Speculum* 17 (1942): 1–32.

Matsen, Patricia P., Philip Rollinson, and Marion Sousa, eds. *Readings in Classical Rhetoric*. Carbondale: Southern Illinois University Press, 1990. PA3637.R5 R4 1990

Miller, Joseph M., et al. *Readings in Medieval Rhetoric*. Bloomington: Indiana University Press, 1973. PN185.M5

Miriam Joseph, Sister. *Shakespeare's Use of the Arts of Language*. New York: Columbia University Press, 1947. PN3072.M5 1947a

Murphy, James J. *Rhetoric in the Middle Ages: A History of Rhetorical Theory from St. Augustine to the Renaissance*. Berkeley, Los Angeles, London: University of California Press, 1974. PN173.M8

———, ed. *Medieval Eloquence: Studies in the Theory and Practice of Medieval Rhetoric*. Berkeley, Los Angeles, London: University of California Press, 1978. PN183.M4

———, ed. *Rhetorical Tradition and Modern Writing*. New York: MLA, 1982. PE1404.R5 1982

———, ed. *Synoptic History of Classical Rhetoric*. Davis, Calif.: Hermagoras Press, 1983. PA3265.M8 1983

Norden, Eduard. *Die antike Kunstprosa vom VI. Jahrhundert vor Christi bis in die Zeit der Renaissance*. 2 vols. Leipzig: Teubner, 1898. PA3035.N6 1898

Ong, Walter J. *Ramus, Method, and the Decay of Dialogue: From the Art of Discourse to the Art of Reason*. Cambridge: Harvard University Press, 1958.

Plett, Heinrich F. *Rhetorik der Affekte: Englische Wirkungsästhetik in Zeitalter der Renaissance*. Tübingen: Niemeyer, 1975. PN88.P6

Roberts, W. Rhys. *Greek Rhetoric and Literary Criticism*. New York: Longmans, Green, 1928. PA3265.R6

Sanford, William E. *English Theories of Public Address, 1530–1828*. Columbus, Ohio: H. L. Hedrick, 1931. PN4036.S3 1929

Scaglione, Aldo. *Classical Theory of Composition from Its Origins to the Present: An Historical Survey*. Chapel Hill: University of North Carolina Press, 1972. PN86.S4

Schwartz, Joseph, and John A. Rycenga. *Province of Rhetoric*. New York: Ronald Press, 1965. PN175.S35

Seigel, Jerrold E. *Rhetoric and Philosophy in Renaissance Humanism: The Union of Eloquence and Wisdom, Petrarch to Valla*. Princeton, N.J.: Princeton University Press, 1968. B775.S4

Trousdale, Marion. *Shakespeare and the Rhetoricians*. Chapel Hill: University of North Carolina Press, 1982. PR2976.T77

Vickers, Brian. *Classical Rhetoric in English Poetry*. New York: St. Martin's, 1970. PN86.V5

———. *In Defense of Rhetoric*. Oxford: Clarendon Press, 1988. PN175.V53 1988

———, ed. *Rhetoric Revalued: Papers from the International Society for the History of Rhetoric*. Binghamton, N.Y.: Center for Medieval and Early Renaissance Studies, 1982. PN171.6.R5 1982

Yates, Frances A. *Art of Memory*. London: Routledge and Kegan Paul, 1966. BF381.Y3 1966

Zielinski, Thadeusz. *Cicero im Wandel der Jahrhunderte*. 4th ed. Leipzig: Teubner, 1929. PA6346.Z5 1929

X–120 **Kinneavy, James L. *Theory of Discourse: The Aims of Discourse*.** Englewood Cliffs, N.J.: Prentice-Hall, 1971. PE1408.K664

Each of the six chapters in this standard work in the field of rhetorical and discourse theory concludes with a substantial bibliography of references relevant to the subject of the chapter. The chapters are: Discourse and the Field of English; The Aims of Discourse; Reference Discourse; Persuasive Discourse; Literary Discourse; and Expressive Discourse. The volume concludes with an index of names and subjects; boldface entries designate references in the bibliographies.

X–124 **Tannacito, Dan J. *Discourse Studies: A Multidisciplinary Bibliography of Research on Text, Discourse and Prose Writing*.** Indiana, Pa.: Indiana University of Pennsylvania, 1981. Z7004.O57 T36 1981

This computer-compiled unannotated bibliography excludes non-English items, most conference papers, and most ERIC documents. It lists entries in three series: Festschriften and Collections; Dissertations; and Books, Articles, Reports, and Papers. Entries are in alphabetical order by author within the three sections. Each is identified by code for the discipline(s) with which it is associated. These include artificial intelligence, anthropology, applied linguistics, cognitive studies, cognitive anthropology, cognitive psychology, communications, computer science, developmental studies, education, educational psychology, English, linguistics, literature, psycholinguistics, psychology, reading research, rhetoric, sociolinguistics, sociology, social psychology, and writing research and pedagogy.

X–125 Dressler, Wolfgang U., and Siegfried J. Schmidt, comps. *Textlinguistik: Kommentierte Bibliographie.* Munich: Wilhelm Fink, 1973.   Z7004.D57 D73

This descriptive and evaluatively annotated bibliography is in three sections: A. Studies in Text Linguistics; B. Studies in Applied Text Linguistics; and C. Related Studies. A total of 117 entries include an appendix of five unannotated items. The volume concludes with a list of periodicals and a list of the annotators with initials.

X–129 Some Frequently Recommended Works on Rhetoric, Communications, and Discourse Theory.

Allport, Alan, et al. *Language Perception and Production: Relationships between Listening, Speaking, Reading, and Writing.* London: Academic Press, 1987.
P37.L365 1987

Austin, J. L. *How to Do Things with Words.* Cambridge: Harvard University Press, 1962.   P106.A9 1962

Bazerman, Charles. *Shaping Written Knowledge: The Genre and Activity of the Experimental Article in Science.* Madison: University of Wisconsin Press, 1988.
T11.B375 1988

Bitzer, Lloyd F., and Edwin Black, eds. *Prospect of Rhetoric.* Englewood Cliffs, N.J.: Prentice-Hall, 1971.
PN4061.P74

Black, Edwin. *Rhetorical Criticism: A Study in Method.* New York: Macmillan, 1965.   PN4061.B55

Booth, Wayne. *Modern Dogma and the Rhetoric of Assent.* Chicago: University of Chicago Press, 1974.
PE1408.B613

Brooke-Rose, Christine. *Grammar of Metaphor.* London: Secker and Warburg, 1958.   PR508.M43 B7

Brown, Gillian, and George Yule. *Discourse Analysis.* Cambridge: Cambridge University Press, 1983.
P302.B76 1983

Brown, Richard Harvey. *Society as Text: Essays on Rhetoric, Reason, and Reality.* Chicago: University of Chicago Press, 1987.   P40.B76 1987

Bryant, Donald C. *Rhetorical Dimensions in Criticism.* Baton Rouge: Louisiana State University Press, 1973.
PN4061.B7

————, ed. *Rhetorical Idiom: Essays in Rhetoric, Oratory, Language, and Drama.* Ithaca, N.Y.: Cornell University Press, 1958.   PN4012.B7

Burke, Kenneth. *Grammar of Motives.* New York: Prentice-Hall, 1945.   B945.B773 G7

————. *Rhetoric of Motives.* New York: Prentice-Hall, 1950.   B840.B8

Burks, Don M., ed. *Rhetoric, Philosophy, and Literature: An Exploration.* West Lafayette, Ind.: Purdue University Press, 1978.   PN175.R48

Burton, Deirdre. *Dialogue and Discourse: A Sociolinguistic Approach to Modern Drama Dialogue and Naturally Occurring Conversation.* London: Routledge and Kegan Paul, 1980.   PR736.B87 1980

Carpenter, P. A., and M. A. Just, eds. *Cognitive Processes in Comprehension.* Hillsdale, N.J.: Erlbaum, 1977.
BF325.S87 1976

Connors, Robert J., Lisa S. Ede, and Andrea Lunsford, eds. *Essays on Classical Rhetoric and Modern Discourse.* Carbondale: Southern Illinois University Press, 1984.
PN175.E84 1984

Coulthard, R. M. *Introduction to Discourse Analysis.* London: Longman, 1977.   P302.C68

Crothers, Edward. *Paragraph Structure Inference.* Norwood, N.J.: Ablex, 1979.   P302.C7

D'Angelo, Frank. *Conceptual Theory of Rhetoric.* Cambridge, Mass.: Winthrop, 1975.   PN187.D3

De Beaugrande, Robert A. *Text, Discourse, and Process: Toward a Multidisciplinary Science of Texts.* Norwood, N.J.: Ablex, 1980.   P302.D5

————. *Text Production: Toward a Science of Composition.* Norwood, N.J.: Ablex, 1983.   P211.D35 1984

————, and Wolfgang Dressler. *Introduction to Text Linguistics.* London: Longman, 1981.   P302.D34

Dijk, Teun A. van. *Pragmatics of Language and Literature.* Amsterdam: North-Holland, 1976.   P302.P7

————. *Some Aspects of Text Grammars: A Study in Theoretical Linguistics and Poetics.* The Hague: Mouton, 1972.   P302.D47 1972

————. *Text and Context.* London: Longman, 1977.
P302.D5

————, ed. *Handbook of Discourse Analysis.* 4 vols. Orlando, Fla.: Academic Press, 1985. Vol. 1, *Disciplines of Discourse.* Vol. 2, *Dimensions of Discourse.* Vol. 3, *Discourse and Dialogue.* Vol. 4, *Discourse Analysis in Society.*   P302.H343 1985

Dillon, George L. *Constructing Texts: Elements of a Theory of Composition and Style.* Bloomington: Indiana University Press, 1981.   PE1404.D5

————. *Language Processing and the Reading of Literature: Toward a Model of Comprehension.* Bloomington: Indiana University Press, 1978. P302.D54 1978

————. *Rhetoric as Social Imagination: Explorations in the Interpersonal Function of Language.* Bloomington: Indiana University Press, 1986.   P106.D46 1986

Ehninger, Douglas, ed. *Contemporary Rhetoric: A Reader's Coursebook.* Glenview, Ill.: Scott, Foresman, 1972.
PN175.E35

Elliott, Robert C. *Literary Persona.* Chicago: University of Chicago Press, 1982.   PN218.E48 1982

Fine, Jonathan, and Roy O. Freedle. *Developmental Issues in Discourse.* Norwood, N.J.: Ablex, 1983.
P118.D47 1983

Finocchiaro, Maurice A. *Galileo and the Art of Reasoning: Rhetorical Foundations of Logic and Scientific Method.* Dordrecht: D. Reidel, 1980.   B785.G24 F56

Fogarty, Daniel. *Roots for a New Rhetoric.* New York: Bureau of Publications, Teachers College, Columbia University, 1959.   PN175.F6 1959

Foss, Sonja K., Karen A. Foss, and Robert Trapp. *Contemporary Perspectives on Rhetoric.* Prospect Heights, Ill.: Waveland Press, 1985.   PN187.F67 1985

Fowler, Roger. *Literature as Social Discourse: The Practice of Linguistic Criticism.* Bloomington: Indiana University Press, 1981.   P302.F63

Freedle, Roy O., ed. *Discourse Production and Comprehension.* Norwood, N.J.: Ablex, 1979.   P302.D56

————, ed. *New Directions in Discourse Processing.* Norwood, N.J.: Ablex, 1979.   P302.N4

Goffman, Erving. *Forms of Talk.* Philadelphia: University of Pennsylvania Press, 1981.   P95.G58

Golden, James L., et al., eds. *Rhetoric of Western Thought.* 3d ed. Dubuque, Iowa: Kendall Hunt, 1983.
PN183.G6 1983

Gorrell, Robert M., ed. *Rhetoric: Theories for Application.* Champaign, Ill.: NCTE, 1967.   PE1408.N34

Grassi, Ernesto. *Rhetoric as Philosophy: The Humanist Tradition.* University Park: Pennsylvania State University Press, 1980.   PN175.G8

Grimes, Joseph E. *Thread of Discourse.* The Hague: Mouton, 1975.   P302.G7

————, ed. *Papers on Discourse.* Dallas: Summer Institute of Linguistics, 1978.   P302.P3

Halliday, M. A. K., and Ruqaiya Hasan. *Cohesion in English.* London: Longman, 1976.   PE1375.H3

Honeck, Richard P., and Robert R. Hoffman, eds. *Cognition and Figurative Language.* Hillsdale, N.J.: Erlbaum, 1980.   BF455.C6727

Hovland, Carl I., et al. *Order of Presentation in Persuasion.* New Haven: Yale University Press, 1957.   BF637.P4 O7

Kneupper, Charles W., ed. *Oldspeak/Newspeak: Rhetorical Transformations.* Arlington, Texas: Rhetoric Society of America, 1985.

————, ed. *Visions of Rhetoric: History, Theory, and Criticism.* Arlington, Texas: Rhetoric Society of America, 1987.

Johannesen, Richard L., ed. *Contemporary Theories of Rhetoric: Selected Readings.* New York: Harper and Row, 1971. Bibliography.   PN175.J57

————, et al., eds. *Language Is Sermonic: Richard M. Weaver on the Nature of Rhetoric.* Baton Rouge: Louisiana State University Press.   PN175.W37 1970

LeFevre, Karen Burke. *Invention as a Social Act.* Carbondale: Southern Illinois University Press, 1987.   PN221.L44 1987

————, and Mary Jane Dickerson. *Until I See What I Say: Teaching Writing in All Disciplines.* Burlington, Vt.: IDC Publications, 1981.

Levin, Samuel. *Semantics of Metaphor.* Baltimore: Johns Hopkins University Press, 1977.   P325.L44

Levinson, Stephen C. *Pragmatics.* Cambridge: Cambridge University Press, 1983.   P99.4.P72

Longacre, R. E. *Anatomy of Speech Notions.* Lisse: Peter de Ridder Press, 1976.   P153.L6

McCloskey, Donald N. *Rhetoric of Economics.* Madison: University of Wisconsin Press, 1985.   HB71.M38 1985

McKeon, Richard. *Rhetoric: Essays in Invention and Discovery.* Woodbridge, Conn.: Ox Bow Press, 1988.   PN175.M3 1987

McKerrow, Ray E., ed. *Explorations in Rhetoric: Studies in Honor of Douglas Ehninger.* Glenview, Ill.: Scott, Foresman, 1982.   PN175.E96

Matsuhashi, Ann. *Writing in Real Time: Modeling Production Processes.* Norwood, N.J.: Ablex, 1987.   PS301.W74 1987

Miller, George A., ed. *Communication, Language, and Meaning: Psychological Perspectives.* New York: Basic Books, 1973.   P90.M48

Mohrmann, G. P., Charles J. Stewart, and Donovan J. Ochs, eds. *Explorations in Rhetorical Criticism.* University Park: Pennsylvania State University Press, 1973.   PN4061.M6

Natanson, Maurice, and Henry W. Johnstone, Jr., eds. *Philosophy, Rhetoric and Argumentation.* University Park: Pennsylvania State University Press, 1965.   PN4061.N5

Nebergall, Roger E., ed. *Dimensions of Rhetorical Scholarship.* Norman: University of Oklahoma Press, 1963.

Nelson, John S., Allan Megill, and Donald N. McCloskey, eds. *Rhetoric of the Human Sciences: Language and Argument in Scholarship and Public Affairs.* Madison: University of Wisconsin Press, 1987.   P301.R465 1987

Nichols, Maurice Hochmuth. *Rhetoric and Criticism.* Baton Rouge: Louisiana State University Press, 1963.   PN175.N5

Ong, Walter J. *Orality and Literacy: The Technologizing of the Word.* London: Methuen, 1982.   P35.O5

Perelman, Chaim. *Idea of Justice and the Problem of Argument.* London: Routledge and Kegan Paul, 1963.   BJ1533.J9 P443 1963

————. *Realm of Rhetoric.* Translation by William Kluback of *L'empire rhétorique* (Paris: Vrin, 1977). Notre Dame, Ind.: University of Notre Dame Press, 1982.   BC177.P38413 1982

Perelman, Chaim, and L. Olbrechts-Tyteca. *New Rhetoric: A Treatise on Argumentation.* Translation by John Wilkinson and Purcell Weaver of *Traité de l'argumentation: La nouvelle rhétorique* (Paris: Presses universitaires de France, 1958). Notre Dame, Ind.: University of Notre Dame Press, 1969.   BC177.P4213

————. *Rhétorique et philosophie: Pour une théorie de l'argumentation en philosophie.* Paris: Presses universitaires de France, 1952.   BC177.P4

Richards, I. A. *Philosophy of Rhetoric.* New York: Oxford University Press, 1936.   PN175.R45

Rockas, Leo. *Modes of Rhetoric.* New York: St. Martin's Press, 1964.   PN203.R57

Schramm, Wilbur, ed. *Science of Human Communication: New Directions and New Findings in Communication Research.* New York: Basic Books, 1963.   P87.S35

Schwartz, Joseph, and John Rycenga, eds. *Province of Rhetoric.* New York: Ronald Press, 1965.   PN175.S35

Searle, John S. *Speech Acts: An Essay in the Philosophy of Language.* Cambridge: Cambridge University Press, 1969.   B840.S4

Shannon, Claude E., and Warren Weaver. *Mathematical Theory of Communication.* Urbana: University of Illinois Press, 1949.   TK5101.S45

Simons, Herbert W., ed. *Rhetoric in the Human Sciences.* Newbury Park, Calif.: Sage, 1989.

Sinclair, Jo Muh, and M. Coulthard. *Towards an Analysis of Discourse: The English Used by Teachers and Pupils.* Oxford: Oxford University Press, 1975.   LB1576.S45

Spiro, Rand J., et al. *Theoretical Issues in Reading Comprehension.* Hillsdale, N.J.: Erlbaum, 1980.   LB1050.45.T48

Steinmann, Martin, Jr. *New Rhetorics.* New York: Scribner's, 1967.   PE1408.S727

Tanner, William E., J. Dean Bishop, and Turner S. Kobler, eds. *Symposium in Rhetoric.* Denton: Texas Women's University Press, 1976.   PN171.6.S9 1975

Toulmin, Stephen. *Uses of Argument.* Cambridge: Cambridge University Press, 1958.   BC177.T6 1958

Wallace, Karl R. *Understanding Discourse: The Speech Act and Rhetorical Action.* Baton Rouge: Louisiana State University Press, 1970.   PN4061.W28

Weathers, Winston, and Otis Winchester. *Attitudes of Rhetoric.* Englewood Cliffs, N.J.: Prentice-Hall, 1970.   PE1417.W38

Weaver, Richard M. *Ethics of Rhetoric.* Chicago: Regnery, 1953.   PN4061.W4

White, Eugene F., ed. *Rhetoric in Transition: Studies in the Nature and Uses of Rhetoric.* University Park: Pennsylvania State University Press, 1980.   PN4061.R47

Winterowd, W. Ross., ed. *Contemporary Rhetoric: A Conceptual Background with Readings.* New York: Harcourt Brace Jovanovich, 1975.   P301.C57

Young, Richard E., Alton L. Becker, and Kenneth L. Pike. *Rhetoric: Discovery and Change.* New York: Harcourt, Brace and World, 1970.   PE1408.Y64

V.   STYLE AND STYLISTICS

See also entries at T–53, T–58, T–59; U–67, U–68; W–26, W–27, W–28, and W–127.

X–130 **Milic, Louis T. *Style and Stylistics: An Analytical Bibliography.*** New York: The Free Press, 1967.   Z6514.S8 M49

This descriptively annotated bibliography contains 755 numbered items, in addition to others interpolated in the series. Secondary materials only are provided. Entries are in five divisions, as follows: Theoretical, Methodological, Applied, Bibliographies, and General Works. Within divisions they are arranged chronologically. There are indexes of literary authors as subjects, scholars, and subjects and topics. In addition, there is a glossary of key terms.

X–131 **Bailey, Richard W., and Dolores M. Burton. *English Stylistics: A Bibliography.*** Cambridge: MIT Press, 1968.
Z2015.S7 B2

This work defines the field of stylistics to include any linguistic study of literary texts. A brief introduction summarizes the work being done in stylistics, thus broadly defined, in the mid-twentieth century. Entries are in three main divisions: Bibliographies and Sources; Studies of Language and Style before 1900 (with chronological divisions); Twentieth Century Stylistics (with subdivisions for defining creativity and "style," modes of stylistic investigation, statistical approaches to style, problems in translation, prose stylistics, and style in poetry). Within each section are listed first major works and commentaries and then general secondary sources. The volume concludes with two indexes, the first of literary authors whose styles are being studied, and the second of the critics who study them.

X–132 **Bailey, Richard W., and Lubomír Doležel, comps. *Annotated Bibliography of Statistical Stylistics.*** Ann Arbor: University of Michigan, Department of Slavic Languages and Literatures, 1968.   Z6514.S8 B34

After an introduction and an annotated list of major works in general stylistics, this volume presents a total of 615 descriptively annotated entries on statistical stylistics. It is international in scope and includes books, articles, and papers. Entries are in six sections, as follows: The Theory of Statistical Stylistics; Stylistic Characteristics; Poetics, Metrics, and Prosody; Individual Styles and the History of Literary Styles; Problems of Chronology and Disputed Authorship; Stylistics and the Computer. A series of unnumbered entries follow in an addenda, and an index of authors concludes this work.

X–133 **Hatzfeld, Helmut. *Critical Bibliography of the New Stylistics, Applied to the Romance Literatures, 1900–1952.*** Chapel Hill: University of North Carolina Press, 1953.
Z6514.S8 H36

This work includes a total of serially numbered entries on books and articles published 1900–1952 concerned with style and stylistics, particularly (though not exclusively) as these impinge upon the study of Romance literature. The entries, accompanied by trenchant descriptive and evaluative annotations, are disposed into nine chapters, as follows: 1, Theory of Style and Stylistics; 2, "Explication de Texte"; 3, Stylistic Manuals; 4, Translations, Stylistic Parallels, Variants; 5,

Style and Structure of Literary Works (subdivided into national literatures, periods, and then alphabetically by the name of the author under scrutiny); 6, Particular Aspects of Style (Lexicological Aspects, Grammatical Elements, Rhetorical Elements, Elements of Rhythm and Melody, Metalinguistic Style Elements); 7, Motives; 8, Collective Styles; and 9, Languages as Styles. The volume concludes with an index of investigators; an index of authors, titles, and terms; and some pages of addenda.

This work, enlarged and translated into Spanish by Emilio Criado, was published under the title *Bibliografía crítica de la nueva estilística, aplicada a las literaturas románicas* (Madrid: Gredos, 1955) [No LC number]. A French supplement, by Hatzfeld and Yves Le Hir, provides additional entries published during the period 1955–1960: *Essai de bibliographie critique de stilistique française et romane (1955–1960)* (Paris: Presses universitaires de France, 1961) [Z7031.H33]. An English-language sequel volume covering the period 1953–1965 was published under the original title by Hatzfeld (Chapel Hill: University of North Carolina Press, 1966) [Z6514.S8 H35].

X–134 **Kluewer, Jeffrey Dane. "An Annotated Checklist of Writings on Linguistics and Literature in the Sixties."** *Bulletin of the New York Public Library* 76 (1972): 36–91.
Z881.N6B

This bibliography contains a total of 288 serially numbered entries with trenchant descriptive annotations, arranged alphabetically by author. These are followed by a series of indexes grouping the entries in various ways. The indexes include I. A List of Bibliographies; II. A List of Collections; III. Works on Theories of Language (A. Metaphor, B. Poetics, C. Semantics, D. Form and Effect / Structure and Meaning, E. Discourse Analysis); IV. Linguistics and Literary Criticism; V. Linguistic Schools (A. "Traditional" Grammar, B. Descriptive-Structural Grammar, C. Transformational-Generative Grammar); VI. Prosody (A. Meter and Rhythm, B. Phonology-Sound Texture, C. Sound and Meaning, D. Suprasegmentals-Performance, E. Prosodic Analysis— authors and titles of analyzed texts); VII. Psycholinguistics; VIII. Quantitative Studies; IX. Style and Stylistics; X. Syntax and Grammar (A. Grammaticalness); XI. Non-prosodic Analyses of Literary Periods and of Authors and Their Works.

An earlier bibliography with similar coverage was compiled by Thomas J. Roberts, "Literary-Linguistics: A Bibliography, 1946–1961," *TSLL* 4 (1962): 625–629.

X–135 **Enkvist, Nils Erik. *Linguistic Stylistics.*** The Hague: Mouton, 1973.   P301.E6

This introduction to linguistic stylistics is disposed into nine chapters, as follows: 1, Introductory; 2, Style and Literary Study; 3, Style, Langue and Parole, Competence and Performance; 4, Context Parameters; 5, Grammatical Models in the Description of Style Markers; 6, Deviance; 7, Linguistic Style Markers beyond the Sentence; 8, Style Statistics; 9, Conclusion and Summary. The tenth chapter is a twenty-five-page bibliography disposed into a section on bibliographies and one on books and articles. The last section of the volume is an index of names.

X–136 **"Annual Bibliography for [1966–]."** *Style*, vol. 1–. Fayetteville: University of Arkansas, 1968–.   PE1.S89

This annual bibliography contains descriptively annotated entries identifying books, articles, and dissertations on style, arranged alphabetically within each of seven sections, as follows: I. Bibliographical Resources; II. Theoretical Orientations; III. Rhythm and Sound; IV. Imagery, Diction, and Figures of Speech; V. Syntax; VI. Beyond the Sentence; Discourse and Rhetoric; and VII. Language, Culture and Style.

In addition, the journal *Style* has published two bibliographies in the form of "Methodological Guides" to books reviewed and articles published in *Style*. The first, treating books reviewed in volumes 1–5 and articles published in volumes 1–6, appeared in vol. 6 (1972), pp. 317–343. The second, treating books reviewed in volumes 6–10 and articles published in volumes 7–10, appeared in vol. 10 (1976), pp. 519–544.

Further, *Style* has published since 1973 various special bibliographies, including indexes to style studies in other journals such as *Le français moderne* (1974), *Poétique* (1974), *Change* (1974), and *Sub-Stance* (1976); bibliographies on important stylisticians such as Genette (1974) and Todorov (1974); and bibliographies on various topics, such as Prose Style (1973); Period Style (1974); Beginnings and Endings (1976); the Paragraph (1977); and Typography and Style (1977).

X–137 **Bennett, James R. "A Stylistics Checklist."** *Style* 10 (1976): 350–401; 11 (1977): 425–445.   PE1.S89

This checklist and its supplement are meant as a guide to contemporary developments in literary stylistics. What are offered are succinct accounts of current terms, methods, theories, and schools in the study of style. A list of bibliographies, dictionaries, encyclopedias, and surveys and a list of journals precede the checklist proper. It consists of alphabetically arranged key terms, with definitions and important books and articles cited. Abundant use of cross-references is a main feature of both the original checklist and the supplement.

X–138 **Bennett, James R. *Bibliography of Stylistics and Related Criticism, 1967–1983.*** New York: Modern Language Association, 1986.   Z6514.S8 B46 1986

This volume contains a total of 1,484 serially numbered, classified, annotated entries on all aspects of style and stylistic analysis. The introduction includes an essay on Linguistics, Literature, and Society; a full Description of the Bibliography; and a Master List of Periodicals in Alphabetical Order by Acronym. Entries are organized according to the following system of classification: 1.0 Bibliographical Resources (A. Annual Bibliographies and Selected Journals; B. Single Bibliographies, Dictionaries, Checklists, Handbooks); 2.0 General Theory and Concepts of Style (A. Collections by Diverse Authors; B. Individual, Dual, or Group Authorship); 3.0 Culture, History, and Style: The Period, the Nation, the Genre (3.1 Theory; 3.2 Practice [3.21 Diction, Imagery, Tropes; 3.22 Syntax, Schemes; 3.23 Prosody, Sound Patterns in Prose; 3.24 Studies on Several Linguistic Levels]); 4.0 Habitual Usage: The Author (4.1 Theory; 4.2 Practice [4.21 Diction, Imagery, Tropes; 4.22 Syntax, Schemes; 4.23 Prosody, Sound Patterns in Prose; 4.24 Studies on Several Linguistic Levels]); 5.0 Individual Choice: The Text (5.1 Theory; 5.2 Practice [5.21 Diction, Imagery, Tropes; 5.22 Syntax, Schemes; 5.23 Prosody, Sound Patterns in Prose; 5.24 Studies on Several Linguistic Levels]); and 6.0 Individual Response: The Reader (6.1 Theory; 6.2 Practice).

Within each subsection, entries are arranged chronologically by the author of the study. In addition to bibliographical information and descriptive annotation, entries cite reviews (often with brief excerpts).

The volume concludes with three appendixes and four indexes. Appendix 1. Chronology enumerates dates and events of importance in the history of stylistics, including the publication of works of major importance. Appendix 2. Approaches: A Classification of Critics by Theory and Method is an alphabetical list of approaches with references to critics associated with that approach and cross-references to related approaches. Appendix 3. Introductory Reading List on Stylistics is divided into the following sections: General, Narrative, Poetry, Nonfiction Prose, and Critiques of Traditional English Studies. Index 1. Terms; Index 2. Authors and Works Studied; Index 3. Critics Discussed; and Index 4. Contributors (i.e., authors of studies) conclude this very well organized and extremely useful volume.

X–139 **Some Frequently Recommended Works on Style and Stylistics.** (See also entries at I–16, T–58, U–67, W–27, and W–127, along with many references cited at X–119, X–129, and X–164.)

Babb, Howard, ed. *Essays in Stylistic Analysis.* New York: Harcourt Brace Jovanovich, 1972.   PN203.B22

Barthes, Roland. *Writing Degree Zero and Elements of Semiology.* Boston: Beacon, 1970.   PN203.B313 1970

Carter, Ronald, ed. *Language and Literature: An Introductory Reader in Stylistics.* London: George Allen and Unwin, 1982. Bibliography.   PE1421.L29 1982

Chapman, Raymond. *Linguistics and Literature: An Introduction to Literary Stylistics.* London: Edward Arnold, 1973.   PN203.C455

Chatman, Seymour, ed. *Approaches to Poetics: English Institute Essays.* New York: Columbia University, 1973.   PN441.E53

——. *Literary Style: A Symposium.* London: Oxford University Press, 1971.   PN203.S9

Chatman, Seymour, and Samuel R. Levin, eds. *Essays on the Language of Literature.* Boston: Houghton Mifflin, 1967.   PE26.C5

Ching, M. K. C., M. C. Haley, and R. F. Lunsford, eds. *Linguistic Perspectives on Literature.* London: Routledge and Kegan Paul, 1980.   P49.L55

Cluysenaar, Anne. *Introduction to Literary Stylistics: A Discussion of Dominant Structures in Verse and Prose.* London: Batsford, 1976.   PN203.C54

Crystal, David, and Derek Davey. *Investigating English Style.* Bloomington: Indiana University Press, 1969.   PE1421.C7 1969

Cummings, Michael, and Robert Simmons. *Language of Literature: A Stylistic Introduction to the Study of Literature.* Oxford: Pergamon, 1983.   PE1421.C8 1983

Cunningham, J. V., ed. *Problem of Style.* Greenwich, Conn.: Fawcett, 1966.   PN203.C8

Doležel, Lubomír, and Richard L. Bailey, eds. *Statistics and Style.* New York: American Elsevier Publishing Co., 1969.   P123.D6

Dubois, Jacques, et al. [Group Mu]. *Rhétorique générale.* Paris: Larousse, 1970.   PN189.R5

Epstein, Edmund L. *Language and Style.* London: Methuen, 1978.   PE1421.E6

Fowler, Roger, ed. *Essays on Style and Language: Linguistic and Critical Approaches to Literary Style.* London: Routledge and Kegan Paul, 1966.   PN203.F6

——, ed. *Languages of Literature.* London: Routledge and Kegan Paul, 1971.   P47.F6

——, ed. *Style and Structure in Literature: Essays in the New Stylistics.* London: B. Blackwell, 1975.   PN85.S78

Freeman, Donald C. *Essays in Modern Stylistics.* London: Methuen, 1981. Bibliography.   PR83.E87 1981

——, ed. *Linguistics and Literary Style.* New York: Holt, Rinehart and Winston, 1970.   PN203.F67

Guirard, Pierre. *La stylistique.* 5th ed. Paris: Presses universitaires de France, 1967.   PC2410.G8 1967

Hendricks, William D. *Grammars of Style and Styles of Grammar.* Amsterdam: North-Holland, 1976.   P301.H43

Hildick, Wallace. *Word for Word: A Study of Authors' Alterations.* London: Faber and Faber, 1965.   PN203.H54

Hough, Graham. *Style and Stylistics.* London: Routledge and Kegan Paul, 1969. Select Bibliography.   PN203.H65 1969

Joos, Martin. *Five Clocks: A Linguistic Excursion into the Five Styles of English Usage.* New York: Harcourt, Brace and World, 1967.   PE1421.J65 1967

Kachru, Braji B., and Herbert F. Stahlke, eds. *Current Trends in Stylistics.* Edmonton, Alberta: Linguistic Research, Inc. 1972.   P301.K3

Lang, Berel, ed. *Concept of Style.* Philadelphia: University of Pennsylvania Press, 1979.   B105.S7 C66

Lanham, Richard A. *Analyzing Prose.* New York: Scribner, 1983.   PE1421.L295 1983

———. *Style: An Anti-Textbook.* New Haven: Yale University Press, 1974.   PE1421.L3

Leed, Jacob, ed. *Computer and Literary Style: Introductory Essays and Studies.* Kent, Ohio: Kent State University Press, 1967.   PN98.E4 L4

Love, Glen, and Michael Payne, eds. *Contemporary Essays on Style, Rhetoric, Linguistics, and Criticism.* Chicago: Scott, Foresman, 1969.   PE1421.L68

Lucas, Frank L. *Style.* London: Cassell, 1974.
                                            PN203.L8 1974

Miles, Josephine. *Style and Proportion: The Language of Prose and Poetry.* Boston: Little, Brown, 1967.
                                            PE1421.M5

Milic, Louis T. *Quantitative Approach to the Style of Jonathan Swift.* The Hague: Mouton, 1967.
                                            PR3728.S8 M5

———. *Stylists on Style: A Handbook with Selections for Analysis.* New York: Scribner, 1969.   PE1421.M53

Murray, J. Middleton. *Problem of Style.* London: Oxford University Press, 1922.   PN203.M8

Quinn, Arthur. *Figures of Speech: 60 Ways to Turn a Phrase.* Salt Lake City, Utah: Gibbs M. Smith, Inc. 1982.   PN227.Q5 1982

Sebeok, Thomas Albert, ed. *Style in Language.* Cambridge: MIT Press, 1960. List of References.
                                            PN203.C61958

Shapiro, Michael, and Marianne Shapiro. *Figuration in Verbal Art.* Princeton, N.J.: Princeton University Press, 1988.   PN227.S54 1988

Spitzer, Leo. *Linguistics and Literary History: Essays in Stylistics.* Princeton, N.J.: Princeton University Press, 1948.   PN511.S674

Stacy, R. H. *Defamiliarization in Language and Literature.* Syracuse: Syracuse University Press, 1977.
                                            PN227.S7

Taylor, Talbot J. *Linguistic Theory and Structural Stylistics.* Oxford: Pergamon, 1981.   P301.T34 1981

Turner, G. W. *Stylistics.* Harmondsworth, England: Penguin, 1973.   P301.T8

Ullman, Stephen. *Language and Style.* Oxford: Blackwell, 1964.   PN203.U4 1964

———. *Meaning and Style.* Oxford: Blackwell, 1973.
                                            PN203.U42 1973

Widdowson, H. G. *Stylistics and the Teaching of Literature.* London: Longman, 1975. Bibliography.   PR35.W5

Yule, G. Udny. *Statistical Study of Literary Vocabulary.* Cambridge: Cambridge University Press, 1944.
                                            BV4829.Y8

VI. COMPOSITION AND THE TEACHING OF WRITING

X–140 **Scott, Patrick. "Bibliographical Problems in Research on Composition."** *College Composition and Communication* 37 (May 1986): 167–177.   PE1001.C6

This essay identifies a series of problems complicating the process of gaining bibliographical control of the burgeoning field of composition. Identified and discussed are issues of Field Demarcation; Taxonomy and Terminology; Publication Format, Purpose, and Intended Audience; and Professional Segmentation. Prospects for the Future and Precautions for the Present conclude the discussion.

Scott's earlier essay, "Reference Sources for Composition Research: A Practical Survey," *College English* 45 (December 1983): 756–768 [PE1.C6], serves as the nearest the field of composition has come to a bibliography of bibliographies, in that the article cites and describes a total of seventeen bibliographies in Historical Rhetoric and eighteen bibliographies in Modern Composition Studies.

X–141 *Teaching Composition: Twelve Bibliographical Essays.* Rev. and enl ed. Edited by Gary Tate. Fort Worth: Texas Christian University Press, 1987.   PE1403.T39 1987

The aim of this collection of retrospective bibliographical review essays is to bring together in one place a record of the most important work done in areas relevant to teaching composition. The individual essays in this edition are as follows: Recent Developments in Rhetorical Invention (Richard Young); Structure and Form in Non-Narrative Prose (Richard L. Larson); Approaches to the Study of Style (Edward P. J. Corbett); Aims, Modes, and Forms of Discourse (Frank J. D'Angelo); Tests of Writing Ability (Richard Lloyd-Jones); Basic Writing (Mina P. Shaughnessy); Basic Writing Update (Andrea Lunsford); Language Varieties and Composition (Jenefer M. Giannasi); Literacy, Linguistics and Rhetoric (W. Ross Winterowd); Literary Theory and Composition (Joseph J. Comprone); Studying Rhetoric and Literature (Jim W. Corder); Writing Across the Curriculum (James L. Kinneavy); and Computers and Composition (Hugh Burns). The volume concludes with an index of names and an index of subjects.

X–142 **Moran, Michael G., and Ronald F. Lunsford, eds.** *Research in Composition and Rhetoric: A Bibliographical Sourcebook.* Westport, Conn.: Greenwood Press, 1984.
                                            Z2015.R5 R47 1984

This volume contains a total of eighteen review essays, divided into three parts and two appendixes. Essays discuss the literature and conclude with sheer lists of references cited. Part I, Current Research, contains essays on The Writing Process (John Warnock): Cross-Sections in an Emerging Psychology of Composition (Louise Wetherbee Phelps); Research on Writing Blocks, Writing Anxiety, and Writing Apprehension (Lynn Z. Bloom); Philosophy and Rhetoric (John C. Briggs); Literature, Literary Theory, and the Teaching of Composition (William L. Stull); Reading and Writing: A Survey of the Questions about Texts (Jasper Neel). Part II, Major Issues, contains essays on Research Methods in Composition (Christopher C. Burnham); Grading and Evaluation (Robert W. Reising and Benjamin J. Stewart); and Assignment Making (Lynn Diane Beene). Part III, The Basics, contains essays on research in Basic Writing (Glynda A. Hull and David J. Bartholomae); The Sentence (Frank J. D'Angelo); The Role of Spelling in Composition for Older Students (James S. Beggs); Vocabulary Development (Mary Hurley Moran); Punctuation (Greta D. Little); Usage (Marvin K. L. Ching); and The English Paragraph (Michael G. Moran). Appendix A contains the review, Textbooks Revisited (Donald C. Stewart); Appendix B treats Evaluating Usage Manuals

(Marvin K. L. Cing). The work concludes with an author index and a subject index.

X–143 McClelland, Ben W., and Timothy R. Donovan, eds. *Perspectives on Research and Scholarship in Composition.* New York: Modern Language Association, 1985.
PE1404.P45 1985

This volume contains a series of thirteen review essays on topics of current interest in composition research. The essays are as follows: Where are English Departments Going? (Ben W. McClelland and Timothy R. Donovan); Toward a Theory of Composition (Lil Brannon); Modern Rhetorical Theory and Its Future Directions (C. H. Knoblauch); Composition Theory and Literary Theory (John Clifford and John Schib); Linguistics and Writing (William Strong); Collaborative Learning and Teaching Writing (John Trimbur); Empirical Research in Composition (Anne Ruggles Gere); Forming Research Communities among Naturalistic Researchers (Lucy McCormick Calkins); Cognitive Studies and Teaching Writing (Andrea A. Lunsford); Research on Error and Correction (Glynda Hull); The Competence of Young Writers (Thomas Newkirk and Nancie Atwell); Technical Communication in the Information Economy (Michael L. Keene); and The Promise of Artificial-Intelligence Research for Composition (Hugh Burns). A twenty-five page enumeration of Works Consulted and an index of names and subjects concludes this volume.

X–144 Hillocks, George. *Research on Written Composition: New Directions for Teaching.* Urbana, Ill.: ERIC Clearinghouse on Reading and Communication, 1986.
PE1404.E55 1986

This volume offers a comprehensive review of empirical research on composition at all educational levels, one that is meant to summarize the twenty-three years of work since the publication of *Research in Written Composition* by Richard Braddock, Richard Lloyd-Jones, and L. Schoer (Urbana, Ill.: NCTE, 1963 [PE1066.B7]), a work which is generally regarded as laying the foundation for the field of composition studies. This volume is organized in nine chapters, with numerous subdivisions. The chapter headings are as follows: Research on the Composing Process; The Writer's Repertoire; Experimental Studies: Introduction to the Meta-Analysis [of seventy-three research studies, designed to assess the validity of a particular class of study]; Modes of Instruction; Grammar and the Manipulation of Syntax; Criteria for Better Writing; Invention; Results of the Meta-Analysis; Validity, Implications, and Recommendations. A Bibliography of 102 pages includes the more than 2,000 research studies which are reported on in this volume, along with several pages of Additional Bibliographic Resources.

X–145 Bizzell, Patricia, and Bruce Herzberg. *Bedford Bibliography for Teachers of Writing.* New York: St. Martin's Press, 1987.
No LC number

Designed as an advertising vehicle for the Bedford Books division of St. Martin's Press, this work includes a useful selective bibliography of 267 annotated entries which is classified into thirteen sections, as follows: Periodicals; Bibliographies; Collections; The Rhetorical Tradition (Primary Texts, Secondary Texts); Modern Rhetorical Theory; The Composing Process; Invention: Heuristics and Pre-Writing; Arrangement and Argument; Revision; Style; Basic Writing, Error Analysis, and Usage; Teaching Composition (Curriculum Development, Writing Across the Curriculum, Evaluating Student Writing, Peer Tutoring and Conference Teaching, Personal Writing, Media and Computers); and Related Fields (Bibliographies, Literary Criticism, Philosophy of Language, Linguistics and Literacy, Education Theory, Psychology, Other Fields). A Brief History of Rhetoric and Composition precedes the Bibliography, and an Index of Authors Cited follows it, preceding the section of the volume devoted to advertising current titles of Bedford Books.

X–146 Lindemann, Erika. *Longman Bibliography of Composition and Rhetoric.* Volume 1: 1984–1985. Volume 2: 1986. New York: Longman, 1987–1988.   Z5818.E5 L55 1987

This bibliography, compiled by some 152 bibliographers and researchers, presents an annual, classified, descriptively annotated listing of research in composition and related fields. It treats books, articles, dissertations, ERIC documents, software programs, videotapes, and sound recordings. More than 275 journals are analyzed for inclusion. The bibliography for 1984–1985 contains nearly 4,000 items; that for 1986 a comparable number. Serially numbered entries are disposed into a classified arrangement as follows (using the subheadings from volume 2 for 1986): 1. Bibliographies and Checklists; 2. Theory and Research (Rhetorical Theory, Discourse Theory, and Composing; Rhetorical History; Political, Religious, and Judicial Rhetoric; Literacy Studies; Advertising, Public Relations, and Business; Literature and Film; Reading; Linguistics, Grammatical Theory, and Semantics; Psychology; Education; Journalism and Publishing; Cross-Disciplinary Studies; Other); 3. Teacher Education, Administration, Social Roles; 4. Curriculum; 5. Textbooks and Instructional Materials; 6. Testing, Measurement, and Evaluation. The volumes end with an author index.

X–147 Larson, Richard L. "Selected Bibliography of Research and Writing about the Teaching of Composition, 1973 and 1974–77." *College Composition and Communication*, vols. 26–30. Urbana, Ill.: NCTE, 1975–1979.   PE1001.C6

This annual annotated selective bibliography of materials excludes textbooks, reviews, teacher preparation materials, works concerned primarily with administrative problems, works that cover familiar territory (unless in a new or a particularly helpful way), and works that are concerned with local or temporary matters. Entries have brief, precise, and helpful descriptive annotations. Beginning with the bibliography for 1976, items published in previous years which were missed are included whenever they are discovered. These bibliographies may be used to update the presentations in *Teaching Composition: Twelve Bibliographical Essays* (X–141). A volume cumulating the annual bibliographies 1973–1977 was to have been published by the National Council of Teachers of English. In its stead, see Larson's "Selected Bibliography of Recent Writings on Composition Arranged according to a Model for Viewing Composition as a Pedagogical Discipline," in *Proceedings of the Inaugural Conference of the University of Maryland Junior Writing Program*, eds. Michael Marcuse and Susan Kleimann (College Park: University of Maryland, 1981), pp. 151–158 [no LC number].

X–148 Burns, Shannon, Mark W. Govoni, M. D. McGee, and Lois Burns, comps. *Annotated Bibliography of Texts on Writing Skills: Grammar and Usage, Composition, Rhetoric, and Technical Writing.* New York: Garland, 1976.
Z2015.R5 A55

This volume contains 443 serially numbered entries arranged alphabetically by author. Included are a selection of the texts that were in print in 1975. Extended descriptive annotations indicate the range, limits, and probable uses of each text. The main author list is preceded by a brief guide to the text types with the following divisions: Grammars and Basic Usage; Handbook/Reference; Workbook; Programmed; Fundamental Composition; Standard Composition; Advanced Composition/Rhetoric; Writing about Literature; Readers/Source Books; Language/Style; Technical Writing; Miscellaneous. A title index concludes the volume.

X–150 Moran, Michael G., and Debra Journet, eds. *Research in Technical Communication: A Bibliographic Sourcebook.* Westport, Conn.: Greenwood Press, 1985.   T10.5.R47 1985

This volume contains a total of eighteen bibliographical review essays on topics associated with technical communication, disposed into four parts and two appendixes. Part I: A Theoretical Examination of Technical Communication contains essays on Technical and Scientific Writing and the Humanities (Philip M. Rubens); The History of Technical and Scientific Writing (Michael G. Moran); Communication Theory and Technical Communication (George A. Barnett and Carol Hughes); and Teaching Technical Writing (Anthony O'Keeffe). Part II: Technical Communication and Rhetorical Concerns contains essays on Invention in Technical and Scientific Discourse: A Prospective Survey (Carolyn R. Miller); Audience Analysis and Adaptation (Michael Keene and Marilyn Barnes-Ostrander); Modes of Organization (Victoria M. Winkler); and Style in Technical and Scientific Writing (Glenn J. Broadhead).

Part III: Specific Types of Technical Communication contains essays on Proposals (Mark P. Haselkorn); Technical Reports (Judith Stanton); Business Letters, Memoranda, Resumes (Mary Hurley Moran and Michael G. Moran). Part IV: Related Concerns and Specialized Forms of Technical Communication contains essays on Computing and the Future of Technical Communication (William L. Benzon); Oral Presentation and Presence in Business and Industry (Bertie E. Fearing); Resources for Teaching Legal Writing (Russel Rutter); and Writing for the Government (Robert Scott Kellner). Three Appendixes present a Guide to Textbooks in Technical Communication (Susan Hilligoss); A Selection of Style Manuals (Caroline R. Goforth); and an essay on The Technical Writing Profession (Julie Lepick Ling). The volume concludes with an index of authors and subjects.

X–151 **Bankston, Dorothy, et al. "[1974–] Bibliography of Technical Writing."** *Technical Writing Teacher*, vol. 3–. Morehead, Ky.: Association of Teachers of Technical Writing, 1975–. No LC number

Preceded by Donald Cunningham's "[Bibliography of] Bibliographies of Technical Writing Material," *Technical Writing Teacher* 1 (1974): 9–10, the annual bibliographies of technical writing are unannotated but classified currently into the following descriptive categories: Bibliographies; Books, Reviews; Articles on Theory and Philosophy, on Pedagogy; on Writing Technical Articles and Reports, on Research, on Technical Writing and the Computer, on Graphic/Visual Aids, on Correspondence; Technical Speech; and Designing Degree Programs.

X–152 **Philler, Theresa A., et al., eds.** *Annotated Bibliography on Technical Writing, Editing, Graphics and Publishing, 1950–1965.* Washington, D.C.: Society of Technical Writers and Publishers; Pittsburgh, Pa.: Carnegie Library, 1966. Z7405.T4 S6

This computer-compiled, briefly annotated bibliography contains some 2,000 continuously numbered entries arranged more or less alphabetically by author or title in a series A for articles and B for books. To this list is added a permuted title index in which the titles are listed in alphabetical order by each significant word, and an author index, as well as a list of periodicals analyzed.

X–153 **Balachandran, Sarojini, ed.** *Technical Writing: A Bibliography.* Urbana, Ill.: American Business Communication Association; Washington, D.C.: Society for Technical Communication, 1977. Z7405.T4 B34

The bibliography, which treats publications 1965–1976, was compiled by a search of abstracts, indexes, and other finding aids under the following rubrics: Communication of Technical Information, Engineering Writing, Report Writing, Science Writing, Technical Manuals, Technical Reports, and Technical Writing. Entries thus culled are descriptively annotated and are arranged in an unnumbered list alphabetically by author. A subject index is provided in lieu of a classified arrangement of entries.

X–155 **Alred, Gerald J., Diana C. Reep, and Mohan R. Limaye.** *Business and Technical Writing: An Annotated Bibliography of Books 1880–1980.* Metuchen, N.J.: Scarecrow Press, 1981. Z7164.C81

This volume contains a list of 874 serially numbered books, including bibliographies, textbooks, anthologies, and books on teaching business and technical writing. Extended annotations describe the purpose, scope, contents, use, and interest of the book, along with any special features it may have. The compilers claim that the volume also provides an overview of the history of business and technical writing; entries are, however, arranged alphabetically by author rather than chronologically.

X–156 **Bowman, Mary Ann, and Joan D. Stamas.** *Written Communication in Business: A Selective Bibliography, 1967–1977.* Champaign, Ill.: American Business Communication Association, 1980. No LC number

This bibliography lists more than 800 books and articles concerned with business correspondence, other forms of business writing, and the teaching of business writing, to the exclusion of work on technical writing. Entries are very briefly annotated and presented in alphabetical order by author, with a subject index in lieu of a classified arrangement.

Recently published is the collection *Abstracts of Studies in Business Communication 1900-1970* by Jane F. White and Patty G. Campbell (Urbana, Ill.: American Business Communication Association, 1983) with abstracts drawn from the following subject areas: Business and Economics, Educational Administration, Journalism, English-Language Studies; Mass Communication, Political Science, Psychology, Sociology, and Speech and Theatre.

Also available are annual collections by Raymond Falcione and Howard Greenbaum, *Organizational Communication Abstracts* (Urbana, Ill.: American Business Communication Association, 1974–) with abstracts arranged in nine categories including Research Methods in Organizational Communication, Texts, Anthologies, Reviews, and General Bibliographies.

X–157 **Walsh, Ruth M., and Stanley J. Birkin, eds.** *Business Communication: An Annotated Bibliography.* Westport, Conn.: Greenwood Press, 1980. Z7164.C81 W24

This computer-generated volume contains more than 1,657 entries referring to books, articles, and dissertations written in the 1960s and 1970s on topics related to business communication. Entries may be located by way of an author-title list, a keyword-in-context list, and a final section providing serially numbered main entries with annotations and abstracts.

X–158 **Hull, Debra L.** *Business and Technical Communication: A Bibliography, 1975–1985.* Metuchen: N.J., Scarecrow Press, 1987. Z7164.C81 H7 1987

This well-annotated bibliography which excludes legal writing and medical writing is divided into three parts covering pedagogy, rhetorical problems, and the impact of technology respectively. Entries are disposed under subheadings that designate such topics as Grading Techniques, Readability, Audience Analysis, Graphics, and Computer Documentation. A section of Selected Books and Selected Bibliographies follows Part III. These enumerations are uneven, with surprising omissions which may be the result of limiting inclusion to items found in the author's local academic library. There are author and subject indexes.

X–159 Burkett, Eva M., comp. *Writing in Subject-Matter Fields: A Bibliographic Guide, with Annotations and Writing Assignments.* Metuchen, N.J.: Scarecrow Press, 1977. Z6514.A9 B87

This volume, with serially numbered and annotated entries, is disposed into seven sections, as follows: 1. About Writing; 2. Writing and Literature; 3. Writing in History, Autobiography and Biography, Law; 4. Writing in Science; 5. Technical and Business Writing; 6. Interdisciplinary Writing (Literature and Other Disciplines, History and Other Disciplines, Languages and Politics); 7. Writing Articles for Newspapers and Magazines. Selection of entries is uneven, as is the quality of annotations, but the work still has value for the number of studies it has brought together which are concerned, directly or indirectly, with what it means to write history, or physics.

X–160 Sides, Charles H., ed. *Technical and Business Communication: Bibliographic Essays for Teachers and Corporate Trainers.* Urbana, Ill.: National Council of Teachers of English, and Washington, D.C.: Society for Technical Communication, 1989.

This 360-page volume presents a series of seventeen essays divided into two parts. Part I, Issues and Abilities in Technical Communication, includes essays on such matters as ethics, the use of visuals, interpersonal communication, consulting work, and professional presentations. Part II, Technical Communication Genres, covers various forms and formats, such as annual reports, letters, memos, and computer documentation.

X–164 Some Frequently Recommended Works on Composition and the Teaching of Writing.

Anderson, Paul V., et al., eds. *New Essays in Technical and Scientific Communication: Research, Theory, Practice.* Farmingdale, N.Y.: Baywood Publishing, 1983. T11.N46 1983

Anson, Chris M., ed. *Writing and Response: Theory, Practice, and Research.* Urbana, Ill.: NCTE, 1989. PE1404.W6934 1989

Bailey, Richard W., and Robin Melanie Fosheim, eds. *Literacy for Life: The Demand for Reading and Writing.* New York: MLA, 1983. LC149.L4985 1983

Beach, Richard, and Lillian S. Bridwell, eds. *New Directions in Composition Research.* New York: Guilford Press, 1984. PE1404.N48 1984

Beene, Lynn Dianne, and Peter White, eds. *Solving Problems in Technical Writing.* New York: Oxford University Press, 1988.

Bennett, James R. "The Paragraph: An Annotated Bibliography." *Style* 11 (Spring 1977): 107–118.

Bereiter, Carol, and Marlene Scardamalia. *Psychology of Written Composition.* Hillsdale, N.J.: Erlbaum, 1987. P301.5 P75 B47 1987

Berthoff, Ann E. *Making of Meaning: Metaphors, Models, and Maxims for Writing Teachers.* Montclair, N.J.: Boynton/Cook, 1981. PE1404.B47

Bogel, Fredric V., and Katherine K. Gottschalk, eds. *Teaching Prose: A Guide for Writing Instructors.* New York: W. W. Norton, 1988. PE1404.T396 1988

Britton, James, et al. *Development of Writing Abilities (11–18).* London: Macmillan Education, 1975. LB1631.G727 1975a

Broadhead, Glenn J., and Richard C. Freed. *Variables of Composition: Process and Product in a Business Setting.* Carbondale: Southern Illinois University Press, 1986. PE1479.B87 B76 1986

Brown, Rollo Walter. *How the French Boy Learns to Write.* Cambridge: Harvard University Press, 1915. LB1577.F7 B7

Christensen, Francis. *Notes toward a New Rhetoric: Nine Essays for Teachers.* Edited by Bonniejean Christensen. 2d ed. New York: Harper and Row, 1978. PE1403.C45 1978

——, et al. *Sentence and the Paragraph.* Urbana, Ill.: NCTE, 1963.

Coles, William E., Jr. *Plural I: The Teaching of Writing.* New York: Holt, Rinehart and Winston, 1978. PE1404.C59

Cooper, Charles R., ed. *Nature and Measurement of Competency in English.* Urbana, Ill.: NCTE, 1981. LB1576. N33

——, and Lee Odell, eds. *Evaluating Writing: Describing, Measuring, Judging.* Urbana, Ill.: NCTE, 1977. PE1464.E9

——, eds. *Research on Composing: Points of Departure.* Urbana, Ill.: NCTE, 1978. PE1404.R4

Couture, Barbara, ed. *Functional Approaches to Writing: Research Perspectives.* Norwood, N.J.: Ablex, 1986. P211.C68 1986

Cunningham, Donald H., and Herman A. Estrin, eds. *Teaching of Technical Writing.* Urbana, Ill.: NCTE, 1975. T11.T29

Diederich, Paul B. *Measuring Growth in English.* Urbana, Ill.: NCTE, 1974. LB1631.D47

Donovan, Timothy R., and Ben W. McClelland. *Eight Approaches to Teaching Composition.* Urbana, Ill.: NCTE, 1980. LB1576.E34

Douglas, George H., ed. *Teaching of Business Communication.* Champaign, Ill.: American Business Communication Association, 1978. No LC number

Emig, Janet. *Composing Processes of Twelfth Graders.* Urbana, Ill.: NCTE, 1971. PE1011.N295 no. 13

Fahnestock, Jeanne, and Marie Secor. *Rhetoric of Argument.* New York: Random House, 1982. PE1431.F3

Faigley, Lester, et al. *Assessing Writers' Knowledge and Processes of Composing.* Norwood, N.J.: Ablex, 1985. PE1404.A85 1985

Flesch, Rudolph. *Art of Readable Writing.* Rev. ed. New York: Harper and Row, 1974. PE1408. F4773 1974

Flower, Linda. *Problem-Solving Strategies for Writing.* 2d ed. New York: Harcourt, Brace, 1985. PN187.F56 1985

Frank, Francine Wattman, and Paula A. Treichler. *Language, Gender, and Professional Writing: Theoretical Approaches and Guidelines for Nonsexist Usage.* New York: Modern Language Association, 1989. PE1460.F64 1989

Freedman, Aviva, and Ian Pringle, eds. *Reinventing the Rhetorical Tradition.* Conway, Ariz.: L & S Books for the Canadian Council of Teachers of English, 1980. No LC number

Freedman, Sarah Warshauer. *Response to Student Writing.* Urbana, Ill.: NCTE, 1987. PE1011.N295 no. 23

Fulweiler, Toby, and Art Young, eds. *Language Connection: Writing and Reading across the Curriculum.* Urbana, Ill.: NCTE, 1982. No LC number

Gebhardt, Richard C., ed. *Composition and Its Teaching: Articles from College Composition and Communication during the Editorship of Edward P. J. Corbett.* Findlay, Ohio: Ohio Council of Teachers of English Language Arts, 1979. PE1404.C62

Gould, Jay R., ed. *Directions in Technical Writing and Communication.* Farmingdale, N.Y.: Baywood Publishing, 1978. T11.D54

Graves, Richard L., ed. *Rhetoric and Composition: A Sourcebook for Teachers.* 2d ed., rev. Upper Montclair, N.J.: Boynton/Cook, 1984. PE1065.R48 1984

Greenberg, Karen, Harvey S. Wiener, and Richard A. Donovan, eds. *Writing Assessment: Issues and Strategies.* New York: Longman, 1986.   PE1404.W694 1986

Gregg, Lee W., and Erwin R. Steinberg. eds. *Cognitive Processes in Writing.* Hillside, N.J.: Erlbaum, 1980.   BF456.W8 C63

Griffin, C. Williams, ed. *Teaching Writing in All Disciplines.* San Francisco: Jossey-Bass, 1982.   PE1404.T42 1982

Halpern, Jeanne W. *Teaching Business Writing: Approaches, Plans, Pedagogy, Research.* Urbana, Ill.: American Business Communication Association, 1983.   HF5721.T4 1983

Halpern, Jeanne W., and Sarah Liggett. *Computers and Composing: How the New Technologies Are Changing Writing.* Carbondale: Southern Illinois University Press, 1984.   PE1404.H34 1984

Hammond, Eugene. *Teaching Writing.* New York: McGraw-Hill, 1983.   PE1401.H35 1983

Haring-Smith, Tori. *Guide to Writing Programs: Writing Centers, Writing-across-the-Curriculum, Peer Tutoring.* Glenview, Ill.: Scott-Foresman, 1984.   PE1405.U6 G8 1985

Hirsch, E. D., Jr. *Philosophy of Composition.* Chicago: University of Chicago Press, 1977.   PE1403.H57

Holdstein, Deborah H. *On Composition and Computers.* New York: Modern Language Association, 1987.   PE1404.H64 1987

Horner, Winifred Bryan, ed. *Composition and Literature: Bridging the Gap.* Chicago: University of Chicago Press, 1983.   PE1404.C618 1983

Horning, Alice S. *Teaching Writing as a Second Language.* Carbondale: Southern Illinois University Press, 1987.   PE1404.H67 1987

Irmscher, William F. *Teaching Expository Writing.* New York: Holt, Rinehart and Winston, 1979.   PE1404.I7

Judy, Stephen N., and Susan J. Judy. *Introduction to the Teaching of Writing.* New York: Wiley, 1981.   PE1404.T35 1981

Kasden, Lawrence N., and Daniel R. Hoeber, eds. *Basic Writing: Essays for Teachers, Researchers, Administrators.* Urbana, Ill.: NCTE, 1980.   PE1404.B3

Knoblauch, C. H., and Lil Brannon. *Rhetorical Traditions and the Teaching of Writing.* Upper Montclair, N.J.: Boynton/Cook, 1984.   PE1404.K58 1983

Kogen, Myra, ed. *Writing in the Business Professions.* Urbana, Ill.: NCTE, 1989.   HF5718.3.W75 1989

Kroll, Barry M., and Roberta J. Vann, eds. *Exploring Speaking-Writing Relationships: Connections and Contrasts.* Urbana, Ill.: NCTE, 1981.   P95.E9

Krull, Robert, ed. *Word Processing for Technical Writers.* Amityville, N.Y.: Baywood, 1988.   T11.W67 1987

Langer, Judith A., and Arthur N. Applebee. *How Writing Shapes Thinking: A Study of Teaching and Learning.* Urbana, Ill.: NCTE, 1987.   PE1011.N295 no. 22

Lauer, Janice, and J. William Asher. *Composition Research: Empirical Designs.* New York: Oxford University Press, 1988.   PE1404.L34 1988

LeFevre, Karen Burke. *Invention as a Social Act.* Carbondale: Southern Illinois University Press, 1987.   PN221.L44 1987

Lindemann, Erica. *Rhetoric for Writing Teachers.* New York: Oxford University Press, 1982.   PE1404.L53 1982

Macorie, Ken. *Telling Writing.* 4th ed. Upper Montclair, N.J.: Boynton/Cook, 1985.   PE1408.M33255 1985

McQuade, Donald, ed. *Linguistics, Stylistics, and the Teaching of Composition.* 2d ed., enl. Carbondale: Southern Illinois University Press, 1984.   PE1404.L56 1984

Martin, Harold, Richard Ohmann, and James Wheatley. *Logic and Rhetoric of Exposition.* 3d ed. New York: Holt, Rinehart and Winston, 1969.   PE1429.M3 1969

Matalene, Carolyn B., ed. *Worlds of Writing: Teaching and Learning in Discourse Communities of Work.* New York: Random House, 1989.   PE1404.W67 1989

Moffit, James. *Teaching the Universe of Discourse.* Boston: Houghton Mifflin, 1968.   PE1408.M5 93

Murphy, James J., ed. *Rhetorical Tradition and Modern Writing.* New York: Modern Language Association, 1982.   PE1404.R5

Murray, Donald M. *Writer Teaches Writing.* 2d ed. Boston: Houghton Mifflin, 1985.   PN181.M8 1985

Neel, Jasper. *Options for the Teaching of English: Freshman Composition.* New York: MLA, 1978.   PE1068.U5 F68

North, Stephen M. *Making of Knowledge in Composition: Portrait of an Emerging Field.* Upper Montclair, N.J.: Boynton/Cook, 1987.   PE1404.N67 1987

Newkirk, Thomas, ed. *Only Connect: Uniting Reading and Writing.* Upper Montclair, N.J.: Boynton/Cook, 1986.   PE1404.O48 1986

O'Dell, Lee, and Dixie Goswami, eds. *Writing in Nonacademic Settings.* New York: Guilford Press, 1985.   PE1404.W726 1985

O'Hare, Frank. *Sentence-Combining: Improving Student Writing without Formal Grammar Instruction.* Urbana, Ill.: NCTE, 1973.   PE1011.N295 no. 15

Ohmann, Richard, and W. B. Coley, eds. *Ideas for English 101: Teaching Writing in College.* Urbana, Ill.: NCTE, 1975.   PE1404.I3

Olson, Gary A., ed. *Writing Centers: Theory and Administration.* Urbana, Ill.: NCTE, 1984.   PE1404.W695 1984

Ponsot, Marie, and Rosemary Deen. *Beat Not the Poor Desk: Writing: What to Teach, How to Teach It, and Why.* Upper Montclair, N.J.: Boynton/Cook, 1982.   PE1404.P6

Raymond, James C., ed. *Literacy as a Human Problem.* University: University of Alabama Press, 1982.   LC149.L498 1982

Rose, Mike. *Writer's Block: The Cognitive Dimension.* Carbondale: Southern Illinois University Press, 1984.   BF456.W8 R67 1984

———, ed. *When a Writer Can't Write: Studies in Writer's Block and Other Composing Process Problems.* New York: Guilford, 1985.   PN171.W74 W48 1985

Shaughnessey, Mina P. *Errors and Expectations: A Guide for the Teacher of Basic Writing.* New York: Oxford University Press, 1977.   PE1404.S5

Stevenson, Dwight W., ed. *Courses, Components, and Exercises in Technical Communication.* Urbana, Ill.: NCTE, 1981.   T11.C68

Stock, Patricia L., ed. *Forum: Essays on Theory and Practice in the Teaching of Writing.* Upper Montclair, N.J.: Boynton/Cook, 1983.   PE1404.F4 1983

Sudol, Ronald A., ed. *Revising: New Essays for Teachers of Writing.* Urbana, Ill.: NCTE, 1982.   PE1404.R45 1982

Summerfield, Judith, and Geoffrey Summerfield. *Texts & Contexts: A Contribution to the Theory and Practice of Teaching Composition.* New York: Random House, 1986.   PE1404.S86 1986

Tate, Gary, and Edward P. J. Corbett, eds. *Writing Teacher's Sourcebook.* New York: Oxford University Press, 1981. Bibliographies.   PE1404.W74

Tchudi, Stephen. See Judy, Stephen.

Turk, Christopher, and John Kirkman. *Effective Writing: Improving Scientific, Technical and Business Communication.* New York: E. and F. Spon, 1982.   T11.T75

Walvoord, Barbara E. Fassler. *Helping Students Write Well: A Guide for Teachers in All Disciplines*. New York: MLA, 1983. PE1408.W31336 1982

Williams, Joseph M. Style: *Ten Lessons in Clarity and Grace*. Glenview, Ill.: Scott, Foresman, 1981. PE1421.W545

Witte, Stephen P., and Lester Faigley. *Evaluating College Writing Programs*. Carbondale: Southern Illinois University Press, 1983. PE1404.W57 1983

Wresch, William ed. *Computer in Composition Instruction*. Urbana, Ill.: NCTE, 1984. PE1404.C63 1984

X–165 Scholarly Journals in Rhetoric, Communications, and Discourse Theory, Stylistics, and Composition.

ABCA Bulletin, Vol. 1–. Urbana, Ill.: American Business Communication Association, 1973–. 4/yr. Indexes. No LC number

ACA Bulletin. Vol. 1–. Annandale, Va.: Association for Communication Administration, 1972–. 4/yr. Indexed in Matlon (X–104). PN4073.A8512

Argumentation: An International Journal on Reasoning. Vol. 1–. Dordrecht: D. Reidel, 1987–. 4/yr. BC1.A74

Central States Speech Journal. Vol. 1–. West Lafayette, IN: Central States Speech Association, 1949–. Indexed in Matlon (X–104). No LC number

CCC *College Composition and Communication*. Vol. 1–. Urbana, Ill.: NCTE, 1950–. 4/yr. Reviews. Bibliographies. See X–147. PE1001.C6

CE *College English*. Vol. 1–. Urbana, Ill.: NCTE, 1939–. 8/yr. Reviews. Bibliographical notices. PE1.C6

CEd *Communication Education* [former title: *Speech Teacher, 1952–1975*]. Vol. 1–. Falls Church, Va.: Speech Communication Association, 1952–. 4/yr. Reviews. Indexed in Matlon (X–104). PN4071.S74

ComM *Communication Monographs* [former title: *Speech Monographs 1934–1975*]. Vol. 1–. Falls Church, Va.: Speech Communication Association, 1934. 4/yr. Annual Bibliography (X–103). Indexed in Matlon (X–104). PN4077.S6

ComQ *Communication Quarterly* [former title: *Today's Speech 1953–1975*]. Vol. 1–. University Park, Pa.: Eastern Communication Association, 1953–. Indexed in Matlon (X–104). PN4071.T6

Communication Research. Vol. 1–. Newbury Park, Calif.: Sage, 1973–. 4–6/yr. P91.C56

Communicator of Scientific and Technical Information. Vol. 1–. Hatfield, Eng.: Institute of Scientific and Technical Communicators, 1976–. 4/yr. No LC number

Composition and Teaching. Vol. 1–. Towson, Md.: Goucher College, 1978–. 2/yr. No LC number

Composition Chronicle: Newsletter for Writing Teachers. Vol. 1–. LeRoy, N.Y.: Viceroy Publications, 1987–. 9/yr. Reviews. No LC number

Discourse Processes: A Multidisciplinapy Jouplal. Vol. 1–. Norwood, N.J.: Ablex, 1978–. 4/yr. P302.D55

ESP *English for Specific Purposes Journal*. Vol. 1 –. New York: Pergamon, 1980–. 2/yr. Reviews. PE1128.A2 E76

EJ *English Journal*. Vol. 1–. Urbana, Ill.: NCTE, 1912–. 8/yr. Reviews. PE1.E5

FEN *Freshman English News*. Vol. 1–. Fort Worth: Texas Christian University, 1972–. 3/yr. No LC number

Human Communication Research. Vol. 1–. New Brunswick, N.J.: International Communication Association, 1974–. 4/yr. Indexed in Matlon (X–104). P91.3.H85

Issues in Writing. Vol. 1–. Stevens Point, Wisc.: University of Wisconsin—Stevens Point, 1988–. 2/yr. No LC number

JBTC: Iowa State Journal of Business and Technical Communication. Vol. 1–. Ames: Iowa State University, 1987–. 2/yr. Reviews. No LC number

JAC *Journal of Advanced Composition*. Vol. 1–. Tampa: University of South Florida for the Association of Teachers of Advanced Composition, 1980–. 2/yr. Reviews. Bibliographical notices. No LC number

Journal of Basic Writing. Vol. 1–. New York: City University of New York, Instructional Resource Center, 1975–. 2/yr. PE1404.J68

Journal of Broadcasting. Vols. 1–28. Washington, D.C.: Broadcast Education Association, 1957-1984. 4/yr. Indexed in Matlon (X–104). PN1991.J6

Journal of Business Communication. Vol. 1–. Urbana, Ill.: American Business Communication Association, 1963–. 4/yr. Reviews. Bibliographical notices. Indexes to vols. 1–10 (in vol. 13), 11–16 (in vol. 17) and annually thereafter. HF5718.J6

JC *Journal of Communication*. Vol. 1–. Oxford: Oxford University Press for the Annenberg School of Communications and the International Communication Association, 1951–. 4/yr. Reviews. Indexed in Matlon (X–104). P87.J6

Journal of Teaching Writing. Indianapolis: Indiana Teachers of Writing, 1982–. 2/yr. PE1404.J69

JTWC *Journal of Technical Writing and Communication*. Vol. 1–. Farmingdale, N.Y.: Baywood Publishing, 1971–. 4/yr. Reviews. T11.J66

Journal of the American Forensic Association. Vol. 1–. Columbia, Mo.: American Forensic Association, 1964. 4/yr. Varies. Indexed in Matlon (X–104). No LC number

Journalism Quarterly: Devoted to Research in Mass Communication. Vol. 1–. Athens, Ohio: Association for Education in Journalism, 1924–. 4/yr. Reviews. "Articles on Mass Communication in U.S. and Foreign Journals: A Selected Bibliography [1930–]." Indexed in Matlon (X–104). PN4700.J7

Language and Communication. Vol. 1–. Oxford: Pergamon Press, 1981–. P87.L36

Language and Style: An International Journal. Vol. 1–. Carbondale: Southern Illinois University, 1968–. 4/yr. Reviews. PN203.L35

LNL *Linguistics in Literature*. Vols. 1–6. San Antonio, Tex.: Trinity University, 1975–1981. 3/yr. PB1.L56

P & R *Philosophy and Rhetoric*. Vol. 1–. University Park: Pennsylvania State University Press, 1968–. 4/yr. Reviews. Indexed in Matlon (X–104). B1.P572

P/T *Pre/Text: An Inter-Disciplinary Journal of Rhetoric*. Vol. 1–. Charleston: Eastern Illinois University, Department of English, 1980–. 2–4/yr. Reviews. P301.P68

QJS   *Quarterly Journal of Speech*. Vol. 1–. Falls Church, Va.: Speech Communication Association, 1915–. 4/yr. Reviews. Bibliography (see X–103). Indexed in Matlon (X–104).

No LC number

Quarterly Review of Doublespeak. Vol. 1–. Urbana, Ill.: NCTE, 1980–. 4/yr. Reviews.

PE1460.A2 Q37

RTE   *Research in the Teaching of English*. Vol. 1–. Urbana, Ill.: NCTE, 1967–. 3/yr. Reviews. Bibliography (see Z–129).

RR   *Rhetoric Review*. Vol. 1–. Dallas: Southern Methodist University, 1982–. 2/yr.   PN171.4.R44

RSQ   *Rhetoric Society Quarterly* [former title: *Rhetoric Society Newsletter, 1968–1975*]. Vol. 1–. St. Cloud, Minn.: St. Cloud State University for the Rhetoric Society of America, 1968–. 4/yr. Reviews. Bibliographies. Annual Bibliography [see X–106].

Rhetorica: A Journal of the History of Rhetoric. Vol. 1–. Berkeley, Los Angeles, London: University of California Press, 1983–. 2/yr. Reviews. Bibliographical notices.

Rhetorik: Ein internationales Jahrbuch. Vol. 1–. Stuttgart: Frommann-Holzboog, 1980–. 1/yr. Reviews. Annual Bibliography.   PN171.4.R47

Sage Written Communication Annual: An International Survey of Current Research and Theory. Vol. 1–. Beverly Hills, Calif.: Sage, 1984–.

Southern Speech Communication Journal [former title: *Southern Speech Journal, 1935–1971*]. Vol. 1–. Knoxville, Tenn.: Southern Speech Communication Association, 1935–. 4/yr. Reviews. Annual "Bibliography of Speech, Theatre, and Mass Communication for South," 1954–. Indexed in Matlon (X–104).   PN4071.S65

Speech Communication Abstracts (see U–13).

SM   *Speech Monographs* (see *Communication Monographs*).

Style   *Style*. Vol. 1–. Fayetteville: University of Arkansas, 1967–. 4/yr. Reviews. Bibliographies. Annual Bibliography (see X–136).   PE1.S89

TETYC   *Teaching English in the Two-Year College*. Vol. 1–. Greenville, N.C.: East Carolina University, Department of English, 1974–. 3–4/yr.   PE1065.T4

Technical Communication: Journal of the Society for Technical Communication. Vol. 1–. Washington, D.C.: The Society, 1953–. 4/yr. Reviews. Bibliography "Recent and Relevant." Abstracts of Articles.   T11.S2

TWT   *Technical Writing Teacher*. Vol. 1–. Morehead, Ky.: Association of Teachers of Technical Writing, 1973–. 3/yr. Reviews. Bibliography (see X–151).   No LC number

Text: An Interdisciplinary Journal for the Study of Discourse. Vol. 1–. Berlin: de Gruyter, 1980–. 4/yr.

TS   *Today's Speech* (see *Communication Quarterly*).

Visible Language: Journal for Research on the Visual Media of Language Expression [former title: *Journal of Typographic Research, 1967–1970*]. Vol. 1–. Cleveland, Ohio: The Cleveland Museum of Art. 1967–. 4/yr.   Z119.J88

WJSC   *Western Journal of Speech Communication* [former title: *Western Speech*]. Portland, Ore.: Western Speech Communication Association, 1937–. 4/yr. Indexed in Matlon (X–104).   PN4071.W45

Writing Center Journal. Vol. 1–. Albany: State University of New York at Albany, Department of English, 1979–. 2/yr.   No LC number

WI   *Writing Instructor*. Vol. 1–. Los Angeles: University of Southern California, Freshman Writing Program, 1981–. 4/yr.   PE1001.W74

WPA   *Writing Program Administration*. Vol. 1–. New York: Council of Writing Program Administrators, 1979–. 2/yr. Bibliographies.   PE1404.W18

Written Communication: A Quarterly Journal of Research, Theory, and Application. Vol. 1–. Beverly Hills, Calif.: Sage Publications, 1984–. 4/yr.

No LC number

Written Communication Annual: An International Survey of Research and Theory. Vol. 1–. Beverly Hills, Calif.: Sage, 1986–.

See the account by Robert J. Connors of "Journals in Composition Studies," *College English* 46 (April 1984).

BIBLIOGRAPHY

I.   GENERAL BIBLIOGRAPHIES AND GUIDES

Y–1   **Howard-Hill, T. H.   *British Bibliography and Textual Criticism: A Bibliography*. Vols. 4–6 of the *Index to British Literary Bibliography*.** Oxford: Clarendon Press, 1979–1980.   Z2011.A1 H68 vols. 4–6

These volumes continue the work begun ten years earlier with the *Bibliography of British Literary Bibliographies* (M–1) and *Shakespearean Bibliography and Textual Criticism* (0–45). Volume 4 is a bibliography of English-language writings published from 1890 through 1969 which concern the bibliographical aspects of works printed or published in Britain from 1475 to the present, along with works concerning the circumstances of printing and publishing during that period. Works attending to literary, historical, or linguistic values are included only if they also present significant bibliographical or textual discussion.

A total of 8,221 serially numbered entries, occasionally annotated (e.g., contents are described for composite volumes), are disposed in a classified arrangement, within the subdivisions of which they are in chronological order. The main divisions are as follows: Bibliography and Textual Criticism (with subdivisions including Bibliographical Description; Bibliography—Manuals; Bibliography—Terms and Concepts; Textual Criticism and Editing); General and Periodical Bibliography (with subdivisions including Books—Auctions and Sales; Books, Lost); Regional Bibliography (with geographic subdivisions); Book Production and Distribution (with subdivisions including Bookbinding; Book Collecting and Libraries; Book Production and Distribution; Paper and Papermaking; Printing; Publishing; Type and Typography); and Forms, Genres, and Subjects (with an alphabetical list of subdivisions including Anonyma, Ballads, The Bible, Books in Series, Children's Literature, Drama, Illustrated Books, Newspapers and Periodicals, Poetry, School Books, Sermons, and Travel Books, among many others).

The last section of the table of contents, Authors, occupies all of volume 5, in which are located entries 8,222 to 14,616. The true entry count, it is noted, is 15,159. These entries are also chronologically arranged under an alphabetical list of authors. When there are only one or two items concerning an author, they have been located within the Forms, Genres, and Subjects classification rather than under a separate author entry. It should be remembered that actual bibliographies of authors, as of regions and subjects, are enumerated in volume 1, the *Bibliography of British Literary Bibliographies* (M–1), or, in the case of Shakespeare along with bibliographical and tex-

tual studies, in volume 2, *Shakespearean Bibliography and Textual Criticism* (0–45). As the second volume contained an important supplement to the first, so volume 5 does contain on pages 374–388 under "Shakespeare" a supplement to volume 2.

All four published volumes (volume 3, to contain material on bibliography and textual criticism published *before* 1890, will not appear for some time) are indexed in volume 6, *British Bibliography and Textual Criticism*: *1890–1969*: *An Index*, designed as an interim cumulative index to the entire series. Two indexes are provided; to authors, editors, compilers, and titles, and to subjects. Entries refer to items in the forthcoming second edition of volume 1 (into which the supplement originally published in volume 2 has been incorporated, along with additional materials gathered during the 1970s), the original edition of volume 2 (and its supplement in volume 5), and all materials in volumes 4 and 5.

Y–2   **"Recent Books." and "Recent Periodicals." *Library: The Transactions of the Bibliographical Society*,** 5th ser., vol. 20–. London: Bibliographical Society, 1965–.
Z671.L69

The "Recent Books" list in each quarterly issue gives brief descriptive summaries with evaluations of recent studies in analytical and descriptive bibliography. Entries are arranged alphabetically by author. The "Recent Periodicals" feature selectively lists bibliographically interesting current contents of various European and American literary, historical, and bibliographical journals.

Y–3   **"A Selective Check List of Bibliographical Scholarship for [1948–1972]." *Studies in Bibliography*,** vols. 3–27. Charlottesville: University Press of Virginia for the Bibliographical Society of the University of Virginia, 1950–1974.
Z1008.V55

This annual bibliography was divided into two separately edited sections, Part I: Incunabula and Early Renaissance (which featured more general European scholarship) and Part II: Later Renaissance to the Present (which tended to have most of the scholarship of interest to students of English and American literary texts). The serially numbered entries in Part I are not further subdivided but are listed alphabetically. The organization of Part II is as follows: 1. Bibliographies, Check Lists, Enumerations (A. English and General, B. United States); 2. Printing, Publishing, Bibliography and Textual Scholarship (A. English and General, B. United States). Within subheadings entries are alphabetical, by author.

There have been two cumulations: *Studies in Bibliography*,

vol. 10 (1957) has the title *Selective Check Lists of Bibliographical Scholarship* [Series A], *1949–1955*, ed. Howell J. Heaney and Rudolph Hitsch [Z1002.V59]. The same editors were also responsible for the separately published *Selective Check List of Bibliographical Scholarship, Series B, 1956-1962* (1967) [Z1002.V59]. Both cumulations reprint the annual lists, but with the addition of a detailed cumulated index. Note that the numeration of entries begins again with each series.

Because of unnecessary duplication, the "Selective Check List" was discontinued in 1974 with the checklist for 1972, and users have been referred to the *Annual Bibliography of the History of the Printed Book and Libraries* (Y–7). The serially numbered Check Lists for 1963–1972, known as "Series C," have not yet been cumulated. In its entirety this bibliography listed a total of 12,554 items: 3,416 in Series A, 3,934 in Series B, and 5,204 in Series C.

Y–4 ***Bibliography in Britain*** [1962–1967]. Vols. 1–6. Oxford: Oxford Bibliographical Society, 1963–1968.   Z1002.B617

This annual bibliography listed works published in the United Kingdom in the fields of analytical and descriptive bibliography and in the related fields of printing and librarianship. Books, articles, and book reviews were cited in a detailed classification that was subsequently revised in the *Annual Bibliography of the History of the Printed Book* (Y–7).

Y–5 **"The Register of Current Publications [1970–]."** *Proof: The Yearbook of American Bibliographical and Textual Studies*, vols. 1–7. Columbia, S.C.: University of South Carolina, 1971–1977.   Z1219.P73

The annual, selective checklist of in-print books, monographs, and pamphlets in bibliographical and textual studies (including facsimile and reprint editions of earlier works) contained descriptively annotated entries disposed into thirteen sections, as follows: 1. Edited Primary Works; 2. Reprinted Primary Works; 3. Author Bibliographies and Checklists; 4. Subject Bibliographies and Checklists; 5. National Bibliographies and Checklists; 6. Writing and Autographs; 7. Printing, Binding, Publishing, and Bookselling; 8. Copyright and Intellectual Property; 9. Libraries and Book Collecting; 10. Bibliographical and Textual Theory and Practice; 11. Concordances and Indexes; 12. Dictionaries, Rhetorics, and Guides to Language; and 13. Miscellaneous. An analytical index of authors, titles, and subjects concluded each volume, treating entries in the bibliography as well as articles in the yearbook.

Y–6 **Reviews of Research in Bibliography and Textual Criticism.**

1923. Childs, James B. "Sixteenth Century Books: A Bibliography of Literature Describing Books Printed between 1501 and 1601." *PBSA* 17 (1923): 75–152.

1929. Cole, George W. "A Survey of the Bibliography of English Literature, 1470–1640, with Special References to the Work of the Bibliographical Society of London." *PBSA* 23 (1929): 1–95.

1945. Francis, F. C., et al. *Bibliographical Society, 1892–1942: Studies in Retrospect*. London: Bibliographical Society, 1945 [No LC number]. Includes the following surveys: 1. The Bibliographical Society: A Sketch of the First Fifty Years (F. C. Francis); 2. Bibliography: A Retrospect (W. W. Greg); 3. Early Printed Books (Victor Scholderer); 4. English Books before 1640 (F. S. Ferguson); Shakespeare and the "New Bibliography" (F. P. Wilson); 6. The Eighteenth Century (Harold Williams); 7. The Development during the Last Fifty Years of Bibliographical

Study of Books of the Nineteenth Century (Michael Sadleir); 8. The Bibliographical Society's Contribution to Foreign Bibliography (H. Thomas); 9. The Study of Bookbinding (E. P. Goldschmidt); 10. America (W. A. Jackson); 11. List of Officers and Members of the Society, 1892–1942; and 12. List of Bibliographical Society Publications, 1892–1942.

1959. Neill, D. G. "Printed Books, 1640–1800." *Library Trends* 7 (1959): 537–553.

1959. Roberts, Julian. "Printed Books to 1640." *Library Trends* 7 (1959): 517–536.

1975. Heaney, Howell J. "Analytical and Descriptive Bibliography since 1947, with a Checklist." *College and Research Libraries*, November 1975.

To these surveys may be added the recent collection of review essays by G. Thomas Tanselle, *Textual Criticism Since Greg: A Chronicle 1950–1985* (Y–29).

Y–7 ***ABHB: Annual Bibliography of the History of the Printed Book and Libraries*** [1970–]. The Hague: Nijhoff, 1973–.   Z117.A55

This annual, international bibliography of books, articles, and reviews concerned with printing history and all associated arts, crafts, economic, social, and cultural institutions and phenomena is prepared by some twenty-five national committees. Some 1,900 periodicals are analyzed. Entries are serially numbered each year and disposed into a twelve-part subject classification scheme, paralleling that used for *Bibliography in Britain* (Y–4): A. General Works about the History of the Printed Book and Library; B. Paper, Inks, Printing Materials; C. Calligraphy, Type Design, Type Founding; D. Layout, Composing, Printing, Presses, Printed Books, including Incunabula, etc.; E. Book Illustration; F. Bookbinding; G. Book Trade, Publishing; H. Bibliophily, Book Collecting; J. Libraries, Librarianship, Scholarship, Institutions; K. Legal, Economic, Social Aspects; L. Newspapers, Journalism; M. Relation to Secondary Subjects Mainly in Order of [their Dewey] Decimal Classifications. Within sections, there are subdivisions by country. Two indexes conclude each annual, an index of author's names and an index of geographical and personal names (and pseudonyms) as subjects.

Because specifically textual studies are excluded, *ABHB* does not really replace the "Selective Checklists" in *SB* (Y–53). And, indeed, there are more extensive limitations to the satisfactoriness of its coverage, for which see B. J. McMullin, "Indexing the Periodical Literature of Anglo-American Bibliography," *SB* 33 (1980): 1–17. Available supplements are the bibliographical entries in the *MLA International Bibliography* (L–50) and in the MHRA *Annual Bibliography* (M–21), both of which should be consulted.

Y–8 ***Bibliographie des Bibliotheks- und Buchwesens*** [1904-1912, 1922–1926]. 13 vols. Leipzig: Harrassowitz, 1905–1927. Neue Folge, under the title ***Internationale Bibliographie des Buch- und Bibliothekswesens, mit besonderer Berücksichtigung der Bibliographie*** [1926–1940]. 15 vols. Leipzig: Zentralblatt für Bibliothekswesen, 1928–1941.   Z671.C39B

These annual, indexed volumes cumulate the lists of primarily separately published current works that appeared in the *Zentralblatt für Bibliothekswesen* [Z671.C39]. Because the new series includes a number of prominent British and American bibliographical journals, it is a major source of information on bibliographical research during the 1920s and 1930s, prior to the inception of the *SB* checklists (see Y–3).

Additional serially published indexes useful in locating bibliographical materials include the annual *MLA International Bibliography* (L–50), the MHRA *Annual Bibliography*

(M–21), and the general periodical indexes, including Poole (D–10), the *Reader's Guide* (D–50), the *Humanities Index* (D–16), the *British Humanities Index* (D–17), and the *IBZ* (D–13).

Y–9 **Winckler, Paul A., ed.** *History of Books and Printing: A Guide to Information Sources.* Detroit: Gale Research Corp., 1979.   Z117.W54

The 776 serially numbered entries in this bibliographical guide are accompanied by long descriptive and evaluative annotations. They are disposed into nine sections, as follows: 1. General Bibliographies; 2. General Information Sources; 3. Materials and Techniques Used in Graphic Communication (with subdivisions); 4. The History of Books and Printing (with period subdivisions); 5. Non-print Media (with subdivisions for each medium); 6. Periodicals and Annals; 7. Associations, Societies, and Clubs; 8. Libraries, Special Collections, and Museums; and 9. Book Dealers. The volume concludes with indexes of authors, titles, and subjects.

Y–10 **International Bibliography of the Book Trade and Librarianship / Fachliteratur zum Buch- und Bibliothekswesen.** 12th ed. 1976–1979. Munich: Saur; New York: R. R. Bowker, 1981.   Z279.I57

This edition, along with its predecessor editions, the tenth and eleventh (both of which have the German language title as their primary title) [Z279.F3], provide a subject classification of some 25,000 monographs (including pamphlets) published 1969–1979 in all languages and countries on all aspects of the history of writing, book production, printing, the book trade, book collecting, and librarianship. Entries in the tenth edition were published 1969–1973; those in the eleventh, 1973–1975. Bibliographies, catalogs, histories, and studies are included, along with works in such allied fields as information science and archivistics. The volumes are organized by regions and then by country. The tenth edition is in two parts (Europe; Africa, the Americas, Asia, Oceania, and Indexes). Within countries, entries are in a subject classification with the following main divisions: 1. Script and History of the Book; 2. Authors; 3. Book Publishing and Trades; 4. Printing and Bookbinding; 5. Library Science; 6. Information and Documentation Science; 7. Archives. There are several levels of subclassifications. Serially numbered entries give titles, translations into German or English as appropriate, the name of the author, editor, the frequency and first year of publication of serials, the place, publisher and year, pagination, whether illustrated, the series and number in the series, if applicable, ISBN or ISSN, and the price.

Y–11 *Bibliographie der Buch- und Bibliotheksgeschichte [BBB]* [1980/81–]. Vol. 1–. Bad Iburg: Bibliographischer Verlag Dr. Horst Meyer, 1982–.   Z4.B54

This annual provides an analysis of more than 300 periodicals (listed at the beginning of each volume) in the fields of the history of books, the history of the book trades, the history of bibliography, and the history of libraries. There is an emphasis on German-language materials. Serially numbered entries are disposed in a classified arrangement as follows: 1. Allgemeines; 2. Der Autor (2.1 Textüberlieferung, 2.2 Edition); 3. Buchherstellung (3.1 Buchgestaltung, 3.2 Schrift, Typographie, 3.3 Satzherstellung, 3.4 Druckverfahren, 3.5 Papier, 3.6 Buchdruck, 3.7 Illustration, 3.8 Einband, 3.9 Konservierung, Restaurierung); 4. Buchgattungen und- formen (4.1 Kinder- und Jugendbuch, 4.2 Zeitschrift, 4.3 Zeitung, 4.4 Printed Ephemera [sic]); 5. Vermittlung des Buches (5.1 Buchmarkt, 5.2 Verlagswesen, 5.3 Buchhandel, 5.4 Antiquariatsbuchhandel, 5.5 Rechtsfragen, 5.6 Zensur, 5.7 Bibliotheken, 5.8 Bibliophilie, Privatbibliotheken, 5.9 Ex

Libris); 6. Der Leser; 7. Kuriosa; 8. Rezensionen. Each volume ends with indexes of compilers, editors, and contributors; of reviewed authors; of names; of places; and of subjects.

Y–12 *BiN: Bibliography Newsletter.* Vol. 1–. Blacksburg, Va.: The Walrus Press, 1973–.   Z1219.B5

Founded and originally published by Terry Belanger, this newsletter appeared monthly (except in the summer). It now appears quarterly (i.e., the monthly numbers are grouped). Featured are articles on American and British developments in all fields of bibliography; news of lectures, conferences, work-in-progress; reviews of new publications; and lists of remaindered books of interest to bibliographers.

Y–13 **"A Review of the Year's Research."** *Direction Line: A Newsletter for Bibliographers and Textual Critics.* Nos. 1–10. Austin, Tex.: Warner Barnes, Department of English, University of Texas, 1975–1980.   No LC number

This bibliographic essay appeared in each semiannual issue of this newsletter, along with information on work proposed or in progress and other notices of interest to working bibliographers and textual critics.

Y–14 *Literary Research: A Journal of Scholarly Method and Technique [LR]* [former title 1976–1985, *Literary Research Newsletter*]. Vol. 1–. College Park, Md.: Literary Research Association, The University of Maryland, 1976–.
                                      PN73.L57

This quarterly journal carries articles on aspects of literary research, reviews of new works of reference for literary studies, updates on new editions and supplements of already existing reference works, brief descriptions of new publications that are worthy of notice, and news and notes of interest to bibliographers and researchers and to students of bibliographic and research methods. Since 1986 a sheer list "Record of Current Publication" has enumerated current reference works including bibliographies, handbooks, concordances, editions, and ancillary tools in all branches of English studies.

Y–15 *AEB: Analytical and Enumerative Bibliography.* Vol. 1–. Dekalb: Department of English, Northern Illinois University, Department of English, for the Bibliographical Society of Northern Illinois, 1977–.   Z1007.A115

This quarterly journal contains articles on problems of analytical or enumerative bibliography, occasional bibliographies, and reviews and notices of publications in analytical or enumerative bibliography. Originally, the fourth issue was the *Index to Reviews of Bibliographical Publications*, which is now published separately (Y–18).

Y–17 **Harner, James.** *On Compiling an Annotated Bibliography.* New York: Modern Language Association, 1985.
                                      Z1001.H33

This brief guide treats planning, organizing, researching, writing, editing, and indexing both selective and comprehensive bibliographies of literary authors and subjects.

For treatment of bibliographies, including but not limited to literary bibliographies, see D. W. Krummel, *Bibliographies: Their Aims and Methods* (London: Mansell, 1984) [Z1001 .K86 1984].

Y–18 *Index to Reviews of Bibliographical Publications* [1976–].
Boston: G. K. Hall, 1977–.   Z1002.I57

The first of these annual indexes, covering 1976 reviews of
publications, was published in 1977 as vol. 1, no. 4 of *Analytical and Enumerative Bibliography* (Y–15). Subsequently,
the index has been published separately. It consists of an alphabetical author list of publications in analytical and descriptive bibliography, enumerative bibliography, and textual criticism, including editions. Each entry locates American reviews, giving authors' names when known. A very general
subject index concludes each volume. This index can also be
used as a checklist of current bibliographical scholarship on
the grounds that all significant work will be reviewed and
therefore cited in due course.

Y–19 **Downs, Robert B., and Frances B. Jenkins, eds. *Bibliography: Current State and Future Trends.*** Urbana: University of Illinois Press, 1967.   Z1002.D62

This volume brings together a collection of thirty-seven essays by authorities which originally appeared in 1967 issues of
Library Trends. They survey the State of Bibliography in
General; National Bibliography; The Bibliography of Periodicals, Newspapers, Manuscripts and Archives, and Incunabula
and Sixteenth-Century Imprints; as well as bibliography in the
following subject areas: Philosophy and Religion; Architecture and the Fine Arts; Music Literature, Music, and Sound
Recordings; English Literature; American Literary Bibliography in the Twentieth century; Continental European Literature; Latin American Books and Periodicals; Anglo-American
Law; Political Science; Education; Psychology; Anthropology; Geography; Cartography; American History; East European History; Far Eastern History; History and Culture of Southeast Asia; The History of Science; General Science; Geology;
Biology; Chemistry; Physics; Mathematical Literature; Engineering; Agriculture; and Medicine. The volume concludes
with a full index of authors or articles, subjects, and titles of
works cited in the essay.

II.   ANALYTICAL AND DESCRIPTIVE BIBLIOGRAPHY AND TEXTUAL CRITICISM: BASIC WORKS OF REFERENCE

Y–20 **Williams, William Proctor, and Craig S. Abbott. *Introduction to Bibliographical and Textual Studies.*** 2nd ed.
New York: MLA, 1989.   Z1001.W58 1989

This slim volume, first published in 1985, is a densely
packed introduction to the fields of Analytical Bibliography,
Historical Bibliography, Descriptive Bibliography, and Textual Criticism. It is disposed into five chapters: Introduction,
Analytical Bibliography, Descriptive Bibliography, A Text
and Its Embodiments, and Textual Criticism. Four examples
of pages taken from the textual apparatuses of Bowers's edition of Dekker; Edwards and Gibson's edition of Massinger;
Hayford, Parker, and Tanselle's edition of Melville's *Mardi*;
and Nathalia Wright's documentary edition of Irving's *Journals and Notebooks* complete the body of this work.
An Appendix on Textual Notation precedes a topically organized Reference Bibliography in the form of brief bibliographical essays. An Index concludes this useful introductory survey.

Y–21 **McKerrow, Ronald B. *Introduction to Bibliography for
Literary Students.*** 2d impression, with corrections. Oxford: Clarendon Press, 1928.   Z1001.M161

Originally published in 1927, this work is a revised and enlarged version of the author's "Notes on Bibliographical Evidence for Literary Students and Editors of English Works of
the Sixteenth and Seventeenth Centuries," which were published in the *Transactions of the Bibliographical Society*, vol.
12 (1914) [Z1008.B587]. The work is in three parts. Part I
consists of eleven chapters describing the process of making a
book during the handpress period, with examples here and later drawn primarily from sixteenth- and seventeenth-century
English works. Part II consists of ten chapters on the analysis
of books with respect to evidence about their production.
Part III, finally, consists of two chapters that discuss aspects
of the bookmaking process most likely to introduce errors into
texts and therefore of particular interest for textual criticism.
Among the eight appendixes is "A Note on Printing, Its Origin
and Spread: Some Famous Presses and Publishing Houses";
an account of printing types; and "A Note on Elizabethan
Handwriting." The volume concludes with a brief subject index.

Y–22 **Gaskell, Philip. *New Introduction to Bibliography.*** Oxford: Clarendon Press, 1972. Reprinted with corrections.
1974.   Z116.A2 G27 1974

This volume, designed as a successor to McKerrow (Y–20),
does not entirely replace its original. But it does bring together the massive literature of analytical and descriptive bibliography published since the 1920s and its scope is extended to
include the machine press, thus making it the work of first resort. What Gaskell does not do is to present bibliographical
information from the point of view of its use to the literary student. This changed focus is compensated for by Gaskell's sequel volume *From Writer to Reader* (Y–32) more adequately
than it is by the brief section on "Bibliographical Applications"
at the end of this volume.
The *New Introduction* is in five sections. The two main
parts treat Book Production. The first covers the Hand-press
Period 1500–1800 in eleven chapters (The Hand-printed
Book; Printing Type; Composition; Paper; Imposition; Presswork; The Warehouse; Binding; Decoration and Illustration;
Patterns of Production; and The English Book Trade to 1800).
The second part treats the Machine-Press Period 1800–1950
in eleven chapters (Introduction; Survival and Change; Plates;
Type 1800–1875; Paper in the Machine-press Period; Edition
Binding; Printing Machines; Processes of Reproduction; Mechanical Composition and Type 1875–1950; Printing Practice
in the Machine-press Period; and The Book Trade in Britain
and America since 1800). The third section, a brief account
of bibliographical applications, discusses aspects of bibliographical identification, bibliographical description, and textual bibliography in about fifty pages. The fourth section
presents three appendixes: McKerrow's "Note on Elizabethan
Handwriting"; a set of four specimen bibliographical descriptions; and two examples of textual transmission, one from
Shakespeare and one from Dickens. The final section, a Reference Bibliography, presents brief bibliographical essays
identifying works to consult on each topic treated in the volume. A detailed subject index concludes the work.

Y–23 **Esdaile, Arundell. *Manual of Bibliography.*** 4th ed. Revised by Roy Stokes. London: George Allen and Unwin,
1967.   Z1001.E75 1967

An additional introductory textbook designed for the student
librarian, this volume is a useful supplement to both McKerrow and Gaskell's accounts, with convenient recommendations for further reading at the end of each of the twelve chap-

ters. These are organized after an introductory chapter into a six-chapter sequence on book production (The Parts of a Book; Papyrus, Parchment, Vellum, Paper; Typography; Composition and Press Work; Illustration; Binding) followed by chapters on Landmarks in the Development of the Book; The Collation of Books; The Description of Books; The Arrangement of Bibliographies; and Bibliographical Tools. This last chapter is a bibliographical essay that discusses a total of 146 reference works from bibliographies of bibliographies to universal bibliographies and the catalogs of major libraries, bibliographies of incunabula, English literature, American literature, serial publications, and academic writings. A brief subject index concludes the volume.

A more recent volume similarly designed is by E. W. Padwick, *Bibliographical Method: An Introductory Survey* (Cambridge: James Clarke and Co., 1969) [Z1001.P145]. It is in four parts, an introduction in two chapters; Part II on Fifteenth Century Books in six chapters, 3–8; Part III on the Sixteenth to Eighteenth Centuries in chapters 9–14; and Part IV on the Nineteenth and Twentieth Centuries in chapters 15–17. Throughout are extensive bibliographical notes; a brief subject index concludes the survey.

Y–24 **Aldis, Harry G. *Printed Book*.** 3d ed. Revised by John Carter and Brooke Crutchley. Cambridge: University Press, 1951.   Z4.A63 1951

This short work, which combines an account of the history of the book and the technique of book production in one compact volume, was first published in 1916, with a second edition, revised by Carter and Crutchley in 1941. The first six chapters sketch printing history (The Advent of Printing; The Spread of The Art; The Fifteenth-Century Book; The Scholar-Printers of the Sixteenth Century; English Books, 1500–1800; The Modern Book). They are followed by chapters on the construction of a book, illustrations, bookbinding, and the handling and mishandling of books. An appendix on the development of typefaces is followed by a brief list of books for further reading and an index of names and subjects.

Y–25 **Bowers, Fredson. *Principles of Bibliographical Description*.** Princeton, N.J.: Princeton University Press, 1949.
                                                        Z1001.B78

This volume provides a single and central authoritative rationale for a standardized system of bibliographical description for use with all printed books of all periods and the rules of that system. It includes definitions of the key terms, *edition, impression, issue,* and *state*; standards of title-page transcription and related matters; procedures and formulas for collation; rules for statements of signing, pagination, foliation, inserts, lists of contents, typography, notes and annotations. A separate chapter discusses the description of incunabula, and a series of three chapters treats the description of nineteenth- and twentieth-century books. The work concludes with appendixes giving an overview of the descriptive formulas, some sample descriptions, and a brief author-title-subject index.

Other works of importance in the study of descriptive bibliography include Curt F. Bühler et al., *Standards of Bibliographical Description* (Philadelphia: University of Pennsylvania Press, 1949) [Z1001.B9 1949], which focuses on problems in the description of incunabula and works of early English and early American literature. See also the critique by David F. Foxon, *Thoughts on the History and Future of Bibliographical Description* (Los Angeles: School of Library Service, University of California, 1970) [Z1005.F65]. There is also a handy collection of post-Bowers readings by John Bush Jones, *Readings in Descriptive Bibliography* (Kent, Ohio: Kent State University Press, 1974) [Z1001.J79], which has its own "Checklist of Further Readings" appended.

Among articles of importance, see many of the collected and separate essays by G. Thomas Tanselle (Y–29). *Workbook of Analytical and Descriptive Bibliography* by M. J. Pearce (Hamden, Conn.: Archon, 1970) [Z1001.P34] is an attempt to reduce to a basic set of rules the Bowers principles of description.

Y–26 **Leif, Irving P. *International Sourcebook of Paper History*.** Hamden, Conn.: Archon Books, 1978.   Z7914.P2L4

This volume is divided into sections on general histories of paper and watermarks; the history of paper and papermaking in Asia and Australia; in Europe and the Soviet Union; in North and South America; and the story of paper history. Though there are many omissions, the work does include 2,185 entries, treating modern books and articles on the subject through the early 1970s.

For work on paper useful for bibliographical study, see B. L. Browning, *Analysis of Paper*, 2d ed. (New York: Marcel Dekker, 1977) [TS1109.B77 1977].

Y–27 **Briquet, Charles M. *Les filigranes: Dictionnaire historique des marques du papier des leur apparition vers 1282 jusqu'en 1600*.** Geneva: A. Jullien, 1907. New ed. Edited by Allan H. Stevenson. 4 vols. Amsterdam: Paper Publications Society, 1968.   Z237.B845 1968

Originally published in 1907, this volume presents a total of 16,112 tracings of watermarks on paper produced on the Continent before 1600. Excluded are papers of Spain, Portugal, Scandinavia, and Britain. Tracings are arranged chronologically under their design or subject matter (Veronica's Veil, Fleur-de-lis, Fool's Cap, etc.). Additional tracings will be found in W. A. Churchill, *Watermarks in Paper in Holland, England, France, etc. in the XVII and XVIII Centuries and Their Interconnections* (Amsterdam: M. Hertzberger, 1935) [Z237.C56 1967], which contains a total of 578 tracings, and Edward Heawood, *Watermarks: Mainly of the 17th and 18th Centuries* (Hilversum: Paper Publications Society, 1950) [TS1080.P183 vol. 1], which contains 4,028 tracings. For English paper see Alfred H. Shorter, *Paper Mills and Paper Makers in England, 1495–1800* (Amsterdam: Paper Publications Society, 1957) [TS1080.P183 vol. 6], which contains a total of 217 tracings. For American paper see the new volume by Thomas L. Gravell and George Miller, *Catalogue of American Watermarks, 1690–1835* (New York: Garland, 1979) [TS1115.G7]. For additional titles see the *Short Guide to Books on Watermarks* (Hilversum: Paper Publications Society, 1955) [Z7914.P2 P3].

Standard reference works on paper and papermaking include E. J. Labarre, *Dictionary and Encyclopedia of Paper and Paper-Making with Equivalents of the Technical Terms in French, German, Dutch, Italian, Swedish and Spanish*, 2d ed. (Oxford: Oxford University Press, 1952) [TS1085.L3 1952], with a *Supplement* (Amsterdam: Swets en Zeitlinger, 1967) [TS1085.L3 1952 suppl.]; the *Dictionary of Paper*, 3d ed. (New York: American Paper and Pulp Association, 1965) [TS1085.A6 1965]; and Dard Hunter's *Papermaking: The History and Technique of an Ancient Craft*, 2d ed. (New York: Knopf, 1978) [TS1090.H818]. The brief, well-illustrated volume published by the Library of Congress, *Papermaking: Art and Craft* (Washington, D.C., 1968) [TS1090.U5] is also recommended.

The most distinguished work on the use of paper as evidence in the solution of bibliographical and textual problems is by Allan Stevenson. Among his works see *Observations on Paper as Evidence* (Lawrence: University of Kansas Press, 1961) [Z237.S76]; "New Uses of Watermarks as Bibliographical Evidence," *SB* (1948–1949): 151–182; "Watermarks Are Twins," *SB* 4 (1951–1952): 47–91; "Chain-Indentations in Paper as Evidence," *SB* 6 (1954): 181–195; and "Paper as

Bibliographical Evidence," *Library*, 5th ser., 17 (1962): 197–212. His solution of the *Problem of the Missale Speciale* (London: Bibliographical Society, 1967) [Z241.M67 S7] combines evidence of paper and type.

Y–28 **Bowers, Fredson.** *Essays in Bibliography, Text, and Editing.* Charlottesville: University Press of Virginia for the Bibliographical Society, 1975.   Z1005.B68 1975

This volume reprints a total of twenty-six essays by Bowers, the dean of American bibliographical and textual studies. The contents are in four sections. General articles include "Bibliography and the University" (1949); "Some Relations of Bibliography to Editorial Problems" (1949); "Bibliography, Pure Bibliography, and Literary Studies" (1952); "The Bibliographical Way" (1948); "Bibliography and Modern Librarianship" (1966); and "Four Faces of Bibliography" (1971). Articles in Descriptive Bibliography are: "Purposes of Descriptive Bibliography, with Some Remarks on Methods" (1952); "Bibliography and Restoration Drama" (1966); and "Bibliography Revisited" (1969).

Articles in Analytical Bibliography are: "The Headline in Early Books" (1941); "An Examination of the Method of Proof Correction in *King Lear* Q1" (1947); "Elizabethan Proofing" (1948); "Running Title Evidence for Determining Half-Sheet Imposition" (1948); "Bibliographical Evidence for the Printer's Measure" (1949); and "Motteux's *Love's a Jest* (1696): A Running-Title and Presswork Problem" (1954).

Finally, articles in Textual Criticism and Editing are: "Current Theories of Copy-Text, with an Illustration from Dryden" (1950); "Old-Spelling Editions of Dramatic Texts" (1957); "Textual Criticism and the Literary Critic" (1958); "The Folio *Othello*: Compositor E" (1959); "Established Texts and Definitive Editions" (1962); "The Text of Johnson" (1964); "Old Wine in New Bottles: Problems of Machine Printing" (1966); "Practical Texts and Definitive Editions" (1968); "The Facsimile of Whitman's Blue Book" (1969); "Multiple Authority: New Problems and Concepts of Copy-Text" (1972); and "Remarks on Eclectic Texts" (1973). The volume concludes with a checklist of Bowers's publications, disposed into sections on Books, Pamphlets, Editions, Articles and Notes, Correspondence, Reviews, and Miscellaneous Contributions.

Among Bowers's separately published works in bibliography and textual criticism, the most important are *Principles of Bibliographical Description* (Y–25); *Textual and Literary Criticism* (Cambridge: Cambridge University Press, 1959) [P47.B6], which contains the text of four lectures, "Textual Criticism and the Literary Critic," "The Walt Whitman Manuscript of *Leaves of Grass* (1860)," "The New Textual Criticism of Shakespeare," and "Principle and Practice in the Editing of Early Dramatic Texts"; *Bibliography and Textual Criticism* (Oxford: Clarendon Press, 1964) [Z1001.B775]; and *On Editing Shakespeare* (Charlottesville: University Press of Virginia, 1966) [PR3071.B59].

Recent, uncollected articles include "Greg's Rationale of Copy-Text Revisited," *SB* 3 (1978): 90–161; "The Historical Collation in an Old-Spelling Shakespeare Edition: Another View," *SB* 35 (1982): 234–258; and "Regularization and Normalization in Modern Critical Texts," *SB* 42 (1989): 79–102.

Y–29 **Tanselle, G. Thomas.** *Selected Studies in Bibliography.* Charlottesville: University Press of Virginia for the Bibliographical Society of the University of Virginia, 1979.   Z1005.T336 1979

This volume includes eleven of Tanselle's essays examining principles and procedures of analytical and descriptive bibliography and textual criticism. The essays and their original dates of publication are as follows: "Bibliography and Science" (1974); "Descriptive Bibliography and Library Cataloging" (1977); "Copyright Records and the Bibliographer"

(1969); "A System of Color Identification for Bibliographical Description" (1967); "The Bibliographical Description of Patterns" (1970); "The Bibliographical Description of Paper" (1971); "Greg's Theory of Copy Text and the Editing of American Literature" (1975); "The Editorial Problem of Final Authorial Intention" (1976); "External Fact as an Editorial Problem" (1979); "Some Principles for Editorial Apparatus" (1972); and "The Editing of Historical Documents" (1978).

In addition to these pieces, all of which were originally published in *Studies in Bibliography*, a number of Tanselle's other essays are frequently recommended. These include: "The Identification of Type Faces in Bibliographical Description," *PBSA* (1966): 186–202; "The Recording of Press Figures," *Library* 5th ser., 21 (1966): 318–325; "Tolerances in Bibliographical Description," *Library*, 5th ser., 23 (1968): 1–12; "Book-Jackets, Blurbs, and Bibliographers," *Library*, 5th ser., 26 (1971): 91–134; "Problems and Accomplishments in the Editing of the Novel," *Studies in the Novel* 7 (1975): 323–360; "The Concept of *Ideal Copy*" *SB* 33 (1980): 18–53; "The Description of Non-Letterpress Material in Books," *SB* 35 (1982): 1–42; "Classical, Biblical, and Medieval Textual Criticism and Modern Editing," *SB* 36 (1983): 21–68; "The Arrangement of Descriptive Bibliographies," *SB* 37 (1984): 1–38; "Title-Page Transcription and Signature Collation Reconsidered," *SB* 38 (1985): 45–81; "A Sample Bibliographical Description, with Commentary," *SB* 40 (1987): 1–30; "Bibliographical History as a Field of Study," *SB* 41 (1988): 33–63; and "Reproductions and Scholarship," *SB* 42 (1989): 25–54.

A collection of Tanselle's review essays, *Textual Criticism Since Greg: A Chronicle, 1950–1985* (Charlottesville: University Press of Virginia for the Bibliographical Society of the University of Virginia, 1987) [PR77.T36 1987] contains the following pieces: "Greg's Theory of Copy-Text and the Editing of American Literature, 1950–1974," (1975); "Recent Editorial Discussion and the Central Questions of Editing, 1974–1979" (1981); and "Historicism and Critical Editing, 1979–1985" (1986). His Rosenbach lectures have also been published: *Rationale of Textual Criticism* (Philadelphia: University of Pennsylvania Press, 1989) [PN81.T318 1989].

Y–30 **Thorpe, James E.** *Principles of Textual Criticism.* San Marino, Calif.: Huntington Library, 1972.   PR65.T5

This introduction to the art of textual criticism, designed primarily for the use of students of English and American literature, is disposed into six chapters, several of which were published earlier in somewhat different forms. The chapters are: 1, The Aesthetics of Textual Criticism; 2, The Ideal of Textual Criticism; 3, The Province of Textual Criticism; 4, Textual Analysis; 5, The Treatment of Accidentals; and 6, The Establishment of the Text. Examples are taken from English and American literary texts; extensive footnotes refer readers to a wide range of related scholarship. An index of topics, literary authors, and scholars concludes the volume.

Y–31 **Dearing, Vinton A.** *Principles and Practice of Textual Analysis.* Berkeley, Los Angeles, London: University of California Press, 1974.   P47.D43

This volume presents a formal theory of textual analysis, the discipline concerned with comparing and determining the derivation of variant copies of a document. It is organized in six chapters: 1, Preliminary Distinctions; 2, Algorithms and a Calculus; 3, The Formal Theory of Textual Analysis; 4, Probabilistic Methods in Textual Criticism; 5, Editing Texts and Documents; and 6, Examples (from literary research and from historical research). There are three appendixes treating the use of an abacus to assist in the analysis, the use of a computer, and the use of Dearing's method of determining derivation to study variants of motifs in folklore.

Dearing's earlier work, *Manual of Textual Analysis* (Berkeley and Los Angeles: University of California Press, 1959) [P47.04], is subsumed as far as possible in the later work, which is the more developed statement of his views.

Y–32 **Gaskell, Philip. *From Writer to Reader: Studies in Editorial Method.*** Oxford: Clarendon Press, 1978.   PN162.G3

This volume is meant to improve upon the brief illustrations of the theory and practice of textual criticism in Gaskell's *New Introduction to Bibliography* (Y–22). It presents an introduction to basic questions in the theory of textual criticism, followed by chapters that gather the available evidence regarding the text of extracts from each of twelve works of literature, along with discussion of how that evidence might be used to produce editions for various groups of readers. The introduction discusses special problems associated with editing works of literature, the problem of author's intentions, the question of copy-text, problems of presentation and annotation, regularization and modernization, and the editing of works not intended for publication as printed books. The literary works from which the examples are given are Harrington's translation of Ariosto's *Orlando Furioso*; Milton, *A Maske* (Comus); Richardson, *Pamela*; Swift, *Directions to Servants*; Scott, *The Heart of Midlothian*; Tennyson, "Oenone"; Dickens, *David Copperfield*; Thackeray, *Henry Esmond*; Hawthorne, *The Marble Faun*; Hardy, *The Woodlanders*; Joyce, *Ulysses*; and Stoppard, *Travesties*. The volume concludes with an index of authors, titles, and subjects.

Y–33 **Brack, O. M., Jr., and Warner Barnes, eds. *Bibliography and Textual Criticism: English and American Literature, 1700 to the Present.*** Chicago: University of Chicago Press, 1969.   PR77.B7

This volume presents a collection of seventeen essays preceded by a historical introduction and followed by a bibliography listing selected articles on the bibliography of eighteenth-, nineteenth-, and twentieth-century literary texts, and an index. The essays include Bruce Harkness, "Bibliography and the Novelistic Fallacy" (1959); W. W. Greg, "The Rationale of Copy-Text" (1949); Fredson Bowers, "Current Theories of Copy-Text, with an Illustration from Dryden" (1950); Vinton A. Dearing, "Methods of Textual Editing" (1962); James Thorpe, "The Aesthetics of Textual Criticism" (1965); William B. Todd, "Bibliography and the Editorial Problem in the Eighteenth Century" (1950), "On the Use of Advertisements in Bibliographical Studies" (1953), and "Early Editions of *The Tatler*" (1962); along with essays by Arthur Friedman on Goldsmith; Bowers on scholarly editions of nineteenth-century American authors; Todd on editing Twain; John M. Robson on Mill; Matthew J. Bruccoli on Hawthorne and on Transatlantic Texts (works published in both Britain and the United States); David Hayman on Joyce; Russell K. Alspach on Yeats; and James B. Meriwether on Hemingway.

Y–34 **Gottesman, Ronald, and Scott Bennett, eds. *Art and Error: Modern Textual Editing.*** Bloomington: Indiana University Press, 1970.   PN162.G63

This volume presents a collection of fifteen essays concerning the editing of English and American literature, followed by a highly selective, annotated bibliography of further readings. The essays are as follows: A. E. Housman, "The Application of Thought to Textual Criticism"; W. W. Greg, "The Rationale of Copy-Text"; R. C. Bald, "Editorial Problems—A Preliminary Survey"; Fredson Bowers, "Some Principles for Scholarly Editions of Nineteenth-Century American Authors"; James Thorpe, "The Aesthetics of Textual Criticism"; David Veith on editing Rochester; Robert Halsband, "Editing the Letters of Letter-Writers"; Thomas H.

Johnson on editing Emily Dickinson; John Butt on editing Dickens; Dennis Welland on editing Twain; Russell K. Alspach on editing Yeats; Harry M. Geduld on editing Shaw; James B. Meriwether on editing Faulkner; Vinton A. Dearing on computer-aided editing of Dryden; and William M. Gibson and George R. Petty, Jr. on "The Ordered Computer Collation of Unprepared Literary Text."

Y–35 **Shillingsburg, Peter L. *Scholarly Editing in the Computer Age.*** Athens: University of Georgia Press, 1986.
PN162.S45 1986

Originally a set of lectures delivered at the University of New South Wales, this work combines an exposition on Shillingsburg's thought on central topics in the theory of textual criticism with an analysis of the effects on editorial process which such thought has, and an introduction to the practical aids furnished by computer technology in both preparing and typesetting scholarly editions. Four appendixes give further information about TEX typesetting software and about generic typesetting codes. A Glossary and an Index conclude this generally well received exposition.

Y–36 **MLA. Center for Editions of American Authors [CEAA]. *Statement of Editorial Principles and Procedures.*** Rev. ed. New York: MLA, 1972.   PN162.M6 1972

The pamphlet, originally published in 1967 with the title *Statement of Editorial Principles: A Working Manual for Editing Nineteenth Century American Texts* [PN162.M6], gives a general statement of the editorial principles adopted by the CEAA which govern such questions as the choice of copytext, the collation of texts, the recording of variants, standards for explanatory or historical notes, introductions, proofreading, and the division of editorial responsibility. These principles make clear the conditions under which an edition may qualify for the seal of CEAA approval. A bibliographical essay, "Relevant Textual Scholarship," is appended.

The work of the CEAA has been controversial; indeed, the Center was transformed into the Center for Scholarly Editions in 1976. An introductory statement about the new CSE will be found in *PMLA* 92 (1977): 583–597. The most recent account of the CEAA and its controversial history is in G. Thomas Tanselle's "Recent Editorial Discussion and the Central Question of Editing," *SB* 34 (1981): 23–65. Other valuable treatments include Herschel Parker's "The CEAA: An Interim Assessment," *PBSA* 68 (1974): 129–148, and Tom Davis, "The CEAA and Modern Textual Editing," *Library*, 5th ser., 32 (1977): 61–74.

Y–37 **The Conference on Editorial Problems, The University of Toronto.** Toronto: University of Toronto Press; New York: Garland; and New York: AMS Press, 1966–.
LC numbers vary

These volumes contain papers generally by practicing editors given at the annual Toronto editing conference, which is focused each year on a particular set of problems or body of texts. Some of the volumes include bibliographies on the conference topic. The series to date is as follows:

1st (1965). *Editing Sixteenth-Century Texts*. Edited by R. J. Schoeck. 1966.   PN162.E3 1965aa

2d (1966). *Editing Nineteenth-Century Texts*. Edited by John M. Robson. 1967.   PN162.E3 1966aa

3d (1967). *Editing Eighteenth-Century Texts*. Edited by D. I. B. Smith. 1968.   PN162.E2 1967aa

4th (1968). *Editor, Author, and Publisher*. Edited by William J. Howard. 1969.   PN155.E3 1968aa

5th (1969). *Editing Twentieth-Century Texts*. Edited by Francess G. Halpenny. 1972.   PN162.E3 1969

6th (1970). *Editing Seventeenth-Century Prose*. Edited by D. I. B. Smith. 1972.   PN162.C62 1970

7th (1971). *Editing Texts of the Romantic Period*. Edited by John D. Baird. 1972.   PN162.C62 1971

8th (1972). *Editing Canadian Texts*. Edited by Francess G. Halpenny. 1975.   PN162.C62 1972

9th (1973). *Editing Eighteenth-Century Novels*. Edited by G. E. Bentley, Jr. 1975.   PN162.C62 1973

10th (1974). *Editing British and American Literature, 1880–1920*. Edited by Eric Domville. 1976.   PN162.C62 1974

11th (1975). *Editing Renaissance Dramatic Texts: English, Italian, Spanish*. Edited by Anne Lancashire. 1976.   PN162.C62 1975

12th (1976). *Editing Medieval Texts: English, French and Latin Written in England*. Edited by A. G. Rigg. 1977.   PN162.C62 1976

13th (1977). *Editing Nineteenth-Century Fiction*. Edited by Jane Millgate. 1978.   PN162.C62 1977

14th (1978). *Editing Correspondence*. Edited by J. A. Dainard. 1979.   PN162.C62 1978

15th (1979). *Editing Illustrated Books*. Edited by William F. Blissett. 1980.   PN162.C62 1979

16th (1980). *Editing Poetry from Spenser to Dryden*. Edited by A. H. de Quehen. 1981.   PN543.C6 1980

17th (1981). *Editing Texts in the History of Science and Medicine*. Edited by Trevor H. Levere. 1982.   T11.4.C66 1981

18th (1982). *Editing Polymaths Erasmus to Russell*.

19th (1983). *Editing Early English Drama: Special Problems and New Directions*. Edited by A. F. Johnston. 1987.   PR641.C66 1983

20th (1984). *Editing, Publishing, and Computer Technology*. Edited by Sharon Butler and William P. Stoneman, 1988.   PN162.C62 1984

21st (1985). *Editing and Editors: A Retrospect*. Edited by Richard Landon.   PN162.C62 1985

22d (1986). *Editing Modern Economists*. Edited by D. E. Moggridge. 1988.   HB199.C64 1986

23d (1987). *Editing Greek and Latin Texts*. Edited by John N. Grant.   PA47.C6 1987

24th (1988). *Crisis in Editing: Texts of the English Renaissance*. Edited by Randall McLeod.   PR418.T48 C66 1988

Y–38   Scholarly Journals in Bibliography and Textual Criticism and in the History of Printing and the Book Trade.

American Book Collector. Vol. 1–. New York: Moretus Press, 1980–. Reviews.   Z990.A52

AEB   *Analytical and Enumerative Bibliography*. Vol. 1–. DeKalb: Northern Illinois University Press for the Northern Illinois University Bibliographical Society, 1977–. 4/yr. Reviews. Bibliographical notices (see Y–15).   Z1007.A115

Bibliographical Society of America. Papers. See *Papers of the Bibliographical Society of America*.

Bibliography, Documentation, Terminology. Vol. 1–. 1961–. 6/yr.   Q223.U46a

Bibliography in Britain. Vols. 1–6. Oxford: Oxford Bibliographical Society, 1963–1968 (see Y–4).   Z1002.B617

BiN   *Bibliography Newsletter*. Vol. 1–. New York: Terry Belanger, 1973–. 12/yr. then 4/yr. Reviews. Bibliographical notices (see Y–12).   Z1219.B5

Bibliothek: A Scottish Journal of Bibliography and Allied Topics. Vol. 1–. Edinburgh: Library Association, Scottish Group, 1956–. 3/yr. plus annual supplement. Bibliography (see M–75). Z2057.A65

BC   *Book Collector*. Vol. 1–. London: Queen Anne Press, 1952–. 4/yr. Reviews.   Z990.B6

British Printer. Vol. 1–. London: Maclean Hunter, 1888–. 12/yr.   Z119.B86

BB   *Bulletin of Bibliography and Magazine Notes*. Vol. 1–. Boston: F. W. Faxon, 1897–. 4/yr. (see A–7).   Z1007.B94

Direction Line. No. 1–. Austin: Warner Barnes, Department of English, The University of Texas, 1975– (see Y–13).   No LC number

De gulden passer. Vol. 1–. Antwerp: Vereeniging der Antwerpsche Bibliophielen, 1923–.   Z1007.G93

Gutenberg Jahrbuch. Vol. 1–. Mainz: Gutenberg Gesellschaft, 1926–. 1/yr.   Z1008.G98

Het boek. Vol. 1–. The Hague: 1912–1969.

RIB   *Inter-American Review of Bibliography / Revista Interamericana de Bibliografia*. Vol. 1–. Washington, D.C.: Pan-American Union, 1951–. 4/yr.   Z1007.R4317

Journal of the Printing Historical Society [former title: *Printing Historical Society Newsletter, 1965-1980*]. Vol. 1–. London: Printing Historical Society, 1965–. 4/yr.   Z119.P95613

Library   *Library: A Quarterly Review of Bibliography* [the title has varied over the years]. 1st ser., 10 vols., 1889–1899; 2d ser., 10 vols., 1900–1909; 3d ser., 10 vols., 1910–1919; 4th ser., 26 vols., 1920–1946; 5th ser., 33 vols., 1946–1978; 6th ser., vol. 1–, 1979–. London and Oxford: Bibliographical Society, 1889–. 4/yr. Reviews. Bibliography of "Recent Books" and "Recent Periodicals" (see Y–2). *Index to the Bibliographical Papers Published by the Bibliographical Society* [London] *and the Library Association, London, 1877–1932*, by George W. Cole (Chicago: University of Chicago Press, for the Bibliographical Society of America, 1933).   Z1008.B585

LR   *Literary Research: A Journal of Scholarly Method and Technique* [former title, *Literary Research Newsletter, 1976–1985*]. Vol. 1–. College Park, Md.: Literary Research Association, The University of Maryland, 1976–. 4/yr. Reviews. Bibliographical notices (see Y–14).   PN73.L57

PBSA   *Papers of the Bibliographical Society of America*. Vol. 1–. New York: The Bibliographical Society of America, 1899–. 4/yr. Reviews. Indexes to volumes 1–25 (Chicago: The Society, 1931) and 26–45 (New York: The Society, 1954).   Z1008.B51P

Printing History: The Journal of the American Printing History Association. Vol. 1–. New York: The Association, 1979–.   No LC number

Proceedings and Papers of the Oxford Bibliographical Society. Vol. 1–. Oxford: Oxford University Press, 1923. 1/yr.   Z1008.O98

Proof   *Proof: Yearbook of American Bibliographical and Textual Studies*. Vol. 1–7. Columbia: University of South Carolina, 1971–1977. Reviews. "The Register of Current Publications" (see Y–5).   Z1219.P73

Publishing History: The Social, Economic, and Literary History of Book, Newspaper, and Magazine Publishing. Vol. 1–. Cambridge: Chadwyck-Healey, 1977–. 2/yr. Index 1977–1981 in issue 10.
Z280.P8

Quarendo. Vol. 1–. Amsterdam: Theatrum Orbis Terrarum, 1971–. 4/yr.

RQ   *R.Q. [Reference Quarterly].* Vol. 1–. Chicago: Reference Services Division, American Library Association, 1960–. 4/yr. Reviews. Bibliographical notices. Z671.R23

Scriptorium: Revue internationale des études relatifs aux manuscrits. Vol. 1–. Ghent: E. Story-Scientia, 1946/47–. 2/yr. (see H–8). Z108.S35

Studi e problemi di critica testuale. Vol. 1–. Bologna: Casa de Risparmio, 1970–. 2/yr. P47.S7

SB   *Studies in Bibliography: Papers of the Bibliographical Society of Virginia.* Vol. 1–. Charlottesville: Bibliographical Society of the University of Virginia, 1946–. 1/yr. Reviews. Annual Bibliography (see Y–3). Z1008.V55

Text: Transactions of the Society for Textual Scholarship. Vol. 1–. New York: AMS Press, 1983–. 1/yr.

Transactions of the Bibliographical Society, London. Vols. 1–15. London: Bibliographical Society, 1893–1920. From 1920, incorporated into the *Library.* Z1008.B587

TCBS   *Transactions of the Cambridge Bibliographical Society.* Vol. 1–. Cambridge: Cambridge University Press, 1949–. 1/yr. Z1008.C2

Transactions of the Edinburgh Bibliographical Society [former title: *Publications of the ... , 1896-1935].* Vol. 16–. Edinburgh: For the Society, 1938–. Z1008.E24

Visible Language [former title, *Journal of Typographic Research*, vols. 1–4, 1967–1970]. Vol. 1–. Cleveland: Press of Case Western Reserve University, 1967–. 4/yr. Z119.J88

For a list of other journals, both current and defunct, concerned with bibliography and textual criticism, along with information about their inclusion in available indexes, see G. Thomas Tanselle, "The Periodical Literature of English and American Bibliography," *SB* 26 (1973): 167–191.

Y–39 Some Frequently Recommended Works in Analytical and Descriptive Bibliography and in Textual Criticism.

Bieler. Ludwig. "The Grammarian's Craft," Rev. ed. *Folia: Studies in the Christian Perpetuation of the Classics* 10 (1958): 3–42.

Bloy, Colin H. *History of Printing Ink, Balls, and Rollers, 1440–1850.* Barnet, Herts: Wynkyn de Worde Society, 1967. TP949.B55

Carter, H. *View of Early Typography [to ca. 1600].* Oxford: Clarendon Press, 1969. Z250.A2 C36

Chapman, R. W. *Cancels: With Eleven Facsimiles in Collotype.* London: Constable and Co., 1930.
Z242.C2 C4

Chaytor, H. J. *From Script to Print: An Introduction to Medieval Vernacular Literature.* Cambridge: W. Heffer, 1966. PN671.C5 1966

Clark, A. C. *Descent of Manuscripts.* Oxford: Clarendon Press, 1918. PA47.C45

D'Amico, John F. *Theory and Practice in Renaissance Textual Criticism: Beatus Rhenanus between Conjecture and History.* Berkeley and Los Angeles: University of California Press, 1988. PA47.D35 1988

Diehl, Edith. *Bookbinding: Its Background and Technique.* 2 vols. New York: Rinehart, 1946. Z266.D5

Foxon, David H. *Thomas J. Wise and the Pre-Restoration Drama: A Study in Theft and Sophistication.* London: Bibliographical Society, 1959. See also the supplement by Foxon and William B. Todd, *Library*, 5th ser., 16 (1961): 287–293. Z989.W8 F6

Froger, Dom J. *La Critique des textes et son automatisation.* Paris: Dunod, 1968. PN98.E4 F7

Gabler, Hans Walter. "The Synchrony and Diachrony of Texts: Practice and Theory of the Critical Edition of James Joyce's *Ulysses* [see M–60]," *Text* 1 (1981): 305–326.

Greg, W. W. *Calculus of Variants: An Essay on Textual Criticism.* Oxford: Clarendon Press, 1927. PA47.G7

––––––. *Collected Papers.* Edited by J. C. Maxwell. Oxford: Clarendon Press, 1966.
PR99.G6845 A16 1966

––––––. *Editorial Problem in Shakespeare: A Survey of the Foundations of the Text.* 3d ed. Oxford: Clarendon Press, 1954.

Haebler, Konrad. *Study of Incunabula.* [Poor] translation by Lucy E. Osborne of *Handbuch der Inkunabel-Kunde* (Leipzig: Hiersemann, 1925). New York: Grolier Club, 1933. Z240.H132E

Hill, T. H. "Spelling and the Bibliographer." *Library*, 5th ser., 18 (1963): 1–28.

Hinman, Charlton. *Printing and Proof-reading of the First Folio of Shakespeare.* 2 vols. Oxford: Clarendon Press, 1963. Z8813.H5

Honigman, E. A. J. *Stability of Shakespeare's Text.* London: E. Arnold, 1965. PR3071.H6 1965a

Hosley, Richard, et al. *Shakespeare Variorum Handbook: A Manual of Editorial Practice.* New York: MLA, 1971. PR3071.H8055

Housman, A. E. "Application of Thought to Textual Criticism" (1972), in *Classical Papers of A. E. Housman*, ed. by J. Diggle and F. R. D. Goodyear. 3 vols. Cambridge: Cambridge University Press, 1972.
PA27.H7 1972

––––––. *Selected Prose.* Edited by John Carter. Cambridge: Cambridge University Press, 1961.
PR4809.H15 A6 1961

Jackson, W. A. *Bibliography and Literary Studies.* Los Angeles: School of Librarianship, University of California, 1962. Z1005.J3

Kenney, E. J. *Classical Text: Aspects of Editing in the Age of the Printed Book.* Berkeley, Los Angeles and London: University of California Press, 1974. P47.K45

Kline, Mary-Jo. *Guide to Documentary Editing.* Baltimore: Johns Hopkins University Press, 1987.
Z113.3.K55 1987

Luck, Georg. "Textual Criticism Today." *American Journal of Philology* 102 (1981): 164–194.

Maas, Paul. *Textual Criticism.* Translation by Barbara Flower of *Textkritik*, 3d ed. (Leipzig: Teubner, 1957). Oxford: Clarendon Press, 1958. PA47.M213

McGann, Jermoe J. *Critique of Modern Textual Criticism.* Chicago: University of Chicago Press, 1983.
P47.M34 1983

———, ed. *Textual Criticism and Literary Interpretation.* Chicago: University of Chicago Press, 1985.
PR7.T49 1985

McKenzie, D. F. *Bibliography and the Sociology of Texts.* The Panizzi Lectures 1985. London: The British Library, 1986.
No LC number

———. *Cambridge University Press, 1696–1712.* 2 vols. Cambridge: Cambridge University Press, 1966.
Z325.C26 M3

———. "Printers of the Mind: Some Notes on Bibliographical Theories and Printing-House Practices." *SB* 22 (1969): 1–75.

McKerrow, R. B. *Prolegomena for the Oxford Shakespeare.* Oxford: Clarendon Press, 1939.   PR3071.M248

Metzger, Bruce M. *Text of the New Testament.* Oxford: Clarendon Press, 1968.   BS2325.M4 1968b

Moorman, Charles. *Editing the Middle English Manuscript.* Jackson: University Press of Mississippi, 1975. Use with caution; adversely reviewed.   PR275.T45 M6

Moyles, R. G. *Text of* Paradise Lost: *A Study in Editorial Procedure.* Toronto: University of Toronto Press, 1985.   PR3562.M67 1985

Paper, Herbert H., ed. *Language and Texts: The Nature of Linguistic Evidence.* Ann Arbor: Center for Coordination of Ancient and Modern Studies, University of Michigan, 1975.   No LC number

Parker, Hershel. *Flawed Texts and Verbal Icons: Literary Authority in American Fiction.* Evanston, Ill.: Northwestern University Press, 1984.
PS374.T48 P37 1984

Pasquali, Giorgio. *Storia della tradizione e critica del testo.* 2d ed. Florence: Le Monnier, 1952.   PA47.P3 1952

Pearsall, Derek, ed. *Manuscripts and Texts: Editorial Problems in Later Middle English Literature.* Cambridge, Eng.: D. S. Brewer, 1989.   PR275.T45 M37 1987

Peckham, Morse. "Reflections on the Foundations of Modern Textual Editing." *Proof* 1 (1971): 122–155.

Povey, Kenneth. "A Century of Press Figures." *Library,* 5th ser., 14 (1959): 251–273.

Quentin, Dom Henri. *Essais de critique textuelle.* Paris, 1926.

———. *Mémoire sur l'établissement du texte de la vulgate.* Rome: Desder et cie, 1922.   BS85.Q4

Reynolds, L. D., and N. G. Wilson. *Scribes and Scholars: A Guide to the Transmission of Greek and Latin Literature.* 2d ed., rev. and enl. Oxford: Clarendon Press, 1974.   Z40.R4 1974

Ruggiers, Paul G. *Editing Chaucer: The Great Tradition.* Norman, Okla.: Pilgrim Books, 1984.
PR1939.E3 1984

Simpson, Percy. *Proof-reading in the Sixteenth, Seventeenth, and Eighteenth Centuries.* Oxford: Clarendon Press, 1935.   Z254.S625

Stählin, Otto. *Editionstechnik.* 2d ed. Leipzig: Teubner, 1914.

Thorpe, James. *Watching the P's and Q's: Editorial Treatment of Accidentals.* Lawrence: University of Kansas, 1971.   P47.T52

Timpanaro, S. *Die Entstehung der Lachmannschen Methode.* 2d ed., rev. Translation by Dieter Irmer of *La genesi del metado del Lachmann* (Florence: Le Monnier, 1958). Hamburg: Helmut Buske Verlag, 1971. Bibliography.   PT67.L2 T4

Todd, William B. "Observations on the Incidence and Interpretation of Press Figures," *SB* 3 (1950/51): 171–205.

Turner, Robert K., Jr. "Reappearing Types as Bibliographical Evidence." *SB* 19 (1966): 198–209.

Updike, Daniel B. *Printing Types: Their History, Forms, and Use: A Study in Survivals.* 3d ed. 2 vols. Cambridge: Harvard University Press, 1962. Extremely out-of-date.   Z250.A2 U6 1962

Vander Meulen, David L. "The Identification of Paper Without Watermarks: The Example of Pope's *Dunciad.*" *SB* 37 (1984): 58–81.

Wells, Stanley. *Modernizing Shakespeare's Spelling.* Oxford: Clarendon Press, 1979.   PR3071.W4 1979

West, Martin l. *Textual Criticism and Editorial Technique Applicable to Greek and Latin Texts.* Stuttgart: Teubner, 1973.   PA47.W4

Willis, James. *Latin Textual Criticism.* Urbana: University of Illinois Press, 1972.   PA3013.W5

Wilson, F. P. *Shakespeare and the New Bibliography.* Rev. ed. Edited by Helen Gardner. Oxford: Clarendon Press, 1970.   PR3071.W5 1970

Zeller, Hans. "A New Approach to the Critical Constitution of Literary Texts." *SB* 28 (1975): 231–264.

III.   THE HISTORY OF PRINTING AND THE BOOK TRADE

The references cited in section C, National Bibliography, are indispensable to study of the book trade. See also works on the history of taste and related matters in K–92 and on the sociology of literature in X–65, X–66, and X–69.

Y–40   **Glaister, Geoffrey A.   *Glaister's Glossary of the Book: Terms Used in Papermaking, Printing, Bookbinding and Publishing with Notes on Illuminated Manuscripts and Private Presses.*** 2d ed. Berkeley, Los Angeles, London: University of California Press, 1979.   Z118.G55 1979

Originally published in 1960, this massive volume presents a total of 3,932 long, well-illustrated, documented articles on persons, societies, terms, techniques, tools, and processes associated with the production and distribution of books. This series of articles from the letter H will illustrate the volume's range: Half-bound; Half-tone process; Hand composition; Hand press; Harley, Robert; Hawthorden Prize; Headline; Hebrew printing before 1600; Heraldic colors; Hic nullus est defectus; Historische Kommission des Börsenvereins des deutschen Buchhandels; Hoe; Holbein, Hans; Hogarth Press; Humanistic scripts. There are four appendixes: Some Type Specimens: Latin Place Names As Used in the Imprints of Early Printed Books; Proof Correction Symbols; and a Short Reading List (disposed into sections on The Manuscript Book, Calligraphy, Illumination; The Book Trade, Publishing, Bookselling, Reading; Printing History; Printing Technology and Management; Book Design, Typography, Illustration, Private Presses; Bookbinding; and Paper Technology).

Y–41   **Feather, John.   *Dictionary of Book History.*** New York: Oxford University Press, 1987.   Z1006.F38 1986

This volume contains sixty-five articles on such broad general topics as bibliographies and bibliographical societies; the history of printing, publishing, and bookselling; famous books; bestiaries; Bibles; and writing in the ancient world.

Y–42   **Bigmore, Edward C., and Charles William Henry Wyman.   *Bibliography of Printing with Notes and Illustrations.*** 3 vols. London: Quaritch, 1880–1886.   Z117.B59

This bibliography remains the standard work for materials to 1800. Entries are arranged alphabetically by author and contain biographical, historical, and descriptive annotations. For nineteenth- and twentieth-century publications see Douglas C. McMurtrie, ed., *Invention of Printing: A Bibliography* (Chicago: Chicago Club of Printing House Craftsmen, 1942) [Z117.M18] which contains a total of 3,228 items disposed into eight sections and numerous subdivisions. It concludes with an index of authors.

The catalogs of the major special collections on the history of printing provide another source of bibliography. Of these, the most important are the *Catalogue of the Technical Reference Library of Works on Printing and the Allied Arts of the St. Bride Institute* (London: The Institute, 1919) [Z117.S216]; the *Catalogue of Periodicals Relating to Printing and Allied Subjects in the Technical Library of the St. Bride Institute* (London: The Institute, 1951) [Z119.S3]; and the *Dictionary Catalog of the History of Printing from the John M. Wing Foundation in the Newberry Library*, 6 vols. (Boston: G. K. Hall, 1961) [Z117.N54]. See also the *History of Printing from Its Beginnings to 1930: The Subject Catalogue of the American Type Founders Company in the Columbia University Libraries*, 4 vols. (Milwood, N.Y.: Kraus International, 1980) [Z117.C65 1980].

Y–43 **Steinberg, S. H.** *Five Hundred Years of Printing.* 3d ed. Revised by James Moran. Harmondsworth: Penguin Books, 1974. Z124.S8 1974

This volume, first published in 1955, is written from the perspective of a historian of culture. A standard work, it is generally regarded as the most satisfactory available history of printing. It is in three main parts, treating the first century of printing, the era of consolidation, and the nineteenth century and after. The third edition includes coverage of recent technological advances including web-offset lithography and computerized composition. A brief bibliography, bibliographical notes, and an index of names conclude the work.

Another, older single-volume history is by Svend Dahl, *History of the Book*, 2d English ed., rev. (Metuchen, N.J.: Scarecrow Press, 1968) [Z4.D133 1968], which treats the history of printing in the context of bookmaking from classical antiquity to the mid-twentieth century. It concludes with a classified bibliography and an index of names, titles, and subjects. Other histories include Douglas C. McMurtrie, the *Book: The Story of Printing and Bookmaking*, 3d ed., rev. (New York: Oxford University Press, 1943) [Z4.M15]; and Norman E. Binn, an *Introduction to Historical Bibliography*, 2d ed., rev. (London: Association of Assistant Librarians, 1962) [Z4.B55], which contains bibliographies at the end of each chapter.

The most recent chronology is by Colin Clair, *Chronology of Printing* (London: Cassell, 1969) [Z124.C6 1969b], which records events by year from A.D. 105 through 1967 and concludes with an index of names, titles, and subjects. Other chronologies include W. Turner Berry and H. E. Poole, *Annals of Printing: A Chronological Encyclopaedia from the Earliest Times to 1950* (London: Blandford Press, 1966) [Z124.B45], which must, however, be used with caution. It contains both a bibliography and an index.

Clair has also prepared a *History of European Printing* (London: Academic Press, 1976) [Z124.C614], which contains thirty-three chapters. This work stresses Renaissance developments and has a somewhat abbreviated account of developments in Britain because they are more fully treated in Clair's *History of Printing in Britain* (Y–48). There are appendixes on fifteenth-century presses and on when and where the first books were printed; a classified bibliography; and an index of names, titles, and subjects.

For contemporary printing see Victor Strauss, the *Printing Industry: An Introduction to Its Many Branches, Processes, and Products* (Washington, D.C.: Printing Industries of America, 1967) [Z244.S873], which contains a series of arti-

cles on broad topics including modern printing processes and methods, printing presses, and other aspects of contemporary technology. Extensively illustrated, the volume contains both a selected bibliography and bibliographical notes, as well as a detailed subject index.

Y–44 **Mumby, Frank Arthur, and Ian Norrie.** *Publishing and Bookselling: A History from the Earliest Times to the Present Day.* 5th ed., rev. London: Cape, 1974. Z323.M95 1974

Originally published in 1910 as the *Romance of Bookselling*, this work is in two parts: part 1, From the Earliest Times to 1870, is by Mumby; part 2, by Ian Norrie, treats the period 1820–1970. The first part is in thirteen chapters; the second in four sections treating 1820–1901, 1901–1939, 1939–1950, and 1950–1970 respectively. The focus is on the book trade in Britain. A series of appendixes, a ninety-page "Bibliography of Publishing and Bookselling" by William Peet with additions by F. A. Mumby, and an index of names and titles conclude the volume. The bibliography is alphabetical by author, with brief annotations.

Y–45 **Brenni, Vito Joseph.** *Book Printing in Britain and America: A Guide to the Literature and a Directory of Printers.* Westport, Conn.: Greenwood Press, 1983. Z151.B68

This work presents a selective bibliography of works concerned with the history of printing. There are separate sections for Britain and America, and within sections, entries are grouped by type of reference work (printing manuals, type specimen books, etc.) or by historical period covered. There are sections treating the printing of music, religious and scientific publishing, writing, and calligraphy. The directory of printers, typographers, calligraphers, and book designers gives an identifying phrase and dates when known. Three checklists follow: General Works on Writing, Printing and Typography; Selected Titles on British Printing, Typography, Book Design, and Writing; and Selected Titles on American Printing, Typography, Book Design, and Writing. Author and subject indexes conclude the volume.

Y–46 **Myers, Robin.** *British Book Trade from Caxton to the Present Day: A Bibliographical Guide Based on the Libraries of the National Book League and St. Bride Institute.* London: Deutsch in association with the National Book League, 1973. Z324.M9

This volume is valuable for the trenchant descriptive and evaluative annotations of its entries, which are disposed into an elaborate classification containing thirteen main sections, as follows: I. Authorship; II. Bookbinding; III. Bookselling (A. History of New Bookselling, B. Bookselling Practice and Organization, C. Antiquarian Bookselling); IV. Book Design and Production; V. Book Illustration; VI. History of the Book Trade; VII. Children's Books; VIII. Law Relating to the Book Trade; IX. The Net Book Agreement; X. Paper for Bookwork and Printing Ink; XI. The Printing of Books (with extensive subdivisions); XII. Private Presses; and XIII. Publishing (A. The History of Publishing, B. Practical Publishing). Elaborate subdivisions include general and specific sections, treating, for example, book illustration in general, and then works on particular illustrators. The volume concludes with an analytical index of names and titles.

Y–47 **Plant, Marjorie.** *English Book Trade: An Economic History of the Making and Sale of Books.* 3d ed. London: Allen and Unwin, 1974.   Z152.E5 P55 1974

This work, the first edition of which was published in 1939, is in two main parts. The first, The Age of Hand Printing, contains chapters on such matters as the demand for books, the division of labor in the printing industry, the structure of the industry, and the supply of paper. Part 2, The Application of Mechanical Power, contains chapters on such issues as modern labor conditions, the rise of trade unions, the cost of books, and copyright and competition. The total of twenty-one chapters are provided with end references; a subject index concludes the volume.

Y–48 **Clair, Colin.** *History of Printing in Britain.* London: Oxford University Press, 1965.   Z151.C55 1965

This outline history of the development of printing since Caxton is disposed in fourteen chapters with notes, and index of names, titles, and subjects. See also Clair's *Chronology of Printing* and *History of European Printing* (Y–43).

Y–49 **Guide to English Book-Trade Lists** [in chronological order].

Duff, E. Gordon. *Century of the English Book Trade: Short Notices of all Printers, Stationers, Book-Binders, and Others Connected with It from the Issue of the First Dated Book in 1457 to the Incorporation of the Company of Stationers in 1557.* London: Bibliographical Society, 1905.   Z151.2.D83

————. *English Provincial Printers, Stationers and Book-Binders to 1557.* Cambridge: Cambridge University Press, 1912.   Z151.D87

Duff, E. Gordon, et al. *Hand-Lists of Books Printed by English Printers, 1501–1556.* 4 parts in 1 vol. London: For the Bibliographical Society, 1895–1913.
                    Z152.L8 B5

McKerrow, R. B. *Dictionary of Printers and Booksellers in England, Scotland, and Ireland, and of Foreign Printers of English Books, 1557–1640.* London: Bibliographical Society, 1910.   Z151.D51

Plomer, Henry R. *Dictionary of the Booksellers and Printers Who Were at Work in England, Scotland, and Ireland from 1641 to 1667.* London: Bibliographical Society, 1907.   Z151.D52

————, et al. *Dictionary of the Printers and Booksellers Who Were at Work in England, Scotland, and Ireland from 1668 to 1725.* Edited by Arundell Esdaile. London: Oxford University Press for the Bibliographical Society, 1922.   Z151.D53

————, et al. *Dictionary of the Printers and Booksellers Who Were at Work in England, Scotland, and Ireland from 1726 to 1775.* London: Oxford University Press for the Bibliographical Society, 1932.   Z151.D54

Alden, John. "Pills and Publishing: Some Notes on the English Book Trade 1660–1715." *Library,* 5th ser., 7 (1957): 21–37.

Carnie, Robert Hay, and Ronald Patterson Doig. "Scottish Printers and Booksellers, 1668–1775: A Supplement." *SB* 12 (1959): 131–159; "A Second Supplement." *SB* 14 (1961): 81–96; *SB* 15 (1962): 105–120.

Maxted, Ian. *British Book Trades, 1710–1777: An Index of the Masters and Apprentices Recorded in the Inland Revenue Registers at the Public Record Office, Kew.* Exeter, Devon: I. Maxted, 1983.   Z325.M39 1983

————. *London Book Trades, 1735–1775: A Checklist of Members in Trade Directories and in Musgrave's "Obituary."* Exeter, Devon: I. Maxted, 1984.
                    Z330.6.L6 M39 1984

————. *London Book Trades 1775–1800: A Preliminary Checklist of Members.* Folkestone: Dawson, 1977.
                    Z152.L8 M39

Todd, William B. "London Printers' Imprints, 1800–1840." *Library,* 5th ser., 21 (1966): 46–59.

See also the Indexes by Paul G. Morrison to printers, publishers, and booksellers cited in the *STC* (C–5) and in Wing (C–7).

The "British Book Trade Index" project now under way at the Library of the University of Newcastle-upon-Tyne will convert all records of persons working in the book trade in Britain to 1850 into machine-readable form. Chairman of the project, from whom further information can be obtained, is Professor Peter Isaac at the University of Newcastle-upon-Tyne.

Y–50 **Lehman-Haupt, Hellmut, et al.** *Book in America: A History of the Making and Selling of Books in the United States.* 2d ed. New York: R. R. Bowker, 1951. Z473.L522

Originally published in 1939, this volume is in three sections. Part 1, Book Production and Distribution from the Beginning to the American Revolution, is by Lawrence C. Wroth. Part 2, Book Production and Distribution from the American Revolution to the War between the States, is by Wroth and Rollo G. Silver. Part 3, by Lehman-Haupt, concerns Book Production and Distribution from 1860 to the Present Day. A bibliography prepared by Janet Bogardus is divided into five main sections, Cultural History, Bibliography, Printing and Book Making, Book Illustration, and Bookselling and Publishing, with numerous subdivisions. It occupies forty-two double-column pages. An index concludes the volume. Note that some sections published in the first edition have been deleted from the second.

See also the separately published volumes by Lawrence C. Wroth, *Colonial Printer* (Portland, Me.: The Southworth-Anthoensen Press, 1938) [Z208.W95 1938], and by Rollo G. Silver, *American Printer 1787–1825* (Charlottesville: University Press of Virginia, 1967) [Z208.S5].

Y–51 **Tebbel, John W.** *History of Book Publishing in the United States.* 4 vols. New York: R. R. Bowker, 1972–1981.
                    Z473.T42

These volumes present the most elaborate and comprehensive treatment available of American publishing. Volume 1, the *Creation of an Industry, 1630–1865,* is in four parts: Colonial Beginnings, 17th Century Printing and Publishing, Printing and Publishing in the 18th Century, and The Rise of Modern Publishing. Volume 2, the *Expansion of an Industry, 1865–1919,* gives a general overview of nineteenth- and early-twentieth-century publishing and then focuses on individual regions, publishing houses, and types of special publishers. Similar movement from general to particular characterizes volume 3, the *Golden Age between Two Wars, 1920–1940.* Volume 4 chronicles the *Great Change, 1940–1980.* Each volume has extensive bibliographical footnotes and an index of authors, titles, and subjects.

Y–52 **Guide to American Book-Trade Lists.**

See the index by R. P. Bristol of printers, publishers, and booksellers cited in Evans (C–22): as well as the enumeration of American book trade bibliographies in Tanselle's *Guide to the Study of United States Imprints* (C–20).

Y–53 **Dzwonkoski, Peter, ed.** *American Literary Publishing Houses, 1638–1899, Dictionary of Literary Biography.* vol. 49 in 2 parts (Part 1: A-M; Part 2: N-Z). Detroit: Gale Research, 1986. Z479.A448 1986

These volumes contain historical and publishing information on more than three hundred firms that have had some literary impact on American culture, including publishers of fiction, poetry, criticism, drama, literary biography, and reference works.

Y–54 **Dzwonkoski, Peter, ed.** *American Literary Publishing Houses, 1900–1980: Trade and Paperback. Dictionary of Literary Biography,* vol. 46. Detroit: Gale Research, 1986. Z479.A45 1986

This work traces the history of twentieth-century trade, mass market, and children's book publishers.

Y–56 **Carter, John.** *ABC For Book Collectors.* 6th ed. with corr. and add. by Nicholas Barker. London: Granada, 1980. Z1006.C37 1980

This volume presents in alphabetical order articles on terms concerning bibliography, textual studies, printing, book illustration, bookbinding, and booktrade history which are of interest to book collectors, along with terms special to the art of book collecting. Foreign terms are not included; cross-references are made from articles to terms defined elsewhere which are used in those articles. An example of the scope of this dictionary will be seen in this list of entries under the letter H: Hain, Half Bound, Half Cloth, Half-Sheets, Half-Title, Halkett and Laing, Hand-List, Hard-Grain Morocco, Harlian Style of Binding, Headband, Headline, Head-Piece, High-Spots, Hinges, Historiated, Hollow Backs, Holograph, Horae or Books of Hours, Horn-Book.

Among other dictionaries of terms may be mentioned the *Dictionary of Printing Terms* (Prague: SNTL, 1976) [Z118.D52 1976]; Jean Peters, *Bookman's Glossary*, 6th ed., rev. and enl. (New York: Bowker, 1983) [Z118.B75 1983]; *Bookbinding and the Conservation of Books*: *A Dictionary of Descriptive Terminology* by Matt Roberts and Don Etherington (Washington, D.C.: Library of Congress, 1982) [Z266.7.R62 1982]; and Horst Kunze and Gotthard Rückl, *Lexikon des Bibliothekswesens* (Leipzig: VEB Verlag für Buch- und Bibliothekswesen, 1969) [Z1006.L46].

Y–57 **Orne, Jerrold.** *Language of the Foreign Book Trade: Abbreviations, Terms, Phrases.* 3d ed. Chicago: American Library Association, 1976. Z1006.07 1976

This volume, the first edition of which appeared in 1949, treats some 26,000 terms taken from the following languages: French, German, Italian, Spanish, Dano-Norwegian, Swedish, Dutch, Russian, Finnish, Hungarian, Rumanian. Terms are listed alphabetically in individual language sections; there are no cross-references among terms, so that this is not a polyglot dictionary but a dictionary of English equivalents for foreign book-trade terms. More comprehensive than Orne is C. G. Allen, *Manual of European Languages for Librarians* (New York: Bowker, 1975) [P380.A4].

For a polyglot dictionary of the book trade see Menno Hertzberger, ed., *Dictionary for the Antiquarian Booktrade in French, English, German, Swedish, Danish, Italian, Spanish, and Dutch and Japanese.* (Tokyo: Antiquarian Booksellers Association, 1977) [Z282.5.D5 1977], a Japanese revised edition of a dictionary first published by the International League of Antiquarian Booksellers in Paris, 1956 [Z282.D5].

Y–59 **Some Frequently Recommended Works on the History of Printing and the Book Trade and on the Cultural Significance of the Book.**

Archives of British and American Publishers on Microfilm with Printed Indexes. Cambridge, Eng.: Chadwyck-Healey.

Bidwell, John, ed. *Nineteenth-Century Book Arts and Printing History.* 23 vols. New York: Garland, 1979–1981. LC numbers vary

Bland, David. *History of Book Illustration.* 2d ed. London: Faber and Faber, 1969. NC760.B62 1969

———. *Illustration of Books.* 3d ed. London: Faber and Faber, 1962. Z1023.B63 1962

Bühler, Curt F. *Fifteenth Century Book.* Philadelphia: University of Pennsylvania Press, 1960.

Z240.B924 1960

Carpenter, Kenneth E., ed. *Books and Society in History.* New York: Bowker, 1983. Z280.B66 1983

Clanchy, Michael T. *From Memory to Written Record: England 1066–1307.* Cambridge: Harvard University Press, 1979. DA185.C52

Coser, Lewis, et al. *Books: The Culture and Commerce of Publishing.* New York: Basic Books, 1982.

Z471.C69

Cressy, David. *Literacy and the Social Order: Reading and Writing in Tudor and Stuart England.* Cambridge: Cambridge University Press, 1980. LC156.G7 C73

Darnton, Robert. *Business of Enlightenment: A Publishing History of the Encyclopédie, 1775–1800.* Cambridge: Belknap Press of Harvard University Press, 1979.

AE25.E6 D37

Dictionary Catalogue of the History of Printing from the John M. Wing Foundation in the Newberry Library. 9 vols. Boston: G. K. Hall, 1961, 1970. Z117.N54

Diringer, David. *Hand-Produced Book.* London: Hutchinson's Scientific and Technical Publications, 1953. Z6.D57

Dudek, Louis. *Literature and the Press: A History of Printing, Printed Media, and Their Relation to Literature.* Toronto: Ryerson Press, 1960. Z151.D83 1960

Eisenstein, Elizabeth. *Printing Press as an Agent of Change: Communications and Cultural Transformations in Early Modern Europe.* 2 vols. Cambridge: Cambridge University Press, 1979. Extensive bibliographical index. Z124.E37

———. *Printing Revolution in Early Modern Europe.* Cambridge: Cambridge University Press, 1983. An abridgement of *Printing Press.* . . . Z124.E374 1983

Febvre, Lucien P.V., and Henri-Jean Martin. *Coming of the Book: The Impact of Printing, 1450–1800.* Translation by David Gerard of *L'apparition du livre* (Paris: Editions A. Michel, 1958). New ed. Edited by Geoffrey Nowell-Smith and David Wooton. Atlantic Highlands, N.J.: Humanities Press, 1976.

Z4.F413 1976

Gaskell, Philip, G. Barber, and G. Warrilow. "An Annotated List of Printers' Manuals to 1850." *Journal of the Printing Historical Society* 4 (1968): 11–32.

Goldschmidt, E. P. *Printed Book of the Renaissance.* Cambridge: Cambridge University Press, 1950.

Graff, Haney J. *Literacy Myth: Literacy and the Social Structure in the Nineteenth-Century City.* New York: Academic Press, 1979. LC154.2.O6 G72

Hirsch, R. *Printing, Selling, and Reading, 1450–1550.* Wiesbaden: Harrassowitz, 1967. Z126.H65

Joyce, William L., et al., eds. *Printing and Society in Early America.* Worcester, Mass.: American Antiquarian Society, 1983. Z208.P74 1983

McLuhan, Marshall. *Gutenberg Galaxy: The Making of Typographic Man.* Toronto: University of Toronto Press, 1962. Z116.M15

Moran, James. *Composition of Reading Matter.* London: Wace, 1965. Z253.M78

———. *Printing Presses: History and Development from the 15th Century to Modern Times.* Berkeley, Los Angeles, London: University of California Press, 1973. Bibliography. Z249.M748 1973

Pollard, H. G., and A. Ehrman. *Distribution of Books by Catalogue from the Invention of Printing to A.D. 1800.* Cambridge: Privately printed, 1965. PR1105.R7 1965

Resnick, Daniel P. *Literacy in Historical Perspective.* Washington, D.C.: Library of Congress, 1983. LC149.L499 1983

Vervliet, Hendrik D. L., ed. *Book through Five Thousand Years: A Survey by Fernand Baudin et al.* London: Phaidon, 1972. Z4.V46

Wiles, Roy M. *Serial Publication in England Before 1750.* Cambridge: Cambridge University Press, 1957. Z323.W5

IV. RARE AND USED BOOK TRADE—CATALOGS AND SALE RECORDS

Y–60 **British Museum. Department of Printed Books. *List of Catalogues of English Book Sales, 1676–1900, Now in the British Museum.*** Compiled by Harold Mattingly and A. K. Burnett. London: Milford, 1915. Z988.B87

This volume presents a chronological list of about 8,000 catalogs listed under the names of their owners or the sale catalog titles if their owners are not known. Entries give the dates of sales and the names of auction firms and indicate whether pricing has been noted in the catalogs or not. There is a supplementary list on pages 441–447. The whole of this list is supplemented by the *Union List* compiled by Munby and Coral (Y–61).

Y–61 **Munby, A. N. L., and Lenore Coral. *British Book Sale Catalogues, 1676–1800: A Union List.*** London: Mansell, 1977. Z999.5.M86

This volume supplements but does not supersede the list of sale catalogs in the British Museum (Y–60). For the period from 1676, the date of the first known sale by auction, to 1800, it enlarges the original list's coverage by several thousand additional items. Entries are chronological by the date of the sale's commencement. Identified are the name of the consignor, a brief title of the sale, information on the conduct of the sale if it was not an auction, the name of the auctioneer or seller, the location of the sale, sigla identifying collections holding a copy of the catalog, and information on the catalog's inclusion in other published bibliographies and on whether it has been reprinted. The volume concludes with some addenda, an index of consignors, and an auctioneers and booksellers index. Volumes treating nineteenth-century sale catalogs are in preparation.

Y–63 **McKay, George L. *American Book Auction Catalogues, 1713–1934: A Union List.*** New York: New York Public Library, 1937. Reprinted with additions from the *Bulletin of the New York Public Library* 50 (1945): 177–184, and 52 (1948): 401–412. Detroit: Gale Research Co., 1967. Z999.M15 1967

The original list and its supplements cite a total of 10,361 sale catalogs. An appendix lists a total of 482 seventeenth- and eighteenth-century sales for which catalogs are not known to have been compiled. Entries, arranged chronologically, give the names of owners, sale dates, and names of auction firms, indicate the presence or absence of pricing in the catalog, give the numbers of pages and lots in the catalogs, and indicate whether names of owners of copies are given. Reference is made to newspaper and book accounts of sales for which catalogs are no longer extant and to articles about sales for which there were presumably no catalogs issued. A list of auctioneers and auction firms with their various names, addresses, and dates of business are given, along with an index of owners. The supplementary lists are not indexed.

Y–65 **Munby, A. N. L., ed. *Sale Catalogues of the Libraries of Eminent Persons.*** 12 vols. London: Mansell and Sotheby-Parke-Bernet, 1971–1975. Z988.S25

These volumes present reprints of rare catalogs of the sales of libraries of persons of note, accompanied with introductions by specialists. Where possible, the catalog copy chosen for reproduction is annotated with prices paid and purchasers, thus facilitating the tracing of copies. The individual volumes and their contents are as follows: vol. 1, *Poets and Men of Letters*, ed. A. N. L. Munby (Waller, Thomson, Bloomfield, Scott, Hazlitt, Peacock, Byron, Macaulay, Fitzgerald, Wilde); vol. 2, *Poets and Men of Letters*, ed. A. N. L. Munby; vol. 3, *Poets and Men of Letters*, ed. Robert J. Gemmett (William Beckford); vol. 4, *Architects*, ed. D. J. Watkins (Wren, Hawkesmoor, Chambers, Adam, Dance, Smirke, Pugin); vol. 5, *Poets and Men of Letters*, ed. Stephen Parks (John Dunton, Elijah Fenton, Joseph Spence, Sterne, Dodd, Hester Lynch Piozzi); vol. 6, *Poets and Men of Letters*, ed. John Woolford (Browning, Ruskin, Swinburne, Theodore Watts-Dunton); vol. 7, *Poets and Men of Letters*, ed. Hugh Amory (Atterbury, Lady Mary Wortley Montague, David Mallet, Fielding, Hugh Blair, Goldsmith); vol. 8, *Politicians*, ed. Seamus Deane (Thomas Hollis, John Wilkes, Edmund Burke, Warren Hastings, William Godwin, David O'Connell); vol. 9, *Poets and Men of Letters*, ed. Roy Park (Wordsworth, Southey, Thomas Moore, Bernard Barton, and Benjamin Haydon); vol. 10, *Antiquaries*, ed. Stuart Piggot (Ralph Thoresby, Thomas Hearne, George Vertue, William Stuckeley, Francis Grose); vol. 11, *Scientists*, ed. H. A. Feisenberger (Elias Ashmole, Robert Hooke, John Ray, Edmund Halley); and vol. 12, *Actors*, ed. James F. Arnott (David Garrick, John Phillip Kemble, Edmund Kean, Charles Kean, William Charles Macready, Henry Irving).

For an overview of the reconstruction of the libraries of English men of letters, using sale catalogs and other means, see A. N. L. Munby's survey, *Libraries of English Men of Letters* (London: Library Association, 1964) [Z987.M838].

Y–69 **Guide to Works on the Private Libraries of English and American Authors.**

Boswell

Bibliotheca Boswelliana. London: J. Compton, 1825. Z997.B755

Browning

Kelley, Philip, and Betty A. Coley. *Browning Collections: A Reconstruction with Other Memorabilia: The Library,*

First Works, Presentation Volumes, Manuscripts, Likenesses, Works of Art, Household and Personal Effects, and Other Association Items of Robert and Elizabeth Barrett Browning. Waco, Tex.: The Armstrong Browning Library of Baylor University, 1984.
PR4235.K44 1984

Coleridge (See also Wordsworth, below)

Coffman, Ralph J. *Coleridge's Library: A Bibliography of Books Owned or Read by Samuel Taylor Coleridge.* Boston: G. K. Hall, 1987.   Z997.C6655 1987

Taylor, William F., ed. *Critical Annotations: Being Marginal Notes Inscribed in Volumes Formerly in the Possession of Coleridge.* Harrow: W. F. Taylor, 1889.
PR4472.T3

Dickinson

Capps, Jack L. *Emily Dickinson's Reading, 1836–1886.* Cambridge: Harvard University Press, 1966.
PS1541.Z5 C3

Lowenberg, Carlton. *Emily Dickinson's Textbooks.* Lafayette, Calif.: C. Lowenberg, 1986.
PS1541.Z5 L66 1986

Eliot, G.

Baker, William. *George Eliot / George Henry Lewes Library: An Annotated Catalogue of Their Books at Dr. Williams's Library, London.* New York: Garland, 1977.   Z997.A1 B34

Emerson

Harding, Walter, ed. *Emerson's Library.* Charlottesville: University Press of Virginia, 1967.   PS1631.H35

Faulkner

Blotner, Joseph L., ed. *William Faulkner's Library: A Catalogue.* Charlottesville: University Press of Virginia, 1964.   Z997.F25

Gibbon

Keynes, Geoffrey, ed. *Library of Edward Gibbon: A Catalogue.* 2d ed. Godalming; St. Paul's Bibliographies; Charlottesville: University Press of Virginia, 1980.
Z997.K433 1980

Hardy

Stevens-Cox, James. *Library of Thomas Hardy, O.M.* St. Peter Port: Toucan Press, 1969. PR4752.A25 no. 52

Hemingway

Brasch, James D., and Joseph Sigman. *Hemingway's Library: A Composite Record.* New York: Garland, 1981.   Z989.H47 B72 1981

Johnson

Fleeman, J. D. *Preliminary Handlist of Copies of Books Associated with Dr. Samuel Johnson.* Oxford: Oxford Bibliographical Society, Bodleian Library, 1984.
Z997.J69 F48 1984

————, ed. *Sale Catalogue of Samuel Johnson's Library.* Facsimile edition. Victoria, B.C.: English Literary Studies, 1975.   Z997.J69 J63 1975

Greene, Donald. *Samuel Johnson's Library: An Annotated Guide.* Victoria, B.C.: English Literary Studies, 1975.   Z997.J69 G73

Joyce

Connolly, Thomas E. *Personal Library of James Joyce: A Descriptive Bibliography.* 2d ed. Buffalo, N.Y.: University Bookstore, University of Buffalo, 1957.
Z997.J86

Keats

Owings, Frank N., Jr. *Keats Library [a descriptive catalog].* London: Keats-Shelley Memorial Association, 1978.
Z8461.O95

Milton

Boswell, Jackson Campbell. *Milton's Library: A Catalogue of the Remains of John Milton's Library and an Annotated Reconstruction of Milton's Library and Ancillary Readings.* New York: Garland, 1975.
Z997.M65 B67

O'Neill

Olson, Sarah M. *Eugene O'Neill National Historical Site, California.* Harpers Ferry, W.Va.: National Park Service, U.S. Department of the Interior, 1983.
PS3529.N5 Z754 1983

Scott

Catalogue of the Library at Abbotsford, Edinburgh, 1838. Bannantyne Club Publications, 60. Reprint. New York: AMS Press, 1971.   Z997.S43 1971

Sterne

Facsimile Reproduction of a Unique Catalogue of Laurence Sterne's Library. London: J. Tregaskis, 1930.
Z997.S839

Swift

Williams, Harold H. *Dean Swift's Library, with a Facsimile of the Original Sale Catalogue and Some Account of Two Manuscript Lists of His Books.* Cambridge: Cambridge University Press, 1932.   Z997.S977

Thoreau

Sattelmeyer, Robert. *Thoreau's Reading: A Study in Intellectual History with Bibliographical Catalogue.* Princeton: Princeton University Press, 1988.
PS3057.B64 S27 1988

Twain

Gribben, Alan. *Mark Twain's Library: A Reconstruction.* 2 vols. Boston: G. K. Hall, 1980.   PS1342.B6 G7

Walpole

Hazen, Allen Tracy. *Catalogue of Horace Walpole's Library.* 3 vols. New Haven: Yale University Press, 1969.   Z997.W24 H38

Woolf

Catalogue of Books From the Library of Leonard and Virginia Woolf, Taken from Monks House, Rodmell, Sussex and 24 Victoria Square, London and Now in the Possession of Washington State University, Pullman, U.S.A. Brighton: Holleyman and Treacher, 1975.
Z997.W92 H65 1975

Wordsworth

Shaver, Chester L., and Alice C. Shaver. *Wordsworth's Library: A Catalogue, Including a List of Books Housed by Wordsworth for Coleridge from c. 1810 to c. 1830.* New York: Garland, 1979.   Z8985.S46

Yeats

O'Shea, Edward. *Descriptive Catalog of W. B. Yeats' Library.* New York: Garland, 1985.
Z997.Y39 074 1985

Y–70 ***Book-Prices Current: A Record of Prices at Which Books Have Been Sold at Auction [in London, 1887–1956].*** 64 vols. London: Stock et al., 1888–1957.   Z1000.B87

This annual presented a record of the books, manuscripts, and autograph letters sold at auction in London and in some

New York auctions. Volumes 1–27 (1888–1913) are arranged by the date of the sales; volumes 28 ff. (1914 ff.) are arranged by the name of the author, with some titles. Entries give the name of the firm, with information given about the name of the purchaser, the date of the sale, and the price paid. There are three cumulative indexes covering the periods 1887–1896, 1897–1906, 1907–1916 (London: Stock, 1901–1920).

Y–71   *Book-Auction Records: A Priced and Annotated Annual Record of London, New York, Montreal, Edinburgh, and Glasgow Book Auctions* [1902–]. Vol. 1–. London: Dawson [publisher has varied], 1903–.   Z1000.B65

This rival, which has now replaced *Book Prices Current* (Y–70): is published annually (since 1976, quarterly with an annual cumulation). Its subtitle and coverage vary from year to year. Arrangement in volumes 1–38 was by sale; since volume 39, arrangement is alphabetical by author. Entries include title, bibliographic information, the auction firm, date of sale, name of purchaser, and price paid. Unlike *Book Prices Current*, *Book Auction Records* has been continuously indexed. To date, there are a total of nine general indexes, covering volumes 1–69 (1902–1973).

Y–72   *American Book Prices Current: A Record of Books, Manuscripts, and Autographs Sold at Auction in New York, Boston, and Philadelphia, with the Prices Realized.* Vol. 1–. New York: Bancroft-Parkman [publisher varies], 1895–.   Z1000.A51

After volume 1, which was arranged chronologically by sale date, subsequent volumes have been alphabetical by author and title. Each volume has two lists, the first of books, broadsides, maps, charts, and related materials; the second of manuscripts and autographs. In addition to bibliographic information, entries give name of firm, date of sale, and price realized, but omit names of purchasers until 1959, after which date, purchasers' names are cited. To date, there have been ten cumulative indexes published, covering the years 1916–1975.

A recent project of *ABC* is *BAMBAM: Bookline Alert: Missing Books and Manuscripts*, vol. 1– (New York: ABPC/Bancroft-Parkman, 1982–) [Z1000.5.B66 1982], which provides a single, central, computer-generated list of missing books, manuscripts, autographs, documents, signed photographs, bookplates, and other valuable books and manuscripts.

Y–73   *Jahrbuch der Bücherpreise: Alphabetische Zusammenstellung der wichtigsten auf dem europäischen Auktionen (mit Ausschluss der englischen) verkauften Bücher mit den erzielten Preisen.* Vols. 1–34 [1906–1939]. Leipzig: Harrassowitz, 1907–1940.   Z1000.J25

This yearly account of prices at which books were sold at Continental auctions included sales in Germany, Austria, Holland, Switzerland, Scandinavia, Czechoslovakia, and Hungary. It is arranged by authors and anonymous titles, with separate lists of manuscripts and autographs. It has been revived under the title *Jahrbuch der Auktionspreise für Bücher, Handschriften und Autographen: Ergebnisse der Auktionen in Deutschland, Holland, Österreich und der Schweiz*, vol. 1– (Hamburg: Hauswedell, 1950–) [Z1000 .J235]. There are indexes to volumes 1–10 (1950- 1959) and volumes 11–20 (1960–1969).

The French series is the biennial *Catalogue bibliographique des ventes publiques (livres et manuscrits)* [1964–] (Paris: Éditions Mayer, 1966–) [Z1000.C34], which was preceded by a series of short-lived catalogs published under a number of different auspices.

Y–74   *Bookman's Price Index: An Annual Guide to the Values of Rare and Other Out-of-Print Books.* Vol. 1–. Detroit, Gale Research Co., 1964–.   Z1000.B74

This index analyzes catalogs published by some fifty leading antiquarian and out-of-print dealers in the United States, England, and Western Europe. Entries are divided into two sections, the first treating books in alphabetical order by author or title, the second treating periodicals. The following information is found in the entries: author, title, place and date of publication, description of the book including its current condition, the year offered, the price at which offered, the name of the dealer, and the number of the catalog and item number within the catalog where the book will be found.

A related volume is Mildred S. Mandeville, the *Used Book Price Guide*, 2d ed., 2 vols. (Kenmore, Wash.: Price Guide Publishers, 1972–1973) [no LC number], which gives prices of some 74,000 entries, located in catalogs issued from 1967 through 1973. Similar though more specialized is J. Norman Heard et al., eds. *Bookman's Guide to Americana*, 9th ed. (Metuchen, N.J.: Scarecrow, 1986) [Z1207.H43 1986] which gives prices derived from catalogs.

Y–76   *Directory of Dealers in Secondhand and Antiquarian Books in the British Isles.* London: Sheppard Press, 1951–.   Z327.D57

See also the *Annual Directory of Booksellers in the British Isles Specialising in Antiquarian and Out-of-Print Books* (Birmingham: The Clique, 1970–) [Z327.A6], and Roy Harley Lewis, *Book Browser's Guide: Britain's Secondhand and Antiquarian Bookshops* (London: David and Charles, 1975) [Z326.L48].

Further directories include the *International Directory of Antiquarian Booksellers*, 6th ed. (London: International League of Antiquarian Booksellers, 1977) [Z282.I58], and *European Bookdealers: A Directory of Dealers in Second-Hand and Antiquarian Books on the Continent of Europe* (London: Sheppard Press, 1967–) [Z291.5.E96]. See also the *Antiquarian Booktrade: An International Directory of Subject Specialists* compiled by E. Donald Grose (Metuchen, N.J.: Scarecrow, 1972) [Z286.A55 G74]; the *AB Bookman's Yearbook: The Specialist Book World Annual for all Bookmen: Dealers and Publishers, Librarians and Collectors* (Clifton, N.J.: Bookman's Weekly, 1949–) [Z990.A18], which includes a subject directory of antiquarian and specialist dealers; and the three-volume *Book Trade of the World* edited by Sigfred Taubert (New York: Bowker, 1972–1978) [Z278.T34].

Y–77   **Antiquarian Booksellers Association of America.** *ABAA Membership Directory.* New York: ABAA, 1979.
   No LC number

See, in addition, *Bookdealers in North America: A Directory of Dealers in Secondhand and Antiquarian Books in Canada and the United States of America* (London: Sheppard Press, 1954–) [no LC number], as well as the *Comprehensive American Book Trade Directory*, 24th ed. (New York: Bowker, 1978) [no LC number].

Y–78   *Annual Report of the American Rare, Antiquarian and Out-of-Print Book Trade.* Vol. 1–. New York: BCAR, 1979–.   Z479.A56

This annual is disposed into six parts. Part VI, "Trends in Bibliography," contains review articles that summarize scholarship on major American bibliographic tools, on trends in codicology, on analytical and historical bibliography, and on analytical bibliography in literary study.

Y–79 Schreyer, Alice D., ed. *Rare Books, 1983–84: Trends, Collections, Sources.* New York: R. R. Bowker, 1984.
Z1029.R36 1984

This volume is the first in a new series to be published by Bowker, the goal of which is to review developments in the field of rare books and manuscript and to identify information sources. The review is in the form of essays on such topics as the antiquarian book trade, the auction year, the Center for the Book at the Library of Congress, recent work in automation of rare book and manuscript records, major institutional collections in the United States, rare periodicals, and trends in the preservation of rare and special materials.

The directory of sources includes lists of associations, auctioneers, rare book and manuscript libraries in the United States and Canada, North American dealers in antiquarian books and manuscripts, and a subject index of dealer specialties.

V.   BOOK COLLECTING

Y–80 Peters, Jean, ed. *Book Collecting: A Modern Guide.* New York: R. R. Bowker, 1977.
Z987.B68

This volume contains an introduction and a total of twelve essays on book collecting by noted specialists. The essays and their contributors are as follows: 1. What Book Collecting Is All About (William Matheson): 2. Buying Books from Dealers (Robin G. Halwas); 3. Buying at Auction (Robert A. Wilson); 4. The Antiquarian Book Market (Robert Rosenthal); 5. The Art and Craft of Collecting Manuscripts (Lola L. Szladits); 6. Descriptive Bibliography (Terry Belanger); 7. Fakes, Forgeries, Facsimiles, and Other Oddities (Joan M. Friedman); 8. Physical Care of Books and Manuscripts (William Spawn); 9. Organizing a Collection (Jean Peters): 10. Appraisal (Katharine Kyes Leab and Daniel J. Leab); 11. The Book Collector and the World of Scholarship (Susan O. Thompson); and 12. The Literature of Book Collecting (G. Thomas Tanselle). The volume closes with notes on the contributors, an appendix of some useful addresses, and an index of authors, titles, and subjects.

Tanselle's bibliographical essay is disposed into sections treating General Introductions and Manuals; Historical Studies and Memoirs; Periodicals; Bibliographies and Checklists (subdivided according to the principle of arrangement); Catalogs (subdivided according to the issuing organization); Price Records and Guides; Directories of Dealers and Collectors; Works on Conservation, Bookplates, and Manuscripts; and Guides to Further Reading.

Jean Peters also edited a sequel volume with the title *Collectible Books: Some New Paths* (New York: R. R. Bowker, 1979) [Z987.C58].

Earlier manuals include John Carter, *Taste and Technique in Book-Collecting; A Study of Recent Development in Great Brtain and the United States* (Cambridge: Cambridge University Press, 1948) [Z987.C35].

Y–82 Berkeley, Edmund, Jr., ed. *Autographs and Manuscripts: A Collector's Manual.* New York: Charles Scribner's Sons, 1978.
Z41.A92

This volume, sponsored by the Manuscript Society, contains a total of I. The Fundamentals, II. Rudiments, and III. Some Areas in Which to Collect. The majority of chapters are in this third part and include advice about collecting American Literary Autographs, English Literary Autographs, French Literary Autographs, European and World Literatures, British Theatre and Dance, American Theatre, and so on. An anno-

tated bibliography, glossary, and index conclude this work. The bibliography is divided into nine sections, as follows: Works of General or Specific Usefulness, General Guides to Collecting, Facsimiles and Handwriting, Memoirs and Reminiscences, Musical Autographs, Periodicals, Preservation and Restoration, Theatre and Dance, and Changing Handwriting.

Earlier guides include Charles Hamilton, *Collecting Autographs and Manuscripts* (Norman: University of Oklahoma Press, 1961) [Z41.H34], which contains discussion of the full range of topics from how to build an important collection to the future of autograph collecting, and ends with a bibliography of the best books in the field and an index. Also recommended is the volume by Mary A. Benjamin, *Autographs: A Key to Collecting*, rev. ed. (New York: Benjamin, 1966) [Z41.B4], and the work of Jerry E. Patterson, *Autographs: A Collector's Guide* (New York: Crown, 1973) [Z41.P36 1973].

Y–85 Dickinson, Donald C. *Dictionary of American Book Collectors.* Westport, Conn.: Greenwood Press, 1986.
Z989.A1 D53 1986

A biographical reference work, this volume presents information on 359 significant American book collectors. Each entry comprises a short biographical synopsis followed by auction sale information marked Collection Disposition, a narrative discussion in which the collector's chief interest is identified, the development of the collection is described, and its influence is noted. Entries conclude with a selective bibliography. There are cross-references between entries and two appendixes. The first identifies areas of collector specialization; the second lists notable American book auctions. An index concludes the volume.

Y–88 Some Frequently Recommended Works on the History of Book and Manuscript Collecting.

Adams, Frederick B. *Uses of Provenance.* School of Librarianship, University of California, 1969.
Z1033.A84 A33

Cannon, Carl L. *American Book Collectors and Collecting from Colonial Times to the Present.* New York: H. W. Wilson, 1941.
Z989.A1 C36 1941

Cole, George Watson. "Book-Collectors as Benefactors of Public Libraries." *PBSA* 9 (1915): 47–110.

de Ricci, Seymour. *English Collectors of Books and Manuscripts (1530–1930) and Their Marks of Ownership.* Cambridge: Cambridge University Press, 1930.
Z987.5.G7 R5 1930

Dickinson, Donald C. *Dictionary of American Book Collectors.* New York: Greenwood Press, 1986.
Z989.A1 D53 1986

Elton, Charles I., and Mary A. Elton. *Great Book-Collectors.* London: Kegan Paul, 1893.
Z989.A1 E45 1893

Fletcher, William Y. *English Book Collectors.* London: Kegan Paul, 1902.
Z989.A1 F55

James, M. R. *Wanderings and Homes of Manuscripts.* London: SPCK, 1919.
Z105.J23

Munby, A. N. L. *Essays and Papers.* Edited with an introduction by Nicholas Barker. London: Scolar Press, 1977.
Z992.M958

Quaritch, Bernard, ed. *Contributions towards a Dictionary of English Book-Collectors.* 14 parts in 1 vol. London: B. Quaritch, 1892–1921.
Z989.Q1C

Raymond, Joseph H. *Pegasus International Book Collectors Directory: A Cornucopia for Booklovers*. Vashond Island, Wash.: Pegasus Press, 1983.
Z989.A1 R39 1983

Y–89 Some Catalogues of Famous Private Collections Relating to English and American Language and Literature.

Adam, R. B. (1863–1940)

R. B. Adam Library Relating to Dr. Samuel Johnson and His Era. 3 vols. London: Oxford University Press, 1929.
Z8455.8.A21

Berg (see B–30)

Brinley, George (1817–1875)

Catalogue of the American Library of the Late Mr. George Brinley, of Hartford Connecticut. Compiled by James H. Trumbull and William I. Fletcher. 5 vols. Hartford: Press of the Case Lockwood and Brainard Co., 1878–1893. With author and subject indexes.
Z1207.B858

Church, E. D. (1835–1908)

Catalogue of Books Relating to the Discovery and Early History of North and South America Forming a Part of the Library of E. D. Church. Compiled by George Watson Cole. 5 vols. New York: Dodd, Mead, 1907.
Z997.C561

Catalogue of Books, Consisting of English Literature and Miscellanea, Including Many Original Editions of Shakespeare, Forming a Part of the Library of E. D. Church. Compiled by George Watson Cole. 2 vols. New York: Dodd, Mead, 1909.   Z997.C56

Cotton (see H–11)

Devonshire, Dukes of

Catalogue of the Library of Chatsworth. Compiled by Sir James Philip. 4 vols. London: Chiswick Press, 1879.   Z997.D511

Folger (see B–22)

Harley, Sir Robert (see H–11)

Wright, Cyril E. *Fontes Harleiani: A Study of the Sources of the Harleian Collection of Manuscripts*. London: British Museum, 1971.   Z6621.B85 H37

Harris (see S–67)

Hoe, Robert (1839–1909)

Library of Robert Hoe: A Contribution to the History of Bibliophilism in America. Compiled by Oscar Bierstadt. New York: Duprat, 1895.   Z997.H69

Catalogue of the Library of Robert Hoe of New York. 8 vols. in 4. New York: D. Taylor and Co., 1911.
Z997.H69 1911

Houghton (see B–26)

Huntington (see B–20)

Huth, Henry (1815–1878)

Catalogue of the Famous Library of Printed Books, Illuminated Manuscripts, Autograph Letters and Engravings Collected by Henry Huth. 9 vols. London: J. Daly and Sons, 1911–1920.   Z997.H97 1911

Isham, Ralph (1890–1955)

Buchanan, David. *Treasure of Anchinleck: The Story of the Boswell Papers*. New York: McGraw-Hill, 1974.
PR3325.B8

Pottle, Frederick R. *Pride and Negligence: A History of the Boswell Papers*. New York: McGraw-Hill, 1982.
PR3325.P617 1982

Lewis, Wilmarth (1895–1979)

Catalogue of Horace Walpole's Library. Compiled by Allen T. Hazen. 3 vols. New Haven: Yale University Press, 1969.   Z997.W24 H38

Collector's Progress. New York: Knopf, 1951.   Z989.L5

Morgan, (see B–31)

Newberry (see B–25)

Pforzheimer, Carl H. (1879–1957)

Carl H. Pforzheimer Library, English Literature, 1475–1700. Compiled by William A. Jackson and Emma V. Unger. 3 vols. New York: Privately printed, 1940.
Z997.P49

Phillipps, Sir Thomas, Bart (1792–1872)

Barker, Nicolas. *Portrait of an Obsession: The Life of Sir Thomas Phillipps, the World's Greatest Book Collector*. London: Constable, 1967.   Z989.P49 M8 1967

Munby, A. N. L. *Phillipps Studies*. 5 vols. *The Catalogues of Manuscripts and Printed Books; The Foundations of the Phillipps Library; and The Dispersal of the Phillipps Library*. Cambridge: Cambridge University Press, 1951–1960.   Z997.P553 M8

Quinn, John (1870–1924)

Library of John Quinn. 5 pts. in 1 vol. Compiled by Charles Vale. New York: The Anderson Galleries, 1923–1924.   Z997.Q75

Rosenwald (see B–23)

Rothschild, Nathaniel Mayer Victor, Baron (1910—)

Rothschild Library: A Catalogue of the Collection of Eighteenth Century Printed Books and Manuscripts Formed by Lord Rothschild. Compiled by John Hayward. 2 vols. Cambridge: Cambridge University Press, 1954. Additions and corrections by Harold Williams, *Library*, 5th ser., 10 (1955): 284–287.
Z997.R85

Sadleir, Michael (see Q–76)

Schomburg, Arthur Alfonso (1874–1938)

Sinnette, Elinor Des Verney. *Arthur Alfonso Schomburg: Black Bibliophile and Collector: A Biography*. Detroit: Wayne State University Press, 1989.
Z989.S36 S56 1989

Streeter, Thomas W. (1883–1965)

Celebrated Collection of Americana Formed by the Late Thomas Winthrop Streeter. 7 vols. New York: Parke-Bernet Galleries, 1966–1969.   Z999.P25

White, William A. (1843–1927)

Catalogue of Early English Books Chiefly of the Elizabethan Period. Compiled by Henrietta C. Bartlett. New York: Privately printed, 1926.   Z997.W594

Handlist of the William A. White Collection. New York, 1914.   No LC number

Widener (see B–26)

Wise, T. J. (1859–1937)

Ashley Library; A Catalogue of Printed Books, Manuscripts, and Autograph Letters Collected by Thomas J. Wise. 11 vols. London: Dawsons, 1922–1936. Z997.W82

VI. LIBRARIES AND LIBRARIANSHIP

See also section B, guides to libraries and descriptions of major research libraries in the United States, Britain and Ireland.

Y–90 **Kent, Allen, and Harold Lancour, eds.** *Encyclopedia of Library and Information Science.* 37 vols. New York: M. Dekker, 1968–1984. Z1006.E57

This international work contains long, authoritative, signed articles with bibliographies on all aspects of librarianship, library history, information science, and related fields including analytical, descriptive, and enumerative bibliography, archivistics, manuscripts, paleography, and many of the arts and crafts of bookmaking and distribution. Volume 35 contains a detailed index to the entire work; volumes 36 and 37 are supplements 1 and 2.

Y–93 *Library and Information Science Abstracts.* London: Library Association, 1969–. Z671.L6

This bimonthly collection of abstracts, which supersedes the earlier *Library Science Abstracts*, 1950–1968 [Z671.L617], treats current articles on bibliography, library collections, manuscripts, and archives drawn from the analysis of some 300 journals. Entries are in a classified arrangement, with annual author and subject indexes. A cumulative index, 1969–1973, was published in 1975.

A second source of current information is *Library Literature: An Index to Library and Information Science* (New York: Wilson, 1921) [Z666.L69], also published bimonthly. This comprehensive, international index to books, pamphlets, and some 175 periodicals is arranged as a single alphabet and subject list.

A third source of information is the "current contents" format of *CALL: Current Awareness Library Literature* (Framingham, Mass: Goldstein Associates, 1972–1974, 1976–) [Z666.C15], also published bimonthly, which cites the tables of contents of current library periodicals and newsletters, along with abstracts of selected articles.

Y–95 **Taylor, Archer.** *Book Catalogues: Their Varieties and Uses.* Chicago, 1957. Z1001.T34

This volume is divided into six chapters, as follows: 1, Varieties of Book Catalogues; 2, Uses of Catalogues; 3, Bibliographies of Catalogues: 4, A List of Catalogues of Private Libraries That Have Been Recommended for Reference Use; 5, Books and Articles Listed by Authors' Names and Short Titles; 6, Indexes of Dealers, Institutions, Owners, and Publishers Whose Books Have Been Listed in Manuscript or Printed Catalogues. Catalogs are cited in the historical order of their appearance, thus making possible an overview of the history of cataloging as well as a taxonomy of catalogs.

A number of other volumes by Taylor provide similar historical perspective on aspects of enumerative bibliography. See, in particular, *Catalogues of Rare Books: A Chapter in Bibliographical History* (Lawrence: University of Kansas, 1958) [Z721.T3].

Y–98 **Scholarly Journals on Libraries and Librarianship.** (See also the journals listed under individual libraries in section B.)

American Libraries: Bulletin of the American Library Association. Vols. 1–63; n.s. vol. 1–. Chicago: American Library Association, 1907–1969; 1970–. 11/yr. Reviews. Z673.A5 B8

American Society for Information Science Journal [former title: *American Documentation: A Quarterly Review of Ideas, Techniques, Problems, and Achievements in Documentation*]. Vol. 1–. Washington, D.C.: American Documentation Institute, 1950–. 4/yr. Reviews. Z1007.A477

British Library Journal. Vol. 1–. London: Oxford University Press, 1975–. 2/yr. Z921.B854 B73

Colby Library Quarterly. Vol. 1–. Waterville, Me.: Colby College, 1943–. 4/yr. Z881.W336

College and Research Libraries. Vol. 1–. Chicago: American Library Association, 1939–. 6/yr. Reviews. Bibliographical notices, including notices of book, manuscript, and collection acqusitions by United States and Canadian libraries. Annual index. Z671.C6

Indiana University Bookman. Vol. 1–. Bloomington: Indiana University, 1956–. Z1007.I513

Journal of Documentation, Devoted to the Recording, Organization, and Dissemination of Specialized Knowledge. Vol. 1–. London: Association of Libraries and Special Information Bureaux, 1945–. 4/yr. Z1007.J9

Journal of Librarianship. London: Library Association, 1969–. 4/yr. Z671.J66

Journal of Library History, Philosophy, and Comparative Librarianship. Vol. 1–. Austin: University of Texas Press, 1966–. 4/yr. Reviews. Annual Bibliographical Essay, "The Year's Work in American Library History." Z671.J67

Library Chronicle. Vol. 1–. Philadelphia: Friends of the Library, University of Pennsylvania, 1934–. Z733.P418

Library History. Vol. 1–. London: Library Association, Library History Group, 1967–. 2/yr. Z721.L634

LJ *Library Journal.* Vol. 1–. New York: R. R. Bowker, 1876–. 6–12/yr. Z671.L7

Library Quarterly: A Journal of Investigation and Discussion in the Field of Library Science. Vol. 1–. Chicago: University of Chicago Press, 1931–. Z671.L713

Library Trends. Vol. 1–. Urbana: University of Illinois Library School, 4/yr. Z671.L6173

Outlook on Research Libraries. Vol. 1–. Lausanne: Elsevier Sequoia, 1978–. 12/yr. Z675.R45 O8x

Princeton University Library Chronicle. Vol. 1–. Princeton, N.J.: The Library, 1939–. 4/yr. Index to vols. 1–25 (1939–1964) in 1 vol. Z733.P93 C5

Private Library: Quarterly Journal of the Private Libraries Association. Vol. 1–. Pinner, England: Private Libraries Association, 1957–. 4/yr. Z990.P7

Special Libraries. Vol. 1–. New York: Special Libraries Association, 1910–. 10/yr. Reviews. *Cumulative Index*, 1971–1980 (1982). Z671.S72

Wilson Library Bulletin. Vol. 1–. New York: Wilson, 1914–. 10/yr. Z1217.W75

For further information about these and other periodicals, see Mary Ann Bowman, *Library and Information Science Journals and Serials: An Analytical Guide* (Westport, Conn.: Greenwood, 1985) [Z666.B64 1985].

Y–99 Some Frequently Recommended Works on the History of Libraries and Librarianship. (See also section B and K–98, Guide to Some Frequently Recommended Studies in the History of Learning.)

Clark, J. W. *Care of Books: An Essay on the Development of Libraries and Their Fittings, from the Earliest Times to the End of the Eighteenth Century.* Rev. ed. Cambridge: Cambridge University Press, 1909. Z721.C61

Harris, Michael H. *Guide to Research in American Library History.* Metuchen, N.J.: Scarecrow, 1968. Z731.H3

Hessel, Alfred. *History of Libraries.* Translation of *Geschichte der Bibliotheken* (Göttingen: Hochschulverlag, 1925). New Brunswick, N.J.: Scarecrow Press, 1955. Z721.H582 1955

Irwin, Raymond. *English Library: Sources and History.* London: Allen and Unwin, 1966. Z791.I67

Jackson, Sidney L. *Libraries and Librarianship in the West: A Brief History.* New York: McGraw-Hill, 1974. Z721.J245

Johnson, Elmer D., and Michael H. Harris. *History of Libraries in the Western World.* 3d ed., rev. Metuchen, N.J.: Scarecrow Press, 1976. Z721.J63 1976

Keeling, Dennis F., ed. *British Library History: A Bibliography 1962–80.* 3 vols. London: Library Association, Library History Group, 1972–1983. Z791.A1 K43

Kelly, Thomas. *Early Public Libraries.* London: Library Association, 1966. Z791.K37

Olle, J. G. *Library History: An Examination Guide Book.* 2d ed., rev. London: Bingley, 1971. Z721.O48 1971

Parsons, Edward A. *Alexandrian Library, Glory of the Hellenic World.* New York: Elsevier, 1952. Z722.5.P3 1952a

Platthy, Jeno. *Sources on the Earliest Greek Libraries with the Testimonia.* Amsterdam: Hakkert, 1968. Z722.P55

Predeek, A. *History of Libraries in Great Britain and North America.* Chicago: American Library Association, 1947. Z721.P72

Richardson, E. C. *Biblical Libraries: A Sketch of Library History from 3400 B.C. to A.D. 150.* Princeton, N.J.: Princeton University Press, 1914. Z722.R53

Savage, Ernest A. *Old English Libraries.* London: Methuen, 1911. Z723.S27

Streeter, B. H. *Chained Library.* London: Macmillan, 1931. Z791.S91

Thompson, James W. *Ancient Libraries.* Berkeley: University of California Press, 1940. Z722.T47

———. *Medieval Library.* New York: Hafner, 1957. Z723.T47 1957

Thornton, John L. *Chronology of Librarianship.* London: Grafton and Co., 1911. Z721.T53 1911

Weimann, Karl-Heinz. *Bibliotheksgeschichte: Lehrbuch zur Entwicklung und Topographie des Bibliothekswesens.* Munich: Verlag Dokumentation, 1975. Z721.W44

Wormald, F., ed. *English Library before 1700.* London: University of London, Athlone Press, 1958. Z791.W7

THE PROFESSION OF ENGLISH

I.   ENGLISH STUDIES

See also references in section M and in section S particularly.

Z–1   **Palmer, David J.** *Rise of English Studies: An Account of the Study of English Language and Literature from Its Origins to the Making of the Oxford English School.* London: Oxford University Press for the University of Hull, 1965.
PE68.G5 1965

This volume, a critical history of English studies in the nineteenth and earlier twentieth centuries, is in nine chapters, as follows: 1, Rhetoric and Belles Lettres; 2, The London Colleges; 3, An Education for the Industrial Classes; 4, The Muse in Chains; 5, The Reform Movement in Oxford; 6, John Churton Collins and the Attack on Oxford; 7, The Founding of the Oxford English School; 8, Walter Raleigh and the Years of the English Fund; 9, From Cambridge to Brighton. There are two appendixes, the first on early study of English Literature in Scottish Universities and the second on the 1921 Report of the Board of Education, "The Teaching of English in England." An index concludes the work.

Z–2   **Harrison, G. B.** *Profession of English.* New York: Harcourt, Brace and World, 1962.
LB2321.H282

This volume is a brief, personal introduction to English literature as a profession. It is designed as a response to a graduate student inquiry: "I wish you would tell me what you are trying to accomplish in your teaching and study of English literature. And Why?" A set of definitions of literature, English, study, scholarship, and criticism is followed by (1) a "Fantastic Interlude: English at the University of New Atlantis," which is then contrasted with things as they are, (2) publication requirements, (3) the structure of English departments, (4) prejudices, and (5) a discussion of Shakespeare in the classroom. Harrison's own answers to the questions posed conclude the volume.
Similar, more or less personal volumes of reminiscence and reflection by distinguished professors of English include the following additional titles:

Baldwin, T. W., et al.   Personal statements published in a series in the *CEA Critic*, November 1961 and March 1962.

Canby, Henry Seidel.   *Alma Mater: The Gothic Age of the American College.* New York: Farrar and Rinehart, 1936.
LA226.C25

Krutch, Joseph Wood.   *More Lives Than One.* New York: William Morrow, 1962.
CT275.K89 A3

Millet, Fred B.   *Professor: Problems and Rewards in College Teaching.* New York: Macmillan, 1961.   LB1778.M5

Mott, Frank Luther.   *Time Enough! Essays in Autobiography.* Chapel Hill: University of North Carolina Press, 1962.
PN4874.M59 A3

Perry, Bliss.   *And Gladly Teach.* Boston: Houghton Mifflin, 1935.
PS2545.P4 Z52

Phelps, William Lyon.   *Autobiography.* London: Oxford University Press, 1939.
PS3531.H4Z5 1939

Z–3   **Allen, Don Cameron.** *Ph.D. in English and American Literature: A Report to the Profession and the Public.* New York: Holt, Rinehart and Winston, 1968.   PE66.A4

This report widely influenced the proliferation of graduate programs in English in the late 1960s and the subsequent glut of English Ph.D.'s in the academic marketplace. It is based on a study performed in the mid–1960s under the auspices of the MLA. Extensive questionnaires were sent out to all departments granting doctoral degrees; a copy of the questionnaire is given in appendix 3 of this volume. The main body is arranged in a series of nine chapters. The first two sketch out the history of graduate departments of English before 1900 and the current (i.e. mid–1960s) set of problems confronting graduate study in English. Chapters 3 through 8 summarize the questionnaires on the subjects of the personnel of departments of English; the recruiting and admission of candidates for the doctorate; the initial training of doctoral candidates; the doctoral dissertation and beyond; the professional career and its problems; and the purpose of doctoral training and some proposals. The final chapter offers some suggestions by way of a conclusion. Appendix 1 provides bibliographical notes for chapters 1 and 2 while Appendix 2 presents the tabulations for chapters 3–8.

Z–4   **Shugrue, Michael.** *English in a Decade of Change.* New York: Pegasus, 1968.   PE1068.U5 855

This volume, on English studies in America in the 1960s by the then Secretary for English Studies of the Modern Language Association, is in three sections, treating The English Curriculum; The Teacher of English; and English, Education, and Change, respectively. Discussed are such issues as what is the subject matter actually being taught; developments in theory, linguistics, methodology, and technology; who is teaching; and what sort of dialogue is possible between British, Canadian, and United States scholars. Notes, a list of works cited, and an index conclude this work.

Z–5 Kampf, Louis. *"English: The Scandal of Literary Scholarship,"* pp. 43–61. In Theodore Roszak, ed., *Dissenting Academy.* New York: Pantheon, 1968.   LC1011.R7

This essay (by one of the leading figures in such activities as the 1970 restructuring of the MLA) is a part of the mid–1960s critique of the American academic community. It is the first in a series of radical critiques of the profession of English which include Ohmann's *English in America* (Z–7). A total of seven additional essays in this volume criticize the teaching of the humanities in American universities in the fields of economics, history, international relations, anthropology, philosophy, social science, and political science. The penultimate essay is a critique of the Catholic university; an essay titled "The Responsibility of Intellectuals" by Noam Chomsky concludes the volume.

Z–6 Kampf, Louis, and Paul Lauter, eds. *Politics of Literature: Dissenting Essays on the Teaching of English.* New York: Pantheon Books, 1970.   PR37.P6

This collection of eleven essays, some of which were originally published elsewhere, presents a summary of the 1960s critique of the English establishment in the wake of the 1968 MLA meeting. It is in three sections, preceded by an introduction from the editors. Part I, "'Thy Hand, Great Anarch . . .': Notes on the Literary Profession," contains the following essays: "Why Teach Literature? An Account of How I Came to Ask That Question" (Ellen Cantarow); "The Teaching of Literature in the Highest Academies of the Empire" (Bruce Franklin); "Teaching and Studying Literature at the End of Ideology" (Richard Ohmann); and "Arnold's Other Axiom" (Katherine Ellis). Part II, "The Laying Off of 'Culture': or, 'Ain't No Black God That's Doin' That Bullshit,'" contains the following essays: "Free, Classless, and Urbane?" (Barbara Bailey Kessell); "The Logic of Nonstandard English" (William Labov); and "The Politics of Bidialectalism" (Wayne O'Neil). Part III, "'But All This Is So—So Unpoetical': or, Toward a New Literary Practice," contains the following essays: "Why Teach Poetry? An Experiment" (Florence Howe); "Up against the Great Tradition" (Sheila Delaney); "The Study of Nineteenth-Century British Working-Class Poetry" (Martha Vicinus); and "Who's Afraid of a Room of One's Own?" (William S. Robinson). The volume concludes with notes, bibliographical references, and an index.

Z–7 Ohmann, Richard. *English in America: A Radical View of the Profession.* New York: Oxford University Press, 1976.   PE68.U5 O36

This work consists of twelve chapters in five sections, as follows: Part I, Introduction (1. Working in English in America about 1965); Part II, Literature and the Rites of Passage (2. MLA: Professors of Literature in a Group; 3. Advanced Placement on the Ladder of Success; 4. Teaching and Studying Literature at the End of Ideology); Part III, English 101 and the Military-Industrial Complex (5. Rhetoric for the Meritocracy—chapter contributed by Wallace Douglas; 6. Freshman Composition and Administered Thought; 7. Writing, Out in the World); Part IV, The Professional Ethos (8. What English Departments Do; 9. Why They Do It); Part V, Past and Future (10. Culture, Knowledge, and Machines; 11. Universities and Industrial Culture; 12. The Politics of Knowledge: A Polemic). The volume concludes with an index of authors, titles, and subjects.

A number of articles responding to the Ohmann critique appeared in the *New York Review of Books*. See issues for 27 May 1976 (pp. 29–32); 5 August 1976 (p. 45); and 30 September 1976 (p. 42).

Z–8 Finestone, Harry, and Michael F. Shugrue, eds. *Prospects for the 70's: English Departments and Multidisciplinary Study.* New York: MLA, 1973.   PE66.F5

This volume reprints a series of essays, reports, and resolutions prepared under the auspices of the Association of Departments of English and originally published in either the *ADE Bulletin* or *PMLA*. All are concerned with the development of interdisciplinary or multidisciplinary studies that might enhance or regenerate the teaching and study of language and literature. Among contributors are John C. Gerber, Maynard Mack, Theodore L. Gross, Alan M. Hollingsworth, and John H. Fisher.

Z–9 Neel, Jasper P., ed. *State of the Discipline, 1970s–1980s.* New York: Modern Language Association, 1979.   PE68.U5 A86a no. 62

This volume is a special double issue of the *ADE Bulletin* highlighting major issues of the 1970s and 1980s. The overall state of the discipline is discussed by J. Paul Hunter. The nature of literary criticism is dealt with by J. Hillis Miller, Jonathan Culler, Murray Krieger, and Carolyn G. Heilbrun. The state of the English major is examined by Geoffrey Hartman and George L. Geckle. Teaching of writing is treated by Paula Johnson, Richard A. Lanham, E. D. Hirsch, Jr., and Norman S. Grabo. The role of the departmental chairman is discussed by Carol Smith, Joel O. Connarroe, Arthur B. Coffin, and Gale H. Carrithers, Jr. Finally, Ward Hellstrom and Vicki Mahaffey treat the job market.

Z–10 *Profession [77–]: Selected Articles from the Bulletins of the Association of Departments of English [ADE] and the Association of Departments of Foreign Languages [ADFL].* New York: Modern Language Association, 1977–.   P57.U7 P75

These annual selections of reprints from the quarterly issues of the *ADE Bulletin* and the *ADFL Bulletin* are collected for distribution to the full MLA membership because of their general professional significance. Topics treated in articles gathered over the last several years include the job crisis, the politics of language teaching, the state of foreign-language studies, undergraduate and graduate curricula, literacy, the teaching of writing, teacher training, and the state of the humanities at the present time, among other matters of current discussion and debate.

Z–15 Gross, John. *Rise and Fall of the Man of Letters: A Study of the Idiosyncratic and the Humane in Modern Literature.* New York: Macmillan, 1969.   PR63.G7 1969b

This history of the man of letters in Britain since 1800 is disposed into ten chapters and an epilogue. The chapters with some of the major figures discussed are as follows: 1, The Rise of the Reviewer (Jeffrey, Lockhart); 2, Heroes and Men of Letters (Carlyle, Mill, Arnold); 3, The Higher Journalism (Lewes, Bagehot, Stephen); 4, Some Liberal Practitioners; 5, The Bookmen (Lang, Saintsbury, Dobson, Gosse); 6, Early English; 7, Popular Approaches; 8, Edwardians; 9, Modern Times; and 10, Cross-Currents of the Thirties (Caudwell, Orwell, Leavis). A selected bibliography, divided into sections that parallel the chapters, and an index of authors, titles, and subjects conclude the volume.

Z–18 **Professional Journals in English Studies.** (Most newsletters and many scholarly journals also have sections with professional news and notes.)

AAUP Bulletin. Vol. 1–. Washington, D.C.: American Association of University Professors, 1915–. 4/yr.
No LC number

ADE Bulletin. No. 1–. New York: Association of Departments of English, MLA, 1963. 4/yr.   PE68.U5 A86a

CEA Forum. Vol. 1–. College Station: Texas A&M University for the College English Association, 1939–. 4/yr.
PE11.C6513

College English. Vol. 1–. Urbana: NCTE, 1939–. 8/yr. Reviews.   PE1.C6

English Studies in Canada. Downsview, Ont.: University of Toronto Press for the Association of Canadian University Teachers of English, 1975–. 4/yr. Reviews.
No LC number

Z–19 **Some Frequently Recommended Works on the Profession of English.** (See also Z–139, Some Frequently Recommended Works on Teaching, the Teaching of English, and Research in the Teaching of English.)

Abbs, Peter. *English for Diversity: A Polemic.* London: Heinemann Educational, 1969.   LB1631.A33

———. *Root and Blossom: Essays in the Philosophy, Practice, and Politics of English Teaching.* London: Heinemann, 1976.   PR33.A2

Baldick, Chris. *Social Mission of English Criticism, 1848-1932.* Oxford: Clarendon Press, 1983.
PR63.B35 1983

Bate, Walter Jackson, *"The Crisis in English Studies," Harvard Magazine* 85 (Sept.-Oct. 1982): 46–53.

Bateson, F. W. *Essays in Critical Dissent.* London: Longman, 1972.   PR403.B3

Bergonzi, Bernard. *Exploding English: Criticism, Theory, Culture.* Oxford: Clarendon Press, 1990.
PE68.G5 B47 1990

Cawley, A. C. "'English Language': English Language and Medieval Literature as University Studies." In D. A. Pearsall and R. A. Waldron, eds., *Medieval Literature and Civilization; Studies in Memory of G. N. Garmonsway,* pp. 322–332. London: University of London, Athlone Press, 1969.   PN681.M4

Chambers, R. W. *Teaching of English in the Universities of England.* London: English Association, 1922.
PE1068.G5 C5

Collins, John Churton. *Study of English Literature.* London, 1891.

Crews, Frederick: "Do Literary Studies Have an Ideology?" *PMLA* 85 (1970): 423–428. Also other articles in this issue.

Curti, Merle, ed. *American Scholarship in the Twentieth Century.* Cambridge: Harvard University Press, 1953. Chapter by René Wellek on Literary Scholarship.
AZ505.C8

Daiches, David, ed. *Idea of a New University: An Experiment in Sussex.* 2d ed. London: Deutsch, 1970. Chapter on English Studies by Daiches.
LF55.D3 1970

Fish, Stanley. "Profession Despise Thyself: Fear and Self-Loathing in Literary Studies." *CI* 10 (1983).

Fisher, John Hurt. "Remembrance and Reflection: PMLA 1884–1982." *PMLA* 99 (1984): 398–406.

Gardner, Helen. "The Academic Study of English Literature." *Critical Quarterly* 1 (1959): 106–115.

Graff, Gerald, and Michael Warner, eds. *Origins of Literary Studies in America: A Documentary Anthology.* New York: Routledge, 1989.   PR51.U507 1988

Hoggart, Richard. *Uses of Literacy.* London: Chatto and Windus, 1957.   DA115.H6

Holloway, John. *Establishment of English.* Cambridge: Cambridge University Press, 1972.   PR37.H6

Latimer, Dan. "The Politics of Literary Theory: An Evanston Memoir." *Southern Humanities Review* 18 (1984).

Lauter, Paul. "Society and the Profession, 1958–1983." *PMLA* 99 (1984): 414–425. Also other articles in this issue.

Leavis, F. R. *Education and the University: A Sketch for an "English School."* 1943.   LB2321.L4

———. *English Literature in Our Time and the University.* London: Chatto and Windus, 1969.

"Literary History in the University," a series on the curricula of major English departments published in *New Literary History,* 1970–1973.

Lowes, John Livingston. "The MLA and Humane Scholarship." *PMLA* 48 (1933): 1403–1408.

McKerrow, R. B. *Note on the Teaching of "English Language and Literature," with Some Suggestions.* London: English Association, 1921.

McMurty, Jo. *English Language, English Literature: The Creation of an Academic Discipline.* Hamden, Conn.: Archon, 1985.   PE1065.M373 1985

Mandel, Barrett J. *Literature and the English Department.* Champaign, Ill.: NCTE, 1970.   PN70.M3

Newbolt, Sir Henry, et al. *Teaching of English in England: Board of Education Report.* London: HMSO, 1921.
PE1068.G5 A5

Parker, William Riley. "Where Do English Departments Come From?" *College English* 28 (1967): 339–351.

Partridge, Astley C. *Landmarks in the History of English Scholarship, 1500–1970.* Cape Town, South Africa: Nasou Limited, n.d.   AZ614.P37

Potter, Stephen. *Muse in Chains: A Study in Education.* London: J. Cape, 1937.   PR51.G7 P6

Robinson, Ian. *Survival of English.* Cambridge: Cambridge University Press, 1973.   PE1072.R57

Robson, W. W. *English as a University Subject.* The F. R. Leavis Lecture, 1965. Cambridge: Cambridge University Press, 1965.   AS121.F18 1965

Saunders, John W. *Profession of English Letters.* London: Routledge and Kegan Paul, 1964.   PR401.S36

Schultze, Martin. *Academic Illusions in the Field of Letters and Arts.* Chicago: University of Chicago Press, 1933.
PN45.S27

Sutherland, James. *English in the Universities.* Cambridge: Cambridge University Press, 1945.   PR37.S8

Tate, Alan. *Man of Letters in the Modern World.* New York: Meridian, 1955.   PN37.T32

Tillyard, E. M. W. *Muse Unchained: An Intimate Account of the Revolution in English Studies at Cambridge.* London: Bowes and Bowes, 1958.   PR53.C3 T5

Vanderbilt, Kermit. *American Literature and the Academy: The Roots, Growth, and Maturity of a Profession.* Philadelphia: University of Pennsylvania Press, 1986.
PS47.O6 V36 1986

Wellek, René. *Rise of English Literary History*. Chapel Hill: University of North Carolina Press, 1941. PR401.W4

Whalley, George. "Scholarship and Criticism." *UTQ* 29 (1959): 33–45.

Whittock, Trevor. *English as a University Subject*. Cape Town, South Africa: University of Cape Town, 1974. PE65.W5

Widdowson, Peter, ed. *Re-reading English*. London: Methuen, 1982. PR51.G7 R4 1982

Wilcox, Thomas. *Anatomy of College English*. San Francisco: Jossey-Bass, 1973. LB2365.E5 W54 1973

II.   DIRECTORIES OF SCHOLARS

See also materials on contemporary biography in section G.

Z–20   *World of Learning.* 2 vols. London: Europa Publications, 1947–. AS2.W6

This directory provides names, addresses, and other pertinent information about more than 26,000 academies, learned societies, libraries and archives, museums and art galleries, research institutes, and universities around the world, arranged alphabetically by country. It also provides names for more than 150,000 professors, academicians, university chancellors and vice-chancellors, deans, bursars, presidents, rectors, curators, and other officials. An opening section treats over 400 international organizations concerned with the field of education.

Z–21   *Directory of American Scholars: A Biographical Directory.* 8th ed. 4 vols. Tempe, Ariz.: Jacques Cattell Press, Division of Bowker, 1982. LA2311.C32

This directory, the first edition of which appeared in 1942, includes biographical articles on some 37,000 living American scholars. The disciplines covered are as follows: vol. 1, History; vol. 2, English, Speech and Drama; vol. 3, Foreign Languages, Linguistics, and Philology; vol. 4, Philosophy, Religion, and Law. Within volumes, entries are arranged alphabetically; each volume concludes with a geographical index; a complete index to the four-volume set concludes volume 4. Entries include name, discipline(s), personal data, education, former and current positions, other scholarly activities, memberships in scholarly societies, research interests, significant publications, and current address. Entries are prepared, revised, and corrected by direct survey of the individual scholars themselves.

Z–23   *PMLA Directory.* Now published as the September issue no. 4, of *PMLA*. New York: Modern Language Association. PB6.M6

The Directory issue of *PMLA* contains lists of the various officers, committees, and staff members of the Modern Language Association; statistics about MLA members; various documents including regional association reports and the constitution of the organization; and lists of honorary members and honorary fellows. The bulk of the directory consists of an alphabetical list of current members with their addresses. A necrology is followed by lists of the department chairmen of English and foreign-language departments; ethnic studies programs; language and area programs; and women's studies programs. These lists are alphabetically arranged by names of all the universities and four-year, junior, and community colleges with the department or program in question. An enum-

eration of Fellowships and Grants (see Z–85); a list of forthcoming meetings and conferences of general interests, a section of professional notes and comment, and a directory of useful addresses conclude this annual.

Z–25   **Gibaldi, Joseph, and Walter S. Achtert, comps.** *Guide to Professional Organizations for Teachers of Language and Literature.* New York: MLA, 1978. P11.G5

This pamphlet records the results of a survey of American organizations directly related to the study and teaching of language and literature. A total of fifty-six organizations are described. Entries give the name, acronym, address, and name of the executive officer of the organizations; its membership; general information about it, including history, purpose, and membership characteristics; its publications; its meetings; and its other activities. A checklist of acronyms concludes the work.

Among organizations most important for English studies (with founding date in parentheses) are the following (those included in the Gibaldi-Achtert pamphlet are marked with an asterisk).

American Antiquarian Society (1812)

*American Comparative Literature Association [ACLA] (1960)

American Dialect Society (1889)

American Folklore Society (1888)

American Name Society (1951)

American Philological Association (1869)

*American Printing History Association [APHA] (1974)

American Society for Aesthetics (1942)

*American Society for Eighteenth Century Studies [ASECS] (1969)

*American Society for Theatre Research [ASTR] (1956)

American Studies Association (1950)

Association for Business Communication [ABC] (1935)

Association for Computers and the Humanities (1978)

Association for Documentary Editing (1978)

Association for Literary and Linguistic Computing (1973)

*Association of Departments of English [ADE] (1963)

Association of Teachers of Advanced Composition [ATAC] (1979)

*Association of Teachers of English as a Second Language [ATESL] (1964)

Association of Teachers of Technical Writing [ATTW] (1973)

Bibliographical Society of America (1904)

Children's Literature Association [CLA] (1972)

*College English Association [CE] (1939)

*College Language Association [CLA] (1937)

Conference on College Composition and Communications [CCCC] (1949)

International Research Society for Children's Literature / Société internationale de recherches pour littérature enfantine / Internationale Forschungsgesellschaft für Kind- und Jungendliteratur (1970)

International Society for Humor Studies (1989)

*Linguistic Society of America [LSA] (1924)

Medieval Academy of America (1925)

*Midwest Modern Language Association [MMLA] (1959)

Modern Humanities Research Association [MHRA] (1918)

*Modern Language Association of America [MLA] (1883)

*National Council of Teachers of English [NCTE] (1911)

*Northeast Modern Language Association [NEMLA] (1967)

*Philological Association of the Pacific Coast [PAPC] (1899)

Renaissance Society of America (1954)

Research Society for Victorian Periodicals [RSVP] (1969)

Rhetoric Society of America (1968)

Rocky Mountain Modern Language Association [RMMLA] (1947)

Shakespeare Association of America (1972)

Society for Literature and Science (1985)

Society for Textual Scholarship (1979)

Society for the Study of the Multi-ethnic Literature of the United States (1974)

Society for the Study of Southern Literature [SSSL] (1968)

Society for Utopian Studies (1975)

*South Atlantic Modern Language Association [SAMLA] (1928)

*South Central Modern Language Association [SCMLA] (1940)

*Speech Communication Association [SCA] (1914)

*Teachers of English to Speakers of Other Languages [TESOL] (1966)

Z–26 *English Association Handbook of Societies and Collections.* Edited by Alicia C. Percival. London: The Library Association for the English Association, 1977. PE11.E423

This volume is divided into two sections. The first lists and describes the work of societies in the United Kingdom of interest to students of English language and literature. It is in five parts, treating general societies, societies devoted to individual authors and literary figures, local groups, special fields, and writers' associations. The aims, foundation, history, membership, officers, address, meeting schedule, and publications of each society are described.

The second section describes United Kingdom libraries and collections of interest to students of English. It is in three parts, treating public libraries, academic libraries, and specialist and notable libraries. The scope, librarian, access, catalogs, classification scheme, stocks, and services available are discussed for each library included.

A supplement lists some further useful Groups and Associations in ancillary disciplines and related fields. It and the two main sections treat a total of 381 serially numbered societies and collections.

The volume ends with an index keyed to the serial numbers of entries. It combines names, subjects, topics, and places in one alphabet.

Z–28 **Guide to Sources of Information about Associations, Societies, and Organizations.**

General and International

Directory of European Associations. Detroit: Gale, 1971–.
AS98.D55

Research Centers Directory. Detroit: Gale, 1960–. Biennial.
AS25.D5

North American (United States and/or Canada)

Encyclopedia of Associations [EA]. 3 vols. Detroit: Gale, 1956–. Biennial. Vol. 1, National Organizations of the U.S.; Vol. 2, Geographic and Executive Indexes; Vol. 3, New Associations and Projects. HS17.G334

Guide to Humanities Centers in the United States. Edited by D. Lydia Brontë. New York: Rockefeller Foundation Working Papers, 1980. AZ507.G84

Great Britain and Ireland

Directory of British Associations. 5th ed. London: C.B.D. Research, 1977–1978. AS118.D56

Scientific and Learned Societies of Great Britain: A Handbook Compiled from Official Sources. London: Allen and Unwin, 1884–1939, 1951–. [former title: *Yearbook of the Scientific and Learned Societies of Great Britain*]. AS115.S313

Z–29 **Guide to the Publications of Learned Societies.**

The oldest guide to the publications of learned societies is the sixteen-volume *Repertorium commentationum a societatibus litterariis editarum secundum disciplinarum ordinem digessit I. D. Reuss,* published in Göttingen by Diederich, 1801-1821, which indexes the publications of learned societies throughout Europe to 1800 [Z5051.R44]. In this series, volume 9 lists the publications of philological and literary societies.

For publications of learned societies through the nineteenth century, see the five-volume separate section in the 1885 British Museum *Catalogue of Printed Books,* which lists all publications of learned societies under the generic heading "Academies." Publications are in alphabetical order by place-name and then by the name of the society. More recent British Museum / British Library catalogs disperse these listings throughout the alphabet. The publications of American learned societies through the nineteenth century will be found listed in Richard Rogers Bowker, *Publications of Societies: A Provisional List of the Publications of American Scientific, Literary, and Other Societies from Their Organization* (New York: Publisher's Weekly, 1899) [Z5055 .U39 B7].

A valuable study of the publications of learned societies through the nineteenth century is Harrison R. Steeves, *Learned Societies and English Literary Scholarship in Great Britain and the United States* (New York: Columbia University Press, 1913) [PN22.A2], which contains both a bibliography and an index of authors, societies, titles, and subjects.

III. PURPOSES AND METHODS OF LITERARY SCHOLARSHIP

See also references in section L, Comparative, General, and World Literature, as well as those in sections pertaining to the particular form of scholarship in question. Many entries in section X, Theory, Rhetoric, and Composition, and in section Y, Bibliography, address fundamental questions of method.

Z–30 **Gibaldi, Joseph, ed. *Introduction to Scholarship in Modern Languages and Literature.*** New York: MLA, 1981.
PB35.I57

This volume, sponsored by the MLA Committee on Research Activities, contains a set of six essays by noted scholars introducing fundamental issues of modern linguistic and literary scholarship. The authors treat purposes, problems, presuppositions, and methods and procedures characterizing contemporary scholarship in each related field of study. Essays, written from an international point of view, cite pertinent sources for further reading in appended selected bibliographies. The individual essays and their authors are as follows: Linguistics (Winfred P. Lehmann); Textual Scholarship

(G. Thomas Tanselle); Historical Scholarship (Barbara Kiefer Lewalski); Literary Criticism (Lawrence Lipking); Literary Theory (Paul Hernadi); and The Scholar in Society (Wayne C. Booth). There is a brief introduction by Joel Connaroe which relates this volume to the earlier introductions edited by Thorpe (Z–31) and Foerster (Z–34). There is no index.

English: An Outline for the Intending Student, ed. Angus Ross (London: Routledge and Kegan Paul, 1971) [PE68 .G5 R6] presents a similar series of essays directed to the British student. The titles and authors are as follows: Introduction: English Studies in British Universities (Angus Ross); The Discipline of Literary Criticism (G. K. Hunter); The Historical Study of English Literature (D. J. Palmer); English Studies and European Culture (Gabriel Josipovici); The Study of the English Language (R. B. Le Page); Literature in English in Overseas Societies (Gerald Moore); The Place of American Literature (Andrew Hook); and Literature and Society (Laurence Lerner). A series of three appendixes discuss Undergraduate Courses in English Studies at British Universities, Degree Courses in Institutions Other Than Universities, and Postgraduate Studies in English in British Universities. A brief bibliography is followed by an index of authors, titles, and subjects.

Z–31 **Thorpe, James, ed. *Aims and Methods of Scholarship in Modern Languages and Literatures.*** 2d ed. New York: MLA, 1970.   PB21.T5 1970

This pamphlet, prepared under the auspices of the Committee on Research Activities of the MLA, contains four essays on the primary forms of scholarship: Linguistics (by William G. Moulton); Textual Criticism (by Fredson Bowers); Literary History (by Robert E. Spiller); and Literary Criticism (by Northrop Frye), accompanied by an introduction by the editor. The introduction stresses the interdependence of these forms and the implication that all literary scholars must be versed in all four forms of inquiry.

Z–32 **Leary, Lewis, ed. *Contemporary Literary Scholarship: A Critical Review.*** New York: Appleton-Century-Crofts, 1958.   PR77.N3

This volume contains a series of surveys of scholarship through the mid–1950s prepared for the Committee on Literary Scholarship and the Teaching of English of the NCTE. The essays present summaries of contemporary research directed to the high school and college teacher who is unable to keep abreast of developments. The essays are in four sections. Two essays, "The Scholar-Critic" by Jacques Barzun and "Literary Scholarship and the Teaching of English" by Lewis Leary, set out The Problem to which this volume is addressed. There follow essays 3–11 on The Periods: "Beowulf, Chaucer and Their Backgrounds" by George K. Anderson; "Shakespeare and His Times" by Gerald E. Bentley; "The Seventeenth Century" by Merritt Y. Hughes; "The Eighteenth Century" by James L. Clifford; "The Romantic Movement" by Richard Hartel Fogle; "The Victorian Period" by Lionel Stevenson; "American Literature" by Leslie A. Fiedler; "Contemporary British Literature" by Fred B. Millett; and "Contemporary American Literature" by R. W. B. Lewis. The third section, with essays 12–16, concerns The Genres: "Modern Literary Criticism" by William Van O'Connor; "Poetry" by George Arms; "The Novel" by Bradford A. Booth; "The Drama" by Henry Popkin; and "Comparative Literature" by Charlton Laird. Essays 17 and 18 are on The Audience: "The Public Arts and the Private Sensibility" by Patrick D. Hazard, and "Literary Audience" by Lennox Grey. The Selected Bibliography reviews fifty outstanding recent literary studies recommended by all or most of those surveyed. An index of subjects, including authors-as-subjects, concludes the volume.

Z–34 **Foerster, Norman, et al. *Literary Scholarship: Its Aims and Methods.*** Chapel Hill: University of North Carolina Press, 1941.   PN45.L5

This volume contains five essays on aspects of literary scholarship as practiced in the late 1930s and early 1940s. Its intent is to provide a historically sound and theoretically adequate rationale for literary scholarship in all of its aspects and relations. The essays and their authors are as follows: The Study of Letters (Norman Foerster); Language (John C. McGalliard); Literary History (René Wellek); Literary Criticism (Austin Warren); and Imaginative Writing (Wilbur H. Schramm). Notes and a chronologically organized, briefly annotated bibliography of works dealing with the aims and methods of literary scholarship are followed by a detailed index of authors, titles, and subjects.

Z–37 **Black, Max, ed. *Morality of Scholarship.*** Ithaca, N.Y.: Cornell University Press, 1967.   AZ103.F75

This volume contains three papers read at the inauguration on 27 October 1966 of the Society for the Humanities at Cornell University. The papers and their authors are: "The Knowledge of Good and Evil" by Northrop Frye; "Commitment and Imagination" by Stuart Hampshire; and "Politics and the Morality of Scholarship" by Conor Cruise O'Brien. All three discuss aspects of the potential conflict between scholarly detachment and social, political, and moral commitment.

Z–39 **Kaplan, Charles, ed. *Overwrought Urn: A Potpourri of Parodies of Critics Who Triumphantly Present the Real Meaning of Authors from Jane Austen to J. D. Salinger.*** New York: Pegasus, 1969.   PN6231.C75 K3

This volume offers a total of twenty-five parodies by a variety of authors including Borges, Robert Manson Myers, Richard Armour, Wayne Booth, Theodore Spencer, Bruce Harkness, Douglas Bush, Frederick C. Crews, Robert Benchley, James Thurber, and Edmund Wilson. The parodies are divided into groups mocking historical scholarship, close readings of poems, interpretations of prose fiction, scholarly method, and the literary world. With a parodic foreword and preface and a coda containing a parody of the list of contributors to a composite academic volume, scholarly publishing also takes its place among the targets.

Other parodic volumes include the numerous works by Richard Armour: *American Lit Relit: A Short History of American Literature for Long-suffering Students, for Teachers Who Manage to Keep One Chapter Ahead of the Class, and for All Who, No Longer Being in School, Can Happily Sink Back into Illiteracy* (New York: McGraw-Hill, 1964) [PS138.A7]; *Classics Reclassified: In Which Certain Famous Books Are Not So Much Digested As Indigested, Together with Mercifully Brief Biographies of Their Authors, a Few Unnecessary Footnotes, and Questions Which It Might Be Helpful Not to Answer* (New York: McGraw-Hill, 1960) [PS3501.R55 C55] (with chapters on *The Iliad, Julius Caesar, Ivanhoe, The Scarlet Letter, Moby Dick, Silas Marner,* and *David Copperfield*); *English Lit Relit: A Short History of English Literature from the Precursors (Before Swearing) to the Pre-Raphaelites and a Little After . . .* (New York: McGraw-Hill, 1969) [PR86.A7] [No LC number]; *Going Around in Academic Circles: A Low View of Higher Education* (New York: McGraw-Hill, 1965) [no LC number]; *It All Started with Freshman English* (New York: McGraw-Hill, 1973) [PR86.A72]; and *Twisted Tales from Shakespeare* (New York: McGraw-Hill, 1957) [PR2877.A7].

See also the twelve brilliant parodies, each of a different school of modern criticism, in Frederick C. Crews, the *Pooh Perplex: In Which It Is Discovered That the True Meaning of the Pooh Stories Is Not As Simple As Is Usually Believed, but for Proper Elucidation Requires the Combined Efforts of Several Academicians of Varying Critical Persuasions* (New York: Dutton, 1963) [PR6025.I65 W65], and the delightful volume by Robert Manson Myers, *From Beowulf to Virginia Woolf: An Astounding and Wholly Unauthorized History of English Literature*, new edition, thoroughly devised (Urbana: University of Illinois Press, 1984) [PR86.M9 1984].

IV.   GUIDES TO RESEARCH

Z–40   **Altick, Richard D.** *Art of Literary Research.* **3d ed.   Revised by John J. Fenstermaker.** New York: W. W. Norton, 1981.   PR56.A68 1981

This volume, first published in 1963, with a second edition in 1975, is a traditional introduction to the purposes, methods, and procedures of literary research.   It is divided into nine chapters, treating the following topics: Vocation; The Spirit of Scholarship (Error: Its Prevalence, Progress and Persistence; Examining the Evidence; Two Applications of the Critical Spirit: Fixing Dates and Testing Genuineness); Some Scholarly Occupations (Textual Study; Problems of Authorship; The Search for Origins; Tracing Reputation and Influence; Cultivating a Sense of the Past); The Task; Finding Materials; Libraries; Making Notes; The Philosophy of Composition; and The Scholar's Life.   An annotated bibliography of works for further reading is followed by a list of research exercises and an index of names, titles, and subjects.   The 3d edition updates citations, but it does not bring the volume up-to-date in the sense of covering the newer fields and approaches to literary research found in English Studies in the 1980s.

Z–41   **Altick, Richard D.** *Scholar Adventures.* New York: Macmillan, 1950.   PR99.A6

This volume narrates the stories of some of the most interesting and arresting scholarly investigations of the past half-century.   Included are fourteen chapters chronicling such themes as the story of the Boswell papers; the discovery of the forgeries of Thomas J. Wise; the uncovering of Malory's jail record; the discovery of important new manuscripts of Poe, Dickinson, and Mrs. Hester Lynch Thrale Piozzi, among others; the unmasking of forged literary works; scientific aid in establishing the date of Chaucer's *Troilus and Criseyde* and some Shakespearean quartos; the decoding of the cipher system used by Pepys in his diary; and the narrow escape from total loss of the Beowulf text.   This volume was reprinted with a new preface by the Ohio State University Press in 1987 [PR56.A7 1987].

Among additional sources of anecdotes about the adventures of scholars, see Rudolph Altrocchi, *Sleuthing in the Stacks* (Cambridge: Harvard University Press, 1944) [PN710.A54]; James L. Clifford's *From Puzzles to Portraits: Problems of a Literary Biographer* (Chapel Hill: University of North Carolina Press, 1970) [CT21.C553]; and Kathleen Coburn, *In Pursuit of Coleridge* (Oxford: Oxford University Press, 1977) [PR4485.C6].

Z–42   **Morize, André.** *Problems and Methods of Literary History.* 2d ed.   Boston: Ginn and Co., 1950.   PN59.M6

Originally published in 1922, this work focuses attention on specifics of French literary history.   But the author's presentation of questions of method is of such value as to warrant the use of the volume for methodological purposes by students of English or American literary history.   There are twelve chapters, in addition to an introduction and conclusion.   They are: 1, Objects and Methods of Literary History; 2, Implements and Tools: Bibliography; 3, The Preparation of an Edition; 4, Establishing a Critical Bibliography; 5, Investigation and Interpretation of Sources; 6, Chronology in Literary History; 7,

Problems of Authenticity and Attribution; 8, Questions of Versification; 9, Treatment of Biographical Material in the History of Literature; 10, Questions of Success and of Influence; 11, The History of Literature in Connection with the History of Ideas and of Manners; 12, Preparation and Redaction of a Thesis.   Throughout the text are extensive bibliographical references, further bibliographical notes, and reading lists.   The volume concludes with an index of authors, titles, and subjects.

Z–43   **Sanders, Chauncey.** *Introduction to Research in English Literary History.* **With a Chapter on Research in Folklore by Stith Thompson.** New York: Macmillan, 1952. PR56.S3

This volume, the examples for which are drawn exclusively from English and American literary history, is in four parts. They treat The Materials of Research; The Tools of Research; The Methods of Research; and Suggestions on Thesis-Writing, respectively.   The part on methods is in ten chapters regarding Problems in Editing, Biography, Authenticity and Attribution, Source Study, Chronology, Success and Influence, Interpretation, Technique, The History of Ideas, and Folklore.   After bibliographical notes keyed to each part and chapter, there are three appendixes.   The first presents a total of fourteen Specimen Bibliographies on the following topics: works on bibliography and methods of research; heuristics; paper; ink; printing; bindings; the care and preservation of books and manuscripts; paleography and abbreviations; chronology; epigraphy; heraldry; diplomatics; sphragistics (the science of seals); and the application of science to research. Appendixes 2 and 3 offer Specimen [research] Notes and Thesis Pages respectively.   A brief index concludes the volume.

Z–44   **Bateson, F. W.** *Scholar-Critic: An Introduction to Literary Research.* London: Routledge and Kegan Paul, 1972.
                                                            PN73.B3

This volume, somewhat outdated in its treatment of specific research techniques and methodologies, is disposed into eight chapters treating The Sense of Fact, Works of Reference, The Literary Object, Style, Interpretation, Textual Criticism, Literary History, and [scholarly] Presentation, respectively. The select bibliography is an abbreviated version of chapter 12 of Bateson's *Guide to English Literature* (A–13).

Z–45   **Barzun, Jacques, and Henry F. Graff.** *Modern Researcher.* 4th ed.   San Diego: Harcourt, Brace and World, 1985.   D13.B334 1985

Originally published in 1957, with a revised edition in 1970 and a 3d edition in 1977, this volume has become a standard guide for anyone engaged in research and report writing.   It is in three parts: First Principles; Research; and Writing.   Part I consists of chapters 1, Research and Report as Historian's Work, and 2, The ABC of Technique.   Part II includes chapters 3, The Searcher: His Mind and His Virtues; 4, Finding the Facts; 5, Verification; 6, Handling Ideas; 7, Truth and Causation; 8, Pattern, Bias, and the Great Systems; 9, Historians in Europe and America; and 10, The Sister Disciplines.   Part III, Writing, contains chapters 11, Organizing: Paragraph, Chapter, and Part; 12, Plain words: The War on Jargon and Cliches; 13, Clear Sentences: Right Emphasis and Right Rhythm; 14, The Arts of Quoting and Translating; 15, The Rules of Citing: Footnotes and Bibliography; and 16, Revising for Printer and Public.   An Afterword concerned with practical advice for progressing in writing is followed by a list of books for further reading, classified as follows: I. On the Historian's Work (Method, Fact Finding and Verification, Truth and Causation, Schools of Thought, The Great Historians, and The Sister Disciplines); II. On Writing and Composition (Diction and Style, Forms, Translations); III. Guides and

Bibliographies (General and Special, then alphabetically by discipline from Aeronautics to Typography and Allied Arts).

Z–46 **Winks, Robin W., ed.** *Historian as Detective: Essays on Evidence.* New York: Harper and Row, 1968.   D13.W65

This volume contains a total of twenty-six essays divided into six sections, all of which concern and explore, if only implicitly, the analogy between historical method and the inquiries of detectives in fiction. In particular, attention is paid to problems of evidence. Each of the anthologized essays is introduced by a discussion of the particular issue of inquiry and argument that it will illustrate. Included are materials dealing with questions of testimony, tracing lost documents, dealing with forgeries, suppressing evidence, committing inadvertent errors, using medical and psychological evidence, using psychoanalytic evidences, and so on. Each concludes with references to additional illustrative essays and materials. The volume concludes with a brief bibliographical essay on standard works on historical methodology. There is no index.

Z–47 **Beaurline, Lester A., ed.** *Mirror for Modern Scholars: Essays in Methods of Research in Literature.* New York: Odyssey Press, 1966.   PN85.B34

This volume contains twenty-four exemplary articles both illustrating and discussing methods of research in literary studies. They are disposed into ten sections as follows: [Analytical] Bibliography, Textual Studies, Authorship and Dating, Biography, Sources and Analogues, Style, Historical Periods, History of Ideas, Historical Interpretation, Form and Convention. Appended are R. B. McKerrow's classic essay "Form and Matter in the Publication of Research" (see Z–99) and a brief bibliography of suggested further readings which is classified according to the same ten divisions used in the main body of the volume.

Z–48 **Zitner, Sheldon P., ed.** *Practice of Modern Literary Scholarship.* Glenview, Ill.: Scott, Foresman, 1966.   PN85.Z5

This volume presents a total of thirty-one exemplary articles discussing and illustrating theoretical issues and research methods in literary studies. The articles are disposed into five sections as follows: I. Contexts of Scholarship (the nature and uses of literary scholarship; literary history and literary theory; the history of ideas and literary theory; and scholarship as argument); II. The Cycle of the Work (the discovery of works and documents; authorship and attribution; dating and chronology; composition and revision; source and influence; conditions of publication and problems of editing; conditions of performance; the audience; reception and reputation); III. Toward Criticism (definition and terminology; literature and biography; literature and society; literature and ideas; varieties of literary history; varieties of scholarly interpretation); IV. Newer Directions (linguistics and literature; the use of statistical methods; computer studies); and V. Caveats (the unreliabllility of texts; the limitations of transcripts; criticism and scholarship once again). An introduction by the editor includes references to numerous other studies dealing with the same or similar questions of theory or method. There is, regrettably, no index.

Z–49 **Some Frequently Recommended Works on Historical Method and on Research Design and Methodology.**

Bloch, Marc. *Historian's Craft: Reflections on the Nature and Uses of History and the Techniques and Methods of the Men Who Write It.* Translation by Peter Putnam of *Apologie pour l'historie: ou, Métier d'historien*

(Paris, 1949). New York: Alfred A. Knopf, 1953.   D13.B5262

Boeckh, August. *Encyklopädie und Methodologie der philologischen Wissenschaften.* 2d ed. Leipzig: Teubner, 1886.   PA91.B7 1886

Boulton, Marjorie. *Anatomy of Literary Studies: An Introduction to the Study of English Literature.* London: Routledge and Kegan Paul, 1980.   PR51.E5 B68

Buchler, Justus. *Concept of Method.* New York: Columbia University Press, 1961.   BD241.B8

Carr, E. H. *What Is History?* New York: Knopf, 1962.   D16.8.C33 1962

Clark, G. Kitson. *Guide for Students Working on Historical Subjects.* 2d ed. Cambridge: Cambridge University Press, 1968.

Crane, R. S. *Critical and Historical Principles of Literary History.* Chicago: University of Chicago Press, 1971. Reprinted from *Idea of the Humanities,* etc., 1967.   PN441.C7 1971

Fling, Fred Morrow. *Writing of History: An Introduction to Historical Method.* New Haven: Yale University Press, 1920.   D16.F63

Gottschalk, Louis. *Understanding History: A Primer of Historical Method.* 2d ed. New York: Knopf, 1969.   D13.G75 1969

Gray, Wood, et al. *Historian's Handbook: A Primer of Historical Method.* 2d ed. Boston: Houghton Mifflin, 1964.   D13.G78 1964

Greenlaw, Edwin. *Province of Literary History.* Baltimore: Johns Hopkins University Press, 1931.   PN441.G7

Hillway, Tyrus. *Introduction to Research.* 2d ed. Boston: Houghton Mifflin, 1964.   Q180.A1 H5 1964

Hockett, Homer C. *Critical Method in Historical Research and Writing.* New York: Macmillan, 1955.   E175.7.H6446

Johnson, Allen. *Historian and Historical Evidence.* New York: Scribners, 1926.   D13.J57

Langlois, Charles Victor, and Charles Seignobos. *Introduction to the Study of History.* Translation by G. G. Berry of *Introduction aux études historiques* (Paris: Hachette, 1895). New York: Holt, 1898.   D16.L29

Lyon, Harvey T. *Keats' Well-read Urn: An Introduction to Literary Method.* New York: Holt, 1958.   PR4834.05 L9

Mann, Thomas. *Guide to Library Research Methods.* New York: Oxofrd University Press, 1987.   Z710.M23 1987

Moyles, R. G. *Basic Methods of Research for the Student of English Literature.* Rev. ed. Edited by David Jackel. Edmonton: Athabascan Publishing Co., 1975.   PR56.M6 1975

O'Toole, Simon [pseud.]. *Confessions of an American Scholar.* Minneapolis, 1970.

Schiff, Hilda, ed. *Contemporary Approaches to English Studies.* London: Heinemann Educational for the English Association, 1977.   PE25.C6

Sears, Donald A. *Discipline of English: A Guide to Literary Research.* New York: Harcourt, Brace and World, 1963.   PR33.S4 1963

Sertillanges, A. D., O. P. *Intellectual Life: Its Spirit, Conditions, Methods.* Translation by Mary Ryan of *La vie intellectuelle* (Paris, 1920). Westminster, Md.: Newman Press, 1948.   AZ101.S412

Shafer, R. J., ed. *Guide to Historical Method.* Rev. ed. Homewood, Ill.: The Dorsey Press, 1974.

> D16.G37 1974

Thorpe, James E. *Literary Scholarship. A Handbook for Advanced Students of English and American Literature.* Boston: Houghton Mifflin, 1964. PR33.T5

Watson, George. *Discipline of English.* London: Macmillan, 1978. PR21.W3 1978

————. *Literary Thesis: A Guide to Research.* London: Longman, 1970. LB2369.W33

————. *Study of Literature: A New Rationale of Literary History.* New York: Charles Scribner's Sons, 1970.

> PN81.W3 1970

V. METHODS AND TECHNIQUES

See also many references in section F, History; section G, Biography; section I, Language, Linguistics, and Philology; section K, Literary Materials and Contexts; section L, General, Comparative, and World Literature; and both sections M, English Literature, and S, American Literature.

Z–50 Erdman, David V., and Ephim G. Fogel, eds. *Evidence for Authorship: Essays on Problems of Attribution with an Annotated Bibliography of Selected Readings.* Ithaca, N.Y.: Cornell University Press, 1966. PR61.E7

This volume contains a total of thirty-one articles, the first eight of which, gathered as Part I, The Case for Internal Evidence, reprint papers from a symposium held at the English Institute in 1958. To these are added further articles on the topic published in the *Bulletin of the New York Public Library.* To these are gathered additional articles of methodological interest, disposed into four further parts, as follows: II. Studies in Attribution; English Literature to 1660; III. 1660 to 1775; IV. English and American Literature since 1775; V. Detections of Forgery.

These are followed by an elaborately annotated bibliography in the form of discursive essays describing the history of deliberations over disputed works of Chaucer and Shakespeare as well as citing and summarizing work concerned with attributions to less celebrated authors. The bibliography is in seven sections, discussing readings on attribution of English Literature to 1500; 1500 to 1600; 1660 to 1789; English Literature since 1789; American Literature; Detections of Forgery; and Statistical Studies and Computer Applications. Within sections, subdivisions are by author or title, as appropriate. The bibliography is followed by a list of contributors, an index of names and titles, and an index of subjects.

Z–53 Madden, David, and Richard Powers. *Writer's Revisions: An Annotated Bibliography of Articles and Books about Writers' Revisions and Their Comments on the Creative Process.* Metuchen, N.J.: Scarecrow, 1981.

> Z6519.M28

This volume, the first reference work that brings together studies on the subject of authors' revisions, is in two parts, preceded by an Introduction also in two parts. The first part of the introduction, "What is the Value of Studying Revision," is followed by a listing of "Books and Articles" on the subject. Part One, "Articles and Books about Writers' Revisions" presents 350 annotated entries covering thirty-seven British and American authors, with special attention to Faulkner, Hardy, James, Joyce, Richardson, Whitman, and Yeats. Entries give the name of the author, the work or works dis-

cussed, the extent to which the work under study is reprinted in the book or article, the method used to compare or display versions, the conclusions drawn by the scholar, the order of the discussion, the kinds of revision discussed, and whether the author's published work need be on hand to derive maximum benefit from the discussion.

Part Two, "Writers Talk about the Creative Process," augments Part One with an enumeration of over 120 entries for articles and books in which writers talk about writing in general and their own in particular. Revision is not always a subject of these items. The work concludes with five indexes, as follows: genre, revision problems at issue (point-of-view, style, etc.), scholars and titles of their books and articles, writers and works in which they comment on the creative process, and writers and the titles of works revised.

Z–54 Some Frequently Recommended Studies in Dating, Attribution, Authenticity, and Composition.

Baker, Donald C. "The Date of *Mankind*" *PQ* 42 (1963): 90–91.

Beaty, Jerome. *"Middlemarch" from Notebook to Novel: A Study of George Eliot's Creative Method.* Urbana: University of Illinois Press, 1960. Composition.

> PR4662.B4

Bennett, Josephine W. *Evolution of "The Faerie Queene."* Chicago: University of Chicago Press, 1942. Composition. PR2358.B4

Benson, Larry D. "The Authorship of St. Erkenwald." *JEGP* 64 (1965): 393–405.

Bentley, G. E., Jr. "The Date of Blake's *Vala* or *The Four Zoas*" *MLN* 71 (1956): 487–491.

Bradford, Curtis. *Yeats at Work.* Carbondale: Southern Illinois University Press, 1965. Composition.

> PR5907.B72

Butt, John, and Kathleen Tillotson. *Dickens at Work.* London: Methuen, 1957. Composition. PR4591.B8

Carter, John, and Graham Pollard. *Enquiry into the Nature of Certain Nineteenth Century Pamphlets, and A Sequel . . . by Nicholas Barker John Collins.* London: Constable and Co., 1934. Authenticity. Z1024.C32

Crane, Ronald S. *New Essays by Oliver Goldsmith.* Chicago: University of Chicago Press, 1927. Attribution.

> PR3487.E9 1927

Dawson, Giles. "Authenticity and Attribution of Written Matter" In *English Institute Annual,* 1942, pp. 77–100. New York: Columbia University Press, 1943. PE1010.E5

Ellegård, Alvar. *Statistical Method for Determining Authorship: The Junius Letters, 1769–1772. Gothenburg Studies in English,* no. 13, Gothenburg, 1962.

> DA508.A6 E4

Gilbert, Allan H. *On the Composition of "Paradise Lost."* Chapel Hill: University of North Carolina Press, 1947.

> PR3562.G5

Houghton, Walter E. *Introduction to The Wellesley Index to Victorian Periodicals.* Attribution. (See D–12.)

Hoy, Cyrus. "The Shares of Fletcher and His Collaborators in the Beaumont and Fletcher Canon" *SB* 16 (1962): 71–90.

Jonson, Linck C. *Thoreau's Complex Weave: The Writing of A Week on the Concord and Merrimack Rivers with the Text of the First Draft.* Charlottesville: University Press of Virginia, 1986. F72.M7 T533 1986

Kane, George. *Piers Plowman: The Evidence for Authorship.* London: University of London, Athlone Press, 1965. PR2015.K3 1965

Lowes, John Livingston. *Road to Xanadu: A Study in the Ways of the Imagination*. Rev. ed. Cambridge: Harvard University Press, 1930. Composition.
PR4484.L6 1930

Mosteller, Frederick, and David L. Wallace. *Inference and Disputed Authorship: The Federalist Papers*. Reading, Mass.: Addison-Wesley, 1964. JK155.M6

Rader, Ralph W. *Tennyson's "Maud": The Biographical Genesis*. Berkeley and Los Angeles: University of California Press, 1963. PR5567.R3

Rogers, Neville. *Shelley at Work*. 2d ed. Oxford: Clarendon Press, 1967. Composition. PR5431.R65 1967

Schoenbaum, Samuel. *Internal Evidence and Elizabethan Dramatic Authorship: An Essay in Literary History and Method*. Evanston, Ill.: Northwestern University Press, 1966. Extensive bibliography. PR658.A9 S3

Stallworthy, Jon. *Between the Lines: Yeats's Poetry in the Making*. Oxford: Clarendon Press, 1963. PR5907.S75

———. *Vision and Revision in Yeats's "Last Poems."* Oxford: Clarendon Press, 1969. PR5907.S758

Stone, Harry, *Dickens' Working Notes for His Novels*. Chicago: University of Chicago Press, 1986.
PR4586.D5 1987

Vieth, David M. *Attribution in Restoration Poetry: A Study of Rochester's "Poems" of 1680*. New Haven: Yale University Press, 1963. PR3669.R2 V5

West, James L. W., III, Sister Carrie *Portfolio*. Charlottesville: University Press of Virginia, 1985.
PS3507.R55 S597 1985

Woods, Charles B. "Fielding and the Authorship of *Shamela*." *PQ* 25 (1956): 248–272.

Yule, G. Udny. *Statistical Study of Literary Vocabulary*. Cambridge: Cambridge University Press, 1944. Attribution. BV4829.Y8

Z–58 Scholarly Journals Publishing Research Notes and Queries.

AN&Q   *American Notes and Queries* Vol. 1–. Owingsville, Ky.: Erasmus, 1962–. 10/yr. Reviews. Bibliography of "Recent [foreign reference] Books" with brief descriptive annotations. Eight volumes of an earlier series with this title were published 1941–1950 at North Bennington, Vt. AG305.A4

Archiv   *Archiv für das Studium der neueren Sprachen und Literaturen* (L–57)

Bulletin of the New York Public Library [now *Bulletin of Research in the Humanities*] [*BNYPL*] (B–30)

HLB   *Harvard Library Bulletin* (B–26)

HLQ   *Huntington Library Quarterly* (B–20)

JNL   *Johnsonian Newsletter* (P–9)

MLN   *Modern Language Notes* (L–57)

NM   *Neuphilologische Mitteilungen* (N–25)

N&Q   *Notes and Queries: For Readers and Writers, Collectors and Librarians*. Vol. 1–. Oxford: Oxford University Press, 1849–. Original series, 198 vols., 1849–1953. New series, vol. 1–, 1954–. Reviews. There are a total of fifteen cumulative indexes through 1947. AG305.N7

OEN   *Old English Newsletter* (N–22)

Restoration (P–7)

SCN   *Seventeenth Century News* (0–9)

Scriblerian (P–8)

ShN   *Shakespeare Newsletter* (0–53)

TLS   *Times Literary Supplement* (Z–151)

Many general literary journals do regularly publish scholarly notes among other articles. Reference to the *MLA Directory of Periodicals* (Z–100) will generally indicate whether a particular journal does publish such items.

Z–59 Some Frequently Recommended Works on Annotation.

Friedman, Arthur. "Principles of Historical Annotation in Critical Editions of Modern Texts." In *English Institute Annual*, 1941, pp. 115–128. New York: Columbia University Press, 1942. PE1010.E5

Menapace, John. "Some Approaches to Annotation." *Scholarly Publishing*, 1 (1970): 194–205. Z286.S37 S33

Morize, *Problems and Methods of Literary History*. (Z–42), pp. 62–65.

Z–60 Hermerén, Göran. *Influence in Art and Literature.* Princeton, N.J.: Princeton University Press, 1975.
BH301.J8 H47 1975

This volume is the first book-length, systematic study of the framework used in making claims and judgments about influence in art and literature. A series of twenty-nine chapters are disposed into four parts treating 1. Problems and Distinctions; 2. Conditions for Influence, Measurement of Influence; 3. Consequences; and 4. Conclusions. A bibliography of works quoted or referred to concludes the volume, along with an index of names, titles, and subjects.

Z–61 Primeau, Ronald, ed. *Influx: Essays on Literary Influence.* Port Washington, N.Y.: Kennikat Press, 1977.
PN45.I45

This small volume conveniently reprints ten essays concerned with the matter of influence both as an historical fact and as a matter of theoretical interest. The essays are in ten sections. Part 1, Literary History and Tradition, includes essays by Eliot, Trilling, and Hassan. Part 2, An Aesthetics of Origins and Revisionism, includes discussions by Guillen, Block, Bloom, and Bate. Part 3, Reader as Participant, includes essays by Rosenblatt, Holland, and Fish. A brief select bibliography and an even briefer index conclude the volume.

Z–64 Some Frequently Recommended Studies of Sources and Influences.

Allen, Michael J. B., and Daniel G. Calder. *Sources and Analogues of Old English Poetry: The Major Latin Texts in Translation*. Cambridge, Eng.: D. S. Brewer, 1976. PA6164.A5

Allen, Michael J. B., Daniel G. Calder, et al. *Sources and Analogues of Old English Poetry II: The Major Germanic and Celtic Texts in Translation*. Cambridge, Eng.: D. S. Brewer, 1983. PR182.S66 1983

Bate, Walter Jackson. *Burden of the Past and the English Poet*. Cambridge: Belknap Press of Harvard University Press, 1970. PR99.B19

Bloom, Harold. *Anxiety of Influence: A Theory of Poetry*. London: Oxford University Press, 1973. PN1031.B53

Bryan, William F., and Germaine Dempster. *Sources and Analogues of Chaucer's Canterbury Tales*. Chicago: University of Chicago Press, 1940. PR1912.A2 B7

Bullough, Geoffrey. *Narrative and Dramatic Sources of Shakespeare*. 8 vols. New York: Columbia University Press, 1957–1975.   PR2952.5.B8

Craig, Hardin. "Shakespeare and Wilson's *Arte of Rhetorique*: An Inquiry into the Criteria for Determining Sources." *SP* 28 (1931): 618–630.

Crane, Ronald S. *Vogue of Medieval Chivalric Romance in the Renaissance*. Menasha, Wis.: George Banta Publishing Co., 1919.   PR418.R7 C7

Curtius, Ernst Robert. *European Literature and the Latin Middle Ages*. Translation by Willard Trask of *Europäische Literatur und lateinisches Mittelalter*. New York: Harper and Row, 1953.   PN674.C82

Dent, R. W. *John Webster's Borrowing*. Berkeley and Los Angeles: University of California Press, 1960.   PR3187.D4

Goodwin, K. L. *Influence of Ezra Pound*. London: Oxford University Press, 1966.   PS3531.082 Z64

Hassan, Ihab H. "The Problem of Influence in Literary History: Notes toward a Definition." *JAAC* 14 (1955/56): 66–76 (reprinted in Z–61).

Havens, Raymond D. *Influence of Milton on English Poetry*. Cambridge: Harvard University Press, 1922.   PR3588.H3 1961

Hughes, Merritt Y. *Virgil and Spenser*. Berkeley: University of California Press, 1929.   PR2366.H8

Lowes, John Livingston. *Road to Xanadu: A Study in the Ways of the Imagination*. Rev. ed. Cambridge: Harvard University Press, 1930.   PR4484.L6 1930

Morris, Lynn King. *Chaucer Source and Analogue Criticism: A Cross-Referenced Guide*. New York: Garland, 1984.   Z8164.M67 1984

Muir, Kenneth, and F. W. Bateson. "Editorial Commentary" [concerning Gittings, *John Keats: The Living Year*, and source study], *Essays in Criticism* 4 (1954): 432–440.

Smith, Grover. *T. S. Eliot, Poetry and Plays: A Study in Sources and Meaning*. 2d ed. Chicago: University of Chicago Press, 1974.   PS3509.L43 Z868 1974

Stallman, R. W. "The Scholar's Net: Literary Sources." *CE* 17 (1955): 20–27.

Taylor, George C. "Montaigne-Shakespeare and the Deadly Parallel." *PQ* 22 (1943): 330–337.

Williams, Arnold. "Methods and Achievements in the Study of Milton's Sources: A Defense." *Papers of the Michigan Academy of Science, Arts and Letters* 32 (1948): 471–480.

Z–66 Aids for Locating Contemporary Reviews.

A convenient sampling of contemporary response to an author will be found in the volumes of the *Critical Heritage Series* which have been published by Routledge since 1968. Authors covered by one (or multiple volumes) in the series included Addison and Steele, Arnold, Auden, Beckett, Bennett, Blake, the Brontës, Burns, Byron, Carlyle, Chaucer (2 vols.), Chekhov, Clare, Clough, Coleridge, Collins, Congreve, Conrad, Cooper, Crabbe, Crane, Dante, Defoe, Dickens, Donne, Dos Passos, Dryden, George Eliot, T. S. Eliot, Faulkner, Fielding, Ford Maddox Ford, Forster, Gissing, Goldsmith, Hardy, Hawthorne, Hemingway, Herbert, Hopkins, Huxley, Ibsen, James, Johnson, Jonson, Joyce, Keats, Kipling, Lawrence, Marlowe, Marvell, Maugham, Melville, Meredith, Milton, Morris, Nabokov, Orwell, Pater, Plath, Poe, Pope, Pound, Proust, Rochester, Ruskin, Scott, Shakespeare (6 vols.), Shaw, Shelley, Skelton, Smollett, Southey, Spenser, Sterne, Stevens, Stevenson, Swift, Swinburne, Tennyson, Thackeray, Tolstoy, Trollope, Twain, Walpole, Waugh, Webster, Wells, Whitman, Wilde, Williams, Woolf, Wyatt, and Yeats.

By virtue of their chronological arrangement of secondary literature, the volumes of the *CBEL* (M–10) and the *NCBEL* (M–11) often include some separately published contemporary responses to works of literature among the earlier items in their enumerations of the secondary literature on various works and authors.

For contemporary reviews of eighteenth-century works, see the new *Index to Book Reviews in England, 1749–1774* compiled by Antonia Forster (Carbondale: Southern Illinois University Press, 1989) [Z1035.A1 F67 1989]. This volume provides access to 3,021 reviews of contemporary poetry, fiction, and drama during the first quarter-century of formal book reviewing in England. Analyzed are the *Monthly Review*, the *Critical Review*, the *Gentleman's Magazine*, and the *London Magazine*, along with eleven other periodicals. Also available is the index by Paul Van Tieghem of *L'anneé littéraire (1754–1790)* (Paris: F. Rieder, 1917) [PN3.A6].

For the later eighteenth and early nineteenth centuries, see Donald Reiman, *Romantics Reviewed: Contemporary Reviews of British Romantic Poets*, in three parts: *Part A: Lake Poets*, 2 vols.; *Part B: Byron and Regency Society Poets*, 5 vols.; and *Part C: Shelley, Keats, and London Radical Writers*, 2 vols. (New York: Garland, 1972) [PR590.R43]. Reiman reproduces contemporary British periodical reviews of major and some minor authors. Each part is arranged alphabetically by title of the periodical covered, and then chronologically for the reviews published in that periodical.

Also useful are William S. Ward's three compilations: *Literary Reviews in British Periodicals, 1789–1797* (New York: Garland, 1979) [Z2013.W36 1979]; *Literary Reviews in British Periodicals 1789–1820: A Bibliography*, 2 vols. (New York: Garland, 1972) [Z2013.W36]; and *Literary Reviews in British Periodicals, 1821–1826* (New York: Garland, 1977) [Z2013.W36 1977], each of which presents a checklist of thousands of reviews arranged alphabetically by author reviewed, with citations given beneath each author's name and the title of the work reviewed. An appendix lists citations to reviews of operas.

For later nineteenth century reviews, see *Poole's Index to Periodical Literature* (D–10), the *Nineteenth Century Reader's Guide to Periodical Literature* (D–11), the *Wellesley Index* (D–12), and the *Combined Retrospective Index to Humanities Journals* (E–78).

For late nineteenth and early twentieth century reviews of American fiction, see Eichelberger, et al., *Guide to Critical Reviews of United States Fiction* (S–88). For general reviews in the earlier twentieth century, see the *Cumulated Magazine Subject Index* (D–12), the *Reader's Guide to Periodical Literature* (D–15), the *Combined Retrospective Index to Humanities Journals* (E–78), and the *Book Review Digest* (E–76). For twentieth century film and theater reviews, see Samples, *How to Locate Reviews of Plays and Films* (U–57). For twentieth century theater reviews, see Salem, *Guide to Critical Reviews* (U–58): the "Dramatic Index" section of the *Bulletin of Bibliography* from 1909 through 1953 (A–7); the special index to theater reviews in the *New York Times*, *New York Times Directory of the Theatre* (U–59); and *New York Times Film Reviews* (U–127).

For additional reviews of twentieth century works, see the *New York Times Book Review Index* (Z–150).

For additional aids to locating contemporary book review citations, see Gray's *Guide to Book Review Citations: A Bibliography of Sources* (E–72).

Z–67 **Some Frequently Recommended Reception Studies.** (See also works on Reader Response Theory in X–23, and on Literature and Society in X–65, X–66, and X–69.)

Baym, Nina. *Novels, Readers and Reviewers: Responses to Fiction in Antebellum American.* Ithaca, N.Y.: Cornell University Press, 1984.   PS377.B37 1984

Bender, Todd K. *Gerard Manley Hopkins: The Classical Background and Critical Reception of His Work.* Baltimore: Johns Hopkins University Press, 1966.
PR4803.H44 Z58

Bentley, G. E. *Shakespeare and Jonson: Their Reputation in the Seventeenth Century Compared.* 2 vols. Chicago: University of Chicago Press, 1945.   PR2959.B4

Bronson, Bertrand H. "The Double Tradition of Dr. Johnson" *ELH* 18 (1951): 90–106.

Bryer, Jackson R., ed. *F. Scott Fitzgerald: The Critical Reception.* New York: B. Franklin, 1978.
PS3511.I9 Z614

Duncan, Joseph E. *Revival of Metaphysical Poetry: The History of a Style, 1800 to the Present.* Minneapolis: University of Minnesota Press, 1959.   PR581.D8

Ford, George H. *Dickens and His Readers: Aspects of Novel Criticism since 1836.* Princeton, N.J.: Princeton University Press, 1955.   PR4588.F6

———. *Keats and the Victorians: A Study of His Influence and Rise to Fame, 1821–95.* New Haven: Yale University Press, 1944.   PR4837.F6

Frost, David. "Shakespeare in the Seventeenth Century." *SQ* 16 (1965): 81–89.

Gallason, Thomas A. *Stephen Crane's Career: Perspectives and Evaluations.* New York: New York University Press, 1972.   PS1449.C85 Z643

Haass, Sabine. *Gedichts-Anthologien der viktorianischen Zeit: Eine buchgeschichtliche Untersuchung zum Wandel des literarischen Geschmacks.* Nurnberg: H. Carl, 1986.   Z326.H33 1986

Hayden, John O. *Romantic Reviewers: 1802–1824.* Chicago: University of Chicago Press, 1968.   PR457.H3

Hetherington, Hugh W. *Melville's Reviewers, British and American, 1846–1891.* Chapel Hill: University of North Carolina Press, 1961.   PS2387.H45

Howes, A. B. *Yorick and the Critics: Sterne's Reputation in England, 1760–1868.* New Haven: Yale University Press, 1958.   PR3716.H6

Lubbers, Klaus. *Emily Dickinson: The Critical Revolution.* Ann Arbor: University of Michigan Press, 1968.
PS1541.Z5 L8

Morgan, Peter F. *Literary Critics and Reviewers in Early 19th Century Britain.* London: Croom Helm, 1983.
PR75.M67 1983

Patten, Robert L. *Charles Dickens and His Publishers.* Oxford: Clarendon Press, 1978.   PR4583.P29

Rodden, John. *Politics of Literary Reputation: The Making and Claiming of "St. George" Orwell.* New York: Oxford University Press, 1989.
PR6029.R8 Z776 1989

Rollins, Hyder Edward. *Keats' Reputation in America to 1848.* Cambridge: Harvard University Press, 1946.
PR4837.R56

Salzman, Jack, ed. *Theodore Dreiser: The Critical Reception.* New York: D. Lewis, 1972.   PS3507.R55 Z816

Schwartz, Lawrence H. *Creating Faulkner's Reputation: The Politics of Modern Literary Criticism.* Knoxville: University of Tennessee Press, 1988.
PS3511.A86 Z9663 1988

Spurgeon, Caroline. *Five Hundred Years of Chaucer Criticism and Allusion, 1357–1900.* 3 vols. Cambridge: Cambridge University Press, 1925. PR1924.A2 1925

Stephens, Robert O., ed. *Ernest Hemingway: The Critical Reception.* New York: B. Franklin, 1977.
PS3515.E37 Z5868

Van Egmond, Peter. *Critical Reception of Robert Frost.* Boston: G. K. Hall, 1974.   Z8317.78.V35

Voigt, Milton. *Swift and the Twentieth Century.* Detroit: Wayne State University Press, 1964.   PR3726.V6

Wagner, Linda W., ed. *Robert Frost: The Critical Reception.* New York: Burt Franklin, 1977.
PS3511.R94 Z9185

Z–68 **Some Frequently Recommended Works on Specific Research Methods, Techniques, or Projects.**

Colainne, A. J. "The Aims and Methods of Annotated Bibliography." *Scholarly Publishing* 11 (July 1980): 321–331.

Harner, James L. *On Compiling an Annotated Bibliography.* New York: MLA, 1985.   Z1001.H33 1985

Howard-Hill, T. H. *Literary Concordances: A Guide to the Preparation of Manual and Computer Concordances.* Oxford: Pergamon, 1979. Bibliography, glossary.
Z695.92.H68 1979

Hunnisett, R. F. *Editing Records for Publication.* London: British Records Association, 1977.   Z286.H5 H86

Robinson, A. M. Lewin. *Systematic [enumerative] Bibliography: A Practical Guide to the Work of Compilation.* With an Additional Chapter by C. D. Batty. 3d ed. Hamden, Conn.: Linnet Books, 1971.
Z1001.R66 1971

Z–69 **Bindoff, Stanley Thomas, and James T. Boulton, eds. *Research in Progress in English and History in Britain, Ireland, Canada, Australia, and New Zealand.*** London: St. James Press, 1976.   Z6201.B59 1976

This volume, which does not cover research pursued by degree candidates, does nevertheless bring together in one place work in progress by scholars established in universities and other institutions. The work of some 3,800 individuals is listed. Entries are classified by discipline, and within English and Historical studies, by period and then by author or historical topic. The volume concludes with addresses of universities and institutions surveyed and an index of scholars with their institutional affiliation.

From 1979–1984 was published the annual *Research in British Universities, Polytechnics, and Colleges,* whose title since 1985 has been *Current Research in Britain: The Humanities* (Boston Spa: British Library Document Supply Center, 1985– [AZ188.G7.C87], which lists work in progress by faculty and graduate students. Organized by institution, department, and researcher, the guide gives a brief project description with expected dates, publication plans, and grants or other support. Indexes by researchers, subjects, and keywords in descriptions conclude the annual volume.

No comparable volume exists for the work in progress of American scholars. In lieu of such, one must consult a broad variety of sources that record work in progress for a limited field of English studies. It should be noted that MLA and FLIN are planning an on-line work in progress database. In its earliest form, it will cite articles accepted for publication from cooperating journals.

VI. COMPUTER-BASED RESEARCH

See also the *MLA International Bibliography* (L–50) under "Computer-Assisted Research," the MHRA *Annual Bibliography of English Language and Literature* (M–21) under "Language, Literature, and Computers," and many references in section X and section Y.

Z–70 Hockey, Susan. *Guide to Computer Application in the Humanities.* Baltimore: Johns Hopkins University Press, 1980.   AZ105.H63 1980

This introduction is intended for the uninitiated potential computer user among researchers in language, literature, history, and bibliography. A lengthy introduction to computers and computer terminology precedes a discussion of the various nonnumerical tasks that computers can be programmed to perform; these include the compilation of indexes, catalogs, word counts, concordances, stylistic analyses, and textual collations. Various general all-purpose programs are introduced, including BABEL (a translation program); COCOA (a word-count and concordance-producing program); SNOBOL (the acronym for String Oriented Symbolic Language, a computer language that permits text collation and editing) and its related program, SPITBOL (the acronym for Speedy Implementation of SNOBOL). The volume concludes with advice about starting up a computer-assisted research project, a directory of useful addresses, a general bibliography, and a comprehensive glossary of computer terms and acronyms.

Z–71 Oakman, Robert L. *Computer Methods for Literary Research.* Rev. ed. Columbia: University of South Carolina Press, 1984.   PN73.O24 1984

This volume, originally published in 1979, is designed as an introduction to computers for the literary scholar or student without computer experience. An introduction to the revised edition describes trends in the use of computers for literary research. It is organized into eight chapters in two parts, as follows: Part I, Fundamentals of Literary Computing (1. Computers for Information Processing; 2. Getting Literary Material In and Out of the Machine; 3. Flowcharting and Programming for Literary Analysis); Part II, Computers in Literary Research (4. Concordances; 5. Information Retrieval: Historical Dictionaries and Scholarly Bibliographies; 6. Textual Editing with a Computer; 7. Stylistic Analysis; 8. Further Considerations; Archives, Packages, and Future Prospects). Each chapter is extensively documented, and to it is appended an annotated list of Further Readings. The volume concludes with A Selected Bibliography for Literary Computing and an Index of authors, titles, and subjects. The bibliography, which excludes items listed in the Further Readings addenda to chapters, is in ten sections, as follows: I. General; II. Hardware Considerations—Input and Output; III. Software Considerations—Programming Languages, Techniques, and Packages; IV. Concordances; V. Information Retrieval; Lexicography; VI. Information Retrieval; Bibliography and Indexes; VII. Textual Criticism and Editing; VIII. Stylistics: Authorship Studies; IX. Content Analysis; and X. Stylistics: Studies of Form.

Z–73 Feldman, Paula R., and Buford Norman. *Wordworthy Computer: Classroom and Research Applications in Language and Literature.* New York: Random House, 1987.   PR73.F44

This volume is an introduction to both classroom and research uses of the computer. Part one treats classroom applications. Part two surveys research applications, with chapters on databases, concordances, interpreting statistical data,

stylistic analysis, and scholarly publishing. There are four valuable appendixes: (1) sources of information, including computer networks, bibliographical databases, repositories of machine-readable texts, and professional organizations; (2) selected journals and periodicals; (3) selected bibliography preceded by a subject index; (4) glossary. The work is indexed by titles, subjects, and persons.

Z–74 McKenzie, Alan T. *Grin on the Interface: Word Processing for the Academic Humanist.* New York: MLA, 1984.   Z52.4.G74 1984

This small volume presents an introduction to word processors and word processing in six chapters, three appendixes, a glossary, and a brief bibliography. Chapters cover the use of a system by an uninitiated humanist; basic functions and features of various systems; the design of a departmental system; various systems and their strengths, shortcomings, and costs; use of word processing in scholarly editing and in the production of a scholarly journal. Among titles included in the brief bibliography are:

Brown, Eric D. *Writing with a Word Processor: Communication in the Computer Age.* Reston, Va.: Reston Publishing Co., 1984.   HF5548.115.B76 1984

Fluegelman, Andrew, and Jeremy Joan Hewes. *Writing in the Computer Age: Word Processing Skills and Style for Every Writer.* New York: Anchor, 1983.   PN171.D37 F58 1983

McCunn, Donald H. *Write, Edit & Print: Word Processing with Personal Computers.* San Francisco: Design Enterprises of San Francisco, 1982.   Z52.4.M35 1982

Zinsser, William. *Writing with a Word Processor.* New York: Harper and Row, 1983.   PN171.D37 Z56 1983

Z–75 "Annual Bibliography for [1965–]." *Computers and the Humanities.* Vol. 1–. Elmsford, N.Y.: Pergamon, 1966–. 6/yr. Reviews.   Z699.5.H8065

This annual bibliography of books, parts of books, and articles concerning computer studies, as well as bibliographies, concordances, editions, and other publications that depended upon computer-assisted research, is disposed into sections, as follows: I. General; II. Language and Literature; III. Archaeology; IV. History; V. Music. Within sections, arrangement is alphabetical by author.

Twice a year, *Computers and the Humanities* also publishes a "Directory of Scholars Active," which reports on studies planned or in progress, giving the title or subject of the study, the name of the chief investigator and institutional affiliation, the scope, method, type of computer being used, and additional technical information. This directory is organized by the same headings as are used in the annual bibliography. A recent separately published volume edited by Joseph Raben, *Computer-Assisted Research in the Humanities: A Directory of Scholars Active* (Elmsford, N.Y.: Pergamon, 1977) [A58.C63 1977], brings much of this information together. In addition to both these features, the journal also includes abstracts and other bibliographic notes in each issue.

There are a number of other scholarly journals concerned with computers and the humanities. These include:

BALLC   *Bulletin of the Association for Literary and Linguistic Computing.* Vol. 1–. Cambridge: Literary and Linguistic Computing Centers, 1973–. 3/yr.   P98.A75a

CSHVB   *Computer Studies in the Humanities and Verbal Behavior.* Vol. 1–. The Hague: Mouton, 1968–. 4/yr. Reviews.   Z699.5.H8 C63

Computers and Education: An International Jour-

nal. Vol. 1–. Oxford: Pergamon Press, 1976–. 4/yr.   LB2845.C578

Hephaistos: A Quarterly Devoted to Computer Research in the Humanities. Vol. 1–. Philadelphia, Pa.: St. Joseph's College, 1970–. 4/yr.
AZ105.H38

Language and Automation. Vol. 1–. Washington, D.C.: Center for Applied Linguistics, 1970–. 4/yr. Reviews. Abstracts.   Z7004.L3 L35

Literary and Linguistic Computing: Journal of the Association for Literary and Linguistic Computing. Oxford: Oxford University Press, 1986–. 4/yr. Reviews.   P98.L568

Newsletter of the Institute for Computer Research in the Humanities. 4 vols. New York: New York University, 1965–1969.   No LC number

Newsletter of the Special Interest Group on Language Analysis and Studies in the Humanities, Association for Computing Machinery [SIGLASH]. Vol. 1–. 1967–. 4/yr.   No LC number

RELO   *Revue de l'Organization internationale pour l'étude des langues anciennes par ordinateur.* No. 1–. Liége, Belgium, 1964–. 4/yr.   P98.I57a

Z–76   Pritchard, Alan.   *Guide to Computer Literature: An Introductory Survey of the Sources of Information.* 2d ed., rev. and enl. Hamden, Conn.: Linnet, 1972.   Z6654.C17 P7

This bibliographical guide, originally published in 1969, includes chapters on primary works reporting the results of original research; on secondary works including abstracts, indexes, and bibliographies; and on sources of information about hardware and software. A statistical appendix on the growth of computer literature and a list of the most important serial publications in the field, along with an index of authors and titles, conclude the volume.

Current publications in the field may be followed through the monthly issues of *Computer Abstracts* (London: Technical Information, 1957–) [Z6654.C17 C64], in which are classified abstracts of books, articles, conference proceedings, government reports, and patents, with indexes of authors, and monthly and annual indexes of authors and subjects. Also useful are the monthly issues of *Computing Reviews* (New York: Association for Computing Machinery, 1960–) [QA76.C5854], in which are classified reviews of books, articles, conference proceedings, government reports, and patents.

Z–77   The MLA Software Evaluation and Distribution Project.

This project has been organized by the Modern Language Association of America in cooperation with IBM to implement peer review for both educational software and research-oriented software in the modern languages and literatures. This project aims both to support the development of high quality software and to disseminate evaluative information about it. An advisory committee is collecting information about IBM-compatible software in foreign language instruction, English composition, writing, rhetoric, and tutorials for literary analysis. In the area of research-oriented software, the committee is studying text retrieval and analysis programs, concordance and index generators, specialized spelling checkers and thesauri, machine-readable texts, and specialized word processing, bibliography-generating, and indexing packages.

Among software programs which have received endorsement from the MLA are the following items:

Bibliography Generator (in MLA style).

Nota Bene 3.0 (a word-processing, text-retrieval, and indexing program).

Pro-Cite (bibliographic database and bibliography generator in multiple formats).

Word Cruncher (a text-indexing and retrieval program).

Z–78   Guide to Computerized Data-bases Used in Literary Research.

The following on-line services supply a number of computerized data-bases of use in literature searches, and likely to be of interest to students of language and literature.

BRS

BRS Information Technologies.   1200 Route 7, Lathan, N.Y. 12110.   800–345–4277. This data-base includes:

Arts and Humanities Citation Index (D–19)

Books in Print (C–29)

Comprehensive Dissertation Index (E–5)

Dissertation Abstracts On-line (E–7)

ERIC (Z–124)

LC MARC and REMARC (see below)

Language and Language Behavior Abstracts (I–7)

Psychological Abstracts (X–63)

Sociological Abstracts (X–67)

Ulrich's International Periodicals Directory (D–100)

BLAISE-LINE

The British Library Bibliographic Services Division, 2 Sheraton St., London, England W1V 4BH.   This data-base includes:

British Library, Department of Printed Books, Catalogue of works published since 1971 and acquired since 1976 (B–41)

Conference Proceedings Index

Eighteenth-Century Short-Title Catalogue, ESTC (C–12)

Incunable Short Title Catalogue, ISTC (C–4)

LC MARC and REMARC (see below)

SIGLE, a "grey literature" file which includes theses, proceedings, and research reports.

UK Marc, the on-line *British National Bibliography* (C–16)

DIALOG

Lockheed Information Services, Inc. 3460 Hillview Ave., Palo Alto, Calif.   94304.   800–227–1960.   This data-base includes:

America: History and Life (F–54)

Biography Master Index (G–6)

Book Review Index (E–74)

Books in Print (C–29)

Bowker's International Serials Database

Comprehensive Dissertation Index (E–5)

Dissertation Abstracts on-line (E–7)

Encyclopedia of Associations (Z–28)

ERIC (Z–124)

Foundation Directory (Z–89)

Foundation Grants Index (Z–89)

Grants (Z–83)

Historical Abstracts (F–5)

LC MARC and REMARC (see below)

Language and Language Behavior Abstracts (I–7)

Magazine Index (D–15)

Marquis Who's Who data-base (G–56, G–57, G–58)

MLA International Bibliography (L–50)

National Newspaper Index

Philosopher's Index (X–57)

Psychological Abstracts (X–63)

RILM Abstracts (X–40)

Sociological Abstracts (X–67)

Ulrich's International Periodicals Directory (D–100)

Washington Post Index (D–23)

MARC

Machine Readable Cataloging. These data files are available in both an American (LC MARC) and a British (BL MARC) version. The LC MARC file includes all books and serials cataloged by the Library of Congress, where this system was developed to provide a set of conventions for use in machine-cataloging all materials. MARC contains records for books in English cataloged since 1968; French since 1973; German, Spanish, and Portuguese since 1975; other European languages in the Roman alphabet since 1976; and Romanized Cyrillic and South Asian languages since 1979. In recent years the system has been further expanded to include motion pictures, filmstrips, music, rare books, and manuscripts.

The REMARC file contains the cataloged Library of Congress collection from 1897–1980. The BL MARC file is the on-line equivalent of the *British National Bibliography* (C–16).

OCLC

Online Computer Library Center. 656 Frantz Rd., Dublin, Ohio 43017. (Former name: Ohio College Library Center.) This data-base is a central computerized union catalog of books and serials held by several thousand participating libraries throughout the United States and Canada. Also available on OCLC are the LC MARC and REMARC (see above) files.

RLIN

Research Libraries Information Network. Research Libraries Group, Jordan Quadrangle, Stanford, Calif. 94305. 415–328–1920. This data-base provides shared cataloging for the large libraries who belong to the Research Libraries Group. The Group, organized to promote sharing of resources and to prevent duplication of effort, includes Columbia University, the New York Public Library, the Hoover Institution of Stanfrod University, the University of Michigan, the University of Pennsylvania, Princeton University, Rutgers University, Brigham Young University, Brown University, Cornell, the University of Minnesota, the University of Toronto, and the University of Chicago.

Among the special features of this databse are the archive and manuscript file, the *Eighteenth-Century Short Title Catalogue* (C–12) file, and a file of machine-readable texts.

WILSONLINE

H. W. Wilson Co., 950 University Avenue, Bronx, N.Y. 10452. 800–622–4002. This data-base includes:

Bibliographic Index (B–2)

Biography Index (G–6)

Book Review Digest (E–76)

Cumulative Book Index (C–30)

Education Index (Z–128)

Essay and General Literature Index (E–81)

Humanities Index (D–16)

Library Literature (Y–93)

MLA International Bibliography (L–50)

Reader's Guide to Periodical Literature (D–15)

Social Sciences Index (D–16)

Useful guides to these and other databases include James L. Hall and Marjorie J. Brown, *Online Bibliographic Databases: An International Directory*, 2d ed. (London: ASLIB, 1981) [Z599.22 H34 1981]; Matthew Lesko, *Computer Data and Database Source Book* (New York: Avon, 1984) [QA76.9 .D32 L47 1984]; and the quarterly *Directory of Online Databases* (New York: Cuadra/Elsevier, 1977–) [Z699.22.D56].

For an introduction to the use of databases, see Alfred Glossbrenner, *Complete Handbook of Personal Computer Communications*, 3d ed. (New York: St. Martin's Press, 1989) [QA76.5.G535 1989]; Barbara Newlin, *Answers Online: Your Guide to Informational Databases* (Berkeley, Calif.: Osborne/McGraw-Hill, 1985) [QA76.55.N49 1985]; Carol Hanser, *Microcomputer User's Guide to Information Online* (Hasbrook Heights, N.J.: Hayden Book Co., 1984) [QA76.5.H3546 1984]; and Nahum Goldman, *Online Research and Retrieval with Microcomputers* (Blue Ridge Summit, Penna.: TAB Professional and Reference Books, 1985) [QA76.55.G65 1985].

For help with on-line search strategies, the following works may be consulted: Peter J. Vigil, *Online Retrieval: Analysis and Strategy* (New York: Wiley, 1988) [Z699.3.V53 1988]; R. J. Hartley, et al., *Online Searching: Principles and Practice* (New York: Bowker-Saur, 1989) [Z699.35 .O55 1989]; Greg Byerly, *Online Searching: A Directory and Bibliographic Guide* (Littleton, Co.: Libraries Unlimited, 1983) [Z699.2.B9 1983]; Ryan E. Hoover, *Online Search Strategies* (White Plains, N.Y.: Knowledge Industry Publications, 1982) [Z699.3.O538 1982]; Carol Fenichel and Thomas H. Hogan, *Online Searching: A Primer* (Marlton, N.J.: Learned Information, 1981) [Z699.F38 1981]; and W. M. Henry, et al., *Online Searching: An Introduction* (London: Butterworths, 1980) [Z699.3.O54].

Z–79 **Some Frequently Recommended Works on Computers and the Humanities.**

Abercrombie, John R. *Computer Programs for Literary Analysis*. Philadelphia: University of Pennsylvania Press, 1984. P302.A24 1984

Aitken, A. J., R. W. Bailey, and N. Hamilton-Smith, eds. *Computer and Literary Studies: Proceedings of the Edinburgh International Symposium, 1972*. Edinburgh: Edinburgh University Press, 1973. PN73.S9 1972

Bessinger, Jess B., et al., eds. *Proceedings: IBM Literary Data Processing Conference, 9–11 September 1964*. White Plains, N.Y.: IBM Corp., Data Processing Division, 1964. P98.L57

Bowles, Edmund A., ed. *Computers in Humanistic Research: Readings and Perspectives*. Englewood Cliffs, N.J.: Prentice-Hall, 1967. AZ105.B6

Butler, Christopher. *Computers in Linguistics*. Oxford: Blackwell, 1985. P98.B84 1985

Garson, G. David. *Academic Microcomputing: A Resource Guide*. Beverly Hills, Calif.: Sage Publications, 1986. LB1028.42.G37 1986

Hockey, Susan. *SNOBOL Programming for the Humanities*. Oxford: Clarendon Press, 1985. QA76.73.S6 H63 1985

Ide, Nancy M. *Pascal for the Humanities*. Philadelphia: University of Pennsylvania Press, 1987. QA76.73.P2 I33 1987

Jones, Alan, and R. F. Churchhouse, eds. *Computer in Literary and Linguistic Studies.* Cardiff: University of Wales Press, 1976.   P98.I58 1974

Lawlor, Joseph. *Computers in Composition Instruction.* Los Alamitos, Calif.: SWRL Educational Research and Development, 1982.

Lawrence, John Shelton. *Electronic Scholar: A Guide to Academic Microcomputing.* Norwood, N.J.: Ablex, 1984.   QA76.5.L3729 1984

Leed, Jacob, ed. *Computer and Literary Style: Introductory Essays and Studies.* Kent, Ohio: Kent State University Press, 1966.   PN98.E4 L4

Lusignan, Serge, and John S. North, eds. *Computing in the Humanities: Proceedings of the Third International Conference on Computing in the Humanities, University of Waterloo, 1977.* Waterloo: University of Waterloo Press, 1977.   AZ105.I57 1977

Machina Analytica: Occasional Papers on Computer-assisted Scholarship. No. 1–. Los Angeles: William Andrews Clark Memorial Library, 1984–.

Mitchell, J. L., ed. *Computers in the Humanities: Proceedings of the International Conference on Computers in the Humanities, University of Minnesota, 1973.* Edinburgh: Edinburgh University Press, 1974.   NX458.I57 1973a

Olsen, Solveig, ed. *Computer-Aided Instruction in the Humanities.* New York: MLA, 1985.   LC1022.2.C66 1985

Patton, Peter C., and Renee A. Haloien, eds. *Computing in the Humanities.* Lexington, Mass.: Lexington Books, 1981.   AZ105.C59

Potter, Rosanne G. *Literary Computing and Literary Criticism: Theoretical and Practical Essays on Theme and Rhetoric.* Philadelphia: University of Pennsylvania Press, 1989.   PR21.L58 1989

Raben, Joseph. *Computer-Assisted Research in the Humanities.* New York: Pergamon Press, 1977.
                    A58.C63 1977

———. "Haste, Scope, and Certainty: The Role of Computers in Humanities Research." *Drexel Library Quarterly* 5 (1969): 290–321.   Z671.D7

Rudall, B. H., and T. N. Corns. *Computers and Literature: A Practical Guide.* Cambridge, Mass.: Abacus Press, 1987.   PN73.R83

Schneider, Ben R., Jr. *Travels in Computerland; or, Incompatibilities and Interfaces: A Full and True Account of the Implementation of The London Stage Information Bank.* Reading, Mass.: Addison-Wesley, 1974.
                    QA76.S3588

Turkle, Sherry. *Second Self: Computers and the Human Spirit.* New York: Simon and Schuster, 1984.
                    QA76.T85 1984

Wisbey, R. A., ed. *Computer in Literary and Linguistic Research: Papers from a Cambridge Symposium.* Cambridge: Cambridge University Press, 1971.   P25.C66

Wresch, William, ed. *Computer in Composition Instruction: A Writer's Tool.* Urbana, Ill.: NCTE, 1984.
                    PE1404.C63 1984

VII. GRANTS AND FELLOWSHIPS

Z–80 *Annual Register of Grant Support.* Chicago: Marquis Academic Media, 1967–.   AS911.A2 A67

This annual listing provides extended descriptions by disciplines of grants awarded during the previous year. Programs are listed in four categories (general, humanities, social sciences, sciences), with subdivisions by discipline in all but the first part. Each annual volume concludes with indexes by subject, funding source, and geographic location of the funding source.

Z–82 *Grants Register.* New York: St. Martin's Press, 1970–.
                    LB2338.G7

This biennial volume (7th ed., 1981–1983) provides information on scholarships, grants, prizes, and awards made in many countries and fields for graduate students, teachers, and professional scholars. Arrangement is alphabetical by funding institution; awards are briefly described. There are indexes by subjects (subdivided by country) and by titles of awards and awarding bodies.

Z–83 **GRANTS Data-base.**

This data-base is produced by the Oryx Press and made available through DIALOG (see Z–78). The most comprehensive source of current information on grants offered by government, corporate, and private funding sources, this data-base is updated monthly. It offers access to the same grant information published in the annual *Directory of Research Grants* (Phoenix, Ariz.: Oryx Press, 1975–) [LB2338.D57]. A guide to the 1,700 item list of subject index terms used in the data-base is available in the *Grants Thesaurus: A Guide to the GRANTS Data-base* (Phoenix, Ariz.: Oryx Press, 1986) [no LC number].

Based on the GRANTS data-base, the annual *Directory of Grants in the Humanities* (Phoenix, Ariz.: Oryx Press, 1986–) provides a convenient print guide to funding sources for research in the arts, education in the humanities, history, languages, and literatures. More than half of the entries cover federal funding sources; others cite important corporate, foundation, state government, and university-sponsored sources. The work is divided into four sections. The first lists the grant programs and includes information on the amount of money available, application deadlines, restrictions and requirements, renewal information, and sponsoring organization name and address. The second section is a subject index to the work, the third is a sponsoring organization index, and the last is an index of sponsoring organizations by organization type.

Z–84 **Coleman, William Emmet. *Grants in the Humanities: A Scholars Guide to Funding Sources.*** 2d ed. New York: Neal-Schuman Publishers, 1984.   AZ188.U5 C64 1984

This work is a guide to humanities grantsmanship. Chapter 1, The Art of Grantsmanship includes discussion of sources and offers both "A Descriptive Bibliography of Research Grants and Fellowships" (General, Foreign Foundations, Study and Research Abroad, Women's Studies and Projects), and "A Descriptive Bibliography of Grantsmanship." Chapter 2, Writing the Proposal, and Chapter 3, The Sample Proposal and Sample Budget, together provide a handy overview of the proposal writing process. Chapter 3 concludes with "A Descriptive Bibliography of Proposal Writing." A concluding fourth chapter discusses supplementary grants, what to do with unsuccessful proposals, and income tax advice, including a bibliography on "The Scholar's Income Tax."

The heart of the volume is Appendix A, Granting Agencies, which describes a total of 197 alphabetically listed granting agencies under eight headings: name, type, purpose, support, conditions, duration, deadline, and inquiries. Appendix B lists deadlines by date; Appendix C lists Federal Information Centers by state; Appendix D lists reference collections operated by The Foundation Center by state; and Appendix E lists state humanities committees by state. An index to subjects in the humanities, which is essentially an index to Appendix A, concludes this useful volume.

Z–85 **"Fellowships and Grants" in the annual Directory published as the September issue, no. 4, of *PMLA*.** New York: Modern Language Association.   PB6.M6

Preceded by a brief bibliography of more inclusive lists, this section of the annual directory lists source organizations alphabetically, describing their various programs, and giving information about qualifications sought in recipients, application procedures, deadlines, and addresses for further information.

Z–87 ***Cultural Directory II: Federal Funds and Services for the Arts and Humanities.*** Washington, D.C.: Smithsonian Institution Press, 1980.   NX735.F42 1980

This volume, sponsored by the Federal Council on the Arts and Humanities, describes some 300 programs administered by thirty-eight federal agencies. Programs of financial support (grants, loans, contracts, stipends), technical assistance, managerial counseling, information services, research and reference collections and services, training, and employment opportunities are described. Included are programs supporting all aspects of the visual and performing arts including traditional and contemporary forms, architecture and design, crafts and folk art, photography and filmmaking, and radio and television. The humanities include the disciplines of archaeology, comparative religion, history, law, classical and modern languages, linguistics, literature, philosophy, aspects of the social sciences, and the history, theory, and criticism of the arts.

Entries are arranged alphabetically by agency and within agency by program title. They are serially numbered and include an identification of the type of assistance and the individuals and organizations for whom the aid is intended; a description of the purpose and scope of a program; specific examples of activities that have been assisted; general comments about past and future prospects; and offices and officers to be contacted for further information. Appendixes give local and regional addresses of various federal agencies. Primary access to the information in the volumes is through the detailed index, which includes disciplines (film, literature), potential users (libraries, low-income persons), types of support (fellowships, residencies), types of agencies, and names of agencies.

An earlier, similarly conceived work is the *MLA Guide to Federal Programs: An Analysis of Current Government Financial Assistance Programs for Students, Teachers, Researchers, and Scholars in the Fields of English and Foreign Languages*, ed. Kenneth W. Mildenberger (New York: MLA, 1969) [no LC number].

Z–89 **Some Additional Guides to Securing Fellowships and Grants.**

Information about Sources

Complete Grants Sourcebook for Higher Education. Washington, D.C.: American Council on Education, 1984.
                                    LB2336.P8 1984

Directory of Grant-Making Trusts. 4th compilation. London: National Council of Social Service, 1975.
                                    AS911.AZ C45 1975

Foundation Directory. 12th ed. New York: Columbia University Press for the Foundation Center, 1989. First edition, 1960. Biennial.   AS911.A2 F65

Foundation Grants Index [1970/71–]: A Cumulative Listing of Foundation Grants. New York: Foundation Center, 1972–. Annual.   AS911.A2 F66

Foundation Grants to Individuals. 6th ed. New York: Foundation Center, 1988. Biennial.   LB2336.F596 1984

Foundations. Westport, Conn.: Greenwood, 1984.
                                    HV88,F68 1984

Grants for Women and Girls. New York: The Foundation Center, 1898.   No LC number

Grants Survival Library, ed. Donald Levitan. Monticello, Ill.: Vance Bibliographies, 1980.
                                    Z7164.A2 P84 no.476

International Foundation Directory. Detroit: Gale Research, 1983.   HV7.I57 1983

On Applications

Ammon-Wexler, Jill, and Catherine Carmel. *How to Create a Winning Proposal: A Complete Step-by-Step Guide to the Art of Successful Proposal.* 2d ed. Santa Cruz, Calif.: Mercury Communications, 1978.
                                    HF5718.5.A48 1978

Casebook of Grant Proposals in the Humanities. New York: Neal Schuman, 1982.   AZ188.U5 C37 1982

Conrad, Daniel. *New Grants Planner.* San Francisco: Public Management Institute, 1980.   HV41.C639 1980

Holtz, Herman, and Terry Schmidt. *Winning Proposal: How to Write It.* New York: McGraw-Hill, 1981.
                                    HF5718.5.H64

Kurzig, Carol. *Foundation Fundamentals: A Guide for Grantseekers.* New York: Foundation Center, 1980.
                                    HV41.K87

Lauffer, Armand. *Grantsmanship.* 2d ed. Beverly Hills, Calif.: Sage Publications, 1983.   HG177.L375 1983

Locke, Lawrence F., et al. *Proposals That Work: A Guide for Planning Dissertations and Grant Proposals.* 2d ed. Newbury Park, Calif.: Sage Publications, 1987.
                                    Q180.55.P7 L63 1987

Margolin, Judith B. *Individual's Guide to Grants.* New York: Plenum Press, 1983.   AZ188.U5 M37 1983

Proposal Writer's Swipe File: Twelve Professionally Written Grant Proposals—Prototypes of Approaches, Styles, and Structures. Edited by Jean Brodsky. Washington, D.C.: Taft Products, 1973.   H91.T33 1973

Proposal Writer's Swipe File III: Fifteen Professionally Written . . . . Edited by Susan Ezell et al. Washington, D.C.: Taft Corporation, 1981.   H91.P76 1981

White, Virginia P. *Grants: How to Find Out About Them and What to Do Next.* New York: Plenum, 1975.
                                    Q180.U5 W47

VIII. SCHOLARLY WRITING

Z–90 **Barzun, Jacques. *On Writing, Editing, and Publishing: Essays Explicative and Hortatory.*** 2d ed. Chicago: University of Chicago Press, 1985.   PN149.B295 1985

This volume, gathered with a foreword by Morris Philipson,

includes nine essays, along with an introductory section and an envoy. The pieces include the introductory "Advice to a Young Writer," "A Writer's Discipline," "English As She's Not Taught," "The Bibliographer and His Absence of Mind," "Paradoxes of Publishing," and the envoy, "Of Making Books."

Z–91 Luey, Beth. *Handbook for Academic Authors.* Cambridge: Cambridge University Press, 1987.   PN146.L84 1987

This volume, designed to be of use to both new and experienced scholarly authors in all fields, is disposed into ten chapters as follows: The publishing partnership; Journal articles; Revising a dissertation; Finding a publisher for the scholarly book; Working with your publisher; Multiauthor books and anthologies; Finding a publisher for the college textbook; Working with your textbook publisher; The mechanics of authorship; Costs and prices. It concludes with a useful, classified Bibliography and an index of subjects.

Among volumes about scholarly writing focused specifically on the needs of the graduate student, see David Sternberg, *How to Complete and Survive a Doctoral Dissertation* (New York: St Martin's Press, 1982) [LB2386.S75] and David Madsen, *Successful Dissertations and Theses: A Guide to Graduate Student Research from Proposal to Completion* (San Francisco: Jossey-Bass, 1983) [LB2369.M32 1983]. Chapter 7 of the *MLA Style Manual* (see Z–94) is also specially addressed to the writers of theses and dissertations.

Z–92 *Chicago Manual of Style.* 13th ed., rev. and exp. Chicago: University of Chicago Press, 1982.   Z253.C57

This work, originally published in 1906, is the standard reference tool for authors, editors, copywriters, and proofreaders. It records the stylistic preferences of the University of Chicago Press, which have become the standards of most university presses and the great majority of book publishers in America. It is in twenty chapters. Part 1, Bookmaking, contains chapters on 1, The Parts of a Book; 2, Manuscript Preparation; 3, Proofs; and 4, Rights and Permissions. Part 2, Style, contains chapters on 5, Punctutation; 6, Spelling and Distinctive Treatment of Words; 7, Names and Terms; 8, Numbers; 9, Foreign Languages in Type; 10, Quotations; 11, Illustrations, Captions, and Legends; 12, Tables; 13, Mathematics in Type; 14, Abbreviations; 15, Notes and Footnotes; 16, Bibliographies; 17, Citing Public Documents; and 18, Indexes. Part 3, Production and Printing, has chapters on 19, Design and Typography; and 20, Composition, Printing, and Binding. A Glossary of Technical Terms, a Bibliography and an Index conclude the volume. The current edition is changed primarily by incorporating information on the revolution in publishing resulting from technological advances including word processing and computerized typesetting. It is also expanded in the detail and examples it provides for authors and editors who are following its instructions.

Z–93 Turabian, Kate L. *Manual for Writers of Term Papers, Theses, and Dissertations.* 5th ed. Revised and expanded by Bonnie Birtwistle Honigsblum. Chicago: University of Chicago Press, 1987.   LB2369.T8 1987

Based on the thirteenth edition of the *Chicago Manual of Style* (1982), this work is a handy compendium of information likely to be needed by the student writer, particularly the graduate student writer. It must be supplemented for more complex problems by the Chicago *Manual* (Z–92), though its extensive examples, abbreviated form, and full index make it the style guide of first recourse for the dissertation writer.

Also available is Turabian's *Student's Guide for Writing College Papers*, 3d ed. (Chicago: University of Chicago Press, 1977) [LB2369.T82], which is addressed specifically to the substantive and explanatory needs of the undergraduate student writer.

Z–94 *MLA Handbook for Writers of Research Papers, Theses, and Dissertations.* Edited by Joseph Gibaldi and Walter S. Achtert. 2d ed. New York: MLA, 1984.
                              PE1478.M57 1984

This volume, addressed to students, is a second edition of the successor to the *MLA Style Sheet* (1951) and its revised version (1970), and was first published in 1977. That first edition offered an expanded version with more detailed explanations and more extensive examples of the various footnote and bibliographical forms found in the original style sheet. This new edition, in contrast, presents an entirely new, streamlined documentation style. In it, the bibliography is renamed "Works Cited" and required forms are altered somewhat from the earlier practice. More drastic are the changes in footnote and/or endnote style from notes to the use of parenthetical references in the text proper to the list of works cited. In addition, the handbook contains sections on research and writing, on the mechanics of writing, and on preparing the manuscript, and has an appendix on thesis and dissertation preparation. A detailed index is followed by sample pages of a research paper to demonstrate correct layout. The conventions of style observed here are those preferred by *PMLA* and many scholarly journals in the humanities, especially in the fields of language and literature.

To supplement the *MLA Handbook* with material suited more to the needs of professional scholars, Walter S. Achtert and Joseph Gibaldi have also prepared the *MLA Style Manual* (New York: MLA, 1985) [PN147.A28 1985]. This volume offers comprehensive and extremely useful guidance to scholarly writers interested in publication in the humanities. It is disposed into seven chapters, as follows: Writing and Publication; Mechanics of Writing; Preparing the Scholarly Manuscript; Preparing the List of Works Cited; Documenting Sources; Abbreviations, Reference Words, Proofreading Symbols; and Preparation of Theses and Dissertations. Numerous subsections treat such matters as guidelines for author-publisher relations, copyright and other legal considerations; most subsections include examples; there are lists of common scholarly abbreviations and the like; and the work concludes with a rather full subject index.

An abbreviated version of the MLA's documentation rules has been prepared by Joseph F. Trimmer, *Guide to MLA Documentation* (Boston: Houghton Mifflin, 1988) [PN147.T75 1988], which includes an appendix on APA (American Psychological Association) style. Complementing the MLA guides is the *MHRA Style Book: Notes for Authors, Editors, and Writers of Dissertations*, edited by A. S. Maney and R. S. Smallwood, 2d ed. (Cambridge: MHRA 1978) [PN147.M65 1978], which was designed for use with publications of the MHRA. First published in 1971, this guide gives an account of conventions to observe in preparing a manuscript for publication in a British journal.

There are a number of other style guides governing journals in other disciplines. 226 of them are described in John Bruce Howell, *Style Manuals of the English-Speaking World: A Guide* (Phoenix, Ariz.: Oryx Press, 1983) [Z5165 .H68 1983]. The guide is divided into two sections, the first treating general manuals and the second treating those in various disciplines. Entries include complete bibliographical citations, descriptions of contents, and observations on the bibliographic style. The volume concludes with an index, preceded by two appendixes citing manuals concerning disabled persons and nonsexist language.

An elaborate study of sexism in language, combined with guidelines for nondiscriminatory usage, *Language, Gender, and Professional Writing: Theoretical Approaches and Guidelines for Nonsexist Usage* by Francine Wattman Frank and Paula A. Treichler (New York: MLA, 1989)

[PE1460.F64 1989] is divided into three parts. Preceded by an introduction, "Scholarship, Feminism, and Language Change," Part 1 collects a series of five essays on Language and Sexual Equality. Part 2 presents Guidelines for Nonsexist Usage, and Part 3 offers a Bibliography.

Z–95 Butcher, Judith. *Copy-editing: The Cambridge Handbook.* 2d ed. New York: Cambridge University Press, 1981. First published in 1975.   PN162.B86 1981

First published in 1975, this volume has a primary focus on the procedure of copyediting rather than on the system of conventions to which the copy editor must make a manuscript conform. It does present those conventions, with a British emphasis (and reference made to American departures from it), but that presentation is secondary. It is organized into fifteen chapters, as follows: 1, Introduction; 2, Estimate and Specimen Pages; 3, Preparing the Typescript for Setting; 4, Illustrations; 5, Proofs; 6, House Styles; 7, Preliminary Pages; 8, Indexes; 9, Other Parts of a Book; 10, Bibliographical References; 11, Literary Material; 12, Multi-author and Multivolume Books; 13, Scientific and Mathematics Books; 14, Other [typographically] Special Subjects; 15, Reprints and New Editions. A total of eight appendixes include a glossary, a select bibliography, and a detailed index.

Other volumes on copyediting include Karen Judd, *Copyediting: A Practical Guide* (Los Altos, Calif.: Kaufmann, 1982) [PN162.J8 1982], which is a textbook for potential copy editors rather than a handbook for the practicing editor. It begins with a chapter on "What Is Copyediting?" and concludes with a chapter on "Getting Work." It has a valuable annotated bibliography of reference books in the field, a checklist for copyediting, and a useful index.

For the author/editor, a useful volume is Bruce Ross-Larson, *Edit Yourself: A Manual for Everyone Who Works with Words* (New York: Norton, 1982) [PE1408.R725 1982]. Other works include Arthur Plotnick, *Elements of Editing: A Modern Guide for Editors and Journalists* (New York: McGraw-Hill, 1982) [PN4778.P59 1982]; R. Thomas Berner, *Editing* (New York: Holt, Rinehart and Winston, 1982) [PN4778.B4 1982]; and the earlier volume by Harry H. McNaughton, *Proofreading and Copyediting: A Practical Guide to Style for the 1970's* (New York: Hastings House, 1973) [Z254.M23].

Z–96 Collison, Robert L. *Indexes and Indexing: Guide to the Indexing of Books and Collections of Books, Periodicals, Music, Readings, Films, and Other Material.* 4th rev. ed. London: E. Benn, 1972.   Z695.9.C63 1972

Originally published in 1953, this volume is in three parts, The Indexing of Books, Including General Principles; Wider Indexing; and a Reference Section, including standard proof correction marks, twenty basic rules, a bibliography of reference works, and a sample examination. Prepared for the Society of Indexers, this work also includes an appendix giving an outline of the rules of the society as well as an outline of answers to the sample examination paper presented in part 3. The work concludes with an index, of course.

Collison has also prepared the briefer and more elementary volume, *Indexing Books* (New York: John de Graf, 1962) [Z695.9.C64], which provides step-by-step procedures with abundant examples from the materials needed and the planning process to starting the index, the handling of personal and other names, subject entries, indexing ideas, sorting and editing, preparing for the printer, and revising.

Other frequently recommended works on indexing include the following titles:

Anderson, Margaret D. *Book Indexing.* Cambridge Authors' and Publishers' Guides. Cambridge: Cambridge University Press, 1971.   Z695.9.A57

Borko, Harold. *Indexing Concepts and Methods.* New York: Academic Press, 1978.   Z695.9.B653

Butcher, Judith. *Typescripts, Proofs, and Indexes.* Cambridge: Cambridge University Press, 1980. PN160.B8

Carey, G. V. *Making an Index.* 3d ed. Cambridge Authors' and Publishers' Guides. Cambridge: Cambridge University Press, 1963.

Foskett, Anthony Charles. *Subject Approach to Information.* Hamden, Conn.: Linnet Books, 1977.   Z695.F66 1977

Harrod, Leonard Montague, ed. *Indexers on Indexing: A Selection of Articles Published in* The Indexer. New York: Bowker, 1978.   Z695.9.I52

Knight, G. Norman. *Indexing, The Art of. Guide to the Indexing of Books and Periodicals.* London: Allen and Unwin, 1979.   Z695.9.K58

————, ed. *Training in Indexing: A Course of the Society of Indexers.* Cambridge: MIT Press, 1969.   Z695.9.T7

Ramsden, Michael J. *Introduction to Index Language Construction.* Hamden, Conn.: Linnet Books, 1974.   Z695.9.R35

Spiker, Sina. *Indexing Your Book: A Practical Guide for Authors.* 2d ed. Madison: University of Wisconsin Press, 1954.   Z695.9.W77 1954

Z–97 Borko, Harold, and Charles L. Bernier. *Abstracting Concepts and Methods.* New York: Academic Press, 1975.   Z695.9.B65

This volume presents an exhaustive discussion of abstracts in nine chapters that are disposed into three parts, as follows: I. The Nature of Abstracts (1. Characteristics and Types of Abstracts; 2. Historical Review of Abstracting Services; 3. Criteria, Instructions, and Standards); II. Abstracting Procedures (4. Contents and Format; 5. Editing; 6. Publishing); III. Management, Automation, and Personnel (7. Abstracting Services; 8. Automatic Abstracting; 9. Career Opportunities). Appendixes include exercises, references, a glossary, and a subject index.

Additional works on abstracting and related topics include the following titles:

Alexander, L. C. *Sixty Steps to Precis.* Munich: Langenscheidt, 1970.   PE1477.A4

Bongartz, Joseph. *Summary and Precis Writing.* Groningen: L. B. Wolters, 1976.   PE1477.B6

Collison, Robert. *Abstracts and Abstracting Services.* Santa Barbara, Calif.: ABC-Clio, 1971. Includes a valuable, though no longer current bibliography of abstracting services and of readings on abstracting and abstracting services.   Z695.9.C625

Cremmins, Edward T. *Art of Abstracting.* Philadelphia: ISI Press, 1982.   PE1477.C7 1982

For a full bibliography of works on abstracting and indexing, see Hans H. Wellisch, *Indexing and Abstracting: An International Bibliography* (Santa Barbara, Calif.: ABC-Clio, 1980) [Z695.9.W44], which includes a total of 2,383 elaborately classified, descriptively and evaluatively annotated entries on books and articles treating the history, theory, and practice of both activities.

Z–98 **Pilpel, Harriet, and Morton David Goldberg.** *Copyright Guide.* 4th ed. New York: R. R. Bowker, 1969.
KF2995.P5 1969

This brief guide to the complexities of copyright law is recommended as a starting point for anyone needing to work with this subject. A guide to whether that is now the case will be found in the summarizing article by Walter S. Achtert, "The New Copyright Law," *PMLA* 93 (1978): 572–577, which includes a bibliography of works to consult. Also helpful is the final section of James Thorpe's *Use of Manuscripts in Literary Research* (H–1).

An extensive, lucid presentation of current law is the recent volume by William S. Strong, *Copyright Book: A Practical Guide*, 2d ed. (Cambridge: MIT Press, 1984) [KF2994 .S75 1984]. Another brief treatment is Mary Hutchings Reed, *Copyright Primer for Librarians and Educators* published jointly by the ALA and the NEA (Chicago: American Library Association, 1987) [Z649.F35 R44 1987]. For British practice see J. M. Cavendish, *Handbook of Copyright in British Publishing Practice*, 2d ed. (London: Cassell, 1974) [KP1300.C38 1984], and the brief work of Christopher Scarles, *Copyright*, in the series of Cambridge Authors' and Publishers' Guides (Cambridge: Cambridge University Press, 1980) [K1420.5.S26].

The standard works in the field of copyright law are *Copinger and Skone James on Copyright*, 12th ed. (London: Mansell, 1980) [KD1289.C6 1980] and Melville B. Nimmer's looseleaf series, *Nimmer on Copyright*, 4 vols. (New York: M. Bender, 1978) [KF2991.5.N5 1978]. The standard bibliography is by Henriette Mertz, *Copyright Bibliography* (Washington, D.C.: United States Copyright Office, 1950) [Z552.A1 US]; current bibliography will be found in the *Bulletin of the Copyright Society of the U.S.A.* (1953–) [KF2987.C66]. Another useful title is Donald F. Johnston, *Copyright Handbook* (New York: Bowker, 1982) [KF2994.J63 1982].

More general, academic volumes include Benjamin Kaplan's discursive series of lectures, *Unhurried View of Copyright* (New York: Columbia University Press, 1967) [KF2995.K37]; Philip Wittenberg's *Law of Literary Property* (Cleveland: World Publishing, 1957) [KF3020.W58]; Ralph R. Shaw, *Literary Property in the United States* (Washington, D.C.: Scarecrow Press, 1950) [KF2994.S47]; the collection edited by Allen Kent and Harold Lancour, *Copyright: Current Viewpoints on History, Laws, Legislation* (New York: Bowker, 1972) [KF2994.A2 C64]; and the historical study by James J. Barnes, *Authors, Publishers, and Politicians: The Quest for an Anglo-American Copyright Agreement, 1815-1854* (Columbus: Ohio State University Press, 1974) [no LC number].

Z–99 **Some Frequently Recommended Works on Scholarly Writing.**

Becker, Howard S. *Writing for Social Scientists: How to Start and Finish Your Thesis, Book, or Article.* Chicago: University of Chicago Press, 1986. H91.B4 1986

Bernstein, Theodore M. *Careful Writer: A Modern Guide to English Usage.* New York: Atheneum, 1965.
PE1460.B4617

———. *Do's, Don'ts and Maybe's of English Usage.* New York: Time Books, 1977. BE1460.B4618

———. *Miss Thistlebottom's Hobgoblins: The Careful Writer's Guide to the Taboos, Bugbears and Outmoded Rules of English Usage.* New York: Farrar, Strauss and Giroux, 1971. PE1460.B4619

Follett, Wilson. *Modern American Usage: A Guide* (I–52).

Fowler, H. W. *Dictionary of Modern English Usage* (I–34).

Gowers, Sir Ernest. *Complete Plain Words.* 2d ed. Revised by Sir Bruce Fraser. London: HMSO, 1973.
PE1421.G592 1973

Harman, Eleanor, and Ian Montagnes, eds. *Thesis and the Book.* Toronto: University of Toronto Press, 1976. Reprints a set of ten articles from *Scholarly Publishing* about revising the doctoral dissertation for publication. Z286.S37 T53

McCartney, Eugene S. *Recurrent Maladies in Scholarly Writing.* Ann Arbor: University of Michigan Press, 1953. PN147.M28

McKerrow, R. B. "Form and Matter in the Publication of Research." *RES* 16 (1940): 116–121. Reprinted in *On the Publication of Research.* New York: MLA, 1964.

Menzel, Donald H., Howard Mumford Jones, and Lyle G. Boyd. *Writing a Technical Paper.* New York: McGraw-Hill, 1961. PE1475.M4

O'Connor, Maeve, and Peter Woodford. *Writing Scientific Papers in English.* Amsterdam: Elsevier, 1975.
T11.03

Silver, Henry M. "Putting It on Paper." In *On the Publication of Research.* New York: MLA, 1964.

Strunk, William, Jr., and E. B. White, *Elements of Style.* 3d ed. New York: Macmillan, 1979. PE1421.S7 1979

Thomas, David St. John. *Non-fiction: A Guide to Writing and Publishing.* Newton Abbot: David and Charles, 1970. PN14.T37

Wiles, Roy McKeen. *Scholarly Publishing in the Humanities.* 4th ed. Toronto: University of Toronto Press, 1970. PN147.W52

Zinsser, William. *On Writing Well.* 2d ed. New York: Harper and Row, 1980. PE1429.Z5

———. *Writing with a Word Processor.* New York: Harper and Row, 1983. PN171.D37256 1983

IX. SCHOLARLY PUBLISHING

Z–100 ***MLA Directory of Periodicals: A Guide to Journals and Series in Languages and Literatures.*** New York: MLA, 1969–. P1.A1 M62a

This volume, published biennially by the MLA, contains descriptions of the more than 3,000 journals and series that are indexed in the MLA *International Bibliography* (L–50). Serially numbered entries are arranged alphabetically by title and currently give the following information (if it has been provided to the MLA by the journal's editor and/or publisher): editor and address, date of first publication, sponsoring organization, international standard serial number, and MLA acronym. Subscription information follows, including frequency of publication, circulation size, microform availability, subscription price, and the year to which the price refers. Advertising information follows, giving policy and rates. Next is an editorial description that includes a statement of the journal's scope, whether it reviews books, what languages it accepts, and whether it prints abstracts. Finally, submission requirements are detailed. Restrictions on contributors, submission fee, and page charges (if any) are given; governing style is specified; number of copies that must be submitted and any other special requirements are noted; copyright information, disposition policy for rejected manuscripts, time requirements for manuscript review and between acceptance and publication, and the number of referees used—all are provided. Publication statistics conclude the entry: the number of submissions per year, the total number of articles published, and the total number of book reviews published. The volume concludes with indexes of subject matter, sponsoring organizations, editorial personnel, and languages in which articles and monographs are published.

A paperback edition of the *Directory* is also available, and cites over 1,000 United States and Canadian journals and series from the larger work.

Z–101 **Gerstenberger, Donna L., and George Hendrick.** *Fourth Directory of Periodicals Publishing Articles in English and American Literature and Language.* Chicago: Swallow Press, 1974.   Z2015.P4 D56

First published in 1960, this directory includes more than 600 journals. Entries give information on editorial address, major fields of interest, manuscript submission preferences (length, style), and time period needed for review of submissions.

Another similar volume is Milton Bruce Byrd and Arnold L. Goldsmith's compilation, *Publication Guide for Literary and Linguistic Scholars* (Detroit: Wayne State University Press, 1958) [Z6951.B9], which presents in alphabetical order the titles of more than 180 periodicals giving subscription data, names of editors, editorial policy, data regarding the length and character of manuscripts the editors are prepared to consider, limits on the contributors from whom the editors are prepared to receive materials, and information as to the disposition of submitted manuscripts.

See also *Women in Print II: Opportunities for Women's Studies Publication in Language and Literature*, ed. Ellen Messer-Davidow and Joan E. Hartman (New York: MLA, 1982) [PN481.W656 1982].

Z–102 **Harmon, Gary L., and Susanna M. Harmon.** *Scholar's Market: An International Directory of Periodicals Publishing Literary Scholarship.* Columbus: Ohio State University Libraries, 1974.   Z6513.H37

This work includes nearly 850 journals. Information provided for each includes the editorial address, the scope and orientation of the journal, article topics preferred, manuscript length and style, time required for review, time required for publication, and disposition of rejected manuscripts.

Z–103 **Woods, William F., ed.** *Directory of Publishing Opportunities for Teachers of Writing.* Charlottesville, Va.: Community Collaborators, 1979.   PE1128.W759

This work describes more than 120 journals that publish articles on college composition, primary and secondary school level language arts, business and technical writing, creative writing, and applied linguistics. The journals are listed alphabetically in a total of six sections: The Teaching of Writing: General (Language Arts, Composition, Rhetoric, Research and Bibliographical); Creative Writing; Business and Technical Writing; Speech Communication and Journalism; Teacher Education; Language Study and the Teaching of Writing. An introduction begins the volume, and indexes of journals by geographical location and by subject area conclude it. Annotations for each entry give the journal title, the editor's name, and address. Information about the subject areas covered, the level of treatment, and the journal's readership is given next. Finally, limitations on manuscript size and other submission requirements are described. Frequency of publication and approximate number of articles per issue is often noted, as is whether or not the journal is refereed.

See also Sidney B. Katz, et al., *Resources for Writing for Publication in Education* (New York: Teachers College Press, Columbia University, 1980) [Z286.E3 K37].

Z–104 **Kefauver, Weldon A., ed.** *Scholars and Their Publishers.* New York: MLA, 1977.   Z286.S37 S34

This guide to the current state of publishing, emphasizing university presses, contains three papers by university press administrators treating scholarly standards and economic factors in publishers' decisions; the scholar as a publishing author; the publisher's reader; the publishing contract; new methods of printing; and academic pressures on he academic publishing scene.

Z–105 *One Book / Five Ways: The Publishing Procedures of Five University Presses.* **Introduction by Chandler Grannis.** Los Altos, Calif.: Kaufman, 1978.   Z479.063

This volume, originally published as a workbook for use at the 1977 annual meeting of the Association of American University Presses, contains case studies of how five different university presses handle the publication of one manuscript. The acquisitions, editorial, production, and marketing procedures followed by each press are revealed, with contract offers, pertinent author-editor correspondence, budgets, promotion plans, design layouts, manufacturing specifications, and appropriate interoffice forms reproduced in full. The work concludes with an annotated bibliography.

Z–106 *Scholarly Communication: The Report of the National Inquiry.* Baltimore: Johns Hopkins University Press, 1979.   Z286.S37 N37 1979

This volume presents the results of a three-year study taken under the initiative of the National Endowment for the Humanities and the American Council of Learned Societies, with NEH and Rockefeller, Mellon, and Ford Foundation funding. The study staff was directed by Edward Booker. The report addresses the issues of (bibliographical) access; scholar entry into the publication system through sufficient places to publish; quality control; timeliness of the system of submissions, review, and return or publication; coordination of the various elements in the system; the adaptability of the system; and its financial viability.

Z–107 *Scholarly Publishing: A Journal for Authors and Publishers.* Vol. 1–.   Toronto: University of Toronto Press, 1967/68–.   Z286.S37 S33

This quarterly journal contains articles on the history of scholarly publishing, on scholarly publishing in various countries, on various scholarly publishers, and on all aspects of the business of publishing scholarly works. Author-publisher relations, author-publisher contracts, questions about the publishability of various classes of scholarly works, costs and other management questions, marketing, and aspects of the publishing process from paper and typesetting to copyediting, indexing, and proofreading—all these and other topics find their place in the pages of this journal. In addition, reviews of books, reports on meetings, and other news and notes are included in most issues.

A new journal devoted to assisting individuals with publishing is the *Academic Publishing Journal [APJ]* (Lincoln, Nebr.: Theraplan Inc., 1989–) [no LC number], a quarterly which features discussions of journals, desk-top publishing issues, profiles of academic publishing houses, and publishing and editing textbooks and non-fiction materials.

Z–108 **Clark, Charles, ed.** *Publishing Agreements: A Book of Precedents.* London: Allen and Unwin, 1980.   KD1340.A65 P8

This volume provides a set of standard agreements that may be used in contractual arrangements with publishers. Though written from the perspective of British publishing, much in the volume will prove useful to the American author in learning about the legal issues in publishing a book. The contents are as follows: General Book Author-publisher Agreement; Educational Book Author-publisher Agreement; Paperback Rights Agreement; Translator's Agreement; Agreement for Sale of Translation Rights; Same-language License Agreement with Developing Countries; Book Club Rights Agreement; Illustration and Artwork Agreement; Merchandising Rights Agreement; Sound Reproduction Rights Agreement; Microform Licensing Agreement; Agreement for Sale of Rights to USA. Appendixes include Permission Fees; Reversionary Provisions of the Copyright Act of 1911; U.S. Copyright Law; Charitable Rights; Royalty Statements; Taxation and the Author; and Territories of the World.

Z–109   Some Frequently Recommended Works on Scholarly Publishing.

Anderson, Dorothy. *Guide to Information Sources for the Preparation, Editing, and Production of Documents.* Brookfield, Vt.: Gower, 1989.   Z5165.A5 1989

Batts, Michael S. *Handbook for Editors of Scholarly Journals in the Humanities.* Ottawa: Canadian Federation for the Humanities [CFH], 1980.   PN4836.B37 1980

Bingley, Clive. *Book Publishing Practice.* London: Bingley, 1966.   Z278.B5

Butcher, Judith. *Typescript, Proofs, and Indexes.* Cambridge Authors' and Publishers' Guides. Cambridge: Cambridge University Press, 1980.   PN160.B8

Cargill, Oscar, William Charvat, and Donald D. Walsh. *Publication of Academic Writing.* New York: MLA, 1966.

Chicago Guide to Preparing Electronic Manuscripts For Authors and Publishers. Chicago: University of Chicago Press, 1987.   Z286.E43 C48 1987

Dennison, Sally. *Alternative Literary Publishing: Five Modern Histories.* Iowa City: University of Iowa Press, 1984.   Z231.5.L5 D47 1984

Dessauer, John P. *Book Publishing: What It Is, What It Does.* 2d ed. Los Altos, Calif.: William Kaufmann, 1981.   Z278.D47 1981

Gibson, Martin L. *Editing in the Electronic Era.* 2d ed. Ames, Iowa: Iowa State University Press, 1984.   PN4784.C75 G5 1984

Gill, Robert S. *Author-Publisher-Printer Complex.* 3d ed. Baltimore: Williams and Wilkins Co., 1958.   PN155.G5 1958

Grannis, Chandler B., ed. *What Happens in Book Publishing?* 3d ed. New York: Columbia University Press, 1976. Bibliographies.   Z471.G7 1976

Gross, Gerald, ed. *Editors on Editing.* New York: Grosset and Dunlap, 1962.   PN162.E35

Hawes, Gene R. *To Advance Knowledge: A Handbook on American University Press Publishing.* New York: Association of American University Presses, 1967.   Z231.5.U6 H3

Howard, William J., ed. *Editor, Author, and Publisher.* 1969. (See Y–37.)

Lavelle, John. "Facts of Journal Publishing, IV." *PMLA* 81 (1967): 3–12.

Machlup, Fritz, et al. *Information through the Printed Word: The Dissemination of Scholarly, Scientific, and Intellectual Knowledge.* 4 vols. *Treating respectively Book Publishing; Journals; Libraries; and Books, Journals, and Bibliographic Services.* New York: Praeger, 1978–1980.   Z286.S37 M3

MLA. *Handbook for Editors of Learned Journals.* New York: MLA, 1969.   PN162.C6

Pell, William. "Facts of Scholarly Publishing." *PMLA* 88 (1973): 639–670.

Powell, Walter W. *Getting Into Print: The Decision-Making Process in Scholarly Publishing.* Chicago: University of Chicago Press, 1985.   Z479.P68 1985

Unwin, Stanley. *Truth about Publishing.* 8th ed. Revised and partly rewritten by Philip Unwin. London: Allen and Unwin, 1976.   Z278.U63 1976

Welter, Rush. *Problems of Scholarly Publication in the Humanities and Social Sciences.* New York: ACLS, 1959.   Z479.W4

X.   THE ACADEMIC JOB MARKET

Z–110   Fox, Marcia R. *Put Your Degree to Work: A Career-planning and Job-hunting Guide for the New Professional.* 2d ed. New York: W. W. Norton, 1988.

HD8038.A1 F69 1988

This thorough and practical guide offers a step-by-step account of the job-hunting process, with chapters on career planning during student years; the effective job search; the résumé; the cover letter; and the interview. A thorough subject index concludes the volume.

Z–111   Brod, Richard I., Elizabeth Cowan, and Neal Woodruff, eds. *English and Foreign Languages: Employment and the Profession.* New York: Modern Language Association, 1976.   No LC number

This volume, a special joint issue of the *ADE Bulletin* and the *ADFL Bulletin*, contains a total of seventeen essays describing the late–1970s job market in the modern languages and literatures from a number of differing vantage points. Several departmental chairmen and several job candidates describe their experiences; there are articles on the special problems of women and part-timers; articles on job-seeking in community colleges and in experimental education programs; and several pieces on nonacademic careers.

Z–112   *MLA Guide for Job Candidates and Department Chairmen in English and Foreign Languages.* Rev. ed. New York: Modern Language Association, 1978.   No LC number

Originally published in 1973 and first revised in 1975, this pamphlet describes the job market, gives advice to job candidates as well as advice to department chairmen (both in placing former students and in hiring new colleagues), describes specific features of the job-seeking process in two-year colleges, and includes an expanded discussion of nonacademic employment. Appendixes enumerate sources of job information and offer sample letters of application, response letters, academic *vitae*, and business résumés.

Z–116   *MLA/ADE Job Information List.* New York: Modern Language Association, 1972–.   No LC number

This list, which appears in October, December, February, and April of each academic year, describes all reported openings in Departments of English, Comparative Literature, and Linguistics. Individual subscriptions may be ordered from the MLA in late summer; most departments also have copies available for consultation.

Z–117 **Wallace, M. Elizabeth, ed.** *Part-time Academic Employment in the Humanities: A Sourcebook for Just Policy.* New York: MLA, 1984.   LB2331.72.P37 1984

This volume presents materials on the needs of part-time faculty, model policies developed at some institutions for the fair employment of part-time instructors, and the impact of part-time hiring practices on the teaching of foreign languages and the teaching of writing.

Other works on part-time teaching include Judith M. Gappa, *Part-time Faculty: Higher Education at a Crossroads* (Washington, D.C.: Association for the Study of Higher Education, the George Washington University, 1984) [LB2335.35 .G37 1984]; David W. Leslie, *Employing Part-time Faculty* (San Francisco: Jossey-Bass, 1978) [LB2335.35 .E46]; David W. Leslie, et al., *Part-time Faculty in American Higher Education* (New York: Praeger, 1982) [LB2335.35.L47 1982]; and Donald Greive, ed., *Teaching in College: A Resource for Adjunct and Part-time Faculty* (Cleveland, Ohio: Info-Tec, 1983) [LB2331.T39 1983].

Z–118 *Chronicle of Higher Education.* Vol 1–. Washington, D.C.: Chronicle of Higher Education, 1966–. 48/yr. Reviews.   No LC number

Published every two weeks during the academic year and monthly during the summer, this newsmagazine, in addition to news and feature articles on all aspects of higher education, contains a "Bulletin Board: Positions Available" section. Advertised are academic, administrative, and nonacademic positions for which academic applicants are sought.

The Sunday edition of the *New York Times* carries some advertisements of education positions, as do several pages of each quarterly issue of *Academe*, the newsletter of the American Association of University Professors.

Z–119 **Some Frequently Recommended Works on Academic Employment and Related Topics.**

Bowen, Howard Rothmann. *American Professors: A National Resource Imperiled.* New York: Oxford University Press, 1986.   LB2331.72.B67 1986

Deneef, A. Leigh, et al., eds. *Academic's Handbook.* Durham, N.C.: Duke University Press, 1988.   LB1778.A24 1988

DeSole, Gloria, and Leonore Hoffman, eds. *Rocking the Boat: Academic Women and Academic Processes.* New York: MLA, 1981.   LB2332.3.R62

Entering the Profession: Advice for the Untenured. Washington, D.C.: The National Education Association, 1988.   No LC number

Franklin, Phyllis, et al. *Sexual and Gender Harassment in the Academy: A Guide for Faculty, Students, and Administrators.* New York: MLA, 1981.   LB2332.3.S49

Furniss, W. Todd. *Reshaping Faculty Careers.* Washington, D.C.: American Council on Education, 1981.   LB2331.72.F87

Hoffman, Leonore, and Gloria DeSole, eds. *Careers and Couples: An Academic Question.* New York: MLA, 1976.   No LC number

Krannich, Ronald L. *Moving Out of Education: The Educator's Guide to Career Management and Change.* Chesapeake, Va.: Progressive Concepts, Inc., 1981.   LB2331.72.K7

Licata, Christine M. *Post-tenure Faculty Evaluation: Threat or Opportunity.* Washington, D.C. Association for the Study of Higher Education, 1986. LB2333.L53 1986

Lunsford, Andrea, et al. *Future of Doctoral Studies in English.* New York: MLA, 1989.   PE68.U5 F88 1989

Miller, Richard I. *Evaluating Faculty for Promotion and Tenure.* San Francisco: Jossey-Bass, 1987.   LB2333.M468 1987

Patton, Carl V. *Academic in Transition: Mid-career Change or Early Retirement.* Cambridge, Mass.: Abt Books, 1979.   LB2331.P364

Seldin, Peter. *Changing Practices in Faculty Evaluation: A Critical Assessment and Recommendations for Improvement.* San Francisco: Jossey-Bass, 1984.   LB2333.S437 1984

Tinsley, Adrian, et al. *Academic Women, Sex Discrimination, and the Law.* Rev. ed. New York: MLA, 1975.   No LC number

XI. PEDAGOGY

Z–120 **Cahn, Steven M., ed.** *Scholars Who Teach: The Art of College Teaching.* Chicago: Nelson-Hall, 1978.   LB2331.S355

This volume consists of a total of seven essays. The second, by Edward B. Partridge, is on "Teaching English." Another piece in the volume, the Appendix on "The Uses and Abuses of Grades and Examinations," may be particularly recommended, though essays in teaching history, social science, foreign language and literature, and music are likely also to be of interest to English teachers.

A more recent volume is edited by Margaret Morganroth Gullette *Art and Craft of Teaching* (Cambridge: Harvard University Press, 1982) [LB2331.A646 1984]. Sponsored by the Harvard-Danforth Center for Teaching and Learning, the volume contains nine essays on such topics as The First Day of Class, The Theory and Practice of Lectures, Questioning, The Rhythms of the Semester, and Grading and Evaluation. An index concludes the work.

Z–121 **Highet, Gilbert.** *Art of Teaching.* New York: Alfred A. Knopf, 1950.   LB1025.H63 1950

This volume is on teaching methods drawn from practice. After an introduction about teaching in general, part 2 describes The Qualities and Abilities of the Good Teacher. Part 3, The Teacher's Methods, reviews preparation, communication (by way of lecturing, tutoring, and recitation), and fixing the impression. Part 4, Great Teachers and Their Pupils, reviews the history of education from the Sophists to our time. The last part, Teaching in Everyday Life, describes the variety of persons who do teach others from parents and spouses to authors and artists. Bibliographical notes are followed by an index of names and subjects.

Z–122 **Cowan, Elizabeth Wooten.** *Options for the Teaching of English: The Undergraduate Curriculum.* New York: Modern Language Association, 1975.   No LC number

This volume presents a collection of reports from twenty-three college and university English departments on their undergraduate curricula. Both traditional and highly innovative curricula are included, as are programs at a wide variety of different types of institutions.

A volume of the series, Harvard English Studies, *Teaching Literature: What is Needed Now*, edited by James Engell and David Perkins (Cambridge: Harvard University Press, 1988) [PN70.T35 1988], brings together a set of essays meant to address present circumstances in the discipline of English.

Contributions include essays on Teaching Poetry; The Crisis of Interpretation; Deconstruction, Feminism, and Pedagogy; The Function of Rhetorical Study at the Present Time; Why Teach Political Theory; and Reflections on the Freshman English Course. The essays are mostly by persons associated with Harvard, are mostly personal and descriptive rather than prescriptive in their thrust.

Z–123   **Neel, Jasper F., comp.** ***Options for the Teaching of English: Freshman Composition.*** New York: Modern Language Association, 1978.   PE1068.U5 F68

This 120-page volume presents fairly detailed descriptions of the composition programs at eighteen different and widely varying colleges in the United States. The selection is meant to offer a representative cross section of the sorts of writing programs currently available throughout the country, with discussion of the theory and practice that characterize them. Preceding each description is a statistical summary identifying the department responsible for the composition program, the number of full-time faculty in it, the enrollment policies for composition classes (maximum, minimum, and average number of students), the staffing of the courses, and the size of the composition program (number of students, number of sections, and number of all sections taught by the department).

Z–124   **Modern Language Association of America. Approaches to Teaching World Literature Series.**

The volumes in this series survey materials and feature a range of critical approaches that have proven effective when teaching the works in undergraduate classrooms. The volumes published to date are as follows:

Bessinger, Jess B., Jr., and Robert F. Yeager, eds. *Approaches to Teaching* Beowulf. 1984.

Bickman, Martin, ed. *Approaches to Teaching Melville's* Moby-Dick. 1985.

Bjornson, Richard, ed. *Approaches to Teaching Cervantes'* Don Quixote, 1984.

Crump, Galbraith M., ed. *Approaches to Teaching Milton's* Paradise Lost. 1986.

Dunn, Richard J., ed. *Approaches to Teaching Dickens'* David Copperfield. 1984.

Fast, Robin Riley, and Christine Mack Gordon, eds. *Approaches to Teaching Dickinson's Poetry.* 1989.

Gibaldi, Joseph, ed. *Approaches to Teaching Chaucer's* Canterbury Tales. 1980.

Gleckner, Robert F., and Mark L. Greenberg, eds. *Approaches to Teaching Blake's* Songs of Innocence and of Experience. 1989.

Hall, Spencer, with Jonathan Ramsey, eds. *Approaches to Teaching Wordsworth's Poetry.* 1986.

Kaplan, Carey, and Ellen Cronon Rose, eds. *Approaches to Teaching Lessing's* The Golden Notebook. 1989.

Kellman, Steven G., ed. *Approaches to Teaching Camus's* The Plague. 1985.

McMillan, Douglas J., ed. *Approaches to Teaching Goethe's* Faust. 1987.

Miller, Miriam Youngerman, and Jane Chance, eds. *Approaches to Teaching* Sir Gawain and the Green Knight. 1986.

Myrsiades, Kostas, ed. *Approaches to Teaching Homer's* Iliad *and* Odyssey. 1987.

New, Melvyn, ed. *Approaches to Teaching Sterne's* Tristram Shandy. 1989.

Olshen, Barry N., and Yael Feldman, eds. *Approaches to Teaching the Hebrew Bible as Literature in Translation.* 1989.

Parr, Susan Resneck, and Pancho Savery, eds. *Approaches to Teaching Ellison's* Invisible Man. 1989.

Ray, Robert H., ed. *Approaches to Teaching Shakespeare's* King Lear. 1986.

Rielly, Edward J., ed. *Approaches To Teaching Swift's* Gulliver's Travels. 1988.

Rosowski, Susan J., ed. *Approaches to Teaching Cather's* My Antonia. 1989.

Shafer, Yvonne, ed. *Approaches to Teaching Ibsen's* A Doll House. 1985.

Slade, Carole, ed. *Approaches to Teaching Dante's* Divine Comedy. 1982.

Waldinger, Renee, ed. *Approaches to Teaching Voltaire's* Candide. 1987.

Z–125   ***Current Index to Journals in Education.*** Vol. 1–. Phoenix, Ariz.: Oryx, 1969–.   Z5813.C8

This international, comprehensive monthly index, sponsored by the U.S. Department of Education and the Educational Resources Information Center (ERIC), analyzes approximately 700 journals. It is in four parts. The first cites articles in chronological order by their accession number, providing bibliographic information and a brief résumé of each article. The second part is a subject index that arranges all the terms used for each article from the *Thesaurus of ERIC Descriptors*. The third part is an author index, while the fourth presents tables of contents of each of the indexed journals. The indexes cumulate biennially. Records in this bibliographical system are available for computer search through the Lockheed DIALOG system (see Z–78).

Z–126   ***Resources in Education*** [former title: ***Research in Education***]. Washington, D.C.: National Institute of Education, 1956–.   Z5811.E42

This monthly publication of the Educational Resources Information Center (ERIC) provides abstracts for some 1,000 new, unpublished educational materials received by ERIC. Included are research and development reports, evaluative studies, speech and conference papers, reviews of research, and bibliographies. Most, but not all, of the items identified are available in the ERIC microfiche collection that is held by most libraries and are filed by ERIC Document (ED) number (see below). The monthly publication is in five sections. Document Résumés, arranged numerically by the ERIC accession number (the ED number), provide bibliographic information and abstracts of the document in question. This section also includes notice whether the document is available in microfiche and, if not, how it may be acquired. Entries also list all of the descriptor terms used for this particular document in the subject index. The other four sections provide a subject index, an author index, an institutional index, and an access-number cross-reference index to the first section. The subject index is an alphabetically arranged list of all terms from the *Thesaurus of ERIC Descriptors* used in connection with the documents reported in each issue. The indexes all cumulate semiannually. These bibliographical records are available for computer search through the Lockheed system (see Z–78).

Z–127 **Drazan, Joseph Gerald.** *Annotated Bibliography of ERIC Bibliographies, 1966–1980.* Westport, Conn.: Greenwood Press, 1982. Z5811.D73 1982

This bibliography collects over 3,200 individual bibliographies which are permanently stored and available for reproduction in the ERIC system's microfiche file. They are indexed in *Resources in Education* (Z–126) from which the bibliography was compiled and briefly annotated. All entries contain the document's ED (ERIC document) number to facilitate ordering. The volume begins with a section titled "How to Order a Bibliography from ERIC."

Citations are arranged in about 600 broad and narrow subject categories which are arranged alphabetically. They are also indexed by subject terms and keywords, and there are cross-references throughout to facilitate access. The volume concludes with an author index along with the previously mentioned subject index.

Z–128 *Education Index* [1929–]. New York: H. W. Wilson, 1932–. Z5813.E23

This index is now published ten times a year with an annual cumulation. From 1929 through 1961 the index analyzed both books and periodicals by author and subject and included book reviews. From 1961 through 1968 it excluded reviews and provided a subject index only to some 250 journals in education. From 1969 on, book review citations were resumed and authors, as well as subjects, were included. Currently some 350 North American English-language periodicals, some yearbooks and composite volumes, and some monographs are analyzed. It is available for search on WILSONLINE (Z–78).

Further indexes for journals in education include the quarterly *British Education Index* (London: Library Association, 1954–) [Z5813.B7]. Now published by the British Library (London, 1961–), which indexes by author and subject some 175 periodicals published or distributed in Great Britain. Also available is the quarterly *Bulletin signalétique 520*: *Pédagogie* (Paris: CNRS, 1948–) [Z5813.B84], which provides abstracts of articles from some 750 periodicals and author and subject indexes. The indexes are cumulated annually.

Z–129 **"Annotated Bibliography of Research in the Teaching of English [for 1966–]."** In *Research in the Teaching of English [RTE].* Urbana, Ill.: NCTE, 1967–. PE1066.R47

This semiannual bibliography compiled at the ERIC Clearinghouse on Reading and Communication Skills (ERIC/RCS) includes books, articles, dissertations, and unpublished documents. Brief, descriptively annotated entries are classified in six main sections as follows: 1. Bilingual and Bidialectical Studies; 2. Language and Verbal Learning; 3. Literature, Humanities, and Media; 4. Teacher Education; 5. Testing and Education; and 6. Written and Oral Communication. Subdivisions in each section are designated with decimal numeration as follows: .1 Preschool and Elementary; .2 Secondary; .3 College and Adult; .4 Status Surveys; and .5 Reviews of Research. Within subdivisions, entries are serially numbered. There are occasional cross-references. The Eric Document (ED) number with an entry indicates that the item so identified is indexed with a complete abstract in *Resources in Education* (Z–126) and is available through the Eric Document Reproduction Service.

Z–130 **Mitzel, Harold E., ed.** *Encyclopedia of Educational Research.* 5th ed. 4 vols. New York: Free Press, 1982. LB15.E48 1982

Sponsored by the American Educational Research Association, these volumes consist of reviews by specialists summarizing research in various fields and placing it in perspective. Extensive bibliographies are appended to each review article. Entries in the encyclopedia are supplemented by information provided in the quarterly issues of the *Review of Educational Research* (Washington, D.C.: American Educational Research Association, 1931–) [L11.R35].

Z–131 **Manheim, Theodore, et al.** *Sources in Educational Research: A Selected and Annotated Bibliography.* 10 parts. Detroit: Wayne State University Press, 1969. Z5811.M25

This work contains ten bibliographical guides for the use of graduate and advanced undergraduate students. Entries are descriptively annotated. The ten parts are as follows. Part 1, General, discusses pertinent guides, dictionaries and encyclopedias, bibliographies and indexes, research series, yearbooks and reports, handbooks, periodicals, and directories. Parts 2–10 are subject-matter oriented. Part 4 concerns research in Library Science education; part 5 is on Comparative Education. Part 9 treats references for research in Language Arts—Reading. Part 10, finally, treats references for Language Arts—Composition, Grammar, and Handwriting.

Another recommended bibliographical guide is by Dorothea M. Berry, *Bibliographical Guide to Educational Research*, 2d ed. (Metuchen, N.J.: Scarecrow, 1980) [Z5811.B39 1980], first published in 1975, which contains a total of 772 descriptively annotated entries emphasizing recently published reference works. Entries are disposed into seven sections, as follows: Books (including catalogs, trade and subject bibliographies); Periodicals (including directories, indexes, abstract journals, and book review indexes); Research Studies (including ERIC documents and dissertations); Government Publications; Special Materials (including children's literature, textbooks, instructional materials—print and nonprint, and texts and measurements); Other Reference Works (encyclopedias, dictionaries, thesauri, handbooks, statistical sources, directories, yearbooks, and biographical sources); and Research Papers (references on research methodology, and manuscript form and style). An appendix describing other reference guides includes general, social science, and education-oriented works. Indexes of authors and editors, titles, and subjects conclude this guide.

Z–132 **Menges, Robert J., and B. Claude Mathis.** *Key Resources on Teaching, Learning, Curriculum, and Faculty Development: A Guide to the Higher Education Literature.* San Francisco: Jossey-Bass, 1988. Z5814.U7 M45 1988

This volume presents a total of 680 annotated, alphabetically arranged and consecutively numbered entries. There are seven chapters, as follows: 1. An Overview of Literature in Teaching, Faculty, Learning, and Curriculum; 2. Teaching and Teaching Effectiveness; 3. Learners and the Learning Process; 4. College and University Curricula: Traditions, Tensions, and Directions; 5. Faculty and Staff Development: Goals, Trends, and Approaches; 6. Periodicals and Reference Tools on Teaching, Learning, Curriculum, and Faculty Development; 7. Trends and Issues for Research and Practice. The last chapter is a summary essay, not a bibliography. Name and subject indexes conclude the work.

Z–133 **Applebee, Arthur N. *Tradition and Reform in the Teaching of English: A History*.** Urbana, Ill.: NCTE, 1974.

LB1576.A63

This history is in a total of nine chronologically ordered chapters, the titles of which are Early Traditions; The Birth of a Subject; A School for the People; Science and the Teaching of English; A Framework for Teaching; Normal Goals; An Academic Model for English; Words of Usage; and Afterword: The Problems Remaining. A selected, briefly annotated bibliography and a series of six appendixes (including ones on important dates, on college entrance requirements, and on most frequently anthologized works), along with an index of authors, titles, and subjects, conclude this work.

Z–134 **Barzun, Jacques. *Teacher in America*.** Boston: Little, Brown, 1944.

LB2331.B374

This volume about the state of higher education in America, circa 1944, is surprisingly informative about many aspects of American college and university teaching nearly half a century later. A total of twenty-one chapters with titles like "Profession: Teacher," "Two Minds, One Thought," "The Ph.D. Octopus," "Our Nation of Highbrows," "The Little Money," and "To a Young Man Who—," were written for a general audience and are expressive of Barzun's own experience as a teacher at Columbia University. A brief bibliographical note is appended.

Z–135 **Goldstein, Wallace L. *Teaching English as a Second Language: An Annotated Bibliography*.** 2d ed. New York: Garland, 1984.

Z5818.E5 G64 1984

This work, first published in 1978, which emphasizes publications 1965–1975, contains more than 1,200 annotated entries representing books, articles, speeches, ERIC documents, dissertations, and unpublished writings on ESL teaching and related topics. Entries are disposed into fifteen topic sections alphabetically arranged as follows: Audio-visual, Bilingual, General Curriculum, Grammar, Language Learning, Reading, Reference (with subdivisions for bibliographies, checklists, basic textbooks, dictionaries, and directories), Sociocultural Studies, Special Purposes, Spoken English, Teacher Preparation, Teaching Aids, Testing and Evaluation, Vocabulary, and Writing. Author and keyword indexes conclude the bibliography.

See also a number of frequently recommended works cited among those on the history, character, and teaching of the English language (I–17).

Z–136 **ACTFL *Annual Bibliography of Books and Articles on Pedagogy in Foreign Languages*** [for 1975–]. New York: American Council on the Teaching of Foreign Languages, 1978–.

Z5818.L35 A44a

This annual classified bibliography of books and articles has had a complex history until its current publishing arrangement. It has been both variously published and variously arranged. "Work on the Teaching of Modern Languages [1875–1912]" by Charles H. Handschin appeared in *Teaching of Modern Languages in the United States* (Washington, D.C.: GPO, 1913) [no LC number], pp. 107–149. An "Annotated Bibliography of Modern Language Methodology [1915–1959]" appeared annually in the *Modern Language Journal*, vols. 1–45 (1916–1961). A retrospective coverage of much of this material was made by Emma Maire Birkmaier and Dale L. Lange and published as "A Selective Bibliography on the Teaching of Foreign Languages, 1920–1966," *Foreign Language Annals* 1 (1967): 318–353. This journal, published by the ACTFL, housed the ACTFL Annual Bibliography for 1967–1972, with those for 1969–1972 also ap-

pearing as volume 4 of the *MLA International Bibliography* (see L–50). The annual bibliography for 1973 was published separately by the ACTFL and is available also in the ERIC system (document 134002), while the bibliography for 1974 is available only in the ERIC system (document 125268).

Z–137 **Gibaldi, Joseph, and James V. Mirollo, eds. *Teaching Apprentice Programs in Language and Literature*.** New York: MLA, 1981.

P91.5.U5 T4

This volume is in two parts. The first gives by topic the results of a national survey of the training provided to graduate students in preparing them for college teaching. A statistical overview is followed by sections discussing, among other topics, the nature and structure of programs, funding, selection of apprentices and duration of appointments, contracts, compensation, role in the governance and daily life of departments, prior and concurrent training, responsibilities, teaching materials and equipment, supervision and evaluation. Part 2 presents descriptions of eighteen programs that represent the variety of teacher apprentice programs in departments of various sizes and in various sorts of institutions.

Z–138 **Scholarly Journals Concerned with College-Level Education and English Education.** (See also journals concerned with teaching rhetoric and composition listed in X–165.)

ADE Bulletin. Vol. 1–. New York: Association of Departments of English, MLA, 1962–. 3/yr. Reviews.

No LC number

ADFL Bulletin. Vol. 1–. New York: Association of Departments of Foreign Languages, 1969–. 3/yr. Reviews.

P57.U7 A77a

CEA Critic. Vol. 1–. College Station: Texas A&M University for the College English Association, 1939–. 4/yr. Reviews.

PE1011.C22

Change: The Magazine of Higher Learning. Vol. 1–. Washington, D.C.: Heldref, The Chronicle of Higher Education (see Z–118). 8/yr.

LB2300.C4

College Literature. Vol. 1–. West Chester, Pa.: West Chester State College, 1973–. 4/yr. Reviews.

PR1.C65

College Teaching. Vol. 1–. Washington, D.C.: Heldref Publications, 1985–. 4/yr.

L11.I4

Educational Record: The Magazine of Higher Education. Vol. 1–. Washington, D.C.: American Council of Education, 1920–. 4/yr.

L11.E46

EFL Gazette [English as a Foreign/Second Language]. Vol. 1–. Oxford: Pergamon Press, 1979–. 10/yr.

No LC number

EE   *English Education*. Vol. 1–. Urbana, Ill.: NCTE, 1969–. 3–4/yr. Reviews.

LA632.E52

EJ   *English Journal*. Vol. 1–. Urbana, Ill.: NCTE, 1912–. 10/yr. Reviews.

PE1.E5

ELT   *English Language Teaching Journal*. Vol. 1–. London: Oxford University Press, 1946–. 3–4/yr.

PE1128.A2 E5

English Quarterly. Vol. 1–. Toronto: Canadian Council of Teachers of English, 1968–. 4/yr.

PR31.E53

ESP Journal: An International Journal of English for Specific Purposes. Vol. 1–. Oxford: Pergamon Press, 1981–. 2/yr. Reviews.

Exercise Exchange: A Journal for Teachers of English in High Schools and Colleges. Vol. 1–. Murray, Ky.: Department of English, Murray State University, 1953–.

No LC number

Harvard Educational Review. Vol. 1–. Cambridge: Harvard University, 1931–. 4/yr. Reviews.
L11.H3

Improving College and University Teaching. Vol. 1–. Washington, D.C.: Heldref, 1953–. 4/yr.
L11.I4

JGE   *Journal of General Education*. Vol. 1–. University Park: Pennsylvania State University Press, 1946–. 4/yr. Reviews.
L11.J775

Journal of Teacher Education. Vol. 1–. Washington, D.C.: American Association of Colleges for Teacher Education, 1950–. 6/yr.
LB1705.N27

LA   *Language Arts* [former title: *Elementary English*]. Vol. 1–. Urbana, Ill.: NCTE, 1924–. 8/yr. Reviews.
LB1576.A1 E6

Modern English Teacher. Vol. 1–. Oxford: Pergamon Press, 1981–.

Radical Teacher. Vol. 1–. Cambridge, Mass.: Boston Women's Teachers' Group, 1975—. 4 then 3/yr.
L11.R21

RRQ   *Reading Research Quarterly*. Vol. 1–. Newark, Del.: International Reading Association, 1965–. 4/yr. Bibliographies.
LB1050.R42

RTE   *Research in the Teaching of English*. Vol. 1–. Urbana, Ill.: NCTE, 1967–. 4/yr. Reviews. Bibliography (see Z–129).
PE1066.R47

RER   *Review of Educational Research*. Washington, D.C.: American Educational Research Association, 1931–. 4–5/yr. Reviews. Bibliography (see Z–130).
L11.R35

Teaching English in the Two-Year College. Vol. 1–. Greenville, N.C.: Department of English, East Carolina University, 1974–. 3/yr.
PE1065.T4

Teaching Professor. Vol. 1–. Madison, Wisc.: Magna Publications, Inc., 1987–. 12/yr. Reviews. Bibliographies. Checklists.
No LC number

TESOL Quarterly. Washington, D.C.: Georgetown University for the Teachers of English as a Second Language, 1967–. 4/yr.
PE1128.A2 T454

Times Higher Education Supplement. No. 1–. London: The Times, 1971–. Reviews.
LA637.T554

Use of English. Vol. 1–. Edinburgh: Scottish Academic Press, 1949–. 4/yr.
PE1001.U4

World Language English. Vol. 1–. Oxford: Pergamon Press, 1981–. 4/yr. Reviews.
PE1128.A2 W67

For additional titles see William Camp and Bryan L. Schwark, *Guide to Periodicals in Education and Its Academic Disciplines*, 2d ed. (Metuchen, N.J.: Scarecrow, 1975) [Z5813.C28 1975], which is classified and provides addresses, publication information, and editorial policy.

Z–139   **Some Frequently Recommended Works on Teaching, the Teaching of English, and Research in the Teaching of English.** (See also entries at X–164 on the teaching of English composition.)

Brereton, John, ed. *Traditions of Inquiry*. New York: Oxford University Press, 1985.
PE1405.U6 T73 1985

Campbell, Oscar James. *Teaching of College English*. New York: Appleton Century Co., 1934.
LB2365.E5 C3

Craig, David, and Margot Heinemann, eds. *Experiments in English Teaching: New York in Higher and Further Education*. London: Edward Arnold, 1976.
PE68.G5 E9 1976

Diamond, Robert M. *Designing and Improving Courses and Curricula in Higher Education: A Systematic Approach*. San Francisco: Jossey-Bass, 1989.
LB2361.5.D5 1989

Douglas, Wallace. "Some Questions about the Teaching of Works of Literary Art." *ADE Bulletin*, no. 25 (1969): 31–45.

Eble, Kenneth. *Craft of Teaching: A Guide to Mastering the Professor's Art*. 2d ed. San Francisco: Jossey-Bass, 1988.
LB2331.E328 1988

———. *Recognition and Evaluation of Teaching*. Salt Lake City, Utah: Project to Improve College Teaching, 1970.
LB2331.E34

Edens, Walter, ed. *Teaching Shakespeare*. Princeton, N.J.: Princeton University Press, 1977.
PR2987.T35

Enright, Dennis J. *Memoirs of a Mendicant Professor*. London: Chatto and Windus, 1969.
PR6009.N6 Z5

Ericksen, Stanford C. *Essence of Good Teaching: Helping Students Learn and Remember What They Learn*. San Francisco: Jossey-Bass, 1984.
LB2331.E75 1984

Fowler, Mary Elizabeth. *Teaching Language, Composition, and Literature*. New York: McGraw-Hill, 1965.
LB1631.F69

Gerber, John C., et al., ed. *College Teaching of English*. New York: Appleton-Century-Crofts, 1965.
PE1065.N295

Gordon, Edward J., and Edward S. Noyes, eds. *Essays on the Teaching of English*. New York: Appleton-Century-Crofts, 1960.
PE1065.G6

Gray, Donald J., et al. *Department of English at Indiana University, Bloomington, 1868–1970*. Bloomington: Indiana University Press, 1974.

Hart, Francis Russell. *Literature in the Classroom: Teaching Students to Learn*. Columbus: Ohio State University Press, 1989.
PN59.H36 1989

Heilman, Robert B. *Ghost on the Ramparts and Other Essays in the Humanities*. Athens: University of Georgia Press, 1973.
PE27.H4

Holbrook, David. *Exploring Word: Creative Disciplines in the Education of Teachers of English*. Cambridge: Cambridge University Press, 1967.
PE1066.H58

Kohl, Herbert. *Growing Minds: On Becoming a Teacher*. New York: Harper and Row, 1984.
LA2317.K64 A33 1984

Leary, Lewis, ed. *Teacher and American Literature*. Champaign, Ill.: NCTE, 1965.
PS41.L4

Loban, Walter, et al. *Teaching Language and Literature*. Grades Seven-Twelve. 2d ed. New York: Harcourt, Brace and World, 1969. Bibliographies.
LB1631.L45 1969

Lowman, Joseph. *Mastering the Techniques of Teaching*. San Francisco: Jossey-Bass, 1984.
LB2331.L68 1984

Morse, Joseph Mitchell. *Irrelevant English Teacher*. Philadelphia: Temple University Press, 1972.
PE65.M65

Muller, Herbert J. *Uses of English: Guidelines for the Teaching of English from the Anglo-American Conference at Dartmouth College*. New York: Holt Rinehart and Winston, 1967.
PE1065.M78

Ohmann, Richard, ed. *Teaching English in Two-Year Colleges: Three Successful Programs*. Urbana, Ill.: NCTC, 1974.
PE68.U5 T44

Peterson, Houston, ed. *Great Teachers, Portrayed by Those Who Studied under Them.* New Brunswick, N.J.: Rutgers University Press, 1946.   CT105.P44

Quirk, Randolph. *Use of English.* New York: St. Martin's Press, 1968.   PE1072.Q5 1968

———, and A. H. Smith, eds. *Teaching of English.* New ed. London: Oxford University Press, 1975.
          PE1065.Q5 1975

Richardson, G., ed. *Teaching Modern Languages.* New York: Nichols, 1983.   PB35.T43 1983

Ryan, Kevin, ed. *Don't Smile until Christmas: Accounts of the First Year of Teaching.* Chicago: University of Chicago Press, 1970.   LB2844.1.N4 R95

Thompson, Irene, and Audrey Roberts. *Road Retaken: Women Reenter the Academy.* New York: MLA, 1985.
          LB2331.72 .R6 1985

Wilcox, Thomas, W. *Anatomy of College English*, San Francisco: Jossey-Bass, 1973.   LB2365.E5 W54 1973

XII. ALTERNATIVE CAREERS

Z–140 **Bestor, Dorothy K.** *Aside from Teaching English, What in the World Can You Do?* Rev. and exp. version. Seattle: University of Washington Press, 1977.   HF5381.B412 1977

This volume, one of the most extensive responses to the "job crisis" of the 1970s, is disposed into thirteen chapters, which take readers from the diagnosis of the job market crisis through self- and skills-analysis, and job-seeking strategies in general, to descriptions of employment possibilities in nontraditional teaching, in noninstructional academic life, free-lance editing, institutional editing, media and related fields, book publishing, writing and research in the business community, and local and federal government. A series of five appendixes offer some useful courses and programs; questionnaires used to survey job possibilities; more detailed information about publishers' views; a note on internships, and a list of resource organizations. Bibliographical notes to the book's chapters are followed by an annotated bibliography of useful works and an index primarily of employers and job classifications.

Z–141 **Donaldson, Christine F., and Elizabeth A. Flynn.** *Alternative Careers for Ph.D.'s in the Humanities: A Selected Bibliography.* New York: MLA, 1982.
          Z7164.U56 D66 1982

This bibliography is in four sections. The first lists materials related to the job search in general. The second lists materials on a wide range of alternative career fields including publishing, communications, research and consulting, nonprofit organizations, libraries, museums, archives, government, academic administration, technical writing, business, computer science, personnel, public relations, accounting, and law. The third section lists materials on international careers, while the fourth lists materials on careers that require competence in foreign languages. A list of useful addresses is appended.

Z–142 **Trzyna, Thomas N., ed.** *Careers for Humanities/Liberal Arts Majors: A Guide to Programs and Resources.* Columbus, Ohio: Humanities Research Group, 1980.
          HF5382.5.U5 C34

This volume presents a critical review of career options open to humanities and liberal arts majors. Sections treat the questions of where humanities majors find work; where the job al-

ternatives are; what the skills are which a humanities major has and how those skills can be marketed; what career-directed supplemental course work is useful for the humanities/liberal arts major; what certification and training programs short of an M.A. program are available; what second B.A. or professional M.A. programs have proved valuable for humanities and liberal arts majors; and what projections are for the job market of the future. Indexes of authors, subjects, books, schools, organizations, commissions, programs, and degrees make access to the contents of this volume relatively easy. Research bibliographies and guides to further reading at the end of each chapter are useful sources of supplementary information.

Z–143 **Entine, Alan D., and Ana L. Zambrano.** *Guide to Career Alternatives for Academics.* New Rochelle, N.Y.: Change Magazine Press, 1976.   No LC number

This brief pamphlet is frequently recommended as a starting point for academics of all fields who are for the first time considering nonacademic employment.

Z–144 **Solmon, Lewis, Nancy L. Ochsner, and Margo-Lea Hurwicz.** *Alternative Careers for Humanities Ph.D.'s: Perspectives of Students and Graduates.* New York: Praeger, 1979.   HD6278.U5 S64

This volume is the result of a multiyear research program conducted at the Higher Education Research Institute of the University of California, Los Angeles. Extensive survey results are here presented and analyzed along with sample questionnaires for both graduate students and graduate alumni. There are numerous tables of data and a brief bibliography of related materials.

Z–145 **May, Ernest R., and Dorothy G. Blaney.** *Careers for Humanists.* New York: Academic Press, 1981.   LC1011.M32

This work reports on a series of investigations designed to explore the present and future job market for persons with humanities Ph.D.'s. The report is disposed into four chapters: 1, How Many Can Teach [now and in the future]? 2, Who Will Go to Graduate School? Why? Where? 3, Humanists Outside Academe [reports of questionnaires and interviews of persons working in alternative careers]; 4, What Is to Be Done? An appendix presenting additional statistical tables concludes the volume.

Z–147 **Gross, Ronald.** *Independent Scholar's Handbook.* Reading, Mass.: Addison-Wesley, 1982.   AZ103.G75 1982

This volume, subtitled "How to Turn Your Interest in Any Subject into Expertise," addresses problems facing the nonacademic scholar. Gross assumes a reader unskilled in research whom he leads through such processes as choosing a topic, finding library resources, accessing data-bases, networking with other scholars, obtaining financial help, and getting work published.
The book is divided into three parts: Starting Out, The Practice of Independent Scholarship, and Independent Scholars in Action. A short bibliographical section enumerates and annotates books which are particularly inspiring or useful or both. Also included are five appendixes: 1. Gourmet Shops for Scholars: Specialized Bookstores; 2. Foundation Funding, Where to Go for Information (listing reference collections operated by libraries and foundations by state); 3. Tax Deductions for Independent Scholarship as a Business; 4. University Presses in America (alphabetical by state); and 5. Copyrighting Your Work. An index concludes the work.
Another work by Gross, *Independent Scholarship: Promise,*

Problems, and Prospects (New York: College Entrance Examination Board, 1983) [LB1048.G75 1983], was produced by the Office of Adult Learning of the College Entrance Examination Board with a grant from the Fund for the Improvement of Post-Secondary Education. It presents the findings and recommendations of a major two-year project intended to identify and help meet the needs of independent scholars. The study opens with a preliminary survey of independent scholarshp. The two succeeding chapters discuss the relationship between independent scholars and academia, offering a presentation on the independent scholar's needs and a discussion of the recommendations of the National Conference on Independent Scholars. A large bibliography and an appendix of supporting data conclude the volume.

Z–148 Associations and Newsletters for Independent Scholars.

Further information about these organizations and contact addresses may be found in the Directory Issue of *PMLA*.

Alliance of Independent Scholars. Boston, Mass.

Center for Independent Study. New Haven, Conn.

Independent Scholars' Association of the North Carolina Triangle. Durham, N.C.

Independent Scholars in Language and Literature. New York, N.Y.

International Association of Independent Scholars.

Northwest Independent Scholars' Association. Portland, Ore.

Princeton Research Forum. Princeton, N.J.

Providence Roundtable. Providence, R.I.

Z–149 Some Frequently Recommended Works on Alternative Careers.

Abel, Emily K. *Terminal Degrees: The Job Crisis in Higher Education*. New York: Praeger, 1984.
LB2335.3.A24 1984

Bolles, Richard Nelson. *What Color Is Your Parachute? A Practical Manual for Job-Hunters and Career Changers*. Rev. ed. Berkeley: Ten Speed Press, 1984.
HF5383.B56 1984

Carter, Allan M. *Ph.D.'s and the Academic Labor Market: A Report Prepared for the Carnegie Commission on Higher Education*. New York: McGraw-Hill, 1976.
LB2386.C37

Harwood, John T. "From Genre Theory to the Want Ads." *ADE Bulletin* 44 (1975): 21–24.

———. "Non-academic Job Hunting." *AAUP Bulletin* 60 (1974): 313–316.

Harrison, Dorothy G. "Aristotle and the Corporate Structure." *Change: The Magazine of Higher Learning* 8 (1976): 9, 64.

Hawkins, James E. *Uncle Sam Connection*. Chicago: Follett Publications, 1978.
JK716.H38 1978

Irish, Richard K. *Go Hire Yourself an Employer*. Rev. and exp. ed. Garden City, N.Y.: Anchor Press, 1978.
HF5383.I75 1978

Jessup, Claudia, and Genie Chipps. *Woman's Guide to Starting a Business*. Rev. ed. New York: Holt, Rinehart and Winston, 1980.
HD69.N3 J47 1980

Lukowski, Susan, and Margaret Piton. *Strategy and Tactics for Getting a Government Job*. Washington, D.C.: Potomac Books, 1972.
JK716.L9

Matthews, Kathy. *On Your Own: 99 Alternatives to a 9-to-5 Job*. New York: Vintage, 1977.
HF5382.M36 1976

Maxfield, Betty D., and Susan M. Henn. *Employment of Humanities Ph.D.'s: A Departure from Traditional Jobs*. Washington D.C.: National Academy of Sciences, 1980.
HD6278.U5 M38 1980

Munschauer, John L. *Jobs for English Majors and Other Smart People*. Princeton, N.J.: Peterson Guides, 1981.
HF5382.7.M86 1981

Orange, Linwood E. *English: The Pre-Professional Major*. New York: MLA, 1972. Originally published in the *ADE Bulletin* 32 (February 1972): 49–51.

Pinkerneil, Dietrich, ed. *Alternativen: Die Berufsaussichten des Geisteswissenschaftlers ausserhalb der Schule*. Kronberg/Taunus: Scriptor, 1973.
HD6278.G4 P56

Rudenstein, Gail M. "The Ph.D. in the Nonacademic Marketplace." In Brad et al. *English and Foreign Languages: Employment and the Profession*. New York: MLA, 1976. (See Z–111.)

Ruland, Richard. "Why English?" *ADE Bulletin.* 42 (September 1974): 27.

Terkel, Studs. *Working: People Talk about What They Do All Day and How They Feel about What They Do*. New York: Random House, 1974.
HD8072.T4

Turpin, Elizabeth R. "Alternatives to Teaching for English Professors in Journalism, Public Relations, and Editing." *ADE Bulletin* 40 (March 1974): 40–44.

Wolfe, Dael, and Charles V. Kidd. "The Future Market for Ph.D.'s." *AAUP Bulletin* 58 (March 1972): 5–16.

Wyman, Roger E., and Nancy A. Risser. *Humanities Ph.D.'s and Nonacademic Careers: A Guide for Faculty Advisors*. Evanston, Ill.: Committee on Institutional Cooperation, 1983.
AZ183.U5 W95 1983

XIII. KEEPING CURRENT

Z–150 *New York Times Book Review*. New York: *The Times*, 1896–.
AP2.N658

The weekly *Book Review* section is published with the Sunday edition of the *New York Times* and is also available separately in most bookstores. Reviewed are a variety of important new books of all sorts, including academic titles on occasion. Reviews tend to be less extensive than those of the *New York Review of Books* (Z–151) or *TLS* (Z–152) and are written for a literate general audience.

In addition to its use in keeping current, the *Times Book Review* is a major source for studying the general reception of individual works and authors and for tracing more general changes in taste through the course of the twentieth century. The five volume *New York Times Book Review Index, 1896–1970* (New York: Arno, 1973) [no LC number] provides access to more than 800,000 reviews by authors, titles, reviewers, subject, and category of publication (e.g., children's books). In addition, a cumulated multivolume reprint of the reviews themselves is available covering 1896–1979.

Z–151 *TLS: The Times Literary Supplement*. London: The Times, 1902–.
AP4.T45

Published weekly as a supplement to the *London Times* but also available separately, *TLS* is the most distinguished review organ of the British intelligentsia. New publications in all branches of learning are discussed at greater or lesser length in its pages, with some works receiving the briefest mention and others treated in extensive review articles that are distinguished essays in their own right. In addition to reviews, *TLS* has become a forum for exchange and debate through its letters columns, and over the years many a literary controversy has flared up in its pages. Other features include an "Information Please" notes-and-queries section and commissioned articles on topics of general cultural interest. A number of special issues during the course of the year focus attention on a particular class of publications, from children's books to new works of bibliography and reference.

In addition to its value as the most inclusive reviewing organ for current publications, *TLS* has value for historical inquiries. The recent *Times Literary Supplement Index*, in two parts, covers the *TLS* for 1902–1939 and 1940–1980. Part 1, in two volumes (1980), contains over 350,000 references to personal names, titles, and subjects of reviews, articles, and letters published through 1939. Part 2 will cover 1940–1980 in some four volumes and will contain over 650,000 references.

Z–152 *New York Review of Books [NYRB].* New York: New York Review, 1963–.   AP2.N6552

Published twenty-two times a year, the *New York Review of Books* has become the preeminent general American forum for review of major academic publications in the humanities and social sciences. Review articles are long, often brilliant essays in their own right, and they frequently treat several related titles. It is unlikely that important new work in any branch of the *sciences humaines* would escape the notice of regular readers of the *New York Review of Books*. A cumulative index is available for 1963–1975.

Z–153 *London Review of Books [LRB].* London: London Review, 1979–.   No LC number

Published twenty-four times a year, the *London Review of Books* has become an eminent British forum for review of major academic publications, along with works of fiction and poetry, essays, memoirs and letters. Only full length reviews are included, and they are written by distinguished British and American intellectuals.

Z–154 *American Scholar.* Washington, D.C.: Phi Beta Kappa, 1932–.   AP2.A4572

This quarterly prints literary essays for a general intellectual audience including both members of Phi Beta Kappa and others. Articles are generally without academic accoutrements such as footnotes, though they are often written by academics and have some degree of importance in specific fields. Most issues include a number of fairly long book reviews.

Z–155 *Daedalus: Journal of the American Academy of Arts and Sciences.* Cambridge: American Academy of Arts and Sciences, 1958–.   Q11.B7

This quarterly is published both for members of the Academy and for a general readership of men and women of learning. In contrast with *American Scholar*, issues focus generally on one topic, articles are academic in character, and the resulting volume may well constitute a major contribution to inquiry in that particular subject matter.

Z–156 *Review.* Vol. 1–. Charlottesville: University Press of Virginia, 1979–.   PR1.R32

This annual presents a set of from twenty to thirty review essays of major scholarly works in English and American language and literature. Scholarly monographs, editions, and

bibliographies are reviewed, as are groups of works and even the state of scholarship in whole fields of study. Essays are extensive, expansive, rigorous, and meticulous, scrutinizing the book or works under review closely, with the aim of delivering a definitive critique. The journal's editors contrast its reviewing policy with that of many current journals that seem less critical than they ought to be; the editors point to the nineteenth century practice of *Blackwoods* or *Edinburgh Review* as a model for the kind of reviewing they seek to provide.

Z–157 **Hoge, James O., ed.** *Literary Reviewing.* Charlottesville: University Press of Virginia, 1987.   PN441.L487 1987

This volume brings together nine essays on the subject of writing reviews. Some of the essays give guidelines to would-be reviewers; others lament the inadequacy of reviews; still others comment on the place of reviews and reviewing in the profession. The essays and their contributors are as follows: Reviewing Criticism: Literary Theory (Ralph Cohen); Reviewing Literary History (Medieval) (Derek Pearsall); Reviewing Literary Biography: Apprehending the *Daimon* (Stanley Weintraub); Reviewing Editions: Letters, Journals, Diaries (Angus Easson); Bibliographies: How Much Should a Reviewer Tell? (Richard D. Altick); Descriptive Bibliography, Detective Fiction, and Knowing the Rules (James L. W. West III); Reviewing Reviewing: From the Editor's Desk (Robert L. Patten); Book Reviews and the Scholarly Publisher (Bruce D. Macphail); and Reflections on Star Wars and Scholarly Reviewing (Michael West).

Z–158 **Journals of Particular Interest to Humanists.**

Annals of Scholarship: Metastudies of the Humanities and Social Sciences. Vol. 1–. New York: Humanities Press, 1982–. 4/yr.

BRH   *Bulletin of Research in the Humanities* [former title: *Bulletin of the New York Public Library*] Vol. 1–. New York: New York Public Library, 1897–. 4/yr.   Z881.N6B

Centennial Review. Vol. 1–. East Lansing; Michigan State University, 1952–.   No LC number

Cultural Critique: An International Journal of Cultural Studies. Vol. 1–. Minneapolis: University of Minnesota Department of English, 1985–. 3/yr.   AC5.C84

Dalhousie Review. Vol. 1–. Dalhousie University Press, 1920–. 4/yr.   AP5.D3

Formations. Vol. 1–. Wilmette, Ill.: Northwestern University Press, 1984–. 3/yr.   No LC number

Georgia Review. Vol 1–. Athens: University of Georgia, 1947–. 4/yr. Reviews.   AP2.G375

Gettysburg Review. Vol. 1–. Gettysburg, Pa.: Gettysburg College, 1988–. Reviews.   AS30.G48

Granta. Vol. 1–. Cambridge, Eng.: Granta Publications, 1980–. 4/yr.   PN2.G68

HudR   *Hudson Review.* Vol. 1–. New York: Hudson Review, Inc., 1946–. 4/yr.   AP2.H886

Humanities in Review. Vol. 1–. New York: Cambridge University Press for the New York Institute for the Humanities, 1982–.   AC5.H82 1982

HIS   *Humanities in the South: Newsletter of the Southern Humanities Conference.* No. 1–. Houston: University of Houston for the Southern Humanities Conference, 19–. 2/yr. Reviews.   No LC number

Interpretation: A Journal of Political Philosophy. Vol. 1–. Flushing, N.Y.: Queens College, 1982–.

Journal of Thought: An Interdisciplinary Quarterly. Vol. 1–. Norman: University of Oklahoma, College of Education, 1983–. 4/yr. Reviews.

Massachusetts Review: A Quarterly of Literature, the Arts, and Public Affairs. Vol. 1–. Amherst: University of Massachusetts, 1959–.   AS30.M3 A22

Michigan Quarterly Review. Vol. 1–. Ann Arbor: University of Michigan, 1961–. 4/yr.   AS30.M48

Midwest Quarterly: A Journal of Contemporary Thought. Vol. 1–. Pittsburgh: Kansas State College, 1959–. 4/yr.   AS30.M5

Minnesota Review. Vol. 1–. Bloomington: Indiana University, 1960–. 4/yr.   AP2.M5598

New Formations. Vol. 1–. London: Methuen, 1987–. 3/yr. Reviews.   No LC number

October. Vol. 1–. Cambridge: MIT Press, 1976–. 4/yr.   NX1.027

Ontario Review: A North-American Journal of the Arts. Vol. 1–. Windsor, Ont., 1974–. 2/yr. Reviews.   NX1.O57

PR   *Partisan Review.* Vol. 1–. New Brunswick, N.J.: Rutgers University Press, 1934–. 4/yr.   HX1.P3

Raritan: A Quarterly Review. Vol. 1–. New Brunswick: Rutgers University Press, 1982–. 4/yr. Reviews.   AS30.R37

Representations. Vol. 1–. Berkeley and Los Angeles: University of California Press, 1983. 4/yr.   NX1.R46

Salmagundi: A Quarterly of the Humanities and Social Sciences. Vol. 1–. Saratoga Springs, N.Y.: Skidmore College, 1965–.   No LC number

STTH   *Science Technology & the Humanities.* Vol. 1–. Melbourne: Florida Institute of Technology, 1978–. 3/yr.   AS30.S16

SR   *Sewanee Review.* Vol. 1–. Sewanee, Tenn.: University of the South, 1892–. 4/yr. Reviews.   AP2.S4

SAQ   *South Atlantic Quarterly.* Vol. 1–. Durham, N.C.: Duke University Press, 1902–. 4/yr.   AP2.S75

South Carolina Review. Vol. 1–. Clemson, S.C.: Clemson University, 1968–.   PS558.S6 S67

Southern Humanities Review. Vol. 1–. Auburn: Auburn University, 1967–.   AS36.A86 A35

Southern Review. 7 vols. 1935–1942. New series, vol. 1–. Baton Rouge: Louisiana State University, 1965–. 4/yr. Reviews.   AP2.S8555

Studies in the Humanities. Vol. 1–. Indiana, Pa.: Indiana University of Pennsylvania, 1971–.   No LC number

Texas Quarterly. Vol. 1–. Austin: University of Texas, 1957–. 4/yr.   AP2.T269

Textual Practice. Vol. 1–. London: Methuen, 1987–. Reviews.   No LC number

Thought: A Review of Culture and Ideas. Vol. 1–. Bronx, N.Y.: Fordham University Press, 1926–.   AP2.T333

Tikkun: A Bimonthly Jewish Critique of Politics, Culture, and Society. Vol. 1–. Oakland, Calif.: Institute for Labor and Mental Health, 1986. 4 then 6/yr.   DS101.T54

Topic: A Journal of the Liberal Arts. Vol. 1–. Washington, Pa.: Washington and Jefferson College, 1960/61–.   AS30.T6

UTQ   *University of Toronto Quarterly.* Vol. 1–. Toronto: University of Toronto Press, 1930–. 4/yr. Reviews.   No LC number

VQR   *Virginia Quarterly Review: A National Journal of Literature and Discussion.* Vol. 1–. Charlottesville: University of Virginia, 1925–. 4/yr.   AP2.V76

YR   *Yale Review: A National Quarterly.* Vol. 1–. New Haven: Yale University, 1910–. 4/yr.   AP2.Y2

Z–159 **Some Frequently Recommended Works on the Humanities in Our Time.**

Adler, Mortimer J. *How to Read a Book: The Art of Getting a Liberal Education.* Rev. and updated ed. New York: Simon and Schuster, 1972.   PN83.A43 1972

Berlin, Isaiah. "The Divorce between the Sciences and the Humanities." *Salmagundi* 27 (1974): 9–39.

Bird, Otto A. *Cultures in Conflict: An Essay on the Philosophy of the Humanities.* Notre Dame, Ind.: University of Notre Dame Press, 1976.   AZ101.B57

Booth, Wayne, ed. *Knowledge Most Worth Having.* Chicago: University of Chicago Press, 1967.   LB7.K73

Crane, Ronald S. *Idea of the Humanities and Other Essays.* 2 vols. Chicago: University of Chicago Press, 1967.   PN50.C7

Elliott, Robert C. "Literature and the Good Life: A Dilemma." *Yale Review* 65 (1975): 24–37.

Finn, Chester E., et al., eds. *Against Mediocrity: The Humanities in America's High Schools.* New York: Holmes and Meier, 1984.   LC1011.A2 1984

Gardner, John W. *Excellence: Can We Be Equal and Excellent Too?* Rev. ed. New York: Norton, 1984.   HM146.G29 1984

Grenander, M. E. "The Camel and the Needle's Eye: Science and the Humanist." *Southern Quarterly* 15 (1977): 245–261.

Hardison, E. B., Jr. *Toward Freedom and Dignity: The Humanities and the Idea of Humanity.* Baltimore: Johns Hopkins University Press, 1972.   LC1011.H263

Hartman, Geoffrey. "Humanistic Study and the Social Sciences." *College English* 38 (1976): 219–223.

Hassan, Ihab. "Beyond Arcadians and Technophiles: New Convergences in Culture?" *Midwest Review* 17 (1976): 7–18.

Humanities in American Life: Report of the Commission on the Humanities. Berkeley, Los Angeles, London: University of California Press, 1980.   AZ103.O54 1980

Jones, Howard Mumford. *One Great Society. Humane Learning in the United States.* New York: Harcourt, Brace and World, 1959.   AZ507.J6

Laidlaw, J. C., ed. *Future of the Humanities: The Papers Delivered at the Jubilee Congress of the Modern Humanities Research Association in August 1968.* Cambridge: MHRA, 1969.   AZ103.M65

Murphy, William M., and D. J. R. Bruckner, eds. *Idea of the University of Chicago . . . 1891 to 1975.* Chicago: University of Chicago Press, 1976.   LD906.5.I33

Niblett, W. Roy, ed. *Sciences, the Humanities and the Technological Threat.* London: University of London Press, 1975.   LC1011.S38 1975b

Priestley, F. E. L. "Science and the Humanities—Are There Two Cultures?" *Humanities Association Bulletin* 23 (1972): 12–22.

————. "Science and the Humanities." *Humanities Association Bulletin*. 27 (1976): 353–366.

Rieff, David, ed. *Humanities in Review*. Vol. 1–. Cambridge: Cambridge University Press, 1982–.   AC.H82 1982

Ritsch, Frederick F. *Humanities: The Contemporary Scene*. Spartanburg, S.C.: Southern Humanities Conference, 1983.   AZ361.H78 1983

Sabine, Gordon, and Patricia Sabine. *Books That Made the Difference: What People Told Us*. Hamden, Conn.: Library Professional Books, 1983.   Z1003.2.S2 1983

Ulich, Robert, ed. *Education and the Idea of Mankind*. New York: Harcourt, Brace and World, 1964.   LC191.U4

Woolf, Robert Paul. *Ideal of the University*. Boston: Beacon Press, 1969.   LA227.3.W63 1969

INDEX OF AUTHORS, COMPILERS, CONTRIBUTORS, AND EDITORS

This index excludes authors, compilers, contributors, and editors of works cited in the "Frequently Recommended" enumerations. Access to those items is through the tables of contents and the subject index only. Names included below are keyed to entry numbers; asterisked entry numbers indicate that the name is associated with the main entry.

INDEX OF TITLES

This index *excludes* titles of works cited in the "Frequently Recommended" enumerations. Access to those items is through the tables of contents and the subject index only. Titles included below are keyed to entry numbers; asterisked entry numbers indicate that the title is the main entry.

Authors and Areas of Canada. [PR9127.J6] M–147

Authors: Critical and Biographical References: A Guide to 4,700 Critical and Biographical Passages in Books. [PN524.C58] L–30

Authors, Publishers, and Politicians: The Quest for an Anglo-American Copyright Agreement, 1815–1854. Z–98

Autobiography [William Lyon Phelps]. [PS3531.H4Z5 1939] Z–2

Autograph Collectors Journal. H–8

Autograph Letters and Manuscripts. [Z6621.P6512 vol.3] H–27

Autograph Letters and Manuscripts [in the Pierpont Morgan Library]. [Z6621.P6512] B–31

Autograph Poetry in the English Language: Facsimiles of Original Manuscripts from the Fourteenth to the Twentieth Century. [PR1174.C75 1973] H–111*

Autographs: A Collector's Guide. [Z41.P36 1973] Y–82

Autographs: A Key to Collecting. [Z41.B4] Y–82

Autographs and Manuscripts: A Collector's Manual. [Z41.A92] Y–82*

Avviamento allo studio critico delle lettere italiane. [Z2351.M47 1971] L–80

Avviamento allo studio della lingua e della letteratura francese. [Z2171.C67] L–70

Ayers Directory of Publications. [Z6951.A97] D-l03*

Ba Shiru: A Journal of African Languages and Literatures. L–135

Babel: Révue internationale de traduction/International Journal of Translation. [PN241.A1 B15] I–106

Baconiana: The Journal of the Francis Bacon Society. [PR2941.A3] M–60

Baker's Biographical Dictionary of Musicians [ML105.B16 1984] A–75

BAMBAM: Bookline Alert: Missing Books and Manuscripts. [Z1000.5.B66 1982] Y- 72

Bantu Studies. L–135

Barker's Continuation of Egerton's Theatrical Remembrancer. [Z2014.D7 B38] U–35

Barock. [Z2232.M4] L–114

Basic Russian Publications: An Annotated Bibliography on Russia and the Soviet Union. [Z2491.H6] L–123

Basic Tools of Biblical Exegesis: A Student's Manual. [Z7770.M33 1976] K–35*

Baudelaire to Beckett: A Century of French Art and Literature [an Exhibition at the Humanities Research Center, University of Texas]. [Z732.T25 T46] B–35

Beats: Literary Bohemians in Postwar America. [PS228.B6 B47 1983] M–58

Beautiful, the Sublime, and the Picturesque in Eighteenth-Century British Aesthetic Theory. [BH221 .G72 H5] L–15

Bedford Bibliography for Teachers of Writing. X–145*

Bedfordshire [Victoria County History]. [DA670.B3 V6] F–102

Beginnings of English Literature to Skelton, 1509. [PR83.I615 vol. 1] N–12*

Beginnings of English Society (from the Anglo-Saxon Invasion). F–18

Beinecke Rare Book and Manuscript Library: A Guide to Its Collections. [Z733.Y18 1974] B–21, H–27

Beiplatt zur Anglia. M–25

Beiträge aus der Thesaurus-Arbeit. [PA2320.B44] I–67

Beiträge zur deutschen Philologie. L–108

Beiträge zur Geschichte der deutschen Sprache und Literatur. [PF3003.B52] L–108

Beiträge zur Kinder- und Jugendliteratur. L–179

Beiträge zur romanischen Philologie. [PC3.B4] L–60, L–63

Ben Jonson: A Quadricentennial Bibliography. [Z8456 .6.B75] M–60

Ben Jonson Companion. [PR2630.B7] M–60

Ben Jonson of Westminster. [PR2631.C53] M–60

Ben Jonson's London: A Jacobean Place Name Dictionary. [PR2645.C4354] M–60

Benjamin Franklin. [E302.F8 V32] S–50

Benjamin Franklin: A Reference Guide. [Z8313.B89 1983] S–50

Beowulf: An Edition with Manuscript Spacing Notation and Graphotactic Analyses. [PR1580.S8 1975] M–60

Beowulf and Judith. M–60

Beowulf and the Fight at Finnsburgh. [PR1580.K5 1950] M–60

Beowulf and the Fight at Finnsburgh: A Bibliography. [Z2012.F83] M–60

Beowulf Scholarship: An Annotated Bibliography. [Z2012.S53] M–60

BEPI: A Bibliography of English Publications in India. [Z3201.B18] M–154*

Berkshire [Victoria County History]. [DA670.B4 V6] F–102

Bernard Shaw Companion. [PR5367.H35 1974] M–60

Best [American] Short Stories . . . and the Yearbook of the American Short Story. [PZ1.B446235] W–57*

Best of Children's Books 1964–1978, Including 1979 Addenda. [Z1037.H358 1981] L–170

Best Plays, 1894–99–. U–40

Bianco e nero. U–129

Bible as Literature: A Selective Bibliography. [Z7770.G68] K–46*

Biblical Methodology: A Student's Manual of Basic Tools. K–35

Biblio: Cataloque des ouvrages parus en langue française dans le monde entier [covering 1933–1970]. [Z2165.B565] C–56*

Bibliografía crítica de la neuva estilística, aplicada a las literaturas romanicas. X–133

Bibliografía de escritores hispanoamericanos/A Bibliography of Spanish American Writers, 1609–1974. [Z1609.L7 F55] L–100

"*Bibliografía [de filogía hispánica].*" [PC4008.N84] L–93*

Bibliografía de la literatura hispánica. [Z2691.S5] L–92

Bibliografía de la literatura picaresca desde sus origenes hasta el presente/A Bibliography of Picaresque Literature from Its Origins to the Present. [Z5917.P5 L35] W–61*

Bibliografia della linguistica italiana. [Z2355.A2 H315] L–82

"*Bibliografia delle pubblicazioni italiane [1945–].*" [PN5.R5] L–9

Bibliografía general de la literatura hispanoamericana. [Z1609.L7 L4 1954] L–98

Bibliografía general de la literatura latinoamericana. [Z1609.L7 B5] L–98*

Bibliografia generale del cinema/Bibliographie général du cinéma/General Bibliography of Motion Pictures. [Z5784.M9 V5 1972] U–90*

"*Bibliografía hispánica.*" [PQ6001.R47] L–93

Bibliografia nazionale italiana: nuova serie del Bollettino della pubblicazioni italiane ricevute per diritto di stampa. [Z2345.F63] C–73*

British Poets, 1880–1914. [PR581.B7 1983] M–58

British Poets, 1914–1945. [PR610.B7 1983] M–58

British Printer. [Z119.B86] Y–38

British Public Record Office. [CD3560.V53 no.25/28] H–70

British Studies Monitor. [DA4.B75] M–25

British Technology Index. [Z7913.B7] D–17

British Union Catalogue of Periodicals: A Record of the Periodicals of the World, from the Seventeenth Century to the Present Day, in British Libraries. [Z6945.B87] D–95*

British Union Catalogue of Periodicals, Incorporating World List of Scientific Periodicals; New Periodical Titles. [Z6945.B874] D–96*

British Union Catalogue of Periodicals–New Serial Titles. C–16

British Writers. [PR85.B688] M–53*

British Writers: Edited under the Auspices of the British Council. [PR85.B688] M–53*

Brockhaus Enzyklopädie in zwanzig Bänden. [AE27.G672] A–45*

Brontë Bibliography. [Z8122.Y3] M–60

Brontë Companion: Literary Assessment, Background, and Reference. [PR4168.P5] M–60

Brontë Society, Transactions. [PR4168.A4] M–60

Brontës. M–60

Browning Collections: A Reconstruction with Other Memorabilia: The Library, First Works, Presentation Volumes, Manuscripts, Likenesses, Works of Art, Household and Personal Effects, and Other Association Items of Robert and Elizabeth Barrett Browning. [PR4235.K44 1984] Y–69

Browning Cyclopaedia: A Guide to the Study of the Works of Robert Browning, with Copious Explanatory Notes and References on All Difficult Passages. [PR4230.B4] M–60

Browning Handbook. [PR4231.D45 1955] M–60

Browning Institute Studies. [PR4229.B77a] M–60

Browning Newsletter. M–60

Bücherkunde für Germanisten: Studienausgabe. [Z2235.A2H3] A–18*

Bücherkunde zur Weltgeschichte vom Untergang des römischen Weltreiches bis zur Gegenwart. [Z6201.F68] F–1

Buckinghamshire [Victoria County History]. [DA670.B9 V6] F–102

Bucknell Review. X–38

Bulletin [of the National Register of Archives]. H–62

Bulletin analytique. L–6

Bulletin analytique de linguistique française. [Z2175.A2 B85] L–74

Bulletin bibliographique de la Société internationale arthurienne/Bibliographical Bulletin of the International Arthurian Society. [Z8045.I5] N–57*

Bulletin bibliographique pour l' étude des épopées romanes. [PQ201.S66a] N–57

Bulletin de la Bibliothèque nationale. [Z927.P22 B84] B–61

Bulletin de la Société de linguistique de Paris. [P12.S45] I–15

Bulletin de philosophie médiévale. [B721.I57a] N–18

Bulletin hispanique: Annales de la Faculté des lettres de Bordeaux. [PQ6001.B8] L–95

Bulletin of Bibliography [1897–1900; vols. 1–4]. D–10

Bulletin of Bibliography [and Magazine Notes]. [Z1007.B94] A–7*, U–55, W–73, Y–38

Bulletin of Bibliography [and Magazine Notes]. Cumulative Index (1976–1980). A–7

Bulletin of Bibliography [and Magazine Notes]. Cumulative Index (1897–1975). A–7

Bulletin of Black Theatre: Newsletter of the AETA Black Theatre Project. U–18

"Bulletin of Far Eastern Bibliography." L–144

Bulletin of Hispanic Studies. [PC4008.B8] L–95

Bulletin of Literary Semiotics. X–13

Bulletin of Reprints. [Z1033.R4 B5] E–63*

Bulletin of Research in the Humanities. [Z881.N6B] Z–158

"Bulletin of Scandinavian Philology." L–108

Bulletin of Spanish Studies. L–95

Bulletin of the Association for African Literature in English. L–135

Bulletin of the Association for Literary and Linguistic Computing [BALLC]. [P98.A75a] Z–75

Bulletin of the Comediantes. [PQ6098.C64a] L–95

Bulletin of the Copyright Society of the U.S.A. [KF2987.C66] Z–98

Bulletin of the History of Medicine. [R11.B93] X–38, X–91

Bulletin of the Institute of Historical Research. [D1.L65] F–10, G–10, G–26*

Bulletin of the John Rylands University Library of Manchester. [Z921.M18 B] B–47

Bulletin of the New York Public Library. [Z881.N6B] B–30, X–134*, Y–63, Z–50, Z–158

Bulletin of the School of Oriental (and African) Studies. [PJ3.L6] L–135, L–148

Bulletin of the Shakespeare Association of America [PR2887.N5] O–50

Bulletin of the Society of Archivists. [CD23.S6 A3] H–8

Bulletin signalétique (19–24): sciences humaines. L–6

Bulletin signalétique 519: Philosophie. [Z7751.F7118] X–56

Bulletin signalétique 520: Pédagogie. [Z5813.B84] Z–128

Bulletin signalétique 521: Sociologie, ethnologie. X–67*

Bulletin signalétique 523: Histoire et sciences de la littérature: Révue trimestrielle. [Z6513.B82] L–6*

Bulletin signalétique 524: Sciences du langage. [P2.B84] I–10*

Bulletin signalétique 527: Sciences religieuses. [Z7751.B85] X–51

Bulletin signalétique: Philosophie, sciences humaines. L–6

Burke Newsletter. P–18

Burke's Family Index. [Z5035.G7 B87] G–20*

Burke's Genealogical and Heraldic History of the Landed Gentry of Great Britain and Ireland. [CS425.B8] G–19*

Burke's Genealogical and Heraldic History of the Landed Gentry of Ireland. [CS490.B8] G–19

Burke's Genealogical and Heraldic History of the Peerage, Baronetage, and Knightage. [CS420.B85] G–18*

Burke's Guide to Country Homes. [NA7620.B86] G–19

Burke's Landed Gentry. G–19

Burney MSS #1–524 [with Arundel MSS] [British Library]. [Z6621.B85 1823] H–11

Burns Mantle Best Plays. U–40

Burns Mantle Yearbook. U–40

Business and Technical Communication: A Bibliography, 1975–1985. [Z7164.C81 H7 1987] X–158*

Business and Technical Writing: An Annotated Bibliography of Books 1880–1980. [Z7164.C81] X–155*

Business Communications: An Annotated Bibliography. [Z7164.C81 W24] X–157*

Chaucer's Lyrics and Anelida and Arcite: An Annotated Bibliography, 1900–1980. [Z8164.P42 1983] N–45

Chaucer's Romaunt of the Rose and Boece, Treatise on the Astrolabe, Equatorie of the Planetis, Lost Works and Apocrypha: An Annotated Bibliography, 1900–1985. [PR1905.Z99 P43x 1988] N–45

Check-List of Eighteenth-Century Books Containing Lists of Subscribers. [Z1016.A47] C–12

Check List of English Plays, 1641–1700. [Z2014.D7 W6] P–33*

Check List of English Prose Fiction, 1700–1739. [Z2014.F4 M3] P–44*

"Check List of Explication for 1943–." [PR1.E9] T–31*

Check List of Historical Records Survey Publications. H–80

Check-List of Medieval Studies. O–6

Check-List of Middle English Prose Writings of Spiritual Guidance. [Z2014.P795 J64] N–65*

Check List of Prose Fiction Published in England 1740–1749. [Z2014.F4 B37] P–45*

Checklist of American Copies of "Short Title Catalogue" Books. [Z2002.P772 B5] C–5

"Checklist of American Critical Works in Science Fiction: 1972–1973." W–112

Checklist of American Imprints for 1820 [through 1829]. [Z1215.S5]. C–25*

"Checklist of American Literary Manuscripts in Australia, Canada, India, Israel, Japan, and New Zealand." H–51

Checklist of Canadian Literature and Background Materials, 1628–1960: In Two Parts: First a Comprehensive List of the Books Which Constitute Canadian Literature Written in English; and Second, a Selective List of Other Books by Canadian Authors Which Reveal the Backgrounds of That Literature. [Z1375.W 1972] M–131*

Checklist of Cumulative Indexes to Individual Periodicals in the New York Public Library. [Z6293.N45] D–6*

"Checklist of D. H. Lawrence Criticism and Scholarship." [PR6023.A93 Z6234] M–60

Checklist of Emerson Criticism 1951–1961, with Detailed Index. [Z8265.B7] S–50

"Checklist of English Newspapers and Periodicals before 1801 in the Huntington Library." D–50

"Checklist of English Women in Print, 1475–1640." L–202

Checklist of Fantastic Literature: A Bibliography of Fantasy, Weird, and Science Fiction Books Published in the English Language. [Z5917.F3 B55 1978] W–103*

Checklist of Hawthorne Criticism, 1951–1966. [Z8393.J6] S–50

Checklist of Interpretation since 1940 of Classical and Continental Plays. U–53

Checklist of Non-Italian Humanists, 1300–1800. [PA83.C6 1969] G–70

Checklist of Printed Materials Relating to French-Canadian Literature 1763–1968/Liste de référence d'imprimés relatifs à la littérature canadienne-française. [Z1377.F8 B72 1973] L–70

"Checklist of Scholarship on Southern Literature." [AS30.M58 A2] S–18, S–103

Checklist of Serials for African Studies. [Z3503.D8] L–135

Cheshire [Victoria County History]. [DA670.C6 H52] F–102

Chester. [PN2596.C48 C4] N–54

Chicago Manual of Style. [Z253.C57] Z–92*, Z–93

Chicago Tribune [index]. [AI21.C45 C47] D–23

Chicano Literature: A Reference Guide. [PS153.M4 C46] S–160*

Chicano Writers, First Series. M–58

Chicorel Index Series. U–49

Chicorel Index to Abstracting and Indexing Services: Periodicals in Humanities and the Social Sciences. [Z6293.C54 1978] D–5*

Chicorel Index to Film Literature. [Z5784.M9 C48] U–125*

Chicorel Index to Poetry in Anthologies and Collections in Print. [PN1022.C55] T–23*

Chicorel Index to Poetry in Anthologies and Collections: Retrospective Index to Out-of-Print Titles. [PN1022.C54] T–24*

Chicorel Index to Poetry in Collections in Print on Discs and Tapes. [PR1175.8.C4] E–105

Chicorel Index to Short Stories in Anthologies and Collections. [Z5917.S5 C44] W–56*

Chicorel Index to the Spoken Arts on Discs, Tapes, and Cassettes. [ML156.2.C52] E–105*

Chicorel Theater Index to Plays in Anthologies and Collections, 1970–1976. [Z5781.C4846] U–49

Chicorel Theater Index to Plays in Anthologies, Periodicals, and Discs in England. [Z5781.C486] U–49

Chicorel Theater Index to Plays in Anthologies, Periodicals, Discs, and Tapes. [Z5781.C485] U–49*

Chicorel Theater Index to Plays in Periodicals. [Z5781.C487] U–49

Child and His Book: Some Account of the History and Progress of Children's Literature in England. [Z1037.F45] L–176

Children and Literature: Views and Reviews. [PN1009.A1 H27] L–170

Children's Book Review Index. [Z1037.A1 C475] L–179

Children's Books in England and America in the 17th Century: A History and Checklist. [Z1037.S62] L–177

Children's Books in England: Five Centuries of Social Life. [PN1009.A1 D35 1982] L–176*

Children's Literature: A Guide to Reference Sources. [Z1037.A1 H35] L–170*

Children's Literature: A Guide to the Criticism. [Z2014.5.H46 1987] L–175*

Children's Literature Abstracts. [Z1037.C5446] L–179

Children's Literature: An Annotated Bibliography of the History and Criticism. [Z1037 R15 1981] L–174*

Children's Literature: An International Journal. [PN1009.A1 C514] L–179

Children's Literature Association Quarterly. [PN1008.2.C48] L–179

Children's Literature in Education: An International Quarterly. [Z1037.A1 C5] L–179

Children's Literature Review. [PN1009.A1 C5139] L–179

Children's Literature Review: Excerpts from Reviews, Criticism, and Commentary on Books for Children and Young People. [Z1037.A1 C475] L–179

China: A Critical Bibliography. [Z3101.H8] L–162

China in Western Literature. [Z3101.Y8] I–161

China in Western Literature: A Continuation of Cordier's Bibliotheca Sinica. [Z3101.Y8] L–162*

China Quarterly: An International Journal for the Study of China. [DS701.C472] L–148

Chinese Literature. [DS777.55.C45] L–148

Chinese Literature: Essays, Articles, and Reviews. [PL2250.C533] L–148

Christian Science Monitor. [AI21.C462 B44] D–23

Christian Science Monitor (1960–). [AI21.C46] D–23

Literature and Theatre of the States and Regions of the U.S.A.: An Historical Bibliography. [Z1225.G63] S–100*

Literature and Theology. X–38

Literature by and about the American Indian: An Annotated Bibliography. [Z1209.S73 1979] S–141*

Literature Criticism from 1400 to 1800. [PN86.L53 1984] X–29

Literature East and West: The Journal of the Conference on Oriental-Western Literary Relations of the MLA. [PN2.L67] L–9, L–148

Literature, English and American: A Bibliography of Bibliographies. [Z2011.A1B47] A–1

Literature/Film Quarterly. [PN1995.3.L57] U–129

Literature of Australia. [PR9609.6.D8 1976] M–120

Literature of Fantasy: A Comprehensive, Annotated Bibliography of Modern Fantasy Fiction. [Z2014.F4 S33] W–107*

Literature of Geography: A Guide to Its Organization and Use. [Z6001.B74 1978] F–90*

Literature of Journalism: An Annotated Bibliography [to 1957]. [Z6940.P7] D–40*

Literature of Medieval History 1930–1975: A Supplement to Louis John Paetow's A Guide to the Study of Medieval History. [Z6203.P25 1980 suppl.] F–21

Literature of Slang. [Z2015.S6 B9] I–42

Literature of Spain in English Translation. [Z2694.T7 R83] I–130

Literature of the American People: An Historical and Critical Survey. [PS88.Q5] S–33*

Literature of the English Renaissance, 1484–1660. M–36

Literature of the Film: A Bibliographical Guide to the Film as Art and Entertainment, 1936–1970. [Z5784.M9 D9] U–95

"Literature of the New South." [PS55.F53 1984] S–21

Literature of the Nineteenth and Early Twentieth Centuries. M–36

"Literature of the Old South." [PS55.F53 1984] S–21

Literature of the Restoration and Eighteenth Century, 1660–1798. M–36

Literature of the United States. M–39

Literature of the United States. [PS92.C8 1986] S–32*

Literatures of Asia and Africa. I–108

Literatures of the East: An Appreciation. [PJ307.C4] L–142*

Literatures of the World in English Translation: A Bibliography. I–108*, I–120*, I–130*

Litteraturblatt für germanische und romanische Philologie. [Z7037.L7] L–57

Littérature générale et littérature comparée: Essai d'orientation. [PN873.J4] L–4

Little Magazine: A History and Bibliography. [PN4836.H6] D–80*

Little Magazine: A Study of Six Editors. [PN 4878.3.H3] D–80

Little Magazine in America, 1950–1975. D–75

Little Magazine in America: A Modern Documentary History. [PN 4878.3.L5] D–27, D–80

Lively Arts Information Directory: A Guide to the Fields of Music, Dance, Theatre, Film, Radio, and Television for the United States and Canada, Covering National, International, State, and Regional Organizations, Government Grant Sources, Foundations, Consultants, Special Libraries, Research and Information Centers, Education Programs, Journals and Periodicals, Festivals and Awards. [PN2289.L55 1982] U–2

Lives and Characters of the English Dramatick Poets. [Z2014.D7 L23] U–29

LLINQUA: Language and Literature Index Quarterly. [Z7003.L35] L–7*

"Local Archives of Great Britain." [CD1.B7] H–8

Local Government Records: An Introduction to Their Management, Presentation, and Use. [CD3024.J66] H–80

Local Historian: The Quarterly Journal of the Standing Conference for Local History. [DA20.A44] F–10

Local Historian's Encyclopedia. [DA34.R53] F–104

Local History Collections. [Z688.L8 T48] F–117

Local Indexes in American Libraries: A Union List of Unpublished Indexes. [Z6293.A5] D–4

Local Record Sources in Print and in Progress. [Z2023.Y68] H–76

Lochlann: A Review of Celtic Studies. [PB1001.L625] M–93

Locke Newsletter. P–18

Loeb Classical Library. L–46*

Logic and Rhetoric in England, 1500–1700. [BC38.H6] X–8

Logic, Philosophy, Epistemology, Universal Language [Bibliography of]. I–12

London Book Trades 1775–1800: A Preliminary Checklist of Members. [Z152.L8 M39] Y–49

London Booktrades, 1735–1775: A Checklist of Members in Trade Directories and in Musgrave's "Obituary." [Z330.6.L6 M39 1984] Y–49

London Catalogue of Books in All Languages, Arts and Sciences, That Have Been Printed in Great Britain, Since the Year MDCC. Properly classed under the Several Branches of Literature and Alphabetically disposed under each Head. With their sizes and prices. Carefully compiled and corrected, with innumerable additions. [Z2001.E5] C-11*

London, including London within the Bars, Westminster, and Southwark [Victoria County History]. [DA677.V6] F–102

London Library. [Z792.L6 L65 1978] B–45

London Magazine. [Z2002.M64] C–10, Z–66

London of Charles Dickens. [PR4584.L6] M–60

"London Printers' Imprints, 1800–1840." Y–49

London Review of Books. Z–153*

London Stage, 1660–1800. A Calendar of Plays, Entertainments, and Afterpieces, Together with Casts, Box-Receipts, and Contemporary Comment Compiled from the Playbills, Newspapers, and Theatrical Diaries of the Period. [PN2592.L6] U–77*

London Stage, 1800–1900. U–78*

London Stage, 1890–1899: A Calendar of Plays and Players. [PN2596.L6 W37] U–79*

London Stage, 1900–1909. [PN2596.L6 W38] U–79

London Stage, 1910–1919. [PN2596.L6 W383] U–79

London Stage, 1920–1929. [PN2596.L6 W384 1984] U–79

London Theatres and Music Halls, 1850–1950. [PN2596.L6 H595] U–78

London Times. Z–151

Longman Bibliography of Composition and Rhetoric. [Z5818.E5 L55 1987] X–146*

Longman Companion to English Literature. [PR19.G54 1977] M–44*

Longman Companion to Twentieth Century Literature. [PN771.W28 1981] R–25*

Longman Literature in English Series. M–35*

Lord Chamberlain's Plays, 1824–1851 [British Library]. H–11

Nelson's Complete Concordance of the Revised Standard Version Bible. K–45

Neohelicon: Acta Comparationis Litterarum Universarum. [PN851.N46] L–9

"Neo-Latin News." O–71

Neo-Latin News. [PR1.S47] O–18, O–78

Neophilologus: A Quarterly Devoted to the Study of the Modern and Medieval Languages and Literature, Including General Linguistics, Literary Theory and Comparative Literature. [PB5.N4] L–57, R–11

Neue deutsche Biographie. [CT1053.N4] G–61*

Neuer Bildniskatalog. [N7575.S56] G–81

Neues Handbuch der Literaturwissenschaft. [PN553.N48] L–29*

Neunzehntes Jahrhundert (1830–80). L–114

Neuphilologische Mitteilungen/Bulletin de la Société néophilologique/Bulletin of the Modern Language Society. [PB10.N415] L–57, N–18, N–25*, N–36, N–40, N–47*

New American Literature, 1890–1930. [PS221.P3] S–38

New American Nation Series. F–60

New and Complete Concordance or Verbal Index to Words, Phrases, and Passages in the Dramatic Works of Shakespeare with a Supplementary Concordance to the Poems. [PR2892.B34] O–55

New Bibliography of African Literature. [Z3508.L5 P37] L–133

New Book of Forms: A Handbook of Poetics. [PN1042.T78 1986] T–67*

New Cambridge Bibliography of English Literature. [Z2011.N45] I–104, M–11*, N–11*, O–11*, P–11*, Q–11*

New Cambridge Modern History. [D208.N4] F–14*

New Cassell's French Dictionary. [PC2640.C3 1962] I–70

New Catholic Encyclopedia. [BX841.N44] A–52*

New Century Classical Handbook. [DE5.N4] L–45*

New Century Handbook of Classical Geography. [DE25.N48] L–45

New Century Handbook of English Literature. [PR19.N4 1967] M–42*

New Century Handbook of Greek Art and Architecture. [N5633.N39] L–45

New Century Handbook of Greek Literature. [PA31.N4] L–45

New Century Handbook of Greek Mythology and Legend. [BL782.N45] L–45

New Century Handbook of Leaders of the Classical World. [D55.N48] L–45

New Columbia Encyclopedia. [AG5.C725 1975] A–49*

New Commentary on the Poems of W. B. Yeats. [PR5907.J39 1984] M–60

"New Copyright Law." Z–98

New Dictionary of American Slang. I–55

New Encyclopedia of Science Fiction. [PN3433.4.N48 1988] W–111*

New England Quarterly: A Historical Review of New England Life and Letters. [F1.N62] S–18, S–101*

New English Dictionary on Historical Principles. [PE1625.N53 1888] I–33

New Extinct Peerage, 1884–1971: Containing Extinct, Abeyant, Dormant, and Suspended Peerages with Genealogies and Arms. [CS422.P56] G–18

New Feminist Scholarship: A Guide to Bibliographies. [Z7161.A1 W54] L–183*

New Film Index: A Bibliography of Magazine Articles in English, 1930–1970. [Z5784.M9 M29 1975] U–122*

New Formations. X–13, Z–158

New Grants Planner. [HV41.C639 1980] Z–89

New Grove Composer Biography Series. A–75

New Grove Dictionary of Music and Musicians. [ML100.N4B] A–75*

New Grove Dictionary of Musical Instruments. [ML102.I5N48 1984] A–75

New History of England [1460–1960]. F–19

New Intellectuals: A Survey and Bibliography of Recent Studies in English Renaissance Drama. [Z2014.D7 N29] O–37*

New International Atlas. [G1019.R355] F–93

New Introduction to Bibliography. [Z116.A2 G27 1974] Y–22*, Y–32

New Larousse Encyclopedia of Mythology. [BL311.L33] K–27*

New Left Review. [HX3.N36] X–38

New Literary History: A Journal of Theory and Interpretation. [PR1.N44] X–13

New Literary History International Bibliography of Literary Theory and Criticism. [Z6514.C97 C65 1988] X–20*

New Orleans Times-Picayune. [AI21.T66] D–23

"New Orthodoxy: Ideology and the Institution of American Literary History." S–36

New Oxford Annotated Bible with the Apocrypha, Revised Standard Version Containing the Second Edition of the New Testament and an Expanded Edition of the Apocrypha. [BS191.A1 N4] K–38*

New Oxford Companion to Music. [ML100.N5 1983] A–75

New Oxford English Dictionary. I–33

New Oxford History of Music. [ML160.N44] A–75

New Oxford Illustrated Dickens. M–60

New Pelican Guide to English Literature. [PR83.N49 1982] M–39*

New Periodicals Index. D–15

New Rambler: Journal of the Johnson Society of London. [PR3532.A16] M–60, P–18

New Reader's Guide to African Literature. [PN849.A35 Z44 1983] L–130*

New Readings vs. Old Plays: Recent Trends in the Reinterpretation of English Renaissance Drama. [PR651.L48] O–2

New Revised Velázquez Spanish and English Dictionary. [PC4640.V5] I–75*

New Sabin: Books Described by Joseph Sabin and His Successors, Now Described Again on the Basis of Examination of Originals, and Fully Indexed by Title, Subject, Joint Authors, and Institutions and Agencies. [Z1201.T45 E18] C–21

New Serial Titles: 1950–1970, Subject Guide. [Z6945.N42] D–92

New Serial Titles: A Union List of Serials Commencing Publication after December 31, 1949. [Z6945.U5 S42] D–92*

New Serial Titles–Classed Subject Arrangement. [Z6945.U5 N38] D–92

New Standard Jewish Encyclopedia. [DS102.8.S73] A–51

New Testament Abstracts: A Record of Current Literature. [BS410.N35] K–37

New Thoreau Handbook. [PS3053.H32 1980] S–50

"New Uses of Watermarks as Bibliographical Evidence." Y–27

New Walt Whitman Handbook. [PS3231.A7 1980] S–50

New Wessex Edition of the Works of Thomas Hardy. M–60

Poems of Charlotte Brontë: A New Text and Commentary.
[PR4166.N48 1985] M–60

Poems of Edgar Allan Poe, Edited with an Introduction, Variant Readings, and Textual Notes.
[PS2605.A1 1965a] S–50

Poems of Edward Taylor. [PS850.T2 A6 1960] S–50

Poems of Emily Dickinson, Including Variant Readings Critically Compared with All Known Manuscripts.
[PS1541.A1 1955] S–50

Poems of Emily Dickinson: An Annotated Guide to Commentary Published in English, 1890–1977. PS1541.Z5 D8] S–50

Poems of Gerard Manley Hopkins.
[PR4803.H44 A17 1967] M–60

Poems of John Donne. [PR2245.A5G6] M–60

Poems of John Keats. [PR4831.A4] M–60

Poems of John Keats. [PR4831.S75 1978] M–60

Poems of Jonathan Swift. [PR3721.W5] M–60

Poems of Matthew Arnold. [PR4021.A45 1979] M–60

Poems of Tennyson. [PR5550.F69] M–60

Poems of W. B. Yeats: A New Edition.
[PR5900.A3 1983] M–60

Poems of William Blake. [PR4141.S8] M–60

Poet and Critic. T–8

Poetica: Zeitschrift für Sprach und Literaturwissenschaft.
[P3.P6] X–13

Poetical Works of Edmund Spenser. [PR2350 1909] M–60

Poetical Works of Edward Taylor. [PS850.T2 1939] S–50

Poetical Works of John Keats. [PR4830.F58] M–60

Poetical Works of Robert Browning.
[PR4203.J3 1983] M–60

Poetical Works of William Wordsworth, Edited from the Manuscripts, with Textual and Critical Notes.
[PR5850.F40] M–60

Poetics: International Review for the Theory of Literature.
[PN45.P58] X–13

Poetics Today: A Central Interim Final Quarterly for Theory of Literature and Related Fields. X–13

Poétique: Revue de théorie et d'analyse littéraires.
[PN3.P64] X–13, X–136

Poetry. [PS301.P6] T–8

Poetry Explication: A Checklist of Interpretation since 1925 of British and American Poems Past and Present.
[Z2014.P7K8 1980] T–30*

Poetry Handbook: A Dictionary of Terms.
[PN44.5.D4 1974b] T–50*

Poetry Index Annual: A Title, Author, First Line, and Subject Index to Poetry in Anthologies (1981–].
[PN1022.P63] T–21*

Poetry of Matthew Arnold: A Commentary.
[PR4024.T5] M–60

Poetry of Robert Frost. [PS3511.R94 1969] S–50

Poetry of Samuel Taylor Coleridge: An Annotated Bibliography of Criticism, 1935–1970. [Z8182.M54] M–60

Poetry of the Romantic Period. [PR502.R58] T–43

Poetry of Thomas Hardy: A Handbook and Commentary.
[PR4753.B27] M–60

Poetry Themes: A Bibliographical Index to Subject Anthologies and Related Criticism in the English Language, 1875–1975. [PN1022.M3] T–25*

Poets of Great Britain and Ireland, 1945–1960.
[PR610.P56 1984] M–58

Poets of Great Britain and Ireland since 1960.
[PR611.P58 1985] M–58

Poets of Ireland: A Biographical and Bibliographical Dictionary. [Z2037.026] M–89

Polish Books in English, 1945–1971.
[Z2528.L5 H37] I–150

Polish Literature in English Translation: A Bibliography.
I–150

Polish Literature Recently Translated.
[Z2528.L5 C68] I–150

Polish Plays in English Translations: A Bibliography.
[Z2528.L5 T3] I–150

Polish Short Story in English: A Guide and Critical Bibliography. [Z2528.T7 M33] I–150

"Political Consciousness in the Age of Johnson: A Review Article." P–3

Politics of Literature: Dissenting Essays on the Teaching of English. [PR37.P6] Z–6*

Polyglot Dictionaries and Grammars: Treatises on English Written for Speakers of French, German, Dutch, Danish, Swedish, Portuguese, Italian, Hungarian, Persian, Bengali, and Russian [Bibliography of]. I–12

Pooh Perplex: In Which It Is Discovered That the True Meaning of the Pooh Stories Is Not As Simple As It Usually Believed, but for Proper Elucidation Requires the Combined Effort of Several Academicians of Varying Critical Persuasions. [PR6025.I65 W65] Z–39

Poole's Index, Date and Volume Key.
[Z674.A75 no. 19] D–10

Poole's Index to Periodical Literature [1802–1881].
[AI3.P7] D–10*

Popular Antiquities of Great Britain, Comprising Notices of the Moveable and Immoveable Feasts, Customs, Superstitions and Amusements Past and Present.
[DA110.B82 1870] K–20

Popular Periodical Index. [AI3.P76] D–15

Popular School: A Survey and Bibliography of Recent Studies in English Renaissance Drama.
[Z2014.D7 L82] O–36*

Portrait of an Obsession: The Life of Sir Thomas Phillipps, the World's Greatest Book Collector.
[Z989.P49 M8 1967] Y–89

Portrait of the Artist as a Young Man: Text, Criticism, and Notes. [PZ3.J853 P23] M–60

Portraits and Daguerreotypes of Edgar Allan Poe.
[PS2635.D4 1989] S–50

Post-Symbolist Bibliography. [Z6520.S9 K7] R–35*

Powre above Powres. [PR9080.P6] M–108

Practice of Modern Literary Scholarship. [PN85.Z5] Z–48*

Praeger Encyclopedia of Art. [N33.P68] A–71

Pragmatics: An Annotated Bibliography.
[Z7004.P73 V47] I–6*

Praxis: A Journal of Radical Perspectives on the Arts. X–38

Pre-Raphaelitism: A Bibliographical Study.
[Z5948.P9 F7] Q–55*

Pre/Text: An Inter-Disciplinary Journal of Rhetoric.
[P301.P68] X–165

Predecessors of Shakespeare: A Survey and Bibliography of Recent Studies in English Renaissance Drama.
[Z2014.D7 L83] O–35*, O–36

"Preliminary Guide to Indexed Newspapers in the United States, 1850–1900." [Z6293.B7] D–20

Preliminary Handlist of Copies of Books Associated with Dr. Samuel Johnson. [Z997.J69 F48 1984] Y–69

Preliminary Handlist of Documents and Manuscripts of Samuel Johnson. [Z8455.8.F55] M–60

Preliminary Inventories, nos. 1–153 (1941–1963) [U.S. National Archives and Records Service]. H–85

"Proverb and Anglo-American Literature." K–60

Proverb Literature: A Bibliography of Works Relating to Proverbs. [Z7191.S83] K–51*

Proverbium. K–60

Proverbs in Literature: An International Bibliography. [Z6514.P76 M53] K–60*

Proverbs, Sentences, and Proverbial Phrases from English Writings Mainly before 1500. [PN6083.W45] K–55*

Psychiatry and Psychology in the Visual Arts and Aesthetics: A Bibliography. [Z5931.K5] X–60

Psychiatry: Journal for the Study of Interpersonal Processes. [RC321.P93] X–38

Psychoanalysis, Psychology, and Literature: A Bibliography. [Z6511.K5 1982] X–60*

Psychoanalytic Study of Literature. [PN56.P92 P74] X–38

Psychocriticism: An Annotated Bibliography. [Z6514.P78 P89 1984] X–60

Psychological Abstracts: Nonevaluative Summaries of the World's Literature in Psychology and Related Disciplines. [BF1.P65] X–61, X–63*

PTL: A Journal for Descriptive Poetics and Theory of Literature. X–13

Publication Guide for Literary and Linguistic Scholars. [Z6951.B9] Z–101

Publication of American Historical Manuscripts. [Z286.H5 P83] H–21

Publications of Societies: A Provisional List of the Publications of American Scientific, Literary, and Other Societies from Their Organization. [Z5055.U39 B7] Z–29

Publications of the American Dialect Society. [PE1702.A5] I–30, I–54

Publications of the Royal Commission on Historical Manuscripts. H–61

"Publications on Dutch Language and Literature in Languages Other Than Dutch." [PF1.D85] L–108

Published Comment on William Dean Howells through 1920: A Research Bibliography. [Z8420.25.E38] S–50

Published Library Catalogues: An Introduction to Their Contents and Use. [Z695.87.C6] B–15*

Published Screenplays: A Checklist. [Z5784.M9 M3] U–113*

Publisher: The Journal of the Publishing Industry [1967–1970]. [Z2005.P97] C–13

Publishers' Circular and Booksellers' Record of British and Foreign Literature [1837–1958]. C–12

Publishers' Trade List Annual. [Z1215.P97] C–29*

Publishers' Weekly: The Book Industry Journal. [Z1219.P98] C–27*

Publishing Agreements: A Book of Precedents. [KD1340.A65 P8] Z–108*

Publishing and Bookselling: A History from the Earliest Times to the Present Day. [Z323.M95 1974] Y–44*

Publishing History: The Social, Economic, and Literary History of Book, Newspaper, and Magazine Publishing. [Z280.P8] Y–38

Put Your Degree to Work: A Career-Planning and Job-hunting Guide for the New Professional. [HD8038.A1 F69 1988] Z–110*

Quarendo. Y–38

Quarterly Checklist of Classical Studies: An International Index of Current Books, Monographs, Brochures, and Separates. [Z7016.Q35] L–47

Quarterly Check-List of Linguistics: An International Index of Current Books, Monographs, Brochures, and Separates. [Z7003.Q35] I–8*

Quarterly Checklist of Medievalia: An International Index of Current Books, Monographs, Brochures, and Separates. [Z6203.Q34] F–23

Quarterly Checklist of Oriental Studies. [Z3001.O34] L–144

Quarterly Check-List of Renaissance Studies: An International Index of Current Books, Monographs, Brochures, and Separates. [Z6207.R4 Q34] O–6*

Quarterly Index Islamicus: Current Books, Articles, and Papers on Islamic Studies. [Z3013.Q34] L–151

Quarterly Journal of Speech. I–15, X–102, X–103*, X–104, X–165

Quarterly Journal of the Library of Congress. [Z663.A5] B–23, H–23

Quarterly of Film, Radio, and Television. U–129

Quarterly Review of Doublespeak. [PE1460.A2 Q37] X–165

Quarterly Review of Film Studies. [PN1994.Q34] U–129

Quellenverzeichnis. [PF3625.G72] I–85

Quest. [AP8.Q4] M–158

Quest for Nationality. S–36

R. B. Adam Library Relating to Dr. Samuel Johnson and His Era. [Z8455.8.A21] Y–89

R. Q. [Reference Quarterly]. [Z671.R23] Y–38

Radical Teacher. [L11.R21] Z–138

Ralph Waldo Emerson: A Descriptive Bibliography. [Z8265.M94 1982] S–50

Ralph Waldo Emerson and the Critics: A Checklist of Criticism, 1900–1977. [Z8265.B64] S–50

Random House Dictionary of the English Language. I–49

Rare Books, 1983–84: Trends, Collections, Sources. [Z1029.R36 1984] Y–79*

Raritan: A Quarterly Review. [AS30.R37] Z–158

"Rassegna bibliografia." [PQ5.S75] L–75*

Rassegna della letteratura italiana. L–83, L–88

Rationale of Textual Criticism. [PN81.T318 1989] Y–29

Reader: Essays in Reader-Oriented Theory, Criticism, and Pedagogy. X–13

Reader-Response Criticism: From Formalism to Post-Structuralism. [PN98.R38 R4] X–23*

Reader's Companion to World Literature. [PN41.R4 1973] L–23

Reader's Encyclopedia: An Encyclopedia of World Literature and the Arts. [PN41.B4 1965] L–23*

Reader's Encyclopedia of American Literature. [PS21.R4] S–41*

Reader's Encyclopedia of World Drama. [PN1625.G3] U–23*

Reader's Guide to Books on the Cinema. [Z1035.L7 no. 21] U–94

Reader's Guide to Charles Dickens. [PR4588.H54 1972] M–60

Reader's Guide to D. H. Lawrence. [PR6023.A93 Z63137] M–60

Reader's Guide to English and American Literature. [Z2011.W73] M–5*

Reader's Guide to Ernest Hemingway. [PS3515.E37 Z92] S–50

Reader's Guide to Finnegan's Wake. [PR6019.09.F938] M–60

Reader's Guide to Geoffrey Chaucer. [PR1924.B6] M–60

Reader's Guide to Herman Melville. [PS2387.M5] S–50

Reader's Guide to James Joyce. [PR6019.09.Z833] M–60

Reader's Guide to Joseph Conrad. [PR6005.04 Z76] M–60

with Historical Introduction, Facsimilies, Portraits, and Other Illustrations. [Z8811.J21] O–46*

Shakespeare Bibliography: The Catalogue of the Birmingham Shakespeare Library. [Z8813.B5] O–49*

Shakespeare Head Brontë [edition].
  [PR4165.A2 1931] M–60

Shakespeare [in the National Library of Scotland]. B–54

Shakespeare in the Theatre, 1701–1800. [PR3097.H6] U–77

Shakespeare Jahrbuch. [PR2889.D4] O–54*, O–54, O–58

Shakespeare Jahrbuch (Heidelberg). O–58

Shakespeare Jahrbuch (Weimar). O–58

Shakespeare Newsletter. [PR2885.S48] O–53*, O–58

Shakespeare on Film Newsletter. O–58

Shakespeare Quarterly. [PR2885.S63] B–22, O–50*, O–54, O–58

Shakespeare: Select Bibliographical Guides.
  [Z8811.W44] O–40*

Shakespeare Studies: An Annual Gathering of Research, Criticism, and Reviews. [PR2885.S64] O–52*, O–58

Shakespeare Studies (Tokyo). [PR2885.S63] O–58

Shakespeare Survey. [PR2888.C3] O–51*, O–58

Shakespeare's England. [PR2910.S 1917] H–96

Shakespeare's Lives. [PR2894.S3] M–60

Shakespeare's World: Renaissance Intellectual Contexts: A Selective, Annotated Guide, 1966–71.
  [PR8813.E38] O–53

Shakespearean Bibliography and Textual Criticism: A Bibliography. [Z2011.A1 H68] M–1, O–45*, Y–1

Shakespearean Criticism. [PR2965.S43 1984] X–29

Shakespearean Research and Opportunities.
  [PR2885.S8] O–53, O–58

Shakespearean Stage, 1574–1642. [PN2589.G8 1980] U–74

"Shakespearean Work in Progress." O–53

Shavian: The Journal of the Shaw Society. M–60

Shaw Bulletin, 1951–1956. M–60

Shaw Review. M–60

Shaw: The Annual of Bernard Shaw Studies.
  [PR5366.A15] M–60

Shaw's Music: The Complete Musical Criticism in Three Volumes. [ML60.55175 1981b] M–60

Shelley Library: An Essay in Bibliography: I. Shelley's Own Books, Pamphlets, and Broadsides, Posthumous Separate Issues, and Posthumous Books Wholly or Mainly by Him. [PR5426.L6 4th series no. 1] M–60

Shelley: The Pursuit. [PR5431.H65 1975] M–60

Shock of Recognition: The Development of Literature in the United States Recorded by Men Who Made It.
  [PS55.W 1955] S–38

Short Dictionary of Anglo-Saxon Poetry in a Normalized Early West-Saxon Orthography. [PE279.B4] I–37

Short Fiction Criticism 1928–1958. S–89

Short Fiction Criticism: A Checklist of Interpretation since 1925 of Stories and Novelettes (American, British, Continental), 1800–1958. [Z5917.S5 T5] W–50*

Short Guide to Books on Watermarks. [Z7914.P2 P3] Y–27

Short History of American Poetry. [PS303.S67] T–46

Short History of English Literature. [PR85.E8 1963] M–38

Short History of English Literature. [PR85.S3 1929] M–38

Short History of English Poetry. [PR502.F7 1981] T–45

Short History of English Versification. [PE1505.K33] T–61

Short Story Index: An Index to 60,000 Stories in 4320 Collections. [Z5917.S5 C6] W–55*

Short-Title Alphabetical Catalogue of Plays Produced or Printed in England from 1660 to 1900 (1959). U–71

Short Title Catalogue of Books Printed in England, Scotland, and Ireland and of English Books Printed Abroad 1475–1640. [Z2002.P77] C–5*

Short-Title Catalogue of Books Printed in England, Scotland, Ireland, Wales and British America and of English Books Printed in Other Countries, 1641–1700.
  [Z2002.W5] C–7*

Short-Title Catalogue of Books Printed in England, Scotland, Ireland, Wales, and British America and of English Books Printed in Other Countries 1641–1700. 2nd. ed. [Z2002.W52] C–7*

Short-Title Catalogue of Books Printed in France and of French Books Printed in Other Countries from 1470 to 1600 [in the Library of the British Museum].
  [Z2162.B86] B–40

Short-Title Catalogue of Books Printed in German-speaking Countries and German Books Printed in other Countries from 1455 to 1600 [in the Library of the British Museum]. [Z2222.B73] B–40

Short-Title Catalogue of Books Printed in Italy and of Books in Italian Printed Abroad, 1501–1600, Held in Selected North American Libraries. [Z2342.S56] C–71

Short-Title Catalogue of Books Printed in Italy and of Italian Books Printed in Other Countries from 1465 to 1600 [in the Library of the British Museum].
  [Z2342.B7] B–40

Short-Title Catalogue of Books Printed in the Netherlands and Belgium and of Dutch and Flemish Books Printed in Other Countries from 1470 to 1600 [in the Library of the British Museum]. [Z2402.B7] B–40

Short-Title Catalogue of French Books, 1601–1700, in the Library of the British Museum.
  [Z2162.B87 1973] B–40, C–52

Short-Title Catalogues of Spanish, Spanish-American and Portuguese Books Printed Before 1601 [in the Library of the British Museum]. [Z2682.B87] B–40

Short-Title List of Additions: Books Printed 1471–1700 [in the John Carter Brown Library].
  [Z881.P9665 1973] B–33

Shorter Cambridge Medieval History. [D117.P75] F–13

Shorter Encyclopaedia of Islam. [DS37.E52] A–53

Shorter New Cambridge Bibliography of English Literature.
  [Z2011.S417] M–11

Shorter Oxford English Dictionary on Historical Principles.
  [PE1625.L53 1973] I–33

Shropshire [Victoria County History].
  [DA670.S4 V6] F–102

Sibley's Harvard Graduates: Biographical Sketches of Those Who Attended Harvard College [title varies].
  [LD2139.S5] G–45

Sight and Sound. [PN1993.S56] U–129

Signal: Approaches to Children's Literature.
  [PN1009.A1 S39] L–179

"Significant Articles, Monographs, and Reviews [*Shakespeare Studies*]." [PR2885.S64] O–52*

Signs: Journal of Women in Culture and Society.
  [HQ1101.S5] L–189

Singing Tradition of Child's Popular Ballads. [ML3650.B82 1976] K–21

"Sir Gawain and the Green Knight: An Appraisal." N–42

Sir Thomas Malory and the Morte D'Arthur: A Survey of Scholarship and Annotated Bibliography.
  [Z8545.5.L53] M–60

Sir Thomas Malory: His Turbulent Career: A Biography.
  [PR2045.H5] M–60

Sir Walter Scott: A Reference Guide. [Z8802.R82] M–60

Sir Walter Scott: An Index Placing the Short Poems in His Novels and in His Long Poems and Dramas.
  [PR5331.B8 1936] M–60

Sir Walter Scott [in the National Library of Scotland].
  [PR5339.S5 1971] B–54

Utopian Literature: A Bibliography, with a Supplementary Listing of Works Influential in Utopian Thought. [Z7164.U8 M43] W–117

Variety Film Reviews, 1907–1980. [PN1995.V34 1983] U–127

Variorum Commentary on the Poems of John Milton. [PR3595.V3] M–60

Variorum Edition of Tennyson's Idylls of the King. [PR5558.A1 1973] M–60

Variorum Edition of the Complete Poems of Thomas Hardy. [PR4741.G5 1979] M–60

Variorum Edition of the Plays of W. B. Yeats. [PR5900.A4] M–60

Variorum Edition of the Poems of W. B. Yeats. [PR5900.A3 1966] M–60

Variorum Edition of the Works of Geoffrey Chaucer. M–60

Verbatim: The Language Quarterly. [P1.V472] I–15

Vergleichende Zeittafel der Weltliteratur, vom Mittelalter bis zur Neuzeit (1150–1939). [PN554.S63] F–80

Verseform: A Comparative Bibliography. [Z7156.V6 B76 1988] T–63*

Versification: Major Language Types. [PN1942.W52] T–62*

Verzeichnis der im deutschen Sprachbereich erschienenen Drucke des XVI. Jahrhunderts: VD16. [Z1014.V47] C–60

Verzeichnis der Märchentypen. K–1

Verzeichnis laufend erscheinender Bibliographien. [Z1002.D4] A–8

Verzeichnis Lieferbarer Bücher/German Books in Print. [Z2221.V47] C–66*

Victoria History of the Counties of England. F–102*

Victoria History of the Counties of England: General Introduction. [DA670.A1 P83] F–102

"*Victorian Bibliography for [1932–1956].*" [PB1.M7] Q–38*

"*Victorian Bibliography for [1957–].*" [PB1.V5] Q–38*

Victorian England, 1837–1901. [Z2019.A56] F–42*

Victorian Fiction: A Guide to Research. [PR873.S8] Q–43*

Victorian Fiction: A Second Guide to Research. [PR871.V5 1978] Q–43, Q–44*

Victorian Newsletter. [PR1.V48] Q–18, Q–38

Victorian: Newsletter of the Victorian Society in America. Q–18

Victorian Novelists after 1885. [PR871.V54 1983] M–58

Victorian Novelists before 1885. [PR871.V55 1983] M–58

Victorian Novels in Serial. [Z2014.F4 V36 1985] Q–45*

Victorian Period: The Intellectual and Cultural Context of English Literature, 1830–1890. M–35

"*Victorian Periodicals [1971/72–]: A Checklist of Scholarship and Criticism.*" [PN5124.P4 V52] Q–48*

Victorian Periodicals: A Guide to Research. [PN5124.P4 V5] Q–47*

Victorian Periodicals Newsletter. D–56, Q–18, Q–47, Q–48*

Victorian Periodicals Review. [PN5124.P4 V52] Q–18, Q–48*

Victorian Poetry: A Critical Journal of Victorian Literature. [PR500.V5] Q–18, Q– 39*, Q–40, Q–42

Victorian Poets: A Guide to Research. [PR593.F3 1968] Q–40*

Victorian Poets after 1850. [PR591.V5 1985] M–58

Victorian Poets and Prose Writers. [Z2013.B8 1978] Q–37*

Victorian Poets before 1850. [PR591.V53 1984] M–58

Victorian Prose: A Guide to Research. [PR785.D4] Q–42*

Victorian Prose Writers after 1867. [PR781.V52 1987] M–58

Victorian Prose Writers before 1867. [PR781.V53 1987] M–58

Victorian Studies: A Quarterly Journal of the Humanities, Arts, and Sciences. [PR1.V5] Q–18, Q–38

Victorians. [PR463.P6 1970] M–34

Victorians and After, 1830–1914, with a Chapter on the Economic Background. [PR85.I615 vol. 4] Q–30*

Victorians: Historical Figures Born between 1800 and 1860. [N7598.05 1979] G–85

Victorians Institute Journal. [AS36.V45] Q–18

Virginia Quarterly Review: A National Journal of Literature and Discussion. [AP2.V76] Z–158

Virginia Woolf: A Biography. [PR6045.072 2545] M–60

Virginia Woolf: An Annotated Bibliography of Criticism, 1915–1974. [Z8984.2.M33] M–60

Virginia Woolf Quarterly. [PR6045.072 Z894] M–60

Virginia Woolf's Literary Sources and Allusions: A Guide to the Essays. [Z8984.2.S74 1983] M–60

Visible Language: The Journal for Research on the Visual Media of Language Expression. [Z119.J88] I–15, X–165, Y–38

Visitation of the Seats and Arms of the Noblemen and Gentlemen of Great Britain. [CS419.B88] G–19

Vocabulaire du cinema/Film Vocabulary/Film Woordenliist. [PN1993.45.V6 1973] U–109

Volkskundliche Bibliographie. K–15

Vollständiges Bücher-Lexikon, enthaltend alle von 1750 bis zu Ende des Jahres [1910] in Deutschland und in den angrenzenden Ländern gedruckten Bücher. [Z2221.K23] C–62*

Von der Anfklärung zur Romantik (1961–62). U–70

Vox Romanica: Annales Helvetici Explorandis Linguis Romanicis Destinati. [PC1.A1 V6] L–63

W. B. Yeats: A Classified Bibliography of Criticism, Including Additions to Allan Wade's Bibliography of the Writings of W. B. Yeats and a Section on the Irish Literary and Dramatic Revival. [Z8992.J59 1978] M–60

W. B. Yeats: Interviews and Recollections. [PR5906.W2 1977b] M–60

W. H. Auden: A Bibliography, 1924–1969. [Z8057.55.B5] M–60

W. H. Auden: A Reference Guide. [Z8047.55.G55] M–60

W. H. Auden: The Life of a Poet. [PS3501.U55 Z83] M–60

Wake Newslitter [sic]. [PR6019.09.F594] M–60

Walden Edition of the Writings of Henry David Thoreau. [PS3040.F82] S–50

Wall Street Journal (1958–). [HG1.W258] D–23

Wallace Stevens: A Descriptive Bibliography. [Z8842.7.E35] S–50

Wallace Stevens Checklist and Bibliography of Stevens Criticism. [Z8842.7.M63] S–50

Wallace Stevens Journal: A Publication of the Wallace Stevens Society. S–50

Wallace Stevens: Musing the Obscure: Readings, an Interpretation, and a Guide to the Collected Poetry. [PS3537.T4753 Z768] S–50

Walt Whitman, 1838–1939: A Reference Guide. [Z8981.5.G5 1981] S–50

Walt Whitman, 1940–1975: A Reference Guide. [Z8981.5.K85 1982] S–50

INDEX OF SUBJECTS AND AUTHORS-AS-SUBJECTS